ATTENTION:
BAR CODE IS LOCATED
INSIDE OF BOOK

✓ **Y0-CYP-702**

Need additional copies?

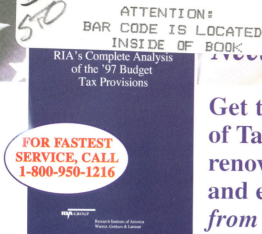

RIA's Complete Analysis
of the '97 Budget
Tax Provisions

**FOR FASTEST
SERVICE, CALL
1-800-950-1216**

RIA GROUP
Research Institute of America
Warren, Gorham & Lamont

Get the complete text of Tax Law '97 plus RIA's renowned clear analysis and expert guidance – *all from one convenient source!*

Now you can make your job a lot easier with *RIA's Tax Law '97 Books*.

They give you expert examples and put practical planning advice at your fingertips, including RIA's unique, reader-friendly features:

- **cautions** save you from misinterpreting the law's text . You'll avoid pitfalls that could waste hours of your time.
- **illustrations** give you step-by-step examples that clarify complex provisions – another big time saver!
- **recommendations** include expert guidance you can't find anywhere else.

- **action alerts** advise you of limited-time, tax-saving opportunities and their deadlines.

BONUS BENEFIT: You also get Code as amended and excerpts of Committee Reports linked back to paragraphs of explanation. This allows you to answer client questions *–fast–* with clear, accurate answers.

With this easy-to-use resource, you'll impress your clients with timely, expert service. So reserve your copy of the very best reporting and analysis of the new tax law available anywhere.

Mail the **REPLY FORM** below or call **1-800-950-1216** right now.

▼ DETACH HERE AND MAIL TODAY▼

STAY CURRENT – REPLY TODAY!

☐ **YES!** Please send me a **FREE** copy of **RIA's Tax Law '97 Highlights Booklet** and *RIA's TAX LAW '97 COMPLETE PACKAGE* for a **FREE** trial examination. Within 30 days I'll either pay your invoice for $100 plus postage, handling and applicable sales tax or I will return the Package and owe nothing. I can keep the Conference Bill Highlights booklet even if I return the Complete Package.

☐ **NO,** I do not need the Complete Package, but please send me _____ additional copies of RIA's Complete Analysis. ($45 per copy, plus postage, handling and applicable sales tax.)

Signature _____
(ALL ORDERS MUST BE SIGNED AND HAVE A PHONE NUMBER)

Phone ( ) _____ ☐ Office ☐ Home

Charge my: ☐ VISA ☐ MasterCard
☐ AmEx ☐ Discover
☐ Diners Club

Card No. _____ Exp: _____

D9708CANBI

Name ☐ Mr. ☐ Ms. _____

Title _____

Firm _____

Address _____

City/State/Zip _____

RIA's TAX LAW '97 COMPLETE PACKAGE includes...full text and highlights booklets for the **House Ways and Means Bill, Senate Bill, and Conference Bill and Report...RIA's Complete Analysis...** and all future RIA Tax Law '97 Client Guides. You save 40%.

Individual books from the Complete Package can be purchased separately.

CALL 1-800-950-1216 TO ORDER NOW

Yours **FREE** when ordering RIA's Tax Law '97 Complete Package

RIA's Tax Law '97 Highlights Booklet gives you a quick overview of this important new law. In just a few minutes, you discover all the important changes along with RIA's *observations, illustrations and cautions* that make it so easy to use.

Best of all, **RIA's Tax Law '97 Highlights Booklet** will be sent to you **ABSOLUTELY FREE**, when you return the **REPLY FORM** on the other side and order RIA's Tax Law '97 Complete Package.

Order now while supplies last!

---

4 EASY WAYS TO ORDER

MAIL the Business Reply Form below
FAX 1-800-452-9009
E-MAIL www.riatax.com

CALL TOLL FREE: 1-800-950-1216

SAVE 40%
BY ORDERING
THE COMPLETE
PACKAGE!

▼ DETACH HERE AND MAIL TODAY▼

 GROUP

117 East Stevens Avenue
Valhalla, New York 10595-9901

Th... Ta... 7

Self-Study and Videocourse

AICPA

Available within 30 days of enactment...Your first-hand look at the landmark changes to the Federal Tax Code!

The AICPA takes the lead again with the latest, authoritative tax training. Coming out within 30 days of President Clinton signing the tax bill into law, *The AICPA Experts' Taxpayer Relief Act of 1997* Self-Study Course (8 CPE credits) and Videocourse by Sid Kess (8 CPE credits) will be the only CPE source you'll need on the new tax legislation.

Let the AICPA's experience and expertise keep your practice on the cutting-edge. Acquire an in-depth understanding of the sweeping changes in the Federal tax code that will provide the deepest tax cuts in 16 years. Both courses are packed with the newest strategies and tips on tax planning and compliance.

Stay current and competitive, enhance your skills, and take advantage of big savings on your order today!

Place your order NOW and get 15% OFF!

Risk-free, money back guarantee

Tear here →

Fold here

The AICPA Experts' Taxpayer Relief Act of 1997

YES! I want to get the most complete, comprehensive instruction available on the latest tax information. Please send me:

☐ **Self-Study Course** *(8 CPE credits)*
Includes: AICPA manual and RIA Complete Analysis
(No. 730330II) $119.00

☐ **Videocourse** *(8 CPE credits)*
Includes: One VHS tape, AICPA manual and RIA Complete Analysis (No. 113330II) $129.00

☐ Additional AICPA manual and RIA Complete Analysis (No.113345II) $80.00

☐ Additional AICPA manual (No. 113335II) $40.00

Full payment must accompany order.

Charge my ☐ VISA   ☐ MasterCard   ☐ Discover   ☐ Bill me
(AICPA member only)

LAST NAME _____ FIRST ___ MI ___   CARD NO. _____ EXP. ___

FIRM NAME OR AFFILIATION _____   SIGNATURE _____ AMOUNT ___

STREET ADDRESS _____   PHONE _____ FAX ___

CITY _____ STATE ___ ZIP ___   E-MAIL ADDRESS _____

AICPA member? ☐ Yes ☐ No

Phone: (800) 862–4272   **FAX:** (800) 362–5066   **E-mail: http:**//www.aicpa.org

Ask about our quantity discounts!

RIA's complete analysis of the Taxpayer Relief Act of 1997

RIA's Complete Analysis of the Taxpayer Relief Act of 1997

(and other budget tax provisions)

With Code Sections as Amended and Committee Reports

To place an order for this or any other RIA publication, or to contact customer service regarding this or any other RIA publication, please call 1 800 950-1216.

To obtain the name and telephone number of your local account representative, please call 1 800 431-9025, ext. 3.

This publication is designed to provide accurate and authoritative information in regard to the subject matter covered. It is sold with the understanding that the publisher is not engaged in rendering legal, accounting or other professional service. If legal advice or other expert assistance is required, the services of a competent professional person should be sought.

AS WE WENT TO PRESS—

On Aug. 11, '97, President Clinton exercised the authority granted to the President by the Line Item Veto Act (PL 104-130, 4/9/96) to veto sections 968 and 1175 of the Taxpayer Relief Act of 1997 (PL 105-34, 8/5/97).

- For the analysis of section 968, which relates to the nonrecognition of gain on the sale of stock to certain farmers' cooperatives, see ¶ 208 of RIA's Complete Analysis of the Taxpayer Relief Act of 1997 (and other budget tax provisions).

- For the analysis of section 1175, which relates to the exemption from foreign personal holding company income for active financing income, see ¶ 1610 of RIA's Complete Analysis of the Taxpayer Relief Act of 1997 (and other budget tax provisions).

The Public Law numbers for the three Acts signed into law on Aug. 5, '97 are:

- the Taxpayer Relief Act of 1997—PL 105-34;

- the Balanced Budget Act of 1997—PL 105-33; and

- the Taxpayer Browsing Protection Act—PL 105-35.

RIA's Complete Analysis of the Taxpayer Relief Act of 1997

Research Institute of America

Euan Menzies, *President and Chief Executive Officer* **RIA** GROUP

Publishing Staff

Steven A. Zelman (LL.M., NY, NJ Bar) *Vice President and General Manager*

Joseph Trapani (J.D., NY Bar) *Vice President and Publisher*

Linda Scheffel (LL.M., NY Bar) *Director, Federal Taxation*

Todd Gordon (J.D., NY Bar) *Director, Primary Law*

Rick Beardsley *Director, Budgeting/ Scheduling*

Mark Jeanette *Director, Production*

Robert Rywick (J.D., NY Bar) *Executive Editor*

Raymond W. Hadrick (J.D., C.P.A., MA, FL, NY Bar) *Managing Editor*

Andrew Katz (LL.M., C.P.A., NY, NJ Bar) *Managing Editor*

Richard S. Nadler (LL.M., NY Bar) *Managing Editor*

Jeffrey N. Pretsfelder (C.P.A.) *Managing Editor*

Kersten Behrens (J.D., NY, NJ Bar) *Manager*

Cornell R. Fuerst (J.D., NY Bar) *Senior Editor*

Stanley Gladstone (LL.M., C.P.A., NY, MD Bar) *Senior Editor*

Dennis P. McMahon (LL.M., NY, MA Bar) *Senior Editor*

Robert P. Rothman (J.D., NY Bar) *Senior Editor*

Frederick M. Stein (LL.M., PA Bar) *Senior Editor*

Sidney Weinman (J.D., NY, NJ Bar) *Senior Editor*

Laurie Asch (LL.M., NY Bar)

Stanley V. Baginski (LL.M., NY Bar)

Meredith L. Berman (J.D., NY, NJ Bar)

Thomas J. Carroll (J.D., NY, NJ Bar)

John G. Clark (LL.M., NY Bar)

Gregory J. Evanella (J.D., NJ Bar)

David Freid (J.D., NY Bar)

Dawn R. Hansen (J.D., NY Bar)

Michael A. Levin (J.D., NY Bar)

Thomas Long (LL.M., NY, NJ Bar)

Carla M. Martin (LL.M., AL, FL Bar)

Betsy McKenny (J.D., NY, NJ Bar)

John M. Melazzo (J.D., NJ Bar)

Peter Ogrodnik (LL.M., NJ Bar)

Michael E. Overton (LL.M., NY, VA Bar)

Julie S. Rose (J.D., CT Bar)

Arthur Rosenberg (J.D., NJ Bar)

Roger M. Ross (LL.M., NY Bar)

E.H. Rubinsky (LL.M., NY Bar)

Rosemary Saldan-Pawson (J.D., NY, KS Bar)

Suzanne B. Schmitt (LL.M., NY Bar)

Simon Schneebalg (LL.M., NY, DC Bar)

Bernard Schneider (LL.M., NY, NJ, DC Bar)

Kristina G. Smith (J.D., NY, DC Bar)

Richard H. Sternberg (LL.M., NY Bar)

Steven Sulsky (LL.M., NY, MA Bar)

Scott E. Weiner (J.D., NY Bar)

Primary Law

Christine Carr, *Manager*
Peter Durham, *Manager*
Lisa Rosa, *Manager*
Claudie Peterfreund, *Project Manager*
Velma Goodwine-McDermon, *Supervisor*
Regan Bullers

Giuseppina Cambareri
Sandra Crowder
Daniel Cubias
Janie Davis
Virginia Gercich
Andrew Glicklin
Charyn Johnson
Pat Link
Ed Mack
Evelyn Manschal

Adam Mantell
David McAndrew
Jessye Mee
Laura Navarro
Anne Nicoletti
Pamela Perez
Jackie Sain
Terry Scherne
Gerard Sullivan
Peggy Taylor

Xiomara Tejeda
Veronica Torres
Janee Trotman
Danny Wang
Holly Yue

Paralegals

Benjamin Clark
Catherine Daleo
Marcia Sam

Table of Contents

¶ 1. Organization of the Book

This book contains RIA's complete analysis of H.R. 2014, the Taxpayer Relief Act of 1997 ('97 Act), and of the tax provisions of both H.R. 2015, the Balanced Budget Act of 1997 (Budget Act), and of H.R. 1226, the Taxpayer Browsing Protection Act (Privacy Act). It also contains the text of the Internal Revenue Code sections that were amended by any of these Acts (Code as amended), and committee reports relating to the above tax provisions. The President signed all three Acts into law on Aug 5, '97. Although the '97 Act and the Budget Act have been signed into law, the President has five days from the date of signing in which to exercise the line-item veto. There are about 80 provisions in the '97 Act and the Budget Act that are subject to the line-item veto. As we go to press, the President is still considering whether to exercise the line-item veto with respect to any of those provisions. For a list of those provisions, see ¶ s 4253 and 4804.

Contents   A complete list of topics discussed, arranged by paragraph title and number . . . . ¶ 2

Complete Analysis of the Tax Provisions of the '97 Act   The analysis of all three Acts is arranged in topical order. Each analysis paragraph starts with a boldface title. That is followed by a list of the Code sections substantively affected by the change, the Act section that caused the change, the generally effective date for the change, and the paragraph in the book where the relevant committee reports may be found. Each analysis paragraph discusses the background for the change, the new law change, and the effective date for that change. Included in the analysis paragraphs are illustrations and observations, which provide practical insight into the effects of the change. Also included are action alert items, which indicate when a taxpayer must take certain action by a specific date or lose the ability to take that action, e.g., make an election, file a statement with IRS, etc. Cites in the analysis paragraphs to the appropriate House, Senate, and Conference Committee reports are cited as Com Rept, with a reference to the paragraph number in the book where those committee reports are reproduced . . . . p. 1

Code as Amended   All Code sections that were amended, added, repealed, or redesignated by all three Acts appear in Code order as amended, added, repealed, or redesignated. New matter is shown in italics. Deleted material and effective dates are shown in footnotes . . . . p. 901

Committee Reports   This section reproduces all important parts of the official explanation of the legislation. The material comes from the following House, Senate, and Conference Committee Reports . . . . p. 1,901

Taxpayer Relief Act ('97 Act)	House	105-148
	Senate	105-33
	Conference	105-220
Budget Act	House	105-149
	Senate	105-30 (S. Prt.)
	Conference	105-217
Privacy Act	House	105-51

Act Section Cross Reference Table Arranged in Act section order, this table shows substantive section(s) amended, added, or repealed, the topic involved, the generally effective date of the amendment, the relevant paragraph number for the analysis in this book, and the paragraph in this book where the relevant committee reports are reproduced . . . . p. 2,901

Code Section Cross Reference Table Arranged in Code section order, this table shows the amending Act section(s) for all three acts, the topic involved, the generally effective date of the amendment, the relevant paragraph number for the analysis in this book, and the paragraph in this book where the relevant committee reports are reproduced . . . . p. 2,972

Code Sections Amended by '97 Act Table Arranged in Code section order, this table shows all changes to the Internal Revenue Code made by all three Acts, including conforming amendments . . . . p. 3,042

'97 Act Sections Amending Code Table Arranged in Act section order, this table shows all changes to the Internal Revenue Code made by all three Acts, including conforming amendments . . . . p. 3,058

Federal Tax Coordinator 2d ¶s Affected by '97 Act Arranged in FTC 2d ¶ order, this table shows the FTC 2d ¶s that have been affected by all three Acts . . . . p. 3,074

United States Tax Reporter ¶s Affected by '97 Act Arranged in USTR ¶ order, this table shows the USTR ¶s that have been affected by all three Acts . . . . p. 3,079

Tax Desk ¶s Affected by '97 Act Arranged in Tax Desk ¶ order, this table shows the Tax Desk ¶s that have been affected by all three Acts . . . . p. 3,082

Pension Coordinator and Pension & Benefits Expert/Advisor ¶s Affected by '97 Act Arranged in Pension Coordinator and Pension CD-ROM ¶ order, this table shows the Pension Coordinator and Pension CD-ROM ¶s that have been affected by all three Acts . . . . p. 3,085

Pension and Profit Sharing 2d ¶s Affected by '97 Act Arranged in Pension and Profit Sharing 2nd ¶ order, this table shows the Pension and Profit Sharing 2nd ¶s that have been affected by all three Acts . . . . p. 3,086

Estate Planning & Taxation Coordinator and Estate Planning Advisor ¶s Affected by '97 Act Arranged in Estate Planning & Taxation Coordinator and Estate Planning Advisor ¶s that have been affected by all three Acts . . . . p. 3,087

Table of Action Alert Items Arranged in chronological order, this table shows actions (elections, amended returns, etc.) that must be taken by a certain date or the

¶ 2. Contents

CONTENTS

CONTENTS

CONTENTS

DEPRECIATION AND EXPENSING   800

Depreciation

Expensing

QUALIFIED RETIREMENT PLANS   900

Distribution Provisions

Excise Tax Reform

CONTENTS

CONTENTS

Disclosure of Returns and Return Information

Other Procedural and Administrative Rules

INTEREST AND PENALTIES   2400

Interest

Penalties

CONTENTS

¶ 100. Individuals

Child Tax Credit

¶ 101. Child tax credit of up to $400 in '98, $500 in '99 and later years, for each qualifying child under age 17

Code Sec. 24, as added by '97 Act § 101(a)
Code Sec. 32(m)(3), as amended by '97 Act § 101(b)
Code Sec. 6213(g)(2)(I), as amended by '97 Act § 101(d)(2)
Generally effective: Tax years beginning after Dec. 31, '97
Committee Reports, see ¶ 5001

Taxpayers with dependent children are generally allowed to claim a personal exemption for each of these dependents. The total amount of personal exemption is subtracted from adjusted gross income in arriving at taxable income. The amount of each personal exemption is $2,650 for '97 and is adjusted annually for inflation. The amount of personal exemption is phased out for high income taxpayers, e.g. starting at $181,600 for married couples filing joint returns. (FTC 2d/FIN ¶ A-3501; USTR ¶ 1514; TaxDesk ¶ 56,240) However, under pre-'97 Act law, there was no tax credit based solely on the number of dependent children of the taxpayer. (Com Rept, see ¶ 5001)

Taxpayers are allowed certain nonrefundable credits against their income tax, e.g., for child and dependent care and for adoption expenses. The aggregate amount of personal nonrefundable tax credits can't exceed the excess of the taxpayer's regular tax liability over his tentative minimum tax (determined without regard to the alternative minimum tax foreign tax credit). (FTC 2d/FIN ¶ L-18100; USTR ¶ 264; TaxDesk ¶ 56,961)

New Law. For tax years beginning after '97 ('97 Act §101(e)), the Act allows a tax credit against the taxpayer's income for the tax year with respect to each qualifying child (defined below) of the taxpayer an amount equal to $500. (Code Sec. 24(a) as added by '97 Act §101(a)) Thus, generally, the amount of the child credit equals $500 times the number of qualifying children. (Com Rept, see ¶ 5001) For tax years beginning in '98, the credit is limited to $400 per qualifying child. (Code Sec. 24(a))

Phase out of credit. For taxpayers with modified adjusted gross income (defined below) above certain thresholds, the otherwise allowable child tax credit is phased out. (Com Rept, see ¶ 5001) The amount of the credit allowable under Code Sec. 24(a) is reduced (but not below zero) by $50 for each $1,000 (or fraction thereof) by which the taxpayer's modified adjusted gross income exceeds the threshold amount. (Code Sec. 24(b)(1)) The threshold amount is:

FTC 2d References are to Federal Tax Coordinator 2d
FIN References are to RIA's Analysis of Federal Taxes: Income
USTR References are to United States Tax Reporter: Income, Estate & Gift, and Excise
PCA References are to Pension Coordinator and Pension & Benefits Expert/Advisor
PE References are to Pension and Profit Sharing 2nd
EP References are to Estate Planning & Taxation Coordinator and Estate Planning Advisor

... $110,000 in the case of a joint return; (Code Sec. 24(b)(2)(A))

... $75,000 in the case of an individual who isn't married; (Code Sec. 24(b)(2)(B)) and

... $55,000 in the case of a married individual filing a separate return. (Code Sec. 24(b)(2)(C))

These threshold amounts aren't indexed for inflation. (Com Rept, see ¶ 5001)

> **✔ observation:** Pegging the phaseout in $50 increments means that for some taxpayers a $1 increase in AGI (from an increment of $1,000 over the threshold to $1,001 over) can trigger a $50 increase in tax liability (through a corresponding reduction in the credit).

> **✔ observation:** In a year when the credit is $500, a couple with one qualifying child who file jointly are entitled to a credit of $450 if their modified adjusted gross income is more than $110,000 but less than $111,000. They lose the credit completely if their modified AGI is more than $119,000. A single taxpayer with one qualifying child isn't entitled to any credit if modified AGI is more than $84,000.

Modified adjusted gross income is adjusted gross income increased by any amount excluded from gross income under Code Sec. 911 (exclusion of income of U.S. citizens or residents living abroad), Code Sec. 931 (exclusion for bona fide residents of Guam, American Samoa, and the Northern Mariana Islands), or Code Sec. 933 (exclusion of income of residents of Puerto Rico). (Code Sec. 24(b)(2)(A))

For purposes of the phaseout, marital status is determined under the normal Code Sec. 7703 rules. (Code Sec. 24(b)(2)(B))

Identification requirement. The child tax credit is not allowed to a taxpayer with respect to any qualifying child unless the taxpayer includes the name and tax identification number (TIN) of the qualifying child on the return of tax for the tax year. (Code Sec. 24(e)) For purposes of the summary assessment procedure applicable to returns which contain mathematical or clerical errors (FTC 2d/FIN ¶ T-3622; USTR ¶ 62134.02; TaxDesk ¶ 83,615) , the definition of mathematical or clerical error includes an omission of a correct TIN that's required under Code Sec. 24(e), above, to be included on a return. (Code Sec. 6213(g)(2)(I) as amended by '97 Act §101(d)(2))

> **✔ observation:** Thus, if a taxpayer claiming the child tax credit omits the TIN of a qualifying child, IRS can recompute the tax liability (i.e., deny the credit) under the summary assessment procedure.

Periods of less than 12 months. No credit is allowed for a tax year covering a period of less than 12 months, except where a tax year is closed by reason of the death of the taxpayer. (Code Sec. 24(f))

Refundable child credit amount. In the case of a taxpayer with three or more qualifying children for any tax year, the amount of the child tax credit is equal to the greater of (Code Sec. 24(d)(1)):

(a) the amount of the credit determined under the above rules, without regard to this Code Sec. 24(d) and after application of the Code Sec. 26 limitation (aggregate credits can't exceed the excess of regular tax liability over tentative minimum tax determined without regard to alternative minimum tax foreign tax credit) (Code Sec. 24(d)(1)(A)), or

(b) the alternative credit amount (defined below). (Code Sec. 24(d)(1)(B))

If the amount of the credit under (b) is more than the amount of the credit under (a), the excess is treated as a refundable credit. But the rule of Code Sec. 32(h) (reducing the credit by the amount of the taxpayer's alternative minimum tax for the tax year) applies to the excess. (Code Sec. 24(d)(4))

The alternative credit amount is the amount of the child tax credit allowed by applying the following limitation rather than the limitation under Code Sec. 26. (Code Sec. 24(d)(2)) For purposes of the alternative credit amount, the limitation is the limitation under Code Sec. 26 (without regard to this Code Sec. 24(d) (Code Sec. 24(d)(3)), increased by the taxpayer's social security taxes (defined below) for the tax year (Code Sec. 24(d)(3)(A)), and reduced by the sum of (Code Sec. 24(d)(3)(B)) —

. . . the credits against tax allowed by Part IV of Subchapter A of Chapter 1 of the Code (Code Sec. 21 *et seq.*) other than the refundable credits under Subpart C of Part IV (Code Sec. 31 through Code Sec. 35) and the child tax credit (Code Sec. 24(d)(3)(B)(i)), and

. . . the earned income credit allowed under Code Sec. 32 without regard to the supplemental child credit, see below. (Code Sec. 24(d)(3)(B)(ii))

The following are social security taxes:

. . . FICA and Tier 1 Railroad Retirement Tax Act taxes imposed on employees under Code Sec. 3101 and Code Sec. 3201(a) on amounts received during the calendar year in which the tax year begins. (Code Sec. 24(d)(5)(A)(i)) These include equivalent taxes paid under an agreement under Code Sec. 3132l(l), relating to agreements entered into by American employers with respect to foreign affiliates (Code Sec. 24(d)(5)(C)),

. . . 50% of the self-employment tax imposed on the self-employment income of the taxpayer for the tax year (Code Sec. 24(d)(5)(A)(ii)), and

. . . 50% of the Tier 1 Railroad Retirement Tax Act taxes imposed on employee representatives under Code Sec. 3211(a)(1) on amounts received during the calendar year in which the tax year begins. (Code Sec. 24(d)(5)(A)(iii))

Social security taxes don't include any taxes to the extent the taxpayer had more than one employer during the year and had wages in excess of the contribution base by reason of which the taxpayer is entitled to a refund under Code Sec. 6413(c). (Code Sec. 24(d)(5)(B))

Thus, for a taxpayer with three or more qualifying children the maximum child tax credit for a year can't exceed the greater of:

(1) the excess of the taxpayer's regular tax liability (net of applicable credits other than the earned income credit) over the taxpayer's tentative minimum tax liability (determined without regard to the alternative minimum foreign tax credit), or

(2) an amount equal to the excess of the sum of the taxpayer's regular income tax liability (net of applicable credits other than the earned income credit) and the employee's share of FICA (and half of any self-employment tax liability) reduced by the earned income credit.

To the extent the amount determined under (1) is greater than the amount determined under (2), the difference is treated as a supplemental child credit amount.

If the amount of the credit determined under this computation is more than the taxpayer's regular tax liability, the excess is a refundable tax credit. (Com Rept, see ¶ 5001)

It is anticipated that IRS will determine if a simplified method of calculating the credit, consistent with the statutory formula, can be achieved. (Com Rept, see ¶ 5001)

A taxpayer to whom the child tax credit is allowed for the tax year is allowed a credit under the earned income credit rules equal to the taxpayer's supplemental child credit, if any, for the tax year. This supplemental credit is in addition to the earned income credit allowed under Code Sec. 32(a). (Code Sec. 32(m)(1) as amended by '97 Act §101(b)) This treatment of a portion of the child tax credit as a supplemental child credit amount is available to a taxpayer with one or two qualifying children. (Com Rept, see ¶ 5001) The amount of the child tax credit under Code Sec. 24 is reduced by any supplemental child credit. (Code Sec. 32(m)(3))

The supplemental child credit is an amount equal to the excess (if any) of the amount determined under Code Sec. 24(d)(1)(A), above, over the amount determined under Code Sec. 24(d)(1)(B), above. These amounts are determined as if Code Sec. 24(d) applied to all taxpayers (Code Sec. 32(m)(2)) i.e., not limited to taxpayers with three or more qualifying children. Thus, the supplemental child credit equals the excess of:

(1) $500 times the number of qualifying children up to the excess of the taxpayer's regular tax liability (net of applicable credits other than the earned income credit) over the taxpayer's tentative minimum tax liability (determined without regard to the alternative minimum foreign tax credit), over

(2) the sum of the taxpayer's regular income tax liability (net of applicable credits other than the earned income credit) and the employee share of FICA (and half of any self-employment tax liability) reduced by any earned income credit amount. (Com Rept, see ¶ 5001)

The total amount of the allowable child tax credit can't exceed the amount that results from its calculation as a nonrefundable personal credit. (Com Rept, see ¶ 5001)

Who is a qualifying child. For an individual to qualify as a qualifying child:

. . . the taxpayer must be entitled to a dependency deduction under Code Sec. 151 for the individual for the tax year (Code Sec. 24(c)(1)(A);

. . . the individual must bear a relationship to the taxpayer described in Code Sec. 32(c)(3)(B) (Code Sec. 24(c)(1)(C)), i.e. be a son or daughter of the taxpayer (or a descendant of either), a stepson or stepdaughter, or an eligible foster child (Com Rept, see ¶ 5001); and

. . . the individual must be under the age of 17 as of the close of the calendar year in which the tax year of the taxpayer begins. (Code Sec. 24(c)(1)(B))

> *observation:* Although the taxpayer must be entitled to a dependency deduction under Code Sec. 151, that deduction is not reduced or otherwise modified because of the child tax credit. Thus, an individual with a qualifying child can claim both the dependency deduction and the child tax credit.

A qualifying child does not include an individual who would not be a dependent if the first sentence of Code Sec. 152(b)(3) were applied without the reference to a country contiguous to the U.S. (Code Sec. 24(c)(2))

> *observation:* Thus, a qualifying child must be a citizen, national, or resident of the U.S.

☐ **Effective:** For tax years beginning after '97. ('97 Act §101(e)) For tax years beginning in '98, the credit is limited to $400. (Code Sec. 24(a))

Exclusions from Income

¶ 102. Replacement of rollover rules and the one-time exclusion that applied to sales of a principal residence with an exclusion of gain of up to $250,000 ($500,000 for joint filers)

Code Sec. 121, as amended by '97 Act § 312(a)
Code Sec. 1034, repealed by '97 Act § 312(b)
Generally effective: Sales and exchanges after May 6, '97
Committee Reports, see ¶ 5020

Under pre-'97 Act law, no gain was recognized on the sale of a principal residence if a taxpayer bought a new residence at least equal in cost to the sales price of the old residence and used the new residence as his or her principal residence within a specified period of time (i.e., taxpayer rolls over his gain from the sale). The period within which the new residence had to be purchased generally began two years before and en-

FTC 2d References are to Federal Tax Coordinator 2d
FIN References are to RIA's Analysis of Federal Taxes: Income
USTR References are to United States Tax Reporter: Income, Estate & Gift, and Excise
PCA References are to Pension Coordinator and Pension & Benefits Expert/Advisor
PE References are to Pension and Profit Sharing 2nd
EP References are to Estate Planning & Taxation Coordinator and Estate Planning Advisor

ded two years after the date of sale of the old residence. The basis of the replacement residence was reduced by the amount of any gain not recognized on the sale of the old residence by reason of the gain rollover rule. (FTC 2d/FIN ¶ I-4600 *et seq.*; USTR ¶ 10,344; TaxDesk ¶ 22,580)

An individual, on a one-time basis, could also exclude from gross income up to $125,000 of gain from the sale or exchange of a principal residence if the taxpayer had attained age 55 before the sale, and had owned the property and used it as a principal residence for three or more of the five years preceding the sale. (FTC 2d/FIN ¶ I-4700 *et seq.*; USTR ¶ 1214; TaxDesk ¶ 22,650)

Congress was concerned that calculating capital gain from the sale of a principal residence under the pre-'97 Act rollover provisions and the pre-'97 Act $125,000 one-time exclusion was among the most complex tasks faced by a typical taxpayer. Even though most homeowners never paid any income tax on the capital gain on their principal residences, as a result of the pre-'97 Act rollover provisions and the $125,000 one-time exclusion, the taxpayers had to keep detailed records of transactions (i.e., appropriately adjust the basis of their current home to reflect untaxed gains from previous housing transactions) and expenditures on home improvements for many decades. Congress felt that by excluding from taxation capital gains on principal residences below a relatively high threshold, few taxpayers would have to refer to records in determining income tax consequences of transactions related to their house. (Com Rept, see ¶ 5020)

Congress also felt that the pre-'97 Act rollover rules promoted an inefficient use of taxpayer's financial resources by encouraging some taxpayers to buy larger and more expensive houses than they otherwise would in order to avoid a tax liability, particularly those who moved from areas where housing costs are high to lower-cost areas. In addition, the pre-'97 Act law discouraged some older taxpayers from selling their homes. Taxpayers who would realize a capital gain in excess of $125,000 if they sold their home and taxpayers who have already used the exclusion may choose to stay in their homes even though the home no longer suits their needs. By raising the $125,000 limit and by allowing multiple exclusions, Congress removed this constraint to the mobility of the elderly. (Com Rept, see ¶ 5020)

New Law. The exclusion of gain from the sale of a principal residence (described below) replaces the pre-'97 Act rollover and one-time exclusion provisions that applied to sales or exchanges of principal residences. (Com Rept, see ¶ 5020) Under the '97 Act, gross income does not include gain from the sale or exchange of property if, during the five-year period ending on the date of the sale or exchange, the property has been *owned and used* by the taxpayer as the taxpayer's principal residence for periods aggregating two years or more. (Code Sec. 121(a) as amended by '97 Act §312(a))

> ✐ *observation:* Code Sec. 121 doesn't provide a definition of "principal residence." Presumably, the definition will be similar to the definition of principal residence that applied under the pre-'97 Act rollover rules (FTC 2d/FIN ¶ I-4602; USTR ¶ 10,344.01; TaxDesk ¶ 22,655) and the one-time exclusion (FTC 2d/FIN ¶ I-4717; USTR ¶ 1214; TaxDesk ¶ 22,637).

Limitations.

Dollar limitations. The amount of gain excluded from gross income with respect to any sale or exchange cannot exceed $250,000. (Code Sec. 121(b)(1)) The $250,000 limitation is applied by substituting "$500,000" for "$250,000" if: (Code Sec. 121(b)(2))

... a husband and wife make a joint return for the tax year of the sale or exchange of the property (Code Sec. 121(b)(2)(A)),

... *either* spouse meets the ownership requirements (described in Code Sec. 121(a)) with respect to the property (Code Sec. 121(b)(2)(B)),

... *both* spouses meet the use requirements (described in Code Sec. 121(a)) with respect to the property (Code Sec. 121(b)(2)(C)), and

... neither spouse is ineligible for the benefits of the exclusion with respect to the property by reason of the one sale every two years rule (contained in Code Sec. 121(b)(3), see below). (Code Sec. 121(b)(2)(D))

In the case of joint filers not sharing a principal residence, an exclusion of $250,000 is available on a qualifying sale or exchange of the principal residence of one of the spouses. (Com Rept, see ¶ 5020)

One sale or exchange every two years. The exclusion does not apply to any sale or exchange by the taxpayer if, during the two-year period ending on the date of the sale or exchange, there was any other sale or exchange by the taxpayer to which the exclusion applied. (Code Sec. 121(b)(3)(A)) The exclusion is allowed each time a taxpayer selling or exchanging a residence meets the eligibility requirements, but generally no more frequently than once every two years. (Com Rept, see ¶ 5020) This limit of one sale every two years is applied without regard to any sale or exchange before May 7, '97. (Code Sec. 121(b)(3)(B))

If a single taxpayer who is otherwise eligible for an exclusion marries someone who has used the exclusion within the two years before the marriage, the newly married taxpayer is allowed a maximum exclusion of $250,000. Once both spouses satisfy the eligibility rules and two years have passed since the last exclusion was allowed to either of them, the taxpayers may exclude $500,000 of gain on their joint return. (Com Rept, see ¶ 5020)

Reduced exclusion for certain taxpayers failing to meet the ownership and use requirements or for taxpayers who have sold or exchanged principal residences within two years.

In the case of certain sales or exchanges (described below), the ownership and use requirements (see above) do not apply and the limit of one sale every two years does not apply; but the amount of the gain excluded from gross income is reduced. (Code Sec. 121(c)(1)) For the amount of the reduced exclusion, see below.

FTC 2d References are to Federal Tax Coordinator 2d
FIN References are to RIA's Analysis of Federal Taxes: Income
USTR References are to United States Tax Reporter: Income, Estate & Gift, and Excise
PCA References are to Pension Coordinator and Pension & Benefits Expert/Advisor
PE References are to Pension and Profit Sharing 2nd
EP References are to Estate Planning & Taxation Coordinator and Estate Planning Advisor

This rule limiting the exclusion to one sale every two years by the taxpayer does not prevent a husband and a wife filing a joint return from each excluding up to $250,000 of gain from the sale or exchange of each spouse's principal residence provided that each spouse would be permitted to exclude up to $250,000 of gain if they filed separate returns. (Com Rept, see ¶ 5020)

Sales and exchanges eligible for the reduced exclusion. The reduced exclusion applies to any sale or exchange if: (Code Sec. 121(c)(2))

... the exclusion would not (but for these rules relating to the reduced exclusion) apply to the sale or exchange by reason of: (Code Sec. 121(c)(2)(A))

(1) a failure to meet the ownership and use requirements (see above), (Code Sec. 121(c)(2)(A)(i)) *or*

(2) the limit of only one sale every two years (see above), *and* (Code Sec. 121(c)(2)(A)(ii))

... the sale or exchange is by reason of a change in place of employment, health, or (to the extent provided in regs), unforeseen circumstances. (Code Sec. 121(c)(2)(B))

Amount of reduced exclusion. For taxpayers subject to the reduced exclusion, the amount of gain excluded from gross income with respect to the sale of exchange cannot exceed: (Code Sec. 121(c)(1))

... the amount which bears the same ratio to the amount which would be so excluded if the ownership and use requirements had been met, as (Code Sec. 121(c)(1)(A))
... the *shorter* of: (Code Sec. 121(c)(1)(B))

(1) the aggregate periods, during the five-year period ending on the date of the sale or exchange, the property has been owned and used by the taxpayer as the taxpayer's principal residence, (Code Sec. 121(c)(1)(B)(i)) *or*

(2) the period after the date of the most recent earlier sale or exchange by the taxpayer to which the exclusion applied and before the date of the sale or exchange, (Code Sec. 121(c)(1)(B)(ii))

bears to two years. (Code Sec. 121(c)(1))

> **observation:** If the taxpayer has never excluded gain under the exclusion described above, he would use the ratio described in (1) above.

> **observation:** Code Sec. 121(c)(1) does not specify whether the ratio should be computed using days or months.

> **illustration:** S sells her principal residence because she has a new job in another city. On the date of the sale, S has used and owned her principal residence for the last 18 months. S has never excluded gain under the Code Sec. 121(a) exclusion. If S had used her principal residence for two years, the entire amount of the gain ($250,000) would be excluded. Since S fails to meet the use and ownership requirements for the exclusion by reason of a change in S's place of employment, health, or other unforeseen circumstances, the amount of gain excluded by S could not exceed the amount determined under

the following ratio (computed using months, see observation above): $\frac{187,500}{250,000} = \frac{18 \text{ months}}{24 \text{ months}}$. Therefore, S could exclude \$187,500 of her gain on the sale of her principal residence.

Husband and wife rules.

Joint returns. If a husband and wife make a joint return for the tax year of the sale or exchange of property, the exclusion and the reduced exclusion (that applies to certain sales by reason of a change in place of employment, health or unforeseen circumstances, see above) apply, if *either* spouse meets the ownership and use requirements for the exclusion with respect to the property. (Code Sec. 121(d)(1))

> **observation:** However, the husband and wife won't qualify for the \$500,000 exclusion unless both spouses meet the *use* requirement.

Transfers between spouses or transfers incident to a divorce. In the case of an individual holding property transferred to that individual in a transaction described in Code Sec. 1041(a) (i.e., transfers between spouses or transfers incident to a divorce, see FTC 2d/FIN ¶ I-3600; USTR ¶ 10,414; TaxDesk ¶ 22,822), the period the individual *owns* the property includes the period the transferor *owned* the property. (Code Sec. 121(d)(3)(A))

> **observation:** Under Code Sec. 121(d)(3)(A), the period that the transferor spouse or former spouse *used* the property is not included in the period that the individual used the property. Presumably, the transferee spouse would still have to satisfy the use requirement in order to qualify for the exclusion.

Solely for purposes of the exclusion described in Code Sec. 121, an individual is treated as using property as the individual's principal residence during any period of ownership while the individual's spouse or former spouse is granted use of the property under a divorce or separation instrument (as defined in Code Sec. 71(b)(2), see FTC 2d/FIN ¶ K-6013; USTR ¶ 714; TaxDesk ¶ 34,157). (Code Sec. 121(d)(3)(B))

> **observation:** Thus, if a spouse (H) continues to own the home after a divorce and his former spouse (W) is granted use of the property under a divorce instrument, the exclusion could be available when H sells the house if H meets the ownership requirements and W meets the use requirements.

> **observation:** Since divorced individuals can't file a joint return, the above rules don't appear to help a taxpayer qualify for the \$500,000 dollar limitation (under Code Sec. 121(b)(2), see above) because Code Sec. 121(b)(2)(A) requires that a couple file a joint return.

FTC 2d References are to Federal Tax Coordinator 2d
FIN References are to RIA's Analysis of Federal Taxes: Income
USTR References are to United States Tax Reporter: Income, Estate & Gift, and Excise
PCA References are to Pension Coordinator and Pension & Benefits Expert/Advisor
PE References are to Pension and Profit Sharing 2nd
EP References are to Estate Planning & Taxation Coordinator and Estate Planning Advisor

Research Institute of America 9

Deceased spouse's property. In the case of an unmarried individual whose spouse is deceased on the date of the sale or exchange of property, the period the unmarried individual owned and used the property includes the period the deceased spouse owned and used the property before death. (Code Sec. 121(d)(2))

observation: Thus, if a decedent (D) leaves his principal residence (that he has owned and used as his principal residence for more than two years) to his surviving spouse (SS), a sale or exchange of the residence by SS within five years of D's death would qualify for the exclusion even if SS has not used the house as her principal residence.

observation: Presumably, a surviving spouse filing a joint return with the deceased spouse for the year of death would be entitled to an exclusion of up to $500,000 where (1) either the surviving spouse and the deceased spouse satisfied the ownership requirements; (2) both spouses satisfied the use requirement within the five-year period ending on the date of the sale; and (3) neither spouse had excluded gain from the sale of a principal residence during the two-year period ending on the date of the sale or exchange.

Rules for the application of the exclusion.

Residences acquired in rollovers. In the case of property the acquisition of which by the taxpayer resulted under Code Sec. 1034 (as in effect on the day before Aug. 5, '97, see FTC 2d/FIN ¶ I-4600; USTR ¶ 10,344; TaxDesk ¶ 22,580) in the nonrecognition of any part of the gain realized on the sale or exchange of another residence, in determining the period for which the taxpayer has owned and used the property as the taxpayer's principal residence, there is included the aggregate periods for which the other residence (and each earlier residence taken into account under Code Sec. 1223(7) in determining the holding period of the property, see FTC 2d/FIN ¶ I-8941; USTR ¶ 12,234.08; TaxDesk ¶ 22,359.30) had been so owned and used. (Code Sec. 121(g))

Determination of use during periods of out-of-residence care. In the case of a taxpayer who (Code Sec. 121(d)(7))

. . . becomes physically or mentally incapable of self-care, and (Code Sec. 121(d)(7)(A))

. . . owns property and uses the property as the taxpayer's principal residence during the five-year period described in Code Sec. 121(a) (see discussion above) for periods aggregating at least one year (Code Sec. 121(d)(7)(B)),

then the taxpayer is treated as using the property as the taxpayer's principal residence during any time during the five-year period in which the taxpayer owns the property and resides in any facility (including a nursing home) licensed by a state or political subdivision to care for an individual in the taxpayer's condition. (Code Sec. 121(d)(7))

Tenant-stockholder in cooperative housing corporation. If the taxpayer holds stock as a tenant-stockholder (as defined in Code Sec. 216, see FTC 2d/FIN ¶ E-1078; USTR ¶ 2164.01; TaxDesk ¶ 26,520) in a cooperative housing corporation (as defined in Code Sec. 216, see FTC 2d/FIN ¶ E-1059; USTR ¶ 2164.01; TaxDesk ¶ 26,519) (Code Sec. 121(d)(4)), then—

... the holding requirements for the exclusion apply to the holding of the stock (Code Sec. 121(d)(4)(A)), and

> *observation:* Presumably, the reference to the "holding requirements" in Code Sec. 121(d)(4)(A) means the requirement in Code Sec. 121(a) that the property be owned by the taxpayer as the taxpayer's principal residence for periods aggregating two years or more.

... the use requirements for the exclusion apply to the house or apartment which the taxpayer was entitled to occupy as the stockholder. (Code Sec. 121(d)(4)(B))

Involuntary conversions. For purposes of the exclusion, the destruction, theft, seizure, requisition, or condemnation of property is treated as the sale of the property. (Code Sec. 121(d)(5)(A))

In applying Code Sec. 1033 (relating to involuntary conversions, see FTC 2d/FIN ¶ I-3700; USTR ¶ 10,334; TaxDesk ¶ 22,790), the amount realized from the sale or exchange of property is treated as being the amount determined without regard to this exclusion, reduced by the amount of gain not included in gross income under the exclusion. (Code Sec. 121(d)(5)(B))

If the basis of the property sold or exchanged is determined (in whole or in part) under Code Sec. 1033(b) (relating to basis of property acquired through involuntary conversion, see FTC 2d/FIN ¶ P-1154; USTR ¶ 10,334.33; TaxDesk ¶ 21,137), then the holding and use by the taxpayer of the converted property is treated as holding and use by the taxpayer of the property sold or exchanged. (Code Sec. 121(d)(5)(C))

> *observation:* Presumably, the reference to "holding" in Code Sec. 121(d)(5)(C) means the requirement in Code Sec. 121(a) that the property be owned by the taxpayer as the taxpayer's principal residence for periods aggregating two years or more.

Sales of remainder interests. At the election of the taxpayer, the exclusion will not fail to apply to the sale or exchange of an interest in a principal residence by reason of the interest being a remainder interest in the residence, but the exclusion does not apply to any other interest in the residence which is sold or exchanged separately. (Code Sec. 121(d)(8)(A))

> *observation:* Code Sec. 121 does not provide rules as to how and when a taxpayer makes the election to have the exclusion apply to the sale of a remainder interest.

FTC 2d References are to Federal Tax Coordinator 2d
FIN References are to RIA's Analysis of Federal Taxes: Income
USTR References are to United States Tax Reporter: Income, Estate & Gift, and Excise
PCA References are to Pension Coordinator and Pension & Benefits Expert/Advisor
PE References are to Pension and Profit Sharing 2nd
EP References are to Estate Planning & Taxation Coordinator and Estate Planning Advisor

But, the rule permitting taxpayers to elect to have the exclusion apply to sales of remainder interests (described in Code Sec. 121(d)(8)(A), above) does not apply to any sale to, or exchange with, any person who bears a relationship to the taxpayer which is described in Code Sec. 267(b) (relating to the disallowance of losses incurred in transactions between related persons, see FTC 2d/FIN ¶ I-3504; USTR ¶ 2674.03; TaxDesk ¶ 22,790) or Code Sec. 707(b) (relating to the disallowance of losses incurred between a partner and a partnership, see FTC 2d/FIN ¶ B-2016; USTR ¶ 7074.03; TaxDesk ¶ 58,450). (Code Sec. 121(d)(8)(B))

Exceptions.

Recognition of gain attributable to depreciation. The exclusion does not apply to so much of the gain from the sale of any property as does not exceed the portion of the depreciation adjustments (as defined in Code Sec. 1250(b)(3) (depreciation deductions subject to recapture to the extent they exceed straight-line depreciation deductions, see FTC 2d/FIN ¶ I-10404; USTR ¶ 12,504.06; TaxDesk ¶ 22,308.7)) attributable to periods after May 6, '97, in respect of the property. (Code Sec. 121(d)(6)) Thus, a taxpayer would recognize gain to the extent of any depreciation allowable with respect to the rental or business use of the principal residence for periods after May 6, '97. (Com Rept, see ¶ 5020)

Denial of exclusion for expatriates. The exclusion does not apply to any sale or exchange by an individual if the treatment provided by Code Sec. 877(a)(1) (rules related to expatriation to avoid tax, see FTC 2d/FIN ¶ O-11701; USTR ¶ 8774; TaxDesk ¶ 64,470) applies to the individual. (Code Sec. 121(e))

Election out of the exclusion. The exclusion does not apply to any sale or exchange with respect to which the taxpayer elects not to have the exclusion apply. (Code Sec. 121(f))

> *observation:* It could be beneficial for a taxpayer to elect not to have the exclusion apply where a taxpayer has owned and used two residences as principal residences at different times during the five-year period and he is planning to sell both of the residences within two years of each other. If the sale of one residence would generate a smaller gain and he expects the sale of the second residence to generate a larger gain, he may want to elect out of the exclusion for the sale of the first residence with the smaller gain in order to preserve the benefits of the exclusion for the second sale.

Repeal of nonrecognition of gain on rollover of principal residence. Code Sec. 1034 (relating to rollover of gain on sale of principal residence) is repealed. (Code Sec. 1034 repealed by '97 Act §312(b))

> *observation:* In addition to the repeal of the rollover rules, the one-time $125,000 exclusion that applied to individuals that had attained age 55 is also effectively repealed by virtue of the amendments to Code Sec. 121.

> *observation:* Although most taxpayers will benefit from the $250,000 ($500,000 for joint filers) exclusion provided under the '97 Act, taxpayers who sell their principal residences and have gains in excess of the dollar limi-

tations may pay more tax than they would have paid under pre-'97 Act rules (where they could rollover the gain on the sale of a principal residence by buying a more expensive house). In particular, taxpayers who have moved repeatedly and always traded up to more expensive houses (and deferred paying tax on the gain by rolling over the gain) may owe more tax under '97 Act law when they sell those homes.

☐ **Effective:** Sales and exchanges after May 6, '97. ('97 Act §312(d)(1))

     observation: There are two subsection "(d)"s in Act §312.

At the taxpayer's election, the exclusion and repeal of the rollover rules will not apply to any sale or exchange before Aug. 5, '97. ('97 Act §312(d)(2))

At the taxpayer's election, the exclusion and repeal of the rollover rules will not apply to a sale or exchange after Aug. 5, '97 ('97 Act §312(d)(4)), if:

... the sale or exchange is under a contract which was binding on Aug. 5, '97 ('97 Act §312(d)(4)(A)), or

... without regard to exclusion and repeal of the rollover rules, gain would not be recognized under the rollover rules of Code Sec. 1034 (as in effect on the day before Aug. 5, '97) on that sale or exchange by reason of a new residence acquired on or before the day before Aug. 5, '97 or with respect to the acquisition of which by the taxpayer a binding contract was in effect on the day before Aug. 5, '97. ('97 Act §312(d)(4)(B))

     observation: In light of the way Act §312(d)(2) and (4) have been drafted, presumably, these elections are not available for sales or exchanges *on* Aug. 5, '97.

     observation: Making either of these two elections could be advantageous for taxpayers who have a gain in excess of the dollar limitations that apply to the exclusion ($500,000 for joint filers and $250,000 for other taxpayers) and who meet the requirements for rolling over the gain under pre-'97 Act Code Sec. 1034. Since no dollar limitations applied to the pre-'97 Act rollover rules, the taxpayer could then rollover his entire gain. In deciding whether to make this election, the taxpayer should also consider the effect of the basis reduction rules that applied to pre-'97 Act rollovers and the need to buy a new residence at a substantial cost.

The binding contract election does not apply to any sale or exchange by an individual if the treatment provided by Code Sec. 877(a)(1) (rules related to expatriation to avoid tax, see FTC 2d/FIN ¶ O-11701; USTR ¶ 8774; TaxDesk ¶ 64,470) applies to

FTC 2d References are to Federal Tax Coordinator 2d
FIN References are to RIA's Analysis of Federal Taxes: Income
USTR References are to United States Tax Reporter: Income, Estate & Gift, and Excise
PCA References are to Pension Coordinator and Pension & Benefits Expert/Advisor
PE References are to Pension and Profit Sharing 2nd
EP References are to Estate Planning & Taxation Coordinator and Estate Planning Advisor

that individual. ('97 Act §312(d)(4))

The exclusion is applied without regard to Code Sec. 121(c)(2)(B) (rules requiring that a sale or exchange occur by reason of a change in place of employment, health, or other unforeseen circumstances in order to qualify for the reduced exclusion, see *Sales and exchanges eligible for the reduced exclusion* above) in the case of any sale or exchange of property during the two-year period beginning on Aug. 5, '97 if the taxpayer held the property on Aug. 5, '97 and fails to meet the ownership and use requirements (described in Code Sec. 121(a), see above) with respect to the property. ('97 Act §312(d)(3))

> *observation:* Thus, even if the sale or exchange of a taxpayer's residence doesn't occur by reason of a change in place of employment, health, or other unforeseen circumstances, a taxpayer who held the residence on Aug. 5, '97 can still qualify for the reduced exclusion during the two-year period beginning on Aug. 5, '97.

¶ 103. Exclusion from income for cancellation of student loans expanded to cover cancellation of loans under nongovernment sponsored programs

Code Sec. 108(f), as amended by '97 Act § 225
Generally effective: Aug. 5, '97
Committee Reports, see ¶ 5011

No amount from the discharge (in whole or in part) of certain student loans is included in an individual's gross income, if the discharge is contingent on the individual's working for a certain period of time in certain professions for any of a broad class of employers.

The loan must be made to an individual to assist the individual in attending an educational organization described in Code Sec. 170(b)(1)(A)(ii) (an educational institution that has a regular faculty and curriculum, and a regularly enrolled body of students in attendance where its education activities are regularly carried on). Pre-'97 Act law didn't otherwise limit the use of the loan proceeds; they could be used not only for tuition and required fees, but also to cover room and board expenses. However, there was no specific provision for student loan refinancings.

Under pre-'97 Act law, a loan made by an educational organization qualified only if the organization had originally received the funds from which the loan was made from the U.S., a state, or a tax-exempt public benefit corporation. Loans made with private, nongovernmental funds didn't qualify for the exclusion. (FTC 2d/FIN ¶ J-7508; USTR ¶ 1084.04; TaxDesk ¶ 18,806)

New Law. In order to promote the establishment of programs that encourage students to use their education and training in valuable community service (Com Rept, see ¶ 5011), the '97 Act expands the income exclusion for student loan cancellations by including in the definition of "student loan" any loan made by a Code Sec. 170(b)(1)(A)(ii) educational organization where the funds used to provide the loan didn't come from the government, as long as the loan is made under a program of that educational organization that's designed to encourage the organization's students to serve in occupations with unmet needs or in areas with unmet needs. In addition, the services provided by the students (or former students) must be for or under the direction of a governmental unit or a Code Sec. 501(c)(3) organization that's exempt from tax under Code Sec. 501(a). (Code Sec. 108(f)(2)(D)(ii) as amended by '97 Act §225(a)(1)) Thus, the student's work must fulfill a public service requirement. (Com Rept, see ¶ 5011)

As with student loans made with government funds (including loans made by Code Sec. 170(b)(1)(A)(ii) educational organizations with government funds), a student loan made by a tax-exempt educational institution out of nongovernment funds qualifies for the income exclusion only if the discharge is contingent on the student's working for a certain period of time in certain professions for any of a broad class of employers. (Com Rept, see ¶ 5011)

The Act also expands the definition of "student loan" to include any loan made by a Code Sec. 170(b)(1)(A)(ii) educational organization or by an organization exempt from tax under Code Sec. 501(a) to refinance a loan that met the requirements for exclusion from income. (Code Sec. 108(f)(2)) Thus, an individual's gross income doesn't include the forgiveness of a loan made by a tax-exempt charitable organization (e.g., educational organizations or private foundations), where the proceeds of the loan are used to refinance an outstanding student loan. (Com Rept, see ¶ 5011)

However, the income exclusion doesn't apply to the discharge of a loan made by a tax-exempt educational institution described in Code Sec. 108(f)(2)(D) (i.e., a Code Sec. 170(b)(1)(A)(ii) educational organization), or by an organization described in Code Sec. 108(f)(2)(E) from funds provided by a tax-exempt educational organization, if the discharge is on account of services performed for either organization. (Code Sec. 108(f)(3) as amended by '97 Act §225(a)(2)) That is, the student can't be employed by the lender organization. (Com Rept, see ¶ 5011)

observation: Code Sec. 108(f)(3) refers to organizations described in Code Sec. 108(f)(2)(D) and Code Sec. 108(f)(2)(E) (which doesn't exist). Presumably, based on the Committee Reports, the reference should be to Code Sec. 108(f)(2)(D) and the flush language of Code Sec. 108(f)(2) (which, as discussed above, refers to an organization exempt from tax under Code Sec. 501(a)).

☐ **Effective:** Discharges of indebtedness after Aug. 5, '97. ('97 Act §225(b))

¶ 104. Tax exemption for annuities paid to survivors of public safety officers killed in the line of duty

Code Sec. 101(h), as amended by '97 Act § 1528(a)
Generally effective: Amounts received in tax years beginning after Dec. 31, '96,
  with respect to officers dying after that date
Committee Reports, see ¶ 5350

Under pre-'97 Act law, survivor annuity benefits paid under a governmental retirement plan to a survivor of a law enforcement officer killed in the line of duty were generally includible in income. However, amounts contributed to the plan by the officer and previously included in the officer's income weren't includible in the survivor's income. (Com Rept, see ¶ 5350) (FTC 2d/FIN ¶ J-5000 *et seq.*; USTR ¶ 724 *et seq.*; TaxDesk ¶ 14,650 *et seq.*)

New Law. The '97 Act excludes from gross income (except as provided below) any amount paid as a survivor annuity on account of the death of a public safety officer (defined below) killed in the line of duty (Code Sec. 101(h)(1) as amended by '97 Act §1528(a)):

. . . if the annuity is provided under a governmental plan which meets the requirements of Code Sec. 401(a), to the spouse (or a former spouse) of the public safety officer or to a child of that officer (Code Sec. 101(h)(1)(A)); and

. . . to the extent the annuity is attributable to the officer's service as a public safety officer. (Code Sec. 101(h)(1)(B))

The Code Sec. 101(h)(1) exclusion described above doesn't apply with respect to the death of any public safety officer if, as determined under the provisions of the Omnibus Crime Control and Safe Streets Act of '68 (Code Sec. 101(h)(2)):

. . . the death was caused by the intentional misconduct of the officer (Code Sec. 101(h)(2)(A));

. . . the death was caused by the officer's intention to bring about the officer's death (Code Sec. 101(h)(2)(A));;

. . . the officer was voluntarily intoxicated (as defined in Sec. 1204 of the Omnibus Crime Control and Safe Streets Act of '68) at the time of death (Code Sec. 101(h)(2)(B)); or

. . . the officer was performing his or her duties in a grossly negligent manner at the time of death. (Code Sec. 101(h)(2)(C))

In addition, the Code Sec. 101(h)(1) exclusion described above doesn't apply to any payment to an individual whose actions were a substantial contributing factor to the death of the officer. (Code Sec. 101(h)(2)(D))

The determination as to whether any of the circumstances listed by Code Sec. 101(h)(2) (above) apply with respect to the death of a public safety officer is to be made by the appropriate supervising authority. (Com Rept, see ¶ 5350)

For purposes of the above rules, "public safety officer" has the definition given by Sec. 1204 of the Omnibus Crime Control and Safe Streets Act of '68. (Code Sec. 101(h)(1)) Public safety officers include law enforcement officers, firefighters, rescue squad workers and ambulance crew members. (Com Rept, see ¶ 5350)

> **◆/ observation:** Under Sec. 1204 of the Omnibus Crime Control and Safe Streets Act of '68 (42 USC 3796b), a law enforcement officer is an individual involved in crime and juvenile delinquency control or reduction, or enforcement of the law, including, but not limited to, police, corrections, probation, parole, and judicial officers.

☐ **Effective:** Amounts received in tax years beginning after Dec. 31, '96, with respect to individuals dying after that date. ('97 Act §1528(b))

> **◆/ recommendation:** Since the exclusion applies retroactively with respect to individuals dying after '96, any beneficiary who is receiving annuity payments that now qualify for exclusion and from which income tax is being withheld, should notify the payor to end the withholding.

¶ 105. Rural mail carriers can exclude full equipment maintenance allowance; 150% standard mileage rate deduction repealed

Code Sec. 162(o), as amended by '97 Act § 1203(a)
Generally effective: For tax years beginning after Dec. 31, '97
Committee Reports, see ¶ 5203

Rural letter carriers are paid an equipment maintenance allowance (EMA) to compensate them for the use of their personal automobiles in delivering the mail. Under pre-'97 Act law, the carrier's tax treatment of the EMA depended on the automobile expense deduction that he was allowed to claim. A mail carrier could deduct either his actual expenses or 150% of the standard mileage rate (47.25¢ per mile for '97). If the EMA exceeded the carrier's allowable automobile expense deductions, the excess generally was subject to tax. If the EMA was less than those allowable expenses, a deduction was allowed for the automobile expense, but only to the extent the sum of this shortfall and all other miscellaneous itemized deductions exceeded 2% of his adjusted gross income (AGI). (Com Rept, see ¶ 5203) (FTC 2d/FIN ¶ L-1911, ¶ A-2604; USTR ¶ 2744.17, ¶ 624.02; TaxDesk ¶ 29,317, ¶ 56,101)

New Law. A United States Postal Service employee who receives "qualified reimbursements" (defined below) for the expenses the employee incurs for the use of a vehicle in performing services involving the collection and delivery of mail on a rural route, gets a deduction for the use of the vehicle in performing those services equal to

---

FTC 2d References are to Federal Tax Coordinator 2d
FIN References are to RIA's Analysis of Federal Taxes: Income
USTR References are to United States Tax Reporter: Income, Estate & Gift, and Excise
PCA References are to Pension Coordinator and Pension & Benefits Expert/Advisor
PE References are to Pension and Profit Sharing 2nd
EP References are to Estate Planning & Taxation Coordinator and Estate Planning Advisor

the amount of the qualified reimbursements. (Code Sec. 162(o)(1)(A) as amended by '97 Act §1203(a)) Thus, the '97 Act provides that the rate of reimbursement provided by the U.S. Postal Service to rural letter carriers is considered to be equivalent to their expenses. (Com Rept, see ¶ 5203) And for purposes of the Code Sec. 62(a)(2)(A) rules (which treat a deduction for expenses reimbursed under a reimbursement or other expense allowance arrangement—i.e., under an "accountable plan"—as a deduction from gross income), the qualified reimbursements are treated as paid under a reimbursement or other expense allowance arrangement, except that Code Sec. 62(c) (which requires the employee to substantiate the expenses covered by the arrangement and prohibits the employee from retaining any amount in excess of the substantiated expenses) doesn't apply to the qualified reimbursements. (Code Sec. 162(o)(1)(A)) Thus, since the income and expenses wash, rural mail carriers don't have to report either on their tax returns. (Com Rept, see ¶ 5203)

observation: Although the Code Sec. 62(a)(2)(A) accountable plan rules speak of a deduction from gross income, there's no "deduction" in the normal sense. Instead, the employee excludes the reimbursed expenses and takes no deduction—there's simply a wash. But since the "deduction" is from gross income, the employee doesn't have to itemize, and the 2%-of-AGI floor doesn't apply.

The term "qualified reimbursement" means the amount paid by the U.S. Postal Service to employees as an EMA under its '91 collective bargaining agreement with the National Rural Letter Carriers' Association. Amounts paid under later collective bargaining agreements that supersede the '91 one will "qualify" if they don't exceed the amounts that would have been paid under the '91 agreement, as adjusted for inflation under the Consumer Price Index since '91. (Code Sec. 162(o)(2))

The '97 Act also repeals the pre-'97 Act 150% standard mileage rate deduction for U.S. Postal Service employees. ('88 Act § 6008 repealed by '97 Act § 1203(b))

☐ **Effective:** Tax years beginning after Dec. 31, '97. ('97 Act §1203(c))

Nonbusiness Deductions and Credits

¶ 106. Standard mileage rate for computing charitable deduction for use of a car is increased from 12¢ to 14¢ per mile

Code Sec. 170(i), as amended by '97 Act § 973(a)
Generally effective: Tax years beginning after Dec. 31, '97
Committee Reports, see ¶ 5096

For purposes of computing the charitable deduction for the use of a passenger automobile, the standard mileage rate under pre-'97 Act law was 12¢ per mile. (FTC 2d/FIN ¶ K-3629; USTR ¶ 1704.37; TaxDesk ¶ 33,272)

New Law. The '97 Act increases the standard mileage rate for computing the charitable deduction for the use of a passenger automobile to 14¢ per mile. (Code

Sec. 170(i) as amended by '97 Act §973(a))

The 14¢-per-mile rate isn't indexed for inflation. (Com Rept, see ¶ 5096)

> *◆observation:* Since there's no indexing, the 14¢ rate won't increase unless and until changed by future legislation.

☐ **Effective:** Tax years beginning after Dec. 31, '97. ('97 Act §973(b))

¶ 107. Full deduction for contributions of qualified appreciated stock to private foundations restored for period June 1, '97 to June 30, '98

Code Sec. 170(e)(5)(D)(ii), as amended by '97 Act § 602(a)
Generally effective: Contributions made after May 31, '97
Committee Reports, see ¶ 5037

The deduction for charitable contributions of appreciated property to a private foundation is generally limited to the adjusted basis of the property, rather than the full fair market value of the property. An exception, allowing a deduction equal to the full fair market value, was provided for contributions of qualified appreciated stock (stock which is traded on an established securities market) to private foundations. This exception did not apply to contributions made after May 31, '97 (as well as to contributions made after Dec. 31, '94 and before July 1, '96). Contributions of qualified appreciated stock which are carried over (because of the annual percentage limitation on contributions) from years in which the exception did apply to years in which the exception doesn't apply, qualify for the exception in the carryover year. ((FTC 2d/FIN ¶ K-3176; USTR ¶ 1704.42; TaxDesk ¶ 33,176))

New Law. The '97 Act extends the termination date for the exception allowing a full fair market value deduction for contributions of qualified appreciated stock to private foundations from May 31, '97 to June 30, '98 (Code Sec. 175(e)(5)(D)(ii) as amended by '97 Act §602(a)) for contributions made after May 31, '97. ('97 Act §602(b)) Thus, the Act extends the exception for contributions of qualified appreciated stock to private foundations during the period June 1, '97 through June 30, '98. (Com Rept, see ¶ 5037)

> *◆observation:* Thus, taxpayers who didn't make contributions of qualified appreciated stock by May 31, '97, or who did but want to make additional contributions this year, have until Dec. 31 to make '97 contributions that will be fully deductible; for '98, taxpayer will have only the six months until June 30 to make such contributions.

FTC 2d References are to Federal Tax Coordinator 2d
FIN References are to RIA's Analysis of Federal Taxes: Income
USTR References are to United States Tax Reporter: Income, Estate & Gift, and Excise
PCA References are to Pension Coordinator and Pension & Benefits Expert/Advisor
PE References are to Pension and Profit Sharing 2nd
EP References are to Estate Planning & Taxation Coordinator and Estate Planning Advisor

action alert: Taxpayers who want to get a deduction for the full fair market value of qualified appreciated stock contributed to a private foundation must have the foundation in existence and make the contribution by June 30, '98.

observation: Neither the Act nor the committee report says whether contributions that are made from June 1, '97 through June 30, '98, but that are carried over to later years will still qualify for the full deduction in the carryover years. Presumably the rule under prior law that permits a full deduction in the carryover years (see above) will also apply to contributions made in and carried over from the June 1, '97 through June 30, '98 periods.

☐ **Effective:** For contributions made after May 31, '97 ('97 Act §602(b)) through June 30, '98. (Com Rept, see ¶ 5037)

observation: Taxpayers who contributed qualified appreciated stock after May 31, '97 but before the Act became law will get a deduction in '97 for the full fair market value of the stock.

¶ 108. No earned income credit allowed for ten years for taxpayers who fraudulently claimed credit (two years for taxpayers who recklessly claimed credit)

Code Sec. 32(k), as amended by '97 Act § 1085(a)(1)
Code Sec. 6213(g)(2)(J), as amended by '97 Act § 1085(a)(3)
Generally effective: Tax years beginning after Dec. 31 '96
Committee Reports, see ¶ 5162

An individual must meet certain specified requirements to be eligible to claim the earned income credit (see FTC 2d/FIN ¶ A-4206; USTR ¶ 324.02; TaxDesk ¶ 56,911). Where a taxpayer claims the earned income credit improperly, the taxpayer can become subject to the accuracy-related penalty or the fraud penalty, but under pre-'97 Act law there was no specific rule preventing the taxpayer from claiming the earned income credit in future years. (FTC 2d/FIN ¶ V-2000; USTR ¶ 66,624; TaxDesk ¶ 86,300)

In addition, if the individual who claims the earned income credit fails to provide a correct taxpayer identification number (TIN) or, if the credit is claimed with respect to net earnings from self-employment, fails to pay the proper amount of self-employment tax, the failure is treated as a mathematical or clerical error. (FTC 2d/FIN ¶ T-3628; USTR ¶ 62,134.02; TaxDesk ¶ 83,616) This means that IRS may summarily assess any additional tax due as a result of the error (i.e., because the credit is denied) without sending the taxpayer a notice of deficiency (90-day letter) and giving him an opportunity to contest the denial in Tax Court. (FTC 2d/FIN ¶ T-3622; USTR ¶ 62,134.02; TaxDesk ¶ 83,615)

New Law. The '97 Act imposes restrictions on the availability of the earned income credit for taxpayers who improperly claimed the credit in earlier years. (Com

Rept, see ¶ 5162)

Denial of earned income credit for earlier acts of fraud or recklessness. A taxpayer may not claim an earned income credit for any tax year during the "disallowance period" (defined below). (Code Sec. 32(k)(1)(A) as amended by '97 Act §1085(a)(1))

Where there is a final determination that a taxpayer's claim of an earned income credit was due to fraud, the disallowance period is the period of ten tax years after the most recent tax year for which the final determination was made. (Code Sec. 32(k)(1)(B)(i))

Where there is a final determination that a taxpayer's claim of an earned income credit was due to reckless or intentional disregard of rules and regulations (but not fraud), the disallowance period is the period of two tax years after the most recent tax year for which the final determination was made. (Code Sec. 32(k)(1)(B)(ii))

> ✪ *observation:* The disallowance period begins in the year after the year in which the credit was claimed improperly, even if the final determination is not made until a later year.

> ✪ *illustration (1):* B claimed the earned income credit for each of Years 1 to 5. During Year 5, a court makes a final determination that B's claiming the credit for Years 1 and 2 was due to a reckless or intentional disregard of rules and regulations. B's credit for Years 3 and Year 4 is disallowed retroactively.

The denial of the credit is in addition to any other applicable penalties. (Com Rept, see ¶ 5162)

> ✪ *observation:* A taxpayer who thus is denied the earned income credit may also be subject to the accuracy-related penalty or the fraud penalty.

The determination of fraud or of reckless or intentional disregard of rules or regulations is made in a deficiency proceeding which provides for judicial review. (Com Rept, see ¶ 5162)

Recertification of eligibility for earned income credit where credit was denied in an earlier year. In the case of an taxpayer who is denied an earned income credit for any tax year as a result of the deficiency procedures under the Code, no earned income credit is allowed for any later tax year unless the taxpayer provides information required by IRS to demonstrate eligibility for the credit. (Code Sec. 32(k)(2)) The taxpayer must demonstrate that he is eligible to claim the credit for the later year, by meeting evidentiary requirements established by IRS. (Com Rept, see ¶ 5162)

FTC 2d References are to Federal Tax Coordinator 2d
FIN References are to RIA's Analysis of Federal Taxes: Income
USTR References are to United States Tax Reporter: Income, Estate & Gift, and Excise
PCA References are to Pension Coordinator and Pension & Benefits Expert/Advisor
PE References are to Pension and Profit Sharing 2nd
EP References are to Estate Planning & Taxation Coordinator and Estate Planning Advisor

Congress believes that requiring additional information to determine that a taxpayer is eligible for the earned income credit claimed for a year is prudent for taxpayers who incorrectly claimed the credit in earlier years. (Com Rept, see ¶ 5162)

> *illustration (2):* Same facts as illustration (1). B must provide the information required by IRS in order to claim the credit for Year 5.

If a taxpayer is thus recertified as eligible for the credit, the taxpayer is not required to provide the information in later years unless IRS again denies the earned income credit as a result of a deficiency procedure. (Com Rept, see ¶ 5162)

> *illustration (3):* Same facts as illustration (2). B provides the required information for Year 5, and so is eligible to claim the credit for that year. Assuming B's credit is not again denied as a result of a deficiency proceeding, B does not have to provide the information to claim the credit for later years.

Failure to provide the required information when claiming the earned income credit for the later year is treated as a mathematical or clerical error. (Code Sec. 6213(g)(2)(J) as amended by '97 Act §1085(a)(3))

> *observation:* This means that where the taxpayer doesn't provide the information, IRS can deny the credit without going through the normal deficiency procedures.

Ineligibility for the earned income credit for failure to meet these evidentiary requirements is subject to review by the courts. (Com Rept, see ¶ 5162)

☐ **Effective:** Tax years beginning after Dec. 31, '96. ('97 Act §1085(e)(1))

¶ 109. Definition of AGI for phasing out the earned income credit is modified by increasing the percentage of certain losses disregarded from 50% to 75%, and adding tax-exempt interest and nontaxable pension and annuity distributions

Code Sec. 32(c)(5)(B)(iv), as amended by '97 Act § 1085(b)
Code Sec. 32(c)(5)(B)(v), as amended by '97 Act § 1085(d)(3)
Code Sec. 32(c)(5)(B)(vi), as amended by '97 Act § 1085(d)(3)
Code Sec. 32(c)(5)(B), as amended by '97 Act § 1085(d)(4)
Generally effective: Tax years beginning after Dec. 31, '97
Committee Reports, see ¶ 5162

The earned income credit is reduced, or eliminated, under a phaseout rule that is based, in part, on the individual's modified adjusted gross income (modified AGI). For individuals with earned income (or AGI, if greater) in excess of the beginning of a phase-out range, the credit is reduced by a phase-out rate multiplied by the amount of that excess. The definition of AGI used for the phase-out disregards certain losses, including: (1) net capital losses (if greater than zero), (2) net losses from trusts and estates, and (3) net losses from nonbusiness rents and royalties. Under pre-'97 Act law, 50% of the net losses from business, computed separately with respect to sole proprietorships (other than in farming), sole proprietorships in farming, and other businesses was also disregarded. The list of items disregarded did not include tax-exempt interest, or nontaxable pension or annuity distributions. (FTC 2d/FIN ¶ A-4203; USTR ¶ 324.01; TaxDesk ¶ 56,904)

New Law. The amount of net losses from carrying on trades or businesses, as separately computed with respect to sole proprietorships (other than in farming), sole proprietorships in farming, and other businesses, that is disregarded in determining modified AGI is increased from 50% to 75%. (Code Sec. 32(c)(5)(B)(iv) as amended by '97 Act §1085(b))

The '97 Act also expands the list of items that are disregarded in determining modified AGI to include:

(1) interest received or accrued during the tax year which is exempt from federal income tax (Code Sec. 32(c)(5)(B)(v) as amended by '97 Act §1085(d)(3)), and

(2) amounts received as a pension or annuity, and any distributions or payments received from an individual retirement plan, by the taxpayer during the tax year to the extent not included in gross income. (Code Sec. 32(c)(5)(B)(vi))

The pension, etc., amounts described in (2), above, don't include any amount which is not includible in gross income by reason of Code Sec. 402(c) (relating to tax-free rollovers from qualified employee plans), Code Sec. 403(a)(4) (relating to tax-free rollovers from qualified employee annuity plans), Code Sec. 403(b) (relating to tax-sheltered annuities for employees of exempt Code Sec. 501(c)(3) organizations and public schools), Code Sec. 408(d)(3), (4) or (5) (relating to rollovers and distributions from individual retirement accounts, or Code Sec. 457(e)(10) (relating to tax-free transfers between eligible deferred compensation plans of state and local governments and tax-exempt organizations). (Code Sec. 32(c)(5)(B))

Thus, the definition of modified AGI used in determining the earned income credit phase-out is modified by adding two items of nontaxable income: (1) tax-exempt interest and (2) nontaxable distributions from pensions, annuities, and individual retirement arrangements (but only if not rolled over into similar vehicles during the applicable rollover period). (Com Rept, see ¶ 5162)

observation: Although '97 Act § 1085(d) adds the tax-exempt interest and nontaxable pension and annuity distributions to the Code Sec. 32(c)(5)(B) list of items that are disregarded in determining modified AGI, it appears that Congress intended the opposite—i.e., to *include* those nontaxable income items (which aren't included in AGI) in modified AGI. The title of that Act subsection ("Certain Nontaxable Income Included in Modified Adjusted Gross

---

FTC 2d References are to Federal Tax Coordinator 2d
FIN References are to RIA's Analysis of Federal Taxes: Income
USTR References are to United States Tax Reporter: Income, Estate & Gift, and Excise
PCA References are to Pension Coordinator and Pension & Benefits Expert/Advisor
PE References are to Pension and Profit Sharing 2nd
EP References are to Estate Planning & Taxation Coordinator and Estate Planning Advisor

Income") supports this. Also, the Committee Reports refer to the two nontaxable income items as items "added" to modified AGI. The only change Congress intended for the disregarded items was to increase the percentage with respect to the disregarded losses. Also, the definition of modified AGI for other Code purposes (e.g., Code Sec. 86, relating to the taxation of Social Security benefits) specifically provide for the inclusion of nontaxable items such as tax-exempt interest.

☐ **Effective:** Tax years beginning after Dec. 31, '97. ('97 Act §1085(e)(2))

¶ 110. Workfare payments not included in earned income for earned income credit purposes

Code Sec. 32(c)(2)(B)(v), as amended by '97 Act § 1085(c)
Generally effective: Tax years beginning after Dec. 31, '97
Committee Reports, see ¶ 5162

An individual's earned income credit is generally determined by multiplying the credit rate (which depends on whether the individual has one, more than one, or no qualifying children) by the individual's earned income. For individuals with earned income (or modified adjusted gross income (modified AGI), if greater) in excess of a phase-out amount, the credit is reduced by a phase-out rate multiplied by the amount of that excess. For these purposes, both earned income and modified AGI are defined to include wages. (FTC 2d/FIN ¶ A-4216; USTR ¶ 324.05; TaxDesk ¶ 56,908)

Under the Personal Responsibility and Work Opportunity Act of '96, the receipt of certain government assistance payments is denied unless the recipient meets certain work requirements. Pre-'97 Act law did not specify the tax treatment for these "workfare payments." There was no explicit provision as to whether workfare payments were wages for purposes of the earned income credit. (Com Rept, see ¶ 5162)

New Law. For purposes of the earned income credit, earned income does not include any amount received for service performed in work activities as defined in paragraph (4) or (7) of Sec. 407(d) of the Social Security Act to which the taxpayer is assigned under any state program under Part A of Title IV of that Act, but only to the extent the amount is subsidized under the state program. (Code Sec. 32(c)(2)(B)(v) as amended by '97 Act §1085(c))

This means that workfare payments are not wages for purposes of the earned income credit. (Com Rept, see ¶ 5162)

There is no inference intended with respect to whether workfare payments otherwise qualify as wages for purposes of income and employment taxes, or for purposes of an employer's eligibility for the work opportunity tax credit and the welfare-to-work tax credit. (Com Rept, see ¶ 5162)

☐ **Effective:** Tax years beginning after Dec. 31, '97. ('97 Act §1085(e)(2)) The Committee reports provide that the provision is effective on Aug. 5, '97, and that no inference is intended with respect to whether workfare payments are wages for purposes of the earned income credit before Aug. 5, '97. (Com Rept, see ¶ 5162) *observation:* Presumably, Congress intends the "no inference" language to apply with respect to workfare payments in tax years beginning before Jan. 1, '98, since the statute provides that the provision is effective for tax years beginning after '97.

¶ 111. IRS authorized to permit appraisals used to get federal disaster relief to also be used to establish amount of disaster loss

Code Sec. 165(i)(4), as amended by '97 Act § 912(a)
Generally effective: Aug. 5, '97
Committee Reports, see ¶ 5062

A taxpayer who suffers a loss from a Presidentially-declared disaster can take the deduction in the tax year the disaster occurs or the immediately preceding year. In order to claim a deduction for a disaster loss, the taxpayer must (as with losses in general) establish the amount of the loss. The amount of the loss may be determined through the use of an appraisal. (FTC 2d/FIN ¶ M-2000 *et seq.*; USTR ¶ 1654.520; TaxDesk ¶ 36,910)

New Law. The '97 Act provides for the use of alternate types of acceptable appraisals that may be used to establish the amount of a disaster loss. (Com Rept, see ¶ 5062) Under the Act, nothing in the Code should be construed as prohibiting IRS from prescribing regulations or other guidelines under which an appraisal that's made for the purpose of getting a loan of federal funds or a loan guarantee from the federal government as a result of a Presidentially-declared disaster (as defined in Code Sec. 1033(h)(3)) could be used to establish the amount of any disaster loss. (Code Sec. 165(i)(4) as amended by '97 Act §912(a)) In other words, IRS can issue guidance that would permit taxpayers to use an appraisal made for the purpose of getting a federal loan or federal loan guarantee as a result of a Presidentially-declared disaster, to establish the amount deductible as a disaster loss. (Com Rept, see ¶ 5062)

☐ **Effective:** Aug. 5, '97 ('97 Act §912(b))

observation: Although the change made by the Act is effective Aug. 5, '97, taxpayers must wait for IRS to prescribe the regs or other guidelines to determine exactly how to take advantage of the alternative appraisals.

FTC 2d References are to Federal Tax Coordinator 2d
FIN References are to RIA's Analysis of Federal Taxes: Income
USTR References are to United States Tax Reporter: Income, Estate & Gift, and Excise
PCA References are to Pension Coordinator and Pension & Benefits Expert/Advisor
PE References are to Pension and Profit Sharing 2nd
EP References are to Estate Planning & Taxation Coordinator and Estate Planning Advisor

¶ 112. Adoption expense credit allowed for expenses paid after the year adoption becomes final and conformed to exclusion for employer adoption assistance payments

Code Sec. 23(a)(2), as amended by '97 Act § 1601(h)(2)(A)
Code Sec. 23(b)(2)(B), as amended by '97 Act § 1601(h)(2)(B)
Code Sec. 137(b)(1), as amended by '97 Act § 1601(h)(2)(C)
Code Sec. 414(n)(3)(C), as amended by '97 Act § 1601(h)(2)(D)(i)
Code Sec. 414(t)(2), as amended by '97 Act § 1601(h)(2)(D)(ii)
Code Sec. 6039D(d)(1), as amended by '97 Act § 1601(h)(2)(D)(iii)
Generally effective: Tax years beginning after Dec. 31, '96
Committee Reports, see ¶ 5368, 5369

Taxpayers are allowed an income tax credit for qualified adoption expenses paid or incurred by the taxpayer. Taxpayers are also allowed an exclusion from gross income for amounts paid or expenses incurred by an employer for qualified adoption expenses under an adoption assistance program. Qualified adoption expenses are reasonable and necessary adoption fees, court costs, attorneys' fees, and other expenses that are directly related to the legal adoption of an eligible child.

Year of credit. The credit for qualified adoption expenses paid or incurred in one tax year is allowed in the next tax year, unless the expenses are paid or incurred in the tax year the adoption becomes final. The credit for expenses paid or incurred in the tax year in which the adoption becomes final is allowed for that year. Under pre-'97 Act law, it wasn't clear when the credit was allowed for qualified adoption expenses paid or incurred in a tax year after the tax year in which the adoption becomes final.

Limitations on credit and exclusion. Both the credit for qualified adoption expenses and the exclusion for qualified adoption expenses are subject to a dollar limitation and an income limitation.

Under the *dollar limitation,* the total amount of qualified adoption expenses that may be taken into account for purposes of the credit is $5,000 ($6,000 in the case of certain children with special needs). Under pre-'97 Act law, the total amount excludable from gross income for qualified adoption expenses was limited to $5,000 ($6,000 in the case of certain children with special needs).

Under the *income limitation,* both the credit for qualified adoption expenses and the exclusion for qualified adoption expenses are generally phased out ratably for taxpayers with modified adjusted gross income (AGI) above $75,000, and are fully phased out at $115,000 of modified AGI.

Modified AGI for purposes of the exclusion of qualified adoption expenses is computed without applying Code Sec. 137 (the exclusion for qualified adoption expenses).

Under pre-'97 Act law, however, modified AGI for purposes of the credit for qualified adoption expenses was determined *after* applying Code Sec. 137 (the exclusion for qualified adoption expenses). (FTC 2d/FIN ¶ A-4401.1, ¶ A-4402, ¶ H-1451; USTR ¶ 1374; TaxDesk ¶ 13,369.2 *et seq.,* ¶ 56,959.1 *et seq.*)

New Law. The '97 Act makes it clear when the credit is allowed for qualified adoption expenses paid or incurred in a tax year after the tax year in which the adoption becomes final. The Act also conforms the income limitation for the credit to the income limitation for the exclusion, and makes certain other changes.

Credit for qualified adoption expenses. The treatment of otherwise qualified adoption expenses paid or incurred in years after the year the adoption becomes final is conformed to the treatment of expenses paid or incurred in the year the adoption becomes final. (Com Rept, see ¶ 5368) Thus, in the case of an expense paid or incurred during or after the tax year in which the adoption becomes final, the credit is allowed for the tax year in which the expense is paid or incurred. (Code Sec. 23(a)(2)(B) as amended by '97 Act §1601(h)(2)(A))

The definition of modified AGI for purposes of the income limitation of the credit is conformed to the definition of modified AGI for purposes of the income limitation of the exclusion by repealing an ordering rule inadvertently included in the credit (Com Rept, see ¶ 5368) that required modified AGI to be determined after applying Code Sec. 86, Code Sec. 135, Code Sec. 137, Code Sec. 219, and Code Sec. 469. (Code Sec. 23(b)(2)(B))

> *observation:* Thus, modified AGI for purposes of the income limitation of the credit is determined without applying Code Sec. 137 (the exclusion for qualified adoption expenses).

Exclusion of qualified adoption expenses from gross income. Instead of applying the dollar limitation to the total amount excludable from gross income, the '97 Act applies the dollar limitation to the total of the amounts taken into account. Under the Act, the total of the amounts paid or expenses incurred that may be taken into account for purposes of the exclusion of qualified adoption expenses is limited to $5,000 ($6,000 in the case of certain children with special needs). (Code Sec. 137(b)(1) as amended by '97 Act §1601(h)(2)(C))

> *observation:* This change doesn't appear to affect the actual amount of the exclusion.

"Leased employees" are treated as employees of the service recipient under the leased employee rules of Code Sec. 414(n) (see FTC 2d/FIN ¶ H-5600 *et seq.*; USTR ¶ 4144) for purposes of the exclusion of qualified adoption expenses. (Code Sec. 414(n)(3)(C) as amended by '97 Act §1601(h)(2)(D)(i))

> *observation:* Thus, leased employees qualify for the exclusion from gross income of employer provided adoption assistance payments.

FTC 2d References are to Federal Tax Coordinator 2d
FIN References are to RIA's Analysis of Federal Taxes: Income
USTR References are to United States Tax Reporter: Income, Estate & Gift, and Excise
PCA References are to Pension Coordinator and Pension & Benefits Expert/Advisor
PE References are to Pension and Profit Sharing 2nd
EP References are to Estate Planning & Taxation Coordinator and Estate Planning Advisor

All employees of a controlled group of businesses who are treated as employed by a single employer under Code Sec. 414(b), (c), or (m) (see FTC 2d/FIN ¶ H-7900 *et seq.*; USTR ¶ 4144) are treated as employed by a single employer for purposes of the exclusion of qualified adoption expenses. (Code Sec. 414(t)(2) as amended by '97 Act §1601(h)(2)(D)(ii))

> *observation:* An employee of a controlled group of businesses treated as a single employer because of the above rule would apparently be able to exclude from gross income qualified adoption assistance payments received from any business in the group.

Every employer maintaining a "specified fringe benefit plan" must file an annual information return with respect to the plan (see FTC 2d/FIN ¶ S-3412; USTR ¶ 60,39D4). The '97 Act adds an adoption assistance program to the list of plans included in the definition of a specified fringe benefit plan. Thus, any employer that maintains an adoption assistance program must file an information return with respect to the plan. (Code Sec. 6039(D)(d)(1) as amended by '97 Act §1601(h)(2)(D)(iii))

> *observation:* IRS has excused employers otherwise required to file information returns for certain specified fringe benefit plans from filing until it provides further guidance.

☐ **Effective:** Tax years beginning after Dec. 31, '96. ('97 Act §1601(j)(1))

¶ 113. Limit on basic standard deduction for certain dependents increased from greater of $500 (indexed) or earned income to greater of $500 (indexed) or earned income plus $250 (indexed)

Code Sec. 63(c)(5), as amended by '97 Act § 1201(a)(1)
Code Sec. 63(c)(4), as amended by '97 Act § 1201(a)(2)
Generally effective: Tax years beginning after Dec. 31, '97
Committee Reports, see ¶ 5201

Under pre-'97 Act law, the basic standard deduction for an individual who can be claimed as a dependent by another taxpayer was limited to the greater of $500 (adjusted for inflation) or the individual's earned income (wages and other compensation received for personal services), but not more than the regular basic standard deduction amount (generally $4,150 for '97 in the case of such an individual). The $500 amount is adjusted for inflation using the '87 Consumer Price Index (CPI), and rounding to the next lowest $50. The $500 amount, as adjusted for inflation, is $650 for '97. (FTC 2d/FIN ¶ A-2811, ¶ A-2809; USTR ¶ 634; TaxDesk ¶ 56,208)

New Law. The '97 Act increases the limitation on the basic standard deduction for an individual who can be claimed as a dependent by another taxpayer. Under the '97 Act, the basic standard deduction of such an individual is limited to the greater of $500 (Code Sec. 63(c)(5)(A) as amended by '97 Act §1201(a)(1)), or the sum of $250 and the individual's earned income (Code Sec. 63(c)(5)(B)), but not more than the regular basic standard deduction amount for such an individual. (Com Rept, see ¶ 5201)

As in the case of the $500 amount, the $250 amount is adjusted for inflation by increasing the $250 amount by a cost-of-living adjustment determined under Code Sec. 1(f)(3) (inflation adjustments for tax rate brackets, see FTC 2d/FIN ¶ A-1103; USTR ¶ 14). (Code Sec. 63(c)(4) as amended by '97 Act §1201(a)(2)) The $500 amount is adjusted for inflation as under pre-'97 Act law. (Com Rept, see ¶ 5201) The $250 amount is adjusted for inflation after '98 (Com Rept, see ¶ 5201), using the '97 Consumer Price Index. (Code Sec. 63(c)(4)(B)(ii)) As in the case of the $500 amount, any increase in the $250 amount that is not a multiple of $50 will be rounded to the next lowest $50 under the rule of Code Sec. 1(f)(6)(A), see FTC 2d/FIN ¶ A-2809; USTR ¶ 634.

The $500 amount, as adjusted for inflation, is projected to be $700 for '98, and the regular basic standard deduction is projected to be generally $4,250 for '98 in the case of an individual who can be claimed as a dependent by another taxpayer. (Com Rept, see ¶ 5201)

illustration: The following illustration shows what the basic standard deduction of a child who can be claimed as a dependent would be under pre-'97 Act law (the current rule for '97) and under the '97 Act, assuming the $500 amount will be $700 for '98 and the regular basic standard deduction will be $4,250 for '98. Assume that A is single and can be claimed as a dependent on his parent's tax return. He has interest income of $850 and earned income as indicated below. He has no itemized deductions. His basic standard deduction for the year is shown in the last column below.

'97 Standard Deduction
(reflecting current, pre-'97 Act rule)

(1) $500 amount as indexed	(2) Earned income	(3) Larger of (1) or (2)	(4) Regular basic standard deduction	(5) Smaller of (3) or (4)
$650	$ 0	$ 650	$4,150	$ 650
$650	$ 450	$ 650	$4,150	$ 650
$650	$ 500	$ 650	$4,150	$ 650
$650	$ 750	$ 750	$4,150	$ 750
$650	$4,100	$4,100	$4,150	$4,100

FTC 2d References are to Federal Tax Coordinator 2d
FIN References are to RIA's Analysis of Federal Taxes: Income
USTR References are to United States Tax Reporter: Income, Estate & Gift, and Excise
PCA References are to Pension Coordinator and Pension & Benefits Expert/Advisor
PE References are to Pension and Profit Sharing 2nd
EP References are to Estate Planning & Taxation Coordinator and Estate Planning Advisor

'98 Standard Deduction
(reflecting '97 Act changes)

(1) $500 amount as indexed	(2) Earned income	(3) Earned income plus $250	(4) Larger of (1) or (3)	(5) Regular basic standard deduction	(6) Smaller of (4) or (5)
$700	$ 0	$ 250	$ 700	$4,250	$ 700
$700	$ 450	$ 700	$ 700	$4,250	$ 700
$700	$ 500	$ 750	$ 750	$4,250	$ 750
$700	$ 750	$1,000	$1,000	$4,250	$1,000
$700	$4,100	$4,350	$4,350	$4,250	$4,250

> *observation:* Assuming the $500 limitation amount on the basic standard deduction will be $700 for '98, the increased limitation under the '97 Act doesn't result in a basic standard deduction larger than $700 until the dependent's earned income exceeds $450.

> *observation:* The figures at the bottom of the table for '98 illustrate the situation where the regular basic standard deduction acts as the limit. Although the greater of $700 and A's earned income plus $250 ($4,100 plus $250 equals $4,350) is $4,350, this can't be more than A's regular basic standard deduction for '98 which is projected to be $4,250.

> *observation:* Under the "kiddie tax" rules of Code Sec. 1(g) (see FTC 2d/FIN ¶ A-1300; USTR ¶ 14), the net unearned (investment) income of a child under age 14 may be taxed at the parent's tax rate instead of the child's tax rate. Net unearned income is defined by reference to the $500 amount (as indexed) in the limitation on the basic standard deduction. Since the above change made by the '97 Act doesn't change the $500 part of the basic standard deduction, the change discussed above has no effect on the "kiddie tax" rules.

☐ **Effective:** Tax years beginning after Dec. 31, '97. ('97 Act §1201(c))

Business Deductions

¶ 114. Deduction allowed after '98 where home office is used for administrative or management activities; result in *Soliman* overturned

Code Sec. 280A(c)(1), as amended by '97 Act § 932(a)
Generally effective: Tax years beginning after Dec. 31, '98
Committee Reports, see ¶ 5069

A taxpayer's business use of his or her home may give rise to a deduction for the business portion of expenses related to operating the home (e.g., a portion of rent or depreciation and repairs). Code Sec. 280A(c)(1) provides, however, that business deductions generally are allowed only with respect to a portion of a home that's used exclusively and regularly in one of the following ways:

. . . as the principal place of business for a trade or business;

. . . as a place of business used to meet with patients, clients, or customers in the normal course of the taxpayer's trade or business; or

. . . in connection with the taxpayer's trade or business, if the portion so used is a separate structure not attached to the dwelling unit.

In the case of an employee, the Code further requires that the business use of the home must be for the convenience of the employer.

The Code doesn't define "principal place of business" for purposes of the first rule above.

In *Com. v. Soliman* (1993, S Ct) 71 AFTR 2d 93-463, 506 US 168, 121 L Ed 2d 634, 93-1 USTC ¶ 50014, the Supreme Court disallowed a home office deduction for a self-employed anesthesiologist who practiced at several hospitals but wasn't provided office space at the hospitals. The court held that the two primary considerations in deciding whether a home office is the taxpayer's principal place of business are: (1) the relative importance of the activities performed at each business location; and (2) the time spent at each place. This two-part test superseded a "facts and circumstances" test and a "focal point" test used by the Tax Court and various Courts of Appeals to determine a taxpayer's "principal place of business."

In *Soliman,* although the anesthesiologist used a room in his home exclusively to perform administrative and management activities for his profession (i.e., he spent two or three hours a day in his home office on bookkeeping, correspondence, reading medical journals, and communicating with surgeons, patients, and insurance companies), the Supreme Court held that the "principal place of business" for the taxpayer wasn't the home office, because the taxpayer performed the "essence of the professional service" at the hospitals. Because the taxpayer didn't meet with patients at his home office and the room wasn't a separate structure, a deduction wasn't available under either of the other two provisions of Code Sec. 280A(c)(1) (described above).

> ☙ *observation:* Under *Soliman,* a taxpayer's use of a home office to perform management or administrative functions of his trade or business, where the "essence" of that trade or business must be performed elsewhere, is insufficient to make the home office the "principal place of business," and thus the requirement of Code Sec. 280A(c)(1)(A) wouldn't be met.

(FTC 2d/FIN ¶ L-1300 *et seq.*; USTR ¶ 280A4.014; TaxDesk ¶ 25,809 *et seq.*)

New Law. Congress believes that the Supreme Court's decision in *Soliman* unfairly denies a home office deduction to a growing number of taxpayers who manage

FTC 2d References are to Federal Tax Coordinator 2d
FIN References are to RIA's Analysis of Federal Taxes: Income
USTR References are to United States Tax Reporter: Income, Estate & Gift, and Excise
PCA References are to Pension Coordinator and Pension & Benefits Expert/Advisor
PE References are to Pension and Profit Sharing 2nd
EP References are to Estate Planning & Taxation Coordinator and Estate Planning Advisor

☙ Research Institute of America 31

their business activities from their homes. (Com Rept, see ¶ 5069) Therefore, for tax years beginning after '98, the '97 Act amends Code Sec. 280A(c)(1) to provide that the term "principal place of business" includes a place of business which is used by the taxpayer for the administrative or management activities of any trade or business of the taxpayer if there's no other fixed location of that trade or business where the taxpayer conducts substantial administrative or management activities of that trade or business. (Code Sec. 280A(c)(1) as amended by '97 Act §932(a)) However, deductions will be allowed for a home office meeting this two-part test only if the office is exclusively used on a regular basis as a place of business by the taxpayer and, in the case of an employee, only if that exclusive use is for the convenience of the employer. (Com Rept, see ¶ 5069) The change made by the Act is intended to reduce the pre-Act bias in favor of taxpayers who manage their business activities from outside their home, thereby enabling more taxpayers to work efficiently at home, save commuting time and expenses, and spend additional time with their families. Moreover, the amendment is an appropriate response to the computer and information revolution, which has made it more practical for taxpayers to manage trade or business activities from a home office. (Com Rept, see ¶ 5069)

> *observation:* Under Code Sec. 280A(c)(1), as amended by the '97 Act, the taxpayer in *Soliman* would be entitled to a home office deduction because he used his home office exclusively and regularly for administrative and management activities of his trade or business as an anesthesiologist, and he had no other fixed business location to conduct those activities.

> *observation:* The amendment of Code Sec. 280A(c)(1) doesn't fully "repeal" the Supreme Court's decision in *Soliman*. The amendment only provides that a home office used for administrative and management activities of the taxpayer's trade or business will qualify as a principal place of business if certain requirements are satisfied. It doesn't otherwise displace *Soliman's* two-part test for determining whether a home office is a principal place of business, and it doesn't resurrect either the "facts and circumstances" test or the "focal point" test that were in use before *Soliman*.

A home office deduction is allowed under the Act (subject to the "convenience of the employer" rule governing employees) if a portion of a taxpayer's home is exclusively and regularly used to conduct administrative or management activities for a trade or business of the taxpayer, who doesn't conduct substantial administrative or management activities at any other fixed location of the trade or business, regardless of whether administrative or management activities connected with his trade or business (e.g., billing activities) are performed by others at other locations. The fact that a taxpayer also carries out administrative or management activities at sites that aren't fixed locations of the business, such as a car or hotel room, doesn't affect the taxpayer's ability to claim a home office deduction under the above rules. Moreover, if a taxpayer conducts some administrative or management activities at a fixed location of the business outside the home, the taxpayer would still be eligible to claim a deduction so long as the administrative or management activities conducted at any fixed location of the business outside the home aren't substantial (e.g., the taxpayer occasionally does minimal paperwork at another fixed location of the business). In addition, a taxpayer's eligibility to claim a home office deduction under the above rules isn't affected by the fact that the taxpayer conducts substantial non-administrative or non-management business activities at a fixed location of the business outside the home (e.g., meeting with, or providing services to, customers, clients, or patients at a fixed location of the business away from home). (Com Rept, see ¶ 5069)

If a taxpayer in fact doesn't perform substantial administrative or management activities at any fixed location of the business away from home, then the second part of the test will be satisfied, regardless of whether or not the taxpayer opted not to use an office away from home that was available for the conduct of such activities. (Com Rept, see ¶ 5069)

However, in the case of an employee, the question whether an employee chose not to use suitable space made available by the employer for administrative activities is relevant to determining whether the "convenience of the employer" test is satisfied. (Com Rept, see ¶ 5069)

In cases where a taxpayer's use of a home office doesn't satisfy the two-part test described above, the taxpayer nonetheless may be able to claim a home office deduction if he can otherwise establish that the home office is his "principal place of business" or if he can satisfy any other relevant provision of Code Sec. 280A. (Com Rept, see ¶ 5069)

☐ **Effective:** Tax years beginning after Dec. 31, '98. ('97 Act §932(b))

> *observation:* As a result of this effective date, *Soliman* still controls whether a home office qualifies as a "principal place of business" through the end of '98. However, taxpayers who satisfy the new rules will be entitled to a deduction in '99.

¶ 115. One-year limit on away-from-home travel expenses doesn't apply to certified federal investigators

Code Sec. 162(a), as amended by '97 Act § 1204(a)
Generally effective: For amounts paid or incurred for tax years ending after Aug. 5, '97
Committee Reports, see ¶ 5204

An employee temporarily away from home on business can deduct, subject to the 2% floor on miscellaneous itemized deductions, his unreimbursed travel expenses that are ordinary and necessary. Expenses that can be deducted include 50% of the cost of meals. FTC 2d/FIN ¶ L-1700; USTR ¶ 1624.114; TaxDesk ¶ 29,100 However, an employee can't deduct any of these travel expenses if the away-from-home employment is

FTC 2d References are to Federal Tax Coordinator 2d
FIN References are to RIA's Analysis of Federal Taxes: Income
USTR References are to United States Tax Reporter: Income, Estate & Gift, and Excise
PCA References are to Pension Coordinator and Pension & Benefits Expert/Advisor
PE References are to Pension and Profit Sharing 2nd
EP References are to Estate Planning & Taxation Coordinator and Estate Planning Advisor

Research Institute of America 33

indefinite. If an employee's employment away from home at a single location lasts for more than one year, it's automatically treated as indefinite, rather than temporary. (FTC 2d/FIN ¶ L-1811; USTR ¶ 1624.130; TaxDesk ¶ 29,213)

New Law. The one-year limitation doesn't apply to any federal employee during any period during which the employee is certified by the Attorney General (or the Attorney General's designee) as traveling on behalf of the United States in temporary duty status to investigate, or provide support services for the investigation of, a federal crime. (Code Sec. 162(a) as amended by '97 Act §1204(a))

☝observation: Thus, FBI Agents, and other federal criminal investigators, who are certified by the Attorney General as traveling in temporary duty status, are covered by this provision.

Expenses for these individuals during these periods are fully deductible, regardless of the length of the period for which certification is given (if the other requirements for deductibility are satisfied). (Com Rept, see ¶ 5204)

☝illustration: Taxpayer A and B are both CPAs who reside in Washington, D.C. Taxpayer A is employed by a multinational corporation with its home office in Seattle. B is employed as a criminal investigator by the federal government. In the course of an extended criminal investigation of A's employer, B is certified by the Attorney General's designee as traveling on behalf of the federal government on a temporary duty status and is assigned to the government office in Seattle. A also travels to Seattle to advise his employer about accounting matters related to the ongoing investigation. While it was anticipated that the investigation of the records of B's employer would last only six months, in fact both A and B remain in Seattle for 13 months until the investigation is concluded. As a result, because of the one-year bar, A is unable to deduct his away-from-home expenses. B is unaffected by the one-year bar and can deduct, subject to the 2% floor on miscellaneous itemized deductions, his unreimbursed travel expenses that are ordinary and necessary.

☐ **Effective:** For amounts paid or incurred with respect to tax years ending after Aug. 5, '97. ('97 Act §1204(b))

☝observation: Thus, presumably amounts paid or incurred before Aug. 5, '97 but "with respect to" the tax year ending after Aug. 5, '97, i.e., calendar '97, are deductible by a certified federal investigator for '97.

¶ 116. Above-the-line (and therefore an AMT) deduction for business expenses of state and local government officials who are compensated on a fee basis

Code Sec. 62(a)(2)(C), as amended by '97 Act § 975(a)

Generally effective: Expenses paid or incurred in tax years beginning after Dec. 31, '86

Committee Reports, see ¶ 5098

Employee business expenses are generally deductible, but only as miscellaneous itemized deductions subject to a 2%-of-AGI "floor." Because miscellaneous itemized deductions aren't allowable in computing a taxpayer's alternative minimum tax (AMT) liability, employee business expenses aren't deductible for AMT purposes. However, deductions that are allowed in arriving at adjusted gross income (AGI) under Code Sec. 62(a) aren't miscellaneous itemized deductions, and are deductible in computing AMT liability. (FTC 2d/FIN ¶ A-2600 *et seq.*, ¶ A-2700 *et seq.*, ¶ A-2707 *et seq.*, ¶ A-8310, ¶ L-3900 *et seq.*, ¶ L-4700 *et seq.*; USTR ¶ 564.02, ¶ 624 *et seq.*, ¶ 634, ¶ 674 *et seq.*, ¶ 1624.067; TaxDesk ¶ 25,664 *et seq.*, ¶ 35,150 *et seq.*, ¶ 56,070 *et seq.*, ¶ 56,120 *et seq.*, ¶ 56,160 *et seq.*, ¶ 69,712)

New Law. Retroactive to tax years beginning after '86, the '97 Act adds to the list of deductions allowed in arriving at adjusted gross income under Code Sec. 62(a) the following: the deductions allowed by Code Sec. 162 which consist of expenses paid or incurred with respect to services performed by an official as an employee of a state or a political subdivision of a state in a position compensated in whole or in part on a fee basis. (Code Sec. 62(a)(2)(C) as amended by '97 Act §975(a))

Under this provision, employee business expenses relating to service as an official of a state or local government (or a political subdivision of a state or local government) are deductible in computing AGI ("above the line"), if the official is compensated in whole or in part on a fee basis. The officials intended to be covered by this provision are those who provide certain services to the government, and who hire employees and incur expenses in connection with their official duties. (Com Rept, see ¶ 5098)

The expenses covered by Code Sec. 62(a)(2)(C) are also deductible for AMT purposes. (Com Rept, see ¶ 5098)

> *observation:* Under the '97 Act, the deductions affected by Code Sec. 62(a)(2)(C) are deductible for AMT purposes because they are, under Code Sec. 62(a)(2)(C), allowed in arriving at adjusted gross income, and hence no longer fall within the definition of miscellaneous itemized deductions. Hence, they are deductible in computing AMT liability.

☐ **Effective:** Expenses paid or incurred in tax years beginning after Dec. 31, '86. ('97 Act §975(b))

> *recommendation:* Taxpayers who paid AMT in open years should consider filing amended returns to claim refunds for those years.

¶ 117. Business meals deduction increased from 50% to 80% (over 10 years) for individuals subject to DOT hours of service limitations

Code Sec. 274(n)(3), as amended by '97 Act § 969(a)
Generally effective: Tax years beginning after Dec. 31, '97
Committee Reports, see ¶ 5092

The amount allowable as a deduction for any expense for food or beverages is generally limited to 50% of the amount otherwise allowable as a deduction. Exceptions to this 50% rule apply for food or beverages provided to crew members of certain commercial vehicles and for food or beverages provided on certain offshore oil or gas platforms or drilling rigs. (FTC 2d/FIN ¶ L-2135, ¶ L-2141; USTR ¶ 2744.01; TaxDesk ¶ 29,455)

New Law. The '97 Act increases to 80% (over a ten year period) the deductible percentage of the cost of food and beverages consumed while away from home by individuals subject to the hours of service limitations of the Department of Transportation. These individuals (see below) are frequently forced to eat meals away from home in circumstances where their choice is limited, prices comparatively high and the opportunity for lavish meals remote. (Com Rept, see ¶ 5092)

The Act provides that in the case of any expenses for food or beverages consumed by an individual while away from home (within the meaning of Code Sec. 162(a)(2)) during, or incident to, the period of duty subject to the hours of service limitations of the Department of Transportation, the amount allowable as a deduction for any expenses for food or beverages is the "applicable percentage" (see below), instead of 50%. (Code Sec. 274(n)(3)(A) as amended by '97 Act §969(a))

The "applicable percentage" will be 80% for tax years beginning in calendar year 2008 or later, but will be phased in as follows:

. . . 55% for tax years beginning in calendar year 1998 or 1999,

. . . 60% for tax years beginning in calendar year 2000 or 2001,

. . . 65% for tax years beginning in calendar year 2002 or 2003,

. . . 70% for tax years beginning in calendar year 2004 or 2005,

. . . 75% for tax years beginning in calendar year 2006 or 2007, and

. . . 80% for tax years beginning in calendar year 2008 or later.   (Code Sec. 274(n)(3)(B))

Individuals subject to the hours of service limitations of the Department of Transportation for purposes of the above rule include:

. . . certain air transportation employees such as pilots, crew, dispatchers, mechanics, and control tower operators under Federal Aviation Administration regulations,

. . . interstate truck operators and interstate bus drivers under Department of Transportation regulations,

. . . certain railroad employees such as engineers, conductors, train crews, dispatchers and control operations personnel under Federal Railroad Administration regulations, and

. . . certain merchant mariners under Coast Guard regulations. (Com Rept, see ¶ 5092)

☐ **Effective:** Tax years beginning after Dec. 31, '97. ('97 Act §969(b))

FTC 2d References are to Federal Tax Coordinator 2d
FIN References are to RIA's Analysis of Federal Taxes: Income
USTR References are to United States Tax Reporter: Income, Estate & Gift, and Excise
PCA References are to Pension Coordinator and Pension & Benefits Expert/Advisor
PE References are to Pension and Profit Sharing 2nd
EP References are to Estate Planning & Taxation Coordinator and Estate Planning Advisor

Research Institute of America 37

¶ 200. Capital Gains and Losses

¶ 201. Capital gains tax rates for individuals reduced from 28% to 20% and 15% to 10% for post-May 6, '97 gains

Code Sec. 1(h), as amended by '97 Act § 311(a)

Generally effective: Tax years ending after May 6, '97, but without regard to pre-May 7, '97 gains

Committee Reports, see ¶ 5019

On the sale or exchange of capital assets, the net capital gain is included in income and taxed at the same rate as ordinary income, except that noncorporate taxpayers are subject to a maximum marginal rate of 28% on the net capital gain. (FTC 2d/FIN ¶ I-5110; USTR ¶ 14; TaxDesk ¶ 23,332)   Capital assets generally include any property except:

... inventory, stock in trade, or property held primarily for sale to customers in the ordinary course of taxpayer's trade or business,

... depreciable or real property used in taxpayer's trade or business,

... certain literary or artistic property,

... business accounts or notes receivable, and

... certain publications of the U.S. government.

(FTC 2d/FIN ¶ I-6001; USTR ¶ 12,214; TaxDesk ¶ 24,901)

New Law. For a taxpayer with net capital gain for any tax year, the tax for the year cannot be more than the sum of (Code Sec. 1(h)(1) as amended by '97 Act §311(a)):

(A) a tax, computed at the rates and in the same manner as if there was no maximum capital gains rate, on the greater of:

... taxable income reduced by the net capital gain, or

... the lesser of (1) the amount of taxable income taxed at a rate below 28%, or (2) taxable income reduced by the adjusted net capital gain (defined below) (Code Sec. 1(h)(1)(A)), plus

(B) 25% of the excess (if any) of:

... the unrecaptured section 1250 gain (defined below) (or, if less, the net capital gain), over

... the excess (if any) of (1) the sum of the amount on which tax is determined under (A), above, plus the net capital gain, over (2) taxable income (Code Sec. 1(h)(1)(B)),

FTC 2d References are to the Federal Tax Coordinator 2d
FIN References are to RIA's Analysis of Federal Taxes: Income
USTR References are to the United States Tax Reporter: Income, Estate & Gift, and Excise
PCA References are to Pension Coordinator and Pension & Benefits Expert/Advisor
PE References are to Pension and Profit Sharing 2nd
EP References are to Estate Planning & Taxation Coordinator and Estate Planning Advisor

Research Institute of America

plus

    (C) 28% of the amount of taxable income in excess of the sum of:

... the adjusted net capital gain, plus

... the sum of the amounts on which tax is determined under (A) and (B) above (Code Sec. 1(h)(1)(C)), plus

    (D) 10% of so much of the taxpayer's adjusted net capital gain (or taxable income, if less) as does not exceed the excess (if any) of—

... the amount of taxable income which would (without regard to this Code Sec. 1(h)(1)) be taxed at a rate below 28%, over

... the taxable income reduced by the adjusted net capital gain (Code Sec. 1(h)(1)(D)), plus

    (E) 20% of the taxpayer's adjusted net capital gain (or taxable income, if less) in excess of the amount on on which a tax is determined under (D), above. (Code Sec. 1(h)(1)(E))

> *illustration:* Tom, a single individual, has taxable income of $70,000 for '97, which includes $50,000 of post-May 6, '97 net capital gain. Tom's tax is $12,535, determined as follows:
>
> (a) tax on $20,000 at 15% ((A) in above formula) . . . . $ 3,000
> (b) 10% of $4,650—the amount otherwise taxed at a rate below 28% for '97 ($24,650) less taxable income reduced by adjusted net capital gain ($20,000) ((D) in above formula)   465
> (c) 20% of $45,350—the adjusted net capital gain ($50,000) above the amount from (b) ($4,650) ((E) in above formula)   9,070
> $12,535

For purposes of this computation, net capital gain for any tax year is reduced (but not below zero) by the amount which the taxpayer takes into account as investment income under Code Sec. 163(d)(4)(B)(iii). (Code Sec. 1(h)(3))

Under this computation, any net capital gain which would otherwise be taxed at 15% is taxed at 10%. Individuals in higher tax brackets pay tax at a maximum rate of 20% on net capital gains. (Com Rept, see ¶ 5019)

> *observation:* Under the pre-'97 Act rules, only taxpayers in a 31% or higher tax bracket derived a tax saving from the 28% top rate on net capital gain. The '97 Act provides a lower rate on net capital gain for all taxpayers with taxable income, regardless of their tax bracket.

> *illustration:* Sam is a taxpayer in the 15% tax bracket. His income includes $1,000 of net capital gain. Sam's tax on the capital gain portion of his income is $100. Under pre-'97 Act rules, his tax on the capital gain was $150,

FTC 2d References are to Federal Tax Coordinator 2d
FIN References are to RIA's Analysis of Federal Taxes: Income
USTR References are to United States Tax Reporter: Income, Estate & Gift, and Excise
PCA References are to Pension Coordinator and Pension & Benefits Expert/Advisor
PE References are to Pension and Profit Sharing 2nd
EP References are to Estate Planning & Taxation Coordinator and Estate Planning Advisor

the same as it would have been on an additional $1,000 of ordinary income.

☙ *illustration:* Sue, a taxpayer in the 39.6% tax bracket has net capital gain of $10,000. Sue's tax on the capital gain is $2,000, a saving of $1,960 over the tax on a comparable amount of ordinary income. Under pre-'97 Act rules, her tax on the capital gain was $2,800, a saving of $1,160 over the tax on a comparable amount of ordinary income.

☙ *observation:* The entire net capital gain is still included in the computation of adjusted gross income. Thus, it continues to be taken into account in determining the floor on certain itemized deductions (medical expenses, casualty losses, miscellaneous itemized deductions), computing the phaseout of itemized deductions and personal exemptions, and determining the amount of social security benefits that must be included in gross income. In effect, this means that for some taxpayers the maximum effective tax rate on net capital gain is higher than 20%, i.e., $100 of net capital gain will increase tax liability by more than $20.

Adjusted net capital gain. Adjusted net capital is net capital gain determined without regard to—

... collectibles gain (Code Sec. 1(h)(4)(A)),

... unrecaptured section 1250 gain (Code Sec. 1(h)(4)(B)),

... section 1202 gain (Code Sec. 1(h)(4)(C)), and

... mid-term gain. (Code Sec. 1(h)(4)(D)).

Collectibles gain is gain from the sale or exchange of a collectible, as that term is defined in Code Sec. 408(m), (FTC 2d/FIN ¶ H-12259; USTR ¶ 4084.03; TaxDesk ¶ 28,394) (but without regard to the exception for coins), which is a capital asset held for more than one year but only to the extent the gain is taken into account in computing gross income. (Code Sec. 1(h)(5)(A)) Any gain from the sale of an interest in a partnership, S corporation, or trust which is attributable to unrealized appreciation in the value of collectibles is treated as gain from the sale or exchange of a collectible. For this purpose, rules similar to Code Sec. 751 (dealing with sales of interests in partnerships holding unrealized receivables and appreciated inventory) (FTC 2d/FIN ¶ B-3901; USTR ¶ 7514; TaxDesk ¶ 59,101) apply. (Code Sec. 1(h)(5)(B)) The tax on the net capital gain attributable to any long-term capital gain from the sale or exchange of collectibles remains at the pre-'97 Act maximum rate of 28%. (Com Rept, see ¶ 5019)

Unrecaptured section 1250 gain is the amount of long-term capital gain that would be treated as ordinary income if—

... Code Sec. 1250(b)(1) included all depreciation and the applicable percentage under Code Sec. 1250(a) were 100%, and

... in the case of gain properly taken into after July 28, '97, only gain from section 1250 property held for more than 18 months were taken into account.

(Code Sec. 1(h)(6)(A))

The maximum rate of tax on gain attributable to the depreciation of section 1250 property is 25%. (Com Rept, see ¶ 5019)

The amount of unrecaptured section 1250 gain from sales, exchanges, and conversions described in Code Sec. 1231(a)(3)(A) for any tax year cannot exceed the excess of the net section 1231 gain (as defined in Code Sec. 1231(c)(3)) for the year over the amount treated as ordinary income under Code Sec. 1231(c)(1) for the year. (Code Sec. 1(h)(6)(B))

For a tax year that includes May 7, '97, the rule for determining unrecaptured section 1250 gain is applied by taking into account only the gain properly taken into account for the portion of the tax year after May 6, '97. (Code Sec. 1(h)(6)(C))

> **illustration:** Martha, a calendar year taxpayer, owns an office building and land. Due to $500,000 of depreciation claimed over the years, her basis in the building is zero. Her basis in the land is $100,000. Martha sells the land and building on July 1, '97 for $2,100,000. She has no other gains or losses in '97. Of the 2,000,000 gain ($2,100,000 − $100,000), $500,000 (the extent to which, because of depreciation allowable, the gain would have been treated as ordinary income if the property had been section 1245 property) is taxed at a maximum rate of 25%; the balance of the gain ($1,500,000) is taxed at a maximum rate of 20%.

Section 1202 gain is an amount equal to the gain excluded from gross income under Code Sec. 1202(a). (Code Sec. 1(h)(7))

Mid-term gain is the amount which would be adjusted net capital gain for the tax year if—

... adjusted net capital gain were determined by taking into account only the gain or loss properly taken into account after July 28, 97, from property held for more than one year but not more than 18 months (Code Sec. 1(h)(8)(A)), and

... Code Sec. 1(h)(3), above, and Code Sec. 1212 did not apply. (Code Sec. 1(h)(8)(B))

18-Month holding period. The lower '97 Act capital gain rates do not apply to the sale or exchange of assets held for 18 months or less, effective for amounts properly taken into account after July 28, '97. The pre-'97 Act 28% maximum rate continues to apply to the sale or exchange of capital assets held more than one year but not more than 18 months. (Com Rept, see ¶ 5019)

> **observation:** Capital gain is thus subject to tax at various rates, depending on the type of asset and the length of time the asset is held.

FTC 2d References are to Federal Tax Coordinator 2d
FIN References are to RIA's Analysis of Federal Taxes: Income
USTR References are to United States Tax Reporter: Income, Estate & Gift, and Excise
PCA References are to Pension Coordinator and Pension & Benefits Expert/Advisor
PE References are to Pension and Profit Sharing 2nd
EP References are to Estate Planning & Taxation Coordinator and Estate Planning Advisor

... Assets held one year or less are taxed at the taxpayer's regular tax rate, i.e., up to 39.6%.

... Assets held more than one year but less than 18 months are taxed at a maximum rate of 28%.

... Assets held more than 18 months are taxed at 10% or 20%.

... Gain on the sale of collectibles is taxed at a maximum rate of 28%.

... Gain attributable to depreciation of section 1250 property is taxed at a maximum rate of 25%.

IRS may issue such regulations as are appropriate to apply these rules in the case of sales and exchanges by pass-through entities (defined below) and of interests in such entities. These regs may also deal with reporting requirements. (Code Sec. 1(h)(11)) These regs may coordinate the capital gains provisions with other rules involving the treatment of sales and exchanges by pass-through entities and of interests in pass-through entities. (Com Rept, see ¶ 5019)

Pre-May 7, 97 gain in a tax year which includes May 7, '97. In a tax year which includes May 7, '97, gains and losses properly taken into account for the portion of the year before May 7, '97 are taken into account in determining mid-term gains as if the gains and losses were described in Code Sec. 1(h)(1)(A), above. (Code Sec. 1(h)(10)(A))

In the case of a pass-through entity, the determination of when gain and loss are properly taken into account (i.e., pre-May 7, 97 or post-May 6, '97) is made at the entity level. (Code Sec. 1(h)(10)(B)) Thus, gain taken into account by a pass-through entity before May 7, '97 is not eligible for the lower '97 Act maximum rate. (Com Rept, see ¶ 5019) For this purpose, the following are pass-through entities:

... a regulated investment company,

... a real estate investment trust,

... an S corporation,

... a partnership,

... an estate or trust, and

... a common trust fund.

(Code Sec. 1(h)(10)(C))

observation: Since the determination of pre-May 7, 97 gain is made at the entity level, IRS will presumably require mutual funds and other pass-through entities to separately report their pre-May 7, '97 and post-May 6, '97 gains. Form 1099-DIV for '97, which has already been released, does not make provision for this. To achieve separate reporting, the '97 Form 1099 and K-1 schedules used by partnerships, S corporations, and estates and trusts will have to be revised and adjusted to permit separate reporting of the two amounts.

Reduced rates for post-2000 qualified 5-year gain. In tax years beginning after Dec. 31, 2000, the 10% rate under Code Sec. 1(h)(1)(D), above, is 8% with respect to so much of the amount to which the 10% rate would otherwise apply as does not exceed qualified 5-year gain (defined below), and 10% with respect to the remainder of the amount. (Code Sec. 1(h)(2)(A)) The 20% rate under Code Sec. 1(h)(1)(E), above, is 18% with respect to so much of the amount to which the 20% rate would otherwise apply as does not exceed the lesser of—

. . . the excess of qualified 5-year gain over the amount of such gain taken into account under Code Sec. 1(h)(2)(A), above, or

. . . the amount of qualified 5-year gain (determined by taking into account only property the holding period for which begins after Dec. 31, 2000. (Code Sec. 1(h)(2)(B)) Thus, the 18% rate only applies to assets the holding period for which begins after Dec. 31, 2000. (Com Rept, see ¶ 5019)

The rate for the remainder of the amount is 20%. (Code Sec. 1(h)(2)(B))

To determine whether the holding period of property begins after Dec. 31, 2000, the holding period of property acquired pursuant to the exercise of an option (or other right or obligation to acquire property) includes the period the option (or other right or obligation) was held. (Code Sec. 1(h)(2)(B))

Qualified 5-year gain is the amount of long-term capital gain which would be computed for the tax year taking into account only gains from the sale or exchange of property held by the taxpayer for more than five years. This determination is made without regard to collectibles gain, unrecaptured section 1250 gain (determined without regard to the limitation in Code Sec. 1(h)(6)(B), above), section 1202 gain, or midterm gain. (Code Sec. 1(h)(9))

> *observation:* The lower 8% rate applies to post-2000 gain on assets held for more than five years, regardless of when the holding period began. Thus, starting in 2001, some gain may be taxed at this 8% rate. To qualify for the 18% rate, the holding period must begin after 2000. As a result, the 18% rate is not available with respect to gain realized before 2006.

Election to recognize gain on assets held held on Jan. 1, 2001. A taxpayer, other than a corporation, may elect to treat any readily tradable stock (i.e., stock which, as of Jan. 1, 2001 is readily tradable on an established securities market or otherwise ('97 Act §311(e)(4))) (which is a capital asset) held by the taxpayer on Jan. 1, 2001 (and not sold before the next business day after that date) as having been sold on the next business day for an amount equal to its closing market price on that date, and as having been reacquired on that date for an amount equal to the closing market price. ('97 Act §311(e)(1)(A)) A taxpayer, other than a corporation, may also elect to treat any other capital asset or property used in a trade or business (as defined in Code Sec.

1231(b)) and held by the taxpayer on Jan. 1, 2001 as having been sold on that date for an amount equal to its fair market value on that date and reacquired on that date for an amount equal to its fair market value. ('97 Act §311(e)(1)(B))

Any gain resulting from the election is treated as received or accrued on the date the asset is treated as sold. The gain is recognized notwithstanding any other Code provision. ('97 Act §311(e)(2)(A)) Any loss resulting from the election is not allowed for any tax year. ('97 Act §311(e)(2)(B))

> **observation:** A taxpayer might want to make this election for an asset which as of Jan. 1, 2001 hasn't appreciated substantially (so that no or only a small amount of gain is recognized) but which the taxpayer expects to hold for at least five more years and which he expects to appreciate further.

IRS is to specify the manner in which the election is to be made. An electing taxpayer must specify the assets for which the election is made. The election, once made with respect to an asset, is irrevocable. ('97 Act §311(e)(3))

☐ **Effective:** For tax years ending after May 6, '97. ('97 Act §311(d)(1)) For a tax year that includes May 7, '97, the lower '97 Act rates for net capital gain (10%/20%) don't apply to an amount equal to the net capital gain determined by including only the net capital gain for the portion of the tax year before May 7, '97. Any net capital gain not eligible for the new rates is subject to the pre-'97 Act maximum rate of 28%. (Com Rept, see ¶ 5019)

¶ 202. Constructive sales treatment for appreciated financial positions

Code Sec. 1259, as added by '97 Act § 1001(a)
Generally effective: Any constructive sale after June 8, '97
Committee Reports, see ¶ 5111

Under pre-'97 Act law, a taxpayer generally did not realize gain on open transactions such as short sales (when a taxpayer sold borrowed property—gain wouldn't be recognized until the taxpayer closed the sale by returning identical property to the lender) or short sales against the box (see below). (FTC 2d/FIN ¶ I-7700; USTR ¶ 12,334.01; TaxDesk ¶ 22,890) Taxpayers could also lock in gain on certain property by entering into offsetting positions in the same or similar property. Under the straddle rules, when a taxpayer realized a loss on one offsetting position in actively-traded personal property, the taxpayer could generally deduct this loss only to the extent that the loss exceeded the unrecognized gain in the other positions in the straddle. (FTC 2d/FIN ¶ I-7500; USTR ¶ 10,924; TaxDesk ¶ 22,840) Taxpayers could also engage in other arrangements, such as "futures contracts," "forward contracts," "equity swaps" and other "notional principal contracts" where the risk of loss and opportunity for gain with respect to property are shifted to another party (the "counterparty"). Under pre-'97 Act law, these arrangements did not result in the recognition of gain by the taxpayer. (Com Rept, see ¶ 5111)

Congress was concerned that in recent years, several financial transactions have been developed or popularized which allow taxpayers to reduce substantially or eliminate their risk of loss (and opportunity for gain) without a taxable disposition. Like most taxable dispositions, many of these transactions also provide the taxpayer with cash or other property in return for the interest that the taxpayer has given up. These transactions include: short sales against the box (see below), notional principal contracts or futures or forward contracts to deliver the same stock and equity swaps (see below). (Com Rept, see ¶ 5111)

One of these transactions is the "short sale against the box." In this transaction, a taxpayer borrows and sells shares identical to the shares the taxpayer holds. Under pre-'97 Act law, the form of the transaction was respected for income tax purposes and gain on the substantially identical property was not recognized at the time of the short sale. By holding two precisely offsetting positions, the taxpayer was insulated from economic fluctuations in the value of the stock. While the short against the box was in place, the taxpayer generally could borrow a substantial portion of the value of the appreciated long stock so that, economically, the transaction strongly resembled a sale of the long stock. (Com Rept, see ¶ 5111)

A taxpayer holding appreciated stock could also enter into an "equity swap" which required the taxpayer to make payments equal to the dividends and any increase in the stock's value for a specified period, and entitled the taxpayer to receive payments equal to any depreciation in value. The terms of the swaps also frequently entitled the shareholder to receive payments during the swap period of a market rate of return (e.g., the Treasury bill rate) on a notional principal amount equal to the value of the shareholder's appreciated stock, making the transaction strongly resemble a taxable exchange of the appreciated stock for an interest-bearing asset. (Com Rept, see ¶ 5111)

New Law. The '97 Act requires a taxpayer to recognize gain (but not loss) upon entering into a constructive sale of any appreciated position in stock, a partnership interest or certain debt instruments as if the position were sold, assigned or otherwise terminated at its fair market value on the date of the constructive sale. (Com Rept, see ¶ 5111)

If there is a constructive sale (defined below) of an "appreciated financial position" (defined below): (Code Sec. 1259(a) as added by '97 Act §1001(a))

(1) the taxpayer has to recognize gain as if the position were sold, assigned, or otherwise terminated at its fair market value on the date of the constructive sale (and any gain must be taken into account for the tax year which includes that date), and (Code Sec. 1259(a)(1))

(2) for purposes of applying the Code for periods after the constructive sale, (Code Sec. 1259(a)(2)) proper adjustment must be made in the amount of any gain or loss later realized with respect to the position for any gain taken into account by reason of

FTC 2d References are to Federal Tax Coordinator 2d
FIN References are to RIA's Analysis of Federal Taxes: Income
USTR References are to United States Tax Reporter: Income, Estate & Gift, and Excise
PCA References are to Pension Coordinator and Pension & Benefits Expert/Advisor
PE References are to Pension and Profit Sharing 2nd
EP References are to Estate Planning & Taxation Coordinator and Estate Planning Advisor

(1) above, (Code Sec. 1259(a)(2)(A)) and the holding period of the position is determined as if the position were originally acquired on the date of the constructive sale. (Code Sec. 1259(a)(2)(B))

Except as IRS may provide in regs, a constructive sale would generally not be treated as a sale for other Code purposes. (Com Rept, see ¶ 5111)

Constructive sale. A taxpayer is treated as having made a constructive sale of an appreciated financial position (defined below) if the taxpayer (or a related person, see below)): (Code Sec. 1259(c)(1))

(1) enters into a short sale of the same or substantially identical property, (Code Sec. 1259(c)(1)(A))

(2) enters into an "offsetting notional principal contract" (defined below) with respect to the same or substantially identical property, (Code Sec. 1259(c)(1)(B))

(3) enters into a futures or "forward contract" (defined below) to deliver the same or substantially identical property, (Code Sec. 1259(c)(1)(C))

(4) in the case of an appreciated financial position that is a short sale or a contract described in (2) or (3) above with respect to any property, acquires the same or substantially identical property, or (Code Sec. 1259(c)(1)(D))

(5) to the extent prescribed by IRS in regs, enters into one or more other transactions (or acquires one or more positions) that have substantially the same effect as a transaction described in (1), (2), (3), or (4) above. (Code Sec. 1259(c)(1)(E)) Under this rule, more than one appreciated financial position or more than one offsetting transaction can be aggregated to determine whether a constructive sale has occurred. For example, it is possible that no constructive sale would result if one appreciated financial position and one offsetting transaction were considered in isolation, but that a constructive sale would result if the appreciated financial position were considered in combination with two transactions. (Com Rept, see ¶ 5111)

> **observation:** Thus, the constructive sale rules do not apply to a short sale of stock that the seller borrows if he does not hold substantially identical property at the time of the sale or until he enters into a transaction that would diminish his risk of loss on the sale.

> **observation:** Code Sec. 1259 does not define the term "substantially identical". The same phrase is used in Code Sec. 1091 (rules relating to the treatment of wash sales, see FTC 2d/FIN ¶ I-3900; USTR ¶ 10,914; TaxDesk ¶ 22,700). It seems likely that IRS would provide in regs that "substantially identical" for purposes of Code Sec. 1259 has the same meaning as in Code Sec. 1091.

Sales of non-marketable securities that are closed within one year. A constructive sale does not include any contract for sale of any stock, debt instrument, or partnership interest which is not a marketable security (as defined in Code Sec. 453(f), see FTC 2d/FIN ¶ G-6410; USTR ¶ 4534.05; TaxDesk ¶ 46,461) if the contract settles within one year after the date the contract is entered into. (Code Sec. 1259(c)(2))

Exception for certain sales closed within 30 days after the close of the tax year. For purposes of the constructive sale rules, any transaction (which would otherwise be treated as a constructive sale) during the tax year will be *disregarded* if: (Code Sec. 1259(c)(3)(A))

(1) the transaction is closed before the end of the 30th day after the close of the tax year, (Code Sec. 1259(c)(3)(A)(i))

(2) the taxpayer holds the appreciated financial position throughout the 60-day period beginning on the date the transaction is closed, *and* (Code Sec. 1259(c)(3)(A)(ii))

(3) at no time during that 60-day period is the taxpayer's risk of loss with respect to the position reduced by reason of a circumstance which would be described in Code Sec. 246(c)(4) (rules relating to suspension of the holding period where the risk of loss is diminished for purposes of the dividends received deduction, see FTC 2d/FIN ¶ D-2264; USTR ¶ 2434.04; TaxDesk ¶ 60,067) if references to stock included references to the position. (Code Sec. 1259(c)(3)(A)(iii))

Thus, this exception is available only if, for the sixty days after closing a transaction, the taxpayer holds the appreciated position and at no time is the taxpayer's risk of loss reduced by holding certain other positions. (Com Rept, see ¶ 5111)

observation: As long as a taxpayer meets the requirements for the exception described in Code Sec. 1259(c)(3)(A), the taxpayer can engage in transactions such as "short sales against the box" without a constructive sale occurring.

observation: If a taxpayer fails to meet the requirements for the exception (i.e., by not closing the transaction within 30 days of the close of the tax year), the constructive sale occurs on the date the taxpayer entered into the transaction.

observation: Presumably, a taxpayer's gain on a transaction qualifying for the exception would be short-term capital gain.

Positions that are reestablished. If: (Code Sec. 1259(c)(3)(B))

(1) a transaction, which would otherwise be treated as a constructive sale of an appreciated financial position, is closed during the tax year or during the 30 days after the close of the tax year, and (Code Sec. 1259(c)(3)(B)(i))

(2) another substantially similar transaction is entered into during the 60-day period beginning on the date the transaction (described in (1) above) is closed: (Code Sec. 1259(c)(3)(B)(ii))

FTC 2d References are to Federal Tax Coordinator 2d
FIN References are to RIA's Analysis of Federal Taxes: Income
USTR References are to United States Tax Reporter: Income, Estate & Gift, and Excise
PCA References are to Pension Coordinator and Pension & Benefits Expert/Advisor
PE References are to Pension and Profit Sharing 2nd
EP References are to Estate Planning & Taxation Coordinator and Estate Planning Advisor

. . . which also would otherwise be treated as a constructive sale of the position, (Code Sec. 1259(c)(3)(B)(ii)(I))

. . . which is closed before the 30th day after the close of the tax year in which the transaction (described in (1) above) occurs, and (Code Sec. 1259(c)(3)(B)(ii)(II))

. . . which meets the requirements of Code Sec. 1259(c)(3)(A)(ii) and Code Sec. 1259(c)(3)(A)(iii) (see above), (Code Sec. 1259(c)(3)(B)(ii)(III))
the transaction (described in (2) above) is disregarded for purposes of determining whether the requirements of Code Sec. 1259(c)(3)(A)(iii) (i.e., whether at any time during the 60-day period, the taxpayer's risk of loss with respect to that position is diminished for purposes of the exception for sales closed within 30 days after the close of the tax year, see above) are met with respect to that transaction (described in (2) above). (Code Sec. 1259(c)(3)(B))

Thus, if a transaction that is closed is reestablished in a substantially similar position, the exception for sales closed within 30 days after the close of the tax year (see above) applies provided that the reestablished position is closed before the end of the tax year and the other requirements (i.e., if for the 60 days after closing a transaction the taxpayer holds the appreciated financial position and at no time is the taxpayer's risk of loss diminished by holding other positions) are met after the closing. (Com Rept, see ¶ 5111)

Constructive sales of a pro-rata portion of a taxpayer's appreciated financial position. Where the standard for a constructive sale is met with respect to only a pro rata portion of a taxpayer's appreciated financial position (e.g., some, but not all, shares of stock), that portion would be treated as constructively sold. If there is a constructive sale of less than all of any type of property held by the taxpayer, the specific property considered sold would be determined under the rules governing actual sales, after adjusting for previous constructive sales. Under the regs to be issued by IRS (see below), either a taxpayer's appreciated financial position or its offsetting transaction might in some circumstances be disaggregated on a non-pro rata basis for purposes of the constructive sale determination. Congress intends that IRS should only use this authority where the disaggregated treatment reflects the economic reality of the transaction and is administratively feasible. For example, one transaction for which disaggregated treatment might be appropriate is an equity swap that references a small group of stocks, where the transaction is entered into by a taxpayer owning only one of the stocks. A standard similar to Reg § 1.246-5 (rules for determining whether the holding period is reduced for any period in which a taxpayer has diminished its risk of loss by holding one or more other positions with respect to substantially similar or related property, see FTC 2d/FIN ¶ D-2268 *et seq.*; USTR ¶ 2434.04; TaxDesk ¶ 60,065) would be be appropriate for determining whether the relationship between the stock held and the group of stocks shorted is sufficient for constructive sale purposes. (Com Rept, see ¶ 5111)

Appreciated financial position. Except as discussed below, an appreciated financial position is any position (defined below) with respect to any stock, debt instrument, or partnership interest if there would be gain were that position sold, assigned, or otherwise terminated at its fair market value. (Code Sec. 1259(b)(1))

Debt instruments (other than debt qualifying for the exception described below), including those identified as part of a hedging or straddle transaction, are appreciated financial positions. (Com Rept, see ¶ 5111) For how the constructive sale rules apply to transactions that are identified as hedges and straddles, see below.

Exceptions. An appreciated financial position does *not* include: (Code Sec. 1259(b)(2))

. . . any position with respect to debt if (Code Sec. 1259(b)(2)(A)) the debt unconditionally entitles the holder to receive a specified principal amount, (Code Sec. 1259(b)(2)(A)(i)) the interest payments (or other similar amounts) with respect to the debt meet the requirements of Code Sec. 860G(a)(1)(B)(i) (i.e., interest payments or other similar amounts payable at a fixed rate or payable at a variable rate (to the extent permitted in the regs), see FTC 2d/FIN ¶ E-6904; USTR ¶ 860A4.01; TaxDesk ¶ 16,102), and (Code Sec. 1259(b)(2)(A)(ii)) the debt is not convertible (directly or indirectly) into stock of the issuer or any related person. (Code Sec. 1259(b)(2)(A)(iii))

. . . any position which is marked to market under any Code section or the regs under those Code sections. (Code Sec. 1259(b)(2)(B)) Thus, a constructive sale does not include a transaction involving an appreciated financial position that is marked to market, including positions governed by Code Sec. 475 (mark-to-market for securities dealers, see FTC 2d/FIN ¶ I-7650; USTR ¶ 4754) or Code Sec. 1256 (mark-to-market for futures contracts, options and currency contracts, see FTC 2d/FIN ¶ I-7600; USTR ¶ 12,564; TaxDesk ¶ 22,870). (Com Rept, see ¶ 5111)

🖉 *observation:* If securities traders, commodities traders, and commodities dealers make the election to be subject to the mark-to-market rules under Code Sec. 475 (¶ 2001), the positions of those traders and commodities dealers will not be appreciated financial positions and therefore will not be subject to the constructive sale rules.

How the constructive sale rules apply to transactions that are identified as hedging or straddle transactions. Congress intended that the constructive sale rules generally will apply to transactions that are identified as hedging or straddle transactions under other Code provisions such as Code Sec. 1092(a)(2) (tax straddles, see FTC 2d/FIN ¶ I-7527; USTR ¶ 10,924; TaxDesk ¶ 22,856), Code Sec. 1092(b)(2) (identified mixed straddles, see FTC 2d/FIN ¶ I-7545; USTR ¶ 10,924), Code Sec. 1092(e) (hedging transactions, see FTC 2d/FIN ¶ I-7620; USTR ¶ 10,924; TaxDesk ¶ 22,883), Code Sec. 1221 (hedging transactions, see FTC 2d/FIN ¶ I-6218.09N; USTR ¶ 12,214.80; TaxDesk ¶ 25,011), and Code Sec. 1256(e) (hedging transactions, see FTC 2d/FIN ¶ I-7622; USTR ¶ 12,564.05; TaxDesk ¶ 22,883). Where either position in an identified transaction is an appreciated financial position and a constructive sale of that position results from the other position, Congress intends that the construc-

FTC 2d References are to Federal Tax Coordinator 2d
FIN References are to RIA's Analysis of Federal Taxes: Income
USTR References are to United States Tax Reporter: Income, Estate & Gift, and Excise
PCA References are to Pension Coordinator and Pension & Benefits Expert/Advisor
PE References are to Pension and Profit Sharing 2nd
EP References are to Estate Planning & Taxation Coordinator and Estate Planning Advisor

tive sale will be treated as having occurred immediately before the identified transaction. The constructive sale will not, however, prevent qualification of the transaction as an identified hedging or straddle transaction. Where, after the establishment of an identified hedging or straddle transaction, there is a constructive sale of either position in the transaction, gain will generally be recognized and accounted for under the relevant hedging or straddle provision. However, Congress intends that future IRS regs may except certain transactions from the constructive sale provision where the gain recognized would be deferred under an identified hedging or straddle provision (e.g. Reg. § 1.446-4(b), i.e., rules relating to the clear reflection of income for hedging transactions, see FTC 2d/FIN ¶ G-2524; TaxDesk ¶ 44,753). (Com Rept, see ¶ 5111)

Definitions.

Related person. A person is related to another person with respect to a transaction if (Code Sec. 1259(c)(4)) the relationship is described in Code Sec. 267(b) (relating to the disallowance of losses incurred in transactions between related persons, see FTC 2d/FIN ¶ G-2707; USTR ¶ 2674.03; TaxDesk ¶ 22,790) or Code Sec. 707(b) (relating to the disallowance of losses incurred between a partner and a partnership, see FTC 2d/FIN ¶ B-2016; USTR ¶ 7074.03; TaxDesk ¶ 58,450), *and* (Code Sec. 1259(c)(4)(A)) the transaction is entered into with a view toward avoiding the purposes of the constructive sale rules. (Code Sec. 1259(c)(4)(B))

Forward contract. A forward contract is a contract to deliver a substantially fixed amount of property for a substantially fixed price. (Code Sec. 1259(d)(1)) An agreement that is not a contract for purposes of applicable contract law is not treated as a forward contract. Thus, contingencies to which the contract is subject will be taken into account. A forward contract providing for delivery of an amount of property, such as shares of stock, that is subject to significant variation under the contract terms is not a forward contract that results in a constructive sale. (Com Rept, see ¶ 5111)

Offsetting notional principal contract. An offsetting notional principal contract is, with respect to any property, an agreement which includes: (Code Sec. 1259(d)(2))

. . . a requirement to pay (or provide credit for) all or substantially all of the investment yield (including appreciation) on the property for a specified period, and (Code Sec. 1259(d)(2)(A))

. . . a right to be reimbursed for (or receive credit for) all or substantially all of any decline in the value of the property. (Code Sec. 1259(d)(2)(B))

observation: Presumably, an equity swap would be considered to be offsetting notional principal contract under the above rules.

Position. For purposes of the above rules, a position is an interest, including a futures or forward contract, short sale, or option. (Code Sec. 1259(b)(3))

Treatment of later sale of a position which was considered sold. If there is a constructive sale of any appreciated financial position, (Code Sec. 1259(e)(1)(A)) the position is later disposed of, and (Code Sec. 1259(e)(1)(B)) at the time of the disposition, the transaction resulting in the constructive sale of the position is open with respect to the taxpayer or any related person, (Code Sec. 1259(e)(1)(C)) then solely for purposes of determining whether the taxpayer has entered into a constructive sale of any other appreciated financial position held by the taxpayer, the taxpayer is treated as entering into the transaction immediately after the disposition. For purposes of this rule, an assignment or other termination is treated as a disposition. (Code Sec. 1259(e)(1))

Thus, a transaction that has resulted in a constructive sale of an appreciated financial position (e.g., a short sale) is not treated as resulting in a constructive sale of another appreciated financial position so long as the taxpayer holds the position which was treated as constructively sold. However, when the taxpayer assigns, terminates, or disposes of that position, the taxpayer, immediately after the assignment, termination, or disposition, is treated as entering into the transaction that resulted in the constructive sale (e.g., the short sale) if it remains open at that time. Thus, the transaction can cause a constructive sale of another appreciated financial position at any time after the assignment, termination, or disposition. For example, assume a taxpayer holds two stock positions and one offsetting short sale, and the taxpayer identifies the short sale as offsetting one of the stock positions. If the taxpayer then sells the stock position that was identified, the identified short position would cause a constructive sale of the taxpayer's other stock position at that time. (Com Rept, see ¶ 5111)

Certain trust instruments treated as stock. For purposes of the constructive sale rules, an interest in a trust which is actively traded (within the meaning of Code Sec. 1092(d)(1), i.e., for which there is an established financial market, see FTC 2d/FIN ¶ I-7506.1; USTR ¶ 10,924) is treated as stock unless substantially all (by value) of the property held by the trust is debt described in Code Sec. 1259(b)(2)(A) (see above). (Code Sec. 1259(e)(2)) Thus, a trust instrument will not be treated as stock if substantially all (by value) of the property held by the trust is debt that qualifies for the exception to the definition of appreciated financial position for certain debt instruments. (Com Rept, see ¶ 5111)

> *observation:* An interest in a trust will be treated as stock under Code Sec. 1259(e)(2)(see above) even if all the property held by the trust is debt if that debt is *not* debt described in Code Sec. 1259(b)(2)(A)).

Multiple positions in property. If a taxpayer holds multiple positions in property, the determination of whether a specific transaction is a constructive sale and, if so, which appreciated financial position is considered sold is made in the same manner as actual sales. (Code Sec. 1259(e)(3))

Regulations. IRS may issue whatever regs may be necessary or appropriate to carry out the purposes of the constructive sale rules. (Code Sec. 1259(f)) Congress expects IRS to issue prompt guidance, including safe harbors, with respect to common transactions entered into by taxpayers. (Com Rept, see ¶ 5111)

FTC 2d References are to Federal Tax Coordinator 2d
FIN References are to RIA's Analysis of Federal Taxes: Income
USTR References are to United States Tax Reporter: Income, Estate & Gift, and Excise
PCA References are to Pension Coordinator and Pension & Benefits Expert/Advisor
PE References are to Pension and Profit Sharing 2nd
EP References are to Estate Planning & Taxation Coordinator and Estate Planning Advisor

Under this rule, IRS may treat as constructive sales certain transactions that have substantially the same effect as those specified (i.e., short sales, offsetting notional principal contracts and futures or forward contracts to deliver the same or substantially similar property). Under Code Sec. 7805(b)(2) (see FTC 2d/FIN ¶ T-10103; USTR ¶ 79,006.78), IRS generally is prohibited from issuing regs that are retroactive unless IRS issues the regs within 18 months of the date of enactment of the provision. (Com Rept, see ¶ 5111)

> **⚫ observation:** Thus, IRS would have until 18 months from Aug. 5, '97 to issue retroactive regs relating to Code Sec. 1259.

Congress anticipates that IRS will use the authority to issue regs to treat as constructive sales other financial transactions that, like those specified in the constructive sale rules, have the effect of eliminating substantially all of the taxpayer's risk of loss and opportunity for income or gain with respect to the appreciated financial position. Because this standard requires reduction of both risk of loss and opportunity for gain, Congress intends that transactions that reduce only risk of loss or only opportunity for gain will not be covered. Thus, for example, Congress does not intend that a taxpayer who holds an appreciated financial position in stock will be treated as having made a constructive sale when the taxpayer enters into a put option with an exercise price equal to the current market price (an "at the money" option). Because that type of option reduces only the taxpayer's risk of loss, and not its opportunity for gain, the test may not be met. (Com Rept, see ¶ 5111)

For purposes of the constructive sale rules, Congress does not intend that risk of loss and opportunity for gain be considered separately. Thus, if a transaction has the effect of eliminating a portion of the taxpayer's risk of loss and a portion of the taxpayer's opportunity for gain with respect to an appreciated financial position which, taken together, are substantially all of the taxpayer's risk of loss and opportunity for gain, Congress intends that IRS regs will treat this transaction as a constructive sale of the position. (Com Rept, see ¶ 5111)

Congress anticipates that IRS regs, when issued, will provide specific standards for determining whether several common transactions (such as collars and in-the-money options, see below) will be treated as constructive sales. (Com Rept, see ¶ 5111)

Collars. In a collar, a taxpayer commits to an option requiring him to sell a financial position at a fixed price (the "call strike price") and has the right to have his position purchased at a lower fixed price (the "put strike price"). A collar can be a single contract or can be effected by using a combination of put and call options. (Com Rept, see ¶ 5111)

> **Illustration:** A shareholder may enter into a collar for a stock currently trading at $100 with a put strike price of $95 and a call strike price of $110. The effect of the transaction is that the seller has transferred the rights to all gain above the $110 call strike price and all loss below the $95 put strike price. The seller has retained all risk of loss and opportunity for gain in the range price between $95 and $110. (Com Rept, see ¶ 5111)

To determine whether collars have substantially the same effect as the transactions specified in the constructive sale rules, Congress anticipates that IRS regs will provide specific standards that take into account various factors with respect to the appreciated financial position, including its volatility. Similarly, Congress expects that several aspects of the collar transaction will be relevant, including the spread between the put and call prices, the period of the transaction, and the extent to which a taxpayer retains the right to periodic payments on the appreciated financial position (e.g., the dividends on collared stock). Congress expects that any regs with respect to collars will be applied prospectively, except in cases to prevent abuse. (Com Rept, see ¶ 5111)

"In-the-money" options. A specific regulatory standard may also be appropriate for a so-called "in-the-money" option, i.e., a put option where the strike price is significantly above the current market price or a call option where the strike price is significantly below the current market price. (Com Rept, see ¶ 5111)

> ***Illustration:*** If a shareholder purchases a put option exercisable at a future date (a so-called "European" option) with a strike price of $120 with respect to stock currently trading at $100, the shareholder has eliminated all risk of loss on the position for the option period and assured himself of all yield and gain on the stock for any appreciation up to $120. (Com Rept, see ¶ 5111)

In determining whether an "in-the-money" option will be treated as a constructive sale, Congress anticipates that IRS regs will provide a specific standard that takes into account many of the factors described above with respect to collars, including the yield and volatility of the stock and the period and other terms of the option. (Com Rept, see ¶ 5111)

Approaches IRS might adopt in regs. For collars, options, and some other transactions, one approach that IRS might take in issuing regs is to rely on option prices and option pricing models. The price of an option represents the payment the market requires to eliminate risk of loss (for a put option) and to purchase the right to receive yield and gain (for a call option). Thus, option pricing offers one model for quantifying both the total risk of loss and opportunity for gain with respect to an appreciated financial position, as well as the proportions of these total amounts that the taxpayer has retained. (Com Rept, see ¶ 5111)

In addition to setting specific standards for treatment of these and other transactions, it may be appropriate for IRS regs to establish "safe harbor" rules for common financial transactions that do not result in constructive sale treatment. An example might be a collar with a sufficient spread between the put and call prices, a sufficiently limited period and other relevant terms so that, regardless of the particular characteristics of the stock, the collar probably would not transfer substantially all risk of loss and opportunity for gain. (Com Rept, see ¶ 5111)

FTC 2d References are to Federal Tax Coordinator 2d
FIN References are to RIA's Analysis of Federal Taxes: Income
USTR References are to United States Tax Reporter: Income, Estate & Gift, and Excise
PCA References are to Pension Coordinator and Pension & Benefits Expert/Advisor
PE References are to Pension and Profit Sharing 2nd
EP References are to Estate Planning & Taxation Coordinator and Estate Planning Advisor

☐ **Effective:** Any constructive sale after June 8, '97. ('97 Act §1001(d)(1))

If before June 9, '97, the taxpayer entered into any transaction which is a constructive sale of any appreciated financial position, and ('97 Act §1001(d)(2)(A)) before the close of the 30-day period beginning on Aug. 5, '97 or before a later date as may be specified by IRS, the transaction and position are clearly identified in the taxpayer's records as offsetting, ('97 Act §1001(d)(2)(B)) the transaction and position are not taken into account in determining whether any other constructive sale after June 8, '97, has occurred. This rule ceases to apply as of the date the transaction is closed or the taxpayer ceases to hold the position. ('97 Act §1001(d)(2))

 ✔ action alert: Within 30 days of Aug. 5, '97, the taxpayer must identify any transaction or position entered into before June 9, '97 which is a constructive sale of any appreciated financial position in order for that transaction to be grandfathered under the transitional rules that apply to constructive sales of appreciated financial positions.

Income in respect of a decedent. In the case of a decedent dying after June 8, '97, if: ('97 Act §1001(d)(3))

. . . there was a constructive sale on or before June 8, '97 of any appreciated financial position, ('97 Act §1001(d)(3)(A))

. . . the transaction resulting in the constructive sale of the position remains open (with respect to the decedent or any related person) ('97 Act §1001(d)(3)(B)) for not less than two years after the date of the transaction (whether the period is before or after June 8, '97), and ('97 Act §1001(d)(3)(B)(i)) and at any time during the three-year period ending on the date of the decedent's death, and ('97 Act §1001(d)(3)(B)(ii))

. . . the transaction is not closed within the 30-day period beginning on Aug. 5, '97, ('97 Act §1001(d)(3)(C))

then, for purposes of the Code, the position (and the transaction resulting in the constructive sale) is treated as property constituting rights to receive an item of income in respect of a decedent under Code Sec. 691 (FTC 2d/FIN ¶ C-9500; USTR ¶ 6914; TaxDesk ¶ 57,850). ('97 Act §1001(d)(3)) Thus, no amount will be treated as income in respect of a decedent under the above rule unless the requirement that the position be open at some time during the three-year period ending on the decedent's death is met, as well as the requirements that the transaction remain open for not less than two years and that the transaction is not closed within 30 days after Aug. 5, '97. (Com Rept, see ¶ 5111)

Code Sec. 1014(c) (rule prohibiting a step-up in basis for property consisting of a right to receive income in respect of a decedent, see FTC 2d/FIN ¶ P-4003; USTR ¶ 10,144.02; TaxDesk ¶ 21,572) does not apply to so much of the position's or property's value (as included in the decedent's estate for estate tax purposes) as exceeds its fair market value as of the date the transaction is closed. ('97 Act §1001(d)(3)) Thus, gain with respect to a position that accrues after the transaction is closed will not be included in income in respect of a decedent. (Com Rept, see ¶ 5111)

¶ 203. Substantial worthlessness of short sale property is a gain recognition event; regs are to provide similar rules for other transactions similar to short sales

Code Sec. 1233(h), as amended by '97 Act § 1003(b)(1)
Generally effective: Property which becomes substantially worthless after Aug. 5, '97
Committee Reports, see ¶ 5113

Gain or loss on a short sale is the difference between the short sale price and the basis of the property used to close the short sale. According to regs issued under pre-'97 Act law, a short sale isn't treated as completed until delivery of property to close the short sale. (FTC 2d/FIN ¶ I-7706; USTR ¶ 12,334.01; TaxDesk ¶ 22,893)

New Law. Under the '97 Act, if the taxpayer enters into a short sale of property, and that property becomes substantially worthless, the taxpayer recognizes gain in the same manner as if the short sale were closed when the property becomes substantially worthless. (Code Sec. 1233(h)(1) as amended by '97 Act §1003(b)(1)).

To the extent provided in regs, this rule will also apply for any option with respect to property, any offsetting notional principal contract w ith respect to property, any futures or forward contract to deliver any property, and any other similar transaction. (Code Sec. 1233(h)(1)). Thus, to the extent provided in those regs, similar gain recognition rules will apply to the transactions listed in the preceding sentence and to any similar position that becomes substantially worthless. (Com Rept, see ¶ 5113)

In enacting the above rules, Congress intended no inference as to the proper treatment of the above transactions or similar transactions or positions under pre-'97 Act law. (Com Rept, see ¶ 5113)

Statute of limitations. Where property becomes substantially worthless during a tax year and any short sale of the property remains open at the time the property becomes substantially worthless: (Code Sec. 1233(h)(2))

... the statutory period for the assessment of any deficiency attributable to any part of the gain on the transaction doesn't expire before the earlier of: (Code Sec. 1233(h)(2)(A))

• the date which is 3 years after the date IRS is notified by the taxpayer (in a manner that IRS may prescribe by regs) of the substantial worthlessness of the property, or (Code Sec. 1233(h)(2)(A)(i))
• the date which is 6 years after the date the return for the tax year during which the position became substantially worthless is filed, and (Code Sec. 1233(h)(2)(A)(ii))

. . . the deficiency may be assessed before the expiration of the assessment period in Code Sec. 1233(h)(2)(A) (described immediately above) despite the existence of any other law or rule of law which would otherwise prevent the assessment. (Code Sec. 1233(h)(2)(B))

> *observation:* Presumably, Congress intends that the IRS regs which are to address options, notional principal contracts, futures contracts, forward contracts and similar transactions and positions (see above) are also to provide statute of limitation rules similar to those for short sales. The Committee Report isn't explicit on this point, but the Committee Report's discussion (referred to above) of IRS's authority to issue regs prescribing "similar gain recognition rules" immediately follows the Committee Report's discussion of the statute of limitation rules for short sales.

☐ **Effective:** Property which becomes substantially worthless after Aug. 5, '97. ('97 Act §1003(b)(2))

¶ 204. Sale treatment for cancellations, lapses, expirations and other terminations is expanded to all property which is a capital asset

Code Sec. 1234A(1), as amended by '97 Act § 1003(a)(1)
Generally effective: Terminations more than 30 days after Aug. 5, '97
Committee Reports, see ¶ 5113

Among the requirements for characterizing a gain or loss as a capital gain or loss is that there be a "sale or exchange" of a capital asset.

Several court decisions interpret a "sale or exchange" to not include a disposition that occurs as a result of a lapse or cancellation of a contract right. However, this result is changed, for some dispositions, by Code provisions. For example, under Code Sec. 1234A, gains and losses attributable to a cancellation, lapse, expiration or other termination covered by that Code section are treated as gains or losses from the sale of a capital asset.

Under pre-'97 Act law, in order that Code Sec. 1234A apply to a cancellation, lapse, expiration or other termination, the cancellation, lapse, expiration or other termination had to be of:

. . . a right or obligation with respect to personal property (other than certain stock) of a type which is actively traded and which is, or would be on acquisition, a capital asset in the hands of the taxpayer or

. . . a Code Sec. 1256 contract which is a capital asset in the hands of the taxpayer. (FTC 2d/FIN ¶ I-1403 *et seq.*, ¶ I-1409 *et seq.*, ¶ I-7619; USTR ¶ 12,224.07, ¶ 12,224.22, ¶ 1234A4; TaxDesk ¶ 22,122 *et seq.*, ¶ 22,128 *et seq.*)

New Law. In general, Congress believed that pre-'97 Act law is deficient because (1) it taxes similar economic transactions differently, (2) it effectively provides some, but not all, taxpayers with an election and (3) its lack of certainty (i.e., conflicting case law) makes the tax laws unnecessarily difficult to administer. (Com Rept, see ¶ 5113) Accordingly, the '97 Act expands the class of property with respect to which a cancellation, lapse, expiration or other termination of a right or obligation is, under Code Sec. 1234A, treated as a sale. Under the '97 Act, that class is expanded to include *all* property which is (or on acquisition would be) a capital asset in the hands of the taxpayer. (Code Sec. 1234A(1) as amended by '97 Act §1003(a)(1))

> **observation:** The '97 Act didn't change the rule in Code Sec. 1234A(2) regarding Code Sec. 1256 contracts.

Property covered by Code Sec. 1234A because of the expansion of the scope of that provision by the '97 Act includes (1) interests in real property and (2) non-actively traded personal property. (Com Rept, see ¶ 5113)

An example of the first type of property interest affected by the expansion of Code Sec. 1234A is the receipt of amounts from a lessee to release the lessee from a requirement that premises be restored (to their pre-lease condition) on termination of a lease. An example of the second type of property interest affected by the expansion of Code Sec. 1234A is the forfeiture of a down payment under a contract to purchase stock. (Com Rept, see ¶ 5113)

> **observation:** Also, stock—other than stock which was part of certain straddles or stock in a corporation formed or availed of to offset positions in personal property taken by any shareholder—even if actively traded, was not covered by Code Sec. 1234A, before its expansion by the '97 Act, and is covered by that provision, as expanded by the '97 Act.

The amendment of Code Sec. 1234A doesn't affect whether a right is "property" or whether property is a capital asset. (Com Rept, see ¶ 5113)

> **observation:** Thus, the requirement, under pre-'97 Act law, for application of Code Sec. 1234A(1), that a right or obligation be with respect to property "which is (or, on acquisition, would be) a capital asset in the hands of the taxpayer," isn't removed or changed by the '97 Act.

Congress believed that, to the extent that pre-'97 Act law treated modifications of property rights as not being a sale or exchange, pre-'97 Act law effectively provided, in many cases, taxpayers with an election to treat the transaction as giving rise to capital gain, subject to more favorable rates than ordinary income, or an ordinary loss that can offset higher-taxed ordinary income and not be subject to limitations on use of capital losses. The effect of an election could be achieved by selling the property right if the resulting transaction results in a gain or providing for the extinguishment of the right if the resulting transaction results in a loss. Thus, Congress believed that a major effect of the expansion of Code Sec. 1234A by the '97 Act is to remove the effective ability of a taxpayer to elect the character of gains and losses from certain transactions. (Com Rept, see ¶ 5113)

> **(RIA) action alert:** For many taxpayers, the last day on which there can occur a cancellation, lapse, expiration or other termination (of a right or obligation with respect to real property interests, non-actively traded personal property or certain stock) eligible to give rise to an ordinary loss, rather than a capital loss, is 30 days after Aug. 5, '97.

> **(RIA) observation:** Code Sec. 1234A doesn't cover retirements of debt instruments. For retirements of debt instruments, see ¶ 205.

☐ **Effective:** Terminations more than 30 days after Aug. 5, '97. ('97 Act § 1003(a)(2))

¶ 205. Sale-or-exchange treatment for retirement of debt instruments is expanded to include instruments issued by natural persons

Code Sec. 1271(b), as amended by '97 Act § 1003(c)

Generally effective: Sales, exchanges and retirements after Aug. 5, '97 for obligations issued by individuals issued or purchased after June 8, '97 and for sales, exchanges and retirements after Aug. 5, '97 for obligations issued before July 2, '82 by an issuer which isn't a corporation or government (or political subdivision) which are purchased after June 8, '97

Committee Reports, see ¶ 5113

Among the requirements for characterizing a gain or loss as a capital gain or loss is that there be a "sale or exchange" of a capital asset.

Court decisions interpret "sale or exchange" to not include the retirement of a debt instrument.

Code Sec. 1271 changed this result for debt instruments to which it applies by providing that amounts received on the retirement of a debt instrument are treated as amounts received in exchange for the debt instrument.

However, under pre-'97 Act law, Code Sec. 1271 didn't apply to (1) debt instruments issued by individuals (natural persons) and (2) debt instruments, issued before July 2, '82, by non-individuals other than corporations or governments (or political subdivisions); i.e., by partnerships, estates or trusts.

As a result of this exemption from the application of the rules of Code Sec. 1271, the character of gain or loss realized on retirement of an obligation issued by a natural person, under pre-'97 law, is governed by case law. (Com Rept, see ¶ 5113) (FTC 2d/FIN ¶ I-1800 *et seq.*, ¶ I-1900 *et seq.*; USTR ¶ 12,714; TaxDesk ¶ 22,151)

New Law. Congress believed that the debt of natural persons and other taxpayers is sufficiently economically similar to be similarly taxed upon retirement of the debt. Accordingly, Congress believed that the pre-'97 Act exception in Code Sec. 1271(b) to the deemed-sale-or-exchange rule in Code Sec. 1271(a) on retirement of debt of a natural person should be repealed. (Com Rept, see ¶ 5113)

Thus, the '97 Act extends the deemed-sale-or-exchange rule of Code Sec. 1271 to include (1) debt instruments issued by natural persons after June 8, '97, (Code Sec. 1271(b)(1)(A) as amended by '97 Act §1003(c)(1)) (2) debt instruments, issued before July 2, '82, by issuers other than corporations or governments (or political subdivisions), which are "purchased" (as defined below) after June 8, '97 (Code Sec. 1271(b)(1)(B)), (Code Sec. 1271(b)(2)) and (3) debt instruments, issued before June 9, '97, by natural persons, which are "purchased" (as defined below) after June 8, '97. (Code Sec. 1271(b)(1)(A)), (Code Sec. 1271(b)(2))

> *observation:* Thus, under the '97 Act, (1) debt instruments issued by individuals and (2) debt instruments, issued before July 2, '82, by partnerships, trusts and estates are no longer excepted from the rule, in Code Sec. 1271(a)(1), which treats amounts received on the retirement of a debt instrument as received in exchange for the debt instrument. Therefore, if a debt instrument described in (1) or (2) is a capital asset in the hands of the taxpayer (and not excepted from application of the '97 Act under the rules which pertain to date of issuance or date of purchase of the debt instrument), gain or loss on retirement of the debt instrument is a capital gain or loss.

> *observation:* Even where a retirement of a debt instrument is treated as an exchange and otherwise qualifies as a capital gain transaction, some portion of the gain may be treated as ordinary income because of market discount or original issue discount rules. See FTC 2d/FIN ¶s I-8000 *et seq.*, J-4550 *et seq.*; USTR ¶s 12,714, 12,764.01; TaxDesk ¶s 15,400 *et seq.*, 27,761.

"Purchase" has the same meaning as in Code Sec. 1271(d)(1) and, thus, means any acquisition of a debt instrument where the basis of the debt instrument is *not* determined in whole or part by reference to the adjusted basis of the debt instrument in the hands of the person from whom acquired. (Code Sec. 1271(b)(2))

☐ **Effective:** Sales, exchanges and retirements after Aug. 5, '97 ('97 Act §1003(c)(2)), for obligations issued by natural persons which are (a) issued after June 8, '97, (Code Sec. 1271(b)(1)(A) as amended by '97 Act §1003(c)(1)) or (b) purchased (within the meaning of Code Sec. 1271(d)(1), see above) after June 8, '97. (Code Sec. 1271(b)(1)(A)), (Code Sec. 1271(b)(2)) Sales, exchanges and retirements after Aug. 5, '97 ('97 Act §1003(c)(2)) for obligations, issued before July 2, '82, by an issuer which isn't a corporation or a government (or political subdivision), which are purchased (within the meaning of Code Sec. 1271(d)(1), see above) after June 8, '97. (Code Sec. 1271(b)(1)(B)), (Code Sec. 1271(b)(2))

¶ 206. Elective rollover of gain from qualified small business stock to other qualified small business stock

Code Sec. 1045, as added by '97 Act § 313(a)
Code Sec. 1223(15), as amended by '97 Act § 313(b)(2)
Generally effective: Sales after Aug. 5, '97
Committee Reports, see ¶ 5021

50% of the gain from the sale or exchange of qualified small business stock held for more than five years by taxpayers other than C corporations is excluded from income. (FTC 2d/FIN ¶ I-9100.1; USTR ¶ 12,024; TaxDesk ¶ 24,661)

New Law. The '97 Act makes available to taxpayers an elective rollover of capital gain from the sale of qualified small business stock held for more than six months. (Code Sec. 1045(a) as added by '97 Act §313(a))

observation: Neither the '97 Act nor its legislative history provide any guidance as to how or when to make the election, whether or not the election is revocable or whether the election can be made for only part of the stock sold in a single sale.

"Qualified small business stock" has the definition provided in Code Sec. 1202(c), see FTC 2d/FIN ¶ I-9101 et seq.; USTR ¶ 12,024 et seq.; TaxDesk ¶ 24,660 et seq. (Code Sec. 1045(b)(1))

Calculating the nonrecognized gain. If the rollover is elected, *capital* gain from the sale of qualified small business stock is recognized only to the extent that the amount realized from the sale exceeds:

. . . the cost of any qualified small business stock "purchased" (defined below) during the 60-day period beginning on the date of the sale, reduced by

. . . any portion of the cost previously taken into account under this rollover rule. (Code Sec. 1045(a))

observation: Presumably, the reference to "cost previously taken into account" means that the cost of stock purchased is applied against the amount realized on qualified small business stock sales, for which an election was made and which occurred during the 59 days preceding the purchase, in the chronological order in which the sales occurred.

illustration (1): On Apr. 1, T sells qualified small business stock in corporation A, held by T for more than six months and a capital asset in T's hands, and realizes an amount of $500,000 from the sale. T's basis in the stock sold on Apr. 1 is $100,000.

On Apr. 2, T sells qualified small business stock in corporation B, held by T for more than six months and a capital asset in T's hands, and realizes an amount of $300,000 from that sale. T's basis in the stock sold on Apr. 2 is $50,000.

On May 30, T purchases qualified small business stock in corporation C at a cost of $700,000. T purchases no other qualified business stock in the period beginning Apr. 1 and ending May 31.

If T elects to rollover gain from the sale on Apr. 1, none of the $400,000 of gain from that sale is recognized (because the amount realized, $500,000, doesn't exceed, $700,000). If T also elects to rollover gain from the sale on Apr. 2, the amount of gain that wouldn't be recognized is $150,000 and the amount of gain recognized would be $100,000 (which is the amount by which $300,000—the amount realized on the sale—exceeds $200,000, which is the amount left after the $700,000 cost of the purchased stock is reduced by the $500,000 of cost applied against the earlier sale.) If the B corporation stock had been held by T for more than five years, fifty percent of that $100,000 of recognized gain (i.e., $50,000) would be excluded from gross income under the 50% exclusion rule of Code Sec. 1202.

A taxpayer is treated as having "purchased" property if the unadjusted basis of the property—determined without taking into account the basis adjustment rule (of Code Sec. 1045(b)(3)) discussed below—is the cost of the property. (Code Sec. 1045(b)(2))

Basis reduction for purchased stock. If gain from any sale isn't recognized because of a rollover election, that gain is applied to reduce (in the order acquired) the basis for determining gain or loss of any qualified business stock which is purchased by the taxpayer during the 60-day period beginning on the date of the sale. (Code Sec. 1045(b)(3))

illustration (2): On Apr. 1, T sells qualified small business stock in corporation A, held by T for more than six months and a capital asset in T's hands, and realizes an amount of $500,000 from the sale. T's basis in the stock sold on Apr. 1 is $100,000.

On May 29, T purchases qualified small business stock in corporation B at a cost of $150,000, and on May 30, T purchases qualified small business stock in corporation C at a cost of $600,000.

T's basis in the corporation B stock is zero and T's basis in the corporation C stock is $350,000 ($600,000 minus $250,000 (the amount left after $400,000 of unrecognized gain on the corporation A stock is reduced by the $150,000 of that unrecognized gain applied against the basis of the corporation B stock)).

FTC 2d References are to Federal Tax Coordinator 2d
FIN References are to RIA's Analysis of Federal Taxes: Income
USTR References are to United States Tax Reporter: Income, Estate & Gift, and Excise
PCA References are to Pension Coordinator and Pension & Benefits Expert/Advisor
PE References are to Pension and Profit Sharing 2nd
EP References are to Estate Planning & Taxation Coordinator and Estate Planning Advisor

Active business requirement for purchased stock. For purposes of determining whether the nonrecognition of gain, under the elective rollover provision, applies to stock which is sold (Code Sec. 1045(b)(4)), only the first six months of the taxpayer's holding period for stock purchased during the 60 day period is taken into account for purposes of applying Code Sec. 1202(c)(2) (which requires that, to be qualified small business stock, stock meet active business requirements for substantially all of the taxpayer's holding period for the stock, see FTC 2d/FIN ¶ I-9104; USTR ¶ 12,024.02; TaxDesk ¶ 24,699). (Code Sec. 1045(b)(4)(B)) Thus, for purposes of the rollover provision, the replacement stock must meet the active business requirement for the six month period following the purchase. (Com Rept, see ¶ 5021)

> ☙ *illustration (3):* On Jan. 1, T sells qualified small business stock in corporation A which he has held for more than six months and which is a capital asset in his hands. On Feb. 15, T purchases stock in corporation B. In determining whether the corporation B stock purchased on Feb. 15 will be treated as qualified small business stock for purposes of qualifying the Jan. 1 sale of the stock in corporation A for an elective rollover of gain under Code Sec. 1045, the stock in corporation B must meet the active business requirements referred to in Code Sec. 1202(c)(2) for the six month period following the Feb. 15 purchase. Whether the stock in corporation B continues to meet the active business requirements referred to in Code Sec. 1202(c)(2) *after* the six month period following the Feb. 15 purchase will determine whether the stock in corporation B is qualified small business stock only for purposes *other than* qualifying the Jan. 1 sale of the A corporation stock for the Code Sec. 1045 elective rollover of gain (e.g, for the purpose of determining whether a future sale by T of the corporation B stock can qualify for an elective rollover of gain under Code Sec. 1045 or the 50% exclusion of gain under Code Sec. 1202.)

The effect of the elective rollover on holding periods. The '97 Act amends Code Sec. 1223 to provide that, in determining the period for which the taxpayer held property, the acquisition of which resulted, under the qualified small business stock rollover provision, in the nonrecognition of any part of the gain realized on the sale of other property, there is included the period for which the other property was held by the taxpayer as of the date of the sale. (Code Sec. 1223(15) as amended by '97 Act §313(b)(2)) However, for purposes of determining whether the nonrecognition of gain, under the elective rollover provision, applies to stock which is sold (Code Sec. 1045(b)(4) as amended by '97 Act §313(a)), the taxpayer's holding period for the stock sold and the stock purchased is determined without regard to Code Sec. 1223. (Code Sec. 1045(b)(4)(A)) Thus, the holding period of the stock purchased will include the holding period of the stock sold except for purposes of determining whether the six-month holding period requirement is met. (Com Rept, see ¶ 5021)

Code paragraph redesignated by '97 Act. In addition to making the substantive changes described above, the '97 Act redesignated Code Sec. 1223(15) as Code Sec. 1223(16). ('97 Act §313(b)(2))

☐ **Effective:** For sales after Aug. 5, '97. ('97 Act §313(c))

¶ 207. Involuntary conversion nonrecognition rules exception for replacement property acquired from a related party is expanded to cover all taxpayers

Code Sec. 1033(i), as amended by '97 Act § 1087(a)
Generally effective: Involuntary conversions occurring after June 8, '97
Committee Reports, see ¶ 5164

C corporations and certain partnerships with corporate partners can't defer gain realized on an involuntary conversion if they acquire the replacement property from a related person. For this purpose, a person is treated as related to another person if the person bears a relationship to the other person described in Code Sec. 267(b) (relating to the disallowance of losses incurred in transactions between related parties, see FTC 2d/FIN ¶ G-2707; USTR ¶ 2674.03; TaxDesk ¶ 22,790) or Code Sec. 707(b)(1) (relating to the disallowance of losses incurred in transactions between partners and partnerships, see FTC 2d/FIN ¶ B-2016; USTR ¶ 7074.03; TaxDesk ¶ 58,450). The rule does not apply to the extent the related party acquired the replacement property or stock from an unrelated party within the period allowed for the acquisition of replacement property or stock. (FTC 2d/FIN ¶ I-3733.1; USTR ¶ 10,334.221; TaxDesk ¶ 22,974.4)

New Law. Congress believed that, except for de minimis cases, individuals should be subject to the same rules with respect to the acquisition of replacement property from a related person as are other taxpayers. (Com Rept, see ¶ 5164)

The '97 Act provides that the denial of nonrecognition under Code Sec. 1033 for purchases of replacement property from related parties also applies to any other taxpayer (including an individual) if, with respect to the property which is involuntarily converted during the tax year, the aggregate of the amount of realized gain on the property on which there is realized gain exceeds $100,000. (Code Sec. 1033(i)(2)(C) as amended by '97 Act §1087(a))

> *observation:* Since the $100,000 limitation is based on "realized gain on the property on which there is a realized gain", the taxpayer can't offset his gains with any losses sustained as a result of the involuntary conversion for purposes of determining whether his gain exceeds the limitation.

In the case of a partnership, this denial of nonrecognition rule applies with respect to the partnership and with respect to each partner. A similar rule applies in the case of an S corporation and its shareholders. (Code Sec. 1033(i)(2)) Thus, the annual $100,000 limitation applies to both the partnership (or S corporation) and each partner (or S corporation shareholder). (Com Rept, see ¶ 5164)

☐ **Effective:** Involuntary conversions occurring after June 8, '97. ('97 Act §1087(b))

FTC 2d References are to Federal Tax Coordinator 2d
FIN References are to RIA's Analysis of Federal Taxes: Income
USTR References are to United States Tax Reporter: Income, Estate & Gift, and Excise
PCA References are to Pension Coordinator and Pension & Benefits Expert/Advisor
PE References are to Pension and Profit Sharing 2nd
EP References are to Estate Planning & Taxation Coordinator and Estate Planning Advisor

¶ 208. Gain may be deferred on the sale to eligible farmers' cooperatives of stock of qualified agricultural refiners or processors

Code Sec. 1042(g), as amended by '97 Act § 968
Generally effective: Sales after Dec. 31, '97
Committee Reports, see ¶ 5091

Gain on the sale of "qualified securities" to an employee stock ownership plan (ESOP) or an "eligible worker-owned cooperative" (EWOC) may be deferred if the taxpayer (other than a C corporation) elects nonrecognition of gain and buys "qualified replacement property" within the replacement period, and certain requirements are met. One of the requirements for deferral is that, immediately after the sale of qualified securities to the ESOP or EWOC, the ESOP or EWOC must own at least 30 percent of each class of the corporation's outstanding stock, or 30 percent of the total value of all of the corporation's outstanding stock. "Qualified securities" are employer securities issued by a domestic C corporation that has no stock outstanding that is readily tradable on an established securities market. (FTC 2d/FIN ¶ H-12103; USTR ¶ 10,424; PCA ¶ 33,204; PE ¶ 1042-4)

> ⚡ *observation:* The approach available to taxpayers for deferral of the gain on the sale of qualified securities to ESOPs and EWOCs was not available to the sale of the stock of agricultural refiners and processors to farmers' cooperatives.

New Law. The Act extends the deferral of "qualified securities" under Code Sec. 1042 to the sale of stock of a "qualified refiner or processor" to an "eligible farmers' cooperative." (Code Sec. 1042(g)(1) as amended by '97 Act §968(a)) In applying the deferral rules to this situation, an "eligible farmers' cooperative" is treated like an EWOC. (Code Sec. 1042(g)(4)(A))

A "qualified refiner or processor" is a domestic corporation:

(1) substantially all of the activities of which consist of the active conduct of the trade or business of refining or processing agricultural or horticultural products, and (Code Sec. 1042(g)(2)(A))

(2) which, during the one-year period ending on the date of sale, buys more than one-half of the products to be refined or processed from: (a) farmers who make up the "eligible farmers' cooperative" which is buying the stock of the corporation in a transaction to which the deferral applies, and (b) the cooperative. (Code Sec. 1042(g)(2)(B))

An "eligible farmers' cooperative" is a cooperative (i.e., an organization to which Code Sec. 1381 *et seq.* applies) which is engaged in the marketing of agricultural or horticultural products. (Code Sec. 1042(g)(3))

The deferral of gain under Code Sec. 1042 applies to the sale of qualified securities to eligible farmers' cooperatives only if, immediately after the sale, the eligible farmers' cooperative owns 100 percent (rather than 30 percent, as for EWOCs) of the qualified refiner or processor. (Code Sec. 1042(g)(4)(B))

In addition, the following rules apply to expand the applicability of the deferral of gain (as compared with the sale of qualifying stock to an ESOP or EWOC):

(1) the determination as to whether any stock is a "qualified security" is made without regard to whether the refiner's or processor's stock has any stock outstanding that is readily tradable on an established securities market, or whether the stock consists of employer securities; (Code Sec. 1042(g)(4)(C))

(2) C corporations can defer gain on the sale of qualified securities to an eligible farmers' cooperative; and

(3) the eligible farmers' cooperative need not elect a majority of the board of directors on the basis of one person, one vote. (Code Sec. 1042(g)(4)(D))

☐ **Effective:** Sales after Dec. 31, '97. ('97 Act §968(b))

¶ 209. Personal property used predominantly in the U.S. is treated as not property of a like-kind with respect to personal property used predominantly outside the U.S. for purposes of the like-kind exchange rules

Code Sec. 1031(h)(2), as amended by '97 Act § 1052(a)
Generally effective: Transfers after June 8, '97, in tax years ending after June 8, '97
Committee Reports, see ¶ 5144

Under pre-'97 Act law, if a taxpayer exchanges personal property that is predominantly used outside the U.S. for personal property that is used predominantly within the U.S., the exchange could have qualified as a tax-free like-kind exchange. (FTC 2d/FIN ¶ I-3060; USTR ¶ 10,314; TaxDesk ¶ 22,360) Tangible personal property that is used predominantly outside the U.S. is accorded a less favorable depreciation regime than is property that is used predominantly within the U.S. (FTC 2d/FIN ¶ L-9402; USTR ¶ 1684.03; TaxDesk ¶ 22,360) Thus, if a taxpayer exchanges depreciable U.S. property with a low adjusted basis (relative to its fair market value) for similar property situated outside the U.S., the adjusted basis of the acquired property is the same as the basis of the relinquished property, but the acquired property will be subject to different depreciation rules than the depreciation rules that applied to the relinquished property. (Com Rept, see ¶ 5144)

New Law. Congress believes that the depreciation rules applicable to foreign use property and domestic use property are sufficiently dissimilar so as to treat the depreciable property as not like-kind property for purposes of the tax-free like-kind exchange rules. (Com Rept, see ¶ 5144)

FTC 2d References are to Federal Tax Coordinator 2d
FIN References are to RIA's Analysis of Federal Taxes: Income
USTR References are to United States Tax Reporter: Income, Estate & Gift, and Excise
PCA References are to Pension Coordinator and Pension & Benefits Expert/Advisor
PE References are to Pension and Profit Sharing 2nd
EP References are to Estate Planning & Taxation Coordinator and Estate Planning Advisor

Under the '97 Act, personal property predominantly used (discussed below) within the U.S. and personal property used predominantly outside the U.S. are not property of like-kind. (Code Sec. 1031(h)(2)(A) as amended by '97 Act §1052(a))

> *observation:* Exchanges of personal property used predominantly outside the U.S. for other personal property used predominantly outside the U.S. can still qualify as like-kind.

How predominant use is determined. Except as discussed below, the predominant use of any property is determined based on: (Code Sec. 1031(h)(2)(B))

. . . in the case of the property *relinquished* in the exchange, the two-year period ending on the date of the relinquishment, (Code Sec. 1031(h)(2)(B)(i)) and

. . . in the case of the property *acquired* in the exchange, the two-year period beginning on the date of the acquisition. (Code Sec. 1031(h)(2)(B)(ii))

Thus, the property received in the exchange must continue in the same use (i.e., foreign or domestic) for the 24 months immediately after the exchange. (Com Rept, see ¶ 5144)

Except in the case of an exchange which is part of a transaction (or series of transactions) structured to avoid the purposes of these rules (Code Sec. 1031(h)(2)(C)), only the periods the property was held by the person relinquishing the property (or any related person) are taken into account for purposes of determining the predominant use of the property relinquished (Code Sec. 1031(h)(2)(C)(i)), and only the periods the property was held by the person acquiring the property (or any related person) are taken into account for purposes of determining the predominant use of the property acquired. (Code Sec. 1031(h)(2)(C)(ii)) Thus, the 24-month period is reduced to the lesser time as the taxpayer held the property, unless the shorter holding period is a result of a transaction (or series of transactions) structured to avoid the purposes of this rule. (Com Rept, see ¶ 5144)

> *observation:* Code Sec. 1031(h)(2)(C) doesn't define who is a related person for purposes of these rules.

> *observation:* Except as discussed below relating to property described in Code Sec. 168(g)(4), Code Sec. 1031(h)(2)(C) doesn't specifically define what is considered to be predominant use of property outside the U.S.

Property described in Code Sec. 168(g)(4) (generally, property used both within and without the U.S. that is eligible for accelerated depreciation as if used in the U.S., see FTC 2d/FIN ¶ L-9406; USTR ¶ 1684.03; TaxDesk ¶ 26,754) is treated as used predominantly in the U.S. (Code Sec. 1031(h)(2)(D))

> *observation:* Thus, a taxpayer can engage in tax-free like-kind exchanges of property described in Code Sec. 168(g)(4) that is actually used predominantly *outside* the U.S. for property used predominantly within the U.S.

☐ **Effective:** Transfers after June 8, '97, in tax years ending after June 8, '97. ('97 Act §1052(b)(1))

But, the above rules do not apply to any transfer under a written binding contract in effect on June 8, '97, and at all times thereafter before the disposition of the property. A contract does not fail to meet these requirements solely because: ('97 Act §1052(b)(2))

... it provides for a sale in lieu of an exchange ('97 Act §1052(b)(2)(A)), or

... the property to be acquired as replacement property was not identified under the contract before June 9, '97. ('97 Act §1052(b)(2)(B))

¶ 210. Tax on nonqualified withdrawals from capital gain account under Merchant Marine capital construction fund reduced from 28% to 20%

Code Sec. 7518(g)(6)(A), as amended by '97 Act § 311(c)(2)
Generally effective: Tax years ending after May 6, '97
Committee Reports, see ¶ 5019

Under the Merchant Marine Act of '36, tax incentives are provided for deposits in a capital construction fund (CCF) established by agreement with the Secretary of Transportation or the Secretary of Commerce. A CCF must maintain three accounts, one of which is a capital gain account. Qualified withdrawals from this account reduce the basis in the vessel, barge, or container for which the withdrawal is made. Nonqualified withdrawals from the capital gain account are taxed at a rate which, in the case of noncorporate taxpayers, couldn't exceed 28%. (FTC 2d/FIN ¶ J-1360; USTR ¶ 75,184)

New Law. With respect to nonqualified withdrawals from the capital gain account by a noncorporate taxpayer, the rate of tax can't exceed 20%. (Code Sec. 7518(g)(6)(A) as amended by '97 Act §311(c)(2))

✔️*observation:* This reduction is in conformity with the reduction in the maximum capital gains tax rate for individuals from 28% to 20%, see ¶ 201.

☐ **Effective:** For tax years ending after May 6, '97. ('97 Act §311(d)(1))

¶ 211. Estate and beneficiaries treated as related for loss and capital gain treatment on sale of depreciable property

Code Sec. 267(b), as amended by '97 Act § 1308(a)
Code Sec. 1239(b), as amended by '97 Act § 1308(b)
Generally effective: Tax years beginning after Aug. 5, '97
Committee Reports, see ¶ 5268

FTC 2d References are to Federal Tax Coordinator 2d
FIN References are to RIA's Analysis of Federal Taxes: Income
USTR References are to United States Tax Reporter: Income, Estate & Gift, and Excise
PCA References are to Pension Coordinator and Pension & Benefits Expert/Advisor
PE References are to Pension and Profit Sharing 2nd
EP References are to Estate Planning & Taxation Coordinator and Estate Planning Advisor

Code Sec. 267 disallows any loss deduction on most sales or exchanges of assets between related persons and imposes special tax accounting rules on those related persons. Code Sec. 1239 disallows capital gain treatment on the sale or exchange of depreciable property between related persons. Under pre-'97 Act law, neither Code Sec. 267 nor Code Sec. 1239 treated an estate and a beneficiary of that estate as related persons. (FTC 2d/FIN ¶ G-2707, ¶ I-3504, ¶ I-3527, ¶ I-8703; USTR ¶ 4534.17, ¶ 12,354.06, ¶ 12,394.01, ¶ 27,044.02, ¶ 44,614, ¶ 79,006.03; TaxDesk ¶ 22,793, ¶ 22,806)

New Law. An estate and a beneficiary of that estate are treated as related persons for purposes of Code Sec. 267 and Code Sec. 1239, except in the case of a sale or exchange in satisfaction of a pecuniary bequest. (Code Sec. 267(b) as amended by '97 Act §1308(a)), (Code Sec. 1239(b) as amended by '97 Act §1308(b))

illustration: Ten shares of stock with a basis of $100/share are held by an estate. The personal representative of the estate sells this stock to a beneficiary of the estate for $90/share. The estate's $10 loss is not deductible.

observation: Where under a definition of a related person, a revocable trust is treated as a related person, there is no exception under Code Sec. 267 or Code Sec. 1239 for distributions from a revocable trust in satisfaction of a pecuniary bequest. It would seem, however, that this result can be achieved by electing to treat the revocable trust as part of the estate (see ¶ 526).

☐ **Effective:** Tax years beginning after Aug. 5, '97. ('97 Act §1308(c))

¶ 212. Loss deferrals under the Code Sec. 267 related party rules are treated as loss disallowances for purposes of the non-Code Sec. 267 related party rules

Code Sec. 267(f)(4), as amended by '97 Act § 1604(e)
Generally effective: Transactions after Dec. 31, '83 in tax years ending after Dec. 31, '83
Committee Reports, see ¶ 5386

Code Sec. 267(a)(1) disallows losses arising from most sales or exchanges between persons that are related, as defined in Code Sec. 267(b). Code Sec. 267(b)(3) includes two corporations which are members of the same controlled group among those persons that are related persons for purposes of Code Sec. 267(a). However, under Code Sec. 267(f)(2), the disallowance rule of Code Sec. 267(a)(1) doesn't apply to losses arising in sales or exchanges between related persons that are members of the same controlled group of corporations, and, under Code Sec. 267(f)(2), those losses are, instead, deferred. Several Code provisions, in defining related persons, incorporate relationships defined in Code Sec. 267 by referring to relationships which would cause a disallowance of loss under Code Sec. 267. (FTC 2d/FIN ¶ C-4107.1, ¶ F-11904, ¶ G-4751, ¶ J-3280, ¶ L-9926, ¶ L-16925, ¶ N-2420, ¶ N-7028; USTR ¶ 1444.01, ¶ 1474.02, ¶ 269A4, ¶ 613A4, ¶ 6314.04, ¶ 6434.10, ¶ 58,814; TaxDesk ¶ 26,866, ¶ 27,126)

New Law. For purposes of any Code section other than Code Sec. 267 which refers to a relationship which would result in a disallowance of losses under Code Sec. 267, *deferral* under Code Sec. 267(f)(2) is treated as a disallowance. (Code Sec. 267(f)(4) as amended by '97 Act §1604(e)(1))

> *illustration:* Under Code Sec. 643(i), a loan of cash or marketable securities made by a foreign trust to a person related to a U.S. grantor or beneficiary may be treated by IRS as a distribution to the grantor or beneficiary. For this purpose, Code Sec. 643(i)(2) says, in relevant part, that a person is related to another person if the relationship would result in a disallowance of losses under section 267.
>
> A is a beneficiary of foreign trust T. A and B are members of the same controlled group of corporations. Therefore, losses on sales or exchanges between A and B would be *deferred*, under Code Sec. 267(f)(2), rather than *disallowed*, under Code Sec. 267(a)(1). Nevertheless, for purposes of Code Sec. 643(i), A and B are treated as persons which have a relationship which would result in a *disallowance* of losses under Code Sec. 267. Thus, if T makes a loan to B, IRS can treat the loan as a trust distribution to A.

☐ **Effective:** Transactions after Dec. 31, '83 in tax years ending after Dec. 31, '83, except for property transferred to a foreign corporation before Mar. 2, '84. ('97 Act §1604(e)(2))

¶ 300. Individual Retirement Accounts

¶ 301. New nondeductible Roth IRA allows tax-free withdrawal of earnings

Code Sec. 408A, as added by '97 Act § 302(a)
Code Sec. 4973(b), as amended by '97 Act § 302(b)
Code Sec. 219(c)(1)(B), as amended by '97 Act § 302(c)
Code Sec. 408(i), as amended by '97 Act § 302(d)
Generally effective: Taxable years beginning after Dec. 31, '97
Committee Reports, see ¶ 5016

Under pre-'97 Act law, there was only one type of individual retirement account (IRA). Contributions to an IRA were deductible in computing adjusted gross income if the taxpayer was not an active participant in an employer-sponsored plan or if the taxpayer's income was below a specified level. Contributions were partly deductible for active participants whose income fell within a specified phase-out range. Taxpayers who could not make a deductible contribution could make a nondeductible contribution. Total contributions (deductible and nondeductible) for a tax year could not exceed the greater of $2,000 or earned income. Earnings on IRA contributions (whether deductible or nondeductible) were includible in gross income when distributed. Distributions from an IRA were required to begin by Apr. 1 of the year after a taxpayer attained age 70½ and were subject to a minimum distribution excise tax. Contributions to IRAs could not be made after age 70½. Distributions to beneficiaries were generally required to begin within five years of the death of the IRA owner. (FTC 2d/FIN ¶ H-12238; USTR ¶ 4084.01; TaxDesk ¶ 28,350; PCA ¶ 35,101; PE ¶ 408-4.01)

New Law. The '97 Act creates the "Roth IRA." Except as provided below, a Roth IRA is treated in the same manner under the Code as a Code Sec. 219 IRA (regular IRA). (Code Sec. 408A(a) as added by '97 Act §302(a)) Contributions to a Roth IRA are nondeductible, and, if certain specified conditions are met, distributions are tax-free. (Com Rept, see ¶ 5016)

Contributions. After '97, an individual can make an annual nondeductible contribution to a Roth IRA up to the excess of:

(1) the lesser of $2,000 or 100% of the individual's annual compensation (Code Sec. 408A(c)(1)), over

(2) the aggregate amount of contributions for the tax year to all other IRAs (other than Roth IRAs) maintained for the benefit of that individual. (Code Sec. 408A(c)(2))

However, the allowable contribution to a Roth IRA is limited for individuals whose AGI exceeds the applicable dollar amount. For those individuals, the allowable contri-

FTC 2d References are to the Federal Tax Coordinator 2d
FIN References are to RIA's Analysis of Federal Taxes: Income
USTR References are to the United States Tax Reporter: Income, Estate & Gift, and Excise
PCA References are to Pension Coordinator and Pension & Benefits Expert/Advisor
PE References are to Pension and Profit Sharing 2nd
EP References are to Estate Planning & Taxation Coordinator and Estate Planning Advisor

Research Institute of America

bution is calculated by reducing the maximum contribution by the same ratio as the amount of the excess of the taxpayer's AGI for the tax year, over the applicable dollar amount, bears to $15,000 ($10,000 for a joint return). (Code Sec. 408A(c)(3)(A)) The applicable dollar amount is $150,000 for a taxpayer filing a joint return and $95,000 for any other taxpayer other than a married taxpayer filing separately. The applicable dollar amount for a taxpayer filing separately is zero. (Code Sec. 408A(c)(3)(C)(ii))

This means that the contribution that can be made to a Roth IRA is phased out for individuals with AGI between $95,000 and $110,000 and for joint filers with AGI between $150,000 and $160,000. (Com Rept, see ¶ 5016)

> *observation:* The limits on contributions to a Roth IRA under the phaseout rules described above apply regardless of whether the IRA owner is an active participant in an employer-sponsored plan.

An individual who cannot or (does not) make deductible contributions, to a regular IRA or nondeductible contributions to a Roth IRA, can make nondeductible contributions to a regular IRA. However, in no case can contributions to all an individual's IRAs for a tax year exceed $2,000. (Com Rept, see ¶ 5016)

> *observation:* There seems to be no reason why an individual would make a nondeductible contribution to a regular IRA if that individual were eligible to make either a deductible contribution to a regular IRA or a nondeductible contribution to a Roth IRA.

> *observation:* There are still no AGI limits on the right to make a deductible contribution to a regular IRA by an individual who is not an active participant in an employer-sponsored plan. Similarly, there are no AGI limits on the right of an active participant to make a nondeductible contribution to a regular IRA. However, unlike the Roth IRA (see below), withdrawals from a regular IRA will be taxed except to the extent the withdrawal is treated as made from nondeductible contributions.

AGI is determined in the same way as for regular IRAs under Code Sec. 219(g)(3) except that the amount included in gross income does not take into account the amount included in gross income for the portion of an endowment contract allocable to life insurance under Code Sec. 219(d)(3). Also, the deduction for a contribution to a regular IRA is allowed as a deduction in computing AGI. (Code Sec. 408A(c)(3)(C)(i))

The same definition of marital status that is used for IRAs under Code Sec. 219(g)(4) is used for the Roth IRA. (Code Sec. 408A(c)(3)(D))

No reduction below $200 is required until the permitted contribution is zero. Any maximum contribution which is not a multiple of $10 must be rounded to the next

FTC 2d References are to Federal Tax Coordinator 2d
FIN References are to RIA's Analysis of Federal Taxes: Income
USTR References are to United States Tax Reporter: Income, Estate & Gift, and Excise
PCA References are to Pension Coordinator and Pension & Benefits Expert/Advisor
PE References are to Pension and Profit Sharing 2nd
EP References are to Estate Planning & Taxation Coordinator and Estate Planning Advisor

lowest $10. (Code Sec. 408A(c)(3)(A))

Contributions to a Roth IRA may be made even after the individual IRA owner has reached age 70½. (Code Sec. 408A(c)(4)) Contributions for the preceding tax year may be made no later than April 15 of the current year. (Code Sec. 408A(c)(7))

The maximum contribution an *individual and spouse* may make in a tax year to all their IRAs in the aggregate, including Roth IRAs, is the lesser of 100% of their combined compensation or $4,000 annually. (Code Sec. 219(c)(1)(B)(ii) as amended by '97 Act §302(c))

A Roth IRA must be designated as a Roth IRA at the time it is established in a manner to be prescribed by IRS. (Code Sec. 408A(b))

Excess contributions. Code Sec. 4973 imposes a 6% tax on excess contributions to medical savings accounts, certain 403(b) annuities, and certain individual retirement accounts, including a Roth IRA. For a Roth IRA the term "excess contributions" means the sum of:

(1) the excess (if any) of:

(A) the amount contributed for the tax year to a Roth IRA(s) (other than a qualified rollover distribution), over

(B) the amount allowed as a contribution to a Roth IRA , and

(2) the excess contribution to a Roth IRA(s) for the preceding tax year, reduced by the sum of:

(A) the distributions out of the Roth IRA(s) for the the tax year, and

(B) the excess of the maximum amount allowed as a contribution to a Roth IRA for the tax year over the amount contributed to the account for the tax year. (Code Sec. 4973(b) as amended by '97 Act §302(b)).

Contributions returned to the individual before April 15 (for the preceding tax year) are not considered excess contributions. (Code Sec. 4973(b))

Rollovers. Distributions from a regular IRA may be rolled over to a Roth IRA without any penalty (Code Sec. 408A(d)(3)(A)(ii)) that would otherwise apply to a distribution from a regular IRA if the distribution meets the requirements for a qualified rollover contribution under Code Sec. 408(d)(3). (Code Sec. 408A(c)(6)(A)) However, only taxpayers whose AGI is not more than $100,000 in a tax year are eligible to make a qualified rollover contribution to a Roth IRA from a regular IRA during that tax year. (Code Sec. 408A(c)(3)(B)(i)) A married taxpayer filing a separate return may not make a rollover contribution to a Roth IRA from a regular IRA. (Code Sec. 408A(c)(3)(B)(ii)) Amounts rolled over are not counted towards the $2,000 annual limit. (Code Sec. 408A(c)(6)(B))

On a rollover distribution from a regular IRA to a Roth IRA, there is included in the taxpayer's gross income any amount which would be included if it were not part of a qualified rollover distribution. (Code Sec. 408A(d)(3)(A)(i)) However, if all or any part of a regular IRA is converted into a Roth IRA after Dec. 31, '97 and before Jan.1, '99, the amount that would have been includible in gross income if the individual had withdrawn the converted amount is included in gross income ratably over the four tax-year period beginning with the tax year in which the conversion is made. (Code Sec. 408A(d)(3)(A)(iii))

> **action alert:** In '98, all or any part of a regular IRA may be converted into a Roth IRA and receive special tax treatment.

> **observation:** Amounts required to be included in gross income on a rollover distribution would presumably be included in AGI for purposes of determining whether AGI is more than $100,000.

Conversion of excess contributions. An individual who makes an excess contribution to a regular IRA in any tax year may transfer the excess contribution (plus earnings) to a Roth IRA before Apr. 15. The amount transferred is not includible in the individual's gross income if no deduction was allowed for the transferred excess contribution. (Code Sec. 408A(d)(3)(D))

Distributions. Distributions from a Roth IRA aren't includible in income if the contribution to which the distribution relates is a *"qualified distribution"*. (Code Sec. 408A(d)(1)(A)). A qualified distribution is a distribution that is not made within the five-tax-year period beginning with the first tax year in which the individual (or the individual's spouse) made a contribution to the Roth IRA, and which is made:

... on or after the individual becomes 59½,

... after the death of the individual,

... on account of the individual becoming disabled, or

... for a "qualified special purpose distribution," (Code Sec. 408A(d)(2)), i.e., a distribution for first time home buyer expenses under Code Sec. 72(t)(2)(F). (Code Sec. 408A(d)(5))

> **observation:** Because assets must be held in a Roth IRA for five *tax* years (instead of calendar years), it appears that the waiting period for a qualified distribution may be shorter than five calendar years especially if a contribution made on the last day permitted (April 15) for the preceding tax year may be counted as contributed in that preceding year.

> **illustration:** Mark Rice, age 57, makes a $2,000 contribution to his Roth IRA on April, 15 '99 for the '98 tax year. On Jan 2, 2003 Rice withdraws $2,000 from his Roth IRA when he is over 59½. This withdrawal should be a "qualified distribution" and thus not includible in Rice's gross income since it was not made within the five-tax-year period beginning with the first tax year for which a contribution was made to a Roth IRA, and it was made after Mark was 59 ½. Presumably, '98 would count as the first year in which the

FTC 2d References are to Federal Tax Coordinator 2d
FIN References are to RIA's Analysis of Federal Taxes: Income
USTR References are to United States Tax Reporter: Income, Estate & Gift, and Excise
PCA References are to Pension Coordinator and Pension & Benefits Expert/Advisor
PE References are to Pension and Profit Sharing 2nd
EP References are to Estate Planning & Taxation Coordinator and Estate Planning Advisor

Research Institute of America 73

contribution was contributed and the five-tax-year period would end with 2002.

Roth IRAs are not subject to the minimum distribution rules before death or to the incidental death benefit rules of Code Sec. 401(a). (Code Sec. 408A(c)(5))

Distributions that do not meet the requirements for qualified distributions are includible in income to the extent of earnings on contributions. Distributions from a Roth IRA are treated as made from contributions first. All of an individual's Roth IRAs are aggregated for this purpose. (Code Sec. 408A(d)(1)(B)) For purposes of applying Code Sec. 72 (taxation of distributions rules) Roth IRAs and regular IRAs are treated separately. (Code Sec. 408A(d)(4))

> ⚡ *illustration:* Harry Jones (age 70) contributes $2,000 in '98 to Roth IRA Number 1 and $2,000 in '99 to Roth IRA Number 2. In 2001, Roth IRA Number 1 has a balance of $2,200 and Roth IRA Number 2 has a balance of $2,100. Jones closes Roth IRA Number 1 in 2001 and takes a distribution of $2,200 which he does not rollover into any other Roth IRA. Because Jones' aggregated nondeductible contributions ($4,000) exceeds the distribution ($2,200), the distribution is not includible in Jones' gross income even though the distribution is not a "qualified distribution".

Reporting requirements. Trustees of Roth IRAs are required to make reports required under Code Sec. 408(i) to ensure that amounts required to be included in gross income are reported. (Code Sec. 408(i) as amended by '97 Act §302(d))

☐ **Effective:** Taxable years beginning after Dec. 31,'97. ('97 Act §301(f))

¶ 302. Increased availability of IRA deductions for active pension plan participants and spouses

Code Sec. 219(g)(3)(B), as amended by '97 Act § 301(a)
Code Sec. 219(g), as amended by '97 Act § 301(b)
Generally effective: Taxable years beginning after Dec. 31, '97
Committee Reports, see ¶ 5015

The maximum deductible contribution that can be made to an IRA is the lesser of $2,000 or 100% percent of an individual's compensation (earned income in the case of self-employed individuals). A married taxpayer filing a joint return may be permitted to make the maximum deductible IRA contribution of up to $2,000 for each spouse (including, for example, a homemaker who does not work outside the home) if the combined compensation of both spouses is at least equal to the contributed amount. A single taxpayer is permitted to make the maximum deductible IRA contribution for a year if the individual is not an active participant in an employer-sponsored retirement plan for the year or the individual has adjusted gross income ("AGI") of less than $25,000. A married taxpayer filing a joint return is permitted to make the maximum deductible IRA contribution for a year if neither spouse is an active participant in an employer-sponsored plan or the couple has combined AGI of less than $40,000.

If a single taxpayer or either spouse (in the case of a married couple) was an active participant in an employer-sponsored retirement plan, the maximum IRA deduction was phased out over certain AGI levels (the "applicable dollar amount"). For single taxpayers, the maximum IRA deduction was phased out between $25,000 and $35,000 of AGI. For married taxpayers, the maximum deduction was phased out between $40,000 and $50,000 of AGI. (FTC 2d/FIN ¶ H-12215; USTR ¶ 2194.01; TaxDesk ¶ 28,352; PCA ¶ 35,116; PE ¶ 219-4.01)

New Law. The '97 Act increases the IRA/AGI limits. The "applicable dollar amount" (of AGI) used to calculate the permissible deduction for an IRA contribution for individuals who are active participants in an employer-sponsored retirement plan is increased as provided in the tables that follow. The first table applies to taxpayers filing a joint return. The second table (labeled "single" in the discussion and tables that follow) applies to any other taxpayer, other than a married individual filing a separate return. (Code Sec. 219(g)(3)(B) as amended by '97 Act §301(a)(1))

Joint Returns

For taxable years beginning in:	The applicable dollar amount is:
1998	$50,000
1999	$51,000
2000	$52,000
2001	$53,000
2002	$54,000
2003	$60,000
2004	$65,000
2005	$70,000
2006	$75,000
2007 and thereafter	$80,000

"Single" Taxpayers

For taxable years beginning in:	The applicable dollar amount is:
1998	$30,000
1999	$31,000
2000	$32,000
2001	$33,000
2002	$34,000
2003	$40,000
2004	$45,000
2005 and thereafter	$50,000

illustration (1): In 2000, Hal Marx, an unmarried, active participant in a qualified retirement plan, has AGI for the taxable year of $30,000 and files an individual return. The applicable dollar amount for 2000 for Hal is $32,000. Because Hal's AGI is less than the applicable dollar amount, there is no

FTC 2d References are to Federal Tax Coordinator 2d
FIN References are to RIA's Analysis of Federal Taxes: Income
USTR References are to United States Tax Reporter: Income, Estate & Gift, and Excise
PCA References are to Pension Coordinator and Pension & Benefits Expert/Advisor
PE References are to Pension and Profit Sharing 2nd
EP References are to Estate Planning & Taxation Coordinator and Estate Planning Advisor

"phaseout" of his IRA deduction, and he may take the maximum deduction of $2,000 for his contribution to his IRA.

observation: The '97 Act does not change the formula for computing the phaseout for "single" taxpayers. Only the "applicable dollar amount" has changed. The same is true for taxpayers filing a joint return *before 2007.* Thus, for "single" taxpayers, and for married taxpayers filing a joint return before 2007, the maximum IRA deduction is still reduced by an amount which bears the same ratio to $2,000 as the taxpayer's AGI minus the applicable dollar limitation bears to $10,000. So, the formula for reducing the maximum deduction ($2,000) for these taxpayers is:

$$\$2,000 \times \frac{\text{adjusted gross income minus applicable dollar amount}}{\$10,000}$$

illustration (2): Assume the same facts as in illustration 1 above, except that Hal has AGI of $40,000 for the taxable year. The maximum IRA deduction ($2,000) must be reduced by the proportionate amount by which AGI exceeds $32,000, as follows. [2,000 x ((40,000 - 32,000) ÷ 10,000) = 2,000 x (8,000 ÷ 10,000) = 2,000 × ⅘ = 1,600]. This $1,600 reduction reduces the $2,000 maximum IRA deduction to $400. Thus, Hal's maximum deductible IRA contribution is $400.

Under the '97 Act, for a married individual filing a separate return, the applicable dollar amount remains zero. (Code Sec. 219(g)(3)(B))

For each individual on a *joint return,* the '97 Act provides that *for taxable years beginning after Dec. 31, 2006,* the maximum IRA deduction is reduced by an amount which bears the same ratio to $2,000 as the taxpayers' (combined) AGI minus the applicable dollar amount bears to *$20,000.* (Code Sec. 219(g)(2)(A)(ii) as amended by '97 Act §301(a)(2))

observation: The amount of the reduction in the maximum deduction ($2,000) for each individual on a joint return for a taxable year *beginning after Dec. 31, 2006* is:

$$\$2,000 \times \frac{\text{adjusted gross income minus applicable dollar amount}}{\$20,000}$$

Deductible contributions for spouses of active participants. Under the '97 Act, the limits on deductible IRS contributions no longer apply to the *spouse* of an active participant. (Code Sec. 219(g)(1) as amended by '97 Act §301(b)) Instead, the maximum deductible IRA contribution for an individual who is not an active participant, but whose spouse is an active participant, is phased out for the nonactive participant if their (combined) AGI is between $150,000 and $160,000. (Com Rept, see ¶ 5015) This is accomplished technically by making the "applicable dollar amount" $150,000 and the denominator in the formula for joint returns (above) $10,000. (Code Sec. 219(g)(7))

Illustration (3): W is an active participant in an employer-sponsored retirement plan, and W's husband, H, is not. The combined AGI of H and W for the year is $200,000. Neither W nor H is entitled to make deductible contributions to an IRA for the year (because their combined AGI exceeds $160,000). (Com Rept, see ¶ 5015)

Illustration (4): The facts are the same as in illustration 3, above, except that the combined AGI of W and H is $125,000. H, who is not an active participant, can make a deductible contribution to an IRA (because combined AGI is under $150,000). However, a deductible contribution can not be made for W (because combined AGI exceeds the applicable dollar amount for an active participant filing jointly, e.g., $80,000 for 2007). (Com Rept, see ¶ 5015)

☐ **Effective:** Taxable years beginning after Dec. 31, '97. ('97 Act §301(c))

¶ 303. No penalty for early withdrawal of IRA funds for "first-time homebuyers"—$10,000 lifetime limitation

Code Sec. 72(t), as amended by '97 Act § 303
Generally effective: Payments and distributions made after '97
Committee Reports, see ¶ 5017

Under current law, if a taxpayer takes an "early withdrawal" (before reaching age 59½) from a qualified retirement plan, including an IRA, a 10% early withdrawal penalty tax applies. However, there are exceptions to this rule, e.g., if the withdrawal is due to death or disability or is part of a periodic payment. (FTC 2d/FIN ¶ H-11101; USTR ¶ 724.22; TaxDesk ¶ 14,552; PCA ¶ 32,202; PE ¶ 72-4.22)

New Law. Congress believes that home ownership is a fundamental part of the "American Dream" and has added another exception to the 10% penalty tax rules. (Com Rept, see ¶ 5017) The '97 Act provides that the 10% penalty does not apply to withdrawals from an IRA (including the new Code Sec. 408A "Roth IRA" added by the '97 Act, see ¶ 301) for up to $10,000 of first-time homebuyer expenses. (Code Sec. 72(t)(2)(F) as amended by '97 Act §303(a)); (Code Sec. 72(t)(8)(B) as amended by '97 Act §303(b))

To escape the 10% penalty tax, the distribution must be a "qualified first-time homebuyer distribution," i.e., any payment or distribution received by an individual to the extent the payment or distribution is used to pay the "qualified acquisition costs" of acquiring the "principal residence" of a "first-time homebuyer". The distribution must be used *within 120 days,* i.e., before the close of the 120th day after the day on which the payment or distribution is received. The first-time homebuyer can be the individual, a spouse, or any child, grandchild, or ancestor of the individual or spouse.

FTC 2d References are to Federal Tax Coordinator 2d
FIN References are to RIA's Analysis of Federal Taxes: Income
USTR References are to United States Tax Reporter: Income, Estate & Gift, and Excise
PCA References are to Pension Coordinator and Pension & Benefits Expert/Advisor
PE References are to Pension and Profit Sharing 2nd
EP References are to Estate Planning & Taxation Coordinator and Estate Planning Advisor

(Code Sec. 72(t)(8)(A))

The term "qualified acquisition costs" means the costs of acquiring, constructing, or reconstructing a residence. Qualified acquisition costs include any usual or reasonable settlement, financing, or other closing costs. (Code Sec. 72(t)(8)(C))

"Principal residence" is defined under the Code Sec. 121 rules on the exclusion of gain from the sale of a principal residence (as amended by the '97 Act, see ¶ 102). (Code Sec. 72(t)(8)(D)(ii))

The withdrawals eligible for "first-time homebuyers" can not exceed $10,000 during the individual's lifetime. (Com Rept, see ¶ 5017) Specifically, under the '97 Act, the aggregate amount of payments or distributions received by an individual which may be treated as qualified first-time homebuyer distributions for any taxable year can not exceed the excess (if any) of:

- $10,000, over

- the aggregate amounts treated as qualified first-time homebuyer distributions for the individual for all prior taxable years. (Code Sec. 72(t)(8)(B))

> *observation:* Neither the '97 Act nor the committee reports indicate whether the $10,000 is *per individual* if two (or more) individuals *together* purchase a home for the first time. But it seems permissible that, for example, a husband and wife purchasing their first home together *can* each withdraw up to $10,000 from each of their respective IRAs without incurring any penalty for early withdrawal.

The term "first-time homebuyer" means any individual if—

(1) the individual (*and* spouse, if any) had no present ownership interest in a principal residence during the two-year period ending on the "date of acquisition" of the principal residence at issue; and

(2) Code Sec. 1034(h) or Code Sec. 1034(k) (as in effect on the day before these first-time-homebuyer rules went into effect (see below), and as relating to the special rules on the rollover of gain on the sale of a principal residence by members of the armed forces and individuals having a tax home outside the U.S.) did not suspend the running of any period of time specified in Code Sec. 1034 (as so in effect) for the individual on the day before the date the distribution is applied under Code Sec. 72(t)(8)(A) (above). (Code Sec. 72(t)(8)(D)(i))

The "date of acquisition" is: (a) the date when a binding contract to purchase a "principal residence" is executed, or (b) the date when construction or reconstruction of a "principal residence" begins. (Code Sec. 72(t)(8)(D)(iii))

For the requirement that a first-time homebuyer be an individual who has not owned a home for two years (item 1, above), the '97 Act requires that the individual's spouse must also meet this requirement when the contract is executed or construction begins. (Com Rept, see ¶ 5017) *observation:* Thus, a "first-time homebuyer" under these rules is not necessarily a person buying a home for the first time.

Any amount withdrawn for the purchase of a principal residence is required to be used within 120 days of the date of withdrawal. (Code Sec. 72(t)(8)(A)) If this 120-day rule cannot be satisfied due to a delay or cancellation of the purchase or construction of the residence, the taxpayer may recontribute all or part of the amount withdrawn to the same or another IRA before the end of the 120-day period without suffering adverse tax consequences. (Com Rept, see ¶5017) The Code Sec. 408(d)(3)(B) limitation on IRA rollover contributions (which provides a one-year waiting period between rollovers from one IRA into another) doesn't apply to this recontribution, and the recontribution is not taken into account in determining whether the Code Sec. 408(d)(3)(B) limitation applies to any other amount. (Code Sec. 72(t)(8)(E))

The exception to the 10% penalty tax rules for first-time homebuyers is not available: (a) if the withdrawal qualifies for one of the other exceptions available under Code Sec. 72(t)(2)(A), Code Sec. 72(t)(2)(C), Code Sec. 72(t)(2)(D), or Code Sec. 72(t)(2)(E) (e.g., if the withdrawal is due to death or disability or is part of a periodic payment.), or (b) to the extent that the distribution is excepted from the penalty under Code Sec. 72(t)(2)(B) (relating to a withdrawal to pay medical expenses). (Code Sec. 72(t)(2)(F))

☐ **Effective:** Payments and distributions made in taxable years beginning after '97. ('97 Act §303(c))

¶304. No penalty for early withdrawal of IRA funds to pay higher education expenses

Code Sec. 72(t), as amended by '97 Act § 203
Generally effective: Distributions made after '97
Committee Reports, see ¶5004

Under current law, if a taxpayer takes an "early withdrawal" (before reaching age 59½) from a qualified retirement plan, including an IRA, a 10% early withdrawal penalty tax applies. However, there are exceptions to this rule, e.g., if the withdrawal is due to death or disability or is part of a periodic payment. (FTC 2d/FIN ¶H-11101; USTR ¶724.22; TaxDesk ¶14,552; PCA ¶32,202; PE ¶72-4.22)

New Law. Congress wants to allow individuals to receive distributions from their IRAs to pay higher education expenses without incurring the 10% early withdrawal penalty, and so has added another exception to the 10% penalty tax rules. (Com Rept, see ¶5004) The '97 Act provides that the 10% penalty does not apply to a distribution from an IRA (including the "Roth IRA" added by the '97 Act, see ¶301 (Com Rept,

FTC 2d References are to Federal Tax Coordinator 2d
FIN References are to RIA's Analysis of Federal Taxes: Income
USTR References are to United States Tax Reporter: Income, Estate & Gift, and Excise
PCA References are to Pension Coordinator and Pension & Benefits Expert/Advisor
PE References are to Pension and Profit Sharing 2nd
EP References are to Estate Planning & Taxation Coordinator and Estate Planning Advisor

see ¶ 5004)), if the taxpayer uses the money to pay "qualified higher education expenses." (Code Sec. 72(t)(2)(E) as amended by '97 Act §203(a))

"Qualified higher education expenses" include tuition at a post-secondary educational institution, as well as room and board, fees, books, supplies, and equipment required for enrollment or attendance. Expenses for graduate level courses are also covered. (Com Rept, see ¶ 5004) Qualified higher education expenses can be incurred by the taxpayer, the taxpayer's spouse, or any child, or grandchild of the taxpayer or his spouse. (Code Sec. 72(t)(7)(A) as amended by '97 Act §203(b))

A "child" is defined (under Code Sec. 151(c)(3)) as the son, stepson, daughter, or stepdaughter of the taxpayer or the taxpayer's spouse. (Code Sec. 72(t)(7)(A)(iii))

> **⊘ observation:** Thus, the taxpayer's child (or grandchild) need not be a dependent.

> **⊘ illustration:** Ward (age 50) marries June, a widow with a 27 year old son (Theodore). If so inclined, after '97, Ward can withdraw money from his IRA—without incurring the 10% penalty on early withdrawals—to pay for Theodore's graduate school education (assuming, of course, that the expenses qualify as qualified higher education expenses).

As a technical matter, "higher education expenses" are defined in Code Sec. 529(e)(3) (which relates to the rules on qualified state tuition programs, as amended by the '97 Act). Also, "*qualified* higher education expenses" must be incurred at an "eligible educational institution" as defined in Code Sec. 529(e)(5), also amended by the '97 Act. (Code Sec. 72(t)(7)(A)) For a discussion of these amended provisions, see ¶ 406.

The exception to the 10% penalty tax rules for "qualified higher education expenses" is not available: (a) if the withdrawal qualifies for one of the other exceptions available under Code Sec. 72(t)(2)(A), Code Sec. 72(t)(2)(C), or Code Sec. 72(t)(2)(D) (e.g., if the withdrawal is due to death or disability or is part of a periodic payment.), or (b) to the extent that the distribution is excepted from the penalty under Code Sec. 72(t)(2)(B) (relating to a withdrawal to pay medical expenses). (Code Sec. 72(t)(2)(E))

The amount of qualified higher education expenses for any taxable year must be reduced as provided in Code Sec. 25A(g)(2) (which relates to the reductions for certain scholarships, veterans benefits, etc. under the '97 Act's new "Hope Scholarship Credit" for higher education tuition and related expenses, see ¶ 401). (Code Sec. 72(t)(7)(B))

☐ **Effective:** Distributions made after Dec. 31, 1997, for expenses paid after '97 in taxable years ending after '97, for education furnished in academic periods beginning after '97. ('97 Act §203(c))

¶ 305. Individual retirement accounts and individually-directed plan accounts may be invested in certain bullion

Code Sec. 408(m)(3), as amended by '97 Act § 304(a)
Generally effective: Tax years beginning after Dec. 31, '97
Committee Reports, see ¶ 5018

The acquisition of "collectibles" by an individual retirement account or an individually-directed account in a qualified plan is treated as a distribution in an amount equal to the cost of the collectible. Certain gold and silver coins are excepted from the definition of collectibles. (FTC 2d/FIN ¶ H-12259; USTR ¶ 4084.03; TaxDesk ¶ 14,312, ¶ 28,394; PCA ¶ 35,160; PE ¶ 408-4.03)

New Law. The Act provides that the term "collectible" does not include a platinum coin described in 31 USCS §5112(k). (Code Sec. 408(m)(3)(A)(iii) as amended by '97 Act §304(a))

Under the Act, the term "collectible" also does not include any gold, silver, platinum, or palladium bullion (other than bullion made into a coin that is considered a "collectible") if the bullion is:

... of a fineness equal to or exceeding the minimum fineness that a "contract market" (as described in the Commodity Exchange Act, 7 USCS §7) requires for metals which may be delivered in satisfaction of a regulated futures contract, and

... in the physical possession of a trustee that meets the requirements for trustees of IRAs (under Code Sec. 408(a)). (Code Sec. 408(m)(3)(B))

☐ **Effective:** Tax years beginning after Dec. 31, '97. ('97 Act §304(b))

FTC 2d References are to Federal Tax Coordinator 2d
FIN References are to RIA's Analysis of Federal Taxes: Income
USTR References are to United States Tax Reporter: Income, Estate & Gift, and Excise
PCA References are to Pension Coordinator and Pension & Benefits Expert/Advisor
PE References are to Pension and Profit Sharing 2nd
EP References are to Estate Planning & Taxation Coordinator and Estate Planning Advisor

 Research Institute of America 81

¶ 400. Education: Expenses, Credits, Exclusions

¶ 401. "Hope Scholarship Credit," up to $1,500 per year, and "Lifetime Learning Credit," up to $1,000 per year, allowed for higher education expenses

Code Sec. 25A, as added by '97 Act § 201(a)
Code Sec. 6213(g)(2), as amended by '97 Act § 201(b)
Generally effective: Expenses paid after Dec. 31, '97
Committee Reports, see ¶ 5002

Under pre-'97 Act law, no credit was allowed for higher education expenses paid by taxpayers for themselves, their spouses or dependents.

New Law. Under the '97 Act, individual taxpayers (as specified below) are allowed as an income tax credit (the Code Sec. 25A credit) the amount equal to the sum of the Hope Scholarship Credit (up to $1,500 per year per student, see below) and the Lifetime Learning Credit (per taxpayer, up to $1,000 per year through 2002, up to $2,000 per year thereafter, see below). (Code Sec. 25A(a) as added by '97 Act §201(a)) The Code Sec. 25A credit is phased out for taxpayers with modified adjusted gross income of $40-50,000 ($80-100,000 for joint return filers). These amounts are to be adjusted for inflation after 2001. (See below.) The Code Sec. 25A credit is not allowed for any expense for which a deduction is allowed under any other provision of Chapter 1 of the Code (Code Sec. 1 through Code Sec. 1399). (Code Sec. 25A(g)(5))

The Code Sec. 25A credit is not allowed for a tax year with respect to the qualified tuition and related expenses of an individual unless the taxpayer elects to have Code Sec. 25A apply with respect to that individual for that tax year. (Code Sec. 25A(e)(1)) But the Code Sec. 25A credit election may not be made with respect to an individual (the student) for any tax year if, for that tax year, there is in effect an election under Code Sec. 530(d)(2)(C), by the taxpayer or any other individual, to exclude from gross income distributions from an education individual retirement account used to pay qualified higher education expenses of the student (see ¶ 403). (Code Sec. 25A(e)(2)) Similarly, as explained below, the Hope Scholarship Credit and the Lifetime Learning Credit may not be claimed in the same tax year for the same expenses. As a result, for a tax year, a taxpayer may elect with respect to an eligible student the Hope Scholarship credit, the Lifetime Learning Credit, or the exclusion from gross income for certain distributions from an education individual retirement account as provided by Code Sec. 530(d)(2)(C). In other words, a taxpayer may (for example) claim the Lifetime Learning Credit for a tax year with respect to one or more students, even though the taxpayer also claims a Hope Scholarship Credit (or claims an exclusion from gross income for certain distributions from qualified State tuition programs or education IRAs)

FTC 2d References are to the Federal Tax Coordinator 2d
FIN References are to RIA's Analysis of Federal Taxes: Income
USTR References are to the United States Tax Reporter: Income, Estate & Gift, and Excise
PCA References are to Pension Coordinator and Pension & Benefits Expert/Advisor
PE References are to Pension and Profit Sharing 2nd
EP References are to Estate Planning & Taxation Coordinator and Estate Planning Advisor

⊘ Research Institute of America

for that same tax year with respect to other students. If, for a tax year, a taxpayer claims a Hope Scholarship Credit with respect to a student (or claims an exclusion for certain distributions from an education IRA with respect to a student), then the Lifetime Learning Credit will not be available with respect to that same student for that year (although the Lifetime Learning Credit may be available with respect to that same student for other tax years). (Com Rept, see ¶ 5002)

The Code Sec. 25A credit is allowed only if the student's name and taxpayer identification number (TIN) are provided on the tax return of the person claiming the credit. (See below.)

The Code Sec. 25A credit is nonrefundable, and may not be used to reduce any alternative minimum tax (AMT) liability of the taxpayer. (Com Rept, see ¶ 5002)

Refunds of qualified tuition and related expenses may result in recapture of the credit. (See below.)

Who is entitled to the Code Sec. 25A credit. As noted above, individuals are entitled to claim the Code Sec. 25A credit, but with the following limitations.

Code Sec. 25A credit not allowed to persons claimed as dependents on another's tax return, but is allowed to the persons claiming them as dependents. As explained below, the Code Sec. 25A credit is allowed for qualified tuition and related expenses of (among others) any dependent of the taxpayer with respect to whom the taxpayer is allowed a personal exemption deduction under Code Sec. 151. However, if a personal exemption deduction under Code Sec. 151 with respect to an individual is allowed to another taxpayer for a tax year beginning in the calendar year in which that individual's tax year begins (Code Sec. 25A(g)(3)):

. . . the Code Sec. 25A credit is not allowed to that individual for that individual's tax year (Code Sec. 25A(g)(3)(A)), and;

. . . qualified tuition and related expenses paid by that individual during that individual's tax year must be treated as paid by the taxpayer to whom the personal exemption deduction referred to above is allowed. (Code Sec. 25A(g)(3)(B))

In other words, a taxpayer may claim the Code Sec. 25A credit with respect to an eligible student who is not the taxpayer or the taxpayer's spouse (e.g., in cases where the student is the taxpayer's child) only if the taxpayer claims the student as a dependent for the tax year for which the credit is claimed. If a student is claimed as a dependent by the parent or other taxpayer, the eligible student him- or herself is not entitled to claim a Code Sec. 25A credit for that tax year on the student's own tax return. If a parent (or other taxpayer) claims a student as a dependent, any qualified tuition and related expenses paid by the student are treated as paid by the parent (or other taxpayer) for purposes of the provision. (Com Rept, see ¶ 5002)

FTC 2d References are to Federal Tax Coordinator 2d
FIN References are to RIA's Analysis of Federal Taxes: Income
USTR References are to United States Tax Reporter: Income, Estate & Gift, and Excise
PCA References are to Pension Coordinator and Pension & Benefits Expert/Advisor
PE References are to Pension and Profit Sharing 2nd
EP References are to Estate Planning & Taxation Coordinator and Estate Planning Advisor

illustration: B is a college student and is the dependent of A. While at school, B works and contributes towards the payment of her qualified tuition and related expenses. A pays the remainder of those expenses. Although B files her own income tax return, A is entitled to, and does, claim a personal exemption deduction for B under Code Sec. 151. Under these circumstances, B is not permitted to claim a Code Sec. 25A credit for the qualified tuition and related expenses that she paid. A, however, is entitled to claim a Code Sec. 25A credit not only for the qualified tuition and related expenses of B that he (A) paid, but also for those expenses that B paid as well.

Credit denied for married individuals filing separate returns. If the taxpayer claiming the Code Sec. 25A credit is a married individual (within the meaning of Code Sec. 7703), the credit is allowed only if the taxpayer and the taxpayer's spouse file a joint return for the tax year. (Code Sec. 25A(g)(6))

Credit available to nonresident aliens only if residency election is in effect. If the taxpayer claiming the Code Sec. 25A credit is a nonresident alien individual for any portion of the tax year, the credit is allowed only if that individual is treated as a resident alien of the U.S. by reason of an election under Code Sec. 6013(g) (allowing nonresident alien individuals to elect to be treated as U.S. residents) or Code Sec. 6013(h) (allowing nonresident alien individuals who become U.S. residents during the tax year and who are married to U.S. citizens or residents to elect to be treated as residents for the entire tax year). (Code Sec. 25A(g)(7))

Code Sec. 25A credit phased out for taxpayers with modified adjusted gross income of $40-50,000 ($80-100,000 for joint return filers). The amount which would, but for the phase-out rules described below, be taken into account under Code Sec. 25A(a) (the first amount) must be reduced (but not below zero) by the amount determined under Code Sec. 25A(d)(2) (the reduction amount). (Code Sec. 25A(d)(1)) The reduction amount is the amount which bears the same ratio to the first amount as (Code Sec. 25A(d)(2)):

. . . the excess of (Code Sec. 25A(d)(2)(A))

• the taxpayer's modified adjusted gross income (defined below) for the tax year, over (Code Sec. 25A(d)(2)(A)(i))

• $40,000 ($80,000 in the case of a joint return) (Code Sec. 25A(d)(2)(ii)),
bears to

. . . $10,000 ($20,000 in the case of a joint return). (Code Sec. 25A(d)(2)(B))

observation: The only "amount" mentioned specifically by Code Sec. 25A(a) is "the amount equal to the sum of— (1) the Hope Scholarship Credit, plus (2) the Lifetime Learning Credit." The "first amount" would therefore appear to be the Code Sec. 25A credit computed without regard to the phase-out rules imposed by Code Sec. 25A(d) described above.

As a result of the reductions required by the above rules, the Code Sec. 25A credit amount that a taxpayer may otherwise claim is phased out ratably for taxpayers with modified AGI between $40,000 and $50,000 ($80,000 and $100,000 for taxpayers filing joint returns). (Com Rept, see ¶ 5002)

"Modified adjusted gross income" means the adjusted gross income of the taxpayer for the tax year increased by any amount excluded from gross income under Code Sec. 911 (the foreign earned income exclusion), Code Sec. 931 (exclusion of income derived from certain U.S. possessions), or Code Sec. 933 (Puerto Rican income exclusion). (Code Sec. 25A(d)(3))

For tax years beginning after 2001, the $40,000 and $80,000 amounts referred to above are each increased by an amount equal to:

... those amounts, multiplied by

... the cost-of-living adjustment determined under Code Sec. 1(f)(3) for the calendar year in which the tax year begins, determined by substituting "calendar year 2000" for "calendar year '92" in Code Sec. 1(f)(3)(b). (Code Sec. 25A(h)(2)A))

If any amount as adjusted under Code Sec. 25A(h)(2)(A) (above) is not a multiple of $1,000, that amount is rounded to the next lowest multiple of $1,000. (Code Sec. 25A(h)(2)(B))

Under the above rule, the first tax year for which the inflation adjustment may be made to increase the income phase-out ranges will be 2002. (Com Rept, see ¶ 5002)

TIN requirement. The Code Sec. 25A credit is allowed to a taxpayer with respect to the qualified tuition and related expenses of an individual only if the taxpayer includes the name and taxpayer identification number (TIN) of that individual on the tax return for the tax year for which the credit is claimed. (Code Sec. 25A(g)(1))

The '97 Act makes omission of a correct TIN that must be included on a return under the above rule a "mathematical or clerical error" subject to summary assessment procedures. (Code Sec. 6213(g)(2)(J) as amended by '97 Act §201(b))

IRS regulatory authority; recapture of the Code Sec. 25A credit. IRS may prescribe any regulations necessary or appropriate to carry out the Code Sec. 25A credit provisions, including regulations providing for a recapture of the credit in cases where there is a refund in a later tax year of any amount which was taken into account in determining the amount of the credit. (Code Sec. 25A(i)) These regulations may address the information reports that eligible educational institutions will be required to file (see ¶ 410) to assist students and the IRS in calculating the amount of the Lifetime Learning Credit potentially available. (Com Rept, see ¶ 5002)

Hope Scholarship Credit. In the case of any eligible student (defined below) for whom an election is in effect for any tax year, the Hope Scholarship Credit is an amount equal to the sum of (Code Sec. 25A(b)(1)):

FTC 2d References are to Federal Tax Coordinator 2d
FIN References are to RIA's Analysis of Federal Taxes: Income
USTR References are to United States Tax Reporter: Income, Estate & Gift, and Excise
PCA References are to Pension Coordinator and Pension & Benefits Expert/Advisor
PE References are to Pension and Profit Sharing 2nd
EP References are to Estate Planning & Taxation Coordinator and Estate Planning Advisor

(1) 100% of so much of the qualified tuition and related expenses (defined below) paid by the taxpayer during the tax year (for education furnished to the eligible student during any academic period beginning in that tax year) as does not exceed $1,000 (Code Sec. 25A(b)(1)(A)), plus

(2) 50% of the expenses so paid as exceeds $1,000 but does not exceed the applicable limit . (Code Sec. 25A(b)(1)(B)) The applicable limit for any tax year is an amount equal to two times the dollar amount in effect under Code Sec. 25A(b)(1)(A) (above) for that tax year. (Code Sec. 25A(b)(4))

> ⓇⒾⒶ *observation:* Because there is no inflation adjustment for tax years beginning before 2002 (see below), for tax years beginning in '98 through tax years beginning in 2001 the applicable limit is $2,000 ($1,000 × 2). Therefore, for those years, the item (2) amount is $500—i.e., $2,000 – $1,000, or $1,000, × 50%. Consequently, for those years, the maximum available Hope Scholarship Credit is equal to $1,500—100% of the $1,000 of qualified tuition and related expenses allowed under item (1); plus the $500 item (2) amount.

> ⓇⒾⒶ *observation:* A taxpayer who is paying (or who, under Code Sec. 25A(g)(3), discussed above, is treated as paying) the qualified tuition and related expenses of more than one eligible student is entitled to the maximum Hope Scholarship Credit allowed for the qualified tuition and related expenses of *each* and *all* of those eligible students. For example, a taxpayer who is paying the qualified tuition and related expenses of two children in college (or a spouse and a child) is entitled (if otherwise qualified) to claim the maximum Hope Scholarship Credit for the expenses of each child (or for the expenses of the spouse and the expenses of the child). This is not the case with respect to the Lifetime Learning Credit, see below.

If qualified tuition and related expenses are paid by the taxpayer during a tax year for an academic period which begins during the first three months following that tax year, the academic period is treated as beginning during that tax year. (Code Sec. 25A(g)(4)) In other words, the Code Sec. 25A credit is available in the tax year the expenses are paid, subject to the requirement that the education commence or continue during that year or during the first three months of the next year. (Com Rept, see ¶ 5002)

> ⓇⒾⒶ *illustration:* In December of Year 1, X pays College for qualified tuition and related expenses for College's spring semester, which begins in Jan. of Year 2. For purposes of the HOPE credit rules, because X has paid for the spring semester in Year 1, that semester is treated as beginning in Year 1. Therefore X is entitled to the HOPE credit in Year 1 for the expenses of the spring semester.

> ⓇⒾⒶ *observation:* In the above RIA *Illustration,* if X waited until Jan. of Year 2 to pay for the spring semester, he would be entitled to the HOPE credit for Year 2, rather than Year 1. Thus, in this situation, X may effectively elect the year in which to claim the credit—but the "election" is made by the timing

of the payment.

For tax years beginning after 2001, each of the $1,000 amounts under Code Sec. 25A(b)(1) (above) is increased by an amount equal to (Code Sec. 25A(h)(1)(A)):

... that dollar amount, multiplied by (Code Sec. 25A(h)(1)(A)(i))

... the cost-of-living adjustment determined under Code Sec. 1(f)(3) for the calendar year in which the tax year begins, determined by substituting "calendar year 2000" for "calendar year '92" in Code Sec. 1(f)(3)(B). (Code Sec. 25A(h)(1)(A)(ii))

If any amount as adjusted as indicated above is not a multiple of $100, that amount is rounded to the next lowest multiple of $100. (Code Sec. 25A(h)(1)(B))

Hope Scholarship Credit election allowed only for first two years of postsecondary education. A Code Sec. 25A credit election with respect to any eligible student for purposes of the Hope Scholarship Credit may not be made for any tax year if such an election (by the taxpayer or any other individual) is in effect with respect to that student for any two earlier tax years. (Code Sec. 25A(b)(2)(A))

Moreover, the Hope Scholarship Credit is not allowed for a tax year with respect to the qualified tuition and related expenses of an eligible student if the student has completed (before the beginning of that tax year) the first two years of postsecondary education at an eligible educational institution (as defined below). (Code Sec. 25A(b)(2)(C))

> *observation:* Thus, the Hope Scholarship Credit is allowed only for the qualified tuition and related expenses of the first two years of undergraduate education. It is not allowed for the expenses of later years of undergraduate education, nor for the expenses of any graduate or advanced degree programs.

Hope Scholarship Credit allowed only for students qualifying as eligible students during one academic period during the tax year. The Hope Scholarship Credit is not allowed for a tax year with respect to the qualified tuition and related expenses of an individual unless that individual is an eligible student (defined below) for at least one academic period which begins during that tax year. (Code Sec. 25A(b)(2)(B))

Hope Scholarship Credit denied if student convicted of a felony drug offense. The Hope Scholarship credit is not allowed for qualified tuition and related expenses for the enrollment or attendance of a student for any academic period if that student has been convicted of a federal or state felony offense consisting of the possession or distribution of a controlled substance before the end of the tax year with or within which that period ends. (Code Sec. 25A(b)(2)(D))

Eligible student defined. With respect to any academic period, "eligible student" means a student who (Code Sec. 25A(d)(3)):

FTC 2d References are to Federal Tax Coordinator 2d
FIN References are to RIA's Analysis of Federal Taxes: Income
USTR References are to United States Tax Reporter: Income, Estate & Gift, and Excise
PCA References are to Pension Coordinator and Pension & Benefits Expert/Advisor
PE References are to Pension and Profit Sharing 2nd
EP References are to Estate Planning & Taxation Coordinator and Estate Planning Advisor

... meets the requirements of Sec. 484(a)(1) of the Higher Education Act of '65 (20 U.S.C. 1091(a)(1)), as in effect on Aug. 5, '97 (Code Sec. 25A(d)(3)(A)), and

... is carrying at least one-half the normal full-time workload (defined below) for the course of study the student is pursuing. (Code Sec. 25A(d)(3)(B))

Under these rules, an eligible student for purposes of the Hope Scholarship Credit is an individual who is enrolled in a degree, certificate, or other program (including a program of study abroad approved for credit by the institution at which such student is enrolled) leading to a recognized educational credential at an eligible educational institution. The student must pursue a course of study on at least a half-time basis. (In other words, for at least one academic period which begins during the tax year, the student must carry at least one-half the normal full-time work load for the course of study the student is pursuing.) (Com Rept, see ¶ 5002)

Lifetime Learning Credit. The Lifetime Learning Credit for any taxpayer for any tax year is an amount equal to 20% of so much of the qualified tuition and related expenses paid by the taxpayer during the tax year for education furnished to an individual during any academic period beginning in that tax year as does not exceed $5,000 ($10,000 in the case of tax years beginning after Dec. 31, 2002). (Code Sec. 25A(c)(1)) Thus, for tax years beginning before Jan. 1, 2003, the maximum credit per taxpayer return is $1,000; and for tax years beginning after Dec. 31, 2002, the maximum credit per taxpayer return is $2,000. (Com Rept, see ¶ 5002)

For purposes of computing the Lifetime Learning Credit for a tax year, the qualified tuition and related expenses with respect to an individual who is an eligible student and for whom a Hope Scholarship Credit is allowed for that tax year are not taken into account. (Code Sec. 25A(c)(2)(A))

> *observation:* The Hope Scholarship Credit is allowed with respect to the qualified tuition and related expenses of a student only if elected, see above. Therefore, if this election is not made, the Lifetime Learning Credit may be claimed with respect to those expenses. If the Hope Scholarship Credit *is* elected with respect to those expenses, the expenses are disregarded in computing the Lifetime Learning Credit for which the taxpayer is eligible.

In contrast to the Hope Scholarship Credit (which may be elected only with respect to the first two years of undergraduate education, see above), the Lifetime Learning Credit may be claimed with respect to tuition and fees incurred with respect to undergraduate or graduate-level (and professional degree) courses. In addition to allowing a credit for the tuition and fees of a student who attends classes on at least a half-time basis as part of a degree or certificate program, the Lifetime Learning Credit also is available with respect to any course of instruction at an eligible educational institution (whether enrolled in by the student on a full-time, half-time, or less than half-time basis) to acquire or improve job skills of the student. (Com Rept, see ¶ 5002)

If qualified tuition and related expenses are paid by the taxpayer during a tax year for an academic period which begins during the first three months following that tax year, the academic period is treated as beginning during that tax year. (Code Sec. 25A(g)(4)) The Lifetime Learning Credit is available in the tax year the expenses are paid, subject to the requirement that the education commence or continue during that year or during the first three months of the next year. Qualified tuition and fees paid with the proceeds of a loan generally are eligible for the Lifetime Learning Credit (rather than repayment of the loan itself). (Com Rept, see ¶ 5002)

In contrast to the Hope Scholarship Credit, a taxpayer may claim the Lifetime Learning Credit for an unlimited number of tax years. Also in contrast to the Hope Scholarship Credit, the maximum amount of the Lifetime Learning Credit that may be claimed on a taxpayer's return will not vary based on the number of students in the taxpayer's family. (Com Rept, see ¶ 5002)

Qualified tuition and related expenses defined. Except as noted below, "qualified tuition and related expenses" means (for purposes of both the Hope Scholarship Credit and the Lifetime Learning Credit) tuition and fees required for the enrollment or attendance of

. . . the taxpayer,

. . . the taxpayer's spouse, or

. . . any dependent of the taxpayer with respect to whom the taxpayer is allowed a personal exemption deduction under Code Sec. 151

at an eligible educational institution (defined below) for courses of instruction of that individual at that institution. (Code Sec. 25A(f)(1)(A)) Neither the Hope Scholarship Credit nor the Lifetime Learning Credit is available for expenses incurred to purchase books. (Com Rept, see ¶ 5002)

For purposes of computing the Lifetime Learning Credit, qualified tuition and related expenses include expenses with respect to any course of instruction at an eligible educational institution to acquire or improve job skills of the individual. (Code Sec. 25A(c)(2)(B))

"Qualified tuition and related expenses" does not include:

. . . expenses with respect to any course or other education involving sports, games, or hobbies, unless the course or other education is part of the individual's degree program (Code Sec. 25A(f)(1)(B)); or

. . . student activity fees, athletic fees, insurance expenses, or other expenses unrelated to an individual's academic course of instruction. (Code Sec. 25A(f)(1)(C)) Other expenses unrelated to an individual's academic course of instruction are room and board expenses, transportation, and similar personal, living or family expenses. (Com Rept, see ¶ 5002)

The amount of qualified tuition and related expenses otherwise taken into account under Code Sec. 25A with respect to an individual for an academic period must be reduced by the sum of any amounts paid for the benefit of that individual which are allo-

FTC 2d References are to Federal Tax Coordinator 2d
FIN References are to RIA's Analysis of Federal Taxes: Income
USTR References are to United States Tax Reporter: Income, Estate & Gift, and Excise
PCA References are to Pension Coordinator and Pension & Benefits Expert/Advisor
PE References are to Pension and Profit Sharing 2nd
EP References are to Estate Planning & Taxation Coordinator and Estate Planning Advisor

 Research Institute of America 89

cable to that period as (Code Sec. 25A(g)(2)):

... a qualified scholarship which is excludable from gross income under Code Sec. 117 (Code Sec. 25A(g)(2)(A));

... an educational assistance allowance under the following chapters of Title 38 of the United States Code (relating to veterans' benefits)—

- Chapter 30, All-Volunteer Force Education Assistance Program;

- Chapter 31, Training and Rehabilitation for Veterans with Service-Connected Disabilities;

- Chapter 32, Post-Vietnam Era Veterans' Educational Assistance;

- Veterans' Educational Assistance;

- Survivors' and Dependents' Educational Assistance (Code Sec. 25A(g)(2)(B));

... an educational assistance allowance under Chapter 1606 of title 10 of the United States Code (Educational Assistance for Members of the Selected Reserve) (Code Sec. 25A(g)(2)(B)); or

... a payment (other than a gift, bequest, devise, or inheritance within the meaning of Code Sec. 102(a)) for that individual's educational expenses, or attributable to that individual's enrollment at an eligible educational institution, which is excludable from gross income under any law of the United States. (Code Sec. 25A(g)(2)(C))

The reduction required by Code Sec. 25A(g)(2), described above, must be done *before* the application of Code Sec. 25A(b) (relating to the Hope Scholarship Credit, see above), Code Sec. 25A(c) (relating to the Lifetime Learning Credit, see above) and Code Sec. 25A(d) (phasing out the Code Sec. 25A credit for taxpayers with modified adjusted gross income above certain levels, see above). (Code Sec. 25A(g)(2))

Under the above rules, qualified tuition and related expenses generally include only out-of-pocket expenses. Qualified tuition and related expenses do not include expenses covered by educational assistance that is not required to be included in the gross income of either the student or the taxpayer claiming the credit. Thus, total qualified tuition and related expenses are reduced by any scholarship or fellowship grants excludable from gross income under Code Sec. 117 and any other tax-free educational benefits received by the student during the tax year. No reduction of qualified tuition and related expenses is required for a gift, bequest, devise, or inheritance within the meaning of Code Sec. 102(a). (Com Rept, see ¶ 5002)

Qualified tuition expenses paid with the proceeds of a loan generally are eligible for the Code Sec. 25A credit (rather than repayment of the loan itself). (Com Rept, see ¶ 5002)

"Eligible educational institution" means an institution (Code Sec. 25A(f)(2)):

... which is described in Sec. 481 of the Higher Education Act of '65 (20 U.S.C. 1088), as in effect on Aug. 5, '97 (Code Sec. 25A(f)(2)(A)), and

... which is eligible to participate in a program under title IV of that act. (Code Sec. 25A(f)(2)(B))

Under these rules, eligible institutions generally are accredited post-secondary educational institutions offering credit toward a bachelor's degree, an associate's degree, or another recognized post-secondary credential. Certain proprietary institutions and post-secondary vocational institutions also are eligible educational institutions. The institution must be eligible to participate in Department of Education student aid programs. (Com Rept, see ¶ 5002)

☐ **Effective:** Expenses paid after Dec. 31, '97, in tax years ending after that date, for education furnished in academic periods beginning after that date. ('97 Act §201(f)(1)) However, the Lifetime Learning Credit allowed by Code Sec. 25A(a)(2) is allowed only for expenses paid after June 30, '98, in tax years ending after that date, for education furnished in academic periods beginning after that date. ('97 Act §201(f)(2))

recommendation: Because payments made before '98 don't qualify for the Hope Scholarship Credit, wait until '98 to pay bills for qualified tuition and related expenses received in '97 for the first semester of '98.

observation: Because of the Act's effective date, and because the Hope Scholarship Credit is only available with respect to the first two years of post-secondary education (see above), the Hope Scholarship Credit is not available to persons who have completed their first two years of undergraduate education before '98. However, this restriction does not apply to the Lifetime Learning Credit, and that credit is available, for expenses paid after June 30, '98, to persons beyond the first two years of secondary education (see above).

¶ 402. Above-the-line deduction allowed for up to $1,000 of interest paid on higher education loans in '98, increasing over four years to $2,500 for interest paid in 2001

Code Sec. 221, as added by '97 Act § 202(a)
Code Sec. 62(a)(17), as amended by '97 Act § 202(b)
Generally effective: Any loan interest payment due and paid after Dec. 31, '97
Committee Reports, see ¶ 5003

Individual taxpayers aren't allowed any deduction for personal interest. Personal interest is any interest that is not home mortgage interest, investment interest, or business interest. Student loan interest is treated as personal interest and thus isn't deductible. (FTC 2d/FIN ¶ K-5510 *et seq.*; USTR ¶ 1634; TaxDesk ¶ 31,400 *et seq.*)

New Law. The '97 Act allows a deduction for interest payments due and paid after Dec. 31, '97 on any qualified education loan. Certain individuals who have paid interest on qualified education loans may claim an above-the-line deduction for the interest expenses. The maximum deduction is phased in over four years, with a $1,000 maximum deduction in '98, $1,500 in '99, $2,000 in 2000, and $2,500 in 2001. No deduction is allowed to an individual if that individual is claimed as a dependent on another taxpayer's return for the tax year. The maximum deduction amount is phased out ratably for individual taxpayers with modified adjusted gross income (AGI) of $40,000 to $55,000 ($60,000 to $75,000 for joint returns). These income ranges will be indexed for inflation after 2002. (Com Rept, see ¶ 5003)

General rule. An individual taxpayer is allowed a deduction for the amount of interest paid by the taxpayer during the tax year on any qualified education loan (generally, indebtedness to pay qualified higher education expenses, i.e., tuition, room and board, and related expenses for attending post-secondary educational institutions, including certain vocational schools, and certain institutions offering postgraduate training, see below). (Code Sec. 221(a) as added by '97 Act §202(a))

Maximum deduction. Subject to the phaseout based on modified AGI discussed below, the deduction allowed under this provision for the tax year may not exceed: (Code Sec. 221(b)(1))

... $1,000 for tax years beginning in '98,

... $1,500 for tax years beginning in '99,

... $2,000 for tax years beginning in 2000, and

... $2,500 for tax years beginning in 2001 or later.

The maximum deduction is not indexed for inflation. (Com Rept, see ¶ 5003)

60-month limitation on period deduction allowed. The deduction is allowed only with respect to interest paid on a qualified education loan during the first 60 months (whether or not consecutive) in which interest payments are required. (Code Sec. 221(d)) Months during which the qualified education loan is in deferral or forbearance do not count against the 60-month period. (Com Rept, see ¶ 5003) For purposes of this rule, any loan and all refinancings of the loan are treated as one loan. (Code Sec. 221(d))

> *observation:* In the case of a qualified education loan incurred before Aug. 5, '97, loan interest payments due after Dec. 31, '97 qualify for the deduction only to the extent the 60-month period referred to above has not expired. See the discussion of the effective date rules below. Thus, except as noted above, months during which interest was paid before Jan. 1, '98 count against the 60-month period for which interest can be deducted.

Phaseout of deduction. The deduction is phased out ratably for taxpayers with modified adjusted gross income (AGI), see below, between $40,000 and $55,000 ($60,000 and $75,000 for joint returns). (Com Rept, see ¶ 5003)

Under the phaseout, the amount that would otherwise be allowable as a deduction under this Code section must be reduced (but not below zero) by the amount determined under a phaseout formula. (Code Sec. 221(b)(2)(A)) The amount determined under this formula is the amount which bears the same ratio to the amount that would otherwise be taken into account as the excess of the taxpayer's modified AGI for the tax year over $40,000 ($60,000 in the case of a joint return), bears to $15,000. (Code Sec. 221(b)(2)(B))

The $40,000 and $60,000 phaseout amounts are indexed for inflation after 2002, see below.

Modified adjusted gross income. For the purpose of the income limitation, modified adjusted gross income means adjusted gross income determined without regard to this deduction for qualified education loan interest, Code Sec. 135 dealing with the exclusion of income from U.S. Savings Bonds used to pay higher education expenses (FTC 2d/FIN ¶ J-3015; USTR ¶ 1354), Code Sec. 137 dealing with the exclusion of employer-provided benefits under an adoption assistance program (FTC 2d/FIN ¶ H-1450; USTR ¶ 1374), Code Sec. 911 dealing with the foreign earned income exclusion (FTC 2d/FIN ¶ O-1200; USTR ¶ 9114), Code Sec. 931 dealing with the exclusion of income from U.S. possessions (FTC 2d/FIN ¶ O-1383; USTR ¶ 9314), and Code Sec. 933 dealing with the exclusion of income from Puerto Rico (FTC 2d/FIN ¶ O-1450; USTR ¶ 9334). (Code Sec. 221(b)(2)(C)(i)) Also, adjusted gross income is determined after the application of Code Sec. 86 dealing with the inclusion in income of Social Security and tier 1 railroad retirement benefits (FTC 2d/FIN ¶ J-1455; USTR ¶ 864), Code Sec. 219 dealing with the deduction for qualified retirement contributions (FTC 2d/FIN ¶ H-12200; USTR ¶ 2194), and Code Sec. 469 dealing with the limitations on passive activity losses and credits (FTC 2d/FIN ¶ M-4600; USTR ¶ 4694). (Code Sec. 221(b)(2)(C)(ii))

For purposes of Code Sec. 86, Code Sec. 135, Code Sec. 137, Code Sec. 219, and Code Sec. 469, adjusted gross income is determined without regard to the deduction allowed under this section for qualified education loan interest. (Code Sec. 221(b)(2)(C))

Dependents not eligible for deduction. No deduction is allowed under this provision to an individual for the tax year if a dependency exemption with respect to the individual is allowed to another taxpayer for the tax year beginning in the calendar year in which the individual's tax year begins. (Code Sec. 221(c))

Double benefit denied. No deduction is allowed under this provision for any amount for which a deduction is allowable under any other provision of the Code. (Code Sec. 221(f)(1))

> *observation:* An example of when a deduction might be allowable under another provision of the Code is where a home equity loan is taken out to pay education expenses. Interest on the home equity loan would be deductible as an itemized deduction, provided the amount of the debt doesn't exceed $100,000 ($50,000 in the case of a separate return by a married individual) and all mortgages on the home total no more than its fair market value. See FTC 2d/FIN ¶ K-5470; USTR ¶ 1634.052. Interest on the home equity loan

FTC 2d References are to Federal Tax Coordinator 2d
FIN References are to RIA's Analysis of Federal Taxes: Income
USTR References are to United States Tax Reporter: Income, Estate & Gift, and Excise
PCA References are to Pension Coordinator and Pension & Benefits Expert/Advisor
PE References are to Pension and Profit Sharing 2nd
EP References are to Estate Planning & Taxation Coordinator and Estate Planning Advisor

couldn't also be deducted under Code Sec. 221 as interest on a qualified education loan.

observation: If a deduction for interest on a loan taken out to pay education expenses is allowable under another provision of the Code, apparently the taxpayer must claim the deduction under that provision. The deduction must be claimed under the other provision even though it may be less valuable if taken under that provision because it's not allowable in determining adjusted gross income, as it would be if it were deducted under Code Sec. 221, and thus doesn't reduce the floor for claiming certain itemized deductions.

observation: If an individual takes out two separate education loans and the interest on one loan qualifies for deduction under Code Sec. 221, while the interest on the other loan qualifies for deduction under some other Code provision, presumably the individual could still take an above-the-line deduction for the maximum amount allowed under Code Sec. 221, and the interest deductible under the other provision would not be taken into account in determining whether the maximum deduction allowed under Code Sec. 221 is reached.

Married couples must file joint return. If the taxpayer is married at the close of the tax year, the deduction under this provision is allowed only if the taxpayer and his or her spouse file a joint return for the tax year. (Code Sec. 221(f)(2)) Marital status is determined under the normal Code Sec. 7703 rules. (Code Sec. 221(f)(3))

How deduction for qualified education loan interest is claimed. The deduction for qualified education loan interest allowed by Code Sec. 221 is deductible from gross income in determining adjusted gross income. (Code Sec. 62(a)(17) as amended by '97 Act §202(b)) Thus, it's an above-the-line deduction. (Com Rept, see ¶ 5003)

observation: This means the deduction for interest on qualified education loans is allowed whether or not the taxpayer itemizes other deductions.

Qualified education loan. Qualified education loan means any indebtedness incurred to pay qualified higher education expenses (see below) that are:

(1) incurred on behalf of the taxpayer, the taxpayer's spouse, or any dependent (as defined in Code Sec. 152 (Code Sec. 221(e)(4))) of the taxpayer as of the time the indebtedness was incurred (Code Sec. 221(e)(1)(A)),

(2) paid or incurred within a reasonable period of time before or after the indebtedness is incurred (Code Sec. 221(e)(1)(B)), and

(3) attributable to education furnished during a period when the recipient was an eligible student (see below). (Code Sec. 221(e)(1)(C))

A qualified education loan includes indebtedness used to refinance indebtedness that qualifies as a qualified education loan. A qualified education loan doesn't include any indebtedness owed to a person who is related to the taxpayer within the meaning of Code Sec. 267(b) (barring deduction of losses from sales or exchanges between related persons, see FTC 2d/FIN ¶ I-3500; USTR ¶ 2674) or Code Sec. 707(b)(1) (disallowing losses on sales of property with respect to controlled partnerships, see FTC 2d/FIN ¶ B-2000; USTR ¶ 7074). (Code Sec. 221(e)(1))

Qualified higher education expenses. Qualified higher education expenses means the cost of attendance (as defined in section 472 of the Higher Education Act of 1965, as in effect on the day before Aug. 5, '97) at an eligible educational institution (see below). (Code Sec. 221(e)(2)) Qualified higher education expenses include tuition, fees, room and board, and related expenses. (Com Rept, see ¶ 5003)

Qualified higher education expenses must be reduced by the sum of

(1) the amount excluded from gross income by reason of such expenses under Code Sec. 127 (exclusion of employer-provided educational assistance benefits, see FTC 2d/FIN ¶ H-2064; USTR ¶ 1274), Code Sec. 135 (exclusion of income from U.S. Savings Bonds used to pay higher education expenses, see FTC 2d/FIN ¶ J-3015; USTR ¶ 1354), or Code Sec. 530 (distribution from an education IRA, see ¶ 403) (Code Sec. 221(e)(2)(A)); and

(2) the amount of any scholarship, allowance, or payment described in Code Sec. 25A(g)(2) (the HOPE credit for higher education expenses, see ¶ 401), (Code Sec. 221(e)(2)(B)), i.e., the amount of any scholarship or fellowship grants excludable from gross income under Code Sec. 117 (see FTC 2d/FIN ¶ J-1230; USTR ¶ 1174), as well as any other tax-free educational benefits. (Com Rept, see ¶ 5003)

Eligible education institution. The term "eligible educational institution" has the same meaning given that term by Code Sec. 25A(f)(2) for purposes of the HOPE credit for higher education expenses (see ¶ 401). Thus, the term includes post-secondary educational institutions and certain vocational schools. (Com Rept, see ¶ 5003) In addition, however, for purposes of the deduction for interest on education loans, the term also includes an institution conducting an internship or residency program leading to a degree or certificate awarded by an institution of higher education, a hospital, or a health care facility which offers postgraduate training. (Code Sec. 221(e)(2))

Eligible student. The term "eligible student" has the meaning given that term by Code Sec. 25A(b)(3) for purposes of the HOPE credit for higher education expenses (see ¶ 401). (Code Sec. 221(e)(3)) Thus, the qualified education expenses must be attributable to a period when the student is at least a half-time student. (Com Rept, see ¶ 5003)

Inflation adjustments. In the case of a tax year beginning after 2002, the $40,000 and $60,000 phaseout amounts in Code Sec. 221(b)(2) (see above) are each increased by an amount equal to such dollar amount, multiplied by the cost-of-living adjustment determined under Code Sec. 1(f)(3) for the calendar year in which the tax year begins, determined by substituting "calendar year 2001" for "calendar year 1992" in Code

FTC 2d References are to Federal Tax Coordinator 2d
FIN References are to RIA's Analysis of Federal Taxes: Income
USTR References are to United States Tax Reporter: Income, Estate & Gift, and Excise
PCA References are to Pension Coordinator and Pension & Benefits Expert/Advisor
PE References are to Pension and Profit Sharing 2nd
EP References are to Estate Planning & Taxation Coordinator and Estate Planning Advisor

Sec. 1(f)(3)(B). (Code Sec. 221(g)(1)) If any amount as adjusted is not a multiple of $5,000, the amount is rounded to the next lowest multiple of $5,000. (Code Sec. 221(g)(2))

Reporting requirement. For information return reporting requirements that apply to any person engaged in a trade or business and receiving interest on qualified education loans, see ¶ 410.

☐ **Effective:** Any qualified education loan incurred on, before, or after Aug. 5, '97, but only with respect to (1) any loan interest payment due and paid after Dec. 31, '97, and (2) the portion of the 60-month period referred to in Code Sec. 221(d) (limitation on period the deduction is allowed, see above) after Dec. 31, '97. ('97 Act §202(e))

Thus, in the case of already existing qualified education loans, interest payments qualify for the deduction to the extent that the 60-month period has not expired. For purposes of counting the 60 months, any qualified education loan and all refinancing (that is treated as a qualified education loan) of that loan are treated as a single loan. (Com Rept, see ¶ 5003)

observation: This 60-month rule means that interest payments on loans taken out many years ago will still be deductible in '98. For example, if payments on a loan started in Jan. '94 (48 months before Jan. '98), the taxpayer/borrower will still be able to deduct a full 12 months of interest in '98 before the 60-month period runs out. And if the taxpayer/borrower wasn't required to start repaying the loan until after graduation, interest payments on loans taken out even before '94 may still be deducted in '98.

recommendation: Practitioners may have clients who took out student loans long ago and who may still be paying off those loans. Practitioners should find out which of their clients are still paying off student loans and how long they have been making the payments, so the client will get all the deduction for interest to which he's entitled.

¶ 403. Tax-exempt education IRAs allowed

Code Sec. 530, as added by '97 Act § 213(a)
Code Sec. 4973(e), as amended by '97 Act § 213(d)
Code Sec. 4975(c), as amended by '97 Act § 213(b)
Code Sec. 6693, as amended by '97 Act § 213(c)
Generally effective: Tax years beginning after Dec. 31, '97
Committee Reports, see ¶ 5005

Under pre-'97 Act law, there was no provision for tax-exempt education individual retirement accounts.

New Law. The '97 Act creates the "education individual retirement account"—a U.S. trust designated as an education IRA created exclusively for the purpose of paying the trust beneficiary's "qualified higher education expenses." (Code Sec. 530(b)(1) as added by '97 Act §213(a)) An education IRA is exempt from income tax except for the Code Sec. 511 tax on unrelated business income of charitable organizations. (Code

Sec. 530(a))

Contributions.

> ⓇⒾⒶ *observation:* Apparently, the '97 Act does not provide a deduction for a contribution to an education IRA. Although neither the '97 Act nor the committee reports specifically state that education IRA contributions are *not* deductible, deductions must be specifically granted by law, and cannot be presumed. Also, as detailed below, the taxation of distributions from education IRAs is consistent with the contributions being nondeductible.

The education IRA beneficiary doesn't include in gross income either contributions to or earnings of an education IRA. (Com Rept, see ¶ 5005)

The education IRA trust document must prohibit contributions that:

. . . aren't made in cash;

. . . are made after the account holder attains age 18; or,

. . . total more than $500 for a year (except for rollover contributions). (Code Sec. 530(b)(1)(A))

The annual $500 contribution per beneficiary is available in full only to a contributor with modified adjusted gross income ("modified AGI") of $95,000 or less ($150,000 or less for joint return filers). (Code Sec. 530(c)(1)) The annual $500 contribution limit per beneficiary is phased out ratably for contributors with modified AGI between $95,000 and $110,000 (between $150,000 and $160,000 for joint filers). Individuals with modified AGI above $110,000 ($160,000 for joint filers) can not contribute to education IRAs. (Com Rept, see ¶ 5005) For this purpose, modified AGI is AGI increased by non-U.S. income excluded under Code Sec. 911, Code Sec. 931, or Code Sec. 933. (Code Sec. 530(c)(2))

> ⓇⒾⒶ *observation:* Apparently, the annual $500 contribution limit is measured on a calendar year basis. The Act doesn't specifically allow a contribution made after the end of a calendar year, but before the due date of the contributor's income tax return for that year, to be considered a contribution for the previous year. (Thus, education IRA contributors—unlike regular IRA contributors—with modified AGI near the phase-out limits must make the difficult calculation of the amount they can contribute by the end of the calendar year, without the benefit of the post-year-end tax filing period to determine the permissible contribution amount.)

An excise tax is imposed on excess contributions to education IRAs. (Code Sec. 4973(a)(4) as amended by '97 Act §213(d)) An "excess contribution" to an education IRA is the amount of any contribution over $500, and any contribution in a year in

---

FTC 2d References are to Federal Tax Coordinator 2d
FIN References are to RIA's Analysis of Federal Taxes: Income
USTR References are to United States Tax Reporter: Income, Estate & Gift, and Excise
PCA References are to Pension Coordinator and Pension & Benefits Expert/Advisor
PE References are to Pension and Profit Sharing 2nd
EP References are to Estate Planning & Taxation Coordinator and Estate Planning Advisor

ⓇⒾⒶ Research Institute of America   97

which a contribution to a "qualified state tuition program" (see ¶ 406) is made for the beneficiary. But the excess contribution tax doesn't apply to:

... contributions returned before the due date of the contributor's income tax return under Code Sec. 530(d)(4)(C);

... contributions to a qualified state tuition program described in Code Sec. 530(b)(2)(B); or

... rollover contributions. (Code Sec. 4973(e))

Other requirements. The following rules also apply to education IRAs:

• Upon the death of the designated beneficiary, the account balance must be distributed within 30 days after the beneficiary's death to his estate. (Code Sec. 530(b)(1)(E))

• The trust can't invest in life insurance contracts. (Code Sec. 530(b)(1)(C))

• Trust assets can't be commingled except in common trust or investment funds. (Code Sec. 530(b)(1)(D))

• The trustee must be a bank or other person that demonstrates to the satisfaction of the IRS that it will administer the trust as required. (Code Sec. 530(b)(1)(B))

A custodial account can be treated as a trust (and a custodian as a trustee) if the bank or other custodian demonstrates to the IRS that it will administer the account in a manner consistent with the education IRA requirements. (Code Sec. 530(g))

Treatment of distributions.   The distributee of a distribution from an education IRA is generally taxed under rules similar to the Code Sec. 72(b) annuity rules. (Code Sec. 530(d)(1)) Thus, distributions generally will be considered to consist of principal (which, under all circumstances, are excludable from gross income) and earnings (which *may* be excludable from gross income under the education IRA rules). (Com Rept, see ¶ 5005)

If the beneficiary's qualified higher education expenses in a year equal or exceed total education IRA distributions for that year, the distributions are entirely excluded from the beneficiary's gross income. (Code Sec. 530(d)(2)(A)) (The Code Sec. 529(e)(3) definition of "qualified higher education expenses" (see ¶ 406) is used for this purpose, reduced as provided in Code Sec. 25A(g)(2) under the HOPE and Lifetime Learning credit provisions (see ¶ 401).) (Code Sec. 530(b)(2))

> *illustration (1):* Dad contributes $500 a year to an education IRA for his 8-year-old son for 10 years, starting in '98. In 2008, when the account balance is $8,000, the son withdraws the entire amount to pay part of his qualified higher education expenses for the year. The son's 2008 taxable income does not include the $3,000 earnings in the account because the distribution is less than his qualified higher education expenses for the year.

But if education IRA distributions exceed higher education expenses in a year, the amount includible bears the same ratio to the amount which would be *includible* in gross income as the expenses bear to the distribution. (Code Sec. 530(d)(2)(B)) The beneficiary can elect to waive this special rule for a year, and instead be taxed on the distributions under the Code Sec. 530(d)(1) general rule. (Code Sec. 530(d)(2)(C))

observation: It seems likely that the drafters, contrary to congressional intent, mistakenly provided for the *inclusion* of the portion of the earnings portion of a distribution that the distributee uses for qualified higher education expenses. The statute should have provided for the *exclusion* of the portion of the earnings portion of the distribution used for education expenses.

illustration (2): In 2008, Son withdraws $8,000 from an education IRA, of which $3,000 are attributable to earnings (and taxable under generally applicable Code Sec. 72(b) annuity rules). But son's qualified higher education expenses in 2008 are only $6,000. Three-quarters ($6,000 education expenses/$8,000 distribution) of the $3,000 earnings—$2,250—are attributable to education expenses. If that $2,250 attributable to education expenses was excluded in accordance with congressional intent, then only $750 ($3,000 - $2,250) would be included in the son's income.

observation: However, under a literal reading of Code Sec. 530(d)(2)(B), then the $2,250 attributable to education expenses is included in the son's 2008 income.

A distribution from an education IRA is not included in income to the extent the amount is paid into another education IRA for the beneficiary, or member of the beneficiary's family as defined in Code Sec. 529(e)(2) (see ¶ 406), within 60 days of the distribution. Only one distribution from an education IRA can be rolled over to another education IRA in a 12-month period. (Code Sec. 529(d)(5)) A change in the education IRA beneficiary is not a distribution as long as the new beneficiary is a member of the family of the old beneficiary. (Code Sec. 529(d)(6))

An additional tax of 10% of the amount of an education IRA distribution included in the distributee's income is imposed unless the distribution is:

... made after the death of the education IRA's designated beneficiary to the beneficiary or estate of the designated beneficiary;

... attributable to the designated beneficiary's disability; or

... made on account of a scholarship, allowance, or payment described in Code Sec. 25A(g)(2) to the extent the amount of the distribution doesn't exceed the amount of the Code Sec. 25A(g)(2) payment. (Code Sec. 529(d)(4))

The additional tax doesn't apply to distributions of contributions in excess of $500 if the excess amount is returned, along with net income attributable to the excess contribution, on or before the due date of the contributor's income tax return. The net income is included in the distributee's gross income for the year of the contribution.

(Code Sec. 529(d)(4)(C))

observation: This additional tax exception doesn't cover situations in which a $500 (or less) contribution becomes an excess contribution solely as a result of the contributor's $500 limit being reduced because the contributor's modified AGI exceeded the limit.

illustration (3): Bob and Brenda Brown, a couple with '98 modified AGI of more than $160,000, contribute $500 to their daughter Beth's education IRA in '98. When the Browns discovered in '99 (before their '98 return due date) that their '98 modified AGI was too high to allow their '98 education IRA contribution, the $550 education IRA account balance was distributed to Beth. Beth's '98 gross income includes the $50 earnings on the education IRA contribution. Also, the exception to the 10% additional tax on the $50 earnings apparently does *not* apply since the excess contribution did not exceed $500.

Rules similar to the rules of Code Sec. 220(f)(7) and Code Sec. 220(f)(8) rules on the income tax consequences of a medical savings account holder's death or divorce apply to education IRAs. (FTC 2d/FIN ¶ H-1341; FTC 2d/FIN ¶ H-1342; FTC 2d/FIN ¶ 1342.1; USTR ¶ 2204.1) (Code Sec. 529(d)(7))

observation: Thus, the transfer of an educational IRA to a spouse or former spouse under a divorce decree isn't a taxable transfer. The transfer of an education IRA to a surviving spouse at the death of the beneficiary isn't a taxable transfer. But if an education IRA is transferred at the beneficiary's death to anyone other than the surviving spouse, the account ceases to be an education IRA as of the death of the education IRA beneficiary, and the value of the account is taxable to the recipient.

Other rules. Rules similar to the Code Sec. 529(c)(2), Code Sec. 529(c)(4) and Code Sec. 529(c)(5) rules on the estate and gift tax treatment of contributions to and distributions from qualified tuition programs apply to education IRAs (see ¶ 405). (Code Sec. 530(d)(3)) And rules similar to the Code Sec. 408(e)(2) and Code Sec. 408(e)(4) rules on individual retirement accounts (IRA) (FTC 2d/FIN ¶ H-12250; USTR ¶ 4084.03; PCA ¶ 35,151; PE ¶ 408-4.03) apply to education IRAs. (Code Sec. 530(e))

observation: Thus, an education IRA loses its status as an education IRA if the account holder or his beneficiary engages in a prohibited transaction with the account. And an individual's use of an education IRA as security for a loan is treated as distribution of the amount used as security.

The education IRA is treated as a qualified retirement plan for the purpose of determining whether a transaction involving the account is a prohibited transaction, but the Code Sec. 4975 excise tax on prohibited transaction isn't imposed on the contributor or beneficiary if the transaction is a distribution to which Code Sec. 530(d) applies. (Code Sec. 4975 as amended by '97 Act §213(b))

The trustee of an education IRA must report to the IRS and the beneficiary on contributions, distributions and other matters at the time and in the manner to be determined by IRS. (Code Sec. 530(h)) The $50 penalty for each failure to file an IRA or a medical savings account report without reasonable cause also applies to a failure to file an education IRA report. (Code Sec. 6693(a)(2)(D) as amended by '97 Act §213(c))

The new Code Sec. 530 rules on tax-exempt education individual retirement accounts apply without regard to community property laws. (Code Sec. 530(f))

☐ **Effective:** Tax years beginning after Dec. 31, '97. ('97 Act §213(f))

¶ 404. Exclusion for employer-provided educational assistance extended through 2000

Code Sec. 127(d), as amended by '97 Act § 221
Generally effective: Years beginning after Dec. 31, '96
Committee Reports, see ¶ 5007

An employee's annual wages don't include up to $5,250 of amounts paid by an employer for educational assistance under a program that meets certain requirements. The exclusion was set to terminate for tax years beginning after May 31, '97. For the '97 calendar tax year, the exclusion applied only for courses that began before July 1, '97. (FTC 2d/FIN ¶ H-2064; USTR ¶ 1274; TaxDesk ¶ 13,676)

New Law. The '97 Act extends the exclusion for educational assistance to amounts paid for undergraduate courses beginning before June 1, 2000. (Com Rept, see ¶ 5007) The exclusion won't apply for courses beginning after May 31, 2000. (Code Sec. 127(d) as amended by '97 Act §221(a))

> ⊘ *observation:* The exclusion is now available for courses that begin at any time in '97, not only for courses that began before July 1, '97.

☐ **Effective:** Tax years beginning after Dec. 31, '96. ('97 Act §221(b))

¶ 405. Tax treatment of contributions to and distributions from qualified tuition programs modified

Code Sec. 529(c), as amended by '97 Act § 211(b)(3)
Code Sec. 529(e), as amended by '97 Act § 211(b)(1)
Code Sec. 135(c)(2)(C), as amended by '97 Act § 211(e)
Generally effective: Jan. 1, '98
Committee Reports, see ¶ 5005

Contributions to a qualified state tuition program were treated as incomplete gifts for federal gift tax purposes, and thus, didn't qualify for the annual gift tax exclusion. The federal gift tax consequences were determined at the time of the *distribution* from the program for the payment (or waiver) of the beneficiary's higher educational expenses, and could qualify for the Code Sec. 2503(e) exclusion from taxable gifts for tuition payments. Amounts contributed to a qualified state tuition program, plus earnings, that hadn't been distributed under the program at the time of the contributor's death were included in the contributor's taxable estate for estate tax purposes. Qualified U.S. savings bonds could be redeemed tax-free to pay qualified higher education expenses under certain circumstances, but redemption proceeds couldn't be transferred tax-free to a qualified state tuition program. (FTC 2d/FIN ¶ D-6258, ¶ J-3017, ¶ J-5401FTC 2d ¶ Q-1910.1, ¶ Q-5255.1, ¶ R-2058.1; USTR ¶ 5294.02, ¶ 5294.03, ¶ 25034; EP ¶ 43,159.1, ¶ 47,161.1, ¶ 48,276.1)

New Law. A contribution to a qualified state tuition program is treated as a completed gift which is not a gift of a future interest, and not a transfer excluded from taxable gifts as a tuition payment under Code Sec. 2503(e). (Code Sec. 529(c)(2)(A) as amended by '97 Act §211(b)(3)(A)) Thus, the contribution is a completed gift of a present interest from the contributor to the beneficiary eligible for the annual $10,000 per donee gift tax exclusion under Code Sec. 2503(b) (to be increased for inflation after '98, see ¶ 503). (Com Rept, see ¶ 5005)

The '97 Act allows a donor who makes total contributions that exceed the Code Sec. 2503(b) limit for a year to elect to take the contributions into account ratably over the 5-year period starting with the year of the contributions. (Code Sec. 529(c)(2)(B)) To do so, the donor must file a gift tax return for the year of the contribution, and the 5-year averaging election must be made on the return. (Com Rept, see ¶ 5005) If a donor who makes the 5-year averaging election dies before the end of the 5-year period, the portion of the contribution allocable to the post-death period is included in his gross estate for estate tax purposes. (Code Sec. 529(c)(4)(C))

> ✔ *illustration:* A donor contributes $30,000 to a qualified state tuition program for her daughter in '98. The donor can elect on her gift tax return to treat the gift as 5 annual contributions of $6,000 starting in '98. As a result of the election, the donor could make an additional gift of $4,000 to her daughter in '98 (and each of the next 4 years) without exceeding the $10,000 annual gift tax exclusion. If the donor dies in '99, $6,000 would be allocated to '98 and '99 for gift tax purposes, and the remaining $18,000 would be included in the donor's estate for estate tax purposes.

A distribution from a qualified state tuition program isn't a taxable gift. A change in the beneficiary under the program, or the rollover to the account of a new beneficiary, will be a taxable gift and a generation-skipping transfer from the old beneficiary to the new beneficiary only if the new beneficiary is assigned to a generation below the old beneficiary under Code Sec. 2651. (Code Sec. 529(c)(5))

No interest in a qualified state tuition program is included in the estate of any person for estate tax purposes, except amounts distributed on account of the beneficiary's death are included in the beneficiary's estate. Thus, if the beneficiary's interest is rolled over to another beneficiary, there are no transfer tax consequences if the beneficiaries are in the same generation. If the new beneficiary is in a lower generation than the deceased beneficiary, the five-year averaging rule may be applied to exempt up to $50,000 of the transfer from the gift tax. (Com Rept, see ¶ 5005)

Redemption of U.S. savings bond. In determining whether a redemption of qualified U.S. savings bonds is tax-free under Code Sec. 135, the transfer of the redemption proceeds to a qualified tuition program for the taxpayer (or his spouse or dependent) is considered a qualified higher education expense. The contribution does not increase the investment in the contract for Code Sec. 72 purposes. (Code Sec. 135(c)(2)(C) as amended by '97 Act §211(c))

☐ **Effective:** The amendment regarding educational savings bonds applies to tax years beginning after Dec. 31, '97. ('97 Act §211(f)(4)) The gift tax changes apply to transfers after Aug. 5, '97. ('97 Act §211(f)(5)(A)) The estate tax changes apply to estates of decedents dying after June 8, '97. ('97 Act §211(f)(5)(B)) All other changes take effect on Jan. 1, '98. ('97 Act §211(f)(1))

¶ 406. Qualified state tuition program expanded

Code Sec. 529(e)(3), as amended by '97 Act § 211(a)
Code Sec. 529(e)(5), as amended by '97 Act § 211(b)(2)
Code Sec. 529(d), as amended by '97 Act § 211(e)(2)(A)
Generally effective: Jan. 1, '98
Committee Reports, see ¶ 5005

A qualified state tuition program for the prepayment of post-secondary higher education expenses, not including room and board, on a tax-favored basis can be maintained by a state or its agencies or instrumentalities. Most accredited colleges, junior colleges and area vocational education schools are eligible higher educational institutions. State officials must report distributions from the program to the IRS and the beneficiary. (FTC 2d/FIN ¶ D-6260, ¶ J-3018; USTR ¶ 5294, ¶ 1354.02; TaxDesk ¶ 67,230)

New Law. The category of "qualified higher education expenses" that can be prepaid under a qualified state tuition program has been expanded to include the reasonable room and board costs incurred by an eligible student (see ¶ 401) while attending an "eligible educational institution" during an academic period. The amount treated as reasonable room and board costs for an academic period can't exceed the minimum amount included in the cost of attendance at the institution applicable to the student under §472 of the Higher Education Act of 1965. (Code Sec. 529(e)(3)(B) as amended by '97 Act §211(a))

An "eligible educational institution" is an institution described in §481 of the Higher Education Act of 1965 that is eligible to participate in a program under title IV

FTC 2d References are to Federal Tax Coordinator 2d
FIN References are to RIA's Analysis of Federal Taxes: Income
USTR References are to United States Tax Reporter: Income, Estate & Gift, and Excise
PCA References are to Pension Coordinator and Pension & Benefits Expert/Advisor
PE References are to Pension and Profit Sharing 2nd
EP References are to Estate Planning & Taxation Coordinator and Estate Planning Advisor

of that Act. (Code Sec. 529(e)(5) as amended by '97 Act §211(c)(2)) The term "eligible educational institution" is meant to include accredited post-secondary educational institutions offering credit towards a bachelor's degree, an associate's degree, a graduate-level or professional degree, or another recognized post-secondary credential. And certain proprietary institutions and post-secondary vocational education institutions that are eligible to participate in Department of Education student aid programs are eligible educational institutions. (Com Rept, see ¶ 5005)

An officer or employee having control of a qualified tuition program must report to the IRS and the designated beneficiaries on contributions, distributions and other matters at the time and in the manner to be determined by IRS regulations. (Code Sec. 529(d) as amended by '97 Act §211(e)(2)(A)) There's a $50 penalty for each failure to provide a required report without reasonable cause. (Code Sec. 6693(a)(2)(C) as amended by '97 Act §S211(e)(2)(B))

The '97 Act specifies that contributors and beneficiaries cannot direct a qualified state tuition program's investments, either directly or indirectly. (Code Sec. 529(b)(5) as amended by '97 Act §211(b)(4))

The '97 Act also expands the definition of "member of the family" for qualified state tuition program purposes. A member of the family is a relative described in paragraphs (1)-(8) of Code Sec. 152(a), or a spouse of such relative. (Code Sec. 529(e)(2) as amended by '97 Act §211(b)(1))

> ⓥ *caution:* The Code Sec. 152(a) list of family members does not include the taxpayer's own spouse as a possible recipient of a non-taxable transfer or rollover from the taxpayer.

☐ **Effective:** The allowance of room and board costs as qualified higher education expenses applies to tax years beginning after Aug. 20, '96. ('97 Act §211(f)(2)) The other changes take effect on Jan. 1, '98. ('97 Act §211(f)(1))

¶ 407. Definition of "designated beneficiary" expanded for purposes of rules on qualified state tuition programs

Code Sec. 529(e)(1)(C), as amended by '97 Act § 1601(h)(1)(B)
Generally effective: Tax years ending after Aug. 20, '96
Committee Reports, see ¶ 5367

Code Sec. 529 provides tax-exempt status to certain qualified state tuition programs and provides rules for the tax treatment of distributions from those programs. The term "qualified state tuition program" means a program established and maintained by a state, or an agency or instrumentality of a state, under which a person (a) may purchase tuition credits or certificates on behalf of a designated beneficiary that entitle the beneficiary to the waiver or payment of qualified higher education expenses of the beneficiary, or (b) may make contributions to an account that is established for the sole purpose of meeting the qualified higher education expenses of the beneficiary of the account. (FTC 2d/FIN ¶ D-6252; USTR ¶ 5294; TaxDesk ¶ 67,232)

Under pre-'97 Act law, the term "designated beneficiary" meant:

(1) the individual designated at the commencement of participation in the qualified state tuition program as the beneficiary of amounts paid (or to be paid) to the program,

(2) in the case of a change in beneficiaries where the new beneficiary is a member of the same family (as defined below) as the old beneficiary, the individual who is the new beneficiary, and

(3) in the case of an interest in a qualified state tuition program purchased by a state or local government or an organization described in Code Sec. 501(c)(3) and exempt from taxation under Code Sec. 501(a) as part of a scholarship program operated by such government or organization, the individual receiving the interest as a scholarship. (FTC 2d/FIN ¶ D-6259; USTR ¶ 5294; TaxDesk ¶ 67,239)

New Law. The reference in part (3), above, of the definition of "designated beneficiary" to "a state or local government" is expanded to provide that, in the case of an interest in a qualified state tuition program purchased by a state or local government *(or agency or instrumentality of a state or local government)* or an organization described in Code Sec. 501(c)(3) and exempt from taxation under Code Sec. 501(a) as part of a scholarship program operated by such government or organization, the individual receiving the interest as a scholarship is a designated beneficiary. (Code Sec. 529(e)(1)(C) as amended by '97 Act §1601(h)(1)(B))

> *observation:* Parts (1) and (2), above, of the definition of "designated beneficiary" are not changed by the '97 Act.

☐ **Effective:** Tax years ending after Aug. 20, '96. ('97 Act §1601(j)(1))

¶ 408. State program under which persons may purchase tuition credits will be treated as a qualified state tuition program if it meets the qualified state tuition program requirements within a specified time period

Code Sec. None, '97 Act § 1601(h)(1)(C)
Generally effective: Tax years ending after Aug. 20, '96
Committee Reports, see ¶ 5367

Code Sec. 529 provides tax-exempt status to certain qualified state tuition programs and provides rules for the tax treatment of distributions from those programs. The term "qualified state tuition program" means a program established and maintained by a state, or an agency or instrumentality of a state, under which a person (a) may purchase tuition credits or certificates on behalf of a designated beneficiary that entitle the beneficiary to the waiver or payment of qualified higher education expenses of the beneficiary, or (b) may make contributions to an account that is established for the sole purpose of meeting the qualified higher education expenses of the beneficiary of the account. (FTC 2d/FIN ¶ D-6252; USTR ¶ 5294; TaxDesk ¶ 67,232) For the definition of "qualified higher education expenses", see ¶ 406.

Code Sec. 529 is effective for tax years ending after Aug. 20, '96 (the date of enactment of the Small Business Job Protection Act of 1996). Under pre-'97 Act law, a special transition rule provided that if—

(1) a state maintained (on Aug. 20, '96) a program under which persons could purchase tuition credits on behalf of, or make contributions for educational expenses of, a designated beneficiary, and

(2) that program met the requirements of a qualified state tuition program before the later of (a) Aug. 20, '97, or (b) the first day of the first calendar quarter after the close of the first regular session of the State legislature that began after Aug. 20, '96,

then Code Sec. 529 applied to contributions (and earnings allocable to those contributions) made before the date the program met the requirements of a qualified state tuition program, without regard to whether the requirements of a qualified state tuition program were satisfied with respect to those contributions and earnings. (FTC 2d/FIN ¶ D-6251; USTR ¶ 5294; TaxDesk ¶ 67,231)   For example, Code Sec. 529 applied to contributions to programs that met requirements (1) and (2), above, even if the interest in the tuition or educational savings program covered not only qualified higher education expenses but also room and board expenses (Com Rept, see ¶ 5367)

New Law. The '97 Act clarifies that, if a state program under which persons may purchase tuition credits comes into compliance with the requirements of a "qualified state tuition program" as defined in Code Sec. 529 within a specified time period, then that program will be treated as a qualified state tuition program with respect to any contributions (and earnings allocable to those contributions) made under a contract entered into under the program before the date on which the program comes into compliance with the pre-'97 Act requirements of a qualified state tuition program under Code Sec. 529. ('97 Act §1601(h)(1)(C))

☐ **Effective:** Tax years ending after Aug. 20, '96. ('97 Act §1601(j)(1))

¶ 409. Higher education expenses used to compute exclusion of redemption proceeds of U.S. savings bonds must be reduced by higher education expenses for which Hope/Lifetime Learning credit is claimed

Code Sec. 135(d)(2), as amended by '97 Act § 201(d)
Generally effective: Expenses paid after Dec. 31, '97
Committee Reports, see ¶ 5002

Under Code Sec. 135(a), if, during the tax year, a taxpayer pays qualified higher education expenses, no amount is includible in the taxpayer's gross income by reason of the redemption during that tax year of any qualified U.S. savings bond (i.e., certain Series EE savings bonds), subject to various limits set by Code Sec. 135(b). The amount of qualified higher education expenses taken into account in computing this exclusion must be reduced by:

... a qualified scholarship which is excludable from gross income under Code Sec. 117;

... an educational assistance allowance under specified chapters of Title 38 of the United States Code (relating to veterans' benefits);

... a payment (other than a gift, bequest, devise, or inheritance within the meaning of Code Sec. 102(a)) for educational expenses, or attributable to attendance at an eligible educational institution, which is exempt from income taxation under any law of the U.S.

(FTC 2d/FIN ¶ J-3015 *et seq.*; USTR ¶ 1354 *et seq.*; TaxDesk ¶ 1354 *et seq.*)

New Law. Under the '97 Act, the amount of qualified higher education expenses otherwise taken into account in determining the amount of redemption proceeds of qualified U.S. savings bonds excluded from gross income under Code Sec. 135(a) with respect to the education of an individual must also be reduced by the amount of those expenses which are taken into account in determining the Hope and Lifetime Learning credit allowable to the taxpayer or any other person under Code Sec. 25A (see ¶ 401) with respect to those expenses. This reduction is made before applying the limitation provisions of Code Sec. 135(b) (which reduce the excluded amount where redemption proceeds exceed the higher education expenses and where taxpayer's modified adjusted gross income exceeds specified dollar amounts). (Code Sec. 135(d)(2) as amended by '97 Act §201(d))

In other words, the amount of qualified higher education expenses taken into account in determining the exclusion allowed under Code Sec. 135(a) must be reduced by the amount of those expenses that are taken into account in determining the Code Sec. 25A credit allowed to any taxpayer with respect to the student for the tax year. (Com Rept, see ¶ 5002)

☐ **Effective:** Expenses paid after Dec. 31, '97, in tax years ending after that date, for education furnished in academic periods beginning after that date. ('97 Act §201(f)(1))

¶ 410. Educational institutions receiving, and businesses paying, higher education expenses must furnish information returns

Code Sec. 6050S, as added by '97 Act § 201(c)(1)
Code Sec. 6724(d)(1)(B)(ix), as amended by '97 Act § 201(c)(2)(A)
Code Sec. 6724(d)(2)(Z), as amended by '97 Act § 201(c)(2)(B)
Generally effective: Expenses paid after Dec. 31, '97
Committee Reports, see ¶ 5002

FTC 2d References are to Federal Tax Coordinator 2d
FIN References are to RIA's Analysis of Federal Taxes: Income
USTR References are to United States Tax Reporter: Income, Estate & Gift, and Excise
PCA References are to Pension Coordinator and Pension & Benefits Expert/Advisor
PE References are to Pension and Profit Sharing 2nd
EP References are to Estate Planning & Taxation Coordinator and Estate Planning Advisor

Under pre-'97 Act law, educational institutions were not required to file information returns with regard to payments received for tuition and related expenses.

Similarly, under pre-'97 law, persons engaged in trades or businesses were not required to file information returns with regards to payments they made to other persons that were reimbursements or refunds of tuition and related expenses, unless those reimbursements or refunds were wages or other taxable compensation. (FTC 2d/FIN ¶ V-1803 et seq., ¶ V-1814 et seq.; USTR ¶ 67,214, ¶ 67,224, ¶ 67,244; TaxDesk ¶ 86,125 et seq., ¶ 86,133 et seq., ¶ 86,153, ¶ 86,164)

New Law. Under the '97 Act, the following persons must make the information returns described below, at such time as IRS may prescribe by regs: (Code Sec. 6050S(a) as added by '97 Act §201(c)(1))

... any person which is an eligible educational institution which receives payments for qualified tuition and related expenses with respect to any individual for any calendar year (Code Sec. 6050S(a)(1)), or

... any person which is engaged in a trade or business and which, in the course of that trade or business (Code Sec. 6050S(a)(2))

• makes payments during any calendar year to any individual which are reimbursements or refunds (or similar amounts) of qualified tuition and related expenses of that individual (Code Sec. 6050S(a)(2)); or

• except as provided in IRS regulations, receives from any individual interest aggregating $600 or more for any calendar year on one or more qualified education loans. (Code Sec. 6050S(a)(2)(B))

The terms "eligible educational institution" and "qualified tuition and related expenses" have the meanings set forth by Code Sec. 25A (see ¶ 401). Except as provided in regulations, the term "qualified education loan" has the meaning given by Code Sec. 221(e)(1) (as added by the '97 Act, see ¶ 402). (Code Sec. 6050S(e))

Except to the extent provided in to-be-prescribed regulations, in the case of any amount received by any person on behalf of another person, only the person first receiving the amount must make the return. (Code Sec. 6050S(f))

The return referred to above must be in the form prescribed by IRS. (Code Sec. 6050S(b)(1)) The return must contain the following information (Code Sec. 6050S(b)(2)):

... the name, address, and TIN of the individual—

• from whom, or with respect to whom, the payments of qualified tuition and related expenses or interest on qualified education loans (referred to above) were received (Code Sec. 6050S(b)(2)(A)), or

• to whom, or with respect to whom, those payments were paid (Code Sec. 6050S(b)(2)(A));

... the name, address, and TIN of any individual certified by the individual described in Code Sec. 6050S(b)(2)(A) (above) as the taxpayer who will claim the individual as a dependent for purposes of the personal exemption deduction allowable under Code Sec. 151 for any tax year ending with or within the calendar year (Code Sec.

6050S(b)(2)(B));

> **✔️ observation:** In other words, for any tax year, the student for whom qualified tuition and related expenses are received or reimbursed, must "certify" to the eligible educational institution or to the employer making the information return that he or she is being claimed as a dependent on another person's tax return, and must provide the name, address and TIN of that other person to the eligible educational institution or employer. The legislative history of this provision doesn't explain what "certification" means or how it's to be accomplished.

> **✔️ observation:** The requirement to show the name, address, and TIN of the taxpayer who will claim the student as a dependent means the educational institution or employer that has to file the information return must adopt procedures—to get the certification—that go beyond normal information reporting compliance efforts.

... the aggregate amount of payments (if received) for qualified tuition and related expenses received with respect to the individual described in Code Sec. 6050S(b)(2)(A) (above) during the calendar year (Code Sec. 6050S(b)(2)(C)(i));

... the aggregate amount of reimbursements or refunds (or similar amounts) (if paid), paid to the individual described in Code Sec. 6050S(b)(2)(A) (above) during the calendar year (Code Sec. 6050S(b)(2)(C)(ii));

... the aggregate amount of interest received for the calendar year from that individual (Code Sec. 6050S(b)(2)(C)(iii)); and

... any other information prescribed by IRS. (Code Sec. 6050S(b)(2)(D))

For purposes of the above rules (Code Sec. 6050S(c)):

... a governmental unit or any agency or instrumentality of a governmental unit is treated as a person (Code Sec. 6050S(c)(1)); and

... any return required under Code Sec. 6050S(a) (above) by that governmental entity must be made by the officer or employee appropriately designated for the purpose of making that return. (Code Sec. 6050S(c)(2))

Return information must be furnished to the individuals with respect to whom the information is required. Every person required to make a return under the above rules must furnish to each individual whose name is required to be set forth in the return a written statement showing (Code Sec. 6050S(d)):

... the name, address, and phone number of the information contact of the person required to make the return (Code Sec. 6050S(d)(1)); and

---

FTC 2d References are to Federal Tax Coordinator 2d
FIN References are to RIA's Analysis of Federal Taxes: Income
USTR References are to United States Tax Reporter: Income, Estate & Gift, and Excise
PCA References are to Pension Coordinator and Pension & Benefits Expert/Advisor
PE References are to Pension and Profit Sharing 2nd
EP References are to Estate Planning & Taxation Coordinator and Estate Planning Advisor

... the aggregate amounts described in Code Sec. 6050S(b)(2)(C) (above). (Code Sec. 6050S(d)(2))

The statement must be furnished on or before Jan. 31 of the year following the calendar year for which the return under Code Sec. 6050S(a) was required to be made. (Code Sec. 6050S(d))

Regulations. IRS is to prescribe such regulations as may be necessary to carry out the provisions described above. (Code Sec. 6050S(g)) IRS will have authority to issue regulations providing appropriate rules for recordkeeping and information reporting. (Com Rept, see ¶ 5002) In addition, IRS is to issue regulations that require lenders separately to report to borrowers the amount of interest that's deductible student loan interest (i.e., interest on a qualified education loan during the first 60 months in which interest payments are required, see ¶ 402). In this regard the regulations should include a method for borrower certification to a lender that the loan proceeds are being used to pay for qualified higher education expenses. (Com Rept, see ¶ 5003)

Failure to file penalties. The '97 Act makes the information return required by Code Sec. 6050S(a), described above, an information return defined by Code Sec. 6724(d)(1). (Code Sec. 6724(d)(1)(B)(ix) as amended by '97 Act §201(c)(2)(A)) Similarly, the '97 Act makes the payee statement required by Code Sec. 6050S(d), described above, a payee statement defined by Code Sec. 6724(d)(2). (Code Sec. 6724(d)(2)(Z) as amended by '97 Act §201(c)(2)(B))

> *observation:* As a result, failure to file the the information return or the payee statement results in the imposition of penalties under Code Sec. 6721 (with respect to information returns) or Code Sec. 6722 (with respect to payee statements). Generally, there is a $50 penalty for each return or statement that isn't filed or furnished as required, subject to certain exceptions and limitations.

However, no penalties are to be imposed under part II of subchapter B of Chapter 68 of the Code (i.e., Code Sec. 6721–Code Sec. 6724) with respect to any return or statement required under these rules until IRS issues the regulations above. (Code Sec. 6050S(g))

☐ **Effective:** Expenses paid after Dec. 31, '97, in tax years ending after that date, for education furnished in academic periods beginning after that date, except as noted below. ('97 Act §201(f)(1))

However, Code Sec. 6050S(a)(2)(B), the reference to "interest" in Code Sec. 6050S(b)(2)(A), and Code Sec. 6050S(b)(2)(C)(iii) apply to any qualified education loan, as defined by Code Sec. 221(e)(1) (as added by the '97 Act, see ¶ 402) incurred on, before, or after Aug. 5, '97, but only with respect to ('97 Act §202(e)):

... any loan interest payment due and paid after Dec. 31, '97 ('97 Act §202(e)(1)); and

... the portion of the 60-month period referred to in Code Sec. 221(d) (as added by the '97 Act, see ¶ 402) after Dec. 31, '97. ('97 Act §202(e)(2))

¶ 500. Estates, Trusts and Gifts

¶ 501. Exemption equivalent amount of unified estate and gift tax credit is increased to $1 million on a phased-in schedule through 2006

Code Sec. 2001(c)(2), as amended by '97 Act § 501(a)(1)(D)
Code Sec. 2010(a), as amended by '97 Act § 501(a)(1)(A)
Code Sec. 2010(c), as amended by '97 Act § 501(a)(1)(B)
Code Sec. 2102(c)(3)(A), as amended by '97 Act § 501(a)(1)(E)
Code Sec. 2505(a)(1), as amended by '97 Act § 501(a)(2)
Code Sec. 6018(a)(1), as amended by '97 Act § 501(a)(1)(C)
Generally effective: Applies to estates of decedents dying, and gifts made, after Dec. 31, '97
Committee Reports, see ¶ 5026

Under pre-'97 Act law, a unified credit of $192,800 was allowed in computing the estate and gift tax of a U.S. citizen or resident. The unified credit effectively exempted a total of $600,000 in cumulative taxable transfers from the estate and gift tax. (FTC 2d ¶ Q-8005; R-7101; USTR ¶ 20,104; 25,054; TaxDesk ¶ 74,404; 78,181; EP ¶ 45,102; 48,555)

Under pre-'97 Act law, estates of U.S. citizens or residents were required to file an estate tax return if the gross estate exceeded $600,000. (FTC 2d ¶ S-2301; USTR ¶ 60,184; TaxDesk ¶ 78,351; EP ¶ 83,052)

The benefits of the unified credit, and of the graduated estate and gift tax rates, are phased out for taxable transfers that exceed $10 million. Under pre-'97 Act law, this was accomplished by increasing the tentative tax determined under the estate and gift tax rate schedule by an amount equal to 5% of so much of the taxable amount as exceeded $10 million but did not exceed $21,040,000. (FTC 2d ¶ R-7008, R-7102; USTR ¶ 20,014; TaxDesk ¶ 78,058; 78,182; EP ¶ 44,909; 45,103)

To the extent required by any obligation of the U.S. under an estate tax treaty with a foreign country, the unified credit allowed to the estate of a nonresident alien under pre-'97 Act law was the amount that bore the same ratio to $192,800 as the part of the gross estate situated in the U.S. bore to the entire gross estate, wherever situated. (FTC 2d ¶ R-8028; USTR ¶ 21,024; TaxDesk ¶ 78,606; EP ¶ 45,529)

New Law. A credit of the "applicable credit amount" is allowed in computing the estate tax (Code Sec. 2010(a) as amended by '97 Act §501(a)(1)(A)) or gift tax (Code Sec. 2505(a)(1) as amended by '97 Act §501(a)(2)) of a U.S. citizen or resident. The applicable credit amount is the amount of the tentative tax that would be determined

FTC 2d References are to Federal Tax Coordinator 2d
FIN References are to RIA's Analysis of Federal Taxes: Income
USTR References are to United States Tax Reporter: Income, Estate & Gift, and Excise
PCA References are to Pension Coordinator and Pension & Benefits Expert/Advisor
PE References are to Pension and Profit Sharing 2nd
EP References are to Estate Planning & Taxation Coordinator and Estate Planning Advisor

under the unified estate and gift tax rate schedule if the amount with respect to which the tentative tax is to be computed were the applicable exclusion amount determined in accordance with the following table: (Code Sec. 2010(c))

In the case of estates of decedents dying, and gifts made, during:	The applicable exclusion amount is:
'98	$ 625,000
'99	$ 650,000
2000 and 2001	$ 675,000
2002 and 2003	$ 700,000
2004	$ 850,000
2005	$ 950,000
2006 or thereafter	$1,000,000

illustration: Under the estate and gift tax rate schedule, the tax on $625,000 is $202,050. Thus, the amount of the unified credit for estates of decedents dying, and gifts made, in '98 will be $202,050.

The applicable exclusion amount of the unified credit is *not* indexed for inflation. (Com Rept, see ¶ 5026)

Estate tax return filing requirements. Estates of U.S. citizens or residents are required to file an estate tax return if the gross estate exceeds the applicable exclusion amount for the calendar year that includes the date of death. (Code Sec. 6018(a)(1) as amended by '97 Act §501(a)(1)(C))

illustration: The estate of a U.S. citizen or resident who dies in '98 will be required to file an estate tax return if the gross estate exceeds $625,000.

Phase-out of benefits of unified credit and graduated rates for certain large estates. The phase-out of the benefits of the unified credit, and of the graduated estate and gift tax rates, is accomplished by increasing the tentative tax determined under the estate and gift tax rate schedule by an amount equal to 5% of so much of the taxable amount as exceeds $10 million but does not exceed the amount at which the average estate tax rate is 55%. (Code Sec. 2001(c)(2) as amended by '97 Act §501(a)(1)(D))

Unified credit for estates of nonresident aliens who were residents of certain treaty countries. To the extent required by any obligation of the U.S. under an estate tax treaty with a foreign country, the unified credit allowed to the estate of a nonresident alien is the amount that bears the same ratio to the applicable credit amount for the calendar year that includes the date of death, as the part of the gross estate situated in the U.S. bears to the entire gross estate, wherever situated. (Code Sec. 2102(c)(3)(A) as amended by '97 Act §501(a)(1)(E))

☐ **Effective:** Applies to estates of decedents dying, and gifts made, after Dec. 31, '97. ('97 Act §501(f))

¶ 502. $750,000 limit on estate tax special use valuation reduction will be adjusted for inflation after '98

Code Sec. 2032A(a)(3), as amended by '97 Act § 501(b)
Generally effective: Applies to estates of decedents dying in a calendar year after '98
Committee Reports, see ¶ 5026

If certain conditions are met, the executor of a decedent's estate may elect to value qualified farm or other closely held business real property included in a decedent's estate on the basis of its actual use as a farm or in the business, rather than at its fair market value based on its highest and best use. Under pre-'97 Act law, the total decrease in the value of property that resulted from a special use valuation election could not exceed $750,000. (FTC 2d ¶ R-5204; USTR ¶ 20,32A4; TaxDesk ¶ 77,141; EP ¶ 44,005)

Individual income tax brackets are indexed for inflation by means of an annual cost-of-living adjustment. Under Code Sec. 1(f)(3), the cost-of-living adjustment for any calendar year is the percentage (if any) by which the consumer price index (CPI) for the preceding calendar year exceeds the CPI for calendar year '92. (FTC 2d/FIN ¶ A-1103; USTR ¶ 14; TaxDesk ¶ 56,821)

New Law. For estates of decedents dying in a calendar year after '98, the $750,000 limit on the decrease in value that can result from a special use valuation election will be increased by an inflation adjustment. The amount of the adjustment will be $750,000, multiplied by (Code Sec. 2032A(a)(3)(A) as amended by '97 Act §501(b)) the cost-of-living adjustment determined under Code Sec. 1(f)(3) by substituting "calendar year 1997" for "calendar year 1992". (Code Sec. 2032A(a)(3)(B))

> *observation:* Thus, the amount of the limit will be indexed for inflation occurring after '97.

If the amount of the limit, as adjusted, is not a multiple of $10,000, the amount will be rounded to the next lowest multiple of $10,000. (Code Sec. 2032A(a)(3))

☐ **Effective:** Applies to estates of decedents dying in a calendar year after '98. (Code Sec. 2032A(a)(3))

¶ 503. Gift tax annual exclusion of $10,000 will be adjusted for inflation after '98

Code Sec. 2503(b)(2), as amended by '97 Act § 501(c)(3)
Generally effective: Applies to gifts made in a calendar year after '98
Committee Reports, see ¶ 5026

FTC 2d References are to Federal Tax Coordinator 2d
FIN References are to RIA's Analysis of Federal Taxes: Income
USTR References are to United States Tax Reporter: Income, Estate & Gift, and Excise
PCA References are to Pension Coordinator and Pension & Benefits Expert/Advisor
PE References are to Pension and Profit Sharing 2nd
EP References are to Estate Planning & Taxation Coordinator and Estate Planning Advisor

For gift tax purposes, an annual exclusion is allowed for gifts (other than gifts of a future interest) made to any person by a donor during a calendar year. Under pre-'97 Act law, the amount of the gift tax annual exclusion was $10,000. (FTC 2d ¶ Q-5002; USTR ¶ 25,034; TaxDesk ¶ 73,102; EP ¶ 48,203)

Individual income tax brackets are indexed for inflation by means of an annual cost-of-living adjustment. Under Code Sec. 1(f)(3), the cost-of-living adjustment for any calendar year is the percentage (if any) by which the consumer price index (CPI) for the preceding calendar year exceeds the CPI for calendar year '92. (FTC 2d/FIN ¶ A-1103; USTR ¶ 14; TaxDesk ¶ 56,821)

New Law. For gifts made in a calendar year after '98, the $10,000 amount of the gift tax annual exclusion will be increased by an inflation adjustment. The amount of the adjustment will be $10,000, multiplied by (Code Sec. 2503(b)(2)(A) as amended by '97 Act §501(c)(3)) the cost-of-living adjustment determined under Code Sec. 1(f)(3) for the calendar year by substituting "calendar year 1997" for "calendar year 1992". (Code Sec. 2503(b)(2)(B))

> *observation:* Thus, the amount of the gift tax annual exclusion will be indexed for inflation occurring after '97.

If the amount of the annual exclusion, as adjusted, is not a multiple of $1,000, the amount will be rounded to the next lowest multiple of $1,000. (Code Sec. 2503(b)(2))

> *observation:* Thus, the amount of the annual exclusion will not increase from $10,000 to $11,000 until the cost-of-living adjustment is at least 10%. At current levels of inflation, it may be several years before the annual exclusion rises to $11,000.

☐ **Effective:** Applies to gifts made in a calendar year after '98. (Code Sec. 2503(b)(2))

¶ 504. Generation-skipping transfer exemption of $1 million will be adjusted for inflation after '98

Code Sec. 2631(c), as amended by '97 Act § 501(d)
Generally effective: Applies to individuals who die in any calendar year after '98
Committee Reports, see ¶ 5026

A generation-skipping transfer (GST) tax is imposed on certain transfers to beneficiaries who are more than one generation below the transferor's generation. Every individual is allowed a GST exemption of $1 million. (FTC 2d ¶ R-9551; USTR ¶ 26,314; TaxDesk ¶ 79,106; EP ¶ 46,092)

Individual income tax brackets are indexed for inflation by means of an annual cost-of-living adjustment. Under Code Sec. 1(f)(3), the cost-of-living adjustment for any calendar year is the percentage (if any) by which the consumer price index (CPI) for the preceding calendar year exceeds the CPI for calendar year '92. (FTC 2d/FIN ¶ A-1103; USTR ¶ 14; TaxDesk ¶ 56,821)

New Law. For individuals who die in a calendar year after '98, the $1 million amount of the GST exemption will be increased by an inflation adjustment. The amount of the adjustment will be $1 million, multiplied by (Code Sec. 2631(c)(1) as amended by '97 Act §501(d)) the cost-of-living adjustment determined under Code Sec. 1(f)(3) for the calendar year by substituting "calendar year 1997" for "calendar year 1992". (Code Sec. 2631(c)(2))

observation: Thus, the amount of the GST exemption will be indexed for inflation occurring after '97.

If the amount of the exemption, as adjusted, is not a multiple of $10,000, the amount will be rounded to the next lowest multiple of $10,000. (Code Sec. 2631(c))

☐ **Effective:** Applies to individuals who die in any calendar year after '98. (Code Sec. 2631(c))

¶ 505. Estate tax exclusion allowed for qualified family-owned business interests—exclusion amount, plus exemption equivalent of unified credit, can't exceed $1.3 million

Code Sec. 2033A, as added by '97 Act § 502(a)
Generally effective: Applies to estates of decedents dying after Dec. 31, '97
Committee Reports, see ¶ 5027

Under pre-'97 Act law, there were no special estate tax rules for qualified family-owned businesses. All taxpayers were allowed a unified credit in computing the tax-payer's estate and gift tax, which (for U.S. citizens and residents) effectively exempted a total of $600,000 in cumulative taxable transfers from the estate and gift tax. (FTC 2d ¶ Q-8005; R-7101; USTR ¶ 20,104; 25,054; TaxDesk ¶ 74,404; 78,181; EP ¶ 45,102; 48,555) As discussed at ¶ 501, the '97 Act increases the unified credit from an effective exemption of $600,000 to an effective exemption of $1 million, on a phased-in schedule through 2006.

An executor may also elect, under Code Sec. 2032A, to value certain qualified real property used in farming or another qualifying closely-held trade or business at its value as a farm or in the business, rather than its value based on its highest and best use. (FTC 2d ¶ R-5200; USTR ¶ 20,32A4; TaxDesk ¶ 77,100; EP ¶ 44,001) (For a change made by the '97 Act in the amount of the maximum reduction that may result from a special use valuation election, see ¶ 502.)

In addition, an executor may elect to pay the federal estate tax attributable to a qualified closely-held business in installments over, at most, a 14-year period. (FTC 2d ¶ S-6000; USTR ¶ 61,664; TaxDesk ¶ 78,400; EP ¶ 83,201) (For changes made by the '97 Act in the rate at which interest is imposed on estate tax that an executor elects to

FTC 2d References are to Federal Tax Coordinator 2d
FIN References are to RIA's Analysis of Federal Taxes: Income
USTR References are to United States Tax Reporter: Income, Estate & Gift, and Excise
PCA References are to Pension Coordinator and Pension & Benefits Expert/Advisor
PE References are to Pension and Profit Sharing 2nd
EP References are to Estate Planning & Taxation Coordinator and Estate Planning Advisor

Research Institute of America 115

pay in installments, see ¶ 507. For the deductibility of interest on estate tax paid in installments under Code Sec. 6166, see ¶ 508.)

New Law. An estate tax exclusion is provided for "qualified family-owned business interests", as defined below. If the exclusion applies to a decedent's estate, the value of the gross estate does not include the lesser of (1) the adjusted value (as defined below, under **"Definitions"**) of the decedent's qualified family-owned business interests otherwise includible in the estate, or (Code Sec. 2033A(a)(1) as added by '97 Act §502(a)) (2) the excess of $1.3 million over the applicable exclusion amount of the unified credit with respect to the estate. (Code Sec. 2033A(a)(2)) Thus, the exclusion for family-owned business interests may be taken only to the extent that (1) the exclusion for family-owned business interests, plus (2) the amount effectively exempted by the unified credit, does not exceed $1.3 million. (Com Rept, see ¶ 5027)

> *illustration:* The estate of a decedent who dies in '98 (when the amount effectively exempted by the unified credit is $625,000, see ¶ 501) includes a qualified family-owned business interest with an adjusted value of $1 million. The amount that may be excluded from the gross estate under the exclusion for family-owned business interests is $675,000 ($1.3 million − $625,000).

The estate tax benefit of the exclusion is subject to recapture if certain events occur within ten years of the decedent's death. For a discussion of the recapture rules, see ¶ 506.

The exclusion for qualified family-owned business interests is provided in addition to the special use valuation provisions of Code Sec. 2032A and the installment payment provisions of Code Sec. 6166. (Com Rept, see ¶ 5027)

The exclusion is intended to prevent the liquidation of family farms and other family-owned enterprises in order to pay estate taxes. (Com Rept, see ¶ 5027)

> *observation:* The exclusion is an *estate tax* exclusion only; no comparable gift tax exclusion is provided. This is presumably because the exclusion is intended to prevent forced sales of family businesses to pay the estate tax due on the death of the business owner.

"Qualified family-owned business interest". A "qualified family-owned business interest" is:

(1) an interest as a proprietor in a trade or business carried on as a proprietorship (Code Sec. 2033A(e)(1)(A)) or

(2) an interest in an entity carrying on a trade or business, if at least: (Code Sec. 2033A(e)(1)(B)(i))

(a) 50% of the entity is owned (directly or indirectly) by the decedent and members of the decedent's family (as defined below, under **"Definitions"**), (Code Sec. 2033A(e)(1)(B)(i)(I))

(b) 70% of the entity is owned (directly or indirectly) by members of two families, (Code Sec. 2033A(e)(1)(B)(i)(II)) or

(c) 90% of the entity is owned (directly or indirectly) by members of three families. (Code Sec. 2033A(e)(1)(B)(i)(III))

For an interest to qualify under the 70% test or the 90% test, at least 30% of the entity must be owned (directly or indirectly) by the decedent and members of the decedent's family. (Code Sec. 2033A(e)(1)(B)(ii))

Rules regarding ownership. An interest owned, directly or indirectly, by or for an entity described above is considered as being owned proportionately by or for the entity's shareholders, partners, or beneficiaries. A person is treated as a beneficiary of any trust only if that person has a present interest in the trust. (Code Sec. 2033A(e)(3)(C))

For purposes of determining whether the 50%, 70%, or 90% ownership requirements described above are met, ownership of a corporation is determined by the holding of stock possessing the appropriate percentage of the total combined voting power of all classes of stock entitled to vote and the appropriate percentage of the total value of shares of all classes of stock. (Code Sec. 2033A(e)(3)(A)(i)) Thus, for purposes of applying the ownership tests in the case of a corporation, the decedent and members of the decedent's family are required to own the requisite percentage of the total combined voting power of all classes of stock entitled to vote *and* the requisite percentage of the total value of all shares of all classes of stock of the corporation. (Com Rept, see ¶ 5027) For the same purpose, ownership of a partnership is determined by the owning of the appropriate percentage of the capital interest in the partnership. (Code Sec. 2033A(e)(3)(A)(ii)) Thus, in the case of a partnership, the decedent and members of the decedent's family are required to own the requisite percentage of the capital interest, and the requisite percentage of the profits interest, in the partnership. (Com Rept, see ¶ 5027)

In the case of a trade or business that owns an interest in another trade or business ("tiered entities"), special look-through rules apply. (Com Rept, see ¶ 5027) Those rules provide that if, by reason of holding an interest in a trade or business, a decedent, any member of the decedent's family, any qualified heir, or any member of the qualified heir's family is treated as holding an interest in any other trade or business— (Code Sec. 2033A(e)(3)(B))

... the ownership interest in the other trade or business is disregarded in determining if the ownership interest in the first trade or business is a qualified family-owned business interest (Code Sec. 2033A(e)(3)(B)(i)) and

... the rules on qualified family-owned businesses will be applied separately in determining if the ownership interest in the other trade or business is a qualified family-owned business interest. (Code Sec. 2033A(e)(3)(B)(ii))

In the case of a multi-tiered entity, the above rules are sequentially applied to look through each separate tier of the entity. (Com Rept, see ¶ 5027)

> *Illustration:* If a holding company owns interests in two other companies, each of the three entities will be separately tested under the qualified family-owned business interest rules. In determining whether the holding company is a qualified family-owned business interest, its ownership interest in the other two companies is disregarded. Even if the holding company itself does not qualify as a family-owned business interest, the other two companies still may qualify if the direct and indirect interests held by the decedent and his family members satisfy the requisite ownership percentages and other requirements of a qualified family-owned business interest. If either (or both) of the lower-tier entities qualify, the value of the qualified family-owned business interests owned by the holding company are treated as proportionately owned by the holding company's shareholders. (Com Rept, see ¶ 5027)

Limitations on qualified family-owned business interests.   A "qualified family-owned business interest" does *not* include:

(1) any interest in a trade or business, if the principal place of business of the trade or business is not located in the U.S. (Code Sec. 2033A(e)(2)(A))

(2) any interest in an entity, if the stock or debt of the entity or a controlled group, as defined in Code Sec. 267(f)(1) (FTC 2d/FIN ¶ G-2708; USTR ¶ 2674.05; TaxDesk ¶ 44,229) of which the entity was a member was readily tradable on an established securities market or secondary market at any time within three years of the decedent's death (Code Sec. 2033A(e)(2)(B))

(3) any interest in a trade or business (other than a bank or a domestic building and loan association), if more than 35% of the adjusted ordinary gross income of the trade or business for the tax year which includes the date of the decedent's death would qualify as personal holding company income under Code Sec. 543(a) (FTC 2d/FIN ¶ D-3507; USTR ¶ 5434; TaxDesk ¶ 60,155) (Code Sec. 2033A(e)(2)(C))

(4) the portion of an interest in a trade or business that is attributable to cash or marketable securities, or both, in excess of the reasonably expected day-to-day working capital needs of the trade or business (Code Sec. 2033A(e)(2)(D)(i))

(5) the portion of an interest in a trade or business that is attributable to any other assets of the trade or business (other than assets used in the active conduct of a bank or a domestic building and loan association), the income of which is described in Code Sec. 543(a) (dealing with personal holding company income) (FTC 2d/FIN ¶ D-3507; USTR ¶ 5434; TaxDesk ¶ 60,155) or Code Sec. 954(c)(1) (dealing with foreign personal holding company income) (FTC 2d/FIN ¶ O-2432; USTR ¶ 9544.02), determined without regard to Code Sec. 954(c)(1)(A) and by substituting "trade or business" for "controlled foreign corporation". (Code Sec. 2033A(e)(2)(D)(ii))

Thus, an interest in a trade or business does not qualify for the exclusion if the business's (or a related entity's) stock or securities were publicly traded at any time within three years of the decedent's death. An interest in a trade or business also does not qualify if more than 35% of the adjusted ordinary gross income of the business for the year of the decedent's death was personal holding company income. This personal holding company restriction does not apply to banks or domestic building and loan associations. (Com Rept, see ¶ 5027)

The value of a trade or business qualifying as a family-owned business interest is reduced to the extent the business holds passive assets or excess cash or marketable securities. The value of qualified family-owned business interests does not include any cash or marketable securities in excess of the reasonably expected day-to-day working capital needs of the trade or business. For this purpose, Congress intended that day-to-day working capital needs be determined based on a historical average of the business's working capital needs in the past, using an analysis similar to that set forth in *Bardahl Mfg. Corp.* (FTC 2d/FIN ¶ D-2840; USTR ¶ 5374; TaxDesk ¶ 60,132) Congress further intended that accumulations for capital acquisitions not be considered "working capital" for this purpose. (Com Rept, see ¶ 5027)

The value of the qualified family-owned business interests also does not include certain other passive assets. For this purpose, passive assets include any assets that:

. . . produce dividends, interest, rents, royalties, annuities and certain other types of passive income, as described in Code Sec. 543(a) (FTC 2d/FIN ¶ D-3507; USTR ¶ 5434; TaxDesk ¶ 60,155)

. . . are an interest in a trust, partnership or REMIC, as described in Code Sec. 954(c)(1)(B)(ii) (FTC 2d/FIN ¶ O-2448; USTR ¶ 9544.02)

. . . produce no income, as described in Code Sec. 954(c)(1)(B)(iii) (FTC 2d/FIN ¶ O-2449; USTR ¶ 9544.02)

. . . give rise to income from commodities transactions or foreign currency gains, as described in Code Sec. 954(c)(1)(C) (FTC 2d/FIN ¶ O-2457; USTR ¶ 9544.02) and Code Sec. 954(c)(1)(D) (FTC 2d/FIN ¶ O-2459; USTR ¶ 9544.02)

. . . produce income equivalent to interest, as described in Code Sec. 954(c)(1)(E), (FTC 2d/FIN ¶ O-2473; USTR ¶ 9544.02) or

. . . produce income from notional principal contracts or payments in lieu of dividends (as described in Code Sec. 954(c)(1)(F) and Code Sec. 954(c)(1)(G), also added by the '97 Act, see ¶ 1609). (Com Rept, see ¶ 5027)

In the case of a regular dealer in property, the property is not considered to produce passive income under these rules, and thus, is not considered to be a passive asset. (Com Rept, see ¶ 5027)

Qualifying estates. An estate qualifies for the exclusion only if the decedent was a U.S. citizen or resident at the date of his death. (Code Sec. 2033A(b)(1)(A))

The executor must elect to have the exclusion apply, and must file an agreement (Code Sec. 2033A(b)(1)(B)) signed by each person in being who has an interest (whether or not in possession) in any property designated in the agreement, consenting to the application of the recapture rules (see ¶ 506) to the property. (Code Sec. 2033A(h)) Rules similar to Code Sec. 2032A(d)(1) and Code Sec. 2032A(d)(3) (relating to the special use valuation election) apply for purposes of the election of the qualified family-owned business exclusion. (Code Sec. 2033A(i)(3)(H))

> ✐ *observation:* The special use valuation election is made on the estate tax return (Form 706) filed for the decedent's estate. (FTC 2d ¶ R-5248; USTR ¶ 20,32A4; TaxDesk ¶ 77,131; EP ¶ 44,049) Presumably, when Form 706 is revised to reflect the exclusion for qualified family-owned business interests, the revised form will also provide a way to elect to have the exclusion apply.

To qualify for the exclusion, an estate must also meet two additional requirements: a requirement (described in detail under *"50% liquidity test"*, below), that the aggregate value of the decedent's qualified family-owned business interests that are passed to qualified heirs exceeds 50% of the decedent's adjusted gross estate (Code Sec. 2033A(b)(1)(C)), and a requirement (described in detail under *"Participation requirements"*, below) that the decedent or a member of the decedent's family must have owned and materially participated in the trade or business for at least five of the eight years preceding the date of the decedent's death. (Code Sec. 2033A(b)(1)(D))

50% liquidity test. For an estate to qualify for the exclusion, the sum of (a) the "includible qualified family-owned business interests", plus (Code Sec. 2033A(b)(1)(C)(i)) (b) the amount of "includible gifts of qualified family-owned business interests", must exceed 50% of the "adjusted gross estate" (as defined below, under **"Definitions"**). (Code Sec. 2033A(b)(1)(C)(ii))

For this purpose, "includible qualified family-owned business interests" are the qualified family-owned business interests (as defined above) that (a) are included in determining the value of the gross estate (without regard to the exclusion for qualified family-owned business interests), (Code Sec. 2033A(b)(2)(A)) and (b) are acquired by any qualified heir (as defined below, under **"Definitions"**) from, or passed to any qualified heir from, the decedent (within the meaning of Code Sec. 2032A(e)(9)). (FTC 2d ¶ R-5207; USTR ¶ 20,32A4; TaxDesk ¶ 77,103; EP ¶ 44,008) (Code Sec. 2033A(b)(2)(B))

For this purpose, the amount of "includible gifts of qualified family-owned business interests" is the excess of—

(1) the sum of (a) the amount of gifts of qualified family-owned business interests from the decedent to members of the decedent's family taken into account as adjusted taxable gifts (FTC 2d ¶ R-7002; USTR ¶ 20,014.02; TaxDesk ¶ 78,053; EP ¶ 44,903) for estate tax purposes (Code Sec. 2033A(b)(3)(A)(i)) plus (b) the amount of gifts of qualified family-owned business interests from the decedent to members of the decedent's family otherwise excluded under the gift tax annual exclusion, to the extent those interests are continuously held by members of the decedent's family (other than the decedent's spouse) between the date of the gift and the date of the decedent's death (Code Sec. 2033A(b)(3)(A)(ii)) over

(2) the amount of gifts of qualified family-owned business interests from the decedent to members of the decedent's family otherwise included in the gross estate. (Code Sec. 2033A(b)(3)(B))

Thus, the 50% liquidity test generally is applied by adding all transfers of qualified family-owned business interests made by the decedent to qualified heirs at the time of the decedent's death, plus certain lifetime gifts of qualified family-owned business interests made to members of the decedent's family, and comparing this total to the decedent's adjusted gross estate. To the extent that a decedent held qualified family-owned business interests in more than one trade or business, all such interests are aggregated for purposes of applying the 50% liquidity test. (Com Rept, see ¶ 5027)

The 50% liquidity test is calculated using a ratio, the numerator and denominator of which are described below. (Com Rept, see ¶ 5027)

The numerator is determined by aggregating the value of all qualified family-owned business interests that are includible in the decedent's gross estate and are passed from the decedent to a qualified heir, plus any lifetime transfers of qualified business interests that are made by the decedent to members of the decedent's family (other than the decedent's spouse), provided those interests have been continuously held by members of the decedent's family and were not otherwise includible in the decedent's gross estate. For this purpose, qualified business interests transferred to members of the decedent's family during the decedent's lifetime are valued as of the date of the transfer. This amount is then reduced by all indebtedness of the estate, except for the following: (a) indebtedness on a qualified residence of the decedent, determined in accordance with the requirements for deductibility of mortgage interest set forth in Code Sec. 163(h)(3) (FTC 2d/FIN ¶ K-5470; USTR ¶ 1634.052; TaxDesk ¶ 31,452), (b) indebtedness incurred to pay the educational or medical expenses of the decedent, the decedent's spouse, or the decedent's dependents, and (c) other indebtedness of up to $10,000. (Com Rept, see ¶ 5027)

The denominator is equal to the decedent's gross estate, reduced by any indebtedness of the estate, and increased by the amount of the following transfers, to the extent not already included in the decedent's gross estate: (a) any lifetime transfers of qualified business interests that were made by the decedent to members of the decedent's family (other than the decedent's spouse), provided those interests have been continuously held by members of the decedent's family, plus (b) any other transfers from the decedent to the decedent's spouse that were made within 10 years of the date of the decedent's death, plus (c) any other transfers made by the decedent within three years of the decedent's death, except non-taxable transfers made to members of the decedent's family. IRS is granted authority to disregard de minimis gifts. In determining the amount of gifts made by the decedent, any gift that the donor and the donor's spouse elected to have treated as a split gift under Code Sec. 2513 (FTC 2d ¶ Q-7000;

FTC 2d References are to Federal Tax Coordinator 2d
FIN References are to RIA's Analysis of Federal Taxes: Income
USTR References are to United States Tax Reporter: Income, Estate & Gift, and Excise
PCA References are to Pension Coordinator and Pension & Benefits Expert/Advisor
PE References are to Pension and Profit Sharing 2nd
EP References are to Estate Planning & Taxation Coordinator and Estate Planning Advisor

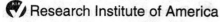 **Research Institute of America** 121

USTR ¶ 25,134; TaxDesk ¶ 74,300; EP ¶ 48,501) is treated as made one-half by each spouse for purposes of this provision. (Com Rept, see ¶ 5027)

Participation requirements. During the eight-year period ending on the date of the decedent's death, there must have been periods aggregating five years or more during which (a) the qualified family-owned business interests were owned by the decedent or a member of the decedent's family (Code Sec. 2033A(b)(1)(D)(i)) and (b) there was material participation, within the meaning of Code Sec. 2032A(e)(6) (FTC 2d ¶ R-5224; USTR ¶ 20,32A4; TaxDesk ¶ 77,119; EP ¶ 44,025) by the decedent or a member of the decedent's family in the operation of the business to which the interests relate. (Code Sec. 2033A(b)(1)(D)(ii))

Under the regs on the special use valuation rules, no one factor is determinative of the presence of material participation, and the uniqueness of the particular industry (e.g., timber, farming, manufacturing) must be considered. Physical work and participation in management decisions are the principal factors to be considered. For example, an individual generally is considered to be materially participating in the business if he or she personally manages the business fully, regardless of the number of hours worked, as long as any necessary functions are performed. (Com Rept, see ¶ 5027)

If a qualified heir rents qualifying property to a member of the qualified heir's family on a net cash basis, and that family member materially participates in the business, the material participation requirement will be considered to have been met with respect to the qualified heir for purposes of the exclusion for qualified family-owned business interests. (Com Rept, see ¶ 5027)

Definitions.

• *Adjusted gross estate.* For purposes of the exclusion for qualified family-owned business interests, the term "adjusted gross estate" means the value of the gross estate (determined without regard to the exclusion) (Code Sec. 2033A(c)) (1) reduced by any amount deductible for estate tax purposes under Code Sec. 2053(a)(3) (relating to claims against the estate) (FTC 2d ¶ R-5456; USTR ¶ 20,534.07; TaxDesk ¶ 77,642; EP ¶ 44,207) or Code Sec. 2053(a)(4) (relating to unpaid mortgages on, or indebtedness in respect of, property includible in the gross estate) (FTC 2d ¶ R-5497; USTR ¶ 20,534.16; TaxDesk ¶ 77,669; EP ¶ 44,248), (Code Sec. 2033A(c)(1)) and (2) increased by the excess of—

(a) the sum of (i) the amount of includible gifts of qualified family-owned business interests (as defined above) (Code Sec. 2033A(c)(2)(A)(i)) (ii) the amount (if more than de minimis) of other transfers from the decedent to the decedent's spouse (at the time of the transfer) within 10 years of the date of the decedent's death, (Code Sec. 2033A(c)(2)(A)(ii)) plus (iii) the amount of other gifts (not included under (i) or (ii)) from the decedent within three years of the date of the decedent's death, other than gifts to members of the decedent's family otherwise excluded under the gift tax annual exclusion (Code Sec. 2033A(c)(2)(A)(iii)) over

(b) the sum of the amounts described in (a), above, which are otherwise includible in the gross estate. (Code Sec. 2033A(c)(2)(B))

Research Institute of America

For purposes of the definition of "adjusted gross estate", IRS may provide that de minimis gifts to persons other than members of the decedent's family won't be taken into account. (Code Sec. 2033A(c))

• *Adjusted value.* For purposes of the exclusion for qualified family-owned business interests, the "adjusted value" of any qualified family-owned business interest is the value of that interest for estate tax purposes (determined without regard to the exclusion), reduced by the excess of (1) any amount deductible for estate tax purposes under Code Sec. 2053(a)(3) (relating to claims against the estate) (FTC 2d ¶ R-5456; USTR ¶ 20,534.07; TaxDesk ¶ 77,642; EP ¶ 44,207) or Code Sec. 2053(a)(4) (relating to unpaid mortgages on, or indebtedness in respect of, property includible in the gross estate), (FTC 2d ¶ R-5497; USTR ¶ 20,534.16; TaxDesk ¶ 77,669; EP ¶ 44,248) (Code Sec. 2033A(d)(1)) over (2) the sum of—

(a) any indebtedness on any qualified residence of the decedent, the interest on which is deductible under Code Sec. 163(h)(3) (FTC 2d/FIN ¶ K-5470; USTR ¶ 1634.052; TaxDesk ¶ 31,452), (Code Sec. 2033A(d)(2)(A)) plus

(b) any indebtedness to the extent the estate establishes that the proceeds of the indebtedness were used for the payment of educational and medical expenses of the decedent, the decedent's spouse, or the decedent's dependents, within the meaning of Code Sec. 152 (FTC 2d/FIN ¶ A-3606; USTR ¶ 1524; TaxDesk ¶ 56,261), (Code Sec. 2033A(d)(2)(B)) plus

(c) any indebtedness not described in (a) or (b), above, to the extent the indebtedness does not exceed $10,000. (Code Sec. 2033A(d)(2)(C))

• *"Member of the family"* is defined, for purposes of the family-owned business exclusion, in the same way as it is defined in Code Sec. 2032A(e)(2) (FTC 2d ¶ R-5211; USTR ¶ 20,32A4; TaxDesk ¶ 77,106; EP ¶ 44,012). (Code Sec. 2033A(i)(2)) Under that definition, members of an individual's family include (1) the individual's spouse, (2) the individual's ancestors, (3) lineal descendants of the individual, of the individual's spouse, or of the individual's parents, and (4) the spouses of any lineal descendant described in (3). (Code Sec. 2032A(e)(2))

• *"Qualified heir"* (1) means a qualified heir as that term is defined in Code Sec. 2032A(e)(1) (FTC 2d ¶ R-5210; USTR ¶ 20,32A4; TaxDesk ¶ 77,105; EP ¶ 44,011). (Code Sec. 2033A(i)(1)(A)), and (2) includes any active employee of the trade or business to which the qualified family-owned business interest relates if the employee has been employed by the trade or business for a period of at least 10 years before the decedent's death. (Code Sec. 2033A(i)(1)(B)) Under the Code Sec. 2032A(e)(1) definition, a qualified heir is a member of the decedent's family (as defined above) who acquired the property (or to whom the property passed) from the decedent.

FTC 2d References are to Federal Tax Coordinator 2d
FIN References are to RIA's Analysis of Federal Taxes: Income
USTR References are to United States Tax Reporter: Income, Estate & Gift, and Excise
PCA References are to Pension Coordinator and Pension & Benefits Expert/Advisor
PE References are to Pension and Profit Sharing 2nd
EP References are to Estate Planning & Taxation Coordinator and Estate Planning Advisor

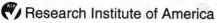

Other applicable rules. For purposes of the exclusion for qualified family-owned business interests, rules similar to the following rules apply:

. . . Code Sec. 2032A(b)(4) (relating to decedents who are retired or disabled under the special use valuation rules) (FTC 2d ¶ R-5233; USTR ¶ 20,32A4; TaxDesk ¶ 77,127; EP ¶ 44,034) (Code Sec. 2033A(i)(3)(A))

. . . Code Sec. 2032A(b)(5) (relating to special rules for surviving spouses under the special use valuation rules) (FTC 2d ¶ R-5230; USTR ¶ 20,32A4; TaxDesk ¶ 77,124; EP ¶ 44,031) (Code Sec. 2033A(i)(3)(B))

. . . Code Sec. 2032A(e)(10) (relating to community property under the special use valuation rules) (Code Sec. 2033A(i)(3)(I)) (FTC 2d ¶ R-5219; USTR ¶ 20,32A4; TaxDesk ¶ 77,114; EP ¶ 44,020)

. . . Code Sec. 2032A(e)(14) (relating to treatment under the special use valuation rules of replacement property acquired in Code Sec. 1031 or Code Sec. 1033 transactions) (FTC 2d ¶ R-5223; USTR ¶ 20,32A4; TaxDesk ¶ 77,118; EP ¶ 44,024) (Code Sec. 2033A(i)(3)(J))

. . . Code Sec. 6166(b)(3) (relating to farmhouses and certain other structures taken into account for purposes of the extension for payment of the estate tax on closely held business interests) (FTC 2d ¶ S-6014; USTR ¶ 61,664.01; TaxDesk ¶ 78,416; EP ¶ 83,215) (Code Sec. 2033A(i)(3)(L))

☐ **Effective:** Applies to estates of decedents dying after '97. ('97 Act §502(c))

¶ 506. Estate tax benefit of qualified family-owned business exclusion may be recaptured if certain events occur

Code Sec. 2033A(f), as added by '97 Act § 502(a)
Code Sec. 2033A(g), as added by '97 Act § 502(a)
Generally effective: Applies to estates of decedents dying after Dec. 31, '97
Committee Reports, see ¶ 5027

Under pre-'97 Act law, there were no special estate tax rules for qualified family-owned businesses. However, under Code Sec. 2032A, an executor may elect, for estate tax purposes, to value certain qualified real property used in farming or another qualifying closely-held trade or business at its value as a farm or in the business, rather than its highest and best use value. (FTC 2d ¶ R-5200; USTR ¶ 20,32A4; TaxDesk ¶ 77,100; EP ¶ 44,001) If, after the special use valuation election is made, the heir who acquired the real property ceases to use it in its qualified use within 10 years of the decedent's death, an additional estate tax is imposed in order to "recapture" the benefit of the special use valuation. The qualified heir is allowed a two-year grace period immediately after the decedent's death to commence the qualified use of the property. But if this grace period applies, the recapture period is extended. (FTC 2d ¶ R-5300; USTR ¶ 20,32A4; TaxDesk ¶ 77,153; EP ¶ 44,101)

Under Code Sec. 2032A(c)(6)(B), specially valued property ceases to be used for the qualified use if, during any period of eight years ending after the date of the decedent's death (but before the death of the qualified heir), there were periods totaling more than three years during which (1) for periods during which the property was held by the decedent, there was no material participation by the decedent or any member of his family in the operation of the farm or other business, and (2) for periods during which the property was held by any qualified heir, there was no material participation by the qualified heir or any member of his family in the operation of the farm or other business. (FTC 2d ¶ R-5306; USTR ¶ 20,32A4; TaxDesk ¶ 77,157; EP ¶ 44,107)

The amount of any additional estate tax imposed under the special use valuation rules is the lesser of (1) the "adjusted tax difference" attributable to the interest or (2) the excess of the amount realized with respect to the interest over the special use value of the interest. Under Code Sec. 2032A(c)(2)(B), the "adjusted tax difference" attributable to any interest is computed by multiplying the excess of what would have been the estate tax if special use valuation had not been elected by a fraction, (a) whose numerator is the excess of the estate tax value of the interest determined without regard to special use valuation over the special use value of the interest, and (b) whose denominator is the excess of the estate tax value of *all* qualified real property determined without regard to special use valuation over the special use value of *all* qualified real property. (FTC 2d ¶ R-5314; USTR ¶ 20,32A4; TaxDesk ¶ 77,165; EP ¶ 44,115)

New Law. An estate tax exclusion is provided for "qualified family-owned business interests". For a discussion of the exclusion, see ¶ 505. However, an additional estate tax is imposed if the exclusion is allowed and any of the following events ("recapture events") occurs within ten years after the decedent's death and before the death of the qualified heir (Code Sec. 2033A(f)(1) as added by '97 Act §502(a)) (the family member or employee to whom the qualified family-owned business interest passed, see ¶ 505):

(1) The material participation requirements described in the special use valuation rules of Code Sec. 2032A(c)(6)(B) (FTC 2d ¶ R-5306; USTR ¶ 20,32A4; TaxDesk ¶ 77,157; EP ¶ 44,107) are not met with respect to the qualified family-owned business interest which was acquired from the decedent (Code Sec. 2033A(f)(1)(A)), i.e., if neither the qualified heir nor any member of his or her family has materially participated in the trade or business for at least five years of any eight-year period. (Com Rept, see ¶ 5027)

(2) The qualified heir disposes of any portion of a qualified family-owned business interest, other than by a disposition to a member of the qualified heir's family or through a qualified conservation contribution (see ¶ 517 *et seq.*). (Code Sec. 2033A(f)(1)(B))

(3) The qualified heir loses U.S. citizenship, within the meaning of the expatriation rules of Code Sec. 877) (FTC 2d/FIN ¶ O-11701; USTR ¶ 8774; TaxDesk ¶ 64,471), or an event described in Code Sec. 877(e)(1)(A) or Code Sec. 877(e)(1)(B) (FTC 2d/FIN ¶ O-11701; TaxDesk ¶ 64,471) occurs with respect to the qualified heir, and

FTC 2d References are to Federal Tax Coordinator 2d
FIN References are to RIA's Analysis of Federal Taxes: Income
USTR References are to United States Tax Reporter: Income, Estate & Gift, and Excise
PCA References are to Pension Coordinator and Pension & Benefits Expert/Advisor
PE References are to Pension and Profit Sharing 2nd
EP References are to Estate Planning & Taxation Coordinator and Estate Planning Advisor

the qualified heir does not comply with the security requirements described below (Code Sec. 2033(f)(1)(C)) or

(4) The principal place of business of a trade or business of the qualified family-owned business interest ceases to be located in the U.S. (Code Sec. 2033A(f)(1)(D))

If one of the above recapture events occurs, an additional tax is imposed on the date of the event. (Com Rept, see ¶ 5027)

A sale or disposition, in the ordinary course of business, of assets such as inventory or a piece of equipment used in the business (e.g., the sale of crops or a tractor) will not result in recapture of the benefits of the qualified family-owned business exclusion. (Com Rept, see ¶ 5027)

Rules similar to Code Sec. 2032A(c)(5) (relating to liability for the tax and the furnishing of a bond) (FTC 2d ¶ R-5318; USTR ¶ 20,32A4; TaxDesk ¶ 77,169; EP ¶ 44,119) apply for purposes of the qualified family-owned business exclusion. (Code Sec. 2033A(i)(3)(F)) Thus, each qualified heir is personally liable for the portion of the recapture tax that is imposed with respect to his interest in the qualified family-owned business. (Com Rept, see ¶ 5027)

> *Illustration:* If a brother and sister inherit a qualified family-owned business from their father, and only the sister materially participates in the business, her participation will cause both her and her brother to meet the material participation test. If she ceases to materially participate in the business within 10 years after her father's death (and the brother still does not materially participate), the sister and brother would both be liable for the recapture tax; that is, each would be liable for the recapture tax attributable to his or her interest. (Com Rept, see ¶ 5027)

Amount of the additional estate tax. The amount of the additional estate tax is (1) the applicable percentage (determined as described below) of the adjusted tax difference attributable to the qualified family-owned business interest, determined under rules similar to the rules of Code Sec. 2032A(c)(2)(B)) (FTC 2d ¶ R-5314; TaxDesk ¶ 77,165; EP ¶ 44,115) (Code Sec. 2033A(f)(2)(A)(i)) plus (2) interest on the amount in (1) at the Code Sec. 6621 underpayment rate (FTC 2d/FIN ¶ V-1101; USTR ¶ 66,214; TaxDesk ¶ 85,101; EP ¶ 87,353) for the period beginning on the date the estate tax liability was due and ending on the date the additional estate tax is due. (Code Sec. 2033A(f)(2)(A(ii)))

The "applicable percentage" used in determining the amount of the additional estate tax depends on when the recapture event occurs. (Com Rept, see ¶ 5027) If the recapture event occurs in year 1 through 6 of material participation, then the applicable percentage is 100%. If the recapture event occurs in:

... Year 7, the applicable percentage is 80%.

... Year 8, the applicable percentage is 60%.

... Year 9, the applicable percentage is 40%.

... Year 10, the applicable percentage is 20%. (Code Sec. 2033A(f)(2)(B))

In general, there is no requirement that the qualified heir (or members of his family) continue to hold or participate in the trade or business more than ten years after the decedent's death. (Com Rept, see ¶ 5027) However, rules similar to Code Sec. 2032A(c)(7) (allowing the qualified heir a two-year grace period immediately after the decedent's death to start use of the property in a qualified use) (FTC 2d ¶ R-5302; USTR ¶ 20,32A4; TaxDesk ¶ 77,154; EP ¶ 44,103) apply for purposes of the qualified family-owned business exclusion. (Code Sec. 2033A(i)(3)(G)) Thus, the ten-year recapture period may be extended for a period of up to two years if the qualified heir does not begin to use the property for a period of up to two years after the decedent's death. (Com Rept, see ¶ 5027)

If a recapture event occurs with respect to any qualified family-owned business interest (or portion thereof), the amount of reduction in estate taxes attributable to that interest is determined on a proportionate basis. (Com Rept, see ¶ 5027)

> *Illustration:* The decedent's estate included $2 million in qualified family-owned business interests, and $1 million of those interests received beneficial treatment under the exclusion. One-half of the value of the interest disposed of is considered to have received the benefits provided under the exclusion. (Com Rept, see ¶ 5027)

Security requirements for noncitizen qualified heirs. If a qualified heir is not a U.S. citizen, any interest held by that heir at a time when the heir is not a U.S. citizen or an event described in Code Sec. 877(e)(1)(A) or Code Sec. 877(e)(1)(B) (FTC 2d/FIN ¶ O-11701; TaxDesk ¶ 64,471) has occurred with respect to the heir is generally treated as a qualified family-owned business interest only if the interest passes or is acquired (or is held) in a "qualified trust". (Code Sec. 2033A(g)(1)) (as defined below). This rule does not apply if a bond is furnished under rules similar to the rules of Code Sec. 2032A(c)(5) (relating to the payment of tax and furnishing of a bond under the special use valuation rules, see FTC 2d ¶ R-5318; USTR ¶ 20,32A4; TaxDesk ¶ 77,169; EP ¶ 44,119) (Code Sec. 2033A(g)(1)) and (Code Sec. 2033A(i)(3)(F)) or if payment of the recapture tax is accelerated under rules similar to Code Sec. 6166(g)(1)(B) (FTC 2d ¶ S-6110; USTR ¶ 61,664.03; TaxDesk ¶ 78,431; EP ¶ 83,311), Code Sec. 6166(g)(1)(C) (FTC 2d ¶ S-6107; USTR ¶ 61,664.03; EP ¶ 83,308), or Code Sec. 6166(g)(1)(D) (FTC 2d ¶ S-6118 and S-6119; USTR ¶ 61,664.03; TaxDesk ¶ 78,432; EP ¶ 83,319 and 83,320) (relating to the payment in installments of the estate tax attributable to closely held business interests). (Code Sec. 2033A(g)(1)) and (Code Sec. 2033A(i)(3)(M))

A qualified trust is a trust that is organized under, and governed by, the laws of the U.S. or a state (Code Sec. 2033A(g)(2)(A)) and (except as otherwise provided in regs) with respect to which the trust instrument requires that at least one trustee of the trust be an individual citizen of the U.S. or a domestic corporation. (Code Sec.

FTC 2d References are to Federal Tax Coordinator 2d
FIN References are to RIA's Analysis of Federal Taxes: Income
USTR References are to United States Tax Reporter: Income, Estate & Gift, and Excise
PCA References are to Pension Coordinator and Pension & Benefits Expert/Advisor
PE References are to Pension and Profit Sharing 2nd
EP References are to Estate Planning & Taxation Coordinator and Estate Planning Advisor

2033A(g)(2)(B)) Thus, a qualified heir who loses U.S. citizenship may avoid recapture by placing the qualified family-owned business assets into a trust meeting requirements similar to a qualified domestic trust (QDOT) under Code Sec. 2056A (FTC 2d ¶ R-6200; USTR ¶ 20,56A4.01; TaxDesk ¶ 77,829; EP ¶ 44,551), or through certain other security arrangements. (Com Rept, see ¶ 5027)

Other applicable rules. Rules similar to the following rules apply for purposes of the recapture of the estate tax benefit of the qualified family-owned business exclusion:

. . . Code Sec. 2032A(c)(2)(D) (relating to partial dispositions) (FTC 2d ¶ R-5316; TaxDesk ¶ 77,167; EP ¶ 44,117) (Code Sec. 2033A(i)(3)(C))

. . . Code Sec. 2032A(c)(3) (relating to only one additional tax imposed with respect to any one portion) (FTC 2d ¶ R-5312; TaxDesk ¶ 77,163; EP ¶ 44,113) (Code Sec. 2033A(i)(3)(D))

. . . Code Sec. 2032A(c)(4) (relating to the due date of the recapture tax) (FTC 2d ¶ R-5317; TaxDesk ¶ 77,168; EP ¶ 44,118) (Code Sec. 2033A(i)(3)(E))

. . . Code Sec. 2032A(f) (relating to the statute of limitations with respect to the recapture tax) (FTC 2d ¶ T-4223; TaxDesk ¶ 83,822; EP ¶ 87,170) (Code Sec. 2033A(i)(3)(K))

. . . Code Sec. 6166(g)(1)(B) (FTC 2d ¶ S-6110; USTR ¶ 61,664.03; TaxDesk ¶ 78,431; EP ¶ 83,311), Code Sec. 6166(g)(1)(C) (FTC 2d ¶ S-6107; USTR ¶ 61,664.03; EP ¶ 83,308), and Code Sec. 6166(g)(1)(D) (FTC 2d ¶ S-6118 and S-6119; USTR ¶ 61,664.03; TaxDesk ¶ 78,432; EP ¶ 83,319 and 83,320) (relating to acceleration of payment) (Code Sec. 2033A(i)(3)(M))

. . . Code Sec. 6324B (relating to the special lien for the recapture tax under Code Sec. 2032A) (FTC 2d ¶ V-6051; USTR ¶ 63,24B4; TaxDesk ¶ 91,110; EP ¶ 87,441) (Code Sec. 2033A(i)(3)(N))

☐ **Effective:** Applies to estates of decedents dying after '97. ('97 Act §502(c))

¶ 507. Interest imposed on estate tax deferred under Code Sec. 6166 is reduced

Code Sec. 6601(j)(1), as amended by '97 Act § 503(a)
Code Sec. 6601(j)(2), as amended by '97 Act § 503(a)
Code Sec. 6601(j)(3), as amended by '97 Act § 501(e)
Generally effective: Applies to estates of decedents dying after Dec. 31, '97
Committee Reports, see ¶ 5028

If certain requirements are met, the executor of an estate that includes an interest in a closely held business may elect to pay the estate tax attributable to the closely held business interest in two or more annual installments. (FTC 2d ¶ S-6000; USTR ¶ 61,664; TaxDesk ¶ 78,401; EP ¶ 83,201)

Under pre-'97 Act law, a special 4% interest rate applied to part of the estate tax, payment of which was deferred under Code Sec. 6166. The portion of the deferred estate tax eligible for the 4% interest rate (the "4% portion") was $345,800, less the amount of the unified credit allowable (except that the 4% portion couldn't exceed the amount of the tax that was subject to an installment payment election).

> **✓ observation:** $345,800 is the tentative tax on the first $1 million of a decedent's taxable estate under the unified estate and gift tax rate schedule.

Under pre-'97 Act law, the deferred estate tax that was *not* eligible for the 4% interest rate was subject to interest at the underpayment rate described in Code Sec. 6621. (FTC 2d ¶ S-6009; USTR ¶ 66,014; TaxDesk ¶ 85,106; EP ¶ 83,210)

Code Sec. 6601(a) provides that, if any tax is not paid when due, interest is imposed on the unpaid amount at the underpayment rate established under Code Sec. 6621. The underpayment rate established under Code Sec. 6621 equals the federal short-term rate plus three percentage points. (FTC 2d/FIN ¶ V-1101; USTR ¶ 66,214; TaxDesk ¶ 85,101; EP ¶ 87,353)

Under pre-'97 Act law, a unified credit of $192,800 was allowed in computing the estate and gift tax liability of a U.S. citizen or resident. The unified credit effectively exempted a total of $600,000 in cumulative taxable transfers from the estate and gift tax. (FTC 2d ¶ R-7101; USTR ¶ 20,104; TaxDesk ¶ 78,181; EP ¶ 45,102) As discussed in ¶ 501, the $192,800 amount of the unified credit has been replaced, for estates of decedents dying after '97, by an "applicable credit amount". The "applicable credit amount" is the equivalent of the tax on the "applicable exclusion amount". The "applicable exclusion amount" will be $625,000 for decedents dying in '98, and it will be increased to $1 million on a phased-in schedule through 2006 (see ¶ 501 for complete details).

Individual income tax brackets are indexed for inflation by means of an annual cost-of-living adjustment. Under Code Sec. 1(f)(3), the cost-of-living adjustment for any calendar year is the percentage (if any) by which the consumer price index (CPI) for the preceding calendar year exceeds the CPI for calendar year '92. (FTC 2d/FIN ¶ A-1103; USTR ¶ 14; TaxDesk ¶ 56,821)

New Law. If the time for payment of an amount of estate tax is extended under Code Sec. 6166, then, instead of the annual interest rate provided by Code Sec. 6601(a), (1) interest at the rate of 2% is imposed on the "2-percent portion" (as defined below) of that amount (Code Sec. 6601(j)(1)(A) as amended by '97 Act §503(a)), and (2) interest on any portion of the deferred estate tax that exceeds the "2-percent portion" is imposed at a rate equal to 45% of of the annual rate provided by Code Sec. 6601(a). (Code Sec. 6601(j)(1)(B)) For this purpose, the amount of any deficiency which is prorated to installments payable under Code Sec. 6166 is treated as an amount of tax payable in installments under that section. (Code Sec. 6601(j)(1))

The term "2-percent portion" means the lesser of—

FTC 2d References are to Federal Tax Coordinator 2d
FIN References are to RIA's Analysis of Federal Taxes: Income
USTR References are to United States Tax Reporter: Income, Estate & Gift, and Excise
PCA References are to Pension Coordinator and Pension & Benefits Expert/Advisor
PE References are to Pension and Profit Sharing 2nd
EP References are to Estate Planning & Taxation Coordinator and Estate Planning Advisor

(1) (a) the amount of the tentative tax that would be determined under the estate tax rate schedule if the amount on which the tentative tax is to be computed were the sum of $1 million (indexed for inflation for estates of decedents dying after '98, as discussed below) and the applicable exclusion amount provided by the unified credit, reduced by (Code Sec. 6601(j)(2)(A)(i)) (b) the applicable credit amount of the unified credit, (Code Sec. 6601(j)(2)(A)(ii)) or

(2) the amount of the estate tax extended under Code Sec. 6166. (Code Sec. 6601(j)(2)(B))

Thus, interest at the rate of 2% is imposed on the amount of deferred estate tax attributable to the first $1 million in *taxable* value of the closely held business interest (i.e., the first $1 million in value in excess of the effective exemption provided by the unified credit and any other exclusions). (Com Rept, see ¶ 5028)

> *Illustration:* If the estate of a decedent dying in '98 (before the $1 million amount is indexed for inflation, see below) qualifies for the qualified family-owned business exclusion (see ¶ 505), the amount of estate tax attributable to the value of the closely held business between $1.3 million and $2.3 million is eligible for the 2% interest rate. (Com Rept, see ¶ 5028)

> *observation:* Under the unified estate and gift tax rate schedule, the tax on the amount between $1.3 million and $2.3 million is $458,000. Thus, the estate in the above Illustration would pay interest at 2% on the first $458,000 of deferred tax.

> *observation:* The unified credit is applied at the bottom of the estate and gift tax rate schedule. For example, in '98, when the effective exemption provided by the unified credit is $625,000, the unified credit will eliminate the estate tax on the *first* $625,000 in value of the taxable estate. The definition of the "2-percent portion" contained in the '97 Act ensures that an estate will get the benefit of paying interest at 2% on the tax on $1 million of taxable property, determined at the higher rates that apply to amounts above the exemption amount of the unified credit (and the qualified family-owned business exclusion, if applicable).

For the deductibility, for income and estate tax purposes, of interest paid on estate taxes deferred under Code Sec. 6166, see ¶ 508.

Cost-of-living adjustment. For estates of decedents dying in a calendar year after '98, the $1 million amount in the definition of the "2-percent portion" will be increased by an inflation adjustment. (Code Sec. 6601(j)(3) as amended by '97 Act §501(e)) The amount of the adjustment will be $1 million, multiplied by (Code Sec. 6601(j)(3)(A)) the cost-of-living adjustment determined under Code Sec. 1(f)(3) for the calendar year but substituting "calendar year 1997" for "calendar year 1992". (Code Sec. 6601(j)(3)(B)) If the amount as adjusted is not a multiple of $10,000, the amount will be rounded to the next lowest multiple of $10,000. (Code Sec. 6601(j)(3))

Estates of pre-'98 decedents may elect to have amendments made by '97 Act apply. In the case of the estate of any decedent dying before Jan. 1, '98, with respect to which there is an election under Code Sec. 6166, the executor may elect to have the amendments described in this paragraph and in ¶ 508 apply with respect to installments due after the effective date of the election, except that the 2-percent portion of those installments will be equal to the amount that would be the 4-percent portion of those installments without regard to the election. ('97 Act §503(d)(2))

Thus, estates deferring estate tax under pre-'97 Act law may make a one-time election to use the lower interest rates and forego the interest deduction (see ¶ 508) for installments due after the date of the election, but those estates do not receive the benefit of the increase in the amount eligible for the Code Sec. 6601(j) interest rate—i.e., only the amount that was previously eligible for the 4-percent rate would be eligible for the 2% rate. (Com Rept, see ¶ 5028)

The election must be made before Jan. 1, '99 in the manner prescribed by IRS and, once made, is irrevocable. ('97 Act §503(d)(2))

> ⚡*action alert:* If the estate of a decedent dying before Jan. 1, '98 has elected under Code Sec. 6166 to make installment payments of the estate tax attributable to a closely held business interest, the estate may elect, before Jan. 1, '99, to have the amendments made by the '97 Act apply with respect to installments due after the effective date of the election to have the '97 Act amendments apply.

☐ **Effective:** Generally applies to estates of decedents dying after Dec. 31, '97 ('97 Act §503(d)(1)), except that (1) estates of decedents dying before Jan. 1, '98 may elect, before Jan. 1, '99, to have the amendments made by the '97 Act apply with respect to installments due after the effective date of the election ('97 Act §503(d)(2)), and (2) the inflation adjustment contained in the definition of the "2-percent portion" applies to estates of decedents dying in a calendar year after '98. ('97 Act §501(e))

¶ 508. No estate tax or income tax deduction allowed for interest paid on estate tax deferred under Code Sec. 6166

Code Sec. 163(h)(2)(E), as amended by '97 Act § 503(b)(2)(B)
Code Sec. 163(k), as amended by '97 Act § 503(b)(2)(A)
Code Sec. 2053(c)(1)(D), as amended by '97 Act § 503(b)(1)
Generally effective: Applies to estates of decedents dying after Dec. 31, '97
Committee Reports, see ¶ 5028

Code Sec. 6166 provides that, if certain requirements are met, the executor of an estate that includes an interest in a closely held business may elect to pay the estate tax

FTC 2d References are to Federal Tax Coordinator 2d
FIN References are to RIA's Analysis of Federal Taxes: Income
USTR References are to United States Tax Reporter: Income, Estate & Gift, and Excise
PCA References are to Pension Coordinator and Pension & Benefits Expert/Advisor
PE References are to Pension and Profit Sharing 2nd
EP References are to Estate Planning & Taxation Coordinator and Estate Planning Advisor

⚡ Research Institute of America 131

attributable to the closely held business interest in two or more annual installments. (FTC 2d ¶ S-6000; USTR ¶ 61,664; TaxDesk ¶ 78,401; EP ¶ 83,201) Interest is imposed on the deferred estate tax during the period in which it remains unpaid. (For the rate of interest on estate taxes deferred under Code Sec. 6166, see ¶ 507.)

Under pre-'97 Act law, interest on unpaid estate tax, the payment of which was deferred under Code Sec. 6166, was a deductible administration expense for estate tax purposes if the expense was allowable under applicable local law. (FTC 2d ¶ R-5450; USTR ¶ 20,534; TaxDesk ¶ 77,636; EP ¶ 44,201) When an estate claimed the deduction, the estate tax had to be recomputed to take the deduction into account. In Rev Proc 81-27, IRS provided a procedure to be followed by an estate when installment payments due under Code Sec. 6166 were recomputed because of a reduction in the estate tax caused by the deduction of interest on the tax due. The procedure set forth in Rev Proc 81-27 called for the estate to file supplemental estate tax returns. (FTC 2d ¶ R-5451; USTR ¶ 20,534; TaxDesk ¶ 77,637; EP ¶ 44,202)

Noncorporate taxpayers may not deduct "personal interest" for income tax purposes. Under pre-'97 Act law, the definition of "personal interest" expressly excluded interest on estate taxes, the payment of which was deferred under Code Sec. 6166. (FTC 2d/FIN ¶ K-5513; USTR ¶ 1634; TaxDesk ¶ 31,402)

     observation: Thus, under pre-'97 Act law, an estate that elected to pay estate tax in installments under Code Sec. 6166 could claim an income tax deduction for interest paid on the deferred tax, provided the estate complied with the requirements of Code Sec. 642(g) (FTC 2d/FIN ¶ C-7226; USTR ¶ 6424; TaxDesk ¶ 77,678; EP ¶ 80,225) by waiving the right to have the interest allowed as an estate tax deduction.

New Law. No *estate tax* administration expense deduction is allowable for any interest payable on any unpaid portion of the estate tax for the period during which an extension of time for payment of the tax is in effect under Code Sec. 6166. (Code Sec. 2053(c)(1)(D) as amended by '97 Act §503(b)(1)) This provision eliminates the need to file supplemental estate tax returns and make complex computations to claim an estate tax deduction for interest paid. (Com Rept, see ¶ 5028)

No *income tax* deduction is allowable for any interest payable on any unpaid portion of the estate tax for the period during which an extension of time for payment of the tax is in effect under Code Sec. 6166. (Code Sec. 163(k) as amended by '97 Act §503(b)(2)(A))

Interest on estate taxes, the payment of which is deferred under Code Sec. 6166, is not excluded from the definition of "personal interest" for income tax purposes. (Code Sec. 163(h)(2)(E))

☐ **Effective:** Applies to estates of decedents dying after Dec. 31, '97. ('97 Act §503(d)(1)) For an election that may be made, by estates of decedents dying before Jan. 1, '98, to have the amendments described above and in ¶ 507 apply, see ¶ 507.

¶ 509. Rules for correcting special use valuation elections eased

Code Sec. 2032A(d)(3), as amended by '97 Act § 1313(a)
Generally effective: Applies to estates of decedents dying after Aug. 5, '97
Committee Reports, see ¶ 5273

For estate tax purposes, an executor may elect to value certain real property used in farming or other closely held business operations at its value as a farm or in the business rather than at its value based on its highest and best use. A written agreement (the "recapture agreement") signed by each person with an interest in the property must be filed with the election. Regs require that a notice of election and certain information be filed with the federal estate tax return. IRS's administrative policy has been to disallow special use valuation elections unless the required information is supplied.

Under an '84 amendment to pre-'97 Act law, an executor who made the election *and substantially complied with the regs* but failed to provide all required information or the signatures of all persons with an interest in the property could supply the missing information within a reasonable period of time (not exceeding 90 days) after notification by IRS. (FTC 2d ¶ R-5254; USTR ¶ 20,32A4; TaxDesk ¶ 77,137; EP ¶ 44,055)

New Law. If an executor makes a timely special use valuation election and submits a recapture agreement, but (1) the notice of election, as filed, doesn't contain all the required information, or (2) the signatures of one or more people required to sign the recapture agreement are not included in the agreement as filed, or the agreement doesn't contain all the required information, then the executor has a reasonable period of time (not exceeding 90 days) after being notified of those failures to provide the missing information or signatures. (Code Sec. 2032A(d)(3) as amended by '97 Act §1313(a))

The '97 Act extends the procedures allowing an executor to perfect a defective election by the later submission of information to any executor who makes the election and submits the recapture agreement, without regard to compliance with the regs. (Com Rept, see ¶ 5273)

Congress believed that IRS has taken an unnecessarily restrictive view of the '84 amendment to the special use valuation rules. Congress intended that, with respect to technically defective special use valuation elections made before Aug. 5, '97, prior law should be applied in a manner consistent with the '97 Act provision. (Com Rept, see ¶ 5273)

☐ **Effective:** Applies to estates of decedents dying after Aug. 5, '97. ('97 Act §1313(b))

FTC 2d References are to Federal Tax Coordinator 2d
FIN References are to RIA's Analysis of Federal Taxes: Income
USTR References are to United States Tax Reporter: Income, Estate & Gift, and Excise
PCA References are to Pension Coordinator and Pension & Benefits Expert/Advisor
PE References are to Pension and Profit Sharing 2nd
EP References are to Estate Planning & Taxation Coordinator and Estate Planning Advisor

¶ 510. Lineal descendant's inter–family cash lease of specially–valued property won't trigger recapture estate tax

Code Sec. 2032A(c)(7), as amended by '97 Act § 504(a)
Code Sec. 2032A(b)(5)(A), as amended by '97 Act § 504(b)
Generally effective: For leases entered into after Dec. 31, '76
Committee Reports, see ¶ 5029

An estate's representative may elect to value certain "qualified real property" used in farming or another qualifying trade or business at its current use value rather than its highest and best use. If, after the special–use valuation election is made, the heir who acquired the real property ceases to use it in its qualified use within 10 years (15 years for individuals dying before 1982) of the decedent's death, an additional estate tax is imposed in order to "recapture" the benefit of the special–use valuation. The surviving spouse is not treated as failing to use the property in a qualified use solely because the spouse rents, on a net cash basis, the property to a member of the spouse's family. But some courts had held that the cash rental of specially–valued property after the death of the decedent by a member of the decedent's family (other than his surviving spouse) was not a qualified use because the heirs no longer bear the financial risk of working the property, and, therefore, it resulted in the imposition of the additional estate tax. (FTC 2d ¶ R-5307.1; USTR ¶ 20,32A4; TaxDesk ¶ 77,158; EP ¶ 44,108.1)

New Law. For purposes of the rules under Code Sec. 2032A for treatment of dispositions and failures to use for a qualified use, a surviving spouse *or* a lineal descendant of the decedent is not treated as failing to use qualified real property in a qualified use solely because the spouse or descendant rents the property to a member of the family of the spouse or descendant on a net cash basis. For this purpose, a legally adopted child of an individual is treated as the child of the individual by blood. (Code Sec. 2032A(c)(7)(E) as amended by '97 Act §504(a))

Thus, the cash lease of specially–valued real property by a lineal descendant of the decedent to a member of the lineal descendant's family, who continues to operate the farm or closely held business, does not cause the qualified use of the property to cease for purposes of imposing the additional estate tax. Cash leasing of farmland among family members is consistent with the purposes of the special–use valuation rules, which are intended to prevent family farms (and other qualifying businesses) from being liquidated to pay estate taxes in cases where members of the decedent's family continue to participate in the business. (Com Rept, see ¶ 5029)

Because of the extension of the cash rental exception to lineal descendants of the decedent (as discussed above), a special rule for surviving spouses under Code Sec. 2032A no longer refers to this exception. (Code Sec. 2032A(b)(5)(A) as amended by '97 Act §504(b))

☐ **Effective:** Applicable to leases entered into after Dec. 31, '76. ('97 Act §504(c))

Research Institute of America

¶ 511. Certain short-term obligations held by nonresident aliens are not subject to U.S. estate tax

Code Sec. 2105(b)(4), as amended by '97 Act § 1304(a)
Generally effective: Applies to estates of decedents dying after Aug. 5, '97
Committee Reports, see ¶ 5264

The U.S. imposes an estate tax on assets of noncitizen nondomiciliaries ("nonresident aliens") that were situated in the U.S. at the time of the individual's death. Debt obligations of a U.S. person, the U.S., a political subdivision of a State, or the District of Columbia are considered property located within the U.S. if held by a nonresident alien. However, special estate tax rules apply to treat certain bank deposits and debt instruments, the income from which qualifies for the portfolio interest exemption provided by Code Sec. 871(h) and the bank deposit interest exemption provided by Code Sec. 871(i)(2)(A), as property from without the U.S. despite the fact that those items are obligations of a U.S. person, the U.S., a political subdivision of a State, or the District of Columbia. (FTC 2d ¶ R-8017; USTR ¶ 21,054; EP ¶ 45,518) Under Code Sec. 871(h) and Code Sec. 871(i)(2)(A), income from those items is exempt from U.S. income tax in the hands of the nonresident alien recipient. (FTC 2d/FIN ¶ O-10204, ¶ O-10220; USTR ¶ 8714; TaxDesk ¶ 63,117, ¶ 63,118)

The effect of the special estate tax rules is to exclude items that qualify for the income tax exemptions provided by Code Sec. 871(h) and Code Sec. 871(i)(2)(A) from the U.S. gross estate of a nonresident alien. However, under pre-'97 Act law, the special estate tax rules did not cover obligations that generate short-term OID (original issue discount) income despite the fact that, under Code Sec. 871(g)(1)(B)(i) (FTC 2d/FIN ¶ O-10226; USTR ¶ 8714) , that income is exempt from U.S. income tax in the hands of the nonresident recipient. (Com Rept, see ¶ 5264)

New Law. Any debt obligation, the income from which would be eligible for the exemption for short-term OID income under Code Sec. 871(g)(1)(B)(i) if that income (if it were received by the decedent on the date of his death) would not be effectively connected with the conduct of a trade or business within the U.S., is treated as property located outside of the U.S. in determining the U.S. estate tax liability of a nonresident alien. (Code Sec. 2105(b)(4) as amended by '97 Act §1304(a)) No inference is intended with respect to the estate tax treatment of those obligations under pre-'97 Act law. (Com Rept, see ¶ 5264)

The change was made because Congress believed that the income and estate tax treatments of short-term OID obligations held by nonresident aliens should conform. A purpose of exempting short-term OID income derived by nonresident aliens from U.S. income tax is to enhance the ability of U.S. borrowers to raise funds from foreign lenders, and that purpose is hindered by the lack of a corresponding exemption for

FTC 2d References are to Federal Tax Coordinator 2d
FIN References are to RIA's Analysis of Federal Taxes: Income
USTR References are to United States Tax Reporter: Income, Estate & Gift, and Excise
PCA References are to Pension Coordinator and Pension & Benefits Expert/Advisor
PE References are to Pension and Profit Sharing 2nd
EP References are to Estate Planning & Taxation Coordinator and Estate Planning Advisor

U.S. estate tax. Moreover, to the extent the interest from such an obligation is exempt from U.S. income tax, the inclusion of the instrument in the nonresident alien's U.S. estate would be a trap for the unwary. (Com Rept, see ¶ 5264)

☐ **Effective:** Applies to estates of decedents dying after Aug. 5, '97. ('97 Act § 1304(b))

¶ 512. Nonparticipant spouse's community property interest in annuity qualifies as QTIP

Code Sec. 2056(b)(7)(C), as amended by '97 Act § 1311(a)
Generally effective: Applies to estates of decedents dying after Aug. 5, '97
Committee Reports, see ¶ 5271

Under state community property laws, each spouse owns an undivided one-half interest in each community property asset. In community property states, a nonparticipant spouse may he treated as having a vested community property interest in his or her spouse's qualified plan, individual retirement arrangement (IRA), or simplified employee pension (SEP) plan.

Under Code Sec. 2033, a decedent's gross estate includes all property in which the decedent had an interest at the time of his death, to the extent of the interest owned by the decedent. (FTC 2d ¶ R-2000; USTR ¶ 20,334; TaxDesk ¶ 76,101; EP ¶ 43,101)

Under Code Sec. 2039, a decedent's gross estate includes annuity payments receivable by any beneficiary to the extent the annuity is attributable to amounts paid by the decedent or his employer. (FTC 2d ¶ R-4400; USTR ¶ 20,394; TaxDesk ¶ 76,852; EP ¶ 43,851)

Property in which a decedent's surviving spouse has a "terminable interest" (e.g., a life estate only) generally does not qualify for the estate tax marital deduction. There is an exception to this general rule for "qualified terminable interest property" (QTIP). Pre-'97 Act law provided that, in the case of an annuity included in the decedent's gross estate under Code Sec. 2039, where only the surviving spouse has the right to receive payments before her death (a "survivor annuity"), the surviving spouse's interest meets the QTIP requirements. (FTC 2d ¶ R-6416; USTR ¶ 20,564; TaxDesk ¶ 77,917; EP ¶ 44,717)

Thus, in noncommunity property states, no estate tax generally is imposed on survivor annuity interests in the estate of the first spouse to die. In contrast, an interest of the non-participant spouse arising under community property laws in an annuity derived from the employment of his spouse is includible in the non-participant spouse's estate under Code Sec. 2033 (not Code Sec. 2039) and therefore, under pre-'97 Act law, might not have qualified as a deductible transfer to his surviving spouse under the QTIP rules.

The Supreme Court has held, in *Boggs v. Boggs,* that ERISA preempted a provision in Louisiana law that allowed a deceased spouse to bequeath her community property interest in her husband's undistributed plan benefits. (PCA ¶ 52,020)

New Law. Eligibility for QTIP treatment is extended to survivor annuities included in the decedent's gross estate under Code Sec. 2033, in the case of an interest in an annuity arising under state community property laws. (Code Sec. 2056(b)(7)(C) as amended by '97 Act §1311(a))

This provision clarifies that the transfer at death of a survivorship interest in an annuity to a surviving spouse is deductible under the QTIP rules regardless of whether the decedent's annuity interest arose out of his employment or arose under community property laws by reason of the employment of his spouse. (Com Rept, see ¶ 5271)

> *Illustration:* The marital deduction is available with respect to a nonparticipant spouse's interest in an annuity attributable to community property laws where he predeceases the participant spouse. (Com Rept, see ¶ 5271)

The '97 Act provision is not intended to create an inference regarding the treatment, under pre-'97 Act law, of a transfer to a surviving spouse of the decedent spouse's interest in an annuity arising under community property laws. Nor is it intended to modify the result of the Supreme Court's decision in *Boggs v. Boggs.* (Com Rept, see ¶ 5271)

☐ **Effective:** Applies to estates of decedents dying after Aug. 5, '97. ('97 Act §1311(b))

¶ 513. Recovery right for QTIP and retained life estate property waived only if specific intent indicated

Code Sec. 2207A(a)(2), as amended by '97 Act § 1302(a)
Code Sec. 2207B(a)(2), as amended by '97 Act § 1302(b)
Generally effective: Applies to estates of decedents dying after Aug. 5, '97
Committee Reports, see ¶ 5262

For estate and gift tax purposes, a marital deduction is allowed for qualified terminable interest property (QTIP). Under Code Sec. 2044, QTIP property generally is included in the surviving spouse's gross estate upon his or her death. Under Code Sec. 2207A, the surviving spouse's estate is entitled to recover from the person receiving the QTIP property the portion of the estate tax attributable to the inclusion of the property, unless the spouse directs otherwise by will. Under pre-'97 Act law, a will provision specifying that all taxes shall be paid by the estate was sufficient to waive the right of recovery. (FTC 2d ¶ R-6439; USTR ¶ 22,07A4; TaxDesk ¶ 77,926; EP ¶ 44,740)

A decedent's gross estate includes the value of previously transferred property in which the decedent retains enjoyment or the right to income. Under Code Sec. 2207B, the estate is entitled to recover from the person receiving the property a portion of the

FTC 2d References are to Federal Tax Coordinator 2d
FIN References are to RIA's Analysis of Federal Taxes: Income
USTR References are to United States Tax Reporter: Income, Estate & Gift, and Excise
PCA References are to Pension Coordinator and Pension & Benefits Expert/Advisor
PE References are to Pension and Profit Sharing 2nd
EP References are to Estate Planning & Taxation Coordinator and Estate Planning Advisor

Research Institute of America 137

estate tax attributable to the inclusion. Under pre-'97 Act law, this right could be waived only by a provision in the will (or revocable trust) specifically referring to Code Sec. 2207B. (FTC 2d ¶ R-2457; USTR ¶ 22,07B4; TaxDesk ¶ 76,439; EP ¶ 43,329)

New Law. The right of recovery with respect to QTIP property is waived to the extent that the decedent in his will (or a revocable trust) specifically indicates an intent to waive the right of recovery with respect to the property. (Code Sec. 2207A(a)(2) as amended by '97 Act §1302(a)) Thus, a general provision specifying that all taxes be paid by the estate is no longer sufficient to waive the right of recovery with respect to QTIP property. (Com Rept, see ¶ 5262)

> *recommendation:* Review the tax apportionment clauses in all your clients' wills and revocable trust agreements to determine if any changes are necessary as a result of the change made by the '97 Act. If a client intends to waive the right of recovery with respect to QTIP property, but the tax apportionment clause in the client's will states only that all taxes be paid by the estate, the client should execute a new will (or codicil) specifically indicating his intent to waive the right of recovery with respect to QTIP property.

> *observation:* There is no provision in the '97 Act excluding wills and trust agreements executed by individuals who have become incompetent—and who are therefore unable to execute new wills or trust agreements—from the application of the rule provided by the '97 Act. Thus, the change made by the '97 Act may cause unintended estate tax consequences in the estates of those individuals.

The right of contribution for property over which the decedent retained enjoyment or the right to income is waived to the extent that the decedent in his will (or a revocable trust) specifically indicates an intent to waive the right of recovery with respect to the property. (Code Sec. 2207B(a)(2) as amended by '97 Act §1302(b)) Specific reference to Code Sec. 2207B is no longer required. (Com Rept, see ¶ 5262)

☐ **Effective:** Applies to estates of decedents dying after Aug. 5, '97. ('97 Act §1302(c))

¶ 514. Entities other than trusts may be eligible for qualified domestic trust (QDOT) treatment

Code Sec. 2056A(c)(3), as amended by '97 Act § 1312(a)
Generally effective: Applies to estates of decedents dying after Aug. 5, '97
Committee Reports, see ¶ 5272

The estate tax marital deduction is generally not allowed if the decedent's surviving spouse is not a U.S. citizen. There is an exception to this rule for property passing to the surviving spouse in a qualified domestic trust (QDOT). (FTC 2d ¶ R-6203; USTR ¶ 20,56A4; TaxDesk ¶ 77,829; EP ¶ 44,554) An estate tax generally is imposed on corpus distributions from a QDOT. (FTC 2d ¶ R-7080; USTR ¶ 20,56A4; TaxDesk

¶ 78,151; EP ¶ 45,051)

Trusts are not permitted in some countries (e.g., many civil law countries). As a result, it was not possible, under pre-'97 Act law, to create a QDOT in those countries. In some civil law states (e.g., Louisiana), an entity similar to a trust, called a usufruct, exists. (Com Rept, see ¶ 5272)

New Law. IRS has the authority to issue regs that provide that, for purposes of the QDOT rules, the term "trust" includes other arrangements that have substantially the same effect as a trust. (Code Sec. 2056A(c)(3) as amended by '97 Act §1312(a))

In giving IRS the authority to issue those regs, Congress anticipated that any regs would permit a marital deduction only with respect to non-trust arrangements under which the U.S. would retain jurisdiction and adequate security to impose U.S. transfer tax on transfers by the surviving spouse of the property transferred by the decedent. Possible arrangements include the adoption of a bilateral treaty that provides for the collection of U.S. transfer tax from the noncitizen surviving spouse or a closing agreement process under which the surviving spouse waives treaty benefits, allows the U.S. to retain taxing jurisdiction, and provides adequate security with respect to U.S. transfer taxes. (Com Rept, see ¶ 5272)

☐ **Effective:** Applies to estates of decedents dying after Aug. 5, '97. ('97 Act §1312(b))

¶ 515. IRS given authority to waive U.S. trustee requirement for qualified domestic trusts (QDOTs)

Code Sec. 2056A(a)(1)(A), as amended by '97 Act § 1314(a)
Generally effective: Estates of decedents dying after Aug. 5, '97
Committee Reports, see ¶ 5274

The purpose of the qualified domestic trust (QDOT) is to ensure that U.S. estate tax is collected upon the death of a noncitizen spouse who has reaped the benefit of a U.S. marital deduction. In order for a trust to be a QDOT, the trust instrument must require that at least one trustee of the trust be an individual citizen of the United States or a domestic corporation. In addition, the U.S. trustee must have the power to approve all corpus distributions from the trust. In some countries, trusts cannot have any U.S. trustees. As a result, trusts established in those countries could not qualify as QDOTs. (FTC 2d ¶ R-6203; USTR ¶ 20,56A4.01; TaxDesk ¶ 77,829; EP ¶ 44,554)

New Law. The '97 Act gives IRS the regulatory authority to waive the requirement that a QDOT have a U.S. trustee. (Code Sec. 2056A(a)(1)(A) as amended by '97 Act §1314(a)) The purpose of this provision is to allow estates to qualify for the marital deduction where the use of a U.S. trustee is prohibited by another country. It is anticipated that regs promulgated under this provision, if any, will provide an alternative mechanism under which the U.S. would retain jurisdiction and adequate security to impose U.S. transfer tax on transfers by the surviving spouse of the property transferred by the decedent. For example, one possible mechanism would be a closing agreement process under which the surviving spouse waives treaty benefits, allows the U.S. to retain taxing jurisdiction, and provides adequate security with respect to the transfer taxes. (Com Rept, see ¶ 5274)

> **observation:** Adequate security could mean that the surviving spouse will be required to post a bond as security for payment of tax.

☐ **Effective:** For estates of decedents dying after Aug. 5, '97. ('97 Act §1314(b))

¶ 516. Trusts created before Nov. 5, '90 are treated as meeting the qualified domestic trust (QDOT) requirements if they meet the QDOT requirements that were in effect before Nov. 5, '90

Code Sec. None, '97 Act § 1303
Generally effective: Applies to estates of decedents dying after Nov. 10, '88
Committee Reports, see ¶ 5263

The estate tax marital deduction is generally not allowed if the decedent's surviving spouse is not a U.S. citizen. There is an exception to this rule for property passing to the surviving spouse in a qualified domestic trust (QDOT). An estate tax generally is imposed on corpus distributions from a QDOT.

A QDOT was originally defined as a trust that, among other things, required all trustees be U.S. citizens or domestic corporations. This provision was later modified (in the Revenue Reconciliation Act of 1990) to require that at least one trustee be a U.S. citizen or domestic corporation and that no corpus distribution be made unless that trustee has the right to withhold any estate tax imposed on the distribution (the "withholding requirement"). (FTC 2d ¶ R-6203; USTR ¶ 20,56A4; TaxDesk ¶ 77,829; EP ¶ 44,554)

New Law. A trust created under an instrument executed before the date of the enactment of the Revenue Reconciliation Act of 1990 is treated as meeting the withholding requirement if its governing instrument requires that all trustees of the trust be U.S. citizens or domestic corporations. ('97 Act §1303(a))

> **observation:** The date of enactment of the Revenue Reconciliation Act of 1990 was Nov. 5, '90.

☐ **Effective:** Applies to estates of decedents dying after Nov. 10, '88. ('97 Act §1303(b))

¶ 517. Estate tax exclusion for up to 40% of value of land subject to qualified conservation easement

Code Sec. 2031(c), as amended and redesignated by '97 Act § 508(a)
Generally effective: For estates of decedents dying after Dec. 31, '97
Committee Reports, see ¶ 5033

A deduction is allowed for estate and gift tax purposes for a contribution of a qualified real property interest to a charity (or other qualified organization) exclusively for conservation purposes. The same definition of qualified conservation contribution also applies for purposes of determining whether such a contribution qualifies as a charitable deduction for income tax purposes. Under Code Sec. 170(h), a qualified real property interest means the entire interest of the transferor in real property (other than certain mineral interests, see ¶ 520), a remainder interest in real property, or a perpetual restriction on the use of real property. A "conservation purpose" is (1) preservation of land for outdoor recreation for use by, or for the education of, the general public, (2) preservation of natural habitat, (3) preservation of open space for scenic enjoyment of the general public or to further a governmental conservation policy, and (4) preservation of historically important land or certified historic structures. A contribution is treated as "exclusively for conservation purposes" only if the conservation purpose is protected in perpetuity. Under pre-'97 Act law, there was no estate tax exclusion for the value of land subject to a qualified conservation easement. (FTC 2d/FIN ¶ K-3478 *et seq.*; USTR ¶ 1704.45; EP ¶ 41,734 *et seq.*)

New Law. An executor is allowed to elect to exclude from the gross estate 40% of the value of any "land subject to a qualified conservation easement" (Code Sec. 2031(c)(1) as amended by '97 Act §508(a)) (as defined below). A reduction in estate taxes for land subject to a qualified conservation easement will ease existing pressures to develop or sell off open spaces in order to raise funds to pay estate taxes, and will thereby help to preserve environmentally significant land. (Com Rept, see ¶ 5033)

For the basis of land subject to a qualified conservation easement that is excluded from the gross estate, see ¶ 518.

For the treatment of a qualified conservation contribution for estate tax special use valuation purposes, see ¶ 519.

For the income and estate tax charitable deduction for a qualified conservation contribution where a mineral interest has been retained, see ¶ 520.

Limits on estate tax exclusion. The exclusion from the gross estate is the lesser of— (Code Sec. 2031(c)(1))

(1) the applicable percentage (as defined below) of the value of land subject to a qualified conservation easement, reduced by the amount of any charitable deduction al-

lowed for a contribution of land exclusively for conservation purposes under Code Sec. 2055(f) (FTC 2d ¶ R-5758; EP ¶ 44,359), or (Code Sec. 2031(c)(1)(A))

(2) the exclusion limitation (as defined below). (Code Sec. 2031(c)(1)(B))

The exclusion for land subject to a qualified conservation easement may be taken in addition to the maximum exclusion for qualified family-owned business interests (see ¶ 505). (Com Rept, see ¶ 5033)

"Applicable percentage" defined. For purposes of the estate tax exclusion, the term "applicable percentage" means 40% reduced (but not below zero) by two percentage points for each percentage point (or fraction of a percentage point) by which the value of the qualified conservation easement is less than 30% of the value of the land, determined without regard to the value of the easement and reduced by the value of any "retained development right" (as defined below). (Code Sec. 2031(c)(2))

If the value of the conservation easement is less than 30% of (a) the value of the land without the easement, reduced by (b) the value of any retained development rights, then the 40% exclusion percentage is reduced. The reduction in the exclusion percentage is equal to two percentage points for each point that the ratio of the value of the conservation easement to the value of the land (with the adjustments described above) falls below 30%. (Com Rept, see ¶ 5033)

> *Illustration:* If the value of a conservation easement is 25% of the value of the land before the easement reduced by the value of any retained development rights, the exclusion percentage is 30%: 40% − (2 × (30% − 25%)). (Com Rept, see ¶ 5033)

Under this calculation, if the value of the easement is 10% or less of the value of the land before the easement reduced by the value of the retained development rights, the exclusion percentage is equal to zero. (Com Rept, see ¶ 5033)

Exclusion limitation. The exclusion limitation is determined using the following table: (Code Sec. 2031(c)(3))

In the case of estates of decedents dying during:	The exclusion limitation is:
1998	$100,000
1999	$200,000
2000	$300,000
2001	$400,000
2002 or thereafter	$500,000

Treatment of certain indebtedness. The estate tax exclusion does not apply to the extent that the land is debt−financed property. (Code Sec. 2031(c)(4)(A)) Debt-financed property is eligible for this provision to the extent of the net equity in the property. (Com Rept, see ¶ 5033)

> *Illustration:* If a $1 million property is subject to an outstanding debt balance of $100,000, it is treated as if it were a $900,000 property that is not debt-financed. (Com Rept, see ¶ 5033)

For these purposes, the term "debt–financed property" means any property with respect to which there is an acquisition indebtedness (as defined below) on the date of the decedent's death. (Code Sec. 2031(c)(4)(B)(i))

For these purposes, the term "acquisition indebtedness" means, with respect to debt–financed property, the unpaid amount of: (Code Sec. 2031(c)(4)(B)(ii))

. . . the indebtedness incurred by the donor in acquiring the property (Code Sec. 2031(c)(4)(B)(ii)(I))

. . . the indebtedness incurred before the acquisition of the property if the indebtedness would not have been incurred but for the acquisition (Code Sec. 2031(c)(4)(B)(ii)(II))

. . . the indebtedness incurred after the acquisition of the property if the indebtedness would not have been incurred but for the acquisition and the incurrence of the indebtedness was reasonably foreseeable at the time of such acquisition, and (Code Sec. 2031(c)(4)(B)(ii)(III))

. . . the extension, renewal, or refinancing of an acquisition indebtedness. (Code Sec. 2031(c)(4)(B)(ii)(IV))

Treatment of "retained development rights." The estate tax exclusion does not apply to the value of any development right (as defined below) retained by the donor in the conveyance of a qualified conservation easement. (Code Sec. 2031(c)(5)(A))

If every person in being who has an interest (whether or not in possession) in the land executes an agreement to extinguish permanently some or all of any development rights retained by the donor on or before the date for filing the estate tax return, then any estate tax is reduced accordingly. The agreement must be filed with the estate tax return. The agreement must be in the form prescribed by IRS. (Code Sec. 2031(c)(5)(B))

An additional tax, in the amount of the tax that would have been due on the retained development rights subject to the agreement, will be imposed on any failure to implement the agreement not later than the earlier of— (Code Sec. 2031(c)(5)(C))

. . . the date that is two years after the date of the decedent's death, or (Code Sec. 2031(c)(5)(C)(i))

. . . the date of the sale of the land subject to the qualified conservation easement (Code Sec. 2031(c)(5)(C)(ii))

The additional tax will be due and payable on the last day of the sixth month following that date. (Code Sec. 2031(c)(5)(C))

Thus, payment for estate taxes on retained development rights may be deferred for up to two years, or until the disposition of the property, whichever is earlier. (Com Rept, see ¶ 5033)

FTC 2d References are to Federal Tax Coordinator 2d
FIN References are to RIA's Analysis of Federal Taxes: Income
USTR References are to United States Tax Reporter: Income, Estate & Gift, and Excise
PCA References are to Pension Coordinator and Pension & Benefits Expert/Advisor
PE References are to Pension and Profit Sharing 2nd
EP References are to Estate Planning & Taxation Coordinator and Estate Planning Advisor

For these purposes, the term "development right" means any right to use the land subject to the qualified conservation easement in which the right is retained for any commercial purpose that is not subordinate to, and directly supportive of, the use of the land as a farm for farming purposes. (Code Sec. 2031(c)(5)(D)) Examples of use of the land as a farm for farming purposes include tree farming, ranching, viticulture, and the raising of other agricultural or horticultural commodities. (Com Rept, see ¶ 5033)

Election. The election to exclude from the gross estate the value of land subject to a qualified conservation easement is made on the estate tax return. Once made, the election is irrevocable. (Code Sec. 2031(c)(6))

Calculation of estate tax due. An executor making the above–described election must, for purposes of calculating the amount of estate tax, include the value of any development right retained by the donor in the conveyance of the qualified conservation easement. The computation of tax on any retained development right must be done in the manner and on the forms prescribed by IRS. (Code Sec. 2031(c)(7))

Thus, the exclusion amount is calculated based on the value of the property after the conservation easement has been placed on the property. (Com Rept, see ¶ 5033)

"Land subject to a qualified conservation easement" defined. The term "land subject to a qualified conservation easement" means land: (Code Sec. 2031(c)(8)(A))

• that is located—(Code Sec. 2031(c)(8)(A)(i))

. . . in or within 25 miles of an area that, on the date of the decedent's death, is a metropolitan area (as defined by the Office of Management and Budget) (Code Sec. 2031(c)(8)(A)(i)(I))

. . . in or within 25 miles of an area that, on the date of the decedent's death, is a national park or wilderness area designated as part of the National Wilderness Preservation System (unless it is determined by IRS that land in or within 25 miles of such a park or wilderness area is not under significant development pressure), or (Code Sec. 2031(c)(8)(A)(i)(II))

. . . in or within 10 miles of an area that, on the date of the decedent's death, is an Urban National Forest (as designated by the Forest Service) (Code Sec. 2031(c)(8)(A)(i)(III))

• that was owned by the decedent or a member of the decedent's family (as defined below), at all times during the three–year period ending on the date of the decedent's death, and (Code Sec. 2031(c)(8)(A)(ii))

• with respect to which a "qualified conservation easement" (as defined below) has been made, as of the date of the election (described above), by the decedent, a member of the decedent's family, the executor of the decedent's estate, or the trustee of a trust the corpus of which includes the land to be subject to the qualified conservation easement. (Code Sec. 2031(c)(8)(A)(iii))

"Qualified conservation easement" defined. The term "qualified conservation easement" means a qualified conservation contribution (as defined in Code Sec.

170(h)(1)) (FTC 2d ¶ R-5758; EP ¶ 44,359) of a qualified real property interest (as defined in Code Sec. 170(h)(2)(C) (FTC 2d/FIN ¶ K-3479; EP ¶ 41,735)), except that clause (iv) of Code Sec. 170(h)(4)(A) (relating to the preservation of an historically important land area or a certified historic structure) (FTC 2d/FIN ¶ K-3484; EP ¶ 41,740) does not apply, and the restriction on the use of the interest described in Code Sec. 170(h)(2)(C) (relating to a restriction granted in perpetuity) includes a prohibition on more than a de minimis use for a commercial recreational activity. (Code Sec. 2031(c)(8)(B))

Congress anticipated that IRS will provide guidance as to the definition of "de minimis" commercial recreational activities. For purposes of the exclusion, preservation of an historically important land area or a certified historic structure does not qualify as a conservation purpose. (Com Rept, see ¶ 5033)

> *observation:* Thus, the definition of "qualified conservation easement" is generally the same as the definition of "qualified conservation contribution of a qualified real property interest" for purposes of the estate and gift tax deduction for a contribution of land exclusively for conservation purposes, with two exceptions: (1) the preservation of a historically important land area or a certified historic structure does not qualify as a conservation purpose for purposes of the estate tax exclusion; and (2) a perpetual restriction on the use of real property must include, for purposes of the estate tax exclusion, a prohibition on more than a de minimis use for commercial recreational activity.

"Member of the decedent's family" defined. The term "member of the decedent's family" means any member of the family (as defined in Code Sec. 2032A(e)(2)) of the decedent. (Code Sec. 2031(c)(8)(D)) A member of the decedent's family includes—

. . . an ancestor of the individual,

. . . the spouse of the individual,

. . . a lineal descendant of the individual, of the individual's spouse, or of a parent of the individual, or

. . . the spouse of any lineal descendant described immediately above. (Com Rept, see ¶ 5033)

Exclusion applies to interests in partnerships, corporations, or trusts. The estate tax exclusion applies to an interest in a partnership, corporation, or trust if at least 30% of the entity is owned (directly or indirectly) by the decedent, as determined under the rules described in Code Sec. 2033A(e)(3) (see ¶ 505 *et seq.*). (Code Sec. 2031(c)(9))

FTC 2d References are to Federal Tax Coordinator 2d
FIN References are to RIA's Analysis of Federal Taxes: Income
USTR References are to United States Tax Reporter: Income, Estate & Gift, and Excise
PCA References are to Pension Coordinator and Pension & Benefits Expert/Advisor
PE References are to Pension and Profit Sharing 2nd
EP References are to Estate Planning & Taxation Coordinator and Estate Planning Advisor

☐ **Effective:** Applicable to the estates of decedents dying after Dec. 31, '97. ('97 Act §508(e)(1))

¶ 518. No step–up in basis for land subject to a qualified conservation easement that is excluded from the gross estate

Code Sec. 1014(a)(4), '97 Act § 508(b)
Generally effective: For estates of decedents dying after Dec. 31, '97
Committee Reports, see ¶ 5033

Under pre-'97 Act law, there was no estate tax exclusion for the value of land subject to a qualified conservation easement.

New Law. To the extent that the value of land subject to a qualified conservation easement is excluded from the gross estate (see ¶ 517), the basis of the land acquired at death is the basis in the hands of the decedent. (Code Sec. 1014(a)(4) as amended by '97 Act §508(b))

This means that the basis is a carryover basis, i.e., it is not stepped–up to its fair market value at death. (Com Rept, see ¶ 5033)

For the estate tax exclusion for land subject to a qualified conservation easement, see ¶ 517.

For the treatment of a qualified conservation contribution for estate tax special use valuation purposes, see ¶ 519.

For the income and estate tax charitable deduction for a qualified conservation contribution where a mineral interest has been retained, see ¶ 520.

☐ **Effective:** Applicable to the estates of decedents dying after Dec. 31, '97. ('97 Act §508(e)(1))

¶ 519. Qualified conservation contribution is not a disposition for estate tax special use valuation purposes

Code Sec. 2032A(c)(8), as amended by '97 Act § 508(c)
Generally effective: For easements granted after Dec. 31, '97
Committee Reports, see ¶ 5033

A deduction is allowed for estate and gift tax purposes for a contribution of a qualified real property interest to a charity (or other qualified organization) exclusively for conservation purposes. The same definition of a qualified conservation contribution also applies for purposes of determining whether such a contribution qualifies as a charitable deduction for income tax purposes. Under Code Sec. 170(h), a qualified real property interest means the entire interest of the transferor in real property (other than certain mineral interests, see ¶ 520), a remainder interest in real property, or a perpetual restriction on the use of real property. A "conservation purpose" is (1) preservation of land for outdoor recreation for use by, or for the education of, the general public, (2) preservation of natural habitat, (3) preservation of open space for scenic enjoyment of the general public or to further a governmental conservation policy, and (4) preservation of historically important land or certified historic structures. A contribution is treated as "exclusively for conservation purposes" only if the conservation purpose is protected in perpetuity. (FTC 2d/FIN ¶ K-3478 *et seq.*; USTR ¶ 1704.45; EP ¶ 41,734 *et seq.*)

If certain conditions are met, an executor may elect, under Code Sec. 2032A, to value qualified farm or other closely held business real property included in a decedent's estate on the basis of its actual use as a farm or in the business, rather than its fair market value based on highest and best use. However, if the qualified real property is disposed of to a non–family member or ceases to be used for a qualified use within ten years after the decedent's death, all or part of the estate tax savings resulting from this special use valuation election may be recaptured. (FTC 2d ¶ R-5200 *et seq.*; USTR ¶ 2032A4; TaxDesk ¶ 77,153; EP ¶ 44,001 *et seq.*)

New Law. A qualified conservation contribution (as defined in Code Sec. 170(h)) is not treated as a disposition triggering the recapture provisions of Code Sec. 2032A. (Code Sec. 2032A(c)(8) as amended by '97 Act §508(c))

Thus, the granting of a qualified conservation easement (see ¶ 517) is not treated as a disposition triggering the recapture provisions of Code Sec. 2032A. In addition, the existence of a qualified conservation easement does not prevent the property from later qualifying for special use valuation treatment under Code Sec. 2032A. (Com Rept, see ¶ 5033)

For the estate tax exclusion for land subject to a qualified conservation easement, see ¶ 517.

For the basis of land subject to a qualified conservation easement that is excluded from the gross estate, see ¶ 518.

For the income and estate tax charitable deduction for a qualified conservation contribution where a mineral interest has been retained, see ¶ 520.

☐ **Effective:** Applicable to easements granted after Dec. 31, '97. ('97 Act §508(e)(2))

¶ 520. Income and estate tax charitable deduction for a qualified conservation contribution where a mineral interest has been retained

Code Sec. 170(h)(5)(B)(ii), '97 Act § 508(d)
Generally effective: For easements granted after Dec. 31, '97
Committee Reports, see ¶ 5033

FTC 2d References are to Federal Tax Coordinator 2d
FIN References are to RIA's Analysis of Federal Taxes: Income
USTR References are to United States Tax Reporter: Income, Estate & Gift, and Excise
PCA References are to Pension Coordinator and Pension & Benefits Expert/Advisor
PE References are to Pension and Profit Sharing 2nd
EP References are to Estate Planning & Taxation Coordinator and Estate Planning Advisor

A deduction is allowed for estate and gift tax purposes for a contribution of a qualified real property interest to a charity (or other qualified organization) exclusively for conservation purposes. The same definition of a qualified conservation contribution also applies for purposes of determining whether such a contribution qualifies as a charitable deduction for income tax purposes. Under Code Sec. 170(h), a donor making a qualified conservation contribution generally is not allowed to retain an interest in minerals which may be extracted or removed by any surface mining method. However, a deduction for a contribution of a conservation interest satisfying all of the requirements discussed at ¶ 517 is permitted if two conditions are satisfied. First, the surface and mineral estates in the property with respect to which the contribution is made must have been separated before June 13, '76 (and remain separated) and, second, the probability of surface mining on the property with respect to which a contribution is made must be so remote as to be negligible. Thus, under pre-'97 Act law, a charitable deduction was allowed in such a case only if the mineral interests had been separated from the land before June 13, '76. (FTC 2d/FIN ¶ K-3503; EP ¶ 41,759)

New Law. Under the special rule with respect to a qualified conservation contribution in which the ownership of the surface estate and mineral interests are separated, the requirement that a contribution must be exclusively for conservation purposes is treated as met if the probability of surface mining occurring on the property is so remote as to be negligible. (Code Sec. 170(h)(5)(B)(ii) as amended by '97 Act §508(d))

Thus, a charitable deduction (for income or estate tax purposes) is allowed to taxpayers making a contribution of a permanent conservation easement on property where a mineral interest has been retained and surface mining is possible, but its probability is so remote as to be negligible, regardless of when the mineral interests had been separated. (Com Rept, see ¶ 5033)

For the estate tax exclusion for land subject to a qualified conservation easement, see ¶ 517.

For the basis of land subject to a qualified conservation easement that is excluded from the gross estate, see ¶ 518.

For the treatment of a qualified conservation contribution for estate tax special use valuation purposes, see ¶ 519.

☐ **Effective:** Applicable to easements granted after Dec. 31, '97. ('97 Act §508(e)(2))

¶ 521. Gifts may not be revalued for estate tax purposes after gift tax statute of limitations expires

Code Sec. 2001(f), as amended by '97 Act § 506(a)
Code Sec. 2504(c), as amended by '97 Act § 506(d)
Generally effective: For gifts made after Aug. 5, '97
Committee Reports, see ¶ 5031

The estate and gift taxes are unified so that a single progressive rate schedule is applied to an individual's cumulative gifts and bequests. The tax on gifts made in a particular year is computed by determining the tax on the sum of the taxable gifts made that year and all previous years and then subtracting the tax on the previous years' taxable gifts and the unified credit. Similarly, the estate tax is computed by determining the tax on the sum of the taxable gifts and the taxable estate and then subtracting the tax on taxable gifts and the unified credit. Under a special rule applicable to the computation of the gift tax, the value of gifts made in previous years is the value that was used to determine the previous year's gift tax. Under pre–'97 Act law, there was no comparable rule for the computation of the estate tax. But most courts permitted IRS to redetermine the value of a gift for which the gift tax statute of limitations period had expired in order to determine the appropriate tax rate bracket and unified credit for the estate tax. (FTC 2d ¶ R-7005; USTR ¶ 25,045; TaxDesk ¶ 78,055; EP ¶ 44,906)

New Law. For purposes of computing the estate tax, the value of a gift is the value of the gift as finally determined for gift tax purposes if—

- the time has expired within which a gift tax may be assessed on the transfer of property by gift made during a preceding calendar period, and

- the value of the gift is shown on the return for the preceding calendar period or is disclosed in the return, or in a statement attached to the return, in a manner adequate to apprise IRS of the nature of the gift. (Code Sec. 2001(f) as amended by '97 Act §506(a))

Thus, a gift for which the gift tax statute of limitations period has expired cannot be revalued for purposes of determining the applicable estate tax bracket and available unified credit. Revaluation of lifetime gifts at the time of death requires the taxpayer to retain records for a potentially lengthy period. Rules that encourage a determination within the gift tax statute of limitations ease transfer tax administration by eliminating reliance on stale evidence and reducing the period for which retention of records is required. (Com Rept, see ¶ 5031)

Congress intended that, in order to revalue a gift that has been adequately disclosed on a gift tax return (see ¶ 522), IRS must issue a final notice of redetermination of value within the statute of limitations period applicable to the gift for gift tax purposes. This rule is applicable even where the value of the gift as shown on the return does not result in any gift tax being owed (e.g., through use of the unified credit). (Com Rept, see ¶ 5031)

Because of new procedures relating to the revaluation of adequately disclosed gifts (see ¶ 523), there is no requirement, under the special gift tax rule applicable to the computation of the gift tax, that there be a gift tax assessment or payment. (Code Sec. 2504(c) as amended by '97 Act §506(d))

observation: Although the revaluation of gifts for estate tax purposes was often used by IRS to increase the estate tax, revaluation could also benefit a

FTC 2d References are to Federal Tax Coordinator 2d
FIN References are to RIA's Analysis of Federal Taxes: Income
USTR References are to United States Tax Reporter: Income, Estate & Gift, and Excise
PCA References are to Pension Coordinator and Pension & Benefits Expert/Advisor
PE References are to Pension and Profit Sharing 2nd
EP References are to Estate Planning & Taxation Coordinator and Estate Planning Advisor

decedent's estate. If an executor could show that a decedent had overstated the value of a taxable gift on his gift tax return, the executor could have used the lower value to determine adjusted taxable gifts for estate tax purposes. This is not possible under the '97 Act.

For the statute of limitations for inadequately disclosed gifts, see ¶ 522.

☐ **Effective:** Applicable to gifts made after Aug. 5, '97. ('97 Act §506(e)(1))

¶ 522. Statute of limitations will not run on inadequately disclosed gift

Code Sec. 6501(c)(9), as amended by '97 Act § 506(b)
Generally effective: For gifts made in calendar years after Aug. 5, '97
Committee Reports, see ¶ 5031

Generally, any estate or gift tax must be assessed within three years after the filing of the return. No proceeding in a court for the collection of an estate or gift tax can be begun without an assessment within the three–year period. If no return is filed, the tax may be assessed, or a suit commenced to collect the tax without assessment, at any time. If an estate or gift tax return is filed, and the amount of unreported items exceeds 25% of the amount of the reported items, the tax may be assessed or a suit commenced to collect the tax without assessment, within six years after the return was filed. Commencement of the statute of limitations generally did not require that a particular gift be disclosed. A special rule, however, applied to certain gifts that were valued under the special valuation rules of Chapter 14. The gift tax statute of limitations ran for a Chapter 14 gift only if it was disclosed on a gift tax return in a manner adequate to apprise IRS of the nature of the item. (FTC 2d ¶ T-4001, ¶ T-4101, ¶ T-4222, ¶ T-4147 *et seq.*; USTR ¶ 65,014, ¶ 65,014.05, ¶ 25,045; TaxDesk ¶ 83,801, ¶ 83,812, ¶ 78,055; EP ¶ 87,151 *et seq.*)

New Law. The value of any item that is disclosed in a gift tax return, or in a statement attached to the return, in a manner adequate to apprise IRS of the nature of the item may not be redetermined after the expiration of the three–year statute of limitations period. However, gift tax on a gift may be assessed, or a proceeding in court for the collection of the gift tax may be begun without assessment, at any time in the case of:

. . . any gift of property the value of which is required to be shown on a gift tax return (without regard to the annual exclusion from gift tax) and is not shown on the return; or

. . . any increase in taxable gifts that is required under the provision for the transfer tax treatment of cumulative but unpaid distributions under the special valuation rules of Chapter 14 and that is required to be shown on a gift tax return (without regard to the annual exclusion from gift tax) and is not shown on the return.

(Code Sec. 6501(c)(9) as amended by '97 Act §506(b))

                                             Research Institute of America

Amended Code Sec. 6501(c)(9), which extends to *all* gifts the rule previously governing only gifts valued under Chapter 14, provides that the statute of limitations will not run on an inadequately disclosed transfer, regardless of whether a gift tax return was filed for other transfers in that same year. (Com Rept, see ¶ 5031)

For the finality of gift tax value for estate tax purposes, see ¶ 521.

For new procedures relating to the revaluation of adequately disclosed gifts, see ¶ 523.

☐ **Effective:** Applicable to gifts made in calendar years ending after Aug. 5, '97. ('97 Act §506(e)(2))

¶ 523. Donor may petition the Tax Court for a declaratory judgment relating to the value of certain gifts

Code Sec. 7477, as added by '97 Act § 506(c)(1)
Generally effective: For gifts made after Aug. 5, '97
Committee Reports, see ¶ 5031

Under pre–'97 Act law, there was no provision for a declaratory judgment relating to the value of gifts.

New Law. In a case of an actual controversy involving a determination by IRS of the value of any gift shown on a gift tax return or disclosed on the return or in any statement attached to the return, upon the filing of an appropriate pleading, the Tax Court may make a declaration of the value of the gift. This declaratory judgment relating to the value of the gift has the force and effect of a decision of the Tax Court and is reviewable as such. (Code Sec. 7477(a) as added by '97 Act §506(c)(1))

Only the donor of the gift may petition for this relief. (Code Sec. 7477(b)(1)) The donor/petitioner must have first exhausted all available administrative remedies within IRS. (Code Sec. 7477(b)(2)) The donor/petitioner must file his pleading before the 91st day after the date of any mailing, by certified or registered mail, to him of the IRS notice of determination. (Code Sec. 7477(b)(3))

The statute of limitations is tolled during the pendency of the Tax Court proceeding. (Com Rept, see ¶ 5031)

> *observation:* This provision gives a taxpayer a remedy similar to the one available to a taxpayer who receives a notice of deficiency ("90–day letter") from IRS.

Congress anticipated that IRS will develop an administrative appeals process whereby a taxpayer can challenge a redetermination of value by the IRS before issuance of a final notice of redetermination of value. (Com Rept, see ¶ 5031)

FTC 2d References are to Federal Tax Coordinator 2d
FIN References are to RIA's Analysis of Federal Taxes: Income
USTR References are to United States Tax Reporter: Income, Estate & Gift, and Excise
PCA References are to Pension Coordinator and Pension & Benefits Expert/Advisor
PE References are to Pension and Profit Sharing 2nd
EP References are to Estate Planning & Taxation Coordinator and Estate Planning Advisor

For the finality of gift tax value for estate tax purposes, see ¶ 521.

☐ **Effective:** Applicable to gifts made after Aug. 5, '97. ('97 Act §506(e)(1))

¶ 524. Annual exclusion gifts from revocable trusts within three years of grantor's death are not includible in gross estate

Code Sec. 2035(e), as amended by '97 Act § 1310(a)
Generally effective: Applies to estates of decedents dying after Aug. 5, '97
Committee Reports, see ¶ 5270

The first $10,000 of gifts of present interests to each donee during any one calendar year is excluded from federal gift tax. (FTC 2d ¶ Q-5002; USTR ¶ 25,034; TaxDesk ¶ 73,102; EP ¶ 48,203)

Under Code Sec. 2038, the value of the gross estate includes the value of any previously transferred property if the decedent retained the power to revoke the transfer. (FTC 2d ¶ R-2600; USTR ¶ 20,384; TaxDesk ¶ 76,551; EP ¶ 43,401) Under Code Sec. 2035, the gross estate also includes the value of any property with respect to which a power to revoke is relinquished during the three years before the transferor's death. (FTC 2d ¶ R-2201; USTR ¶ 20,354; TaxDesk ¶ 76,301; EP ¶ 43,252) Under pre-'97 Act law, there was significant litigation as to whether these rules required that certain transfers made from a revocable trust within three years of death be includible in the gross estate. For example, in *Jalkut,* transfers from a revocable trust were held to be includible in the gross estate, while in *McNeely* and *Kisling,* transfers from revocable trusts were held not to be includible in the gross estate. The inclusion of those transfers causes gifts that would otherwise qualify under the annual $10,000 exclusion to be subject to estate tax. (FTC 2d ¶ R-2202; USTR ¶ 20,385.01(15); TaxDesk ¶ 76,302; EP ¶ 43,253)

Code Sec. 676 provides that the grantor of a trust is treated as the owner of the trust for income tax purposes if the grantor reserves the power to revest in himself title to the trust property (e.g., by revoking the trust). (FTC 2d/FIN ¶ C-5300; USTR ¶ 6764; TaxDesk ¶ 65,717; EP ¶ 85,701) For purposes of this rule, Code Sec. 672(e) provides that the grantor is treated as holding any power held by his spouse. (FTC 2d/FIN ¶ C-5204; USTR ¶ 6724; TaxDesk ¶ 65,703; EP ¶ 85,675)

New Law. Any transfer from any portion of a trust during any period that the portion was treated under Code Sec. 676 as owned by the decedent by reason of a power in the grantor (determined without regard to the spousal attribution rule of Code Sec. 672(e)) is treated as a transfer made directly by the decedent for purposes of Code Sec. 2035 and Code Sec. 2038. (Code Sec. 2035(e) as amended by '97 Act §1310(a))

The '97 Act codifies the rule set forth in *McNeely* and *Kisling* to provide that a transfer from a revocable trust (i.e., a trust described in Code Sec. 676) is treated as if made directly by the grantor. Thus, an annual exclusion gift from a revocable trust is not included in the gross estate. Congress did not intend this rule to modify the result reached in *Kisling.* (Com Rept, see ¶ 5270)

The inclusion of certain property transferred during the three years before death is directed at transfers that would otherwise reduce the amount subject to estate tax by more than the amount subject to gift tax, disregarding appreciation between the date of the gift and the date of death. Because all amounts transferred from a revocable trust are subject to the gift tax, Congress believed that inclusion of those amounts is unnecessary where the transferor has retained no power over the property transferred out of the trust. (Com Rept, see ¶ 5270)

The '97 Act also revises Code Sec. 2035 to improve its clarity. (Com Rept, see ¶ 5270)

> **✔ observation:** The changes made to Code Sec. 2035 by the '97 Act for the sake of improving its clarity do not substantively change the rules provided in that section.

☐ **Effective:** Applies to estates of decedents dying after Aug. 5, '97. ('97 Act §1310(c))

¶ 525. "Deceased parent exception" to generation–skipping transfer (GST) tax is expanded

Code Sec. 2651(e), as amended and redesignated by '97 Act § 511(a)
Code Sec. 2612(c)(2), as amended by '97 Act § 511(b)(1)
Code Sec. 2612(c)(3), as amended and redesignated by '97 Act § 511(b)(2)
Generally effective: For generation–skipping transfers occurring after Dec. 31, '97
Committee Reports, see ¶ 5034

There is an exception to the general rule for assigning beneficiaries to generations for generation–skipping transfer (GST) tax purposes, which is known as the "predeceased parent exception" (or the "generation step–up rule"). Under the exception, a direct skip transfer to a transferor's grandchild is not subject to the GST tax if the child of the transferor who was the grandchild's parent is deceased at the time of the transfer. Under pre–'97 Act law, the "predeceased parent exception" to the GST tax was not applicable to (1) transfers to collateral heirs (e.g., grandnieces or grandnephews), or (2) taxable terminations or taxable distributions. (FTC 2d ¶ R-9514; USTR ¶ 26,124; TaxDesk ¶ 79,101; EP ¶ 46,045)

New Law. The predeceased parent exception does not apply with respect to a transfer to any individual who is not a lineal descendant of the transferor (or the transferor's spouse or former spouse) if, at the time of the transfer, the transferor has any living lineal descendant. (Code Sec. 2651(e)(2) as amended and redesignated by '97 Act §511(a))

FTC 2d References are to Federal Tax Coordinator 2d
FIN References are to RIA's Analysis of Federal Taxes: Income
USTR References are to United States Tax Reporter: Income, Estate & Gift, and Excise
PCA References are to Pension Coordinator and Pension & Benefits Expert/Advisor
PE References are to Pension and Profit Sharing 2nd
EP References are to Estate Planning & Taxation Coordinator and Estate Planning Advisor

Thus, the predeceased parent exception is extended to collateral heirs under certain circumstances—if the decedent has no living lineal descendants at the time of the transfer, a transfer to a collateral relative whose parent is dead qualifies for the exception. (Com Rept, see ¶ 5034)

> ***Illustration:*** An individual with no living lineal heirs makes a transfer to a grandniece where the transferor's niece who is the parent of the grandniece is deceased at the time of the transfer. The predeceased parent exception applies. (Com Rept, see ¶ 5034)

For purposes of determining whether a transfer is a GST, an individual is treated as if the individual were a member of the generation that is one generation below the lower of the transferor's generation or the generation assignment of the youngest living ancestor of the individual who is also a descendant of the parent of the transferor (or the transferor's spouse or former spouse), and the generation assignment of any descendant of the individual will be adjusted accordingly, if—(Code Sec. 2651(e)(1))

- that individual is a descendant of a parent of the transferor (or the transferor's spouse or former spouse), and (Code Sec. 2651(e)(1)(A))

- the individual's parent who is a lineal descendant of the parent of the transferor (or the transferor's spouse or former spouse) is deceased at the time the transfer (from which an interest of the individual is established or derived) is subject to an estate or gift tax imposed upon the transferor (and if there is more than one time, then at the earliest time). (Code Sec. 2651(e)(1)(B))

Thus, the predeceased parent exception is extended to taxable terminations and taxable distributions under certain circumstances—if the parent of a particular beneficiary is deceased at the earliest time that the transfer (from which the beneficiary's interest in the property was established) was subject to estate or gift tax, the transfer qualifies for the exception (as modified by the change described above in connection with collateral heirs). This treatment removes an impediment to the establishment of charitable lead trusts (CLTs). (Com Rept, see ¶ 5034)

> ***Illustration:*** A CLT is established to pay an annuity to a charity for a term of years with a remainder interest granted to a grandson. The termination of the term for years will not be a taxable termination subject to the GST tax if the grandson's parent (who is the child of the transferor) is deceased at the time the trust was created and the transfer creating the trust was subject to estate or gift tax. (Com Rept, see ¶ 5034)

Because of the extension of the deceased parent exception to taxable terminations and taxable distributions (as discussed above), the special rule for direct skip transfers to grandchildren has been deleted. (Code Sec. 2612(c)(2) as amended by '97 Act §511(b)(1)) And the reference to the deceased parent exception of " Code Sec. 2651(e)(2)" in the entity look–thru rule (which provides a special rule for the generation assignment of individuals having a beneficial interest in certain entities) has been changed to "Code Sec. 2651(f)(2)." (Code Sec. 2612(c)(3) as amended and redesignated by '97 Act §511(b)(2))

☐ **Effective:** For terminations, distributions, and transfers occurring after Dec. 31, '97. ('97 Act §511(c))

Income Taxes of Trusts and Estates

¶ 526. Election to treat revocable trust as part of estate for income and generation–skipping transfer (GST) tax purposes

Code Sec. 646, as added by '97 Act § 1305(a)
Code Sec. 2652(b)(1), as amended by '97 Act § 1305(b)
Generally effective: For estates of decedents dying after Aug. 5, '97
Committee Reports, see ¶ 5265

Both estates and revocable *inter vivos* trusts can function to wind up the affairs of a decedent/grantor and distribute assets to heirs. While both estates and revocable trusts perform essentially the same function after the death of the testator or grantor, there are a number of ways in which an estate and a revocable trust operate in different ways: (1) there can be only one estate per decedent while there can be more than one revocable trust; and (2) estates are in existence for only a reasonable period of administration; revocable trusts can perform the same winding up functions as an estate, but may continue in existence thereafter as testamentary trusts. Moreover, a number of differences exist between the income tax treatment of estates and revocable trusts, including the following: (1) estates are allowed a charitable deduction for amounts permanently set aside for charitable purposes while post–death revocable trusts are allowed a charitable deduction only for amounts paid to charities; (2) the active participation requirement under the passive loss rules is waived in the case of estates (but not revocable trusts) for two years after the owner's death; and (3) estates can qualify for amortization of reforestation expenditures, while trusts do not. (FTC 2d/FIN ¶ C-1000 *et seq.*, ¶ C-7000 *et seq.*; USTR ¶ 6409; TaxDesk ¶ 65,101, ¶ 66,101; EP ¶ 85,001 *et seq.*, ¶ 80,051 *et seq.*)

New Law.

Income tax. For income tax purposes, if both the executor (if any) of an estate and the trustee of a qualified revocable trust (defined below) so elect, the trust will be treated and taxed as part of the estate (and not as a separate trust) for all tax years of the estate ending after the date of the decedent's death (Code Sec. 646(a) as added by '97 Act §1305(a)) and before—

. . . the date that is two years after the date of the decedent's death (if no estate tax return is required), or (Code Sec. 646(b)(2)(A))

FTC 2d References are to Federal Tax Coordinator 2d
FIN References are to RIA's Analysis of Federal Taxes: Income
USTR References are to United States Tax Reporter: Income, Estate & Gift, and Excise
PCA References are to Pension Coordinator and Pension & Benefits Expert/Advisor
PE References are to Pension and Profit Sharing 2nd
EP References are to Estate Planning & Taxation Coordinator and Estate Planning Advisor

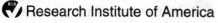

... the date that is six months after the date of the final determination of estate tax liability (if an estate tax return is required). (Code Sec. 646(b)(2)(B))

> *observation:* Presumably, where there is no probate estate (because all of the decedent's assets were transferred to the revocable trust before the decedent's death), the election can be made for the revocable trust to be treated as the estate.

The election must be made no later than the time for filing the income tax return for the first tax year of the estate (taking into account any extensions). Once made, the election is irrevocable. (Code Sec. 646(c))

For purposes of the election, a "qualified revocable trust" is any trust a portion or all of which was treated under Code Sec. 676 (the grantor trust rule relating to revocable trusts) as owned by the decedent with respect to whom the election is being made, by reason of a power in the grantor determined without regard to Code Sec. 672(e) (which treats a grantor as holding a power or interest of the grantor's spouse). (Code Sec. 646(b)(1))

The separate share rule (see ¶ 528) may apply when a qualified revocable trust is treated as part of the decedent's estate. (Com Rept, see ¶ 5265)

> *observation:* The treatment of accumulation distributions had also been different for estates (which were not subject to the throwback rules) and trusts (which were subject to the throwback rules). But the throwback rules have now been repealed for domestic trusts, see ¶ 530.

For another provision that minimizes the differences between estates and trusts, see ¶ 211.

Generation–skipping transfer (GST) tax. For GST tax purposes, the term "trust" does not include any trust during any period in which the trust is treated as part of an estate under Code Sec. 646. (Code Sec. 2652(b)(1) as amended by '97 Act §1305(b))

☐ **Effective:** Applicable to estates of decedents dying after Aug. 5, '97. ('97 Act §1305(d))

¶ 527. Election to treat distributions during first 65 days of estate's tax year as made in previous tax year

Code Sec. 663(b), as amended by '97 Act § 1306
Generally effective: For tax years beginning after Aug. 5, '97
Committee Reports, see ¶ 5266

In general, trusts and estates are treated as conduits for income tax purposes: income received by a trust or estate that is distributed to a beneficiary in the trust or estate's tax year "ending with or within" the tax year of the beneficiary is taxable to the beneficiary in that year; income that is retained by the trust or estate is initially taxable to the trust or estate. Under the "65–day rule," a trustee may elect to treat distributions paid from the trust within 65 days after the close of its tax year as paid on the last day of its tax year. Under pre–'97 Act law, the 65–day rule was not applicable to estates. (FTC 2d/FIN ¶ C-2713; USTR ¶ 6634.03; TaxDesk ¶ 65,448; EP ¶ 85,364)

New Law. The application of the 65–day rule is extended to distributions by estates so that an executor may elect to treat distributions paid within 65 days after the close of the estate's tax year as having been paid on the last day of that tax year. (Code Sec. 663(b) as amended by '97 Act §1306)

Extending the 65–day rule to estates is one way to minimize the tax differences between estates and trusts. (Com Rept, see ¶ 5266)

For other provisions that minimize the tax differences between estates and trusts, see ¶ 526, ¶ 528, and ¶ 211.

☐ **Effective:** For tax years beginning after Aug. 5, '97. ('97 Act §1306(c))

¶ 528. Separate share rule is extended to estates

Code Sec. 663(c), as amended by '97 Act § 1307(a)
Generally effective: For estates of decedents dying after Aug. 5, '97
Committee Reports, see ¶ 5267

Trusts with more than one beneficiary must use the "separate share" rule under which different tax treatment of distributions to different beneficiaries is provided to reflect the income earned by substantially separate and independent shares of the trust's corpus. The application of the separate share rule to a trust will generally depend upon whether distributions of the trust are to be made in substantially the same manner as if separate trusts had been created. Under pre–'97 Act law, the separate share rule did not apply to estates. (FTC 2d/FIN ¶ C-2711; USTR ¶ 6634.01; TaxDesk ¶ 65,446; EP ¶ 85,362)

New Law. For purposes of determining an estate's deduction for distributions to beneficiaries and the income taxable to the beneficiaries, the separate share rule applies where there are substantially separate and independent shares of different beneficiaries in an estate having more than one beneficiary. (Code Sec. 663(c) as amended by '97 Act §1307(a)) As in the case of trusts, the application of the separate share rule to estates is mandatory where separate shares exist. (Com Rept, see ¶ 5267)

There are separate shares in an estate where the will or local law creates separate economic interests in one beneficiary or class of beneficiaries such that the economic interests of those beneficiaries (e.g., rights to income or gains from specified items of property) are not affected by economic interests accruing to another separate beneficiary or class of beneficiaries. (Com Rept, see ¶ 5267)

> *Illustration:* The decedent's will provides that all of the shares of a closely held corporation are bequeathed to one beneficiary. The will also provides

FTC 2d References are to Federal Tax Coordinator 2d
FIN References are to RIA's Analysis of Federal Taxes: Income
USTR References are to United States Tax Reporter: Income, Estate & Gift, and Excise
PCA References are to Pension Coordinator and Pension & Benefits Expert/Advisor
PE References are to Pension and Profit Sharing 2nd
EP References are to Estate Planning & Taxation Coordinator and Estate Planning Advisor

 Research Institute of America 157

that any dividends paid to the estate by that corporation should be paid only to that beneficiary and any dividends would not affect any other amounts that the beneficiary would receive under the will. A separate share in the estate exists. (Com Rept, see ¶ 5267)

☐ **Effective:** Applicable to estates of decedents dying after Aug. 5, '97. ('97 Act §1307(c))

¶ 529. IRS regs can allow nongrantor trusts to elect to continue to be U.S. trusts despite '96 Act provision that would treat them as foreign

Code Sec. 7701(a)(30)(E), '97 Act § 1161(a)
Generally effective: Tax years beginning after Dec. 31, '96
Committee Reports, see ¶ 5190

The Small Business Job Protection Act of '96 (Sec. 1907(a)(1), PL 104-188, 8/20/96) redefined what trusts qualify as "U.S. persons." Under the two-part test of Code Sec. 7701(a)(30)(E) (as amended by the '96 Act), a trust is a U.S. person if: (1) a court within the U.S. is able to exercise primary supervision over the administration of the trust, and (2) one or more U.S. fiduciaries of the trust have the authority to control all substantial decisions of the trust. A trust that does not satisfy both of these tests is a foreign trust. These definitions apply to tax years that beginning after Dec. 31, '96, unless the trustee elects to apply them for tax years ending after Aug. 20, '96. (FTC 2d/FIN ¶ C-5602.1; USTR ¶ 77,014.45; TaxDesk ¶ 65,806) One effect of Code Sec. 7701(a)(30)(E) (as amended by the '96 Act) was that domestic trusts that became foreign trusts solely by operation of law were subject to the 35% excise tax under Code Sec. 1491 (dealing with transfers of appreciated property to a foreign entity). Recognizing this problem, IRS in Notice 96-65 gave domestic trusts that were in existence on Aug. 20, '96, and that met certain other requirements, until two years after the due date (including extensions) for filing the trust's tax return for its first tax year that began after Dec. 31, '96 to comply with the post-'96 rules. (FTC 2d/FIN ¶ O-3701.2; USTR ¶ 14,914)

New Law. IRS is authorized to issue regulations which can provide that any trust which was in existence on Aug. 20, '96 and which was treated as a U.S. person on Aug. 19, '96 (the day before the date of enactment of the Small Business Job Protection Act of '96) may elect to continue to be treated as a U.S. person notwithstanding the requirements of Code Sec. 7701(a)(30)(E) (as amended by the '96 Act). However, the authority to allow trusts to make this election doesn't include trusts treated as owned by the grantor under Code Sec. 671 through Code Sec. 679. (Small Business Job Protection Act § 1907(a)(3) as amended by '97 Act § 1161(a)) Thus, IRS is granted regulatory authority to allow nongrantor trusts that had been treated as U.S. trusts under the law before the Small Business Job Protection Act of '96 to elect to continue to be treated as U.S. trusts, notwithstanding the criteria added by the '96 Act for qualification as a U.S. trust. (Com Rept, see ¶ 5190)

Congress is concerned that the change in the criteria for qualification as a U.S. trust could cause large numbers of existing domestic trusts to become foreign trusts, unless they are able to make the modifications necessary to satisfy the changed criteria. Accordingly, Congress believes an election is appropriate for those existing domestic trusts that prefer to continue to be subject to tax as U.S. trusts. (Com Rept, see ¶5190)

☐ **Effective:** Tax years beginning after Dec. 31, '96, or where elected by the trustee, tax years ending after Aug. 20, '96. ('97 Act §1161(b))

¶530. Throwback rules repealed for U.S. trusts

Code Sec. 665(c), as amended by '97 Act § 507(a)(1)
Generally effective: For distributions made in tax years beginning after Aug. 5, '97
Committee Reports, see ¶5032

A nongrantor trust is treated as a separate taxpayer for income tax purposes. Using the mechanisms of distributable net income (DNI) and the deduction for amounts distributed to beneficiaries, the trust is treated as a conduit with respect to amounts distributed currently and taxed with respect to any income that is accumulated in the trust rather than distributed. A separate graduated tax rate structure, which historically has permitted accumulated trust income to be taxed at lower rates than the rates applicable to trust beneficiaries, applies to trusts. This benefit was often compounded through the creation of multiple trusts.

The throwback rules were intended to limit this benefit by providing that the distribution of previously accumulated trust income to a beneficiary is subject to an additional tax (in addition to any tax paid by the trust on that income) when the beneficiary's average top marginal rate in the previous five years is higher than those of the trust.

The throwback rules apply differently to accumulation distributions from a foreign trust than to accumulation distributions from U.S. trusts. For example, under Code Sec. 668 interest is charged on accumulation distributions from foreign trusts. IRS ruled in Rev Rul 91-6 that, if a foreign trust accumulates income, changes its situs so as to become a U.S. trust, and then makes a distribution that is thrown back to a year in which the trust was a foreign trust, the distribution is treated as a distribution from a foreign trust for purposes of the accumulation distribution rules. (FTC 2d/FIN ¶C-4004; USTR ¶6654; TaxDesk ¶65,603; EP ¶85,505)

New Law. The '97 Act provides that distributions from qualified trusts shall be computed without regard to any undistributed income. (Code Sec. 665(c)(1) as amended by '97 Act §507(a)(1)) For this purpose, a qualified trust is any trust other than:

(1) a foreign trust; (Code Sec. 665(c)(2)(A))

FTC 2d References are to Federal Tax Coordinator 2d
FIN References are to RIA's Analysis of Federal Taxes: Income
USTR References are to United States Tax Reporter: Income, Estate & Gift, and Excise
PCA References are to Pension Coordinator and Pension & Benefits Expert/Advisor
PE References are to Pension and Profit Sharing 2nd
EP References are to Estate Planning & Taxation Coordinator and Estate Planning Advisor

(2) except as IRS may provide in regs, a U.S. trust that at any time was a foreign trust; (Code Sec. 665(c)(2)(A)) or

(3) a trust created before Mar. 1, '84, unless it is established that the trust would not be aggregated with other trusts under the anti-multiple trust rule of Code Sec. 643(f). (Code Sec. 665(c)(2)(B))

Thus, amounts distributed by a qualified trust are exempt from the throwback rules. The treatment of foreign trusts, including the treatment of foreign trusts that become domestic trusts as set forth in Rev Rul 91-6, remains the same. (Com Rept, see ¶ 5032)

> *observation:* Foreign trusts that become U.S. trusts will not be subject to the throwback rules if Rev Rul 91-6 doesn't apply, i.e., if the distribution is not thrown back to a year in which the trust was a foreign trust.

The throwback rules were intended to eliminate the potential tax reduction arising from taxation of income at the trust, rather than the beneficiary, level. However, in '84, Congress curtailed the tax avoidance uses of multiple trusts by means of Code Sec. 643(f), and, in '86, Congress supplied a new compressed rate schedule for trusts that leaves little opportunity for saving tax by having the trust, rather than the beneficiary, taxed on the income. Thus, the complex throwback rules are unnecessary to deal with the insignificant tax reduction potential. (Com Rept, see ¶ 5032)

The special rule for gain on property transferred to a trust at less than fair market value is repealed for all trusts. See ¶ 531.

☐ **Effective:** For distributions made in tax years beginning after Aug. 5, '97. ('97 Act §507(c)(1))

¶ 531. Special rule for gain on property transferred to trust at less than fair market value is repealed

Code Sec. 644, repealed by '97 Act § 507(b)(1)
Generally effective: For sales or exchanges after the Aug. 5, '97
Committee Reports, see ¶ 5032

The Code had several rules intended to limit the benefit that would otherwise occur from using the lower tax rates available to one or more trusts. If property was sold within two years of its contribution to a trust, the gain that would have been recognized had the contributor sold the property was taxed at the contributor's, rather than the trust's, marginal tax rates. In effect, the gains realized by the trust were treated as if the contributor had realized the gain and then transferred the net after-tax proceeds from the sale to the trust as corpus. (FTC 2d/FIN ¶ C-2016; USTR ¶ 6444; TaxDesk ¶ 65,122; EP ¶ 85,067)

New Law. The two-year rule taxing precontribution gain on the sale of property by a trust at the contributor's marginal income tax rates is repealed. (Code Sec. 644 repealed by '97 Act §507(b)(1))

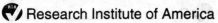 *observation:* Thus, the gain on the sale of property by a trust is taxed at the trust's marginal rates.

Code Sec. 644 was intended to eliminate the potential tax reduction arising from taxation of the gain at the trust, rather than the contributor, level. However, in '84, Congress curtailed the tax avoidance uses of multiple trusts in Code Sec. 643(f), and, in '86, Congress supplied a new compressed rate schedule for trusts that leaves little opportunity for saving tax by having the trust recognize gain on the sale of appreciated property. (Com Rept, see ¶ 5032)

Other rules intended to eliminate the benefit of using a trust's lower tax rates, the throwback rules, have been repealed for U.S. trusts. See ¶ 530.

☐ **Effective:** For sales or exchanges after Aug. 5, '97. ('97 Act §507(c)(2))

¶ 532. Limitation on charitable remainder trust (CRT) eligibility for trusts with greater than 50% payout and less than 10% charitable remainder

Code Sec. 664(d), as amended by '97 Act § 1089
Code Sec. 2055(e)(3)(J), as amended by '97 Act § 1089(b)(3)
Generally effective: For transfers in trust after June 18, '97
Committee Reports, see ¶ 5166

A charitable deduction is disallowed for income, estate, and gift tax purposes where the donor transfers an interest in property to a charity (e.g., a remainder) while also either retaining an interest in that property (e.g., an income interest) or transferring an interest in that property to a non-charity for less than full and adequate consideration. Exceptions to this general rule are provided for (1) remainder interests in charitable remainder annuity trusts (CRATs), charitable remainder unitrusts (CRUTs), pooled income funds, farms, and personal residences; (2) present interests in the form of a guaranteed annuity or a fixed percentage of the annual value of the property; (3) an undivided portion of the donor's entire interest in the property; and (4) a qualified conservation easement (see ¶ 517 *et seq.*).

Under Code Sec. 664(d)(1), a CRAT is a trust that is required to pay, at least annually, a fixed dollar amount of at least 5% of the initial value of the trust (the annuity amount) to a non-charity for the life of an individual or period of less than 20 years, with the remainder passing to charity. And under Code Sec. 664(d)(2), a CRUT is a trust that generally is required to pay, at least annually, a fixed percentage of at least 5% of the fair market value of the trust's assets determined at least annually (the unitrust amount) to a non-charity for the life of an individual or period less than 20 years, with the remainder passing to charity.

FTC 2d References are to Federal Tax Coordinator 2d
FIN References are to RIA's Analysis of Federal Taxes: Income
USTR References are to United States Tax Reporter: Income, Estate & Gift, and Excise
PCA References are to Pension Coordinator and Pension & Benefits Expert/Advisor
PE References are to Pension and Profit Sharing 2nd
EP References are to Estate Planning & Taxation Coordinator and Estate Planning Advisor

Distributions from a CRAT or CRUT are treated in the following order as: (1) ordinary income to the extent of the trust's current and previously undistributed ordinary income for the trust's year in which the distribution occurred; (2) capital gains to the extent of the trust's current capital gain and previously undistributed capital gain for the trust's year in which the distribution occurred; (3) other income (e.g., tax–exempt income) to the extent of the trust's current and previously undistributed other income for the trust's year in which the distribution occurred; and (4) corpus.

Distributions are includible in the income of the beneficiary for the year that the annuity or unitrust amount is required to be distributed even though the annuity or unitrust amount is not distributed until after the close of the trust's tax year.

On April 18, '97, IRS proposed regs providing additional rules under Code Sec. 664 to address perceived abuses involving distributions from charitable remainder trusts (CRTs). One of those proposed rules would require that payment of any required annuity or unitrust amount by a CRT be made by the close of the trust's tax year in which the payments are due.

However, under pre–'97 Act law, there was no limit imposed on a CRAT or CRUT's maximum annual payout and no minimum imposed on the value of the charitable remainder. (FTC 2d/FIN ¶ K-3261 *et seq.*, ¶ K-3291 *et seq.*; USTR ¶ 6644.01; TaxDesk ¶ 33,211; EP ¶ 41,514 *et seq.*, ¶ 41,544)

If a deduction for a remainder interest passing to charity in a trust with both charitable and noncharitable beneficiaries is not allowable for estate tax purposes at the time of a decedent's death because it fails to meet the requirements of a CRAT or a CRUT, an estate tax deduction is allowed if the governing instrument is reformed so that the interest passing to charity satisfies those requirements. (FTC 2d ¶ R-5766 *et seq.*; USTR ¶ 20,554.16; TaxDesk ¶ 77,759 *et seq.*; EP ¶ 44,367 *et seq.*)

New Law.

50% payout test. A trust does not qualify as a CRAT if the annuity amount for a year is greater than 50% of the initial fair market value of the trust's assets. (Code Sec. 664(d)(1)(A) as amended by '97 Act §1089(a)(1)) A trust does not qualify as a CRUT if the percentage of assets that are required to be distributed at least annually is greater than 50%. (Code Sec. 664(d)(2)(A))

The interplay of the rules governing the timing of income from distributions from CRTs and the rules governing the character of distributions have created opportunities for abuse where the required annual payments are a large portion of the trust and realization of income and gain can be postponed until a year later than the accrual of the large payments. For example, some taxpayers have been creating CRUTs with a required annual payout of 80% of the trust's assets and then funding the trust with highly–appreciated nondividend–paying stock that the trust sells in a later year when the required distribution is includible in the beneficiary's income, and using proceeds from that sale to pay the required distribution attributable to the previous year. Those taxpayers have treated the distribution of 80% of the trust's assets attributable to the trust's first required distribution as non–taxable distributions of corpus because the trust had not realized any income in its first tax year. Congress believed that this treatment is abusive and is inconsistent with the purpose of the CRT rules. In order to limit this kind of abuse, a trust can no longer be a CRT if the required payout is greater than 50% of the initial fair market value of the trusts assets (in the case of a CRAT) or 50% of the annual value of the trusts assets (in the case of a CRUT). Any trust that violates this 50% rule will not be a CRT whose taxation is governed under Code Sec. 664, but will be treated as a complex trust (FTC 2d/FIN ¶ C-2601; USTR ¶ 6434.02; TaxDesk ¶ 65,429; EP ¶ 85,302), and, accordingly, all of its income will be taxed to its beneficiaries or to the trust. (Com Rept, see ¶ 5166)

10% charitable remainder test. A trust does not qualify as a CRUT unless the value of the charitable remainder with respect to any transfer to the trust is at least 10% of the initial net fair market value of all property transferred to the trust. (Code Sec. 664(d)(1)(D) as amended by '97 Act §1089(b)(1)) A trust does not qualify as a CRAT unless the value of the charitable remainder with respect to each transfer to the trust is at least 10% of the net fair market value of the property transferred to the trust. (Code Sec. 664(d)(2)(D) as amended by '97 Act §1089(b)(2)) The 10% test is measured on each transfer to the CRT and, consequently, a charitable remainder trust that meets the 10% test on the date of transfer will not later fail to meet that test if interest rates have declined between the trust's creation and the death of a measuring life. Similarly, when a CRT is created for the joint lives of two individuals with a remainder to charity, the trust will not cease to qualify as a CRT because the value of the charitable remainder is less than 10% of the trust's assets at the first death of those two individuals. (Com Rept, see ¶ 5166)

Relief for trusts not meeting the 10% rule. For a CRT that fails the 10% test, the trust may be (1) treated as void from its inception or (2) treated as meeting the 10% requirement if the governing instrument of the trust is changed by reformation, amendment, or otherwise to meet the 10% requirement by reducing the payout rate or the duration (or both) of any noncharitable beneficiary's interest to the extent necessary to satisfy the 10% test. If a trust is treated as void (under (1), above), no estate, gift or income tax deduction is allowed for a transfer to the trust and any transactions entered into by the trust before it was declared void will be treated as if they were entered into by the trust's transferor. The reformation proceeding (under (2), above) must be begun no later than (a) the 90th day after the last date (including extensions) that an estate tax return is required to be filed or, (b) if no estate tax return is required to be filed, the last date (including extensions) for filing the income tax return for the first tax year of the CRT. (Code Sec. 2055(e)(3)(J) as amended by '97 Act §1089(b)(3))

A transfer to a trust will be treated as if the transfer had never been made when a court having jurisdiction over the trust subsequently declares the trust void because, for example, the application of the 10% test frustrates the purposes for which the trust was created, and judicial proceedings to revoke the trust are commenced within the period permitted for reformations of CRTs. Under this provision, the effect of "unwinding" the trust is that any transactions made by the trust with respect to the property trans-

FTC 2d References are to Federal Tax Coordinator 2d
FIN References are to RIA's Analysis of Federal Taxes: Income
USTR References are to United States Tax Reporter: Income, Estate & Gift, and Excise
PCA References are to Pension Coordinator and Pension & Benefits Expert/Advisor
PE References are to Pension and Profit Sharing 2nd
EP References are to Estate Planning & Taxation Coordinator and Estate Planning Advisor

ferred, including income earned on the assets transferred to the trust and capital gains generated by the sales of the property transferred, would be income and capital gain of the donor (or the donor's estate if the trust was testamentary), and the donor (or the donor's estate if the trust was testamentary) would not be permitted a charitable deduction with respect to the transfer. (Com Rept, see ¶ 5166)

The statute of limitations applicable to a deficiency of any tax resulting from reformation of the trust shall not expire before the date one year after IRS is notified that the trust has been reformed or revoked. (Code Sec. 2055(e)(3)(G) as amended by '97 Act §1089(b)(5))

If an additional transfer is made to a CRUT and the CRUT would be disqualified because it no longer meets the 10-percent requirement after the additional contribution, the additional contribution will be treated, under regulations to be issued by IRS, as if it had been made to a separate trust. (Code Sec. 664(d)(4)) The new trust that does not meet the 10% requirement does not affect the qualified status of the original CRUT. (Com Rept, see ¶ 5166)

The provision is not intended to limit or alter the validity of the regs proposed by IRS on April 18, '97, or IRS's authority to address this or other abuses of the rules governing the taxation of CRTs or their beneficiaries. (Com Rept, see ¶ 5166)

☐ **Effective:** The provision limiting the annuity or payout percentage to 50% is applicable to transfers in trust after June 18, '97. ('97 Act §1089(a)(2))

The requirement that the value of the charitable remainder with respect to any transfer to a CRT be at least 10% of the fair market value of the assets transferred in trust applies to transfers to a trust made after July 28, '97. ('97 Act §1089(b)(6)(A)) However, the 10% requirement does not apply to a CRT created by a will or other testamentary instrument executed before July 29, '97, if (1) the instrument is not modified, by codicil or otherwise, after that date and the transferor dies before Jan. 1, '99, ('97 Act §1089(b)(6)(B)(i)) or (2) the transferor could not modify the instrument after July 28, '97, because he was under a mental disability on that date and all times thereafter. ('97 Act §1089(b)(6)(B)(ii)) For this purpose, a testamentary instrument includes a revocable trust. (Com Rept, see ¶ 5166)

¶ 533. Election to have income of qualified funeral trust taxed to the trust

Code Sec. 685, as added by '97 Act § 1309(a)
Generally effective: For tax years ending after Aug. 5, '97
Committee Reports, see ¶ 5269

A pre–need funeral trust is an arrangement where an individual purchases funeral services or merchandise from a funeral home or cemetery in advance of the individual's death. The individual enters into a contract with the provider of the services or merchandise whereby the individual selects the services or merchandise to be provided upon his death, and agrees to pay for them in advance of his death. These amounts (or a portion of them) are held in trust during the individual's lifetime and are paid to the seller (the provider of the services or merchandise) upon the individual's death. Under pre–'97 Act law, pre–need funeral trusts generally were treated as grantor trusts, and the annual income earned by the trusts was taxed to the purchaser/grantor of the trust. Any amount received from the trust by the seller (as payment for services or merchandise) was includible in the gross income of the seller. (FTC 2d/FIN ¶ C-5215; TaxDesk ¶ 65,711; EP ¶ 85,686)

New Law. The trustee of a pre–need funeral trust that is a "qualified funeral trust" may elect special income tax treatment for the trust, to the extent the trust would otherwise be treated as a grantor trust. (Com Rept, see ¶ 5269)

"Qualified funeral trust" defined. A "qualified funeral trust" is any trust (other than a foreign trust) if the following six requirements are satisfied: (Code Sec. 685(b) as added by '97 Act §1312(a))

(1) The trust arises as a result of a *contract* with a person engaged in the trade or business of providing funeral or burial services or property necessary to provide the services. (Code Sec. 685(b)(1))

(2) The sole purpose of the trust is to hold, invest, and reinvest funds in the trust and to use the funds solely to make payments for the services or property for the benefit of the beneficiaries of the trust. (Code Sec. 685(b)(2))

(3) The only *beneficiaries* of the trust are individuals with respect to whom services or property are to be provided at their death under contracts (as described in requirement (1), above). (Code Sec. 685(b)(3))

(4) The only *contributions* to the trust are contributions by or for the benefit of the beneficiaries. (Code Sec. 685(b)(4))

(5) The trustee makes an *election*. (Code Sec. 685(b)(5))

(6) The trust would (except for the election described in requirement (5), above) be treated as owned by the *purchasers* of the contracts (as described in requirement (1), above) under the grantor trust rules. (Code Sec. 685(b)(6))

For the dollar limit on contributions to a qualified funeral trust, see below.

Income tax treatment of qualified funeral trust, beneficiaries, etc. The rules for simple and complex trusts, the throwback rules, and the grantor trust rules do not apply to a qualified funeral trust. (Code Sec. 685(a)(1))

The income tax rate schedule generally applicable to estates and trusts under Code Sec. 1(e) is applied to each qualified funeral trust by treating the interest of each beneficiary (referred to in requirement (3), above, for a qualified funeral trust) in each trust as a separate trust. (Code Sec. 685(d)) However, no deduction for a personal exemption under Code Sec. 642(b) is allowed. (Code Sec. 685(a)(2))

No gain or loss is recognized to a purchaser of a contract (as described in requirement (1), above, for a qualified funeral trust) because of any payment from the trust to

---

FTC 2d References are to Federal Tax Coordinator 2d
FIN References are to RIA's Analysis of Federal Taxes: Income
USTR References are to United States Tax Reporter: Income, Estate & Gift, and Excise
PCA References are to Pension Coordinator and Pension & Benefits Expert/Advisor
PE References are to Pension and Profit Sharing 2nd
EP References are to Estate Planning & Taxation Coordinator and Estate Planning Advisor

the purchaser by reason of cancellation of a contract. If any payment consists of property other than money, the basis of the property in the hands of the beneficiary is the same as the trust's basis in the property immediately before the payment. (Code Sec. 685(e))

The trustee's election is to be made separately with respect to each purchaser's trust. If the election is made, the trust is not treated as a grantor trust and the amount of tax paid with respect to each purchaser's trust is determined in accordance with the income tax rate schedule generally applicable to estates and trusts, but no deduction for a personal deduction is allowed. The tax on the annual earnings of the trust is payable by the trustee. As under pre-'97 Act law, amounts received from the trust by the seller are treated as payments for services and merchandise and are includible in the gross income of the seller. No gain or loss is recognized to the beneficiary of the trust for payments from the trust to the beneficiary upon cancellation of the contract, and the beneficiary takes a carryover basis in any assets received from the trust upon cancellation. (Com Rept, see ¶ 5269)

Simplified income tax reporting for a qualified funeral trust. IRS may prescribe rules for simplified reporting of all qualified funeral trusts having a single trustee. (Code Sec. 685(f))

To the extent that pre–need funeral trusts were treated as grantor trusts under pre-'97 Act law, numerous individual taxpayers were required to account for the earnings of the trusts on their tax returns, even though the earnings with respect to any one taxpayer were small. Taxing qualified funeral trusts at the entity level, with one simplified annual return filed by the trustee reporting the aggregate income from all the trusts administered by the trustee and separately listing the amount of income earned with respect to each purchase, is intended to ease the recordkeeping burden on individuals and improve compliance with the tax laws. Congress anticipated that IRS will issue prompt guidance with respect to the simplified reporting. (Com Rept, see ¶ 5269)

Limit on contributions to a qualified funeral trust. A qualified funeral trust may not accept aggregate contributions by or for the benefit of an individual in excess of $7,000. (Code Sec. 685(c)(1)) For this purpose, "contributions" include all amounts transferred to the trust, regardless of how denominated in the contract (as described in requirement (1), above, for a qualified funeral trust). However, contributions do not include income or gain earned with respect to property in the trust. (Com Rept, see ¶ 5269)

For purposes of the limit on contributions to a qualified funeral trust, all trusts having trustees that are related persons are treated as one trust. (Code Sec. 685(c)(2)) For this purpose, persons are related if—

...the relationship between the persons is described in Code Sec. 267 (relating to losses, expenses, and interest with respect to transactions between related taxpayers, see FTC 2d/FIN ¶ I-3500; USTR ¶ 2674.03; TaxDesk ¶ 22,793) or Code Sec. 707(b) (relating to certain sales or exchanges of property with respect to controlled partnerships, see FTC 2d/FIN ¶ B-2016; USTR ¶ 7074.03; TaxDesk ¶ 58,464) (Code Sec. 685(c)(2)(A))

... the persons are treated as a single employer under Code Sec. 52(a) (relating to a controlled group of corporations, see FTC 2d/FIN ¶ L-17787; USTR ¶ 514; TaxDesk ¶ 38,086) or Code Sec. 52(b) (relating to employees of partnerships, proprietorships, etc. that are under common control, see FTC 2d/FIN ¶ L-17787; USTR ¶ 514; TaxDesk ¶ 38,086) (Code Sec. 685(c)(2)(B)) or

... IRS determines that treating the persons as related is necessary to prevent avoidance of the limitation on contributions to a qualified funeral trust. (Code Sec. 685(c)(2)(C))

Thus, for purposes of applying the $7,000 contribution limit, if a purchaser has more than one contract with a single trustee (or related trustees), all the trusts are treated as one trust. And if IRS determines that a purchaser has entered into separate contracts with unrelated trustees to avoid the $7,000 limit, IRS may require that the trusts be treated as one trust. (Com Rept, see ¶ 5269)

In the case of any contract that is entered into during any calendar year after '98, the dollar amount of the limit on contributions will be increased by an amount equal to (Code Sec. 685(c)(3))

... the dollar amount, multiplied by (Code Sec. 685(c)(3)(A))

... the cost-of-living adjustment determined under Code Sec. 1(f)(3) for the calendar year, by substituting "calendar year '97" for "calendar year '92" in Code Sec. 1(f)(3)(B). (Code Sec. 685(c)(3)(B))

If any dollar amount, after being so increased, is not a multiple of $100, the dollar amount must be rounded to the nearest multiple of $100. (Code Sec. 685(c)(3)) Thus, for contracts entered into after '98, the $7,000 contribution limit is indexed annually for inflation. (Com Rept, see ¶ 5269)

☐ **Effective:** For tax years ending after Aug. 5, '97. ('97 Act §1309(c))

FTC 2d References are to Federal Tax Coordinator 2d
FIN References are to RIA's Analysis of Federal Taxes: Income
USTR References are to United States Tax Reporter: Income, Estate & Gift, and Excise
PCA References are to Pension Coordinator and Pension & Benefits Expert/Advisor
PE References are to Pension and Profit Sharing 2nd
EP References are to Estate Planning & Taxation Coordinator and Estate Planning Advisor

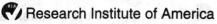

¶ 600. Alternative Minimum Tax

¶ 601. Alternative minimum tax (AMT) repealed for small corporations after '97

Code Sec. 55(e), as amended by '97 Act § 401(a)
Generally effective: Tax years beginning after Dec. 31, '97
Committee Reports, see ¶ 5023

Under pre-'97 Act law, all corporations (except S corporations) were subject to the alternative minimum tax. (FTC 2d/FIN ¶ A-8104, ¶ A-8115, ¶ A-8132; USTR ¶ 554, ¶ 534; TaxDesk ¶ 69,153, ¶ 69,401)

New Law. The '97 Act repeals the corporate AMT for small business corporations for tax years beginning after Dec. 31, '97. (Com Rept, see ¶ 5023) The Act provides that the tentative minimum tax of a corporation is zero for any tax year if the corporation:

(1) met the $5,000,000 gross receipts test of Code Sec. 448(c) (relating to the exemption of certain corporations from the rule barring use of the cash method of accounting, see FTC 2d/FIN ¶ G-2069; USTR ¶ 4484) for its first tax year beginning after Dec. 31, '96 (Code Sec. 55(e)(1)(A) as amended by '97 Act §402(a)), and

(2) would meet that test for the tax year and all prior tax years beginning after such first tax year if that test were applied by substituting $7,500,000 for $5,000,000. (Code Sec. 55(e)(1)(B))

> ✔ *observation:* Under the gross receipts test of Code Sec. 448(c), the rule barring the use of the cash method of accounting by certain corporations doesn't apply for a tax year of a corporation if, for all earlier tax years the corporation met the $5,000,000 gross receipts test. A corporation meets that test for any earlier tax year if the average annual gross receipts of the entity for the three-tax-year period ending with the earlier tax year does not exceed $5,000,000. See FTC 2d/FIN ¶ G-2069; USTR ¶ 4484.

Under the above rule exempting small corporations from the AMT, a corporation that had average gross receipts of less than $5,000,000 for the three-year period beginning after Dec. 31, '94, is a small business corporation (and its tentative minimum tax is zero) for any tax year beginning after Dec. 31, '97. A corporation that meets the $5,000,000 gross receipts test will continue to be treated as a small business corporation exempt from the AMT so long as its average gross receipts don't exceed $7,500,000. (Com Rept, see ¶ 5023)

✔ **Research Institute of America**

Prospective application of AMT if corporation ceases to meet gross receipts test. If a corporation's tentative minimum tax is zero for any prior tax year because it met the above gross receipts test (and the corporation later ceases to meet that test), the AMT for tax years beginning with the first tax year the corporation ceases to meet the test will be determined with the following modifications: (Code Sec. 55(e)(2))

. . . Code Sec. 56(a)(1) (adjustment for depreciation, see FTC 2d/FIN ¶ A-8209; USTR ¶ 564.01) and Code Sec. 56(a)(5) (adjustment for pollution control facilities, see FTC 2d/FIN ¶ A-8228; USTR ¶ 564.01) apply only to property placed in service on or after the change date (see below). (Code Sec. 55(e)(2)(A))

. . . Code Sec. 56(a)(2) (adjustment for mining exploration and development costs, see FTC 2d/FIN ¶ A-8226; USTR ¶ 564.01) applies only to costs paid or incurred on or after the change date. (Code Sec. 55(e)(2)(B))

. . . Code Sec. 56(a)(3) (adjustment for long-term contracts, see FTC 2d/FIN ¶ A-8237; USTR ¶ 564.01) applies only to contracts entered into on or after the change date. (Code Sec. 55(e)(2)(C))

. . . Code Sec. 56(a)(4) (adjustment for alternative tax net operating loss deduction, see FTC 2d/FIN ¶ A-8201; USTR ¶ 564.01) applies in the same manner as if, in Code Sec. 56(d)(2) (adjustments to the net operating loss computation, see FTC 2d/FIN ¶ A-8603 et seq.; USTR ¶ 564.01), the change date were substituted for Jan. 1, '87 and the day before the change date were substituted for Dec. 31, '86 each place it appears. (Code Sec. 55(e)(2)(D))

. . . Code Sec. 56(g)(2)(B) (relating to limitation on allowance of negative adjustments based on adjusted current earnings, see FTC 2d/FIN ¶ A-8401; USTR ¶ 564.03) applies only to prior tax years beginning on or after the change date. (Code Sec. 55(e)(2)(E))

. . . Code Sec. 56(g)(4)(A) (adjustment for depreciation to adjusted current earnings, see FTC 2d/FIN ¶ A-8416; USTR ¶ 564.03) does not apply. (Code Sec. 55(e)(2)(F))

. . . Code Sec. 56(g)(4)(D) and Code Sec. 56(g)(4)(F) (relating to other earnings and profits adjustments and depletion, see FTC 2d/FIN ¶ A-8400 et seq.; USTR ¶ 564.03) apply in the same manner as if the day before the change date were substituted for Dec. 31, '89 each place it appears in those sections. (Code Sec. 55(e)(2)(G))

The above modifications don't apply to (a) any item acquired by the corporation in a transaction to which Code Sec. 381 (carryover of tax items in liquidations and reorganizations, see FTC 2d/FIN ¶ F-7000; USTR ¶ 3814) applies, and (b) any property the basis of which in the hands of the corporation is determined by reference to the basis of the property in the hands of the transferor, if such item or property was subject to any provision referred to in the above list of modifications while held by the transferor. (Code Sec. 55(e)(3))

The term "change date" for purposes of the above modifications is the first day of the first tax year for which the taxpayer ceases to meet the above gross receipts test. (Code Sec. 55(e)(4))

Limitation on use of credit for prior year minimum tax. The '97 Act provides that if a corporation's tentative minimum tax for any tax year is zero because it met the above gross receipts test, then in computing the limitation on the corporations's credit for prior year minimum tax allowable for any tax year under Code Sec. 53(c) (the excess of the corporation's regular tax for the tax year, over its tentative minimum tax for the tax year, see FTC 2d/FIN ¶ A-8132; USTR ¶ 534), the regular tax otherwise taken into account under Code Sec. 53(c)(1) must be reduced by 25% of so much of such amount as exceeds $25,000. (Code Sec. 55(e)(5))

The $25,000 amount is apportioned among members of a controlled group of corporations under rules similar to the rules of Code Sec. 38(c)(3)(B) for purposes of computing the limit on the general business credit (see FTC 2d/FIN ¶ L-15205; USTR ¶ 384). (Code Sec. 55(e)(5))

☐ **Effective:** Tax years beginning after Dec. 31, '97. ('97 Act §401(b))

¶ 602. Alternative minimum tax rate on net capital gain for noncorporate taxpayers reduced from 26%/28% to 20% or 10%

Code Sec. 55(b)(3), as amended by '97 Act § 311(b)
Generally effective: Tax years ending after May 6, '97, but without regard to pre-May 7, '97 gains
Committee Reports, see ¶ 5019

The starting point for the computation of the alternative minimum tax is taxable income. Various adjustments and preferences are added or subtracted to arrive at alternative minimum taxable income. For noncorporate taxpayers, the taxable excess, determined after subtraction of an exemption amount, is subject to a tentative minimum tax of 26% or 28% (subject to reduction for any alternative minimum tax foreign tax credit). In making these computations under pre-'97 Act rules, no distinction was made between income consisting of net capital gain (otherwise taxed at a maximum rate of 28% for regular tax purposes) and other ordinary income (taxed for regular tax purposes at rates up to 39.6%). (FTC 2d/FIN ¶ A-8115; USTR ¶ 554.01; TaxDesk ¶ 69,152)

New Law. The amount determined under the first sentence of Code Sec. 55(b)(1)(A)(i) (a noncorporate taxpayer's tentative minimum tax) cannot be more than the sum of: (Code Sec. 55(b)(3) as amended by '97 Act §311(b))

(A) the amount determined under that first sentence (computed at the 26% and 28% rates and in the same manner as if this Code Sec. 55(b)(3) had not been enacted) on the taxable excess reduced by the lesser of (1) the net capital gain, or (2) the sum of—

... the adjusted net capital gain (as defined in Code Sec. 1(h)(4), see ¶ 201), plus

. . . the unrecaptured section 1250 gain (as defined in Code Sec. 1(h)(6), see ¶ 201 (Code Sec. 55(b)(3)(A)), plus

(B) 25% of the lesser of (1) the unrecaptured section 1250 gain , or (2) the amount of taxable excess in excess of the sum of—

. . . the adjusted net capital gain, plus

. . . the amount on which a tax is determined under (A), above, (Code Sec. 55(b)(3)(B)) plus

(C) 10% of so much of the taxpayer's adjusted net capital gain (or, if less, taxable excess) as does not exceed the amount on which a tax is determined under Code Sec. 1(h)(1)(D), see ¶ 201 (Code Sec. 55(b)(3)(C)), plus

(D) 20% of the taxpayer's adjusted net capital gain (or, if less, taxable excess) in excess of the amount on which tax is determined under (C), above. (Code Sec. 55(b)(3)(D))

The effect of this formula is to apply the same rates (10% for net capital gain that would otherwise be taxed at 15% for regular tax purposes, and 20% for net capital gain that would otherwise be taxed at 28%, see ¶ 201) to net capital gain for both regular and minimum tax purposes. (Com Rept, see ¶ 5019)

Under Code Sec. 1(h)(2), see ¶ 201, for tax years beginning after Dec. 31, 2000 the maximum capital gain rates for assets held for more than five years are 8% and 18% (rather than 10% and 20%). Rules similar to the rules of Code Sec. 1(h)(2), will apply for purposes of (C) and (D) above. (Code Sec. 55(b)(3))

☐ **Effective:** For tax years ending after May 6, '97. ('97 Act §311(d)(1)) For a tax year that includes May 7, '97, the lower '97 Act rates for net capital gain (10%/20%) don't apply to an amount equal to the net capital gain determined by including only the net capital gain for the portion of the year before May 7, '97. (Com Rept, see ¶ 5019)

¶ 603. Amount of net capital gain taken into account in computing alternative tax on net capital gain for corporations is limited to taxable income

Code Sec. 1201(a)(2), as amended by '97 Act § 314(a)
Generally effective: Tax years ending after Dec. 31, '97
Committee Reports, see ¶ 5022

Under pre-'97 Act law, the Code Sec. 1201 alternative tax on the net capital gain of corporations was equal to the sum of (1) a tax, at the generally applicable graduated rates for corporations, computed on the corporation's taxable income reduced by the

FTC 2d References are to Federal Tax Coordinator 2d
FIN References are to RIA's Analysis of Federal Taxes: Income
USTR References are to United States Tax Reporter: Income, Estate & Gift, and Excise
PCA References are to Pension Coordinator and Pension & Benefits Expert/Advisor
PE References are to Pension and Profit Sharing 2nd
EP References are to Estate Planning & Taxation Coordinator and Estate Planning Advisor

net capital gain and (2) 35 percent of the corporation's net capital gain. (FTC 2d/FIN ¶ D-1004, ¶ D-6928, ¶ E-9458, ¶ I-5117 *et seq.*; USTR ¶ 5114, ¶ 12,014; TaxDesk ¶ 22,388, ¶ 68,102)

New Law. The '97 Act changes the portion of the Code Sec. 1201 alternative tax on the net capital gain of corporations that, under pre-'97 Act law, equaled 35 percent of the corporation's net capital gain to a portion that equals 35 percent of the corporation's net capital gain *or, if less, taxable income.* (Code Sec. 1201(a)(2) as amended by '97 Act §314(a)).

Thus, the amount of gain subject to the alternative rate of tax can't exceed the corporation's taxable income. However, because the Code Sec. 1201 alternative tax on net capital gain doesn't apply under pre-'97 Act law, the change made by the '97 Act has no effect under the rate structure of pre-'97 Act law. (Com Rept, see ¶ 5022)

> *observation:* The Code Sec. 1201 alternative tax on net capital gain doesn't presently apply under pre-'97 Act law (or under '97 Act law) because, by its terms, Code Sec. 1201 applies only where there is a corporate tax rate, calculated *without* regard to the surtaxes imposed by the last two sentences of Code Sec. 11(b)(1), which exceeds 35 percent. However, unless those two sentences are taken into account, no corporate tax rate, under pre-'97 Act law (or under '97 Act law) presently exceeds 35 percent. Thus, the change made by the '97 Act won't have an effect unless corporate tax rates are amended to establish one or more corporate tax rates, calculated without regard to the surtaxes discussed above, in excess of 35 percent.

☐ **Effective:** Tax years ending after Dec. 31, '97. ('97 Act §314(b))

¶ 604. Limit on AMT exemption for under-age-14 child increased from sum of earned income plus twice the $500 limit on basic standard deduction to sum of earned income plus $5,000; limit on child's AMT repealed

Code Sec. 59(j), as amended by '97 Act § 1201(b)(1)
Code Sec. 6103(e)(1)(A)(iv), as amended by '97 Act § 1201(b)(2)
Generally effective: Tax years beginning after Dec. 31, '97
Committee Reports, see ¶ 5201

Under the "kiddie" tax rules, the net unearned (investment) income of a child under age 14 may be taxed at the parent's tax rate instead of the child's tax rate. The alternative minimum tax (AMT) of a child under the age of 14 is computed the same as that of any other individual, except as indicated below.

Limit on child's AMT exemption. Under pre-'97 Act law, if the "kiddie" tax applied, the child's AMT exemption was limited to the sum of the child's earned income for the tax year, plus the greater of (1) twice the inflation adjusted $500 limitation ($650 for '97) on the basic standard deduction allowable to an individual who can be claimed as a dependent by another taxpayer, or (2) the child's share of the parents' unused parental minimum tax exemption (excess of the parent's exemption amount over the parent's alternative minimum taxable income). But the exemption computed under this limitation can't be more than the child's regular AMT exemption ($33,750 before a phaseout).

Limit on child's AMT. Also, under pre-'97 Act law, if the "kiddie" tax applied, the child's AMT couldn't exceed the child's share of the allocable parental minimum tax. The allocable parental minimum tax was (1) the AMT that would be imposed on the parent if his tentative minimum tax were increased by the tentative minimum taxes of all his children under age 14 who had investment income taxed at the parents' rates, and if the parent's regular tax were increased by the regular taxes of all those children, minus (2) the AMT imposed on the parents without regard to the tentative minimum tax or regular tax of his children under age 14. Each child's share of the allocable parental minimum tax was determined under rules similar to the regular tax "kiddie" tax rules.

Disclosure of parent's return and return information to under-age-14 child. Under pre-'97 Act law, a child under age 14 (or the child's legal representative) could make a written request to IRS for disclosure of the child's parent's return and return information in order to compute the child's AMT. (FTC 2d/FIN ¶ A-8107, ¶ A-8124, ¶ S-6302; USTR ¶ 594, ¶ 61,034.08; TaxDesk ¶ 69,104, ¶ 69,155)

New Law. The '97 Act increases the limitation on the AMT exemption for a child under age 14 who is subject to the "kiddie" tax. The larger AMT exemption that results from the increased limitation simplifies the existing income tax system because a child with alternative minimum taxable income less than the exemption will not be required to compute and pay the AMT. (Com Rept, see ¶ 5201) The '97 Act also repeals the limitation on the child's AMT. The rule authorizing disclosure of the parent's return and return information in order to compute the child's AMT has also been repealed.

Limit on child's AMT exemption. The '97 Act provides that in the case of a child to whom the "kiddie" tax applies, the AMT exemption cannot exceed the sum of (a) the child's earned income for the tax year (Code Sec. 59(j)(1)(A) as amended by '97 Act §1201(b)), plus (b) $5,000 (as adjusted for inflation, see below). (Code Sec. 59(j)(1)(B)) But the exemption computed under this limitation can't be more than the child's regular AMT exemption ($33,750 before a phaseout). (Com Rept, see ¶ 5201)

Since the limitation on the child's AMT exemption no longer refers to the unused parental minimum tax exemption, the '97 Act repeals the rule for computing the unused parental minimum tax exemption. (Code Sec. 59(j))

illustration: The following illustration shows how the AMT exemption amount for a child under age 14 would be computed under the limitation for '97, reflecting the current pre-'97 Act rule, and for '98, reflecting the '97 Act changes. Assume that for both '97 and '98 the child has earned income of

FTC 2d References are to Federal Tax Coordinator 2d
FIN References are to RIA's Analysis of Federal Taxes: Income
USTR References are to United States Tax Reporter: Income, Estate & Gift, and Excise
PCA References are to Pension Coordinator and Pension & Benefits Expert/Advisor
PE References are to Pension and Profit Sharing 2nd
EP References are to Estate Planning & Taxation Coordinator and Estate Planning Advisor

Research Institute of America 173

$25,000, alternative minimum taxable income of $55,000, and the child's parents have zero unused minimum tax exemption.

AMT exemption amount for '97 reflecting current pre-'97 Act rule

(1) Regular AMT exemption (before phaseout)	$33,750
(2) Twice the inflation adjusted $500 limit ($650 for '97) on basic standard deduction of a dependent	$ 1,300
(3) Child's earned income	$25,000
(4) Add lines 2 and 3	$26,300
(5) AMT exemption—smaller of line 1 or line 4	$26,300

AMT exemption amount for '98 reflecting '97 Act changes

(1) Regular AMT exemption (before phaseout)	$33,750
(2) Amount in (b) above	$ 5,000
(3) Child's earned income	$25,000
(4) Add lines 2 and 3	$30,000
(5) AMT exemption—smaller of line 1 or line 4	$30,000

Inflation adjustment. In the case of any tax year beginning in a calendar year after '98, the $5,000 amount in (b) above is increased by an amount equal to the product of (1) such dollar amount, and (2) the cost-of-living adjustment determined under Code Sec. 1(f)(3) (adjustments in tax tables, see FTC 2d/FIN ¶ A-1103; USTR ¶ 14) for the calendar year in which the tax year begins, but using the consumer price index (CPI) for '97 instead of the CPI for '92. Any increase determined under this rule that isn't a multiple of $50 is rounded to the nearest multiple of $50. (Code Sec. 59(j)(2))

> *observation:* The amount could be rounded to the next highest or next lowest multiple of $50, depending upon which is "nearest."

Limit on child's AMT. The '97 Act repeals the limitation on the child's AMT based on the child's share of the allocable parental minimum tax. (Code Sec. 59(j))

> *observation:* The committee reports don't address why the limitation on the child's AMT based on the child's share of the allocable parental minimum tax was repealed. This limitation on the child's AMT was presumably repealed since the alternative minimum taxable income of most children subject to the "kiddie" tax will be less than the AMT exemption amount, and thus they won't be required to compute and pay the AMT.

Disclosure of parent's return and return information to under-age-14 child. The '97 Act repeals the rule authorizing disclosure of the parent's return and return information to a child under age 14 (or to the child's legal representative) in order to compute the child's AMT. (Code Sec. 6103(e)(1)(A)(iv) as amended by '97 Act §1201(b)(2))

> *observation:* As a result of the above changes made by the '97 Act in the computation of the AMT of a child under age 14, the parent's return and return information are no longer needed to compute the child's AMT. Disclosure of the parent's return and return information are still authorized, however, if necessary to compute the child's "kiddie" tax under Code Sec. 1(g).

☐ **Effective:** Tax years beginning after Dec. 31, '97. ('97 Act §1201(c))

¶ 605. AMT preference for portion of gain on sale of qualified small business stock reduced from 50% to 42%

Code Sec. 57(a)(7), as amended by '97 Act § 311(b)(2)(B)
Generally effective: Tax years ending after May 6, '97
Committee Reports, see ¶ 5019

Under Code Sec. 1202, a taxpayer who satisfies certain requirements may exclude from gross income 50% of the gain that he realizes on the disposition of "qualified small business stock." One-half of the amount excluded from gross income under this rule (i.e. 25% of the total gain) was treated as a preference item for alternative minimum tax purposes. (FTC 2d/FIN ¶ A-8316; USTR ¶ 574; TaxDesk ¶ 69,702)

New Law. The amount of the AMT preference is 42% of the amount excluded from gross income under Code Sec. 1202, rather than one-half of the amount excluded. (Code Sec. 57(a)(7) as amended by '97 Act §311(b)(2)(B))

> **⚫️observation:** Thus, the AMT preference is 21% of the total gain, instead of 25% under pre-'97 Act law.

☐ **Effective:** For tax years ending after May 6, '97. ('97 Act §311(d)(1))

¶ 606. The alternative minimum tax adjustment for depreciation of property placed in service after '98 is computed using the 150% declining balance method (and switching to the straight line method)

Code Sec. 56(a)(1)(A)(i), as amended by '97 Act § 402(a)
Generally effective: Aug. 5, '97
Committee Reports, see ¶ 5024

In determining alternative minimum taxable income (AMTI) for purposes of computing the alternative minimum tax, the most significant alternative minimum tax adjustment relates to depreciation. In computing AMTI, with some exceptions, Code Sec. 56(a)(1)(i) prescribed that depreciation on property placed in service after '86 was computed under the alternative depreciation system of Code Sec. 168(g) for Code Sec. 1250 property (i.e., most depreciable real property), and for property for which depreciation for purposes of the regular income tax was computed using the straight line method; and Code Sec. 56(a)(1)(ii) prescribed that depreciation on all other property placed in service after '86 was computed using the 150% declining balance method

FTC 2d References are to Federal Tax Coordinator 2d
FIN References are to RIA's Analysis of Federal Taxes: Income
USTR References are to United States Tax Reporter: Income, Estate & Gift, and Excise
PCA References are to Pension Coordinator and Pension & Benefits Expert/Advisor
PE References are to Pension and Profit Sharing 2nd
EP References are to Estate Planning & Taxation Coordinator and Estate Planning Advisor

(but switching to straight line in the year necessary to maximize the allowance). For regular income tax purposes, depreciation on tangible personal property generally is computed using shorter recovery periods and more accelerated methods than are allowed for alternative minimum tax purposes. (Com Rept, see ¶ 5024) (FTC 2d/FIN ¶ A-8209; USTR ¶ 564.01; TaxDesk ¶ 69,659)

New Law. Congress believes that the alternative minimum tax inhibits capital formation and business enterprise and is administratively complex. To help remedy this, Congress has eliminated the depreciation adjustment under Code Sec. 56(a)(1)(i)) for new investment in depreciable property by all businesses for property placed in service after '98. (Com Rept, see ¶ 5024) More specifically, under the '97 Act, the alternative minimum tax adjustment of Code Sec. 56(a)(1)(i) (see above) doesn't apply to property placed in service after Dec. 31, '98. (Code Sec. 56(a)(1)(A)(i) as amended by '97 Act §402(a)) However, the alternative minimum tax adjustment of Code Sec. 56(a)(1)(ii) (see above) continues to apply to property placed in service after Dec. 31, '98. (Code Sec. 56(a)(1)(A)(i))

> *observation:* Thus, as a result of the '97 Act, the alternative minimum tax adjustment for depreciation, unless an exception otherwise applies, is computed using the 150% declining balance method (switching to straight line in the year necessary to maximize the allowance) for all property placed in service after Dec. 31, '98.

According to Congress, this will mean that for property placed in service after '98, the recovery period used for purposes of the alternative minimum tax depreciation adjustment will conform to the recovery period used for purposes of the regular tax. (Com Rept, see ¶ 5024)

☐ **Effective:** Aug. 5, '97. As indicated above, the repeal of the alternative minimum tax adjustment under Code Sec. 56(a)(1)(i) is effective for property placed in service after Dec. 31, '98. (Com Rept, see ¶ 5024)

> *observation:* Although the depreciation adjustment under Code Sec. 56(a)(1)(i) is eliminated for property placed in service after '98, with respect to property placed in service before '99, taxpayers will still have to compute and apply this depreciation adjustment for as long as the taxpayer continues to own that property.

¶ 607. Alternative minimum tax on installment sales repealed retroactively for dispositions in tax years beginning after '87

Code Sec. 56(a)(6), repealed by '97 Act § 403(a)
Generally effective: Dispositions in tax years beginning after Dec. 31, '87
Committee Reports, see ¶ 5025

The installment method allows a taxpayer to recognize gain from the disposition of property over the period during which the payments for the property are received.

Dealers in personal property can't use the installment method for regular income tax purposes. However, farmers disposing of property used or produced in the trade or business of farming can use the installment method for regular tax purposes.

For purposes of computing alternative minimum taxable income (AMTI), the installment method isn't allowed for dispositions after Mar. 1, '86 of stock in trade, other property of a kind that would properly be included in inventory if on hand at the close of the year, or property held primarily for sale to customers. As a result of this rule, an AMT adjustment is required. An exception to this rule is provided in the case of certain dispositions on the installment plan of timeshares and residential lots if the taxpayer elects to pay interest on the taxes deferred.

Under pre-'97 Act law, no explicit exception to this rule was provided for dispositions of farm property. And, even though farmers disposing of farm property could use the installment method for regular tax purposes, IRS took the position in IRS Letter Ruling 9640003 that where a cash basis farmer sells farm property under a deferred payment sales contract, the installment method can't be used for purposes of computing AMTI. However, in Notice 97-13, IRS announced that it generally won't enforce this position for prior tax years, so long as the farmer changes his method of accounting for installment sales for tax years beginning after Dec. 31, '96, by attaching a change of accounting method Form 3115 to his timely filed '97 return (due in '98). (FTC 2d/FIN ¶ A-8242; USTR ¶ 564; TaxDesk ¶ 69,657)

New Law. The '97 Act retroactively repeals, for dispositions in tax years beginning after '87, the rule requiring AMTI to be computed without regard to the installment method. (Code Sec. 56(a)(6) repealed by '97 Act §403(a)) Thus, for purposes of computing AMTI, taxpayers may use the installment method of accounting. (Com Rept, see ¶ 5025) For tax years beginning in '87, however, an exception to this rule is provided for cash basis farmers, see below.

> *observation:* A taxpayer who disposes of timeshares and residential lots on the installment plan and elects to pay interest on the taxes deferred, can still use the installment method for AMT purposes, just as under prior law. Under pre-Act law, those sales were an exception to the then prohibition on using the installment method for AMT purposes; now the prohibition is repealed.

☐ **Effective:** Dispositions in tax years beginning after Dec. 31, '87. ('97 Act §403(b)(1))

For tax years beginning in '87, the rule requiring AMTI to be computed without regard to the installment method doesn't apply, in the case of a cash basis taxpayer, to any disposition described in Code Sec. 453C(e)(1)(B)(ii) as in effect for such years (i.e., a disposition under the installment method of property used or produced in the trade or business of farming). ('97 Act §403(b)(2))

FTC 2d References are to Federal Tax Coordinator 2d
FIN References are to RIA's Analysis of Federal Taxes: Income
USTR References are to United States Tax Reporter: Income, Estate & Gift, and Excise
PCA References are to Pension Coordinator and Pension & Benefits Expert/Advisor
PE References are to Pension and Profit Sharing 2nd
EP References are to Estate Planning & Taxation Coordinator and Estate Planning Advisor

☙ observation: This repeal creates a refund opportunity for farmers who paid AMT as a result of IRS's position under pre-'97 Act law, as well as for other taxpayers who paid AMT on installment sales. Also, farmers who didn't follow IRS's position for open tax years no longer have to change their method of accounting, and thus shouldn't file change-of-accounting Form 3115 with their '97 returns.

¶ 608. Simplified foreign tax credit limitation may be elected for alternative minimum tax purposes

Code Sec. 59(a)(3), as amended by '97 Act § 1103(a)
Generally effective: Tax years beginning after Dec. 31, '97
Committee Reports, see ¶ 5172

Computing the foreign tax credit limitation requires the allocation and apportionment of deductions between foreign source income and U.S. source income. The foreign tax credit limitation must be computed both for regular tax purposes and for purposes of the alternative minimum tax (AMT). Thus, the allocation and apportionment of deductions must be done separately for regular tax foreign tax credit limitation purposes and AMT foreign tax credit limitation purposes.

Under pre-'97 Act law, the foreign tax credit limitation for AMT purposes had to be computed on the basis of the taxpayer's alternative minimum taxable income instead of taxable income. Thus, the allocation and apportionment of deductions had to be based on the taxpayer's foreign source alternative minimum taxable income. Taxpayers that allocated and apportioned deductions for regular tax purposes generally had to reallocate and reapportion the same deductions for AMT foreign tax credit purposes, based on assets and income that reflected AMT adjustments (including depreciation). (FTC 2d/FIN ¶ A-8126; USTR ¶ 594; TaxDesk ¶ 69,302)

☙ observation: Taxpayers that were subject to the AMT and that claimed a foreign tax credit for regular tax purposes were required to complete and attach to their AMT forms an additional foreign tax credit form recomputing the foreign tax credit limitation based on foreign source alternative minimum taxable income.

New Law. The '97 Act permits taxpayers to use foreign source regular taxable income in computing their AMT foreign tax credit limitation. (Com Rept, see ¶ 5172) The Act provides that in determining the AMT foreign tax credit for any tax year to which an election applies (see below), the above rule requiring alternative minimum taxable income to be substituted for regular taxable income in computing the foreign tax credit limitation for AMT purposes doesn't apply. (Code Sec. 59(a)(3)(A)(i) as amended by '97 Act §1103(a)) Instead, if the election applies, the foreign tax credit limitation is based on the proportion that (a) the taxpayer's regular taxable income from sources outside the U.S. (but not in excess of the taxpayer's entire alternative minimum taxable income), bears to (b) the taxpayer's entire alternative minimum taxable income for the tax year. (Code Sec. 59(a)(3)(A)(ii)) This eliminates the need to reallocate and reapportion every deduction. (Com Rept, see ¶ 5172)

If foreign source regular taxable income does exceed the taxpayer's entire alternative minimum taxable income, and the taxpayer has income in more than one foreign tax credit limitation category, it is intended that the foreign source taxable income in each such category generally would be reduced by a pro rata portion of that excess. (Com Rept, see ¶ 5172)

If the election isn't made, the foreign tax credit limitation for AMT purposes would be based on the proportion that the taxpayer's foreign source alternative minimum taxable income bears to the taxpayer's entire alternative minimum taxable income. (Com Rept, see ¶ 5172)

An election under this rule may be made only for the taxpayer's first tax year that begins after Dec. 31, '97, and for which the taxpayer claims an AMT foreign tax credit. (Code Sec. 59(a)(3)(B)(i)) A taxpayer will be treated, for this purpose, as claiming an AMT foreign tax credit for any tax year for which the taxpayer chooses to have the benefits of the foreign tax credit and in which the taxpayer is subject to the AMT or would be subject to the AMT but for the availability of the AMT foreign tax credit. (Com Rept, see ¶ 5172)

> ⓡ *action alert:* A taxpayer who wants to use the simplified limitation to compute the AMT foreign tax credit must elect to do so for the taxpayer's first tax year that begins after Dec. 31,'97 for which the taxpayer claims an AMT foreign tax credit.

Once made, the election applies to the tax year for which made and all later tax years, unless revoked with IRS consent. (Code Sec. 59(a)(3)(B)(ii))

> ⓡ *observation:* The '97 Act adds new Code Sec. 59(a)(3). Since the current Code already has a Code Sec. 59(a)(3), apparently Code Sec. 59(a)(4) was intended.

☐ **Effective:** Tax years beginning after Dec. 31, '97. ('97 Act §1103(b))

¶ 609. Exception for certain domestic corporations from limitation on use of foreign tax credits to reduce alternative minimum tax is repealed

Code Sec. 59(a)(2)(C), repealed by '97 Act § 1057(a)
Generally effective: Tax years beginning after Aug. 5, '97
Committee Reports, see ¶ 5149

FTC 2d References are to Federal Tax Coordinator 2d
FIN References are to RIA's Analysis of Federal Taxes: Income
USTR References are to United States Tax Reporter: Income, Estate & Gift, and Excise
PCA References are to Pension Coordinator and Pension & Benefits Expert/Advisor
PE References are to Pension and Profit Sharing 2nd
EP References are to Estate Planning & Taxation Coordinator and Estate Planning Advisor

An alternative minimum tax (AMT) is imposed on a corporation to the extent that the corporation's minimum tax liability exceeds its regular income tax liability. The corporation can use the alternative minimum tax federal tax credit (AMTFTC—i.e., the foreign tax credit as modified for purposes of the AMT) to reduce its AMT liability. However, the reduction in AMT is subject to this limitation: The combination of the corporation's net operating loss carryover and AMTFTCs cannot reduce the corporation's AMT liability by more than 90% of the amount determined without these items. If the AMTFTC exceeds the limitation, the excess may be applied to reduce AMT for other years.

This limitation was designed to prevent U.S. taxpayers with substantial income from using the foreign tax credit to avoid all U.S. tax liability. However, under pre-'97 Act law, a domestic corporation was excepted from this limitation if: (1) more than 50% of the corporation's stock (by vote and value) was owned by U.S. persons who were not members of an affiliated group which included the corporation; (2) all of the corporation's activities were conducted in one foreign country with which the U.S. had an income tax treaty in effect and which provided for the exchange of information between the two countries; (3) the corporation distributed all current earnings and profits (except certain amounts used for normal maintenance or capital expenditures relating to its existing business); *and* (4) all of those distributions which were received by U.S. persons were utilized by them in a U.S. trade or business. (FTC 2d/FIN ¶ A-8128; USTR ¶ 594; TaxDesk ¶ 69,304)

New Law. The '97 Act repeals the exception to the limitation on using foreign tax credits to reduce AMT, that was available to certain domestic corporations. (Code Sec. 59(a)(2)(C) repealed by '97 Act §1057(a))

> **☯ *observation:*** This means that for all corporations (foreign and all domestic), the combination of the corporation's net operating loss carryover and AMTFTCs cannot reduce the AMT liability by more than 90% of the amount determined without these items.

Congress believes that taxpayers should be treated the same with respect to the foreign tax credit limitation under the alternative minimum tax. (Com Rept, see ¶ 5149)

☐ **Effective:** Tax years beginning after Aug. 5, '97. ('97 Act §1057(b))

¶ 610. The AMT adjustment for pollution control facilities is determined for facilities placed in service after '98 by using straight line depreciation

Code Sec. 56(a)(5), as amended by '97 Act § 402(b)
Generally effective: Aug. 5, '97
Committee Reports, see ¶ 5024

In determining alternative minimum taxable income (AMTI) for purposes of computing the alternative minimum tax, an alternative minimum tax adjustment is required for the amortization deduction under Code Sec. 169 for certified pollution control facilities. In computing AMTI, the amortization deduction for certified pollution control facilities placed in service after '86 was determined under the alternative depreciation system of Code Sec. 168(g). (FTC 2d/FIN ¶ A-8228; USTR ¶ 564.01; TaxDesk ¶ 69,681)

New Law. For facilities placed in service after Dec. 31, '98, the alternative minimum tax adjustment for the deduction under Code Sec. 169 for certified pollution control facilities is determined under Code Sec. 168 using the straight line method of depreciation. (Code Sec. 56(a)(5) as amended by '97 Act §402(b))

According to Congress, this will mean that for facilities placed in service after '98, the recovery period used for purposes of the alternative minimum tax adjustment for pollution control facilities will conform to the recovery period used for purposes of the regular tax. (Com Rept, see ¶ 5024)

☐ **Effective:** Aug. 5, '97. As indicated above, computation of the alternate minimum tax adjustment under under Code Sec. 168 using the straight line method of depreciation. is effective for facilities placed in service after Dec. 31, '98. (Com Rept, see ¶ 5024)

> 🅡🄸🄰 *observation:* Although the depreciation adjustment required under pre-'97 Act law does not apply to pollution control facilities placed in service after '98, taxpayers will still have to compute and apply that adjustment for facilities placed in service before '99, for as long as the taxpayer continues to own that property.

¶ 611. Property and casualty insurance companies electing to be taxed only on taxable investment income compute ACE for AMT purposes without regard to underwriting income or expenses

Code Sec. 56(g)(4)(B)(i), as amended by '97 Act § 1212(a)
Generally effective: Tax years beginning after Dec. 31, '97
Committee Reports, see ¶ 5207

Certain small property and casualty insurance companies may elect under Code Sec. 831(b) to be taxed only on taxable investment income (interest, dividends, and rent) for regular tax purposes, instead of being taxed on both investment income and underwriting income (premiums earned on insurance contracts less underwriting losses and expenses). Eligible property and casualty insurance companies are those whose net written premiums (or if greater, direct written premiums) for the tax year exceed $350,000 but do not exceed $1,200,000.

All corporations including insurance companies are subject to the alternative minimum tax. Alternative minimum taxable income (AMTI) of corporations is adjusted by

FTC 2d References are to Federal Tax Coordinator 2d
FIN References are to RIA's Analysis of Federal Taxes: Income
USTR References are to United States Tax Reporter: Income, Estate & Gift, and Excise
PCA References are to Pension Coordinator and Pension & Benefits Expert/Advisor
PE References are to Pension and Profit Sharing 2nd
EP References are to Estate Planning & Taxation Coordinator and Estate Planning Advisor

🄁 Research Institute of America   181

the ACE adjustment. The ACE adjustment provides that AMTI is increased by 75% of the excess of adjusted current earnings (ACE) over AMTI (determined without regard to this adjustment and without regard to the alternative tax net operating deduction).

Any amount which is excluded from gross income for purposes of computing AMTI, but which is taken into account in computing earnings and profits (E&P), is added in the calculation of ACE. And, any deduction that is not allowable for any year for AMT purposes solely because it relates to such an excludable item of income is subtracted.

Under pre-'97 Act law, property and casualty insurance companies that elected to be taxed only on taxable investment income for regular tax purposes, instead of being taxed on both investment income and underwriting income, nevertheless had to take underwriting income (less underwriting losses and expenses) into account for purposes of computing ACE. (FTC 2d/FIN ¶ A-8404, ¶ A-8405; USTR ¶ 564; TaxDesk ¶ 69,803)

New Law. Property and casualty insurance companies eligible to simplify their regular tax computation by electing to be taxed only on taxable investment income are accorded comparable simplicity in the calculation of their AMT. (Com Rept, see ¶ 5207)

The '97 Act provides that if an insurance company elects under Code Sec. 831(b) to be taxed only on taxable investment income (see FTC 2d/FIN ¶ E-5503; USTR ¶ 8314), the ACE adjustment described above for amounts taken into account for E&P purposes doesn't apply to any amount not described in Code Sec. 834(b) (the definition of gross investment income for purposes of computing taxable investment under the Code Sec. 831(b) election, see FTC 2d/FIN ¶ E-5504; USTR ¶ 8344). (Code Sec. 56(g)(4)(B)(i) as amended by '97 Act §1212(a))

Thus, the ACE of an electing company is determined without regard to underwriting income (or underwriting expense). (Com Rept, see ¶ 5207) This obviates the need for electing companies to calculate underwriting income for tax purposes under the AMT. (Com Rept, see ¶ 5207)

☐ **Effective:** Tax years beginning after Dec. 31,'97. ('97 Act §1212(b))

¶ 700. Business Deductions and Credits

Business Credits

¶ 701. Carryback period for unused business credits reduced from 3 years to 1; carryforward period extended from 15 years to 20

Code Sec. 39(a), as amended by '97 Act § 1083(a)
Generally effective: Credits arising in tax years beginning after Dec. 31, '97
Committee Reports, see ¶ 5160

The alcohol fuel credit, contributions to community development corporations (CDCs) credit, disabled access credit, employer social security credit, empowerment zone employment credit, enhanced oil recovery credit, incremental research credit, Indian employment credit, investment tax credit, low-income housing credit, orphan drug credit, and work opportunity credit, are combined into a general business credit for purpose of determining each credit's allowance limitation for the tax year, as well as carrybacks and carryovers into past and future years. Under pre-'97 Act rules, there was a three-year carryback and 15-year carryforward for the current year unused business credit. (FTC 2d/FIN ¶ L-15209; USTR ¶ 394.01; TaxDesk ¶ 38,059)

New Law. The time period for carryback of unused business credits is reduced from the 3 preceding tax years to the 1 preceding tax year. The time period for carryforward of unused business credits is extended from 15 to 20 tax years. (Code Sec. 39(a) as amended by '97 Act §1083(b)) (For changes made by the '97 Act to the time periods to which a net operating loss can be carried, see ¶ 1510.)

☐ **Effective:** For credits arising in tax years beginning after Dec. 31, '97. ('97 Act §1083(b))

observation: Unused credits that arise in tax years beginning before '98 can still be carried back three years. Thus, such credits that arise in '97 can be carried back to '94, '95, and '96. But unused credits that arise in '98 can only be carried back to '97. As a result, taxpayers who paid tax in '95 and/or '96 will lose the opportunity to recover those taxes by credit carryback unless they generate a large enough unused credit in '97.

FTC 2d References are to Federal Tax Coordinator 2d
FIN References are to RIA's Analysis of Federal Taxes: Income
USTR References are to United States Tax Reporter: Income, Estate & Gift, and Excise
PCA References are to Pension Coordinator and Pension & Benefits Expert/Advisor
PE References are to Pension and Profit Sharing 2nd
EP References are to Estate Planning & Taxation Coordinator and Estate Planning Advisor

Research Institute of America   183

¶ 702. Work opportunity credit is modified and extended through June 30, '98

Code Sec. 51(a), as amended by '97 Act § 603(d)(1)
Code Sec. 51(c)(4)(B), as amended by '97 Act § 603(a)(1)
Code Sec. 51(d)(1)(H), as amended by '97 Act § 603(c)(1)
Code Sec. 51(d)(2)(A), as amended by '97 Act § 603(b)(1)
Code Sec. 51(d)(3)(A), as amended by '97 Act § 603(b)(2)
Code Sec. 51(d)(9), as amended by '97 Act § 603(c)(2)
Code Sec. 51(i)(3), '97 Act § 603(d)(2)
Generally effective: Individuals who begin work for the employer after Sept. 30,
* '97, but before July 1, '98*
Committee Reports, see ¶ 5038

A work opportunity credit is available on an elective basis for a percentage of first-year wages (subject to a per-employee dollar limitation) paid or incurred by an employer to an individual who belongs to a "targeted group."

Under pre-'97 Act law, the work opportunity credit was available for wages paid or incurred to an individual who began work for the employer after Sept. 30, '96 but *not* after Sept. 30, '97.

Also, under pre-'97 Act law, there were seven "targeted groups" and the percentage of wages eligible for the credit was 35%.

One requirement for getting the credit was that the individual to which the wages were paid or incurred had to meet a minimum employment requirement of either (i) employment by the employer for at least 180 days (20 days for a qualified summer youth employee) or (ii) completion of at least 400 hours (120 hours for a qualified summer youth employee) of work for the employer. An individual qualifies as a member of the targeted group consisting of "qualified IV-A recipients" if that individual is certified by the designated local agency as being a member of a family receiving assistance under a IV-A program—a state plan approved under Part A of Title IV of the Social Security Act (assistance for needy families with minor children) or a successor program. Under pre-'97 Act law, the family had to receive assistance under a IV-A program for at least a 9-month period ending during the *9-month* period ending on the hiring date. One of the ways a military veteran could qualify as a member of the targeted group consisting of "qualified veterans" was to be certified by the designated local agency as a member of a family receiving assistance under a IV-A program (as defined above) for at least a 9-month period ending during the 12-month period ending on the hiring date. (FTC 2d/FIN ¶ L-17775, ¶ L-17776, ¶ L-17777, ¶ L-17778, ¶ L-17779, ¶ L-17785, ¶ L-17785.1; USTR ¶ 514; TaxDesk ¶ 38,070, ¶ 38,071, ¶ 38,072, ¶ 38,079, ¶ 38,080)

New Law. Under the '97 Act, the work opportunity credit is modified and extended as described below.

Extension of the credit. The date on or before which an individual must begin work for the employer—in order that wages paid or incurred to that individual qualify for the credit—is extended to June 30, '98. (Code Sec. 51(c)(4)(B) as amended by '97 Act §603(a)) Thus, the credit is extended for nine months. (Com Rept, see ¶ 5038)

> **action alert:** The last day a taxpayer can employ a qualifying individual and be eligible to get a credit for that individual is June 30, '98.

Qualified SSI recipients are a targeted group. The '97 Act increases the number of "targeted groups" to eight by making a "qualified SSI recipient" a member of a targeted group. (Code Sec. 51(d)(1)(H) as amended by '97 Act §603(c)(1)) A "qualified SSI recipient" is an individual certified by the designated local agency as receiving supplemental security income benefits under Title XVI of the Social Security Act (including supplemental security income benefits of the type described in section 1616 of the Social Security Act or section 212 of Public Law 93-66) for any month ending within the 60-day period ending on the hiring date. (Code Sec. 51(d)(9) as amended by '97 Act §603(c)(2))

Percentage of wages eligible for the credit. The percentage of wages eligible for the credit is increased to 40%. (Code Sec. 51(a) as amended by '97 Act §603(d)(1)) However, if an individual performs at least 120 hours, but less than 400 hours, of service for the employer, the percentage is reduced to 25%. (Code Sec. 51(i)(3)(A) as amended by '97 Act §603(d)(2)) Congress says that, under these rules, the percentage is 25% for the first 400 hours and 40% thereafter. (Com Rept, see ¶ 5038)

> **illustration:** T hires W who works 600 hours at $5 per hour and has qualified wages of $3,000. According to Congress, T's credit would be 25% of $2,000 or $500, plus 40% of $1,000 or $400, for a total of $900 (not 40% of $3,000, or $1,200).

Minimum employment period. The minimum employment period for credit eligibility related to the wages of any employee is reduced to 120 hours of service performed for the employer. The pre-'97 Act alternative for satisfying the minimum employment requirement—working a minimum number of days for the employer—is eliminated. (Code Sec. 51(i)(3)(B))

IV-A program participation requirement. The minimum period for which an individual's family must be certified as receiving benefits under a IV-A program—as the requirement for being a "qualified IV-A recipient"—is any 9 months during the 18-month period ending on the individual's hiring date. (Code Sec. 51(d)(2)(A) as amended by '97 Act §603(b)(1)) The expansion of the 9-month period under pre-'97 Act law to any 9 months during the 18 month period ending on the hiring date applies whether or not the individual is a qualified veteran. (Com Rept, see ¶ 5038) The '97 Act eliminates, as one of the ways in which an individual who is a military veteran

FTC 2d References are to Federal Tax Coordinator 2d
FIN References are to RIA's Analysis of Federal Taxes: Income
USTR References are to United States Tax Reporter: Income, Estate & Gift, and Excise
PCA References are to Pension Coordinator and Pension & Benefits Expert/Advisor
PE References are to Pension and Profit Sharing 2nd
EP References are to Estate Planning & Taxation Coordinator and Estate Planning Advisor

Research Institute of America 185

can qualify as a member of the targeted group consisting of "qualified veterans," certification as a member of a family receiving assistance under a IV-A program. (Code Sec. 51(d)(3)(A) as amended by '97 Act §603(b)(2))

> *observation:* However, a veteran—as well as anyone else—can qualify as a "qualified IV-A recipient" under the '97 Act under the "9 month of 18 month" test. In some situations that test, as applied to veterans, is more liberal than the pre-'97 Act "9 months ending within 12 months" test for "qualified veterans"—for example, where a family receives assistance for 9 nonconsecutive months during the 18 month period before the hiring date. In other situations, the "9 month of 18 month" test is less liberal—for example, where a family receives assistance for a 9 month period ending more than 9 months before the hiring date.

Redesignations of Code paragraphs by '97 Act. The '97 Act redesignated pre-'97 Act Code Sec. 51(d)(9) through (11) as Code Sec. 51(d)(10) through (12). ('97 Act §603(c)(2))

☐ **Effective:** Individuals who begin work for the employer after Sept. 30, '97. ('97 Act §603(e)) However, the credit isn't available with respect to wages paid or incurred to an individual who begins work for the employer after June 30, '98. (Code Sec. 51(c)(4)(B) as amended by '97 Act §603(a))

¶ 703. Work opportunity credit not allowed to tax-exempt organizations

Code Sec. 52(c), as amended by '97 Act § 1601(b)
Generally effective: Individuals who begin work for the employer after Sept. 30, '96

A credit called the targeted jobs credit was available on an elective basis for employers hiring individuals who belonged to one of nine targeted groups (generally economically disadvantaged) and began work for the employer before Jan. 1, '95. The '96 Small Business Job Protection Act replaced the targeted jobs credit with an elective work opportunity credit.

The targeted jobs credit wasn't allowed to tax-exempt organizations, other than farmers' cooperatives exempt from tax under Code Sec. 521. Under pre-'97 Act law, there was no similar rule applicable to the work opportunity credit. (FTC 2d/FIN ¶ L-17775; USTR ¶ 524; TaxDesk ¶ 38,070)

New Law. Under the '97 Act, the work opportunity credit isn't allowed to tax-exempt organizations, other than farmers' cooperatives exempt from tax under Code Sec. 521. (Code Sec. 52(c) as amended by '97 Act §1601(b)) For the application of this disallowance rule to the welfare-to-work credit, see ¶ 704.

☐ **Effective:** As to individuals who begin work for the employer after Sept. 30, '96. ('97 Act §1601(j)(1))

¶ 704. New welfare-to-work credit is available to employers of long-term family assistance recipients

Code Sec. 51A, as added by '97 Act § 801(a)
Generally effective: Individuals who begin work for the employer after Dec. 31, '97, but before May 1, '99
Committee Reports, see ¶ 5050

A work opportunity credit is available to employers who hire individuals who belong to groups targeted by the credit. One of the groups targeted by the credit is families receiving assistance under the Aid to Families with Dependent Children program or a successor program. However, under pre-'97 Act law, there was no credit specifically targeted to the hiring of long-term public assistance recipients. (FTC 2d/FIN ¶ L-15202, ¶ L-15202.1, ¶ L-15208, ¶ L-15209, ¶ L-15635, ¶ L-17775; USTR ¶ 384, ¶ 394, ¶ 514, ¶ 280C4, ¶ 13,964; TaxDesk ¶ 29,753, ¶ 38,416, ¶ 38,432, ¶ 38,052, ¶ 38,053, ¶ 38,058, ¶ 38,059, ¶ 38,071, ¶ 57,622)

New Law. The '97 Act makes available to employers a new welfare-to-work credit. (Code Sec. 51A as added by '97 Act §801(a)) Congress believes that the welfare-to-work credit will provide to employers an additional incentive to hire categories of individuals who were or are receiving welfare assistance. This incentive is intended to ease the transition from welfare to work for the targeted categories of individuals (described below) by increasing access to employment. It is also intended to provide certain employee benefits to these individuals to encourage training, health coverage, dependent care and ultimately better job attachment. (Com Rept, see ¶ 5050)

The credit is one of the current year business credits under Code Sec. 38(b) which is a component of the Code Sec. 38 general business credit. (Code Sec. 51A(d)(2)) The welfare-to-work credit is elective (that is, a taxpayer may elect to have the rules *not* apply for any tax year) under rules similar to the rules of Code Sec. 51(j), which apply to the work opportunity credit. (Code Sec. 51A(d)(1)) If the welfare-to-work credit is allowed to an employer with respect to an individual for a tax year, then for purposes of applying the rules applicable to the work opportunity credit to that employer, that individual isn't treated as a member of a targeted group for that tax year. (Code Sec. 51A(e))

    observation: Because an employer may only take a work opportunity credit with respect to an individual if that individual is a member of a targeted group, the rule in Code Sec. 51A(e) means that if a welfare-to-work credit is allowed to an employer with respect to an individual for any tax year, the employer can't also take a work opportunity credit with respect to that individual for that tax year. Presumably, "allowed" means actually allowed (not "allowable"). As discussed above, the welfare-to-work credit is allowed unless the

FTC 2d References are to Federal Tax Coordinator 2d
FIN References are to RIA's Analysis of Federal Taxes: Income
USTR References are to United States Tax Reporter: Income, Estate & Gift, and Excise
PCA References are to Pension Coordinator and Pension & Benefits Expert/Advisor
PE References are to Pension and Profit Sharing 2nd
EP References are to Estate Planning & Taxation Coordinator and Estate Planning Advisor

taxpayer elects to *not* have the welfare-to-work credit apply.

Computation of the credit. The amount of the welfare-to work credit is equal, for a tax year, to 35% of the "qualified first-year wages" (defined below) for the year, (Code Sec. 51A(a)(1)), and 50% of the "qualified second-year wages" (defined below) for the year. (Code Sec. 51A(a)(2))

"Qualified first-year wages," with respect to an individual, are "qualified wages" (defined below) attributable to service rendered during the 1-year period beginning with the day the individual begins work for the employer. (Code Sec. 51A(b)(2))

"Qualified second-year wages," with respect to an individual, are "qualified wages" (defined below) attributable to service rendered during the 1-year period beginning with the day after the last day of the 1-year period beginning with the day the individual begins work for the employer. (Code Sec. 51A(b)(3))

> *illustration:* W begins work for T on Jan. 10, '98. "Qualified second-year wages" are qualified wages attributable to services rendered in the period beginning on Jan. 10, '99 and ending on Jan. 9, 2000.

"Qualified wages" are "wages" (defined below) paid or incurred by the employer during the tax year to individuals who are "long-term family assistance recipients" (defined below). (Code Sec. 51A(b)(1))

"Wages" has the meaning given in Code Sec. 51(c) for purposes of the work opportunity credit (see FTC 2d/FIN ¶ L-17783; USTR ¶ 514; TaxDesk ¶ 38,076), except that (1) the credit termination date rules in Code Sec. 51(c)(4) don't apply, (Code Sec. 51A(b)(5)(A)), and (2) wages include amounts paid or incurred by the employer which are excludable from the recipient's gross income under:

(1) Code Sec. 105 (relating to amounts received under accident and health plans), (Code Sec. 51A(b)(5)(B)(i)),

(2) Code Sec. 106 (relating to contributions by the employer to accident and health plans), (Code Sec. 51A(b)(5)(B)(ii)),

(3) Code Sec. 127 (relating to educational assistance programs)—or would be so excludable but for the termination date of that Code section described in Code Sec. 127(d)—but only to the extent paid or incurred to a person not related to the employer, (Code Sec. 51A(b)(5)(B)(iii)), or

(4) Code Sec. 129 (relating to dependent care assistance programs). (Code Sec. 51A(b)(5)(B)(iv))

The amount which is treated as excludable wages under Code Sec. 105 or Code Sec. 106 for any period is based on the reasonable cost of coverage for the period, but cannot exceed the "applicable premium" (as that term is defined under Code Sec. 4980B(f)(4), see FTC 2d/FIN ¶ H-1282; USTR ¶ 49,80B4) for the period. (Code Sec. 51A(b)(5))

The amount of qualified first-year wages and the amount of qualified second-year wages which may be taken into account with respect to any individual cannot exceed

$10,000 per year. (Code Sec. 51A(b)(4)) Thus, employers may get a credit on the first $20,000 of eligible wages paid to an eligible individual during the first two years of employment. Therefore, the maximum credit is $8,500 per qualified employee— 35% of the first $10,000 of eligible wages in the first year of employment plus 50% of the first $10,000 of eligible wages in the second year of employment. (Com Rept, see ¶ 5050)

> *illustration:* W begins work for T (a cash-basis calendar-year taxpayer) on Dec. 1, '98. W earns and T pays to W $1,000 of wages in Dec. '98 and $11,000 of wages in the period beginning Jan. 1, '99 and ending Nov. 30, '99. Effective Dec. 1, '99, T gives W a raise. Thus, W earns and T pays to W $1,200 in Dec. '99. T's welfare-to-work credit, in respect of W, for '98 is $350 ($1,000 × 35%) T's welfare-to-work credit, in respect of W, for '99 is $3,750 ($9,000 × 35% plus $1,200 × 50%).

Eligible employees. A "long-term family assistance recipient" means any individual who is certified by a designated local agency (i.e., a State employment security agency established in accordance with the Act of June 6, '33, as amended [29 U.S.C. 4949n]) as satisfying one of the following three tests:

(1) being a member of a family receiving assistance under a IV-A program (an Aid to Families with Dependent Children or successor program, as further described in Code Sec. 51(d)(2)(B), which relates to the work opportunity credit) for at least the 18-month period ending on the day the individual is hired by the employer. (Code Sec. 51A(c)(1)(A)), (Code Sec. 51A(c)(2)) Under this test, the 18-month period consists of consecutive months. (Com Rept, see ¶ 5050),

(2) being a member of a family receiving IV-A program assistance for 18 months beginning after Aug. 5, '97, (Code Sec. 51A(c)(1)(B)(i)), and having been hired by the employer on a date which isn't more than 2 years after the end of the earliest such 18-month period. (Code Sec. 51A(c)(1)(B)(ii)), (Code Sec. 51A(c)(2)) Under this test, the 18 months needn't be consecutive, but the individual must be hired within two years after the date that the 18-month total is reached. (Com Rept, see ¶ 5050),

(3) being a member of a family which ceased to be eligible after Aug. 5, '97 for IV-A program assistance by reason of any limitation imposed by Federal or State law on the maximum period that the assistance is payable to a family, (Code Sec. 51A(c)(1)(C)(i)), and having been hired by the employer on a date which isn't more than 2 years after the date of that cessation. (Code Sec. 51A(c)(1)(C)(ii)), (Code Sec. 51A(c)(2))

The required certification is made in accordance with rules similar to the rules which, under Code Sec. 51(d)(11), apply to the work opportunity credit. (Code Sec. 51A(d)(1))

FTC 2d References are to Federal Tax Coordinator 2d
FIN References are to RIA's Analysis of Federal Taxes: Income
USTR References are to United States Tax Reporter: Income, Estate & Gift, and Excise
PCA References are to Pension Coordinator and Pension & Benefits Expert/Advisor
PE References are to Pension and Profit Sharing 2nd
EP References are to Estate Planning & Taxation Coordinator and Estate Planning Advisor

No credit is available with respect to an individual unless the individual satisfies a minimum employment period test imposed under rules similar to the ones imposed, in the instance of the work opportunity credit, by Code Sec. 51(i), as in effect on the day before Aug. 5, '97.   (Code Sec. 51A(d)(1))

Similarity to work opportunity credit rules.   Rules similar to the rules (with respect to the work opportunity credit) in the following Code sections apply to the welfare-to-work credit:

- Code Sec. 52, which provides rules for (1) allocating the amount of the work opportunity credit among entities or businesses under common control, (2) allocating the amount of the work opportunity credit among a trust and its beneficiaries or an estate and its beneficiaries, (3) prohibiting the work opportunity credit (¶ 703) to most tax-exempt organizations and (4) limiting the amount of the work opportunity credit allowable to regulated investment companies, real estate investment trusts and certain cooperatives, see FTC 2d/FIN ¶ L-17787 et seq.; USTR ¶ 524; TaxDesk ¶s 38,086, 38,130, 38,131.

- Code Sec. 51(f), which permits remuneration paid to an employee during a tax year to be taken into account by the employer only if more than 50% of the remuneration paid during that year is for services performed in a trade or business of the employer, see FTC 2d/FIN ¶ L-17783.1; USTR ¶ 514; TaxDesk ¶ 38,076.

- Code Sec. 51(k), which provides rules applicable to successor employers, and rules which prohibit credit, in some circumstances, for remuneration for work performed by an individual for a person other than the employer, see FTC 2d/FIN ¶s L-17784, L-17790; USTR ¶ 514; TaxDesk ¶s 38,117, 38,133.

- Code Sec. 51(g), which requires the U.S. Employment Service, in consultation with IRS, to take necessary or appropriate steps to keep employers apprised of the availability of the work opportunity credit, see FTC 2d/FIN ¶ L-17784.1; USTR ¶ 514.   (Code Sec. 51A(d)(1))

If a qualified recipient is an agricultural employee to whom Code Sec. 51(h)(A) applies (see FTC 2d/FIN ¶ L-17783.2; USTR ¶ 514; TaxDesk ¶ 38,076), rules similar to the rules in Code Sec. 51(h)(A) apply, except that the rules are applied by substituting "$10,000" for "$6,000."   (Code Sec. 51A(b)(5)(C)(i))

If a qualified recipient is a railroad employee to whom Code Sec. 51(h)(B) applies, rules similar to the rules in Code Sec. 51(h)(B) apply (see FTC 2d/FIN ¶ L-17783.2; USTR ¶ 514; TaxDesk ¶ 38,076), except that the rules are applied by substituting "$833.33" for "$500."   (Code Sec. 51A(b)(5)(C)(ii))

> **observation:** The substitution of "$10,000" (per calendar year) for '$6,000" (per calendar year) in applying the rules of Code Sec. 51(h)(A) and "$833.33" (per month) for "$500" (per month) in applying the rules of Code Sec. 51(h)(B) is necessary because the annual limit on wages which may be taken into account for the welfare-to-work credit is $10,000 and the annual limit on wages (for other than summer youth employees) which may be taken into account under the work opportunity credit is $6,000.

No deduction for expenses for which credit is allowable. Code Sec. 280C(a) applies to the welfare-to-work credit. Thus, no deduction is allowed for the portion of the wages and salaries, paid or incurred in the tax year, equal to the amount of the welfare-to-work credit determined for the tax year. (Code Sec. 51A(d)(2)) For additional rules for the application of Code Sec. 280C(a), see FTC 2d/FIN ¶ L-17780; USTR ¶ 514; TaxDesk ¶ 38,073.

Coordination with empowerment zone employment credit. Code Sec. 1396(c)(3) applies to the welfare-to-work credit. Thus, (1) wages taken into account in determining the welfare-to-work credit cannot be taken into account in determining the empowerment zone employment credit and (2) the $15,000 per-calendar-year per-worker limitation on the empowerment zone employment credit is reduced by the wages paid or incurred during the calendar year which are taken into account in determining the welfare-to-work credit. (Code Sec. 51A(d)(2))

☐ **Effective:** Individuals who begin work for the employer after Dec. 31, '97 ('97 Act §801(c)), but before May 1, '99. (Code Sec. 51A(f))

🅡🅘🅐 *action alert:* The last day for hiring an employee with respect to whom the welfare-to-work credit is allowable is Apr. 30, '99.

¶ 705. Certain financial institutions holding qualified zone academy bonds are entitled to nonrefundable tax credit

Code Sec. 1397E, as added by '97 Act § 226(a)
Generally effective: Obligations issued after Dec. 31, '97
Committee Reports, see ¶ 5012

Interest on bonds issued for general governmental purposes, including public schools, is exempt from federal income tax. (see FTC 2d/FIN ¶ J-3000; USTR ¶ 1034; TaxDesk ¶ 15,801)

New Law. Certain qualified financial institutions (described below) that hold "qualified zone academy bonds" (defined below) on the "credit allowance date" (defined below) of the bond which occurs during the tax year are entitled to a nonrefundable tax credit for that tax year. (Code Sec. 1397E(a) as added by '97 Act §226(a)) The credit is includable in gross income (Code Sec. 1397E(g)), but may be claimed against regular income tax and alternative minimum tax liability. (Code Sec. 1397E(c)(1)).

Amount of the credit. The amount of the credit equals the credit rate (defined below) determined by Treasury for the month in which the bond was issued, multiplied by the face amount of the bond held by the taxpayer on the credit allowance date.

(Code Sec. 1397E(b)(1)) The credit allowance date is the last day of the one-year period starting with the date of issuance and the last day of each successive one-year period thereafter. (Code Sec. 1397E(f)(1)) The taxpayer is entitled to a credit for each year the taxpayer holds the bond. (Com Rept, see ¶ 5012)

Credit rate. The percentage rate for calculating the credit will be set by Treasury each calendar month for bonds to be issued in the next month. (Code Sec. 1397E(b)(2)) The rate will be set so that the bonds can be issued without discount and without interest cost to the issuer. (Code Sec. 1397E(b)(2)) This credit rate applies to all qualified zone academy bonds purchased in each month. (Com Rept, see ¶ 5012)

Limitation based on tax amount. The allowable credit cannot exceed the excess of the taxpayer's regular tax liability plus AMT over the credits allowed under Part IV of subchapter A (disregarding subpart C, relating to refundable credits). (Code Sec. 1397E(c))

Qualified financial institutions. Institutions that qualify for the credit are:

. . . Banks (and domestic building and loan associations) that fall under the definition of Code Sec. 581,

. . . Insurance companies to which subchapter L applies (pertaining to life insurance companies and certain mutual insurance companies), and

. . . Corporations actively engaged in the business of lending money. (Code Sec. 1397E(d)(6))

Qualified zone academy bond. A qualified zone academy bond is any bond issued as part of an issue if: (Code Sec. 1397E(d)(1))

(1) 95% or more of the proceeds of the issue are to be used for a qualified purpose with respect to a qualified zone academy established by an eligible local education agency, (Code Sec. 1397E(d)(1)(A))

(2) the bond is issued by a state or local government within the jurisdiction of which the academy is located, (Code Sec. 1397E(d)(1)(B))

(3) the issuer—

• designates the bond for purposes of this provision,

• certifies that it has written assurances that the private business contribution requirement (discussed below) will be satisfied with respect to the academy, and

• certifies that it has the written approval of the eligible local education agency for the bond issuance, and (Code Sec. 1397E(d)(1)(C))

(4) the term of each bond which is part of the issue does not exceed the maximum term permitted in the term requirement (discussed below). (Code Sec. 1397E(d)(1)(D))

Private business contribution requirement. The private business contribution requirement is satisfied with respect to any issue if the eligible local education agency that established the qualified zone academy has written commitments from private entities to make qualified contributions (defined below) having a present value (as of the date of issuance of the issue) of not less than 10% of the proceeds of the issue. (Code Sec.

1397E(d)(2)(A))

A qualified contribution means any contribution (of a type and quality acceptable to the eligible local education agency) of:

... equipment for use in the qualified zone academy (including state-of-the-art technology and vocational equipment),

... technical assistance in developing curriculum or training teachers to promote appropriate market-driven technology in the classroom,

... services of employees as volunteer mentors,

... internships, field trips, or other educational opportunities outside the academy for students, or

... other property or services specified by the eligible local education agency. (Code Sec. 1397E(d)(2)(B))

Term requirement. During each calendar month, IRS will determine the maximum term permitted for bonds issued during the following calendar month. The maximum term will be the term which IRS estimates will result in the present value of the obligation to repay the principal on the bond being equal to 50% of the face amount of the bond. The present value is determined using as a discount rate the average annual interest rate of tax exempt obligations having a term of ten years or more which are issued during the month. If the term as so determined is not a multiple of a whole year, the term is rounded to the next highest whole year. (Code Sec. 1397E(d)(3))

Qualified zone academy. A qualified zone academy is a public school, or an academic program within a public school, that is established and operated under the supervision of an eligible local education agency to provide education or training below the post-secondary level if:

... the public school or program (as the case may be) is designed in cooperation with business to enhance the academic curriculum, increase graduation and employment rates, and better prepare students for the rigors of college and the increasingly complex workforce,

... students in the public school or program (as the case may be) will be subject to the same academic standards and assessments as other students educated by the eligible local education agency,

... the comprehensive education plan of the public school or program is approved by the eligible local education agency, and

... the public school is either (1) located in an empowerment zone or enterprise community (existing now or designated after Aug. 5, '97) or (2) reasonably expected, at the date of issuance of the bonds, to have at least 35% of its students eligible for free or reduced-cost lunches under the National School Lunch Act. (Code Sec.

FTC 2d References are to Federal Tax Coordinator 2d
FIN References are to RIA's Analysis of Federal Taxes: Income
USTR References are to United States Tax Reporter: Income, Estate & Gift, and Excise
PCA References are to Pension Coordinator and Pension & Benefits Expert/Advisor
PE References are to Pension and Profit Sharing 2nd
EP References are to Estate Planning & Taxation Coordinator and Estate Planning Advisor

 Research Institute of America   193

1397E(d)(4)(A))

An eligible local education agency is any local education agency as defined in section 14101 of the Elementary and Secondary Education Act of '65. (Code Sec. 1397E(d)(4)(B))

Qualified purpose. Qualified purposes for which a bond may be issued are to:

. . . rehabilitate or repair the public school facility in which the academy is established,

. . . provide equipment for use at the academy,

. . . develop educational course materials for use at the academy, or

. . . train teachers and other school personnel in the academy. (Code Sec. 1397E(d)(5))

Nationwide bond limitation. A total of $400 million of bonds can be issued in each of '98 and '99. Except for carryovers, the limit will be zero after '99. (Code Sec. 1397E(e)(1)) This bond cap of $800 million will be allocated by Treasury to the states based on the percentage of their population below the poverty line (as defined by the Office of Management and Budget). (Code Sec. 1397E(e)(2)) Allocation to the individual schools will be determined by the state education agency. (Code Sec. 1397E(e)(2)) The maximum aggregate face amount of bonds issued during any calendar year with respect to any qualified zone academy cannot exceed the limitation amount allocated to that school by the state education agency. (Code Sec. 1397E(e)(3))

There is a carryover of any unused limitation. The limitation amount for the state for the following calendar year is increased by the amount of the excess if the limitation amount for any state exceeds the amount of bonds issued during the year which are designated with respect to the qualified zone academies within the state. (Code Sec. 1397E(e)(4))

Other definitions. The term "credit allowance date" means with respect to any issue, the last day of the one-year period beginning on the date of issuance of the issue and the last day of each successive one-year period thereafter. (Code Sec. 1397E(f)(1))

A "bond" includes any obligation. (Code Sec. 1397E(f)(2))

The term "state" includes the District of Columbia and any U.S. possession. (Code Sec. 1397E(f)(3))

Gross Income. The amount of the credit allowed to the taxpayer is included in gross income. (Code Sec. 1397E(g))

☐ **Effective:** Obligations issued after Dec. 31, '97. ('97 Act §226(c))

¶ 706. Research credit is retroactively restored and extended until June 30, '98

Code Sec. 41(h)(1), as amended by '97 Act § 601(a)(1)
Code Sec. 41(c)(4)(B), as amended by '97 Act § 601(b)(1)
Generally effective: Amounts paid or incurred after May 31, '97
Committee Reports, see ¶ 5036

Before May 31, '97, a taxpayer was entitled to a research tax credit equal to 20% of the amount by which the taxpayer's qualified research expenditures for a tax year exceeded a specified base amount for that year. In addition, a separate university basic research credit was available. The Small Business Job Protection Act of '96 ('96 Act) extended the research credit for the period July 1, '96 through May 31, '97 (an eleven-month period).

Taxpayers could elect a somewhat differently computed alternative incremental research credit for a taxpayer's first tax year beginning after June 30, '96. If a taxpayer elected to be subject to the alternative regime for its first tax year beginning after June 30, '96 and before July 1, '97, then all qualified research expenses paid or incurred during the first eleven months of the tax year were treated as qualified research expenses for purposes of computing the credit. Thus, if a calendar year taxpayer elected the alternative credit for '97, qualified research expenses paid or incurred from Jan. 1, '97 through Nov. 30, '97 would be creditable, although for nonelecting taxpayers the credit expired on May 31, '97. (FTC 2d/FIN ¶ L-15300 et seq.; USTR ¶ 414 et seq.; TaxDesk ¶ 38,401 et seq.)

New Law. The '97 Act strikes the May 31, '97 expiration date of the research credit (including the university basic research credit) and replaces that date with June 30, '98. (Code Sec. 41(h)(1)(B) as amended by '97 Act §601(a)(1)) Thus, the research tax credit is extended for thirteen months (generally for the period June 1, '97 through June 30, '98). (Com Rept, see ¶ 5036)

The requirement under pre-'97 Act law that the taxpayer could only make the election of the alternative incremental research credit for the taxpayer's first tax year beginning after June 30, '96 no longer applies. (Code Sec. 41(c)(4)(B)) Thus, taxpayers may elect the alternative incremental research credit regime for any tax year beginning after June 30, '96, and the election will apply to that taxable year and all subsequent taxable years unless revoked with IRS's consent. (Com Rept, see ¶ 5036)

Even though the research credit does not apply to amounts paid or incurred after June 30, '98, if a taxpayer elects the alternative incremental credit for its first tax year beginning after June 30, '96, and before July 1, '97, then the research credit applies to all qualified research expenses paid or incurred during the 24-month period beginning with the first month of the year. (Code Sec. 41(h)(1)) Thus, the alternative incremental research credit is available during the entire 24-month period (i.e., the equivalent of the 11-month extension of the credit provided for by the '96 Small Business Job Protection Act plus the additional 13-month extension provided for by the '97 Act) beginning with the first month of that tax year. (Com Rept, see ¶ 5036)

illustration (1): P Corporation, a calendar year taxpayer, makes the election for '97 (its first tax year beginning after June 30, '96 and before July 1, '97). Before '97, P hasn't paid or incurred any amount taken into account in determining the credit. The credit applies to all qualified research expenses paid or incurred by P during the 24-month period commencing with Jan. of '97 (Jan. 1, '97 through Dec. 31, '98). If P does not make the election, it can't claim the credit after June 30, '98.

However, the 24 months is reduced by the number of full months after June '96 (and before the first month of the first tax year) during which the taxpayer paid or incurred any amount which is taken into account in determining the credit. (Code Sec. 41(h)(1)) This rule prevents taxpayers from effectively obtaining more than 24 months of research credits from the '96 Act and the '97 Act and reduces the 24-month period for taxpayers electing the alternative incremental research credit regime by the number of months (if any) after June '96 with respect to which the taxpayer claimed research credit amounts under the regular 20% credit rules. (Com Rept, see ¶ 5036)

> *illustration (2):* The facts are the same as in Illustration (1) except that P, in Nov. and Dec. of '96, paid or incurred research expenses that were taken into account in determining the credit. The credit applies to all qualified research expenses paid or incurred by P during the 22-month period commencing with Jan. of '97 (Jan. 1, '97 through Oct. 31, '98).

☐ **Effective:** Amounts paid or incurred after May 31, '97. ('97 Act §601(c))

¶ 707. Orphan drug tax credit is retroactively restored and permanently extended

Code Sec. 45C, as amended by '97 Act § 604(a)
Generally effective: Amounts paid or incurred after May 31, '97
Committee Reports, see ¶ 5039

Under pre-'97 Act law, the orphan drug credit (a nonrefundable tax credit for qualified expenses incurred in the testing of certain drugs to cure rare diseases or conditions) was not available for amounts of clinical testing expenses paid or incurred after May 31, '97. (FTC 2d/FIN ¶ L-15600.1; USTR ¶ 45C4; TaxDesk ¶ 38,051)

> *observation:* Thus, under pre-'97 Act law, the orphan drug credit had expired.

New Law. In order to encourage the socially optimal level of research to develop drugs to treat rare diseases and conditions, and because the research and clinical testing of these types of drugs has to be conducted over several years, Congress believed that the orphan drug credit should be permanently extended. (Com Rept, see ¶ 5039)

The '97 Act strikes the rule providing that the orphan drug tax credit is not available for amounts of clinical testing expenses paid or incurred after May 31, '97. (Code Sec. 45C(e) as amended by '97 Act §604(a)) Thus, the orphan drug credit is permanently extended. (Com Rept, see ¶ 5039).

☐ **Effective:** Amounts paid or incurred after May 31, '97. ('97 Act §604(b)) *observation:* Since the permanent extension of the orphan drug credit is retroactive (i.e., covers qualified clinical expenses paid or incurred after May 31, '97), there is no period of time since July 1, '96 that otherwise qualified expenses would not qualify for the credit.

Business Deductions

¶ 708. No deduction for interest allocable to unborrowed policy cash values ("inside buildup") on life insurance contracts

Code Sec. 264(f), as amended by '97 Act § 1084(c)
Generally effective: Contracts issued after June 8, '97
Committee Reports, see ¶ 5161

No federal income tax generally is imposed on a policyholder with respect to the earnings under a life insurance contract ("inside buildup"), unless the life insurance contracts fails to meet the requirements of Code Sec. 7702(a) (requiring that a contract satisfy a cash value accumulation test, or guideline premium requirements coupled with a "cash value corridor"). (Com Rept, see ¶ 5161) FTC 2d/FIN ¶ J-4900 *et seq.*; USTR ¶s 77,024.07, 77,02A4; TaxDesk ¶ 14,854

New Law. Under the '97 Act, with the exceptions discussed below, no deduction is allowed for that portion of the taxpayer's interest expense that's allocable (as explained below) to unborrowed policy cash values (as defined below). (Code Sec. 264(f)(1) as amended by '97 Act §1084(c))

observation: In other words, unless a taxpayer meets one of the exceptions described below, if a taxpayer owns a life insurance policy, or an annuity or endowment contract, with "inside buildup"—i.e., where the policy's or contract's cash surrender value exceeds the amount of any loans taken out with respect to the policy or contract—the taxpayer will lose an allocable portion of any interest deduction to which he would otherwise be entitled.

Exceptions. *Policies and contracts covering 20% owners, officers, directors, employees.* The disallowance rule of Code Sec. 264(f)(1) doesn't apply to any policy or contract owned by an entity engaged in a trade or business if that policy or contract covers only one individual and if that individual is (at the time first covered by the policy or contract) (Code Sec. 264(f)(4)(A)):

... a 20% owner of the entity. (Code Sec. 264(f)(4)(A)(i)) ("20% owner" has the definition given by Code Sec. 264(e)(4) [Code Sec. 264(d)(4) before redesignation by ('97 Act §1084(a)(2))]) (Code Sec. 264(f)(4)(D)); or

---

FTC 2d References are to Federal Tax Coordinator 2d
FIN References are to RIA's Analysis of Federal Taxes: Income
USTR References are to United States Tax Reporter: Income, Estate & Gift, and Excise
PCA References are to Pension Coordinator and Pension & Benefits Expert/Advisor
PE References are to Pension and Profit Sharing 2nd
EP References are to Estate Planning & Taxation Coordinator and Estate Planning Advisor

... an individual (who isn't a 20% owner of the entity) who is an officer, director, or employee of the trade or business. (Code Sec. 264(f)(4)(A)(ii))

A policy or contract covering a 20% owner of an entity isn't treated as failing to meet the just-described requirements because the policy or contract covers the joint lives of the 20% owner and the owner's spouse. (Code Sec. 264(f)(4)(A)) But a joint-life contract under which the sole insureds are a 20% owner and his or her spouse is the only type of policy or contract with more than one insured that comes within the Code Sec. 264(f)(4)(A) rule described above. Thus, for example, if the insureds under a contract include an individual described in Code Sec. 264(f)(4)(A) (e.g., an employee, officer, director, or 20% owner) and any individual who isn't described in Code Sec. 264(f)(4)(A) (e.g., a debtor of the entity), then Code Sec. 264(f)(4)(A) doesn't apply to the policy or contract. (Com Rept, see ¶ 5161)

Annuities held by other than natural persons, other policies and contracts held by natural persons. The disallowance rule of Code Sec. 264(f)(1) doesn't apply to:

... any annuity contract to which Code Sec. 72(u) applies (i.e., annuity contracts held by other than natural persons) (Code Sec. 264(f)(4)(B));

... any policy or contract held by a natural person (Code Sec. 264(f)(5)(A)(i)), except as noted below.

Insurance companies. The disallowance rule of Code Sec. 264(f)(1) doesn't apply to an insurance company subject to tax under Subchapter L of the Code (i.e., Code Sec. 801–Code Sec. 848). (Code Sec. 264(f)(8)(B)) (Instead, the '97 Act modifies the rules governing certain deductions and income inclusions of insurance companies, see ¶ 1716.)

For treatment of controlled groups, partnerships and S corporations, see below.

Allocating interest expense to unborrowed policy cash values. The portion of the taxpayer's interest expense (defined below) that's allocable to unborrowed policy cash values (also defined below) is an amount that bears the same ratio to that interest expense as (Code Sec. 264(f)(2)):

... the taxpayer's average unborrowed policy cash values of life insurance policies, and annuity and endowment contracts, issued after June 8, '97, bears to (Code Sec. 264(f)(2)(A))

... the sum of (Code Sec. 264(f)(2)(B))

(1) in the case of the taxpayer's assets that are life insurance policies or annuity or endowment contracts, the average unborrowed policy cash values of such policies and contracts (Code Sec. 264(f)(2)(B)(i)); and

(2) in the case of the taxpayer's assets that aren't described in (1) above, the average adjusted bases (within the meaning of Code Sec. 1016) of those assets. (Code Sec. 264(f)(2)(B)(ii))

> *observation:* The Act doesn't specify how the taxpayer is to compute its average unborrowed policy cash values or average adjusted bases of all assets.

However, any policy or contract to which the disallowance rule of Code Sec. 264(f)(1) doesn't apply by reason of Code Sec. 264(f)(4) isn't taken into account in computing the portion of the taxpayer's interest expense allocable to unborrowed policy cash values. (Code Sec. 264(f)(4)(C)) In other words, any policy or contract that isn't subject to the pro rata interest disallowance rule of Code Sec. 264(f)(1) by reason of the Code Sec. 264(f)(2) exceptions (for 20% owners, their spouses, employees, officers and directors, and in the case of an annuity contract to which Code Sec. 72(u) applies) isn't taken into account in the applying the ratio to determine the portion of the taxpayer's interest expense that's allocable to unborrowed policy cash values. (Com Rept, see ¶ 5161)

> ✔️ *observation:* Policies or contracts to which the disallowance rule of Code Sec. 264(f)(1) doesn't apply by reason of Code Sec. 264(f)(4) are all those listed in **Exceptions** above, *except* for policies and contracts held by natural persons or insurance companies.

As noted in **Exceptions** above, the disallowance rule doesn't apply to any policy or contract held by a natural person. However, if a trade or business is directly or indirectly the beneficiary under any policy or contract, that policy or contract is treated as held by the trade or business and not by a natural person. (Code Sec. 264(f)(5)(A)(ii)) But this doesn't apply to any trade or business carried on as a sole proprietorship, or to any trade or business of performing services as an employee. (Code Sec. 264(f)(5)(A)(iii)(I)) IRS must require whatever reporting from policyholders and issuers that's necessary to carry out this trade or business rule. Any report required will be treated as an information return under Code Sec. 6724(d)(1). (Code Sec. 264(f)(5)(A)(iv))

If a trade or business is directly or indirectly the beneficiary under any policy or contract, the amount of the unborrowed cash value of that policy or contract taken into account in computing the portion of the taxpayer's interest expense allocable to unborrowed policy cash values can't exceed the benefit to which the trade or business is directly or indirectly entitled under the policy or contract. (Code Sec. 264(f)(5)(A)(iii)(II)) The amount of the benefit is intended to take into account the amount payable to the business under the contract (e.g., as a death benefit) or under another agreement (e.g., under a split-dollar agreement). The amount of the benefit is intended also to include any amount by which liabilities of the business would be reduced by payments under the policy or contract (e.g., when payments under the policy reduce the principal or interest on a liability owed to or by the business). (Com Rept, see ¶ 5161)

Interest expense defined. For purposes of the above rules, "interest expense" means the aggregate amount allowable to the taxpayer as a deduction for interest (within the meaning of Code Sec. 265(b)(4) [and thus including amounts, whether or

FTC 2d References are to Federal Tax Coordinator 2d
FIN References are to RIA's Analysis of Federal Taxes: Income
USTR References are to United States Tax Reporter: Income, Estate & Gift, and Excise
PCA References are to Pension Coordinator and Pension & Benefits Expert/Advisor
PE References are to Pension and Profit Sharing 2nd
EP References are to Estate Planning & Taxation Coordinator and Estate Planning Advisor

✔️ **Research Institute of America** 199

not designated as interest, paid in respect of deposits, investment certificates, or withdrawable or repurchasable shares]) for the tax year, determined without regard to this Code Sec. 264(f), Code Sec. 265(b) (barring a deduction for interest on indebtedness incurred to purchase or carry tax-exempt obligations), and Code Sec. 291 (corporate preference items). (Code Sec. 264(f)(7)) (However, where interest expense has been disallowed under Code Sec. 264(a) or Code Sec. 265, see below.)

Unborrowed policy cash value defined. The term "unborrowed policy cash value" means, with respect to any life insurance policy or annuity or endowment contract, the excess of (Code Sec. 264(f)(3))

. . . the cash surrender value of the policy or contract determined without regard to any surrender charge, over (Code Sec. 264(f)(3)(A))

. . . the amount of any loan with respect to the policy or contract. (Code Sec. 264(f)(3)(B))

The cash surrender value is to be determined without regard to any other contractual or noncontractual arrangement that artificially depresses the cash value of a contract. (Com Rept, see ¶ 5161)

Coordination with Code Sec. 264(a) and Code Sec. 265. If interest on any indebtedness is disallowed under Code Sec. 264(a) (limiting deduction of interest on debt incurred with respect to life insurance policies and endowment or annuity contracts), or Code Sec. 265 (prohibiting deduction for expenses and interest relating to tax-exempt income):

. . . the disallowed interest must not be taken into account in computing the portion of the taxpayer's interest expense allocable to unborrowed policy cash values (Code Sec. 264(f)(6)(A)(i)) and

. . . the amount otherwise taken into account under Code Sec. 264(f)(2)(B) (i.e., the sum of the average unborrowed policy cash values of life insurance policies, annuity or endowment contracts, and the average adjusted bases for all of the taxpayer's other assets, see above), must be reduced (but not below zero) by the amount of that indebtedness. (Code Sec. 264(f)(6)(A)(ii))

Coordination with uniform capitalization rules. The above rules must be applied before the application of the Code Sec. 263A uniform capitalization rules. (Code Sec. 264(f)(6)(B))

Controlled groups. In applying the above rules, all members of a controlled group (within the meaning of Code Sec. 264(d)(5)(B)) are treated as one taxpayer (Code Sec. 264(f)(8)(A)), except that any member of an affiliated group which is an insurance company isn't taken into account. (Code Sec. 264(f)(8)(B))

The above rule is intended to prevent taxpayers from avoiding the pro rata interest limitation by owning life insurance, endowment or annuity contracts, while incurring interest expense through a related person. (Com Rept, see ¶ 5161)

Partnerships and S corporations. In the case of a partnership or S corporation, the above rules apply at the partnership and corporate levels. (Code Sec. 264(f)(5)(B))

☐ **Effective:** Contracts issued after June 8, '97, in tax years ending after that date. Any material increase in the death benefit or other material change in the contract is treated as a new contract. However, the addition of covered lives is treated as a new contract only with respect to those additional covered lives. For purposes of these effective date rules, an increase in the death benefit under a policy or contract issued in connection with a lapse described in Sec. 501(d)(2) of the Health Insurance Portability and Accountability Act of '96 isn't treated as a new contract. ('97 Act §1084(d))

¶ 709. Limit on deductibility of interest to carry COLI policies extended to policies covering taxpayer's former officers or employees and persons formerly financially interested in taxpayer's current or former trade or business

Code Sec. 264(a)(4), as amended by '97 Act § 1602(f)(1)
Generally effective: Interest paid or accrued after Oct. 13, '95
Committee Reports, see ¶ 5375

For interest paid or accrued after Oct. 13, '95 (subject to phase-in rules), the '96 Health Insurance Portability and Accountability Act amended Code Sec. 264(a)(4) to prohibit a deduction for interest paid or accrued on any indebtedness with respect to one or more life insurance policies or annuity or endowment contracts owned by the taxpayer covering any individual who (1) is an officer or employee of, or (2) is financially interested in, any trade or business carried on by the taxpayer. (This is the "company-owned life insurance," or COLI, rule.) An exception is provided for interest on indebtedness with respect to life insurance policies covering up to 20 key persons, subject to an interest rate cap.

According to the "Blue Book" issued by the staff of the Joint Committee on Taxation (the "General Explanation of Tax Legislation Enacted in the 104th Congress"), the above rule was also intended to apply to policies or contracts covering individuals who were, in the past, officers or employees of, or financially interested in, any trade or business carried on the by taxpayer. (FTC 2d/FIN ¶ K-5351; USTR ¶ 2644; TaxDesk ¶ 31,681)

New Law. The '97 Act retroactively amends Code Sec. 264(a)(4) to prohibit a deduction for interest paid or accrued after Oct. 13, '95 (subject to the phase-in rules of Sec. 501(c)(2) of the '96 Health Insurance Portability and Accountability Act) on any indebtedness with respect to one or more life insurance policies or annuity or endowment contracts owned by the taxpayer covering any individual:

. . . who is *or was* an officer or employee (Code Sec. 264(a)(4)(A) as amended by '97 Act §1602(f)(1)), or

---

FTC 2d References are to Federal Tax Coordinator 2d
FIN References are to RIA's Analysis of Federal Taxes: Income
USTR References are to United States Tax Reporter: Income, Estate & Gift, and Excise
PCA References are to Pension Coordinator and Pension & Benefits Expert/Advisor
PE References are to Pension and Profit Sharing 2nd
EP References are to Estate Planning & Taxation Coordinator and Estate Planning Advisor

... who is *or was* financially interested in (Code Sec. 264(a)(4)(B)), any trade or business carried on *(currently or formerly)* by the taxpayer. (Code Sec. 264(a)(4)) (Changes made by the '97 Act are shown in italics.)

The above provision is intended to prevent unintended avoidance of the COLI rule. Thus, for example, the provision would clarify the treatment of interest on debt with respect to contracts covering former employees of the taxpayer. As another example, the provision would clarify the treatment of interest on debt with respect to a business formerly conducted by the taxpayer and transferred to an affiliate of the taxpayer. (Com Rept, see ¶ 5375)

> ✐*caution:* For contracts entered into after June 8, '97, the '97 Act removes Code Sec. 264(a)(4)'s restriction regarding officers or employees of the taxpayer, or persons financially interested in any trade or business carried on by the taxpayer, described above. As a result, for those contracts, with certain exceptions, Code Sec. 264(a)(4) prohibits a deduction for interest paid or accrued on any indebtedness with respect to one or more life insurance policies owned by the taxpayer covering the life of any individual, or any endowment or annuity contracts owned by the taxpayer covering any individual. See ¶ 710

☐ **Effective:** For interest paid or accrued after Oct. 13, '95, subject to the phase-in rules of Sec. 501(c)(2) of the '96 Health Insurance Portability and Accountability Act. ('97 Act §1602(i))

The amendment of Code Sec. 264(a)(4), described above, is treated as having been enacted immediately before the amendment of Code Sec. 264(a)(4) by Sec. 1084(b)(1) of the '97 Act (discussed at ¶ 710). ('97 Act §1600)

No inference is intended as the interpretation of this provision under prior law. (Com Rept, see ¶ 5375)

¶ 710. Rules disallowing premium and interest deductions on life insurance of officers and employees extended to life insurance on debtors and others

Code Sec. 264(a)(1), as amended by '97 Act § 1084(a)(1)
Code Sec. 264(b), as amended by '97 Act § 1084(a)(2)
Code Sec. 264(a)(4), as amended by '97 Act § 1084(b)(1)
Generally effective: Contracts issued after June 8, '97
Committee Reports, see ¶ 5161

Deductibility of premiums on company-owned life insurance (COLI). A taxpayer may not deduct premiums paid on any life insurance policy covering the life of any of its officers or employees if the taxpayer is directly or indirectly a beneficiary under the policy. Similarly, a taxpayer may not deduct premiums on any life insurance policy covering the life of any person financially interested in the taxpayer's trade or business, if the taxpayer is directly or indirectly a beneficiary under the policy. These rules apply with respect to all life insurance policies, including group life and so-called "split-dollar" policies.

Deductibility of interest on debt incurred on company-owned life insurance, endowment or annuity contracts. Under Code Sec. 264(a)(4), as in effect before the '97 Act, a taxpayer may not deduct interest on debt incurred with respect to life insurance policies, endowment or annuity contracts owned by the taxpayer, but this prohibition is restricted to policies and contracts covering any officer or employee of the taxpayer, or any person who is financially interested in any trade or business carried on by the taxpayer. (The '97 Act retroactively expands Code Sec. 264(a)(4)'s interest prohibition to cover interest on life insurance policies, endowment or annuity contracts owned by the taxpayer and covering former officers and employees of, and persons formerly financially interest in, any trade or business currently or formerly carried on by the taxpayer. See ¶ 709.) An exception to this rule applies to contracts purchased before June 20, '86, and (for contracts purchased after that date) to a limited number of "key person" policies. In addition, for interest paid or accrued after '95 and before '99 on debt incurred before '96 on post-June 20, '86 contracts (before '97 on contracts entered into in '94 or '95), the prohibition was phased in.

(FTC 2d/FIN ¶ H-4035 *et seq.*, ¶ H-4109, ¶ K-5351, ¶ L-3402; USTR ¶ 2644; TaxDesk ¶ 27,855 *et seq.*, ¶ 30,402, ¶ 31,681, ¶ 31,684)

New Law. Deductibility of premiums for life insurance policies, endowment, and annuity contracts. The '97 Act repeals the prohibition on the deduction of premiums on life insurance policies, described above, and replaces it with a more expansive prohibition on the deduction of premiums for life insurance policies, endowment, and annuity contracts. Specifically, with the exceptions noted below, the '97 Act prohibits a deduction for premiums on any life insurance policy, or endowment or annuity contract, if the taxpayer is directly or indirectly a beneficiary under the policy or contract. (Code Sec. 264(a)(1) as amended by '97 Act §1084(a)(1))

However, the above deduction prohibition does not apply to: (Code Sec. 264(b) as amended by '97 Act §1084(a)(2))

. . . any annuity contract described in Code Sec. 72(s)(5) (relating to certain qualified pension plans, certain retirement annuities, individual retirement annuities and qualified funding assets) (Code Sec. 264(b)(1)); and

. . . any annuity contract to which Code Sec. 72(u) (governing treatment of annuity contracts held by other than natural persons) applies. (Code Sec. 264(b)(2))

In other words, the premium deduction limitation of Code Sec. 264(a)(1) does not apply to premiums with respect to any annuity contract described in Code Sec. 72(s)(5) nor to premiums with respect to any annuity to which Code Sec. 72(u) applies. (Com Rept, see ¶ 5161)

Deductibility of interest on debt incurred on company-owned life insurance, endowment or annuity contracts. The '97 Act removes Code Sec. 264(a)(4)'s restriction regarding officers or employees of the taxpayer, or persons financially interested in any trade or business carried on by the taxpayer, described above. (The '97 Act also removes Code Sec. 264(a)(4)'s restriction, retroactively added by the Act [see above], regarding former officers and employees of, and persons formerly financially interested in, any trade or business currently or formerly carried on by the taxpayer.) As a result, while retaining the exception for pre-June 20, '86 contracts and the limited exception for later "key person policies" (as well as the transitional phase-in rules noted above), the '97 Act prohibits a deduction for interest paid or accrued on any indebtedness with respect to one or more life insurance policies owned by the taxpayer covering the life of any individual, or any endowment or annuity contracts owned by the taxpayer covering any individual. (Code Sec. 264(a)(4) as amended by '97 Act §1084(b)(1)) Thus, the '97 Act limits interest deductibility in the case of a contract covering any individual in whom the taxpayer has an insurable interest when the contract is first issued under applicable state law, except as otherwise provided under pre-'97 Act law with respect to key persons and pre-June 20, '86 contracts. (Com Rept, see ¶ 5161)

The reason for the expansion of the prohibitions is that, under state laws, businesses are treated as having insurable interests in the lives of their debtors, as well as in the lives of individuals with other relationships to the taxpayer such as shareholders, employees or officers. In addition, insurable interest laws in many states have been expanded in recent years, and states could decide in the future to expand further the range of persons in whom a taxpayer has an insurable interest. For example, a business could purchase cash value life insurance on the lives of its debtors, and increase the investment in these contracts as the debt diminishes and even after the debt is repaid. If a mortgage lender can (under applicable state law and banking regulations) buy a cash value life insurance policy on the lives of mortgage borrowers, the lender may be able to deduct premiums or interest on debt with respect to such a contract, if no other deduction disallowance rule or principle of tax law applies to limit the deductions. The premiums or interest could be deductible even after the individual's mortgage loan is sold to another lender or to a mortgage pool. If the loan were sold to a second lender, the second lender might also be able to buy a cash value life insurance contract on the life of the same borrower, and to deduct premiums or interest with respect to that contract. The '97 Act addresses this issue by providing that no deduction is allowed for premiums on any life insurance policy, or endowment or annuity contract, if the taxpayer is directly or indirectly a beneficiary under the policy or contract, and by providing that no deduction is allowed for interest paid or accrued on any indebtedness with respect to a life insurance policy, or endowment or annuity contract, covering the life of any individual, except as otherwise provided under pre-'97 Act law with respect to key persons and pre-June 20, '86 contracts. (Com Rept, see ¶ 5161)

For treatment of the interest disallowed under the rules described above as a death benefit excludable from gross income where the underlying life insurance contract has been transferred for valuable consideration, see ¶ 711.

☐ **Effective:** Contracts issued after June 8, '97, in tax years ending after that date. Any material increase in the death benefit or other material change in the contract is treated as a new contract. However, the addition of covered lives is treated as a new contract only with respect to those additional covered lives. For purposes of these effective date rules, an increase in the death benefit under a policy or contract issued in connection with a lapse described in Sec. 501(d)(2) of the Health Insurance Portability and Accountability Act of '96 isn't treated as a new contract. ('97 Act §1084(d))

The amendment of Code Sec. 264(a)(4), described above, is treated as having been enacted immediately after the amendment of Code Sec. 264(a)(4) by Sec. 1602(f)(1) of the '97 Act (discussed at ¶ 709). ('97 Act §1600)

¶ 711. Nondeductible interest on transferred company-owned life insurance policies taken into account in determining amount of excludible death benefits under those policies

Code Sec. 101(a)(2), as amended by '97 Act § 1084(b)(2)
Generally effective: Contracts issued after June 8, '97
Committee Reports, see ¶ 5161

Under Code Sec. 101(a), with various exceptions, benefits paid under a life insurance contract by reason of the death of the insured are not includible in the gross income of the recipient. FTC 2d/FIN ¶ J-4700 *et seq.*; USTR ¶ 1014 *et seq.*; TaxDesk ¶ 14,850 *et seq.* One of the exceptions governs the treatment of death benefits paid under a life insurance contract if the contract, or any interest in the contract, was transferred for valuable consideration. In this case, under Code Sec. 101(a)(2), the death benefits paid on the life insurance contract are excludable from gross income only to the extent of the actual value of the consideration paid by the transferee to acquire the contract (or interest), plus "the premiums and other amounts" paid by the transferee after the transfer. (FTC 2d/FIN ¶ J-4729 *et seq.*; USTR ¶ 1014.02; TaxDesk ¶ 14,877 *et seq.*)

New Law. The '97 Act amends Code Sec. 101(a)(2) to provide that the term "other amounts," as used in that section, includes interest paid or accrued by the transferee on indebtedness with respect to a life insurance contract or any interest in a life insurance contract that was transferred for valuable consideration, if the interest paid or accrued is not allowable as a deduction by reason of Code Sec. 264(a)(4). (Code Sec. 101(a)(2) as amended by '97 Act §1084(b)(2))

> *observation:* As amended by the '97 Act, Code Sec. 264(a)(4) prohibits a deduction for interest paid or accrued on any indebtedness with respect to one or more life insurance policies owned by the taxpayer covering the life of any individual, or any endowment or annuity contracts owned by the taxpayer covering any individual. See ¶ 710.

FTC 2d References are to Federal Tax Coordinator 2d
FIN References are to RIA's Analysis of Federal Taxes: Income
USTR References are to United States Tax Reporter: Income, Estate & Gift, and Excise
PCA References are to Pension Coordinator and Pension & Benefits Expert/Advisor
PE References are to Pension and Profit Sharing 2nd
EP References are to Estate Planning & Taxation Coordinator and Estate Planning Advisor

Thus, under the '97 Act, in the case of a transfer for valuable consideration of a life insurance contract or any interest in a life insurance contract described in Code Sec. 101(a)(2), the amount of the death benefit excluded from gross income under Code Sec. 101(a) may not exceed an amount equal to the sum of the actual value of the consideration, premiums, interest disallowed as a deduction under Code Sec. 264(a)(4) as amended by the '97 Act, and other amounts later paid by the transferee. (Com Rept, see ¶ 5161)

☐ **Effective:** Contracts issued after June 8, '97, in tax years ending after that date. Any material increase in the death benefit or other material change in the contract is treated as a new contract. However, the addition of covered lives is treated as a new contract only with respect to those additional covered lives. For purposes of these effective date rules, an increase in the death benefit under a policy or contract issued in connection with a lapse described in Sec. 501(d)(2) of the Health Insurance Portability and Accountability Act of '96 isn't treated as a new contract. ('97 Act §1084(d))

¶ 712. For company-owned life insurance (COLI) rules, noncorporate "key person" definition clarified to refer to taxpayer, not employer

Code Sec. 264(d)(4)(B), as amended by '97 Act § 1602(f)(3)
Code Sec. 264(d), redesignated by '97 Act § 1084(a)(2)
Generally effective: Interest paid or accrued after Oct. 13, '95
Committee Reports, see ¶ 5377

For interest paid or accrued after Oct. 13, '95, Code Sec. 264(a)(4) prohibits a deduction for interest paid or accrued on any indebtedness with respect to one or more life insurance policies or annuity or endowment contracts owned by the taxpayer covering any individual who is (1) an officer or employee of, or (2) is financially interested in, any trade or business carried on by the taxpayer. (This is the "company-owned life insurance," or COLI, rule.)

🖋️ *caution:* The '97 Act retroactively expands Code Sec. 264(a)(4)'s interest prohibition to cover interest on life insurance policies, endowment or annuity contracts owned by the taxpayer and covering former officers and employees of, and persons formerly financially interest in, any trade or business currently or formerly carried on by the taxpayer. See ¶ 709.

An exception is provided for interest on indebtedness with respect to life insurance policies or annuity or endowment contracts covering up to 20 key persons, subject to an interest rate cap. A key person includes a 20% owner. If the taxpayer isn't a corporation, Code Sec. 264(d)(4)(B), as in effect before the '97 Act, defined 20% owner as any person who owns 20% or more of the capital or profits interest in the "employer." However, the "Blue book" explanation of the change—the General Explanation of Tax Legislation Enacted in the 104th Congress, prepared by the staff of the Joint Committee on Taxation—indicates that "taxpayer" was intended rather than "employer."(FTC 2d/FIN ¶ K-5353; USTR ¶ 2644; TaxDesk ¶ 31,682)

New Law. The '97 Act redesignates Code Sec. 264(d) as Code Sec. 264(e). ('97 Act §1084(a)(2))

The '97 Act retroactively changes the word "employer" to the word "taxpayer" in Code Sec. 264(e)(4)(B)'s (as redesignated) definition of 20% owner. (Code Sec. 264(d)(4)(B) as amended by '97 Act §1602(f)(3)); (Code Sec. 264(d) redesignated by '97 Act §1084(a)(2))

The change clarifies that, in determining a key person, if the taxpayer isn't a corporation, a 20% owner is an individual who directly owns 20% or more of the capital or profits interest of the taxpayer. (Com Rept, see ¶ 5377)

☐ **Effective:** For interest paid or accrued after Oct. 13, '95, subject to the phase-in rules of Sec. 501(c)(2) of the '96 Health Insurance Portability and Accountability Act. ('97 Act §1602(i))

The amendment of Code Sec. 264(d)(4)(B) is treated as having been enacted immediately before the redesignation of Code Sec. 264(d) as Code Sec. 264(e). ('97 Act §1600)

¶ 713. "Lapse" safe harbor rules for single-premium and "plan of purchase" life insurance contract rules corrected to refer to lapses occurring because of failure to pay premiums, rather than failure to pay premiums occurring because of lapses

Code Sec. 264(a)(2), '97 Act § 1602(f)(5)
Code Sec. 264(c)(1), '97 Act § 1602(f)(5)
Generally effective: Interest paid or accrued after Oct. 13, '95
Committee Reports, see ¶ 5379

No deduction is allowed for any amount paid or accrued on indebtedness incurred or continued to purchase or carry a single premium life insurance, endowment or annuity contract. A single premium contract is one on which substantially all the premiums are paid within four years from the date on which the contract is purchased, or one with respect to which an amount has been deposited with the insurer for payment of a substantial number of future premiums on the contract.

No deduction is allowed for interest on debt incurred or continued to purchase or carry a life insurance, endowment, or annuity contract pursuant to a plan of purchase that contemplates the systematic direct or indirect borrowing of part or all of the increases in the cash value of the contract. However, this rule does not apply with respect to interest on bona fide debt that is part of such a plan, if no part of four of the annual premiums due during the first seven years is paid by means of debt (the "4-out-

FTC 2d References are to Federal Tax Coordinator 2d
FIN References are to RIA's Analysis of Federal Taxes: Income
USTR References are to United States Tax Reporter: Income, Estate & Gift, and Excise
PCA References are to Pension Coordinator and Pension & Benefits Expert/Advisor
PE References are to Pension and Profit Sharing 2nd
EP References are to Estate Planning & Taxation Coordinator and Estate Planning Advisor

Research Institute of America 207

of-7" rule).

Under Sec. 501(d)(2) of the '96 Health Insurance Portability and Accountability Act, a contract may not be treated as a single premium contract, or as failing to meet the 4-out-of-7 rule "solely by reason of no additional premiums being received under the contract by reason of a lapse occurring after Oct. 13, '95." (FTC 2d/FIN ¶ K-5570 *et seq.*, ¶ K-5580 *et seq.*, ¶ J-5307.1; USTR ¶ 2644; TaxDesk ¶ 31,685, ¶ 31,720 *et seq.*, ¶ 31,750 *et seq.*)

New Law. The '97 Act retroactively changes the language of Sec. 501(d)(2) of the '96 Health Insurance Portability and Accountability Act by removing the phrase, "solely by reason of no additional premiums being received under the contract by reason of a lapse occurring after Oct. 13, '95," and replacing it with the phrase, "solely by reason of a lapse occurring after Oct. 13, '95 by reason of no additional premiums being received under the contract." ('96 Health Act § 501(d)(2) as amended by '97 Act § 1602(f)(5))

The change clarifies that the 4-out-of-7 rule and the single premium rule are not to apply solely by reason of a lapse occurring after Oct. 13, '95 by reason of no additional premiums being received under the contract. (Com Rept, see ¶ 5379)

☐ **Effective:** Interest paid or accrued after Oct. 13, '95. ('97 Act §1602(i))

¶ 714. Interest paid or accrued after Dec. 31, '95, on pre-June 21, '86 COLI contracts is subject to '96 Health Act grandfather rules—conflict with Oct. 13, '95 date eliminated

Code Sec. 264(d)(2)(A), '97 Act § 1602(f)(4)
Generally effective: Interest paid or accrued after Oct. 13, '95
Committee Reports, see ¶ 5378

For interest paid or accrued after Oct. 13, '95 (subject to phase-in rules), the '96 Health Insurance Portability and Accountability Act amended Code Sec. 264(a)(4) to prohibit a deduction for interest paid or accrued on any indebtedness with respect to one or more life insurance policies or annuity or endowment contracts owned by the taxpayer covering any individual who is (1) an officer or employee of, or (2) is financially interested in, any trade or business carried on by the taxpayer. (This is the "company-owned life insurance," or COLI, rule.)

> ✐ *caution:* The '97 Act retroactively expands Code Sec. 264(a)(4)'s interest prohibition to cover interest on life insurance policies, endowment or annuity contracts owned by the taxpayer and covering former officers and employees of, and persons formerly financially interest in, any trade or business currently or formerly carried on by the taxpayer. See ¶ 709.

An exception to the above rule is provided for interest on indebtedness with respect to life insurance policies covering up to 20 key persons (as defined by Code Sec. 264(d)(3)), subject to an interest rate cap.

The above rules generally do not apply to interest on debt with respect to contracts purchased before June 21, '86. However, if the policy loan interest rate under such a contract does not provide for a fixed rate of interest, then interest on such a contract paid or accrued after Dec. 31, '95, is allowable only to the extent the rate of interest for each fixed period selected by the taxpayer does not exceed Moody's Corporate Bond Yield Average—Monthly Average Corporates, for the third month preceding the first month of the fixed period. The fixed period must be 12 months or less.

caution: The '97 Act has changed the manner in which the "fixed period selected by the taxpayer" is selected. See ¶715

Code Sec. 264(d)(2)(A), as amended by the '96 Health Insurance Portability and Accountability Act, makes the interest rate cap on key persons and pre-June 21, 86 contracts effective "with respect to interest paid or accrued for any month beginning after December 31, 1995." However, the special effective date provision in Sec. 501(c)(3) of that same '96 health insurance act makes that same interest rate cap (on key employees and pre-June 21, '86 contracts) effective with respect to interest paid or accrued after a different date—namely, Oct. 13, '95. (FTC 2d/FIN ¶ K-5354 *et seq.*; USTR ¶ 2644; TaxDesk ¶ 31,683)

New Law. The '97 Act retroactively repeals Sec. 501(c)(3) of the '96 Health Insurance Portability and Accountability Act, as of the date of its original enactment. ('97 Act § 1602(f)(4))

The repeal clarifies that the interest rate cap on key persons and pre-June 21, '86 contracts applies to interest paid or accrued for any month beginning after Dec. 31, '95, thus eliminating the discrepancy between the October and the December dates in the grandfather rule for pre-June 21, '86 contracts. (Com Rept, see ¶ 5378)

☐ **Effective:** For interest paid or accrued after Oct. 13, '95, subject to the phase-in rules of Sec. 501(c)(2) of the '96 Health Insurance Portability and Accountability Act. ('97 Act §1602(i))

¶ 715. "Applicable period" changed for interest-rate cap rules on pre-'86 key person life insurance contracts

Code Sec. 264(d)(2)(B)(ii), as amended by '97 Act § 1602(f)(2)
Code Sec. 264(d), redesignated by '97 Act § 1084(a)(2)
Generally effective: Interest paid or accrued after Oct. 13, '95
Committee Reports, see ¶ 5376

For debt on life insurance contracts covering key persons (as defined by Code Sec. 264(d)(3)) bought before June 21, '86, no deduction is allowed for interest paid or accrued for any month beginning after Dec. 31, '95 to the extent the amount of that in-

FTC 2d References are to Federal Tax Coordinator 2d
FIN References are to RIA's Analysis of Federal Taxes: Income
USTR References are to United States Tax Reporter: Income, Estate & Gift, and Excise
PCA References are to Pension Coordinator and Pension & Benefits Expert/Advisor
PE References are to Pension and Profit Sharing 2nd
EP References are to Estate Planning & Taxation Coordinator and Estate Planning Advisor

terest exceeds the amount that would have been allowable using the applicable rate of interest for that month.

For purposes of this rule, under Code Sec. 264(d)(2)(B)(ii)(II), if the contract provides for a variable rate of interest, the applicable rate of interest for any month in an "applicable period" is the Moody's rate for the third month before the first month in that period. For purposes of this rule, under pre-'97 Act law, the applicable period for a contract was a period that the taxpayer had to elect on its income tax return for its first tax year ending on or after Oct. 13, '95. However, the applicable period could be for any number of months (not greater than 12) specified in the election. The applicable period couldn't be changed by the taxpayer without IRS consent. (FTC 2d/FIN ¶ K-5355; USTR ¶ 2644; TaxDesk ¶ 31,683)

New Law. The '97 Act redesignates Code Sec. 264(d) as Code Sec. 264(e). ('97 Act §1084(a)(2))

The '97 Act retroactively removes the rules, described above, that determine the "applicable period" for purposes of Code Sec. 264(e)(2)(B)(ii)(II) (as redesignated by the '97 Act). The Act retroactively substitutes the following rule: for purposes of Code Sec. 264(e)(2)(B)(ii)(II) (as redesignated), the term "applicable period" means the 12-month period beginning on the date the policy is issued (and each successive 12-month period after that) unless the taxpayer elects a number of months (not greater than 12) other than that 12-month period to be its applicable period. That election may not be later than the 90th day after Aug. 5, '97 and, if made, applies to the taxpayer's first tax year ending on or after Oct. 13, '95, and all later tax years unless revoked with the consent of IRS. (Code Sec. 264(d)(2)(B)(ii) as amended by '97 Act §1602(f)(2)); (Code Sec. 264(d) redesignated by '97 Act §1084(a)(2))

In other words, an election of an applicable period for purposes of applying the interest rate for a variable rate contract can be made no later than the 90th day after Aug. 5, '97, and applies to the taxpayer's first tax year ending on or after Oct. 13, '95. If no election is made, the applicable period is the policy year. The policy year is the 12-month period beginning on the anniversary date of the policy. (Com Rept, see ¶ 5376)

action alert: For purposes of deducting interest on debt incurred with respect to company-owned life insurance policies, endowment or annuity contracts on key persons, the election to use an "applicable period" different from the 12-month policy year period specified by Code Sec. 264(e)(2)(B)(ii) (as redesignated) must be made no later than the 90th day after Aug. 5, '97.

☐ **Effective:** For interest paid or accrued after Oct. 13, '95, subject to the phase-in rules of Sec. 501(c)(2) of the '96 Health Insurance Portability and Accountability Act. ('97 Act §1602(i))

The amendment of Code Sec. 264(d)(2)(B)(ii) is treated as having been enacted immediately before the redesignation of Code Sec. 264(d) as Code Sec. 264(e). ('97 Act §1600)

¶ 800. Depreciation and Expensing

Depreciation

¶ 801. Property qualifying for the income forecast method of depreciation is limited; rent-to-own consumer durables are ineligible

Code Sec. 167(g)(6), as amended by '97 Act § 1086(a)
Generally effective: Property placed in service after Aug. 5, '97
Committee Reports, see ¶ 5163

The income forecast method of depreciation is permissible for some property which is either expressly excluded, under the Code, from depreciation under the Modified Accelerated Cost Recovery System (MACRS) or for which the taxpayer elects to not apply MACRS. Under the income forecast method, the depreciation deduction for a tax year for a property is determined by multiplying the cost of the property (less estimated salvage value) by a fraction, the numerator of which is the income generated by the property during the year and the denominator of which is the total forecasted or estimated income from the property over the property's useful life or the period ending with the end of the 10th tax year beginning after the tax year the property was placed in service. If the full cost of the property hasn't been recovered by the beginning of that 10th year, any remaining basis is deducted in that 10th year. There are special rules for costs incurred after property is placed in service and for certain types of income. Also, in some instances, a "look-back" calculation applies and either pays to the taxpayer or charges the taxpayer with interest arising from the difference in the timing of depreciation deductions caused by the difference between the estimated and actual income from the property.

Under pre-'97 Act law, the question of which types of property were eligible for the income forecast method was a matter of some judicial disagreement. For instance, the Tax Court and the Fifth Circuit held that rent-to-own consumer durables weren't permitted to be depreciated under the income forecast method. On the other hand, the Tenth Circuit held that, if certain conditions were met, the income forecast method could be permissibly applied to rent-to-own consumer durables. (FTC 2d/FIN ¶ L-8214, ¶ L-10704, ¶ L-10704.1, ¶ L-10705 *et seq.*; USTR ¶ 1674.100, ¶ 1684; TaxDesk ¶ 26,804, ¶ 26,805 *et seq.*)

New Law. Congress believes that the availability of the income forecast method should be limited to instances where the economic depreciation of the property cannot be adequately reflected by the passage of time alone or where the income stream from the property is sufficiently unpredictable or uneven such that the application of another depreciation method may result in the distortion of income. (Com Rept, see ¶ 5163)

FTC 2d References are to Federal Tax Coordinator 2d
FIN References are to RIA's Analysis of Federal Taxes: Income
USTR References are to United States Tax Reporter: Income, Estate & Gift, and Excise
PCA References are to Pension Coordinator and Pension & Benefits Expert/Advisor
PE References are to Pension and Profit Sharing 2nd
EP References are to Estate Planning & Taxation Coordinator and Estate Planning Advisor

Thus, the '97 Act limits the types of property for which the income forecast method (or any similar method) of depreciation may be used to the following: (Code Sec. 167(g)(6) as amended by '97 Act §1086(a))

(1) any motion picture film or video tape, (Code Sec. 167(g)(6)(A)),

(2) sound recordings, (Code Sec. 168(g)(6)(A)),

(3) copyrights, (Code Sec. 168(g)(6)(B)),

(4) books, (Code Sec. 168(g)(6)(C)),

(5) patents, (Code Sec. 168(g)(6)(D)), and

(6) other property specified in regs. (Code Sec. 168(g)(6)(E))

> **observation:** Thus, the '97 Act codifies existing case law and IRS rulings which approved the income forecast method for depreciation of the property listed in Code Sec. 167(g)(6)(A) through (D) (items (1) through (5) above).

An income forecast or similar method may not be used with respect to any amortizable Code Sec. 197 intangible, as defined in Code Sec. 197(c). (Code Sec. 168(g)(6)) Thus, the income forecast method is not applicable to property to which Code Sec. 197 applies. (Com Rept, see ¶ 5163) For what is an amortizable Code Sec. 197 intangible, see FTC 2d/FIN ¶ L-7951.1; USTR ¶ 1974; TaxDesk ¶ 26,902.

Congress clarified that the income forecast method is available for television films and taped shows. Congress expects that IRS will exercise the authority, referred to above, to specify other property eligible for the income forecast method, to allow the method to be available to property (1) the economic depreciation of which cannot be adequately measured by the passage of time alone or (2) the income from which is sufficiently unpredictable or uneven so as to result in the distortion of income. The mere fact that property is subject to a lease shouldn't make the property eligible for the income forecast method. (Com Rept, see ¶ 5163)

Also, Congress said that consumer durables subject to rent-to-own contracts are not eligible for the income forecast method. (Com Rept, see ¶ 5163)

For discussion of the recovery period and MACRS class life for consumer durables subject to rent-to-own contracts, see ¶ 803.

> **observation:** The exclusion by the '97 Act of consumer durables subject to rent-to-own contracts from eligibility for the income forecast method effectively overturns the Tenth Circuit decision (discussed above) which had held that the method could, in appropriate situations, be applied to rent-to-own consumer durables.

☐ **Effective:** Property placed in service after Aug. 5, '97. ('97 Act §1086(c))

Research Institute of America

¶ 802. Luxury automobile depreciation limits are removed for clean-fuel vehicle property and tripled for electric vehicles

Code Sec. 280F(a)(1)(C), as amended by '97 Act § 971(a)

Generally effective: Property placed in service after Aug. 5, '97, but before Jan. 1, 2005

Committee Reports, see ¶ 5094

The maximum amount a taxpayer may claim as a depreciation deduction for any business passenger automobile is limited by Code Sec. 280F, which provides dollar limitations on the amount of the depreciation deduction which is indexed for inflation after Oct. '87. For automobiles subject to these limitations which are first placed in service during calendar year '97, the depreciation deduction is limited to: $3,160 for the first tax year of the recovery period, $5,000 for the second tax year of the recovery period, $3,050 for the third tax year of the recovery period and $1,775 for each succeeding tax year in the recovery period. (FTC 2d/FIN ¶ L-10004, ¶ L-10012; USTR ¶ 280F4; TaxDesk ¶ 26,761, ¶ 26,767)

> **observation:** The term "luxury" (as in luxury automobiles) appears in the statutory heading of Code Sec. 280F, but not in the statute's tests. The term isn't defined in Code Sec. 280F and there is no rule expressed in terms of "luxury".

New Law. Congress believed that the price of a clean-burning fuel vehicle or an electric vehicle doesn't necessarily represent the purchase of a luxury. Rather, the higher price of those vehicles often represents the cost of the technology required to provide an automobile designed to provide certain environmental benefits. Therefore, for certain clean-burning fuel vehicles and electric vehicles, Congress believed it appropriate to modify the limitation on depreciation that applies to passenger automobiles. (Com Rept, see ¶ 5094)

Qualified clean-fuel vehicle property. Where "qualified clean-fuel vehicle property" (defined below) is installed on a passenger automobile which is propelled by a fuel which isn't a "clean-burning fuel" (defined below), and the purpose of the installation is to permit the vehicle to be propelled by a "clean-burning fuel," the dollar limits on depreciation deductions for automobiles don't apply to the cost of the installed "qualified clean burning vehicle property." (Code Sec. 280F(a)(1)(C)(i) as amended by '97 Act §971(a))

> **observation:** Code Sec. 280F provides no definition of "qualified clean burning vehicle property." Furthermore, the term is not mentioned in the

FTC 2d References are to Federal Tax Coordinator 2d
FIN References are to RIA's Analysis of Federal Taxes: Income
USTR References are to United States Tax Reporter: Income, Estate & Gift, and Excise
PCA References are to Pension Coordinator and Pension & Benefits Expert/Advisor
PE References are to Pension and Profit Sharing 2nd
EP References are to Estate Planning & Taxation Coordinator and Estate Planning Advisor

committee reports which explain the enactment of Code Sec. 280F(a)(C)(1)(i). It would therefore seem that the term is used in error and that the intended term is "qualified clean-fuel vehicle property." That term is used elsewhere in Code Sec. 280F(a)(1)(C)(i) (see above) and, as discussed immediately below, is a defined term.

"Qualified clean-fuel vehicle property" (as defined in pre-'97 Act Code Sec. 179A(c)(1)(A)) is property which has the following characteristics:

. . . the property is acquired for use by the taxpayer, and not for resale;

. . . the original use of the property begins with the taxpayer;

. . . the motor vehicle of which the property is a part meets any applicable Federal or State emission standards for each fuel by which the vehicle is designed to be propelled;

. . . the property meets applicable Federal and State emissions-related certification, testing, and warranty requirements;

. . . the property ("retrofit parts and components") is an engine (or modification of an engine) which may use a "clean-burning fuel" *or* is used in the storage or delivery to the engine of "clean-burning fuel" or in the exhaust of gases from combustion of "clean-burning fuel," see FTC 2d/FIN ¶ K-7012; USTR ¶ 179A4; TaxDesk ¶ 30,704 (Code Sec. 280F(a)(C)(1)(i))

"Clean-burning fuel" (as defined in pre-'97 Act Code Sec. 179A(e)(1)) is either: (1) natural gas, (2) liquefied natural gas, (3) liquefied petroleum gas, (4) hydrogen, (5) electricity or (6) any other fuel at least 85% of which is one or more of the following: methanol, ethanol, any other alcohol, or ether. (Code Sec. 280F(a)(1)(C)(i))

Thus, the '97 Act generally modifies pre-'97 Act law by applying the pre-'97 Act depreciation deduction limitation of Code Sec. 280F(a)(1)(A) to that portion of the vehicle's cost not represented by the installed qualified clean-burning fuel property. The taxpayer may claim an amount otherwise allowable as a depreciation deduction on the installed qualified-clean burning fuel property, without regard to the Code Sec. 280F(a)(1)(A) limitation. (Com Rept, see ¶ 5094)

> *Illustration:* A taxpayer purchases a clean-burning fuel vehicle for $43,000. Had the taxpayer purchased the identical vehicle, without having had certain components replaced to qualify it as clean burning, the price paid would have been $39,000. The cost of the qualified retrofit parts and components is $4,000. The depreciation that the taxpayer may claim for this vehicle in any year is the sum of (1) the depreciation for the $39,000 portion as limited by the dollar limitations on depreciation deductions for automobiles (as under pre-'97 Act law) and (2) the depreciation that can be claimed under Code Sec. 168 for the $4,000 worth of qualified retrofit parts and components. (Com Rept, see ¶ 5094)

Purpose built passenger vehicles. For a "purpose built passenger vehicle," each of the annual limitations on depreciation deductions for automobiles is tripled. (Code

Sec. 280F(a)(1)(C)(ii))

A "purpose built passenger vehicle" is a passenger vehicle produced by an original equipment manufacturer and designed so that the vehicle may be propelled primarily by electricity. (Code Sec. 280F(a)(1)(C)(ii))

The tripled limitations are computed as follows:

(1) the base-year limitation amounts of $2,560 for the first tax year in the recovery period, $4,100 for the second tax year in the recovery period, $2,450 for the third tax year in the recovery period and $1,475 for each succeeding tax year in the recovery period are tripled to $7,680, $12,300, $7,350 and $4,425 respectively and

(2) then adjusted for inflation after Oct. '87 by the automobile component of the Consumer Price Index. (Com Rept, see ¶ 5094)

☐ **Effective:** Property placed in service after Aug. 5, '97, but before Jan. 1, 2005. ('97 Act §971(b))

¶ 803. Qualified rent-to-own property is designated as MACRS 3-year property with a 4-year class life

Code Sec. 168(3(A)(iii), as amended by '97 Act § 1086(b)(1)
Code Sec. 168(g)(3)(B), as amended by '97 Act § 1086(b)(2)
Code Sec. 168(i)(14), as amended by '97 Act § 1086(b)(3)
Generally effective: Property placed in service after Aug. 5, '97
Committee Reports, see ¶ 5163

Under the Modified Accelerated Cost Recovery System (MACRS) under Code Sec. 168, property is grouped into classes. A property's class determines, among other things, its recovery period under the general depreciation system (GDS) of Code Sec. 168. Classes are usually assigned to property by reference to the property's "class life" (i.e., anticipated useful life), as determined under the "class life" system referred to in Code Sec. 168(i)(1). However, the Code specifically assigns some types of property to a class without reference to the property's class life.

Taxpayers may be required or may elect to depreciate property under an alternative depreciation system (ADS) instead of under the GDS. For most personal property, the recovery period under the ADS is equal to the property's class life.

Property in the 3-year property class is property with a class life of 4-years or less, and also includes some types of property specifically assigned to that class by the Code. Property in the 5-year property class is property with a class life of more than 4 years, but less than 10 years, and also includes some types of property specifically assigned to that class by the Code.

FTC 2d References are to Federal Tax Coordinator 2d
FIN References are to RIA's Analysis of Federal Taxes: Income
USTR References are to United States Tax Reporter: Income, Estate & Gift, and Excise
PCA References are to Pension Coordinator and Pension & Benefits Expert/Advisor
PE References are to Pension and Profit Sharing 2nd
EP References are to Estate Planning & Taxation Coordinator and Estate Planning Advisor

Under pre-'97 Act law, IRS took the position that rent-to-own consumer durables had a class life of 9 years. Accordingly, this property (1) had to be treated as 5-year property, for purposes of determining the recovery period under the general depreciation system, and (2) had a recovery period of 9 years for ADS purposes. (FTC 2d/FIN ¶ L-8204, ¶ L-8205, ¶ L-9403; USTR ¶ 1684.01, ¶ 1684.03; TaxDesk ¶ 26,623, ¶ 26,624, ¶ 26,753)

New Law. Under the '97 Act, "qualified rent-to-own property" (defined below) is assigned to the 3-year property class. (Code Sec. 168(e)(3)(A)(iii) as amended by '97 Act §1086(b)(1))

> **observation:** Thus, for GDS purposes, the recovery period of qualified rent-to-own property is 3 years.

Also, qualified rent-to-own property is assigned a class life, for purposes of determining the property's ADS recovery period, of 4 years. (Code Sec. 168(g)(3)(B) as amended by '97 Act §1086(b)(2)) Congress says that 4 years is the class life of qualified rent-to-own property for MACRS purposes. (Com Rept, see ¶ 5163)

> **observation:** An example of a MACRS purpose (other than determination of recovery period for GDS or ADS purposes) for which a property's class life is relevant is the determination of eligibility for the short-term lease exception to treatment as tax-exempt use property, see FTC 2d/FIN ¶ L-9616; USTR ¶ 1684.06.

"Qualified rent-to-own property" is property held by a "rent-to-own dealer" (defined below) for purposes of being subject to a "rent-to-own contract" (defined below). (Code Sec. 168(i)(14)(A) as amended by '97 Act §1086(b)(3))

A "rent-to-own dealer" is a person that, in the ordinary course of business, regularly enters into rent-to-own contracts with customers for the use of "consumer property" (defined below), if a substantial portion of those contracts terminate and the property is returned to that person before the receipt of all payments required to transfer ownership of the property from that person to the customer. (Code Sec. 168(i)(14)(B))

A "rent-to-own contract" is any lease for the use of "consumer property" (defined below) between a rent-to-own dealer and a customer who is an individual, where the lease satisfies *all* of the following requirements: (Code Sec. 168(i)(14)(D))

... is titled "Rent-to-Own Agreement" or "Lease Agreement with Ownership Option" or uses other similar language, (Code Sec. 168(i)(14)(D)(i)),

... provides for level (or decreasing where no payment is less than 40% of the largest payment), regular periodic payments (for a payment period which is a week or month), (Code Sec. 168(i)(14)(D)(ii)),

... provides that legal title to the property remains with the rent-to-own dealer until the customer makes all the payments described in Code Sec. 168(i)(14)(D)(ii) (above) or early purchase payments required under the contract to acquire legal title to the item of property, (Code Sec. 168(i)(14)(D)(iii)),

... provides a beginning date and a maximum period of time for which the contract may be in effect that doesn't exceed 156 weeks or 36 months from that beginning date (including renewals or options to extend), (Code Sec. 168(i)(14)(D)(iv)),

... provides for payments within the 156-week or 36-month period that, in the aggregate, generally exceed the normal retail price of the consumer property plus interest, (Code Sec. 168(i)(14)(D)(v)),

... provides for payments under the contract that, in the aggregate, don't exceed $10,000 per item of consumer property, (Code Sec. 168(i)(14)(D)(vi)),

... provides that the customer doesn't have any legal obligation to make all the payments referred to in Code Sec. 168(i)(14)(D)(ii) (above) set forth under the contract, and that at the end of each payment period the customer may either continue to use the consumer property by making the payment for the next payment period or return the property to the rent-to-own dealer in good working order, in which case the customer doesn't incur any further obligations under the contract and isn't entitled to a return of any payments previously made under the contract, (Code Sec. 168(i)(14)(D)(vii)), *and*

... provides that the customer has no right to sell, sublease, mortgage, pawn, pledge, encumber, or otherwise dispose of the consumer property until all the payments stated in the contract have been made. (Code Sec. 168(i)(14)(D)(viii))

"Consumer property" is tangible personal property of a type generally used within the home for personal use, (Code Sec. 168(i)(14)(C)), but not business use. (Com Rept, see ¶ 5163) Congress understands that certain rent-to-own property, including computer and peripheral equipment, may be used in the home for either personal or business purposes, and the taxpayer may not be aware of how its customers may use the property. Thus, so as not to increase the administrative burdens of taxpayers, Congress intends that if dual-use property doesn't represent a significant portion of a taxpayer's leasing property, and if other leasing property predominantly is qualified rent-to-own property, the dual-use property is to be treated as qualified rent-to-own property. However, if the dual-use property represents a significant portion of the taxpayer's leasing property, it is intended that the burden of proof be placed on the taxpayer to show that the property is qualified rent-to-own property. (Com Rept, see ¶ 5163)

Congress says that consumer durables subject to rent-to-own contracts are generally described in Rev Proc 95-38. (Com Rept, see ¶ 5163) For discussion of Rev Proc 95-38, see FTC 2d/FIN ¶s J-2209.1, J-2209.2; USTR ¶ 614.086; TaxDesk ¶ 12,113.1.

Congress also clarifies that the 3-year recovery period for qualified rent-to-own property applies only to property subject to leases and that no inference is intended as to whether any arrangement is a lease for tax purposes. (Com Rept, see ¶ 5163)

☐ **Effective:** Property placed in service after Aug. 5, '97. ('97 Act §1086(c))

FTC 2d References are to Federal Tax Coordinator 2d
FIN References are to RIA's Analysis of Federal Taxes: Income
USTR References are to United States Tax Reporter: Income, Estate & Gift, and Excise
PCA References are to Pension Coordinator and Pension & Benefits Expert/Advisor
PE References are to Pension and Profit Sharing 2nd
EP References are to Estate Planning & Taxation Coordinator and Estate Planning Advisor

¶ 804. Amounts expensed as the cost of qualified clean-fuel vehicle property and qualified clean-fuel refueling property are items considered to be depreciation for purposes of computing recomputed basis in determining Code Sec. 1245 recapture

Code Sec. 1245(a)(2)(C), as amended by '97 Act § 1604(a)(3)
Generally effective: Property placed in service after June 30, '93

The Energy Policy Act of '92 (P.L. 102-486) provided an election to expense the cost of certain qualified clean-fuel vehicle property and qualified clean-fuel refueling property under Code Sec. 179A. Under pre-'97 Act law, there was no specific rule indicating that an amount expensed with respect to qualified clean-fuel vehicle property and qualified clean-fuel refueling property was considered to be an item of depreciation for purposes of computing recomputed basis in determining Code Sec. 1245 recapture. (FTC 2d/FIN ¶ I-10204; USTR ¶ 12,454.05; TaxDesk ¶ 22,308.3)

New Law. The '97 Act retroactively provides that amounts which are expensed with respect to the cost of qualified clean-fuel vehicle property and qualified clean-fuel refueling property under Code Sec. 179A are items of depreciation that affect the computation of recomputed basis in determining Code Sec. 1245 recapture. (Code Sec. 1245(a)(2)(C) as amended by '97 Act §1604(a)(3))

⚡*observation:* Thus, if a taxpayer realized a gain upon the disposition of real property whose basis had been reduced by a deduction under Code Sec. 179A and the taxpayer did not treat the Code Sec. 179A expense as an item of depreciation that affected the computation of recomputed basis for the recapture rules, he should apply the recapture rules (treating the Code Sec. 179A expense as an item of depreciation affecting the computation of recomputed basis) to determine whether he should have reported any of the gain as ordinary income. If the application of the recapture rules results in a portion (or all) of the gain being recharacterized as ordinary income and the taxpayer previously reported that gain as capital gain, the taxpayer should consider amending his return to reflect the recharacterization of the gain as ordinary income.

☐ **Effective:** Property placed in service after June 30, '93. ('97 Act §1604(a)(4))

¶ 805. Code Sec. 1245 property includes real property whose basis has been reduced by deductions made under an election to expense the cost of qualified clean-fuel vehicle property and qualified clean-fuel refueling property

Code Sec. 1245(a)(3)(C), as amended by '97 Act § 1604(a)(3)
Generally effective: Property placed in service after June 30, '93

The Energy Policy Act of '92 (P.L. 102-486) provided an election to expense the cost of certain qualified clean-fuel vehicle property and qualified clean-fuel refueling property under Code Sec. 179A. Under pre-'97 Act law, there was no specific rule indicating that the definition of Code Sec. 1245 property included the portion of any real property whose basis had been reduced by a deduction made under an election to expense the cost of qualified clean-fuel vehicle property and qualified clean-fuel refueling property under Code Sec. 179A. (FTC 2d/FIN ¶ I-10106; USTR ¶ 12,454.01; TaxDesk ¶ 22,308.5)

New Law. The '97 Act retroactively provides that the definition of Code Sec. 1245 property includes the portion of any real property whose basis had been reduced by a deduction made under an election to expense the cost of qualified clean-fuel vehicle property and qualified clean-fuel refueling property under Code Sec. 179A. (Code Sec. 1245(a)(3)(C) as amended by '97 Act §1604(a)(3))

> *observation:* Thus, if a taxpayer realized a gain upon the disposition of real property whose basis had been reduced by a deduction under Code Sec. 179A and the taxpayer did not treat the disposition as a disposition of Code Sec. 1245 property (i.e., property subject to the recapture rules), he should apply the recapture rules to determine whether he should report any part of that gain as ordinary income. If the application of the recapture rules results in a portion (or all) of the gain being recharacterized as ordinary income and the taxpayer previously reported that gain as capital gain, the taxpayer should consider amending his return to reflect the recharacterization of the gain as ordinary income.

☐ **Effective:** Property placed in service after June 30, '93. ('97 Act §1604(a)(4))

¶ 806. Definition of Indian reservation clarified for depreciation and incremental credit purposes

Code Sec. 168(j)(6), as amended by '97 Act § 1604(c)(1)
Generally effective: Property placed in service after Dec. 31, '93
Committee Reports, see ¶ 5388

Code Sec. 168(j)(6) provides accelerated depreciation for certain property located on Indian reservations. Under pre-'97 Act law, an Indian reservation was a reservation as defined in section 3(d) of the '74 Indian Financing Act (as in effect on Aug. 10, '93) or section 4(10) of the '78 Indian Child Welfare Act (as in effect on Aug. 10, '93). (FTC 2d/FIN ¶ L-8807; USTR ¶ 1684.01; TaxDesk ¶ 26,708) Section 3(d) of the '74 Indian Financing Act includes not only officially designated Indian reservations and public domain Indian allotments, but also all "former Indian reservations in Oklahoma", which covers most of the state of Oklahoma even though parts of the for-

FTC 2d References are to Federal Tax Coordinator 2d
FIN References are to RIA's Analysis of Federal Taxes: Income
USTR References are to United States Tax Reporter: Income, Estate & Gift, and Excise
PCA References are to Pension Coordinator and Pension & Benefits Expert/Advisor
PE References are to Pension and Profit Sharing 2nd
EP References are to Estate Planning & Taxation Coordinator and Estate Planning Advisor

mer Indian reservations may no longer have a significant nexus to an Indian tribe. (Com Rept, see ¶ 5388)

In addition, the incremental Indian employment credit provided in Code Sec. 45A incorporates by reference the definition of Indian reservation provided in Code Sec. 168(j)(6) for purposes of determining who is a qualified employee under the credit. (FTC 2d/FIN ¶ L-15684; USTR ¶ 45A4; TaxDesk ¶ 38,433)

New Law. For purposes of the definition of Indian reservation in Code Sec. 168(j)(6), section 3(d) of the '74 Indian Financing Act is applied by treating the term "former Indian reservations in Oklahoma" as including only lands which are within the jurisdictional area of an Oklahoma Indian tribe (as determined by the Secretary of the Interior) and are recognized by the Secretary of the Interior as eligible for trust land status under 25 CFR Part 151 (as in effect on Aug. 5, '97). (Code Sec. 168(j)(6) as amended by '97 Act §1604(c)(1))

☐ **Effective:** Property placed in service after Dec. 31, '93, except that the portion of the definition of Indian reservation relating to "former Indian reservations in Oklahoma" does not apply: ('97 Act §1604(c)(2))

. . . with respect to property (with an applicable recovery period under Code Sec. 168(j) of six years or less) held by the taxpayer if the taxpayer claimed the benefits of accelerated depreciation under Code Sec. 168(j) with respect to the property on a return filed before Mar. 18, '97, but only if the return was the first return of tax filed for the tax year in which the property was placed in service ('97 Act §1604(c)(2)(A)), or

. . . with respect to wages for which the taxpayer claimed the benefits of the incremental Indian employment credit (Code Sec. 45A) for a tax year on a return filed before Mar. 18, '97, but only if the return was the first return of tax filed for that tax year. ('97 Act §1604(c)(2)(B))

Expensing

¶ 807. Amounts expensed as the cost of qualified clean-fuel vehicle property and qualified clean-fuel refueling property deducted in connection with clean-fuel vehicles are not capital expenditures

Code Sec. 263(a)(1)(H), as amended by '97 Act § 1604(a)(1)
Generally effective: Property placed in service after June 30, '93

The Energy Policy Act of '92 (P.L. 102-486) provided an election to expense the cost of certain qualified clean-fuel vehicle property and qualified clean-fuel refueling property under Code Sec. 179A. Under pre-'97 Act law, there was no specific rule indicating that amounts expensed with respect to qualified clean-fuel vehicle property and qualified clean-fuel refueling property were not capital expenditures. (FTC 2d/FIN ¶ L-5800 et seq.; USTR ¶ 2634; TaxDesk ¶ 26,520 et seq.)

New Law. The '97 Act makes it clear that the rule that capital expenditures are not deductible does not apply to amounts expensed with respect to the cost of qualified clean-fuel vehicle property and qualified clean-fuel refueling property. (Code Sec. 263(a)(1)(H) as amended by '97 Act §1604(a)(1))

☐ **Effective:** For property placed in service after June 30, '93. ('97 Act §1604(a)(4))

¶ 808. Election to treat certain environmental remediation costs as deductible ("brownfields")

Code Sec. 198, as added by '97 Act § 941
Generally effective: Expenditures paid or incurred after Aug. 5, '97 in tax years
ending after Aug. 5, '97
Committee Reports, see ¶ 5073

The tax treatment of environmental cleanup costs was governed by the normal tax rules relating to the deduction or capitalization of expenses. Thus, the cost was deductible if it was an ordinary and necessary expense paid or incurred in carrying on a trade or business. However, the cost had to be capitalized if it was the cost of acquiring or constructing buildings, machinery, equipment, etc., that had a useful life extending beyond the tax year, or if it resulted in a permanent improvement or betterment made to increase the value of property. The cost was deductible if for an incidental repair that merely maintained property in an ordinary, efficient operating condition, and neither materially added to the property's value nor materially prolonged its life), but it had to be capitalized if needed to *place* property in an ordinarily efficient operating condition, or if the expenditure added to the property's value, substantially prolonged its useful life, or adapted it to a new or different use. (FTC 2d/FIN ¶ L-6151; USTR ¶ 1627.117; TaxDesk ¶ 30,811)

In *Plainfield Union Water Co. v. Comm'r., (1962) 39 TC 333*, the Tax Court determined that if a taxpayer acquired property in clean condition, and contaminated the property in the course of its everyday business operations, restoring the property to its approximate condition at the time of acquisition did not result in a permanent improvement that increased the property's value, and the restoration costs were deductible. The appropriate test for determining whether cleanup expenditures increased the value of property (and thus must be capitalized) was to compare the status of the property after the expenditure with the status of the asset before the condition arose that necessitated the expenditure—i.e., before the property was contaminated by taxpayer's operations. This is called the restoration principle. (FTC 2d/FIN ¶ L-6154; USTR ¶ 1627.177(3); TaxDesk ¶ 30,811)

In several Technical Advice Memoranda, IRS declined to apply the *Plainfield Union* valuation analysis, indicating that the analysis represented just one of several alternative methods of determining increases in the value of an asset. (Com Rept, see ¶ 5073) In one ruling, a taxpayer acquired a boiler house and a warehouse that contained as-

FTC 2d References are to Federal Tax Coordinator 2d
FIN References are to RIA's Analysis of Federal Taxes: Income
USTR References are to United States Tax Reporter: Income, Estate & Gift, and Excise
PCA References are to Pension Coordinator and Pension & Benefits Expert/Advisor
PE References are to Pension and Profit Sharing 2nd
EP References are to Estate Planning & Taxation Coordinator and Estate Planning Advisor

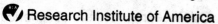 Research Institute of America

221

bestos. In order to secure a loan, the taxpayer was required to remove all asbestos from the boiler house, and to abate exposed and damaged asbestos-containing pipe insulation in the warehouse. After removing the asbestos from the boiler house, taxpayer converted it into a garage and office space, and rented the office space to a related freight company. IRS ruled that—because the property was acquired in an asbestos-containing condition—the asbestos removal resulted in an improvement, and the restoration principle did not apply. IRS also found that there was an improvement based on the following factors: the removal of the asbestos resulted in the permanent elimination of any health risks; it created better operating conditions; it prevented further contamination of employees or lessees; it made the property significantly more attractive to potential buyers, investors, lenders and customers; it enhanced the usefulness and capacity of the property by enabling the taxpayer to turn the space into an office and garage. The asbestos removal thus did not return the property to the state that it was in before the condition necessitating the expenditures arose, and the costs of the removal were capital expenditures.

In another case, IRS ruled that the costs of removing asbestos insulation from machinery and replacing it with other insulation in order to comply with federal and state legal requirements were capital expenditures. As in the ruling discussed above, IRS found that the removal resulted in an improvement in the property because the removal reduced or eliminated human health risks and thus increased the value of the property. In addition, IRS rejected taxpayer's argument that the restoration principle of *Plainfield Union* applied to make the removal costs deductible. It did so on the grounds that *Plainfield Union* applied only to repairs necessitated by the progressive deterioration of property. It also ruled that modifications to property made to bring it into compliance with the law increased the property's value and consequently were capital expenditures. (FTC 2d/FIN ¶ L-6157; USTR ¶ 1627.177(3); TaxDesk ¶ 30,811)

In *Rev Rul 94-38, 1994-1 CB 35,* IRS applied the restoration principle from *Plainfield Union Water Co.* to allow a deduction for most of a taxpayer's environmental cleanup costs in the following situation. Taxpayer built a manufacturing plant on land that it acquired in uncontaminated condition. Taxpayer's manufacturing operations produced hazardous wastes, which taxpayer buried on portions of this land. The waste contaminated the soil and groundwater. In order to comply with applicable and anticipated legal requirements, taxpayer removed and properly disposed of the contaminated soil, replaced it with uncontaminated soil, and constructed groundwater treatment facilities to purify the groundwater. Taxpayer's soil remediation and groundwater treatment activities restored the land to its precontamination condition. IRS ruled that, except for the costs of constructing a groundwater treatment facility with a useful life of several years, taxpayer's cleanup expenditures—the costs of removing and replacing the contaminated soil, and the ongoing groundwater treatment expenditures—were not capital expenditures and were currently deductible. The cost of the groundwater treatment facility, however, had to be capitalized. (FTC 2d/FIN ¶ L-6154; USTR ¶ 1627.177(3); TaxDesk ¶ 30,811)

IRS ruled privately that the restoration principle of *Rev Rul 94-38* would apply to make deductible the costs of restoring the land to its approximate original uncontaminated condition. IRS concluded that the interim break in ownership resulting from the land's donation to and repurchase from the county did not affect the applicability of the principle. Because the same taxpayer contaminated the property and would incur the remediation costs, that interim break in ownership should not, in and of itself, operate to disallow a deduction under the restoration principle. The contamination and taxpayer's liability for remediation were unchanged during the break in ownership. (FTC 2d/FIN ¶ L-6155; USTR ¶ 1627.177(3); TaxDesk ¶ 30,811)

New Law. A taxpayer may elect to treat any "qualified environmental remediation expenditure" (as defined below) which is paid or incurred by the taxpayer as an expense which is not chargeable to capital account. Any expenditure which is treated as not chargeable to capital account is allowed as a deduction for the tax year in which it is paid or incurred. (Code Sec. 198(a) as added by '97 Act §941(a)) The deduction applies for both regular and alternative minimum tax purposes. (Com Rept, see ¶ 5073)

Solely for purposes of Code Sec. 1245 (gain from the disposition of depreciable property), in the case of property to which a qualified environmental remediation expenditure would have been capitalized but for this provision—

• the deduction allowed for the expenditure is treated as a deduction for depreciation (Code Sec. 198(e)(1)), and

• the property (if not otherwise Code Sec. 1245 property) is treated as Code Sec. 1245 property solely for purposes of applying Code Sec. 1245 to the deduction. (Code Sec. 198(e)(2))

Thus, deductions for qualified environmental remediation expenditures are subject to recapture as ordinary income upon sale or other disposition of the property. (Com Rept, see ¶ 5073)

The following provisions do not apply to amounts which are treated as expenses by this provision:

• Code Sec. 280B, which provides rules for the demolition of structures, and

• Code Sec. 468, which provides rules for mining and solid waste reclamation and closing costs. (Code Sec. 198(f))

IRS is required to prescribe the regulations that may be necessary or appropriate to carry out the purposes of this provision. (Code Sec. 198(g))

Termination. This provision will not apply to expenditures paid or incurred after Dec. 31, 2000. (Code Sec. 198(h)) Thus, the provision sunsets after three years. (Com Rept, see ¶ 5073)

Definitions.

Qualified environmental remediation expenditure. A "qualified environmental remediation expenditure" is any expenditure which is:

FTC 2d References are to Federal Tax Coordinator 2d
FIN References are to RIA's Analysis of Federal Taxes: Income
USTR References are to United States Tax Reporter: Income, Estate & Gift, and Excise
PCA References are to Pension Coordinator and Pension & Benefits Expert/Advisor
PE References are to Pension and Profit Sharing 2nd
EP References are to Estate Planning & Taxation Coordinator and Estate Planning Advisor

- otherwise chargeable to capital account (Code Sec. 198(b)(1)(A)), and

- paid or incurred in connection with the abatement or control of "hazardous substances" (as defined below) at a "qualified contaminated site" (as defined below). (Code Sec. 198(b)(1)(B))

With a limited exception, "qualified environmental remediation expenditure" does not include any expenditure for the acquisition of property of a character subject to the allowance for depreciation which is used in connection with the abatement or control of hazardous substances at a qualified contaminated site. However, the portion of the allowance under Code Sec. 167 for the property which is otherwise allocated to the site is treated as a qualified environmental remediation expenditure. (Code Sec. 198(b)(2)) Thus, depreciation deductions allowable for property used in connection with the abatement or control of hazardous substances at a qualified contaminated site which would otherwise be allocated to the site under principles set forth in *Comm'r v. Idaho Power Co., 418 U.S. 1 (1974)* and Code Sec. 263A are treated as qualified environmental remediation expenditures. In *Comm'r v. Idaho Power Co.,* the Court held that equipment depreciation allocable to the taxpayer's construction of capital facilities must be capitalized under Code Sec. 263(a)(1). (Com Rept, see ¶ 5073)

Qualified contaminated site.   A "qualified contaminated site" is any area:

- which is held by the taxpayer for use in a trade or business, for the production of income, or is property described in Code Sec. 1221(1) that is included in inventory in the taxpayer's hands (Code Sec. 198(c)(1)(A)(i)),

- which is within a targeted area (see below) (Code Sec. 198(c)(1)(A)(ii)), and

- at or on which there has been a release (or threat of release) or disposal of any hazardous substance. (Code Sec. 198(c)(1)(A)(iii))

In addition to the above definition of "qualified contaminated site," an area is treated as a qualified contaminated site for expenditures paid or incurred during any tax year only if the taxpayer receives a statement that the area meets certain requirements from the appropriate agency of the state in which the area is located. The requirements that the state agency must certify are that the area —

- is within a targeted area, and

- is an area at or on which there has been a release (or threat of release) or disposal of any hazardous substance. (Code Sec. 198(c)(1)(B))

For purposes of the requirements for statements from the state environmental agency, the chief executive officer of each State may, in consultation with the Administrator of the Environmental Protection Agency, designate the appropriate State environmental agency within 60 days of Aug. 5, '97 . If the chief executive officer of a State has not designated an appropriate State environmental agency within the 60-day period, the appropriate environmental agency for the State must be designated by the Administrator of the Environmental Protection Agency. (Code Sec. 198(c)(1)(C))

Targeted area. The term "targeted area" means —

• any population census tract with a poverty rate of not less than 20% (Code Sec. 198(c)(2)(A)(i)),

• a population census tract with a population of less than 2,000 if more than 75% of the tract is zoned for commercial or industrial use, and the tract is contiguous to one or more other population census tracts which satisfy the requirement of a poverty rate of not less than 20% without regard to to the fact that it is contiguous to the other tracts (Code Sec. 198(c)(2)(A)(ii)),

• any empowerment zone or enterprise community (and any supplemental zone designated on Dec. 21, '94) (Code Sec. 198(c)(2)(A)(iii)), and

• any site announced before Feb. 1, '97, as being included as a Brownfields Pilot Project of the Environmental Protection Agency. (Code Sec. 198(c)(2)(A)(iv))

Both urban and rural sites qualify. (Com Rept, see ¶ 5073) Twenty additional empowerment zones authorized to be designated under the '97 Act (¶ 2606) as well as the D.C. Enterprize Zone (¶ 2601) are targeted areas for these purposes. (Com Rept, see ¶ 5073)

The term targeted area doesn't include National Priorities listed sites. That is, a targeted area does not include any site which is on, or proposed for, the national priorities list under §105(a)(8)(B) of the Comprehensive Environmental Response, Compensation, and Liability Act of 1980 (as in effect on the Aug. 5, '97). (Code Sec. 198(c)(2)(B))

> ⚡ *observation:* The national priorities list is a list provided by the President at least annually. Each state establishes and submits priorities for remedial action among known releases and potential releases in the state for consideration by the President. In assembling or revising the national list, the President is instructed to consider any priorities established by the states.

For purposes of determining targeted areas the rules contained in the following Code sections apply:

• Code Sec. 1392(b)(4), regarding areas that are not within census tracts, and

• Code Sec. 1393(a)(9), regarding the use of decennial census data to determine population and poverty rates. (Code Sec. 198(c)(2)(C))

Hazardous substance. The term "hazardous substance" means —

• any substance which is a hazardous substance as defined in §101(14) of the Comprehensive Environmental Response, Compensation, and Liability Act of 1980 (CERCLA) (Code Sec. 198(d)(1)(A)), and

FTC 2d References are to Federal Tax Coordinator 2d
FIN References are to RIA's Analysis of Federal Taxes: Income
USTR References are to United States Tax Reporter: Income, Estate & Gift, and Excise
PCA References are to Pension Coordinator and Pension & Benefits Expert/Advisor
PE References are to Pension and Profit Sharing 2nd
EP References are to Estate Planning & Taxation Coordinator and Estate Planning Advisor

• any substance which is designated as a hazardous substance under §102 of CER-CLA. (Code Sec. 198(d)(1)(B))

The term hazardous substance does not include any substance with respect to which a removal or remedial action is not permitted under §104 of the CERCLA, by reason of §104(a)(3) of that Act. (Code Sec. 198(d)(2))

⚓ *observation:* CERCLA §104(a)(3) provides that the President will not provide for removal or remedial action in response to a release or threat of release:

    (A) of a naturally occurring substance in its unaltered form, or altered solely through naturally occurring processes or phenomena, from a location where it is naturally found;

    (B) from products which are part of the structure of, and result in exposure within, residential buildings or business or community structures; or

    (C) into public or private drinking water supplies due to deterioration of the system through ordinary use.

Thus, under CERCLA §104(a)(3), the definition of hazardous substance is subject to additional limitations applicable to asbestos and similar substances within buildings, certain naturally occurring substances such as radon, and certain other substances released into drinking water supplies due to deterioration through ordinary use. (Com Rept, see ¶ 5073)

Providing current deductions for certain environmental remediation expenditures in the '97 Act creates no inference as to the proper treatment of other remediation expenditures not described in the agreement. (Com Rept, see ¶ 5073)

☐ **Effective:** Expenditures paid or incurred after Aug. 5, '97, in tax years ending after Aug. 5, '97. ('97 Act §941(c))

¶ 900. Qualified Retirement Plans
Distribution Provisions

¶ 901. Qualified retirement plans may receive rollovers from plans intended to have a qualified trust

Code Sec. None, '97 Act § 1509
Generally effective: Aug. 5, '97
Committee Reports, see ¶ 5315

A qualified plan that accepts rollover contributions from other plans won't be disqualified just because the plan making the distribution was not qualified at the time of the distribution, if, before accepting the distribution, the receiving plan reasonably concluded that the distributing plan was qualified. The receiving plan can reasonably conclude that the distributing plan was qualified if, before accepting the rollover, the distributing plan provided a statement from the distributing plan that it had received a favorable determination letter from IRS. The receiving plan isn't required to verify this information. (FTC 2d/FIN ¶ H-8251.2; USTR ¶ 4014.27; TaxDesk ¶ 14,405; PCA ¶ 26,652.2; PE ¶ 401-4.27)

New Law. Under the '97 Act, it is not necessary for a distributing plan to have a determination letter on the distributing plan's status as a qualified plan for the administrator of the receiving plan to reasonably conclude that the contribution is a valid rollover contribution. IRS is directed to clarify this rule under regulations protecting pension plans from disqualification because of the receipt of invalid rollover contributions (under Code Sec. 402(c)). ('97 Act §1509)

> *observation:* The '97 Act does not provide an effective date for Sec. 1509. But Congress's direction to IRS to *clarify* the rule (that a receiving plan doesn't need a determination letter from a distributing plan for a rollover to be valid) seems to indicate that this is the rule and that it already has been in effect.

☐ **Effective:** Aug. 5, '97.

¶ 902. Maximum involuntary pension "cash-out" amount increased from $3,500 to $5,000

Code Sec. 411(a)(11)(A), as amended by '97 Act § 1071(a)(1)
Code Sec. 417(e), as amended by '97 Act § 1071(a)(2)
Code Sec. 457(e)(9), as amended by '97 Act § 1071(a)(2)
Generally effective: Plan years beginning after Aug. 5, '97
Committee Reports, see ¶ 5153

FTC 2d References are to Federal Tax Coordinator 2d
FIN References are to RIA's Analysis of Federal Taxes: Income
USTR References are to United States Tax Reporter: Income, Estate & Gift, and Excise
PCA References are to Pension Coordinator and Pension & Benefits Expert/Advisor
PE References are to Pension and Profit Sharing 2nd
EP References are to Estate Planning & Taxation Coordinator and Estate Planning Advisor

When an employee terminates participation in a qualified plan (including a government plan), the plan may "cash out" the vested accrued benefits in that employee's account without the employee's consent and, in the case of joint and survivor annuity benefits, also without the consent of the surviving spouse, if the present value of those benefits does not exceed $3,500. Cash-outs are only allowed if the plan provides that any participant who later returns to employment will be able to repay the distribution and have his forfeited benefit reinstated. (FTC 2d/FIN ¶ H-3303, ¶ H-7510, ¶ H-8701; USTR ¶ 4114.15, ¶ 4174.06, ¶ 4574; TaxDesk ¶ 14,453; PCA ¶ 25,511, ¶ 27,202, ¶ 40,404; PE ¶ 411-4.15, ¶ 417-4.06, ¶ 457-4)

🖐 *observation:* The $3,500 is not indexed for inflation.

New Law. The '97 Act increases the limit on involuntary cash outs to $5,000. (Code Sec. 411(a)(11)(A) as amended by '97 Act §1071(a)) This increase also applies to involuntary cash outs of joint and survivor annuity benefits (Code Sec. 417(e)) and to cash outs under government plans. (Code Sec. 457(e)(9)) Corresponding changes are made to ERISA §§203(e)(1), 204(d)(1) and 204 (g). ('97 Act §1071(b))

🖐 *observation:* As under pre-'97 law, the dollar limit is fixed, without any adjustment for inflation in later years.

☐ **Effective:** Effective for plan years beginning after Aug. 5, '97. ('97 Act §1071(c))

¶ 903. Separate table provided for figuring basis recovery for annuities based on more than one life

Code Sec. 72(d)(1)(B)(iii), '97 Act § 1075(b)
Code Sec. 72(d)(1)(B)(iv), '97 Act § 1075(a)
Generally effective: Annuity starting dates beginning after '97
Committee Reports, see ¶ 5157

Amounts received as an annuity under a qualified pension plan generally are includible in income in the year received, except to the extent the amount received represents return of the recipient's investment in the contract (i.e., basis). The portion of each annuity payment that represents a return of basis is determined by a simplified method which provides that this portion is equal to the employee's total basis as of the annuity starting date, divided by the number of anticipated payments under a specified table (reproduced below). The number of anticipated payments listed in the table is based on the age of the primary annuitant on the annuity starting date. There was no separate table for joint and survivor annuities, which are based on the life of more than one person.

Age of Primary Annuitant	Number of Payments
55 or less	360
56–60	310
61–65	260
66–70	210
71 or more	160

If the number of payments is fixed under the terms of the annuity, that number is used instead of the number of anticipated payments listed in the table. The simplified method is not available if the primary annuitant is 75 or older on the annuity starting date, unless there are fewer than 5 years of guaranteed payments under the annuity. If, in connection with commencement of annuity payments, the recipient gets a lump-sum payment that is not part of the annuity stream, the payment is taxable under the rules relating to annuities as if received before the annuity starting date, and the investment in the contract used to calculate the simplified exclusion ratio for the annuity payments is reduced by the amount of the payment. In no event can the total amount that is excluded from income as a nontaxable return of basis be greater than the recipient's total investment in the contract. (FTC 2d/FIN ¶ H-11012; USTR ¶ 4024.02; TaxDesk ¶ 14,110; PCA ¶ 32,113; PE ¶ 402-4.02)

New Law. The pre-'97 Act table (reproduced above) now applies only to benefits based on the life of one annuitant. (Code Sec. 72(d)(1)(B)(iii) as amended by '97 Act §1075(b)) The '97 Act provides a separate table, reproduced below, which applies to benefits based on the life of more than one annuitant. (Code Sec. 72(d)(1)(B)(iv))

Combined Age of Annuitants	Number of Payments
110 or less	410
111–120	360
121–130	310
131–140	260
141 or more	210

Applying the pre-'97 Act table for single life annuities to joint and survivor annuities understated the expected payments under a joint and survivor annuity. (Com Rept, see ¶ 5157)

✪ observation: This understatement permitted faster recovery of the basis in the annuity; thus the taxable amount in those years was smaller.

☐ **Effective:** For annuity starting dates beginning after Dec. 31, 1997. ('97 Act §1075(c))

FTC 2d References are to Federal Tax Coordinator 2d
FIN References are to RIA's Analysis of Federal Taxes: Income
USTR References are to United States Tax Reporter: Income, Estate & Gift, and Excise
PCA References are to Pension Coordinator and Pension & Benefits Expert/Advisor
PE References are to Pension and Profit Sharing 2nd
EP References are to Estate Planning & Taxation Coordinator and Estate Planning Advisor

¶ 904. Judgment or settlement amounts for certain participant crimes and ERISA violations may be offset against his benefits

Code Sec. 401(a)(13)(C), as amended by '97 Act § 1502(b)
Generally effective: Judgments, orders, and decrees issued, and settlements entered into, on or after Aug. 5, '97
Committee Reports, see ¶ 5308

A pension plan must provide that qualified retirement plan benefits may not be assigned or alienated. As an exception, a plan may permit a participant to make a voluntary revocable assignment of an amount not in excess of 10% of any benefit payment (other than for defraying plan administration costs). Also, even if a participant is not in pay status, a plan may comply with a state court's qualified domestic relations order requiring benefit payments to former spouses or other alternate payees. In addition, the prohibition on assignment and alienation of plan benefits doesn't preclude the collection of tax by the U.S. through tax levies and court judgments.

Courts have been divided as to whether the prohibition on alienation and assignment of plan benefits permits an offset of a participant's benefits against amounts owed to the plan as a result of the participant's breach of fiduciary duty to the plan or criminality involving the plan. Some courts have said that the purpose of the anti-alienation provision to ensure that plan assets are used only for the payment of benefits would be undermined by prohibiting an offset where fiduciary-beneficiaries were found to have violated their fiduciary duties. Other courts have held that there is no exception in ERISA for the offset of a participant's benefit to make a plan whole. (FTC 2d/FIN ¶ H-8201; USTR ¶ 4014.14; PCA ¶ 26,602, ¶ 51,211; PE ¶ 401-4.14)

New Law. The offset of a participant's accrued benefit in an employee pension benefit plan against an amount that the participant is ordered or required to pay to the plan won't violate the required plan prohibition against assignment or alienation of benefits if:

(1) the order or requirement to pay arises under a judgment, order, decree, or settlement stemming from certain crimes or violations of ERISA (see below);

(2) the judgment, order, decree, or settlement agreement expressly provides for the offset of all or part of the amount ordered or required to be paid to the plan against the participant's plan benefits; and

(3) where the survivor annuity requirements apply to plan distributions to the participant (under Code Sec. 401(a)(11)), the rights of the participant's spouse to survivor benefits are preserved (see below). (Code Sec. 401(a)(13)(C) as amended by '97 Act §1502(b))

An offset is includible in income on the date of the offset. (Com Rept, see ¶ 5308)

Violations for which offset is allowable. The amount of a judgment or settlement may be offset against a participant's plan benefits if the participant is ordered or required to pay under either:

(1) a judgment of conviction for a crime involving the plan; (Code Sec. 401(a)(13)(C)(i)(I))

(2) a civil judgment (including a consent order or decree) entered by a court in an action brought in connection with a violation (or an alleged violation) of ERISA's fiduciary responsibility provisions; or (Code Sec. 401(a)(13)(C)(i)(II))

(3) a settlement agreement between IRS and the participant, or a settlement agreement between the Pension Benefit Guaranty Corporation (PBGC) and the participant, in connection with a violation (or alleged violation) of ERISA's fiduciary responsibility provisions by a fiduciary or any other person. (Code Sec. 401(a)(13)(C)(i)(III))

Rights of a participant's spouse. If the participant has a spouse at the time at which offset is made against the participant's plan benefits and the survivor annuity requirements apply, then:

(1) either: (a) the spouse must consent in writing to the offset, and the consent must be witnessed by a notary public or plan representative (or it is established that there is no spouse, the spouse cannot be located, etc.) or (b) an election to waive the spouse's right to a qualified joint and survivor annuity (QJSA) or a qualified preretirement survivor annuity (QPSA) is in effect; or (Code Sec. 401(a)(13)(C)(iii)(I))

(2) the spouse must have been ordered or required in the judgment, order, decree, or settlement to pay an amount to the plan in connection with the violation of fiduciary duties; or (Code Sec. 401(a)(13)(C)(iii)(II))

(3) in the judgment, order, decree, or settlement, the spouse must retain the right to receive the survivor annuity under a QJSA and under a QPSA (as determined below). (Code Sec. 401(a)(13)(C)(iii)(III))

Spouse's survivor annuity. The survivor annuity that a participant's spouse retains the right to receive despite the offset against the participant's plan benefits (under Code Sec. 401(a)(13)(C)(iii)(III), item (3) above) must be determined as if:

(1) the participant terminated employment on the date of the offset; (Code Sec. 401(a)(13)(D)(i)(I))

(2) there was no offset; (Code Sec. 401(a)(13)(D)(i)(II))

(3) the plan permitted commencement of benefits only on or after normal retirement age; (Code Sec. 401(a)(13)(D)(i)(III))

(4) the plan provided only the "minimum-required qualified joint and survivor annuity"; and (Code Sec. 401(a)(13)(D)(i)(IV))

(5) the amount of the qualified preretirement survivor annuity under the plan is equal to the amount of the survivor annuity payable under the "minimum-required qualified joint and survivor annuity." (Code Sec. 401(a)(13)(D)(i)(V))

The "minimum-required qualified joint and survivor annuity" is the qualified joint and survivor annuity: (i) which is the actuarial equivalent of the participant's accrued benefit, and (ii) under which the survivor annuity is 50% of the amount of the annuity which is payable during the joint lives of the participant and the spouse. (Code Sec. 401(a)(13)(D)(ii))

Pension offset under other rules. A plan won't fail the rules for qualified plans (under Code Sec. 401(a)), 401(k) plans, tax-sheltered annuities (under Code Sec. 403(b)) and employee stock ownership plans (under Code Sec. 409(d)), solely because of an offset of a participant's accrued benefit described in Code Sec. 401(a)(13)(C). (Code Sec. 401(a)(13)(C))

☐ **Effective:** Judgments, orders, and decrees issued, and settlement agreements entered into, on or after Aug. 5, '97. ('97 Act §1502(c))

¶ 905. Interest and mortality rate rules in Retirement Protection Act of '94 corrected

Code Sec. None, as amended by '97 Act § 1604(b)(3)
Generally effective: Dec. 8, '94
Committee Reports, see ¶ 5385

The Retirement Protection Act of '94, enacted as part of the Uruguay Round Agreements Act (PL 103-465, 12/8/94), modified the actuarial assumptions that must be used to adjust benefits and limitations for defined benefit pension plans. In general, in adjusting the Code Sec. 415 limit on a benefit payable in a form other than a straight life annuity, and in adjusting the defined benefit dollar limit for benefits beginning before age 62, the interest rate cannot be less than 5% or, if greater, the plan rate.

However, if the benefit form is subject to the cash-out rules of Code Sec. 417(e)(3) (e.g., a lump-sum distribution), the interest rate on 30-year Treasury securities is substituted for 5% in adjusting the Code Sec. 415 limits, even if the participant has not reached age 62. (FTC 2d/FIN ¶ H-5957.1; USTR ¶ 4154.03; TaxDesk ¶ 28,268; PCA ¶ 23,708.1; PE ¶ 415-4.03) For purposes of adjusting any benefit or limit, a mortality table prescribed by IRS must be used. (FTC 2d/FIN ¶ H-5957.2; USTR ¶ 4154.03; PCA ¶ 23,708.2; PE ¶ 415-4.03)

The above rules are generally effective for plan years and limitation years beginning after '94. However, the Small Business Job Protection Act of '96 (PL 104-188, 8/20/96) conformed this effective date to the effective date of similar changes by generally allowing defined benefit plans adopted and in effect before Dec. 8, '94, to disregard the above interest rate and mortality assumptions for benefits accrued before the earlier of (1) the later of the adoption date or effective date of the applicable plan amendment, or (2) the first day of the first limitation year beginning after Dec. 31, '99. (FTC 2d/FIN ¶ H-5957.1; USTR ¶ 4154.03; PCA ¶ 23,708.1; PE ¶ 415-4.03)

Sec. 767(d)(3)(A) of PL 103-465, as amended by Sec. 1449(a) of PL 104-188, provides that "Determinations under Code Sec. 415(b)(2)(E) before such earlier date shall be made with respect to such benefits on the basis of such section as in effect on Dec. 7, '94 (except that the modification made by section 1449(b) of the Small Business Job

Protection Act of '96 shall be taken into account), and the provisions of the plan as in effect on Dec. 7, '94, but only if such provisions of the plan meet the requirements of such section (as so in effect)." This provision was intended to permit plans to apply prior law under Code Sec. 415(b)(2)(E) for a transition period. (Com Rept, see ¶ 5385)

New Law. The '97 Act deletes from the above transitional rule the parenthetical phrase "(except that the modification made by section 1449(b) of the Small Business Job Protection Act of '96 shall be taken into account)." (§ 767(d)(3)(A) of PL 103-465 as amended by '97 Act § 1604(b)(3)) Thus, Sec. 767(d)(3)(A) of PL 103-465 now provides that interest rate and mortality determinations under Code Sec. 415(b)(2)(E) before the earlier of (1) the later of the adoption date or effective date of the applicable plan amendment or (2) the first day of the first limitation year beginning after Dec. 31, '99, with respect to benefits accrued before that earlier date, are to be made on the basis of Code Sec. 415(b)(2)(E) as in effect on Dec. 7, '94 (i.e., before the Retirement Protection Act of '94 amendments) and plan provisions in effect on Dec. 7, '94, but only if the plan provision met the Code Sec. 415(b)(2)(E) requirements as in effect on Dec. 7, '94. This change conforms the statute to the intent of Congress. (Com Rept, see ¶ 5385)

☐ **Effective:** Dec. 8, '94. ('97 Act §1604(b)(4))

¶ 906. Permissible rollovers from certain 403(b) plans maintained by Indian tribal governments

Code Sec. None, '97 Act § 1601(d)(4)
Generally effective: Aug. 20, '96
Committee Reports, see ¶ 5390

In applying Code Sec. 403(b) to any tax-sheltered annuity contract bought in a plan year beginning before Jan. 1, '95, an Indian tribal government is treated as an organization that is tax-exempt under Code Sec. 501(c)(3).

> ✔ *observation:* Remedial legislation provided by the Small Business Job Protection Act of '96 put to rest any doubts about the tax-qualified status of tax-sheltered annuity plans adopted by Indian tribes before Jan. 1, '95.

Amounts invested in an annuity contract bought by an Indian tribal government before '95 may be rolled over tax-free to a 401(k) plan maintained by the tribal government. (FTC 2d/FIN ¶ H-12436; USTR ¶ 4034.04; PCA ¶ 36,037; PE ¶ 403-4.04)

New Law. The '97 Act clarifies the treatment of rollovers from pre-'95 tribal government annuity contracts to tribal government 401(k) plans. Rollovers (including trustee-to-trustee direct rollovers) of distributions made before Jan. 1, '98 are permitted

FTC 2d References are to Federal Tax Coordinator 2d
FIN References are to RIA's Analysis of Federal Taxes: Income
USTR References are to United States Tax Reporter: Income, Estate & Gift, and Excise
PCA References are to Pension Coordinator and Pension & Benefits Expert/Advisor
PE References are to Pension and Profit Sharing 2nd
EP References are to Estate Planning & Taxation Coordinator and Estate Planning Advisor

without regard to the early withdrawal restrictions prohibiting distributions before attainment of age 59 1/2, separation from service, death, disability or hardship. ('97 Act §1601(d)(4)(A)(i)) These rollovers are permissible whether or not the annuity contract has terminated. (Com Rept, see ¶ 5390) The early withdrawal restrictions (above) are also inapplicable to any distributions made on or after Jan. 1, '98 to the extent that the distribution is not includible in income by reason of Code Sec. 403(b)(1) (relating to the taxation of employee annuities). ('97 Act §1601(d)(4)(A)(ii))

> *observation:* Thus, Indian tribal governments can effectuate rollovers between their 403(b) plans and 401(k) plans, as provided in the '96 SBJPA, without jeopardizing the tax-qualified status of these plans.

> *observation:* Neither the '97 Act nor the committee reports explain the significance of the Jan. 1, '98 cut-off date.

☐ **Effective:** Aug. 20, '96. ('97 Act §1601(j)(1))

Excise Tax Reform

¶ 907. Repeal of excess distribution and excess retirement accumulation tax

Code Sec. 4980A, as amended by '97 Act § 1073(a)
Generally effective: After Dec. 31, '96
Committee Reports, see ¶ 5155

The Small Business Job Protection Act of '96 suspended the 15% excise tax on excess distributions received in '97, '98 and '99. The excise tax applied to excess distributions from qualified retirement plans, tax-sheltered annuities, and individual retirement arrangements. An excess distribution is the aggregate amount of retirement distributions to an individual, during any calendar year, which exceed a threshold amount that is adjusted for inflation ($160,000 for '97). For certain lump-sum distributions, the dollar amount is five times the threshold amount ($800,000 for '97). Excess distributions received on or after Jan. 1, 2000 were scheduled to be subject to the excise tax. (FTC 2d/FIN ¶ H-11300; USTR ¶ 49,80A4; TaxDesk ¶ 14,560; PCA ¶ 32,701; PE ¶ 4980A-4)

Certain retirement plan distributions made after death were subject to an excise tax equalling 15% of any excess retirement accumulation. The excess retirement accumulation is the excess (if any) of the value of the decedent's interest in all qualified retirement plans, tax-sheltered annuities and IRAs over the present value of a single life annuity that would not be subject to the 15% tax on excess distributions. (FTC 2d/FIN ¶ R-7041; USTR ¶ 49,80A4; TaxDesk ¶ 78,121; PCA ¶ 34,252; PE ¶ 4980A-4; EP ¶ 45,002)

> *observation:* The SBJPA of '96 did not affect the continued operation of the 15% excise tax on excess retirement accumulations.

New Law. The '97 Act repeals both the 15% excise tax on excess distributions and the 15% estate tax on excess retirement accumulations. (Code Sec. 4980A as amended by '97 Act §1073(a)) These excise taxes were designed to place limitations on the total amount that a person could keep in tax-deferred savings, while at the same time help make sure that these monies were saved for retirement planning purposes. However, Congress believes that the amount of tax-deferred savings can be limited by existing rules that restrict contributions and benefits. Thus, Congress views these excise taxes as unnecessary additional penalties that may also thwart retirement saving and inappropriately penalize favorable returns on investment. (Com Rept, see ¶ 5155)

☐ **Effective:** The excess distribution tax is repealed for excess distributions received after Dec. 31, '96. ('97 Act §1073(c)(1)) The excess retirement accumulation tax is repealed for estates of decedents dying after Dec. 31, '96. ('97 Act §1073(c)(2))

¶ 908. First-tier excise tax on prohibited transactions increased from 10% to 15%

Code Sec. 4975(a), as amended by '97 Act § 1074(a)
Generally effective: For prohibited transactions after Aug. 5, '97
Committee Reports, see ¶ 5156

Certain transactions between a qualified plan and a disqualified person are prohibited in order to prevent persons with a close relationship to the qualified plan from using that relationship to the detriment of plan participants and beneficiaries. For example, a plan fiduciary cannot deal with the income or assets of a plan in his own interest or for his own account. A two-tier excise tax is imposed on prohibited transactions. The first-tier tax was equal to 10 percent of the amount involved with respect to a transaction. If the transaction is not corrected within the taxable period, a second-tier excise tax equal to 100 percent of the amount involved may be imposed. (FTC 2d/FIN ¶ H-12501; USTR ¶ 49,754; TaxDesk ¶ 28,751; PCA ¶ 53,802; PE ¶ 4975-4)

New Law. The '97 Act increases the first-tier excise tax on prohibited transactions from 10 percent to 15 percent. (Code Sec. 4975(a) as amended by '97 Act §1074(a)) Congress believed it was appropriate to increase the first-tier tax to discourage disqualified persons from engaging in prohibited transactions. (Com Rept, see ¶ 5156)

☐ **Effective:** For prohibited transactions occurring after Aug. 5, '97. ('97 Act §1074(b))

FTC 2d References are to Federal Tax Coordinator 2d
FIN References are to RIA's Analysis of Federal Taxes: Income
USTR References are to United States Tax Reporter: Income, Estate & Gift, and Excise
PCA References are to Pension Coordinator and Pension & Benefits Expert/Advisor
PE References are to Pension and Profit Sharing 2nd
EP References are to Estate Planning & Taxation Coordinator and Estate Planning Advisor

¶ 909. Statutory exemptions from prohibited transaction rules extended to S corporations

Code Sec. 4975(f)(6), as amended by '97 Act § 1506(b)(1)
Generally effective: Taxable years beginning after Dec. 31, 1997
Committee Reports, see ¶ 5312

Certain transactions between a qualified plan and a party in interest are strictly prohibited. However, Code Sec. 4975(d)(1) through (15) provide exemptions to the prohibited transaction rules. All but two of the exemptions ((9) and (12)) don't apply to "owner-employee" plans. Because a shareholder-employee is treated as an "owner-employee", qualified plans maintained by S corporations are subject to most aspects of the prohibited transaction rules, including the prohibition against sales of stock by a shareholder-employee to an ESOP sponsored by the S corporation. (FTC 2d/FIN ¶ H-12566; USTR ¶ 49,754; TaxDesk ¶ 28,751; PCA ¶ 53,867; PE ¶ 4975-4)

New Law. To facilitate the operation of an ESOP by an S corporation (Com Rept, see ¶ 5312), shareholder-employees are exempted from the prohibition against the sale of employer securities to an ESOP maintained by an S corporation. This exemption also extends to a family member of a shareholder-employee as well as to a corporation controlled by the shareholder-employee. (Code Sec. 4975(f)(6)(B)(ii) as amended by '97 Act §1506(b)(1)) The '97 Act defines "shareholder-employee" to mean an employee or officer of an S corporation who owns (or constructively owns) more than 5% of the S corporation's stock on any day of the corporation's taxable year. (Code Sec. 4975(f)(6)(C))

> **observation:** This exemption will permit an ESOP maintained by an S corporation to purchase employer stock from plan participants (shareholder-employees) who are taking cash distributions from the plan in an amount equal to the value of their stock. See ¶ 910 for a discussion of the '97 Act provision that allows ESOPs maintained by S corporations to distribute cash to participants in lieu of employer securities.

> **observation:** This exemption is already available to parties in interest (i.e., employee-participants) of ESOPs maintained by C corporations.

> **observation:** This provision of the '97 Act should not be construed to extend other exemptions from the prohibited transaction rules. Thus, shareholder-employees of an S corporation continue to be ineligible to borrow against their account balances, unless they apply for and receive an administrative exemption from the Department of Labor for such participant loan.

However, an ESOP maintained by an S corp can obtain a loan (or guarantee a loan) in connection with a transaction involving the sale of employer securities by a shareholder-employee to the ESOP. (Com Rept, see ¶ 5312)

ERISA §408(d) is also amended by the '97 Act to provide that shareholder-employees are exempt from the prohibition against selling employer securities to the ESOP.

(ERISA §408(d) as amended by '97 Act §1506(b)(2))

☐ **Effective:** Taxable years beginning after Dec. 31, '97. ('97 Act §1506(c))

¶ 910. Certain cash distributions permitted by ESOPs maintained by S corporations

Code Sec. 409(h)(2)(B), as amended by '97 Act § 1506(a)
Generally effective: Taxable years beginning after Dec. 31, 1997
Committee Reports, see ¶ 5312

The pay-out policy of an ESOP must provide eligible participants with an election to take their distributions in the form of employer securities. However, an ESOP may prevent a participant from demanding a distribution in the form of employer securities if the employer's corporate charter (or a bylaw) restricts the ownership of substantially all outstanding employer securities to employees or to a trust under a qualified plan, as long as participants entitled to a distribution have a right to receive the distribution in cash. As an alternative, the ESOP may distribute employer securities subject to a requirement that they be resold to the employer under terms meeting the fair valuation requirements of Code Sec. 409(h)(1)(B). (FTC 2d ¶ H-9329; USTR ¶ 4094.10; TaxDesk ¶ 28,062; PCA ¶ 28,630; PE ¶ 409-4.10)

Because S corporations can have no more than 75 shareholders, distributions from an ESOP maintained by an S corporation present a unique issue. If participants of an ESOP maintained by an S corp were to receive their distributions in the form of stock of the S corporation, then the number of shareholders could grow to more than 75 and the S corporation would lose its status as an S corp. (Com Rept, see ¶ 5312)

> *observation:* The Small Business Job Protection Act of '96 provided that starting in tax years beginning after Dec. 31, '97, certain tax-exempt organizations, including qualified retirement plan trusts, will be allowed to own shares in S corporations. As a result, an S corporation will be permitted to establish an ESOP that invests in its own stock. The ESOP is counted as one shareholder, but if shares in the S corporation are distributed from the ESOP into the hands of individual plan participants, then each distributee-participant is counted as an individual shareholder. As a result, the total number of shareholders could grow to exceed the 75-shareholder limit, causing the S corporation to lose its S corp status.

New Law. The '97 Act provides that an ESOP maintained by an S corporation doesn't have to give participants the right to demand employer securities upon distribution, as long as participants are entitled to receive their distribution in cash equal to the stock's fair market value. (Code Sec. 409(h)(2)(B) as amended by '97 Act §1506(a))

FTC 2d References are to Federal Tax Coordinator 2d
FIN References are to RIA's Analysis of Federal Taxes: Income
USTR References are to United States Tax Reporter: Income, Estate & Gift, and Excise
PCA References are to Pension Coordinator and Pension & Benefits Expert/Advisor
PE References are to Pension and Profit Sharing 2nd
EP References are to Estate Planning & Taxation Coordinator and Estate Planning Advisor

The rationale for this is based on the 75-shareholder limit on S corporations. Distributions of cash, instead of employer stock, will help prevent the possibility that the S corporation will lose its status as an S corp by going over the limit of 75 shareholders. (Com Rept, see ¶ 5312)

> *observation:* Because the effective dates for both the SBJPA '96 provision and the '97 Act provision coincide, there is no gap period during which an ESOP maintained by an S corporation would be required to give participants the right to demand employer securities upon distribution of their accounts.

> *recommendation:* The anti-cutback rules should be considered when drafting an ESOP for an S corporation. Thus, it may be prudent not to allow employer stock as an optional form of distribution right from the start, rather than as an amendment later.

> *caution:* If the status of the plan sponsor changes from an S corporation to a C corporation, appropriate action may be necessary to prevent plan disqualification. For example, if ownership of employer securities in the C corporation is not restricted to employees or to a qualified trust, then the plan would have to be amended to provide participants with the right to take distributions in the form of employer securities.

☐ **Effective:** Taxable years beginning after Dec. 31, '97. ('97 Act §1506(c))

¶ 911. New exception to 10-percent excise tax on nondeductible contributions for contributions to 401(k) plan

Code Sec. 4972(c)(6)(B), as amended by '97 Act § 1507(a)
Generally effective: Tax years after '97
Committee Reports, see ¶ 5313

Employer contributions to qualified pension plans are deductible within certain limits. In the case of a single-employer defined benefit plan which has more than 100 participants during the year, the maximum amount deductible is not less than the plan's unfunded current liability as determined under the minimum funding rules. Limits are also imposed on the amount of annual deductible contributions if an employer sponsors both a defined benefit plan and a defined contribution plan that covers some of the same employees. Under the combined plan limitation, the total deduction for all plans for a plan year is generally limited to the greater of (1) 25 percent of compensation, or (2) the contribution necessary to meet the minimum funding requirements of the defined benefit plan for the year.

A 10-percent nondeductible excise tax is imposed on contributions that are not deductible. There are two exceptions to this tax. Under one exception, the excise tax does not apply to contributions to one or more defined contribution plans that are nondeductible because they exceed the combined plan deduction limit, to the extent the contributions do not exceed 6 percent of compensation paid to beneficiaries under the plans in the year for which the contributions are made. (FTC 2d/FIN ¶ H-10303.2;

USTR ¶ 49,724; TaxDesk ¶ 28,203.2; PCA ¶ 30,404.2; PE ¶ 4972-4)

New Law. Congress believes that prior law unfairly penalized employers by imposing an excise tax on employer plan contributions that were required to be made and that were not deductible because the employer was fully funding its pension plan. In particular, Congress did not believe that the excise tax on nondeductible contributions should have been imposed when an employer was required to make contributions attributable to elective deferrals under a 401(k) plan and employer matching contributions. (Com Rept, see ¶ 5313) So, the '97 Act adds another exception to the 10-percent excise tax on nondeductible contributions. The excise tax does not apply to contributions to one or more defined contribution plans that are not deductible because they exceed the combined plan deduction limit to the extent the contributions do not exceed the sum of: (1) the elective deferral contributions to a 401(k) plan, plus (2) the employer's matching contributions. (Code Sec. 4972(c)(6)(B) as amended by '97 Act §1507(a))

☐ **Effective:** Tax years beginning after Dec. 31, '97. ('97 Act §1507(b))

¶ 912. UBIT no longer applies to S corporation ESOPs

Code Sec. 512(e)(3), '97 Act § 1523(a)
Generally effective: Taxable years beginning after Dec. 31, '97
Committee Reports, see ¶ 5345

For taxable years beginning after Dec. 31, '97, certain tax-exempt organizations, including employee stock ownership plans ("ESOPs") can be a shareholder in an S corporation. Items of income or loss of the S corporation will flow through to qualified tax-exempt shareholders, including ESOP shareholders, as unrelated business taxable income ("UBTI"). (FTC 2d/FIN ¶ D-1452; USTR ¶ 13,614.03)

New Law. Congress said that the treatment of S corporation income as UBTI is not appropriate because it subjects the income to tax at the ESOP level and again when benefits are distributed by the ESOP to participants. (Com Rept, see ¶ 5345) So, the '97 Act repeals application of the unrelated business income tax (UBIT) to S corporation ESOPs. Specifically, an S corporation's income or loss generated by employer securities (as defined in Code Sec. 409(l)) held by an ESOP maintained by the S corporation won't be taxed as UBTI. (Code Sec. 512(e)(3) as amended by '97 Act §1523(a))

☐ **Effective:** Taxable years beginning after Dec. 31, '97. ('97 Act §1523(b))

FTC 2d References are to Federal Tax Coordinator 2d
FIN References are to RIA's Analysis of Federal Taxes: Income
USTR References are to United States Tax Reporter: Income, Estate & Gift, and Excise
PCA References are to Pension Coordinator and Pension & Benefits Expert/Advisor
PE References are to Pension and Profit Sharing 2nd
EP References are to Estate Planning & Taxation Coordinator and Estate Planning Advisor

SIMPLE Plans

¶ 913. Employers that maintain a plan for collectively bargained employees can maintain a SIMPLE plan for noncollectively bargained employees

Code Sec. 408(p)(2)(D)(i), as amended by '97 Act § 1601(d)(1)(E)
Generally effective: Tax years beginning after Dec. 31, '96
Committee Reports, see ¶ 5361

An employer's salary reduction arrangement isn't treated as "qualified" under the SIMPLE plan rules if the employer maintained a qualified plan for which contributions were made, or benefits were accrued, for service performed during the period a SIMPLE plan has been established. (FTC 2d/FIN ¶ H-12353; USTR ¶ 4084.06; TaxDesk ¶ 28,331; PCA ¶ 35,554; PE ¶ 408-4.06)

> *observation:* Thus, if an employer's collectively bargained employees were covered under a qualified plan, the employer was prevented from maintaining a SIMPLE plan not only for employees covered under the collectively bargained plan, but for employees not covered under any qualified plan.

New Law. A salary reduction arrangement may be "qualified" under the SIMPLE plan rules despite an employer's maintaining a qualified plan for which contributions are made, or benefits accrued, if: (1) the employees eligible to participate in that qualified plan are covered by a collective bargaining agreement for which retirement benefits were the subject of good faith bargaining, and (2) the only individuals who are eligible to participate in the salary reduction arrangement are those employees who are *not* covered by a collective bargaining agreement for which retirement benefits were the subject of good faith bargaining. (Code Sec. 408(p)(2)(D)(i) as amended by '97 Act §1601(d)(1)(E))

> *observation:* Thus, employees in the collective bargaining unit who are not covered under the collectively bargained plan cannot be eligible to participate in the SIMPLE plan.

☐ **Effective:** Tax years beginning after Dec. 31, '96. ('97 Act §1601(j)(1))

¶ 914. Grace period for employers that maintain both a qualified plan and a SIMPLE plan as a result of a merger or acquisition

Code Sec. 408(p)2)(D)(iii), as amended by '97 Act § 1601(d)(1)(F)
Generally effective: Tax years beginning after Dec. 31, '96
Committee Reports, see ¶ 5361

An employer can adopt a SIMPLE plan only if the employer: (1) employs 100 or fewer employees who received at least $5,000 of compensation from the employer in the preceding year, and (2) does not maintain a qualified retirement plan (including a SIMPLE IRA) to which contributions were made or benefits accrued while the SIMPLE plan was maintained.

A grace period is provided, but only for the failure to meet the first requirement. With the grace period, an employer that previously maintained a SIMPLE plan is treated as satisfying the "100-employee limitation" for the two calendar years immediately following the calendar year for which it last satisfied the "100-employee limitation." If the failure to be an eligible employer is due to any acquisition, disposition, or similar transaction, then the grace period applies only under rules similar to those providing a transition period after changes in the membership of a controlled group (under Code Sec. 410(b)(6)(C)).

There was no parallel provision providing a grace period for an employer that, because of an acquisition, disposition, or similar transaction, maintained a qualified plan and a SIMPLE plan at the same time. (FTC 2d/FIN ¶ H-12352; USTR ¶ 4084.06; TaxDesk ¶ 28,331; PCA ¶ 35,553; PE ¶ 408-4.06)

New Law. The Act adds a parallel provision. If an employer establishes and maintains a SIMPLE plan for at least one year, and then fails to meet any of the SIMPLE plan requirements because of an acquisition, disposition, or similar transaction involving another employer that maintained a SIMPLE plan for at least one year, then rules apply that are similar to those providing a transition period after changes in the membership of a controlled group (under Code Sec. 410(b)(6)(C)). (Code Sec. 408(p)(2)(D)(iii) as amended by '97 Act §1601(d)(1)(F)) Thus, if an employer maintained a qualified plan and a SIMPLE plan in the same year due to an acquisition, disposition, or similar transaction, the SIMPLE plan's salary reduction arrangement may be treated as qualified for the year of the transaction and the following calendar year. (Com Rept, see ¶ 5361)

☐ **Effective:** Tax years beginning after Dec. 31, '96. ('97 Act §1601(j)(1))

¶ 915. Maximum dollar limitation on IRA contributions conformed to allow maximum contributions to SIMPLE IRAs

Code Sec. 408((p)(8), as amended by '97 Act § 1601(d)(1)(D)
Generally effective: Tax years beginning after Dec. 31, '96
Committee Reports, see ¶ 5361

A SIMPLE plan permits employees to make elective contributions of up to $6,000 a year (as adjusted for changes in the cost of living) to their SIMPLE IRAs. Under a SIMPLE plan, employers are required to contribute to employees' SIMPLE IRAs under either of two contribution formulas. Thus, it is possible for contributions of up

FTC 2d References are to Federal Tax Coordinator 2d
FIN References are to RIA's Analysis of Federal Taxes: Income
USTR References are to United States Tax Reporter: Income, Estate & Gift, and Excise
PCA References are to Pension Coordinator and Pension & Benefits Expert/Advisor
PE References are to Pension and Profit Sharing 2nd
EP References are to Estate Planning & Taxation Coordinator and Estate Planning Advisor

 Research Institute of America 241

to $12,000 a year to be made to an employee's SIMPLE IRA under the SIMPLE plan rules. But the maximum amount that can be contributed to an IRA in a tax year (other than from certain rollover contributions) is $2,000. (FTC 2d/FIN ¶ H-12201, ¶ H-12357; USTR ¶ 4084.01, ¶ 4084.06; TaxDesk ¶ 28,388, ¶ 28,333; PCA ¶ 35,102, ¶ 35,558; PE ¶ 408-4.01, ¶ 408-4.06)

New Law. The maximum amount that can be contributed to an IRA for a tax year is increased to the limitations in effect for contributions made under a qualified salary reduction arrangement under a SIMPLE plan. This includes both employee elective contributions and required employer contributions under either contribution formula. (Code Sec. 408(p)(8) as amended by '97 Act §1601(d)(1)(D))

> *observation:* The maximum elective contribution that can be made for '97 is $6,000.

☐ **Effective:** Tax years beginning after Dec. 31, '96. ('97 Act §1601(j)(1))

¶ 916. Notification requirements and penalties for SIMPLE IRAs apply also to issuers of SIMPLE IRA annuities

Code Sec. 408(l)(2)(B), as amended by '97 Act § 1601(d)(1)(C)(i)
Code Sec. 6693(c)(2), as amended by '97 Act § 1601(d)(1)(C)(ii)
Generally effective: Tax years beginning after Dec. 31, '96
Committee Reports, see ¶ 5361

A SIMPLE IRA may be either an individual retirement account, or an individual retirement annuity, that meets specified requirements. The trustee of a SIMPLE IRA that is an individual retirement account must: (1) provide the employer maintaining the SIMPLE plan a summary plan description containing basic information about the plan, (2) furnish an account statement to each individual maintaining a SIMPLE IRA, and (3) file an annual report with IRS. A trustee who fails to provide any of these reports is subject to a penalty of $50 per day until the failure is corrected, unless the failure is due to reasonable cause. Issuers of SIMPLE IRAs that are individual retirement annuities were not subject to the notification requirements or the penalty for failure to comply with these requirements. (FTC 2d/FIN ¶ S-3399.1, ¶ S-3399.2, ¶ S-3399.3, ¶ V-1955.2; USTR ¶ 4084.06, ¶ 66,934; TaxDesk ¶ 28,345, ¶ 28,346, ¶ 86,137; PCA ¶ 56,153.1, ¶ 56,153.2, ¶ 56,153.3, ¶ 56,174.3A; PE ¶ 408-4.06, ¶ 6693-4)

New Law. Issuers of individual retirement annuities as SIMPLE IRAs are subject to the same reporting requirements, (Code Sec. 408(l)(2)(B) as amended by '97 Act §1601(d)(1)(C)(i)) and subject to the same penalty for failure to comply with these requirements, as SIMPLE IRA trustees. (Code Sec. 6693(c)(2) as amended by '97 Act §1601(d)(1)(C)(ii))

☐ **Effective:** Tax years beginning after Dec. 31, '96. ('97 Act §1601(j)(1))

¶917. Trustees' SIMPLE IRA reports to individuals now due on Jan. 31

Code Sec. 408(i), as amended by '97 Act § 1601(d)(1)(A)
Generally effective: Tax years beginning after Dec. 31, '96
Committee Reports, see ¶5361

The trustee of a SIMPLE IRA had through Jan. 30 to furnish each individual maintaining a SIMPLE IRA with a statement of the account balance at the close of the previous calendar year, and the account activity for that year. The trustee of a non-SIMPLE IRA and the issuer of an individual retirement annuity have until Jan. 31 to furnish reports for the previous calendar year to the individual for whom the account was maintained. (FTC 2d/FIN ¶ S-3399.3; USTR ¶ 4084.06; TaxDesk ¶ 28,346; PCA ¶ 56,153.3; PE ¶ 408-4.06)

New Law. Trustees of SIMPLE IRAs must furnish reports to individuals maintaining SIMPLE IRAs by Jan. 31 following the calendar year covered by the report. (Code Sec. 408(i) as amended by '97 Act §1601(d)(1)(A)) This conforms the time for providing reports for SIMPLE IRAs to that for IRA reports generally. (Com Rept, see ¶ 5361)

☐ **Effective:** Tax years beginning after Dec. 31, '96. ('97 Act §1601(j)(1))

¶918. Employer contributions to SIMPLE 401(k) plans are not subject to the 15 percent limits on contributions to profit-sharing or stock bonus plans

Code Sec. 404(a)(3)(A), as amended by '97 Act § 1601(d)(2)(C)
Generally effective: Tax years beginning after Dec. 31, '96
Committee Reports, see ¶5361

SIMPLE 401(k) plans are not subject to the nondiscrimination tests or the top-heavy rules, but they are subject to other qualified plan rules. Contributions paid by an employer to a profit-sharing or stock bonus plan are deductible by an employer only to the extent that the contributions do not exceed 15 percent of the compensation otherwise paid or accrued during the tax year to all employees participating in the plan. The excess contributions may be carried over to succeeding tax years, and the limit applies to contributions for the carryover year. An employer that pays contributions to a profit-sharing or stock bonus plan that are not deductible because they are in excess of the 15 percent limit is subject to a 10 percent excise tax. (FTC 2d/FIN ¶ H-9087, ¶ H-10202, ¶ H-10214, ¶ H-10300; USTR ¶ 4014.1735, ¶ 4044.08, ¶ 4044.12, ¶ 49,724; TaxDesk ¶ 28,182, ¶ 28,194, ¶ 28,200, ¶ 28,403.1; PCA ¶ 28,238, ¶ 30,303, ¶ 30,315, ¶ 30,401;

PE ¶ 404-4.08, ¶ 404-4.12, ¶ 4972-4)

New Law. Employer contributions to a SIMPLE 401(k) that meet the SIMPLE 401(k) contribution requirements are deductible by the employer for the tax year. (Code Sec. 404(a)(3)(A) as amended by '97 Act §1601(d)(2)(C))

observation: Since contributions that meet the SIMPLE 401(k) contribution rules are deductible, they are not subject to the excise tax on nondeductible contributions.

☐ **Effective:** Tax years beginning after Dec. 31, '96. ('97 Act §1601(j)(1))

¶ 919. Limit on contributions to SIMPLE 401(k) plans will be adjusted for changes in the cost-of-living

Code Sec. 401(k)(11)(E), as amended by '97 Act § 1601(d)(2)(B)
Generally effective: Tax years beginning after Dec. 31, '96
Committee Reports, see ¶ 5361

Under a SIMPLE 401(k) plan, an employee must be able to elect to have the employer make contributions on his behalf in an amount not to exceed $6,000 for the year. Although there is no cost-of-living adjustment to the SIMPLE 401(k) contribution limits, the parallel $6,000 limit on elective contributions to SIMPLE IRAs is subject to a cost-of-living adjustment. (FTC 2d/FIN ¶ H-9087, ¶ H-12357; USTR ¶ 4014.1735, ¶ 4084.06; TaxDesk ¶ 28,333, ¶ 28,403.1; PCA ¶ 28,238, ¶ 35,558; PE ¶ 401-4.1735, ¶ 408-4.06) (Com Rept, see ¶ 5361)

New Law. The $6,000 annual limit on the amount of elective contributions that may be made under a SIMPLE 401(k) plan will be adjusted for changes in the cost of living, in the same manner as for contributions under a SIMPLE plan. (Code Sec. 401(k)(11)(E) as amended by '97 Act §1601(d)(2)(B))

☐ **Effective:** Tax years beginning after Dec. 31, '96. ('97 Act §1601(j)(1))

¶ 920. Employers must provide timely notice of SIMPLE 401(k) plan elective contribution rules to eligible employees

Code Sec. 401(k)(11)(B)(iii), as amended by '97 Act § 1601(d)(2)(D)
Generally effective: Calendar years beginning after Aug. 5, '97
Committee Reports, see ¶ 5361

An employer maintaining a SIMPLE 401(k) plan had only to notify eligible employees of the employer's election to make nonelective two-percent contributions, rather than matching contributions of up to three percent of compensation for employees making elective contributions. In contrast, an employer maintaining a SIMPLE plan is required to notify each employee of the employee's opportunity to make or modify salary reduction contributions, as well as the contribution alternative chosen by the employer, within a reasonable period of time before the employee's election period. (FTC

2d/FIN ¶ H-9087, ¶ H-12378; USTR ¶ 4014.1735, ¶ 4084.06; TaxDesk ¶ 28,340, ¶ 28,403.1; PCA ¶ 28,238, ¶ 35,579; PE ¶ 401-4.1735, ¶ 408-4.06)

New Law. The election requirements that apply to SIMPLE plans are extended to SIMPLE 401(k)s. Thus, under a SIMPLE 401(k) plan:

(1) an employee may elect to terminate participation in the salary reduction election at any time during the year. The plan may provide that an employee who terminates may not elect to resume participation until the next year; and

(2) each employee eligible to participate may elect, during the 60-day period before the beginning of any year, to reduce salary and have the elective amounts contributed to the plan, or to modify the amounts subject to the election, for that year. For employees who first become eligible, the election period is the 60-day period before eligibility. (Code Sec. 401(k)(11)(B)(iii)(I) as amended by '97 Act §1601(d)(2)(D))

The employer must notify each employee eligible to participate, within a reasonable period of time before the 60th day before the beginning of the year, of the rules for electing to participate (under the rules described in (2) above). An employee first becoming eligible must be notified within a reasonable period of time before the 60th day before the first day the employee is eligible. (Code Sec. 408(k)(11)(B)(iii)(II))

☐ **Effective:** Calendar years beginning after Aug. 5, '97. ('97 Act §1601(j)(2))

¶ 921. Only SIMPLE 401(k) plans are exempt from the top-heavy rules

Code Sec. 401(k)(11)(D)(ii), as amended by '97 Act § 1601(d)(2)(A)
Generally effective: Tax years beginning after Dec. 31, '96
Committee Reports, see ¶ 5361

A plan that meets the SIMPLE 401(k) requirements for any year is not treated as a top-heavy plan for the year. This exemption was not worded to confine the exemption from the top-heavy rules to SIMPLE 401(k)s. (FTC 2d/FIN ¶ H-9087; USTR ¶ 4014.1735; TaxDesk ¶ 28,403.1; PCA ¶ 28,238; PE ¶ 401-4.1735)

New Law. The top-heavy exemption applies to a plan which permits only contributions required to satisfy the SIMPLE 401(k) requirements. (Code Sec. 401(k)(11)(D)(ii) as amended by '97 Act §1601(d)(2)(A)) This exemption applies only to SIMPLE 401(k)s, and not to other plans maintained by the employer. (Com Rept, see ¶ 5361)

☐ **Effective:** Tax years beginning after Dec. 31, '96. ('97 Act §1601(j)(1))

FTC 2d References are to Federal Tax Coordinator 2d
FIN References are to RIA's Analysis of Federal Taxes: Income
USTR References are to United States Tax Reporter: Income, Estate & Gift, and Excise
PCA References are to Pension Coordinator and Pension & Benefits Expert/Advisor
PE References are to Pension and Profit Sharing 2nd
EP References are to Estate Planning & Taxation Coordinator and Estate Planning Advisor

Plans of Tax-Exempt Employers

¶ 922. Dollar limitation on defined benefit plan payments is no longer reduced for police and firefighters whose benefits begin before age 65

Code Sec. 415(b)(2)(G), as amended by '97 Act § 1527(a)
Generally effective: Years beginning after Dec. 31, '96
Committee Reports, see ¶ 5349

Generally, a defined benefit plan must provide that the annual benefit starting at an employee's social security retirement age will not exceed the lesser of (1) $125,000 (adjusted for the cost of living) or (2) 100% of average compensation for the participant's high three years of compensation. Governmental plans, however, are not subject to the 100% of compensation limitation. If benefits begin before the participant reaches social security retirement age, the dollar limitation is actuarially reduced. If benefits begin after reaching social security retirement age, the limitation is actuarially increased.

For a government plan, "age 62" is substituted for "social security retirement age." If payments begin at age 55 or later, the benefit limitation can't be reduced below $75,000. If the benefit begins before age 55, the benefit limitation is the actuarial equivalent of the $75,000 limitation at age 55. The dollar limitation is increased if benefits begin after age 65.

For a plan covering police and firefighters, special limitation rules apply to "qualified participants" under pre-'97 Act law. The rules generally applicable to government plans applied, but the dollar limitation at early retirement could not be reduced below $50,000, as adjusted for the cost of living. A "qualified participant" includes an employee who has at least 15 years of service with a police or fire department organized and operated by a state or local subdivision, or a member of the U.S. Armed Services, and who is a participant in a pension plan maintained by a state or local subdivision. (FTC 2d/FIN ¶ H-5960; USTR ¶ 4154.03; TaxDesk ¶ 28,271; PCA ¶ 23,711; PE ¶ 415-4.03)

New Law. The defined benefit dollar limitation is not reduced when qualified police or firefighters or members of the armed forces retire early. (Code Sec. 415(b)(2)(G) as amended by '97 Act §1527(a)) The defined benefit dollar limitation still applies, though. If benefits begin after age 65, the dollar limit is actuarially increased, the same as under pre-'97 Act law. (Com Rept, see ¶ 5349)

> *observation:* Thus, under the '97 Act, whether payments begin at age 65 or at any younger age, defined benefit plan payouts to qualified police and fire personnel and members of the U.S. armed forces are subject to the same dollar limitation ($125,000 for '97).

☐ **Effective:** Years beginning after Dec. 31, '96. ('97 Act §1527(b))

¶ 923. Limits on contributions for purchasing permissive service credit under governmental plans

Code Sec. 415(n), as amended by '97 Act § 1526(a)
Code Sec. 415(k), as amended by '97 Act § 1526(b)
Generally effective: Years beginning after Dec. 31, '97
Committee Reports, see ¶ 5348

Many state and local government plans allow employees to purchase credit for service with another governmental employer. Employee contributions made to purchase service credit are subject to the applicable qualified plan limits on contributions and benefits. For a defined contribution plan, the limit on annual additions is the lesser of $30,000 (indexed) or 25% of compensation. Annual additions include both employer contributions and after-tax employee contributions. (FTC 2d/FIN ¶ H-6003; USTR ¶ 4154.06; TaxDesk ¶ 28,278; PCA ¶ 23,754; PE ¶ 415-4.06) Generally, for a defined benefit plan, the maximum annual benefit payable is the lesser of (1) 100% of compensation or (2) $125,000 (indexed). Governmental plans, however, are not subject to the 100% of compensation limitation. (FTC 2d/FIN ¶ H-5950.1; USTR ¶ 4154.02; PCA ¶ 23,701.1; PE ¶ 415-4.02) Employee contributions "picked up" by the governmental employer are treated as employer contributions. (FTC 2d/FIN ¶ H-9554; USTR ¶ 4144.16; TaxDesk ¶ 14,180; PCA ¶ 29,005; PE ¶ 414-4.16)

There were no restrictions on the amount of the service credit an employee could purchase other than the limits on contributions and benefits.

New Law. The '97 Act modifies the limits on contributions and benefits to encourage portability of benefits for employees changing jobs from one government employer to another. (Com Rept, see ¶ 5348)

Under the '97 Act: (i) contributions by a participant in a governmental plan to purchase "permissive service credit" must satisfy one of two limits, applied by taking these contributions into account (see below); and (ii) limits are placed on the amount of permissive service credit that may be purchased or taken into account for "nonqualified service" (see below).

Under the '97 Act, if a participant in a state or local governmental defined benefit plan makes a contribution to the plan in order to purchase "permissive service credit," then either one of the two following limitations will apply to the contribution:

(1) the defined benefit plan limit (under Code Sec. 415(b)), as determined by treating the accrued benefit derived from all of the employee's contributions to purchase "permissive service credit" as an annual benefit; or (Code Sec. 415(n)(1)(A) as amended by '97 Act §1526(a))

FTC 2d References are to Federal Tax Coordinator 2d
FIN References are to RIA's Analysis of Federal Taxes: Income
USTR References are to United States Tax Reporter: Income, Estate & Gift, and Excise
PCA References are to Pension Coordinator and Pension & Benefits Expert/Advisor
PE References are to Pension and Profit Sharing 2nd
EP References are to Estate Planning & Taxation Coordinator and Estate Planning Advisor

(2) the defined contribution plan limit (under Code Sec. 415(c)), as determined by treating all of the employee's contributions to purchase "permissive service credit" as annual additions, (Code Sec. 415(n)(1)(B)) and taking into account any other of the participant's annual additions. (Com Rept, see ¶ 5348)

In applying the Code Sec. 415(b) plan limit ((1) above), the plan won't fail the reduced limit for early retirement under Code Sec. 415(b)(2)(C) solely by reason of the application of the permissive service credit rules. (Code Sec. 415(n)(2)(A)) The plan won't fail the 25% of compensation limit under the Code Sec. 415(c) limit ((2) above) solely by reason of the application of the permissive service credit rules. (Code Sec. 415(n)(2)(B)) Thus, when the Code Sec. 415(c) limit is applied, contributions to purchase "permissive service credit" are considered only toward the $30,000 limit. (Com Rept, see ¶ 5348)

For purposes of these rules, "permissive service credit" means credit for a period of service recognized by the governmental plan, but not received under the plan, if the employee voluntarily contributes to the plan an amount (as determined by the plan) which does not exceed the amount necessary to fund the benefit attributable to the period of service and which is in addition to the regular employee contributions, if any, under the plan. (Code Sec. 415(n)(3)(A))

Limits for "nonqualified service" A plan will not comply with Code Sec. 415 if more than five years of permissive service credit is purchased for "nonqualified service." Also, Code Sec. 415 is violated if nonqualified service is taken into account for an employee with less than five years of plan participation. (Code Sec. 415(n)(3)(B)) "Nonqualified service" is service *other than* service as an employee of:

(1) a federal, state or local government;

(2) an association representing federal, state or local employees;

(3) an elementary or secondary educational institution; or

(4) the military services (other than military service under the rules relating to veterans' reemployment rights under Code Sec. 414(u)).

Service under items (1), (2) or (3), above, is not qualified if it enables a participant to receive a retirement benefit for the same service under more than one plan. (Code Sec. 415(n)(3)(C))

If a participant repays to a governmental plan any contributions or earnings that were previously refunded upon a forfeiture of service credit under the plan (or another plan maintained by a state or local government employer within the same state), then the repayment can't be taken into account for purposes of Code Sec. 415. (Code Sec. 415(k)((3) as amended by '97 Act §1526(b)) Any service credit obtained as a result of the repayment cannot be considered permissive service credit. (Com Rept, see ¶ 5348)

The '97 Act is not intended to affect the application of "pick up" contributions to purchase permissive service credit or the treatment of pick up contributions under Code Sec. 415. (Com Rept, see ¶ 5348)

Transition rule The amendments made by this provision of the '97 Act generally apply to permissive service credit contributions made in years beginning after Dec. 31,

'97. A transitional rule applies to plans that allow participants to purchase permissive service credit before the '97 Act is enacted. Under this rule, the defined contribution plan limits under Code Sec. 415(c)(1) don't reduce the amount of permissive service credit of an eligible participant allowed under the terms of the plan as in effect on the date of enactment. For this purpose, an "eligible participant" is an individual who first became a participant in the plan before the first plan year beginning after the last day of the calendar year in which the next regular session (following Aug. 5, '97) of the governing body with authority to amend the plan ends. ('97 Act §1526(c))

☐ **Effective:** Years beginning after Dec. 31, '97. ('97 Act §1526(c))

¶ 924. Qualified plan nondiscrimination and minimum participation rules made permanently inapplicable to state and local governmental plans

Code Sec. 401(a)(5), as amended by '97 Act § 1505(a)(1)
Code Sec. 401(a)(26)(H), as amended by '97 Act § 1505(a)(2)
Code Sec. 410(c)(2), as amended by '97 Act § 1505(a)(3)
Code Sec. 401(k)(3)(G), as amended by '97 Act § 1505(b)
Code Sec. 403(b)(12)(C), as amended by '97 Act § 1505(c)
Generally effective: Tax years beginning on or after Aug. 5, '97
Committee Reports, see ¶ 5311

Nondiscrimination and minimum participation rules for various retirement plans require that a plan not discriminate in favor of highly compensated employees with regard to plan contribution and benefits. These nondiscrimination rules apply to all governmental plans, including 401(k) plans in effect before May 6, '86, and 403(b) annuity plans. The effective date by which government plans must comply with the nondiscrimination and minimum participation rules has been extended to plan years beginning on or after the later of: (1) Jan. 1, '99, or (2) 90 days after the opening of the first legislative session beginning on or after Jan. 1, '99, of the governing body with authority to amend the plan (if that body doesn't meet continuously). For plan years beginning before the extended effective date, governmental plans are considered to satisfy the nondiscrimination requirements. (FTC 2d/FIN ¶ H-5406, ¶ H-5754, ¶ H-6104, ¶ H-6512, ¶ H-9051, ¶ H-12420; USTR ¶ 4014, ¶ 4014.173, ¶ 4014.19, ¶ 4014.21, ¶ 4014.25, ¶ 4034.04, ¶ 4104.1021; TaxDesk ¶ 28,403, ¶ 28,418, ¶ 28,070, ¶ 28,606; PCA ¶ 23,207, ¶ 23,505, ¶ 23,905, ¶ 24,613, ¶ 28,202, ¶ 36,021; PE ¶ 401-4, ¶ 401-4.173, ¶ 401-4.19, ¶ 401-4.21, ¶ 401-4.25, ¶ 403-4.04, ¶ 410-4.1021)

New Law. The '97 Act makes permanent the moratorium on state and local governmental plans' compliance with several nondiscrimination rules. (Com Rept, see ¶ 5311) Thus, the following nondiscrimination rules and minimum participation requirements do not apply to state and local governmental plans:

FTC 2d References are to Federal Tax Coordinator 2d
FIN References are to RIA's Analysis of Federal Taxes: Income
USTR References are to United States Tax Reporter: Income, Estate & Gift, and Excise
PCA References are to Pension Coordinator and Pension & Benefits Expert/Advisor
PE References are to Pension and Profit Sharing 2nd
EP References are to Estate Planning & Taxation Coordinator and Estate Planning Advisor

(1) the nondiscrimination rules under Code Sec. 401(a)(4) and the minimum participation standards of Code Sec. 410 (as required under Code Sec. 401(a)(3)), (Code Sec. 401(a)(5)(G) as amended by '97 Act §1505(a)(1)) including the requirement that plans not exclude employees who have attained a specified age; (Code Sec. 410(c)(2) as amended by '97 Act §1505(a)(3))

(2) the additional participation requirements (under Code Sec. 401(a)(26)); (Code Sec. 401(a)(26)(H))

(3) the minimum coverage requirements as applied to 401(k) plans; and (Code Sec. 401(k)(3)(G))

(4) for contributions to 403(b) plans other than under a salary reduction agreement, the nondiscrimination rules of Code Sec. 401(a)(4), Code Sec. 401(a)(5), Code Sec. 401(a)(26), and Code Sec. 410. (Code Sec. 403(b)(12)(C) as amended by '97 Act §1505(c))

For years beginning before these nondiscrimination and minimum participation rules were made permanent, a state or local governmental plan is treated as satisfying the requirements of Code Sec. 401(a)(3), Code Sec. 401(a)(4), Code Sec. 401(a)(26), Code Sec. 401(k), Code Sec. 401(m), Code Sec. 403(b)(1)(D), Code Sec. 403(b)(12), and Code Sec. 410, for all tax years beginning before Aug. 5, '97. ('97 Act §1505(d)(2))

☐ **Effective:** Tax years beginning on or after Aug. 5, '97. ('97 Act §1505(d)(1))

¶ 925. Exclusion allowance rules for 403(b) annuities modified to conform to earlier Code Sec. 415 changes

Code Sec. 403(b)(3), as amended by '97 Act § 1504(a)(1)
Code Sec. None, '97 Act § 1504(b)
Generally effective: Years beginning after Dec. 31, '97
Committee Reports, see ¶ 5310

Annual contributions to a section 403(b) annuity cannot exceed the "exclusion allowance," which can be determined under either of two methods.

Under one method, the exclusion allowance for a tax year is the excess (if any) of: (1) 20 percent of an employee's "includible compensation" multiplied by his years of service, over (2) the aggregate employer contributions for an annuity excludable for any prior tax years. Before the '97 Act, "includible compensation" was the amount of compensation from the employer that was includible in gross income for the most recent year that can be counted as a year of service.

Under an alternative method, an employee can elect to have the exclusion allowance determined under the rules relating to tax-qualified defined contribution plans (under Code Sec. 415). Under these rules, the maximum annual addition that can be made to a defined contribution plan is the lesser of: (1) $30,000, or (2) 25 percent of compensation.

Under Code Sec. 415, "compensation" includes certain of an employee's elective deferrals.

Also, under Code Sec. 415, an overall limitation applies if the employee is a participant in both a defined contribution plan and a defined benefit plan of the same employer. This overall limitation may further reduce the maximum annual addition that can be made to a defined contribution plan. But this overall limitation has been repealed for years beginning after Dec. 31, '99. (FTC 2d/FIN ¶ H-12439, ¶ H-12443, ¶ H-12457; USTR ¶ 4034.04; TaxDesk ¶ 28,070; PCA ¶ 36,040, ¶ 36,044, ¶ 36,058; PE ¶ 403-4.04)

New Law. The Act conforms the exclusion allowance to the way in which the Code Sec. 415 limit is calculated. (Com Rept, see ¶ 5310) Thus, "includible compensation" for determining the exclusion allowance is modified to also include:

(1) any elective deferral, and

(2) any amount which is contributed or deferred by the employer at the employee's election under (i) a cafeteria plan, or (ii) an unfunded deferred compensation plan of a state or local government (i.e., a section 457 plan), and which is not includible in the employee's income. (Code Sec. 403(b)(3) as amended by '97 Act §1504(a)(1))

IRS is directed to modify its regulations on the exclusion allowance to reflect the fact that the overall limit on benefits and contributions under Code Sec. 415(e) has been repealed (effective for years beginning after Dec. 31, '99). IRS's modified regs are to take effect for years beginning after Dec. 31, '99. ('97 Act §1504(b)) The revised regs are to relate to the election to have the exclusion allowance determined under Code Sec. 415. (Com Rept, see ¶ 5310)

☐ **Effective:** Years beginning after Dec. 31, '97. ('97 Act §1504(a)(2))

¶ 926. Exclusion of ministers from discrimination testing of non-church retirement plans is expanded

Code Sec. 414(e)(5)(C), as amended by '97 Act § 1522(a)(1)
Generally effective: Years beginning after '97
Committee Reports, see ¶ 5344

A minister who is employed by an organization other than a church is treated as if employed by the church and may participate in the church's retirement plan. If the organization employing the minister also sponsors a retirement plan, the plan did not have to include the minister as an employee for purposes of satisfying the nondiscrimination rules applicable to qualified plans provided the organization was *not eligible to participate* in the church plan. (FTC 2d/FIN ¶ H-9556; USTR ¶ 4144.13; PCA ¶ 29,007; PE ¶ 414-4.13)

New Law. The '97 Act provides that if a minister is employed by an organization other than a church, and the organization is *not otherwise participating* in the church

---

FTC 2d References are to Federal Tax Coordinator 2d
FIN References are to RIA's Analysis of Federal Taxes: Income
USTR References are to United States Tax Reporter: Income, Estate & Gift, and Excise
PCA References are to Pension Coordinator and Pension & Benefits Expert/Advisor
PE References are to Pension and Profit Sharing 2nd
EP References are to Estate Planning & Taxation Coordinator and Estate Planning Advisor

plan, then the minister does not have to be included as an employee under the retirement plan of the organization for purposes of the nondiscrimination rules. (Code Sec. 414(e)(5)(C) as amended by '97 Act §1522(a)(1)) In other words, an organization that may be part of a church plan but chooses not to be is subject to the same rule as an organization that cannot participate in a church plan. Congress believed that it was appropriate to extend the same relief to non-church organizations that may be eligible to participate in a church plan but elect not to do so as it had to organizations that could not participate in church plans. (Com Rept, see ¶ 5344)

☐ **Effective:** Years beginning after Dec. 31, '97. ('97 Act §1522(b))

¶ 927. Contributions to church plan on behalf of self-employed minister are excluded from income

Code Sec. 415(e)(5)(E), as amended by '97 Act § 1522(a)(2)
Generally effective: Years beginning after '97
Committee Reports, see ¶ 5344

Contributions made to retirement plans by ministers who are self-employed are deductible to the extent such contributions do not exceed certain limitations applicable to retirement plans. These limitations include the limit on elective deferrals, the exclusion allowance, and the limit on annual additions to a retirement plan. There was no income exclusion for contributions to church plans made on behalf of a self-employed minister. (FTC 2d/FIN ¶ H-9556; USTR ¶ 4144.13; PCA ¶ 29,007; PE ¶ 414-4.13)

New Law. The unique characteristics of church plans and the procedures associated with contributions made by ministers who are self-employed create particular problems with respect to plan administration. (Com Rept, see ¶ 5344) The '97 Act provides that for a contribution made on behalf of a self-employed minister to a church plan, the contribution is excluded from the minister's gross income. However, the exclusion is available only to the extent that the contribution would be excluded if the minister was an employee of the church and the contribution was made to the church's plan. (Code Sec. 414(e)(5)(E) as amended by '97 Act §1522(a)(2))

☐ **Effective:** Years beginning after Dec. 31, '97. ('97 Act §1522(b))

¶ 928. Transitional relief for certain bus companies from some minimum funding requirements

Code Sec. None, '97 Act § 1508
Generally effective: Plan years beginning after Dec. 31, '96
Committee Reports, see ¶ 5314

Defined benefit plans are required to meet regular minimum funding rules. Additional funding requirements, providing for faster funding, are imposed on certain plans because, even if the plan meets the regular minimum funding requirements, there may not be sufficient assets available to pay all promised benefits to participants if the plan were terminated. These additional funding requirements do not apply for plans with a "funded current liability percentage" of at least 90%.

The amount to be charged to the funding standard account (in satisfying the regular minimum funding rules) is limited to the amount of the "full funding limitation." The "full funding limitation" may not be less than: (1) 90% of the plan's current liability, over (2) the value of the plan's assets.

The Pension Benefit Guaranty Corporation (PBGC) insures benefits under most defined benefit pension plans, paying specified benefits in the event the plan is terminated with insufficient funds to pay for plan benefits. PBGC is funded in part by a flat-rate premium per plan participant, and a variable rate premium based on plan underfunding. (FTC 2d/FIN ¶ H-7644.1, ¶ H-7629.1; USTR ¶ 4124.10; PCA ¶ 25,645.1; PE ¶ 412-4.10)

New Law. Certain interstate bus companies have pension plans that are closed to new participants, and the rate of mortality of the participants in these plans has been significantly greater than that predicted by the mortality tables that the plans are required to use for minimum funding purposes. As a result, the sponsors of these plans have been required to make contributions that cause the plan to be substantially overfunded. Congress believes that it is appropriate to modify the minimum funding requirements for these plans, while at the same time ensuring that pension benefits are adequately funded. (Com Rept, see ¶ 5314)

The Act provides transitional relief for plans of certain bus companies from "additional" funding requirements applicable to underfunded plans. Under the rule, a plan meeting specified requirements is treated as having a "funded current liability percentage" of at least 90% for plan years beginning after '95 (see below). Also, the floor for the amount of the "full funding limitation" is reduced (see below). (Sec. 769(c), PL 103-465, 12/8/94, as amended by '97 Act §1508(a))

> *observation:* Thus, for years in which eligible plans satisfy the transition rule, the additional funding requirements do not apply. Also, the "full funding limitation" may be lower than it otherwise could be (so that the required contribution to the funding standard account would be reduced).

The "funded current liability percentage" for plans to which the transition rule applies (see below), is treated as at least 90% for any plan year beginning:

(1) after '95 and before 2005, if, for the plan year, the "funded current liability percentage" for the plan year is at least 85%; and

(2) after 2004 and before 2009, if the "funded current liability percentage" for the plan year is at least the minimum percentage determined according to the table below. (Sec. 769(c)(2)(A), PL 103-465, 12/8/94, as amended by '97 Act §1508(a))

In determining the floor below which the "full funding limitation" cannot be less than, "90 percent" is replaced:

FTC 2d References are to Federal Tax Coordinator 2d
FIN References are to RIA's Analysis of Federal Taxes: Income
USTR References are to United States Tax Reporter: Income, Estate & Gift, and Excise
PCA References are to Pension Coordinator and Pension & Benefits Expert/Advisor
PE References are to Pension and Profit Sharing 2nd
EP References are to Estate Planning & Taxation Coordinator and Estate Planning Advisor

Research Institute of America

(1) after '95 and before 2005, with 85%, and

(2) after 2004 and before 2010, with the minimum percentage in the table below. (Sec. 769(c)(2)(B), PL 103-465, 12/8/94, as amended by '97 Act §1508(a))

Plan year beginning in:	Minimum percentage
2005	86
2006	87
2007	88
2008	89
2009 and thereafter	90

If "funded current liability percentage" falls to less than 85%. If the "funded current liability percentage" falls to less than 85%, the transitional relief described above will continue to apply if contributions for the plan year are made to the plan:

(1) for any plan year beginning after '95 and before 2005, in an amount equal to the lesser of:

(a) the amount necessary to result in a "funded current liability percentage" of 85%, or

(b) the greater of: (i) 2% of the plan's current liability as of the beginning of the plan year, or (ii) the amount necessary to result in a "funded current liability percentage" of 80% as of the end of the plan year.

(2) for the plan year beginning in 2005 and for each of the next three plan years, in an amount equal to at least the expected increase in current liability due to benefits accruing during the plan year. (Sec. 769(c)(2)(C), PL 103-465, 12/8/94, as amended by '97 Act §1508(a))

Plans eligible for relief. The transition rule described above may apply for a plan that:

(1) was not required to pay a variable rate premium for the plan year beginning in '96;

(2) has not, in any plan year beginning after 2005 and before 2009, merged with another plan (other than a plan sponsored by an employer that was in '96 within the plan sponsor's controlled group); and

(3) is sponsored by a company that is engaged primarily in the interurban or interstate passenger bus service. (Sec. 769(c)(1)(C), PL 103-465, 12/8/94, as amended by '97 Act §1508(a))

☐ **Effective:** Plan years beginning after Dec. 31, '96. ('97 Act §1508(b))

¶ 929. Certain church health plans can discriminate based on health status

Code Sec. 9802(c), as amended by '97 Act § 1532
Generally effective: Plan years beginning after June 30, '97
Committee Reports, see ¶ 5354

Group health plans can not establish rules that base eligibility or premium contributions on any of a list of factors related to an individual's health status (*e.g.*, medical condition, claims experience or medical history). There is no exception for group health plans that are church plans. (FTC 2d/FIN ¶ H-1325.14, ¶ H-1325.15; USTR ¶ 98,024; PE ¶ 9802-4)

New Law. A church plan (as defined in Code Sec. 414(e)) is not treated as discriminating based on health status solely because it requires evidence of good health for coverage of:

... an employee of an employer with 10 or less employees;

... a self-employed individual; or,

... an individual who enrolls in the health plan more than 90 days after initial eligibility under the plan.

This exception to the discrimination rules applies to a church health plan only if the plan included the provision requiring evidence of good health on July 15, '97, and at all times thereafter. (Code Sec. 9802(c) as amended by '97 Act §1532(a))

> ⚡ *caution:* Although this exception allows church health plans to take health status into account in some *coverage* determinations, it does not allow these plans to consider the health status of an individual in setting an individual's *premium contribution* requirements.

☐ **Effective:** As if included in §401(a) of the Health Reform Act of '96 (which was generally effective for plan years beginning after June 30, '97). ('97 Act §1532(b))

¶ 930. Rural irrigation and water conservation entities can have 401(k) plans

Code Sec. 401(k)(7)(B)(iv), as amended by '97 Act § 1525
Generally effective: Years beginning after Dec. 31 '97
Committee Reports, see ¶ 5347

Taxable and tax-exempt entities, including rural cooperatives, can adopt qualified cash or deferred arrangements, but state and local governments cannot. For this purpose, the term "rural cooperative" includes a cooperative telephone company described in Code Sec. 501(c)(12). But the term "rural cooperative" didn't include a mutual ditch or irrigation company, whether or not it qualified for tax-exempt status under Code Sec. 501(c)(12) by receiving at least 85% of its income from members. (FTC 2d/FIN ¶ H-8969; USTR ¶ 4014.17; PCA ¶ 28,120; PE ¶ 401-4.17)

New Law. The definition of "rural cooperative" has been expanded to include any organization which is: (1) a mutual irrigation or ditch company under Code Sec.

FTC 2d References are to Federal Tax Coordinator 2d
FIN References are to RIA's Analysis of Federal Taxes: Income
USTR References are to United States Tax Reporter: Income, Estate & Gift, and Excise
PCA References are to Pension Coordinator and Pension & Benefits Expert/Advisor
PE References are to Pension and Profit Sharing 2nd
EP References are to Estate Planning & Taxation Coordinator and Estate Planning Advisor

501(c)(12) (without regard to the 85% requirement), or (2) an irrigation, water conservation or drainage district organized as a municipal corporation under state law. (Code Sec. 401(k)(7)(B)(iv) as amended by '97 Act §1525(a)) This allows mutual irrigation or ditch companies or districts organized under state law to maintain 401(k) plans even if the organization is a state or local government organization. (Com Rept, see ¶ 5347)

> **⊘ observation:** Under the '97 Act, a mutual irrigation or ditch company can have a 401(k) plan even if it doesn't meet the 85% requirement for tax-exempt status under Code Sec. 501(c)(12). But a cooperative telephone company that doesn't meet the 85% requirement for tax-exempt status can't have a 401(k) plan since it presumably isn't "described" in Code Sec. 501(c)(12).

☐ **Effective:** Years beginning after Dec. 31, '97. ('97 Act §1525(b))

Other Qualified Plan Rules

¶ 931. Increase in current liability funding limit and new special amortization rule

Code Sec. 412(c)(7)(A)(i)(I), as amended by '97 Act § 1521(a)
Code Sec. 412(c)(7)(F), as amended by '97 Act § 1521(a)
Code Sec. 412(b)(2)(E), as amended by '97 Act § 1521(c)(1)
Generally effective: Plan years beginning after Dec. 31, '98
Committee Reports, see ¶ 5343

Defined benefit plans and money purchase plans (including target benefit plans) must meet certain minimum funding requirements. The minimum funding rules require that these plans conform to a minimum "funding standard." A funding standard is a formula or calculation that determines the minimum contribution the employer must make each year in order to fund promised benefits payable under the plan. The amount of the plan contribution is also subject to a maximum limit. Before the '97 Act, the maximum limit, or "full funding limitation", was the lesser of a plan's accrued liability or 150% of current liability. Accrued liability refers to projected benefits; current liability refers to the benefits accrued to date. To the extent that amounts can't be contributed because of the full funding limit, they can be amortized over a 10-year period. (Com Rept, see ¶ 5343) (FTC 2d/FIN ¶ H-7629; USTR ¶ 4124.07; TaxDesk ¶ 28,156; PCA ¶ 25,630; PE ¶ 412-4.07)

New Law. Congress believes that the 150% full funding limit unduly restricts funding. (Com Rept, see ¶ 5343) The percentage of current liability that may be considered for purposes of determining the maximum funding limit is increased from 150% to the following applicable percentages: (Code Sec. 412(c)(7)(A)(i)(I) as amended by '97 Act §1521(a))

For plan years beginning	% of current liability
1999 or 2000	155
2001 or 2002	160
2003 or 2004	165
2005 and later	170

observation: To the extent that the amount of the tax deduction that an employer can claim for the year is tied to the full funding limitation (under Code Sec. 404(a)(1)(A)), an employer will be able to increase both its permissible contribution to the plan and thus, its deductible amount for the year.

In addition, the amount necessary to fund the minimum funding standard account is amended to include the amount necessary to amortize over a 20-year period the contributions which would be required to be made under the plan but for the provisions of the current liability funding limit under Code Sec. 412(c)(7)(A)(i)(I) (above). (Code Sec. 412(b)(2)(E) as amended by '97 Act §1521(c)(1))

Although this new amortization rule is effective for plan years beginning after Dec. 31, '98 (see below), a special rule is provided for amortization bases remaining at the end of the '98 plan year. Any unamortized balance left over from before '99 which is part of an amortization base established under Code Sec. 412(c)(7)(D)(iii) and ERISA §302(c)(7)(D)(iii) (the ERISA companion section) must be amortized in equal annual installments (until fully amortized) over a 20-year period reduced by the number of years since the amortization base had been established. ('97 Act §1521(d)(2))(Code Sec. 412(c)(7)(D)(iii) and ERISA §302(c)(7)(D)(iii) refer to contributions which would be required to be made under the plan but for the current liability funding limit. Both of these provisions are repealed by the '97 Act, effective after '98. ('97 Act §1521(c))) No amortization is required for funding methods that do not provide for amortization bases. (Com Rept, see ¶ 5343)

Both ERISA §302(c)(7)(A)(i)(I) (the companion provision to Code Sec. 412(c)(7)(A)(i)(I)) and ERISA §302(b)(2) (the companion provision to Code Sec. 412(b)(2)) are also amended by the '97 Act to provide, respectively, for the same increase (as in the Code) in the allowable ceiling on the current liability full funding limitation ('97 Act §1521(b)) and the special amortization rule ('97 Act §1521(c)(2)).

☐ **Effective:** Plan years beginning after Dec. 31, '98. ('97 Act §1521(d)(1))

¶ 932. Window period for amending plans and annuity contracts to reflect the '97 Act

Code Sec. None, '97 Act § 1541
Generally effective: Aug. 5, '97
Committee Reports, see ¶ 5355

Plan amendments to reflect legislative changes generally must be made by the due date for filing the employer's income tax return for the employer's tax year in which the law change occurs. A plan sponsor may not be able to amend the plan as readily as required or desired, but may need or want to operate the plan consistently with an anticipated amendment before that amendment is formally adopted. Also, under the "anti-cutback" rules, a plan amendment must not reduce or eliminate a participant's accrued plan benefits (except under limited exceptions). The anti-cutback rules could complicate the administration of a plan that is to be operated as if an anticipated plan amendment was already adopted. (FTC 2d/FIN ¶ H-7301, ¶ H-8751; USTR ¶ 4014, ¶ 4114.45; TaxDesk ¶ 28,617, ¶ 28,635; PCA ¶ 25,302, ¶ 27,302; PE ¶ 401-4, ¶ 411-4.45)

New Law. The '97 Act provides that, if certain conditions (see below) are met, an amendment to a plan or annuity contract that is made in response to the '97 Act's pension and benefit provisions: ('97 Act §1541(b)(1)(A))

(1) doesn't have to be made before the first day of the first plan year beginning after Dec. 31, '98 (or beginning after Dec. 31, 2000, for governmental plans); and ('97 Act §1541(b)(1)(B))

(2) whether or not the amendment is required:

(a) won't cause the plan or contract to be treated as not operated under its terms for the period before an amendment would be required, merely because the plan or contract is operated in a manner consistent with the anticipated amendment, and ('97 Act §1541(a)(1))

(b) won't cause the plan to fail to meet the anti-cutback rules ('97 Act §1541(a)(2)) as a result of the plan amendment. (Com Rept, see ¶ 5355)

Conditions. For the rules allowing a delay in the amendment (in response to the '97 Act) of a plan or annuity contract to apply (see above), the plan or contract must be operated as if the amendment were in effect during, and applied retroactively for, the period:

(i) beginning on: (A) the effective date of the legislative change in response to which the amendment was made, or (B) if the amendment was not *required* by the legislative change, the effective date specified in the plan; and

(ii) ending on the date that is the earlier of: (A) the first day of the first plan year beginning after Dec. 31, '98 (or beginning after Dec. 31, 2000, for governmental plans), or (B) the date the plan or contract amendment is adopted. ('97 Act §1541(b)(2))

☐ **Effective:** Effective date of the legislative change in the '97 Act in response to which the plan or contract amendment was made. ('97 Act §1541(b)(2)(A))

¶ 933. Matching contributions of self-employed individuals are not treated as elective employer contributions

Code Sec. 402(g)(9), as amended by '97 Act § 1501(a)
Code Sec. 408(p)(8), as amended by '97 Act § 1501(b)
Generally effective: Years beginning after Dec. 31, '97
Committee Reports, see ¶ 5307

An employee can elect to make pre-tax contributions, i.e., "elective deferrals," to a qualified 401(k) plan or a SIMPLE plan. The amount of an individual's "elective deferrals" for any tax year over the applicable dollar limit (which is adjusted for changes in the cost of living) is includible in the individual's income. For '97, the applicable dollar limit is $9,500.

Employers may make matching contributions, which include any employer contributions to a defined contribution plan on behalf of an employee on account of the employee's elective deferral. Matching contributions generally are not subject to the annual limit on elective deferrals. But matching contributions made for a self-employed individual are treated as additional elective contributions for that individual. Thus, both elective and matching contributions for self-employed individuals are applied towards the limit on the annual deferral limits for elective deferrals. (FTC 2d/FIN ¶ H-6526, ¶ H-9152, ¶ H-9155; USTR ¶ 4014.17, ¶ 4014.171, ¶ 4024, ¶ 4084.06; TaxDesk ¶ 28,413, ¶ 28,420; PCA ¶ 24,627, ¶ 28,403, ¶ 28,406; PE ¶ 401-4.17, ¶ 401-4.171, ¶ 402-4, ¶ 408-4.06)

New Law. Under the '97 Act, the treatment of matching contributions for self-employed individuals is the same as for other employees. (Com Rept, see ¶ 5307) That is, a matching contribution made on behalf of a self-employed individual is not treated as an elective employer contribution under a qualified 401(k) plan. (Code Sec. 402(g)(9) as amended by '97 Act §1501(a)) Thus, matching contributions on behalf of self-employed individuals are not subject to the elective contribution limit. (Com Rept, see ¶ 5307)

But qualified matching contributions that a self-employed individual treats as elective contributions for purposes of satisfying the ADP test *are* treated as elective contributions and *are* subject to the elective contribution limits. (Code Sec. 402(g)(9))

Any matching contribution which is made to a SIMPLE IRA on behalf of a self-employed individual is not treated as an elective employer contribution. (Code Sec. 408(p)(8) as amended by '97 Act §1501(b))

> *observation:* Thus, matching contributions under a SIMPLE plan on behalf of a self-employed individual do not count towards the limit on elective deferrals.

FTC 2d References are to Federal Tax Coordinator 2d
FIN References are to RIA's Analysis of Federal Taxes: Income
USTR References are to United States Tax Reporter: Income, Estate & Gift, and Excise
PCA References are to Pension Coordinator and Pension & Benefits Expert/Advisor
PE References are to Pension and Profit Sharing 2nd
EP References are to Estate Planning & Taxation Coordinator and Estate Planning Advisor

observation: Matching contributions made on behalf of self-employed individuals are not treated as elective contributions for any purposes of the Code. Thus, this provision clarifies that matching contributions for a self-employed individual are not taken into account in applying the actual deferral percentage test (ADP) for 401(k) plans.

☐ **Effective:** Years beginning after Dec. 31, '97, for elective deferrals under 401(k) plans. ('97 Act §1501(c)(1))

Years beginning after Dec. 31, '96, for elective deferrals under SIMPLE plans. ('97 Act §1501(c)(2))

¶ 934. ERISA limit on investments in employer securities applies to 401(k) plan deferrals

Code Sec. None, as amended by '97 Act § 1524
Generally effective: Plan years beginning after '98
Committee Reports, see ¶ 5346

Under the Employee Retirement Income Security Act (ERISA), an "eligible individual account plan"—unlike other pension plans—may hold more than 10% of its assets in qualifying employer securities and real property. The term "eligible individual account plan" includes profit-sharing plans (that may include Code Sec. 401(k) cash or deferred arrangements) and employee stock ownership plans (ESOPs). (PCA ¶ 54,111; PE ¶ ER407-4.07)

New Law. The '97 Act amends ERISA § 407(b)(2) to treat the portion of an "eligible individual account plan" that consists of "applicable elective deferrals" (and earnings) as a separate non-eligible individual account plan if the deferrals are *required* to be invested in qualifying employer securities or qualifying employer real property under the terms of the plan, or at the direction of anyone other than the participant (or his beneficiary). An "applicable elective deferral" is an elective deferral made under a Code Sec. 401(k) qualified cash or deferred arrangement. (ERISA Sec. 407(b)(2) as amended by '97 Act §1524(a))

observation: Thus, a 401(k) plan trustee can't invest more than 10% of a 401(k) plan's assets attributable to elective deferrals in company stock. The 10% limit doesn't apply to investments in company stock made at the direction of the participant.

observation: This provision was enacted in response to recent well-publicized cases where employees of failing employers lost not only their jobs, but also a significant portion of their 401(k) plan account balances that were heavily invested in stock of the failing employers.

The category of "eligible individual account plans" not subject to the 10% limit on investments in employer securities and employer real property still includes:

... ESOPs;

. . . individual account plans if, on the last day of the preceding plan year, the fair market value of the assets of all of the employer's individual account plans is no more than 10% of the fair market value of all of the assets of all of the employer's pension plans (other than multiemployer plans); and,

. . . individual account plans that don't require the investment in employer securities and employer real property of more than 1% of an employee's compensation that is eligible for deferral. (ERISA Sec. 407(b)(2)(B))

☐ **Effective:** For elective deferrals for plan years beginning after '98. ('97 Act §1524(b)) The provision doesn't apply to *earnings* on pre-'99 elective deferrals. (Com Rept, see ¶ 5346)

observation: Thus, the 10% limit on a 401(k) plan's investment in company stock will apply after '98 to all of a 401(k) plan's assets attributable to elective deferrals, except for earnings on pre-'99 deferrals.

illustration: The '98 year-end value of the assets in Widget Co.'s 401(k) plan is $10 million, attributable entirely to the elective deferrals of Widget's employees. Of the plan's $10 million in assets, Widget employee deferrals totalled $2 million, with the other $8 million attributable to the 401(k) plan's successful investment of most of its assets in Widget stock. The post-'98 10% limit on the plan's investment in Widget stock will apply to the $2 million attributable to deferrals, but not to the $8 million attributable to plan earnings, according to the conference report. (The plan trustees may be able to maximize the plan's post-'98 investment in Widget stock by transferring Widget stock from the portion of the plan attributable to elective deferrals to the portion of the plan attributable to pre-'99 earnings—subject to their fiduciary duties to plan participants.)

¶ 935. ERISA plan descriptions, summary plan descriptions, and material modifications no longer filed with DOL, except on request

Code Sec. None, '97 Act § 1503
Generally effective: Aug. 5, '97
Committee Reports, see ¶ 5309

The Employee Retirement Income Security Act (ERISA) is designed to protect the interests of participants in employee benefit plans, and their beneficiaries. Employers are required to prepare ERISA employee benefit plan descriptions, summary plan descriptions ("SPDs"), and summaries of material modifications ("SMMs") to ERISA

FTC 2d References are to Federal Tax Coordinator 2d
FIN References are to RIA's Analysis of Federal Taxes: Income
USTR References are to United States Tax Reporter: Income, Estate & Gift, and Excise
PCA References are to Pension Coordinator and Pension & Benefits Expert/Advisor
PE References are to Pension and Profit Sharing 2nd
EP References are to Estate Planning & Taxation Coordinator and Estate Planning Advisor

plans. The SPDs and SMMs generally provide information on the benefits provided by the plan, as well as the participants' rights and obligations under the plan. The SPDs (in place of plan descriptions) and SMMs must be furnished to plan participants and beneficiaries. Before the '97 Act, the SPDs (in place of plan descriptions) and SMMs also had to be filed with the Secretary for the Department of Labor (DOL). (PCA ¶ 56,210; PE ¶ ER101-4)

New Law. Congress wants to alleviate the cost and burden of paperwork associated with employee benefit plans. (Com Rept, see ¶ 5309) To this end, the '97 Act eliminates the requirement that plan descriptions, SPDs and SMMs be filed with DOL. (ERISA § 101(b) as amended by '97 Act § 1503(a); ERISA § 102(a) as amended by '97 Act § 1503(b); ERISA § 104(a)(1) as amended by '97 Act § 1503(c)(1)) Instead, the plan administrator must furnish plan descriptions, SPDs, and SMMs (as well as any documents relating to the plan, e.g., bargaining agreement, trust agreement, contract, or other instrument under which the plan is established or operated) to DOL *only if* DOL requests the plan administrator to do so. (ERISA § 104(a)(6) as amended by '97 Act § 1503(c)(2)(A))

DOL can impose a civil penalty on the plan administrator for failure to comply (within 30 days) with requests to provide plan descriptions, SPDs, and SMMs and other plan related documents. The penalty is up to $100 per day for each failure, up to a maximum of $1,000 per request. No penalty applies if the failure was due to matters reasonably outside the control of the plan administrator. (ERISA § 502(c)(6) as amended by '97 Act § 1503(c)(2)(B))

☐ **Effective:** Aug. 5, '97. (Com Rept, see ¶ 5309)

¶ 936. Congress directs IRS and DOL to facilitate retirement plan administrators' use of electronic technologies

Code Sec. None, '97 Act § 1510
Generally effective: Aug. 5, '97
Committee Reports, see ¶ 5316

Under the law, it is not clear if sponsors of employee benefit plans may use new technologies (telephonic response systems, computers, e-mail) to satisfy the various ERISA requirements for providing notices, making elections, issuing consent forms, keeping records, and disclosing information. (Com Rept, see ¶ 5316)

New Law. Congress wants a review of existing agency guidance as a prelude for letting retirement plans use electronic technologies to satisfy ERISA requirements for providing notices, making elections, issuing consent forms, keeping records, and disclosing information. (Com Rept, see ¶ 5316) So, the '97 Act directs that, not later than Dec. 31, '98, the Secretary of the Treasury and the Secretary of the Department of Labor (DOL) must *each* issue guidance designed to interpret the retirement-plan notice, election, consent, disclosure, and time requirements, and the related recordkeeping requirements, that exist under the Internal Revenue Code and the Employee Retirement Income Security Act (ERISA). IRS and DOL must determine how plan sponsors and administrators can meet these requirements while still protecting the rights of participants and beneficiaries. The guidance must also clarify the extent to which the Code's writing requirements relating to retirement plans can be interpreted to permit paperless transactions. ('97 Act §1510(a))

Final regulations on the use of new technologies can't be made effective until the first plan year beginning at least six months after IRS and DOL issue final regulations. ('97 Act §1510(b))

☐ **Effective:** Aug. 5, '97. (Com Rept, see ¶ 5316)

¶ 937. Grandfather rule with respect to pension business of TIAA-CREF and Mutual of America is repealed

Code Sec. None, '97 Act § 1042
Generally effective: Tax years beginning after '97
Committee Reports, see ¶ 5142

Under Code Sec. 501(m) (which was enacted in '86), an organization described in Code Sec. 501(c)(3) or Code Sec. 501(c)(4) is exempt from tax only if no substantial part of its activities consists of providing commercial-type insurance. (FTC 2d/FIN ¶ D-6830; USTR ¶ 5014.35; TaxDesk ¶ 67,061; 67,251)

The '86 Act provided grandfather rules relating to the changes made by the '86 Act. Section 1012(c)(4)(A) of the '86 Act provided that the changes made by the '86 Act did not apply with respect to that portion of the business of Mutual of America which was attributable to pension business. Section 1012(c)(4)(B) of the '86 Act provided that the changes made by the '86 Act did not apply to that portion of the business of the Teachers Insurance Annuity Association-College Retirement Equities Fund (TIAA-CREF) which was attributable to pension business. "Pension business" meant the administration of any plan described in Code Sec. 401(a) which included a trust exempt from tax under Code Sec. 501(a), any plan under which amounts are contributed by an individual's employer for an annuity contract described in Code Sec. 403(b), any individual retirement plan described in Code Sec. 408, and any eligible deferred compensation plan to which Code Sec. 457(a) applied.

For those organizations which became taxable organizations under the provision added by the '86 Act, a fresh start was provided with respect to changes in accounting methods resulting from the change from tax-exempt to taxable status. Thus, no adjustment was made under Code Sec. 481 (FTC 2d/FIN ¶ G-2290; USTR ¶ 4814; TaxDesk ¶ 44,331) on account of an accounting method change. Such an organization was required to compute its ending '86 loss reserves without artificial changes that would reduce '87 income. Thus, any reserve weakening after Aug. 16, '86 was treated as occurring in the organization's first tax year beginning after Dec. 31, '86. The basis of such an organization's assets was deemed to be equal to the amount of the assets' fair mar-

FTC 2d References are to Federal Tax Coordinator 2d
FIN References are to RIA's Analysis of Federal Taxes: Income
USTR References are to United States Tax Reporter: Income, Estate & Gift, and Excise
PCA References are to Pension Coordinator and Pension & Benefits Expert/Advisor
PE References are to Pension and Profit Sharing 2nd
EP References are to Estate Planning & Taxation Coordinator and Estate Planning Advisor

 Research Institute of America 263

ket value on the first day of the organization's tax year beginning after Dec. 31, '86, for purposes of determining gain or loss (but not for determining depreciation or for other purposes). (FTC 2d/FIN ¶ E-5627)

Under Code Sec. 843, an insurance company is generally required to use the calendar year as the tax year. (FTC 2d/FIN ¶ E-4888; USTR ¶ 8434)

New Law. Section 1012(c)(4)(A) and Section 1012(c)(4)(B) of the '86 Act do not apply to any tax year beginning after Dec. 31, '97. ('97 Act §1042(a)) Thus, the grandfather rules applicable to that portion of the business of TIAA-CREF which is attributable to pension business, and that portion of the business of Mutual of America which is attributable to pension business are repealed. TIAA-CREF and Mutual of America are to be treated for federal tax purposes as life insurance companies. (Com Rept, see ¶ 5142)

Congress was concerned that the continued tax-exempt status of TIAA-CREF and Mutual of America, organizations that engage in insurance activities, gave those organizations an unfair competitive advantage. Congress believed that the provision of insurance at a price sufficient to cover the costs of insurance generally constituted an activity that was commercial. Thus, Congress believed it was no longer appropriate to continue the grandfather rule that permitted TIAA-CREF and Mutual of America to retain tax-exempt status with respect to pension business that constituted commercial-type insurance. (Com Rept, see ¶ 5142)

Fresh start provided for changes in accounting methods. In the case of an organization to which Code Sec. 501(m) applies solely by reason of the repeal, by the '97 Act, of the grandfather rules provided by the '86 Act, no adjustment will be made under Code Sec. 481 (or any other provision of the Code) on account of a change in its method of accounting for its first tax year beginning after Dec. 31, '97. ('97 Act §1042(b)(1)) Thus, a fresh start is provided with respect to changes in accounting methods resulting from the change from tax-exempt to taxable status. (Com Rept, see ¶ 5142)

Special rule with respect to basis for purposes of gain or loss. In the case of an organization to which Code Sec. 501(m) applies solely by reason of the repeal, by the '97 Act, of the grandfather rules provided by the '86 Act, for purposes of determining gain or loss, the adjusted basis of any asset held on the first day of the organization's first tax year beginning after Dec. 31, '97 will be treated as equal to its fair market value as of that day. ('97 Act §1042(b)(2)) This rule does not apply for determining depreciation or for other purposes. (Com Rept, see ¶ 5142)

Treatment of reserve weakening after June 8, '97. Any reserve weakening after June 8, '97 by an organization to which Code Sec. 501(m) applies solely by reason of the repeal, by the '97 Act, of the grandfather rules provided by the '86 Act is treated as occurring in that organization's first tax year beginning after Dec. 31, '97. ('97 Act §1042(c)) This rule requires TIAA-CREF and Mutual of America to compute ending '97 loss reserves without artificial changes that would reduce '98 income. (Com Rept, see ¶ 5142)

IRS may provide adjustments for short tax years beginning in '98. IRS is authorized to issue regs providing proper adjustments for organizations to which Code

Sec. 501(m) applies solely by reason of the repeal, by the '97 Act, of the grandfather rules provided by the '86 Act, with respect to short tax years that begin in '98 by reason of Code Sec. 843. ('97 Act §1042(d))

☐ **Effective:** Tax years beginning after Dec. 31, '97 ('97 Act §1042(a))

¶ 938. Limited transfer of qualified employer securities by charitable remainder trusts to ESOPs is permitted

Code Sec. 664(d), as amended by '97 Act § 1530(b)
Code Sec. 664(g), as amended by '97 Act § 1530(b)
Code Sec. 2055(a), as amended by '97 Act § 1530(c)(7)
Generally effective: Aug. 5, '97
Committee Reports, see ¶ 5352

An employee stock ownership plan (ESOP) is a qualified stock bonus plan or a combination stock bonus and money purchase pension plan under which employer securities are held for the benefit of employees. The securities are held by one or more tax-exempt trusts under the plan.

An estate tax deduction is allowed for transfers by a decedent to charitable, religious, scientific, etc. organizations. In the case of a transfer of a remainder interest to a charity, the remainder interest must be in a charitable remainder trust. A charitable remainder trust generally is a trust that is required to pay, no less often than annually, a fixed dollar amount (charitable remainder annuity trust) or a fixed percentage of the fair market value of the trust's assets determined at least annually (charitable remainder unitrust) to noncharitable beneficiaries, and, after the expiration of the noncharitable beneficiaries' interest in the trust, the remainder of the trust to a charitable, religious, scientific, etc. organization. (FTC 2d/FIN ¶ K-3283, ¶ K-3324, ¶ R-5701; USTR ¶ 6644.01, ¶ 20,554; TaxDesk ¶ 33,211, ¶ 77,710; EP ¶ 41,536, ¶ 41,577, ¶ 44,302)

New Law. The '97 Act provides a limited window of opportunity for decedents dying before Jan. 1, '99. "Qualified gratuitous transfers" of "qualified employer securities" by charitable remainder trusts to ESOPs are permitted without adversely affecting the status of the charitable remainder trusts. (Code Sec. 664(d) as amended by '97 Act §1530(a)) Thus, the '97 Act provides that the present value of the remainder interest in a charitable remainder trust holding qualified employer securities to be transferred to an ESOP qualifies for an estate tax deduction. (Code Sec. 2055(a)(5) as amended by '97 Act §1530(c)(7)) Further, an ESOP will not fail to be a qualified plan if it meets the requirements of this provision because the transfer of the securities is a "qualified gratuitous transfer." (Code Sec. 664(g)(3) as amended by '97 Act §1530(b))

Qualified gratuitous transfer. A transfer of securities is a qualified gratuitous transfer if:

FTC 2d References are to Federal Tax Coordinator 2d
FIN References are to RIA's Analysis of Federal Taxes: Income
USTR References are to United States Tax Reporter: Income, Estate & Gift, and Excise
PCA References are to Pension Coordinator and Pension & Benefits Expert/Advisor
PE References are to Pension and Profit Sharing 2nd
EP References are to Estate Planning & Taxation Coordinator and Estate Planning Advisor

(1) the securities transferred previously passed from a decedent dying before Jan. 1, '99 to a charitable remainder trust;

(2) no deduction for the employer is allowable for the contribution of the stock to the ESOP;

(3) the ESOP contains certain requirements (see below);

(4) the ESOP treats the transferred securities as attributable to employer contributions but without regard to the limitations on deduction of employer contributions;

(5) the employer files with IRS a statement consenting to the application of the excise taxes on dispositions of stock by ESOPs and prohibited allocations of qualified securities (Code Sec. 664(g)(1) as amended by '97 Act §1530(b));

(6) the ESOP was in existence on Aug. 1, '96;

(7) at the time of the transfer to the ESOP, family members of the decedent own (directly or indirectly) no more than ten percent of the value of the outstanding stock of the company;

(8) immediately after the transfer to the ESOP, the ESOP owns at least 60 percent of the value of outstanding stock of the company. (Code Sec. 664(g)(2))

Excise taxes. To prevent erosion of the 60-percent ownership requirements , an excise tax is imposed on the employer maintaining the ESOP on dispositions of the transferred stock within three years of the transfer. (Code Sec. 4978(a) as amended by '97 Act §1530(c)(11)) (Com Rept, see ¶ 5352) Additionally, an excise tax is imposed if, during a three-year period from the date of the transfer to the ESOP, any of the transferred securities are allocated to the account of any person who is related to the decedent or any person who at the time of the allocation, or during the one-year period ending on the date of the acquisition of the employer securities, is a five-percent owner of the employer. (Code Sec. 4979A(a) as amended by '97 Act §1530(c)(15))

Plan requirements. For a transfer to qualify as a gratuitous transfer, the ESOP must provide that:

• the qualified employer securities transferred must be allocated to the plan participants in a way that does not discriminate in favor of highly compensated employees.

• plan participants are entitled to direct the manner in which the transferred stock that is allocated to their accounts is to be voted. Transferred securities that have not yet been allocated to participants must be voted by a trustee who is not a five-percent shareholder of the company or a family member of the decedent.

• an independent trustee votes the transferred securities not allocated to participants.

• participants entitled to a distribution have the right to receive distributions in the form of stock and, if the employer securities are not readily tradable on an established market, that the participant can require the employer to repurchase any shares distributed under a fair valuation formula.

• the transferred securities must be held in a suspense account under the plan to be allocated each year up to the contribution limitations under Code Sec. 415, after first allocating all other annual additions for the limitation year.

• on plan termination, all transferred securities which are not allocated to plan participants are to be transferred to one or more charitable organizations. (Code Sec. 664(g)(3))

The employer is subject to an excise tax designed to recapture the estate taxes that would have been due had the transfer to the ESOP not occurred if the plan is terminated and any unallocated shares are not transferred to charitable organizations. (Code Sec. 664(g)(6))

This provision does not fail to apply merely because the ESOP is amended after Aug. 1, '96, for example, in order to conform to the plan requirements necessary to obtain the charitable deduction. (Com Rept, see ¶ 5352)

Qualified employer securities. "Qualified employer securities" are employer securities under the ESOP rules (Code Sec. 409(l) FTC 2d/FIN ¶ H-9303; USTR ¶ 4094.05; PE ¶ 409-4.05), issued by a domestic corporation that has no outstanding stock that is readily tradable on an established securities market and that has only one class of stock. (Code Sec. 664(g)(4))

Effect on other pension rules. The employer gets no deduction for the transfer of the qualified employer securities from the charitable remainder trust to the ESOP. (Code Sec. 404(a)(9) as amended by '97 Act §1530(c)(2)) Qualified gratuitous transfers are neither taken into account in determining whether any other contributions satisfy the contributions limit under (Code Sec. 415 FTC 2d/FIN ¶ H-5900 et seq.; USTR ¶ 4154; TaxDesk ¶ 28,250 et seq.; PE ¶ 415-4) (Code Sec. 415(c)(6) as amended by '97 Act §1530(c)(3)) nor are they taken into account in calculating the contributions limit. (Code Sec. 415(e)(6) as amended by '97 Act §1530(c)(4))

☐ **Effective:** For transfers made by trusts to, or for the use of, an ESOP after Aug. 5, '97. ('97 Act §1530(d))

¶ 939. D.C. Federal Pension Liability Trust Fund to be treated as qualified plan

Code Sec. None, Budget Act § 11034
Generally effective: Aug. 5, '97

Under pre-'97 Act law there was no provision for the District of Columbia Federal Pension Liability Trust Fund.

New Law. The '97 Act creates on the books of the Treasury the District of Columbia Federal Pension Liability Trust Fund (Trust Fund). (Budget Act §11031) The Trust Fund replaces and will acquire all the assets of the District Retirement Fund. (Budget Act §11033)

FTC 2d References are to Federal Tax Coordinator 2d
FIN References are to RIA's Analysis of Federal Taxes: Income
USTR References are to United States Tax Reporter: Income, Estate & Gift, and Excise
PCA References are to Pension Coordinator and Pension & Benefits Expert/Advisor
PE References are to Pension and Profit Sharing 2nd
EP References are to Estate Planning & Taxation Coordinator and Estate Planning Advisor

The Trust Fund will be treated as a qualified plan under Code Sec. 401(a), and, therefore, will be exempt from income taxes under Code Sec. 501(a). (Budget Act §11034(a)(1)) Any transfer to or distribution from the Trust Fund will be treated as a transfer to or distribution from a qualified plan. (Budget Act §11034(a)(2)) The benefits provided by the Trust Fund will be treated as benefits provided under a governmental plan maintained by the District of Columbia for purposes of both the Code (Budget Act §11034(a)(3)) and ERISA. (Budget Act §11034(b))

To the extent that any provision of the Code governing qualified plans (Code Sec. 401 *et seq.*) is amended after the creation of the Trust Fund, the amended provision will apply to the Trust Fund only to the extent that the Secretary determines that application of the amended Code section would be consistent with the administration of the Trust Fund. (Budget Act §11034(c))

The Trust Fund is being created to relieve the District of Columbia from responsibility for its underfunded pension liabilities, which were transferred to it by the federal government. The retirement programs for the police, firefighters, teachers and judges of the District of Columbia had significant unfunded pension liabilities of $1.9 billion when the federal government transferred those programs to the District, and those liabilities increased to nearly $4.8 billion before the enactment of the Budget Act. The federal government is assuming the responsibility for paying pension benefits, including unfunded pension liabilities as they existed before enactment of the Budget Act, for the retirement plans of teachers, police, and firefighters. (Budget Act §11002)

☐ **Effective:** Aug. 5, '97.

¶ 1000. Health and Other Employee Benefits

¶ 1001. Clarification of de minimis fringe benefit rules to no-charge employee meals

Code Sec. 132(e)(2), as amended by '97 Act § 970(a)
Generally effective: For tax years beginning after Dec. 31, '97
Committee Reports, see ¶ 5093

In general, subject to several exceptions, only 50% of business meal and entertainment expenses are allowed as a deduction under Code Sec. 274(n). Under one exception, the value of meals that are excludable from employees' incomes, under Code Sec. 132 (relating to certain fringe benefits), as a *de minimis* fringe is fully deductible by the employer. If meals are provided to employees at an employer–operated eating facility, their value is excludable from gross income as a *de minimis* fringe if several requirements are met, including a requirement that the facility's annual revenue must equal or exceed its direct operating costs. In addition, the courts that have considered the issue have held that if meals are provided for the convenience of the employer under Code Sec. 119 (relating to meals or lodging furnished for the convenience of the employer), they are fully deductible. (FTC 2d/FIN ¶ H-1821, ¶ H-1931; USTR ¶ 1324.06, ¶ 1324.01; TaxDesk ¶ 13,160, ¶ 13,377)

New Law. The '97 Act provides that for purposes of the rule that an eating facility's annual revenue must equal or exceed its direct operating costs, an employee entitled under Code Sec. 119 to exclude the value of a meal provided at the facility is treated as having paid an amount for the meal equal to the direct operating costs of the facility attributable to the meal. (Code Sec. 132(e)(2) as amended by '97 Act §970(a))

Thus, business meals that are excludable from employees' incomes under Code Sec. 119, because they are provided for the convenience of the employer at an employer–operated eating facility, are excludable as a *de minimis* fringe and therefore are fully deductible by the employer. This is consistent with the pre-'97 Act case law. (Com Rept, see ¶ 5093)

> *observation:* This is limited to meals at company cafeterias that are *not* subsidized.

No inference is intended as to whether the meals are fully deductible under prior law. (Com Rept, see ¶ 5093)

☐ **Effective:** Applicable to tax years beginning after Dec. 31, '97. ('97 Act §970(b))

FTC 2d References are to Federal Tax Coordinator 2d
FIN References are to RIA's Analysis of Federal Taxes: Income
USTR References are to United States Tax Reporter: Income, Estate & Gift, and Excise
PCA References are to Pension Coordinator and Pension & Benefits Expert/Advisor
PE References are to Pension and Profit Sharing 2nd
EP References are to Estate Planning & Taxation Coordinator and Estate Planning Advisor

¶ 1002. Retroactive exclusion from certain retired firefighters' and police officers' income for amounts received because of heart disease or hypertension

Code Sec. None, '97 Act § 1529
Generally effective: Aug. 5, '97
Committee Reports, see ¶ 5351

Amounts received under a workers' compensation act as compensation for personal injuries or sickness are excluded from gross income if the injuries or sickness are incurred in the course of employment. Some state statutes create a presumption that certain injuries are work-related (e.g., heart disease related to work as a policeman). If the presumption is irrebuttable, and the injuries or disease for which compensation is paid under the statute are prevalent in the general population (e.g., heart disease), then the statute doesn't restrict payments to occupational sickness or injuries, and the payments are not excludable as workers' compensation. (FTC 2d/FIN ¶ H-1355; USTR ¶ 1044.01; TaxDesk ¶ 53,217)

New Law. Certain payments made on behalf of full-time employees of any police or fire department ('97 Act §1529(b)(1)(A)) because of (1) heart disease or (2) hypertension, are treated as personal injuries or sickness in the course of employment ('97 Act §1529(a)) so that the payments are excludable from gross income as workers' compensation. (Com Rept, see ¶ 5351)

This treatment applies to any amount which:

(1) is payable to an individual (or the individual's survivors) who was a full-time employee of any police or fire department which is organized and operated by a state or the state's political subdivision, or its agency or instrumentality ('97 Act §1529(b)(1)(A));

(2) is payable under a state law (as amended on May 19, '92) which irrebuttably presumed that heart disease and hypertension are work-related illnesses, but only for employees separating from service before July 1, '92 ('97 Act §1529(b)(1)(B)); and

(3) were received in '89, '90, or '91. ('97 Act §1529(b)(2))

A claim for credit or refund of any overpayment of tax resulting from the retroactive treatment of the payments described above as workers' compensation will not be barred in the one-year period beginning on Aug. 5, '97 by: (i) any otherwise applicable statute of limitations, or (ii) res judicata (i.e., the rule that a matter once judicially decided cannot be relitigated), if the claim is filed before the date one year after Aug. 5, '97. ('97 Act §1529(c))

✐ action alert: Claims for credit or refund should be filed in the one-year period beginning on Aug. 5, '97.

☐ **Effective:** Aug. 5, '97. (Com Rept, see ¶ 5351)

¶ 1003. Election to receive taxable cash compensation in place of nontaxable parking benefits

Code Sec. 132(f)(4), as amended by '97 Act § 1072(a)
Generally effective: Tax years beginning after Dec. 31, '97
Committee Reports, see ¶ 5154

Employer-provided parking cannot be provided as part of a cafeteria plan. Under pre-'97 Act law, up to $170 per month of employer-provided parking was excludable from gross income. In order for the exclusion to have applied, the parking had to be a "qualified transportation fringe," a grouping of employer-provided benefits that included transit passes, van pools, and "qualified parking" (e.g., access to parking on a lot on the employer's business premises with the employer making payments directly to the lot operator or reimbursing the employee). Under Code Sec. 132(f)(4), the exclusion from gross income is not allowed for the value of any qualified transportation fringe unless the benefit is provided in addition to, and not in place of, any compensation that was otherwise payable to the employee. (FTC 2d/FIN ¶ 2205; USTR ¶ 1324; TaxDesk ¶ 13489)

New Law. The rule under Code Sec. 132(f)(4) barring the exclusion of a qualified transportation fringe from gross income unless it is provided in addition to (and not in place of) compensation does not apply to qualified parking when the parking benefit is provided in place of compensation that otherwise would have been includible in the gross income of the employee. No amount will be included in the gross income of the employee solely because the employee may choose between the qualified parking and compensation. (Code Sec. 134(f)(4) as amended by '97 Act §1072(a))

The amount of cash offered is includible in income only if the employee chooses the cash instead of parking. (Com Rept, see ¶ 5154)

According to Congress, the reason for the change in the rule for employee parking was because prior law resulted in an overuse of parking as a fringe benefit. By permitting employers to offer cash compensation in place of parking, employees will be more likely to elect to receive cash compensation, which will increase the electing employees' taxable income. In addition, the election to take cash may promote sound energy policy by increasing the use of mass transit and by reducing the amount of commuting by automobile. (Com Rept, see ¶ 5154)

☐ **Effective:** Taxable years beginning after Dec. 31, '97. ('97 Act §1072(b))

FTC 2d References are to Federal Tax Coordinator 2d
FIN References are to RIA's Analysis of Federal Taxes: Income
USTR References are to United States Tax Reporter: Income, Estate & Gift, and Excise
PCA References are to Pension Coordinator and Pension & Benefits Expert/Advisor
PE References are to Pension and Profit Sharing 2nd
EP References are to Estate Planning & Taxation Coordinator and Estate Planning Advisor

¶ 1100. Health Care Insurance

¶ 1101. Group health plans that fail to comply with the Newborns' and Mothers' Health Protection Act of 1996 are subject to Code Sec. 4980D excise tax

Code Sec. 9811, as added by '97 Act § 1531(a)(4)
Generally effective: Plan years beginning after Dec. 31, '97
Committee Reports, see ¶ 5353

The Newborns' and Mothers' Health Protection Act of 1996 amended ERISA and the Public Health Service Act to impose certain requirements on group health plans with respect to coverage of newborns and mothers, including a requirement that a group health plan cannot restrict benefits for a hospital stay in connection with childbirth for the mother or newborn to less than 48 hours following a normal vaginal delivery or less than 96 hours following a caesarean section. These provisions are effective with respect to plan years beginning on or after January 1, 1998.

Under the Code, group health plans must meet certain requirements with respect to limitations on exclusions of preexisting conditions, and group health plans may not discriminate against individuals based on health status. An excise tax of $100 per day during the period of noncompliance is imposed on the employer sponsoring the plan if the plan fails to meet these requirements. During a tax year, the maximum tax that can be imposed due to failures that are due to reasonable cause and not willful neglect cannot exceed the lesser of 10 percent of the employer's group health plan expenses for the prior year or $500,000. No tax is imposed if IRS determines that the employer did not know, and exercising reasonable diligence would not have known, that the failure existed. (FTC 2d/FIN ¶ H-1325.1 *et seq.*; USTR ¶ 4980D4)

New Law. The '97 Act incorporates into the Code, as Code Sec. 9811, the provisions of the Newborns' and Mothers' Health Protection Act of 1996 relating to group health plans. Failures to comply with those provisions are subject to the excise tax under Code Sec. 4980D, applicable to failures to comply with group health requirements. (Com Rept, see ¶ 5353) Code Sec. 9811 doesn't apply to any group health plan that does not provide benefits for hospital lengths of stay in connection with childbirth for a mother or her newborn child. (Code Sec. 9811(c)(2) as added by '97 Act §1531(a)(4))

Requirements for minimum hospital stay following birth. A group health plan may not—

(1) (a) restrict benefits for any hospital length of stay in connection with childbirth for the mother or newborn child, following a normal or vaginal delivery, to less than

---

FTC 2d References are to the Federal Tax Coordinator 2d
FIN References are to RIA's Analysis of Federal Taxes: Income
USTR References are to the United States Tax Reporter: Income, Estate & Gift, and Excise
PCA References are to Pension Coordinator and Pension & Benefits Expert/Advisor
PE References are to Pension and Profit Sharing 2nd
EP References are to Estate Planning & Taxation Coordinator and Estate Planning Advisor

48 hours, or (Code Sec. 9811(a)(1)(A)(i)) (b) restrict benefits for any hospital length of stay in connection with childbirth for the mother or newborn child, following a caesarean section, to less than 96 hours, (Code Sec. 9811(a)(1)(A)(ii)), except where the decision to discharge the mother or her newborn child before the expiration of the minimum length of stay otherwise required is made by the attending provider in consultation with the mother, (Code Sec. 9811(a)(2)) or

(2) require that a provider obtain authorization from the plan or the issuer for prescribing any length of stay required under (1), above. (Code Sec. 9811(a)(1)(B))

Nothing in Code Sec. 9811 will be construed to require a mother who is a participant or beneficiary to give birth in a hospital, (Code Sec. 9811(c)(1)(A)) or to stay in the hospital for a fixed period of time following the birth of her child. (Code Sec. 9811(c)(1)(B))

Prohibitions.   A group health plan may not—

... deny to the mother or her newborn child eligibility, or continued eligibility, to enroll or to renew coverage under the terms of the plan, solely for the purpose of avoiding the requirements of Code Sec. 9811, (Code Sec. 9811(b)(1))

... provide monetary payments or rebates to mothers to encourage them to accept less than the minimum protections available under Code Sec. 9811, (Code Sec. 9811(b)(2))

... penalize or otherwise reduce or limit the reimbursement of an attending provider because the provider provided care to an individual participant or beneficiary in accordance with Code Sec. 9811, (Code Sec. 9811(b)(3))

... provide incentives (monetary or otherwise) to an attending provider to induce the provider to provide care to an individual participant or beneficiary in a manner inconsistent with Code Sec. 9811, (Code Sec. 9811(b)(4)) or

... subject to the rules on coinsurance and cost-sharing (see below), restrict benefits for any portion of a period within a hospital length of stay required under Code Sec. 9811(a) (see above) in a manner which is less favorable than the benefits provided for any preceding portion of the stay. (Code Sec. 9811(b)(5))

Coinsurance and cost-sharing.   Nothing in Code Sec. 9811 will be construed as preventing a group health plan from imposing deductibles, coinsurance, or other cost-sharing in relation to benefits for hospital lengths of stay in connection with childbirth for a mother or newborn child under the plan, except that the coinsurance or other cost-sharing for any portion of a period within a hospital length of stay required under Code Sec. 9811(a) (see above) may not be greater than the coinsurance or cost-sharing for any preceding portion of the stay. (Code Sec. 9811(c)(3))

Level and type of reimbursements.   Nothing in Code Sec. 9811 will be construed to prevent a group health plan from negotiating the level and type of reimbursement

FTC 2d References are to Federal Tax Coordinator 2d
FIN References are to RIA's Analysis of Federal Taxes: Income
USTR References are to United States Tax Reporter: Income, Estate & Gift, and Excise
PCA References are to Pension Coordinator and Pension & Benefits Expert/Advisor
PE References are to Pension and Profit Sharing 2nd
EP References are to Estate Planning & Taxation Coordinator and Estate Planning Advisor

with a provider for care provided in accordance with Code Sec. 9811. (Code Sec. 9811(d))

Exception for health insurance coverage in certain states. The requirements of Code Sec. 9811 don't apply with respect to health insurance coverage if there is a state law (including a decision, rule, regulation, or other state action having the effect of law) for a state that regulates health insurance coverage that is described in any of the following paragraphs:

• The state law requires health insurance coverage to provide for at least a 48-hour hospital length of stay following a normal vaginal delivery and at least a 96-hour hospital length of stay following a caesarean section. (Code Sec. 9811(f)(1))

• The state law requires health insurance coverage to provide for maternity and pediatric care in accordance with guidelines established by the American College of Obstetricians and Gynecologists, the American Academy of Pediatrics, or other established professional medical associations. (Code Sec. 9811(f)(2))

• The state law requires, in connection with health insurance coverage for maternity care, that the hospital length of stay for such care is left to the decision of (or required to be made by) the attending provider in consultation with the mother. (Code Sec. 9811(f)(3))

    🅡🅘🅐 *observation:* Code Sec. 9811 contains a subsection (f), but no subsection (e).

☐ **Effective:** With respect to group health plans for plan years beginning on or after Jan. 1, '98. ('97 Act §1531(c))

¶ 1102. Mental health benefits under group health plans to have parity with medical benefits

Code Sec. 9812, as added by '97 Act § 1531(a)(4)
Generally effective: For plan years beginning after Dec. 31, '97
Committee Reports, see ¶ 5353

The Mental Health Parity Act of 1996 amended ERISA and the Public Health Service Act to provide that group health plans that provide both medical and surgical benefits and mental health benefits cannot impose limits on mental health benefits that are not imposed on substantially all medical and surgical benefits. The provisions of the Mental Health Parity Act are effective with respect to plan years beginning on or after Jan. 1, '98, but do not apply to benefits for services furnished on or after Sep. 30, 2001.

Under the Code, group health plans must meet certain requirements with respect to limitations on exclusions of preexisting conditions, and group health plans may not discriminate against individuals based on health status. An excise tax of $100 per day during the period of noncompliance is imposed on the employer sponsoring the plan if the plan fails to meet these requirements. During a tax year, the maximum tax that can be imposed due to failures that are due to reasonable cause and not willful neglect cannot exceed the lesser of 10 percent of the employer's group health plan expenses for the prior year or $500,000. No tax is imposed if IRS that the employer did not know, and exercising reasonable diligence would not have known, that the failure existed. (FTC 2d/FIN ¶ H-1325.1 *et seq.*; USTR ¶ 4980D4)

New Law. The '97 Act incorporates into the Code the provisions of the Mental Health Parity Act of 1996 relating to group health plans. Failures to comply with these provisions are subject to the excise tax under Code Sec. 4980D, applicable to failures to comply with group health plan requirements. (Com Rept, see ¶ 5353) This mental health parity provision will not apply to benefits for services furnished after Sep. 29, 2001. (Code Sec. 9812(f) as added by '97 Act §1531(a)(4)) The parity provision does not require a group health plan to provide mental health benefits, (Code Sec. 9812(b)(1)) nor, in the case of plans that do provide mental health benefits, does it affect the terms and conditions (including cost sharing, limits on numbers of visits or days of coverage, and requirements regarding medical necessity) regarding the amount, duration, or scope of the benefits provided by the plans, except to the extent described below. (Code Sec. 9812(b)(2))

Aggregate lifetime limits. A group health plan that provides both medical and surgical benefits (as defined below) and mental health benefits (as defined below), and that does not include an aggregate lifetime limit (as defined below) on substantially all medical and surgical benefits, may not impose any aggregate lifetime limit on mental health benefits. (Code Sec. 9812(a)(1)(A)) If the plan includes an aggregate lifetime limit on substantially all medical and surgical benefits, the plan must either: (1) include mental health benefits in the aggregate lifetime limit on medical and surgical benefits without distinction between the two categories of benefits; or (2) provide a separate but equal lifetime limit on mental health benefits. (Code Sec. 9812(a)(1)(B)) If a plan includes no or different lifetime limits on various categories of medical and surgical benefits, IRS is directed to establish rules applying the rules of the last sentence, but under which an average aggregate lifetime limit, computed taking into account the weighted average of the lifetime limits applicable to the differentiated categories, is substituted for the aggregate lifetime limit. (Code Sec. 9812(a)(1)(C))

Annual limits. If a group health plan does not include an annual limit on substantially all medical and surgical benefits, the plan may not impose any annual limit on mental health benefits. (Code Sec. 9812(a)(2)(A)) If a plan includes an annual limit on substantially all medical and surgical benefits, the plan must either: (1) include mental health benefits in the annual limit for medical and surgical benefits without distinction to the two categories of benefits; or (2) provide a separate but equal annual limit for mental health benefits. (Code Sec. 9812(a)(2)(B)) If a plan includes no or different annual limits on various categories of medical and surgical benefits, IRS is directed to establish rules applying the rules of the last sentence, but under which an average annual limit that takes into account the weighted average of the annual limits

FTC 2d References are to Federal Tax Coordinator 2d
FIN References are to RIA's Analysis of Federal Taxes: Income
USTR References are to United States Tax Reporter: Income, Estate & Gift, and Excise
PCA References are to Pension Coordinator and Pension & Benefits Expert/Advisor
PE References are to Pension and Profit Sharing 2nd
EP References are to Estate Planning & Taxation Coordinator and Estate Planning Advisor

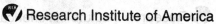 Research Institute of America   275

applicable to the differentiated categories is substituted for the annual limit. (Code Sec. 9812(a)(2)(C))

Exemptions. Small employers, those who employed an average of at least two and not more than 50 employees during the preceding calendar year and who employed at least two employees on the first day of the plan year, are exempted from the mental health parity requirements. Aggregation rules similar to those under Code Sec. 414 apply for purposes of determining which employers are treated as a single employer. The size of an employer that did not exist during the preceding calendar year is determined based on the average number of employees that it is reasonably expected to employ during the current calendar year. (Code Sec. 9812(c)(1))

The parity requirements do not apply to a group health plan if to apply them would cause an increase in the cost under the plan of at least 1%. (Code Sec. 9812(c)(2))

Definitions.

Aggregate lifetime limit. "Aggregate lifetime limit" means a dollar limitation on the total amount of benefits that may be paid under the plan with respect to an individual or other coverage unit. (Code Sec. 9812(e)(1))

Annual limit. "Annual limit" means a dollar limitation on the total amount of benefits that may be paid under the plan during a 12-month period with respect to an individual or other coverage unit. (Code Sec. 9812(e)(2))

Medical or surgical benefits. "Medical or surgical benefits" means benefits with respect to medical or surgical services, as defined under the terms of the plan, but does not include mental health benefits. (Code Sec. 9812(e)(3))

Mental health benefits. "Mental health benefits" are benefits with respect to mental health services, as defined by the applicable plan, but the treatment of substance abuse or chemical dependency is specifically excluded. (Code Sec. 9812(e)(4))

☐ **Effective:** With respect to group health plans for plan years beginning on or after Jan. 1, '98. ('97 Act §1531(c))

¶ 1103. Percentage of health insurance costs deductible by self-employeds gradually increased to 100% by 2007

Code Sec. 162(l)(1)(B), as amended by '97 Act § 934(a)
Generally effective: Tax years beginning after Dec. 31, '96
Committee Reports, see ¶ 5071

A self-employed individual (as defined in Code Sec. 401(c)(1)) can deduct as a business expense the applicable percentage of the amount paid during the tax year for medical insurance for himself, his spouse, and his dependents. The applicable percentage is 40% for '97, and was scheduled to increase to 80% by 2006 and thereafter (see table below in the **New Law** discussion). (FTC 2d/FIN ¶ L-3510; USTR ¶ 1624.403; TaxDesk ¶ 30,459)

New Law. The applicable percentages under the '97 Act are as follows (pre- '97 Act percentages are shown for comparison purposes only):

For tax years beginning in calendar year:	The applicable percentage is:	
	New law	Pre–'97 Act law
1997	40%	40%
1998 and 1999	45%	45%
2000 and 2001	50%	45%
2002	60%	45%
2003	80%	50%
2004	80%	60%
2005	80%	70%
2006	90%	80%
2007 and thereafter	100%	80%

(Code Sec. 162(l)(1)(B) as amended by '97 Act §934(a))

⚫️ *observation:* Thus, the '97 Act doesn't increase the deductible percentage over what it was under pre-Act law until the year 2000 (when 50% becomes deductible instead of 45%).

☐ **Effective:** Tax years beginning after Dec. 31, '96. ('97 Act §934(b))

¶ 1104. Self-employeds can deduct long-term care premiums even if they participate in employer-provided health plan (if the plan doesn't include long-term care coverage)

Code Sec. 162(l)(2)(B), as amended by '97 Act § 1602(c)
Generally effective: Tax years beginning after Dec. 31, '96
Committee Reports, see ¶ 5372

Self-employed individuals are entitled to a deduction in computing adjusted gross income, i.e., above-the-line, for a specified percentage (40% in '97) of amounts paid for health insurance for themselves, their spouses, and their dependents. The deduction isn't available to a taxpayer for any calendar month for which the taxpayer is eligible to participate in any subsidized health plan maintained by any employer of the taxpayer or of the taxpayer's spouse. In the case of a qualified long-term care insurance contract, only eligible long-term care premiums are taken into account in determining the deduction for health insurance expenses of a self-employed individual. ((FTC 2d/FIN ¶ L-3510; USTR ¶ 1624.403; TaxDesk ¶ 56,072))

New Law. The rule barring the above-the-line deduction for individuals eligible to participate in a subsidized plan maintained by an employer is applied separately with respect to:

... plans which include coverage for qualified long-term care services (as defined in Code Sec. 7702B(c)) or are qualified long-term care insurance contracts (as defined in

FTC 2d References are to Federal Tax Coordinator 2d
FIN References are to RIA's Analysis of Federal Taxes: Income
USTR References are to United States Tax Reporter: Income, Estate & Gift, and Excise
PCA References are to Pension Coordinator and Pension & Benefits Expert/Advisor
PE References are to Pension and Profit Sharing 2nd
EP References are to Estate Planning & Taxation Coordinator and Estate Planning Advisor

⚫️ **Research Institute of America** 277

Code Sec. 7702B(b)), (Code Sec. 162(l)(2)(B)(i) as amended by '97 Act §1602(c)) and
. . . plans which don't include such coverage and aren't such contracts. (Code Sec.
162(l)(2)(B)(ii))

Thus, the fact that an individual is eligible for employer-subsidized health insurance
doesn't affect that individual's right to claim an above-the-line deduction for long-term
care insurance premiums, so long as the individual isn't eligible for employer-subsidized long-term care insurance. (Com Rept, see ¶ 5372)

> *observation:* An individual eligible for employer-subsidized health insur-
> ance as well as employer-subsidized long-term care insurance cannot claim
> the above-the-line deduction for any health insurance costs. Subsidized health
> insurance and long-term care insurance need not be provided by the same em-
> ployer for this rule to apply. Thus, for example, the bar to any above-the-line
> deduction would apply if one spouse's employer provided subsidized health
> insurance and the other spouse's employer provided subsidized long-term care
> insurance.

> *observation:* The rule barring an above-the-line deduction where there's an
> employer-provided plan is applied monthly. Thus, if a taxpayer has been pay-
> ing for long-term care coverage on his own and at some point during the year
> his employer starts to provide such coverage, the taxpayer gets the above-the-
> line deduction for the amounts he paid in the earlier months.

☐ **Effective:** For tax years beginning after Dec. 31, '96. ('97 Act §1602(i))

¶ 1105. Definition of "chronically ill" individual modified for qualified long-term care insurance contracts

Code Sec. 7702B(c)(2), as amended by '97 Act § 1602(b)
Generally effective: For contracts issued after Dec. 31, '96
Committee Reports, see ¶ 5371

Amounts paid for insurance that cover qualified long-term care services are deductible up to specific limits. Qualified long-term care services are services provided for a
"chronically ill" individual. A "chronically ill" individual is one who has been certified within the previous 12-months, by a licensed health care practitioner, as

(1) being unable to perform (without substantial assistance) at least two activities of
daily living for at least 90 days due to a loss of functional capacity;

(2) having a level of disability similar to that described in item 1, above, as determined under regulations issued by IRS in consultation with Health and Human Services; or

(3) requiring substantial supervision to protect the individual from threats to health
and safety due to severe cognitive impairment.

A contract is not treated as a qualified long-term care insurance contract unless the
determination of whether an individual is a chronically ill individual takes into account

at least five activities of daily living, i.e. eating, toileting, transferring, bathing, dressing, and continence. (FTC 2d/FIN ¶ K-2141.2; USTR ¶ 77,02B4.01; TaxDesk ¶ 34,634)

New Law. Technical corrections made by the '97 Act clarify that the requirement that a qualified long-term care insurance contact must base a determination of whether an individual is chronically ill by taking into account at least five activities of daily living applies only to item (1) above (being unable to perform at least two activities of daily living). (Code Sec. 7702B(c)(2) as amended by '97 Act §1602(b))

> *illustration:* A long-term care insurance contract that defines a chronically ill individual as an individual who requires substantial supervision to protect him from threats to health and safety due to severe cognitive impairment (such as Alzheimer's disease) is a qualified long-term care insurance contract (in that it satisfies item (3), above)—even if the individual can perform all the activities of daily living.

☐ **Effective:** For contracts issued after Dec. 31, '96. ('97 Act §1602(i))

¶ 1106. Deduction for Blue Cross and Blue Shield organizations clarified to include cost-plus contract liabilities and expenses

Code Sec. 833(b)(1), as amended by '97 Act § 1604(d)(2)(A)
Generally effective: Tax years beginning after Dec. 31, '86
Committee Reports, see ¶ 5387

Qualifying Blue Cross and Blue Shield organizations and other specified health insurance providers are subject to the same tax treatment that is applicable to nonlife insurance companies generally, with certain modifications. One deduction applicable to these organizations is equal to 25% of the sum of: (1) the claims incurred during the tax year, and (2) the expenses incurred during the tax year in connection with the administration, adjustment, or settlement of claims. It has not been clear whether liabilities and expenses incurred during the year under cost-plus contracts, i.e., contracts under which providers get paid for the cost of providing insurance, plus a fixed amount of profit, are taken into account in determining the special deduction. (FTC 2d/FIN ¶ E-5625; USTR ¶ 8334)

New Law. The '97 Act clarifies that, in determining the amount of the 25% deduction for health insurance providers like qualifying Blue Cross and Blue Shield organizations, liabilities incurred during the tax year under cost-plus contracts are added to claims incurred. Also, expenses incurred during the tax year in connection with cost-plus contracts are added to the expenses taken into account in determining the amount

FTC 2d References are to Federal Tax Coordinator 2d
FIN References are to RIA's Analysis of Federal Taxes: Income
USTR References are to United States Tax Reporter: Income, Estate & Gift, and Excise
PCA References are to Pension Coordinator and Pension & Benefits Expert/Advisor
PE References are to Pension and Profit Sharing 2nd
EP References are to Estate Planning & Taxation Coordinator and Estate Planning Advisor

of the 25% deduction. (Code Sec. 833(b)(1) as amended by '97 Act §1604(d)(2)(A))

☐ **Effective:** Tax years beginning after Dec. 31, '86. ('97 Act §1604(d)(2)(B))

¶ 1107. Long-term care insurance contract nonforfeiture provisions subject to state regulatory approval

Code Sec. 7702B(g)(4)(B), as amended by '97 Act § 1602(e)
Generally effective: For contracts issued after '96
Committee Reports, see ¶ 5374

Under the consumer protection provisions for long-term care insurance, the issuer of a contract must offer the policyholder a nonforfeiture provision. The provision must provide that, in the event of a default in the payment of a premium, the amount of the benefit may be adjusted, after being initially granted, only as necessary to reflect changes in claims, persistency, and interest—as reflected in changes of rates for premium paying policies *approved by IRS* for the same contract form. (FTC 2d/FIN ¶ K-2141.3; USTR ¶ 7702B4; TaxDesk ¶ 34,634)

New Law. In a technical correction, the '97 Act substitutes state regulators for IRS as the entity that makes the approval. So, the nonforfeiture provision must provide that, in the event of a default in the payment of a premium, the amount of the benefit may be adjusted, after being initially granted, only as necessary to reflect changes in claims, persistency, and interest—as reflected in changes of rates for premium paying policies *approved by the appropriate state regulatory authority* for the same contract form. (Code Sec. 7702B(g)(4)(B) as amended by '97 Act §1602(e))

☐ **Effective:** For contracts issued after Dec. 31, '96. ('97 Act §1602(i))

¶ 1200. Medical Savings Accounts

¶ 1201. Medicare eligible individuals may choose "Medicare+Choice MSAs" as a Medicare option

Code Sec. 138, as amended by Budget Act § 4006(a)
Code Sec. 220(b), as amended by Budget Act § 4006(b)(2)
Code Sec. 4973(d), as amended by Budget Act § 4006(b)(1)
Generally effective: Taxable years beginning after Dec. 31, '98
Committee Reports, see ¶ 5501

Under Code Sec. 220, a "medical savings account" ("MSA") is defined as a trust or custodial agreement that is created or organized in the United States exclusively for the purpose of paying the qualified medical expenses of the account holder, his spouse and/or dependents. Contributions to an MSA are made by the account holder's employer and are not taxable to the account holder. Distributions from an MSA to pay qualified medical expenses are generally not taxable. Qualified medical expenses are any amounts paid by the account holder for medical care as defined under Code Sec. 213(d) (relating to medical expenses) for the account holder, his spouse, or dependents, but only to the extent the amounts are not reimbursed by insurance or otherwise.

Before the Budget Act, there were no "Medicare+Choice MSAs". Also, individuals covered under Medicare were not eligible to have an MSA. (FTC 2d/FIN ¶ H-1326; USTR ¶ 1245.08; TaxDesk ¶ 28,800)

New Law. The Budget Act provides that individuals who are eligible for Medicare may choose among several types of Medicare coverage, including a "Medicare+Choice MSA". A "Medicare+Choice MSA" is a medical savings account as defined in Code Sec. 220(d), but which is designated as a Medicare+Choice MSA (Code Sec. 138(b)(1) as amended by Budget Act §4006(a)) by the individual account holder. (Com Rept, see ¶ 5501) If an account holder chooses a Medicare+Choice MSA, the Secretary of Health and Human Services will make a contribution directly to the Medicare+Choice MSA designated by the account holder. (Com Rept, see ¶ 5501) No contribution may be made except by the Secretary of Health and Human Services, or by a trustee-to-trustee transfer (see below). (Code Sec. 138(b)(2)) The Medicare+Choice MSA's governing instrument must allow for a trustee-to-trustee transfer. (Code Sec. 138(b)(3))

Contributions made by the Secretary of Health and Human Services are not currently includible in the gross income of the account holder. (Code Sec. 138(a)) Likewise, earnings on amounts held in a Medicare+Choice MSA are not currently includible in the taxable income of the account holder. (Com Rept, see ¶ 5501)

FTC 2d References are to Federal Tax Coordinator 2d
FIN References are to RIA's Analysis of Federal Taxes: Income
USTR References are to United States Tax Reporter: Income, Estate & Gift, and Excise
PCA References are to Pension Coordinator and Pension & Benefits Expert/Advisor
PE References are to Pension and Profit Sharing 2nd
EP References are to Estate Planning & Taxation Coordinator and Estate Planning Advisor

💡*observation:* An individual who selects a Medicare+Choice MSA will not be restricted, as under Medicare, on the amount paid, or the procedures covered, so long as the expense is a qualified medical expense. Nor will the individual need to be concerned whether the health care provider is willing to accept Medicare patients. However, the election of a Medicare+Choice MSA rather than Medicare eliminates Medicare as an option, and effectively places an investment risk on the individual. Only the contribution and earnings of the Medicare+Choice MSA will be available to pay medical expenses traditionally paid for by Medicare. If the Medicare+Choice MSA investments do not perform well, the account holder runs the risk of having insufficient assets to cover medical expenses.

A Medicare+Choice MSA must be established in connection with an MSA plan described in Sec. 1859(b)(2) of the Social Security Act (which contains definitions of terms relating to Medicare+Choice organizations, including MSAs which are used for Medicare+Choice plans). (Code Sec. 138(b)(4))

💡*observation:*　Code Sec. 138 does not specify how an individual creates or designates an MSA as a Medicare+Choice MSA. Nor does it specify how the Secretary of Health and Human Services is notified of the election and designation. Other provisions concerning Medicare under the Balanced Budget Act of '97 address operational issues and limitations on the number of individuals covered and the amount of coverage which may be provided by a Medicare+Choice MSA.

A Medicare+Choice MSA is a tax-exempt trust (or a custodial account), similar to an Individual Retirement Account ("IRA"), created exclusively for the purpose of paying the qualified medical expenses of the account holder. The trustee of a Medicare+Choice MSA can be a bank, insurance company, or other person that demonstrates to the satisfaction of the IRS that the manner in which the person will administer the trust will be consistent with applicable requirements.　No Medicare+Choice MSA assets can be invested in life insurance contracts. Medicare+Choice MSA assets cannot be commingled with other property except in a common trust fund or common investment fund, and an account holder's interest in a Medicare+Choice MSA is nonforfeitable. (Com Rept, see ¶ 5501)

Distributions of qualified medical expenses.　Under Code Sec. 220, distributions from MSAs used to pay the "qualified medical expenses" of the account holder and/or his wife and dependents are not taxable.

Qualified medical expenses of Medicare+Choice MSAs do not include amounts paid for the medical expenses of any individual other than the account holder. (Code Sec. 138(c)(1)(A))　Qualified medical expenses are any amount paid to the account holder for medical care as defined in Code Sec. 213(d) for the individual, but only to the extent the amounts are not reimbursed by insurance, or otherwise. (Code Sec. 220(d)(2)(A))　Qualified medical expenses do not include any insurance premiums other than premiums for long-term care insurance, continuation insurance ("COBRA coverage"), or premiums for coverage while an individual is receiving unemployment compensation. (Com Rept, see ¶ 5501)

Distributions from a Medicare+Choice MSA that are excludable from gross income can not be taken as an itemized deduction for medical expenses. Distributions from a Medicare+Choice MSA for purposes other than qualified medical expenses are includable in taxable income. (Com Rept, see ¶ 5501)

Code Sec. 220(d)(2)(C) does not apply to Medicare+Choice MSAs. (Code Sec. 138(c)(1)(B)) Thus, distributions from a Medicare+Choice MSA that are used to pay the qualified medical expenses of the account holder are excludable from taxable income regardless of whether the account holder is enrolled in the Medicare+Choice MSA at the time of the distribution. (Com Rept, see ¶ 5501)

Additional tax on nonqualified distributions. Distributions for purposes other than qualified medical expenses are not only included in income, but are also subject to an additional tax. The additional tax is 50% of the excess (if any) of:

(1) the amount of the payment or distribution, over

(2) the excess (if any) of:

(A) the fair market value of the assets of the Medicare+Choice MSA as of the close of the calendar year preceding the calendar year in which the taxable year begins, over

(B) an amount equal to 60% of the deductible under the Medicare+Choice MSA plan covering the account holder as of Jan. 1 of the calendar year in which the taxable year begins. (Code Sec. 138(c)(2)(A))

The additional tax does not apply to distributions made on account of the disability or death of the account holder. (Code Sec. 138(c)(2)(B))

For purposes of applying the additional tax, all Medicare+Choice MSAs of the account holder are treated as one account. All payments and distributions which are not used exclusively to pay the qualified medical expenses of the account holder during any taxable year are treated as one distribution. Any distribution of property is taken into account at its fair market value on the date of distribution. (Code Sec. 138(c)(2)(C)).

The 15% additional tax on the amount includible in gross income for non-qualified distributions under Code Sec. 220(f)(4) for MSAs does *not* apply to any payment or distribution from a Medicare+Choice MSA. (Code Sec. 138(c)(2)(A))

Trustee-to-trustee transfers. A direct trustee-to-trustee transfer, i.e. from one Medicare+Choice MSA to another Medicare+Choice MSA, is not a taxable distribution, nor is it subject to the additional penalty on distributions, described above. (Code Sec. 138(c)(4))

FTC 2d References are to Federal Tax Coordinator 2d
FIN References are to RIA's Analysis of Federal Taxes: Income
USTR References are to United States Tax Reporter: Income, Estate & Gift, and Excise
PCA References are to Pension Coordinator and Pension & Benefits Expert/Advisor
PE References are to Pension and Profit Sharing 2nd
EP References are to Estate Planning & Taxation Coordinator and Estate Planning Advisor

Reporting requirements and penalties. A Medicare+Choice MSA trustee must make reports as required by IRS under Code Sec. 220(h). The reports must include the fair market value of the assets in the Medicare+Choice MSA as of the close of each calendar year. The reports must also be furnished to the account holder not later than Jan. 31 following the calendar year to which the report relates. (Code Sec. 138(e))

Distribution of erroneous contributions. If contributions for a year are erroneously made by the Secretary of Health and Human Services, the erroneous contributions can be returned to the Secretary of Health and Human Services (along with any attributable earnings) from the Medicare+Choice MSA. The return of an erroneous contribution is not a taxable distribution, and the additional penalty on distributions does not apply. (Code Sec. 138(c)(3)) Thus, the return of an erroneous contribution has no adverse tax consequences to the account holder. (Com Rept, see ¶ 5501)

⚡*observation:* Apparently the *return* of an erroneous contribution does not have to occur in the same taxable year as the erroneous contribution itself.

Treatment of a Medicare+Choice MSA at death. Under Code Sec. 220(f)(8)(A), if the surviving spouse of an account holder acquires the account holder's interest in an MSA as the designated beneficiary on the account holder's death, the MSA is treated as if the surviving spouse were the account holder. The rules concerning the tax treatment of distributions from MSAs under Code Sec. 220(f) will apply to the treatment of a Medicare+Choice MSA where the spouse of the deceased is the designated beneficiary. (Code Sec. 138(d)) This means that if the beneficiary of a Medicare+Choice MSA is not the account holder's spouse, the Medicare+Choice MSA is no longer treated as a Medicare+Choice MSA, and the value of the Medicare+Choice MSA on the account holder's date of death is included in the taxable income of the beneficiary for the taxable year in which the death occurred. If the account holder fails to name a beneficiary, the value of the Medicare+Choice MSA on the account holder's date of death is included in the taxable income of the account holder's final income tax return. In all cases, the value of the Medicare+Choice MSA is included in the account holder's gross estate for estate tax purposes. (Com Rept, see ¶ 5501)

No limitation on number of Medicare+Choice MSAs. Code Sec. 220(i), relating to the cut-off year for MSAs, after which no new individual can be treated as an eligible individual, does not apply to Medicare+Choice MSAs. Nor are Medicare+Choice MSAs taken into account for purposes of the limitation on the number of taxpayers who may have MSAs under Code Sec. 220(j). (Code Sec. 138(f))

Distribution of excess contributions. The '97 Act provides that, for purposes of computing the Code Sec. 4973 excise tax on excess contributions to MSAs, any withdrawal of an erroneous contribution (under Code Sec. 138(c)(3), see above) is treated as an amount not contributed. (Code Sec. 4973(d) as amended by Budget Act §4006(b)(1))

No deduction for MSA contribution for individuals entitled to Medicare. Under Code Sec. 220(b) the amount that is allowable as a deduction to an individual for a contribution to an MSA cannot exceed the monthly limitations for months during the taxable year that the individual is an eligible individual. The '97 Act provides that for any month an individual is entitled to benefits under Medicare and for each month thereafter, the individual's monthly limitation is zero. (Code Sec. 220(b) as amended by Budget Act §4006(b)(2))

observation: Thus, if an individual is entitled to benefits under Medicare, the amount that is allowable as a deduction for an MSA contribution is zero.

☐ **Effective:** Taxable years beginning after Dec. 31, '98. (Budget Act §4006(c))

¶ 1202. Changes to MSA rules on coverage, distributions, and reporting requirements

Code Sec. 26(b)(2)(P), as amended by '97 Act § 1602(a)
Code Sec. 220, as amended by '97 Act § 1602(a)
Code Sec. 6693(a), as amended by '97 Act § 1602(a)
Generally effective: Taxable years beginning after Dec. 31, '96
Committee Reports, see ¶ 5370

Distributions from an MSA that are not used for medical expenses are includible in gross income and subject to a 15% additional tax unless the distribution is made to an individual after age 65, or on account of disability or death. The 15% additional tax is treated as a tax liability for purposes of the minimum tax.

To be eligible to have an MSA, an individual must be covered under a high deductible health plan and no other health plan, except for plans that provide certain permitted coverage. Among those plans which provide one of the types of permitted coverage are Medicare supplemental plans, even though an individual covered by Medicare is not eligible to have an MSA.

Also, to be eligible to have an MSA plan, an individual must be either self-employed or employed by a small employer. Distributions from an MSA for the medical expenses of the MSA account holder and his spouse or dependents are excludible from income. However, in any year for which a contribution is made to an MSA, withdrawals from the MSA are excludible from income only if the individual for whom the expenses were incurred was an eligible individual for the month in which the expenses were incurred.

Trustees of MSAs are required to provide reports to IRS and account holders as required by IRS. A penalty of $50 applies to each failure to provide a required report. Separate penalties apply to information returns required by the Code. (FTC 2d/FIN ¶ L-18100, ¶ H-12500, ¶ V-1955.1; USTR ¶ 264.01, ¶ 2204.02, ¶ 66,934; TaxDesk ¶ 28,800)

New Law. Under the '97 Act, the 15% tax on nonmedical withdrawals form an MSA is not treated as a tax liability for purposes of the minimum tax. (Code Sec.

26(b)(2)(P) as amended by '97 Act §1602(a)) Also, Medicare supplemental plans are deleted from the types of permitted coverage an individual may have and still be eligible for an MSA. (Code Sec. 220(c)(3))

The '97 Act clarifies that so long as an individual for whom a medical expense was incurred was covered by a high deductible health plan and no other plan (except for those that provide certain permitted coverage) in the month in which the medical expense was incurred, he did not have to be self-employed or employed by a small employer in order for the withdrawal from the MSA to be excluded from income. (Code Sec. 220(d)(2)(C))

The '97 Act provides that the $50 penalty for failure to make required reports does not apply to Code Sec. 6724(d)(1)(C)(i) information returns or Code Sec. 6724(d)(2)(X) payee statements. (Code Sec. 6693(a))

☐ **Effective:** Taxable years beginning after Dec. 31, '96. ('97 Act §1602(i))

¶ 1300. Exempt Organizations

¶ 1301. "Qualified sponsorship payments" excluded from UBIT

Code Sec. 513(i), as amended by '97 Act § 965(a)
Generally effective: Payments solicited or received after Dec 31, '97.
Committee Reports, see ¶ 5086

Tax-exempt organizations are subject to the unrelated business income tax ("UBIT") on income derived from a separate trade or business regularly carried on if the business is not substantially related to the performance of the organization's tax-exempt functions. If an activity is not substantially related to an organization's tax-exempt purpose, it can be subject to UBIT as a separate trade or business. An activity (such as advertising) does not lose its identity as a separate trade or business merely because it is carried on within a larger complex of other endeavors. If a tax-exempt organization receives sponsorship payments in connection with an event or other activity, the solicitation and receipt of the sponsorship payments may be treated as a separate activity. IRS has taken the position that, under some circumstances, these sponsorship payments are subject to the UBIT. (FTC 2d/FIN ¶ D-6800; USTR ¶ 5124; TaxDesk ¶ 68,118)

New Law. Congress said that it is appropriate to distinguish sponsorship payments: (a) for which the donor receives no substantial return benefit, other than the use or acknowledgement of the donor's name or logo as part of a sponsored event (which should not be subject to UBIT), from (b) payments made in exchange for advertising provided by the recipient organization (which should be subject to UBIT). (Com Rept, see ¶ 5086) So, the '97 Act creates a safe-harbor which provides that UBTI does not include the activity of soliciting and receiving "qualified sponsorship payments". (Code Sec. 513(i)(1) as amended by '97 Act §965(a))

"Qualified sponsorship payments" are defined as any payment made by a person engaged in a trade or business with respect to which the person will receive no substantial return benefit other than the use or acknowledgment of the name or logo (or product lines) of the person's trade or business in connection with a tax-exempt organization's activities. This use or acknowledgment does not include advertising of the person's products or services (including qualitative or comparative language), price information or other indications of savings or value, or an endorsement or other inducement to purchase, sell, or use the products or services. (Code Sec. 513(i)(2)(A))

Congress intends that, as provided under Prop. Reg. § 1.513-4, the use of promotional logos or slogans that are an established part of the sponsor's identity does not, by itself, constitute advertising for purposes of determining whether a payment is a qualified sponsorship payment. (Com Rept, see ¶ 5086)

FTC 2d References are to Federal Tax Coordinator 2d
FIN References are to RIA's Analysis of Federal Taxes: Income
USTR References are to United States Tax Reporter: Income, Estate & Gift, and Excise
PCA References are to Pension Coordinator and Pension & Benefits Expert/Advisor
PE References are to Pension and Profit Sharing 2nd
EP References are to Estate Planning & Taxation Coordinator and Estate Planning Advisor

If, in return for receiving a sponsorship payment, a tax-exempt organization promises to use the sponsor's name or logo in acknowledging the sponsor's support for an educational or fund-raising event conducted by the organization, the payment is not subject to UBIT. (Com Rept, see ¶ 5086)

If a tax-exempt organization provides advertising of a sponsor's products, the payment made to the organization by the sponsor in order to receive the advertising is subject to UBIT (provided that the other requirements for UBIT liability are met). (Com Rept, see ¶ 5086)

A qualified sponsorship payment does not include any payment where the amount of the payment is contingent, by contract or otherwise, on the level of attendance at an event, broadcast ratings, or other factors indicating the degree of public exposure to an activity. (Code Sec. 513(i)(2)(B)(i))

However, if a sponsorship payment is contingent on an event actually taking place or being broadcast, the payment can still be a qualified sponsorship payment. Also, simply distributing or displaying a sponsor's products (either by the sponsor or the tax-exempt organization) to the general public at a sponsored event, whether for free or for remuneration, is considered to be "use or acknowledgment" of the sponsor's product lines (as opposed to advertising), and, thus, does not affect the determination of whether a payment made by the sponsor is a qualified sponsorship payment. (Com Rept, see ¶ 5086)

The term "qualified sponsorship payment" does *not* include:

(1) any payment which entitles the payor to the use or acknowledgement of the name or logo (or product lines) of the payor's trade or business in regularly scheduled and printed material (e.g., periodicals) published by or on behalf of the tax-exempt organization—unless the printed material is related to, and primarily distributed in connection with, a specific event conducted by the tax-exempt organization; or

(2) any payment made in connection with any qualified convention or trade show activity (as defined in Code Sec. 513(d)(3)(B)). (Code Sec. 513(i)(2)(B)(ii))

Payments that do not meet the qualified sponsorship payment safe-harbor requirements are governed by the general rules that determine whether the payment is subject to the UBIT. Thus, for example, payments that entitle the payor to a depiction of the payor's name or logo in a tax-exempt organization periodical may or may not be subject to the UBIT depending on the application of the general rules on periodical advertising and nontaxable donor recognition. (Com Rept, see ¶ 5086)

If a portion of a payment would (if made as a separate payment) be a qualified sponsorship payment, that portion of the payment is treated as a separate payment. (Code Sec. 513(i)(3))

Thus, if a sponsorship payment made to a tax-exempt organization entitles the sponsor to both product advertising and the use or acknowledgment of the sponsor's name or logo by the organization, then the UBIT does not apply to the amount of the payment that exceeds the fair market value of the product advertising provided to the sponsor. The provision of facilities, services or other privileges by an exempt organization to a sponsor or the sponsor's designees (e.g., complimentary tickets, pro-am playing spots in golf tournaments, or receptions for major donors) in connection with a sponsorship payment does not affect the determination of whether the payment is a qualified sponsorship payment. Instead, the provision of the goods or services is evaluated as a separate transaction in determining whether the organization has unrelated business taxable income from the event. In general, if the services or facilities do not constitute a substantial return benefit, or if the provision of such services or facilities is a related business activity, then the payments attributable to these services or facilities are not be subject to the UBIT. (Com Rept, see ¶5086)

As with the provision of facilities, services or other privileges provided by a tax-exempt organization to a sponsor or the sponsor's designees (complimentary tickets, pro-am playing spots in golf tournaments, or receptions for major donors) are treated as a separate transaction that does not affect the determination of whether a sponsorship payment is a qualified sponsorship payment. A sponsor's receipt of a license to use an intangible asset (e.g., trademark, logo, or designation) of the tax-exempt organization also is treated as separate from the qualified sponsorship transaction in determining whether the organization has unrelated business income. (Com Rept, see ¶5086)

The exemption provided for qualified sponsorship payments is in addition to other exceptions from the UBIT (e.g., the exceptions for volunteer activities and for activities not regularly carried on). No inference should be drawn from the creation of qualified sponsorship payments as to whether any sponsorship payment received before '98 (the effective date of the '97 Act changes, see below) was subject to the UBIT. (Com Rept, see ¶5086)

☐ **Effective:** For payments solicited or received after Dec. 31, '97. ('97 Act §965(b))

¶1302. UBTI rules apply to second-tier subsidiaries; control test changed

Code Sec. 512(b)(13), as amended by '97 Act § 1041
Generally effective: Aug. 5, '97
Committee Reports, see ¶5141

In general, interest, rents, royalties and annuities are excluded from the unrelated taxable business income ("UBTI") of tax-exempt organizations. However, Code Sec. 512(b)(13) treated otherwise excludable rent, royalty, annuity, and interest income as UBTI if the income was received from a taxable or tax-exempt subsidiary that was 80% controlled by the parent tax-exempt organization. For a stock subsidiary, the 80% control test was met if the parent organization owned 80% or more of the voting stock and all other classes of stock of the subsidiary. For a non-stock subsidiary, IRS looked to factors such as the representation of the parent corporation on the board of directors of the nonstock subsidiary, or the power of the parent corporation to appoint or remove the board of directors of the subsidiary.

The control test under Code Sec. 512(b)(13) did not, however, incorporate any *indirect* ownership rules. Consequently, rents, royalties, annuities and interest derived from second-tier subsidiaries generally did not constitute UBTI to the tax-exempt parent organization. (FTC 2d/FIN ¶ D-6800; USTR ¶ 5124; TaxDesk ¶ 68,106)

New Law. The '97 Act modifies the test for determining whether a tax-exempt organization has sufficient control of a another organization for the tax-exempt organization to have UBTI from the subsidiary. "Control" means (in the case of a stock corporation) ownership by vote or value of more than 50% of the stock. For a partnership or other entity, "control" means ownership of more than 50% of the profits, capital or beneficial interests. (Code Sec. 512(b)(13)(D)(i) as amended by '97 Act §1041(a))

The constructive ownership rules of Code Sec. 318 apply for purposes of Code Sec. 512(b)(13). Thus, a parent exempt organization is deemed to control any subsidiary in which it holds more than 50% of the voting power or value, directly (as in the case of a first-tier subsidiary) or indirectly (as in the case of a second-tier subsidiary). (Code Sec. 512(b)(13)(D)(ii))

Code Sec. 512(b)(13) was enacted to prevent subsidiaries of tax-exempt organizations from reducing their otherwise taxable income by borrowing, leasing, or licensing assets from a tax-exempt parent organization at inflated levels. Because Code Sec. 512(b)(13) was narrowly drafted, organizations were able to circumvent its application through, for example, the issuance of 21% of nonvoting stock with nominal value to a separate friendly party or through the use of tiered or brother/sister subsidiaries. The modifications to the control requirement and inclusion of attribution rules are intended to ensure that Code Sec. 512(b)(13) operate consistent with its intended purpose. (Com Rept, see ¶ 5141) The '97 Act authorizes IRS to prescribe rules to prevent avoidance of the purpose of Code Sec. 512(b)(13) through the use of related persons. (Code Sec. 512(b)(13)(E))

If a controlling organization receives a "specific payment" from a controlled organization, the controlling organization must include the payment as UBTI to the extent that the payment reduces the "net unrelated income", (or increases the "net unrelated loss") of the controlled entity. All deductions of the controlling organization directly connected with the amounts treated as UBTI are allowed. (Code Sec. 512(b)(13)(A))

"Specific payment" means any interest, annuity, royalty, or rent. (Code Sec. 512(b)(13)(C))

"Net unrelated income" means:

• in the case of a controlled entity which is not a tax-exempt organization—the portion of the entity's income which would be UBTI if the organization were tax-exempt and had the same tax-exempt purpose as the controlling organization;

• in the case of a controlled entity which is a tax-exempt organization—the amount of the UBTI of the controlled entity.

"Net unrelated loss" means the net operating loss adjusted in the same manner as net unrelated income. (Code Sec. 512(b)(13)(B))

☐ **Effective:** For taxable years beginning after Aug. 5, '97. ('97 Act §1041(b)(1)) However, the '97 Act's changes to Code Sec. 512(b)(13) do not apply to any payment made during the first two taxable years beginning on or after Aug. 5, '97, if the payment was made under a written binding contract that was in effect on June 8, '97, and the contract was in effect at all times thereafter before the payment was made. ('97 Act §1041(b)(2))

¶ 1303. Cooperative hospital service organizations may purchase patient account receivables

Code Sec. 501(e)(1)(A), as amended by '97 Act § 974(a)
Generally effective: Taxable years beginning after Dec. 31, '96
Committee Reports, see ¶ 5097

Code Sec. 501(e) provides that an organization organized on a cooperative basis by tax-exempt hospitals (a "cooperative hospital service organization") will itself be tax-exempt if it is operated solely to perform, on a centralized basis, one or more of the following tasks: data processing, purchasing (including the purchase of insurance on a group basis), warehousing, billing and collection, food services, clinical services, industrial engineering, laboratory functions, printing services, communications, record maintenance and storage, and personnel services. (FTC 2d/FIN ¶ D-4100; USTR ¶ 5014.10; TaxDesk ¶ 67,073)

New Law. For purposes of Code Sec. 501(e), billing and collection services include the purchase of patron accounts receivable on a recourse basis. Thus, hospital cooperative service organizations are permitted to advance cash on the basis of member accounts receivable, provided that each member hospital retains the risk of nonpayment with respect to its accounts receivable. (Code Sec. 501(e)(1)(A) as amended by '97 Act §974(a)) Congress said that it is important to clarify that permissible billing and collection services that can be carried out by hospital cooperative services organizations under Code Sec. 501(e) include the purchase of patron accounts receivable on a recourse basis. (Com Rept, see ¶ 5097)

☐ **Effective:** Taxable years beginning after Dec. 31, '96. ('97 Act §974(b))

¶ 1304. Hospitals will not loose tax-exempt status by participating in a provider-sponsored organization ("PSO")

Code Sec. 501(o), as amended by Budget Act § 4041
Generally effective: Aug. 5, '97
Committee Reports, see ¶ 5502

FTC 2d References are to Federal Tax Coordinator 2d
FIN References are to RIA's Analysis of Federal Taxes: Income
USTR References are to United States Tax Reporter: Income, Estate & Gift, and Excise
PCA References are to Pension Coordinator and Pension & Benefits Expert/Advisor
PE References are to Pension and Profit Sharing 2nd
EP References are to Estate Planning & Taxation Coordinator and Estate Planning Advisor

A tax-exempt organization may, subject to certain limitations, enter into a joint venture or partnership with a for-profit organization without affecting its tax-exempt status. Tax-exempt hospitals may enter into various arrangements with provider-sponsored organizations ("PSOs"). PSOs are joint venture arrangements between doctors and hospitals that provide health care services under contract to employers and insurers. PSOs may be taxable or tax-exempt entities. These arrangements come in a variety of permutations, such as partnership arrangements, hospital owned primary care physician practices, and HMO arrangements.

IRS examines the facts and circumstances to determine whether the PSO and the participation of a tax-exempt organization in the venture furthers a charitable purpose. If so, the tax-exempt organization's participation in the PSO does not negatively affect its tax-exempt status. However, IRS also examines whether the sharing of profits and losses or other aspects of a for-profit and tax-exempt organization venture results in improper private inurement or private benefit, which can result in the loss of an organization's tax-exempt status. (FTC 2d/FIN ¶ D-4114; USTR ¶ 5014.07; TaxDesk ¶ 67,060)

New Law. The Budget Act provides a limited exception from the Code Sec. 501(c)(3) requirement that a tax-exempt entity must be able to demonstrate that it is organized and operated exclusively for a tax exempt purpose. A hospital does not loose its tax-exempt status under Code Sec. 501(c)(3) for failure to be organized and operated exclusively for a charitable purpose solely because the hospital participates in a PSO, regardless of whether the PSO is taxable or tax-exempt. (Code Sec. 501(o) as amended by Budget Act §4041(a)) Participation by a hospital in a PSO (whether taxable or tax-exempt) is deemed to satisfy the requirement that the venture furthers a charitable purpose. (Com Rept, see ¶ 5502)

The Budget Act does not change the law concerning restrictions on private inurement and private benefit. (Com Rept, see ¶ 5502) However, the Budget Act provides that *any person* with a material financial interest in the PSO is treated as a private shareholder or individual when applying the private inurement prohibition under Code Sec. 501(c)(3). (Code Sec. 501(o)) Thus, the facts and circumstances of each PSO arrangement are evaluated to determine whether the arrangement entails impermissible private inurement or more than incidental private benefit (e.g., where there is a disproportionate allocation of profits and losses to the non-exempt partners, the tax-exempt partner makes loans to the joint venture that are commercially unreasonable, the tax-exempt partner provides property or services to the joint venture at less than fair market value, or a non-exempt partner receives more than reasonable compensation for the sale of property or services to the joint venture). (Com Rept, see ¶ 5502)

☐ **Effective:** Aug. 5, '97 (Budget Act §4041(b))

¶ 1305. Tax-exempt state-sponsored high risk pools can provide health care coverage to spouse and children of high risk individual

Code Sec. 501(c)(26), as amended by '97 Act § 101(c)
Generally effective: Tax years beginning after Dec. 31, '97
Committee Reports, see ¶ 5001

A membership organization (high risk pool) established by a state exclusively to provide coverage for medical care on a not-for-profit basis to certain high-risk individuals is tax-exempt if certain requirements are met. For the organization to qualify, the only individuals eligible to receive coverage must be residents of the state who, because of a pre-existing medical condition, can't get medical coverage for that condition through insurance or from a health maintenance organization (HMO), or are able to acquire coverage only at a rate that's substantially higher than the rate charged for that coverage by the organization (high-risk individuals). (FTC 2d/FIN ¶ D-6322; USTR ¶ 5014.39; TaxDesk ¶ 67,288)

New Law. A spouse and any qualifying child (as defined in Code Sec. 24(c)—the child tax credit, added by the '97 Act, see ¶ 101) of an individual eligible to receive coverage under the pre-'97 Act criteria (without regard to this '97 Act rule for a spouse and qualifying children) are treated as individuals eligible to receive coverage. (Code Sec. 501(c)(26) as amended by '97 Act §101(c)) Thus, the definition of high-risk individual is expanded to include the spouse and children of a high risk individual who meets the pre-97 Act definition of a high-risk individual. For a child to qualify, the taxpayer must be allowed a deduction for a personal exemption for the child for the year, the child must not have attained the age of 17 as of the close of the calendar year in which the tax year of the taxpayer begins, and the child must be a son or daughter of the taxpayer (or a "dependent" of either), a stepson, stepdaughter, or eligible foster child of the taxpayer. (Com Rept, see ¶ 5001)

> *observation:* To qualify under Code Sec. 24(c), the child must also be a citizen, national, or resident of the U.S., see ¶ 101.

> *observation:* The Committee Report, above, in describing the required relationship, refers to a son or daughter of the taxpayer or a "dependent " of either. Code Sec. 32(c)(3)(B), from which the relationship test is derived, says descendant rather than dependent.

☐ **Effective:** For tax years beginning after Dec. 31, '97. ('97 Act §101(e))

FTC 2d References are to Federal Tax Coordinator 2d
FIN References are to RIA's Analysis of Federal Taxes: Income
USTR References are to United States Tax Reporter: Income, Estate & Gift, and Excise
PCA References are to Pension Coordinator and Pension & Benefits Expert/Advisor
PE References are to Pension and Profit Sharing 2nd
EP References are to Estate Planning & Taxation Coordinator and Estate Planning Advisor

¶ 1306. Certain state workmen's compensation act companies are tax–exempt

Code Sec. 501(c)(27)(B), as amended by '97 Act § 963(a)
Generally effective: For tax years after Dec. 31, '97
Committee Reports, see ¶ 5084

In general, IRS takes the position that organizations that provide insurance for their members or other individuals are not considered to be engaged in a tax–exempt activity. IRS maintains that this type of insurance activity is either (1) a regular business of a kind ordinarily carried on for profit, or (2) an economy or convenience in the conduct of members' businesses because it relieves the members from obtaining insurance on an individual basis. Certain insurance risk pools have qualified for tax exemption under Code Sec. 501(c)(6). In general, these organizations (1) assign any insurance policies and administrative functions to their member organizations (although they may reimburse their members for amounts paid and expenses); (2) serve an important common business interest of their members; and (3) must be membership organizations financed, at least in part, by membership dues. State insurance risk pools may also qualify for tax–exempt status under Code Sec. 501(c)(4) as a social welfare organizations or under Code Sec. 115 as serving an essential governmental function of a state. In seeking qualification under Code Sec. 501(c)(4), insurance organizations generally are constrained by the restrictions on the provision of "commercial–type insurance" contained in Code Sec. 501(m). Code Sec. 115 generally provides that gross income does not include income derived from the exercise of any essential governmental function and accruing to a state or any political subdivision of the state. However, under pre–'97 Act law, IRS may have been reluctant to rule that particular state risk–pooling entities satisfied the Code Sec. 501(c)(4) or the Code Sec. 115 requirements for tax–exempt status. (FTC 2d/FIN ¶ D-6341 *et seq.*)

New Law. The new provision relating to membership organizations under workmen's compensation acts is intended to eliminate uncertainty as to the eligibility of certain state workmen's compensation act companies for tax–exempt status, in order to assist states in ensuring workmen's compensation coverage for uninsured employers with respect to employees in the state. (Com Rept, see ¶ 5084)

Any organization (including a mutual insurance company) is tax–exempt if all of the following requirements are met: (Code Sec. 501(c)(27)(B) as amended by '97 Act §963(a))

• The organization is created by state law and organized and operated under state law exclusively to provide the following—(Code Sec. 501(c)(27)(B)(i))

... workmen's compensation insurance which is required by state law or with respect to which state law provides significant disincentives if the insurance is not purchased by an employer (Code Sec. 501(c)(27)(B)(i)(I)), such as loss of exclusive remedy or forfeiture of affirmative defenses such as contributory negligence (Com Rept, see ¶ 5084), and

⊛ **Research Institute of America**

... related coverage incidental to workmen's compensation insurance (Code Sec. 501(c)(27)(B)(i)(II)), such as the liability under federal workmen's compensation laws. (Com Rept, see ¶ 5084)

• The organization must provide workmen's compensation insurance to any employer in the state (for employees in the state or temporarily assigned out–of–state) who seeks the insurance and meets other reasonable requirements. (Code Sec. 501(c)(27)(B)(ii))

• The state makes a financial commitment with respect to the organization either by extending the full faith and credit of the state to the initial debt of the organization or by providing the initial operating capital of the organization. (Code Sec. 501(c)(27)(B)(iii)(I)) For this purpose, the initial operating capital can be provided by providing the proceeds of bonds issued by a state authority; for example, the bonds may be repaid through exercise of the state's taxing authority. (Com Rept, see ¶ 5084)

• In the case of periods after the date of enactment of this provision, the assets of the organization revert to the state upon dissolution or state law does not permit the dissolution of the organization. (Code Sec. 501(c)(27)(B)(iii)(II)) Should dissolution of the organization become permissible under applicable state law, then the requirement that the assets of the organization revert to the state upon dissolution applies. (Com Rept, see ¶ 5084)

• The majority of the board of directors or oversight body of the organization are appointed by the chief executive officer or other executive branch official of the state, by the state legislature, or by both. (Code Sec. 501(c)(27)(B)(iv))

Many organizations described in the '97 Act provision have been operating as organizations that are exempt from tax, for example, as an organization that is exempt from tax because it is serving an essential governmental function of a state. Congress intended no inference that organizations described in the provision are not exempt from tax under pre-'97 Act law. In addition, no inference was intended that the benefit plans of such organizations are not properly maintained by the organization. It is anticipated that federal regulatory agencies will take appropriate action to address transition issues faced by organizations to conform their benefit plans under the provision. For example, Congress intended that an organization that has been maintaining a plan under Code Sec. 457 as an agency or instrumentality of a state could freeze future contributions to that plan and establish a retirement arrangement, for example, a 401(k) plan, that is consistent with the treatment of the organization as a tax-exempt employer under the '97 Act provision. (Com Rept, see ¶ 5084)

☐ **Effective:** Applicable to tax years beginning after Dec. 31, '97. ('97 Act §963(c))

FTC 2d References are to Federal Tax Coordinator 2d
FIN References are to RIA's Analysis of Federal Taxes: Income
USTR References are to United States Tax Reporter: Income, Estate & Gift, and Excise
PCA References are to Pension Coordinator and Pension & Benefits Expert/Advisor
PE References are to Pension and Profit Sharing 2nd
EP References are to Estate Planning & Taxation Coordinator and Estate Planning Advisor

¶ 1400. Partnerships
Electing Large Partnership

¶ 1401. Simplified flow-through for electing large partnerships

Code Sec. 771, as added by '97 Act § 1221(a)
Code Sec. 772, as added by '97 Act § 1221(a)
Code Sec. 773, as added by '97 Act § 1221(a)
Code Sec. 774, as added by '97 Act § 1221(a)
Code Sec. 775, as added by '97 Act § 1221(a)
Code Sec. 776, as added by '97 Act § 1221(a)
Code Sec. 777, as added by '97 Act § 1221(a)
Generally effective: Partnership tax years beginning after Dec. 31, '97
Committee Reports, see ¶ 5209

The taxable income of a partnership is computed in the same manner as that of an individual, with certain modifications. A partnership is generally treated as a conduit, with each partner taking into account separately his distributive share of the partnership's items of income, gain, loss, deduction or credit as if the item had been directly realized or incurred by the partner. Limitations affecting the computation of taxable income generally apply at the partner level and most elections affecting the computation of partnership taxable income are made at the partnership level.

Thus, for instance, a partner's shares of a partnership's net short-term capital gain or loss, net long-term capital gain or loss from portfolio investments and Code Sec. 1231 net gain or loss are separately reported to the partner.

Similarly, miscellaneous itemized deductions (i.e., certain items that are deductible only to the extent that, in the aggregate, they exceed 2% of an individual's adjusted gross income), charitable contributions, tax credits, and foreign taxes are passed through to the partners and the limitations on the use of these items are applied at the partner level. (FTC 2d/FIN ¶ B-1900; USTR ¶ 7024, ¶ 7034; TaxDesk ¶ 58,400)

Oil and gas percentage depletion. The depletion deduction is computed separately by the partners. The limitations on the deduction are applied at the partner level. (FTC 2d/FIN ¶ N-2431; USTR ¶ 860A4.05; TaxDesk ¶ 27,124)

New Law. The '97 Act adds electing large partnership rules that are designed to simplify partnership reporting. The electing large partnership rules override the ordinary partnership rules to the extent the electing large partnership rules are inconsistent with the ordinary partnership rules. (Code Sec. 771 as added by '97 Act §1221(a)) Thus, the character of fewer partnership items passes through to the partners. Instead, many items are netted at the partnership level. (Com Rept, see ¶ 5209)

FTC 2d References are to the Federal Tax Coordinator 2d
FIN References are to RIA's Analysis of Federal Taxes: Income
USTR References are to the United States Tax Reporter: Income, Estate & Gift, and Excise
PCA References are to Pension Coordinator and Pension & Benefits Expert/Advisor
PE References are to Pension and Profit Sharing 2nd
EP References are to Estate Planning & Taxation Coordinator and Estate Planning Advisor

Separately stated items. The tax treatment of an electing large partnership (generally, an electing partnership with at least 100 partners, see below) and its partners is modified so that each partner takes into account separately the partner's distributive share of the following items, which are determined at the partnership level:

(1) taxable income or loss from passive loss limitation activities. (Code Sec. 772(a)(1) as added by '97 Act §1221(a)) Passive loss limitation activities include activities that involve the conduct of a trade or business (Code Sec. 772(d)(1)(A)) (including activities described at Code Sec. 469(c)(5) and Code Sec. 469(c)(6) (Code Sec. 772(d)(1))) and rental activities. (Code Sec. 772(d)(1)(B))

(2) taxable income or loss from other activities (Code Sec. 772(a)(2)) (e.g., portfolio income or loss) (Com Rept, see ¶5209);

(3) net capital gain or loss to the extent allocable to passive loss limitation activities (Code Sec. 772(a)(3)(A)) and other activities (Code Sec. 772(a)(3)(B)). The net capital loss is the excess of the losses from sales or exchanges of capital assets over the gains from sales or exchanges of capital assets (Code Sec. 772(d)(4)(C));

(4) tax-exempt interest (Code Sec. 772(a)(4)) (i.e., interest excludable from gross income under Code Sec. 103 (Code Sec. 772(d)(2)));

(5) net AMT adjustment separately computed for passive loss limitation activities (Code Sec. 772(a)(5)(A)) and for other activities (Code Sec. 772(a)(5)(B));

(6) general credits (Code Sec. 772(a)(6)) (i.e., all credits other the low-income housing credit, the rehabilitation credit, the foreign tax credit and the credit for producing fuel from a nonconventional source (Code Sec. 772(d)(5)));

(7) Code Sec. 42 low-income housing credit (Code Sec. 772(a)(7));

(8) Code Sec. 47 rehabilitation credit (Code Sec. 772(a)(8));

(9) foreign income taxes (Code Sec. 772(a)(9)) (i.e., taxes described in Code Sec. 901 that are paid or accrued to foreign countries or U.S. possessions (Code Sec. 772(d)(6))). The partnership also reports the source of any income, gain, loss or deduction to the partner. (Com Rept, see ¶5209);

(10) Code Sec. 29 credit for producing fuel from a nonconventional source (Code Sec. 772(a)(10)); and

(11) any other items to the extent that IRS determines that separate treatment of such items is appropriate. (Code Sec. 772(a)(11))

Taxable income or loss from passive loss limitation activities and other activities are determined by excluding any net capital gain or loss and any items described in item (11). (Code Sec. 772(d)(4)(A))

> 🖋 *observation:* In contrast, regular partnerships pass through many more items to the partners. Items that are passed through by regular partnerships, but not by large partnerships, include long and short term capital gains and

FTC 2d References are to Federal Tax Coordinator 2d
FIN References are to RIA's Analysis of Federal Taxes: Income
USTR References are to United States Tax Reporter: Income, Estate & Gift, and Excise
PCA References are to Pension Coordinator and Pension & Benefits Expert/Advisor
PE References are to Pension and Profit Sharing 2nd
EP References are to Estate Planning & Taxation Coordinator and Estate Planning Advisor

losses, which are passed through without netting gains and losses, Code Sec. 1231 gains and losses, and certain itemized deductions, including Code Sec. 212 expenses.

In determining the amounts of each item separately taken into account by a partner, these rules are applied separately with respect to the partner by taking into account the partner's distributive share of the partnership items of income, gain, loss, deduction loss or credit. (Code Sec. 772(b)) Thus, if a partnership makes special allocations of particular items, a partner's share of these items is determined by taking the special allocations into account. (Com Rept, see ¶ 5209)

Except as otherwise provided, a partner's distributive share of any of these items is treated as if realized by the partner directly. (Code Sec. 772(c)(1)) The exceptions with regard to income and loss from passive loss activities and other activities, net capital gains and losses, alternative minimum taxable income and tax credits are described below.

Taxable income computations. The taxable income of an electing large partnership is computed in the same manner as that of an individual, except that the items described above are separately stated (Code Sec. 773(a)(1)(A) as added by '97 Act §1221(a)), and certain modifications are made. (Code Sec. 773(a)(1)(B))

The modifications are:

(1) the deduction for personal exemptions is disallowed (Code Sec. 773(b)(1)(A));

(2) the net operating loss deduction is disallowed (Code Sec. 773(b)(1)(B));

(3) the additional itemized deductions described in Code Sec. 211 to Code Sec. 220 (other than the Code Sec. 212 deduction) are disallowed (Code Sec. 773(b)(1)(C));

(4) the deduction for charitable contributions is subject to the limitation that applies to corporations. (Code Sec. 773(b)(2)) Thus, the deduction for charitable contributions is determined at the partnership level and is not separately reported to the partners. (Com Rept, see ¶ 5209)

(5) in lieu of applying the 2% floor on miscellaneous itemized deductions, 70% of the miscellaneous itemized deductions are disallowed. (Code Sec. 773(b)(3))

> **🖉 observation:** The disallowance of 70% of the miscellaneous itemized deductions is disadvantageous to corporate partners, who are normally not subject to any limitation on miscellaneous itemized deductions, and to individuals with large amounts of miscellaneous itemized deductions.

All limitations and other provisions affecting the computation of taxable income or any credit are applied at the partnership (and not the partner) level (Code Sec. 773(a)(3)(A)), except for:

(1) the Code Sec. 68 overall itemized deduction limitation (Code Sec. 773(a)(3)(B)(i)),

(2) the Code Sec. 49 and Code Sec. 465 at-risk limitations (Code Sec. 773(a)(3)(B)(ii)),

(3) the Code Sec. 469 passive loss and credit limitations (Code Sec. 773(a)(3)(B)(iii)), and

(4) any other provision specified in regulations. (Code Sec. 773(a)(3)(B)(iv))

All elections affecting the computation of taxable income or any credit (except for elections relating to the foreign tax credit and to the exclusion of cancellation of indebtedness income) are made by the partnership. (Code Sec. 773(a)(2)) These rules regarding limitations and elections apply notwithstanding any other provisions other than the electing large partnership provisions. (Code Sec. 773(a)(4))

Capital gains. Capital gains and losses are netted at the partnership level and net capital gains or losses are passed through to the partners as long-term capital gain or loss. (Code Sec. 772(c)(4)) Any excess of net short-term capital gain over net long-term capital loss is consolidated with the partnership's other taxable income and is not separately reported. Thus, a partnership cannot use any part of its capital losses to offset ordinary income. (Com Rept, see ¶ 5209)

Any Code Sec. 1231 gains and losses of the partnership are netted at the partnership level, with net gain being treated as long-term capital gain and and net loss being treated as ordinary loss and consolidated with the partnership's other taxable income. (Com Rept, see ¶ 5209)

Discharge of indebtedness income. Discharge of indebtedness income of a partnership is excluded in determining the partnership's income. (Code Sec. 773(c)(1)) Instead, the discharge of indebtedness is treated by each partner as an item that is separately reported to the partner (Code Sec. 773(c)(2)(A)) and the Code Sec. 108 rules relating to the exclusion of cancellation of indebtedness income are applied without regard to the electing large partnership rules. (Code Sec. 773(c)(2)(B)) Partner-level elections under Code Sec. 108 are made by each partner separately. (Code Sec. 773(a)(2)) For instance, the election to exclude discharge of indebtedness income with respect to qualified real property business indebtedness is made at the partner level. (Com Rept, see ¶ 5209)

Basis adjustments under the Code Sec. 108 rules are applied separately to each partner (Code Sec. 774(a)(2) as added by '97 Act §1221(a)) and do not affect partnership level computations. (Code Sec. 774(a)(1))

Passive and nonpassive income and loss. A partner's share of an electing large partnership's taxable income or loss from passive loss limitation activities is treated as income or loss from the conduct of a single passive activity. Similarly, a partner's share of an electing large partnership's net capital gain or loss and net AMT adjustment from passive loss limitation activities is treated as attributable to the conduct of a single passive activity. (Code Sec. 772(c)(2)) Thus, an electing large partnership generally does not have to report separately items from multiple activities. (Com Rept, see

¶ 5209)

The net capital gain is allocated to passive loss limitation activities to the extent that it does not exceed the net capital gain determined by only taking gains and losses from sales and exchanges of property used in connection with such activities into account (Code Sec. 772(d)(4)(B)(i)) and is allocated to other activities to the extent that it exceeds the amount allocated to passive loss limitation activities. (Code Sec. 772(d)(4)(B)(ii)) A similar rule shall apply for purposes of allocating any net capital loss. (Code Sec. 772(d)(4)(B))

A partner's distributive share of a partnership's taxable income or loss from activities other than passive loss limitation activities is treated as an item of income or expense with respect to property held for investment. (Code Sec. 772(c)(3)(A)) Thus, portfolio income (e.g., interest and dividends) is reported separately and is reduced by portfolio deductions and allocable investment interest expense. (Com Rept, see ¶ 5209) Nonbusiness Code Sec. 212 deductions are not treated as miscellaneous itemized deductions subject to the 2% floor. (Code Sec. 772(c)(3)(B)) However, these deductions are subject to the 70% disallowance. (Com Rept, see ¶ 5209)

Where a partner holds an interest in an electing large partnership other than a limited partnership interest, the rule treating the partner's distributive share of the partnership's taxable income or loss from passive loss limitation activities as income or loss from the conduct of a single passive activity does not apply. (Code Sec. 772(f)(1)) Instead, the partner's distributive share of the partnership's items allocable to passive loss limitation activities (other than those allocable to an interest as a limited partner (Code Sec. 772(f))) are taken into account separately to the extent necessary to comply with the passive loss rules. (Code Sec. 772(f)(2)) Thus, for example, income of an electing large partnership is not treated as passive income with respect to the general partnership interest of a partner who materially participates in the partnership's trade or business. (Com Rept, see ¶ 5209)

The rule that the passive loss rules are applied separately to each publicly traded partnership applies to large partnerships. (Com Rept, see ¶ 5209)

Credits. General credits are passed through to the partners as a current year business credit. (Code Sec. 772(c)(6)) The limitations on the business credit are applied at the partner level. (Com Rept, see ¶ 5209) The Code Sec. 34 fuel credit (Code Sec. 774(d)(1)) and the credit for undistributed capital gains of a regulated investment company (Code Sec. 774(d)(2)) are allowed to the partnership and not separately reported to partners.

> ✔️*observation:* The reason why Code Sec. 34 fuel credit and the credit for undistributed capital gains of a regulated investment company are allowed to the partnership is that these credits are refundable. (Com Rept, see ¶ 5209)

Any tax credit recapture is taken into account by the partnership. (Code Sec. 774(b)(1)(A)) This is done by reducing the partnership's current tax credits to the extent of the recapture and subjecting the partnership to tax to the extent of the excess of the recapture over the current tax credits. (Code Sec. 774(b)(2)) The amount of the recapture is determined as if the recaptured credit had been fully utilized to reduce tax.

(Code Sec. 774(b)(1)(B))

Tax credit recapture means the increases in tax described in Code Sec. 42(j) (low-income housing credit recapture) and Code Sec. 50(a) (investment credit recapture). (Code Sec. 774(b)(4)) However, a transfer of an interest in an electing large partnership will not trigger tax credit recapture. (Code Sec. 774(b)(3))

Unrelated business taxable income (UBTI). Each exempt partner subject to tax on UBTI must take its distributive share of any partnership items into account separately to the extent necessary to comply with rules that provides for the pass through of the partnership's UBTI items to the partners. (Code Sec. 772(e))

Alternative minimum tax (AMT). In determining a partner's alternative minimum taxable income, a partner's distributive share of any net AMT adjustment (defined below) is taken into account instead of making separate AMT adjustments under Code Sec. 56, Code Sec. 57, and Code Sec. 58 with respect to partnership items. Except as provided in regs, the applicable net AMT adjustment is treated for purposes of the Code Sec. 53 AMT credit as a deferral preference not specified in Code Sec. 53(d)(1)(B)(ii). (Code Sec. 772(c)(5)) The applicable net AMT adjustment is determined by using the adjustments applicable to individuals (in the case of partners other than corporations) (Code Sec. 772(d)(3)(A)(i)) and by using the adjustments applicable to corporations (in the case of corporate partners). (Code Sec. 772(d)(3)(A)(ii)) The net AMT adjustment is the net adjustment in the items attributable to passive loss activities or other activities which would result if such items were determined with the adjustments of Code Sec. 56, Code Sec. 57, and Code Sec. 58. (Code Sec. 772(d)(3)(B))

Election of optional basis adjustments. Where an electing large partnership makes a Code Sec. 754 election to adjust the basis of partnership assets on transfers of partnership interests, a transferee partner's distributive share of separately stated partnership items will be affected by Code Sec. 743(b) basis adjustments (Code Sec. 774(a)(2)), but the basis adjustments do not affect partnership level computations. (Code Sec. 774(a)(1))

Electing large partnerships that make a Code Sec. 754 election adjust the basis of their property for distributions under Code Sec. 734. (Com Rept, see ¶ 5209)

Installment sales interest charges. Where an electing large partnership is subject to an interest charge with respect to installment sales, the interest charge is imposed at the partnership level. (Code Sec. 774(f)(1)) In determining the amount of the interest charge, the partnership is treated as subject to tax at the highest corporate or noncorporate tax rate. (Code Sec. 774(f)(2))

REMIC residuals. An electing large partnership is subject to the tax imposed on partnerships with disqualified organizations as partners that hold REMIC residual interests as if all the interests in the partnership were held by disqualified organizations.

FTC 2d References are to Federal Tax Coordinator 2d
FIN References are to RIA's Analysis of Federal Taxes: Income
USTR References are to United States Tax Reporter: Income, Estate & Gift, and Excise
PCA References are to Pension Coordinator and Pension & Benefits Expert/Advisor
PE References are to Pension and Profit Sharing 2nd
EP References are to Estate Planning & Taxation Coordinator and Estate Planning Advisor

(Code Sec. 774(e)(1)) The exclusion from tax for instances where the holder provides the partnership with an affidavit that it is not a disqualified organization does not apply. (Code Sec. 774(e)(3)) Thus, the electing large partnership is subject to a tax equal to the excess inclusions multiplied by the highest corporate rate. (Com Rept, see ¶ 5209) In lieu of the deduction allowed under Code Sec. 860E(e)(6)(C), the amount subject to tax is excluded from partnership income. (Code Sec. 774(e)(2))

Oil and gas partnerships. Except as discussed below, an electing large partnership's oil and gas depletion deduction allowance is computed at the partnership level (Code Sec. 776(a)(1) as added by '97 Act §1221(a)) without regard to the 1,000-barrel-per-day limit on the amount of production for which percentage depletion is allowable and without regard to the 65% of taxable income limitation of Code Sec. 613A(d)(1). (Code Sec. 776(a)(2)) The basis of the partners of the partnership is not reduced by the partner's depletion deduction. (Code Sec. 776(a)(3))

The depletion deduction and other oil and gas related items are generally reported to the partners as components of that partner's distributive share of taxable income or loss from passive loss limitation activities. (Com Rept, see ¶ 5209)

The election to deduct intangible drilling costs (IDCs) and the Code Sec. 59(e) election to capitalize and amortize IDCs are made at the partnership level. The reduction of the IDC deduction as a preference item does not apply. (Com Rept, see ¶ 5209)

As described above, electing large partnerships report a single AMT adjustment to the partners as a separate item. For purposes of the Code Sec. 57(a)(2)(E) exception from the preference for excess IDCs, the partnership is the taxpayer. Thus, the exception is applied at the partnership level and the limitation on the reduction in alternative minimum taxable income due to this exception is based on the cumulative reduction in the partnership's alternative minimum taxable income. (Com Rept, see ¶ 5209)

However, the distributive shares of partners who are disqualified persons of all items of income, gain, loss, deduction, or credit attributable to partnership oil or gas properties are determined under the normal partnership rules (rather than the electing large partnership rules) and are excluded from the items passed through under the electing large partnership rules. (Code Sec. 776(b)(1)) For example, in computing the partnership's net income from oil and gas for purposes of determining the IDC preference reported to partners who are not disqualified persons as part of the AMT adjustment, disqualified persons' distributive shares of the partnership's net income from oil and gas are not taken into account. (Com Rept, see ¶ 5209)

A disqualified person's distributive share of non-oil and gas related items is reported under the electing large partnership rules. (Com Rept, see ¶ 5209)

Partners who are disqualified persons are permitted to make their own separate Code Sec. 59(e) elections to capitalize and amortize IDCs. (Com Rept, see ¶ 5209)

A disqualified person is any retailer or refiner described in Code Sec. 613A(d)(2) or Code Sec. 613A(d)(4) (Code Sec. 776(b)(2)(A)) and any other person whose average daily production of domestic crude oil and natural gas during the person's tax year in which the partnership's tax year ends exceeds 500 barrels. (Code Sec. 776(b)(2)(B))

A person's average daily production of domestic crude oil and natural gas for any tax year is computed under the rules described at Code Sec. 613A(c)(2) by (a) taking into account all production of domestic crude oil and natural gas (including the person's proportionate share of any production of a partnership) (Code Sec. 776(b)(3)(A)), (b) treating 6,000 cubic feet of natural gas as a barrel of crude oil (Code Sec. 776(b)(3)(B)), and (c) treating as one taxpayer all persons who are related or among whom allocations are required under Code Sec. 613A(c)(8). (Code Sec. 776(b)(3)(C))

A disqualified person has the responsibility of notifying any large partnership in which it holds an interest directly or indirectly (e.g., through a pass- through entity) of its disqualified person status. Thus, for example, if an integrated producer owns an interest in a partnership which in turn owns an interest in an oil and gas large partnership, it is responsible for providing the the electing large partnership with information regarding its status as a disqualified person and details regarding its indirect interest in the electing large partnership. (Com Rept, see ¶ 5209)

Terminations. An electing large partnership does not terminate for tax purposes on the sale or exchange of a 50% or greater interest within a 12-month period. (Code Sec. 774(c))

Electing large partnership defined. An "electing large partnership" is any partnership with at least 100 partners in any preceding tax year (Code Sec. 775(a)(1)(A) as added by '97 Act §1221(a)) that makes an election to be treated as an electing large partnership. (Code Sec. 775(a)(1)(B)) The number of partners is determined by counting only persons directly holding partnership interests in the taxable year, including persons holding through nominees; persons holding interests indirectly (e.g., through another partnership) are not counted. (Com Rept, see ¶ 5209)

> ⓥ *observation:* It would appear that the 100 partner test would be satisfied by a partnership that has very few partnership interests if the turn over of the partnership interests is sufficiently frequent.

The election applies to the tax year in which it is made and all later tax years unless revoked with IRS consent. (Code Sec. 775(a)(2)) To the extent provided in regs, a partnership will lose its electing large partnership status for any partnership tax year in which it had fewer than 100 partners. (Code Sec. 775(a)(1))

A partnership cannot make the election if substantially all the partners of the partnership are:

(a) individuals performing substantial services in connection with the partnership's activities of such partnership or are personal service corporations (as defined in Code Sec. 269A(b) with owner-employees who (as defined in Code Sec. 269A(b)) who perform such substantial services (Code Sec. 775(b)(2)(A));

FTC 2d References are to Federal Tax Coordinator 2d
FIN References are to RIA's Analysis of Federal Taxes: Income
USTR References are to United States Tax Reporter: Income, Estate & Gift, and Excise
PCA References are to Pension Coordinator and Pension & Benefits Expert/Advisor
PE References are to Pension and Profit Sharing 2nd
EP References are to Estate Planning & Taxation Coordinator and Estate Planning Advisor

(b) retired partners who had performed such substantial services (Code Sec. 775(b)(2)(B)); or

(c) spouses of partners who are performing (or had previously performed) such substantial services. (Code Sec. 775(b)(2)(C))

In addition, for purposes of the 100 partner requirement, individuals performing substantial services in connection with the partnership's activities who hold partnership interests (or individuals who formerly performed substantial services in connection with such activities and held partnership interests at the time the services were performed) are excluded. (Code Sec. 775(b)(1))

For purposes of determining whether a partner is a service partner, the activities of a partnership include the activities of any other partnership in which the partnership owns directly an 80% or more interest in capital and profits. (Code Sec. 775(b)(3))

A partnership cannot make the election if its principal activity is buying and selling commodities (other than inventory described in Code Sec. 1221(1)), or options, futures, or forwards with respect to such commodities. (Code Sec. 775(c))

If a partnership files a return on which it is treated as an electing large partnership, such treatment is binding on the partnership and all its partners partnership, but not IRS. (Code Sec. 775(d))

Regulations. IRS is directed to issue regs as appropriate to carry out the purposes of the electing large partnership rules. (Code Sec. 777 as added by '97 Act §1221(a))

For the due date by which electing large partnerships must provide information to partners, see ¶ 2302.

☐ **Effective:** The large partnership rules apply for partnership tax years beginning after Dec. 31, 1997. ('97 Act §1221(c))

¶ 1402. Consistency rules and audit procedures for electing large partnerships

Code Sec. 6240, as added by '97 Act § 1222(a)
Code Sec. 775(a), as added by '97 Act § 1221(a)
Code Sec. 6255(a), as added by '97 Act § 1222(a)
Code Sec. 6255(g), as added by '97 Act § 1222(a)
Generally effective: Partnership tax years ending after Dec. 30, '97
Committee Reports, see ¶ 5210

Under pre-'97 Act law, all partnerships that are required to file a partnership return and are not covered by a small partnership exception are subject to consistency rules and unified audit rules. (FTC 2d/FIN ¶ T-2100 *et seq.*; USTR ¶ 21,214 *et seq.*; TaxDesk ¶ 82,501 *et seq.*)

New Law. Special consistency and audit rules apply to electing large partnerships and partners in such partnerships. (Code Sec. 6240(a) as added by '97 Act §1222(a)) The special rules for electing large partnerships include:

(1) special consistency rules (see ¶ 1403),

(2) special procedures for adjusting electing large partnership items (see ¶ 1404), and

(3) special rules for taking adjustments into account (see ¶ 1405).

For purposes of these special rules for electing large partnerships, the term "electing large partnership" has the meaning given to the term by Code Sec. 775. (Code Sec. 6255(a)(1) as added by '97 Act §1222(a)) An "electing large partnership" is any partnership with at least 100 partners in the preceding tax year if the partnership elects the application of the part of the Internal Revenue Code including the simplified reporting (or flow-through) rules for electing large partnerships as discussed at ¶ 1401. Thus, the '97 Act defines electing large partnership the same way for audit and reporting purposes. (Com Rept, see ¶ 5210)

> *observation:* The simplified reporting or flow-through rules discussed at ¶ 1401 allow electing large partnerships to flow through items to partners under a simplified system. Since Code Sec. 775 defines an electing large partnership as a partnership that meets the 100-partner numerical requirement and elects the simplified reporting rules, an electing large partnership must elect the simplified reporting rules at ¶ 1401 in order for the simplified large partnership audit procedures to apply.

The electing large partnership audit procedures are intended to simplify the audit process, which is more inefficient and cumbersome for large partnerships than it is for other large entities. (Com Rept, see ¶ 5210)

The partnership consistency rules and unified audit procedures do not apply to any electing large partnership other than in its capacity as a partner in another partnership which is not an electing large partnership. (Code Sec. 6240(b)(1))

If an electing large partnership is a partner in another partnership which is not an electing large partnership, the unified partnership audit procedures will apply to items of the electing large partnership which are partnership items as to the other partnership. (Code Sec. 6240(b)(2)(A)) However, any adjustment under these provisions is taken into account under the electing large partnership audit procedures described at ¶ 1405. (Code Sec. 6240(b)(2)(B)) The term "partnership item" has the same meaning as under the unified audit provisions. (Code Sec. 6255(a)(2))

> *observation:* Thus, under the provisions for electing large partnerships, a partnership item is an item that is more appropriately determined at the partnership level than at the partner level.

FTC 2d References are to Federal Tax Coordinator 2d
FIN References are to RIA's Analysis of Federal Taxes: Income
USTR References are to United States Tax Reporter: Income, Estate & Gift, and Excise
PCA References are to Pension Coordinator and Pension & Benefits Expert/Advisor
PE References are to Pension and Profit Sharing 2nd
EP References are to Estate Planning & Taxation Coordinator and Estate Planning Advisor

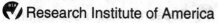

Regulations. IRS is authorized to prescribe regulations necessary to carry out the electing large partnership rules, including regulations (a) to prevent abuse through manipulation of the electing large partnership rules (Code Sec. 6255(g)(1)), and (b) providing that the elective rules will not apply to any case described in Code Sec. 6231(c)(1) or in related regs (i.e., special enforcement areas) where the application of the elective rules to such a case would interfere with the effective and efficient enforcement of the Code. (Code Sec. 6255(g)(2)) In any case to which the electing partnership rules do not apply due to the rule at (b) above, rules similar to the rules of Code Sec. 6229(f) (assessment limits where partnership items become non-partnership items) and to the rules of Code Sec. 6255(f) (suspension of limitations periods, see ¶ 1404) will apply. (Code Sec. 6255(g))

For special enforcement areas that might be covered by the regs, see ¶ 1405.

☐ **Effective:** Partnership taxable years ending after Dec. 30, '97. ('97 Act §1226)

> *observation:* The above statutory effective date is probably a mistake by Congress, based on the following:
>
> . . . . The '97 Act Committee Reports state that the effective date of the above rule is tax years beginning after Dec. 31, '97. (This is a significant difference from the above statutory date, since the Committee Report date does not encompass '97 calendar-year partnerships while the statutory date does.)
>
> . . . The provisions under which a partnership can become an electing large partnership are effective for tax years beginning after Dec. 31, '97, see ¶ 1401.

¶ 1403. Consistency rules for electing large partnerships

Code Sec. 6241, as added by '97 Act § 1222(a)
Generally effective: Partnership tax years ending after Dec. 30, '97
Committee Reports, see ¶ 5210

Under pre-'97 Act law, all partnerships that are required to file a partnership return and are not covered by a small partnership exception are subject to consistency rules and unified audit rules. Under the consistency rules, a partner must report all partnership items consistently with the partnership return or must notify IRS of any inconsistency. If a partner fails to report any partnership item consistently with the partnership return, IRS may make a computational adjustment and immediately assess any additional tax that results. (FTC 2d/FIN ¶ B-1800 *et seq.*; USTR ¶ 62,214.01; TaxDesk ¶ 58,410)

New Law. The following rules apply to electing large partnerships described at ¶ 1402.

A partner in any electing large partnership must, on the partner's return, treat each partnership item attributable to the partnership in a manner which is consistent with the treatment of that partnership item on the partnership return. (Code Sec. 6241(a) as added by '97 Act §1222(a)) This means that a partner is not permitted to report any partnership items inconsistently with the partnership return, even if the partner notifies IRS of the inconsistency. (Com Rept, see ¶ 5210)

> ✔️ *observation:* Thus, the electing large partnership rules differ from the partnership rules, which allow a partner to report partnership items inconsistently with the partnership return if he notifies IRS of any inconsistency.

Any underpayment of tax by a partner due to failure to comply with this consistency requirement is assessed and collected in the same manner as if the underpayment were on account of a mathematical or clerical error on the partner's return. The partnership may not request an abatement of the assessment (as in the deficiency rules for mathematical or clerical errors) for any such assessment of an underpayment. (Code Sec. 6241(b))

Except as provided below (relating to changes in distributive share taken by partners), the above consistency rules apply without regard to any adjustment to the partnership item under the rules at ¶ 1404. (Code Sec. 6241(c)(1)) To the extent that any adjustment under the rules at ¶ 1404 involves a change in the partner's distributive share, under Code Sec. 704, of the amount of any partnership item shown on the partnership return, the adjustment is taken into account in determining the partner's items for tax purposes for the partner's tax year for which the item was required to be taken into account. (Code Sec. 6241(c)(2)(A)) Non-partnership audit procedures will not apply to the assessment or collection of any underpayment of tax attributable to any distributive share adjustment. (Code Sec. 6241(c)(2)(B)(i)) However, notwithstanding any other law, nothing in the non-partnership audit procedures (or in any proceeding under them) will preclude the assessment or collection of any underpayment of tax (or the allowance of any credit or refund of any overpayment of tax) attributable to any distributive share adjustment and the assessment or collection or allowance (or any notice of it) will not preclude any notice, proceeding, or determination under the non-partnership audit procedures. (Code Sec. 6241(c)(2)(B)(ii))

The period for assessing any underpayment of tax, (Code Sec. 6241(c)(2)(C)(i)) or filing a claim for credit or refund of any overpayment of tax, (Code Sec. 6241(c)(2)(C)(ii)) attributable to a distributive share adjustment will not expire before the close of the period prescribed by the electing large partnership audit procedures (see ¶ 1404) for making adjustments with respect to the partnership tax year involved. (Code Sec. 6241(c)(2)(C)) If the partner affected by the distributive share rules is also a partnership or an S corporation, these rules will also apply to persons holding interests in that partnership or S corporation; except that, if the partner is an electing large partnership, the adjustment under the rules will be taken into account in the manner provided under the electing large partnership rules as described at ¶ 1405. (Code Sec. 6241(c)(2)(D))

☐ **Effective:** Partnership taxable years ending after Dec. 30, '97. ('97 Act §1226)

FTC 2d References are to Federal Tax Coordinator 2d
FIN References are to RIA's Analysis of Federal Taxes: Income
USTR References are to United States Tax Reporter: Income, Estate & Gift, and Excise
PCA References are to Pension Coordinator and Pension & Benefits Expert/Advisor
PE References are to Pension and Profit Sharing 2nd
EP References are to Estate Planning & Taxation Coordinator and Estate Planning Advisor

✪ *observation:* The above statutory effective date is probably a mistake by Congress, based on the following:

. . . . The '97 Act Committee Reports state that the effective date of the above rule is tax years beginning after Dec. 31, '97. (This is a significant difference from the above statutory date, since the Committee Report date does not encompass '97 calendar-year partnerships while the statutory date does.)

. . . The provisions under which a partnership can become an electing large partnership are effective for tax years beginning after Dec. 31, '97, see ¶ 1401.

¶ 1404. Partnership-level adjustments under the electing large partnership audit procedures

Code Sec. 6245, as added by '97 Act § 1222(a)
Code Sec. 6246, as added by '97 Act § 1222(a)
Code Sec. 6247, as added by '97 Act § 1222(a)
Code Sec. 6248, as added by '97 Act § 1222(a)
Code Sec. 6251, as added by '97 Act § 1222(a)
Code Sec. 6252, as added by '97 Act § 1222(a)
Code Sec. 6255(b), as added by '97 Act § 1222(a)
Code Sec. 6255(c), as added by '97 Act § 1222(a)
Code Sec. 6255(e), as added by '97 Act § 1222(a)
Code Sec. 6255(f), as added by '97 Act § 1222(a)
Code Sec. 7459(c), as amended by '97 Act § 1222(b)(2)
Code Sec. 7482(b)(1)(E), as amended by '97 Act § 1222(b)(3)
Code Sec. 7485(b), as amended by '97 Act § 1222(b)(4)
Generally effective: Partnership tax years ending after Dec. 30, '97
Committee Reports, see ¶ 5210

Under the unified partnership audit rules, IRS may challenge the reporting position of a partnership by conducting a single administrative proceeding to resolve the issue with respect to all partners. IRS must give notice of the beginning of partnership-level administrative proceedings to all partners except for partners in partnerships with more than 100 partners whose profits interest is less than 1%. IRS must notify the same partners of any resulting partnership-level adjustments (adjustments to partnership items (¶ 1406) made in a proceeding relating to the partnership rather than the individual partner). All partners have the right to participate in the audit. (FTC 2d/FIN ¶ T-2101, ¶ T-2156, ¶ T-2160, ¶ T-2172, ¶ T-2215; USTR ¶ 62,214, ¶ 62,214.02, ¶ 62,214.03; TaxDesk ¶ 82,508, ¶ 82,519)

Assessment and collection of deficiencies determined by the Tax Court in a partnership proceeding (see ¶ 1406) may be stayed if, on or before the time the notice of appeal of that decision is filed, a bond is filed with the Tax Court. (FTC 2d/FIN ¶ T-2211, ¶ T-2242; USTR ¶ 74,824.10; TaxDesk ¶ 82,522, ¶ 82,528)

New Law. Certain large partnerships which elect the status of "electing large partnerships" (defined at ¶ 1402) are subject to special consistency and audit procedures. The electing large partnership audit procedures are intended to allow a less complicated audit process than the process under the unified partnership audit rules, see ¶ 1402. The audit procedures for electing large partnerships include special procedures described below for adjusting partnership items.

Deficiency procedures. Under the electing large partnership audit procedures, IRS is authorized and directed to make adjustments at the partnership level in any partnership item to the extent necessary to have the item treated in the manner required. (Code Sec. 6245(a) as added by '97 Act §1222(a))

> *observation:* The electing large partnership audit procedures generally parallel the non-partnership audit procedures.

If IRS determines that a partnership adjustment is required, IRS is authorized to send a notice of the adjustment to the partnership by certified mail or registered mail. The notice will be sufficient if mailed to the partnership at its last known address even if the partnership has terminated its existence. (Code Sec. 6245(b)(1))

Under the electing large partnership procedures, unlike the unified partnership audit procedures, partners cannot participate individually in settlement conferences or request a refund. In addition, IRS is not required by the electing large partnership audit procedures to give notice to individual partners of the commencement of an administrative proceeding or of a final adjustment. (Com Rept, see ¶ 5210)

If IRS mails a notice of a partnership adjustment to any partnership for any partnership tax year and the partnership files a petition under Code Sec. 6247 for judicial review with respect to the notice, in the absence of a showing of fraud, malfeasance, or misrepresentation of a material fact, IRS may not mail another such notice to that partnership for that taxable year. (Code Sec. 6245(b)(2))

If notice of a partnership adjustment with respect to any taxable year is mailed to the partnership, the running of the three-year limitations period on adjustments (see "Limitations period" below) is suspended for the period during which a Code Sec. 6247 judicial review action may be brought (and, if a petition is filed under Code Sec. 6247 with respect to the notice, until the decision of the court becomes final), and (Code Sec. 6248(d)(1)) for one year after that. (Code Sec. 6248(d)(2))

For purposes of the electing large partnership audit procedures, the principles of Code Sec. 7481(a) (relating to finality of Tax Court decisions) apply in determining the date on which a decision of a district court or the Claims Court becomes final. (Code Sec. 6255(e))

> *observation:* Under Code Sec. 7481(a), a Tax Court decision becomes final when the time allowed for filing a notice of appeal has expired, if no petition for review is filed.

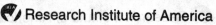

IRS may, with the consent of the partnership, rescind any notice of a partnership adjustment mailed to the partnership. Any notice rescinded is not treated as a notice of a partnership adjustment, for purposes of the partnership-level adjustment rules, and the taxpayer will have no right to bring a proceeding for judicial review with respect to the notice. However, this rule will not affect any suspension of the running of any period of limitations during any period during which the rescinded notice was outstanding. (Code Sec. 6245(b)(3))

Restrictions on partnership adjustments. Except as otherwise provided in Chapter 63 (relating to assessment), no adjustment to any partnership item may be made, and no levy or proceeding in any court for the collection of any amount resulting from the adjustment may be made, begun or prosecuted, before:

. . . the close of the 90th day after the day on which a notice of a partnership adjustment was mailed to the partnership (Code Sec. 6246(a)(1) as added by '97 Act §1222(a)), or

. . . if a Code Sec. 6247 petition for judicial review is filed with respect to the notice, the day the decision of the court has become final. (Code Sec. 6246(a)(2))

Any action by IRS which violates these adjustment limitations may be enjoined in the proper court, including the Tax Court, without regard to the prohibition on suits to restrain assessment and collection in Code Sec. 7421(a). The Tax Court has no jurisdiction to enjoin any action unless a timely petition has been filed under Code Sec. 6247 and then only as to adjustments that are the subject of the petition. (Code Sec. 6246(b))

However, if a partnership is notified that, on account of a mathematical or clerical error appearing on the partnership return, an adjustment to a partnership item is required, rules similar to the deficiency rules on mathematical or clerical errors in Code Sec. 6213(b)(1) and Code Sec. 6213(b)(2) will apply to the adjustment. (Code Sec. 6246(c)(1)(A)) If an electing large partnership is a partner in another electing large partnership, any adjustment on account of the electing partnership's failure to comply with the consistency requirement with respect to its interest in the other partnership will be treated as an adjustment under the mathematical or clerical error rule, except that the rules allowing abatements of such errors, will not apply to the adjustment. (Code Sec. 6246(c)(1)(B))

> *observation:* Thus, adjustments based on mathematical or clerical errors can be abated under the electing large partnership audit procedures under rules similar to Code Sec. 6213(b)(2), which allows a taxpayer to get an abatement of an initial assessment and subjects any reassessment to the non-partnership audit procedures. However, no such abatement rule applies to adjustments based on failure to meet the consistency requirement under the above rule for electing large partnerships which are partners in other electing large partnerships or to the assessment of underpayments due to failure to meet the consistency requirement (see ¶ 1403). These parallel provisions reflect the emphasis on consistent reporting in the electing large partnership procedures.

A partnership may at any time (whether or not a notice of partnership adjustment has been issued) waive the Code Sec. 6246(a) restrictions, described above, on the making of any partnership adjustment by a signed notice in writing filed with IRS. (Code Sec. 6246(c)(2))

For purposes of the Code Sec. 6246 restrictions on partnership adjustments, a rule similar to Code Sec. 6213(f)(2) will apply. (Code Sec. 6255(f)(1) as added by '97 Act §1222(a))

> ✪ *observation:* Code Sec. 6213(f)(2) provides that, for purposes of provisions in Code Sec. 6213 that are analogous to Code Sec. 6246(a) and Code Sec. 6246(b) explained above, the filing of a proof of claim or request for payment (or the taking of any other action) under Title 11 bankruptcy provisions is not treated as an action prohibited by the Code Sec. 6213 rule analogous to Code Sec. 6246(a). Thus, the above provision appears to mean that such an action under Title 11 is not prohibited by Code Sec. 6246(a).

If the partnership doesn't begin a proceeding for judicial review with respect to any notice of a partnership adjustment during the 90-day period after the notice, the amount for which the partnership is liable under the rules at ¶ 1405 (and any increase in any partner's liability for Chapter 1 income tax because of any Code Sec. 6242(a) adjustment under these procedures) cannot exceed the amount determined in accordance with the notice. (Code Sec. 6246(d))

> ✪ *observation:* Where IRS asserts a deficiency and there is reason to fear that a significant additional deficiency could be asserted, it may be better to contest the deficiency by suing for a refund rather than seeking to avoid payment. Following the refund route limits IRS to the assertion of the further deficiency as an offset to the refund claim, and prevents it from increasing its recovery to reflect the further deficiency.

Judicial review of partnership adjustments. Within 90 days after the date on which a notice of a partnership adjustment is mailed to the partnership with respect to any partnership taxable year, the partnership may file a petition for a readjustment of the partnership items for the taxable year with:

. . . the Tax Court (Code Sec. 6247(a)(1) as added by '97 Act §1222(a)),

. . . the district court for the district in which the partnership's principal place of business is located (Code Sec. 6247(a)(2)), or

. . . the Claims Court. (Code Sec. 6247(a)(3))

For purposes of this judicial review provision, a principal place of business located outside the U.S. is treated as located in Washington, D.C. (Code Sec. 6255(c) as added by '97 Act §1222(a))

In a Title 11 bankruptcy case, the running of the 90-day period above is suspended for the period during which the partnership is prohibited by reason of the case from filing a petition for a readjustment and for 60 days after that. (Code Sec. 6255(f)(2) as added by '97 Act §1222(a))

Only the partnership, and not partners individually, can petition for a readjustment of partnership items. (Com Rept, see ¶ 5210)

However, a readjustment petition under the above rules may be filed in a district court or the Claims Court only if the partnership filing the petition makes a deposit with IRS, on or before the date the petition is filed. The amount of the required partnership deposit is the amount of penalties or interest for which the partnership would be liable under the rules at ¶ 1405 (as of the date of the filing of the petition) if the partnership items were adjusted as provided by the notice of partnership adjustment. The court may by order provide that these jurisdictional requirements are satisfied where there has been a good faith attempt to satisfy the requirement and any shortfall of the amount required to be deposited is timely corrected. (Code Sec. 6247(b)(1)) Any amount deposited under this rule, while deposited, will not be treated as a payment of tax for purposes of the Internal Revenue Code (except for the purpose of determining interest). (Code Sec. 6247(b)(2))

A court with which a petition is filed under the above rules has jurisdiction to determine all partnership items of the partnership for the partnership taxable year to which the notice of partnership adjustment relates and the proper allocation of the items among the partners (and the applicability of any penalty, addition to tax, or additional amount for which the partnership may be liable under the rules at ¶ 1405). (Code Sec. 6247(c)) Thus, the court's jurisdiction is not limited to the items adjusted in the notice. (Com Rept, see ¶ 5210)

Any determination by a court under these rules will have the force and effect of a decision of the Tax Court or a final judgment or decree of the district court or the Claims Court, as the case may be, and will be reviewable as such a decision. The date of the determination will be the date of the court's order entering the decision. (Code Sec. 6247(d)) If an action brought under these rules is dismissed other than by reason of a rescission of the notice of partnership adjustment, the decision of the court dismissing the action will be considered as its decision that the notice of partnership adjustment is correct, and an appropriate order will be entered in the records of the court. (Code Sec. 6247(e))

Limitations period. Except as otherwise provided under the rules below, no adjustment under the adjustment rules above to any partnership item for any partnership taxable year may be made after the date which is three years after the later of:

(1) the date on which the partnership return for the taxable year was filed (Code Sec. 6248(a)(1) as added by '97 Act §1222(a)), or

(2) the last day for filing the return for the year (without regard to extensions). (Code Sec. 6248(a)(2))

This limitation period (including an extension period) may be extended by an agreement entered into by IRS and the partnership before the expiration of the period. (Code Sec. 6248(b))

In the case of a false or fraudulent partnership return with intent to evade tax, (Code Sec. 6248(c)(1)) or, in the case of a failure by a partnership to file a return for any tax year, (Code Sec. 6248(c)(3)) the adjustment may be made at any time. (Code Sec. 6248(c)) If any partnership omits from gross income an amount properly includible which is in excess of 25% of the amount of gross income stated in its return, the limitations period is six years instead of three years. (Code Sec. 6248(c)(2)) For purposes of the limitations period rules, a return executed by IRS under Code Sec. 6020(b) (relating to IRS-prepared returns) on behalf of the partnership is not treated as a return. (Code Sec. 6248(c)(4))

In a Title 11 bankruptcy case, the running of any limitations period provided in the electing large partnership audit procedures on making a partnership adjustment (or the period provided by Code Sec. 6501 or Code Sec. 6502 on the assessment or collection of any amount required to be paid under the procedures for taking adjustments into account) is suspended during the period during which IRS is prohibited by reason of the case from making the adjustment (or assessment or collection) until 60 days after the end of the period for adjustment or assessment (Code Sec. 6255(f)(1)(A)) and until six months after the end of the period for collection. (Code Sec. 6255(f)(1)(B))

Partnership representative. Each electing large partnership will designate (in the manner prescribed by IRS) a partner (or other person) who will have the sole authority to act on behalf of such partnership under the electing large partnership audit procedures. In any case in which a designation is not in effect, IRS may select any partner as the partner with such authority. (Code Sec. 6255(b)(1)) After IRS's designation, an electing large partnership may designate a replacement for the IRS-designated partner. (Com Rept, see ¶ 5210)

An electing large partnership and all partners of such partnership are bound by actions taken under the electing large partnership audit procedures by the partnership (Code Sec. 6255(b)(2)(A)) and by any decision in a proceeding brought under the electing large partnership audit procedures. (Code Sec. 6255(b)(2)(B))

> *observation:* Investors in electing large partnerships should consider limiting the discretion of the partnership representative by provisions in the partnership agreement, such as provisions requiring a vote by the partners before agreement to any settlement. Otherwise, there is a danger that the partnership representative might make agreements with IRS with a view to protecting his own interests rather than those of the partners as a whole.

FTC 2d References are to Federal Tax Coordinator 2d
FIN References are to RIA's Analysis of Federal Taxes: Income
USTR References are to United States Tax Reporter: Income, Estate & Gift, and Excise
PCA References are to Pension Coordinator and Pension & Benefits Expert/Advisor
PE References are to Pension and Profit Sharing 2nd
EP References are to Estate Planning & Taxation Coordinator and Estate Planning Advisor

Administrative adjustment requests. A partnership may file a request for an administrative adjustment of partnership items for any partnership taxable year at any time which is within three years after the later of (a) the date on which the partnership return for the year is filed (Code Sec. 6251(a)(1)(A) as added by '97 Act §1222(a)), or (b) the last day for filing the partnership return for the year (determined without extensions). (Code Sec. 6251(a)(1)(B))

observation: These rules generally parallel the non-partnership refund procedures.

This request must be filed before the mailing to the partnership of a notice of a partnership adjustment with respect to the tax year. (Code Sec. 6251(a)(2))

If a partnership files an administrative adjustment request under the above rules, IRS may allow any part of the requested adjustments. (Code Sec. 6251(b)) If the limitations period for deficiencies is extended under agreement between the partnership and IRS, the three-year limit will not expire before the date six months after the expiration of the extension. (Code Sec. 6251(c))

Judicial review where administrative adjustment request not allowed. If any part of an administrative adjustment request filed under the above rules is not allowed by IRS, the partnership may file a petition for an adjustment with respect to the partnership items to which the part of the request relates with

... the Tax Court (Code Sec. 6252(a)(1) as added by '97 Act §1222(a)),

... the district court for the district in which the principal place of business of the partnership is located (Code Sec. 6252(a)(2)), or

... the Claims Court. (Code Sec. 6252(a)(3))

The partnership may file a petition for judicial review with respect to partnership items for a partnership tax year only:

(1) after the expiration of six months from the date of filing of the request for an administrative adjustment (Code Sec. 6252(b)(1)), and

(2) before the date which is two years after the date of the request. (Code Sec. 6252(b)(2)) The two-year period will be extended for the period as may be agreed on in writing by the partnership and IRS. (Code Sec. 6252(b))

In a Title 11 bankruptcy case, the running of the period specified in Code Sec. 6252(b) above is suspended for the period during which the partnership is prohibited by reason of the case from filing a petition for judicial review and for 60 days after that. (Code Sec. 6255(f)(2))

observation: The suspension in bankruptcy cases described above may have been intended to apply only to the period at (2) above, but, by its terms, the suspension provision applies to the periods at both (1) and (2) above.

No petition may be filed under these rules after IRS mails to the partnership a notice of a partnership adjustment for the partnership tax year to which the request for an administrative adjustment relates. (Code Sec. 6252(c)(1)) If IRS mails to the partnership a notice of a partnership adjustment for the partnership taxable year to which the request for administrative adjustment relates after the filing of a petition, but before the hearing of the petition, the petition will be treated as an action for judicial review brought with respect to a notice of partnership adjustment, except that no deposit is required in order to obtain review by a district court or Claims Court. (Code Sec. 6252(c)(2)) A notice of a partnership adjustment for the partnership tax year will be taken into account under these rules only if the notice is mailed by IRS before the expiration of the period for making adjustments to partnership items for the tax year. (Code Sec. 6252(c)(3))

Except where a notice of partnership adjustment is mailed after the filing of a petition for judicial review but before the hearing, a court with which a petition is filed under these rules has jurisdiction to determine only those partnership items to which the part of the Code Sec. 6251 request for an administrative adjustment not allowed by IRS relates and those items for which IRS asserts adjustments as offsets to the adjustments requested by the partnership. (Code Sec. 6252(d)) Any determination by a court under these rules will have the force and effect of a decision of the Tax Court or a final judgment or decree of the district court or the Claims Court, as the case may be, and will be reviewable as such. The date of any the determination will be treated as being the date of the court's order entering the decision. (Code Sec. 6252(e))

For IRS's authority to prescribe regulations necessary to carry out the electing large partnership audit rules, including regulations to prevent abuses by manipulation of the rules, see ¶ 1402.

Conforming amendments relating to judicial review by Tax Court. The following conforming amendments relate to the judicial review provisions in Code Sec. 6247, discussed above under "Judicial review of partnership adjustments," and Code Sec. 6252, discussed above under "Judicial review where administrative adjustment request not allowed":

A decision of the Tax Court under the above judicial review procedures, other than a decision dismissing a proceeding for lack of jurisdiction, is treated as rendered on the date of the court's order entering the decision. Where a proceeding is dismissed for lack of jurisdiction, the decision is treated as rendered on the date an order to that effect is entered in the records of the Tax Court. (Code Sec. 7459(c) as amended by '97 Act §1222(b)(2))

In the case of a petition under the above judicial review procedures, a Tax Court decision is reviewed by the United States court of appeals for the circuit in which the partnership's principal place of business is located, unless IRS and the taxpayer agree on a different court in a written stipulation. (Code Sec. 7482(b)(1)E) as amended by '97 Act §1222(b)(3))

The rules providing for stay, on the filing of a bond with the Tax Court, of assessment and collection of deficiencies determined in a proceeding under the unified partnership audit procedures also apply in Tax Court cases under the above judicial review procedures. (Code Sec. 7485(b) as amended by '97 Act §1222(b)(4))

☐ **Effective:** Partnership taxable years ending after Dec. 30, '97. ('97 Act §1226)

⟳ observation: The above statutory effective date is probably a mistake by Congress, based on the following:

. . . . The '97 Act Committee Reports state that the effective date of the above rule is tax years beginning after Dec. 31, '97. (This is a significant difference from the above statutory date, since the Committee Report date does not encompass '97 calendar-year partnerships while the statutory date does.)

. . . The provisions under which a partnership can become an electing large partnership are effective for tax years beginning after Dec. 31, '97, see ¶ 1401.

¶ 1405. Procedures for taking partnership adjustments into account under the electing large partnership audit procedures

Code Sec. 6242, as added by '97 Act § 1222(a)
Code Sec. 6255(d), as added by '97 Act § 1222(a)
Generally effective: Partnership tax years ending after Dec. 30, '97
Committee Reports, see ¶ 5210

Under pre-'97 Act law, all partnerships that are required to file a partnership return and are not covered by a small partnership exception are subject to consistency rules and unified audit procedures. However, any resulting deficiency is assessed against each of the taxpayers who were partners in the year in which the understatement of tax liability arose. (FTC 2d/FIN ¶ T-2100 *et seq.*; USTR ¶ 21,214 *et seq.*; TaxDesk ¶ 82,501 *et seq.*)

New Law. The following rules apply to electing large partnerships described at ¶ 1402.

Adjustments taken in year of adjustment. If any partnership adjustment (defined below) with respect to any partnership item takes effect as described below during any partnership taxable year and an election not to take an adjustment into account under the rule described below does not apply to that adjustment, the adjustment is taken into account in determining the amount of the item *for the partnership taxable year in which the adjustment takes effect.* For any person who is (directly or indirectly) a partner in the partnership during the partnership taxable year, the adjustment is treated as an item actually arising during the tax year. (Code Sec. 6242(a)(1) as added by '97 Act §1222(a))

This means that the *current-year* partners' share of current-year partnership items of income, gains, losses, deductions, or credits will be adjusted to reflect partnership adjustments that take effect in that year. The adjustments *generally will not affect prior-year returns* of any partners (except in the case of changes to any partner's distributive shares). (Com Rept, see ¶ 5210)

For purposes of these rules the term "partnership adjustment" means any adjustment in the amount of any partnership item of an electing large partnership. (Code Sec. 6242(d)(1))

A partnership adjustment takes effect:

. . . in the case of an adjustment under the decision of a court in a proceeding brought under the adjustment rules at ¶ 1404, when the decision becomes final (Code Sec. 6242(d)(2)(A)),

. . . in the case of an adjustment under any administrative adjustment request, when the adjustment is allowed by IRS (Code Sec. 6242(d)(2)(B)), or

. . . in any other case, when the adjustment is made. (Code Sec. 6242(d)(2)(C))

For when a decision becomes final, see "Finality of decisions" in ¶ 1404.

Amounts taken into account under the above rules for any partnership taxable year will continue to be treated as adjustments for the adjusted year for purposes of determining whether these amounts may be readjusted under the rules at ¶ 1404. (Code Sec. 6242(a)(4))

Partnership liability for adjustments. Under the following circumstances, a partnership is required to make payments as a result of an adjustment under the electing large partnership rules:

. . . where a partnership elects to not take an adjustment into account under the rules described above. (Code Sec. 6242(a)(2)(A) as added by '97 Act §1222(a)) A partnership may make this election only if it meets requirements set forth in regulations designed to ensure payment (for example, in the case of a foreign partnership). (Com Rept, see ¶ 5210)

. . . where a partnership does not make such an election but in filing its return for any partnership taxable year fails to take fully into account any partnership adjustment as required under the rules described above. (Code Sec. 6242(a)(2)(B))

. . . where any partnership adjustment involves a reduction in a credit which exceeds the amount of such credit determined for the partnership taxable year in which the adjustment takes effect. (Code Sec. 6242(a)(2)(C))

The amount the partnership must pay is the amount determined under the imputed underpayment rules below plus the credit adjustment. (Code Sec. 6242(a)(2))

The "imputed underpayment" with respect to any partnership adjustment is the underpayment (if any) which would result:

FTC 2d References are to Federal Tax Coordinator 2d
FIN References are to RIA's Analysis of Federal Taxes: Income
USTR References are to United States Tax Reporter: Income, Estate & Gift, and Excise
PCA References are to Pension Coordinator and Pension & Benefits Expert/Advisor
PE References are to Pension and Profit Sharing 2nd
EP References are to Estate Planning & Taxation Coordinator and Estate Planning Advisor

. . . by netting all adjustments to items of income, gain, loss, or deduction and by treating any net increase in income as an underpayment equal to the amount of the net increase multiplied by the highest rate of tax in effect under Code Sec. 1 or Code Sec. 11 for the adjusted year (Code Sec. 6242(b)(4)(A)), and

. . . by taking adjustments to credits into account as increases or decreases (whichever is appropriate) in the amount of tax. (Code Sec. 6242(b)(4)(B))

For purposes of determining the imputed underpayment, any net decrease in a loss is treated as an increase in income. Similarly, a net increase in a loss is treated as a decrease in income. (Code Sec. 6242(b)(4))

No deduction is allowed for any payment required to be made by an electing large partnership under the above rules. (Code Sec. 6242(e)) This includes taxes, interest, and penalties. (Com Rept, see ¶ 5210)

A partner may not file a claim for credit or refund of his allocable share of the payment. (Com Rept, see ¶ 5210)

Interest and penalties. If a partnership adjustment takes effect during any partnership taxable year and the adjustment results in an imputed underpayment for the adjusted year, the partnership must pay interest (Code Sec. 6242(b)(1)(A)) and penalties, additions to tax, or additional amounts as provided below. (Code Sec. 6242(b)(1)(B)) This rule applies regardless of whether the partnership makes the payments for the adjustments. (Com Rept, see ¶ 5210)

Interest is computed under this rule with respect to any partnership adjustment by applying the rules for underpayments to the "imputed underpayment" with respect to the adjustment, (Code Sec. 6242(b)(2)(A)) for the period beginning on the day after the return due date for the adjusted year and ending on the return due date for the partnership tax year in which the adjustment takes effect (or, if earlier, in the case of an adjustment for which the partnership makes the payments, the date on which the payment required is made). (Code Sec. 6242(b)(2)(B))

The term "return due date" means, with respect to any tax year, the date prescribed for filing the partnership return for the tax year (determined without extensions). (Code Sec. 6242(d)(4)) The term "adjusted year" means the partnership taxable year to which the item being adjusted relates. (Code Sec. 6242(d)(3))

Proper adjustments in the amount determined under this rule must be made for adjustments required for partnership taxable years after the adjusted year and before the year in which the partnership adjustment takes effect by reason of the partnership adjustment. (Code Sec. 6242(b)(2))

A partnership is liable for any penalty, addition to tax, or additional amount for which it would have been liable if the partnership had been an individual subject to income tax for the adjusted year and the imputed underpayment were an actual underpayment (or understatement) for that year. (Code Sec. 6242(b)(3)) Thus, penalties (such as the accuracy and fraud penalties) are determined on a year-by-year basis (without offsets) based on an imputed underpayment. All accuracy penalty criteria and waiver criteria (such as reasonable cause, substantial authority, etc.) are determined as if the partnership were a taxable individual. Accuracy and fraud penalties are assessed and accrue interest in the same manner as if asserted against a taxable individual. (Com Rept, see ¶ 5210)

Offsetting adjustments. If a partnership adjustment requires another adjustment in a taxable year after the adjusted year and before the partnership taxable year in which the partnership adjustment takes effect, the other adjustment is taken into account for the partnership taxable year in which the partnership adjustment takes effect. (Code Sec. 6242(a)(3)) Thus, regardless of whether a partnership adjustment flows through to the partners, an adjustment must be offset if it requires another adjustment in a year after the adjusted year and before the year the offsetted adjustment takes effect. (Com Rept, see ¶ 5210)

> *Illustration:* A partnership expensed a $1,000 item in Year 1, and it is determined in Year 4 that the item should have been capitalized and amortized ratably over 10 years. The adjustment in Year 4 is $700, apart from any interest or penalty, because the $900 adjustment for the improper deduction is offset by $200 of adjustments for amortization deductions. Thus, the Year 4 partners are required to include an additional $700 in income for that year. The partnership may ratably amortize the remaining $700 of expenses in Years 4-10. (Com Rept, see ¶ 5210)

In addition, the partnership, rather than the partners individually, generally is liable for any interest and penalties that result from a partnership adjustment. Interest is computed under rules described above for the period beginning on the return due date for the adjusted year and ending on the earlier of the return due date for the partnership taxable year in which the adjustment takes effect or the date the partnership pays the imputed underpayment. Thus, in the above Illustration, the partnership would be liable for four years' worth of interest (on a declining principal amount). (Com Rept, see ¶ 5210)

Changes in character of items. Under regulations, appropriate adjustments in the application of the above procedures will be made for purposes of taking into account partnership adjustments which involve a change in the character of any item of income, gain, loss, or deduction. (Code Sec. 6242(d)(5))

Termination of partnership. If a partnership ceases to exist before a partnership adjustment under the electing large partnership rules takes effect, the adjustment will be taken into account by the former partners of the partnership under IRS regulations. (Code Sec. 6255(d) as added by '97 Act §1222(a))

Regulations. IRS is authorized to prescribe regulations necessary to carry out the electing large partnership audit rules, including regulations to prevent abuses by manipulation of the rules, see ¶ 1402. The regulations might except some special enforcement areas from these rules. Special enforcement areas that might be the subject of

---

FTC 2d References are to Federal Tax Coordinator 2d
FIN References are to RIA's Analysis of Federal Taxes: Income
USTR References are to United States Tax Reporter: Income, Estate & Gift, and Excise
PCA References are to Pension Coordinator and Pension & Benefits Expert/Advisor
PE References are to Pension and Profit Sharing 2nd
EP References are to Estate Planning & Taxation Coordinator and Estate Planning Advisor

regulations could include partnership bankruptcy. (Com Rept, see ¶ 5210)

observation: The special enforcement areas enumerated in Code Sec. 6231(c)(1) are termination assessments, jeopardy assessments, criminal investigations, indirect methods of proof of income, foreign partnerships, and other areas covered by regs to be issued.

The regulations may include rules that address transfers of partnership interests, in anticipation of a partnership adjustment, to persons who are tax-favored (e.g., corporations with net operating losses, tax-exempt organizations, and foreign partners) or persons who are expected to be unable to pay tax (e.g., shell corporations). For example, if before the time a partnership adjustment takes effect, a taxable partner transfers a partnership interest to a nonresident alien to avoid the tax effect of the partnership adjustment, the rules may provide, among other things, that income related to the partnership adjustment is treated as effectively connected taxable income, that the partnership adjustment is treated as taking effect before the partnership interest was transferred, or that the former partner is treated as a current partner to whom the partnership adjustment is allocated. (Com Rept, see ¶ 5210)

Administrative provisions. Any payment required by Code Sec. 6242(a)(2) (relating to failure to take an adjustment into account and reductions in credits) or Code Sec. 6242(b)(1)(A) (relating to interest) must be assessed and collected in the same manner as if it were a tax imposed by the rules for employment taxes (Code Sec. 6242(c)(1)(A)), and must be paid on or before the return due date for the partnership taxable year in which the partnership adjustment takes effect. (Code Sec. 6242(c)(1)(B))

Amounts required to be paid by a partnership under Code Sec. 6242(a)(2) and interest on such amounts are treated as underpayments of tax subject to interest. (Code Sec. 6242(c)(2)) In the case of any failure by any partnership to pay these required amounts on the date prescribed, a penalty of 10% of the underpayment is imposed on the partnership. For purposes of this rule, the term "underpayment" means the excess of any payment required over the amount (if any) paid on or before the date prescribed for it. (Code Sec. 6242(c)(3)(A)) For purposes of the accuracy related and fraud penalties (Code Sec. 6662 through Code Sec. 6664), any payment required by Code Sec. 6242(a)(2) (relating to failure to take an adjustment into account and reductions in credits) is treated as an underpayment of tax. (Code Sec. 6242(c)(3)(B))

☐ **Effective:** Partnership taxable years ending after Dec. 30, '97. ('97 Act §1226)

observation: The above statutory effective date is probably a mistake by Congress, based on the following:

.... The '97 Act Committee Reports state that the effective date of the above rule is tax years beginning after Dec. 31, '97. (This is a significant difference from the above statutory date, since the Committee Report date does not encompass '97 calendar-year partnerships while the statutory date does.)

... The provisions under which a partnership can become an electing large partnership are effective for tax years beginning after Dec. 31, '97, see ¶ 1401.

Unified Partnership Audit Procedures

¶ 1406. Numerous changes made to unified partnership audit procedures

Under the "unified partnership audit procedures" (also referred to as TEFRA procedures) enacted by the '82 Tax Equity and Fiscal Responsibility Act (TEFRA), P.L. 97-248, 9/3/82, audit proceedings involving partnerships are separate from deficiency proceedings involving the partners in their individual capacities. Such partnership audit proceedings are referred to as "partnership proceedings" or "TEFRA proceedings."

The unified partnership audit procedures apply to all partnerships other than electing large partnerships (see ¶ 1401) and certain small partnerships. The excepted small partnerships must have ten or fewer partners, and the partners cannot include any entities in certain proscribed categories (such as nonresident aliens). Partnerships that are subject to these procedures are sometimes referred to as "TEFRA partnerships." (FTC 2d/FIN ¶ T-2103; USTR ¶ 62,214.10; TaxDesk ¶ 82,504)

Under the unified partnership audit procedures, the tax treatment of any "partnership item" (also referred to as "TEFRA item") is determined at the partnership level. A partnership item with respect to a partnership is any item required to be taken into account for the partnership's tax year for income tax purposes, to the extent IRS regs provide that the item is more appropriately determined at the partnership level than at the partner level. (FTC 2d/FIN ¶s T-2101, T-2110; USTR ¶s 62,214, 62,214.10; TaxDesk ¶ 82,507)

> **✐ observation:** Determination "at the partnership level" is not specifically defined in the tax law, but it refers to determinations that are made in proceedings relating to the partnership rather than to the individual partners.

A nonpartnership item is defined as an item that is (or is treated as) not a partnership item. Under some circumstances, some or all or a partnership's partnership items convert to nonpartnership items. Then their tax treatment is determined in a separate proceeding subject to the procedural rules applicable to taxpayers other than partnerships, except in the case of items which convert to nonpartnership items as a result of a settlement. (FTC 2d/FIN ¶ T-2244; USTR ¶ 62,214.10)

Under the unified partnership audit procedures, IRS may decide, after conducting an audit of a partnership, that adjustments to the partnership's return are necessary. If it does, it issues a final partnership administrative adjustment (FPAA). IRS must send notice of an FPAA resulting from a partnership proceeding to each partner eligible to receive notice under the unified partnership audit procedures. (FTC 2d/FIN ¶ T-2215; USTR ¶ 62,214.02; TaxDesk ¶ 82,518) The tax matters partner (TMP) must notify partners not required to be notified directly by IRS of the FPAA. (FTC 2d/FIN ¶ T-

FTC 2d References are to Federal Tax Coordinator 2d
FIN References are to RIA's Analysis of Federal Taxes: Income
USTR References are to United States Tax Reporter: Income, Estate & Gift, and Excise
PCA References are to Pension Coordinator and Pension & Benefits Expert/Advisor
PE References are to Pension and Profit Sharing 2nd
EP References are to Estate Planning & Taxation Coordinator and Estate Planning Advisor

2219; USTR ¶ 62,214.02; TaxDesk ¶ 82,513)

The TMP of any partnership is the general partner designated as the TMP by the other partners or, if no general partner is so designated, the general partner having the largest profits interest in the partnership at the close of the tax year involved. IRS may select a TMP if there is no general partner designated as TMP and it is impractical to apply the profits interest rule. (FTC 2d/FIN ¶ T-2121; USTR ¶ 62,214.10; TaxDesk ¶ 82,509) The TMP may extend the time limit on assessment for partnership items (FTC 2d/FIN ¶ T-4419; USTR ¶ 62,214.08; TaxDesk ¶ 82,538) and has the right to petition for judicial review of an FPAA. (FTC 2d/FIN ¶ T-2222; USTR ¶ 62,214.05; TaxDesk ¶ 82,523) Also, as indicated above, the TMP must notify partners not required to be notified directly by IRS of an FPAA.

"Computational adjustments" are changes in a partner's tax liability made to properly reflect the treatment of partnership items. Subject to exceptions, the usual (i.e., non-partnership) deficiency assessment procedures don't apply to computational adjustments (and thus, for example, a deficiency notice does not have to be issued to assess a computational adjustment). (FTC 2d/FIN ¶ T-2249; USTR ¶ 62,214.10; TaxDesk ¶ 82,531) Computational adjustments attributable to "affected items" which require partner level determinations are one of the exceptions to the above rule. (FTC 2d/FIN ¶ T-2251; USTR ¶ 62,214.09; TaxDesk ¶ 82,533) The term "affected item" means an item to the extent it is affected by a partnership item. (FTC 2d/FIN ¶ T-2254; USTR ¶ 62,214.10; TaxDesk ¶ 82,533)

A partner can file a request for administrative adjustment (RAA) of partnership items. The RAA is treated as either a substituted return (correcting errors) or as a claim for refund. (FTC 2d/FIN ¶ T-2201; USTR ¶ 62,214.06; TaxDesk ¶ 82,520)

New Law. The '97 Act includes a number of simplification provisions relating to unified partnership audit procedures. One such provision allows IRS to rely on the partnership return in determining if the unified partnership audit procedures should be followed, see ¶ 1407. Another expands the definition of small partnership so that a partnership may have C corporations as partners and may specially allocate items without jeopardizing its exemption from the unified partnership audit procedures, see ¶ 1408.

Other provisions extend the time for filing an RAA where the time limit on assessment is extended (see ¶ 1409) and where the RAA relates to bad debts or worthless securities, see ¶ 1410. These provisions relating to RAAs have the effect of making the special rules relating to unified partnership audit procedures more similar to the general procedural rules of the tax law. Other provisions of the new law which have this effect are provisions that:

... allow suspension of certain statutes of limitations relating to unified partnership audit procedures in untimely petition and bankruptcy situations, see ¶ 1411;

... provide a judicial forum for raising the innocent spouse defense regarding any tax or interest relating to an investment in a partnership subject to the unified partnership audit procedures, see ¶ 1412;

... suspend the running of interest where IRS delays making notice and demand with respect to certain computational adjustments, see ¶ 1413.

Other provisions of the new law:

... exclude some items in partial settlement cases from the one-year limit on assessment that otherwise applies to partnership items that convert to nonpartnership items, see ¶ 1414;

... require that penalties with respect to partnership items are determined at the partnership level, see ¶ 1415;

... simplify the resolution of tax cases by clarifying that: (a) an action to enjoin premature assessments of deficiencies from partnership items may be brought in the Tax Court; (b) a partner may participate in an action or file a petition solely to assert that the time limit for assessing tax from partnership items has expired as to that partner; and (c) the Tax Court has overpayment jurisdiction as to affected items, see ¶ 1416;

... modify the calculation of bond amounts in partnership appeal cases, see ¶ 1417.

... treat premature petitions by partners entitled to notice of an FPAA as timely, see ¶ 1418.

... provide a new set of deficiency procedures with respect to adjustments relating to partnership items on oversheltered returns. (The term "oversheltered return" means an income tax return which shows (a) no taxable income and (b) a net loss from partnership items), see ¶ 1419;

... provide that, for purposes of determining the amount of deficiency for purposes of applying the non-partnership deficiency rules, adjustments to partnership items can only be made as provided by the unified partnership audit procedures, see ¶ 1420.

¶ 1407. IRS can rely on partnership return in determining whether to use partnership audit procedures

Code Sec. 6231(g), as amended by '97 Act § 1232(a)
Generally effective: Partnership tax years ending after Aug. 5, '97
Committee Reports, see ¶ 5216

Contests involving tax treatment of partnership items (¶ 1406) are generally determined at the partnership level under the unified partnership audit provisions (¶ 1406). However, these procedures do not apply to electing large partnerships (see ¶ 1402) and certain small partnerships (see ¶ 1406), which are subject to regular deficiency procedures. The excepted small partnerships must have ten or fewer partners, and the partners must not include any entities in certain proscribed categories (such as nonresident aliens). Under pre-'97 Act law, if IRS made an erroneous determination as to whether to follow the unified audit procedures or the regular deficiency procedures, any assessment it made might have been jeopardized. (FTC 2d/FIN ¶ T-2103; USTR ¶ 62,214.10; TaxDesk ¶ 82,504)

FTC 2d References are to Federal Tax Coordinator 2d
FIN References are to RIA's Analysis of Federal Taxes: Income
USTR References are to United States Tax Reporter: Income, Estate & Gift, and Excise
PCA References are to Pension Coordinator and Pension & Benefits Expert/Advisor
PE References are to Pension and Profit Sharing 2nd
EP References are to Estate Planning & Taxation Coordinator and Estate Planning Advisor

New Law. If, based on the partnership's return for a tax year, IRS reasonably determines that the unified audit provisions should apply to the partnership for the year, but the determination is erroneous, then the unified provisions will be extended to that partnership (and its items) for that tax year and to partners of the partnership. (Code Sec. 6231(g)(1) as amended by '97 Act §1232(a)) Conversely, if, based on the partnership's return for a tax year, IRS reasonably determines that the unified audit procedures should not apply to the partnership for the year, but the determination is erroneous, then the unified provisions will not apply to that partnership (and its items) for that tax year or to partners of the partnership; (Code Sec. 6231(g)(2)) the regular (non-partnership) deficiency procedures will apply. (Com Rept, see ¶ 5216)

☐ **Effective:** Partnership tax years ending after Aug. 5, '97. ('97 Act §1232(b))

¶ 1408. Small partnership exception to unified partnership audit procedures expanded

Code Sec. 6231(a)(1)(B)(i), as amended by '97 Act § 1234(a)
Generally effective: Tax years ending after Aug. 5, '97
Committee Reports, see ¶ 5218

The unified partnership audit procedures (see ¶ 1406) do not apply to (a) electing large partnerships (see ¶ 1402) and (b) small partnerships, i.e., partnerships that meet the requirements of what is often called the "small partnership exception." Under pre-'97 Act law, the small partnership exception applied to partnerships:

• that had ten or fewer partners, all of whom were natural persons (who weren't nonresident aliens) or estates, and

• for which each partner's share of each partnership item was the same as his share of every other item.

Thus, a partnership was subject to the unified partnership audit procedures if it had a C corporation as a partner or if it specially allocated items.

For purposes of qualifying for the small partnership exception, a husband and wife (and their estates) count as one partner. A partnership does not qualify if any partner is a flow-through entity other than an estate (e.g., a partnership or S corporation). (FTC 2d/FIN ¶ T-2103; USTR ¶ 62,214.10; TaxDesk ¶ 82,504)

New Law. The '97 Act changes the small partnership exception to provide that a small partnership is any partnership that has ten or fewer partners, each of whom is an estate of a deceased partner, a C corporation, or a natural person who isn't a nonresident alien. For purposes of this definition, a husband and wife (and their estates) are treated as one partner. (Code Sec. 6231(a)(1)(B)(i) as amended by '97 Act §1234(a)) Thus, a partnership can have a C corporation as a partner and can specially allocate items without jeopardizing its exception from the unified partnership audit procedures. However, the provision retains the prohibition against having a partnership that has a flow-through entity (other than an estate of a deceased partner) as a partner qualify for the small partnership exception. (Com Rept, see ¶ 5218)

　　　　　　　　　　　　　　　　　　　　　　　Research Institute of America

caution: As under pre-'97 Act law, divorce can endanger the eligibility of the partnership for small partnership status since it will result in two partners instead of one for purposes of the ten-partner limit.

☐ **Effective:** Partnership taxable years ending after Aug. 5, '97. ('97 Act §1234(b))

¶ 1409. Extension of assessment period automatically extends time for filing request for administrative adjustment

Code Sec. 6227(b), as added by '97 Act § 1236(a)
Generally effective: Partnership tax years beginning after Sept. 3, '82
Committee Reports, see ¶ 5220

A partner can file a request for administrative adjustment (RAA) of partnership items. An RAA is treated as a claim for refund unless the partnership requests that it be treated as a substituted return and IRS allows such treatment. (FTC 2d/FIN ¶ T-2201 *et seq.*; USTR ¶ 62,214.06; TaxDesk ¶ 82,520 *et seq.*)

For taxpayers not subject to the unified partnership audit procedures (see ¶ 1406), an agreement between IRS and the taxpayer that extends the statute of limitations on assessment also extends the statute of limitations for filing refund claims. (FTC 2d/FIN ¶ T-7574; USTR ¶ 65,114.09; TaxDesk ¶ 80,664) Under pre-'97 Act law, there was no comparable provision for extending the time for filing RAAs with respect to partnership items (¶ 1406) in cases where the statute of limitations on assessments resulting from partnership items was extended. (FTC 2d/FIN ¶ T-2202, ¶ T-4419; USTR ¶ 62,214.06, ¶ 62,214.08; TaxDesk ¶ 82,521) The absence of an extension for filing RAAs in unified partnership audit procedures hindered taxpayers that wanted to agree to extend the statute of limitations but wanted to preserve their option to file an RAA later. (Com Rept, see ¶ 5220)

New Law. The period prescribed for filing an RAA is extended (a) for the period within which an assessment may be made under an agreement (or any extension of it) extending the limitations period for assessments, and (b) for six months after that. (Code Sec. 6227(b) as added by '97 Act §1236(a)) Thus, an agreement extending the statute of limitations on assessments for purposes of the unified partnership audit procedures also extends the statute of limitations for filing RAAs attributable to partnership items or affected items (¶ 1406) until six months after the expiration of the limitations period for assessments. (Com Rept, see ¶ 5220)

☐ **Effective:** Except as otherwise provided in the next sentence, partnership tax years beginning after Sept. 3, '82. Partnership tax years *ending* after Sept. 3, '82 if the partnership, each partner, and each indirect partner requested, and IRS consented to, have the unified partnership audit procedures first take effect in that year. ('97 Act

FTC 2d References are to Federal Tax Coordinator 2d
FIN References are to RIA's Analysis of Federal Taxes: Income
USTR References are to United States Tax Reporter: Income, Estate & Gift, and Excise
PCA References are to Pension Coordinator and Pension & Benefits Expert/Advisor
PE References are to Pension and Profit Sharing 2nd
EP References are to Estate Planning & Taxation Coordinator and Estate Planning Advisor

§1236(b))

> ●/*observation:* Sept. 3 '82 was the enactment date of the legislation which added the unified partnership audit procedures to the tax law.

¶ 1410. Time for filing administrative adjustment requests relating to bad debts or worthless securities extended

Code Sec. 6227(e), as amended by '97 Act § 1243(a)
Generally effective: Partnership tax years beginning after Sept. 3, '82
Committee Reports, see ¶ 5228

With certain exceptions, for all taxes for which a return must be filed, a claim for credit or refund must be filed (a) within three years of the time the return was filed or (b) within two years from the time the tax was paid, if that period ends later. However, an extended period of time, seven years from the date the return was due, is provided for filing a claim for refund of an overpayment resulting from a deduction for a loss from a worthless security or bad debt. This rule applies because the time when a stock or debt becomes worthless is a question of fact that may not be determinable until after the year in which it appears that the loss has occurred. (FTC 2d/FIN ¶ T-7501, ¶ T-7552; USTR ¶ 65,114.01, ¶ 65,114.10; TaxDesk ¶ 80,601, ¶ 80,646)

Under the unified partnership audit procedures applicable to certain large partnerships (see ¶ 1406), a request for administrative adjustment (RAA) (see ¶ 1406) for any partnership tax year must be filed within three years after the later of the date the partnership return was filed or the last day for filing the partnership return for the year (determined without regard to extensions). In addition, the RAA must be filed before IRS mails a notice of final partnership administrative adjustment (FPAA) (¶ 1406) for the tax year to the partnership. (FTC 2d/FIN ¶ T-2202; USTR ¶ 62,214.06; TaxDesk ¶ 82,521) Under pre-'97 Act law, there was no special provision extending the time for filing an RAA relating to a deduction for a worthless security or an entirely worthless bad debt. Moreover, IRS occasionally issued FPAAs that did not adjust the partnership's tax return (Com Rept, see ¶ 5228), which resulted in a shortening of the otherwise available claims period.

A petition for judicial review in regard to an RAA must be filed after the expiration of six months from the date the RAA was filed and before two years after the date the RAA was filed. The petition may not be filed after an IRS notice of the commencement of a partnership proceeding has been mailed to the partnership. A petition by a TMP to review the RAA may not be filed after IRS has mailed notice to the TMP of the FPAA. (FTC 2d/FIN ¶ T-2206 *et seq.*; USTR ¶ 62,214.07; TaxDesk ¶ 82,522 *et seq.*)

New Law.

Extension of claims period. The '97 Act provides that, in the case of that portion of any RAA that relates to the deductibility by the partnership

. . . under Code Sec. 166, of a debt as a debt which became worthless, or

. . . under Code Sec. 165(g), of loss from worthlessness of a security, the period for filing an RAA is seven years from the last day for filing the partnership return for the year with respect to which the request is made (determined without regard to extensions). (Code Sec. 6227(e) as amended by '97 Act §1243(a)) Thus, the '97 Act extends the time for filing an RAA relating to the deduction by a partnership for a worthless security or bad debt so as to allow partners in large partnerships the same opportunity to file a delayed claim for refund as other taxpayers are permitted. (Com Rept, see ¶ 5228)

> *illustration:* In filing its income tax return for Year 1 on Apr. 15, Year 2, a calendar year partnership failed to deduct a bad debt as worthless. It deducted it on its return for Year 2, but IRS disallowed the deduction on the grounds that the debt had become worthless in Year 1. A partner of the partnership may file an RAA on or before Apr. 15, Year 9, for overpayment of its Year 1 tax.

> *observation:* The effect of the new provision is to make the special rules relating to unified partnership audit procedures more similar to the general procedural rules of the tax law. In this respect, the change is similar to several other '97 Act provisions, i.e. those discussed at ¶ 1411, ¶ 1409, ¶ 1412, and ¶ 1413.

Remedy for taxpayers who were adversely impacted by past IRS practice. In the case of that portion of any RAA filed before Aug. 5, '97 for an administrative adjustment which relates to the deductibility of a debt as a debt which became worthless or the deductibility of a loss from the worthlessness of a security:

(1) the rule requiring that the RAA precede the mailing of a notice of FPAA for the tax year does not apply, ('97 Act §1243(b)(2)(A))

(2) the period for filing a petition for judicial review in regard to the RAA does not expire before the date six months after Aug. 5, '97, ('97 Act §1243(b)(2)(B)) and

(3) such a petition for judicial review may be filed without regard to whether there was a notice of the beginning of an administrative proceeding or an FPAA. ('97 Act §1243(b)(2)(C))

Under the '97 Act, the RAA is still required to be filed before the FPAA is mailed for the taxable year. A special rule was necessary to permit partners who may have been adversely impacted by the past IRS practice of issuing FPAAs without adjustments to avail themselves of the extended period irrespective of whether an FPAA has been issued (see (1) above). (Com Rept, see ¶ 5228)

> *illustration:* In filing its income tax return for '94 on Apr. 15, '95, a calendar year partnership failed to take a deduction for a bad debt which became worthless in '94. In Jan. '96, IRS issued an FPAA for '94 without adjustments

to the partnership. In Jan., '97, the partnership determined that the bad debt had become worthless in '94, and a partner of the partnership filed an RAA for overpayment of its '94 tax. Under the above rules, the RAA is valid, even though it was filed after the mailing of the FPAA for '94. Moreover, the period for filing a petition for judicial review in regard to it won't expire before the date six months after Aug. 5, '97.

☐ **Effective:** Except as otherwise provided in the next sentence, partnership tax years beginning after Sept. 3, '82. Partnership tax years *ending* after Sept. 3, '82 if the partnership, each partner, and each indirect partner requested, and IRS consented to, have the unified partnership audit procedures first take effect in that tax year. ('97 Act §1243(b)(1))

observation: Sept. 3 '82 was the enactment date of the legislation which added the unified partnership audit procedures to the tax law.

¶ 1411. Statute of limitations for partnership proceedings suspended by untimely partnership petition and by partner's bankruptcy petition

Code Sec. 6229(d)(1), as amended by '97 Act § 1233(a)
Code Sec. 6229(h), as amended by '97 Act § 1233(b)
Code Sec. 6229(b), as amended by '97 Act § 1233(c)
Generally effective: Partnership tax years for which the partnership assessment limitations period has not expired on or before Aug. 5, '97
Committee Reports, see ¶ 5217

Under pre-'97 Act law, if IRS mailed notice of a final partnership administrative adjustment (FPAA) (¶ 1406) to the tax matters partner (TMP) (¶ 1406), the running of the period for assessment of tax attributable to a partnership item was suspended for:

. . . the period during which an action for review of the FPAA could be brought under Code Sec. 6226 (i.e., 90 days), and if an action relating to the administrative adjustment was brought during that period, until the court decision became final, and

. . . for one year thereafter. (FTC 2d/FIN ¶ T-4316; USTR ¶ 62,214.08; TaxDesk ¶ 82,540)

Under this rule, the running of the statute of limitations in a case under the unified partnership audit procedures (¶ 1406) was only tolled by the filing of a timely petition. If an untimely petition was filed in a unified partnership audit case, the statute of limitations could expire while the case was still pending before the court. To prevent this from occurring, IRS could make assessments against all of the investors during the pendency of the action and, if the action was in the Tax Court, presumably abate such assessments if the court ultimately determined that the petition was timely. (Com Rept, see ¶ 5217)

For partnership items (¶ 1406) that convert to nonpartnership items (¶ 1406), the period for assessing tax does not expire under Code Sec. 6229(f) before the date that is one year after the date that the items become nonpartnership items. Code Sec. 6503(h) provides for the suspension of the assessment and collection limitations periods in Code Sec. 6501 and Code Sec. 6502 during the pendency of a bankruptcy proceeding. (FTC 2d/FIN ¶ T-4320, ¶ T-4323, ¶ V-7332; USTR ¶ 62,214.08, ¶ 65,034; TaxDesk ¶ 83,844, ¶ 83,846) Under pre-'97 Act law, it was uncertain whether Code Sec. 6503(h) suspended the assessment limitations period on converted items in Code Sec. 6229(f) when a petition naming a partner as a debtor in a bankruptcy proceeding was filed. (Com Rept, see ¶ 5217)

The assessment period may be extended for all partners by an agreement entered into by IRS and the TMP or any other person authorized by the partnership in writing to enter into the agreement, before the assessment period expires. But, temporary regs provide that, on the filing of a petition naming a partner as a debtor in a bankruptcy proceeding, that partner's partnership items convert to nonpartnership items, and if the debtor was the TMP, such status terminates. (FTC 2d/FIN ¶ T-2137, ¶ T-4419; USTR ¶ 62,214.08; TaxDesk ¶ 82,511, ¶ 82,538) As a result, under pre-'97 Act law, if a consent to extend the statute of limitations was signed by a person who would be the TMP except that, at the time the agreement was executed, the person was a debtor in a bankruptcy proceeding, the consent wasn't binding on the other partners because the person signing the agreement was no longer the TMP at the time of the agreement. IRS is not automatically notified of bankruptcy filings and cannot easily determine whether a taxpayer is in bankruptcy, especially if the audit of the partnership is being conducted by one district and the taxpayer resides in another district (a frequent situation in cases under the unified partnership audit procedures). If IRS was unaware that a person signing a consent was in bankruptcy, IRS could mistakenly rely on the consent and be precluded from assessing any tax attributable to partnership item adjustments for any of the partners in the partnership. (Com Rept, see ¶ 5217)

New Law. The '97 Act provides rules suspending statutes of limitations relating to partnerships in untimely petition and bankruptcy situations and allowing IRS reliance on apparent TMP status of a person in bankruptcy. (Com Rept, see ¶ 5217)

Suspension of limitations period where untimely petitions filed. If IRS mails notice of a final partnership administrative adjustment (FPAA) to the tax matters partner (TMP), the running of the period for assessment of tax is suspended:

... for the period during which an action for review of the FPAA may be brought (i.e., 90 days), and if a petition is filed under Code Sec. 6226 relating to that administrative adjustment, until the court decision becomes final (Code Sec. 6229(d)(1) as amended by '97 Act §1233(a)), and

... for one year thereafter. (Code Sec. 6229(d)(2))

Thus, the statute of limitations in unified partnership cases is suspended by the filing of any petition under Code Sec. 6226, regardless of whether the petition is timely or

FTC 2d References are to Federal Tax Coordinator 2d
FIN References are to RIA's Analysis of Federal Taxes: Income
USTR References are to United States Tax Reporter: Income, Estate & Gift, and Excise
PCA References are to Pension Coordinator and Pension & Benefits Expert/Advisor
PE References are to Pension and Profit Sharing 2nd
EP References are to Estate Planning & Taxation Coordinator and Estate Planning Advisor

valid. This change conforms the suspension rule for the filing of petitions in cases under the unified partnership rules with the rule under Code Sec. 6503(a) for deficiency cases. Thus, the limitations period will not run and possibly expire while an untimely partnership action is pending before the court. (Com Rept, see ¶ 5217)

Suspension of limitations period during bankruptcy proceeding. If a petition is filed naming a partner as a debtor in a Title 11 bankruptcy proceeding, the running of the period of limitations provided in Code Sec. 6229 with respect to the partner is suspended:

... for the period during which IRS is prohibited by reason of the bankruptcy proceeding from making an assessment, and

... for 60 days after that. (Code Sec. 6229(h) as amended by '97 Act §1233(b))

This change clarifies that the statute of limitations is suspended for a partner who is named in a bankruptcy petition. The ambiguity in pre-'97 Act law made it difficult for IRS to adjust partnership items that converted to nonpartnership items by reason of a partner going into bankruptcy since, if the statute of limitations was not suspended, the Code Sec. 6229(f) limitations period could continue to run during the pendency of the bankruptcy proceeding, although IRS could not make an assessment against the debtor because of the Bankruptcy Code's automatic stay provisions. The uncertainty could have resulted in increased requests for the bankruptcy court to lift the automatic stay to permit IRS to make an assessment with respect to the converted items. This change does not purport to create any inference as to the proper interpretation of pre-'97 Act law. (Com Rept, see ¶ 5217)

> **🔷 observation:** The Committee Report discussion above is misleading since, under 11 USC § 362(b)(9)(D), for bankruptcy cases commenced after Oct. 21, '94, an automatic stay does not prevent IRS from assessing any tax. The language of the Committee Report may reflect the fact that the above provision is only the latest version of a change that was included in proposed legislation in '93.

TMP in bankruptcy proceeding. Notwithstanding any other law or rule of law, if an extension agreement is entered into for all partners and the agreement is signed by a person who would be the TMP but for the fact that, at the time that the agreement is executed, the person is a debtor in a Title 11 bankruptcy proceeding, the agreement is binding on all partners in the partnership unless IRS has been notified of the bankruptcy proceeding in accordance with regulations prescribed by IRS. (Code Sec. 6229(b)(2) as amended by '97 Act §1233(c)) Thus, unless IRS is notified of a bankruptcy proceeding in accordance with regulations, IRS can rely on a limitations period extension signed by a person who is the TMP but for the fact that the person was in bankruptcy at the time that the person signed the agreement. This change is not intended to create any inference as to the proper interpretation of pre-'97 Act law. (Com Rept, see ¶ 5217)

> **🔷 observation:** The statement in the Committee Reports disclaiming any intent to affect the interpretation of pre-'97 Act law seems anomalous since the Committee Reports express no uncertainty about pre-'97 Act law in their dis-

cussion of it. The fact that the problem under pre-'97 Act law, as discussed above, derived partly from temporary regs rather than from the statute may be the reason for the statement.

☐ **Effective:** Partnership tax years for which the period of limitations for assessment (under pre-'97 Act law (Com Rept, see ¶ 5217)) has not expired on or before Aug. 5, '97. ('97 Act §1233(d)(1)) However, the amendment relating to bankruptcy of TMPs applies to agreements entered into after Aug. 5, '97 ('97 Act §1233(d)(2))—i.e., extension agreements entered into after Aug. 5, '97. (Com Rept, see ¶ 5217)

¶ 1412. Innocent spouse relief extended to unified partnership proceedings

Code Sec. 6230(a)(3), as amended by '97 Act § 1237(a)
Code Sec. 6230(a)(3), as amended by '97 Act § 1238(b)(3)
Code Sec. 6230(a)(1), as amended by '97 Act § 1237(c)
Code Sec. 6230(c)(5), as amended by '97 Act § 1237(b)
Code Sec. 6230(c)(5), as amended by '97 Act § 1238(b)(3)(D)
Generally effective: Partnership tax years beginning after Sept. 3, '82
Committee Reports, see ¶ 5221

An innocent spouse may be relieved of liability for tax, penalties, and interest attributable to a joint return if certain conditions are satisfied. Under pre-'97 Act law, the unified partnership audit procedures discussed at ¶ 1406 did not provide a judicial forum to raise the innocent spouse defense regarding any tax or interest relating to an investment in a partnership subject to the unified rules. (FTC 2d/FIN ¶ T-2261.1; TaxDesk ¶ 57,093)

New Law. If a spouse of a partner asserts that the innocent spouse rule applies with respect to a liability attributable to any adjustment of a partnership item (including any penalties or additions to tax relating thereto (Code Sec. 6230(a)(3)(A) as amended by '97 Act §1238(b)(3)(A))) then, notwithstanding Code Sec. 6404(b) (which bars claims for abatement of income, estate and gift taxes), the spouse may file, within 60 days after the notice of computational adjustment is mailed to the spouse, a request that the assessment specified in the notice be abated. Upon receipt of such a request, IRS will abate the assessment, and any reassessment will be subject to the regular (non-unified) deficiency procedures. If an abatement is requested, the statute of limitations for making the reassessment does not expire before the date which is 60 days after the date of the abatement. (Code Sec. 6230(a)(3)(A) as amended by '97 Act §1237(a))

If the spouse files a petition with the Tax Court with respect to the request for an innocent spouse abatement described above, the Tax Court only has jurisdiction to deter-

FTC 2d References are to Federal Tax Coordinator 2d
FIN References are to RIA's Analysis of Federal Taxes: Income
USTR References are to United States Tax Reporter: Income, Estate & Gift, and Excise
PCA References are to Pension Coordinator and Pension & Benefits Expert/Advisor
PE References are to Pension and Profit Sharing 2nd
EP References are to Estate Planning & Taxation Coordinator and Estate Planning Advisor

 Research Institute of America 331

mine whether the requirements of the innocent spouse rule have been satisfied. In making this determination, the treatment of the partnership items (including any penalties or additions to tax relating thereto (Code Sec. 6230(a)(3)(B) as amended by '97 Act §1238(b)(3)(B))) under the settlement, the final partnership administrative adjustment, or the decision of the court (whichever is appropriate) that gave rise to the liability in question is conclusive. (Code Sec. 6230(a)(3)(B))

Rules similar to those of Code Sec. 6230(a)(2)(B) and Code Sec. 6230(a)(2)(C) apply for purposes of the above innocent spouse provisions. (Code Sec. 6230(a)(3)(C))

> ⊘ *observation:* In providing for a rule similar to Code Sec. 6230(a)(2)(B), Congress seems to be providing for a requirement of separate application of the regular deficiency proceedings to each deficiency attributable to each partnership in the case of deficiencies that are covered by the above innocent spouse rules. The reference to Code Sec. 6230(a)(2)(C) seems to mean that, for deficiencies covered by the innocent spouse rules, any proceedings under the regular deficiency proceedings would not preclude or be precluded by any other proceedings relating to the partner's tax liability for a tax year.

Refund claims. Alternatively, the spouse of a partner can assert the innocent spouse rule in a claim for refund. (Code Sec. 6230(c)(5)(A) as amended by '97 Act §1237(b)) The refund claim has to be filed within six months after the day on which IRS mails to the spouse the notice of computational adjustment. (Code Sec. 6230(c)(5)(B)) If the claim is not allowed, the spouse can file a refund suit. The suit must be brought within the refund suit limitations period specified in Code Sec. 6532(a). (Code Sec. 6230(c)(5)(C)) For purposes of any claim or suit under this provision, the treatment of the partnership items (including penalties or additions to tax (Code Sec. 6230(c)(5)(D) as amended by '97 Act §1238(b)(3)(D))) under the settlement or administrative or judicial determination (whichever is appropriate) that gave rise to the liability in question is conclusive. (Code Sec. 6230(c)(5)(D))

Thus, the '97 Act provides both a prepayment forum and a refund forum for raising the innocent spouse defense in cases subject to the unified partnership audit procedures. (Com Rept, see ¶ 5221)

> ⊘ *observation:* The innocent spouse defense is particularly important in partnership cases because the complicated nature of many partnership cases may give credibility to assertion of the defense, particularly where the spouse relying on the defense is relatively unsophisticated.

☐ **Effective:** Partnership tax years beginning after Sep. 3, '82. The rule also applies to partnership tax years ending after Sep. 3, '82 if the partnership, each partner, and each indirect partner requested such an effective for the unified partnership audit provisions and IRS consented. ('97 Act §1237(d)) The changes conforming to the rules requiring penalties to be determined at the partnership level apply to partnership tax years ending after Aug. 5, '97. ('97 Act §1238(b))

¶ 1413. Interest suspended where IRS delays notice and demand with respect to computational adjustment relating to partnership settlement

Code Sec. 6601(c), as amended by '97 Act § 1242(a)
Generally effective: Adjustments for partnership tax years beginning after Aug. 5, '97
Committee Reports, see ¶ 5227

For most deficiencies, if a waiver of restrictions on the assessment of the deficiency has been filed as part of a settlement agreement, and if notice and demand for payment of the deficiency is not made within 30 days after the filing of the waiver, interest is not imposed on the deficiency for the period beginning immediately after the 30th day and ending with the date of notice and demand. However, under pre-'97 Act law, interest on a deficiency that resulted from an adjustment of partnership items (¶ 1406) in unified partnership audit proceedings (¶ 1406) was not suspended. (FTC 2d/FIN ¶ T-3406; USTR ¶ 66,014.02; TaxDesk ¶ 85,311) Processing settlement agreements and assessing the tax due takes a substantial amount of time in unified partnership proceedings. Under pre-'97 Act law, a taxpayer was not afforded any relief from interest during that period. (Com Rept, see ¶ 5227)

Under the unified partnership audit procedures, partnership items are converted to nonpartnership items on the date that IRS enters into a settlement agreement with a partner with respect to the items. (FTC 2d/FIN ¶ T-2244; USTR ¶ 62,214.10)

New Law. In the case of a settlement under the unified partnership audit provisions which results in the conversion of partnership items to nonpartnership items, the above rule that suspends interest will apply to a computational adjustment resulting from the settlement, in the same manner as if the adjustment were a deficiency and the settlement were a waiver of restrictions on assessment. (Code Sec. 6601(c) as amended by '97 Act §1242(a)) Thus, the new provision suspends interest where there is a delay in making a computational adjustment relating to a settlement in a unified partnership proceeding. (Com Rept, see ¶ 5227)

observation: Under the new provision, if notice and demand for payment of a computational adjustment is not made within 30 days after the settlement, interest is not imposed on the adjustment for the period beginning immediately after the 30th day and ending with the date of notice and demand.

☐ **Effective:** Adjustments relating to partnership tax years beginning after Aug. 5, '97. ('97 Act §1242(b))

FTC 2d References are to Federal Tax Coordinator 2d
FIN References are to RIA's Analysis of Federal Taxes: Income
USTR References are to United States Tax Reporter: Income, Estate & Gift, and Excise
PCA References are to Pension Coordinator and Pension & Benefits Expert/Advisor
PE References are to Pension and Profit Sharing 2nd
EP References are to Estate Planning & Taxation Coordinator and Estate Planning Advisor

¶ 1414. Partial settlements excluded from one-year limitation on assessment

Code Sec. 6229(f), as amended by '97 Act § 1235(a)
Generally effective: Settlements entered into after Aug. 5, '97
Committee Reports, see ¶ 5219

For partnership items (¶ 1406) that convert to nonpartnership items (¶ 1406), the period for assessing tax does not expire earlier than one year after the items become nonpartnership items. The partnership items of a partner for a partnership tax year become nonpartnership items as of the date the partner enters into a settlement agreement with IRS with respect to these items. Under pre-'97 Act law, if a partial settlement agreement was entered into, the operation of the above rules could result in an assessment period for the items covered by the agreement that differed from the assessment period for the remaining items. (FTC 2d/FIN ¶ T-4320; USTR ¶ 62,214.08; TaxDesk ¶ 83,844)

New Law. If a partner enters into a settlement agreement with IRS with respect to the treatment of some of the partnership items in dispute for a partnership tax year but other partnership items for that year remain in dispute, the period of limitations for assessing any tax attributable to the settled items is determined as if the agreement had not been entered into. (Code Sec. 6229(f)(2) as amended by '97 Act §1235(a)(3)) Thus, the limitations period that is applicable to the last item to be resolved for the partnership tax year is controlling for all disputed partnership items for the partnership tax year. Congress intends no inference as to the proper interpretation of pre-'97 Act law. (Com Rept, see ¶ 5219)

☐ **Effective:** Settlements entered into after Aug. 5, '97. ('97 Act §1235(b))

observation: Thus, a bifurcated statute of limitations can still apply where partial settlements were entered into on or before Aug. 5, '97, but other items remain in dispute after Aug. 5, '97.

¶ 1415. Certain penalties to be determined at partnership level under unified partnership audit procedures

Code Sec. 6221, as amended by '97 Act § 1238(a)
Code Sec. 6226(f), as amended by '97 Act § 1238(b)
Code Sec. 6230(a), as amended by '97 Act § 1238(b)
Code Sec. 6230(c), as amended by '97 Act § 1238(b)
Generally effective: Partnership tax years ending after Aug. 5, '97
Committee Reports, see ¶ 5223

Under the unified partnership audit procedures that apply for all but certain small (10 or fewer partners) partnerships (see ¶ 1406) and electing large partnerships (see ¶ 1402), the tax treatment of any partnership item is determined at the partnership level rather than at the partner level (see ¶ 1406), except where these procedures provide otherwise. Partnership items include only items that are required to be taken into account for the partnership's tax year under Subtitle A (the income tax subtitle of the tax law). (FTC 2d/FIN ¶ T-2101 *et seq.*; USTR ¶ 62,214 *et seq.*; TaxDesk ¶ 82,501 *et seq.*)

Penalties are not partnership items since they are contained in Subtitle F (relating to procedure and administration). As a result, penalties could only be asserted against a partner by application of the generally applicable deficiency procedures of the tax law, after the completion of the partnership-level proceeding. (Com Rept, see ¶ 5223)

A partner could file a refund claim arising out of an erroneous computation under the unified partnership audit procedures on the following grounds:

(1) IRS erroneously computed the computational adjustment (¶ 1406) necessary to: (a) make the partner's treatment of partnership items consistent with the treatment on the partnership return, or (b) apply a settlement, final partnership administrative adjustment (FPAA) (¶ 1406), or court decision relating to partnership items to a partner; or

(2) IRS failed to allow a credit or refund due the partner in the amount of the overpayment attributable to a settlement, FPAA or court decision.

For purposes of any claim or suit under these erroneous computation rules, the treatment of partnership items on the return, under the settlement, FPAA, or court decision, was conclusive. (FTC 2d/FIN ¶ T-2262; USTR ¶ 62,214.09; TaxDesk ¶ 82,532)

If a petition was properly filed for judicial review of a FPAA, the Tax Court, district court or Claims Court had jurisdiction over all partnership items relating to the FPAA, including allocation of such items to parties. (FTC 2d/FIN ¶ T-2240; USTR ¶ 62,214.05; TaxDesk ¶ 82,530)

The usual (i.e., nonpartnership) deficiency procedures generally don't apply to computational adjustments. Computational adjustments attributable to "affected items" which require partner level determinations are one of the exceptions to the above rule. (The term "affected item" means an item to the extent it is affected by a partnership item. (FTC 2d/FIN ¶ T-2254; USTR ¶ 62,214.10; TaxDesk ¶ 82,533)) (FTC 2d/FIN ¶ T-2251; USTR ¶ 62,214.09, ¶ 65,034; TaxDesk ¶ 82,533)

New Law.

Penalties to be determined at partnership level. The '97 Act provides that the applicability of any penalty which relates to an adjustment to a partnership item is determined at the partnership level. (Code Sec. 6221 as amended by '97 Act §1238(a)) This change reflects Congress' belief that (a) the relevant conduct for which penalties are imposed often occurs at the partnership level and (b) the pre-'97 Act rule of applying penalties at the partner level following the conclusion of the partnership proceedings, increased the administrative burden on IRS and could have significantly increased the Tax Court's inventory. (Com Rept, see ¶ 5223)

FTC 2d References are to Federal Tax Coordinator 2d
FIN References are to RIA's Analysis of Federal Taxes: Income
USTR References are to United States Tax Reporter: Income, Estate & Gift, and Excise
PCA References are to Pension Coordinator and Pension & Benefits Expert/Advisor
PE References are to Pension and Profit Sharing 2nd
EP References are to Estate Planning & Taxation Coordinator and Estate Planning Advisor

Research Institute of America

Refund claims with respect to penalties. The '97 Act expands the grounds on which a partner can make a refund claim to include IRS's erroneous imposition of any penalty which relates to an adjustment to a partnership item. (Code Sec. 6230(c)(1)(C) as amended by '97 Act §1238(b)(4)) A refund claim based on such grounds must be filed within six months after the day on which IRS mails the notice of computational adjustment to the partner. (Code Sec. 6230(c)(2)(A) as amended by '97 Act §1238(b)(5)) For purposes of any claim or suit under the erroneous computation rules, the determination under the FPAA or court decision concerning the applicability of any penalty which relates to an adjustment to a partnership item is conclusive. Notwithstanding this rule, the partner will be allowed to assert any partner level defenses that may apply or to challenge the amount of the computational adjustment. (Code Sec. 6230(c)(4) as amended by '97 Act §1238(b)(6)) Although the partnership-level proceeding includes a determination of the applicability of penalties at the partnership level, partners can raise any partner level defenses in the refund forum. (Com Rept, see ¶ 5223)

🅡🅘🅐 *observation:* Thus, under the rules of Code Sec. 6230(c)(4), it would appear that a determination in the partnership-level proceeding that a penalty applies will not foreclose the partner from contesting its application to him under the refund procedures if he can invoke partner level defenses (e.g., reasonable reliance on a qualified tax adviser).

Expanded scope of judicial review. The '97 Act also provides that, if a petition is properly filed for judicial review of an FPAA, the Tax Court, district court, or Claims Court has jurisdiction over all partnership items relating to the FPAA, the allocation of such items to parties, and the applicability of any penalty which relates to the adjustment of any partnership item. (Code Sec. 6226(f) as amended by '97 Act §1238(b)(1))

🅡🅘🅐 *observation:* This provision amends the jurisdictional rule for judicial review of FPAAs to include the applicability of penalties, etc., in order to conform the rule with the expanded scope of the unified partnership audit procedures.

Deficiency proceedings. The pre-'97 Act rule discussed above, under which the usual (i.e., nonpartnership) deficiency procedures applied to computational adjustments attributable to "affected items" which require partner level determinations, has been changed to apply to such items other than penalties that relate to adjustments to partnership items. (Code Sec. 6230(a)(2)(A) as amended by '97 Act §1238(b)(2))

☐ **Effective:** Partnership tax years ending after Aug. 5, '97. ('97 Act §1238(c))

¶ 1416. Tax Court jurisdiction extended in partnership proceedings

Code Sec. 6225(b), as amended by '97 Act § 1239(a)
Code Sec. 6226(d)(1), as amended by '97 Act § 1239(b)
Code Sec. 6230(d)(6), as amended by '97 Act § 1239(c)(1)
Code Sec. 6512(b)(3), as amended by '97 Act § 1239(c)(2)
Code Sec. 7482(b)(1)(F), as amended by '97 Act § 1239(d)(1)
Code Sec. 7459(c), as amended by '97 Act § 1239(e)(1)
Generally effective: Partnership tax years ending after Aug. 5, '97
Committee Reports, see ¶ 5224

Improper assessment and collection activities by IRS during the 150-day period for filing a petition with the Tax Court relating to a final partnership administrative adjustment ("FPAA," see ¶ 1406) or during the pendency of any Tax Court proceeding may "be enjoined in the proper court." However, under pre-'97 Act law, it was unclear whether the proper court included the Tax Court. (FTC 2d/FIN ¶ T-4015 *et seq.*; USTR ¶ 62,214.04; TaxDesk ¶ 83,803)

For a partner other than the Tax Matters Partner ("TMP," see ¶ 1406) to be eligible to file a petition for redetermination of partnership items in any court or to participate in an existing case, the period for assessing any tax attributable to the partnership items of that partner must not have expired. Since such a partner would only be treated as a party to the action if the statute of limitations with respect to him was still open, pre-'97 Act law was unclear whether the partner would have standing to assert that the statute of limitations had expired with respect to him. (FTC 2d/FIN ¶ T-2236; USTR ¶ 62,214.05; TaxDesk ¶ 82,523)

The non-partnership rules for limitations on credits or refunds in Chapter 66 of the Code do not apply, under Code Sec. 6230(d)(6), to any credit or refund of an overpayment attributable to a partnership item (see ¶ 1406). Under pre-'97 Act law, this rule applied also to overpayments attributable to an affected item (see ¶ 1406).

If the Tax Court finds an overpayment instead of a deficiency, it can determine the amount of overpayment under Code Sec. 6512(b). Refund of an overpayment determined by the Tax Court is conditioned, under Code Sec. 6512(b)(3), on the Tax Court's including as a part of its decision a finding to the effect that the portion to be refunded was paid:

(1) after mailing the notice of deficiency; or

(2) within the look-back period which would be applicable under Code Sec. 6511(b)(2) (the regular period of three years after the return was filed or two years after payment), Code Sec. 6511(c) (the special period for extension agreements), or Code

FTC 2d References are to Federal Tax Coordinator 2d
FIN References are to RIA's Analysis of Federal Taxes: Income
USTR References are to United States Tax Reporter: Income, Estate & Gift, and Excise
PCA References are to Pension Coordinator and Pension & Benefits Expert/Advisor
PE References are to Pension and Profit Sharing 2nd
EP References are to Estate Planning & Taxation Coordinator and Estate Planning Advisor

Sec. 6511(d) (the special period for bad debts, worthless securities, operating loss carrybacks, and foreign tax credits), if a refund claim, stating the grounds upon which the court finds an overpayment, had been filed on the date the deficiency notice was mailed; or

(3) within the applicable look-back period (see (2) above), in respect of a timely refund claim filed before the date of mailing the deficiency notice. However, this rule applies only if (a) the refund claim was not disallowed before the date of mailing the deficiency notice, or (b) if it was disallowed before that date, a timely refund suit could have been filed on that date, or (c) a refund suit had been filed before that date. (FTC 2d/FIN ¶ T-2254, ¶ T-7578; USTR ¶ 62,214.09, ¶ 65,124; TaxDesk ¶ 82,533, ¶ 82,534)

Subject to exceptions, the proper circuit (venue) for a corporate taxpayer to appeal a decision of the Tax Court is the U.S. court of appeals for the circuit in which the corporation's principal place of business or principal office or agency is located. If the corporation has neither a principal place of business nor a principal office or agency in any judicial district, an appeal may be taken to the court of appeals for the circuit in which is located the office where the return for the year or years in issue was filed. (FTC 2d/FIN ¶ U-5201; USTR ¶ 74,824)

Appeal from a decision of the Tax Court is initiated by the filing of a notice of appeal with the clerk of the Tax Court within 90 days after the decision is entered. FTC 2d/FIN ¶ U-5204; USTR ¶ 74,824.09; TaxDesk ¶ 83,205

New Law. The '97 Act specifies that the Tax Court is a "proper court" in which to bring an action to enjoin premature assessment and collection of deficiencies attributable to partnership items. However, the Tax Court will have no jurisdiction to enjoin any action or proceeding unless a timely petition for readjustment of the partnership items for the tax year has been filed, and then only in respect of the adjustments that are the subject of the petition. (Code Sec. 6225(b) as amended by '97 Act §1239(a))

Partner's participation to assert statute of limitations. Notwithstanding the provision restricting participation in a case by partners other than TMPs, a partner is permitted to participate in an action or file a petition for the sole purpose of asserting that the period of limitations for assessing any tax attributable to partnership items has expired for that partner, and the court having jurisdiction of the action will have jurisdiction to consider that assertion. (Code Sec. 6226(d)(1) as amended by '97 Act §1239(b))

Jurisdiction to determine overpayment from affected items. Under the '97 Act, the reference to affected items is removed from the rule in Code Sec. 6230(d)(6) prohibiting application of the nonpartnership credit or refund limitation rules to credits or refunds of overpayments attributable to partnership items or affected items. (Code Sec. 6230(d)(6) as amended by '97 Act §1239(c)(1)) This change clarifies that the Tax Court has overpayment jurisdiction with respect to affected items. (Com Rept, see ¶ 5224)

observation: What the Committee Report seems to mean is that by allowing application of the nonpartnership rules for refunds and credits in the case of affected items, the new law specifically authorizes application of the rules of Code Sec. 6512(b), which provides the Tax Court with jurisdiction to determine overpayments.

Under the '97 Act, the Code Sec. 6512(b)(3) rules for overpayments found by the Tax Court at (1) to (3) above are amended by the addition of a rule providing that where a credit or refund relates to an affected item, the rules are applied by substituting the periods under Code Sec. 6229 and Code Sec. 6230(d) for the periods under Code Sec. 6511(b)(2), Code Sec. 6511(c), and Code Sec. 6511(d), described at (1) to (3) above, which relate to non-partnership proceedings. (Code Sec. 6512(b)(3) as amended by '97 Act §1239(c)(2))

> **✔ *observation:*** Code Sec. 6229 provides the general time limits on assessments under the unified partnership audit procedures and Code Sec. 6230(d) limits credits or refunds of overpayments attributable to a partnership item after the Code Sec. 6229 time limit has expired. Thus, the provisions are the partnership procedure equivalent to the non-partnership rules of Code Sec. 6511. Thus, the above change conforms to the '97 Act rule applying Code Sec. 6512(b) to affected items. The conforming change applies the time limits in the partnership audit rules to a non-partnership provision in Code Sec. 6512(b)(3) which the '97 Act has applied to affected items.

Venue on appeal. In the case of a petition in the Tax Court relating to redetermination of adjustments on an "oversheltered return" (defined below), the decision may be reviewed by the court of appeals for the circuit in which is located the legal residence of the petitioner if the petitioner is not a corporation, and the place or office applicable under the rules described above for corporations if the petitioner is a corporation. (Code Sec. 7482(b)(1)(F) as amended by '97 Act §1239(d)(1)) The decision of the Tax Court in such cases is considered to have been rendered on the date of the court's order entering the decision. (Code Sec. 7459(c) as amended by '97 Act §1239(e)(1))

> **✔ *observation:*** The '97 Act provides a declaratory judgment procedure for oversheltered returns (see ¶ 1419) and thus, the new law also had to establish the above venue rule for appeals relating to the procedure. The term "oversheltered return" means an income tax return which shows no taxable income for the tax year, and shows a net loss from partnership items.

☐ **Effective:** Partnership tax years ending after Aug. 5, '97. ('97 Act §1239(f))

FTC 2d References are to Federal Tax Coordinator 2d
FIN References are to RIA's Analysis of Federal Taxes: Income
USTR References are to United States Tax Reporter: Income, Estate & Gift, and Excise
PCA References are to Pension Coordinator and Pension & Benefits Expert/Advisor
PE References are to Pension and Profit Sharing 2nd
EP References are to Estate Planning & Taxation Coordinator and Estate Planning Advisor

¶ 1417. Calculation of bond amount for stay of assessment and collection pending appeal of Tax Court decision in partnership proceeding is modified

Code Sec. 7485(b), as amended by '97 Act § 1241(a)
Generally effective: Partnership tax years beginning after Sept. 3, '82
Committee Reports, see ¶ 5226

Assessment and collection of deficiencies determined by the Tax Court in a partnership proceeding (see ¶ 1406) may be stayed if, on or before the time the notice of appeal of that decision is filed, a bond is filed with the Tax Court. The bond amount required is based on the total deficiencies attributable to the partnership items (¶ 1406) to which the decision related as finally determined (including interest and penalties).

Under pre-'97 Act law, if the parties did not stipulate to the amount of the total deficiencies, the Tax Court estimated the total based on the "aggregate of such deficiencies" (the total deficiencies attributable to the partnership items to which the decision related). (FTC 2d/FIN ¶ T-2211, ¶ T-2242; USTR ¶ 74,824.10; TaxDesk ¶ 82,522, ¶ 82,528) However, the Tax Court could not easily determine the aggregate changes in tax liability of all of the partners in a partnership who would be affected by the court's decision in the proceeding. (Com Rept, see ¶ 5226)

New Law. The '97 Act replaces the term "aggregate of such deficiencies" in the above provision with "aggregate liability of the parties to the action." (Code Sec. 7485(b)(1) as amended by '97 Act §1241(a)(2)) This change means that the amount of the bond will be based on the Tax Court's estimate of the aggregate liability of the parties to the action (and not of all of the partners in the partnership). After the '97 Act change, the amount of the bond can be estimated by applying the highest individual rate to the total adjustments determined by the Tax Court and doubling that amount to take into account interest and penalties. This change simplifies the Tax Court's task in determining the amount of the bond. (Com Rept, see ¶ 5226)

Under the unified partnership audit procedures, parties to a Tax Court action include any partner who was a partner in the partnership at any time during the partnership tax year in question, unless (a) the statute of limitations has expired for him or (b) his partnership items have been treated as nonpartnership items (see ¶ 1406). (FTC 2d/FIN ¶s T-2210, T-2236; USTR ¶ 62,214.05; TaxDesk ¶ 82,522)

> ⚡ *observation:* The Committee Report indicates that the above change is intended to narrow the scope of the bond calculation rule by applying the calculation rule only to the liability of parties to the action and not to the liability of other partners in the partnership, even if they might be affected by the Tax Court decision. Although the partners affected by the decision for this purpose could, under pre-'97 Act law, include any partner whose deficiencies were attributable to partnership items to which the decision related, in many cases, the parties to the action will be identical to all the affected partners and the change will make no difference in the result of the calculation.

☑️*observation:* The term "aggregate liability of the parties to the action" is not defined either in the unified partnership audit procedures or the '97 Act.

☐ **Effective:** Except as otherwise provided in the next sentence, partnership tax years beginning after Sept. 3, '82. Partnership tax years *ending* after Sept. 3, '82 if the partnership, each partner, and each indirect partner requested, and IRS consented to, have the unified partnership audit procedures first take effect in that year. ('97 Act §1241(b))

☑️*observation:* Sept. 3, '82 was the enactment date of the legislation that added the unified partnership audit provisions to the tax law.

¶ 1418. Premature petitions for judicial review filed by notice partners or 5% groups may be treated as timely

Code Sec. 6226(b)(5), as amended by '97 Act § 1240(a)
Generally effective: Petitions filed after Aug. 5, '97
Committee Reports, see ¶ 5225

Under the unified partnership audit procedures (see ¶ 1406), partners entitled to receive notice of the beginning of a partnership level audit and of a final partnership administrative adjustment ("FPAA") are called "notice partners." Partners that otherwise are not eligible for notice can form a "5% group" and declare one of its members to be a notice partner if they have, in the aggregate, a 5% or more interest in the profits of the partnership. (FTC 2d/FIN ¶ T-2157, ¶ T-2160, ¶ T-2161; USTR ¶ 62,214.02; TaxDesk ¶ 82,512)

Under pre-'97 Act law, the Tax Matters Partner (TMP; see ¶ 1406) was given the exclusive right to file a petition for judicial review of an FPAA (a "petition for a readjustment") within the 90-day period after the issuance of the notice of an FPAA. (Com Rept, see ¶ 5225) If the TMP did not file a petition within the 90-day period, notice partners were permitted to file a petition within the 60-day period after the close of the 90-day period, but a petition that was filed within the 90-day period by a person who was not the TMP was dismissed. If the TMP did not file a petition within the 90-day period and no timely and valid petition was filed during the succeeding 60-day period, judicial review of the adjustments set forth in the notice of FPAA was foreclosed and the adjustments were deemed to be correct. (FTC 2d/FIN ¶ T-2222, ¶ T-2228, ¶ T-2231, ¶ T-2232; USTR ¶ 62,214.05; TaxDesk ¶ 82,523, ¶ 82,526)

New Law. If:

... a petition for a readjustment of partnership items for the tax year involved is filed by a notice partner or a 5% group during the 90-day period,

FTC 2d References are to Federal Tax Coordinator 2d
FIN References are to RIA's Analysis of Federal Taxes: Income
USTR References are to United States Tax Reporter: Income, Estate & Gift, and Excise
PCA References are to Pension Coordinator and Pension & Benefits Expert/Advisor
PE References are to Pension and Profit Sharing 2nd
EP References are to Estate Planning & Taxation Coordinator and Estate Planning Advisor

... and no action (other than an action that is dismissed) is brought during the 60-day period with respect to the tax year,

the petition will be treated as filed on the last day of the 60-day period. (Code Sec. 6226(b)(5) as added by '97 Act §1240(a)) This change provides the partnership with an opportunity for judicial review that was not available under prior law. (Com Rept, see ¶ 5225)

> *observation:* Thus, a petition filed by a notice partner that would otherwise be premature and thus ineffective, can be effective.

> *observation:* This change provides an additional incentive for partners who don't qualify as notice partners to form 5% groups.

☐ **Effective:** Petitions filed after Aug. 5, '97. ('97 Act §1240(b))

¶ 1419. New set of deficiency procedures provided for certain returns of partners that show no taxable income

Code Sec. 6234, as added by '97 Act § 1231(a)
Generally effective: Partnership tax years ending after Aug. 5, '97
Committee Reports, see ¶ 5215

Audit proceedings involving partnerships that are subject to the "unified partnership audit procedures" (see ¶ 1406) are separate from audit proceedings under the general rules that apply to other entities (the "deficiency procedures"). Even if a partnership is subject to the unified partnership audit procedures, the deficiency procedures apply to the determination of deficiencies on returns of individual partners that result from nonpartnership items (i.e., items other than "partnership items," see ¶ 1406). As a result of the Tax Court's ruling in *Munro,* (1989) 92 TC 71, partnership items (whether income, loss, deduction, or credit) included on a partner's return must be completely ignored in determining whether a deficiency that is attributable to nonpartnership items exists with respect to that return.

This Tax Court position created problems for both taxpayers and IRS. For example, a taxpayer was harmed where he (a) invested in a partnership subject to the unified partnership audit procedures whose partnership items were losses and (b) was also subject to the deficiency procedures with respect to nonpartnership item adjustments. *Munro's* requirement that the partnership losses be ignored resulted in a greatly increased deficiency for the nonpartnership items. If, when the partnership proceedings were completed, the taxpayer was ultimately allowed any part of the partnership losses, the taxpayer would get part of the increased deficiency back in the form of an overpayment. Meanwhile, however, the taxpayer would have been subject to assessment and collection of a deficiency inflated by items still in dispute in the partnership proceeding. Basically, a taxpayer in that case would be deprived of a prepayment forum (a way to challenge the deficiency in court before payment) for the partnership item adjustments. And, IRS could have been harmed if a taxpayer's income was primarily from a TEFRA partnership (¶ 1406), since IRS might be unable to adjust nonpartnership items such as medical expense deductions, home mortgage interest deductions or charitable contribution deductions where there was no deficiency because, under the *Munro* rule, the partner's income was ignored. The harm caused under these scenarios was not corrected until after the partnership proceedings were completed. (Com Rept, see ¶ 5215)

New Law.

IRS may issue "notice of adjustment with respect to nonpartnership items." The '97 Act creates a new set of procedures with respect to the tax deficiencies of "oversheltered returns." (Com Rept, see ¶ 5215) An oversheltered return is an income tax return which shows (a) no taxable income, and (b) a net loss from partnership items. (Code Sec. 6234(b) as added by '97 Act §1231(a)) Under these new procedures, if:

. . . a taxpayer files an oversheltered return for a tax year;

. . . IRS makes a determination with respect to the treatment of taxpayer's nonpartnership items for that tax year; and

. . . the adjustments resulting from the determination do not give rise to a deficiency but would give rise to a deficiency if there were no net loss from partnership items,

IRS is authorized to send a notice of adjustment reflecting that determination to the taxpayer by certified or registered mail. (Code Sec. 6234(a)) Thus, IRS is authorized to issue a notice of adjustment with respect to nonpartnership items, notwithstanding that no deficiency would result from the adjustment, but only if a deficiency would have arisen in the absence of the net loss from TEFRA partnerships. (Com Rept, see ¶ 5215)

The above '97 Act provisions overrule *Munro,* described above. The changes eliminate the need to do special computations that involve the removal of partnership items from a taxpayer's return, and will restore to taxpayers a prepayment forum with respect to the partnership items. (Com Rept, see ¶ 5215)

Notice of adjustment subject to judicial review. Within 90 days (150 days if the notice is addressed to a person outside the United States) after the day on which an above described notice of adjustment is mailed to the taxpayer, he may file a petition with the Tax Court for redetermination of the adjustments. On the filing of such a petition, the Tax Court will have jurisdiction to make a declaration with respect to all items for the tax year to which the notice of adjustment relates, except for partnership items and affected items (¶ 1406) which require partner-level determinations. The principles of Code Sec. 6214(a) (the Code section that gives the Tax Court jurisdiction to redetermine deficiencies and to determine if additional amounts should be assessed) apply to these declarations. (Code Sec. 6234(c)) No tax is due on the Tax Court's determination. (Com Rept, see ¶ 5215) Any such declaration will have the force and effect of a Tax Court decision and will be reviewable as such. (Code Sec. 6234(c)) Thus, either IRS or the taxpayer can appeal the declaration. (Com Rept, see ¶ 5215)

An adjustment determined to be correct has the effect of increasing the taxable income that is deemed to have been reported on the taxpayer's return. IRS preserves its ability to collect tax on any increased deficiency attributable to the nonpartnership items. (Com Rept, see ¶ 5215)

> **observation:** IRS will be able to assert the increased deficiency attributable to nonpartnership items, if, for example, partnership losses are disallowed after the statute of limitations for nonpartnership items has expired.

For other rules relating to judicial review of notices of adjustment, see ¶ 1416.

Other ways taxpayer can appeal findings contained in notice of adjustment. If the taxpayer does not file a petition with the Tax Court within the time prescribed above, IRS's determination set out in the notice of adjustment that was mailed to the taxpayer is deemed correct (Code Sec. 6234(d)(1)), but not after the date that the taxpayer (Code Sec. 6234(d)(2)):

(1) files a petition with the Tax Court within the time prescribed above with respect to a subsequent notice of adjustment relating to the same tax year (Code Sec. 6234(d)(2)(A)), or

(2) files a claim for refund of an overpayment of tax under Code Sec. 6511 (i.e., the normal refund claim time limit rules; see FTC 2d/FIN ¶ T-7500 *et seq.*; USTR ¶ 65,114 *et seq.*) for the tax year involved. (Code Sec. 6234(d)(2)(B))

> **observation:** For purposes of (1) above, "notice of adjustment" would seem to mean only a notice of adjustment under Code Sec. 6234(a). The "time prescribed" would seem to be within 90 or 150 days of the second notice of adjustment. Limitations apply to the mailing of subsequent notices of adjustment for a tax year if a petition is filed (see "Limitations on IRS's issuance of notices" below).

Thus, if the taxpayer chooses not to contest the notice of adjustment within the 90-day period, when his partnership items are finally determined he has the right to file a refund claim for tax attributable to the items adjusted by that notice of adjustment. (Com Rept, see ¶ 5215)

Limitations on IRS's issuance of notices. Any notice of adjustment under the above rules must be mailed before the expiration of Code Sec. 6501's statute of limitations on making tax assessments. (Code Sec. 6234(e)(1)) If IRS mails a notice of adjustment to the taxpayer for a tax year and the taxpayer files a petition with the Tax Court within the time prescribed above under "Notice of adjustment subject to judicial review," IRS may not mail another such notice to the taxpayer with respect to the same tax year unless there is fraud, malfeasance, or misrepresentation of a material fact. (Code Sec. 6234(f))

IRS's mailing of a notice of adjustment suspends the statute of limitations on the making of assessments for the longer of:

... the period mentioned in the preceding sentence during which IRS is prohibited from making the assessment;

... if a proceeding in respect of the notice of adjustment is placed on the docket of the Tax Court, until the decision of the Tax Court becomes final,

and for 60 days thereafter. (Code Sec. 6234(e)(2))

Effect of notice of assessment on tax. Except as otherwise provided in the jeopardy and termination assessment rules of Code Sec. 6851, Code Sec. 6852, and Code Sec. 6861, where IRS issues a notice of adjustment, no assessment of income tax deficiency, other than a deficiency attributable to any partnership item or any item affected by a partnership item may be made:

... until the expiration of the applicable 90-day or 150-day period for filing the Tax Court petition mentioned under "Notice of adjustment subject to judicial review" above (Code Sec. 6234(e)(3)(A)) or

... if such a petition has been filed with the Tax Court, until the decision of the Tax Court has become final. (Code Sec. 6234(e)(3)(B))

Conversion of notice of adjustment into notice of deficiency and related rules. A notice of adjustment will be treated as a notice of deficiency and any petition filed in respect of the notice will be treated as a petition for redetermination of a deficiency under Code Sec. 6213 if:

... after the notice of adjustment for a tax year is mailed to a taxpayer but before the expiration of the 90- or 150-day period for filing a petition with the Tax Court that is described below (or, if a petition is filed with the Tax Court, before the Tax Court makes a declaration for that tax year), the treatment of any partnership item for the tax year is "finally determined" or, under Code Sec. 6231(b) rules, any partnership item ceases to be a partnership item, and

... as a result of that final determination or cessation, a deficiency can be determined with respect to the items that are the subject of the notice of adjustment. (Code Sec. 6234(g)(3))

The treatment of partnership items is treated as finally determined if:

... IRS enters into a settlement agreement (within the meaning of Code Sec. 6224) with the taxpayer regarding such items;

... a notice of final partnership administrative adjustment (FPAA) adjustment has been issued and either (a) no petition has been filed under Code Sec. 6226 and the time for doing so has expired, or (b) such a petition has been filed and the decision of the court has become final, or

... the period within which any tax attributable to such items may be assessed against the taxpayer has expired. (Code Sec. 6234(g)(4))

FTC 2d References are to Federal Tax Coordinator 2d
FIN References are to RIA's Analysis of Federal Taxes: Income
USTR References are to United States Tax Reporter: Income, Estate & Gift, and Excise
PCA References are to Pension Coordinator and Pension & Benefits Expert/Advisor
PE References are to Pension and Profit Sharing 2nd
EP References are to Estate Planning & Taxation Coordinator and Estate Planning Advisor

If IRS erroneously mails notice of adjustment instead of notice of deficiency or vice versa. If IRS erroneously determines that the non-partnership deficiency rules do not apply to a tax year of a taxpayer and consistent with that determination timely mails a notice of adjustment to the taxpayer under the above rules, the notice of adjustment will be treated as a notice of deficiency and any petition that is filed in respect of the notice will be treated as a petition for redetermination of a deficiency. (Code Sec. 6234(h)(1))

> *observation:* The above provision seems to mean that if a notice of adjustment (rather than a notice of deficiency) is mailed under circumstances that do not meet the requirements for application of Code Sec. 6234, the notice of adjustment will be treated as a notice of deficiency.

If IRS erroneously determines that the non-partnership deficiency rules apply to a tax year of a taxpayer and consistent with that determination timely mails a notice of deficiency to the taxpayer, the notice of deficiency will be treated as a notice of adjustment under the above rules and any petition that is filed in respect of the notice will be treated as a petition for review of a notice of adjustment. (Code Sec. 6234(h)(2))

> *observation:* The above provision seems to mean that if a notice of deficiency (rather than a notice of adjustment) is mailed under circumstances that meet the requirements for application of Code Sec. 6234, the notice of deficiency will be treated as a notice of adjustment.

> *observation:* In giving IRS some leeway to make mistakes about which procedure to follow, the above provision is similar to another '97 Act rule discussed at ¶ 1407 (relating to the partnership return).

Coordination with other partnership/partner audit, etc. rules. *Calculation of computational adjustments and the amount of deficiency attributable to affected items.* Except as otherwise provided below, if the treatment of any item has been determined under the above rules (either in a Tax Court proceeding or in an IRS notice of adjustment that is deemed correct), it must be taken into account in determining the amount of any computational adjustment (see ¶ 1406) or the amount of any deficiency attributable to affected items in a proceeding under Code Sec. 6230(a)(2) (i.e., a deficiency proceeding), for the tax year involved (i.e., the tax year for which the item was determined). For this purpose, regardless of any other law relating to the period of limitations on assessments, any adjustment made in accordance with the above rules will be taken into account regardless of whether any assessment has been made with respect to the adjustment. (Code Sec. 6234(g)(1)) The application of this rule for computational adjustments is limited to those cases where the computational adjustment is made within the statute of limitations prescribed by Code Sec. 6229 for assessing income tax attributable to any partnership item or affected item for the tax year involved (i.e., the tax year for which the item was determined). (Code Sec. 6234(g)(2))

If a taxpayer who received a notice of adjustment described above does file a claim for refund with respect to the tax year in that notice, then, solely for purposes of determining

. . . the amount of any computational adjustment in connection with a partnership proceeding or

. . . the amount of any deficiency attributable to affected items in a proceeding under Code Sec. 6230(a)(2) (i.e., in a deficiency proceeding),

the items that are the subject of the notice of adjustment will be presumed to have been correctly reported on the taxpayer's return during the pendency of the refund claim and, if within the time prescribed by Code Sec. 6532 the taxpayer commences a civil action for refund under Code Sec. 7422, until the decision in the refund action becomes final. (Code Sec. 6234(d))

> *observation:* Code Sec. 7422 provides general rules applicable to civil actions for refund, including rules requiring prepayment and filing of a refund claim as prerequisites to suit. Code Sec. 6532 provides time limits on when a refund suit can be brought, which are dependent on the time the claim was filed, see FTC 2d/FIN ¶ T-9016 *et seq.*; USTR ¶ 65,324 *et seq.*

> *observation:* The presumption discussed above means that while the refund claim or suit is still undecided, IRS can assume the treatment of the item on the partner's return is correct for purposes of determinations relating to the partner (computational adjustments and deficiencies).

Adjustment of nonpartnership item that causes increase in tax on partnership item. Under the '97 Act provisions, any adjustment with respect to a nonpartnership item that causes an increase in tax liability with respect to a partnership item must be treated as a computational adjustment and assessed after the conclusion of the TEFRA proceeding. Accordingly, deficiency procedures do not apply with respect to this increase in tax liability, and the statute of limitations applicable to TEFRA proceedings applies. (Com Rept, see ¶ 5215)

☐ **Effective:** Partnership tax years ending after Aug. 5, '97. ('97 Act §1231(d))

¶ 1420. Clarification of treatment of partnership items for purposes of computing amount of deficiency under nonpartnership deficiency procedures

Code Sec. 6211(c), as amended by '97 Act § 1231(b)
Generally effective: Partnership tax years ending after Aug. 5, '97
Committee Reports, see ¶ 5215

If a partnership is subject to the unified partnership audit procedures (¶ 1406), the tax treatment of any partnership item (¶ 1406) is determined in a proceeding at the partnership level. (FTC 2d/FIN ¶s T-2101, T-2110; USTR ¶s 62,214, 62,214.10;

FTC 2d References are to Federal Tax Coordinator 2d
FIN References are to RIA's Analysis of Federal Taxes: Income
USTR References are to United States Tax Reporter: Income, Estate & Gift, and Excise
PCA References are to Pension Coordinator and Pension & Benefits Expert/Advisor
PE References are to Pension and Profit Sharing 2nd
EP References are to Estate Planning & Taxation Coordinator and Estate Planning Advisor

TaxDesk ¶ 82,507) The tax treatment of items that are not partnership items (except in the case of items that are converted from partnership item status in a settlement) is determined in a separate proceeding under the non-partnership deficiency procedures (the procedures for determining deficiencies that apply to entities not subject to the unified partnership audit procedures or the large partnership audit procedures discussed at ¶ 1402). (FTC 2d/FIN ¶ T-2245; USTR ¶ 62,214.10; TaxDesk ¶ 82,517)

New Law. The '97 Act provides that, in determining the amount of any deficiency for purposes of the non-partnership deficiency procedures, adjustments to partnership items can be made only as provided under the unified partnership audit procedures. (Code Sec. 6211(c) as amended by '97 Act §1231(b))

observation: This provision is apparently intended to improve coordination between the non-partnership deficiency procedures and the unified partnership audit procedures by clarifying that partnership items are always adjusted only under the partnership procedures. Although the unified partnership audit procedures only apply to determinations at the partnership level, adjustments under those procedures often affect determinations under the non-partnership procedures (e.g., a partnership loss can be passed through to a partner and affect the computation of the partner's deficiency).

☐ **Effective:** Partnership taxable years ending after Aug. 5, '97. ('97 Act §1231(d))

¶ 1421. Deductions denied to partners of nonfiling partnerships with non-U.S. tax matters partner or books kept outside U.S.

Code Sec. 6231(f), as amended by '97 Act § 1141(b)
Generally effective: Tax years beginning after Aug. 5, '97
Committee Reports, see ¶ 5182

Except to the extent that IRS provides otherwise in regulations, for any foreign or domestic partnership whose tax matters partner resides outside the U.S. or whose books are kept outside the U.S., no loss or credit is allowable to any partner unless, for the partnership's tax year in which the loss or credit arose, the partnership complies with the return filing requirements. (FTC 2d/FIN ¶ B-3507, ¶ S-3643.1; USTR ¶ 62,314; TaxDesk ¶ 58,907)

New Law. Deductions, as well as losses and credits, are disallowed to partners of a partnership whose tax matters partner resides outside the U.S. or whose books are kept outside the U.S. unless the partnership complies with the return filing requirements for the tax year in which the deduction, loss, or credit arose. (Code Sec. 6231(f) as amended by '97 Act §1141(b))

☐ **Effective:** Tax years beginning after Aug. 5, '97. ('97 Act §1141(c))

Other Partnership Provisions

¶ 1422. Allocation of basis among properties distributed by partnerships

Code Sec. 732(c), as amended by '97 Act § 1061
Generally effective: Partnership distributions after Aug. 5, '97
Committee Reports, see ¶ 5150

Partnership distributions are generally tax-free to the partners. A partner who received property in a non-liquidating distribution generally takes the property with a basis equal to the partnership's basis in the distributed property. However, the partner's basis in the property cannot exceed his basis in his partnership interest before the distribution. The basis of property distributed in liquidation of a partner's interest is equal to the partner's adjusted basis in its partnership interest (reduced by any cash distributed in the same transaction).

Where multiple properties are distributed in a liquidating distribution or where the total carryover basis of the distributed properties exceeds the partner's basis in its partnership interest, the partner's basis in his partnership interest must be allocated among the distributed properties. Under pre-'97 Act law, the partner's basis was allocated first to unrealized receivables (as defined in Code Sec. 751(c)) and inventory items (as defined in Code Sec. 751(d)(2)) up to their basis in the hands of the partnership (in proportion to the partnership's basis in these assets), and any excess was allocated among other properties in proportion to their adjusted bases to the partnership. (FTC 2d/FIN ¶ B-3700; USTR ¶ 7324.01; TaxDesk ¶ 58,950)

> **✐ observation:** Under pre-'97 Act law, taxpayers tried to increase the basis of distributed properties artificially in order to get increased depreciation deductions or artificial losses. (Com Rept, see ¶ 5150) IRS has tried to recast these transactions as inconsistent with the purposes of Subchapter K under the partnership anti-abuse rules.

New Law. Where multiple properties are distributed in a liquidating distribution or where the total carryover basis of the distributed properties exceed the partner's basis in its partnership interest, the partner's basis in his partnership interest is allocated as follows:

(1) first, to any unrealized receivables and inventory items in an amount equal to the adjusted basis of each such property to the partnership. (Code Sec. 732(c)(1)(A)(i) as amended by '97 Act §1061) If the basis to be allocated is less than the sum of the adjusted bases of these properties in the hands of the partnership, a basis decrease is applied as described below. (Code Sec. 732(c)(1)(A)(ii))

FTC 2d References are to Federal Tax Coordinator 2d
FIN References are to RIA's Analysis of Federal Taxes: Income
USTR References are to United States Tax Reporter: Income, Estate & Gift, and Excise
PCA References are to Pension Coordinator and Pension & Benefits Expert/Advisor
PE References are to Pension and Profit Sharing 2nd
EP References are to Estate Planning & Taxation Coordinator and Estate Planning Advisor

(2) to the extent any basis is not allocated under (1), basis is allocated to other distributed properties. This allocation is made by assigning to each property its adjusted basis in the hands of the partnership (Code Sec. 732(c)(1)(B)(i)) and then increasing or decreasing the basis to the extent any increase or decrease in basis is required in order for the adjusted bases of the other distributed properties to equal the remaining basis under the rules described below. (Code Sec. 732(c)(1)(B)(ii))

Any basis *increase* required under the above rules is allocated (i) first to properties with unrealized appreciation in proportion to their respective amounts of unrealized appreciation before such increase (but only to the extent of each property's unrealized appreciation) (Code Sec. 732(c)(2)(A)) and (ii) to the extent the required increase is not allocated under (i), in proportion to the respective fair market values of the properties. (Code Sec. 732(c)(2)(B))

Any basis *decrease* required under the above rules is allocated (a) first to properties with unrealized depreciation in proportion to their respective amounts of unrealized appreciation before such decrease (but only to the extent of each property's unrealized depreciation) (Code Sec. 732(c)(3)(A)) and (b) to the extent the required decrease is not allocated under (a), in proportion to the respective bases of the properties (as adjusted under (a)). (Code Sec. 732(c)(3)(B))

> **Illustration (1):** A partnership distributes both its assets, A and B, in liquidation of a partner whose basis in its interest is $55. Neither asset consists of inventory or unrealized receivables. A has a basis to the partnership of $5 and a fair market value of $40, and B has a basis to the partnership of $10 and a fair market value of $10. Basis is first allocated $5 to A and $10 to B (their adjusted bases to the partnership). The $40 basis increase (the partner's $55 basis minus the partnership's total basis in distributed assets of $15) is first allocated to A in the amount of $35, its unrealized appreciation, and the remaining basis adjustment of $5 is allocated according to the assets' fair market values, i.e., $4 to A (for a total basis of $44) and $1 to B (for a total basis of $11). (Com Rept, see ¶ 5150)

> **Illustration (2):** A partnership distributes both its assets, C and D, in liquidation of a partner whose basis in its interest is $20. Neither asset consists of inventory or unrealized receivables. C has a basis to the partnership of $15 and a fair market value of $15, and D has a basis to the partnership of $15 and a fair market value of $5. Basis is first allocated to C and D to the extent of the partnership's basis in C and D, or $15 to each. Because the partner's basis in its interest is only $20, a decrease of $10 ($30 minus $20) is required. The $10 decrease is allocated to D, reducing its basis to $5. Thus, C has a $15 basis and D has a $5 basis in the hands of the distributee partner. (Com Rept, see ¶ 5150)

> **illustration (3):** Same facts as Illustration (2), except that the distribution is not a liquidating distribution. The result is the same as that of Illustration (2). Thus, basis is allocated to C and D to the extent of the partnership's basis in C and D, or $15 to each. The basis of C and is then decreased by $10 ($30

basis of assets minus $20 partner's basis). The $10 decrease is allocated to D, reducing its basis to $5. Thus, C has a $15 basis and D has a $5 basis in the hands of the distributee partner.

☐ **Effective:** Distributions after Aug. 5, '97. ('97 Act §1061(b))

¶ 1423. Code Sec. 751 rules apply to non-appreciated inventory where partnership interests are sold or exchanged

Code Sec. 751(a)(2), as amended by '97 Act § 1062(a)
Code Sec. 751(b)(1), as amended by '97 Act § 1062(b)(1)(A)
Generally effective: Partnership sales, exchanges, and distributions after Aug. 5, '97.
Committee Reports, see ¶5151

Under pre-'97 Act law, amounts received on a sale or exchange of a partnership interest that were attributable to unrealized receivables or substantially appreciated inventory were treated as realized from the sale or exchange of property that is not a capital asset. A similar rule applies where a partnership makes a distribution in which a partner receives substantially appreciated inventory or unrealized receivables in exchange for its interest in certain other partnership property (or receives certain other property in exchange for its interest in substantially appreciated inventory or unrealized receivables). These rules are sometimes referred to as the "collapsible partnership rules." Substantially appreciated inventory is generally inventory with a fair market value exceeding 120% of its adjusted basis. (FTC 2d/FIN ¶ B-3900; USTR ¶ 7514; TaxDesk ¶ 59,100)

New Law. The '97 Act eliminates the requirement that inventory be substantially appreciated in order to give rise to ordinary income under the rules relating to *sales and exchanges* of partnership interests under Code Sec. 751(a). Thus, all inventory is subject to the collapsible partnership rules with respect to Code Sec. 751(a) sales and exchanges. (Code Sec. 751(a)(2) as amended by '97 Act §1062(a)) However, no change has been made with respect to *distributions* under Code Sec. 752(b), with the result that the requirement that inventory be substantially appreciated continues to apply to such distributions. (Code Sec. 751(b)(1) as amended by '97 Act §1062(b)(1)(A))

☐ **Effective:** Partnership sales, exchanges, and distributions after Aug. 5, '97. ('97 Act §1062(c)(1)) However, the new rule doesn't apply to sales and exchanges under written binding contracts in effect on June 8, '97 and at all times thereafter before the sale or exchange. ('97 Act §1062(c)(2))

FTC 2d References are to Federal Tax Coordinator 2d
FIN References are to RIA's Analysis of Federal Taxes: Income
USTR References are to United States Tax Reporter: Income, Estate & Gift, and Excise
PCA References are to Pension Coordinator and Pension & Benefits Expert/Advisor
PE References are to Pension and Profit Sharing 2nd
EP References are to Estate Planning & Taxation Coordinator and Estate Planning Advisor

¶ 1424. Seven-year period for taxing pre-contribution gain or loss

Code Sec. 704(c)(1)(B), as amended by '97 Act § 1063(a)
Code Sec. 737(b)(1), as amended by '97 Act § 1063(a)
Generally effective: Property contributed to a partnership after June 8, '97
Committee Reports, see ¶ 5152

If a partner contributes appreciated property to a partnership, no gain or loss is recognized to the contributing partner at the time of the contribution. The pre-contribution gain or loss must be allocated to the contributing partner. Thus, income, gain, loss, and deduction with respect to the contributed property must be shared among the partners so as to take account of the variation between the basis of the property to the partnership and its fair market value at the time of contribution

Under pre-'97 Act law, in order to ensure that pre-contribution gain or loss was taxed to the contributing partner, if the contributed property was distributed to another partner within five years of the contribution, the pre-contribution gain or loss was generally recognized to the contributing partner as if the property had been sold for its fair market value at the time of the distribution. In addition, where property was distributed to a partner who contributed appreciated property to a partnership, the contributing partner generally included the net pre-contribution gain on property contributed within five years in income to the extent that the value of the property distributed by the partnership to the contributing partner exceeded the contributing partner's adjusted basis in its partnership interest. (FTC 2d/FIN ¶ B-3125; USTR ¶ 7044.09, ¶ 7374; TaxDesk ¶ 58,818)

New Law. The '97 Act extends the period during which a distribution of contributed property to another partner triggers recognition of the pre-contribution gain or loss to within seven years of the contribution. (Code Sec. 704(c)(1)(B) as amended by '97 Act §1063(a)) Similarly, the net precontribution gain that is triggered on a property distribution to a partner who contributed appreciated property to a partnership includes the precontribution gain on property contributed within seven years of the contribution. (Code Sec. 737(b)(1) as amended by '97 Act §1063(a))

☐ **Effective:** Contributions to a partnership after June 8, '97. ('97 Act §1063(b)(1)) However, the amendment does not apply to property contributed pursuant to a binding written contract in effect on June 8, '97 and at all times thereafter, if such contract provides for the contribution of a fixed amount of property. ('97 Act §1063(b)(2))

¶ 1425. Partnership tax year closes with respect to interest of deceased partner

Code Sec. 760(c)(2)(A), as amended by '97 Act § 1246(a)
Generally effective: Partnership tax years beginning after Dec. 31, '97.
Committee Reports, see ¶ 5229

Under pre-'97 Act law, the tax year of a partnership was closed with respect to a partner whose entire interest was sold, exchanged or liquidated, but did not terminate with respect to a partner upon the death of the partner. Thus, a deceased partner's share of partnership items for the partnership year in which he dies was taxed to his successor, rather than on the deceased partner's final return. (FTC 2d/FIN ¶ B-4200; USTR ¶ 7064.02; TaxDesk ¶ 59,250)

New Law. The partnership year terminates with respect to a partner whose interest terminates by death, liquidation, or otherwise. (Code Sec. 706(c)(2)(A) as amended by '97 Act §1246(a)) The '97 Act does not change the effect of a transfer of a partnership interest by a debtor to the debtor's estate under the Chapters 7 or 11 of the Bankruptcy Code. (Com Rept, see ¶ 5229)

> *observation:* Where the partnership tax year is not a calendar year, the closing of the partnership tax year with respect to the deceased partner may cause a "bunching" of income, i.e., the deceased partner's final return will have to include more than one full year's income.

> *illustration:* A, a calendar year individual partner in a partnership that has a Feb. 28 tax year, dies on July 4, Year 2. The partnership's tax year closes on July 4, Year 2 with respect to A. A's final return is required to include the income earned by the partnership in its full fiscal tax year ending Feb. 28, Year 2 and the income earned in the short period Mar. 1-July 4, Year 2.

☐ **Effective:** For partnership tax years beginning after Dec. 31, '97('97 Act §1246(c))

¶ 1426. IRS regs can treat a domestic partnership as a foreign partnership

Code Sec. 7701(a)(4), as amended by '97 Act § 1151(a)
Generally effective: For partnerships created after regulations are filed or a notice published
Committee Reports, see ¶ 5182

A partnership is a domestic partnership if it was created or organized in the U.S. or under the laws of the U.S. or any State. A foreign partnership is any partnership that isn't a domestic partnership. Pre-'97 Act law didn't grant IRS specific authority to issue regulations under which an otherwise domestic partnership could be classified as a foreign partnership where that treatment would be more appropriate. (FTC 2d/FIN ¶ O-1006.1)

New Law. The definition of what is a domestic partnership (i.e., one created or organized in the U.S. under the laws of the U.S. or a State) is modified to provide that this categorization as a domestic partnership won't apply if IRS regulations provide

FTC 2d References are to Federal Tax Coordinator 2d
FIN References are to RIA's Analysis of Federal Taxes: Income
USTR References are to United States Tax Reporter: Income, Estate & Gift, and Excise
PCA References are to Pension Coordinator and Pension & Benefits Expert/Advisor
PE References are to Pension and Profit Sharing 2nd
EP References are to Estate Planning & Taxation Coordinator and Estate Planning Advisor

Research Institute of America 353

otherwise. (Code Sec. 7701(a)(4) as amended by '97 Act §1151(a)) Thus, IRS is granted regulatory authority to provide rules treating a partnership as a domestic or foreign partnership where that treatment is more appropriate without regards to where the partnership is created or organized. (Com Rept, see ¶ 5182)

Congress expects that a recharacterization of a partnership as foreign rather than domestic under regulations will be based only on material factors such as the residence of the partners and the extent to which the partnership is engaged in business in the U.S. or earns U.S. source income. Congress expects that any regulations will provide guidance regarding the determination of whether an entity that's a partnership for federal income tax purposes is to be considered to be created or organized in the U.S. or under the law of the U.S. or any state. Congress also expects that any regulations will avoid a period-by-period reclassification of partnerships. (Com Rept, see ¶ 5182).

Congress intends that the general rule for classifying a partnership as domestic or foreign will continue to be determined by the place where the partnership is created or organized (or the law under which it's created or organized). These regulations are expected to provide a different classification result only in unusual cases. (Com Rept, see ¶ 5182)

☐ **Effective:** Any regulation issued with respect to this provision will apply to partnerships created or organized after the date determined under Code Sec. 7805(b) (dealing with when regulations can be issued retroactively), without regard to Code Sec. 7805(b)(2) (which provides an exception to the general prohibition against issuing retroactively effective regs for promptly issued regulations). ('97 Act §1151(b)) Thus, regulations issued under this regulatory authority will apply only to partnerships created or organized after the date these regulations are filed with the Federal Register (or, if earlier, the dated of a public notice substantially describing the expected contents of the regulations). These regulations won't apply to pre-existing partnerships. (Com Rept, see ¶ 5182)

¶ 1427. "Electing 1987 partnerships" continue exception from treatment as corporations but must pay 3.5% tax on gross income

Code Sec. 7704(g), as amended by '97 Act § 964(a)
Generally effective: Tax years beginning after Dec. 31, '97
Committee Reports, see ¶ 5085

For tax purposes, a publicly traded partnership (also known as a master limited partnership) is treated as a corporation. There are exceptions for publicly traded partnerships that have substantial amounts of passive-type income and for "existing publicly traded partnerships," i.e., publicly traded partnerships that were in existence on Dec. 17, '87 and that don't acquire a substantial new line of business. An existing publicly traded partnership won't be treated as a corporation until tax years beginning after Dec. 31, '97. (FTC 2d/FIN ¶ D-1322; USTR ¶ 77,044.03)

New Law. The rule treating a publicly traded partnership as a corporation doesn't apply to an electing 1987 partnership (defined below). (Code Sec. 7704(g)(1) as amended by '97 Act §964(a)) An electing 1987 partnership pays a tax equal to 3.5% of its gross income for the tax year from the active conduct of trades or businesses by the partnership. (Code Sec. 7704(g)(3)(A)) This 3.5% gross income tax is intended to approximate the corporate tax that would be imposed if the electing 1987 partnership was treated as a corporation. (Com Rept, see ¶ 5085)

Although the tax is imposed under Code Sec. 7704, which is in Chapter 29 of the Code, the tax is treated as imposed under Chapter 1 (normal taxes and surtaxes) other than for purposes of determining the amount of any credit allowable under Chapter 1. (Code Sec. 7704(g)(3)(C)) Thus, this gross income tax cannot be offset by tax credits. (Com Rept, see ¶ 5085)

In the case of a partnership which is a partner in another partnership (a tiered partnership), the gross income upon which the 3.5% tax is imposed includes the partnership's distributive share of the gross income of the other partnership from the active conduct of trades and businesses of the other partnership. A similar rule applies in the case of lower-tiered partnerships. (Code Sec. 7704(g)(3)(B))

Electing 1987 partnership defined. An electing 1987 partnership is any publicly-traded partnership if—

. . . the partnership is an existing partnership as defined in Sec. 10211(c)(2) of the Revenue Reconciliation Act of 1987 (Code Sec. 7704(g)(2)(A)), see (FTC 2d/FIN ¶ D-1323; USTR ¶ 77,044.03)

. . . the rule in Code Sec. 7704(a) treating a publicly traded partnership as a corporation hasn't applied (and without regard to the passive-type income exception of Code Sec. 7704(c)(1) wouldn't have applied) to the partnership for all prior tax years beginning after Dec. 31, '87, and before Jan. 1, '98 (Code Sec. 7704(g)(2)(B)), and

. . . the partnership elects to have the '97 Act provision apply and consents to the application of the 3.5% gross income tax for its first tax year beginning after Dec. 31, '97. (Code Sec. 7704(g)(2)(C))

A partnership treated as an electing 1987 partnership ceases to be so treated (and the election to have the '97 Act provision apply ceases to be in effect) as of the first day after Dec. 31, '97 on which there has been an addition of a substantial new line of business with respect to the partnership. (Code Sec. 7704(g)(2))

An election and consent applies to the tax year for which made and all later tax years unless revoked by the partnership. An electing 1987 partnership that wants to revoke its election may do so without IRS consent. However, once an election is revoked it may not be reinstated. (Code Sec. 7704(g)(4))

FTC 2d References are to Federal Tax Coordinator 2d
FIN References are to RIA's Analysis of Federal Taxes: Income
USTR References are to United States Tax Reporter: Income, Estate & Gift, and Excise
PCA References are to Pension Coordinator and Pension & Benefits Expert/Advisor
PE References are to Pension and Profit Sharing 2nd
EP References are to Estate Planning & Taxation Coordinator and Estate Planning Advisor

observation: Neither the statutory language nor the Committee Report explain how the election is made.

☐ **Effective:** For tax years beginning after Dec. 31, '97. ('97 Act §964(b))

¶ 1500. Corporations

Corporate Organizations, Reorganizations, Divisions and Redemptions

¶ 1501. Rules for tax-free divisions modified

Code Sec. 355(e), as amended by '97 Act § 1012(a)
Code Sec. 355(f), as amended by '97 Act § 1012(b)(1)
Code Sec. 358(g), as amended by '97 Act § 1012(b)(2)
Code Sec. 351(c), as amended by '97 Act § 1012(c)(1)
Code Sec. 368(a)(2)(H), as amended by '97 Act § 1012(c)(2)
Generally effective: Distributions after April 16, '97 and transfers after Aug. 5, '97
Committee Reports, see ¶ 5117

Generally, a corporation recognizes gain on property (including stock of a subsidiary) that it distributes to its shareholders, as if the property had been sold for its fair market value. Such a distribution is also taxable to the shareholders. If certain requirements are satisfied, however, an exception is available for corporate divisions where a corporation distributes "control"of a subsidiary corporation to its shareholders. For this purpose, "control" is the ownership of 80% of the voting stock of all classes of stock entitled to vote and 80% of the total number of shares of all other classes of stock ("80% control"). If the requirements for a tax-free division are satisfied, the distribution is tax-free to the shareholders and also, generally, to the distributing corporation.

In order to effect such a tax-free division of a business which is not already in a separate subsidiary corporation, the business must first be contributed to such a subsidiary. In that case, the contribution and subsequent distribution will only qualify for tax-free treatment if, after the contribution, the parent corporation is in "control" of the subsidiary. "Control" for this purpose is, however, defined differently than the 80% control which applies to distributions; under pre-'97 Act law, it referred to the ownership (taking into account certain attribution rules) of stock with at least 50% of the total value *or* total voting power of all stock.

Under pre-'97 Act law, it was possible to dispose of one of several businesses on a tax-free basis, by combining a tax-free division with an acquisition of either the distributing corporation or the controlled corporation in a reorganization.

> ✪ *observation:* Transactions which were designed to accomplish this have been popularly referred to as "Morris Trust" transactions, after an early case in which the basic technique was held to result in tax-free treatment. It has been reported that some corporations have used this technique to achieve the

FTC 2d References are to Federal Tax Coordinator 2d
FIN References are to RIA's Analysis of Federal Taxes: Income
USTR References are to United States Tax Reporter: Income, Estate & Gift, and Excise
PCA References are to Pension Coordinator and Pension & Benefits Expert/Advisor
PE References are to Pension and Profit Sharing 2nd
EP References are to Estate Planning & Taxation Coordinator and Estate Planning Advisor

economic equivalent of a cash sale, while still preserving tax-free treatment, by borrowing and then distributing the businesses subject to the debt, while retaining the proceeds of the borrowing.

Under pre-'97 Act law, there was no prohibition on tax-free divisions within an affiliated group. (FTC 2d/FIN ¶ F-4608, ¶ F-2707, ¶ F-4707; USTR ¶ 3554.01, ¶ 3514.05, ¶ 3684.13; TaxDesk ¶ 23,737, 23,754)

New Law.

Tax-free divisions in connection with acquisitions. If stock of a controlled corporation is distributed in a transaction that qualifies as a tax-free corporate division and either the distributing corporation or the controlled corporation is acquired in a transaction to which the rule applies (see below), stock or securities of the controlled corporation are not treated as "qualified property." (Code Sec. 355(e)(1) as amended by '97 Act §1012(a)) This results in recognition of gain by the *distributing* corporation as if it had sold the stock or securities of the controlled corporation for fair market value immediately before the distribution. (Com Rept, see ¶ 5117)

> *illustration (1):* P owns 100% of the stock of S, with a basis of $100,000 and a value of $200,000. It distributes all of the stock to its shareholders in a transaction that qualifies as a tax-free division. S is acquired in a transaction to which the gain recognition rule applies. Under the '97 Act, the stock of S is not treated as qualified property, with the consequence that P recognizes $100,000 of gain immediately before the distribution.

> *illustration (2):* P owns 100% of the stock of S, with a basis of $100,000 and a value of $200,000. It distributes all of the stock to its shareholders in a transaction that qualifies as a tax-free division. P is acquired in a transaction to which the gain recognition rule applies. Under the '97 Act, the stock of S is not treated as qualified property, with the consequence that P recognizes $100,000 of gain immediately before the distribution.

> *observation:* The acquisition of the distributing corporation or the acquired corporation does not affect the tax treatment of the distribution to the shareholders.

> *observation:* Where the business to be retained is not already in a separate corporation from the business which is to be acquired, there is a choice of which business to distribute. Since the gain recognized will always be with respect to stock of the *controlled* corporation, this choice presents significant planning opportunities, particularly where the amount of unrealized gain in each of the two businesses differs.

> *illustration (3):* P corporation operates two businesses, business A and business B. Business A consists of assets with a basis of zero and a fair market value of $100,000. Business B consists of assets with a basis and a fair market value of $100,000. Corporation X wishes to acquire only business A in a transaction to which the gain recognition rules apply.

One approach is for P to contribute business A to newly formed subsidiary S in exchange for S stock, distribute the S stock to P's shareholders, and then have X acquire S. In that case, P will take the S stock with a basis of zero (equal to P's basis in the assets constituting business A), and will therefore recognize $100,000 of gain. Alternatively, P could contribute business B to S, distribute the S stock to P's shareholders, and then have X acquire P. In that case, P will take the S stock with a basis of $100,000 (P's basis in the business B assets), so that no gain is recognized despite application of the new rule.

✐ caution: An acquisition of the *controlled* corporation (S, in the above Illustration), could, under pre-'97 Act law, result in the entire transaction failing to qualify as a tax-free division if the division and the acquisition were integrated under normal step-transaction principles. This is not changed by the '97 Act. Therefore, if it desired to have the controlled corporation acquired, negotiations for the acquisition should not begin until after the separation has been completed.

No adjustment to the basis of the stock or assets of either corporation is allowed by reason of the recognition of gain. However, if the corporation recognizing the gain is an S corporation, the shareholder may be entitled to a step-up in basis under Code Sec. 1367. (Com Rept, see ¶ 5117)

Acquisitions to which the gain recognition rule applies. The gain recognition rule applies if (1) stock of the controlled corporation is distributed in a transaction which qualifies for nonrecognition of gain by the shareholders and security holders in whole or in part, (Code Sec. 355(e)(2)(A)(i)) and (2) the distribution is part of a plan or series of related transactions pursuant to which one or more persons acquire, directly or indirectly, a 50% or greater interest (measured by either vote or value (Code Sec. 355(e)(4)(A))) in either the distributing corporation or any controlled corporation. (Code Sec. 355(e)(2)(A)(ii)) Such an acquisition can occur by virtue of a public offering, if of sufficient size. (Com Rept, see ¶ 5117)

✐ observation: Although the new rule was developed in response to transactions in which a tax-free division was followed by a tax-free acquisition in a reorganization, the rule also applies to tax-free divisions in conjunction with taxable acquisitions. However, even under pre-'97 Act law, a taxable acquisition of either corporation would, if integrated with the distribution, generally disqualify the distribution as a tax-free division, and this result is generally not changed by the '97 Act.

FTC 2d References are to Federal Tax Coordinator 2d
FIN References are to RIA's Analysis of Federal Taxes: Income
USTR References are to United States Tax Reporter: Income, Estate & Gift, and Excise
PCA References are to Pension Coordinator and Pension & Benefits Expert/Advisor
PE References are to Pension and Profit Sharing 2nd
EP References are to Estate Planning & Taxation Coordinator and Estate Planning Advisor

If an acquisition of such an interest actually occurs during the four-year period beginning two years before the distribution, the acquisition is presumed to be pursuant to such a plan, unless the taxpayer establishes to the contrary. (Code Sec. 355(e)(2)(B))

> *observation:* There is no safe-harbor for an acquisition that takes place outside the four-year period. Thus, if an actual plan exists which encompasses both a distribution and an acquisition, the gain recognition rule applies even if the acquisition occurs outside the four-year period.

If the assets of the distributing corporation or the controlled corporation are acquired in an "A" (merger), "C" (assets for voting stock), or "D" (assets for control) reorganization, or in a transaction specified in regs, then, except as provided in regs, shareholders of the acquiring corporation immediately before the acquisition are treated as acquiring stock in the transferor. (Code Sec. 355(e)(3)(B))

> *observation:* Thus, the gain recognition rule also applies where there is a tax-free acquisition of assets, rather than stock, of the distributing or controlled corporation.

Exceptions to gain recognition. The new gain recognition rule does not apply if, immediately after the completion of the plan (or series of related transactions) to acquire a 50% or greater interest, the distributing corporation and all controlled corporations are members of a single "affiliated group" (as defined in Code Sec. 1504 without regard to Code Sec. 1504(b)). (Code Sec. 355(e)(2)(C))

> *observation:* Corporations that are ineligible to join in filing a consolidated return (e.g., foreign corporations or certain insurance companies) are included as members of an "affiliated group" under this definition.

> *observation:* This exception applies even if the distributing corporation is acquired by another corporation, provided that the distributing corporation and the controlled corporation are part of the same group.

> *Illustration:* P owns all of the stock of S and S owns all of the stock of S1. P is merged into X in a transaction in which the former shareholders of P receive 25% of X's only class of stock. As part of the plan, S1 is distributed by S to X. Gain is not recognized, because S (the distributing corporation) and S1 (the controlled corporation) remain part of the same affiliated group. It does not matter that the ownership of the P group has changed. (Com Rept, see ¶ 5117)

> *observation:* In the above Illustration, it would not matter if S or S1 were a foreign corporation or an insurance company and, therefore, ineligible to join in filing a consolidated return.

The new gain recognition rule also does not apply to:

• distributions in bankruptcy or certain non-bankruptcy workout proceedings (Code Sec. 355(e)(4)(B)); or

- distributions to which Code Sec. 355(d) applies. (Code Sec. 355(e)(2)(D))

> **⟲ observation:** Code Sec. 355(d), which applies in certain circumstances where stock has been recently acquired, imposes corporate-level gain recognition on the distributing corporation with respect to appreciation in the controlled corporation. Thus, this exception avoids double-counting of the same gain under two different provisions.

In addition, except as provided in regs, the following acquisitions of stock are not taken into account in determining whether the gain recognition rule applies:

(i) The acquisition of stock in any controlled corporation by the distributing corporation. (Code Sec. 355(e)(3)(A)(i))

> **⟲ observation:** Thus, gain recognition is not triggered under this rule if, shortly before the distribution, the distributing corporation (1) acquired stock for property contributed to a controlled corporation that was organized for purposes of the distribution, or (2) acquired additional stock in a pre-existing controlled corporation.

(ii) The acquisition of stock in any controlled corporation by reason of holding stock or securities in the distributing corporation. (Code Sec. 355(e)(3)(A)(ii))

> **⟲ observation:** This covers the distribution itself, in which shareholders or security holders of the distributing corporation acquire stock of the controlled corporation. Were it not for this exception, all tax-free divisions would become subject to the gain recognition rules.

(iii) The acquisition of stock in a successor corporation of the distributing corporation or a controlled corporation by reason of holding stock or securities in such corporation. (Code Sec. 355(e)(3)(A)(iii))

(iv) The acquisition of stock in a corporation if shareholders who own, directly or indirectly, more than 50% (by both vote and value) of the distributing corporation or the controlled corporation before the acquisition own, directly or indirectly, more than 50% of such distributing or controlled corporation thereafter. (Code Sec. 355(e)(3)(A)(iv))

> **⟲ observation:** Although the Code provides that, for this exception to apply, the same persons must own more than 50% of *either* the controlled corporation or the distributing corporation, the Committee Report appears to state that the ownership requirement must be satisfied with respect to *both* such corporations. (Com Rept, see ¶ 5117)

FTC 2d References are to Federal Tax Coordinator 2d
FIN References are to RIA's Analysis of Federal Taxes: Income
USTR References are to United States Tax Reporter: Income, Estate & Gift, and Excise
PCA References are to Pension Coordinator and Pension & Benefits Expert/Advisor
PE References are to Pension and Profit Sharing 2nd
EP References are to Estate Planning & Taxation Coordinator and Estate Planning Advisor

Illustration (1):   Individual A owns all of the stock of both P corporation and Q corporation. P owns all of the stock of S. P distributes the stock of S to A in a transaction which qualifies as a tax-free division, and, as part of the plan, P merges into Q. Recognition is not required because A owns more than 50% of both Q (the successor to P) and S both before and after the transaction. (Com Rept, see ¶ 5117)

Illustration (2):   Individual A owns all of the stock of P corporation, which in turn owns all of the stock of S. P distributes the stock of S to A in a transaction which qualifies as a tax-free division, and, as part of the plan, A transfers the stock of P to his wholly-owned holding company. Recognition is not required. (Com Rept, see ¶ 5117)

observation: This exception also appears to cover situations where either the distributing corporation or the controlled corporation is acquired by a smaller corporation.

illustration (3):   P corporation distributes all of the stock of S corporation to P shareholders in a transaction which qualifies as a tax-free division. As part of the plan, X corporation (which is otherwise unrelated) acquires all of the stock of P in exchange for X stock (in a B reorganization or otherwise). Because X was smaller than P, P shareholders wind up with X stock which represents an indirect greater than 50% interest in P. There is no acquisition which triggers gain recognition.

However, exceptions (i) through (iv) do not apply to any acquisition if the stock that was held before the acquisition was acquired pursuant to a plan to acquire a 50% or greater interest in the stock of the distributing corporation or the controlled corporation. (Code Sec. 355(e)(3))

Other rules.   In applying the gain recognition rule,

• all persons who are related (within the meaning of Code Sec. 267(b) or Code Sec. 707(b)(1)) are treated as one person   (Code Sec. 355(e)(4)(C)(i)),

• the attribution rules of Code Sec. 318(a)(2) apply, but, except as provided in regs, Code Sec. 318(a)(2)(C) applies without regard to a 50% or more stock threshold (Code Sec. 355(e)(4)(C)(ii)), and

• any reference to a controlled corporation or a distributing corporation includes a reference to a predecessor or successor corporation. (Code Sec. 355(e)(4)(D))

The limitations period for assessing a deficiency on gain recognized by virtue of this rule is extended until the expiration of three years from the date IRS is notified by the taxpayer (as provided in regs) that the distribution occurred (Code Sec. 355(e)(4)(E)(i)), and the deficiency may be assessed within such period notwithstanding any other law or rule of law that would otherwise have prevented the assessment. (Code Sec. 355(e)(4)(E)(ii))

IRS can issue regs necessary to carry out the purposes of this provision (Code Sec. 355(e)(5)), including regs:

- providing for its application where there is more than one controlled corporation, (Code Sec. 355(e)(5)(A))

- treating two or more distributions as one distribution where necessary to prevent avoidance of the purposes of the rule, (Code Sec. 355(e)(5)(B)) and

- providing for the application of rules under which the running of the four-year period would be suspended while a holder's risk of loss is substantially diminished. (Code Sec. 355(e)(5)(C))

Distributions within an affiliated group. A tax-free division is no longer available for distributions from one member of an affiliated group (as defined in Code Sec. 1504(a)) to another member of the group, except as provided in regs, if the distribution is part of a plan under which one or more persons acquire, directly or indirectly, a 50% or greater interest (measured by either vote or value) in either the distributing corporation or the controlled corporation, determined after the application of the gain recognition rules of Code Sec. 355(e) (described above). (Code Sec. 355(f) as amended by '97 Act §1012(b))

> *observation:* The "plan" which results in application of this rule is defined by reference to Code Sec. 355(e)(2)(A)(ii), which applies for purposes of the gain recognition rule for tax-free divisions in connection with acquisitions (see above). It appears, but is not entirely clear, that the four-year presumption for the existence of such a plan (contained in Code Sec. 355(e)(2)(B), which is not specifically incorporated by reference) should apply for this purpose as well.

> *observation:* The definition of "affiliated group" for purposes of this rule is that which applies in determining eligibility to file consolidated returns. Thus, corporations that are ineligible to join in filling such a return (e.g., foreign corporations) are excluded. By contrast, the exception to gain recognition where the distributing corporation and the controlled corporation remain part of the same "affiliated group" (described above) includes such corporations.

> *observation:* This rule is directed, in part, at transactions carried out under pre-'97 Act law in which money was borrowed by a controlled corporation and distributed to its parent as a dividend. The stock of the controlled corporation was then distributed within the consolidated group in a tax-free division. Under the consolidated return regs, (1) the dividend was eliminated in consolidation, (2) to the extent the dividend distribution exceeded the parent's basis in the controlled corporation, it created an excess loss account, and (3) the excess loss account was apparently eliminated when the tax-free division occurred. The net result was that the parent could then dispose of the stock of the controlled corporation effectively free of tax.

FTC 2d References are to Federal Tax Coordinator 2d
FIN References are to RIA's Analysis of Federal Taxes: Income
USTR References are to United States Tax Reporter: Income, Estate & Gift, and Excise
PCA References are to Pension Coordinator and Pension & Benefits Expert/Advisor
PE References are to Pension and Profit Sharing 2nd
EP References are to Estate Planning & Taxation Coordinator and Estate Planning Advisor

illustration: P, the common parent of an affiliated group, owns 100% of the stock of S1 which in turn owns 100% of the stock of S2. P's basis in the stock of S1 is $100,000, and S1's basis in the stock of S2 is $50,000. S1 and S2 both have a value of $500,000. S2 borrows $500,000 and distributes the proceeds to S1 (thus reducing the equity value of S2 to zero). Under the consolidated return regs, the dividend is eliminated from S1's income, reduces S1's basis in S2 to zero, and creates an excess loss account of $450,000. Under pre-'97 Act law, S1 could distribute the stock of S2 to P in a tax-free corporate division. If it did so, P's $100,000 basis in stock of S1 was allocated between stock of S1 and S2 in proportion to relative fair market value, and, under the consolidated return regs, the excess loss account was eliminated. If P later sold the stock of S2 for its nominal equity value (effectively zero) it would recognize no gain. The next result is that S1 would have received $500,000 in loan proceeds totally free of tax. Under the '97 Act, if the disposition of S2 and the distribution are part of a plan this result is precluded because the elimination of the excess loss account is only available if the division is tax-free—which it no longer is.

observation: The application of Code Sec. 355(e) incorporates all of the exceptions to the gain recognition rules. Thus, for example, gain is not recognized if the distributing corporation and the controlled corporations remain part of the same "affiliated group." (Com Rept, see ¶ 5117)

observation: A distribution of a controlled corporation outside the "affiliated group" can disqualify a transaction in its entirety, even with respect to another corporation that is distributed within the group and never leaves the group.

Illustration: Corporation P owns 100% of the stock of S, which owns 100% of the stock of S1. S1 is distributed by S to P, which in turn distributes S to P's shareholders. As part of the same plan, P merges into X, an unrelated corporation. The result is that X owns S1 and P's former shareholders own S. Since S has left the affiliated group, the intragroup distribution of S1 does not qualify as a tax free division. (Com Rept, see ¶ 5117)

IRS has authority to issue regs which would allow transactions which would otherwise be disqualified under these rules to continue to qualify as tax-free divisions. Such regs might be issued in connection with the issuance of basis adjustment regs, as discussed below. (Com Rept, see ¶ 5117)

Basis adjustments. If there is a distribution of stock of a controlled corporation from one member of an "affiliated group" to another member of the group and such distribution does qualify as a tax-free division, IRS may provide adjustments to the adjusted basis of any stock in a corporation which is a member of such group and is held by another member of the group to reflect the proper treatment of the distribution. (Code Sec. 358(g))

Under this authority, IRS may require a carryover basis within the group for stock of the distributed corporation (including a carryover of the excess loss account, if any). IRS may also provide a reduction in the basis of stock of the distributing corporation to reflect the change in the value and basis of the distributing corporation's assets. Also, IRS may determine that the aggregate stock basis of the distributing and controlled corporation after the distribution may be adjusted to an amount that is less than the basis of the stock of the distributing corporation before the distribution to prevent a potential for artificial losses or diminished gain on disposition of any corporation involved. In addition, IRS may provide separate regs for corporations in affiliated groups filling consolidated returns and for affiliated groups not filing a consolidated return. It is expected that the regs will be applied prospectively, except to prevent abuse. (Com Rept, see ¶ 5117)

Determination of "control" in divisive transactions. Where property is transferred to a corporation as part of a plan to distribute stock of that corporation in a tax-free division, the control test which applies in determining whether the transfer of property is tax-free has been modified. Under the '97 act, "control" for this purpose is satisfied if, after the distribution, the shareholders of the distributing corporation (who received stock of the controlled corporation in the distribution) own more than 50% of the stock of the controlled corporation, measured by both vote *and* value (without application of any attribution rules). (Code Sec. 351(c)(2) as amended by '97 Act §1012(c)(1)); (Code Sec. 368(a)(2)(H)(ii) as amended by '97 Act §1012(c)(2)) This does not change the independent requirement that 80% "control" be distributed in order for the *distribution* to be tax-free. It is expected that the new definition of control will be applied in a way that would prevent a tax-free distribution of a less than 80% owned subsidiary, but would not impose additional restrictions on post-distribution restructurings. (Com Rept, see ¶ 5117)

> *observation:* If the transfer of property to the controlled corporation does not satisfy the control requirement, the tax-free nature of the distribution is also likely to be jeopardized.

> *observation:* Effectively, this provision seems designed to conform the treatment of acquisitions of newly-formed controlled corporations (which require a transfer of property to the controlled corporation) to acquisitions of pre-existing subsidiaries.

> *observation:* The change made by the '97 Act both liberalizes and tightens the rules applicable to control. On the one hand, unlike pre-'97 Act law, an integrated disposition or other transaction which causes the shareholders to lose 80% control will not cause the distribution to become taxable unless it also causes the new 50% control test to be violated. On the other hand, the 50% test itself is now more difficult to satisfy, since it requires ownership of

FTC 2d References are to Federal Tax Coordinator 2d
FIN References are to RIA's Analysis of Federal Taxes: Income
USTR References are to United States Tax Reporter: Income, Estate & Gift, and Excise
PCA References are to Pension Coordinator and Pension & Benefits Expert/Advisor
PE References are to Pension and Profit Sharing 2nd
EP References are to Estate Planning & Taxation Coordinator and Estate Planning Advisor

Research Institute of America 365

more than 50% measured by both vote and value. Even if this provision were not present, most transactions which resulted in a loss of 50% control would result in corporate-level taxation upon the distribution, under the rules discussed above relating to tax-free divisions followed by acquisitions. Thus the practical significance of this provision is that, by disqualifying the transfer of property, and hence the distribution, as tax-free, tax is imposed at the shareholder level as well.

illustration (1): Corporation P owns two businesses, Q and R. It contributes business Q to newly-formed corporation S, in exchange for 100% of the sole class of stock of S. It then distributes the S stock to its shareholders in a transaction which otherwise meets the requirements for a tax-free division. The shareholders, pursuant to a pre-existing binding agreement, dispose of 30% of such stock. Under pre-'97 Act law, the disposition was considered to result in a failure to satisfy the requirement that 80% control requirement be distributed. As a result, the distribution did not qualify as a tax-free division, and tax was imposed at both the corporate and shareholder levels.

Under the '97 Act, because shareholders of P continue to own more than 50% of S (measured by both vote and value), the transaction is tax-free.

illustration (2): Corporation P owns two businesses, Q and R. It contributes business Q to newly-formed corporation S, in exchange for 100% of the sole class of stock of S. It then distributes the S stock to its shareholders in a transaction which otherwise meets the requirements for a tax-free division. Pursuant to a pre-arranged plan, S then issues, in a private placement, a second class of stock to a third party. This second class of stock has 75% of the aggregate value, but only 10% of the aggregate voting power, of all S stock. The net result is that P shareholders who received S stock in the distribution wind up with 90% of the voting power and 25% of the value of S.

Under pre-'97 Act law, the 50% control test applicable to the transfer of Q to S was satisfied, since 50% by vote *or* value was sufficient. Moreover, the 80% control test applicable to the distribution was satisfied, since, with respect to voting stock, that test looked (and continues to look) only to voting power. Hence, both the transfer of Q to S and the distribution of S stock were tax-free to both P and its shareholders.

Under the '97 Act, the pre-arranged issuance of S stock causes P shareholders to own less than 50% of the value of S, so the new 50% control test is not satisfied. As a result, the transfer of Q to S results in gain recognition by P. This in turn causes the distribution of S stock to fail to qualify as a tax-free division, so that P shareholders are taxed on the distribution.

☐ **Effective:** The amendments relating to

- divisions in connection with acquisitions, and
- divisions within an affiliated group

apply to distributions after April 16, '97 pursuant to an acquisition plan with the acquisition occurring after such date. ('97 Act §1012(d)(1)). Thus, the amendments do not apply to an acquisition on or before such date, even if there is a distribution after such date that is part of a plan or series of related transactions that would otherwise be subject to the provision. (Com Rept, see ¶ 5117)

The amendments relating to the definition of control apply to transfers after Aug. 5, '97. ('97 Act §1012(d)(2))

However, the amendments do not apply to a distribution pursuant to an acquisition plan (or, in the case of the amendments to the control definition, to a transfer) after April 16, '97, if such acquisition or transfer is

• made pursuant to an agreement which was binding on such date and at all times thereafter; ('97 Act §1012(d)(3)(A))

> *observation:* Any contract that is in fact binding under state law as of April 16, '97, even though not written, is eligible for transition relief. However, it would be expected in such a case that some form of contemporaneous written evidence of the contract would be in existence. If, for example, the acceptance of the terms and conditions of a contract by a corporate board of directors creates a binding contract under state law with an acquirer, the contract and the terms and conditions presented to the board could satisfy the requirement. (Com Rept, see ¶ 5117)

• described in a ruling request submitted to the IRS on or before such date; ('97 Act §1012(d)(3)(B)) or

• described on or before such date in a public announcement or in a filing with the SEC required solely by reason of the acquisition or transfer.('97 Act §1012(d)(3)(C))

However, these exceptions are only available if the agreement, ruling request, or public announcement, or filing identifies the acquirer of the distributing corporation or any controlled corporation, or the transferee, whichever is applicable. ('97 Act §1012(d)(3)) If, before Apr. 17, '97 there was an offer and acceptance and a ruling request was filed which identified the acquirer as one of a list of potential acquirers, the transaction may be entitled to relief under the transition rules. (Com Rept, see ¶ 5117)

FTC 2d References are to Federal Tax Coordinator 2d
FIN References are to RIA's Analysis of Federal Taxes: Income
USTR References are to United States Tax Reporter: Income, Estate & Gift, and Excise
PCA References are to Pension Coordinator and Pension & Benefits Expert/Advisor
PE References are to Pension and Profit Sharing 2nd
EP References are to Estate Planning & Taxation Coordinator and Estate Planning Advisor

¶ 1502. Certain preferred stock treated as boot

Code Sec. 351(g), as amended by '97 Act § 1014(a)
Code Sec. 354(a)(2)(C), as amended by '97 Act § 1014(b)
Code Sec. 355(a)(3)(D), as amended by '97 Act § 1014(c)
Code Sec. 356(e), as amended by '97 Act § 1014(d)
Code Sec. 1036(c), as amended by '97 Act § 1014(e)(3)
Generally effective: Transactions after June 8, '97
Committee Reports, see ¶ 5119

No gain or loss is recognized if property is transferred to a controlled corporation in exchange solely for stock of such corporation. For this purpose, "control" is defined as the ownership of stock with at least 80% of the voting power of all voting stock, and at least 80% of the total number of shares of all other classes of stock. If other property is received (including securities), gain (but not loss) is recognized up to the value of that property.

Under a separate rule, if a transaction qualifies as a reorganization, gain or loss is not recognized if stock is exchanged for stock, or if securities are exchanged for stock or for securities with the same (or a lesser) principal amount. However, if other property is received, gain (but not loss) is recognized in an amount equal to the lesser of (1) the gain realized in the exchange or (2) the value of such other property. Similar rules apply to certain tax-free divisions.

Under pre-'97 Act law, these nonrecognition rules applied to preferred as well as to common stock. In addition, no gain or loss was recognized if preferred stock was exchanged for preferred stock in the same corporation, even if the exchange was not part of a reorganization. (FTC 2d/FIN ¶ F-1004, F-4010; USTR ¶ 3544.06, 3515.04; TaxDesk ¶ 23,105)

New Law. The '97 Act excludes certain preferred stock from nonrecognition treatment in these transactions.

Transfers to controlled corporations. "Nonqualified preferred stock" (defined below) is treated as boot for purposes of recognizing gain when it is received in exchange for property transferred to a controlled corporation. (Code Sec. 351(g)(1) as amended by '97 Act §1014(a))

> *observation:* Therefore, gain (but not loss) is recognized up to the fair market value of the "nonqualified preferred stock."

> *observation:* This effectively precludes the use of so-called "National Starch" acquisitive Code Sec. 351 transactions, which, under pre-'97 Act law, enabled some shareholders of an acquired corporation to receive tax-free treatment even though the overall transaction did not qualify as a reorganization. Under the "National Starch" structure, the shareholders who did not want to recognize gain transferred their target stock to a new holding company in exchange for holding company redeemable preferred stock; simultaneously, the acquiror contributed cash in exchange for holding company common stock.

The holding company then used the cash to acquire the remaining stock of the target. Under pre-'97 Act law, the contribution of target stock to the holding company was tax-free because the transferors (including the acquiror, which contributed cash) were, collectively, in control of the holding company after the transfers. Under the '97 Act, this technique is available only if the preferred stock is not nonqualified preferred stock.

observation: "Nonqualified preferred stock" resembles debt in various ways (see below) and is now treated in similar fashion for purposes of recognizing gain under Code Sec. 351(a).

"Nonqualified preferred stock" continues to be treated as stock for purposes of determining whether the control test of Code Sec. 368(c) is satisfied, unless (and until) regs are issued providing for a different result. Thus, a person who receives "nonqualified preferred stock" and other stock in exchange for property transferred to a corporation is not required to recognize gain on the value of the other stock if, taking the "nonqualified preferred stock" into account, the control test is satisfied. In addition, the "nonqualified preferred stock" may enable other transferors to satisfy the control test. (Com Rept, see ¶ 5119)

Reorganizations. "Nonqualified preferred stock" received in a reorganization in exchange for stock other than "nonqualified preferred stock" is not treated as stock or securities. (Code Sec. 354(a)(2)(C)(i) as amended by '97 Act §1014(b)) Instead, it is other property (i.e., "boot") on which gain (but not loss) is recognized when it is received in a reorganization exchange. (Code Sec. 356(e) as amended by '97 Act §1014(d))

In the case of a reorganization, the treatment of "nonqualified preferred stock" as boot only applies where it is received in exchange for other stock. Thus, it does not apply if "nonqualified preferred stock" is:

- received in exchange for comparable preferred stock (of no greater value),
- transferred in exchange for common stock, or
- received in exchange for debt securities of the same or lesser value. (Com Rept, see ¶ 5119)

observation: The Committee Reports say that "nonqualified preferred stock" received in exchange for "comparable" preferred stock is not boot, without specifying what is "comparable." Based on the statutory language, however, "nonqualified preferred stock" *received* in exchange for any stock which is not also "nonqualified preferred stock" would be a taxable receipt of boot. However, the *transfer* of "nonqualified preferred stock" in exchange for any stock, including common stock and regular preferred stock, would not

FTC 2d References are to Federal Tax Coordinator 2d
FIN References are to RIA's Analysis of Federal Taxes: Income
USTR References are to United States Tax Reporter: Income, Estate & Gift, and Excise
PCA References are to Pension Coordinator and Pension & Benefits Expert/Advisor
PE References are to Pension and Profit Sharing 2nd
EP References are to Estate Planning & Taxation Coordinator and Estate Planning Advisor

produce boot.

observation: Securities received in exchange for other securities in a reorganization are tax-free to the extent that the *principal amount* of the securities received does not exceed that of the securities surrendered. Where nonqualified preferred stock is received in exchange for comparable preferred stock, it is tax-free to the extent the *value* is no greater than that of the stock surrendered. Thus, while the treatment of nonqualified preferred stock is somewhat comparable to that of debt securities, it is not identical.

If "nonqualified preferred stock" is received in a transaction that is both a transfer to a controlled corporation, where its receipt is taxable, and a reorganization, where it may be received tax-free in exchange for like stock, the conflict generally is to be resolved by applying the reorganization provisions. (Com Rept, see ¶ 5119)

illustration: S owns "nonqualified preferred stock" and common stock in T. T transfers substantially all of its properties to P in exchange for common stock and "nonqualified preferred stock" in P. As part of the same transaction, X, an unrelated party, transfers property to P in exchange for P stock. Together, S and X are, immediately after the transfers, in "control" of P. T completely liquidates, distributing to S the common stock and the nonqualified preferred stock of P which it received as consideration. The "nonqualified preferred stock" in P which S receives is equivalent in value to the "nonqualified preferred stock" in T which it surrendered. The transaction is covered by Code Sec. 351(a), under which the receipt of the "nonqualified preferred stock" is taxable to S, and is also a reorganization under Code Sec. 368(a)(1)(C), under which such stock may be received tax-free. The "nonqualified preferred stock" is received tax-free.

The rule which treats "nonqualified preferred stock" as boot does not apply to recapitalizations of family-owned corporations. (Code Sec. 354(a)(2)(C)(ii)(I) as amended by '97 Act §1014(b)) To qualify for this exception, the corporation must satisfy the family-ownership requirements of Code Sec. 447(d)(2)(C) (except as provided in regs) for five years before and three years after the recapitalization. Periods during which a family member's risk of loss in holding the stock is reduced (under the rules of Code Sec. 355(d)(6)(B)) are excluded. (Code Sec. 354(a)(2)(C)(ii)(II))

Tax-free divisions. "Nonqualified preferred stock" received in a tax-free corporate division described in Code Sec. 355(a) as a distribution on stock other than "nonqualified preferred stock" is not treated as stock or securities. (Code Sec. 355(a)(3)(D) as amended by '97 Act §1014(c)) Instead, it is boot. (Code Sec. 356(e))

observation: Consequently, the shareholder recognizes gain (which may be treated as a dividend).

observation: This rule only applies for purposes of Code Sec. 355(a) and Code Sec. 355(b), which govern shareholder-level gain. Corporate-level recognition or nonrecognition is apparently unaffected.

Exchanges of stock in the same corporation. "Nonqualified preferred stock" is treated as property other than stock for purposes of the rule which permits tax-free exchanges of preferred stock for preferred stock of the same corporation. (Code Sec. 1036(b) as amended by '97 Act §1014(e)(3))

> **🅡 *observation:*** Thus, such an exchange is not accorded nonrecognition treatment under this provision.

> **🅡 *observation:*** This provision is apparently intended to cover the receipt of "nonqualified preferred stock" in exchange for "regular" preferred stock. However, there is no exception for "nonqualified preferred stock" received in exchange for other "nonqualified preferred stock" in the same corporation. This provision appears among "conforming amendments" but the result as to an exchange of "nonqualified preferred stock" for like stock of the same corporation is inconsistent with the nonrecognition accorded comparable exchanges in a reorganization. Since the exchange of stock for stock in the same corporation may also qualify as a recapitalization (and hence a reorganization), it is not clear that this result is intended.

Definition of "nonqualified preferred stock." "Nonqualified preferred stock" is preferred stock (defined below) that satisfies any of the following conditions:

(1) The holder of the stock has the right to require the corporation that issued the stock ("the issuer") or a person "related" to the issuer (as defined under Code Sec. 267(b) or Code Sec. 707(b) (Code Sec. 351(g)(3)(B))) to redeem or purchase the stock. (Code Sec. 351(g)(2)(A)(i) as amended by '97 Act §1014(a))

(2) The issuer or a person "related" to the issuer is required to redeem or purchase the stock. (Code Sec. 351(g)(2)(A)(ii))

(3) The issuer or a person "related" to the issuer has the right to redeem or purchase the stock and, as of the issue date of the stock, it is more likely than not that the right will be exercised. (Code Sec. 351(g)(2)(A)(iii))

(4) The dividend rate on the stock varies in whole or in part (directly or indirectly) with reference to interest rates, commodity prices, or other similar indices. (Code Sec. 351(g)(2)(A)(iv))

Congress thought that gain should be recognized on the receipt of "nonqualified preferred stock" because it is often a more secure form of investment than other stock. Thus, a put or call may determine the period within which payment is to occur. Also, a dividend rate that tracks changes in interest rates over the term of the instrument, as in the case of "auction rate" preferred stock, diminishes the risk that there will be a decline in value if interest rates rise. (Com Rept, see ¶ 5119)

FTC 2d References are to Federal Tax Coordinator 2d
FIN References are to RIA's Analysis of Federal Taxes: Income
USTR References are to United States Tax Reporter: Income, Estate & Gift, and Excise
PCA References are to Pension Coordinator and Pension & Benefits Expert/Advisor
PE References are to Pension and Profit Sharing 2nd
EP References are to Estate Planning & Taxation Coordinator and Estate Planning Advisor

observation: The first three conditions relate to the right or obligation to redeem or have stock redeemed, giving it, in effect, a fixed maturity. However, there are exceptions (below) that apply where any fixed maturity is postponed or is unlikely to be operative, or is conditioned on certain events with independent significance.

The first three conditions don't apply (i.e., to make stock "nonqualified preferred stock") if any of the following exceptions applies:

• The right or obligation can't be exercised within the 20-year period beginning on the date the stock is issued.

• The right or obligation is subject to a contingency which, as of the date the stock is issued, makes the likelihood of the redemption or purchase remote. (Code Sec. 351(g)(2)(B))

• The right or obligation may be exercised only upon the death, disability, or mental incompetency of the holder. (Code Sec. 351(g)(2)(C)(i)(I)) This exception does not apply if the stock given or received in the exchange is in a corporation any of whose stock (or stock of a "related" party) is readily tradable on an established securities market or otherwise (Code Sec. 351(g)(2)(C)(ii)(I)), or will be readily tradable as a result of a transaction or series of transactions of which the exchange is a part. (Code Sec. 351(g)(2)(C)(ii)(II))

observation: Congress was concerned that, if "nonqualified preferred stock" can be put or redeemed only at death, the shareholder would obtain a basis step-up and never recognize gain. (Com Rept, see ¶ 5119) Despite this concern, a provision that the stock can be put or redeemed only at the shareholder's death does not make the stock "nonqualified preferred stock."

• The stock was issued as reasonable compensation for services performed for the issuer or a "related" person and the right or obligation to purchase or redeem the stock may only be exercised on the holder's separation from the service of the issuer or the "related person." (Code Sec. 351(g)(2)(C)(i)(II))

"Preferred stock" is defined as stock which is limited and preferred as to dividends and does not participate in corporate growth to any significant extent. (Code Sec. 351(g)(3)(A))

observation: Thus, participating preferred stock is not covered. This is consistent with the definition of preferred stock in Code Sec. 305.

The right to convert stock into other stock of the issuing corporation does not automatically constitute participation in corporate growth to any significant extent. Stock that is convertible or exchangeable into stock of a corporation other than the issuer (e.g., into stock of a parent corporation or stock of another related corporation) is not considered to be stock that participates in corporate growth to any significant extent for purposes of this provision. (Com Rept, see ¶ 5119)

Regulatory authority. IRS has specific authority to issue regs carrying out the purposes of the provisions described above. In addition, consistent with the these sections, IRS may prescribe the treatment of "nonqualified preferred stock" under other income tax provisions (Code Sec. 351(g)(4)), e.g., Code Sec. 304, Code Sec. 306, Code Sec. 318, and Code Sec. 368(c). Until regs are issued, however, "nonqualified preferred stock" remains stock for purposes of these other sections. The regs may apply installment sale rules to "nonqualified preferred stock." (Com Rept, see ¶ 5119)

> **✔️ observation:** "Nonqualified preferred stock" to which installment sale rules apply would be treated like debt. Presumably, regs providing this result would explain how rules such as the interest charge on deferred tax liability under Code Sec. 453A and imputed interest apply in this situation.

☐ **Effective:** The amendments apply to transactions after June 8, '97. ('97 Act §1014(f)(1)) However, they do not apply to a transaction (1) made pursuant to a written agreement agreement binding on June 8, '97 and at all times after that date ('97 Act §1014(f)(2)(A)), (2) described in a ruling request submitted to IRS on or before June 8, '97 ('97 Act §1014(f)(2)(B)), or (3) described on or before June 8, '97 in a public announcement or in a filing with SEC, required solely by reason of the transaction. ('97 Act §1014(f)(2)(C))

¶ 1503. Treatment of extraordinary dividends amended

Code Sec. 1059, as amended by '97 Act § 1011
Generally effective: Distributions after May 3, '95
Committee Reports, see ¶ 5116

A corporation which receives a dividend from another corporation can deduct at least 70%, and possibly as much as 100%, of the dividend, depending on how much stock it owns in the distributing corporation. However, a corporate shareholder which receives an "extraordinary dividend" must reduce the basis of the stock with respect to which the dividend was paid by the portion of the dividend which went untaxed as a result of the dividends received deduction. Under pre-'97 Act law, the reduction in basis occurred immediately before the stock was disposed of. If the reduction in basis exceeded the basis in stock with respect to which an extraordinary dividend was paid, the excess was only taxed as gain when the stock was sold or disposed of.

Under pre-'97 Act law, an extraordinary dividend included certain dividends which were sufficiently large in proportion to the shareholder's basis in the stock with respect to which they were paid. However, such extraordinary dividends gave rise to a basis reduction only if they occurred within two years of the time the stock was acquired. In addition, dividends arising out of redemptions of stock which were part of a partial liquidation or which were not pro rata were treated as extraordinary dividends and gave rise to a basis reduction regardless of how long the stock was held.

FTC 2d References are to Federal Tax Coordinator 2d
FIN References are to RIA's Analysis of Federal Taxes: Income
USTR References are to United States Tax Reporter: Income, Estate & Gift, and Excise
PCA References are to Pension Coordinator and Pension & Benefits Expert/Advisor
PE References are to Pension and Profit Sharing 2nd
EP References are to Estate Planning & Taxation Coordinator and Estate Planning Advisor

In general, a distribution in redemption of stock is treated as a dividend, rather than as a sale of the stock, if it does not result in a sufficiently large reduction in the shareholder's proportionate interest in the distributing corporation. In making this determination, constructive ownership rules, including option attribution rules, apply. (FTC 2d/FIN ¶ P-5101, ¶ P-5103, ¶ P-5108; USTR ¶ 10,594; TaxDesk ¶ 21,622)

New Law. A reduction in basis by virtue of an extraordinary dividend is treated as occurring at the beginning of the ex-dividend date for the extraordinary dividend. (Code Sec. 1059(d)(1) as amended by '97 Act §1011(c))

When the nontaxed portion of an extraordinary dividend exceeds the basis of the stock with respect to which it was paid, gain is recognized to the extent of such excess and is includible in income for the tax year in which the extraordinary dividend is received. (Code Sec. 1059(a)(2) as amended by '97 Act §1011(a))

In addition, the definition of extraordinary dividend is expanded to include a redemption which is treated as a dividend as a result of the option attribution rules. In that case, the basis reduction applies without regard to holding period, and only the basis in the stock actually redeemed is taken into account. (Code Sec. 1059(e)(1)(A) as amended by '97 Act §1011(b))

> *observation:* The reason for the expanded rule is that Congress was concerned about reported transactions (included a widely-discussed transaction involving Seagram Co.) designed to avoid tax on distributions by using the option attribution rules to characterize a redemption as a dividend.

Reorganizations or other exchanges involving amounts that are treated as dividends under Code Sec. 356 are treated as redemptions for purposes of applying the above rules. (Code Sec. 1059(e)(1)(B))) Thus, if a recapitalization or other transaction that involves a dividend under Code Sec. 356 has the effect of a non pro rata redemption or is treated as a dividend due to options being counted as stock, the extraordinary dividend rules apply. (Com Rept, see ¶ 5116)

Redemptions of shares (or other extraordinary dividends on shares) held by a partnership are subject to these rules to the extent there are corporate partners (e.g., appropriate adjustments to the basis of the shares held by the partnership and to the basis of the corporate partner's partnership interest are required). (Com Rept, see ¶ 5116)

Congress intends no inference regarding the treatment under pre-'97 Act law of any transaction within the scope of the above amendments, including transactions utilizing options. In addition, no inference is intended regarding the rules under pre-'97 Act law (or in any case where the treatment is not specified in the '97 Act) for determining the shares of stock with respect to which a dividend is received or that experience a basis reduction. (Com Rept, see ¶ 5116)

☐ **Effective:** The new rules apply to distributions after May 3, '95, ('97 Act §1011(d)(1)) unless made pursuant to the terms of a written binding contract in effect on, or a tender offer outstanding on, that date. ('97 Act §1011(d)(2)) However, for any distribution that is not a partial liquidation, a non pro rata redemption, or a redemption that is treated as a dividend by reason of option attribution, the new rule requiring immediate gain recognition to the extent the non-taxed portion of the dividend exceeds basis applies only to distributions after Sept. 13, '95. ('97 Act §1011(d)(3))

¶ 1504. Expanded definition of investment company for purposes of transfers to partnerships and controlled corporations

Code Sec. 351(e)(1), as amended by '97 Act § 1002
Generally effective: Transfers after June 8, '97
Committee Reports, see ¶ 5112

Generally, no gain or loss is recognized if property is transferred to a controlled corporation in exchange solely for its stock. However, if the corporation is an "investment company" both gain and loss are recognized. A corresponding provision for transfers to partnerships requires recognition of gain, but not loss, on the contribution of property to a partnership that would have been treated as an "investment company" if it were a corporation.

Under pre-'97 Act law, the definition of "investment company" was left solely to regs. These provide that the exception from nonrecognition treatment applies only if the transfer results, directly or indirectly, in a diversification of the transferor's interests, and define an investment company as either (1) a regulated investment company (RIC), (2) a real estate investment trust (REIT), or (3) a corporation more than 80% of whose assets by value (excluding cash and nonconvertible debt instruments) were held for investment and consisted of readily marketable stocks or securities, or interests in RICs or REITs. (FTC 2d/FIN ¶ F-1302; USTR ¶ 3514.06; TaxDesk ¶ 23,212)

New Law. Additional classes of property, as described below, are taken into account in determining whether a corporation is an investment company. (Code Sec. 351(e)(1) as amended by '97 Act §1002(a))

> **observation:** Although the '97 Act only amends Code Sec. 351, which governs transfers to controlled corporations, the exception for transfers to investment companies is incorporated by reference in Code Sec. 721, which governs transfers to partnerships. Therefore, the expanded definition of investment company applies for that purpose as well.

The '97 Act only adds to the types of property that count towards making a corporation an investment company under the 80% test; it does not change other provisions of the regs, including the requirement that the transfer result in the diversification of the transferor's interests. (Com Rept, see ¶ 5112)

> **observation:** Since the definition of investment company (including the 80% test) remains a creature of regs, the effect of the '97 Act is to have pro-

FTC 2d References are to Federal Tax Coordinator 2d
FIN References are to RIA's Analysis of Federal Taxes: Income
USTR References are to United States Tax Reporter: Income, Estate & Gift, and Excise
PCA References are to Pension Coordinator and Pension & Benefits Expert/Advisor
PE References are to Pension and Profit Sharing 2nd
EP References are to Estate Planning & Taxation Coordinator and Estate Planning Advisor

Research Institute of America 375

visions in the Code which apply for purposes of a rule (i.e., the definition) which exists only in the regs.

Congress was concerned that the pre-'97 Act regs' restrictions on the property taken into account enabled a shareholder (or partner) to exchange appreciated property for an interest in a pool of high quality investment assets of determinable value (e.g., nonconvertible debt instruments or foreign currency) without recognizing gain. Congress thought that the receipt of an interest in these financial assets had the effect of a taxable exchange. Also, Congress was concerned about swap funds that encouraged these transactions. (Com Rept, see ¶ 5112)

Under the '97 Act, in applying the investment company definition, all stock and securities are taken into account. (Code Sec. 351(e)(1)(A))

observation: Thus, unlike pre-'97 Act law, they do not have to be marketable.

For this purpose, the following property is treated as stock and securities: (Code Sec. 351(e)(1)(B))

(i) money, (Code Sec. 351(e)(1)(B)(i))

observation: Although money is listed, the Code Sec. 351(e)(1) regs give effect to a plan in existence at the time of the transfer to the corporation to change an entity's assets. Therefore, if there is a plan to use money contributed to the corporation to purchase an asset that is not taken into account under the 80% test, the money should similarly not be taken into account.

recommendation: A taxpayer who transfers cash to a corporation or partnership with the understanding that the cash will be used to purchase assets other than those treated as stock or securities for purposes of the investment company definition should carefully document the intended use of the cash in order to avoid having the cash count against the 80% test. Preferably, the subscription agreement or other contract which governs the terms of the transfer should require the corporation to use the money for that purpose.

(ii) stocks and other equity interests in a corporation, evidences of indebtedness, options, forward or futures contracts, notional principal contracts and derivatives, (Code Sec. 351(e)(1)(B)(ii))

(iii) foreign currency, (Code Sec. 351(e)(1)(B)(iii))

(iv) any interest in a REIT, common trust fund, RIC, publicly traded partnership (as defined in Code Sec. 7704(b)), or any other equity interest (which is not an equity interest in a corporation) that by its terms or any other arrangement is readily convertible into or exchangeable for, any other asset described in (i) through (v) or in (viii). (Code Sec. 351(e)(1)(B)(iv))

illustration: X Corp. has a 5% interest in partnership P, which is not an asset included in the list. X currently has the right to exchange its interest for P's interest in a REIT that comprises less than 10% of P's assets. X's interest in P is the type of exchangeable equity interest covered and X must take its value into account.

observation: In the above Illustration, because the interest in the REIT represents less than 20% of P's assets, it is not covered by the entity-look-through rules in (vi) and (vii) below.

observation: A partnership agreement may provide for the purchase of a partner's interest by the partnership under various circumstances. If this in effect gives the partner a readily exercisable put, the interest would seem to be covered, unless it is a type of arrangement excepted by regs. A right of a partner, under state law, to withdraw and be paid the value of the interest arguably is not covered because it would not be "readily" exercisable and, also, might not be pursuant to an "arrangement."

(v) any interest in a precious metal, unless it is used or held in the active conduct of a trade or business after the contribution (or regs narrow this category), (Code Sec. 351(e)(1)(B)(v))

(vi) except as provided in regs, interests in any entity if substantially all of the assets of the entity consist (directly or indirectly) of any assets listed in (i) through (v) or (viii), (Code Sec. 351(e)(1)(B)(vi))

observation: Until regs are issued, the regs that were issued under Code Sec. 731(c)(2) will apply under (vi). (Com Rept, see ¶ 5112) Under those regs, an entity meets the substantially all requirement if 90% or more of its assets are listed assets.

illustration: X Corp. has a 10% interest in partnership P, 90% of whose assets consist of money, stocks and bonds. The entire value of P, not just 90%, is counted.

(vii) to the extent provided in regs, an interest in an entity not described in (vi), to the extent of the value of the interest that is attributable to assets listed in (i) through (v), or (viii), (Code Sec. 351(e)(1)(B)(vii))

observation: Regs that were issued under Code Sec. 731(c)(2) will apply here until regs are issued under (vii). (Com Rept, see ¶ 5112) Under those regs, if 20% or more, but less than 90%, of an entity's assets are listed assets, a pro rata portion of its assets is taken into account.

illustration: Corp X has an interest in partnership P, 40% of whose assets consist of stocks and bonds, and the balance are not listed property. X takes into account 40% of the value of the interest.

FTC 2d References are to Federal Tax Coordinator 2d
FIN References are to RIA's Analysis of Federal Taxes: Income
USTR References are to United States Tax Reporter: Income, Estate & Gift, and Excise
PCA References are to Pension Coordinator and Pension & Benefits Expert/Advisor
PE References are to Pension and Profit Sharing 2nd
EP References are to Estate Planning & Taxation Coordinator and Estate Planning Advisor

observation: Under existing regs which define an investment company, the assets of a subsidiary are considered to be owned proportionately by its parent if the parent owns 50% or more of the stock of the subsidiary. The Committee Reports state that the '97 Act does not override this provision. (Com Rept, see ¶ 5112). However, since all stock is now covered, the regs' look-through rule in effect becomes irrelevant. Moreover, the 50% threshold is inconsistent with the 20% threshold in the Code Sec. 731(c)(2) regs that Congress said should be applied to interests in noncorporate entities.

(viii) any other asset specified in regs. (Code Sec. 351(e)(1)(B)(viii))

IRS may treat any asset described in (i) through (v) as not so described. (Code Sec. 351(e)(1))

☐ **Effective:** Transfers after June 8, '97 in tax years ending after that date ('97 Act §1002(b)(1)), unless the transfer is pursuant to a written binding contract in effect on that date and at all times thereafter before such transfer if such contract provides for the transfer of a fixed amount of property. ('97 Act §1002(b)(2))

¶ 1505. Treatment of dividend from related-party stock purchase amended

Code Sec. 304(a)(1), as amended by '97 Act § 1013(a)
Code Sec. 1059(e)(1)(A)(iii), as amended by '97 Act § 1013(b)
Code Sec. 304(b)(5), as amended by '97 Act § 1013(c)
Generally effective: Distributions or acquisitions after June 8, '97
Committee Reports, see ¶ 5118

If a person in control of each of two sister corporations sells stock in one of the corporations to the other corporation, the sale proceeds are treated as distributions in redemption of the stock of the purchasing corporation. The proceeds of such a deemed redemption are treated either as being from a sale or exchange or from a non-exchange distribution (generally a dividend, assuming adequate earnings and profits), depending on whether there has been a sufficient reduction in ownership of the corporation whose stock was sold. Attribution rules apply in determining whether "control" exists, and also in determining whether the deemed redemption is treated as an exchange or a dividend, based on the reduction in ownership of the corporation whose stock was sold. Under these rules, stock of the purchaser which is owned by the person in common control may be attributed to the seller.

Under pre-'97 Act law, if a distribution in such a transfer was considered to be a dividend, the stock that was sold was treated as having been transferred to the buyer as a contribution to its capital. However, if the seller did not actually own any stock in the buyer, the seller's basis in the shares that were sold was added to the basis of its remaining shares in that corporation.

A corporation which receives a dividend from another corporation is generally entitled to a dividends-received deduction of at least 70%, and in some cases as much as 100%, of the amount of the dividend. However, in the case of an "extraordinary dividend," the recipient corporation is required to reduce its basis in the stock of the paying corporation by the amount of the dividend which effectively went untaxed as a result of the dividends-received deduction. Under pre-'97 Act law, in the context of a related-party sale of stock treated as a dividend under the above rules, this basis reduction may not have applied to require a reduction in the control person's basis in the remaining shares of the corporation whose stock was sold.

If a related party sale of stock to which the above rules apply is treated as a distribution which is not a sale or exchange, under pre-'97 Act law in determining the portion that was treated as a dividend, the earnings and profits of both the acquiring corporation and the corporation whose stock was sold were taken into account, regardless of whether the purchaser was a U.S. or a foreign corporation. If the purchaser was a foreign corporation and the distribution was a dividend, the seller was not barred from claiming foreign tax credits for foreign taxes paid by the purchaser. (FTC 2d/FIN ¶ F-11710 *et seq.*; USTR ¶ 3044.03; TaxDesk ¶ 24,336 et seq.)

New Law. If a deemed distribution to a seller arising out of the sale of stock of one controlled corporation to a sister controlled corporation is treated as a distribution which is not a sale or exchange, two additional exchanges are deemed to occur:

(1) The stock that was sold is deemed to have been transferred by the seller to the buyer for stock of the buyer in a tax-free transfer to a controlled corporation.

(2) The buyer is deemed to have redeemed the stock that it is treated as having issued to the seller in the constructive transfer. (Code Sec. 304(a)(1) as amended by '97 Act §1013(a))

> *illustration:* X Corp owns 75% of the stock of S and 100% of the stock of B. S owns all the stock of T (100 shares). S sells 99 shares of T to B for $1,000 (their fair market value). The $1,000 is, as under pre-'97 Act law, treated as a distribution from B to S in redemption of B stock. Under the attribution rules, S is deemed to own the B stock which X actually owns, and the deemed distribution is not treated as a sale or exchange. Under the '97 Act, S is treated as transferring the 99 shares of T to B in exchange for shares of B which are then treated as having been redeemed by B.

> *observation:* Under Code Sec. 358, S's basis for the T shares that it transferred to B becomes the initial basis of the shares that S is deemed to receive from B, instead of being added to the basis of its one remaining share of T stock. The basis of the B shares that S is deemed to receive from B is reduced if the dividends received deduction applies (see below).

The '97 Act expands the definition of an extraordinary dividend to include a redemption that is treated as a dividend as a result of a related-party sale. (Code Sec.

FTC 2d References are to Federal Tax Coordinator 2d
FIN References are to RIA's Analysis of Federal Taxes: Income
USTR References are to United States Tax Reporter: Income, Estate & Gift, and Excise
PCA References are to Pension Coordinator and Pension & Benefits Expert/Advisor
PE References are to Pension and Profit Sharing 2nd
EP References are to Estate Planning & Taxation Coordinator and Estate Planning Advisor

Research Institute of America

379

1059(e)(1)(A)(iii)(II) as amended by '97 Act §1013(b))

✔ observation: This makes the dividend that S receives an extraordinary dividend for purposes of the dividends received deduction, without regard to the holding period for the shares of B that S is deemed to receive (which includes the holding period of the T shares). Therefore, the basis of the B shares which are treated as having been issued and immediately redeemed is reduced by the portion of the distribution which is not taxed because of the dividends received deduction. Under Code Sec. 1059(e)(1)(A) (see ¶ 1503), the reduction is applied only to the basis of the B shares which are treated as actually redeemed and, if the reduction exceeds S's basis in those shares, gain is recognized immediately.

Congress was concerned about S being able to add the basis of the T shares that it had sold to B to its basis for its remaining share(s) of T, without having had that basis reduced by the amount of the sales proceeds which were treated as a dividend from B but were effectively not taxed because of the dividends received deduction, and then claiming a loss when it sold its remaining T share(s). (Com Rept, see ¶ 5118) This result is no longer possible under the '97 Act, since S's basis in the T stock that it sold to B is transferred to the basis of the B stock that it is deemed to receive from B and is then reduced by the amount of any dividend from B which is effectively not taxed because of the dividends received deduction.

✔ observation: The '97 Act does not specify what happens to any remaining basis that S has in the "phantom" B shares after the above reduction. If the redemption proceeds are a dividend, the basis in the shares that are redeemed is added to the basis of any remaining shares. Therefore, if S owned B stock before the transaction, any remaining basis would be added to those shares. If, however, S did not own any stock of B before the transaction, there is an issue as to whether S (or even X) can benefit from the remaining basis or whether it simply "disappears."

✔ recommendation: If the basis reduction on account of the extraordinary dividend is less than S's original (pre-reduction) basis in the T stock being sold, S can avoid having basis disappear if it owns at least one real share of B before the transaction.

✔ illustration: Before selling shares of T stock to B, S owns 1% of the stock of B. The sale proceeds are treated as a dividend from B to S. S's basis in the T stock that it sold is transferred to the B shares which B is treated as issuing to it and then redeeming. S's basis for these B shares is reduced by the amount of the dividends received deduction that S is entitled to, but this may not be sufficient to wipe out its basis for the B shares. Any remaining basis is added to the 1% of the B stock that S owned before the transaction. If S did not own any B stock before the transaction, it might not be able to recover the remaining basis.

Acquisitions by foreign corporations. If, in a related-party stock sale described above, the purchasing corporation is a foreign corporation, the earnings and profits that are taken into account in determining the amount of the distribution that is a dividend are limited to earnings and profits of the purchaser, and further restricted to those that satisfy all of the following conditions:

... they are attributable (under regs) to stock of the purchaser "owned" by the seller, or a person "related" to the seller, that is a "U. S. shareholder" of the purchaser. (Code Sec. 304(b)(5)(A)(i) as amended by '97 Act §1013(c))

... they were accumulated while the purchaser was a controlled foreign corporation and the seller or "related" person owned the shares. (Code Sec. 304(b)(5)(A)(ii))

... they are not excluded under Code Sec. 1248(d) (except as provided in regs). (Code Sec. 304(b)(5)(B))

applying these rules, "U. S. shareholder" is defined in Code Sec. 951(b) and ownership of stock is determined under Code Sec. 958(a). Whether persons are "related" is determined under Code Sec. 267(b) or Code Sec. 707(b). (Code Sec. 304(b)(5)(A)(i)) IRS is to issue regs to carry out the purposes of the new rules on acquisitions by foreign persons. (Code Sec. 304(b)(5)(C))

> *observation:* Congress was particularly concerned about a situation where (in the illustration above) X and B were foreign corporations. Stock of B actually owned by X was attributed to S. Therefore, under pre-'97 Act law, S claimed an indirect foreign tax credit for foreign taxes paid by B when it was treated as receiving a dividend from B, even though, if B had actually paid a dividend, it would have gone to X and S could not have claimed the credit. (Com Rept, see ¶ 5118)
>
> Under the '97 Act, the deemed distribution which S has by virtue of the sale is not treated as a dividend (and hence does not entitle S to claim an indirect foreign tax credit), because S is not a "U. S. shareholder" which "owns" stock of B, as determined under the more limited CFC attribution rules of Code Sec. 958.

☐ **Effective:** The new rules apply to distributions or acquisitions after June 8, '97 ('97 Act §1013(d)(1)), unless made pursuant to the terms of a written binding contract in effect on such date and at all times thereafter, or described in a ruling request submitted to IRS, or described in a public announcement or filing with the SEC, on or before, such date. ('97 Act §1013(d)(2))

FTC 2d References are to Federal Tax Coordinator 2d
FIN References are to RIA's Analysis of Federal Taxes: Income
USTR References are to United States Tax Reporter: Income, Estate & Gift, and Excise
PCA References are to Pension Coordinator and Pension & Benefits Expert/Advisor
PE References are to Pension and Profit Sharing 2nd
EP References are to Estate Planning & Taxation Coordinator and Estate Planning Advisor

S Corporations

¶ 1506. Charitable remainder trusts may not be electing small business trust shareholders

Code Sec. 1361(e)(1)(B)(iii), as amended by '97 Act § 1601(c)(1)
Generally effective: Tax years beginning after Dec. 31, '96
Committee Reports, see ¶ 5357

Electing small business trusts that may be S corporation shareholders may not, among other things, have made a qualified subchapter S trust (QSST) election with respect to any stock held by the trust and may not be tax-exempt trusts. (FTC 2d/FIN ¶ D-1479.1; USTR ¶ 13,614.03; TaxDesk ¶ 61,116.1)

New Law. The '97 Act provides that a charitable remainder annuity trust and charitable remainder unitrust cannot be electing small business trusts. (Code Sec. 1361(e)(1)(B)(iii) as amended by '97 Act §1601(c)(1))

☐ **Effective:** Tax years beginning after Dec. 31, '96. ('97 Act §1601(j)(1))

¶ 1507. Effective date of '96 Act changes to post-termination transition period (PTTP) of S corporations

Code Sec. None, '97 Act § 1601(c)(2)(A)
Code Sec. None, '97 Act § 1601(c)(2)(B)
Generally effective: Determination after Dec. 31, '96
Committee Reports, see ¶ 5358

The Small Business Job Protection Act of '96 expanded the post-termination transition period (PTTP) to include the 120-day period after a determination with respect to an audit of the corporation that affects Subchapter S items of income, gain, loss, or deduction of the corporation after the termination of the corporation's S election. In addition, the definition of a "determination" was expanded to include any determination under Code Sec. 1313(a) and an agreement between the corporation and IRS that the corporation failed to qualify as an S corporation. These changes were effective for tax years beginning after Dec. 31, '96. (FTC 2d/FIN ¶ D-1788; USTR ¶ 13,774; TaxDesk ¶ 61,485.1)

New Law. The '97 Act makes the PTTP changes effective for determinations made after Dec. 31, '96. ('97 Act §1601(c)(2)(A)) In addition, the 120-day period after a determination with respect to an audit of a corporation after the termination of the corporation's S election will not expire before the end of the 120-period beginning after Aug. 5, '97. ('97 Act §1601(c)(2)(B))

☐ **Effective:** Determinations after Dec. 31, '96. ('97 Act §1601(c)(2)(A))

¶ 1508. Treatment of qualified Subchapter S subsidiaries (QSSSs) as separate corporations

Code Sec. 1361(b)(3)(A), as amended by '97 Act § 1601(c)(3)
Generally effective: Tax years beginning after Dec. 31, '96
Committee Reports, see ¶ 5359

The Small Business Job Protection Act of '96 allowed S corporations to have wholly-owned qualified Subchapter S subsidiaries (QSSSs) that are not treated as separate corporations. Instead, the assets, liabilities and items of income, deduction and credit of the QSSS are treated as those of the parent S corporation. (FTC 2d/FIN ¶ D-1452.1; USTR ¶ 13,614.05; TaxDesk ¶ 61,485.1)

New Law. IRS may issue regs under which QSSSs are treated as separate corporations. (Code Sec. 1361(b)(3)(A) as amended by '97 Act §1601(c)(3)) Under this rule, it is expected that where a bank is a QSSS, the bank will be treated as a separate corporation for purposes of rules that apply specifically to banks, such as the special bad debt rules. (Com Rept, see ¶ 5359)

IRS regs may also provide exceptions to the general rule that the QSSS election results in a deemed Code Sec. 332 subsidiary liquidation in certain cases. In addition, if the effect of a QSSS election is to invalidate an election to join in a consolidated return filing for a group of subsidiaries that formerly so filed, IRS regs may provide guidance regarding the consolidated return effects of the QSSS election. (Com Rept, see ¶ 5359)

☐ **Effective:** Tax years beginning after Dec. 31, '96. ('97 Act §1601(j)(1))

Deductions and Other Corporate Provisions

¶ 1509. Holding period for dividends-received deduction modified

Code Sec. 246(c), as amended by '97 Act § 1015
Generally effective: Dividends received or accrued after the 30th day after Aug. 5, '97
Committee Reports, see ¶ 5120

A corporation that receives a dividend from another corporation is generally allowed to deduct a portion (or in some cases the full amount) of the dividend. This dividends-received deduction is only available if the shareholder satisfies a more-than-45-day holding period for the dividend-paying stock (or a more-than-90-day period where dividends attributable to a period of more that 366 days are received on preferred stock).

FTC 2d References are to Federal Tax Coordinator 2d
FIN References are to RIA's Analysis of Federal Taxes: Income
USTR References are to United States Tax Reporter: Income, Estate & Gift, and Excise
PCA References are to Pension Coordinator and Pension & Benefits Expert/Advisor
PE References are to Pension and Profit Sharing 2nd
EP References are to Estate Planning & Taxation Coordinator and Estate Planning Advisor

Research Institute of America 383

In determining whether the applicable holding period has been satisfied, any period during which the shareholder is protected from the risk of loss of the ownership of the stock (e.g., where the shareholder made a short sale or owns a put option on the stock) is not taken into account. Under pre-'97 Act law, the holding period had to be satisfied only once, rather than with respect to each dividend received. (FTC 2d/FIN ¶ D-2263; USTR ¶ 2434.04; TaxDesk ¶ 60,066)

> ✅ *observation:* This meant that once the holding period requirement was met the dividends-received deduction remained available even if the shareholder was protected from the risk of loss at the time the dividend was received.

New Law. A shareholder does not qualify for a dividends-received deduction on a dividend on stock that is held for 45 days or less during the 90-day period beginning on the date that is 45 days before the date on which the stock becomes ex-dividend with respect to the dividend. (Code Sec. 246(c)(1) as amended by '97 Act §1015(a)) A similar rule provides that dividends attributable to a period of more than 366 days that are received on preferred stock will not qualify for the dividends-received deduction if the stock is held for 90 days or less during the 180-day period beginning on the date that is 90 days before the date on which the stock becomes ex-dividend with respect to the dividend. (Code Sec. 246(c)(2) as amended by '97 Act §1015(b)(1)) These rules allow a dividends-received deduction only if the taxpayer's holding period for the dividend-paying stock is satisfied over a period immediately before or immediately after the taxpayer becomes entitled to receive the dividend. (Com Rept, see ¶ 5120)

The '97 Act removes the rule that excluded holding periods after the 45-day period (or 90-day period) as unnecessary. (Code Sec. 246(c)(3)(B) as amended by '97 Act §1015(b)(2))

☐ **Effective:** Dividends received or accrued after the 30th day after Aug. 5, '97. ('97 Act §1015(c)(1)) However, these rules do not apply to dividends received or accrued during the two-year period beginning on Aug. 5, '97 if:

(1) the dividend is paid with respect to stock held by the taxpayer on June 8, '97, and all times thereafter until the dividend is received ('97 Act §1015(c)(2)(A));

(2) the stock is continuously subject to a position that causes the holding period of the stock to be reduced because of a diminished risk of loss on June 8, '97, and all times thereafter until the dividend is received. ('97 Act §1015(c)(2)(B)) Stock will not meet this requirement if the position is sold, closed, or otherwise terminated and reestablished ('97 Act §1015(c)(2)); and

(3) the stock and position are clearly identified in the taxpayer's records within 30 days after Aug. 5, '97. ('97 Act §1015(c)(2)(C))

> ✅ *action alert:* A corporation which has owned stock in another corporation continuously since June 8, '97, which stock has been subject to a diminished risk of loss by virtue of holding another position at all times since such date, should clearly identify the stock and the position on its books or records within 30 days after Aug. 5, '97 in order to be entitled to the two-year transition rule for the more stringent holding period requirement applicable to the

dividends received deduction.

¶1510. NOL carryback period reduced from three to two years; carryforward period extended from 15 to 20 years

Code Sec. 172(b)(1)(A), as amended by '97 Act § 1082(a)
Code Sec. 172(b)(1)(F), as amended by '97 Act § 1082(b)
Generally effective: Tax years beginning after Aug. 5, '97
Committee Reports, see ¶5159

Under pre-'97 Act law, the general rule was that a net operating loss (NOL) could be carried back three years and forward 15 years. NOLs arising from casualty losses of individuals were subject to the three-year carryback period for NOLs generally.

Certain NOLs are subject to specific carryback period rules (although the general carryforward period applies). For example, any part of an NOL that is attributable to a "specified liability loss" (i.e., a product liability loss) may be carried back 10 years. And certain NOLs cannot be carried back at all—e.g., NOLs attributable to interest allocable to a corporate equity reduction transaction (CERT) (so-called "excess interest losses"). An NOL of a real estate investment trust (REIT) can't be carried back to any year in which the trust qualified as a REIT. (FTC 2d/FIN ¶M-4301; USTR ¶1724.31; TaxDesk ¶35,601)

New Law. The '97 Act modifies the carryover periods for NOLs generally. (Com Rept, see ¶5159)

NOL carrybacks. The '97 Act reduces the general NOL carryback period to two years (from three years) (Com Rept, see ¶5159) by substituting 2 for 3 in the provision under the general rule that provides for the number of tax years an NOL for a tax year can be carried back. (Code Sec. 172(b)(1)(A)(i) as amended by '97 Act §1082(a))

The allowance of NOL carryovers is based on the fact that taxpayers are required to report income and file federal income tax returns based on a 12-month period even if their natural business exceeds 12 months. Congress believes that a two-year carryback period is sufficient to account for a natural business cycle that exceeds the 12-month tax reporting period. This is partly because many deductions that are allowed for tax purposes relate to future, rather than past, income streams. And while certain deductions do relate to past income streams, those deductions aren't subject to the general carryback period, but are instead granted longer carryback periods under rules unaffected by the Act. (Com Rept, see ¶5159)

The reduction in the NOL carryback period doesn't apply to certain NOLs. (Com Rept, see ¶5159) The three-year carryback period is retained for certain "eligible

FTC 2d References are to Federal Tax Coordinator 2d
FIN References are to RIA's Analysis of Federal Taxes: Income
USTR References are to United States Tax Reporter: Income, Estate & Gift, and Excise
PCA References are to Pension Coordinator and Pension & Benefits Expert/Advisor
PE References are to Pension and Profit Sharing 2nd
EP References are to Estate Planning & Taxation Coordinator and Estate Planning Advisor

 Research Institute of America 385

losses" (defined below). The portion of an NOL for a tax year that's an eligible loss with respect to the taxpayer may be carried back to the three preceding tax years. (Code Sec. 172(b)(1)(F)(i) as amended by '97 Act §1082(b))

In the case of an individual, "eligible losses" are property losses arising from fire, storm, shipwreck, or other casualty, or from theft. (Code Sec. 172(b)(1)(F)(ii)(I)) Thus, a three-year carryback period applies to NOLs arising from casualty losses of individuals. (Com Rept, see ¶ 5159)

> ⊘ *observation:* The three-year carryback period is also retained for NOLs arising from an individual's theft loss.

In the case of a taxpayer that's a "small business" (defined below) (Code Sec. 172(b)(1)(F)(ii)(II)), or engaged in the trade or business of farming (as defined in Code Sec. 263A(e)(4)), "eligible losses" are NOLs attributable to Presidentially declared disasters (as defined in Code Sec. 1033(h)(3)). (Code Sec. 172(b)(1)(F)(ii)(III)) Thus, taxpayers engaged in a small business or a farming business have a three-year carryback period for their NOLs attributable to losses incurred in Presidentially declared disaster areas. (Com Rept, see ¶ 5159)

A "small business" for this purpose is a corporation or partnership that meets the gross receipts test of Code Sec. 448(c) for the tax year in which the loss arose, or a sole proprietorship that would meet that test if the proprietorship were a corporation. (Code Sec. 172(b)(1)(F)(iii)) This means any trade or business (including one conducted in or through a corporation, partnership, or sole proprietorship) whose average annual gross receipts (under Code Sec. 448(c)) are $5 million or less. (Com Rept, see ¶ 5159)

The '97 Act doesn't modify the carryback rules relating to specified liability losses (10-year carryback), REITs (no carryback) and excess interest losses (no carryback), and corporate capital losses. (Com Rept, see ¶ 5159)

NOL carryforwards. The '97 Act extends the NOL carryforward period to 20 years (from 15 years) (Com Rept, see ¶ 5159) by substituting 20 for 15 in the provision under the general rule that provides for the number of tax years an NOL for a tax year can be carried forward. (Code Sec. 172(b)(1)(A)(ii))

> ⊘ *observation:* The extension of the carryforward period to 20 years applies to NOLs with respect to specified liability losses, REITs, and excess interest losses. Those NOLs were subject to the pre-'97 Act law 15-year carryforward period.

☐ **Effective:** NOLs for tax years beginning after Aug. 5, '97. ('97 Act §1082(c)) This means NOLs arising in tax years beginning after that date. (Com Rept, see ¶ 5159)

> ⊘ *observation:* Thus, NOLs for '97 can still be carried back three years (to '94), but NOLs for '98 can only be carried back two years (to '96). No carryback is available to '95, except for a carryback from '97 that's large enough to carry from '94 to '95. Taxpayers who paid tax in '95 and anticipate losses in '98 may therefore want to, if possible, accelerate the '98 losses into '97 if

that would create a '97 NOL that wouldn't all be used up in '94 and so could reach '95.

The changes made by the Act don't apply to NOLs carried forward from tax years beginning on or before Aug. 5, '97. (Com Rept, see ¶ 5159)

observation: Thus, NOLs from pre-'98 tax years still expire after 15 carryforward years.

¶ 1511. No deduction for interest on corporate debt payable in stock of the issuer or a related party

Code Sec. 163(l), as amended by '97 Act § 1005(a)
Generally effective: Debt instruments issued after June 8, '97
Committee Reports, see ¶ 5115

The tax treatment of an instrument as debt or equity can be significant for the issuer. Interest on indebtedness, including original issue discount (OID), is generally deductible by the issuer. Dividends paid on equity (stock) are not deductible. Determining whether an instrument is debt or equity is based on a number of factors, including intent of the parties and economic reality. (FTC 2d/FIN ¶ K-5790; USTR ¶ 3854; TaxDesk ¶ 31,351)

New Law. Under the '97 Act, no deduction is allowed for any interest paid or accrued on a disqualified debt instrument. (Code Sec. 163(l)(1) as amended by '97 Act §1005(a)) The bar to deduction also applies to OID on a disqualified instrument. (Com Rept, see ¶ 5115) A disqualified debt instrument is any indebtedness of a corporation (or indebtedness issued by a partnership to the extent of its corporate partners (Com Rept, see ¶ 5115)) that is payable in equity (i.e., stock (Com Rept, see ¶ 5115)) of the issuer or a related party (defined below). (Code Sec. 163(l)(2))

observation: If the debt is issued by a partnership, the equity involved would have to be stock of a related party such as a corporate partner or a corporation owned by the partners of the partnership.

Indebtedness is treated as payable in equity of the issuer or a related party only if—

(A) a substantial amount of the principal or interest is required to be paid or converted, or at the option of the issuer or a related party, is payable in, or convertible into, the equity (Code Sec. 163(l)(3)(A)),

(B) a substantial amount of the principal or interest is required to be determined, or at the option of the issuer or a related party is determined, by reference to the value of the equity (Code Sec. 163(l)(3)(B)), or

(C) the indebtedness is part of an arrangement which is reasonably expected to result in a transaction described in (A) or (B) (Code Sec. 163(l)(3)(C)), such as in the case of certain issuances of a forward contract in connection with the issuance of debt, nonrecourse debt that is secured principally by stock, or certain debt instruments that are convertible at the holder's option when it is substantially certain that the right will be exercised. (Com Rept, see ¶ 5115)

For purposes of (A), (B), and (C) above, principal or interest is treated as required to be so paid, converted, or determined if it may be required at the option of the holder or a related party and there is a substantial certainty that the option will be exercised. (Code Sec. 163(l)(3))

It is not expected that these rules will affect debt with a conversion feature where the conversion price is significantly higher than the market price of the stock on the issue date of the debt. (Com Rept, see ¶ 5115)

A person is a related party with respect to another person if the person bears a relationship to the other person described in Code Sec. 267(b) or Code Sec. 707(b). (Code Sec. 163(l)(4))

IRS is to issue such regulations as may be necessary or appropriate to carry out the purposes of these rules, including regulations to prevent avoidance of these rules through the use of an issuer other than a corporation. (Code Sec. 163(l)(5))

These rules deal only with the deduction by the issuer. They do not affect the treatment of a holder of an instrument. (Com Rept, see ¶ 5115)

> *observation:* The fact that an instrument is treated as a disqualified debt instrument for purposes of denying an interest deduction to the issuer doesn't mean that the instrument is treated as equity so as to permit a corporate holder a dividends received deduction for amounts paid on the instrument.

> *observation:* Presumably the holder can still apply the usual debt-equity rules to claim that the instrument was equity for purposes of the dividends received deduction.

☐ **Effective:** For disqualified debt instruments issued after June 8, '97. ('97 Act §1005(b)(1)) However, under a transition rule, these rules don't apply to instruments issued after June 8, '97, if the instrument:

. . . is issued under a written agreement which was binding on June 8, '97 and at all times thereafter ('97 Act §1005(b)(2)(A)),

. . . is described in a ruling request submitted to IRS on or before June 8, '97 ('97 Act §1005(b)(2)(B)), or

. . . is described on or before June 8, '97 in a public announcement or in a filing with the Securities and Exchange Commission required solely by reason of the issuance. ('97 Act §1005(b)(2)(C))

The provision is not intended to affect the characterization of instruments as debt or equity under pre-'97 Act rules. No inference is intended as to the treatment of any instrument under pre-'97 Act rules. (Com Rept, see ¶ 5115)

¶ 1512. Corporate gifts of computer technology and equipment to elementary and secondary schools before 2000 get charitable deduction tax break

Code Sec. 170(e)(6), as amended by '97 Act § 224(a)
Generally effective: Tax years beginning after '97
Committee Reports, see ¶ 5010

The amount deductible for property contributed to a charitable organization is generally the fair market value of the property at the time of the contribution. However, for a charitable contribution of inventory or other ordinary-income property, or short-term capital gain property, the deduction is reduced and limited to the taxpayer's basis in the property. (FTC 2d/FIN ¶ K-3160; USTR ¶ 1704.42; TaxDesk ¶ 33,169) This reduction doesn't apply for certain corporate contributions of inventory and other property for the care of the ill, the needy, or infants and certain corporate contributions of scientific equipment constructed by the taxpayer to be used for research. In these situations, the reduction in the deduction is limited, and instead the amount of the charitable contribution deduction is the lesser of the property's basis plus one half of the amount of non-long-term capital gain income that it would incur on the property's sale, or two times the contributed property's basis. FTC 2d/FIN ¶ K-3179; USTR ¶ 1704.42; TaxDesk ¶ 33,179

New Law. Congress believes that providing an incentive for businesses to invest their computer equipment and software for the benefit of primary and secondary school students will help to provide America's schools with the technological resources necessary to prepare both teachers and students for a technologically advanced present and future. (Com Rept, see ¶ 5010) The '97 Act therefore provides that for tax years beginning after '97 and before 2000 (see below), the Code Sec. 170(e)(1)(A) reduction in fair market value (by the gain that wouldn't have been long-term capital gain had the contributed property been sold) in the case of a qualified elementary or secondary educational contribution (defined below) is no greater than the amount determined under Code Sec. 170(e)(3)(B) (the limitation on the reduction for corporate contributions of inventory, etc. for the care of the ill, needy and infants). (Code Sec. 170(e)(6)(A) as amended by '97 Act §224(a)) Accordingly, a qualified elementary or secondary educational contribution, like a contribution of inventory or other property for the care of the ill, the needy, or infants under Code Sec. 170(e)(3) and a contribution of scientific equipment constructed by the taxpayer to be used for research under Code Sec. 170(e)(4), qualifies for the "augmented deduction" available under Code Sec. 170(e)(3)(B). (Com Rept, see ¶ 5010)

FTC 2d References are to Federal Tax Coordinator 2d
FIN References are to RIA's Analysis of Federal Taxes: Income
USTR References are to United States Tax Reporter: Income, Estate & Gift, and Excise
PCA References are to Pension Coordinator and Pension & Benefits Expert/Advisor
PE References are to Pension and Profit Sharing 2nd
EP References are to Estate Planning & Taxation Coordinator and Estate Planning Advisor

⚫observation: Thus, the amount of its charitable contribution deduction for a qualified elementary or secondary educational contribution as computed under Code Sec. 170(e)(3)(B) is the lesser of: (1) the property's basis plus one half of the amount of non-long-term capital gain income which it would incur on the property's sale, or (2) two times the contributed property's basis.

A qualified elementary or secondary educational contribution is a charitable contribution by a corporation (defined below) of any computer technology or equipment (defined below), if certain requirements are met. (Code Sec. 170(e)(6)(B)) The computer technology or equipment that is contributed can be inventory or depreciable trade or business property in the hands of the donor. (Com Rept, see ¶ 5010)

To qualify as a qualified elementary or secondary educational contribution, the following requirements must be met:

(1) The contribution must be made no later than two years after either the date the taxpayer acquired the property or, in the case of property constructed by the taxpayer, the date the construction of the property was substantially completed. (Code Sec. 170(e)(6)(B)(ii)) Whether or nor property is constructed by the taxpayer is determined under the rules of Code Sec. 170(e)(4)(C). (Code Sec. 170(e)(6)(D)) Thus, property is constructed by the taxpayer only if the cost of the parts used in the construction of the property (other than parts manufactured by the taxpayer or a related person) do not exceed 50% of the taxpayer's basis in the property;

(2) The original use of of the property must be by the donor or the donee (Code Sec. 170(e)(6)(B)(iii));

(3) Substantially all of the use of the property by the donee must be for use within the U.S. for educational purposes in any of the grades K through 12 that are related to the purpose or function of the organization or entity (Code Sec. 170(e)(6)(B)(iv));

(4) The property can't be transferred by the donee in exchange for money, other property, or services, except for shipping, installation and transfer costs. (Code Sec. 170(e)(6)(B)(v)) Thus, payment by the donee organization of shipping, transfer, and installation costs is permitted. (Com Rept, see ¶ 5010) In the case of contributions made through private foundations (see below), payment by the private foundation of shipping, transfer, and installation costs is permitted (Com Rept, see ¶ 5010);

(5) The property must fit productively into the entity's education plan (Code Sec. 170(e)(6)(B)(vi)); and

(6) The entity's use and disposition of the property must be in accordance with the provisions of (3) and (4), above. (Code Sec. 170(e)(6)(B)(vii))

Except for certain contributions to a private foundation (see below), the contribution must be made to either an educational organization described in Code Sec. 170(b)(1)(A)(ii) (Code Sec. 170(e)(6)(B)(i)(I)), i.e., any educational organization that normally maintains a regular faculty and curriculum and has a regularly enrolled body of pupils in attendance at the place where its educational activities are regularly carried on (Com Rept, see ¶ 5010), or to an entity described in Code Sec. 501(c)(3) and exempt from tax under Code Sec. 501(a) that's organized primarily for purposes of supporting elementary and secondary education. (Code Sec. 170(e)(6)(B)(i)(II))

A qualified contribution can also be made to a private foundation, if the contribution to the private foundation satisfies the requirements of (1) and (4), see above, (Code Sec. 170(e)(6)(C)(i)) and that within 30 days after the contribution, the private foundation:

... contributes the property to an educational organization as described in Code Sec. 170(e)(6)(B)(i) (see above), that satisfies the requirements of (3), (4), (5), and (6), see above (Code Sec. 170(e)(6)(C)(ii)(I)), and

... notifies the donor of the contribution. (Code Sec. 170(e)(6)(C)(ii)(II))

Corporation defined. A "corporation" for purpose of a qualified elementary or secondary educational contribution is defined the same as in Code Sec. 170(e)(4)(D) (which excludes S corporations, personal holding companies, and service organizations). (Code Sec. 170(e)(6)(E)(ii)) Thus, only a C corporations can make a qualified elementary or secondary educational contribution. (Com Rept, see ¶ 5010)

Computer technology or equipment defined. Computer technology or equipment for this purpose is:

... computer software as defined in Code Sec. 197(e)(3)(B) (Code Sec. 170(e)(6)(E)(i)), i.e., any program designed to cause a computer to perform a desired function, but usually not including data bases;

... computer or peripheral equipment as defined in Code Sec. 168(i)(2)(B) (Code Sec. 170(e)(6)(E)(i)), i.e., a computer and any auxiliary machine designed to be placed under the control of the central processing unit, but not typewriters, calculators, or copiers, and not any equipment used primarily for the user's amusement or entertainment; and

... fiber optic cable related to computer use. (Code Sec. 170(e)(6)(E)(i))

☐ **Effective:** Tax years beginning after Dec. 31, '97. ('97 Act §224(b)) The augmented deduction for a qualified elementary or secondary educational contribution doesn't apply for any contribution made during any tax year beginning after Dec. 31, '99. (Code Sec. 170(e)(6)(F))

¶ 1513. Corporations, including financial institutions, must compute nondeductible "interest expense" allocable to tax-exempt interest without regard to interest disallowed under Code Sec. 264

Code Sec. 265(b)(4)(A), as amended by '97 Act § 1084(c) [sic]
Generally effective: Contracts issued after June 8, '97
Committee Reports, see ¶ 5161

FTC 2d References are to Federal Tax Coordinator 2d
FIN References are to RIA's Analysis of Federal Taxes: Income
USTR References are to United States Tax Reporter: Income, Estate & Gift, and Excise
PCA References are to Pension Coordinator and Pension & Benefits Expert/Advisor
PE References are to Pension and Profit Sharing 2nd
EP References are to Estate Planning & Taxation Coordinator and Estate Planning Advisor

Under Code Sec. 265(b)(1), in the case of a financial institution, no deduction is allowed for that portion of the taxpayer's interest expense that's allocable to tax-exempt interest. For this purpose, Code Sec. 265(b)(4)(A) defines interest expense as the total amount allowable to the taxpayer as an interest deduction for the tax year, without regard to Code Sec. 265(b) (disallowing a deduction for interest allocable to tax-exempt interest, as just described), and without regard to Code Sec. 291 (requiring a 20% reduction of deductions with respect to "financial institution preference items," which include interest on debt incurred to acquire or carry certain tax-exempt obligations).

✔observation: In other words, for purposes of Code Sec. 265(b)(1), interest expense means the total amount of the taxpayer's deductible interest for the tax year, *plus* amounts that couldn't be deducted as interest because of the limitations of Code Sec. 265(b) or Code Sec. 291.

(FTC 2d/FIN ¶ E-3108, ¶ E-3111; USTR ¶ 2654)

New Law. The '97 Act adds Code Sec. 264 (disallowing deductions for amounts paid or accrued on indebtedness incurred or continued to buy or carry, or paid or accrued with respect to, specified life insurance, endowment or annuity contracts) to the list of Code sections that must be disregarded in determining "interest expense" for purposes of Code Sec. 265(b)(1). (Code Sec. 265(b)(4)(A) as amended by '97 Act §1084(c) [sic])

✔observation: In other words, the '97 Act requires financial institutions to add interest disallowed under Code Sec. 264 to the "interest expense" used to compute the amount of nondeductible interest allocable to tax-exempt interest.

☐ **Effective:** Contracts issued after June 8, '97, in tax years ending after that date. Any material increase in the death benefit or other material change in the contract is treated as a new contract. However, the addition of covered lives is treated as a new contract only with respect to those additional covered lives. For purposes of these effective date rules, an increase in the death benefit under a policy or contract issued in connection with a lapse described in Sec. 501(d)(2) of the Health Insurance Portability and Accountability Act of '96 isn't treated as a new contract. ('97 Act §1084(d))

¶ 1514. Amounts deducted in connection with clean-fuel vehicles amortized over five years in computing earnings and profits

Code Sec. 312(k)(3)(B), as amended by '97 Act § 1604(a)(2)
Generally effective: Qualified clean-fuel property placed in service after June 30, '93

Code Sec. 179 provides an election to expense the cost of certain property which would otherwise be depreciated. The Energy Policy Act of '92 (P.L. 102-486) added a similar rule for the cost of qualified clean-fuel vehicle property and qualified clean-fuel refueling property.

In determining a corporation's earnings and profits (E&P), amounts deductible under the Code Sec. 179 expensing election are treated as though they were amortized ratably over five years. However, under pre-'97 Act law, amounts which are deductible with respect to qualified clean-fuel vehicle property and qualified clean-fuel refueling property were not subject to a similar rule for determining E&P. (FTC 2d/FIN ¶ F-10304; USTR ¶ 3124.04; TaxDesk ¶ 17,123)

New Law. The rule which provides for 5-year straight-line amortization in computing E&P is extended to apply to amounts which are expensed for the cost of qualified clean-fuel vehicle property and qualified clean-fuel refueling property. (Code Sec. 312(k)(3)(B) as amended by '97 Act §1604(a)(2))

☐ **Effective:** For property placed in service after June 30, '93. ('97 Act §1604(a)(4))

FTC 2d References are to Federal Tax Coordinator 2d
FIN References are to RIA's Analysis of Federal Taxes: Income
USTR References are to United States Tax Reporter: Income, Estate & Gift, and Excise
PCA References are to Pension Coordinator and Pension & Benefits Expert/Advisor
PE References are to Pension and Profit Sharing 2nd
EP References are to Estate Planning & Taxation Coordinator and Estate Planning Advisor

¶ 1600. International

Foreign Tax Credit

¶ 1601. Indirect foreign tax credit extended to sixth-tier corporations

Code Sec. 902(b), as amended by '97 Act § 1113(a)
Code Sec. 960(a)(1), as amended by '97 Act § 1113(b)
Generally effective: Tax years beginning after Aug. 5, '97
Committee Reports, see ¶ 5175

A U.S. corporation that owns at least 10% of the voting stock of a foreign corporation is treated as if it had paid a share of the foreign income taxes paid by the foreign corporation (and hence is entitled to claim an "indirect" credit for such taxes) in the year in which the foreign corporation's earnings and profits become subject to U.S. tax as dividend income of the U.S. shareholder.

An indirect foreign tax credit is available to a U.S. corporate shareholder meeting the requisite ownership threshold with respect to inclusions of subpart F income from controlled foreign corporations (CFCs). The U.S. corporation claiming the credit must own indirectly at least 5%, calculated as the product of the percentages of voting stock owned by each corporation in the chain, of the voting stock of the other foreign corporation through a chain of foreign corporations connected through stock ownership of at least 10% of their voting stock.

Under pre-'97 Act law, the indirect credit was available for taxes paid by a second-tier or third-tier foreign corporation. Foreign taxes paid below the third tier of foreign corporations, however, were not eligible for the indirect foreign tax credit. (FTC 2d/FIN ¶ O-4804, ¶ O-4901; USTR ¶ 9024.01)

New Law. The indirect foreign tax credit is extended to taxes paid or accrued by fourth-tier, fifth-tier and sixth-tier foreign corporations. (Code Sec. 902(b) as amended by '97 Act §1113(a)(1)) Under the '97 Act, if any foreign corporation is a member of a "qualified group," and that foreign corporation owns 10% or more of the voting stock of another member of the same qualified group from which it receives dividends in any tax year, the foreign corporation is deemed to have paid the same proportion of the other member's foreign income taxes as would be the case if the foreign corporation were a domestic corporation. (Code Sec. 902(b)(1))

For purposes of these rules, "qualified group" means the foreign corporation referred to in the preceding paragraph (referred to below as the "first foreign corporation") (Code Sec. 902(b)(2)(A)) and any other foreign corporation, if all of the following requirements are met:

FTC 2d References are to the Federal Tax Coordinator 2d
FIN References are to RIA's Analysis of Federal Taxes: Income
USTR References are to the United States Tax Reporter: Income, Estate & Gift, and Excise
PCA References are to Pension Coordinator and Pension & Benefits Expert/Advisor
PE References are to Pension and Profit Sharing 2nd
EP References are to Estate Planning & Taxation Coordinator and Estate Planning Advisor

• The U.S. corporation claiming the credit owns at least 5% of the voting stock of the other foreign corporation indirectly through a chain of foreign corporations connected through stock ownership of at least 10% of their voting stock. (Code Sec. 902(b)(2)(B)(i))

> *illustration:* U.S. corporation P owns 80% of F1's voting stock. F1 owns 80% of F2's voting stock, which in turn owns 50% of F3's voting stock. F3 owns 25% of F4's voting stock. F1, F2, F3 and F4 are all foreign corporations. The requirement that the chain of foreign corporations be connected through stock ownership of at least 10% is satisfied, since each corporation in the chain, other than F4, owns at least 10% of the voting stock of the corporation in the tier immediately below it. Also, P indirectly owns at least 5% of the voting stock in each of the three lower tier subs: In the case of F2, 80% times 80% (64%); in the case of F3, 80% times 80% times 50% (32%); in the case of F4, 80% times 80% times 50% times 25% (8%). As a result, P can claim an indirect foreign tax credit for taxes paid by all four foreign corporations.

• The first foreign corporation is the first tier corporation in the chain of foreign corporations. (Code Sec. 902(b)(2)(B)(ii))

• The other foreign corporation is not below the sixth tier of the chain of corporations. (Code Sec. 902(b)(2)(iii))

A "qualified group" does not include any corporation below the third tier unless the corporation is a CFC and the U.S. corporation claiming the credit is a U.S. shareholder of that corporation. The application of the indirect foreign tax credit below the third tier is limited to taxes paid in tax years during which the member below the third tier was a CFC. (Code Sec. 902(b)(2))

Any amount included in gross income of the U.S. corporation as a distribution from earnings and profits of a CFC which is part of a "qualified group" is, except to the extent provided in regs, treated for purposes of the indirect foreign tax credit as a dividend paid by the CFC. (Code Sec. 960(a)(1) as amended by '97 Act §1113(b))

The provisions ease arbitrary limitations on the operation of the indirect foreign tax credit that may have resulted in taxpayers undergoing burdensome and costly corporate restructuring or may have contributed to decisions by U.S. corporations against acquiring foreign subsidiaries. (Com Rept, see ¶ 5175)

☐ **Effective:** Taxes of foreign corporations for tax years beginning after Aug. 5, '97. ('97 Act §1113(c)(1))

In the case of any chain of foreign corporations which meets the requirements of Code Sec. 902(b)(2)(i) and Code Sec. 902(b)(2)(ii) (above), no liquidation, reorganization or similar transaction in a tax year beginning after Aug. 5, '97 will allow taxes to be taken into account under the indirect foreign tax credit provisions that wouldn't have been taken into account under those provisions but for that transaction. ('97 Act §1113(c)(2)) This rule applies in the case of any chain of foreign corporations which would be eligible for the indirect foreign tax credit, under pre-'97 Act law or under the '97 Act, but for the denial of indirect credits below the third or sixth tier, as the case may be. (Com Rept, see ¶ 5175)

🅡 *illustration:* A chain of corporations meeting the requirements of Code Sec. 902(b)(2)(i) and Code Sec. 902(b)(2)(ii) consists of F1, F2, F3 F4, F5, F6 and F7. During a tax year that begins after Aug. 5, '97, F7 is liquidated into F6, its 100% owner, and the business formerly carried on by F7 is taken over by F6. Under the effective date provisions discussed above, foreign taxes paid with respect to income earned by what had formerly been F7's business, though now paid by F6, apparently would not qualify for the indirect foreign tax credit.

¶ 1602. Certain individuals exempt from foreign tax credit limitation

Code Sec. 904(j), as amended by '97 Act § 1101(a)
Generally effective: Tax years starting after Dec. 31, '97.
Committee Reports, see ¶ 5170

A U.S. taxpayer who also pays taxes to a foreign country may generally claim a credit against U.S. tax for the amount of foreign taxes. The foreign tax credit is generally limited to the lesser of (1) the ratio that foreign-source income bears to worldwide income multiplied by the U.S. income taxes on worldwide income, or (2) the actual foreign taxes paid (and deemed paid) on the income. (FTC 2d/FIN ¶ O-4401; USTR ¶ 9044.01; TaxDesk ¶ 39,412)

New Law.   The limitation on the foreign tax credit does not apply to certain taxpayers that are entitled to credit relatively small amounts of foreign tax imposed at modest effective tax rates on foreign source investment income.   Specifically, individuals with no more than $300 ($600 in the case of married persons filing jointly) of creditable foreign taxes (Code Sec. 904(j)(2)(B) as amended by '97 Act §1101(a)) and no foreign source income other than qualified passive income (Code Sec. 904(j)(2)(A)) may elect for the tax year (Code Sec. 904(j)(2)(C)) to be exempt from the foreign tax credit limitation (Code Sec. 904(j)(1)(A)). If this election is made, the taxpayer is not required to file Form 1116. (Com Rept, see ¶ 5170).

No carryover. An individual making this election is not entitled to any carryover of excess foreign taxes to (Code Sec. 904(j)(1)(C)) or from (Code Sec. 904(j)(1)(B)) a tax year to which the election applies.

Qualified passive income. Qualified passive income includes foreign personal holding company income under the subpart F rules, plus income inclusions from foreign personal holding companies and passive foreign investment companies that are qualified electing funds (Code Sec. 904(j)(3)(A)(i)), provided that the income is shown on a payee statement furnished to the individual. (Code Sec. 904(j)(3)(A)(ii))

Creditable foreign taxes. Creditable foreign taxes under this provision are any taxes for which a foreign tax credit is allowed under Code Sec. 901, but only if the taxes are shown on a payee statement furnished to the individual. (Code Sec. 904(j)(3)(B))

> *observation:* The significance of this definition of creditable foreign taxes is not entirely clear, and a literal reading of the Code suggests an apparently unintended result. The requirement that a tax be shown on a payee statement in order to be a "creditable foreign tax" does not affect whether the tax is entitled to a credit under Code Sec. 901. Rather, the only consequence of being a creditable foreign tax is that it is taken into account in applying the $300 limitation of Code Sec. 904(j)(2)(B). Consider the case of a taxpayer who meets the passive income requirement and who pays (1) $250 in foreign taxes that are shown on a payee statement, and (2) $5,000 in foreign taxes that are not reflected on a payee statement. The $5,000 in foreign taxes relate to an item which is not income for U.S. tax purposes, so that the failure to reflect that amount on a payee statement does not cause the qualified passive income requirement to be violated. Reading the Code literally, one would reach the conclusion that the taxpayer has only $250 of "creditable foreign taxes" and, therefore, satisfies the conditions for exemption from the foreign tax credit limitation. The additional $5,000 does not constitute "creditable foreign taxes" (since it is not shown on a payee statement), but nothing in the Code changes the rule of Code Sec. 901, which allows the taxpayer to claim a credit for it. The seemingly absurd result is that the taxpayer gets a full credit for $5,250, which is not subject to the limitation.
>
> Clearly, this result cannot have been intended by Congress, which intended merely to provide taxpayers with small amounts of foreign taxes with relief from the complex limitation rules. The Congressional intent may have been that a taxpayer who wishes to take advantage of the exemption may claim a credit only for foreign taxes that are reflected on a payee statement. However, technically, this result is not achieved by defining "creditable foreign tax," but would require an operative provision to the effect that a credit may be claimed only for "creditable foreign taxes."

Estates and trusts. Estates and trusts are not eligible for the exemption from the foreign tax credit limitation. (Code Sec. 904(j)(3)(D))

☐ **Effective:** Tax years starting after Dec. 31, '97. ('97 Act §1101(b))

FTC 2d References are to Federal Tax Coordinator 2d
FIN References are to RIA's Analysis of Federal Taxes: Income
USTR References are to United States Tax Reporter: Income, Estate & Gift, and Excise
PCA References are to Pension Coordinator and Pension & Benefits Expert/Advisor
PE References are to Pension and Profit Sharing 2nd
EP References are to Estate Planning & Taxation Coordinator and Estate Planning Advisor

¶ 1603. Treatment of noncontrolled Code Sec. 902 corporations for purposes of foreign tax credit limitation

Code Sec. 904(d)(1)(E), as amended by '97 Act § 1105(a)(1)
Code Sec. 904(d)(2)(E), as amended by '97 Act § 1105(a)(2)
Code Sec. 904(d)(2)(C)(iii)(II), as amended by '97 Act § 1105(a)(3)
Code Sec. 904(d)(2)(D), as amended by '97 Act § 1105(a)(3)
Code Sec. 904(d)(4), as amended by '97 Act § 1105(b)
Generally effective: Tax years beginning after Dec. 31, 2002.
Committee Reports, see ¶ 5174

A noncontrolled Code Sec. 902 corporation is a foreign corporation at least 10% of the stock of which is owned by the taxpayer and which is not a controlled foreign corporation (CFC) (sometimes called a 10/50 company). Under pre-'97 Act law, dividends received from each 10/50 company were subject to a separate foreign tax credit limitation. (FTC 2d/FIN ¶ O-4332; USTR ¶ 9044.01; TaxDesk ¶ 39,401)

New Law. *Dividends from 10/50 companies out of earnings and profits accumulated in tax years beginning before Jan. 1, 2003* are subject to a separate foreign tax credit limitation. (Code Sec. 904(d)(1)(E) as amended by '97 Act §1105(a)(1)) For this purpose, all 10/50 companies which are not passive foreign investment companies (PFICs) are treated as one 10/50 company. (Code Sec. 904(d)(2)(E)(iv) as amended by '97 Act §1105(a)(2))

In the case of dividends from a 10/50 company out of earnings and profits accumulated in tax years beginning after Dec. 31, 2002, (Code Sec. 904(d)(4)(B)) a "look-through" rule applies. Under this rule, for purposes of determining the separate application of the limitations on the foreign tax credit, any such dividend is treated as income in a separate category in proportion to the ratio of: (Code Sec. 904(d)(4)(A))

- the portion of such post-2002 earnings and profits which is attributable to income in such category (Code Sec. 904(d)(4)(A)(i)), to

- the total amount of such earnings and profits. (Code Sec. 904(d)(4)(A)(ii))

For purposes of these rules, Code Sec. 316 applies. (Code Sec. 904(d)(4)(C)(ii)(I) as amended by '97 Act §1105(b))

✔ observation: Under Code Sec. 316, dividends are generally deemed to be paid first out of the most recently accumulated earnings and profits.

IRS may prescribe regs regarding the treatment of distributions out of earnings and profits for periods before the taxpayer's acquisition of the stock. (Code Sec. 904(d)(4)(C)(ii)(II)) Congress expects that, to the extent regs treat distributions from a foreign corporation out of pre-acquisition earnings as subject to a separate foreign tax credit limitation, taxpayers could elect to apply such separate foreign tax credit limitation to all distributions by that corporation, including distributions out of post-acquisition earnings. (Com Rept, see ¶ 5174)

Rules similar to the look-through rules that are applied to controlled foreign corporations with respect to defining what types of income are in a "separate category" also apply for purposes of the look-through rules applicable to 10/50 companies with respect to dividends paid out of earnings and profits accumulated in tax years beginning after Dec. 31, 2002. (Code Sec. 904(d)(4)(C)(i))

For purposes of the separate foreign tax credit limitations, dividends from 10/50 companies are excluded from financial services income (Code Sec. 904(d)(2)(C)(iii)(II)) and shipping income (Code Sec. 904(d)(2)(D)) only to the extent they are out of earnings and profits accumulated in tax years beginning before Jan. 1, 2003.

☐ **Effective:** Tax years beginning after Dec. 31, 2002. ('97 Act §1105(c))

¶ 1604. Holding period requirement for certain foreign taxes

Code Sec. 901(k), as amended by '97 Act § 1053(a)
Code Sec. 853(c), as amended by '97 Act § 1053(b)
Generally effective: Dividends paid or accrued more than 30 days after Aug. 5, '97.
Committee Reports, see ¶ 5145

A U.S. taxpayer which pays taxes to a foreign country is, subject to certain limitations, entitled to claim the amount of the taxes as a credit against its U.S. tax liability. In addition, a U.S. corporation that receives a dividend from a foreign corporation in which it is a 10% or more shareholder may be entitled to an "indirect" credit for foreign taxes paid by the foreign corporation. Under pre-'97 Act law, there was no minimum holding period for stock which paid a dividend with respect to which the credit was claimed. (FTC 2d/FIN ¶ O-4000 *et seq.*, ¶ O-4800 *et seq.*; USTR ¶ 902.01, ¶ 9604)

New Law. In order to claim a foreign tax credit for certain taxes imposed on dividends, or for income, war profits and excess profits taxes deemed paid with respect to certain stock, a taxpayer must hold the stock for a minimum holding period. (Code Sec. 901(k) as amended by '97 Act §1053(a))

If a foreign tax credit is disallowed under these rules, (1) the deduction disallowance under Code Sec. 275 for foreign income, war profits and excess profits taxes for which a foreign tax credit is claimed and (2) the Code Sec. 78 gross-up of foreign taxes deemed paid do not apply. (Code Sec. 901(k)(7)) Thus, a taxpayer is entitled to a deduction for the foreign taxes for which the credit is disallowed, even if the taxpayer claims the foreign tax credit for other taxes in the same tax year. (Com Rept, see ¶ 5145)

No inference is intended as to the treatment under pre-'97 Act law of tax-motivated transactions intended to transfer foreign tax credit benefits. (Com Rept, see ¶ 5145)

Withholding taxes. No credit is allowed for any "withholding tax" (as defined below) on a dividend (1) with respect to stock in a corporation, if the stock is held by the recipient of the dividend for 15 days or less during the 30 day period beginning on the date which is 15 days before the date on which the shares become ex-dividend with respect to the dividend (Code Sec. 901(k)(1)(A)(i)), or (2) to the extent the recipient of the dividend is required, under a short sale or otherwise, to make payments with respect to substantially similar or related property. (Code Sec. 901(k)(1)(A)(ii))

In the case of dividends on preferred stock which are attributable to a period in excess of 366 days, the credit is not allowed if the stock is held by the recipient of the dividend for 45 days or less during the 90-day period beginning on the date which is 45 days before the date on which the shares become ex-dividend with respect to the dividend. (Code Sec. 901(k)(3))

The 16 day or 46 day holding period, whichever applies, must be satisfied over the period immediately before or immediately after the shareholder becomes entitled to receive each dividend. For purposes of determining whether the minimum holding period is met, any period during which the shareholder has protected itself from risk of loss is not included. (Com Rept, see ¶ 5145)

> *Illustration:* The day after foreign common stock is purchased, the taxpayer enters into an equity swap under which the taxpayer is entitled to receive payments equal to the losses on the stock, and the taxpayer retains the swap position for the entire period it holds the stock. The taxpayer is not able to claim any foreign tax credits with respect to dividends on the stock because the taxpayer's holding period is limited to the single day during which the loss on the stock was not protected. (Com Rept, see ¶ 5145)

For purposes of these rules, "withholding tax" includes any tax determined on a gross basis but does not include any tax which is a prepayment of a tax imposed on a net basis. (Code Sec. 901(k)(1)(B))

> ⚡ *observation:* Thus, the definition of withholding tax is not limited to taxes actually collected by means of withholding.

Indirect foreign tax credit. The same minimum holding period rules also apply to the stock of *each* corporation in a chain of corporations for which an indirect foreign tax credit is claimed. Thus, in the case of taxes deemed paid under Code Sec. 902 or Code Sec. 960, no credit is available if any stock of any corporation in the chain of ownership fails to satisfy the minimum holding period rules (Code Sec. 901(k)(2)(A)) or is subject to an obligation to make related payments. (Code Sec. 901(k)(2)(B))

> ⚡ *illustration:* U.S. corporation P owns 20% of F1, which owns 30% of F2, which owns 50% of F3. F1, F2 and F3 are foreign corporations. F1 distributes a dividend to P. F3 pays income tax to Country X. At the time the F1 stock becomes ex-dividend with respect to the dividend paid to P, P has held its position in F1 and F1 has held its position in F2 for more than 90 days.

However, F2 has held its position in F3 for only 10 days before such ex-dividend date, and F2 disposes of its F3 stock the day after such ex-dividend date. Even though P has satisfied the minimum holding period with respect to its F1 stock, it can not claim the indirect foreign tax credit for the income taxes paid by F3 because F2 has not satisfied the minimum holding period with respect to its F3 stock.

observation: The literal language of Code Sec. 901(k)(2)(A) suggests that a failure to satisfy the holding period for *any* stock, even one share, anywhere in the chain of ownership results in the loss of the indirect foreign tax credit with respect to dividends paid on *all* stock.

For a discussion of the extension of the Code Sec. 902 indirect foreign tax credit to sixth-tier foreign corporations, see ¶ 1601.

Taxes passed through regulated investment companies. The same minimum holding period rules also apply to stock in a regulated investment company (RIC) for which an indirect foreign tax credit is claimed. Thus, in the case of taxes deemed paid by shareholders of a RIC under a Code Sec. 853 election by the RIC to treat its foreign taxes as paid by its shareholders, no credit is available if any stock of any corporation in the chain fails to satisfy the minimum holding period rules (Code Sec. 901(k)(2)(A)) or is subject to an obligation to make related payments. (Code Sec. 901(k)(2)(B))

The notice which a RIC must send to its shareholders informing them of their proportionate share of certain taxes and gross income must also include the amount of taxes which would not be allowed as a foreign tax credit because of the minimum holding period rules. (Code Sec. 853(c) as amended by '97 Act §1053(b))

Exception for securities dealers. The minimum holding period rules do not apply to any "qualified tax" on a security held in the active conduct in a foreign country (the first foreign country) of a securities business of any person (1) registered as a securities broker or dealer under section 15(a) of the Securities Exchange Act of '34, (Code Sec. 901(k)(4)(A)(i)) (2) registered as a government securities broker or dealer under section 15C(a) of the Securities Exchange Act of '34 (Code Sec. 901(k)(4)(A)(ii)) or (3) licensed or authorized in the first foreign country to conduct securities activities in the first foreign country and subject to bona fide regulation by a securities regulating authority of the first foreign country. (Code Sec. 901(k)(4)(A)(iii)) "Qualified tax" means a tax paid to a second foreign country, if the dividend to which the tax is attributable is subject to tax on a net basis by the first foreign country (Code Sec. 901(k)(4)(B)(i)) and the first foreign country allows a credit against its net basis tax for the full amount of the tax paid to the second foreign country. (Code Sec. 901(k)(4)(B)(ii)) IRS may prescribe regs appropriate to carry out the rules of Code

FTC 2d References are to Federal Tax Coordinator 2d
FIN References are to RIA's Analysis of Federal Taxes: Income
USTR References are to United States Tax Reporter: Income, Estate & Gift, and Excise
PCA References are to Pension Coordinator and Pension & Benefits Expert/Advisor
PE References are to Pension and Profit Sharing 2nd
EP References are to Estate Planning & Taxation Coordinator and Estate Planning Advisor

 Research Institute of America 401

Sec. 901(k)(4), including regs to prevent abuse of the exception for foreign securities businesses and to treat other taxes as "qualified taxes." (Code Sec. 901(k)(4)(C)) The regs are to provide guidance as to the determination of whether stock is held in a tax-payer's capacity as a dealer or in connection with its securities trading activities. The authority to treat other foreign taxes as "qualified taxes" may be used to address internal withholding taxes imposed by a foreign country on persons that do business in the foreign country. (Com Rept, see ¶ 5145)

Rules for determining holding period. In applying the minimum holding period rules, (1) the date of disposition of the stock, but not the date of acquisition, is taken into account, (2) any day more than 45 days after the date on which the share becomes ex-dividend (or more than 90 days after in the case of dividends on preferred stock) is not taken into account, (3) Code Sec. 1223(4), regarding holding periods for property involved in wash sales, does not apply and (4) the holding period is reduced for any period during which the risk of loss is diminished, by the use of options or otherwise. (Code Sec. 901(k)(5))

If the taxpayer's holding period under Code Sec. 901(k) is reduced because of a diminished risk of loss resulting from a contract for the bona fide sale of stock, the determination of whether the taxpayer's holding period satisfies the minimum holding period rules for the indirect foreign tax credit under Code Sec. 902 or Code Sec. 960 is made as of the date the sales contract is entered into. (Code Sec. 901(k)(6))

☐ **Effective:** For dividends paid or accrued more than 30 days after Aug. 5, '97. ('97 Act §1053(c))

¶ 1605. Translation of foreign taxes simplified

Code Sec. 905(c), as amended by '97 Act § 1102(a)(2)
Code Sec. 986(a), as amended by '97 Act § 1102(a)(1)
Code Sec. 986(a)(3), as amended by '97 Act § 1102(b)(1)
Code Sec. 989(c)(6), as amended by '97 Act § 1102(b)(2)
Generally effective: Tax years starting after Dec. 31, '97.
Committee Reports, see ¶ 5171

Under pre-'97 Act law, an accrual method taxpayer determined the foreign tax credit (including the indirect credit) by translating the amount of foreign income taxes into U.S. dollar amounts using the currency exchange rate as of the last day of the tax year of accrual. If the dollar exchange value of foreign income taxes when paid differed from the value when accrued, a redetermination was required. A foreign tax redetermination could also occur in certain other cases. For this purpose, "income taxes" included income, war profits, or excess profits taxes paid to a foreign country or U.S. possession. (FTC 2d/FIN ¶ O-5300 *et seq.*; USTR ¶ 9864.01; TaxDesk ¶ 39,437)

New Law. The '97 Act simplifies the translation of income taxes denominated in foreign currency and reduces the number of instances requiring reconsideration. For accrual method taxpayers, foreign taxes are translated at the average exchange rate for the tax year to which the taxes relate (Code Sec. 986(a)(1)(A) as amended by '97 Act

§1102(a)(1)), rather than the rate at the end of the tax year of accrual. However, this rule does not apply to

- taxes paid more than two years after the close of the tax year to which these taxes relate (Code Sec. 986(a)(1)(B)(i)),

- taxes paid in a tax year prior to the year to which they relate (Code Sec. 986(a)(1)(B)(ii)), or

- taxes denominated in an inflationary currency (as determined under regs). (Code Sec. 986(a)(1)(C)).

Foreign income taxes to which the above rule does not apply are translated into U.S. dollars using the exchange rates as of the time the taxes are paid. (Code Sec. 986(a)(2)(A)). Any adjustment to the amount of the taxes is translated using the exchange rate at the time the adjustment is paid to the foreign country. (Code Sec. 986(a)(2)(B)(i)). In the case of any refund or credit of foreign taxes, the exchange rate to be used is that at the time when the original payment of the foreign income taxes was made. (Code Sec. 986(a)(2)(B)(ii)). IRS has authority to issue regulations that would allow these foreign tax payments to be translated into U.S. dollar amounts using an average exchange rate for a specified period. (Code Sec. 986(a)(3) as amended by '97 Act §1102(b)(1)); (Code Sec. 989(c)(6) as amended by '97 Act §1102(b)(2))

For purposes of these rules, "foreign income taxes" means foreign income, war profits, or excess profits taxes paid or accrued to a foreign country or to a U.S. possession. (Code Sec. 986(a)(4) as amended by '97 Act §1102(a))

Redeterminations. The taxpayer must notify IRS, and a redetermination will be made (Code Sec. 905(c)(1)) if:

- accrued taxes when paid differ from the amounts claimed as credits by the taxpayer, (Code Sec. 905(c)(1)(A)).

- accrued taxes are not paid before the date two years after the close of the tax year to which the taxes relate, (Code Sec. 905(c)(1)(B)) or

- any tax paid is refunded in whole or in part. (Code Sec. 905(c)(1)(C)).

However, instead of requiring redetermination in such cases, IRS may instead require appropriate adjustments to the pools of post-'86 foreign income taxes and the pools of post-'86 undistributed earnings which apply in determining the indirect foreign tax credit. (Code Sec. 905(c)(1) as amended by '97 Act §1102(a)(2))

Taxes not paid within two years. In the case of taxes not paid within two years from the close of the year in which they were accrued, no credit is permitted. (Code Sec. 905(c)(2)(A) as amended by '97 Act §1102(a)(2)) The following rules apply for taxes paid after the two-year period:

- If they are deemed paid taxes, they are taken into account for the tax year in which they are paid (without the requirement of a redetermination) (Code Sec. 905(c)(2)(B)(i)(I)).
- All other taxes are taken into account for the tax year to which they relate (Code Sec. 905(c)(2)(B)(i)(II)).

In both cases, the taxes are translated into U.S. dollars at the exchange rate in effect at the time they are paid to the foreign country. (Code Sec. 905(c)(2)(B)).

> *Illustration:* Assume that (1) in Year 1 a taxpayer accrues 1,000 units of foreign tax that relate to Year 1 and (2) the currency involved is not inflationary. Further assume that as of the end of Year 1 the tax is unpaid. The taxpayer translates 1,000 units of accrued foreign tax into U.S. dollars at the average exchange rate for Year 1. If the 1,000 units of tax are paid by the taxpayer in either Year 2 or Year 3, no redetermination of foreign tax is required. If any portion of the tax so accrued remains unpaid as of the end of Year 3, however, the taxpayer is required to redetermine its foreign tax accrued in Year 1 to eliminate the accrued but unpaid tax, thereby reducing its foreign tax credit for such year. If the taxpayer pays the disallowed taxes in Year 4, the taxpayer again redetermines its foreign taxes (and foreign tax credit) for Year 1, but the taxes paid in Year 4 are translated into U.S. dollars at the exchange rate for Year 4. (Com Rept, see ¶ 5171)

> *observation:* The foregoing Illustration sheds some light on the proper interpretation of the rule of Code Sec. 905(c)(1)(A), which requires redetermination whenever accrued taxes, when paid, differ from the amounts previously claimed as credits. On its face, this rule could be interpreted as requiring redetermination, whenever *the U.S. dollar value* of foreign taxes changes between the time of accrual and the time of payment—a reading which is similar to pre-'97 Act law and would seem inconsistent with Congress's intention to reduce the number of redeterminations that must be made.

> The Illustration suggests that Code Sec. 905(c)(1)(A) should instead be read to require redetermination only when the amount of the taxes *as denominated in foreign currency* has changed.

☐ **Effective:** The provision that changes the rate at which foreign taxes are translated is effective for taxes paid or accrued in tax years starting after Dec. 31, '97. ('97 Act §1102(c)(1)) The changes to the foreign tax redetermination rules apply to foreign taxes that relate to tax years beginning after Dec. 31, '97. ('97 Act §1102(c)(2))

¶ 1606. Clarification of determination of foreign taxes deemed paid

Code Sec. 902(c)(2)(B), as amended by '97 Act § 1163(a)
Generally effective: Aug. 5, '97
Committee Reports, see ¶ 5192

In determining the amount of the indirect foreign tax credit, a U.S. corporation that receives a dividend from a foreign corporation is deemed to have paid a portion of the foreign corporation's post-'86 foreign income taxes. For this purpose, under pre-'97 Act law, post-'86 foreign taxes included (1) current year foreign income taxes, plus (2) foreign income taxes with respect to prior post-'86 years to the extent such taxes were not *deemed paid with respect to* dividends distributed in prior years. (FTC 2d/FIN ¶ O-5003; USTR ¶ 9024.03; TaxDesk ¶ 39,404)

New Law. The '97 Act clarifies that, for purposes of the deemed paid credit for a tax year, a foreign corporation's post-'86 foreign income taxes includes foreign income taxes with respect to prior post-'86 tax years only to the extent those taxes are not *attributable to* (rather than *deemed paid with respect to*) dividends distributed by the foreign corporation in prior tax years. (Code Sec. 902(c)(2)(B) as amended by '97 Act §1163(a)) Congress intends no inference regarding the determination of foreign taxes paid under present law. (Com Rept, see ¶ 5192)

☐ **Effective:** Aug. 5, '97. ('97 Act §1163(c))

¶ 1607. Clarification of foreign tax credit limitation for financial services income

Code Sec. 904(d)(2)(C)(i)(II), as amended by '97 Act § 1163(b)
Generally effective: Aug. 5, '97
Committee Reports, see ¶ 5192

Separate foreign tax credit limitations apply to various categories of income. Two of these separate limitation categories are passive income and financial services income. Certain income that is treated as high-taxed income is excluded from the definition of passive income for purposes of the separate foreign tax credit limitation. For purposes of the separate limitation applicable to financial services income, the definition generally incorporates passive income as defined for purposes of the separate limitation applicable to passive income. (FTC 2d/FIN ¶ O-4325; USTR ¶ 9044.01)

New Law. The '97 Act clarifies that the exclusion of high-taxed income from passive income does not apply for purposes of the separate foreign tax credit limitation applicable to financial services income. (Code Sec. 904(d)(2)(C)(i)(II) as amended by '97 Act §1163(b))

Congress intends no inference regarding the treatment of high-taxed income for purposes of the separate foreign tax credit limitation applicable to financial services income under present law. (Com Rept, see ¶ 5192)

☐ **Effective:** Aug. 5, '97. ('97 Act §1163(c))

¶ 1608. IRS can modify rule for determining foreign source income attributable to capital gains to properly reflect capital gain rate differential and computation of net capital gain

Code Sec. 904(b)(2)(C), as amended by '97 Act § 311(c)(3)
Generally effective: For tax years ending after May 6, '97

For purposes of computing the foreign tax credit limitation, taxable income from sources outside the U.S. includes capital gain only to the extent of foreign source capital gain net income. This is the lesser of capital gain net income from foreign sources or capital gain net income from all sources. Capital gain net income is the excess of capital gains over capital losses and includes net section 1231 gain. But this rule doesn't apply if there is a capital gain rate differential, i.e., if the maximum tax rate on the ordinary income of individual taxpayers is higher than the maximum rate on the net capital gains of the taxpayers. If there is a capital gain rate differential, taxable income from sources outside the U.S. includes capital gain only in an amount equal to foreign source capital gain net income reduced by the rate differential portion of foreign source net capital gain. (FTC 2d/FIN ¶ O-4404; USTR ¶ 9044.01)

New Law. IRS may by regulations modify the pre-'97 Act rule to properly reflect any capital gain rate differential under Code Sec. 1(h), see ¶ 201, or Code Sec. 1201(a), and the computation of net capital gain. (Code Sec. 904(b)(2)(C) as amended by '97 Act §311(c)(3))

☐ **Effective:** For tax years ending after May 6, '97. ('97 Act §311(d)(1))

Controlled Foreign Corporations

¶ 1609. Definition of foreign personal holding company income expanded

Code Sec. 954(c)(1)(B), as amended by '97 Act § 1051(a)(2)
Code Sec. 954(c)(1)(F), as amended by '97 Act § 1051(a)(1)
Code Sec. 954(c)(1)(G), as amended by '97 Act § 1051(a)(1)
Code Sec. 954(c)(2)(C), as amended by '97 Act § 1051(b)
Generally effective: Tax years starting after Aug. 5, '97
Committee Reports, see ¶ 5143

Under pre-'97 Act law, for purposes of applying the controlled foreign corporation (CFC) rules, foreign personal holding company income did not include income from notional principal contracts, but did include income from transactions in commodities or foreign currency as well as income that is equivalent to interest. It also did not include stock-lending transactions, although it did include economically equivalent transactions involving transfers of debt securities. (FTC 2d/FIN ¶ O-2432; USTR ¶ 9544.02)

Income earned by a CFC that is a regular dealer in the property sold or exchanged generally is excluded from the definition of foreign personal holding company income. No exception, however, was available for a CFC that is a regular dealer in financial instruments referenced to commodities. (FTC 2d/FIN ¶ O-2448; USTR ¶ 9544.02)

New Law. The '97 Act adds two new categories to the definition of foreign personal holding company income:

• net income from notional principal contracts (Code Sec. 954(c)(1)(F) as amended by '97 Act §1051(a)(1)), and

• payments in lieu of dividends in connection with stock-lending transactions (Code Sec. 954(c)(1)(G)).

Any item of income, gain, deduction, or loss from a notional principal contract entered into for purposes of hedging any other item listed in another subsection of the definition is taken into account only under that other subsection. (Code Sec. 954(c)(1)(F)) Thus, because gains and losses from transactions in inventory property are excluded from personal holding company income, income from a notional principal contract entered into to hedge inventory property is similarly excluded. (Com Rept, see ¶ 5143)

In the case of a CFC that is a regular dealer in property, forward contracts, option contracts, or similar financial instruments (including notional principal contracts and all instruments referenced to commodities), foreign personal holding company income does not include any item of income, gain, deduction, or loss from any transaction (including hedging transactions) entered into in the ordinary course of the dealer's trade or business, except for dividends (or payments in lieu thereof), interest (or income equivalent thereto), royalties, rents, and annuities. (Code Sec. 954(c)(2)(C) as amended by '97 Act §1051(b))

☐ **Effective:** Tax years starting after Aug. 5, '97. ('97 Act §1051(c))

¶ 1610. Temporary exception from foreign personal holding company income for active financing income

Code Sec. 954(h), as amended by '97 Act § 1175(a)
Code Sec. 954(e)(2), as amended by '97 Act § 1175(b)
Generally effective: Tax years of foreign corporations beginning after Dec. 31, '97 and before Jan. 1, '99, and tax years of U.S. shareholders with or within such tax years of foreign corporations end.
Committee Reports, see ¶ 5197

U.S. 10% shareholders of a foreign personal holding company are required to include in income their pro rata share of foreign personal holding company income

---

FTC 2d References are to Federal Tax Coordinator 2d
FIN References are to RIA's Analysis of Federal Taxes: Income
USTR References are to United States Tax Reporter: Income, Estate & Gift, and Excise
PCA References are to Pension Coordinator and Pension & Benefits Expert/Advisor
PE References are to Pension and Profit Sharing 2nd
EP References are to Estate Planning & Taxation Coordinator and Estate Planning Advisor

Ⓡ Research Institute of America 407

(FPHCI), whether or not the income is distributed to the shareholders. FPHCI includes dividends, interest, income equivalent to interest, rents, royalties and annuities. Under pre-'97 Act law, there was no exception for banking or insurance income. (FTC 2d/FIN ¶ O-2432 *et seq.*, ¶ O-3600 *et seq.*; USTR ¶ 5514, ¶ 9544.02)

New Law. *For tax years beginning in '98 only,* FPHCI does not include income that is:

(1) derived in the active conduct by a controlled foreign corporation (CFC) of a banking, financing or similar business, if the corporation is "predominantly engaged" (as defined below) in the active conduct of such business, (Code Sec. 954(h)(1)(A) as amended by '97 Act §1175(a))

(2) received from a person other than a related person (within the meaning of Code Sec. 954(d)(3), which pertains to the definition of foreign base company sales income) and derived from investments made by a "qualifying insurance company" (as defined below) of its reserves or of 80% of its unearned premiums (as determined in the manner described below), (Code Sec. 954(h)(1)(B)) or

(3) received from a person other than a related person (within the meaning of Code Sec. 954(d)(3)) and derived from investments made by a qualifying insurance company of a specified amount of its assets. (Code Sec. 954(h)(1)(C)) The specified amount is equal to:

- one-third of its premiums earned on insurance contracts during the tax year, in the case of contracts regulated in the country in which sold as property, casualty or health insurance contracts (Code Sec. 954(h)(1)(C)(i)), and
- the greater of 10% of insurance reserves or (with respect to "start-up companies," as defined below) $10,000,000, in the case of contracts regulated in the country in which sold as life insurance or annuity contracts. (Code Sec. 954(h)(1)(C)(ii))

Income described in (1) is also excluded from the definition of foreign base company service income. (Code Sec. 954(e)(2)(C) as amended by '97 Act §1175(b))

Applicable income. For purposes of determining whether banking, financing or similar income is subject to the exception described in item (1) above, the principles of Code Sec. 904(d)(2)(C)(ii) (which apply to financial services income for purposes of the foreign tax credit limitation) are followed, except that income from all leases entered into in the ordinary course of the active conduct of a banking, financing or similar business is included. (Code Sec. 954(h)(2)(A)(i)) In the case of a corporation that satisfies the "predominately engaged" requirement under the special rules described in Code Sec. 954(h)(3)(B) (see below), the determination of income to which the exception applies is made in accordance with the principles of Code Sec. 1296(b) (pertaining to passive foreign investment companies) as in effect before the enactment of the '97 Act. (Code Sec. 954(h)(2)(A)(ii)) Thus, income that is treated as nonpassive income under Prop. Reg. §§ 1.1296-4 and 1.1296-6 will be eligible for the exclusion. In particular, income or gains with respect to foreclosed property incident to the active conduct of a banking business is eligible. (Com Rept, see ¶ 5197)

In determining whether insurance income is entitled to the exception under items (2) and (3) above, the following rules apply. In the case of separate account-type contracts (including variable contracts that don't meet the requirements of Code Sec. 817), only income specifically allocable to such contracts is taken into account. (Code Sec. 954(h)(2)(B)(i)) In the case of other contracts, income is allocated ratably. (Code Sec. 954(h)(2)(B)(ii))

IRS is to prescribe regs consistent with the principles of Code Sec. 904(d)(3), providing look-through treatment for dividends, interest, income equivalent to interest, rents and royalties received or accrued from a related person (within the meaning of Code Sec. 954(d)(3)). (Code Sec. 954(h)(2)(C))

"Predominantly engaged" requirement. A corporation is considered "predominantly engaged" in the active conduct of a banking, financing or similar business only if:

(1) more than 70% of its gross income is derived from such business from transactions with unrelated persons (as defined in Code Sec. 954(d)(3), which pertains to the definition of foreign base company sales income) "located" (as specially defined below) within the country under the laws of which the CFC is created or organized (Code Sec. 954(h)(3)(A)), or

(2) the corporation is engaged in the active conduct of a banking or securities business within the meaning of Code Sec. 1296(b) (pertaining to passive foreign investment companies) as in effect before the enactment of the '97 Act, or is a qualified bank affiliate or a qualified securities affiliate within the meaning of proposed regs issued under pre-'97 Act Code Sec. 1296(b). (Code Sec. 954(h)(3)(B))

Reserves and unearned premiums. For purposes of applying the exclusion to the income of an insurance company derived from the investment of its reserves and unearned premiums, the following methods are to be used. The reserves and unearned premiums of a qualifying insurance company (as defined below) with respect to property, casualty or health insurance contracts are determined using the same methods and insurance rates that would be used if the company were taxed under Subchapter L (Code Sec. 801 through Code Sec. 848, pertaining to insurance companies). (Code Sec. 954(h)(4)(A))

The reserves of a qualifying insurance company with respect to life insurance or annuity contracts are determined, electively, under a "U.S.," "foreign" or "cash surrender value method." (Code Sec. 954(h)(4)(B)) The "U.S. method" is the method that would apply under Subchapter L except that the interest rate used is a rate determined for the foreign country in which the company is created or organized, and calculated in the same manner as the Federal mid-term rate under Code Sec. 1274(d). (Code Sec. 954(h)(5)(A)) The "foreign method" is a preliminary term method, except that the interest rate used is the rate determined for the foreign country in which the company is created or organized, and calculated in the same manner as the Federal mid-term rate under Code Sec. 1274(d). If a qualifying insurance company uses a preliminary term method for contracts insuring risks in the foreign country, that method shall apply if the foreign method is elected. (Code Sec. 954(h)(5)(B)) The "cash surrender value method" is a method under which reserves are equal to the net surrender value of the contract as defined in Code Sec. 807(e)(1)(A). (Code Sec. 954(h)(5)(C)) A taxpayer's election of one of these methods is to be made when, and in the manner, prescribed by IRS, and once made is irrevocable without IRS consent. (Code Sec. 954(h)(4)(B))

In no case may a reserve determined under these rules (including Code Sec. 954(h)(4)(A) above) for any contract as of any time exceed the amount that would be taken into account with respect to the contract in determining foreign annual statement reserves (less any catastrophe or deficiency reserves). (Code Sec. 954(h)(4)(C))

"Qualifying insurance company" defined. A "qualifying insurance company" is any entity:

. . . subject to regulation as an insurance company under the laws of its country of incorporation, (Code Sec. 954(h)(6)(A)(i)(I))

. . . which realizes at least 50% of its net written premiums from the insurance or reinsurance of risks located in the country in which the entity is created or organized, (Code Sec. 954(h)(6)(A)(i)(II))

. . . is engaged in the active conduct of an insurance business, and

. . . would be subject to tax under Subchapter L if it were a U.S. corporation. (Code Sec. 954(h)(6)(A)(i)(III))

When person "located" in foreign country. For purposes of Code Sec. 954(h)(3)(A) (above), a person (other than a natural person) is treated as located in the country in which it maintains an office or other fixed place of business through which it engages in a trade or business, and by which the transaction is affected. (Code Sec. 954(h)(6)(B)(i)(I)) A natural person is located in the country in which that person is physically located at the time of the transaction. (Code Sec. 954(h)(6)(B)(i)(II))

A special rule applies to "qualified business units" (as defined in Code Sec. 989(a)). Gross income derived by a corporation's qualified business unit (QBU) from transactions with persons that aren't related persons under Code Sec. 954(d)(3), and who are located in the country in which the QBU maintains its principal office and conducts substantial business activity, are treated as derived from transactions with unrelated persons located in the country under the laws of which the CFC is created or organized. (Code Sec. 954(h)(6)(B)(ii))

Anti-abuse rules. Any item of income, gain, loss, or deduction is disregarded under Code Sec. 954(h) if it is with respect to any transaction or series of transactions one of the principal purposes of which is to qualify income or gain for the exclusion. This includes any change in the method of computing reserves or any other transaction a principal purpose of which is the acceleration or deferral of any item in order to claim the exclusion. (Code Sec. 954(h)(7))

Start-up companies. A qualifying insurance company will be treated as a start-up company if the company (and any predecessor) hasn't been engaged in the active conduct of an insurance business for more than 5 years as of the beginning of the company's tax year. (Code Sec. 954(h)(6)(A)(ii)) If the foreign company was formed before being acquired by the U.S. shareholder, the 5-year period begins when the company was first engaged in the active conduct of an insurance business. In the event of the acquisition of a book of business from another company through an assumption or indemnity reinsurance transaction, the 5-year period begins when the acquiring company first engages in the active conduct of an insurance business, except that if more than a substantial part (e.g. 80%) of the business of the ceding company is acquired, the period begins when the ceding company first engaged in the active conduct of an insurance business. Also, it's not intended that reinsurance transactions among related persons be used to multiply the number of 5-year periods. (Com Rept, see ¶5197)

Other rules. The Code Sec. 954(h) exclusion doesn't apply to investment income allocable to contracts that insure related party risks, or risks located in a foreign country other than the country in which the qualifying insurance company is created or organized. (Code Sec. 954(h)(8))

Investment income of a CFC that is attributable to the issuing or reinsuring of any insurance or annuity contract related to risks outside its country of organization remains taxable as subpart F insurance income. (Com Rept, see ¶5197)

☐ **Effective:** The first *full* tax year of a foreign corporation that begins after '97 and before '99, (Code Sec. 954(h)(9)) and tax years of U.S. shareholders with or within such tax years of foreign corporations end. ('97 Act §1175(c))

> *observation:* This means, presumably, that if the foreign corporation has a short tax year beginning in '98, followed by a full tax year also beginning in '98, Code Sec. 954(h) will apply to the full year and not to the short year.

¶1611. U.S. property does not include certain assets acquired by a dealer in securities or commodities in the ordinary course of a trade or business

Code Sec. 956(c)(2), as amended by '97 Act § 1173(a)
Generally effective: Tax years of foreign corporations beginning after Dec. 31, '97, and to tax years of U.S. shareholders with or within which such tax years of foreign corporations end.
Committee Reports, see ¶5195

A U.S. shareholder of a controlled foreign corporation (CFC) is taxed on an amount equal to the lesser of (1) the U.S. shareholder's pro rata share of the average amount of U.S. property held, directly or indirectly, by the CFC as of the close of each quarter, less that portion of the CFC's earnings and profits attributable to amounts included previously in that shareholder's gross income on account of investment in U.S. property, or (2) that shareholder's pro rata share of the CFC's applicable earnings.

Under pre-'97 Act law, there was no exclusion from the definition of U.S. property for deposits of collateral or margin and repurchase agreements made in the ordinary course of business. (FTC 2d/FIN ¶ O-2546; USTR ¶ 9564.01)

New Law. U.S. property does not include deposits of cash or securities made or received on commercial terms in the ordinary course of a U.S. or foreign person's business as a dealer in securities or commodities, to the extent the deposits are made or received as collateral or margin for (1) a securities loan, notional principal contract, options contract, forward contract or futures contract or (2) any other financial transaction in which IRS determines it is customary to post collateral or margin. (Code Sec. 956(c)(2)(J) as amended by '97 Act §1173(a))

U.S. property also does not include an obligation of a U.S. person to the extent the principal amount of the obligation does not exceed the fair market value of readily marketable securities sold or purchased under a sale and repurchase agreement or otherwise posted or received as collateral for the obligation in the ordinary course of the business of a U.S. or foreign person which is a dealer in securities or commodities. (Code Sec. 956(c)(2)(K))

The term "dealer in securities" has the same meaning given that term in Code Sec. 475(c)(1) (mark-to-market accounting rules for securities dealers). The term "dealer in commodities" has the same meaning given that term in Code Sec. 475(e) (as amended by '97 Act §1001(b), see ¶ 2001), except that the term includes a futures commission merchant. (Code Sec. 956(c)(2))

No inference is intended regarding the treatment of an obligation of a U.S. person to return stock that is borrowed pursuant to a securities loan. (Com Rept, see ¶ 5195)

☐ **Effective:** Tax years of foreign corporations beginning after Dec. 31, '97, and tax years of U.S. shareholders with or within which such tax years of foreign corporations end. ('97 Act §1173(b))

¶ 1612. Gain on certain stock sales by CFCs treated as dividends

Code Sec. 964(e), as amended by '97 Act § 1111(a)
Code Sec. 904(d)(2)(E)(i), as amended by '97 Act § 1111(b)
Generally effective: Aug. 5, '97
Committee Reports, see ¶ 5175

For purposes of applying the foreign tax credit limitations, receipt of a dividend from a lower-tier controlled foreign corporation (CFC) by an upper-tier CFC may result in subpart F income for the U.S. shareholder that is treated as income in the same foreign tax credit limitation category as the income of the lower-tier CFC (the "look-through" rule). If, on the other hand, the upper-tier CFC sells stock of a lower-tier CFC, then under pre-'97 Act law the look-through rule did not apply; instead, gain on the sale generally was treated as passive income.

The look-through rule does not apply to dividends received from a "noncontrolled Section 902 corporation." Instead, such dividends are treated as a separate foreign tax credit limitation category. Under pre-'97 Act law, a noncontrolled Section 902 corporation did not include a CFC with respect to any distribution out of its earnings and profits for periods during which it was a CFC and, except as provided in regulations, the recipient of the distribution was a U.S. shareholder in the corporation. (FTC 2d/FIN ¶ O-4343, ¶ O-4351; USTR ¶ 9044.01)

New Law. Gain recognized by a CFC from the sale or exchange of stock in a foreign corporation is treated as a dividend to the same extent that it would have been so treated under Code Sec. 1248 if the CFC were a U.S. person. This provision, however, does not affect the determination of whether the corporation whose stock is sold or exchanged is a CFC. (Code Sec. 964(e)(1) as added by '97 Act §1111(a))

> **☢️observation:** Code Sec. 1248 characterizes as a dividend gain recognized by a *U.S. person* on certain sales of CFC stock.

> **Illustration:** D, a U.S. corporation, owns 100% of the stock of F1, a foreign corporation, which owns 100% of the stock of F2, a foreign corporation. Gain recognized by F1 on a sale or exchange of stock of F2 is treated as a dividend for purposes of subpart F income inclusions to D, to the extent of earnings and profits of F2 attributable to periods in which F1 owned the stock of F2 while F2 was a CFC with respect to the U.S. shareholder. (Com Rept, see ¶ 5175)

The provision reduces complexities and eliminates uncertainties and gaps in the pre-'97 Act statutory regime by rationalizing the rules for taxing gains on dispositions of stock in CFCs as dividend income or subpart F income. (Com Rept, see ¶ 5175)

Same-country exception does not apply. Gain on disposition of stock in a related corporation created or organized under the laws of, and having a substantial part of its assets in a trade or business in, the same foreign country as the gain recipient is not excluded from foreign personal holding company income under the same-country exception that applies to actual dividends, even if such gain is recharacterized as a dividend under the above rule. (Code Sec. 964(e)(2))

For purposes of the above rule, a CFC is treated as having sold or exchanged stock if, under any provision of subtitle A of the Code, the CFC is treated as having gain from the sale or exchange of such stock. (Code Sec. 964(e)(3))

> **Illustration:** A CFC distributes to its shareholder stock in a foreign corporation, and the distribution results in gain being recognized by the CFC under Code Sec. 311(b) as if the stock were sold to the shareholder for fair market value. For purposes of Code Sec. 964(e), the CFC is treated as having sold or exchanged the stock. (Com Rept, see ¶ 5175)

FTC 2d References are to Federal Tax Coordinator 2d
FIN References are to RIA's Analysis of Federal Taxes: Income
USTR References are to United States Tax Reporter: Income, Estate & Gift, and Excise
PCA References are to Pension Coordinator and Pension & Benefits Expert/Advisor
PE References are to Pension and Profit Sharing 2nd
EP References are to Estate Planning & Taxation Coordinator and Estate Planning Advisor

Noncontrolled section 902 corporation redefined. A CFC is not treated as a noncontrolled section 902 corporation with respect to any distribution out of its earnings and profits for periods during which it was a CFC, whether or not the recipient of the distribution was a U.S. shareholder of the corporation when the earnings and profits giving rise to the distribution were generated. (Code Sec. 904(d)(2)(E)(i) as amended by '97 Act §1111(b))

☐ **Effective:** Transactions (or, in the case of the amendment to the definition of noncontrolled Section 902 corporation, distributions) after Aug. 5, '97. ('97 Act §1111(c))

¶ 1613. Pro rata share of subpart F income takes into account previous shareholders' Code Sec. 1248 gain

Code Sec. 951(a)(2), as amended by '97 Act § 1112(a)
Generally effective: Dispositions after Aug. 5, '97
Committee Reports, see ¶ 5175

Subpart F income earned by a foreign corporation during a tax year is taxed to the persons who are U.S. shareholders of the corporation on the last day, in that year, on which the corporation is a controlled foreign corporation (CFC). In the case of a U.S. shareholder who acquired stock in a CFC during the year, the inclusion is reduced by the lesser of (1) the amount of dividends with respect to such stock received by other persons during the year, or (2) the amount determined by multiplying the subpart F income for the year by the proportion of the year during which the acquiring shareholder did not own the stock.

Under pre-'97 Act law, the Code did not provide a similar rule to reflect gain recognized by other holders of the stock which was treated as a dividend under Code Sec. 1248. (FTC 2d/FIN ¶ O-2609.2, ¶ O-2800.1; USTR ¶ 9514.01)

New Law. If a U.S. shareholder acquires the stock of a CFC from another U.S. shareholder during a tax year of the CFC in which it earns subpart F income, the acquirer's subpart F income inclusion for that year is reduced by a portion of the amount of the dividend deemed under Code Sec. 1248 to be received by the transferor. (Code Sec. 951(a)(2) as amended by '97 Act §1112(a)(1))

> ✔️*observation:* As a result of the amendment, an inclusion based on the treatment of gain as a dividend under Code Sec. 1248 is reduced by the lesser of (1) the amount of dividends with respect to the stock deemed received under Code Sec. 1248 by other persons during the year, or (2) the amount determined by multiplying the subpart F income for the year by the proportion of the year during which the acquiring shareholder did not own the stock.

> ✔️*observation:* The amount of the reduction is the same as applied under pre-'97 Act law (and which continues to apply) where an actual dividend was paid to the previous owner of the stock.

For a discussion of the new rule treating CFC gain on the sale of stock in a foreign corporation as a dividend under Code Sec. 1248, see ¶ 1612.

☐ **Effective:** Dispositions after Aug. 5, '97. ('97 Act §1112(a)(2))

¶ 1614. Adjustments to basis of stock in lower-tier CFCs

Code Sec. 961(c), as amended by '97 Act § 1112(b)
Generally effective: Tax years beginning after Dec. 31, '97
Committee Reports, see ¶ 5175

If subpart F income of a lower-tier controlled foreign corporation (CFC) is included in the gross income of a U.S. shareholder, the U.S. shareholder increases its basis in stock of the upper-tier CFC. Under pre-'97 Act law, no provision permitted adjustment of the basis of the upper-tier CFC's stock in the lower-tier CFC. (FTC 2d/FIN ¶ O-2613; USTR ¶ 9614.01)

New Law. Under regs to be issued by IRS, when a lower-tier CFC earns subpart F income, and stock in that corporation is later disposed of by an upper-tier CFC, the upper-tier CFC's basis in the stock of the lower-tier CFC is adjusted to account for previous income inclusions, in a manner similar to the adjustments to the basis of stock in a first-tier CFC. However, the basis adjustment only applies for purposes of determining the amount included in income of the U.S. shareholder under the CFC rules, or in income of a successor to the U.S. shareholder, to the extent of the interest of the U.S. shareholder acquired by the successor and subject to proof of the identity of the interest as prescribed by regs. (Code Sec. 961(c) as amended by '97 Act §1112(b)(1))

Thus, just as the basis of a U.S. shareholder in a first-tier CFC rises when subpart F income is earned and falls when previously taxed income is distributed, so as to avoid double taxation of the income on a later disposition of the stock of that company, the subpart F income from gain on the disposition of the stock of a lower-tier CFC is reduced by income inclusions of earnings that were not subsequently distributed by the lower-tier CFC. (Com Rept, see ¶ 5175)

> **Illustration:** A, a U.S. person, is the owner of all of the stock of F1, a first-tier CFC which, in turn, is the sole shareholder of F2, a second-tier CFC. In year 1, F2 earns $100 of subpart F income which is included in A's gross income for that year. In year 2, F1 disposes of its F2 stock and recognizes $300 of income with respect to the disposition. All of that income is subpart F foreign personal holding company income. IRS has regulatory authority to reduce A's year 2 subpart F inclusion by $100—the amount of year 1 subpart F income of F2 that was included, in that year, in A's gross income. Such an adjustment would, in effect, allow for a step-up in the basis of the stock of F2 to the extent of its subpart F income previously included in A's gross income. (Com Rept, see ¶ 5175)

☐ **Effective:** For determining income inclusions for tax years of U.S. shareholders beginning after Dec. 31, '97. ('97 Act §1112(b)(2))

¶ 1615. Treatment of exemptions from branch profits tax clarified

Code Sec. 952(b), as amended by '97 Act § 1112(c)
Generally effective: Tax years beginning after Dec. 31, '86
Committee Reports, see ¶ 5175

Generally, subpart F income of a controlled foreign corporation (CFC) does not include income earned from sources within the U. S. if the income is effectively connected with the conduct of a U.S. trade or business by the CFC. Under pre-'97 Act law, this general rule did not apply if the income was exempt from, or subject to a reduced rate of, U.S. tax under a treaty. (FTC 2d/FIN ¶ O-2602; USTR ¶ 9524.01)

New Law. An exemption or reduction by treaty of the branch profits tax on a CFC is not taken into account for the general statutory exemption from subpart F income for U.S. source effectively connected income. (Code Sec. 952(b) as amended by '97 Act §1112(c)(1))

> *Illustration:* A CFC earns income of a type that generally would be subpart F income, and that income is earned from sources within the U. S. in connection with business operations therein. Repatriation of that income is exempted from the U.S. branch profits tax under a provision of an applicable U.S. income tax treaty. Notwithstanding the treaty's effect on the branch tax, the income is not treated as subpart F income as long as it is not exempt from U.S. taxation (or subject to a reduced rate of tax) under any other treaty provision. (Com Rept, see ¶ 5175)

☐ **Effective:** Tax years beginning after Dec. 31, '86. ('97 Act §1112(c)(2))

¶ 1616. Clarification of earnings and profits definition for purposes of CFC rules

Code Sec. 956(b)(1)(A), as amended by '97 Act § 1601(e)
Generally effective: Tax years of CFCs beginning after '96, and tax years of U.S. shareholders within which or with which such years end
Committee Reports, see ¶ 5362

A U.S. shareholder of a controlled foreign corporation (CFC) is required to include in income the lesser of (1) the shareholder's pro rata share of the corporation's increase in earnings invested in U.S. property, or (2) the shareholder's pro rata share of the corporation's "applicable earnings." Under pre-'97 Act law, "applicable earnings" specifically included both earnings and profits (E&P) for the current year and accumulated E&P (without taking into account any deficit). This formulation could be read to suggest that E&P for the current year was taken into account twice. (FTC 2d/FIN ¶ O-2546; USTR ¶ 9564.01)

New Law. For purposes of the definition of applicable earnings, accumulated E&P includes only amounts accumulated in prior tax years. (Code Sec. 956(b)(1)(A) as amended by '97 Act §1601(e))

> ☝ *observation:* Amounts accumulated during the current year are still included in applicable earnings as *current* E&P. By specifically excluding such amounts from *accumulated* E&P, the amendment clarifies that they are not counted twice.

☐ **Effective:** Tax years of CFCs beginning after '96, and tax years of U.S. shareholders within which or with which such years end ('97 Act §1601(j))

Passive Foreign Investment Companies

¶ 1617. 10% U.S. shareholders of a CFC are not subject to PFIC rules

Code Sec. 1296(e), as amended by '97 Act § 1121
Generally effective: Tax years of U.S. persons beginning after Dec. 31, '97.
Committee Reports, see ¶ 5178

A foreign corporation that is a controlled foreign corporation (CFC) can also be a passive foreign investment company (PFIC). If an item of income of a foreign corporation is includable in the gross income of a 10% U.S. shareholder both under the CFC rules and the PFIC rules, that item of income is included only under the CFC rules if the PFIC is also a qualified electing fund (QEF). Under pre-'97 Act law, if a PFIC was not a QEF, and the shareholder was a 10% U.S. shareholder, the shareholder could be subject to both the CFC and the PFIC rules, but with certain adjustments made to the PFIC's excess distributions taxed under the CFC rules in order to avoid double taxation. (FTC 2d/FIN ¶ O-2201; USTR ¶ 12,914.05)

New Law. A PFIC is not treated as a PFIC with respect to a shareholder during the "qualified portion" of the shareholder's holding period. (Code Sec. 1296(e)(1) as amended by '97 Act §1121) "Qualified portion" means the portion of the shareholder's holding period after Dec. 31, '97 during which the shareholder is a 10% U.S. shareholder and the corporation is a CFC. (Code Sec. 1296(e)(2)) In other words, a PFIC isn't treated as a PFIC with respect to a shareholder's holding period after Dec. 31, '97 during which the shareholder is subject to the CFC current inclusion rules with respect to that corporation. (Com Rept, see ¶ 5178)

The PFIC provisions continue to apply in the case of a PFIC that is also a CFC with respect to shareholders that are not subject to the CFC rules, namely less than 10% U.S. shareholders. (Com Rept, see ¶ 5178)

FTC 2d References are to Federal Tax Coordinator 2d
FIN References are to RIA's Analysis of Federal Taxes: Income
USTR References are to United States Tax Reporter: Income, Estate & Gift, and Excise
PCA References are to Pension Coordinator and Pension & Benefits Expert/Advisor
PE References are to Pension and Profit Sharing 2nd
EP References are to Estate Planning & Taxation Coordinator and Estate Planning Advisor

The change was prompted by the unnecessary complexity in the overlap of the CFC and PFIC rules under pre-'97 Act law. (Com Rept, see ¶ 5178)

If the "qualified portion" of the U.S. shareholder's holding period ends after Dec. 31, '97, then solely for purposes of the PFIC rules, the U.S. shareholder's holding period is treated as beginning as of the first day following such period. (Code Sec. 1296(e)(3)(A)) In other words, if a shareholder is not subject to the PFIC provisions because the CFC rules apply, and the shareholder later ceases to be subject to the CFC rules, then for purposes of the PFIC rules, the shareholder's holding period is treated as beginning immediately after such cessation. Accordingly, in applying the rules for PFICs that are not QEFs, the earnings of the corporation are not attributed to the period during which the corporation was treated as a CFC with respect to the shareholder and not as a PFIC. (Com Rept, see ¶ 5178)

Code Sec. 1296(e)(3)(A) does not apply if the shareholder's stock in the corporation was stock in a PFIC at any time before the "qualified portion" of the U.S. shareholder's holding period and no election is made to make the corporation a QEF. (Code Sec. 1296(e)(3)(B)) If a shareholder of a PFIC is subject to the rules that apply to nonqualified funds before becoming subject to the new provision for shareholders subject to the CFC rules, stock held by that shareholder continues to be treated as PFIC stock unless the shareholder makes an election to pay tax and an interest charge with respect to the unrealized appreciation in the stock or the accumulated earnings of the corporation. (Com Rept, see ¶ 5178)

☐ **Effective:** Tax years of U.S. persons beginning after Dec. 31, '97, and tax years of foreign corporations ending with or within such tax years of U.S. persons. ('97 Act §1124)

¶ 1618. Mark-to-market election for PFIC stock

Code Sec. 1296, as added by '97 Act § 1122(a)
Generally effective: Tax years of U.S. persons beginning after Dec. 31, '97 and tax years of foreign corporations ending with or within such tax years of U.S. persons.
Committee Reports, see ¶ 5178

A U.S. person who is a shareholder in a passive foreign investment company (PFIC) that is not a qualified electing fund (QEF) pays U.S. tax and an interest charge based on the value of the tax deferral at the time the shareholder disposes of stock in the PFIC or upon receipt of an excess distribution (interest charge method). However, if a U.S. person elects that the PFIC be treated as a QEF with respect to that shareholder, the shareholder currently includes in gross income the shareholder's pro rata share of the PFIC's total earnings and profits (current inclusion method). The QEF election, which is made at the shareholder level, is available only where the PFIC complies with requirements to determine the income of the PFIC and provides other necessary information.

Under pre-'97 Act law, there was no current income inclusion method for shareholders of a PFIC who were unable to make the QEF election because they could not obtain the necessary information from the PFIC. (FTC 2d/FIN ¶ O-2200; USTR ¶ 12,914.02, ¶ 12,914.04)

New Law. A shareholder of a PFIC may make a mark-to-market election for marketable PFIC stock. (Code Sec. 1296(a) as added by '97 Act §1122(a)) If the election is made, the shareholder includes in income each year an amount equal to the excess, if any, of the fair market value of the PFIC stock as of the close of the tax year over the shareholder's adjusted basis in the stock. (Code Sec. 1296(a)(1)) The shareholder is allowed a deduction for the lesser of the excess, if any, of the adjusted basis of the PFIC stock over its fair market value as of the close of the tax year, or the "unreversed inclusions" with respect to the PFIC stock. (Code Sec. 1296(a)(2)) The "unreversed inclusions" are the excess, if any, of the mark-to-market gains for the stock included by the shareholder for earlier tax years, including any amount which would have been included for any prior tax year but for the Code Sec. 1291 interest on tax deferral rules, over the mark-to-market losses for the stock that were allowed as deductions for earlier tax years. (Code Sec. 1296(d))

The interest charge method is a substantial source of complexity for PFIC shareholders. The mark-to-market election makes a fair alternative to the current income inclusion method available to a shareholder who prefers such a method, even where the shareholder is unable to make a QEF election because the shareholder could not obtain the necessary information from the PFIC, under which circumstances the interest charge method would otherwise apply. (Com Rept, see ¶ 5178)

If the election is made, the general rules for a PFIC that is not a QEF do not apply. (Com Rept, see ¶ 5178)

The shareholder's adjusted basis in the PFIC stock is increased or decreased to reflect the amounts included or deducted under the election. (Code Sec. 1296(b)(1)) Where the PFIC stock is constructively owned through ownership of certain foreign entities, similar adjustments are made to the adjusted basis of the property by reason of which the U.S. person is treated as owning the PFIC stock. Such adjustments are also made to the PFIC stock in the hands of the person who actually owns the PFIC stock, but only for purposes of determining the treatment of the U.S. person with respect to the PFIC stock. (Code Sec. 1296(b)(2)) Basis in PFIC stock subject to a mark-to-market election acquired from a decedent is the lesser of the adjusted basis of the stock in the hands of the decedent immediately before death or the basis as determined under Code Sec. 1014. (Code Sec. 1296(i)) For an individual PFIC shareholder who becomes a U.S. person in a tax year beginning after Dec. 31, '97, for purposes of the mark-to-market election, the adjusted basis of the PFIC stock on the first day of the tax year is the greater of its fair market value on that day or its adjusted basis on that day. (Code Sec. 1296(l))

FTC 2d References are to Federal Tax Coordinator 2d
FIN References are to RIA's Analysis of Federal Taxes: Income
USTR References are to United States Tax Reporter: Income, Estate & Gift, and Excise
PCA References are to Pension Coordinator and Pension & Benefits Expert/Advisor
PE References are to Pension and Profit Sharing 2nd
EP References are to Estate Planning & Taxation Coordinator and Estate Planning Advisor

PFIC stock is considered marketable if it is regularly traded on: (1) a national securities exchange that is registered with the Securities and Exchange Commission, (2) the national market system established under section 11A of the Securities and Exchange Act of '34, or (3) any exchange or market that IRS determines has rules sufficient to ensure that the market price represents a legitimate and sound fair market value. Any option on stock that is considered marketable under these rules is treated as marketable stock. (Code Sec. 1296(e)(1))

If the mark-to-market election is made after the beginning of the holding period, the Code Sec. 1291 election regarding interest on tax deferral on an excess distribution with respect to PFIC stock applies to any distribution with respect to or disposition of such stock in the first tax year of the taxpayer for which the election is made and any amount which would have been included in gross income under the mark-to-market election but for the tax deferral election unless, with respect to each of the corporation's tax years beginning after Dec. 31, '86 for which the corporation was a PFIC, the corporation was a QEF with respect to the taxpayer. (Code Sec. 1296(j)(1)) This rule ensures that the interest charge on amounts attributable to periods before the election is not avoided. (Com Rept, see ¶ 5178)

Amounts included in income or deducted under the mark-to-market election, as well as gain or loss on the actual sale or other disposition of the PFIC stock, are treated as ordinary income or loss. (Code Sec. 1296(c)(1)) An amount so treated is allowable in computing adjusted gross income. (Code Sec. 1296(c)(1)(B)) The source of the gain or loss produced by the election is determined as if the amounts were gain or loss from the sale of stock in the PFIC. (Code Sec. 1296(c)(2))

Stock owned, directly or indirectly, by or for a foreign partnership, trust or estate is treated as owned proportionately by its partners or beneficiaries. (Code Sec. 1296(g)(1)) A disposition which results in the U.S. person being treated as not owning PFIC stock constructively is treated as a disposition by the U.S. person of the PFIC stock. (Code Sec. 1296(g)(2)) In addition, a controlled foreign corporation (CFC) that owns stock in a PFIC is treated as a U.S. person that may make the election with respect to the PFIC stock, and the amount included in gross income or allowed as a deduction is treated as foreign personal holding company income. (Code Sec. 1296(f)) The source of such amounts is determined by reference to the actual residence of the CFC. (Com Rept, see ¶ 5178)

The mark-to-market election applies to the tax year for which the election is made and to all later tax years, unless the PFIC stock ceases to be marketable or IRS consents to the revocation of the election. (Code Sec. 1296(k))

observation: The procedure for making the election is not explained. Presumably, IRS will issue guidance that explains how and when to make the election.

Treatment of regulated investment companies PFIC stock owned directly or indirectly by a regulated investment company (RIC) whose stock is outstanding or offered for sale and is redeemable at its net asset value is treated as marketable stock. Except as provided in regs, similar treatment as marketable stock applies in the case of any RIC which publishes net asset valuations at least annually. (Code Sec. 1296(e)(2)) Where there is regular reporting under the securities laws, inaccurate valuation may bring exposure to legal liability, and this exposure may ensure the reliability of the values the RIC assigns to its PFIC stock. (Com Rept, see ¶5178)

For purposes of the income limitations for determining whether a corporation is a RIC, any amount included in gross income under the mark-to market election is treated as a dividend. (Code Sec. 1296(h))

If a RIC makes the mark-to-market election after the beginning of the taxpayer's holding period, the Code Sec. 1291 election regarding interest on tax deferral on an excess distribution with respect to PFIC stock does not apply to any distribution with respect to or disposition of such stock in the first tax year of the taxpayer for which the election is made. The RIC's tax for the first tax year is increased by the interest which would have been charged under Code Sec. 1291, unless the mark-to-market election is made on the last day of the preceding year. No deductions are allowed to the RIC for the increase in tax based on the interest charge. (Code Sec. 1296(j)(2))

☐ **Effective:** Tax years of U.S. persons beginning after Dec. 31, '97, and tax years of foreign corporations ending with or within such tax years of U.S. persons. ('97 Act §1124)

¶1619. Valuation of assets for passive foreign investment company determination

Code Sec. 1297(e), as amended by '97 Act § 1123(a)
Generally effective: Tax years of U.S. persons beginning after Dec. 31. '97.
Committee Reports, see ¶5178

A passive foreign investment company (PFIC) is any foreign corporation if (1) 75% or more of the corporation's gross income for its tax year is passive income or (2) the average percentage of assets held by the corporation during the tax year which produce, or are held for the production of, passive income is at least 50% (50% asset test). (Code Sec. 1296) If a foreign corporation is a controlled foreign corporation (CFC), the 50% asset test is applied based on the adjusted basis of the corporation's assets, as determined for purposes of computing earnings and profits. If a foreign corporation is not a CFC, the 50% asset test is applied on the basis of the value of the corporation's assets, unless the corporation elects to use the adjusted basis of the corporation's assets, as determined for purposes of computing earnings and profits. (FTC 2d/FIN ¶O-2202; USTR ¶12,914.01)

New Law. Code Sec. 1296 was redesignated by the '97 Act as Code Sec. 1297 ('97 Act §1122(a)) The 50% asset test is applied on the basis of the value of the corporation's assets if (1) the corporation is publicly traded for the tax year or (2) the test

FTC 2d References are to Federal Tax Coordinator 2d
FIN References are to RIA's Analysis of Federal Taxes: Income
USTR References are to United States Tax Reporter: Income, Estate & Gift, and Excise
PCA References are to Pension Coordinator and Pension & Benefits Expert/Advisor
PE References are to Pension and Profit Sharing 2nd
EP References are to Estate Planning & Taxation Coordinator and Estate Planning Advisor

Research Institute of America 421

is not required to be applied based on the adjusted basis of the corporation's assets. (Code Sec. 1297(e)(1) as amended by '97 Act §1123(a)) The 50% asset test is required to be applied based on the adjusted basis, as determined for the purposes of computing earnings and profits, of the corporation's assets, if the corporation is not publicly traded and (1) is a CFC or (2) elects to have the test applied based on the adjusted basis of the corporation's assets. An election, once made, may be revoked only with the consent of IRS. (Code Sec. 1297(e)(2))

The 50% asset test rules applicable to non-publicly traded foreign corporations remain unchanged. Accordingly, CFCs that are not publicly traded continue to be required to apply the test based on the adjusted basis of the corporation's assets, and other foreign corporations that are not publicly traded continue to be required to apply the test on the basis of the fair market value of the corporation's assets, unless they elect to use the adjusted basis of the corporation's assets. (Com Rept, see ¶ 5178)

A foreign corporation is treated as a publicly traded corporation if the stock in the corporation is regularly traded on

(1) a national securities exchange which is registered with the SEC or the national market system established pursuant to section 11A of the Securities and Exchange Act of 1934, or

(2) any exchange or other market which IRS determines has rules adequate to carry out the purposes of Code Sec. 1297(e) (Code Sec. 1297(e)(3)), that is, to ensure that the market price represents a sound fair market value. (Com Rept, see ¶ 5178)

In applying the 50% asset test, it is intended that the total value of a publicly traded foreign corporation's assets generally be treated as equal to the sum of the aggregate value of its outstanding stock plus its liabilities. (Com Rept, see ¶ 5178)

Because the 50% asset test is applied on the basis of quarterly measurements of a foreign corporation's assets, it is intended that a corporation the stock of which is publicly traded on each quarterly measurement date during the tax year be eligible to use the fair market value of its assets in applying the 50% asset test for the tax year. (Com Rept, see ¶ 5178)

☐ **Effective:** Tax years of U.S. persons beginning after Dec. 31, '97, and tax years of foreign corporations ending with or within such tax years of U.S. persons. ('97 Act §1124)

Other International Provisions

¶ 1620. Simplification of the stock and securities trading safe harbor for foreign corporations

Code Sec. 864(b)(2)(A)(ii), as amended by '97 Act § 1162(a)
Generally effective: Tax years starting after Dec. 31, '97
Committee Reports, see ¶ 5191

A nonresident alien individual or foreign corporation engaged in a trade or business in the U.S. is subject to U.S. taxation on its net income that is effectively connected with the trade or business. Under a safe harbor rule, foreign persons that trade in stocks or securities for their own account are not treated as engaged in a U.S. trade or business. To qualify under this safe harbor, a foreign person trading in stock or securities for its own account must not be a dealer in stock or securities. In addition, under pre-'97 Act law, a foreign corporation was entitled to the safe harbor only if its principal office was not in the U.S. (FTC 2d/FIN ¶ O-10516; USTR ¶ 8644.01; TaxDesk ¶ 64,166)

New Law. The '97 Act eliminates the requirement that a foreign corporation not have its principal office in the U.S. to qualify for the safe harbor. (Code Sec. 864(b)(2)(A)(ii) as amended by '97 Act §1162(a))

☐ **Effective:** Tax years starting after Dec. 31, '97. ('97 Act §1162(b))

¶ 1621. FSC export property treatment extended to computer software licensed for reproduction abroad

Code Sec. 927(a)(2)(B), as amended by '97 Act § 1171
Generally effective: Gross receipts attributable to periods after Dec. 31, '97, in tax years ending after that date.
Committee Reports, see ¶ 5193

For purposes of the foreign sales corporation (FSC) provisions, proceeds from sales of export property are treated as foreign trading gross receipts, which may be partially exempt from U.S. taxes. Intangible property generally is excluded from the definition of export property for purposes of the FSC provisions. The exclusion applies to copyrights other than films, tapes, records or similar reproductions for commercial or home use. Regs provide that a copyright on computer software is not export property, but that mass marketed computer software is export property if the software is not accompanied by a right to reproduce for external use. Under pre-'97 Act law, the statutory exclusion for intangible property did not contain any specific reference to computer software. (FTC 2d/FIN ¶ O-1840 *et seq.*, ¶ O-1894; USTR ¶ 9214.02)

New Law. Computer software licensed for reproduction abroad is explicitly included in the definition of export property for purposes of the FSC provisions. (Code Sec. 927(a)(2)(B) as amended by '97 Act §1171(a))

Under pre-'97 Act law, for purposes of the FSC provisions, films, tapes, records and similar reproductions were already included explicitly in the definition of export property. In light of technological developments, computer software is virtually indistinguishable from films, tapes and records. Accordingly, the benefits of the FSC provisions also should be available to computer software. (Com Rept, see ¶ 5193)

In light of the rapid innovations in the computer and software industries, the term computer software is to be construed broadly to accommodate technological changes in

FTC 2d References are to Federal Tax Coordinator 2d
FIN References are to RIA's Analysis of Federal Taxes: Income
USTR References are to United States Tax Reporter: Income, Estate & Gift, and Excise
PCA References are to Pension Coordinator and Pension & Benefits Expert/Advisor
PE References are to Pension and Profit Sharing 2nd
EP References are to Estate Planning & Taxation Coordinator and Estate Planning Advisor

✔ Research Institute of America   423

the products of both industries. No inference is intended regarding the qualification as export property of computer software licensed for reproduction abroad under pre-'97 Act law. (Com Rept, see ¶ 5193)

☐ **Effective:** Gross receipts attributable to periods after Dec. 31, '97, in tax years ending after that date. ('97 Act §1171(b)) Accordingly, in the case of a multi-year license, the provision applies to gross receipts attributable to the period of the license after Dec. 31, '97. (Com Rept, see ¶ 5193)

¶ 1622. Increase in dollar limitation on foreign earned income exclusion

Code Sec. 911(b)(2), as amended by '97 Act § 1172
Generally effective: Tax years starting after Dec. 31, '97.
Committee Reports, see ¶ 5194

A taxpayer whose tax home is in a foreign country and who meets certain other requirements may exclude foreign earned income from income. Under pre-'97 Act law, this exclusion was limited, for any tax year, to the amount of foreign earned income computed on a daily basis at an annual rate of $70,000. (FTC 2d/FIN ¶ O-1102; USTR ¶ 9114.06; TaxDesk ¶ 19,104)

New Law. The '97 Act increases the $70,000 maximum exclusion amount to $80,000, to be phased in in $2,000 increments each year beginning in '98. Thus, for any tax year, the maximum foreign earned income exclusion is based on the "exclusion amount" for the calendar year in which such tax year begins. (Code Sec. 911(b)(2)(A) as amended by '97 Act §1172(a)(1)) The exclusion amount for '98 through 2002 is as follows:

For calendar year	The exclusion is
1998	$72,000
1999	74,000
2000	76,000
2001	78,000
2002 and after	80,000 (Code Sec. 911(b)(2)(D)(i))

For tax years starting after 2007, the $80,000 will be indexed to the cost-of-living adjustment, rounded to the nearest $100. (Code Sec. 911(b)(2)(D)(ii)).

☐ **Effective:** Tax years starting after Dec. 31, '97. ('97 Act §1172(b))

¶ 1623. Simplification of treatment of personal transactions in foreign currency

Code Sec. 988(e), as amended by '97 Act § 1104(a)
Generally effective: Tax years starting after Dec. 31, '97.
Committee Reports, see ¶ 5173

Foreign currency is generally treated as property. Thus, like any other property, a taxpayer who acquires foreign currency and then disposes of it realizes gain or loss on any change in value. For this purpose, a taxpayer who uses foreign currency to buy goods or services is treated as having exchanged the currency for those goods or services, and realizes gain or loss to the extent the value of the currency has shifted relative to the U.S. dollar.

Pre-'97 Act law had no exception to these rules for small amounts of foreign currency acquired and used in personal transactions. (FTC 2d/FIN ¶ G-7047; USTR ¶ 9884.01)

New Law. The regular foreign currency rules do not apply to personal transactions of individuals. (Code Sec. 988(e)(1) as amended by '97 Act §1104(a)) An individual U.S. taxpayer who disposes of foreign currency in a personal transaction does not recognize gain by reason of fluctuations in exchange rates during the period the taxpayer held the currency, unless the gain that would, absent this provision, otherwise be taken into account exceeds $200. (Code Sec. 988(e)(2))

> *observation:* The gain that is entitled to nonrecognition is only the gain that occurs by virtue of changes in the exchange rate while the taxpayer held the foreign currency. In unusual situations (for example, if a taxpayer acquires currency for less than its full value under a contract that was already entered into, or if the currency is acquired in a transaction that gives rise to a basis other than cost), a portion of the gain might not be entitled to nonrecognition.

> *observation:* It appears that the $200 limit applies on a transaction-by-transaction, rather than an annual, basis.

> *observation:* The provision does not specifically address the basis of property acquired with foreign currency in a transaction on which no gain was recognized. It also does not address the treatment of transactions in which one foreign currency is exchanged for another, which is then used to purchase goods or something else. This might occur, for example, where a taxpayer travels through several countries and exchanges currency as each border is crossed.

A "personal transaction" is any transaction entered into by an individual to the extent that there are no expenses associated with the transaction that meet the requirements for deductibility as a trade or business expense (other than travel expenses in connection with a business trip) or as an expense for the production of income. (Code Sec. 988(e)(3)) Thus, transactions entered into in connection with a business trip are personal transactions under this provision. (Com Rept, see ¶ 5173)

The provision does not change the treatment of resulting exchange losses. (Com Rept, see ¶ 5173)

FTC 2d References are to Federal Tax Coordinator 2d
FIN References are to RIA's Analysis of Federal Taxes: Income
USTR References are to United States Tax Reporter: Income, Estate & Gift, and Excise
PCA References are to Pension Coordinator and Pension & Benefits Expert/Advisor
PE References are to Pension and Profit Sharing 2nd
EP References are to Estate Planning & Taxation Coordinator and Estate Planning Advisor

observation: Although the nonrecognition rule by its terms only applies to gains, losses from personal transactions are generally nondeductible. (Com Rept, see ¶ 5173)

☐ **Effective:** Tax years starting after Dec. 31, '97. ('97 Act §1104(b))

¶ 1624. Nonresident alien crew member's income not U.S. source income

Code Sec. 861(a)(3), as amended by '97 Act § 1174(a)(1)
Code Sec. 863(c)(2)(B), as amended by '97 Act § 1174(a)(2)
Code Sec. 7701(b)(7)(D), as amended by '97 Act § 1174(b)
Generally effective: Tax years beginning after Dec. 31, '97
Committee Reports, see ¶ 5196

Compensation for labor and personal services performed within the U.S. is U.S. source income that is subject to U.S. tax unless the income qualifies for a $3,000 de minimis exception. Compensation for personal services that is transportation income between the U.S. and a U.S. possession is treated as 50% U.S. source income and 50% foreign source income.

An individual is treated as a U.S. resident (who is subject to U.S. tax on worldwide income) if, among other things, the individual satisfies a "substantial presence test," i.e., was present in the U.S. during the tax year for at least 31 days and was present in the U.S. for 183 or more days under a three-year weighted average test.

Pre-'97 Act law did not provide any special exceptions from the above rules for crew members of foreign ships. (FTC 2d/FIN ¶ O-1057, ¶ O-10931.1; USTR ¶ 8614.15, ¶ 8714; TaxDesk ¶ 63,305, ¶ 19,060)

New Law. Compensation for labor or services performed in the U.S. by a nonresident alien individual in connection with the individual's temporary presence in the U.S. as a regular crew member of a foreign vessel engaged in transportation between the U.S. and a foreign country or a U.S. possession is not U.S. source income. However, this rule doesn't apply for purposes of:

• Code Sec. 79, which pertains to group-term life insurance purchased for employees.

• Code Sec. 105, which pertains to amounts received under accident and health plans.

• Subchapter D (Code Sec. 401 through Code Sec. 424), pertaining to deferred compensation, retirement plans and other employee benefits. (Code Sec. 861(a)(3) as amended by '97 Act §1174(a)(1))

In addition, the rule that personal services transportation income between the U.S. and a U.S. possession is 50% U.S. source income and 50% foreign source income applies, in the case of income derived from or in connection with a vessel, only where the personal services are performed by a U.S. citizen or resident. (Code Sec. 863(c)(2)(B) as amended by '97 Act §1174(a)(2))

The '97 Act also provides that for purposes of determining whether an individual is a U.S. resident under the substantial presence test, the individual is not treated as present in the U.S. on any day that he is temporarily present as a member of the regular crew of a foreign vessel engaged in transportation between the U.S. and a foreign country or a U.S. possession, unless on that day the individual otherwise engages in a trade or business in the U.S. (Code Sec. 7701(b)(7)(D) as amended by '97 Act §1174(b)(1))

☐ **Effective:** The rules governing compensation of crew members apply to remuneration for services performed in tax years beginning after Dec. 31, '97. ('97 Act §1174(c)(1)) The rules regarding whether an individual is present in the U.S. apply for tax years beginning after Dec. 31, '97('97 Act §1174(c)(2))

¶ 1625. Treaty benefits denied for certain payments through hybrid entities

Code Sec. 894(c), as amended by '97 Act § 1054
Generally effective: Aug. 5, '97
Committee Reports, see ¶ 5146

Many income tax treaties between the U.S. and foreign countries provide benefits to foreign persons who derive income from U.S. sources. One of the most important treaty benefits is a reduced withholding tax rate imposed on this income.

New Law. Foreign persons are not entitled under any U.S. income tax treaty to any reduced withholding tax rate on income derived through an entity that is treated as a partnership (or otherwise as fiscally transparent) for purposes of U.S. taxes if:

(1) The income is not treated for purposes of taxation in the foreign country as income of the person,

(2) The treaty contains no provision relating to the applicability of the treaty to income derived through a partnership, and

(3) The foreign country imposes no tax on the distribution of the income from the entity to the person. (Code Sec. 894(c)(1) as amended by '97 Act §1054(a))

IRS is directed to prescribe whatever regulations are necessary or appropriate to determine to what extent a taxpayer to which the above rule does not apply is denied benefits under any U.S. income tax treaty with regard to payments to, or income attributable to, an entity organized in any jurisdiction, including the U.S., that is treated as a partnership or otherwise as fiscally transparent for U.S. tax purposes (including, for example, common investment trusts, grantor trusts, and entities disregarded for U.S. federal income tax purposes), but is not so treated under the tax laws of the jurisdiction of residence of the taxpayer. (Code Sec. 894(c)(2))

FTC 2d References are to Federal Tax Coordinator 2d
FIN References are to RIA's Analysis of Federal Taxes: Income
USTR References are to United States Tax Reporter: Income, Estate & Gift, and Excise
PCA References are to Pension Coordinator and Pension & Benefits Expert/Advisor
PE References are to Pension and Profit Sharing 2nd
EP References are to Estate Planning & Taxation Coordinator and Estate Planning Advisor

observation: After a bill including a provision similar to that in the '97 Act was passed by the two houses of Congress, but before Aug. 5, '97, IRS issued proposed and temporary regs dealing with eligibility of certain entities (including fiscally transparent entities) for treaty benefits (TD 8722). These temporary and proposed regulations are consistent with the new law. (Com Rept, see ¶ 5146)

☐ **Effective:** Aug. 5, '97. ('97 Act §1054(b))

¶ 1626. Expatriate tax rules clarified

Code Sec. 877(d)(2)(B), as amended by '97 Act § 1602(g)(1)
Code Sec. 877(d)(2)(D), as amended by '97 Act § 1602(g)(2)
Code Sec. 877(d)(3), as amended by '97 Act § 1602(g)(3)
Code Sec. 877(d)(4)(A), as amended by '97 Act § 1602(g)(4)
Code Sec. 2107(c)(2)(B)(i), as amended by '97 Act § 1602(g)(6)(A)
Code Sec. 2107(c)(2)(C), as amended by '97 Act § 1602(g)(6)(B)
Generally effective: For individuals giving up U.S. citizenship or U.S. residency after Feb. 5, '95
Committee Reports, see ¶ 5380

A U.S. citizen who gives up U.S. citizenship and a long-term U.S. resident who terminates U.S. residency must recognize gain, under certain circumstances, on what would otherwise be nonrecognition exchanges during a specified period. Under pre-'97 Act law, this special gain recognition rule applied to exchanges made during the 10-year period immediately preceding the close of the tax year. The 10-year period was subject to suspension during any period in which the expatriate's risk of loss was substantially diminished. IRS has the authority to issue regs making the special gain recognition rule apply to a 15-year period beginning five years before the expatriate's loss of U.S. citizenship or residency. (FTC 2d/FIN ¶ O-11713; USTR ¶ 8774; TaxDesk ¶ 64,471)

Under another special income tax rule, if an expatriate contributes property to a corporation that would have been a controlled foreign corporation (CFC) of which the expatriate was a U.S. shareholder if the individual in question had remained a U.S. citizen or resident and hadn't become an expatriate, any income or gain from that property received by the corporation is treated as having been received by the expatriate. Under pre-'97 Act law, this special rule applied during the 10-year period immediately preceding the close of the tax year (also subject to suspension during any period in which the expatriate's risk of loss was substantially diminished), and applied to any property the income from which was U.S. source income. (FTC 2d/FIN ¶ O-11712; USTR ¶ 8774; TaxDesk ¶ 64,471)

A credit against the expatriate estate tax is available for foreign death taxes. The credit is limited to the lesser of (1) an amount that bears the same ratio to death taxes paid to the foreign country that property included in the expatriate's U.S. gross estate under the expatriation provision bears to all of the property taxed by the foreign country, or (2) such property's "proportionate share" of the excess of the expatriate's U.S.

estate tax over the U.S. estate tax that would have been due if the expatriate provision hadn't applied. Under pre-'97 Act law, "proportionate share" was defined as "the percentage of the value of the property which is included in the gross estate solely by reason of [the expatriation provision] bears to the total value of the gross estate." (FTC 2d ¶ R-8033.5; USTR ¶ 21,074.02; TaxDesk ¶ 64,471)

> ⟨*observation:* Under pre-'97 Act law, it was unclear, with respect to part (2) of the credit limitation, what the term "such property" referred to—the property included in the expatriate's U.S. gross estate solely under the expatriation provision, or the property taxed by the foreign country.

New Law. The rules described above have been retroactively clarified in several respects. The rules governing gain recognition on what would otherwise be nonrecognition transactions (Code Sec. 877(d)(2) as amended by '97 Act §1602(g)(1)), and treating a CFC's gain or income on contributed property as the gain or income of the expatriate (Code Sec. 877(d)(4) as amended by '97 Act §1602(g)(4)), are both clarified to provide that the 10-year period begins on the date that U.S. citizenship or U.S. residency is lost. The 10-year period beginning on the date that U.S. citizenship or residency is lost is subject to suspension during any period in which the expatriate's risk of loss is substantially diminished. (Code Sec. 877(d)(3) as amended by '97 Act §1602(g)(3))

If, under regs, the extended 15-year period applies, then in the case of any exchange that occurs during the five years before the loss of U.S. citizenship or residency, any gain that must be recognized on a nonrecognition transaction is recognized immediately after the loss of U.S. citizenship or residency. (Code Sec. 877(d)(2)(D) as amended by '97 Act §1602(g)(2))

The special rule for property contributed to foreign corporations that would otherwise have been CFCs has been amended to provide that it applies to property *contributed during the 10-year period* to a corporation that would otherwise have been treated as a CFC, and to specify that it applies only to property income from which *immediately before the contribution* was from U.S. sources. (Code Sec. 877(d)(4)(A) as amended by '97 Act §1602(g)(4))

> ⟨*observation:* Under pre-'97 Act law, the language of Code Sec. 877(d)(4)(A) was somewhat ambiguous, and could be read as applying only to income or gain received by the corporation during the 10-year period, and without regard to when the property was contributed. The '97 Act specifies that these rules apply to property that the expatriate has contributed to the corporation during the 10-year period, with no explicit limitation as to when the income or gain must be received by the corporation in order for that income or gain to be subject to Code Sec. 877(d)(4)(A). Apparently, if the property is contributed within the 10-year period, income or gain received with respect

FTC 2d References are to Federal Tax Coordinator 2d
FIN References are to RIA's Analysis of Federal Taxes: Income
USTR References are to United States Tax Reporter: Income, Estate & Gift, and Excise
PCA References are to Pension Coordinator and Pension & Benefits Expert/Advisor
PE References are to Pension and Profit Sharing 2nd
EP References are to Estate Planning & Taxation Coordinator and Estate Planning Advisor

⟨*Research Institute of America*   429

to the property, including income or gain received by the corporation after the end of the 10-year period, would remain subject to Code Sec. 877(d)(4)(A).

Credit for foreign estate taxes clarified.   The formula for determining the amount of foreign estate taxes creditable against U.S. estate taxes has been clarified. Under the '97 Act, the credit can't exceed the lesser of:

(1) an amount bearing the same ratio to death taxes actually paid to the foreign country as the value of the property subjected to death taxes by the foreign country and included in the U.S. gross estate by reason of the expatriation provision bears to the value of all property subjected to death taxes by the foreign country, or

(2) such property's "proportionate share" of the excess of the expatriate's U.S. estate tax over the U.S. estate tax that would have been due if the expatriate provision hadn't applied. (Code Sec. 2107(c)(2)(B)(i) as amended by '97 Act §1602(g)(6)(A))

This change makes it clear that the term "such property" in part (2) of the credit limitation refers to property that was subject to the foreign country's estate tax *and* was also included in the expatriate's estate for U.S. estate tax purposes on account of the expatriation provision. (Com Rept, see ¶ 5380)

The "proportionate share" of "such property" is redefined as the percentage that the value of "such property" bears to the total value of all property included in the U.S. gross estate solely on account of the expatriation provision. (Code Sec. 2107(c)(2)(C) as amended by '97 Act §1602(g)(6)(B))

In other words, the credit is generally limited to the lesser of (1) foreign death taxes attributable to property includible in the expatriate's U.S. estate solely by reason of the expatriation provisions, or (2) the U.S. estate tax attributable to property that is subject to estate tax in the foreign country and also includible in the U.S. estate solely by reason of the expatriation tax provisions. The amount of taxes attributable to such property is determined on a pro rata basis. (Com Rept, see ¶ 5380)

☐ **Effective:** For individuals giving up U.S. citizenship or U.S. residency after Feb. 5, '95. ('97 Act §1602(i))

¶ 1627. Obligations issued by owner are disregarded in determining whether transfer to foreign trust is for fair market value

Code Sec. 679(a)(3)(C), as amended by '97 Act § 1601(i)(2)
Generally effective: Property transfers made after Feb. 6, '95
Committee Reports, see ¶ 5363

A U.S. person who transfers property to a foreign trust that has U.S. beneficiaries is generally treated as the owner of that trust. An exception to this rule applies to transfers for fair market value. In determining whether the transferor has received fair market value, obligations issued (or, to the extent provided in regs, guaranteed) by the trust, or by any grantor or beneficiary of the trust, or by any person related to any such grantor or beneficiary, are generally disregarded.   (FTC 2d/FIN ¶ C-5603; USTR

¶ 6794; TaxDesk ¶ 65,752)

New Law. The rule under which certain obligations are disregarded is extended to also include obligations issued or guaranteed by any owner of the trust, or by any person related to such owner. (Code Sec. 679(a)(3)(C) as amended by '97 Act §1601(i)(2))

☐ **Effective:** Property transfers made after Feb. 6, '95. ('97 Act §1601(j)(1))

¶ 1628. Definition of trust as U.S. person clarified

Code Sec. 7701(a)(30)(E), as amended by '97 Act § 1601(i)(3)(A)
Code Sec. 641(b), as amended by '97 Act § 1601(i)(3)(B)
Generally effective: Tax years beginning after '96
Committee Reports, see ¶ 5364

Under pre-'97 Act law, a trust was considered to be a U.S. person if a court in the U.S. has primary jurisdiction over the trust's administration, and one or more U.S. fiduciaries have control over all substantial trust decisions. Although the Code provided that this rule is to apply to tax years beginning after '96, IRS has announced that a U.S. trust that was in existence on Aug. 20, '96 may continue to file returns as a U.S. trust for tax years beginning after '96 if (1) the trustee begins to modify the trust to conform to the post-'96 standards by the due date for filing the trust's return for its first tax year beginning after '96, (2) modifications are completed within two years after such due date, and (3) a statement is attached to the trust's returns for tax years beginning after '96. (FTC 2d/FIN ¶ C-5602; USTR ¶ 77,014.45; TaxDesk ¶ 65,806)

New Law. A trust is treated as a U.S. person if a court in the U.S. has primary jurisdiction over the trust's administration, and one or more U. S. *persons* have control over all substantial trust decisions. (Code Sec. 7701(a)(30)(E) as amended by '97 Act §1601(i)(3)(A)) Thus, the fact that a substantial decision is controlled by a U.S. person who isn't a fiduciary won't cause the trust not to be treated as a U.S. person. (Com Rept, see ¶ 5364)

For purposes of computing the amount of tax imposed on a foreign estate or trust, such an estate or trust is treated as a nonresident alien individual who isn't present in the U.S. at any time. (Code Sec. 641(b) as amended by '97 Act §1601(i)(3)(B))

IRS has been given authority to issue regs or other guidance under which certain trusts may be given a reasonable period to comply with the post-'96 standards. Trusts qualifying for this relief are those that:

(1) were in existence on Aug. 20, '96 and were U.S. persons on that date under the pre-'97 standards,

(2) haven't elected to apply the post-'96 standards retroactively,

---

FTC 2d References are to Federal Tax Coordinator 2d
FIN References are to RIA's Analysis of Federal Taxes: Income
USTR References are to United States Tax Reporter: Income, Estate & Gift, and Excise
PCA References are to Pension Coordinator and Pension & Benefits Expert/Advisor
PE References are to Pension and Profit Sharing 2nd
EP References are to Estate Planning & Taxation Coordinator and Estate Planning Advisor

(3) make what modifications are needed to comply with the post-'96 standards and be treated as a U.S. person before the expiration of the reasonable period, and

(4) meet such other conditions as IRS may require. ('97 Act §1601(i)(4))

> 🖐 *observation:* The '97 Act doesn't give any guidance on what a "reasonable period" might be for this purpose. However, the two-year period specified in the guidance IRS has already issued would presumably qualify as "a reasonable period."

☐ **Effective:** Tax years beginning after '96. ('97 Act §1601(j)(1))

¶ 1629. Transfer of property to foreign estate, trust, corporation or partnership triggers gain; excise tax on transfers to foreign entities repealed

Code Sec. 684, as added by '97 Act § 1131(b)
Code Sec. 1491, repealed by '97 Act § 1131(a)
Code Sec. 1492, repealed by '97 Act § 1131(a)
Code Sec. 1494, repealed by '97 Act § 1131(a)
Code Sec. 1057, repealed by '97 Act § 1131(c)
Code Sec. 1035(c), as amended by '97 Act § 1131(b)(1)
Generally effective: Aug. 5, '97
Committee Reports, see ¶ 5182

Under pre-'97 Act rules, an excise tax was imposed on transfers of property by a U.S. person to a foreign corporation as paid-in surplus or as a contribution to capital, or to a foreign partnership, estate or trust. The tax was 35 percent of the amount of gain inherent in the transferred property but not recognized for income tax purposes at the time of the transfer. An election could be made to treat the transfer as a sale or exchange. Several exceptions to the excise tax were available. A substantial penalty applied in the case of a failure to report a transfer subject to the excise tax. (FTC 2d/FIN ¶ O-3701; USTR ¶ 14,914)

New Law. The '97 Act repeals the excise tax rules of Code Sec. 1491, Code Sec. 1492, and Code Sec. 1494 that applied to transfers of appreciated property by a U.S. person to a foreign entity, and the penalty under Code Sec. 1494(c) for failure to report a transfer subject to the excise tax ('97 Act §1131(a)), as well as Code Sec. 1057, which provided the election to treat a transfer to a foreign entity as a sale or exchange, ('97 Act §1131(c)(2)) and replaces them with a variety of gain recognition provisions applicable to transfers to foreign corporations, estates, trusts and partnerships, and to transfers of insurance contracts to foreign persons.

Gain on transfer to foreign trust or estate. In place of the excise tax that applied to transfers to a foreign estate or trust, except as provided in regs, gain is recognized upon a transfer of appreciated property by a U.S. person to a foreign estate or trust. The transfer is treated as a sale or exchange for an amount equal to the fair market value of the property transferred. Gain is recognized in the amount of the excess of the fair market value of the property over the adjusted basis of the property in the hands of the transferor. (Code Sec. 684(a) as added by '97 Act §1131(b))

☯ observation: The '97 Act has two subsections labeled §1131(b).

Gain not recognized if any person is treated as the owner of the transferee trust under the grantor trust rules. (Code Sec. 684(b))

☯ observation: This would exclude, from gain recognition, trusts where a person other than the grantor of the trust is treated as an owner under Code Sec. 678 because that person holds a power over the corpus or income of the trust.

If a U.S. trust becomes a foreign trust, the trust is treated as having transferred, immediately before it becomes a foreign trust, all of its assets to a foreign trust. (Code Sec. 684(c))

Transfers to foreign corporations and partnerships. Instead of the excise tax that applied to certain transfers to foreign corporations, regulatory authority is granted to deny nonrecognition treatment to a transfer to a foreign corporation as paid-in surplus or as a contribution to capital (in a transaction that is not otherwise described in Code Sec. 367, such as transfers to foreign controlled corporations, certain corporate reorganizations involving foreign corporations and the liquidation of 80%-owned foreign corporate subsidiaries). The transfer will be treated as a sale or exchange for an amount equal to the fair market value of the transferred property and the transferor must recognize gain on the excess of (1) the fair market value of the transferred property over (2) the adjusted basis of the property in the hands of the transferor. (Code Sec. 367(f) as amended by '97 Act §1313(b)(2)) Instead of the excise tax that applied to transfers to foreign partnerships, regulatory authority is granted to provide for gain recognition on a transfer of appreciated property to a partnership in cases where such gain otherwise would be transferred to a foreign partner. (Code Sec. 721(c) as amended by '97 Act §1313(b)(3))

Exchange of insurance policies. When the transferor of an insurance policy is a foreign person, IRS has regulatory authority to deny the nonrecognition treatment that is provided to certain exchanges of insurance, endowment and annuity contracts. (Code Sec. 1035(c) as amended by '97 Act §1313(b)(1))

☐ **Effective:** Aug. 5, '97. ('97 Act §1313(d))

However, the penalty under Code Sec. 1494(c) won't apply to transfers made after Aug. 20, '96, if all applicable reporting requirements of Code Sec. 6038B, as amended by the '97 Act (see ¶ 2315), are satisfied. ('97 Act §1144(d)(2)) Thus, taxpayers can avoid the Code Sec. 1494(c) penalty by electing to apply the '97 Act amendments to Code Sec. 6038B to transfers after Aug. 20, '96. (Com Rept, see ¶ 5186) Congress has given IRS permission to prescribe simplified reporting requirements for these cases.

FTC 2d References are to Federal Tax Coordinator 2d
FIN References are to RIA's Analysis of Federal Taxes: Income
USTR References are to United States Tax Reporter: Income, Estate & Gift, and Excise
PCA References are to Pension Coordinator and Pension & Benefits Expert/Advisor
PE References are to Pension and Profit Sharing 2nd
EP References are to Estate Planning & Taxation Coordinator and Estate Planning Advisor

('97 Act §1144(d)(2))

observation: Code Sec. 1494(c) applies to transfers to foreign corporations, trusts, and estates as well as to foreign partnerships. However, the reporting requirements added to Code Sec. 6038B by '97 Act § 1144(d)(2) only apply to transfers to partnerships. It is therefore likely that the above election will only enable taxpayers to avoid the Code Sec. 1494(c) penalty with respect to transfers to partnerships.

¶ 1630. U.S. source treatment of deemed royalties repealed

Code Sec. 367(d)(2), as amended by '97 Act § 1131(b)(4)
Code Sec. 367(d)(3), as amended by '97 Act § 1131(b)(5)
Code Sec. 721(d), as amended by '97 Act § 1131(b)(5)
Generally effective: Aug. 5, '97
Committee Reports, see ¶ 5182

A U.S. person that contributes intangible property to a foreign corporation is treated as having sold the property to the corporation and is treated as receiving deemed royalty payments from the corporation. These deemed royalty payments were treated as U.S. source income. A U.S. person could elect to apply similar rules to a transfer of intangible property to a foreign partnership that otherwise would have been subject to the 35% excise tax on transfers to foreign partnerships (see ¶ 1629). (FTC 2d/FIN ¶ F-6501; USTR ¶ 3,674.03)

New Law. The '97 Act repeals the rule that treats any deemed royalty arising as a result of a transfer of intangible property to a foreign corporation as U.S. source income. Instead, the deemed royalty payments are treated as foreign source income to the same extent that an actual royalty payment would be treated as foreign source income. The '97 Act accomplishes this by labeling the deemed royalty payments as ordinary income (rather than U.S. source income under pre-'97 Act law), which means that they are subject to the usual rules governing when income is treated as foreign source income. (Code Sec. 367(d)(2)(C) as amended by '97 Act §1131(b)(4)) IRS is given regulatory authority to provide similar treatment in the case of a transfer of intangible property to a foreign partnership. (Code Sec. 367(d)(3) as amended by '97 Act §1131(b)(5))   (Code Sec. 721(d) as amended by '97 Act §1131(d)(5))

observation: The '97 Act contains two §§ 1131(b).

☐ **Effective:** Aug. 5, '97. ('97 Act §1131(d))

¶ 1700. Financial Intermediaries

REITs

¶ 1701. REITs may elect to retain capital gains and pass-through to shareholders credit for capital gains taxes paid like RICs

Code Sec. 857(b)(3)(D), as amended and redesignated by '97 Act § 1254(a)
Code Sec. 857(b)(7)(A), as amended by '97 Act § 1254(b)(1)
Generally effective: For tax years beginning after Aug. 5, '97
Committee Reports, see ¶ 5230

A REIT that has a net capital gain for a tax year generally is subject to tax on this capital gain in the same manner as corporations are subject to tax on capital gains. However, a REIT may reduce or eliminate its tax liability attributable to capital gains by paying a capital gain dividend to its shareholders. A capital gain dividend is any dividend or part of a dividend that is designated by the REIT as a capital gain dividend in a written notice mailed to the shareholders of the REIT. Shareholders who receive capital gain dividends treat the amount of these dividends as long-term capital gain regardless of their holding period for the stock. Thus, REITs can pass through their capital gains to their shareholders.

Because REITs pass through the capital gains character of their income that is distributed to shareholders, absent a specific provision it would be possible for REIT shareholders to purchase REIT shares before the REIT dividend is paid and recognize capital gain income. After the distribution, the REIT shares could be sold at a loss (since the distribution reduces the value of the REIT shares) and that loss would, absent specific provisions, be a short-term capital loss. To prevent the use of short-term capital losses attributable to capital gains dividends, Code Sec. 857(b)(7)(A) provides that if a shareholder receives a capital gains dividend on shares held for six months or less, any loss on the sale of those shares (within the six-month period) is treated as a long-term capital loss to the extent of the capital gains dividend. (FTC 2d/FIN ¶ E-6616, ¶ E-6617, ¶ E-6619; USTR ¶ 8574.01; TaxDesk ¶ 17,306)

New Law. REITs may elect to retain and pay income tax on net long-term capital gains received by the REIT during the tax year. At the close of a REIT's tax year, its shareholders must include, in computing their long-term capital gains for their tax year in which the last day of the REIT's tax year falls, the amount that the trust designates as long-term capital gains in respect of such shares. This designation must be made in a written notice mailed to the REIT's shareholders at any time before the expiration of 60 days after the close of the REIT's tax year, or mailed to the REIT's shareholders or holders of beneficial interests with its annual report for the tax year. However, the

FTC 2d References are to Federal Tax Coordinator 2d
FIN References are to RIA's Analysis of Federal Taxes: Income
USTR References are to United States Tax Reporter: Income, Estate & Gift, and Excise
PCA References are to Pension Coordinator and Pension & Benefits Expert/Advisor
PE References are to Pension and Profit Sharing 2nd
EP References are to Estate Planning & Taxation Coordinator and Estate Planning Advisor

 Research Institute of America   435

amount includible by a shareholder is limited to that part of the amount subject to tax under Code Sec. 857(b)(3)(A)(ii) as a capital gain dividend that the shareholder would have received if it had been distributed as capital gain dividends by the REIT to the shareholders at the close of the tax year. (Code Sec. 857(b)(3)(D)(i) as amended by '97 Act §1254(a)) For this purpose, "shares" and "shareholders" include beneficial interests and holders of beneficial interests, respectively. (Code Sec. 857(b)(3)(D)(vi))

In allowing for a REIT to retain and pay income tax on net long-term capital gains, Congress intended to grant to REITs the same tax advantages granted to regulated investment companies (RICs). Congress indicates that as a pass-through entity, REITs should be permitted to retain the proceeds of realized capital gains in a manner comparable to RICs. (Com Rept, see ¶ 5230)

> *observation:* There is a considerable investment advantage to having the proceeds of net long-term capital gain remain within the REIT so that it can be reinvested by the professional managers of the fund, rather than having the gain distributed to shareholders. Presumably, many investors would prefer to have their share of the capital gains remain subject to reinvestment by the REIT's financial managers.

For purposes of determining income tax liability, every shareholder of a REIT is considered to have paid, for their tax year at issue, the capital gain tax imposed by Code Sec. 857(b)(3)(A)(ii) on the amounts required to be included in respect of such shares in computing the shareholder's long-term capital gains for that year. The REIT shareholders are allowed a credit or refund for the tax that they are deemed to have paid. (Code Sec. 857(b)(3)(D)(ii))

The shareholder's adjusted basis of shares for which deemed capital gain treatment was obtained is increased with respect to the amounts required to be included in computing his long-term capital gains, by the difference between the amount of the includible capital gains and the tax on the capital gains that is deemed paid by the shareholder. (Code Sec. 857(b)(3)(D)(iii))

> *illustration:* A REIT has $200,000 of undistributed net capital gains for tax year 1, which it elects to retain. The REIT pays $70,000 in capital gains taxes on those gains (assuming a 35% maximum rate on corporate capital gains), for which its shareholders receive a corresponding credit of $70,000. The shareholders' basis in the shares of the REIT is increased by the difference between he amount of the includible capital gains from the dividend ($200,000) and the tax that the shareholder is deemed to have paid with respect to those shares ($70,000). The upward basis adjustment in this case is equal to $130,000.

Upon designation by the REIT, the capital gains tax imposed under Code Sec. 857(b)(3)(A)(ii) must be paid by the REIT within 30 days after the close of its taxable year. (Code Sec. 857(b)(3)(D)(iv))

The earnings and profits of the REIT, and the earnings and profits of a REIT shareholder that is a corporation, are to be appropriately adjusted in accordance with regs to be issued by IRS. (Code Sec. 857(b)(3)(D)(v))

Long-term capital loss treatment on shares held for six-months or less. Where a shareholder receives a capital gains dividend under Code Sec. 857(b)(3)(B) or a deemed long-term capital gain distribution under Code Sec. 857(b)(3)(D) on shares held for six months or less, any loss on the sale of those shares (within the six-month period) is treated as a long-term capital loss to the extent of the capital gains dividend or deemed long-term capital gain distribution. (Code Sec. 857(b)(7)(A)(i) as amended by '97 Act §1254(b)(1))

☐ **Effective:** For tax years beginning after Aug. 5, '97. ('97 Act §1263)

¶ 1702. Increase in shareholder's basis for undistributed capital gains passed through a RIC is adjusted

Code Sec. 852(b)(3)(D)(iii), as amended by '97 Act § 1254(b)(2)
Generally effective: Tax years beginning after Aug. 5, '97
Committee Reports, see ¶ 5230

A RIC may pass through undistributed capital gains to its shareholders by designating an amount which it could have distributed as capital gains dividends in a notice sent to its shareholders not more than 60 days after the close of the RIC's tax year. FTC 2d/FIN ¶ E-6154 The undistributed net capital gain will be deemed to have been constructively distributed to the shareholders in proportion to their interest in the RIC and is included in their income as long term capital gain for the shareholder's tax year in which the last day of the RIC's tax year falls.   The RIC pays the tax on the undistributed capital gains, and the shareholders are deemed to have paid their proportionate shares of the tax paid by the RIC and are allowed a credit or refund (at a maximum 35% rate) for the tax paid by the RIC. Under pre-'97 Act law, each shareholder's adjusted basis in his shares is increased by 65% of the amount subject to the tax. (FTC 2d/FIN ¶ E-6155; USTR ¶ 8524.02)

New Law. The 65% rule is no longer applicable. The adjusted basis of each shareholder's shares in the RIC is increased by the difference between the amount of the includible capital gains from the dividend and the tax that the shareholder is deemed to have paid with respect to those shares. (Code Sec. 852(b)(3)(D)(iii) as amended by '97 Act §1254(b)(2))

☐ **Effective:** Tax years beginning after Aug. 5, '97. ('97 Act §1263)

¶ 1703. Failure by REIT to maintain shareholder records results in monetary penalties, not disqualification

Code Sec. 857(a)(2), repealed by '97 Act § 1251(a)(1)
Code Sec. 857(a)(3), redesignated by '97 Act § 1251(a)(1)
Code Sec. 857(f), as amended by '97 Act § 1251(a)(2)
Generally effective: Tax years beginning after Aug. 5, '97
Committee Reports, see ¶ 5230

Under pre-'97 Act law, for a corporation or other entity to qualify to be taxed as a REIT, the entity was required to keep permanent records showing actual ownership of its stock or certificates. A REIT that failed to comply with the recordkeeping requirements was disqualified and lost all of the tax benefits of REIT status with respect to the tax year for which the REIT failed to comply. The regs provided that the ownership records must be kept in the IRS district in which the REIT filed its return, and had to be retained for as long as the records might become material in the administration of any tax law. The actual owner of the REIT's stock (or certificates) was the person required to include in his income the dividends received on the stock or certificates. This was normally the record owner. However, where the record owner was not the actual owner, the REIT's records of its shareholders might not have disclosed the actual owner. Therefore, the regs required the REIT to demand written statements from record holders as to actual owners. The statements had to be demanded not later than 30 days after the close of the REIT's tax year. (FTC 2d/FIN ¶ E-6620; USTR ¶ 8574.01)

New Law. The requirement that an entity follow the recordkeeping requirements and issue demand statements to qualify as a REIT is repealed. (Code Sec. 857(a)(2) repealed by '97 Act §1251(a)(1)) However, REITs must continue to comply with the regs issued by the IRS for the purpose of determining the actual ownership of outstanding shares, or certificates of beneficial interest, of the REIT. (Code Sec. 857(f)(1) as amended by '97 Act §1251(a)(2))

> 🅡🅘🅐 *observation:* Presumably, the regs referred to in Code Sec. 857(f)(1) are the existing regs that were issued under prior law governing a REIT's recordkeeping obligation with respect to its shareholders.

The failure to comply with the recordkeeping and shareholder demand letter requirements results in a monetary penalty rather than disqualification of the REIT. Accordingly, if a REIT fails to comply with the recordkeeping requirements of Code Sec. 871(f)(1) for a tax year, the trust must, on notice and demand by the IRS in the manner applicable to taxes, pay a $25,000 penalty. (Code Sec. 857(f)(2)(A)) If the failure to comply is due to intentional disregard of the recordkeeping requirements, the penalty is increased to $50,000. ((Code Sec. 857(f)(2)(B)) The IRS may require a REIT to take such actions as the IRS determines to be appropriate to determine actual ownership if the trust fails to meet the recordkeeping requirements of Code Sec. 871(f)(1). If the trust fails to take such actions, the trust must, on notice and demand by the IRS in the manner applicable to taxes, pay an additional penalty equal to the penalty determined under Code Sec. 871(f)(2)(A) or Code Sec. 871(f)(2)(B), whichever is applicable. (Code Sec. 857(f)(2)(C)) The REIT may be required, for instance, to send curative demand letters when requested by the IRS. (Com Rept, see ¶ 5230)

No penalty is imposed under Code Sec. 871(f)(2) with respect to any failure to comply with the recordkeeping requirements if it is shown that this failure is due to reasonable cause and not willful neglect. (Code Sec. 857(f)(2)(D))

☐ **Effective:** For tax years beginning after Aug. 5, '97. ('97 Act §1263)

¶ 1704. Requirement that REIT not be closely held is met where adequate shareholder records are maintained and REIT has no knowledge to contrary

Code Sec. 856(k), as amended by '97 Act § 1251(b)(1)
Code Sec. 856(a)(6), as amended by '97 Act § 1251(b)(2)
Generally effective: Tax years beginning after Aug. 5, '97
Committee Reports, see ¶ 5230

A REIT must be a corporation, trust or association which, among other requirements, isn't closely held. FTC 2d/FIN ¶ E-6506 An entity is considered to be closely held if more than 50% in value of the outstanding shares or certificates of beneficial ownership is held directly or indirectly by or for five or fewer individuals at any time during the last half of a tax year. To determine that the REIT is not disqualified because it is closely held, the regs require that a REIT's permanent records must show the maximum number of shares of the REIT (including number and face value of securities convertible into stock of the REIT) to be considered as actually or constructively owned by each of the actual owners of the REIT's stock at any time during the last half of its tax year. (FTC 2d/FIN ¶ E-6511, ¶ E-6620; USTR ¶ 8564.01)

New Law. A corporation, trust or association is deemed to have satisfied the requirement that it not be closely held where it satisfies the recordkeeping requirements of Code Sec. 857(f)(1) and the pre-'97 Act regs (see ¶ 1703) during the tax year, and does not know, or by exercising reasonable diligence would not have known, if the REIT failed to satisfy the requirement that it not be closely held. (Code Sec. 856(k) as amended by '97 Act §1251(b)(1))

> **⊘** *observation:* Accordingly, under Code Sec. 856(k), even if a REIT is in fact a closely held corporation, as long as the REIT meets the recordkeeping requirements, and doesn't know that it was in fact closely held, or by exercising reasonable diligence wouldn't have known that it was closely held, it will nevertheless be treated as satisfying the requirement that it not be closely held.

FTC 2d References are to Federal Tax Coordinator 2d
FIN References are to RIA's Analysis of Federal Taxes: Income
USTR References are to United States Tax Reporter: Income, Estate & Gift, and Excise
PCA References are to Pension Coordinator and Pension & Benefits Expert/Advisor
PE References are to Pension and Profit Sharing 2nd
EP References are to Estate Planning & Taxation Coordinator and Estate Planning Advisor

☐ **Effective:** Tax years beginning after Aug. 5, '97 ('97 Act §1263)

¶ 1705. REITs may render de minimis amount of tenant services and still treat income from property as rent

Code Sec. 856(d)(2)(C), as amended by '97 Act § 1252(a)
Code Sec. 856(d)(7), as amended by '97 Act § 1252(b)
Generally effective: Tax years beginning after Aug. 5, '97
Committee Reports, see ¶ 5230

To qualify as a REIT, an entity must satisfy various tests that are intended to insure that the income is primarily derived from passive real estate investments. One of these tests requires that at least 95% of the REIT's gross income be derived from passive investments such as dividends, interest and rents from real property. Additionally, 75% of the REIT's gross income must be derived specifically from various types of investments in real property, such as rents from real property.

Under pre-'97 Act law, rents from real property did not include amounts received or accrued with respect to real property if the REIT furnished or rendered services to the tenants of the property, or managed or operated the property, other than through an independent contractor from whom the REIT did not derive or receive any income. Notwithstanding this rule, under pre-'97 Act law a REIT could include in rents from real property any amount that would be excluded from unrelated business taxable income under Code Sec. 512(b)(3) if they were received by an organization described in Code Sec. 511(a)(2). Accordingly, the rule that the REIT must use an independent contractor didn't apply to these amounts, and those services could be provided directly by the REIT. FTC 2d/FIN ¶ E-6515; FTC 2d/FIN ¶ E-6529; FTC 2d/FIN ¶ E-6529.1; USTR ¶ 8564.04

New Law. The '97 Act permits a REIT to render a de minimis amount of services to tenants, or in connection with the management of property, and still treat amounts received with respect to that property as rent, although the services are of such a nature that all of the rent from the property would have been disqualified under pre-'97 Act law. (Com Rept, see ¶ 5230) Income received for such services is called "impermissible tenant service income," but the receipt of such income won't disqualify the treatment of income from a property as rents from real property if it doesn't exceed 1% of all the income from the property during the tax year. (Code Sec. 856(d)(7) as amended by '97 Act §1252(b))

"Impermissible tenant service income" means, with respect to any real or personal property, any amount received or accrued directly or indirectly by a REIT for services furnished or rendered by the REIT to the tenants of the property, or for managing or operating the property. (Code Sec. 856(d)(7)(A))

"Impermissible tenant service income" is excluded from qualifying rents from real property. (Code Sec. 856(d)(2)(C) as amended by '97 Act §1252(a))

If the amount of "impermissible tenant service income" with respect to a property for any tax year exceeds 1% of all amounts received or accrued during the tax year directly or indirectly by the REIT from that property, the REIT's impermissible tenant service income with respect to the property includes all such amounts. (Code Sec. 856(d)(7)(B))

observation: Presumably, the term "all such amounts," as used in Code Sec. 856(d)(7)(B), refers to all amounts received or accrued with respect to the property, including all of the rent as well as all of the income from services. Thus, as happens under pre-'97 Act law, if any amount of impermissible services are rendered, all of the income from the property is disqualified under the '97 Act if the de minimis amount is exceeded.

observation: Regardless of whether or not the de minimis amount is exceeded, the entire amount of any "impermissible tenant service income" is excluded from qualifying real property rents. For instance, if the gross income from a property is $100,000, of which $99,000 is rent and $1,000 is "impermissible tenant service income," the $99,000 in rent won't be disqualified, because the 1% de minimis limit won't have been exceeded, but the $1,000 in "impermissible tenant service income" will nonetheless be excluded from qualifying rents.

For purposes of determining the amount of impermissible tenant service income, the following rules also apply:

• services furnished or rendered, or management or operation provided, through an independent contractor from whom the trust itself does not derive or receive any income shall not be treated as furnished, rendered, or provided by the trust, and

• no amount is taken into account if it would be excluded from unrelated business taxable income under Code Sec. 512(b)(3) if received by a tax-exempt organization described in Code Sec. 511(a)(2). (Code Sec. 856(d)(7)(C))

observation: Thus, the rules applicable under pre-'97 Act law with respect to services rendered by an independent contractor on behalf of a REIT, and for amounts that would be excludable from unrelated business taxable income of a tax-exempt organization continue to apply for purposes of determining the amount of a REIT's impermissible rental services income.

In addition, the amount treated as received for services (or management or operation) cannot be less than 150% of the direct cost of the trust in furnishing or rendering the service (or providing the management or operation). (Code Sec. 856(d)(7)(D)) This prohibits REIT from valuing the services at less than 150% of its direct cost of providing the services. (Com Rept, see ¶ 5230)

For purposes of determining whether a REIT satisfies the 95% gross income test of Code Sec. 856(c)(2), or the 75% gross income test of Code Sec. 856(c)(3), amounts of impermissible tenant services income as determined under Code Sec. 856(d)(7)(A) are included in the gross income of the REIT. (Code Sec. 856(d)(7)(E))

☐ **Effective:** For tax years beginning after Aug. 5, '97. ('97 Act §1263)

¶ 1706. Election by REIT to treat real estate as foreclosure property made revocable, election grace periods extended, definition of independent contractor conformed

Code Sec. 856(e)(2), as amended by '97 Act § 1257(a)(1)
Code Sec. 856(e)(3), as amended by '97 Act § 1257(a)(2)
Code Sec. 856(e)(4), as amended by '97 Act § 1257(c)
Code Sec. 856(e)(5), as amended by '97 Act § 1257(b)
Generally effective: Tax years beginning after Aug. 5, '97
Committee Reports, see ¶ 5230

To qualify as a REIT, at least 95% of an entity's income must be derived from passive investment sources such as interest, dividends and rents from real property, and at least 75% of the entity's income must be derived from sources related to real estate, such rental income. Rents from real property do not include any amount received or accrued with respect to real property if the REIT furnishes services to the tenants of the property, or manages the property, other than through an independent contractor from whom the REIT does not derive income. An independent contractor is defined for this purpose as an entity that cannot own more than 35% or more of the REIT's shares or certificates at any time during the tax year. FTC 2d/FIN ¶ E-6529

Income and gain from foreclosure property qualifies for both the 95% and 75% tests. FTC 2d/FIN ¶ E-6515 Foreclosure property includes real property (including interests in real property), and any personal property incident to real property, acquired by the REIT as the result of the REIT having bid in the property at foreclosure, or having otherwise reduced the property to ownership or possession by agreement or process of law, after there was a default (or default was imminent) on a lease of the property or on an indebtedness which the property secured. FTC 2d/FIN ¶ E-6537

Under pre-'97 Act law, real property was treated as foreclosure property only if the REIT made an irrevocable election to so treat the real property. Pre-'97 Act law also gave REITs a two-year grace period in which property was treated as foreclosure property for two years after the election. A REIT could obtain extensions of time on the grace period for as much as four additional years.

Furthermore, under pre-'97 Act law, the election to treat real property as foreclosure property terminated if the REIT used the foreclosure property in a trade or business at any time more than 90 days after the property was acquired, and conducted the business itself rather than through an independent contractor from whom the REIT did not derive or receive income. An independent contractor was also defined for this purpose as an entity that cannot own more than 35% or more of the REIT's shares or certificates at any time during the tax year. (FTC 2d/FIN ¶ E-6538, ¶ E-6540, ¶ E-6541, ¶ E-6545; USTR ¶ 8564.11)

New Law. An election to treat real property as foreclosure property is no longer irrevocable. A REIT may revoke the election for a tax year by filing the revocation (in a manner to be provided by the IRS) on or before the due date (including any extension of time) for filing the REIT's tax return for that tax year. If a REIT revokes an election to treat real property as foreclosure property, no election may be made by the REIT with respect to that real property for any subsequent tax year. (Code Sec. 856(e)(5) as amended by '97 Act §1257(b))

Grace periods extended. The initial grace period for treatment of real property as foreclosure property is extended from two years after the date that the trust acquires the property to the close of the third tax year following the tax year in which the trust acquires the real property. (Code Sec. 856(e)(2) as amended by '97 Act §1257(a)(1)) The available extension of the grace period is limited to the close of the third tax year following the last tax year of the initial grace period. (Code Sec. 856(e)(3) as amended by '97 Act §1257(a)(2))

> ⚡ *observation:* Thus, the maximum available extension of the grace period is the close of the sixth tax year following the tax year in which the trust acquired the property. Under pre-'97 Act law, a REIT could also obtain a maximum extension of six years from the date that the property was acquired. However, under pre-'97 Act law, the last four of those years were subject to IRS discretion, while under the current version of Code Sec. 856(e)(3) only the final three years are subject to IRS discretion.

Definition of independent contractor conformed. For purposes of determining whether a REIT is engaging in business activity which results in the disqualification of the election to treat real property as foreclosure property, real property shall not be treated as used in a trade or business by reason of any activities of the REIT with respect to the real property to the extent that these activities would not result in amounts received or accrued, directly or indirectly, with respect to such property being treated as other than rents from real property. (Code Sec. 856(e)(4)(C) as amended by '97 Act §1257(c)) The purpose of this change is to expressly conform the definition of independent contractor for purposes of the treatment of foreclosure property to the definition of independent contractor for purposes of the general rules under Code Sec. 856(d)(2)(C) regarding the definition of rents from real property. (Com Rept, see ¶ 5230)

> ⚡ *observation:* Under pre-'97 Act law, there was no Code provision that expressly conformed the definition of an independent contractor for purposes of the rule for disqualifying foreclosure property with the definition of independent contractor for purposes of determining whether rents were qualifying rents from real property. As a result of the law change, both references to independent contractor are now expressly subject to the same standards under

FTC 2d References are to Federal Tax Coordinator 2d
FIN References are to RIA's Analysis of Federal Taxes: Income
USTR References are to United States Tax Reporter: Income, Estate & Gift, and Excise
PCA References are to Pension Coordinator and Pension & Benefits Expert/Advisor
PE References are to Pension and Profit Sharing 2nd
EP References are to Estate Planning & Taxation Coordinator and Estate Planning Advisor

⚡ Research Institute of America 443

Code Sec. 856(e)(4)(C).

☐ **Effective:** For tax years beginning after Aug. 5, '97. ('97 Act §1263)

¶ 1707. REIT's "excess noncash income" includes coupon interest and OID under both cash and accrual methods, as well as income from debt cancellation

Code Sec. 857(e)(2)(B), as amended and redesignated by '97 Act § 1259
Code Sec. 857(e)(2)(C), as amended and redesignated by '97 Act § 1259
Generally effective: Tax years beginning after Aug. 5, '97
Committee Reports, see ¶ 5230

For an entity to be taxed as a REIT for a tax year, it must distribute deductible dividends (other than capital gains dividends) to its shareholders equal to at least the sum of:

- 95% of its real estate investment trust income for the tax year exclusive of net capital gains (and before the dividends-paid deduction), plus 95% of the excess of its net income from foreclosure property over the tax imposed on such income, minus

- its "excess noncash income."

Under pre-'97 Act law, "excess noncash income" consisted of certain amounts of income from rental agreements involving deferred rents, from original issue discount and coupon interest on loans subject to Code Sec. 1274 (for cash basis REITs only), and from certain realty dispositions the gain from which was subject to nonrecognition under Code Sec. 1031, reduced by 5% of real estate trust taxable income (exclusive of capital gains and before the dividends-paid deduction). In the case of a cash basis REIT, the amount of OID and coupon interest that had to be taken into account with respect to Code Sec. 1274 was reduced by the amount of money and fair market value of other property received during the tax year under these instruments. (FTC 2d/FIN ¶ E-6602, ¶ E-6603; USTR ¶ 8574.03)

New Law. The definition of excess noncash income is expanded to include debt cancellation income, and the treatment provided for cash method REITs for OID income and coupon interest is both modified and extended to accrual basis REITs. Accordingly, excess noncash income, for both cash and accrual basis REITs, includes the amount (if any) by which the amounts includible in gross income with respect to instruments to which Code Sec. 860E(a) (relating to residual interests in a real estate mortgage investment conduit (REMIC)) or Code Sec. 1272 (relating to OID debt obligations) applies, exceeds the amount of money and the fair market value of other property received during the taxable year under such instruments. (Code Sec. 857(e)(2)(C) as amended and redesignated by '97 Act §1259)

This provision extends excess noncash item treatment for coupon interest and OID income to REIT's that use the accrual method of tax accounting. (Com Rept, see ¶ 5230)

Excess noncash income also includes amounts includible in income by reason of cancellation of indebtedness. (Code Sec. 857(e)(2)(D))

> **✔observation:** Accordingly, items of income described in new Code Sec. 857(e)(2)(C) and income from cancellation of indebtedness, along with the two existing categories for income from deferred rental arrangements and realty dispositions that qualify under Code Sec. 1031, are excluded from the 95% distribution requirements otherwise applicable to income of a REIT. This gives a REIT the ability to retain income from these items without jeopardizing its tax status as a flow-through entity.

☐ **Effective:** For tax years beginning after Aug. 5, '97. ('97 Act §1263)

¶ 1708. Favorable treatment of REIT income from interest rate swaps and caps is extended to income from all types of hedging agreements

Code Sec. 856(c)(6)(G), as amended and redesignated by '97 Act § 1258
Code Sec. 856(c)(6)(G), as amended and redesignated by '97 Act § 1255(b)(1)
Generally effective: For tax years beginning after Aug. 5, '97
Committee Reports, see ¶ 5230

To qualify as a REIT, an entity must satisfy a number of tests that are intended to insure that the income of a REIT is primarily derived from passive real estate investments. One of these tests requires that at least 95% of gross income is derived from passive investments such as dividends and interest, or gains from the sale of assets other than assets that would qualify as inventory under Code Sec. 1221(1).

Under pre-'97 Act law, except to the extent provided by IRS regs, payments made to a REIT by virtue of an interest rate swap or cap agreement entered into by a REIT to hedge against its variable interest rate indebtedness incurred to acquire or hold real estate assets, and any gain from its sale or other disposition of such an agreement, qualified for purposes of the 95% gross income test. Pre-'97 Act law also provided that the interest rate swap or cap agreement itself was treated as a security for purposes of the 30% gross income test. An entity qualified as a REIT under the 30% gross income test if less than 30% of its gross income was derived from certain transactions such as the sale of stock or securities held for less than one year. FTC 2d/FIN ¶ E-6515;(FTC 2d/FIN ¶ E-6522; USTR ¶ 8564.03)

New Law. Except to the extent provided by IRS regs, the favorable treatment for payments made to a REIT under an interest rate swap or cap agreement is extended to hedging agreements. Specifically, any payment to a real estate investment trust under an option, futures contract, forward rate agreement, or any similar financial instrument,

---

FTC 2d References are to Federal Tax Coordinator 2d
FIN References are to RIA's Analysis of Federal Taxes: Income
USTR References are to United States Tax Reporter: Income, Estate & Gift, and Excise
PCA References are to Pension Coordinator and Pension & Benefits Expert/Advisor
PE References are to Pension and Profit Sharing 2nd
EP References are to Estate Planning & Taxation Coordinator and Estate Planning Advisor

entered into by the trust in a transaction to reduce the interest rate risks with respect to any indebtedness incurred or to be incurred by the trust to acquire or carry real estate assets, as well as the gain from the sale or other disposition of such financial instruments, is treated as qualified income for purposes of the 95% gross income test. (Code Sec. 856(c)(5)(G) as amended and redesignated by '97 Act §1258) Thus, the income from all hedges that reduce the interest rate risk of REIT liabilities, not just from interest rate swaps and caps, are treated as qualifying income for purposes of the 95% test. Congress indicated that this modification was made to provide flexibility to REITs in managing risk for their shareholders. (Com Rept, see ¶ 5230)

The 30% gross income test is repealed (see ¶ 1709). (Code Sec. 856(c)(4) repealed by '97 Act §1255(a)(2))   Accordingly, the interest rate swap, cap or hedging agreement is no longer treated as a security for purposes of the 30% gross income test. (Code Sec. 856(c)(5)(G) as amended and redesignated by '97 Act §1255(b)(1))

☐ **Effective:** Tax years beginning after Aug. 5, '97. ('97 Act §1263)

¶ 1709. Repeal of requirement that no more than 30% of REIT's gross income can be derived from sales or other dispositions

Code Sec. 856(c)(4), repealed by '97 Act § 1255(a)(2)
Code Sec. 856(c)(8), repealed by '97 Act § 1255(a)(2)
Code Sec. 856(c), redesignated by '97 Act § 1255(a)(3)
Generally effective: Tax years beginning after Aug. 5, '97
Committee Reports, see ¶ 5230

Under pre-'97 Act law, for an entity to qualify as a REIT, less than 30% of the entity's gross income must have been derived from the sale or other disposition of:

• stock or securities held for less than one year;

• property in a transaction that was a prohibited transaction (the sale or other disposition of property held by a REIT primarily for sale to customers in the ordinary course of a REIT's business), and

• real property (including interests in real property and interests in mortgages on real property) held for less than four years other than involuntarily converted property subject to Code Sec. 1033 or foreclosure property. Foreclosure property is property acquired by a REIT by way of a bid in a foreclosure proceeding.

For purposes of the 30% test, no gain from the sale, exchange, or other disposition of any property was taken into account after the adoption of a plan of complete liquidation during the taxable year in which the REIT was completely liquidated.   (FTC 2d/FIN ¶ E-6515, ¶ E-6517; USTR ¶ 8564.03)

New Law. The 30% gross income test is repealed. (Code Sec. 856(c)(4) repealed by '97 Act §1255(a)(2)) The exception for gain from the sale or exchange of property after the adoption of a plan of complete liquidation is also repealed. (Code Sec. 865(c)(8) repealed by '97 Act §1255(a)(2)) Congress indicates that the various asset requirements applicable to REITs ensure that the REIT acts as a pass-through entity for taxpayers wishing to invest in real estate. As a result, the 30% gross income test is seen as unnecessary and administratively burdensome. (Com Rept, see ¶ 5230)

> **⊘ observation:** The repeal of the 30% gross income test give REITs additional flexibility in the management of the real estate held in the REIT. For example, a REIT could act within a single tax year to dispose of a number of unproductive properties without concern of whether the income from this activity would cause the entity to fail to qualify as a REIT.

☐ **Effective:** For tax years beginning after Aug. 5, '97. ('97 Act §1263)

¶ 1710. REIT property that is involuntarily converted is excluded from prohibited transaction 100% tax

Code Sec. 857(b)(6)(C)(iii), as amended by '97 Act § 1260
Generally effective: Tax years beginning after Aug. 5, '97
Committee Reports, see ¶ 5230

A 100% tax is imposed on the net income of a REIT that is derived from prohibited transactions. Prohibited transactions include the sale or other disposition of property (other than foreclosure property) that is held by a REIT primarily for sale to customers in the ordinary course of the REIT's trade or business. FTC 2d/FIN ¶ E-6613; USTR ¶ 8574.01

Under pre-'97 Act law, sales of property which were real estate assets were excluded from the definition of prohibited transactions if, among other requirements, the REIT didn't make more than seven sales of property (other than foreclosure property) during the tax year, or the aggregate adjusted basis, as determined for purposes of computing earnings and profit, of property (other than foreclosure property) sold during the tax year didn't exceed 10% of the aggregate bases of all the REIT's assets as of the beginning of the tax year. (FTC 2d/FIN ¶ E-6614; USTR ¶ 8574.01)

New Law. In addition to the sale of foreclosure property, the sale of property that was involuntarily converted in a transaction that is subject to Code Sec. 1033 is disregarded for purposes of determining whether the REIT made seven sales of property during the tax year, or whether the aggregate adjusted basis of property sold during the tax year exceeds 10% of the aggregate basis of all of the REIT's assets as of the beginning of the tax year. (Code Sec. 857(b)(6)(C)(iii) as amended by '97 Act §1260) Accordingly, property that is involuntarily converted is not subject to the prohibited transaction 100% tax. (Com Rept, see ¶ 5230)

☐ **Effective:** Tax years beginning after Aug. 5, '97 ('97 Act §1263)

FTC 2d References are to Federal Tax Coordinator 2d
FIN References are to RIA's Analysis of Federal Taxes: Income
USTR References are to United States Tax Reporter: Income, Estate & Gift, and Excise
PCA References are to Pension Coordinator and Pension & Benefits Expert/Advisor
PE References are to Pension and Profit Sharing 2nd
EP References are to Estate Planning & Taxation Coordinator and Estate Planning Advisor

¶ 1711. Existing corporation in which a REIT acquires a 100% ownership interest is a qualified subsidiary

Code Sec. 856(i)(2), as amended by '97 Act § 1262
Generally effective: Tax years beginning after Aug. 5, '97
Committee Reports, see ¶ 5230

A corporation that is a qualified REIT subsidiary is not treated as a separate corporation for tax reporting purposes. All assets, liabilities, and items of income, deduction and credit of a qualified REIT subsidiary are treated as assets, liabilities, and items of income, deduction and credit of the REIT.

Under pre-'97 Act law, a qualified REIT subsidiary was any corporation (or entity that was taxed as a corporation) if 100% of the stock of that corporation was held by the REIT at all times during the corporation's existence. The IRS had privately ruled, however, that the 100% rule did not prevent a REIT from acquiring the stock of a pre-existing corporation. In such a situation, the IRS said that for tax purposes the subsidiary was deemed to have been liquidated under Code Sec. 332 and to have been formed as a new corporation. Thus, after a deemed Code Sec. 351 exchange, the subsidiary became a qualified REIT subsidiary. It wasn't necessary for the REIT to actually liquidate the C corporation to achieve this result. (FTC 2d/FIN ¶ E-6553, ¶ E-6553.1; USTR ¶ 8564.07)

New Law. A qualified REIT subsidiary includes any corporation if 100% of the stock of the corporation is owned by a REIT. (Code Sec. 856(i)(2) as amended by '97 Act §1262) Accordingly, any corporation that is wholly-owned by a REIT may be treated as a qualified subsidiary, regardless of whether the corporation had always been owned by the REIT. Where the REIT acquires an existing corporation, that corporation is treated as if it is liquidated at the time of the acquisition by the REIT, and then reincorporated. Accordingly, the subsidiary's pre-REIT built-in gain is subject to tax under the rules that apply to distributions of property by a corporation completely liquidating in a subsidiary liquidation under Code Sec. 337. In addition, all earnings and profits of the subsidiary that were accumulated before it was acquired by the REIT must be distributed before the end of the REIT's tax year. (Com Rept, see ¶ 5230)

> **☑ observation:** The Committee Reports indicate that pre-REIT built-in gain would be subject to tax on complete liquidation of the subsidiary under Code Sec. 337, which is generally a nonrecognition provision for the liquidation of a subsidiary. However, Code Sec. 337(d) provides that the IRS will issue regulations to prevent the circumvention of the rule requiring the recognition of net built-in gain on appreciated property held by a C corporation by use of a REIT. Specifically, the regulations to be issued by the IRS will require that when the assets of a C corporation become the assets of a REIT, the C corporation is treated as if it sold all of its assets at their respective fair market values and immediately liquidated. This rule causes the recognition of the C corporation's net built-in gain. FTC 2d/FIN ¶ E-6851

⊘ *observation:* The deemed liquidation discussed in the Committee Reports apparently adopts the position taken by the IRS in private letter rulings and in the regulations to be issued under Code Sec. 337(d).

☐ **Effective:** Tax years beginning after Aug. 5, '97. ('97 Act §1263)

¶ 1712. REITs provided safe harbor from prohibited transaction tax for shared appreciation mortgages disposed of under bankruptcy court jurisdiction

Code Sec. 856(j)(4), redesignated by '97 Act § 1261(a)
Code Sec. 856(j)(4), as amended by '97 Act § 1261(a)
Code Sec. 856(j)(4)(A), as amended by '97 Act § 1261(b)
Generally effective: For tax years beginning after Aug. 5, '97
Committee Reports, see ¶ 5230

Income that is derived from a shared appreciation provision is treated as gain recognized on the sale of the secured property for the purpose of applying the prohibited transaction tax under Code Sec. 857(b)(6). FTC 2d/FIN ¶ E-6612 A "shared appreciation provision" means any provision that:

• is in connection with an obligation that is held by the REIT and is secured by an interest in real property; and

• entitles the REIT to receive a specified portion of the gain realized on the sale or exchange of the real property (or of the gain that would be realized if the property were sold on a specified date).

Under Code Sec. 856(b)(6)(C), an exception to the prohibited transaction tax applies to sales of property, which, among other requirements, had been held by a REIT for four or more years. Under pre-'97 Act law, the REIT was treated as holding the secured property for the period during which it actually held the shared appreciation provision or, if shorter, for the period during which the secured property was held by the person holding the secured property. (FTC 2d/FIN ¶ E-6546, ¶ E-6614; USTR ¶ 8564.08)

New Law. For purposes of determining whether a REIT qualifies for the four-year holding period exception to the prohibited transaction tax, if a REIT is treated as having sold secured property as a result of its having received income under a shared appreciation mortgage, the REIT is treated as having held the shared appreciation mortgage for at least four years if:

• the secured property is sold or otherwise disposed of under a Title 11 bankruptcy case;

FTC 2d References are to Federal Tax Coordinator 2d
FIN References are to RIA's Analysis of Federal Taxes: Income
USTR References are to United States Tax Reporter: Income, Estate & Gift, and Excise
PCA References are to Pension Coordinator and Pension & Benefits Expert/Advisor
PE References are to Pension and Profit Sharing 2nd
EP References are to Estate Planning & Taxation Coordinator and Estate Planning Advisor

• the seller is under the jurisdiction of the bankruptcy court in such case; and

• the disposition is required by the bankruptcy court or is made under a plan approved by the bankruptcy court.

(Code Sec. 856(j)(4)(A) as amended by '97 Act §1261(a))

The bankruptcy safe harbor rule does not apply where (1) the secured property was acquired by the seller with the intent to evict or foreclose or (2) the REIT knew or had reason to know that default on the shared appreciation mortgage would occur. (Code Sec. 856(j)(4)(B))

The definition of a shared appreciation provision is also extended to include a provision that (1) is in connection with an obligation that is held by the REIT and secured by an interest in real property, as under pre-'97 Act law, and (2) provides that the REIT is entitled to receive the appreciation in value of the property subject to the shared appreciated provision as of any specified date. (Code Sec. 856(j)(5)(A) as amended and redesignated by '97 Act §1261(b))

☐ **Effective:** For tax years beginning after Aug. 5, '97. ('97 Act §1263)

¶ 1713. For purposes of applying the related party test or the independent contractor test to REIT rental income, the attribution rules apply to partnerships only where a partner owns 25% or more interest in the partnership

Code Sec. 856(d)(5), as amended by '97 Act § 1253
Generally effective: Tax years beginning after Aug. 5, '97
Committee Reports, see ¶ 5230

To qualify as a REIT, an entity must satisfy a series of tests of its income that is intended to insure that the income is primarily derived from passive investments One of these tests requires that at least 95% of gross income is derived from passive investments, such as dividends, interest and rents from real property.   Another test requires that at least 75% of gross income of the REIT is derived from investments connected with real property, such as rents from real property. FTC 2d/FIN ¶ E-6515 However, rents from real property do not include amounts received from related parties, such as a corporate tenant in which the REIT owns 10% or more of the combined voting power of all classes of stock entitled to vote, or from a noncorporate tenant such as a partnership, in which the REIT owns, directly or indirectly, an interest in 10% or more of the assets or net profits.   FTC 2d/FIN ¶ E-6527 Furthermore, where a REIT furnishes or renders services to tenants, amounts received or accrued with respect to the property generally are not treated as qualifying rents from real property, unless the services are furnished through an independent contractor. FTC 2d/FIN ¶ E-6529 An independent contractor is a person who does not own more than a 35% interest in the REIT, and in which no more than a 35% interest is held by persons with a 35% or greater interest in the REIT.   FTC 2d/FIN ¶ E-6530

In determining whether rents are paid by a related party, or whether a person qualifies as an independent contractor, the REIT's ownership of stock, assets and net profits is determined by applying the constructive ownership rules of Code Sec. 318(a). However, in applying these rules to attribute ownership of stock from a REIT to a shareholder under Code Sec. 318(a)(2)(C), or from the shareholder to the REIT under Code Sec. 318(a)(3)(C), attribution is made where the REIT shareholder owns 10% (instead of 50%) or more in value of the REIT's stock. Similarly, attribution of stock under Code Sec. 318(a)(2)(C) to a REIT from another corporation in which the REIT owns stock occurs where the REIT owns 10% or more of the other corporation's stock.

Under pre-'97 Act law, in applying the attribution rules with respect to a partnership, a partner (including a REIT) was considered to own stock or assets owned by a partnership in proportion to the partner's ownership interest in the partnership. Furthermore, stock or assets owned by a REIT or any other partner were attributed to a partnership in which the REIT or other partner held any ownership interest. Under pre-'97 Act law, in applying the attribution rules from a partner (including a REIT) to a partnership, the partner's percentage ownership was disregarded and the entire amount of stock or assets owned by the partner was attributed to the partnership. (FTC 2d/FIN ¶ E-6527, ¶ E-6531; USTR ¶ 8564.04)

> **Illustration (1):** If 10% or more of a REIT's shares were owned by a partnership, and a partner owning a one-percent interest in that partnership also owned a 10% or greater interest in a person that was a tenant of the REIT, rents paid by the tenant to the REIT were not qualifying rents to the REIT. The 10% interest in the tenant was considered to be owned by the partnership, and was therefore also attributable to the REIT since the partnership is a 10% stockholder in the REIT. (Com Rept, see ¶ 5230)

> **☞ observation:** In Illustration 1, the interest that the partnership holds in the tenant is attributable to the REIT under Code Sec. 318(a)(3)(C). Under that provision, a corporation (such as the REIT) is deemed to own stock held by a person (such as the partnership) who holds at least 50% in value of the stock of the corporation (at least 10% in the case of a REIT). Thus, the interest in the tenant is attributable to the REIT because the partnership holds a 10% stock interest in the REIT.

> **Illustration (2):** If a REIT owns a 30% interest in a partnership that owns a 40% interest in a person that was a tenant of the REIT, rents paid by that person to the REIT were not qualifying rents to the REIT because under the attribution rules the REIT was considered to own more than a 10% interest in the tenant. (Com Rept, see ¶ 5230)

> **Illustration (3):** Where more than 35% of a REIT's shares were owned by a partnership and a partner owning a one-percent interest in that partnership also owned a more than 35% of a contractor, that contractor was not considered to

FTC 2d References are to Federal Tax Coordinator 2d
FIN References are to RIA's Analysis of Federal Taxes: Income
USTR References are to United States Tax Reporter: Income, Estate & Gift, and Excise
PCA References are to Pension Coordinator and Pension & Benefits Expert/Advisor
PE References are to Pension and Profit Sharing 2nd
EP References are to Estate Planning & Taxation Coordinator and Estate Planning Advisor

be an independent contractor because the partnership owned more than 35% of the REIT's shares and was also considered to own more than a 35% interest in the contractor. The partnership's 35% interest in the contractor was attributable to the REIT as a partner of the partnership. (Com Rept, see ¶ 5230)

Illustration (4): If more than 35% of a REIT's shares were owned by a person who owned a one-percent interest in a partnership and another one-percent partner in that partnership owned more than 35% of the interests in a contractor, the independent contractor test was not satisfied because the partnership was considered to own more than a 35% interest in both the REIT and the contractor. (Com Rept, see ¶ 5230)

New Law. For purposes of determining whether rental payments received by a REIT qualify as "rents from real property," the attribution rules applicable with respect to corporations continue to apply as under prior law, with attribution occurring from a REIT to a shareholder, from a shareholder to a REIT, or to a REIT from a corporation in which the REIT is a shareholder, if a 10% (instead of 50%) ownership requirement is met. (Code Sec. 856(d)(5)(A) as amended by '97 Act §1253) With respect to partnerships, attribution of stock, assets or net profits from a partner to a partnership under Code Sec. 318(a)(3)(A) is applicable only if the partner owns (directly or indirectly) 25% or more of the capital interest or profits interest in the partnership. (Code Sec. 856(d)(5)(B)) Thus, a REIT and a tenant are not related (and, therefore, rents paid by the tenant to the REIT would be qualifying rents) if the REIT's shares are owned by a partnership and a partner owning (directly or indirectly) less than a 25% interest in that partnership also owns an interest in the tenant. In addition, there would be no violation of the related tenant rule where owners of the REIT and owners of the tenant are partners in a partnership and either the owners of the REIT or the owners of the tenant own (directly or indirectly) less than a 25% interest in the partnership. (Com Rept, see ¶ 5230)

❷ **illustration (5):** Assuming the same facts as in Illustration 1, above, the rents paid by the tenant to the REIT would be qualifying rents from real property. Since the partner owns less than a 25% interest in the partnership, his ownership in the tenant would not be attributable to the partnership, and therefore, would not be attributable to the REIT.

❷ **illustration (6):** Assuming the same facts as in Illustration 2, above, the result in this illustration does not change under the new law. The partnership's 40% interest in the tenant is attributable to the REIT to the extent of the REIT's 30% ownership interest in the partnership.

The conference agreement also clarifies that the modified attribution rules for partnerships apply both for the purpose of determining whether rents are paid by a related party and whether rents are paid to a REIT for services provided by an independent contractor. Thus, a person providing services will qualify as an independent contractor (and, therefore, amounts received or accrued by the REIT with respect to the property serviced by the independent contractor will be qualifying rents) where the REIT's shares are owned by a partnership and a partner owning less than a 25% interest in the partnership (either directly or indirectly) also owns an interest in a contractor. Similarly, a contractor qualifies as an independent contractor where owners of the REIT and owners of the contractor are partners in a partnership and either the owners of the REIT or the owners of the tenant own (directly or indirectly) less than a 25% interest in the partnership. (Com Rept, see ¶ 5230)

illustration (7): Assuming the same facts as in Illustration 3, above, the contractor would qualify as an independent contractor for purposes of determining whether rents paid for services performed by the contractor would be qualifying rents from real property. Since the partner owns less than a 25% interest in the partnership, his ownership in the contractor would not be attributable to the partnership, and therefore, would not be attributable to the REIT as a partner of the partnership.

illustration (8): Assuming the same facts as in Illustration 4, above, the contractor would qualify as an independent contractor for purposes of determining whether rents paid for services performed by the contractor would be qualifying rents from real property. Since the "one-percent partner" owns less than a 25% interest in the partnership, his ownership in the contractor would not be attributable to the partnership. Furthermore, the interest in the REIT is also not attributable to the partnership, because the partner holding the interest in the REIT is also a one-percent partner.

observation: The limitation of the attribution rules to a partnership to instances where a partner holds a 25% or greater ownership interest will make it easier for REITs to participate in real estate ventures by being a partner in a partnership. A REIT which invests in real estate through a partnership is referred to as an umbrella partnership REIT (or "UPREIT"). An UPREIT holding an ownership interest in a partnership will not have interests in other entities attributed to the UPREIT through the partnership unless the other entities hold at least a 25% interest in the partnership.

☐ **Effective:** Tax years beginning after Aug. 5, '97 ('97 Act §1263)

FTC 2d References are to Federal Tax Coordinator 2d
FIN References are to RIA's Analysis of Federal Taxes: Income
USTR References are to United States Tax Reporter: Income, Estate & Gift, and Excise
PCA References are to Pension Coordinator and Pension & Benefits Expert/Advisor
PE References are to Pension and Profit Sharing 2nd
EP References are to Estate Planning & Taxation Coordinator and Estate Planning Advisor

Research Institute of America · 453

¶ 1714. Distributions by newly electing REITs to reduce pre-REIT earnings and profits are deemed to reduce earliest acquired earnings and profits before current earnings and profits

Code Sec. 857(a)(3), redesignated by '97 Act § 1251(a)(1)
Code Sec. 857(d)(3), as amended by '97 Act § 1256
Generally effective: For tax years beginning after Aug. 5, '97
Committee Reports, see ¶ 5230

A corporation is not eligible for REIT treatment for a tax year unless as of the close of the tax year, the corporation has no earnings and profits accumulated in a non-REIT year. A non-REIT year is any tax year in which the REIT provisions did not apply to the corporation. Thus, a C corporation which has accumulated earnings and profits must distribute those earnings and profits during its first tax year as a REIT to qualify to make an election to become a REIT with respect to that first tax year. Distributions by an entity are generally treated as being made from the most recently accumulated earnings and profits under the rules that apply to distributions by regulated investment companies (RICs). (FTC 2d/FIN ¶ E-6615, ¶ E-6622; USTR ¶ 8574.01)

illustration (1): A C corporation that has a tax year that ends on June 30 makes a decision to become a REIT in tax year 1. The C corporation has $150,000 of earnings and profits that were accumulated in tax years before it became subject to the REIT provisions (non-REIT E&P). By June 1 of tax year 1, the REIT generates $75,000 of earnings and profits that are subject to the REIT provisions. On June 15 of tax year 1, the REIT makes a distribution of $220,000 to its shareholders. Under pre-'97 Act law, the distribution would have been treated as being made first from the most recently accumulated earnings and profits before reducing the non-REIT E&P. Accordingly, if this was the only distribution during tax year 1 the C corporation would fail to qualify as a REIT, because it would have $5,000 of non-REIT E&P remaining at the end of tax year 1 ($220,000 minus $75,000 of current E&P leaves only $145,000 to reduce non-REIT E&P).

New Law. A distribution by an entity that is made to comply with the requirement in Code Sec. 857(a)(2)(B) that a REIT have no earnings and profits accumulated in a non-REIT year is treated for this purpose as being made from the earliest accumulated earnings and profits rather than from the most recently accumulated earnings and profits. (Code Sec. 857(d)(3)(A) as amended by '97 Act §1256)

observation: Accordingly, a newly-electing REIT entity can make distributions to eliminate its non-REIT accumulated earnings and profits during its first tax year while also generating current earnings and profits relating to the tax period that the entity is a REIT. The entity would not be required to first eliminate current earnings and profits before making a distribution to eliminate pre-REIT earnings and profits.

illustration (2): Assume the same facts as in illustration 1, except that tax year 1 is a tax year beginning after Aug. 5, '97. In addition, assume that when the C corporation makes its distribution on June 15 that it designates the distribution as being made to comply with the requirements of Code Sec. 857(a)(2)(B). The distribution will first reduce the non-REIT E&P from $150,000 to zero. The remaining $70,000 will apply to reduce current E&P to $5,000. Accordingly, the C corporation would have satisfied the requirements of Code Sec. 857(a)(2)(B), because it would have no non-REIT E&P at the end of tax year 1. Thus, the C corporation qualifies as a REIT for tax year 1.

To the extent that a distribution is treated as being made from accumulated earnings and profits, the distribution is not treated as a distribution for purposes of calculating the dividends paid deduction allowable to a REIT under Code Sec. 857(b)(2)(B). (Code Sec. 857(d)(3)(B))

observation: Since the dividends paid deduction otherwise allowable to a REIT is not applicable, the distributions of non-REIT accumulated earnings and profits will not reduce the taxable income of the REIT.

☐ **Effective:** Tax years beginning after Aug. 5, '97. ('97 Act §1263)

RICs

¶ 1715. 30% gross income limitation (short-short test) for RICs is repealed

Code Sec. 851(b)(3), repealed by '97 Act § 1271
Generally effective: Tax years beginning after Aug. 5, '97
Committee Reports, see ¶ 5247

Under pre-'97 Act law, in order to qualify as a regulated investment company (RIC), a corporation, among other requirements, had to derive less than 30% of its gross income from the sale or disposition of stock, securities, options, futures, and forward contracts, and certain foreign currencies (and currency related options, futures, and forward contracts), that were held for less than three months (the "short-short test"). (FTC 2d/FIN ¶ E-6006; USTR ¶ 8514.03)

New Law. The short-short test has been repealed. Thus, RICs do not have to satisfy the 30% gross income requirement. (Code Sec. 851(b)(3) repealed by '97 Act §1271(a))

The '97 Act removes the designated hedge rules (Code Sec. 851(g) repealed by '97 Act §1271(b)(6)), and the abnormal redemption rules for series funds under the short-

FTC 2d References are to Federal Tax Coordinator 2d
FIN References are to RIA's Analysis of Federal Taxes: Income
USTR References are to United States Tax Reporter: Income, Estate & Gift, and Excise
PCA References are to Pension Coordinator and Pension & Benefits Expert/Advisor
PE References are to Pension and Profit Sharing 2nd
EP References are to Estate Planning & Taxation Coordinator and Estate Planning Advisor

Research Institute of America   455

short test. (Code Sec. 851(g)(3) repealed by '97 Act §1271(b)(7)).

☐ **Effective:**   Tax years begining after Aug. 5, '97. ('97 Act §1271(c))

Insurance Companies

¶ 1716. Insurance company deductions and reserves modified to take into account cash value increases of life insurance policies, annuity or endowment contracts held by those companies

Code Sec. 805(a)(4)(C)(ii), as amended by '97 Act § 1084(b)[sic]
Code Sec. 805(a)(4)(D)(iii), as amended by '97 Act § 1084(b)[sic]
Code Sec. 807(a)(2)(B), as amended by '97 Act § 1084(b)[sic]
Code Sec. 807(b)(1)(B), as amended by '97 Act § 1084(b)[sic]
Code Sec. 812(d)(1)(D), as amended by '97 Act § 1084(b)[sic]
Code Sec. 832(b)(5)(B)(iii), as amended by '97 Act § 1084(b)[sic]
Generally effective: Contracts issued after June 8, '97
Committee Reports, see ¶ 5161

A company that qualifies as a life insurance company is given special tax treatment because of the reserves it must carry for policyholder claims. It's subject to the same tax rates as corporations in general, but its income and deductions are computed under special rules. A company that qualifies as a nonlife insurance company is subject to the same tax rates as corporations in general. However, because of the nature of its business, its income and deductions are computed differently from both a life insurance company and a regular corporation.

Life insurance companies.   A life insurance company treats a decrease in its reserves as gross income, and an increase in its reserves as a deduction from gross income. There's a decrease if the closing balance of reserve items reduced by the amount of policyholders' allocated share of tax-exempt interest and further reduced by certain deductions that only apply to mutual life insurance companies is less than the opening balance of the reserve items for the tax year. There's an increase if the closing balance, reduced as described above, is greater than the opening balance.

Like regular corporations, life insurance companies are entitled to a 100% deduction for dividends received from certain other corporations ("100% dividends"). However, the deduction isn't allowed for a dividend from a corporation that isn't an insurance company to the extent the dividend is paid out of tax-exempt interest, or dividends that aren't themselves 100% dividends (determined under life insurance company rules). In the case of dividends received from other life insurance companies, the amount of the deduction is reduced with respect to "prorated amounts"—i.e., tax-exempt interest, and dividends that aren't themselves 100% dividends.

Also like regular corporations, life insurance companies are allowed a deduction for certain dividends received from other corporations that don't qualify for the 100% dividends received deduction. The deduction is computed based, in part, on the life insurance company's gross investment income. Gross investment income, includes, among other things, interest, including tax-exempt interest, dividends, rent, royalties, income from a lease, mortgage or other instrument or agreement, income from altering or terminating such an instrument or agreement, the excess of net short-term capital gain over net long-term capital loss, and certain noninsurance trade or business income.

Nonlife insurance companies. In computing the taxable income of nonlife insurance companies, a deduction is allowed for "losses incurred" on insurance contracts. The deduction is reduced by 15% of the sum of tax-exempt interest and deductible dividends received by the company.

(FTC 2d/FIN ¶ E-4821 *et seq.*, ¶ E-4826, ¶ E-4950 *et seq.*, ¶ E-5535 *et seq.*; USTR ¶ 8054, ¶ 8074, ¶ 8124, ¶ 8324.01)

New Law. In connection with changes in the tax treatment of interest on debt incurred with respect to life insurance policies, endowment and annuity contracts (by means of new Code Sec. 264(f), see ¶ 708), the '97 Act makes certain changes in the treatment of insurance companies that incur debt with respect to life insurance policies, endowment and annuity contracts that they hold. Under the '97 Act, the rules reducing certain deductions for losses incurred, in the case of property and casualty companies, and reducing reserve deductions or dividends received deductions of life insurance companies, are modified to take into account the increase in cash values of life insurance policies or annuity or endowment contracts held by insurance companies. (Com Rept, see ¶ 5161) These changes are explained in detail below.

Life insurance companies. *Reserves.* For purposes of computing a life insurance company's decrease in reserves, the '97 Act adds to those items that reduce the closing balance of reserve items the amount of the policyholder's share of the increase for the tax year in policy cash values (within the meaning of Code Sec. 805(a)(4)(F), see below) of life insurance policies and annuity and endowment contracts to which Code Sec. 264(f) applies (see ¶ 708). (Code Sec. 807(a)(2)(B) as amended by '97 Act §1084(b)[sic](2)(A))

For purposes of computing a life insurance company's increase in reserves, the '97 Act adds to those items that reduce the closing balance of reserve items the amount of the policyholder's share of the increase for the tax year in policy cash values (within the meaning of Code Sec. 805(a)(4)(F)) of life insurance policies and annuity and endowment contracts to which Code Sec. 264(f) applies. (Code Sec. 807(b)(1)(B) as amended by '97 Act §1084(b)[sic](2)(B))

Dividends received deduction. The '97 Act adds to the list of dividends that *aren't* qualified for 100% dividend treatment, a dividend received by a life insurance company from a corporation that isn't an insurance company to the extent the distribution is out of the increase for the tax year in policy cash values, within the meaning of Code Sec. 805(a)(4)(F) (see below), of life insurance polices and annuity and endowment contracts to which Code Sec. 264(f) applies. (Code Sec. 805(a)(4)(C)(ii) as amended by '97 Act §1084(b)[sic](1)(A))

For purposes of computing the deduction for 100% dividends received by life insurance companies from other life insurance companies, the '97 Act adds to the items treated as "prorated amounts" the increase for the tax year in policy cash values, within the meaning of Code Sec. 805(a)(4)(F), of life insurance polices and annuity and endowment contracts to which Code Sec. 264(f) applies. (Code Sec. 805(a)(4)(D)(iii))

> **✓** *observation:* Therefore, as a result of the '97 Act, prorated amounts include tax-exempt interest, dividends that aren't themselves 100% dividends, and the increase for the tax year in policy cash values.

For purposes of computing the deduction for dividends received by life insurance companies that aren't 100% dividends, the '97 Act adds to the items treated as gross investment income the increase for any tax year in the policy cash values, within the meaning of Code Sec. 805(a)(4)(F), of life insurance polices and annuity and endowment contracts to which Code Sec. 264(f) applies. (Code Sec. 812(d)(1)(D) as amended by '97 Act §1084(b)[sic](3))

Nonlife insurance companies. In computing a nonlife insurance company's deduction for "losses incurred" on insurance contracts, the '97 Act adds to the items that reduce the amount of the deduction the increase for the tax year in policy cash values, within the meaning of Code Sec. 805(a)(4)(F), of life insurance polices and annuity and endowment contracts to which Code Sec. 264(f) applies. (Code Sec. 832(b)(5)(B)(iii) as amended by '97 Act §1084(b)[sic](4))

> **✓** *observation:* Therefore, as a result of the '97 Act, the deduction for "losses incurred" is reduced by 15% of the sum of tax-exempt interest, deductible dividends, and the increase for the tax year in policy cash values.

Increase in policy cash values. The increase in the policy cash value for any tax year with respect to a policy or contract is the amount of the increase in the adjusted cash value (as defined below) during that tax year determined without regard to (Code Sec. 805(a)(4)(F)(i) as amended by '97 Act §1084(b)[sic](1)(C)):

... gross premiums paid during that tax year (Code Sec. 805(a)(4)(F)(i)(I)); and

... distributions (other than amounts includible in the policyholder's gross income) during that tax year to which Code Sec. 72(e) applies. (Code Sec. 805(a)(4)(F)(i)(II))

In other words, an increase in the policy cash value for any policy or contract is (1) the amount of the increase in the adjusted cash value, reduced by (2) the gross premiums received with respect to the policy or contract during the taxable year, and increased by (3) distributions under the policy or contract to which Code Sec. 72(e) apply (other than amounts includable in the policyholder's gross income). (Com Rept, see ¶ 5161)

The term "adjusted cash value" means the cash surrender value of the policy or contract increased by the sum of (Code Sec. 805(a)(4)(F)(ii)):

. . . commissions payable with respect to that policy or contract for the tax year (Code Sec. 805(a)(4)(F)(ii)(I)); and

. . . asset management fees, surrender charges, mortality and expense charges, and any other fees or charges specified in IRS regulations which are imposed (or which would be imposed were the policy or contract canceled) with respect to that policy or contract for the tax year. (Code Sec. 805(a)(4)(F)(ii)(II))

☐ **Effective:** Contracts issued after June 8, '97, in tax years ending after that date. Any material increase in the death benefit or other material change in the contract is treated as a new contract. However, the addition of covered lives is treated as a new contract only with respect to those additional covered lives. For purposes of these effective date rules, an increase in the death benefit under a policy or contract issued in connection with a lapse described in Sec. 501(d)(2) of the Health Insurance Portability and Accountability Act of '96 isn't treated as a new contract. ('97 Act §1084(d))

Thrift Institutions

¶ 1717. Rules modified on recapture of bad debt reserve by thrift institutions

Code Sec. 593(e)(1)(A), as amended by '97 Act § 1601(f)(5)(A)
Code Sec. 1374(d)(7), as amended by '97 Act § 1601(f)(5)(B)
Generally effective: Tax years beginning after Dec. 31, '95
Committee Reports, see ¶ 5365

The Small Business Job Protection Act of '96 repealed the percentage-of-taxable income method for deducting the bad debts of thrift institutions. Adjustments required by resulting changes in the method of accounting which are applicable to pre-'88 reserves are generally not restored to income unless the institution makes a distribution to shareholders under Code Sec. 593(e). Code Sec. 593(e) provides that if an institution makes a nonliquidating distribution in an amount in excess of its post-'51 accumulated earnings and profits, the excess will be treated as a distribution of the post-'87 reserve for bad-debts, requiring recapture of the amount.

Thus, when a thrift institution makes a nonliquidating distribution and has pre-'88 reserves, the source of the distribution (other than a distribution which is entitled to the dividends paid deduction) is determined in the following order:

(1) earnings and profits accumulated in post-'51 years;

(2) pre-'88 reserves;

(3) the supplemental reserve for losses on loans;

(4) other accounts. (FTC 2d/FIN ¶ E-3318; USTR ¶ 5934.01)

S corporations that have converted from C corporations to S corporation status, or that have acquired appreciated assets of a C corporation in a carryover basis transaction, may be subject to a corporate-level tax on built-in gains. The recognition period during which transactions are subject to the tax is the 10-year period beginning on the first day the corporation is an S corporation or the day the S corporation acquires appreciated assets from a C corporation. (FTC 2d/FIN ¶ D-1655; USTR ¶ 13,744.01)

New Law. The '97 Act clarifies the treatment of pre-'88 bad debt reserves of a thrift institution that is organized as an S corporation. The accumulated adjustments account of an S corporation is treated the same as post-'51 earnings and profits. (Code Sec. 593(e)(1)(A) as amended by '97 Act §1601(f)(5))

observation: Thus, an S-corporation thrift institution with pre-'88 reserves would make nonliquidating distributions out of its accumulated adjustments account first.

The recognition period over which the built-in gains on the recapture of distributions of pre-'88 reserves are subject to the built-in gains tax begins with the first day of the first tax year the corporation is an S corporation and continues without limitation on time. (Code Sec. 1374(d)(7) as amended by '97 Act §1601(f)(5))

☐ **Effective:** Tax years beginning after Dec. 31, '95. ('97 Act §1601(j))

FASITs

¶ 1718. Rules for regular interests in FASITs apply to interests issued on or after the starting date

Code Sec. 860L(b)(1), as amended by '97 Act § 1601(f)(6)(A)
Generally effective: Sep. 1, '97
Committee Reports, see ¶ 5366

Under pre-'97 Act law, a "regular interest" in a financial asset securitization investment trust (FASIT) was defined as any interest which was issued *after* the startup date and which met certain additional requirements. (FTC 2d/FIN ¶ E-7304; USTR ¶ 860H4.01)

New Law. A regular interest is any interest in a FASIT which is issued *on or after* the startup date and which meets the same requirements as under pre-'97 Act law. (Code Sec. 860L(b)(1) as amended by '97 Act §1601(f)(6)(A))

☐ **Effective:** Sep. 1, '97 ('97 Act §1601(j)(1))

¶ 1719. Certain transactions exempted from FASIT prohibited transaction rules

Code Sec. 860L(e)(2)(B), as amended by '97 Act § 1601(f)(6)(C)
Code Sec. 860L(e)(3)(A), as amended by '97 Act § 1601(f)(6)(D)
Code Sec. 860L(e)(3)(D), as amended by '97 Act § 1601(f)(6)(E)
Generally effective: Sep. 1, '97
Committee Reports, see ¶ 5366

The owner of a financial asset securitization investment trust (FASIT) is subject to a penalty excise tax equal to 100% percent of net income derived from prohibited transactions. Under pre-'97 Act law, a prohibited transaction was (1) the receipt of income from any asset other than a "permitted asset," (2) any disposition of a permitted asset (except as specifically provided), (3) the receipt of any income attributable to loans originated by the FASIT, and (4) the receipt of compensation for services (other than fees for a waiver, amendment, or consent under permitted assets not acquired through foreclosure). Certain exceptions were provided, including an exception for dispositions of permitted assets which would not be prohibited transactions if the FASIT were a real estate mortgage investment conduit (REMIC) and certain debt instruments held by the FASIT were treated as qualified mortgages. (FTC 2d/FIN ¶ E-7357; USTR ¶ 860H4.01)

New Law. The rule which treats dispositions of permitted assets as prohibited transactions does not apply to dispositions of foreclosure property. (Code Sec. 860L(e)(2)(B) as amended by '97 Act §1601(f)(6)(C))

The exception for dispositions of permitted assets which would not be prohibited transactions if the FASIT were a REMIC applies if all permitted assets of the FASIT (other than cash and cash equivalents) were treated as qualified mortgages. (Code Sec. 860L(e)(3)(A) as amended by '97 Act §1601(f)(6)(D))

A new exception is provided for dispositions of former hedge assets. Under this exception, the rule which treats income from assets other permitted assets does not apply to income from the disposition of an asset which, when first acquired by the FASIT, was a permitted asset because it was an interest rate or foreign currency hedge, but which no longer so qualified at the time of disposition. (Code Sec. 860L(e)((3)(D)(i) as amended by '97 Act §1601(f)(6)(E)(i)) The same rule applies to dispositions of contract rights to acquire such assets. (Code Sec. 860L(e)(3)(D)(ii))

☐ **Effective:** Sep. 1, '97. ('97 Act §1601(j))

¶ 1800. Estimated Taxes

¶ 1801. No penalty for underpayment of pre-'98 estimated tax caused by '97 Act

Code Sec. None, '97 Act § 1(d)
Generally effective: Aug. 5, '97
Committee Reports, see ¶ 5168

Individuals, corporations, and most other entities that are subject to income tax are subject to a penalty on any underpayment of estimated tax. To avoid the underpayment of estimated tax penalty, these entities must pay taxes, generally equal to 25% of their "required annual payment," in quarterly installments. Failure to pay an installment, or the making of an insufficient or late payment, will result in a penalty. However, no penalty is imposed if certain exceptions apply or a waiver is granted by IRS. (FTC 2d/FIN ¶ S-5200 *et seq.*, ¶ S-5320 *et seq.*; USTR ¶ 66,544, ¶ 66,555; TaxDesk ¶ 57,130 *et seq.*, ¶ 60,920 *et seq.*)

New Law. No estimated tax penalty will be imposed with respect to any underpayment of an installment to the extent the underpayment was created or increased by the '97 Act, if the period covered by the installment is before Jan. 1, '98 and the due date of the payment is before Jan. 16, '98. ('97 Act §1(d))

☐ **Effective:** Aug. 5, '97.

¶ 1802. Increase in de minimis threshold for individuals' estimated taxes

Code Sec. 6654(e)(1), as amended by '97 Act § 1202(a)
Generally effective: Tax years beginning after Dec. 31, '97
Committee Reports, see ¶ 5202

The penalty for underpayment of individual estimated taxes was not imposed for any tax year with respect to which the total tax liability, reduced by any withheld tax for the year, was less than $500. (FTC 2d/FIN ¶ S-5266; USTR ¶ 66,544 *et seq.*; TaxDesk ¶ 57,186)

New Law. The '97 Act increases the above $500 amount to $1,000. (Code Sec. 6654(e)(1) as amended by '97 Act §1202(a))

observation: Therefore, no penalty is imposed if the total tax liability for the year, reduced by any withheld tax, is less than $1,000.

☐ **Effective:** Tax years beginning after Dec. 31, '97. ('97 Act §1202(b))

FTC 2d References are to the Federal Tax Coordinator 2d
FIN References are to RIA's Analysis of Federal Taxes: Income
USTR References are to the United States Tax Reporter: Income, Estate & Gift, and Excise
PCA References are to Pension Coordinator and Pension & Benefits Expert/Advisor
PE References are to Pension and Profit Sharing 2nd
EP References are to Estate Planning & Taxation Coordinator and Estate Planning Advisor

¶1803. Estimated tax 110%-of-prior-year's-tax safe harbor for high income individuals changed to 100% for '98, 105% for '99–2001, 112% for 2002

Code Sec. 6654(d)(1)(C)(i), '97 Act § 1091(a)
Generally effective: Tax years ending after Dec. 31, '97
Committee Reports, see ¶5168

To avoid penalties for underpayment of tax, Code Sec. 6654 requires individuals to make timely payments of estimated tax. The general rule requires annual payments of the lesser of:

... 90% of the tax shown on the return for the current tax year, or

... 100% of the tax shown on the return for the preceding year.

However, if the adjusted gross income of the individual for the preceding tax year exceeds $150,000 ($75,000 for a married individual filing a separate return), the required annual payment is the lesser of:

... 90% of the tax shown on the return for the current tax year, or

... 110% of the tax shown on the return of the individual for the preceding tax year. (FTC 2d/FIN ¶ S-5204.1; USTR ¶ 66,544; TaxDesk ¶ 57,135)

The estimated tax rules applicable to individuals also apply to certain trusts and estates. (FTC 2d/FIN ¶ S-5301; USTR ¶ 66,544(h); TaxDesk ¶ 66,606)

New Law. The '97 Act substitutes "the applicable percentage" (defined below) for "110%" for purposes of determining the preceding-year's-tax safe harbor for individuals whose adjusted gross income for the preceding tax year exceeds $150,000. (Code Sec. 6654(d)(1)(C)(i) as amended by '97 Act §1091(a)) However, the new applicable percentage rule doesn't apply if the preceding tax year begins in calendar year '97. (Code Sec. 6654(d)(1)(C)(i)) That means that for '98, the applicable percentage is 100%. (Com Rept, see ¶ 5168)

> *observation:* By not requiring payments of the applicable percentage where the preceding tax year begins in '97, the general rule (above) that requires annual payments of only 100% of the preceding year's tax applies. Thus, individuals can base their '98 estimated taxes on 100% of the tax shown on the '97 return regardless of their adjusted gross income for '97.

For tax years beginning after '98, the applicable percentage is determined as follows:

... for '99 (the preceding tax year begins in '98) the applicable percentage is 105%;

FTC 2d References are to Federal Tax Coordinator 2d
FIN References are to RIA's Analysis of Federal Taxes: Income
USTR References are to United States Tax Reporter: Income, Estate & Gift, and Excise
PCA References are to Pension Coordinator and Pension & Benefits Expert/Advisor
PE References are to Pension and Profit Sharing 2nd
EP References are to Estate Planning & Taxation Coordinator and Estate Planning Advisor

... for 2000 (the preceding tax year begins in '99) the applicable percentage is 105%;

... for 2001 (the preceding tax year begins in 2000) the applicable percentage is 105%;

... for 2002 (the preceding tax year begins in 2001) the applicable percentage is 112%;

... for 2003 or later (the preceding tax year begins in 2002 or later) the applicable percentage is 110%. (Code Sec. 6654(d)(1)(C)(i))

Thus, under the '97 Act, the required percentage of preceding year's tax that must be paid in a tax year to meet the safe harbor is as follows:

Tax year beginning in	Required percentage of prior-years tax
'98	100%
'99	105
2000	105
2001	105
2002	112
2003 or later	110

(Com Rept, see ¶ 5168)

observation: Since the estimated tax requirements for estates and trusts are the same as for individuals, the above rules also apply to estates and trusts.

☐ **Effective:** For any installment payment for tax years beginning after Dec. 31, '97. ('97 Act §1091(b))

observation: For '97 estimated payments (including the Jan. '98 payment), the pre-'97 Act 110% safe harbor continues to apply.

For '97 estimated tax underpayments due to '97 Act changes, see ¶ 1801.

¶ 1804. Extension of private foundation's first quarter estimated tax payment due date

Code Sec. 6655(g)(3), as amended by '97 Act § 1461(a)
Generally effective: For tax years beginning after Aug. 5, '97
Committee Reports, see ¶ 5304

Private foundations are subject to estimated tax payment rules with respect to their taxable income, unrelated business taxable income, and net investment income. They are treated as corporations subject to the regular corporate income tax are treated and must pay their estimated tax in quarterly installments. Under Pre-'97 Act law, a calendar-year foundation's first quarterly installment was due on April 15th. (FTC 2d/FIN ¶ S-5422; USTR ¶ 66,554; TaxDesk ¶ 68,901)

New Law. A calendar-year foundation's first-quarter estimated tax payment is due on May 15th. (Code Sec. 6655(g)(3) as amended by '97 Act §1461(a)) This is the same day that its annual return, Form 990-PF, for the preceding year is due. (Com

Rept, see ¶ 5304) Fiscal year foundations will be required to make their first-quarter estimated tax payment no later than the 15th day of the fifth month of their taxable year. (Com Rept, see ¶ 5304)

☐ **Effective:** Tax years beginning after Aug. 5, '97. ('97 Act §1461(b))

FTC 2d References are to Federal Tax Coordinator 2d
FIN References are to RIA's Analysis of Federal Taxes: Income
USTR References are to United States Tax Reporter: Income, Estate & Gift, and Excise
PCA References are to Pension Coordinator and Pension & Benefits Expert/Advisor
PE References are to Pension and Profit Sharing 2nd
EP References are to Estate Planning & Taxation Coordinator and Estate Planning Advisor

¶ 1900. Employment Taxes

¶ 1901. Rules on self-employed ministers clarified

Code Sec. 414(e)(5)(A), as amended by '97 Act § 1601(d)(6)(A)
Code Sec. 403(b)(1)(A), as amended by '97 Act § 1601(d)(6)(B)
Generally effective: Years beginning after Dec. 31, '96
Committee Reports, see ¶ 5344

Under the Small Business Job Protection Act of 1996, a self-employed minister covered under a church plan is treated as his own employer. A minister employed by an organization that is not tax-exempt under Code Sec. 501(c)(3) was treated as if employed by a tax-exempt 501(c)(3) employer, and thus could participate in a church plan, whether or not he shared a common religious bond with the organization. (FTC 2d/FIN ¶ H-9556; USTR ¶ 4144.13; PCA ¶ 29,007; PE ¶ 414-4.13)

New Law. The '97 Act clarifies provisions of the '96 Act dealing with self-employed ministers and ministers employed by non-501(c)(3) exempt organizations. (Code Sec. 414(e)(5)(A) as amended by '97 Act §1601(d)(6)(A)) First, the '97 Act provides that a minister will be treated as employed by a tax-exempt 501(c)(3) organization if he is employed by an organization that is not tax-exempt under Code Sec. 501(c)(3) only if he shares common religious bonds with the organization. (Code Sec. 414(e)(5)(A)(i)(II))

> **🔖 illustration:** A rabbi who works for a Jewish burial society/cemetery (an organization exempt from federal income tax under Code Sec. 501(c)(13)) has a common religious bond with the organization. Thus, the rabbi is treated as employed by an exempt 501(c)(3) organization and is eligible to participate in a church plan. But a rabbi employed by a tax-exempt cemetery with no religious affiliation does not share a common religious bond with the organization, and thus is not treated as employed by an exempt 501(c)(3) organization under the '97 Act.

Next, the '97 Act clarifies that self-employed ministers and ministers working for non-501(c)(3) organizations with whom they share a common bond are employees for purposes of the church plan rules. (Code Sec. 414(e)(5)(A)(i))

Further, the '97 Act clarifies that for purposes of the rules relating to tax-sheltered annuities purchased by tax-exempt 501(c)(3) organizations or public schools, and the rules providing ministers with a deduction for their contributions to their own retirement income accounts, a self-employed minister is treated as employed by the minister's own employer, which is an exempt 501(c)(3) organization. (Code Sec. 414(e)(5)(A)(ii))

FTC 2d References are to the Federal Tax Coordinator 2d
FIN References are to RIA's Analysis of Federal Taxes: Income
USTR References are to the United States Tax Reporter: Income, Estate & Gift, and Excise
PCA References are to Pension Coordinator and Pension & Benefits Expert/Advisor
PE References are to Pension and Profit Sharing 2nd
EP References are to Estate Planning & Taxation Coordinator and Estate Planning Advisor

Finally, the '97 Act clarifies that tax-sheltered annuities can be purchased by self-employed ministers, or for a minister employed by an organization that is not tax-exempt under Code Sec. 501(c)(3), in the same manner as annuities purchased for employees of exempt 501(c)(3) organizations and public schools. (Code Sec. 403(b)(1)(A) as amended by '97 Act §1601(d)(6)(B))

☐ **Effective:** Years beginning after Dec. 31, '96. ('97 Act §1601(j))

¶ 1902. In determining the employment status of retail securities brokers, instructions to ensure compliance with government investor protection standards are disregarded

Code Sec. 3121(d), '97 Act § 921(a)
Generally effective: For services performed after Dec. 31, '97
Committee Reports, see ¶ 5066

Generally, the employment status of a worker, i.e., whether he is an employee or independent contractor, is determined under a common law facts and circumstances test. An employment relationship exists if the person engaging the worker not only has the right to control the result to be accomplished, but also the means by which the result are accomplished. The amount of instructions given by the person for whom the work is done to the person who does the work is an important factor in determining whether or not a worker is an employee. A worker who is required to comply with another person's instructions about when, where, and how he is to work is ordinarily an employee. However, IRS realizes that it's important to consider the weight to be given those instructions if they are imposed only in compliance with government regulations. Accordingly, IRS's training manual provides that if a business requires its workers to comply with rules established by a third party (e.g., municipal building codes related to construction), the fact that these rules are imposed should be given little weight in determining the worker's status (Com Rept, see ¶ 5066) (FTC 2d/FIN ¶ H-4260; USTR ¶ 34,014.37; TaxDesk ¶ 53,510)

New Law. In determining for purposes of the Code whether a registered representative of a securities broker-dealer is an employee (as defined in Code Sec. 3121(d), which defines who is an employee for purposes of the Federal Insurance Contribution Act (FICA)), no weight is to be given to instructions from the service recipient which are imposed only in compliance with investor protection standards imposed by the state or federal government or by a governing body under a delegation by a the state or federal agency. ('97 Act § 921(a))

Congress believes that because brokerage houses are required to monitor compliance with certain investor protection laws, this monitoring shouldn't be taken into account in determining the status of a broker for federal tax purposes. (Com Rept, see ¶ 5066)

FTC 2d References are to Federal Tax Coordinator 2d
FIN References are to RIA's Analysis of Federal Taxes: Income
USTR References are to United States Tax Reporter: Income, Estate & Gift, and Excise
PCA References are to Pension Coordinator and Pension & Benefits Expert/Advisor
PE References are to Pension and Profit Sharing 2nd
EP References are to Estate Planning & Taxation Coordinator and Estate Planning Advisor

☐ **Effective:** For services performed after Dec. 31, '97. ('97 Act §921(b)) No inference is intended that the new rule wasn't the pre-'97 Act law. (Com Rept, see ¶ 5066)

¶ 1903. Exemption from self-employment tax for termination payments received by former insurance salesmen

Code Sec. 1402(k), as amended by '97 Act § 922(a)
Generally effective: Payments made after Dec. 31, '97
Committee Reports, see ¶ 5067

Under the self-employment contributions act ("SECA"), taxes are imposed on an individual's net earnings from self employment. In general, net earnings from self employment means the gross income derived by an individual from any trade or business carried on by the individual, less the deductions attributable to the trade or business. The SECA tax rate is the same as the combined employer and employee FICA rates (i.e., 12.4% for old-age, survivors and disability insurance (OASDI) and 2.9% for hospital insurance (HI)). The maximum amount of earnings subject to the OASDI portion of SECA taxes is coordinated with and is set at the same level as the maximum level of wages and salaries subject to the OASDI portion of FICA taxes. There is no limit on the amount of self-employment income subject to the HI portion of the tax.

Certain insurance salesmen are independent contractors and therefore, subject to tax under SECA. Under case law, certain payments received by former insurance salesmen who had sold insurance as independent contractors are not net earnings from self employment and therefore are not subject to SECA. (FTC 2d/FIN ¶ A-6032; USTR ¶ 14,024)

New Law. The '97 Act codifies the case law on insurance salesmen by providing that net earnings from self employment do not include any amount received during the taxable year from an insurance company on account of services performed by an individual as an insurance salesman for the company if:

(1) the amount is received after termination of the individual's agreement to perform services for the company;

(2) the individual performs no services for the company after the agreement ends and before the close of the taxable year;

(3) the payments are conditioned on the salesman's agreeing not to compete with the company for at least one year following termination of the agreement; and

(4) the amount of the payment depends primarily on: (a) policies sold by, or credited to the account of, the individual during the last year of the agreement, and/or (b) the extent to which the policies remain in force for some period after the agreement ends. The *amount of the payment* can not depend on the length of service or overall earnings from services performed for the company. However, *eligibility for payment* can depend on length of service (Code Sec. 1402(k) as amended by '97 Act §922(a)) and/or overall earnings. (Com Rept, see ¶ 5067)

Congress said that no inference is intended with respect to the SECA tax treatment of payments that are not described in the '97 Act. Nor is any inference intended that the provisions contained in the '97 Act were not the law before the effective date. (Com Rept, see ¶ 5067)

☐ **Effective:** Payments made after Dec. 31, '97. ('97 Act §922(c))

¶ 1904. Wages paid for services by inmates in a penal institution are exempt from FUTA tax

Code Sec. 3306(c)(21), as amended by Budget Act § 5406(a)(3)
Generally effective: Service performed after Jan. 1, '94
Committee Reports, see ¶ 5506

Federal Unemployment Tax (FUTA) applies to wages paid for services performed by an employee. Wages are generally defined to include all remuneration for employment except for certain enumerated types of services which are exempted from the definition of employment. (FTC 2d/FIN ¶ H-4760; USTR ¶ 33,014; TaxDesk ¶ 55,102) States can exclude from coverage services performed for a government agency by inmates of custodial or penal institutions, but under pre-Budget Act law there was no blanket FUTA tax exemption for wages paid to persons committed to penal institutions. Thus, work performed by inmates under work-release programs or other cooperative arrangements between prison authorities and private employers weren't exempt. (Com Rept, see ¶ 5506)

New Law. The term "employment" for FUTA purposes doesn't include service performed by a person committed to a penal institution. (Code Sec. 3306(c)(21) as amended by Budget Act §5406(a)(3)) Thus, wages paid to persons committed to penal institutions are exempt from the definition of wages for FUTA tax purposes. This includes wages paid to inmates who participate in prison work programs other than directly for the prison. As a result, wages paid to inmates are exempt from FUTA tax whether the wages are paid by the prison or a private employer. Inmates are also ineligible to claim unemployment benefits with respect to these wages. (Com Rept, see ¶ 5506)

observation: "Penal institution" isn't otherwise defined.

☐ **Effective:** For service performed after Jan. 1, '94. (Budget Act §5406(b))

recommendation: Employers who have made payments of FUTA tax with respect to post-Jan. 1, '94 services performed by persons committed to penal institutions should consider filing refund claims to recover the tax.

FTC 2d References are to Federal Tax Coordinator 2d
FIN References are to RIA's Analysis of Federal Taxes: Income
USTR References are to United States Tax Reporter: Income, Estate & Gift, and Excise
PCA References are to Pension Coordinator and Pension & Benefits Expert/Advisor
PE References are to Pension and Profit Sharing 2nd
EP References are to Estate Planning & Taxation Coordinator and Estate Planning Advisor

¶ 1905. FUTA surtax extended through 2007

Code Sec. 3301, as amended by '97 Act § 1035
Generally effective: For labor performed on or after Jan. 1, '99
Committee Reports, see ¶ 5133

The Federal Unemployment Tax Act (FUTA) imposes a 6.2% gross tax rate on the first $7,000 paid annually by covered employers to each employee. Employers in States with programs approved by the Federal Government and with no delinquent Federal loans may credit 5.4 percentage points against the 6.2% tax rate, making the minimum, *net* Federal unemployment tax rate 0.8% (6.2% − 5.4% = 0.8%). (FTC 2d/FIN ¶ H-4801; USTR ¶ 35,014.07; TaxDesk ¶ 55,052; PCA ¶ 34,123; PE ¶ 3501-4.07)

Since all States have approved programs, 0.8% is the Federal tax rate that generally applies. The resulting Federal revenue finances administration of the system, half of the Federal-State extended benefits program, and a Federal account for State loans. The States use the revenue turned back to them via the 5.4% credit to finance their regular State programs and half of the Federal-State extended benefits program.

In '76, Congress passed a temporary surtax of 0.2% of taxable wages to be added to the permanent FUTA tax rate. Before the '97 Act, the temporary 0.2% surtax rate was scheduled to expire after '98. In '99, the FUTA tax rate was scheduled to return to 6%. (Com Rept, see ¶ 5133)

New Law. The '97 Act extends the temporary 0.2% surtax rate (and the resulting 6.2% FUTA tax rate) through 2007. In 2008, the FUTA tax rate is scheduled to return to 6%. (Code Sec. 3301 as amended by '97 Act §1035) Congress says that the surtax extension will increase the Federal Unemployment Trust Fund to provide a cushion against future expenditures. The monies retained in the Federal Unemployment Account of the Federal Unemployment Trust Fund can then be used to make loans to the 53 State Unemployment Compensation benefit accounts as needed. (Com Rept, see ¶ 5133)

☐ **Effective:** For labor performed on or after Jan. 1, '99. (Com Rept, see ¶ 5133)

¶ 1906. Prohibition issued on regulatory definition of a limited partner for self-employment tax purposes

Code Sec. None, '97 Act § 935
Generally effective: Aug. 5, '97

In Jan. '97, for self-employment tax purposes, IRS issued Prop. Reg. 1.1402(a)-2 on the definition of a limited partner under Code Sec. 1402(a)(13). The proposed reg, which was to go into effect if and when it became a final reg, would have provided that a partner would not be treated as a limited partner if he had personal liability for partnership debts, had authority to contract on behalf of the partnership, or participated in the partnership's trade or business for more than 500 hours during the taxable year. Also, the proposed reg would have provided that an individual who met one of these criteria would have been treated as a general partner and net earnings from self-employment would have included the partner's distributive share of partnership income and loss. (FTC 2d/FIN ¶ A-6156.1; USTR ¶ 14,024.16; TaxDesk ¶ 57,653)

New Law. The '97 Act provides that no temporary or final regulation can be issued or made effective by IRS on the definition of a limited partner under Code Sec. 1402(a)(13) before July 1, '98. ('97 Act § 935)

Under a "Sense of the Senate" provision in the Senate-passed version of the '97 Act (H.R. 2014, § 734), the Senate had expressed its concern that Prop. Reg. 1.1402(a)-2 exceeded IRS's regulatory authority and would effectively change the law administratively without congressional action. The Senate also expressed it's concern that the proposed regulation would have a substantial impact on the tax liability of certain individuals and affect those individuals' entitlement to social security benefits.

☐ **Effective:** Aug. 5, '97

FTC 2d References are to Federal Tax Coordinator 2d
FIN References are to RIA's Analysis of Federal Taxes: Income
USTR References are to United States Tax Reporter: Income, Estate & Gift, and Excise
PCA References are to Pension Coordinator and Pension & Benefits Expert/Advisor
PE References are to Pension and Profit Sharing 2nd
EP References are to Estate Planning & Taxation Coordinator and Estate Planning Advisor

¶ 2000. Tax Accounting

¶ 2001. Commodities dealers and traders in securities and commodities can elect the mark-to-market rules

Code Sec. 475(e), as amended by '97 Act § 1001(b)
Code Sec. 475(f), as amended by '97 Act § 1001(b)
Generally effective: Tax years ending after Aug. 5, '97
Committee Reports, see ¶ 5111

Under pre-'97 Act law, the mark-to-market method of accounting that applies to securities dealers did not apply to traders in securities or to dealers in other property. Traders in securities generally are taxpayers who engage in a trade or business involving active sales or exchanges of securities on the market, rather than to customers. (FTC 2d/FIN ¶ I-7650; USTR ¶ 4754)

New Law. Congress believes that mark-to-market accounting generally provides a clear reflection of income with respect to assets that are traded in established markets. For market-valued assets, mark-to-market accounting imposes few burdens and offers few opportunities for manipulation. Securities and exchange-traded commodities have determinable market values, and securities traders and commodities traders and dealers regularly calculate year-end values of their assets in determining their income for financial statement purposes. Many commodities dealers also utilize year-end values in adjusting their inventory using the lower-of-cost-or-market method for federal income tax purposes. (Com Rept, see ¶ 5111)

The '97 Act allows commodities dealers and securities traders and commodities traders to elect application of the mark-to-market accounting rules, which applied only to securities dealers under pre-'97 Act law. (Com Rept, see ¶ 5111)

Dealers in commodities. In the case of a dealer in commodities (defined below) who makes an election, the mark-to-market rules apply to commodities held by that dealer in the same manner as the mark-to-market rules apply to securities held by a dealer in securities. (Code Sec. 475(e)(1)) Any gain or loss recognized by an electing taxpayer is ordinary gain or loss. (Com Rept, see ¶ 5111)

> *observation:* This means that exceptions to the mark-to-market rules that apply to securities dealers also apply to dealers in commodities. For example, any commodities held for investment by an electing commodities dealer would not be subject to the mark-to-market rules under Code Sec. 475(b)(1) (FTC 2d/FIN ¶ I-7659; USTR ¶ 4754) if the commodities dealer complies with the identification requirements of Code Sec. 475(b)(2) (FTC 2d/FIN ¶ I-7660.1; USTR ¶ 4754).

FTC 2d References are to the Federal Tax Coordinator 2d
FIN References are to RIA's Analysis of Federal Taxes: Income
USTR References are to the United States Tax Reporter: Income, Estate & Gift, and Excise
PCA References are to Pension Coordinator and Pension & Benefits Expert/Advisor
PE References are to Pension and Profit Sharing 2nd
EP References are to Estate Planning & Taxation Coordinator and Estate Planning Advisor

Commodity defined. For purposes of the election to be subject to the mark-to-market rules by either a commodities dealer (see above) or a trader in securities or commodities (see below), commodity means (Code Sec. 475(e)(2))

(1) any commodity which is actively traded (within the meaning of Code Sec. 1092(d)(1)) (i.e., personal property for which there is an established financial market, see FTC 2d/FIN ¶ I-7506.1; USTR ¶ 10,924); (Code Sec. 475(e)(2)(A))

(2) any notional principal contract with respect to any commodity described in (1), above; (Code Sec. 475(e)(2)(B))

(3) any evidence of an interest in, or a derivative instrument in, any commodity (described in (1) or (2) above), including any option, forward contract, futures contract, short position, and any similar instrument in a commodity; and (Code Sec. 475(e)(2)(C))

(4) any position which: (Code Sec. 475(e)(2)(D))

... is not a commodity described in (1), (2), or (3) above, (Code Sec. 475(e)(2)(D)(i))

... is a hedge with respect to a commodity (described in (1), (2), or (3) above), and (Code Sec. 475(e)(2)(D)(ii))

... is clearly identified in the taxpayer's records as being described in Code Sec. 475(e)(2)(D) (i.e., as a hedge with respect to commodities described in (1), (2), or (3)) before the close of the day on which it was acquired or entered into (or any other time as IRS may by regs prescribe). (Code Sec. 475(e)(2)(D)(iii))

How to make the election. An election by a dealer in commodities to be subject to the mark-to-market rules may be made without IRS's consent. (Code Sec. 475(e)(3)) The election is made in the time and manner to be prescribed by IRS. (Com Rept, see ¶ 5111) The election, once made, applies to the tax year for which made and all later tax years unless revoked with IRS's consent. (Code Sec. 475(e)(3))

Traders in securities and traders in commodities.

Securities traders. In the case of a person who is engaged in a trade or business as a trader in securities and who elects to have the mark-to-market rules apply to the trade or business: (Code Sec. 475(f)(1)(A))

... the person recognizes gain or loss on any security held in connection with the trade or business at the close of any tax year as if the security were sold for its fair market value on the last business day of the tax year, and (Code Sec. 475(f)(1)(A)(i))

... any gain or loss is taken into account for the tax year. (Code Sec. 475(f)(1)(A)(ii))

Any gain or loss recognized by an electing taxpayer is ordinary gain or loss. (Com Rept, see ¶ 5111)

FTC 2d References are to Federal Tax Coordinator 2d
FIN References are to RIA's Analysis of Federal Taxes: Income
USTR References are to United States Tax Reporter: Income, Estate & Gift, and Excise
PCA References are to Pension Coordinator and Pension & Benefits Expert/Advisor
PE References are to Pension and Profit Sharing 2nd
EP References are to Estate Planning & Taxation Coordinator and Estate Planning Advisor

A security that hedges another security that is held in connection with the taxpayer's trade or business as a trader will be treated as so held. (Com Rept, see ¶ 5111)

> ✔️ *observation:* Thus, an electing taxpayer will recognize gain or loss under the above rules from a security that hedges another security that is held in connection with the taxpayer's trade or business.

Congress does not intend that an electing taxpayer can mark-to-market loans made to customers or receivables or debt instruments acquired from customers that are not received or acquired in connection with a trade or business as a securities trader. (Com Rept, see ¶ 5111)

Proper adjustment is made in the amount of any gain or loss subsequently realized for gain or loss taken into account under the above rule (described in Code Sec. 475(f)(1)(A)(i) and Code Sec. 475(f)(1)(A)(ii)). IRS may provide by regs for the application of the above rules (i.e., the recognition of gain or loss) at times other than the times provided in the above rule (i.e. at times other than the last business day of the tax year). (Code Sec. 475(f)(1)(A))

Traders in commodities. In the case of a person who is engaged in a trade or business as a trader in commodities (defined above) and who elects to have the mark-to-market rules apply to the trade or business, the rules described in Code Sec. 475(f)(1) (see above) for securities traders who make the mark-to-market election also apply to commodities held by that trader in connection with the trade or business in the same manner as those rules apply to securities held by a trader in securities. (Code Sec. 475(f)(2))

Exception for certain securities that are not connected to the trader's activities and are clearly identified in the trader's records. The election of the mark-to-market rules by a securities trader does *not* apply to any security: (Code Sec. 475(f)(1)(B))

(1) which is established to IRS's satisfaction as having *no* connection to the activities of the person as a trader, and (Code Sec. 475(f)(1)(B)(i))

(2) which is clearly identified in the person's records as having *no* connection to the activities of the person as a trader (see (1) above) before the close of the day on which it was acquired, originated, or entered into (or any other time as IRS may by regs prescribe). (Code Sec. 475(f)(1)(B)(ii))

Because Congress was concerned with issues of taxpayer selectivity, Congress intends that an electing taxpayer must be able to demonstrate by clear and convincing evidence that a security bears *no* relation to activities as a trader in order to be identified as not subject to the mark-to-market regime. (Com Rept, see ¶ 5111)

If a security ceases to have no connection to the activities of the person as a trader (as described in (1) above) at any time after it was identified as having no connection (under (2) above), the election applies to any changes in value of the security occurring after the cessation. (Code Sec. 475(f)(1)(B))

Coordination with the constructive sale rules. Any security which is subject to a securities trader's election to have the mark-to-market rules apply and which was acquired in the normal course of the taxpayer's activities as a trader in securities is not taken into account in applying Code Sec. 1259 (constructive sales treatment for certain appreciated financial positions, see ¶ 202) to any position to which the election does not apply. (Code Sec. 475(f)(1)(C))

observation: Any securities held by a taxpayer that are subject to the mark-to-market rules are exempt from the constructive sale rules, see ¶ 202.

Application of other mark-to-market rules. Rules similar to the rules of Code Sec. 475(b)(4) (rules preventing a securities dealer from treating certain notional principal contracts and other derivative financial instruments as held for investment, see FTC 2d/FIN ¶ I-7659.2; USTR ¶ 4754), Code Sec. 475(d)(1) (rules coordinating the mark-to-market rules with other tax rules (see FTC 2d/FIN ¶ I-7663; USTR ¶ 4754), Code Sec. 475(d)(2) (rules relating to securities improperly identified as qualifying for an exception to the mark-to-market rules, see FTC 2d/FIN ¶ I-7662; USTR ¶ 4754), and Code Sec. 475(d)(3) (rules relating to the character of gain or loss under the mark-to-market rules, see FTC 2d/FIN ¶ I-7654; USTR ¶ 4754) apply to securities held by a person in any trade or business with respect to which an election by a securities or commodities trader to have the mark-to-market rules apply is in effect. (Code Sec. 475(f)(1)(D)) In the case of a commodities trader or dealer, Congress anticipates that Code Sec. 475(b)(4) (see above) will apply only to contracts and instruments referenced to commodities. (Com Rept, see ¶ 5111)

How to make the election. The elections for traders in securities (see above) and traders in commodities (see above) to be subject to the mark-to-market rules can be made separately for each trade or business and without IRS's consent. (Code Sec. 475(f)(3)) Thus, a taxpayer that is both a commodities dealer and a securities trader may make the election with respect to one business, but not the other business. (Com Rept, see ¶ 5111)

The election is made in the time and manner to be prescribed by IRS. (Com Rept, see ¶ 5111) The election, once made, applies to the tax year for which made and all later tax years unless revoked with IRS's consent. (Code Sec. 475(f)(3))

Four-year spread for Code Sec. 481 adjustments. In the case of a taxpayer who elects to have the mark-to-market rules under Code Sec. 475(e) (election for commodities dealers, see above) or Code Sec. 475(f) (election for securities traders and commodities traders) to change its method of accounting for the tax year which includes Aug. 5, '97, ('97 Act §1001(d)(4)(B)) the net amount of the adjustments required to be taken into account by the taxpayer under Code Sec. 481 as a result of the change in accounting method is taken into account ratably over the four tax year period beginning with the first tax year. ('97 Act §1001(d)(4)(B)(ii)) This rule only applies to taxpayers making the election for the tax year which includes Aug. 5, '97. Any elections made after the tax year which includes Aug. 5, '97 will be governed by rules and pro-

FTC 2d References are to Federal Tax Coordinator 2d
FIN References are to RIA's Analysis of Federal Taxes: Income
USTR References are to United States Tax Reporter: Income, Estate & Gift, and Excise
PCA References are to Pension Coordinator and Pension & Benefits Expert/Advisor
PE References are to Pension and Profit Sharing 2nd
EP References are to Estate Planning & Taxation Coordinator and Estate Planning Advisor

cedures established by IRS. (Com Rept, see ¶ 5111)

☐ **Effective:** Tax years ending after Aug. 5, '97. ('97 Act §1001(d)(4)(A))

In the case of a taxpayer who elects to have the mark-to-market rules under Code Sec. 475(e) (election for commodities dealers, see above) or Code Sec. 475(f) (election for securities traders and commodities traders) to change its method of accounting for the tax year which includes Aug. 5, '97: ('97 Act §1001(d)(4)(B)) any identification required under the elections with respect to securities and commodities held on Aug. 5, '97 is treated as timely made if made on or before the 30th day after Aug. 5, '97, ('97 Act §1001(d)(4)(B)(i))

> *action alert:* Securities and commodities traders and dealers in commodities must identify the securities or commodities, to which the election to be subject to the mark-to-market rules will apply, within 30 days of Aug. 5, '97.

¶ 2002. Repeal of exception to the installment sale rules for sales of property by a manufacturer to a dealer

Code Sec. None, '97 Act § 1088(a)
Generally effective: Tax years beginning more than one year after Aug. 5, '97
Committee Reports, see ¶ 5165

The installment sales method of accounting generally does not apply to sales by dealers in personal property. However, under pre-'97 Act law, there was an exception that permitted the use of the installment method for installment obligations arising from the sale of tangible personal property by a manufacturer of the property (or an affiliate of the manufacturer) to a dealer, but only if the dealer was obligated to make payments of principal only when the dealer resold (or rented) the property, the manufacturer had the right to repurchase the property at a fixed (or ascertainable) price after no longer than a nine month period following the sale to the dealer, and certain other conditions were met. In order to meet the other conditions, the aggregate face amount of the installment obligations that otherwise qualified for the exception had to equal at least 50% of the total sales to dealers that gave rise to the receivables (the 50% test) in both the tax year and the preceding tax year, except that, if the taxpayer met all of the requirements for the exception in the preceding tax year, the taxpayer would not have been treated as failing to meet the 50% test before the second consecutive year in which the taxpayer did not actually meet the test. For purposes of applying the 50% test, the aggregate face amount of the taxpayer's receivables was computed using the weighted average of the taxpayer's receivables outstanding at the end of each month during the taxpayer's tax year. In addition, these requirements had to be met by the taxpayer in its first tax year beginning after Oct. 22, '86, except that obligations issued before that date were treated as meeting the applicable requirements if the obligations were conformed to the requirements for the exception within 60 days of Oct. 22, '86. (FTC 2d/FIN ¶ G-6611, ¶ G-6736 *et seq.*; USTR ¶ 4534, ¶ 453C8.400; TaxDesk ¶ 46,609)

New Law. Congress believed that the exception that permitted certain dealers to use the installment method is no longer necessary or appropriate and the installment sale method of accounting should not be available to those dealers. (Com Rept, see ¶ 5165)

The '97 Act repeals the exception that permitted the use of the installment method for certain sales (described above) by manufacturers to dealers. ('97 Act §1088(a))

In the case of any taxpayer required by the repeal of the exception to change its method of accounting for any tax year: ('97 Act §1088(b)(2))

... the changes are treated as initiated by the taxpayer, ('97 Act §1088(b)(2)(A))

... the changes are treated as made with IRS's consent, and ('97 Act §1088(b)(2)(B))

... the net amount of the Code Sec. 481(a) adjustments resulting from the required accounting method change must be taken into account ratably over the four tax year period beginning with the first tax year beginning after Aug. 5, '97. ('97 Act §1088(b)(2)(C))

☐ **Effective:** Tax years beginning more than one year after Aug. 5, '97. ('97 Act §1088(b)(1))

¶ 2003. Look-back method as applied to long-term contracts isn't required in de minimis situations

Code Sec. 460(b)(6), as amended by '97 Act § 1211(a)
Generally effective: Contracts completed in tax years ending after Aug. 5, '97
Committee Reports, see ¶ 5206

Taxpayers who manufacture, build, install or construct property under most long-term contracts must compute income from the contract under the percentage-of-completion method. Subject to an exception which can be elected for tax years ending before 10% of the estimated contract costs have been incurred, the method requires a taxpayer to include in gross income for a tax year an amount that is based on the product of (a) the gross contract price and (b) the percentage of the contract completed as of the end of the year. That percentage is determined by dividing costs incurred with respect to the contract as of the end of the year by estimated total contract costs.

The percentage-of-completion method relies upon estimated, rather than actual, contract price and costs to determine gross income for any tax year. Thus, for most contracts subject to the percentage-of-completion method, a "look-back method" is applied in the year a contract is completed in order to compensate the taxpayer (or IRS) for the acceleration (or deferral) of taxes paid over the contract term.

The look-back method also applies to items of cost and income which are properly taken into account after the contract is completed.

There is an election available to not apply the look-back method in years after the completion of the contract where increases or decreases in contract cost or contract price after the most recent previous application of the look-back method are relatively small.

However, under pre-'97 Act law, there was no election available to not apply the look-back method—either in the year of contract completion or in years after the year of contract completion—even though there existed a relatively small difference in taxable income or loss caused by the difference between applying and not applying the look-back method.   (FTC 2d/FIN ¶ G-3156, ¶ G-3157, ¶ G-3166, ¶ G-3167, ¶ G-3204; USTR ¶ 4604; TaxDesk ¶ 44,542, ¶ 44,546, ¶ 44,555, ¶ 44,556, ¶ 44,582)

New Law. The '97 Act makes available to the taxpayer an election which eliminates the need to apply the look-back method under the circumstances described below. The election applies to all long-term contracts completed during the tax year for which the election is made and to all long-term contracts completed in later tax years. The election is revocable only with IRS consent. (Code Sec. 460(b)(6)(D) as amended by '97 Act §1211(a)).

If a taxpayer makes the election, the taxpayer doesn't apply the look-back method to a long-term contract for a year in which the look-back method would otherwise have to be applied if (Code Sec. 460(b)(6)(B)) at the close of each "contract year" before the tax year in which the method would otherwise have to be applied, the cumulative taxable income or loss under the contract (as determined using estimated contract price and costs (Com Rept, see ¶ 5206)) is within (Code Sec. 460(b)(6)(B)(i)) 10% of the cumulative "look-back income (or loss)" under the contract as of the close of that earlier year. (Code Sec. 460(b)(6)(B)(ii))

For purposes of the above rule:

... a "contract year" is any tax year for which income is taken into account under the contract, (Code Sec. 460(b)(6)(C)(i)); and

... "look-back income (or loss)" is the amount which would be the taxable income (or loss) under the contract if the method of allocating income required by the look-back method were used in determining taxable income. (Code Sec. 460(b)(6)(C)(ii)) Thus, "look-back income (or loss)" is determined using actual contract price and costs. (Com Rept, see ¶ 5206)

> *Illustration:* A taxpayer enters into a three-year contract and, upon completion of the contract, determines that annual net income under the contract using actual contract price and costs is $100,000, $150,000, and $250,000, respectively, for Years 1, 2, and 3 under the percentage of completion method. An electing taxpayer need not apply the look-back method to the contract if it had reported cumulative net taxable income under the contract, using estimated contract price and costs, of between $90,000 and $110,000 as of the end of Year 1 and between $225,000 and $275,000 as of the end of Year 2. (Com Rept, see ¶ 5206)

Additionally, if the taxpayer makes an election referred to above, the look-back method won't apply to a tax year beginning after the tax year in which the contract is completed if (Code Sec. 460(b)(6)(A)): the cumulative taxable income (or loss) under the contract as of the close of that tax year is within (Code Sec. 460(b)(6)(A)(i)) 10% of the cumulative look-back taxable income or (loss) under the contract as of the close of the most recent tax year in which the look-back method was applied (or would have applied but for the calculation in Code Sec. 460(b)(6)(B) discussed above). (Code Sec. 460(b)(6)(A)(ii))

For purposes of the calculation immediately above, "look-back income (or loss)" has the same meaning as discussed above in connection with the calculation in Code Sec. 460(b)(6)(B). (Code Sec. 460(b)(6)(C)(ii))

Illustration: A taxpayer enters into a three-year contract and reports taxable income of $12,250, $15,000 and $12,750, respectively, for Years 1 through 3 with respect to the contract. Upon completion of the contract, cumulative look-back income with respect to the contract is $40,000, and 10% of that amount is $4,000. After the completion of the contract, the taxpayer incurs additional costs of $2,500 in each of the next three succeeding years (Years 4, 5, and 6) with respect to the contract. Under the Code Sec. 460(b)(6)(A) de minimis exception, an electing taxpayer doesn't reapply the look-back method for Year 4 because the cumulative amount of contract taxable income ($37,500) is within 10% of contract look-back income as of the completion of the contract ($40,000). However, the look-back method must be applied for Year 5 because the cumulative amount of contract taxable income ($35,000) is not within 10% of contract look-back income as of the completion of the contract ($40,000). Finally, the taxpayer doesn't reapply the look-back method for Year 6 because the cumulative amount of contract taxable income ($32,500) is within 10% of contract look-back income as of the last application of the look-back method ($35,000). (Com Rept, see ¶ 5206)

For purposes of the above rules, amounts taken into account after completion of the contract *aren't* discounted under the discounting rule in Code Sec. 460(b)(2) (relating to using a Federal rate under Code Sec. 1274(d)). (Code Sec. 460(b)(6)(C)(iii))

☐ **Effective:** Contracts completed in tax years ending after Aug. 5, '97. ('97 Act §1211(c)(1))

FTC 2d References are to Federal Tax Coordinator 2d
FIN References are to RIA's Analysis of Federal Taxes: Income
USTR References are to United States Tax Reporter: Income, Estate & Gift, and Excise
PCA References are to Pension Coordinator and Pension & Benefits Expert/Advisor
PE References are to Pension and Profit Sharing 2nd
EP References are to Estate Planning & Taxation Coordinator and Estate Planning Advisor

¶ 2004. Interest calculation changed in the look-back methods used in long-term contract accounting and in income forecast depreciation

Code Sec. 460(b)(2)(C), as amended by '97 Act § 1211(b)(1)

Code Sec. 460(b)(7), as amended by '97 Act § 1211(b)(2)

Generally effective: For long-term contract accounting, contracts completed in tax years ending after Aug. 5, '97. For income forecast depreciation, property placed in service after Sept. 13, '95

Committee Reports, see ¶ 5206

The look-back methods used in the percentage-of-completion method of long-term contract accounting and in the income forecast method of depreciation each require taxpayers to make interest calculations over the look-back period. Under pre-'97 Act law, interest was calculated under the look-back methods in the same way that interest was calculated, under Code Sec. 6621, on tax overpayments. Therefore, the interest rate used was subject to quarterly adjustment, with the result that taxpayers doing a look-back period calculation could have to divide single years into two or more periods in order to calculate interest. (FTC 2d/FIN ¶ G-3161, ¶ G-3171, ¶ L-10707.4; USTR ¶ 1674.100, ¶ 4604; TaxDesk ¶ 26,806.4, ¶ 44,549, ¶ 44,559)

New Law. Congress believed that the use of multiple interest rates complicates the mechanics of the look-back calculation, and wished to address this concern. (Com Rept, see ¶ 5206) Thus, the '97 Act changes the interest calculation used in applying the look-back method for purposes of the percentage-of-completion method of accounting for long-term contracts, (Code Sec. 460(b)(2)(C) as amended by '97 Act §1211(b)(1)) and the income forecast method of depreciation.

> 🅥 *observation:* The '97 Act didn't amend the Code's income forecast method of depreciation provision— Code Sec. 167(g)—in order to apply the interest calculation change made by Code Sec. 460(b)(7), discussed below, to income forecast method depreciation. No amendment was necessary because pre-'97 Act Code Sec. 167(g)(2)(C) referenced "the adjusted overpayment rate (as described in section 460(b)(7))." Apparently, the drafters of the Small Business Job Protection Act of '96 (the '96 Act) anticipated, in drafting Code Sec. 167(g)(2)(C), that Code Sec. 460(b)(7) would also be included in the '96 Act. Instead, Code Sec. 460(b)(7) was enacted as part of the '97 Act.

Under the '97 Act, for purposes of the look-back method, only one rate of interest applies for each accrual period. (Com Rept, see ¶ 5206) The adjusted overpayment rate for any "interest accrual period" is the overpayment rate in effect under Code Sec. 6621 for the calendar quarter in which that interest accrual period begins. (Code Sec. 460(b)(7)(A) as amended by '97 Act §1211(b)(2))

An "interest accrual period" means the period (Code Sec. 460(b)(7)(B)):

. . . beginning on the day after the "return due date" for any tax year of the taxpayer (Code Sec. 460(b)(7)(B)(i)), and

... ending on the "return due date" for the following tax year. (Code Sec. 460(b)(7)(B)(ii))

The "return due date" means the date prescribed for filing the income tax return, determined without regard to extensions. (Code Sec. 460(b)(7)(B)).

> 📩 *observation:* The above way of calculating interest assures that taxpayers needn't break single years into two or more periods in calculating interest over a look-back period.

☐ **Effective:** For long-term contract accounting, contracts completed in tax years ending after Aug. 5, '97. ('97 Act §1211(c)(1)) For income forecast depreciation, property placed in service after Sept. 13, '95. ('97 Act §1211(c)(2))

¶ 2005. Rules for estimating inventory shrinkage are provided

Code Sec. 471(b), as amended by '97 Act § 961(a)
Generally effective: Tax years ending after Aug. 5, '97
Committee Reports, see ¶ 5082

Under Code Sec. 471(a), where, in the opinion of IRS, a taxpayer must maintain inventories in order to clearly determine income, IRS may require a taxpayer to maintain inventories under a method which most clearly reflects income. Under Reg. § 1.471-2(d), where a taxpayer maintains book inventories in accordance with a sound accounting system, the net value of the inventory will be deemed to be the cost basis of the inventory, provided that the book inventories are verified by physical inventories at reasonable intervals and are adjusted to conform with the physical inventories.

Under pre-'97 Act law, there was uncertainty as to whether a taxpayer was in compliance with the rules discussed above where the taxpayer made adjustments to year-end inventory for estimated "shrinkage"—that is, inventory decrease due to items such as undetected theft, breakage and bookkeeping errors—based on physical counts taken on other than the last day of the tax year. (FTC 2d/FIN ¶ G-5120; USTR ¶ 4714, ¶ 4714.21; TaxDesk ¶ 45,113)

New Law. A method of determining inventories won't be deemed not to clearly reflect income solely because it uses estimates of inventory shrinkage that are confirmed by a physical count only after the last day of the tax year if: (Code Sec. 471(b) as amended by '97 Act §961(a))

• (1) the taxpayer normally does a physical count of inventories at each location on a regular and consistent basis, and (Code Sec. 471(b)(1)),

• (2) the taxpayer makes proper adjustments to those inventories and to its estimating methods to the extent those estimates are greater than or less than the actual

FTC 2d References are to Federal Tax Coordinator 2d
FIN References are to RIA's Analysis of Federal Taxes: Income
USTR References are to United States Tax Reporter: Income, Estate & Gift, and Excise
PCA References are to Pension Coordinator and Pension & Benefits Expert/Advisor
PE References are to Pension and Profit Sharing 2nd
EP References are to Estate Planning & Taxation Coordinator and Estate Planning Advisor

📩 **Research Institute of America** 481

shrinkage.　(Code Sec. 471(b)(2))

According to Congress, in order for a taxpayer to be covered by the Code provision discussed above, (1) estimates must be based on actual physical counts, (2) ending inventory must be adjusted to take into account all physical counts performed through the end of the taxpayer's tax year and (3) the taxpayer is required to take a physical count of inventories at each location on a regular and consistent basis. (Com Rept, see ¶ 5082)

Congress said that, under the Code provision discussed above, a method of keeping inventories will not be considered unsound, or to fail to clearly reflect income, solely because it includes an adjustment for the shrinkage estimated to occur through year-end based on inventories taken other than at year-end. (Com Rept, see ¶ 5082)

🔷*observation:*　By saying that a method of keeping inventories will not be considered "unsound" solely because of an adjustment for estimated shrinkage based on pre-year end inventories, Congress appears to intend that an adjustment for estimated shrinkage based on pre-year-end inventories, but in compliance with the Code provision discussed above, won't cause non-compliance with Reg. § 1.471-2(d). That reg says that where a taxpayer maintains book inventories in accordance with a "sound" accounting system (which follows certain other guidelines discussed in the reg), verifies book inventory balances by physical inventories at reasonable intervals and adjusts the balances in accordance with the physical inventories, the net value as shown by the inventory accounts will be deemed to be the cost of the goods on hand.

Safe harbor methods in general.　Congress expects that IRS will issue guidance establishing one or more safe harbor methods for the estimation of inventory shrinkage treated as resulting in a clear reflection of income, provided that the safe harbor method is consistently applied and the taxpayer's inventory methods otherwise satisfy the clear reflection of income standard. (Com Rept, see ¶ 5082)

Safe harbors methods for retail trade.　For taxpayers primarily engaged in retail trade (the resale of personal property to the general public), where physical inventories are normally taken at each location at least annually, Congress anticipates that a safe harbor method will be established that will use a historical ratio of shrinkage to sales, multiplied by total sales between the date of the last physical inventory and year-end. This historical ratio is based on the actual shrinkage established by all physical inventories taken during the most recent three tax years and the sales for related periods. The historical ratio should be separately determined for each store (or department in a store) of the taxpayer. The historical ratio, or estimated shrinkage determined using the historical ratio, cannot be adjusted by judgmental or other factors (for example, floors or caps). Congress expects that estimated shrinkage determined in accordance with the consistent application of the safe harbor method won't be required to be recalculated, through a lookback adjustment or otherwise, to reflect the results of physical inventories taken after year end. (Com Rept, see ¶ 5082)

For a new store or department in a store that hasn't verified shrinkage by a physical inventory in each of the most recent three tax years, the historical ratio is the average of the historical ratios of the retailer's other stores or departments. Retailers using last-in, first-out (LIFO) methods of inventory are expected to be required to allocate shrinkage among their various inventory pools in a reasonable and consistent manner. (Com Rept, see ¶ 5082)

Accounting method change. Where any taxpayer is permitted by the Code provision discussed above to change, for any tax year, to a permissible method of accounting, the change to the permissible method is treated as initiated by the taxpayer ('97 Act §961(b)(2)(A)), and made with the consent of IRS. ('97 Act §961(b)(2)(B)) A taxpayer is considered permitted to change its method of accounting by the Code provision discussed above if the taxpayer is using a method that doesn't use estimates of inventory shrinkage and wishes to change to a method for inventories that includes shrinkage estimates based on physical inventories taken other than at year-end. (Com Rept, see ¶ 5082). The period for taking into account any adjustment required under Code Sec. 481 by reason of a change permitted by the Code provision discussed above is 4 years. ('97 Act §961(b)(2)(C))

Congress expects that procedures will be provided allowing an automatic election of a method of accounting described above for a taxpayer's first tax year ending after Aug. 5, '97. (Com Rept, see ¶ 5082)

By adoption of the Code provisions discussed above, Congress intended no inference as to the validity of any method of accounting for inventories under pre-'97 Act law. (Com Rept, see ¶ 5082)

Redesignation of Code subsection. Pre-'97 Act Code Sec. 471(b) is redesignated as Code Sec. 471(c). ('97 Act §961(a))

☐ **Effective:** For tax years ending after Aug. 5, '97. ('97 Act §961(b)(1))

¶ 2006. Interest must be accrued on credit card receivables during payment grace period

Code Sec. 1272(a)(6)(C), as amended by '97 Act § 1004(a)
Generally effective: Tax years beginning after Aug. 5, '97
Committee Reports, see ¶ 5114

A taxpayer (creditor) generally must include in gross income the amount of interest received or accrued within the tax year on indebtedness held by the taxpayer. Under pre-'97 Act law, if the principal amount of an indebtedness may be paid without interest by a specified date (as is the case with certain credit card balances), the holder of the indebtedness wasn't required to accrue interest until after the specified date had passed.

FTC 2d References are to Federal Tax Coordinator 2d
FIN References are to RIA's Analysis of Federal Taxes: Income
USTR References are to United States Tax Reporter: Income, Estate & Gift, and Excise
PCA References are to Pension Coordinator and Pension & Benefits Expert/Advisor
PE References are to Pension and Profit Sharing 2nd
EP References are to Estate Planning & Taxation Coordinator and Estate Planning Advisor

However, a different regime applies with respect to holders of debt instruments with original issue discount (OID). The holder of an OID instrument generally accrues and includes in gross income, as interest, the OID over the life of the obligation, even though the amount of the interest may not be received until the maturity of the instrument. In any particular tax year, the amount includible in these circumstances is the sum of the "daily portions" of OID on the debt instrument attributable to the days during the tax year that the holder held the instrument.

Under Code Sec. 1272(a)(6)(C), the rules described below (the REMIC daily portion rules) apply to determine the daily portion of OID for:

. . . any regular interest in a real estate mortgage investment conduit (REMIC) or qualified mortgage held by a REMIC, or

. . . any other debt instrument if payments under that debt instrument may be accelerated by reason of prepayments of other obligations securing that debt instrument (or, to the extent provided in regulations, by reason of other events).

With respect to those interests and instruments, the daily portion of OID is determined by allocating to each day in any accrual period its ratable part of the excess (if any) of:

. . . the sum of (1) the present value (see below) of all remaining payments under the debt instrument as of the close of that accrual period, and (2) the payments during the accrual period of amounts included in the stated redemption price of the debt instrument, over

. . . the adjusted issue price of the debt instrument at the beginning of the accrual period.

The present value of the remaining payments under the debt instrument at the close of an accrual period is determined on the basis of:

. . . the original yield to maturity (determined on the basis of compounding at the close of each accrual period and properly adjusted for the length of the accrual period), and

. . . events that have occurred before the close of the accrual period, and

. . . a prepayment assumption determined under regs to be issued.

The prepayment assumption to be used is that used by the parties in pricing the particular transaction. Prepayment assumptions used must not be unreasonable based on comparable transactions if there are comparable transactions. In addition, in determining whether a prepayment assumption is reasonable, the nature of the debt instruments on which prepayments are being assumed, and the availability of information about prepayments on those debt instruments is taken into account.

(Com Rept, see ¶ 5114) (FTC 2d/FIN ¶ J-4343 et seq.; USTR ¶ 12,714.01; TaxDesk ¶ 15,308 et seq.)

New Law. To the types of interests and instruments subject to the REMIC daily portion rules, except as noted below, the '97 Act adds any pool of debt instruments the yield on which may be affected by reason of prepayments, or, to the extent provided by regulations, by reason of other events. (Code Sec. 1272(a)(6)(C)(iii) as amended by

'97 Act §1004(a))

However, to the extent provided in regulations to be prescribed by IRS, in the case of a small business engaged in the trade or business of selling tangible personal property at retail, the REMIC daily portion rules won't apply to debt instruments incurred in the ordinary course of that trade or business while held by that business. (Code Sec. 1272(a)(6)(C)) In other words, IRS is authorized to provide appropriate exemptions, including exemptions for taxpayers that hold a limited amount of debt instruments, such as small retailers. (Com Rept, see ¶ 5114)

Thus, under the '97 Act, if a taxpayer holds a pool of credit card receivables that require borrowers to pay interest if they don't pay their accounts by a specified date, the taxpayer is required to accrue interest or OID on the pool based upon a reasonable assumption regarding the timing of the payments of the accounts in the pool. In cases where the payments in the pool occur soon after year-end and before the taxpayer files its tax return for that year-end, the taxpayer may accrue interest based on its actual experience rather than based upon reasonable assumptions. (Com Rept, see ¶ 5114)

> **Illustration:** A calendar year taxpayer issues credit cards, the terms of which provide that if charges for a calendar month are paid within 30 days after the close of the month, no interest will accrue with respect to such charges. However, if the balances aren't paid within this 30-day grace period, interest will accrue from the date of the charge until the balance is paid. The taxpayer issues a significant number of such credit cards and the card holders incur charges of $10 million in December of Year 1. In computing its taxable income for Year 1, the taxpayer is required to make a reasonable assumption as to what portion of the $10 million balances won't be paid off within the 30-day grace period and is required to accrue interest income through December 31 of Year 1 with respect to that portion. The taxpayer must then adjust the accrual in Year 2 to reflect the extent to which the prepayment assumption reflected the actual payments received in January. (Com Rept, see ¶ 5114)

Changes of accounting method. In the case of any taxpayer required, as a result of the above provisions, to change its method of accounting for its first tax year beginning after Aug. 5, '97 ('97 Act §1004(b)(2)):

... the change will be treated as initiated by the taxpayer ('97 Act §1004(b)(2)(A));

... the change will be treated as made with IRS consent ('97 Act §1004(b)(2)(B)); and

... the net amount of the adjustments required to be taken into account by the taxpayer under Code Sec. 481 will be taken into account ratably over the four-tax year period beginning with that first tax year. (Code Sec. 1004(b)(2)(C))

FTC 2d References are to Federal Tax Coordinator 2d
FIN References are to RIA's Analysis of Federal Taxes: Income
USTR References are to United States Tax Reporter: Income, Estate & Gift, and Excise
PCA References are to Pension Coordinator and Pension & Benefits Expert/Advisor
PE References are to Pension and Profit Sharing 2nd
EP References are to Estate Planning & Taxation Coordinator and Estate Planning Advisor

action alert: Calendar-year taxpayers holding a pool of debt instruments the yield on which may be reduced by reason of prepayments who are required to change their method of accounting for interest earned on those instruments to conform to the requirements of Code Sec. 1272(a)(6)(C)(iii) must file the change request no later than Dec. 31, '98.

According to the legislative history of the above provisions, it's understood that some taxpayers presently use a method of accounting similar to the method required to be used under the '97 Act, and have asked IRS for permission to change to a different method for pre-Aug. 5, '97 years. So as not to require taxpayers to change methods of accounting multiple times, it's expected that IRS won't grant these pending requests. However, IRS does have discretion to grant changes of methods of accounting that are pending for pre-Aug. 5, '97 years. (Com Rept, see ¶ 5114)

☐ **Effective:** Tax years beginning after Aug. 5, '97. ('97 Act §1004(b)(1))

¶ 2100. Farming

¶ 2101. Cash basis farmers may elect to defer gain from forced sales of livestock due to floods or other weather-related conditions

Code Sec. 451(e)(1), as amended by '97 Act § 913(a)(1)
Generally effective: Sales and exchanges after Dec. 31, '96
Committee Reports, see ¶ 5063

A cash method taxpayer whose principal trade or business is farming and who is forced to sell livestock due to drought conditions may elect to include the income from the sale of the livestock in the tax year following the tax year of the sale. This elective deferral of income is only available if the taxpayer establishes that, under the taxpayer's usual business practices, the sale would not have occurred but for the drought conditions that resulted in the area being designated as eligible for federal assistance. (FTC 2d/FIN ¶ N-1031; USTR ¶ 4514.176; TaxDesk ¶ 11,803) The purpose of this rule is to put taxpayers who receive an unusually high amount of income in one year in the position that they would have been in absent the drought. (Com Rept, see ¶ 5063)

New Law. The '97 Act amends the gain recognition rule that applies to livestock sold or exchanged on account of a drought to also apply to sales or exchanges of livestock on account of a flood or other weather-related conditions. (Code Sec. 451(e)(1) as amended by '97 Act §913(a)(1))

Thus, a cash basis farmer who otherwise meets the tests of Code Sec. 451(e) can elect to defer income recognition from the sale or exchange of livestock due not only to drought, but also to floods or other weather-related conditions, to the tax year following the tax year of the sale or exchange. (Com Rept, see ¶ 5063)

> ⓡ *observation:* The livestock sale must be compelled by drought, flood or other weather-related conditions in a tax year different from the tax year in which the livestock would otherwise have been sold. Thus, if it is a calendar year farmer's usual business practice to sell livestock in November, but drought, flood, or other weather-related conditions forces the sale of the livestock in February of the same year, the farmer does not qualify for the deferral.

> ⓡ *observation:* Notwithstanding that the purpose of this elective rule is to prevent the bunching of income in the year of sale (Year 1) by postponing income recognition until the following year (Year 2), the taxpayer's particular situation may be that he expects to realize more income (i.e., be in a higher

FTC 2d References are to Federal Tax Coordinator 2d
FIN References are to RIA's Analysis of Federal Taxes: Income
USTR References are to United States Tax Reporter: Income, Estate & Gift, and Excise
PCA References are to Pension Coordinator and Pension & Benefits Expert/Advisor
PE References are to Pension and Profit Sharing 2nd
EP References are to Estate Planning & Taxation Coordinator and Estate Planning Advisor

income tax bracket) in Year 2 than in Year 1. In the event that this is the case, the taxpayer presumably will *not* want to elect to postpone income recognition regarding sales due to weather-related conditions to Year 2.

☐ **Effective:** Sales and exchanges of livestock after Dec. 31, '96. ('97 Act §913(c))

¶ 2102. Forced sales of livestock due to floods or other weather conditions are treated as involuntary conversions

Code Sec. 1033(e), as amended by '97 Act § 913(b)(1)
Generally effective: Sales and exchanges after Dec. 31, '96
Committee Reports, see ¶ 5063

The sale of livestock (other than poultry) that is held for draft, breeding, or dairy purposes in excess of the number of livestock that would have been sold but for drought conditions is treated as an involuntary conversion under Code Sec. 1033. Consequently, gain from the sale of that livestock can be deferred by reinvesting the proceeds of the sale in similar property within a two-year period. (FTC 2d/FIN ¶ N-1216; USTR ¶ 10,334.08)

New Law. The '97 Act amends the rule treating sales or exchanges of livestock solely on account of a drought as involuntary conversions to also apply to sales or exchanges of livestock solely on account of a flood or other weather-related conditions. (Code Sec. 1033(e) as amended by '97 Act §913(b)(1))

Thus, the sale or exchange of livestock (other than poultry) that are held for draft, breeding or dairy purposes in excess of the number of livestock that would have been sold but for the drought (as under pre-'97 Act law), flood or other weather-related conditions is treated as an involuntary conversion. (Com Rept, see ¶ 5063)

☐ **Effective:** Sales and exchanges of livestock after Dec. 31, '96. ('97 Act §913(c))

¶ 2103. Farm income averaging over a three-year period is permitted for individuals

Code Sec. 1301, as added by '97 Act § 933
Generally effective: Tax years beginning after Dec. 31, '97 and before Jan. 1, 2001
Committee Reports, see ¶ 5070

No averaging of farm income existed under pre-'97 Act law. Earlier provisions that allowed income averaging for individuals were repealed by the Tax Reform Act of '86 effective for tax years beginning after '86.

New Law. At the election of an individual engaged in a farming business, the tax imposed by Code Sec. 1 (relating to, among other things, income tax on individuals) for the tax year will be equal to the sum of:

- a tax computed under Code Sec. 1 on taxable income reduced by "elected farm income" (as defined below) plus, (Code Sec. 1301(a)(1) as added by '97 Act

§933(a))

• the increase in tax imposed by Code Sec. 1 which would result if taxable income for the three prior tax years were increased by an amount equal to one-third of the "elected farm income". (Code Sec. 1301(a)(2))

The provision operates so that an electing eligible taxpayer:

(1) designates all or a portion of his taxable income from the trade or business of farming from the current year as "elected farm income;"

(2) allocates one-third of the "elected farm income" to each of the prior three tax years; and

(3) determines his or her current year Code Sec. 1 tax liability by determining the sum of —

• his or her current year Code Sec. 1 liability without the elected farm income allocated to the three prior tax years, plus

• the increases in the Code Sec. 1 tax for each of the three prior tax years by taking into account the allocable share of the elected farm income for those years.

(Com Rept, see ¶ 5070)

Any adjustment under this provision for any tax year is taken into account in applying this provision for any later tax year. (Code Sec. 1301(a)) That is, if a taxpayer elects the operation of the provision for a tax year, the allocation of elected farm income among tax years under the election applies for purposes of any election in a later tax year. (Com Rept, see ¶ 5070)

The term "individual" does not include any estate or trust. (Code Sec. 1301(b)(2)) Thus, the provision does not apply to an estate or a trust. (Com Rept, see ¶ 5070)

The term "elected farm income" means so much of the taxable income for the tax year—

• which is attributable to any "farming business;" and (Code Sec. 1301(b)(1)(A)(i))

• which is specified in the election to average farm income. (Code Sec. 1301(b)(1)(A)(ii))

For purposes of the definition of elected farm income, gain from the sale or other disposition of property (other than land) regularly used by the taxpayer in a farming business for a substantial period is treated as attributable to that farming business. (Code Sec. 1301(b)(1)(B))

The term "farming business" has the meaning given to the term by Code Sec. 263A(e)(4) (i.e., the business of farming, including operating a nursery or sod farm or raising or harvesting certain types of trees). (Code Sec. 1301(b)(3))

FTC 2d References are to Federal Tax Coordinator 2d
FIN References are to RIA's Analysis of Federal Taxes: Income
USTR References are to United States Tax Reporter: Income, Estate & Gift, and Excise
PCA References are to Pension Coordinator and Pension & Benefits Expert/Advisor
PE References are to Pension and Profit Sharing 2nd
EP References are to Estate Planning & Taxation Coordinator and Estate Planning Advisor

The provision applies neither for employment tax purposes nor for purposes of the alternative minimum tax under Code Sec. 55. In addition, the provision does not require the recalculation of the tax liability of any other taxpayer, including a minor child required to use the tax rates of his or her parents under Code Sec. 1(g). (Com Rept, see ¶ 5070)

IRS is instructed to prescribe the regulations that may be appropriate to carry out the purposes of this provision, including regulations regarding:

• the order and manner in which items of income, gain, deduction, or loss, or limitations on tax, are to be taken into account in computing the tax imposed on the income of any taxpayer to whom this provision applies for any tax year, and (Code Sec. 1301(c)(1))

• the treatment of any short tax year. (Code Sec. 1301(a)(2))

Congress expects that the regulations will deny the multiple application of items that carryover from one tax year to the next (e.g., net operating loss or tax credit carryovers). (Com Rept, see ¶ 5070)

The election must be made in the manner prescribed by IRS and, except as provided by IRS, will be irrevocable. (Com Rept, see ¶ 5070)

> ⓡ*observation:* The provision does not specify how the election is to be made, but, presumably a computation to claim income averaging can be made when the individual files an income tax return for the tax year.

☐ **Effective:** Tax years beginning after Dec. 31, '97 and before Jan. 1, 2001. ('97 Act §933(c))

¶ 2104. Suspense accounts prohibited for family corporations required to change to the accrual method of accounting for farming income

Code Sec. 447(i)(3), repealed by '97 Act § 1081
Code Sec. 447(i)(4), repealed by '97 Act § 1081
Code Sec. 447(i)(5), as amended by '97 Act § 1081
Generally effective: Tax years ending after June 8, '97
Committee Reports, see ¶ 5158

A corporation (or a partnership with a corporate partner) engaged in the trade or business of farming must use an accrual method to account for taxable income from farming unless the corporation (or any predecessor corporation) for each prior tax year beginning after Dec. 31, '75 doesn't have gross receipts exceeding $1 million. If a farm corporation is required to change its method of accounting because of the $1 million rule, the Code Sec. 481 adjustment resulting from the change is included in gross income ratably over a 10-year period beginning with the year of change.

The above rules don't apply to a family corporation (or a partnership with a family corporation as a partner) engaged in the trade or business of farming. Instead, that kind of corporation (or partnership) must use an accrual method to account for its taxable income from farming unless, for each prior tax year beginning after Dec. 31, '85, the corporation (or any predecessor corporation) doesn't have gross receipts exceeding $25 million. (Com Rept, see ¶ 5158)

Under pre-'97 Act law, if a family corporation changed its method of accounting because of the $25 million rule, the family corporation—instead of making a Code Sec. 481 adjustment—had to establish a suspense account. The initial balance of the suspense account equaled the lesser of (1) the Code Sec. 481 adjustment otherwise required for the year of change or (2) the Code Sec. 481 adjustment computed as if the change in method of accounting had occurred as of the beginning of the tax year preceding the year of change. (Com Rept, see ¶ 5158)

The amount of the suspense account is required to be included in gross income if the corporation ceases to be a family corporation. (Com Rept, see ¶ 5158)

Under pre-'97 Act law, if the gross receipts of the corporation attributable to farming for a tax year declined to an amount below the lesser of (1) the gross receipts attributable to farming for the last tax year for which an accrual method of accounting wasn't required or (2) the gross receipts attributable to farming for the most recent tax year for which a portion of the suspense account was required to be included in income, a portion of the suspense account was required to be included in gross income. (FTC 2d/FIN ¶ N-1045, ¶ N-1047; USTR ¶ 4474; TaxDesk ¶ 11,813)

New Law.

Suspense accounts prohibited. Under the '97 Act, suspense accounts can't be established by any family corporation required, for any tax year ending after June 8, '97, to change its method of accounting for taxable income from farming because of the $25 million rule. (Code Sec. 447(i)(5)(A) as amended by '97 Act §1081(a)) Thus, any family corporation required, because of the $25 million rule, to change to an accrual method of accounting for any tax year ending after June 8, '97 must restore the Code Sec. 481 adjustment applicable to the change in gross income ratably over a 10-year period beginning with the year of change. (Com Rept, see ¶ 5158) The availability of suspense accounts was ended because Congress believed that suspense accounts may effectively provide an exclusion for, rather than a deferral of, amounts otherwise included in income under a Code Sec. 481 adjustment. (Com Rept, see ¶ 5158).

Suspense accounts established under pre-'97 Act law phased-out. For suspense accounts established under pre-'97 Act law, Congress believed that requiring their recognition as income may impose liquidity concerns upon family corporations. Thus, for those suspense accounts, the '97 Act provides phase-out rules under which the accounts are restored to income over an extended period, with further deferral where the corporation has insufficient income. (Com Rept, see ¶ 5158)

FTC 2d References are to Federal Tax Coordinator 2d
FIN References are to RIA's Analysis of Federal Taxes: Income
USTR References are to United States Tax Reporter: Income, Estate & Gift, and Excise
PCA References are to Pension Coordinator and Pension & Benefits Expert/Advisor
PE References are to Pension and Profit Sharing 2nd
EP References are to Estate Planning & Taxation Coordinator and Estate Planning Advisor

Under the '97 Act, existing suspense accounts are reduced (but not below zero) for each tax year beginning after June 8, '97 by an amount equal to the lesser of (1) the "applicable portion" (defined below) of the account, (Code Sec. 447(i)(5)(B)(i)(I)), or (2) 50% of the taxable income of the corporation for the tax year, or, if the corporation has no taxable income for the tax year, the amount of any net operating loss (as defined in Code Sec. 172(c)) for the tax year. (Code Sec. 447(i)(5)(B)(i)(II)) Thus, the amount required to be restored to income for a tax year cannot exceed the net operating loss for the year (in a year where there is a net operating loss) or 50% of the net income of the taxpayer for the year (in a year where there is net income). (Com Rept, see ¶ 5158)   For purposes of this calculation, taxable income and net operating loss are determined without regard to the calculation. (Code Sec. 447(i)(5)(B)(i))   Any reduction in a suspense account under the calculation is included in gross income for the tax year of the reduction. (Code Sec. 447(i)(5)(B)(iv)). Where a family corporation elects to be an S corporation for a tax year, the net operating loss and 50%-of-taxable-income limitations in the calculation are determined by taking into account all the items of income, gain, deduction and loss of the corporation, whether or not the items are separately stated under Code Sec. 1366 (under which an S corporation must separately state items which could affect the tax liability of any shareholder, see FTC 2d/FIN ¶ D-1765; USTR ¶ 13,664; TaxDesk ¶ 61,451). (Com Rept, see ¶ 5158)

"Applicable portion" means, for any tax year, the amount which would ratably reduce the amount in the account (after taking into account prior reductions) to zero over the period consisting of the tax year and the remaining tax years in the first 20 tax years. (Code Sec. 447(i)(5)(C))   However, it is possible that the restoration period may extend beyond 20 years. (Com Rept, see ¶ 5158)   In that circumstance, any amount in the account as of the close of the 20th tax year is treated as the applicable portion for each year after the 20th year, to the extent not reduced for any prior tax year after the 20th year. (Code Sec. 447(i)(5)(D))   Amounts that are still in the suspense account at the end of the 20-year period remain subject to the net operating loss and 50%-of-taxable-income rules. (Com Rept, see ¶ 5158)

According to Congress, the requirement of restoring the suspense account to income under the calculation discussed above is subject to any pre-'97 Act law requirements to restore the account more rapidly. (Com Rept, see ¶ 5158)   Thus, the amount of the applicable portion for any tax year is reduced (but not below zero) by the amount of any reduction in the suspense account required for the tax year under any provision of Code Sec. 447(i) other than the calculation discussed above. (Code Sec. 447(i)(5)(B)(ii))

observation: In view of the repeal, discussed immediately below, of the rule requiring reduction of a suspense account where gross receipts decline below certain levels, the only apparent applicability of Code Sec. 447(i)(5)(B)(ii)—which coordinates the 20-year reduction rule with other required reductions in a suspense account—appears to be where, under Code Sec. 447(i)(3), as redesignated by §1081(a) of the '97 Act, the entire remaining balance of the suspense account is required to be included in gross income if the corporation ceases to be a family corporation, see FTC 2d/FIN ¶ N-1046; USTR ¶ 4474; TaxDesk ¶ 11,813.

Repeal of rules reducing suspense account and requiring income inclusion if farming business contracts. The '97 Act repeals the rule which required that the suspense account be reduced if gross receipts declined to an amount below the lesser of (1) the gross receipts attributable to farming for the last tax year for which an accrual method of accounting wasn't required or (2) the gross receipts attributable to farming for the most recent tax year for which a portion of the suspense account was required to be included in income. (Code Sec. 447(i)(3) repealed by '97 Act §1081(a)) The '97 Act also repeals the rule which required the inclusion in income of the amount by which the suspense account was reduced under repealed Code Sec. 447(i)(3). (Code Sec. 447(i)(4) repealed by '97 Act §1081(a))

Code Sections redesignated by '97 Act. In addition to making the substantive changes described above, the '97 Act redesignated pre-'97 Act Code Sec. 447(i)(5) and (6) as Code Sec. 447(i)(3) and Code Sec. 447(i)(4). ('97 Act §1081(a))

🅡 *observation:* In Code Sec. 447(i)(5)(B), as amended by '97 Act § 1081(a), the numbering of clauses skips from Code Sec. 447(i)(5)(B)(ii) to Code Sec. 447(i)(5)(B)(iv); i.e., there is no Code Sec. 447(i)(5)(B)(iii).

☐ **Effective:** Tax years ending after June 8, '97. ('97 Act §1081(b))

FTC 2d References are to the Federal Tax Coordinator 2d
FIN References are to RIA's Analysis of Federal Taxes: Income
USTR References are to United States Tax Reporter: Income, Estate & Gift, and Excise
PCA References are to Pension Coordinator and Pension & Benefits Expert/Advisor
PE References are to Pension and Profit Sharing 2nd
EP References are to Estate Planning & Taxation Coordinator and Estate Planning Advisor

¶ 2200. Excise Taxes

Air Transportation and Communications Taxes

¶ 2201. Airport and airway trust fund taxes extended through Sept. 30, 2007

Code Sec. 4041(c)(3)(B), as amended by '97 Act § 1031(a)(3)
Code Sec. 4081(d)(2)(B), as amended by '97 Act § 1031(a)(2)
Code Sec. 4091(b)(3)(A)(ii), as amended by '97 Act § 1031(a)(1)
Code Sec. 4261(g)(1)(A)(ii), as amended by '97 Act § 1031(b)(1)
Code Sec. 4271(d)(1)(A)(ii), as amended by '97 Act § 1031(b)(2)
Generally effective: Oct. 1, '97
Committee Reports, see ¶ 5129

The following excise taxes that fund the Federal Airport and Airway Trust Fund program were scheduled to expire after Sept. 30, '97:

(1) The 10% tax on domestic air passenger tickets. (FTC 2d ¶ W-5103; USTR ¶ 42,614.01)

(2) The $6-per person tax on international departures. (FTC 2d ¶ W-5101; USTR ¶ 42,614.01)

(3) The 6.25% tax on domestic air transportation of property. (FTC 2d ¶ W-5201; USTR ¶ 42,714)

(4) 17.5 cents per gallon of the tax on aviation fuel used in noncommercial aviation that is imposed on producers, importers or retail sellers. (FTC 2d ¶ W-1607, ¶ W-1713; USTR ¶ 40,414, ¶ 40,914)

(5) 15 cents per gallon of the tax imposed on aviation gasoline upon its removal from the terminal. (FTC 2d ¶ W-1501; USTR ¶ 40,814)

New Law. The '97 Act extends the Airport and Airway Trust Fund taxes through Sept 30, 2007. (Code Sec. 4041(c)(3)(B) as amended by '97 Act §1031(a)(3)) (Code Sec. 4081(d)(2)(B) as amended by '97 Act §1031(a)(2)) (Code Sec. 4091(b)(3)(A)(ii) as amended by '97 Act §1031(a)(1)) (Code Sec. 4261(g)(1)(A)(ii) as amended by '97 Act §1031(b)(1)) (Code Sec. 4271(d)(1)(A)(ii) as amended by '97 Act §1031(b)(2))

> *observation:* Other '97 Act provisions (see ¶ 2203 and ¶ 2202) make changes to the rates at which and the conditions under which items (1) and (2) above are imposed. Thus, the '97 Act extends those taxes but changes their rates and application.

FTC 2d References are to the Federal Tax Coordinator 2d
FIN References are to RIA's Analysis of Federal Taxes: Income
USTR References are to the United States Tax Reporter: Income, Estate & Gift, and Excise
PCA References are to Pension Coordinator and Pension & Benefits Expert/Advisor
PE References are to Pension and Profit Sharing 2nd
EP References are to Estate Planning & Taxation Coordinator and Estate Planning Advisor

Research Institute of America

☐ **Effective:** With respect to the air transportation taxes described at (1) through (3) above: transportation beginning after Sept. 30, '97. ('97 Act §1031(e)(2)(A))

With respect to the fuel taxes described at (4) and (5) above: Oct. 1, '97. ('97 Act §1031(e)(1))

¶ 2202. Domestic air passenger transportation tax restructured; tax imposed on right to make mileage awards

Code Sec. 4261(a), as amended by '97 Act § 1031(c)(1)
Code Sec. 4261(b), as amended by '97 Act § 1031(c)(1)
Code Sec. 4261(e), as amended by '97 Act § 1031(c)(2)
Generally effective: Transportation beginning after Sept. 30, '97
Committee Reports, see ¶ 5129

Domestic air passenger transportation was subject to a 10% excise tax (the "domestic air transportation tax"). (FTC 2d ¶ W-5103; USTR ¶ 42,614.01)

Except as provided at "However, the 10% tax isn't imposed" below, the tax is imposed on "taxable transportation," which is defined for this purpose as:

(1) transportation that begins and ends within the U.S. or points in Canada or Mexico that are within 225 miles of the U.S. border (the "225-mile zone") (see FTC 2d ¶ W-5117 et seq.; USTR ¶ 42,614.02); and

(2) transportation that isn't described in (1), but that is directly or indirectly from one port or station in the U.S. to another, unless such transportation is a connecting flight for transportation that begins or ends outside the U.S. or the 225-mile zone (i.e., a connecting flight for an international destination) and for which the stopover at the intermediate U.S. point is scheduled to be 12 hours or less. (FTC 2d ¶ W-5121 et seq.; USTR ¶ 42,614.02).

However, the 10% tax isn't imposed on amounts paid outside the U.S. for taxable transportation that didn't both begin and end in the U.S. (FTC 2d ¶ W-5125, ¶ W-5126; USTR ¶ 42,614.03)

Any transportation that began in the U.S., other than transportation that was taxable transportation subject to the 10% domestic air transportation tax, was subject to a flat $6 per person international departure tax, see ¶ 2203.

Because the domestic air transportation tax was imposed only on transportation for which an amount was paid, no tax was imposed on free travel (e.g., frequent flyer travel and airline employee travel for which the employee wasn't directly charged), even if a third party (e.g., a credit card company) made cash or in-kind payments for the right to award such "free-travel" or reduced-rate travel to their customers. (FTC 2d

¶ W-5103.1, ¶ W-5103.2)

A 10% tax also applied to any amounts paid for seating or sleeping accommodations in connection with taxable transportation. (FTC 2d ¶ W-5103; USTR ¶ 42,614.01)

New Law. As discussed below, the '97 Act restructures the tax rate imposed on domestic air passenger transportation, provides reduced rates for flights to and from rural airports, expands the exemption for amounts paid outside the U.S. and extends the tax to certain previously exempt travel.

Tax rate restructured. The 10% tax on the amount paid for taxable transportation is reduced to:

. . . 9% for transportation beginning after Sept. 30, '97 and before Oct. 1, '98 (Code Sec. 4261(e)(5)(A) as amended by '97 Act §1031(c)(2)),

. . . 8% for transportation beginning after Sept. 30, '98 and before Oct. 1, '99 (Code Sec. 4261(e)(5)(B)), and

. . . 7.5% thereafter. (Code Sec. 4261(a) as amended by '97 Act §1031(c)(1))

In addition to the above 9%, 8% or 7.5% tax, the '97 Act imposes a fixed dollar amount per "domestic segment." (Code Sec. 4261(b)(1))

A "domestic segment" means any segment consisting of one takeoff and one landing and which is taxable transportation as described at (1) above. (Code Sec. 4261(b)(2)) For example, travel from New York to San Francisco, with an intermediate stop in Chicago, would consist of two segments, without regard to whether the passenger changed aircraft in Chicago. (Com Rept, see ¶ 5129)

The fixed-dollar-per-segment tax applies as follows:

For segments beginning:	The tax is:
After Sept. 30, '97 and before Oct. 1, '98	$1.00
After Sept. 30, '98 and before Oct. 1, '99	$2.00
After Sept. 30, '99 and before Jan. 1, 2000	$2.25
During 2000	$2.50
During 2001	$2.75
During 2002	$3.00
(Code Sec. 4261(b)(1))	

Illustration: Thus, for example, for taxable transportation beginning after Sept. 30, '97 and before Oct. 1, '98, the domestic air passenger tax would equal 9% of the fare, plus $1.00 per domestic flight segment. (Com Rept, see ¶ 5129)

For segments that begin (Code Sec. 4261(e)(4)(C) as amended by '97 Act §1031(c)(2)) in 2003 or thereafter (Code Sec. 4261(e)(4)(B)(i) as amended by '97 Act §1031(c)(2)), the fixed-dollar-per-segment amount is indexed annually as follows: Multiply the 2002 rate, $3.00, by the percentage (if any) by which (a) the consumer price index (CPI) for the preceding calendar year exceeds (b) the CPI for 2001. Round the resulting amount to the nearest multiple of 10 cents, and add it to the $3.00 fixed amount. (Code Sec. 4261(e)(4)(A) as amended by '97 Act §1031(c)(2))

The fixed-dollar-per-segment tax is determined without regard to changes in route in the following case: (a) transportation is purchased between two locations on specified flights; (b) and there is a change in the route taken which changes the number of domestic segments, but (c) there is no change in the amount charged for the transportation, (Code Sec. 4261(b)(3) as amended by '97 Act §1031(c)(1)) including no imposition of any additional administrative or other fee. (Com Rept, see ¶ 5129) Thus, there is no change in the number of flight segments for which a passenger is charged (i.e., no increase or decrease) where the origin and destination stay the same but, for example, there is a flight change due to aircraft mechanical problems or a diversion to another intermediate or destination airport as a result of inclement weather conditions. (Com Rept, see ¶ 5129)

The '97 Act also deletes the rule providing for imposition of the domestic air transportation tax on amounts paid for seating or sleeping accommodations in connection with taxable transportation. ('97 Act §1031(c)(1))

> ⓥ *observation:* Deletion of the provision makes no substantive change to how domestic passenger air transportation is taxed since air carriers no longer charge separately for seating or offer sleeping accommodations.

Reduced rates apply for flight segments to or from rural airport. In the case of any domestic segment beginning or ending at an airport that is a "rural airport" for the calendar year in which that segment begins or ends (as the case may be):

. . . The fixed-dollar-per segment tax described above does not apply. (Code Sec. 4261(e)(1)(A) as amended by '97 Act §1031(c)(2));

. . . The 7.5% tax rate applies to all tax years. I.e., the 9% and 8% tax rates described above don't apply. (Code Sec. 4261(e)(1)(C)(i))

For transportation that begins before Oct. 1, '99 and that involves more than one domestic segment at least one of which does not begin or end at a rural airport: (a) the 7.5% tax is applied only to the amount that bears the same ratio to the amount paid for the transportation as the number of specified miles in the domestic segments beginning or ending at rural airports bear to the total number of specified miles for the transportation (Code Sec. 4261(e)(1)(C)(ii)); (b) the 9% or 8% tax applies to the remainder of the amount paid for the transportation (Code Sec. 4261(e)(5)), and (c) the applicable fixed-dollar-segment tax applies for each domestic segment (Code Sec. 4261(b)) that is not a flight segment to or from a rural airport. (Code Sec. 4261(e)(1)(A))

> ⓥ *observation:* The term "specified miles," as used in the preceding paragraph, is not defined in the '97 Act. However, it was defined in Sec. 841(c)(2) of the Senate-passed version of the Act as: the "Great Circle miles" (as speci-

FTC 2d References are to Federal Tax Coordinator 2d
FIN References are to RIA's Analysis of Federal Taxes: Income
USTR References are to United States Tax Reporter: Income, Estate & Gift, and Excise
PCA References are to Pension Coordinator and Pension & Benefits Expert/Advisor
PE References are to Pension and Profit Sharing 2nd
EP References are to Estate Planning & Taxation Coordinator and Estate Planning Advisor

fied by IRS between the two points of each segment), except that IRS may specify mileage that will apply instead of Great Circle miles with respect to any two points if IRS determines that the mileage on the route customarily traveled by air between such points is different from the Great Circle miles.

It would appear that Congress means for this definition to apply.

Great Circle miles are based on the shortest distance (i.e., "as the crow flies") between two points. In general, this mileage calculation is identical to that which is used by frequent flyer programs offered by all major U.S. airlines. Computer programs are readily available for calculating Great Circle miles between origin and destination points for flights. (Com Rept, see ¶ 5129)

A rural airport means, with respect to any calendar year, any airport if: (1) there are fewer than 100,000 commercial passengers departing by air during the second preceding calendar year from the airport, and (2) the airport (i) isn't located within 75 miles of another airport which doesn't meet the description in (1), or (ii) is receiving essential air service subsidies as of the date of enactment of this provision. (Code Sec. 4261(e)(1)(B) as amended by '97 Act §1031(c)(2)) Congress has directed IRS to publish an annual list of qualified rural airports, based on passenger enplanements for the requisite calendar year. (Com Rept, see ¶ 5129)

Exemption for amounts paid outside the U.S. expanded. The '97 Act provided that the pre-'97 Act rule that exempted from tax amounts paid outside the U.S. for taxable transportation that didn't both begin and end in the U.S. applies to the 9%, 8% and 7.5% taxes and to the fixed-dollar-per-segment tax. (Code Sec. 4261(e)(2) as amended by '97 Act §1031(c)(2))

> ⚫*observation:* Thus, for example, for transportation beginning after Sept. 30, '97 and before Oct. 1, '98, neither the 9% tax nor the $1.00 fixed-dollar-per-segment tax is imposed in the case of travel between the U.S. and the 225-mile zone where such travel is paid for outside the U.S.

Extension of tax to certain previously exempt travel (the "right-to-make-mileage-award rules"). Except otherwise provided at "For purposes of the above rule" below (Com Rept, see ¶ 5129), any amount paid (and the value of any benefit provided) to an air carrier or related person for the right to provide mileage awards for (or other reductions in the cost of) any transportation of persons by air, is treated as an amount paid for taxable transportation and is subject to the 9%, 8% or 7.5% tax, notwithstanding any other air transportation tax provision. (Code Sec. 4261(e)(3)(A) as amended by '97 Act §1031(c)(2)) Examples of such amounts include (1) payments for frequent flyer miles (including other rights to air transportation) purchased by credit card companies, telephone companies, rental car companies, television networks, restaurants and hotels, air carriers and related parties, and other businesses and (2) amounts received by air carriers (or related parties) pursuant to joint venture credit card or other marketing arrangements. Congress says that taxpayers should make no inferences from the addition of this provision as to the proper treatment of such payments under pre-'97 Act law. (Com Rept, see ¶ 5129) *observation:* No domestic segment tax is imposed on the right to provide mileage awards.

observation: Under the above provision, even where the flight actually taken with the mileage award is an international flight, the domestic air transportation tax is imposed.

For purposes of the above rule, a corporation and all wholly owned subsidiaries of that corporation are treated as one corporation. (Code Sec. 4261(e)(3)(B)) That is, Code Sec. 4261(e)(3)(A) (see above) doesn't apply to payments for air transportation rights between corporations that are members of a 100% commonly owned controlled group. (Com Rept, see ¶ 5129)

Illustration: For example, transportation purchased from an air carrier by a 100% commonly owned corporation operating a frequent flyer award program for the air carrier wouldn't be subject to tax. (Com Rept, see ¶ 5129)

IRS is directed to prescribe rules which reallocate items of income, deduction, credit, exclusion or other allowance to the extent necessary to prevent avoidance of tax imposed under these right to award mileage rules. (Code Sec. 4261(e)(3)(C))

IRS is granted the authority to prescribe rules that exclude from the 9%, 8%, or 7.5% tax, amounts that are attributable to mileage awards but that are used for purposes other than passenger air transportation. (Code Sec. 4261(e)(3)(C)) However, Congress intends that IRS issue such regs only if IRS determines that there is a consistent pattern of non-air-transportation use of awarded mileage by consumers that indicates that a significant amount of mileage that was taxable under the right-to-make mileage award rules is being used for non-air-transportation purposes.

Congress says that it recognizes that (a) consumers accrue mileage awards from numerous sources, including (i) actual air travel and (ii) mileage award programs subject to the above right-to-award-mileage provision; (b) once awarded, such miles are commingled in consumer accounts; and (c) therefore, any given miles may not be traceable to their source. Congress authorizes IRS to have the above mentioned regs exclude from the tax base any portion of otherwise taxable payments with respect to awarded frequent flyer miles that IRS determines can be properly allocated (traced) to miles which are used for other than air passenger transportation purposes. Congress provides IRS with the following additional guidance with respect to the regs:

... They should provide that unused miles are not to be treated as if they were used for purposes other than air passenger transportation.

... They should treat mileage used for non-air transportation purposes as coming first from mileage awarded to consumers from actual air travel (and other sources not sub-

FTC 2d References are to Federal Tax Coordinator 2d
FIN References are to RIA's Analysis of Federal Taxes: Income
USTR References are to United States Tax Reporter: Income, Estate & Gift, and Excise
PCA References are to Pension Coordinator and Pension & Benefits Expert/Advisor
PE References are to Pension and Profit Sharing 2nd
EP References are to Estate Planning & Taxation Coordinator and Estate Planning Advisor

Research Institute of America 499

ject to tax under the above taxation-of-rights-to-award-mileage-award rules). (Com Rept, see ¶ 5129)

☐ **Effective:** Except as otherwise provided below: for amounts paid after Sept. 30, '97 ('97 Act §1031(e)(2)(B)) for transportation beginning after Sept. 30, '97. ('97 Act §1031(e)(2)(A))

For amounts paid for rights-to-award-mileage awards described above: amounts paid (and other benefits provided) after Sept. 30, '97. ('97 Act §1031(e)(2)(C)(i)) For this purpose, where an amount is paid after June 11, '97 and before Oct. 1, '97 by a member of a controlled group for a right to award mileage awards, and that right is furnished by another member of the group after Sept. 30, '97, the amount is treated as having been paid after Sept. 30, '97. All persons treated as a single employer for purposes of Code Sec. 52(a) or Code Sec. 52(b) (relating to the work opportunity credit, see FTC 2d/FIN ¶ L-17787; USTR ¶ 514) are treated as members of a controlled group. ('97 Act §1031(e)(2)(C)(ii))

> *observation:* The rule of § 1031(e)(2)(C)(ii) applies to controlled groups that meet the above definition but that aren't treated as one corporation under the rule of Code Sec. 4261(e)(3)(B) described under "Extension of tax to certain previously exempt travel" above.

¶ 2203. Air passenger tax on international departures increased; international arrivals taxed

Code Sec. 4261(c), as amended by '97 Act § 1031(c)(1)
Code Sec. 4261(e)(4), as amended by '97 Act § 1031(c)(2)
Generally effective: Transportation beginning after Sept. 30, '97
Committee Reports, see ¶ 5129

Any transportation that began in the U.S., other than "taxable transportation" (i.e., other than transportation that is subject to the domestic air transportation tax, see ¶ 2202), transportation on small aircraft on nonestablished lines and transportation by members of an affiliated group, was subject to a flat $6 per person tax (the "international departure tax"). No tax was imposed on passengers arriving in the U.S. from other countries. (FTC 2d ¶ W-5101; USTR ¶ 42,614.01)

The tax applied to travel between the 48 contiguous states and Alaska or Hawaii, and travel between Alaska and Hawaii. (The domestic air transportation tax (see ¶ 2202) is also imposed on that travel.) (FTC 2d ¶ W-5114 et seq.; USTR ¶ 42,614.02)

New Law. Tax on international departures increased; international arrivals taxed. The '97 Act increases the international departure tax to $12.00 per departure, and imposes an identical $12.00 tax on international arrivals. (Com Rept, see ¶ 5129) That is, subject to the same exceptions as applied to the pre-'97 Act tax on international departures (Code Sec. 4261(c)(2) as amended by '97 Act §1031(c)(1)), tax applies on any amount paid, whether paid in the U.S. or outside the U.S., for air transportation that begins or ends in the U.S. (Code Sec. 4261(c)(1)) The $12.00 international departure and arrival tax is indexed for inflation for transportation beginning in calendar years after '98. (Code Sec. 4261(e)(4)(B)(ii) as amended by '97 Act §1031(c)(2)) The inflation adjustment is calculated each year after '98 as follows: Multiply the $12.00 by the percentage (if any) by which (a) the consumer price index (CPI) for the preceding calendar year exceeds (b) the CPI for '97. Round the resulting amount to the nearest multiple of 10 cents, and add it to the $12.00 fixed amount. (Code Sec. 4261(e)(4)(A) as amended by '97 Act §1031(c)(2))

Transportation between the 48 contiguous states and Alaska or Hawaii, or between Alaska and Hawaii. The pre-'97 Act law rules classifying transportation between the 48 contiguous states and Alaska or Hawaii (or between Alaska and Hawaii) as part domestic flight and part international flight are retained. (Com Rept, see ¶ 5129) But the '97 Act adds that in any case where the $12.00 tax applies to a domestic segment (as defined in Code Sec. 4261(b)(2), see ¶ 2202) beginning or ending in Alaska or Hawaii, the tax is reduced to $6.00, and it applies only to departures. (Code Sec. 4261(c)(3) as amended by '97 Act §1031(c)(1)) As a result of this rule, in the case of a single flight segment between the 48 continuous states and Alaska or Hawaii, only one $6.00 per passenger international tax applies, despite the fact that the flight both departs into and arrives from international airspace.(Com Rept, see ¶ 5129)

The $6-per-passenger rate is indexed for inflation. (Com Rept, see ¶ 5129) The inflation described above applies, except that each reference to "$12" is replaced with "$6." (Code Sec. 4261(e)(4)(A))

observation: Unlike with respect to the domestic air transportation tax (see ¶ 2202), the '97 Act doesn't impose any international departure or arrival tax on amounts paid to air carriers for the right to award mileage awards.

☐ **Effective:** Amounts paid after Aug. 12, '97 for transportation beginning after Sept. 30, '97. ('97 Act §1031(e)(2)(B)(i))

¶ 2204. Air carriers made secondarily liable for passenger air transportation taxes; due date for certain deposits of passenger and property air transportation taxes delayed

Code Sec. 4263(c), as amended by '97 Act § 1031(c)(3)
Code Sec. 6302, '97 Act § 1031(g)
Generally effective: Transportation beginning after Sept. 30, '97
Committee Reports, see ¶ 5129

Where a passenger air transportation tax (see ¶ 2203 and ¶ 2202) was not paid at the time payment for the transportation was made, then, under regulations prescribed by IRS, to the extent that the taxes were not collected under any other air transportation tax provision: (1) the taxes had to be paid by the person who paid for the transporta-

FTC 2d References are to Federal Tax Coordinator 2d
FIN References are to RIA's Analysis of Federal Taxes: Income
USTR References are to United States Tax Reporter: Income, Estate & Gift, and Excise
PCA References are to Pension Coordinator and Pension & Benefits Expert/Advisor
PE References are to Pension and Profit Sharing 2nd
EP References are to Estate Planning & Taxation Coordinator and Estate Planning Advisor

tion, or the person who used the transportation; (2) the taxes had to be paid, as prescribed by regs, by the time the rights to the transportation expired, or the transportation became subject to tax, whichever occurred first; and (3) payment of the tax had to be made to either (a) IRS, (b) the party to whom payment for the transportation was made, or (c) for transportation other than transportation between points in the U.S., between a point in the U.S. and the 225-mile zone (see ¶ 2202) or between two points within the 225-mile zone, any person who furnished any portion of the transportation. (FTC 2d ¶ W-5146; USTR ¶ 42,614.03)

Air transportation providers must, generally, deposit with IRS the passenger air transportation tax and the property air transportation tax (FTC 2d ¶ W-5201; USTR ¶ 42,714) that they collect, or that they treat as collected, for a semi-monthly period. Accelerated due dates for these deposits apply for certain amounts collected, or treated as collected, in Sept. (FTC 2d ¶ S-5719, ¶ S-5721; USTR ¶ 63,014)

New Law. As discussed below, the '97 Act makes air carriers secondarily liable for unpaid air passenger transportation taxes and delays the due dates for certain deposits of passenger and property air transportation taxes.

Carriers made secondarily liable for unpaid passenger air transportation taxes. The pre-'97 Act passenger air transportation tax liability and payment rules described in items (1) through (3) above are replaced with the following rule: where tax is not paid at the time payment for transportation is made, then, under regs to be prescribed by IRS, to the extent the air transportation tax isn't collected under any other air transportation tax provision, the carrier who provides the initial segment of the transportation which begins or ends in the U.S. must pay the tax. (Code Sec. 4263(c) as amended by '97 Act §1031(c)(3)) Thus, the pre-'97 Act provision imposing liability for air passenger transportation tax on passengers (with transportation providers being liable for collecting and remitting revenues to IRS) is modified to impose secondary liability on air carriers. (Com Rept, see ¶ 5129)

Certain deposit due dates for passenger and property air transportation taxes delayed. The '97 Act delays deposit due dates as follows:

(1) deposits of passenger air transportation taxes otherwise required to be made after Aug. 14, '97 and before Oct. 1, '97, are due Oct. 10, '97 ('97 Act §1031(g)(1)), and

(2) deposits of passenger air transportation taxes otherwise due after Aug. 14, '98 and before Oct. 1, '98, are due Oct. 5, '98. ('97 Act §1031(g)(2))

(3) deposits of property air transportation taxes otherwise due after Jul. 31, '98 and before Oct. 1, '98, are due Oct. 5, '98. ('97 Act §1031(g)(3))

☐ **Effective:** Except as otherwise provided below: for amounts paid after Sept. 30, '97 ('97 Act §1031(e)(2)(B)) for transportation beginning after Sept. 30, '97, ('97 Act §1031(e)(2)(A))

However, the above changes to Code Sec. 4263(c), to the extent related to the international air passenger transportation taxes as modified by the '97 Act (¶ 2203), apply to amounts paid after Aug. 12, '97, for transportation beginning after Sept. 30, '97. ('97 Act §1031(e)(2)(B)(ii))

¶ 2205. Exemption from air transportation of persons tax for fixed-wing aircraft used for emergency medical services applied retroactively to aviation fuel taxes; definition of fixed-wing aircraft is modified

Code Sec. 4041(l), as amended by '97 Act § 1601(f)(4)(A)(i)
Code Sec. 4261(f), as amended by '97 Act § 1601(f)(4)(D)
Generally effective: Aug. 27, '96

The Small Business Job Protection Act of '96 ("the '96 Act") expanded an exemption from the excise tax on air transportation of persons for transportation on helicopters for purposes of providing emergency medical services to also apply to transportation for such purposes on fixed-wing aircraft equipped for and exclusively dedicated to acute care emergency medical services. The excise taxes on noncommercial aviation fuel imposed on producers or importers, or alternatively, retailers provide for an exemption from tax for fuel used in helicopters that are used for the purposes described under the air-transportation-of-persons tax exemption provisions. The '96 Act, however, did not also modify the aviation fuel tax exemptions to apply to the above described fixed-wing aircraft. (FTC 2d ¶ W-1617, ¶ W-1728, ¶ W-5141; USTR ¶ 40,414.09, ¶ 40,914, ¶ 42,614.02)

New Law. The '97 Act retroactively corrects the aviation fuel tax rules to exempt from tax noncommercial aviation fuel sold for use, or used in, a helicopter or fixed-wing aircraft that meets the requirements for exemption from the air-transportation-of-persons tax. (Code Sec. 4041(l) as amended by '97 Act §1601(f)(4)(A)(i))

Further, the '97 Act retroactively modifies the above-mentioned fixed-wing aircraft exemption to the air-transportation-of-persons tax so that it applies with respect to a fixed-wing aircraft that is equipped for and exclusively dedicated *on that flight* to acute care emergency medical services. (Code Sec. 4261(f) as amended by '97 Act §1601(f)(4)(D))

> *observation:* Because, as described above, the aviation fuel tax exemptions apply if the air-transportation-of-persons tax exemption requirements are met, this change to the description of a qualifying fixed-wing aircraft also applies for purposes of those exemptions.

> *observation:* Neither the '96 Act nor the '97 Act amended the retail fuel tax refund provision under Code Sec. 6427(d). That provision continues to refer only to helicopters used for emergency medical services (see FTC 2d ¶ W-1738; USTR ¶ 64,274). Thus, persons who, after Aug. 26, '96 (see below), purchased noncommercial aviation fuel for use in a fixed-wing aircraft as de-

FTC 2d References are to Federal Tax Coordinator 2d
FIN References are to RIA's Analysis of Federal Taxes: Income
USTR References are to United States Tax Reporter: Income, Estate & Gift, and Excise
PCA References are to Pension Coordinator and Pension & Benefits Expert/Advisor
PE References are to Pension and Profit Sharing 2nd
EP References are to Estate Planning & Taxation Coordinator and Estate Planning Advisor

 Research Institute of America 503

scribed above on which the retail tax was imposed cannot obtain a refund of that tax. However, if the producers/importers fuel tax, rather than the retail tax, was imposed on such fuel, a refund or credit may be claimed under Code Sec. 6427(l) since that provision applies if producers/importers tax is paid on fuel used for a "nontaxable use," which is defined for this purpose as a use exempt from the retail tax (see FTC 2d ¶ W-1641; USTR ¶ 64,274).

☐ **Effective:** Aug. 27, '96. ('97 Act §1601(j)(1))

¶ 2206. Skydiving flights are exempted from air transportation taxes; fuel used in such flights taxed as fuel used in noncommercial aviation

Code Sec. 4261(h), as amended by '97 Act § 1435(a)
Code Sec. 4041(c)(2), as amended by '97 Act § 1435(b)
Generally effective: Oct. 1, '97
Committee Reports, see ¶ 5293

Air transportation taxes are imposed on domestic air passenger fares, international departures, and domestic freight waybills. These taxes apply to commercial transportation, i.e., they apply to transportation for hire. Small aircraft operating on nonestablished lines and affiliated group-owned and used aircraft are specifically exempted from these taxes (see FTC 2d ¶ W-5138 and W-5142; USTR ¶ 42,814.01 and 42,814.02). Where an air transportation tax isn't imposed, the transportation is treated as "noncommercial aviation" and an excise tax on the aviation fuel used in the aircraft applies instead (see FTC 2d ¶ W-1717; USTR ¶ 40,414).

Under pre-'97 Act law, it wasn't clear whether skydiving flights were commercial or noncommercial, and thus which tax applied. In general, such flights were treated as commercial unless instruction was offered. However, many skydiving flights provide instruction to some passengers and not to others. (Com Rept, see ¶ 5293)

New Law. The '97 Act exempts air transportation exclusively for the purpose of skydiving from the air transportation taxes (Code Sec. 4261(h) as amended by '97 Act §1435(a)), whether or not instruction is offered to any of the passengers. (Com Rept, see ¶ 5293) The '97 Act also makes use of an aircraft for such purposes noncommercial aviation for purposes of the fuel tax rules. (Code Sec. 4041(c)(2))

⊘ *observation:* As a result of the '97 Act changes, air transportation exclusively for skydiving is exempt from air transportation tax, but the fuel used in such aircraft is subject to fuel excise tax.

☐ **Effective:** For the exemption from air transportation tax: amounts paid after Sept. 30, '97. ('97 Act §1435(c)(1)) For change to fuel tax rules: Oct. 1, '97. ('97 Act §1435(c)(2))

¶ 2207. Prepaid telephone cards and similar arrangements are subject to communications excise tax

Code Sec. 4251(d), as amended by '97 Act § 1034(a)
Generally effective: Amounts paid in calendar months beginning more than 60 days after Aug. 5, '97
Committee Reports, see ¶ 5132

A 3% excise tax is imposed on amounts paid for communications services, i.e., local telephone, toll (long-distance) telephone and teletypewriter exchange services. The communications service provider collects the tax from the consumer and pays it over to IRS. The tax is imposed on the "amounts paid" for the communications service. (FTC 2d ¶ W-5001; USTR ¶ 42,514) Pre-'97 Act law didn't include a rule for determining the amount paid for phone services acquired by means of a prepaid phone card. Also, there was no rule for determining the time at which that amount was treated as paid.

New Law. The '97 Act adds rules for the application of the communications excise tax to communications services acquired by means of a "prepaid telephone card." A prepaid telephone card, for this purpose, is any card or other similar arrangement that permits its holder to obtain communications services and pay for those services in advance. (Code Sec. 4251(d)(3) as amended by '97 Act §1043(a))

Where communications services are acquired by means of a prepaid telephone card, the face amount of the card (Code Sec. 4251(d)(1)(A)), i.e., the retail value of the service provided by the use of the card or arrangement (Com Rept, see ¶ 5132), is treated as the amount paid for the communications services. That amount is treated as paid when the card is transferred by any telecommunications carrier to any person who is not a carrier. (Code Sec. 4251(d)(1)(B))

Thus, where a telecommunications carrier sells units of local or toll telephone service to a third party (not a carrier) who, in turn, resells or distributes the units to the ultimate customer in the form of prepaid telephone cards, the face amount of the cards is treated as an amount paid for taxable communication services at the time of the sale to the third party.

Under the above rule, the communications excise tax applies in the following cases:

... prepaid telephone cards offered through service stations, convenience stores and other businesses to their customers and others and

... amounts received by communications service providers by reason of joint venture credit cards or other marketing arrangements.

FTC 2d References are to Federal Tax Coordinator 2d
FIN References are to RIA's Analysis of Federal Taxes: Income
USTR References are to United States Tax Reporter: Income, Estate & Gift, and Excise
PCA References are to Pension Coordinator and Pension & Benefits Expert/Advisor
PE References are to Pension and Profit Sharing 2nd
EP References are to Estate Planning & Taxation Coordinator and Estate Planning Advisor

No inference is intended from the above rules as to the proper treatment under pre-'97 Act law of payments received by communications service providers for prepaid telephone cards or pursuant to joint venture credit card or other marketing arrangements. (Com Rept, see ¶ 5312)

> *observation:* It appears, based on the above Committee Report rules, that, for purposes of the prepaid telephone card rules, the terms "telecommunication carrier" and "communications service provider" are synonomous.

> *illustration (1):* A, a telephone carrier that owns telephone transmission and switching equipment and offers telephone service to the public, sells for $X a block of long-distance message units to B, a telephone carrier that doesn't own transmission or switching equipment and that acts as a reseller of long-distance telephone service. B resells for $Y all or part of the message units to C, a retail convenience store chain. C, in turn, resells some of the message units to its customers in the form of prepaid telephone cards and makes some message units available to employees as a benefit in the form of pre-paid telephone cards. The cards have a face amount (i.e., retail value) of $Z. The amount paid for communications services (i.e., the tax base) is $Z, and it is treated as paid when B sold the message units to C.

> *illustration (2):* If, in Illustration (1), C had purchased a block of message units directly from A for $X, the taxable amount would be treated as paid at the time of the sale to C. However, the taxable amount would still be $Z (the face amount of the cards).

"Unit" or "minute" cards. In the case of a "unit card" or "minute card," the final customer buys a card or account that allows the use of a certain number of units or minutes (rather than a dollar amount) of telephone service provided by an underlying telecommunications carrier. (Com Rept, see ¶ 5312) The "face amount" of a prepaid telephone card that doesn't entitle the user to a specified dollar amount of use will be determined under IRS regs. (Code Sec. 4251(d)(2)) It is intended that IRS use this regulatory authority to determine the retail value of the telephone service offered to a consumer. (Com Rept, see ¶ 5312)

Retail value based on FCC tariffs. Presently, the Federal Communications Commission generally requires telecommunications carriers to file tariffs listing the prices of units or minutes offered through prepaid telephone cards. In that case, the "amount paid" for a prepaid telephone card is the number of units or minutes on the card multiplied by their tariffed price at the time the card is sold by a telecommunications carrier to a person who isn't a carrier. While this value may not always correspond to the over-the-counter price paid by the final customer, using the tariffed price as the tax base is presently the best way to achieve neutral treatment of unit or minute cards and cards that offer a dollar amount of telephone service.

If no underlying tariff applies to a particular card, it is intended that tariffs for comparable telephone service be applied, if applicable. If, in the future, tariffs aren't generally filed for service offered via prepaid telephone cards, IRS is authorized to determine the appropriate retail value of the units or minutes of service offered on such cards. (Com Rept, see ¶ 5312)

Certain prepayments treated as deposits. Communications service providers may require prepayment from certain customers as assurance of payment for future services. If the customer is entitled to a full cash refund of the value of any unused services, this arrangement is a deposit, and not a payment that is subject to the above prepaid telephone card provisions. (Com Rept, see ¶ 5132)

> **☜** *observation:* Communications excise tax under the pre-'97 Act rules would presumably be imposed if and when such a deposit were converted into a payment, i.e., when the customer was no longer entitled to a refund.

☐ **Effective:** Amounts paid in calendar months beginning more than 60 days after Aug. 5, '97. ('97 Act §1034(b))

Fuel Taxes

¶ 2208. Diesel fuel removal-at-terminal excise tax rules generally made applicable to kerosene

Code Sec. 4081(a)(2)(A)(iii), as amended by '97 Act § 1032(b)
Code Sec. 4082, as amended by '97 Act § 1032(c)(1) and 1032(c)(2)
Code Sec. 4083(a), as amended by '97 Act § 1032(a)
Code Sec. 4083(b), as amended by '97 Act § 1032(e)(4)
Code Sec. 4101(e), as amended by '97 Act § 1032(d)
Code Sec. 6427(f), as amended by '97 Act § 1032(e)(7) and 1032(e)(8)
Code Sec. 6427(i)(3)(A), as amended by '97 Act § 1032(e)(9)
Code Sec. 6427(i)(5)(A)(i), as amended by '97 Act § 1032(c)(3)(E)
Code Sec. 6427(l), as amended by '97 Act § 1032(c)(3)
Code Sec. 6715(c)(1), as amended by '97 Act § 1032(e)(11)
Code Sec. 7232, as amended by '97 Act § 1032(e)(12)(A)
Generally effective: July 1, '98
Committee Reports, see ¶ 5130

Diesel fuel used as a transportation motor fuel is taxed at a rate of 24.4 cents per gallon (after Sept. 30, '97, see ¶ 2211) upon removal of the fuel from a terminal or pipeline, removal from a refinery, entry into the U.S. or sale to an unregistered person (the "removal-at-terminal tax"). Diesel fuel removed, etc., for use in producing a qualified alcohol mixture (10% alcohol-diesel fuel, which is also called "diesohol") is subject to a reduced removal-at-terminal tax rate. (FTC 2d ¶ W-1501.1, ¶ W-1522.1; USTR ¶ 40,814, ¶ 40,814.01)

FTC 2d References are to Federal Tax Coordinator 2d
FIN References are to RIA's Analysis of Federal Taxes: Income
USTR References are to United States Tax Reporter: Income, Estate & Gift, and Excise
PCA References are to Pension Coordinator and Pension & Benefits Expert/Advisor
PE References are to Pension and Profit Sharing 2nd
EP References are to Estate Planning & Taxation Coordinator and Estate Planning Advisor

Diesel fuel is exempt from removal-at-terminal tax if it (1) is destined for a nontaxable use (e.g., use for a non-highway purpose, on a farm, by a state or local government or as heating oil) and (2) is indelibly dyed as required by IRS. Use of diesel fuel in trains and intercity buses is nontaxable for purposes of the removal-at-terminal tax, but fuel so used is taxed, at reduced rates, at the retail level (see FTC 2d ¶ W-1707; USTR ¶ 40,414). (FTC 2d ¶ W-1515.2, ¶ W-1707.1; USTR ¶ 40,414.01, ¶ 40,824) IRS has the authority to issue, and has issued, regs requiring the conspicuous labeling of retail diesel fuel pumps and other delivery facilities so that it is clear which diesel fuel is available only for nontaxable uses. (FTC 2d ¶ W-1515.4; USTR ¶ 40,824)

Code Sec. 4101 provides that various persons that may be subject to the diesel fuel removal-at-terminal tax, e.g., terminal operators, are required to be registered with IRS. (See FTC 2d ¶ W-1527; USTR ¶ 41,014)

The exemptions or reduced rates described above can also be realized by credit or refund where undyed diesel fuel is taxed at the full rate but is later used in a nontaxable use or to produce an alcohol-fuel mixture. An accelerated refund procedure is available for certain alcohol-fuel mixture claims. The ultimate purchaser is generally the party who may claim a nontaxable-use refund or credit. However, a registered ultimate vendor, rather than the ultimate purchaser, claims the refund or credit for diesel fuel used on a farm or by a state or local government. The minimum refund amount that may be claimed by a registered vendor is $200, and the minimum period with respect to which a registered vendor can receive a refund is one week. (FTC 2d ¶ W-1564.2 *et seq.*, ¶ W-1564.3 *et seq.*, ¶ W-1565, ¶ W-1566; USTR ¶ 64,274, ¶ 64,274.01)

Kerosene is used as a transportation motor fuel and as an aviation fuel. It is also blended with diesel fuel destined for both taxable (highway) and nontaxable (heating oil) uses to, among other things, prevent the gelling of the diesel fuel in colder temperatures. Under pre-'97 Act law, kerosene was not subject to removal-at-terminal tax unless it was blended with diesel fuel. Kerosene sold for use as aviation fuel was taxed under the aviation fuel tax provisions—i.e., sale by a producer or importer, or, alternatively, a retailer, for use in noncommercial aviation was taxed at 21.8 cents per gallon, and sale by a producer or importer for use in commercial aviation, was taxed at 4.3 cents per gallon. Nontaxable uses of kerosene include use of kerosene as a feedstock in the petrochemical industry and use of clear low-sulphur kerosene (K-1) in space heaters. (FTC 2d ¶ W-1509, ¶ W-1601, ¶ W-1607, ¶ W-1625, ¶ W-1713; USTR ¶ 40,414, ¶ 40,814, ¶ 40,914)

New Law. The '97 Act adds kerosene to the list of "taxable fuels" subject to the removal-at-terminal tax (Code Sec. 4083(a) as amended by '97 Act §1032(a)) and imposes the same rate on its removal at the terminal, entry into the U.S., etc., as is imposed on diesel fuel—i.e., 24.4 cents per gallon. (Code Sec. 4081(a)(2)(A)(iii) as amended by '97 Act §1032(b)) (Code Sec. 4081(a)(2)(B)) (Code Sec. 4081(d)(3) as amended by '97 Act §1033) Use of kerosene, other than in the production of (a) fuel that is subject to removal-at-terminal tax or (b) special fuels (as defined in Code Sec. 4041(a)(2) (FTC 2d ¶ W-1712; USTR ¶ 40,414)), is treated as a removal. (Code Sec. 4083(b) as amended by '97 Act §1032(e)(4)) *observation:* The above-mentioned change in the definition of taxable fuels makes various diesel fuel removal-at-terminal tax rules applicable to kerosene. For example, the following rules discussed above apply to kerosene: the removal-at-terminal tax registration requirements under Code Sec. 4101; and the reduced rate rules for removals, etc., for use in producing qualified alcohol mixtures. Thus, for example, a 10% alcohol-kerosene mixture is a qualified alcohol mixture, and kerosene removed, etc., for use in producing such a mixture is subject to the same reduced rate as applies to removals, etc., of diesel fuel for use in producing diesohol.

Exemptions; aviation-grade and feedstock kerosene exempted from dyeing requirements. The '97 Act provides that all of the diesel fuel nontaxable use exemption rules and IRS's authority to require retail pump and delivery facility labeling apply to kerosene. (Code Sec. 4082 as amended by '97 Act §1032(c)(1))

However, whereas all diesel fuel must be dyed to qualify for exemption, the '97 Act exempts from the dyeing requirements:

. . . aviation-grade kerosene (as determined under regs to be prescribed by IRS) removed, entered or sold, if the person receiving the kerosene is a registered aviation fuel producer (Code Sec. 4082(d)(1) as amended by '97 Act §1032(c)(2))

observation: Although aviation-grade kerosene is exempt from the removal-at-terminal tax, other changes made by the '97 Act clarify that the pre-'97 Act rules under which kerosene sold for use as aviation fuel was taxed under the aviation fuel tax provisions (see above) continue to apply to such kerosene.

. . . kerosene that is: (Code Sec. 4082(d)(2) as amended by '97 Act §1032(c)(2))

(1) received by pipeline or vessel for use by the receiver in the manufacture or production of any substance other than gasoline, diesel fuel or special fuels referred to under the retail fuel tax rules (Code Sec. 4082(d)(2)(A)); or

(2) to the extent provided in regulations, removed or entered for such use by the person removing or entering the kerosene, or for resale for such use by the purchaser (Code Sec. 4082(d)(2)(B)), where the person receiving, removing or entering the kerosene and the purchaser (if any) are registered with IRS for purposes of the removal-at-terminal tax. (Code Sec. 4082(d)(2))

Thus, feedstock kerosene that a registered industrial user receives by pipeline or vessel is exempt from dyeing requirements, as is other feedstock kerosene to the extent and under the conditions (including satisfaction of registration and certification requirements) IRS prescribes. (Com Rept, see ¶ 5130)

FTC 2d References are to Federal Tax Coordinator 2d
FIN References are to RIA's Analysis of Federal Taxes: Income
USTR References are to United States Tax Reporter: Income, Estate & Gift, and Excise
PCA References are to Pension Coordinator and Pension & Benefits Expert/Advisor
PE References are to Pension and Profit Sharing 2nd
EP References are to Estate Planning & Taxation Coordinator and Estate Planning Advisor

. . . to the extent provided in regulations, removal, entry, or sale of kerosene to a wholesale distributor of kerosene, if the distributor: (Code Sec. 4082(d)(3) as amended by '97 Act §1032(c)(2))

(a) is registered with IRS under Code Sec. 4101 with respect to the removal-at-terminal tax on kerosene, and (Code Sec. 4082(d)(3)(A))

(b) sells kerosene exclusively to registered ultimate vendors (retailers) (i) for any use if the vendor's sale is from a pump which (as determined under regulations prescribed by IRS) is not suitable for use in fueling any diesel-powered highway vehicle or train, or (ii) to the extent provided by IRS, for blending with heating oil to be used during extreme or unseasonable cold. (Code Sec. 4082(d)(3)(B))

Refunds and credits. Except as otherwise provided below, the nontaxable use refund and credit provisions that apply for diesel fuel are also made applicable to kerosene, including the rules for registered ultimate vendor refund claims for sales of fuel for use on a farm or by a state or local government. (Code Sec. 6427(l) as amended by '97 Act §1042(c)(3)(A)) The exception provides that, for kerosene, the minimum refund permitted to be claimed by a registered ultimate vendor is reduced to $100. (Code Sec. 6427(i)(5)(A) as amended by '97 Act §1032(c)(3)(E))

In addition, under the '97 Act, the registered ultimate vendor of kerosene, rather than the purchaser, is required to claim any refund (Code Sec. 6427(l)(5) as amended by '97 Act §1042(c)(3)(A) and 1042(c)(3)(C)) with respect to kerosene sold by the vendor (a) for any use if the sale is from a pump which (as determined under regulations prescribed by IRS) is not suitable for use in fueling any diesel-powered highway vehicle or train, or (b) to the extent provided by IRS, for blending with heating oil to be used during extreme or unseasonable cold. (Code Sec. 6427(l)(5)(B) as amended by '97 Act §1042(c)(3)(B)) This refund procedure is intended to accommodate state safety regulations that require the use of clear (K-1) kerosene in certain space heaters. (Com Rept, see ¶ 5130)

The '97 Act also provides that the pre-'97 Act alcohol-fuel mixture refund/credit, including the accelerated refund procedure (Code Sec. 6427(i)(3)(A) as amended by '97 Act §1042(e)(9)), is also available with respect to kerosene taxed at the regular removal-at-terminal tax rate that is later used to produce a qualifying alcohol-fuel mixture. (Code Sec. 6427(f)(1) as amended by '97 Act §1042(e)(7)) The refund equals the difference between the regular removal-at-terminal tax rate imposed on the kerosene and the reduced tax rate for kerosene sold for use in producing a qualified alcohol-fuel mixture. (Code Sec. 6427(f)(1)) (Code Sec. 6427(f)(2) as amended by '97 Act §1042(e)(8))

New requirement in order that a facility be allowed to store nontaxed fuel. The '97 Act provides that, except as provided below, a terminal for kerosene or diesel fuel may not be an approved facility for storage of non-tax-paid diesel fuel or kerosene unless the terminal operator offers dyed diesel fuel and kerosene for removal for nontaxable use, in accordance with the dyeing and marking requirements of Code Sec. 4082(a). (Code Sec. 4101(e)(1) as amended by '97 Act §1032(d)) That is, registration as a terminal facility eligible to handle non-tax-paid diesel fuel and kerosene is conditional on the facility offering its customers dyeing for nontaxable sales of diesel fuel and kerosene. (Com Rept, see ¶ 5130) However, this rule doesn't apply to any terminal exclusively providing aviation-grade kerosene by pipeline to an airport. (Code Sec. 4101(e)(2))

Penalties. The '97 Act makes the following penalties applicable with respect to kerosene:

. . . the civil penalty for the sale or use of dyed fuel for a taxable use (see FTC 2d ¶ V-2723; USTR ¶ 67,154) (Code Sec. 6715(c)(1) as amended by '97 Act §1042(e)(11)); and

. . . the criminal penalty for failure to register for fuel tax purposes, falsely representing that one is registered, or willfully making a false statement on the registration application (see FTC 2d ¶ V-3503). (Code Sec. 7232 as amended by '97 Act §1042(e)(12)(A))

Related taxes. For discussion of the '97 Act floor stocks tax on kerosene held on July 1, '98, see ¶ 2209.

For discussion of the '97 Act reimposition of the 0.1 cent per gallon Leaking Underground Storage Trust Fund Financing tax on most fuels used for highway transportation, see ¶ 2211.

☐ **Effective:** July 1, '98 ('97 Act §1042(f)), i.e., for kerosene removed from facilities after June 30, '98. (Com Rept, see ¶ 5130)

¶ 2209. Floor stocks tax imposed on kerosene held on July 1, '98

Code Sec. None, '97 Act § 1032(g)
Generally effective: July 1, '98
Committee Reports, see ¶ 5130

The '97 Act imposes a floor stocks tax of 24.4 cents per gallon on kerosene held by any person on July 1, '98 ('97 Act §1032(g)(1)), except that no floor stocks tax is imposed on kerosene to the extent that the Code Sec. 4081 removal-at-terminal tax on motor transportation fuels or the Code Sec. 4091 producers importers tax on aviation fuel has been or will be imposed. ('97 Act §1032(g)(7))

Liability for tax. The person holding the kerosene on July 1, '98, is liable for the tax. ('97 Act §1032(g)(2)(A)) Kerosene is considered to be "held by a person" if title to the kerosene has passed to that person (whether or not delivery to the person has been made). ('97 Act §1032(g)(3)(A))

FTC 2d References are to Federal Tax Coordinator 2d
FIN References are to RIA's Analysis of Federal Taxes: Income
USTR References are to United States Tax Reporter: Income, Estate & Gift, and Excise
PCA References are to Pension Coordinator and Pension & Benefits Expert/Advisor
PE References are to Pension and Profit Sharing 2nd
EP References are to Estate Planning & Taxation Coordinator and Estate Planning Advisor

Payment of tax. The floor stocks tax must be paid on or before Aug. 31, '98 ('97 Act §1032(g)(2)(C)), in the manner prescribed by IRS. ('97 Act §1032(g)(2)(B))

Exceptions to tax. *Fuel held for an exempt use.* The floor stocks tax doesn't apply to kerosene held by any person exclusively for any use to the extent a credit or refund of the Code Sec. 4081 removal-at-terminal tax is allowable for such use. ('97 Act §1032(g)(4))

Fuel held in vehicle tank. The floor stocks tax also doesn't apply to kerosene held in the tank of a motor vehicle or motorboat. ('97 Act §1032(g)(5))

No more than 2,000 gallons of fuel held. In addition, the tax isn't imposed on kerosene held by any person, if the aggregate amount of kerosene held on July 1, '98 by that person doesn't exceed 2,000 gallons. This exception will only apply if the person submits to IRS (at the time and in the manner required by IRS) information IRS requests. ('97 Act §1032(g)(6)(A)) Kerosene held by any person which is exempt from the floor stocks tax by reason of the exempt use of the fuel or the fact that the fuel is held in a vehicle's tank is not taken into account in determining whether a person holds more than 2,000 gallons of fuel. ('97 Act §1032(g)(6)(B))

All persons treated as a controlled group are treated as one person. ('97 Act §1032(g)(6)(C)(i)(I)) The term "controlled group" has the meaning given to that term in Code Sec. 1563(a) (relating to the definition of controlled group for purposes of the limitations on the tax benefits of the members of the group (FTC 2d/FIN ¶ E-10700 et seq.; USTR ¶ 15,634)), except that the phrase "more than 50 percent" is substituted for the phrase "at least 80 percent" each place that the latter appears. ('97 Act §1032(g)(6)(C)(i)(II)) Under regulations to be issued by IRS, principles similar to the controlled group rules for corporations will apply to a group of persons under common control where one or more of those persons isn't a corporation. ('97 Act §1032(g)(6)(C)(ii))

Applicability of removal-at-terminal, etc., tax rules. All provisions of law, including penalties, that are applicable with respect to the removal-at-terminal, etc., tax imposed by Code Sec. 4081 are, to the extent applicable and not inconsistent with the floor stocks tax provisions discussed above, applicable to the floor stock tax. Those provisions apply to the same extent as if the floor stocks tax were imposed by Code Sec. 4081. ('97 Act §1032(g)(8))

☐ **Effective:** July 1, '98. ('97 Act §1032(f))

¶ 2210. Suspended excise tax on diesel fuel used in recreational motorboats is repealed

Code Sec. 4041(a)(1)(A), as amended by '97 Act § 902(b)(1)
Code Sec. 4083(a)(3), as amended by '97 Act § 902(b)(3)
Code Sec. 6421(e)(2)(B), as amended by '97 Act § 902(a)
Generally effective: Jan. 1, '98
Committee Reports, see ¶ 5052

Before enactment of the Small Business Job Protection Act of '96 ("the '96 Act"), there was a 24.4 cents per gallon excise tax on diesel fuel sold for use or used in a motorboat; the tax was imposed either on removal of the fuel at the terminal or at the retail level. (FTC 2d ¶ W-1515.1, ¶ W-1707; USTR ¶ 40,414, ¶ 40,814) There was an exemption from this tax for diesel fuel that was dyed in accordance with IRS regulations and that was used in any trade or business, except where the boat was used predominantly in an entertainment, amusement or recreational activity. (FTC 2d ¶ W-1551, ¶ W-1724; USTR ¶ 40,414, ¶ 64,204.2)

Many marinas found it uneconomical to carry both undyed (taxed) and dyed (untaxed) diesel fuel because the majority of their market was for non-taxed uses. Thus, some recreational boaters experienced difficulty finding fuel. Because of this, Congress, as part of the '96 Act, suspended the tax through Dec. 31, '97.

New Law. Congress has concluded that it cannot find an alternative method for collecting the retail tax on diesel fuel used in a recreational motorboat. It therefore concluded that the competing needs for boat fuel availability and preservation of the integrity of the diesel fuel compliance structure were best served by repealing the tax. (Com Rept, see ¶ 5052) So, the '97 Act repeals both the retail (Code Sec. 4041(a)(1)(A) as amended by '97 Act §902(b)(1)) and removal-at-terminal taxes on diesel fuel used in motorboats. (Code Sec. 4083(a)(3) as amended by '97 Act §902(b)(3))

The Act also deletes the above-described pre-'97 Act exemption for trade or business use. (Code Sec. 6421(e)(2)(B) as amended by '97 Act §902(a))

observation: Because the taxes on motorboats have been repealed, the exemption is no longer needed.

observation: Under both pre-'97 Act law and after enactment of the '97 Act, where tax-paid diesel fuel is later used for a nontaxable use, a refund is allowed to the ultimate purchaser (see FTC 2d ¶s W-1564.2, W-1739.1; USTR ¶ 64,274). Thus, as a result of the above '97 Act changes, diesel fuel used as motorboat fuel is a nontaxable use and where tax is imposed on diesel fuel and such fuel is later used as fuel in a motorboat, a refund will be available.

☐ **Effective:** Jan. 1, '98. ('97 Act §902(c))

¶ 2211. Leaking underground storage tank trust fund financing tax reimposed

Code Sec. 4081(d)(3), as amended by '97 Act § 1033
Generally effective: Oct. 1, '97
Committee Reports, see ¶ 5131

Before Jan. 1, '96, an excise tax of 0.1 cent per gallon was imposed, in addition to various other excise fuel taxes, on gasoline, diesel fuel, special motor fuels other than liquefied petroleum gas, aviation fuels, and inland waterway fuels. The revenue from the tax was paid into the Leaking Underground Storage Tax Trust Fund to finance cleanups of leaking underground storage tanks. (FTC 2d ¶ W-1501, ¶ W-1501.1, ¶ W-1607, ¶ W-1707, ¶ W-1711, ¶ W-1713, ¶ W-1720, ¶ W-3201; USTR ¶ 40,414, ¶ 40,424, ¶ 40,814, ¶ 40,914)

New Law. The 0.1 cent tax is reimposed for the period Oct. 1, '97 through Mar. 31, 2005. (Code Sec. 4081(d)(3) as amended by '97 Act §1033)

☐ **Effective:** Oct. 1, '97. ('97 Act §1033)

¶ 2212. Tax rates on propane, liquefied natural gas and methanol produced from natural gas decreased

Code Sec. 4041(a)(2), as amended by '97 Act § 907(a)(1)
Code Sec. 4041(d)(1), as amended by '97 Act § 907(a)(2)
Code Sec. 4041(m)(1)(A)(i), as amended by '97 Act § 907(b)
Generally effective: Oct. 1, '97
Committee Reports, see ¶ 5057

An excise tax is imposed on the retail sale of special motor fuels used in highway transportation. These special motor fuels include liquefied petroleum gas ("propane"), liquefied natural gas ("LNG") and methanol fuel produced from natural gas. The tax on special motor fuels was generally imposed at the same rate as the tax on gasoline upon its removal at the terminal: 18.3 cents per gallon through Sept. 30, '99, and 4.3 cents thereafter. (FTC 2d ¶ W-1501; USTR ¶ 40,814) However, reduced rates applied for certain fuels. Methanol from natural gas was taxed at 11.3 cents per gallon through Sept. 30, '99, and at 4.3 cents rate thereafter. A large portion of the revenue from these taxes finances federal highway programs through the Highway Trust Fund. (FTC 2d ¶ W-1711, ¶ W-1726; USTR ¶ 40,414)

New Law. The '97 Act decreases the rates of tax imposed on propane, LNG and methanol from natural gas, as follows:

. . . Propane is taxed at 13.6 cents per gallon (Code Sec. 4041(a)(2)(B)(ii) as amended by '97 Act §907(a)(1)) through Sept. 30, '99, and at 3.2 cents per gallon thereafter. (Code Sec. 4041(a)(2)(B))

. . . LNG is taxed at 11.9 cents per gallon (Code Sec. 4041(a)(2)(B)(iii)) through Sept. 30, '99, and at 2.8 cents per gallon thereafter. (Code Sec. 4041(a)(2)(B))

. . . Methanol from natural gas is taxed at 9.15 cents per gallon after Sept. 30, '97 through Sept. 30, '99 (Code Sec. 4041(m)(1)(A)(i)(I) as amended by '97 Act §907(b)), and at 2.15 cents per gallon thereafter. (Code Sec. 4041(m)(1)(A)(ii)(I))

    🖋 *observation:* Another '97 Act provision (see ¶ 2211) reimposes the 0.1 cent per gallon Leaking Underground Storage Trust Fund Financing tax on most fuels used for highway transportation—including special motor fuels. This tax applies in addition to other excise taxes imposed on the applicable fuels.

The '97 Act also excepts liquefied natural gas from the 0.1 cent-per-gallon Leaking Underground Storage Trust Fund Financing tax. (Code Sec. 4041(d)(1) as amended by '97 Act §907(a)(2))

The decreases in tax rates on these fuels reflect the respective energy equivalence of the fuels to gasoline. Consumers must purchase more gallons of these lower-energy-content fuels than of gasoline in order to travel a given distance. Thus, the rate decreases will cause highway users of these fuels to be taxed in relation with their use of the federal highway system. (Com Rept, see ¶ 5057)

☐ **Effective:** Oct. 1, '97. ('97 Act §907(c))

¶ 2213. Period for claiming refund for gasoline or diesel fuel used to produce alcohol fuel for period Sept. 30, '95 through Oct. 1, '96 is extended

Code Sec. None, '97 Act § 1601(g)(1)
Generally effective: Jan. 1, '94

Where gasoline or diesel fuel that was taxed at the regular removal-at-terminal excise tax rate is used to produce a qualified fuel-alcohol mixture (gasohol or diesohol) which is sold or used in the blender's trade or business, an "accelerated" refund, equal to the difference between the regular tax rate imposed and the reduced rate applicable for gasoline or diesel fuel used to produce gasohol or diesohol is available to blenders who meet certain requirements. One of those requirements is that the blender file a refund claim on or before the last day of the first quarter following the earliest quarter included in the claim.

The alcohol fuel refund provisions had expired on Oct. 1, '95, but were retroactively extended by the Small Business Job Protection Act of '96. However, because that Act wasn't enacted until Aug. 20, '96, the above "on or before last day of the quarter following..." rule prevented blenders from getting accelerated refunds with respect to sales or uses of mixtures occurring after Sept. 30, '95 and before Apr. 1, '96. (FTC 2d ¶ W-1566; USTR ¶ 64,274.01)

New Law. The '97 Act provides that, notwithstanding the above "on or before last day of the quarter following..." rule, an alcohol fuel mixture refund claim for any period after Sept. 30, '95 and before Oct. 1, '96, will be treated as timely filed if it is filed before the 60th day after Aug. 5, '97. ('97 Act §1601(g)(1))

☐ **Effective:** Jan. 1, '94. ('97 Act §1601(j))

FTC 2d References are to Federal Tax Coordinator 2d
FIN References are to RIA's Analysis of Federal Taxes: Income
USTR References are to United States Tax Reporter: Income, Estate & Gift, and Excise
PCA References are to Pension Coordinator and Pension & Benefits Expert/Advisor
PE References are to Pension and Profit Sharing 2nd
EP References are to Estate Planning & Taxation Coordinator and Estate Planning Advisor

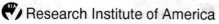

¶ 2214. Multiple-outlet gasoline retailers may claim gasoline tax refunds

Code Sec. 6416(a)(4)(B), as amended by '97 Act § 905(a)
Generally effective: Sales after Aug. 5, '97
Committee Reports, see ¶ 5055

Tax on gasoline removed from a terminal facility or registered pipeline (the "removal-at-terminal tax") is paid upon its removal by the "position holder" of the gasoline (generally, the owner of the gasoline when it is removed). (FTC 2d ¶ W-1510; USTR ¶ 40,814) This tax is passed on to gasoline users by inclusion in the price they pay for gasoline. However, some uses of gasoline are tax-exempt (e.g., exclusive use by a state or local government). Where gasoline is sold at a tax-included price to any person for an exempt use, the Code provides for a credit or refund of the tax. Where a wholesale distributor purchases gasoline at a tax-included price and sells it at a tax-excluded price directly to a user who uses it for an exempt purpose, the wholesale distributor is the party who is owed the credit or refund. Under pre-'97 Act law, the term "wholesale distributor" didn't include retailers. (FTC 2d ¶ W-1564; USTR ¶ 64,164)

New Law. The '97 Act expands the definition of a "wholesale distributor" who can claim a gasoline removal-at-terminal tax refund to include any person who makes retail sales of gasoline at 10 or more retail motor fuel outlets. (Code Sec. 6416(a)(4)(B) as amended by '97 Act §905(a))

The '97 Act adapts the law to current market conditions, in which state and local governments increasingly purchase gasoline for their fleets by credit card from retail outlets. In the past, they had purchased gasoline through bulk deliveries by wholesalers to tanks that supplied private pumps at government installations. (Com Rept, see ¶ 5055)

As a result of this change, "wholesale distributor" has the same definition as it had before '87, when the excise tax on gasoline was collected at the wholesale distribution level rather than upon removal from a terminal facility. (Com Rept, see ¶ 5055)

☐ **Effective:** Sales after Aug. 5, '97. ('97 Act §905(b))

¶ 2215. Registered aviation fuel producers who buy and resell tax-paid fuel are allowed a refund to prevent double taxation

Code Sec. 4091(d), as amended by '97 Act § 1436(a)
Code Sec. 6416(d), as amended by '97 Act § 1436(b)
Generally effective: Fuel acquired by the producer after Sept. 30, '97
Committee Reports, see ¶ 5294

An excise tax is imposed on the sale of aviation fuel by an aviation fuel producer (the "producers/importers tax"). A producer for this purpose is defined to include a wholesale distributor. Sales by one producer to another, however, are exempt from tax if both producers are registered with IRS. (FTC 2d ¶s W-1601 *et seq.*, W-1615; USTR

¶ 40,914)

Fuel sold at many rural airports is sold by retail dealers who do not qualify as wholesale distributors. These retailers purchase the fuel at a tax-included price. In certain instances, fuel that is purchased tax-paid by a retailer is resold to a producer, e.g., to enable the producer to serve one of its customers at the airport. When the producer resells such fuel, the fuel is taxed a second time. Under pre-'97 Act law, the Code contained no provision for refunding the first tax in these circumstances. (Com Rept, see ¶ 5294)

Where payments of a Chapter 32 excise tax—including the producers/importers tax—are treated as overpayments of tax, excise tax refunds, or credits against Chapter 32 excise taxes due on a later return, are available. To claim such a refund or credit of producers/importers tax, the person who paid the tax must prove that he (a) hasn't included that tax in the price at which he resells the fuel and hasn't otherwise collected the tax from the purchaser, (b) has repaid the tax to the ultimate purchaser, or (c) has filed with IRS a consent from the purchaser of the fuel from him that allows him to take the credit or claim the refund. (FTC 2d ¶ W-2416, ¶ W-2417; USTR ¶ 40,914, ¶ 64,164)

New Law. The '97 Act provides that where

(1) an aviation fuel producer is registered with IRS, and (Code Sec. 4091(d)(1) as amended by '97 Act §1436)

(2) the producer establishes to IRS's satisfaction that a prior tax was paid (and not credited or refunded) on aviation fuel held by the producer (Code Sec. 4091(d)(2)),

than an amount equal to the tax so paid will be allowed as a refund (without interest) to that producer in the same manner as if it were an overpayment of producers/importers tax. (Code Sec. 4091(d))

That is, a refund is permitted for tax previously paid on aviation fuel when a producer acquires the fuel, resells it, and pays tax on the second sale. (Com Rept, see ¶ 5294)

However, the '97 Act does not permit a credit against Chapter 32 excise taxes due on a later return to be taken in lieu of the refund described above. (Code Sec. 6416(d) as amended by '97 Act §1436(b))

☐ **Effective:** Fuel acquired by the producer after Sept. 30, '97. ('97 Act §1436(c))

¶ 2216. Exemption from floor stocks tax on aviation fuel held on Aug. 27, '96 is retroactively expanded

Code Sec. None, '97 Act § 1601(f)(4)(F)
Generally effective: Aug. 27, '96

FTC 2d References are to Federal Tax Coordinator 2d
FIN References are to RIA's Analysis of Federal Taxes: Income
USTR References are to United States Tax Reporter: Income, Estate & Gift, and Excise
PCA References are to Pension Coordinator and Pension & Benefits Expert/Advisor
PE References are to Pension and Profit Sharing 2nd
EP References are to Estate Planning & Taxation Coordinator and Estate Planning Advisor

The Small Business Job Protection Act of '96 ("the '96 Act") imposed a 17.5 cents per gallon tax on aviation fuel floor stocks held on Aug. 27, '96. The '96 Act provided an exemption from this tax for fuel held exclusively for a use for which a full refund or credit of producers/importers aviation fuel tax (currently imposed at a 21.8 cent per gallon rate) could be claimed if the fuel were bought for such use after Aug. 26, '96. Producers/importers tax imposed on aviation fuel sold for use, or used, in commercial aviation (other than as supplies for vessels or aircraft) is refundable, but only for the amount of any tax imposed in excess of 4.3 cents per gallon. Therefore, such "partially taxable" fuel couldn't qualify for this exemption from floor stocks tax. (FTC 2d ¶ W-1647.06; USTR ¶ 40,914)

New Law. The '97 Act expands the floor stocks tax exemption to make it also apply to fuel held exclusively for the partially taxable commercial aviation fuel use described above. ('96 Act § 1609(h)(4) as amended by '97 Act § 1601(f)(4)(F))

> *recommendation:* The floor stocks tax had to be paid by Mar. 1, '97, and the aviation fuel's title holder on Aug. 27, '96 was liable for that tax. Any person who paid the floor stocks tax on above-described commercial aviation fuel should file a claim for refund with IRS. Excise tax refund claims are filed on Form 8849, unless the person is otherwise required to file a Form 720 excise tax return, in which case a refund may be claimed on that form.

☐ **Effective:** Aug. 27, '96. ('97 Act §1601(j)(1))

¶ 2217. Deposit due dates for certain fuel excise taxes delayed

Code Sec. 6302, '97 Act § 901(e) and 1031(g)(3)
Generally effective: July 31, '98
Committee Reports, see ¶ 5051

Generally, the excise taxes imposed for a semimonthly period on: (1) the removal at the terminal, refinery, etc, of gasoline, aviation gasoline, diesel fuel, and (after June 30, '98, see ¶ 2208) kerosene, (2) a producer's or importer's sale or use of aviation fuels, and (3) the retail sale or use of diesel fuel, special motor fuels, noncommercial aviation fuel or compressed natural gas, must be deposited with IRS by the 9th day following the semimonthly period ("9-day rule" deposits). (FTC 2d ¶ S-5711.0; USTR ¶ 63,014)   Certain "qualified persons," however, are permitted to deposit removal-at-terminal taxes by electronic funds transfer, by the 14th day after the semimonthly period ("14-day rule" deposits). (FTC 2d ¶ S-5722; USTR ¶ 63,014)   In addition, special accelerated deposit due dates apply for 9-day rule and 14-day-rule deposits for taxes imposed for certain periods in Sept. (FTC 2d ¶ S-5711.1, ¶ S-5722.1; USTR ¶ 63,014)

New Law. The '97 Act provides that deposits of the fuel taxes described above that are otherwise required to be made after July 31, '98 and before Oct. 1, '98, are due on Oct. 5, '98. ('97 Act §901(e)) ('97 Act §1031(g)(3))

☐ **Effective:** July 31, '98. ('97 Act §901(e)) ('97 Act §1031(g)(3))

Retail Taxes on Luxury Vehicles and Heavy Trucks

¶ 2218. Purchase price triggering imposition of luxury excise tax is increased for electric and other clean-burning fuel vehicles

Code Sec. 4001(a), as amended by '97 Act § 906(a)
Code Sec. 4001(e)(1), as amended by '97 Act § 906(b)(1)
Code Sec. 4003(a)(1)(A), as amended by '97 Act § 906(b)(3)
Code Sec. 4003(a)(2)(B), as amended by '97 Act § 906(b)(4)
Generally effective: For sales and installations occurring after Aug. 5, '97
Committee Reports, see ¶ 5056

The luxury excise tax is imposed on the amount by which the sale price of an automobile exceeds a threshold amount of $30,000 plus an inflation adjustment. For '97, this threshold amount is $36,000. Amounts paid for vehicle parts and accessories installed within six months of a vehicle's purchase are taxed where the sum of the original purchase price and the separate purchases exceeds the threshold amount. However, any tax on the separate installation of parts and accessories is limited to an amount equal to the applicable luxury tax rate (see ¶ 2219), multiplied by an amount equal to (I) the sum of (a) the price of such parts and accessories and their installation, (b) the aggregate price of earlier installed parts and accessories and their installation, and (c) the price paid for the vehicle, minus (II) the appropriate applicable threshold amount for that vehicle. (FTC 2d ¶ W-2971, ¶ W-2972, ¶ W-2980; USTR ¶ 40,014, ¶ 40,034)

New Law. The '97 Act provides that the threshold amount for a "purpose built passenger vehicle" is 150% of $30,000 (Code Sec. 4001(a)(2)(C)(i) as amended by '97 Act §906(a)), increased by an annual inflation adjustment. (Code Sec. 4001(e)(1) as amended by '97 Act §906(b)(1)) A purpose built passenger vehicle is a passenger vehicle produced by an original equipment manufacturer and designed so that it may be propelled primarily by electricity. (Code Sec. 4001(a)(2)(C)(ii))

The '97 Act also provides that, where "qualified clean-fuel property" (as defined in Code Sec. 179A(c)(1)(A)) is installed on a passenger vehicle which is propelled by a fuel which is not a clean-burning fuel, for purposes of permitting the vehicle to be propelled by a clean-burning fuel, the threshold amount is increased to the sum of (a) $30,000 (Code Sec. 4001(a)(2)(B) as amended by '97 Act §906(a)), adjusted for inflation (Code Sec. 4001(e)(1)) and (b) the increase in price for which the vehicle is sold due to the installation of such property. (Code Sec. 4001(a)(2)(B))

illustration (1): A buys a clean-burning fuel vehicle for $43,000. In its original form, the vehicle wasn't clean-burning, but qualifying components were installed to make it clean-burning. Without those components, the vehi-

FTC 2d References are to Federal Tax Coordinator 2d
FIN References are to RIA's Analysis of Federal Taxes: Income
USTR References are to United States Tax Reporter: Income, Estate & Gift, and Excise
PCA References are to Pension Coordinator and Pension & Benefits Expert/Advisor
PE References are to Pension and Profit Sharing 2nd
EP References are to Estate Planning & Taxation Coordinator and Estate Planning Advisor

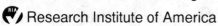 Research Institute of America   519

cle would have cost A $39,000. Thus, the price increase attributable to installation of the qualified clean-burning fuel property is $4,000. The threshold amount for A's purchase (assuming a $36,000 base threshold as adjusted for inflation) is, therefore, $40,000 ($36,000 plus $4,000), and the luxury tax would apply to $3,000 of the sales price ($43,000 minus the $40,000 threshold).

Separate purchase of vehicle parts and accessories. The '97 Act exempts from the separate parts and accessories tax that applies to installations made within six-month of the date a vehicle is placed in service, installations of qualified clean-fuel vehicle property as defined above. (Code Sec. 4003(a)(1)(A) as amended by '97 Act §906(b)(3))

The '97 Act also adjusts the rule limiting the amount of luxury tax that may be imposed on the separate installation of parts and accessories to account for the new applicable threshold amounts for electric and clean-burning fuel vehicles. (Code Sec. 4003(a)(2)(B) as amended by '97 Act §906(b)(4))

> *illustration (2):* Four months after A purchases the vehicle described in Illustration (1) for $43,000 and places that vehicle in service, he has parts and accessories (other than qualified clean-fuel property) installed costing $3,000 (including installation). Assuming an 8% separate parts and accessories tax rate, A's tax is $240. This result is reached by first computing the possible tax, 8% of $3,000 ($240), and then determining whether that tax exceeds the limitation on how much tax may be imposed. The limitation amount equals 8% of the sum of $3,000 plus $43,000 (the parts and the original purchase price) minus $40,000 (the applicable threshold, see Illustration (1) above)— i.e., 8% of $6,000 ($480). Since the $240 tax is less than the limitation amount, A must pay that full tax.

☐ **Effective:** Sales and installations occurring after Aug. 5, '97. ('97 Act §906(c))

¶ 2219. Luxury tax on separate installation of auto parts and accessories is conformed to tax on auto sales

Code Sec. 4001(f), as amended by '97 Act § 1601(f)(3)(A)
Code Sec. 4001(g), as amended by '97 Act § 1601(f)(3)(B)
Generally effective: Sales after Aug. 5, '97
Committee Reports, see ¶ 5387

The Small Business Job Protection Act of '96 ("the '96 Act") reduced the tax rate imposed on the sale of luxury passenger vehicles from 10% to 9% effective for sales after Aug. 27, '96, reduced that tax by an additional percentage point in each following calendar year through 2002, and terminated the tax thereafter. Luxury tax is also imposed on the installation of parts and accessories on a luxury passenger vehicle that are installed within six months of the date the vehicle was first placed in service. The '96 Act did not also reduce this 10% tax or provide for its termination. (FTC 2d ¶ W-2971, ¶ W-2980; USTR ¶ 40,014, ¶ 40,034)

New Law. The '97 Act reduces the luxury tax rate on the separate installation of vehicle parts and accessories to be the same as the rate applicable to the purchase of a vehicle. (Code Sec. 4001(f) as amended by '97 Act §1601(f)(3)(A)) It also provides for the termination of the tax after 2002. (Code Sec. 4001(g) as amended by '97 Act §1601(f)(3)(B))

☐ **Effective:** Sales after Aug. 5, '97. ('97 Act §1601(f)(3)(C))

¶ 2220. De minimis exceptions to retail heavy truck and luxury taxes on separate purchase and installation of parts and accessories are increased

Code Sec. 4003(a)(3)(C), as amended by '97 Act § 1401(a)
Code Sec. 4051(b)(2)(B), as amended by '97 Act § 1401(a)
Generally effective: Installations on vehicles sold after Aug. 5, '97
Committee Reports, see ¶ 5275

Excise taxes are imposed on the first retail sale of truck chassis and bodies suitable for use on vehicles with a gross weight of over 33,000 pounds and luxury passenger automobiles. In addition, with certain exceptions, these taxes also apply to the separate purchase and installation of parts and accessories within six months of the placing in service of a heavy truck that contains a taxable chassis or body or a taxable luxury vehicle. However, the installation of parts and accessories within these applicable six-month periods that totals $200 or less in price (including installation) was excepted from imposition of each tax.

Retailers are, generally, liable for payment to IRS of the retail heavy truck tax and the luxury tax, and must file excise tax returns reporting these taxes. However, in the case of subsequent installations of parts and accessories the owner or operator of the vehicle is responsible for paying the tax attributable to the installation and the installer is secondarily liable. (FTC 2d ¶ W-2983, ¶ W-3118; USTR ¶ 40,034, ¶ 40,514)

New Law. To reduce the number of excise tax return filers and relieve many people from the administrative burden of filing an excise tax return reporting a very small amount of tax (Com Rept, see ¶ 5275), the '97 Act increases both of the de minimis exceptions described above to permit an aggregate $1,000 in parts, accessories and installation costs to be incurred, within the applicable six-month period, without imposition of tax. (Code Sec. 4003(a)(3)(C) as amended by '97 Act §1401(a)) (Code Sec. 4051(b)(2)(B) as amended by '97 Act §1401(a))

Congress says that parts and accessories installed on a vehicle on or before the effective date of the above '97 Act provision are taken into account in determining whether the $1,000 threshold is exceeded. (Com Rept, see ¶ 5275)

FTC 2d References are to Federal Tax Coordinator 2d
FIN References are to RIA's Analysis of Federal Taxes: Income
USTR References are to United States Tax Reporter: Income, Estate & Gift, and Excise
PCA References are to Pension Coordinator and Pension & Benefits Expert/Advisor
PE References are to Pension and Profit Sharing 2nd
EP References are to Estate Planning & Taxation Coordinator and Estate Planning Advisor

🅡✓observation: The immediately preceding sentence is incorrect because, as indicated at "Effective" below, this '97 Act provision doesn't apply to vehicles sold before the effective date of the provision.

☐ **Effective:** Installations on vehicles sold after Aug. 5, '97. ('97 Act §1401(b))

¶ 2221. Exclusion of tire value from retail heavy truck excise tax replaced by credit for manufacturers' excise tax on tires

Code Sec. 4051(e), as amended by '97 Act § 1402(a)
Code Sec. 4052(b)(1)(B)(iii), as amended by '97 Act § 1402(b)
Generally effective: Jan. 1, '98
Committee Reports, see ¶ 5276

A tax is imposed on the first retail sale of truck chassis and bodies suitable for use on vehicles with a gross weight of over 33,000 pounds. The tax equals 12% of the purchase price of the taxable article. Tires are subject to a separate manufacturers' excise tax based on the tire's weight.

Under pre-'97 Act law, the fair market value at retail of any tires (including any manufacturers' excise tax imposed), not including any metal rim or rim base, was excluded from the taxable sales price of an article subject to the 12% retail tax. (FTC 2d ¶ W-3140; USTR ¶ 40,514) This rule gave rise to many audit challenges, because the value of tires was a factual question. (Com Rept, see ¶ 5276)

New Law. To simplify the application of the 12% retail tax (Com Rept, see ¶ 5276), the '97 Act eliminates the rule that excluded the value of tires from the taxable sales price of an article. (Code Sec. 4052(b)(1)(B)(iii) as amended by '97 Act §1402(b)) Instead, if tires are sold on or in connection with the sale of an article, and the 12% retail tax applies on the sale of such tires, a credit equal to the manufacturers' excise tax (if any) imposed on the tires is allowed against the retail tax. (Code Sec. 4051(e) as amended by '97 Act §1402(a))

☐ **Effective:** Jan. 1, '98. ('97 Act §1402(c))

¶ 2222. Retail heavy truck tax modified for wrecked vehicle remanufacturing and resale registration requirement replaced with certification procedure

Code Sec. 4052(d), as amended by '97 Act § 1434(b)(1)
Code Sec. 4052(f), as amended by '97 Act § 1434(a)
Code Sec. 4052(g), as amended by '97 Act § 1434(b)(2)
Generally effective: Jan. 1, '98
Committee Reports, see ¶ 5292

A tax is imposed on the first retail sale of truck chassis and bodies suitable for use on vehicles with a gross vehicle weight of over 33,000 pounds, and truck trailer, semitrailer and tractor chassis and bodies suitable for use with trailers or semi-trailers with a gross vehicle weight of 26,000 pounds or less (the "retail heavy truck tax") (FTC 2d ¶ W-3101 and W-3130; USTR ¶ 40,514). The first retail sale is the first sale, other than for resale or for leasing for a term of one year or more, after manufacture, production or importation (FTC 2d ¶ W-3134; USTR ¶ 40,514). Determination of whether a particular modification to a vehicle constitutes a taxable remanufacture or a nontaxable repair is generally based on whether the function of the vehicle is changed or, in the case of worn vehicles, whether the cost of the modification exceeds 75% of the value of the modified vehicle. (FTC 2d ¶ W-3135; USTR ¶ 40,514)

Where a tax-free sale for resale or long-term leasing is made, the purchaser is liable for the tax on the resale or lease of the vehicle. In order to make a tax-free purchase under pre-'97 Act law, the purchaser had to be registered with IRS. (FTC 2d ¶ W-3163; USTR ¶ 40,514)

New Law. The '97 Act provides that an otherwise taxable article will not be treated as manufactured or produced solely by reason of repairs or modifications to the article (including any modification which changes the transportation function of the article or restores a wrecked article to a functional condition), if the cost of such repairs and modifications does not exceed 75% of the retail price of a comparable new article. (Code Sec. 4052(f)(1) as amended by '97 Act §1434(a)) This change makes clear that the 75%-of-value threshold applies in determining whether repairs to a wrecked vehicle constitute remanufacture. (Com Rept, see ¶ 5292) The above rule does not apply if the article (as repaired or modified) would, if new, be subject to the retail heavy truck tax and the article when new was not taxable under this repair or modification provision or the corresponding provision of prior law. (Code Sec. 4052(f)(2))

In addition, the '97 Act repeals the registration requirement for tax-free sales (Code Sec. 4052(d) as amended by '97 Act §1434(b)(1)) and replaces it with direction to IRS to prescribe regulations that permit, in lieu of any other certification, persons who are purchasing taxable articles for resale or long-term leasing to execute a statement (made under penalties of perjury) on the sale invoice that indicates that the sale is for resale. Further, IRS is not to impose any registration requirement as a condition of using this certification procedure. (Code Sec. 4052(g) as added by '97 Act §1434(b)(2))

☐ **Effective:** Jan. 1, '98. ('97 Act §1434(c))

FTC 2d References are to Federal Tax Coordinator 2d
FIN References are to RIA's Analysis of Federal Taxes: Income
USTR References are to United States Tax Reporter: Income, Estate & Gift, and Excise
PCA References are to Pension Coordinator and Pension & Benefits Expert/Advisor
PE References are to Pension and Profit Sharing 2nd
EP References are to Estate Planning & Taxation Coordinator and Estate Planning Advisor

Manufacturers Excise Taxes

¶ 2223. Uniform vaccine excise tax rate replaces various vaccine-specific rates; three new vaccines taxed

Code Sec. 4131(b), as amended by '97 Act § 904(a)
Code Sec. 4132(a), as amended by '97 Act § 904(c)
Code Sec. 4132(a)(1), as amended by '97 Act § 904(b)
Code Sec. 4132(b), '97 Act § 904(e)
Generally effective: Day after Aug. 5, '97
Committee Reports, see ¶ 5054

An excise tax is imposed on manufacturers', producers' and importers' sales or use of: DPT (diphtheria, petussis, tetanus) vaccine; DT (diphtheria, tetanus) vaccine; MMR (measles, mumps or rubella) vaccine; and polio vaccine. Tax was imposed on a per dose basis at the following rates: $4.56 for DPT vaccine, $0.06 for DT vaccine, $4.44 for MMR vaccine, and $0.29 for polio vaccine. Except as otherwise provided below, if any vaccine was administered by combining more than one listed taxable vaccine, the tax imposed equaled the sum of the tax on each of the separate taxable component vaccines. Under the exception, only one tax (at the MMR rate) was imposed by reason of a vaccine being administered against one or more of the following: measles; mumps; or rubella. (FTC 2d ¶ W-2952, ¶ W-2953; USTR ¶ 41,314)

New Law. The '97 Act replaces the various vaccine-specific excise tax rates with a single $0.75 per dose rate (Code Sec. 4131(b)(1) as amended by '97 Act §904(a)) and adds three vaccines against the following diseases to the list of taxable vaccines— any HIB vaccine; any vaccine against Hepatitis B and any vaccine against chicken pox (Code Sec. 4132(a)(1) as amended by '97 Act §904(b)), i.e., HIB (hemophilus influenza type B), Hepatitis B and varicella (chicken pox) vaccines. (Com Rept, see ¶ 5054)

In addition, the '97 Act eliminates the pre-Act MMR exception (see above) to the rule involving vaccines that combine more than one taxable vaccine. (Code Sec. 4132(a) as amended by '97 Act §904(c)) Thus, under the '97 Act, the tax on any vaccine that is a combination of vaccine components is $0.75 times the number of taxable components in the combined vaccine. (Com Rept, see ¶ 5054)

> *illustration:* For example, an MMR vaccine (for measles, mumps or rubella) will be taxed at a rate of $2.25 per dose and a DT vaccine (for diphtheria and tetanus) will be taxed at a rate of $1.50 per dose.

☐ **Effective:** Day after Aug. 5, '97 ('97 Act §904(d)) (i.e., for vaccine purchases after Aug. 5, '97). (Com Rept, see ¶ 5054)

No floor stocks tax is to be collected or floor stocks refund permitted for amounts held on the above effective date. (Com Rept, see ¶ 5054)

> *observation:* The new uniform $0.75 rate reduces the tax on some vaccines and increases the tax on others. The Committee Report makes clear that

(1) for vaccines purchased before the effective date of the rate change at a lower than $0.75 rate, which the purchaser (e.g., a hospital or clinic) still holds for sale as of that effective date, Congress isn't imposing a floor stocks tax to capture the increase in tax, and (2) for vaccines purchased before the effective date of the rate change at a higher than $0.75 rate, which the purchaser still holds for sale as of the effective date, Congress isn't making available any special refunds for the decrease in tax.

For purposes of applying Code Sec. 4132(b) (relating to the credit or refund of vaccine tax paid on vaccines that are returned to the manufacturer or that are destroyed, see FTC 2d ¶ W-2955; USTR ¶ 41,314) with respect to any claim for credit or refund filed before Jan. 1, '99, the amount of tax taken into account is not to exceed the tax computed under the rate in effect on the above effective date. ('97 Act §904(e)) That is, for returns to manufacturers occurring after the above effective date and before Jan. 1, '99, the amount of tax assumed to have been paid on the initial purchase of the returned vaccine shall not exceed $0.75 per dose. (Com Rept, see ¶ 5054)

¶ 2224. IRS authority to waive purchaser registration requirements for excise-tax-free sales is expanded

Code Sec. 4222(b)(2), as amended by '97 Act § 1431(a)
Generally effective: Aug. 5, '97
Committee Reports, see ¶ 5289

Certain types of sales (e.g., sales for use in further manufacture, sales for export and sales for use by a state or local government or a nonprofit educational organization) that are otherwise subject to particular manufacturers' or retailers' excise taxes may be exempt from tax. Generally, a requirement for making these tax-free sales is that the seller, purchaser and any person to whom the article is resold by the purchaser (the "second purchaser") must register with IRS. The Code, however, authorizes IRS to relieve a purchaser or second purchaser from the registration requirements in the case of any sale or resale for export. (FTC 2d ¶ W-2261; USTR ¶ 42,214)

New Law. To permit more efficient administration of these exemptions (Com Rept, see ¶ 5289), the '97 Act authorizes IRS to relieve any purchaser or second purchaser from the registration requirements, whether or not the sale or resale was made for export. (Code Sec. 4222(b)(2) as amended by '97 Act §1431(a))

☐ **Effective:** Aug. 5, '97. ('97 Act §1431(b))

FTC 2d References are to Federal Tax Coordinator 2d
FIN References are to RIA's Analysis of Federal Taxes: Income
USTR References are to United States Tax Reporter: Income, Estate & Gift, and Excise
PCA References are to Pension Coordinator and Pension & Benefits Expert/Advisor
PE References are to Pension and Profit Sharing 2nd
EP References are to Estate Planning & Taxation Coordinator and Estate Planning Advisor

¶ 2225. Manufacturers' tax on completed arrows is replaced with tax on arrow's component parts

Code Sec. 4161(b), as amended by '97 Act § 1433(a)
Generally effective: Articles sold by the manufacturer, producer or importer after Sept. 30, '97
Committee Reports, see ¶ 5291

A tax was imposed on a manufacturer's, producer's or importer's sale of bows having a draw weight of more than 10 pounds and arrows that were either 18 inches or more in length, or that were suitable for use with a taxable bow. The tax equalled 11% of the sales price of the bow or arrow. (FTC 2d ¶ W-2751 *et seq.*; USTR ¶ 41,614)

New Law. The '97 Act replaces the tax on arrows described above with separate taxes on each of the four component parts of an arrow, i.e., the shaft, point, nock and vane. (Com Rept, see ¶ 5291) Tax is imposed at a rate of 12.4% of the sales price on the manufacturer's, importer's or producer's sale of any shaft, point, nock, or vane of a type used to produce an arrow which after assembly either (1) measures 18 inches or more in length (Code Sec. 4161(b)(2)(A) as amended by '97 Act §1433(a)) or (2) is suitable for use with a taxable bow. (Code Sec. 4161(b)(2)(B) as amended by '97 Act §1433(a))

The tax rate on the component parts of an arrow was increased in order to offset the reduction in aggregate value taxed, as compared to the value of the completed arrow taxed under pre-'97 Act law. (Com Rept, see ¶ 5291) The tax on bows remains at 11%. (Code Sec. 4161(b)(1)(A) as amended by '97 Act §1433(a))

☐ **Effective:** For articles sold by the manufacturer, producer or importer after Sept. 30, '97. ('97 Act §1433(b))

Ozone Depleting Chemicals Tax

¶ 2226. Scheduled exemption from ozone-depleting-chemicals tax for imported recycled halon-1211 is repealed

Code Sec. 4682(d)(1), as amended by '97 Act § 903(a)
Generally effective: Aug. 5, '97
Committee Reports, see ¶ 5053

An excise tax is imposed on manufacturers' or importers' sales and uses of certain ozone-depleting chemicals (ODCs), including halon-1211, halon-1301 and halon-2402. However, domestically recycled halons are exempt from tax. In addition, recycled halon-1301 and halon-2402 imported from countries that are signatories of the "Montreal Protocol on Substances that Deplete the Ozone Layer" are exempt from tax. Exemption from tax for recycled halon-1211 imported from such countries was scheduled to take effect on Jan. 1, '98. (FTC 2d ¶ W-4328; USTR ¶ 46,814.01)

New Law. The scheduled exemption for imported recycled halon-1211 is repealed. (Code Sec. 4682(d)(1) as amended by '97 Act §903(a))

☐ **Effective:** Aug. 5, '97. ('97 Act §903(b))

Alcohol and Tobacco Taxes

¶ 2227. Tax-free removal of alcoholic beverages from bonded premises and refund or credit on return to bonded premises allowed

Code Sec. 5008(c)(1), as amended by '97 Act § 1411(a)
Code Sec. 5044(a), as amended by '97 Act § 1416(a)
Code Sec. 5053(f), as amended by '97 Act § 1414(b)
Code Sec. 5053(g), as amended by '97 Act § 1418(a)
Code Sec. 5053(h), as amended by '97 Act § 1419(a)
Code Sec. 5056(c), as amended by '97 Act § 1414(c)(1)
Code Sec. 5056(d), as amended by '97 Act § 1414(c)(2)
Code Sec. 5222(b)(2), as amended by '97 Act § 1414(a)
Code Sec. 5361, as amended by '97 Act § 1416(b)(1)
Code Sec. 5364, as added by '97 Act § 1422(a)
Code Sec. 5418, as added by '97 Act § 1421(a)
Generally effective: The first day of the first calendar quarter beginning at least 180 days after Aug. 5, '97.
Committee Reports, see ¶ 5277

The pre-'97 Act rules governing the tax-free removal of alcoholic beverages from bonded premises (or the refund or credit of tax on the return of alcoholic beverages to bonded premises) drew inappropriate distinctions between different types of alcoholic beverages, and limited the ways taxpayers could comply with environmental rules governing the destruction of alcoholic beverages. (Com Rept, see ¶ 5277)

New Law. The '97 Act liberalizes the above rules, as follows:

Credit or refund for imported bottled distilled spirits returned to bonded premises. Distilled spirits do not have to be withdrawn from bonded premises before the tax on the distilled spirits is refunded, abated or credited when the distilled spirits are returned to bonded premises for destruction, denaturation, redistillation, reconditioning or rebottling. (Code Sec. 5008(c)(1) as amended by '97 Act §1411(a))

> ✔ *observation:* The change means the rule now applies to imported bottled distilled spirits as well as to domestically produced and imported bulk distilled spirits. It didn't apply to imported bottled distilled spirits before because they are withdrawn from the custody of customs rather than from bonded premises.

FTC 2d References are to Federal Tax Coordinator 2d
FIN References are to RIA's Analysis of Federal Taxes: Income
USTR References are to United States Tax Reporter: Income, Estate & Gift, and Excise
PCA References are to Pension Coordinator and Pension & Benefits Expert/Advisor
PE References are to Pension and Profit Sharing 2nd
EP References are to Estate Planning & Taxation Coordinator and Estate Planning Advisor

Refund of tax on wine returned to bond not limited to unmerchantable wine. The '97 Act repeals the requirement that domestic wine returned to bonded premises be unmerchantable in order for tax to be refunded or credited. (Code Sec. 5044(a) as amended by '97 Act §1416(a)) A parallel change allows bonded wine cellars to receive tax-paid wine, even though it isn't unmerchantable. (Code Sec. 5361 as amended by '97 Act §1416(b)(1))

Beer may be transferred tax-free from a brewery to a distilled spirits plant. Subject to any regulations IRS may prescribe, an exemption is provided to the tax on beer, for beer removed from any brewery to a distilled spirits plant for use as distilling material. (Code Sec. 5053(f) as amended by '97 Act §1414(b))

In parallel changes,

. . . refunds or credits are allowed for taxes paid by a brewer on beer that is removed from the brewery to a distilled spirits plant for use as distilling material (Code Sec. 5056(c) as amended by '97 Act §1414(c)(1)),

. . . refund claims must be made within six months of the time the beer is delivered to the distilled spirits plant (Code Sec. 5056(d) as amended by '97 Act §1414(c)(2)), and

. . . the list of items that may be received on the bonded premises of a distilled spirits plant is extended to include (a) beer conveyed without payment of tax from brewery premises, and (b) beer that has been lawfully removed from brewery premises on determination of tax. (Code Sec. 5222(b)(2) as amended by '97 Act §1414(a))

Imported beer transferred in bulk to brewery and imported wine transferred in bulk to bonded wine cellar without payment of tax. Imported beer brought into the United States in bulk containers can be transferred from customs custody to brewery premises in those bulk containers without payment of tax, subject to regulations that may be prescribed. The brewery becomes liable for the tax on the beer when it is released from customs, and the importer, or person bringing the beer into the country, is then relieved from liability for the tax. (Code Sec. 5418 as added by '97 Act §1421(a))

Imported wine brought into the United States in bulk containers can be transferred from customs custody to a bonded wine cellar premises in those bulk containers without payment of tax, under rules that parallel those above for the transfer of imported beer in bulk to a brewery. (Code Sec. 5364 as added by '97 Act §1422(a))

Beer may be withdrawn tax-free for destruction. Beer may be removed from a brewery for destruction without payment of tax, subject to regulations that may be prescribed. (Code Sec. 5053(h) as amended by '97 Act §1419(a))

Domestic beer is tax-free for foreign embassies, legations, etc. Subject to regulations that may be issued, domestic beer may be withdrawn tax-free from a brewery for transfer to a customs bonded warehouse for further tax-free withdrawal by foreign governments, organizations and individuals who can withdraw imported beer from customs warehouses without tax. (Code Sec. 5053(g) as amended by '97 Act §1418(a))

☐ **Effective:** The first day of the first calendar quarter beginning at least 180 days after Aug. 5, '97. ('97 Act §1411(b), 1414(d), 1416(c), 1418(b), 1419(b), 1421(c), 1422(c)).

¶ 2228. Alcohol excise tax on hard cider reduced

Code Sec. 5041(b)(6), as amended by '97 Act § 908(a)
Code Sec. 5041(c), as amended by '97 Act § 908(b)
Generally effective: Oct. 1, '97
Committee Reports, see ¶ 5058

Under pre-'97 Act law, hard cider was taxed as wine. The tax on still wine of 14% alcohol or less is $1.07 per gallon. (USTR ¶ 50,009)

New Law. The '97 Act reduces the tax on hard cider to 22.6 cents per gallon for cider (1) derived primarily from apples or apple concentrate and water, (2) containing no other fruit product, and (3) containing at least one-half of 1% and less than 7% alcohol by volume. (Code Sec. 5041(b)(6) as amended by '97 Act §908(a)) This puts the tax on low-alcohol hard cider on a par with the tax paid on beer by small brewers. (Com Rept, see ¶ 5058)

Cider subject to the reduced tax is counted as part of the 100,000 gallons of wine for which small producers (i.e. producers of not more than 250,000 gallons of wine) get a credit. (Com Rept, see ¶ 5058) But the credit is calculated on the basis of 5.6 cents per gallon, rather than the 90 cents per gallon applicable to other wine. (Code Sec. 5041(c)(1) as amended by '97 Act §908(b))

☐ **Effective:** Oct. 1, '97. ('97 Act §908(c))

Under the Senate Report, which was adopted by the Conference Report, the change in the tax on hard cider is effective for cider removed after Sept. 30. '97. (Com Rept, see ¶ 5058)

¶ 2229. Alcoholic beverage taxes paperwork and administration eased

Code Sec. 5027(c), as amended by '97 Act § 1413(a)
Code Sec. 5055, as amended by '97 Act § 1420(a)
Code Sec. 5175(c), as amended by '97 Act § 1412(a)
Generally effective: The first day of the first calender quarter beginning at least 180 says after Aug. 5, '97
Committee Reports, see ¶ 5277

New Law. The '97 Act made a number of changes to reduce paperwork and ease administration. They include:

(1) repealing the requirement that records and reports of the activities at a distilled spirits plant be kept on the plant premises. (Code Sec. 5207(c) as amended by '97 Act

§1413(a))

(2) allowing a drawback of tax paid on beer that is subsequently exported on proof of exportation required by regulations. (Code Sec. 5055 as amended by '97 Act §1420(a)) Pre-'97 Act law required that proof be based on records, evidence, and certificates required by regulations. (Code Sec. 5055 before amended by '97 Act §1420(a))

(3) permitting the cancellation (or crediting) of export bonds on proof of exportation required by regulations. (Code Sec. 5175(c) as amended by '97 Act §1412(a)) Pre-'97 Act law required that proof be based on records, evidence, and certificates required by regulations. (Code Sec. 5175(c) before amended by '97 Act §1412(a))

☐ **Effective:** The first day of the first calendar quarter beginning at least 180 days after Aug. 5, '97. ('97 Act §1412(b), 1413(b), 1420(b))

¶ 2230. Regs on geographic appellations codified; sign-posting requirement for wholesale liquor dealers repealed; up to 60% added sugar allowed in acidic wines

Code Sec. 5115, repealed by '97 Act § 1415(a)
Code Sec. 5384(b)(2)(D), as amended by '97 Act § 1417(a)
Code Sec. 5388(c), as amended by '97 Act § 910(a)
Generally effective: various
Committee Reports, see ¶ 5277, 5060

New Law. The '97 Act made changes to the alcoholic beverage tax provisions that:

(1) incorporate into the Code labeling regulations on the use of geographic appellations, such as burgundy, as semi-generic wine designations, with a requirement that certain names, such as burgundy, are to be semi-generic wine designations. (Code Sec. 5388(c) as amended by '97 Act §910(a))

(2) repeal the requirement that wholesale liquor dealers post signs outside their places of business showing their name and identifying themselves as wholesale liquor dealers. (Code Sec. 5115 repealed by '97 Act §1415(a))

(3) allow wines made with any fruit or berry with a natural fixed acid of 20 parts per thousand or more to have up to 60% sugar added. (Code Sec. 5384(b)(2)(D) as amended by '97 Act §1417(a)) Under pre-'97 Act law, this provision applied only to wine made from currants, loganberries, or gooseberries. (Code Sec. 5384(b)(2)(D) before amended by '97 Act §1417(a))

☐ **Effective:** The codification of regulations on wine labeling and the repeal of the sign requirement for wholesale liquor dealers are effective on Aug. 5, '97. ('97 Act §910(b), 1415(c)).

The provision on adding sugar to wines is effective the first day of the first calendar quarter beginning at least 180 days after Aug. 5, '97. ('97 Act §1417(b)).

¶ 2231. Taxes on cigarettes and other tobacco products rise

Code Sec. 5701(a), as amended by Budget Act § 9302(b)
Code Sec. 5701(b), as amended by Budget Act § 9302(a)
Code Sec. 5701(c), as amended by Budget Act § 9302(c)
Code Sec. 5701(d), as amended by Budget Act § 9302(d)
Code Sec. 5701(f), as amended by Budget Act § 9302(f)
Code Sec. 5701(g), as amended by Budget Act § 9302(g)
Code Sec. None, as amended by Budget Act § 9302(j)
Generally effective: Products removed after Dec. 31, '99
Committee Reports, see ¶ 5509

New Law. Cigarettes and other tobacco products are subject to excise taxes when removed from the factory, internal revenue bond or the custody of customs. Taxes on these products are increased to the amounts shown below:

. . . small cigarettes, $19.50 per thousand ($17 per thousand on cigarettes removed during 2000 and 2001) (Code Sec. 5701(b)(1) as amended by Budget Act §9302(a)) (formerly $12 per thousand).

. . . large cigarettes, $40.95 per thousand ($35.70 per thousand on cigarettes removed during 2000 and 2001) (Code Sec. 5701(b)(2)) (formerly $25.20 per thousand).

. . . small cigars, $1.828 per thousand ($1.594 per thousand on cigars removed during 2000 and 2001) (Code Sec. 5701(a)(1) as amended by Budget Act §9302(b)) (formerly $1.125 per thousand).

. . . large cigars, 20.719% (18.063% on cigars removed during 2000 and 2001) of the price for which paid but not more than S48.75 per thousand ($42.50 per thousand on cigars removed during 2000 or 2001) (Code Sec. 5701(a)(2)) (formerly 12.75% of the price per thousand but not more than $30 per thousand).

. . . pipe tobacco, $1.0969 per pound (95.67 cents per pound on pipe tobacco removed during 2000 or 2001) (Code Sec. 5701(f) as amended by Budget Act §9302(f)) (formerly 67.5 cents per pound).

. . . snuff, 58.5 cents per pound (51 cents per pound on snuff removed from during 2000 and 2001 (Code Sec. 5701(e)(1) as amended by Budget Act §9302(e)) (formerly 36 cents per pound).

. . . chewing tobacco, 19.5 cents per pound (17 cents per pound on chewing tobacco removed during 2000 or 2001) (Code Sec. 5701(e)(2)) (formerly 12 cents per pound).

. . . roll-your-own tobacco, $1.0969 cents per pound (95.67 cents per pound on roll-you-own tobacco removed during 2000 and 2001) (Code Sec. 5701(g) as amended by Budget Act §9302(g)) (new provision).

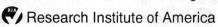

. . . cigarette papers (each package or book containing more than 25 papers), 1.22 cents per 50 papers or part thereof (1.06 cents on cigarette paper removed during 2000 or 2001) (Code Sec. 5701(c) as amended by Budget Act §9302(c)) (formerly .75 cent per 50 papers or part thereof).

. . . cigarette tubes, 2.44 cents per 50 tubes (2.13 cents on cigarette tubes removed during 2000 or 2001 (Code Sec. 5701(d) as amended by Budget Act §9302(d)) (formerly 1.5 cents per 50 tubes).

Floor stocks tax. The '97 Act imposes a floor stocks tax on any of the tobacco products discussed above that are removed from the factory, internal revenue bond or the custody of customs before—and held for sale on—Jan. 1, 2000 and Jan. 1, 2002. (Budget Act §9302(j)(1)) (Budget Act §9302(j)(6)(B)) The tax is the difference between the '97 Act tax and the prior tax, if any, on the product. (Budget Act §9302(j)(1))

☐ **Effective:** For tobacco products removed from the factory, internal revenue bond or the custody of customs after Dec. 31, '99. (Budget Act §9302(i)(1))

¶ 2300. Procedure and Administration

Reporting Requirements

¶ 2301. Large partnerships' tax returns must be filed on magnetic media and are subject to information return reporting penalties

Code Sec. 6011(e)(2), as amended by '97 Act § 1224
Code Sec. 6724(e), as amended by '97 Act § 1223(b)
Generally effective: Partnership tax years ending after Dec. 30, '97
Committee Reports, see ¶ 5211, 5212

Partnerships were allowed, but not required, to use magnetic media to file their partnership returns (Form 1065) and the copies of the Form K-1 schedules sent to their partners, with IRS. (FTC 2d/FIN ¶ S-1302; USTR ¶ 60,114.07; TaxDesk ¶ 59,625)

Partnerships that fail to file their partnership return (including the copies of Form K-1) are liable for a monthly penalty equal to $50 multiplied by the number of persons who were partners during any part of the taxable year, for each month or fraction of a month for which the failure continues. However, the total penalty can not be imposed for more than five months. (FTC 2d/FIN ¶ V-1762; USTR ¶ 66,984; TaxDesk ¶ 59,625)

Taxpayers are required to file information returns with respect to a large variety of types of payments and transfers. Failing to file those returns results in a penalty, the amount of which depends on a number of factors but which can equal up to $50 for each failure up to a maximum of $250,000 per calendar year. (FTC 2d/FIN ¶ V-1803, V-1804, V-1805; USTR ¶ 67,214; TaxDesk ¶ 86,125, 86,126)

New Law. The '97 Act provides that IRS must require partnerships with more than 100 partners to file returns on magnetic media. (Code Sec. 6011(e)(2) as amended by '97 Act §1224) This requirement applies to Form 1065 partnership tax returns and to the copies of Form K-1 that must be sent to IRS. (Com Rept, see ¶ 5212) This change conforms the reporting provisions for large partnerships with those for other entities that file large numbers of documents with IRS. Most such entities already must file on magnetic media. (Com Rept, see ¶ 5212)

Penalty for failing to file on magnetic media. The '97 Act also provides that, for partnerships that are required under the above rule to file their partnership return with IRS on magnetic media, each schedule required to be included with the return for each partner is treated as a separate information return, for purposes of the above penalty rules. (Code Sec. 6724(e) as amended by '97 Act §1223(b)) Thus, each Form K-1 is treated as a separate information return under this rule. (Com Rept, see ¶ 5211)

FTC 2d References are to Federal Tax Coordinator 2d
FIN References are to RIA's Analysis of Federal Taxes: Income
USTR References are to United States Tax Reporter: Income, Estate & Gift, and Excise
PCA References are to Pension Coordinator and Pension & Benefits Expert/Advisor
PE References are to Pension and Profit Sharing 2nd
EP References are to Estate Planning & Taxation Coordinator and Estate Planning Advisor

❤️ *observation:* The above penalty is in addition to the Code Sec. 6698 penalty for failure to timely file a partnership return (see FTC 2d/FIN ¶ V-1762; USTR ¶ 66,984; TaxDesk ¶s 86,141, 86,142); the Code Sec. 6698 penalty applies to both taxpayers who are required to file magnetically and to taxpayers who aren't required to file magnetically.

☐ **Effective:** Partnership tax years ending after Dec. 30, '97. ('97 Act §1226)

❤️ *observation:* The above statutory effective date is probably a mistake by Congress, based on the following:

. . . . The '97 Act Committee Reports state that the effective date of the above rule is tax years beginning after Dec. 31, '97. (This is a significant difference from the above statutory date, since the Committee Report date does not encompass '97 calendar year partnerships while the statutory date does).

. . . The provisions under which a partnership can become an electing large partnership are effective for tax years beginning after Dec. 31, '97, see ¶ 1401.

¶ 2302. Electing large partnerships must file K-1s by Mar. 15

Code Sec. 6031(b), as amended by '97 Act § 1223(a)
Generally effective: Partnership tax years ending after Dec. 30, '97
Committee Reports, see ¶ 5211

Partnerships required to file income tax returns must also furnish a Form K-1 payee statement to each partner on or before the day on which the income tax return for the tax year is required to be filed, including extensions. Unless it obtains an extension, a partnership must file its income tax return on or before the fifteenth day of the fourth month following the end of the partnership's taxable year. Thus, for calendar year partnerships, unextended returns must be filed on or before April 15, the same day most individual partners must file their tax returns. (FTC 2d/FIN ¶ S-2710; USTR ¶ 60,314; TaxDesk ¶ 59,608)

New Law. The '97 Act adds a requirement that an electing large partnership (as defined in new Code Sec. 775, explained at ¶ 1401) must furnish Form K-1 payee statements to partners on or before the first March 15 following the close of the partnership's taxable year. (Code Sec. 6031(b) as amended by '97 Act §1223(a))

The new provision was created because Congress felt that information returns received shortly before, on or after Apr. 15 are difficult for individuals to use in preparing returns or computing their payments that are due on Apr. 15. (Com Rept, see ¶ 5211)

❤️ *observation:* This new requirement applies in addition to the pre-'97 Act provision that requires K-1s to be filed on or before the extended due date of Form 1065.

⟪RIA⟫ *illustration:* Thus, an electing large partnership with a June 30 year end must still file its K-1s by the following Oct. 15 unless it obtains an extension for filing its Form 1065.

⟪RIA⟫ *caution:* Extensions for filing returns exist only to the extent provided for by the Code or by IRS regulation, ruling, etc. The Code contains no such extension provision with respect to the new Mar. 15 deadline, so no extension of the Mar. 15 deadline is available.

⟪RIA⟫ *illustration:* Partnership X, an electing large partnership which has an Oct. 31 year end, gets a three month extension for filing its Year 1 Form 1065, from its normal Feb. 15, Year 2 due date to May 15, Year 2. It must furnish K-1s to its partners by Mar. 15, Year 2.

⟪RIA⟫ *caution:* Under current law, many tax return preparers somewhat routinely put off preparing calendar year partnership returns until after Apr. 15, to alleviate the "tax season crunch." The fact that calendar year electing large partnership K-1s must be filed by Mar. 15 will mean that the great majority of the work involved in preparing calendar year electing large partnership returns must be done before Mar. 15. This factor should be taken into consideration before making the electing large partnership election.

☐ **Effective:** Partnership tax years ending after Dec. 30, '97. ('97 Act §1226)

⟪RIA⟫ *observation:* The above statutory effective date is probably a mistake by Congress, based on the following:

.... The '97 Act Committee Reports state that the effective date of the above rule is tax years beginning after Dec. 31, '97. (This is a significant difference from the above statutory date, since the Committee Report date does not encompass '97 calendar year partnerships while the statutory date does).

... The provisions under which a partnership can become an electing large partnership are effective for tax years beginning after Dec. 31, '97, see ¶ 1401.

¶ 2303. Return requirements of foreign partnerships clarified

Code Sec. 6031(e), as amended by '97 Act § 1141(a)
Generally effective: Tax years beginning after Aug. 5, '97
Committee Reports, see ¶ 5182

FTC 2d References are to Federal Tax Coordinator 2d
FIN References are to RIA's Analysis of Federal Taxes: Income
USTR References are to United States Tax Reporter: Income, Estate & Gift, and Excise
PCA References are to Pension Coordinator and Pension & Benefits Expert/Advisor
PE References are to Pension and Profit Sharing 2nd
EP References are to Estate Planning & Taxation Coordinator and Estate Planning Advisor

Partnerships must file annual information returns showing the partnership's gross income, deductions, etc., and each partner's distributive share of income. The partnership must also give each partner a copy of the information provided to IRS. (FTC 2d/FIN ¶ S-2700 et seq.; USTR ¶ 60,314; TaxDesk ¶ 59,601)

Some foreign partnerships are required to file annual partnership returns. (FTC 2d/FIN ¶ S-2717.1; USTR ¶ 60,314; TaxDesk ¶ 58,907) For the definition of "foreign partnership," see ¶ 1426.

New Law. The '97 Act requires a foreign partnership to file a partnership return only for a tax year in which it has:

... gross income from sources within the U.S., or

... gross income that is effectively connected with the conduct of a trade or business within the U.S. (Code Sec. 6031(e)(2) as amended by '97 Act §1141(a))

observation: Under pre-'97 Act law, Reg. §1.6031-1(c) required every partnership engaged in trade or business within the U.S. or having income from U.S. sources to file a partnership return, even if its main place of business was outside the U.S. and its members were nonresident aliens.

IRS regs can provide exceptions to the above filing requirement. (Code Sec. 6031(e)(2)) IRS can also provide simplified filing procedures for foreign partnerships that are required to file returns. (Code Sec. 6031(e)(2))

☐ **Effective:** Tax years beginning after Aug. 5, '97. ('97 Act §1141(c))

¶ 2304. Estate and trust beneficiaries must report items in manner consistent with estate or trust return or notify IRS of inconsistency

Code Sec. 6034A(c), as amended by '97 Act § 1027(a)
Code Sec. 6048(d), as amended by '97 Act § 1027(b)
Generally effective: Returns of beneficiaries and owners filed after Aug. 5, '97
Committee Reports, see ¶ 5127

An S corporation must file a return for the tax year (FTC 2d/FIN ¶ S-1905; USTR ¶ 60,374; TaxDesk ¶ 60,985) and furnish to its shareholders a copy of certain information shown on the return. (FTC 2d/FIN ¶ S-1906; USTR ¶ 60,374; TaxDesk ¶ 60,985) And the shareholder's income tax return must be consistent with the information received from the S corporation, unless the shareholder identifies the inconsistency on a statement filed with IRS. (FTC 2d/FIN ¶ D-1801; USTR ¶ 60,374; TaxDesk ¶ 58,410) Similar rules apply to partnerships and their partners. (FTC 2d/FIN ¶ B-1800 et seq.; USTR ¶ 62,224; TaxDesk ¶ 58,410)

The fiduciary of an estate or trust that is required to file a return must furnish to beneficiaries certain information shown on the return, generally on a Schedule K-1. (FTC 2d/FIN ¶ S-2018; USTR ¶ 60,34A4; TaxDesk ¶ 65,920) Also, a U.S. person that is treated as the owner of a portion of a foreign trust must ensure that the trust files a return and furnishes certain required information to each U.S. person who is treated as an owner of a portion of the trust or who receives a distribution from the trust. (FTC 2d/FIN ¶ S-3645; USTR ¶ 60,484) However, under pre-'97 Act law, rules similar to the S corporation and partnership consistency rules did not apply to beneficiaries of estates and trusts.

If the tax is underreported on a return due to a mathematical or clerical error, IRS can make a summary assessment without issuing a 90-day letter. The taxpayer can ask IRS to abate the assessment within 60 days after IRS sends the taxpayer notice of the assessment. Collection of the tax is stayed during this 60-day period. (FTC 2d/FIN ¶ T-3622 *et seq.*; USTR ¶ 62,134)

New Law. Except as otherwise provided below, the '97 Act requires beneficiaries of estates and trusts to treat any "reported item" on the beneficiary's own return in a manner that is consistent with the treatment of that item on the return of the estate or trust. (Code Sec. 6034A(c)(1) as amended by '97 Act §1027(a)) A "reported item" is any item for which the estate or trust must furnish information to the beneficiary. (Code Sec. 6034A(c)(4)(A))

The exception to this rule applies where:

... the beneficiary's treatment of any reported item is (or may be) inconsistent with the treatment of the item on the return of the estate or trust, or

... the estate or trust didn't file a return. (Code Sec. 6034A(c)(2)(A)(i))

and the beneficiary identifies the inconsistency on a statement filed with IRS. (Code Sec. 6034A(c)(2)(A)(ii))

A beneficiary is treated as having complied with the identification requirement if (1) he demonstrates to IRS's satisfaction that his treatment of the item on his return is consistent with the treatment of the item on a schedule furnished to him by the estate or trust, and (2) he elects to have this rule apply. (Code Sec. 6034A(c)(2)(B))

> **observation:** The above election comes into play where the schedule furnished to the beneficiary by the estate or trust disagrees with the estate or trust return. It is apparently intended to protect beneficiaries who file their returns according to the schedules they receive. The beneficiary may be unaware that his return is inconsistent with the estate or trust return, in which case he can't identify the inconsistency to IRS. Were it not for the above election, IRS could make a summary assessment (see below).

IRS adjustment of inconsistent items. If a beneficiary treats an item inconsistently, and doesn't file a statement identifying the inconsistency, any IRS adjustment required to make the beneficiary's treatment of the item consistent with the treatment of the item on the estate or trust return is treated as resulting from a mathematical or

FTC 2d References are to Federal Tax Coordinator 2d
FIN References are to RIA's Analysis of Federal Taxes: Income
USTR References are to United States Tax Reporter: Income, Estate & Gift, and Excise
PCA References are to Pension Coordinator and Pension & Benefits Expert/Advisor
PE References are to Pension and Profit Sharing 2nd
EP References are to Estate Planning & Taxation Coordinator and Estate Planning Advisor

clerical error, in that IRS can make a summary assessment of the deficiency without issuing a 90-day letter. However, unlike in the case of mathematical or clerical errors: (a) the rule allowing the taxpayer to request abatement of the assessment within 60 days doesn't apply and (b) IRS collection of the tax isn't stayed for 60 days. (Code Sec. 6034A(c)(3))

Foreign trusts. Consistency rules similar to those described above apply to U.S. persons that are treated as the owner of a portion of a foreign trust or that receive a distribution from the trust. (Code Sec. 6048(d)(5) as amended by '97 Act §1027(b))

Accuracy-related penalty. For the penalty that may apply in the case of a benefici-ary's negligence in connection with, or disregard of, the consistency rules, see the ac-curacy-related and fraud penalty rules in Code Sec. 6662 through Code Sec. 6664. (Code Sec. 6034A(c)(5))

☐ **Effective:** Returns of beneficiaries and owners filed after Aug. 5, '97. ('97 Act §1027(c))

observation: The effective date of the above provision depends on the date on which the return is filed, and not on its due date. Thus, a late return that was due before Aug. 5, '97 but filed after that date is subject to the consis-tency rules. Similarly, an amended return filed after Aug. 5, '97 that relates to an earlier tax year is subject to those rules.

¶ 2305. Reporting by public charities on excise tax penalties coordinated with the penalties

Code Sec. 6033(b)(10), as amended by '97 Act § 1603(b)(1)
Code Sec. 6033(b)(11), as amended by '97 Act § 1603(b)(2)
Generally effective: Returns for tax years beginning after July 30, '96
Committee Reports, see ¶ 5384

A penalty excise tax is imposed under Code Sec. 4911 on public charities making excess lobbying expenditures. The tax is imposed on the organization itself. A penalty excise tax is also imposed under Code Sec. 4912 on certain public charities that make disqualifying lobbying expenditures and another such tax is imposed under Code Sec. 4955 on political expenditures of public charities. Both of these penalty taxes are im-posed not only on the affected organization, but also on organization managers who agree to an expenditure knowing that it is improper.

IRS has authority under Code Sec. 4962 to abate some first-tier taxes (including taxes under Code Sec. 4955) if the taxable event was due to reasonable cause and not to willful neglect (or was not willful and flagrant in the case of Code Sec. 4955 taxes) and the event was corrected within the applicable correction period. (FTC 2d/FIN ¶ D-6429, ¶ D-8201; USTR ¶ 49,624; TaxDesk ¶ 68,566)

Penalty excise taxes are imposed under Code Sec. 4958 as an "intermediate sanc-tion" on "disqualified persons" who improperly benefit from an "excess benefit trans-action" of an organization exempt from tax under Code Sec. 501(c)(3) (i.e., religious, charitable, scientific, and educational organizations) or Code Sec. 501(c)(4) (civic leagues and social welfare organizations) that is not a private foundation. An additional penalty excise tax may be imposed on organization managers who participate in a transaction knowing that it is improper. No tax is imposed on the organization itself. (FTC 2d/FIN ¶ D-6651; USTR ¶ 49,584; TaxDesk ¶ 67,650)

Code Sec. 501(c)(3) organizations, with certain exceptions, must annually report the following taxes paid by the organization during the tax year:

(1) the Code Sec. 4911 tax on excess lobbying expenditures,

(2) the Code Sec. 4912 tax on disqualifying lobbying expenditures, and

(3) the Code Sec. 4955 tax on political expenditures of Code Sec. 501(c)(3) organizations.

Although Code Sec. 4912 and Code Sec. 4955 impose excise taxes on organization managers, organizations technically were not required to report any such excise taxes paid by such managers.

Code Sec. 501(c)(3) organizations, subject to exceptions, must also annually report the amount of Code Sec. 4958 excess benefit transaction taxes paid by the organization or by "disqualified persons" with respect to the organization during the tax year. The tax law did not explicitly require the reporting of any excess benefit excise taxes paid by an organization manager solely in his or her capacity as such (i.e., an organization manager might also be a disqualified person with respect to an excess benefit transaction, in which case any tax paid would be reported). (FTC 2d/FIN ¶ S-2857.1, ¶ S-2857.2; USTR ¶ 60,334)

New Law. The '97 Act makes the penalty excise tax reporting requirements consistent with the tax provisions to which they relate. Thus, the '97 Act requires reporting of taxes imposed on organization managers, as well as taxes imposed on the organization and on disqualified persons. In addition, the '97 Act requires reporting of reimbursements paid by the organization with respect to taxes imposed on organization managers and disqualified persons, and clarifies that no reporting is required with respect to first-tier taxes abated under Code Sec. 4962. (Com Rept, see ¶ 5384)

Reporting of taxes on lobbying and political expenditures. Except to the extent that the Code Sec. 4955 tax wasn't required to be paid, or was credited or refunded, under the Code Sec. 4962 abatement rule, Code Sec. 501(c)(3) organizations, subject to exceptions, must annually report the respective amounts of any:

. . . taxes under Code Sec. 4911, Code Sec. 4912, and Code Sec. 4955 imposed during the tax year on the organization or any organization manager of the organization, and

. . . reimbursements that the organization paid during the tax year with respect to any of those taxes that were imposed on any organization manager of the organization. (Code Sec. 6033(b)(10) as amended by '97 Act §1603(b)(1))

FTC 2d References are to Federal Tax Coordinator 2d
FIN References are to RIA's Analysis of Federal Taxes: Income
USTR References are to United States Tax Reporter: Income, Estate & Gift, and Excise
PCA References are to Pension Coordinator and Pension & Benefits Expert/Advisor
PE References are to Pension and Profit Sharing 2nd
EP References are to Estate Planning & Taxation Coordinator and Estate Planning Advisor

observation: The above expansion of the reporting rules to cover taxes on organization managers only affects the Code Sec. 4912 and Code Sec. 4955 taxes, since the Code Sec. 4911 tax does not apply to organization managers.

Reporting of excess benefit transaction taxes. Except to the extent that the Code Sec. 4958 tax wasn't required to be paid, or was credited or refunded, under the Code Sec. 4962 abatement rule, Code Sec. 501(c)(3) organizations, subject to exceptions, must annually report the respective amounts of any:

. . . Code Sec. 4958 excess benefit transaction taxes imposed during the tax year with respect to the organization on any organization manager or any disqualified person, and

. . . reimbursements that the organization paid during the tax year with respect to taxes under Code Sec. 4958. (Code Sec. 6033(b)(11) as amended by '97 Act §1603(b)(2))

☐ **Effective:** Returns for tax years beginning after July 30, '96. ('97 Act §1603(c))

¶ 2306. Unrelated business income tax return requirements for IRAs liberalized

Code Sec. 6012(b)(6), as amended by '97 Act § 1225
Generally effective: Partnership tax years ending after Dec. 30, '97
Committee Reports, see ¶ 5213

An IRA must file Form 990-T, Exempt Organization Business Income Tax Return, for each taxable year in which it has gross income of $1,000 or more that is included in computing unrelated business taxable income. (FTC 2d/FIN ¶ S-2010; USTR ¶ 60,124.04; TaxDesk ¶ 65,905) In calculating unrelated business taxable income, IRAs are permitted deductions for expenses, etc., that are directly connected to the unrelated business and an additional $1,000 deduction. (FTC 2d/FIN ¶ D-6921; USTR ¶ 5124; TaxDesk ¶ 68,112)

Many partnerships are subject to unified audit rules that require the tax treatment of those items that are more appropriately determined at the partnership, rather than the partner, level be determined at the partnership level. There are two sets of partnership level audit rules: (a) the unified partnership audit procedures, which existed before the '97 Act; (FTC 2d/FIN ¶ T-2100 *et seq.*; USTR ¶ 62,214 *et seq.*; TaxDesk ¶ 82,500) (see also ¶ 1406) and (b) the electing large partnership audit procedures, which were added by the '97 Act, see ¶ 1402.

New Law. The '97 Act provides that, for purposes of determining whether it meets the above $1,000 gross income filing threshold, an IRA is to treat its share of *taxable income* of any partnership that it is a partner in and that is subject to either of the above sets of partnership level audit procedures, as if it were its share of the partnership's *gross income* and gains. (Code Sec. 6012(b)(6) as amended by '97 Act §1225) Thus, for example, an IRA that receives taxable income of less than $1,000 from a partnership that is subject to partnership-level audit rules and that does not have any other income from an unrelated trade or business, is not required to file an income tax return. (Com Rept, see ¶ 5213)

The new rule reflects Congress' belief that requiring an IRA to file a Form 990-T is unnecessary to the extent that the IRA's income comes from a partnership that is subject to a partnership-level audit. In such circumstances, the validity of any deductions may be determined at the partnership level, and an additional filing to facilitate that determination is unnecessary. (Com Rept, see ¶ 5213)

☐ **Effective:** Partnership tax years ending after Dec. 30, '97. ('97 Act §1226)

> ✐ *observation:* The above statutory effective date may be a mistake by Congress, based on the following:
>
> . . . . The '97 Act Committee Reports state that the effective date of the above rule is tax years beginning after Dec. 31, '97. (This is a significant difference from the above statutory date, since the Committee Report date does not encompass '97 calendar year partnerships while the statutory date does).
>
> . . . The provisions under which a partnership can become an electing large partnership are effective for tax years beginning after Dec. 31, '97, see ¶ 1401.

¶ 2307. Gift tax return requirement eliminated for many charitable donations

Code Sec. 6019(3), as amended by '97 Act § 1301(a)
Generally effective: Gifts made after Aug. 5, '97
Committee Reports, see ¶ 5261

With limited exceptions, gifts of more than $10,000 made to any one donee in a calendar year must be reported on a gift tax return. There was no exception to this rule with respect to charitable gifts, including those charitable gifts that qualified for the gift tax charitable deduction. (FTC 2d ¶ S-2201; USTR ¶ 25,224, ¶ 60,194; TaxDesk ¶ 74,601)

Code Sec. 2522(a) and Code Sec. 2522(b) provide the general rules for the gift tax charitable deduction for citizens and residents and for nonresidents, respectively. (FTC 2d/FIN ¶ Q-6000; USTR ¶ 25,224) A gift tax charitable deduction is also available for "qualified conservation contributions," i.e., gifts to qualified organizations of perpetual easements for conservation purposes that meet the requirements of Code Sec. 2522(d). (FTC 2d ¶ Q-6079; USTR ¶ 25,224; TaxDesk ¶ 33,207)

New Law. The '97 Act provides that a transfer of property that qualifies for the gift tax charitable deduction need not be reported on a gift tax return, if either: (Code Sec. 6019(3) as amended by '97 Act §1301)

FTC 2d References are to Federal Tax Coordinator 2d
FIN References are to RIA's Analysis of Federal Taxes: Income
USTR References are to United States Tax Reporter: Income, Estate & Gift, and Excise
PCA References are to Pension Coordinator and Pension & Benefits Expert/Advisor
PE References are to Pension and Profit Sharing 2nd
EP References are to Estate Planning & Taxation Coordinator and Estate Planning Advisor

... the gift qualifies for the qualified conservation contribution deduction described above; (Code Sec. 6019(3)(B)), *or*

... (A) the gift is of the donor's entire interest in the property (Code Sec. 6019(3)(A)(i)), and (B) the donor is not making (and has never made) a transfer of any interest in that property that both (i) was for less than adequate and full consideration and (ii) did not qualify for a charitable deduction under Code Sec. 2522(a) or Code Sec. 2522(b). (Code Sec. 6019(3)(A)(ii))

☐ **Effective:** Gifts made after Aug. 5, '97. ('97 Act §1301(b))

¶ 2308. Five-year test of joint Montana-Federal employment tax reporting is authorized

Code Sec. None, '97 Act § 976(a)
Code Sec. None, '97 Act § 976(b)
Code Sec. 6103(d)(5), as amended by '97 Act § 976(c)
Generally effective: Aug. 5, '97
Committee Reports, see ¶ 5099

Traditionally, Federal tax returns are filed with the Federal government and state tax returns with the individual states. This necessitates duplication of items common to both returns. Some states are working with IRS to combine state and Federal reporting of certain items to reduce taxpayers' compliance burden.

The state of Montana and IRS have developed a system for reporting state and Federal employment taxes on one form. The form would contain Federal and state information and the following information common to both: the taxpayers' names, addresses, taxpayer identification numbers (TINs), and signatures.

Code Sec. 6103 prohibits the disclosure of tax returns and return information, except as specifically authorized by the Code (see ¶ 2407). Implementation of the Montana-IRS project has been hindered because IRS maintains that Code Sec. 6103 bars it from disclosing taxpayer information to the state. (Com Rept, see ¶ 5099)

New Law. The '97 Act authorizes a demonstration project to assess the feasibility and desirability of expanding combined Federal and state tax reporting. ('97 Act §976(a)) The project is to be carried out between IRS and Montana and is limited to (1) a period to end five years after Aug. 5, '97 ('97 Act §976(b)(1)), (2) the reporting of employment taxes ('97 Act §976(b)(2)), and (3) the disclosure of the taxpayers' names, mailing addresses, TINs and signatures ('97 Act §976(b)(3)). Code Sec. 6103 is amended to authorize IRS to disclose this information for purposes of the demonstration project. (Code Sec. 6103(d)(5) as amended by '97 Act §976(c))

☐ **Effective:** Aug. 5, '97. (Com Rept, see ¶ 5099)

¶ 2309. Sales and exchanges of certain principal residences exempted from real estate reporting requirements

Code Sec. 6045(e), as amended by '97 Act § 312(c)
Generally effective: Sales and exchanges after May 6, '97
Committee Reports, see ¶ 5020

In most cases, a "real estate reporting person" must file an information return with IRS and must furnish a written statement to the transferor with respect to the sale or exchange of real estate. The "real estate reporting person" is either (i) the person responsible for closing the real estate transaction or (ii) if no one is responsible for closing the transaction, the mortgage lender, a broker, the transferee, etc.

There is no exception from these requirements for sales and exchanges of principal residences. (FTC 2d/FIN ¶ S-3800; USTR ¶ 60,454.04; TaxDesk ¶ 81,439)

New Law. The '97 Act provides an exception from the above reporting requirements for any sale or exchange of a residence for $250,000 or less, if the real estate reporting person receives written assurance, in a form acceptable to IRS, from the seller that: (a) the residence is the seller's principal residence (within the meaning of Code Sec. 121), (b) if the real estate sale or exchange information return requires disclosure as to whether there is federally subsidized mortgage financing assistance with respect to the mortgage on residences, there is no such assistance with respect to the mortgage on the residence, and (c) the full amount of the gain on the sale or exchange is excludable from gross income under Code Sec. 121, see ¶ 102. If the assurance described above includes an assurance that the seller is married, the exception applies to a sale or exchange for $500,000 or less. (Code Sec. 6045(e)(5)(A) as amended by '97 Act §312(c))

IRS may issue regulations that increase the above $250,000 and $500,000 amounts if it determines that such an increase will not materially reduce tax revenues. (Code Sec. 6045(e)(5)(A))

For purposes of the above rules, the term "seller" includes the person relinquishing the residence in an exchange. (Code Sec. 6045(e)((5)(B))

> *observation:* With respect to requirement (b) above, the statutory language does not specify whether the mortgage in question is the seller's old mortgage or the buyer's new mortgage. Logic suggests that it is the seller's as (1) this would discourage sellers from using low-cost federally subsidized mortgages to finance multiple sales to take advantage of the exclusion; and (2) the seller generally would not be able to effectively make any assurances as to the buyer's financing source.

FTC 2d References are to Federal Tax Coordinator 2d
FIN References are to RIA's Analysis of Federal Taxes: Income
USTR References are to United States Tax Reporter: Income, Estate & Gift, and Excise
PCA References are to Pension Coordinator and Pension & Benefits Expert/Advisor
PE References are to Pension and Profit Sharing 2nd
EP References are to Estate Planning & Taxation Coordinator and Estate Planning Advisor

As a result of this provision, information returns will generally not be required with respect to sales of personal residences where the sales price does not exceed the amount eligible to be excluded from income under the rules in ¶ 102. (Com Rept, see ¶ 5020)

☐ **Effective:** The effective date of the above provisions is the same as the effective date at ¶ 102. ('97 Act §312(d))

observation: The above cite to '97 Act §312(d) is to the second §312(d)). Due to a drafting error there are two subsection "(d)"s in Act §312.

¶ 2310. Information reporting required for trade or business payments to attorneys after '97

Code Sec. 6045(f), as amended by '97 Act § 1021(a)
Generally effective: Payments made after Dec. 31, '97
Committee Reports, see ¶ 5121

Under Code Sec. 6041(a), each person engaged in a trade or business who, in the course of that trade or business, makes a payment of $600 or more of rent, salaries, wages, or other fixed or determinable gains, profits, or income must report that payment on an information return. Form 1099-MISC is used for this purpose. (FTC 2d/FIN ¶ S-3656; USTR ¶ 60,414; TaxDesk ¶ 81,401)

Attorneys' fees are covered by this rule. (FTC 2d/FIN ¶ S-3675; USTR ¶ 60,414.05; TaxDesk ¶ 81,418) However, if a payment to an attorney was for a gross amount and it wasn't known what portion was for fees, none of the payment had to be reported. (Com Rept, see ¶ 5121)

With certain exceptions, Reg. §1.6041-3(c) exempted payments to corporations from these reporting requirements. Salaries and profits paid or distributed by a partnership to the individual partners are also exempt from information reporting. (FTC 2d/FIN ¶ S-3676; USTR ¶ 60,414.05; TaxDesk ¶ 81,406)

Under Code Sec. 6051, an employer must furnish each employee with a written statement reporting the amount of the employee's wages and the tax withheld. Form W-2 is used for this purpose. (FTC 2d/FIN ¶ S-3151; USTR ¶ 60,514; TaxDesk ¶ 81,203)

A person with respect to whom a return is required to be made by another person must give his TIN to that person on request. (FTC 2d/FIN ¶ S-1541; USTR ¶ 61,094) Failure to comply with this requirement results in a $50 penalty (FTC 2d/FIN ¶ V-1821; USTR ¶ 67,234; TaxDesk ¶ 86,149) and causes the payment involved to be subject to backup withholding. (FTC 2d/FIN ¶ J-9001; USTR ¶ 34,064; TaxDesk ¶ 55,451)

New Law. The '97 Act provides that any person engaged in a trade or business who makes a payment described below to an attorney in the course of that trade or business must (1) report that payment on an information return filed with IRS and (2) furnish a written statement to the recipient of the payment. (Code Sec. 6045(f)(1) as amended by '97 Act §1021(a)) Form 1099-B is to be used for these returns and statements. (Com Rept, see ¶ 5121)

The above reporting requirement applies to any payment to an attorney in connection with legal services, whether or not the services are performed for the payor (Code Sec. 6045(f)(2)(A) as amended by '97 Act §1021(a)), but it doesn't apply to the portion of any payment that:

. . . must be reported under Code Sec. 6041(a) (trade or business payments reported on Form 1099-MISC);

. . . would have to be reported under Code Sec. 6041(a) but for the $600 limitation; or

. . . must be reported under Code Sec. 6051 (wages reported on Form W-2). (Code Sec. 6045(f)(2)(B) as amended by '97 Act §1021(a))

The provision applies whether or not the attorney is the exclusive payee. Payments to law firms are considered payments to attorneys, and therefore must be reported under this new rule. (Com Rept, see ¶ 5121)

Congress wants IRS to administer this provision so that there is no overlap between reporting under Code Sec. 6041 and Code Sec. 6045. (Com Rept, see ¶ 5121)

> *Illustration:* Two simultaneous payments are made to an attorney, one representing the attorney's fee and the other a settlement with the attorney's client. The fee must be reported under Code Sec. 6041. The settlement need not be reported under either Code Sec. 6041 or Code Sec. 6045, since none of it is income to the attorney. (Com Rept, see ¶ 5121)

Payments to corporations. The '97 Act also provides that the exemption from information reporting under Reg §1.6041-3(c) for payments to corporations doesn't apply to attorneys' fees. ('97 Act §1021(b)) Payments to corporations that provide legal services must be reported under both Code Sec. 6041 and Code Sec. 6045(f). (Com Rept, see ¶ 5121)

Payments by partnerships to their partners. The pre-'97 Act rule exempting salaries and profits paid or distributed by a partnership to the individual partners from information reporting will continue to apply for purposes of both the Code Sec. 6041 and Code Sec. 6045 reporting rules, since these amounts must be reported on Schedule K-1. (Com Rept, see ¶ 5121)

Attorneys must provide TINs to payors. Attorneys must promptly supply their TINs to persons required to file the information return described above. Failure to do so could result in the attorney being subject to a $50 penalty for each failure and the payments being subject to backup withholding. (Com Rept, see ¶ 5121)

FTC 2d References are to Federal Tax Coordinator 2d
FIN References are to RIA's Analysis of Federal Taxes: Income
USTR References are to United States Tax Reporter: Income, Estate & Gift, and Excise
PCA References are to Pension Coordinator and Pension & Benefits Expert/Advisor
PE References are to Pension and Profit Sharing 2nd
EP References are to Estate Planning & Taxation Coordinator and Estate Planning Advisor

☐ **Effective:** Payments made after Dec. 31, '97. ('97 Act §1021(c)) Thus, the first information returns will be filed with IRS (and copies will be provided to payees) in '99, with respect to payments made in '98. (Com Rept, see ¶ 5121)

¶ 2311. Information reporting required for federal agency payments of $600 or more to corporations

Code Sec. 6041A(d), as amended by '97 Act § 1022(a)

Generally effective: Returns with due dates (determined without regard to any extension) more than 90 days after Aug. 5, '97

Committee Reports, see ¶ 5122

Governmental entities, agencies, etc. that make payments of remuneration for services performed must file with IRS an annual information return reporting such payments (and the name, address, and taxpayer identification number of the recipient) with respect to each person for whom the remuneration during the calendar year was $600 or more. They must also furnish a written statement containing similar information (a "payee statement") to each person to whom such payment was made. However, IRS regs provided that none of these requirements applied to payments made to corporations. (FTC 2d/FIN ¶ S-3656, S-3659, S-3660; USTR ¶ 60,41A4; TaxDesk ¶ 81,401, 81,405)

A "federal executive agency" is any executive agency other than the General Accounting Office, any military department, the United States Postal Service and the Postal Rate Commission. (FTC 2d/FIN ¶ S-3681; USTR ¶ 60,50M4.01; TaxDesk ¶ 81,620)

New Law. The '97 Act provides that, except as otherwise provided below and notwithstanding any regulation in existence before the date this rule is enacted, the above information return and payee statement requirements apply to all payments of $600 or more made by a federal executive agency to a corporation for services. (Code Sec. 6041A(d)(3)(A) as amended by '97 Act §1022(a)) (Code Sec. 6041A(e)) Exempted from these new reporting requirements are: (1) services under certain classified or confidential contracts described in Code Sec. 6050M(e)(3) that meet the reporting requirement of Code Sec. 6050M(e)(2) (Code Sec. 6041A(d)(3)(B)(i) as amended by '97 Act §1022(a)), and (2) such other services as IRS may specify by regulation. (Code Sec. 6041A(d)(3)(B)(ii))

observation: Federal executive agency payments of $600 or more to corporations are subject to the two above-mentioned exemptions, but such payments to noncorporations are not.

☐ **Effective:** Returns with due dates (determined without regard to any extension) more than 90 days after Aug. 5, '97. ('97 Act §1022(b))

Research Institute of America

¶ 2312. U.S. partners that control foreign partnerships subject to information reporting

Code Sec. 6038(a)(1), as amended by '97 Act § 1142(a)
Code Sec. 6038(e), as amended by '97 Act § 1142(b)
Code Sec. 6038(b), as amended by '97 Act § 1142(c)
Code Sec. 6038(a)(5), as amended by '97 Act § 1142(d)
Generally effective: Annual accounting periods beginning after Aug. 5, '97
Committee Reports, see ¶ 5182

Every U.S. person must furnish, with respect to any foreign corporation which that person controls, information prescribed by IRS regs relating to:

. . . the foreign corporation's name, its main place of business, the nature of its business, and the country under whose laws it is incorporated;

. . . the foreign corporation's post-'86 undistributed earnings;

. . . a balance sheet for the foreign corporation listing assets, liabilities, and capital;

. . . transactions between the foreign corporation and the U.S. person, any other corporation which that person controls, and any other U.S. person that owns, at the time the transaction takes place, 10% or more of the value of any class of the foreign corporation's stock;

. . . a description of the various classes of stock outstanding, and a list showing the name and address of, and number of shares held by, each U.S. person who is a shareholder of record owning at any time during the annual accounting period 5% or more in value of any class of the foreign corporation's stock; and

. . . other information required by IRS that is similar or related to the above information or that IRS determines to be appropriate to carry out the provisions of the Code. (FTC 2d/FIN ¶ S-3585 *et seq.*; USTR ¶ 60,384; TaxDesk ¶ 81,553)

The information return described above covers the annual accounting period of the foreign corporation ending with or within the U.S. person's tax year. No information return is required for any annual accounting period unless the information was required to be furnished under regs in effect on the first day of that period. (FTC 2d/FIN ¶ S-3593.2; USTR ¶ 60,384)

Where two or more U.S. persons would be required to furnish information with respect to the same foreign corporation for the same period, IRS regs provide that the information is only required from one person. (FTC 2d/FIN ¶ S-3597 *et seq.*; USTR ¶ 60,384; TaxDesk ¶ 81,553)

Also under pre-'97 Act law, a $1,000 penalty was imposed for the failure of a U.S. person to furnish the above information on time. For failures that continued for more

---

FTC 2d References are to Federal Tax Coordinator 2d
FIN References are to RIA's Analysis of Federal Taxes: Income
USTR References are to United States Tax Reporter: Income, Estate & Gift, and Excise
PCA References are to Pension Coordinator and Pension & Benefits Expert/Advisor
PE References are to Pension and Profit Sharing 2nd
EP References are to Estate Planning & Taxation Coordinator and Estate Planning Advisor

than 90 days after IRS mailed notice to the U.S. person, additional $1,000 penalties applied for each 30-day period (or fraction thereof) during which the failure continued, up to a maximum penalty of $24,000.

Another penalty applies which reduces the U.S. person's foreign tax credit where the U.S. person fails to timely furnish any information required with respect to any foreign corporation. Foreign taxes paid or deemed paid by the U.S. person for any tax year with or within which the foreign corporation's annual accounting period ended are reduced by 10%. If the failure continues for 90 days or more after IRS mails a written notice, an additional 5% reduction is made for each 3-month period (or fraction thereof) during which the failure continues. The foreign tax credit reduction for each failure can't exceed the greater of (1) $10,000 or (2) the foreign corporation's income for the period for which the U.S. person fails to file the return. (FTC 2d/FIN ¶ V-1950; USTR ¶ 60,384; TaxDesk ¶ 86,143)

There was no comparable information-reporting requirement with respect to controlled foreign partnerships.

New Law. The '97 Act adds reporting rules for U.S. partners that control foreign partnerships similar to those that apply in the case of controlled foreign corporations. (Com Rept, see ¶ 5182) A U.S. partner that controls (as defined below) (Code Sec. 6038(a)(1) as amended by '97 Act §1142(a)) a foreign partnership (Code Sec. 6038(e)(1) as amended by '97 Act §1142(b)(1)) must file an annual information return with respect to that partnership that includes information prescribed by IRS relating to (Code Sec. 6038(a)(1)):

. . . the foreign partnership's name, its main place of business, the nature of its business, and the country under whose laws it is organized (Code Sec. 6038(a)(1)(A));

. . . a balance sheet of the foreign partnership listing assets, liabilities, and capital (Code Sec. 6038(a)(1)(C));

. . . transactions between the foreign partnership and the U.S. partner (Code Sec. 6038(a)(1)(D)(i)), any corporation or partnership which that partner controls (Code Sec. 6038(a)(1)(D)(ii)), and any other U.S. person that owns, at the time the transaction takes place (Code Sec. 6038(a)(1)(D)(iii)), a 10% or more interest in the foreign partnership (Code Sec. 6038(a)(1)(D)(iii)(II));

. . . information about the foreign partnership that is comparable to the information required in the case of a foreign corporation (above) regarding the classes of stock outstanding, and the names, addresses, and number of shares held by each U.S. person who is a 5% shareholder (Code Sec. 6038(a)(1)(E)(ii)); and

. . . other information required by IRS that is similar or related to the above information or that IRS determines to be appropriate to carry out the provisions of the Code (Code Sec. 6038(a)(1)).

"Control" defined. For this purpose, a U.S. partner controls a foreign partnership if that partner owns, directly or indirectly, a 50% percent or greater interest in the partnership's capital, profits, or (to the extent provided in IRS regs) deductions or losses. Rules similar to the constructive stock ownership rules of Code Sec. 267(c) (see FTC 2d/FIN ¶ G-2711; USTR ¶ 2674.04; TaxDesk ¶ 44,230) apply for this purpose, except for the rule of Code Sec. 267(c)(3) that provides for constructive ownership of interests owned by a partner. (Code Sec. 6038(e)(3) as amended by '97 Act §1142(b)(1)(C))

> ❧*observation:* Under the above-described Code Sec. 267(c) rules, an individual is deemed to own stock owned, directly or indirectly, by or for his brothers and sisters (whether whole or half blood), spouse, ancestors and lineal descendants. An individual is also deemed to own a proportionate part of stock owned, directly or indirectly, by or for a corporation of which he is a shareholder, a partnership of which he is a partner, or an estate or trust of which he is a beneficiary. The '97 Act makes similar constructive ownership rules apply in determining whether a U.S. person controls a foreign partnership.

> ❧*illustration:* A U.S. person holds a 40% interest in a foreign partnership, and his 50%-owned Delaware corporation holds a 20% interest in the same partnership. Since ownership by the corporation is attributed proportionately to its shareholders, the U.S. person is deemed to hold a 50% interest in the foreign partnership, 40% individually and 10% (50% of 20%) through the corporation. The U.S. person therefore controls the foreign partnership.

Reporting by 10% partners. If a foreign partnership is controlled (as defined above) by U.S. persons that each hold a 10% or greater interest, but not by any one U.S. person, IRS may require each U.S. person that holds a 10% interest to furnish information about the partnership, including information about the partner's ownership interests and allocations to the partner of partnership items. (Code Sec. 6038(a)(5) as amended by '97 Act §1142(d)) The same rules described above that are used to determine control of the partnership are also used to determine a 10% interest, but with "10%" substituted for "50%." (Code Sec. 6038(e)(3)(C))

Reporting with respect to controlled foreign corporations expanded. As a result of the '97 Act changes, a U.S. person who controls a foreign corporation must furnish information prescribed by IRS regs relating to transactions between the foreign corporation and any partnership which the U.S. person controls. (Code Sec. 6038(a)(1)(D)(ii))

> ❧*observation:* This is an expansion of the pre-'97 Act rule, which only required reporting of transactions between the foreign corporation and the U.S. person, any other corporation which the U.S. person controlled, and any other U.S. person owning 10% or more of the foreign corporation's stock.

Penalties for failure to furnish information. The '97 Act provides that a U.S. person who fails to furnish the required information with respect to a controlled foreign partnership or corporation on time is subject to a $10,000 penalty for each annual accounting period for which the failure exists. For failures that continue for more than 90 days after IRS mails notice to the U.S. person, additional $10,000 penalties apply for each 30-day period (or fraction thereof) during which the failure continues, up to a maximum penalty of $50,000. (Code Sec. 6038(b) as amended by '97 Act §1142(c))

♥ observation: Thus, the '97 Act, in addition to imposing these penalties with respect to controlled foreign partnership reporting, increases the penalties for failure to report information with respect to controlled foreign corporations.

Other rules made applicable to controlled foreign partnerships. The '97 Act also makes the following above-described controlled foreign corporation reporting rules applicable to controlled foreign partnerships:

... information returns must cover the foreign partnership's annual accounting period ending with or within the U.S. person's tax year (Code Sec. 6038(a)(2) as amended by '97 Act §1142(e)(1)(A));

... no information return is required unless required under regs in effect on the first day of the annual accounting period (Code Sec. 6038(a)(3));

... the foreign tax credit is reduced where a U.S. person fails to furnish on time any information required with respect to a foreign partnership (Code Sec. 6038(c) as amended by '97 Act §1142(e)(1)(C));

... where two or more U.S. persons would be required to furnish information with respect to the same foreign partnership, regs may require that only one provide the information. (Code Sec. 6038(d) as amended by '97 Act §1142(e)(1)(D))

☐ **Effective:** Annual accounting periods beginning after Aug. 5, '97. ('97 Act §1142(f))

¶ 2313. Change of interest in foreign partnership need not be reported unless change involves 10% interest

Code Sec. 6046A(a), as amended by '97 Act § 1143(a)(1)
Code Sec. 6046A(d), as amended by '97 Act § 1143(a)(2)
Generally effective: Transfers and changes after Aug. 5, '97
Committee Reports, see ¶ 5182

An information return had to be filed by any U.S. person:

... who acquired any interest in a foreign partnership;

... who disposed of any portion of his interest in a foreign partnership; or

... whose proportional interest in a foreign partnership changed substantially. (FTC 2d/FIN ¶ S-3643; USTR ¶ 60,46A4)

New Law. Under the '97 Act, reporting by a U.S. person of an acquisition or disposition of an interest in a foreign partnership is required only if the U.S. person holds, directly or indirectly, a 10% or greater interest in the partnership either before or after the acquisition or disposition. Reporting by a U.S. person of a change in that person's proportional interest in the partnership is required only if the change is equivalent to a 10% or greater interest in the partnership. (Code Sec. 6046A(a) as amended by '97 Act §1143(a)(1))

illustration (1): A U.S. person holds an 8% interest in a foreign partnership. He acquires an additional 4%, for a total partnership interest of 12%. Because his interest is 10% or greater after the acquisition, he must report the acquisition on an information return.

illustration (2): A U.S. person holds a 12% interest in a foreign partnership. She disposes of 4%, leaving her with a partnership interest of 8%. Because her interest was 10% or greater before the disposition, she must report the disposition on an information return.

illustration (3): A U.S. person holds a 15% interest in a foreign partnership. A person holding a 40% interest withdraws from the partnership. Assuming that the partnership continues in existence, the U.S. person now holds a 25% interest. Because the change in the U.S. person's interest is equivalent to a 10% interest in the partnership, he must report the change on an information return.

A 10% interest in a partnership is defined in the same manner as under the information-reporting rules for controlled foreign partnerships. Thus, the rules at ¶ 2312 under "'Control' defined" apply, except that "10%" is substituted for "50%." (Code Sec. 6046A(d) as amended by '97 Act §1143(a)(2))

For an increase in the penalty for failure to comply with the above reporting requirement, see ¶ 2411.

☐ **Effective:** Transfers and changes after Aug. 5, '97. ('97 Act §1143(c))

¶ 2314. Reporting threshold for stock ownership in a foreign corporation increased from 5% to 10%

Code Sec. 6046(a), as amended by '97 Act § 1146(a)
Generally effective: Jan. 1, '98
Committee Reports, see ¶ 5188

Certain U.S. persons must file information returns with respect to a foreign corporation upon the occurrence of certain events. Under pre-'97 Act law, the U.S. persons required to file these information returns were:

... each U.S. citizen or resident who became an officer or director of a foreign corporation if a U.S. person owned 5% by value of the stock of that corporation; (FTC

FTC 2d References are to Federal Tax Coordinator 2d
FIN References are to RIA's Analysis of Federal Taxes: Income
USTR References are to United States Tax Reporter: Income, Estate & Gift, and Excise
PCA References are to Pension Coordinator and Pension & Benefits Expert/Advisor
PE References are to Pension and Profit Sharing 2nd
EP References are to Estate Planning & Taxation Coordinator and Estate Planning Advisor

2d/FIN ¶ S-3602; USTR ¶ 60,464; TaxDesk ¶ 88,551)

. . . each U.S. person who acquired stock that, when added to any stock owned on the date of the acquisition, equaled 5% by value of the stock of a foreign corporation;

. . . each U.S. person who acquired 5% by value of the stock of a foreign corporation (regardless of any stock already owned); (FTC 2d/FIN ¶ S-3606; USTR ¶ 60,464; TaxDesk ¶ 88,551) and

. . . each person who became a U.S. person while owning 5% by value of the stock of a foreign corporation. (FTC 2d/FIN ¶ S-3607; USTR ¶ 60,464; TaxDesk ¶ 88,551)

New Law. The '97 Act increases the threshold of stock ownership in a foreign corporation at which information reporting is required from 5% (based on value) to 10% (based on vote or value). (Code Sec. 6046(a)(2) as amended by '97 Act §1146(a)) The 10% threshold is generally parallel to thresholds that apply to other reporting requirements involving foreign corporations. This change is intended to reduce the compliance burden on taxpayers. (Com Rept, see ¶ 5188)

Under the '97 Act, an information return must be filed by:

. . . each U.S. citizen or resident who becomes an officer or director of a foreign corporation if a U.S. person owns 10% of the stock of that corporation;

. . . each U.S. person who acquires stock that, when added to any stock owned on the date of the acquisition, equals 10% of the stock of a foreign corporation;

. . . each U.S. person who acquires 10% of the stock of a foreign corporation (regardless of any stock already owned); and

. . . each person who becomes a U.S. person while owning 10% of the stock of a foreign corporation. (Code Sec. 6046(a)(1))

A person meets the 10% stock ownership requirement if the person owns 10% or more of:

. . . the total combined voting power of all classes of stock of the corporation entitled to vote, or

. . . the total value of the stock of the corporation. (Code Sec. 6046(a)(2))

See ¶ 2411 for an increase in the penalty for failure to comply with the above reporting requirement.

☐ **Effective:** Jan. 1, '98. ('97 Act §1146(b))

¶ 2315. U.S. persons must report contributions to foreign partnerships

Code Sec. 6038B(a)(1), as amended by '97 Act § 1144(a)
Code Sec. 6038B(b), as amended by '97 Act § 1144(b)
Code Sec. 6038B(b)(1), as amended by '97 Act § 1144(c)(1)
Code Sec. 6038B(b)(3), as amended by '97 Act § 1144(c)(2)
Generally effective: Transfers made after Aug. 5, '97
Committee Reports, see ¶ 5186

Each U.S. person who transfers property to a foreign corporation as part of certain exchanges, or who distributes property to a foreign person as part of a complete liquidation, must furnish to IRS, at the time and in the manner that IRS regs prescribe, any information about the exchange or distribution that the regs require. (FTC 2d/FIN ¶s S-3629, S-3630; USTR ¶ 60,38B4; TaxDesk ¶ 81,556)

A penalty is imposed on a U.S. person who fails to furnish the required information, unless the U.S. person shows that the failure is due to reasonable cause and not willful neglect. Under pre-'97 Act law, the penalty was equal to 25% of the gain realized on the exchange. (FTC 2d/FIN ¶ V-1901.2; USTR ¶ 60,38B4)

Under pre-'97 Act law, there was no information-reporting requirement in the case of transfers to a foreign partnership.

New Law. Subject to the exceptions and special rules described below, the '97 Act provides that the above-described reporting rules apply to transfers by U.S. persons of property to a foreign partnership in a contribution described in Code Sec. 721 (i.e., a contribution of property to the partnership in exchange for a partnership interest) and to transfers in any other contribution described in IRS regs. (Code Sec. 6038B(a)(1)(B) as amended by '97 Act §1144(a))

These reporting rules apply in the case of a transfer to a foreign partnership only if: (1) immediately after the transfer, the U.S. person holds, directly or indirectly, a 10% or greater interest in the partnership or (2) the value of the property transferred, when added to the value of the property that the U.S. person (or a related person) transferred to the foreign partnership (or a related partnership) during the 12-month period ending on the date of the transfer, exceeds $100,000. The transferred property is valued at its fair market value at the time of the transfer. (Code Sec. 6038B(b)(1) as amended by '97 Act §1144(b))

> **observation:** Congress has not defined "related person" as that term is used at (2), above.

If a U.S. person is deemed to have made a contribution to a foreign partnership on account of a Code Sec. 482 adjustment (i.e., an allocation of income, deductions, etc., among commonly-controlled entities, see FTC 2d/FIN ¶ G-4000 et seq.; USTR ¶ 4824) or otherwise, the contribution is treated as having been made no earlier than the date specified by IRS. (Code Sec. 6038B(b)(2))

The '97 Act changes the penalty for failing to comply with the above-described reporting requirements to be as follows: A U.S. person who fails to comply with these reporting requirements, whether for a transfer to a foreign corporation or a foreign partnership, is liable for a penalty equal to 10% of the fair market value of the transferred property at the time of the exchange. In the case of a transfer to a foreign partnership, a U.S. person who fails to comply must also recognize gain as if the contrib-

FTC 2d References are to Federal Tax Coordinator 2d
FIN References are to RIA's Analysis of Federal Taxes: Income
USTR References are to United States Tax Reporter: Income, Estate & Gift, and Excise
PCA References are to Pension Coordinator and Pension & Benefits Expert/Advisor
PE References are to Pension and Profit Sharing 2nd
EP References are to Estate Planning & Taxation Coordinator and Estate Planning Advisor

 Research Institute of America   553

uted property had been sold for its fair market value at the time of the contribution. (Code Sec. 6038B(b)(1) as amended by '97 Act §1144(c)(1))

> 📙 *illustration:* X, a U.S. person, contributes property worth $100,000 to a foreign partnership in exchange for a partnership interest. X had a basis of $70,000 in that property at the time of the contribution. If X fails to file the required information return, he is subject to a penalty of $10,000 (10% of the $100,000 fair market value) and recognizes $30,000 of gain (as if the property had been sold for $100,000 at the time of the contribution).

The penalty is limited to $100,000 per exchange, except with respect to any exchange for which the failure was due to intentional disregard. (Code Sec. 6038B(b)(3) as amended by '97 Act §1144(c)(2))

☐ **Effective:** Transfers made after Aug. 5, '97. ('97 Act §1144(d)(1))

However, taxpayers can elect to apply the above '97 Act reporting rules to transfers after Aug. 20, '96, and thereby avoid the pre-'97 Act Code Sec. 1494(c) penalty (for failure to file certain information returns). (Com Rept, see ¶ 5186) For further discussion of that election, see ¶ 1629.

¶ 2316. Information return requirements for purchasers of fish for resale expanded

Code Sec. 6050R(c)(1), as amended by '97 Act § 1601(a)(1)
Generally effective: Payments made after Dec. 31, '97
Committee Reports, see ¶ 5356

Pre-'97 Act law provides that, after Dec. 31, '97, every person who is engaged in the trade or business of purchasing fish for resale ("fish purchaser") from persons engaged in the trade or business of catching fish ("sellers"), must file an information return with respect to each seller to whom he makes payments in cash of $600 or more during a calendar year. The fish purchaser must also furnish a written statement to each such seller. One requirement for this statement is that it include the name and address of the person required to make the return. (FTC 2d/FIN ¶ S-3695.1; USTR ¶ 60,50R4)

New Law. The '97 Act changes the above-described requirement for the statement furnished to the seller to provide that that statement must include the name, address, and phone number of the information contact of the person required to make the return. (Code Sec. 6050R(c)(1) as amended by '97 Act §1601(a))

☐ **Effective:** Payments made after Dec. 31, '97. ('97 Act §1601(j)(1))

¶ 2317. Information return requirements for payors of long-term care benefits expanded

Code Sec. 6050Q(b)(1), as amended by '97 Act § 1602(d)(1)
Generally effective: Benefits paid after Dec. 31, '96
Committee Reports, see ¶ 5373

Payors of long-term care benefits, i.e, long-term care insurance payments and accelerated death benefits excluded from gross income under Code Sec. 101(g), must file an information return with respect to the amount of benefits paid to any individual during any calendar year. The payor must also furnish a written statement to each individual whose name is required to be shown such an information return. Included in the information that must be on this written statement is the name of the payor. (FTC 2d/FIN ¶ S-3441, ¶ S-3442; USTR ¶ 60,50Q4; TaxDesk ¶ 86,164)

New Law. The '97 Act requires that the written statement described above contain not only the payor's name but his address and the phone number of an information contact. (Code Sec. 6050Q(b)(1) as amended by '97 Act §1602(d)(1))

☐ **Effective:** Benefits paid after Dec. 31, '96. ('97 Act §1602(i))

¶ 2318. Tax shelter registration requirements extended to certain "confidential corporate tax shelters"

Code Sec. 6111(d), as amended by '97 Act § 1028(a)
Code Sec. 6111(e), as amended by '97 Act § 1028(a)
Code Sec. 6707(a), as amended by '97 Act § 1028(b)
Generally effective: Tax shelter interests offered after IRS issues guidance
Committee Reports, see ¶ 5128

Tax shelter organizers are generally required to register their shelters with IRS by the day on which interests in the shelter are first offered for sale. Generally, if the organizer does not register, the duty falls upon any other participant in the organization of the shelter, or any person participating in its sale or management. (FTC 2d ¶ S-4400 *et seq.*; USTR ¶ 61,114, ¶ 61,124; TaxDesk ¶ 81,700 *et seq.*)

IRS assigns an identification number to a registered tax shelter. This number must be furnished to each investor who buys or otherwise acquires an interest in the shelter. Any person claiming a deduction, credit, or tax benefit by reason of a tax shelter must include the identification number on the return claiming the deduction, credit, etc. (FTC 2d ¶ S-4413; USTR ¶ 61,114; TaxDesk ¶ 81,708)

New Law.

Registration requirements. The above tax shelter registration requirements have been extended to certain "confidential corporate tax shelters," (Code Sec. 6111(d)(1) as amended by '97 Act §1028(a)) and an offer to participate in such a shelter is treated as an offer for sale for purposes of the above rule. (Code Sec. 6111(d)(4)) Confidential corporate tax shelters are entities, plans, arrangements, or transactions:

(1) a significant purpose of the structure of which is the avoidance or evasion of tax by a corporation (including a corporation that participates indirectly, e.g., through a

---

FTC 2d References are to Federal Tax Coordinator 2d
FIN References are to RIA's Analysis of Federal Taxes: Income
USTR References are to United States Tax Reporter: Income, Estate & Gift, and Excise
PCA References are to Pension Coordinator and Pension & Benefits Expert/Advisor
PE References are to Pension and Profit Sharing 2nd
EP References are to Estate Planning & Taxation Coordinator and Estate Planning Advisor

partnership, trust, or other non-corporate entity);

(2) which are offered to any potential participant under "conditions of confidentiality;" and

(3) for which the tax shelter promoters may receive total fees of more than $100,000 in the aggregate. (Code Sec. 6111(d)(1))

> *observation:* Although the term "confidential corporate tax shelter" isn't used in the Code, it is used in the '97 Act Committee Report to describe the above arrangements and will be used in this explanation to represent the entities subject to these requirements.

> *observation:* Congress has provided no guidance as to how to determine whether a promoter *may* receive more than $100,000 in fees.

The term "promoter," for purposes of the above rules, means any person or any related person (within the meaning of Code Sec. 267 (FTC 2d/FIN ¶ I-3504 *et seq.*; USTR ¶ 2674 *et seq.*; TaxDesk ¶ 22,790 *et seq.*) or Code Sec. 707 (FTC 2d/FIN ¶ B-2016 *et seq.*; USTR ¶ 7074 *et seq.*; TaxDesk ¶ 58,464)) who participates in the organization, management, or sale of the tax shelter. (Code Sec. 6111(d)(2)(B))

> *observation:* It would appear that Congress erred in drafting the above rule, and that it should read "...any person who participates in the organization, management, or sale of the tax shelter, or any related person (within the meaning of...)"

An offer is made under "conditions of confidentiality" if either:

(A) the potential participant (or a person acting for him) has an understanding or agreement with or for the benefit of any promoter of the tax shelter that the participant will limit disclosure of the tax shelter or any significant tax features of the tax shelter; or (Code Sec. 6111(d)(2)(A))

(B) any promoter:

... claims, knows, or has reason to know, or

... knows or has reason to know that any other person (other than the potential participant) claims, or

... causes another person to claim,

that the shelter is proprietary to any person other than the potential participant or is otherwise protected from disclosure to or use by others. (Code Sec. 6111(d)(2)(B))

An offer can be made under conditions of confidentiality if one or more aspects of the shelter's structure is claimed to be proprietary. (Com Rept, see ¶ 5128)

If no promoter registers the tax shelter by the day on which the first offering for sale of interests in the shelter occurs and there is not at least one promoter who is a U.S. person, then, except as provided in the next sentence, each U.S. person who discussed participation in the shelter must register. Under the exception to this rule, any U.S. person who does not actually participate in the shelter and who notifies the promoter in writing, by the end of the 90th day after the beginning of their discussions, that he is not participating, does not have to register. (Code Sec. 6111(d)(3))

Registration will require the submission of information identifying and describing the tax shelter and its tax benefits, as well as any other information required by IRS. The promoter must maintain lists of those who have signed confidentiality agreements or who otherwise have been subjected to nondisclosure requirements. Additionally, promoters must retain lists of those paying fees with respect to plans or arrangements that have previously been registered (even though the particular party may not have been subject to confidentiality restrictions). Registrations will be treated as taxpayer information under Code Sec. 6103 and will therefore not be subject to any public disclosure. (Com Rept, see ¶ 5128)

For tax shelter identification number purposes, an offer to participate in a tax shelter described above is treated as an offer for sale. (Code Sec. 6111(d)(4))

Penalty for failure to register. Except as provided in the next paragraph (Code Sec. 6707(a)(3)(B) as amended by '97 Act §1028(b)) and except to the extent the failure is due to reasonable cause (Code Sec. 6707(a)(1)), a person who is responsible for, but fails to, register a confidential corporate tax shelter, or who provides false or incomplete information to IRS, must pay a penalty of 50% (or 75% in the case of intentional acts) of the fees paid to all promoters of the shelter with respect to offerings made before the date it is registered, or $10,000, whichever is the greater amount. (Code Sec. 6707(a)(3)(A))

> *observation:* The '97 Act erroneously amends Code Sec. 6707(a)(1)(A) instead of Code Sec. 6707(a)(1). It placed the conforming amendment that should have appeared in Code Sec. 6707(a)(1), to direct the reader to the amount of the penalty mentioned above, in Code Sec. 6707(a)(1)(A), which details when a tax shelter must be registered. It is likely that a technical correction will be made to formally correct this error.

The above penalty rule applies as follows to persons required to register under the rules of Code Sec. 6111(d)(3) (see above): (Code Sec. 6707(a)(3)(B))

. . . It doesn't apply to such a person who does not actually participate in the shelter. (Code Sec. 6707(a)(3)(B)(i))

. . . The term "fees paid by such person" is substituted for "fees paid to all promoters of the shelter." (Code Sec. 6707(a)(3)(B)(ii))

. . . The penalty is in addition to the penalty imposed on any other person for failing to register the shelter. (Code Sec. 6707(a)(3)(B)(iii))

Treasury Report. Congress has directed the Treasury Department, in consultation with the Department of Justice, to issue a report to Congress' tax-writing committees on the following tax shelter issues: (1) a description of enforcement efforts under Code Sec. 7408 (relating to actions to enjoin promoters of abusive tax shelters) with respect to corporate tax shelters and the lawyers, accountants, and others who provide opinions (whether or not directly addressed to the taxpayer) regarding aspects of corporate tax shelters; (2) an evaluation of whether the penalties regarding corporate tax shelters are generally sufficient; and (3) an evaluation of whether confidential arrangement tax shelter registration should be extended to transactions where the investor (or potential investor) is not a corporation. The report is due one year after Aug. 5, '97. (Com Rept, see ¶ 5128)

☐ **Effective:** Tax shelters in which interests are offered after IRS prescribes guidance for meeting the above reporting requirements. ('97 Act §1028(e)(1))

Tax Payments, Assessments, Refunds, Collection

¶ 2319. Methods by which taxes may be paid expanded

Code Sec. 6311, as amended by '97 Act § 1205(a)
Code Sec. 6103(k)(8), as amended by '97 Act § 1205(c)(1)
Code Sec. 6103(p)(3)(A), as amended by '97 Act § 1205(c)(3)
Code Sec. 7431(g), as amended by '97 Act § 1205(c)(2)
Generally effective: Nine months after Aug. 5, '97
Committee Reports, see ¶ 5205

IRS accepts checks, money orders, and drafts in payment of taxes. If a check, money order or draft is not paid, the taxpayer is liable for the tax and all penalties to the same extent as if the instrument had not been tendered. Moreover, IRS has a lien against a financial institution in the amount of an unpaid certified, treasurer's or cashier's check or other guaranteed draft drawn on the institution. And it has a lien in the amount of an unpaid money order on the issuer of the money order. The liens are preferred claims. (FTC 2d/FIN ¶ S-5754; USTR ¶ 63,114; TaxDesk ¶ 32,902)

New Law.

Expansion of payment methods. The '97 Act expands the methods that can be used to pay taxes to include any commercially acceptable means that IRS deems appropriate, to the extent and under the conditions provided in regs. (Code Sec. 6311(a) as amended by '97 Act §1205(a)) Congress has directed IRS to issue regulations on receiving payment by commercially acceptable means, including regulations that: (Code Sec. 6311(d)(1))

. . . specify acceptable methods of payment (Code Sec. 6311(d)(1)(A));

. . . specify when payments by these means will be considered received (Code Sec. 6311(d)(1)(B));

. . . identify the types of nontax matters related to payment by these means that are to be resolved by the taxpayer and financial intermediaries without involving IRS (Code Sec. 6311(d)(1)(C)); and

. . . ensure that tax matters will be resolved by IRS, without the involvement of financial intermediaries. (Code Sec. 6311(d)(1)(D))

The pre-'97 Act law rules governing the ultimate liability of the taxpayer if a check or money order is not paid and the liability of financial institutions who guarantee a check or money order are extended to other methods of payment. Thus, if a check, money order or other method of payment, including payment by credit card, debit card, or charge card is not honored or is honored and charged back to IRS, the taxpayer remains liable for the tax and for all legal penalties and additions, as if the payment had not been tendered. (Code Sec. 6311(b))

In addition, if any certified, treasurer's, or cashier's check (or other guaranteed draft), money order or any other method of payment is guaranteed by a financial institution (including a credit card, debit card, or charge card transaction expressly guaranteed by the institution) and is not paid, IRS has a lien for the amount of the check (or draft) on all the assets of the financial institution on which drawn (Code Sec. 6311(c)(1)), for the amount of the money order on all the assets of the issuer (Code Sec. 6311(c)(2)), or for the guaranteed amount of any other transaction on all the assets of the institution making the guarantee (Code Sec. 6311(c)(3)). As under pre-'97 law, the lien is a preferred claim. (Code Sec. 6311(c))

Credit and debit card dispute resolution. In the course of processing credit and debit card transactions, it will be necessary to resolve billing errors and other disputes. The Code contains mechanisms for the determination of tax liability, defenses and other taxpayer protections, and the resolution of disputes with respect to those liabilities. The Truth-in-Lending Act (TILA) contains provisions for determination of credit card liabilities, defenses and other consumer protections, and the resolution of disputes with respect to these liabilities. The Electronic Funds Transfer Act (EFTA) contains corresponding defenses and billing error provisions applicable to debit cards. (Com Rept, see ¶ 5205)

The '97 Act provides that if a credit card is accepted for tax payment:

(1) a tax payment made by credit card is not subject to the TILA provision on the correction of billing errors (15 USC §1666), or to any similar provision of State law, if the alleged error relates to the underlying tax liability, as opposed to relating to the credit card account. Examples for this purpose, of errors relating to the credit card account are (a) computational errors or numerical transpositions in the credit card transactions, and (b) questions as to whether the taxpayer authorized payment by credit card. (Code Sec. 6311(d)(3)(A)) This provision prevents a taxpayer from contesting his tax liability by putting the charge that appears on his credit card bill in dispute. The above TILA provision, however, does apply to disputes involving the errors referred to at (a) and (b) above, as well as to disputes involving postings to the wrong cardholder's account. (Com Rept, see ¶ 5205)

(2) the rules at (1) above also apply to tax payments by debit card, except that "the Electronic Funds Transfer Act" and "15 USC §1693f" are substituted for "TILA" and "15 USC §1666," respectively. (Code Sec. 6311(d)(3)(C)); (Com Rept, see ¶ 5205)

FTC 2d References are to Federal Tax Coordinator 2d
FIN References are to RIA's Analysis of Federal Taxes: Income
USTR References are to United States Tax Reporter: Income, Estate & Gift, and Excise
PCA References are to Pension Coordinator and Pension & Benefits Expert/Advisor
PE References are to Pension and Profit Sharing 2nd
EP References are to Estate Planning & Taxation Coordinator and Estate Planning Advisor

(3) a tax payment is not subject to the TILA provision on claims by the cardholder against the card issuer (15 USC §1666i) or to any similar provision of State law. (Code Sec. 6311(d)(3)(B)) This provision prevents a cardholder from defending a collection action by the card issuer by asserting that IRS incorrectly computed his tax liability. (Com Rept, see ¶ 5205)

Thus, the '97 Act excludes credit card, debit card and charge card issuers and processing mechanisms from the resolution of tax liability, but makes IRS subject to the TILA and EFTA provisions that impose obligations and responsibilities with regard to the "billing error" resolution process. It is not the intention of the above provisions that consumers obtain additional ways to dispute their tax liabilities, i.e., via TILA or EFTA provisions. (Com Rept, see ¶ 5205)

The '97 Act also provides that:

. . . notwithstanding any other provision of law, if IRS owes a taxpayer money because of a correction of a billing error under 15 USC §1666 (TILA) or 15 USC §1693(f) (EFTA), it can credit the amount owed to the taxpayer's credit card account (Code Sec. 6311(d)(3)(E)), rather than crediting it directly to the taxpayer. (Com Rept, see ¶ 5205)

. . . IRS not does come under the TILA definition of a creditor (15 USC §1602(f)), with respect to credit card transactions in payment of taxes. (Code Sec. 6311(d)(3)(D))

observation: Thus, IRS is not subject to the various obligations and deadlines that TILA and its regulations impose on "creditors."

Confidentiality of information. *Limitations on IRS's disclosure of information.* The '97 Act provides that IRS may disclose returns or return information to financial institutions and others to the extent it finds that is necessary for the administration of the above rules. Disclosures made for purposes other than to accept payments by checks or money orders are to be made only to the extent they are authorized by written IRS procedures. (Code Sec. 6103(k)(8) as amended by '97 Act §1205(c)(1))

IRS will have to disclose tax information to financial institutions to obtain payment by credit card charges and to resolve billing disputes. To obtain payment, IRS will have to disclose, at least, the dollar amount of the payment and the taxpayer's credit card number. The resolution of billing disputes may require the disclosure of additional tax information; in these cases, financial institutions could conceivably require some information regarding the underlying tax liability. In lieu of disclosing further information, IRS may elect to allow disputed amounts to be charged back to IRS and to reinstate the corresponding tax liability. (Com Rept, see ¶ 5205) IRS is not required to keep records of requests for information or disclosure of information made under the above rules. (Code Sec. 6103(p)(3)(A) as amended by '97 Act §1205(c)(3))

Limitations on persons who received information from IRS. Except as otherwise provided below, no person can use or disclose information relating to debit or credit card transactions that is received from IRS under Code Sec. 6103(k)(8) (see above) other than for purposes directly related to the processing of the transactions or the billing or collection of amounts charged or debited under the transaction. (Code Sec.

6311(e)(1) as amended by '97 Act §1205(a)) The exceptions to this rule allow:

(i) debit and credit card issuers and others acting for them to use and disclose this information for purposes directly relating to servicing an issuer's account. (Code Sec. 6311(e)(2)(A))

(ii) debit and credit care issuers or others directly involved in the processing of credit or debit card transactions or the billing or collection of charged or debited amounts to use and disclose this information for purposes directly related to: (Code Sec. 6311(e)(2)(B))

... statistical risk and profitability assessment (Code Sec. 6311(e)(2)(B)(i));

... transferring receivables, accounts, or interests therein (Code Sec. 6311(e)(2)(B)(ii));

... auditing the account information (Code Sec. 6311(e)(2)(B)(iii));

... complying with Federal, State, or local law (Code Sec. 6311(e)(2)(B)(iv)); and

... properly authorized civil, criminal, or regulatory investigations by Federal, State or local authorities. (Code Sec. 6311(e)(2)(B)(v))

The '97 Act provides that the use and disclosure of credit or debit card transaction information obtained from IRS can be made only to the extent authorized by written IRS procedures. (Code Sec. 6311(e)(3)) Congress expects that these written procedures will prohibit the use of tax transaction information for marketing tax-related services by the issuer or any marketing that targets only those who use their credit card to pay taxes. Congress also expects that written procedures will ban the sale of tax transaction information to a third-party. (Com Rept, see ¶ 5205)

The '97 Act also provides that Code Sec. 7431, which provides for civil damages for unauthorized disclosure of returns and return information (FTC 2d/FIN ¶ S-6501; USTR ¶ 74,314) , applies to the violation of the above limitations on persons who receive information from IRS. (Code Sec. 7431(g) as amended by '97 Act §1205(c)(2))

☐ **Effective:** Nine months after Aug. 5, '97. ('97 Act §1205(d))

¶ 2320. Assessment limitations period stays open where information returns aren't filed with respect to certain foreign transactions

Code Sec. 6501(c)(8), as amended by '97 Act § 1145(a)
Generally effective: Information returns due after Aug. 5, '97
Committee Reports, see ¶ 5187

Generally, any tax imposed by the Code must be assessed within three years of the date the return was filed (or the return due date if later). (FTC 2d/FIN ¶ T-4001; USTR ¶ 65,014.01; TaxDesk ¶ 83,801) But the period for assessing tax on exchanges

---

FTC 2d References are to Federal Tax Coordinator 2d
FIN References are to RIA's Analysis of Federal Taxes: Income
USTR References are to United States Tax Reporter: Income, Estate & Gift, and Excise
PCA References are to Pension Coordinator and Pension & Benefits Expert/Advisor
PE References are to Pension and Profit Sharing 2nd
EP References are to Estate Planning & Taxation Coordinator and Estate Planning Advisor

and distributions made in connection with certain transfers of property by U.S. persons to foreign persons or corporations won't expire before the date that is three years after the date on which the U.S. transferor files an information return under Code Sec. 6038B (FTC 2d/FIN ¶ S-3629; USTR ¶ 60,38B4; TaxDesk ¶ 81,556) with respect to the exchange or distribution. (FTC 2d/FIN ¶ T-4146; USTR ¶ 65,014.28(d))

Besides the information return required under Code Sec. 6038B (above), the following information returns are required with respect to foreign transactions:

. . . return of U.S. person who controls foreign corporation—Code Sec. 6038 (FTC 2d/FIN ¶ S-3585; USTR ¶ 60,384; TaxDesk ¶ 81,553);

. . . 25% foreign-owned corporation's return of transactions with related parties—Code Sec. 6038A (FTC 2d/FIN ¶ S-3510; USTR ¶ 60,38A4; TaxDesk ¶ 81,554);

. . . return of officer, director, or 5% shareholder of foreign corporation—Code Sec. 6046 (FTC 2d/FIN ¶ S-3602 *et seq.*; USTR ¶ 60,464; TaxDesk ¶ 81,551);

. . . return of person who acquires, disposes of, or has substantial changes in, interests in foreign partnership— Code Sec. 6046A (FTC 2d/FIN ¶ S-3643; USTR ¶ 60,46A4); and

. . . return regarding transfer to or creation of foreign trust—Code Sec. 6048 (FTC 2d/FIN ¶ S-3644; USTR ¶ 60,484; TaxDesk ¶ 81,564).

There was no special assessment period with respect to these returns.

New Law. Under the '97 Act, in the case of any information required to be reported under Code Sec. 6038, Code Sec. 6038A, Code Sec. 6038B, Code Sec. 6046, Code Sec. 6046A, or Code Sec. 6048, the statute of limitations with respect to any event or period to which that information relates won't expire before the date that is three years after the date on which the required information is furnished to IRS. (Code Sec. 6501(c)(8) as amended by '97 Act §1145(a))

> *observation:* Thus, a statute of limitations rule similar to the pre-'97 Act rule that applied with respect to transactions reportable under Code Sec. 6038B now applies with respect to additional foreign transactions.

> *observation:* Under this new provision, the assessment period remains open with respect to the "event or period" to which the required information relates. Most of the information returns listed above relate to discrete events, in which case the assessment period will remain open only with respect to that event. The Code Sec. 6038 return of a U.S. person who controls a foreign corporation relates to the foreign corporation's annual accounting period that ends with or within the U.S. person's tax year. Thus, in the case of a failure to report required information under Code Sec. 6038, the statute of limitations will remain open with respect to that period.

☐ **Effective:** Information the due date for the reporting of which is after Aug. 5, '97. ('97 Act §1145(b))

¶ 2321. Limitations period for passthrough items starts running with filing of taxpayer's return

Code Sec. 6501(a), as amended by '97 Act § 1284(a)
Generally effective: Tax years beginning after Aug. 5, '97
Committee Reports, see ¶ 5251

Certain "passthrough" entities such as S corporations (FTC 2d/FIN ¶ D-1420; USTR ¶ 13,614; TaxDesk ¶ 61,450), partnerships (FTC 2d/FIN ¶ B-1000; USTR ¶ 7614; TaxDesk ¶ 58,400), and certain trusts (FTC 2d/FIN ¶ C-1000; USTR ¶ 6414; TaxDesk ¶ 65,100) generally pass through their items of income, gain, loss, deduction, and credit to their shareholders or beneficial owners, who are liable for any tax due.

Taxes generally must be assessed within three years after the return was filed. (FTC 2d/FIN ¶ T-4001; USTR ¶ 65,014.01; TaxDesk ¶ 83,801) In '93, the Supreme Court held in *Bufferd* that the limitations period for assessing the income tax liability of an S corporation shareholder runs from the date the shareholder's return is filed. (FTC 2d/FIN ¶ T-4021; USTR ¶ 65,014.04; TaxDesk ¶ 83,805) Before that decision, courts were divided on whether the limitations period for adjustments arising from passthrough items runs from the filing date of the passthrough entity's return or the shareholder or beneficial owner's return. (FTC 2d/FIN ¶ T-4020, ¶ T-4021, ¶ T-4023; USTR ¶ 65,014.04; TaxDesk ¶ 83,803, ¶ 83,805, ¶ 83,806)

New Law. The '97 Act provides that the return that starts the running of the statute of limitations for a taxpayer is the return of the taxpayer and not the return of another person from whom the taxpayer has received an item of income, gain, loss, deduction, or credit. (Code Sec. 6501(a) as amended by '97 Act §1284(a))

> *observation:* The above '97 Act provision codifies the holding in *Bufferd* and makes it clear that the same rule applies to partnerships and trusts. *Bufferd* continues to apply for tax years beginning on or before Aug. 5, '97.

> *illustration:* Taxpayer is a partner in ABC partnership. ABC filed its Year 1 partnership return on Mar. 15 of Year 2. Taxpayer filed her Year 1 individual return on Apr. 15 of Year 2. On Apr. 1 of Year 5, IRS sent Taxpayer a notice of deficiency contesting certain partnership items reported on her return. The notice was timely because it was sent within three years of the filing of Taxpayer's return, although more than three years after ABC filed its return.

> *observation:* Many partnerships are subject to a unified audit and review procedure (¶ 1406), under which the tax treatment of partnership items is determined at the partnership level. (FTC 2d/FIN ¶ T-2100 *et seq.*; USTR

FTC 2d References are to Federal Tax Coordinator 2d
FIN References are to RIA's Analysis of Federal Taxes: Income
USTR References are to United States Tax Reporter: Income, Estate & Gift, and Excise
PCA References are to Pension Coordinator and Pension & Benefits Expert/Advisor
PE References are to Pension and Profit Sharing 2nd
EP References are to Estate Planning & Taxation Coordinator and Estate Planning Advisor

¶ 62,214 *et seq.*; TaxDesk ¶ 82,501 *et seq.*) For those partnerships, the period for assessing tax with respect to any person that is attributable to a partnership item won't expire before the end of a special limitations period. That period is generally three years from the later of the date the partnership return was filed or the return due date (FTC 2d/FIN ¶ T-4018; USTR ¶ 62,214.08; TaxDesk ¶ 83,803), but it can be extended by agreement (FTC 2d/FIN ¶ T-4419; USTR ¶ 62,214.08; TaxDesk ¶ 82,538) or suspended if IRS makes an administrative adjustment (FTC 2d/FIN ¶ T-4316; USTR ¶ 62,214.08; TaxDesk ¶ 83,844). Thus, tax attributable to a partnership item can sometimes be assessed against a partner even after that partner's general assessment period has expired.

illustration: Taxpayer is a partner in XYZ partnership, a large partnership subject to the unified audit and review procedure. XYZ filed its Year 1 partnership return on Mar. 15 of Year 2. Taxpayer filed his Year 1 individual return on Apr. 15 of Year 2. The limitations period on assessment against Taxpayer expired as scheduled on Apr. 15 of Year 5. However, the tax matters partner of XYZ agreed, on behalf of all partners, to extend the statute of limitations with respect to partnership items. As a result, tax attributable to XYZ partnership items can be assessed against Taxpayer until the end of the extended limitations period, even after Apr. 15 of Year 5.

☐ **Effective:** Tax years beginning after Aug. 5, '97. ('97 Act §1284(b))

¶ 2322. Special limitations period for credits or refunds for self-employment taxes resulting from Tax Court employment status cases

Code Sec. 6511(d)(7), as amended by '97 Act § 1454(b)
Generally effective: Aug. 5, '97
Committee Reports, see ¶ 5303

In order for a claim for a refund or credit to be effective, a taxpayer must file it with IRS within a certain time period; generally, this period is the later of the period that ends three years after the relevant return was filed or two years after the tax was paid. (FTC 2d/FIN ¶ T-7501; USTR ¶ 65,114.01; TaxDesk ¶ 80,601)

New Law. If a credit or refund claim relates to an overpayment of self-employment tax attributable to a Tax Court employment status proceeding under new Code Sec. 7436 (¶ 2329), and the credit or refund is otherwise prevented by the operation of any law other than an offer in compromise under Code Sec. 7122, such credit or refund may be allowed or made if a claim is filed on or before the last day of the second year after the calendar year in which the Tax Court decision becomes final. (Code Sec. 6511(d)(7) as amended by '97 Act §1454(b)(1))

observation: The '97 Act thus provides a special limitations period for self-employment tax claims attributable to Tax Court employment status proceedings.

☐ **Effective:** Aug. 5, '97. ('97 Act §1454(c))

¶ 2323. Limitations period on refund claim attributable to foreign tax credit begins on due date of return for year in which foreign taxes were paid or accrued

Code Sec. 6511(d)(3)(A), as amended by '97 Act § 1056(a)
Generally effective: Taxes paid or accrued in tax years beginning after Aug. 5, '97
Committee Reports, see ¶ 5148

U.S. persons may credit foreign taxes against U.S. tax on foreign source income. (FTC 2d/FIN ¶ O-4000 *et seq.*; USTR ¶ 9014; TaxDesk ¶ 39,101 *et seq.*) The amount of foreign tax credits that can be claimed in a year is subject to a limitation that prevents taxpayers from using foreign tax credits to offset U.S. tax on U.S. source income. (FTC 2d/FIN ¶ O-4400 *et seq.*; USTR ¶ 9044; TaxDesk ¶ 39,412) Separate limitations are applied to specific categories of income. (FTC 2d/FIN ¶ O-4300 *et seq.*; USTR ¶ 9044.01; TaxDesk ¶ 39,401 *et seq.*) The amount of creditable taxes paid or accrued in any tax year that exceeds the foreign tax credit limitation can be carried back two years and forward five years. (FTC 2d/FIN ¶ O-4600 *et seq.*; USTR ¶ 9044.02; TaxDesk ¶ 39,429 *et seq.*)

For refund claims relating to an overpayment attributable to foreign tax credits, the limitations period on filing a claim was ten years from the due date of the return "for the year with respect to which the claim is made." (FTC 2d/FIN ¶ T-7569; USTR ¶ 65,114.12; TaxDesk ¶ 80,660) IRS's position was that, in the case of a foreign tax credit carryforward, the limitations period is determined by reference to the year in which the foreign taxes were paid or accrued. However, the Court of Federal Claims held in *Ampex Corp.* that the limitations period is determined by reference to the year to which the foreign tax credits are carried. (FTC 2d/FIN ¶ T-7570; USTR ¶ 65,115.12; TaxDesk ¶ 80,661)

New Law. The '97 Act changes the limitations period for a refund claim relating to an overpayment attributable to foreign tax credits from (a) ten years from the due date of the return for the year with respect to which the claim is made to (b) ten years from the due date of the return for the year in which the foreign taxes were actually paid or accrued. (Code Sec. 6511(d)(3)(A) as amended by '97 Act §1056(a)) Thus, the year to which the foreign tax credits are carried is not considered for purposes of this rule. (Com Rept, see ¶ 5148)

> *illustration:* Taxpayer pays creditable foreign taxes in Year 1. Those taxes are carried forward to, and create an overpayment in, Year 4. Taxpayer's Year 1 return was due on Mar. 15 of Year 2. Taxpayer may file a refund claim relating to the Year 4 overpayment attributable to the foreign tax credit carryfor-

---

FTC 2d References are to Federal Tax Coordinator 2d
FIN References are to RIA's Analysis of Federal Taxes: Income
USTR References are to United States Tax Reporter: Income, Estate & Gift, and Excise
PCA References are to Pension Coordinator and Pension & Benefits Expert/Advisor
PE References are to Pension and Profit Sharing 2nd
EP References are to Estate Planning & Taxation Coordinator and Estate Planning Advisor

ward on or before Mar. 15 of Year 12, which is ten years from the due date of Taxpayer's return for the tax year in which the foreign taxes were paid.

☐ **Effective:** Foreign taxes paid or accrued in tax years beginning after Aug. 5, '97. ('97 Act §1056(b)) No inference is intended regarding the limitations period for foreign taxes paid or accrued in tax years beginning on or before Aug. 5, '97. (Com Rept, see ¶ 5148)

¶ 2324. IRS may levy on certain wage replacement and annuity payments

Code Sec. 6331(h), as amended by '97 Act § 1024(a)
Code Sec. 6334(f), as amended by '97 Act § 1025(a)
Generally effective: Levies issued after Aug. 5, '97
Committee Reports, see ¶ 5124, 5125

If any person fails to pay a tax within 10 days of notice and demand for payment, IRS may collect the tax by levy on all property and rights to property belonging to that person, unless an explicit statutory exemption from levy applies. Property exempt from levy included a minimum amount of salary and wages, workmen's compensation payments, annuity or pension payments under the Railroad Retirement Act and benefits under the Railroad Unemployment Insurance Act, unemployment benefits, and certain means-tested public assistance.

In general, a levy does not apply to property acquired after the date of levy. However, a continuous levy, i.e., a levy that is effective from the day it is first made until the day it is fully paid or unenforceable, applies to salary and wages above the minimum amount exempted from levy. (FTC 2d/FIN ¶ V-5200 *et seq.*; USTR ¶ 63,314.03; TaxDesk ¶ 90,201)

New Law. The '97 Act extends the continuous levy provisions to permit a continuous levy to attach to up to 15% of the following payments due to the taxpayer (Code Sec. 6331(h)(1) as amended by '97 Act §1024(a)) (Code Sec. 6334(f) as amended by '97 Act §1025(a)):

(1) any federal payment for which eligibility isn't based on a payee's income or assets (or both),

(2) the minimum exempted amount of salary and wages,

(3) workmen's compensation payments,

(4) annuity or pension payments under the Railroad Retirement Act and benefits under the Railroad Unemployment Insurance Act,

(5) unemployment benefits, and

(6) certain means-tested public assistance payments. (Code Sec. 6331(h)(2))

Included in item (1) above are Social Security payments, which were subject to levy under pre-'97 Act law and are now subject to continuous levy. (Com Rept, see ¶ 5124) (Com Rept, see ¶ 5125)

Congress has explained this provision by saying that it believes that because wages are subject to levy, wage replacement payments should also be subject to levy. Congress also believes that it is inappropriate to exempt from levy one type of annuity or pension payment while most other types of these payments are subject to levy. (Com Rept, see ¶ 5124) (Com Rept, see ¶ 5125)

☐ **Effective:** Levies issued after Aug. 5, '97. ('97 Act §1024(b), 1025(b))

Tax Court Procedures

¶ 2325. Tax Court order requiring IRS to refund overpayment may be appealed; Tax Court jurisdiction over refund offset is limited

Code Sec. 6512(b)(2), as amended by '97 Act § 1451(a)
Code Sec. 6512(b)(4), as amended by '97 Act § 1451(b)
Generally effective: Aug. 5, '97
Committee Reports, see ¶ 5300

If IRS fails to refund an overpayment determined by the Tax Court, plus interest, within 120 days after the decision determining the overpayment becomes final, the Tax Court may, on the taxpayer's motion, order IRS to refund the overpayment plus interest. (FTC 2d/FIN ¶ U-2133; USTR ¶ 65,124; TaxDesk ¶ 80,743) Under pre-'97 Act law, it was not clear whether the Tax Court's order in this situation could be appealed. (Com Rept, see ¶ 5300)

Before making a refund or crediting a taxpayer's overpayment, IRS must first offset the overpayment by the following liabilities of the taxpayer: (a) past-due child support, (b) any debts owed to federal agencies, and (c) any past-due state tax obligations (in that order). (FTC 2d/FIN ¶ T-6001; USTR ¶ 64,024; TaxDesk ¶ 80,312) Under pre-'97 Act law, it was not clear whether the Tax Court had jurisdiction over the validity or merits of these offsets. (Com Rept, see ¶ 5300)

New Law. The '97 Act provides that a Tax Court order disposing of a taxpayer's motion to force a refund from IRS is reviewable in the same manner as a decision of the Tax Court, but only with respect to the matters determined in the order. (Code Sec. 6512(b)(2) as amended by '97 Act §1451(a))

> *observation:* The review is limited to the Tax Court's grant or denial of the taxpayer's motion for a Tax Court order requiring IRS to make the refund; it doesn't apply to the Tax Court's overpayment determination itself.

The procedures for appealing the order are the same as for appealing a Tax Court decision. (Com Rept, see ¶ 5300)

FTC 2d References are to Federal Tax Coordinator 2d
FIN References are to RIA's Analysis of Federal Taxes: Income
USTR References are to United States Tax Reporter: Income, Estate & Gift, and Excise
PCA References are to Pension Coordinator and Pension & Benefits Expert/Advisor
PE References are to Pension and Profit Sharing 2nd
EP References are to Estate Planning & Taxation Coordinator and Estate Planning Advisor

The '97 Act also denies the Tax Court jurisdiction to determine the validity or merits of the offsets for (a) past-due child support, (b) any debts owed to federal agencies, and (c) any past-due state tax obligations, that may reduce or eliminate a taxpayer's refund or credit. (Code Sec. 6512(b)(4) as amended by '97 Act §1451(b))

Congress believes this clarification of the jurisdiction of the Tax Court and the ability to appeal orders of the Tax Court will provide greater certainty for taxpayers and the government in conducting cases before the Tax Court. This clarification will also reduce litigation. (Com Rept, see ¶ 5300)

☐ **Effective:** Aug. 5, '97. ('97 Act §1451(c))

¶ 2326. Nonfilers can get Tax Court refund of overpayments paid within three years before deficiency notice

Code Sec. 6512(b)(3), as amended by '97 Act § 1282(a)
Generally effective: Claims for credit or refund for tax years ending after Aug. 5, '97
Committee Reports, see ¶ 5249

The Code provides limitations on both the time period in which a claim for refund can be made and the amount that can be refunded. In general, a refund claim must be filed within three years of the date of when the return was filed (or the due date, if the return was filed early) or two years of the date the tax was paid, whichever period ends later. (FTC 2d/FIN ¶ T-7501; USTR ¶ 65,114.01; TaxDesk ¶ 80,601) If a claim was filed within three years from the time the return was filed, the taxpayer can recover amounts paid during the three years before the claim was filed (the "three-year lookback period"). (FTC 2d/FIN ¶ T-7537; USTR ¶ 65,114.07; TaxDesk ¶ 80,634) If a claim wasn't filed within three years from the time the return was filed (FTC 2d/FIN ¶ T-7546; USTR ¶ 65,114.07), or if no return was filed (FTC 2d/FIN ¶ T-7547; USTR ¶ 65,114.07), the taxpayer can recover amounts paid during the two years before the claim was filed (the "two-year lookback period").

If the taxpayer contests a deficiency in the Tax Court, and the court determines an overpayment instead of a deficiency, the taxpayer can obtain a refund of the portion of the overpayment that was paid within the two- or three-year lookback period that would apply if a refund claim had been filed on the date of mailing of the notice of deficiency. (FTC 2d/FIN ¶ T-7578; USTR ¶ 65,124; TaxDesk ¶ 80,668)

In *Lundy,* the taxpayer hadn't filed a return, but received a notice of deficiency within three years after the date the return was due and challenged the deficiency in Tax Court. The Supreme Court held that the taxpayer couldn't recover overpayments attributable to withholding during the tax year. The two-year lookback rule applied because no return had been filed. Since overwithheld amounts are deemed paid as of the due date the taxpayer's return, which was more than two years before the notice of deficiency was issued, the overpayments couldn't be recovered. (FTC 2d/FIN ¶ T-7578.1; USTR ¶ 65,124; TaxDesk ¶ 80,668) If the same taxpayer had filed a return on the date the notice of deficiency was issued and then claimed a refund, the three-year lookback rule would have applied, and the taxpayer could have obtained a refund.

(Com Rept, see ¶ 5249)

New Law. The '97 Act permits taxpayers who fail to file a return and are sent a notice of deficiency during the third year after the return due date (with extensions) to obtain a refund of an overpayment found by the Tax Court that was paid within the three-year period prior to the date of the notice of deficiency. (Code Sec. 6512(b)(3) as amended by '97 Act §1282(a))

> 🖝 *illustration:* Taxpayer's Year 1 return was due on Apr. 15 of Year 2. Taxpayer didn't file a return for Year 1, but did pay tax for that year through wage withholding. IRS sent Taxpayer a notice of deficiency for Year 1 on Oct. 15 of Year 4, which was during the third year after the due date of the Year 1 return. If Taxpayer contests the deficiency in the Tax Court, and the court finds that there was actually an overpayment for Year 1, Taxpayer can get a refund of any overpayment paid within the three-year period prior to the date of the notice of deficiency. Here, since the overwithheld amounts were deemed paid on Apr. 15 of Year 2 (the due date of the Year 1 return), Taxpayer can get a refund of the entire overpayment.

☐ **Effective:** Claims for credit or refund for tax years ending after Aug. 5, '97. ('97 Act §1282(b))

¶ 2327. Taxpayers may motion, instead of petition, for interest redeterminations in Tax Court; Tax Court given jurisdiction over IRS interest underpayments

Code Sec. 7481(c), as amended by '97 Act § 1452(a)
Generally effective: Aug. 5, '97
Committee Reports, see ¶ 5301

After the Tax Court determines a deficiency, IRS may assess and collect interest on the deficiency. If the taxpayer disagrees with IRS's computation of interest on such a deficiency, he can pay the entire deficiency and interest and, within one year after the date the Tax Court decision becomes final, petition the Tax Court for a determination that he had overpaid the interest. Any overpayment of interest determined by the Court as a result of these procedures is treated the same as a Tax Court-determined overpayment of tax (under the rules of Code Sec. 6512(b)(1)), and the order of the Tax Court that redetermines the interest, when entered in the records of the court, is reviewable in the same manner as a decision of the Tax Court. (FTC 2d/FIN ¶ U-3421; USTR ¶ 74,814)

New Law. The '97 Act changes the above rule so that, instead of petitioning the Tax Court, a taxpayer must file a motion in the Tax Court. (Code Sec. 7481(c)(1) as

FTC 2d References are to Federal Tax Coordinator 2d
FIN References are to RIA's Analysis of Federal Taxes: Income
USTR References are to United States Tax Reporter: Income, Estate & Gift, and Excise
PCA References are to Pension Coordinator and Pension & Benefits Expert/Advisor
PE References are to Pension and Profit Sharing 2nd
EP References are to Estate Planning & Taxation Coordinator and Estate Planning Advisor

amended by '97 Act §1452(a))

The '97 Act also provides comparable rules in cases where, in the original Tax Court case, the court determines that there was an overpayment. (Code Sec. 7481(c)(2)(B)) If the taxpayer disagrees with IRS's computation of interest on the overpayment, then, within one year after the date the Tax Court decision becomes final, he can file a motion with the Tax Court for a determination that IRS had underpaid the interest. (Code Sec. 7481(c)(1)) Any underpayment of interest determined by the Court as a result of the above procedures is treated the same as a Tax Court-determined overpayment of tax (under the rules of Code Sec. 6512(b)(1), and the order of the Tax Court that redetermines the interest, when entered in the records of the court, is reviewable in the same manner as a decision of the Tax Court. (Code Sec. 7481(c)(3))

> *observation:* The '97 Act contains a drafting error. There should be an "or", not an "and", between Code Sec. 7481(c)(2)(A)(ii) and Code Sec. 7481(c)(2)(B).

☐ **Effective:** Aug. 5, '97. ('97 Act §1452(b))

¶ 2328. Tax Court authorized to issue declaratory judgments on eligibility for deferral of estate tax from closely-held business

Code Sec. 7479, as added by '97 Act § 505
Generally effective: Estates of decedents dying after Aug. 5, '97
Committee Reports, see ¶ 5030

Under Code Sec. 6166, an executor may elect to pay the estate tax attributable to an interest in a closely-held business in up to ten annual installments. (FTC 2d/FIN ¶ S-6000 *et seq.*; USTR ¶ 61,664; TaxDesk ¶ 78,401 *et seq.*) If certain events occur during the repayment period (e.g., the closely-held business is sold), the election is terminated, and the future installments are accelerated. (FTC 2d/FIN ¶ S-6100 *et seq.*; USTR ¶ 61,664.03; TaxDesk ¶ 78,427 *et seq.*)

Under pre-'97 Act law, in order to obtain judicial review of an IRS determination that an estate wasn't eligible for deferral under Code Sec. 6166 or had lost its eligibility, the estate had to pay the full estate tax asserted by IRS. (FTC 2d/FIN ¶ U-2108; USTR ¶ 74,424) This could necessitate liquidation of the business assets that Code Sec. 6166 is designed to protect. (Com Rept, see ¶ 5030)

New Law. The '97 Act authorizes the Tax Court to issue declaratory judgments where there is an actual controversy about an IRS determination (or IRS's failure to make a determination) of an estate's initial or continuing eligibility for deferral under Code Sec. 6166. (Code Sec. 7479(a) as added by '97 Act §505(a))

> *observation:* In a declaratory judgment action, the court declares the parties' legal rights and relations before a claim has accrued, but where it is likely that a claim would arise if no declaration were issued.

> ☙ *observation:* The Code doesn't define "actual controversy," but the term is used in the federal court system to mean a real dispute between adverse parties involving substantial legal interests. The requirement of an "actual controversy" also applies in other cases in which the Tax Court is empowered to issue declaratory judgments (see FTC 2d/FIN ¶s U-3704, U-3803).

Upon the filing of an appropriate pleading, the Tax Court can declare whether the estate was initially eligible for deferral or whether it has ceased to be eligible. The court's declaration has the force and effect of a Tax Court decision and is reviewable as such. (Code Sec. 7479(a))

Who can bring action. Only the executor or a person who has assumed an obligation to make installment payments with respect to the estate can file a pleading for a declaratory judgment of the type described above. If a person who assumed a payment obligation files a pleading, he must join each other such person as a party. (Code Sec. 7479(b)(1))

Exhaustion of administrative remedies. In order for the Tax Court to issue a declaratory judgment, it must determine that the petitioner has exhausted all available administrative remedies within IRS. A petitioner is deemed to have exhausted administrative remedies if IRS fails to make a determination of an estate's initial or continuing eligibility for deferral within 180 days after a determination was requested, but only if the petitioner has taken, in a timely manner, all reasonable steps to secure the determination. (Code Sec. 7479(b)(2))

> ☙ *observation:* This implies that a petitioner is also deemed to have exhausted administrative remedies if IRS makes a determination of the estate's initial or continuing eligibility for deferral.

Time limit on bringing action. If IRS sends notice to the petitioner, by certified or registered mail, of IRS's determination with respect to the estate's initial or continuing eligibility for deferral, any petition for a declaratory judgment must be filed before the 91st day after the date of the mailing. (Code Sec. 7479(b)(3))

> ☙ *observation:* While Code Sec. 7479(b)(3) (above) speaks of sending notice to "the petitioner," in certain cases more than one party is eligible to file a petition (see "Who can bring action," above). It's not clear, in such cases, whether notice sent to one petitioner starts the 90-day period running against other parties who are eligible to file a petition but didn't receive notice.

☐ **Effective:** Estates of decedents dying after Aug. 5, '97. ('97 Act §505(c))

FTC 2d References are to Federal Tax Coordinator 2d
FIN References are to RIA's Analysis of Federal Taxes: Income
USTR References are to United States Tax Reporter: Income, Estate & Gift, and Excise
PCA References are to Pension Coordinator and Pension & Benefits Expert/Advisor
PE References are to Pension and Profit Sharing 2nd
EP References are to Estate Planning & Taxation Coordinator and Estate Planning Advisor

¶ 2329. Tax Court given jurisdiction to review certain IRS determinations of employment status

Code Sec. 7436, as added by '97 Act § 1454(a)
Code Sec. 7421(a), as amended by '97 Act § 1454(b)(2)
Code Sec. 7453, as amended by '97 Act § 1454(b)(3)
Code Sec. 7481(b), as amended by '97 Act § 1454(b)(3)
Generally effective: Aug. 5, '97
Committee Reports, see ¶ 5303

If certain requirements of Section 530(a) of the Revenue Act of '78 ("Sec. 530(a)") are satisfied, an employer can treat a worker as an independent contractor rather than as an employee for employment tax purposes. Where Sec. 530(a) allows an employer to treat a worker as an independent contractor, the employer is not liable for social security (FICA), railroad retirement, federal unemployment (FUTA), federal railroad unemployment, and federal income tax withholding taxes. In addition, a taxpayer who is under IRS audit or involved in administrative or judicial processes and meets the requirements of Sec. 530(a) can get an unpaid assessment abated, refunds of employment taxes paid, and automatic forgiveness of any interest or penalties. Under pre-'97 Act law, IRS's determination as to the employment status of an individual or the taxpayer's entitlement to relief under Sec. 530(a) wasn't subject to review by the Tax Court. (FTC 2d/FIN ¶ H-4300 *et seq.*; USTR ¶ 34,014.375; TaxDesk ¶ 53,700 *et seq.*)

IRS has an early referral program for employment tax issues. Under this program a taxpayer can request the transfer of developed, unagreed employment tax issues to the Appeals Office while other issues in the case continue to be examined. (FTC 2d/FIN ¶ T-1801.1 *et seq.*; USTR ¶ 76,557)

If a taxpayer's deficiency or overpayment (including penalties) does not exceed $10,000 and the taxpayer has filed a timely Tax Court petition, he may elect to have his case tried under a special procedure for small tax cases. Under pre-'97 Act law, there was no small tax case procedure for cases specifically concerning Sec. 530(a) relief. (FTC 2d/FIN ¶ U-3600 *et seq.*; USTR ¶ 34,014.375)

New Law. The '97 Act permits a taxpayer, upon filing an appropriate pleading, to obtain Tax Court review of an "actual controversy" involving an IRS determination, as part of an examination, that: (1) one or more individuals performing services for the taxpayer are employees for employment tax purposes (Code Sec. 7436(a)(1) as added by '97 Act §1454(a)), or (2) the taxpayer is not entitled to relief under Sec. 530(a) with respect to such an individual (Code Sec. 7436(a)(2)).

> ✪ *observation:* The Code doesn't define "actual controversy," but the term is used in the federal court system to mean a real dispute between adverse parties involving substantial legal interests. The requirement of an "actual controversy" also applies in other cases in which the Tax Court is empowered to issue declaratory judgments (see FTC 2d/FIN ¶s U-3704, U-3803).

> ✪ *observation:* For the sake of brevity in this analysis, items (1) and (2) above will be referred to as "employment status" matters.

A pleading described above can only be filed by the person for whom the services are performed. (Code Sec. 7436(b)(1)) If IRS sends by certified or registered mail notice to the taxpayer of the above described determination, no proceeding may be initiated in Tax Court with respect to the determination unless the pleading is filed before the 91st day after the date of such mailing. (Code Sec. 7436(b)(2))

Congress notes that IRS could make the determination mentioned above that must precede the Tax Court review through a mechanism similar to the employment tax early referral procedures mentioned above. (Com Rept, see ¶ 5303)

> *observation:* It seems the Committee Report is suggesting that IRS institute a program similar to the employment tax early referral program in order to hasten Tax Court review of eligible cases.

If during the Tax Court proceeding, the taxpayer changes his employment tax treatment of any individual whose employment status as an employee is at issue in the proceeding (or of any individual holding a substantially similar position) to treatment as an employee, such change will not be taken into account in the Tax Court's decision. (Code Sec. 7436(b)(3))

Assessment and collection of tax is suspended while the matter is pending in the Tax Court. (Com Rept, see ¶ 5303)

Congress intends that Tax Court reviews of employment status cases be de novo reviews rather than reviews of IRS's administrative records. (Com Rept, see ¶ 5303)

> *observation:* In a de novo review, the Tax Court reviews the case anew without considering IRS's findings in the administrative record.

Small case procedures. If the amount of employment taxes disputed is $10,000 or less for each calendar quarter involved and the taxpayer and the Tax Court agree before the case begins, the case can be conducted under the rules of evidence, practice, and procedure applicable to small tax cases mentioned above. (Code Sec. 7436(c)(1)) (Code Sec. 7453 as amended by '97 Act §1454(b)(3)) Decisions entered under the small tax case rules will not be reviewed in any other court and will not be treated as precedent for any other case not involving the same petitioner and the same determinations. (Code Sec. 7436(c)(2)) A Tax Court decision together with a brief summary of the court's reasons for its decision will satisfy requirements for reports on Tax Court proceedings, hearings and determinations. Additionally, rules similar to the small case rules dealing with limitation of jurisdiction, discontinuances, and the amount of deficiency in dispute will apply to employment status cases. (Code Sec. 7436(c)(3))

Effect of Tax Court's decision. The Tax Court's determination has the force and effect of a Tax Court decision and is reviewable as such. (Code Sec. 7436(a)(2) as added by '97 Act §1454(a)) Thus, it would be binding on the parties. (Com Rept, see

FTC 2d References are to Federal Tax Coordinator 2d
FIN References are to RIA's Analysis of Federal Taxes: Income
USTR References are to United States Tax Reporter: Income, Estate & Gift, and Excise
PCA References are to Pension Coordinator and Pension & Benefits Expert/Advisor
PE References are to Pension and Profit Sharing 2nd
EP References are to Estate Planning & Taxation Coordinator and Estate Planning Advisor

 Research Institute of America 573

¶ 5303)

Tax Court decisions become final 90 days after a decision is entered. (Code Sec. 7481(b) as amended by '97 Act §1454(b)(3))

Procedural rules. The principles of the following assessment and collection rules apply to employment status cases in the same manner as if the IRS determination described at Code Sec. 7436(a) (see above) were a notice of deficiency:

... restrictions on IRS assessments or collections of any tax deficiency until a final Tax Court decision;

... the Tax Court's jurisdiction to redetermine a deficiency;

... assessments of deficiencies found by the Tax Court due on notice and demand;

... the suspension of the limitations period for assessment by levy or court proceeding;

... the limitation on taxpayer refund suits after a Tax Court case has been started; and

... the date when a Tax Court decision becomes final. (Code Sec. 7436(d)(1))

The prohibition on suits to restrain assessment or collection does not apply to employment status cases. (Code Sec. 7421(a) as amended by '97 Act §1454(b)(2))

Employment status cases are also eligible for awards of administrative or litigation costs under Code Sec. 7430. (Code Sec. 7436(d)(2) as added by '97 Act §1454(a))

☐ **Effective:** Aug. 5, '97. ('97 Act §1454(c))

Disclosure of Returns and Return Information

¶ 2330. Repeal of IRS authority to disclose whether prospective juror has been audited

Code Sec. 6103(h)(5), as amended by '97 Act § 1283(a)
Generally effective: Judicial proceedings commenced after Aug. 5, '97
Committee Reports, see ¶ 5250

In connection with a civil or criminal tax proceeding to which the U.S. is a party, IRS had to disclose, upon the written request of either party to the lawsuit, whether a prospective juror had been the subject of an IRS audit or other tax investigation. (FTC 2d/FIN ¶ S-6348; USTR ¶ 61,035.10(43))

New Law. The '97 Act repeals the requirement that IRS disclose, upon the written request of either party to the lawsuit, whether a prospective juror had been the subject of an audit or other IRS tax investigation. (Code Sec. 6103(h)(5) as amended by '97 Act §1283(a))

> ✪ *observation:* Information about whether a taxpayer's return was subject to audit or other IRS investigation is "return information." (FTC 2d/FIN ¶ S-6206; USTR ¶ 61,034.03) Therefore, where IRS has no authority to disclose whether it has investigated a prospective juror, such disclosure falls within the general prohibition of unauthorized disclosure of return information. (FTC 2d/FIN ¶ S-6200; USTR ¶ 61,034)

The committee report cites as reasons for this change the following significant difficulties that the disclosure requirement had created for civil and criminal tax litigation: First, litigation could be substantially slowed while IRS compiled the necessary information. (Some courts had required searches going back as far as 25 years.) Second, releasing the list of potential jurors to defendants earlier than usual (as some courts had required, to give defendants time to get disclosure information from IRS) could allow harassment and intimidation of potential jurors in organized crime, drug, and some tax protester cases. Third, significant judicial resources were expended in interpreting the provision. Fourth, differing judicial interpretations of the provision had caused confusion. Some convictions for criminal tax offenses had been reversed because of failure to comply with the disclosure requirement. (Com Rept, see ¶ 5250)

☐ **Effective:** Judicial proceedings commenced after Aug. 5, '97. ('97 Act §1283(c))

¶ 2331. IRS authorized to disclose return information when levying on certain federal payments

Code Sec. 6103(k), as amended by '97 Act § 1026(a)
Code Sec. 6103(p)(3)(A), as amended by '97 Act § 1026(b)(1)(A)
Code Sec. 6103(p)(4), as amended by '97 Act § 1026(b)(1)(B)
Generally effective: Levies issued after Aug. 5, '97
Committee Reports, see ¶ 5126

IRS is generally prohibited from disclosing tax returns and return information (as defined at ¶ 2407), except as authorized by statute. (FTC 2d/FIN ¶ S-6200; USTR ¶ 61,034) Under one such exception, IRS can disclose certain information for tax administration purposes. (FTC 2d/FIN ¶ S-6325; USTR ¶ 61,034.01)

IRS must maintain a permanent system of standardized records on requests for and disclosures of returns and return information. However, disclosures to certain persons need not be included in this system.

In addition, certain agencies that request information from IRS must maintain a permanent system of standardized records that accounts for all disclosure requests. These agencies must also safeguard the information disclosed. (FTC 2d/FIN ¶ S-6411; USTR ¶ 61,034.02)

New Law. The '97 Act provides that, in serving a notice of levy or a release of levy with respect to any "applicable government payment," IRS may disclose the following information to officers and employees of the Treasury Department's Financial Management Service (FMS):

... return information, including taxpayer identity information (i.e., the taxpayer's name, mailing address, and TIN) (Code Sec. 6103(k)(8)(A)(i) as amended by '97 Act §1026(a)),

---

FTC 2d References are to Federal Tax Coordinator 2d
FIN References are to RIA's Analysis of Federal Taxes: Income
USTR References are to United States Tax Reporter: Income, Estate & Gift, and Excise
PCA References are to Pension Coordinator and Pension & Benefits Expert/Advisor
PE References are to Pension and Profit Sharing 2nd
EP References are to Estate Planning & Taxation Coordinator and Estate Planning Advisor

¶ 2332   **Procedure and Administration**

. . . the amount of any unpaid tax liability (including penalties and interest) (Code Sec. 6103(k)(8)(A)(ii)), and

. . . the type of tax and tax period to which the unpaid tax liability relates. (Code Sec. 6103(k)(8)(A)(iii))

> ✪ *observation:* FMS is the U.S. government's financial manager, central disburser, and collections agent, as well as its accountant and reporter of financial information.

Applicable government payment. An applicable government payment is:

. . . any federal payment that is certified to FMS for disbursement, if eligibility for the payment isn't based on a payee's income or assets (or both) (Code Sec. 6103(k)(8)(C)(i)), and

. . . any other payment that is certified to FMS for disbursement and that IRS designates by published notice. (Code Sec. 6103(k)(8)(C)(ii))

Restriction on use of disclosed information. Return information disclosed for this purpose can be used by officers and employees of the FMS only for the purpose of, and to the extent necessary in:

. . . transferring levied funds to satisfy the levy,

. . . maintaining appropriate agency records about the levy or its release,

. . . notifying the taxpayer and the agency certifying the payment that the levy has been honored, or

. . . defending any litigation resulting from the levy. (Code Sec. 6103(k)(8)(B))

Recordkeeping and safeguards. Information disclosed under the above provision need not be included in IRS's system of records on requests for and disclosures of returns and return information. (Code Sec. 6103(p)(3)(A) as amended by '97 Act §1026(b)(1)(A)) However, FMS must maintain a system of records that accounts for all disclosure requests and must safeguard the information disclosed. (Code Sec. 6103(p)(4) as amended by '97 Act §1026(b)(1)(B))

☐ **Effective:** Levies issued after Aug. 5, '97. ('97 Act §1026(c))

¶ 2332. Rules on disclosure of return information to Veterans Affairs Department extended through 2003

Code Sec. 6103(l)(7)(D), as amended by '97 Act § 1023(a)
Generally effective: Aug. 5, '97
Committee Reports, see ¶ 5123

The Commissioner of Social Security and IRS must, upon written request, disclose to the Department of Veterans Affairs ("DVA") certain tax information supplied to IRS and the Social Security Administration by third parties. Disclosure is permitted to assist DVA in determining eligibility for, and establishing correct benefit amounts under, certain of its needs-based pension, health care, and other programs. The DVA must comply with the safeguards currently contained in the Internal Revenue Code and the Social Security Act governing the use of disclosed tax information. The DVA disclosure rules were scheduled to expire after Sept. 30, '98. (FTC 2d/FIN ¶ S-6362; USTR ¶ 61,034.06)

New Law. The '97 Act extends the above DVA disclosure provision for five years. It is now scheduled to expire after Sept. 30, 2003. (Code Sec. 6103(l)(7)(D) as amended by '97 Act §1023(a))

☐ **Effective:** Aug. 5, '97. ('97 Act §1023(b))

¶ 2333. Medicare secondary payer program disclosure rules made permanent

Code Sec. 6103(l)(12)(F), as amended by Budget Act § 4631(c)(2)
Generally effective: Aug. 5, '97
Committee Reports, see ¶ 5503

Medicare is a secondary payer under specified circumstances where individuals are covered by other third-party payers, e.g., employer health plans. Thus, for example, where an employer health plan pays part of an individual's medical bill, Medicare becomes liable, as a secondary payer, for the remainder of the bill.

To assist in the administration of these secondary-payer situations, there are so-called "secondary-payer" rules under which IRS must, upon a written request from the Social Security Administration (SSA), disclose to SSA available filing status and tax-payer identity information from IRS's individual master files relating to whether any Medicare beneficiary identified by SSA was a married individual for any specified year after '86, and, if so, the name of the spouse and his or her taxpayer identification number (i.e., "TIN" or social security number). Similarly, the SSA must, upon written request from the Health Care Financing Administration (HCFA), disclose certain information to HCFA with respect to Medicare benefits.

Under pre-'97 Act law, the rules on disclosure of taxpayer information by IRS to SSA did not apply to any request made after Sept. 30, '98, or to any request made before Sept. 30, '98 for information relating to '97 or thereafter. The rules on disclosures from the SSA to HCFA did not apply to any request made after Sept. 30, '98, or to any request made before Sept. 30, '98 for information relating to '98 or thereafter. (FTC 2d/FIN ¶ S-6363; USTR ¶ 61,034.06)

New Law. The Budget Act permanently extends the above disclosure provisions. (Code Sec. 6103(l)(12)(F) as amended by Budget Act §4631(c)(2))

☐ **Effective:** Aug. 5, '97.

Other Procedural and Administrative Rules

¶ 2334. IRS authority to extend tax deadlines for taxpayers affected by Presidentially-declared disasters expanded

Code Sec. 7508A, as added by '97 Act § 911
Generally effective: With respect to periods for performing acts that have not expired before Aug. 5, '97
Committee Reports, see ¶ 5061

IRS can grant reasonable extensions of time for filing returns and other documents. (FTC 2d/FIN ¶ S-5001; USTR ¶ 60,814) On a showing of undue hardship, IRS can grant an extension of time for the payment of tax. (FTC 2d/FIN ¶ S-5851; USTR ¶ 61,614; TaxDesk ¶ 57,046)

IRS has exercised this authority in aid of taxpayers affected by Presidentially-declared disasters. Alternatively, IRS has assisted these taxpayers by waiving late-filing and late-payment penalties. (FTC 2d/FIN ¶s S-5049, S-5606, V-1657; USTR ¶ 60,815.08; TaxDesk ¶ 86,881)

However, under pre-'97 Act law, IRS didn't have authority to extend certain other tax-related deadlines (Com Rept, see ¶ 5061), such as the deadline for filing a Tax Court petition. (FTC 2d/FIN ¶ U-2301)

Individuals serving in the U.S. armed forces in a combat zone are given extra time to:

... file any return of income, estate or gift tax (except withholding and payroll taxes);
... pay any income, estate, gift tax or installment thereof (except withholding and payroll taxes);
... file a petition in the Tax Court for redetermination of a deficiency;
... file a claim for credit or refund of any tax;
... bring a suit for refund or credit upon any claim for refund; and
... perform any other act permitted or required under the Code that is specified in IRS regs to be issued. (FTC 2d/FIN ¶ V-8012; USTR ¶ 75,084; TaxDesk ¶ 85,305)

In general, the amount of any refund or credit is limited to the amount of tax paid during two or three years (depending on the circumstances) immediately preceding the filing of the claim for refund or credit. (FTC 2d/FIN ¶ T-7537 *et seq.*; USTR ¶ 65,114.07; TaxDesk ¶ 80,634) In the case of a member of the armed forces serving in a combat zone, the period of the extension is disregarded in determining the amount of any credit or refund to which the taxpayer may be entitled. (FTC 2d/FIN ¶ V-8013; USTR ¶ 75,084)

New Law. The '97 Act expands IRS's authority to extend deadlines (Com Rept, see ¶ 5061) by authorizing IRS to prescribe regs under which, for taxpayers that IRS determines to be affected by a Presidentially-declared disaster, a period of up to 90 days may be disregarded in determining, with respect to the taxpayer's tax liability (including penalties):

... whether the taxpayer timely performed any of the acts for which an extension is available under the combat-zone rules discussed above, (Code Sec. 7508A(a)(1) as added by '97 Act §911(a)).and

... the amount of any credit or refund. (Code Sec. 7508A(a)(2))

observation: As a result of Code Sec. 7508A(a)(1), IRS may permit a taxpayer an extra 90 days to file a claim for refund. It appears that the intent of the rule of Code Sec. 7508A(a)(2) is to provide that the limit on the amount of a such a refund claim would be the amount of tax paid within the two-or-three-year-*plus-90-day* period that preceded the date that claim is filed. However, it is unclear whether the above '97 Act provision actually fulfills this intent.

illustration: Taxpayer filed his Year 1 return and paid his Year 1 tax on the due date, Apr. 15 of Year 2. He therefore had until Apr. 15 of Year 5 to file a refund claim for Year 1. (See FTC 2d/FIN ¶ T-7501; USTR ¶ 65,114.01; TaxDesk ¶ 80,601) On Apr. 1 of Year 5, taxpayer is affected by a Presidentially-declared disaster for which IRS grants a 90-day extension. Taxpayer's refund claim will be timely if filed by the extended due date. However, it is unclear whether, in determining the amount of the refund, the taxpayer can, for example, include amounts he paid on Apr. 15 of Year 2.

However, the up-to-90-day extension doesn't apply for purposes of determining interest on any overpayment or underpayment. (Code Sec. 7508A(b)).

observation: A special provision waives taxpayer interest in cases of relief afforded for disasters occurring in '97, see ¶ 2401.

illustration: Taxpayer's Year 1 return and tax payment are due on Apr. 15 of Year 2. On Apr. 1 of Year 2, taxpayer is affected by a Presidentially-declared disaster for which IRS grants a 90-day extension. Taxpayer has until the extended due date to file her return and pay her tax. She won't be liable for any late-filing or late-payment penalty if she files and pays by the extended due date. She will, however, be liable for interest on any underpayment that isn't paid by Apr. 15.

observation: While the combat-zone rules don't permit an extension to file payroll or withholding tax returns or to pay those taxes, IRS has granted taxpayers affected by Presidentially-declared disasters extensions to file these returns and pay the taxes (or waived late filing and payment penalties). The '97 Act should not be taken to limit IRS's authority to continue to do so.

FTC 2d References are to Federal Tax Coordinator 2d
FIN References are to RIA's Analysis of Federal Taxes: Income
USTR References are to United States Tax Reporter: Income, Estate & Gift, and Excise
PCA References are to Pension Coordinator and Pension & Benefits Expert/Advisor
PE References are to Pension and Profit Sharing 2nd
EP References are to Estate Planning & Taxation Coordinator and Estate Planning Advisor

☐ **Effective:** With respect to any period for performing an act that has not expired before Aug. 5, '97. ('97 Act §911(c))

illustration: On Aug. 5, '97, a taxpayer had 80 days left to file a Tax Court petition for redetermination of a deficiency. Pursuant to the above provision, IRS issues regs that extend by 90 days the time for taxpayers affected by a Presidentially-declared disaster to file their Tax Court petitions and determines that the taxpayer was affected by a Presidentially-declared disaster. Thus the taxpayer has 170 days from the Aug. 5, '97 to file his petition.

¶ 2335. Net worth requirements for awards of litigation, etc. costs to estates, trusts, and joint return filers clarified

Code Sec. 7430(c)(4)(D), as amended by '97 Act § 1453(a)
Generally effective: Proceedings commenced after Aug. 5, '97
Committee Reports, see ¶ 5302

Persons who substantially prevail in any action brought by or against IRS, in connection with the determination, collection, or refund of any tax, interest, or penalty may recover reasonable administrative costs and/or litigation costs that they incur in connection with any administrative or court proceeding. However, one must meet certain net worth requirements in order to be eligible for recovery of those costs. Under these requirements, at the time the action begins, an individual's net worth cannot exceed $2,000,000, and a corporation's or partnership's net worth cannot exceed $7,000,000. (FTC 2d/FIN ¶ U-1282; USTR ¶ 74,304.01) The Code provided no net worth requirement rules for estates, trusts, and individuals filing joint returns; although regs and the courts provided net worth rules with respect to estates and with respect to individuals filing joint returns. (FTC 2d/FIN ¶ U-1283, U-1283.1; USTR ¶ 74,304.01)

An innocent spouse is relieved from liability for tax, interest, and penalties on a joint return if there is a substantial understatement of tax attributable to a grossly erroneous item of the other spouse. The innocent spouse must demonstrate that he or she didn't know and had no reason to know there was a substantial understatement and that it would be inequitable to hold the innocent spouse liable. (FTC 2d/FIN ¶ V-8506 *et seq.*; USTR ¶ 60,134.05; TaxDesk ¶ 57,093)

New Law. The '97 Act provides that the net worth limitation rules applicable to individuals also apply to:

. . . estates, except that, instead of using net worth at the time the action begins, net worth on the decedent's date of death is used. (Code Sec. 7430(c)(4)(D)(i)(I) as amended by '97 Act §1453(a))

. . . trusts, except that, instead of using net worth at the time the action begins, net worth on the last day of the trust's tax year that it is involved in the proceeding is used. (Code Sec. 7430(c)(4)(D)(i)(II))

The '97 Act also provides that individuals filing a joint return will be treated as separate individuals for purposes of the $2,000,000 net worth limitation, (Code Sec. 7430(c)(4)(D)(ii)) resulting in a net worth limitation of $4,000,000 for individuals who file a joint return. (Com Rept, see ¶ 5302)

☐ **Effective:** Proceedings commenced after Aug. 5, '97. ('97 Act §1453(b))

> ⚫*observation:* In the recent *Maggie Management Co.* ((1997) 108 TC No.
> 21) case, the Tax Court ruled that, for purposes of Code Sec. 7430, a Tax
> Court "proceeding" is commenced by the filing of the Tax Court petition, not
> by the filing of a motion for attorney's fees. This Tax Court ruling should
> also apply for purposes of the above effective date.

¶ 2336. Taxpayers' right to seek administrative cost awards from IRS subjected to time limits

Code Sec. 7430(b)(5), as amended by '97 Act § 1285(b)
Code Sec. 7430(f)(2), as amended by '97 Act § 1285(c)
Code Sec. 7430(f)(3), as amended by '97 Act § 1285(a)
Generally effective: Civil actions or proceedings commenced after Aug. 5, '97
Committee Reports, see ¶ 5252

A taxpayer who substantially prevails (the "prevailing party") in an administrative
proceeding before IRS involving the determination, collection or refund of any tax, interest, or penalty may be awarded reasonable administrative costs. In order to obtain
such an award, the prevailing party must first file a written request for recovery of
costs with IRS. If IRS denies the request, the prevailing party may appeal that decision
to the Tax Court.

Under pre-'97 Act law, the Code didn't specify a time limit for the prevailing party
to file the request with IRS or the appeal with the Tax Court. However, Reg §
301.7430-2(c)(5) (see FTC 2d/FIN ¶ U-1286) provides that a claim for administrative
costs must be filed with IRS within 90 days of IRS's final decision with respect to all
taxes and penalties at issue in the administrative proceeding. (FTC 2d/FIN ¶ U-1285,
¶ U-1286, ¶ U-1287, ¶ U-1289; USTR ¶ 74,304.02)

New Law. The '97 Act provides that, in order to obtain an administrative costs
award, the prevailing party must file an application for such costs with IRS before the
91st day after the date on which IRS mails to the prevailing party its final decision as
to the determination of the tax, interest or penalty. (Code Sec. 7430(b)(5) as amended
by '97 Act §1285(b))

> ⚫*observation:* This change merely codifies the Reg § 301.7430-2(c)(5) time
> limit for filing a claim for administrative costs with IRS.

The '97 Act also provides that where IRS sends the prevailing party, by certified or
registered mail, notice of its administrative costs award decision, the prevailing party

FTC 2d References are to Federal Tax Coordinator 2d
FIN References are to RIA's Analysis of Federal Taxes: Income
USTR References are to United States Tax Reporter: Income, Estate & Gift, and Excise
PCA References are to Pension Coordinator and Pension & Benefits Expert/Advisor
PE References are to Pension and Profit Sharing 2nd
EP References are to Estate Planning & Taxation Coordinator and Estate Planning Advisor

⚫ Research Institute of America 581

cannot initiate a Tax Court appeal of that decision unless it files a petition with the Tax Court before the 91st day after the date of IRS's mailing of its decision notice. (Code Sec. 7430(f)(2) as amended by '97 Act §1285(c))

Finally, the '97 Act provides that an order of the Tax Court disposing of a prevailing party's petition for review of IRS's denial of an administrative costs award is reviewable in the same manner as a decision of the Tax Court, but only with respect to the matters determined in that order. (Code Sec. 7430(f)(3) as amended by '97 Act §1285(a))

☐ **Effective:** Civil actions or proceedings commenced after Aug. 5, '97. ('97 Act §1285(d))

¶ 2337. IRS required to notify taxpayers of unlawful inspection or disclosure of their returns or return information

Code Sec. 7431(e), as amended by Privacy Act § 3(b)
Generally effective: Inspections and disclosures occurring on or after Aug. 5, '97
Committee Reports, see ¶ 5551

Unauthorized willful disclosure of tax returns and return information by Federal employees, IRS contractors (Code Sec. 7213(a)(1)) and state and certain other employees (Code Sec. 7213(a)(2)) is a felony. (FTC 2d/FIN ¶ V-3304, ¶ V-3305; USTR ¶ 72,134) The '97 Act has added Code Sec. 7213A, which makes unauthorized willful *inspection* of returns or return information a felony, see ¶ 2407.

Unauthorized inspection of information of any U.S. department or agency (including IRS) via computer is a crime under 18 U.S.C. § 1030(a)(2)(B).

There was no requirement that IRS notify taxpayers of unauthorized inspection or disclosure of the taxpayer's tax return or return information.

New Law. If any person is criminally charged (by indictment or information) with inspection or disclosure of a taxpayer's return or return information in violation of Code Sec. 7213(a)(1), Code Sec. 7213(a)(2), new Code Sec. 7213A(a), or 18 U.S.C. § 1030(a)(2)(B)), IRS must notify that taxpayer as soon as practicable of the inspection or disclosure. (Code Sec. 7431(e) as amended by Privacy Act §3(b))

☐ **Effective:** Inspections and disclosures occurring on and after Aug. 5, '97. (Privacy Act §3(e))

¶ 2400. Interest and Penalties

Interest

¶ 2401. Interest abated when due date for tax extended in '97 disaster areas

Code Sec. None, '97 Act § 915
Generally effective: Disasters declared after Dec. 31, '96
Committee Reports, see ¶ 5065

IRS has authority to extend the date for filing an income tax return and the date for paying tax, and it has exercised this authority for taxpayers in disaster areas. But even if IRS has exercised this authority, under pre-'97 Act law none of these taxpayers are excused from paying interest on their taxes from the original (unextended) due date until the taxes are paid. (FTC 2d/FIN ¶ S-5001, ¶ S-5851, ¶ V-1002; USTR ¶ 60,814, ¶ 61,614, ¶ 66,014; TaxDesk ¶ 57,046)

New Law. When IRS extends the due date for filing an income tax return and paying the tax, and waives the related failure to file and failure to pay penalties, for any individual located in a Presidentially declared disaster area, it must also abate the assessment of underpayment interest for the period of the extension. ('97 Act §915(a)) For purposes of this rule, Presidentially declared disaster areas are areas the President has determined during '97 warrant federal assistance under the Robert T. Stafford Disaster Relief and Emergency Assistance Act. ('97 Act §915(b)) Estates and trusts are not treated as "individuals" for purposes of this abatement of interest rule. ('97 Act §915(c))

The above specific waiver-of-interest rule for '97 disasters applies notwithstanding the rule in new Code Sec. 7508A(b) that interest is not abated when taxpayers are afforded disaster relief (¶ 2334). ('97 Act §915(a))

☐ **Effective:** Applicable to disasters declared after Dec. 31, '96. ('97 Act §915(d))

¶ 2402. Interest accrual period with respect to tax underpayment not reduced by foreign tax credit carryback

Code Sec. 6601(d)(2), as amended by '97 Act § 1055(a)
Code Sec. 6611(f)(2), as amended by '97 Act § 1055(b)(1)
Code Sec. 6611(f)(4)(B)(ii)(II), as amended by '97 Act § 1055(b)(2)
Generally effective: Foreign tax credit carrybacks arising in tax years beginning after Aug. 5, '97
Committee Reports, see ¶ 5147

FTC 2d References are to Federal Tax Coordinator 2d
FIN References are to RIA's Analysis of Federal Taxes: Income
USTR References are to United States Tax Reporter: Income, Estate & Gift, and Excise
PCA References are to Pension Coordinator and Pension & Benefits Expert/Advisor
PE References are to Pension and Profit Sharing 2nd
EP References are to Estate Planning & Taxation Coordinator and Estate Planning Advisor

Subject to a statutorily-defined limitation, U.S. persons may take a credit, the foreign tax credit, for the amount of foreign taxes they pay or accrue. (FTC 2d/FIN ¶ O-4000 *et seq.*; USTR ¶ 9014; TaxDesk ¶ 39,101 *et seq.*) The amount of creditable taxes paid or accrued in any tax year that exceeds this foreign tax credit limitation may be carried back two years and forward five years. (FTC 2d/FIN ¶ O-4600 *et seq.*; USTR ¶ 9044.02; TaxDesk ¶ 39,429 *et seq.*)

If an underpayment for a tax year is reduced or eliminated by a carryback of a net operating loss or net capital loss incurred in a later year, that reduction or elimination doesn't affect the interest computation for the period ending with the filing date for the tax year in which the net operating loss or net capital loss arises. Similarly, if a general business credit allowed for a tax year is increased by a credit carryback, that increase won't affect the computation of interest for the period ending with the filing date for the tax year in which the credit carryback arises.

However, the Code didn't provide any similar provision with respect to foreign tax credit carrybacks, and in *Fluor Corp,* the Court of Federal Claims held that, where an underpayment for a tax year is eliminated by a foreign tax credit carryback from a later year, no interest accrues on the underpayment that is eliminated by the foreign tax credit carryback. (FTC 2d/FIN ¶ V-1220; USTR ¶ 66,014.03; TaxDesk ¶ 85,314)

In computing interest on tax overpayments, if an overpayment for a tax year results from a foreign tax credit carryback from a later year, the overpayment is deemed not to arise before the filing date for the tax year in which the foreign taxes were paid or accrued. Accordingly, interest doesn't start accruing until that date. (FTC 2d/FIN ¶ T-8059; TaxDesk ¶ 80,740)

No interest is payable on overpayments refunded within 45 days after the due date of the return or, if the return is filed late, within 45 days after filing. (FTC 2d/FIN ¶ T-8024; USTR ¶ 66,014; TaxDesk ¶ 80,710) Also, no interest is payable on overpayments refunded within 45 days after the taxpayer filed a refund claim. (FTC 2d/FIN ¶ T-8027; USTR ¶ 66,014; TaxDesk ¶ 80,737) If a refund claim is based on an overpayment caused by a carryback of a net operating loss, net capital loss, or general business credit, the overpayment is treated as an overpayment for the year in which the loss or credit carryback arises (the "loss year"), and the return for the loss year is treated as not filed until the claim is filed. Thus, IRS won't pay any interest if it makes the refund within 45 days of the date on which the refund claim was filed. (FTC 2d/FIN ¶ T-8054; TaxDesk ¶ 80,738)

New Law. The '97 Act provides that, if an underpayment for a tax year is reduced or eliminated by a foreign tax credit carryback from a later tax year, the carryback doesn't affect the computation of interest on that underpayment for the period ending with the filing date for the tax year in which the foreign taxes were paid or accrued. (Code Sec. 6601(d)(2) as amended by '97 Act §1055(a)) i.e., interest continues to accrue on the underpayment until that date. This change makes the interest rules that apply in the case of a underpayment that is reduced or eliminated by a foreign tax credit carryback consistent with the rules (described above) that apply where an overpayment results from a foreign tax credit carryback. (Com Rept, see ¶ 5147)

illustration: Taxpayer had an underpayment for Year 1. For Year 2, it had a foreign tax credit that, when carried back to Year 1, eliminated the entire Year 1 underpayment. Taxpayer's Year 2 return was due on Mar. 15 of Year 3. Interest continues to accrue on the Year 1 underpayment until Mar. 15 of Year 3.

Foreign tax credit carryback triggered by loss carryback.   The '97 Act also provides that, where a foreign tax credit carryback is triggered by a net operating loss or net capital loss carryback, an underpayment is not considered to have been reduced until the filing date for the year in which the loss carryback arose. (Code Sec. 6601(d)(2)) Similarly, an overpayment caused by the foreign tax credit carryback is not considered to have been created until the filing date for the year in which the loss carryback arose. (Code Sec. 6611(f)(2) as amended by '97 Act §1055(b)(1))

illustration: Taxpayer had an underpayment for Year 1. For Year 3, it had a net operating loss that, when carried back to Year 2, triggered a Year 2 foreign tax credit that, in turn, was carried back to Year 1 and reduced the Year 1 underpayment. Taxpayer's Year 3 return was due on Mar. 15 of Year 4. The Year 1 underpayment isn't considered to have been reduced until Mar. 15 of Year 4. Likewise, if the foreign tax credit carryback had created a Year 1 overpayment, that overpayment would not be considered to have been created until Mar. 15 of Year 4.

Interest-free period.   With respect to the 45-day interest-free period, in the case of a foreign tax credit carryback, the "loss year" is the tax year in which the foreign taxes were actually paid or accrued. (Code Sec. 6611(f)(4)(B)(ii)(II) as amended by '97 Act §1055(b)(2)(B))

observation: Thus, if a refund claim is based on an overpayment caused by a foreign tax credit carryback, the overpayment is treated as an overpayment for the year in which the foreign taxes were actually paid or accrued and the return for that year is treated as not filed until the claim is filed. Accordingly, IRS won't pay any interest if it makes the refund within 45 days of the date on which the refund claim was filed.

For any portion of the carryback attributable to a net operating loss or capital loss carryback from a later tax year, the "loss year" is that later year. (Code Sec. 6611(f)(4)(B)(ii)(II))

☐ **Effective:** Foreign tax credit carrybacks arising in tax years beginning after Aug. 5, '97. ('97 Act §1055(c)) Thus, the '97 Act changes are effective for foreign taxes actually paid or accrued in tax years beginning after Aug. 5, '97. (Com Rept, see ¶ 5147)

FTC 2d References are to Federal Tax Coordinator 2d
FIN References are to RIA's Analysis of Federal Taxes: Income
USTR References are to United States Tax Reporter: Income, Estate & Gift, and Excise
PCA References are to Pension Coordinator and Pension & Benefits Expert/Advisor
PE References are to Pension and Profit Sharing 2nd
EP References are to Estate Planning & Taxation Coordinator and Estate Planning Advisor

No inference is intended regarding the interest computation under pre-'97 Act law in the case of a foreign tax credit carryback (including a foreign tax credit carryback that is triggered by a net operating loss or net capital loss carryback). (Com Rept, see ¶ 5147)

¶ 2403. Notices involving less than $100,000 disregarded under rule increasing interest rate on large corporate underpayments

Code Sec. 6621(c)(2)(B)(iii), as amended by '97 Act § 1463(a)
Generally effective: Interest for periods after Dec. 31, '97
Committee Reports, see ¶ 5306

The interest rate on a large corporate underpayment of tax is the Federal short-term rate plus five percentage points (2% more than the regular underpayment rate). A large corporate underpayment is any underpayment by a subchapter C corporation of any tax imposed for any taxable period, if the amount of the underpayment for the period exceeds $100,000. The large corporate underpayment rate applies to periods after the "applicable date." In the case of any underpayment of tax to which the deficiency procedures apply, the applicable date is the 30th day following the earlier of the date on which IRS sends (a) the first letter of proposed deficiency that allows the taxpayer an opportunity for administrative review in IRS's Office of Appeals (the 30-day letter) or (b) the statutory notice of deficiency (90-day letter). In the case of any underpayment of tax to which the deficiency procedures do not apply (e.g., excise taxes), the applicable date is 30 days after the date on which IRS sends the first letter or notice that notifies the taxpayer of the assessment or proposed assessment. (FTC 2d/FIN ¶ V-1110, ¶ V-1111; USTR ¶ 66,214; TaxDesk ¶ 85,105)

Under pre-'97 Act law, the large corporate underpayment rate could apply where an underpayment of tax for a taxable period exceeded $100,000 even if the initial letter or notice of deficiency, proposed deficiency, assessment, or proposed assessment was for an amount less than $100,000. Thus, for example, a nondeficiency notice relating to a relatively minor mathematical error by the taxpayer could result in the application of the large corporate underpayment rate to a subsequently identified income tax deficiency. (Com Rept, see ¶ 5306)

New Law. If the amount of a deficiency, proposed deficiency, assessment, or proposed assessment set forth in a letter or notice is not greater than $100,000 (determined by not taking into account any interest, penalties, or additions to tax) the letter or notice is disregarded for purposes of the definition of "applicable date" under the large corporate underpayment rules (Code Sec. 6621(c)(2)(B)(iii) as amended by '97 Act §1463(a)) (i.e. for purposes of determining the period to which the large corporate underpayment rate applies). (Com Rept, see ¶ 5306)

☐ **Effective:** Interest for periods after Dec. 31, 1997. ('97 Act §1463(b))

¶ 2404. Definition of "taxable period" for reduced interest rate on large corporate overpayments corrected

Code Sec. 6621(a)(1), as amended by '97 Act § 1604(b)(1)
Generally effective: Periods after Dec. 31, '94

The interest rate on overpayments is generally the federal short-term rate plus two percentage points. However, to the extent that a corporate overpayment exceeds $10,000 for any taxable period, the interest rate is the federal short-term rate plus 0.5 of a percentage point. (FTC 2d/FIN ¶ T-8002; USTR ¶ 66,214; TaxDesk ¶ 80,701)

In the case of corporate overpayments of income tax, "taxable period" means the corporation's tax year. In the case of overpayments of other taxes (e.g., excise taxes), the Internal Revenue Code defined "taxable period" as "the period to which the underpayment relates." This was a mistake, because the provision relates to corporate overpayments, not underpayments.

New Law. The '97 Act corrects the definition of "taxable period" for purposes of determining whether a corporate overpayment of a tax other than income tax exceeds $10,000. That definition is now "the period to which the overpayment relates." (Code Sec. 6621(a)(1) as amended by '97 Act §1604(b)(1))

☐ **Effective:** Interest determinations for periods after Dec. 31, '94. ('97 Act §1604(b)(4))

Penalties

¶ 2405. Penalty for failure by small businesses to make electronic tax deposits waived through June 30, '98

Code Sec. None, '97 Act § 931
Generally effective: Aug. 5, '97
Committee Reports, see ¶ 5068

Absent reasonable cause, a taxpayer required to deposit federal taxes through IRS's electronic funds transfer system is subject to the failure to deposit penalty if he deposits the tax by other means. For a large group of smaller taxpayers the requirement to make electronic tax payments went into effect on July 1, '97. (This group consists of taxpayers who meet all of the following requirements: they are required to deposit employment taxes; all of their tax deposits for calendar year '95 totalled more than $50,000; and all of their tax deposits for calendar year '94 did not exceed $47,000,000.) IRS announced that it would waive the penalty for these smaller taxpayers through Dec. 31, '97, if they make timely deposits using paper coupons. (FTC

FTC 2d References are to Federal Tax Coordinator 2d
FIN References are to RIA's Analysis of Federal Taxes: Income
USTR References are to United States Tax Reporter: Income, Estate & Gift, and Excise
PCA References are to Pension Coordinator and Pension & Benefits Expert/Advisor
PE References are to Pension and Profit Sharing 2nd
EP References are to Estate Planning & Taxation Coordinator and Estate Planning Advisor

2d/FIN ¶ V-1656.1; USTR ¶ 66,564.01; TaxDesk ¶ 55,986)

New Law. Congress believes smaller businesses should have more time to get ready for electronic tax deposits. (Com Rept, see ¶ 5068) Thus, the '97 Act waives penalties for failure to use IRS's electronic funds transfer system to make a tax deposit with respect to all such failures occurring through June 30, '98, by taxpayers who were first required to make electronic deposits after June 30, '97. ('97 Act §931)

observation: The waiver applies only to the failure to make the deposit by electronic funds transfer. A timely tax deposit must still be made to avoid a late deposit penalty.

☐ **Effective:** Aug. 5, '97.

¶ 2406. Reasonable cause exception provided for various civil penalties

Code Sec. 6652(g), as amended by '97 Act § 1281(a)
Code Sec. 6652(k), as amended by '97 Act § 1281(b)
Code Sec. 6683, as amended by '97 Act § 1281(c)
Code Sec. 7519(f)(4)(A), as amended by '97 Act § 1281(d)
Generally effective: Tax years beginning after Aug. 5, '97
Committee Reports, see ¶ 5248

Civil penalties are imposed in the case of:

. . . a failure by a plan administrator to make a report of voluntary employee contributions to a retirement savings plan (FTC 2d/FIN ¶ V-1956; USTR ¶ 66,524) ;

. . . a failure by a corporation that issues qualified small business stock to make prescribed reports to IRS (FTC 2d/FIN ¶ V-1919; USTR ¶ 66,524) ;

. . . a failure by a foreign corporation to file a true and accurate return of personal holding company tax (FTC 2d/FIN ¶ V-1764; USTR ¶ 66,834) ; and

. . . a failure to make timely required payments for partnerships or S corporations electing not to have the required tax year. (FTC 2d/FIN ¶ G-1573; USTR ¶ 4444; TaxDesk ¶ 43,408)

Many civil tax penalties have "reasonable cause" exceptions. For example, the accuracy-related and fraud penalties generally don't apply to any portion of an underpayment for which reasonable cause and the taxpayer's good faith are shown. (FTC 2d/FIN ¶ V-2060; USTR ¶ 66,644; TaxDesk ¶s 86,301, 86,501) However, under pre-'97 Act law, there was no "reasonable cause" exception to the four penalties listed above.

New Law. The '97 Act provides that the following four penalties won't be imposed if the failure is shown to be due to reasonable cause and not willful neglect:

. . . the penalty for failure by a plan administrator to make a report of voluntary employee contributions to a retirement savings plan (Code Sec. 6652(g) as amended by '97 Act §1281(a));

... the penalty for failure by a corporation that issues qualified small business stock to make prescribed reports to IRS (Code Sec. 6652(k) as amended by '97 Act §1281(b));

... the penalty for failure by a foreign corporation to file a true and accurate return of personal holding company tax (Code Sec. 6683 as amended by '97 Act §1281(c)); and

... the penalty for failure to make timely required payments for partnerships or S corporations electing not to have the required tax year (Code Sec. 7519(f)(4)(A) as amended by '97 Act §1281(d)).

☐ **Effective:** Tax years beginning after Aug. 5, '97. ('97 Act §1281(e))

¶ 2407. Criminal penalty imposed on "browsing" of tax returns or return information

Code Sec. 7213A, as added by Privacy Act § 2(a)
Code Sec. 7213(a)(2), as amended by Privacy Act § 2(b)(1)
Generally effective: Violations occurring on or after Aug. 5, '97
Committee Reports, see ¶ 5551

Returns and return information are confidential and may not be disclosed except as specifically authorized by the Code. (FTC 2d/FIN ¶ S-6200; USTR ¶ 61,034) Unauthorized willful disclosure is a felony. (FTC 2d/FIN ¶s V-3304, V-3305; USTR ¶ 72,134)

A "return" means any tax return, estimated tax declaration, information return or refund claim, including any amendment, schedule, or attachment. (FTC 2d/FIN ¶ S-6205; USTR ¶ 61,034.03)

"Return information" means a taxpayer's identity, the nature, source or amount of income, payments, receipts, deductions, exemptions, credits, assets, liabilities, net worth, tax liability, tax withheld, deficiencies, overassessments and tax payments, whether the return is, was or will be examined or investigated, or any other data with respect to a return or the determination of any person's tax liability. It also includes any written determination or related background file document that isn't open to public inspection. (FTC 2d/FIN ¶ S-6206; USTR ¶ 61,034.03)

The Code authorizes inspection of returns or return information in certain cases. For example, the following may inspect returns or return information: (a) an officer or employee of the Treasury Department (including IRS) whose official duties require such inspection; (b) officers and employees of the Justice Department, under certain conditions. (FTC 2d/FIN ¶ S-6335; USTR ¶ 61,034.01)

An IRS Declaration of Privacy Principles prohibits unauthorized inspection (without disclosure) of tax returns and return information, a practice known as "browsing." However, under pre-Privacy Act law, there was no criminal penalty in the Internal Revenue Code for such inspection.

FTC 2d References are to Federal Tax Coordinator 2d
FIN References are to RIA's Analysis of Federal Taxes: Income
USTR References are to United States Tax Reporter: Income, Estate & Gift, and Excise
PCA References are to Pension Coordinator and Pension & Benefits Expert/Advisor
PE References are to Pension and Profit Sharing 2nd
EP References are to Estate Planning & Taxation Coordinator and Estate Planning Advisor

New Law. The Privacy Act creates a new criminal penalty for willful inspection of any tax return or return information, except as authorized by the Code, by:

... any Federal officer or employee (Code Sec. 7213A(a)(1)(A) as added by Privacy Act §2(a));

... any IRS contractor, or an officer or employee of an IRS contractor, to whom returns and return information may be disclosed to the extent necessary to process, store, transmit, and reproduce the returns or return information, to program, maintain, repair, test, and procure equipment, or to provide other tax administration services (Code Sec. 7213A(a)(1)(B)); or

... any other person, if the return or return information was acquired (by the person making the inspection or by another person) under the disclosure rules applicable to state tax officials, state and local law enforcement agencies, Federal law enforcement officials when imminent danger of death or physical injury is involved, child support enforcement agencies, certain welfare and Social Security Administration officials, administrators of state alcohol laws, creditor agencies entitled to a portion of a taxpayer's tax refund, the blood donor locator service, and government employees receiving disclosure of cash transaction reporting information. (Code Sec. 7213A(a)(2)) The mailing address, acquired under Code Sec. 6103(m)(5) (see FTC 2d/FIN ¶ S-6358; USTR ¶ 61,034.06), of a taxpayer who has defaulted on a student loan administered by the Department of Health and Human Services is added to the list of information for which a criminal penalty may be imposed, both for unauthorized inspection and unauthorized disclosure. (Code Sec. 7213(a)(2) as amended by Privacy Act §2(b)(1))

The term "inspection" means any examination of a return or return information. "Return" and "return information" are defined as under the rules prohibiting unauthorized disclosure (see above). (Code Sec. 7213A(c))

The penalty upon conviction is a fine not exceeding $1,000 or imprisonment for not more than one year, or both, together with the costs of prosecution. (Code Sec. 7213A(b)(1)) Under 18 USC § 3571, the amount of the fine is not more than the greater of the amount specified in Code Sec. 7213A ($1,000) or $100,000. (Com Rept, see ¶ 5551)

In addition, upon conviction, a Federal officer or employee will be dismissed from office or discharged from employment. (Code Sec. 7213A(b)(2))

This new criminal penalty reflects Congress' view that unauthorized inspection of tax return information is a very serious offense. Congress believes that the very serious personnel sanction of dismissal is warranted against IRS employees who engage in unauthorized inspection. (Com Rept, see ¶ 5551)

☐ **Effective:** Violations occurring on or after Aug. 5, '97. (Privacy Act §2(c))

¶ 2408. Civil damages made available for unauthorized inspection of returns or return information

Code Sec. 7431(a), as amended by Privacy Act § 3(a)
Code Sec. 7431(b), as amended by Privacy Act § 3(c)
Code Sec. 7431(c), as amended by Privacy Act § 3(d)(1) and (2)
Code Sec. 7431(f), as amended by Privacy Act § 3(d)(3)
Generally effective: Inspections and disclosures occurring on or after Aug. 5, '97
Committee Reports, see ¶ 5551

An action for civil damages may be brought for unauthorized disclosure of tax returns and return information (see ¶ 2407) that occurs knowingly or negligently. However, no civil liability arises from a disclosure that results from a good faith but erroneous interpretation of the disclosure rules (Code Sec. 6103). (FTC 2d/FIN ¶ S-6501; USTR ¶ 74,314)

Taxpayers can recover the cost of the action plus the greater of (1) $1,000 for each act of unauthorized disclosure or (2) the sum of (a) the actual damages sustained by the taxpayer as a result of the unauthorized disclosure plus (b) punitive damages, in the case of a willful or grossly negligent disclosure. (FTC 2d/FIN ¶ S-6506; USTR ¶ 74,314)

Under pre-Privacy Act law, civil damages weren't available for unauthorized *inspection* without disclosure.

New Law. The Privacy Act provides for civil damages for unauthorized inspection that occurs knowingly or negligently. (Code Sec. 7431(a) as amended by Privacy Act §3(a)) Thus, damages can't be recovered for accidental or inadvertent inspection, such as where an error is made in typing in a TIN. (Com Rept, see ¶ 5551)

> ⚡*observation:* Thus, an IRS employee who is authorized to inspect the file of Taxpayer X, but mistakenly types Taxpayer Y's TIN into a computer and views Y's return information, is not liable to the extent he accidentally inspects Y's return information..

The term "inspection" means any examination of a return or return information. (Code Sec. 7431(f) as amended by Privacy Act §3(d)(3))

Damages are computed under the formula described above, but with "inspection" substituted for "disclosure." (Code Sec. 7431(c) as amended by Privacy Act §3(d)(1) and (2))

The Privacy Act also provides that a taxpayer can't recover damages for an inspection or disclosure that the taxpayer requested. And, it provides that the exception for

FTC 2d References are to Federal Tax Coordinator 2d
FIN References are to RIA's Analysis of Federal Taxes: Income
USTR References are to United States Tax Reporter: Income, Estate & Gift, and Excise
PCA References are to Pension Coordinator and Pension & Benefits Expert/Advisor
PE References are to Pension and Profit Sharing 2nd
EP References are to Estate Planning & Taxation Coordinator and Estate Planning Advisor

good faith but erroneous interpretations of Code Sec. 6103 (above) applies in the case of unauthorized inspections as well as unauthorized disclosures. (Code Sec. 7431(b) as amended by Privacy Act §3(c))

> **☙ observation:** A new notification provision (¶ 2337) may assist taxpayers in learning of violations of the rules against unauthorized disclosure or inspection and thus facilitate their seeking civil damages.

☐ **Effective:** Inspections and disclosures occurring on and after Aug. 5, '97. (Privacy Act §3(e))

¶ 2409. IRS authorized to make reasonable cause abatements of first-tier penalty taxes on charitable organization excess benefit transactions

Code Sec. 4962(b), as amended by '97 Act § 1603(a)
Generally effective: Excess benefit transactions occurring after Sept. 13, '95
Committee Reports, see ¶ 5384

Penalty excise taxes are imposed as an "intermediate sanction" in cases where organizations exempt from tax under Code Sec. 501(c)(3) (charitable, religious, etc. organizations) or Code Sec. 501(c)(4) (civic leagues and social welfare organizations) that are not private foundations engage in an "excess benefit transaction." The penalty tax may be imposed on certain disqualified persons who improperly benefit from an excess benefit transaction and on organization managers who participate in such a transaction knowing that it is improper. If a disqualified person benefits from the transaction, he is subject to a "first-tier" penalty tax equal to 25% of the excess benefit. If an organization manager participates in the transaction, he is subject to a first-tier penalty tax equal to 10% of the excess benefit. Additional "second-tier" taxes equal to 200% of the excess benefit may be imposed on a disqualified person if there is no correction of the transaction within a specified period.

IRS has the authority to abate some first-tier taxes relating to private foundations and other exempt organizations where the transaction was due to reasonable cause and not to willful neglect and was corrected within the required time period. Congress intended, when it added the first-tier intermediate penalty taxes on excess benefit transactions, to give IRS abatement authority for those taxes. But Code Sec. 4962, which contains the abatement rules, applied only to qualified first-tier taxes imposed by subchapter A or C of Chapter 42 of the Internal Revenue Code. Because the intermediate penalty tax on excess benefit transactions is in subchapter D of Chapter 42, IRS didn't have authority to abate that tax. (FTC 2d/FIN ¶ D-6651 *et seq.*, ¶ D-8201; USTR ¶ 49,584, ¶ 49,614; TaxDesk ¶ 67,650, ¶ 68,566)

New Law. The '97 Act modifies the abatement rules to make them also apply to first-tier taxes imposed by subchapter D. (Code Sec. 4962(b) as amended by '97 Act §1603(a)) Thus, IRS has authority to abate the first-tier excise taxes on excess benefit transactions involving charities in cases where it is established that the violation was due to reasonable cause and not due to willful neglect and the transaction at issue was corrected within the specified period. (Com Rept, see ¶ 5384)

> ✪*observation:* The penalty tax on excess benefit transactions is the only provision in subchapter D. Thus, the '97 Act change has no effect on any other rules.

☐ **Effective:** Excess benefit transactions occurring after Sept. 13, '95. However, benefits arising from a transaction under a written contract binding on Sept. 13 '95 and until the transaction date are not affected where the terms of contract have not materially changed. ('97 Act §1603(c))

¶ 2410. $100 penalty for lack of due diligence by preparers of returns claiming earned income credit

Code Sec. 6695(g), as amended by '97 Act § 1085(a)(2)
Generally effective: Tax years beginning after Dec. 31 '96.
Committee Reports, see ¶ 5162

Paid income tax return preparers may be subject to various penalties. Under pre-'97 Act law there were no specific penalties for income tax preparers with regard to returns claiming the earned income credit. (FTC 2d/FIN ¶ V-2630; USTR ¶ 66,944; TaxDesk ¶ 86,700)

New Law. An income tax preparer with respect to any return or claim for refund who fails to comply with due diligence requirements imposed under IRS regs with respect to determining eligibility for, or the amount of, an earned income credit must pay a $100 penalty for each failure. (Code Sec. 6695(g) as amended by '97 Act §1085(a)(2))

> ✪*observation:* There is no calendar year maximum on the $100 due diligence penalty, unlike certain other return preparer penalties (e.g., the $25,000 calendar year maximum on the $50 penalty for each failure to furnish a copy of the return or refund claim to the taxpayer).

This penalty is in addition to any other applicable penalties. (Com Rept, see ¶ 5162)

☐ **Effective:** Tax years beginning after Dec. 31, '96. ('97 Act §1085(e)(1))

> ✪*observation:* Assuming that IRS issues the due diligence regs in time, preparers will have to comply with the due diligence requirements when preparing '97 returns.

¶ 2411. Penalty for failure to file certain information returns relating to foreign partnerships and corporations increased from $1,000 to $10,000; additional penalties imposed on continuing failures

Code Sec. 6679(a), as amended by '97 Act § 1143(b)
Generally effective: Transfers and changes after Aug. 5, '97
Committee Reports, see ¶ 5185

Information returns must be filed under Code Sec. 6046 in the case of the organization or reorganization of a foreign corporation or the acquisition of its stock by a U.S. person (see ¶ 2314), and under Code Sec. 6046A in the case of an acquisition or disposition of, or substantial change in, an interest in a foreign partnership (see ¶ 2313).

Under pre-'97 Act law, failure to comply with either of these filing requirements without reasonable cause resulted in a civil penalty of $1,000. No additional penalty was imposed in the case of continuing failures. (FTC 2d/FIN ¶ V-1901.2; USTR ¶ 60,46A4; TaxDesk ¶ 86,145, ¶ 86,148)

New Law. A person required to file a return under Code Sec. 6046 or Code Sec. 6046A who, without reasonable cause, fails to file a timely return containing the required information is liable for a $10,000 civil penalty. (Code Sec. 6679(a)(1) as amended by '97 Act §1143(b)) If the failure continues for more than 90 days after IRS mails notice to the U.S. person, additional $10,000 penalties apply for each 30-day period (or fraction of one) that the failure continues after the 90-day period, up to a maximum penalty of $50,000. (Code Sec. 6679(a)(2))

☐ **Effective:** Transfers and changes after Aug. 5, '97. ('97 Act §1143(c))

¶ 2412. Substantial understatement penalty modified

Code Sec. 6662(d)(2)(B), as amended by '97 Act § 1028(c)(1)
Code Sec. 6662(d)(2)(C)(iii), as amended by '97 Act § 1028(c)(2)
Generally effective: Transactions entered into after Aug. 5, '97
Committee Reports, see ¶ 5128

An accuracy-related penalty of 20% applies to the portion of any tax underpayment that is attributable to, among other things, any substantial understatement of income tax. A substantial understatement exists if the taxpayer's correct income tax liability for a tax year exceeds that reported by the greater of 10% of the correct tax or $5,000 ($10,000 in the case of most corporations). Except with respect to tax shelter items (see below), understatements are reduced, for this purpose, to the extent that they are attributable to either: (1) the treatment of items by the taxpayer for which there is or was substantial authority, or (2) items that meet both of the following tests: (a) relevant facts affecting the items' tax treatment are adequately disclosed in the return or in a statement attached to it and (b) there was a reasonable basis for the tax treatment of the items.

For tax shelter items of non-corporate taxpayers,

Research Institute of America

... (1) above does not apply unless the taxpayer also establishes that he reasonably believed that the treatment claimed was more likely than not the proper treatment of the item, and

... (2) above doesn't apply.

For tax shelter items of corporations, neither factor (1) or (2) above is applicable. (FTC 2d/FIN ¶ V-2154; USTR ¶ 66,624.04; TaxDesk ¶ 86,316)

For purposes of the above rules, a "tax shelter" is a partnership or other entity, any investment plan or arrangement, or any other plan or arrangement, if the principal purpose of the partnership, entity, plan, or arrangement is the avoidance or evasion of federal income tax. (FTC 2d/FIN ¶ V-2178; USTR ¶ 66,624.04; TaxDesk ¶ 86,316)

New Law. The '97 Act provides that for purposes of factor (2) above, a corporation will in no event be treated as having a "reasonable basis" for its tax treatment of an item attributable to a "multiple-party financing transaction" if that treatment does not clearly reflect the income of the corporation. (Code Sec. 6662(d)(2)(B) as amended by '97 Act §1028(c)(1))

> *observation:* Although the '97 Act doesn't define the term "multiple-party financing transaction, " regs dealing with tax avoidance by use of conduit financing arrangements do define a "financing transaction." Under Reg. §1.881-3(a) (2)(ii), a "financing transaction" is: debt, stock (only if the stock issuer or holder has rights, or payments that are ensured by other means), interests in a partnership or trust, any lease or license, other advances of money or property or rights to use property (other than collateral in certain cases) that the recipient must repay or return (or its equivalent in value). Therefore, the similarity of terms and issues would permit one to speculate that a multiple-party financing transaction is a financing transaction, as defined above, involving multiple parties.

No inference is intended that such a multiple-party financing transaction could not also be a tax shelter for purposes of the above tax shelter rules. (Com Rept, see ¶ 5128)

The '97 Act also modifies the above definition of a "tax shelter" to substitute "a significant purpose" for "the principal purpose." (Code Sec. 6662(d)(2)(C)(iii) as amended by '97 Act §1028(c)(2))

This modification conforms the definition of tax shelter for purposes of the substantial understatement penalty to the definition of tax shelter for purposes of the confidential corporate tax shelter registration requirements (see ¶ 2318). (Com Rept, see ¶ 5128)

FTC 2d References are to Federal Tax Coordinator 2d
FIN References are to RIA's Analysis of Federal Taxes: Income
USTR References are to United States Tax Reporter: Income, Estate & Gift, and Excise
PCA References are to Pension Coordinator and Pension & Benefits Expert/Advisor
PE References are to Pension and Profit Sharing 2nd
EP References are to Estate Planning & Taxation Coordinator and Estate Planning Advisor

🅡🅘🅐 *observation:* This Committee Report rule means the following: The '97 Act has changed the above definition of tax shelter so that both it and the definition of the term that we've called "confidential corporate tax shelters" at ¶ 2318 require that the avoidance or evasion of federal income tax be "a significant purpose," not "the principal purpose" of the entity.

☐ **Effective:** Items with respect to transactions entered into after Aug. 5, '97. ('97 Act §1028(e)(2))

¶ 2500. Tax-Exempt Bonds

¶ 2501. First-time home buyer, purchase price, and mortgagor's income requirements waived for mortgage bond financing for residences located in disaster areas

Code Sec. 143(k)(11), as amended by '97 Act § 914
Generally effective: Bonds issued after Dec. 31, '96 and before Jan. 1, '99
Committee Reports, see ¶ 5064

State and local bonds that are "qualified mortgage bonds" qualify for tax-exempt status. Qualified mortgage bonds are private activity bonds issued by state and local governments acting as conduits to provide mortgage loans. The bond must be part of a qualified mortgage issue. This means the issue must satisfy certain specified requirements, including the following:

- *First-time home buyer requirement (a/k/a three-year requirement)*. Code Sec. 143(d) requires that at least 95% of the net proceeds of the issue must be used to finance the residences of mortgagors who had no present ownership interest in their principal residences (other than the residence for which the financing is being provided) during the three-year period ending on the date the mortgage is executed. This requirement is waived in the case of loans made to finance homes in statutorily prescribed economically distressed areas—so-called "target areas."
- *Purchase price requirement*. Code Sec. 143(e) requires that the acquisition cost of each residence for which owner-financing is provided can't be more than 90% of the average area purchase price applicable to the residence. The percentage applicable to targeted area residences is 110%.
- *Mortgagor's income requirement*. Code Sec. 143(f) requires that all owner-financing provided under the issue must be provided to mortgagors whose family income is 115% or less of the applicable median family income. In the case of any financing provided for targeted area residences, one-third of the financing may be provided without regard to this income requirement, and the remainder may be provided to mortgagors whose family income is 140% or less of the applicable median family income.

(FTC 2d/FIN ¶ J-3187, ¶ J-3191, ¶ J-3193, ¶ J-3211; USTR ¶ 1434.012, ¶ 1434.013, ¶ 1434.014; TaxDesk ¶ 15,810)

New Law. In order to help survivors of Presidentially-declared disasters rebuild their homes (Com Rept, see ¶ 5064), the '97 Act provides that, in the case of financing provided with respect to a residence located in an area determined by the President to warrant assistance from the federal government under the Robert T. Stafford Disaster

---

FTC 2d References are to Federal Tax Coordinator 2d
FIN References are to RIA's Analysis of Federal Taxes: Income
USTR References are to United States Tax Reporter: Income, Estate & Gift, and Excise
PCA References are to Pension Coordinator and Pension & Benefits Expert/Advisor
PE References are to Pension and Profit Sharing 2nd
EP References are to Estate Planning & Taxation Coordinator and Estate Planning Advisor

Relief and Emergency Assistance Act (as in effect on Aug. 5, '97), a modified version of the qualified mortgage bond requirements will apply to any financing that is provided with respect to those residences within two years after the date of the disaster declaration. (Code Sec. 143(k)(11) as amended by '97 Act §914) Specifically:

The three-year requirement of Code Sec. 143(d) won't apply to any financing that's provided with respect to the residence during this two-year period. (Code Sec. 143(k)(11)(A)) The Act thus waives the first-time home buyer requirement with respect to the proceeds of a qualified mortgage bond issue that are used to finance homes located in target areas. (Com Rept, see ¶ 5064)

The purchase price requirement of Code Sec. 143(e) will be applied during the two-year period following the disaster declaration as if the residence were a targeted area residence. (Code Sec. 143(k)(11)(B))

> **✐** *observation:* Thus, the acquisition cost of each residence for which owner-financing is provided during this two-year period will be subject to the 110% limit, rather than the 90% limit.

The mortgagor's income requirement of Code Sec. 143(f) will be applied during the two-year period following the disaster declaration as if the residence were a targeted area residence. (Code Sec. 143(k)(11)(B))

> **✐** *observation:* One-third of the financing that's provided during this two-year period may be provided without regard to the mortgagors' income levels, and the remainder may be provided to mortgagors whose family income is 140% or less of the applicable median family income.

These waivers apply only during the two-year period following the date of the disaster declaration. (Com Rept, see ¶ 5064)

> **✐** *observation:* Since the three-year requirement generally doesn't apply to financing that is provided with respect to a targeted area residence, the effect of this '97 Act rule is to treat the residence as if it were a targeted area residence during this two-year period, for purposes of all three of the above requirements.

☐ **Effective:** Bonds issued after Dec. 31, '96 and before Jan. 1, '99. ('97 Act §914) This means loans financed with bonds issued after Dec. 31, '96 and before Jan. 1, '99. (Com Rept, see ¶ 5064)

¶ 2502. Up to $5 million in bonds used to finance public school capital expenditures after '97 exempted from arbitrage rebate requirements

Code Sec. 148(f)(4)(D)(vii), as amended by '97 Act § 223(a)
Generally effective: Bonds issued after Dec. 31, '97
Committee Reports, see ¶ 5009

State or local bonds are not tax-exempt if they are arbitrage bonds. An arbitrage bond is a bond issued as part of an issue any portion of the proceeds of which are reasonably expected to be used to acquire higher yielding investments or to replace funds which were used to acquire higher yielding investments. Bonds will also be considered to be arbitrage bonds if the issuer uses an artifice or device to circumvent this definition. Under Code Sec. 148(f)(1), bonds are not treated as arbitrage bonds if certain "rebate to the U.S." requirements, set forth by Code Sec. 148(f)(2) and Code Sec. 148(f)(3), are satisfied.

Small issuer exception. Under Code Sec. 148(f)(4)(D)(i), the above rebate requirements are treated as satisfied with respect to an issue if the issue is issued by a governmental unit with general taxing powers; the aggregate face amount of all tax-exempt bonds (other than private activity bonds) issued by that unit during the calendar year in which the issue is issued is not reasonably expected, as of the issue date, to exceed $5 million; and certain other requirements are satisfied.

Under Code Sec. 148(f)(4)(D)(iv), for purposes of the small issuer rules, an issue issued by a subordinate entity of a government unit with general taxing powers is treated as itself a government unit with general taxing powers if the aggregate face amount of the issue does not exceed the lesser of: (i) $5 million, or (ii) the amount which, when added to the aggregate face amount of other issues issued by that subordinate entity, does not exceed the portion of the $5 million limitation under Code Sec. 148(f)(4)(D)(i) (see above), that the superior governmental unit allocates to the subordinate entity.

Code Sec. 148(f)(4)(D)(v) and Code Sec. 148(f)(4)(D)(vi) set forth requirements for applying the small issuer exception to "refunding issues" — i.e., bond issues used to refund outstanding bonds. One of these requirements is set forth by Code Sec. 148(f)(4)(D)(v)(I): the aggregate face amount of the issue that includes the refunding portion may not exceed $5 million. Another of these requirements is set forth by Code Sec. 148(f)(4)(D)(vi)(III): for refunded bonds issued before Aug. 16, '86, the aggregate face amount of all tax-exempt bonds issued by the issuer during the calendar year in which the refunded bond was issued could not have exceeded $5 million.

(FTC 2d/FIN ¶ J-3400 *et seq.*, ¶ J-3462 *et seq.*; USTR ¶ 1484 *et seq.*; TaxDesk ¶ 15,813 *et seq.*)

New Law. Under the '97 Act, each of the $5 million amounts mentioned in the provisions described above is increased by the lesser of:

... $5 million, or

... so much of the aggregate face amount of the bonds as are attributable to financing the construction (as defined by Code Sec. 148(f)(4)(C)(iv)) of public school facilities.

(Code Sec. 148(f)(4)(d)(vii) as amended by '97 Act §223(a))

FTC 2d References are to Federal Tax Coordinator 2d
FIN References are to RIA's Analysis of Federal Taxes: Income
USTR References are to United States Tax Reporter: Income, Estate & Gift, and Excise
PCA References are to Pension Coordinator and Pension & Benefits Expert/Advisor
PE References are to Pension and Profit Sharing 2nd
EP References are to Estate Planning & Taxation Coordinator and Estate Planning Advisor

Thus, the '97 Act provides that up to $5 million dollars of bonds used to finance public school capital expenditures are excluded from application of the various $5 million limits under the small issuer exception. As a result, small issuers will continue to benefit from the small issue exception from arbitrage rebate if they issue no more than $10 million in governmental bonds per calendar year and no more than $5 million of the bonds is used to finance expenditures other than for public school capital expenditures. This provision is intended to address the needs of the U.S.'s crumbling public school infrastructure by reducing the compliance costs of issuers of tax-exempt debt issued for public school construction. (Com Rept, see ¶ 5009)

☐ **Effective:** Bonds issued after Dec. 31, '97. ('97 Act §223(b))

¶ 2503. Repeal of 150%-of-debt-service limit on investment in nonpurpose investments under arbitrage bond rules

Code Sec. 148(d), as amended by '97 Act § 1443
Generally effective: Bonds issued after Aug. 5, '97
Committee Reports, see ¶ 5297

All state and local bonds (including private activity bonds) are subject to restrictions limiting the arbitrage profits from investment of the bond proceeds. In addition to the requirement that arbitrage profits from investing the proceeds in investments unrelated to the governmental purpose of the financing must be rebated to the federal government (the "arbitrage rebate requirement," see ¶ 2504), the bond must also meet certain yield restrictions.

For a state or local bond to satisfy the arbitrage yield restrictions, the bond proceeds must be invested at a yield that isn't materially higher (generally 0.125 percentage points) than the bond yield. There are exceptions for investments during any of several "temporary periods" pending use of the proceeds and, throughout the term of the issue, for proceeds invested as part of a reasonably required reserve or replacement fund and for investments of a "minor" portion of the proceeds.

Under pre-'97 Act law, the amount of proceeds of private activity bonds (other than qualified 501(c)(3) bonds) that could be invested at materially higher yields at any time during a bond year was limited to 150% of the debt service on the issue for that bond year—i.e., 150% of the scheduled amount of interest and amortization of principal payable with respect to the issue for the bond year. This limitation didn't apply to temporary period investments and amounts held pending use to pay current debt service. It primarily affected investments in reasonably required reserves or replacement funds. Investments in these reserve funds are further restricted in that the amount of proceeds from the sale of bonds that can be invested in the funds is limited to 10% of the proceeds. (Com Rept, see ¶ 5297) (FTC 2d/FIN ¶ J-3620; USTR ¶ 1484.03; TaxDesk ¶ 15,813)

New Law. The '97 Act repeals the 150%-of-debt-service limit on investment in reasonably required reserve or replacement funds. (Code Sec. 148(d) as amended by '97 Act §1443) This limit, which was intended to eliminate arbitrage-motivated activities available from investment of these reserve funds, was enacted before the arbitrage rules were modified to include the rebate requirement and the ten percent limit on the size of reasonably required reserve or replacement funds. In view of the comprehensive yield restrictions and rebate requirements under the arbitrage rules, and the overall size limit on reserve funds, the 150%-of-debt-service yield restriction is duplicative. (Com Rept, see ¶ 5297)

☐ **Effective:** Bonds issued after Aug. 5, '97. ('97 Act §1445)

¶ 2504. Arbitrage bond rebate requirement: repeal of $100,000 limitation on unspent proceeds under six-month spending exception; exemption for earnings on bona fide debt service funds under construction issue exception

Code Sec. 148(f)(4)(B)(ii)(I), as amended by '97 Act § 1441
Code Sec. 148(f)(4)(C)(xvii), as amended by '97 Act § 1442
Generally effective: Bonds issued after Aug. 5, '97
Committee Reports, see ¶ 5295, 5296

The exemption from federal income tax for interest on bonds issued by state or local governments does not apply unless certain requirements, including restrictions relating to arbitrage, are met. The arbitrage restrictions limit the profits (and later earnings on those profits) derived from investing the bond proceeds in investments that have a materially higher yield than the bonds, and that are unrelated to the governmental purpose of the financing ("nonpurpose investments").

In addition to satisfying certain arbitrage yield restrictions (see ¶ 2503), a bond issue must also satisfy an arbitrage rebate requirement. The arbitrage profits from investing the bond proceeds in nonpurpose investments must be rebated to the federal government. However, there are certain exceptions to this rebate requirement, including a "six-month spending exception" and a "construction issue exception."

Six-month spending exception. No rebate is required if the gross proceeds of an issue are spent for the governmental purpose of the borrowing within six months after issuance. Specifically, an issue is treated as satisfying the arbitrage rebate requirements if (1) the gross proceeds of the issue (other than amounts held in a bona fide debt service fund) are spent for the governmental purpose for which the bond was issued within six months after the issuance, and (2) all of the rebate requirements are met with respect to amounts not required to be spent for government purposes (other than earnings on amounts in any bona fide debt service fund). Pre-'97 Act law provided that issuers of governmental bonds (other than tax and revenue anticipation notes) and qualified 501(c)(3) bonds met this six-month spending exception if (a) all of the issue proceeds other than an amount not exceeding the lesser of five percent of the proceeds or $100,000 were spent for the governmental purpose within six months after the issu-

FTC 2d References are to Federal Tax Coordinator 2d
FIN References are to RIA's Analysis of Federal Taxes: Income
USTR References are to United States Tax Reporter: Income, Estate & Gift, and Excise
PCA References are to Pension Coordinator and Pension & Benefits Expert/Advisor
PE References are to Pension and Profit Sharing 2nd
EP References are to Estate Planning & Taxation Coordinator and Estate Planning Advisor

ance, and (b) the remaining proceeds (other than earnings on debt service amounts) were spent for the governmental purpose within one year after the bonds were issued. (FTC 2d/FIN ¶ J-3446; USTR ¶ 1484.04; TaxDesk ¶ 15,813)

Construction issue exception. There is an exception to the arbitrage rebate requirement for certain construction bond issues if the bonds are governmental bonds, qualified 501(c)(3) bonds, or exempt-facility private activity bonds for governmentally-owned property. If the available construction proceeds (defined below) of the issue are spent at minimum specified rates during the 24-month period after the bonds are issued, no rebate is required with respect to those proceeds. Issuers of construction bonds also may elect to pay a penalty instead of rebating arbitrage profits if they fail to satisfy the 24-month spending requirements.

The term "available construction proceeds" for a construction issue means an amount equal to the sum of: the issue price of the issue, earnings on the issue price, earnings on amounts in any reasonably required reserve or replacement fund (so-called "4R funds") not funded from the issue, plus earnings on all the foregoing amounts; reduced by the amount of the issue price invested in any 4R fund (e.g., in a bona fide debt service fund), and by the issuance costs financed by the issue. Thus, the "issue price" that enters into the available construction proceeds doesn't include any amount that is invested in a bona fide debt service fund, although the earnings on those amounts *are* included. Also, "available construction proceeds" don't include amounts earned on any 4R fund after the earlier of (a) the close of the 24-month period or (b) the date the construction is substantially completed (see FTC 2d/FIN ¶s J-3458, J-3625; USTR ¶ 1484.04; TaxDesk ¶ 15,813).

Thus, the construction issue exception does not apply to bond proceeds invested after the 24-month expenditure period as part of a 4R fund, or to certain other investments (e.g., sinking funds). Nor does the exception apply to proceeds invested in a bona fide debt service fund (and so not included in available construction proceeds). However, pre-'97 Act law did not provide an exemption for the earnings on the amounts so invested. (FTC 2d/FIN ¶ J-3448; USTR ¶ 1484.04; TaxDesk ¶ 15,813)

New Law. The '97 Act modifies the six-month spending exception (Com Rept, see ¶ 5295) and the construction issue exception (Com Rept, see ¶ 5296) to the arbitrage rebate requirements.

Six-month spending exception. The '97 Act repeals the $100,000 limitation on proceeds that may remain unspent after six months for certain governmental and qualified 501(c)(3) bonds to be exempt from the arbitrage rebate requirement. (Com Rept, see ¶ 5295) Specifically, the bond issue is considered to satisfy the six-month spending exception if (1) all of the issue proceeds other than an amount not exceeding five percent of the proceeds are spent for the governmental purpose within six months after the issuance, and (2) the remaining proceeds (other than earnings on debt service amounts) are spent for the governmental purpose within one year after the bonds are issued. (Code Sec. 148(f)(4)(B)(ii)(I) as amended by '97 Act §1441) If at least 95% of the proceeds of the bonds is spent within six months after their issuance, and the remainder is spent within one year, the six-month spending exception is considered to be satisfied. (Com Rept, see ¶ 5295)

💡observation: Thus, no rebate is required for a bond issue if at least 95% of the bond proceeds are spent for the governmental purpose within the first six months after the issuance, and the remaining proceeds are spent for that purpose within one year after the issuance.

Congress believes that if at least 95% of the proceeds of an issue is spent within six months, and the remainder is spent within one year, opportunities for arbitrage profit are significantly limited. (Com Rept, see ¶ 5295)

Construction issue exception. The '97 Act provides an exemption from the arbitrage rebate requirements, for earnings on construction bond issue proceeds that are invested in bona fide debt service funds. (Com Rept, see ¶ 5296) If the available construction proceeds of a construction issue are spent as required over the prescribed 24-month period, the rebate requirements will not apply to the earnings on a bona fide debt service fund for the issue. (Code Sec. 148(f)(4)(C)(xvii) as amended by '97 Act §1442) The issuer will not have to rebate the arbitrage profits attributable to those earnings, or comply with the alternative penalty provisions. (Com Rept, see ¶ 5296)

Congress believes it is appropriate to exempt the earnings on bond proceeds invested in a bona fide debt service fund from the arbitrage rebate requirements. Bond proceeds that are invested in these funds generally must be spent at least annually for current debt service. The short-term nature of these investments results in only limited potential for generating arbitrage profits. If the spending requirements of the 24-month construction issue exception are satisfied, the administrative complexity of calculating rebate on these proceeds outweighs the other federal policy concerns addressed by the rebate requirement. (Com Rept, see ¶ 5296)

☐ **Effective:** Bonds issued after Aug. 5, '97. ('97 Act §1445)

¶ 2505. $150 million limitation on 501(c)(3) bonds repealed

Code Sec. 145(b)(1), as amended by '97 Act § 222(a)
Generally effective: Aug. 5, '97
Committee Reports, see ¶ 5008

Interest on bonds issued by state and local governments to provide financing for private purposes—i.e., "private activity bonds"—isn't eligible for the exemption from federal income tax otherwise applicable to interest on state and local bonds *unless* the bond meets certain requirements, and is one of seven specified types of "qualified bonds." One type of qualified bond is a "501(c)(3) bond." A qualified 501(c)(3) bond is a bond used to finance activities of private charitable organizations described in Code Sec. 501(c)(3), where the activities aren't a taxable unrelated trade or business. However, under Code Sec. 145(b), as in effect before the '97 Act, bonds (other than qualified hospital bonds) weren't treated as qualified 501(c)(3) bonds if they were allo-

FTC 2d References are to Federal Tax Coordinator 2d
FIN References are to RIA's Analysis of Federal Taxes: Income
USTR References are to United States Tax Reporter: Income, Estate & Gift, and Excise
PCA References are to Pension Coordinator and Pension & Benefits Expert/Advisor
PE References are to Pension and Profit Sharing 2nd
EP References are to Estate Planning & Taxation Coordinator and Estate Planning Advisor

💡 **Research Institute of America** 603

cated to any 501(c)(3) organization which met certain requirements, and the total amount of outstanding tax-exempt non-hospital bonds allocated to that organization (including all other 501(c)(3) organizations under the same management or control) exceeded $150 million. As a result, under pre-'97 Act law, a public university generally had unlimited access to tax-exempt bond financing, while a private, non-profit university was subject to the $150 million limitation on outstanding bonds from which it could benefit. (Com Rept, see ¶ 5008) (FTC 2d/FIN ¶ J-3248.2; USTR ¶ 1454.02)

New Law. Congress believes a distinguishing feature of American society is the singular degree to which the U.S. maintains a private, non-profit sector of private higher education and other charitable institutions in the public service. It's important to assist these private institutions in their advancement of the public good. Congress finds particularly inappropriate the restrictions which place these section 501(c)(3) organizations at a financial disadvantage relative to substantially identical governmental institutions. Congress is concerned that this and other restrictions inhibit the ability of America's private, non-profit institutions to modernize their educational facilities. Congress believes the tax-exempt bond rules should treat more equally state and local governments and those private organizations which are engaged in similar actions advancing the public good. (Com Rept, see ¶ 5008)

Therefore, the '97 Act makes the provisions of Code Sec. 145(b) inapplicable with respect to bonds issued after Aug. 5, '97, as part of an issue 95% or more of the net proceeds of which are to be used to finance capital expenditures incurred after that date. (Code Sec. 145(b)(5) as amended by '97 Act §222)

> *observation:* In other words, the '97 Act repeals the $150 million amount limitation on non-hospital 501(c)(3) bonds issued after Aug. 5, '97 that are allocable to 501(c)(3) organizations, if at least 95% of the net proceeds of the relevant bond issue are to be used to finance capital expenditures .

Because the above provision of '97 Act applies only to bonds issued with respect to capital expenditures incurred after Aug. 5, '97, the $150 million limit will continue to govern issuance of other non-hospital qualified 501(c)(3) bonds (e.g., refunding bonds or new-money bonds for capital expenditures incurred before Aug. 5, '97). Thus, bond issuers will continue to need Treasury Department guidance on the application of this limit in the future and expect that the Treasury will continue to provide interpretative rules on this limit. (Com Rept, see ¶ 5008)

☐ **Effective:** For bonds issued after Aug. 5, '97. (Com Rept, see ¶ 5008)

¶ 2506. Certain Virgin Islands bonds allowed one additional refinancing if Virgin Islands priority first lien requirement is repealed

Code Sec. 149(d)(3)(A)(i)(I), '97 Act § 967
Generally effective: Aug. 5, '97
Committee Reports, see ¶ 5090

The interest on a state or local bond doesn't qualify for the exemption from federal income tax that applies to governmental bonds generally, if the bond is part of an issue that violates the Code restrictions on advance refundings. A bond is treated as issued to advance refund another bond if it is issued more than 90 days before the redemption of the refunded bond. An issue generally violates the advance refunding restrictions if any bond that is part of the issue is issued to advance refund a bond. However, Code Sec. 149(d)(3)(A)(i)(I) does allow for one advance refunding of bonds that were originally issued after '85. The refunding bond must be part of the first advance refunding of the original bond. (FTC 2d/FIN ¶ J-3660; USTR ¶ 1493.03; TaxDesk ¶ 15,814)

In addition, governmental bonds may be subject to statutory restrictions other than those imposed by the Code. For example, the Virgin Islands is required to secure its bonds with a priority first lien claim on specified revenue streams; it isn't permitted to issue multiple bond issues secured on a parity basis by a common pool of revenues. A proposed non-tax law change would repeal this priority lien requirement. (Com Rept, see ¶ 5090)

> **✔️ observation:** Presumably, Congress is referring to H.R. 1152, which proposes amendments to the bond priority requirements under 48 U.S.C. 1574 (the Revised Organic Act of the Virgin Islands).

New Law. The '97 Act permits an additional advance refunding of bonds issued by the Virgin Islands, in the event that the priority first lien requirement is repealed. (Com Rept, see ¶ 5090) Specifically, if the debt provisions of the refunding bonds are changed to repeal the priority first lien requirement of the refunded bonds, the Code Sec. 149(d)(3)(A)(i)(I) rule that a refunding bond must be part of the first advance refunding of the original bonds won't apply to the second advance refunding of any issue of the Virgin Islands that was first advance refunded before June 9, '97. ('97 Act §967) This means that governmental bonds issued by the Virgin Islands that were advance refunded before June 9, '97 will be allowed one additional advance refunding if the priority first lien requirement is repealed. (Com Rept, see ¶ 5090)

☐ **Effective:** Aug. 5, '97. (Com Rept, see ¶ 5090)

¶ 2507. Repeal as deadwood two exceptions to arbitrage rebate and temporary period pooled financing rules for qualified student loan bonds issued before '89

Code Sec. 148(c)(2)(B), repealed by '97 Act § 1444(a)
Code Sec. 148(f)(4)(E), repealed by '97 Act § 1444(b)
Generally effective: Bonds issued after Aug. 5, '97
Committee Reports, see ¶ 5298

FTC 2d References are to Federal Tax Coordinator 2d
FIN References are to RIA's Analysis of Federal Taxes: Income
USTR References are to United States Tax Reporter: Income, Estate & Gift, and Excise
PCA References are to Pension Coordinator and Pension & Benefits Expert/Advisor
PE References are to Pension and Profit Sharing 2nd
EP References are to Estate Planning & Taxation Coordinator and Estate Planning Advisor

The issuer of state or local bonds must rebate the arbitrage profits earned from investing the bond proceeds in higher-yielding investments for purposes other than the governmental purpose for the issuance. The amount of the rebate that is required with respect to these nonpurpose investments is the excess of the amount earned on all nonpurpose investments, minus the amount that would have been earned if the nonpurpose investments had been invested at a rate equal to the yield on the issue, plus any income attributable to that excess. However, no rebate is required with respect to nonpurpose investments made during a reasonable temporary period. For pooled financing issues where the proceeds are to be used to make or finance loans (other than nonpurpose investments) to two or more persons, the temporary period is six months.

Pre-'97 Act law included two exceptions to the arbitrage rebate and pooled financing temporary period rules, for certain qualified student loan bonds. The "amount earned" on nonpurpose investments that was used in computing the required arbitrage rebate did not include certain reasonable administrative costs for the program, or the issuance costs of the issuance. Also, the temporary period was 18 months (rather than six months). These exceptions applied only to qualified student loan bonds issued before Jan. 1, '89, in connection with the Federal Guaranteed Student Loan (GSL) and Parents' Loans for Undergraduate Students (PLUS) programs. (FTC 2d/FIN ¶ J-3614, ¶ J-3621; USTR ¶ 1484.04; TaxDesk ¶ 15,813)

New Law. The '97 Act repeals (as "deadwood" (Com Rept, see ¶ 5298)) the exceptions that applied to qualified student loan bonds issued before Jan. 1, '89, with respect to computing the "amount earned" on nonpurpose investments for purposes of computing the arbitrage rebate (Code Sec. 148(c)(2)(B) repealed by '97 Act §1444(a)) and with respect to the temporary period. (Code Sec. 148(f)(4)(E) repealed by '97 Act §1444(b))

> *observation:* Unless another exception applies, for all qualified student loan bonds, the arbitrage rebate computation includes reasonable administrative costs and issuance costs. The temporary period during which the proceeds may be invested in nonpurpose investments with no rebate required is reduced from 18 months to the six-month temporary period that applies to pooled financings generally.

☐ **Effective:** Bonds issued after Aug. 5, '97. ('97 Act §1445) The repeal has no effect on bonds issued before that date. (Com Rept, see ¶ 5298)

¶ 2600. District of Columbia and Empowerment Zones

DC Tax Incentives

¶ 2601. Designation of DC Enterprise Zone as an empowerment zone

Code Sec. 1400, as added by '97 Act § 701(a)
Code Sec. 39(d)(8), as amended by '97 Act § 701(b)(1)
Generally effective: Aug. 5, '97
Committee Reports, see ¶ 5040

The following tax incentives apply to areas designated as empowerment zones:

... an increased Code Sec. 179 expensing election is allowed for certain depreciable business property used by an enterprise zone business in an empowerment zone (FTC 2d/FIN ¶ L-9950 *et seq.*; USTR ¶ 13,97A4; TaxDesk ¶ 26,842)

... employers are allowed a credit equal to 20% of the first $15,000 of qualified wages paid annually to each employee who lives and works in an empowerment zone. In 2002, the credit is reduced to 15%. (FTC 2d/FIN ¶ L-15630 *et seq.*; USTR ¶ 13,964; TaxDesk ¶ 38,412)

... the issuance of tax-exempt enterprise zone facility bonds that can be used to finance facilities used by an enterprise zone business in an empowerment zone. (FTC 2d/FIN ¶ J-3350 *et seq.*; USTR ¶ 13,944)

Under pre-'97 Act law, areas of the District of Columbia were not designated as the DC Enterprise Zone and treated as an empowerment zone.

New Law. Congress believed that one of the key problems faced by the District of Columbia is insufficient economic activity. To this end, Congress has provided certain tax incentives to encourage economic development in those areas of the District where development has been inadequate. (Com Rept, see ¶ 5040)

Under the '97 Act, specified economically depressed census tracts within the District of Columbia are designated as the "DC Enterprise Zone," within which businesses and individual residents are eligible for certain tax incentives. (Com Rept, see ¶ 5040) The '97 Act designates the "applicable DC area" (defined below) as the District of Columbia Enterprise Zone. (Code Sec. 1400(a)(1) as added by '97 Act §701(a)) Except as discussed below and in ¶ 2604 (relating to tax-exempt economic development bonds for the District of Columbia), ¶ 2602 (zero percent capital gains rate that applies to sales of certain District of Columbia assets), and ¶ 2603 (the first-time homebuyer credit for the District of Columbia), the District of Columbia Enterprise Zone is treated

---

FTC 2d References are to Federal Tax Coordinator 2d
FIN References are to RIA's Analysis of Federal Taxes: Income
USTR References are to United States Tax Reporter: Income, Estate & Gift, and Excise
PCA References are to Pension Coordinator and Pension & Benefits Expert/Advisor
PE References are to Pension and Profit Sharing 2nd
EP References are to Estate Planning & Taxation Coordinator and Estate Planning Advisor

as an empowerment zone designated under Code Sec. 1391 through Code Sec. 1397D. (Code Sec. 1400(a)(2))

Thus, the following tax incentives that are available, under pre-'97 Act law, in empowerment zones are available in the DC Enterprise Zone (modified as described below):

. . . empowerment zone employment credit. With respect to the DC Enterprise Zone, Code Sec. 1396(d)(1)(B) (relating to the requirement under the empowerment zone employment credit that the principal place of abode of the employee performing the services is within the empowerment zone) is applied by substituting "the District of Columbia" for "such empowerment zone." (Code Sec. 1400(d)(1)) Thus, the wage credit is available with respect to all residents of the District of Columbia and is not limited to residents of the DC Enterprise Zone. (Com Rept, see ¶ 5040)

> *observation:* Although the employee does not have to live in the DC Enterprise Zone, the services would still have to be performed in the DC Enterprise Zone (as required by Code Sec. 1396(d)(1)(A)).

In the case of the District of Columbia Enterprise Zone, Code Sec. 1396 (relating to the empowerment zone employment credit) is applied by substituting "20%" for "15%" as the applicable percentage of the amount of qualified wages (up to $15,000 per year) which may be taken into account as an empowerment zone credit for wages paid or incurred during the calendar year 2002. This rule applies only with respect to qualified zone employees (as defined in Code Sec. 1396(d)), determined by treating no area other than the DC Zone as an empowerment zone or enterprise community. (Code Sec. 1400(d)(2)) Thus, for wages paid to these employees, the wage credit rate remains at 20% for the DC Enterprise Zone for the period '98 through 2002 (and does not phase down to 15% in the year 2002 as under Code Sec. 1396). (Com Rept, see ¶ 5040)

> *observation:* In 2002, a credit can be claimed for 20% of wages paid to employees who reside in the DC Enterprise Zone and 15% of wages paid to employees who reside elsewhere in the District of Columbia.

No portion of the unused business credit for any tax year which is attributable to the empowerment zone employment credit under Code Sec. 1396 by reason of the designation of DC Zone as an empowerment zone (see above) can be carried back to a tax year ending before Aug. 5, '97. (Code Sec. 39(d)(8) as amended by '97 Act §701(b)(1))

. . . the additional $20,000 of expensing under Code Sec. 179 and Code Sec. 1397A(a)(1)(A) (which was available under pre-'97 Act law) for qualified zone property. Thus, qualified DC Zone property placed in service in tax years beginning in '98 is eligible for up to $38,500 of expensing. (Com Rept, see ¶ 5040)

. . . tax-exempt financing as described in ¶ 2604.

Modifications to the definition of enterprise zone business. For purposes of the above rules and for purposes of applying Code Sec. 1391 through Code Sec. 1397D (see FTC 2d/FIN ¶ J-3375 *et seq.*; USTR ¶ 13,914 *et seq.*) with respect to the DC

Zone, Code Sec. 1397B (the definition of an enterprise zone business) is applied without regard to the requirement that at least 35% of the business's employees must be residents of an empowerment zone provided in Code Sec. 1397B(b)(6) and Code Sec. 1397B(c)(5). (Code Sec. 1400(e)) For other changes to the definition of enterprise zone business under the '97 Act, see ¶ 2610 and ¶ 2611.

Applicable DC area defined. For purposes of the designation of the District of Columbia Enterprise Zone (see above), the applicable DC area is the area consisting of: (Code Sec. 1400(b))

(1) the census tracts located in the District of Columbia which are part of an enterprise community designated under Code Sec. 1391 through Code Sec. 1397D (see FTC 2d/FIN ¶ J-3375 *et seq.*; USTR ¶ 13,914 *et seq.*) before Aug. 5, '97 (Code Sec. 1400(b)(1)), and

(2) all other census tracts (Code Sec. 1400(b)(2)) which are located in the District of Columbia (Code Sec. 1400(b)(2)(A)), *and* for which the poverty rate is at least 20%. (Code Sec. 1400(b)(2)(B))

Thus, the DC Enterprise Zone consists of (1) all census tracts that presently are part of the DC enterprise community designated under Code Sec. 1391 (i.e., portions of Anacostia, Mt. Pleasant, Chinatown, and the easternmost part of the District) and (2) all additional census tracts within the District of Columbia where the poverty rate is at least 20%. (Com Rept, see ¶ 5040)

Time for which designation of the District of Columbia Enterprise Zone applies. The designation of the District of Columbia Enterprise Zone (see above) applies for the period beginning on Jan. 1, '98, and ending on Dec. 31, 2002. (Code Sec. 1400(f)(1)) Thus, the Code Sec. 1396 empowerment zone wage credit is effective for wages paid (or incurred) to a qualified individual after Dec. 31, '97, and before Jan. 1, 2003 and the increased expensing under Code Sec. 179 is effective for property placed in service in tax years beginning after Dec. 31, '97, and before Jan. 1, 2003. (Com Rept, see ¶ 5040)

When the enterprise community designation of certain census tracts in the applicable DC area terminates. The designation as an enterprise community, under Code Sec. 1391 through Code Sec. 1397D, of the census tracts referred to in Code Sec. 1400(b)(1) (see definition of the applicable DC area, above) terminates on Dec. 31, 2002. (Code Sec. 1400(f)(2))

☐ **Effective:** Aug. 5, '97. ('97 Act §701(d))

FTC 2d References are to Federal Tax Coordinator 2d
FIN References are to RIA's Analysis of Federal Taxes: Income
USTR References are to United States Tax Reporter: Income, Estate & Gift, and Excise
PCA References are to Pension Coordinator and Pension & Benefits Expert/Advisor
PE References are to Pension and Profit Sharing 2nd
EP References are to Estate Planning & Taxation Coordinator and Estate Planning Advisor

¶ 2602. Zero percent capital gains rate applies to certain sales of DC Zone assets held for more than five years

Code Sec. 1400B, as added by '97 Act § 701(a)
Generally effective: Aug. 5, '97
Committee Reports, see ¶ 5040

Under pre-'97 Act law, there were no special capital gains rules related to sales or exchanges of DC Zone assets.

New Law. Congress believed that one of the key problems faced by the District of Columbia is insufficient economic activity. To this end, Congress has provided certain tax incentives to encourage economic development in those areas of the District where development has been inadequate. (Com Rept, see ¶ 5040)

The '97 Act provides a zero percent capital gains rate for capital gains from the sale of certain DC Zone assets held for more than five years. (Com Rept, see ¶ 5040) Gross income does not include qualified capital gain (defined below) from the sale or exchange of any "DC Zone" (defined at ¶ 2601 and as modified below) asset (defined below) held for more than five years. (Code Sec. 1400B(a) as added by '97 Act §701(a))

Qualified capital gain. Except as discussed below, qualified capital gain is any gain recognized on the sale or exchange of: (Code Sec. 1400B(e)(1))

. . . a capital asset, or (Code Sec. 1400B(e)(1)(A))

. . . property used in the trade or business (as defined in Code Sec. 1231(b), see FTC 2d/FIN ¶ I-9008; USTR ¶ 12,314; TaxDesk ¶ 22,318). (Code Sec. 1400B(e)(1)(B))

But, qualified capital gain does *not* include any gain:

. . . attributable to periods before Jan. 1, '98, or after Dec. 31, 2007; (Code Sec. 1400B(e)(2))

> *observation:* Although qualified capital gain does not include gain attributable to periods after Dec. 31, 2007, it appears that there is no requirement that the taxpayer sell the DC Zone asset before Dec. 31, 2007. Where a taxpayer continues to hold his DC Zone asset after Dec. 31, 2007, he should consider having the DC Zone asset appraised as of Dec. 31, 2007 so that he will be able to demonstrate what gain is attributable to periods before Dec. 31, 2007 (i.e., what gain qualifies for the zero capital gains rate).

. . . which would be treated as ordinary income under the recapture rules of Code Sec. 1245 (pertaining to the disposition of certain depreciable property) (see FTC 2d/FIN ¶ I-10100 *et seq.*; USTR ¶ 12,454 *et seq.*; TaxDesk ¶ 22,308.2 *et seq.*) or Code Sec. 1250 (pertaining to the disposition of certain depreciable realty) (see FTC 2d/FIN ¶ I-10400 *et seq.*; USTR ¶ 12,504 *et seq.*; TaxDesk ¶ 22,308.7 *et seq.*) if Code Sec. 1250 applied to all depreciation rather than the additional depreciation; (Code Sec. 1400B(e)(3))

... which is attributable to real property, or an intangible asset, which is not an integral part of a DC Zone business (defined below); or (Code Sec. 1400B(e)(4))

... attributable, directly or indirectly, in whole or in part, to a transaction with a related person. For purposes of this rule, persons are related to each other if the persons are described in Code Sec. 267(b) (relating to the disallowance of losses incurred in transactions between related persons, see FTC 2d/FIN ¶ I-3504; USTR ¶ 2674.03; TaxDesk ¶ 22,790) or Code Sec. 707(b)(1) (relating to the disallowance of losses incurred between a partner and a partnership or between related partnerships, see FTC 2d/FIN ¶ B-2016; USTR ¶ 7074.03; TaxDesk ¶ 58,450). (Code Sec. 1400B(e)(5))

Sales and exchanges of interests in partnerships and S corporations which are DC Zone businesses. In the case of the sale or exchange of an interest in a partnership, or of stock in an S corporation, which was a DC Zone business during substantially all of the period the taxpayer held the interest or stock, the amount of qualified capital gain (defined above) is determined *without* regard to: (Code Sec. 1400B(g))

... any gain which is attributable to real property, or an intangible asset, which is not an integral part of a DC Zone business, and (Code Sec. 1400B(g)(1))

... any gain attributable to periods before Jan. 1, '98, or after Dec. 31, 2007. (Code Sec. 1400B(g)(2))

But, in the case of a sale or exchange of an interest in a pass-thru entity that was *not* a qualified DC business during substantially all of the period that the taxpayer held the interest, the zero-percent capital gains rate applies to the extent that the gain is attributable to amounts that would have been qualified capital gain had the underlying assets been sold for their fair market value on the date of the sale or exchange of the interest in the pass-thru entity. (Com Rept, see ¶ 5040)

> **⊘ observation:** Interests in pass-thru entities are also subject to rules similar to those provided in Code Sec. 1202(g) (relating to the treatment of holders of interests in a partnership, S corporation, regulated investment company (RIC), or any common trust fund (i.e., pass-thru entities) for purposes of the 50% exclusion for gain from certain small business stock), see the discussion under **Other operating rules** below and in FTC 2d/FIN ¶ I-9116; USTR ¶ 12,024.03; TaxDesk ¶ 24,671.

Thus, the above rule relating to sales and exchanges of interests in partnerships and S corporations applies only if the interest in the pass-thru entity were held by the taxpayer for more than five years. In addition, the rule applies apply only to qualified DC assets that were held by the pass-thru entity for more than five years, and throughout the period that the taxpayer held the interest in the pass-thru entity. (Com Rept, see ¶ 5040)

FTC 2d References are to Federal Tax Coordinator 2d
FIN References are to RIA's Analysis of Federal Taxes: Income
USTR References are to United States Tax Reporter: Income, Estate & Gift, and Excise
PCA References are to Pension Coordinator and Pension & Benefits Expert/Advisor
PE References are to Pension and Profit Sharing 2nd
EP References are to Estate Planning & Taxation Coordinator and Estate Planning Advisor

DC Zone asset. A DC Zone asset is any: (Code Sec. 1400B(b)(1))

... DC Zone business stock (defined below), (Code Sec. 1400B(b)(1)(A))

... DC Zone partnership interest (defined below), and (Code Sec. 1400B(b)(1)(B))

... DC Zone business property (defined below). (Code Sec. 1400B(b)(1)(C))

DC Zone business stock. DC Zone business stock is any stock in a domestic corporation which is originally issued after Dec. 31, '97, if: (Code Sec. 1400B(b)(2)(A))

... the stock is acquired by the taxpayer, before Jan. 1, 2003, at its original issue (directly or through an underwriter) solely in exchange for cash, (Code Sec. 1400B(b)(2)(A)(i))

... as of the time the stock was issued, the corporation was a DC Zone business (defined below) (or, in the case of a new corporation, the corporation was being organized for purposes of being a DC Zone business), and (Code Sec. 1400B(b)(2)(A)(ii))

... during substantially all of the taxpayer's holding period for the stock, the corporation qualified as a DC Zone business. (Code Sec. 1400B(b)(2)(A)(iii))

A rule similar to the rule provided in Code Sec. 1202(c)(3) (rules related to purchases by a corporation of its own stock for purposes of the 50% gain exclusion from small business stock, see FTC 2d/FIN ¶ I-9102; USTR ¶ 12.024; TaxDesk ¶ 24,696) applies for purposes of the rules related to what constitutes DC business stock. (Code Sec. 1400B(b)(2)(B)) Thus, qualified DC business stock does not include any stock acquired from a corporation which made a substantial stock redemption or distribution (without a bona fide business purpose for the redemption or distribution) in an attempt to avoid the rules defining what is qualified DC business stock. (Com Rept, see ¶ 5040)

DC Zone business. A DC Zone business means any entity which is an enterprise zone business (as defined in Code Sec. 1397B, see FTC 2d/FIN ¶ L-9954; USTR ¶ 13,97B4; TaxDesk ¶ 26,871), determined: (Code Sec. 1400B(c))

... after the application of Code Sec. 1400(e) ('97 Act rule requiring that the definition of enterprise zone business is applied without regard to the requirement that at least 35% of a business's employees must be residents of an empowerment zone, see ¶ 2601) (Code Sec. 1400B(c)(1))

... by substituting "80%" for "50%" in Code Sec. 1397B(b)(2) ('97 Act rule relating to the definition of an enterprise zone business that requires at least 50% of a qualified business entity's total gross income be derived from the active conduct of a qualified business, see ¶ 2610) and Code Sec. 1397B(c)(1) (similar '97 Act rule relating to qualified proprietorships, see ¶ 2611), and (Code Sec. 1400B(c)(2))

... by treating the entire District of Columbia as an empowerment zone and as if no other area is an empowerment zone or enterprise community. (Code Sec. 1400B(c)(3))

Thus, for purposes of the zero-percent capital gains rate, the definition of qualified DC Zone business generally is the same as the definition applicable for purposes of the increased expensing (discussed at ¶ 2601). However, solely for purposes of the zero-percent capital gains rate, a qualified DC Zone business must derive at least 80% (as opposed to 50%, see ¶ 2610 and ¶ 2611) of its total gross income from the active conduct of a qualified business within the DC Enterprise Zone. In addition to the 80% requirement, a corporation or partnership is treated as a qualified DC business if: (1) its sole trade or business is the active conduct of a "qualified business" within the District of Columbia; (2) substantially all of the business's tangible property is used within the District of Columbia; (3) substantially all of the business's intangible property is used in, and exclusively related to, the active conduct of the business; (4) substantially all of the services performed by employees are performed within the District of Columbia; and (5) no more than 5% of the average of the aggregate unadjusted bases of the property owned by the business is attributable to (a) certain financial property, or (b) collectibles not held primarily for sale to customers in the ordinary course of an active trade or business. (Com Rept, see ¶ 5040)

A "qualified business" means any trade or business other than a trade or business that consists predominantly of the development or holding of intangibles for sale or license. A qualified business does not include certain facilities described in Code Sec. 144(c)(6)(B) (such as a massage parlor, hot tub facility, or liquor store, see FTC 2d/FIN ¶ J-3247; USTR ¶ 1444.02; TaxDesk ¶ 26,871) or certain large farms. In addition, the leasing of real property that is located within the District of Columbia to others is treated as a qualified business only if (1) the leased property is not residential property, and (2) at least 50% of the gross rental income from the real property is from qualified DC businesses. The rental of tangible personal property to others is not a qualified business unless substantially all of the rental of the property is by qualified DC businesses or by residents of the District of Columbia. (Com Rept, see ¶ 5040)

DC Zone partnership interest. A DC Zone partnership interest is any capital or profits interest in a domestic partnership which is originally issued after Dec. 31, '97, if: (Code Sec. 1400B(b)(3))

... the interest is acquired by the taxpayer, before Jan. 1, 2003, from the partnership solely in exchange for cash, (Code Sec. 1400B(b)(3)(A))

... as of the time the interest was acquired, the partnership was a DC Zone business (defined above) (or, in the case of a new partnership, the partnership was being organized for purposes of being a DC Zone business), and (Code Sec. 1400B(b)(3)(B))

... during substantially all of the taxpayer's holding period for the interest, the partnership qualified as a DC Zone business. (Code Sec. 1400B(b)(3)(C))

A rule similar to the rule that applies to corporate redemptions and distributions (described in Code Sec. 1400B(b)(2)(B), see above) applies for purposes of determining whether a partnership interest is a DC Zone partnership interest. (Code Sec. 1400B(b)(3))

DC Zone business property. DC Zone business property is tangible property if: (Code Sec. 1400B(b)(4)(A))

FTC 2d References are to Federal Tax Coordinator 2d
FIN References are to RIA's Analysis of Federal Taxes: Income
USTR References are to United States Tax Reporter: Income, Estate & Gift, and Excise
PCA References are to Pension Coordinator and Pension & Benefits Expert/Advisor
PE References are to Pension and Profit Sharing 2nd
EP References are to Estate Planning & Taxation Coordinator and Estate Planning Advisor

. . . the property was acquired by the taxpayer by purchase (as defined in Code Sec. 179(d)(2) (i.e., any acquisition of property other than from a related party or in a carryover basis transaction, see FTC 2d/FIN ¶ L-9925; USTR ¶ 1794.01; TaxDesk ¶ 26,866) after Dec. 31, '97, and before Jan. 1, 2003, (Code Sec. 1400B(b)(4)(A)(i))

. . . the original use of the property in the DC Zone commences with the taxpayer, and (Code Sec. 1400B(b)(4)(A)(ii))

. . . during substantially all of the taxpayer's holding period for the property, substantially all of the use of the property was in a DC Zone business of the taxpayer. (Code Sec. 1400B(b)(4)(A)(iii))

When substantially improved buildings are considered to be DC Zone business property. The requirements for DC Zone business property relating to the acquisition of the property by purchase after Dec. 31, '97 and before Jan. 1, 2003 (described in Code Sec. 1400B(b)(4)(A)(i), see above) and that the original use of the property commence with the taxpayer (described in Code Sec. 1400B(b)(4)(A)(ii), see above) is treated as met with respect to: (Code Sec. 1400B(b)(4)(B)(i))

. . . property which is substantially improved by the taxpayer before Jan. 1, 2003, and (Code Sec. 1400B(b)(4)(B)(i)(I))

. . . any land on which that property is located. (Code Sec. 1400B(b)(4)(B)(i)(II))

Thus, substantially renovated real estate located in the District of Columbia enterprise zone can constitute DC Zone business property. But, land that is not an integral part of a DC Zone business is excluded from the definition of DC Zone business property. (Com Rept, see ¶ 5040)

Substantially improved. Property will be treated as substantially improved by the taxpayer only if, during any 24-month period beginning after Dec. 31, '97, additions to basis with respect to the property in the hands of the taxpayer exceed the *greater* of: (Code Sec. 1400B(b)(4)(B)(ii))

. . . an amount equal to the adjusted basis of the property at the beginning of the 24-month period in the hands of the taxpayer, or (Code Sec. 1400B(b)(4)(B)(ii)(I))

. . . $5,000. (Code Sec. 1400B(b)(4)(B)(ii)(II))

Treatment of subsequent purchasers. A DC Zone asset includes any property which would be a DC Zone asset but for the rules relating to (1) that stock be acquired before Jan. 1, 2003, at its original issue (directly or through an underwriter) solely in exchange for cash (described in Code Sec. 1400B(b)(2)(A)(i)) to be considered to be DC Zone stock, (2) that a partnership interest acquired before Jan. 1, 2003, from the partnership solely in exchange for cash (described in Code Sec. 1400B(b)(3)(A)) to be considered to be a DC Zone partnership interest, or (3) that the original use of the property commence with the taxpayer (described in Code Sec. 1400B(b)(4)(A)(ii)) to be considered to be a DC Zone business property, in the hands of the taxpayer if the property was a DC Zone asset in the hands of a previous holder. (Code Sec. 1400B(b)(6)) Thus, qualified DC Zone assets include property that was a qualified DC Zone asset in the hands of a prior owner, provided that at the time of acquisition, and during substantially all of the subsequent purchaser's holding period, either (1) substantially all of the use of the property is in a qualified DC Zone business, or (2) the property is an ownership interest in a qualified DC Zone business. (Com Rept, see ¶ 5040)

observation: In Code Sec. 1400B, there is no Code Sec. 1400B(b)(5) (i.e., the numbering of the section skips from Code Sec. 1400B(b)(4) to Code Sec. 1400C(b)(6)).

5-year safe harbor for property ceasing to be a DC Zone asset. If any property ceases to be a DC Zone asset because property is no longer used in a DC Zone business under the rules of Code Sec. 1400B(b)(2)(A)(iii) (during substantially all of the taxpayer's holding period for the DC Zone business stock, the corporation qualified as a DC Zone business, see above), Code Sec. 1400B(b)(3)(C) (during substantially all of the taxpayer's holding period for the DC Zone partnership interest, the partnership qualified as a DC Zone business, see above), or Code Sec. 1400B(b)(4)(A)(iii) (during substantially all of the taxpayer's holding period for the DC Zone business property, substantially all the use of the property was in a DC Zone business, see above) after the 5-year period beginning on the date the taxpayer acquired the property, the property will continue to be treated as a DC Zone asset; except that the amount of gain subject to the exclusion from gross income (under Code Sec. 1400B(a)) on any sale or exchange of the property does not exceed the amount which would be qualified capital gain had the property been sold on the date of that cessation. (Code Sec. 1400B(b)(7))

Treatment of DC Zone as including census tracts with 10% poverty rate. For purposes of applying the zero capital gains rate (and for purposes of applying Code Sec. 1400 through Code Sec. 1400C (see ¶ 2601 and ¶ 2604) and the empowerment zone rules provided in Code Sec. 1391 through Code Sec. 1397D (see FTC 2d/FIN ¶ J-3375 *et seq.*; L-9950 *et seq.*; ; USTR ¶ 13,914 *et seq.*; TaxDesk ¶ 26,842; 38,412 for purposes of the zero capital gains rate), the DC Zone is treated as including all census tracts: (Code Sec. 1400B(d))

... which are located in the District of Columbia, and (Code Sec. 1400B(d)(1))

... for which the poverty rate is not less than 10%. (Code Sec. 1400B(d)(2))

Other operating rules. Rules similar to Code Sec. 1202(g) (relating to the treatment of holders of interests in a partnership, S corporation, regulated investment company (RIC) or any common trust fund (i.e., pass-thru entities), see FTC 2d/FIN ¶ I-9116; USTR ¶ 12,024.03; TaxDesk ¶ 24,671), Code Sec. 1202(h) (relating to certain tax-free transfers such as transfers by gift and transfers at death, see FTC 2d/FIN ¶ I-9117 *et seq.*; USTR ¶ 12,024.03; TaxDesk ¶ 24,672 *et seq.*), Code Sec. 1202(i)(2) (regarding treatment of contributions to capital after the original stock issuance date, see FTC 2d/FIN ¶ I-9114; USTR ¶ 12,024; TaxDesk ¶ 24,668), and Code Sec. 1202(j) (regarding treatment of certain short positions, see FTC 2d/FIN ¶ I-9115; TaxDesk

FTC 2d References are to Federal Tax Coordinator 2d
FIN References are to RIA's Analysis of Federal Taxes: Income
USTR References are to United States Tax Reporter: Income, Estate & Gift, and Excise
PCA References are to Pension Coordinator and Pension & Benefits Expert/Advisor
PE References are to Pension and Profit Sharing 2nd
EP References are to Estate Planning & Taxation Coordinator and Estate Planning Advisor

¶ 24,669) apply for purposes of the zero capital gains rate rules discussed above. (Code Sec. 1400B(f)) Thus, in the case of a transfer of a qualified DC Zone asset by gift, at death, or from a partnership to a partner that held an interest in the partnership at the time that the qualified DC Zone asset was acquired, (1) the transferee is to be treated as having acquired the asset in the same manner as the transferor, and (2) the transferee's holding period includes that of the transferor. (Com Rept, see ¶ 5040)

☐ **Effective:** Aug. 5, '97. ('97 Act §701(d)) However, as described above, the rules do not apply to capital gains attributable to periods before '98 or to property acquired before '98.

¶ 2603. $5,000 credit for first-time home buyers in the District of Columbia

Code Sec. 1400C, as added by '97 Act § 701(a)
Generally effective: Aug. 5, '97
Committee Reports, see ¶ 5040

Under pre-'97 Act law, there was no first-time homebuyer credit for the District of Columbia.

New Law. Congress believed that one key problem faced by the District of Columbia is the inability to attract and retain a stable residential base. To this end, Congress has provided certain tax incentives to attract new homeowners to the District of Columbia. (Com Rept, see ¶ 5040)

An individual who is a first-time homebuyer (defined below) of a principal residence (defined below) in the District of Columbia during any tax year is permitted a credit against income tax liability for the tax year. The amount of the credit is the lesser of (1) $5,000 or (2) the purchase price (defined below) of the residence. (Code Sec. 1400C(a) as added by '97 Act §701(a))

> **✪** *observation:* Presumably, the first-time homebuyer credit applies to a purchase of a residence located anywhere in the District of Columbia (e.g., Georgetown).

Phaseout of the credit based on a homebuyer's modified adjusted gross income. The amount allowable as the first-time homebuyer credit (determined without regard to this rule) for the tax year is reduced (but not below zero) by the amount which bears the same ratio to the credit so allowable as: (Code Sec. 1400C(b)(1))

. . . the excess (if any) of: (Code Sec. 1400C(b)(1)(A))

(1) the taxpayer's modified adjusted gross income (defined below) for the tax year, *over* (Code Sec. 1400C(b)(1)(A)(i))

(2) $70,000 ($110,000 in the case of a joint return), bears to (Code Sec. 1400C(b)(1)(A)(ii))

. . . $20,000. (Code Sec. 1400C(b)(1)(B))

Thus, the credit phases out for individual taxpayers with modified adjusted gross income between $70,000 and $90,000 ($110,000 and $130,000 for joint filers). (Com Rept, see ¶ 5040)

Modified adjusted gross income. For purposes of the phaseout rule, modified adjusted gross income is the taxpayer's adjusted gross income for the tax year increased by any amount excluded from gross income as a result of the foreign earned income exclusion or the possessions exclusion. (Code Sec. 1400C(b)(2))

Allocation of dollar limitation.

Married individuals filing separately. Married individuals filing separate returns can claim a maximum credit of $2,500 each. (Code Sec. 1400C(e)(1)(A))

Unmarried taxpayers buying a principal residence together. If two or more individuals who are not married purchase (defined below) a principal residence, the amount of the first-time homebuyer credit allowed is allocated among the unmarried individuals in the manner as IRS may prescribe, but the total amount of the credits allowed to all the individuals cannot exceed $5,000. (Code Sec. 1400C(e)(1)(B))

First-time homebuyer defined. The term "first-time homebuyer" has the same meaning as when used in Code Sec. 72(t)(8)(D)(i) (definition under '97 Act rule providing that no penalty applies to early withdrawals of IRA funds by first-time homebuyers, see ¶ 303), except that "principal residence in the District of Columbia during the 1-year period'" is substituted for "principal residence during the 2-year period" in Code Sec. 72(t)(8)(D)(i)(I). (Code Sec. 1400C(c)(1)) Thus, to qualify as a "first-time homebuyer," neither the individual (nor the individual's spouse, if married) can have had a present ownership interest in a principal residence (defined below) in the District of Columbia for the one-year period before the date of acquisition of the principal residence. (Com Rept, see ¶ 5040) There are special rules for determining whether members of the Armed Forces and certain individuals with tax homes outside the U.S. qualify as first-time homebuyers, see ¶ 303.

⊘ *observation:* Under these rules, a first-time homebuyer is not necessarily a person buying a home for the first time.

Principal residence. The term "principal residence" has the same meaning as when used in Code Sec. 121 (rules relating to the exclusion of gain from the sale of a principal residence, see ¶ 102). (Code Sec. 1400C(c)(3))

Purchase price. Purchase price is the adjusted basis of the principal residence on the date of acquisition (within the meaning of Code Sec. 72(t)(8)(D)(iii), see ¶ 303). (Code Sec. 1400C(e)(3)) Thus, the date of acquisition is the date on which a binding contract to purchase the principal residence is entered into or the date on which construction or reconstruction of the residence commences. (Com Rept, see ¶ 5040)

FTC 2d References are to Federal Tax Coordinator 2d
FIN References are to RIA's Analysis of Federal Taxes: Income
USTR References are to United States Tax Reporter: Income, Estate & Gift, and Excise
PCA References are to Pension Coordinator and Pension & Benefits Expert/Advisor
PE References are to Pension and Profit Sharing 2nd
EP References are to Estate Planning & Taxation Coordinator and Estate Planning Advisor

observation: This statement in the Committee Report is somewhat puzzling. In most cases, a taxpayer who purchases a home does not become the owner for tax purposes until the title closing. Since closing typically does not occur until some period of time after a contract of sale is executed, the buyer generally has no basis in the residence at the time of contract. It therefore seems unlikely that Congress intended to limit the amount of the credit to the taxpayer's basis on that date.

Purchase defined. A purchase is any acquisition (including construction by the taxpayer, (Code Sec. 1400C(e)(2)(B))), but only if: (Code Sec. 1400C(e)(2)(A))

... the property is not acquired from a person whose relationship to the person acquiring it would result in the disallowance of losses under Code Sec. 267 (relating to the disallowance of losses incurred in transactions between related persons) or Code Sec. 707(b) (relating to the disallowance of losses incurred between a partner and a partnership). However, in applying Code Sec. 267(b) and Code Sec. 267(c) for purposes of the first-time homebuyer credit, an individual's family is limited to his spouse, ancestors, and lineal descendants, and (Code Sec. 1400C(e)(2)(A)(i))

observation: Thus, for purposes of the above rule, brothers and sisters (including half-brothers and half-sisters) aren't considered to be family members, and a purchase which otherwise would qualify the first-time homebuyer for the credit will not be disqualified merely because the acquisition transaction occurred between siblings.

... the basis of the property in the hands of the person acquiring it is not determined (Code Sec. 1400C(e)(2)(A)(ii)) in whole or in part by reference to the adjusted basis of the property in the hands of the person from whom acquired (Code Sec. 1400C(e)(2)(A)(ii)(I)), or under Code Sec. 1014(a) (relating to property acquired from a decedent). (Code Sec. 1400C(e)(2)(A)(ii)(II))

One-time only claim of credit. If an individual is treated as a first-time homebuyer with respect to any principal residence, the individual may not be treated as a first-time homebuyer with respect to any other principal residence. (Code Sec. 1400C(c)(2)) Thus, the credit may be claimed one time only. (Com Rept, see ¶ 5040)

Basis adjustment. If a first-time homebuyer credit is allowed with respect to the purchase of any residence, the basis of the residence is reduced by the amount of the credit so allowed. (Code Sec. 1400C(h))

Credit treated as nonrefundable personal credit. The first-time homebuyer credit is treated as a nonrefundable personal credit. (Code Sec. 1400C(g))

Carryover of credit. If the amount of the first-time homebuyer credit exceeds the taxpayer's tax liability for the tax year (reduced by other nonrefundable personal credits), the excess is carried to the succeeding tax year and added to the first-time homebuyer credit allowable for the tax year. (Code Sec. 1400C(d)) Thus, the homebuyer may carry forward any excess credit indefinitely to succeeding tax years. (Com Rept, see ¶ 5040)

Reporting requirements. If IRS requires information reporting under Code Sec. 6045 to verify the eligibility of taxpayers for the first-time homebuyer credit, the exception to the reporting rules for sales and exchanges of a residence for $250,000 or less under the '97 Act (Code Sec. 6045(e)(5), see ¶ 2309) will not apply. (Code Sec. 1400C(f)) Thus, this exception to the reporting rules would not apply to these sales of personal residences in the District of Columbia. Also, Congress anticipates that IRS will require any information as may be necessary to verify eligibility for the District of Columbia first-time homebuyer credit. (Com Rept, see ¶ 5040)

Expiration of the credit. The first-time homebuyer credit does not apply to any property bought after Dec. 31, 2000. (Code Sec. 1400C(i)) Thus, the credit is available with respect to property bought after Aug. 5, '97 and before Jan. 1, 2001. (Com Rept, see ¶ 5040)

☐ **Effective:** Aug. 5, '97. ('97 Act §701(d))

¶ 2604. Tax-exempt bonds for District of Columbia

Code Sec. 1400A, as added by '97 Act § 701(a)
Generally effective: Aug. 5, '97
Committee Reports, see ¶ 5040

Tax-exempt private activity bonds may be issued to finance certain facilities in empowerment zones. These bonds, along with most private activity bonds, are subject to an annual private activity bond state volume cap equal to $50 per resident of each state, or (if greater) $150 million per state.

Qualified enterprise zone facility bonds are bonds 95% or more of the net proceeds of which are used to finance (1) qualified zone property the principal user of which is an enterprise zone business or (2) functionally related and subordinate land located in the empowerment zone or enterprise community. These bonds may only be issued while an empowerment zone is in effect.

The aggregate face amount of all qualified enterprise zone bonds for each qualified enterprise zone business may not exceed $3 million per zone or community. In addition, total qualified enterprise zone bond financing for each principal user of these bonds may not exceed $20 million for all zones and communities. (FTC 2d/FIN ¶ J-3350 *et seq.*; USTR ¶ 13,944)

Before the '97 Act, the District of Columbia Enterprise Zone (or DC Zone, see ¶ 2601) did not qualify for tax-exempt financing that was available in empowerment zones.

New Law. Congress believed that one of the key problems faced by the District of Columbia is insufficient economic activity. To this end, Congress has provided cer-

FTC 2d References are to Federal Tax Coordinator 2d
FIN References are to RIA's Analysis of Federal Taxes: Income
USTR References are to United States Tax Reporter: Income, Estate & Gift, and Excise
PCA References are to Pension Coordinator and Pension & Benefits Expert/Advisor
PE References are to Pension and Profit Sharing 2nd
EP References are to Estate Planning & Taxation Coordinator and Estate Planning Advisor

tain tax incentives to encourage economic development in those areas of the District where development has been inadequate. Thus, the '97 Act provides special tax-exempt financing for specified economically depressed census tracts within the District of Columbia. (Com Rept, see ¶ 5040)

In the case of the District of Columbia Enterprise Zone (or the DC Zone), Code Sec. 1394(c)(1)(A) (relating to the limitation on the amount of bonds, see FTC 2d/FIN ¶ J-3355; USTR ¶ 13,944) is applied by substituting "$15,000,000" for "$3,000,000". (Code Sec. 1400A(a) as added by '97 Act §701(a)) Thus, the amount of outstanding bond proceeds that can be borrowed by any qualified District business cannot exceed $15,000,000 (rather than $3,000,000). (Com Rept, see ¶ 5040)

> ✔ *observation:* The principal user would still be subject to the $20 million limit on a principal user's total qualified enterprise zone bond financing (described above).

For modifications to the definition of enterprise zone business that applies to tax-exempt financing in the DC Enterprise Zone, see ¶ 2601.

Period over which bonds may be issued. The above rules apply to bonds issued during the period beginning on Jan. 1, '98, and ending on Dec. 31, 2002. (Code Sec. 1400A(c))

☐ **Effective:** Aug. 5, '97. ('97 Act §701(d)) As noted above, the above rules only apply to bonds issued during the period beginning on Jan. 1, '98, and ending on Dec. 31, 2002.

¶ 2605. Disclosure of return information authorized for purposes of administering District of Columbia retirement provisions

Code Sec. 6103(l), as amended by Budget Act § 11024(b)
Code Sec. 6103(p), as amended by Budget Act § 11024(b)
Code Sec. 6103(a)(3), as amended by Budget Act § 11024(b)
Code Sec. 6103(i)(7), as amended by Budget Act § 11024(b)
Code Sec. 7213(a)(2), as amended by Budget Act § 11024(b)
Generally effective: Oct 1, '97 or, if later, the date certified by the District of Columbia Financial Responsibility and Management Assistance Authority

"Returns" and "return information" (defined below) are confidential, and except as provided in the Code, no

(1) officer or employee of the U.S., or

(2) officer or employee of any state, any local child support enforcement agency, or any local agency administering one of certain enumerated programs who has or had access to returns or return information, or

(3) other person who has or had access to such material under certain enumerated disclosure provisions, or officers or employees of such persons,

may disclose any return or return information that he obtained via his employment. (FTC 2d/FIN ¶ S-6200; USTR ¶ 61,034) However, the Code provides numerous exceptions to the nondisclosure rule. (FTC 2d/FIN ¶ S-6300 *et seq.*; USTR ¶ 61,034.01)

A "return" is any tax return, estimated tax declaration, information return or refund claim which is filed by, on behalf of, or with respect to any person. A return also includes any amendment or supplement to the return, including supporting schedules, attachments, or lists that are supplemental to, or part of, the return. (FTC 2d/FIN ¶ S-6205; USTR ¶ 61,034.03)

Subject to an exception for data that cannot be associated with a particular taxpayer, "return information" means a taxpayer's identity, the nature, source or amount of his income, payments, receipts, deductions, exemptions, credits, assets, liabilities, net worth, tax liability, tax withheld, deficiencies, over-assessments and tax payments, whether his return is, was or will be examined or investigated, or any other data with respect to a return or the determination of the existence of the liability of any person for any tax, penalty, interest, fine, forfeiture, or other imposition, or offense. It also includes any part of any written determination or any background file document relating to such written determination which is not open to public inspection.

The term "taxpayer identity" means the taxpayer's name, mailing address, taxpayer identifying number, or a combination of these three items. (FTC 2d/FIN ¶ S-6206; USTR ¶ 61,034.03)

IRS must maintain a standardized system of permanent records on the use and disclosure of returns and return information. These records must contain copies of all requests and a record of all inspections and disclosures of return and return information. However, certain disclosures need not be part of this recordkeeping system.

Agencies can obtain tax information from IRS only if they set up safeguards. The law requires a permanent system of records, a secure place to store the information, restrictions on access, protection of confidentiality, reports to IRS, and the return or destruction of used material. IRS reviews safeguards established by the agencies. If IRS determines that any agency, body, or commission or the General Accounting Office (GAO) has failed to, or does not, meet the safeguard requirements, it may, after any required review proceeding, take actions necessary to ensure the requirements are met, including refusing to disclose returns or return information to the agency, body or commission or the GAO until it determines that the requirements have been or will be met. In the case of an agency that receives information under certain specified disclosure rules and discloses it to any agent, the safeguard rules will apply to the agency and each such agent (except that, in the case of an agent, any report to IRS or other action taken with respect to IRS must be made or taken through the agency). (FTC 2d/FIN ¶ S-6411; USTR ¶ 61,034.02)

FTC 2d References are to Federal Tax Coordinator 2d
FIN References are to RIA's Analysis of Federal Taxes: Income
USTR References are to United States Tax Reporter: Income, Estate & Gift, and Excise
PCA References are to Pension Coordinator and Pension & Benefits Expert/Advisor
PE References are to Pension and Profit Sharing 2nd
EP References are to Estate Planning & Taxation Coordinator and Estate Planning Advisor

Subject to exceptions, the GAO may, on written request by the Comptroller General, obtain returns and return information that are necessary to perform audits of IRS or the Bureau of Alcohol, Tobacco and Firearms (ATF), or the procedures used by other agencies, etc., to safeguard returns and return information that are disclosed to the agencies, etc. The nondisclosure rules do not prohibit returns and return information obtained by any federal agency (other than IRS or the Bureau of Alcohol, Tobacco and Firearms) for use in any program or activity from being open for inspection by, or disclosure to, officers or employees of the GAO if the inspection and disclosure is (a) for purposes of, and to the extent necessary in, making an audit that is authorized by law, of the program or activity and (b) under a written request by the Comptroller General of the U.S. to the head of the agency. (FTC 2d/FIN ¶ S-6352; USTR ¶ 61,034.06)

It is unlawful for any officer or employee of the U.S. or certain other persons to willfully disclose to any person, except as authorized in the Code, any return, or returns or return information. It is unlawful for any other employee (including a state employee) to willfully disclose to any person any return or return information acquired under certain specified disclosure rules. Any violation of these rules is a felony punishable by a fine in an amount not exceeding $5,000, or imprisonment of not over five years, or both, together with the costs of prosecution. (FTC 2d/FIN ¶ V-3304; USTR ¶ 72,134)

New Law. Solely for the purpose of, and to the extent necessary in, determining an individual's eligibility for, or the correct amount of benefits under, the District of Columbia Retirement Protection Act ("the Act") (Subtitle A of Title XI of the Budget Act), certain return information may be disclosed on written request to any duly authorized officer or employee of the Treasury Department, or a Trustee, or any designated officer or employee of a Trustee or any actuary engaged by a Trustee under the terms of the Act, whose official duties require such disclosure. Disclosure can be made by the Commissioner of Social Security, or to the extent not available from the Social Security Administration (SSA), by the Treasury Secretary. Information that can be disclosed under the above rule includes information disclosed to the SSA under Code Sec. 6103(l)(1) to (5) (i.e., disclosures relating to criminal investigations and cases). (Code Sec. 6103(l)(16)(A) as amended by Budget Act §11024(b)(1)) The term "Trustee" means the person or persons selected by the Secretary of the Treasury to administer the District of Columbia Federal Pension Liability Trust Fund. (Budget Act §11003(16))

Under the above rule, information can be disclosed that relates to the amount of wage income, the name, address, and identifying number of payors of wage income, taxpayer identity, and the occupational status reflected on any return filed by, or with respect to, any individual with respect to whom eligibility for, or the correct amount of, benefits under the Act, is sought to be determined. Taxpayer identity for this purpose is defined as in the definition of "return information" above. (Code Sec. 6103(l)(16)(A))

Return information that is disclosed to any person under the above rules may be disclosed in a judicial or administrative proceeding relating to the determination of the individual's eligibility for, or the correct amount of, benefits under the Act. (Code Sec. 6103(l)(16)(B))

Research Institute of America

IRS is not required to maintain a record or accounting of requests for inspection or disclosure of returns and return information, and of returns and return information inspected or disclosed under the authority of the above rules. Any agency authorized to receive disclosure under the above rules can obtain the information only if it meets the safeguard standards described above, which require a permanent system of records, a secure place to store the information, restrictions on access, protection of confidentiality, reports to IRS, and the return or destruction of used material.

If IRS determines that any agency, body, or commission, including any agency or any other person described in Code Sec. 6103(l)(16), or the GAO has failed to, or does not, meet the safeguard requirements, it may, after any required review proceeding, take actions necessary to ensure the requirements are met, including refusing to disclose returns or return information to the agency, body or commission, until it determines that the requirements have been or will be met. In the case of an agency that receives information under certain specified disclosure rules (including the disclosure rules described above) and discloses it to any agent or any person including an agent described in Code Sec. 6103(l)(16), the safeguard rules will apply to the agency and each such agent or other person (except that, in the case of an agent or any person including an agent described in Code Sec. 6103(l)(16), any report to IRS or other action taken with respect to IRS must be made or taken through the agency). (Code Sec. 6103(p) as amended by Budget Act §11024(b))

The above disclosure rules are included in the provisions enumerated as covered by the nondisclosure rule for non-government employees at (3) above. Thus, except as authorized under the disclosure rules, no person (or officer or employee of one) who has or had access to returns or return information under the above rules can disclose any return or return information obtained by him in any way through his employment. (Code Sec. 6103(a)(3) as amended by Budget Act §11024(b)(2))

The rule described above allowing disclosure of returns and return information by agencies other than IRS or ATF to GAO employees applies to information obtained by a Trustee as well as to information obtained by federal agencies. (Code Sec. 6103(i)(7)(B)(i) as amended by Budget Act §11024(b)(3))

The disclosure rules above have been included in the rules specifically enumerated under Code Sec. 7213(a)(2) (providing a criminal penalty for disclosures by state and other non-federal employees of information acquired under the specifically enumerated rules). (Code Sec. 7213(a)(2) as amended by Budget Act §11024(b)(8))

> ✐ *observation:* The '97 Act provides that unauthorized inspection of information acquired under the rules listed in Code Sec. 7213(a)(2) is subject to a new criminal penalty for "browsing," see ¶ 2407. Thus, unauthorized inspection of information acquired under the above disclosure rules is also subject to that penalty.

FTC 2d References are to Federal Tax Coordinator 2d
FIN References are to RIA's Analysis of Federal Taxes: Income
USTR References are to United States Tax Reporter: Income, Estate & Gift, and Excise
PCA References are to Pension Coordinator and Pension & Benefits Expert/Advisor
PE References are to Pension and Profit Sharing 2nd
EP References are to Estate Planning & Taxation Coordinator and Estate Planning Advisor

☐ **Effective:** The later of Oct. 1, '97 or the day the District of Columbia Financial Responsibility and Management Assistance Authority certifies that the financial plan and budget for the District government for fiscal year '98 meets the requirements of section 201(d)(1) of the District of Columbia Financial Responsibility and Management Assistance Act of '95, as amended by the Budget Act. (Budget Act §11721)

Empowerment Zones

¶ 2606. Authorization of 20 new empowerment zones meeting different eligibility criteria and eligible for different tax incentives

Code Sec. 1391(g), as amended by '97 Act § 952(a)
Code Sec. 1396(e), as amended by '97 Act § 952(b)
Code Sec. 1397A(c), as amended by '97 Act § 952(c)
Generally effective: Upon designations to be made after Aug. 5, '97 but before Jan. 1, '99
Committee Reports, see ¶ 5081

A nominated area which meets all of the criteria specified in Code Sec. 1391, Code Sec. 1392 and Code Sec. 1393 is eligible, subject to selection by the appropriate U.S. Secretary, to become an empowerment zone.

Under pre-'97 Act law, the appropriate U.S. Secretary was authorized to select nine empowerment zones, of which no more than six could be designated in urban areas and no more than three in rural areas.

The criteria specified in Code Sec. 1391, Code Sec. 1392 and Code Sec. 1393 include, but aren't limited to, poverty criteria, size criteria, an aggregate limitation on the population of empowerment zones in urban areas, a required certification that no portion of a nominated area is already included in an enterprise community, a prohibition on the inclusion of Indian reservations in empowerment zones, and a requirement that an area be nominated by one or more local governments and the State or States in which it is located.

The poverty criteria require that the poverty rate (1) for each population census tract within the nominated area isn't less than 20%, (2) for at least 90% of the population census tracts within the nominated area isn't less than 25% and (3) for at least 50 percent of the population census tracts within the nominated area isn't less than 35%. Population census tracts with no population are treated as satisfying the requirements of (1) and (2) and as failing (3). A population census tract with a population of less than 2,000 is treated as satisfying (1) and (2) if more than 75% of the tract is zoned for commercial or industrial use. Also, the appropriate U.S. Secretary has authority to lower the poverty thresholds in (1), (2) and (3) under rules specified in the Code. Where a nominated area includes a non-contiguous parcel, each parcel must satisfy (1), (2) and (3). For an area not tracted for population census tracts, the equivalent county divisions (as defined by the Bureau of the Census for purposes of defining poverty areas) are used for purposes of determining poverty rates (see FTC 2d/FIN ¶ J-3387; USTR ¶ 13,914).

The size criteria include, but aren't limited to, the following requirements: (1) that the nominated area be no more than 20 square miles if an urban area or 1,000 square miles if a rural area and (2) that the nominated area either have a continuous boundary or, if the nominated area is a rural area located in more than one State, consist of not more than three noncontiguous parcels (see FTC 2d/FIN ¶ J-3387; USTR ¶ 13,914).

Empowerment zones which meet all of the criteria specified in Code Sec. 1391, Code Sec. 1392 and Code Sec. 1393 are eligible for Federal grants and tax-exempt financing not available to other areas. Additionally, employers in those empowerment zones are eligible for a special wage credit (see FTC 2d/FIN ¶ L-15630; USTR ¶ 13,964; TaxDesk ¶ 38,412) and businesses in those empowerment zones are eligible for an additional $20,000 of Code Sec. 179 expense deductions, see FTC 2d/FIN ¶ L-9950; USTR ¶ 1794.05; TaxDesk ¶ 26,870. (FTC 2d/FIN ¶ J-3377, ¶ J-3379, ¶ J-3384, ¶ J-3387, ¶ L-9950, ¶ L-15630; USTR ¶ 1794.05, ¶ 13,914, ¶ 13,964; TaxDesk ¶ 26,870, ¶ 38,412)

New Law. The '97 Act authorizes the appropriate U.S. Secretary to designate an additional 20 nominated areas as empowerment zones. Of that number, not more than 15 may be designated in urban areas and not more than 5 may be designated in rural areas. (Code Sec. 1391(g)(1) as amended by '97 Act §952(a))

> **✔ observation:** In addition to the 20 additional empowerment zones referred to above, the '97 Act authorizes two other additional empowerment zones, which differ from the 20 additional empowerment zones referred to above, both as to eligibility criteria and available tax incentives, see ¶ 2607.

With respect to the 20 additional empowerment zones, the eligibility criteria for empowerment zones are expanded slightly (Com Rept, see ¶ 5081), as described below.

Different poverty criteria. The three-part poverty rate test (discussed above) which applies to empowerment zones other than the 20 additional zones doesn't apply to the 20 additional empowerment zones. (Code Sec. 1391(g)(3)(A)(iv)) Also so much of the rules (discussed above) for census tracts with no population, census tracts with less than 2,000 people and the authority of an appropriate U.S. Secretary to lower poverty thresholds as relates to the three-part poverty test doesn't apply to the 20 additional empowerment zones. (Code Sec. 1391(g)(3)(A)(iv))

Instead, a nominated area is eligible for designation only if the poverty rate for each population census tract within the nominated area isn't less than 20% and the poverty rate for at least 90% of the population census tracts within the nominated area isn't less than 25%. (Code Sec. 1391(g)(3)(A)(i)) Thus, the rule applicable to other empowerment zones, which requires that at least half of the nominated area (sic) consist of census tracts with poverty rates of 35% or more doesn't apply to the 20 additional empowerment zones. (Com Rept, see ¶ 5081)

FTC 2d References are to Federal Tax Coordinator 2d
FIN References are to RIA's Analysis of Federal Taxes: Income
USTR References are to United States Tax Reporter: Income, Estate & Gift, and Excise
PCA References are to Pension Coordinator and Pension & Benefits Expert/Advisor
PE References are to Pension and Profit Sharing 2nd
EP References are to Estate Planning & Taxation Coordinator and Estate Planning Advisor

observation: The Committee Report discussion immediately above appears to state the 35% rule incorrectly. The rule is that at least half of the *census tracts* in the nominated area must have poverty rates of 35% or more.

A population census tract with a population of less than 2,000 is treated as having a poverty rate of not less than 25% if (Code Sec. 1391(g)(3)(A)(ii)):

... more than 75% of the tract is zoned for commercial or industrial use *and,* (Code Sec. 1391(g)(3)(A)(ii)(I))

... the tract is contiguous to one or more other population census tracts which have a poverty rate of not less than 25 % (determined without regard to this rule) (Code Sec. 1391(g)(3)(A)(ii)(II)); i.e, the one or more other population tracts must *actually* have a poverty rate of 25% or more. (Com Rept, see ¶ 5081)).

Also, the 20%-and-25% test, in Code Sec. 1391(g)(3)(A)(i), discussed above, doesn't apply to 3 or fewer noncontiguous parcels which may be developed for commercial or industrial use. The total area of the noncontiguous parcels to which this exception (referred to below as the developable site exception) can apply cannot exceed 2,000 acres. (Code Sec. 1391(g)(3)(A)(iii))

Furthermore, the U.S. Secretary of Agriculture may designate one empowerment zone in a rural area without regard to the 20%-and-25% test if the area satisfies emigration criteria specified by the U.S. Secretary of Agriculture. (Code Sec. 1391(g)(3)(A)(v))

Different size criteria. The size criteria which apply to empowerment zones other than the 20 additional empowerment zones apply to the 20 additional zones, but with the following modifications.

In determining whether either of the 20-square-miles or 1,000-square-miles requirements (discussed above) is satisfied and in determining whether either of the continuous-boundary or not-more-than-three-noncontiguous-parcels requirements (discussed above) is satisfied, parcels which satisfy the developable site exception (see discussion of Code Sec. 1391(g)(3)(A)(iii) above) aren't taken into account. (Code Sec. 1391(g)(3)(B)(i)) Thus, the 20 additional empowerment zones can include an additional 2,000 acres and these acres can consist of up to three non-contiguous parcels. (Com Rept, see ¶ 5081)

Also, if a population census tract (or equivalent county division in an area not tracted for population census tracts) in a rural area exceeds 1,000 square miles or includes a substantial amount of land owned by the Federal, state or local government, an area nominated to be one of the 20 additional empowerment zones may exclude that excess square mileage or governmentally owned land, and the exclusion of that area won't be treated as violating the continuous-boundary requirement (discussed above). (Code Sec. 1391(g)(3)(B)(ii))

Other different criteria. The criteria for the 20 additional empowerment zones also differ from the criteria for other empowerment zones in the ways described below.

The aggregate 1,000,000 population limit, imposed by Code Sec. 1391(b)(2), for all empowerment zones in urban areas doesn't apply to the 20 additional empowerment zones. (Code Sec. 1391(g)(3)(C))

> **☑ observation:** Code Sec. 1391(g)(3)(C) refers to a paragraph (1)(B). No such paragraph exists in Code Sec. 1391(g). The correct reference appears to be to paragraph (1) of Code Sec. 1391(g), which, as discussed above, is the paragraph authorizing the designation of the 20 additional empowerment zones.

The rule, in Code Sec. 1391(e)(5), which requires the applicable State (or States) and local governments to certify that no portion of a nominated area is already included in an enterprise community doesn't apply to the 20 additional empowerment zones. (Code Sec. 1391(g)(3)(D))

The rule, in Code Sec. 1393(a)(4), which prohibits the inclusion of Indian reservations in empowerment zones doesn't apply to the 20 additional empowerment zones. (Code Sec. 1391(g)(3)(E)(i)) Thus, areas located within Indian reservations can be included in the 20 additional empowerment zones. (Com Rept, see ¶ 5081) Furthermore, an area in an Indian reservation is treated, for purposes of satisfying the nomination requirement in Code Sec. 1391(e)(1), as an area nominated by a State and by a local government if it is nominated by the reservation's governing body (as determined by the U.S. Secretary of the Interior). (Code Sec. 1391(g)(3)(E)(ii))

Different availability of tax incentives. Tax-exempt financing benefits are available within the 20 additional empowerment zones. So too is the "brownfields" incentive, i.e, the environmental remediation incentive under Code Sec. 198 (see ¶ 808). (Com Rept, see ¶ 5081)

However, the special wage credit (discussed above) for empowerment zones doesn't apply to any of the 20 additional empowerment zones. (Code Sec. 1396(e) as amended by '97 Act §952(b))

Also, the additional Code Sec. 179 expense deductions (discussed above) aren't available for any property substantially all of the use of which is in parcels described in the developable site exception (see discussion of Code Sec. 1391(g)(3)(A)(iii) above). (Code Sec. 1397A(c) as amended by '97 Act §952(c)) Thus, the additional Code Sec. 179 expense deductions aren't available within the 2,000 additional acres allowed to be included in the 20 additional empowerment zones because of the developable site exception. (Com Rept, see ¶ 5081) However, subject to this limitation regarding parcels described in the developable site exception, the additional Code Sec. 179 expense deductions are available within the 20 additional empowerment zones. (Com Rept, see ¶ 5081)

Period for which designation is in effect. The designations of new empowerment zones under the above provisions will generally remain in effect for 10 years. (Com Rept, see ¶ 5081)

FTC 2d References are to Federal Tax Coordinator 2d
FIN References are to RIA's Analysis of Federal Taxes: Income
USTR References are to United States Tax Reporter: Income, Estate & Gift, and Excise
PCA References are to Pension Coordinator and Pension & Benefits Expert/Advisor
PE References are to Pension and Profit Sharing 2nd
EP References are to Estate Planning & Taxation Coordinator and Estate Planning Advisor

observation: Based on the Committee Report referred to immediately above, it would appear that Congress intends the designations to remain in effect for periods defined by the rules in Code Sec. 1391(d), under which a designation generally remains in effect from the date of designation to the close of the 10th calendar year beginning after that date (unless the period is shortened under other rules in Code Sec. 1391(d)), see FTC 2d/FIN ¶ J-3382; USTR ¶ 13,914.

☐ **Effective:** Upon the respective designations of the 20 additional empowerment zones; those designations are to be made after Aug. 5, '97, but before Jan. 1, '99. (Code Sec. 1391(g)(2) as amended by '97 Act §952(a))

¶ 2607. Authorization of two additional urban empowerment zones meeting the same criteria and eligible for the same tax incentives as existing empowerment zones

Code Sec. 1391(b)(2), as amended by '97 Act § 951(a)

Code Sec. 1396(b)(2), as amended by '97 Act § 951(b)(2)

Generally effective: Aug. 5, '97, except that designations of new empowerment zones will be made in the 180-day period after Aug. 5, '97, and no designation takes effect before Jan. 1, 2000

Committee Reports, see ¶ 5081

A nominated area which meets all of the criteria specified in Code Sec. 1391, Code Sec. 1392 and Code Sec. 1393 is eligible, subject to selection by the appropriate U.S. Secretary, to become an empowerment zone. Empowerment zones which meet all of those criteria are eligible for Federal grants and tax-exempt financing not available to other areas. Additionally, employers in those empowerment zones are eligible for a special wage credit (see FTC 2d/FIN ¶ L-15630; USTR ¶ 13,964; TaxDesk ¶ 38,412) and businesses in those empowerment zones are eligible for an additional $20,000 of Code Sec. 179 expense deductions, see FTC 2d/FIN ¶ L-9950; USTR ¶ 1794.05; TaxDesk ¶ 26,870.

Under pre-'97 Act law, the appropriate U.S. Secretary was authorized to select nine empowerment zones, of which no more than six could be designated in urban areas and no more than three in rural areas. The aggregate population of the six urban zones couldn't exceed 750,000.

For empowerment zones designated under pre-'97 Act law, the special wage credit for employers in empowerment zones applied to 20% of the qualified zone wages paid or incurred in '94 through 2001, 15% of those wages paid or incurred in 2002, 10% of those wages paid or incurred in 2003 and 5% of those wages paid or incurred in 2004. (FTC 2d/FIN ¶ J-3377, ¶ L-15632; USTR ¶ 13,914, ¶ 13,964; TaxDesk ¶ 38,413)

New Law. The '97 Act increases to eleven the total number of empowerment zones which can be designated (Code Sec. 1391(b)(2) as amended by '97 Act §951(a)(1)), and to eight the number of empowerment zones in urban areas which can be designated. (Code Sec. 1391(b)(2) as amended by '97 Act §951(a)(2)) Thus, the

'97 Act authorizes two additional urban empowerment zones. (Com Rept, see ¶ 5081) The two additional urban empowerment zones are subject to the same eligibility criteria under Code Sec. 1392 (see FTC 2d/FIN ¶ J-3387; USTR ¶ 13,914) that apply to the original six urban empowerment zones and are eligible for the same tax incentives (i.e, wage credit, additional Code Sec. 179 expense deductions and special tax-exempt financing). (Com Rept, see ¶ 5081).

> ⓥ *observation:* In addition to the two additional empowerment zones discussed above, the '97 Act authorizes 20 other additional empowerment zones, which differ from the two empowerment zones discussed above, both as to eligibility criteria and available tax incentives, see ¶ 2606.

The aggregate population limit for the eight urban empowerment zones is increased to $1,000,000. (Code Sec. 1391(b)(2) as amended by '97 Act §951(a)(3)) Congress raised the population limit in order to permit the designation of the two additional urban zones. The designations of the new empowerment zones will be made during the 180-day period beginning on Aug. 5, '97 and no designation will take effect before Jan. 1, 2000. ('97 Act §951(c)). The designations will generally remain in effect for 10 years. (Com Rept, see ¶ 5081)

> ⓥ *observation:* Based on the Committee Report referred to immediately above, it would appear that Congress intends the designations to remain in effect for 10 years, subject to the possible shortening effect of any rules in Code Sec. 1391(d). For those rules, see FTC 2d/FIN ¶ J-3382; USTR ¶ 13,914.

For the two new urban empowerment zones authorized by the '97 Act, the special wage credit percentages applicable to empowerment zones designated under pre-'97 Act law don't apply and the applicable special wage credit percentages are, instead, 20% of the qualified zone wages paid or incurred in 2000 through 2004, 15% of those wages paid or incurred in 2005, 10% of those wages paid or incurred in 2006 and 5% of those wages paid or incurred in 2007. (Code Sec. 1396(b)(2) as amended by '97 Act §951(b)(2)) No wage credit is available in the two new urban empowerment zones after 2007. (Com Rept, see ¶ 5081).

☐ **Effective:** Aug. 5, '97, except that designations of the new empowerment zones will be made during the 180-day period beginning on Aug. 5, '97. No designation will take effect before Jan. 1, 2000. ('97 Act §951(c)).

¶ 2608. Enterprise zone facility bond rules are modified

Code Sec. 1394(b)(2), as amended by '97 Act § 955(b)
Code Sec. 1394(b)(3), as amended by '97 Act § 955(a)
Generally effective: Obligations issued after Aug. 5, '97
Committee Reports, see ¶ 5081

The term "enterprise zone business" for purposes of the enterprise zone facility bond requirements has the same meaning as in Code Sec. 1397B for purposes of the increased Code Sec. 179 expensing election for qualified zone property of an enterprise zone business with two exceptions.

First, references to empowerment zones in Code Sec. 1397B are treated as including references to enterprise communities.

Second, enterprise zone business for purposes of the enterprise zone facility bond requirements includes any trades or businesses that would qualify as an enterprise zone business (after taking into account the above modification concerning references to enterprise communities) if the trades or businesses were separately incorporated. (FTC 2d/FIN ¶ J-3354; USTR ¶ 13,944)

Qualified zone property has the same meaning for purposes of the enterprise zone facility bond requirements as in Code Sec. 1397C for purposes of the increased Code Sec. 179 expensing election for qualified zone property of an enterprise zone business, except that references to empowerment zones in Code Sec. 1397C are treated as including enterprise communities. (FTC 2d/FIN ¶ J-3353; USTR ¶ 13,944)

New Law. The '97 Act provides that except as provided below, the term "enterprise zone business" for purposes of the tax-exempt enterprise facility bond rules, has the meaning given to the term by Code Sec. 1397B (the definitional provision, see ¶ 2610, ¶ 2611). (Code Sec. 1394(b)(3)(A) as amended by '97 Act §955(a))

The modifications to the definition of the term enterprise zone business that apply for these purposes are:

(1) References to empowerment zones in Code Sec. 1397B are treated as including references to enterprise communities. (Code Sec. 1394(b)(3)(B)(i))

(2) A business will not fail to be treated as an enterprise zone business during the startup period (defined below) if—

• as of the beginning of the startup period, it is reasonably expected that the business will be an enterprise zone business (as defined in Code Sec. 1397B as modified by these rules) at the end of the period, and

• the business makes bona fide efforts to be an enterprise zone business. (Code Sec. 1394(b)(3)(B)(ii))

(3) A business will not fail to be treated as an enterprise zone business for any tax year beginning after the testing period (defined below) by reason of failing to satisfy any requirement of the rules for qualified business entities in Code Sec. 1397B(b) or the rules for qualified proprietorships in Code Sec. 1397B(c) if at least 35% of the employees of the business for the year are residents of an empowerment zone or an enterprise community. This rule does not apply to any business which is not a qualified business by reason of—

• failing to satisfy the general requirements for qualified businesses in Code Sec. 1397B(d)(1),

• failing to satisfy the requirements for treatment of businesses holding intangibles in Code Sec. 1397B(d)(4), or

• failing to satisfy the requirements for excluded businesses in Code Sec. 1397B(d)(5).

(Code Sec. 1394(b)(3)(B)(iii))

Portions of businesses may be enterprise zone businesses. The term enterprise zone business includes any trades or businesses which would qualify as an enterprise zone business (determined after the modifications discussed above) if the trades or businesses were separately incorporated. (Code Sec. 1394(b)(3)(D))

Startup period and testing period defined. The term startup period means, with respect to any property being provided for any business, the period before the first tax year beginning more than two years after the later of:

• the date of issuance of the issue providing the property, or

• the date the property is first placed in service after the issuance (or, if earlier, the date which is three years after the date of issuance of the issue providing the property). (Code Sec. 1394(b)(3)(C)(i))

The "testing period" is the first three tax years beginning after the startup period. (Code Sec. 1394(b)(3)(C)(ii))

Qualified zone property. For purposes of the tax-exempt enterprise zone facility bond rules, except as provided below, "qualified zone property" has the meaning given to the term by Code Sec. 1397C (see FTC 2d/FIN ¶ L-9953; USTR ¶ 13,97A4), except that:

• the references to empowerment zones are treated as including references to enterprise communities, and

• the rule for substantial renovations in Code Sec. 1397C(a)(2) is applied requiring only that the additions to basis exceed 15% of the taxpayer's adjusted basis at the beginning of the period (or $5,000 if that is greater). (Code Sec. 1394(b)(2) as amended by '97 Act §955(b))

☐ **Effective:** Obligations issued after Aug. 5, '97. ('97 Act §955(c))

¶ 2609. State private activity bond volume caps and $3 million/$20 million limits on issue amounts do not apply to new empowerment zone facility bonds

Code Sec. 1394(f), as amended by '97 Act § 953(a)
Generally effective: Obligations issued after Aug. 5, '97
Committee Reports, see ¶ 5081

FTC 2d References are to Federal Tax Coordinator 2d
FIN References are to RIA's Analysis of Federal Taxes: Income
USTR References are to United States Tax Reporter: Income, Estate & Gift, and Excise
PCA References are to Pension Coordinator and Pension & Benefits Expert/Advisor
PE References are to Pension and Profit Sharing 2nd
EP References are to Estate Planning & Taxation Coordinator and Estate Planning Advisor

Qualified enterprise zone facility bonds are a category of tax-exempt facility private activity bonds that may be issued to finance certain facilities in empowerment zones and enterprise communities. Specifically, qualified enterprise zone facility bonds are bonds 95% or more of the net proceeds of which are used to provide an enterprise zone facility. These bonds are subject to state private activity "volume cap" limitations, which limit the amount of tax-exempt private activity bonds that a state may issue. (FTC 2d ¶ J-3351; USTR ¶ 13,944) Thus, under Code Sec. 146(d), these bonds are subject to an annual private activity bond state volume cap equal to $50 multiplied by the state population, or (if greater) $150 million per state. (FTC 2d ¶ J-3252.1; USTR ¶ 13,944)

Further, under Code Sec. 1394(c), tax-exempt status doesn't apply to any issue of enterprise zone facility bonds if the aggregate amount of outstanding enterprise zone facility bonds allocable to any person (taking into account that issue) exceeds: (1) $3 million for any one empowerment zone or enterprise community, or (2) $20 million for all empowerment zones and enterprise communities. (FTC 2d ¶ J-3355; USTR ¶ 13944)

New Law. For a "new empowerment zone facility bond" (defined below), the bond will not be treated as a private activity bond for purposes of Code Sec. 146, and the limitation on bond amounts under Code Sec. 1394(c) will not apply. (Code Sec. 1394(f)(1) as amended by '97 Act §953(a)) Thus, new empowerment zone facility bonds that are to be issued for qualified enterprise zone businesses in the additional 20 empowerment zones (see ¶ 2606) are not subject to the state private activity bond volume caps or the Code Sec. 1394(c) limitations. (Com Rept, see ¶ 5081)

This rule applies to a new empowerment zone facility bond only if the bond is "designated" by the local government which nominated the area to which the bond relates. (Code Sec. 1394(f)(2)(A))

Limitation on bonds designated. The aggregate face amount of bonds which may be designated with respect to any empowerment zone cannot exceed:

... $60 million if the zone is in a rural area (Code Sec. 1394(f)(2)(B)(i));

... $130 million if the zone is in an urban area and the zone has a population of less than 100,000 (Code Sec. 1394(f)(2)(B)(ii)); and

... $230 million if the zone is in an urban area and the zone has a population of at least 100,000. (Code Sec. 1394(f)(2)(B)(iii))

Coordination with Code Sec. 1394(c) limitations. New empowerment zone facility bonds will not be taken into account in applying the limitations in Code Sec. 1394(c) to other bonds. (Code Sec. 1394(f)(2)(C)(i))

Current refundings. For a refunding (or series of refundings) of a bond designated under Code Sec. 1394(f)(2), the refunding obligation will be treated as designated (and will not be taken into account in applying the Code Sec. 1394(f)(2)(B) limitations (see above)) if: ((Code Sec. 1394(f)(2)(C)(ii))

... the amount of the refunding bond does not exceed the outstanding amount of the refunded bond (Code Sec. 1394(f)(2)(C)(ii)(I)), and

... the refunded bond is redeemed not later than 90 days after the date of issuance of the refunding bond. (Code Sec. 1394(f)(2)(C)(ii)(II))

New empowerment zone facility bond defined. The term "new empowerment zone facility bond" means any bond which would be described in Code Sec. 1394(a) (relating to bonds issued as part of an issue 95% or more of the net proceeds of which are to be used to provide any enterprise zone facility) if only empowerment zones designated under Code Sec. 1391(g) (see ¶ 2606) were taken into account under Code Sec. 1397B (dealing with the definition of enterprise zone businesses, see ¶ 2610) and Code Sec. 1397C (dealing with the definition of qualified zone property).

☐ **Effective:** Obligations issued after Aug. 5, '97. ('97 Act §953(b))

¶ 2610. Definition of business entity for enterprise zone business rules is liberalized

Code Sec. 1397B(b), as amended by '97 Act § 956(a)
Generally effective: Tax years beginning on or after Aug. 5, '97
Committee Reports, see ¶ 5081

Under pre-'97 Act law, for purposes of the definition of an enterprise zone business, a qualified business entity meant any corporation or partnership if all of the following requirements are satisfied for the tax year:

(1) Every trade or business of the entity is the active conduct of a qualified business within an empowerment zone.

(2) At least 80% of the entity's total gross income is derived from the active conduct of the qualified business.

(3) Substantially all of the use of the entity's tangible property (whether owned or leased) is in an empowerment zone.

(4) Substantially all of the entity's intangible property is used in, and exclusively related to, the active conduct of any such business.

(5) Substantially all of the services performed for the entity by its employees are performed in an empowerment zone.

(6) At least 35% of the entity's employees are residents of an empowerment zone.

(7) Less than 5% of the average of the aggregate unadjusted bases of the entity's property is attributable to collectibles not held primarily for sale to customers in the ordinary course of such business.

(8) Less than 5% of the average of the aggregate unadjusted bases of the entity's property is attributable to nonqualified financial property.

(FTC 2d/FIN ¶ L-9955; USTR ¶ 13,97A4; TaxDesk ¶ 26,870)

New Law. For purposes of the active trade or business requirement ((2) above), a qualified business entity must have at least 50% of the total gross income of the entity derived from the active conduct of the business. (Code Sec. 1397B(b)(2) as amended by '97 Act §956(a)(1)) Thus, the '97 Act liberalizes this requirement by reducing the percentage threshold so that an entity could qualify as an enterprise zone business if at least 50% of the total gross income of the entity is derived from the active conduct of a qualified business within an empowerment zone or enterprise community (assuming that the other criteria of the provision are satisfied). (Com Rept, see ¶ 5081)

For purposes of the rules for tangible property ((3) above), a substantial portion of the use of the entity's tangible property (whether owned or leased) must be in an empowerment zone. (Code Sec. 1397B(b)(3) as amended by '97 Act §956(a)(2)) Thus, rather than requiring that substantially all tangible property of an enterprise zone business be used within a designated zone or community, a substantial portion of the tangible property would be required to be used within a designated zone or community. (Com Rept, see ¶ 5081)

For purposes of the rules for intangible property ((4) above), a substantial portion of the entity's intangible property must be used in the active conduct of any such business. (Code Sec. 1397B(b)(4)) Thus, rather than requiring that substantially all of the intangible property of an enterprise zone business be used within a designated zone or community, a substantial portion of the intangible property would be required to be used within a designated zone or community. (Com Rept, see ¶ 5081) Further, there is no need to determine whether the use of the assets is "exclusively related to" the business. (Code Sec. 1397B(b)(4) as amended by '97 Act §956(a)(3))

For purposes of the rules for services performed for the entity ((5) above), a substantial portion of the services performed for the entity by its employees must be performed in an empowerment zone. (Code Sec. 1397B(b)(5)) Thus, rather than requiring that substantially all employee services of an enterprise zone business be performed within a designated zone or community, a substantial portion of the employee services must be performed within a designated zone or community. (Com Rept, see ¶ 5081)

This modified "enterprise zone business" definition applies to all previously designated empowerment zones and enterprise communities, the two urban empowerment zones designated under the '97 Act, (see ¶ 2607) as well as to the twenty additional empowerment zones authorized to be designated under the '97 Act (see ¶ 2606). In addition, the modifications to the enterprise zone business definition will apply for purposes of defining a D.C. Zone business under certain provisions of the '97 Act that provide certain tax incentives for the District of Columbia. (see ¶ 2602) (Com Rept, see ¶ 5081)

☐ **Effective:** Tax years beginning on or after Aug. 5, '97. ('97 Act §956(b)(1)) For purposes of the special rules for enterprize zone facility bonds provided in Code Sec. 1394(b), these amendments apply to obligations issued after Aug. 5, '97. ('97 Act §956(b)(2))

¶ 2611. Definition of qualified proprietorship for enterprise zone business rules is liberalized

Code Sec. 1397B(c), as amended by '97 Act § 956(a)
Generally effective: Tax years beginning on or after Aug. 5, '97
Committee Reports, see ¶ 5081

Under pre-'97 Act law, a qualified proprietorship means any qualified business carried on by an individual as a proprietorship if all of the following requirements are satisfied for the tax year:

(1) At least 80% of the total gross income of the individual from the qualified business is derived from the active conduct of the business in an empowerment zone.

(2) Substantially all of the use of the tangible property of the individual in the business (whether owned or leased) is in an empowerment zone.

(3) Substantially all of the intangible property of the business is used in, and exclusively related to, the active conduct of the business.

(4) Substantially all of the services performed for the individual in the business by its employees are performed in an empowerment zone.

(5) At least 35% of the employees are residents of an empowerment zone.

(6) Less than 5% of the average of the aggregate unadjusted bases of the individual's property that is used in the business is attributable to collectibles not held primarily for sale to customers in the ordinary course of the business.

(7) Less than 5% of the average of the aggregate unadjusted bases of the individual's property that is used in the business is attributable to nonqualified financial property.

(FTC 2d/FIN ¶ L-9956; USTR ¶ 13,97A4; TaxDesk ¶ 26,870)

New Law. For purposes of the gross income requirement ((1) above), the '97 Act requires that at least 50% of the total gross income of the individual from the qualified business must be derived from the active conduct of the business in an empowerment zone. (Code Sec. 1397B(c)(1) as amended by '97 Act §956(a)(1)) Thus, the '97 Act liberalizes this requirement by reducing the percentage threshold so that an entity could satisfy the requirements of a qualified proprietorship if at least 50% of the total gross income of the individual from the business is derived from the active conduct of the business within an empowerment zone (assuming that the other criteria of the provision are satisfied). (Com Rept, see ¶ 5081)

The '97 Act amends the rules for tangible property ((2) above) so that a substantial portion of the use of the tangible property of the individual in the business (whether owned or leased) must be in an empowerment zone. (Code Sec. 1397B(c)(2) as

FTC 2d References are to Federal Tax Coordinator 2d
FIN References are to RIA's Analysis of Federal Taxes: Income
USTR References are to United States Tax Reporter: Income, Estate & Gift, and Excise
PCA References are to Pension Coordinator and Pension & Benefits Expert/Advisor
PE References are to Pension and Profit Sharing 2nd
EP References are to Estate Planning & Taxation Coordinator and Estate Planning Advisor

amended by '97 Act §956(a)(2)) Thus, rather than requiring that substantially all of the use of tangible property of the individual in the business be used within a designated zone, a substantial portion of the tangible property would be required to be used within a designated zone. (Com Rept, see ¶ 5081)

The '97 Act also amends the rules for intangible property ((3) above). A substantial portion of the intangible property of the business must be used in the active conduct of the business. (Code Sec. 1397B(c)(3)) Thus, rather than requiring that substantially all of the intangible property of a business be used in the active conduct of the business, a substantial portion of the intangible property of the business must be used in the active conduct of the business. (Com Rept, see ¶ 5081) Further, there is no need to determine whether the use of the assets is "exclusively related to" the business. (Code Sec. 1397B(c)(3) as amended by '97 Act §956(a)(3))

Also amended are the rules for services performed ((4) above). A substantial portion of the services performed for the individual in the business by its employees must be performed in an empowerment zone. (Code Sec. 1397B(c)(4)) Thus, rather than requiring that substantially all employee services performed for the individual be performed within a designated zone, a substantial portion of the employee services must be performed within a zone. (Com Rept, see ¶ 5081)

This modified "enterprise zone business" definition applies to all previously designated empowerment zones and enterprise communities, the two urban empowerment zones designated under the '97 Act, (see ¶ 2607) as well as to the twenty additional empowerment zones authorized to be designated under the '97 Act (see ¶ 2606). In addition, the modifications to the enterprise zone business definition will apply for purposes of defining a D.C. Zone business under certain provisions of the '97 Act that provide certain tax incentives for the District of Columbia. (see ¶ 2602) (Com Rept, see ¶ 5081)

☐ **Effective:** Tax years beginning on or after Aug. 5, '97. ('97 Act §956(b)(1)) For purposes of the special rules for enterprize zone facility bonds provided in Code Sec. 1394(b), these amendments apply to obligations issued after Aug. 5, '97. ('97 Act §956(b)(2))

¶ 2612. Property rental rules are modified for enterprize zone business definition

Code Sec. 1397B(d), as amended by '97 Act § 956(a)(4)
Generally effective: Tax years beginning on or before Aug. 5, '97
Committee Reports, see ¶ 5081

The rental of real property located in an empowerment zone to others is a qualified business if and only if (1) the property is not residential rental property (as defined in Code Sec. 168(e)(2) for purposes of the accelerated depreciation rules), and (2) at least 50% of the gross rental income from the property is from enterprise zone businesses. (FTC 2d/FIN ¶ L-9958; USTR ¶ 13,97A4; TaxDesk ¶ 26,871)

The rental of tangible personal property to others is a qualified business if and only if substantially all of the rental of the property is by enterprise zone businesses or by residents of an empowerment zone. (FTC 2d/FIN ¶ L-9959; USTR ¶ 13,97A4; TaxDesk ¶ 26,871)

New Law. For purposes of the requirement that 50% of the gross rental income from the property be from an enterprise zone business ((2) above), the lessor of the property may rely on a lessee's certification that the lessee is an enterprise zone business. (Code Sec. 1397B(d)(2) as amended by '97 Act §956(a)(4))

The rental of tangible personal property to others is a qualified business if and only if at least 50% of the rental of the property is by enterprise zone businesses or by residents of an empowerment zone. (Code Sec. 1397B(d)(3))

This modified enterprise zone business definition applies to all previously designated empowerment zones and enterprise communities, the two urban empowerment zones designated under the '97 Act, (see ¶ 2607) as well as to the twenty additional empowerment zones authorized to be designated under the '97 Act (see ¶ 2606). In addition, the modifications to the enterprise zone business definition will apply for purposes of defining a D.C. Zone business under certain provisions of the '97 Act that provide certain tax incentives for the District of Columbia. (see ¶ 2602) (Com Rept, see ¶ 5081)

☐ **Effective:** Tax years beginning on or after Aug. 5, '97. ('97 Act §956(b)(1)) For purposes of the special rules for enterprize zone facility bonds provided in Code Sec. 1394(b), these amendments apply to obligations issued after Aug. 5, '97. ('97 Act §956(b)(2))

¶ 2613. Treatment of businesses straddling census tract lines for enterprise zone business definition

Code Sec. 1397B(f), as amended by '97 Act § 956(a)(6)
Generally effective: Tax years beginning on or after Aug. 5, '97
Committee Reports, see ¶ 5081

Under pre-'97 Act law, there is no provision in the definition of enterprise zone business for businesses straddling census tract lines.

New Law. For purposes of the definition of enterprise zones, if certain requirements are satisfied, then all the services performed by employees, all business activities, all tangible property, and all intangible property of the business entity or proprietorship that occur in or are located on the real property straddling census tract lines is treated as occurring or situated in an empowerment zone. (Code Sec. 1397B(f) as amended by '97 Act §956(a)(6)): The requirements are that:

• a business entity or proprietorship uses real property located within an empowerment zone, (Code Sec. 1397B(f)(1))

FTC 2d References are to Federal Tax Coordinator 2d
FIN References are to RIA's Analysis of Federal Taxes: Income
USTR References are to United States Tax Reporter: Income, Estate & Gift, and Excise
PCA References are to Pension Coordinator and Pension & Benefits Expert/Advisor
PE References are to Pension and Profit Sharing 2nd
EP References are to Estate Planning & Taxation Coordinator and Estate Planning Advisor

Research Institute of America 637

• the business entity or proprietorship also uses real property located outside the empowerment zone, (Code Sec. 1397B(f)(2))

• the amount of real property that is used and located within the empowerment zone is substantial compared to the amount of real property used and located outside of the empowerment zone, and (Code Sec. 1397B(f)(3))

• the real property that is used and located outside of the empowerment zone is contiguous to part or all of the real property located in the empowerment zone. (Code Sec. 1397B(f)(4))

This modified "enterprise zone business" definition applies to all previously designated empowerment zones and enterprise communities, the two urban empowerment zones designated under the '97 Act, (see ¶ 2607) as well as to the twenty additional empowerment zones authorized to be designated under the '97 Act (see ¶ 2606). In addition, the modifications to the enterprise zone business definition will apply for purposes of defining a D.C. Zone business under certain provisions of the '97 Act that provide certain tax incentives for the District of Columbia. (see ¶ 2602) (Com Rept, see ¶ 5081)

☐ **Effective:** Tax years beginning on or after Aug. 5, '97. ('97 Act §956(b)(1)) For purposes of the special rules for enterprize zone facility bonds provided in Code Sec. 1394(b), these amendments apply to obligations issued after Aug. 5, '97. ('97 Act §956(b)(2))

¶ 2614. Empowerment zone and enterprise community eligibility criteria for nominated areas in Alaska or Hawaii are relaxed

Code Sec. 1392(d), as amended by '97 Act § 954
Generally effective: Aug. 5, '97
Committee Reports, see ¶ 5081

A nominated area which meets criteria specified in the Code is eligible, subject to selection by the appropriate U.S. Secretary, to become an empowerment zone or enterprise community. Empowerment zones and enterprise communities are eligible for tax incentives not available to other areas. (FTC 2d/FIN ¶ J-3387; USTR ¶ 13,914)

New Law. In view of the unique characteristics of the states of Alaska and Hawaii, and the economically depressed areas within those states, Congress believed that the generally applicable criteria for empowerment zones and enterprise communities should be modified in the event that Congress decides to provide for additional designations of those zones or communities. (Com Rept, see ¶ 5081)

Under the '97 Act, a nominated area in Alaska or Hawaii is treated as meeting the requirements of Code Sec. 1392(a)(2) (economic distress), Code Sec. 1392(a)(3) (size, contiguity and the absence of a central business district) and Code Sec. 1392(a)(4) (poverty rate) if, for each census track or block group within the area, 20% or more of the families have income which is 50% or less of the statewide median family income. (Code Sec. 1392(d) as amended by '97 Act §954) For what is statewide median family income, see FTC 2d/FIN ¶ J-3193; USTR ¶ 1434.014. Nominated areas in Alaska or Hawaii continue to be subject to the population limitations imposed by Code Sec. 1392(a)(1). (Com Rept, see ¶ 5081) Nominated areas in Alaska or Hawaii which meet the criteria, modified as described above, of Code Sec. 1392, will be eligible for designation as an empowerment zone or enterprise community. (Com Rept, see ¶ 5081)

☐ **Effective:** Aug. 5, '97. (Com Rept, see ¶ 5081)

FTC 2d References are to Federal Tax Coordinator 2d
FIN References are to RIA's Analysis of Federal Taxes: Income
USTR References are to United States Tax Reporter: Income, Estate & Gift, and Excise
PCA References are to Pension Coordinator and Pension & Benefits Expert/Advisor
PE References are to Pension and Profit Sharing 2nd
EP References are to Estate Planning & Taxation Coordinator and Estate Planning Advisor

¶ 2700. Miscellaneous

¶ 2701. Tax rate changes made by '97 Act are not subject to "tax-straddle" computation

Code Sec. None, '97 Act § 1(c)
Generally effective: Aug. 5, '97

A "straddle computation" is required by Code Sec. 15 when an income tax rate changes during a taxpayer's tax year. The computation is made as follows: (1) a tentative tax is computed using the rates in effect before the change; (2) a tentative tax is computed using the rates in effect after the change; (3) the amount computed in (1) is multiplied by the number of days in the tax year before the change, divided by the number of days in the year; (4) the amount computed in (2) is multiplied by the number of days in the tax year after the change, divided by the number of days in the year; (5) the tax due is the sum of (3) and (4). (FTC 2d/FIN ¶ A-1104 *et seq.*; USTR ¶ 154.02; TaxDesk ¶ 56,822)

New Law. The '97 Act provides, however, that no section of the '97 Act will be considered to change a rate for purposes of Code Sec. 15. ('97 Act §1(c))

> **⚡ observation:** Thus, none of the '97 Act rate changes will require the straddle computation discussed above.

> **⚡ illustration:** A taxpayer in the 31% bracket sells stock held for 18 months on Oct. 20, '97 for a gain of $30,000. The tax rate on the gain is the '97 Act rate of 20% ($6,000) and not a rate that blends the 20% rate with the pre-'97 Act rate of 28%, see ¶ 602.

☐ **Effective:** Aug. 5, '97.

¶ 2702. Income exclusion of construction allowances received by lessees for qualified lessee construction related to short-term leases of retail space

Code Sec. 110, as added by '97 Act § 1213(a)
Code Sec. 6724(d)(1)(A)(ix), as amended by '97 Act § 1213(b)
Generally effective: Leases entered into after Aug. 5, '97
Committee Reports, see ¶ 5208

Issues have arisen as to the proper treatment of amounts provided to a lessee by a lessor for property to be constructed and used by the lessee under a lease ("construction allowances"). In some cases, lessees have had to include incentive payments in

FTC 2d References are to the Federal Tax Coordinator 2d
FIN References are to RIA's Analysis of Federal Taxes: Income
USTR References are to the United States Tax Reporter: Income, Estate & Gift, and Excise
PCA References are to Pension Coordinator and Pension & Benefits Expert/Advisor
PE References are to Pension and Profit Sharing 2nd
EP References are to Estate Planning & Taxation Coordinator and Estate Planning Advisor

640   ⚡ Research Institute of America

gross income. (FTC 2d/FIN ¶ F-1908; USTR ¶ 1185.01(20); TaxDesk ¶ 23,238) However, IRS issued a coordinated issue paper that provided that amounts received by a lessee from a lessor and expended by the lessee on assets owned by the lessor were not includible in the lessee's gross income. The issue paper provided that tax ownership was determined by applying a "benefits and burdens of ownership" test and includes an examination of the following factors: (1) whether legal title passes; (2) how the parties treat the transaction; (3) whether an equity interest was acquired in the property; (4) whether the contract creates present obligations on the seller to execute and deliver a deed and on the buyer to make payments; (5) whether the right of possession is vested; (6) who pays property taxes; (7) who bears the risk of loss or damage to the property; (8) who receives the profits from the operation and sale of the property; (9) who carries insurance with respect to the property; (10) who is responsible for replacing the property; and (11) who has the benefits of any remainder interests in the property. (Com Rept, see ¶ 5208)

New Law. Congress was concerned that the traditional factors (cited by IRS in the coordinated issue paper) in making the determination of who is the tax owner of the property could be applied differently by the lessor and the lessee and could lead to controversies between IRS and taxpayers. (Com Rept, see ¶ 5208)

The '97 Act provides a safe harbor for the exclusion of certain construction allowances (see below) from the lessee's gross income and provides safeguards to ensure that lessors and lessees consistently treat the property subject to the construction allowance as nonresidential real property. (Com Rept, see ¶ 5208)

No inference, however, is intended as to the treatment of amounts that are not subject to the provisions of the '97 Act discussed below, and provisions of the IRS coordinated issue paper and pre-'97 Act law (including case law) continue to apply where applicable. (Com Rept, see ¶ 5208)

Exclusion of construction allowances from the lessee's gross income. Gross income of a lessee does not include any amount received in cash (or treated as a rent reduction) by a lessee from a lessor: (Code Sec. 110(a) as added by '97 Act §1213(a))

... under a short-term lease (defined below) of retail space (defined below), and (Code Sec. 110(a)(1))

... for the purpose of the lessee's constructing or improving qualified long-term real property (defined below) for use in the lessee's trade or business at the retail space, (Code Sec. 110(a)(2))

but only to the extent that the amount does not exceed the amount expended by the lessee for the construction or improvement. (Code Sec. 110(a))

observation: Thus, if the amount of the cash payment or rent reduction exceeds the actual amount spent by the lessee, the lessee must include the ex-

FTC 2d References are to Federal Tax Coordinator 2d
FIN References are to RIA's Analysis of Federal Taxes: Income
USTR References are to United States Tax Reporter: Income, Estate & Gift, and Excise
PCA References are to Pension Coordinator and Pension & Benefits Expert/Advisor
PE References are to Pension and Profit Sharing 2nd
EP References are to Estate Planning & Taxation Coordinator and Estate Planning Advisor

Research Institute of America 641

cess amount in gross income.

Consistent treatment by the lessor. Qualified long-term real property (defined below) constructed or improved in connection with any amount excluded from a lessee's income under the exclusion (see above) is treated as nonresidential real property of the lessor (including for purposes of Code Sec. 168(i)(8)(B), dealing with the treatment of lessor improvements which are abandoned at the termination of a lease). (Code Sec. 110(b)) (Code Sec. 168(i)(8)(B) allows lessors to take losses with respect to certain leasehold improvements abandoned at the end of the term of the lease. (Com Rept, see ¶ 5208) However, the lessee's exclusion is not dependent upon the lessor's treatment of the property as nonresidential real property. (Com Rept, see ¶ 5208)

Definitions.

Short-term lease. A short-term lease is a lease (or other agreement for occupancy or use) of retail space for fifteen years or less (as determined under the rules of Code Sec. 168(i)(3), relating to when the term of a lease includes renewal options, see FTC 2d/FIN ¶ L-9612.1; USTR ¶ 1684.06; TaxDesk ¶ 26,787). (Code Sec. 110(c)(2))

Retail space. Retail space means real property leased, occupied, or otherwise used by a lessee in its trade or business of selling tangible personal property or services to the general public. (Code Sec. 110(c)(3))

Qualified long-term real property. Qualified long-term real property is nonresidential real property which is part of, or otherwise present at, the retail space (see above) and which reverts to the lessor at the termination of the lease. (Code Sec. 110(c)(1))

Information reporting. Under regs, the lessee and lessor will, at the times and in the manner as may be provided in the regs, furnish to IRS: (Code Sec. 110(d))

... information concerning the amounts received (or treated as a rent reduction) and expended in a manner that qualified for the exclusion of the amounts from the lessee's gross income (see above), and (Code Sec. 110(d)(1))

... any other information which IRS considers necessary to carry out these rules related to the exclusion of the amounts from the lessee's gross income and the lessor's consistent treatment of those amounts. (Code Sec. 110(d)(2))

Congress expects that IRS, in promulgating the regs, will attempt to minimize the administrative burdens of taxpayers while ensuring compliance with the rules related to the exclusion of the amounts from the lessee's gross income and the lessor's consistent treatment of those amounts. (Com Rept, see ¶ 5208)

The information required to be furnished to IRS will be furnished on an information return. (Code Sec. 6724(d)(1)(A)(ix) as amended by '97 Act §1213(b))

Treatment of amounts not subject to the exclusion for construction allowances. Congress did not intend any inference as to the treatment of amounts that are not subject to the rules provided in Code Sec. 110 (exclusion for construction allowances, described above). (Com Rept, see ¶ 5208)

☐ **Effective:** Leases entered into after Aug. 5, '97. ('97 Act §1213(e))

¶2703. Commonwealth income taxes can be withheld from federal employees' wages

Code Sec. None, '97 Act § 1462(a)
Generally effective: Jan. 1, '98
Committee Reports, see ¶5305

At the request of a state that imposes income tax withholding, the Secretary of the Treasury will enter into an agreement for withholding state income tax from the wages of federal employees in the state. The definition of "state" for this purpose includes a U.S. territory or possession. However, the Court of Appeals for the Federal Circuit held in *Romero v. U.S.*, 38 F.3d 1204 (1994), that Puerto Rico, a commonwealth, wasn't included in this definition of "state." The court invalidated an agreement between the Secretary of the Treasury and Puerto Rico that provided for withholding Puerto Rico income taxes from the wages of federal employees.

New Law. The '97 Act expands the above definition of "state" to include a commonwealth. (5 USC §5517(c) as amended by '97 Act §1462(a)) Thus, the Secretary of the Treasury can enter into an agreement with a commonwealth for withholding commonwealth income tax from the wages of federal employees. (Com Rept, see ¶5305)

☐ **Effective:** Jan. 1, '98. ('97 Act §1462(b))

¶2704. 100%-of-net-income limitation on percentage depletion is suspended for production from marginal oil and gas wells after '97 and before 2000

Code Sec. 613A(c)(6)(H), as amended by '97 Act § 972
Generally effective: Tax years beginning after Dec. 31, '97
Committee Reports, see ¶5095

The amount of a taxpayer's percentage depletion deduction could not exceed 100% of the taxable income from the oil and gas property with respect to which the deduction was claimed. (FTC 2d/FIN ¶N-2700 *et seq.*; USTR ¶6134.009; TaxDesk ¶27,101)

Oil and gas production from marginal properties is subject to an increased percentage depletion rate. Marginal production is defined as domestic crude oil and natural gas production from stripper well property or from property substantially all of the production from which during the calendar year is heavy oil. Stripper well property is property from which the average daily production is 15 barrel equivalents or less, determined by dividing the average daily production of domestic crude oil and domestic natural gas from producing wells on the property for the calendar year by the number

FTC 2d References are to Federal Tax Coordinator 2d
FIN References are to RIA's Analysis of Federal Taxes: Income
USTR References are to United States Tax Reporter: Income, Estate & Gift, and Excise
PCA References are to Pension Coordinator and Pension & Benefits Expert/Advisor
PE References are to Pension and Profit Sharing 2nd
EP References are to Estate Planning & Taxation Coordinator and Estate Planning Advisor

of wells. (FTC 2d/FIN ¶ N-2424 *et seq.*; USTR ¶ 613A4; TaxDesk ¶ 27,120)

New Law. Under the '97 Act, the 100%-of-net-income limitation that applies to depletion deductions with respect to domestic oil and gas properties will not apply to so much of the allowance for depletion as is determined under the rules related to oil and gas produced from marginal properties for any tax year beginning after Dec. 31, '97 and before Jan. 1, 2000. (Code Sec. 613A(c)(6)(H) as amended by '97 Act §972(a))

> **✐ observation:** The suspension of this limit may also have an effect on the calculation of depletion for alternative minimum tax purposes. The depletion deduction for corporations, for example, is refigured for AMT purposes. Income and deductions allowed when refiguring the limit based on taxable income from the property under Code Sec. 613(a) and the limit based on taxable income from the property with respect to adjustments under Code Sec. 613A(d)(1) are used.

☐ **Effective:** Tax years beginning after Dec. 31, '97 ('97 Act §972(b))

¶ 2705. Exclusion for amounts received for agreeing to a qualified assignment is extended to amounts received for assuming a workers' compensation liability

Code Sec. 130(c), as amended by '97 Act § 962(a)
Generally effective: Claims filed after Aug. 5, '97
Committee Reports, see ¶ 5083

Amounts received by the assignee of a qualified assignment for agreeing to make payments under the assignment are excluded from gross income under Code Sec. 130 to the extent of the total cost of the qualified funding assets. A qualified assignment is any assignment of a liability to make periodic payments as damages (whether by lawsuit or by agreement) on account of personal physical injury or physical sickness, if certain requirements are met. An assignment of a liability to make workers' compensation payments wasn't eligible to be a qualified assignment, even though these amounts were also received on account of personal injury or sickness. The following requirements must be met to qualify as a qualified assignment: (1) the assignee assumes the liability from a person who is a party to the suit or agreement, (2) the periodic payments are fixed and determinable with respect to the amount and time of payment, (3) the periodic payments cannot be accelerated, deferred, increased, or decreased by the recipient of the payments, (4) the assignee's obligation on account of the personal injuries or sickness is no greater than was the obligation of the person who assigned the liability, and (5) the periodic payments are excludible from the gross income of the recipient under Code Sec. 104(a)(2) (as damages for injury to personal rights). (FTC 2d/FIN ¶ J-5833, ¶ J-5834; USTR ¶ 1304.01; TaxDesk ¶ 18,207)

New Law. The exclusion for qualified assignments under Code Sec. 130 is expanded to include amounts received for assuming a liability to pay compensation under any workers' compensation act. (Code Sec. 130(c) as amended by '97 Act §962(a))

This change provides additional economic security to workers' compensation claimants by permitting periodic payments to be made through state-regulated structured settlement companies instead of self-insured employers that may not be subject to comparable solvency-related regulations. (Com Rept, see ¶ 5083)

To qualify as a qualified assignment the assignee must assume liability from a person who is a party to the workers' compensation claim. (Code Sec. 130(c)(1)) The other requirements for a qualified assignment (described above) continue to apply (Com Rept, see ¶ 5083), except that in (5), above, the periodic payments must be excludable from the recipient's gross income under Code Sec. 104(a)(1) (as amounts received under workers' compensation acts for personal injuries or sickness) or Code Sec. 104(a)(2). (Code Sec. 130(c)(2)(D))

☐ **Effective:** For claims under workers' compensation acts filed after Aug. 5, '97. ('97 Act §962(b))

¶ 2706. Timeshare associations may elect to be taxed like other homeowner associations

Code Sec. 528(c)(1), as amended by '97 Act § 966(a)(1)
Code Sec. 528(c)(4), as amended by '97 Act § 966(a)(2)
Code Sec. 528(d)(3), as amended by '97 Act § 966(b)
Code Sec. 528(c)(5), as amended by '97 Act § 966(c)
Generally effective: Tax years beginning after Dec. 31, '96
Committee Reports, see ¶ 5089

Condominium management associations and residential real estate management associations may elect under Code Sec. 528 to be treated as "tax-exempt organizations" for certain purposes, and to be subject to tax on "homeowners association income" at a 30% rate. "Homeowners association income" is the excess of: (1) the association's gross income, excluding "exempt function income," over (2) allowable deductions directly connected with non-exempt function gross income. "Exempt function income" includes membership dues, fees, and assessments for a common activity undertaken by association members or owners of residential units in the condominium or subdivision.

For an association to qualify for treatment as a "homeowners association": (1) at least 60 percent of the association's gross income must consist of membership dues, fees, or assessments on owners; (2) at least 90% of the association's expenditures must be for the acquisition, management, maintenance, or care of "association property;" and (3) no part of the association's net earnings can inure to the benefit of any private shareholder.

"Association property" is all property: (1) held by the association; (2) commonly held by association members; (3) within the association privately held by association

FTC 2d References are to Federal Tax Coordinator 2d
FIN References are to RIA's Analysis of Federal Taxes: Income
USTR References are to United States Tax Reporter: Income, Estate & Gift, and Excise
PCA References are to Pension Coordinator and Pension & Benefits Expert/Advisor
PE References are to Pension and Profit Sharing 2nd
EP References are to Estate Planning & Taxation Coordinator and Estate Planning Advisor

 Research Institute of America 645

members; and (4) held by a governmental unit for the benefit of association members. In addition, the association's units must be used for residential purposes. Use is not considered "residential" if for more than half of the association's tax year the unit is occupied for periods of less than 30 days.

Homeowners associations that do not (or cannot) make the Code Sec. 528 election are taxed either as regular C corporations, or as tax-exempt social welfare organizations (under Code Sec. 501(c)(4)). To qualify as a tax-exempt social welfare organization, a homeowners association must: (1) serve a "community" which bears a reasonable relationship to an area ordinarily identified as a governmental unit; (2) not conduct activities directed to the exterior maintenance of any private residence; and (3) have common areas or facilities for use by the general public.

Non-exempt homeowners associations are taxed as C corporations except that: (1) an association may exclude excess assessments that it refunds to its members or applies to the next year's assessments; (2) gross income does not include special assessments held in a special bank account; and (3) assessments for capital improvements are treated as nontaxable contributions to capital.

Timeshare associations were taxed as regular C corporations because they: (1) could not meet the requirement for the Code Sec. 528 "homeowners association" election that the units be used for residential purposes (i.e., the 30-day rule), and (2) could not meet any of the requirements for tax-exempt status as a social welfare organization. (FTC 2d/FIN ¶ D-5106, ¶ D-5700 *et seq.*, ¶ F-1906, ¶ F-1907; USTR ¶ 5014.13, ¶ 5284; TaxDesk ¶ 23,236, ¶ 23,237, ¶ 60,991, ¶ 68,854) IRS has challenged the exclusions from gross income of timeshare associations that apply to non-exempt homeowners associations. (Com Rept, see ¶ 5089)

New Law. Congress believes that the activities of timeshare associations are similar to those of homeowners associations and should be taxed similarly. (Com Rept, see ¶ 5089) Thus, under the '97 Act, a "timeshare association" may qualify as a "homeowner association." (Code Sec. 528(c)(1) as amended by '97 Act §966(a)(1))

A "timeshare association" is any organization (other than a condominium management association):

... that is organized and operated to provide for the acquisition, construction, management, maintenance, and care of "association property," and

... whose members hold a timeshare right to use, or a timeshare ownership interest in, real property that is "association property," (Code Sec. 528(c)(4)) i.e., property of the timeshare association. (Com Rept, see ¶ 5089)

"Timeshare associations" that are "homeowners associations" are taxable on their "homeowners association income" at the rate of 32%. (Code Sec. 528(b))

For a timeshare association to qualify as a homeowners association under Code Sec. 528:

(1) the association must receive at least 60% of its income from membership dues, fees, or assessments from either: (i) owners of timeshare rights to use of, or (ii) timeshare ownership in, association property; (Code Sec. 528(c)(1)(B)(iii))

(2) at least 90% of the association's expenditures must be for activities provided by the association for the acquisition, construction, management, maintenance, and care of association property, and for activities to, or on behalf of, members of the timeshare association. (Code Sec. 528(c)(1)(C)) "Activities provided to, or on behalf of, members of the timeshare association" include events located on association property, e.g., members' meetings at the association's meeting room, parties at the association's swimming pool, golf lessons on the association's golf range, transportation to and from association property, etc. (Com Rept, see ¶ 5089)

(3) no part of the net earnings of the timeshare association can inure to the benefit of any private shareholder or individual (other than from the exempt functions of a homeowners association, or by a rebate of excess membership dues, fees, or assessments); and (Code Sec. 528(c)(1)(D))

(4) the association elects to be treated as a homeowners association under Code Sec. 528. (Code Sec. 528(c)(1)(E))

"Exempt function income," as applied to timeshare associations, is any amount received as membership dues, fees, or assessments from owners of timeshare rights to use, or timeshare ownership interests in, real property. (Code Sec. 528(d)(3)(C))

"Association property," for a timeshare association, includes property in which the timeshare association, or members of the association, have rights arising out of recorded easements, covenants, or other recorded instruments to use property related to the timeshare project. (Code Sec. 528(c)(5))

☐ **Effective:** Tax years beginning after Dec. 31, '96. ('97 Act §966(e))

FTC 2d References are to Federal Tax Coordinator 2d
FIN References are to RIA's Analysis of Federal Taxes: Income
USTR References are to United States Tax Reporter: Income, Estate & Gift, and Excise
PCA References are to Pension Coordinator and Pension & Benefits Expert/Advisor
PE References are to Pension and Profit Sharing 2nd
EP References are to Estate Planning & Taxation Coordinator and Estate Planning Advisor

[¶ 3000] *Code As Amended*

This section reproduces new law enacted by the Taxpayer Relief Act of 1997, H.R. 2014, the Taxpayer Browsing Protection Act, H.R. 1226, and tax provisions of the Balanced Budget Act of 1997, H.R. 2015. Code sections appear as amended, added or repealed starting at ¶ 3001. They are in Code section order. New matter is shown in italics. All changes and effective dates are shown in the endnotes. To aid in distinguishing between which changes were made by each particular bill, a "B" is added to the footnotes for H.R. 2015 and a "P" is added to the footnotes for H.R. 1226.

Act sections that do not amend Code sections start at ¶ 4000 for H.R. 2014, ¶ 4700 for H.R. 2015 and ¶ 4800 for H.R. 1226.

Cross references at the end of each Code section refer to both the paragraph in the Analysis section where the law change is explained, and the paragraph in the Committee Report sections of this book.

[¶ 3001]   **Code Sec. 1.**   **Tax imposed.**

* * * * * * * * * * * *

[1]*(h) Maximum capital gains rate.*

(1) In general. If a taxpayer has a net capital gain for any taxable year, the tax imposed by this section for such taxable year shall not exceed the sum of—

(A) a tax computed at the rates and in the same manner as if this subsection had not been enacted on the greater of—

(i) taxable income reduced by the net capital gain, or

(ii) the lesser of—

(I) the amount of taxable income taxed at a rate below 28 percent, or

(II) taxable income reduced by the adjusted net capital gain, plus

(B) 25 percent of the excess (if any) of—

(i) the unrecaptured section 1250 gain (or, if less, the net capital gain), over

(ii) the excess (if any) of—

(I) the sum of the amount on which tax is determined under subparagraph (A) plus the net capital gain, over

(II) taxable income, plus

(C) 28 percent of the amount of taxable income in excess of the sum of—

(i) the adjusted net capital gain, plus

(ii) the sum of the amounts on which tax is determined under subparagraphs (A) and (B), plus

(D) 10 percent of so much of the taxpayer's adjusted net capital gain (or, if less, taxable income) as does not exceed the excess (if any) of—

(i) the amount of taxable income which would (without regard to this paragraph) be taxed at a rate below 28 percent, over

(ii) the taxable income reduced by the adjusted net capital gain, plus

(E) 20 percent of the taxpayer's adjusted net capital gain (or, if less, taxable income) in excess of the amount on which a tax is determined under subparagraph (D).

(2) Reduced capital gain rates for qualified 5-year gain.

(A) Reduction in 10-percent rate. In the case of any taxable year beginning after December 31, 2000, the rate under paragraph (1)(D) shall be 8 percent with respect to so much of the amount to which the 10-percent rate would otherwise apply as does not exceed qualified 5-year gain, and 10 percent with respect to the remainder of such amount.

(B) *Reduction in 20-percent rate.* The rate under paragraph (1)(E) shall be 18 percent with respect to so much of the amount to which the 20-percent rate would otherwise apply as does not exceed the lesser of—

(i) the excess of qualified 5-year gain over the amount of such gain taken into account under subparagraph (A) of this paragraph, or

(ii) the amount of qualified 5-year gain (determined by taking into account only property the holding period for which begins after December 31, 2000), and 20 percent with respect to the remainder of such amount. For purposes of determining under the preceding sentence whether the holding period of property begins after December 31, 2000, the holding period of property acquired pursuant to the exercise of an option (or other right or obligation to acquire property) shall include the period such option (or other right or obligation) was held.

(3) Net capital gain taken into account as investment income. For purposes of this subsection, the net capital gain for any taxable year shall be reduced (but not below zero) by the amount which the taxpayer takes into account as investment income under section 163(d)(4)(B)(iii).

(4) Adjusted net capital gain. For purposes of this subsection, the term "adjusted net capital gain" means net capital gain determined without regard to—

(A) collectibles gain,

(B) unrecaptured section 1250 gain,

(C) section 1202 gain, and

(D) mid-term gain.

(5) Collectibles gain. For purposes of this subsection—

(A) *In general.* The term "collectibles gain" means gain from the sale or exchange of a collectible (as defined in section 408(m) without regard to paragraph (3) thereof) which is a capital asset held for more than 1 year but only to the extent such gain is taken into account in computing gross income.

(B) *Partnerships, etc.* For purposes of subparagraph (A), any gain from the sale of an interest in a partnership, S corporation, or trust which is attributable to unrealized appreciation in the value of collectibles shall be treated as gain from the sale or exchange of a collectible. Rules similar to the rules of section 751 shall apply for purposes of the preceding sentence.

(6) Unrecaptured section 1250 gain. For purposes of this subsection—

(A) *In general.* The term "unrecaptured section 1250 gain" means the amount of long-term capital gain which would be treated as ordinary income if—

(i) section 1250(b)(1) included all depreciation and the applicable percentage under section 1250(a) were 100 percent, and

(ii) in the case of gain properly taken into account after July 28, 1997, only gain from section 1250 property held for more than 18 months were taken into account.

(B) *Limitation with respect to section 1231 property.* The amount of unrecaptured section 1250 gain from sales, exchanges, and conversions described in section 1231(a)(3)(A) for any taxable year shall not exceed the excess of the net section 1231 gain (as defined in section 1231(c)(3)) for such year over the amount treated as ordinary income under section 1231(c)(1) for such year.

(C) *Pre-may 7, 1997, gain.* In the case of a taxable year which includes May 7, 1997, subparagraph (A) shall be applied by taking into account only the gain properly taken into account for the portion of the taxable year after May 6, 1997.

(7) Section 1202 gain. For purposes of this subsection, the term "section 1202 gain" means an amount equal to the gain excluded from gross income under section 1202(a).

(8) Mid-term gain. For purposes of this subsection, the term "mid-term gain" means the amount which would be adjusted net capital gain for the taxable year if—

(A) adjusted net capital gain were determined by taking into account only the gain or loss properly taken into account after July 28, 1997, from property held for more than 1 year but not more than 18 months, and

(B) paragraph (3) and section 1212 did not apply.

(9) Qualified 5-year gain. For purposes of this subsection, the term "qualified 5-year gain" means the amount of long-term capital gain which would be computed for the taxable year if only gains from the sale or exchange of property held by the taxpayer for more than 5 years were taken into account. The determination under the preceding sentence shall be made without regard to collectibles gain, unrecaptured section 1250 gain (determined without regard to subparagraph (B) of paragraph (6)), section 1202 gain, or mid-term gain.

(10) Pre-effective date gain.

(A) In general. In the case of a taxable year which includes May 7, 1997, gains and losses properly taken into account for the portion of the taxable year before May 7, 1997, shall be taken into account in determining mid-term gain as if such gains and losses were described in paragraph (8)(A).

(B) Special rules for pass-thru entities. In applying subparagraph (A) with respect to any pass-thru entity, the determination of when gains and loss are properly taken into account shall be made at the entity level.

(C) Pass-thru entity defined. For purposes of subparagraph (B), the term "pass-thru entity" means—

(i) a regulated investment company,

(ii) a real estate investment trust,

(iii) an S corporation,

(iv) a partnership,

(v) an estate or trust, and

(vi) a common trust fund.

(11) Treatment of pass-thru entities. The Secretary may prescribe such regulations as are appropriate (including regulations requiring reporting) to apply this subsection in the case of sales and exchanges by pass-thru entities (as defined in paragraph (10)(C)) and of interests in such entities.

[For analysis, see ¶ 201. For text of Committee Report see ¶ 5019.]

[Endnote Code Sec. 1]

Matter in *italics* in Code Sec. 1(h) added by Sec. 311(a) of the Taxpayer Relief Act of 1997, H.R. 2014, 8/5/97, which struck out:

1. "(h) If a taxpayer has a net capital gain for any taxable year, then the tax imposed by this section shall not exceed the sum of—

"(1) a tax computed at the rates and in the same manner as if this subsection had not been enacted on the greater of—

"(A) taxable income reduced by the amount of the net capital gain, or

"(B) the amount of taxable income taxed at a rate below 28 percent, plus

"(2) a tax of 28 percent of the amount of taxable income in excess of the amount determined under paragraph (1).

For purposes of the preceding sentence, the net capital gain for any taxable year shall be reduced (but not below zero) by the amount which the taxpayer elects to take into account as investment income for the taxable year under section 163(d)(4)(B)(iii)."

Effective Date (Sec. 311(d)(1), H.R. 2014, 8/5/97) effective for tax. yrs. end. after 5/6/97. Sec. 311(e) of this Act provides:

"(e) Election To Recognize Gain on Assets Held on January 1, 2001.—For purposes of the Internal Revenue Code of 1986—

"(1) In general.—A taxpayer other than a corporation may elect to treat—

"(A) any readily tradable stock (which is a capital asset) held by such taxpayer on January 1, 2001, and not sold before the next business day after such date, as having been sold on such next business day for an amount equal to its closing market price on such next business day (and as having been reacquired on such next business day for an amount equal to such closing market price), and

"(B) any other capital asset or property used in the trade or business (as defined in section 1231(b) of the Internal Revenue Code of 1986) held by the taxpayer on January 1, 2001, as having been sold on such date for an amount equal to its fair market value on such date (and as having been reacquired on such date for an amount equal to such fair market value).

"(2) Treatment of gain or loss.—

"(A) Any gain resulting from an election under paragraph (1) shall be treated as received or accrued on the date the asset is treated as sold under paragraph (1) and shall be recognized notwithstanding any provision of the Internal Revenue Code of 1986.

"(B) Any loss resulting from an election under paragraph (1) shall not be allowed for any taxable year.

"(3) Election.—An election under paragraph (1) shall be made in such manner as the Secretary of the Treasury or his delegate may prescribe and shall specify the assets for which such election is made. Such an election, once made with respect to any asset, shall be irrevocable.

"(4) Readily tradable stock.—For purposes of this subsection, the term 'readily tradable stock' means any stock which, as of January 1, 2001, is readily tradable on an established securities market or otherwise."

[¶ 3002]   Code Sec. 23.   Adoption expenses.

(a) **Allowance of credit.**

* * * * * * * * * * * *

[1](2) *Year credit allowed. The credit under paragraph (1) with respect to any expense shall be allowed—*

(A) *in the case of any expense paid or incurred before the taxable year in which such adoption becomes final, for the taxable year following the taxable year during which such expense is paid or incurred, and*

(B) *in the case of an expense paid or incurred during or after the taxable year in which such adoption becomes final, for the taxable year in which such expense is paid or incurred.*

* * * * * * * * * * *

(b) **Limitations.**

* * * * * * * * * * * *

(2) **Income limitation.**

* * * * * * * * * * *

(B) Determination of adjusted gross income. For purposes of subparagraph (A), adjusted gross income shall be [2]*determined without regard to sections 911, 931, and 933.*

* * * * * * * * * * *

[Endnote Code Sec. 23]

Matter in *italics* in Code Sec. 23(a)(2) and Code Sec. 23(b)(2)(B) added by Sec. 1601(h)(2)(A) and (B) of the Taxpayer Relief Act of 1997, H.R. 2014, 8/5/97, which struck out:

1. "(2) Year credit allowed. The credit under paragraph (1) with respect to any expense shall be allowed—

"(A) for the taxable year following the taxable year during which such expense is paid or incurred, or

"(B) in the case of an expense which is paid or incurred during the taxable year in which the adoption becomes final, for such taxable year."

2. "determined—

"(i) without regard to sections 911, 931, and 933, and

"(ii) after the application of sections 86, 135, 137, 219, and 469."

Effective Date (Sec. 1601(j)(1), H.R. 2014, 8/5/97) effective for tax. yrs. begin. after 12/31/96.

[¶ 3003]   Code Sec.[1] 24.

CAUTION.   Code Sec. 24, following, is effective for tax. yrs. begin. after 12/31/97.

Child tax credit.

(a) **Allowance of credit.** There shall be allowed as a credit against the tax imposed by this chapter for the taxable year with respect to each qualifying child of the taxpayer an amount equal to $500 ($400 in the case of taxable years beginning in 1998).

(b) **Limitation based on adjusted gross income.**

(1) **In general.** The amount of the credit allowable under subsection (a) shall be reduced (but not below zero) by $50 for each $1,000 (or fraction thereof) by which the taxpayer's modified adjusted gross income exceeds the threshold amount. For purposes of the preceding sentence, the term "modified adjusted gross income" means adjusted gross income increased by any amount excluded from gross income under section 911, 931, or 933.

(2) **Threshold amount.** For purposes of paragraph (1), the term "threshold amount" means—

(A) $110,000 in the case of a joint return,

(B) $75,000 in the case of an individual who is not married, and

(C) $55,000 in the case of a married individual filing a separate return. For purposes of this paragraph, marital status shall be determined under section 7703.

(c) Qualifying child. For purposes of this section—

(1) In general. The term "qualifying child" means any individual if—

(A) the taxpayer is allowed a deduction under section 151 with respect to such individual for the taxable year,

(B) such individual has not attained the age of 17 as of the close of the calendar year in which the taxable year of the taxpayer begins, and

(C) such individual bears a relationship to the taxpayer described in section 32(c)(3)(B).

(2) Exception for certain noncitizens. The term "qualifying child" shall not include any individual who would not be a dependent if the first sentence of section 152(b)(3) were applied without regard to all that follows "resident of the United States".

(d) Additional credit for families with 3 or more children.

(1) In general. In the case of a taxpayer with 3 or more qualifying children for any taxable year, the amount of the credit allowed under this section shall be equal to the greater of—

(A) the amount of the credit allowed under this section (without regard to this subsection and after application of the limitation under section 26), or

(B) the alternative credit amount determined under paragraph (2).

(2) Alternative credit amount. For purposes of this subsection, the alternative credit amount is the amount of the credit which would be allowed under this section if the limitation under paragraph (3) were applied in lieu of the limitation under section 26.

(3) Limitation. The limitation under this paragraph for any taxable year is the limitation under section 26 (without regard to this subsection)—

(A) increased by the taxpayer's social security taxes for such taxable year, and

(B) reduced by the sum of—

(i) the credits allowed under this part other than under subpart C or this section, and

(ii) the credit allowed under section 32 without regard to subsection (m) thereof.

(4) Unused credit to be refundable. If the amount of the credit under paragraph (1)(B) exceeds the amount of the credit under paragraph (1)(A), such excess shall be treated as a credit to which subpart C applies. The rule of section 32(h) shall apply to such excess.

(5) Social security taxes. For purposes of paragraph (3)—

(A) In general. The term "social security taxes" means, with respect to any taxpayer for any taxable year—

(i) the amount of the taxes imposed by sections 3101 and 3201(a) on amounts received by the taxpayer during the calendar year in which the taxable year begins,

(ii) 50 percent of the taxes imposed by section 1401 on the self-employment income of the taxpayer for the taxable year, and

(iii) 50 percent of the taxes imposed by section 3211(a)(1) on amounts received by the taxpayer during the calendar year in which the taxable year begins.

(B) Coordination with special refund of social security taxes. The term "social security taxes" shall not include any taxes to the extent the taxpayer is entitled to a special refund of such taxes under section 6413(c).

(C) Special rule. Any amounts paid pursuant to an agreement under section 3121(l) (relating to agreements entered into by American employers with respect to foreign affiliates) which are equivalent to the taxes referred to in subparagraph (A)(i) shall be treated as taxes referred to in such subparagraph.

(e) Identification requirement. No credit shall be allowed under this section to a taxpayer with respect to any qualifying child unless the taxpayer includes the name and taxpayer identification number of such qualifying child on the return of tax for the taxable year.

(f) Taxable year must be full taxable year. Except in the case of a taxable year closed by reason of the death of the taxpayer, no credit shall be allowable under this section in the case of a taxable year covering a period of less than 12 months.

[For analysis, see ¶ 101. For text of Committee Report see ¶ 5001.]

[Endnote Code Sec. 24]

Code Sec. 24 was added by Sec. 101(a) of the Taxpayer Relief Act of 1997, H.R. 2014, 8/5/97.
1. added Code Sec. 24
Effective Date (Sec. 101(e), H.R. 2014, 8/5/97) effective for tax. yrs. begin. after 12/31/97.

[¶ 3004]   Code Sec. 25.   Interest on certain home mortgages.

* * * * * * * * * * *

(e) **Special rules and definitions.** For purposes of this section—

* * * * * * * * * * * *

(7) **Principal residence.** The term "principal residence" has the same meaning as when used in [1]*section 121.*

* * * * * * * * * * *

[Endnote Code Sec. 25]
Matter in *italics* in Code Sec. 25(e)(7) added by Sec. 312(d)(1) of the Taxpayer Relief Act of 1997, H.R. 2014, 8/5/97, which struck out:
1. "section 1034"
Effective Date (Sec. 312(d) [sic (e)], H.R. 2014, 8/5/97) effective for sales and exchanges after 5/6/97, except as provided in Secs. 312(d)(2)-(4) [sic (e)(2)-(4)] of this Act which read as follows:
"(2) Sales before 8/5/97.—At the election of the taxpayer, the amendments made by this section shall not apply to any sale or exchange before the date of the enactment of this Act.
"(3) Certain sales within 2 years after 8/5/97. Section 121 of the Internal Revenue Code of 1986 (as amended by this section) shall be applied without regard to subsection (c)(2)(B) thereof in the case of any sale or exchange of property during the 2-year period beginning on the date of the enactment of this Act if the taxpayer held such property on the date of the enactment of this Act and fails to meet the ownership and use requirements of subsection (a) thereof with respect to such property.
"(4) Binding contracts.—At the election of the taxpayer, the amendments made by this section shall not apply to a sale or exchange after the date of the enactment of this Act, if—
"(A) such sale or exchange is pursuant to a contract which was binding on such date, or
"(B) without regard to such amendments, gain would not be recognized under section 1034 of the Internal Revenue Code of 1986 (as in effect on the day before the date of the enactment of this Act) on such sale or exchange by reason of a new residence acquired on or before such date or with respect to the acquisition of which by the taxpayer a binding contract was in effect on such date.
"This paragraph shall not apply to any sale or exchange by an individual if the treatment provided by section 877(a)(1) of the Internal Revenue Code of 1986 applies to such individual."

[¶ 3005]   Code Sec.[1] 25A.

CAUTION.   Code Sec. 25A, following, is effective for expenses paid after 12/31/97 (in tax. yrs. end. after 12/31/97), for education furnished in academic periods begin. after 12/31/97.

Hope and lifetime learning credits.
(a) **Allowance of credit.** In the case of an individual, there shall be allowed as a credit against the tax imposed by this chapter for the taxable year the amount equal to the sum of—
(1) the Hope Scholarship Credit, plus

CAUTION.   Para. (a)(2), following, is effective for expenses paid after 6/30/98 (in tax. yrs. end. after 6/30/98), for education furnished in academic periods begin. after 6/30/98.

(2) the Lifetime Learning Credit.
(b) **Hope Scholarship Credit.**
(1) **Per student credit.** In the case of any eligible student for whom an election is in effect under this section for any taxable year, the Hope Scholarship Credit is an amount equal to the sum of—
(A) 100 percent of so much of the qualified tuition and related expenses paid by the taxpayer during the taxable year (for education furnished to the eligible student during any academic period beginning in such taxable year) as does not exceed $1,000, plus

(B) 50 percent of such expenses so paid as exceeds $1,000 but does not exceed the applicable limit.

(2) Limitations applicable to hope scholarship credit.

(A) Credit allowed only for 2 taxable years. An election to have this section apply with respect to any eligible student for purposes of the Hope Scholarship Credit under subsection (a)(1) may not be made for any taxable year if such an election (by the taxpayer or any other individual) is in effect with respect to such student for any 2 prior taxable years.

(B) Credit allowed for year only if individual is at least 1/2 time student for portion of year. The Hope Scholarship Credit under subsection (a)(1) shall not be allowed for a taxable year with respect to the qualified tuition and related expenses of an individual unless such individual is an eligible student for at least one academic period which begins during such year.

(C) Credit allowed only for first 2 years of postsecondary education. The Hope Scholarship Credit under subsection (a)(1) shall not be allowed for a taxable year with respect to the qualified tuition and related expenses of an eligible student if the student has completed (before the beginning of such taxable year) the first 2 years of postsecondary education at an eligible educational institution.

(D) Denial of credit if student convicted of a felony drug offense. The Hope Scholarship Credit under subsection (a)(1) shall not be allowed for qualified tuition and related expenses for the enrollment or attendance of a student for any academic period if such student has been convicted of a Federal or State felony offense consisting of the possession or distribution of a controlled substance before the end of the taxable year with or within which such period ends.

(3) Eligible student. For purposes of this subsection, the term "eligible student" means, with respect to any academic period, a student who—

(A) meets the requirements of section 484(a)(1) of the Higher Education Act of 1965 (20 U.S.C. 1091(a)(1)), as in effect on the date of the enactment of this section, and

(B) is carrying at least 1/2 the normal full-time work load for the course of study the student is pursuing.

(4) Applicable limit. For purposes of paragraph (1)(B), the applicable limit for any taxable year is an amount equal to 2 times the dollar amount in effect under paragraph (1)(A) for such taxable year.

(c) Lifetime Learning Credit.

(1) Per taxpayer credit. The Lifetime Learning Credit for any taxpayer for any taxable year is an amount equal to 20 percent of so much of the qualified tuition and related expenses paid by the taxpayer during the taxable year for education furnished to an individual during any academic period beginning in such taxable year as does not exceed $10,000 ($5,000 in the case of taxable years beginning before January 1, 2003).

(2) Special rules for determining expenses.

(A) Coordination with hope scholarship. The qualified tuition and related expenses with respect to an individual who is an eligible student for whom a Hope Scholarship Credit under subsection (a)(1) is allowed for the taxable year shall not be taken into account under this subsection.

(B) Certain additional expenses eligible for lifetime learning credit. For purposes of paragraph (1), qualified tuition and related expenses shall include expenses with respect to any course of instruction at an eligible educational institution to acquire or improve job skills of the individual.

(d) Limitation Based on Modified Adjusted Gross Income.

(1) In general. The amount which would (but for this subsection) be taken into account under subsection (a) for the taxable year shall be reduced (but not below zero) by the amount determined under paragraph (2).

(2) Amount of reduction. The amount determined under this paragraph is the amount which bears the same ratio to the amount which would be so taken into account as—

(A) the excess of—

(i) the taxpayer's modified adjusted gross income for such taxable year, over

(ii) $40,000 ($80,000 in the case of a joint return), bears to

(B) $10,000 ($20,000 in the case of a joint return).

(3) Modified adjusted gross income. The term "modified adjusted gross income" means the adjusted gross income of the taxpayer for the taxable year increased by any amount excluded from gross income under section 911, 931, or 933.

(e) Election To Have Section Apply.

(1) In general. No credit shall be allowed under subsection (a) for a taxable year with respect to the qualified tuition and related expenses of an individual unless the taxpayer elects to have this section apply with respect to such individual for such year.

(2) Coordination with exclusions. An election under this subsection shall not take effect with respect to an individual for any taxable year if there is in effect for such taxable year an election under section 530(d)(2)(C) (by the taxpayer or any other individual) to exclude from gross income distributions from an education individual retirement account used to pay qualified higher education expenses of the individual.

(f) Definitions. For purposes of this section—

(1) Qualified tuition and related expenses.

(A) In general. The term "qualified tuition and related expenses" means tuition and fees required for the enrollment or attendance of—

(i) the taxpayer,

(ii) the taxpayer's spouse, or

(iii) any dependent of the taxpayer with respect to whom the taxpayer is allowed a deduction under section 151,

at an eligible educational institution for courses of instruction of such individual at such institution.

(B) Exception for education involving sports, etc. Such term does not include expenses with respect to any course or other education involving sports, games, or hobbies, unless such course or other education is part of the individual's degree program.

(C) Exception for nonacademic fees. Such term does not include student activity fees, athletic fees, insurance expenses, or other expenses unrelated to an individual's academic course of instruction.

(2) Eligible educational institution. The term "eligible educational institution" means an institution—

(A) which is described in section 481 of the Higher Education Act of 1965 (20 U.S.C. 1088), as in effect on the date of the enactment of this section, and

(B) which is eligible to participate in a program under title IV of such Act.

(g) Special rules.

(1) Identification requirement. No credit shall be allowed under subsection (a) to a taxpayer with respect to the qualified tuition and related expenses of an individual unless the taxpayer includes the name and taxpayer identification number of such individual on the return of tax for the taxable year.

(2) Adjustment for certain scholarships, etc. The amount of qualified tuition and related expenses otherwise taken into account under subsection (a) with respect to an individual for an academic period shall be reduced (before the application of subsections (b), (c) and (d)) by the sum of any amounts paid for the benefit of such individual which are allocable to such period as—

(A) a qualified scholarship which is excludable from gross income under section 117,

(B) an educational assistance allowance under chapter 30, 31, 32, 34, or 35 of title 38, United States Code, or under chapter 1606 of title 10, United States Code, and

(C) a payment (other than a gift, bequest, devise, or inheritance within the meaning of section 102(a)) for such individual's educational expenses, or attributable to such individual's enrollment at an eligible educational institution, which is excludable from gross income under any law of the United States.

(3) Treatment of expenses paid by dependent. If a deduction under section 151 with respect to an individual is allowed to another taxpayer for a taxable year beginning in the calendar year in which such individual's taxable year begins—

(A) no credit shall be allowed under subsection (a) to such individual for such individual's taxable year, and

(B) qualified tuition and related expenses paid by such individual during such individual's taxable year shall be treated for purposes of this section as paid by such other taxpayer.

(4) Treatment of certain prepayments. If qualified tuition and related expenses are paid by the taxpayer during a taxable year for an academic period which begins during the first 3 months following such taxable year, such academic period shall be treated for purposes of this section as beginning during such taxable year.

(5) Denial of double benefit. No credit shall be allowed under this section for any expense for which a deduction is allowed under any other provision of this chapter.

(6) No credit for married individuals filing separate returns. If the taxpayer is a married individual (within the meaning of section 7703), this section shall apply only if the taxpayer and the taxpayer's spouse file a joint return for the taxable year.

(7) Nonresident aliens. If the taxpayer is a nonresident alien individual for any portion of the taxable year, this section shall apply only if such individual is treated as a resident alien of the United States for purposes of this chapter by reason of an election under subsection (g) or (h) of section 6013.

(h) Inflation adjustments.

(1) Dollar limitation on amount of credit.

(A) In general. In the case of a taxable year beginning after 2001, each of the $1,000 amounts under subsection (b)(1) shall be increased by an amount equal to—

(i) such dollar amount, multiplied by

(ii) the cost-of-living adjustment determined under section 1(f)(3) for the calendar year in which the taxable year begins, determined by substituting "calendar year 2000" for "calendar year 1992" in subparagraph (B) thereof.

(B) Rounding. If any amount as adjusted under subparagraph (A) is not a multiple of $100, such amount shall be rounded to the next lowest multiple of $100.

(2) Income limits.

(A) In general. In the case of a taxable year beginning after 2001, the $40,000 and $80,000 amounts in subsection (d)(2) shall each be increased by an amount equal to—

(i) such dollar amount, multiplied by

(ii) the cost-of-living adjustment determined under section 1(f)(3) for the calendar year in which the taxable year begins, determined by substituting "calendar year 2000" for "calendar year 1992" in subparagraph (B) thereof.

(B) Rounding. If any amount as adjusted under subparagraph (A) is not a multiple of $1,000, such amount shall be rounded to the next lowest multiple of $1,000.

(i) Regulations. The Secretary may prescribe such regulations as may be necessary or appropriate to carry out this section, including regulations providing for a recapture of the credit allowed under this section in cases where there is a refund in a subsequent taxable year of any amount which was taken into account in determining the amount of such credit.

[For analysis, see ¶ 401. For text of Committee Report see ¶ 5002.]

[Endnote Code Sec. 25A]

Code Sec. 25A was added by Sec. 201(a) of the Taxpayer Relief Act of 1997, H.R. 2014, 8/5/97.

1. added Code Sec. 25A

Effective Date (Sec. 201(f)(1) and (2), H.R. 2014, 8/5/97) effective for expenses paid after 12/31/97 (in tax. yrs. end. after 12/31/97), for education furnished in academic periods begin. after 12/31/97, except for Sec. 25A(a)(2), which is effective for expenses paid after 6/30/98 (in tax. yrs. end. after 6/30/98), for education furnished in academic periods begin. after 6/30/98.

[¶ 3006]   Code Sec. 26.   Limitation based on tax liability; definition of tax liability.

* * * * * * * * * * * *

(b) **Regular tax liability.** For purposes of this part—

* * * * * * * * * * * *

(2) **Exception for certain taxes.** For purposes of paragraph (1), any tax imposed by any of the following provisions shall not be treated as tax imposed by this chapter:

* * * * * * * * * * * *

CAUTION.   Subparas. (b)(2)(E)-(P), following, are effective before 1/1/98. For subpara. (b)(2)(E)-(Q), effective after 12/31/97, see below.

(E) section 531 (relating to accumulated earnings tax),

(F) section 541 (relating to personal holding company tax),

(G) section 1351(d)(1) (relating to recoveries of foreign expropriation losses),

(H) section 1374 (relating to tax on certain built-in gains of S corporations),

(I) section 1375 (relating to tax imposed when passive investment income of corporation having subchapter C earnings and profits exceeds 25 percent of gross receipts),

(J) subparagraph (A) of section 7518(g)(6) (relating to nonqualified withdrawals from capital construction funds taxed at highest marginal rate),

(K) sections 871(a) and 881 (relating to certain income of nonresident aliens and foreign corporations),

(L) section 860E(e) (relating to taxes with respect to certain residual interests),

(M) section 884 (relating to branch profits tax),

(N) sections 453(l)(3) and 453A(c) (relating to interest on certain deferred tax liabilities),[1]

(O) section 860K (relating to treatment of transfers of high-yield interests to disqualified holders)[2], *and*

[3]*(P) section 220(f)(4) (relating to additional tax on medical savings account distributions not used for qualified medical expenses).*

CAUTION.   Subparas. (b)(2)(E)-(Q), following, are effective after 12/31/97. For subparas. (b)(2)(F)-(P), effective before 1/1/98, see above.

[4]*(E) section 530(d)(3) (relating to additional tax on certain distributions from education individual retirement accounts),*

[5]*(F) section 531 (relating to accumulated earnings tax),*

[6]*(G) section 541 (relating to personal holding company tax),*

[7]*(H) section 1351(d)(1) (relating to recoveries of foreign expropriation losses),*

[8]*(I) section 1374 (relating to tax on certain built-in gains of S corporations),*

[9]*(J) section 1375 (relating to tax imposed when passive investment income of corporation having subchapter C earnings and profits exceeds 25 percent of gross receipts),*

[10]*(K) subparagraph (A) of section 7518(g)(6) (relating to nonqualified withdrawals from capital construction funds taxed at highest marginal rate),*

[11]*(L) sections 871(a) and 881 (relating to certain income of nonresident aliens and foreign corporations),*

[12]*(M) section 860E(e) (relating to taxes with respect to certain residual interests),*

[13]*(N) section 884 (relating to branch profits tax),*

[14]*(O) sections 453(l)(3) and 453A(c) (relating to interest on certain deferred tax liabilities), and*

[15]*(P) section 860K (relating to treatment of transfers of high-yield interests to disqualified holders).*

[16]*(Q)* section 220(f)(4) (relating to additional tax on medical savings account distributions not used for qualified medical expenses).

* * * * * * * * * * * *

[For analysis, see ¶ 1202. For text of Committee Report see ¶ 5370.]

[Endnote Code Sec. 26]

Matter in *italics* in Code Sec. 26(b)(2)(N), Code Sec. 26(b)(2)(O) and Code Sec. 26(b)(2)(P) added by Sec. 1602(a)(1) of the Taxpayer Relief Act of 1997, H.R. 2014, 8/5/97, which struck out:

   1. "and"
   2. "."
   3. added subpara. (b)(2)(P)

Effective Date (Sec. 1602(i), H.R. 2014, 8/5/97) 12/31/96.

Matter in *italics* in Code Sec. 26(b)(2)(E), Code Sec. 26(b)(2)(F), Code Sec. 26(b)(2)(G), Code Sec. 26(b)(2)(H), Code Sec. 26(b)(2)(I), Code Sec. 26(b)(2)(K), Code Sec. 26(b)(2)(L), Code Sec. 26(b)(2)(M), Code Sec. 26(b)(2)(N), Code Sec. 26(b)(2)(O), Code Sec. 26(b)(2)(P) and Code Sec. 26(b)(2)(Q) added by Sec. 211(g)(1), H.R. 2014, 8/5/97, which struck out:

   4. added subpara. (b)(2)(E)
   5. "(E)"
   6. "(F)"
   7. "(G)"
   8. "(H)"
   9. "(I)"
   10. "(J)"
   11. "(K)"
   12. "(L)"
   13. "(M)"
   14. "(N)"
   15. "(O)"
   16. "(P)"

Effective Date (Sec. 211(h)(1), H.R. 2014, 8/5/97) effective 1/1/98.

**[¶ 3007]   Code Sec. 30A.   [1]*Puerto Rico economic activity credit.*

* * * * * * * * * * * *

[Endnote Code Sec. 30A]

Matter in *italics* in Code Sec. 30A added by Sec. 1601(f)(1)(A) of the Taxpayer Relief Act of 1997, H.R. 2014, 8/5/97, which struck out:

   1. "SEC. 30A. PUERTO RICAN ECONOMIC ACTIVITY CREDIT."

Effective Date (Sec. 1601(j)(1), H.R. 2014, 8/5/97) effective for tax. yrs. begin. after 12/31/95. Secs. 1601(c)(2) and (c)(3), of P.L. 104-188, provide special rules, reproduced below.

"(2) Special rule for qualified possession source investment income. The amendments made by this section shall not apply to qualified possession source investment income received or accrued before July 1, 1996, without regard to the taxable year in which received or accrued.

"(3) Special transition rule for payment of estimated tax installments. In determining the amount of any installment due under section 6655 of the Internal Revenue Code of 1986 after the date of the enactment of this Act and before October 1, 1996, only 1/2 of any increase in tax (for the taxable year for which such installment is made) by reason of the amendments made by subsections (a) and (b) shall be taken into account. Any reduction in such installment by reason of the preceding sentence shall be recaptured by increasing the next required installment for such year by the amount of such reduction."

[¶ 3008]   Code Sec. 32.   Earned income.

* * * * * * * * * * * *

  (c) Definitions and special rules. For purposes of this section—

* * * * * * * * * * * *

   (2) Earned income.

* * * * * * * * * * * *

    (B) For purposes of subparagraph (A)—

* * * * * * * * * * * *

CAUTION.   Clauses (c)(2)(B)(iii) and (iv), following, are effective for tax. yrs. begin. before 1/1/98. For clause (c)(2)(B)(iii)-(v), effective for tax. yrs. begin. after 12/31/97, see below.

(iii) no amount to which section 871(a) applies (relating to income of nonresident alien individuals not connected with United States business) shall be taken into account, and

(iv) no amount received for services provided by an individual while the individual is an inmate at a penal institution shall be taken into account.

CAUTION.   Clauses (c)(2)(B)(iii)-(v), following, are effective for tax. yrs. begin. after 12/31/97. For clause (c)(2)(B)(iii) and (iv), effective for tax. yrs. begin. before 1/1/98, see above.

(iii) no amount to which section 871(a) applies (relating to income of nonresident alien individuals not connected with United States business) shall be taken into account,[1]

(iv) no amount received for services provided by an individual while the individual is an inmate at a penal institution shall be taken into account[2], *and*

[3]*(v) no amount described in subparagraph (A) received for service performed in work activities as defined in paragraph (4) or (7) of section 407(d) of the Social Security Act to which the taxpayer is assigned under any State program under part A of title IV of such Act, but only to the extent such amount is subsidized under such State program.*

* * * * * * * * * * * *

(4) Treatment of military personnel stationed outside the United States. For purposes of paragraphs (1)(A)(ii)(I) and (3)(E), the principal place of abode of a member of the Armed Forces of the United States shall be treated as in the United States during any period during which such member is stationed outside the United States while serving on extended active duty[4] with the Armed Forces of the United States. [5]*For purposes of the preceding sentence, the term "extended active duty" means any period of active duty pursuant to a call or order to such duty for a period in excess of 90 days or for an indefinite period.*

(5) Modified adjusted gross income.

* * * * * * * * * * * *

CAUTION.   Subpara. (c)(5)(B), following, is effective for tax. yrs. begin. before 1/1/98. For subpara. (c)(5)(B), effective for tax. yrs. begin. after 12/31/97, see below.

(B) Certain amounts disregarded. An amount is described in this subparagraph if it is—

(i) the amount of losses from sales or exchanges of capital assets in excess of gains from such sales or exchanges to the extent such amount does not exceed the amount under section 1211(b)(1),

(ii) the net loss from estates and trusts,

(iii) the excess (if any) of amounts described in subsection (i)(2)(C)(ii) over the amounts described in subsection (i)(2)(C)(i) (relating to nonbusiness rents and royalties), and

(iv) 50 percent of the net loss from the carrying on of trades or businesses, computed separately with respect to—

(I) trades or businesses (other than farming) conducted as sole proprietorships,

(II) trades or businesses of farming conducted as sole proprietorships, and

(III) other trades or businesses.

For purposes of clause (iv), there shall not be taken into account items which are attributable to a trade or business which consists of the performance of services by the taxpayer as an employee.

CAUTION.   Subpara. (c)(5)(B), following, is effective for tax. yrs. begin. after 12/31/97. For subpara. (c)(5)(B), effective for tax. yrs. begin. before 1/1/98, see above.

(B) Certain amounts disregarded. An amount is described in this subparagraph if it is—

(i) the amount of losses from sales or exchanges of capital assets in excess of gains from such sales or exchanges to the extent such amount does not exceed the amount under section 1211(b)(1),

(ii) the net loss from estates and trusts,

(iii) the excess (if any) of amounts described in subsection (i)(2)(C)(ii) over the amounts described in subsection (i)(2)(C)(i) (relating to nonbusiness rents and royalties),[6]

(iv) [7]*75 percent* of the net loss from the carrying on of trades or businesses, computed separately with respect to—

(I) trades or businesses (other than farming) conducted as sole proprietorships,

(II) trades or businesses of farming conducted as sole proprietorships, and

(III) other trades or businesses[8]

[9]*(v) interest received or accrued during the taxable year which is exempt from tax imposed by this chapter, and*

(vi) amounts received as a pension or annuity, and any distributions or payments received from an individual retirement plan, by the taxpayer during the taxable year to the extent not included in gross income.

For purposes of clause (iv), there shall not be taken into account items which are attributable to a trade or business which consists of the performance of services by the taxpayer as an employee. [10]*Clause (vi) shall not include any amount which is not includible in gross income by reason of section 402(c), 403(a)(4), (403(b), 408(d)(3), (4), or (5), or 457(e)(10).*

* * * * * * * * * * * *

[11]**(k) Restrictions on taxpayers who improperly claimed credit in prior year.**

(1) Taxpayers making prior fraudulent or reckless claims.

(A) In general. No credit shall be allowed under this section for any taxable year in the disallowance period.

(B) Disallowance period. For purposes of paragraph (1), the disallowance period is—

(i) the period of 10 taxable years after the most recent taxable year for which there was a final determination that the taxpayer's claim of credit under this section was due to fraud, and

(ii) the period of 2 taxable years after the most recent taxable year for which there was a final determination that the taxpayer's claim of credit under this section was due to reckless or intentional disregard of rules and regulations (but not due to fraud).

(2) Taxpayers making improper prior claims. In the case of a taxpayer who is denied credit under this section for any taxable year as a result of the deficiency procedures under subchapter B of chapter 63, no credit shall be allowed under this section for any subsequent taxable year unless the taxpayer provides such information as the Secretary may require to demonstrate eligibility for such credit.

[12]**(l) Coordination with certain means-tested programs.** For purposes of—

(1) the United States Housing Act of 1937,

(2) title V of the Housing Act of 1949,

(3) section 101 of the Housing and Urban Development Act of 1965,

(4) sections 221(d)(3), 235, and 236 of the National Housing Act, and

(5) the Food Stamp Act of 1977,

any refund made to an individual (or the spouse of an individual) by reason of this section, and any payment made to such individual (or such spouse) by an employer under section 3507, shall not be treated as income (and shall not be taken into account in determining resources for the month of its receipt and the following month).

[13]**(m) Identification numbers.** Solely for purposes of subsections (c)(1)(F) and (c)(3)(D), a taxpayer identification number means a social security number issued to an individual by the Social Security Administration (other than a social security number issued pursuant to clause (II)

(or that portion of clause (III) that relates to clause (II)) of section 205(c)(2)(B)(i) of the Social Security Act).

CAUTION.   Subsec. (m) [sic (n)' is effective for tax. yrs. begin. after 12/31/97.

[14]*(m) [sic (n)] Supplemental Child Credit.*

(1) In general. In the case of a taxpayer with respect to whom a credit is allowed under section 24 for the taxable year, there shall be allowed as a credit under this section an amount equal to the supplemental child credit (if any) determined for such taxpayer for such taxable year under paragraph (2). Such credit shall be in addition to the credit allowed under subsection (a).

(2) Supplemental child credit. For purposes of this subsection, the supplemental child credit is an amount equal to the excess (if any) of—

(A) the amount determined under section 24(d)(1)(A), over

(B) the amount determined under section 24(d)(1)(B).

The amounts referred to in subparagraphs (A) and (B) shall be determined as if section 24(d) applied to all taxpayers.

(3) Coordination with section 24. The amount of the credit under section 24 shall be reduced by the amount of the credit allowed under this subsection.

[For analysis, see ¶s 101, 108, 109, 110. For text of Committee Report see ¶s 5001, 5162.]

[Endnote Code Sec. 32]

Matter in *italics* in Code Sec. 32(c)(2)(B)(iii), Code Sec. 32(c)(2)(B)(iv) and Code Sec. 32(c)(2)(B)(v) added by Sec. 1085(c) of the Taxpayer Relief Act of 1997, H.R. 2014, 8/5/97, which struck out:

1. "and"
2. "."
3. added clause (c)(2)(B)(v)

Effective Date (Sec. 1085(e)(2), H.R. 2014, 8/5/97) effective for tax. yrs. begin. after 12/31/97.

Matter in *italics* in Code Sec. 32(c)(4) added by Sec. 312(d)(2), H.R. 2014, 8/5/97, which struck out:

4. "(as defined in section 1034(h)(3))"
5. added matter in para. (c)(4)

Effective Date (Sec. 312(d) [sic (e)], H.R. 2014, 8/5/97) Sec. 312(d) [sic (e)], H.R. 2014, 8/5/97, provides:

"(d) Effective date.

"(1) In general. The amendments made by this section shall apply to sales and exchanges after May 6, 1997.

"(2) Sales before 8/5/97. At the election of the taxpayer, the amendments made by this section shall not apply to any sale or exchange before the date of the enactment of this Act.

"(3) Certain sales within 2 years after 8/5/97. Section 121 of the Internal Revenue Code of 1986 (as amended by this section) shall be applied without regard to subsection (c)(2)(B) thereof in the case of any sale or exchange of property during the 2-year period beginning on the date of the enactment of this Act if the taxpayer held such property on the date of the enactment of this Act and fails to meet the ownership and use requirements of subsection (a) thereof with respect to such property.

"(4) Binding contracts. At the election of the taxpayer, the amendments made by this section shall not apply to a sale or exchange after the date of the enactment of this Act, if—

"(A) such sale or exchange is pursuant to a contract which was binding on such date, or

"(B) without regard to such amendments, gain would not be recognized under section 1034 of the Internal Revenue Code of 1986 (as in effect on the day before the date of the enactment of this Act) on such sale or exchange by reason of a new residence acquired on or before such date or with respect to the acquisition of which by the taxpayer a binding contract was in effect on such date.

This paragraph shall not apply to any sale or exchange by an individual if the treatment provided by section 877(a)(1) of the Internal Revenue Code of 1986 applies to such individual."

Matter in *italics* in Code Sec. 32(c)(5)(B), Code Sec. 32(c)(5)(B)(iii), Code Sec. 32(c)(5)(B)(iv), Code Sec. 32(c)(5)(B)(iv)(III), Code Sec. 32(c)(5)(B)(v) and Code Sec. 32(c)(5)(B)(vi) added by Sec. 1085(b) and (d)(1)-(4), H.R. 2014, 8/5/97, which struck out:

6. "and"
7. "50 percent"
8. "."
9. added clauses (c)(5)(B)(v) and (vi)
10. added matter in subpara. (c)(5)(B)

Effective Date (Sec. 1085(e)(2), H.R. 2014, 8/5/97) effective for tax. yrs. begin. after 12/31/97.

Matter in *italics* in Code Sec. 32(k), Code Sec. 32(l) and Code Sec. 32(m) added by Sec. 1085(a)(1), H.R. 2014, 8/5/97, which struck out:

11. added subsec. (k)
12. "(k)"
13. "(l)"
Effective Date (Sec. 1085(e)(1), H.R. 2014, 8/5/97) effective for tax. yrs. begin. after 12/31/96.

Code Sec. 1085(m) [sic (n)], in *italics,* was added by Sec. 101(b), H.R. 2014, 8/5/97.
14. added subsec. (m) [sic (n)]
Effective Date (Sec. 101(e), H.R. 2014, 8/5/97) effective for tax. yrs. begin. after 12/31/97.

[¶ 3009] Code Sec. 39.   Carryback and carryforward of unused credits.

CAUTION.   Subsec. (a), following, is effective for credits arising in tax. yrs. begin. before 1/1/98. For subsec. (a) effective for credits arising in tax. yrs. begin. after 12/31/97, see below.

(a) In general.

(1) 3-year carryback and 15-year carryforward. If the sum of the business credit carryforwards to the taxable year plus the amount of the current year business credit for the taxable year exceeds the amount of the limitation imposed by subsection (c) of section 38 for such taxable year (hereinafter in this section referred to as the "unused credit year"), such excess (to the extent attributable to the amount of the current year business credit) shall be—

(A) a business credit carryback to each of the 3 taxable years preceding the unused credit year, and

(B) a business credit carryforward to each of the 15 taxable years following the unused credit year,

and, subject to the limitations imposed by subsections (b) and (c), shall be taken into account under the provisions of section 38(a) in the manner provided in section 38(a).

(2) Amount carried to each year.

(A) Entire amount carried to first year. The entire amount of the unused credit for an unused credit year shall be carried to the earliest of the 18 taxable years to which (by reason of paragraph (1)) such credit may be carried.

(B) Amount carried to other 17 years. The amount of the unused credit for the unused credit year shall be carried to each of the other 17 taxable years to the extent that such unused credit may not be taken into account under section 38(a) for a prior taxable year because of the limitations of subsections (b) and (c).

CAUTION.   Subsec. (a), following, is effective for credits arising in tax. yrs. begin. after 12/31/97. For subsec. (a) effective for credits arising in tax. yrs. begin. before 1/1/98, see above.

(a) In general.

(1) [1]1-year carryback and [2]20-year carryforward. If the sum of the business credit carryforwards to the taxable year plus the amount of the current year business credit for the taxable year exceeds the amount of the limitation imposed by subsection (c) of section 38 for such taxable year (hereinafter in this section referred to as the "unused credit year"), such excess (to the extent attributable to the amount of the current year business credit) shall be—

(A) a business credit carryback to each of the [3]1 taxable years preceding the unused credit year, and

(B) a business credit carryforward to each of the [4]20 taxable years following the unused credit year,

and, subject to the limitations imposed by subsections (b) and (c), shall be taken into account under the provisions of section 38(a) in the manner provided in section 38(a).

(2) Amount carried to each year.

(A) Entire amount carried to first year. The entire amount of the unused credit for an unused credit year shall be carried to the earliest of the [5]22 taxable years to which (by reason of paragraph (1)) such credit may be carried.

(B) Amount carried to other [6]21 years. The amount of the unused credit for the unused credit year shall be carried to each of the other [7]21 taxable years to the extent that such unused credit may not be taken into account under section 38(a) for a prior taxable year because of the limitations of subsections (b) and (c).

* * * * * * * * * * * *

(d) **Transitional rules.**

* * * * * * * * * * * *

[8]*(8) No carryback of DC zone credits before effective date. No portion of the unused business credit for any taxable year which is attributable to the credits allowable under subchapter U by reason of section 1400 may be carried back to a taxable year ending before the date of the enactment of section 1400.*

[For analysis, see ¶s 701, 2601. For text of Committee Report see ¶s 5040, 5160.]

[Endnote Code Sec. 39]

Matter in *italics* in Code Sec. 39(a)(1) and Code Sec. 39(a)(2) added by Secs. 1083(a)(1) and (2) of the Taxpayer Relief Act of 1997, H.R. 2014, 8/5/97, which struck out:

1. "3"
2. "15"
3. "3"
4. "15"
5. "18"
6. "17"
7. "17"

Effective Date (Sec. 1083(b), H.R. 2014, 8/5/97) effective for credits arising in tax. yrs. begin. after 12/31/97.

Matter in *italics* in Code Sec. 39(d)(8) added by Sec. 701(b)(2), H.R. 2014, 8/5/97.
8. added para. (d)(8)

Effective Date (Sec. 701(d), H.R. 2014, 8/5/97) effective 8/5/97.

[¶ 3010]   Code Sec. 41.   Credit for increasing research activities.

* * * * * * * * * * * *

(c) **Base amount.**

* * * * * * * * * * * *

(4) **Election of alternative incremental credit.**

* * * * * * * * * * * *

[1]*(B) Election. An election under this paragraph shall apply to the taxable year for which made and all succeeding taxable years unless revoked with the consent of the Secretary.*

* * * * * * * * * * * *

* * * * * * * * * * * *

(h) **Termination.**

(1) **In general.** This section shall not apply to any amount paid or incurred—

* * * * * * * * * * * *

(B) after [2]*June 30, 1998.*

Notwithstanding the preceding sentence, in the case of a taxpayer making an election under subsection (c)(4) for its first taxable year beginning after June 30, 1996, and before July 1, 1997, this section shall apply to amounts paid or incurred [3]*during the 24-month period beginning with the first month of such year. The 24 months referred to in the preceding sentence shall be reduced by the number of full months after June 1996 (and before the first month of such first taxable year) during which the taxpayer paid or incurred any amount which is taken into account in determining the credit under this section.*

* * * * * * * * * * * *

[For analysis, see ¶ 706. For text of Committee Report see ¶ 5036.]

[Endnote Code Sec. 41]

Matter in *italics* in Code Sec. 41(c)(4)(B), and Code Sec. 41(h)(1) added by Sec. 601(a)(1), (a)(2), and (b)(1) of the Taxpayer Relief Act of 1997, H.R. 2014, 8/5/97, which struck out:

1. "(B) Election. An election under this paragraph may be made only for the first taxable year of the taxpayer beginning after June 30, 1996. Such an election shall apply to the taxable year for which made and all succeeding taxable years unless revoked with the consent of the Secretary."

2. "May 31, 1997"

3. "during the first 11 months of such taxable year"

Effective Date (Sec. 601(c), H.R. 2014, 8/5/97) effective for amounts paid or incurred after 5/31/97.

[¶ 3011]   Code Sec. 45C.   Clinical testing expenses for certain drugs for rare diseases or conditions.

* * * * * * * * * * * *

(b) Qualified clinical testing expenses. For purposes of this section—

(1) Qualified clinical testing expenses.

* * * * * * * * * * * *

(D) Special rule. For purposes of this paragraph, section 41 shall be deemed to remain in effect for periods after June 30, 1995, and before July 1, 1996, and periods after [1]*June 30, 1998.*

* * * * * * * * * * * *

[2]**(e) [Repealed]**

[For analysis, see ¶ 707. For text of Committee Report see ¶ 5039.]

[Endnote Code Sec. 45C]

Matter in *italics* in Code Sec. 45C(b)(1) added by Sec. 601(b)(2) of the Taxpayer Relief Act of 1997, H.R. 2014, 8/5/97, which struck out:

1. "May 31, 1997"

Effective Date (Sec. 601(c), H.R. 2014, 8/5/97) effective for amounts paid or incurred after 5/31/97.

Matter in Code Sec. 45C(e) deleted by Sec. 604(a), H.R. 2014, which struck out:

2. "(e) Termination.

"This section shall not apply to any amount paid or incurred—

"(1) after December 31, 1994, and before July 1, 1996, or

"(2) after May 31, 1997."

Effective Date (Sec. 604(b), H.R. 2014, 8/5/97) effective for amounts paid or incurred after 5/31/97.

[¶ 3012]   Code Sec. 51.   Amount of credit.

(a) **Determination of amount.** For purposes of section 38, the amount of the work opportunity credit determined under this section for the taxable year shall be equal to [1]*40 percent* of the qualified first-year wages for such year.

* * * * * * * * * * * *

(c) **Wages defined.** For purposes of this subpart—

* * * * * * * * * * * *

(4) Termination. The term "wages" shall not include any amount paid or incurred to an individual who begins work for the employer—

* * * * * * * * * * * *

(B) after [2]*June 30, 1998.*

(d) **Members of targeted groups.** For purposes of this subpart—

(1) **In general.** An individual is a member of a targeted group if such individual is—

* * * * * * * * * * * *

(F) a qualified summer youth employee, [3]

(G) a qualified food stamp recipient[4], *or*

[5]*(H) a qualified SSI recipient.*

(2) Qualified IV-A recipient.

(A) In general. The term "qualified IV-A recipient" means any individual who is certified by the designated local agency as being a member of a family receiving assistance under a IV-A program [6]*for any 9 months during the 18-month period ending on the hiring date.*

* * * * * * * * * * *

(3) Qualified veteran.

[7]*(A) In general. The term "qualified veteran" means any veteran who is certified by the designated local agency as being a member of a family receiving assistance under a food stamp program under the Food Stamp Act of 1977 for at least a 3-month period ending during the 12-month period ending on the hiring date.*

* * * * * * * * * * *

[8]*(9) Qualified SSI recipient. The term "qualified SSI recipient" means any individual who is certified by the designated local agency as receiving supplemental security income benefits under title XVI of the Social Security Act (including supplemental security income benefits of the type described in section 1616 of such Act or section 212 of Public Law 930966) for any month ending within the 60- day period ending on the hiring date.*

CAUTION. Sec. 603(c)(2) of H.R. 2014 redesignates para. (d)(9) as para. (d)(10). However, incompatible amendments were made to para. (d)(9) by P.L. 104-188 and P.L. 104-193, and both versions of para. (d)(9), now para. (d)(10) , appear below.

CAUTION. Para. following, was amended by the Small Business Job Protection Act of 1996, P.L. 104-188, effective for individuals who begin work for the employer after 9/30/96.

[9]*(10) Hiring date.* The term "hiring date" means the day the individual is hired by the employer.

CAUTION. Para. following, is amended by Sec. 110(l)(1) of the Personal Responsibility and Work Opportunity Reconciliation Act of 1996, P.L. 104-193, effective 7/1/97.

[10]*(10) Eligible work incentive employees.* The term "eligible work incentive employee" means an individual who has been certified by the designated local agency as being eligible for financial assistance under part A of title IV of the Social Security Act and as having continually received such financial assistance during the 90-day period which immediately precedes the date on which such individual is hired by the employer.

[11]*(11) Designated local agency.* The term "designated local agency" means a State employment security agency established in accordance with the Act of June 6, 1933, as amended (29 U.S.C. 4949n).

[12]*(12) Special rules for certifications.*

(A) In general. An individual shall not be treated as a member of a targeted group unless—

(i) on or before the day on which such individual begins work for the employer, the employer has received a certification from a designated local agency that such individual is a member of a targeted group, or

(ii) (I) on or before the day the individual is offered employment with the employer, a pre-screening notice is completed by the employer with aspect to such individual, and

(II) not later than the 21st day after the individual begins work for the employer, the employer submits such notice, signed by the employer and the individual under penalties of perjury, to the designated local agency as part of a written request for such a certification from such agency.

For purposes of this paragraph, the term "pre-screening notice" means a document (in such form as the Secretary shall prescribe) which contains information provided by the individual on the basis of which the employer believes that the individual is a member of a targeted group.

(B) Incorrect certifications. If—

(i) an individual has been certified by a designated local agency as a member of a targeted group, and

(ii) such certification is incorrect because it was based on false information provided by such individual,

the certification shall be revoked and wages paid by the employer after the date on which notice of revocation is received by the employer shall not be treated as qualified wages.

(C) Explanation of denial of request. If a designated local agency denies a request for certification of membership in a targeted group, such agency shall provide to the person making such request a written explanation of the reasons for such denial.

* * * * * * * * * *

(i) Certain individuals ineligible.

* * * * * * * * * * * * *

[13]*(3) Individuals not meeting minimum employment periods.*

(A) Reduction of credit for individuals performing fewer than 400 hours of services. In the case of an individual who has completed at least 120 hours, but less than 400 hours, of service for the employer, subsection (a) shall be applied by substituting "25 percent" for "40 percent".

(B) Denial of credit for individuals performing fewer than 120 hours of services. No wages shall be taken into account under subsection (a) with respect to any individual unless such individual has completed at least 120 hours of services performed for the employer.

* * * * * * * * * * * *

[For analysis, see ¶ 702. For text of Committee Report see ¶ 5038.]

[Endnote Code Sec. 51]

Matter in *italics* in Code Sec. 51(a), Code Sec. 51(c)(4)(B), Code Sec. 51(d)(1)(F), Code Sec. 51(d)(1)(G), Code Sec. 51(d)(1)(H), Code Sec. 51(d)(2)(A), Code Sec. 51(d)(3)(A), Code Sec. 51(d)(9), Code Sec. 51(d)(10), Code Sec. 51(d)(11), Code Sec. 51(d)(12) and Code Sec. 51(i)(3) added by Sec. 603(a)-(d) of the Taxpayer Relief Act of 1997, H.R. 2014, 8/5/97, which struck out:

1. "35 percent"
2. "September 30, 1997"
3. "or"
4. "."
5. added subpara. (d)(1)(H)
6. "for at least a 9-month period ending during the 9-month period ending on the hiring date."
7. "(A) In general. The term 'qualified veteran' means any veteran who is certified by the designated local agency as being—

"(i) a member of a family receiving assistance under a IV-A program (as defined in paragraph (2)(B)) for at least a 9-month period ending during the 12-month period ending on the hiring date, or

"(ii) a member of a family receiving assistance under a food stamp program under the Food Stamp Act of 1977 for at least a 3-month period ending during the 12-month period ending on the hiring date."
8. added para. (d)(9)
9. "(9)"
10. "(9)"
11. "(10)"
12. "(11)"
13. "(3) Individuals not meeting minimum employment period. No wages shall be taken into account under subsection (a) with respect to any individual unless such individual either—

"(A) is employed by the employer at least 180 days (20 days in the case of a qualified summer youth employee), or

"(B) has completed at least 400 hours (120 hours in the case of a qualified summer youth employee) of services performed for the employer."

Effective Date (Sec. 603(e), H.R. 2014, 8/5/97) effective for individuals who begin. work for the employer after 9/30/97.

[¶ 3013]   Code Sec.[1] 51A.

CAUTION.   Code Sec. 51A, following, is effective for individuals who begin work for the employer after 12/31/97.

Temporary incentives for employing long-term family assistance recipients.

(a) **Determination of amount.** For purposes of section 38, the amount of the welfare-to-work credit determined under this section for the taxable year shall be equal to—

(1) 35 percent of the qualified first-year wages for such year, and

(2) 50 percent of the qualified second-year wages for such year.

(b) **Qualified wages defined.** For purposes of this section—

(1) **In general.** The term "qualified wages" means the wages paid or incurred by the employer during the taxable year to individuals who are long-term family assistance recipients.

(2) **Qualified first-year wages.** The term "qualified first-year wages" means, with respect to any individual, qualified wages attributable to service rendered during the 1-year period beginning with the day the individual begins work for the employer.

(3) **Qualified second-year wages.** The term "qualified second-year wages" means, with respect to any individual, qualified wages attributable to service rendered during the 1-year period beginning on the day after the last day of the 1-year period with respect to such individual determined under paragraph (2).

(4) **Only the first $10,000 of wages per year taken into account.** The amount of the qualified first-year wages, and the amount of qualified second-year wages, which may be taken into account with respect to any individual shall not exceed $10,000 per year.

(5) **Wages.**

(A) In general. The term "wages" has the meaning given such term by section 51(c), without regard to paragraph (4) thereof.

(B) Certain amounts treated as wages. The term "wages" includes amounts paid or incurred by the employer which are excludable from such recipient's gross income under—

(i) section 105 (relating to amounts received under accident and health plans),

(ii) section 106 (relating to contributions by employer to accident and health plans),

(iii) section 127 (relating to educational assistance programs) or would be so excludable but for section 127(d), but only to the extent paid or incurred to a person not related to the employer, or

(iv) section 129 (relating to dependent care assistance programs).

The amount treated as wages by clause (i) or (ii) for any period shall be based on the reasonable cost of coverage for the period, but shall not exceed the applicable premium for the period under section 4980B(f)(4).

(C) Special rules for agricultural and railway labor. If such recipient is an employee to whom subparagraph (A) or (B) of section 51(h)(1) applies, rules similar to the rules of such subparagraphs shall apply except that—

(i) such subparagraph (A) shall be applied by substituting "$10,000" for "$6,000", and

(ii) such subparagraph (B) shall be applied by substituting "$833.33" for "$500".

(c) **Long-term family assistance recipients.** For purposes of this section—

(1) **In general.** The term "long-term family assistance recipient" means any individual who is certified by the designated local agency (as defined in section 51(d)(10))—

(A) as being a member of a family receiving assistance under a IV-A program (as defined in section 51(d)(2)(B)) for at least the 18-month period ending on the hiring date,

(B)

(i) as being a member of a family receiving such assistance for 18 months beginning after the date of the enactment of this section, and

(ii) as having a hiring date which is not more than 2 years after the end of the earliest such 18-month period, or

(C)

(i) as being a member of a family which ceased to be eligible after the date of the enactment of this section for such assistance by reason of any limitation imposed by Federal or State law on the maximum period such assistance is payable to a family, and

(ii) as having a hiring date which is not more than 2 years after the date of such cessation.

(2) Hiring date. The term "hiring date" has the meaning given such term by section 51(d).

(d) Certain rules to apply.

(1) In general. Rules similar to the rules of section 52, and subsections (d)(11), (f), (g), (i) (as in effect on the day before the date of the enactment of the Taxpayer Relief Act of 1997), (j), and (k) of section 51, shall apply for purposes of this section.

(2) Credit to be part of general business credit, etc. References to section 51 in section 38(b), 280C(a), and 1396(c)(3) shall be treated as including references to this section.

(e) Coordination with work opportunity credit. If a credit is allowed under this section to an employer with respect to an individual for any taxable year, then for purposes of applying section 51 to such employer, such individual shall not be treated as a member of a targeted group for such taxable year.

(f) Termination. This section shall not apply to individuals who begin work for the employer after April 30, 1999.

[For analysis, see ¶ 704. For text of Committee Report see ¶ 5050.]

[Endnote Code Sec. 51A]

Code Sec. 51A was added by Sec. 801(a) of the Taxpayer Relief Act of 1997, H.R. 2014, 8/5/97.

1. added Code Sec. 51A

Effective Date (Sec. 801(c), H.R. 2014, 8/5/97) effective for individuals who begin work for the employer after 12/31/97.

[¶ 3014]   Code Sec. 52.   Special rules.

* * * * * * * * * * * *

(c) Tax-exempt organizations. No credit shall be allowed under section 38 for any [1]*work opportunity credit* determined under this subpart to any organization (other than a cooperative described in section 521) which is exempt from income tax under this chapter.

* * * * * * * * * * * *

[Endnote Code Sec. 52]

Matter in *italics* in Code Sec. 52(c) added by Sec. 1601(b) of the Taxpayer Relief Act of 1997, H.R. 2014, 8/5/97, which struck out:

1. "targeted jobs credit"

Effective Date (Sec. 1601(j)(1), H.R. 2014, 8/5/97) effective for individuals who begin work for the employer after 9/30/96.

[¶ 3015]   Code Sec. 55.   Alternative minimum tax imposed.

* * * * * * * * * * * *

(b) Tentative minimum tax. For purposes of this part—

* * * * * * * * * * * *

(1) Amount of tentative tax.

(A) Noncorporate taxpayers.

* * * * * * * * * * * *

(ii) **Taxable excess.** For purposes of [1]*this subsection,* the term "taxable excess" means so much of the alternative minimum taxable income for the taxable year as exceeds the exemption amount.

* * * * * * * * * * * *

[2]*(3) **Maximum rate of tax on net capital gain of noncorporate taxpayers.** The amount determined under the first sentence of paragraph (1)(A)(i) shall not exceed the sum of—*

(A) the amount determined under such first sentence computed at the rates and in the same manner as if this paragraph had not been enacted on the taxable excess reduced by the lesser of—

(i) the net capital gain, or

(ii) the sum of—

(I) the adjusted net capital gain, plus

(II) "(II) the unrecaptured section 1250 gain, plus

(B) 25 percent of the lesser of—

(i) the unrecaptured section 1250 gain, or

(ii) the amount of taxable excess in excess of the sum of—

(I) the adjusted net capital gain, plus

(II) the amount on which a tax is determined under subparagraph (A), plus

(C) 10 percent of so much of the taxpayer's adjusted net capital gain (or, if less, taxable excess) as does not exceed the amount on which a tax is determined under section 1(h)(1)(D), plus

(D) 20 percent of the taxpayer's adjusted net capital gain (or, if less, taxable excess) in excess of the amount on which tax is determined under subparagraph (C).

In the case of taxable years beginning after December 31, 2000, rules similar to the rules of section 1(h)(2) shall apply for purposes of subparagraphs (C) and (D). Terms used in this paragraph which are also used in section 1(h) shall have the respective meanings given such terms by section 1(h).

(c) Regular tax.

CAUTION. Para. (c)(1), following, is effective for tax. yrs. begin. before 1/1/2000 [as amended by Sec. 1601(b)(2)(A), of this Act, see below]. For para. (c)(1) effective for tax. yrs. begin. after 12/31/99, see below. For transitional rules, see Sec. 1401(c)(2), of this Act, reproduced in note following Code Sec. 55.

(1) In general. For purposes of this section, the term "regular tax" means the regular tax liability for the taxable year (as defined in section 26(b)) reduced by the foreign tax credit allowable under section 27(a), the section 936 credit allowable under section 27(b), and the [3]*Puerto Rico* economic activity credit under section 30A. Such term shall not include any tax imposed by section 402(d) and shall not include any increase in tax under section 49(b) or 50(a) or subsection (j) or (k) of section 42.

CAUTION. Para. (c)(1), following, is effective for tax. yrs. begin. after 12/31/99 [as amended by Sec. 1601(b)(2)(A), of this Act, see below]. For transitional rules, see Sec. 1401(c)(2), of this Act, reproduced in note following Code Sec. 55. For para. (c)(1) effective for tax. yrs. begin. before 1/1/2000, see above.

(1) In general. For purposes of this section, the term "regular tax" means the regular tax liability for the taxable year (as defined in section 26(b)) reduced by the foreign tax credit allowable under section 27(a), the section 936 credit allowable under section 27(b), and the [3]*Puerto Rico* economic activity credit under section 30A. Such term shall not include any increase in tax under section 49(b) or 50(a) or subsection (j) or (k) of section 42.

* * * * * * * * * * *

CAUTION. Subsec. (e), following, is effective for tax. yrs. begin. after 12/31/97.

[4](e) *Exemption for small corporations.*

(1) In general. The tentative minimum tax of a corporation shall be zero for any taxable year if—

(A) such corporation met the $5,000,000 gross receipts test of section 448(c) for its first taxable year beginning after December 31, 1996, and

(B) such corporation would meet such test for the taxable year and all prior taxable years beginning after such first taxable year if such test were applied by substituting "$7,500,000" for "$5,000,000".

(2) Prospective application of minimum tax if small corporation ceases to be small. In the case of a corporation whose tentative minimum tax is zero for any prior taxable year by reason of paragraph (1), the application of this part for taxable years beginning with the first taxable year such corporation ceases to be described in paragraph (1) shall be determined with the following modifications:

(A) Section 56(a)(1) (relating to depreciation) and section 56(a)(5) (relating to pollution control facilities) shall apply only to property placed in service on or after the change date.

(B) Section 56(a)(2) (relating to mining exploration and development costs) shall apply only to costs paid or incurred on or after the change date.

(C) Section 56(a)(3) (relating to treatment of long-term contracts) shall apply only to contracts entered into on or after the change date.

(D) Section 56(a)(4) (relating to alternative net operating loss deduction) shall apply in the same manner as if, in section 56(d)(2), the change date were substituted for "January 1, 1987" and the day before the change date were substituted for "December 31, 1986" each place it appears.

(E) Section 56(g)(2)(B) (relating to limitation on allowance of negative adjustments based on adjusted current earnings) shall apply only to prior taxable years beginning on or after the change date.

(F) Section 56(g)(4)(A) (relating to adjustment for depreciation to adjusted current earnings) shall not apply.

(G) Subparagraphs (D) and (F) of section 56(g)(4) (relating to other earnings and profits adjustments and depletion) shall apply in the same manner as if the day before the change date were substituted for "December 31, 1989" each place it appears therein.

(3) Exception. The modifications in paragraph (2) shall not apply to—

(A) any item acquired by the corporation in a transaction to which section 381 applies, and

(B) any property the basis of which in the hands of the corporation is determined by reference to the basis of the property in the hands of the transferor,

if such item or property was subject to any provision referred to in paragraph (2) while held by the transferor.

(4) Change date. For purposes of paragraph (2), the change date is the first day of the first taxable year for which   the taxpayer ceases to be described in paragraph (1).

(5) Limitation on use of credit for prior year minimum tax liability. In the case of a taxpayer whose tentative minimum tax for any taxable year is zero by reason of paragraph (1), section 53(c) shall be applied for such year by reducing the amount otherwise taken into account under section 53(c)(1) by 25 percent of so much of such amount as exceeds $25,000. Rules similar to the rules of section 38(c)(3)(B) shall apply for purposes of the preceding sentence.

[For analysis, see ¶s 601, 602. For text of Committee Report see ¶s 5019, 5023.]

[Endnote Code Sec. 55]

Matter in *italics* in Code Sec. 55(b)(1)(A)(ii) and Code Sec. 55(b)(3) added by Sec. 311(b)(1) and (2)(A) of the Taxpayer Relief Act of 1997, H.R. 2014, 8/5/97, which struck out:

1. "clause (i)"
2. added para. (b)(3)

Effective Date (Sec. 311(d)(1), H.R. 2014, 8/5/97) effective for tax. yrs. end. after 5/6/97.

Matter in *italics* in Code Sec. 55(c)(1) added by Sec. 1601(f)(1)(C), H.R. 2014, 8/5/97, which struck out:

3. "Puerto Rican"

Effective Date (Sec. 1601(j)(1), H.R. 2014, 8/5/97) effective for tax. yrs. begin. after 12/31/95. For special rules, see Sec. 1601(c)(2)-(3), of the Small Job Business Protection Act of 1996, P.L. 104-188, 8/20/96, which reads as follows:

"(2) Special rule for qualified possession source investment income. The amendments made by this section shall not apply to qualified possession source investment income received or accrued before July 1, 1996, without regard to the taxable year in which received or accrued.

"(3) Special transition rule for payment of estimated tax installments. In determining the amount of any installment due under section 6655 of the Internal Revenue Code of 1986 after the date of the enactment of this Act and before October 1, 1996, only ½ of any increase in tax (for the taxable year for which such installment is made) by reason of the amendments made by subsections (a) and (b) shall be taken into account. Any reduction in such installment by reason of the preceding sentence shall be recaptured by increasing the next required installment for such year by the amount of such reduction."

Code Sec. 55(e) in *italics* was added by Sec. 401(a), H.R. 2014, 8/5/97.
  4. added subsec. (e)
Effective Date (Sec. 401(b), H.R. 2014, 8/5/97) effective for tax. yrs. begin. after 12/31/97

[¶ 3016]   Code Sec. 56.   Adjustments in computing alternative minimum taxable income.

(a) **Adjustments applicable to all taxpayers.** In determining the amount of the alternative minimum taxable income for any taxable year the following treatment shall apply (in lieu of the treatment applicable for purposes of computing the regular tax):

(1) **Depreciation.**

(A) In general.

(i) Property other than certain personal property. Except as provided in clause (ii), the depreciation deduction allowable under section 167 with respect to any tangible property placed in service after December 31, 1986, shall be determined under the alternative system of section 168(g). [1]*In the case of property placed in service after December 31, 1998, the preceding sentence shall not apply but clause (ii) shall continue to apply.*

* * * * * * * * * * *

* * * * * * * * * * *

(5) **Pollution control facilities.** In the case of any certified pollution control facility placed in service after December 31, 1986, the deduction allowable under section 169 (without regard to section 291) shall be determined under the alternative system of section 168(g). [2]*In the case of such a facility placed in service after December 31, 1998, such deduction shall be determined under section 168 using the straight line method.*

[3](6) **Adjusted basis.** The adjusted basis of any property to which paragraph (1) or (5) applies (or with respect to which there are any expenditures to which paragraph (2) or subsection (b)(2) applies) shall be determined on the basis of the treatment prescribed in paragraph (1), (2), or (5), or subsection (b)(2), whichever applies.

[4](7) **Section 87 not applicable.** Section 87 (relating to alcohol fuel credit) shall not apply.

* * * * * * * * * * *

(e) **Qualified housing interest.** For purposes of this part—

(1) **In general.** The term "qualified housing interest" means interest which is qualified residence interest (as defined in section 163(h)(3)) and is paid or accrued during the taxable year on indebtedness which is incurred in acquiring, constructing, or substantially improving any property which—

(A) is the principal residence (within the meaning of [5]*section 121*) of the taxpayer at the time such interest accrues, or

(B) is a qualified dwelling which is a qualified residence (within the meaning of section 163(h)(4)).

Such term also includes interest on any indebtedness resulting from the refinancing of indebtedness meeting the requirements of the preceding sentence; but only to the extent that the amount of the indebtedness resulting from such refinancing does not exceed the amount of the refinanced indebtedness immediately before the refinancing.

* * * * * * * * * * *

(3) Special rule for indebtedness incurred before July 1, 1982. The term "qualified housing interest" includes interest which is qualified residence interest (as defined in section 163(h)(3)) and is paid or accrued on indebtedness which—

* * * * * * * * * * *

(B) is secured by property which, at the time such indebtedness was incurred, was—

(i) the principal residence (within the meaning of [6]*section 121*) of the taxpayer, or

(ii) a qualified dwelling used by the taxpayer (or any member of his family (within the meaning of section 267(c)(4))).

* * * * * * * * * * *

(g) Adjustments based on adjusted current earnings.

* * * * * * * * * * *

(4) Adjustments. In determining adjusted current earnings, the following adjustments shall apply:

(B) Inclusion of items included for purposes of computing earnings and profits.

CAUTION. Clause (g)(4)(B)(i), following, is effective for tax. yrs. begin. before 1/1/98. For clause (g)(4)(B)(i), effective for tax. yrs. begin. after 12/31/97, see below.

(i) In general. In the case of any amount which is excluded from gross income for purposes of computing alternative minimum taxable income but is taken into account in determining the amount of earnings and profits—

(I) such amount shall be included in income in the same manner as if such amount were includible in gross income for purposes of computing alternative minimum taxable income, and

(II) the amount of such income shall be reduced by any deduction which would have been allowable in computing alternative minimum taxable income if such amount were includible in gross income.

The preceding sentence shall not apply in the case of any amount excluded from gross income under section 108 (or the corresponding provisions of prior law).

CAUTION. Clause (g)(4)(B)(i), following, is effective for tax. yrs. begin. after 12/31/97. For clause (g)(4)(B)(i), effective for tax. yrs. begin. before 1/1/98, see above.

(i) In general. In the case of any amount which is excluded from gross income for purposes of computing alternative minimum taxable income but is taken into account in determining the amount of earnings and profits—

(I) such amount shall be included in income in the same manner as if such amount were includible in gross income for purposes of computing alternative minimum taxable income, and

(II) the amount of such income shall be reduced by any deduction which would have been allowable in computing alternative minimum taxable income if such amount were includible in gross income.

The preceding sentence shall not apply in the case of any amount excluded from gross income under section 108 (or the corresponding provisions of prior law). [7]*In the case of any insurance company taxable under section 831(b), this clause shall not apply to any amount not described in section 834(b).*

* * * * * * * * * * *

[For analysis, see ¶ 606, ¶ 607, ¶ 610, and ¶ 611. For text of Committee Report see ¶s 5024, 5025, 5207.]

[Endnote Code Sec. 56]

Matter in *italics* in Code Sec. 56(a)(1)(A)(i) and Code Sec. 56(a)(5) added by Sec. 402(a) and (b) of the Taxpayer Relief Act of 1997, H.R. 2014, 8/5/97.

1. added matter in clause (a)(1)(A)(i)
2. added matter in para. (a)(5)

Effective Date Effective 8/5/97.

Matter in *italics* in Code Sec. 56(a)(6), Code Sec. 56(a)(7) added by Sec. 403(a), H.R. 2014, 8/5/97, which struck out:

3. "(6) Installment sales of certain property.

" In the case of any disposition after March 1, 1986, of any property described in section 1221(1), income from such disposition shall be determined without regard to the installment method under section 453. This paragraph shall not apply to any disposition with respect to which an election is in effect under section 453(1)(2)(B)."

"(7)"

4. "(8)"

Effective Date (Sec. 403(b), H.R. 2014, 8/5/97) effective for dispositions in tax. yrs. begin. after 12/31/97, except as provided in Sec. 403(b)(2) of this Act, which reads as follows:

"(2) Special rule for 1987.— In the case of taxable years beginning in 1987, the last sentence of section 56(a)(6) of the Internal Revenue Code of 1986 (as in effect for such taxable years) shall be applied by inserting 'or in the case of a taxpayer using the cash receipts and disbursements method of accounting, any disposition described in section 453C(e)(1)(B)(ii)' after 'section 453C(e)(4)."

Matter in *italics* in Code Sec. 56(e)(1)(A) and Code Sec. 56(e)(3)(B)(i) added by Sec. 312(d)(1) of the, H.R. 2014, 8/5/97, which struck out:

5. "section 1034"

6. "section 1034"

Effective Date (Sec. 312(d)[sic (e)], H.R. 2014, 8/5/97) effective for sales and exchanges after 5/6/97, except as provided in Secs. 312(d)(2)-(4) [sic (e)(2)-(4)], which read as follows:

"(2) Sales before 8/5/97. At the election of the taxpayer, the amendments made by this section shall not apply to any sale or exchange before the date of the enactment of this Act.

"(3) Certain sales within 2 years after 8/5/97. Section 121 of the Internal Revenue Code of 1986 (as amended by this section) shall be applied without regard to subsection (c)(2)(B) thereof in the case of any sale or exchange of property during the 2-year period beginning on the date of the enactment of this Act if the taxpayer held such property on the date of the enactment of this Act and fails to meet the ownership and use requirements of subsection (a) thereof with respect to such property.

"(4) Binding contracts. At the election of the taxpayer, the amendments made by this section shall not apply to a sale or exchange after the date of the enactment of this Act, if—

"(A) such sale or exchange is pursuant to a contract which was binding on such date, or

"(B) without regard to such amendments, gain would not be recognized under section 1034 of the Internal Revenue Code of 1986 (as in effect on the day before the date of the enactment of this Act) on such sale or exchange by reason of a new residence acquired on or before such date or with respect to the acquisition of which by the taxpayer a binding contract was in effect on such date.

This paragraph shall not apply to any sale or exchange by an individual if the treatment provided by section 877(a)(1) of the Internal Revenue Code of 1986 applies to such individual."

Matter in *italics* in Code Sec. 56(g)(4)(B)(i) added by Sec. 1212(a), H.R. 2014, 8/5/97.

7. added matter in clause (g)(4)(B)(i)

Effective Date (Sec. 1212(b), H.R. 2014, 8/5/97) effective for tax. yrs. begin. after 12/31/97.

[¶ 3017]   Code Sec. 57.   Items of tax preference.

(a) **General rule.** For purposes of this part, the items of tax preference determined under this section are—

* * * * * * * * * * *

(7) **Exclusion for gains on sale of certain small business stock.** An amount equal to [1]*42 percent* of the amount excluded from gross income for the taxable year under section 1202.

* * * * * * * * * * * *

[For analysis, see ¶ 605. For text of Committee Report see ¶ 5019.]

[Endnote Code Sec. 57]

Matter in *italics* in Code Sec. 57(a)(7) added by Sec. 311(b)(2)(B) of the Taxpayer Relief Act of 1997, H.R. 2014, 8/5/97, which struck out:

1. "one-half"

Effective Date (Sec. 311(d)(1), H.R. 2014, 8/5/97) effective for tax. yrs. end. after 5/6/97.

[¶ 3018]   Code Sec. 59.   Other definitions and special rules.

(a) **Alternative minimum tax foreign tax credit.** For purposes of this part—

* * * * * * * * * * *

(2) Limitation to 90 percent of tax.

* * * * * * * * * * * *

(C) [1]Repealed.

* * * * * * * * * * * *

CAUTION.   Para. (a)(3) [sic (4)], following, is effective for tax. yrs. begin. after 12/31/97.

[2]**(3) [sic (4)] Election to use simplified section 904 limitation.**

(A) In general. In determining the alternative minimum tax foreign tax credit for any taxable year to which an election under this paragraph applies—

(i) subparagraph (B) of paragraph (1) shall not apply, and

(ii) the limitation of section 904 shall be based on the proportion which—

(I) the taxpayer's taxable income (as determined for purposes of the regular tax) from sources without the United States (but not in excess of the taxpayer's entire alternative minimum taxable income), bears to

(II) the taxpayer's entire alternative minimum taxable income for the taxable year.

(B) Election.

(i) In general. An election under this paragraph may be made only for the taxpayer's first taxable year which begins after December 31, 1997, and for which the taxpayer claims an alternative minimum tax foreign tax credit.

(ii) Election revocable only with consent. An election under this paragraph, once made, shall apply to the taxable year for which made and all subsequent taxable years unless revoked with the consent of the Secretary.

* * * * * * * * * * *

CAUTION.   Subsec. (j), following, is effective for tax. yrs. begin. before 1/1/98. For subsec. (j), effective for tax. yrs. begin. after 12/31/97, see below.

(j) Treatment of unearned income of minor children.

(1) Limitation on exempt amount. In the case of a child to whom section 1(g) applies, the exemption amount for purposes of section 55 shall not exceed the sum of—

(A) such child's earned income (as defined in section 911(d)(2)) for the taxable year, plus

(B) twice the amount in effect for the taxable year under section 63(c)(5)(A) (or, if greater, the child's share of the unused parental minimum tax exemption).

(2) Limitation based on parental minimum tax.

(A) In general. In the case of a child to whom section 1(g) applies, the amount of the tax imposed by section 55 shall not exceed such child's share of the allocable parental minimum tax.

(B) Allocable parental minimum tax. For purposes of this paragraph, the term "allocable parental minimum tax" means the excess of—

(i) the tax which would be imposed by section 55 on the parent if—

(I) the amount of the parent's tentative minimum tax were increased by the aggregate of the tentative minimum taxes of all children of the parent to whom section 1(g) applies, and

(II) the amount of the parent's regular tax were increased by the aggregate of the regular taxes of all children of the parent to whom section 1(g) applies, over

(ii) the tax imposed by section 55 on the parent without regard to this subparagraph.

(C) Child share. A child's share of any allocable parental minimum tax shall be determined under rules similar to the rules of section 1(g)(3)(B).

(D) Other rules made applicable. For purposes of this paragraph, rules similar to the rules of paragraphs (3)(D), (5), and (6) of section 1(g) shall apply.

(3) Unused parental minimum tax exemption.

(A) In general. For purposes of this subsection, the term "unused parental minimum tax exemption" means the excess (if any) of—

(i) the exemption amount applicable to the parent under section 55(d), over

(ii) the parent's alternative minimum taxable income.

(B) Certain rules made applicable. A child's share of any unused parental minimum tax exemption shall be determined under rules similar to the rules of section 1(g)(3)(B), and rules similar to the rules of paragraphs (3)(D) and (5) of section 1(g) shall apply for purposes of this paragraph.

CAUTION.   Subsec. (j), following, is effective for tax. yrs. begin. after 12/31/97. For subsec. (j), effective for tax. yrs. begin. before 1/1/98, see above.

³*(j) Treatment of unearned income of minor children.*

(1) In general. In the case of a child to whom section 1(g) applies, the exemption amount for purposes of section 55 shall not exceed the sum of—

(A) such child's earned income (as defined in section 911(d)(2)) for the taxable year, plus

(B) $5,000.

(2) Inflation adjustment. In the case of any taxable year beginning in a calendar year after 1998, the dollar amount in paragraph (1)(B) shall be increased by an amount equal to the product of—

(A) such dollar amount, and

(B) the cost-of-living adjustment determined under section 1(f)(3) for the calendar year in which the taxable year begins, determined by substituting "1997" for "1992" in subparagraph (B) thereof.

If any increase determined under the preceding sentence is not a multiple of $50, such increase shall be rounded to the nearest multiple of $50.

[For analysis, see ¶s 604, 608, 609. For text of Committee Report see ¶s 5149, 5172, 5201.]

[Endnote Code Sec. 59]

Code Sec. 59(a)(2)(C) was deleted by Sec. 1057(a) of the Taxpayer Relief Act of 1997, H.R. 2014, 8/5/97, which struck out:

1. "(C) Exception. Subparagraph (A) shall not apply to any domestic corporation if—

"(i) more than 50 percent of the stock of such domestic corporation (by vote and value) is owned by United States persons who are not members of an affiliated group (as defined in section 1504 of such Code) which includes such corporation,

"(ii) all of the activities of such corporation are conducted in 1 foreign country with which the United States has an income tax treaty in effect and such treaty provides for the exchange of information between such foreign country and the United States,

"(iii) all of the current earnings and profits of such corporation are distributed at least annually (other than current earnings and profits retained for normal maintenance or capital replacements or improvements of an existing business), and

"(iv) all of such distributions by such corporation to United States persons are used by such persons in a trade or business conducted in the United States."

Effective Date (Sec. 1057(b), H.R. 2014, 8/5/97) effective for tax. yrs. begin. after 8/5/97.

Code Sec. 59(a)(3) [sic (4)], in *italics*, was added by Sec. 1103(a), H.R. 2014, 8/5/97.

2. added paragraph (a)(3) [sic (4)]

Effective Date (Sec. 1103(b), H.R. 2014, 8/5/97) effective for tax. yrs. begin. after 12/31/97.

Matter in *italics* in Code Sec. 59(j) added by Sec. 1201(b), H.R. 2014, 8/5/97, which struck out:

3. "(j) Treatment of unearned income of minor children.

"(1) Limitation on exemption amount. In the case of a child to whom section 1(g) applies, the exemption amount for purposes of section 55 shall not exceed the sum of—

"(A) such child's earned income (as defined in section 911(d)(2)) for the taxable year, plus

"(B) twice the amount in effect for the taxable year under section 63(c)(5)(A) (or, if greater, the child's share of the unused parental minimum tax exemption).

"(2) Limitation based on parental minimum tax.

"(A) In general. In the case of a child to whom section 1(g) applies, the amount of the tax imposed by section 55 shall not exceed such child's share of the allocable parental minimum tax.

"(B) Allocable parental minimum tax. For purposes of this paragraph, the term 'allocable parental minimum tax' means the excess of—

"(i) the tax which would be imposed by section 55 on the parent if—

"(I) the amount of the parent's tentative minimum tax were increased by the aggregate of the tentative minimum taxes of all children of the parent to whom section 1(g) applies, and

"(II) the amount of the parent's regular tax were increased by the aggregate of the regular taxes of all children of the parent to whom section 1(g) applies, over

"(ii) the tax imposed by section 55 on the parent without regard to this subparagraph.

"(C) Child share. A child's share of any allocable parental minimum tax shall be determined under rules similar to the rules of section 1(g)(3)(B).

"(D) Other rules made applicable. For purposes of this paragraph, rules similar to the rules of paragraphs (3)(D), (5), and (6) of section 1(g) shall apply.

"(3) Unused parental minimum tax exemption.

"(A) In general. For purposes of this subsection, the term 'unused parental minimum tax exemption' means the excess (if any) of—

"(i) the exemption amount applicable to the parent under section 55(d), over

"(ii) the parent's alternative minimum taxable income.

"(B) Certain rules made applicable. A child's share of any unused parental minimum tax exemption shall be determined under rules similar to the rules of section 1(g)(3)(B), and rules similar to the rules of paragraphs (3)(D) and (5) of section 1(g) shall apply for purposes of this paragraph."

Effective Date (Sec. 1201(c), H.R. 2014, 8/5/97) effective for tax. yrs. begin. after 12/31/97.

[¶ 3019] Code Sec. 62.   Adjusted gross income defined.

(a) **General rule.** For purposes of this subtitle, the term "adjusted gross income" means, in the case of an individual, gross income minus the following deductions:

* * * * * * * * * * * *

(2) **Certain trade and business deductions of employees.**

* * * * * * * * * * * *

[1]*(C) Certain expenses of officials. The deductions allowed by section 162 which consist of expenses paid or incurred with respect to services performed by an official as an employee of a State or a political subdivision thereof in a position compensated in whole or in part on a fee basis.*

* * * * * * * * * * *

[2]*(17) Interest on education loans. The deduction allowed by section 221.*

Nothing in this section shall permit the same item to be deducted more than once.

* * * * * * * * * * *

[For analysis, see ¶s 116, 402. For text of Committee Report see ¶s 5003, 5098.]

[Endnote Code Sec. 62]

Code Sec. 62(a)(2)(C), in *italics*, was added by Sec. 975(a) the Taxpayer Relief Act of 1997, H.R. 2014, 8/5/97.

1. added subpara. (a)(2)(C)

Effective Date (Sec. 975(b), H.R. 2014, 8/5/97) effective for expenses paid or incurred in tax. yrs. begin. after 12/31/86.

Code Sec. 62(a)(17), in *italics*, was added by Sec. 202(b) of H.R. 2014, 8/5/97.

2. added para. (a)(17)

Effective Date (Sec. 202(e), H.R. 2014, 8/5/97) effective for any qualified education loan, as defined by Code Sec. 221(d), with respect to Sec. 202(e)(1) and (2) of this Act, which read as follows:

"(1) any loan interest payment due and paod after December 31, 1997, and

"(2) the portion of the 60-month period referred to in section 221(d) of the Internal Revenue Code of 1986 (as added by this section) after December 31, 1997."

[¶ 3020] Code Sec. 63.   Taxable income defined.

* * * * * * * * * * *

(c) **Standard deduction.** For purposes of this subtitle—

* * * * * * * * * * * *

CAUTION.   Paras. (c)(4) and (5), following, are effective for tax. yrs. begin. before 1/1/98. For paras. (c)(4) and (5), effective for tax. yrs. begin. after 12/31/97, see below.

(4) Adjustments for inflation. In the case of any taxable year beginning in a calendar year after 1988, each dollar amount contained in paragraph (2) or (5)(A) or subsection (f) shall be increased by an amount equal to—

(A) such dollar amount, multiplied by

(B) the cost-of-living adjustment determined under section 1(f)(3) for the calendar year in which the taxable year begins, by substituting "calendar year 1987" for "calendar year 1992 " in subparagraph (B) thereof.

(5) Limitation on basic standard deduction in the case of certain dependents. In the case of an individual with respect to whom a deduction under section 151 is allowable to another taxpayer for a taxable year beginning in the calendar year in which the individual's taxable year begins, the basic standard deduction applicable to such individual for such individual's taxable year shall not exceed the greater of—

(A) $500, or

(B) such individual's earned income.

CAUTION.   Paras. (c)(4) and (5), following, are effective for tax. yrs. begin. after 12/31/97. For paras. (c)(4) and (5), effective for tax. yrs. begin. before 1/1/98, see above.

(4) Adjustments for inflation. In the case of any taxable year beginning in a calendar year after 1988, each dollar amount contained in paragraph (2) or [1](5) or subsection (f) shall be increased by an amount equal to—

(A) such dollar amount, multiplied by

(B) the cost-of-living adjustment determined under section 1(f)(3) for the calendar year in which the taxable year begins, [2]*by substituting "calendar year 1992" in subparagraph (B) thereof—*

(i) *"calendar year 1987" in the case of the dollar amounts contained in paragraph (2) of (5)(A) or subsection (f), and*

(ii) *"calendar year 1997" in the case of the dollar amount contained in paragraph (5)(B).*

(5) Limitation on basic standard deduction in the case of certain dependents. In the case of an individual with respect to whom a deduction under section 151 is allowable to another taxpayer for a taxable year beginning in the calendar year in which the individual's taxable year begins, the basic standard deduction applicable to such individual for such individual's taxable year [3]*shall not exceed the greater of—*

(A) *$500, or*

(B) *the sum of $250 and such individual's earned income.*

* * * * * * * * * * * *

[For analysis, see ¶ 113. For text of Committee Report see ¶ 5201.]

[Endnote Code Sec. 63]

Matter in *italics* in Code Sec. 63(c)(4), Code Sec. 63(c)(4)(B) and Code Sec. 63(c)(5) added by Sec. 1201(a)(1), and (2) of the Taxpayer Relief Act of 1997, H.R. 2014, 8/5/97, which struck out:

1. "(5)(A)"

2. "by substituting 'calendar year 1987' for 'calendar year 1992' in subparagraph (B) thereof."

3. "shall not exceed the greater of—

"(A) $500, or

"(B) such individual's earned income."

Effective Date (Sec. 1201(c), H.R. 2014, 8/5/97) effective for tax. yrs. begin. after 12/31/97.

[¶ 3021] Code Sec. 72.   Annuities; certain proceeds of endowment and life insurance contracts.

* * * * * * * * * *

(d) **Special rules for qualified employer retirement plans.**
   (1) **Simplified method of taxing annuity payments.**

* * * * * * * * * * *

   (B) Method of recovering investment in contract.

* * * * * * * * * * *

CAUTION.   Clause (d)(1)(B)(iii), following, is effective for annuity starting dates begin. before 1/1/98. For clause (d)(1)(B)(iii), effective for annuity starting dates begin. after 12/31/97, see below.

   (iii) Number of anticipated payments.

If the age of the primary annuitant on the annuity starting date is:	The number of anticipated payments is:
Not more than 55	360
More than 55 but not more than 60	310
More than 60 but not more than 65	260
More than 65 but not more than 70	210
More than 70	160

CAUTION.   Clause (d)(1)(B)(iii), following, is effective for annuity starting dates begin. after 12/31/97. For clause (d)(1)(B)(iii), effective for annuity starting dates begin. before 1/1/98, see above.

   (iii) Number of anticipated payments. [1]*If the annuity is payable over the life of a single individual, the number of anticipated payments shall be determined as follows:*

If the age of the[2] annuitant on the annuity starting date is:	The number of anticipated payments is:
Not more than 55	360
More than 55 but not more than 60	310
More than 60 but not more than 65	260
More than 65 but not more than 70	210
More than 70	160

CAUTION.   Clause (d)(1)(B)(iv), following, is effective for annuity starting dates begin. after 12/31/97.

   [3]*(iv) Number of anticipated payments where more than one life. If the annuity is payable over the lives of more than 1 individual, the number of anticipated payments shall be determined as follows:*

If the combined ages of annuitants are:	The number is:
Not more than 110	410
More than 110 but not more than 120	360
More than 120 but not more than 130	310
More than 130 but not more than 140	260
More than 140	210.

* * * * * * * * * * * *

931

(t) 10-percent additional tax on early distributions from qualified retirement plans.

* * * * * * * * * * *

(2) Subsection not to apply to certain distributions. Except as provided in paragraphs (3) and (4), paragraph (1) shall not apply to any of the following distributions:

* * * * * * * * * * *

CAUTION. Subpara. (t)(2)(E), following, is effective for distributions after 12/31/97, with respect to expenses paid after such date (in tax. yrs. end. after such date), for education furnished in academic periods begin. after such date.

[4]*(E) Distributions from individual retirement plans for higher education expenses. Distributions to an individual from an individual retirement plan to the extent such distributions do not exceed the qualified higher education expenses (as defined in paragraph (7)) of the taxpayer for the taxable year. Distributions shall not be taken into account under the preceding sentence if such distributions are described in subparagraph (A), (C), or (D) or to the extent paragraph (1) does not apply to such distributions by reason of subparagraph (B).*

CAUTION. Subpara. (t)(2)(F), following, is effective for payments and distributions in tax. yrs. begin. after 12/31/97.

[5]*(F) Distributions from certain plans for first home purchases. Distributions to an individual from an individual retirement plan which are qualified first-time homebuyer distributions (as defined in paragraph (8)). Distributions shall not be taken into account under the preceding sentence if such distributions are described in subparagraph (A), (C), (D), or (E) or to the extent paragraph (1) does not apply to such distributions by reason of subparagraph (B).*

* * * * * * * * * * *

CAUTION. Para. (t)(7), following, is effective for distributions after 12/31/97, with respect to expenses paid after such date (in tax. yrs. end. after such date), for education furnished in academic periods begin. after such date.

[6]*(7) Qualified higher education expenses. For purposes of paragraph (2)(E)—*

(A) In general. The term "qualified higher education expenses" means qualified higher education expenses (as defined in section 529(e)(3)) for education furnished to—

(i) the taxpayer,

(ii) the taxpayer's spouse, or

(iii) any child (as defined in section 151(c)(3)) or grandchild of the taxpayer or the taxpayer's spouse,

at an eligible educational institution (as defined in section 529(e)(5)).

(B) Coordination with other benefits. The amount of qualified higher education expenses for any taxable year shall be reduced as provided in section 25A(g)(2).

CAUTION. Para. (t)(8), following, is effective for payments and distributions in tax. yrs. begin. after 12/31/97.

[7]*(8) Qualified first-time homebuyer distributions. For purposes of paragraph (2)(F)—*

(A) In general. The term "qualified first-time homebuyer distribution" means any payment or distribution received by an individual to the extent such payment or distribution is used by the individual before the close of the 120th day after the day on which such payment or distribution is received to pay qualified acquisition costs with respect to a principal residence of a first-time homebuyer who is such individual, the spouse of such individual, or any child, grandchild, or ancestor of such individual or the individual's spouse.

(B) Lifetime dollar limitation. The aggregate amount of payments or distributions received by an individual which may be treated as qualified first-time homebuyer distributions for any taxable year shall not exceed the excess (if any) of—

(i) $10,000, over

(ii) the aggregate amounts treated as qualified first-time homebuyer distributions with respect to such individual for all prior taxable years.

(C) Qualified acquisition costs. For purposes of this paragraph, the term "qualified acquisition costs" means the costs of acquiring, constructing, or reconstructing a residence. Such term includes any usual or reasonable settlement, financing, or other closing costs.

(D) First-time homebuyer; other definitions. For purposes of this paragraph—

(i) First-time homebuyer. The term "first-time homebuyer" means any individual if—

(I) such individual (and if married, such individual's spouse) had no present ownership interest in a principal residence during the 2-year period ending on the date of acquisition of the principal residence to which this paragraph applies, and

(II) subsection (h) or (k) of section 1034 (as in effect on the day before the date of the enactment of this paragraph) did not suspend the running of any period of time specified in section 1034 (as so in effect) with respect to such individual on the day before the date the distribution is applied pursuant to subparagraph (A).

(ii) Principal residence. The term "principal residence" has the same meaning as when used in section 121.

(iii) Date of acquisition. The term "date of acquisition" means the date—

(I) on which a binding contract to acquire the principal residence to which subparagraph (A) applies is entered into, or

(II) on which construction or reconstruction of such a principal residence is commenced.

(E) Special rule where delay in acquisition. If any distribution from any individual retirement plan fails to meet the requirements of subparagraph (A) solely by reason of a delay or cancellation of the purchase or construction of the residence, the amount of the distribution may be contributed to an individual retirement plan as provided in section 408(d)(3)(A)(i) (determined by substituting "120 days" for "60 days" in such section), except that—

(i) section 408(d)(3)(B) shall not be applied to such contribution, and

(ii) such amount shall not be taken into account in determining whether section 408(d)(3)(B) applies to any other amount.

* * * * * * * * * * *

[For analysis, see ¶s 303, 304, 903. For text of Committee Report see ¶s 5004, 5017, 5157.]

[Endnote Code Sec. 72]

Matter in *italics* in Code Sec. 72(d)(1)(B)(iii) and Code Sec. 72(d)(1)(B)(iv) added by Sec. 1075(a), (b)(1), and (b)(2) of the Taxpayer Relief Act of 1997, H.R. 2014, 8/5/97, which struck out:

1. added matter in clause (d)(1)(B)(iii)
2. "primary"
3. added clause (d)(1)(B)(iv)

Effective Date (Sec. 1075(c), H.R. 2014, 8/5/97) effective for annuity starting dates begin. after 12/31/97.

Code Sec. 72(t)(2)(E), in *italics*, was added by Sec. 203(a), H.R. 2014, 8/5/97.

4. added subpara. (t)(2)(E)

Effective Date (Sec. 203(c), H.R. 2014, 8/5/97) effective for distributions after 12/31/97, with respect to expenses paid after 12/31/97 (in tax. yrs. end. after 12/31/97), for education furnished in academic periods begin. after 12/31/97.

Code Sec. 72(t)(2)(F), in *italics*, was added by Sec. 303(a), H.R. 2014, 8/5/97.

5. added subpara. (t)(2)(F)

Effective Date (Sec. 303(c), H.R. 2014, 8/5/97) effective for payments and distributions in tax. yrs. begin. after 12/31/97.

Code Sec. 72(t)(7), in *italics*, was added by Sec. 203(b), H.R. 2014, 8/5/97.

6. added para. (t)(7)

Effective Date (Sec. 203(c), H.R. 2014, 8/5/97) effective for distributions after 12/31/97, with respect to expenses paid after 12/31/97 (in tax. yrs. end. after 12/31/97), for education furnished in academic periods begin. after 12/31/97.

Code Sec. 72(t)(8), in *italics*, was added by Sec. 303(b), H.R. 2014, 8/5/97.

7. added para. (t)(8)
Effective Date (Sec. 303(c), H.R. 2014, 8/5/97) effective for payments and distributions in tax. yrs. begin. after 12/31/97.

[¶ 3022]   Code Sec. 101.   Certain death benefits.
(a) Proceeds of life insurance contracts payable by reason of death.

* * * * * * * * * * *

(2) Transfer for valuable consideration. In the case of a transfer for a valuable consideration, by assignment or otherwise, of a life insurance contract or any interest therein, the amount excluded from gross income by paragraph (1) shall not exceed an amount equal to the sum of the actual value of such consideration and the premiums and other amounts subsequently paid by the transferee. The preceding sentence shall not apply in the case of such a transfer—

(A) if such contract or interest therein has a basis for determining gain or loss in the hands of a transferee determined in whole or in part by reference to such basis of such contract or interest therein in the hands of the transferor, or

(B) if such transfer is to the insured, to a partner of the insured, to a partnership in which the insured is a partner, or to a corporation in which the insured is a shareholder or officer.

[1] *The term "other amounts" in the first sentence of this paragraph includes interest paid or accrued by the transferee on indebtedness with respect to such contract or any interest therein if such interest paid or accrued is not allowable as a deduction by reason of section 264(a)(4).*

* * * * * * * * * * *

[2] *(h) Survivor benefits attributable to service by a public safety officer who is killed in the line of duty.*

(1) In general. Gross income shall not include any amount paid as a survivor annuity on account of the death of a public safety officer (as such term is defined in section 1204 of the Omnibus Crime Control and Safe Streets Act of 1968) killed in the line of duty—

(A) if such annuity is provided, under a governmental plan which meets the requirements of section 401(a), to the spouse (or a former spouse) of the public safety officer or to a child of such officer; and

(B) to the extent such annuity is attributable to such officer's service as a public safety officer.

(2) Exceptions. Paragraph (1) shall not apply with respect to the death of any public safety officer if, as determined in accordance with the provisions of the Omnibus Crime Control and Safe Streets Act of 1968—

(A) the death was caused by the intentional misconduct of the officer or by such officer's intention to bring about such officer's death;

(B) the officer was voluntarily intoxicated (as defined in section 1204 of such Act) at the time of death;

(C) the officer was performing such officer's duties in a grossly negligent manner at the time of death; or

(D) the payment is to an individual whose actions were a substantial contributing factor to the death of the officer.

[For analysis, see ¶s 104, 711. For text of Committee Report see ¶s 5161, 5350.]

[Endnote Code Sec. 101]

Matter in *italics* in Code Sec. 101(a)(2) added by Sec. 1084(b)(2) of the Taxpayer Relief Act of 1997, H.R. 2014, 8/5/97.
1. added matter in para. (a)(2)
Effective Date (Sec. 1084(d) [sic (f)], H.R. 2014, 8/5/97) provides as follows:

"(d) [sic (f)] Effective date. The amendments made by this section shall apply to contracts issued after June 8, 1997, in taxable years ending after such date. For purposes of the preceding sentence, any material increase in the death benefit or other material change in the contract shall be treated as a new contract but the addition of covered lives shall be treated as a new contract only with respect to such additional covered lives. For purposes of this subsection, an increase in the death benefit under a policy or contract issued in connection with a lapse described in section 501(d)(2) of the Health Insurance Portability and Accountability Act of 1996 shall not be treated as a new contract."

Code Sec. 101(h), in *italics*, was added by Sec. 1528(a), H.R. 2014, 8/5/97.

2. added subsec. (h)

Effective Date (Sec. 1528(b), H.R. 2014, 8/5/97) effective for amounts received in tax. yrs. begin. after 12/31/96, with respect to individuals dying after 12/31/96.

[¶ 3023]   Code Sec. 108.   Income from discharge of indebtedness.

* * * * * * * * * * *

(f) Student loans.

* * * * * * * * * * *

(2) Student loan. For purposes of this subsection, the term "student loan" means any loan to an individual to assist the individual in attending an educational organization described in section 170(b)(1)(A)(ii) made by—

* * * * * * * * * * *

(B) a State, territory, or possession of the United States, or the District of Columbia, or any political subdivision thereof, [1]

* * * * * * * * * * *

[2]*(D) any educational organization described in section 170(b)(1)(A)(ii) if such loan is made—*

(i) pursuant to an agreement with any entity described in subparagraph (A), (B), or (C) under which the funds from which the loan was made were provided to such educational organization, or

(ii) pursuant to a program of such educational organization which is designed to encourage its students to serve in occupations with unmet needs or in areas with unmet needs and under which the services provided by the students (or former students) are for or under the direction of a governmental unit or an organization described in section 501(c)(3) and exempt from tax under section 501(a).

The term "student loan" includes any loan made by an educational organization so described or by an organization exempt from tax under section 501(a) to refinance a loan meeting the requirements of the preceding sentence.

[3]*(3) Exception for discharges on account of services performed for certain lenders. Paragraph (1) shall not apply to the discharge of a loan made by an organization described in paragraph (2)(D) (or by an organization described in paragraph (2)(E) from funds provided by an organization described in paragraph (2)(D)) if the discharge is on account of services performed for either such organization.*

* * * * * * * * * * *

[For analysis, see ¶ 103. For text of Committee Report see ¶ 5011.]

[Endnote Code Sec. 108]

Matter in *italics* in Code Sec. 108(f)(2) and Code Sec. 108(f)(3) added by Secs. 225(a)(1) and (2) of the Taxpayer Relief Act of 1997, H.R. 2014, 8/5/97, which struck out:

1. "or"

2. "(D) any educational organization so described pursuant to an agreement with any entity described in subparagraph (A), (B), or (C) under which the funds from which the loan was made were provided to such educational organization."

3. added para. (f)(3)

Effective Date (Sec. 225(b), H.R. 2014, 8/5/97) effective for discharges of indebtedness after 8/5/97.

[¶ 3024] Code Sec.[1] 110.   Qualified lessee construction allowances for short-term leases.

(a) In general. Gross income of a lessee does not include any amount received in cash (or treated as a rent reduction) by a lessee from a lessor—

(1) under a short-term lease of retail space, and

(2) for the purpose of such lessee's constructing or improving qualified long-term real property for use in such lessee's trade or business at such retail space,

but only to the extent that such amount does not exceed the amount expended by the lessee for such construction or improvement.

(b) Consistent treatment by lessor. Qualified long-term real property constructed or improved in connection with any amount excluded from a lessee's income by reason of subsection (a) shall be treated as nonresidential real property of the lessor (including for purposes of section 168(i)(8)(B)).

(c) Definitions. For purposes of this section—

(1) **Qualified long-term real property.** The term "qualified long-term real property" means nonresidential real property which is part of, or otherwise present at, the retail space referred to in subsection (a) and which reverts to the lessor at the termination of the lease.

(2) **Short-term lease.** The term "short-term lease" means a lease (or other agreement for occupancy or use) of retail space for 15 years or less (as determined under the rules of section 168(i)(3)).

(3) **Retail space.** The term "retail space" means real property leased, occupied, or otherwise used by a lessee in its trade or business of selling tangible personal property or services to the general public.

(d) Information required to be furnished to Secretary. Under regulations, the lessee and lessor described in subsection (a) shall, at such times and in such manner as may be provided in such regulations, furnish to the Secretary—

(1) information concerning the amounts received (or treated as a rent reduction) and expended as described in subsection (a), and

(2) any other information which the Secretary deems necessary to carry out the provisions of this section.

[For analysis, see ¶ 2702. For text of Committee Report see ¶ 5208.]

[Endnote Code Sec. 110]

Code Sec. 110 was added by Sec. 1213(a) of the Taxpayer Relief Act of 1997, H.R. 2014, 8/5/97.

1. added Code Sec. 110

Effective Date (Sec. 1213(e), H.R. 2014, 8/5/97) effective for leases entered into after 8/5/97.

[¶ 3025] *Code Sec.[1] 121.*   *Exclusion of gain from sale of principal residence.*

(a) Exclusion. Gross income shall not include gain from the sale or exchange of property if, during the 5-year period ending on the date of the sale or exchange, such property has been owned and used by the taxpayer as the taxpayer's principal residence for periods aggregating 2 years or more.

(b) Limitations.

(1) In general. The amount of gain excluded from gross income under subsection (a) with respect to any sale or exchange shall not exceed $250,000.

(2) $500,000 limitation for certain joint returns. Paragraph (1) shall be applied by substituting "$500,000" for "$250,000" if—

(A) a husband and wife make a joint return for the taxable year of the sale or exchange of the property,

(B) either spouse meets the ownership requirements of subsection (a) with respect to such property,

(C) both spouses meet the use requirements of subsection (a) with respect to such property, and

(D) neither spouse is ineligible for the benefits of subsection (a) with respect to such property by reason of paragraph (3).

(3) Application to only 1 sale or exchange every 2 years.

(A) In general. Subsection (a) shall not apply to any sale or exchange by the taxpayer if, during the 2-year period ending on the date of such sale or exchange, there was any other sale or exchange by the taxpayer to which subsection (a) applied.

(B) Pre-May 7, 1997, sales not taken into account. Subparagraph (A) shall be applied without regard to any sale or exchange before May 7, 1997.

(c) Exclusion for taxpayers failing to meet certain requirements.

(1) In general. In the case of a sale or exchange to which this subsection applies, the ownership and use requirements of subsection (a) shall not apply and subsection (b)(3) shall not apply; but the amount of gain excluded from gross income under subsection (a) with respect to such sale or exchange shall not exceed—

(A) the amount which bears the same ratio to the amount which would be so excluded under this section if such requirements had been met, as

(B) the shorter of—

(i) the aggregate periods, during the 5-year period ending on the date of such sale or exchange, such property has been owned and used by the taxpayer as the taxpayer's principal residence, or

(ii) the period after the date of the most recent prior sale or exchange by the taxpayer to which subsection (a) applied and before the date of such sale or exchange,

bears to 2 years.

(2) Sales and exchanges to which subsection applies. This subsection shall apply to any sale or exchange if—

(A) subsection (a) would not (but for this subsection) apply to such sale or exchange by reason of—

(i) a failure to meet the ownership and use requirements of subsection (a), or

(ii) subsection (b)(3), and

(B) such sale or exchange is by reason of a change in place of employment, health, or, to the extent provided in regulations, unforeseen circumstances.

(d) Special rules.

(1) Joint returns. If a husband and wife make a joint return for the taxable year of the sale or exchange of the property, subsection (a) and (c) shall apply if either spouse meets the ownership and use requirements of subsection (a) with respect to such property.

(2) Property of deceased spouse. For purposes of this section, in the case of an unmarried individual whose spouse is deceased on the date of the sale or exchange of property, the period such unmarried individual owned and used such property shall include the period such deceased spouse owned and used such property before death.

(3) Property owned by spouse or former spouse. For purposes of this section—

(A) Property transferred to individual from spouse or former spouse. In the case of an individual holding property transferred to such individual in a transaction described in section 1041(a), the period such individual owns such property shall include the period the transferor owned the property.

(B) Property used by former spouse pursuant to divorce decree, etc. Solely for purposes of this section, an individual shall be treated as using property as such individual's principal residence during any period of ownership while such individual's spouse or former spouse is granted use of the property under a divorce or separation instrument (as defined in section 71(b)(2)).

(4) Tenant-stockholder in cooperative housing corporation. For purposes of this section, if the taxpayer holds stock as a tenant-stockholder (as defined in section 216) in a cooperative housing corporation (as defined in such section), then—

(A) the holding requirements of subsection (a) shall be applied to the holding of such stock, and

(B) the use requirements of subsection (a) shall be applied to the house or apartment which the taxpayer was entitled to occupy as such stockholder.

(5) Involuntary conversions.

(A) In general. For purposes of this section, the destruction, theft, seizure, requisition, or condemnation of property shall be treated as the sale of such property.

(B) Application of section 1033. In applying section 1033 (relating to involuntary conversions), the amount realized from the sale or exchange of property shall be treated as being the amount determined without regard to this section, reduced by the amount of gain not included in gross income pursuant to this section.

(C) Property acquired after involuntary conversion. If the basis of the property sold or exchanged is determined (in whole or in part) under section 1033(b) (relating to basis of property acquired through involuntary conversion), then the holding and use by the taxpayer of the converted property shall be treated as holding and use by the taxpayer of the property sold or exchanged.

(6) Recognition of gain attributable to depreciation. *Subsection (a) shall not apply to so much of the gain from the sale of any property as does not exceed the portion of the depreciation adjustments (as deemed in section 1250(b)(3)) attributable to periods after May 6, 1997, in respect of such property.*

(7) Determination of use during periods of out-of-residence care. *In the case of a taxpayer who—*

(A) becomes physically or mentally incapable of self-care, and

(B) owns property and uses such property as the taxpayer's principal residence during the 5-year period described in subsection (a) for periods aggregating at least 1 year,

then the taxpayer shall be treated as using such property as the taxpayer's principal residence during any time during such 5- year period in which the taxpayer owns the property and resides in any facility (including a nursing home) licensed by a State or political subdivision to care for an individual in the taxpayer's condition.

(8) Sales of remainder interests. *For purposes of this section—*

(A) In general. At the election of the taxpayer, this section shall not fail to apply to the sale or exchange of an interest in a principal residence by reason of such interest being a remainder interest in such residence, but this section shall not apply to any other interest in such residence which is sold or exchanged separately.

(B) Exception for sales to related parties. Subparagraph (A) shall not apply to any sale to, or exchange with, any person who bears a relationship to the taxpayer which is described in section 267(b) or 707(b).

(e) Denial of exclusion for expatriates. *This section shall not apply to any sale or exchange by an individual if the treatment provided by section 877(a)(1) applies to such individual.*

(f) Election to have section not apply. *This section shall not apply to any sale or exchange with respect to which the taxpayer elects not to have this section apply.*

(g) Residences acquired in rollovers under section 1034. *For purposes of this section, in the case of property the acquisition of which by the taxpayer resulted under section 1034 (as in effect on the day before the date of the enactment of this section) in the nonrecognition of any part of the gain realized on the sale or exchange of another residence, in determining the period for which the taxpayer has owned and used such property as the taxpayer's principal residence, there shall be included the aggregate periods for which such other residence (and each prior residence taken into account under section 1223(7) in determining the holding period of such property) had been so owned and used.*

[For analysis, see ¶ 102. For text of Committee Report see ¶ 5020.]

[Endnote Code Sec. 121]

Code Sec. 121 was amended by Sec. 312(a) of the Taxpayer Relief Act of 1997, H.R. 2014, 8/5/97, which struck out:

1. " SEC. 121. ONE-TIME EXCLUSION OF GAIN FROM SALE OF PRINCIPAL RESIDENCE BY INDIVIDUAL WHO HAS ATTAINED AGE 55.

"(a) General rule. At the election of the taxpayer, gross income does not include gain from the sale or exchange of property if—

"(1) the taxpayer has attained the age of 55 before the date of such sale or exchange, and

"(2) during the 5-year period ending on the date of the sale or exchange, such property has been owned and used by the taxpayer as his principal residence for periods aggregating 3 years or more.

"(b)Limitations.

"(1) Dollar limitation. The amount of the gain excluded from gross income under subsection (a) shall not exceed $125,000 ($62,500 in the case of a separate return by a married individual).

"(2) Application to only 1 sale or exchange. Subsection (a) shall not apply to any sale or exchange by the taxpayer if an election by the taxpayer or his spouse under subsection (a) with respect to any other sale or exchange is in effect.

"(3) Additional election if prior sale was made on or before July 26, 1978. In the case of any sale or exchange after July 26, 1978, this section shall be applied by not taking into account any election made with respect to a sale or exchange on or before such date.

"(c) Election. An election under subsection (a) may be made or revoked at any time before the expiration of the period for making a claim for credit or refund of the tax imposed by this chapter for the taxable year in which the sale or exchange occurred, and shall be made or revoked in such manner as the Secretary shall by regulations prescribe. In the case of a taxpayer who is married, an election under subsection (a) or a revocation thereof may be made only if his spouse joins in such election or revocation.

"(d) Special rules.

"(1) Property held jointly by husband and wife. For purposes of this section, if—

"(A) property is held by a husband and wife as joint tenants, tenants by the entirety, or community property,

"(B) such husband and wife make a joint return under section 6013 for the taxable year of the sale or exchange, and

"(C) one spouse satisfies the age, holding, and use requirements of subsection (a) with respect to such property,

then both husband and wife shall be treated as satisfying the age, holding, and use requirements of subsection (a) with respect to such property.

"(2) Property of deceased spouse. For purposes of this section, in the case of an unmarried individual whose spouse is deceased on the date of the sale or exchange of property, if—

"(A) the deceased spouse (during the 5-year period ending on the date of the sale or exchange) satisfied the holding and use requirements of subsection (a)(2) with respect to such property, and

"(B) no election by the deceased spouse under subsection (a) is in effect with respect to a prior sale or exchange,

then such individual shall be treated as satisfying the holding and use requirements of subsection (a)(2) with respect to such property.

"(3) Tenant-stockholder in cooperative housing corporation. For purposes of this section, if the taxpayer holds stock as a tenant-stockholder (as defined in section 216) in a cooperative housing corporation (as defined in such section), then—

"(A) the holding requirements of subsection (a)(2) shall be applied to the holding of such stock, and

"(B) the use requirements of subsection (a)(2) shall be applied to the house or apartment which the taxpayer was entitled to occupy as such stockholder.

"(4) Involuntary conversions. For purposes of this section, the destruction, theft, seizure, requisition, or condemnation of property shall be treated as the sale of such property.

"(h) Property used in part as principal residence. In the case of property only a portion of which, during the 5-year period ending on the date of the sale or exchange,has been owned and used by the taxpayer as his principal residence for periods aggregating 3 years or more, this section shall apply with respect to so much of the gain from the sale or exchange of such property as is determined, under regulations prescribed by the Secretary, to be attributable to the portion of the property so owned and used by the taxpayer.

"(6) Determination of marital status. In the case of any sale or exchange, for purposes of this section—

"(A) the determination of whether an individual is married shall be made as of the date of the sale or exchange; and

"(B) an individual legally separated from his spouse under a decree of divorce or of separate maintenance shall not be considered as married.

"(7) Application of sections 1033 and 1034. In applying sections 1033 (relating to involuntary conversions) and 1034 (relating to sale or exchange of residence), the amount realized from the sale or exchange of property shall be treated as being the amount determined without regard to this section, reduced by the amount of gain not included in gross income pursuant to an election under this section.

"(8) Property acquired after involuntary conversion. If the basis of the property sold or exchanged is determined (in whole or in part) under subsection (b) of section 1033 (relating to basis of property acquired through involuntary conversion), then the holding and use by the taxpayer of the converted property shall be treated as holding and use by the taxpayer of the property sold or exchanged.

"(9) Determination of use during periods of out-of-residence care. In the case of a taxpayer who—

"(A) becomes physically or mentally incapable of self-care, and

"(B) owns property and uses such property as the taxpayer's principal residence during the 5-year period described in subsection (a)(2) for periods aggregating at least 1 year,

then the taxpayer shall be treated as using such property as the taxpayer's principal residence during any time during such 5-year period in which the taxpayer owns the property and resides in any facility (including a nursing home) licensed by a State or political subdivision to care for an individual in the taxpayer's condition."

Effective Date (Sec. 312(d) [sic (e)], H.R. 2014, 8/5/97) effective for sales and exchanges after 5/6/97, except as provided by Sec. 312(d)(2)-(4) [sic (e)(2)-(4)], of this Act, which reads as follows:

"(2) Sales before 8/5/97. At the election of the taxpayer, the amendments made by this section shall not apply to any sale or exchange before the date of the enactment of this Act.

"(3) Certain sales within 2 years after 8/5/97. Section 121 of the Internal Revenue Code of 1986 (as amended by this section) shall be applied without regard to subsection (c)(2)(B) thereof in the case of any sale or exchange of property during the 2-year period beginning on the date of the enactment of this Act if the taxpayer held such property on the date of the enactment of this Act and fails to meet the ownership and use requirements of subsection (a) thereof with respect to such property.

"(4) Binding contracts. At the election of the taxpayer, the amendments made by this section shall not apply to a sale or exchange after the date of the enactment of this Act, if—

"(A) such sale or exchange is pursuant to a contract which was binding on such date, or

"(B) without regard to such amendments, gain would not be recognized under section 1034 of the Internal Revenue Code of 1986 (as in effect on the day before the date of the enactment of this Act) on such sale or exchange by reason of a new residence acquired on or before such date or with respect to the acquisition of which by the taxpayer a binding contract was in effect on such date.

This paragraph shall not apply to any sale or exchange by an individual if the treatment provided by section 877(a)(1) of the Internal Revenue Code of 1986 applies to such individual."

[¶ 3026]   Code Sec. 127.   Educational assistance programs.

* * * * * * * * * * *

[1](d) *Termination. This section shall not apply to expenses paid with respect to courses beginning after May 31, 2000.*

* * * * * * * * * * *

[For analysis, see ¶ 404. For text of Committee Report see ¶ 5007.]

[Endnote Code Sec. 127]

Matter in *italics* in Code Sec. 127(d) added by Sec. 221(a) of the Taxpayer Relief Act of 1997, H.R. 2014, 8/5/97, which struck out:

1. "(d) Termination. This section shall not apply to taxable years beginning after May 31, 1997. In the case of any taxable year beginning in 1997, only expenses paid with respect to courses beginning before July 1, 1997, shall be taken into account in determining the amount excluded under this section."

Effective Date (Sec. 221(b), H.R. 2014, 8/5/97) effective for tax. yrs. begin. after 12/31/96.

[¶ 3027]   Code Sec. 130.   Certain personal injury liability assignments.

* * * * * * * * * * *

(c) Qualified assignment. For purposes of this section, the term "qualified assignment" means any assignment of a liability to make periodic payments as damages (whether by suit or agreement)[1], *or as compensation under any workmen's compensation act,* on account of personal injury or sickness (in a case involving physical injury or physical sickness)—

(1) if the assignee assumes such liability from a person who is a party to the suit or agreement, [2]*or the workmen's compensation claim,* and

(2) if—

* * * * * * * * * * *

(D) such periodic payments are excludable from the gross income of the recipient under [3]*paragraph (1) or (2) of* section 104(a).

The determination for purposes of this chapter of when the recipient is treated as having received any payment with respect to which there has been a qualified assignment shall be made without regard to any provision of such assignment which grants the recipient rights as a creditor greater than those of a general creditor.

* * * * * * * * * * *

[For analysis, see ¶ 2705. For text of Committee Report see ¶ 5083.]

[Endnote Code Sec. 130]

Matter in *italics* in Code Sec. 130(c), Code Sec. 130(c)(1) and Code Sec. 130(c)(2)(D) added by Sec. 962(a)(1)-(3) of the Taxpayer Relief Act of 1997, H.R. 2014, 8/5/97, which struck out:

1. added matter in subsection (c)
2. added matter in paragraph (c)(1)
3. "section 104(a)(2)"

Effective Date (Sec. 962(b), H.R. 2014, 8/5/97) effective for claims under workmen's compensation acts filed after 8/5/97.

[¶ 3028]   Code Sec. 132.   Certain fringe benefits.

* * * * * * * * * * *

(e) **De minimis fringe defined.** For purposes of this section—

* * * * * * * * * * *

CAUTION. Para. (e)(2), following, is effective for tax. yrs. begin. before 1/1/98. For para. (e)(2), effective for tax. yrs. begin. after 12/31/97, see below.

(2) **Treatment of certain eating facilities.** The operation by an employer of any eating facility for employees shall be treated as a de minimis fringe if—

(A) such facility is located on or near the business premises of the employer, and

(B) revenue derived from such facility normally equals or exceeds the direct operating costs of such facility.

The preceding sentence shall apply with respect to any highly compensated employee only if access to the facility is available on substantially the same terms to each member of a group of employees which is defined under a reasonable classification set up by the employer which does not discriminate in favor of highly compensated employees.

CAUTION. Para. (e)(2), following, is effective for tax. yrs. begin. after 12/31/97. For para. (e)(2), effective for tax. yrs. begin. before 1/1/98, see above.

(2) **Treatment of certain eating facilities.** The operation by an employer of any eating facility for employees shall be treated as a de minimis fringe if—

(A) such facility is located on or near the business premises of the employer, and

(B) revenue derived from such facility normally equals or exceeds the direct operating costs of such facility.

The preceding sentence shall apply with respect to any highly compensated employee only if access to the facility is available on substantially the same terms to each member of a group of employees which is defined under a reasonable classification set up by the employer which does not discriminate in favor of highly compensated employees. [1]*For purposes of subparagraph (B), an employee entitled under section 119 to exclude the value of a meal provided at such facility shall be treated as having paid an amount for such meal equal to the direct operating costs of the facility attributable to such meal.*

(f) **Qualified transportation fringe.**

* * * * * * * * * * * *

CAUTION. Para. (f)(4), following, is effective for tax. yrs. begin. before 1/1/98. For para. (f)(4), effective for tax. yrs. begin. after 12/31/97, see below.

(4) **Benefit not in lieu of compensation.** Subsection (a)(5) shall not apply to any qualified transportation fringe unless such benefit is provided in addition to (and not in lieu of) any compensation otherwise payable to the employee.

CAUTION. Para. (f)(4), following, is effective for tax. yrs. begin. after 12/31/97. For para. (f)(4), effective for tax. yrs. begin. before 1/1/98, see above.

(4) **Benefit not in lieu of compensation.** Subsection (a)(5) shall not apply to any qualified transportation fringe unless such benefit is provided in addition to (and not in lieu of) any compensation otherwise payable to the employee. [2]*This paragraph shall not apply to any qualified parking provided in lieu of compensation which otherwise would have been includible in gross income of the employee, and no amount shall be included in the gross income of the employee solely because the employee may choose between the qualified parking and compensation.*

* * * * * * * * * * *

[For analysis, see ¶s 1001, 1003. For text of Committee Report see ¶s 5093, 5154.]

[Endnote Code Sec. 132]
Matter in *italics* in Code Sec. 132(e)(2) added by Sec. 970(a) of the Taxpayer Relief Act of 1997, H.R. 2014, 8/5/97.
1. added matter in para. (e)(2)
Effective Date (Sec. 970(b), H.R. 2014, 8/5/97) effective for tax. yrs. begin. after 12/31/97.

Matter in *italics* in Code Sec. 132(f)(4) added by Sec. 1072(a), H.R. 2014, 8/5/97.
2. added matter in para. (f)(4)
Effective Date (Sec. 1072(b), H.R. 2014, 8/5/97) effective for tax. yrs. begin. after 12/31/97.

[¶ 3029] Code Sec. 135.   Income from United States savings bonds used to pay higher education tuition and fees.

* * * * * * * * * * *

(c) Definitions. For purposes of this section—

* * * * * * * * * * *

(2) Qualified higher education expenses.

* * * * * * * * * * *

CAUTION.   Subparagraph (c)(2)(C), following, is effective for tax. yrs. begin. after 12/31/97.

[1]*(C) Contributions to qualified State tuition program. Such term shall include any contribution to a qualified State tuition program (as defined in section 529) on behalf of a designated beneficiary (as defined in such section)*[2]*, or to an education investment, account (as defined in section 530) on behalf of an account beneficiary, who is an individual described in subparagraph (A); but there shall be no increase in the investment in the contract for purposes of applying section 529(c)(3)(A) by reason of any portion of such a contribution which is not includible in gross income by reason of this subparagraph.*

* * * * * * * * * * *

(d) Special rules.

* * * * * * * * * * *

CAUTION.   Paragraphs (d)(2) and (3), following, are effective for expenses paid before 1/1/98 (in tax. yrs. end. before 1/1/98), for education furnished in academic periods begin. before 1/1/98. For paragraphs (d)(2)-(4) effective for expenses paid after 12/31/97 (in tax. yrs. begin. after 12/31/97), for education furnished in academic periods begin. after 12/31/97, see below.

(2) No exclusion for married individuals filing separate returns. If the taxpayer is a married individual (within the meaning of section 7703), this section shall apply only if the taxpayer and his spouse file a joint return for the taxable year.

(3) Regulations. The Secretary may prescribe such regulations as may be necessary or appropriate to carry out this section, including regulations requiring record keeping and information reporting.

CAUTION.   Paragraphs (d)(2)-(4), following, are effective for expenses paid after 12/31/97 (in tax. yrs. begin. after 12/31/97), for education furnished in academic periods beginning after 12/31/97. For paragraphs (d)(2) and (3) effective for expenses paid before 1/1/98 (in tax. yrs. end. before 1/1/98), for education furnished in academic periods begin. before 1/1/98, see below.

[3]*(2) Coordination with higher education credit. The amount of the qualified higher education expenses otherwise taken into account under subsection (a) with respect to the education of an individual shall be reduced (before the application of subsection (b)) by the amount*

of such expenses which are taken into account in determining the credit allowable to the taxpayer or any other person under section 25A with respect to such expenses.

[4](3) **No exclusion for married individuals filing separate returns.** If the taxpayer is a married individual (within the meaning of section 7703), this section shall apply only if the taxpayer and his spouse file a joint return for the taxable year.

[5](4) **Regulations.** The Secretary may prescribe such regulations as may be necessary or appropriate to carry out this section, including regulations requiring record keeping and information reporting.

[For analysis, see ¶s 405, 409. For text of Committee Report see ¶s 5002, 5005.]

[Endnote Code Sec. 135]

Matter in *italics* in Code Sec. 135(c)(2)(C) added by Sec. 211(c) of the Taxpayer Relief Act of 1997, H.R. 2014, 8/5/97.

1. added clause (c)(2)(C)

Effective Date (Sec. 211(f)(4) and (6), H.R. 2014, 8/5/97) effective for tax. yrs. begin. after 12/31/97, except as provided in Sec. 211(f)(6), which reads as follows:

"(6) Transition rule for pre-August 20, 1996 contracts. In the case of any contract issued prior to August 20, 1996, section 529(c)(3)(C) of the Internal Revenue Code of 1986 shall be applied for taxable years ending after August 20, 1996, without regard to the requirement that a distribution be transferred to a member of the family or the requirement that a change in beneficiaries may be made only to a member of the family."

Matter in *italics* in Code Sec. 135(c)(2)(C) [as added by Sec. 211(c) of this Act] added by Sec. 213(e)(2), H.R. 2014.

2. added "; or an education investment account (as defined in section 530) on behalf of an account beneficiary," in clause (c)(2)(C)

Effective Date (Sec. 212(f), H.R. 2014, 8/5/97) effective for tax. yrs. begin. after 12/31/97.

Matter in *italics* in Code Sec. 135(d)(2), Code Sec. 135(d)(3), and Code Sec. 135(d)(4) added by Sec. 201(d), H.R. 2014, which struck out:

3. added para. (d)(2)

4. "(2)"

5. "(3)"

Effective Date (Sec. 201(f)(1), H.R. 2014, 8/5/97) effective for expenses paid after 12/31/97 (in tax. yrs end. after 12/31/97), for education furnished in academic periods begin. after 12/31/97.

[¶ 3030]   Code Sec. 137.   **Adoption assistance programs.**

* * * * * * * * * * *

(b) **Limitations.**

(1) **Dollar limitation.** The aggregate [1]*of the amounts paid or expenses incurred which may be taken into account* under subsection (a) for all taxable years with respect to the adoption of a child by the taxpayer shall not exceed $5,000 ($6,000, in the case of a child with special needs).

* * * * * * * * * * *

[Endnote Code Sec. 137]

Matter in *italics* in Code Sec. 137(b)(1) added by Sec. 1601(h)(2)(C) of the Taxpayer Relief Act of 1997, H.R. 2014, 8/5/97, which struck out:

1. "amount excludable from gross income"

Effective Date (Sec. 1601(j)(1), H.R. 2014, 8/5/97) effective for tax. yrs. begin. after 12/31/96.

[¶ 3031]   *Code Sec.*[1-B] *138.*

CAUTION.   Code Sec. 138, following, is effective for tax. yrs. begin. after 12/31/98. For Code Sec. 138, effective for tax. yrs. begin. before 1/1/99, see above.

Medicare+Choice MSA.

(a) Exclusion. Gross income shall not include any payment to the Medicare+Choice MSA of an individual by the Secretary of Health and Human Services under part C of title XVIII of the Social Security Act.

(b) Medicare+Choice MSA. For purposes of this section, the term "Medicare+Choice MSA" means a medical savings account (as defined in section 220(d))—

(1) which is designated as a Medicare+Choice MSA,

(2) with respect to which no contribution may be made other than—

(A) a contribution made by the Secretary of Health and XVIII of the Social Security Act, or

(B) a trustee-to-trustee transfer described in subsection (c)(4),

(3) the governing instrument of which provides that trustee-to-trustee transfers described in subsection (c)(4) may be made to and from such account, and

(4) which is established in connection with an MSA plan described in section 1859(b)(3) of the Social Security Act.

(c) Special rules for distributions.

(1) Distributions for qualified medical expenses. In applying section 220 to a Medicare+Choice MSA—

(A) qualified medical expenses shall not include amounts paid for medical care for any individual other than the account holder, and

(B) section 220(d)(2)(C) shall not apply.

(2) Penalty for distributions from Medicare+Choice MSA not used for qualified medical expenses if minimum balance not maintained.

(A) In general. The tax imposed by this chapter for any taxable year in which there is a payment or distribution from a Medicare+Choice MSA which is not used exclusively to pay the qualified medical expenses of the account holder shall be increased by 50 percent of the excess (if any) of—

(i) the amount of such payment or distribution, over

(ii) the excess (if any) of—

(I) the fair market value of the assets in such MSA as of the close of the calendar year preceding the calendar year in which the taxable year begins, over

(II) an amount equal to 60 percent of the deductible under the Medicare+Choice MSA plan covering the account holder as of January 1 of the calendar year in which the taxable year begins.

Section 220(f)(4) shall not apply to any payment or distribution from a Medicare+Choice MSA.

(B) Exceptions. Subparagraph (A) shall not apply if the payment or distribution is made on or after the date the account holder—

(i) becomes disabled within the meaning of section 72(m)(7), or

(ii) dies.

(C) Special rules. For purposes of subparagraph (A)—

(i) all Medicare+Choice MSAs of the account holder shall be treated as 1 account,

(ii) all payments and distributions not used exclusively to pay the qualified medical expenses of the account holder during any taxable year shall be treated as 1 distribution, and

(ii) any distribution of property shall be taken into account at its fair market value on the date of the distribution.

(3) Withdrawal of erroneous contributions. Section 220(f)(2) and paragraph (2) of this subsection shall not apply to any payment or distribution from a Medicare+Choice MSA to the Secretary of Health and Human Services of an erroneous contribution to such MSA and of the net income attributable to such contribution.

(4) Trustee-to-trustee transfers. Section 220(f)(2) and paragraph (2) of this subsection shall not apply to any trustee-to-trustee transfer from a Medicare+Choice MSA of an account holder to another Medicare+Choice MSA of such account holder.

(d) Special rules for treatment of account after death of account holder. In applying section 220(f)(8)(A) to an account which was a Medicare+Choice MSA of a decedent, the rules of section 220(f) shall apply in lieu of the rules of subsection (c) of this section with respect to the spouse as the account holder of such Medicare+Choice MSA.

(e) Reports. In the case of a Medicare+Choice MSA, the report under section 220(h)—

(1) shall include the fair market value of the assets in such Medicare+Choice MSA as of the close of each calendar year, and

(2) shall be furnished to the account holder—

(A) not later than January 31 of the calendar year following the calendar year to which such reports relate, and

(B) in such manner as the Secretary prescribes in such regulations.

(f) Coordination with limitation on number of taxpayers having medical savings accounts. Subsection (i) of section 220 shall not apply to an individual with respect to a Medicare+Choice MSA, and Medicare+Choice MSA's shall not be taken into account in determining whether the numerical limitations under section 220(j) are exceeded.

[For analysis, see ¶ 1201. For text of Committee Report see ¶ 5501.]

[Endnote Code Sec. 138]

H.R. 2015. Code Sec. 138 was added by Sec. 4006(a) of the Balanced Budget Act of 1997, H.R. 2015, 8/5/97.

1_B. added Code Sec. 138 [H.R. 2015]

Effective Date (Sec. 4006(c), H.R. 2015, 8/5/97) effective for tax. yrs. begin. after 12/31/98.

[¶ 3032]   *Code Sec.1_B 139.*

CAUTION.   Code Sec. 139 is effective for tax. yrs. begin. after 12/31/98.

Cross references to other acts.

(a) For exemption of—

(1) Allowances and expenditures to meet losses sustained by persons serving the United States abroad, due to appreciation of foreign currencies, see section 5943 of title 5, United States Code.

(2) Amounts credited to the Maritime Administration under section 9(b)(6) of the Merchant Ship Sales Act of 1946, see section 9(c)(1) of that Act (50 U.S.C. App. 1742).

(3) Benefits under laws administered by the Veterans' Administration, see section 5301 of title 38, United States Code.

(4) Earnings of ship contractors deposited in special reserve funds, see section 607(d) of the Merchant Marine Act, 1936 (46 U.S.C. 1177).

(5) Income derived from Federal Reserve banks, including capital stock and surplus, see section 7 of the Federal Reserve Act (12 U.S.C. 531).

(6) Special pensions of persons on Army and Navy medal of honor roll, see 38 U.S.C. 562(a)–(c).

(b) For extension of military income-tax-exemption benefits to commissioned officers of Public Health Service in certain circumstances, see section 212 of the Public Health Service Act (42 U.S.C. 213).

[Endnote Code Sec. 139]

H.R. 2015. Code Sec. 138 was redesignated as Code Sec. 139 by Sec. 4006(a) of the Balanced Budget Act of 1997, H.R. 2015, 8/5/97.

1. "IRC §138" [H.R. 2015]

Effective Date (Sec. 4006(c), H.R. 2015, 8/5/97) effective for tax. yrs. begin. after 12/31/98.

[¶ 3033]   Code Sec. 143.   Mortgage revenue bonds: qualified mortgage bond and qualified veterans' mortgage bond.

* * * * * * * * * * * *

(i) Other requirements.

(1) Mortgages must be new mortgages.

* * * * * * * * * * * *

(C) Exception for certain contract for deed agreements.

(i) In general. In the case of land possessed under a contract for deed by a mortgagor—

(I) whose principal residence (within the meaning of [1]*section 121*) is located on such land, and

* * * * * * * * * * *

(k) Other definitions and special rules. For purposes of this section—

* * * * * * * * * * *

[2]*(11) Special rules for residences located in disaster areas. In the case of a residence located in an area determined by the President to warrant assistance from the Federal Government under the Robert T. Stafford Disaster Relief and Emergency Assistance Act (as in effect on the date of the enactment of the Taxpayer Relief Act of 1997), this section shall be applied with the following modifications to financing provided with respect to such residence within 1 year after the date of the disaster declaration:*

(A) Subsection (d) (relating to 3-year requirement) shall not apply.

(B) Subsections (e) and (f) (relating to purchase price requirement and income requirement) shall be applied as if such residence were a targeted area residence.

The preceding sentence shall apply only with respect to bonds issued after December 31, 1996, and before January 1, 1999.

* * * * * * * * * * *

(m) Recapture of portion of federal subsidy from use of qualified mortgage bonds and mortgage credit certificates.

* * * * * * * * * * *

(6) Special rules relating to limitation on recapture amount based on gain realized.

(A) In general. For purposes of paragraph (1), gain shall be taken into account whether or not recognized, and the adjusted basis of the taxpayer's interest in the residence shall be determined without regard to sections 1033(b) and 1034(e) [3]*(as in effect on the day before the date of the enactment of the Taxpayer Relief Act of 1997)* for purposes of determining gain.

* * * * * * * * * * *

[For analysis, see ¶ 2501. For text of Committee Report see ¶ 5064.]

[Endnote Code Sec. 143]

Matter in *italics* in Code Sec. 143(i)(1)(C)(i)(I) added by Sec. 312(d)(1) of the Taxpayer Relief Act of 1997, H.R. 2014, 8/5/97, which struck out:

1. "section 1034"

Effective Date (Sec. 312(d) [sic (e)], H.R. 2014, 8/5/97) effective for sales and exchanges after 5/6/97, except as provided in Secs. 312(d)(2)-(4) [sic (e)(2)-(4)] of this Act, which read as follows:

"(2) Sales before 8/5/97.—At the election of the taxpayer, the amendments made by this section shall not apply to any sale or exchange before the date of the enactment of this Act.

"(3) Certain sales within 2 years after 8/5/97. Section 121 of the Internal Revenue Code of 1986 (as amended by this section) shall be applied without regard to subsection (c)(2)(B) thereof in the case of any sale or exchange of property during the 2-year period beginning on the date of the enactment of this Act if the taxpayer held such property on the date of the enactment of this Act and fails to meet the ownership and use requirements of subsection (a) thereof with respect to such property.

"(4) Binding contracts.—At the election of the taxpayer, the amendments made by this section shall not apply to a sale or exchange after the date of the enactment of this Act, if—

"(A) such sale or exchange is pursuant to a contract which was binding on such date, or

"(B) without regard to such amendments, gain would not be recognized under section 1034 of the Internal Revenue Code of 1986 (as in effect on the day before the date of the enactment of this Act) on such sale or exchange by reason of a new residence acquired on or before such date or with respect to the acquisition of which by the taxpayer a binding contract was in effect on such date.

This paragraph shall not apply to any sale or exchange by an individual if the treatment provided by section 877(a)(1) of the Internal Revenue Code of 1986 applies to such individual."

Code Sec. 143(k)(11), in *italics*, was added by Sec. 914, H.R. 2014.

2. added para. (k)(11)

Effective Date Effective 8/5/97.

Matter in *italics* in Code Sec. 143(m)(6)(A) added by Sec. 312(d)(3), H.R. 2014.

3. added matter to para. (m)(6)(A)

Effective Date (Sec. 312(d) [sic (e)], H.R. 2014, 8/5/97) effective for sales and exchanges after 5/6/97, except as provided in Secs. 312(d)(2)-(4) [sic (e)(2)-(4)] of this Act, reproduced above.

[¶ 3034]   Code Sec. 145.   Qualified 501(c)(3) bond.

* * * * * * * * * * *

(b) $150,000,000 limitation on bonds other than hospital bonds.

* * * * * * * * * * *

[1]*(5) Termination of limitation. This subsection shall not apply with respect to bonds issued after the date of the enactment of this paragraph as part of an issue 95 percent or more of the net proceeds of which are to be used to finance capital expenditures incurred after such date.*

* * * * * * * * * * *

[For analysis, see ¶ 2505. For text of Committee Report see ¶ 5008.]

[Endnote Code Sec. 145]

Code Sec. 145(b)(5), in *italics*, added by Sec. 222 of the Taxpayer Relief Act of 1997, H.R. 2014, 8/5/97.

1. added para. (b)(5)

Effective Date Effective 8/5/97.

[¶ 3035]   Code Sec. 148.   Arbitrage.

* * * * * * * * * * *

(c) Temporary period exception.

* * * * * * * * * * *

(2) Limitation on temporary period for pooled financings.

* * * * * * * * * * *

[1]*(B)* Shorter temporary period for loan repayments, etc. Subparagraph (A) shall be applied by substituting "3 months" for "6 months" with respect to the proceeds from the sale or repayment of any loan which are to be used to make or finance any loan. For purposes of the preceding sentence, a nonpurpose investment shall not be treated as a loan.

[2]*(C)* Bonds used to provide construction financing. In the case of an issue described in subparagraph (A) any portion of which is used to make or finance loans for construction expenditures (within the meaning of subsection (f)(4)(C)(iv))—

(i) rules similar to the rules of subsection (f)(4)(C)(v) shall apply, and

(ii) subparagraph (A) shall be applied with respect to such portion by substituting "2 years" for "6 months".

[3]*(D)* Exception for mortgage revenue bonds. This paragraph shall not apply to any qualified mortgage bond or qualified veterans' mortgage bond.

(d) Special rules for reasonably required reserve or replacement fund.

* * * * * * * * * * *

(3) [4]**Repealed.**

* * * * * * * * * * *

(f) Required rebate to the United States.

* * * * * * * * * * *

(4) Special rules for applying paragraph (2).

* * * * * * * * * * *

(B) Temporary investments. Under regulations prescribed by the Secretary—

* * * * * * * * * * *

(ii) Additional period for certain bonds.

(I) In general. In the case of an issue described in subclause (II), clause (i) shall be applied by substituting "1 year" for "6 months" each place it appears with respect to the portion of the proceeds of the issue which are not expended in accordance with clause (i) if such portion does not exceed [5]*the lesser of 5 percent of the proceeds of the issue.*

* * * * * * * * * * *

(C) Exception from rebate for certain proceeds to be used to finance construction expenditures.—

* * * * * * * * * * *

[6]*(xvii) Treatment of bona fide debt service funds. If the spending requirements of clause (ii) are met with respect to the available construction proceeds of a construction issue, then paragraph (2) shall not apply to earnings on a bona fide debt service fund for such issue.*

(D) Exception for governmental units issuing $5,000,000 or less of bonds.—

* * * * * * * * * * *

CAUTION. Clause (f)(4)(D)(vii), following, is effective for bonds issued after 12/31/97.

[7]*(vii) Increase in exception for bonds financing public school capital expenditures. Each of the $5,000,000 amounts in the preceding provisions of this subparagraph shall be increased by the lesser of $5,000,000 or so much of the aggregate face amount of the bonds as are attributable to financing the construction (within the meaning of subparagraph (C)(iv)) of public school facilities.*

(E) [8]Repealed.

* * * * * * * * * * *

[For analysis, see ¶s 2502, 2503, 2507. For text of Committee Report see ¶s 5009, 5297, 5298.]

[Endnote Code Sec. 148]

Matter in *italics* in Code Sec. 148(c)(2)(B), Code Sec. 148(c)(2)(C), Code Sec. 148(c)(2)(D), Code Sec. 148(d), Code Sec. 148(f)(4), Code Sec. 148(f)(4)(B)(ii)(I) and Code Sec. 148(f)(4)(C)(xvii) added by Secs. 1441-1443 and Sec. 1444(a) of the Taxpayer Relief Act of 1997, H.R. 2014, 8/5/97, which struck out:

1. "(B) Special rule for certain student loan pools. In the case of the proceeds of an issue to be used to make or finance loans under a program described in section 144(b)(1)(A), subparagraph (A) shall be applied by substituting '18 months' for '6 months'. The preceding sentence shall not apply to any bond issued after December 31, 1988."

"(C)

2. "(D)"

3. "(E)"

4. "(3) Limitation on investment in nonpurpose investments.

"(A) In general. A bond which is part of an issue which does not meet the requirements of subparagraph (B) shall be treated as an arbitrage bond.

"(B) Requirements. An issue meets the requirements of this subparagraph only if—

"(i) at no time during any bond year may the amount invested in nonpurpose investments with a yield materially higher than the yield on the issue exceed 150 percent of the debt service on the issue for the bond year, and

"(ii) the aggregate amount invested as provided in clause (i) is promptly and appropriately reduced as the amount of outstanding bonds of the issue is reduced (or, in the case of a qualified mortgage bond or a qualified veterans' mortgage bond, as the mortgages are repaid).

"(C) Exceptions for temporary period. Subparagraph (B) shall not apply to—

"(i) proceeds of the issue invested for an initial temporary period until such proceeds are needed for the governmental purpose of the issue, and

"(ii) temporary investment periods related to debt service.

"(D) Debt service defined. For purposes of this paragraph, the debt service on the issue for any bond year is the scheduled amount of interest and amortization of principal payable for such year with respect to such issue. For purposes of the preceding sentence, there shall not be taken into account amounts scheduled with respect to any bond which has been redeemed before the beginning of the bond year.

"(E) No disposition in case of loss. This paragraph shall not require the sale or disposition of any investment if such sale or disposition would result in a loss which exceeds the amount which, but for such sale or disposition, would at the time of such sale or disposition—

"(i) be paid to the United States, or,

"(ii) in the case of a qualified veterans' mortgage bond, be paid or credited mortgagors under section 143(g)(3)(A).

"(F) Exception for governmental use bonds and qualified 501(c)(3) bonds. This paragraph shall not apply to any bond which is not a private activity bond or which is a qualified 501(c)(3) bond."

5. "the lesser of 5 percent of the proceeds of the issue or $100,000"

6. added clause (f)(4)(C)(xvii)

Effective Date (Sec. 1445, H.R. 2014, 8/5/97) effective for bonds issued after 8/5/97.

Code Sec. 148(f)(4)(D)(vii) was added by Sec. 223(a), H.R. 2014, 8/5/97.

7. added clause (f)(4)(D)(vii)

Effective Date (Sec. 223(b), H.R. 2014, 8/5/97) effective for bonds issued after 12/31/97.

Code Sec. 148(f)(4)(E) deleted by Sec. 1444(b), H.R. 2014, 8/5/97, which struck out:

8. "(E) Exception for certain qualified student loan bonds.

"(i) In general. In determining the aggregate amount earned on nonpurpose investments acquired with gross proceeds of an issue of bonds for a program described in section 144(b)(1)(A), the amount earned from investment of net proceeds of such issue during the initial temporary period under subsection (c) shall not be taken into account to the extent that the amount so earned is used to pay the reasonable—

"(I) administrative costs of such program attributable to such issue and the costs of carrying such issue, and

"(II) costs of issuing such issue,

but only to the extent such costs were financed with proceeds of such issue and for which the issuer was not reimbursed. Amounts designated as interest on student loans shall not be taken into account in determining whether the issuer is reimbursed for such costs. Except as otherwise hereafter provided in regulations prescribed by the Secretary, costs described in subclause (I) paid from amounts earned as described in the first sentence of this clause may also be taken into account in determining the yield on the student loans under a program described in section 144(b)(1)(A).

"(ii) Only arbitrage on amounts loaned during temporary period taken into account for administrative costs, etc. The amount earned from investment of net proceeds of an issue during the initial temporary period under subsection (c) shall be taken into account under clause (i)(I) only to the extent attributable to proceeds which were used to make or finance (not later than the close of such period) student loans under a program described in section 144(b)(1)(A).

"(iii) Election. This subparagraph shall not apply to any issue if the issuer elects not to have this subparagraph apply to such issue.

"(iv) Termination. This subparagraph shall not apply to any bond issued after December 31, 1988."

Effective Date (Sec. 1445, H.R. 2014, 8/5/97) effective for bonds issued after 8/5/97.

[¶ 3036]   Code Sec. 162.   Trade or business expenses.

(a) In general. There shall be allowed as a deduction all the ordinary and necessary expenses paid or incurred during the taxable year in carrying on any trade or business, including—

(1) a reasonable allowance for salaries or other compensation for personal services actually rendered;

(2) traveling expenses (including amounts expended for meals and lodging other than amounts which are lavish or extravagant under the circumstances) while away from home in the pursuit of a trade or business; and

(3) rentals or other payments required to be made as a condition to the continued use or possession, for purposes of the trade or business, of property to which the taxpayer has not taken or is not taking title or in which he has no equity.

For purposes of the preceding sentence, the place of residence of a Member of Congress (including any Delegate and Resident Commissioner) within the State, congressional district, or possession which he represents in Congress shall be considered his home, but amounts expended by such Members within each taxable year for living expenses shall not be deductible for income tax purposes in excess of $3,000. For purposes of paragraph (2), the taxpayer shall not be treated as being temporarily away from home during any period of employment if such period exceeds 1 year. [1]*The preceding sentence shall not apply to any Federal employee during any period for which such employee is certified by the Attorney General (or the designee thereof) as traveling on behalf of the United States in temporary duty status to investigate, or provide support services for the investigation of, a Federal crime.*

* * * * * * * * * * *

(l) Special rules for health insurance costs of self-employed individuals.

(1) Allowance of deduction.

* * * * * * * * * * * *

(B) Applicable percentage. For purposes of subparagraph (A), the applicable percentage shall be determined under the following table:

For taxable years beginning in calendar year—	The applicable percentage is—
1997	40 percent
1998 and 1999	45 percent
2000 and 2001	50 percent
2002	60 percent
2003 through 2005	80 percent
2006	90 percent
2007 and thereafter	100 percent

(2) Limitations.

* * * * * * * * * * * *

(B) Other coverage. Paragraph (1) shall not apply to any taxpayer for any calendar month for which the taxpayer is eligible to participate in any subsidized health plan maintained by any employer of the taxpayer or of the spouse of the taxpayer. [2]*The preceding sentence shall be applied separately with respect to—*

(i) *plans which include coverage for qualified long-term care services (as defined in section 7702B(c)) or are qualified long-term care insurance contracts (as defined in section 7702B(b)), and*

(ii) *plans which do not include such coverage and are not such contracts.*

* * * * * * * * * * * *

CAUTION.   Subsec. (o), following, is effective for tax. yrs. begin. after 12/31/97.

[3]*(o) Treatment of certain reimbursed expenses of rural mail carriers.*

(1) General rule. In the case of any employee of the United States Postal Service who performs services involving the collection and delivery of mail on a rural route and who receives qualified reimbursements for the expenses incurred by such employee for the use of a vehicle in performing such services—

(A) the amount allowable as a deduction under this chapter for the use of a vehicle in performing such services shall be equal to the amount of such qualified reimbursements; and

(B) such qualified reimbursements shall be treated as paid under a reimbursement or other expense allowance arrangement for purposes of section 62(a)(2)(A) (and section 62(c) shall not apply to such qualified reimbursements).

(2) Definition of qualified reimbursements. For purposes of this subsection, the term "qualified reimbursements" means the amounts paid by the United States Postal Service to employees as an equipment maintenance allowance under the 1991 collective bargaining agreement between the United States Postal Service and the National Rural Letter Carriers' Association. Amounts paid as an equipment maintenance allowance by such Postal Service under later collective bargaining agreements that supersede the 1991 agreement shall be considered qualified reimbursements if such amounts do not exceed the amounts that would have been paid under the 1991 agreement, adjusted for changes in the Consumer Price Index (as defined in section 1(f)(5)) since 1991.

CAUTION.   Subsec. (o), effective for services provided after 2/2/93, and on or before 12/31/95, has been redesignated by Sec. 1204(a) of H.R. 2014 as subsec. (p), which follows. This redesignation is effective for tax. yrs. begin. after 12/31/97.

[4]*(p)* **Cross reference.**

(1) For special rule relating to expenses in connection with subdividing real property for sale, see section 1237.

(2) For special rule relating to the treatment of payments by a transferee of a franchise, trademark, or trade name, see section 1253.

(3) For special rules relating to—

(A) funded welfare benefit plans, see section 419, and

(B) deferred compensation and other deferred benefits, see section 404.

[For analysis, see ¶s 105, 115, 1103, 1104. For text of Committee Report see ¶s 5071, 5203, 5204, 5372.]

[Endnote Code Sec. 162]
Matter in *italics* in Code Sec. 162(a) added by Sec. 1204(a) of the Taxpayer Relief Act of 1997, H.R. 2014, 8/5/97
1. added matter at the end of subsec. (a)
Effective Date (Sec. 1204(b), H.R. 2014, 8/5/97) effective for amounts paid or incurred for tax. yrs. end. after 8/5/97.

Matter in *italics* in Code Sec. 162(l)(2)(B), Code Sec. 162(l)(2)(B)(i) and Code Sec. 162(l)(2)(B)(ii) added by Sec. 1602(c), H.R. 2014, 8/5/97.
2. added matter in subpara. (l)(2)(B) and added clauses (l)(2)(B)(i) and (ii)
Effective Date (Sec. 1602(i), H.R. 2014, 8/5/97) effective for tax. yrs. begin. after 12/31/96.

Matter in *italics* in Code Sec. 162(o) and Code Sec. 162(p) added by Sec. 1203(a), H.R. 2014, 8/5/97, which struck out:
3. added subsec. (o)
4. "(o)"
Effective Date (Sec. 1203(c), H.R. 2014, 8/5/97) effective for tax. yrs. begin. after 12/31/97.

[¶ 3037]   Code Sec. 163.   Interest.

* * * * * * * * * * *

(h) Disallowance of deduction for personal interest.

* * * * * * * * * * * *

(2) Personal interest. For purposes of this subsection, the term "personal interest" means any interest allowable as a deduction under this chapter other than—

* * * * * * * * * * *

CAUTION.   Subpara. (h)(2)(E), following, is effective for estates of decedents dying before 1/1/98, except as provided in Sec. 503(d)(2) of H.R. 2014, reproduced in notes following this Code Sec. For subpara. (h)(2)(E), effective for estates of decedents dying after 12/31/97, except as provided in Sec. 503(d)(2) of H.R. 2014, reproduced in notes following this Code Sec., see below.

(E) any interest payable under section 6601 on any unpaid portion of the tax imposed by section 2001 for the period during which an extension of time for payment of such tax is in effect under section 6163 or 6166 or under section 6166A (as in effect before its repeal by the Economic Recovery Tax Act of 1981).

CAUTION.   Subpara. (h)(2)(E), following, is effective for estates of decedents dying after 12/31/97, except as provided in Sec. 503(d)(2) of H.R. 2014, reproduced in notes following this Code Sec.. For subpara. (h)(2)(E), effective for estates of decedents dying before 1/1/98, except as provided in Sec. 503(d)(2) of H.R. 2014, reproduced in notes following this Code Sec., see above.

(E) any interest payable under section 6601 on any unpaid portion of the tax imposed by section 2001 for the period during which an extension of time for payment of such tax is in effect under section 6163[1].

* * * * * * * * * * * *

(4) Other definitions and special rules. For purposes of this subsection—

(A) Qualified residence.

(i) In general. The term "qualified residence" means—

(I) the principal residence (within the meaning of [2]*section 121*) of the taxpayer, and

(II) 1 other residence of the taxpayer which is selected by the taxpayer for purposes of this subsection for the taxable year and which is used by the taxpayer as a residence (within the meaning of section 280A(d)(1)).

* * * * * * * * * * * *

(j) Limitation of deduction for interest on certain indebtedness.

* * * * * * * * * * * *

(2) Corporations to which subsection applies.

* * * * * * * * * * * *

(B) Excess interest expense.

* * * * * * * * * * * *

(iii) Excess limitation. For purposes of [3]*clause (ii)*, the term "excess limitation" means the excess (if any) of—

(I) 50 percent of the adjusted taxable income of the corporation, over

(II) the corporation's net interest expense.

* * * * * * * * * * * *

CAUTION. Subsec. (k), following, is is effective for estates of decedents dying before 1/1/98, except as provided in Sec. 503(d)(2) of H.R. 2014, reproduced in notes following this Code Sec. For subsec. (k) effective for estates of decedents dying after 12/31/97, except as provided in Sec. 503(d)(2) of H.R. 2014, reproduced in notes following this Code Sec., see below.

(k) Cross references.

(1) For disallowance of certain amounts paid in connection with insurance, endowment, or annuity contracts, see section 264.

(2) For disallowance of deduction for interest relating to tax-exempt income, see section 265(a)(2).

(3) For disallowance of deduction for carrying charges chargeable to capital account, see section 266.

(4) For disallowance of interest with respect to transactions between related taxpayers, see section 267.

(5) For treatment of redeemable ground rents and real property held subject to liabilities under redeemable ground rents, see section 1055.

CAUTION. Subsec. (k), following, is effective for estates of decedents dying after 12/31/97, except as provided in Sec. 503(d)(2) of H.R. 2014, reproduced in notes following this Code Sec. For subsec. (k), effective for estates of decedents dying before 1/1/98, except as provided in Sec. 503(d)(2) of H.R. 2014, reproduced in notes following this Code Sec., see above.

[4]*(k) Section 6166 interest. No deduction shall be allowed under this section for any interest payable under section 6601 on any unpaid portion of the tax imposed by section 2001 for the period during which an extension of time for payment of such tax is in effect under section 6166.*

[5](l) **Disallowance of deduction on certain debt instruments of corporations.**

(1) **In general.** No deduction shall be allowed under this chapter for any interest paid or accrued on a disqualified debt instrument.

(2) **Disqualified debt instrument.** For purposes of this subsection, the term "disqualified debt instrument" means any indebtedness of a corporation which is payable in equity of the issuer or a related party.

(3) **Special rules for amounts payable in equity.** For purposes of paragraph (2), indebtedness shall be treated as payable in equity of the issuer or a related party only if—

(A) a substantial amount of the principal or interest is required to be paid or converted, or at the option of the issuer or a related party is payable in, or convertible into, such equity,

(B) a substantial amount of the principal or interest is required to be determined, or at the option of the issuer or a related party is determined, by reference to the value of such equity, or

(C) the indebtedness is part of an arrangement which is reasonably expected to result in a transaction described in subparagraph (A) or (B).

For purposes of this paragraph, principal or interest shall be treated as required to be so paid, converted, or determined if it may be required at the option of the holder or a related party and there is a substantial certainty the option will be exercised.

(4) **Related party.** For purposes of this subsection, a person is a related party with respect to another person if such person bears a relationship to such other person described in section 267(b) or 707(b).

(5) **Regulations.** The Secretary shall prescribe such regulations as may be necessary or appropriate to carry out the purposes of this subsection, including regulations preventing avoidance of this subsection through the use of an issuer other than a corporation.

CAUTION.   Subsec. (m), following was subsec. (l) as redesignated from subsec. (k) by Sec. 503(b)(2)(A), H.R. 2014. See notes following this Code Sec. for effective date of this amendment. Subsec (l), as redesignated from (k), was further redesignated as subsec. (m) by Sec. 1005(a) of H.R. 2014, effective for disqualified debt instruments issued after 6/8/97, except as provided in Sec. 1005(b)(2) of H.R. 2014, reproduced in notes following this Code Sec..

[6](m) **Cross references.**

(1) For disallowance of certain amounts paid in connection with insurance, endowment, or annuity contracts, see section 264.

(2) For disallowance of deduction for interest relating to tax-exempt income, see section 265(a)(2).

(3) For disallowance of deduction for carrying charges chargeable to capital account, see section 266.

(4) For disallowance of interest with respect to transactions between related taxpayers, see section 267.

(5) For treatment of redeemable ground rents and real property held subject to liabilities under redeemable ground rents, see section 1055.

[For analysis, see ¶s 506, 1511. For text of Committee Report see ¶s 5028, 5115.]

[Endnote Code Sec. 163]

Sec. 503(b)(2)(B) of the Taxpayer Relief Act of 1997, H.R. 2014, 8/5/97, struck out from Code Sec. 163(h)(2)(E):

1. "or 6166 or under section 6166A (as in effect before its repeal by the Economic Recovery Tax Act of 1981)"

Effective Date (Sec. 503(d), H.R. 2014, 8/5/97) effective for estates of decedents dying after 12/31/97, except as provided in Sec. 503(d)(2) of this Act, which reads as follows:

"(2) Election.—In the case of the estate of any decedent dying before January 1, 1998, with respect to which there is an election under section 6166 of the Internal Revenue Code of 1986, the executor of the estate may elect to have the amendments made by this section apply with respect to installments due after the effective date of the election; except that the 2-percent portion of such installments shall be equal to the amount which would be the 4-percent portion of such installments without regard to such election. Such an election shall be made before January 1, 1999 in the manner prescribed by the Secretary of the Treasury and, once made, is irrevocable."

Matter in *italics* in Code Sec. 163(h)(4)(A)(i)(I) added by Sec. 312(d)(1), H.R. 2014, 8/5/97, which struck out:
2. "section 1034"
Effective Date (Sec. 312(d) [sic (e)], H.R. 2014, 8/5/97) effective for sales and exchanges after 5/6/97, except as provided by Secs. 312(d)(2)-(4) [sic (e)(2)-(4)] of this Act, which read as follows:
"(2) Sales before 8/5/97. At the election of the taxpayer, the amendments made by this section shall not apply to any sale or exchange before the date of the enactment of this Act.
"(3) Certain sales within 2 years after 8/5/97. Section 121 of the Internal Revenue Code of 1986 (as amended by this section) shall be applied without regard to subsection (c)(2)(B) thereof in the case of any sale or exchange of property during the 2-year period beginning on the date of the enactment of this Act if the taxpayer held such property on the date of the enactment of this Act and fails to meet the ownership and use requirements of subsection (a) thereof with respect to such property.
"(4) Binding contracts. At the election of the taxpayer, the amendments made by this section shall not apply to a sale or exchange after the date of the enactment of this Act, if—
"(A) such sale or exchange is pursuant to a contract which was binding on such date, or
"(B) without regard to such amendments, gain would not be recognized under section 1034 of the Internal Revenue Code of 1986 (as in effect on the day before the date of the enactment of this Act) on such sale or exchange by reason of a new residence acquired on or before such date or with respect to the acquisition of which by the taxpayer a binding contract was in effect on such date.
This paragraph shall not apply to any sale or exchange by an individual if the treatment provided by section 877(a)(1) of the Internal Revenue Code of 1986 applies to such individual."

Matter in *italics* in Code Sec. 163(j)(2)(B)(iii) added by Sec. 1604(g)(1), H.R. 2014, 8/5/97, which struck out:
3. "clause (i)"
Effective Date Effective 8/5/97.

Code Sec. 163(k) in *italics* was added by Sec. 503(b)(2)(A), H.R. 2014, 8/5/97. Sec. 503(b)(2)(A), H.R. 2014, 8/5/97, also redesignated the existing Code Sec. 163(k) as Code Sec. 163(l) which was further redesignated as Code Sec. 163(m) by Sec. 1005(a), H.R. 2014, 8/5/97, see below.
4. added subsec. (k)
Effective Date (Sec. 503(d), H.R. 2014, 8/5/97) effective for estates of decedents dying after 12/31/97, except as provided in Sec. 503(d)(2) of this Act, reproduced above.

Matter in *italics* in Code Sec. 163(l) and Code Sec. 163(m) added by Sec. 1005(a), H.R. 2014, 8/5/97, which struck out:
5. added subsec. (l)
6. "(l)"
Effective Date (Sec. 1005(b), H.R. 2014, 8/5/97) effective for disqualified debt instruments issued after 6/8/97, except as provided in Sec. 1005(b)(2) of this Act, which reads as follows:
"(2) Transition rule.—The amendment made by this section shall not apply to any instrument issued after June 8, 1997, if such instrument is—
"(A) issued pursuant to a written agreement which was binding on such date and at all times thereafter,
"(B) described in a ruling request submitted to the Internal Revenue Service on or before such date, or
"(C) described on or before such date in a public announcement or in a filing with the Securities and Exchange Commission required solely by reason of the issuance."

[¶ 3038]   Code Sec. 165.   Losses.

* * * * * * * * * * * *

(i) Disaster losses.

* * * * * * * * * * * *

[1]*(4) Use of disaster loan appraisals to establish amount of loss. Nothing in this title shall be construed to prohibit the Secretary from prescribing regulations or other guidance under which an appraisal for the purpose of obtaining a loan of Federal funds or a loan guarantee from the Federal Government as a result of a Presidentially declared disaster (as defined by section 1033(h)(3)) may be used to establish the amount of any loss described in paragraph (1) or (2).*

* * * * * * * * * * * *

[For analysis, see ¶ 111. For text of Committee Report see ¶ 5062.]

[Endnote Code Sec. 165]
Code Sec. 165(i)(4), in *italics*, was added by Sec. 912(a) of the Taxpayer Relief Act, H.R. 2014, 8/5/97.
1. added para. (i)(4)
Effective Date (Sec. 912(b), H.R. 2014, 8/5/97) effective 8/5/97.

[¶ 3039]   Code Sec. 167.   Depreciation.

* * * * * * * * * * *

(g) Depreciation under income forecast method.

* * * * * * * * * *

[1]*(6) Limitation on property for which income forecast method may be used. The depreciation deduction allowable under this section may be determined under the income forecast method or any similar method only with respect to—*

    (A) property described in paragraph (3) or (4) of section 168(f),

    (B) copyrights,

    (C) books,

    (D) patents, and

    (E) other property specified in regulations.

Such methods may not be used with respect to any amortizable section 197 intangible (as defined in section 197(c)).

* * * * * * * * * * * *

[For analysis, see ¶ 801. For text of Committee Report see ¶ 5163.]

[Endnote Code Sec. 167]
Code Sec. 167(g)(6), in *italics,* was added by Sec. 1086(a) of the Taxpayer Relief Act of 1997, H.R. 2014, 8/5/97.
1. added para. (g)(6)
Effective Date (Sec. 1086(c), H.R. 2014, 8/5/97) effective for property placed in service after 8/5/97.

[¶ 3040]   Code Sec. 168.   Accelerated cost recovery system.

* * * * * * * * * * *

(e) Classification of property. For purposes of this section—

* * * * * * * * * * * *

(3) Classification of certain property.

    (A) 3-year property. The term "3-year property" includes—

        (i) any race horse which is more than 2 years old at the time it is placed in service,[1]

        (ii) any horse other than a race horse which is more than 12 years old at the time it is placed in service[2], *and*

    [3]*(iii) any qualified rent-to-own property.*

* * * * * * * * * * *

(g) Alternative depreciation system for certain property.

* * * * * * * * * * * *

(3) Special rules for determining class life.

* * * * * * * * * * *

    (B) Special rule for certain property assigned to classes. For purposes of paragraph (2), in the case of property described in any of the following subparagraphs of subsection (e)(3), the class life shall be determined as follows:

If property is described in subparagraph:	The class life is:
[4](A)(iii)	4
(B)(ii)...	5
(B)(iii)	9.5
(C)(i)	10

* * * * * * * * * * *

(i) Definitions and special rules. For purposes of this section—

* * * * * * * * * * *

(8) Treatment of leasehold improvements.

* * * * * * * * * * *

[5]*(C) Cross reference. For treatment of qualified long-term real property constructed or improved in connection with cash or rent reduction from lessor to lessee, see section 110(b).*

* * * * * * * * * * *

[6]*(14) Qualified rent-to-own property.*
    (A) In general. The term "qualified rent-to-own property" means property held by a rent-to-own dealer for purposes of being subject to a rent-to-own contract.
    (B) Rent-to-own dealer. The term "rent-to-own dealer" means a person that, in the ordinary course of business, regularly enters into rent-to-own contracts with customers for the use of consumer property, if a substantial portion of those contracts terminate and the property is returned to such person before the receipt of all payments required to transfer ownership of the property from such person to the customer.
    (C) Consumer property. The term "consumer property" means tangible personal property of a type generally used within the home for personal use.
    (D) Rent-to-own contract. The term "rent-to-own contract" means any lease for the use of consumer property between a rent-to-own dealer and a customer who is an individual which—
        (i) is titled "Rent-to-Own Agreement" or "Lease Agreement with Ownership Option," or uses other similar language,
        (ii) provides for level (or decreasing where no payment is less than 40 percent of the largest payment), regular periodic payments (for a payment period which is a week or month),
        (iii) provides that legal title to such property remains with the rent-to-own dealer until the customer makes all the payments described in clause (ii) or early purchase payments required under the contract to acquire legal title to the item of property,
        (iv) provides a beginning date and a maximum period of time for which the contract may be in effect that does not exceed 156 weeks or 36 months from such beginning date (including renewals or options to extend),
        (v) provides for level payments within the 156-week or 36-month period that, in the aggregate, generally exceed the normal retail price of the consumer property plus interest,
        (vi) provides for payments under the contract that, in the aggregate, do not exceed $10,000 per item of consumer property,
        (vii) provides that the customer does not have any legal obligation to make all the payments referred to in clause (ii) set forth under the contract, and that at the end of each payment period the customer may either continue to use the consumer property by making the payment for the next payment period or return such property to the rent-to-own dealer in good working order, in which case the customer does not incur any further obligations under the contract and is not entitled to a return of any payments previously made under the contract, and
        (viii) provides that the customer has no right to sell, sublease, mortgage, pawn, pledge, encumber, or otherwise dispose of the consumer property until all the payments stated in the contract have been made.

(j) Property on Indian reservations.

* * * * * * * * * * *

(6) Indian reservation defined. For purposes of this subsection, the term "Indian reservation" means a reservation, as defined in—

(A) section 3(d) of the Indian Financing Act of 1974 (25 U.S.C. 1452(d)), or

(B) section 4(10) of the Indian Child Welfare Act of 1978 (25 U.S.C. 1903(10)). [7]

For purposes of the preceding sentence, such section 3(d) shall be applied by treating the term "former Indian reservations in Oklahoma" as including only lands which are within the jurisdictional area of an Oklahoma Indian tribe (as determined by the Secretary of the Interior) and are recognized by such Secretary as eligible for trust land status under 25 CFR Part 151 (as in effect on the date of the enactment of this sentence).

* * * * * * * * * * *

[For analysis, see ¶s 803, 806. For text of Committee Report see ¶s 5163, 5388.]

[Endnote Code Sec. 168]

Matter in *italics* in Code Sec. 168(e)(3)(A)(i), Code Sec. 168(e)(3)(A)(ii), Code Sec. 168(e)(3)(A)(iii) and Code Sec. 168(g)(3)(B) added by Sec. 1086(b)(1) and (2) of the Taxpayer Relief Act of 1997, H.R. 2014, 8/5/97, which struck out:
1. "and"
2. "."
3. added clause (e)(3)(A)(iii)
4. added matter in subpara. (g)(3)(B)
Effective Date (Sec. 1086(c), H.R. 2014, 8/5/97) effective for property placed in service after 8/5/97.

Code Sec. 168(i)(8)(C), in *italics*, was added by Sec. 1213(c), H.R. 2014, 8/5/97.
5. added subpara. (i)(8)(C)
Effective Date (Sec. 1213(e), H.R. 2014, 8/5/97) effective for leases entered into after 8/5/97.

Code Sec. 168(i)(14), in *italics*, was added by Sec. 1086(b)(3), H.R. 2014, 8/5/97.
6. added para. (i)(14)
Effective Date (Sec. 1086(c), H.R. 2014, 8/5/97) effective for property placed in service after 8/5/97.

Matter in *italics* in para. (j)(6) was added by Sec. 1604(c)(1), H.R. 2014, 8/5/97.
7. added matter in para. (j)(6)
Effective Date (Sec. 1604(c)(2), H.R. 2014, 8/5/97) effective for property placed in service after 12/31/93, except as provided in Sec. 1604(c)(2)(A) and (B) of this Act, which reads as follows:
"(A) with respect to property (with an applicable recovery period under section 168(j) of the Internal Revenue Code of 1986 of 6 years or less) held by the taxpayer if the taxpayer claimed the benefits of section 168(j) of such Code with respect to such property on a return filed before March 18, 1997, but only if such return is the first return of tax filed for the taxable year in which such property was placed in service, or
"(B) with respect to wages for which the taxpayer claimed the benefits of section 45A of such Code for a taxable year on a return filed before March 18, 1997, but only if such return was the first return of tax filed for such taxable year."

[¶ 3041]   Code Sec. 170.   Charitable, etc., contributions and gifts.

* * * * * * * * * * *

(e) Certain contributions of ordinary income and capital gain property.

* * * * * * * * * * *

(5) Special rule for contributions of stock for which market quotations are readily available.

* * * * * * * * * * *

(D) Termination. This paragraph shall not apply to contributions made—

* * * * * * * * * * *

(ii) after [1]*June 30, 1998.*

CAUTION.   Para. (e)(6), following, is effective for tax. yrs. begin. after 12/31/97.

[2]*(6) Special rule for contributions of computer technology and equipment for elementary or secondary school purposes.*

(A) Limit on reduction. In the case of a qualified elementary or secondary educational contribution, the reduction under paragraph (1)(A) shall be no greater than the amount determined under paragraph (3)(B).

(B) Qualified elementary or secondary educational contribution. For purposes of this paragraph, the term "qualified elementary or secondary educational contribution" means a charitable contribution by a corporation of any computer technology or equipment, but only if —

　(i) the contribution is to—

　　(I) an educational organization described in subsection (b)(1)(A)(ii), or

　　(II) an entity described in section 501(c)(3) and exempt from tax under section 501(a) (other than an entity described in subclause (I)) that is organized primarily for purposes of supporting elementary and secondary education,

　(ii) the contribution is made not later than 2 years after the date the taxpayer acquired the property (or in the case of property constructed by the taxpayer, the date the construction of the property is substantially completed),

　(iii) the original use of the property is by the donor or the donee,

　(iv) substantially all of the use of the property by the donee is for use within the United States for educational purposes in any of the grades K-12 that are related to the purpose or function of the organization or entity,

　(v) the property is not transferred by the donee in exchange for money, other property, or services, except for shipping, installation and transfer costs,

　(vi) the property will fit productively into the entity's education plan, and

　(vii) the entity's use and disposition of the property will be in accordance with the provisions of clauses (iv) and (v).

(C) Contribution to private foundation. A contribution by a corporation of any computer technology or equipment to a private foundation (as defined in section 509) shall be treated as a qualified elementary or secondary educational contribution for purposes of this paragraph if—

　(i) the contribution to the private foundation satisfies the requirements of clauses (ii) and (v) of subparagraph (B), and

　(ii) within 30 days after such contribution, the private foundation—

　　(I) contributes the property to an entity described in clause (i) of subparagraph (B) that satisfies the requirements of clauses (iv) through (vii) of subparagraph (B), and

　　(II) notifies the donor of such contribution.

(D) Special rule relating to construction of property. For the purposes of this paragraph, the rules of paragraph (4)(C) shall apply.

(E) Definitions. For the purposes of this paragraph—

　(i) Computer technology or equipment. The term "computer technology or equipment" means computer software (as defined by section 197(e)(3)(B)), computer or peripheral equipment (as defined by section 168(i)(2)(B)), and fiber optic cable related to computer use.

　(ii) Corporation. The term "corporation" has the meaning given to such term by paragraph (4)(D).

(F) Termination. This paragraph shall not apply to any contribution made during any taxable year beginning after December 31, 1999.

* * * * * * * * * * * *

(h) Qualified conservation contribution.

* * * * * * * * * * * * *

(5) Exclusively for conservation purposes. For purposes of this subsection—

　(B) No surface mining permitted.

CAUTION. Clause (h)(5)(B)(ii), following, is effective for easements granted before 1/1/98. For clause (h)(5)(B)(ii), effective for easements granted after 12/31/97, see below.

(ii) Special rule. With respect to any contribution of property in which the ownership of the surface estate and mineral interests were separated before June 13, 1976, and remain so separated, subparagraph (A) shall be treated as met if the probability of surface mining occurring on such property is so remote as to be negligible.

CAUTION. Clause (h)(5)(B)(ii), following, is effective for easements granted after 12/31/97. For clause (h)(5)(B)(ii), effective for easements granted before 1/1/98, see above.

[3]*(ii) Special rule. With respect to any contribution of property in which the ownership of the surface estate and mineral interests has been and remains separated, subparagraph (A) shall be treated as met if the probability of surface mining occurring on such property is so remote as to be negligible.*

* * * * * * * * * * * *

CAUTION. Subsec. (i), following, is effective for tax. yrs. begin. before 1/1/98. For subsec. (i), effective for tax. yrs. begin. after 12/31/97, see below.

(i) Standard mileage rate for use of passenger automobile. For purposes of computing the deduction under this section for use of a passenger automobile the standard mileage rate shall be 12 cents per mile.

CAUTION. Subsec. (i), following, is effective for tax. yrs. begin. after 12/31/97. For subsec. (i), effective for tax. yrs. begin. before 1/1/98, see above.

[4]*(i) Standard mileage rate for use of passenger automobile. For purposes of computing the deduction under this section for use of a passenger automobile, the standard mileage rate shall be 14 cents per mile.*

* * * * * * * * * * * *

[For analysis, see ¶s 106, 107, 520, 1512. For text of Committee Report see ¶s 5010, 5033, 5037, 5096.]

[Endnote Code Sec. 170]
   Matter in *italics* in Code Sec. 170(e)(5)(D)(ii) added by Sec. 602(a) of the Taxpayer Relief Act of 1997, H.R. 2014, 8/5/97, which struck out:
   1. "May 31, 1997"
Effective Date (Sec. 602(a), H.R. 2014, 8/5/97) effective for contributions after 5/31/97.

   Code Sec. 170(e)(6), in *italics*, was added by Sec. 224(a), H.R. 2014, 8/5/97.
   2. added para. (e)(6)
Effective Date (Sec. 224(b), H.R. 2014, 8/5/97) effective for tax. yrs. begin. after 12/31/97.

   Matter in *italics* in Code Sec. 170(h)(5)(B)(ii) added by Sec. 508(d), H.R. 2014, 8/5/97, which struck out:
   3. "(ii) Special rule. With respect to any contribution of property in which the ownership of the surface estate and mineral interests were separated before June 13, 1976, and remain so separated, subparagraph (A) shall be treated as met if the probability of surface mining occurring on such property is so remote as to be negligible."
Effective Date (Sec. 508(e)(2), H.R. 2014, 8/5/97) effective for easements granted after 12/31/97.

   Matter in *italics* in Code Sec. 170(i) added by Sec. 973(d), H.R. 2014, 8/5/97, which struck out:
   4. "(i) Standard mileage rate for use of passenger automobile. For purposes of computing the deduction under this section for use of a passenger automobile the standard mileage rate shall be 12 cents per mile."
Effective Date (Sec. 973(b), H.R. 2014, 8/5/97) effective for tax. yrs. begin. after 12/31/97.

[¶ 3042] Code Sec. 172.   Net operating loss deduction.

* * * * * * * * * * * *

(b) Net operating loss carrybacks and carryovers.

(1) Years to which loss may be carried.

(A) General rule. Except as otherwise provided in this paragraph, a net operating loss for any taxable year—

(i) shall be a net operating loss carryback to each of the [1]2 taxable years preceding the taxable year of such loss, and

(ii) shall be a net operating loss carryover to each of the [2]20 taxable years following the taxable year of the loss.

* * * * * * * * * * * *

[3]*(F) Retention of 3-year carryback in certain cases.*

(i) In general. Subparagraph (A)(i) shall be applied by substituting "3 years" for "2 years" with respect to the portion of the net operating loss for the taxable year which is an eligible loss with respect to the taxpayer.

(ii) Eligible loss. For purposes of clause (i), the term "eligible loss" means—

(I) in the case of an individual, losses of property arising from fire, storm, shipwreck, or other casualty, or from theft,

(II) in the case of a taxpayer which is a small business, net operating losses attributable to Presidentially declared disasters (as defined in section 1033(h)(3)), and

(III) in the case of a taxpayer engaged in the trade or business of farming (as defined in section 263A(e)(4)), net operating losses attributable to such Presidentially declared disasters.

(iii) Small business. For purposes of this subparagraph, the term "small business" means a corporation or partnership which meets the gross receipts test of section 448(c) for the taxable year in which the loss arose (or, in the case of a sole proprietorship, which would meet such test if such proprietorship were a corporation).

* * * * * * * * * * * *

[For analysis, see ¶ 1510. For text of Committee Report see ¶ 5159.]

[Endnote Code Sec. 172]

Matter in *italics* in Code Sec. 172(b)(1)(A)(i), Code Sec. 172(b)(1)(A)(ii) and Code Sec. 172(b)(1)(F) added by Sec. 1082(a) and (b) of the Taxpayer Relief Act of 1997, H.R. 2014, 8/5/97, which struck out:

1. "3"
2. "15"
3. added subparagraph (b)(1)(F)

Effective Date (Sec. 1082(c), H.R. 2014, 8/5/97) effective for net operating losses for tax. yrs. begin. after 8/5/97.

[¶ 3043] Code Sec.[1] 198.   Expensing of environmental remediation costs.

(a) In general. A taxpayer may elect to treat any qualified environmental remediation expenditure which is paid or incurred by the taxpayer as an expense which is not chargeable to capital account. Any expenditure which is so treated shall be allowed as a deduction for the taxable year in which it is paid or incurred.

(b) Qualified environmental remediation expenditure. For purposes of this section—

(1) In general. The term "qualified environmental remediation expenditure" means any expenditure—

(A) which is otherwise chargeable to capital account, and

(B) which is paid or incurred in connection with the abatement or control of hazardous substances at a qualified contaminated site.

(2) Special rule for expenditures for depreciable property. Such term shall not include any expenditure for the acquisition of property of a character subject to the allowance for depreciation which is used in connection with the abatement or control of hazardous substances at a qualified contaminated site; except that the portion of the allowance under section 167 for such property which is otherwise allocated to such site shall be treated as a qualified environmental remediation expenditure.

(c) Qualified contaminated site. For purposes of this section—

(1) Qualified contaminated site.

(A) In general. The term "qualified contaminated site" means any area—

(i) which is held by the taxpayer for use in a trade or business or for the production of income, or which is property described in section 1221(1) in the hands of the taxpayer,

(ii) which is within a targeted area, and

(iii) at or on which there has been a release (or threat of release) or disposal of any hazardous substance.

(B) Taxpayer must receive statement from state environmental agency. An area shall be treated as a qualified contaminated site with respect to expenditures paid or incurred during any taxable year only if the taxpayer receives a statement from the appropriate agency of the State in which such area is located that such area meets the requirements of clauses (ii) and (iii) of subparagraph (A).

(C) Appropriate state agency. For purposes of subparagraph (B), the chief executive officer of each State may, in consultation with the Administrator of the Environmental Protection Agency, designate the appropriate State environmental agency within 60 days of the 8/5/97 of this section. If the chief executive officer of a State has not designated an appropriate State environmental agency within such 60-day period, the appropriate environmental agency for such State shall be designated by the Administrator of the Environmental Protection Agency.

(2) Targeted area.

(A) In general. The term "targeted area" means—

(i) any population census tract with a poverty rate of not less than 20 percent,

(ii) a population census tract with a population of less than 2,000 if—

(I) more than 75 percent of such tract is zoned for commercial or industrial use, and

(II) such tract is contiguous to 1 or more other population census tracts which meet the requirement of clause (i) without regard to this clause,

(iii) any empowerment zone or enterprise community (and any supplemental zone designated on December 21, 1994), and

(iv) any site announced before February 1, 1997, as being included as a brownfields pilot project of the Environmental Protection Agency.

(B) National priorities listed sites not included. Such term shall not include any site which is on, or proposed for, the national priorities list under section 105(a)(8)(B) of the Comprehensive Environmental Response, Compensation, and Liability Act of 1980 (as in effect on the date of the enactment of this section).

(C) Certain rules to apply. For purposes of this paragraph the rules of sections 1392(b)(4) and 1393(a)(9) shall apply.

(d) Hazardous substance. For purposes of this section—

(1) In general. The term "hazardous substance" means—

(A) any substance which is a hazardous substance as defined in section 101(14) of the Comprehensive Environmental Response, Compensation, and Liability Act of 1980, and

(B) any substance which is designated as a hazardous substance under section 102 of such Act.

(2) Exception. Such term shall not include any substance with respect to which a removal or remedial action is not permitted under section 104 of such Act by reason of subsection (a)(3) thereof.

(e) Deduction recaptured as ordinary income on sale, etc. Solely for purposes of section 1245, in the case of property to which a qualified environmental remediation expenditure would have been capitalized but for this section—

(1) the deduction allowed by this section for such expenditure shall be treated as a deduction for depreciation, and

(2) such property (if not otherwise section 1245 property) shall be treated as section 1245 property solely for purposes of applying section 1245 to such deduction.

(f) Coordination with other provisions. Sections 280B and 468 shall not apply to amounts which are treated as expenses under this section.

(g) Regulations. The Secretary shall prescribe such regulations as may be necessary or appropriate to carry out the purposes of this section.

(h) Termination. This section shall not apply to expenditures paid or incurred after December 31, 2000.

[For analysis, see ¶ 808. For text of Committee Report see ¶ 5073.]

[Endnote Code Sec. 198]
Code Sec. 198 was added by Sec. 941(a) of the Taxpayer Relief Act of 1997, H.R. 2014, 8/5/97.
1. added Code Sec. 198
Effective Date (Sec. 941(c), H.R. 2014, 8/5/97) effective for expenditures paid or incurred after 8/5/97, in tax. yrs. end. after 8/5/97.

[¶ 3044]   Code Sec. 216.   Deduction of taxes, interest, and business depreciation by cooperative housing corporation tenant-stockholder.

* * * * * * * * * * * *

(e) Distributions by cooperative housing corporations. Except as provided in regulations no gain or loss shall be recognized on the distribution by a cooperative housing corporation of a dwelling unit to a stockholder in such corporation if such distribution is in exchange for the stockholder's stock in such corporation and [1]*such dwelling unit is used as his principal residence (within the meaning of section 121).*

[Endnote Code Sec. 216]
Matter in *italics* in Code Sec. 216(e) added by Sec. 312(d)(4) of the Taxpayer Relief Act of 1997, H.R. 2014, 8/5/97, which struck out:
1. "such exchange qualifies for nonrecognition of gain under section 1034(f)"
Effective Date (Sec. 312(d) [sic (e)], H.R. 2014, 8/5/97) effective for sales and exchanges after 5/6/97, except as provided in Sec. 312(d)(2)-(4) [(e)(2)-(4)] of this Act, which reads as follows:
"(2) Sales before 8/5/97. At the election of the taxpayer, the amendments made by this section shall not apply to any sale or exchange before the date of the enactment of this Act.
"(3) Certain sales within 2 years after 8/5/97. Section 121 of the Internal Revenue Code of 1986 (as amended by this section) shall be applied without regard to subsection (c)(2)(B) thereof in the case of any sale or exchange of property during the 2-year period beginning on the date of the enactment of this Act if the taxpayer held such property on the date of the enactment of this Act and fails to meet the ownership and use requirements of subsection (a) thereof with respect to such property.
"(4) Binding contracts. At the election of the taxpayer, the amendments made by this section shall not apply to a sale or exchange after the date of the enactment of this Act, if—
"(A) such sale or exchange is pursuant to a contract which was binding on such date, or
"(B) without regard to such amendments, gain would not be recognized under section 1034 of the Internal Revenue Code of 1986 (as in effect on the day before the date of the enactment of this Act) on such sale or exchange by reason of a new residence acquired on or before such date or with respect to the acquisition of which by the taxpayer a binding contract was in effect on such date.
This paragraph shall not apply to any sale or exchange by an individual if the treatment provided by section 877(a)(1) of the Internal Revenue Code of 1986 applies to such individual."

[¶ 3045]   Code Sec. 219.   Retirement savings.

* * * * * * * * * * * *

(c) Special rules for certain married individuals.

(1) In general. In the case of an individual to whom this paragraph applies for the taxable year, the limitation of paragraph (1) of subsection (b) shall be equal to the lesser of—

* * * * * * * * * * * *

(B) the sum of—

* * * * * * * * * * *

CAUTION. Clause (c)(1)(B)(ii), following, is effective for tax. yrs. begin. before 1/1/98. For clause (c)(1)(B)(ii), effective for tax. yrs. begin. after 12/31/97, see below.

(ii) the compensation includible in the gross income of such individual's spouse for the taxable year reduced by the amount allowed as a deduction under subsection (a) to such spouse for such taxable year.

CAUTION. Clause (c)(1)(B)(ii), following, is effective for tax. yrs. begin. after 12/31/97. For clause (c)(1)(B)(ii), effective for tax. yrs. begin. before 1/1/98, see above.

[1]*(ii) the compensation includible in the gross income of such individual's spouse for the taxable year reduced by—*

(I) the amount allowed as a deduction under subsection (a) to such spouse for such taxable year, and

(II) the amount of any contribution on behalf of such spouse to a Roth IRA under section 408A for such taxable year.

* * * * * * * * * * *

(g) Limitation on deduction for active participants in certain pension plans.

CAUTION. Para. (g)(1), following, is effective for tax. yrs. begin. before 1/1/98. For para. (g)(1), effective for tax. yrs. begin. after 12/31/97, see below.

(1) In general. If (for any part of any plan year ending with or within a taxable year) an individual or the individual's spouse is an active participant, each of the dollar limitations contained in subsections (b)(1)(A) and (c)(1)(A) for such taxable year shall be reduced (but not below zero) by the amount determined under paragraph (2).

CAUTION. Para. (g)(1), following, is effective for tax. yrs. begin. after 12/31/97. For para. (g)(1), effective for tax. yrs. begin. before 1/1/98, see above.

(1) In general. If (for any part of any plan year ending with or within a taxable year) an individual[2] is an active participant, each of the dollar limitations contained in subsections (b)(1)(A) and (c)(1)(A) for such taxable year shall be reduced (but not below zero) by the amount determined under paragraph (2).

(2) Amount of reduction.

(A) In general. The amount determined under this paragraph with respect to any dollar limitation shall be the amount which bears the same ratio to such limitation as—

* * * * * * * * * * *

CAUTION. Clause (g)(2)(A)(ii), following, is effective for tax. yrs. begin. before 1/1/98. For clause (g)(2)(A)(ii), effective for tax. yrs. begin. after 12/31/97, see below.

(ii) $10,000.

CAUTION. Clause (g)(2)(A)(ii), following, is effective for tax. yrs. begin. after 12/31/97. For clause (g)(2)(A)(ii), effective for tax. yrs. begin. before 1/1/98, see above.

(ii) $10,000 [3]($20,000 in the case of a joint return for a taxable year beginning after December 31, 2006).

* * * * * * * * * * *

(3) Adjusted gross income; applicable dollar amount. For purposes of this subsection—

* * * * * * * * * * *

CAUTION. Subpara. (g)(3)(B), following, is effective for tax. yrs. begin. before 1/1/98. For subpara. (g)(3)(B), effective for tax. yrs. begin. after 12/31/97, see below.

(B) Applicable dollar amount. The term "applicable dollar amount" means—

(i) in the case of a taxpayer filing a joint return, $40,000,

(ii) in the case of any other taxpayer (other than a married individual filing a separate return), $25,000, and

(iii) in the case of a married individual filing a separate return, zero.

CAUTION. Subpara. (g)(3)(B), following, is effective for tax. yrs. begin. after 12/31/97. For subpara. (g)(3)(B), effective for tax. yrs. begin. before 1/1/98, see above.

[4](B) *Applicable dollar amount. The term "applicable dollar amount" means the following:*

(i) In the case of a taxpayer filing a joint return:

For taxable years beginning in:	The applicable dollar amount is:
1998	$ 50,000
1999	$ 51,000
2000	$ 52,000
2001	$ 53,000
2002	$ 54,000
2003	$ 60,000
2004	$ 65,000
2005	$ 70,000
2006	$ 75,000
2007 and thereafter	$ 80,000

(ii) In the case of any other taxpayer (other than a married individual filing a separate return):

For taxable years beginning in:	The applicable dollar amount is:
1998	$ 30,000
1999	$ 31,000
2000	$ 32,000
2001	$ 33,000
2002	$ 34,000
2003	$ 40,000
2004	$ 45,000
2005 and thereafter	$ 50,000

(iii) In the case of a married individual filing a separate return, zero.

* * * * * * * * * * * *

CAUTION. Para. (g)(7), following, is effective for tax. yrs. begin. after 12/31/97.

[5]*(7) Special rule for certain spouses. In the case of an individual who is an active participant at no time during any plan year ending with or within the taxable year but whose spouse is an active participant for any part of any such plan year—*

(A) the applicable dollar amount under paragraph (3)(B)(i) with respect to the taxpayer shall be $150,000, and

(B) the amount applicable under paragraph (2)(A)(ii) shall be $10,000.

* * * * * * * * * * * *

[For analysis, see ¶s 301, 302. For text of Committee Report see ¶s 5015, 5016.]

Matter in *italics* in Code Sec. 219(c)(1)(B)(ii) added by Sec. 302(c) of the Taxpayer Relief Act of 1997, H.R. 2014, 8/5/97, which struck out:

1. "(ii) the compensation includible in the gross income of such individual's spouse for the taxable year reduced by the amount allowed as a deduction under subsection (a) to such spouse for such taxable year."
Effective Date (Sec. 302(f), H.R. 2014, 8/5/97) effective for tax. yrs. begin. after 12/31/97.

Matter in *italics* in Code Sec. 219(g)(1), Code Sec. 219(g)(2)(A)(ii), Code Sec. 219(g)(3)(B) and Code Sec. 219(g)(7) added by Sec. 301(a)(1), (a)(2), (b)(1), and (b)(2), H.R. 2014, 8/5/97, which struck out:

2. "or the individual's spouse"
3. added matter in clause (g)(2)(A)(ii)
4. "(B) Applicable dollar amount. The term 'applicable dollar amount' means —
"(i) in the case of a taxpayer filing a joint return, $40,000,
"(ii) in the case of any other taxpayer (other than a married individual filing a separate return), $25,000, and
"(iii) in the case of a married individual filing a separate return, zero."
5. added para. (g)(7)
Effective Date (Sec. 301(c), H.R. 2014, 8/5/97) effective for tax. yrs. begin. after 12/31/97.

[¶ 3046]   Code Sec. 220.   Medical savings accounts.

* * * * * * * * * * * *

(b) Limitations.

* * * * * * * * * * * *

[1-B]*(7) Medicare eligible individuals. The limitation under this subsection for any month with respect to an individual shall be zero for the first month such individual is entitled to benefits under title XVIII of the Social Security Act and for each month thereafter.*

(c) Definitions. For purposes of this section —

* * * * * * * * * * * *

(3) Permitted insurance. The term "permitted insurance" means —

[2]*(A)* insurance if substantially all of the coverage provided under such insurance relates to —

    (i) liabilities incurred under workers' compensation laws,

    (ii) tort liabilities,

    (iii) liabilities relating to ownership or use of property, or

    (iv) such other similar liabilities as the Secretary may specify by regulations,

[3]*(B)* insurance for a specified disease or illness, and

[4]*(C)* insurance paying a fixed amount per day (or other period) of hospitalization.

* * * * * * * * * * * *

(d) Medical savings account. For purposes of this section —

* * * * * * * * * * * *

(2) Qualified medical expenses.

* * * * * * * * * * * *

(C) Medical expenses of individuals who are not eligible individuals. Subparagraph (A) shall apply to an amount paid by an account holder for medical care of an individual who is not [5]*described in clauses (i) and (ii) of subsection (c)(1)(A)* for the month in which the expense for such care is incurred only if no amount is contributed (other than a rollover contribution) to any medical savings account of such account holder for the taxable year which includes such month. This subparagraph shall not apply to any expense for coverage described in subclause (I) or (III) of subparagraph (B)(ii).

* * * * * * * * * * * *

[For analysis, see ¶s 1201, 1202. For text of Committee Report see ¶s 5370, 5501.]

Code Sec. 220(b)(7) in *italics* was added by Sec. 4006(b) of the Balanced Budget Act of 1997, H.R. 2014, 8/5/97.
1_B. added para. (b)(7)
Effective Date (Sec. 4006(c), H.R. 2015, 8/5/97) effective for tax. yrs. begin. after 12/31/98.

Matter in *italics* in Code Sec. 220(c)(3)(A), Code Sec. 220(c)(3)(B), Code Sec. 220(c)(3)(C), Code Sec. 220(c)(3)(D), and Code Sec. 220(d)(2)(C) added by Secs. 1602(a)(2) and (3) of the Taxpayer Relief Act of 1997, H.R. 2014, 8/5/97, which struck out:
2. "(A) Medicare supplemental insurance,
"(B)"
3. "(C)"
4. "(D)"
5. "an eligible individual"
Effective Date (Sec. 1602(i), H.R. 2014, 8/5/97) effective for tax. yrs. begin. after 12/31/96.

[¶ 3047]   Code Sec.[1] 221.   Interest on education loans.

(a) **Allowance of deduction.** In the case of an individual, there shall be allowed as a deduction for the taxable year an amount equal to the interest paid by the taxpayer during the taxable year on any qualified education loan.

(b) **Maximum Deduction.**

(1) **In general.** Except as provided in paragraph (2), the deduction allowed by subsection (a) for the taxable year shall not exceed the amount determined in accordance with the following table:

In the case of taxable years beginning in:	The dollar amount is:
1998	$1,000
1999	$1,500
2000	$2,000
2001 or thereafter	$2,500

(2) **Limitation based on modified adjusted gross income.**

(A) In general. The amount which would (but for this paragraph) be allowable as a deduction under this section shall be reduced (but not below zero) by the amount determined under subparagraph (B).

(B) Amount of reduction. The amount determined under this subparagraph is the amount which bears the same ratio to the amount which would be so taken into account as—

(i) the excess of—

(I) the taxpayer's modified adjusted gross income for such taxable year, over

(II) $40,000 ($60,000 in the case of a joint return), bears to

(ii) $15,000.

(C) Modified adjusted gross income. The term "modified adjusted gross income" means adjusted gross income determined—

(i) without regard to this section and sections 135, 137, 911, 931, and 933, and

(ii) after application of sections 86, 219, and 469.

For purposes of sections 86, 135, 137, 219, and 469, adjusted gross income shall be determined without regard to the deduction allowed under this section.

(c) **Dependents Not Eligible for Deduction.** No deduction shall be allowed by this section to an individual for the taxable year if a deduction under section 151 with respect to such individual is allowed to another taxpayer for the taxable year beginning in the calendar year in which such individual's taxable year begins.

(d) **Limit on Period Deduction Allowed.** A deduction shall be allowed under this section only with respect to interest paid on any qualified education loan during the first 60 months (whether or not consecutive) in which interest payments are required. For purposes of this paragraph, any loan and all refinancings of such loan shall be treated as 1 loan.

(e) **Definitions.** For purposes of this section—

(1) **Qualified education loan.** The term "qualified education loan" means any indebtedness incurred to pay qualified higher education expenses—

(A) which are incurred on behalf of the taxpayer, the taxpayer's spouse, or any dependent of the taxpayer as of the time the indebtedness was incurred,

(B) which are paid or incurred within a reasonable period of time before or after the indebtedness is incurred, and

(C) which are attributable to education furnished during a period during which the recipient was an eligible student.

Such term includes indebtedness used to refinance indebtedness which qualifies as a qualified education loan. The term "qualified education loan" shall not include any indebtedness owed to a person who is related (within the meaning of section 267(b) or 707(b)(1)) to the taxpayer.

(2) Qualified higher education expenses. The term "qualified higher education expenses" means the cost of attendance (as defined in section 472 of the Higher Education Act of 1965, 20 U.S.C. 1087ll, as in effect on the day before the date of the enactment of this Act) at an eligible educational institution, reduced by the sum of—

(A) the amount excluded from gross income under section 127, 135, or 530 by reason of such expenses, and

(B) the amount of any scholarship, allowance, or payment described in section 25A(g)(2).

For purposes of the preceding sentence, the term "eligible educational institution" has the same meaning given such term by section 25A(f)(2), except that such term shall also include an institution conducting an internship or residency program leading to a degree or certificate awarded by an institution of higher education, a hospital, or a health care facility which offers postgraduate training.

(3) Eligible student. The term "eligible student" has the meaning given such term by section 25A(b)(3).

(4) Dependent. The term "dependent" has the meaning given such term by section 152.

(f) Special Rules.

(1) Denial of double benefit. No deduction shall be allowed under this section for any amount for which a deduction is allowable under any other provision of this chapter.

(2) Married couples must file joint return. If the taxpayer is married at the close of the taxable year, the deduction shall be allowed under subsection (a) only if the taxpayer and the taxpayer's spouse file a joint return for the taxable year.

(3) Marital status. Marital status shall be determined in accordance with section 7703.

(g) Inflation Adjustments.

(1) In general. In the case of a taxable year beginning after 2002, the $40,000 and $60,000 amounts in subsection (b)(2) shall each be increased by an amount equal to—

(A) such dollar amount, multiplied by

(B) the cost-of-living adjustment determined under section 1(f)(3) for the calendar year in which the taxable year begins, determined by substituting "calendar year 2001" for "calendar year 1992" in subparagraph (B) thereof.

(2) Rounding. If any amount as adjusted under paragraph (1) is not a multiple of $5,000, such amount shall be rounded to the next lowest multiple of $5,000.

[For analysis, see ¶ 402. For text of Committee Report see ¶ 5003.]

[Endnote Code Sec. 221]
  Code Sec. 221 was added by Sec. 202(a) of the Taxpayer Relief Act of 1997, H.R. 2014, 8/5/97.
  1. added Code Sec. 221
Effective Date (Sec. 202(e), H.R. 2014, 8/5/97) effective for any qualified education loan (as defined in Code Sec. 221(e)(1) as added by this section) incurred on, before, or after 8/5/97, but only with respect to any loan interest payment due and paid after 12/31/97, and the portion of the 60-month period referred to in Code Sec. 221(d) (as added by this section) after 12/31/97.

[¶ 3048]   Code Sec.[1] 222.   Cross reference.
For deductions in respect of a decedent, see section 691.

[Endnote Code Sec. 222]
    Code Sec. 221 is redesignated as Code Sec. 222 by Sec. 202(a) of the Taxpayer Relief Act of 1997, H.R. 2014, 8/5/97.
1. redesignated Code Sec. 221
Effective Date (Sec. 202(e), H.R. 2014, 8/5/97) effective for any qualified education loan (as defined in Code Sec. 221(e)(1) as added by this section) incurred on, before, or after 8/5/97, but only with respect to any loan interest payment due and paid after 12/31/97, and the portion of the 60-month period referred to in Code Sec. 221(d) (as added by this section) after 12/31/97.

[¶ 3049]   Code Sec. 246.   Rules applying to deductions for dividends received.

* * * * * * * * * * * *

(c) Exclusion of certain dividends.

(1) In general. No deduction shall be allowed under section 243, 244, or 245, in respect of any dividend on any share of stock—

    [1]*(A) which is held by the taxpayer for 45 days or less during the 90-day period beginning on the date which is 45 days before the date on which such share becomes ex-dividend with respect to such dividend, or*

* * * * * * * * * * * *

    [2]*(2) 90-day rule in the case of certain preference dividends. In the case of stock having preference in dividends, if the taxpayer receives dividends with respect to such stock which are attributable to a period or periods aggregating in excess of 366 days, paragraph (1)(A) shall be applied—*

    (A) by substituting "90 days" for "45 days" each place it appears, and

    (B) by substituting "180-day period" for "90-day period".

    (3) Determination of holding periods. For purposes of this subsection, in determining the period for which the taxpayer has held any share of stock—

    (A) the day of disposition, but not the day of acquisition, shall be taken into account, [3]*and*

    [4]*(B) paragraph (4) of section 1223 shall not apply.*

* * * * * * * * * * * *

    [For analysis, see ¶ 1509. For text of Committee Report see ¶ 5120.]

[Endnote Code Sec. 246]
    Matter in *italics* in Code Sec. 246(c)(1)(A), Code Sec. 246(c)(2), Code Sec. 246(c)(3)(A), Code Sec. 246(c)(3)(B), and Code Sec. 246(c)(3)(C) added by Secs. 1015(a), (b)(1) and (2) of the Taxpayer Relief Act of 1997, H.R. 2014, 8/5/97, which struck out:
1. "(A) which is held by the taxpayer for 45 days or less, or"
2. "(2) 90-day rule in the case of certain preference dividends. In the case of any stock having preference in dividends, the holding period specified in paragraph (1) (A) shall be 90 days in lieu of 45 days if the taxpayer receives dividends with respect to such stock which are attributable to a period or periods aggregating in excess of 366 days."
3. added matter in subpara. (c)(3)(A)
4. "(B) there shall not be taken into account any day which is more than 45 days (or 90 days in the case of stock to which paragraph (2) applies) after the date on which such share becomes ex-dividend, and"
    "(C)"
Effective Date (Sec. 1015(c), H.R. 2014, 8/5/97) effective for dividends received or accrued after the 30th day after 8/5/97. For transitional rule, see Sec. 1015(c)(2) of this Act, which provides:
    "(2) Transitional rule.—The amendments made by this section shall not apply to dividends received or accrued during the 2-year period beginning on the date of the enactment of this Act if—
    "(A) the dividend is paid with respect to stock held by the taxpayer on June 8, 1997, and all times thereafter until the dividend is received,
    "(B) such stock is continuously subject to a position described in section 246(c)(4) of the Internal Revenue Code of 1986 on June 8, 1997, and all times thereafter until the dividend is received, and

"(C) such stock and position are clearly identified in the taxpayer's records within 30 days after the date of the enactment of this Act.
"Stock shall not be treated as meeting the requirement of subparagraph (B) if the position is sold, closed, or otherwise terminated and reestablished."

[¶ 3050]   Code Sec. 263.   Capital expenditures.

(a) **General rule.** No deduction shall be allowed for—

(1) Any amount paid out for new buildings or for permanent improvements or betterments made to increase the value of any property or estate. This paragraph shall not apply to—

* * * * * * * * * * *

(F) expenditures for tertiary injectants with respect to which a deduction is allowed under section 193;[1]

(G) expenditures for which a deduction is allowed under section 179[2]; or

[3]*(H) expenditures for which a deduction is allowed under section 179A.*

* * * * * * * * * * *

[Endnote Code Sec. 263]
Matter in *italics* in Code Sec. 263(a)(1)(F), Code Sec. 263(a)(1)(G), and Code Sec. 263(a)(1)(H) added by Sec. 1604(a)(1) of the Taxpayer Relief Act of 1997, H.R. 2014, 8/5/97, which struck out:
1. "or"
2. ";"
3. added subpara. (a)(1)(F)
Effective Date (Sec. 1604(a)(4), H.R. 2014, 8/5/97) effective for property placed in service after 6/30/93.

[¶ 3051]   Code Sec. 264.   Certain amounts paid in connection with insurance contracts.

(a) **General rule.** No deduction shall be allowed for—

[1]*(1) Premiums on any life insurance policy, or endowment or annuity contract, if the taxpayer is directly or indirectly a beneficiary under the policy or contract.*

* * * * * * * * * * *

(4) Except as provided in subsection (d), any interest paid or accrued on any indebtedness with respect to 1 or more life insurance policies owned by the taxpayer covering the life of any individual, or any endowment or annuity contracts owned by the taxpayer covering any [2]*individual.*[3]

Paragraph (2) shall apply in respect of annuity contracts only as to contracts purchased after March 1, 1954. Paragraph (3) shall apply only in respect of contracts purchased after August 6, 1963. Paragraph (4) shall apply with respect to contracts purchased after June 20, 1986.

[4]*(b) Exceptions to subsection (a)(1). Subsection (a)(1) shall not apply to—*

(1) any annuity contract described in section 72(s)(5), and

(2) any annuity contract to which section 72(u) applies.

[5]*(c) Contracts treated as single premium contracts.* For purposes of subsection (a)(2), a contract shall be treated as a single premium contract—

(1) if substantially all the premiums on the contract are paid within a period of 4 years from the date on which the contract is purchased, or

(2) if an amount is deposited after March 1, 1954, with the insurer for payment of a substantial number of future premiums on the contract.

[6]*(d) Exceptions.* Subsection (a)(3) shall not apply to any amount paid or accrued by a person during a taxable year on indebtedness incurred or continued as part of a plan referred to in subsection (a)(3)—

(1) if no part of 4 of the annual premiums due during the 7-year period (beginning with the date the first premium on the contract to which such plan relates was paid) is paid under such plan by means of indebtedness,

(2) if the total of the amounts paid or accrued by such person during such taxable year for which (without regard to this paragraph) no deduction would be allowable by reason of subsection (a)(3) does not exceed $100,

(3) if such amount was paid or accrued on indebtedness incurred because of an unforeseen substantial loss of income or unforeseen substantial increase in his financial obligations, or

(4) if such indebtedness was incurred in connection with his trade or business.

For purposes of applying paragraph (1), if there is a substantial increase in the premiums on a contract, a new 7-year period described in such paragraph with respect to such contract shall commence on the date the first such increased premium is paid.

[7]**(e) Special rules for application of subsection (a)(4).**

(1) Exception for key persons. Subsection (a)(4) shall not apply to any interest paid or accrued on any indebtedness with respect to policies or contracts covering an individual who is a key person to the extent that the aggregate amount of such indebtedness with respect to policies and contracts covering such individual does not exceed $50,000.

(2) Interest rate cap on key persons and pre-1986 contracts.

(A) In general. No deduction shall be allowed by reason of paragraph (1) or the last sentence of subsection (a) with respect to interest paid or accrued for any month beginning after December 31, 1995, to the extent the amount of such interest exceeds the amount which would have been determined if the applicable rate of interest were used for such month.

(B) Applicable rate of interest. For purposes of subparagraph (A)—

(i) In general. The applicable rate of interest for any month is the rate of interest described as Moody's Corporate Bond Yield Average-Monthly Average Corporates as published by Moody's Investors Service, Inc., or any successor thereto, for such month.

(ii) Pre-1986 contracts. In the case of indebtedness on a contract purchased on or before June 20, 1986—

(I) which is a contract providing a fixed rate of interest, the applicable rate of interest for any month shall be the Moody's rate described in clause (i) for the month in which the contract was purchased, or

(II) which is a contract providing a variable rate of interest, the applicable rate of interest for any month in an applicable period shall be such Moody's rate for the third month preceding the first month in such period.

[8]*For purposes of subclause (II), the term "applicable period" means the 12-month period beginning on the date the policy is issued (and each successive 12-month period thereafter) unless the taxpayer elects a number of months (not greater than 12) other than such 12-month period to be its applicable period. Such an election shall be made not later than the 90th day after the date of the enactment of this sentence and, if made, shall apply to the taxpayer's first taxable year ending on or after October 13, 1995, and all subsequent taxable years unless revoked with the consent of the Secretary.*

(3) Key person. For purposes of paragraph (1), the term "key person" means an officer or 20-percent owner, except that the number of individuals who may be treated as key persons with respect to any taxpayer shall not exceed the greater of—

(A) 5 individuals, or

(B) the lesser of 5 percent of the total officers and employees of the taxpayer or 20 individuals.

(4) 20-percent owner. For purposes of this subsection, the term "20-percent owner" means—

(A) if the taxpayer is a corporation, any person who owns directly 20 percent or more of the outstanding stock of the corporation or stock possessing 20 percent or more of the total combined voting power of all stock of the corporation, or

(B) if the taxpayer is not a corporation, any person who owns 20 percent or more of the capital or profits interest in [9]*the taxpayer.*

(5) Aggregation rules.

(A) In general. For purposes of paragraph (4)(A) and applying the $50,000 limitation in paragraph (1)—

(i) all members of a controlled group shall be treated as 1 taxpayer, and

(ii) such limitation shall be allocated among the members of such group in such manner as the Secretary may prescribe.

(B) Controlled group. For purposes of this paragraph, all persons treated as a single employer under subsection (a) or (b) of section 52 or subsection (m) or (o) of section 414 shall be treated as members of a controlled group.

[10]*(f) Pro rata allocation of interest expense to policy cash values*

(1) In general. No deduction shall be allowed for that portion of the taxpayer's interest expense which is allocable to unborrowed policy cash values.

(2) Allocation. For purposes of paragraph (1), the portion of the taxpayer's interest expense which is allocable to unborrowed policy cash values is an amount which bears the same ratio to such interest expense as—

(A) the taxpayer's average unborrowed policy cash values of life insurance policies, and annuity and endowment contracts, issued after June 8, 1997, bears to

(B) the sum of—

(i) in the case of assets of the taxpayer which are life insurance policies or annuity or endowment contracts, the average unborrowed policy cash values of such policies and contracts, and

(ii) in the case of assets of the taxpayer not described in clause (i), the average adjusted bases (within the meaning of section 1016) of such assets.

(3) Unborrowed policy cash value. For purposes of this subsection, the term "unborrowed policy cash value" means, with respect to any life insurance policy or annuity or endowment contract, the excess of—

(A) the cash surrender value of such policy or contract determined without regard to any surrender charge, over

(B) the amount of any loan in respect of such policy or contract.

(4) Exception for certain policies and contracts.

(A) Policies and contracts covering 20-percent owners, officers, directors, and employees. Paragraph (1) shall not apply to any policy or contract owned by an entity engaged in a trade or business if such policy or contract covers only 1 individual and if such individual is (at the time first covered by the policy or contract)—

(i) a 20-percent owner of such entity, or

(ii) an individual (not described in clause (i)) who is an officer, director, or employee of such trade or business.

A policy or contract covering a 20-percent owner of such entity shall not be treated as failing to meet the requirements of the preceding sentence by reason of covering the joint lives of such owner and such owner's spouse.

(B) Contracts subject to current income inclusion. Paragraph (1) shall not apply to any annuity contract to which section 72(u) applies.

(C) Coordination with paragraph (2). Any policy or contract to which paragraph (1) does not apply by reason of this paragraph shall not be taken into account under paragraph (2).

(D) 20-percent owner. For purposes of subparagraph (A), the term "20-percent owner" has the meaning given such term by subsection (e)(4).

(5) Exception for policies and contracts held by natural persons; treatment of partnerships and S corporations.

(A) Policies and contracts held by natural persons.

(i) In general. This subsection shall not apply to any policy or contract held by a natural person.

(ii) Exception where business is beneficiary. If a trade or business is directly or indirectly the beneficiary under any policy or contract, such policy or contract shall be treated as held by such trade or business and not by a natural person.

(iii) Special rules.

(I) Certain trades or businesses not taken into account. Clause (ii) shall not apply to any trade or business carried on as a sole proprietorship and to any trade or business performing services as an employee.

(II) Limitation on unborrowed cash value. The amount of the unborrowed cash value of any policy or contract which is taken into account by reason of clause (ii) shall not exceed the benefit to which the trade or business is directly or indirectly entitled under the policy or contract.

(iv) Reporting. The Secretary shall require such reporting from policyholders and issuers as is necessary to carry out clause (ii). Any report required under the preceding sentence shall be treated as a statement referred to in section 6724(d)(1).

(B) Treatment of partnerships and S corporations. In the case of a partnership or S corporation, this subsection shall be applied at the partnership and corporate levels.

(6) Special rules.

(A) Coordination with subsection (a) and section 265. If interest on any indebtedness is disallowed under subsection (a) or section 265—

(i) such disallowed interest shall not be taken into account for purposes of applying this subsection, and

(ii) the amount otherwise taken into account under paragraph 2(B) shall be reduced (but not below zero) by the amount of such indebtedness.

(B) Coordination with section 263A. This subsection shall be applied before the application of section 263A (relating to capitalization of certain expenses where taxpayer produces property).

(7) Interest expense. The term "interest expense" means the aggregate amount allowable to the taxpayer as a deduction for interest (within the meaning of section 265(b)(4)) for the taxable year (determined without regard to this subsection, section 265(b), and section 291).

(8) Aggregation rules.

(A) In general. All members of a controlled group (within the meaning of subsection (d)(5)(B)) shall be treated as 1 taxpayer for purposes of this subsection.

(B) Treatment of insurance companies. This subsection shall not apply to an insurance company subject to tax under subchapter L, and subparagraph (A) shall be applied without regard to any member of an affiliated group which is an insurance company.

[For analysis, see ¶s 708, 709, 710, 712, 713, 714, 715. For text of Committee Report see ¶ 5161, 5375, 5376, 5377, 5378, 5379.]

[Endnote Code Sec. 264]

Matter in *italics* in Code Sec. 264(a)(1) and Code Sec. 264(a)(4) [as amended by Sec. 1602(f)(1) of this Act, see below] added by Secs. 1084(a)(1) and (b)(1) of the Taxpayer Relief Act of 1997, H.R. 2014, 8/5/97, which struck out:

1. "(1) Premiums paid on any life insurance policy covering the life of any officer or employee, or of any person financially interested in any trade or business carried on by the taxpayer, when the taxpayer is directly or indirectly a beneficiary under such policy."

2. "individual, who—

"(A) is or was an officer or employee, or

"(B) is or was financially interested in,

any trade or business carried on (currently or formerly) by the taxpayer."

Effective Date (Sec. 1084(d)[sic (f)], H.R. 2014, 8/5/97) effective as provided in Sec. 1084(d)[sic (f)] of this Act, which reads:

"(d)[sic (f)] Effective date. The amendments made by this section shall apply to contracts issued after June 8, 1997, in taxable years ending after such date. For purposes of the preceding sentence, any material increase in the death benefit or other material change in the contract shall be treated as a new contract but the addition of covered lives shall be treated as a new contract only with respect to such additional covered lives. For purposes of this subsection, an increase in the death benefit under a policy or contract issued in connection with a lapse described in section 501(d)(2) of the Health Insurance Portability and Accountability Act of 1996 [P.L. 104-191] shall not be treated as a new contract."

Matter in footnote #2 added to Code Sec. 264(a)(4) [before amendment by Sec. 1084(b)(1) of this Act, see above] added by Sec. 1602(f)(1), H.R. 2014, which struck out:

3. "(A) is an officer or employee of, or

"(B) is financially interested in,

any trade or business carried on by the taxpayer."

Matter in *italics* in Code Sec. 264(b), Code Sec. 264(c), Code Sec. 264(d), Code Sec. 264(e) added by Sec. 1084(a)(2)

4. added subsec. (b)

5. "(b)"

6. "(c)"

7. "(d)"

Effective Date (Sec. 1084(d) [sic (f)], H.R. 2014, 8/5/97) see above.

Matter in *italics* in Code Sec. 264(e)(2)(B)(ii), and Code Sec. 264(e)(4)(B) added by Secs. 1602(f)(2) and (3), [to redesignation from (d) to (e) by Sec. 1084(a)(2)] of this Act, which struck out:

8. "For purposes of subclause (II), the taxpayer shall elect an applicable period for such contract on its return of tax imposed by this chapter for its first taxable year ending on or after October 13, 1995. Such applicable period shall be for any number of months (not greater than 12) specified in the election and may not be changed by the taxpayer without the consent of the Secretary."

9. "the employer"

Effective Date (Sec. 1602(i), H.R. 2014, 8/5/97) effective for interest paid or accrued after 10/13/95. For other rules, see Secs. 501(c)(2) and (d), of P.L. 104-191, [as amended by H.R. 2014, Sec. 1602(f)(4) and (5)] which read as follows:

"(2) Transition rule for existing indebtedness.

"(A) In general. In the case of—

"(i) indebtedness incurred before January 1, 1996, or

"(ii) indebtedness incurred before January 1, 1997 with respect to any contract or policy entered into in 1994 or 1995, the amendments made by this section shall not apply to qualified interest paid or accrued on such indebtedness after October 13, 1995, and before January 1, 1999.

"(B) Qualified interest. For purposes of subparagraph (A), the qualified interest with respect to any indebtedness for any month is the amount of interest (otherwise deductible) which would be paid or accrued for such month on such indebtedness if—

"(i) in the case of any interest paid or accrued after December 31, 1995, indebtedness with respect to no more than 20,000 insured individuals were taken into account, and

"(ii) the lesser of the following rates of interest were used for such month:

"(I) The rate of interest specified under the terms of the indebtedness as in effect on October 13, 1995 (and without regard to modification of such terms after such date).

"(II) The applicable percentage of the rate of interest described as Moody's Corporate Bond Yield Average-Monthly Average Corporates as published by Moody's Investors Service, Inc., or any successor thereto, for such month.

For purposes of clause (i), all persons treated as a single employer under subsection (a) or (b) of section 52 of the Internal Revenue Code of 1986 or subsection (m) or (o) of section 414 of such Code shall be treated as 1 person. Subclause (II) of clause (ii) shall not apply to any month before January 1, 1996.

"(C) Applicable percentage. For purposes of subparagraph (B), the applicable percentage is as follows:

For calendar year:	The percentage is:
1996	100 percent
1997	90 percent
1998	80 percent

*

"(d) Spread of income inclusion on surrender, etc. of contracts.

"(1) In general. If any amount is received under any life insurance policy or endowment or annuity contract described in paragraph (4) of section 264(a) of the Internal Revenue Code of 1986—

"(A) on the complete surrender, redemption, or maturity of such policy or contract during calendar year 1996, 1997, or 1998, or

"(B) in full discharge during any such calendar year of the obligation under the policy or contract which is in the nature of a refund of the consideration paid for the policy or contract.

then (in lieu of any other inclusion in gross income) such amount shall be includible in gross income ratably over the 4-taxable year period beginning with the taxable year such amount would (but for this paragraph) be includible. The preceding sentence shall only apply to the extent the amount is includible in gross income for the taxable year in which the event described in subparagraph (A) or (B) occurs.

"(2) Special rules for applying section 264. A contract shall not be treated as—

"(A) failing to meet the requirement of section 264(c)(1) of the Internal Revenue Code of 1986, or

"(B) a single premium contract under section 264(b)(1) of such Code, solely by reason of an occurrence described in subparagraph (A) or (B) of paragraph (1) of this subsection or

solely by reason of ***a lapse occurring after October 13, 1995, by reason of no additional premiums being received under the contract.*

"(3) Special rule for deferred acquisition costs. In the case of the occurrence of any event described in subparagraph (A) or (B) of paragraph (1) of this subsection with respect to any policy or contract—

"(A) section 848 of the Internal Revenue Code of 1986 shall not apply to the unamortized balance (if any) of the specified policy acquisition expenses attributable to such policy or contract immediately before the insurance company's taxable year in which such event occurs, and

"(B) there shall be allowed as a deduction to such company for such taxable year under chapter 1 of such Code an amount equal to such unamortized balance."

Code Sec. 264(f), in *italics*, was added by Sec. 1084(c), H.R. 2014.
10. added subsec. (f)
Effective Date (Sec. 1084(d)[sic (f)], H.R. 2014, 8/5/97) see above.

Sec. 501(c)(3), of P.L. 104-191, was deleted by Sec. 1602(f)(4), H.R. 2014. Prior to deletion, Sec. 501(c)(3) of P.L. 104-191, read as follows:
*. "(3) Special rule for grandfathered contracts. This section shall not apply to any contract purchased on or before June 20, 1986, except that section 264(d)(2) of the Internal Revenue Code of 1986 shall apply to interest paid or accrued after October 13, 1995."
Matter in *italics* in Sec. 501(d), of P.L. 104-191, above was added by Sec. 1602(f)(5), H.R. 2014, which struck out:
**. "no additional premiums being received under the contract by reason of a lapse occurring after October 13, 1995."

[¶ 3052]   Code Sec. 265.   Expenses and interest relating to tax-exempt income.

* * * * * * * * * * *

(b) Pro rata allocation of interest expense of financial institutions to tax-exempt interest.

* * * * * * * * * * * *

(4) Definitions. For purposes of this subsection—

(A) Interest expense. The term "interest expense" means the aggregate amount allowable to the taxpayer as a deduction for interest for the taxable year (determined without regard to this subsection[1], *section 264*, and section 291). For purposes of the preceding sentence, the term "interest" includes amounts (whether or not designated as interest) paid in respect of deposits, investment certificates, or withdrawable or repurchasable shares.

* * * * * * * * * * *

[Endnote Code Sec. 265]
Matter in *italics* in Code Sec. 265(b)(4)(A) added by Sec. 1084(c) [sic (e)] of the Taxpayer Relief Act of 1997, H.R. 2014, 8/5/97.
1. added matter in subpara. (b)(4)(A)
Effective Date (Sec. 1084(d) [sic (f)], H.R. 2014, 8/5/97) effective for contracts issued after 6/8/97, in tax. yrs. end after such date. For purposes of the preceding sentence, any material increase in the death benefit or other material change in the contract shall be treated as a new contract but the addition of covered lives shall be treated as a new contract only with respect to such additional covered lives. For purposes of this subsection, an increase in the death benefit under a policy or contract issued in connection with a lapse described in section 501(d)(2) of the Health Insurance Portability and Accountability Act of 1996 shall not be treated as a new contract.

[¶ 3053]   Code Sec. 267.   Losses, expenses, and interest with respect to transactions between related taxpayers.

* * * * * * * * * * *

(b) Relationships. The persons referred to in subsection (a) are:

* * * * * * * * * * *

(11) An S corporation and another S corporation if the same persons own more than 50 percent in value of the outstanding stock of each corporation;[1]

(12) An S corporation and a C corporation, if the same persons own more than 50 percent in value of the outstanding stock of each corporation[2]; or

[3]*(13) Except in the case of a sale or exchange in satisfaction of a pecuniary bequest, an executor of an estate and a beneficiary of such estate.*

* * * * * * * * * * *

(f) Controlled group defined; special rules applicable to controlled groups.

* * * * * * * * * * *

⁴*(4) Determination of relationship resulting in disallowance of loss, for purposes of other provisions. For purposes of any other section of this title which refers to a relationship which would result in a disallowance of losses under this section, deferral under paragraph (2) shall be treated as disallowance.*

* * * * * * * * * * *

[For analysis, see ¶s 211, 212. For text of Committee Report see ¶s 5268, 5386.]

[Endnote Code Sec. 267]

Matter in *italics* in Code Sec. 267(b)(11), Code Sec. 267(b)(12), and Code Sec. 267(b)(13) added by Sec. 1308(a) of the Taxpayer Relief Act of 1997, H.R. 2014, 8/5/97, which struck out:

1. "or"
2. "."
3. added Code Sec. 267(b)(13)

Effective Date (Sec. 1308(c), H.R. 2014, 8/5/97) effective for tax. yrs. begin. after 8/5/97.

Matter in *italics* in Code Sec. 267(f)(4) was added by Sec. 1604(e)(1), H.R. 2014.

4. added Code Sec. 267(f)(4)

Effective Date (Sec. 1604(e)(2), H.R. 2014, 8/5/97) effective for transactions after 12/31/83, in tax. yrs. end. after such date, excepting property transferred to a foreign corporation on or before 3/1/84.

[¶ 3054]   Code Sec. 274.   Disallowance of certain entertainment, etc., expenses.

* * * * * * * * * * *

(n) Only 50 percent of meal and entertainment expenses allowed as deduction.

* * * * * * * * * * *

CAUTION. Para. (n)(3), following, is effective for tax. yrs. begin. after 12/31/97.

³*(3) Special rule for individuals subject to federal hours of service.*

(A) In general. In the case of any expenses for food or beverages consumed while away from home (within the meaning of section 162(a)(2)) by an individual during, or incident to, the period of duty subject to the hours of service limitations of the Department of Transportation, paragraph (1) shall be applied by substituting "the applicable percentage" for "50 percent".

(B) Applicable percentage. For purposes of this paragraph, the term "applicable percentage" means the percentage determined under the following table:

For taxable years beginning in calendar year—	The applicable percentage is—
1998 or 1999	55
2000 or 2001	60
2002 or 2003	65
2004 or 2005	70
2006 or 2007	75
2008 or thereafter	80

* * * * * * * * * * *

[For analysis, see ¶ 117. For text of Committee Report see ¶ 5092.]

[Endnote Code Sec. 274]

Matter in *italics* in Code Sec. 274(n)(3) was added by Sec. 969(a) of the Revenue Reconciliation Act of 1997, H.R. 2014, 8/5/97.

1. added para. (n)(3)

Effective Date (Sec. 969(b), H.R. 2014, 8/5/97) effective for tax. yrs. begin. after 12/31/97.

[¶ 3055]   Code Sec. 280A.   Disallowance of certain expenses in connection with business use of home, rental of vacation homes, etc.

* * * * * * * * * * *

(c) Exceptions for certain business or rental use; limitation on deductions for such use.

CAUTION.   Para. (c)(1), following, is effective for tax. yrs. begin. before 1/1/99. For para. (c)(1), effective for tax. yrs. begin. after 12/31/98, see below.

(1) Certain business use. Subsection (a) shall not apply to any item to the extent such item is allocable to a portion of the dwelling unit which is exclusively used on a regular basis—

(A) as the principal place of business for any trade or business of the taxpayer,

(B) as a place of business which is used by patients, clients, or customers in meeting or dealing with the taxpayer in the normal course of his trade or business, or

(C) in the case of a separate structure which is not attached to the dwelling unit, in connection with the taxpayer's trade or business.

In the case of an employee, the preceding sentence shall apply only if the exclusive use referred to in the preceding sentence is for the convenience of his employer.

CAUTION.   Para. (c)(1), following, is effective for tax. yrs. begin. after 12/31/98. For para. (c)(1), effective for tax. yrs. begin. before 1/1/99, see above.

(1) Certain business use. Subsection (a) shall not apply to any item to the extent such item is allocable to a portion of the dwelling unit which is exclusively used on a regular basis—

(A) as the principal place of business for any trade or business of the taxpayer,

(B) as a place of business which is used by patients, clients, or customers in meeting or dealing with the taxpayer in the normal course of his trade or business, or

(C) in the case of a separate structure which is not attached to the dwelling unit, in connection with the taxpayer's trade or business.

In the case of an employee, the preceding sentence shall apply only if the exclusive use referred to in the preceding sentence is for the convenience of his employer. [1]*For purposes of subparagraph (A), the term "principal place of business" includes a place of business which is used by the taxpayer for the administrative or management activities of any trade or business of the taxpayer if there is no other fixed location of such trade or business where the taxpayer conducts substantial administrative or management activities of such trade or business.*

* * * * * * * * * * *

(d) Use as residence.

* * * * * * * * * * *

(4) Rental of principal residence.

(A) In general. For purposes of applying subsection (c)(5) to deductions allocable to a qualified rental period, a taxpayer shall not be considered to have used a dwelling unit for personal purposes for any day during the taxable year which occurs before or after a qualified rental period described in subparagraph (B)(i), or before a qualified rental period described in subparagraph (B)(ii), if with respect to such day such unit constitutes the principal residence (within the meaning of [2]*section 121*) of the taxpayer.

* * * * * * * * * * *

[For analysis, see ¶ 113. For text of Committee Report see ¶ 5069].

[Endnote Code Sec. 280A]

Matter in *italics* in Code Sec. 280A(c)(1) added by Sec. 932(a) of the Taxpayer Relief Act of 1997, H.R. 2014, 8/5/97.
1. added matter in para. (c)(1)

Effective Date (Sec. 932(b), H.R. 2014, 8/5/97) effective for tax. yrs. begin. after 12/31/98.

Matter in *italics* in Code Sec. 280A(d)(4)(A) added by Sec. 312(d)(1), H.R. 2014, 8/5/97, which struck out:
2. "section 1034"
Effective Date (Sec. 312(d) [sic (e)], H.R. 2014, 8/5/97) Sec. 312(d) [sic (e)], H.R. 2014, 8/5/97, reads as follows:
"(d) Effective date.
"(1) In general. The amendments made by this section shall apply to sales and exchanges after May 6, 1997.
"(2) Sales before 8/5/97. At the election of the taxpayer, the amendments made by this section shall not apply to any sale or exchange before the date of the enactment of this Act.
"(3) Certain sales within 2 years after 8/5/97. Section 121 of the Internal Revenue Code of 1986 (as amended by this section) shall be applied without regard to subsection (c)(2)(B) thereof in the case of any sale or exchange of property during the 2-year period beginning on the date of the enactment of this Act if the taxpayer held such property on the date of the enactment of this Act and fails to meet the ownership and use requirements of subsection (a) thereof with respect to such property.
"(4) Binding contracts. At the election of the taxpayer, the amendments made by this section shall not apply to a sale or exchange after the date of the enactment of this Act, if—
"(A) such sale or exchange is pursuant to a contract which was binding on such date, or
"(B) without regard to such amendments, gain would not be recognized under section 1034 of the Internal Revenue Code of 1986 (as in effect on the day before the date of the enactment of this Act) on such sale or exchange by reason of a new residence acquired on or before such date or with respect to the acquisition of which by the taxpayer a binding contract was in effect on such date.
This paragraph shall not apply to any sale or exchange by an individual if the treatment provided by section 877(a)(1) of the Internal Revenue Code of 1986 applies to such individual."

[¶ 3056] Code Sec. 280F.   Limitation on depreciation for luxury automobiles; limitation where certain property used for personal purposes.
(a) **Limitation on amount of depreciation for luxury automobiles.**
(1) **Depreciation.**

* * * * * * * * * * * *

CAUTION.   Subpara. (c)(1)(C), following, is effective for property placed in service on or after 8/5/97 and before 1/1/2005.

¹*(C) Special rule for certain clean-fuel passenger automobiles.*
(i) Modified automobiles. In the case of a passenger automobile which is propelled by a fuel which is not a clean-burning fuel to which is installed qualified clean-fuel vehicle property (as defined in section 179A(c)(1)(A)) for purposes of permitting such vehicle to be propelled by a clean burning fuel (as defined in section 179A(e)(1)), subparagraph (A) shall not apply to the cost of the installed qualified clean burning vehicle property.
(ii) Purpose built passenger vehicles. In the case of a purpose built passenger vehicle (as defined in section 4001(a)(2)(C)(ii)), each of the annual limitations specified in subparagraph (A) shall be tripled.

* * * * * * * * * * * *

[For analysis, see ¶ 802. For text of Committee Report see ¶ 5094].

[Endnote Code Sec. 280F]
Code Sec. 280F(a)(1)(C), in *italics* was added by Sec. 971(a) of the Taxpayer Relief Act of 1997, H.R. 2014, 8/7/97.
1. added subpara. (a)(1)(C)
Effective Date (Sec. 971(b), H.R. 2014, 8/5/97) effective for property placed in service after 8/5/97 and before 1/1/2005.

[¶ 3057] Code Sec. 304.   Redemption through use of related corporations.
(a) **Treatment of certain stock purchases.**
(1) **Acquisition by related corporation (other than subsidiary).** For purposes of sections 302 and 303, if—
(A) one or more persons are in control of each of two corporations, and
(B) in return for property, one of the corporations acquires stock in the other corporation from the person (or persons) so in control,

then (unless paragraph (2) applies) such property shall be treated as a distribution in redemption of the stock of the corporation acquiring such stock. [1]*To the extent that such distribution is treated as a distribution to which section 301 applies, the transferor and the acquiring corporation shall be treated in the same manner as if the transferor had transferred the stock so acquired to the acquiring corporation in exchange for stock of the acquiring corporation in a transaction to which section 351(a) applies, and then the acquiring corporation had redeemed the stock it was treated as issuing in such transaction.*

* * * * * * * * * * *

(b) Special rules for application of subsection (a).

* * * * * * * * * * *

[2]*(5) Acquisitions by foreign corporations.*

(A) In general. In the case of any acquisition to which subsection (a) applies in which the acquiring corporation is a foreign corporation, the only earnings and profits taken into account under paragraph (2)(A) shall be those earnings and profits —

(i) which are attributable (under regulations prescribed by the Secretary) to stock of the acquiring corporation owned (within the meaning of section 958(a)) by a corporation or individual which is —

(I) a United States shareholder (within the meaning of section 951(b)) of the acquiring corporation, and

(II) the transferor or a person who bears a relationship to the transferor described in section 267(b) or 707(b), and

(ii) which were accumulated during the period or periods such stock was owned by such person while the acquiring corporation was a controlled foreign corporation.

(B) Application of section 1248. For purposes of subparagraph (A), the rules of section 1248(d) shall apply except to the extent otherwise provided by the Secretary.

(C) Regulations. The Secretary shall prescribe such regulations as are appropriate to carry out the purposes of this paragraph.

* * * * * * * * * * *

[For analysis, see ¶ 1505. For text of Committee Report see ¶ 5118].

[Endnote Code Sec. 304]

Matter in *italics* in Code Sec. 304(a)(1) and Code Sec. 304(b)(5) was added by Sec. 1013(a) and (c) of the Taxpayer Relief Act of 1997, H.R. 2014, 8/5/97, which struck out:

1. "To the extent that such distribution is treated as a distribution to which section 301 applies, the stock so acquired shall be treated as having been transferred by the person from whom acquired, and as having been received by the corporation acquiring it, as a contribution to the capital of such corporation."

2. added para. (b)(5)

Effective Date (Sec. 1013(d), H.R. 2014, 8/5/97) reads as follows:

"(d) Effective date.

"(1) In general. The amendments made by this section shall apply to distributions and acquisitions after June 8, 1997.

"(2) Transition rule. The amendments made by this section shall not apply to any distribution or acquisition after June 8, 1997, if such distribution or acquisition is —

"(A) made pursuant to a written agreement which was binding on such date and at all times thereafter,

"(B) described in a ruling request submitted to the Internal Revenue Service on or before such date, or

"(C) described in a public announcement or filing with the Securities and Exchange Commission on or before such date."

[¶ 3058] Code Sec. 312.   Effect on earnings and profits.

* * * * * * * * * * *

(k) Effect of depreciation on earnings and profits.

* * * * * * * * * * *

(3) Exception for tangible property.

* * * * * * * * * * *

(B) Treatment of amounts deductible under section [1]*179 or 179A*. For purposes of computing the earnings and profits of a corporation, any amount deductible under section [2]*179 or 179A* shall be allowed as a deduction ratably over the period of 5 taxable years (beginning with the taxable year for which such amount is deductible under section [3]*179 or 179A, as the case may be*).

* * * * * * * * * * *

[Endnote Code Sec. 312]
Matter in *italics* in Code Sec. 312(k)(3)(B) added by Secs. 1604(a)(2)(A) and (B) of the Taxpayer Relief Act of 1997, H.R. 2014, 8/5/97, which struck out:
1. "179"
2. "179"
3. "179"
Effective Date (Sec. 1604(a)(4), H.R. 2014, 8/5/97) effective for property placed in service after 6/30/93.

[¶ 3059] Code Sec. 318. Constructive ownership of stock.

* * * * * * * * * * *

(b) Cross references. For provisions to which the rules contained in subsection (a) apply, see—

* * * * * * * * * * *

(8) [1]*section 6038(d)(2)* (relating to information with respect to certain foreign corporations).

[Endnote Code Sec. 318]
Matter in *italics* in Code Sec. 318(b)(8) added by Sec. 1142(e)(3) of the Taxpayer Relief Act of 1997, H.R. 2014, 8/5/97, which struck out:
1. "section 6038(d)(1)"
Effective Date (Sec. 1142(f), H.R. 2014, 8/5/97) effective for annual accounting periods begin. after 8/5/97.

[¶ 3060] Code Sec. 351. Transfer to corporation controlled by transferor.

* * * * * * * * * * *

[1]*(c) Special rules where distribution to shareholders. In determining control for purposes of this section—*

(1) the fact that any corporate transferor distributes part or all of the stock in the corporation which it receives in the exchange to its shareholders shall not be taken into account, and

(2) if the requirements of section 355 are met with respect to such distribution, the shareholders shall be treated as in control of such corporation immediately after the exchange if the shareholders own (immediately after the distribution) stock possessing—

(A) more than 50 percent of the total combined voting power of all classes of stock entitled to vote, and

(B) more than 50 percent of the total value of shares of all classes of stock of such corporation.

* * * * * * * * * * *

(e) Exceptions. This section shall not apply to—

(1) Transfer of property to an investment company. A transfer of property to an investment company. [2]*For purposes of the preceding sentence, the determination of whether a company is an investment company shall be made—*

(A) by taking into account all stock and securities held by the company, and

(B) by treating as stocks and securities:

(i) money,

(ii) stocks and other equity interests in a corporation, evidences of indebtedness, options, forward or futures contracts, notional principal contracts and derivatives,

(iii) any foreign currency,

(iv) any interest in a real estate investment trust, a common trust fund, a regulated investment company, a publicly-traded partnership (as defined in section 7704(b)) or any other equity interest (other than in a corporation) which pursuant to its terms or any other arrangement is readily convertible into, or exchangeable for, any asset described in any preceding clause, this clause or clause (v) or (viii),

(v) except to the extent provided in regulations prescribed by the Secretary, any interest in a precious metal, unless such metal is used or held in the active conduct of a trade or business after the contribution,

(vi) except as otherwise provided in regulations prescribed by the Secretary, interests in any entity if substantially all of the assets of such entity consist (directly or indirectly) of any assets described in any preceding clause or clause (viii),

(vii) to the extent provided in regulations prescribed by the Secretary, any interest in any entity not described in clause (vi), but only to the extent of the value of such interest that is attributable to assets listed in clauses (i) through (v) or clause (viii), or

(viii) any other asset specified in regulations prescribed by the Secretary. The Secretary may prescribe regulations that, under appropriate circumstances, treat any asset described in clauses (i) through (v) as not so listed.

* * * * * * * * * * *

[3](g) **Nonqualified preferred stock not treated as stock.**

(1) In general. In the case of a person who transfers property to a corporation and receives nonqualified preferred stock—

(A) subsection (a) shall not apply to such transferor,

(B) subsection (b) shall apply to such transferor, and

(C) such nonqualified preferred stock shall be treated as other property for purposes of applying subsection (b).

(2) Nonqualified preferred stock. For purposes of paragraph (1)—

(A) In general. The term "nonqualified preferred stock" means preferred stock if—

(i) the holder of such stock has the right to require the issuer or a related person to redeem or purchase the stock,

(ii) the issuer or a related person is required to redeem or purchase such stock,

(iii) the issuer or a related person has the right to redeem or purchase the stock and, as of the issue date, it is more likely than not that such right will be exercised, or

(iv) the dividend rate on such stock varies in whole or in part (directly or indirectly) with reference to interest rates, commodity prices, or other similar indices.

(B) Limitations. Clauses (i), (ii), and (iii) of subparagraph (A) shall apply only if the right or obligation referred to therein may be exercised within the 20-year period beginning on the issue date of such stock and such right or obligation is not subject to a contingency which, as of the issue date, makes remote the likelihood of the redemption or purchase.

(C) Exceptions for certain rights or obligations.

(i) In general. A right or obligation shall not be treated as described in clause (i), (ii), or (iii) of subparagraph (A) if—

(I) it may be exercised only upon the death, disability, or mental incompetency of the holder, or

(II) in the case of a right or obligation to redeem or purchase stock transferred in connection with the performance of services for the issuer or a related person (and which represents reasonable compensation), it may be exercised only upon the holder's separation from service from the issuer or a related person.

(ii) Exception. Clause (i)(I) shall not apply if the stock relinquished in the exchange, or the stock acquired in the exchange is in—

(I) a corporation if any class of stock in such corporation or a related party is readily tradable on an established securities market or otherwise, or

(II) any other corporation if such exchange is part of a transaction or series of transactions in which such corporation is to become a corporation described in subclause (I).

(3) Definitions. *For purposes of this subsection—*

(A) Preferred stock. The term "preferred stock" means stock which is limited and preferred as to dividends and does not participate (including through a conversion privilege) in corporate growth to any significant extent.

(B) Related person. A person shall be treated as related to another person if they bear a relationship to such other person described in section 267(b) or 707(b).

(4) Regulations. *The Secretary may prescribe such regulations as may be necessary or appropriate to carry out the purposes of this subsection and sections 354(a)(2)(C), 355(a)(3)(D), and 356(e). The Secretary may also prescribe regulations, consistent with the treatment under this subsection and such sections, for the treatment of nonqualified preferred stock under other provisions of this title.*

[4](h) Cross references.

(1) For special rule where another party to the exchange assumes a liability, or acquires property subject to a liability, see section 357.

(2) For the basis of stock or property received in an exchange to which this section applies, see sections 358 and 362.

(3) For special rule in the case of an exchange described in this section but which results in a gift, see section 2501 and following.

(4) For special rule in the case of an exchange described in this section but which has the effect of the payment of compensation by the corporation or by a transferor, see section 61(a)(1).

(5) For coordination of this section with section 304, see section 304(b)(3).

[For analysis, see ¶s 1501, 1502, 1504. For text of Committee Report see ¶s 5112, 5117, 5119].

[Endnote Code Sec. 351]

Matter in *italics* in Code Sec. 351(c) was added by Sec. 1012(c)(1) of the Taxpayer Relief Act of 1997, H.R. 2014, 8/5/97, which struck out:

1. "(c) Special rule. In determining control, for purposes of this section, the fact that any corporate transferor distributes part or all of the stock which it receives in the exchange to its shareholders shall not be taken into account."

Effective Date (Sec. 1012(d)(2) and (3), H.R. 2014, 8/5/97) effective for transfers after date of enactment, except as provided in Sec. 1012(d)(3) of this Act, which reads as follows:

"(3) Transition rule. The amendments made by this section shall not apply to any distribution pursuant to a plan (or series of related transactions) which involves an acquisition described in section 355(e)(2)(A)(ii) of the Internal Revenue Code of 1986 (or, in the case of the amendments made by subsection (c), any transfer) occurring after April 16, 1997, if such acquisition or transfer is—

"(A) made pursuant to an agreement which was binding on such date and at all times thereafter,

"(B) described in a ruling request submitted to the Internal Revenue Service on or before such date, or

"(C) described on or before such date in a public announcement or in a filing with the Securities and Exchange Commission required solely by reason of the acquisition or transfer.

"This paragraph shall not apply to any agreement, ruling request, or public announcement or filing unless it identifies the acquirer of the distributing corporation or of any controlled corporation, or the transferee, whichever is applicable."

Matter in *italics* in Code Sec. 351(e)(1) added by Sec. 1002(a)(1), H.R. 2014, 8/5/97.

2. added matter to para. (e)(1).

Effective Date (Sec. 1002(b), H.R. 2014, 8/5/97) effective for transfers after 6/8/97, in tax. yrs. end. after such date, except as provided in Sec. 1002(b)(2) of this Act, which reads as follows:

"(2) Binding contracts. The amendment made by subsection (a) shall not apply to any transfer pursuant to a written binding contract in effect on June 8, 1997, and at all times thereafter before such transfer if such contract provides for the transfer of a fixed amount of property."

Matter in *italics* in Code Sec. 351(g) and Code Sec. 351(h) was added by Sec. 1014(a), H.R. 2014, 8/5/97, which struck out:

3. added subsec. (g).

4. "(g)"

Effective Date (Sec. 1014(f), H.R. 2014, 8/5/97) effective for transactions after 6/8/97, except as provided in Sec. 1014(f)(2) of this Act, which reads as follows:

"(2) Transition rule. The amendments made by this section shall not apply to any transaction after June 8, 1997, if such transaction is—

"(A) made pursuant to a written agreement which was binding on such date and at all times thereafter,

"(B) described in a ruling request submitted to the Internal Revenue Service on or before such date, or

"(C) described on or before such date in a public announcement or in a filing with the Securities and Exchange Commission required solely by reason of the transaction."

[¶ 3061]   Code Sec. 354.   Exchanges of stock and securities in certain reorganizations.

(a) General rule.

* * * * * * * * * * * *

(2) Limitations.

* * * * * * * * * * * *

(B) Property attributable to accrued interest. Neither paragraph (1) nor so much of section 356 as relates to paragraph (1) shall apply to the extent that any stock [1]*(including nonqualified preferred stock, as defined in section 351(g)(2)),* securities, or other property received is attributable to interest which has accrued on securities on or after the beginning of the holder's holding period.

[2]*(C) Nonqualified preferred stock.*

(i) In general. Nonqualified preferred stock (as defined in section 351(g)(2)) received in exchange for stock other than nonqualified preferred stock (as so defined) shall not be treated as stock or securities.

(ii) Recapitalizations of family-owned corporations.

(I) In general. Clause (i) shall not apply in the case of a recapitalization under section 368(a)(1)(E) of a family-owned corporation.

(II) Family-owned corporation. For purposes of this clause, except as provided in regulations, the term "family-owned corporation" means any corporation which is described in clause (i) of section 447(d)(2)(C) throughout the 8-year period beginning on the date which is 5 years before the date of the recapitalization. For purposes of the preceding sentence, stock shall not be treated as owned by a family member during any period described in section 355(d)(6)(B).

(3) Cross references.

(A) For treatment of the exchange if any property is received which is not permitted to be received under this subsection (including an excess principal amount of securities received over securities surrendered, but not including [3]*nonqualified preferred stock and property* to which paragraph (2)(B) applies), see section 356.

* * * * * * * * * * * *

[For analysis, see ¶ 1502. For text of Committee Report see ¶ 5119].

[Endnote Code Sec. 354]

Matter in *italics* in Code Sec. 354(a)(2)(B), Code Sec. 354(a)(2)(C) and Code Sec. 354(a)(3)(A) was added by Sec. 1014(b) and (e) of the Taxpayer Relief Act of 1997, H.R. 2014, 8/5/97.

1. added matter in subpara. (a)(2)(B).

2. added subpara. (a)(2)(C).

3. added matter in subpara. (a)(3)(A).

Effective Date (Sec. 1014(f), H.R. 2014, 8/5/97) provides:

"(f) Effective date.

"(1) In general. The amendments made by this section shall apply to transactions after June 8, 1997.

"(2) Transition rule. The amendments made by this section shall not apply to any transaction after June 8, 1997, if such transaction is—

"(A) made pursuant to a written agreement which was binding on such date and at all times thereafter,

"(B) described in a ruling request submitted to the Internal Revenue Service on or before such date, or

"(C) described on or before such date in a public announcement or in a filing with the Securities and Exchange Commission required solely by reason of the transaction."

[¶ 3062]   Code Sec. 355.   Distribution of stock and securities of a controlled corporation.
(a) Effect on distributees.

* * * * * * * * * * * *

(3) Limitations.

(C) Property attributable to accrued interest. Neither paragraph (1) nor so much of section 356 as relates to paragraph (1) shall apply to the extent that any stock [1]*(including nonqualified preferred stock, as defined in section 351(g)(2))*, securities, or other property received is attributable to interest which has accrued on securities on or after the beginning of the holder's holding period.

[2]*(D) Nonqualified preferred stock. Nonqualified preferred stock (as defined in section 351(g)(2)) received in a distribution with respect to stock other than nonqualified preferred stock (as so defined) shall not be treated as stock or securities.*

(4) Cross references.

(A) For treatment of the exchange if any property is received which is not permitted to be received under this subsection (including an excess principal amount of securities received over securities surrendered, but not including [3]*nonqualified preferred stock and prop-*erty to which paragraph (3)(C) applies), see section 356.

* * * * * * * * * * * *

[4]*(e) Recognition of gain on certain distributions of stock or securities in connection with acquisition.*

(1) General rule. If there is a distribution to which this subsection applies, any stock or securities in the controlled corporation shall not be treated as qualified property for purposes of subsection (c)(2) of this section or section 361(c)(2).

(2) Distributions to which subsection applies.

(A) In general. This subsection shall apply to any distribution—

(i) to which this section (or so much of section 356 as relates to this section) applies, and

(ii) which is part of a plan (or series of related transactions) pursuant to which 1 or more persons acquire directly or indirectly stock representing a 50- percent or greater interest in the distributing corporation or any controlled corporation.

(B) Plan presumed to exist in certain cases. If 1 or more persons acquire directly or indirectly stock representing a 50-percent or greater interest in the distributing corporation or any controlled corporation during the 4-year period beginning on the date which is 2 years before the date of the distribution, such acquisition shall be treated as pursuant to a plan described in subparagraph (A)(ii) unless it is established that the distribution and the acquisition are not pursuant to a plan or series of related transactions.

(C) Certain plans disregarded. A plan (or series of related transactions) shall not be treated as described in subparagraph (A)(ii) if, immediately after the completion of such plan or transactions, the distributing corporation and all controlled corporations are members of a single affiliated group (as defined in section 1504 without regard to subsection (b) thereof).

(D) Coordination with subsection (d). This subsection shall not apply to any distribution to which subsection (d) applies.

(3) Special rules relating to acquisitions.

(A) Certain acquisitions not taken into account. Except as provided in regulations, the following acquisitions shall not be treated as described in paragraph (2)(A)(ii):

(i) The acquisition of stock in any controlled corporation by the distributing corporation.

(ii) The acquisition by a person of stock in any controlled corporation by reason of holding stock in the distributing corporation.

(iii) The acquisition by a person of stock in any successor corporation of the distributing corporation or any controlled corporation by reason of holding stock in such distributing or controlled corporation.

(iv) The acquisition of stock in a corporation if shareholders owning directly or indirectly stock possessing—

(I) more than 50 percent of the total combined voting power of all classes of stock entitled to vote, and

(II) more than 50 percent of the total value of shares of all classes of stock, in the distributing corporation or any controlled corporation before such acquisition own directly or indirectly stock possessing such vote and value in such distributing or controlled corporation after such acquisition.

This subparagraph shall not apply to any acquisition if the stock held before the acquisition was acquired pursuant to a plan (or series of related transactions) described in subparagraph (2)(A)(ii).

(B) Asset acquisitions. Except as provided in regulations, for purposes of this subsection, if the assets of the distributing corporation or any controlled corporation are acquired by a successor corporation in a transaction described in subparagraph (A), (C), or (D) of section 368(a)(1) or any other transaction specified in regulations by the Secretary, the shareholders (immediately before the acquisition) of the corporation acquiring such assets shall be treated as acquiring stock in the corporation from which the assets were acquired.

(4) Definition and special rules. *For purposes of this subsection—*

(A) 50-percent or greater interest. The term "50-percent or greater interest" has the meaning given such term by subsection (d)(4).

(B) Distributions in title 11 or similar case. Paragraph (1) shall not apply to any distribution made in a title 11 or similar case (as defined in section 368(a)(3)).

(C) Aggregation and attribution rules.

(i) Aggregation. The rules of paragraph (7)(A) of subsection (d) shall apply.

(ii) Attribution. Section 318(a)(2) shall apply in determining whether a person holds stock or securities in any corporation. Except as provided in regulations, section 318(a)(2)(C) shall be applied without regard to the phrase "50 percent or more in value" for purposes of the preceding sentence.

(D) Successors and predecessors. For purposes of this subsection, any reference to a controlled corporation or a distributing corporation shall include a reference to any predecessor or successor of such corporation.

(E) Statute of limitations. If there is an acquisition to which paragraph (1) applies—

(i) the statutory period for the assessment of any deficiency attributable to any part of the gain recognized under this subsection by reason of such distribution shall not expire before the expiration of 3 years from the date the Secretary is notified by the taxpayer (in such manner as the Secretary may by regulations prescribe) that such distribution occurred, and

(ii) such deficiency may be assessed before the expiration of such 3-year period notwithstanding the provisions of any other law or rule of law which would otherwise prevent such assessment.

(5) Regulations. *The Secretary shall prescribe such regulations as may be necessary to carry out the purposes of this subsection, including regulations—*

(A) providing for the application of this subsection where there is more than 1 controlled corporation,

(B) treating 2 or more distributions as 1 distribution where necessary to prevent the avoidance of such purposes, and

(C) providing for the application of rules similar to the rules of subsection (d)(6) where appropriate for purposes of paragraph (2)(B).

⁵**(f) Section not to apply to certain intragroup transactions.** *Except as provided in regulations, this section (or so much of section 356 as relates to this section) shall not apply to the distribution of stock from 1 member of an affiliated group (as defined in section 1504(a)) to an-*

other member of such group if such distribution is part of a plan (or series of related transactions) described in subsection (e)(2)(A)(ii) (determined after the application of subsection (e)).

[For analysis, see ¶s 1501, 1502. For text of Committee Report see ¶s 5117, 5119].

[Endnote Code Sec. 355]
    Matter in *italics* in Code Sec. 355(a)(3)(C), Code Sec. 355(a)(3)(D) and Code Sec. 355(a)(4)(A) added by Sec. 1014(c) and (e) of the Taxpayer Relief Act of 1997, H.R. 2014, 8/5/97.
    1. added matter in subpara. (a)(3)(C).
    2. added subpara. (a)(3)(D).
    3. added matter in subpara. (a)(4)(A)
Effective Date (Sec. 1013(f), H.R. 2014, 8/5/97) reads as follows:
    "(f) Effective date.
    "(1) In general. The amendments made by this section shall apply to transactions after June 8, 1997.
    "(2) Transition rule. The amendments made by this section shall not apply to any transaction after June 8, 1997, if such transaction is—
    "(A) made pursuant to a written agreement which was binding on such date and at all times thereafter,
    "(B) described in a ruling request submitted to the Internal Revenue Service on or before such date, or
    "(C) described on or before such date in a public announcement or in a filing with the Securities and Exchange Commission required solely by reason of the transaction."

    Code Sec. 355(e) and Code Sec. 355(f) in *italics* were added by Sec. 1012(a) and (b)(1), H.R. 2014, 8/5/97.
    4. added subsec. (e).
    5. added subsec. (f).
Effective Date (Sec. 1012(d)(1), H.R. 2014, 8/5/97) effective for distributions after 4/16/97, pursuant to a plan (or series of related transactions) which involved an acquisition described in section 355(e)(2)(A)(ii) occurring after 4/16/97. Sec. 1012(d)(3), H.R. 2014, 8/5/97, provides:
    "(3) Transition rule. The amendments made by this section shall not apply to any distribution pursuant to a plan (or series of related transactions) which involves an acquisition described in section 355(e)(2)(A)(ii) of the Internal Revenue Code of 1986)or, in the case of the amendments made by subsection (c), any transfer) occurring after April 16, 1997, if such acquisition or transfer is—
    "(A) made pursuant to a written agreement which was binding on such date and at all times thereafter,
    "(B) described in a ruling request submitted to the Internal Revenue Service on or before such date, or
    "(C) described on or before such date in a public announcement or in a filing with the Securities and Exchange Commission required solely by reason of the acquisition or transfer.
"This paragraph shall not apply to any agreement, ruling request, or public announcement or filing unless it identifies the unrelated acquirer of the distributing corporation or of any controlled corporation, or the transferee, whichever is applicable."

[¶ 3063]   Code Sec. 356.   Receipt of additional consideration.

* * * * * * * * * * * *

[1]*(e) Nonqualified preferred stock treated as other property. For purposes of this section—*

    (1) In general. Except as provided in paragraph (2), the term "other property" includes nonqualified preferred stock (as defined in section 351(g)(2)).

    (2) Exception. The term "other property" does not include nonqualified preferred stock (as so defined) to the extent that, under section 354 or 355, such preferred stock would be permitted to be received without the recognition of gain.

[2]*(f)* **Exchanges for section 306 stock.** Notwithstanding any other provision of this section, to the extent that any of the other property (or money) is received in exchange for section 306 stock, an amount equal to the fair market value of such other property (or the amount of such money) shall be treated as a distribution of property to which section 301 applies.

[3]*(g)* **Transactions involving gift or compensation.** For special rules for a transaction described in section 354, 355, or this section, but which—

    (1) results in a gift, see section 2501 and following, or

    (2) has the effect of the payment of compensation, see section 61(a)(1).

[For analysis, see ¶ 1502. For text of Committee Report see ¶ 5119].

[Endnote Code Sec. 356]

Matter in *italics* in Code Sec. 356(e), Code Sec. 356(f) and Code Sec. 356(g) added by Sec. 1014(d) of the Taxpayer Relief Act of 1997, H.R. 2014, 8/5/97, which struck out:

1. added subsec. (e).
2. "(e)"
3. "(f)"

Effective Date (Sec. 1014(f), H.R. 2014, 8/5/97) effective as provided in Sec. 1014(f), H.R. 2014, 8/5/97, which reads as follows:

"(f) Effective date.

"(1) In general. The amendments made by this section shall apply to transactions after June 8, 1997.

"(2) Transition rule. The amendments made by this section shall not apply to any transaction after June 8, 1997, if such transaction is—

"(A) made pursuant to a written agreement which was binding on such date and at all times thereafter,

"(B) described in a ruling request submitted to the Internal Revenue Service on or before such date, or

"(C) described on or before such date in a public announcement or in a filing with the Securities and Exchange Commission required solely by reason of the transaction."

[¶ 3064]   Code Sec. 358.   Basis to distributees.

* * * * * * * * * * *

[1](g) *Adjustments in intragroup transactions involving section 355.* In the case of a distribution to which section 355 (or so much of section 356 as relates to section 355) applies and which involves the distribution of stock from 1 member of an affiliated group (as defined in section 1504(a) without regard to subsection (b) thereof) to another member of such group, the Secretary may, notwithstanding any other provision of this section, provide adjustments to the adjusted basis of any stock which—*

(1) is in a corporation which is a member of such group, and

(2) is held by another member of such group, to appropriately reflect the proper treatment of such distribution.

[For analysis, see ¶ 1501. For text of Committee Report see ¶ 5117].

[Endnote Code Sec. 358]

Code Sec. 358(g), in *italics*, added by Sec. 1012(b)(2) of the Taxpayer Relief Act of 1997, H.R. 2014, 8/5/97.

1. added subsec. (g)

Effective Date (Sec. 1012(d)(1) and (3), H.R. 2014, 8/5/97) effective for distributions after 4/16/97 pursuant to a plan (or series of related transactions) which involves an acquisition described in section 355(e)(2)(A)(ii) of the Internal Revenue Code of 1986 occurring after 4/16/97. For exceptions, see Sec. 1012(d)(3) of this Act, which provides:

"(3) Transition rule.—The amendments made by this section shall not apply to any distribution pursuant to a plan (or series of related transactions) which involves an acquisition described in section 355(e)(2)(A)(ii) of the Internal Revenue Code of 1986 (or, in the case of the amendments made by subsection (c), any transfer) occurring after April 16, 1997, if such acquisition or transfer is—

"(A) made pursuant to an agreement which was binding on such date and at all times thereafter,

"(B) described in a ruling request submitted to the Internal Revenue Service on or before such date, or

"(C) described on or before such date in a public announcement or in a filing with the Securities and Exchange Commission required solely by reason of the acquisition or transfer.

This paragraph shall not apply to any agreement, ruling request, or public announcement or filing unless it identifies the acquirer of the distributing corporation or any controlled corporation, or the transferee, whichever is applicable."

[¶ 3065]   Code Sec. 367.   Foreign corporations.

* * * * * * * * * * *

(d) Transfers of intangibles.

* * * * * * * * * * *

(2) Transfer of intangibles treated as transfer pursuant to sale of contingent payments.

* * * * * * * * * * *

986

[1](C) Amounts received treated as ordinary income. For purposes of this chapter, any amount included in gross income by reason of this subsection shall be treated as ordinary income.

[2](3) **Regulations relating to transfers of intangibles to partnerships.** The Secretary may provide by regulations that the rules of paragraph (2) also apply to the transfer of intangible property by a United States person to a partnership in circumstances consistent with the purposes of this subsection.

* * * * * * * * * * *

[3](f) **Other transfers.** To the extent provided in regulations, if a United States person transfers property to a foreign corporation as paid-in surplus or as a contribution to capital (in a transaction not otherwise described in this section), such transfer shall be treated as a sale or exchange for an amount equal to the fair market value of the property transferred, and the transferor shall recognize as gain the excess of—

[3](1) the fair market value of the property so transferred, over

[3](2) the adjusted basis (for purposes of determining gain) of such property in the hands of the transferor.

[For analysis, see ¶ 1630. For text of Committee Report see ¶ 5182].

[Endnote Code Sec. 367]

Matter in *italics* in Code Sec. 367(d)(2)(C), Code Sec. 367(d)(3) and Code Sec. 367(f) was added by Secs. 1131(b)(2) [sic (c)(2)], (b)(4) [sic (c)(4)] and (b)(5)(A) [sic (c)(5)(A)] of the Taxpayer Relief Act of 1997, H.R. 2014, 8/5/97, which struck out:

1. "(C) Amounts received treated as United States source ordinary income. For purposes of this chapter, any amount included in gross income by reason of this subsection shall be treated as ordinary income from sources within the United States."

2. added para. (d)(3).

3. added subsec. (f).

Effective Date (Sec. 1131(d) [sic (e)], H.R. 2014, 8/5/97) effective 8/5/97.

[¶ 3066]   Code Sec. 368.   Definitions relating to corporate reorganizations.

(a) Reorganization.

* * * * * * * * * * *

(2) Special rules relating to paragraph (1).

[1](H) Special rules for determining whether certain transactions are qualified under paragraph (1)(D). For purposes of determining whether a transaction qualifies under paragraph (1)(D)—

(i) in the case of a transaction with respect to which the requirements of subparagraphs (A) and (B) of section 354(b)(1) are met, the term "control" has the meaning given such term by section 304(c), and

(ii) in the case of a transaction with respect to which the requirements of section 355 are met, the shareholders described in paragraph (1)(D) shall be treated as having control of the corporation to which the assets are transferred if such shareholders own (immediately after the distribution) stock possessing—

(I) more than 50 percent of the total combined voting power of all classes of stock of such corporation entitled to vote, and

(II) more than 50 percent of the total value of shares of all classes of stock of such corporation.

* * * * * * * * * * *

[For analysis, see ¶ 1501. For text of Committee Report see ¶ 5117].

[Endnote Code Sec. 368]

Matter in *italics* in Code Sec. 368(a)(2)(H) added by Sec. 1012(c)(2) of the Taxpayer Relief Act of 1997, H.R. 2014, 8/5/97, which struck out:

1. "(H) Special rule for determining whether certain transactions are qualified under paragraph (1)(D). In the case of any transaction with respect to which the requirements of subparagraphs (A) and (B) of section 354(b)(1) are met, for purposes of determining whether such transaction qualifies under subparagraph (D) of paragraph (1), the term 'control' has the meaning given to such term by section 304(c)."

Effective Date (Sec. 1012(d)(2) and (3) of H.R. 2014, 8/5/97) effective for transfers after 8/5/97, except as provided in Sec. 1012(d)(3) of this Act which reads as follows:

"(3) Transition rule. The amendments made by this section shall not apply to any distribution pursuant to a plan (or series of related transactions) which involves an acquisition described in section 355(e)(2)(A)(ii) of the Internal Revenue Code of 1986 (or, in the case of the amendments made by subsection (c), any transfer) occurring after April 16, 1997, if such acquisition or transfer is—

"(A) made pursuant to an agreement which was binding on such date and at all times thereafter,

"(B) described in a ruling request submitted to the Internal Revenue Service on or before such date, or

"(C) described on or before such date in a public announcement or in a filing with the Securities and Exchange Commission required solely by reason of the acquisition or transfer.

This paragraph shall not apply to any agreement, ruling request, or public announcement or filing unless it identifies the acquirer of the distributing corporation or any controlled corporation, or the transferee, whichever is applicable."

[¶ 3067]   Code Sec. 401.   Qualified pension, profit-sharing, and stock bonus plans.

(a) **Requirements for qualification.** A trust created or organized in the United States and forming part of a stock bonus, pension, or profit-sharing plan of an employer for the exclusive benefit of his employees or their beneficiaries shall constitute a qualified trust under this section—

(1) if contributions are made to the trust by such employer, or employees, or both, or by another employer who is entitled to deduct his contributions under section 404(a)(3)(B) (relating to deduction for contributions to profit-sharing and stock bonus plans), [1]*or by a charitable remainder trust pursuant to a qualified gratuitous transfer (as defined in section 664(g)(1)) for the purpose of distributing to such employees or their beneficiaries the corpus and income of the fund accumulated by the trust in accordance with such plan;*

* * * * * * * * * * *

(5) **Special rules relating to nondiscrimination requirements.**

* * * * * * * * * * * *

[2]*(G) State and local governmental plans. Paragraphs (3) and (4) shall not apply to a governmental plan (within the meaning of section 414(d)) maintained by a State or local government or political subdivision thereof (or agency or instrumentality thereof).*

* * * * * * * * * * * *

(13) **Assignment and alienation.**

* * * * * * * * * * *

[3]*(C) Special rule for certain judgments and settlements. Subparagraph (A) shall not apply to any offset of a participant's benefits provided under a plan against an amount that the participant is ordered or required to pay to the plan if—*

(i) the order or requirement to pay arises—

(I) (I) under a judgment of conviction for a crime involving such plan,

(II) under a civil judgment (including a consent order or decree) entered by a court in an action brought in connection with a violation (or alleged violation) of part 4 of subtitle B of title I of the Employee Retirement Income Security Act of 1974, or

(III) pursuant to a settlement agreement between the Secretary of Labor and the participant, or a settlement agreement between the Pension Benefit Guaranty Corporation and the participant, in connection with a violation (or alleged violation) of part 4 of such subtitle by a fiduciary or any other person,

(ii) the judgment, order, decree, or settlement agreement expressly provides for the offset of all or part of the amount ordered or required to be paid to the plan against the participant's benefits provided under the plan, and

(iii) in a case in which the survivor annuity requirements of section 401(a)(11) apply with respect to distributions from the plan to the participant, if the participant has a spouse at the time at which the offset is to be made —

(I) either such spouse has consented in writing to such offset and such consent is witnessed by a notary public or representative of the plan (or it is established to the satisfaction of a plan representative that such consent may not be obtained by reason of circumstances described in section 417(a)(2)(B)), or an election to waive the right of the spouse to either a qualified joint and survivor annuity or a qualified preretirement survivor annuity is in effect in accordance with the requirements of section 417(a),

(II) such spouse is ordered or required in such judgment, order, decree, or settlement to pay an amount to the plan in connection with a violation of part 4 of such subtitle, or

(III) in such judgment, order, decree, or settlement, such spouse retains the right to receive the survivor annuity under a qualified joint and survivor annuity provided pursuant to section 401(a)(11)(A)(i) and under a qualified preretirement survivor annuity provided pursuant to section 401(a)(11)(A)(ii), determined in accordance with subparagraph (D).

A plan shall not be treated as failing to meet the requirements of this subsection, subsection (k), section 403(b), or section 409(d) solely by reason of an offset described in this subparagraph.

(D) Survivor annuity.

(i) In general. The survivor annuity described in subparagraph (C)(iii)(III) shall be determined as if—

(I) the participant terminated employment on the date of the offset,

(II) there was no offset,

(III) the plan permitted commencement of benefits only on or after normal retirement age,

(IV) the plan provided only the minimum-required qualified joint and survivor annuity, and

(V) the amount of the qualified preretirement survivor annuity under the plan is equal to the amount of the survivor annuity payable under the minimum-required qualified joint and survivor annuity.

(ii) Definition. For purposes of this subparagraph, the term "minimum-required qualified joint and survivor annuity" means the qualified joint and survivor annuity which is the actuarial equivalent of the participant's accrued benefit (within the meaning of section 411(a)(7)) and under which the survivor annuity is 50 percent of the amount of the annuity which is payable during the joint lives of the participant and the spouse.

* * * * * * * * * * *

(26) Additional participation requirements.

* * * * * * * * * * *

[4](H) Exception for state and local governmental plans. This paragraph shall not apply to a governmental plan (within the meaning of section 414(d)) maintained by a State or local government or political subdivision thereof (or agency or instrumentality thereof)

(k) Cash or deferred arrangements.

* * * * * * * * * * *

(3) Application of participation and discrimination standards.

* * * * * * * * * * *

[5](G) *A governmental plan (within the meaning of section 414(d)) maintained by a State or local government or political subdivision thereof (or agency or instrumentality thereof) shall be treated as meeting the requirements of this paragraph.*

* * * * * * * * * * *

(7) Rural cooperative plan. For purposes of this subsection—

* * * * * * * * * * *

(B) Rural cooperative defined. For purposes of subparagraph (A), the term "rural cooperative" means—

* * * * * * * * * * *

CAUTION. Clauses (k)(7)(B)(iii) and (iv), following, is effective for yrs. begin. before 1/1/98. For clause (k)(7)(B)(iii)-(v) effective for yrs. begin. after 12/31/97, see below.

(iii) a cooperative telephone company described in section 501(c)(12), and

(iv) an organization which is a national association of organizations described in clause (i), (ii), or (iii).

CAUTION. Clauses (k)(7)(B)(iii) and (iv), following, are effective for yrs. begin. before 1/1/98. For clause (k)(7)(B)(iii)-(v) effective for yrs. begin. after 12/31/97, see below.

(iii) a cooperative telephone company described in section 501(c)(12), and

(iv) an organization which is a national association of organizations described in clause (i), (ii), or (iii).

CAUTION. Clauses (k)(7)(B)(iii)-(v), following, are effective for yrs. begin. after 12/31/97. For clauses (k)(7)(B)(iii) and (iv) effective for yrs. begin. before 1/1/98, see above.

(iii) a cooperative telephone company described in section 501(c)(12), [6]

[7]*(iv) any organization which—*

(I) is a mutual irrigation or ditch company described in section 501(c)(12) (without regard to the 85 percent requirement thereof), or

(II) is a district organized under the laws of a State as a municipal corporation for the purpose of irrigation, water conservation, or drainage, and

[8]*(v) an organization which is a national association of organizations described in clause (i), (ii), [9](iii), or (iv).*

* * * * * * * * * * *

(11) Adoption of simple plan to meet nondiscrimination tests.

* * * * * * * * * * *

(B) Contribution requirements.

* * * * * * * * * * *

[10]*(iii) Administrative requirements.*

(I) In general. Rules similar to the rules of subparagraphs (B) and (C) of section 408(p)(5) shall apply for purposes of this subparagraph.

(II) Notice of election period. The requirements of this subparagraph shall not be treated as met with respect to any year unless the employer notifies each employee eligible to participate, within reasonable period of time before the 60th day before the beginning of such year (and, for the first year the employee is so eligible, the 60th day before the first day such employee is so eligible), of the rules similar to the rules of section 408(p)(5)(C) which apply by reason of subclause (I).

* * * * * * * * * * *

(D) Definitions and special rule.

* * * * * * * * * * * *

(ii) Coordination with top-heavy rules. A plan meeting the requirements of this paragraph for any year shall not be treated as a top-heavy plan under section 416 for such year [11]*if such plan allows only contributions required under this paragraph.*

[12]*(E) Cost-of-living adjustment. The Secretary shall adjust the $6,000 amount under subparagraph (B)(i)(I) at the same time and in the same manner as under section 408(p)(2)(E).*

* * * * * * * * * * *

(m) Nondiscrimination test for matching contributions and employee contributions.

* * * * * * * * * * *

(11) [13]*Additional alternative* **method of satisfying tests.**

(A) In general. A defined contribution plan shall be treated as meeting the requirements of paragraph (2) with respect to matching contributions if the plan—

(i) meets the contribution requirements of subparagraph (B) or (C) of subsection (k)(12),

(ii) meets the notice requirements of subsection (k)(12)(D), and

(iii) meets the requirements of subparagraph (B).

(B) Limitation on matching contributions. The requirements of this subparagraph are met if—

(i) matching contributions on behalf of any employee may not be made with respect to an employee's contributions or elective deferrals in excess of 6 percent of the employee's compensation.

(ii) the rate of an employer's matching contribution does not increase as the rate of an employee's contributions or elective deferrals increase, and

(iii) the matching contribution with respect to any highly compensated employee at any rate of an employee contribution or rate of elective deferral is not greater than that with respect to an employee who is not a highly compensated employee.

* * * * * * * * * * *

[For analysis, see ¶s 904, 919, 920, 921, 924, 930. For text of Committee Report see ¶s 5308, 5311, 5347, 5361].

[Endnote Code Sec. 401]

Matter in *italics* in Code Sec. 401(a)(1) added by Sec. 1530(c)(1) of the Taxpayer Relief Act of 1997, H.R. 2014, 8/5/97.

1. added matter in para. (a)(1)

Effective Date (Sec. 1530(d), H.R. 2014, 8/5/97) effective for transfers made by trusts to, or for the use of, an employee stock ownership plan after 8/5/97.

Code Sec. 401(a)(5)(G) in *italics* was added by Sec. 1505(a)(1), H.R. 2014, 8/5/97.

2. added subpara. (a)(5)(G)

Effective Date (Sec. 1505(d), H.R. 2014, 8/5/97) effective for tax. yrs. begin. on or after date of enactment. Sec. 1505(d)(2) of this Act provides:

"(2) Treatment for years beginning before 8/5/97.—A governmental plan (within the meaning of section 414(d) of the Internal Revenue Code of 1986) maintained by a State or local government or political subdivision thereof (or agency or instrumentality thereof) shall be treated as satisfying the requirements of sections 401(a)(3), 401(a)(4), 401(a)(26), 401(k), 401(m), 403 (b)(1)(D) and (b)(12), and 410 of such Code for all taxable years beginning before the 8/5/97 of this Act."

Code Sec. 401(a)(13)(C) and Code Sec. 401(a)(13)(D) in *italics* were added by Sec. 1502(b), H.R. 2014, 8/5/97.

3. added subparas. (a)(13)(C) and (D)

Effective Date (Sec. 1502(c), H.R. 2014, 8/5/97) effective for judgments, orders, and decrees issued, and settlement agreements entered into, on or after 8/5/97.

Matter in *italics* in Code Sec. 401(a)(26)(H) and Code Sec. 401(k)(3)(G) added by Sec. 1505(a)(2) and (b), H.R. 2014, 8/5/97, which struck out:

4. "(H) Special rule for certain police or firefighters.

"(i) In general. An employer may elect to have this paragraph applied separately with respect to any classification of qualified public safety employees for whom a separate plan is maintained.

"(ii) Qualified public safety employee. For purposes of this subparagraph, the term 'qualified public safety employee' means any employee of any police department or fire department organized and operated by a State or political subdivision if the employee provides police protection, firefighting services, or emergency medical services for any area within the jurisdiction of such State or political subdivision."

5. added subpara. (k)(3)(G)

Effective Date (Sec. 1505(d), H.R. 2014, 8/5/97) effective for tax. yrs. begin. on or after date of enactment. See Sec. 1505(d)(2) of this Act reproduced above.

Matter in *italics* in Code Sec. 401(k)(7)(B)(iii), Code Sec. 401(k)(7)(B)(iv), and Code Sec. 401(k)(7)(B)(v), added by Sec. 1525(a)(1) and (2), H.R. 2014, 8/5/97, which struck out:
6. "and"
7. added clause (k)(7)(B)(iv)
8. "(iv)"
9. "or (iii)"
Effective Date (Sec. 1525(b), H.R. 2014, 8/5/97) effective for yrs. begin. after 12/31/97.

Code Sec. 401(k)(11)(B)(iii) in *italics* was , added by Sec. 1601(d)(2)(D), H.R. 2014, 8/5/97, which struck out:
10. added clause (k)(11)(B)(iii)
Effective Date (Sec. 1601(j)(2), H.R. 2014, 8/5/97) effective for calendar yrs. begin. after 8/5/97.

Matter in *italics* in Code Sec. 401(k)(11)(D)(ii) and Code Sec. 401(k)(11)(E) added by Sec. 1601(d)(2)(A) and (d)(2)(B), H.R. 2014, 8/5/97, which struck out:
11. "."
12. added subpara. (k)(11)(E)
Effective Date (Sec. 1601(j)(1), H.R. 2014, 8/5/97) effective for plan. yrs. begin. after 12/31/96.

Matter in *italics* in Code Sec. 401(m)(11) added by Sec. 1601(d)(3), H.R. 2014, 8/5/97, which struck out:
13. "Alternative"
Effective Date (Sec. 1601(j)(1), H.R. 2014, 8/5/97) effective for yrs. begin. after 12/31/98.

Sec. 1509, H.R. 2014, 8/5/97, relating to the clarification of disqualification rules relating to acceptance of rollover contributions, provides:
"Sec. 1509. Clarification of disqualification rules relating to acceptance of rollover contributions. The Secretary of the Treasury or his delegate shall clarify that, under the Internal Revenue Service regulations protecting pension plans from disqualification by reason of the receipt of invalid rollover contributions under section 402(c) of the Internal Revenue Code of 1986, in order for the administrator of the plan receiving any such contribution to reasonably conclude that the contribution is a valid rollover contribution it is not necessary for the distributing plan to have a determination letter with respect to its status as a qualified plan under section 401 of such Code."

[¶ 3068]   Code Sec. 402.   Taxability of beneficiary of employees' trust.

* * * * * * * * * * * *

(g) Limitation on exclusion for elective deferrals.

* * * * * * * * * * * *

CAUTION.   Para. (g)(9), following, is effective for tax. yrs. begin. after 12/31/97.

[1]*(9) Matching contributions on behalf of self-employed individuals not treated as elective employer contributions. Except as provided in section 401(k)(3)(D)(ii), any matching contribution described in section 401(m)(4)(A) which is made on behalf of a self-employed individual (as defined in section 401(c)) shall not be treated as an elective employer contribution under a qualified cash or deferred arrangement (as defined in section 401(k)) for purposes of this title.*

* * * * * * * * * * * *

[For analysis, see ¶ 933. For text of Committee Report see ¶ 5307].

[Endnote Code Sec. 402]
Code Sec. 402(g)(9), in *italics*, was added by Sec. 1501(a) of the Taxpayer Relief Act of 1997, H.R. 2014, 8/5/97.
1. added para. (g)(9)
Effective Date (Sec. 1501(c), H.R. 2014, 8/5/97) effective for tax. yrs. begin. after 12/31/97.

Sec. 1509, H.R. 2014, 8/5/97, relating to the clarification of disqualification rules relating to acceptance of rollover contributions is reproduced in notes following Code Sec. 401.

[¶ 3069]   Code Sec. 403.   Taxation of employee annuities.

* * * * * * * * * * *

(b) Taxability of beneficiary under annuity purchased by section 501(c)(3) organization or public school.

(1) General rule. If—

(A) an annuity contract is purchased—

(i) for an employee by an employer described in section 501(c)(3) which is exempt from tax under section 501(a), [1]

(ii) for an employee (other than an employee described in clause (i)), who performs services for an educational organization described in section 170(b)(1)(A)(ii), by an employer which is a State, a political subdivision of a State, or an agency or instrumentality of any one or more of the foregoing,[2] or

[3] *(iii) for the minister described in section 414(e)(5)(A) by the minister or by an employer,*

* * * * * * * * * * * *

CAUTION.   Para. (b)(3), following, is effective for yrs. begin. before 1/1/98. For para. (b)(3) effective for yrs. begin. after 12/31/97, see below.

(3) Includible compensation. For purposes of this subsection, the term "includible compensation" means, in the case of any employee, the amount of compensation which is received from the employer described in paragraph (1)(A), and which is includible in gross income (computed without regard to section 911) for the most recent period (ending not later than the close of the taxable year) which under paragraph (4) may be counted as one year of service.

CAUTION.   Para. (b)(3), following, is effective for yrs. begin. after 12/31/97. For para. (b)(3) effective for yrs. begin. before 1/1/98, see above.

(3) Includible compensation. For purposes of this subsection, the term "includible compensation" means, in the case of any employee, the amount of compensation which is received from the employer described in paragraph (1)(A), and which is includible in gross income (computed without regard to section 911) for the most recent period (ending not later than the close of the taxable year) which under paragraph (4) may be counted as one year of service.[4] *Such term does not include any amount contributed by the employer for any annuity contract to which this subsection applies. Such term includes—*

(A) any elective deferral (as defined in section 402(g)(3)), and

(B) any amount which is contributed or deferred by the employer at the election of the employee and which is not includible in the gross income of the employee by reason of section 125 or 457.

* * * * * * * * * * * *

(12) Nondiscrimination requirements.

* * * * * * * * * * * *

[5]*(C) State and local governmental plans. For purposes of paragraph (1)(D), the requirements of subparagraph (A)(i) (other than those relating to section 401(a)(17)) shall not apply to a governmental plan (within the meaning of section 414(d)) maintained by a State or local government or political subdivision thereof (or agency or instrumentality thereof).*

* * * * * * * * * * * *

[For analysis, see ¶s 924, 925, 1901. For text of Committee Report see ¶s 5310, 5311, 5344].

[Endnote Code Sec. 403]

Matter in *italics* in Code Sec. 403(b)(1)(A)(i), Code Sec. 403(b)(1)(A)(ii) and Code Sec. 403(b)(1)(A)(iii), added by Sec. 1601(d)(6)(B) of the Taxpayer Relief Act of 1997, H.R. 2014, 8/5/97, which struck out:
"or"
added material in clause (b)(1)(A)(ii)
added clause (b)(1)(A)(iii)
Effective Date (Sec. 1601(j)(1), H.R. 2014, 8/5/97) effective for yrs. begin. after 12/31/96.

Matter in *italics* in Code Sec. 403(b)(3) was added by Sec. 1504(a)(1), H.R. 2014, 8/5/97.
added material in para. (b)(3)
Effective Date (Sec. 1504(a)(2), H.R. 2014, 8/5/97) effective for yrs. begin. after 12/31/97. Sec. 1504(b) of this Act, reads as follows:
"(b) Repeal of Rules in Section 415(e).—The Secretary of the Treasury shall modify the regulations regarding the exclusion allowance under section 403(b)(2) of the Internal Revenue Code of 1986 to reflect the amendment made by section 1452(a) of the Small Business Job Protection Act of 1996. Such modification shall take effect for years beginning after December 31, 1999."

Code Sec. 403(b)(12)(C), in *italics*, was added by Sec. 1505(c), H.R. 2014, 8/5/97.
5. added subpara. (b)(12)(C)
Effective Date (Sec. 1505(d), H.R. 2014, 8/5/97) effective for tax. yrs. begin. on or after 8/5/97, except as provided in Sec. 1505(d)(2) of this Act, which reads as follows:.
"(2) Treatment for years beginning before 8/5/97.—A governmental plan (within the meaning of section 414(d) of the Internal Revenue Code of 1986) maintained by a State or local government or political subdivision thereof (or agency or instrumentality thereof) shall be treated as satisfying the requirements of sections 401(a)(3), 401(a)(4), 401(a)(26), 401(k), 401(m), 403 (b)(1)(D) and (b)(12), and 410 of such Code for all taxable years beginning before the 8/5/97 of this Act."
Sec. 1604(d)(4) of H.R. 2014 provides:
"(4) Clarification of section 1450.—
"(A) Section 403(b)(11) of the Internal Revenue Code of 1986 shall not apply with respect to a distribution from a contract described in section 1450(b)(1) of such Act to the extent that such distribution is not includible in income by reason of—
"(i) in the case of distributions before January 1, 1998, section 403 (b)(8) or (b)(10) of such Code (determined after the application of section 1450(b)(2) of such Act), and
"(ii) in the case of distributions on and after such date, such section 403(b)(1).
"(B) This paragraph shall apply as if included in section 1450 of the Small Business Job Protection Act of 1996."

[¶ 3070]   Code Sec. 404.   Deduction for contributions of an employer to an employees' trust or annuity plan and compensation under a deferred-payment plan.

(a) General rule. If contributions are paid by an employer to or under a stock bonus, pension, profit-sharing, or annuity plan, or if compensation is paid or accrued on account of any employee under a plan deferring the receipt of such compensation, such contributions or compensation shall not be deductible under this chapter; but, if they would otherwise be deductible, they shall be deductible under this section, subject, however, to the following limitations as to the amounts deductible in any year:

* * * * * * * * * * * *

(3) Stock bonus and profit-sharing trusts.
(A) Limits on deductible contributions.
(i) In general. In the taxable year when paid, if the contributions are paid into a stock bonus or profit-sharing trust, and if such taxable year ends within or with a taxable year of the trust with respect to which the trust is exempt under section 501(a), in an amount [1]*not in excess of the greater of—*
(I) 15 percent of the compensation otherwise paid or accrued during the taxable year to the beneficiaries under the stock bonus or profit-sharing plan, or
(II) the amount such employer is required to contribute to such trust under section 401(k)(11) for such year.
(ii) Carryover of excess contributions. Any amount paid into the trust in any taxable year in excess of the limitation of clause (i) (or the corresponding provision of prior law) shall be deductible in the succeeding taxable years in order of time, but the amount so deductible under this clause in any 1 such succeeding taxable year together with the amount allowable under clause (i) shall not exceed [2]*the amount described in subclause (I) or (II) of clause (i), whichever is greater, with respect to such taxable year.*

(9) Certain contributions to employee stock ownership plans.

* * * * * * * * * * *

CAUTION.   Subpara. (a)(9)(C), following, is effective for tax. yrs. begin. after 12/31/97.

(C) S corporations. This paragraph shall not apply to an S corporation.

³(C[sic (D)]) *A qualified gratuitous transfer (as defined in section 664(g)(1)) shall have no effect on the amount or amounts otherwise deductible under paragraph (3) or (7) or under this paragraph.*

* * * * * * * * * * *

[For analysis, see ¶ 918. For text of Committee Report see ¶ 5361].

[Endnote Code Sec. 404]

Matter in *italics* in Code Sec. 404(a)(3)(A)(i) and Code Sec. 404(a)(3)(A)(ii) added by Sec. 1601(d)(2)(C)(i) and (ii) of the Taxpayer Relief Act of 1997, H.R. 2014, 8/5/97, which struck out:

1. "not in excess of 15 percent of the compensation otherwise paid or accrued during the taxable year to the beneficiaries under the stock bonus or profit-sharing plan."

2. "15 percent of the compensation otherwise paid or accrued during such taxable year to the beneficiaries under the plan."

Effective Date (Sec. 1601(j)(1), H.R. 2014, 8/5/97) effective for plan yrs. begin. after 12/31/96.

Subpara (a)(9)(C)[sic (D)] in *italics* was added by Sec. 1530(c)(2), H.R. 2014, 8/5/97.

3. added subpara. (a)(9)(C)[sic (D)]

Effective Date (Sec. 1530(d), H.R. 2014, 8/5/97) effective for transfers made by trusts to, or for the use of, an employee stock ownership plan after 8/5/97.

[¶ 3071]   Code Sec. 408.   Individual retirement accounts.

* * * * * * * * * * *

CAUTION.   Subsec. (i), following, is effective for tax. yrs. begin. before 1/1/98. For subsec. (i) effective for tax. yrs. begin. after 12/31/97, see below.

(i) Reports. The trustee of an individual retirement account and the issuer of an endowment contract described in subsection (b) or an individual retirement annuity shall make such reports regarding such account, contract, or annuity to the Secretary and to the individuals for whom the account, contract, or annuity is, or is to be, maintained with respect to contributions (and the years to which they relate), distributions aggregating $10 or more in any calender year and such other matters as the Secretary may require under regulations. The reports required by this subsection—

(1) shall be filed at such time and in such manner as the Secretary prescribes in such regulations, and

(2) shall be furnished to individuals—

(A) not later than January 31 of the calendar year following the calendar year to which such reports relate, and

(B) in such manner as the Secretary prescribes in such regulations.

In the case of a simple retirement account under subsection (p), only one report under this subsection shall be required to be submitted each calendar year to the Secretary (at the time provided under paragraph (2)) but, in addition to the report under this subsection, there shall be furnished, within ¹31 *days* after each calendar year, to the individual on whose behalf the account is maintained a statement with respect to the account balance as of the close of, and the account activity during, such calendar year.

CAUTION.   Subsec. (i), following, is effective for tax. yrs. begin. after 12/31/97. For subsec. (i) effective for tax. yrs. begin. before 1/1/98, see above.

(i) Reports. The trustee of an individual retirement account and the issuer of an endowment contract described in subsection (b) or an individual retirement annuity shall make such reports regarding such account, contract, or annuity to the Secretary and to the individuals for whom the account, contract, or annuity is, or is to be, maintained with respect to contributions (and the years to which they relate), distributions aggregating $10 or more in any calender year and such other matters as the Secretary may require[2]. The reports required by this subsection—

(1) shall be filed at such time and in such manner as the Secretary prescribes[3], and

(2) shall be furnished to individuals—

(A) not later than January 31 of the calendar year following the calendar year to which such reports relate, and

(B) in such manner as the Secretary prescribes[4].

In the case of a simple retirement account under subsection (p), only one report under this subsection shall be required to be submitted each calendar year to the Secretary (at the time provided under paragraph (2)) but, in addition to the report under this subsection, there shall be furnished, within 31 days after each calendar year, to the individual on whose behalf the account is maintained a statement with respect to the account balance as of the close of, and the account activity during, such calendar year.

* * * * * * * * * * *

(k) Simplified employee pension defined.

* * * * * * * * * * *

(6) Employee may elect salary reduction arrangement.

(H) Termination. This paragraph shall not apply to years beginning after December 31, 1996. The preceding sentence shall not apply to a simplified employee pension [5]*of an employer if the terms of simplified employee pensions of such employer*, as in effect on December 31, 1996, provide that an employee may make the election described in subparagraph (A).

* * * * * * * * * * *

(l) Simplified employer reports.

* * * * * * * * * * *

(2) Simple retirement accounts.

* * * * * * * * * * *

(B) Summary description. The trustee of any simple retirement account established pursuant to a qualified salary reduction arrangement under subsection (p) [6]*and the issuer of an annuity established under such an arrangement* shall provide to the employer maintaining the arrangement, each year a description containing the following information:

(i) The name and address of the employer and the trustee [7]*or issuer.*

* * * * * * * * * * *

(m) Investment in collectibles treated as distributions.

* * * * * * * * * * *

CAUTION. Para. (m)(3), following, is effective for tax. yrs. begin. after 12/31/97. For para. (m)(3) effective for tax. yrs. begin. before 1/1/98, see below.

(3) Exception for certain coins. In the case of an individual retirement account, paragraph (2) shall not apply to—

(A) any gold coin described in paragraph (7), (8), (9), or (10) of section 5112(a) of title 31,

(B) any silver coin described in section 5112(e) of title 31, or

(C) any coin issued under the laws of any State.

CAUTION. Para. (m)(3), following, is effective for tax. yrs. begin. after 12/31/97. For para. (m)(3) effective for tax. yrs. begin. before 1/1/98, see above.

[8]**(3) Exception for certain coins and bullion.** *For purposes of this subsection, the term "collectible" shall not include—*

(A) any coin which is—

(i) a gold coin described in paragraph (7), (8), (9), or (10) of section 5112(a) of title 31, United States Code,

(ii) a silver coin described in section 5112(e) of title 31, United States Code,

(iii) a platinum coin described in section 5112(k) of title 31, United States Code, or

(iv) a coin issued under the laws of any State, or

(B) any gold, silver, platinum, or palladium bullion of a fineness equal to or exceeding the minimum fineness that a contract market (as described in section 7 of the Commodity Exchange Act, 7 U.S.C. 7) requires for metals which may be delivered in satisfaction of a regulated futures contract,

if such bullion is in the physical possession of a trustee described under subsection (a) of this section.

* * * * * * * * * * * *

(p) Simple retirement accounts.

* * * * * * * * * * * *

(2) Qualified salary reduction arrangement.

* * * * * * * * * * * *

(D) Arrangement may be only plan of employer.

(i) In general. An arrangement shall not be treated as a qualified salary reduction arrangement for any year if the employer (or any predecessor employer) maintained a qualified plan with respect to which contributions were made, or benefits were accrued, for service in any year in the period beginning with the year such arrangement became effective and ending with the year for which the determination is being made. [9]*If only individuals other than employees described in subparagraph (A) or (B) of section 410(b)(3) are eligible to participate in such arrangement, then the preceding sentence shall be applied without regard to any qualified plan in which only employees so described are eligible to participate.*

* * * * * * * * * * * *

[10]*(iii) Grace period. In the case of an employer who establishes and maintains a plan under this subsection for 1 or more years and who fails to meet any requirement of this subsection for any subsequent year due to any acquisition, disposition, or similar transaction involving another such employer, rules similar to the rules of section 410(b)(6)(C) shall apply for purposes of this subsection.*

* * * * * * * * * * * *

(5) Administrative requirements. The requirements of this paragraph are met with respect to any [11]*simple* retirement account if, under the qualified salary reduction arrangement—

(A) an employer must—

(i) make the elective employer contributions under paragraph (2)(A)(i) not later than the close of the 30-day period following the last day of the month with respect to which the contributions are to be made, and

(ii) make the matching contributions under paragraph (2)(A)(iii) or the nonelective contributions under paragraph (2)(B) not later than the date described in section 404(m)(2)(B).

(B) an employee may elect to terminate participation in such arrangement at any time during the year, except that if an employee so terminates, the arrangement may provide that the employee may not elect to resume participation until the beginning of the next year, and

(C) each employee eligible to participate may elect, during the 60-day period before the beginning of any year (and the 60-day period before the first day such employee is eligible to participate), to participate in the arrangement, or to modify the amounts subject to such arrangement, for such year.

* * * * * * * * * * * *

[12](8) **Coordination with maximum limitation under subsection (a).** *In the case of any simple retirement account, subsections (a)(1) and (b)(2) shall be applied by substituting "the sum of the dollar amount in effect under paragraph (2)(A)(ii) of this subsection and the employer contribution required under subparagraph (A)(iii) or (B)(i) of paragraph (2) of this subsection, whichever is applicable" for "$2.000".*

[13](8) [sic (9)] **Matching contributions on behalf of self-employed individuals not treated as elective employer contributions.** *Any matching contribution described in paragraph (2)(A)(iii) which is made on behalf of a self-employed individual (as defined in section 401(c)) shall not be treated as an elective employer contribution to a simple retirement account for purposes of this title.*

* * * * * * * * * * * *

[For analysis, see ¶s 301, 305, 913, 914, 915, 916, 917, 933. For text of Committee Report see ¶s 5016, 5018, 5307, 5361].

[Endnote Code Sec. 408]

Matter in *italics* in Code Sec. 408(i) added by Sec. 1601(d)(1)(A) of the Taxpayer Relief Act of 1997, H.R. 2014, 8/5/97, which struck out:

1. "30 days"

Effective Date (Sec. 1601(j)(1), H.R. 2014, 8/5/97) effective for tax. yrs. begin. after 12/31/96.

In Code Sec. 401(i)Sec. 302(d)(1) and (2) struck out:

2. "under regulations"
3. "in such regulations"
4. "in such regulations"

Effective Date (Sec. 302(f), H.R. 2014, 8/5/97) effective for tax. yrs. begin. after 12/31/97.

Matter in *italics* in Code Sec. 408(k)(6)(H), Code Sec. 408(l)(2)(B) and Code Sec. 408(l)(2)(B)(i) added by Sec. 1601(d)(1)(B) and (C), H.R. 2014, 8/5/97, which struck out:

5. "if the terms of such pension"
6. added matter in subpara. (l)(2)(B)
7. added matter in clause (l)(2)(B)(i)

Effective Date (Sec. 1601(j)(1), H.R. 2014, 8/5/97) effective for tax. yrs. begin. after 12/31/96.

Matter in *italics* in Code Sec. 408(m)(3) added by Sec. 304(a), H.R. 2014, 8/5/97, which struck out:

8. "(3) Exception for certain coins.
"In the case of an individual retirement account, paragraph (2) shall not apply to—
"(A) any gold coin described in paragraph (7), (8), (9), or (10) of section 5112(a) of title 31,
"(B) any silver coin described in section 5112(e) of title 31, or
"(C) any coin issued under the laws of any State."

Effective Date (Sec. 304(b), H.R. 2014, 8/5/97) effective for tax. yrs. begin. after 12/31/97.

Matter in *italics* in Code Sec. 408(p)(2)(D)(i), Code Sec. 408(p)(2)(D)(iii), Code Sec. 408(p)(5) and Code Sec. 408(p)(8) added by Sec. 1601(d)(1)(D) and (G), H.R. 2014, 8/5/97, which struck out:

9. added matter in clause (p)(2)(D)(i)
10. added clause (p)(2)(D)(iii)
11. "simplified"
12. added paragraph (p)(8)

Effective Date (Sec. 1601(j)(1), H.R. 2014, 8/5/97) effective for tax. yrs. begin. after 12/31/96.

Code Sec. 408(p)(8)[sic (9)] was added by Sec. 1501(b), H.R. 2014, 8/5/97:

13. added para. (p)(8)[sic (9)]

Effective Date (Sec. 1501(c)(2), H.R. 2014, 8/5/97) effective for yrs. begin. after 12/31/96.

[¶ 3072] Code Sec.[1] 408A.

CAUTION.   Code Sec. 408A, following, is effective for tax. yrs. begin. after 12/31/97.

Roth IRAs.

(a) General rule. Except as provided in this section, a Roth IRA shall be treated for purposes of this title in the same manner as an individual retirement plan.

(b) Roth IRA. For purposes of this title, the term "Roth IRA" means an individual retirement plan (as defined in section 7701(a)(37)) which is designated (in such manner as the Secretary may prescribe) at the time of the establishment of the plan as a Roth IRA. Such designation shall be made in such manner as the Secretary may prescribe.

(c) Treatment of contributions.

(1) No deduction allowed. No deduction shall be allowed under section 219 for a contribution to a Roth IRA.

(2) Contribution limit. The aggregate amount of contributions for any taxable year to all Roth IRAs maintained for the benefit of an individual shall not exceed the excess (if any) of —

(A) the maximum amount allowable as a deduction under section 219 with respect to such individual for such taxable year (computed without regard to subsection (d)(1) or (g) of such section), over

(B) the aggregate amount of contributions for such taxable year to all other individual retirement plans (other than Roth IRAs) maintained for the benefit of the individual.

(3) Limits based on modified adjusted gross income.

(A) Dollar limit. The amount determined under paragraph (2) for any taxable year shall be reduced (but not below zero) by the amount which bears the same ratio to such amount as —

(i) the excess of—

(I) the taxpayer's adjusted gross income for such taxable year, over

(II) the applicable dollar amount, bears to

(ii) $15,000 ($10,000 in the case of a joint return). The rules of subparagraphs (B) and (C) of section 219(g)(2) shall apply to any reduction under this subparagraph.

(B) Rollover from ira. A taxpayer shall not be allowed to make a qualified rollover contribution to a Roth IRA from an individual retirement plan other than a Roth IRA during any taxable year if—

(i) the taxpayer's adjusted gross income for such taxable year exceeds $100,000, or

(ii) the taxpayer is a married individual filing a separate return.

(C) Definitions. For purposes of this paragraph—

(i) adjusted gross income shall be determined in the same manner as under section 219(g)(3), except that any amount included in gross income under subsection (d)(3) shall not be taken into account and the deduction under section 219 shall be taken into account, and

(ii) the applicable dollar amount is—

(I) in the case of a taxpayer filing a joint return, $150,000,

(II) in the case of any other taxpayer (other than a married individual filing a separate return), $95,000, and

(III) in the case of a married individual filing a separate return, zero.

(D) Marital status. Section 219(g)(4) shall apply for purposes of this paragraph.

(4) Contributions permitted after age 70½ Contributions to a Roth IRA may be made even after the individual for whom the account is maintained has attained age 701/2.

(5) Mandatory distribution rules not to apply before death. Notwithstanding subsections (a)(6) and (b)(3) of section 408 (relating to required distributions), the following provisions shall not apply to any Roth IRA:

(A) Section 401(a)(9)(A).

(B) The incidental death benefit requirements of section 401(a).

(6) Rollover contributions.

(A) In general. No rollover contribution may be made to a Roth IRA unless it is a qualified rollover contribution.

(B) Coordination with limit.—A qualified rollover contribution shall not be taken into account for purposes of paragraph (2).

(7) Time when contributions made. For purposes of this section, the rule of section 219(f)(3) shall apply.

(d) Distribution rules. For purposes of this title—

(1) General rules.

(A) Exclusions from gross income. Any qualified distribution from a Roth IRA shall not be includible in gross income.

(B) Nonqualified distributions. In applying section 72 to any distribution from a Roth IRA which is not a qualified distribution, such distribution shall be treated as made from contributions to the Roth IRA to the extent that such distribution, when added to all previous distributions from the Roth IRA, does not exceed the aggregate amount of contributions to the Roth IRA.

(2) Qualified distribution. For purposes of this subsection—

(A) In general. The term "qualified distribution" means any payment or distribution—

(i) made on or after the date on which the individual attains age 59½,

(ii) made to a beneficiary (or to the estate of the individual) on or after the death of the individual,

(iii) attributable to the individual's being disabled (within the meaning of section 72(m)(7)), or

(iv) which is a qualified first-time homebuyer distribution.

(B) Certain distributions within 5 years. A payment or distribution shall not be treated as a qualified distribution under subparagraph (A) if—

(i) it is made within the 5-taxable year period beginning with the 1st taxable year for which the individual made a contribution to a Roth IRA (or such individual's spouse made a contribution to a Roth IRA) established for such individual, or

(ii) in the case of a payment or distribution properly allocable (as determined in the manner prescribed by the Secretary) to a qualified rollover contribution from an individual retirement plan other than a Roth IRA (or income allocable thereto) , it is made within the 5-taxable year period beginning with the taxable year in which the rollover contribution was made.

(3) Rollovers from an ira other than a Roth IRA.

(A) In general. Notwithstanding section 408(d)(3), in the case of any distribution to which this paragraph applies—

(i) there shall be included in gross income any amount which would be includible were it not part of a qualified rollover contribution,

(ii) section 72(t) shall not apply, and

(iii) in the case of a distribution before January 1, 1999, any amount required to be included in gross income by reason of this paragraph shall be so included ratably over the 4-taxable year period beginning with the taxable year in which the payment or distribution is made.

(B) Distributions to which paragraph applies. This paragraph shall apply to a distribution from an individual retirement plan (other than a Roth IRA) maintained for the benefit of an individual which is contributed to a Roth IRA maintained for the benefit of such individual in a qualified rollover contribution.

(C) Conversions. The conversion of an individual retirement plan (other than a Roth IRA) to a Roth IRA shall be treated for purposes of this paragraph as a distribution to which this paragraph applies.

(D) Conversion of excess contributions. If, no later than the due date for filing the return of tax for any taxable year (without regard to extensions), an individual transfers, from an individual retirement plan (other than a Roth IRA), contributions for such taxable year (and any earnings allocable thereto) to a Roth IRA, no such amount shall be includible in gross income to the extent no deduction was allowed with respect to such amount.

(E) Additional reporting requirements. Trustees of Roth IRAs, trustees of individual retirement plans, or both, whichever is appropriate, shall include such additional information in reports required under section 408(i) as the Secretary may require to ensure that amounts required to be included in gross income under subparagraph (A) are so included.

(4) Coordination with individual retirement accounts. Section 408(d)(2) shall be applied separately with respect to Roth IRAs and other individual retirement plans.

(5) Qualified special purpose distribution. For purposes of this section, the term "qualified special purpose distribution" means any distribution to which subparagraph (F) of section 72(t)(2) applies.

(e) Qualified rollover contribution. For purposes of this section, the term "qualified rollover contribution" means a rollover contribution to a Roth IRA from another such account, or from an individual retirement plan, but only if such rollover contribution meets the requirements of section 408(d)(3). For purposes of section 408(d)(3)(B), there shall be disregarded any qualified rollover contribution from an individual retirement plan (other than a Roth IRA) to a Roth IRA.

[For analysis, see ¶ 301. For text of Committee Report see ¶ 5016].

[Endnote Code Sec. 408A]
  Code Sec. 408A was added by Sec. 302(a) of the Taxpayer Relief Act of 1997, H.R. 2014, 8/5/97.
  1. added Code Sec. 408A
Effective Date (Sec. 302(f), H.R. 2014, 8/5/97) effective for tax. yrs. begin. after 12/31/97.

[¶ 3073]   Code Sec. 409.   Qualifications for tax credit employee stock ownership plans.

* * * * * * * * * * *

(h) Right to demand employer securities; put option.

* * * * * * * * * * *

CAUTION.   Para. (h)(2), following, is effective for tax. yrs. end. before 1/1/98. For para. (h)(2), effective for tax yrs. end. after 12/31/97, see below.

(2) Plan may distribute cash in certain cases. A plan which otherwise meets the requirements of this subsection or of section 4975(e)(7) shall not be considered to have failed to meet the requirements of section 401(a) merely because under the plan the benefits may be distributed in cash or in the form of employer securities. In the case of an employer whose charter or bylaws restrict the ownership of substantially all outstanding employer securities to employees or to a trust described in section 401(a), a plan which otherwise meets the requirements of this subsection or section 4975(e)(7) shall not be considered to have failed to meet the requirements of this subsection or of section 401(a) merely because it does not permit a participant to exercise the right described in paragraph (1)(A) if such plan provides that participants entitled to a distribution from the plan shall have a right to receive such distribution in cash, except that such plan may distribute employer securities subject to a requirement that such securities may be resold to the employer under terms which meet the requirements of paragraph (1)(B).

CAUTION.   Para. (h)(2), following, is effective for tax. yrs. end. after 12/31/97. For para. (h)(2), effective for tax. yrs. end. before 1/1/98, see above.

(2) Plan may distribute cash in certain cases.

¹(A) *In general. A plan which* otherwise meets the requirements of this subsection or of section 4975(e)(7) shall not be considered to have failed to meet the requirements of section 401(a) merely because under the plan the benefits may be distributed in cash or in the form of employer securities. ²

³(B) *Exception for certain plans restricted from distributing securities.*

  (i) *In general. A plan to which this subparagraph applies shall not be treated as failing to meet the requirements of this subsection or section 401(a) merely because it does not permit a participant to exercise the right described in paragraph (1)(A) if such plan provides that the participant entitled to a distribution has a right to receive the distribution in cash, except that such plan may distribute employer securities subject to a requirement that such securities may be resold to the employer under terms which meet the requirements of paragraph (1)(B).*

(ii) Applicable plans. This subparagraph shall apply to a plan which otherwise meets the requirements of this subsection or section 4975(e)(7) and which is established and maintained by—

(I) an employer whose charter or bylaws restrict the ownership of substantially all outstanding employer securities to employees or to a trust described in section 401(a), or

(II) an S corporation.

* * * * * * * * * * * *

[For analysis, see ¶ 910. For text of Committee Report see ¶ 5312].

[Endnote Code Sec. 409]

Matter in *italics* in Code Sec. 409(h)(2) was added by Sec. 1506(a) of the Taxpayer Relief Act of 1997, H.R. 2014, 8/5/97, which struck out:

1. "A plan which"

2. "In the case of an employer whose charter or bylaws restrict the ownership of substantially all outstanding employer securities to employees or to a trust described in section 401(a), a plan which otherwise meets the requirements of this subsection or section 4975(e)(7) shall not be considered to have failed to meet the requirements of this subsection or of section 401(a) merely because it does not permit a participant to exercise the right described in paragraph (1)(A) if such plan provides that participants entitled to a distribution from the plan shall have a right to receive such distribution in cash, except that such plan may distribute employer securities subject to a requirement that such securities may be resold to the employer under terms which meet the requirements of paragraph (1)(B)."

3. added subpara. (h)(2)(B)

Effective Date (Sec. 1506(c), H.R. 2014, 8/5/97) effective for tax. yrs. begin. after 12/31/97.

[¶ 3074] Code Sec. 410. Minimum participation standards.

* * * * * * * * * * * *

(c) Application of participation standards to certain plans.

* * * * * * * * * * * *

[1](2) A plan described in paragraph (1) shall be treated as meeting the requirements of this section for purposes of section 401(a), except that in the case of a plan described in subparagraph (B), (C), or (D) of paragraph (1), this paragraph shall apply only if such plan meets the requirements of section 401(a)(3) (as in effect on September 1, 1974).

* * * * * * * * * * * *

[For analysis, see ¶ 924. For text of Committee Report see ¶ 5311].

[Endnote Code Sec. 410]

Matter in *italics* in Code Sec. 410(c)(2) added by Sec. 1505(a)(3) of the Taxpayer Relief Act of 1997, H.R. 2014, 8/5/97, which struck out::

1. "(2) A plan described in paragraph (1) shall be treated as meeting the requirements of this section, for purposes of section 401(a), if such plan meets the requirements of section 401(a)(3) as in effect on September 1, 1974."

Effective Date (Sec. 1505(d), H.R. 2014, 8/5/97) Sec. 1505(d), H.R. 2014, 8/5/97, reads as follows:

"(d) Effective dates.

"(1) In general. The amendments made by this section shall apply to taxable years beginning on or after 8/5/97.

"(2) Treatment for years beginning before 8/5/97. A governmental plan (within the meaning of section 414(d) of the Internal Revenue Code of 1986) maintained by a State or local government or political subdivision thereof (or agency or instrumentality thereof) shall be treated as satisfying the requirements of sections 401(a)(3), 401(a)(4), 401(a)(26), 401(k), 401(m), 403(b)(1)(D) and (b)(12), and 410 of such Code for all taxable years beginning before the 8/5/97 of this Act."

[¶ 3075] Code Sec. 411. Minimum vesting standards.

(a) General rule. A trust shall not constitute a qualified trust under section 401(a) unless the plan of which such trust is a part provides that an employee's right to his normal retirement benefit is nonforfeitable upon the attainment of normal retirement age (as defined in paragraph (8)) and in addition satisfies the requirements of paragraphs (1), (2), and (11) of this subsection and the requirements of subsection (b)(3), and also satisfies, in the case of a defined benefit plan, the requirements of subsection (b)(1) and, in the case of a defined contribution plan, the requirements of subsection (b)(2).

* * * * * * * * * * *

(7) Accrued benefit.

* * * * * * * * * * *

(B) Effect of certain distributions. Notwithstanding paragraph (4), for purposes of determining the employee's accrued benefit under the plan, the plan may disregard service performed by the employee with respect to which he has received—

(i) a distribution of the present value of his entire nonforfeitable benefit if such distribution was in an amount (not more than [1]*the applicable limit under section 411(a)(11)(D))* permitted under regulations prescribed by the Secretary, or

(ii) a distribution of the present value of his nonforfeitable benefit attributable to such service which he elected to receive.

Clause (i) of this subparagraph shall apply only if such distribution was made on termination of the employee's participation in the plan. Clause (ii) of this subparagraph shall apply only if such distribution was made on termination of the employee's participation in the plan or under such other circumstances as may be provided under regulations prescribed by the Secretary.

* * * * * * * * * * *

(11) Restrictions on certain mandatory distributions.

(A) In general. If the present value of any nonforfeitable accrued benefit exceeds [2]*the applicable limit*, a plan meets the requirements of this paragraph only if such plan provides that such benefit may not be immediately distributed without the consent of the participant.

* * * * * * * * * * *

[For analysis, see ¶ 902. For text of Committee Report see ¶ 5153].

[Endnote Code Sec. 411]

Matter in *italics* in Code Sec. 411(a)(7)(B)(i), Code Sec. 411(a)(11)(A) and Code Sec. 411(a)(11)(D) was added by Sec. 917(a), 917(b) and 917(c)(1) of the Revenue Reconciliation Act of 1997, H.R. 2014, 8/5/97, which struck out:

1. "$3,500"
2. "$3,500"
3. added subpara. (a)(11)(D)

Effective Date (Sec. 917(d), H.R. 2014, 8/5/97) effective for plan yrs. begin. after 8/5/97.

[¶ 3076]   Code Sec. 412.   Minimum funding standards.

* * * * * * * * * * *

(b) Funding standard account.

* * * * * * * * * * *

(2) Charges to account. For a plan year, the funding standard account shall be charged with the sum of—

* * * * * * * * * * *

CAUTION.   Subparas. (b)(2)(C) and (D), following, are effective for plan yrs. begin. before 1/1/99. For subparas. (b)(2)(C)-(E), effective for plan yrs. begin. after 12/31/98, see below.

(C) the amount necessary to amortize each waived funding deficiency (within the meaning of subsection (d)(3)) for each prior plan year in equal annual installments (until fully amortized) over a period of 5 plan years (15 plan years in the case of a multiemployer plan), and

(D) the amount necessary to amortize in equal annual installments (until fully amortized) over a period of 5 plan years any amount credited to the funding standard account under paragraph (3)(D).

CAUTION. Subparas. (b)(2)(C)-(E), following, are effective for plan yrs. begin. after 12/31/98. For subparas. (b)(2)(C) and (D), effective for plan yrs. begin. before 1/1/99, see above.

(C) the amount necessary to amortize each waived funding deficiency (within the meaning of subsection (d)(3)) for each prior plan year in equal annual installments (until fully amortized) over a period of 5 plan years (15 plan years in the case of a multiemployer plan),[1]

(D) the amount necessary to amortize in equal annual installments (until fully amortized) over a period of 5 plan years any amount credited to the funding standard account under paragraph (3)(D)[2], *and*

[3]*(E) the amount necessary to amortize in equal annual installments (until fully amortized) over a period of 20 years the contributions which would be required to be made under the plan but for the provisions of subsection (c)(7)(A)(i)(I).*

For additional requirements in the case of plans other than multiemployer plans, see subsection (l).

* * * * * * * * * * * *

(c) Special rules.

* * * * * * * * * * * *

(7) Full-funding limitation.

(A) In general. For purposes of paragraph (6), the term "full-funding limitation" means the excess (if any) of—

CAUTION. Clause (c)(7)(A)(i), following, is effective for plan yrs. begin. before 1/1/99. For clause (c)(7)(A)(i), effective for plan yrs. begin. after 12/31/98, see below.

(i) the lesser of (I) 150 percent of current liability (including the expected increase in current liability due to benefits accruing during the plan year), or (II) the accrued liability (including normal cost) under the plan (determined under the entry age normal funding method if such accrued liability cannot be directly calculated under the funding method used for the plan), over

CAUTION. Clause (c)(7)(A)(i), following, is effective for plan yrs. begin. after 12/31/98. For clause (c)(7)(A)(i), effective for plan yrs. begin. before 1/1/99, see above.

(i) the lesser of (I) [4]the applicable percentage of current liability (including the expected increase in current liability due to benefits accruing during the plan year), or (II) the accrued liability (including normal cost) under the plan (determined under the entry age normal funding method if such accrued liability cannot be directly calculated under the funding method used for the plan), over

* * * * * * * * * * * *

CAUTION. Subpara. (c)(7)(D), following, is effective for plan yrs. begin. before 1/1/99. For subpara. (c)(7)(D), effective for plan yrs. begin. after 12/31/98, see below.

(D) Regulatory authority. The Secretary may by regulations provide—

(i) for adjustments to the percentage contained in subparagraph (A)(i) to take into account the respective ages or lengths of service of the participants,

(ii) alternative methods based on factors other than current liability for the determination of the amount taken into account under subparagraph (A)(i), and

(iii) for the treatment under this section of contributions which would be required to be made under the plan but for the provisions of subparagraph (A)(i)(I).

CAUTION. Subpara. (c)(7)(D), following, is effective for plan yrs. begin. after 12/31/98. For subpara. (c)(7)(D), effective for plan yrs. begin. before 1/1/99, see above.

(D) Regulatory authority. The Secretary may by regulations provide—

(i) for adjustments to the percentage contained in subparagraph (A)(i) to take into account the respective ages or lengths of service of the participants, [5]*and*

(ii) alternative methods based on factors other than current liability for the determination of the amount taken into account under subparagraph (A)(i)[6].

(iii) [7]Repealed.

* * * * * * * * * * *

CAUTION.   Subpara. (c)(7)(F) is effective for plan yrs. begin. after 12/31/98.

[8]*(F) Applicable percentage. For purposes of subparagraph (A)(i)(I), the applicable percentage shall be determined in accordance with the following table:*

In the case of any plan year beginning in—	The applicable percentage is—
1999 or 2000	155
2001 or 2002	160
2003 or 2004	165
2005 and succeeding years	170.

* * * * * * * * * * *

(m) **Quarterly contributions required.**

* * * * * * * * * * *

(5) **Liquidity requirement.**

* * * * * * * * * * *

(E) Definitions. For purposes of this paragraph:

* * * * * * * * * * *

(ii) Base amount.

* * * * * * * * * * *

(II) Special rule. If the amount determined under [9]*subclause (I)* exceeds an amount equal to 2 times the sum of the adjusted disbursements from the plan for the 36 months ending on the last day of the quarter and an enrolled actuary certifies to the satisfaction of the Secretary that such excess is the result of nonrecurring circumstances, the base amount with respect to such quarter shall be determined without regard to amounts related to those nonrecurring circumstances.

* * * * * * * * * * *

[For analysis, see ¶ 931. For text of Committee Report see ¶ 5343].

[Endnote Code Sec. 412]

Matter in *italics* in Code Sec. 412(b)(2)(C), Code Sec. 412(b)(2)(D), Code Sec. 412(b)(2)(E), Code Sec. 412(c)(7)(A)(i), Code Sec. 412(c)(7)(D)(i), Code Sec. 412(c)(7)(D)(ii) and Code Sec. 412(c)(7)(F) added by Sec. 1521(a)(A) [sic (a)(1)], (a)(B) [sic (a)(2)], (c)(1), and (c)(3)(A) of the Taxpayer Relief Act of 1997, H.R. 2014, 8/5/97, which struck out:

1. "and"

2. ".".

3. added subpara. (b)(2)(E)

4. "150 percent"

5. added matter in clause (c)(7)(D)(i)

6. ", and"

7. "(iii) for the treatment under this section of contributions which would be required to be made under the plan but for the provisions of subparagraph (A)(i)(I)."

8. added subpara. (c)(7)(F)

Effective Date (Sec. 1521(d), H.R. 2014, 8/5/97) Sec. 1521(d), H.R. 2014, 8/5/97, reads as follows:

"(d) Effective dates.

"(1) In general. The amendments made by this section shall apply to plan years beginning after December 31, 1998.

"(2) Special rule for unamortized balances under existing law. The unamortized balance (as of the close of the plan year preceding the plan's first year beginning in 1999) of any amortization base established under section 412(c)(7)(D)(iii) of such Code and section 302(c)(7)(D)(iii) of such Act (as repealed by subsection (c)(3)) for any plan year beginning before 1999 shall be amortized in equal annual installments (until fully amortized) over a period of years equal to the excess of—

"(A) 20 years, over

"(B) the number of years since the amortization base was established."

Matter in *italics* in Code Sec. 412(m)(5)(E)(ii)(II) added by Sec. 1604(b)(2)(A), H.R. 2014, 8/5/97, which struck out:

9. "clause (i)"

Effective Date (Sec. 1604(b)(4), H.R. 2014, 8/5/97) effective for plan yrs. begin. after 12/31/94.

Sec. 1508(a), H.R. 2014, add subsec. (c) to P.L. 103-465, Sec. 769, reproduced below:

"Sec. 769. Special funding rules for certain plans.

"(a) Funding rules not to apply to certain plans. Any changes made by this Act to section 412 of the Internal Revenue Code of 1986 or to part 3 of subtitle B of title I of the Employee Retirement Income Security Act of 1974 shall not apply to—

"(1) a plan which is, on the 8/5/97 of this Act, subject to a restoration payment schedule order issued by the Pension Benefit Guaranty Corporation that meets the requirements of section 1.412(c)(1)-3 of the Treasury Regulations, or

"(2) a plan established by an affected air carrier (as defined under section 4001(a)(14)(C)(ii)(I) of such Act) and assumed by a new plan sponsor pursuant to the terms of a written agreement with the Pension Benefit Guaranty Corporation dated January 5, 1993, and approved by the United States Bankruptcy Court for the District of Delaware on December 30, 1992.

"(b) Change in actuarial method. Any amortization installments for bases established under section 412(b) of the Internal Revenue Code of 1986 and section 302(b) of the Employee Retirement Income Security Act of 1974 for plan years beginning after December 31, 1987, and before January 1, 1993, by reason of nonelective changes under the frozen entry age actuarial cost method shall not be included in the calculation of offsets under section 412(l)(1)(A)(ii) of such Code and section 302(d)(1)(A)(ii) of such Act for the 1st 5 plan years beginning after December 31, 1994.

"(c) Transition rules for certain plans.

"(1) In general. In the case of a plan that—

"(A) was not required to pay a variable rate premium for the plan year beginning in 1996;

"(B) has not, in any plan year beginning after 1995 and before 2009, merged with another plan (other than a plan sponsored by an employer that was in 1996 within the controlled group of the plan sponsor); and

"(C) is sponsored by a company that is engaged primarily in the interurban or interstate passenger bus service, the transition rules described in paragraph (2) shall apply for any plan year beginning after 1996 and before 2010.

"(2) Transition rules. The transition rules described in this paragraph are as follows:

"(A) For purposes of section 412(l)(9)(A) of the Internal Revenue Code of 1986 and section 302(d)(9)(A) of the Employee Retirement Income Security Act of 1974—

"(i) the funded current liability percentage for any plan year beginning after 1996 and before 2005 shall be treated as not less than 90 percent if for such plan year the funded current liability percentage is at least 85 percent, and

"(ii) the funded current liability percentage for any plan year beginning after 2004 and before 2010 shall be treated as not less than 90 percent if for such plan year the funded current liability percentage satisfies the minimum percentage determined according to the following table:

"In the case of a plan year beginning in:	The minimum percentage is:
2005	86 percent
2006	87 percent
2007	88 percent
2008	89 percent
2009 and thereafter	90 percent.

"(B) Sections 412(c)(7)(E)(i)(I) of such Code and 302(c)(7)(E)(i)(I) of such Act shall be applied—

"(i) by substituting '85 percent' for '90 percent' for plan years beginning after 1996 and before 2005, and

"(ii) by substituting the minimum percentage specified in the table contained in subparagraph (A)(ii) for '90 percent' for plan years beginning after 2004 and before 2010.

"(C) In the event the funded current liability percentage of a plan is less than 85 percent for any plan year beginning after 1996 and before 2005, the transition rules under subparagraphs (A) and (B) shall continue to apply to the plan if contributions for such a plan year are made to the plan in an amount equal to the lesser of—

"(i) the amount necessary to result in a funded current liability percentage of 85 percent, or

"(ii) the greater of—

"(I) 2 percent of the plan's current liability as of the beginning of such plan year, or

"(II) the amount necessary to result in a funded current liability percentage of 80 percent as of the end of such plan year. For the plan year beginning in 2005 and for each of the 3 succeeding plan years, the transition rules under subparagraphs (A) and (B) shall continue to apply to the plan for such plan year only if contributions to the plan for such plan year equal at least the expected increase in current liability due to benefits accruing during such plan year."

Effective Date (Sec. 1508(b), H.R. 2014, 8/5/97) effective for plan yrs. begin. after 12/31/96.

[¶ 3077]   Code Sec. 414.   Definitions and special rules.

* * * * * * * * * * *

(e) Church plan.

* * * * * * * * * * *

(5) Special rules for chaplains and self-employed ministers.[1]

[1]*(A) Certain ministers may participate. For purposes of this part—*

(i) In general. A duly ordained, commissioned, or licensed minister of a church is described in paragraph (3)(B) if, in connection with the exercise of their ministry, the minister—

(I) is a self-employed individual (within the meaning of section 401(c)(1)(B), or

(II) is employed by an organization other than an organization which is described in section 501(c)(3) and with respect to which the minister shares common religious bonds.

(ii) Treatment as employer and employee. For purposes of sections 403(b)(1)(A) and 404(a)(10), a minister described in clause (i)(I) shall be treated as employed by the minister's own employer which is an organization described in section 501(c)(3) and exempt from tax under section 501(a).

* * * * * * * * * * *

CAUTION.   Subpara. (e)(5)(C), following, is effective for yrs. begin. before 1/1/98. For subpara. (e)(5)(C), effective for yrs. begin. after 12/31/97, see below.

(C) Effect on non-denominational plans. If a duly ordained, commissioned, or licensed minister of a church in the exercise of his or her ministry participates in a church plan (within the meaning of this section) and in the exercise of such ministry is employed by an employer not eligible to participate in such church plan, then such employer may exclude such minister from being treated as an employee of such employer for purposes of applying sections 401(a)(3), 401(a)(4), and 401(a)(5), as in effect on September 1, 1974, and sections 401(a)(4), 401(a)(5), 401(a)(26), 401(k)(3), 401(m), 403(b)(1)(D) (including section 403(b)(12)), and 410 to any stock bonus, pension, profit-sharing, or annuity plan (including an annuity described in section 403(b) or a retirement income account described in section 403(b)(9)). The Secretary shall prescribe such regulations as may be necessary or appropriate to carry out the purpose of, and prevent the abuse of, this subparagraph.

CAUTION.   Subpara. (e)(5)(C), following, is effective for yrs. begin. after 12/31/97. For subpara. (e)(5)(C), effective for yrs. begin. before 1/1/98, see above.

(C) Effect on non-denominational plans. If a duly ordained, commissioned, or licensed minister of a church in the exercise of his or her ministry participates in a church plan (within the meaning of this section) and in the exercise of such ministry is employed by an employer [2]*not otherwise participating* in such church plan, then such employer may exclude such minister from being treated as an employee of such employer for purposes of applying sections 401(a)(3), 401(a)(4), and 401(a)(5), as in effect on September 1, 1974, and sections 401(a)(4), 401(a)(5), 401(a)(26), 401(k)(3), 401(m), 403(b)(1)(D) (including section 403(b)(12)), and 410 to any stock bonus, pension, profit-sharing, or annuity plan (including an annuity described in section 403(b) or a retirement income account described in section 403(b)(9)). The Secretary shall prescribe such regulations as may be necessary or appropriate to carry out the purpose of, and prevent the abuse of, this subparagraph.

* * * * * * * * * * *

CAUTION.   Subpara. (e)(5)(E), following, is effective for yrs. begin. after 12/31/97.

³*(E) Exclusion. In the case of a contribution to a church plan made on behalf of a minister described in subparagraph (A)(i)(II), such contribution shall not be included in the gross income of the minister to the extent that such contribution would not be so included if the minister was an employee of a church.*

* * * * * * * * * *

(n) Employee leasing.

* * * * * * * * * *

(3) Requirements. For purposes of this subsection, the requirements listed in this paragraph are—

* * * * * * * * * * *

(C) sections 79, 106, 117(d), 120, 125, 127, 129, 132, ⁴*137*, 274(j), 505, and 4980B.

* * * * * * * * * *

(q) Highly compensated employee.

* * * * * * * * * *

⁵*(9)* **Certain employees not considered highly compensated and excluded employees under pre-ERISA rules for church plans.** In the case of a church plan (as defined in subsection (e)), no employee shall be considered an officer, a person whose principal duties consist of supervising the work of other employees, or a highly compensated employee for any year unless such employee is a highly compensated employee under paragraph (1) for such year.

* * * * * * * * * *

(t) Application of controlled group rules to certain employee benefits.

* * * * * * * * * *

(2) Applicable section. For purposes of this subsection, the term "applicable section" means section 79, 106, 117(d), 120, 125, 127, 129, 132, ⁶*137*, 274(j), 505, or 4980B.

* * * * * * * * * *

[For analysis, see ¶s 926, 1901. For text of Committee Report see ¶ 5344].

[Endnote Code Sec. 414]

Matter in *italics* in Code Sec. 414(e)(5)(A) was added by Sec. 1601(d)(6)(A) of the Taxpayer Relief Act of 1997, H.R. 2014, 8/5/97.

1.

"(A) Certain ministers may participate. For purposes of this part—

"(i) In general. An employee of a church or a convention or association of churches shall include a duly ordained, commissioned, or licensed minister of a church who, in connection with the exercise of his or her ministry—

"(I) is a self-employed individual (within the meaning of section 401(c)(1)(B)), or

"(II) is employed by an organization other than an organization described in section 501(c)(3).

"(ii) Treatment of employer and employee.

"(I) Self-employed. A minister described in clause (i)(I) shall be treated as his or her own employer which is an organization described in section 501(c)(3) and which is exempt from tax under section 501(a).

"(ii) Others. A minister described in clause (i)(II) shall be treated as employed by an organization described in section 501(c)(3) and exempt from tax under section 501(a)."

Effective Date (Sec. 1601(j)(1), H.R. 2014, 8/5/97) effective for yrs. begin. after 12/31/96.

Matter in *italics* in Code Sec. 414(e)(5)(C) and Code Sec. 414(e)(5)(E) added by Sec. 1522(a)(1) and (2), H.R. 2014, 8/5/97, which struck out:

2. "not eligible to participate"

3. added subpara. (e)(5)(E)

Effective Date (Sec. 1522(b), H.R. 2014, 8/5/97) effective for yrs. begin. after 12/31/96.

Matter in *italics* in Code Sec. 414(n)(3)(C) added by Sec. 1601(h)(2)(D)(i) of the Taxpayer Relief Act of 1997, H.R. 2014, 8/5/97.

4. added matter in subpara. (n)(3)(C)

Effective Date (Sec. 1601(j)(1), H.R. 2014, 8/5/97) effective for tax. yrs. begin. after 12/31/96.

Matter in *italics* in Code Sec. 414(q)(9) added by Sec. 1601(d)(7), H.R. 2014, 8/5/97, which struck out:

5. "(7)[sic (9)]"
Effective Date (Sec. 1601(j)(1), H.R. 2014, 8/5/97) effective for yrs. begin. after 12/31/96.

Matter in *italics* in Code Sec. 414(t)(2) added by Sec. 1601(h)(2)(D)(ii), H.R. 2014, 8/5/97.
6. added matter in para. (t)(2)
Effective Date (Sec. 1601(j)(1), H.R. 2014, 8/5/97) effective for tax. yrs. begin. after 12/31/96.

[¶ 3078]   Code Sec. 415.   Limitations on benefits and contributions under qualified plans.

* * * * * * * * * * *

(b) Limitation for defined benefit plans.

* * * * * * * * * * *

(2) Annual benefit.

* * * * * * * * * * *

(G) Special limitation for qualified police or firefighters. In the case of a qualified [1]*participant, subparagraph (C) of this paragraph shall not apply.*

* * * * * * * * * * *

(c) Limitation for defined contribution plans.

* * * * * * * * * * *

(6) Special rule for employee stock ownership plans. If no more than one-third of the employer contributions to an employee stock ownership plan (as described in section 4975(e)(7)) for a year which are deductible under paragraph (9) of section 404(a) are allocated to highly compensated employees (within the meaning of section 414(q)), the limitations imposed by this section shall not apply to—

(A) forfeitures of employer securities (within the meaning of section 409) under such an employee stock ownership plan if such securities were acquired with the proceeds of a loan (as described in section 404(a)(9)(A)), or

(B) employer contributions to such an employee stock ownership plan which are deductible under section 404(a)(9)(B) and charged against the participant's account.

[2]*The amount of any qualified gratuitous transfer (as defined in section 664(g)(1)) allocated to a participant for any limitation year shall not exceed the limitations imposed by this section, but such amount shall not be taken into account in determining whether any other amount exceeds the limitations imposed by this section.*

* * * * * * * * * * *

CAUTION.   Subsec. (e), following, is effective for limitation yrs. begin. before 1/1/2000. Subsec. (e) is repealed effective for limitation yrs. begin. after 12/31/99, see below.

(e) Limitation in case of defined benefit plan and defined contribution plan for same employee.

* * * * * * * * * * *

[3]*(6) Special rule for qualified gratuitous transfers. Any qualified gratuitous transfer of qualified employer securities (as defined by section 664(g)) shall not be taken into account in calculating, and shall not be subject to, the limitations provided in this subsection.*

[4]*(7) Special transition rule for defined contribution fraction for years ending after December 31, 1982.*

(A) In general. At the election of the plan administrator, in applying paragraph (3) with respect to any year ending after December 31, 1982, the amount taken into account under paragraph (3)(B) with respect to each participant for all years ending before January 1, 1983, shall be an amount equal to the product of—

(i) the amount determined under paragraph (3)(B) (as in effect for the year ending in 1982) for the year ending in 1982, multiplied by

(ii) the transition fraction.

(B) Transition fraction. The term "transition fraction" means a fraction—

(i) the numerator of which is the lesser of—

(I) $51,875, or

(II) 1.4, multiplied by 25 percent of the compensation of the participant for the year ending in 1981, and

(ii) the denominator of which is the lesser of—

(I) $41,500, or

(II) 25 percent of the compensation of the participant for the year ending in 1981.

(C) Plan must have been in existence on or before July 1, 1982. This paragraph shall apply only to plans which were in existence on or before July 1, 1982.

CAUTION. Subsec. (e), following, is repealed effective for limitation yrs. begin. after 12/31/99. For subsec. (e) effective for limitation yrs. begin. before 1/1/2000, see above.

(e) Repealed.

* * * * * * * * * * *

(k) Special rules.

* * * * * * * * * * *

CAUTION. Para. (k)(3), following, is effective for permissive service credit contributions made in yrs. begin. after 12/31/97.

[5]*(3) Repayments of cashouts under governmental plans. In the case of any repayment of contributions (including interest thereon) to the governmental plan with respect to an amount previously refunded upon a forfeiture of service credit under the plan or under another governmental plan maintained by a State or local government employer within the same State, any such repayment shall not be taken into account for purposes of this section.*

* * * * * * * * * * *

CAUTION. Subsec. (n), following, is effective for permissive service credit contributions made in yrs. begin. after 12/31/97.

[6]*(n) Special rules relating to purchase of permissive service credit.*

(1) In general. If an employee makes 1 or more contributions to a defined benefit governmental plan (within the meaning of section 414(d)) to purchase permissive service credit under such plan, then the requirements of this section shall be treated as met only if—

(A) the requirements of subsection (b) are met, determined by treating the accrued benefit derived from all such contributions as an annual benefit for purposes of subsection (b), or

(B) the requirements of subsection (c) are met, determined by treating all such contributions as annual additions for purposes of subsection (c).

(2) Application of limit. For purposes of—

(A) applying paragraph (1)(A), the plan shall not fail to meet the reduced limit under subsection (b)(2)(C) solely by reason of this subsection, and

(B) applying paragraph (1)(B), the plan shall not fail to meet the percentage limitation under subsection (c)(1)(B) solely by reason of this subsection.

(3) Permissive service credit. For purposes of this subsection—

(A) In general. The term "permissive service credit' means service credit—

(i) recognized by the governmental plan for purposes of calculating a participant's benefit under the plan,

(ii) which such participant has not received under such governmental plan, and

(iii) which such participant may receive only by making a voluntary additional contribution, in an amount determined under such governmental plan, which does not exceed the amount necessary to fund the benefit attributable to such service credit.

(B) Limitation on nonqualified service credit.—A plan shall fail to meet the requirements of this section if—

(i) more than 5 years of permissive service credit attributable to nonqualified service are taken into account for purposes of this subsection, or

(ii) any permissive service credit attributable to nonqualified service is taken into account under this subsection before the employee has at least 5 years of participation under the plan.

(C) Nonqualified service. For purposes of subparagraph (B), the term "nonqualified service" means service for which permissive service credit is allowed other than—

(i) service (including parental, medical, sabbatical, and similar leave) as an employee of the Government of the United States, any State or political subdivision thereof, or any agency or instrumentality of any of the foregoing (other than military service or service for credit which was obtained as a result of a repayment described in subsection (k)(3)),

(ii) service (including parental, medical, sabbatical, and similar leave) as an employee (other than as an employee described in clause (i)) of an educational organization described in section 170(b)(1)(A)(ii) which is a public, private, or sectarian school which provides elementary or secondary education (through grade 12), as determined under State law,

(iii) service as an employee of an association of employees who are described in clause (i), or

(iv) military service (other than qualified military service under section 414(u)) recognized by such governmental plan.

In the case of service described in clauses (i), (ii), or (iii), such service will be nonqualified service if recognition of such service would cause a participant to receive a retirement benefit for the same service under more than one plan.

[For analysis, see ¶s 922, 923, 927. For text of Committee Report see ¶s 5344, 5348, 5349].

[Endnote Code Sec. 415]

Matter in *italics* in Code Sec. 415(b)(2)(G) added by Sec. 1527(a) of the Taxpayer Relief Act of 1997, H.R. 2014, 8/5/97, which struck out:

1. "participant—

"(i) subparagraph (C) shall not reduce the limitation of paragraph (1)(A) to an amount less than $50,000, and

"(ii) the rules of subparagraph (F) shall apply.

The Secretary shall adjust the $50,000 amount in clause (i) at the same time and in the same manner as under section 415(d)."

Effective Date (Sec. 1527(b), H.R. 2014, 8/5/97) effective for yrs. begin. after 12/31/96.

Matter in *italics* in Code Sec. 415(c)(6), Code Sec. 415(e)(6) and Code Sec. 415(e)(7) added by Sec. 1530(c)(3), (c)(4)(A), and (c)(4)(B), H.R. 2014, 8/5/97, which struck out:

2. added matter in para. (c)(6)

3. added para. (e)(6)

4. "(6)"

Effective Date (Sec. 1530(d), H.R. 2014, 8/5/97) effective for transfers made by trusts to, or for the use of, an employee stock ownership plan after 8/5/97.

Code Sec. 415(k)(3) and Code Sec. 415(n), in *italics*, were added by Sec. 1526(a) and (b), H.R. 2014, 8/5/97.

5. added para. (k)(3)

6. added subsec. (n)

Effective Date (Sec. 1526(c), H.R. 2014, 8/5/97) Sec. 1526(c), H.R. 2014, 8/5/97, reads as follows:

"(c) Effective dates.

"(1) In general. The amendments made by this section shall apply to permissive service credit contributions made in years beginning after December 31, 1997.

"(2) Transition rule.

"(A) In general. In the case of an eligible participant in a governmental plan (within the meaning of section 414(d) of the Internal Revenue Code of 1986), the limitations of section 415(c)(1) of such Code shall not be applied to reduce the amount of permissive service credit which may be purchased to an amount less than the amount which was allowed to be purchased under the terms of the plan as in effect on the date of the enactment of this Act.

"(B) Eligible participant. For purposes of subparagraph (A), an eligible participant is an individual who first became a participant in the plan before the first plan year beginning after the last day of the calendar year in which the next regular session (following the date of the enactment of this Act) of the governing body with authority to amend the plan ends."

[¶ 3079] Code Sec. 417.   Definitions and special rules for purposes of minimum survivor annuity requirements.

* * * * * * * * * * * *

(e) Restrictions on cash-outs.

(1) **Plan may require distribution if present value not in excess of** [1]*dollar limit.* A plan may provide that the present value of a qualified joint and survivor annuity or a qualified preretirement survivor annuity will be immediately distributed if such value does not exceed [2]*the dollar limit under section 411(a)(11)(A).* No distribution may be made under the preceding sentence after the annuity starting date unless the participant and the spouse of the participant (or where the participant has died, the surviving spouse) consents in writing to such distribution.

(2) **Plan may distribute benefit in excess of** [3]*dollar limit* **only with consent.** If—

(A) the present value of the qualified joint and survivor annuity or the qualified preretirement survivor annuity exceeds [4]*the applicable limit under section 411(a)(11)(D),* and

(B) the participant and the spouse of the participant (or where the participant has died, the surviving spouse) consent in writing to the distribution,

the plan may immediately distribute the present value of such annuity.

* * * * * * * * * * * *

[For analysis, see ¶ 902. For text of Committee Report see ¶ 5153].

[Endnote Code Sec. 417]

Matter in *italics* in Code Sec. 417(e)(1) and Code Sec. 417(e)(2) added by Secs. 1071(a)(2)(A) and (a)(2)(B) of the Taxpayer Relief Act of 1997, H.R. 2014, 8/5/97, which struck out:

1. "$3,500"
2. "$3,500"
3. "$3,500"
4. "$3,500"

Effective Date (Sec. 1071(c), H.R. 2014, 8/5/97) effective for plan yrs. begin. after 8/5/97.

[¶ 3080]   Code Sec. 447.   Method of accounting for corporations engaged in farming.

* * * * * * * * * * *

(i) Suspense account for family corporations.

* * * * * * * * * * *

[1]*(3)* **Inclusion where corporation ceases to be a family corporation.**

(A) In general. If the corporation ceases to be a family corporation during any taxable year, the amount in the suspense account (after taking into account prior reductions) shall be included in gross income for such taxable year.

(B) Special rule for certain transfers. For purposes of subparagraph (A), any transfer in a corporation after December 15, 1987, shall be treated as a transfer to a person whose ownership could not qualify such corporation as a family corporation unless it is a transfer—

(i) to a member of the family of the transferor, or

(ii) in the case of a corporation described in subsection (h), to a member of a family which on December 15, 1987, held stock in such corporation which qualified the corporation under subsection (h).

[2]*(4)* **Subchapter C transactions.** The application of this subsection with respect to a taxpayer which is a party to any transaction with respect to which there is nonrecognition of gain

or loss to any party by reason of subchapter C shall be determined under regulations prescribed by the Secretary.

[3] **(5) Termination.**

(A) *In general.* No suspense account may be established under this subsection by any corporation required by this section to change its method of accounting for any taxable year ending after June 8, 1997.

(B) *Phaseout of existing suspense accounts.*

(i) *In general.* Each suspense account under this subsection shall be reduced (but not below zero) for each taxable year beginning after June 8, 1997, by an amount equal to the lesser of—

(I) the applicable portion of such account, or

(II) 50 percent of the taxable income of the corporation for the taxable year, or, if the corporation has no taxable income for such year, the amount of any net operating loss (as defined in section 172(c)) for such taxable year.

For purposes of the preceding sentence, the amount of taxable income and net operating loss shall be determined without regard to this paragraph.

(ii) *Coordination with other reductions.* The amount of the applicable portion for any taxable year shall be reduced (but not below zero) by the amount of any reduction required for such taxable year under any other provision of this subsection.

(iv) [sic (iii)] *Inclusion in income.* Any reduction in a suspense account under this paragraph shall be included in gross income for the taxable year of the reduction.

(C) *Applicable portion.* For purposes of subparagraph (B), the term "applicable portion" means, for any taxable year, the amount which would ratably reduce the amount in the account (after taking into account prior reductions) to zero over the period consisting of such taxable year and the remaining taxable years in such first 20 taxable years.

(D) *Amounts after 20th year.* Any amount in the account as of the close of the 20th year referred to in subparagraph (C) shall be treated as the applicable portion for each succeeding year thereafter to the extent not reduced under this paragraph for any prior taxable year after such 20th year.

[*For analysis, see ¶ 2104. For text of Committee Report see ¶ 5158*].

[Endnote Code Sec. 447]

Matter in *italics* in Code Sec. 447(i)(3), Code Sec. 447(i)(4) and Code Sec. 447(i)(5) added by Sec. 1081(a) of the Taxpayer Relief Act of 1997, H.R. 2014, 8/5/97, which struck out:

1. "(3) Reduction in account if farming business contracts. If—

"(A) the gross receipts of the corporation from the trade or business of farming for the year of the change or any subsequent taxable year, is less than

"(B) such gross receipts for the taxpayer's last taxable year beginning before the year of the change (or for the most recent taxable year for which a reduction in the suspense account was made under this paragraph),

the amount in the suspense account (after taking into account prior reductions) shall be reduced by the percentage by which the amount described in subparagraph (A) is less than the amount described in subparagraph (B).

"(4) Income inclusion. Any reduction in the suspense account under paragraph (3) shall be included in gross income for the taxable year of the reduction.

"(5)"

2. "(6)"

3. added para. (i)(5)

Effective Date (Sec. 1081(b), H.R. 2014, 8/5/97) effective for tax. yrs. end. after 6/8/97.

[¶ 3081] Code Sec. 451. General rule for taxable year of inclusion.

* * * * * * * * * * * *

(e) **Special rule for proceeds from livestock sold on account of drought**[1]**, *flood, or other weather-related conditions.***

(1) **In general.** In the case of income derived from the sale or exchange of livestock in excess of the number the taxpayer would sell if he followed his usual business practices, a taxpayer reporting on the cash receipts and disbursements method of accounting may elect to include such income for the taxable year following the taxable year in which such sale or

exchange occurs if he establishes that, under his usual business practices, the sale or exchange would not have occurred in the taxable year in which it occurred if it were not for [2]*drought, flood, or other weather-related conditions, and that such conditions* had resulted in the area being designated as eligible for assistance by the Federal Government.

* * * * * * * * * * *

[For analysis, see ¶ 2101. For text of Committee Report see ¶ 5063].

[Endnote Code Sec. 451]

Matter in *italics* in Code Sec. 451(e) added by Sec. 913(a)(1) and (2) of the Taxpayer Relief Act of 1997, H.R. 2014, 8/5/97, which struck out:

  1. added matter in subsec. (e) heading
  2. "drought conditions, and that these drought conditions"

Effective Date (Sec. 913(c), H.R. 2014, 8/5/97) effective for sales and exchanges after 12/31/96.

[¶ 3082] Code Sec. 457.   Deferred compensation plans of state and local governments and tax-exempt organizations.

* * * * * * * * * * *

(e) Other definitions and special rules. For purposes of this section—

* * * * * * * * * * *

(9) Benefits not treated as made available by reason of certain elections, etc.

(A) Total amount payable is [1]*dollar limit* or less. The total amount payable to a participant under the plan shall not be treated as made available merely because the participant may elect to receive such amount (or the plan may distribute such amount without the participant's consent) if—

(i) such amount does not exceed [2]*the dollar limit under section 411(a)(11)(A),* and

(ii) such amount may be distributed only if—

(I) no amount has been deferred under the plan with respect to such participant during the 2-year period ending on the date of the distribution and

(II) there has been no prior distribution under the plan to such participant to which this subparagraph applied.

A plan shall not be treated as failing to meet the distribution requirements of subsection (d) by reason of a distribution to which this subparagraph applies.

(B) Election to defer commencement of distributions. The total amount payable to a participant under the plan shall not be treated as made available merely because the participant may elect to defer commencement of distributions under the plan if—

(i) such election is made after amounts may be available under the plan in accordance with subsection (d)(1)(A) and before commencement of such distributions, and

(ii) the participant may make only 1 such election.

* * * * * * * * * * *

[For analysis, see ¶ 902. For text of Committee Report see ¶ 5153].

[Endnote Code Sec. 457]

Matter in *italics* in Code Sec. 457(e)(9)(A) heading and Code Sec. 457(e)(9)(A)(i) was added by Sec. 1071(a)(2)(A) and (a)(2)(B) of the Taxpayer Relief Act of 1997, H.R. 2014, 8/5/97, which struck out:

  1. "$3,500"
  2. "$3,500"

Effective Date (Sec. 1071(c), H.R. 2014, 8/5/97) effective for plan yrs. begin. after 8/5/97.

[¶ 3083] Code Sec. 460.   Special rules for long-term contracts.

* * * * * * * * * * *

(b) Percentage of completion method.

* * * * * * * * * * *

(2) Look-back method. The interest computed under the look-back method of this paragraph shall be determined by—

* * * * * * * * * * *

(C) then using [1]*the adjusted overpayment rate (as defined in paragraph (7)),* compounded daily, on the overpayment or underpayment determined under subparagraph (B).

For purposes of the preceding sentence, any amount properly taken into account after completion of the contract shall be taken into account by discounting (using the Federal midterm rate determined under section 1274(d) as of the time such amount was properly taken into account) such amount to its value as of the completion of the contract. The taxpayer may elect with respect to any contract to have the preceding sentence not apply to such contract.

* * * * * * * * * * *

[2]*(6) Election to have look-back method not apply in de minimis cases.*

(A) *Amounts taken into account after completion of contract. Paragraph (1)(B) shall not apply with respect to any taxable year (beginning after the taxable year in which the contract is completed) if—*

    (i) *the cumulative taxable income (or loss) under the contract as of the close of such taxable year, is within*

    (ii) *10 percent of the cumulative look-back taxable income (or loss) under the contract as of the close of the most recent taxable year to which paragraph (1)(B) applied (or would have applied but for subparagraph (B)).*

(B) *De minimis discrepancies. Paragraph (1)(B) shall not apply in any case to which it would otherwise apply if—*

    (i) *the cumulative taxable income (or loss) under the contract as of the close of each prior contract year, is within*

    (ii) *10 percent of the cumulative look-back income (or loss) under the contract as of the close of such prior contract year.*

(C) *Definitions. For purposes of this paragraph—*

    (i) *Contract year. The term "contract year" means any taxable year for which income is taken into account under the contract.*

    (ii) *Look-back income or loss. The look-back income (or loss) is the amount which would be the taxable income (or loss) under the contract if the allocation method set forth in paragraph (2)(A) were used in determining taxable income.*

    (iii) *Discounting not applicable. The amounts taken into account after the completion of the contract shall be determined without regard to any discounting under the 2nd sentence of paragraph (2).*

(D) *Contracts to which paragraph applies. This paragraph shall only apply if the taxpayer makes an election under this subparagraph. Unless revoked with the consent of the Secretary, such an election shall apply to all long-term contracts completed during the taxable year for which election is made or during any subsequent taxable year.*

[3]*(7) Adjusted overpayment rate.*

(A) *In general. The adjusted overpayment rate for any interest accrual period is the overpayment rate in effect under section 6621 for the calendar quarter in which such interest accrual period begins.*

(B) Interest accrual period. For purposes of subparagraph (A), the term "interest accrual period" means the period—

> *(i) beginning on the day after the return due date for any taxable year of the taxpayer, and*

> *(ii) ending on the return due date for the following taxable year.*

For purposes of the preceding sentence, the term "return due date" means the date prescribed for filing the return of the tax imposed by this chapter (determined without regard to extensions).

* * * * * * * * * * * *

[For analysis, see ¶s 2003, 2004. For text of Committee Report see ¶ 5206].

[Endnote Code Sec. 460]

Matter in *italics* in Code Sec. 460(b)(2)(C) was added by Sec. 1211(b)(1) of the Taxpayer Relief Act of 1997, H.R. 2014, 8/5/97, which struck out:

1. "the overpayment rate established by section 6621"

Effective Date (Sec. 1211(c)(2), H.R. 2014, 8/5/97) effective for purposes of section 167(g) of the Internal Revenue Code of 1986 for property placed in service after 9/13/95.

Code Sec. 460(b)(6), in *italics*, was added by Sec. 1211(a), H.R. 2014, 8/5/97.

2. added para. (b)(6)

Effective Date (Sec. 1211(c)(1), H.R. 2014, 8/5/97) effective for contracts completed in tax. yrs. end. after 8/5/97.

Code Sec. 460(b)(7), in *italics*, was added by Sec. 1211(a), H.R. 2014, 8/5/97.

3. added para. (b)(7)

Effective Date (Sec. 1211(c)(2), H.R. 2014, 8/5/97) effective for purposes of section 167(g) of the Internal Revenue Code of 1986 for property placed in service after 9/13/95.

[¶ 3084]   Code Sec. 464.   Limitations on deductions for certain farming.

* * * * * * * * * * * *

(f) Subsections (a) and (b) to apply to certain persons prepaying 50 percent or more of certain farming expenses.

* * * * * * * * * * * *

(3) Qualified farm-related taxpayer.

* * * * * * * * * * * *

(B) Farm-related taxpayer. For purposes of this paragraph, the term "farm-related taxpayer" means any taxpayer—

> *(i) whose principal residence (within the meaning of* ¹*section 121) is on a farm,*

* * * * * * * * * * * *

[Endnote Code Sec. 464]

Matter in *italics* in Code Sec. 464(f)(3)(B)(i) added by Sec. 312(d)(1) of the Taxpayer Relief Act of 1997, H.R. 2014, 8/5/97, which struck out:

1. "section 1034"

Effective Date (Sec. 312(d) [sic (e)], H.R. 2014, 8/5/97) effective for sales and exchanges after 5/6/97, except as provided in Secs. 313(d)(2)-(4) [sic (e)(2)-(4)] of this Act, which read as follows:

"(2) Sales before 8/5/97.—At the election of the taxpayer, the amendments made by this section shall not apply to any sale or exchange before the date of the enactment of this Act.

"(3) Certain sales within 2 years after 8/5/97. Section 121 of the Internal Revenue Code of 1986 (as amended by this section) shall be applied without regard to subsection (c)(2)(B) thereof in the case of any sale or exchange of property during the 2-year period beginning on the date of the enactment of this Act if the taxpayer held such property on the date of the enactment of this Act and fails to meet the ownership and use requirements of subsection (a) thereof with respect to such property.

"(4) Binding contracts.—At the election of the taxpayer, the amendments made by this section shall not apply to a sale or exchange after the date of the enactment of this Act, if—

"(A) such sale or exchange is pursuant to a contract which was binding on such date, or

"(B) without regard to such amendments, gain would not be recognized under section 1034 of the Internal Revenue Code of 1986 (as in effect on the day before the date of the enactment of this Act) on such sale or exchange by reason of a new residence acquired on or before such date or with respect to the acquisition of which by the taxpayer a binding contract was in effect on such date.

This paragraph shall not apply to any sale or exchange by an individual if the treatment provided by section 877(a)(1) of the Internal Revenue Code of 1986 applies to such individual."

[¶ 3085]   Code Sec. 471.   General rule for inventories.

* * * * * * * * * * * * *

[1]*(b) Estimates of inventory shrinkage permitted. A method of determining inventories shall not be treated as failing to clearly reflect income solely because it utilizes estimates of inventory shrinkage that are confirmed by a physical count only after the last day of the taxable year if—*

(1) the taxpayer normally does a physical count of inventories at each location on a regular and consistent basis, and

(2) the taxpayer makes proper adjustments to such inventories and to its estimating methods to the extent such estimates are greater than or less than the actual shrinkage.

[2]*(c) Cross reference.* For rules relating to capitalization of direct and indirect costs of property, see section 263A.

[For analysis, see ¶ 2005. For text of Committee Report see ¶ 5082].

[Endnote Code Sec. 471]

Matter in *italics* in Code Sec. 471(b) and Code Sec. 471(c) was added by Sec. 961(a) of the Taxpayer Relief Act of 1997, H.R. 2014, 8/5/97, which struck out:

1. added subsec. (b)
2. "(b)"

Effective Date (Sec. 961(b), H.R. 2014, 8/5/97) effective for tax. yrs. end. after 8/5/97. Sec. 961(b)(2) provides:

"(2) Coordination with section 481. In the case of any taxpayer permitted by this section to change its method of accounting to a permissible method for any taxable year—

"(A) such changes shall be treated as initiated by the taxpayer,

"(B) such changes shall be treated as made with the consent of the Secretary of the Treasury, and

"(C) the period for taking into account the adjustments under section 481 by reason of such change shall be 4 years."

[¶ 3086]   Code Sec. 475.   Mark to market accounting method for dealers in securities.

* * * * * * * * * * * *

[1]*(e) Election of Mark to Market For Dealers in Commodities.*

(1) In general. In the case of a dealer in commodities who elects the application of this subsection, this section shall apply to commodities held by such dealer in the same manner as this section applies to securities held by a dealer in securities.

(2) Commodity. For purposes of this subsection and subsection (f), the term "commodity" means—

(A) any commodity which is actively traded (within the meaning of section 1092(d)(1));

(B) any notional principal contract with respect to any commodity described in subparagraph (A);

(C) any evidence of an interest in, or a derivative instrument in, any commodity described in subparagraph (A) or (B), including any option, forward contract, futures contract, short position, and any similar instrument in such a commodity; and

(D) any position which—

(i) is not a commodity described in subparagraph (A), (B), or (C),

(ii) is a hedge with respect to such a commodity, and

(iii) is clearly identified in the taxpayer's records as being described in this subparagraph before the close of the day on which it was acquired or entered into (or such other time as the Secretary may by regulations prescribe).

1,017

(3) Election. An election under this subsection may be made without the consent of the Secretary. Such an election, once made, shall apply to the taxable year for which made and all subsequent taxable years unless revoked with the consent of the Secretary.

[2]*(f) Election of Mark to Market For Traders in Securities or Commodities.*

(1) Traders in securities.

    (A) In general. In the case of a person who is engaged in a trade or business as a trader in securities and who elects to have this paragraph apply to such trade or business—

      (i) such person shall recognize gain or loss on any security held in connection with such trade or business at the close of any taxable year as if such security were sold for its fair market value on the last business day of such taxable year, and

      (ii) any gain or loss shall be taken into account for such taxable year.

    Proper adjustment shall be made in the amount of any gain or loss subsequently realized for gain or loss taken into account under the preceding sentence. The Secretary may provide by regulations for the application of this subparagraph at times other than the times provided in this subparagraph.

    (B) Exception. Subparagraph (A) shall not apply to any security—

      (i) which is established to the satisfaction of the Secretary as having no connection to the activities of such person as a trader, and

      (ii) which is clearly identified in such person's records as being described in clause (i) before the close of the day on which it was acquired, originated, or entered into (or such other time as the Secretary may by regulations prescribe).

    If a security ceases to be described in clause (i) at any time after it was identified as such under clause (ii), subparagraph (A) shall apply to any changes in value of the security occurring after the cessation.

    (C) Coordination with section 1259.—Any security to which subparagraph (A) applies and which was acquired in the normal course of the taxpayer's activities as a trader in securities shall not be taken into account in applying section 1259 to any position to which subparagraph (A) does not apply.

    (D) Other rules to apply. Rules similar to the rules of subsections (b)(4) and (d) shall apply to securities held by a person in any trade or business with respect to which an election under this paragraph is in effect.

(2) Traders in commodities. In the case of a person who is engaged in a trade or business as a trader in commodities and who elects to have this paragraph apply to such trade or business, paragraph (1) shall apply to commodities held by such trader in connection with such trade or business in the same manner as paragraph (1) applies to securities held by a trader in securities.

(3) Election. The elections under paragraphs (1) and (2) may be made separately for each trade or business and without the consent of the Secretary. Such an election, once made, shall apply to the taxable year for which made and all subsequent taxable years unless revoked with the consent of the Secretary.

[3]*(g) Regulatory authority.* The Secretary shall prescribe such regulations as may be necessary or appropriate to carry out the purposes of this section, including rules—

    (1) to prevent the use of year-end transfers, related parties, or other arrangements to avoid the provisions of this section, and

    (2) to provide for the application of this section to any security which is a hedge which cannot be identified with a specific security, position, right to income, or liability.

    [For analysis, see ¶ 2001. For text of Committee Report see ¶ 5111].

[Endnote Code Sec. 475]

    Matter in *italics* in Code Sec. 475(e), Code Sec. 475(f), and Code Sec. 475(g) added by Sec. 1001(b) of the Taxpayer Relief Act of 1997, H.R. 2014, 8/5/97, which struck out:

  1. added subsec. (e)

  2. added subsec. (f)

  3. "(e)"

Effective Date (Sec. 1001(d)(1), H.R. 2014, 8/5/97) effective for any constructive sale after 6/8/97, except as provided in Secs. 1001(d)(2)-(4), which read as follows:

"(2) Exception for sales of positions, etc. held before June 9, 1997. If—

"(A) before June 9, 1997, the taxpayer entered into any transaction which is a constructive sale of any appreciated financial position, and

"(B) before the close of the 30-day period beginning on the date of the enactment of this Act, or before such later date as may be specified by the Secretary of the Treasury, such transaction and position are clearly identified in the taxpayer's records as offsetting,

such transaction and position shall not be taken into account in determining whether any other constructive sale after June 8, 1997, has occurred. The preceding sentence shall cease to apply as of the date such transaction is closed or the taxpayer ceases to hold such position.

"(3) Special rule.—In the case of a decedent dying after June 8, 1997, if—

"(A) there was a constructive sale on or before such date of any appreciated financial position,

"(B) the transaction resulting in such constructive sale of such position remains open (with respect to the decedent or any related person)—

"(i) for not less than 2 years after the date of such transaction (whether such period is before or after June 8, 1997), and

"(ii) at any time during the 3-year period ending on the date of the decedent's death, and

"(C) such transaction is not closed within the 30-day period beginning on the date of the enactment of this Act,

then, for purposes of such Code, such position (and the transaction resulting in such constructive sale) shall be treated as property constituting rights to receive an item of income in respect of a decedent under section 691 of such Code. Section 1014(c) of such Code shall not apply to so much of such position's or property's value (as included in the decedent's estate for purposes of chapter 11 of such Code) as exceeds its fair market value as of the date such transaction is closed.

"(4) Election of mark to market by securities traders and traders and dealers in commodities.—

"(A) In general.—The amendments made by subsection (b) shall apply to taxable years ending after the date of the enactment of this Act.

"(B) 4-year spread of adjustments.—In the case of a taxpayer who elects under subsection (e) or (f) of section 475 of the Internal Revenue Code of 1986 (as added by this section) to change its method of accounting for the taxable year which includes the date of the enactment of this Act—

"(i) any identification required under such subsection with respect to securities and commodities held on the date of the enactment of this Act shall be treated as timely made if made on or before the 30th day after such 8/5/97, and

"(ii) the net amount of the adjustments required to be taken into account by the taxpayer under section 481 of such Code shall be taken into account ratably over the 4-taxable year period beginning with such first taxable year."

[¶ 3087] Code Sec. 501.   **Exemption from tax on corporations, certain trusts, etc.**

* * * * * * * * * * *

(c) **List of exempt organizations.** The following organizations are referred to in subsection (a):

* * * * * * * * * *

(26) Any membership organization if—

(A) such organization is established by a State exclusively to provide coverage for medical care (as defined in section 213(d)) on a not-for-profit basis to individuals described in subparagraph (B) through—

(i) insurance issued by the organization, or

(ii) a health maintenance organization under an arrangement with the organization,

(B) the only individuals receiving such coverage through the organization are individuals—

(i) who are residents of such State, and

(ii) who, by reason of the existence or history of a medical condition—

(I) are unable to acquire medical care coverage for such condition through insurance or from a health maintenance organization, or

(II) are able to acquire such coverage only at a rate which is substantially in excess of the rate for such coverage through the membership organization,

(C) the composition of the membership in such organization is specified by such State, and

(D) no part of the net earnings of the organization inures to the benefit of any private shareholder or individual.

CAUTION.   The following sentence is effective for tax. yrs. begin. after 12/31/97.

[1] A spouse and any qualifying child (as defined in section 24(c)) of an individual described in subparagraph (B) (without regard to this sentence) shall be treated as described in subparagraph (B).

CAUTION. Para. (c)(27), following, is effective for tax. yrs. begin. before 1/1/98. For para. (c)(27), effective for tax. yrs. begin. after 12/31/97, see below.

(27) Any membership organization if—

(A) such organization is established before June 1, 1996, by a State exclusively to reimburse its members for losses arising under workmen's compensation acts,

(B) such State requires that the membership of such organization consist of—

(i) all persons who issue insurance covering workmen's compensation losses in such State, and

(ii) all persons and governmental entities who self-insure against such losses, and

(C) such organization operates as a non-profit organization by—

(i) returning surplus income to its members or workmen's compensation policyholders on a periodic basis, and

(ii) reducing initial premiums in anticipation of investment income.

CAUTION. Para. (c)(27), following, is effective for tax. yrs. begin. after 12/31/97. For para. (c)(27), effective for tax. yrs. begin. before 1/1/98, see above.

(27)   [2]*(A) Any membership organization if—*

[3]*(i) such organization is established before June 1, 1996, by a State exclusively to reimburse its members for losses arising under workmen's compensation acts,*

[4]*(ii) such State requires that the membership of such organization consist of—*

[5]*(I) all persons who issue insurance covering workmen's compensation losses in such State, and*

[6]*(II) all persons and governmental entities who self-insure against such losses, and*

[7]*(iii) such organization operates as a non-profit organization by—*

[8]*(I) returning surplus income to its members or workmen's compensation policyholders on a periodic basis, and*

[9]*(II) reducing initial premiums in anticipation of investment income.*

[10]*(B) Any organization (including a mutual insurance company) if—*

(i) such organization is created by State law and is organized and operated under State law exclusively to—

(I) provide workmen's compensation insurance which is required by State law or with respect to which State law provides significant disincentives if such insurance is not purchased by an employer, and

(II) provide related coverage which is incidental to workmen's compensation insurance,

(ii) such organization must provide workmen's compensation insurance to any employer in the State (for employees in the State or temporarily assigned out-of-State) which seeks such insurance and meets other reasonable requirements relating thereto,

(iii) (I) the State makes a financial commitment with respect to such organization either by extending the full faith and credit of the State to debt of such organization or by providing the initial operating capital of such organization and (II) in the case of periods after the date of enactment of this subparagraph, the assets of such organization revert to the State upon dissolution, and

(iv) the majority of the board of directors or oversight body of such organization are appointed by the chief executive officer or other executive branch official of the State, by the State legislature, or by both.

* * * * * * * * * * *

(e) Cooperative hospital service organizations. For purposes of this title, an organization shall be treated as an organization organized and operated exclusively for charitable purposes, if—

(1) such organization is organized and operated solely—

(A) to perform, on a centralized basis, one or more of the following services which, if performed on its own behalf by a hospital which is an organization described in subsection (c)(3) and exempt from taxation under subsection (a), would constitute activities in exercising or performing the purpose or function constituting the basis for its exemption: data processing, purchasing (including the purchasing of insurance on a group basis), warehousing, billing and collection [11]*(including the purchase of patron accounts receivable on a recourse basis)*, food, clinical, industrial engineering, laboratory, printing, communications, record center, and personnel (including selection, testing, training, and education of personnel) services; and

* * * * * * * * * * * *

[12]_B*(o) Treatment of hospitals participating in provider-sponsored organizations. Asn organization shall not fail to be treated as organized and operated exclusively for a charitable purpose for purposes of subsection (c)(3) solely because a hospital which is owned and operated by such organization participates in a provider-sponsored organization (as defined in section 1853(e) of the Social Security Act), whether or not the provider-sponsored organization is exempt from tax. For purposes of subsection (c)(3), any person with a material financial interest in such a provider-sponsored organization shall be treated as a private shareholder or individual with respect to the hospital.*

[13]_B*(p)* **Cross reference.** For nonexemption of Communist-controlled organizations, see section 11(b) of the Internal Security Act of 1950 (64 Stat 997; 50 U.S.C. 790(b)).

[For analysis, see ¶s 1303, 1304, 1305, 1306. For text of Committee Report see ¶s 5001, 5084, 5097, 5502].

[Endnote Code Sec. 501]

Matter in *italics* in Code Sec. 501(c)(26) was added by Sec. 101(c) of the Taxpayer Relief Act of 1997, H.R. 2014, 8/5/97.

1. added matter in para. (c)(26)

Effective Date (Sec. 101(e), H.R. 2014, 8/5/97) effective for tax. yrs. begin. after 12/31/97.

Matter in *italics* in Code Sec. 501(c)(27)(A), Code Sec. 501(c)(27)(A)(i), Code Sec. 501(c)(27)(A)(ii), Code Sec. 501(c)(27)(A)(ii)(I), Code Sec. 501(c)(27)(A)(ii)(II), Code Sec. 501(c)(27)(A)(iii), Code Sec. 501(c)(27)(A)(iii)(I), Code Sec. 501(c)(27)(A)(iii)(II) and Code Sec. 501(c)(27)(B) added by Sec. 963(a) and (b), H.R. 2014, 8/5/97, which struck out:

2. added matter in subpara. (c)(27)(A)
3. "(A)"
4. "(B)"
5. "(i)"
6. "(ii)"
7. "(C)"
8. "(i)"
9. "(ii)"
10. added subpara. (c)(27)(B)

Effective Date (Sec. 963(c), H.R. 2014, 8/5/97) effective for tax. yrs. begin. after 12/31/97.

Matter in *italics* in Code Sec. 501(e)(1)(A) was added by Sec. 974(a), H.R. 2014, 8/5/97.

11. added matter in subpara. (e)(1)(A)

Effective Date (Sec. 974(b), H.R. 2014, 8/5/97) effective for tax. yrs. begin. after 12/31/96.

H.R. 2015. Matter in *italics* in Code Sec. 501(o) and Code Sec. 501(p) added by Sec. 4041(a) of the Balanced Budget Act of 1997, H.R. 2015, 8/5/97, which struck out:

12_B. added subsec. (o) [H.R. 2015]
13_B. "(o)" [H.R. 2015]

Effective Date (Sec. 4041(b), H.R. 2015, 8/5/97) effective 8/5/97.

[¶ 3088]   Code Sec. 512.   Unrelated business taxable income.

(a) **Definition.** For purposes of this title—

* * * * * * * * * * * *

(3) Special rules applicable to organizations described in paragraph (7), (9), (17), or (20) of section 501(c).

* * * * * * * * * * *

(D) Nonrecognition of gain. If property used directly in the performance of the exempt function of an organization described in paragraph (7), (9), (17), or (20) of section 501(c) is sold by such organization, and within a period beginning 1 year before the date of such sale, and ending 3 years after such date, other property is purchased and used by such organization directly in the performance of its exempt function, gain (if any) from such sale shall be recognized only to the extent that such organization's sales price of the old property exceeds the organization's cost of purchasing the other property. For purposes of this subparagraph, the destruction in whole or in part, theft, seizure, requisition, or condemnation of property, shall be treated as the sale of such property, and rules similar to the rules provided by subsections (b), (c), (e), and (j) of section 1034 [1]*(as in effect on the day before the date of the enactment of the Taxpayer Relief Act of 1997)* shall apply.

* * * * * * * * * * *

(b) Modifications. The modifications referred to in subsection (a) are the following:

* * * * * * * * * * *

[2]*(13) Special rules for certain amounts received from controlled entities.*

(A) In general. If an organization (in this paragraph referred to as the "controlling organization") receives (directly or indirectly) a specified payment from another entity which it controls (in this paragraph referred to as the "controlled entity"), notwithstanding paragraphs (1), (2), and (3), the controlling organization shall include such payment as an item of gross income derived from an unrelated trade or business to the extent such payment reduces the net unrelated income of the controlled entity (or increases any net unrelated loss of the controlled entity). There shall be allowed all deductions of the controlling organization directly connected with amounts treated as derived from an unrelated trade or business under the preceding sentence.

(B) Net unrelated income or loss. For purposes of this paragraph—

(i) Net unrelated income. The term "net unrelated income" means—

(I) in the case of a controlled entity which is not exempt from tax under section 501(a), the portion of such entity's taxable income which would be unrelated business taxable income if such entity were exempt from tax under section 501(a) and had the same exempt purposes (as defined in section 513A(a)(5)(A)) as the controlling organization, or

(II) in the case of a controlled entity which is exempt from tax under section 501(a), the amount of the unrelated business taxable income of the controlled entity.

(ii) Net unrelated loss. the term "net unrelated loss" means the net operating loss adjusted under rules similar to the rules of clause (i).

(C) Specified payment. For purposes of this paragraph, the term "specified payment" means any interest, annuity, royalty, or rent.

(D) Definition of control. For purposes of this paragraph—

(i) Control. The term "control" means—

(I) in the case of a corporation, ownership (by vote or value) of more than 50 percent of the stock in such corporation,

(II) in the case of a partnership, ownership of more than 50 percent of the profits interests or capital interests in such partnership, or

(III) in any other case, ownership of more than 50 percent of the beneficial interests in the entity.

(ii) Constructive ownership. Section 318 (relating to constructive ownership of stock) shall apply for purposes of determining ownership of stock in a corporation. Similar principles shall apply for purposes of determining ownership of interests in any other entity.

(E) *Related persons.* The Secretary shall prescribe such rules as may be necessary or appropriate to prevent avoidance of the purposes of this paragraph through the use of related persons.

* * * * * * * * * * * *

CAUTION.   Subsec. (e), following, is effective for tax. yrs. begin. after 12/31/97.

(e) Special rules applicable to S corporations.

(1) In general. If an organization described in section [3]*1361(c)(6)* holds stock in an S corporation—

(A) such interest shall be treated as an interest in an unrelated trade or business; and

(B) notwithstanding any other provision of this part—

(i) all items of income, loss, or deduction taken into account under section 1366(a), and

(ii) any gain or loss on the disposition of the stock in the S corporation

shall be taken into account in computing the unrelated business taxable income of such organization.

(2) Basis reduction. Except as provided in regulations, for purposes of paragraph (1), the basis of any stock acquired by purchase ([4]*as defined in section 1361(e)(1)(C)*) shall be reduced by the amount of any dividends received by the organization with respect to the stock.

CAUTION.   Para. (e)(3), following, is effective for tax. yrs. begin. after 12/31/97.

* * * * * * * * * *

[5]**(3) Exception for ESOPs.** This subsection shall not apply to employer securities (within the meaning of section 409(l)) held by an employee stock ownership plan described in section 4975(e)(7).

[For analysis, see ¶s 912, 1302. For text of Committee Report see ¶s 5141, 5345].

[Endnote Code Sec. 512]

Matter in *italics* in Code Sec. 512(a)(3)(D) added by Sec. 312(d)(5) of the Taxpayer Relief Act of 1997, H.R. 2014, 8/5/97.

1. added matter in subpara. (a)(3)(D)

Effective Date (Sec. 312(d) [sic (e)], H.R. 2014, 8/5/97) effective for sales and exchanges after 5/6/97, except as provided in Secs. 312(d)(2)-(4) [sic (e)(2)-(4)] of this Act, which read as follows:

"(2) Sales before 8/5/97. At the election of the taxpayer, the amendments made by this section shall not apply to any sale or exchange before the date of the enactment of this Act.

"(3) Certain sales within 2 years after 8/5/97. Section 121 of the Internal Revenue Code of 1986 (as amended by this section) shall be applied without regard to subsection (c)(2)(B) thereof in the case of any sale or exchange of property during the 2-year period beginning on the date of the enactment of this Act if the taxpayer held such property on the date of the enactment of this Act and fails to meet the ownership and use requirements of subsection (a) thereof with respect to such property.

"(4) Binding contracts. At the election of the taxpayer, the amendments made by this section shall not apply to a sale or exchange after the date of the enactment of this Act, if—

"(A) such sale or exchange is pursuant to a contract which was binding on such date, or

"(B) without regard to such amendments, gain would not be recognized under section 1034 of the Internal Revenue Code of 1986 (as in effect on the day before the date of the enactment of this Act) on such sale or exchange by reason of a new residence acquired on or before such date or with respect to the acquisition of which by the taxpayer a binding contract was in effect on such date.

This paragraph shall not apply to any sale or exchange by an individual if the treatment provided by section 877(a)(1) of the Internal Revenue Code of 1986 applies to such individual."

Matter in *italics* in Code Sec. 512(b)(13) added by Sec. 1041(a), H.R. 2014, 8/5/97, which struck out:

2. "(13) Notwithstanding paragraphs (1), (2), or (3), amounts of interest, annuities, royalties, and rents derived from any organization (in this paragraph called the 'controlled organization') of which the organization deriving such amounts (in this paragraph called the 'controlling organization') has control (as defined in section 368(c)) shall be included as an item of gross income (whether or not the activity from which such amounts are derived represents a trade or business or is regularly carried on) in an amount which bears the same ratio as—

"(A)(i) in the case of a controlled organization which is not exempt from taxation under section 501(a), the excess of the amount of taxable income of the controlled organization over the amount of such organization's taxable income which if derived directly by the controlling organization would not be unrelated business taxable income, or "(ii) in the case of a controlled organization which is exempt from taxation under section 501(a), the amount of unrelated business taxable income of the controlled organization, bears to

"(B) the taxable income of the controlled organization (determined in the case of a controlled organization to which subparagraph (A)(ii) applies as if it were not an organization exempt from taxation under section 501(a)), but not less than the amount determined in clause (i) or (ii), as the case may be, of subparagraph (A),

both amounts computed without regard to amounts paid directly or indirectly to the controlling organization. There shall be allowed all deductions directly connected with amounts included in gross income under the preceding sentence."

Effective Date (Sec. 1041(b), H.R. 2014, 8/5/97) provides:

"(b) Effective date.

"(1) In general. Except as provided in paragraph (2), the amendments made by this section shall apply to taxable years beginning after the date of the enactment of this Act.

"(2) Binding contracts. The amendments made by this section shall not apply to any payment made during the first 2 taxable years beginning on or after the date of the enactment of this Act if such payment is made pursuant to a written binding contract in effect on June 8, 1997, and at all times thereafter before such payment."

Matter in *italics* in Code Sec. 512(e)(1) and Code Sec. 512(e)(1) added by Sec. 1601(c)(4)(A) and (D), H.R. 2014, 8/5/97, which struck out:

3. "section 1361(c)(7)"

4. "within the meaning of section 1012"

Effective Date (Sec. 1601(j)(1), H.R. 2014, 8/5/97) effective for tax. yrs. begin. after 12/31/97.

Code Sec. 512(e)(3) was added by Sec. 1523(a), H.R. 2014, 8/5/97.

5. added para. (e)(3)

Effective Date (Sec. 1523(b), H.R. 2014, 8/5/97) effective for tax. yrs. begin. after 12/31/97.

[¶ 3089]   Code Sec. 513.   Unrelated trade or business.

* * * * * * * * * * * *

CAUTION.   Subsec. (i), following, is effective for payments solicited or received after 12/31/97.

[1]*(i) Treatment of certain sponsorship payments.*

(1) In general. The term "unrelated trade or business" does not include the activity of soliciting and receiving qualified sponsorship payments.

(2) Qualified sponsorship payments. For purposes of this subsection—

(A) In general. The term "qualified sponsorship payment" means any payment made by any person engaged in a trade or business with respect to which there is no arrangement or expectation that such person will receive any substantial return benefit other than the use or acknowledgement of the name or logo (or product lines) of such person's trade or business in connection with the activities of the organization that receives such payment. Such a use or acknowledgement does not include advertising such person's products or services (including messages containing qualitative or comparative language, price information, or other indications of savings or value, an endorsement, or an inducement to purchase, sell, or use such products or services).

(B) Limitations.

(i) Contingent payments. The term "qualified sponsorship payment" does not include any payment if the amount of such payment is contingent upon the level of attendance at one or more events, broadcast ratings, or other factors indicating the degree of public exposure to one or more events.

(ii) Safe harbor does not apply to periodicals and qualified convention and trade show activities. The term "qualified sponsorship payment" does not include—

(I) any payment which entitles the payor to the use or acknowledgement of the name or logo (or product lines) of the payor's trade or business in regularly scheduled and printed material published by or on behalf of the payee organization that is not related to and primarily distributed in connection with a specific event conducted by the payee organization, or

(II) any payment made in connection with any qualified convention or trade show activities (as defined in subsection (d)(3)(B)).

(3) Allocation of portions of single payment. For purposes of this subsection, to the extent that a portion of a payment would (if made as a separate payment) be a qualified sponsorship payment, such portion of such payment and the other portion of such payment shall be treated as separate payments.

[For analysis, see ¶ 1301. For text of Committee Report see ¶ 5086].

[Endnote Code Sec. 513]
Code Sec. 513(i), in *italics*, was added by Sec. 965(a) of the Taxpayer Relief Act of 1997, H.R. 2014, 8/5/97.
1. added subsec. (i)
Effective Date (Sec. 965(b), H.R. 2014, 8/5/97) effective for payments solicited or received after 12/31/97.

[¶ 3090]   Code Sec. 528.   Certain homeowners associations.

* * * * * * * * * * * *

(b) Tax imposed. A tax is hereby imposed for each taxable year on the homeowners association taxable income of every homeowners association. Such tax shall be equal to 30 percent of the homeowners association taxable income [1]*(32 percent of such income in the case of a timeshare association).*

(c) Homeowners association defined. For purposes of this section —

(1) Homeowners association. The term "homeowners association" means an organization which is a condominium management association[2], *a residential real estate management association, or a timeshare association* if —

(A) such organization is organized and operated to provide for the acquisition, construction, management, maintenance, and care of association property,

(B) 60 percent or more of the gross income of such organization for the taxable year consists solely of amounts received as membership dues, fees, or assessments from —

(i) owners of residential units in the case of a condominium management association,[3]

(ii) owners of residences or residential lots in the case of a residential real estate management association[4], *or*

[5]*(iii) owners of timeshare rights to use, or timeshare ownership interests in, association property in the case of a timeshare association,*

(C) 90 percent or more of the expenditures of the organization for the taxable year are expenditures for the acquisition, construction, management, maintenance, and care of association property [6]*and, in the case of a timeshare association, for activities provided to or on behalf of members of the association,*

(D) no part of the net earnings of such organization inures (other than by acquiring, constructing, or providing management, maintenance, and care of association property, and other than by a rebate of excess membership dues, fees, or assessments) to the benefit of any private shareholder or individual, and

(E) such organization elects (at such time and in such manner as the Secretary by regulations prescribes) to have this section apply for the taxable year.

* * * * * * * * * * * *

[7]*(4) Timeshare association. The term "timeshare association" means any organization (other than a condominium management association) meeting the requirement of subparagraph (A) of paragraph (1) if any member thereof holds a timeshare right to use, or a timeshare ownership interest in, real property constituting association property.*

[8]*(5) Association property.* The term "association property" means —

(A) property held by the organization,

(B) property commonly held by the members of the organization,

(C) property within the organization privately held by the members of the organization, and

(D) property owned by a governmental unit and used for the benefit of residents of such unit. [9]

In the case of a timeshare association, such term includes property in which the timeshare association, or members of the association, have rights arising out of recorded easements, covenants, or other recorded instruments to use property related to the timeshare project.

(d) Homeowners association taxable income defined.

* * * * * * * * * * *

(3) Exempt function income. For purposes of this subsection, the term "exempt function income" means any amount received as membership dues, fees, or assessments from—

(A) owners of condominium housing units in the case of a condominium management association, [10]

(B) owners of real property in the case of a residential real estate management association[11], *or*

[12]*(C) owners of timeshare rights to use, or timeshare ownership interests in, real property in the case of a timeshare association.*

[For analysis, see ¶ 2706. For text of Committee Report see ¶ 5089].

[Endnote Code Sec. 528]

Matter in *italics* in Code Sec. 528(b), Code Sec. 528(c)(1) introductory text, Code Sec. 528(c)(1)(B)(i), Code Sec. 528(c)(1)(B)(ii), Code Sec. 528(c)(1)(B)(iii), Code Sec. 528(c)(1)(C), Code Sec. 528(c)(4), Code Sec. 528(c)(5), Code Sec. 528(d)(3)(A), Code Sec. 528(d)(3)(B) and Code Sec. 528(d)(3)(C) added by Sec. 966(a)(1)(A), (a)(1)(B), (a)(1)(C), (a)(2), (b), (c) and (d) of the Taxpayer Relief Act of 1997, H.R. 2014, 8/5/97, which struck out:

1. added matter in subsec. (b)
2. "or a residential real estate management association"
3. "or"
4. "."
5. added clause (c)(1)(B)(iii)
6. added matter in subpara. (c)(1)(C)
7. added para. (c)(4)
8. "(4)"
9. added matter in para. (c)(5)
10. "or"
11. "."
12. added subpara. (d)(3)(C)

Effective Date (Sec. 966(e), H.R. 2014, 8/5/97) effective for tax. yrs. begin. after 12/31/96.

[¶ 3091] Code Sec. 529. Qualified State tuition programs.

* * * * * * * * * * *

(b) Qualified State tuition program. For purposes of this section—

* * * * * * * * * * *

CAUTION. Para. (b)(5), following, is effective before 1/1/98. For para. (b)(5), effective after 12/31/97, see below.

(5) No investment direction. A program shall not be treated as a qualified State tuition program unless it provides that any contributor to, or designated beneficiary under, such program may not direct the investment of any contributions to the program (or any earnings thereon).

CAUTION. Para. (b)(5), following, is effective after 12/31/97. For para. (b)(5), effective before 1/1/98, see above.

(5) No investment direction. A program shall not be treated as a qualified State tuition program unless it provides that any contributor to, or designated beneficiary under, such program may not [1]*directly or indirectly* direct the investment of any contributions to the program (or any earnings thereon).

* * * * * * * * * * *

(c) Tax treatment of designated beneficiaries and contributors.

* * * * * * * * * * *

[2](2) *Gift tax treatment of contributions.* For purposes of chapters 12 and 13—

(A) *In general.* Any contribution to a qualified tuition program on behalf of any designated beneficiary—

(i) shall be treated as a completed gift to such beneficiary which is not a future interest in property, and

(ii) shall not be treated as a qualified transfer under section 2503(e).

(B) *Treatment of excess contributions.* If the aggregate amount of contributions described in subparagraph (A) during the calendar year by a donor exceeds the limitation for such year under section 2503(b), such aggregate amount shall, at the election of the donor, be taken into account for purposes of such section ratably over the 5-year period beginning with such calendar year.

(3) Distributions.

CAUTION.   Subpara. (c)(3)(A), following, is effective before 1/1/98. For subpara. (c)(3)(A), effective after 12/31/97, see below.

(A) *In general.* Any distribution under a qualified State tuition program shall be includible in the gross income of the distributee in the manner as provided under section 72 to the extent not excluded from gross income under any other provision of this chapter.

CAUTION.   Subpara. (c)(3)(A), following, is effective after 12/31/97. For subpara. (c)(3)(A), effective before 1/1/98, see above.

(A) *In general.* Any distribution under a qualified State tuition program shall be includible in the gross income of the distributee in the manner as provided under [3]*section 72(b)* to the extent not excluded from gross income under any other provision of this chapter.

* * * * * * * * * * *

[4](4) *Estate tax treatment.*

(A) *In general.* No amount shall be includible in the gross estate of any individual for purposes of chapter 11 by reason of an interest in a qualified tuition program.

(B) *Amounts includible in estate of designated beneficiary in certain cases.* Subparagraph (A) shall not apply to amounts distributed on account of the death of a beneficiary.

(C) *Amounts includible in estate of donor making excess contributions.* In the case of a donor who makes the election described in paragraph (2)(B) and who dies before the close of the 5-year period referred to in such paragraph, notwithstanding subparagraph (A), the gross estate of the donor shall include the portion of such contributions properly allocable to periods after the date of death of the donor.

[5](5) *Other gift tax rules.* For purposes of chapters 12 and 13—

(A) *Treatment of distributions.* Except as provided in subparagraph (B), in no event shall a distribution from a qualified tuition program be treated as a taxable gift.

(B) *Treatment of designation of new beneficiary.* The taxes imposed by chapters 12 and 13 shall apply to a transfer by reason of a change in the designated beneficiary under the program (or a rollover to the account of a new beneficiary) only if the new beneficiary is a generation below the generation of the old beneficiary (determined in accordance with section 2651).

CAUTION.   Subsec. (d), following, is effective before 1/1/98. For subsec. (d), effective after 12/31/97, see below.

(d) Reporting requirements.

(1) In general. If there is a distribution to any individual with respect to an interest in a qualified State tuition program during any calendar year, each officer or employee having control of the qualified State tuition program or their designee shall make such reports as the Secretary may require regarding such distribution to the Secretary and to the designated beneficiary or the individual to whom the distribution was made. Any such report shall include such information as the Secretary may prescribe.

(2) Timing of reports. Any report required by this subsection—

(A) shall be filed at such time and in such matter as the Secretary prescribes, and

(B) shall be furnished to individuals not later than January 31 of the calendar year following the calendar year to which such report relates.

CAUTION. Subsec. (d), following, is effective after 12/31/97. For subsec. (d), effective before 1/1/98, see above.

[6]*(d) Reports. Each officer or employee having control of the qualified State tuition program or their designee shall make such reports regarding such program to the Secretary and to designated beneficiaries with respect to contributions, distributions, and such other matters as the Secretary may require. The reports required by this subsection shall be filed at such time and in such manner and furnished to such individuals at such time and in such manner as may be required by the Secretary.*

(e) Other definitions and special rules. For purposes of this section—

(1) Designated beneficiary. The term "designated beneficiary" means—

* * * * * * * * * * * *

(B) in the case of a change in beneficiaries described in [7]*subsection (c)(3)(C)*, the individual who is the new beneficiary, and

(C) in the case of an interest in a qualified State tuition program purchased by a State or local government [8]*(or agency or instrumentality thereof)* or an organization described in section 501(c)(3) and exempt from taxation under section 501(a) as part of a scholarship program operated by such government or organization, the individual receiving such interest as a scholarship.

CAUTION. Para. (e)(2), following, is effective before 1/1/98. For para. (e)(2), effective after 12/31/97, see below.

(2) Member of family. The term "member of the family" has the same meaning given such term as section 2032A(e)(2).

CAUTION. Para. (e)(2), following, is effective after 12/31/97. For para. (e)(2), effective before 1/1/98, see above.

[9]*(2) Member of family. The term "member of the family" means—*

(A) an individual who bears a relationship to another individual which is a relationship described in paragraphs (1) through (8) of section 152(a), and

(B) the spouse of any individual described in subparagraph (A).

[10]*(3) Qualified higher education expenses.*

(A) In general. The term "qualified higher education expenses" means tuition, fees, books, supplies, and equipment required for the enrollment or attendance of a designated beneficiary at an eligible educational institution.

(B) Room and board included for students under guaranteed plans who are at least half-time.

(i) In general. In the case of an individual who is an eligible student (as defined in section 25A(b)(3)) for any academic period, such term shall also include reasonable costs for such period (as determined under the qualified State tuition program) incurred by the designated beneficiary for room and board while attending such institution. For purposes of subsection (b)(7), a designated beneficiary shall be treated as meeting the requirements of this clause.

(ii) Limitation. The amount treated as qualified higher education expenses by reason of the preceding sentence shall not exceed the minimum amount (applicable to the student) included for room and board for such period in the cost of attendance (as defined in section 472 of the Higher Education Act of 1965, 20 U.S.C. 1087ll, as in effect on the date of the enactment of this paragraph) for the eligible education institution for such period.

* * * * * * * * * * * *

CAUTION. Para. (e)(5) is effective for distributions after 12/31/97, with respect to expenses paid after such date (in tax. yrs. end. after such date), for education furnished in academic periods begin. after such date.

[11]*(5) Eligible educational institution. The term "eligible educational institution" means an institution—*

    (A) which is described in section 481 of the Higher Education Act of 1965 (20 U.S.C. 1088), as in effect on the date of the enactment of this paragraph, and

    (B) which is eligible to participate in a program under title IV of such Act.

    [For analysis, see ¶s 405, 406, 407. For text of Committee Report see ¶s 5005, 5367].

[Endnote Code Sec. 529]

Matter in *italics* in Code Sec. 529(b)(5) added by Sec. 211(b)(4) of the Taxpayer Relief Act of 1997, H.R. 2014, 8/5/97. 1. added matter in para. (b)(5)

Effective Date (Sec. 211(f)(1), H.R. 2014, 8/5/97) effective 1/1/98. Sec. 211(f)(6), H.R. 2014, 8/5/97, reads as follows:

"(6) Transition rule for pre-August 20, 1996 contracts. In the case of any contract issued prior to August 20, 1996, section 529(c)(3)(C) of the Internal Revenue code of 1986 shall be applied for taxable years ending after August 20, 1996, without regard to the requirement that a distribution be transferred to a member of the family or the requirement that a change in beneficiaries may be made only to a member of the family."

Matter in *italics* in Code Sec. 529(c)(2) added by Sec. 211(b)(3)(A)(i), H.R. 2014, 8/5/97, which struck out:

2. "(2) Contributions. In no event shall a contribution to a qualified State tuition program on behalf of a designated beneficiary be treated as a taxable gift for purposes of chapter 12."

Effective Date (Sec. 211(f)(5)(A), H.R. 2014, 8/5/97) effective for transfers (including designations of new beneficiaries) made after 8/5/97. For Sec. 211(f)(6), H.R. 2014, 8/5/97, see above.

Matter in *italics* in Code Sec. 529(c)(3)(A) added by Sec. 211(d), H.R. 2014, 8/5/97, which struck out:

3. "section 72"

Effective Date (Sec. 211(f)(1), H.R. 2014, 8/5/97) effective 1/1/98. For Sec. 211(f)(6), H.R. 2014, 8/5/97, see above.

Matter in *italics* in Code Sec. 529(c)(4) added by Sec. 211(b)(3)(B), H.R. 2014, 8/5/97, which struck out:

4. "(4) Estate tax inclusion. The value of any interest in any qualified State tuition program which is attributable to contributions made by an individual to such program on behalf of any designated beneficiary shall be includible in the gross estate of the contributor for purposes of chapter 11."

Effective Date (Sec. 211(f)(5)(B), H.R. 2014, 8/5/97) effective for estates of decedents dying after 6/8/97. For Sec. 211(f)(6), H.R. 2014, 8/5/97, see above.

Matter in *italics* in Code Sec. 529(c)(5) added by Sec. 211(b)(3)(A)(ii), H.R. 2014, 8/5/97, which struck out:

5. "(5) Special rule for applying section 2503(e). For purposes of section 2503(e), the waiver (or payment to an educational institution) of qualified higher education expenses of a designated beneficiary under a qualified State tuition program shall be treated as a qualified transfer."

Effective Date (Sec. 211(f)(5)(A), H.R. 2014, 8/5/97) effective for transfers (including designations of new beneficiaries) made after 8/5/97. For Sec. 211(f)(6), H.R. 2014, 8/5/97, see above.

Matter in *italics* in Code Sec. 529(d) added by Sec. 211(e)(2)(A), H.R. 2014, 8/5/97, which struck out:

6. "(d) Reporting requirements.

"(1) In general. If there is a distribution to any individual with respect to an interest in a qualified State tuition program during any calendar year, each officer or employee having control of the qualified State tuition program or their designee shall make such reports as the Secretary may require regarding such distribution to the Secretary and to the designated beneficiary or the individual to whom the distribution was made. Any such report shall include such information as the Secretary may prescribe.

"(2) Timing of reports. Any report required by this subsection—

"(A) shall be filed at such time and in such matter as the Secretary prescribes, and

"(B) shall be furnished to individuals not later than January 31 of the calendar year following the calendar year to which such report relates."

Effective Date (Sec. 211(f)(1), H.R. 2014, 8/5/97) effective 1/1/98. For Sec. 211(f)(6), H.R. 2014, 8/5/97, see above.

Matter in *italics* in Code Sec. 529(e)(1)(B) added by Sec. 1601(h)(1)(A), H.R. 2014, 8/5/97, which struck out:

7. "subsection (c)(2)(C)"

8. added matter in subpara. (e)(1)(C)

Effective Date (Sec. 1601(j)(1), H.R. 2014, 8/5/97) effective for tax. yrs. end. after 8/20/96. Sec. 1806(C)(2), of P.L. 104-188 [as amended by Sec. 1601(h)(1)(C) of this Act] provides:

"(2) Transition rule. If—

"(A) a State or agency or instrumentality thereof maintains, on the date of the enactment of this Act, a program under which persons may purchase tuition credits or certificates on behalf of, or make contributions for education expenses of, a designated beneficiary, and

"(B) such program meets the requirements of a qualified State tuition program before the later of—

"(i) the date which is 1 year after such date of enactment, or

"(ii) the first day of the first calendar quarter after the close of the first regular session of the State legislature that begins after such 8/5/97,

then such program (as in effect on August 20, 1996) shall be treated as a qualified State tuition program with respect to contributions (and earnings allocable thereto) pursuant to contracts entered into under such program before the first date on which such program meets such requirements (determined without regard to this paragraph) and the provisions of such program (as so in effect) shall apply in lieu of section 529(b) of the Internal Revenue Code of 1986 with respect to such contributions and earnings.

For purposes of subparagraph (B)(ii), if a State has a 2-year legislative session, each year of such session shall be deemed to be a separate regular session of the State legislature."

Matter in *italics* in Code Sec. 529(e)(2) added by Sec. 211(b)(1), H.R. 2014, 8/5/97, which struck out:

9. "(2) Member of family. The term 'member of the family' has the same meaning given such term as section 2032A(e)(2)."

Effective Date (Sec. 211(f)(1), H.R. 2014, 8/5/97, see above.

Matter in *italics* in Code Sec. 529(e)(3) added by Sec. 211(a), H.R. 2014, 8/5/97, which struck out:

10. "(3) Qualified higher education expenses. The term 'qualified higher education expenses' means tuition, fees, books, supplies, and equipment required for the enrollment or attendance of a designated beneficiary at an eligible educational institution (as defined in section 135(c)(3))."

Effective Date (Sec. 211(f)(2), H.R. 2014, 8/5/97) effective 1/1/98. effective for tax. yrs. end. after 8/20/96. For Sec. 1806(C)(2), of P.L. 104-188 [as amended by Sec. 1601(h)(1)(C) of this Act], see above. For Sec. 211(f)(6), H.R. 2014, 8/5/97, see above.

Code Sec. 529(e)(5), in *italics*, added by Sec. 211(b)(2), H.R. 2014, 8/5/97.

11. added para. (e)(5)

Effective Date (Sec. 211(f)(3), H.R. 2014, 8/5/97) effective for distributions after 12/31/97, with respect to expenses paid after 12/31/97 (in tax. yrs. end. after 12/31/97), for education furnished in academic periods begin. after 12/31/97. For Sec. 211(f)(6), H.R. 2014, 8/5/97, see above.

[¶ 3092] Code Sec.[1] 530.

CAUTION. Code Sec. 530, following, is effective for tax. yrs. begin. after 12/31/97.

Education individual retirement accounts.

(a) **General rule.** An education individual retirement account shall be exempt from taxation under this subtitle. Notwithstanding the preceding sentence, the education individual retirement account shall be subject to the taxes imposed by section 511 (relating to imposition of tax on unrelated business income of charitable organizations).

(b) **Definitions and special rules.** For purposes of this section—

(1) **Education individual retirement account.** The term "education individual retirement account" means a trust created or organized in the United States exclusively for the purpose of paying the qualified higher education expenses of the designated beneficiary of the trust (and designated as an education individual retirement account at the time created or organized), but only if the written governing instrument creating the trust meets the following requirements:

(A) No contribution will be accepted—

(i) unless it is in cash,

(ii) after the date on which such beneficiary attains age 18, or

(iii) except in the case of rollover contributions, if such contribution would result in aggregate contributions for the taxable year exceeding $500.

(B) The trustee is a bank (as defined in section 408(n)) or another person who demonstrates to the satisfaction of the Secretary that the manner in which that person will administer the trust will be consistent with the requirements of this section or who has so demonstrated with respect to any individual retirement plan.

(C) No part of the trust assets will be invested in life insurance contracts.

(D) The assets of the trust shall not be commingled with other property except in a common trust fund or common investment fund.

(E) Upon the death of the designated beneficiary, any balance to the credit of the beneficiary shall be distributed within 30 days after the date of death to the estate of such beneficiary.

(2) Qualified higher education expenses.

(A) In general. The term "qualified higher education expenses" has the meaning given such term by section 529(e)(3), reduced as provided in section 25A(g)(2).

(B) Qualified state tuition programs. Such term shall include amounts paid or incurred to purchase tuition credits or certificates, or to make contributions to an account, under a qualified State tuition program (as defined in section 529(b)) for the benefit of the beneficiary of the account.

(3) Eligible educational institution. The term "eligible educational institution" has the meaning given such term by section 529(f)(5).

(c) Reduction in permitted contributions based on adjusted gross income.

(1) In general. The maximum amount which a contributor could otherwise make to an account under this section shall be reduced by an amount which bears the same ratio to such maximum amount as—

(A) the excess of—

(i) the contributor's modified adjusted gross income for such taxable year, over

(ii) $95,000 ($150,000 in the case of a joint return), bears to

(B) $15,000 ($10,000 in the case of a joint return).

(2) Modified adjusted gross income. For purposes of paragraph (1), the term "modified adjusted gross income" means the adjusted gross income of the taxpayer for the taxable year increased by any amount excluded from gross income under section 911, 931, or 933.

(d) Tax Treatment of Distributions.

(1) In general. Any distribution shall be includible in the gross income of the distributee in the manner as provided in section 72(b).

(2) Distributions for qualified higher education expenses.

(A) In general. No amount shall be includible under paragraph (1) if the qualified higher education expenses of the designated beneficiary during the taxable year are not less than the aggregate distributions during the taxable year.

(B) Distributions in excess of expenses.—If such aggregate distributions exceed such expenses during the taxable year, the amount includible in gross income under paragraph (1) shall be equal to the amount which bears the same ratio to the amount which would be includible in gross income under paragraph (1) (without regard to this subparagraph) as the qualified higher education expenses bear to such aggregate distributions.

(C) Election to waive exclusion.—A taxpayer may elect to waive the application of this paragraph for any taxable year.

(3) Special rules for applying estate and gift taxes with respect to account. Rules similar to the rules of paragraphs (2), (4), and (5) of section 529(c) shall apply for purposes of this section.

(4) Additional tax for distributions not used for educational expenses.

(A) In general. The tax imposed by this chapter for any taxable year on any taxpayer who receives a payment or distribution from an education individual retirement account which is includible in gross income shall be increased by 10 percent of the amount which is so includible.

(B) Exceptions. Subparagraph (A) shall not apply if the payment or distribution is—

(i) made to a beneficiary (or to the estate of the designated beneficiary) on or after the death of the designated beneficiary,

(ii) attributable to the designated beneficiary's being disabled (within the meaning of section 72(m)(7)), or

(iii) made on account of a scholarship, allowance, or payment described in section 25A(g)(2) received by the account holder to the extent the amount of the payment or distribution does not exceed the amount of the scholarship, allowance, or payment.

(C) Excess contributions returned before due date of return. Subparagraph (A) shall not apply to the distribution of any contribution made during a taxable year on behalf of a designated beneficiary to the extent that such contribution exceeds $500 if—

(i) such distribution is received on or before the day prescribed by law (including extensions of time) for filing such contributor's return for such taxable year, and

(ii) such distribution is accompanied by the amount of net income attributable to such excess contribution.

Any net income described in clause (ii) shall be included in gross income for the taxable year in which such excess contribution was made.

(5) Rollover contributions. Paragraph (1) shall not apply to any amount paid or distributed from an education individual retirement account to the extent that the amount received is paid into another education individual retirement account for the benefit of the same beneficiary or a member of the family (within the meaning of section 529(e)(2)) of such beneficiary not later than the 60th day after the date of such payment or distribution. The preceding sentence shall not apply to any payment or distribution if it applied to any prior payment or distribution during the 12-month period ending on the date of the payment or distribution.

(6) Change in beneficiary. Any change in the beneficiary of an education individual retirement account shall not be treated as a distribution for purposes of paragraph (1) if the new beneficiary is a member of the family (as so defined) of the old beneficiary.

(7) Special rules for death and divorce. Rules similar to the rules of paragraphs (7) and (8) of section 220(f) shall apply.

(e) Tax Treatment of Accounts. Rules similar to the rules of paragraphs (2) and (4) of section 408(e) shall apply to any education individual retirement account.

(f) Community property laws. This section shall be applied without regard to any community property laws.

(g) Custodial accounts. For purposes of this section, a custodial account shall be treated as a trust if the assets of such account are held by a bank (as defined in section 408(n)) or another person who demonstrates, to the satisfaction of the Secretary, that the manner in which he will administer the account will be consistent with the requirements of this section, and if the custodial account would, except for the fact that it is not a trust, constitute an account described in subsection (b)(1). For purposes of this title, in the case of a custodial account treated as a trust by reason of the preceding sentence, the custodian of such account shall be treated as the trustee thereof.

(h) Reports. The trustee of an education individual retirement account shall make such reports regarding such account to the Secretary and to the beneficiary of the account with respect to contributions, distributions, and such other matters as the Secretary may require. The reports required by this subsection shall be filed at such time and in such manner and furnished to such individuals at such time and in such manner as may be required.

[For analysis, see ¶ 403. For text of Committee Report see ¶ 5005].

[Endnote Code Sec. 530]
    Code Sec. 530 was added by Sec. 213(a) of the Taxpayer Relief Act of 1997, H.R. 2014, 8/5/97.
    1. added Code Sec. 530
Effective Date (Sec. 213(f), H.R. 2014, 8/5/97) effective for tax. yrs. begin. after 12/31/97.

[¶ 3093]   Code Sec. 532.   Corporations subject to accumulated earnings tax.

* * * * * * * * * * *

(b) Exceptions. The accumulated earnings tax imposed by section 531 shall not apply to—

* * * * * * * * * * * *

CAUTION.   Para. (b)(4), following, is effective for tax. yrs. of United States persons begin. before 1/1/98, and tax. yrs. of foreign corporations end. with or within such tax. yrs. of United States persons. For para. (b)(4), effective for tax yrs. of United States persons begin. after 12/31/97, and tax. yrs. of foreign corporations end. with or within such tax. yrs. of United States persons, see below.

(4) a passive foreign investment company (as defined in section 1296).

CAUTION.   Para. (b)(4), following, is effective for tax. yrs. of United States persons begin. after 12/31/97, and tax. yrs. of foreign corporations end. with or within such tax. yrs. of United States persons. For para. (b)(4), effective for tax yrs. of United States persons begin. before 1/1/98, and tax. yrs. of foreign corporations end. with or within such tax. yrs. of United States persons, see above.

(4) a passive foreign investment company (as defined in [1]*section 1297*).

* * * * * * * * * * *

[Endnote Code Sec. 532]

Matter in *italics* in Code Sec. 532(b)(4) added by Sec. 1122(d)(1) of the Taxpayer Relief Act of 1997, H.R. 2014, 8/5/97, which struck out:

1. "section 1296"

Effective Date (Sec. 1123, H.R. 2014, 8/5/97) effective for tax. yrs. of United States persons begin. after 12/31/97, and tax. yrs. of foreign corporations end. with or within such tax. yrs. of United States persons.

[¶ 3094]   Code Sec. 542.   Definition of personal holding company.

* * * * * * * * * * *

(c) **Exceptions.** The term "personal holding company" as defined in subsection (a) does not include—

* * * * * * * * * * *

CAUTION.   Para. (c)(10), following, is effective for tax. yrs. of United States persons begin. before 1/1/98, and tax. yrs. of foreign corporations end. with or within such tax. yrs. of United States persons. For para. (c)(10), effective for tax yrs. of United States persons begin. after 12/31/97, and tax. yrs. of foreign corporations end. with or within such tax. yrs. of United States persons, see below.

(10) a passive foreign investment company (as defined in section 1296).

CAUTION.   Para. (c)(10), following, is effective for tax. yrs. of United States persons begin. after 12/31/97, and tax. yrs. of foreign corporations end. with or within such tax. yrs. of United States persons. For para. (c)(10), effective for tax yrs. of United States persons begin. before 1/1/98, and tax. yrs. of foreign corporations end. with or within such tax. yrs. of United States persons, see above.

(10) a passive foreign investment company (as defined in [1]*section 1297*).

* * * * * * * * * * *

[Endnote Code Sec. 542]

Matter in *italics* in Code Sec. 542(c)(10) added by Sec. 1122(d)(1) of the Taxpayer Relief Act of 1997, H.R. 2014, 8/5/97, which struck out:

1. "section 1296"

Effective Date (Sec. 1123, H.R. 2014, 8/5/97) effective for tax. yrs. of United States persons begin. after 12/31/97, and tax. yrs. of foreign corporations end. with or within such tax. yrs. of United States persons.

[¶ 3095]   Code Sec. 551.   Foreign personal holding company income taxed to United States shareholders.

* * * * * * * * * * *

CAUTION. Subsec. (f), following, is effective for tax. yrs. of United States persons begin. before 1/1/98, and tax. yrs. of foreign corporations end. with or within such tax. yrs. of United States persons. For subsec. (f), effective for tax. yrs. of United States persons begin. after 12/31/97, and tax. yrs. of foreign corporations end. with or within such tax. yrs. of United States persons, see below.

(f) Stock held through foreign entity. For purposes of this section, stock of a foreign personal holding company owned (directly or through the application of this subsection) by—

(1) a foreign partnership or an estate or trust which is a foreign estate or trust, or

(2) a foreign corporation which is not a foreign personal holding company,

shall be considered as being owned proportionately by its partners, beneficiaries, or shareholders. In any case to which the preceding sentence applies, the Secretary may by regulations provide that rules similar to the rules of section 1297(b)(5) shall apply, and provide for such other adjustments in the application of this subchapter as may be necessary to carry out the purposes of this subsection.

CAUTION. Subsec. (f), following, is effective for tax. yrs. of United States persons begin. after 12/31/97, and tax. yrs. of foreign corporations end. with or within such tax. yrs. of United States persons. For subsec. (f), effective for tax. yrs. of United States persons begin. before 1/1/98, and tax. yrs. of foreign corporations end. with or within such tax. yrs. of United States persons, see above.

(f) Stock held through foreign entity. For purposes of this section, stock of a foreign personal holding company owned (directly or through the application of this subsection) by—

(1) a foreign partnership or an estate or trust which is a foreign estate or trust, or

(2) a foreign corporation which is not a foreign personal holding company,

shall be considered as being owned proportionately by its partners, beneficiaries, or shareholders. In any case to which the preceding sentence applies, the Secretary may by regulations provide that rules similar to the rules of [1]*section 1298(b)(5)* shall apply, and provide for such other adjustments in the application of this subchapter as may be necessary to carry out the purposes of this subsection.

* * * * * * * * * * * *

[Endnote Code Sec. 551]

Matter in *italics* in Code Sec. 551(f) added by Sec. 1122(d)(2) of the Taxpayer Relief Act of 1997, H.R. 2014, date of enactment, which struck out:

1. "section 1297(b)(5)"

Effective Date (Sec. 1123, H.R. 2014, 8/5/97) effective for tax. yrs. of United States persons begin. after 12/31/97, and tax. yrs. of foreign corporations end. with or within such tax. yrs. of United States persons.

[¶ 3096] Code Sec. 593. Reserves for losses on loans.

* * * * * * * * * * * *

(e) Distributions to shareholders.

(1) In general. For purposes of this chapter, any distribution of property (as defined in section 317(a)) by a taxpayer having a balance described in subsection (g)(2)(A)(ii) to a shareholder with respect to its stock, if such distribution is not allowable as a deduction under section 591, shall be treated as made—

(A) first out of its earnings and profits accumulated in taxable years beginning after December 31, 1951, [1]*(and, in the case of an S corporation, the accumulated adjustments account, as defined in section 1368(e)(1))* to the extent thereof,

* * * * * * * * * * * *

[For analysis, see ¶ 1717. For text of Committee Report see ¶ 5365].

[Endnote Code Sec. 593]

Matter in *italics* in Code Sec. 593(e)(1)(A) added by Sec. 1601(f)(5)(A) of the Taxpayer Relief Act of 1997, H.R. 2014, 8/5/97.

1. added matter in subpara. (e)(1)(A)
Effective Date (Sec. 1601(j)(1), H.R. 2014, 8/5/97) effective for tax. yrs. begin. after 12/31/95.

[¶ 3097]   Code Sec. 613A.   Limitations on percentage depletion in case of oil and gas wells.

* * * * * * * * * * *

(c) Exemption for independent producers and royalty owners.

* * * * * * * * * * *

(6) Oil and natural gas produced from marginal properties.

* * * * * * * * * * *

CAUTION.   Subpara. (c)(6)(H), following, is effective for tax. yrs. begin. after 12/31/97.

¹*(H) Temporary suspension of taxable income limit with respect to marginal production. The second sentence of subsection (a) of section 613 shall not apply to so much of the allowance for depletion as is determined under subparagraph (A) for any taxable year beginning after December 31, 1997, and before January 1, 2000.*

* * * * * * * * * * *

[For analysis, see ¶ 2704. For text of Committee Report see ¶ 5095].

[Endnote Code Sec. 613A]
   Code Sec. 613A(c)(6)(H), in *italics*, was added by Sec. 972(a) of the Taxpayer Relief Act of 1997, H.R. 2014, 8/5/97.
   1. added subpara. (c)(6)(H)
Effective Date (Sec. 972(b), H.R. 2014, 8/5/97) effective for tax. yrs. begin. after 12/31/97.

[¶ 3098]   Code Sec. 641.   Imposition of tax.

* * * * * * * * * * *

(b) Computation and payment. The taxable income of an estate or trust shall be computed in the same manner as in the case of an individual, except as otherwise provided in this part. The tax shall be computed on such taxable income and shall be paid by the fiduciary. ¹*For purposes of this subsection, a foreign trust or foreign estate shall be treated as a nonresident alien individual who is not present in the United States at any time.*

* * * * * * * * * * *

[For analysis, see ¶ 1628. For text of Committee Report see ¶ 5364].

[Endnote Code Sec. 641]
   Matter in *italics* in Code Sec. 641(b) added by Sec. 1601(i)(3)(B) of the Taxpayer Relief Act of 1997, H.R. 2014, 8/5/97.
   1. added matter in subsec. (b)
Effective Date (Sec. 1601(j)(1), H.R. 2014, 8/5/97) effective 8/20/96.

[¶ 3099]   Code Sec.¹ 644.   Taxable year of trusts.
   (a) In general. For purposes of this subtitle, the taxable year of any trust shall be the calendar year.
   (b) Exception for trusts exempt from tax and charitable trusts. Subsection (a) shall not apply to a trust exempt from taxation under section 501(a) or to a trust described in section 4947(a)(1).

[For analysis, see ¶ 531. For text of Committee Report see ¶ 5032].

[Endnote Code Sec. 644]

Code Sec. 645 was redesignated as Code Sec. 644 by Sec. 507(b)(1) of the Taxpayer Relief Act of 1997, H.R. 2014, 8/5/97.
  1. redesignated Code Sec. 645 as Code Sec. 644
Effective Date (Sec. 507(c)(2), H.R. 2014, 8/5/97) effective for sales or exchanges after 8/5/97.

[¶ 3100]   Code Sec. 644.   Repealed

[Endnote Code Sec. 644]
  Code Sec. 644 was repealed by Sec. 507(b)(1) of the Taxpayer Relief Act of 1997, H.R. 2014, 8/5/97, which struck out:
  1. SEC. 644 SPECIAL RULE FOR GAIN ON PROPERTY TRANSFERRED TO TRUST AT LESS THAN FAIR MARKET VALUE.
  "(a) Imposition of tax.
  "(1) In general. If—
  "(A) a trust (or another trust to which the property is distributed) sells or exchanges property at a gain not more than 2 years after the date of the initial transfer of the property in trust by the transferor, and
  "(B) the fair market value of such property at the time of the initial transfer in trust by the transferor exceeds the adjusted basis of such property immediately after such transfer,
there is hereby imposed a tax determined in accordance with paragraph (2) on the includible gain recognized on such sale or exchange.
  "(2) Amount of tax. The amount of the tax imposed by paragraph (1) on any includible gain recognized on the sale or exchange of any property shall be equal to the sum of—
  "(A) the excess of—
  "(i) the tax which would have been imposed under this chapter for the taxable year of the transferor in which the sale or exchange of such property occurs had the amount of the includible gain recognized on such sale or exchange, reduced by any deductions properly allocable to such gain, been included in the gross income of the transferor for such taxable year, over
  "(ii) the tax actually imposed under this chapter for such taxable year on the transferor, plus
  "(B) if such sale or exchange occurs in a taxable year of the transferor which begins after the beginning of the taxable year of the trust in which such sale or exchange occurs, an amount equal to the amount determined under subparagraph (A) multiplied by the underpayment rate established under section 6621.
The determination of tax under clause (i) of subparagraph (A) shall be made by not taking into account any carryback, and by not taking into account any loss or deduction to the extent that such loss or deduction may be carried by the transferor to any other taxable year.
  "(3) Taxable year for which tax imposed. The tax imposed by paragraph (1) shall be imposed for the taxable year of the trust which begins with or within the taxable year of the transferor in which the sale or exchange occurs.
  "(4) Tax to be in addition to other taxes. The tax imposed by this subsection for any taxable year of the trust shall be in addition to any other tax imposed by this chapter for such taxable year.
  "(b) Definition of includible gain. For purposes of this section, the term 'includible gain' means the lesser of—
  "(1) the gain recognized by the trust on the sale or exchange of any property, or
  "(2) the excess of the fair market value of such property at the time of the initial transfer in trust by the transferor over the adjusted basis of such property immediately after such transfer.
  "(c) Character of includible gain. For purposes of subsection (a)—
  "(1) the character of the includible gain shall be determined as if the property had actually been sold or exchanged by the transferor, and any activities of the trust with respect to the sale or exchange of the property shall be deemed to be activities of the transferor, and
  "(2) the portion of the includible gain subject to the provisions of section 1245 and section 1250 shall be determined in accordance with regulations prescribed by the Secretary.
  "(d) Special rules.
  "(1) Short sales. If the trust sells the property referred to in subsection (a) in a short sale within the 2-year period referred to in such subsection, such 2-year period shall be extended to the date of the closing of such short sale.
  "(2) Substituted basis property. For purposes of this section, in the case of any property held by the trust which has a basis determined in whole or in part by reference to the basis of any other property which was transferred to the trust—
  "(A) the initial transfer of such property in trust by the transferor shall be treated as having occurred on the date of the initial transfer in trust of such other property,
  "(B) subsections (a)(1)(B) and (b)(2) shall be applied by taking into account the fair market value and the adjusted basis of such other property, and
  (C) the amount determined under subsection (b)(2) with respect to such other property shall be allocated (under regulations prescribed by the Secretary) among such other property and all properties held by the trust which have a basis determined in whole or in part by reference to the basis of such other property.
  "(e) Exceptions. Subsection (a) shall not apply to property—
  "(1) acquired by the trust from a decedent or which passed to a trust from a decedent (within the meaning of section 1014), or
  "(2) acquired by a pooled income fund (as defined in section 642(c)(5)), or
  "(3) acquired by a charitable remainder annuity trust (as defined in section 664(d)(1)) or a charitable remainder unitrust (as defined in sections 664(d)(2) and (3)), or
  "(4) if the sale or exchange of the property occurred after the death of the transferor.
  "(f) Special rule for installment sales. If the trust reports income under section 453 on any sale or exchange to which subsection (a) applies, under regulations prescribed by the Secretary—

"(1) subsection (a) (other than the 2-year requirement of paragraph (1)(A) thereof) shall be applied as if each installment were a separate sale or exchange of property to which such subsection applies, and

"(2) the term 'includible gain' shall not include any portion of an installment received by the trust after the death of the transferor."

Effective Date (Sec. 507(c)(2), H.R. 2014, 8/5/97) effective for sales or exchanges after 8/5/97.

[¶ 3101]   Code Sec.[1] 646.   Certain revocable trusts treated as part of estate.

(a) **General rule.** For purposes of this subtitle, if both the executor (if any) of an estate and the trustee of a qualified revocable trust elect the treatment provided in this section, such trust shall be treated and taxed as part of such estate (and not as a separate trust) for all taxable years of the estate ending after the date of the decedent's death and before the applicable date.

(b) **Definitions.** For purposes of subsection (a)—

(1) **Qualified revocable trust.** The term "qualified revocable trust" means any trust (or portion thereof) which was treated under section 676 as owned by the decedent of the estate referred to in subsection (a) by reason of a power in the grantor (determined without regard to section 672(e)).

(2) **Applicable date.** The term "applicable date" means—

(A) if no return of tax imposed by chapter 11 is required to be filed, the date which is 2 years after the date of the decedent's death, and

(B) if such a return is required to be filed, the date which is 6 months after the date of the final determination of the liability for tax imposed by chapter 11.

(c) **Election.** The election under subsection (a) shall be made not later than the time prescribed for filing the return of tax imposed by this chapter for the first taxable year of the estate (determined with regard to extensions) and, once made, shall be irrevocable.

[For analysis, see ¶ 526. For text of Committee Report see ¶ 5265].

[Endnote Code Sec. 646]
Code Sec. 646 was added by Sec. 1305(a) of the Taxpayer Relief Act of 1997, H.R. 2014, 8/5/97.
1. added Code Sec. 646
Effective Date (Sec. 1305(d), H.R. 2014, 8/5/97) effective for estates of decedents dying after 8/5/97.

[¶ 3102]   Code Sec. 663.   Special rules applicable to sections 661 and 662.

* * * * * * * * * * * *

(b) **Distributions in first sixty-five days of taxable year.**

(1) **General rule.** If within the first 65 days of any taxable year of [1]*an estate or* a trust, an amount is properly paid or credited, such amount shall be considered paid or credited on the last day of the preceding taxable year.

(2) **Limitation.** Paragraph (1) shall apply with respect to any taxable year of [2]*an estate or* a trust only if [3]*the executor of such estate or the fiduciary of such trust (as the case may be)* elects, in such manner and at such time as the Secretary prescribes by regulations, to have paragraph (1) apply for such taxable year.

(c) **Separate shares treated as separate** [4]*estates or* **trusts.** For the sole purpose of determining the amount of distributable net income in the application of sections 661 and 662, in the case of a single trust having more than one beneficiary, substantially separate and independent shares of different beneficiaries in the trust shall be treated as separate trusts. [5]*Rules similar to the rules of the preceding provisions of this subsection shall apply to treat substantially separate and independent shares of different beneficiaries in an estate having more than 1 beneficiary as separate estates.* The existence of such substantially separate and independent shares and the manner of treatment as separate trusts [6]*or estates,* including the application of subpart D, shall be determined in accordance with regulations prescribed by the Secretary.

[For analysis, see ¶s 527, 528. For text of Committee Report see ¶s 5266, 5267].

[Endnote Code Sec. 663]

Matter in *italics* in Code Sec. 663(b) added by Sec. 1306(a) and (b) of the Taxpayer Relief Act of 1997, H.R. 2014, 8/5/97, which struck out:

1. added matter in subsec. (b)
2. added matter in subsec. (b)
3. "the fiduciary of such trust"

Effective Date (Sec. 1306(c), H.R. 2014, 8/5/97) effective for tax. yrs. begin. after 8/5/97.

Matter in *italics* in Code Sec. 663(c) added by Sec. 1307(a) and (b), H.R. 2014, 8/5/97, which struck out:

4. added matter in the heading of subsec. (c)
5. added matter in subsec. (c)
6. added matter subsec. (c)

Effective Date (Sec. 1307(c), H.R. 2014, 8/5/97) effective for estates of decedents dying after 8/5/97.

[¶ 3103] Code Sec. 664.   Charitable remainder trusts.

* * * * * * * * * * * *

(d) Definitions.

(1) Charitable remainder annuity trust. For purposes of this section, a charitable remainder annuity trust is a trust—

(A) from which a sum certain (which is not less than 5 percent [1]*nor more than 50 percent* of the initial net fair market value of all property placed in trust) is to be paid, not less often than annually, to one or more persons (at least one of which is not an organization described in section 170(c) and, in the case of individuals, only to an individual who is living at the time of the creation of the trust) for a term of years (not in excess of 20 years) or for the life or lives of such individual or individuals,

(B) from which no amount other than the payments described in subparagraph (A) [2]*and other than qualified gratuitous transfers described in subparagraph (C)* may be paid to or for the use of any person other than an organization described in section 170(c),[3]

(C) following the termination of the payments described in subparagraph (A), the remainder interest in the trust is to be transferred to, or for the use of, an organization described in section 170(c) or is to be retained by the trust for such a use [4]*or, to the extent the remainder interest is in qualified employer securities (as defined in subsection (g)(4)), all or part of such securities are to be transferred to an employee stock ownership plan (as defined in section 4975(e)(7)) in a qualified gratuitous transfer (as defined by subsection (g))* [5]

[6]*(D) the value (determined under section 7520) of such remainder interest is at least 10 percent of the initial net fair market value of all property placed in the trust.*

(2) Charitable remainder unitrust. For purposes of this section, a charitable remainder unitrust is a trust—

(A) from which a fixed percentage (which is not less than 5 percent [7]*nor more than 50 percent*) of the net fair market value of its assets, valued annually, is to be paid, not less often than annually, to one or more persons (at least one of which is not an organization described in section 170(c) and, in the case of individuals, only to an individual who is living at the time of the creation of the trust) for a term of years (not in excess of 20 years) or for the life or lives of such individual or individuals,

(B) from which no amount other than the payments described in subparagraph (A) [8]*and other than qualified gratuitous transfers described in subparagraph (C)* may be paid to or for the use of any person other than an organization described in section 170(c),[9]

(C) following the termination of the payments described in subparagraph (A), the remainder interest in the trust is to be transferred to, or for the use of, an organization described in section 170(c) or is to be retained by the trust for such a use [10]*or, to the extent the remainder interest is in qualified employer securities (as defined in subsection (g)(4)), all or part of such securities are to be transferred to an employee stock ownership plan (as defined in section 4975(e)(7)) in a qualified gratuitous transfer (as defined by subsection (g))* [11]

[12](D) with respect to each contribution of property to the trust, the value (determined under section 7520) of such remainder interest in such property is at least 10 percent of the net fair market value of such property as of the date such property is contributed to the trust.

* * * * * * * * * * * * *

[13]**(4) Severance of certain additional contributions.** If—

(A) any contribution is made to a trust which before the contribution is a charitable remainder unitrust, and

(B) such contribution would (but for this paragraph) result in such trust ceasing to be a charitable unitrust by reason of paragraph (2)(D),

such contribution shall be treated as a transfer to a separate trust under regulations prescribed by the Secretary.

* * * * * * * * * * * *

[14]**(g) Qualified gratuitous transfer of qualified employer securities.**

(1) In general. For purposes of this section, the term "qualified gratuitous transfer" means a transfer of qualified employer securities to an employee stock ownership plan (as defined in section 4975(e)(7)) but only to the extent that—

(A) the securities transferred previously passed from a decedent dying before January 1, 1999, to a trust described in paragraph (1) or (2) of subsection (d),

(B) no deduction under section 404 is allowable with respect to such transfer,

(C) such plan contains the provisions required by paragraph (3),

(D) such plan treats such securities as being attributable to employer contributions but without regard to the limitations otherwise applicable to such contributions under section 404, and   "(E) the employer whose employees are covered by the plan described in this paragraph files with the Secretary a verified written statement consenting to the application of sections 4978 and 4979A with respect to such employer.

(2) Exception. The term "qualified gratuitous transfer" shall not include a transfer of qualified employer securities to an employee stock ownership plan unless—

(A) such plan was in existence on August 1, 1996,

(B) at the time of the transfer, the decedent and members of the decedent's family (within the meaning of section 2032A(e)(2)) own (directly or through the application of section 318(a)) no more than 10 percent of the value of the stock of the corporation referred to in paragraph (4), and

(C) immediately after the transfer, such plan owns (after the application of section 318(a)(4)) at least 60 percent of the value of the outstanding stock of the corporation.

(3) Plan requirements. A plan contains the provisions required by this paragraph if such plan provides that—

(A) the qualified employer securities so transferred are allocated to plan participants in a manner consistent with section 401(a)(4),

(B) plan participants are entitled to direct the plan as to the manner in which such securities which are entitled to vote and are allocated to the account of such participant are to be voted,

(C) an independent trustee votes the securities so transferred which are not allocated to plan participants,

(D) each participant who is entitled to a distribution from the plan has the rights described in subparagraphs (A) and (B) of section 409(h)(1),

(E) such securities are held in a suspense account under the plan to be allocated each year, up to the limitations under section 415(c), after first allocating all other annual additions for the limitation year, up to the limitations under sections 415 (c) and (e), and

(F) on termination of the plan, all securities so transferred which are not allocated to plan participants as of such termination are to be transferred to, or for the use of, an organization described in section 170(c).

For purposes of the preceding sentence, the term "*independent trustee*" means any trustee who is not a member of the family (within the meaning of section 2032A(e)(2)) of the decedent or a 5-percent shareholder. A plan shall not fail to be treated as meeting the requirements of section 401(a) by reason of meeting the requirements of this subsection.

(4) Qualified employer securities. For purposes of this section, the term "qualified employer securities" means employer securities (as defined in section 409(l)) which are issued by a domestic corporation—

(A) which has no outstanding stock which is readily tradable on an established securities market, and

(B) which has only 1 class of stock.

(5) Treatment of securities allocated by employee stock ownership plan to persons related to decedent or 5-percent shareholders.—

(A) In general. If any portion of the assets of the plan attributable to securities acquired by the plan in a qualified gratuitous transfer are allocated to the account of—

(i) any person who is related to the decedent (within the meaning of section 267(b)) or a member of the decedent's family (within the meaning of section 2032A(e)(2)), or

(ii) any person who, at the time of such allocation or at any time during the 1-year period ending on the date of the acquisition of qualified employer securities by the plan, is a 5-percent shareholder of the employer maintaining the plan,

the plan shall be treated as having distributed (at the time of such allocation) to such person or shareholder the amount so allocated.

(B) 5-percent shareholder. For purposes of subparagraph (A), the term "5-percent shareholder" means any person who owns (directly or through the application of section 318(a)) more than 5 percent of the outstanding stock of the corporation which issued such qualified employer securities or of any corporation which is a member of the same controlled group of corporations (within the meaning of section 409(l)(4)) as such corporation. For purposes of the preceding sentence, section 318(a) shall be applied without regard to the exception in paragraph (2)(B)(i) thereof.

(C) Cross reference. For excise tax on allocations described in subparagraph (A), see section 4979A.

(6) Tax on failure to transfer unallocated securities to charity on termination of plan. If the requirements of paragraph (3)(F) are not met with respect to any securities, there is hereby imposed a tax on the employer maintaining the plan in an amount equal to the sum of—

(A) the amount of the increase in the tax which would be imposed by chapter 11 if such securities were not transferred as described in paragraph (1), and

(B) interest on such amount at the underpayment rate under section 6621 (and compounded daily) from the due date for filing the return of the tax imposed by chapter 11.

[For analysis, see ¶s 532, 938. For text of Committee Report see ¶s 5166, 5352].

[Endnote Code Sec. 664]

Matter in *italics* in Code Sec. 664(d)(1)(A) added by Sec. 1089(a)(1) of the Tax Relief Act of 1997, H.R. 2014, 8/5/97.
1. added matter subpara. (d)(1)(A)
Effective Date (Sec. 1089(a)(2), H.R. 2014, 8/5/97) effective for transfers in trust after 6/18/97.

Matter in *italics* in Code Sec. 664(d)(1)(B) added by Sec. 1530(c)(5), H.R. 2014, 8/5/97.
2. added matter in subpara. (d)(1)(B)
Effective Date (Sec. 1530(d), H.R. 2014, 8/5/97) effective for transfers made by trusts to, or for the use of, an employee stock ownership plan after 8/5/97.

Matter in *italics* in Code Sec. 664(d)(1)(B) added by Sec. 1089(b)(1), H.R. 2014, 8/5/97, which struck out:
3. "and"
Effective Date (Sec. 1089(b)(6), H.R. 2014, 8/5/97) Sec. 1089(b)(6), H.R. 2014, 8/5/97, reads as follows:
"(6) Effective dates.
"(A) In general. Except as otherwise provided in this paragraph, the amendments made by this subsection shall apply to transfers in trust after July 28, 1997.
"(B) Special rule for certain decedents. The amendments made by this subsection shall not apply to transfers in trust under the terms of a will (or other testamentary instrument) executed on or before July 28, 1997, if the decedent—

"(i) dies before January 1, 1999, without having republished the will (or amended such instrument) by codicil or otherwise, or

"(ii) was on July 28, 1997, under a mental disability to change the disposition of his property and did not regain his competence to dispose of such property before the date of his death."

Matter in *italics* in Code Sec. 664(d)(1)(C) added by Sec. 1530(a), H.R. 2014, 8/5/97, which struck out:
4. "."
Effective Date (Sec. 1530(d), H.R. 2014, 8/5/97) effective for transfers made by trusts to, or for the use of, an employee stock ownership plan after 8/5/97.

Matter in *italics* in Code Sec. 664(d)(1)(C) and Code Sec. 664(d)(1)(D) added by Sec. 1089(b)(1), H.R. 2014, date of enactment, which struck out:
5. "."
6. added subpara. (d)(1)(D)
Effective Date (Sec. 1089(b)(6), H.R. 2014, 8/5/97) see above.

Matter in *italics* in Code Sec. 664(d)(2)(A) added by Sec. 1089(a)(1) of the Tax Relief Act of 1997, H.R. 2014, 8/5/97.
7. added matter subpara. (d)(2)(A)
Effective Date (Sec. 1089(a)(2), H.R. 2014, 8/5/97) effective for transfers in trust after 6/18/97.

Matter in *italics* in Code Sec. 664(d)(2)(B) added by Sec. 1530(c)(5), H.R. 2014, 8/5/97.
8. added matter in subpara. (d)(2)(B)
Effective Date (Sec. 1530(d), H.R. 2014, 8/5/97) effective for transfers made by trusts to, or for the use of, an employee stock ownership plan after 8/5/97.

Matter in *italics* in Code Sec. 664(d)(2)(B) added by Sec. 1089(b)(2), H.R. 2014, 8/5/97, which struck out:
9. "and"
Effective Date (Sec. 1089(b)(6), H.R. 2014, 8/5/97) see above.

Matter in *italics* in Code Sec. 664(d)(2)(C) added by Sec. 1530(a), H.R. 2014, 8/5/97, which struck out:
10. "."
Effective Date (Sec. 1530(d), H.R. 2014, 8/5/97) effective for transfers made by trusts to, or for the use of, an employee stock ownership plan after 8/5/97.

Matter in *italics* in Code Sec. 664(d)(2)(C), Code Sec. 664(d)(2)(D) and Code Sec. 664(d)(4) added by Sec. 1089(b)(2) and (4), H.R. 2014, date of enactment, which struck out:
11. "."
12. added subpara. (d)(2)(D)
13. added para. (d)(4)
Effective Date (Sec. 1089(b)(6), H.R. 2014, 8/5/97) see above.

Code Sec. 664(g), in *italics*, was added by Sec. 1530(b), H.R. 2014, 8/5/97.
14. added subpara. (g)
Effective Date (Sec. 1530(d), H.R. 2014, 8/5/97) effective for transfers made by trusts to, or for the use of, an employee stock ownership plan after 8/5/97.

[¶ 3104]   Code Sec. 665.   Definitions applicable to subpart D.

* * * * * * * * * * * *

(b) Accumulation distribution. For purposes of this subpart, [1]*except as provided in subsection (c),* the term "accumulation distribution" means, for any taxable year of the trust, the amount by which—

   (1) the amounts specified in paragraph (2) of section 661(a) for such taxable year, exceed

   (2) distributable net income for such year reduced (but not below zero) by the amounts specified in paragraph (1) of section 661(a).

For purposes of section 667 (other than subsection (c) thereof, relating to multiple trusts), the amounts specified in paragraph (2) of section 661(a) shall not include amounts properly paid, credited, or required to be distributed to a beneficiary from a trust (other than a foreign trust) as income accumulated before the birth of such beneficiary or before such beneficiary attains the age of 21. If the amounts properly paid, credited, or required to be distributed by the trust for the taxable year do not exceed the income of the trust for such year, there shall be no accumulation distribution for such year.

[2](c) Exception for accumulation distributions from certain domestic trusts. For purposes of this subpart—

(1) In general. In the case of a qualified trust, any distribution in any taxable year beginning after the date of the enactment of this subsection shall be computed without regard to any undistributed net income.

(2) Qualified trust. For purposes of this subsection, the term "qualified trust" means any trust other than—

(A) a foreign trust (or, except as provided in regulations, a domestic trust which at any time was a foreign trust), or

(B) a trust created before March 1, 1984, unless it is established that the trust would not be aggregated with other trusts under section 643(f) if such section applied to such trust.

(d) Taxes imposed on the trust. For purposes of this subpart—

(1) In general. The term "taxes imposed on the trust" means the amount of the taxes which are imposed for any taxable year of the trust under this chapter (without regard to this subpart or part IV of subchapter A) and which, under regulations prescribed by the Secretary, are properly allocable to the undistributed portions of distributable net income and gains in excess of losses from sales or exchanges of capital assets. The amount determined in the preceding sentence shall be reduced by any amount of such taxes deemed distributed under section 666(b) and (c)[3] to any beneficiary.

* * * * * * * * * * * *

[For analysis, see ¶530. For text of Committee Report see ¶5032].

[Endnote Code Sec. 665]

Matter in *italics* in Code Sec. 665(b) and Code Sec. 665(c) added by Sec. 507(a)(1) and (2) of the Taxpayer Relief Act of 1997, H.R. 2014, 8/5/97.
  1. added matter in subsec. (b)
  2. added subsec. (c)
Effective Date (Sec. 507(c)(1), H.R. 2014, 8/5/97) effective for distributions in tax. yrs. begin. after 8/5/97.

Matter in Code Sec. 665(d)(1) deleted by Sec. 1604(g)(2), H.R. 2014, 8/5/97, which struck out:
  3. "or 669(d) and (e)"
Effective Date Effective 8/5/97.

[¶3105] Code Sec. 674.   Power to control beneficial enjoyment.

* * * * * * * * * * * *

(b) Exceptions for certain powers. Subsection (a) shall not apply to the following powers regardless of by whom held:

* * * * * * * * * * * *

(4) Power to allocate among charitable beneficiaries. A power to determine the beneficial enjoyment of the corpus or the income therefrom if the corpus or income is irrevocably payable for a purpose specified in section 170(c) (relating to definition of charitable contributions) [1]*or to an employee stock ownership plan (as defined in section 4975(e)(7)) in a qualified gratuitous transfer (as defined in section 664(g)(1)).*

* * * * * * * * * * * *

[Endnote Code Sec. 674]

Matter in *italics* in Code Sec. 674(b)(4) added by Sec. 1530(c)(6) of the Taxpayer Relief Act of 1997, H.R. 2014, 8/5/97.
  1. added matter in paragraph (b)(4)
Effective Date (Sec. 1530(d), H.R. 2014, 8/5/97) effective for transfers made by trusts to, or for the use of, an employee stock ownership plan after 8/5/97.

[¶ 3106]   Code Sec. 679.   Foreign trusts having one or more United States beneficiaries.
(a) Transferor treated as owner.

* * * * * * * * * * *

(3) Certain obligations not taken into account under fair market value exception.

* * * * * * * * * * *

(C) Persons described. The persons described in this subparagraph are—

* * * * * * * * * * *

(ii) any grantor[1], *owner,* or beneficiary of the trust, and

(iii) any person who is related (within the meaning of section 643(i)(2)(B)) to any grantor[2], *owner,* or beneficiary of the trust.

* * * * * * * * * * *

[For analysis, see ¶ 1627. For text of Committee Report see ¶ 5363].

[Endnote Code Sec. 679]
  Matter in *italics* in Code Sec. 679(a)(3)(C)(ii) and Code Sec. 679(a)(3)(C)(iii) added by Sec. 1601(i)(2) of the Taxpayer Relief Act of 1997, H.R. 2014, 8/5/97.
  1. added matter in clause (a)(3)(C)(ii)
  2. added matter in clause (a)(3)(C)(iii)
Effective Date (Sec. 1601(j)(1), H.R. 2014, 8/5/97) effective for transfers of property after 2/6/95.

[¶ 3107]   Code Sec.[1] 684.   Recognition of gain on certain transfers to certain foreign trusts and estates.
(a) In general. Except as provided in regulations, in the case of any transfer of property by a United States person to a foreign estate or trust, for purposes of this subtitle, such transfer shall be treated as a sale or exchange for an amount equal to the fair market value of the property transferred, and the transferor shall recognize as gain the excess of—
  (1) the fair market value of the property so transferred, over
  (2) the adjusted basis (for purposes of determining gain) of such property in the hands of the transferor.
(b) Exception. Subsection (a) shall not apply to a transfer to a trust by a United States person to the extent that any person is treated as the owner of such trust under section 671.
(c) Treatment of trusts which become foreign trusts. If a trust which is not a foreign trust becomes a foreign trust, such trust shall be treated for purposes of this section as having transferred, immediately before becoming a foreign trust, all of its assets to a foreign trust.

[For analysis, see ¶ 1629. For text of Committee Report see ¶ 5182].

[Endnote Code Sec. 684]
  Code Sec. 684 was added by Sec. 1131(b) of the Taxpayer Relief Act of 1997, H.R. 2014, 8/5/97.
  1. added Code Sec. 684
Effective Date (Sec. 1131(d) [sic (e)], H.R. 2014, 8/5/97) effective 8/5/97.

[¶ 3108]   Code Sec.[1] 685.   Treatment of funeral trusts.
(a) In General. In the case of a qualified funeral trust—
  (1) subparts B, C, D, and E shall not apply, and
  (2) no deduction shall be allowed by section 642(b).
(b) Qualified Funeral Trust. For purposes of this subsection, the term "qualified funeral trust" means any trust (other than a foreign trust) if—
  (1) the trust arises as a result of a contract with a person engaged in the trade or business of providing funeral or burial services or property necessary to provide such services,

(2) the sole purpose of the trust is to hold, invest, and reinvest funds in the trust and to use such funds solely to make payments for such services or property for the benefit of the beneficiaries of the trust,

(3) the only beneficiaries of such trust are individuals with respect to whom such services or property are to be provided at their death under contracts described in paragraph (1),

(4) the only contributions to the trust are contributions by or for the benefit of such beneficiaries,

(5) the trustee elects the application of this subsection, and

(6) the trust would (but for the election described in paragraph (5)) be treated as owned under subpart E by the purchasers of the contracts described in paragraph (1).

(c) **Dollar Limitation on Contributions.** (1) **In general.** The term "qualified funeral trust" shall not include any trust which accepts aggregate contributions by or for the benefit of an individual in excess of $7,000.

(2) **Related trusts.** For purposes of paragraph (1), all trusts having trustees which are related persons shall be treated as 1 trust. For purposes of the preceding sentence, persons are related if—

(A) the relationship between such persons is described in section 267 or 707(b),

(B) such persons are treated as a single employer under subsection (a) or (b) of section 52, or

(C) the Secretary determines that treating such persons as related is necessary to prevent avoidance of the purposes of this section.

(3) **Inflation adjustment.** In the case of any contract referred to in subsection (b)(1) which is entered into during any calendar year after 1998, the dollar amount referred to paragraph (1) shall be increased by an amount equal to—

(A) such dollar amount, multiplied by

(B) the cost-of-living adjustment determined under section 1(f)(3) for such calendar year, by substituting "calendar year 1997" for "calendar year 1992" in subparagraph (B) thereof.

(C) If any dollar amount after being increased under the preceding sentence is not a multiple of $100, such dollar amount shall be rounded to the nearest multiple of $100.

(d) **Application of Rate Schedule.** Section 1(e) shall be applied to each qualified funeral trust by treating each beneficiary's interest in each such trust as a separate trust.

(e) **Treatment of Amounts Refunded to Purchaser on Cancellation.** No gain or loss shall be recognized to a purchaser of a contract described in subsection (b)(1) by reason of any payment from such trust to such purchaser by reason of cancellation of such contract. If any payment referred to in the preceding sentence consists of property other than money, the basis of such property in the hands of such purchaser shall be the same as the trust's basis in such property immediately before the payment.

(f) **Simplified Reporting.** The Secretary may prescribe rules for simplified reporting of all trusts having a single trustee.

[For analysis, see ¶ 533. For text of Committee Report see ¶ 5269].

[Endnote Code Sec. 685]
  Code Sec. 685 was added by Sec. 1309(a) of the Taxpayer Relief Act of 1997, H.R. 2014, 8/5/97.
  1. added Code Sec. 685
Effective Date (Sec. 1309(b), H.R. 2014, 8/5/97) effective for tax. yrs. end. after 8/5/97.

[¶ 3109]   Code Sec. 691.   Recipients of income in respect of decedents.

* * * * * * * * * * * *

(c) **Deduction for estate tax.**
  (1) **Allowance of deduction.**

* * * * * * * * * * * *

(B) Estates and trusts. In the case of an estate or trust, the amount allowed as a deduction under subparagraph (A) shall be computed by excluding from the gross income of the estate or trust the portion (if any) of the items described in subsection (a)(1) which is properly paid, credited, or to be distributed to the beneficiaries during the taxable year.[1]

* * * * * * * * * * * *

[Endnote Code Sec. 691]

Code Sec. 691(c)(1)(C) was deleted by Sec. 1073(b)(1) of the Taxpayer Relief Act of 1997, H.R. 2014, 8/5/97, which struck out:

"(C) Excess retirement accumulation tax. For purposes of this subsection, no deduction shall be allowed for the portion of the estate tax attributable to the increase in such tax under section 4980A(d)."

Effective Date (Sec. 1073(c)(2), H.R. 2014, 8/5/97) effective for estates of decedents dying after 12/31/96.

[¶ 3110]   Code Sec. 704.   Partner's distributive share.

* * * * * * * * * * * *

(c) Contributed property.

   (1) In general. Under regulations prescribed by the Secretary—

* * * * * * * * * * * *

   (B) if any property so contributed is distributed (directly or indirectly) by the partnership (other than to the contributing partner) within [1]*7 years* of being contributed—

      (i) the contributing partner shall be treated as recognizing gain or loss (as the case may be) from the sale of such property in an amount equal to the gain or loss which would have been allocated to such partner under subparagraph (A) by reason of the variation described in subparagraph (A) if the property had been sold at its fair market value at the time of the distribution,

      (ii) the character of such gain or loss shall be determined by reference to the character of the gain or loss which would have resulted if such property had been sold by the partnership to the distributee, and

      (iii) appropriate adjustments shall be made to the adjusted basis of the contributing partner's interest in the partnership and to the adjusted basis of the property distributed to reflect any gain or loss recognized under this subparagraph.

* * * * * * * * * * * *

[For analysis, see ¶ 1424. For text of Committee Report see ¶ 5152].

[Endnote Code Sec. 704]

Matter in *italics* in Code Sec. 704(c)(1)(B) added by Sec. 1063(a) of the Taxpayer Relief Act of 1997, H.R. 2014, 8/5/97, which struck out:

   1. "5 years"

Effective Date (Sec. 1063(b), H.R. 2014, 8/5/97) Sec. 1063(b), H.R. 2014, 8/5/97, reads as follows:

"(b) Effective date.

"(1) In general. The amendment made by subsection (a) shall apply to property contributed after June 8, 1997.

"(2) Binding contracts. The amendments made by subsection (a) shall not apply to any property contributed pursuant to a written binding contract in effect on June 8, 1997, and at all times thereafter before such contribution if such contract provides for the contribution of a fixed amount of property."

[¶ 3111]   Code Sec. 706.   Taxable years of partner and partnership.

* * * * * * * * * * * *

(b) Taxable year.

* * * * * * * * * * * *

   (5) Application with other sections. Except as provided in regulations, for purposes of determining the taxable year to which a partnership is required to change by reason of this subsection, changes in taxable years of other persons required by this subsection, section 441(i), section 584(h), [1]*section 644*, or section 1378(a) shall be taken into account.

(c) Closing of partnership year.

* * * * * * * * * * * *

CAUTION.   Para. (c)(2), following, is effective for partnership tax. yrs. begin. before 1/1/98. For para. (c)(2), effective for partnership tax. yrs. begin. after 12/31/97, see below.

(2) Partner who retires or sells interest in partnership.

(A) Disposition of entire interest. The taxable year of a partnership shall close—

(i) with respect to a partner who sells or exchanges his entire interest in a partnership, and

(ii) with respect to a partner whose interest is liquidated, except that the taxable year of a partnership with respect to a partner who dies shall not close prior to the end of the partnership's taxable year.

(B) Disposition of less than entire interest. The taxable year of a partnership shall not close (other than at the end of a partnership's taxable year as determined under subsection (b)(1)) with respect to a partner who sells or exchanges less than his entire interest in the partnership or with respect to a partner whose interest is reduced (whether by entry of a new partner, partial liquidation of a partner's interest, gift, or otherwise).

CAUTION.   Para. (c)(2), following, is effective for partnership tax. yrs. begin. after 12/31/97. For para. (c)(2), effective for partnership tax. yrs. begin. before 1/1/98, see above.

(2) [2]*Treatment of dispositions.*

[3]*(A) Disposition of entire interest. The taxable year of a partnership shall close with respect to a partner whose entire interest in the partnership terminates (whether by reason of death, liquidation, or otherwise).*

(B) Disposition of less than entire interest. The taxable year of a partnership shall not close (other than at the end of a partnership's taxable year as determined under subsection (b)(1)) with respect to a partner who sells or exchanges less than his entire interest in the partnership or with respect to a partner whose interest is reduced (whether by entry of a new partner, partial liquidation of a partner's interest, gift, or otherwise).

* * * * * * * * * * * *

[Endnote Code Sec. 706]

Matter in *italics* in Code Sec. 706(b)(5) added by Sec. 507(b)(2) of the Taxpayer Relief Act of 1997, H.R. 2014, 8/5/97, which struck out:

1. "section 645"

Effective Date (Sec. 507(c)(2), H.R. 2014, 8/5/97) effective for sales or exchanges after 8/5/97.

Matter in *italics* in Code Sec. 706(c)(2) heading and Code Sec. 706(c)(2)(A) added by Sec. 1246(a) and (b) of the Taxpayer Relief Act of 1997, H.R. 2014, 8/5/97, which struck out:

2. "(2) Partner who retires or sells interest in partnership."

3. "(A) Disposition of entire interest. The taxable year of a partnership shall close—

"(i) with respect to a partner who sells or exchanges his entire interest in a partnership, and

"(ii) with respect to a partner whose interest is liquidated, except that the taxable year of a partnership with respect to a partner who dies shall not close prior to the end of the partnership's taxable year."

Effective Date (Sec. 1246(c), H.R. 2014, 8/5/97) effective for partnership tax. yrs. begin. after 12/31/97.

[¶ 3112]   Code Sec. 721.   Nonrecognition of gain or loss on contribution.

* * * * * * * * * * * *

[1]*(c) Regulations relating to certain transfers to partnerships. The Secretary may provide by regulations that subsection (a) shall not apply to gain realized on the transfer of property to a partnership if such gain, when recognized, will be includible in the gross income of a person other than a United States person.*

[2]*(d) Transfers of intangibles.* For *regulatory authority to treat intangibles transferred to a partnership as sold, see section 367(d)(3).*

[For analysis, see ¶ 1630. For text of Committee Report see ¶ 5182].

[Endnote Code Sec. 721]

Code Sec. 721(c) and Code Sec. 721(d), in *italics*, were added by Sec. 1131(b)(3) [sic (c)(3)] and (5)(B) [sic (c)(5)(B)] of the Taxpayer Relief Act of 1997, H.R. 2014, 8/5/97.

 1. added subsec. (c)

 2. added subsec. (d)

Effective Date (Sec. 1131(d) [sic (e)], H.R. 2014, 8/5/97) effective 8/5/97.

[¶ 3113] Code Sec. 724. Character of gain or loss on contributed unrealized receivables, inventory items, and capital loss property.

* * * * * * * * * * *

 (d) **Definitions.** For purposes of this section—

* * * * * * * * * * * *

  (2) **Inventory item.** The term "inventory item" has the meaning given such term by [1]*section 751(d)* determined by treating any reference to the partnership as referring to the partner and by applying section 1231 without regard to any holding period therein provided).

* * * * * * * * * * *

[Endnote Code Sec. 724]

Matter in *italics* in Code Sec. 724(d)(2) added by Sec. 1062(b)(3) of the Taxpayer Relief Act of 1997, H.R. 2014, 8/5/97, which struck out:

 1. "section 751(d)(2)"

Effective Date (Sec. 1062(c), H.R. 2014, 8/5/97) Sec. 1062(c), H.R. 2014, 8/5/97, reads as follows:

"(c) Effective date.

"(1) The amendments made by this section shall apply to sales, exchanges, and distributions after the date of the enactment of this Act.

"(2) Binding contracts. The amendments made by this section shall apply to sales, exchanges, and distributions after 8/5/97."

[¶ 3114] Code Sec. 731. Extent of recognition of gain or loss on distribution.

 (a) **Partners.** In the case of a distribution by a partnership to a partner—

* * * * * * * * * * *

  (2) loss shall not be recognized to such partner, except that upon a distribution in liquidation of a partner's interest in a partnership where no property other than that described in subparagraph (A) or (B) is distributed to such partner, loss shall be recognized to the extent of the excess of the adjusted basis of such partner's interest in the partnership over the sum of—

   (A) any money distributed, and

   (B) the basis to the distributee, as determined under section 732, of any unrealized receivables (as defined in section 751(c)) and inventory (as defined in [1]*section 751(d)*).

* * * * * * * * * * *

 (c) **Treatment of marketable securities.**

* * * * * * * * * * *

  (6) **Character of gain recognized.** In the case of a distribution of a marketable security which is an unrealized receivable (as defined in section 751(c)) or an inventory item (as defined in [2]*section 751(d)*), any gain recognized under this subsection shall be treated as ordinary income to the extent of any increase in the basis of such security attributable to the gain described in paragraph (4)(A)(ii).

* * * * * * * * * * * *

[Endnote Code Sec. 731]
Matter in *italics* in Code Sec. 731(a)(2)(B) and Code Sec. 731(c)(6) was added by Sec. 1062(b)(3) of the Taxpayer Relief Act of 1997, H.R. 2014, 8/5/97, which struck out:
1. "section 751(d)(2)"
2. "section 751(d)(2)"
Effective Date (Sec. 1062(c), H.R. 2014, 8/5/97) Sec. 1062(c), H.R. 2014, 8/5/97, reads as follows:
"(c) Effective date.
"(1) The amendments made by this section shall apply to sales, exchanges, and distributions after the date of the enactment of this Act.
"(2) Binding contracts. The amendments made by this section shall apply to sales, exchanges, and distributions after 8/5/97."

[¶ 3115]   Code Sec. 732.   Basis of distributed property other than money.

* * * * * * * * * * *

[1]*(c) Allocation of basis.*

(1) In general. The basis of distributed properties to which subsection (a)(2) or (b) is applicable shall be allocated —

(A)

(i) first to any unrealized receivables (as defined in section 751(c)) and inventory items (as defined in [2]*section 751(d)) in an amount equal to the adjusted basis of each such property to the partnership, and*

(ii) if the basis to be allocated is less than the sum of the adjusted bases of such properties to the partnership, then, to the extent any decrease is required in order to have the adjusted bases of such properties equal the basis to be allocated, in the manner provided in paragraph (3), and

(B) to the extent of any basis remaining after the allocation under subparagraph (A), to other distributed properties—

(i) first by assigning to each such other property such other property's adjusted basis to the partnership, and

(ii) then, to the extent any increase or decrease in basis is required in order to have the adjusted bases of such other distributed properties equal such remaining basis, in the manner provided in paragraph (2) or (3), whichever is appropriate.

(2) Method of allocating increase. Any increase required under paragraph (1)(B) shall be allocated among the properties —

(A) first to properties with unrealized appreciation in proportion to their respective amounts of unrealized appreciation before such increase (but only to the extent of each property's unrealized appreciation), and

(B) then, to the extent such increase is not allocated under subparagraph (A), in proportion to their respective fair market values.

(3) Method of allocating decrease. Any decrease required under paragraph (1)(A) or (1)(B) shall be allocated—

(A) first to properties with unrealized depreciation in proportion to their respective amounts of unrealized depreciation before such decrease (but only to the extent of each property's unrealized depreciation), and

(B) then, to the extent such decrease is not allocated under subparagraph (A), in proportion to their respective adjusted bases (as adjusted under subparagraph (A)).

* * * * * * * * * * *

[For analysis, see ¶ 1422. For text of Committee Report see ¶ 5150].

[Endnote Code Sec. 732]
Matter in *italics* in Code Sec. 732(c) added by Sec. 1061(a) of the Taxpayer Relief Act of 1997, H.R. 2014, 8/5/97, which struck out:
1. "(c) Allocation of basis.
"The basis of distributed properties to which subsection (a)(2) or subsection (b) is applicable shall be allocated—

"(1) first to any unrealized receivables (as defined in section 751(c)) and inventory items (as defined in section 751(d)(2)) in an amount equal to the adjusted basis of each such property to the partnership (or if the basis to be allocated is less than the sum of the adjusted bases of such properties to the partnership, in proportion to such bases), and

"(2) to the extent of any remaining basis, to any other distributed properties in proportion to their adjusted bases to the partnership."

Effective Date (Sec. 1061(b), H.R. 2014, 8/5/97) effective for distributions after 8/5/97.

In Code Sec. 732(c)(1)(A) [as amended by Sec. 1061(a)] Sec. 1062(b)(3), H.R. 2014, added "section 751(d)" and struck out:

2. "section 751(d)(2)"

Effective Date (Sec. 1062(c), H.R. 2014, 8/5/97) effective for sales, exchanges, and distributions after 8/5/97. For exceptions, see Sec. 1062(c)(2) of this Act, which provides:

"(2) Binding contracts. The amendments made by this section shall not apply to any sale or exchange pursuant to a written binding contract in effect on June 8, 1997, and at all times thereafter before such sale or exchange."

[¶ 3116]   Code Sec. 735.   Character of gain or loss on disposition of distributed property.

   (a) Sale or exchange of certain distributed property.

* * * * * * * * * * *

   (2) Inventory items. Gain or loss on the sale or exchange by a distributee partner of inventory items (as defined in [1]*section 751(d)*) distributed by a partnership shall, if sold or exchanged within 5 years from the date of the distribution, be considered as ordinary income or as ordinary loss, as the case may be.

* * * * * * * * * * *

   (c) Special rules.

   (1) Waiver of holding periods contained in section 1231. For purposes of this section, [2]*section 751(d)* (defining inventory item) shall be applied without regard to any holding period in section 1231(b).

* * * * * * * * * * *

[Endnote Code Sec. 735]

Matter in *italics* in Code Sec. 735(a)(2) and Code Sec. 735(c)(1) added by Sec. 1062(b)(3) of the Taxpayer Relief Act of 1997, H.R. 2014, 8/5/97, which struck out:

1. "section 751(d)(2)"
2. "section 751(d)(2)"

Effective Date (Sec. 1062(c), H.R. 2014, 8/5/97) Sec. 1062(c), H.R. 2014, 8/5/97, reads as follows:

"(c) Effective date.

"(1) The amendments made by this section shall apply to sales, exchanges, and distributions after the date of the enactment of this Act.

"(2) Binding contracts. The amendments made by this section shall apply to sales, exchanges, and distributions after 8/5/97."

[¶ 3117]   Code Sec. 737.   Recognition of precontribution gain in case of certain distributions to contributing partner.

* * * * * * * * * * *

   (b) Net precontribution gain. For purposes of this section, the term "net precontribution gain" means the net gain (if any) which would have been recognized by the distributee partner under section 704(c)(1)(B) if all property which—

   (1) had been contributed to the partnership by the distributee partner within [1]*7 years* of the distribution, and

* * * * * * * * * * *

[For analysis, see ¶ 1424. For text of Committee Report see ¶ 5152].

[Endnote Code Sec. 737]

Matter in *italics* in Code Sec. 737(b)(1) added by Sec. 1063(a) of the Taxpayer Relief Act of 1997, H.R. 2014, 8/5/97, which struck out:
　1. "5 years"
Effective Date (Sec. 1063(b), H.R. 2014, 8/5/97) Sec. 1063(b), H.R. 2014, 8/5/97, reads as follows:
　"(b) Effective date.
　"(1) In general. The amendment made by subsection (a) shall apply to property contributed to a partnership after June 8, 1997.
　"(2) Binding contracts. The amendment made by subsection (a) shall not apply to any property contributed pursuant to a written binding contract in effect on June 8, 1997, and at all times thereafter before such contribution if such contract provides for the contribution of a fixed amount of property."

[¶ 3118]　Code Sec. 751.　Unrealized receivables and inventory items.
　(a) **Sale or exchange of interest in partnership.** The amount of any money, or the fair market value of any property, received by a transferor partner in exchange for all or a part of his interest in the partnership attributable to—

　　　　　　　* * * * * * * * * * *

　[1]*(2) inventory items of the partnership,*
shall be considered as an amount realized from the sale or exchange of property other than a capital asset.
　(b) **Certain distributions treated as sales or exchanges.**
　　(1) **General rule.** To the extent a partner receives in a distribution—
　　　[2]*(A) partnership property which is—*
　　　　(i) unrealized receivables, or
　　　　(ii) inventory items which have appreciated substantially in value,
　　　in exchange for all or a part of his interest in other partnership property (including money), or
　　　[3]*(B) partnership property (including money) other than property described in subparagraph (A)(i) or (ii) in exchange for all or a part of his interest in partnership property described in subparagraph (A)(i) or (ii),*
　　such transactions shall, under regulations prescribed by the Secretary, be considered as a sale or exchange of such property between the distributee and the partnership (as constituted after the distribution).

　　　　　　　* * * * * * * * * * *

　[4]*(3) Substantial appreciation. For purposes of paragraph (1) —*
　　(A) In general. Inventory items of the partnership shall be considered to have appreciated substantially in value if their fair market value exceeds 120 percent of the adjusted basis to the partnership of such property.
　　(B) Certain property excluded. For purposes of subparagraph (A), there shall be excluded any inventory property if a principal purpose for acquiring such property was to avoid the provisions of this subsection relating to inventory items.

　　　　　　　* * * * * * * * * * *

　[5]*(d) Inventory items. For purposes of this subchapter, the term "inventory items" means—*
　　(1) property of the partnership of the kind described in section 1221(1),
　　(2) any other property of the partnership which, on sale or exchange by the partnership, would be considered property other than a capital asset and other than property described in section 1231,
　　(3) any other property of the partnership which, if sold or exchanged by the partnership, would result in a gain taxable under subsection (a) of section 1246 (relating to gain on foreign investment company stock), and
　　(4) any other property held by the partnership which, if held by the selling or distributee partner, would be considered property of the type described in paragraph (1), (2), or (3).

* * * * * * * * * * * *
[For analysis, see ¶ 1422. For text of Committee Report see ¶ 5151].

[Endnote Code Sec. 751]
Matter in *italics* in Code Sec. 751(a)(2), Code Sec. 751(b)(1)(A), Code Sec. 751(b)(1)(B), Code Sec. 751(b)(3) and Code Sec. 751(d) added by Secs. 1062(a), (b)(1) and (b)(2) of the Taxpayer Relief Act of 1997, H.R. 2014, 8/5/97, which struck out:

1. "(2) inventory items of the partnership which have appreciated substantially in value,"
2. "(A) partnership property described in subsection (a)(1) or (2) in exchange for all or a part of his interest in other partnership property (including money), or"
3. "(B) partnership property (including money) other than property described in subsection (a)(1) or (2) in exchange for all or a part of his interest in partnership property described in subsection (a)(1) or (2),"
4. added para. (b)(3)
5. "(d) Inventory items which have appreciated substantially in value.
"(1) Substantial appreciation.
"(A) In general. Inventory items of the partnership shall be considered to have appreciated substantially in value if their fair market value exceeds 120 percent of the adjusted basis to the partnership of such property.
"(B) Certain property excluded. For purposes of subparagraph (A), there shall be excluded any inventory property if a principal purpose for acquiring such property was to avoid the provisions of this section relating to inventory items.
"(2) Inventory items. For purposes of this subchapter the term 'inventory items' means—
"(A) property of the partnership of the kind described in section 1221(1),
"(B) any other property of the partnership which, on sale or exchange by the partnership, would be considered property other than a capital asset and other than property described in section 1231,
"(C) any other property of the partnership which, if sold or exchanged by the partnership, would result in a gain taxable under subsection (a) of section 1246 (relating to gain on foreign investment company stock), and
"(D) any other property held by the partnership which, if held by the selling or distributee partner, would be considered property of the type described in subparagraph (A), (B), or (C)."
Effective Date (Sec. 1062(c), H.R. 2014, 8/5/97) effective for sales, exchanges, and distributions after 8/5/97. Sec. 1602(c)(2) of this Act provides:
"(2) Binding contracts. The amendments made by this section shall not apply to any sale or exchange pursuant to a written binding contract in effect on June 8, 1997, and at all thereafter before such sale or exchange."

[¶ 3119]   Code Sec.[1] 771.

CAUTION.   Code Sec. 771, following, is effective for partnership tax. yrs. begin. after 12/31/97.

Application of subchapter to electing large partnerships.
The preceding provisions of this subchapter to the extent inconsistent with the provisions of this part shall not apply to an electing large partnership and its partners.

[For analysis, see ¶ 1401. For text of Committee Report see ¶ 5209].

[Endnote Code Sec. 771]
Code Sec. 771 was added by Sec. 1221(a) of the Taxpayer Relief Act of 1997, H.R. 2014, 8/5/97.
1. added Code Sec. 771
Effective Date (Sec. 1221(c), H.R. 2014, 8/5/97) effective for partnership tax. yrs. begin. after 12/31/97.

[¶ 3120]   Code Sec.[1] 772.

CAUTION.   Code Sec. 772, following, is effective for partnership tax. yrs. begin. after 12/31/97.

Simplified flow-through.
(a) **General rule.** In determining the income tax of a partner of an electing large partnership, such partner shall take into account separately such partner's distributive share of the partnership's—
   (1) taxable income or loss from passive loss limitation activities,
   (2) taxable income or loss from other activities,
   (3) net capital gain (or net capital loss)—
      (A) to the extent allocable to passive loss limitation activities, and
      (B) to the extent allocable to other activities,

(4) tax-exempt interest,

(5) applicable net AMT adjustment separately computed for—

(A) passive loss limitation activities, and

(B) other activities,

(6) general credits,

(7) low-income housing credit determined under section 42,

(8) rehabilitation credit determined under section 47,

(9) foreign income taxes,

(10) the credit allowable under section 29, and

(11) other items to the extent that the Secretary determines that the separate treatment of such items is appropriate.

(b) Separate computations. In determining the amounts required under subsection (a) to be separately taken into account by any partner, this section and section 773 shall be applied separately with respect to such partner by taking into account such partner's distributive share of the items of income, gain, loss, deduction, or credit of the partnership.

(c) Treatment at partner level.

(1) In general. Except as provided in this subsection, rules similar to the rules of section 702(b) shall apply to any partner's distributive share of the amounts referred to in subsection (a).

(2) Income or loss from passive loss limitation activities. For purposes of this chapter, any partner's distributive share of any income or loss described in subsection (a)(1) shall be treated as an item of income or loss (as the case may be) from the conduct of a trade or business which is a single passive activity (as defined in section 469). A similar rule shall apply to a partner's distributive share of amounts referred to in paragraphs (3)(A) and (5)(A) of subsection (a).

(3) Income or loss from other activities.

(A) In general. For purposes of this chapter, any partner's distributive share of any income or loss described in subsection (a)(2) shall be treated as an item of income or expense (as the case may be) with respect to property held for investment.

(B) Deductions for loss not subject to section 67. The deduction under section 212 for any loss described in subparagraph (A) shall not be treated as a miscellaneous itemized deduction for purposes of section 67.

(4) Treatment of net capital gain or loss. For purposes of this chapter, any partner's distributive share of any gain or loss described in subsection (a)(3) shall be treated as a long-term capital gain or loss, as the case may be.

(5) Minimum tax treatment. In determining the alternative minimum taxable income of any partner, such partner's distributive share of any applicable net AMT adjustment shall be taken into account in lieu of making the separate adjustments provided in sections 56, 57, and 58 with respect to the items of the partnership. Except as provided in regulations, the applicable net AMT adjustment shall be treated, for purposes of section 53, as an adjustment or item of tax preference not specified in section 53(d)(1)(B)(ii).

(6) General credits. A partner's distributive share of the amount referred to in paragraph (6) of subsection (a) shall be taken into account as a current year business credit.

(d) Operating rules. For purposes of this section—

(1) Passive loss limitation activity. The term "passive loss limitation activity" means—

(A) any activity which involves the conduct of a trade or business, and

(B) any rental activity.

For purposes of the preceding sentence, the term "trade or business" includes any activity treated as a trade or business under paragraph (5) or (6) of section 469(c).

(2) Tax-exempt interest. The term "tax-exempt interest" means interest excludable from gross income under section 103.

(3) Applicable net AMT adjustment.

(A) In general. The applicable net AMT adjustment is—

(i) with respect to taxpayers other than corporations, the net adjustment determined by using the adjustments applicable to individuals, and

(ii) with respect to corporations, the net adjustment determined by using the adjustments applicable to corporations.

(B) Net adjustment. The term "net adjustment" means the net adjustment in the items attributable to passive loss activities or other activities (as the case may be) which would result if such items were determined with the adjustments of sections 56, 57, and 58.

(4) Treatment of certain separately stated items.

(A) Exclusion for certain purposes.—In determining the amounts referred to in paragraphs (1) and (2) of subsection (a), any net capital gain or net capital loss (as the case may be), and any item referred to in subsection (a)(11), shall be excluded.

(B) Allocation rules. The net capital gain shall be treated—

(i) as allocable to passive loss limitation activities to the extent the net capital gain does not exceed the net capital gain determined by only taking into account gains and losses from sales and exchanges of property used in connection with such activities, and

(ii) as allocable to other activities to the extent such gain exceeds the amount allocated under clause (i).

A similar rule shall apply for purposes of allocating any net capital loss.

(C) Net capital loss. The term "net capital loss" means the excess of the losses from sales or exchanges of capital assets over the gains from sales or exchange of capital assets.

(5) General credits. The term "general credits" means any credit other than the low-income housing credit, the rehabilitation credit, the foreign tax credit, and the credit allowable under section 29.

(6) Foreign income taxes. The term "foreign income taxes" means taxes described in section 901 which are paid or accrued to foreign countries and to possessions of the United States.

(e) Special rule for unrelated business tax. In the case of a partner which is an organization subject to tax under section 511, such partner's distributive share of any items shall be taken into account separately to the extent necessary to comply with the provisions of section 512(c)(1).

(f) Special rules for applying passive loss limitations. If any person holds an interest in an electing large partnership other than as a limited partner—

(1) paragraph (2) of subsection (c) shall not apply to such partner, and

(2) such partner's distributive share of the partnership items allocable to passive loss limitation activities shall be taken into account separately to the extent necessary to comply with the provisions of section 469.

The preceding sentence shall not apply to any items allocable to an interest held as a limited partner.

[For analysis, see ¶1401. For text of Committee Report see ¶5209].

[Endnote Code Sec. 772]

Code Sec. 772 was added by Sec. 1221(a) of the Taxpayer Relief Act of 1997, H.R. 2014, 8/5/97.

1. added Code Sec. 772

Effective Date (Sec. 1221(c), H.R. 2014, 8/5/97) effective for partnership tax. yrs. begin. after 12/31/97.

[¶3121] Code Sec.[1] 773.

CAUTION. Code Sec. 773, following, is effective for partnership tax. yrs. begin. after 12/31/97.

Computations at partnership level.

(a) General rule.

(1) Taxable income. The taxable income of an electing large partnership shall be computed in the same manner as in the case of an individual except that—

(A) the items described in section 772(a) shall be separately stated, and

(B) the modifications of subsection (b) shall apply.

(2) Elections. All elections affecting the computation of the taxable income of an electing large partnership or the computation of any credit of an electing large partnership shall be made by the partnership; except that the election under section 901, and any election under section 108, shall be made by each partner separately.

(3) Limitations, etc.

(A) In general. Except as provided in subparagraph (B), all limitations and other provisions affecting the computation of the taxable income of an electing large partnership or the computation of any credit of an electing large partnership shall be applied at the partnership level (and not at the partner level).

(B) Certain limitations applied at partner level. The following provisions shall be applied at the partner level (and not at the partnership level):

(i) Section 68 (relating to overall limitation on itemized deductions).

(ii) Sections 49 and 465 (relating to at risk limitations).

(iii) Section 469 (relating to limitation on passive activity losses and credits).

(iv) Any other provision specified in regulations.

(4) Coordination with other provisions. Paragraphs (2) and (3) shall apply notwithstanding any other provision of this chapter other than this part.

(b) Modifications to determination of taxable income. In determining the taxable income of an electing large partnership—

(1) Certain deductions not allowed. The following deductions shall not be allowed:

(A) The deduction for personal exemptions provided in section 151.

(B) The net operating loss deduction provided in section 172.

(C) The additional itemized deductions for individuals provided in part VII of subchapter B (other than section 212 thereof).

(2) Charitable deductions. In determining the amount allowable under section 170, the limitation of section 170(b)(2) shall apply.

(3) Coordination with section 67. In lieu of applying section 67, 70 percent of the amount of the miscellaneous itemized deductions shall be disallowed.

(c) Special rules for income from discharge of indebtedness. If an electing large partnership has income from the discharge of any indebtedness—

(1) such income shall be excluded in determining the amounts referred to in section 772(a), and

(2) in determining the income tax of any partner of such partnership—

(A) such income shall be treated as an item required to be separately taken into account under section 772(a), and

(B) the provisions of section 108 shall be applied without regard to this part.

[For analysis, see ¶ 1401. For text of Committee Report see ¶ 5209].

[Endnote Code Sec. 773]
 Code Sec. 773 was added by Sec. 1221(a) of the Taxpayer Relief Act of 1997, H.R. 2014, 8/5/97.
 1. added Code Sec. 773
Effective Date (Sec. 1221(c), H.R. 2014, 8/5/97) effective for partnership tax. yrs. begin. after 12/31/97.

[¶ 3122]   Code Sec.[1] 774.

CAUTION.   Code Sec. 774, following, is effective for partnership tax. yrs. begin. after 12/31/97.

Other modifications.

(a) Treatment of certain optional adjustments, etc. In the case of an electing large partnership—

(1) computations under section 773 shall be made without regard to any adjustment under section 743(b) or 108(b), but

(2) a partner's distributive share of any amount referred to in section 772(a) shall be appropriately adjusted to take into account any adjustment under section 743(b) or 108(b) with respect to such partner.

(b) Credit recapture determined at partnership level.

(1) In general. In the case of an electing large partnership—

(A) any credit recapture shall be taken into account by the partnership, and

(B) the amount of such recapture shall be determined as if the credit with respect to which the recapture is made had been fully utilized to reduce tax.

(2) Method of taking recapture into account. An electing large partnership shall take into account a credit recapture by reducing the amount of the appropriate current year credit to the extent thereof, and if such recapture exceeds the amount of such current year credit, the partnership shall be liable to pay such excess.

(3) Dispositions not to trigger recapture. No credit recapture shall be required by reason of any transfer of an interest in an electing large partnership.

(4) Credit recapture. For purposes of this subsection, the term "credit recapture" means any increase in tax under section 42(j) or 50(a).

(c) Partnership not terminated by reason of change in ownership. Subparagraph (B) of section 708(b)(1) shall not apply to an electing large partnership.

(d) Partnership entitled to certain credits. The following shall be allowed to an electing large partnership and shall not be taken into account by the partners of such partnership:

(1) The credit provided by section 34.

(2) Any credit or refund under section 852(b)(3)(D).

(e) Treatment of REMIC residuals. For purposes of applying section 860E(e)(6) to any electing large partnership—

(1) all interests in such partnership shall be treated as held by disqualified organizations,

(2) in lieu of applying subparagraph (C) of section 860E(e)(6), the amount subject to tax under section 860E(e)(6) shall be excluded from the gross income of such partnership, and

(3) subparagraph (D) of section 860E(e)(6) shall not apply.

(f) Special rules for applying certain installment sale rules. In the case of an electing large partnership—

(1) the provisions of sections 453(l)(3) and 453A shall be applied at the partnership level, and

(2) in determining the amount of interest payable under such sections, such partnership shall be treated as subject to tax under this chapter at the highest rate of tax in effect under section 1 or 11.

[For analysis, see ¶ 1401. For text of Committee Report see ¶ 5209].

[Endnote Code Sec. 774]

Code Sec. 774 was added by Sec. 1221(a) of the Taxpayer Relief Act of 1997, H.R. 2014, 8/5/97.

1. added Code Sec. 774

Effective Date (Sec. 1221(c), H.R. 2014, 8/5/97) effective for partnership tax. yrs. begin. after 12/31/97.

[¶ 3123] Code Sec.¹ 775.

CAUTION.   Code Sec. 775, following, is effective for partnership tax. yrs. begin. after 12/31/97.

Electing large partnership defined.

(a) General rule. For purposes of this part—

(1) In general. The term "electing large partnership" means, with respect to any partnership taxable year, any partnership if—

(A) the number of persons who were partners in such partnership in the preceding partnership taxable year equaled or exceeded 100, and

(B) such partnership elects the application of this part.

To the extent provided in regulations, a partnership shall cease to be treated as an electing large partnership for any partnership taxable year if in such taxable year fewer than 100 persons were partners in such partnership.

(2) Election. The election under this subsection shall apply to the taxable year for which made and all subsequent taxable years unless revoked with the consent of the Secretary.

(b) Special rules for certain service partnerships.

(1) Certain partners not counted. For purposes of this section, the term "partner" does not include any individual performing substantial services in connection with the activities of the partnership and holding an interest in such partnership, or an individual who formerly performed substantial services in connection with such activities and who held an interest in such partnership at the time the individual performed such services.

(2) Exclusion. For purposes of this part, an election under subsection (a) shall not be effective with respect to any partnership if substantially all the partners of such partnership—

(A) are individuals performing substantial services in connection with the activities of such partnership or are personal service corporations (as defined in section 269A(b)) the owner-employees (as defined in section 269A(b)) of which perform such substantial services,

(B) are retired partners who had performed such substantial services, or

(C) are spouses of partners who are performing (or had previously performed) such substantial services.

(3) Special rule for lower tier partnerships. For purposes of this subsection, the activities of a partnership shall include the activities of any other partnership in which the partnership owns directly an interest in the capital and profits of at least 80 percent.

(c) Exclusion of commodity pools. For purposes of this part, an election under subsection (a) shall not be effective with respect to any partnership the principal activity of which is the buying and selling of commodities (not described in section 1221(1)), or options, futures, or forwards with respect to such commodities.

(d) Secretary may rely on treatment on return. If, on the partnership return of any partnership, such partnership is treated as an electing large partnership, such treatment shall be binding on such partnership and all partners of such partnership but not on the Secretary.

[For analysis, see ¶s 1401, 1402. For text of Committee Report see ¶s 5209, 5210].

[Endnote Code Sec. 775]
Code Sec. 775 was added by Sec. 1221(a) of the Taxpayer Relief Act of 1997, H.R. 2014, 8/5/97.
1. added Code Sec. 775
Effective Date (Sec. 1221(c), H.R. 2014, 8/5/97) effective for partnership tax. yrs. begin. after 12/31/97.

[¶ 3124]   Code Sec.[1] 776.

CAUTION.   Code Sec. 776, following, is effective for partnership tax. yrs. begin. after 12/31/97.

Special rules for partnerships holding oil and gas properties.

(a) Computation of percentage depletion. In the case of an electing large partnership, except as provided in subsection (b)—

(1) the allowance for depletion under section 611 with respect to any partnership oil or gas property shall be computed at the partnership level without regard to any provision of section 613A requiring such allowance to be computed separately by each partner,

(2) such allowance shall be determined without regard to the provisions of section 613A(c) limiting the amount of production for which percentage depletion is allowable and without regard to paragraph (1) of section 613A(d), and

(3) paragraph (3) of section 705(a) shall not apply.

(b) Treatment of certain partners.

(1) In general. In the case of a disqualified person, the treatment under this chapter of such person's distributive share of any item of income, gain, loss, deduction, or credit attributable to any partnership oil or gas property shall be determined without regard to this part. Such person's distributive share of any such items shall be excluded for purposes of making determinations under sections 772 and 773.

(2) Disqualified person. For purposes of paragraph (1), the term "disqualified person" means, with respect to any partnership taxable year—

(A) any person referred to in paragraph (2) or (4) of section 613A(d) for such person's taxable year in which such partnership taxable year ends, and

(B) any other person if such person's average daily production of domestic crude oil and natural gas for such person's taxable year in which such partnership taxable year ends exceeds 500 barrels.

(3) Average daily production. For purposes of paragraph (2), a person's average daily production of domestic crude oil and natural gas for any taxable year shall be computed as provided in section 613A(c)(2)—

(A) by taking into account all production of domestic crude oil and natural gas (including such person's proportionate share of any production of a partnership),

(B) by treating 6,000 cubic feet of natural gas as a barrel of crude oil, and

(C) by treating as 1 person all persons treated as 1 taxpayer under section 613A(c)(8) or among whom allocations are required under such section.

[For analysis, see ¶ 1401. For text of Committee Report see ¶ 5209].

[Endnote Code Sec. 776]
Code Sec. 776 was added by Sec. 1221(a) of the Taxpayer Relief Act of 1997, H.R. 2014, 8/5/97.
1. added Code Sec. 776
Effective Date (Sec. 1221(c), H.R. 2014, 8/5/97) effective for partnership tax. yrs. begin. after 12/31/97.

[¶ 3125]   Code Sec.[1] 777.

CAUTION.   Code Sec. 777, following, is effective for partnership tax. yrs. begin. after 12/31/97.

Regulations.
The Secretary shall prescribe such regulations as may be appropriate to carry out the purposes of this part.

[For analysis, see ¶ 1401. For text of Committee Report see ¶ 5209].

[Endnote Code Sec. 777]
Code Sec. 777 was added by Sec. 1221(a) of the Taxpayer Relief Act of 1997, H.R. 2014, 8/5/97.
1. added Code Sec. 777
Effective Date (Sec. 1221(c), H.R. 2014, 8/5/97) effective for partnership tax. yrs. begin. after 12/31/97.

[¶ 3126]   Code Sec. 805.   General deductions.

(a) **General rule.** For purposes of this part, there shall be allowed the following deductions:

* * * * * * * * * * * *

(4) **Dividends received by company.**

* * * * * * * * * * * *

(C) 100 percent dividend. For purposes of subparagraph (A)—

* * * * * * * * * * * *

(ii) Treatment of dividends from noninsurance companies. The term "100 percent dividend" does not include any distribution by a corporation which is not an insurance company to the extent such distribution is out of tax-exempt interest[1], *or out of the increase for the taxable year in policy cash values (within the meaning of subparagraph (F)) of life insurance policies and annuity and endowment contracts to which section 264(f) applies* or out of dividends which are not 100 percent dividends (determined with the application of this clause as if it applies to distributions by all corporations including insurance companies).

(D) Special rules for certain dividends from insurance companies.

* * * * * * * * * * *

(iii) Prorated amounts. For purposes of this subparagraph, the term "prorated amounts" means tax-exempt interest[2], *the increase for the taxable year in policy cash values (within the meaning of subparagraph (F)) of life insurance policies and annuity and endowment contracts to which section 264(f) applies, and* dividends other than 100 percent dividends.

* * * * * * * * * * * *

[3](F) Increase in policy cash values. For purposes of subparagraphs (C) and (D)—

(i) In general. The increase in the policy cash value for any taxable year with respect to policy or contract is the amount of the increase in the adjusted cash value during such taxable year determined without regard to—

(I) gross premiums paid during such taxable year, and

(II) distributions (other than amounts includible in the policyholder's gross income) during such taxable year to which section 72(e) applies.

(ii) Adjusted cash value. For purposes of clause (i), the term "adjusted cash value" means the cash surrender value of the policy or contract increased by the sum of—

(I) commissions payable with respect to such policy or contract for the taxable year, and

(II) asset management fees, surrender charges, mortality and expense charges, and any other fees or charges specified in regulations prescribed by the Secretary which are imposed (or which would be imposed were the policy or contract canceled) with respect to such policy or contract for the taxable year.

* * * * * * * * * * *

[Endnote Code Sec. 805]

Matter in *italics* in Code Sec. 805(a)(4)(C)(ii), Code Sec. 805(a)(4)(D)(iii), and Code Sec. 805(a)(4)(F) added by Sec. 1084(b)(1) [sic (d)(1)] of the Taxpayer Relief Act of 1997, H.R. 2014, 8/5/97, which struck out:

1. added matter in clause (a)(4)(C)(ii)
2. "and"
3. added subpara. (a)(4)(F)

Effective Date (Sec. 1084(d) [sic (f)], H.R. 2014, 8/5/97) reads as follows:

"(d) [sic (f)] Effective date. The amendments made by this section shall apply to contracts issued after June 8, 1997, in taxable years ending after such date. For purposes of the preceding sentence, any material increase in the death benefit or other material change in the contract shall be treated as a new contract but the addition of covered lives shall be treated as a new contract only with respect to such additional covered lives. For purposes of this subsection, an increase in the death benefit under a policy or contract issued in connection with a lapse described in section 501(d)(2) of the Health Insurance Portability and Accountability Act of 1996 shall not be treated as a new contract."

[¶ 3127]   Code Sec. 807.   Rules for certain reserves.

(a) **Decrease treated as gross income.** If for any taxable year—

* * * * * * * * * * *

(2)

* * * * * * * * * * *

(B) the sum of (i) the amount of the policyholders' share of tax-exempt [1]*interest and the amount of the policyholder's share of the increase for the taxable year in policy cash values (within the meaning of section 805(a)(4)(F)) of life insurance policies and annuity and endowment contracts to which section 264(f) applies.* plus (ii) any excess described in section 809(a)(2) for the taxable year,

such excess shall be included in gross income under section 803(a)(2).

(b) Increase treated as deduction. If for any taxable year—

(1)

* * * * * * * * * * *

(B) the sum of (i) the amount of the policyholders' share of tax-exempt [2]*interest and the amount of the policyholder's share of the increase for the taxable year in policy cash values (within the meaning of section 805(a)(4)(F)) of life insurance policies and annuity and endowment contracts to which section 264(f) applies,* plus (ii) any excess described in section 809(a)(2) for the taxable year, exceeds

* * * * * * * * * * *

[Endnote Code Sec. 807]

Matter in *italics* in Code Sec. 807(a)(2)(B) and Code Sec. 807(b)(1)(B) added by Sec. 1084(b)(2)(A) [sic (d)(2)(A)] and (b)(2)(B) [sic (d)(2)(B)] of the Taxpayer Relief Act of 1997, H.R. 2014, 8/5/97, which struck out:
 1. "interest,"
 2. "interest,"
Effective Date (Sec. 1084(d) [sic (f), H.R. 2014, 8/5/97. Sec. 1084(d) [sic (f), H.R. 2014, 8/5/97, reads as follows:
 "(d) [sic (f)] Effective date. The amendments made by this section shall apply to contracts issued after June 8, 1997, in taxable years ending after such date. For purposes of the preceding sentence, any material increase in the death benefit or other material change in the contract shall be treated as a new contract but the addition of covered lives shall be treated as a new contract only with respect to such additional covered lives. For purposes of this subsection, an increase in the death benefit under a policy or contract issued in connection with a lapse described in section 501(d)(2) of the Health Insurance Portability and Accountability Act of 1996 shall not be treated as a new contract."

[¶ 3128]   Code Sec. 812.   Definition of company's share and policyholders' share.

* * * * * * * * * * *

(d) Gross investment income. For purposes of this section, the term "gross investment income" means the sum of the following:

(1) Interest, etc. The gross amount of income from—

* * * * * * * * * * *

(B) the entering into of any lease, mortgage, or other instrument or agreement from which the life insurance company derives interest, rents, or royalties,[1]

(C) the alteration or termination of any instrument or agreement described in subparagraph (B)[2], *and*

[3]*(D) the increase for any taxable year in the policy cash values (within the meaning of section 805(a)(4)(F)) of life insurance policies and annuity and endowment contracts to which section 264(f) applies.*

* * * * * * * * * * *

[Endnote Code Sec. 812]

Matter in *italics* in Code Sec. 812(d)(1)(B), Code Sec. 812(d)(1)(C) and Code Sec. 812(d)(1)(D) added by Sec. 1084(b)(5) [sic (d)(5)] of the Taxpayer Relief Act of 1997, H.R. 2014, 8/5/97, which struck out:
 1. "and"
 2. "."
 3. added subpara. (d)(1)(D)
Effective Date (Sec. 1084(d) [sic (f)], H.R. 2014, 8/5/97) reads as follows:
 "(d) [sic (f)] Effective date. The amendments made by this section shall apply to contracts issued after June 8, 1997, in taxable years ending after such date. For purposes of the preceding sentence, any material increase in the death benefit or other material change in the contract shall be treated as a new contract but the addition of covered lives shall be treated as a new contract only with respect to such additional covered lives. For purposes of this subsection, an increase in the death benefit under a policy or contract issued in connection with a lapse described in section 501(d)(2) of the Health Insurance Portability and Accountability Act of 1996 shall not be treated as a new contract."

[¶ 3129]   Code Sec. 814.   Contiguous country branches of domestic life insurance companies.

* * * * * * * * * * * * *

(h) Special rule for domestic stock life insurance companies. At the election of a domestic stock life insurance company which has a contiguous country life insurance branch described in subsection (b) (without regard to the mutual requirement in subsection (b)(3)), the assets of such branch may be transferred to a foreign corporation organized under the laws of the contiguous country without the application of section 367[1]. Subsection (a) shall apply to the stock of such foreign corporation as if such domestic company were a mutual company and as if the stock were an item described in subsection (c). Subsection (e)(2) shall apply to amounts transferred or credited to such domestic company as if such domestic company and such foreign corporation constituted one domestic mutual life insurance company. The insurance contracts which may be transferred pursuant to this subsection shall include only those which are similar to the types of insurance contracts issued by a mutual life insurance company. Notwithstanding the first sentence of this subsection, if the aggregate fair market value of the invested assets and tangible property which are separately accounted for by the domestic life insurance company in the branch account exceeds the aggregate adjusted basis of such assets for purposes of determining gain, the domestic life insurance company shall be deemed to have sold all such assets on the first day of the taxable year for which the election under this subsection applies and the net gain shall be recognized to the domestic life insurance company on the deemed sale, but not in excess of the proportion of such net gain which equals the proportion which the aggregate fair market value of such assets which are transferred pursuant to this subsection is of the aggregate fair market value of all such assets.

[Endnote Code Sec. 814]

   Matter in Code Sec. 814(h) deleted by Sec. 1131(c)(1)[sic (d)(1)] of the Taxpayer Relief Act of 1997, H.R. 2014, 8/5/97, which struck out:
   1. "or 1491"
Effective Date (Sec. 1131(d)[sic (e)], H.R. 2014, 8/5/97) effective 8/5/97.

[¶ 3130]   Code Sec. 817.   Treatment of variable contracts.

* * * * * * * * * * * *

(h) Treatment of certain nondiversified contracts.

* * * * * * * * * * * * *

   (2) Safe harbor for diversification. A segregated asset account shall be treated as meeting the requirements of paragraph (1) for any quarter of a taxable year if as of the close of such quarter—

      (A) it meets the requirements of section [1]*851(b)(3)*, and

      (B) no more than 55 percent of the value of the total assets of the account are assets described in section [2]*851(b)(3)(A)(i)*.

* * * * * * * * * * * *

[Endnote Code Sec. 817]

   Matter in *italics* in Code Sec. 817(h)(2)(A) and Code Sec. 817(h)(2)(B) added by Secs. 1271(b)(8)(A) and (B) of the Taxpayer Relief Act of 1997, H.R. 2014, 8/5/97, which struck out:
   1. "851(b)(4)"
   2. "851(b)(4)(A)(i)"
Effective Date (Sec. 1271(c), H.R. 2014, 8/5/97) effective for tax. yrs. begin. after 8/5/97.

[¶ 3131]   Code Sec. 832.   **Insurance company taxable income.**

* * * * * * * * * * *

(b) **Definitions.** In the case of an insurance company subject to the tax imposed by section 831—

* * * * * * * * * * *

(5) **Losses incurred.**

* * * * * * * * * * *

(B) Reduction of deduction. The amount which would (but for this subparagraph) be taken into account under subparagraph (A) shall be reduced by an amount equal to 15 percent of the sum of—

(i) tax-exempt interest received or accrued during such taxable year,[1]

(ii) the aggregate amount of deductions provided by sections 243, 244, and 245 for—

(I) dividends (other than 100 percent dividends) received during the taxable year, and

(II) 100 percent dividends received during the taxable year to the extent attributable (directly or indirectly) to prorated amounts[2], *and*

[3]*(iii) the increase for the taxable year in policy cash values (within the meaning of section 805(a)(5)(F)) of life insurance policies and annuity and endowment contracts to which section 264(f) applies.*

In the case of a 100 percent dividend paid by an insurance company, the portion attributable to prorated amounts shall be determined under subparagraph (E)(ii).

* * * * * * * * * * *

[Endnote Code Sec. 832]

Matter in *italics* in Code Sec. 832(b)(5)(B)(i), Code Sec. 832(b)(5)(B)(ii), and Code Sec. 832(b)(5)(B)(iii) added by Sec. 1084(b)(4)[sic (d)(4)] of the Taxpayer Relief Act of 1997, H.R. 2014, 8/5/97, which struck out:

1. "and"

2. "."

3. added clause (b)(5)(B)(iii)

Effective Date (Sec. 1084(d)[sic (f)], H.R. 2014, 8/5/97) effective as provided in Sec. 1063(d)[sic (f)] of this Act, which reads:

"(d) Effective date.—The amendments made by this section shall apply to contracts issued after June 8, 1997, in taxable years ending after such date. For purposes of the preceding sentence, any material increase in the death benefit or other material change in the contract shall be treated as a new contract but the addition of covered lives shall be treated as a new contract only with respect to such additional covered lives. For purposes of this subsection, an increase in the death benefit under a policy or contract issued in connection with a lapse described in section 501(d)(2) of the Health Insurance Portability and Accountability Act of 1996 shall not be treated as a new contract."

[¶ 3132]   Code Sec. 833.   **Treatment of blue cross and blue shield organizations, etc.**

* * * * * * * * * * *

(b) **Amount of deduction.**

(1) **In general.** Except as provided in paragraph (2), the deduction determined under this subsection for any taxable year is the excess (if any) of—

(A) 25 percent of the sum of—

(i) the claims incurred during the taxable year [1]*and liabilities incurred during the taxable year under cost-plus contracts,* and

(ii) the expenses incurred during the taxable year in connection with the administration, adjustment, or settlement of claims [2]*or in connection with the administration of cost-plus contracts,* over

* * * * * * * * * * *

[For analysis, see ¶ 1106. For text of Committee Report see ¶ 5387].

[Endnote Code Sec. 833]

Matter in *italics* in Code Sec. 833(b)(1)(A)(i) and Code Sec. 833(b)(1)(A)(ii) added by Sec. 1604(d)(2)(A)(i) and (ii) of the Taxpayer Relief Act of 1997, H.R. 2014, 8/5/97.

1. added matter in clause (b)(1)(A)(i)
2. added matter in clause (b)(1)(A)(ii)

Effective Date (Sec. 1604(d)(2)(B), H.R. 2014, 8/5/97) effective for tax. yrs. begin. after 12/31/86.

[¶ 3133]   Code Sec. 851.   Definition of regulated investment company.

* * * * * * * * * * *

(b) Limitations. A corporation shall not be considered a regulated investment company for any taxable year unless—

* * * * * * * * * * *

(2) at least 90 percent of its gross income is derived from dividends, interest, payments with respect to securities loans (as defined in section 512(a)(5)), and gains from the sale or other disposition of stock or securities (as defined in section 2(a)(36) of the Investment Company Act of 1940, as amended) or foreign currencies, or other income (including but not limited to gains from options, futures, or forward contracts) derived with respect to its business of investing in such stock, securities, or currencies; [1]*and*

[2]*(3)* at the close of each quarter of the taxable year—

(A) at least 50 percent of the value of its total assets is represented by—

(i) cash and cash items (including receivables), Government securities and securities of other regulated investment companies, and

(ii) other securities for purposes of this calculation limited, except and to the extent provided in subsection (e), in respect of any one issuer to an amount not greater in value than 5 percent of the value of the total assets of the taxpayer and to not more than 10 percent of the outstanding voting securities of such issuer, and

(B) not more than 25 percent of the value of its total assets is invested in the securities (other than Government securities or the securities of other regulated investment companies) of any one issuer, or of two or more issuers which the taxpayer controls and which are determined, under regulations prescribed by the Secretary, to be engaged in the same or similar trades or businesses or related trades or businesses.

For purposes of paragraph (2), there shall be treated as dividends amounts included in gross income under section 951(a)(1)(A)(i) or 1293(a) for the taxable year to the extent that, under section 959(a)(1) or 1293(c) (as the case may be), there is a distribution out of the earnings and profits of the taxable year which are attributable to the amounts so included. For purposes of paragraph (2), the Secretary may by regulation exclude from qualifying income foreign currency gains which are not directly related to the company's principal business of investing in stock or securities (or options and futures with respect to stock or securities). For purposes of [3]*paragraph (2),* amounts excludable from gross income under section 103(a) shall be treated as included in gross income. Income derived from a partnership or trust shall be treated as described in paragraph (2) only to the extent such income is attributable to items of income of the partnership or trust (as the case may be) which would be described in paragraph (2) if realized by the regulated investment company in the same manner as realized by the partnership or trust.[4]

(c) Rules applicable to [5]*subsection (b)(3).* For purposes of [6]*subsection (b)(3)* and this subsection—

(1) In ascertaining the value of the taxpayer's investment in the securities of an issuer, for the purposes of subparagraph (B), there shall be included its proper proportion of the investment of any other corporation, a member of a controlled group, in the securities of such issuer, as determined under regulations prescribed by the Secretary.

(2) The term "controls" means the ownership in a corporation of 20 percent or more of the total combined voting power of all classes of stock entitled to vote.

(3) The term "controlled group" means one or more chains of corporations connected through stock ownership with the taxpayer if—

(A) 20 percent or more of the total combined voting power of all classes of stock entitled to vote of each of the corporations (except the taxpayer) is owned directly by one or more of the other corporations, and

(B) the taxpayer owns directly 20 percent or more of the total combined voting power of all classes of stock entitled to vote, of at least one of the other corporations.

(4) The term "value" means, with respect to securities (other than those of majority-owned subsidiaries) for which market quotations are readily available, the market value of such securities; and with respect to other securities and assets, fair value as determined in good faith by the board of directors, except that in the case of securities of majority-owned subsidiaries which are investment companies such fair value shall not exceed market value or asset value, whichever is higher.

(5) All other terms shall have the same meaning as when used in the Investment Company Act of 1940, as amended.

(d) Determination of status. A corporation which meets the requirements of [7]subsections (b)(3) and (c) at the close of any quarter shall not lose its status as a regulated investment company because of a discrepancy during a subsequent quarter between the value of its various investments and such requirements unless such discrepancy exists immediately after the acquisition of any security or other property and is wholly or partly the result of such acquisition. A corporation which does not meet such requirements at the close of any quarter by reason of a discrepancy existing immediately after the acquisition of any security or other property which is wholly or partly the result of such acquisition during such quarter shall not lose its status for such quarter as a regulated investment company if such discrepancy is eliminated within 30 days after the close of such quarter and in such cases it shall be considered to have met such requirements at the close of such quarter for purposes of applying the preceding sentence.

(e) Investment companies furnishing capital to development corporations.

(1) General rule. If the Securities and Exchange Commission determines, in accordance with regulations issued by it, and certifies to the Secretary not earlier than 60 days prior to the close of the taxable year of a management company or a business development company described in subsection (a)(1), that such investment company is principally engaged in the furnishing of capital to other corporations which are principally engaged in the development or exploitation of inventions, technological improvements, new processes, or products not previously generally available, such investment company may, in the computation of 50 percent of the value of its assets under subparagraph (A) of [8]subsection (b)(3) for any quarter of such taxable year, include the value of any securities of an issuer, whether or not the investment company owns more than 10 percent of the outstanding voting securities of such issuer, the basis of which, when added to the basis of the investment company for securities of such issuer previously acquired, did not exceed 5 percent of the value of the total assets of the investment company at the time of the subsequent acquisition of securities. The preceding sentence shall not apply to the securities of an issuer if the investment company has continuously held any security of such issuer (or of any predecessor company of such issuer as determined under regulations prescribed by the Secretary) for 10 or more years preceding such quarter of such taxable year.

* * * * * * * * * * * *

(4) Definitions. The terms used in this subsection shall have the same meaning as in [9]subsections (b)(3) and (c) of this section.

* * * * * * * * * * * *

[10](g) Special rule for series funds.

(1) In general. In the case of a regulated investment company (within the meaning of subsection (a)) having more than one fund, each fund of such regulated investment company shall be treated as a separate corporation for purposes of this title (except with respect to the definitional requirement of subsection (a)).

(2) Fund defined. For purposes of paragraph (1) the term "fund" means a segregated port-folio of assets, the beneficial interests in which are owned by the holders of a class or series of stock of the regulated investment company that is preferred over all other classes or series in respect of such portfolio of assets. [11]

[For analysis, see ¶ 1715. For text of Committee Report see ¶ 5247].

[Endnote Code Sec. 851]

Matter in *italics* in Code Sec. 851(b)(2), Code Sec. 851(b)(3), Code Sec. 851(c), Code Sec. 851(d), Code Sec. 851(e)(1), Code Sec. 851(e)(4), and Code Sec. 851(g) added by Sec. 1271(a), (b)(1)-(7) of the Taxpayer Relief Act of 1997, H.R. 2014, 8/5/97, which struck out:

1. added matter in para. (b)(2)

2. "(3) less than 30 percent of its gross income is derived from the sale or disposition of any of the following which was held for less than 3 months:

"(A) stock or securities (as defined in section 2(a)(36) of the Investment Company Act of 1940, as amended),

"(B) options, futures, or forward contracts (other than options, futures, or forward contracts on foreign currencies), or

"(C) foreign currencies (or options, futures, or forward contracts on foreign currencies) but only if such currencies (or options, futures, or forward contracts) are not directly related to the company's principal business of investing in stock or se-curities (or options and futures with respect to stocks or securities), and"

"(4)"

3. "paragraphs (2) and (3)"

4. In the case of the taxable year in which a regulated investment company is completely liquidated, there shall not be taken into account under paragraph (3) any gain from the sale, exchange, or distribution of any property after the adoption of the plan of complete liquidation."

5. "subsection (b)(4)"

6. "subsection (b)(4)"

7. "subsections (b)(4)"

8. "subsection (b)(4)"

9. "subsections (b)(4)"

10. "(g) Treatment of certain hedging transactions.

"(1) In general. In the case of any designated hedge, for purposes of subsection (b)(3), increases (and decreases) during the period of the hedge in the value of positions which are part of such hedge shall be netted.

"(2) Designated hedge. For purposes of this subsection, there is a designated hedge where—

"(A) the taxpayer's risk of loss with respect to any position in property is reduced by reason of—

"(i) the taxpayer having an option to sell, being under a contractual obligation to sell, or having made (and not closed) a short sale of substantially identical property,

"(ii) the taxpayer being the grantor of an option to buy substantially identical property, or

"(iii) under regulations prescribed by the Secretary, the taxpayer holding 1 or more other positions, and

"(B) the positions which are part of the hedge are clearly identified by the taxpayer in the manner prescribed by regula-tions.

"(h)"

11. "(3) Special rule for abnormal redemptions.

"(A) In general. Any fund treated as a separate corporation under paragraph (1) shall not be disqualified under subsection (b)(3) for any taxable year by reason of sales resulting from abnormal redemptions on any day and occurring before the close of the 5th business day after such day if—

"(i) the sum of the percentages determined under subparagraph (B) for the abnormal redemptions on such day and for ab-normal redemptions on prior days during such taxable year exceeds 30 percent; and

"(ii) the regulated investment company of which such fund is a part would meet the requirements of subsection (b)(3) for such taxable year if all the funds which are part of such company were treated as a single company.

"(B) Abnormal redemptions. For purposes of subparagraph (A), the term 'abnormal redemptions' means redemptions oc-curring on any day if the net redemptions on such day exceed 1 percent of the fund's net asset value.

"(C) Determination of net asset value. For purposes of this paragraph, net asset value for any day shall be determined as of the close of the preceding day.

"(D) Limitation. For purposes of subparagraph (A), any sale or other disposition of stock or securities held less than 3 months occurring during any day shall be deemed to result from abnormal redemptions until the cumulative proceeds from such sales or dispositions occurring during such day, plus the cumulative net positive cash flow of the fund for preceding business days (if any) following the day with abnormal redemptions, exceed the amount of net redemptions on the day with abnormal redemptions."

Effective Date (Sec. 1271(c), H.R. 2014, 8/5/97) effective for tax. yrs. begin. after 8/5/97.

[¶ 3134] Code Sec. 852. Taxation of regulated investment companies and their share-holders.

* * * * * * * * * * * *

(b) Method of taxation of companies and shareholders.

* * * * * * * * * * * *

(3) Capital gains.

* * * * * * * * * * * *

(D) Treatment by shareholders of undistributed capital gains.

* * * * * * * * * * *

(iii) The adjusted basis of such shares in the hands of the shareholder shall be increased, with respect to the amounts required by this subparagraph to be included in computing his long-term capital gains, [1]*by the difference between the amount of such includible gains and the tax deemed paid by such shareholder in respect of such shares under clause (ii).*

* * * * * * * * * * *

CAUTION. Para. (b)(10) is effective for tax, yrs. of U.S. persons begin. after 12/31/97, and tax. yrs. of foreign corporations end. with or within such tax. yrs. of U.S. persons.

[2]*(10) Special rule for certain losses on stock in passive foreign investment company. To the extent provided in regulations, the taxable income of a regulated investment company (other than a company to which an election under section 4982(e)(4) applies) shall be computed without regard to any net reduction in the value of any stock of a passive foreign investment company with respect to which an election under section 1296(k) is in effect occurring after October 31 of the taxable year, and any such reduction shall be treated as occurring on the first day of the following taxable year.*

(c) Earnings and profits.

* * * * * * * * * * * *

CAUTION. Para. (c)(2), following, is effective before 1/1/98. For para. (c)(2), effective for tax, yrs. of U.S. persons begin. after 12/31/97, and tax. yrs. of foreign corporations end. with or within such tax. yrs. of U.S. persons, see below.

(2) Coordination with tax on undistributed income. For purposes of applying this chapter to distributions made by a regulated investment company with respect to any calendar year, the earnings and profits of such company shall be determined without regard to any net capital loss (or net foreign currency loss) attributable to transactions after October 31 of such year and with such other adjustments as the Secretary may by regulations prescribe. The preceding sentence shall apply—

(A) only to the extent that the amount distributed by the company with respect to the calendar year does not exceed the required distribution for such calendar year (as determined under section 4982 by substituting "100 percent" for each percentage set forth in section 4982(b)(1)), and

(B) except as provided in regulations, only if an election under section 4982(e)(4) is not in effect with respect to such company.

CAUTION. Para. (c)(2), following, is effective for tax, yrs. of U.S. persons begin. after 12/31/97, and tax. yrs. of foreign corporations end. with or within such tax. yrs. of U.S. persons. For para. (c)(2), effective before 1/1/98, see above.

(2) Coordination with tax on undistributed income. For purposes of applying this chapter to distributions made by a regulated investment company with respect to any calendar year, the earnings and profits of such company shall be determined without regard to any net capital loss (or net foreign currency loss) attributable to transactions after October 31 of such year[3], *without regard to any net reduction in the value of any stock of a passive foreign investment company with respect to which an election under section 1296(k) is in effect occurring after October 31 of such year,* and with such other adjustments as the Secretary may by regulations prescribe. The preceding sentence shall apply—

(A) only to the extent that the amount distributed by the company with respect to the calendar year does not exceed the required distribution for such calendar year (as determined under section 4982 by substituting "100 percent" for each percentage set forth in section 4982(b)(1)), and

(B) except as provided in regulations, only if an election under section 4982(e)(4) is not in effect with respect to such company.

* * * * * * * * * * * *

[For analysis, see ¶ 1702. For text of Committee Report see ¶ 5230].

[Endnote Code Sec. 852]

Matter in *italics* in Code Sec. 852(b)(3)(D)(iii) added by Sec. 1254(b)(2) of the Taxpayer Relief Act of 1997, H.R. 2014, 8/5/97, which struck out:

1. "by 65 percent of so much of such amounts as equals the amount subject to tax in accordance with section 1201(a)."
Effective Date (Sec. 1263, H.R. 2014, 8/5/97) effective for tax. yrs. begin. after 8/5/97.

Matter in *italics* in Code Sec. 852(b)(10) and Code Sec. 852(c)(2) added by Sec. 1254(c)(2) and (3), H.R. 2014, 8/5/97.
2. added para. (b)(10)
3. added matter in para. (c)(2)
Effective Date (Sec. 1124, H.R. 2014, 8/5/97) effective for tax, yrs. of U.S. persons begin. after 12/31/97, and tax. yrs. of foreign corporations end. with or within such tax. yrs. of U.S. persons.

[¶ 3135]   Code Sec. 853.   Foreign tax credit allowed to shareholders.

* * * * * * * * * * * *

(c) **Notice to shareholders.** The amounts to be treated by the shareholder, for purposes of subsection (b)(2), as his proportionate share of—

(1) taxes paid to any foreign country or possession of the United States, and

(2) gross income derived from sources within any foreign country or possession of the United States,

shall not exceed the amounts so designated by the company in a written notice mailed to its shareholders not later than 60 days after the close of its taxable year. [1]*Such notice shall also include the amount of such taxes which (without regard to the election under this section) would not be allowable as a credit under section 901(a) to the regulated investment company by reason of section 901(k).*

* * * * * * * * * * * *

[For analysis, see ¶ 1604. For text of Committee Report, see ¶ 5145.]

[Endnote Code Sec. 853]

Matter in *italics* in Code Sec. 853(c) added by Sec. 1053(b) of the Taxpayer Relief Act of 1997, H.R. 2014, 8/5/97.
1. added matter in subsec. (c)
Effective Date (Sec. 1053(c), H.R. 2014, 8/5/97) effective for dividends paid or accrued more than 30 days after 8/5/97.

[¶ 3136]   Code Sec. 856.   Definition of real estate investment trust.

(a) **In general.** For purposes of this title, the term "real estate investment trust" means a corporation, trust, or association—

* * * * * * * * * * * *

(6) [1]*subject to the provisions of subsection (k)*, which is not closely held (as determined under subsection (h)); and

* * * * * * * * * * * *

(c) **Limitations.** A corporation, trust, or association shall not be considered a real estate investment trust for any taxable year unless—

* * * * * * * * * * * *

(3) at least 75 percent of its gross income (excluding gross income from prohibited transactions) is derived from—

(A) rents from real property;

(B) interest on obligations secured by mortgages on real property or on interests in real property;

(C) gain from the sale or other disposition of real property (including interests in real property and interests in mortgages on real property) which is not property described in section 1221(1);

(D) dividends or other distributions on, and gain (other than gain from prohibited transactions) from the sale or other disposition of, transferable shares (or transferable certificates of beneficial interest) in other real estate investment trusts which meet the requirements of this part;

(E) abatements and refunds of taxes on real property;

(F) income and gain derived from foreclosure property (as defined in subsection (e));

(G) amounts (other than amounts the determination of which depends in whole or in part on the income or profits of any person) received or accrued as consideration for entering into agreements (i) to make loans secured by mortgages on real property or on interests in real property or (ii) to purchase or lease real property (including interests in real property and interests in mortgages on real property);

(H) gain from the sale or other disposition of a real estate asset which is not a prohibited transaction solely by reason of section 857(b)(6); and

(I) qualified temporary investment income; [2]and

[3](4) at the close of each quarter of the taxable year—

(A) at least 75 percent of the value of its total assets is represented by real estate assets, cash and cash items (including receivables), and Government securities; and

(B) not more than 25 percent of the value of its total assets is represented by securities (other than those includible under subparagraph (A)) for purposes of this calculation limited in respect of any one issuer to an amount not greater in value than 5 percent of the value of the total assets of the trust and to not more than 10 percent of the outstanding voting securities of such issuer.

A real estate investment trust which meets the requirements of this paragraph at the close of any quarter shall not lose its status as a real estate investment trust because of a discrepancy during a subsequent quarter between the value of its various investments and such requirements unless such discrepancy exists immediately after the acquisition of any security or other property and is wholly or partly the result of such acquisition. A real estate investment trust which does not meet such requirements at the close of any quarter by reason of a discrepancy existing immediately after the acquisition of any security or other property which is wholly or partly the result of such acquisition during such quarter shall not lose its status for such quarter as a real estate investment trust if such discrepancy is eliminated within 30 days after the close of such quarter and in such cases it shall be considered to have met such requirements at the close of such quarter for purposes of applying the preceding sentence.

[4](5) For purposes of this part—

(A) The term "value" means, with respect to securities for which market quotations are readily available, the market value of such securities; and with respect to other securities and assets, fair value as determined in good faith by the trustees, except that in the case of securities of real estate investment trusts such fair value shall not exceed market value or asset value, whichever is higher.

(B) The term "real estate assets" means real property (including interests in real property and interests in mortgages on real property) and shares (or transferable certificates of beneficial interest) in other real estate investment trusts which meet the requirements of this part. Such term also includes any property (not otherwise a real estate asset) attributable to the temporary investment of new capital, but only if such property is stock or a debt instrument, and only for the 1-year period beginning on the date the real estate trust receives such capital.

(C) The term "interests in real property" includes fee ownership and co-ownership of land or improvements thereon, leaseholds of land or improvements thereon, options to acquire land or improvements thereon, and options to acquire leaseholds of land or improvements thereon, but does not include mineral, oil, or gas royalty interests.

(D) Qualified temporary investment income.

(i) In general. The term "qualified temporary investment income" means any income which—

(I) is attributable to stock or a debt instrument (within the meaning of section 1275(a)(1)),

(II) is attributable to the temporary investment of new capital, and

(III) is received or accrued during the 1-year period beginning on the date on which the real estate investment trust receives such capital.

(ii) New capital. The term "new capital" means any amount received by the real estate investment trust—

(I) in exchange for stock (or certificates of beneficial interests) in such trust (other than amounts received pursuant to a dividend reinvestment plan), or

(II) in a public offering of debt obligations of such trust which have maturities of at least 5 years.

(E) A regular or residual interest in a REMIC shall be treated as a real estate asset, and any amount includible in gross income with respect to such an interest shall be treated as interest on an obligation secured by a mortgage on real property; except that, if less than 95 percent of the assets of such REMIC are real estate assets (determined as if the real estate investment trust held such assets), such real estate investment trust shall be treated as holding directly (and as receiving directly) its proportionate share of the assets and income of the REMIC. For purposes of determining whether any interest in a REMIC qualifies under the preceding sentence, any interest held by such REMIC in another REMIC shall be treated as a real estate asset under principles similar to the principles of the preceding sentence, except that, if such REMIC's are part of a tiered structure, they shall be treated as one REMIC for purposes of this subparagraph. The principles of the preceding provisions of this subparagraph shall apply to regular interests in a FASIT.

(F) All other terms shall have the same meaning as when used in the Investment Company Act of 1940, as amended (15 U.S.C. 80a-1 and following).

[5](G) Treatment of certain hedging instruments. Except to the extent provided by regulations, any—

(i) payment to a real estate investment trust under an interest rate swap or cap agreement, option, futures contract, forward rate agreement, or any similar financial instrument, entered into by the trust in a transaction to reduce the interest rate risks with respect to any indebtedness incurred or to be incurred by the trust to acquire or carry real estate assets, and

(ii) gain from the sale or other disposition of any such investment,
shall be treated as income qualifying under paragraph (2).

[6](6) A corporation, trust, or association which fails to meet the requirements of paragraph (2) or (3), or of both such paragraphs, for any taxable year shall nevertheless be considered to have satisfied the requirements of such paragraphs for such taxable year if—

(A) the nature and amount of each item of its gross income described in such paragraphs is set forth in a schedule attached to its income tax return for such taxable year;

(B) the inclusion of any incorrect information in the schedule referred to in subparagraph (A) is not due to fraud with intent to evade tax; and

(C) the failure to meet the requirements of paragraph (2) or (3), or of both such paragraphs, is due to reasonable cause and not due to willful neglect. [7]

(d) Rents from real property defined.

* * * * * * * * * * * *

(2) Amounts excluded. For purposes of paragraphs (2) and (3) of subsection (c), the term "rents from real property" does not include—

(A) except as provided in paragraphs (4) and (6), any amount received or accrued, directly or indirectly, with respect to any real or personal property, if the determination of such amount depends in whole or in part on the income or profits derived by any person from such property (except that any amount so received or accrued shall not be excluded from the term "rents from real property" solely by reason of being based on a fixed percentage or percentages of receipts or sales);

(B) any amount received or accrued directly or indirectly from any person if the real estate investment trust owns, directly or indirectly—

(i) in the case of any person which is a corporation, stock of such person possessing 10 percent or more of the total combined voting power of all classes of stock entitled to vote, or 10 percent or more of the total number of shares of all classes of stock of such person; or

(ii) in the case of any person which is not a corporation, an interest of 10 percent or more in the assets or net profits of such person; and

[8]*(C) any impermissible tenant service income (as defined in paragraph (7)).*

* * * * * * * * * * * *

(5) Constructive ownership of stock. For purposes of this subsection, the rules prescribed by section 318(a) for determining the ownership of stock shall apply in determining the ownership of stock, assets, or net profits of any person; [9]*except that—*

(A) "10 percent" shall be substituted for "50 percent" in subparagraph (C) of paragraphs (2) and (3) of section 318(a), and

(B) section 318(a)(3)(A) shall be applied in the case of a partnership by taking into account only partners who own (directly or indirectly) 25 percent or more of the capital interest, or the profits interest, in the partnership.

* * * * * * * * * * *

[10]*(7)* **Impermissible tenant service income.** *For purposes of paragraph (2)(C)—*

(A) In general. The term "impermissible tenant service income" means, with respect to any real or personal property, any amount received or accrued directly or indirectly by the real estate investment trust for—

(i) services furnished or rendered by the trust to the tenants of such property, or

(ii) managing or operating such property.

(B) Disqualification of all amounts where more than de minimis amount. If the amount described in subparagraph (A) with respect to a property for any taxable year exceeds 1 percent of all amounts received or accrued during such taxable year directly or indirectly by the real estate investment trust with respect to such property, the impermissible tenant service income of the trust with respect to the property shall include all such amounts.

(C) Exceptions. For purposes of subparagraph (A)—

(i) services furnished or rendered, or management or operation provided, through an independent contractor from whom the trust itself does not derive or receive any income shall not be treated as furnished, rendered, or provided by the trust, and

(ii) there shall not be taken into account any amount which would be excluded from unrelated business taxable income under section 512(b)(3) if received by an organization described in section 511(a)(2).

(D) Amount attributable to impermissible services. For purposes of subparagraph (A), the amount treated as received for any service (or management or operation) shall not be less than 150 percent of the direct cost of the trust in furnishing or rendering the service (or providing the management or operation).

(E) Coordination with limitations. For purposes of paragraphs (2) and (3) of subsection (c), amounts described in subparagraph (A) shall be included in the gross income of the corporation, trust, or association.

(e) Special rules for foreclosure property.

(1) Foreclosure property defined. For purposes of this part, the term "foreclosure property" means any real property (including interests in real property), and any personal property incident to such real property, acquired by the real estate investment trust as the result of such trust having bid in such property at foreclosure, or having otherwise reduced such property to ownership or possession by agreement or process of law, after there was default (or default was imminent) on a lease of such property or on an indebtedness which such property secured. Such term does not include property acquired by the real estate investment trust as a result of indebtedness arising from the sale or other disposition of property of the trust described in section 1221(1) which was not originally acquired as foreclosure property.

(2) **Grace period.** Except as provided in paragraph (3), property shall cease to be foreclosure property with respect to the real estate investment trust [11] *as of the close of the 3d taxable year following the taxable year in which the trust acquired such property.*

(3) **Extensions.** If the real estate investment trust establishes to the satisfaction of the Secretary that an extension of the grace period is necessary for the orderly liquidation of the trust's interests in such property, the Secretary may grant one [12] *extension* of the grace period for such property. [13] *Any such extension shall not extend the grace period beyond the close of the 3d taxable year following the last taxable year in the period under paragraph (2).*

(4) **Termination of grace period in certain cases.** Any foreclosure property shall cease to be such on the first day (occurring on or after the day on which the real estate investment trust acquired the property) on which—

(A) a lease is entered into with respect to such property which, by its terms, will give rise to income which is not described in subsection (c)(3) (other than subparagraph (F) of such subsection), or any amount is received or accrued, directly or indirectly, pursuant to a lease entered into on or after such day which is not described in such subsection,

(B) any construction takes place on such property (other than completion of a building, or completion of any other improvement, where more than 10 percent of the construction of such building or other improvement was completed before default became imminent), or

(C) if such day is more than 90 days after the day on which such property was acquired by the real estate investment trust and the property is used in a trade or business which is conducted by the trust (other than through an independent contractor (within the meaning of section (d)(3)) from whom the trust itself does not derive or receive any income).

[14] *For purposes of subparagraph (C), property shall not be treated as used in a trade or business by reason of any activities of the real estate investment trust with respect to such property to the extent that such activities would not result in amounts received or accrued, directly or indirectly, with respect to such property being treated as other than rents from real property.*

(5) **Taxpayer must make election.** Property shall be treated as foreclosure property for purposes of this part only if the real estate investment trust so elects (in the manner provided in regulations prescribed by the Secretary) on or before the due date (including any extensions of time) for filing its return of tax under this chapter for the taxable year in which such trust acquires such property. [15] *A real estate investment trust may revoke any such election for a taxable year by filing the revocation (in the manner provided by the Secretary) on or before the due date (including any extension of time) for filing its return of tax under this chapter for the taxable year. If a trust revokes an election for any property, no election may be made by the trust under this paragraph with respect to the property for any subsequent taxable year.*

* * * * * * * * * * * *

(i) Treatment of certain wholly owned subsidiaries.

(1) **In general.** For purposes of this title—

(A) a corporation which is a qualified REIT subsidiary shall not be treated as a separate corporation, and

(B) all assets, liabilities, and items of income, deduction, and credit of a qualified REIT subsidiary shall be treated as assets, liabilities, and such items (as the case may be) of the real estate investment trust.

(2) **Qualified REIT subsidiary.** For purposes of this subsection, the term "qualified REIT subsidiary" means any corporation if 100 percent of the stock of such corporation is held by the real estate investment trust[16].

* * * * * * * * * * * *

(j) Treatment of shared appreciation mortgages.

(1) In general. Solely for purposes of subsection (c) of this section and section 857(b)(6), any income derived from a shared appreciation provision shall be treated as gain recognized on the sale of the secured property.

* * * * * * * * * * *

[17]**(4) Coordination with 4-year holding period.**

(A) In general. For purposes of section 857(b)(6)(C), if a real estate investment trust is treated as having sold secured property under paragraph (3)(A), the trust shall be treated as having held such property for at least 4 years if—

(i) the secured property is sold or otherwise disposed of pursuant to a case under title 11 of the United States Code,

(ii) the seller is under the jurisdiction of the court in such case, and

(iii) the disposition is required by the court or is pursuant to a plan approved by the court.

(B) Exception. Subparagraph (A) shall not apply if—

(i) the secured property was acquired by the seller with the intent to evict or foreclose, or

(ii) the trust knew or had reason to know that default on the obligation described in paragraph (5)(A) would occur.

[18]**(5) Definitions.** For purposes of this subsection—

(A) Shared appreciation provision. The term "shared appreciation provision" means any provision—

(i) which is in connection with an obligation which is held by the real estate investment trust and is secured by an interest in real property, and

(ii) which entitles the real estate investment trust to receive a specified portion of any gain realized on the sale or exchange of such real property (or of any gain which would be realized if the property were sold on a specified date) [19]*or appreciation in value as of any specified date.*

(B) Secured property. The term "secured property" means the real property referred to in subparagraph (A).

[20]*(k) Requirement that entity not be closely held treated as met in certain cases. A corporation, trust, or association—*

(1) which for a taxable year meets the requirements of section 857(f)(1), and

(2) which does not know, or exercising reasonable diligence would not have known, whether the entity failed to meet the requirement of subsection (a)(6),

shall be treated as having met the requirement of subsection (a)(6) for the taxable year.

[For analysis, see ¶ 1704, ¶ 1705, ¶ 1706, ¶ 1708, ¶ 1709, ¶ 1711, ¶ 1712, ¶ 1713. For text of Committee Report, see ¶ 5230.]

[Endnote Code Sec. 856]

Matter in *italics* in Code Sec. 856(a)(6), Code Sec. 856(c)(3), Code Sec. 856(c)(4), Code Sec. 856(c)(5), and Code Sec. 856(c)(5)(G) was added by Sec. 1251(b)(2), 1255(a)(1)-(3) and 1258 of the Taxpayer Relief Act of 1997, H.R. 2014, 8/5/97, which struck out:

1. added matter in para. (a)(6)

2. added matter in subpara. (c)(3)(I)

3. "(4) less than 30 percent of its gross income is derived from the sale or other disposition of—

"(A) stock or securities held for less than 1 year;

"(B) property in a transaction which is a prohibited transaction; and

"(C) real property (including interests in real property and interests in mortgages on real property) held for less than 4 years other than—

"(i) property compulsorily or involuntarily converted within the meaning of section 1033, and

"(ii) property which is foreclosure property within the definition of section 856(e); and

"(5)"

4. "(6)"

"(G) Treatment of certain interest rate agreements. Except to the extent provided by regulations, any—

"(i) payment to a real estate investment trust under a bona fide interest rate swap or cap agreement entered into by the real estate investment trust to hedge any variable rate indebtedness of such trust incurred or to be incurred to acquire or carry real estate assets, and

"(ii) any gain from the sale or other disposition of such agreement,

shall be treated as income qualifying under paragraph (2)*

The principles of the preceding provisions of this subparagraph shall apply to regular interests in a FASIT."

Effective Date (Sec. 1263, H.R. 2014, 8/5/97) effective for tax. yrs. begin. after 8/5/97.

Matter in Code Sec. 856(c)(5)(G) was deleted by Sec. 1255(b)(1), H.R. 2014, 8/5/97, which struck out:

*. "and such agreement shall be treated as a security for purposes of paragraph (4)(A)"

Effective Date (Sec. 1263, H.R. 2014, 8/5/97) effective for tax. yrs. begin. after 8/5/97.

Matter in *italics* in Code Sec. 856(c)(6), Code Sec. 856(c)(7), Code Sec. 856(d)(2)(C), Code Sec. 856(d)(5), Code Sec. 856(d)(7), Code Sec. 856(e)(2), Code Sec. 856(e)(3), Code Sec. 856(e)(4), Code Sec. 856(e)(5), Code Sec. 856(i)(2), Code Sec. 856(j)(4), Code Sec. 856(j)(5), Code Sec. 856(j)(5)(A)(ii) and Code Sec. 856(k) was added by Sec. 1251(b)(1), 1252(a) and (b), 1253, 1255(a)(3), 1257(a)(1), (a)(2)(A), (a)(2)(B), (b) and (c), 1261(a) and (b), and 1262 of the Taxpayer Relief Act of 1997, H.R. 2014, 8/5/97, which struck out:

6. "(7)"

7. "(8) Treatment of liquidating gains. In the case of the taxable year in which a real estate investment trust is completely liquidated, there shall not be taken into account under paragraph (4) any gain from the sale, exchange, or distribution of any property after the adoption of the plan of complete liquidation."

8. "(C) any amount received or accrued, directly or indirectly, with respect to any real or personal property if the real estate investment trust furnishes or renders services to the tenants of such property, or manages or operates such property, other than through an independent contractor from whom the trust itself does not derive or receive any income.

Subparagraph (C) shall not apply with respect to any amount if such amount would be excluded from unrelated business taxable income under section 512(b)(3) if received by an organization described in section 511(a)(2)."

9. "except that '10 percent' shall be substituted for '50 percent' in subparagraph (C) of section 318(a)(2) and 318(a)(3)."

10. added paragraph (d)(7)

11. "on the date which is 2 years after the date the trust acquired such property"

12. "or more extensions"

13. "Any such extension shall not extend the grace period beyond the date which is 6 years after the date such trust acquired such property."

14. added matter in paragraph (e)(4)

15. "Any such election shall be irrevocable."

16. "at all times during the period such corporation was in existence"

17. added paragraph (j)(4)

18. "(4)"

19. added matter in clause (j)(5)(A)(ii)

20. added subsection (k)

Effective Date (Sec. 1263, H.R. 2014, 8/5/97) effective for tax. yrs. begin. after 8/5/97.

[¶ 3137] Code Sec. 857.   Taxation of real estate investment trusts and their beneficiaries.

(a) **Requirements applicable to real estate investment trusts.** The provisions of this part (other than subsection (d) of this section and subsection (g) of section 856) shall not apply to a real estate investment trust for a taxable year unless—

(1) the deduction for dividends paid during the taxable year (as defined in section 561, but determined without regard to capital gains dividends) equals or exceeds—

(A) the sum of—

(i) 95 percent (90 percent for taxable years beginning before January 1, 1980) of the real estate investment trust taxable income for the taxable year (determined without regard to the deduction for dividends paid (as defined in section 561) and by excluding any net capital gain); and

(ii) 95 percent (90 percent for taxable years beginning before January 1, 1980) of the excess of the net income from foreclosure property over the tax imposed on such income by subsection (b)(4)(A); minus

(B) any excess noncash income (as determined under subsection (e)); and

[1](2) either—

(A) the provisions of this part apply to the real estate investment trust for all taxable years beginning after February 28, 1986, or

(B) as of the close of the taxable year, the real estate investment trust has no earnings and profits accumulated in any non-REIT year.

For purposes of the preceding sentence, the term "non-REIT year" means any taxable year to which the provisions of this part did not apply with respect to the entity.

The Secretary may waive the requirements of paragraph (1) for any taxable year if the real estate investment trust establishes to the satisfaction of the Secretary that it was unable to meet such requirements by reason of distributions previously made to meet the requirements of section 4981.

(b) Method of taxation of real estate investment trusts and holders of shares or certificates of beneficial interest.

(1) Imposition of tax on real estate investment trusts. There is hereby imposed for each taxable year on the real estate investment trust taxable income of every real estate investment trust a tax computed as provided in section 11, as though the real estate investment trust taxable income were the taxable income referred to in section 11.

(2) Real estate investment trust taxable income. For purposes of this part, the term "real estate investment trust taxable income" means the taxable income of the real estate investment trust, adjusted as follows:

(A) The deductions for corporations provided in part VIII (except section 248) of subchapter B (section 241 and following, relating to the deduction for dividends received, etc.) shall not be allowed.

(B) The deduction for dividends paid (as defined in section 561) shall be allowed, but shall be computed without regard to that portion of such deduction which is attributable to the amount excluded under subparagraph (D).

(C) The taxable income shall be computed without regard to section 443(b) (relating to computation of tax on change of annual accounting period).

(D) There shall be excluded an amount equal to the net income from foreclosure property.

(E) There shall be deducted an amount equal to the tax imposed by paragraph (5) for the taxable year.

(F) There shall be excluded an amount equal to any net income derived from prohibited transactions.

(3) Capital gains.

(A) Alternative tax in case of capital gains. If for any taxable year a real estate investment trust has a net capital gain, then, in lieu of the tax imposed by subsection (b)(1), there is hereby imposed a tax (if such tax is less than the tax imposed by such subsection) which shall consist of the sum of—

(i) a tax, computed as provided in subsection (b)(1), on the real estate investment trust taxable income (determined by excluding such net capital gain and by computing the deduction for dividends paid without regard to capital gain dividends), and

(ii) a tax determined at the rate provided in section 1201(a) on the excess of the net capital gain over the deduction for dividends paid (as defined in section 561) determined with reference to capital gains dividends only.

(B) Treatment of capital gain dividends by shareholders. A capital gain dividend shall be treated by the shareholders or holders of beneficial interests as a gain from the sale or exchange of a capital asset held for more than 1 year.

(C) Definition of capital gain dividend. For purposes of this part, a capital gain dividend is any dividend, or part thereof, which is designated by the real estate investment trust as a capital gain dividend in a written notice mailed to its shareholders or holders of beneficial interests at any time before the expiration of 30 days after the close of its taxable year (or mailed to its shareholders or holders of beneficial interests with its annual report for the taxable year); except that, if there is an increase in the excess described in subparagraph (A)(ii) of this paragraph for such year which results from a determination (as defined in section 860(e)), such designation may be made with respect to such increase at any time before the expiration of 120 days after the date of such determination. If the aggregate amount so designated with respect to a taxable year of the trust (including capital gain dividends paid after the close of the taxable year described in section 858) is greater than the net capital gain of the taxable year, the portion of each distribution which shall be a capital gain dividend shall be only that proportion of the amount so designated which such net capital gain bears to the aggregate amount so designated. For purposes of this subparagraph, the amount of the net capital gain for any taxable year which is not a calendar year shall be determined without regard to any net capital loss attributable to transactions after December 31 of such year, and any such net capital loss shall be treated as arising on the 1st day of the next taxable year. To the extent provided in regulations, the preceding sentence shall apply also for purposes of computing the taxable income of the real estate investment trust.

[2](D) *Treatment by shareholders of undistributed capital gains.*

(i) Every shareholder of a real estate investment trust at the close of the trust's taxable year shall include, in computing his long-term capital gains in his return for his taxable year in which the last day of the trust's taxable year falls, such amount as the trust shall designate in respect of such shares in a written notice mailed to its shareholders at any time prior to the expiration of 60 days after the close of its taxable year (or mailed to its shareholders or holders of beneficial interests with its annual report for the taxable year), but the amount so includible by any shareholder shall not exceed that part of the amount subjected to tax in subparagraph (A)(ii) which he would have received if all of such amount had been distributed as capital gain dividends by the trust to the holders of such shares at the close of its taxable year.

(ii) For purposes of this title, every such shareholder shall be deemed to have paid, for his taxable year under clause (i), the tax imposed by subparagraph (A)(ii) on the amounts required by this subparagraph to be included in respect of such shares in computing his long-term capital gains for that year; and such shareholders shall be allowed credit or refund as the case may be, for the tax so deemed to have been paid by him.

(iii) The adjusted basis of such shares in the hands of the holder shall be increased with respect to the amounts required by this subparagraph to be included in computing his long-term capital gains, by the difference between the amount of such includible gains and the tax deemed paid by such shareholder in respect of such shares under clause (ii).

(iv) In the event of such designation, the tax imposed by subparagraph (A)(ii) shall be paid by the real estate investment trust within 30 days after the close of its taxable year.

(v) The earnings and profits of such real estate investment trust, and the earnings and profits of any such shareholder which is a corporation, shall be appropriately adjusted in accordance with regulations prescribed by the Secretary.

(vi) As used in this subparagraph, the terms "shares" and "shareholders" shall include beneficial interests and holders of beneficial interests, respectively.

[3](E) Coordination with net operating loss provisions. For purposes of section 172, if a real estate investment trust pays capital gain dividends during any taxable year, the amount of the net capital gain for such taxable year (to the extent such gain does not exceed the amount of such capital gain dividends) shall be excluded in determining—

(i) the net operating loss for the taxable year, and

(ii) the amount of the net operating loss of any prior taxable year which may be carried through such taxable year under section 172(b)(2) to a succeeding taxable year.

(4) Income from foreclosure property.

(A) Imposition of tax. A tax is hereby imposed for each taxable year on the net income from foreclosure property of every real estate investment trust. Such tax shall be computed by multiplying the net income from foreclosure property by the highest rate of tax specified in section 11(b).

(B) Net income from foreclosure property. For purposes of this part, the term "net income from foreclosure property" means the excess of—

(i) gain from the sale or other disposition of foreclosure property described in section 1221(1) and the gross income for the taxable year derived from foreclosure property (as defined in section 856(e)), but only to the extent such gross income is not described in subparagraph (A), (B), (C), (D), (E), or (G) of section 856(c)(3), over

(ii) the deductions allowed by this chapter which are directly connected with the production of the income referred to in clause (i).

(5) Imposition of tax in case of failure to meet certain requirements. If [4]*section 856(c)(6)* applies to a real estate investment trust for any taxable year, there is hereby imposed on such trust a tax in an amount equal to the greater of—

(A) the excess of —

(i) 95 percent (90 percent in the case of taxable years beginning before January 1, 1980) of the gross income (excluding gross income from prohibited transactions) of the real estate investment trust, over

(ii) the amount of such gross income which is derived from sources referred to in section 856(c)(2); or

(B) the excess of—

(i) 75 percent of the gross income (excluding gross income from prohibited transactions) of the real estate investment trust, over

(ii) the amount of such gross income which is derived from sources referred to in section 856(c)(3),

multiplied by a fraction the numerator of which is the real estate investment trust taxable income for the taxable year (determined without regard to the deductions provided in paragraphs (2)(B) and (2)(E), without regard to any net operating loss deduction, and by excluding any net capital gain) and the denominator of which is the gross income for the taxable year (excluding gross income from prohibited transactions; gross income and gain from foreclosure property (as defined in section 856(e), but only to the extent such gross income and gain is not described in subparagraph (A), (B), (C), (D), (E), or (G) of section 856(c)(3)); long-term capital gain; and short-term capital gain to the extent of any short-term capital loss).

(6) Income from prohibited transactions.

(A) Imposition of tax. There is hereby imposed for each taxable year of every real estate investment trust a tax equal to 100 percent of the net income derived from prohibited transactions.

(B) Definitions. For purposes of this part—

(i) the term "net income derived from prohibited transactions" means the excess of the gain from prohibited transactions over the deductions allowed by this chapter which are directly connected with prohibited transactions;

(ii) in determining the amount of the net income derived from prohibited transactions, there shall not be taken into account any item attributable to any prohibited transaction for which there was a loss; and

(iii) the term "prohibited transaction" means a sale or other disposition of property described in section 1221(1) which is not foreclosure property.

(C) Certain sales not to constitute prohibited transactions. For purposes of this part, the term "prohibited transaction" does not include a sale of property which is a real estate asset as defined in [5]*section 856(c)(5)(B)* if—

(i) the trust has held the property for not less than 4 years;

(ii) aggregate expenditures made by the trust, or any partner of the trust, during the 4-year period preceding the date of sale which are includible in the basis of the property do not exceed 30 percent of the net selling price of the property;

(iii) (I) during the taxable year the trust does not make more than 7 sales of property [6]*(other than sales of foreclosure property or sales to which section 1033 applies)*, or (II) the aggregate adjusted bases (as determined for purposes of computing earnings and profits) of property [7]*(other than sales of foreclosure property or sales to which section 1033 applies)* sold during the taxable year does not exceed 10 percent of the aggregate bases (as so determined) of all of the assets of the trust as of the beginning of the taxable year;

(iv) in the case of property, which consists of land or improvements, not acquired through foreclosure (or deed in lieu of foreclosure), or lease termination, the trust has held the property for not less than 4 years for production of rental income; and

(v) if the requirement of clause (iii)(I) is not satisfied, substantially all of the marketing and development expenditures with respect to the property were made through an independent contractor (as defined in section 856(d)(3)) from whom the trust itself does not derive or receive any income.

(D) Special rules. In applying subparagraph (C) the following special rules apply:

(i) The holding period of property acquired through foreclosure (or deed in lieu of foreclosure), or termination of the lease, includes the period for which the trust held the loan which such property secured, or the lease of such property.

(ii) In the case of a property acquired through foreclosure (or deed in lieu of foreclosure), or termination of a lease, expenditures made by, or for the account of, the mortgagor or lessee after default became imminent will be regarded as made by the trust.

(iii) Expenditures (including expenditures regarded as made directly by the trust, or indirectly by any partner of the trust, under clause (ii)) will not be taken into account if they relate to foreclosure property and did not cause the property to lose its status as foreclosure property.

(iv) Expenditures will not be taken into account if they are made solely to comply with standards or requirements of any government or governmental authority having relevant jurisdiction, or if they are made to restore the property as a result of losses arising from fire, storm or other casualty.

(v) The term "expenditures" does not include advances on a loan made by the trust.

(vi) The sale of more than one property to one buyer as part of one transaction constitutes one sale.

(vii) The term "sale" does not include any transaction in which the net selling price is less than $10,000.

(E) Sales not meeting requirements. In determining whether or not any sale constitutes a "prohibited transaction" for purposes of subparagraph (A), the fact that such sale does not meet the requirements of subparagraph (C) of this paragraph shall not be taken into account; and such determination, in the case of a sale not meeting such requirements, shall be made as if subparagraphs (C) and (D) had not been enacted.

(7) **Loss on sale or exchange of stock held 6 months or less.**

(A) In general. If—

(i) [8]*subparagraph (B) or (D)* of paragraph (3) provides that any amount with respect to any share or beneficial interest is to be treated as a long-term capital gain, and

(ii) the taxpayer has held such share or interest for 6 months or less,

then any loss on the sale or exchange of such share or interest shall, to the extent of the amount described in clause (i), be treated as a long-term capital loss.

(B) Determination of holding period. For purposes of this paragraph, the rules of paragraphs (3) and (4) of section 246(c) shall apply in determining the period for which the taxpayer has held any share of stock or beneficial interest; except that "6 months" shall be substituted for the number of days specified in subparagraph (B) of section 246(c)(3).

(C) Exception for losses incurred under periodic liquidation plans. To the extent provided in regulations, subparagraph (A) shall not apply to any loss incurred on the sale or exchange of shares of stock of, or beneficial interest in, a real estate investment trust pursuant to a plan which provides for the periodic liquidation of such shares or interests.

(8) **Time certain dividends taken into account.** For purposes of this title, any dividend declared by a real estate investment trust in October, November, or December of any calendar year and payable to shareholders of record on a specified date in such a month shall be deemed—

(A) to have been received by each shareholder on December 31 of such calendar year, and

(B) to have been paid by such trust on December 31 of such calendar year (or, if earlier, as provided in section 858).

The preceding sentence shall apply only if such dividend is actually paid by the company during January of the following calendar year.

* * * * * * * * * * *

(d) Earnings and profits.

(1) In general. The earnings and profits of a real estate investment trust for any taxable year (but not its accumulated earnings) shall not be reduced by any amount which is not allowable in computing its taxable income for such taxable year. For purposes of this subsection, the term "real estate investment trust" includes a domestic corporation, trust, or association which is a real estate investment trust determined without regard to the requirements of subsection (a).

* * * * * * * * * * *

[9]*(3) Distributions to meet requirements of subsection (a)(2)(B). Any distribution which is made in order to comply with the requirements of subsection (a)(2)(B)—*

(A) shall be treated for purposes of this subsection and subsection (a)(2)(B) as made from the earliest accumulated earnings and profits (other than earnings and profits to which subsection (a)(2)(A) applies) rather than the most recently accumulated earnings and profits, and

(B) to the extent treated under subparagraph (A) as made from accumulated earnings and profits, shall not be treated as a distribution for purposes of subsection (b)(2)(B).

(e) Excess noncash income.

(1) In general. For purposes of subsection (a)(1)(B), the term "excess noncash income" means the excess (if any) of—

(A) the amount determined under paragraph (2) for the taxable year, over

(B) 5 percent of the real estate investment trust taxable income for the taxable year determined without regard to the deduction for dividends paid (as defined in section 561) and by excluding any net capital gain.

(2) Determination of amount. The amount determined under this paragraph for the taxable year is the sum of—

(A) the amount (if any) by which—

(i) the amounts includible in gross income under section 467 (relating to certain payments for the use of property or services), exceed

(ii) the amounts which would have been includible in gross income without regard to such section,

[10]*(B) any income on the disposition of a real estate asset if—*

(i) there is a determination (as defined in section 860(e)) that such income is not eligible for nonrecognition under section 1031, and

(ii) failure to meet the requirements of section 1031 was due to reasonable cause and not to willful neglect[11],

[12]*(C) the amount (if any) by which—*

(i) the amounts includible in gross income with respect to instruments to which section 860E(a) or 1272 applies, exceed

(ii) the amount of money and the fair market value of other property received during the taxable year under such instruments, and

(D) amounts includible in income by reason of cancellation of indebtedness.

[13]*(f) Real estate investment trusts to ascertain ownership.*

(1) In general. Each real estate investment trust shall each taxable year comply with regulations prescribed by the Secretary for the purposes of ascertaining the actual ownership of the outstanding shares, or certificates of beneficial interest, of such trust.

(2) Failure to comply.

(A) In general. If a real estate investment trust fails to comply with the requirements of paragraph (1) for a taxable year, such trust shall pay (on notice and demand by the Secretary and in the same manner as tax) a penalty of $25,000.

(B) *Intentional disregard. If any failure under paragraph (1) is due to intentional disregard of the requirement under paragraph (1), the penalty under subparagraph (A) shall be $50,000.*

(C) *Failure to comply after notice. The Secretary may require a real estate investment trust to take such actions as the Secretary determines appropriate to ascertain actual ownership if the trust fails to meet the requirements of paragraph (1). If the trust fails to take such actions, the trust shall pay (on notice and demand by the Secretary and in the same manner as tax) an additional penalty equal to the penalty determined under subparagraph (A) or (B), whichever is applicable.*

(D) *Reasonable cause. No penalty shall be imposed under this paragraph with respect to any failure if it is shown that such failure is due to reasonable cause and not to willful neglect.*

[14]*(g) Cross reference. For provisions relating to excise tax based on certain real estate investment trust taxable income not distributed during the taxable year, see section 4981.*

[For analysis, see ¶ 1701, ¶ 1703, ¶ 1707, ¶ 1710, ¶ 1714. For text of Committee Report, see ¶ 5230.]

[Endnote Code Sec. 857]

Matter in *italics* in Code Sec. 857(a)(2), Code Sec. 857(b)(3)(D), Code Sec. 857(b)(3)(E), Code Sec. 857(b)(5), Code Sec. 857(b)(6)(C), Code Sec. 857(b)(6)(C)(iii), Code Sec. 857(b)(7)(A)(i), Code Sec. 857(d)(3), Code Sec. 857(e)(2)(B), Code Sec. 857(e)(2)(C), Code Sec. 857(e)(2)(D), Code Sec. 857(f) and Code Sec. 857(g) added by Sec. 1251(a)(1) and (2), 1254(a) and (b)(1), 1255(b)(2) and (3), 1256, 1259(1)-(4), and 1260 of the Taxpayer Relief Act of 1997, H.R. 2014, 8/5/97, which struck out:

1. "(2) the real estate investment trust complies for such year with regulations prescribed by the Secretary for the purpose of ascertaining the actual ownership of the outstanding shares, or certificates of beneficial interest, of such trust, and "(3)"

2. added subpara. (b)(3)(D)

3. "(D)"

4. "section 856(c)(7)"

5. "section 856(c)(6)(B)"

6. "(other than foreclosure property)"

7. "(other than foreclosure property)"

8. "subparagraph (B)"

9. added para. (d)(3)

10. "(B) in the case of a real estate investment trust using the cash receipts and disbursements method of accounting, the amount (if any) by which—

"(i) the amounts includible in gross income with respect to instruments to which section 1274 (relating to certain debt instruments issued for property) applies, exceed

"(ii) the amount of money and the fair market value of other property received during the taxable year under such instruments; plus

"(C)"

11. "."

12. added subparas. (e)(2)(C) and (D)

13. added subsec. (f)

14. "(f)"

Effective Date (Sec. 1263, H.R. 2014, 8/5/97) effective for tax. yrs. begin. after 8/5/97.

[¶ 3138] Code Sec. 860L.

CAUTION.   Code Sec. 860L, following, is effective 9/1/97.

Definitions and other special rules.

(a) FASIT.

(1) In general. For purposes of this title, the terms "financial asset securitization investment trust" and "FASIT" mean any entity—

    (A) for which an election to be treated as a FASIT applies for the taxable year,

    (B) all of the interests in which are regular interests or the ownership interest,

    (C) which has only 1 ownership interest and such ownership interest is held directly by an eligible corporation,

(D) as of the close of the 3rd month beginning after the day of its formation and at all times thereafter, substantially all of the assets of which (including assets treated as held by the entity under section 860I(b)(2)) consist of permitted assets, and

(E) which is not described in section 851(a).

A rule similar to the rule of the last sentence of section 860D(a) shall apply for purposes of this paragraph.

(2) Eligible corporation. For purposes of paragraph (1)(C), the term "eligible corporation" means any domestic C corporation other than—

(A) a corporation which is exempt from, or is not subject to, tax under this chapter,

(B) an entity described in section 851(a) or 856(a),

(C) a REMIC, and

(D) an organization to which part I of subchapter T applies.

(3) Election. An entity (otherwise meeting the requirements of paragraph (1)) may elect to be treated as a FASIT. Except as provided in paragraph (5), such an election shall apply to the taxable year for which made and all subsequent taxable years unless revoked with the consent of the Secretary.

(4) Termination. If any entity ceases to be a FASIT at any time during the taxable year, such entity shall not be treated as a FASIT after the date of such ceasation. [sic]

(5) Inadvertent terminations, etc. Rules similar to the rules of section 860D(b)(2)(B) shall apply to inadvertent failures to qualify or remain qualified as a FASIT.

(6) Permitted assets not treated as interest in FASIT. Except as provided in regulations prescribed by the Secretary, any asset which is a permitted asset at the time acquired by a FASIT shall not be treated at any time as an interest in such FASIT.

(b) Interests in FASIT. For purposes of this part—

(1) Regular interest.

(A) In general. The term "regular interest" means any interest which is issued by a FASIT [1]*on or after the startup date* with fixed terms and which is designated as a regular interest if—

(i) such interest unconditionally entitles the holder to receive a specified principal amount (or other similar amount),

(ii) interest payments (or other similar amounts), if any, with respect to such interest are determined based on a fixed rate, or, except as otherwise provided by the Secretary, at a variable rate permitted under section 860G(a)(1)(B)(i),

(iii) such interest does not have a stated maturity (including options to renew) greater than 30 years (or such longer period as may be permitted by regulations),

(iv) the issue price of such interest does not exceed 125 percent of its stated principal amount, and

(v) the yield to maturity on such interest is less than the sum determined under section 163(i)(1)(B) with respect to such interest.

An interest shall not fail to meet the requirements of clause (i) merely because the timing (but not the amount) of the principal payments (or other similar amounts) may be contingent on the extent that payments on debt instruments held by the FASIT are made in advance of anticipated payments and on the amount of income from permitted assets.

(B) High-yield interests.

(i) In general. The term "regular interest" includes any high-yield interest.

(ii) High-yield interest. The term "high-yield interest" means any interest which would be described in subparagraph (A) but for—

(I) failing to meet the requirements of one or more of clauses (i), (iv), or (v) thereof, or

(II) failing to meet the requirement of clause (ii) thereof but only if interest payments (or other similar amounts), if any, with respect to such interest consist of a specified portion of the interest payments on permitted assets and such portion does not vary during the period such interest is outstanding.

(2) Ownership interest. The term "ownership interest" means the interest issued by a FASIT after the startup day which is designated as an ownership interest and which is not a regular interest.

(c) Permitted assets. For purposes of this part—

(1) In general. The term "permitted asset" means—

(A) cash or cash equivalents,

(B) any debt instrument (as defined in section 1275(a)(1)) under which interest payments (or other similar amounts), if any, at or before maturity meet the requirements applicable under clause (i) or (ii) of section 860G(a)(1)(B).

(C) foreclosure property,

(D) any asset—

(i) which is an interest rate or foreign currency notional principal contract, letter of credit, insurance, guarantee against payment defaults, or other similar instrument permitted by the Secretary, and

(ii) which is reasonably required to guarantee or hedge against the FASIT's risks associated with being the obligor on interests issued by the FASIT,

(E) contract rights to acquire debt instruments described in subparagraph (B) or assets described in subparagraph (D),

(F) any regular interest in another FASIT, and

(G) any regular interest in a REMIC.

(2) Debt issued by holder of ownership interest not permitted asset. The term "permitted asset" shall not include any debt instrument issued by the holder of the ownership interest in the FASIT or by any person related to such holder or any direct or indirect interest in such a debt instrument. The preceding sentence shall not apply to cash equivalents and to any other investment specified in regulations prescribed by the Secretary.

(3) Foreclosure property.

(A) In general. The term "foreclosure property" means property—

(i) which would be foreclosure property under section 856(e) (determined without regard to paragraph (5) thereof) if such property were real property acquired by a real estate investment trust, and

(ii) which is acquired in connection with the default or imminent default of a debt instrument held by the FASIT unless the security interest in such property was created for the principal purpose of permitting the FASIT to invest in such property.

Solely for purposes of subsection (a)(1), the determination of whether any property is foreclosure property shall be made without regard to section 856(e)(4).

(B) Authority to reduce grace period. In the case of property other than real property and other than personal property incident to real property, the Secretary may by regulation reduce for purposes of subparagraph (A) the periods otherwise applicable under paragraphs (2) and (3) of section 856(e).

(d) Startup day. For purposes of this part—

(1) In general. The term "startup day" means the date designated in the election under subsection (a)(3) as the startup day of the FASIT. Such day shall be the beginning of the first taxable year of the FASIT.

(2) Treatment of property held on startup day. All property held (or treated as held under [2]*section 860I(b)(2))* by an entity as of the startup day shall be treated as contributed to such entity on such day by the holder of the ownership interest in such entity.

(e) Tax on prohibited transactions.

(1) In general. There is hereby imposed for each taxable year of a FASIT a tax equal to 100 percent of the net income derived from prohibited transactions. Such tax shall be paid by the holder of the ownership interest in the FASIT.

(2) Prohibited transactions. For purposes of this part, the term "prohibited transaction" means—

(A) [3]*except as provided in paragraph (3),* the receipt of any income derived from any asset that is not a permitted asset,

(B) except as provided in paragraph (3), the disposition of any permitted asset [4]*other than foreclosure property,*

(C) the receipt of any income derived from any loan originated by the FASIT, and

(D) the receipt of any income representing a fee or other compensation for services (other than any fee received as compensation for a waiver, amendment, or consent under permitted assets (other than foreclosure property) held by the FASIT).

(3) Exception for income from certain dispositions.

(A) In general. Paragraph (2)(B) shall not apply to a disposition which would not be a prohibited transaction (as defined in section 860F(a)(2)) by reason of—

(i) clause (ii), (iii), or (iv) of section 860F(a)(2)(A), or

(ii) section 860F(a)(5),

[5]*if the FASIT were treated as a REMIC and permitted assets (other than cash or cash equivalents) were treated as qualified mortgages.*

(B) Substitution of debt instruments: reduction of overcollateralization. Paragraph (2)(B) shall not apply to—

(i) the substitution of a debt instrument described in subsection (c)(1)(B) for another debt instrument which is a permitted asset, or

(ii) the distribution of a debt instrument contributed by the holder of the ownership interest to such holder in order to reduce over-collateralization of the FASIT,

but only if a principal purpose of acquiring the debt instrument which is disposed of was not the recognition of gain (or the reduction of a loss) as a result of an increase in the market value of the debt instrument after its acquisition by the FASIT.

(C) Liquidation of class of regular interests. Paragraph (2)(B) shall not apply to the complete liquidation of any class of regular interests.

[6]*(D) Income from dispositions of former hedge assets. Paragraph (2)(A) shall not apply to income derived from the disposition of—*

(i) an asset which was described in subsection (c)(1)(D) when first acquired by the FASIT but on the date of such disposition was no longer described in subsection (c)(1)(D)(ii), or

(ii) a contract right to acquire an asset described in clause (i).

(4) Net income. For purposes of this subsection, net income shall be determined in accordance with section 860F(a)(3).

(f) Coordination with other provisions.

(1) Wash sales rules Rules similar to the rules of section 860F(d) shall apply to the ownership interest in a FASIT.

(2) Section 475. Except as provided by the Secretary by regulations, if any security which is sold or contributed to a FASIT by the holder of the ownership interest in such FASIT was required to be marked-to-market under section 475 by such holder, section 475 shall continue to apply to such security; except that in applying section 475 while such security is held by the FASIT, the fair market value of such security for purposes of section 475 shall not be less than its value under section 860I(d).

(g) Related person. For purposes of this part, a person (hereinafter in this subsection referred to as the "related person") is related to any person if—

(1) the related person bears a relationship to such person specified in section 267(b) or section 707(b)(1), or

(2) the related person and such person are engaged in trades or businesses under common control (within the meaning of subsections (a) and (b) of section 52).

For purposes of paragraph (1), in applying section 267(b) or 707(b)(1), "20 percent" shall be substituted for "50 percent".

(h) Regulations. The Secretary shall prescribe such regulations as may be necessary or appropriate to carry out the purposes of this part, including regulations to prevent the abuse of the purposes of this part through transactions which are not primarily related to securitization of debt instruments by a FASIT.

[For analysis, see ¶ 1718, ¶ 1719. For text of Committee Report, see ¶ 5366.]

[Endnote Code Sec. 860L]

Matter in *italics* in Code Sec. 860L(b)(1)(A), Code Sec. 860L(d)(2), Code Sec. 860L(e)(2)(A), Code Sec. 860L(e)(2)(B), Code Sec. 860L(e)(3)(A), and Code Sec. 860L(e)(3)(D) added by Sec. 1601(f)(6)(A)-(E) of the Taxpayer Relief Act of 1997, H.R. 2014, 8/5/97, which struck out:

1. "after the startup date"
2. "860I(c)(2)"
3. added matter in subpara. (e)(2)(A)
4. added matter in subpara. (e)(2)(B)
5. "if the FASIT were treated as a REMIC and debt instruments described in subsection (c)(1)(B) were treated as qualified mortgages."
6. added subpara. (e)(3)(D)

Effective Date (Sec. 1601(j)(1), H.R. 2014, 8/5/97) effective 9/1/97.

[¶ 3139]   Code Sec. 861.   Income from sources within the United States.

(a) Gross income from sources within United States. The following items of gross income shall be treated as income from sources within the United States:

* * * * * * * * * * * *

CAUTION.   Para. (a)(3), following, is effective for remuneration for services performed in tax. yrs. begin. before 1/1/98. For para. (a)(3) effective for remuneration for services performed in tax. yrs. begin. after 12/31/97, see below.

(3) Personal services. Compensation for labor or personal services performed in the United States; except that compensation for labor or services performed in the United States shall not be deemed to be income from sources within the United States if—

(A) the labor or services are performed by a nonresident alien individual temporarily present in the United States for a period or periods not exceeding a total of 90 days during the taxable year,

(B) such compensation does not exceed $3,000 in the aggregate, and

(C) the compensation is for labor or services performed as an employee of or under a contract with—

(i) a nonresident alien, foreign partnership, or foreign corporation, not engaged in trade or business within the United States, or

(ii) an individual who is a citizen or resident of the United States, a domestic partnership, or a domestic corporation, if such labor or services are performed for an office or place of business maintained in a foreign country or in a possession of the United States by such individual, partnership, or corporation.

CAUTION.   Para. (a)(3), following, is effective for remuneration for services performed in tax. yrs. begin. after 12/31/97. For para. (a)(3) effective for remuneration for services performed in tax. yrs. begin. before 1/1/98, see above.

(3) Personal services. Compensation for labor or personal services performed in the United States; except that compensation for labor or services performed in the United States shall not be deemed to be income from sources within the United States if—

(A) the labor or services are performed by a nonresident alien individual temporarily present in the United States for a period or periods not exceeding a total of 90 days during the taxable year,

(B) such compensation does not exceed $3,000 in the aggregate, and

(C) the compensation is for labor or services performed as an employee of or under a contract with—

(i) a nonresident alien, foreign partnership, or foreign corporation, not engaged in trade or business within the United States, or

(ii) an individual who is a citizen or resident of the United States, a domestic partnership, or a domestic corporation, if such labor or services are performed for an office or place of business maintained in a foreign country or in a possession of the United States by such individual, partnership, or corporation.

[1]*In addition, except for purposes of section 79 and 105 and subchapter D, compensation for labor or services performed in the United States shall not be deemed to be income from sources within the United States if the labor or services are performed by a nonresident alien individual in connection with the individual's temporary presence in the United States as a regular member of the crew of a foreign vessel engaged in transportation between the United States and a foreign country or a possession of the United States.*

* * * * * * * * * * *

[For analysis, see ¶ 1624. For text of Committee Report, see ¶ 5196.]

[Endnote Code Sec. 861]
    Matter in *italics* in Code Sec. 861(a)(3) added by Sec. 1174(a)(1) of the Taxpayer Relief Act of 1997, H.R. 2014, 8/5/97.
    1. added matter in para. (a)(3)
Effective Date (Sec. 1174(c)(1), H.R. 2014, 8/5/97) effective for remuneration for services performed in tax. yrs. begin. after 12/31/97.

[¶ 3140]   Code Sec. 863.   Special rules for determining source.

* * * * * * * * * * *

(c) Source rule for certain transportation income.
    (1) Transportation beginning and ending in the United States. All transportation income attributable to transportation which begins and ends in the United States shall be treated as derived from sources within the United States.
    (2) Other transportation having United States connection.
        (A) In general. 50 percent of all transportation income attributable to transportation which—
            (i) is not described in paragraph (1), and
            (ii) begins or ends in the United States, shall be treated as from sources in the United States.

CAUTION.   Subpara. (c)(2)(B), following, is effective for remuneration for services performed in tax. yrs. begin. before 1/1/98. For supara. (c)(2)(B) effective for remuneration for services performed in tax. yrs. begin. after 12/31/97, see below.

        (B) Special rule for personal service income. Subparagraph (A) shall not apply to any transportation income which is income derived from personal services performed by the taxpayer, unless such income is attributable to transportation which—
            (i) begins in the United States and ends in a possession of the United States, or
            (ii) begins in a possession of the United States and ends in the United States.

CAUTION.   Subpara. (c)(2)(B), following, is effective for remuneration for services performed in tax. yrs. begin. after 12/31/97. For supara. (c)(2)(B) effective for remuneration for services performed in tax. yrs. begin. before 1/1/98, see above.

        (B) Special rule for personal service income. Subparagraph (A) shall not apply to any transportation income which is income derived from personal services performed by the taxpayer, unless such income is attributable to transportation which—
            (i) begins in the United States and ends in a possession of the United States, or
            (ii) begins in a possession of the United States and ends in the United States.
        [1]*In the case of transportation income derived from, or in connection with, a vessel, this subparagraph shall only apply if the taxpayer is a citizen or resident alien.*

* * * * * * * * * * *

[For analysis, see ¶ 1624. For text of Committee Report, see ¶ 5196.]

[Endnote Code Sec. 863]
    Matter in *italics* in Code Sec. 863(c)(2)(B), added by Sec. 1174(a)(2) of the Taxpayer Relief Act of 1997, H.R. 2014, 8/5/97.
    1. added matter in subpara. (c)(2)(B)

Effective Date (Sec. 1174(c)(1), H.R. 2014, 8/5/97) effective for remuneration for services performed in tax. yrs. begin. after 12/31/97.

[¶ 3141]　Code Sec. 864.　　Definitions and special rules.

＊ ＊ ＊ ＊ ＊ ＊ ＊ ＊ ＊ ＊ ＊ ＊

(b) Trade or business within the United States. For purposes of this part, part II, and chapter 3, the term "trade or business within the United States" includes the performance of personal services within the United States at any time within the taxable year, but does not include—

(1) Performance of personal services for foreign employer. The performance of personal services—

(A) for a nonresident alien individual, foreign partnership, or foreign corporation, not engaged in trade or business within the United States, or

(B) for an office or place of business maintained in a foreign country or in a possession of the United States by an individual who is a citizen or resident of the United States or by a domestic partnership or a domestic corporation,

by a nonresident alien individual temporarily present in the United States for a period or periods not exceeding a total of 90 days during the taxable year and whose compensation for such services does not exceed in the aggregate $3,000.

(2) Trading in securities or commodities.

(A) Stocks and securities.

(i) In general. Trading in stocks or securities through a resident broker, commission agent, custodian, or other independent agent.

CAUTION.　　Clause (b)(2)(A)(ii), following, is effective for tax. yrs. begin. before 1/1/98. For clause (b)(2)(A)(ii) effective for tax. yrs. begin. after 12/31/97, see below.

(ii) Trading for taxpayer's own account. Trading in stocks or securities for the taxpayer's own account, whether by the taxpayer or his employees or through a resident broker, commission agent, custodian, or other agent, and whether or not any such employee or agent has discretionary authority to make decisions in effecting the transactions. This clause shall not apply in the case of a dealer in stocks or securities, or in the case of a corporation (other than a corporation which is, or but for section 542(c)(7), 542(c)(10), or 543(b)(1)(C) would be, a personal holding company) the principal business of which is trading in stocks or securities for its own account, if its principal office is in the United States.

CAUTION.　　Clause (b)(2)(A)(ii), following, is effective for tax. yrs. begin. after 12/31/97. For clause (b)(2)(A)(ii) effective for tax. yrs. begin. before 1/1/98, see above.

(ii) Trading for taxpayer's own account. Trading in stocks or securities for the taxpayer's own account, whether by the taxpayer or his employees or through a resident broker, commission agent, custodian, or other agent, and whether or not any such employee or agent has discretionary authority to make decisions in effecting the transactions. This clause shall not apply in the case of a dealer in stocks or securities.[1]

(B) Commodities.

(i) In general. Trading in commodities through a resident broker, commission agent, custodian, or other independent agent.

(ii) Trading for taxpayer's own account. Trading in commodities for the taxpayer's own account, whether by the taxpayer or his employees or through a resident broker, commission agent, custodian, or other agent, and whether or not any such employee or agent has discretionary authority to make decisions in effecting the transactions. This clause shall not apply in the case of a dealer in commodities.

(iii) Limitation. Clauses (i) and (ii) shall apply only if the commodities are of a kind customarily dealt in on an organized commodity exchange and if the transaction is of a kind customarily consummated at such place.

(C) Limitation. Subparagraphs (A)(i) and (B)(i) shall apply only if, at no time during the taxable year, the taxpayer has an office or other fixed place of business in the United States through which or by the direction of which the transactions in stocks or securities, or in commodities, as the case may be, are effected.

* * * * * * * * * * * *

[For analysis, see ¶ 1620. For text of Committee Report, see ¶ 5191.]

[Endnote Code Sec. 864]

Matter in Code Sec. 864(b)(2)(A)(ii) deleted by Sec. 1162(a) of the Taxpayer Relief Act of 1997, H.R. 2014, 8/5/97, which struck out:

1. ", or in the case of a corporation (other than a corporation which is, or but for section 542(c)(7), 542(c)(10), or 543(b)(1)(C) would be, a personal holding company) the principal business of which is trading in stocks or securities for its own account, if its principal office is in the United States."

Effective Date (Sec. 1162(b), H.R. 2014, 8/5/97) effective for tax. yrs. begin. after 12/31/97.

[¶ 3142]   Code Sec. 877.   Expatriation to avoid tax.

* * * * * * * * * * * *

(d) Special rules for source, etc. For purposes of subsection (b)—

* * * * * * * * * * * *

(2) Gain recognition on certain exchanges.

(A) In general. In the case of any exchange of property to which this paragraph applies, notwithstanding any other provision of this title, such property shall be treated as sold for its fair market value on the date of such exchange, and any gain shall be recognized for the taxable year which includes such date.

(B) Exchanges to which paragraph applies. This paragraph shall apply to any exchange during [1]*the 10-year period beginning on the date the individual loses United States citizenship* if—

(i) gain would not (but for this paragraph) be recognized on such exchange in whole or in part for purposes of this subtitle,

(ii) income derived from such property was from sources within the United States (or, if no income was so derived, would have been from such sources), and

(iii) income derived from the property acquired in the exchange would be from sources outside the United States.

(C) Exception. Subparagraph (A) shall not apply if the individual enters into an agreement with the Secretary which specifies that any income or gain derived from the property acquired in the exchange (or any other property which has a basis determined in whole or part by reference to such property during such 10-year period shall be treated as from sources within the United States. If the property transferred in the exchange is disposed of by the person acquiring such property, such agreement shall terminate and any gain which was not recognized by reason of such agreement shall be recognized as of the date of such disposition.

(D) Secretary may extend period. To the extent provided in regulations prescribed by the Secretary, subparagraph (B) shall be applied by substituting the 15-year period beginning 5 years before the loss of United States citizenship for the 10-year period referred to therein. [2]*In the case of any exchange occurring during such 5 years, any gain recognized under this subparagraph shall be recognized immediately after such loss of citizenship.*

(E) Secretary may require recognition of gain in certain cases. To the extent provided in regulations prescribed by the Secretary—

(i) the removal of appreciated tangible personal property from the United States, and

(ii) any other occurrence which (without recognition of gain) results in a change in the source of the income or gain) from property from sources within the United States to sources outside the United States,

shall be treated as an exchange to which this paragraph applies.

(3) Substantial diminishing of risks of ownership. For purposes of determining whether this section applies to any gain on the sale or exchange of any property the running of the 10-year period described in subsection (a) [3]*and the period applicable under paragraph (2)* shall be suspended for any period during which the individual's risk of loss with respect to the property is substantially diminished by—

(A) the holding of a put with respect to such property (or similar property),

(B) the holding by another person of a right to acquire the property, or

(C) a short sale or any other transaction.

(4) Treatment of property contributed to controlled foreign corporations.

(A) In general. If—

(i) an individual losing United States citizenship contributes property [4]*during the 10-year period beginning on the date the individual loses United States citizenship* to any corporation which, at the time of the contribution, is described in subparagraph (B), and

(ii) income derived from such property [5]*immediately before such contribution* was from sources within the United States (or, if no income was so derived, would have been from such sources),

[6]any income or gain on such property (or any other property which has a basis determined in whole or part by reference to such property) received or accrued by the corporation shall be treated as received or accrued directly by such individual and not by such corporation. The preceding sentence shall not apply to the extent the property has been treated under subparagraph (C) as having been sold by such corporation.

(B) Corporation described. A corporation is described in this subparagraph with respect to an individual if, were such individual a United States citizen—

(i) such corporation would be a controlled foreign corporation (as defined in 957), and

(ii) such individual would be a United States shareholder (as defined in section 951(b)) with respect to such corporation.

(C) Disposition of stock in corporation. If stock in the corporation referred to in subparagraph (A) (or any other stock which has a basis determined in whole or part by reference to such stock) is disposed of during the 10-year period referred to in subsection (a) and while the property referred to in subparagraph (A) is held by such corporation, a pro rata share of such property (determined on the basis of the value of such stock) shall be treated as sold by the corporation immediately before such disposition.

(D) Anti-abuse rules. The Secretary shall prescribe such regulations as may be necessary to prevent the avoidance of the purposes of this paragraph, including where—

(i) the property is sold to the corporation, and

(ii) the property taken into account under subparagraph (A) is sold by the corporation.

(E) Information reporting. The Secretary shall require such information reporting as is necessary to carry out the purposes of this paragraph.

(e) Comparable treatment of lawful permanent residents who cease to be taxed as residents.

(1) In general. Any long-term resident of the United States who—

(A) ceases to be a lawful permanent resident of the United States (within the meaning of section 7701(b)(6)), or

(B) commences to be treated as a resident of a foreign country under the provisions of a tax treaty between the United States and the foreign country and who does not waive the benefits of such treaty applicable to residents of the foreign country,

shall be treated for purposes of this section and sections 2107, 2501, and [7]*6039G* in the same manner as if such resident were a citizen of the United States who lost United States citizenship on the date of such cessation or commencement.

* * * * * * * * * * * * *

[For analysis, see ¶ 1626. For text of Committee Report, see ¶ 5380.]

[Endnote Code Sec. 877]

Matter in *italics* in Code Sec. 877(d)(2)(B), Code Sec. 877(d)(2)(D), Code Sec. 877(d)(3), Code Sec. 877(d)(4)(A)(i), and Code Sec. 877(d)(4)(A) added by Secs. 1602(g)(1)-(4) of the Taxpayer Relief Act of 1997, H.R. 2014, 8/5/97, which struck out:

1. "the 10-year period described in subsection (a)"
2. added matter in subpara. (d)(2)(D)
3. added matter in para. (d)(3)
4. added matter in clause (d)(4)(A)(i)
5. added matter in subpara. (d)(4)(A)
6. "during the 10-year period referred to in subsection (a),"

Effective Date (Sec. 1602(i), H.R. 2014, 8/5/97) effective as provided in P.L. 104-191, Sec. 511(g), which reads as follows:

"(g) Effective date.

"(1) In general. The amendments made by this section shall apply to—

"(A) individuals losing United States citizenship (within the meaning of section 877 of the Internal Revenue Code of 1986) on or after February 6, 1995, and

"(B) long-term residents of the United States with respect to whom an event described in subparagraph (A) or (B) of section 877(e)(1) of such Code occurs on or after February 6, 1995.

"(2) Rulings requests. In no event shall the 1-year period referred to in section 877(c)(1)(B) of such Code, as amended by this section, expire before the date which is 90 days after the date of the enactment of this Act.

"(3) Special rule.

"(A) In general. In the case of an individual who performed an act of expatriation specified in paragraph (1), (2), (3), or (4) of section 349(a) of the Immigration and Nationality Act (8 U.S.C. 1481(a)(1)(4)) before February 6, 1995, but who did not, on or before such date, furnish to the United States Department of State a signed statement of voluntary relinquishment of United States nationality confirming the performance of such act, the amendments made by this section and section 512 shall apply to such individual except that the 10-year period described in section 877(a) of such Code shall not expire before the end of the 10-year period beginning on the date such statement is so furnished.

"(B) Exception. Subparagraph (A) shall not apply if the individual establishes to the satisfaction of the Secretary of the Treasury that such loss of United States citizenship occurred before February 6, 1994."

Matter in *italics* in Code Sec. 877(e)(1) added by Sec. 1602(h)(3), H.R. 2014, which struck out:

7. "6039F"

Effective Date (Sec. 1602(i), H.R. 2014, 8/5/97) effective as provided in P.L. 104-191, Sec. 512(c), which reads as follows:

"(c) Effective date. The amendments made by this section shall apply to—

"(1) individuals losing United States citizenship (within the meaning of section 877 of the Internal Revenue Code of 1986) on or after February 6, 1995, and

"(2) long-term residents of the United States with respect to whom an event described in subparagraph (A) or (B) of section 877(e)(1) of such Code occurs on or after such date.

In no event shall any statement required by such amendments be due before the 90th day after the date of the enactment of this Act."

[¶ 3143]   Code Sec. 894.   Income affected by treaty.

(a) Treaty provisions.

(1) In general. The provisions of this title shall be applied to any taxpayer with due regard to any treaty obligation of the United States which applies to such taxpayer.

(2) Cross reference. For relationship between treaties and this title, see section 7852(d).

(b) Permanent establishment in United States. For purposes of applying any exemption from, or reduction of, any tax provided by any treaty to which the United States is a party with respect to income which is not effectively connected with the conduct of a trade or business within the United States, a nonresident alien individual or a foreign corporation shall be deemed not to have a permanent establishment in the United States at any time during the taxable year. This subsection shall not apply in respect of the tax computed under section 877(b).

¹*(c) Denial of treaty benefits for certain payments through hybrid entities.* *The Secretary shall prescribe such regulations as may be necessary or appropriate to determine the extent to which a taxpayer shall be denied benefits under any income tax treaty of the United States with respect to any payment received by, or income attributable to any activities of, an entity organized in any jurisdiction (including the United States) that is treated as a partnership or is otherwise treated as fiscally transparent for United States Federal income tax purposes (including a common investment trust under section 584, a grantor trust, or an entity that is disregarded for*

United States Federal income tax purposes) and is treated as fiscally nontransparent for purposes of the tax laws of the jurisdiction of residence of the taxpayer.

[For analysis, see ¶ 1625. For text of Committee Report, see ¶ 5146.]

[Endnote Code Sec. 894]
Code Sec. 894(c), in *italics*, added by Sec. 742(a) of the Revenue Reconciliation Act of 1997, H.R. 2014, 8/5/97.
1. added subsec. (c)
Effective Date (Sec. 742(b), H.R. 2014, 8/5/97) effective 8/5/97.

[¶ 3144]   Code Sec. 901.   Taxes of foreign countries and of possessions of United States.

* * * * * * * * * * * *

CAUTION.   Subsec. (k), following, is effective for dividends paid or accrued 30 days or less after 8/5/97. For subsecs. (k) and (l) effective for dividends paid or accrued more than 30 days after 8/5/97, see below.

(k) Cross reference.

(1) For deductions of income, war profits, and excess profits taxes paid to a foreign country or a possession of the United States, see sections 164 and 175.

(2) For right of each partner to make election under this section, see section 703(b).

(3) For right of estate or trust to the credit for taxes imposed by foreign countries and possessions of the United States under this section, see section 642(a).

(4) For reduction of credit for failure of a United States person to furnish certain information with respect to a [1]*foreign corporation or partnership* controlled by him, see section 6038.

CAUTION.   Subsecs. (k) and (l), following, are effective for dividends paid or accrued more than 30 days after 8/5/97. For subsec. (k) effective for dividends paid or accrued 30 days or less after 8/5/97, see above.

[2]*(k) Minimum holding period for certain taxes.*

(1) Withholding taxes.

(A) In general. In no event shall a credit be allowed under subsection (a) for any withholding tax on a dividend with respect to stock in a corporation if—

(i) such stock is held by the recipient of the dividend for 15 days or less during the 30-day period beginning on the date which is 15 days before the date on which such share becomes ex-dividend with respect to such dividend, or

(ii) to the extent that the recipient of the dividend is under an obligation (whether pursuant to a short sale or otherwise) to make related payments with respect to positions in substantially similar or related property.

(B) Withholding tax. For purposes of this paragraph, the term "withholding tax" includes any tax determined on a gross basis; but does not include any tax which is in the nature of a prepayment of a tax imposed on a net basis.

(2) Deemed paid taxes. In the case of income, war profits, or excess profits taxes deemed paid under section 853, 902, or 960 through a chain of ownership of stock in 1 or more corporations, no credit shall be allowed under subsection (a) for such taxes if—

(A) any stock of any corporation in such chain (the ownership of which is required to obtain credit under subsection (a) for such taxes) is held for less than the period described in paragraph (1)(A)(i), or

(B) the corporation holding the stock is under an obligation referred to in paragraph (1)(A)(ii).

(3) 45-day rule in the case of certain preference dividends. In the case of stock having preference in dividends and dividends with respect to such stock which are attributable to a period or periods aggregating in excess of 366 days, paragraph (1)(A)(i) shall be applied—

(A) by substituting "45 days" for "15 days" each place it appears, and

(B) by substituting "90-day period" for "30-day period".

(4) Exception for certain taxes paid by securities dealers.

(A) In general. Paragraphs (1) and (2) shall not apply to any qualified tax with respect to any security held in the active conduct in a foreign country of a securities business of any person—

(i) who is registered as a securities broker or dealer under section 15(a) of the Securities Exchange Act of 1934,

(ii) who is registered as a Government securities broker or dealer under section 15C(a) of such Act, or

(iii) who is licensed or authorized in such foreign country to conduct securities activities in such country and is subject to bona fide regulation by a securities regulating authority of such country.

(B) Qualified tax. For purposes of subparagraph (A), the term "qualified tax" means a tax paid to a foreign country (other than the foreign country referred to in subparagraph (A)) if—

(i) the dividend to which such tax is attributable is subject to taxation on a net basis by the country referred to in subparagraph (A), and

(ii) such country allows a credit against its net basis tax for the full amount of the tax paid to such other foreign country.

(C) Regulations. The Secretary may prescribe such regulations as may be appropriate to carry out this paragraph, including regulations to prevent the abuse of the exception provided by this paragraph and to treat other taxes as qualified taxes.

(5) Certain rules to apply. For purposes of this subsection, the rules of paragraphs (3) and (4) of section 246(c) shall apply.

(6) Treatment of bona fide sales. If a person's holding period is reduced by reason of the application of the rules of section 246(c)(4) to any contract for the bona fide sale of stock, the determination of whether such person's holding period meets the requirements of paragraph (2) with respect to taxes deemed paid under section 902 or 960 shall be made as of the date such contract is entered into.

(7) Taxes allowed as deduction, etc. Sections 275 and 78 shall not apply to any tax which is not allowable as a credit under subsection (a) by reason of this subsection.

³*(l)* **Cross reference.**

(1) For deductions of income, war profits, and excess profits taxes paid to a foreign country or a possession of the United States, see sections 164 and 175.

(2) For right of each partner to make election under this section, see section 703(b).

(3) For right of estate or trust to the credit for taxes imposed by foreign countries and possessions of the United States under this section, see section 642(a).

(4) For reduction of credit for failure of a United States person to furnish certain information with respect to a foreign corporation or partnership controlled by him, see section 6038.

[For analysis, see ¶ 1604. For text of Committee Report, see ¶ 5145.]

[Endnote Code Sec. 901]

Matter in *italics* in Code Sec. 901(k)(4) [before redesignated by Sec. 1053(a) of this Act, see below] added by Sec. 1142(a) of the Taxpayer Relief Act of 1997, H.R. 2014, which struck out:
1. "foreign corporation"
Effective Date (Sec. 1142(f), H.R. 2014, 8/5/97) effective for annual accounting periods begin. after 8/5/97.

Matter in *italics* in Code Sec. 901(k) and Code Sec. 901(l) added by Sec. 1053(a), H.R. 2014, 8/5/97, which struck out:
2. added new subsec. (k)
3. "(k)"
Effective Date (Sec. 1053(c), H.R. 2014, 8/5/97) effective for dividends paid or accrued more than 30 days after 8/5/97.

[Endnote Code Sec. 901]

Matter in *italics* in Code Sec. 901(k)(4) [before redesignated by Sec. 1053(a) of this Act, see below] added by Sec. 1142(a) of the Taxpayer Relief Act of 1997, H.R. 2014, which struck out:
1. "foreign corporation"
Effective Date (Sec. 1142(f), H.R. 2014, 8/5/97) effective for annual accounting periods begin. after 8/5/97.

Matter in *italics* in Code Sec. 901(k) and Code Sec. 901(l) added by Sec. 1053(a), H.R. 2014, 8/5/97, which struck out:
2. added new subsec. (k)
3. "(k)"
Effective Date (Sec. 1053(c), H.R. 2014, 8/5/97) effective for dividends paid or accrued more than 30 days after 8/5/97.

[¶ 3145]   Code Sec. 902.   Deemed paid credit where domestic corporation owns 10 percent or more of voting stock of foreign corporation.

* * * * * * * * * * * *

[1]*(b) Deemed taxes increased in case of certain lower tier corporations.*

(1) In general. If—

(A) any foreign corporation is a member of a qualified group, and

(B) such foreign corporation owns 10 percent or more of the voting stock of another member of such group from which it receives dividends in any taxable year,

such foreign corporation shall be deemed to have paid the same proportion of such other member's post-1986 foreign income taxes as would be determined under subsection (a) if such foreign corporation were a domestic corporation.

(2) Qualified group. For purposes of paragraph (1), the term "qualified group" means—

(A) the foreign corporation described in subsection (a), and

(B) any other foreign corporation if—

(i) the domestic corporation owns at least 5 percent of the voting stock of such other foreign corporation indirectly through a chain of foreign corporations connected through stock ownership of at least 10 percent of their voting stock,

(ii) the foreign corporation described in subsection (a) is the first tier corporation in such chain, and

(iii) such other corporation is not below the sixth tier in such chain.

The term "qualified group" shall not include any foreign corporation below the third tier in the chain referred to in clause (i) unless such foreign corporation is a controlled foreign corporation (as defined in section 957) and the domestic corporation is a United States shareholder (as defined in section 951(b)) in such foreign corporation. Paragraph (1) shall apply to those taxes paid by a member of the qualified group below the third tier only with respect to periods during which it was a controlled foreign corporation.

(c) Definitions and special rules. For purposes of this section—

(1) Post-1986 undistributed earnings. The term "post-1986 undistributed earnings" means the amount of the earnings and profits of the foreign corporation (computed in accordance with sections 964(a) and 986) accumulated in taxable years beginning after December 31, 1986—

(A) as of the close of the taxable year of the foreign corporation in which the dividend is distributed, and

(B) without diminution by reason of dividends distributed during such taxable year.

(2) Post-1986 foreign income taxes. The term "post-1986 foreign income taxes" means the sum of—

(A) the foreign income taxes with respect to the taxable year of the foreign corporation in which the dividend is distributed, and

(B) the foreign income taxes with respect to prior taxable years beginning after December 31, 1986, to the extent such foreign taxes were not [2]*attributable to* dividends distributed by the foreign corporation in prior taxable years.

(3) Special rule [3]*where foreign corporation first qualifies* **after December 31, 1986.**

(A) In general. If the 1st day on which the[4] requirements of subparagraph (B) are met with respect to any foreign corporation is in a taxable year of such corporation beginning after December 31, 1986, the post-1986 undistributed earnings and the post-1986 foreign income taxes of such foreign corporation shall be determined by taking into account only periods beginning on and after the 1st day of the 1st taxable year in which such[5] requirements are met.

(B) Ownership requirements. The[6] requirements of this subparagraph are met with respect to any foreign corporation if—

(i) 10 percent or more of the voting stock of such foreign corporation is owned by a domestic corporation, [7]*or*

[8]*(ii) the requirements of subsection (b)(2) are met with respect to such foreign corporation.*

(4) Foreign income taxes.

(A) In general. The term "foreign income taxes" means any income, war profits, or excess profits taxes paid by the foreign corporation to any foreign country or possession of the United States.

(B) Treatment of deemed taxes. Except for purposes of determining the amount of the post-1986 foreign income taxes of a [9]*sixth tier foreign corporation* referred to in subsection (b)(2), the term "foreign income taxes" includes any such taxes deemed to be paid by the foreign corporation under this section.

* * * * * * * * * * * *

[For analysis, see ¶ 1601, ¶ 1606. For text of Committee Report, see ¶ 5175, ¶ 5192.]

[Endnote Code Sec. 902]

Matter in *italics* in Code Sec. 902(b) was added by Sec. 1113(a)(1) of the Taxpayer Relief Act of 1997, H.R. 2014, 8/5/97, which struck out:

1. "(b) Deemed taxes increased in case of certain 2nd and 3rd tier foreign corporations.

"(1) 2nd tier. If the foreign corporation described in subsection (a) (hereinafter in this section referred to as the '1st tier corporation') owns 10 percent or more of the voting stock of a 2nd foreign corporation from which it receives dividends in any taxable year, the 1st tier corporation shall be deemed to have paid the same proportion of such 2nd foreign corporation's post-1986 foreign income taxes as would be determined under subsection (a) if such 1st tier corporation were a domestic corporation.

"(2) 3rd tier. If such 1st tier corporation owns 10 percent or more of the voting stock of a 2nd foreign corporation which, in turn, owns 10 percent or more of the voting stock of a 3rd foreign corporation from which the 2nd corporation receives dividends in any taxable year, such 2nd foreign corporation shall be deemed to have paid the same proportion of such 3rd foreign corporation's post-1986 foreign income taxes as would be determined under subsection (a) if such 2nd foreign corporation were a domestic corporation.

"(3) 5 percent stock requirement. For purposes of this subpart—

"(A) For 2nd tier. Paragraph (1) shall not apply unless the percentage of voting stock owned by the domestic corporation in the 1st tier corporation and the percentage of voting stock owned by the 1st tier corporation in the 2nd foreign corporation when multiplied together equal at least 5 percent.

"(B) For 3rd tier. Paragraph (2) shall not apply unless the percentage arrived at for purposes of applying paragraph (1) when multiplied by the percentage of voting stock owned by the 2nd foreign corporation in the 3rd foreign corporation is equal to at least 5 percent."

Effective Date (Sec. 1113(c), H.R. 2014, 8/5/97) Sec. 1113(c) of this Act reads as follows:

"(c) Effective date.

"(1) In general. The amendments made by this section shall apply to taxes of foreign corporations for taxable years of such corporations beginning after the 8/5/97 of this Act.

"(2) Special rule. In the case of any chain of foreign corporations described in clauses (i) and (ii) of section 902(b)(2)(B) of the Internal Revenue Code of 1986 (as amended by this section), no liquidation, reorganization, or similar transaction in a taxable year beginning after the date of the enactment of this Act shall have the effect of permitting taxes to be taken into account under section 902 of the Internal Revenue Code of 1986 which could not have been taken into account under such section but for such transaction."

Matter in *italics* in Code Sec. 902(c)(2)(B) was added by Sec. 1163(a), H.R. 2014, 8/5/97, which struck out:

2. "deemed paid with respect to"

Effective Date (Sec. 1163(c), H.R. 2014, 8/5/97) effective 8/5/97.

Matter in *italics* in Code Sec. 902(c)(3)(B)(i), Code Sec. 902(c)(3)(B)(ii) and Code Sec. 902(c)(4)(B) was added by Sec. 1113(a)(2)(A)–(D), H.R. 2014, 8/5/97, which struck out:

3. "where domestic corporation acquires 10 percent of foreign corporation"

4. "ownership"

5. "ownership"

6. "ownership"

7. added matter in clause (c)(3)(B)(i)

8. "(ii) the requirements of subsection (b)(3)(A) are met with respect to such foreign corporation and 10 percent or more of the voting stock of such foreign corporation is owned by another foreign corporation described in clause (i), or

"(iii) the requirements of subsection (b)(3)(B) are met with respect to such foreign corporation and 10 percent or more of the voting stock of such foreign corporation is owned by another foreign corporation described in clause (ii)."

9. "3rd foreign corporation"

Effective Date (Sec. 1113(c), H.R. 2014, 8/5/97) Sec. 1113(c) of this Act, reproduced above.

[¶ 3146]   Code Sec. 904.   Limitation on credit.

* * * * * * * * * * *

(b) Taxable income for purpose of computing limitation.

* * * * * * * * * * *

(2) **Capital gains.** For purposes of this section—

(A) In general. Taxable income from sources outside the United States shall include gain from the sale or exchange of capital assets only to the extent of foreign source capital gain net income.

(B) Special rules where capital gain rate differential. In the case of any taxable year for which there is a capital gain rate differential—

(i) in lieu of applying subparagraph (A), the taxable income from sources outside the United States shall include gain from the sale or exchange of capital assets only in an amount equal to foreign source capital gain net income reduced by the rate differential portion of foreign source net capital gain,

(ii) the entire taxable income shall include gain from the sale or exchange of capital assets only in an amount equal to capital gain net income reduced by the rate differential portion of net capital gain, and

(iii) for purposes of determining taxable income from sources outside the United States, any net capital loss (and any amount which is a short-term capital loss under section 1212(a)) from sources outside the United States to the extent taken into account in determining capital gain net income for the taxable year shall be reduced by an amount equal to the rate differential portion of the excess of net capital gain from sources within the United States over net capital gain.

[1](C) Coordination with capital gains rates. The Secretary may by regulations modify the application of this paragraph and paragraph (3) to the extent necessary to properly reflect any capital gain rate differential under section 1(h) or 1201(a) and the computation of net capital gain.

* * * * * * * * * * *

(d) Separate application of section with respect to certain categories of income.

(1) **In general.** The provisions of subsections (a), (b), and (c) and sections 902, 907, and 960 shall be applied separately with respect to each of the following items of income:

(A) passive income,

(B) high withholding tax interest,

(C) financial services income,

(D) shipping income,

CAUTION.   Subpara. (d)(1)(E), following, is effective for tax. yrs. begin. before 1/1/2003. For subpara. (d)(1)(E), effective for tax. yrs. begin. after 12/31/2002, see below.

(E) in the case of a corporation, dividends from each noncontrolled section 902 corporation,

CAUTION.   Subpara. (d)(1)(E), following, is effective for tax. yrs. begin. after 12/31/2002. For subpara. (d)(1)(E), effective for tax. yrs. begin. before 1/1/2003, see above.

[2](E) in the case of a corporation, dividends from noncontrolled section 902 corporations out of earnings and profits accumulated in taxable years beginning before January 1, 2003,

(F) dividends from a DISC or former DISC (as defined in section 992(a)) to the extent such dividends are treated as income from sources without the United States,

(G) taxable income attributable to foreign trade income (within the meaning of section 923(b)),

(H) distributions from a FSC (or a former FSC) out of earnings and profits attributable to foreign trade income (within the meaning of section 923(b)) or interest or carrying charges (as defined in section 927(d)(1)) derived from a transaction which results in foreign trade income (as defined in section 923(b)), and

(I) income other than income described in any of the preceding subparagraphs.

(2) Definitions and special rules. For purposes of this subsection—

* * * * * * * * * * * *

(C) Financial services income.

(i) In general. Except as otherwise provided in this subparagraph, the term "financial services income" means any income which is received or accrued by any person predominantly engaged in the active conduct of a banking, insurance, financing, or similar business, and which is—

(I) described in clause (ii),

(II) passive income (determined without regard to [3]*subclauses (I) and (III)* of subparagraph (A)(iii)), or

(III) export financing interest which (but for subparagraph (B)(ii)) would be high withholding tax interest.

(ii) General description of financial services income. Income is described in this clause if such income is—

(I) derived in the active conduct of a banking, financing, or similar business,

(II) derived from the investment by an insurance company of its unearned premiums or reserves ordinary and necessary for the proper conduct of its insurance business, or

(III) of a kind which would be insurance income as defined in section 953(a) determined without regard to those provisions of paragraph (1)(A) of such section which limit insurance income to income from countries other than the country in which the corporation was created or organized.

(iii) Exceptions. The term "financial services income" does not include—

(I) any high withholding tax interest,

CAUTION. Subclause (d)(2)(C)(iii)(II), following, is effective for tax. yrs. begin. before 1/1/2003. For subclause (d)(2)(C)(iii)(II), effective for tax. yrs. begin. after 12/31/2002, see below.

(II) any dividend from a noncontrolled section 902 corporation, and

CAUTION. Subclause (d)(2)(C)(iii)(II), following, is effective for tax. yrs. begin. after 12/31/2002. For subclause (d)(2)(C)(iii)(II), effective for tax. yrs. begin. before 1/1/2003, see above.

(II) any dividend from a noncontrolled section 902 corporation [4]*out of earnings and profits accumulated in taxable years beginning before January 1, 2002,* and

(III) any export financing interest not described in clause (i)(III).

CAUTION. Subpara. (d)(2)(D), following, is effective for tax. yrs. begin. before 1/1/2003. For subpara. (d)(2)(D), effective for tax. yrs. begin. after 12/31/2002, see below.

(D) Shipping income. The term "shipping income" means any income received or accrued by any person which is of a kind which would be foreign base company shipping income (as defined in section 954(f)). Such term does not include any dividend from a noncontrolled section 902 corporation and does not include any financial services income.

CAUTION. Subpara. (d)(2)(D), following, is effective for tax. yrs. begin. after 12/31/2002. For subpara. (d)(2)(D), effective for tax. yrs. begin. before 1/1/2003, see above.

(D) Shipping income. The term "shipping income" means any income received or accrued by any person which is of a kind which would be foreign base company shipping income (as defined in section 954(f)). Such term does not include any dividend from a noncontrolled section 902 corporation [5]*out of earnings and profits accumulated in taxable years beginning before January 1, 2002* and does not include any financial services income.

(E) Noncontrolled section 902 corporation.

(i) In general. The term "noncontrolled section 902 corporation" means any foreign corporation with respect to which the taxpayer meets the stock ownership requirements of section 902(a) (or, for purposes of applying paragraph (3), the requirements of section 902(b)). A controlled foreign corporation shall not be treated as a noncontrolled section 902 corporation with respect to any distribution out of its earnings and profits for periods during which it was a controlled foreign corporation[6].

(ii) Special rule for taxes on high-withholding tax interest. If a foreign corporation is a noncontrolled section 902 corporation with respect to the taxpayer, taxes on high withholding tax interest (to the extent imposed at a rate in excess of 5 percent) shall not be treated as foreign taxes for purposes of determining the amount of foreign taxes deemed paid by the taxpayer under section 902.

(iii) Treatment of inclusions under section 1293. If any foreign corporation is a noncontrolled section 902 corporation with respect to the taxpayer, any inclusion under section 1293 with respect to such corporation shall be treated as a dividend from such corporation.

CAUTION.   Clause (d)(2)(E)(iv) is effective for tax. yrs. begin. after 12/31/2002.

[7]*(iv) All non-PFICs treated as one. All noncontrolled section 902 corporations which are not passive foreign investment companies (as defined in section 1297) shall be treated as one noncontrolled section 902 corporation for purposes of paragraph (1).*

* * * * * * * * * * *

CAUTION.   Paras. (d)(4) and (5), following, are effective for tax. yrs. begin. before 1/1/2003. For paras. (d)(4)-(6), effective for tax. yrs. begin. after 12/31/2002, see below.

(4) Controlled foreign corporation; United States shareholder. For purposes of this subsection—

(A) Controlled foreign corporation. The term "controlled foreign corporation" has the meaning given such term by section 957 (taking into account section 953(c)).

(B) United States shareholder. The term "United States shareholder" has the meaning given such term by section 951(b) (taking into account section 953(c)).

(5) Regulations. The Secretary shall prescribe such regulations as may be necessary or appropriate for the purposes of this subsection, including regulations—

(A) for the application of paragraph (3) and subsection (f)(5) in the case of income paid (or loans made) through 1 or more entities or between 2 or more chains of entities,

(B) preventing the manipulation of the character of income the effect of which is to avoid the purposes of this subsection, and

(C) providing that rules similar to the rules of paragraph (3)(C) shall apply to interest, rents, and royalties received or accrued from entities which would be controlled foreign corporations if they were foreign corporations.

CAUTION.   Paras. (d)(4)-(6), following, are effective for tax. yrs. begin. after 12/31/2002. For paras. (d)(4) and (5), effective for tax. yrs. begin. before 1/1/2003, see above.

[8]**(4) Look-thru applies to dividends from noncontrolled section 902 corporations.**

(A) In general. For purposes of this subsection, any applicable dividend shall be treated as income in a separate category in proportion to the ratio of—

(i) the portion of the earnings and profits described in subparagraph (B)(ii) attributable to income in such category, to

(ii) the total amount of such earnings and profits.

(B) Applicable dividend. For purposes of subparagraph (A), the term "applicable dividend" means any dividend—

(i) from a noncontrolled section 902 corporation with respect to the taxpayer, and

(ii) paid out of earnings and profits accumulated in taxable years beginning after December 31, 2002.

(C) Special rules.

(i) In general. Rules similar to the rules of paragraph (3)(F) shall apply for purposes of this paragraph.

(ii) Earnings and profits. For purposes of this paragraph and paragraph (1)(E)—

(I) In general. The rules of section 316 shall apply.

(II) Regulations. The Secretary may prescribe regulations regarding the treatment of distributions out of earnings and profits for periods prior to the taxpayer's acquisition of such stock.

[9]**(5) Controlled foreign corporation; United States shareholder.** For purposes of this subsection—

(A) Controlled foreign corporation. The term "controlled foreign corporation" has the meaning given such term by section 957 (taking into account section 953(c)).

(B) United States shareholder. The term "United States shareholder" has the meaning given such term by section 951(b) (taking into account section 953(c)).

[10]**(6) Regulations.** The Secretary shall prescribe such regulations as may be necessary or appropriate for the purposes of this subsection, including regulations—

(A) for the application of paragraph (3) and subsection (f)(5) in the case of income paid (or loans made) through 1 or more entities or between 2 or more chains of entities,

(B) preventing the manipulation of the character of income the effect of which is to avoid the purposes of this subsection, and

(C) providing that rules similar to the rules of paragraph (3)(C) shall apply to interest, rents, and royalties received or accrued from entities which would be controlled foreign corporations if they were foreign corporations.

* * * * * * * * * * *

CAUTION. Subsec. (j), following, is effective for tax. yrs. begin. before 1/1/98. For subsecs. (j) and (k), effective for tax. yrs. begin. after 12/31/97, see below.

(j) Cross references.

(1) For increase of limitation under subsection (a) for taxes paid with respect to amounts received which were included in the gross income of the taxpayer for a prior taxable year as a United States shareholder with respect to a controlled foreign corporation, see section 960(b).

(2) For modification of limitation under subsection (a) for purposes of determining the amount of credit which can be taken against the alternative minimum tax, see section 59(a).

CAUTION. Subsecs. (j) and (k), following, are effective for tax. yrs. begin. after 12/31/97. For subsec. (j), effective for tax. yrs. begin. before 1/1/98, see above.

[11]*(j) Certain individuals exempt.*

(1) In general. In the case of an individual to whom this subsection applies for any taxable year—

(A) the limitation of subsection (a) shall not apply,

(B) no taxes paid or accrued by the individual during such taxable year may be deemed paid or accrued under subsection (c) in any other taxable year, and

(C) no taxes paid or accrued by the individual during any other taxable year may be deemed paid or accrued under subsection (c) in such taxable year.

(2) Individuals to whom subsection applies. This subsection shall apply to an individual for any taxable year if—

(A) the entire amount of such individual's gross income for the taxable year from sources without the United States consists of qualified passive income,

(B) the amount of the creditable foreign taxes paid or accrued by the individual during the taxable year does not exceed $300 ($600 in the case of a joint return), and

(C) such individual elects to have this subsection apply for the taxable year.

(3) **Definitions.** For purposes of this subsection—

(A) Qualified passive income. The term "qualified passive income" means any item of gross income if—

(i) such item of income is passive income (as defined in subsection (d)(2)(A) without regard to clause (iii) thereof), and

(ii) such item of income is shown on a payee statement furnished to the individual.

(B) Creditable foreign taxes. The term "creditable foreign taxes" means any taxes for which a credit is allowable under section 901; except that such term shall not include any tax unless such tax is shown on a payee statement furnished to such individual.

(C) Payee statement. The term "payee statement" has the meaning given to such term by section 6724(d)(2).

(D) Estates and trusts not eligible. This subsection shall not apply to any estate or trust.

[12]**(k) Cross references.**

(1) For increase of limitation under subsection (a) for taxes paid with respect to amounts received which were included in the gross income of the taxpayer for a prior taxable year as a United States shareholder with respect to a controlled foreign corporation, see section 960(b).

(2) For modification of limitation under subsection (a) for purposes of determining the amount of credit which can be taken against the alternative minimum tax, see section 59(a).

[For analysis, see ¶ 1602, ¶ 1607, ¶ 1612. For text of Committee Report, see ¶ 5170, ¶ 5174, ¶ 5175, ¶ 5192.]

[Endnote Code Sec. 904]
Code Sec. 904(b)(2)(C), in *italics*, was added by Sec. 311(c)(3) of the Taxpayer Relief Act of 1997, H.R. 2014, 8/5/97.
1. added subpara. (b)(2)(C)
Effective Date (Sec. 311(d)(1), H.R. 2014, 8/5/97) effective for tax. yrs. end. after 5/6/97.

Matter in *italics* in Code Sec. 904(d)(1)(E) added by Sec. 1105(a)(1), H.R. 2014, 8/5/97, which stuck out:
2. "(E) in the case of a corporation, dividends from each noncontrolled section 902 corporation,"
Effective Date (Sec. 1105(c), H.R. 2014, 8/5/97) effective for tax. yrs. begin. after 12/31/2002.

Matter in *italics* in Code Sec. 904(d)(2)(C)(i)(II) added by Sec. 1163(b), H.R. 2014, 8/5/97, which stuck out:
3. "subclause (I)"
Effective Date (Sec. 1163(c), H.R. 2014, 8/5/97) effective 8/5/97.

Matter in *italics* in Code Sec. 904(d)(2)(C)(iii)(II) and Code Sec. 904(d)(2)(D) added by Sec. 1105(a)(3), H.R. 2014, 8/5/97.
4. added matter in subclause (d)(2)(C)(iii)(II)
5. added matter in subpara. (d)(2)(D)
Effective Date (Sec. 1105(c), H.R. 2014, 8/5/97) effective for tax. yrs. begin. after 12/31/2002.

Matter in Code Sec. 904(d)(2)(E)(i) deleted by Sec. 1111(b), H.R. 2014, 8/5/97, which struck out:
6. "and except as provided in regulations, the taxpayer was a United States shareholder in such corporation"
Effective Date (Sec. 1111(c)(2), H.R. 2014, 8/5/97) effective for distributions after 8/5/97.

Matter in *italics* in Code Sec. 904(d)(2)(E)(iv), Code Sec. 904(d)(4), Code Sec. 904(d)(5) and Code Sec. 904(d)(6) added by Sec. 1105(a)(2) and (b), H.R. 2014, 8/5/97, which struck out:
7. added subpara. (d)(2)(E)(iv)
8. added para. (d)(4)
9. "(4)"
10. "(5)"
Effective Date (Sec. 1105(c), H.R. 2014, 8/5/97) effective for tax. yrs. begin. after 12/31/2002.

Matter in *italics* in Code Sec. 904(j), and Code Sec. 904(k) added by Sec. 1101(a), H.R. 2014, 8/5/97, which struck out:
11. added subsec. (j)
12. "(j)"
Effective Date (Sec. 1101(b), H.R. 2014, 8/5/97) effective for tax. yrs. begin. after 12/31/97.

[¶ 3147]   Code Sec. 905.   Applicable rules.

* * * * * * * * * * * *

CAUTION.   Subsec. (c), following, is effective for taxes which relate to tax. yrs. begin. before 1/1/98. For subsec. (c) effective for taxes which relate to tax. yrs. begin. after 12/31/97, see below.

(c) Adjustments on payment of accrued taxes. If accrued taxes when paid differ from the amounts claimed as credits by the taxpayer, or if any tax paid is refunded in whole or in part, the taxpayer shall notify the Secretary, who shall redetermine the amount of the tax for the year or years affected. The amount of tax due on such redetermination, if any, shall be paid by the taxpayer on notice and demand by the Secretary, or the amount of tax overpaid, if any, shall be credited or refunded to the taxpayer in accordance with subchapter B of chapter 66 (sec. 6511 and following). In the case of such a tax accrued but not paid, the Secretary, as a condition precedent to the allowance of this credit, may require the taxpayer to give a bond, with sureties satisfactory to and to be approved by the Secretary, in such sum as the Secretary may require, conditioned on the payment by the taxpayer of any amount of tax found due on any such redetermination; and the bond herein prescribed shall contain such further conditions as the Secretary may require. In such redetermination by the Secretary of the amount of tax due from the taxpayer for the year or years affected by a refund, the amount of the taxes refunded for which credit has been allowed under this section shall be reduced by the amount of any tax described in section 901 imposed by the foreign country or possession of the United States with respect to such refund; but no credit under this subpart, and no deduction under section 164 (relating to deduction for taxes) shall be allowed for any taxable year with respect to such tax imposed on the refund. No interest shall be assessed or collected on any amount of tax due on any redetermination by the Secretary, resulting from a refund to the taxpayer, for any period before the receipt of such refund, except to the extent interest was paid by the foreign country or possession of the United States on such refund for such period.

CAUTION.   Subsec. (c), following, is effective for taxes which relate to tax. yrs. begin. after 12/31/97. For subsec. (c) effective for taxes which relate to tax. yrs. begin. before 1/1/98, see above.

[1]*(c) Adjustments to accrued taxes.*

   (1) In general. If—

      (A) accrued taxes when paid differ from the amounts claimed as credits by the taxpayer,

      (B) accrued taxes are not paid before the date 2 years after the close of the taxable year to which such taxes relate, or

      (C) any tax paid is refunded in whole or in part, the taxpayer shall notify the Secretary, who shall redetermine the amount of the tax for the year or years affected. The Secretary may prescribe adjustments to the pools of post-1986 foreign income taxes and the pools of post-1986 undistributed earnings under sections 902 and 960 in lieu of the redetermination under the preceding sentence.

   (2) Special rule for taxes not paid within 2 years.

      (A) In general. Except as provided in subparagraph (B), in making the redetermination under paragraph (1), no credit shall be allowed for accrued taxes not paid before the date referred to in subparagraph (B) of paragraph (1).

      (B) Taxes subsequently paid. Any such taxes if subsequently paid—

         (i) shall be taken into account—

            (I) in the case of taxes deemed paid under section 902 or section 960, for the taxable year in which paid (and no redetermination shall be made under this section by reason of such payment), and

            (II) in any other case, for the taxable year to which such taxes relate, and

         (ii) shall be translated as provided in section 986(a)(2)(A).

*(3) **Adjustments.** The amount of tax (if any) due on any redetermination under paragraph (1) shall be paid by the taxpayer on notice and demand by the Secretary, and the amount of tax overpaid (if any) shall be credited or refunded to the taxpayer in accordance with subchapter B of chapter 66 (section 6511 et seq.).*

*(4) **Bond requirements.** In the case of any tax accrued but not paid, the Secretary, as a condition precedent to the allowance of the credit provided in this subpart, may require the taxpayer to give a bond, with sureties satisfactory to and approved by the Secretary, in such sum as the Secretary may require, conditioned on the payment by the taxpayer of any amount of tax found due on any such redetermination. Any such bond shall contain such further conditions as the Secretary may require.*

*(5) **Other special rules.** In any redetermination under paragraph (1) by the Secretary of the amount of tax due from the taxpayer for the year or years affected by a refund, the amount of the taxes refunded for which credit has been allowed under this section shall be reduced by the amount of any tax described in section 901 imposed by the foreign country or possession of the United States with respect to such refund; but no credit under this subpart, or deduction under section 164, shall be allowed for any taxable year with respect to any such tax imposed on the refund. No interest shall be assessed or collected on any amount of tax due on any redetermination by the Secretary, resulting from a refund to the taxpayer, for any period before the receipt of such refund, except to the extent interest was paid by the foreign country or possession of the United States on such refund for such period.*

[For analysis, see ¶ 1605. For text of Committee Report, see ¶ 5171.]

[Endnote Code Sec. 905]

Matter in *italics* in Code Sec. 905(c) added by Sec. 1102(a)(2) of the Taxpayer Relief Act of 1997, H.R. 2014, 8/5/97, which struck out:

1. "(c) Adjustments on payment of accrued taxes.

"If accrued taxes when paid differ from the amounts claimed as credits by the taxpayer, or if any tax paid is refunded in whole or in part, the taxpayer shall notify the Secretary, who shall redetermine the amount of the tax for the year or years affected. The amount of tax due on such redetermination, if any, shall be paid by the taxpayer on notice and demand by the Secretary, or the amount of tax overpaid, if any, shall be credited or refunded to the taxpayer in accordance with subchapter B of chapter 66 (sec. 6511 and following). In the case of such a tax accrued but not paid, the Secretary, as a condition precedent to the allowance of this credit, may require the taxpayer to give a bond, with sureties satisfactory to and to be approved by the Secretary, in such sum as the Secretary may require, conditioned on the payment by the taxpayer of any amount of tax found due on any such redetermination; and the bond herein prescribed shall contain such further conditions as the Secretary may require. In such redetermination by the Secretary of the amount of tax due from the taxpayer for the year or years affected by a refund, the amount of the taxes refunded for which credit has been allowed under this section shall be reduced by the amount of any tax described in section 901 imposed by the foreign country or possession of the United States with respect to such refund; but no credit under this subpart, and no deduction under section 164 (relating to deduction for taxes) shall be allowed for any taxable year with respect to such tax imposed on the refund. No interest shall be assessed or collected on any amount of tax due on any redetermination by the Secretary, resulting from a refund to the taxpayer, for any period before the receipt of such refund, except to the extent interest was paid by the foreign country or possession of the United States on such refund for such period."

Effective Date (Sec. 1102(c)(2), H.R. 2014, 8/5/97) effective for taxes which relate to tax. yrs. begin. after 12/31/97.

[¶ 3148] Code Sec. 911. Citizens or residents of the United States living abroad.

* * * * * * * * * * *

(b) Foreign earned income.

* * * * * * * * * * *

(2) Limitation on foreign earned income.

CAUTION. Subpara. (b)(2)(A), following, is effective for tax. yrs. begin. before 1/1/98. For subpara. (b)(2)(A), effective for tax. yrs. begin. after 12/31/97, see below.

(A) In general. The foreign earned income of an individual which may be excluded under subsection (a)(1) for any taxable year shall not exceed the amount of foreign earned income computed on a daily basis at an annual rate of $70,000.

CAUTION.   Subpara. (b)(2)(A), following, is effective for tax. yrs. begin. after 12/31/97. For subpara. (b)(2)(A), effective for tax. yrs. begin. before 1/1/98, see above.

(A) In general. The foreign earned income of an individual which may be excluded under subsection (a)(1) for any taxable year shall not exceed the amount of foreign earned income computed on a daily basis at an annual rate [1]*equal to the exclusion amount for the calendar year in which such taxable year begins.*

(B) Attribution to year in which services are performed. For purposes of applying subparagraph (A), amounts received shall be considered received in the taxable year in which the services to which the amounts are attributable are performed.

(C) Treatment of community income. In applying subparagraph (A) with respect to amounts received from services performed by a husband or wife which are community income under community property laws applicable to such income, the aggregate amount which may be excludable from the gross income of such husband and wife under subsection (a)(1) for any taxable year shall equal the amount which would be so excludable if such amounts did not constitute community income.

CAUTION.   Subpara. (b)(2)(D), following, is effective for tax. yrs. begin. after 12/31/97.

[2]*(D) Exclusion amount.*

(i) In general. The exclusion amount for any calendar year is the exclusion amount determined in accordance with the following table (as adjusted by clause (ii)):

For calendar year—	The exclusion amount is:
1998	$72,000
1999	74,000
2000	76,000
2001	78,000
2002 and thereafter	80,000

(ii) Inflation adjustment. In the case of any taxable year beginning in a calendar year after 2007, the $80,000 amount in clause (i) shall be increased by an amount equal to the product of—

(I) such dollar amount, and

(II) the cost-of-living adjustment determined under section 1(f)(3) for the calendar year in which the taxable year begins, determined by substituting "2006" for "1992" in subparagraph (B) thereof.

If any increase determined under the preceding sentence is not a multiple of $100, such increase shall be rounded to the next lowest multiple of $100.

* * * * * * * * * * * *

[For analysis, see ¶ 1622. For text of Committee Report, see ¶ 5194.]

[Endnote Code Sec. 911]

Matter in *italics* in Code Sec. 911(b)(2)(A) and Code Sec. 911(b)(2)(D) added by Sec. 1172(a)(1) and (2) of the Taxpayer Relief Act of 1997, H.R. 2014, 8/5/97, which struck out:

1. "of $70,000"

2. added subparagraph (b)(2)(D)

Effective Date (Sec. 1172(b), H.R. 2014, 8/5/97) effective for tax. yrs. begin. after 12/31/97.

[¶ 3149]   Code Sec. 927.   Other definitions and special rules.

(a) **Export property.** For purposes of this subpart—

(1) **In general.** The term "export property" means property—

(A) manufactured, produced, grown, or extracted in the United States by a person other than a FSC,

(B) held primarily for sale, lease, or rental, in the ordinary course of trade or business, by, or to, a FSC, for direct use, consumption, or disposition outside the United States, and

(C) not more than 50 percent of the fair market value of which is attributable to articles imported into the United States.

For purposes of subparagraph (C), the fair market value of any article imported into the United States shall be its appraised value, as determined by the Secretary under section 402 of the Tariff Act of 1930 (19 U.S.C. 1401a) in connection with its importation.

(2) Excluded property. The term "export property" shall not include—

(A) property leased or rented by a FSC for use by any member of a controlled group of corporations of which such FSC is a member,

CAUTION.   Subpara. (a)(2)(B), following, is effective for gross receipts attributable to periods before 1/1/98, in tax. yrs. end. before 1/1/98. For subpara. (a)(2)(B), effective for gross receipts attributable to periods after 12/31/97, in tax. yrs. end. after 12/31/97, see below.

(B) patents, inventions, models, designs, formulas, or processes whether or not patented, copyrights (other than films, tapes, records, or similar reproductions, for commercial or home use), good will, trademarks, trade brands, franchises, or other like property,

CAUTION.   Subpara. (a)(2)(B), following, is effective for gross receipts attributable to periods after 12/31/97, in tax. yrs. end. after 12/31/97. For subpara. (a)(2)(B), effective for gross receipts attributable to periods before 1/1/98, in tax. yrs. end. after 1/1/98, see above.

(B) patents, inventions, models, designs, formulas, or processes whether or not patented, copyrights (other than films, tapes, records, or similar reproductions[1], *and other than computer software (whether or not patented),* for commercial or home use), good will, trademarks, trade brands, franchises, or other like property,

(C) oil or gas (or any primary product thereof),

(D) products the export of which is prohibited or curtailed to effectuate the policy set forth in paragraph (2)(C) of section 3 of the Export Administration Act of 1979 (relating to the protection of the domestic economy) , or

(E) any unprocessed timber which is a softwood.

For purposes of subparagraph (E), the term "unprocessed timber" means any log, cant, or similar form of timber.

* * * * * * * * * * * *

[For analysis, see ¶ 1621. For text of Committee Report, see ¶ 5193.]

[Endnote Code Sec. 927]

Matter in *italics* in Code Sec. 927(a)(2)(B) added by Sec. 1171(a) of the Taxpayer Relief Act of 1997, H.R. 2014, 8/5/97.
1. added matter in subpara. (a)(2)(B)

Effective Date (Sec. 1171(b), H.R. 2014, 8/5/97) effective for gross receipts attributable to periods after 12/31/97, in tax. yrs. end. 12/31/97.

[¶ 3150]   Code Sec. 951.   Amounts included in gross income of United States shareholders.

(a) Amounts included.

(1) In general. If a foreign corporation is a controlled foreign corporation for an uninterrupted period of 30 days or more during any taxable year, every person who is a United States shareholder (as defined in subsection (b)) of such corporation and who owns (within the meaning of section 958(a)) stock in such corporation on the last day, in such year, on which such corporation is a controlled foreign corporation shall include in his gross income, for his taxable year in which or with which such taxable year of the corporation ends—

(A) the sum of—

(i) his pro rata share (determined under paragraph (2)) of the corporation's subpart F income for such year,

(ii) his pro rata share (determined under section 955(a)(3) as in effect before the enactment of the Tax Reduction Act of 1975) of the corporation's previously excluded subpart F income withdrawn from investment in less developed countries for such year, and

(iii) his pro rata share (determined under section 955(a)(3)) of the corporation's previously excluded subpart F income withdrawn from foreign base company shipping operations for such year; and

(B) the amount determined under section 956 with respect to such shareholder for such year (but only to the extent not excluded from gross income under section 959(a)(2)) .

(2) **Pro rata share of subpart F income.** The pro rata share referred to in paragraph (1)(A)(i) in the case of any United States shareholder is the amount—

(A) which would have been distributed with respect to the stock which such shareholder owns (within the meaning of section 958(a)) in such corporation if on the last day, in its taxable year, on which the corporation is a controlled foreign corporation it had distributed pro rata to its shareholders an amount (i) which bears the same ratio to its subpart F income for the taxable year, as (ii) the part of such year during which the corporation is a controlled foreign corporation bears to the entire year, reduced by

(B) the amount of distributions received by any other person during such year as a dividend with respect to such stock, but only to the extent of the dividend which would have been received if the distribution by the corporation had been the amount (i) which bears the same ratio to the subpart F income of such corporation for the taxable year, as (ii) the part of such year during which such shareholder did not own (within the meaning of section 958(a)) such stock bears to the entire year.

[1]*For purposes of subparagraph (B), any gain included in the gross income of any person as a dividend under section 1248 shall be treated as a distribution received by such person with respect to the stock involved.*

* * * * * * * * * * *

[For analysis, see ¶ 1612. For text of Committee Report, see ¶ 5175.]

[Endnote Code Sec. 951]

Matter in *italics* in Code Sec. 951(a)(2) added by Sec. 1112(a)(1) of the Taxpayer Relief Act of 1997, H.R. 2014, 8/5/97. 1. added matter in para. (a)(2)

Effective Date (Sec. 1112(a)(2), H.R. 2014, 8/5/97) effective for dispositions after 8/5/97.

[¶ 3151]   Code Sec. 952.   Subpart F income defined.

(a) **In general.** For purposes of this subpart, the term "subpart F income" means, in the case of any controlled foreign corporation, the sum of—

(1) insurance income (as defined under section 953),

(2) the foreign base company income (as determined under section 954),

(3) an amount equal to the product of—

(A) the income of such corporation other than income which—

(i) is attributable to earnings and profits of the foreign corporation included in the gross income of a United States person under section 951 (other than by reason of this paragraph), or

(ii) is described in subsection (b),

multiplied by

(B) the international boycott factor (as determined under section 999),

(4) the sum of the amounts of any illegal bribes, kickbacks, or other payments (within the meaning of section 162(c)) paid by or on behalf of the corporation during the taxable year of the corporation directly or indirectly to an official, employee, or agent in fact of a government, and

(5) the income of such corporation derived from any foreign country during any period during which section 901(j) applies to such foreign country.

The payments referred to in paragraph (4) are payments which would be unlawful under the Foreign Corrupt Practices Act of 1977 if the payor were a United States person. For purposes of paragraph (5), the income described therein shall be reduced, under regulations prescribed by the Secretary, so as to take into account deductions (including taxes) properly allocable to such income.

(b) Exclusion of United States income. In the case of a controlled foreign corporation, subpart F income does not include any item of income from sources within the United States which is effectively connected with the conduct by such corporation of a trade or business within the United States unless such item is exempt from taxation (or is subject to a reduced rate of tax) pursuant to a treaty obligation of the United States. For purposes of the preceding sentence, income described in paragraph (2) or (3) of section 921(d) shall be treated as derived from sources within the United States. [1]*For purposes of this subsection, any exemption (or reduction) with respect to the tax imposed by section 884 shall not be taken into account.*

* * * * * * * * * * * *

[For analysis, see ¶ 1615. For text of Committee Report, see ¶ 5175.]

[Endnote Code Sec. 952]

Matter in *italics* in Code Sec. 952(b) added by Sec. 1112(c)(1) of the Taxpayer Relief Act of 1997, H.R. 2014, 8/5/97. 1. added matter in subsec. (b)

Effective Date (Sec. 1112(c)(2), H.R. 2014, 8/5/97) effective for tax. yrs. begin. after 12/31/86.

[¶ 3152]   Code Sec. 954.   Foreign base company income.

* * * * * * * * * * * *

(c) Foreign personal holding company income.

(1) In general. For purposes of subsection (a)(1), the term "foreign personal holding company income" means the portion of the gross income which consists of:

(A) Dividends, etc. Dividends, interest, royalties, rents, and annuities.

(B) Certain property transactions. The excess of gains over losses from the sale or exchange of property—

(i) which gives rise to income described in subparagraph (A) (after application of paragraph (2)(A),

(ii) which is an interest in a trust, partnership, or REMIC, or

(iii) which does not give rise to any income.

[1]Gains and losses from the sale or exchange of any property which, in the hands of the controlled foreign corporation, is property described in section 1221(1)[2] shall not be taken into account under this subparagraph.

(C) Commodities transactions. The excess of gains over losses from transactions (including futures, forward, and similar transactions) in any commodities. This subparagraph shall not apply to gains or losses which—

(i) arise out of bona fide hedging transactions reasonably necessary to the conduct of any business by a producer, processor, merchant, or handler of a commodity in the manner in which such business is customarily and usually conducted by others,

(ii) are active business gains or losses from the sale of commodities, but only if substantially all of the controlled foreign corporation's business is as an active producer, processor, merchant, or handler of commodities, or

(iii) are foreign currency gains or losses (as defined in section 988(b)) attributable to any section 988 transactions.

(D) Foreign currency gains. The excess of foreign currency gains over foreign currency losses (as defined in section 988(b)) attributable to any section 988 transactions. This subparagraph shall not apply in the case of any transaction directly related to the business needs of the controlled foreign corporation.

(E) Income equivalent to interest. Any income equivalent to interest, including income from commitment fees (or similar amounts) for loans actually made.

[3]*(F) Income from notional principal contracts. Net income from notional principal contracts. Any item of income, gain, deduction, or loss from a notional principal contract en-*

tered into for purposes of hedging any item described in any preceding subparagraph shall not be taken into account for purposes of this subparagraph but shall be taken into account under such other subparagraph.

(G) Payments in lieu of dividends. Payments in lieu of dividends which are made pursuant to an agreement to which section 1058 applies.

(2) Exception for certain amounts.

(A) Rents and royalties derived in active business. Foreign personal holding company income shall not include rents and royalties which are derived in the active conduct of a trade or business and which are received from a person other than a related person (within the meaning of subsection (d)(3)).

(B) Certain export financing. Foreign personal holding company income shall not include any interest which is derived in the conduct of a banking business and which is export financing interest (as defined in section 904(d)(2)(G)).

[4]*(C) Exception for dealers. Except as provided in subparagraph (A), (E), or (G) of paragraph (1) or by regulations, in the case of a regular dealer in property (within the meaning of paragraph (1)(B)), forward contracts, option contracts, or similar financial instruments (including notional principal contracts and all instruments referenced to commodities), there shall not be taken into account in computing foreign personal holding income any item of income, gain, deduction, or loss from any transaction (including hedging transactions) entered into in the ordinary course of such dealer's trade or business as such a dealer.*

* * * * * * * * * * * *

(e) Foreign base company services income.

(1) In general. For purposes of subsection (a)(3), the term "foreign base company services income" means income (whether in the form of compensation, commissions, fees, or otherwise) derived in connection with the performance of technical, managerial, engineering, architectural, scientific, skilled, industrial, commercial, or like services which—

(A) are performed for or on behalf of any related person (within the meaning of subsection (d)(3), and

(B) are performed outside the country under the laws of which the controlled foreign corporation is created or organized.

(2) Exception. Paragraph (1) shall not apply to income derived in connection with the performance of services which are directly related to—

CAUTION. Subparas. (e)(2)(A) and (B), following, are effective for the first full tax. yr. of a foreign corporation begin. before 1/1/98, and for tax. yrs. of U.S. shareholders with or within which such tax. yr. of such foreign corporation ends. For subparas. (e)(2)(A)-(C), effective for the first full tax. yr. of a foreign corporation begin. after 12/31/97, and before 1/1/99, and for tax. yrs. of U.S. shareholders with or within which such tax. yr. of such foreign corporation ends, see below.

(A) the sale or exchange by the controlled foreign corporation of property manufactured, produced, grown, or extracted by it and which are performed before the time of the sale or exchange, or

(B) an offer or effort to sell or exchange such property.

CAUTION. Subparas. (e)(2)(A)-(C), following, are effective for the first full tax. yr. of a foreign corporation begin. after 12/31/97, and before 1/1/99, and for tax. yrs. of U.S. shareholders with or within which such tax. yr. of such foreign corporation ends. For subparas. (e)(2)(A) and (B), effective for the first full tax. yr. of a foreign corporation begin. before 1/1/98, and for tax. yrs. of U.S. shareholders with or within which such tax. yr. of such foreign corporation ends, see above.

(A) the sale or exchange by the controlled foreign corporation of property manufactured, produced, grown, or extracted by it and which are performed before the time of the sale or exchange,[5]

(B) an offer or effort to sell or exchange such property[6], *or*

[7](C) *in the case of taxable years described in subsection (h)(8), the active conduct by a controlled foreign corporation of a banking, financing, insurance, or similar business, but only if the corporation is predominantly engaged in the active conduct of such business (within the meaning of subsection (h)(3)) or is a qualifying insurance company.*

* * * * * * * * * * *

CAUTION.   Subsec. (h) is effective for the first full tax. yr. of a foreign corporation begin. after 12/31/97, and before 1/1/99, and for tax. yrs. of U.S. shareholders with or within which such tax. yr. of such foreign corporation ends.

[8]*(h) Special rule for income derived in the active conduct of banking, financing, or similar businesses.*

(1) In general. For purposes of subsection (c)(1), foreign personal holding company income shall not include income which is—

(A) derived in the active conduct by a controlled foreign corporation of a banking, financing, or similar business, but only if the corporation is predominantly engaged in the active conduct of such business,

(B) received from a person other than a related person (within the meaning of subsection (d)(3)) and derived from the investments made by a qualifying insurance company of its reserves or of 80 percent of its unearned premiums (as both are determined in the manner prescribed under paragraph (4)), or

(C) received from a person other than a related person (within the meaning of subsection (d)(3)) and derived from investments made by a qualifying insurance company of an amount of its assets equal to —

(i) in the case of contracts regulated in the country in which sold as property, casualty, or health insurance contracts, one-third of its premiums earned on such insurance contracts during the taxable year (as defined in section 832(b)(4)), and

(ii) in the case of contracts regulated in the country in which sold as life insurance or annuity contracts, the greater of—

(I) 10 percent of the reserves described in subparagraph (B) for such contracts, or

(II) in the case of a qualifying insurance company which is a start-up company, $10,000,000.

(2) Principles for determining applicable income.

(A) Banking and financing income. The determination as to whether income is described in paragraph (1)(A) shall be made—

(i) except as provided in clause (ii), in accordance with the applicable principles of section 904(d)(2)(C)(ii), except that such income shall include income from all leases entered into in the ordinary course of the active conduct of a banking, financing, or similar business, and

(ii) in the case of a corporation described in paragraph (3)(B), in accordance with the applicable principles of section 1296(b) (as in effect on the day before the enactment of the Taxpayer Relief Act of 1997) for determining what is not passive income.

(B) Insurance income. Under rules prescribed by the Secretary, for purposes of paragraphs (1) (B) and (C)—

(i) in the case of contracts which are separate account-type contracts (including variable contracts not meeting the requirements of section 817), only income specifically allocable to such contracts shall be taken into account, and

(ii) in the case of other contracts, income not allocable under clause (i) shall be allocated ratably among such contracts.

(C) Look-thru rules. The Secretary shall prescribe regulations consistent with the principles of section 904(d)(3) which provide that dividends, interest, income equivalent to interest, rents, or royalties received or accrued from a related person (within the meaning of subsection (d)(3)) shall be subject to look-thru treatment for purposes of this subsection.

(3) Predominantly engaged. *For purposes of paragraph (1)(A), a corporation shall be deemed predominantly engaged in the active conduct of a banking, financing, or similar business only if—*

(A) *more than 70 percent of its gross income is derived from such business from transactions with persons which are not related persons (as defined in subsection (d)(3)) and which are located within the country under the laws of which the controlled foreign corporation is created or organized, or*

(B) *the corporation is—*

(i) *engaged in the active conduct of a banking or securities business (within the meaning of section 1296(b), as in effect before the enactment of the Taxpayer Relief Act of 1997), or*

(ii) *a qualified bank affiliate or a qualified securities affiliate (within the meaning of the proposed regulations under such section 1296(b)).*

(4) Methods for determining unearned premiums and reserves. *For purposes of paragraph (1)(B)—*

(A) *Property and casualty contracts. The unearned premiums and reserves of a qualifying insurance company with respect to property, casualty, or health insurance contracts shall be determined using the same methods and interest rates which would be used if such company were subject to tax under subchapter L.*

(B) *Life insurance and annuity contracts. The reserves of a qualifying insurance company with respect to life insurance or annuity contracts shall be determined under the method described in paragraph (5) which such company elects to apply for purposes of this paragraph. Such election shall be made at such time and in such manner as the Secretary may prescribe and, once made, shall be irrevocable without the consent of the Secretary.*

(C) *Limitation on reserves. In no event shall the reserve determined under this paragraph for any contract as of any time exceed the amount which would be taken into account with respect to such contract as of such time in determining foreign annual statement reserves (less any catastrophe or deficiency reserves).*

(5) Methods. *The methods described in this paragraph are as follows:*

(A) *U.S. method. The method which would apply if the qualifying insurance company were subject to tax under subchapter L, except that the interest rate used shall be an interest rate determined for the foreign country in which such company is created or organized and which is calculated in the same manner as the Federal mid-term rate under section 1274(d).*

(B) *Foreign method. A preliminary term method, except that the interest rate used shall be the interest rate determined for the foreign country in which such company is created or organized and which is calculated in the same manner as the Federal mid-term rate under section 1274(d). If a qualifying insurance company uses such a preliminary term method with respect to contracts insuring risks located in such foreign country, such method shall apply if such company elects the method under this clause.*

(C) *Cash surrender value. A method under which reserves are equal to the net surrender value (as defined in section 807(e)(1)(A)) of the contract.*

(6) Definitions. *For purposes of this subsection—*

(A) *Terms relating to insurance companies.*

(i) *Qualifying insurance company. The term "qualifying insurance company" means any entity which—*

(I) *is subject to regulation as an insurance company under the laws of its country of incorporation,*

(II) *realizes at least 50 percent of its net written premiums from the insurance or reinsurance of risks located within the country in which such entity is created or organized, and*

(III) *is engaged in the active conduct of an insurance business and would be subject to tax under subchapter L if it were a domestic corporation.*

(ii) *Start-up company. A qualifying insurance company shall be treated as a start-up company if such company (and any predecessor) has not been engaged in the active con-*

duct of an insurance business for more than 5 years as of the beginning of the taxable year of such company.

(B) Located. For purposes of paragraph (3)(A)—

(i) In general. A person shall be treated as located—

(I) except as provided in subclause (II), within the country in which it maintains an office or other fixed place of business through which it engages in a trade or business and by which the transaction is effected, or

(II) in the case of a natural person, within the country in which such person is physically located when such person enters into a transaction.

(ii) Special rule for qualified business units. Gross income derived by a corporation's qualified business unit (within the meaning of section 989(a)) from transactions with persons which are not related persons (as defined in subsection (d)(3)) and which are located in the country in which the qualified business unit both maintains its principal office and conducts substantial business activity shall be treated as derived from transactions with persons which are not related persons (as defined in subsection (d)(3)) and which are located within the country under the laws of which the controlled foreign corporation is created or organized.

(7) Anti-abuse rules. For purposes of applying this subsection, there shall be disregarded any item of income, gain, loss, or deduction with respect to any transaction or series of transactions one of the principal purposes of which is qualifying income or gain for the exclusion under this section, including any change in the method of computing reserves or any other transaction or series of transactions a principal purpose of which is the acceleration or deferral of any item in order to claim the benefits of such exclusion through the application of this subsection.

(8) Coordination with section 953. This subsection shall not apply to investment income allocable to contracts that insure related party risks or risks located in a foreign country other than the country in which the qualifying insurance company is created or organized.

(9) Application. This subsection shall apply to the first full taxable year of a foreign corporation beginning after December 31, 1997, and before January 1, 1999, and to taxable years of United States shareholders with or within which such taxable year of such foreign corporation ends.

[For analysis, see ¶ 1609, ¶ 1610. For text of Committee Report, see ¶ 5143, ¶ 5197.]

[Endnote Code Sec. 954]

Matter in *italics* in Code Sec. 954(c)(1)(B), Code Sec. 954(c)(1)(F), Code Sec. 954(c)(1)(G) and Code Sec. 954(c)(2)(C) added by Sec. 1051(a)(1), (a)(2)(A), (a)(2)(B), and (b) of the Taxpayer Relief Act of 1997, H.R. 2014, 8/5/97, which struck out:

1. "In the case of any regular dealer in property, gains and losses from the sale or exchange of any such property or arising out of bona fide hedging transactions reasonably necessary to the conduct of the business of being a dealer in such property shall not be taken into account under this subparagraph."
2. "also"
3. added subparas. (c)(1)(F) and (G)
4. added subpara. (c)(2)(C)

Effective Date (Sec. 1051(c), H.R. 2014, 8/5/97) effective for tax. yrs. begin. after 8/5/97.

Matter in *italics* in Code Sec. 954(e)(2)(A), Code Sec. 954(e)(2)(B), Code Sec. 954(e)(2)(C) and Code Sec. 954(h) added by Sec. 1175(a) and (b), H.R. 2014, 8/5/97, which struck out:

5. "or"
6. "."
7. added subpara. (e)(2)(C)
8. added subsec. (h)

Effective Date (Sec. 1175(c), H.R. 2014, 8/5/97) effective for the first full tax. yr. of a foreign corporation begin. after 12/31/97, and before 1/1/99, and for tax. yrs. of U.S. shareholders with or within which such tax. yr. of such foreign corporation ends.

[¶ 3153]   Code Sec. 956.   Investment of earnings in United States property.

(a) **General rule.** In the case of any controlled foreign corporation, the amount determined under this section with respect to any United States shareholder for any taxable year is the lesser of—

   (1) the excess (if any) of—

     (A) such shareholder's pro rata share of the average of the amounts of United States property held (directly or indirectly) by the controlled foreign corporation as of the close of each quarter of such taxable year, over

     (B) the amount of earnings and profits described in section 959(c)(1)(A) with respect to such shareholder, or

   (2) such shareholder's pro rata share of the applicable earnings of such controlled foreign corporation.

The amount taken into account under paragraph (1) with respect to any property shall be its adjusted basis as determined for purposes of computing earnings and profits, reduced by any liability to which the property is subject.

(b) **Special rules.**

   (1) **Applicable earnings.** For purposes of this section, the term "applicable earnings" means, with respect to any controlled foreign corporation, the sum of—

     (A) the amount (not including a deficit) referred to in section 316(a)(1) [1]*to the extent such amount was accumulated in prior taxable years,* and

     (B) the amount referred to in section 316(a)(2),

   but reduced by distributions made during the taxable year and by earnings and profits described in section 959(c)(i).

* * * * * * * * * * * *

(c) **United States property defined.**

   (1) **In general.** For purposes of subsection (a), the term "United States property" means any property acquired after December 31, 1962, which is—

     (A) tangible property located in the United States;

     (B) stock of a domestic corporation;

     (C) an obligation of a United States person; or

     (D) any right to the use in the United States of—

       (i) a patent or copyright,

       (ii) an invention, model, or design (whether or not patented),

       (iii) a secret formula or process, or

       (iv) any other similar property right,

   which is acquired or developed by the controlled foreign corporation for use in the United States.

   (2) **Exceptions.** For purposes of subsection (a), the term "United States property" does not include—

     (A) obligations of the United States, money, or deposits with persons carrying on the banking business;

     (B) property located in the United States which is purchased in the United States for export to, or use in, foreign countries;

     (C) any obligation of a United States person arising in connection with the sale or processing of property if the amount of such obligation outstanding at no time during the taxable year exceeds the amount which would be ordinary and necessary to carry on the trade or business of both the other party to the sale or processing transaction and the United States person had the sale or processing transaction been made between unrelated persons;

     (D) any aircraft, railroad rolling stock, vessel, motor vehicle, or container used in the transportation of persons or property in foreign commerce and used predominantly outside the United States;

(E) an amount of assets of an insurance company equivalent to the unearned premiums or reserves ordinary and necessary for the proper conduct of its insurance business attributable to contracts which are not contracts described in section 953(a)(1);

(F) the stock or obligations of a domestic corporation which is neither a United States shareholder (as defined in section 951(b)) of the controlled foreign corporation, nor a domestic corporation, 25 percent or more of the total combined voting power of which, immediately after the acquisition of any stock in such domestic corporation by the controlled foreign corporation, is owned, or is considered as being owned, by such United States shareholders in the aggregate;

(G) any movable property (other than a vessel or aircraft) which is used for the purpose of exploring for, developing, removing, or transporting resources from ocean waters or under such waters when used on the Continental Shelf of the United States;

CAUTION. Subparas. (c)(2)(H) and (I), following, are effective for tax. yrs. of foreign corporations begin. before 1/1/98. For subparas. (c)(2)(H)-(K), effective for tax. yrs. of foreign corporations begin. after 12/31/97, and for tax. yrs. of U.S. shareholders with or within which such tax. yrs. of foreign corporations end, see below.

(H) an amount of assets of the controlled foreign corporation equal to the earnings and profits accumulated after December 31, 1962, and excluded from subpart F income under section 952(b); and

(I) to the extent provided in regulations prescribed by the Secretary, property which is otherwise United States property which is held by a FSC and which is related to the export activities of such FSC.

CAUTION. Subparas. (c)(2)(H)-(K), following, are effective for tax. yrs. of foreign corporations begin. after 12/31/97, and for tax. yrs. of U.S. shareholders with or within which such tax. yrs. of foreign corporations end. For subparas. (c)(2)(H) and (I), effective for tax. yrs. of foreign corporations begin. before 1/1/98, see above.

(H) an amount of assets of the controlled foreign corporation equal to the earnings and profits accumulated after December 31, 1962, and excluded from subpart F income under section 952(b);[2]

(I) to the extent provided in regulations prescribed by the Secretary, property which is otherwise United States property which is held by a FSC and which is related to the export activities of such FSC[3];

[4]*(J) deposits of cash or securities made or received on commercial terms in the ordinary course of a United States or foreign person's business as a dealer in securities or in commodities, but only to the extent such deposits are made or received as collateral or margin for (i) a securities loan, notional principal contract, options contract, forward contract, or futures contract, or (ii) any other financial transaction in which the Secretary determines that it is customary to post collateral or margin; and*

(K) an obligation of a United States person to the extent the principal amount of the obligation does not exceed the fair market value of readily marketable securities sold or purchased pursuant to a sale and repurchase agreement or otherwise posted or received as collateral for the obligation in the ordinary course of its business by a United States or foreign person which is a dealer in securities or commodities.

For purposes of subparagraphs (J) and (K), the term "dealer in securities" has the meaning given such term by section 475(c)(1), and the term "dealer in commodities" has the meaning given such term by section 475(e), except that such term shall include a futures commission merchant.

* * * * * * * * * * * *

[For analysis, see ¶ 1611, ¶ 1616. For text of Committee Report, see ¶ 5195, ¶ 5362.]

[Endnote Code Sec. 956]

Matter in *italics* in Code Sec. 956(b)(1)(A) added by Sec. 1601(e) of the Taxpayer Relief Act of 1997, H.R. 2014, 8/5/97.
1. added matter in subpara. (b)(1)(A)

Effective Date (Sec. 1601(j)(1), H.R. 2014, 8/5/97) effective for tax. yrs. of foreign corporations begin. after 12/31/96, and for tax. yrs. of U.S. shareholders within which or with which such tax. yrs. of foreign corporations end.

Matter in *italics* in Code Sec. 956(c)(2)(H), Code Sec. 956(c)(2)(I), Code Sec. 956(c)(2)(J) and Code Sec. 956(c)(2)(K) added by Sec. 1173(a), H.R. 2014, 8/5/97, which struck out:
2. "and"
3. "."
4. added subparas. (c)(2)(J) and (K) and flush language in para. (c)(2)
Effective Date (Sec. 1173(b), H.R. 2014, 8/5/97) effective for tax. yrs. of foreign corporations begin. after 12/31/96, and for tax. yrs. of U.S. shareholders within which or with which such tax. yrs. of foreign corporations end.

[¶ 3154]   Code Sec. 960.   Special rules for foreign tax credit.
(a) Taxes paid by a foreign corporation.
   [1]*(1) Deemed paid credit. For purposes of subpart A of this part, if there is included under section 951(a) in the gross income of a domestic corporation any amount attributable to earnings and profits of a foreign corporation which is a member of a qualified group (as defined in section 902(b)) with respect to the domestic corporation, then, except to the extent provided in regulations, section 902 shall be applied as if the amount so included were a dividend paid by such foreign corporation (determined by applying section 902(c) in accordance with section 904(d)(3)(B)).*

* * * * * * * * * * * *

[For analysis, see ¶ 1601. For text of Committee Report, see ¶ 5175.]

[Endnote Code Sec. 960]
   Matter in *italics* in Code Sec. 960(a)(1) added by Sec. 1113(b) of the Taxpayer Relief Act of 1997, H.R. 2014, 8/5/97, which struck out:
   1. "(1) General rule. For purposes of subpart A of this part, if there is included, under section 951(a), in the gross income of a domestic corporation any amount attributable to earnings and profits—
   "(A) of a foreign corporation (hereafter in this subsection referred to as the 'first foreign corporation') at least 10 percent of the voting stock of which is owned by such domestic corporation, or
   "(B) of a second foreign corporation (hereinafter in this subsection referred to as the 'second foreign corporation') at least 10 percent of the voting stock of which is owned by the first foreign corporation, or
   "(C) of a third foreign corporation (hereinafter in this subsection referred to as the 'third foreign corporation') at least 10 percent of the voting stock of which is owned by the second foreign corporation,
then, except to the extent provided in regulations, such domestic corporation shall be deemed to have paid a portion of such foreign corporation's post-1986 foreign income taxes determined under section 902 in the same manner as if the amount so included were a dividend paid by such foreign corporation (determined by applying section 902(c) in accordance with section 904(d)(3)(B)). This paragraph shall not apply with respect to any amount included in the gross income of such domestic corporation attributable to earnings and profits of the second foreign corporation or of the third foreign corporation unless, in the case of the second foreign corporation, the percentage-of-voting-stock requirement of section 902(b)(3)(A) is satisfied, and in the case of the third foreign corporation, the percentage-of-voting-stock requirement of section 902(b)(3)(B) is satisfied."
Effective Date (Sec. 1113(c)(1), H.R. 2014, 8/5/97) effective for taxes of foreign corporations for tax. yrs. of such corporations begin. after 8/5/97. Sec. 1113(c)(2) of this Act provides:
   "(2) Special rule. In the case of any chain of foreign corporations described in clauses (i) and (ii) of section 902(b)(2)(B) of the Internal Revenue Code of 1986 (as amended by this section), no liquidation, reorganization, or similar transactions in a taxable year beginning after the 8/5/97 of this act shall have the effect of permitting taxes to be taken into account under section 902 of the Internal Revenue Code of 1986 which could not have been taken into account under such section but for such transaction."

[¶ 3155]   Code Sec. 961.   Adjustments to basis of stock in controlled foreign corporations and of other property.

* * * * * * * * * * * *

   CAUTION.   Subsec. (c), following, is effective for purposes of determining inclusions for tax. yrs. of United States shareholders begin. after 12/31/97.

   [1]*(c) Basis adjustments in stock held by foreign corporation. Under regulations prescribed by the Secretary, if a United States shareholder is treated under section 958(a)(2) as owning any*

stock in a controlled foreign corporation which is actually owned by another controlled foreign corporation, adjustments similar to the adjustments provided by subsections (a) and (b) shall be made to the basis of such stock in the hands of such other controlled foreign corporation, but only for the purposes of determining the amount included under section 951 in the gross income of such United States shareholder (or any other United States shareholder who acquires from any person any portion of the interest of such United States shareholder by reason of which such shareholder was treated as owning such stock, but only to the extent of such portion, and subject to such proof of identity of such interest as the Secretary may prescribe by regulations).

[For analysis, see ¶ 1614. For text of Committee Report, see ¶ 5175.]

[Endnote Code Sec. 961]
  Code Sec. 961(c), in *italics*, was added by Sec. 1112(b)(1) of the Taxpayer Relief Act of 1997, H.R. 2014, 8/5/97.
  1. added subsec. (c)
Effective Date (Sec. 1112(b)(2), H.R. 2014, 8/5/97) effective for purposes of determining inclusions for tax. yrs. of United States shareholders begin. after 12/31/97.

[¶ 3156] Code Sec. 964. Miscellaneous provisions.

* * * * * * * * * * * *

[1](e) *Gain on certain stock sales by controlled foreign corporations treated as dividends.*
  (1) In general. If a controlled foreign corporation sells or exchanges stock in any other foreign corporation, gain recognized on such sale or exchange shall be included in the gross income of such controlled foreign corporation as a dividend to the same extent that it would have been so included under section 1248(a) if such controlled foreign corporation were a United States person. For purposes of determining the amount which would have been so includible, the determination of whether such other foreign corporation was a controlled foreign corporation shall be made without regard to the preceding sentence.
  (2) Same country exception not applicable. Clause (i) of section 954(c)(3)(A) shall not apply to any amount treated as a dividend by reason of paragraph (1).
  (3) Clarification of deemed sales. For purposes of this subsection, a controlled foreign corporation shall be treated as having sold or exchanged any stock if, under any provision of this subtitle, such controlled foreign corporation is treated as having gain from the sale or exchange of such stock.

[For analysis, see ¶ 1612. For text of Committee Report, see ¶ 5175.]

[Endnote Code Sec. 964]
  Code Sec. 964(e), in *italics*, was added by Sec. 1111(a) of the Taxpayer Relief Act of 1997, H.R. 2014, 8/5/97.
  1. added subsec. (e)
Effective Date (Sec. 1111(c)(1), H.R. 2014, 8/5/97) effective for gain recognized on transactions occurring after 8/5/97.

[¶ 3157] Code Sec. 986. Determination of foreign taxes and foreign corporation's earnings and profits.

  CAUTION. Subsec. (a), following, is effective for taxes paid or accrued in tax. yrs. begin. before 1/1/98. For subsec. (a), effective for taxes paid or accrued in tax. yrs. begin. after 12/31/97, see below.

  (a) Foreign taxes.
    (1) In general. For purposes of determining the amount of the foreign tax credit—
      (A) any foreign income taxes shall be translated into dollars using the exchange rates as of the time such taxes were paid to the foreign country or possession of the United States, and
      (B) any adjustment to the amount of foreign income taxes shall be translated into dollars using—

(i) except as provided in clause (ii), the exchange rate as of the time when such adjustment is paid to the foreign country or possession, or

(i) in the case of any refund or credit of foreign income taxes, using the exchange rate as of the time of original payment of such foreign income taxes.

(2) Foreign income taxes. For purposes of paragraph (1), "foreign income taxes" means any income, war profits, or excess profits taxes paid to any foreign country or to any possession of the United States.

CAUTION.   Subsec. (a), following, is effective for taxes paid or accrued in tax. yrs. begin. after 12/31/97. For subsec. (a), effective for taxes paid or accrued in tax. yrs. begin. before 1/1/98, see above.

[1](a) *Foreign income taxes.*

(1) *Translation of accrued taxes.*

(A) *In general.* For purposes of determining the amount of the foreign tax credit, in the case of a taxpayer who takes foreign income taxes into account when accrued, the amount of any foreign income taxes (and any adjustment thereto) shall be translated into dollars by using the average exchange rate for the taxable year to which such taxes relate.

(B) *Exception for certain taxes.* Subparagraph (A) shall not apply to any foreign income taxes—

(i) paid after the date 2 years after the close of the taxable year to which such taxes relate, or

(ii) paid before the beginning of the taxable year to which such taxes relate.

(C) *Exception for inflationary currencies.* Subparagraph (A) shall not apply to any foreign income taxes the liability for which is denominated in any inflationary currency (as determined under regulations).

(D) *Cross reference.* For adjustments where tax is not paid within 2 years, see section 905(c).

(2) *Translation of taxes to which paragraph (1) does not apply.* For purposes of determining the amount of the foreign tax credit, in the case of any foreign income taxes to which subparagraph (A) of paragraph (1) does not apply—

(A) such taxes shall be translated into dollars using the exchange rates as of the time such taxes were paid to the foreign country or possession of the United States, and

(B) any adjustment to the amount of such taxes shall be translated into dollars using—

(i) except as provided in clause (ii), the exchange rate as of the time when such adjustment is paid to the foreign country or possession, or

(ii) in the case of any refund or credit of foreign income taxes, using the exchange rate as of the time of the original payment of such foreign income taxes.

[2](3) *Authority to permit use of average rates.* To the extent prescribed in regulations, the average exchange rate for the period (specified in such regulations) during which the taxes or adjustment is paid may be used instead of the exchange rate as of the time of such payment.

[3](4) *Foreign income taxes.* For purposes of this subsection, the term "foreign income taxes" means any income, war profits, or excess profits taxes paid or accrued to any foreign country or to any possession of the United States.

(b) Earnings and profits and distributions. For purposes of determining the tax under this subtitle—

(1) of any shareholder of any foreign corporation, the earnings and profits of such corporation shall be determined in the corporation's functional currency, and

(2) in the case of any United States person, the earnings and profits determined under paragraph (1) (when distributed, deemed distributed, or otherwise taken into account under this subtitle) shall (if necessary) be translated into dollars using the appropriate exchange rate.

(c) Previously taxed earnings and profits.

(1) In general. Foreign currency gain or loss with respect to distributions of previously taxed earnings and profits (as described in section 959 or 1293(c)) attributable to movements

in exchange rates between the times of deemed and actual distribution shall be recognized and treated as ordinary income or loss from the same source as the associated income inclusion.

(2) Distributions through tiers. The Secretary shall prescribe regulations with respect to the treatment of distributions of previously taxed earnings and profits through tiers of foreign corporations.

[For analysis, see ¶ 1605. For text of Committee Report, see ¶ 5171.]

[Endnote Code Sec. 986]

Matter in *italics* in Code Sec. 986(a) was added by Sec. 1102(a)(1) and (b)(1) of the Taxpayer Relief Act of 1997, H.R. 2014, 8/5/97, which struck out:

1. added subsec. (a)
2. added para. (a)(3) [as amended above]
3. "(3)"

Effective Date (Sec. 1102(c)(1), H.R. 2014, 8/5/97) effective for taxes paid or accrued in tax. yrs. begin. after 12/31/97.

[¶ 3158]   Code Sec. 988.   Treatment of certain foreign currency transactions.

* * * * * * * * * * * *

CAUTION.   Subsec. (e), following, is effective for tax. yrs. begin. before 1/1/98. For subsec. (e) effective for tax .yrs. begin. after 12/31/97, see below.

(e) Application to individuals. This section shall apply to section 988 transactions entered into by an individual only to the extent expenses properly allocable to such transactions meet the requirements of section 162 or 212 (other than that part of section 212 dealing with expenses incurred in connection with taxes).

CAUTION.   Subsec. (e), following, is effective for tax. yrs. begin. after 12/31/97. For subsec. (e) effective for tax. yrs. begin. before 1/1/98, see above.

[1]*(e) Application to individuals.*

(1) In general. The preceding provisions of this section shall not apply to any section 988 transaction entered into by an individual which is a personal transaction.

(2) Exclusion for certain personal transactions. If—

(A) nonfunctional currency is disposed of by an individual in any transaction, and

(B) such transaction is a personal transaction,

no gain shall be recognized for purposes of this subtitle by reason of changes in exchange rates after such currency was acquired by such individual and before such disposition. The preceding sentence shall not apply if the gain which would otherwise be recognized on the transaction exceeds $200.

(3) Personal transactions. For purposes of this subsection, the term "personal transaction" means any transaction entered into by an individual, except that such term shall not include any transaction to the extent that expenses properly allocable to such transaction meet the requirements of—

(A) section 162 or 212 (other than that part of section 212 dealing with expenses incurred in connection with taxes).

(B) section 212 (other than that part of section 212 dealing with expenses incurred in connection with taxes).

[For analysis, see ¶ 1623. For text of Committee Report, see ¶ 5173.]

[Endnote Code Sec. 988]

Matter in *italics* in Code Sec. 988(e) added by Sec. 1104(a) of the Taxpayer Relief Act of 1997, H.R. 2014, 8/5/97, which struck out:

1. "(e) Application to individuals.

"This section shall apply to section 988 transactions entered into by an individual only to the extent expenses properly allocable to such transactions meet the requirements of section 162 or 212 (other than that part of section 212 dealing with expenses incurred in connection with taxes)."

Effective Date (Sec. 1104(b), H.R. 2014, 8/5/97) effective for tax. yrs. begin. after 12/31/97.

[¶ 3159]   Code Sec. 989.   Other definitions and special rules.

(a) **Qualified business unit.** For purposes of this subpart, the term "qualified business unit" means any separate and clearly identified unit of a trade or business of a taxpayer which maintains separate books and records.

(b) **Appropriate exchange rate.** Except as provided in regulations, for purposes of this subpart, the term "appropriate exchange rate" means—

(1) in the case of an actual distribution of earnings and profits, the spot rate on the date such distribution is included in income,

(2) in the case of an actual or deemed sale or exchange of stock in a foreign corporation treated as a dividend under section 1248, the spot rate on the date the deemed dividend is included in income,

CAUTION.   Paras. (b)(3) and (4), following, are effective for taxes paid or accrued in tax. yrs. begin. before 1/1/98. For paras. (b)(3) and (4), effective for taxes paid or accrued in tax. yrs. begin. after 12/31/97, see below.

(3) in the case of any amounts included in income under section 951(a)(1)(A), 551(a), or 1293(a), the weighted average exchange rate for the taxable year of the foreign corporation, or

(4) in the case of any other qualified business unit of a taxpayer, the weighted average exchange rate for the taxable year of such qualified business unit.

CAUTION.   Paras. (b)(3) and (4), following, are effective for taxes paid or accrued in tax. yrs. begin. after 12/31/97. For paras. (b)(3) and (4), effective for taxes paid or accrued in tax. yrs. begin. before 1/1/98, see above.

(3) in the case of any amounts included in income under section 951(a)(1)(A), 551(a), or 1293(a), the[1] average exchange rate for the taxable year of the foreign corporation, or

(4) in the case of any other qualified business unit of a taxpayer, the[2] average exchange rate for the taxable year of such qualified business unit.

For purposes of the preceding sentence, any amount included in income under section 951(a)(1)(B) shall be treated as an actual distribution made on the last day of the taxable year for which such amount was so included.

(c) **Regulations** The Secretary shall prescribe such regulations as may be necessary or appropriate to carry out the purposes of this subpart including regulations—

(1) setting forth procedures to be followed by taxpayers with qualified business units using a net worth method of accounting before the enactment of this subpart,

(2) limiting the recognition of foreign currency loss on certain remittances from qualified business units,

(3) providing for the recharacterization of interest and principal payments with respect to obligations denominated in certain hyperinflationary currencies,

CAUTION.   Paras. (c)(4) and (5), following, are effective for taxes paid or accrued in tax. yrs. begin. before 1/1/98. For paras. (c)(4)-(6), effective for taxes paid or accrued in tax. yrs. begin. after 12/31/97, see below.

(4) providing for alternative adjustments to the application of section 905(c), and

(5) providing for the appropriate treatment of related party transactions (including transactions between qualified business units of the same taxpayer).

CAUTION.   Paras. (c)(4)-(6), following, are effective for taxes paid or accrued in tax. yrs. begin. after 12/31/97. For paras. (c)(4) and (5), effective for taxes paid or accrued in tax. yrs. begin. before 1/1/98, see above.

(4) providing for alternative adjustments to the application of section 905(c),[3]

(5) providing for the appropriate treatment of related party transactions (including transactions between qualified business units of the same taxpayer)[4], *and*

[5]*(6) setting forth procedures for determining the average exchange rate for any period.*

[For analysis, see ¶ 1605. For text of Committee Report, see ¶ 5171.]

[Endnote Code Sec. 989]

Matter in *italics* in Code Sec. 989(b)(3), Code Sec. 989(b)(4), Code Sec. 989(c)(4), Code Sec. 989(c)(5), and Code Sec. 989(c)(6) was added by Sec. 1102(b)(2) and (3) of the Taxpayer Relief Act of 1997, H.R. 2014, 8/5/97, which struck out:
1. "weighted"
2. "weighted"
3. "and"
4. "."
5. added para. (c)(6)

Effective Date (Sec. 1102(c)(1), H.R. 2014, 8/5/97) effective for taxes paid or accrued in tax. yrs. begin. after 12/31/97.

[¶ 3160] Code Sec. 1014.   Basis of property acquired from a decedent.

    CAUTION.   Subsec. (a), following, is effective for estates of decedents dying before 1/1/98. For subsec. (a), effective for estates of decedents dying after 12/31/97, see below.

    (a) In general. Except as otherwise provided in this section, the basis of property in the hands of a person acquiring the property from a decedent or to whom the property passed from a decedent shall, if not sold, exchanged, or otherwise disposed of before the decedent's death by such person, be—

    (1) the fair market value of the property at the date of the decedent's death, or

    (2) in the case of an election under either section 2032 or section 811(j) of the Internal Revenue Code of 1939 where the decedent died after October 21, 1942, its value at the applicable valuation date prescribed by those sections, or

    (3) in the case of an election under section 2032A, its value determined under such section.

    CAUTION.   Subsec. (a), following, is effective for estates of decedents dying after 12/31/97. For subsec. (a), effective for estates of decedents dying before 1/1/98, see above.

    (a) In general. Except as otherwise provided in this section, the basis of property in the hands of a person acquiring the property from a decedent or to whom the property passed from a decedent shall, if not sold, exchanged, or otherwise disposed of before the decedent's death by such person, be—

    (1) the fair market value of the property at the date of the decedent's death,[1]

    (2) in the case of an election under either section 2032 or section 811(j) of the Internal Revenue Code of 1939 where the decedent died after October 21, 1942, its value at the applicable valuation date prescribed by those sections,[2]

    (3) in the case of an election under section 2032A, its value determined under such section, [3]*or*

    [4]*(4) to the extent of the applicability of the exclusion described in section 2031(c), the basis in the hands of the decedent.*

    (b) Property acquired from the decedent. For purposes of subsection (a), the following property shall be considered to have been acquired from or to have passed from the decedent:

    (1) Property acquired by bequest, devise, or inheritance, or by the decedent's estate from the decedent;

    (2) Property transferred by the decedent during his lifetime in trust to pay the income for life to or on the order or direction of the decedent, with the right reserved to the decedent at all times before his death to revoke the trust;

    (3) In the case of decedents dying after December 31, 1951, property transferred by the decedent during his lifetime in trust to pay the income for life to or on the order or direction of the decedent with the right reserved to the decedent at all times before his death to make any change in the enjoyment thereof through the exercise of a power to alter, amend, or terminate the trust;

    (4) Property passing without full and adequate consideration under a general power of appointment exercised by the decedent by will;

(5) In the case of decedents dying after August 26, 1937, property acquired by bequest, devise, or inheritance or by the decedent's estate from the decedent, if the property consists of stock or securities of a foreign corporation, which with respect to its taxable year next preceding the date of the decedent's death was, under the law applicable to such year, a foreign personal holding company. In such case, the basis shall be the fair market value of such property at the date of the decedent's death or the basis in the hands of the decedent, whichever is lower;

(6) In the case of decedents dying after December 31, 1947, property which represents the surviving spouse's one-half share of community property held by the decedent and the surviving spouse under the community property laws of any State, or possession of the United States or any foreign country, if at least one-half of the whole of the community interest in such property was includible in determining the value of the decedent's gross estate under chapter 11 of subtitle B (section 2001 and following, relating to estate tax) or section 811 of the Internal Revenue Code of 1939;

(7) In the case of decedents dying after October 21, 1942, and on or before December 31, 1947, such part of any property, representing the surviving spouse's one-half share of property held by a decedent and the surviving spouse under the community property laws of any State, or possession of the United States or any foreign country, as was included in determining the value of the gross estate of the decedent, if a tax under chapter 3 of the Internal Revenue Code of 1939 was payable on the transfer of the net estate of the decedent. In such case, nothing in this paragraph shall reduce the basis below that which would exist if the Revenue Act of 1948 had not been enacted;

(8) In the case of decedents dying after December 31, 1950, and before January 1, 1954, property which represents the survivor's interest in a joint and survivor's annuity if the value of any part of such interest was required to be included in determining the value of decedent's gross estate under section 811 of the Internal Revenue Code of 1939;

(9) In the case of decedents dying after December 31, 1953, property acquired from the decedent by reason of death, form of ownership, or other conditions (including property acquired through the exercise or non-exercise of a power of appointment), if by reason thereof the property is required to be included in determining the value of the decedent's gross estate under chapter 11 of subtitle B or under the Internal Revenue Code of 1939. In such case, if the property is acquired before the death of the decedent, the basis shall be the amount determined under subsection (a) reduced by the amount allowed to the taxpayer as deductions in computing taxable income under this subtitle or prior income tax laws for exhaustion, wear and tear, obsolescence, amortization, and depletion on such property before the death of the decedent. Such basis shall be applicable to the property commencing on the death of the decedent. This paragraph shall not apply to—

(A) annuities described in section 72;

(B) property to which paragraph (5) would apply if the property had been acquired by bequest; and

(C) property described in any other paragraph of this subsection.

(10) Property includible in the gross estate of the decedent under section 2044 (relating to certain property for which marital deduction was previously allowed). In any such case, the last 3 sentences of paragraph (9) shall apply as if such property were described in the first sentence of paragraph (9).

(c) **Property representing income in respect of a decedent.** This section shall not apply to property which constitutes a right to receive an item of income in respect of a decedent under section 691.

(d) **Special rule with respect to DISC stock.** If stock owned by a decedent in a DISC or former DISC (as defined in section 992(a)) acquires a new basis under subsection (a), such basis (determined before the application of this subsection) shall be reduced by the amount (if any) which would have been included in gross income under section 995(c) as a dividend if the decedent had lived and sold the stock at its fair market value on the estate tax valuation date. In computing the gain the decedent would have had if he had lived and sold the stock, his basis shall be determined without regard to the last sentence of section 996(e)(2) (relating to reductions of basis of DISC stock). For purposes of this subsection, the estate tax valuation date is the date of the decedent's death or, in the case of an election under section 2032, the applicable valuation date prescribed by that section.

(e) Appreciated property acquired by decedent by gift within 1 year of death.

(1) In general. In the case of a decedent dying after December 31, 1981, if—

(A) appreciated property was acquired by the decedent by gift during the 1-year period ending on the date of the decedent's death, and

(B) such property is acquired from the decedent by (or passes from the decedent to) the donor of such property (or the spouse of such donor),

the basis of such property in the hands of such donor (or spouse) shall be the adjusted basis of such property in the hands of the decedent immediately before the death of the decedent.

(2) Definitions. For purposes of paragraph (1)—

(A) Appreciated property. The term "appreciated property" means any property if the fair market value of such property on the day it was transferred to the decedent by gift exceeds its adjusted basis.

(B) Treatment of certain property sold by estate. In the case of any appreciated property described in subparagraph (A) of paragraph (1) sold by the estate of the decedent or by a trust of which the decedent was the grantor, rules similar to the rules of paragraph (1) shall apply to the extent the donor of such property (or the spouse of such donor) is entitled to the proceeds from such sale.

[For analysis, see ¶ 518. For text of Committee Report, see ¶ 5033.]

[Endnote Code Sec. 1014]

Matter in *italics* in Code Sec. 1014(a)(1), Code Sec. 1014(a)(2), Code Sec. 1014(a)(3) and Code Sec. 1014(a)(4) added by Sec. 508(b) of the Taxpayer Relief Act of 1997, H.R. 2014, 8/5/97, which struck out:

1. "or"
2. "or"
3. "."
4. added para. (a)(4)

Effective Date (Sec. 508(e)(1), H.R. 2014, 8/5/97) effective for estates of decedents dying after 12/31/97.

[¶ 3161]   Code Sec. 1016.   Adjustments to basis.

(a) General rule. Proper adjustment in respect of the property shall in all cases be made—

(1) for expenditures, receipts, losses, or other items, properly chargeable to capital account, but no such adjustment shall be made—

(A) for taxes or other carrying charges described in section 266, or

(B) for expenditures described in section 173 (relating to circulation expenditures),

for which deductions have been taken by the taxpayer in determining taxable income for the taxable year or prior taxable years;

(2) in respect of any period since February 28, 1913, for exhaustion, wear and tear, obsolescence, amortization, and depletion, to the extent of the amount—

(A) allowed as deductions in computing taxable income under this subtitle or prior income tax laws, and

(B) resulting (by reason of the deductions so allowed) in a reduction for any taxable year of the taxpayer's taxes under this subtitle (other than chapter 2, relating to tax on self-employment income), or prior income, war-profits, or excess-profits tax laws,

but not less than the amount allowable under this subtitle or prior income tax laws. Where no method has been adopted under section 167 (relating to depreciation deduction), the amount allowable shall be determined under the straight line method. Subparagraph (B) of this paragraph shall not apply in respect of any period since February 28, 1913, and before January 1, 1952, unless an election has been made under section 1020 (as in effect before the date of the enactment of the Tax Reform Act of 1976). Where for any taxable year before the taxable year 1932 the depletion allowance was based on discovery value or a percentage of income, then the adjustment for depletion for such year shall be based on the depletion which would have been allowable for such year if computed without reference to discovery value or a percentage of income;

(3) in respect of any period—

(A) before March 1, 1913,

(B) since February 28, 1913, during which such property was held by a person or an organization not subject to income taxation under this chapter or prior income tax laws,

(C) since February 28, 1913, and before January 1, 1958, during which such property was held by a person subject to tax under part I of subchapter L (or the corresponding provisions of prior income tax laws), to the extent that paragraph (2) does not apply, and

(D) since February 28, 1913, during which such property was held by a person subject to tax under part II of subchapter L (or the corresponding provisions of prior income tax laws), to the extent that paragraph (2) does not apply,

for exhaustion, wear and tear, obsolescence, amortization, and depletion, to the extent sustained;

(4) in the case of stock (to the extent not provided for in the foregoing paragraphs) for the amount of distributions previously made which, under the law applicable to the year in which the distribution was made, either were tax-free or were applicable in reduction of basis (not including distributions made by a corporation which was classified as a personal service corporation under the provisions of the Revenue Act of 1918 (40 Stat. 1057), or the Revenue Act of 1921 (42 Stat. 227), out of its earnings or profits which were taxable in accordance with the provisions of section 218 of the Revenue Act of 1918 or 1921);

(5) in the case of any bond (as defined in section 171(d)) the interest on which is wholly exempt from the tax imposed by this subtitle, to the extent of the amortizable bond premium disallowable as a deduction pursuant to section 171(a)(2), and in the case of any other bond (as defined in section 171(d)) to the extent of the deductions allowable pursuant to section 171(a)(1) (or the amount applied to reduce interest payments under section 171(e)(2)) with respect thereto;

(6) in the case of any municipal bond (as defined in section 75(b)), to the extent provided in section 75(a)(2);

(7) in the case of a residence the acquisition of which resulted, under section 1034 [1] *(as in effect on the day before the 8/5/97 of the Taxpayer Relief Act of 1997)*, in the nonrecognition of any part of the gain realized on the sale, exchange, or involuntary conversion of another residence, to the extent provided in section 1034(e) [2] *(as so in effect);*

(8) in the case of property pledged to the Commodity Credit Corporation, to the extent of the amount received as a loan from the Commodity Credit Corporation and treated by the taxpayer as income for the year in which received pursuant to section 77, and to the extent of any deficiency on such loan with respect to which the taxpayer has been relieved from liability;

(9) for amounts allowed as deductions as deferred expenses under section 616(b) (relating to certain expenditures in the development of mines) and resulting in a reduction of the taxpayer's taxes under this subtitle, but not less than the amounts allowable under such section for the taxable year and prior years;

(10) **Repealed.**

(11) for deductions to the extent disallowed under section 268 (relating to sale of land with unharvested crops), notwithstanding the provisions of any other paragraph of this subsection;

(12) to the extent provided in section 28(h) of the Internal Revenue Code of 1939 in the case of amounts specified in a shareholder's consent made under section 28 of such code;

(13) to the extent provided in section 551(e) in the case of the stock of United States shareholders in a foreign personal holding company;

(14) for amounts allowed as deductions as deferred expenses under section 174(b)(1) (relating to research and experimental expenditures) and resulting in a reduction of the taxpayers' taxes under this subtitle, but not less than the amounts allowable under such section for the taxable year and prior years;

(15) for deductions to the extent disallowed under section 272 (relating to disposal of coal or domestic iron ore), notwithstanding the provisions of any other paragraph of this subsection;

(16) in the case of any evidence of indebtedness referred to in section 811(b) (relating to amortization of premium and accrual of discount in the case of life insurance companies), to the extent of the adjustments required under section 811(b) (or the corresponding provisions of prior income tax laws) for the taxable year and all prior taxable years;

(17) to the extent provided in section 1367 in the case of stock of, and indebtedness owed to, shareholders of an S corporation;

(18) to the extent provided in section 961 in the case of stock in controlled foreign corporations (or foreign corporations which were controlled foreign corporations) and of property by reason of which a person is considered as owning such stock;

(19) to the extent provided in section 50(c), in the case of expenditures with respect to which a credit has been allowed under section 38;

(20) for amounts allowed as deductions under section 59(e) (relating to optional 10-year writeoff of certain tax preferences);

(21) to the extent provided in section 1059 (relating to reduction in basis for extraordinary dividends);

(22) in the case of qualified replacement property the acquisition of which resulted under section 1042 in the nonrecognition of any part of the gain realized on the sale or exchange of any property, to the extent provided in section 1042(d),

(23) in the case of property the acquisition of which resulted under section 1043[3], *1044, or 1045* in the nonrecognition of any part of the gain realized on the sale of other property, to the extent provided in section 1043(c)[4], *1044(d), or 1045(b)(4)*, as the case may be,

(24) to the extent provided in section 179A(e)(6)(A),

(25) to the extent provided in section 30(d)(1),[5]

(26) to the extent provided in sections 23(g) and 137(e)[6], *and*

[7]*(27) in the case of a residence with respect to which a credit was allowed under section 1400C, to the extent provided in section 1400C(h).*

(b) **Substituted basis.** Whenever it appears that the basis of property in the hands of the taxpayer is a substituted basis, then the adjustments provided in subsection (a) shall be made after first making in respect of such substituted basis proper adjustments of a similar nature in respect of the period during which the property was held by the transferor, donor, or grantor, or during which the other property was held by the person for whom the basis is to be determined. A similar rule shall be applied in the case of a series of substituted bases.

(c) **Increase in basis of property on which additional estate tax is imposed.**

(1) **Tax imposed with respect to entire interest.** If an additional estate tax is imposed under section 2032A(c)(1) with respect to any interest in property and the qualified heir makes an election under this subsection with respect to the imposition of such tax, the adjusted basis of such interest shall be increased by an amount equal to the excess of—

(A) the fair market value of such interest on the date of the decedent's death (or the alternate valuation date under section 2032, if the executor of the decedent's estate elected the application of such section), over

(B) the value of such interest determined under section 2032A(a).

(2) **Partial dispositions.**

(A) In general. In the case of any partial disposition for which an election under this subsection is made, the increase in basis under paragraph (1) shall be an amount—

(i) which bears the same ratio to the increase which would be determined under paragraph (1) (without regard to this paragraph) with respect to the entire interest, as

(ii) the amount of the tax imposed under section 2032A(c)(1) with respect to such disposition bears to the adjusted tax difference attributable to the entire interest (as determined under section 2032A(c)(2)(B)).

(B) Partial disposition. For purposes of subparagraph (A), the term "partial disposition" means any disposition or cessation to which subsection (c)(2)(D), (h)(1)(B), or (i)(1)(B) of section 2032A applies.

(3) Time adjustment made. Any increase in basis under this subsection shall be deemed to have occurred immediately before the disposition or cessation resulting in the imposition of the tax under section 2032A(c)(1).

(4) Special rule in the case of substituted property. If the tax under section 2032A(c)(1) is imposed with respect to qualified replacement property (as defined in section 2032A(h)(3)(B)) or qualified exchange property (as defined in section 2032A(i)(3)), the increase in basis under paragraph (1) shall be made by reference to the property involuntarily converted or exchanged (as the case may be).

(5) Election.

(A) In general. An election under this subsection shall be made at such time and in such manner as the Secretary shall by regulations prescribe. Such an election, once made, shall be irrevocable.

(B) Interest on recaptured amount. If an election is made under this subsection with respect to any additional estate tax imposed under section 2032A(c)(1), for purposes of section 6601 (relating to interest on underpayments), the last date prescribed for payment of such tax shall be deemed to be the last date prescribed for payment of the tax imposed by section 2001 with respect to the estate of the decedent (as determined for purposes of section 6601).

(d) Reduction in basis of automobile on which gas guzzler tax was imposed. If—

(1) the taxpayer acquires any automobile with respect to which a tax was imposed by section 4064, and

(2) the use of such automobile by the taxpayer begins not more than 1 year after the date of the first sale for ultimate use of such automobile,

the basis of such automobile shall be reduced by the amount of the tax imposed by section 4064 with respect to such automobile. In the case of importation, if the date of entry or withdrawal from warehouse for consumption is later than the date of the first sale for ultimate use, such later date shall be substituted for the date of such first sale in the preceding sentence.

(e) Cross reference. For treatment of separate mineral interests as one property, see section 614.

[Endnote Code Sec. 1016]

Matter in *italics* in Code Sec. 1016(a)(7) added by Sec. 312(d)(6) of the Taxpayer Relief Act of 1997, H.R. 2014, 8/5/97.
1. added matter in para. (a)(7)
2. added matter in para. (a)(7)

Effective Date (Sec. 312(d) [sic (e)], H.R. 2014, 8/5/97) effective for sales and exchanges after 5/6/97, except as provided in Sec. 312(d)(2)-(4) [sic (e)(2)-(4)], which reads as follows:

"(2) Sales before 8/5/97. At the election of the taxpayer, the amendments made by this section shall not apply to any sale or exchange before the date of the enactment of this Act.

"(3) Certain sales within 2 years after 8/5/97. Section 121 of the Internal Revenue Code of 1986 (as amended by this section) shall be applied without regard to subsection (c)(2)(B) thereof in the case of any sale or exchange of property during the 2-year period beginning on the date of the enactment of this Act if the taxpayer held such property on the date of the enactment of this Act and fails to meet the ownership and use requirements of subsection (a) thereof with respect to such property.

"(4) Binding contracts. At the election of the taxpayer, the amendments made by this section shall not apply to a sale or exchange after the date of the enactment of this Act, if—

"(A) such sale or exchange is pursuant to a contract which was binding on such date, or

"(B) without regard to such amendments, gain would not be recognized under section 1034 of the Internal Revenue Code of 1986 (as in effect on the day before the date of the enactment of this Act) on such sale or exchange by reason of a new residence acquired on or before such date or with respect to the acquisition of which by the taxpayer a binding contract was in effect on such date.

This paragraph shall not apply to any sale or exchange by an individual if the treatment provided by section 877(a)(1) of the Internal Revenue Code of 1986 applies to such individual."

Matter in *italics* in Code Sec. 1016(a)(23) added by Sec. 313(b)(1)(A) and (B), H.R. 2014, 8/5/97, which struck out:
3. "or 1044"
4. "or 1044(d)"

Effective Date (Sec. 313(c), H.R. 2014, 8/5/97) effective for sales after 8/5/97.

Matter in *italics* in Code Sec. 1016(a)(25), Code Sec. 1016(a)(26) and Code Sec. 1016(a)(27) added by Sec. 701(b)(2), H.R. 2014, 8/5/97, which struck out:
5. "and"
6. "."

7. added para. (a)(27)
Effective Date (Sec. 701(d), H.R. 2014, 8/5/97) effective 8/5/97.

[¶ 3162] Code Sec. 1031. **Exchange of property held for productive use or investment.**
(a) Nonrecognition of gain or loss from exchanges solely in kind.

(1) **In general.** No gain or loss shall be recognized on the exchange of property held for productive use in a trade or business or for investment if such property is exchanged solely for property of like kind which is to be held either for productive use in a trade or business or for investment.

(2) **Exception.** This subsection shall not apply to any exchange of—

(A) stock in trade or other property held primarily for sale,

(B) stocks, bonds, or notes,

(C) other securities or evidences of indebtedness or interest,

(D) interests in a partnership,

(E) certificates of trust or beneficial interests, or

(F) choses in action.

For purposes of this section, an interest in a partnership which has in effect a valid election under section 761(a) to be excluded from the application of all of subchapter K shall be treated as an interest in each of the assets of such partnership and not as an interest in a partnership.

(3) **Requirement that property be identified and that exchange be completed not more than 180 days after transfer of exchanged property.** For purposes of this subsection, any property received by the taxpayer shall be treated as property which is not like-kind property if—

(A) such property is not identified as property to be received in the exchange on or before the day which is 45 days after the date on which the taxpayer transfers the property relinquished in the exchange, or

(B) such property is received after the earlier of—

(i) the day which is 180 days after the date on which the taxpayer transfers the property relinquished in the exchange, or

(ii) the due date (determined with regard to extension) for the transferor's return of the tax imposed by this chapter for the taxable year in which the transfer of the relinquished property occurs.

(b) Gain from exchanges not solely in kind. If an exchange would be within the provisions of subsection (a), of section 1035(a), of section 1036(a), or of section 1037(a), if it were not for the fact that the property received in exchange consists not only of property permitted by such provisions to be received without the recognition of gain, but also of other property or money, then the gain, if any, to the recipient shall be recognized, but in an amount not in excess of the sum of such money and the fair market value of such other property.

(c) Loss from exchanges not solely in kind. If an exchange would be within the provisions of subsection (a), of section 1035(a), of section 1036(a), or of section 1037(a), if it were not for the fact that the property received in exchange consists not only of property permitted by such provisions to be received without the recognition of gain or loss, but also of other property or money, then no loss from the exchange shall be recognized.

(d) Basis. If property was acquired on an exchange described in this section, section 1035(a), section 1036(a), or section 1037(a), then the basis shall be the same as that of the property exchanged, decreased in the amount of any money received by the taxpayer and increased in the amount of gain or decreased in the amount of loss to the taxpayer that was recognized on such exchange. If the property so acquired consisted in part of the type of property permitted by this section, section 1035(a), section 1036(a), or section 1037(a), to be received without the recognition of gain or loss, and in part of other property, the basis provided in this subsection shall be allocated between the properties (other than money) received, and for the purpose of the allocation there shall be assigned to such other property an amount equivalent to its fair market value at the date of the exchange. For purposes of this section, section 1035(a), and section 1036(a), where as part of the consideration to the taxpayer another party to the exchange assumed a liability of the taxpayer or acquired from the taxpayer property subject to a liability, such assumption or acquisition (in the amount of the liability) shall be considered as money received by the taxpayer on the exchange.

(e) Exchanges of livestock of different sexes. For purposes of this section, livestock of different sexes are not property of a like kind.

(f) Special rules for exchanges between related persons.

(1) In general. If—

(A) a taxpayer exchanges property with a related person,

(B) there is nonrecognition of gain or loss to the taxpayer under this section with respect to the exchange of such property (determined without regard to this subsection), and

(C) before the date 2 years after the date of the last transfer which was part of such exchange—

(i) the related person disposes of such property, or

(ii) the taxpayer disposes of the property received in the exchange from the related person which was of like kind to the property transferred by the taxpayer,

there shall be no nonrecognition of gain or loss under this section to the taxpayer with respect to such exchange; except that any gain or loss recognized by the taxpayer by reason of this subsection shall be taken into account as of the date on which the disposition referred to in subparagraph (C) occurs.

(2) Certain dispositions not taken into account. For purposes of paragraph (1)(C), there shall not be taken into account any disposition—

(A) after the earlier of the death of the taxpayer or the death of the related person,

(B) in a compulsory or involuntary conversion (within the meaning of section 1033) if the exchange occurred before the threat or imminence of such conversion, or

(C) with respect to which it is established to the satisfaction of the Secretary that neither the exchange nor such disposition had as one of its principal purposes the avoidance of Federal income tax.

(3) Related person. For purposes of this subsection, the term "related person" means any person bearing a relationship to the taxpayer described in section 267(b) or 707(b)(1).

(4) Treatment of certain transactions. This section shall not apply to any exchange which is part of a transaction (or series of transactions) structured to avoid the purposes of this subsection.

(g) Special rule where substantial diminution of risk.

(1) In general. If paragraph (2) applies to any property for any period, the running of the period set forth in subsection (f)(1)(C) with respect to such property shall be suspended during such period.

(2) Property to which subsection applies. This paragraph shall apply to any property for any period during which the holder's risk of loss with respect to the property is substantially diminished by—

(A) the holding of a put with respect to such property,

(B) the holding by another person of a right to acquire such property, or

(C) a short sale or any other transaction.

[1]**(h) Special rules for foreign real and personal property.** *For purposes of this section—*

(1) Real property. *Real property located in the United States and real property located outside the United States are not property of a like kind.*

(2) Personal property.

(A) In general. Personal property used predominantly within the United States and personal property used predominantly outside the United States are not property of a like kind.

(B) Predominant use. Except as provided in subparagraph (C) and (D), the predominant use of any property shall be determined based on—

(i) in the case of the property relinquished in the exchange, the 2-year period ending on the date of such relinquishment, and

(ii) in the case of the property acquired in the exchange, the 2-year period beginning on the date of such acquisition.

(C) Property held for less than 2 years. Except in the case of an exchange which is part of a transaction (or series of transactions) structured to avoid the purposes of this subsection—

(i) only the periods the property was held by the person relinquishing the property (or any related person) shall be taken into account under subparagraph (B)(i), and

(ii) only the periods the property was held by the person acquiring the property (or any related person) shall be taken into account under subparagraph (B)(ii).

(D) Special rule for certain property. Property described in any subparagraph of section 168(g)(4) shall be treated as used predominantly in the United States.

[For analysis, see ¶209. For text of Committee Report, see ¶5144.]

[Endnote Code Sec. 1031]

Matter in *italics* in Code Sec. 1031(h) added by Sec. 1052(a) of the Taxpayer Relief Act of 1997, H.R. 2014, 8/5/97, which struck out:

1. "(h) Special rule for foreign real property.

"For purposes of this section, real property located in the United States and real property located outside the United States are not property of a like kind."

Effective Date (Sec. 1052(b), H.R. 2014, 8/5/97) effective for transfers after 6/8/97, in tax. yrs. end. after 6/8/97. Sec. 1172(b)(2) of this Act provides:

"(2) Binding contracts.—The amendment made by this section shall not apply to any transfer pursuant to a written binding contract in effect on June 8, 1997, and at all times thereafter before the disposition of property. A contract shall not fail to meet the requirements of the preceding sentence solely because—

"(A) it provides for a sale in lieu of an exchange, or

"(B) the property to be acquired as replacement property was not identified under such contract before June 9, 1997."

[¶3163]   Code Sec. 1033.   Involuntary conversions.

* * * * * * * * * * *

(e) Livestock sold on account of drought[1], *flood, or other weather-related conditions.* For purposes of this subtitle, the sale or exchange of livestock (other than poultry) held by a taxpayer for draft, breeding, or dairy purposes in excess of the number the taxpayer would sell if he followed his usual business practices shall be treated as an involuntary conversion to which this section applies if such livestock are sold or exchanged by the taxpayer solely on account of drought[2], *flood, or other weather-related conditions.*

* * * * * * * * * * *

(h) Special rules for property damaged by Presidentially declared disasters.

* * * * * * * * * * *

(4) Principal residence. For purposes of this subsection, the term "principal residence" has the same meaning as when used in [3]*section 121,* except that such term shall include a residence not treated as a principal residence solely because the taxpayer does not own the residence.

[4]*(i) Replacement property must be acquired from unrelated person in certain cases.*

(1) In general. If the property which is involuntarily converted is held by a taxpayer to which this subsection applies, subsection (a) shall not apply if the replacement property or stock is acquired from a related person. The preceding sentence shall not apply to the extent that the related person acquired the replacement property or stock from an unrelated person during the period applicable under subsection (a)(2)(B).

(2) Taxpayers to which subsection applies. This subsection shall apply to—

(A) a C corporation,

(B) a partnership in which 1 or more C corporations own, directly or indirectly (determined in accordance with section 707(b)(3)), more than 50 percent of the capital interest, or profits interest, in such partnership at the time of the involuntary conversion, and

(C) *any other taxpayer if, with respect to property which is involuntarily converted during the taxable year, the aggregate of the amount of realized gain on such property on which there is realized gain exceeds $100,000.*

In the case of a partnership, subparagraph (C) shall apply with respect to the partnership and with respect to each partner. A similar rule shall apply in the case of an S corporation and its shareholders.

(3) Related person. For purposes of this subsection, a person is related to another person if the person bears a relationship to the other person described in section 267(b) or 707(b)(1).

* * * * * * * * * * *

(k) **Cross references.**

* * * * * * * * * * *

[5]*(3) For exclusion from gross income of gain from involuntary conversion of principal residence, see section 121.*

[For analysis, see ¶ 207, ¶ 2102. For text of Committee Report, see ¶ 5063, ¶ 5164.]

[Endnote Code Sec. 1033]

Matter in *italics* in Code Sec. 1033(e) was added by Sec. 913(b)(1) and (2) of the Taxpayer Relief Act of 1997, H.R. 2014, 8/5/97.

1. added matter in the heading of subsec. (e)
2. added matter in the text of subsec. (e)

Effective Date (Sec. 913(c), H.R. 2014, 8/5/97) effective for sales and exchanges after 12/31/96.

Matter in *italics* in Code Sec. 1033(h)(4) was added by Sec. 312(d)(1), H.R. 2014, 8/5/97, which struck out:

3. "section 1034"

Effective Date (Sec. 312(d)[sic (e)], H.R. 2014, 8/5/97) reads as follows:

"(d) Effective date.

"(1) In general. The amendments made by this section shall apply to sales and exchanges after May 6, 1997.

"(2) Sales before 8/5/97. At the election of the taxpayer, the amendments made by this section shall not apply to any sale or exchange before the date of the enactment of this Act.

"(3) Certain sales within 2 years after 8/5/97. Section 121 of the Internal Revenue Code of 1986 (as amended by this section) shall be applied without regard to subsection (c)(2)(B) thereof in the case of any sale or exchange of property during the 2-year period beginning on the date of the enactment of this Act if the taxpayer held such property on the date of the enactment of this Act and fails to meet the ownership and use requirements of subsection (a) thereof with respect to such property.

"(4) Binding contracts. At the election of the taxpayer, the amendments made by this section shall not apply to a sale or exchange after the date of the enactment of this Act, if—

"(A) such sale or exchange is pursuant to a contract which was binding on such date, or

"(B) without regard to such amendments, gain would not be recognized under section 1034 of the Internal Revenue Code of 1986 (as in effect on the day before the date of the enactment of this Act) on such sale or exchange by reason of a new residence acquired on or before such date or with respect to the acquisition of which by the taxpayer a binding contract was in effect on such date.

This paragraph shall not apply to any sale or exchange by an individual if the treatment provided by section 877(a)(1) of the Internal Revenue Code of 1986 applies to such individual."

Matter in *italics* in Code Sec. 1033(i) was added by Sec. 1087(a), H.R. 2014, 8/5/97, which struck out:

4. "(i) Nonrecognition not to apply if corporation acquires replacement property from related person.

"(1) In general. In the case of—

"(A) a C corporation, or

"(B) a partnership in which 1 or more C corporations own, directly or indirectly (determined in accordance with section 707(b)(3)), more than 50 percent of the capital interest, or profits interest, in such partnership at the time of the involuntary conversion,

subsection (a) shall not apply if the replacement property or stock is acquired from a related person. The preceding sentence shall not apply to the extent that the related person acquired the replacement property or stock from an unrelated person during the period described in subsection (a)(2)(B)."

"(2) Related person. For purposes of this subsection, a person is related to another person if the person bears a relationship to the other person described in section 267(b) or 707(b)(1)."

Effective Date (Sec. 1087(b), H.R. 2014, 8/5/97) effective for involuntary conversions occurring after 6/8/97.

Matter in *italics* in Code Sec. 1033(k)(3) was added by Sec. 312(d)(7), H.R. 2014, 8/5/97, which struck out:

5. "(3) For one-time exclusion from gross income of gain from involuntary conversion of principal residence by individual who has attained age 55, see section 121."

Effective Date (Sec. 312(d)[sic (e)], H.R. 2014, 8/5/97) see above.

[¶ 3164]   Code Sec.[1] 1034.   Repealed.

[For analysis, see ¶ 102. For text of Committee Report, see ¶ 5020.]

[Endnote Code Sec. 1034]

   Code Sec. 1034 was repealed by Sec. 312(b) of the Taxpayer Relief Act of 1997, H.R. 2014, 8/5/97, which struck out:
1. "Sec. 1034. Rollover of gain on sale of principal residence.

"(a) Nonrecognition of gain.

   "If property (in this section called 'old residence') used by the taxpayer as his principal residence is sold by him and, within a period beginning 2 years before the date of such sale and ending 2 years after such date, property (in this section called 'new residence') is purchased and used by the taxpayer as his principal residence, gain (if any) from such sale shall be recognized only to the extent that the taxpayer's adjusted sales price (as defined in subsection (b)) of the old residence exceeds the taxpayer's cost of purchasing the new residence.

"(b) Adjusted sales price defined.

   "(1) In general. For purposes of this section, the term 'adjusted sales price' means the amount realized, reduced by the aggregate of the expenses for work performed on the old residence in order to assist in its sale.

   "(2) Limitations. The reduction provided in paragraph (1) applies only to expenses—

   "(A) for work performed during the 90-day period ending on the day on which the contract to sell the old residence is entered into;

   "(B) which are paid on or before the 30th day after the date of the sale of the old residence; and

   "(C) which are—

   "(i) not allowable as deductions in computing taxable income under section 63 (defining taxable income), and

   "(ii) not taken into account in computing the amount realized from the sale of the old residence.

"(c) Rules for application of section.

   "For purposes of this section:

   "(1) An exchange by the taxpayer of his residence for other property shall be treated as a sale of such residence, and the acquisition of a residence on the exchange of property shall be treated as a purchase of such residence.

   "(2) A residence any part of which was constructed or reconstructed by the taxpayer shall be treated as purchased by the taxpayer. In determining the taxpayer's cost of purchasing a residence, there shall be included only so much of his cost as is attributable to the acquisition, construction, reconstruction, and improvements made which are properly chargeable to capital account, during the period specified in subsection (a).

   "(3) If a residence is purchased by the taxpayer before the date of his sale of the old residence, the purchased residence shall not be treated as his new residence if sold or otherwise disposed of by him before the date of the sale of the old residence.

   "(4) If the taxpayer, during the period described in subsection (a), purchases more than one residence which is used by him as his principal residence at some time within 2 years after the date of the sale of the old residence, only the last of such residences so used by him after the date of such sale shall constitute the new residence. If a principal residence is sold in a sale to which subsection (d)(2) applies within 2 years after the sale of the old residence, for purposes of applying the preceding sentence with respect to the old residence, the principal residence so sold shall be treated as the last residence used during such 2-year period.

"(d) Limitation.

   "(1) In general. Subsection (a) shall not apply with respect to the sale of the taxpayer's residence if within 2 years before the date of such sale the taxpayer sold at a gain other property used by him as his principal residence, and any part of such gain was not recognized by reason of subsection (a).

   "(2) Subsequent sale connected with commencing work at new place. Paragraph (1) shall not apply with respect to the sale of the taxpayer's residence if—

   "(A) such sale was in connection with the commencement of work by the taxpayer as an employee or as a self-employed individual at a new principal place of work, and

   "(B) if the residence so sold is treated as the former residence for purposes of section 217 (relating to moving expenses), the taxpayer would satisfy the conditions of subsection (c) of section 217 (as modified by the other subsections of such section).

"(e) Basis of new residence.

   "Where the purchase of a new residence results, under subsection (a) or under section 112(n) of the Internal Revenue Code of 1939, in the nonrecognition of gain on the sale of an old residence, in determining the adjusted basis of the new residence as of any time following the sale of the old residence, the adjustments to basis shall include a reduction by an amount equal to the amount of the gain not so recognized on the sale of the old residence. For this purpose, the amount of the gain not so recognized on the sale of the old residence includes only so much of such gain as is not recognized by reason of the cost, up to such time, of purchasing the new residence.

"(f) Tenant-stockholder in a cooperative housing corporation.

   "For purposes of this section, section 1016 (relating to adjustments to basis), and section 1223 (relating to holding period), references to property used by the taxpayer as his principal residence, and references to the residence of a taxpayer, shall include stock held by a tenant-stockholder (as defined in section 216, relating to deduction for amounts representing taxes and interest paid to a cooperative housing corporation) in a cooperative housing corporation (as defined in such section) if—

   "(1) in the case of stock sold, the house or apartment which the taxpayer was entitled to occupy as such stockholder was used by him as his principal residence, and

"(2) in the case of stock purchased, the taxpayer used as his principal residence the house or apartment which he was entitled to occupy as such stockholder.

"(g) Husband and wife.

"If the taxpayer and his spouse, in accordance with regulations which shall be prescribed by the Secretary pursuant to this subsection, consent to the application of paragraph (2) of this subsection, then—

"(1) for purposes of this section—

"(A) the taxpayer's adjusted sales price of the old residence is the adjusted sales price (of the taxpayer, or of the taxpayer and his spouse) of the old residence, and

"(B) the taxpayer's cost of purchasing the new residence is the cost (to the taxpayer, his spouse, or both) of purchasing the new residence (whether held by the taxpayer, his spouse, or the taxpayer and his spouse); and

"(2) so much of the gain on the sale of the old residence as is not recognized solely by reason of this subsection, and so much of the adjustment under subsection (e) to the basis of the new residence as results solely from this subsection shall be allocated between the taxpayer and his spouse as provided in such regulations.

This subsection shall apply only if the old residence and the new residence are each used by the taxpayer and his spouse as their principal residence. In case the taxpayer and his spouse do not consent to the application of paragraph (2) of this subsection then the recognition of gain on the sale of the old residence shall be determined under this section without regard to the rules provided in this subsection. For purposes of this subsection, except to the extent provided in regulations, in the case of an individual who dies after the date of the sale of the old residence and is married on the date of death, consent to the application of paragraph (2) by such individual's spouse and use of the new residence as the principal residence of such spouse shall be treated as consent and use by such individual.

"(h) Members of armed forces.

"(1) In general. The running of any period of time specified in subsection (a) or (c) (other than the 2 years referred to in subsection (c)(4)) shall be suspended during any time that the taxpayer (or his spouse if the old residence and the new residence are each used by the taxpayer and his spouse as their principal residence) serves on extended active duty with the Armed Forces of the United States after the date of the sale of the old residence, except that any such period of time as so suspended shall not extend beyond the date 4 years after the date of the sale of the old residence.

"(2) Members stationed outside the United States or required to reside in government quarters. In the case of any taxpayer who, during any period of time the running of which is suspended by paragraph (1)—

"(A) is stationed outside of the United States, or

"(B) after returning from a tour of duty outside of the United States and pursuant to a determination by the Secretary of Defense that adequate off-base housing is not available at a remote base site, is required to reside in on-base Government quarters,

any such period of time as so suspended shall not expire before the day which is 1 year after the last day described in subparagraph (A) or (B), as the case may be, except that any such period of time as so suspended shall not extend beyond the date which is 8 years after the date of the sale of the old residence.

"(3) Extended active duty defined. For purposes of this subsection, the term 'extended active duty' means any period of active duty pursuant to a call or order to such duty for a period in excess of 90 days or for an indefinite period.

"(i) Special rule for condemnation.

"In the case of the seizure, requisition, or condemnation of a residence, or the sale or exchange of a residence under threat or imminence thereof, the provisions of this section, in lieu of section 1033 (relating to involuntary conversions), shall be applicable if the taxpayer so elects. If such election is made, such seizure, requisition, or condemnation shall be treated as the sale of the residence. Such election shall be made at such time and in such manner as the Secretary shall prescribe by regulations.

"(j) Statute of limitations.

"If the taxpayer during a taxable year sells at a gain property used by him as his principal residence, then—

"(1) the statutory period for the assessment of any deficiency attributable to any part of such gain shall not expire before the expiration of 3 years from the date the Secretary is notified by the taxpayer (in such manner as the Secretary may by regulations prescribe) of—

"(A) the taxpayer's cost of purchasing the new residence which the taxpayer claims results in nonrecognition of any part of such gain,

"(B) the taxpayer's intention not to purchase a new residence within the period specified in subsection (a), or

"(C) a failure to make such purchase within such period; and

"(2) such deficiency may be assessed before the expiration of such 3-year period notwithstanding the provisions of any other law or rule of law which would otherwise prevent such assessment.

"(k) Individual whose tax home is outside the United States.

"The running of any period of time specified in subsection (a) or (c) (other than the 2 years referred to in subsection (c)(4)) shall be suspended during any time that the taxpayer (or his spouse if the old residence and the new residence are each used by the taxpayer and his spouse as their principal residence) has a tax home (as defined in section 911(d)(3)) outside the United States after the date of the sale of the old residence; except that any such period of time as so suspended shall not extend beyond the date 4 years after the date of the sale of the old residence.

"(l) Cross reference.

"For one-time exclusion from gross income of gain from sale of principal residence by individual who has attained age 55, see section 121."

Effective Date (Sec. 312(d) [sic (e)], H.R. 2014, 8/5/97) effective for sales and exchanges after 5/6/97 except as provided by Secs. 312(d)(2)-(4) [sic (e)(2)-(4)] of this Act, which read as follows:

"(2) Sales before 8/5/97.—At the election of the taxpayer, the amendments made by this section shall not apply to any sale or exchange before the date of the enactment of this Act.

"(3) Certain sales within 2 years after 8/5/97. Section 121 of the Internal Revenue Code of 1986 (as amended by this section) shall be applied without regard to subsection (c)(2)(B) thereof in the case of any sale or exchange of property during the 2-year period beginning on the date of the enactment of this Act if the taxpayer held such property on the date of the enactment of this Act and fails to meet the ownership and use requirements of subsection (a) thereof with respect to such property.

"(4) Binding contracts.—At the election of the taxpayer, the amendments made by this section shall not apply to a sale or exchange after the date of the enactment of this Act, if—

"(A) such sale or exchange is pursuant to a contract which was binding on such date, or

"(B) without regard to such amendments, gain would not be recognized under section 1034 of the Internal Revenue Code of 1986 (as in effect on the day before the date of the enactment of this Act) on such sale or exchange by reason of a new residence acquired on or before such date or with respect to the acquisition of which by the taxpayer a binding contract was in effect on such date. This paragraph shall not apply to any sale or exchange by an individual if the treatment provided by section 877(a)(1) of the Internal Revenue Code of 1986 applies to such individual."

[¶ 3165]   Code Sec. 1035.   Certain exchanges of insurance policies.

* * * * * * * * * * * *

[1]*(c) Exchanges involving foreign persons. To the extent provided in regulations, subsection (a) shall not apply to any exchange having the effect of transferring property to any person other than a United States person.*

[2]*(d) Cross references.*

(1) For rules relating to recognition of gain or loss where an exchange is not solely in kind, see subsections (b) and (c) of section 1031.

(2) For rules relating to the basis of property acquired in an exchange described in subsection (a), see subsection (d) of section 1031.

[For analysis, see ¶ 1629. For text of Committee Report, see ¶ 5182.]

[Endnote Code Sec. 1035]

Matter in *italics* in Code Sec. 1035(c) and Code Sec. 1035(d) added by Sec. 1131(b)(1) [sic (c)(1)] of the Taxpayer Relief Act of 1997, H.R. 2014, 8/5/97, which struck out:
  1. added subsec. (c)
  2. "(c)"

Effective Date (Sec. 1131(d) [sic (e)], H.R. 2014, 8/5/97) effective 8/5/97.

[¶ 3166]   Code Sec. 1036.   Stock for stock of same corporation.

* * * * * * * * * * * *

[1]*(b) Nonqualified preferred stock not treated as stock. For purposes of this section, nonqualified preferred stock (as defined in section 351(g)(2)) shall be treated as property other than stock.*

[2]*(c) Cross references.*

(1) For rules relating to recognition of gain or loss where an exchange is not solely in kind, see subsections (b) and (c) of section 1031.

(2) For rules relating to the basis of property acquired in an exchange described in subsection (a), see subsection (d) of section 1031.

[For analysis, see ¶ 1502. For text of Committee Report, see ¶ 5119.]

[Endnote Code Sec. 1036]

Matter in *italics* in Code Sec. 1036(b) and Code Sec. 1036(c) added by Sec. 1014(e)(3) of the Taxpayer Relief Act of 1997, H.R. 2014, 8/5/97, which struck out:
  1. added subsec. (b)
  2. "(b)"

Effective Date (Sec. 1014(f), H.R. 2014, 8/5/97) reads as follows:
  "(f) Effective date.
  "(1) In general. The amendments made by this section shall apply to transactions after June 8, 1997.

"(2) Transition rule. The amendments made by this section shall not apply to any transaction after June 8, 1997, if such transaction is—

"(A) made pursuant to a written agreement which was binding on such date and at all times thereafter,

"(B) described in a ruling request submitted to the Internal Revenue Service on or before such date, or

"(C) described on or before such date in a public announcement or in a filing with the Securities and Exchange Commission required solely by reason of the transaction."

[¶ 3167] Code Sec. 1038. Certain reacquisitions of real property.

* * * * * * * * * * * *

[1]*(e) Principal residences. If—*

(1) subsection (a) applies to a reacquisition of real property with respect to the sale of which gain was not recognized under section 121 (relating to gain on sale of principal residence); and

(2) within 1 year after the date of the reacquisition of such property by the seller, such property is resold by him,

then, under regulations prescribed by the Secretary, subsections (b), (c), and (d) of this section shall not apply to the reacquisition of such property and, for purposes of applying section 121, the resale of such property shall be treated as a part of the transaction constituting the original sale of such property.

(f) Repealed.

(g) Acquisition by estate, etc., of seller. Under regulations prescribed by the Secretary, if an installment obligation is indebtedness to the seller which is described in subsection (a), and if such obligation is, in the hands of the taxpayer, an obligation with respect to which section 691(a)(4)(B) applies, then—

(1) for purposes of subsection (a), acquisition of real property by the taxpayer shall be treated as reacquisition by the seller, and

(2) the basis of the real property acquired by the taxpayer shall be increased by an amount equal to the deduction under section 691(c) which would (but for this subsection) have been allowable to the taxpayer with respect to the gain on the exchange of the obligation for the real property.

[Endnote Code Sec. 1038]

Matter in *italics* in Code Sec. 1038(e) added by Sec. 312(d)(8) of the Taxpayer Relief Act of 1997, H.R. 2014, 8/5/97, which struck out:

1. "(e) Principal residences. If—

"(1) subsection (a) applies to a reacquisition of real property with respect to the sale of which—

"(A) an election under section 121 (relating to one-time exclusion of gain from sale of principal residence by individual who has attained age 55) is in effect, or

"(B) gain was not recognized under section 1034 (relating to rollover of gain on sale of principal residence); and

"(2) within one year after the date of the reacquisition of such property by the seller, such property is resold by him, then, under regulations prescribed by the Secretary, subsections (b), (c), and (d) of this section shall not apply to the reacquisition of such property and, for purposes of applying sections 121 and 1034, the resale of such property shall be treated as a part of the transaction constituting the original sale of such property."

Effective Date (Sec. 312(d) [sic (e)], H.R. 2014, 8/5/97) effective for sales and exchanges after 5/6/97, except as provided by Sec. 312(d)(2)-(4) [(e)(2)-(4)] of this Act, which reads as follows:

"(2) Sales before 8/5/97. At the election of the taxpayer, the amendments made by this section shall not apply to any sale or exchange before the date of the enactment of this Act.

"(3) Certain sales within 2 years after 8/5/97. Section 121 of the Internal Revenue Code of 1986 (as amended by this section) shall be applied without regard to subsection (c)(2)(B) thereof in the case of any sale or exchange of property during the 2-year period beginning on the date of the enactment of this Act if the taxpayer held such property on the date of the enactment of this Act and fails to meet the ownership and use requirements of subsection (a) thereof with respect to such property.

"(4) Binding contracts. At the election of the taxpayer, the amendments made by this section shall not apply to a sale or exchange after the date of the enactment of this Act, if—

"(A) such sale or exchange is pursuant to a contract which was binding on such date, or

"(B) without regard to such amendments, gain would not be recognized under section 1034 of the Internal Revenue Code of 1986 (as in effect on the day before the date of the enactment of this Act) on such sale or exchange by reason of a new residence acquired on or before such date or with respect to the acquisition of which by the taxpayer a binding contract was in effect on such date. This paragraph shall not apply to any sale or exchange by an individual if the treatment provided by section 877(a)(1) of the Internal Revenue Code of 1986 applies to such individual."

[¶ 3168] Code Sec. 1042.   Sales of stock to employee stock ownership plans or certain cooperatives.

* * * * * * * * * * * *

CAUTION.   Subsec. (g), following, is effective for sales after 12/31/97.

[1]*(g) Application of section to sales of stock in agricultural refiners and processors to eligible farm cooperatives.*

(1) In general. This section shall apply to the sale of stock of a qualified refiner or processor to an eligible farmers' cooperative.

(2) Qualified refiner or processor. For purposes of this subsection, the term "qualified refiner or processor" means a domestic corporation—

(A) substantially all of the activities of which consist of the active conduct of the trade or business of refining or processing agricultural or horticultural products, and

(B) which, during the 1-year period ending on the date of the sale, purchases more than one-half of such products to be refined or processed from—

(i) farmers who make up the eligible farmers' cooperative which is purchasing stock in the corporation in a transaction to which this subsection is to apply, or

(ii) such cooperative.

(3) Eligible farmers' cooperative. For purposes of this section, the term "eligible farmers' cooperative" means an organization to which part I of subchapter T applies which is engaged in the marketing of agricultural or horticultural products.

(4) Special rules. In applying this section to a sale to which paragraph (1) applies—

(A) the eligible farmers' cooperative shall be treated in the same manner as a cooperative described in subsection (b)(1)(B),

(B) subsection (b)(2) shall be applied by substituting "100 percent" for "30 percent" each place it appears,

(C) the determination as to whether any stock in the domestic corporation is a qualified security shall be made without regard to whether the stock is an employer security or to subsection (c)(1)(A), and

(D) paragraphs (2)(D) and (7) of subsection (c) shall not apply.

[For analysis, see ¶ 208. For text of Committee Report, see ¶ 5091.]

[Endnote Code Sec. 1042]

Code Sec. 1042(g), in *italics*, was added by Sec. 968(a) of the Taxpayer Relief Act of 1997, H.R. 2014, 8/5/97.

1. added subsec. (g)

Effective Date (Sec. 968(b), H.R. 2014, 8/5/97) effective for sales after 12/31/97.

[¶ 3169] Code Sec.[1] 1045.   Rollover of gain from qualified small business stock to another qualified small business stock.

(a) Nonrecognition of gain. In the case of any sale of qualified small business stock held by an individual for more than 6 months and with respect to which such individual elects the application of this section, gain from such sale shall be recognized only to the extent that the amount realized on such sale exceeds—

(1) the cost of any qualified small business stock purchased by the taxpayer during the 60-day period beginning on the date of such sale, reduced by

(2) any portion of such cost previously taken into account under this section.

This section shall not apply to any gain which is treated as ordinary income for purposes of this title.

(b) Definitions and special rules. For purposes of this section—

(1) Qualified small business stock. The term "qualified small business stock" has the meaning given such term by section 1202(c).

(2) Purchase. A taxpayer shall be treated as having purchased any property if, but for paragraph (3), the unadjusted basis of such property in the hands of the taxpayer would be its cost (within the meaning of section 1012).

(3) Basis adjustments. If gain from any sale is not recognized by reason of subsection (a), such gain shall be applied to reduce (in the order acquired) the basis for determining gain or loss of any qualified small business stock which is purchased by the taxpayer during the 60-day period described in subsection (a).

(4) Holding period. For purposes of determining whether the nonrecognition of gain under subsection (a) applies to stock which is sold—

(A) the taxpayer's holding period for such stock and the stock referred to in subsection (a)(1) shall be determined without regard to section 1223, and

(B) only the first 6 months of the taxpayer's holding period for the stock referred to in subsection (a)(1) shall be taken into account for purposes of applying section 1202(c)(2).

[For analysis, see ¶ 206. For text of Committee Report, see ¶ 5021.]

[Endnote Code Sec. 1045]
Code Sec. 1045 was added by Sec. 313(a) of the Taxpayer Relief Act of 1997, H.R. 2014, 8/5/97.
1. added Code Sec. 1045
Effective Date (Sec. 313(c), H.R. 2014, 8/5/97) effective for sales after 8/5/97.

[¶ 3170] Code Sec. 1057. Repealed.[1]
[For analysis, see ¶ 1629. For text of Committee Report, see ¶ 5182.]

[Endnote Code Sec. 1057]
Code Sec. 1057 was repealed by Sec. 1131(c)(2) sic [(d)(2)] of the Taxpayer Relief Act of 1997, H.R. 2014, 8/5/97, which struck out:
1. "SEC. 1057 ELECTION TO TREAT TRANSFER TO FOREIGN TRUST, ETC., AS TAXABLE EXCHANGE.
"In lieu of payment of the tax imposed by section 1491, the taxpayer may elect (for purposes of this subtitle), at such time and in such manner as the Secretary may prescribe, to treat a transfer described in section 1491 as a sale or exchange of property for an amount equal in value to the fair market value of the property transferred and to recognize as gain the excess of—
"(1) the fair market value of the property so transferred, over
"(2) the adjusted basis (for determining gain) of such property in the hands of the transferor."
Effective Date (Sec. 1131(d) sic [(e)], H.R. 2014, 8/5/97) effective 8/5/97.

[¶ 3171] Code Sec. 1059. Corporate shareholder's basis in stock reduced by nontaxed portion of extraordinary dividends.

(a) General rule. If any corporation receives any extraordinary dividend with respect to any share of stock and such corporation has not held such stock for more than 2 years before the dividend announcement date—

* * * * * * * * * * *

[1]*(2) Amounts in excess of basis. If the nontaxed portion of such dividends exceeds such basis, such excess shall be treated as gain from the sale or exchange of such stock for the taxable year in which the extraordinary dividend is received.*

* * * * * * * * * * *

(d) Special rules. For purposes of this section—

[2]*(1) Time for reduction. Any reduction in basis under subsection (a)(1) shall be treated as occurring at the beginning of the ex-dividend date of the extraordinary dividend to which the reduction relates.*

* * * * * * * * * * *

(3) Determination of holding period. For purposes of determining the holding period of stock under [3]*subsection (a)*, rules similar to the rules of paragraphs (3) and (4) of section 246(c) shall apply; except that "2 years" shall be substituted for the number of days specified in subparagraph (B) of section 246(c)(3).

* * * * * * * * * * *

(e) Special rules for certain distributions.

[4]*(1) Treatment of partial liquidations and certain redemptions. Except as otherwise provided in regulations—*

(A) Redemptions. In the case of any redemption of stock—

(i) which is part of a partial liquidation (within the meaning of section 302(e)) of the redeeming corporation,

(ii) which is not pro rata as to all shareholders, or

[5]*(iii) which would not have been treated (in whole or in part) as a dividend if any options had not been taken into account under section 318(a)(4),*

any amount treated as a dividend with respect to such redemption shall be treated as an extraordinary dividend to which paragraphs (1) and (2) of subsection (a) apply without regard to the period the taxpayer held such stock. In the case of a redemption described in clause (iii), only the basis in the stock redeemed shall be taken into account under subsection (a).

(B) Reorganizations, etc. An exchange described in section 356 which is treated as a dividend shall be treated as a redemption of stock for purposes of applying subparagraph (A).

* * * * * * * * * * *

[For analysis, see ¶ 1503, ¶ 1505. For text of Committee Report, see ¶ 5116, ¶ 5118.]

[Endnote Code Sec. 1059]

Matter in *italics* in Code Sec. 1059(a)(2) and Code Sec. 1059(d)(1) added by Sec. 1011(a) and (c) of the Taxpayer Relief Act of 1997, H.R. 2014, 8/5/97, which struck out:

1. "(2) Recognition upon sale or disposition in certain cases. In addition to any gain recognized under this chapter, there shall be treated as gain from the sale or exchange of any stock for the taxable year in which the sale or disposition of such stock occurs an amount equal to the aggregate nontaxed portions of any extraordinary dividends with respect to such stock which did not reduce the basis of such stock by reason of the limitation on reducing basis below zero."

2. "(1) Time for reduction.

"(A) In general. Except as provided in subparagraph (B), any reduction in basis under subsection (a)(1) shall occur immediately before any sale or disposition of the stock.

"(B) Special rule for computing extraordinary dividend. In determining a taxpayer's adjusted basis for purposes of subsection (c)(1), any reduction in basis under subsection (a)(1) by reason of a prior distribution which was an extraordinary dividend shall be treated as occurring at the beginning of the ex-dividend date for such distribution."

Effective Date (Sec. 1011(d), H.R. 2014, 8/5/97) reads as follows:

"(d) Effective dates.

"(1) In general. The amendments made by this section shall apply to distributions after May 3, 1995.

"(2) Transition rule. The amendments made by this section shall not apply to any distribution made pursuant to the terms of—

"(A) a written binding contract in effect on May 3, 1995, and at all times thereafter before such distribution, or

"(B) a tender offer outstanding on May 3, 1995.

"(3) Certain dividends not pursuant to certain redemptions. In determining whether the amendment made by subsection (a) applies to any extraordinary dividend other than a dividend treated as an extraordinary dividend under section 1059(e)(1) of the Internal Revenue Code of 1986 (as amended by this Act), paragraphs (1) and (2) shall be applied by substituting 'September 13, 1995' for 'May 3, 1995'."

Matter in *italics* in Code Sec. 1059(d)(3) added by Sec. 1604(d), H.R. 2014, which struck out:

3. "subsection (a)(2)"

Effective Date Effective 8/5/97.

Matter in *italics* in Code Sec. 1059(e)(1) added by Sec. 1011(b), H.R. 2014, 8/5/97, which struck out:

4. "(1) Treatment of partial liquidations and non-pro rata redemptions. Except as otherwise provided in regulations, in the case of any redemption of stock which is—

"(A) part of a partial liquidation (within the meaning of section 302(e)) of the redeeming corporation, or

"(B) not pro rata as to all shareholders,

any amount treated as a dividend under section 301 with respect to such redemption shall be treated as an extraordinary dividend to which paragraphs (1) and (2) of subsection (a) apply without regard to the period the taxpayer held such stock."

Effective Date (Sec. 1011(d), H.R. 2014, 8/5/97) see above.

Matter in *italics* in Code Sec. 1059(e)(1)(A)(iii) added by Sec. 1013(b), H.R. 2014, [as amended by Sec. 1011(b), H.R. 2014, 8/5/97, see above], which struck out:

5. "(iii) which would not have been treated (in whole or in part) as a dividend if any options had not been taken into account under section 318(a)(4)."

Effective Date (Sec. 1013(d), H.R. 2014, 8/5/97) reads as follows:

"(d) Effective date.

"(1) In general. The amendments made by this section shall apply to distributions and acquisitions after June 8, 1997.

"(2) Transition rule. The amendments made by this section shall not apply to any distribution or acquisition after June 8, 1997, if such distribution or acquisition is—

"(A) made pursuant to a written agreement which was binding on such date and at all times thereafter,

"(B) described in a ruling request submitted to the Internal Revenue Service on or before such date, or

"(C) described in a public announcement or filing with the Securities and Exchange Commission on or before such date."

[¶ 3172]　Code Sec. 1092.　Straddles.

* * * * * * * * * * *

(f) Treatment of gain or loss and suspension of holding period where taxpayer grantor of qualified covered call option. If a taxpayer holds any stock and grants a qualified covered call option to purchase such stock with a strike price less than the applicable stock price—

* * * * * * * * * * *

(2) Suspension of holding period. [1]*The* holding period of such stock shall not include any period during which the taxpayer is the grantor of such option.

* * * * * * * * * * *

[Endnote Code Sec. 1092]

Matter in *italics* in Code Sec. 1092(f)(2) added by Sec. 1271(b)(9) of the Taxpayer Relief Act of 1997, H.R. 2014, 8/5/97, which struck out:

1. "Except for purposes of section 851(b)(3), the"

Effective Date (Sec. 1271(c), H.R. 2014, 8/5/97) effective for tax. yrs. begin. after 8/5/97.

[¶ 3173]　Code Sec. 1201.　Alternative tax for corporations.

(a) General rule. If for any taxable year a corporation has a net capital gain and any rate of tax imposed by section 11, 511, or 831(a) or (b) (whichever is applicable) exceeds 35 percent (determined without regard to the last 2 sentences of section 11(b)(1)), then, in lieu of any such tax, there is hereby imposed a tax (if such tax is less than the tax imposed by such sections) which shall consist of the sum of—

(1) a tax computed on the taxable income reduced by the amount of the net capital gain, at the rates and in the manner as if this subsection had not been enacted, plus

CAUTION.　Para. (a)(2), following, is effective for tax. yrs. end. before 1/1/98. For para. (a)(2) effective for tax. yrs. end. after 12/31/97, see below.

(2) a tax of 35 percent of the net capital gain.

CAUTION.　Para. (a)(2), following, is effective for tax. yrs. end. after 12/31/97. For para. (a)(2) effective for tax. yrs. end. before 1/1/98, see above.

(2) a tax of 35 percent of the net capital gain [1]*(or, if less, taxable income).*

* * * * * * * * * * *

[For analysis, see ¶ 603. For text of Committee Report, see ¶ 5022.]

[Endnote Code Sec. 1201]

Matter in *italics* in Code Sec. 1201(a)(2) added by Sec. 314(a) of the Taxpayer Relief Act of 1997, H.R. 2014, 8/5/97.

1. added matter in para. (a)(2)

Effective Date (Sec. 314(b), H.R. 2014, 8/5/97) effective for tax. yrs. end. after 12/31/97.

[¶ 3174]   Code Sec. 1223.   Holding period of property.
For purposes of this subtitle—

* * * * * * * * * * *

(7) In determining the period for which the taxpayer has held a residence, the acquisition of which resulted under section 1034 [1]*(as in effect on the day before the date of the enactment of the Taxpayer Relief Act of 1997)* in the nonrecognition of any part of the gain realized on the sale or exchange of another residence, there shall be included the period for which such other residence had been held as of the date of such sale or exchange. For purposes of this paragraph, the term "sale or exchange" includes an involuntary conversion occurring after December 31, 1950, and before January 1, 1954.

* * * * * * * * * * *

[2]*(15) In determining the period for which the taxpayer has held property the acquisition of which resulted under section 1045 in the nonrecognition of any part of the gain realized on the sale of other property, there shall be included the period for which such other property has been held as of the date of such sale.*

[3]*(16)* **Cross Reference.** For special holding period provision relating to certain partnership distributions, see section 735(b).

[For analysis, see ¶ 206. For text of Committee Report, see ¶ 5021.]

[Endnote Code Sec. 1223]

Matter in *italics* in Code Sec. 1223(7) added by Sec. 312(d)(9) of the Taxpayer Relief Act of 1997, H.R. 2014, 8/5/97.
1. added matter in para. (7)
Effective Date (Sec. 312(d) [sic (e)], H.R. 2014, 8/5/97) effective for sales and exchanges after 5/6/97, except as provided in Secs. 312(d)(2)-(4) [sic (e)(2)-(4)] of this Act, which read as follows:
  "(2) Sales before 8/5/97.—At the election of the taxpayer, the amendments made by this section shall not apply to any sale or exchange before the date of the enactment of this Act.
  "(3) Certain sales within 2 years after 8/5/97. Section 121 of the Internal Revenue Code of 1986 (as amended by this section) shall be applied without regard to subsection (c)(2)(B) thereof in the case of any sale or exchange of property during the 2-year period beginning on the date of the enactment of this Act if the taxpayer held such property on the date of the enactment of this Act and fails to meet the ownership and use requirements of subsection (a) thereof with respect to such property.
  "(4) Binding contracts.—At the election of the taxpayer, the amendments made by this section shall not apply to a sale or exchange after the date of the enactment of this Act, if—
  "(A) such sale or exchange is pursuant to a contract which was binding on such date, or
  "(B) without regard to such amendments, gain would not be recognized under section 1034 of the Internal Revenue Code of 1986 (as in effect on the day before the date of the enactment of this Act) on such sale or exchange by reason of a new residence acquired on or before such date or with respect to the acquisition of which by the taxpayer a binding contract was in effect on such date. This paragraph shall not apply to any sale or exchange by an individual if the treatment provided by section 877(a)(1) of the Internal Revenue Code of 1986 applies to such individual."

Matter in *italics* in Code Sec. 1223(15) and Code Sec. 1223(16) was added by Sec. 313(b)(2), H.R. 2014.
2. added para. (15)
3. "(15)"
Effective Date (Sec. 313(c), H.R. 2014, 8/5/97) effective for sales after 8/5/97.

[¶ 3175]   Code Sec. 1233.   Gains and losses from short sales.

* * * * * * * * * * *

[1]*(h) Short Sales of Property Which Becomes Substantially Worthless.*
  (1) In general. If—
    (A) the taxpayer enters into a short sale of property, and
    (B) such property becomes substantially worthless, the taxpayer shall recognize gain in the same manner as if the short sale were closed when the property becomes substantially

worthless. To the extent provided in regulations prescribed by the Secretary, the preceding sentence also shall apply with respect to any option with respect to property, any offsetting notional principal contract with respect to property, any futures or forward contract to deliver any property, and any other similar transaction.

(2) Statute of limitations. If property becomes substantially worthless during a taxable year and any short sale of such property remains open at the time such property becomes substantially worthless, then—

(A) the statutory period for the assessment of any deficiency attributable to any part of the gain on such transaction shall not expire before the earlier of—

(i) the date which is 3 years after the date the Secretary is notified by the taxpayer (in such manner as the Secretary may by regulations prescribe) of the substantial worthlessness of such property, or

(ii) the date which is 6 years after the date the return for such taxable year is filed, and

(B) such deficiency may be assessed before the date applicable under subparagraph (A) notwithstanding the provisions of any other law or rule of law which would otherwise prevent such assessment.

[For analysis, see ¶ 203. For text of Committee Report, see ¶ 5113.]

[Endnote Code Sec. 1233]
Code Sec. 1233(h), in *italics*, was added by Sec. 1003(b)(1) of the Taxpayer Relief Act of 1997, H.R. 2014, 8/5/97.
1. added subsec. (h)
Effective Date (Sec. 1003(b)(2), H.R. 2014, 8/5/97) effective for property which becomes substantially worthless after 8/5/97.

[¶ 3176] Code Sec. 1234A.   Gains or losses from certain terminations.
Gain or loss attributable to the cancellation, lapse, expiration, or other termination of—

(1) a right or obligation with respect to [1]*property* which is (or on acquisition would be) a capital asset in the hands of the taxpayer, or

(2) a section 1256 contract (as defined in section 1256) not described in paragraph (1) which is a capital asset in the hands of the taxpayer,

shall be treated as gain or loss from the sale of a capital asset.

The preceding sentence shall not apply to the retirement of any debt instrument (whether or not through a trust or other participation arrangement).

[For analysis, see ¶ 204. For text of Committee Report, see ¶ 5113.]

[Endnote Code Sec. 1234A]
Matter in *italics* in Code Sec. 1234A(1) added by Sec. 1003(a)(1) of the Taxpayer Relief Act of 1997, H.R. 2014, 8/5/97, which struck out:
1. "personal property (as defined in section 1092(d)(1))"
Effective Date (Sec. 1003(a)(2), H.R. 2014, 8/5/97) effective for terminations more than 30 days after 8/5/97.

[¶ 3177] Code Sec. 1239.   Gain from sale of depreciable property between certain related taxpayers.

* * * * * * * * * * *

(b) Related persons. For purposes of subsection (a), the term "related persons" means—

(1) a person and all entities which are controlled entities with respect to such person,

(2) a taxpayer and any trust in which such taxpayer (or his spouse) is a beneficiary, unless such beneficiary's interest in the trust is a remote contingent interest (within the meaning of section 318(a)(3)(B)(i))[1], *and*

[2]*(3) except in the case of a sale or exchange in satisfaction of a pecuniary bequest, an executor of an estate and a beneficiary of such estate.*

* * * * * * * * * * *

[For analysis, see ¶ 211. For text of Committee Report, see ¶ 5268.]

[Endnote Code Sec. 1239]

Matter in *italics* in Code Sec. 1239(b)(2) and Code Sec. 1239(b)(3) added by Sec. 1308(b) of the Taxpayer Relief Act of 1997, H.R. 2014, 8/5/97, which struck out:

1. "."

2. added para. (b)(3)

Effective Date (Sec. 1308(c), H.R. 2014, 8/5/97) effective for tax. yrs. begin. after 8/5/97.

[¶ 3178] Code Sec. 1245. Gain from dispositions of certain depreciable property.
(a) **General rule.**

* * * * * * * * * * * *

(2) **Recomputed basis.** For purposes of this section—

(A) In general. The term "recomputed basis" means, with respect to any property, its adjusted basis recomputed by adding thereto all adjustments reflected in such adjusted basis on account of deductions (whether in respect of the same or other property) allowed or allowable to the taxpayer or to any other person for depreciation or amortization.

(B) Taxpayer may establish amount allowed. For purposes of subparagraph (A), if the taxpayer can establish by adequate records or other sufficient evidence that the amount allowed for depreciation or amortization for any period was less than the amount allowable, the amount added for such period shall be the amount allowed.

(C) Certain deductions treated as amortization. Any deduction allowable under section 179, ¹179A, 190, or 193 shall be treated as if it were a deduction allowable for amortization.

(3) **Section 1245 property.** For purposes of this section, the term "section 1245 property" means any property which is or has been property of a character subject to the allowance for depreciation provided in section 167 and is either—

(A) personal property,

(B) other property (not including a building or its structural components) but only if such other property is tangible and has an adjusted basis in which there are reflected adjustments described in paragraph (2) for a period in which such property (or other property)—

(i) was used as an integral part of manufacturing, production, or extraction or of furnishing transportation, communications, electrical energy, gas, water, or sewage disposal services,

(ii) constituted a research facility used in connection with any of the activities referred to in clause (i), or

(iii) constituted a facility used in connection with any of the activities referred to in clause (i) for the bulk storage of fungible commodities (including commodities in a liquid or gaseous state),

(C) so much of any real property (other than any property described in subparagraph (B)) which has an adjusted basis in which there are reflected adjustments for amortization under section 169, 179, ²179A, 185, 188 (as in effect before its repeal by the Revenue Reconciliation Act of 1990), 190, 193, or 194[,]

(D) a single purpose agricultural or horticultural structure (as defined in section 168(i)(13)),

(E) a storage facility (not including a building or its structural components) used in connection with the distribution of petroleum or any primary product of petroleum, or

(F) any railroad grading or tunnel bore (as defined in section 168(e)(4)).

* * * * * * * * * * * *

[Endnote Code Sec. 1245]

Matter in *italics* in Code Sec. 1245(a)(2)(C) and Code Sec. 1245(a)(3)(C) added by Sec. 1604(a)(3) of the Taxpayer Relief Act of 1997, H.R. 2014, 8/5/97.

1. added matter in subpara. (a)(2)(C)

2. added matter in subpara. (a)(3)(C)

Effective Date (Sec. 1604(a)(4), H.R. 2014, 8/5/97) effective for property placed in service after 6/30/93.

[¶ 3179]   Code Sec. 1250.   Gain from dispositions of certain depreciable realty.

* * * * * * * * * * * *

(d) Exceptions and limitations.

* * * * * * * * * * * *

[1]**(7) Transfers to tax-exempt organization where property will be used in unrelated business.**

(A) In general. The second sentence of paragraph (3) shall not apply to a disposition of section 1250 property to an organization described in section 511(a)(2) or 511(b)(2) if, immediately after such disposition, such organization uses such property in an unrelated trade or business (as defined in section 513).

(B) Later change in use. If any property with respect to the disposition of which gain is not recognized by reason of subparagraph (A) ceases to be used in an unrelated trade or business of the organization acquiring such property, such organization shall be treated for purposes of this section as having disposed of such property on the date of such cessation.

[2]**(8) Foreclosure dispositions.** If any section 1250 property is disposed of by the taxpayer pursuant to a bid for such property at foreclosure or by operation of an agreement or of process of law after there was a default on indebtedness which such property secured, the applicable percentage referred to in paragraph (1)(B), (2)(B), or (3)(B) of subsection (a), as the case may be, shall be determined as if the taxpayer ceased to hold such property on the date of the beginning of the proceedings pursuant to which the disposition occurred, or, in the event there are no proceedings, such percentage shall be determined as if the taxpayer ceased to hold such property on the date, determined under regulations prescribed by the Secretary, on which such operation of an agreement or process of law, pursuant to which the disposition occurred, began.

(e) Holding period. For purposes of determining the applicable percentage under this section, the provisions of section 1223 shall not apply, and the holding period of section 1250 property shall be determined under the following rules:

(1) Beginning of holding period. The holding period of section 1250 property shall be deemed to begin—

(A) in the case of property acquired by the taxpayer, on the day after the date of acquisition, or

(B) in the case of property constructed, reconstructed, or erected by the taxpayer, on the first day of the month during which the property is placed in service.

(2) Property with transferred basis. If the basis of property acquired in a transaction described in paragraph (1), (2), (3), or (5) of subsection (d) is determined by reference to its basis in the hands of the transferor, then the holding period of the property in the hands of the transferee shall include the holding period of the property in the hands of the transferor.

[3]**(3) Repealed.**

* * * * * * * * * * * *

[Endnote Code Sec. 1250]

Matter in *italics* in Code Sec. 1250(d)(7), Code Sec. 1250(d)(8) and Code Sec. 1250(e)(2) added by Sec. 312(d)(10)(A) and (B) of the Taxpayer Relief Act of 1997, H.R. 2014, 8/5/97, which struck out:

1. "(7) Disposition of principal residence. Subsection (a) shall not apply to a disposition of—

"(A) property to the extent used by the taxpayer as his principal residence (within the meaning of section 1034, relating to rollover of gain on sale of principal residence), and

"(B) property in respect of which the taxpayer meets the age and ownership requirements of section 121 (relating to one-time exclusion of gain from sale of principal residence by individual who has attained age 55) but only to the extent that he meets the use requirements of such section in respect of such property.

"(9)"

2. "(10)"

3. "(3) Principal residence. If the basis of property acquired in a transaction described in paragraph (7) of subsection (d) is determined by reference to the basis in the hands of the taxpayer of other property, then the holding period of the property acquired shall include the holding period of such other property."

Effective Date (Sec. 312(d) [sic (e)], H.R. 2014, 8/5/97) Sec. 312(d) [sic (e)], H.R. 2014, 8/5/97, reads as follows:

"(d) Effective date.

"(1) In general. The amendments made by this section shall apply to sales and exchanges after May 6, 1997.

"(2) Sales before 8/5/97. At the election of the taxpayer, the amendments made by this section shall not apply to any sale or exchange before the date of the enactment of this Act.

"(3) Certain sales within 2 years after 8/5/97. Section 121 of the Internal Revenue Code of 1986 (as amended by this section) shall be applied without regard to subsection (c)(2)(B) thereof in the case of any sale or exchange of property during the 2-year period beginning on the date of the enactment of this Act if the taxpayer held such property on the date of the enactment of this Act and fails to meet the ownership and use requirements of subsection (a) thereof with respect to such property.

"(4) Binding contracts. At the election of the taxpayer, the amendments made by this section shall not apply to a sale or exchange after the date of the enactment of this Act, if—

"(A) such sale or exchange is pursuant to a contract which was binding on such date, or

"(B) without regard to such amendments, gain would not be recognized under section 1034 of the Internal Revenue Code of 1986 (as in effect on the day before the date of the enactment of this Act) on such sale or exchange by reason of a new residence acquired on or before such date or with respect to the acquisition of which by the taxpayer a binding contract was in effect on such date.

This paragraph shall not apply to any sale or exchange by an individual if the treatment provided by section 877(a)(1) of the Internal Revenue Code of 1986 applies to such individual."

[¶ 3180]   Code Sec.¹ 1259.   Constructive sales treatment for appreciated financial positions.

(a) In general. If there is a constructive sale of an appreciated financial position—

(1) the taxpayer shall recognize gain as if such position were sold, assigned, or otherwise terminated at its fair market value on the date of such constructive sale (and any gain shall be taken into account for the taxable year which includes such date), and

(2) for purposes of applying this title for periods after the constructive sale—

(A) proper adjustment shall be made in the amount of any gain or loss subsequently realized with respect to such position for any gain taken into account by reason of paragraph (1), and

(B) the holding period of such position shall be determined as if such position were originally acquired on the date of such constructive sale.

(b) Appreciated financial position. For purposes of this section—

(1) **In general.** Except as provided in paragraph (2), the term "appreciated financial position" means any position with respect to any stock, debt instrument, or partnership interest if there would be gain were such position sold, assigned, or otherwise terminated at its fair market value.

(2) **Exceptions.** The term "appreciated financial position" shall not include—

(A) any position with respect to straight debt

(i) the debt unconditionally entitles the holder to receive a specified principal amount,

(ii) the interest payments (or other similar amounts) with respect to such debt meet the requirements of clause (i) of section 860G(a)(1)(B), and

(iii) such debt is not convertible (directly or indirectly) into stock of the issuer or any related person, and

(B) any position which is marked to market under any provision of this title or the regulations thereunder.

(3) **Position.** The term "position" means an interest, including a futures or forward contract, short sale, or option.

(c) Constructive sale. For purposes of this section—

(1) **In general.** A taxpayer shall be treated as having made a constructive sale of an appreciated financial position if the taxpayer (or a related person)—

(A) enters into a short sale of the same or substantially identical property,

(B) enters into an offsetting notional principal contract with respect to the same or substantially identical property,

(C) enters into a futures or forward contract to deliver the same or substantially identical property,

(D) in the case of an appreciated financial position that is a short sale or a contract described in subparagraph (B) or (C) with respect to any property, acquires the same or substantially identical property, or

(E) to the extent prescribed by the Secretary in regulations, enters into 1 or more other transactions (or acquires 1 or more positions) that have substantially the same effect as a transaction described in any of the preceding subparagraphs.

(2) **Exception for sales of nonpublicly traded property.** The term "constructive sale" shall not include any contract for sale of any stock, debt instrument, or partnership interest which is not a marketable security (as defined in section 453(f)) if the contract settles within 1 year after the date such contract is entered into.

(3) **Exception for certain closed transactions.**

(A) In general. In applying this section, there shall be disregarded any transaction (which would otherwise be treated as a constructive sale) during the taxable year if—

(i) such transaction is closed before the end of the 30th day after the close of such taxable year,

(ii) the taxpayer holds the appreciated financial position throughout the 60-day period beginning on the date such transaction is closed, and

(iii) at no time during such 60-day period is the taxpayer's risk of loss with respect to such position reduced by reason of a circumstance which would be described in section 246(c)(4) if references to stock included references to such position.

(B) Treatment of positions which are reestablished.—If—

(i) a transaction, which would otherwise be treated as a constructive sale of an appreciated financial position, is closed during the taxable year or during the 30 days thereafter, and

(ii) another substantially similar transaction is entered into during the 60-day period beginning on the date the transaction referred to in clause (i) is closed—

(I) which also would otherwise be treated as a constructive sale of such position,

(II) which is closed before the 30th day after the close of the taxable year in which the transaction referred to in clause (i) occurs, and

(III) which meets the requirements of clauses (ii) and (iii) of subparagraph (A), the transaction referred to in clause (ii) shall be disregarded for purposes of determining whether the requirements of subparagraph (A)(iii) are met with respect to the transaction described in clause (i).

(4) **Related person.** A person is related to another person with respect to a transaction if—

(A) the relationship is described in section 267(b) or 707(b), and

(B) such transaction is entered into with a view toward avoiding the purposes of this section.

(d) **Other definitions.** For purposes of this section—

(1) **Forward contract.** The term "forward contract" means a contract to deliver a substantially fixed amount of property for a substantially fixed price.

(2) **Offsetting notional principal contract.** The term "offsetting notional principal contract" means, with respect to any property, an agreement which includes—

(A) a requirement to pay (or provide credit for) all or substantially all of the investment yield (including appreciation) on such property for a specified period, and

(B) a right to be reimbursed for (or receive credit for) all or substantially all of any decline in the value of such property.

(e) **Special rules.**

(1) **Treatment of subsequent sale of position which was deemed sold.** If—

(A) there is a constructive sale of any appreciated financial position,

(B) such position is subsequently disposed of, and

(C) at the time of such disposition, the transaction resulting in the constructive sale of such position is open with respect to the taxpayer or any related person,

solely for purposes of determining whether the taxpayer has entered into a constructive sale of any other appreciated financial position held by the taxpayer, the taxpayer shall be treated as entering into such transaction immediately after such disposition. For purposes of the preceding sentence, an assignment or other termination shall be treated as a disposition.

(2) Certain trust instruments treated as stock. For purposes of this section, an interest in a trust which is actively traded (within the meaning of section 1092(d)(1)) shall be treated as stock unless substantially all (by value) of the property held by the trust is debt described in subsection (b)(2)(A).

(3) Multiple positions in property. If a taxpayer holds multiple positions in property, the determination of whether a specific transaction is a constructive sale and, if so, which appreciated financial position is deemed sold shall be made in the same manner as actual sales.

(f) Regulations. The Secretary shall prescribe such regulations as may be necessary or appropriate to carry out the purposes of this section.

[For analysis, see ¶ 202. For text of Committee Report, see ¶ 5111.]

[Endnote Code Sec. 1259]

Code Sec. 1259 was added by Sec. 1001(a) of the Taxpayer Relief Act of 1997, H.R. 2014, 8/5/97.

1. added Code Sec. 1259

Effective Date (Sec. 1001(d), H.R. 2014, 8/5/97) effective for any constructive sale after 6/8/97, except as provided in Secs. 1001(d)(2)-(4) of this Act, which read as follows:

"(2) Exception for sales of positions, etc. held before June 9, 1997. If—

"(A) before June 9, 1997, the taxpayer entered into any transaction which is a constructive sale of any appreciated financial position, and

"(B) before the close of the 30-day period beginning on the date of the enactment of this Act, or before such later date as may be specified by the Secretary of the Treasury, such transaction and position are clearly identified in the taxpayer's records as offsetting,

such transaction and position shall not be taken into account in determining whether any other constructive sale after June 8, 1997, has occurred. The preceding sentence shall cease to apply as of the date such transaction is closed or the taxpayer ceases to hold such position.

"(3) Special rule.—In the case of a decedent dying after June 8, 1997, if—

"(A) there was a constructive sale on or before such date of any appreciated financial position,

"(B) the transaction resulting in such constructive sale of such position remains open (with respect to the decedent or any related person)—

"(i) for not less than 2 years after the date of such transaction (whether such period is before or after June 8, 1997), and

"(ii) at any time during the 3-year period ending on the date of the decedent's death, and

"(C) such transaction is not closed within the 30-day period beginning on the date of the enactment of this Act,

then, for purposes of such Code, such position (and the transaction resulting in such constructive sale) shall be treated as property constituting rights to receive an item of income in respect of a decedent under section 691 of such Code. Section 1014(c) of such Code shall not apply to so much of such position's or property's value (as included in the decedent's estate for purposes of chapter 11 of such Code) as exceeds its fair market value as of the date such transaction is closed.

"(4) Election of mark to market by securities traders and traders and dealers in commodities.—

"(A) In general.—The amendments made by subsection (b) shall apply to taxable years ending after the date of the enactment of this Act.

"(B) 4-year spread of adjustments.—In the case of a taxpayer who elects under subsection (e) or (f) of section 475 of the Internal Revenue Code of 1986 (as added by this section) to change its method of accounting for the taxable year which includes the date of the enactment of this Act—

"(i) any identification required under such subsection with respect to securities and commodities held on the date of the enactment of this Act shall be treated as timely made if made on or before the 30th day after such 8/5/97, and

"(ii) the net amount of the adjustments required to be taken into account by the taxpayer under section 481 of such Code shall be taken into account ratably over the 4-taxable year period beginning with such first taxable year."

[¶ 3181] Code Sec. 1271.   Treatment of amounts received on retirement or sale or exchange of debt instruments.

* * * * * * * * * * * *

[1](b) *Exception for certain obligations.*

(1) *In general. This section shall not apply to—*

(A) *any obligation issued by a natural person before June 9, 1997, and*

(B) any obligation issued before July 2, 1982, by an issuer which is not a corporation and is not a government or political subdivision thereof.

(2) Termination. *Paragraph (1) shall not apply to any obligation purchased (within the meaning of section 1272(d)(1)) after June 8, 1997.*

* * * * * * * * * * *

[For analysis, see ¶205. For text of Committee Report, see ¶5113.]

[Endnote Code Sec. 1271]

Matter in *italics* in Code Sec. 1271(b) added by Sec. 1003(c)(1) of the Taxpayer Relief Act of 1997, H.R. 2014, 8/5/97, which struck out:

1. "(b) Exceptions.

"This section shall not apply to—

"(1) Natural persons. Any obligation issued by a natural person.

"(2) Obligations issued before July 2, 1982, by certain issuers. Any obligation issued before July 2, 1982, by an issuer which—

"(A) is not a corporation, and

"(B) is not a government or political subdivision thereof."

Effective Date (Sec. 1003(c)(2), H.R. 2014, 8/5/97) effective for sales, exchanges and retirements after 8/5/97.

[¶3182] Code Sec. 1272.   Current inclusion in income of original issue discount.

(a) Original issue discount on debt instruments issued after July 1, 1982, included in income on basis of constant interest rate.

* * * * * * * * * * *

(6) Determination of daily portions where principal subject to acceleration.

* * * * * * * * * * *

(C) Debt instruments to which paragraph applies. This paragraph applies to—

(i) any regular interest in a REMIC or qualified mortgage held by a REMIC,[1]

(ii) any other debt instrument if payments under such debt instrument may be accelerated by reason of prepayments of other obligations securing such debt instrument (or, to the extent provided in regulations, by reason of other events)[2], *or*

[3]*(iii) any pool of debt instruments the yield on which may be affected by reason of prepayments (or to the extent provided in regulations, by reason of other events).*

To the extent provided in regulations prescribed by the Secretary, in the case of a small business engaged in the trade or business of selling tangible personal property at retail, clause (iii) shall not apply to debt instruments incurred in the ordinary course of such trade or business while held by such business.

* * * * * * * * * * *

[For analysis, see ¶2006. For text of Committee Report, see ¶5114.]

[Endnote Code Sec. 1272]

Matter in *italics* in Code Sec. 1272(a)(6)(C)(i), Code Sec. 1272(a)(6)(C)(ii) and Code Sec. 1272(a)(6)(C)(iii) added by Sec. 1004(a) of the Taxpaye Relief Act of 1997, H.R. 2014, 8/5/97, which struck out:

1. "or"

2. "."

3. added clause (a)(6)(C)(iii) and matter at the end of subparagraph (a)(6)(C)

Effective Date (Sec. 1004(b), H.R. 2014, 8/5/97) reads as follows:

"(b) Effective dates.

"(1) In general. The amendment made by this section shall apply to taxable years beginning after the date of the enactment of this Act.

"(2) Change in method of accounting. In the case of any taxpayer required by this section to change its method of accounting for its first taxable year beginning after the date of the enactment of this Act—

"(A) such change shall be treated as initiated by the taxpayer,

"(B) such change shall be treated as made with the consent of the Secretary, and

"(C) the net amount of the adjustments required to be taken into account by the taxpayer under section 481 of the Internal Revenue Code of 1986 shall be taken into account ratably over the 4-taxable year period beginning with such first taxable year."

[¶ 3183]   Code Sec. 1274.   Determination of issue price in the case of certain debt instruments issued for property.

* * * * * * * * * * *

(c) Debt instruments to which section applies.

* * * * * * * * * * *

   (3) Exceptions. This section shall not apply to—

* * * * * * * * * * *

      (B) Sales of principal residences. Any debt instrument arising from the sale or exchange by an individual of his principal residence (within the meaning of ¹*section 121*).

* * * * * * * * * * *

[Endnote Code Sec. 1274]

   Matter in *italics* in Code Sec. 1274(c)(3)(B) added by Sec. 312(d)(1) of the Taxpayer Relief Act of 1997, H.R. 2014, 8/5/97, which struck out:

   1. "section 1034"

Effective Date (Sec. 312(d) [sic (e)], H.R. 2014, 8/5/97) effective for sales and exchanges after 5/6/97. Sec. 312(d)(2)-(4) [sic (e)(2)-(4)] of this Act provides:

   "(2) Sales before 8/5/97.—At the election of the taxpayer, the amendments made by this section shall not apply to any sale or exchange before the date of the enactment of this Act.

   "(3) Certain sales within 2 years after 8/5/97. Section 121 of the Internal Revenue Code of 1986 (as amended by this section) shall be applied without regard to subsection (c)(2)(B) thereof in the case of any sale or exchange of property during the 2-year period beginning on the date of the enactment of this Act if the taxpayer held such property on the date of the enactment of this Act and fails to meet the ownership and use requirements of subsection (a) thereof with respect to such property.

   "(4) Binding contracts.—At the election of the taxpayer, the amendments made by this section shall not apply to a sale or exchange after the date of the enactment of this Act, if—

   "(A) such sale or exchange is pursuant to a contract which was binding on such date, or

   "(B) without regard to such amendments, gain would not be recognized under section 1034 of the Internal Revenue Code of 1986 (as in effect on the day before the date of the enactment of this Act) on such sale or exchange by reason of a new residence acquired on or before such date or with respect to the acquisition of which by the taxpayer a binding contract was in effect on such date. This paragraph shall not apply to any sale or exchange by an individual if the treatment provided by section 877(a)(1) of the Internal Revenue Code of 1986 applies to such individual."

[¶ 3184]   Code Sec. 1291.   Interest on tax deferral.

   (a) Treatment of distributions and stock dispositions.

* * * * * * * * * * *

   (3) Definitions. For purposes of this section—

   CAUTION.   Subpara. (a)(3)(A), following, is effective for tax. yrs. of U.S. persons begin. before 1/1/98, and tax. yrs. of foreign corporations end. with or within such tax. yrs. of U.S. persons. For subpara. (a)(3)(A), effective for tax. yrs. of U.S. persons begin. after 12/31/97, and tax. yrs. of foreign corporations end. with or within such tax. yrs. of U.S. persons, see below.

      (A) Holding period. The taxpayer's holding period shall be determined under section 1223; except that, for purposes of applying this section to an excess distribution, such holding period shall be treated as ending on the date of such distribution.

   CAUTION.   Subpara. (a)(3)(A), following, is effective for tax. yrs. of U.S. persons begin. after 12/31/97, and tax. yrs. of foreign corporations end. with or within such tax. yrs. of U.S. persons. For subpara. (a)(3)(A), effective for tax. yrs. of U.S. persons begin. before 1/1/98, and tax. yrs. of foreign corporations end. with or within such tax. yrs. of U.S. persons, see above.

[1](A) Holding period. The taxpayer's holding period shall be determined under section 1223; except that—

(i) for purposes of applying this section to an excess distribution, such holding period shall be treated as ending on the date of such distribution, and

(ii) if section 1296 applied to such stock with respect to the taxpayer for any prior taxable year, such holding period shall be treated as beginning on the first day of the first taxable year beginning after the last taxable year for which section 1296 so applied.

* * * * * * * * * * * *

CAUTION.   Subsec. (d) heading and para. (d)(1), following, are effective for tax. yrs. of U.S. persons begin. before 1/1/98, and tax. yrs. of foreign corporations end. with or within such tax. yrs. of U.S. persons. For subsec. (d) heading and para. (d)(1), effective for tax. yrs. of U.S. persons begin. after 12/31/97, and tax. yrs. of foreign corporations end. with or within such tax. yrs. of U.S. persons, see below.

(d) Coordination with subpart B.

(1) In general. This section shall not apply with respect to any distribution paid by a passive foreign investment company, or any disposition of stock in a passive foreign investment company, if such company is a qualified electing fund with respect to the taxpayer for each of its taxable years—

(A) which begins after December 31, 1986, and for which such company is a passive foreign investment company, and

(B) which includes any portion of the taxpayer's holding period.

CAUTION.   Subsec. (d) heading and para. (d)(1), following, are effective for tax. yrs. of U.S. persons begin. after 12/31/97, and tax. yrs. of foreign corporations end. with or within such tax. yrs. of U.S. persons. For subsec. (d) heading and para. (d)(1), effective for tax. yrs. of U.S. persons begin. before 1/1/98, and tax. yrs. of foreign corporations end. with or within such tax. yrs. of U.S. persons, see above.

(d) Coordination with [2]subparts B and C.

(1) In general. This section shall not apply with respect to any distribution paid by a passive foreign investment company, or any disposition of stock in a passive foreign investment company, if such company is a qualified electing fund with respect to the taxpayer for each of its taxable years—

(A) which begins after December 31, 1986, and for which such company is a passive foreign investment company, and

(B) which includes any portion of the taxpayer's holding period.

[3]Except as provided in section 1296(j), this section also shall not apply if an election under section 1296(k) is in effect for the taxpayer's taxable year.

* * * * * * * * * * * *

[Endnote Code Sec. 1291]

Matter in *italics* in Code Sec. 1291(a)(3)(A), Code Sec. 1291(d), and Code Sec. 1291(d)(1) was added by Sec. 1122(b)(1)-(3) of the Taxpayer Relief Act of 1997, H.R. 2014, 8/5/97, which struck out:

1. "(A) Holding period. The taxpayer's holding period shall be determined under section 1223; except that, for purposes of applying this section to an excess distribution, such holding period shall be treated as ending on the date of such distribution."

2. "subpart B"

3. added matter at the end of para. (d)(1)

Effective Date (Sec. 1124, H.R. 2014, 8/5/97) effective for tax. yrs. of United States persons beginning after 12/31/97, and tax. yrs. of foreign corporations ending with or within such tax. yrs. of United States persons.

[¶ 3185]   Code Sec. 1293.   Current taxation of income from qualified electing funds.
(a) Inclusion.

CAUTION.   Para. (a)(1), following, is effective for tax. yrs. of U.S. persons begin. before 1/1/98 and for tax. yrs. of foreign corporations ending with or within such tax. yrs. of U.S. persons. For para. (a)(1), effective for tax. yrs. of U.S. persons begin. after 12/31/97 and for tax. yrs. of foreign corporations ending with or within such tax. yrs. of U.S. persons, see below.

(1) In general. Every United States person who owns (or is treated under section 1297(a) as owning) stock of a qualified electing fund at any time during the taxable year of such fund shall include in gross income—

(A) as ordinary income, such shareholder's pro rata share of the ordinary earnings of such fund for such year, and

(B) as long-term capital gain, such shareholder's pro rata share of the net capital gain of such fund for such year.

CAUTION.   Para. (a)(1), following, is effective for tax. yrs. of U.S. persons begin. after 12/31/97 and for tax. yrs. of foreign corporations ending with or within such tax. yrs. of U.S. persons. For para. (a)(1), effective for tax. yrs. of U.S. persons begin. before 1/1/98 and for tax. yrs. of foreign corporations ending with or within such tax. yrs. of U.S. persons, see above.

(1) In general. Every United States person who owns (or is treated under [1]*section 1298(a)* as owning) stock of a qualified electing fund at any time during the taxable year of such fund shall include in gross income—

(A) as ordinary income, such shareholder's pro rata share of the ordinary earnings of such fund for such year, and

(B) as long-term capital gain, such shareholder's pro rata share of the net capital gain of such fund for such year.

* * * * * * * * * * * *

CAUTION.   Subsec. (d), following, is effective for tax. yrs. of U.S. persons begin. before 1/1/98 and for tax. yrs. of foreign corporations ending with or within such tax. yrs. of U.S. persons. For subsec. (d), effective for tax. yrs. of U.S. persons begin. after 12/31/97 and for tax. yrs. of foreign corporations ending with or within such tax. yrs. of U.S. persons, see below.

(d) Basis adjustments. The basis of the taxpayer's stock in a passive foreign investment company shall be—

(1) increased by any amount which is included in the income of the taxpayer under subsection (a) with respect to such stock, and

(2) decreased by any amount distributed with respect to such stock which is not includible in the income of the taxpayer by reason of subsection (c).

A similar rule shall apply also in the case of any property if by reason of holding such property the taxpayer is treated under section 1297(a) as owning stock in a qualified electing fund.

CAUTION.   Subsec. (d), following, is effective for tax. yrs. of U.S. persons begin. after 12/31/97 and for tax. yrs. of foreign corporations ending with or within such tax. yrs. of U.S. persons. For subsec. (d), effective for tax. yrs. of U.S. persons begin. before 1/1/98 and for tax. yrs. of foreign corporations ending with or within such tax. yrs. of U.S. persons, see above.

(d) Basis adjustments. The basis of the taxpayer's stock in a passive foreign investment company shall be—

(1) increased by any amount which is included in the income of the taxpayer under subsection (a) with respect to such stock, and

(2) decreased by any amount distributed with respect to such stock which is not includible in the income of the taxpayer by reason of subsection (c).

A similar rule shall apply also in the case of any property if by reason of holding such property the taxpayer is treated under [2]*section 1298(a)* as owning stock in a qualified electing fund.

* * * * * * * * * * * *

[Endnote Code Sec. 1293]

Matter in *italics* in Code Sec. 1293(a)(1) and Code Sec. 1293(d) added by Sec. 1122(d)(3) of the Taxpayer Relief Act of 1997, H.R. 2014, 8/5/97, which struck out:

1. "section 1297(a)"
2. "section 1297(a)"

Effective Date (Sec. 1124, H.R. 2014, 8/5/97) reads as follows:

"SEC. 1124. EFFECTIVE DATE.

"The amendments made by this subtitle shall apply to—

"(1) taxable years of United States persons beginning after December 31, 1997, and

"(2) taxable years of foreign corporations ending with or within such taxable years of United States persons."

[¶ 3186]   Code Sec. 1296.

CAUTION.   Code Sec. 1296, following, is effective for tax. yrs. of United States persons begin. before 1/1/98, and tax. yrs. of foreign corporations end. with or within such tax. yrs. of United States persons. For Code Sec. 1296 effective for tax. yrs. of United States persons begin. after 12/31/97, and tax. yrs. of foreign corporations end. with or within such tax. yrs. of United States persons, see above.

Passive foreign investment company.

(a) **In general.** For purposes of this part, except as otherwise provided in this subpart, the term "passive foreign investment company" means any foreign corporation if—

(1) 75 percent or more of the gross income of such corporation for the taxable year is passive income, or

(2) the average percentage of assets (by value) held by such corporation during the taxable year which produce passive income or which are held for the production of passive income is at least 50 percent.

In the case of a controlled foreign corporation (or any other foreign corporation if such corporation so elects), the determination under paragraph (2) shall be based on the adjusted bases (as determined for purposes of computing earnings and profits) of its assets in lieu of their value. Such an election, once made, may be revoked only with the consent of the Secretary.

(b) **Passive income.** For purposes of this section—

(1) **In general.** Except as provided in paragraph (2), the term "passive income" means any income which is of a kind which would be foreign personal holding company income as defined in section 954(c).

(2) **Exceptions** Except as provided in regulations, the term "passive income" does not include any income—

(A) derived in the active conduct of a banking business by an institution licensed to do business as a bank in the United States (or, to the extent provided in regulations, by any other corporation),

(B) derived in the active conduct of an insurance business by a corporation which is predominantly engaged in an insurance business and which would be subject to tax under subchapter L if it were a domestic corporation,

(C) which is interest, a dividend, or a rent or royalty, which is received or accrued from a related person (within the meaning of section 954(d)(3)) to the extent such amount is properly allocable (under regulations prescribed by the Secretary) to income of such related person which is not passive income , or

(D) which is foreign trade income of a FSC or export trade income of an export trade corporation (as defined in section 971).

1,143

For purposes of subparagraph (C), the term "related person" has the meaning given such term by section 954(d)(3) determined by substituting "foreign corporation" for "controlled foreign corporation" each place it appears in section 954(d)(3).

(3) Treatment of certain dealers in securities.

(A) In general. In the case of any foreign corporation which is a controlled foreign corporation (as defined in section 957(a)), the term "passive income" does not include any income derived in the active conduct of a securities business by such corporation if such corporation is registered as a securities broker or dealer under section 15(a) of the Securities Exchange Act of 1934 or is registered as a Government securities broker or dealer under section 15C(a) of such Act. To the extent provided in regulations, such term shall not include any income derived in the active conduct of a securities business by a controlled foreign corporation which is not so registered.

(B) Application of look-thru rules. For purposes of paragraph (2)(C), rules similar to the rules of subparagraph (A) of this paragraph shall apply in determining whether any income of a related person (whether or not a corporation) is passive income.

(C) Limitation. The preceding provisions of this paragraph shall only apply in the case of persons who are United States shareholders (as defined in section 951(b)) in the controlled foreign corporation.

(c) Look-thru in the case of 25-percent owned corporations. If a foreign corporation owns (directly or indirectly) at least 25 percent (by value) of the stock of another corporation, for purposes of determining whether such foreign corporation is a passive foreign investment company, such foreign corporation shall be treated as if it—

(1) held its proportionate share of the assets of such other corporation, and

(2) received directly its proportionate share of the income of such other corporation.

(d) Section 1247 corporations. For purposes of this part, the term "passive foreign investment company" does not include any foreign investment company to which section 1247 applies.

Code Sec.¹ 1296.

CAUTION. Code Sec. 1296, as part of Subpart C, following, is effective for tax. yrs. of United States persons begin. after 12/31/97, and tax. yrs. of foreign corporations end. with or within such tax. yrs. of United States persons. For Code Sec. 1296 effective for tax. yrs. of United States persons begin. before 1/1/98, and for tax. yrs. of foreign corporations end. with or within such tax. yrs. of United States persons, see below.

Election of mark to market for marketable stock.

(a) General rule. In the case of marketable stock in a passive foreign investment company which is owned (or treated under subsection (g) as owned) by a United States person at the close of any taxable year of such person, at the election of such person—

(1) If the fair market value of such stock as of the close of such taxable year exceeds its adjusted basis, such United States person shall include in gross income for such taxable year an amount equal to the amount of such excess.

(2) If the adjusted basis of such stock exceeds the fair market value of such stock as of the close of such taxable year, such United States person shall be allowed a deduction for such taxable year equal to the lesser of—

(A) the amount of such excess, or

(B) the unreversed inclusions with respect to such stock.

(b) Basis adjustments.

(1) In general. The adjusted basis of stock in a passive foreign investment company—

(A) shall be increased by the amount included in the gross income of the United States person under subsection (a)(1) with respect to such stock, and

(B) shall be decreased by the amount allowed as a deduction to the United States person under subsection (a)(2) with respect to such stock.

(2) Special rule for stock constructively owned. In the case of stock in a passive foreign investment company which the United States person is treated as owning under subsection (g)—

(A) the adjustments under paragraph (1) shall apply to such stock in the hands of the person actually holding such stock but only for purposes of determining the subsequent treatment under this chapter of the United States person with respect to such stock, and

(B) similar adjustments shall be made to the adjusted basis of the property by reason of which the United States person is treated as owning such stock.

(c) Character and source rules.

(1) Ordinary treatment.

(A) Gain. Any amount included in gross income under subsection (a)(1), and any gain on the sale or other disposition of marketable stock in a passive foreign investment company (with respect to which an election under this section is in effect), shall be treated as ordinary income.

(B) Loss. Any—

(i) amount allowed as a deduction under subsection (a)(2), and

(ii) loss on the sale or other disposition of marketable stock in a passive foreign investment company (with respect to which an election under this section is in effect) to the extent that the amount of such loss does not exceed the unreversed inclusions with respect to such stock,

shall be treated as an ordinary loss. The amount so treated shall be treated as a deduction allowable in computing adjusted gross income.

(2) Source. The source of any amount included in gross income under subsection (a)(1) (or allowed as a deduction under subsection (a)(2)) shall be determined in the same manner as if such amount were gain or loss (as the case may be) from the sale of stock in the passive foreign investment company.

(d) Unreversed inclusions. For purposes of this section, the term "unreversed inclusions" means, with respect to any stock in a passive foreign investment company, the excess (if any) of—

(1) the amount included in gross income of the taxpayer under subsection (a)(1) with respect to such stock for prior taxable years, over

(2) the amount allowed as a deduction under subsection (a)(2) with respect to such stock for prior taxable years.

The amount referred to in paragraph (1) shall include any amount which would have been included in gross income under subsection (a)(1) with respect to such stock for any prior taxable year but for section 1291.

(e) Marketable stock. For purposes of this section—

(1) In general. The term "marketable stock" means—

(A) any stock which is regularly traded on—

(i) a national securities exchange which is registered with the Securities and Exchange Commission or the national market system established pursuant to section 11A of the Securities and Exchange Act of 1934, or

(ii) any exchange or other market which the Secretary determines has rules adequate to carry out the purposes of this part,

(B) to the extent provided in regulations, stock in any foreign corporation which is comparable to a regulated investment company and which offers for sale or has outstanding any stock of which it is the issuer and which is redeemable at its net asset value, and

(C) to the extent provided in regulations, any option on stock described in subparagraph (A) or (B).

(2) Special rule for regulated investment companies. In the case of any regulated investment company which is offering for sale or has outstanding any stock of which it is the issuer and which is redeemable at its net asset value, all stock in a passive foreign investment company which it owns directly or indirectly shall be treated as marketable stock for purposes of this section. Except as provided in regulations, similar treatment as marketable stock shall apply in the case of any other regulated investment company which publishes net asset valuations at least annually.

(f) Treatment of controlled foreign corporations which are shareholders in passive foreign investment companies. In the case of a foreign corporation which is a controlled foreign corporation and which owns (or is treated under subsection (g) as owning) stock in a passive foreign investment company—

(1) this section (other than subsection (c)(2)) shall apply to such foreign corporation in the same manner as if such corporation were a United States person, and

(2) for purposes of subpart F of part III of subchapter N—

(A) any amount included in gross income under subsection (a)(1) shall be treated as foreign personal holding company income described in section 954(c)(1)(A), and

(B) any amount allowed as a deduction under subsection (a)(2) shall be treated as a deduction allocable to foreign personal holding company income so described.

(g) Stock owned through certain foreign entities. Except as provided in regulations—

(1) In general. For purposes of this section, stock owned, directly or indirectly, by or for a foreign partnership or foreign trust or foreign estate shall be considered as being owned proportionately by its partners or beneficiaries. Stock considered to be owned by a person by reason of the application of the preceding sentence shall, for purposes of applying such sentence, be treated as actually owned by such person.

(2) Treatment of certain dispositions. In any case in which a United States person is treated as owning stock in a passive foreign investment company by reason of paragraph (1)—

(A) any disposition by the United States person or by any other person which results in the United States person being treated as no longer owning such stock, and

(B) any disposition by the person owning such stock,

shall be treated as a disposition by the United States person of the stock in the passive foreign investment company.

(h) Coordination with section 851(b). For purposes of paragraphs (2) and (3) of section 851(b), any amount included in gross income under subsection (a) shall be treated as a dividend.

(i) Stock acquired from a decedent. In the case of stock of a passive foreign investment company which is acquired by bequest, devise, or inheritance (or by the decedent's estate) and with respect to which an election under this section was in effect as of the date of the decedent's death, notwithstanding section 1014, the basis of such stock in the hands of the person so acquiring it shall be the adjusted basis of such stock in the hands of the decedent immediately before his death (or, if lesser, the basis which would have been determined under section 1014 without regard to this subsection).

(j) Coordination with section 1291 for first year of election.

(1) Taxpayers other than regulated investment companies.

(A) In general. If the taxpayer elects the application of this section with respect to any marketable stock in a corporation after the beginning of the taxpayer's holding period in such stock, and if the requirements of subparagraph (B) are not satisfied, section 1291 shall apply to—

(i) any distributions with respect to, or disposition of, such stock in the first taxable year of the taxpayer for which such election is made, and

(ii) any amount which, but for section 1291, would have been included in gross income under subsection (a) with respect to such stock for such taxable year in the same manner as if such amount were gain on the disposition of such stock.

(B) Requirements. The requirements of this subparagraph are met if, with respect to each of such corporation's taxable years for which such corporation was a passive foreign investment company and which begin after December 31, 1986, and included any portion of the taxpayer's holding period in such stock, such corporation was treated as a qualified electing fund under this part with respect to the taxpayer.

(2) Special rules for regulated investment companies.

(A) In general. If a regulated investment company elects the application of this section with respect to any marketable stock in a corporation after the beginning of the taxpayer's holding period in such stock, then, with respect to such company's first taxable year for which such company elects the application of this section with respect to such stock—

(i) section 1291 shall not apply to such stock with respect to any distribution or disposition during, or amount included in gross income under this section for, such first taxable year, but

(ii) such regulated investment company's tax under this chapter for such first taxable year shall be increased by the aggregate amount of interest which would have been determined under section 1291(c)(3) if section 1291 were applied without regard to this subparagraph.

Clause (ii) shall not apply if for the preceding taxable year the company elected to mark to market the stock held by such company as of the last day of such preceding taxable year.

(B) Disallowance of deduction. No deduction shall be allowed to any regulated investment company for the increase in tax under subparagraph (A)(ii).

(k) Election. This section shall apply to marketable stock in a passive foreign investment company which is held by a United States person only if such person elects to apply this section with respect to such stock. Such an election shall apply to the taxable year for which made and all subsequent taxable years unless—

(1) such stock ceases to be marketable stock, or

(2) the Secretary consents to the revocation of such election.

(l) Transition rule for individuals becoming subject to united states tax. If any individual becomes a United States person in a taxable year beginning after December 31, 1997, solely for purposes of this section, the adjusted basis (before adjustments under subsection (b)) of any marketable stock in a passive foreign investment company owned by such individual on the first day of such taxable year shall be treated as being the greater of its fair market value on such first day or its adjusted basis on such first day.

[For analysis, see ¶ 1617, ¶ 1618. For text of Committee Report, see ¶ 5178.]

[Endnote Code Sec. 1296]
Code Sec. 1296 was added by Sec. 1122(a) of the Taxpayer Relief Act of 1997, H.R. 2014, 8/5/97.

1. added Code Sec. 1296

Effective Date (Sec. 1124, H.R. 2014, 8/5/97) effective for tax. yrs. of United States persons begin. after 12/31/97, and tax. yrs. of foreign corporations end. with or within such tax. yrs. of United States persons.

[¶ 3187]   Code Sec. 1297.

CAUTION.   Code Sec. 1297, following, is effective for tax. yrs. of United States persons begin. before 1/1/98, and tax. yrs. of foreign corporations end. with or within such tax. yrs. of United States persons. For Code Sec. 1297 effective for tax. yrs. of United States persons begin. after 12/31/97, and tax. yrs. of foreign corporations end. with or within such tax. yrs. of United States persons, see below.

Special rules.

(a) Attribution of ownership. For purposes of this part—

(1) Attribution to United States persons. This subsection—

(A) shall apply to the extent that the effect is to treat stock of a passive foreign investment company as owned by a United States person, and

(B) except to the extent provided in regulations, shall not apply to treat stock owned (or treated as owned under this subsection) by a United States person as owned by any other person.

(2) Corporations.

(A) In general. If 50 percent or more in value of the stock of a corporation is owned, directly or indirectly, by or for any person, such person shall be considered as owning the stock owned directly or indirectly by or for such corporation in that proportion which the value of the stock which such person so owns bears to the value of all stock in the corporation.

(B) 50-percent limitation not to apply to PFIC. For purposes of determining whether a shareholder of a passive foreign investment company is treated as owning stock owned directly or indirectly by or for such company, subparagraph (A) shall be applied without regard to the 50-percent limitation contained therein.

(3) **Partnerships, etc.** Stock owned, directly or indirectly, by or for a partnership, estate, or trust shall be considered as being owned proportionately by its partners or beneficiaries.

(4) **Options.** To the extent provided in regulations, if any person has an option to acquire stock, such stock shall be considered as owned by such person. For purposes of this paragraph, an option to acquire such an option, and each one of a series of such options, shall be considered as an option to acquire such stock.

(5) **Successive application.** Stock considered to be owned by a person by reason of the application of paragraph (2), (3), or (4) shall, for purposes of applying such paragraphs, be considered as actually owned by such person.

(b) Other special rules. For purposes of this part—

(1) **Time for determination.** Stock held by a taxpayer shall be treated as stock in a passive foreign investment company if, at any time during the holding period of the taxpayer with respect to such stock, such corporation (or any predecessor) was a passive foreign investment company which was not a qualified electing fund. The preceding sentence shall not apply if the taxpayer elects to recognize gain (as of the last day of the last taxable year for which the company was a passive foreign investment company) under rules similar to the rules of section 1291(d)(2).

(2) **Certain corporations not treated as PFIC's during start-up year.** A corporation shall not be treated as a passive foreign investment company for the first taxable year such corporation has gross income (hereinafter in this paragraph referred to as the "start-up year") if—

(A) no predecessor of such corporation was a passive foreign investment company,

(B) it is established to the satisfaction of the Secretary that such corporation will not be a passive foreign investment company for either of the 1st 2 taxable years following the start-up year, and

(C) such corporation is not a passive foreign investment company for either of the 1st 2 taxable years following the start-up year.

(3) **Certain corporations changing businesses.** A corporation shall not be treated as a passive foreign investment company for any taxable year if—

(A) neither such corporation (nor any predecessor) was a passive foreign investment company for any prior taxable year,

(B) it is established to the satisfaction of the Secretary that—

(i) substantially all of the passive income of the corporation for the taxable year is attributable to proceeds from the disposition of 1 or more active trades or businesses, and

(ii) such corporation will not be a passive foreign investment company for either of the 1st 2 taxable years following such taxable year, and

(C) such corporation is not a passive foreign investment company for either of such 2 taxable years.

(4) **Separate interests treated as separate corporations.** Under regulations prescribed by the Secretary, where necessary to carry out the purposes of this part, separate classes of stock (or other interests) in a corporation shall be treated as interests in separate corporations.

(5) **Application of part where stock held by other entity.**

(A) In general. Under regulations, in any case in which a United States person is treated as owning stock in a passive foreign investment company by reason of subsection (a)—

(i) any disposition by the United States person or the person owning such stock which results in the United States person being treated as no longer owning such stock, or

(ii) any distribution of property in respect of such stock to the person holding such stock,

shall be treated as a disposition by, or distribution to, the United States person with respect to the stock in the passive foreign investment company.

(B) **Amount treated in same manner as previously taxed income.** Rules similar to the rules of section 959(b) shall apply to any amount described in subparagraph (A) and to any amount included in gross income under section 1293(a) (or which would have been so included but for section 951(f)) in respect of stock which the taxpayer is treated as owning under subsection (a).

(6) **Dispositions.** Except as provided in regulations, if a taxpayer uses any stock in a passive foreign investment company as security for a loan, the taxpayer shall be treated as having disposed of such stock.

(7) **Coordination with section 1246.** Section 1246 shall not apply to earnings and profits of any company for any taxable year beginning after December 31, 1986, if such company is a passive foreign investment company for such taxable year.

(8) **Treatment of certain foreign corporations owning stock in 25-percent owned domestic corporation.**

(A) **In general.** If—

(i) a foreign corporation is subject to the tax imposed by section 531 (or waives any benefit under any treaty which would otherwise prevent the imposition of such tax), and

(ii) such foreign corporation owns at least 25 percent (by value) of the stock of a domestic corporation,

for purposes of determining whether such foreign corporation is a passive foreign investment company, any qualified stock held by such domestic corporation shall be treated as an asset which does not produce passive income (and is not held for the production of passive income) and any amount included in gross income with respect to such stock shall not be treated as passive income.

(B) **Qualified stock.** For purposes of subparagraph (A), the term "qualified stock" means any stock in a C corporation which is a domestic corporation and which is not a regulated investment company or real estate investment trust.

(9) **Treatment of certain subpart F inclusions.** Any amount included in gross income under section 951(a)(1)(B) shall be treated as a distribution received with respect to the stock.

(c) **Treatment of stock held by pooled income fund.** If stock in a passive foreign investment company is owned (or treated as owned under subsection (a)) by a pooled income fund (as defined in section 642(c)(5)) and no portion of any gain from a disposition of such stock may be allocated to income under the terms of the governing instrument of such fund—

(1) section 1291 shall not apply to any gain on a disposition of such stock by such fund if (without regard to section 1291) a deduction would be allowable with respect to such gain under section 642(c)(3),

(2) section 1293 shall not apply with respect to such stock, and

(3) in determining whether section 1291 applies to any distribution in respect of such stock, subsection (d) of section 1291 shall not apply.

(d) **Treatment of certain leased property.** For purposes of this part—

(1) **In general.** Any tangible personal property with respect to which a foreign corporation is the lessee under a lease with a term of at least 12 months shall be treated as an asset actually held by such corporation.

(2) **Amount taken into account.**

(A) **In general.** The amount taken into account under section 1296(a)(2) with respect to any asset to which paragraph (1) applies shall be the unamortized portion (as determined under regulations prescribed by he Secretary) of the present value of the payments under the lease for the use of such property.

(B) **Present value.** For purposes of subparagraph (A), the present value of payments described in subparagraph (A) shall be determined in the manner provided in regulations prescribed by the Secretary—

(i) as of the beginning of the lease term, and

(ii) except as provided in such regulations, by using a discount rate equal to the applicable Federal rate determined under section 1274(d)—

(I) by substituting the lease term for the term of the debt instrument, and

(II) without regard to paragraph (2) or (3) thereof.

(3) Exceptions. This subsection shall not apply in any case where—

(A) the lessor is a related person (as defined in section 954(d)(3)) with respect to the foreign corporation, or

(B) a principal purpose of leasing the property was to avoid the provisions of this part.

(e) Special rules for certain intangibles. For purposes of this part—

(1) Research expenditures. The adjusted basis of the total assets of a controlled foreign corporation shall be increased by the research or experimental expenditures (within the meaning of section 174) paid or incurred by such foreign corporation during the taxable year and the preceding 2 taxable years. Any expenditure otherwise taken into account under the preceding sentence shall be reduced by the amount of any reimbursement received by the controlled foreign corporation with respect to such expenditure.

(2) Certain licensed intangibles.

(A) In general. In the case of any intangible property (as defined in section 936(h)(3)(B)) with respect to which a controlled foreign corporation is a licensee and which is used by such foreign corporation in the active conduct of a trade or business, the adjusted basis of the total assets of such foreign corporation shall be increased by an amount equal to 300 percent of the payments made during the taxable year by such foreign corporation for the use of such intangible property.

(B) Exceptions. Subparagraph (A) shall not apply to—

(i) any payments to a foreign person if such foreign person is a related person (as defined in section 954(d)(3)) with respect to the controlled foreign corporation, and

(ii) any payments under a license if a principal purpose of entering into such license was to avoid the provisions of this part.

(3) Controlled foreign corporation. For purposes of this subsection, the term "controlled foreign corporation" has the meaning given such term by section 957(a).

(f) Regulations. The Secretary shall prescribe such regulations as may be necessary or appropriate to carry out the purposes of this part.

Code Sec.[1] 1297.

CAUTION. Code Sec. 1297, following, is effective for tax. yrs. of United States persons begin. after 12/31/97, and tax. yrs. of foreign corporations end. with or within such tax. yrs. of United States persons. For Code Sec. 1297 effective for tax. yrs. of United States persons begin. before 1/1/98, and tax. yrs. of foreign corporations end. with or within such tax. yrs. of United States persons, see above.

Passive foreign investment company.

(a) In general. For purposes of this part, except as otherwise provided in this subpart, the term "passive foreign investment company" means any foreign corporation if—

(1) 75 percent or more of the gross income of such corporation for the taxable year is passive income, or

(2) the average percentage of assets [2](*as determined in accordance with subsection (e)*) held by such corporation during the taxable year which produce passive income or which are held for the production of passive income is at least 50 percent.[3]

(b) Passive income. For purposes of this section—

(1) In general. Except as provided in paragraph (2), the term "passive income" means any income which is of a kind which would be foreign personal holding company income as defined in section 954(c).

(2) Exceptions Except as provided in regulations, the term "passive income" does not include any income—

(A) derived in the active conduct of a banking business by an institution licensed to do business as a bank in the United States (or, to the extent provided in regulations, by any other corporation),

(B) derived in the active conduct of an insurance business by a corporation which is predominantly engaged in an insurance business and which would be subject to tax under subchapter L if it were a domestic corporation.

(C) which is interest, a dividend, or a rent or royalty, which is received or accrued from a related person (within the meaning of section 954(d)(3)) to the extent such amount is properly allocable (under regulations prescribed by the Secretary) to income of such related person which is not passive income, or

(D) which is foreign trade income of a FSC or export trade income of an export trade corporation (as defined in section 971).

For purposes of subparagraph (C), the term "related person" has the meaning given such term by section 954(d)(3) determined by substituting "foreign corporation" for "controlled foreign corporation" each place it appears in section 954(d)(3).

[4](3) Repealed.

(c) **Look-thru in the case of 25-percent owned corporations.** If a foreign corporation owns (directly or indirectly) at least 25 percent (by value) of the stock of another corporation, for purposes of determining whether such foreign corporation is a passive foreign investment company, such foreign corporation shall be treated as if it—

(1) held its proportionate share of the assets of such other corporation, and

(2) received directly its proportionate share of the income of such other corporation.

(d) **Section 1247 corporations.** For purposes of this part, the term "passive foreign investment company" does not include any foreign investment company to which section 1247 applies.

[5](e) *Exception for United States shareholders of controlled foreign corporations.*

(1) In general. For purposes of this part, a corporation shall not be treated with respect to a shareholder as a passive foreign investment company during the qualified portion of such shareholder's holding period with respect to stock in such corporation.

(2) Qualified portion. For purposes of this subsection, the term "qualified portion" means the portion of the shareholder's holding period—

(A) which is after December 31, 1997, and

(B) during which the shareholder is a United States shareholder (as defined in section 951(b)) of the corporation and the corporation is a controlled foreign corporation.

(3) New holding period if qualified portion ends.

(A) In general. Except as provided in subparagraph (B), if the qualified portion of a shareholder's holding period with respect to any stock ends after December 31, 1997, solely for purposes of this part, the shareholder's holding period with respect to such stock shall be treated as beginning as of the first day following such period.

(B) Exception. Subparagraph (A) shall not apply if such stock was, with respect to such shareholder, stock in a passive foreign investment company at any time before the qualified portion of the shareholder's holding period with respect to such stock and no election under section 1298(b)(1) is made.

[6](e) *[sic (f)] Methods for measuring assets.*

(1) Determination using value. The determination under subsection (a)(2) shall be made on the basis of the value of the assets of a foreign corporation if—

(A) such corporation is a publicly traded corporation for the taxable year, or

(B) (B) paragraph (2) does not apply to such corporation for the taxable year.

(2) Determination using adjusted bases. The determination under subsection (a)(2) shall be based on the adjusted bases (as determined for the purposes of computing earnings and profits) of the assets of a foreign corporation if such corporation is not described in paragraph (1)(A) and such corporation—

(A) is a controlled foreign corporation, or

(B) elects the application of this paragraph. An election under subparagraph (B), once made, may be revoked only with the consent of the Secretary.

(3) Publicly traded corporation. For purposes of this subsection, a foreign corporation shall be treated as a publicly traded corporation if the stock in the corporation is regularly traded on—

(A) a national securities exchange which is registered with the Securities and Exchange Commission or the national market system established pursuant to section 11A of the Securities and Exchange Act of 1934, or

(B) any exchange or other market which the Secretary determines has rules adequate to carry out the purposes of this subsection.

[For analysis, see ¶ 1619. For text of Committee Report, see ¶ 5178.]

[Endnote Code Sec. 1297]

Matter in *italics* in Code Sec. 1297, Code Sec. 1297(a), Code Sec. 1297(b)(3), Code Sec. 1297(e), and Code Sec. 1297(e) [sic (f)] added by Secs. 1121, 1122(a) and (d)(4), 1123(a), (b)(1), and (b)(2) of the Taxpayer Relief Act of 1997, H.R. 2014, 8/5/97, which struck out:

1. "1296"

2. "(by value)"

3. "In the case of a controlled foreign corporation (or any other foreign corporation if such corporation so elects), the determination under paragraph (2) shall be based on the adjusted bases (as determined for purposes of computing earnings and profits) of its assets in lieu of their value. Such an election, once made, may be revoked only with the consent of the Secretary."

4. "(3) Treatment of certain dealers in securities.

"(A) In general. In the case of any foreign corporation which is a controlled foreign corporation (as defined in section 957(a)), the term 'passive income' does not include any income derived in the active conduct of a securities business by such corporation if such corporation is registered as a securities broker or dealer under section 15(a) of the Securities Exchange Act of 1934 or is registered as a Government securities broker or dealer under section 15C(a) of such Act. To the extent provided in regulations, such term shall not include any income derived in the active conduct of a securities business by a controlled foreign corporation which is not so registered.

"(B) Application of look-thru rules. For purposes of paragraph (2)(C), rules similar to the rules of subparagraph (A) of this paragraph shall apply in determining whether any income of a related person (whether or not a corporation) is passive income.

"(C) Limitation. The preceding provisions of this paragraph shall only apply in the case of persons who are United States shareholders (as defined in section 951(b)) in the controlled foreign corporation."

5. added subsec. (e)

6. added subsec. (e)[sic (f)]

Effective Date (Sec. 1124, H.R. 2014, 8/5/97) effective for tax. yrs. of United States persons begin. after 12/31/97, and tax. yrs. of foreign corporations end. with or within such tax. yrs. of United States persons.

[¶ 3188]   Code Sec.[1] 1298.

CAUTION.   Code Sec. 1298, following, is effective for tax. yrs. of United States persons begin. after 12/31/97, and tax. yrs. of foreign corporations end. with or within such tax. yrs. of United States persons.

Special rules.

(a) **Attribution of ownership.** For purposes of this part—

(1) **Attribution to United States persons.** This subsection—

(A) shall apply to the extent that the effect is to treat stock of a passive foreign investment company as owned by a United States person, and

(B) except to the extent provided in regulations, shall not apply to treat stock owned (or treated as owned under this subsection) by a United States person as owned by any other person.

(2) **Corporations.**

(A) In general. If 50 percent or more in value of the stock of a corporation is owned, directly or indirectly, by or for any person, such person shall be considered as owning the stock owned directly or indirectly by or for such corporation in that proportion which the value of the stock which such person so owns bears to the value of all stock in the corporation.

(B) 50-percent limitation not to apply to PFIC. For purposes of determining whether a shareholder of a passive foreign investment company is treated as owning stock owned directly or indirectly by or for such company, subparagraph (A) shall be applied without regard to the 50-percent limitation contained therein.

(3) **Partnerships, etc.** Stock owned, directly or indirectly, by or for a partnership, estate, or trust shall be considered as being owned proportionately by its partners or beneficiaries.

(4) Options. To the extent provided in regulations, if any person has an option to acquire stock, such stock shall be considered as owned by such person. For purposes of this paragraph, an option to acquire such an option, and each one of a series of such options, shall be considered as an option to acquire such stock.

(5) Successive application. Stock considered to be owned by a person by reason of the application of paragraph (2), (3), or (4) shall, for purposes of applying such paragraphs, be considered as actually owned by such person.

(b) Other special rules. For purposes of this part—

(1) Time for determination. Stock held by a taxpayer shall be treated as stock in a passive foreign investment company if, at any time during the holding period of the taxpayer with respect to such stock, such corporation (or any predecessor) was a passive foreign investment company which was not a qualified electing fund. The preceding sentence shall not apply if the taxpayer elects to recognize gain (as of the last day of the last taxable year for which the company was a passive foreign investment company [2]*(determined without regard to the preceding sentence))* under rules similar to the rules of section 1291(d)(2).

(2) Certain corporations not treated as PFIC's during start-up year. A corporation shall not be treated as a passive foreign investment company for the first taxable year such corporation has gross income (hereinafter in this paragraph referred to as the "start-up year") if—

(A) no predecessor of such corporation was a passive foreign investment company,

(B) it is established to the satisfaction of the Secretary that such corporation will not be a passive foreign investment company for either of the 1st 2 taxable years following the start-up year, and

(C) such corporation is not a passive foreign investment company for either of the 1st 2 taxable years following the start-up year.

(3) Certain corporations changing businesses. A corporation shall not be treated as a passive foreign investment company for any taxable year if—

(A) neither such corporation (nor any predecessor) was a passive foreign investment company for any prior taxable year,

(B) it is established to the satisfaction of the Secretary that—

(i) substantially all of the passive income of the corporation for the taxable year is attributable to proceeds from the disposition of 1 or more active trades or businesses, and

(ii) such corporation will not be a passive foreign investment company for either of the 1st 2 taxable years following such taxable year, and

(C) such corporation is not a passive foreign investment company for either of such 2 taxable years.

(4) Separate interests treated as separate corporations. Under regulations prescribed by the Secretary, where necessary to carry out the purposes of this part, separate classes of stock (or other interests) in a corporation shall be treated as interests in separate corporations.

(5) Application of part where stock held by other entity.

(A) In general. Under regulations, in any case in which a United States person is treated as owning stock in a passive foreign investment company by reason of subsection (a)—

(i) any disposition by the United States person or the person owning such stock which results in the United States person being treated as no longer owning such stock, or

(ii) any distribution of property in respect of such stock to the person holding such stock,

shall be treated as a disposition by, or distribution to, the United States person with respect to the stock in the passive foreign investment company.

(B) Amount treated in same manner as previously taxed income. Rules similar to the rules of section 959(b) shall apply to any amount described in subparagraph (A) and to any amount included in gross income under section 1293(a) (or which would have been so included but for section 951(f)) in respect of stock which the taxpayer is treated as owning under subsection (a).

(6) Dispositions. Except as provided in regulations, if a taxpayer uses any stock in a passive foreign investment company as security for a loan, the taxpayer shall be treated as having disposed of such stock.

(7) Coordination with section 1246. Section 1246 shall not apply to earnings and profits of any company for any taxable year beginning after December 31, 1986, if such company is a passive foreign investment company for such taxable year.

(8) Treatment of certain foreign corporations owning stock in 25-percent owned domestic corporation.

(A) In general. If—

(i) a foreign corporation is subject to the tax imposed by section 531 (or waives any benefit under any treaty which would otherwise prevent the imposition of such tax), and

(ii) such foreign corporation owns at least 25 percent (by value) of the stock of a domestic corporation,

for purposes of determining whether such foreign corporation is a passive foreign investment company, any qualified stock held by such domestic corporation shall be treated as an asset which does not produce passive income (and is not held for the production of passive income) and any amount included in gross income with respect to such stock shall not be treated as passive income.

(B) Qualified stock. For purposes of subparagraph (A), the term "qualified stock" means any stock in a C corporation which is a domestic corporation and which is not a regulated investment company or real estate investment trust.

(9) Treatment of certain subpart F inclusions. Any amount included in gross income under section 951(a)(1)(B) shall be treated as a distribution received with respect to the stock.

(c) Treatment of stock held by pooled income fund. If stock in a passive foreign investment company is owned (or treated as owned under subsection (a)) by a pooled income fund (as defined in section 642(c)(5)) and no portion of any gain from a disposition of such stock may be allocated to income under the terms of the governing instrument of such fund—

(1) section 1291 shall not apply to any gain on a disposition of such stock by such fund if (without regard to section 1291) a deduction would be allowable with respect to such gain under section 642(c)(3),

(2) section 1293 shall not apply with respect to such stock, and

(3) in determining whether section 1291 applies to any distribution in respect of such stock, subsection (d) of section 1291 shall not apply.

(d) Treatment of certain leased property. For purposes of this part—

(1) In general. Any tangible personal property with respect to which a foreign corporation is the lessee under a lease with a term of at least 12 months shall be treated as an asset actually held by such corporation.

(2) Amount taken into account.

(A) In general. The amount taken into account under section 1296(a)(2) with respect to any asset to which paragraph (1) applies shall be the unamortized portion (as determined under regulations prescribed by he Secretary) of the present value of the payments under the lease for the use of such property.

(B) Present value. For purposes of subparagraph (A), the present value of payments described in subparagraph (A) shall be determined in the manner provided in regulations prescribed by the Secretary—

(i) as of the beginning of the lease term, and

(ii) except as provided in such regulations, by using a discount rate equal to the applicable Federal rate determined under section 1274(d)—

(I) by substituting the lease term for the term of the debt instrument, and

(II) without regard to paragraph (2) or (3) thereof.

(3) Exceptions. This subsection shall not apply in any case where—

(A) the lessor is a related person (as defined in section 954(d)(3)) with respect to the foreign corporation, or

(B) a principal purpose of leasing the property was to avoid the provisions of this part.

(e) **Special rules for certain intangibles.** For purposes of this part—

(1) **Research expenditures.** The adjusted basis of the total assets of a controlled foreign corporation shall be increased by the research or experimental expenditures (within the meaning of section 174) paid or incurred by such foreign corporation during the taxable year and the preceding 2 taxable years. Any expenditure otherwise taken into account under the preceding sentence shall be reduced by the amount of any reimbursement received by the controlled foreign corporation with respect to such expenditure.

(2) **Certain licensed intangibles.**

(A) In general. In the case of any intangible property (as defined in section 936(h)(3)(B)) with respect to which a controlled foreign corporation is a licensee and which is used by such foreign corporation in the active conduct of a trade or business, the adjusted basis of the total assets of such foreign corporation shall be increased by an amount equal to 300 percent of the payments made during the taxable year by such foreign corporation for the use of such intangible property.

(B) Exceptions. Subparagraph (A) shall not apply to—

(i) any payments to a foreign person if such foreign person is a related person (as defined in section 954(d)(3)) with respect to the controlled foreign corporation, and

(ii) any payments under a license if a principal purpose of entering into such license was to avoid the provisions of this part.

(3) **Controlled foreign corporation.** For purposes of this subsection, the term "controlled foreign corporation" has the meaning given such term by section 957(a).

(f) **Regulations.** The Secretary shall prescribe such regulations as may be necessary or appropriate to carry out the purposes of this part.

[Endnote Code Sec. 1298]

Matter in *italics* in Code Sec. 1298 and Code Sec. 1298(b)(1) added by Secs. 1122(a) and (e) of the Taxpayer Relief Act of 1997, H.R. 2014, 8/5/97, which struck out:

1. "1297"

2. added matter in para. (b)(1)

Effective Date (Sec. 1124, H.R. 2014, 8/5/97) effective for tax. yrs. of United States persons begin. after 12/31/97, and tax. yrs. of foreign corporations end. with or within such tax. yrs. of United States persons.

[¶ 3189] Code Sec.[1] 1301.

CAUTION. Code Sec. 1301, following, is effective for tax. yrs. begin. after 12/31/97 and before 1/1/2001.

Averaging of farm income.

(a) **In General.** At the election of an individual engaged in a farming business, the tax imposed by section 1 for such taxable year shall be equal to the sum of—

(1) a tax computed under such section on taxable income reduced by elected farm income, plus

(2) the increase in tax imposed by section 1 which would result if taxable income for each of the 3 prior taxable years were increased by an amount equal to one-third of the elected farm income.

Any adjustment under this section for any taxable year shall be taken into account in applying this section for any subsequent taxable year.

(b) **Definitions.** In this section—

(1) **Elected farm income.** (A) In general. The term "elected farm income" means so much of the taxable income for the taxable year—

(i) which is attributable to any farming business; and

(ii) which is specified in the election under subsection (a).

(B) Treatment of gains. For purposes of subparagraph (A), gain from the sale or other disposition of property (other than land) regularly used by the taxpayer in such a farming business for a substantial period shall be treated as attributable to such a farming business.

(2) Individual. The term "individual" shall not include any estate or trust.

(3) Farming business. The term "farming business" has the meaning given such term by section 263A(e)(4).

(c) Regulations. The Secretary shall prescribe such regulations as may be appropriate to carry out the purposes of this section, including regulations regarding—

(1) the order and manner in which items of income, gain, deduction, or loss, or limitations on tax, shall be taken into account in computing the tax imposed by this chapter on the income of any taxpayer to whom this section applies for any taxable year, and

(2) the treatment of any short taxable year.

[For analysis, see ¶ 2103. For text of Committee Report, see ¶ 5070.]

[Endnote Code Sec. 1301]

Code Sec. 1301 was added as Part I of Subchapter Q of Chapter 1 of Subtitle A, by Sec. 933(a) of the Taxpayer Relief Act of 1997, H.R. 2014, 8/5/97.

1. added Code Sec. 1301

Effective Date (Sec. 933(b), H.R. 2014, 8/5/97) effective for tax. yrs. begin. after 12/31/97 and before 1/1/2001.

[¶ 3190]   Code Sec. 1361.   S corporation defined.

* * * * * * * * * * * *

(b) Small business corporation.

(1) In general. For purposes of this subchapter, the term "small business corporation" means a domestic corporation which is not an ineligible corporation and which does not—

(A) have more than 75 shareholders,

CAUTION.   Subpara. (b)(1)(B), following, is effective for tax. yrs. begin. before 1/1/98. For subpara. (b)(1)(B) effective for tax. yrs. begin. after 12/31/97, see below.

(B) have as a shareholder a person (other than an estate and other than a trust described in subsection (c)(2)) who is not an individual,

CAUTION.   Subpara. (b)(1)(B), following, is effective for tax. yrs. begin. after 12/31/97. For subpara. (b)(1)(B) effective for tax. yrs. begin. before 1/1/98, see above.

(B) have as a shareholder a person (other than an estate, a trust described in subsection (c)(2), or an organization described in [1]*subsection (c)(6)*) who is not an individual,

(C) have a nonresident alien as a shareholder, and

(D) have more than 1 class of stock.

* * * * * * * * * * * *

(3) Treatment of certain wholly owned subsidiaries.

(A) In general. [2]*Except as provided in regulations prescribed by the Secretary, for purposes of this title—*

(i) a corporation which is a qualified subchapter S subsidiary shall not be treated as a separate corporation, and

(ii) all assets, liabilities, and items of income, deduction, and credit of a qualified subchapter S subsidiary shall be treated as assets, liabilities, and such items (as the case may be) of the S corporation.

* * * * * * * * * * * *

(c) Special rules for applying subsection (b).

* * * * * * * * * * * *

CAUTION.   Para. (c)(6), following, is effective for tax. yrs. begin. before 1/1/98. For para. (c)(6) effective for tax. yrs. begin. after 12/31/97, see below.

(6) Repealed.

CAUTION. Para. (c)(6) [as redesignated by H.R. 2014, Sec. 1401(c)(4)(B)], following, is effective for tax. yrs. begin. after 12/31/97. For para. (c)(6) effective for tax. yrs. begin. before 1/1/98, see above.

[3]**(6) Certain exempt organizations permitted as shareholders.** For purposes of subsection (b)(1)(B), an organization which is—
    (A) described in section 401(a) or 501(c)(3), and
    (B) exempt from taxation under section 501(a),
may be a shareholder in an S corporation.

* * * * * * * * * * * *

(e) Electing small business trust defined.
    (1) Electing small business trust. For purposes of this section—
    (A) In general. Except as provided in subparagraph (B), the term "electing small business trust" means any trust if—

CAUTION. Clause (e)(1)(A)(i), following, is effective for tax. yrs. begin. before 1/1/98. For clause (e)(1)(A)(i) effective for tax. yrs. begin. after 12/31/97, see below.

    (i) such trust does not have as a beneficiary any person other than (I) an individual, (II) an estate, or (III) an organization described in paragraph (2), (3), (4), or (5) of section 170(c) which holds a contingent interest and is not a potential current beneficiary,

CAUTION. Clause (e)(1)(A)(i), following, is effective for tax. yrs. begin. after 12/31/97. For clause (e)(1)(A)(i) effective for tax. yrs. begin. before 1/1/98, see above.

    (i) such trust does not have as a beneficiary any person other than (I) an individual, (II) an estate, or (III) an organization described in paragraph (2), (3), (4), or (5) of section 170(c),
    (ii) no interest in such trust was acquired by purchase, and
    (iii) an election under this subsection applies to such trust.
    (B) Certain trusts not eligible. The term "electing small business trust" shall not include—
    (i) any qualified subchapter S trust (as defined in subsection (d)(3)) if an election under subsection (d)(2) applies to any corporation the stock of which is held by such trust,[4]
    (ii) any trust exempt from tax under this subtitle[5], *and*
    [6]*(iii) any charitable remainder annuity trust or charitable remainder unitrust (as defined in section 664(d)).*

* * * * * * * * * * * *

[For analysis, see ¶ 1506, ¶ 1508. For text of Committee Report, see ¶ 5357, ¶ 5359.]

[Endnote Code Sec. 1361]
    Matter in *italics* in Code Sec. 1361(b)(1)(B) added by Sec. 1601(c)(4)(C) of the Taxpayer Relief Act of 1997, H.R. 2014, 8/5/97, which struck out:
    1. "subsection (c)(7)"
Effective Date (Sec. 1601(j)(1), H.R. 2014, 8/5/97) effective for tax. yrs. begin. after 12/31/97.

    Matter in *italics* in Code Sec. 1361(b)(3)(A) added by Sec. 1601(c)(3), H.R. 2014, which struck out:
    2. "For purposes of this title"
Effective Date (Sec. 1601(j)(1), H.R. 2014, 8/5/97) effective for tax. yrs. begin. after 12/31/96.

    Matter in *italics* in Code Sec. 1361(c)(6) added by Sec. 1601(c)(4)(B), H.R. 2014, which struck out:
    3. "(7)"
Effective Date (Sec. 1601(j)(1), H.R. 2014, 8/5/97) effective for tax. yrs. begin. after 12/31/97.

    Matter in *italics* in Code Sec. 1361(e)(1)(B)(i), Code Sec. 1361(e)(1)(B)(ii), and Code Sec. 1361(e)(1)(B)(iii) added by Sec. 1601(c)(1), H.R. 2014, which struck out:
    4. "and"

5. ";"
6. added clause (e)(1)(B)(iii)
Effective Date (Sec. 1601(j)(1), H.R. 2014, 8/5/97) effective for tax. yrs. begin. after 12/31/96.

[¶ 3191]   Code Sec. 1374.   Tax imposed on certain built-in gains.

* * * * * * * * * * *

(d) Definitions and special rules. For purposes of this section—

* * * * * * * * * * *

(7) Recognition period. The term "recognition period" means the 10-year period beginning with the 1st day of the 1st taxable year for which the corporation was an S corporation. *[1]For purposes of applying this section to any amount includible in income by reason of section 593(e), the preceding sentence shall be applied without regard to the phrase "10-year".*

* * * * * * * * * * *

[For analysis, see ¶ 1717. For text of Committee Report, see ¶ 5365.]

[Endnote Code Sec. 1374]

Matter in *italics* in Code Sec. 1374(d)(7) added by Sec. 1601(f)(5)(B) of the Taxpayer Relief Act of 1997, H.R. 2014, 8/5/97.

1. added matter in para. (d)(7)

Effective Date (Sec. 1601(j)(1), H.R. 2014, 8/5/97) effective for tax. yrs. begin. after 12/31/95.

[¶ 3192]   Code Sec. 1391.   Designation procedure.

* * * * * * * * * * *

(b) Number of designations.

* * * * * * * * * * * *

(2) Empowerment zones. The appropriate Secretaries may designate in the aggregate [1]*11* nominated areas as empowerment zones under this section, subject to the availability of eligible nominated areas. Of that number, not more than [2]*8* may be designated in urban areas and not more than 3 may be designated in rural areas. If [3]*8* empowerment zones are designated in urban areas, no less than 1 shall be designated in an urban area the most populous city of which has a population of 500,000 or less and no less than 1 shall be a nominated area which includes areas in 2 States and which has a population of 50,000 or less. The Secretary of Housing and Urban Development shall designate empowerment zones located in urban areas in such a manner that the aggregate population of all such zones does not exceed [4]*1,000,000.*

(c) Period designations may be made. A designation may be made under [5]*subsection (a)* only after 1993 and before 1996.

* * * * * * * * * * *

(e) Limitations on designations. No area may be designated under [6]*this section* unless—

(1) the area is nominated by 1 or more local governments and the State or States in which it is located for designation under this section,

(2) such State or States and the local governments have the authority—

(A) to nominate the area for designation under this section, and

(B) to provide the assurances described in paragraph (3),

(3) such State or States and the local governments provide written assurances satisfactory to the appropriate Secretary that the strategic plan described in the application under subsection (f)(2) for such area will be implemented,

(4) the appropriate Secretary determines that any information furnished is reasonably accurate, and

(5) such State or States and local governments certify that no portion of the area nominated is already included in an   empowerment zone or in an enterprise community or in an area otherwise nominated to be designated under this section.

(f) **Application.** No area may be designated under [7]*this section* unless the application for such designation—

(1) demonstrates that the nominated area satisfies the eligibility criteria described in section 1392,

(2) includes a strategic plan for accomplishing the purposes of this subchapter that—

(A) describes the coordinated economic, human, community, and physical development plan and related activities proposed for the nominated area,

(B) describes the process by which the affected community is a full partner in the process of developing and   implementing the plan and the extent to which local institutions and organizations have contributed to the planning process,

(C) identifies the amount of State, local, and private resources that will be available in the nominated area and the private/public partnerships to be used, which may include participation by, and cooperation with, universities, medical centers, and other private and public entities,

(D) identifies the funding requested under any Federal program in support of the proposed economic, human, community, and physical development and related activities,

(E) identifies baselines, methods, and benchmarks for measuring the success of carrying out the strategic plan, including the extent to which poor persons and families will be empowered to become economically self-sufficient, and

(F) does not include any action to assist any   establishment in relocating from one area outside the nominated area to the nominated area, except that assistance for the expansion of an existing business entity through the establishment of a new branch, affiliate, or subsidiary is permitted if—

(i) the establishment of the new branch, affiliate, or subsidiary will not result in a decrease in employment in the area of original location or in any other area where the existing business entity conducts business operations, and

(ii) there is no reason to believe that the new branch, affiliate, or subsidiary is being established with the intention of closing down the operations of the existing business entity in the area of its original location or in any other area where the existing business entity conducts business operation, and

(3) includes such other information as may be required by the appropriate Secretary.

[8]*(g)* *Additional Designations Permitted.*

(1) *In general.* *In addition to the areas designated under subsection (a), the appropriate Secretaries may designate in the aggregate an additional 20 nominated areas as empowerment zones under this section, subject to the availability of eligible nominated areas. Of that number, not more than 15 may be designated in urban areas and not more than 5 may be designated in rural areas.*

(2) *Period designations may be made and take effect.* *A designation may be made under this subsection after the date of the enactment of this subsection and before January 1, 1999.*

(3) *Modifications to eligibility criteria, etc.*

(A) *Poverty rate requirement.*

(i) *In general.* *A nominated area shall be eligible for designation under this subsection only if the poverty rate for each population census tract within the nominated area is not less than 20 percent and the poverty rate for at least 90 percent of the population census tracts within the nominated area is not less than 25 percent.*

(ii) *Treatment of census tracts with small populations.—A population census tract with a population of less than 2,000 shall be treated as having a poverty rate of not less than 25 percent if—*

(I) *more than 75 percent of such tract is zoned for commercial or industrial use, and*

(II) *such tract is contiguous to 1 or more other population census tracts which have a poverty rate of not less than 25 percent (determined without regard to this clause).*

(iii) Exception for developable sites. Clause *(i)* shall not apply to up to 3 noncontiguous parcels in a nominated area which may be developed for commercial or industrial purposes. The aggregate area of noncontiguous parcels to which the preceding sentence applies with respect to any nominated area shall not exceed 2,000 acres.

(iv) Certain provisions not to apply. Section *1392(a)(4)* (and so much of paragraphs *(1)* and *(2)* of section *1392(b)* as relate to section *1392(a)(4)*) shall not apply to an area nominated for designation under this subsection.

(v) Special rule for rural empowerment zone. The Secretary of Agriculture may designate not more than 1 empowerment zone in a rural area without regard to clause *(i)* if such area satisfies emigration criteria specified by the Secretary of Agriculture.

(B) Size limitation.

(i) In general. The parcels described in subparagraph *(A)(iii)* shall not be taken into account in determining whether the requirement of subparagraph *(A)* or *(B)* of section *1392(a)(3)* is met.

(ii) Special rule for rural areas. If a population census tract (or equivalent division under section *1392(b)(4)*) in a rural area exceeds 1,000 square miles or includes a substantial amount of land owned by the Federal, State, or local government, the nominated area may exclude such excess square mileage or governmentally owned land and the exclusion of that area will not be treated as violating the continuous boundary requirement of section *1392(a)(3)(B)*.

(C) Aggregate population limitation. The aggregate population limitation under the last sentence of subsection *(b)(2)* shall not apply to a designation under paragraph *(1)(B)*.

(D) Previously designated enterprise communities may be included. Subsection *(e)(5)* shall not apply to any enterprise community designated under subsection *(a)* that is also nominated for designation under this subsection.

(E) Indian reservations may be nominated.

(i) In general. Section *1393(a)(4)* shall not apply to an area nominated for designation under this subsection.

(ii) Special rule. An area in an Indian reservation shall be treated as nominated by a State and a local government if it is nominated by the reservation governing body (as determined by the Secretary of Interior).

[*For analysis, see ¶ 2606, ¶ 2607. For text of Committee Report, see ¶ 5081.*]

[Endnote Code Sec. 1391]

Matter in *italics* in Code Sec. 1391(b)(2) added by Sec. 951(a) of the Taxpayer Relief Act of 1997, H.R. 2014, 8/5/97, which struck out:
1. "9"
2. "6"
3. "6"
4. "750,000"

Effective Date (Sec. 951(c), H.R. 2014, 8/5/97) effective 8/5/97, except that designations of new empowerment zones made pursuant to such amendments shall be made during the 180-day period begin. 8/5/97. No designation to such amendments shall take effect before 1/1/2000.

Matter in *italics* in Code Sec. 1391(c), Code Sec. 1391(e), Code Sec. 1391(f), and Code Sec. 1391(g) added by Secs. 952(a) and (d), H.R. 2014, 8/5/97, which struck out:
5. "this section"
6. "subsection (a)"
7. "subsection (a)"
8. added subsec. (g)
Effective Date Effective 8/5/97.

[¶ 3193]   Code Sec. 1392.   Eligibility criteria.

* * * * * * * * * * * *

[1](d) **Special eligibility for nominated areas located in Alaska or Hawaii.** *A nominated area in Alaska or Hawaii shall be treated as meeting the requirements of paragraphs (2), (3), and (4) of subsection (a) if for each census tract or block group within such area 20 percent or more of the families have income which is 50 percent or less of the statewide median family income (as determined under section 143).*

[For analysis, see ¶ 2614. For text of Committee Report, see ¶ 5081.]

[Endnote Code Sec. 1392]
Code Sec. 1392(d), in *italics*, was added by Sec. 954 of the Taxpayer Relief Act of 1997, H.R. 2014, 8/5/97.
1. added subsec. (d)
Effective Date Effective 8/5/97.

[¶ 3194] Code Sec. 1394.   Tax-exempt enterprise zone facility bonds.

* * * * * * * * * * * *

(b) **Enterprise zone facility.** For purposes of this subsection—

(1) **In general.** The term "enterprise zone facility" means any qualified zone property the principal user of which is an enterprise zone business, and any land which is functionally related and subordinate to such property.

[1](2) **Qualified zone property.** The term "qualified zone property" has the meaning given such term by section 1397C; except that—

(A) the references to empowerment zones shall be treated as including references to enterprise communities, and

(B) section 1397C(a)(2) shall be applied by substituting "an amount equal to 15 percent of the adjusted basis" for "an amount equal to the adjusted basis".

[2](3) *Enterprise zone business.*

(A) In general. Except as modified in this paragraph, the term "enterprise zone business" has the meaning given such term by section 1397B.

(B) Modifications. In applying section 1397B for purposes of this section—

(i) Businesses in enterprise communities eligible. References in section 1397B to empowerment zones shall be treated as including references to enterprise communities.

(ii) Waiver of requirements during startup period. A business shall not fail to be treated as an enterprise zone business during the startup period if—

(I) as of the beginning of the startup period, it is reasonably expected that such business will be an enterprise zone business (as defined in section 1397B as modified by this paragraph) at the end of such period, and

(II) such business makes bona fide efforts to be such a business.

(iii) Reduced requirements after testing period. A business shall not fail to be treated as an enterprise zone business for any taxable year beginning after the testing period by reason of failing to meet any requirement of subsection (b) or (c) of section 1397B if at least 35 percent of the employees of such business for such year are residents of an empowerment zone or an enterprise community. The preceding sentence shall not apply to any business which is not a qualified business by reason of paragraph (1), (4), or (5) of section 1397B(d).

(C) Definitions relating to subparagraph (B). For purposes of subparagraph (B)—

(i) Startup period. The term "startup period" means, with respect to any property being provided for any business, the period before the first taxable year beginning more than 2 years after the later of—

(I) the date of issuance of the issue providing such property, or

(II) the date such property is first placed in service after such issuance (or, if earlier, the date which is 3 years after the date described in subclause (I)).

(ii) Testing period. The term "testing period" means the first 3 taxable years beginning after the startup period.

(D) Portions of business may be enterprise zone business. The term "enterprise zone business" includes any trades or businesses which would qualify as an enterprise zone business (determined after the modifications of subparagraph (B)) if such trades or businesses were separately incorporated.

* * * * * * * * * * * *

³**(f) Bonds for empowerment zones designated under section 1391(g).**

(1) In general. In the case of a new empowerment zone facility bond—

(A) such bond shall not be treated as a private activity bond for purposes of section 146, and

(B) subsection (c) of this section shall not apply.

(2) Limitation on amount of bonds.

(A) In general. Paragraph (1) shall apply to a new empowerment zone facility bond only if such bond is designated for purposes of this subsection by the local government which nominated the area to which such bond relates.

(B) Limitation on bonds designated. The aggregate face amount of bonds which may be designated under subparagraph (A) with respect to any empowerment zone shall not exceed—

(i) $60,000,000 if such zone is in a rural area,

(ii) $130,000,000 if such zone is in an urban area and the zone has a population of less than 100,000, and

(iii) $230,000,000 if such zone is in an urban area and the zone has a population of at least 100,000.

(C) Special rules.

(i) Coordination with limitation in subsection (c). Bonds to which paragraph (1) applies shall not be taken into account in applying the limitation of subsection (c) to other bonds.

(ii) Current refunding not taken into account. In the case of a refunding (or series of refundings) of a bond designated under this paragraph, the refunding obligation shall be treated as designated under this paragraph (and shall not be taken into account in applying subparagraph (B)) if—

(I) the amount of the refunding bond does not exceed the outstanding amount of the refunded bond, and

(II) the refunded bond is redeemed not later than 90 days after the date of issuance of the refunding bond.

(3) New empowerment zone facility bond. For purposes of this subsection, the term "new empowerment zone facility bond" means any bond which would be described in subsection (a) if only empowerment zones designated under section 1391(g) were taken into account under sections 1397B and 1397C.

[For analysis, see ¶ 2608, ¶ 2609. For text of Committee Report, see ¶ 5081.]

[Endnote Code Sec. 1394]

Matter in *italics* in Code Sec. 1394(b)(2) and Code Sec. 1394(b)(3) added by Secs. 955(a) and (b) of the Taxpayer Relief Act of 1997, H.R. 2014, 8/5/97, which struck out:

1. "(2) Qualified zone property. The term 'qualified zone property' has the meaning given such term by section 1397C; except that the references to empowerment zones shall be treated as including references to enterprise communities."

2. "(3) Enterprise zone business. The term 'enterprise zone business' has the meaning given to such term by section 1397B, except that—

"(A) references to empowerment zones shall be treated as including references to enterprise communities, and

"(B) such term includes any trades or businesses which would qualify as an enterprise zone business (determined after the modification of subparagraph (A)) if such trades or businesses were separately incorporated."

Effective Date (Sec. 955(c), H.R. 2014, 8/5/97) effective for obligations issued after 8/5/97.

Code Sec. 1394(f), in *italics*, was added by Sec. 953(a), H.R. 2014, 8/5/97.

3. added subsec. (f)

Effective Date (Sec. 953(b), H.R. 2014, 8/5/97) effective for obligations issued after 8/5/97.

[¶ 3195]   Code Sec. 1396.   Empowerment zone employment credit.

* * * * * * * * * * *

(b) [1]*Applicable percentage. For purposes of this section—*
   (1) In general. Except as provided in paragraph (2), the term "applicable percentage" means the percentage determined in accordance with the following table:

In the case of wages paid or incurred during calendar year:	The applicable percentage is:
1994 through 2001	20
2002	15
2003	10
2004	5

   [2]*(2) Special rule. With respect to each empowerment zone designated pursuant to the amendments made by the Taxpayer Relief Act of 1997 to section 1391(b)(2), the following table shall apply in lieu of the table in paragraph (1):*

In the case of wages paid or incurred during calendar year:	The applicable percentage is:
2000 through 2004	20
2005	15
2006	10
2007	5

* * * * * * * * * * *

[3](e) **Credit not to apply to empowerment zones designated under section1 391(g).** This section shall be applied without regard to any empowerment zone designated under section 1391(g).

   [For analysis, see ¶ 2606, ¶ 2607. For text of Committee Report, see ¶ 5081.]

[Endnote Code Sec. 1396]
   Matter in *italics* in Code Sec. 1396(b) added by Sec. 951(b) of the Taxpayer Relief Act of 1997, H.R. 2014, 8/5/97, which struck out:
   1. "Applicable percentage. For purposes of this section, the term 'applicable percentage' means the percentage determined in accordance with the following table:"
   2. added para. (b)(2)
Effective Date (Sec. 951(c), H.R. 2014, 8/5/97) effective 8/5/97, except that designations of new empowerment zones made pursuant to such amendments shall be made during the 180-day period beginning on 8/5/97. No designation pursuant to such amendments shall take effect before 1/1/2000.

   Code Sec. 1396(e) was added by Sec. 952(b), H.R. 2014, 8/5/97.
   3. added subsec. (e)
Effective Date Effective 8/5/97.

[¶ 3196]   Code Sec. 1397A.   Increase in expensing under section 179.

* * * * * * * * * * *

[1](c) *Limitation. For purposes of this section, qualified zone property shall not include any property substantially all of the use of which is in any parcel described in section 1391(g)(2)(A)(iii).*

   [For analysis, see ¶ 2606. For text of Committee Report, see ¶ 5081.]

[Endnote Code Sec. 1397A]

Code Sec. 1397A(c) was added by Sec. 952(c) of the Taxpayer Relief Act of 1997, H.R. 2014, 8/5/97.
  1. added subsec. (c)
Effective Date Effective 8/5/97.

[¶ 3197]   Code Sec. 1397B.   Enterprise zone business defined.

(a) **In general.** For purposes of this part, the term "enterprise zone business" means—

  (1) any qualified business entity, and

  (2) any qualified proprietorship.

(b) **Qualified business entity.** For purposes of this section, the term "qualified business entity" means, with respect to any taxable year, any corporation or partnership if for such year—

  (1) every trade or business of such entity is the active conduct of a qualified business within an empowerment zone,

  (2) at least [1]*50 percent* of the total gross income of such entity is derived from the active conduct of such business,

  (3) [2]*a substantial portion* of the use of the tangible property of such entity (whether owned or leased) is within an empowerment zone,

  (4) [3]*a substantial portion* of the intangible property of such entity is used in[4] the active conduct of any such business,

  (5) [5]*a substantial portion* of the services performed for such entity by its employees are performed in an empowerment zone,

  (6) at least 35 percent of its employees are residents of an empowerment zone,

  (7) less than 5 percent of the average of the aggregate unadjusted bases of the property of such entity is attributable to collectibles (as defined in section 408(m)(2)) other than collectibles that are held primarily for sale to customers in the ordinary course of such business, and

  (8) less than 5 percent of the average of the aggregate unadjusted bases of the property of such entity is attributable to nonqualified financial property.

(c) **Qualified proprietorship.** For purposes of this section, the term "qualified proprietorship" means, with respect to any taxable year, any qualified business carried on by an individual as a proprietorship if for such year—

  (1) at least [6]*50 percent* of the total gross income of such individual from such business is derived from the active conduct of such business in an empowerment zone,

  (2) [7]*a substantial portion* of the use of the tangible property of such individual in such business (whether owned or leased) is within an empowerment zone,

  (3) [8]*a substantial portion* of the intangible property of such business is used in[9] the active conduct of such business,

  (4) [10]*a substantial portion* of the services performed for such individual in such business by employees of such business are performed in an empowerment zone,

  (5) at least 35 percent of such employees are residents of an empowerment zone,

  (6) less than 5 percent of the average of the aggregate unadjusted bases of the property of such individual which is used in such business is attributable to collectibles (as defined in section 408(m)(2)) other than collectibles that are held primarily for sale to customers in the ordinary course of such business, and

  (7) less than 5 percent of the average of the aggregate unadjusted bases of the property of such individual which is used in such business is attributable to nonqualified financial property.

For purposes of this subsection, the term "employee" includes the proprietor.

(d) **Qualified business.** For purposes of this section—

  (1) **In general.** Except as otherwise provided in this subsection, the term "qualified business" means any trade or business.

  (2) **Rental of real property.** The rental to others of real property located in an empowerment zone shall be treated as a qualified business if and only if—

    (A) the property is not residential rental property (as defined in section 168(e)(2)), and

(B) at least 50 percent of the gross rental income from the real property is from enterprise zone businesses.

[11]*For purposes of subparagraph (B), the lessor of the property may rely on a lessee's certification that such lessee is an enterprise zone business.*

(3) **Rental of tangible personal property.** The rental to others of tangible personal property shall be treated as a qualified business if and only if [12]*at least 50 percent of the rental of such property is by enterprise zone businesses or by residents of an empowerment zone.*

* * * * * * * * * * * *

[13]*(f) Treatment of businesses straddling census tract lines. For purposes of this section, if—*

(1) a business entity or proprietorship uses real property located within an empowerment zone,

(2) the business entity or proprietorship also uses real property located outside the empowerment zone,

(3) the amount of real property described in paragraph (1) is substantial compared to the amount of real property described in paragraph (2), and

(4) the real property described in paragraph (2) is contiguous to part or all of the real property described in paragraph (1), then all the services performed by employees, all business activities, all tangible property, and all intangible property of the business entity or proprietorship that occur in or is located on the real property described in paragraphs (1) and (2) shall be treated as occurring or situated in an empowerment zone.

[For analysis, see ¶ 2610, ¶ 2611, ¶ 2612, ¶ 2613. For text of Committee Report, see ¶ 5081.]

[Endnote Code Sec. 1397B]

Matter in *italics* in Code Sec. 1397B(b), Code Sec. 1397B(b)(2), Code Sec. 1397B(b)(4), Code Sec. 1397B(c), Code Sec. 1396B(c)(1), Code Sec. 1397B(c)(3), Code Sec. 1397B(d)(2), Code Sec. 1397B(d)(3), and Code Sec. 1397B(f) added by Sec. 956(a) of the Taxpayer Relief Act of 1997, H.R. 2014, 8/5/97, which struck out:

1. "80 percent"
2. "substantially all"
3. "substantially all"
4. ", and exclusively related to,"
5. "substantially all"
6. "80 percent"
7. "substantially all"
8. "substantially all"
9. ", and exclusively related to,"
10. "substantially all"
11. added matter in para. (d)(2)
12. "substantially all"
13. added subsec. (f)

Effective Date (Sec. 956(b), H.R. 2014, 8/5/97) effective for tax. yrs. begin. on or after 8/5/97. For special rule, see Sec. 956(b)(2) of this Act, which provides:

"(2) Special rule for enterprise zone facility bonds. For purposes of section 1394(b) of the Internal Revenue Code of 1986, the amendments made by this section shall apply to obligations issued after the date of the enactment of this Act."

[¶ 3198] Code Sec.[1] 1397E.

CAUTION. Code Sec. 1397E, following, is effective for obligations issued after 12/31/97.

Credit to holders of qualified zone academy bonds.

(a) **Allowance of Credit.** In the case of an eligible taxpayer who holds a qualified zone academy bond on the credit allowance date of such bond which occurs during the taxable year, there shall be allowed as a credit against the tax imposed by this chapter for such taxable year the amount determined under subsection (b).

(b) Amount of Credit. (1) In general. The amount of the credit determined under this subsection with respect to any qualified zone academy bond is the amount equal to the product of—

(A) the credit rate determined by the Secretary under paragraph (2) for the month in which such bond was issued, multiplied by

(B) the face amount of the bond held by the taxpayer on the credit allowance date.

(2) Determination. During each calendar month, the Secretary shall determine a credit rate which shall apply to bonds issued during the following calendar month. The credit rate for any month is the percentage which the Secretary estimates will permit the issuance of qualified zone academy bonds without discount and without interest cost to the issuer.

(c) Limitation based on amount of tax. The credit allowed under subsection (a) for any taxable year shall not exceed the excess of—

(1) the sum of the regular tax liability (as defined in section 26(b)) plus the tax imposed by section 55, over

(2) the sum of the credits allowable under part IV of subchapter A (other than subpart C thereof, relating to refundable credits).

(d) Qualified zone academy bond. For purposes of this section—

(1) In general. The term "qualified zone academy bond" means any bond issued as part of an issue if—

(A) 95 percent or more of the proceeds of such issue are to be used for a qualified purpose with respect to a qualified zone academy established by an eligible local education agency,

(B) the bond is issued by a State or local government within the jurisdiction of which such academy is located,

(C) the issuer—

(i) designates such bond for purposes of this section,

(ii) certifies that it has written assurances that the private business contribution requirement of paragraph (2) will be met with respect to such academy, and

(iii) certifies that it has the written approval of the eligible local education agency for such bond issuance, and

(D) the term of each bond which is part of such issue does not exceed the maximum term permitted under paragraph (3).

(2) Private business contribution requirement. (A) In general. For purposes of paragraph (1), the private business contribution requirement of this paragraph is met with respect to any issue if the eligible local education agency that established the qualified zone academy has written commitments from private entities to make qualified contributions having a present value (as of the date of issuance of the issue) of not less than 10 percent of the proceeds of the issue.

(B) Qualified contributions. For purposes of subparagraph (A), the term "qualified contribution" means any contribution (of a type and quality acceptable to the eligible local education agency) of—

(i) equipment for use in the qualified zone academy (including state-of-the-art technology and vocational equipment),

(ii) technical assistance in developing curriculum or in training teachers in order to promote appropriate market driven technology in the classroom,

(iii) services of employees as volunteer mentors,

(iv) internships, field trips, or other educational opportunities outside the academy for students, or

(v) any other property or service specified by the eligible local education agency.

(3) Term requirement. During each calendar month, the Secretary shall determine the maximum term permitted under this paragraph for bonds issued during the following calendar month. Such maximum term shall be the term which the Secretary estimates will result in the present value of the obligation to repay the principal on the bond being equal to 50 percent of the face amount of the bond. Such present value shall be determined using as a discount rate the average annual interest rate of tax-exempt obligations having a term of 10 years or more which are issued during the month. If the term as so determined is not a multiple of a whole year, such term shall be rounded to the next highest whole year.

(4) Qualified zone academy. (A) In general. The term "qualified zone academy" means any public school (or academic program within a public school) which is established by and operated under the supervision of an eligible local education agency to provide education or training below the postsecondary level if—

(i) such public school or program (as the case may be) is designed in cooperation with business to enhance the academic curriculum, increase graduation and employment rates, and better prepare students for the rigors of college and the increasingly complex workforce,

(ii) students in such public school or program (as the case may be) will be subject to the same academic standards and assessments as other students educated by the eligible local education agency,

(iii) the comprehensive education plan of such public school or program is approved by the eligible local education agency, and

(iv) (I) such public school is located in an empowerment zone or enterprise community (including any such zone or community designated after the date of the enactment of this section), or

(II) there is a reasonable expectation (as of the date of issuance of the bonds) that at least 35 percent of the students attending such school or participating in such program (as the case may be) will be eligible for free or reduced-cost lunches under the school lunch program established under the National School Lunch Act.

(B) Eligible local education agency. The term "eligible local education agency" means any local education agency as defined in section 14101 of the Elementary and Secondary Education Act of 1965.

(5) Qualified purpose. The term "qualified purpose" means, with respect to any qualified zone academy—

(A) rehabilitating or repairing the public school facility in which the academy is established,

(B) providing equipment for use at such academy,

(C) developing course materials for education to be provided at such academy, and

(D) training teachers and other school personnel in such academy.

(6) Eligible taxpayer. The term "eligible taxpayer" means—

(A) a bank (within the meaning of section 581),

(B) an insurance company to which subchapter L applies, and

(C) a corporation actively engaged in the business of lending money.

(e) Limitation on amount of bonds designated. **(1) National limitation.** There is a national zone academy bond limitation for each calendar year. Such limitation is $400,000,000 for 1998 and 1999, and, except as provided in paragraph (4), zero thereafter.

(2) Allocation of limitation. The national zone academy bond limitation for a calendar year shall be allocated by the Secretary among the States on the basis of their respective populations of individuals below the poverty line (as defined by the Office of Management and Budget). The limitation amount allocated to a State under the preceding sentence shall be allocated by the State education agency to qualified zone academies within such State.

(3) Designation subject to limitation amount. The maximum aggregate face amount of bonds issued during any calendar year which may be designated under subsection (d)(1) with respect to any qualified zone academy shall not exceed the limitation amount allocated to such academy under paragraph (2) for such calendar year.

(4) Carryover of unused limitation. If for any calendar year —

(A) the limitation amount for any State, exceeds

(B) the amount of bonds issued during such year which are designated under subsection (d)(1) with respect to qualified zone academies within such State,

the limitation amount for such State for the following calendar year shall be increased by the amount of such excess.

(f) Other definitions. For purposes of this section—

(1) Credit allowance date. The term "credit allowance date" means, with respect to any issue, the last day of the 1-year period beginning on the date of issuance of such issue and the last day of each successive 1-year period thereafter.

(2) Bond. The term "bond" includes any obligation.

(3) State. The term "State" includes the District of Columbia and any possession of the United States.

(g) Credit included in gross income. Gross income includes the amount of the credit allowed to the taxpayer under this section.

[For analysis, see ¶ 705. For text of Committee Report, see ¶ 5012.]

[Endnote Code Sec. 1397E]

Code Sec. 1397E was added by Sec. 226(a) of the Taxpayer Relief Act of 1997, H.R. 2014, 8/5/97.

1. added Code Sec. 1397E

Effective Date (Sec. 226(c), H.R. 2014, 8/5/97) effective for obligations issued after 12/31/97.

[¶ 3199]   Code Sec.[1] 1400.   Establishment of DC Zone.

(a) In general. For purposes of this title—

(1) the applicable DC area is hereby designated as the District of Columbia Enterprise Zone, and

(2) except as otherwise provided in this subchapter, the District of Columbia Enterprise Zone shall be treated as an empowerment zone designated under subchapter U.

(b) Applicable DC area. For purposes of subsection (a), the term "applicable DC area" means the area consisting of—

(1) the census tracts located in the District of Columbia which are part of an enterprise community designated under subchapter U before the date of the enactment of this subchapter, and

(2) all other census tracts—

   (A) which are located in the District of Columbia, and

   (B) for which the poverty rate is not less than 20 percent.

(c) District of Columbia Enterprise Zone. For purposes of this subchapter, the terms "District of Columbia Enterprise Zone" and "DC Zone" mean the District of Columbia Enterprise Zone designated by subsection (a).

(d) Special rules for application of employment credit.

(1) Employees whose principal place of abode is in district of columbia.—With respect to the DC Zone, section 1396(d)(1)(B) (relating to empowerment zone employment credit) shall be applied by substituting 'the District of Columbia' for 'such empowerment zone'.

(2) No decrease of percentage in 2002.—In the case of the DC Zone, section 1396 (relating to empowerment zone employment credit) shall be applied by substituting '20' for '15' in the table contained in section 1396(b). The preceding sentence shall apply only with respect to qualified zone employees, as defined in section 1396(d), determined by treating no area other than the DC Zone as an empowerment zone or enterprise community.

(e) Special Rule for Application of Enterprise Zone Business Definition. For purposes of this subchapter and for purposes of applying subchapter U with respect to the DC Zone, section 1397B shall be applied without regard to subsections (b)(6) and (c)(5) thereof.

(f) Time For Which Designation Applicable.

(1) In general. The designation made by subsection (a) shall apply for the period beginning on January 1, 1998, and ending on December 31, 2002.

(2) Coordination with dc enterprise community designated under subchapter u. The designation under subchapter U of the census tracts referred to in subsection (b)(1) as an enterprise community shall terminate on December 31, 2002.

[For analysis, see ¶ 2601. For text of Committee Report, see ¶ 5040.]

[Endnote Code Sec. 1400]

Code Sec. 1400 was added by Sec. 701(a) of the Taxpayer Relief Act of 1997, H.R. 2014, 8/5/97.

1. added Code Sec. 1400

Effective Date (Sec. 701(d), H.R. 2014, 8/5/97) effective 8/5/97. For exception, see Sec. 702 of this Act, which provides: "702. Incentives conditioned on other DC reform. The amendments made by section 701 shall not take effect unless an entity known as the Economic Development Corporation is created by Federal law in 1997 as part of the District of Columbia government."

[¶ 3200] Code Sec.[1] 1400A.   Tax-exempt economic development bonds.

(a) In general. In the case of the District of Columbia Enterprise Zone, subparagraph (A) of section 1394(c)(1) (relating to limitation on amount of bonds) shall be applied by substituting "$15,000,000" for "$3,000,000".

(b) Period of applicability. This section shall apply to bonds issued during the period beginning on January 1, 1998, and ending on December 31, 2002.

[For analysis, see ¶ 2604. For text of Committee Report, see ¶ 5040.]

[Endnote Code Sec. 1400A]

Code Sec. 1400A was added by Sec. 701(a) of the Taxpayer Relief Act of 1997, H.R. 2014, 8/5/97.

1. added Code Sec. 1400A

Effective Date (Sec. 701(d), H.R. 2014, 8/5/97) effective 8/5/97. For exception, see Sec. 702 of this Act, which provides: "702. Incentives conditioned on other DC reform. The amendments made by section 701 shall not take effect unless an entity known as the Economic Development Corporation is created by Federal law in 1997 as part of the District of Columbia government."

[¶ 3201] Code Sec.[1] 1400B.   Zero percent capital gains rate.

(a) Exclusion. Gross income shall not include qualified capital gain from the sale or exchange of any DC Zone asset held for more than 5 years.

(b) DC Zone Asset. For purposes of this section—

(1) **In general.** The term "DC Zone asset" means—

(A) any DC Zone business stock,

(B) any DC Zone partnership interest, and

(C) any DC Zone business property.

(2) **DC zone business stock.**

(A) In general. The term "DC Zone business stock" means any stock in a domestic corporation which is originally issued after December 31, 1997, if—

(i) such stock is acquired by the taxpayer, before January 1, 2003, at its original issue (directly or through an underwriter) solely in exchange for cash,

(ii) as of the time such stock was issued, such corporation was a DC Zone business (or, in the case of a new corporation, such corporation was being organized for purposes of being a DC Zone business), and

(iii) during substantially all of the taxpayer's holding period for such stock, such corporation qualified as a DC Zone business.

(B) Redemptions. A rule similar to the rule of section 1202(c)(3) shall apply for purposes of this paragraph.

(3) **DC zone partnership interest.** The term "DC Zone partnership interest" means any capital or profits interest in a domestic partnership which is originally issued after December 31, 1997, if—

(A) such interest is acquired by the taxpayer, before January 1, 2003, from the partnership solely in exchange for cash,

(B) as of the time such interest was acquired, such partnership was a DC Zone business (or, in the case of a new partnership, such partnership was being organized for purposes of being a DC Zone business), and

(C) during substantially all of the taxpayer's holding period for such interest, such partnership qualified as a DC Zone business. A rule similar to the rule of paragraph (2)(B) shall apply for purposes of this paragraph.

(4) DC zone business property.

(A) In general. The term "DC Zone business property" means tangible property if—

(i) such property was acquired by the taxpayer by purchase (as defined in section 179(d)(2)) after December 31, 1997, and before January 1, 2003,

(ii) the original use of such property in the DC Zone commences with the taxpayer, and

(iii) during substantially all of the taxpayer's holding period for such property, substantially all of the use of such property was in a DC Zone business of the taxpayer.

(B) Special rule for buildings which are substantially improved.

(i) In general. The requirements of clauses (i) and (ii) of subparagraph (A) shall be treated as met with respect to—

(I) property which is substantially improved by the taxpayer before January 1, 2003, and

(II) any land on which such property is located.

(ii) Substantial improvement. For purposes of clause (i), property shall be treated as substantially improved by the taxpayer only if, during any 24-month period beginning after December 31, 1997, additions to basis with respect to such property in the hands of the taxpayer exceed the greater of—

(I) an amount equal to the adjusted basis of such property at the beginning of such 24-month period in the hands of the taxpayer, or

(II) $5,000.

(5) [sic 1400B(b)(5)] EDITORIAL NOTE: Paragraph 1400C(b)(5) is missing from the code sections enacted.

(6) Treatment of subsequent purchasers, etc. The term "DC Zone asset" includes any property which would be a DC Zone asset but for paragraph (2)(A)(i), (3)(A), or (4)(A)(ii) in the hands of the taxpayer if such property was a DC Zone asset in the hands of a prior holder.

(7) 5-year safe harbor. If any property ceases to be a DC Zone asset by reason of paragraph (2)(A)(iii), (3)(C), or (4)(A)(iii) after the 5-year period beginning on the date the taxpayer acquired such property, such property shall continue to be treated as meeting the requirements of such paragraph; except that the amount of gain to which subsection (a) applies on any sale or exchange of such property shall not exceed the amount which would be qualified capital gain had such property been sold on the date of such cessation.

(c) DC Zone Business. For purposes of this section, the term "DC Zone business" means any entity which is an enterprise zone business (as defined in section 1397B), determined—

(1) after the application of section 1400(e),

(2) by substituting "80 percent" for "50 percent" in subsections (b)(2) and (c)(1) of section 1397B, and

(3) by treating no area other than the DC Zone as an empowerment zone or enterprise community.

(d) Treatment of Zone as Including Census Tracts With 10 Percent Poverty Rate. For purposes of applying this section (and for purposes of applying this subchapter and subchapter U with respect to this section), the DC Zone shall be treated as including all census tracts—

(1) which are located in the District of Columbia, and

(2) for which the poverty rate is not less than 10 percent.

(e) Other Definitions and Special Rules. For purposes of this section—

(1) Qualified capital gain. Except as otherwise provided in this subsection, the term "qualified capital gain" means any gain recognized on the sale or exchange of—

(A) a capital asset, or

(B) property used in the trade or business (as defined in section 1231(b)).

(2) Gain before 1998 or after 2007 not qualified. The term "qualified capital gain" shall not include any gain attributable to periods before January 1, 1998, or after December 31, 2007.

(3) **Certain gain not qualified.** The term "qualified capital gain" shall not include any gain which would be treated as ordinary income under section 1245 or under section 1250 if section 1250 applied to all depreciation rather than the additional depreciation.

(4) **Intangibles and land not integral part of dc zone business.** The term "qualified capital gain" shall not include any gain which is attributable to real property, or an intangible asset, which is not an integral part of a DC Zone business.

(5) **Related party transactions.** The term "qualified capital gain" shall not include any gain attributable, directly or indirectly, in whole or in part, to a transaction with a related person. For purposes of this paragraph, persons are related to each other if such persons are described in section 267(b) or 707(b)(1).

(f) **Certain Other Rules To Apply.** Rules similar to the rules of subsections (g), (h), (i)(2), and (j) of section 1202 shall apply for purposes of this section.

(g) **Sales and Exchanges of Interests in Partnerships and S Corporations Which Are DC Zone Businesses.** In the case of the sale or exchange of an interest in a partnership, or of stock in an S corporation, which was a DC Zone business during substantially all of the period the taxpayer held such interest or stock, the amount of qualified capital gain shall be determined without regard to—

(1) any gain which is attributable to real property, or an intangible asset, which is not an integral part of a DC Zone business, and

(2) any gain attributable to periods before January 1, 1998, or after December 31, 2007.

[For analysis, see ¶ 2602. For text of Committee Report, see ¶ 5040.]

[Endnote Code Sec. 1400B]
Code Sec. 1400B was added by Sec. 701(a) of the Taxpayer Relief Act of 1997, H.R. 2014, 8/5/97.
1. added Code Sec. 1400B
Effective Date (Sec. 701(d), H.R. 2014, 8/5/97) effective 8/5/97. For exception, see Sec. 702 of this Act, which provides:
"702. Incentives conditioned on other DC reform. The amendments made by section 701 shall not take effect unless an entity known as the Economic Development Corporation is created by Federal law in 1997 as part of the District of Columbia government."

[¶ 3202] Code Sec.[1] 1400C. First-time homebuyer credit for District of Columbia.

(a) **Allowance of credit.** In the case of an individual who is a first-time homebuyer of a principal residence in the District of Columbia during any taxable year, there shall be allowed as a credit against the tax imposed by this chapter for the taxable year an amount equal to so much of the purchase price of the residence as does not exceed $5,000.

(b) **Limitation Based on Modified Adjusted Gross Income.**

(1) **In general.** The amount allowable as a credit under subsection (a) (determined without regard to this subsection) for the taxable year shall be reduced (but not below zero) by the amount which bears the same ratio to the credit so allowable as—

(A) the excess (if any) of—

(i) the taxpayer's modified adjusted gross income for such taxable year, over

(ii) $70,000 ($110,000 in the case of a joint return), bears to

(B) $20,000.

(2) **Modified adjusted gross income.** For purposes of paragraph (1), the term 'modified adjusted gross income' means the adjusted gross income of the taxpayer for the taxable year increased by any amount excluded from gross income under section 911, 931, or 933.

(c) **First-Time Homebuyer.** For purposes of this section—

(1) **In general.** The term "first-time homebuyer" has the same meaning as when used in section 72(t)(8)(D)(i), except that "principal residence in the District of Columbia during the 1-year period" shall be substituted for "principal residence during the 2- year period" in subclause (I) thereof.

(2) **One-time only.** If an individual is treated as a first- time homebuyer with respect to any principal residence, such individual may not be treated as a first-time homebuyer with respect to any other principal residence.

(3) Principal residence. The term "principal residence" has the same meaning as when used in section 121.

(d) Carryover of Credit. If the credit allowable under subsection (a) exceeds the limitation imposed by section 26(a) for such taxable year reduced by the sum of the credits allowable under subpart A of part IV of subchapter A (other than this section), such excess shall be carried to the succeeding taxable year and added to the credit allowable under subsection (a) for such taxable year.

(e) Special Rules. For purposes of this section—

(1) Allocation of dollar limitation.

(A) Married individuals filing separately. In the case of a married individual filing a separate return, subsection (a) shall be applied by substituting "$2,500" for "$5,000".

(B) Other taxpayers. If 2 or more individuals who are not married purchase a principal residence, the amount of the credit allowed under subsection (a) shall be allocated among such individuals in such manner as the Secretary may prescribe, except that the total amount of the credits allowed to all such individuals shall not exceed $5,000.

(2) Purchase.

(A) In general. The term "purchase" means any acquisition, but only if—

(i) the property is not acquired from a person whose relationship to the person acquiring it would result in the disallowance of losses under section 267 or 707(b) (but, in applying section 267 (b) and (c) for purposes of this section, paragraph (4) of section 267(c) shall be treated as providing that the family of an individual shall include only his spouse, ancestors, and lineal descendants), and

(ii) the basis of the property in the hands of the person acquiring it is not determined—

(I) in whole or in part by reference to the adjusted basis of such property in the hands of the person from whom acquired, or

(II) under section 1014(a) (relating to property acquired from a decedent).

(B) Construction. A residence which is constructed by the taxpayer shall be treated as purchased by the taxpayer.

(3) Purchase price. The term "purchase price" means the adjusted basis of the principal residence on the date of acquisition (within the meaning of section 72(t)(8)(D)(iii)).

(f) Reporting. If the Secretary requires information reporting under section 6045 by a person described in subsection (e)(2) thereof to verify the eligibility of taxpayers for the credit allowable by this section, the exception provided by section 6045(e)(5) shall not apply.

(g) Credit Treated as Nonrefundable Personal Credit. For purposes of this title, the credit allowed by this section shall be treated as a credit allowable under subpart A of part IV of subchapter A of this chapter.

(h) Basis Adjustment. For purposes of this subtitle, if a credit is allowed under this section with respect to the purchase of any residence, the basis of such residence shall be reduced by the amount of the credit so allowed.

(i) Termination. This section shall not apply to any property purchased after December 31, 2000.

[For analysis, see ¶ 2603. For text of Committee Report, see ¶ 5040.]

[Endnote Code Sec. 1400C]

Code Sec. 1400C was added by Sec. 701(a) of the Taxpayer Relief Act of 1997, H.R. 2014, 8/5/97.
1. added Code Sec. 1400C

Effective Date (Sec. 701(d), H.R. 2014, 8/5/97) effective 8/5/97. For exception, see Sec. 702 of this Act, which provides: "702. Incentives conditioned on other DC reform. The amendments made by section 701 shall not take effect unless an entity known as the Economic Development Corporation is created by Federal law in 1997 as part of the District of Columbia government."

[¶ 3203]   Code Sec. 1402.   Definitions.

* * * * * * * * * * * *

CAUTION.   Subsec. (k), following, is effective for payments after 12/31/97.

[1]*(k) Codification of treatment of certain termination payments received by former insurance salesmen. Nothing in subsection (a) shall be construed as including in the net earnings from self-employment of an individual any amount received during the taxable year from an insurance company on account of services performed by such individual as an insurance salesman for such company if—*

(1) such amount is received after termination of such individual's agreement to perform such services for such company,

(2) such individual performs no services for such company after such termination and before the close of such taxable year,

(3) such individual enters into a covenant not to compete against such company which applies to at least the 1-year period beginning on the date of such termination, and

(4) the amount of such payment—

(A) depends primarily on policies sold by or credited to the account of such individual during the last year of such agreement or the extent to which such policies remain in force for some period after such termination, or both, and

(B) does not depend to any extent on length of service or overall earnings from services performed for such company (without regard to whether eligibility for payment depends on length of service).

[For analysis, see ¶ 1903. For text of Committee Report, see ¶ 5067.]

[Endnote Code Sec. 1402]
Code Sec. 1402(k) was added by Sec. 922(a) of the Taxpayer Relief Act of 1997, H.R. 2014, 8/5/97.
1. added subsec. (k)
Effective Date (Sec. 922(c), H.R. 2014, 8/5/97) effective for payments after 12/31/97.

Sec. 935 of this Act provides:
"SEC. 935 MORATORIUM ON CERTAIN REGULATIONS.
"No temporary or final regulation with respect to the definition of a limited partner under section 1402(a)(13) of the Internal Revenue Code of 1986 may be issued or made effective before July 1, 1998."

[¶ 3204]   Code Sec. 1441.   Withholding of tax on nonresident aliens.

* * * * * * * * * * * *

(g) Cross reference. For provision treating [1]*85 percent* of social security benefits as subject to withholding under this section, see section 871(a)(3).

[Endnote Code Sec. 1441]
Matter in *italics* in Code Sec. 1441(g) added by Sec. 1604(g)(3) of the Taxpayer Relief Act of 1997, H.R. 2014, 8/5/97, which struck out:
1. "one-half"
Effective Date Effective 8/5/97.

[¶ 3205]   Code Sec. 1445.   Withholding of tax on dispositions of United States real property interests.

* * * * * * * * * * * *

(e) Special rules relating to distributions, etc., by corporations, partnerships, trusts, or estates.

(1) Certain domestic partnerships, trusts, and estates. In the case of any disposition of a United States real property interest as defined in section 897(c) (other than a disposition described in paragraph (4) or 5)) by a domestic partnership, domestic trust, or domestic estate, such partnership, the trustee of such trust, or the executor of such estate (as the case may be) shall be required to deduct and withhold under subsection (a) a tax equal to 35 percent (or, to the extent provided in regulations, [1]*20 percent*) of the gain realized to the extent such gain—

(A) is allocable to a foreign person who is a partner or beneficiary of such partnership, trust, or estate, or

(B) is allocable to a portion of the trust treated as owned by a foreign person under subpart E of part I of subchapter J.

* * * * * * * * * * * *

[Endnote Code Sec. 1445]

Matter in *italics* in Code Sec. 1445(e)(1) added by Sec. 311(c)(1) of the Taxpayer Relief Act of 1997, H.R. 2014, 8/5/97, which struck out:

1. "28 percent"

Effective Date (Sec. 311(d)(2), H.R. 2014, 8/5/97) effective for amounts paid after 8/5/97.

[¶ 3206]   Code Sec.[1] 1491.   Repealed.

[For analysis, see ¶ 1629. For text of Committee Report, see ¶ 5182.]

[Endnote Code Sec. 1491]

Code Sec. 1491 was repealed as part of the repeal of Chapter 5 of Subtitle A, by Sec. 1131(a) of the Taxpayer Relief Act of 1997, H.R. 2014, 8/5/97, which struck out:

1. "Sec. 1491 Imposition of tax.

"There is hereby imposed on the transfer of property by a citizen or resident of the United States, or by a domestic corporation or partnership, or by an estate or trust which is not a foreign estate or trust, to a foreign corporation as paid-in surplus or as a contribution to capital, or to a foreign estate or trust, or to a foreign partnership, an excise tax equal to 35 percent of the excess of—

"(1) the fair market value of the property so transferred, over

"(2) the sum of—

"(A) the adjusted basis (for determining gain) of such property in the hands of the transferor, plus

"(B) the amount of the gain recognized to the transferor at the time of the transfer.

If a trust which is not a foreign trust becomes a foreign trust, such trust shall be treated for purposes of this section as having transferred, immediately before becoming a foreign trust, all of its assets to a foreign trust."

Effective Date (Sec. 1131(d)[sic (e)], H.R. 2014, 8/5/97) effective 8/5/97.

[¶ 3207]   Code Sec.[1] 1492.   Repealed.

[For analysis, see ¶ 1629. For text of Committee Report, see ¶ 5182.]

[Endnote Code Sec. 1492]

Code Sec. 1492 was repealed as part of the repeal of Chapter 5 of Subtitle A, by Sec. 1131(a) of the Taxpayer Relief Act of 1997, H.R. 2014, 8/5/97, which struck out:

1. "Sec. 1492. Nontaxable transfers.

"The tax imposed by section 1491 shall not apply—

"(1) If the transferee is an organization exempt from income tax under part I of subchapter F of chapter 1 (other than an organization described in section 401(a)); or

"(2) To a transfer—

"(A) described in section 367, or

"(B) not described in section 367 but with respect to which the taxpayer elects (before the transfer) the application of principles similar to the principles of section 367, or

"(3) To a transfer for which an election has been made under section 1057."

Effective Date (Sec. 1131(d)[sic (e)], H.R. 2014, 8/5/97) effective 8/5/97.

[¶ 3208] Code Sec. 1494. Repealed.[1]

[For analysis, see ¶ 1629. For text of Committee Report, see ¶ 5182.]

[Endnote Code Sec. 1494]

Code Sec. 1494 was repealed as part of the repeal of chapter 5 of subtitle A of title 26 by Sec. 1131(a) of the Taxpayer Relief Act of 1997, H.R. 2014, 8/5/97, which struck out:

1. "SEC. 1494 PAYMENT AND COLLECTION.

"(a) Time for payment. The tax imposed by section 1491 shall, without assessment or notice and demand, be due and payable by the transferor at the time of the transfer, and shall be assessed, collected, and paid under regulations prescribed by the Secretary.

"(b) Abatement or refund. Under regulations prescribed by the Secretary, the tax may be abated, remitted, or refunded if the taxpayer, after the transfer, elects the application of principles similar to the principles of section 367.

"(c) Penalty. In the case of any failure to file a return required by the Secretary with respect to any transfer described in section 1491, the person required to file such return shall be liable for the penalties provided in section 6677 in the same manner as if such failure were a failure to file a notice under section 6048(a)."

Effective Date (Sec. 1131(d) sic [(e)], H.R. 2014, 8/5/97) effective 8/5/97.

[¶ 3209] Code Sec. 2001. Imposition and rate of tax.

* * * * * * * * * * *

(c) Rate schedule.

* * * * * * * * * * *

CAUTION. Para. (c)(2), following, is effective for estates of decedents dying, and gifts made, before 1/1/98. For para. (c)(2), effective for estates of decedents dying, and gifts made, after 12/31/97, see below.

(2) Phaseout of graduated rates and unified credit. The tentative tax determined under paragraph (1) shall be increased by an amount equal to 5 percent of so much of the amount (with respect to which the tentative tax is to be computed) as exceeds $10,000,000 but does not exceed $21,040,000.

CAUTION. Para. (c)(2), following, is effective for estates of decedents dying, and gifts made, after 12/31/97. For para. (c)(2), effective for estates of decedents dying, and gifts made, before 1/1/98, see above.

(2) Phaseout of graduated rates and unified credit. The tentative tax determined under paragraph (1) shall be increased by an amount equal to 5 percent of so much of the amount (with respect to which the tentative tax is to be computed) as exceeds $10,000,000 but does not exceed [1]*the amount at which the average tax rate under this section is 55 percent.*

* * * * * * * * * * *

[2]*(f) Valuation of gifts. If—*

(1) the time has expired within which a tax may be assessed under chapter 12 (or under corresponding provisions of prior laws) on the transfer of property by gift made during a preceding calendar period (as defined in section 2502(b)), and

(2) the value of such gift is shown on the return for such preceding calendar period or is disclosed in such return, or in a statement attached to the return, in a manner adequate to apprise the Secretary of the nature of such gift,

the value of such gift shall, for purposes of computing the tax under this chapter, be the value of such gift as finally determined for purposes of chapter 12.

[For analysis, see ¶ 501, ¶ 521. For text of Committee Report, see ¶ 5026, ¶ 5031.]

[Endnote Code Sec. 2001]

Matter in *italics* in Code Sec. 2001(c)(2) added by Sec. 501(a)(1)(D) of the Taxpayer Relief Act of 1997, H.R. 2014, 8/5/97, which struck out:

1. "$21,040,000"

Effective Date (Sec. 501(f), H.R. 2014, 8/5/97) effective for estates of decedents dying, and gifts made, after 12/31/97.

Code Sec. 2001(f), in *italics* was added by Sec. 506(a), H.R. 2014, 8/5/97.
2. added subsec. (d)
Effective Date (Sec. 506(e)(1), H.R. 2014, 8/5/97) effective for gifts made after 8/5/97.

[¶ 3210] Code Sec. 2010.   Unified credit against estate tax.

CAUTION.   Subsec. (a), following, is effective for estates of decedents dying, and gifts made, before 1/1/98. For subsec. (a), effective for estates of decedents dying, and gifts made, after 12/31/97, see below.

(a) **General rule.** A credit of $192,800 shall be allowed to the estate of every decedent against the tax imposed by section 2001.

CAUTION.   Subsec. (a), following, is effective for estates of decedents dying, and gifts made, after 12/31/97. For subsec. (a), effective for estates of decedents dying, and gifts made, before 1/1/98, see above.

(a) **General rule.** A credit of [1]*the applicable credit amount* shall be allowed to the estate of every decedent against the tax imposed by section 2001.

* * * * * * * * * * * *

CAUTION.   Subsec. (c), following, is effective for estates of decedents dying, and gifts made, before 1/1/98. For subsecs. (c) and (d), effective for estates of decedents dying, and gifts made, after 12/31/97, see below.

(c) **Limitation based on amount of tax.** The amount of the credit allowed by subsection (a) shall not exceed the amount of the tax imposed by section 2001.

CAUTION.   Subsecs. (c) and (d), following, are effective for estates of decedents dying, and gifts made, after 12/31/97. For subsec. (c), effective for estates of decedents dying, and gifts made, before 1/1/98, see above.

[2]*(c) Applicable credit amount. For purposes of this section, the applicable credit amount is the amount of the tentative tax which would be determined under the rate schedule set forth in section 2001(c) if the amount with respect to which such tentative tax is to be computed were the applicable exclusion amount determined in accordance with the following table:*

In the case of estates of decedents dying, and gifts made, during:	The applicable exclusion amount is:
1998	$ 625,000
1999	$ 650,000
2000 and 2001	$ 675,000
2002 and 2003	$ 700,000
2004	$ 850,000
2005	$ 950,000
2006 or thereafter	$1,000,000

(2) *Cost-of-living adjustment. In the case of any decedent dying, and gift made, in a calendar year after 2007, the $1,000,000 amount set forth in paragraph (1) shall be increased by an amount equal to—*

(A) *$1,000,000, multiplied by*

(B) *the cost-of-living adjustment determined under section 1(f)(3) for such calendar year by substituting "calendar year 2006" for "calendar year 1992" in subparagraph (B) thereof. If any amount as adjusted under the preceding sentence is not a multiple of $10,000, such amount shall be rounded to the next lowest multiple of $10,000.*

[3]*(d) Limitation based on amount of tax.* The amount of the credit allowed by subsection (a) shall not exceed the amount of the tax imposed by section 2001.

[For analysis, see ¶ 501. For text of Committee Report, see ¶ 5026.]

[Endnote Code Sec. 2010]

   Matter in *italics* in Code Sec. 2010(a), Code Sec. 2010(c) and Code Sec. 2010(d) added by Sec. 501(a)(1)(A) and (B) of the Taxpayer Relief Act of 1997, H.R. 2014, 8/5/97, which struck out:
   1. "$192,800"
   2. added subsec. (c)
   3. "(c)"

Effective Date (Sec. 501(f), H.R. 2014, 8/5/97) effective for estates of decedents dying, and gifts made, after 12/31/97.

[¶ 3211]   Code Sec. 2013.   Credit for tax on prior transfers.

* * * * * * * * * * * *

[1]**(g) Repealed.**

[Endnote Code Sec. 2013]

   Code Sec. 2013(g) was deleted by Sec. 1073(b)(2) of the Taxpayer Relief Act of 1997, H.R. 2014, 8/5/97, which struck out:
   1. "(g) Treatment of additional tax under section 4980A. For purposes of this section, the estate tax paid shall not include any portion of such tax attributable to section 4980A(d)."

Effective Date (Sec. 1073(c)(2), H.R. 2014, 8/5/97) effective for estates of decedents dying after 12/31/96.

[¶ 3212]   Code Sec. 2031.   Definition of gross estate.

* * * * * * * * * * * *

CAUTION.   Subsec. (c), following, is effective for estates of decedents dying before 1/1/98. For subsecs. (c) and (d), effective for estates of decedents dying after 12/31/97, see below.

(c) Cross reference. For executor's right to be furnished on request a statement regarding any valuation made by the Secretary within the gross estate, see section 7517.

CAUTION.   Subsecs. (c) and (d), following, are effective for estates of decedents dying after 12/31/97. For subsec. (c), effective for estates of decedents dying before 1/1/98, see above.

[1]*(c) Estate tax with respect to land subject to a qualified conservation easement.*

   (1) In general. If the executor makes the election described in paragraph (6), then, except as otherwise provided in this subsection, there shall be excluded from the gross estate the lesser of—

      (A) the applicable percentage of the value of land subject to a qualified conservation easement, reduced by the amount of any deduction under section 2055(f) with respect to such land, or

      (B) the exclusion limitation.

   (2) Applicable percentage. For purposes of paragraph (1), the term "applicable percentage" means 40 percent reduced (but not below zero) by 2 percentage points for each percentage point (or fraction thereof) by which the value of the qualified conservation easement is less than 30 percent of the value of the land (determined without regard to the value of such easement and reduced by the value of any retained development right (as defined in paragraph (5)).

   (3) Exclusion limitation. For purposes of paragraph (1), the exclusion limitation is the limitation determined in accordance with the following table:

In the case of estates of decedents dying during:	The exclusion limitation is:
1998	$ 100,000
1999	$ 200,000

2000	$ 300,000
2001	$ 400,000
2002 or thereafter	$500,000.

(4) Treatment of certain indebtedness.

(A) In general. The exclusion provided in paragraph (1) shall not apply to the extent that the land is debt-financed property.

(B) Definitions. For purposes of this paragraph—

(i) Debt-financed property. The term "debt-financed property" means any property with respect to which there is an acquisition indebtedness (as defined in clause (ii)) on the date of the decedent's death.

(ii) Acquisition indebtedness. The term "acquisition indebtedness" means, with respect to debt-financed property, the unpaid amount of—

(I) the indebtedness incurred by the donor in acquiring such property,

(II) the indebtedness incurred before the acquisition of such property if such indebtedness would not have been incurred but for such acquisition,

(III) the indebtedness incurred after the acquisition of such property if such indebtedness would not have been incurred but for such acquisition and the incurrence of such indebtedness was reasonably foreseeable at the time of such acquisition, and

(IV) the extension, renewal, or refinancing of an acquisition indebtedness.

(5) Treatment of retained development right.

(A) In general. Paragraph (1) shall not apply to the value of any development right retained by the donor in the conveyance of a qualified conservation easement.

(B) Termination of retained development right. If every person in being who has an interest (whether or not in possession) in the land executes an agreement to extinguish permanently some or all of any development rights (as defined in subparagraph (D)) retained by the donor on or before the date for filing the return of the tax imposed by section 2001, then any tax imposed by section 2001 shall be reduced accordingly. Such agreement shall be filed with the return of the tax imposed by section 2001. The agreement shall be in such form as the Secretary shall prescribe.

(C) Additional tax. Any failure to implement the agreement described in subparagraph (B) not later than the earlier of—

(i) the date which is 2 years after the date of the decedent's death, or

(ii) the date of the sale of such land subject to the qualified conservation easement, shall result in the imposition of an additional tax in the amount of the tax which would have been due on the retained development rights subject to such agreement. Such additional tax shall be due and payable on the last day of the 6th month following such date.

(D) Development right defined. For purposes of this paragraph, the term "development right" means any right to use the land subject to the qualified conservation easement in which such right is retained for any commercial purpose which is not subordinate to and directly supportive of the use of such land as a farm for farming purposes (within the meaning of section 2032(e)).

(6) Election. The election under this subsection shall be made on the return of the tax imposed by section 2001. Such an election, once made, shall be irrevocable.

(7) Calculation of estate tax due. An executor making the election described in paragraph (6) shall, for purposes of calculating the amount of tax imposed by section 2001, include the value of any development right (as defined in paragraph (5)) retained by the donor in the conveyance of such qualified conservation easement. The computation of tax on any retained development right prescribed in this paragraph shall be done in such manner and on such forms as the Secretary shall prescribe.

(6) Definitions. For purposes of this subsection—

(A) Land subject to a qualified conservation easement. The term "land subject to a qualified conservation easement" means land—

(i) which is located—

(I) in or within 25 miles of an area which, on the date of the decedent's death, is a metropolitan area (as defined by the Office of Management and Budget),

(II) *in or within 25 miles of an area which, on the date of the decedent's death, is a national park or wilderness area designated as part of the National Wilderness Preservation System (unless it is determined by the Secretary that land in or within 25 miles of such a park or wilderness area is not under significant development pressure), or*

(III) *in or within 10 miles of an area which, on the date of the decedent's death, is an Urban National Forest (as designated by the Forest Service),*

(ii) *which was owned by the decedent or a member of the decedent's family at all times during the 3-year period ending on the date of the decedent's death, and*

(iii) *with respect to which a qualified conservation easement has been made by an individual described in subparagraph (C), as of the date of the election described in paragraph (6).*

(B) *Qualified conservation easement. The term "qualified conservation easement" means a qualified conservation contribution (as defined in section 170(h)(1)) of a qualified real property interest (as defined in section 170(h)(2)(C)), except that clause (iv) of section 170(h)(4)(A) shall not apply, and the restriction on the use of such interest described in section 170(h)(2)(C) shall include a prohibition on commercial recreational activity.*

(C) *Individual described. An individual is described in this subparagraph if such individual is—*

(i) *the decedent,*

(ii) *a member of the decedent's family,*

(iii) *the executor of the decedent's estate, or*

(iv) *the trustee of a trust the corpus of which includes the land to be subject to the qualified conservation easement.*

(D) *Member of family. The term "member of the decedent's family" means any member of the family (as defined in section 2032A(e)(2)) of the decedent.*

(7) Application of this section to interests in partnerships, corporations, and trusts. *This section shall apply to an interest in a partnership, corporation, or trust if at least 30 percent of the entity is owned (directly or indirectly) by the decedent, as determined under the rules described in section 2033A(e)(3).*

²*(d)* **Cross reference.** For executor's right to be furnished on request a statement regarding any valuation made by the Secretary within the gross estate, see section 7517.

[For analysis, see ¶ 517. For text of Committee Report, see ¶ 5033.]

[Endnote Code Sec. 2031]

Matter in italics in Code Sec. 2031(c) and Code Sec. 2031(d) added by Sec. 508(a) of the Taxpayer Relief Act of 1997, H.R. 2014, 8/5/97, which struck out:

1. added subsec. (c)
2. "(c)"

Effective Date (Sec. 508(e)(1), H.R. 2014, 8/5/97) effective for estates of decedents dying after 12/31/97.

[¶ 3213]   Code Sec. 2032A.   Valuation of certain farm, etc., real property.
(a) Value based on use under which property qualifies.

* * * * * * * * * * * *

CAUTION.   Para. (a)(3) is effective for estates of decedents dying, and gifts made, after 12/31/97.

¹*(3)* **Inflation adjustment.** *In the case of estates of decedents dying in a calendar year after 1998, the $750,000 amount contained in paragraph (2) shall be increased by an amount equal to—*

(A) *$750,000, multiplied by*

(B) *the cost-of-living adjustment determined under section 1(f)(3) for such calendar year by substituting "calendar year 1997" for "calendar year 1992" in subparagraph (B) thereof.*

If any amount as adjusted under the preceding sentence is not a multiple of $10,000, such amount shall be rounded to the next lowest multiple of $10,000.

(b) Qualified real property.

* * * * * * * * * * *

(5) Special rules for surviving spouses.

(A) In general. If property is qualified real property with respect to a decedent (hereinafter in this paragraph referred to as the "first decedent") and such property was acquired from or passed from the first decedent to the surviving spouse of the first decedent, for purposes of applying this subsection and subsection (c) in the case of the estate of such surviving spouse, active management of the farm or other business by the surviving spouse shall be treated as material participation by such surviving spouse in the operation of such farm or business.[2]

* * * * * * * * * * *

(c) Tax treatment of dispositions and failures to use for qualified use.

* * * * * * * * * * *

(7) Special rules.

* * * * * * * * * * *

[3]*(E) Certain rents treated as qualified use. For purposes of this subsection, a surviving spouse or lineal descendant of the decedent shall not be treated as failing to use qualified real property in a qualified use solely because such spouse or descendant rents such property to a member of the family of such spouse or descendant on a net cash basis. For purposes of the preceding sentence, a legally adopted child of an individual shall be treated as the child of such individual by blood.*

CAUTION.   Para. (c)(8), following, is effective for easements granted after 12/31/97.

[4]*(8) Qualified conservation contribution is not a disposition. A qualified conservation contribution (as defined in section 170(h)) by gift or otherwise shall not be deemed a disposition under subsection (c)(1)(A).*

(d) Election; agreement.

* * * * * * * * * * *

[5]*(3) Modification of election and agreement to be permitted. The Secretary shall prescribe procedures which provide that in any case in which the executor makes an election under paragraph (1) (and submits the agreement referred to in paragraph (2)) within the time prescribed therefor, but—*

(A) the notice of election, as filed, does not contain all required information, or

(B) signatures of 1 or more persons required to enter into the agreement described in paragraph (2) are not included on the agreement as filed, or the agreement does not contain all required information,

the executor will have a reasonable period of time (not exceeding 90 days) after notification of such failures to provide such information or signatures.

* * * * * * * * * * *

[For analysis, see ¶ 502, ¶ 509, ¶ 510, ¶ 519. For text of Committee Report, see ¶ 5026, ¶ 5029, ¶ 5033, ¶ 5273.]

[Endnote Code Sec. 2032A]
  Code Sec. 2032A(a)(3), in *italics*, was added by Sec. 501(b) of the Taxpayer Relief Act of 1997, H.R. 2014, 8/5/97.
  1. added paragraph (a)(3)
Effective Date (Sec. 501(f), H.R. 2014, 8/5/97) effective for estates of decedents dying, and gifts made, after 12/31/97.

Matter in *italics* in Code Sec. 2032A(b)(5)(A) and Code Sec. 2032A(c)(7)(E) added by Sec. 504(a) and (b), H.R. 2014, 8/5/97, which struck out:

2. "For purposes of subsection (c), such surviving spouse shall not be treated as failing to use such property in a qualified use solely because such spouse rents such property to a member of such spouse's family on a net cash basis."

3. added subparagraph (c)(7)(E)

Effective Date (Sec. 504(c), H.R. 2014, 8/5/97) effective for leases entered into after 12/31/76.

Code Sec. 2032A(c)(8), in *italics*, was added by Sec. 508(c), H.R. 0214, 8/5/97.

4. added para. (c)(8)

Effective Date (Sec. 508(e)(2), H.R. 2014, 8/5/97) effective for easements granted after 12/31/97.

Matter in *italics* in Code Sec. 2032A(d)(3) added by Sec. 1313(a), H.R. 2014, 8/5/97, which struck out:

5. "(3) Modification of election and agreement to be permitted. The Secretary shall prescribe procedures which provide that in any case in which—

"(A) the executor makes an election under paragraph (1) within the time prescribed for filing such election, and

"(B) substantially complies with the regulations prescribed by the Secretary with respect to such election, but—

"(i) the notice of election, as filed, does not contain all required information, or

"(ii) signatures of 1 or more persons required to enter into the agreement described in paragraph (2) are not included on the agreement as filed, or the agreement does not contain all required information,

the executor will have a reasonable period of time (not exceeding 90 days) after notification of such failures to provide such information or agreements."

Effective Date (Sec. 1313(b), H.R. 2014, 8/5/97) effective for estates of decedents dying after 8/5/97.

[¶ 3214] Code Sec.[1] 2033A.

CAUTION. Code Sec. 2033A, following, is effective for estates of decedents dying after December 31, 1997.

Family-owned business exclusion.

(a) **In general.** In the case of an estate of a decedent to which this section applies, the value of the gross estate shall not include the lesser of—

(1) the adjusted value of the qualified family-owned business interests of the decedent otherwise includible in the estate, or

(2) the excess of $1,300,000 over the applicable amount under section 2010(c) with respect to such estate.

(b) **Estates to which section applies.**

(1) **In general.** This section shall apply to an estate if—

(A) the decedent was (at the date of the decedent's death) a citizen or resident of the United States,

(B) the executor elects the application of this section and files the agreement referred to in subsection (h),

(C) the sum of—

(i) the adjusted value of the qualified family-owned business interests described in paragraph (2), plus

(ii) the amount of the gifts of such interests determined under paragraph (3), exceeds 50 percent of the adjusted gross estate, and

(D) during the 8-year period ending on the date of the decedent's death there have been periods aggregating 5 years or more during which—

(i) such interests were owned by the decedent or a member of the decedent's family, and

(ii) there was material participation (within the meaning of section 2032A(e)(6)) by the decedent or a member of the decedent's family in the operation of the business to which such interests relate.

(2) **Includible qualified family-owned business interests.** The qualified family-owned business interests described in this paragraph are the interests which—

(A) are included in determining the value of the gross estate (without regard to this section), and

(B) are acquired by any qualified heir from, or passed to any qualified heir from, the decedent (within the meaning of section 2032A(e)(9)).

(3) Includible gifts of interests. The amount of the gifts of qualified family-owned business interests determined under this paragraph is the excess of—

(A) the sum of—

(i) the amount of such gifts from the decedent to members of the decedent's family taken into account under subsection 2001(b)(1)(B), plus

(ii) the amount of such gifts otherwise excluded under section 2503(b), to the extent such interests are continuously held by members of such family (other than the decedent's spouse) between the date of the gift and the date of the decedent's death, over

(B) the amount of such gifts from the decedent to members of the decedent's family otherwise included in the gross estate.

(c) Adjusted gross estate. For purposes of this section, the term "adjusted gross estate" means the value of the gross estate (determined without regard to this section)—

(1) reduced by any amount deductible under paragraph (3) or (4) of section 2053(a), and

(2) increased by the excess of—

(A) the sum of—

(i) the amount of gifts determined under subsection (b)(3), plus

(ii) the amount (if more than de minimis) of other transfers from the decedent to the decedent's spouse (at the time of the transfer) within 10 years of the date of the decedent's death, plus

(iii) the amount of other gifts (not included under clause (i) or (ii)) from the decedent within 3 years of such date, other than gifts to members of the decedent's family otherwise excluded under section 2503(b), over

(B) the sum of the amounts described in clauses (i), (ii), and (iii) of subparagraph (A) which are otherwise includible in the gross estate.

For purposes of the preceding sentence, the Secretary may provide that de minimis gifts to persons other than members of the decedent's family shall not be taken into account.

(d) Adjusted value of the qualified family-owned business interests. For purposes of this section, the adjusted value of any qualified family-owned business interest is the value of such interest for purposes of this chapter (determined without regard to this section), reduced by the excess of—

(1) any amount deductible under paragraph (3) or (4) of section 2053(a), over

(2) the sum of—

(A) any indebtedness on any qualified residence of the decedent the interest on which is deductible under section 163(h)(3), plus

(B) any indebtedness to the extent the taxpayer establishes that the proceeds of such indebtedness were used for the payment of educational and medical expenses of the decedent, the decedent's spouse, or the decedent's dependents (within the meaning of section 152), plus

(C) any indebtedness not described in subparagraph (A) or (B), to the extent such indebtedness does not exceed $10,000.

(e) Qualified family-owned business interest.

(1) In general. For purposes of this section, the term "qualified family-owned business interest" means—

(A) an interest as a proprietor in a trade or business carried on as a proprietorship, or

(B) an interest in an entity carrying on a trade or business, if—

(i) at least—

(I) 50 percent of such entity is owned (directly or indirectly) by the decedent and members of the decedent's family,

(II) 70 percent of such entity is so owned by members of 2 families, or

(III) 90 percent of such entity is so owned by members of 3 families, and

(ii) for purposes of subclause (II) or (III) of clause (i), at least 30 percent of such entity is so owned by the decedent and members of the decedent's family.

(2) Limitation. Such term shall not include—

(A) any interest in a trade or business the principal place of business of which is not located in the United States,

(B) any interest in an entity, if the stock or debt of such entity or a controlled group (as defined in section 267(f)(1)) of which such entity was a member was readily tradable on an established securities market or secondary market (as defined by the Secretary) at any time within 3 years of the date of the decedent's death,

(C) any interest in a trade or business not described in section 542(c)(2), if more than 35 percent of the adjusted ordinary gross income of such trade or business for the taxable year which includes the date of the decedent's death would qualify as personal holding company income (as defined in section 543(a)),

(D) that portion of an interest in a trade or business that is attributable to—

(i) cash or marketable securities, or both, in excess of the reasonably expected day-to-day working capital needs of such trade or business, and

(ii) any other assets of the trade or business (other than assets used in the active conduct of a trade or business described in section 542(c)(2)), which produce, or are held for the production of, income of which is described in section 543(a) or in section 954(c)(1) (determined without regard to subparagraph (A) thereof and by substituting "trade or business" for "controlled foreign corporation").

(3) Rules regarding ownership.

(A) Ownership of entities. For purposes of paragraph (1)(B) —

(i) Corporations. Ownership of a corporation shall be determined by the holding of stock possessing the appropriate percentage of the total combined voting power of all classes of stock entitled to vote and the appropriate percentage of the total value of shares of all classes of stock.

(ii) Partnerships. Ownership of a partnership shall be determined by the owning of the appropriate percentage of the capital interest in such partnership.

(B) Ownership of tiered entities. For purposes of this section, if by reason of holding an interest in a trade or business, a decedent, any member of the decedent's family, any qualified heir, or any member of any qualified heir's family is treated as holding an interest in any other trade or business—

(i) such ownership interest in the other trade or business shall be disregarded in determining if the ownership interest in the first trade or business is a qualified family-owned business interest, and

(ii) this section shall be applied separately in determining if such interest in any other trade or business is a qualified family- owned business interest.

(C) Individual ownership rules. For purposes of this section, an interest owned, directly or indirectly, by or for an entity described in paragraph (1)(B) shall be considered as being owned proportionately by or for the entity's shareholders, partners, or beneficiaries. A person shall be treated as a beneficiary of any trust only if such person has a present interest in such trust.

(f) Tax treatment of failure to materially participate in business or dispositions of interests.

(1) In general. There is imposed an additional estate tax if, within 10 years after the date of the decedent's death and before the date of the qualified heir's death—

(A) the material participation requirements described in section 2032A(c)(6)(B) are not met with respect to the qualified family-owned business interest which was acquired (or passed) from the decedent,

(B) the qualified heir disposes of any portion of a qualified family-owned business interest (other than by a disposition to a member of the qualified heir's family or through a qualified conservation contribution under section 170(h)),

(C) the qualified heir loses United States citizenship (within the meaning of section 877) or with respect to whom an event described in subparagraph (A) or (B) of section 877(e)(1) occurs, and such heir does not comply with the requirements of subsection (g), or

(D) the principal place of business of a trade or business of the qualified family-owned business interest ceases to be located in the United States.

(2) Additional estate tax.

(A) In general. The amount of the additional estate tax imposed by paragraph (1) shall be equal to—

(i) the applicable percentage of the adjusted tax difference attributable to the qualified family-owned business interest (as determined under rules similar to the rules of section 2032A(c)(2)(B)), plus

(ii) interest on the amount determined under clause (i) at the underpayment rate established under section 6621 for the period beginning on the date the estate tax liability was due under this chapter and ending on the date such additional estate tax is due.

(B) Applicable percentage. For purposes of this paragraph, the applicable percentage shall be determined under the following table:

(g) Security requirements for noncitizen qualified heirs.

(1) In general. Except upon the application of subparagraph (F) or (M) of subsection (i)(3), if a qualified heir is not a citizen of the United States, any interest under this section passing to or acquired by such heir (including any interest held by such heir at a time described in subsection (f)(1)(C)) shall be treated as a qualified family-owned business interest only if the interest passes or is acquired (or is held) in a qualified trust.

(2) Qualified trust. The term "qualified trust" means a trust—

(A) which is organized under, and governed by, the laws of the United States or a State, and

(B) except as otherwise provided in regulations, with respect to which the trust instrument requires that at least 1 trustee of the trust be an individual citizen of the United States or a domestic corporation.

(h) Agreement. The agreement referred to in this subsection is a written agreement signed by each person in being who has an interest (whether or not in possession) in any property designated in such agreement consenting to the application of subsection (f) with respect to such property.

(i) Other definitions and applicable rules. For purposes of this section—

(1) Qualified heir. The term "qualified heir"—

(A) has the meaning given to such term by section 2032A(e)(1), and

(B) includes any active employee of the trade or business to which the qualified family-owned business interest relates if such employee has been employed by such trade or business for a period of at least 10 years before the date of the decedent's death.

(2) Member of the family. The term "member of the family" has the meaning given to such term by section 2032A(e)(2).

(3) Applicable rules. Rules similar to the following rules shall apply:

(A) Section 2032A(b)(4) (relating to decedents who are retired or disabled).

(B) Section 2032A(b)(5) (relating to special rules for surviving spouses).

(C) Section 2032A(c)(2)(D) (relating to partial dispositions).

(D) Section 2032A(c)(3) (relating to only 1 additional tax imposed with respect to any 1 portion).

(E) Section 2032A(c)(4) (relating to due date).

(F) Section 2032A(c)(5) (relating to liability for tax; furnishing of bond).

(G) Section 2032A(c)(7) (relating to no tax if use begins within 2 years; active management by eligible qualified heir treated as material participation).

(H) Paragraphs (1) and (3) of section 2032A(d) (relating to election; agreement).

(I) Section 2032A(e)(10) (relating to community property).

(J) Section 2032A(e)(14) (relating to treatment of replacement property acquired in section 1031 or 1033 transactions).

(K) Section 2032A(f) (relating to statute of limitations).

(L) Section 6166(b)(3) (relating to farmhouses and certain other structures taken into account).

(M) Subparagraphs (B), (C), and (D) of section 6166(g)(1) (relating to acceleration of payment).

(N) Section 6324B (relating to special lien for additional estate tax).

[For analysis, see ¶ 505, ¶ 506. For text of Committee Report, see ¶ 5027.]

[Endnote Code Sec. 2033A]

Code Sec. 2033A was added by Sec. 502(a) of the Taxpayer Relief Act of 1997, H.R. 2014, 8/5/97.

1. added Code Sec. 2033A

Effective Date (Sec. 502(c), H.R. 2014, 8/5/97) effective for estates of decedents dying after December 31, 1997.

[¶ 3215]   Code Sec. 2035. [1] *Adjustments for certain gifts made within 3 years of decedent's death.*

(a) Inclusion of certain property in gross estate. If—

(1) the decedent made a transfer (by trust or otherwise) of an interest in any property, or relinquished a power with respect to any property, during the 3-year period ending on the date of the decedent's death, and

(2) the value of such property (or an interest therein) would have been included in the decedent's gross estate under section 2036, 2037, 2038, or 2042 if such transferred interest or relinquished power had been retained by the decedent on the date of his death,

the value of the gross estate shall include the value of any property (or interest therein) which would have been so included.

(b) Inclusion of gift tax on gifts made during 3 years before decedent's death. The amount of the gross estate (determined without regard to this subsection) shall be increased by the amount of any tax paid under chapter 12 by the decedent or his estate on any gift made by the decedent or his spouse during the 3-year period ending on the date of the decedent's death.

(c) Other rules relating to transfers within 3 years of death.

(1) In general. For purposes of—

(A) section 303(b) (relating to distributions in redemption of stock to pay death taxes),

(B) section 2032A (relating to special valuation of certain farms, etc., real property), and

(C) subchapter C of chapter 64 (relating to lien for taxes),

the value of the gross estate shall include the value of all property to the extent of any interest therein of which the decedent has at any time made a transfer, by trust or otherwise, during the 3-year period ending on the date of the decedent's death.

(2) Coordination with section 6166. An estate shall be treated as meeting the 35 percent of adjusted gross estate requirement of section 6166(a)(1) only if the estate meets such requirement both with and without the application of paragraph (1).

(3) Marital and small transfers. Paragraph (1) shall not apply to any transfer (other than a transfer with respect to a life insurance policy) made during a calendar year to any donee if the decedent was not required by section 6019 (other than by reason of section 6019(2)) to file any gift tax return for such year with respect to transfers to such donee.

(d) Exception. Subsection (a) shall not apply to any bona fide sale for an adequate and full consideration in money or money's worth.

(e) Treatment of certain transfers from revocable trusts. For purposes of this section and section 2038, any transfer from any portion of a trust during any period that such portion was treated under section 676 as owned by the decedent by reason of a power in the grantor (determined without regard to section 672(e)) shall be treated as a transfer made directly by the decedent.

[For analysis, see ¶ 524. For text of Committee Report, see ¶ 5270.]

[Endnote Code Sec. 2035]

Matter in *italics* in Code Sec. 2035 added by Sec. 1310(a) of the Taxpayer Relief Act of 1997, H.R. 2014, 8/5/97, which struck out:

"SEC. 2035 ADJUSTMENTS FOR GIFTS MADE WITHIN 3 YEARS OF DECEDENT'S DEATH.

"(a) Inclusion of gifts made by decedent. Except as provided in subsection (b), the value of the gross estate shall include the value of all property to the extent of any interest therein of which the decedent has at any time made a transfer, by trust or otherwise, during the 3-year period ending on the date of the decedent's death.

"(b) Exceptions. Subsection (a) shall not apply—

"(1) to any bona fide sale for an adequate and full consideration in money or money's worth, and

"(2) to any gift to a donee made during a calendar year if the decedent was not required by section 6019 (other than by reason of section 6019(2)) to file any gift tax return for such year with respect to gifts to such donee.

Paragraph (2) shall not apply to any transfer with respect to a life insurance policy.

"(c) Inclusion of gift tax on certain gifts made during 3 years before decedent's death. The amount of the gross estate (determined without regard to this subsection) shall be increased by the amount of any tax paid under chapter 12 by the decedent or his estate on any gift made by the decedent or his spouse after December 31, 1976, and during the 3-year period ending on the date of the decedent's death.

"(d) Decedents dying after 1981.

"(1) In general. Except as otherwise provided in this subsection, subsection (a) shall not apply to the estate of a decedent dying after December 31, 1981.

"(2) Exceptions for certain transfers. Paragraph (1) of this subsection and paragraph (2) of subsection (b) shall not apply to a transfer of an interest in property which is included in the value of the gross estate under section 2036, 2037, 2038, or 2042 or would have been included under any of such sections if such interest had been retained by the decedent.

"(3) 3-year rule retained for certain purposes. Paragraph (1) shall not apply for purposes of—

"(A) section 303(b) (relating to distributions in redemption of stock to pay death taxes),

"(B) section 2032A (relating to special valuation of certain farm, etc., real property), and

"(C) subchapter C of chapter 64 (relating to lien for taxes).

"(4) Coordination of 3-year rule with section 6166(a)(1). An estate shall be treated as meeting the 35-percent of adjusted gross estate requirement of section 6166(a)(1) only if the estate meets such requirement both with and without the application of paragraph (1)."

Effective Date (Sec. 1310(c), H.R. 2014, 8/5/97) effective for the estates of decedents dying after 8/5/97.

[¶ 3216] Code Sec. 2053.   Expenses, indebtedness, and taxes.

* * * * * * * * * * * *

(c) Limitations.

(1) Limitations applicable to subsections (a) and (b).

* * * * * * * * * * * *

(B) Certain taxes. Any income taxes on income received after the death of the decedent, or property taxes not accrued before his death, or any estate, succession, legacy, or inheritance taxes, shall not be deductible under this section.[1]

* * * * * * * * * * * *

CAUTION.   Subpara. (c)(1)(D) is effective for estates of decedents dying after 12/31/97.

[2]*(D) Section 6166 interest. No deduction shall be allowed under this section for any interest payable under section 6601 on any unpaid portion of the tax imposed by section 2001 for the period during which an extension of time for payment of such tax is in effect under section 6166.*

* * * * * * * * * * * *

[For analysis, see ¶ 506. For text of Committee Report, see ¶ 5028.]

[Endnote Code Sec. 2053]

Matter in Code Sec. 2053(c)(1)(B) deleted by Sec. 1073(b)(3) of the Taxpayer Relief Act of 1997, H.R. 2014, 8/5/97) which struck out:

1. "This subparagraph shall not apply to any increase in the tax imposed by this chapter by reason of section 4980A(d)."
Effective Date (Sec. 1073(c)(2), H.R. 0214, 8/5/97) effective for estates of decedents dying after 12/31/96.

Code Sec. 2053(c)(1)(D), in *italics,* was added by Sec. 503(b)(1), H.R. 2014, 8/5/97.

2. added subpara. (c)(1)(D)

Effective Date (Sec. 503(c), H.R. 2014, 8/5/97) effective for estates of decedents dying after 12/31/97.

[¶ 3217]   Code Sec. 2055.   Transfers for public, charitable, and religious uses.

(a) In general. For purposes of the tax imposed by section 2001, the value of the taxable estate shall be determined by deducting from the value of the gross estate the amount of all bequests, legacies, devises, or transfers—

* * * * * * * * * * *

(3) to a trustee or trustees, or a fraternal society, order, or association operating under the lodge system, but only if such contributions or gifts are to be used by such trustee or trustees, or by such fraternal society, order, or association, exclusively for religious, charitable, scientific, literary, or educational purposes, or for the prevention of cruelty to children or animals, such trust, fraternal society, order, or association would not be disqualified for tax exemption under section 501(c)(3) by reason of attempting to influence legislation, and such trustee or trustees, or such fraternal society, order, or association, does not participate in, or intervene in (including the publishing or distributing of statements), any political campaign on behalf of (or in opposition to) any candidate for public office;[1]

(4) to or for the use of any veterans' organization incorporated by Act of Congress, or of its departments or local chapters or posts, no part of the net earnings of which inures to the benefit of any private shareholder or individual[2]; or

[3]*(5) to an employee stock ownership plan if such transfer qualifies as a qualified gratuitous transfer of qualified employer securities within the meaning of section 664(g).*

* * * * * * * * * * *

(e) Disallowance of deductions in certain cases.

* * * * * * * * * * *

(3) Reformations to comply with paragraph (2).

* * * * * * * * * * *

(G) Statute of limitations. The period for assessing any deficiency of any tax attributable to the application of this paragraph shall not expire before the date 1 year after the date on which the Secretary is notified that such reformation [4]*(or other proceeding pursuant to subparagraph (J)* has occurred.

* * * * * * * * * * *

[5]*(J) Void or reformed trust in cases of insufficient remainder interests. In the case of a trust that would qualify (or could be reformed to qualify pursuant to subparagraph (B)) but for failure to satisfy the requirement of paragraph (1)(D) or (2)(D) of section 664(d), such trust may be—*

(i) declared null and void ab initio, or

(ii) changed by reformation, amendment, or otherwise to meet such requirement by reducing the payout rate or the duration (or both) of any noncharitable beneficiary's interest to the extent necessary to satisfy such requirement,

pursuant to a proceeding that is commenced within the period required in subparagraph (C)(iii). In a case described in clause (i), no deduction shall be allowed under this title for any transfer to the trust and any transactions entered into by the trust prior to being declared void shall be treated as entered into by the transferor.

* * * * * * * * * * *

[For analysis, see ¶ 532, ¶ 938. For text of Committee Report, see ¶ 5166, ¶ 5352.]

[Endnote Code Sec. 2055]

Matter in *italics* in Code Sec. 2055(a)(3), Code Sec. 2055(a)(4) and Code Sec. 2055(a)(5) added by Sec. 915(c)(7)(i)-(iii) [sic (c)(7)(A)-(C)] of the Taxpayer Relief Act of 1997, H.R. 2014, 8/5/97, which struck out:

1. "or"
2. "."
3. added para. (a)(5)

Effective Date (Sec. 1530(d), H.R. 2014, 8/5/97) effective for transfers made by trusts to, or for the use of, an employee stock ownership plan after 8/5/97.

Matter in *italics* in Code Sec. 2055(e)(3)(G) and Code Sec. 2055(e)(3)(J) added by Sec. 1089(b)(3) and (5), H.R. 2014, 8/5/97.

4. added matter in subpara. (e)(3)(G)

5. added subpara. (e)(3)(J)

Effective Date (Sec. 1089(b)(6)(A), P.L. 105-xxx, 8/5/97) effective for transfers in trust after 7/28/97. For exceptions, see Sec. 1089(b)(6)(B) of this Act, which provides:

"(B) Special rule for certain decedents. The amendments made by this subsection shall not apply to transfers in trust under the terms of a will (or other testamentary instrument) executed on or before July 28, 1997, if the decedent—

"(i) dies before January 1, 1999, without having republished the will (or amended such instrument) by codicil or otherwise, or

"(ii) was on July 28, 1997, under a mental disability to change the disposition of his property and did not regain his competence to dispose of such property before the date of his death."

[¶ 3218]   Code Sec. 2056.   Bequests, etc., to surviving spouse.

* * * * * * * * * * *

(b) Limitation in the case of life estate or other terminable interest.

* * * * * * * * * * *

(7) Election with respect to life estate for surviving spouse.

* * * * * * * * * * *

(C) Treatment of survivor annuities. In the case of an annuity included in the gross estate of the decedent under section 2039 [1]*(or, in the case of an interest in an annuity arising under the community property laws of a State, included in the gross estate of the decedent under section 2033)* where only the surviving spouse has the right to receive payments before the death of such surviving spouse—

(i) the interest of such surviving spouse shall be treated as a qualifying income interest for life, and

(ii) the executor shall be treated as having made an election under this subsection with respect to such annuity unless the executor otherwise elects on the return of tax imposed by section 2001.

An election under clause (ii), once made, shall be irrevocable.

[2]*(8) Special rule for charitable remainder trusts.*

(A) In general. If the surviving spouse of the decedent is the only beneficiary of a qualified charitable remainder trust who is not a charitable beneficiary nor an ESOP beneficiary, paragraph (1) shall not apply to any interest in such trust which passes or has passed from the decedent to such surviving spouse.

(B) Definitions. For purposes of subparagraph (A)—

(i) Charitable beneficiary. The term "charitable beneficiary" means any beneficiary which is an organization described in section 170(c).

(ii) ESOP beneficiary. The term "ESOP beneficiary" means any beneficiary which is an employee stock ownership plan (as defined in section 4975(e)(7)) that holds a remainder interest in qualified employer securities (as defined in section 664(g)(4)) to be transferred to such plan in a qualified gratuitous transfer (as defined in section 664(g)(1)).

(iii) Qualified charitable remainder trust. The term "qualified charitable remainder trust" means a charitable remainder annuity trust or charitable remainder unitrust (described in section 664).

* * * * * * * * * * *

[For analysis, see ¶ 512. For text of Committee Report, see ¶ 5271.]

[Endnote Code Sec. 2056]

Matter in *italics* in Code Sec. 2056(b)(7)(C) added by Sec. 1311(a) of the Taxpayer Relief Act of 1997, H.R. 2014, 8/5/97.

1. added matter in subpara. (b)(7)(C)

Effective Date (Sec. 1311(b), H.R. 2014, 8/5/97) effective for estates of decedents dying after 8/5/97.

Matter in *italics* in Code Sec. 2056(b)(8) added by Sec. 1530(c)(8), H.R. 2014, 8/5/97, which struck out:

2. "(8) Special rule for charitable remainder trusts.

"(A) In general. If the surviving spouse of the decedent is the only noncharitable beneficiary of a qualified charitable remainder trust, paragraph (1) shall not apply to any interest in such trust which passes or has passed from the decedent to such surviving spouse.

"(B) Definitions. For purposes of subparagraph (A)—

"(i) Noncharitable beneficiary. The term 'noncharitable beneficiary' means any beneficiary of the qualified charitable remainder trust other than an organization described in section 170(c).

"(ii) Qualified charitable remainder trust. The term 'qualified charitable remainder trust' means a charitable remainder annuity trust or charitable remainder unitrust (described in section 664)."

Effective Date (Sec. 1530(d), H.R. 2014, 8/5/97) effective for transfers made by trusts to, or for the use of, an employee stock ownership plan after 8/5/97.

[¶ 3219]   Code Sec. 2056A.   Qualified domestic trust.

(a) **Qualified domestic trust defined.** For purposes of this section and section 2056(d), the term "qualified domestic trust" means, with respect to any decedent, any trust if—

(1) the trust instrument—

(A) [1]*except as provided in regulations prescribed by the Secretary,* requires that at least 1 trustee of the trust be an individual citizen of the United States or a domestic corporation, and

* * * * * * * * * * *

(c) **Definitions.** For purposes of this section—

* * * * * * * * * * *

[2]*(3) Trust. To the extent provided in regulations prescribed by the Secretary, the term "trust" includes other arrangements which have substantially the same effect as a trust.*

* * * * * * * * * * *

[For analysis, see ¶ 514, ¶ 515. For text of Committee Report, see ¶ 5272, ¶ 5274.]

[Endnote Code Sec. 2056A]

Matter in *italics* in Code Sec. 2056A(a)(1)(A) added by Sec. 1314(a) of the Taxpayer Relief Act of 1997, H.R. 2014, 8/5/97.

1. added matter in subparagraph (a)(1)(A)

Effective Date (Sec. 1314(b), H.R. 2014, 8/5/97) effective for estates of decedents dying after 8/5/97.

Code Sec. 2056A(c)(3), in *italics*, was added by Sec. 1312(a), H.R. 2014, 8/5/97.

2. added paragraph (c)(3)

Effective Date (Sec. 1312(b), H.R. 2014, 8/5/97) effective for estates of decedents dying after 8/5/97.

Sec. 1303(a), H.R. 2014, 8/5/97, provides:

"(a) General rules. In the case of any trust created under an instrument executed before the date of the enactment of the Revenue Reconciliation Act of 1990, such trust shall be treated as meeting the requirements of paragraph (1) of section 2056A(a) of the Internal Revenue Code of 1986 if the trust instrument requires that all trustees of the trust be individual citizens of the United States or domestic corporations."

Effective Date (Sec. 1303(b), H.R. 2014, 8/5/97) effective for estates of decedents dying after 11/10/88.

[¶ 3220]   Code Sec. 2102.   Credits against tax.

* * * * * * * * * * *

(c) **Unified credit.**

(1) **In general.** A credit of $13,000 shall be allowed against the tax imposed by section 2101.

* * * * * * * * * * *

(3) Special rules.

(A) Coordination with treaties. To the extent required under any treaty obligation of the United States, the credit allowed under this subsection shall be equal to the amount which bears the same ratio to [1]*the applicable credit amount in effect under section 2010(c) for the calendar year which includes the date of death* as the value of the part of the decedent's gross estate which at the time of his death is situated in the United States bears to the value of his entire gross estate wherever situated. For purposes of the preceding sentence, property shall not be treated as situated in the United States if such property is exempt from the tax imposed by this subchapter under any treaty obligation of the United States.

(B) Coordination with gift tax unified credit. If a credit has been allowed under section 2505 with respect to any gift made by the decedent, each dollar amount contained in paragraph (1) or (2) or subparagraph (A) of this paragraph (whichever applies) shall be reduced by the amount so allowed.

* * * * * * * * * * *

[For analysis, see ¶ 501. For text of Committee Report, see ¶ 5026.]

[Endnote Code Sec. 2102]

Matter in *italics* in Code Sec. 2102(c)(3)(A) added by Sec. 501(a)(1)(E) of the Taxpayer Relief Act of 1997, H.R. 2014, 8/5/97, which struck out:

1. "$192,800"

Effective Date (Sec. 501(f), H.R. 2014, 8/5/97) effective for the estates of decedents dying, and gifts made, after 12/31/97.

[¶ 3221]   Code Sec. 2105.   Property without the United States.

* * * * * * * * * * *

(b) Bank deposits and certain other debt obligations. For purposes of this subchapter, the following shall not be deemed property within the United States —

* * * * * * * * * * *

(2) deposits with a foreign branch of a domestic corporation or domestic partnership, if such branch is engaged in the commercial banking business,[1]

(3) debt obligations, if, without regard to whether a statement meeting the requirements of section 871(h)(5) has been received, any interest thereon would be eligible for the exemption from tax under section 871(h)(1) were such interest received by the decedent at the time of his death[2], *and*

[3]*(4) obligations which would be original issue discount obligations as defined in section 871(g)(1) but for subparagraph (B)(i) thereof, if any interest thereon (were such interest received by the decedent at the time of his death) would not be effectively connected with the conduct of a trade or business within the United States.*

* * * * * * * * * * *

[For analysis, see ¶ 511. For text of Committee Report, see ¶ 5264.]

[Endnote Code Sec. 2105]

Matter in *italics* in Code Sec. 2105(b)(2), Code Sec. 2105(b)(3) and Code Sec. 2105(b)(4) added by Sec. 1304(a) of the Taxpayer Relief Act of 1997, H.R. 2014, 8/5/97, which struck out:

1. "and"

2. "."

3. added para. (b)(4)

Effective Date (Sec. 1304(b), H.R. 2014, 8/5/97) effective for estates of decedents dying after 8/5/97.

[¶ 3222]   Code Sec. 2107.   Expatriation to avoid tax.

* * * * * * * * * * * *

(c) Credits.

* * * * * * * * * *

(2) Credit for foreign death taxes.

(A) In general. The tax imposed by subsection (a) shall be credited with the amount of any estate, inheritance, legacy, or succession taxes actually paid to any foreign country in respect of any property which is included in the gross estate solely by reason of subsection (b).

(B) Limitation on credit. The credit allowed by subparagraph (A) for such taxes paid to a foreign country shall not exceed the lesser of—

(i) the amount which bears the same ratio to the amount of such taxes actually paid to [1]*such foreign country as the value of the property subjected to such taxes by such foreign country and* included in the gross estate solely by reason of subsection (b) bears to the value of all property subjected to such taxes by such foreign country, or

(ii) such property's proportionate share of the excess of—

(I) the tax imposed by subsection (a), over

(II) the tax which would be imposed by section 2101 but for this section.

[2]*(C) Proportionate share. In the case of property which is included in the gross estate solely by reason of subsection (b), such property's proportionate share is the percentage which the value of such property bears to the total value of all property included in the gross estate solely by reason of subsection (b).*

* * * * * * * * * * * *

[For analysis, see ¶ 1626. For text of Committee Report, see ¶ 5380.]

[Endnote Code Sec. 2107]

Matter in *italics* in Code Sec. 2107(c)(2)(B)(i) and Code Sec. 2107(c)(2)(C) added by Sec. 1602(g)(6)(A), and (B) of the Taxpayer Relief Act of 1997, H.R. 2014, 8/5/97, which struck out:

1. "such foreign country in respect of property included in the gross estate as the value of the property"

2. "(C) Proportionate share. For purposes of subparagraph (B), a property's proportionate share is the percentage of the value of the property which is included in the gross estate solely by reason of subsection (b) bears to the total value of the gross estate."

Effective Date (Sec. 1602(i), H.R. 2014, 8/5/97) effective as provided in P.L. 104-191, Sec. 1511(g), which reads as follows:

"(g) Effective date.

"(1) In general. The amendments made by this section shall apply to—

"(A) individuals losing United States citizenship (within the meaning of section 877 of the Internal Revenue Code of 1986) on or after February 6, 1995, and

"(B) long-term residents of the United States with respect to whom an event described in subparagraph (A) or (B) of section 877(e)(1) of such Code occurs on or after February 6, 1995.

"(2) Rulings requests. In no event shall the 1-year period referred to in section 877(c)(1)(B) of such Code, as amended by this section, expire before the date which is 90 days after the date of the enactment of this Act.

"(3) Special rule.

"(A) In general. In the case of an individual who performed an act of expatriation specified in paragraph (1), (2), (3), or (4) of section 349(a) of the Immigration and Nationality Act (8 U.S.C. 1481(a)(1)(4)) before February 6, 1995, but who did not, on or before such date, furnish to the United States Department of State a signed statement of voluntary relinquishment of United States nationality confirming the performance of such act, the amendments made by this section and section 512 shall apply to such individual except that the 10-year period described in section 877(a) of such Code shall not expire before the end of the 10-year period beginning on the date such statement is so furnished.

"(B) Exception. Subparagraph (A) shall not apply if the individual establishes to the satisfaction of the Secretary of the Treasury that such loss of United States citizenship occurred before February 6, 1994."

[¶ 3223] Code Sec. 2207A. Right of recovery in the case of certain marital deduction property.

(a) Recovery with respect to estate tax.

(1) In general. If any part of the gross estate consists of property the value of which is includible in the gross estate by reason of section 2044 (relating to certain property for which marital deduction was previously allowed), the decedent's estate shall be entitled to recover from the person receiving the property the amount by which—

(A) the total tax under this chapter which has been paid, exceeds

(B) the total tax under this chapter which would have been payable if the value of such property had not been included in the gross estate.

[1]*(2) Decedent may otherwise direct. Paragraph (1) shall not apply with respect to any property to the extent that the decedent in his will (or a revocable trust) specifically indicates an intent to waive any right of recovery under this subchapter with respect to such property.*

* * * * * * * * * * * *

[For analysis, see ¶ 513. For text of Committee Report, see ¶ 5262.]

[Endnote Code Sec. 2207A]

Matter in *italics* in Code Sec. 2207A(a)(2) added by Sec. 1302(a), of the Taxpayer Relief Act of 1997, H.R. 2014, 8/5/97, which struck out:

1. "(2) Decedent may otherwise direct by will. Paragraph (1) shall not apply if the decedent otherwise directs by will."

Effective Date (Sec. 1302(c), H.R. 2014, 8/5/97) effective for estates of decedents dying after 8/5/97.

[¶ 3224] Code Sec. 2207B. Right of recovery where decedent retained interest.

(a) Estate tax.

(1) In general. If any part of the gross estate on which tax has been paid consists of the value of property included in the gross estate by reason of section 2036 (relating to transfers with retained life estate), the decedent's estate shall be entitled to recover from the person receiving the property the amount which bears the same ratio to the total tax under this chapter which has been paid as—

(A) the value of such property, bears to

(B) the taxable estate.

[1]*(2) Decedent may otherwise direct. Paragraph (1) shall not apply with respect to any property to the extent that the decedent in his will (or a revocable trust) specifically indicates an intent to waive any right of recovery under this subchapter with respect to such property.*

* * * * * * * * * * * *

[For analysis, see ¶ 513. For text of Committee Report, see ¶ 5262.]

[Endnote Code Sec. 2207B]

Matter in *italics* in Code Sec. 2207B(a)(2) added by Sec. 1302(b) of the Taxpayer Relief Act of 1997, H.R. 2014, 8/5/97, which struck out:

1. "(2) Decedent may otherwise direct by will. Paragraph (1) shall not apply if the decedent otherwise directs in a provision of his will (or a revocable trust) specifically referring to this section."

Effective Date (Sec. 1302(c), H.R. 2014, 8/5/97) effective for estates of decedents dying after 8/5/97.

[¶ 3225] Code Sec. 2501. Imposition of tax.

(a) Taxable transfers.

* * * * * * * * * * * *

(3) Exception.

* * * * * * * * * * * *

(C) Exception for certain individuals. Subparagraph (B) shall not apply to a [1]*donor* meeting the requirements of section 877(c)(1).

* * * * * * * * * * * *

[Endnote Code Sec. 2501]
  Matter in *italics* in Code Sec. 2501(a)(3)(C) added by Sec. 1602(g)(5) of the Taxpayer Relief Act of 1997, H.R. 2014, 8/5/97, which struck out:
  1. "decedent"
Effective Date (Sec. 1602(i), H.R. 2014, 8/5/97) effective as provided in P.L. 104-191, Sec. 511(g), which reads as follows:
  "(g) Effective date.
  "(1) In general. The amendments made by this section shall apply to—
  "(A) individuals losing United States citizenship (within the meaning of section 877 of the Internal Revenue Code of 1986) on or after February 6, 1995, and
  "(B) long-term residents of the United States with respect to whom an event described in subparagraph (A) or (B) of section 877(e)(1) of such Code occurs on or after February 6, 1995.
  "(2) Ruling requests. In no event shall the 1-year period referred to in section 877(c)(1)(B) of such Code, as amended by this section, expire before the date which is 90 days after the date of the enactment of this Act.
  "(3) Special rule.
  "(A) In general. In the case of an individual who performed an act of expatriation specified in paragraph (1), (2), (3), or (4) of section 349(a) of the Immigration and Nationality Act (8 U.S.C. 1481(a)(1)-(4)) before February 6, 1995, but who did not, on or before such date, furnish to the United States Department of State a signed statement of voluntary relinquishment of United States nationality confirming the performance of such act, the amendments made by this section and section 512 shall apply to such individual except that the 10-year period described in section 877(a) of such Code shall not expire before the end of the 10-year period beginning on the date such statement is so furnished.
  "(B) Exception. Subparagraph (A) shall not apply if the individual establishes to the satisfaction of the Secretary of the Treasury that such loss of United States citizenship occurred before February 6, 1994."

[¶ 3226] Code Sec. 2503. Taxable gifts.

* * * * * * * * * * *

[1]*(b) Exclusions from gifts.*

(1) In general. In the case of gifts (other than gifts of future interests in property) made to any person by the donor during the calendar year, the first $10,000 of such gifts to such person shall not, for purposes of subsection (a), be included in the total amount of gifts made during such year. Where there has been a transfer to any person of a present interest in property, the possibility that such interest may be diminished by the exercise of a power shall be disregarded in applying this subsection, if no part of such interest will at any time pass to any other person.

[2]*(2) Inflation adjustment. In the case of gifts made in a calendar year after 1998, the $10,000 amount contained in paragraph (1) shall be increased by an amount equal to—*

(A) $10,000, multiplied by

(B) the cost-of-living adjustment determined under section 1(f)(3) for such calendar year by substituting "calendar year 1997" for "calendar year 1992" in subparagraph (B) thereof. If any amount as adjusted under the preceding sentence is not a multiple of $1,000, such amount shall be rounded to the next lowest multiple of $1,000.

* * * * * * * * * * *

[For analysis, see ¶ 503. For text of Committee Report, see ¶ 5026.]

[Endnote Code Sec. 2503]
  Matter in *italics* in Code Sec. 2503(b), Code Sec. 2503(b)(1) and Code Sec. 2503(b)(2) added by Sec. 501(c)(1) and (3) of the Taxpayer Relief Act of 1997, H.R. 2014, 8/5/97, which struck out:
  1. "(b) Exclusions from gifts."
  2. added paragraph (b)(2)
Effective Date (Sec. 501(f), H.R. 2014, 8/5/97) effective for estates of decedents dying, and gifts made, after 12/31/97.

[¶ 3227]   Code Sec. 2504.   Taxable gifts for preceding calendar periods.

* * * * * * * * * * *

(c) **Valuation of certain gifts for preceding calendar periods.** If the time has expired within which a tax may be assessed under this chapter or under corresponding provisions of prior laws on the transfer of property by gift made during a preceding calendar period, as defined in section 2502(b)[1], the value of such gift made in such preceding calendar period shall, for purposes of computing the tax under this chapter for any calendar year, be the value of such gift which was used in computing the tax for the last preceding calendar period for which a tax under this chapter or under corresponding provisions of prior laws was assessed or paid.

* * * * * * * * * * *

[For analysis, see ¶ 521. For text of Committee Report, see ¶ 5031.]

[Endnote Code Sec. 2504]
Matter in Code Sec. 2504(c) deleted by Sec. 506(d) of the Taxpayer Relief Act of 1997, H.R. 2014, 8/5/97, which struck out:
1. ", and if a tax under this chapter or under corresponding provisions of prior laws has been assessed or paid for such preceding calendar period"
Effective Date Effective 8/5/97.

[¶ 3228]   Code Sec. 2505.   Unified credit against gift tax.

(a) **General rule.** In the case of a citizen or resident of the United States, there shall be allowed as a credit against the tax imposed by section 2501 for each calendar year an amount equal to—

(1) [1]*the applicable credit amount in effect under section 2010(c) for such calendar year,* reduced by

(2) the sum of the amounts allowable as a credit to the individual under this section for all preceding calendar periods.

* * * * * * * * * * *

[For analysis, see ¶ 501. For text of Committee Report, see ¶ 5026.]

[Endnote Code Sec. 2505]
Matter in *italics* in Code Sec. 2505(a)(1) added by Sec. 501(a)(2) of the Taxpayer Relief Act of 1997, H.R. 2014, 8/5/97, which struck out:
1. "$192,800"
Effective Date (Sec. 501(f), H.R. 2014, 8/5/97) effective for estates of decedents dying, and gifts made, after 12/31/97.

[¶ 3229]   Code Sec. 2523.   Gift to spouse.

* * * * * * * * * * *

(g) **Special rule for charitable remainder trusts.**

(1) **In general.** If, after the transfer, the donee spouse is the only noncharitable beneficiary (other than the donor) of a [1]*qualified charitable remainder trust,* subsection (b) shall not apply to the interest in such trust which is transferred to the donee spouse.

* * * * * * * * * * *

[Endnote Code Sec. 2523]
Matter in *italics* in Code Sec. 2523(g)(1) added by Sec. 1604(g)(4) of the Taxpayer Relief Act of 1997, H.R. 2014, 8/5/97, which struck out:
1. "qualified remainder trust"
Effective Date Effective 8/5/97.

[¶ 3230]   Code Sec. 2612.   Taxable termination; taxable distribution; direct skip.

* * * * * * * * * * * *

(c) Direct skip. For purposes of this chapter —

* * * * * * * * * * * *

[1]*(2)* **Look-thru rules not to apply.** Solely for purposes of determining whether any transfer to a trust is a direct skip, the rules of [2]*section 2651(f)(2) shall not apply.*

[For analysis, see ¶ 525. For text of Committee Report, see ¶ 5034.]

[Endnote Code Sec. 2612]
Matter in *italics* in Code Sec. 2612(c)(2) added by Secs. 511(b)(1) and (2) of the Taxpayer Relief Act of 1997, H.R. 2014, 8/5/97, which struck out:
   1. "(2) Special rule for transfers to grandchildren. For purposes of determining whether any transfer is a direct skip, if—
   "(A) an individual is a grandchild of the transferor (or the transferor's spouse or former spouse), and
   "(B) as of the time of the transfer, the parent of such individual who is a lineal descendant of the transferor (or the transferor's spouse or former spouse) is dead,
such individual shall be treated as if such individual were a child of the transferor and all of that grandchild's children shall be treated as if they were grandchildren of the transferor. In the case of lineal descendants below a grandchild, the preceding sentence may be reapplied. If any transfer of property to a trust would be a direct skip but for this paragraph, any generation assignment under this paragraph shall apply also for purposes of applying this chapter to transfers from the portion of the trust attributable to such property.
   "(3)"
   2. "section 2651(e)(2)"
Effective Date (Sec. 511(c), H.R. 2014, 8/5/97) effective for terminations, distributions, and transfers occurring after 12/31/97.

[¶ 3231]   Code Sec. 2631.   GST exemption.

* * * * * * * * * * * *

[1]*(c)* **Inflation adjustment.** *In the case of an individual who dies in any calendar year after 1998, the $1,000,000 amount contained in subsection (a) shall be increased by an amount equal to—*

   (1) $1,000,000, multiplied by

   (2) the cost-of-living adjustment determined under section 1(f)(3) for such calendar year by substituting "calendar year 1997" for "calendar year 1992" in subparagraph (B) thereof.

   If any amount as adjusted under the preceding sentence is not a multiple of $10,000, such amount shall be rounded to the next lowest multiple of $10,000.

[For analysis, see ¶ 504. For text of Committee Report, see ¶ 5026.]

[Endnote Code Sec. 2631]
Code Sec. 2631(c), in *italics*, was added by Sec. 501(d) of the Taxpayer Relief Act of 1997, H.R. 2014, 8/5/97.
   1. added subsec. (c)
Effective Date (Sec. 501(f), H.R. 2014, 8/5/97) effective for estates of decedents dying, and gifts made, after 12/31/97.

[¶ 3232]   Code Sec. 2651.   Generation assignment.

* * * * * * * * * * * *

[1]*(e)* **Special rule for persons with a deceased parent.**

   (1) **In general.** *For purposes of determining whether any transfer is a generation-skipping transfer, if—*

(A) an individual is a descendant of a parent of the transferor (or the transferor's spouse or former spouse), and

(B) such individual's parent who is a lineal descendant of the parent of the transferor (or the transferor's spouse or former spouse) is dead at the time the transfer (from which an interest of such individual is established or derived) is subject to a tax imposed by chapter 11 or 12 upon the transferor (and if there shall be more than 1 such time, then at the earliest such time),

such individual shall be treated as if such individual were a member of the generation which is 1 generation below the lower of the transferor's generation or the generation assignment of the youngest living ancestor of such individual who is also a descendant of the parent of the transferor (or the transferor's spouse or former spouse), and the generation assignment of any descendant of such individual shall be adjusted accordingly.

*(2) **Limited application of subsection to collateral heirs.** This subsection shall not apply with respect to a transfer to any individual who is not a lineal descendant of the transferor (or the transferor's spouse or former spouse) if, at the time of the transfer, such transferor has any living lineal descendant.*

²*(f)* **Other special rules.**

* * * * * * * * * * * *

[For analysis, see ¶ 525. For text of Committee Report, see ¶ 5034.]

[Endnote Code Sec. 2651]

Matter in *italics* in Code Sec. 2651(e) and Code Sec. 2651(f) was added by Sec. 511(a) of the Taxpayer Relief Act of 1997, H.R. 2014, 8/5/97, which struck out:

1. added subsec. (e)
2. "(e)"

Effective Date (Sec. 511(c), H.R. 2014, 8/5/97) effective for terminations, distributions, and transfers, occurring after 12/31/97.

[¶ 3233]   Code Sec. 2652.   Other definitions.

* * * * * * * * * * * *

(b) Trust and trustee.

(1) Trust. The term "trust" includes any arrangement (other than an estate) which, although not a trust, has substantially the same effect as a trust. ¹*Such term shall not include any trust during any period the trust is treated as part of an estate under section 646.*

* * * * * * * * * * * *

[For analysis, see ¶ 526. For text of Committee Report, see ¶ 5265.]

[Endnote Code Sec. 2652]

Matter in *italics* in Code Sec. 2652(b)(1) added by Sec. 1305(b) of the Taxpayer Relief Act of 1997, H.R. 2014, 8/5/97.

1. added matter in para. (b)(1)

Effective Date (Sec. 1305(d), H.R. 2014, 8/5/97) effective for estates of decedents dying after 8/5/97.

[Endnote Code Sec. 2652]

Sec. 921 of the Taxpayer Relief Act of 1997, H.R. 2014, 8/5/97, provides:

"Sec. 921 Clarification of standard to be used in determining employment tax status of securities brokers.

"(a) In General.— In determining for purposes of the Internal Revenue Code of 1986 whether a registered representative of a securities broker-dealer is an employee (as defined in section 3121(d) of the Internal Revenue Code of 1986), no weight shall be given to instructions from the service recipient which are imposed only in compliance with investor protection standards imposed by the Federal Government, any State government, or a governing body pursuant to a delegation by a Federal or State agency."

P.L. 104-188. Matter in *italics* in Code Sec. 3121(a)(5)(F) and Code Sec. 3121(a)(5)(G) added by Sec. 1421(b)(8)(A) of the Small Business Job Protection Act of 1996, P.L. 104-188, 8/20/96, which struck out:

1. "or" [P.L. 104-188]
2. added matter to subpara. (a)(5)(G) [deleted by Sec. 1458(b)(1) of this Act, see below] [P.L. 104-188]

Effective Date (Sec. 1421(e), P.L. 104-188, 8/20/96) effective for tax. yrs. begin. after 12/31/96.

P.L. **104-188.** Code Sec. 3121(a)(5)(H) was added by Sec. 1421(b)(8)(A), P.L. 104-188.
3. added subpara. (a)(5)(H) [P.L. 104-188]
Effective Date (Sec. 1421(e), P.L. 104-188, 8/20/96) effective for tax. yrs. begin. after 12/31/96.

P.L. **104-188.** Matter in *italics* in Code Sec. 3121(a)(5)(G), Code Sec. 3121(a)(5)(H) [as added by Sec. 1421(b)(8)(A) of this Act, see above] and Code Sec. 3121(a)(5)(I) added by Sec. 1458(b)(1), P.L. 104-188.
4. "or" [P.L. 104-188]
5. added matter to subpara. (a)(5)(H) [P.L. 104-188]
6. added subpara. (a)(6)(I) [P.L. 104-188]
Effective Date (Sec. 1458(c)(2), P.L. 104-188, 8/20/96) effective for remuneration paid after 12/31/96.

P.L. **104-188.** Matter in *italics* in Code Sec. 3121(b) and Code Sec. 3121(b)(20)(A) added by Secs. 1116(a)(1)(A) and (B), P.L. 104-188, which struck out:
7. "(A) such individual does not receive any cash remuneration (other than as provided in subparagraph (B))," [P.L. 104-188]
8. added matter to subsec. (b) [P.L. 104-188]
Effective Date (Sec. 1116(a)(3)(A), P.L. 104-188, 8/20/96) effective for remuneration paid after 12/31/94, and after 12/31/84 and before 1/1/95 unless the payor treated such remuneration (when paid) as being subject to tax under chapter 21 of the Internal Revenue Code of 1986.

P.L. **104-188.** Sec. 1802, P.L. 104-188, provides:
"Sec. 1802. Treatment of certain university accounts.
"(a) In general. For purposes of subsection (s) of section 3121 of the Internal Revenue Code of 1986 (relating to concurrent employment by 2 or more employers)—
"(1) the following entities shall be deemed to be related corporations that concurrently employ the same individual:
"(A) a State university which employs health professionals as facility members at a medical school, and
"(B) an agency account of a State university which is described in subparagraph (A) and from which there is distributed to such faculty members payments forming a part of the compensation that the State, or such State university, as the case may be, agrees to pay to such faculty members, but only if—
"(i) such agency account is authorized by State law and receives the funds for such payments from a faculty practice plan described in section 501(c)(3) of such Code and exempt from tax under section 501(a) of such Code.
"(ii) such payments are distributed by such agency account to such faculty members who render patient care at such medical school, and
"(iii) such faculty members comprise at least 30 percent of the membership of such faculty practice plan, and
"(2) remuneration which is disbursed by such agency account to any such faculty member of the medical school described in paragraph (1)(A) shall be deemed to have been actually disbursed by the State, or such State university, as the case may be, as a common paymaster and not to have been actually disbursed by such agency account.
"(b) Effective date. The provisions of subsection (a) shall apply to remuneration paid after December 31, 1996."

[¶ 3234]   Code Sec. 3301.   Rate of tax.

There is hereby imposed on every employer (as defined in section 3306(a)) for each calendar year an excise tax, with respect to having individuals in his employ, equal to—

(1) 6.2 percent in the case of calendar years 1988 through [1]*2007*

(2) 6.0 percent in the case of calendar year [2]*2008* and each calendar year thereafter;

of the total wages (as defined in section 3306(b)) paid by him during the calendar year with respect to employment (as defined in section 3306(c)).

[For analysis, see ¶ 1905. For text of Committee Report, see ¶ 5133.]

[Endnote Code Sec. 3301]
Matter in *italics* in Code Sec. 3301(1) and Code Sec. 3301(2) added by Secs. 1035(1) and (2) of the Taxpayer Relief Act of 1997, H.R. 2014, 8/5/97, which struck out:
1. "1998"
2. "1999"
Effective Date Effective 8/5/97.

[¶ 3235]   Code Sec. 3306.   Definitions.

* * * * * * * * * * * *

(c) **Employment.** For purposes of this chapter, the term "employment" means any service performed prior to 1955, which was employment for purposes of subchapter C of chapter 9 of the Internal Revenue Code of 1939 under the law applicable to the period in which such service was performed, and (A) any service, of whatever nature, performed after 1954 by an employee for the person employing him, irrespective of the citizenship or residence of either, (i) within the United States, or (ii) on or in connection with an American vessel or American aircraft under a contract of service which is entered into within the United States or during the performance of which and while the employee is employed on the vessel or aircraft it touches at a port in the United States, if the employee is employed on and in connection with such vessel or aircraft when outside the United States, and (B) any service, of whatever nature, performed after 1971 outside the United States (except in a contiguous country with which the United States has an agreement relating to unemployment compensation) by a citizen of the United States as an employee of an American employer (as defined in subsection (j)(3)), except

* * * * * * * * * * *

(19) service which is performed by a nonresident alien individual for the period he is temporarily present in the United States as a nonimmigrant under subparagraph (F), (J), (M), or (Q) of section 101(a)(15) of the Immigration and Nationality Act, as amended (8 U.S.C. 1101(a)(15)(F), (J), (M), or (Q)), and which is performed to carry out the purpose specified in subparagraph (F), (J), (M), or (Q) as the case may be;[1-B]

(20) service performed by a full time student (as defined in subsection (q)) in the employ of an organized camp

(A) if such camp—

(i) did not operate for more than 7 months in the calendar year and did not operate for more than 7 months in the preceding calendar year, or

(ii) had average gross receipts for any 6 months in the preceding calendar year which were not more than 33⅓ percent of its average gross receipts for the other 6 months in the preceding calendar year; and

(B) if such full time student performed services in the employ of such camp for less than 13 calendar weeks in such calendar year[2-B]; or

[3-B] *(21) service performed by a person committed to a penal institution.*

* * * * * * * * * * *

[For analysis, see ¶ 1904. For text of Committee Report, see ¶ 5506.]

[Endnote Code Sec. 3306]
   H.R. 2015. Matter in *italics* in Code Sec. 3306(c)(19), Code Sec. 3306(c)(20) and Code Sec. 3306(c)(21) added by Sec. 5406(a)(1)-(3) of the Balanced Budget Act of 1997, H.R. 2015, 8/5/97, which struck out:
   1_B. "or" [H.R. 2015]
   2_B. "." [H.R. 2015]
   3_B. added para. (c)(21) [H.R. 2015]
Effective Date (Sec. 5406(b), H.R. 2015, 8/5/97) effective for service performed after 1/1/94.

[¶ 3236]   Code Sec. 3309.   State law coverage of services performed for nonprofit organizations or governmental entities.

* * * * * * * * * * *

(b) **Section not to apply to certain service.** This section shall not apply to service performed—

(1) in the employ of (A) a church or convention or association of churches,[1-B] (B) an organization which is operated primarily for religious purposes and which is operated, supervised, controlled, or principally supported by a church or convention or association of churches[2-B], *or (C) an elementary or secondary school which is operated primarily for religious purposes, which is described in section 501(c)(3), and which is exempt from tax under section 501(a);*

* * * * * * * * * * *

(3) in the employ of a governmental entity referred to in paragraph (7) of section 3306(c), if such service is performed by an individual in the exercise of his duties—

(A) as an elected official;

(B) as a member of a legislative body, or a member of the judiciary, of a State or political subdivision thereof;

(C) as a member of the State National Guard or Air National Guard;

(D) as an employee serving on a temporary basis in case of fire, storm, snow, earthquake, flood, or similar emergency;[3-B]

(E) in a position which, under or pursuant to the State law, is designated as (i) a major nontenured policymaking or advisory position, or (ii) a policymaking or advisory position the performance of the duties of which ordinarily does not require more than 8 hours per week; [4-B]*or*

[5-B]*(F) as an election official or election worker if the amount of remuneration received by the individual during the calendar year for services as an election official or election worker is less than $1,000;*

* * * * * * * * * * *

[Endnote Code Sec. 3309]

H.R. 2015. Matter in *italics* in Code Sec. 3309(b)(1) added by Sec. 5407(a)(1) and (2) of the Balanced Budget Act of 1997, H.R. 2015, 8/5/97, which struck out:

1_B. "or" [H.R. 2015]
2_B. added matter in para. (b)(1) [H.R. 2015]

Effective Date (Sec. 5407(b), H.R. 2015, 8/5/97) effective for service performed after 8/5/97.

H.R. 2015. Matter in *italics* in Code Sec. 3309(b)(3)(D), Code Sec. 3309(b)(3)(E) and Code Sec. 3309(b)(3)(F) added by Sec. 5405(a)(1)-(3), H.R. 2015, 8/5/97, which struck out:

3_B. "or" [H.R. 2015]
4_B. added matter in subpara. (b)(3)(E) [H.R. 2015]
5_B. added subpara. (b)(3)(F) [H.R. 2015]

Effective Date (Sec. 5405(b), H.R. 2015, 8/5/97) effective for service performed after 8/5/97.

[¶ 3237]   Code Sec. 4001.   Imposition of tax.

[1]*(a) Imposition of tax.*

(1) In general. There is hereby imposed on the 1st retail sale of any passenger vehicle a tax equal to 10 percent of the price for which so sold to the extent such price exceeds the applicable amount.

(2) Applicable amount.

(A) In general. Except as provided in subparagraphs (B) and (C), the applicable amount is $30,000.

(B) Qualified clean-fuel vehicle property. In the case of a passenger vehicle which is propelled by a fuel which is not a clean-burning fuel and to which is installed qualified clean-fuel vehicle property (as defined in section 179A(c)(1)(A)) for purposes of permitting such vehicle to be propelled by a clean-burning fuel, the applicable amount is equal to the sum of—

(i) the dollar amount in effect under subparagraph (A), plus

(ii) the increase in the price for which the passenger vehicle was sold (within the meaning of section 4002) due to the installation of such property.

(C) Purpose built passenger vehicle.

(i) In general. In the case of a purpose built passenger vehicle, the applicable amount is equal to 150 percent of the dollar amount in effect under subparagraph (A).

(ii) Purpose built passenger vehicle. For purposes of clause (i), the term "purpose built passenger vehicle" means a passenger vehicle produced by an original equipment manufacturer and designed so that the vehicle may be propelled primarily by electricity.

* * * * * * * * * * *

(e) Inflation adjustment

(1) In general. The $30,000 amount in subsection (a)[2] shall be increased by an amount equal to—

(A) $30,000, multiplied by

(B) the cost-of-living adjustment under section 1(f)(3) for the calendar year in which the vehicle is sold, determined by substituting "calendar year 1990" for "calendar year 1992" in subparagraph (B) thereof.

(2) **Rounding.** If any amount as adjusted under paragraph (1) is not a multiple of $2,000, such amount shall be rounded to the next lowest multiple of $2,000.

(f) **Phasedown** For sales occurring in calendar years after 1995 and before 2003, [3]*subsection (a)(1)* [4]*and section 4003(a)* shall be applied by substituting for "10 percent"[5], *each place it appears,* the percentage determined in accordance with the following table.

If the calendar year is:	The percentage is:
1996	9 percent
1997	8 percent
1998	7 percent
1999	6 percent
2000	5 percent
2001	4 percent
2002	3 percent

(g) **Termination.** The [6]*taxes imposed by this section and section 4003* shall not apply to any sale[7], *use, or installation* after December 31, 2002.

[For analysis, see ¶ 2218 and ¶ 2219. For text of Committee Report, see ¶ 5056 and ¶ 5387.]

[Endnote Code Sec. 4001]

Matter in *italics* in Code Sec. 4001(a), Code Sec. 4001(e)(1) and Code Sec. 4001(f) added by Sec. 906(a), (b)(1), and (b)(2) of the Taxpayer Relief Act of 1997, H.R. 2014, 8/5/97, which struck out:

1. "(a) Imposition of tax. There is hereby imposed on the 1st retail sale of any passenger vehicle a tax equal to 10 percent of the price for which so sold to the extent such price exceeds $30,000."

2. "and section 4003(a)"

3. "subsection (a)"

Effective Date (Sec. 906(c), H.R. 2014, 8/5/97) effective for sales and installations occurring after 8/5/97.

Matter in *italics* in Code Sec. 4001(f) and Code Sec. 4001(g) added by Sec. 1601(f)(3)(A)(i), (f)(3)(A)(ii), and (f)(3)(B), H.R. 2014, 8/5/97, which struck out:

4. added matter in subsec. (f)

5. added matter in subsec. (f)

6. "tax imposed by this section"

7. "or use"

Effective Date (Sec. 1601(j)(1), H.R. 2014, 8/5/97) effective for sales occurring after the date which is 7 days after 8/20/96.

[¶ 3238] Code Sec. 4003. Special rules.

(a) **Separate purchase of vehicle and parts and accessories therefor.** Under regulations prescribed by the Secretary—

(1) **In general.** Except as provided in paragraph (2), if—

(A) the owner, lessee, or operator of any passenger vehicle installs (or causes to be installed) any part or accessory [1]*(other than property described in section 4001(a)(2)(B))* on such vehicle, and

(B) such installation is not later than the date 6 months after the date the vehicle was 1st placed in service,

then there is hereby imposed on such installation a tax equal to 10 percent of the price of such part or accessory and its installation.

(2) **Limitation.** The tax imposed by paragraph (1) on the installation of any part or accessory shall not exceed 10 percent of the excess (if any) of—

(A) the sum of—

(i) the price of such part or accessory and its installation,

(ii) the aggregate price of the parts and accessories (and their installation) installed before such part or accessory, plus

(iii) the price for which the passenger vehicle was sold, over

[2](B) *the appropriate applicable amount as determined under section 4001(a)(2).*

(3) Exceptions. Paragraph (1) shall not apply if—

(A) the part or accessory installed is a replacement part or accessory,

(B) the part or accessory is installed to enable or assist an individual with a disability to operate the vehicle, or to enter or exit the vehicle, by compensating for the effect of such disability, or

(C) the aggregate price of the parts and accessories (and their installation) described in paragraph (1) with respect to the vehicle does not exceed [3]*$1,000* (or such other amount or amounts as the Secretary may by regulation prescribe).

The price of any part or accessory (and its installation) to which paragraph (1) does not apply by reason of this paragraph shall not be taken into account under paragraph (2)(A).

* * * * * * * * * * * *

[For analysis, see ¶ 2218 and ¶ 2220. For text of Committee Report, see ¶ 5056 and ¶ 5257.]

[Endnote Code Sec. 4003]

Matter in *italics* in Code Sec. 4003(a)(1)(A) and Code Sec. 4003(a)(2)(B) added by Sec. 906(b)(3) and (4) of the Tax-payer Relief Act of 1997, H.R. 2014, 8/5/97, which struck out:

  1. added matter in subpara. (a)(1)(A)

  2. "(B) $30,000."

Effective Date (Sec. 906(c), H.R. 2014, 8/5/97) effective for sales and installations occurring after 8/5/97.

Matter in *italics* in Code Sec. 4003(a)(3)(C) added by Sec. 1401(a), H.R. 2014, 8/5/97, which struck out:

  3. "$200"

Effective Date (Sec. 1401(b), H.R. 2014, 8/5/97) effective for installations on vehicles sold after 8/5/97.

[¶ 3239]   Code Sec. 4041.   Imposition of tax.

(a) Diesel fuel and special motor fuels.

(1) Tax on diesel fuel in certain cases.

(A) In general. There is hereby imposed a tax on any liquid other than gasoline (as defined in section 4083)—

(i) sold by any person to an owner, lessee, or other operator of a diesel-powered highway vehicle [1]*or a diesel-powered train* for use as a fuel in such [2]*vehicle or train,* or

(ii) used by any person as a fuel in a diesel-powered highway vehicle [3]*or a diesel-powered train* unless there was a taxable sale of such fuel under clause (i).

* * * * * * * * * * * *

[4]*(D) Repealed.*

CAUTION.   Para. (a)(2), following, is effective before 10/1/97. For para. (a)(2), effective after 9/30/97, see below.

(2) Special motor fuels. There is hereby imposed a tax on benzol, benzene, naphtha, liquefied petroleum gas, casing head and natural gasoline, or any other liquid (other than kerosene, gas oil, or fuel oil, or any product taxable under section 4081)—

(A) sold by any person to an owner, lessee, or other operator of a motor vehicle or motorboat for use as a fuel in such motor vehicle or motorboat, or

(B) used by any person as a fuel in a motor vehicle or motorboat unless there was a taxable sale of such liquid under subparagraph (A).

The rate of the tax imposed by this paragraph shall be the rate of tax specified in [5]*section 4081(a)(2)(A)(i)* on gasoline which is in effect at the time of such sale or use.

CAUTION.   Para. (a)(2), following, is effective after 9/30/97 and before 7/1/98. For para. (a)(2), effective before 10/1/97, see above. For para. (a)(2) effective after 6/30/98, see below.

[6](2) *Special motor fuels.*

(A) *In general.* There is hereby imposed a tax on any liquid (other than kerosene, gas oil, fuel oil, or any product taxable under section 4081)—

(i) sold by any person to an owner, lessee, or other operator of a motor vehicle or motorboat for use as a fuel in such motor vehicle or motorboat, or

(ii) used by any person as a fuel in a motor vehicle or motorboat unless there was a taxable sale of such liquid under clause (i).

(B) *Rate of tax.* The rate of the tax imposed by this paragraph shall be—

(i) except as otherwise provided in this subparagraph, the rate of tax specified in section 4081(a)(2)(A)(i) which is in effect at the time of such sale or use,

(ii) 13.6 cents per gallon in the case of liquefied petroleum gas, and

(iii) 11.9 cents per gallon in the case of liquefied natural gas.

In the case of any sale or use after September 30, 1999, clause (ii) shall be applied by substituting "3.2 cents" for "13.6 cents", and clause (iii) shall be applied by substituting "2.8 cents" for "11.9 cents".

CAUTION. Para. (a)(2), following, is effective after 6/30/98. For para. (a)(2), effective before 7/1/98, see above.

(2) Special motor fuels.

(A) In general. There is hereby imposed a tax on any liquid (other than[7] gas oil, fuel oil, or any product taxable under section 4081)—

(i) sold by any person to an owner, lessee, or other operator of a motor vehicle or motorboat for use as a fuel in such motor vehicle or motorboat, or

(ii) used by any person as a fuel in a motor vehicle or motorboat unless there was a taxable sale of such liquid under clause (i).

(B) Rate of tax. The rate of the tax imposed by this paragraph shall be—

(i) except as otherwise provided in this subparagraph, the rate of tax specified in section 4081(a)(2)(A)(i) which is in effect at the time of such sale or use,

(ii) 13.6 cents per gallon in the case of liquefied petroleum gas, and

(iii) 11.9 cents per gallon in the case of liquefied natural gas.

In the case of any sale or use after September 30, 1999, clause (ii) shall be applied by substituting "3.2 cents" for "13.6 cents", and clause (iii) shall be applied by substituting "2.8 cents" for "11.9 cents".

* * * * * * * * * * * *

(c) Noncommercial aviation.

(1) Tax on nongasoline fuels where no tax imposed on fuel under section 4091. There is hereby imposed a tax upon [8]*kerosene and any other liquid* (other than any product taxable under section 4081)—

(A) sold by any person to an owner, lessee, or other operator of an aircraft, for use as a fuel in such aircraft in noncommercial aviation; or

(B) used by any person as a fuel in an aircraft in noncommercial aviation, unless there was a taxable sale of such liquid under this section. The rate of the tax imposed by this paragraph shall be the rate of tax specified in section 4091(b)(1) which is in effect at the time of such sale or use. No tax shall be imposed by this paragraph on the sale or use of [9]*kerosene and any other liquid* if there was a taxable sale of such liquid under section 4091.

(2) Definition of noncommercial aviation. For purposes of this chapter, the term "noncommercial aviation" means any use of an aircraft, other than use in a business of transporting persons or property for compensation or hire by air. The term also includes any use of an aircraft, in a business described in the preceding sentence, which is properly allocable to any transportation exempt from the taxes imposed by sections 4261 and 4271 by reason of section 4281 or 4282 [10]*or by reason of section 4261(h).*

(3) Termination. The rate of the taxes imposed by paragraph (1) shall be 4.3 cents per gallon—

(A) after December 31, 1996, and before the date which is 7 days after the date of the enactment of the Airport and Airway Trust Fund Reinstatement Act 1997, and

CAUTION.   Subpara. (c)(3)(B), following, is effective before 10/1/97. For subpara. (c)(3)(B), effective after 9/30/97, see below.

(B) after September 30, 1997.

CAUTION.   Subpara. (c)(3)(B), following, is effective after 9/30/97. For subpara. (c)(3)(B), effective before 10/1/97, see above.

(B) after [11]*September 30, 2007.*

(d) Additional taxes to fund leaking underground storage tank trust fund.

(1) Tax on sales and uses subject to tax under subsection (a). In addition to the taxes imposed by subsection (a), there is hereby imposed a tax of 0.1 cent a gallon on the sale or use of any liquid (other than liquefied petroleum gas [12]*and other than liquefied natural gas*) if tax is imposed by subsection (a)(1) or (2), on such sale or use.

* * * * * * * * * * *

(l) Exemption for certain[13] uses. No tax shall be imposed under this section on any liquid sold for use in, or used in, a helicopter [14]*or a fixed-wing aircraft* for purposes of providing transportation with respect to which the requirements of subsection (e) or (f) of section 4261 are met.

(m) Certain alcohol fuels.

(1) In general. In the case of the sale or use of any partially exempt methanol or ethanol fuel—

[15]*(A) the rate of the tax imposed by subsection (a)(2) shall be—*

(i) after September 30, 1997, and before October 1, 1999—

(I) in the case of fuel none of the alcohol in which consists of ethanol, 9.15 cents per gallon, and

(II) in any other case, 11.3 cents per gallon, and

(ii) after September 30, 1999,—

(I) in the case of fuel none of the alcohol in which consists of ethanol, 2.15 cents per gallon, and

(II) in any other case, 4.3 cents per gallon, and

* * * * * * * * * * *

[For analysis, see ¶ 2201, ¶ 2206, ¶ 2210, and ¶ 2212. For text of Committee Report, see ¶ 5052, ¶ 5057, ¶ 5129, and ¶ 5293.]

[Endnote Code Sec. 4041]

Matter in *italics* in Code Sec. 4041(a)(1)(A) and Code Sec. 4041(a)(1)(D) added by Sec. 902(b)(1)(A), (b)(1)(B), and (b)(2) of the Taxpayer Relief Act of 1997, H.R. 2014, 8/5/97, which struck out:

1. ", a diesel-powered train, or a diesel-powered boat"
2. "vehicle, train, or boat"
3. ", a diesel-powered train, or a diesel-powered boat"
4. "(D) Diesel fuel used in motorboats. In the case of any sale for use, or use, of fuel in a diesel-powered motorboat—

"(i) no tax shall be imposed by subsection (a) or (d)(1) during the period beginning on the date which is 7 days after the date of the enactment of the Small Business Job Protection Act of 1996 and ending on December 31, 1997,

"(ii) effective during the period after September 30, 1999, and before January 1, 2000, the rate of tax imposed by this paragraph is 24.3 cents per gallon, and

"(iii) the termination of the tax under subsection (d) shall not occur before January 1, 2000."

Effective Date (Sec. 902(c), H.R. 2014, 8/5/97) effective 1/1/98.

Matter in *italics* in Code Sec. 4041(a)(2) added by Sec. 1601(f)(4)(B), H.R. 2014, 8/5/97, which struck out:

5. "section 4081(a)(2)(A)"

Effective Date (Sec. 1601(j)(1), H.R. 2014, 8/5/97) effective on the 7th calendar day after 8/20/96.

Matter in *italics* in Code Sec. 4041(a)(2) and added by Sec. 907(a)(1), H.R. 2014, 8/5/97, which struck out:

6. "(2) Special motor fuels. There is hereby imposed a tax on benzol, benzene, naphtha, liquefied petroleum gas, casing head and natural gasoline, or any other liquid (other than kerosene, gas oil, or fuel oil, or any product taxable under section 4081)—

"(A) sold by any person to an owner, lessee, or other operator of a motor vehicle or motorboat for use as a fuel in such motor vehicle or motorboat, or

"(B) used by any person as a fuel in a motor vehicle or motorboat unless there was a taxable sale of such liquid under subparagraph (A).

The rate of the tax imposed by this paragraph shall be the rate of tax specified in section 4081(a)(2)(A) on gasoline which is in effect at the time of such sale or use."

Effective Date (Sec. 907(c), H.R. 2014, 8/5/97) effective 10/1/97.

Matter in *italics* in Code Sec. 4041(a)(2)(A) and Code Sec. 4041(c)(1) added by Sec. 1032(e), H.R. 2014, 8/5/97, which struck out:
7. "kerosene,"
8. "any liquid"
9. "any liquid"
Effective Date (Sec. 1032(f), H.R. 2014, 8/5/97) effective 7/1/98.

Matter in *italics* in Code Sec. 4041(c)(2) added by Sec. 1435(c)(2), H.R. 2014, 8/5/97.
10. added matter in para. (c)(2)
Effective Date (Sec. 1435(c)(2), H.R. 2014, 8/5/97) effective 10/1/97.

Matter in *italics* in Code Sec. 4041(c)(3)(B) added by Sec. 1031(a)(3), H.R. 2014, 8/5/97, which struck out:
11. "September 30, 1997"
Effective Date (Sec. 1031(e)(1), H.R. 2014, 8/5/97) effective 10/1/97.

Matter in *italics* in Code Sec. 4041(d)(1) added by Sec. 907(a)(2), H.R. 2014, 8/5/97.
12. added matter in para. (d)(1)
Effective Date (Sec. 907(c), H.R. 2014, 8/5/97) effective 10/1/97.

Matter in *italics* in Code Sec. 4041(l) added by Sec. 1601(f)(4)(A)(i) and (ii), H.R. 2014, 8/5/97, which struck out:
13. "helicopter"
14. added matter in subsec. (l)
Effective Date (Sec. 1601(j)(1), H.R. 2014, 8/5/97) effective on the 7th calendar day after 8/20/96.

Matter in *italics* in Code Sec. 4041(m)(1)(A) added by Sec. 907(b), H.R. 2014, 8/5/97, which struck out:
15. "(A) the rate of the tax imposed by subsection (a)(2) shall be—
"(i) 11.3 cents per gallon after September 30, 1993, and before October 1, 1999, and
"(ii) 4.3 cents per gallon after September 30, 1999, and"
Effective Date (Sec. 907(c), H.R. 2014, 8/5/97) effective 10/1/97.

[¶ 3240]   Code Sec. 4051.   Imposition of tax on heavy trucks and trailers sold at retail.

* * * * * * * * * * * *

(b) Separate purchase of truck or trailer and parts and accessories therefor. Under regulations prescribed by the Secretary—

(1) In general. If—

(A) the owner, lessee, or operator of any vehicle which contains an article taxable under subsection (a) installs (or causes to be installed) any part or accessory on such vehicle, and

(B) such installation is not later than the date 6 months after the date such vehicle (as it contains such article) was first placed in service,

then there is hereby imposed on such installation a tax equal to 12 percent of the price of such part or accessory and its installation.

(2) Exceptions. Paragraph (1) shall not apply if—

(A) the part or accessory installed is a replacement part or accessory, or

(B) the aggregate price of the parts and accessories (and their installation) described in paragraph (1) with respect to any vehicle does not exceed [1]*$1,000* (or such other amount or amounts as the Secretary may by regulations prescribe).

* * * * * * * * * * * *

CAUTION.   Subsec. (d) [which was subsec. (e) prior to amendment by H.R. 2014, Sec. 1432(a)], following, is effective 1/1/98.

[2,3]*(d) Credit against tax for tire tax.* If—

(1) tires are sold on or in connection with the sale of any article, and

(2) tax is imposed by this subchapter on the sale of such tires,

there shall be allowed as a credit against the tax imposed by this subchapter an amount equal to the tax (if any) imposed by section 4071 on such tires.

[For analysis, see ¶ 2220, ¶ 2221. For committee reports, see ¶ 5275, ¶ 5276.]

[Endnote Code Sec. 4051]

Matter in *italics* in Code Sec. 4051(b)(2)(B) added by Sec. 1401(a) of the Taxpayer Relief Act of 1997, H.R. 2014, 8/5/97, which struck out:

1. "$200"

Effective Date (Sec. 1401(b), H.R. 2014, 8/5/97) effective for installations on vehicles sold after 8/5/97.

Matter in *italics* in Code Sec. 4051(d) added by Sec. 1432(a), H.R. 2014, which struck out:

2. "(d) Temporary reduction in tax on certain piggyback trailers.

"(1) In general. In the case of piggyback trailers or semitrailers sold within the 1-year period beginning on July 18, 1984, subsection (a) shall be applied by substituting "6 percent" for "12 percent".

"(2) Piggyback trailers or semitrailers. For purposes of this subsection, the term "piggyback trailers or semitrailers" means any trailer or semitrailer—

"(A) which is designed for use principally in connection with trailer-on-flatcar service by rail, and

"(B)(i) both the seller and the purchaser of which are registered in a manner similar to registration under section 4222, and

"(ii) with respect to which the purchaser certifies (at such time and in such form and manner as the Secretary prescribes by regulations) to the seller that such trailer or semitrailer—

"(I) will be used, or resold for use, principally in connection with such service, or

"(II) will be incorporated into an article which will be so used or resold.

"(3) Additional tax where nonqualified use. If any piggyback trailer or semitrailer was subject to tax under subsection (a) at the 6 percent rate and such trailer or semitrailer is used or resold for use other than for a use described in paragraph (2)—

"(A) such use or resale shall be treated as a sale to which subsection (a) applies,

"(B) the amount of the tax imposed under subsection (a) on such sale shall be equal to the amount of the tax which was imposed on the first retail sale, and

"(C) the person so using or reselling such trailer or semitrailer shall be liable for the tax imposed by subsection (a).

No tax shall be imposed by reason of this paragraph on any use or resale which occurs more than 6 years after the date of the first retail sale.

"(e)"

Effective Date Effective 8/5/97.

Matter in *italics* in Code Sec. 4051(d) added by Sec. 1402(a), H.R. 2014, which struck out:

3. "(e) Transitional rule.

"In the case of any article taxable under subsection (a) on which tax was imposed under section 4061(a), subsection (a) shall be applied by substituting '2 percent' for '12 percent'."

Effective Date (Sec. 1402(c), H.R. 2014, 8/5/97) effective 1/1/98.

[¶ 3241]   Code Sec. 4052.   Definitions and special rules.

* * * * * * * * * * * *

(b) Determination of price.

(1) In general. In determining price for purposes of this subchapter—

(A) there shall be included any charge incident to placing the article in condition ready for use,

(B) there shall be excluded—

(i) the amount of the tax imposed by this subchapter,

(ii) if stated as a separate charge, the amount of any retail sales tax imposed by any State or political subdivision thereof or the District of Columbia, whether the liability for such tax is imposed on the vendor or vendee, [1]*and*

[2]*(iii)* the value of any component of such article if—

(I) such component is furnished by the first user of such article, and

(II) such component has been used before such furnishing, and

(C) the price shall be determined without regard to any trade-in.

* * * * * * * * * * * *

(d) Certain other rules made applicable. Under regulations prescribed by the Secretary, rules similar to the [3]*rules of subsections (c) and (d) of section 4216 (relating to partial payments) shall apply* for purposes of this subchapter.

[4]*(e) Long-term lease.* For purposes of this section, the term "long-term lease" means any lease with a term of 1 year or more. In determining a lease term for purposes of the preceding sentence, the rules of section 168(i)(3)(A) shall apply.

[5]*(f) Certain repairs and modifications not treated as manufacture.*

(1) In general. An article described in section 4051(a)(1) shall not be treated as manufactured or produced solely by reason of repairs or modifications to the article (including any modification which changes the transportation function of the article or restores a wrecked article to a functional condition) if the cost of such repairs and modifications does not exceed 75 percent of the retail price of a comparable new article.

(2) Exception. Paragraph (1) shall not apply if the article (as repaired or modified) would, if new, be taxable under section 4051 and the article when new was not taxable under this section or the corresponding provision of prior law.

[6]*(g) Regulations. The Secretary shall prescribe regulations which permit, in lieu of any other certification, persons who are purchasing articles taxable under this subchapter for resale or leasing in a long-term lease to execute a statement (made   under penalties of perjury) on the sale invoice that such sale is for resale. The Secretary shall not impose any registration requirement as a condition of using such procedure.*

[For analysis, see ¶ 2221, ¶ 2222. For committee reports, see ¶ 5276, ¶ 5292.]

[Endnote Code Sec. 4052]

Matter in *italics* in Code Sec. 4052(b)(1)(B)(ii) and Code Sec. 4052(b)(1)(B)(iii) added by Sec. 1402(b) of the Taxpayer Relief Act of 1997, H.R. 2014, 8/5/97, which struck out:

1. added matter in clause (b)(1)(B)(ii)

2. "(iii) the fair market value (including any tax imposed by section 4071) at retail of any tires (not including any metal rim or rim base), and

"(iv)"

Effective Date (Sec. 1402(c), H.R. 2014, 8/5/97) effective 1/1/98.

Matter in *italics* in Code Sec. 4052(d), Code Sec. 4052(e), Code Sec. 4052(f) and Code Sec. 4052(g) added by Sec. 1434(a), (b)(1), and (b)(2), H.R. 2014, 8/5/97, which struck out:

3. "rules of—

"(1) subsections (c) and (d) of section 4216 (relating to partial payments), and

"(2) section 4222 (relating to registration), shall apply"

4. "(f) [sic (e)]"

5. added subsec. (f)

6. added subsec. (g)

Effective Date (Sec. 1434(c), H.R. 2014, 8/5/97) effective 1/1/98.

[¶ 3242]   Code Sec. 4081.   Imposition of tax.

(a) Tax imposed.

(1) Tax on removal, entry, or sale.

(A) In general. There is hereby imposed a tax at the rate specified in paragraph (2) on—

(i) the removal of a taxable fuel from any refinery,

(ii) the removal of a taxable fuel from any terminal,

(iii) the entry into the United States of any taxable fuel for consumption, use, or warehousing, and

(iv) the sale of a taxable fuel to any person who is not registered under section 4101 unless there was a prior taxable removal or entry of such fuel under clause (i), (ii), or (iii).

(B) Exemption for bulk transfers to registered terminals or refineries. The tax imposed by this paragraph shall not apply to any removal or entry of a taxable fuel transferred in bulk to a terminal or refinery if the person removing or entering the taxable fuel and the operator of such terminal or refinery are registered under section 4101.

(2) Rates of tax.

(A) In general. The rate of the tax imposed by this section is—

(i) in the case of gasoline other than aviation gasoline, 18.3 cents per gallon

(ii) in the case of aviation gasoline, 19.3 cents per gallon, and

(iii) in the case of diesel fuel [1]*or kerosene*, 24.3 cents per gallon.

(B) **Leaking underground storage tank trust fund tax.** The rates of tax specified in subparagraph (A) shall each be increased by 0.1 cent per gallon. The increase in tax under this subparagraph shall in this title be referred to as the Leaking Underground Storage Tank Trust Fund financing rate.

* * * * * * * * * * *

(d) Termination.

(1) In general. The rates of tax specified in clauses (i) and (iii) of subsection (a)(2)(A) shall be 4.3 cents per gallon after September 30, 1999.

(2) Aviation Gasoline. The rate of tax specified in subsection (a)(2)(A)(ii) shall be 4.3 cents per gallon—

(A) after December 31, 1996, and before the date which is 7 days after the date of the enactment of the Airport and Airway Trust Fund Tax Reinstatement Act of 1997, and

(B) after [2]*September 30, 2007*.

(3) Leaking Underground Storage Tank Trust Fund financing rate. The Leaking Underground Storage Tank Trust Fund financing rate under subsection (a)(2) [3]*shall apply after September 30, 1997, and before April 1, 2005.*

* * * * * * * * * * *

[For analysis, see ¶ 2201, ¶ 2208, ¶ 2211 . For committee reports, see ¶ 5129, ¶ 5130, ¶ 5131.]

[Endnote Code Sec. 4081]

  Matter in *italics* in Code Sec. 4081(a)(2)(A)(iii) added by Sec. 1032(b) of the Taxpayer Relief Act of 1997, H.R. 2014, 8/5/97.

  1. added matter in clause (a)(2)(A)(iii)

Effective Date (Sec. 1032(f), H.R. 2014, 8/5/97) effective 7/1/98.

  Matter in *italics* in Code Sec. 4081(d)(2)(B) added by Sec. 1031(a)(2), H.R. 2014, 8/5/97, which struck out:

  2. "September 30, 1997"

Effective Date (Sec. 1032(f), H.R. 2014, 8/5/97) effective 10/1/97.

  Matter in *italics* in Code Sec. 4081(d)(3) added by Sec. 1033, H.R. 2014, 8/5/97, which struck out:

  3. "shall not apply after December 31, 1995"

Effective Date Effective 8/5/97.

[¶ 3243] Code Sec. 4082.   Exemptions for diesel fuel [1]*and kerosene*.

  (a) In general. The tax imposed by section 4081 shall not apply to [2]*diesel fuel and kerosene*—

(1) which the Secretary determines is destined for a nontaxable use,

(2) which is indelibly dyed in accordance with regulations which the Secretary shall prescribe, and

(3) which meets such marking requirements (if any) as may be prescribed by the Secretary in regulations.

  Such regulations shall allow an individual choice of dye color approved by the Secretary or chosen from any list of approved dye colors that the Secretary may publish.

* * * * * * * * * * *

  (c) Exception to dyeing requirements. Paragraph (2) of subsection (a) shall not apply with respect to any [3]*diesel fuel and kerosene*—

(1) removed, entered, or sold in a State for ultimate sale or use in an area of such State during the period such area is exempted from the fuel dyeing requirements under subsection (i) of section 211 of the Clean Air Act (as in effect on the date of the enactment of this sub-

section) by the Administrator of the Environmental Protection Agency under paragraph (4) of such subsection (i) (as so in effect), and

(2) the use of which is certified pursuant to regulations issued by the Secretary.

[4]*(d) Additional exceptions to dyeing requirements for kerosene.*

(1) Aviation-grade kerosene. Subsection (a)(2) shall not apply to a removal, entry, or sale of aviation-grade kerosene (as determined under regulations prescribed by the Secretary) if the person receiving the kerosene is registered under section 4101 with respect to the tax imposed by section 4091.

(2) Use for non-fuel feedstock purposes. Subsection (a)(2) shall not apply to kerosene—

(A) received by pipeline or vessel for use by the person receiving the kerosene in the manufacture or production of any substance (other than gasoline, diesel fuel, or special fuels referred to in section 4041), or

(B) to the extent provided in regulations, removed or entered—

(i) for such a use by the person removing or entering the kerosene, or

(ii) for resale by such person for such a use by the purchaser,

but only if the person receiving, removing, or entering the kerosene and such purchaser (if any) are registered under section 4101 with respect to the tax imposed by section 4081.

(3) Wholesale distributors. To the extent provided in regulations, subsection (a)(2) shall not apply to a removal, entry, or sale of kerosene to a wholesale distributor of kerosene if such distributor—

(A) is registered under section 4101 with respect to the tax imposed by section 4081 on kerosene, and

(B) sells kerosene exclusively to ultimate vendors described in section 6427(l)(5)(B) with respect to kerosene.

[5](e) Regulations. The Secretary shall prescribe such regulations as may be necessary to carry out this section, including regulations requiring the conspicuous labeling of retail [6]*diesel fuel and kerosene* pumps and other delivery facilities to assure that persons are aware of which fuel is available only for nontaxable uses.

[7](f) Cross Reference.   For tax on train and certain bus uses of fuel purchased tax-free, see section 4041(a)(1).

[For analysis, see ¶ 2201, ¶ 2208. For committee reports, see ¶ 5130.]

[Endnote Code Sec. 4082]

Matter in *italics* in the heading of Code Sec. 4082, Code Sec. 4082(a), Code Sec. 4082(c), (d), (e), and (f) added by Secs. 1032(c)(1), (c)(2), and (e)(3)(A) of the Taxpayer Relief Act of 1997, H.R. 2014, 8/5/97, which struck out:
1. added matter in the heading of Code Sec. 4082
2. "diesel fuel"
3. "diesel fuel"
4. added subsec. (d)
5. "(d)"
6. "diesel fuel"
7. "(e)"

Effective Date (Sec. 1032(f), H.R. 2014, 8/5/97) effective 7/1/98.

[¶ 3244]   Code Sec. 4083.   Definitions; special rule; administrative authority.

(a) Taxable fuel. For purposes of this subpart—

(1) In general. The term "taxable fuel" means—

(A) gasoline,[1][sic]

(B) diesel fuel[2][, and

[3](C) kerosene]

(2) **Gasoline.** The term "gasoline" includes, to the extent prescribed in regulations—
    (A) gasoline blend stocks, and
    (B) products commonly used as additives in gasoline.
For purposes of subparagraph (A), the term "gasoline blend stock" means any petroleum product component of gasoline.

(3) **Diesel fuel.** The term "diesel fuel" means any liquid (other than gasoline) which is suitable for use as a fuel in a diesel-powered highway vehicle, [4] *or a diesel-powered train.*

(b) **Certain uses defined as removal.** If any person uses taxable fuel (other than in the production of [5]*taxable fuels* or special fuels referred to in section 4041), such use shall for the purposes of this chapter be considered a removal.

* * * * * * * * * * *

[For analysis, see ¶ 2208, ¶ 2210. For committee reports, see ¶ 5030, ¶ 5052.]

[Endnote Code Sec. 4083]
    Matter in *italics* in Code Sec. 4083(a)[(1)](A), Code Sec. 4083(a)[(1)](B) and Code Sec. 4083(a)[(1)](C) [Ed. note: it was unclear from the law if this section was amending para. (a)(1) or (a)(2), but we believe it was the intent of Congress to amend para. (a)(1)] added by Sec. 1032(e)(4) of the Taxpayer Relief Act of 1997, H.R. 2014, 8/5/97, which struck out:
    1. "and"
    2. "."
    3. added subpara. (a)(1)(C)
Effective Date (Sec. 1032(f), H.R. 2014, 8/5/97) effective 7/1/98.

    Matter in *italics* in para. (a)(3), added by Sec. 902(b)(3), H.R. 2014, 8/5/97, which struck out:
    4. " a diesel-powered train, or a diesel-powered boat"
Effective Date (Sec. 902(c), H.R. 2014, 8/5/97) effective 1/1/98.

    Matter in *italics* in Code Sec. 4083(b), added by Sec. 1032(e)(4), H.R. 2014, 8/5/97, which struck out:
    5. "gasoline, diesel fuel"
Effective Date (Sec. 1032(f), H.R. 2014, 8/5/97) effective 7/1/98.

[¶ 3245]   **Code Sec. 4091.   Imposition of tax.**

* * * * * * * * * * *

    (b) **Rate of tax.**

* * * * * * * * * * *

    (3) **Termination.**
        (A) The rate of tax specified in paragraph (1) shall be 4.3 cents per gallon—
            (i) after December 31, 1996, and before the date which is 7 days after the date of the enactment of the Airport and Airway Trust Fund Tax Reinstatement Act of 1997, and
            (ii) after [1]*September 30, 2007.*
        (B) The Leaking Underground Storage Tank Trust Fund financing rate shall not apply during any period during which the Leaking Underground Storage Tank Trust Fund financing rate under section 4081 does not apply.

* * * * * * * * * * *

[2]*(d) **Refund of tax-paid aviation fuel to registered producer of fuel.** If—*
    (1) a producer of aviation fuel is registered under section 4101, and
    (2) such producer establishes to the satisfaction of the Secretary that a prior tax was paid (and not credited or refunded) on aviation fuel held by such producer,
    then an amount equal to the tax so paid shall be allowed as a refund (without interest) to such producer in the same manner as if it were an overpayment of tax imposed by this section.

[For analysis, see ¶ 2201, ¶ 2215. For committee reports, see ¶ 5129, ¶ 5294.]

[Endnote Code Sec. 4091]

Matter in *italics* in Code Sec. 4091(b)(3)(A)(ii) added by Sec. 1031(a)(1) of the Taxpayer Relief Act of 1997, H.R. 2014, 8/5/97, which struck out:
   1. "September 30, 1997"
Effective Date (Sec. 1031(e)(1), H.R. 2014, 8/5/97) effective 10/1/97.

Code Sec. 4091(d), in *italics*, added by Sec. 1436(a), H.R. 2014, 8/5/97.
   2. added subsec. (d)
Effective Date (Sec. 1436(c), H.R. 2014, 8/5/97) effective for fuel acquired by the producer after 9/30/97.

[¶ 3246] Code Sec. 4092.   Exemptions.

* * * * * * * * * * * *

(b) No exemption from certain taxes on fuel used in commercial aviation. In the case of fuel sold for use in commercial aviation (other than supplies for vessels or aircraft within the meaning of section 4221(d)(3)), subsection (a) shall not apply to so much of the tax imposed by section 4091 as is attributable to—

   (1) the Leaking Underground Storage Tank Trust Fund financing rate imposed by such section, and

   (2) in the case of fuel sold after September 30, 1995, 4.3 cents per gallon of the rate specified in section 4091(b)(1).

For purposes of the preceding sentence, the term "commercial aviation" means any use of an aircraft other than in noncommercial aviation (as defined in [1]*section 4041(c)(2)*).

* * * * * * * * * * * *

[Endnote Code Sec. 4092]
   Matter in *italics* in Code Sec. 4092(b) added by Sec. 1601(f)(4)(C) of the Taxpayer Relief Act of 1997, H.R. 2014, 8/5/97, which struck out:
   1. "section 4041(c)(4)"
Effective Date (Sec. 1601(j)(1), H.R. 2014, 8/5/97) effective on the 7th calendar day after 8/20/96.

[¶ 3247] Code Sec. 4093.   Definitions.

   (a) Aviation fuel. For purposes of this subpart, the term "aviation fuel" means [1]*kerosene and any other liquid* (other than any product taxable under section 4081) which is suitable for use as a fuel in an aircraft.

* * * * * * * * * * * *

[Endnote Code Sec. 4093]
   Matter in *italics* in Code Sec. 4093(a) added by section 1032(e)(5) of the Taxpayer Relief Act of 1997, H.R. 2014, 8/5/97, which struck out:
   1. "any liquid"
Effective Date (Sec. 1032(f), H.R. 2014, 8/5/97) effective 7/1/98.

[¶ 3248] Code Sec. 4101.   Registration and bond.

* * * * * * * * * * * *

[1]*(e) Certain approved terminals of registered persons required to offer dyed diesel fuel and kerosene for nontaxable purposes.*

   (1) In general. A terminal for kerosene or diesel fuel may not be an approved facility for storage of non-tax-paid diesel fuel or kerosene under this section unless the operator of such terminal offers dyed diesel fuel and kerosene for removal for nontaxable use in accordance with section 4082(a).

   (2) Exception. Paragraph (1) shall not apply to any terminal exclusively providing aviation grade kerosene by pipeline to an airport.

[For analysis, see ¶ 2208. For committee reports, see ¶ 5130.]

[Endnote Code Sec. 4101]
Code Sec. 4101(e), in *italics*, was added by Sec. 1032(d) of the Taxpayer Relief Act of 1997, H.R. 2014, 8/5/97.
1. added subsec. (e)
Effective Date (Sec. 1032(f), H.R. 2014, 8/5/97) effective 7/1/98.

[¶ 3249]   Code Sec. 4131.   Imposition of tax.

* * * * * * * * * * *

[1]*(b) Amount of tax.*

(1) In general. The amount of the tax imposed by subsection (a) shall be 75 cents per dose of any taxable vaccine.

(2) Combinations of vaccines. If any taxable vaccine is described in more than 1 subparagraph of section 4132(a)(1), the amount of the tax imposed by subsection (a) on such vaccine shall be the sum of the amounts for the vaccines which are so included.

* * * * * * * * * * *

[For analysis, see ¶ 2223. For committee reports, see ¶ 5054.]

[Endnote Code Sec. 4131]
Matter in *italics* in Code Sec. 4131(b) added by Sec. 904(a) of the Taxpayer Relief Act of 1997, H.R. 2014, 8/5/97, which struck out:
1. "(b) Amount of tax.
"(1) In general. The amount of the tax imposed by subsection (a) shall be determined in accordance with the following table:

If the taxable vaccine is:	The tax per dose is:
DPT vaccine	$4.56
DT vaccine	0.06
MMR vaccine	4.44
Polio vaccine	0.29

"(2) Combinations of vaccines. If any taxable vaccine is included in more than 1 category of vaccines in the table contained in paragraph (1), the amount of the tax imposed by subsection (a) on such vaccine shall be the sum of the amounts determined under such table for each category in which such vaccine is so included."
Effective Date (Sec. 904(d), H.R. 2014, 8/5/97) effective on the day after 8/5/97.

[¶ 3250]   Code Sec. 4132.   Definitions and special rules.
(a) **Definitions relating to taxable vaccines.** For purposes of this subchapter—
[1]*(1) Taxable vaccine. The term "taxable vaccine" means any of the following vaccines which are manufactured or produced in the United States or entered into the United States for consumption, use, or warehousing:*
   (A) Any vaccine containing diphtheria toxoid.
   (B) Any vaccine containing tetanus toxoid.
   (C) Any vaccine containing pertussis bacteria, extracted or partial cell bacteria, or specific pertussis antigens.
   (D) Any vaccine against measles.
   (E) Any vaccine against mumps.
   (F) Any vaccine against rubella.
   (G) Any vaccine containing polio virus.
   (H) Any HIB vaccine.
   (I) Any vaccine against hepatitis B.
   (J) Any vaccine against chicken pox.

[2](2) **Vaccine.** The term "vaccine" means any substance designed to be administered to a human being for the prevention of 1 or more diseases.

[3](3) **United States.** The term "United States" has the meaning given such term by section 4612(a)(4).

[4](4) **Importer.** The term "importer" means the person entering the vaccine for consumption, use, or warehousing.

* * * * * * * * * * *

[For analysis, see ¶ 2223. For committee reports, see ¶ 5054.]

[Endnote Code Sec. 4132]

Matter in *italics* in Code Sec. 4132(a)(1), Code Sec. 4132(a)(2), Code Sec. 4132(a)(3), Code Sec. 4132(a)(4), Code Sec. 4132(a)(5), and Code Sec. 4132(a)(6) added by Sec. 904(b) and (c) of the Taxpayer Relief Act of 1997, H.R. 2014, 8/5/97, which struck out:

1. "(1) Taxable vaccine. The term 'taxable vaccine' means any vaccine—

"(A) which is listed in the table contained in section 4131(b)(1), and

"(B) which is manufactured or produced in the United States or entered into the United States for consumption, use, or warehousing."

2. "(2) DPT vaccine. The term 'DPT vaccine' means any vaccine containing pertussis bacteria, extracted or partial cell bacteria, or specific pertussis antigens.

"(3) DT vaccine. The term 'DT vaccine' means any vaccine (other than a DPT vaccine) containing diphtheria toxoid or tetanus toxoid.

"(4) MMR vaccine. The term 'MMR vaccine' means any vaccine against measles, mumps, or rubella. Not more than 1 tax shall be imposed by section 4131 on any MMR vaccine by reason of being a vaccine against more than 1 of measles, mumps, or rubella.

"(5) Polio vaccine. The term 'polio vaccine' means any vaccine containing polio virus."

"(6)"

3. "(7)"

4. "(8)"

Effective Date (Sec. 904(d), H.R. 2014, 8/5/97) effective on the day after 8/5/97. Sec. 904(e) of this Act provides:

"(e) Limitation on certain credits or refunds.

"For purposes of applying section 4131(b) of the Internal Revenue Code of 1986 with respect to any claim for credit or refund file before January 1, 1999, the amount of tax taken into account shall not exceed the tax computed under the rate in effect on the day after the date of the enactment of this Act."

[¶ 3251]   Code Sec. 4161.   Imposition of tax.

* * * * * * * * * * *

[1](b) *Bows and arrows, etc.*

   (1) Bows.

      (A) In general. There is hereby imposed on the sale by the manufacturer, producer, or importer of any bow which has a draw weight of 10 pounds or more, a tax equal to 11 percent of the price for which so sold.

      (B) Parts and accessories. There is hereby imposed upon the sale by the manufacturer, producer, or importer—

         (i) of any part of accessory suitable for inclusion in or attachment to a bow described in subparagraph (A), and

         (ii) of any quiver suitable for use with arrows described in paragraph (2), a tax equivalent to 11 percent of the price for which so sold.

   (2) Arrows. There is hereby imposed on the sale by the manufacturer, producer, or importer of any shaft, point, nock, or vane of a type used in the manufacture of any arrow which after its assembly—

      (A) measures 18 inches overall or more in length, or

      (B) measures less than 18 inches overall in length but is suitable for use with a bow described in paragraph (1)(A),

      a tax equal to 12.4 percent of the price for which so sold.

   (3) Coordination with subsection (a). No tax shall be imposed under this subsection with respect to any article taxable under subsection (a).

[For analysis, see ¶ 2225. For committee reports, see ¶ 5291.]

[Endnote Code Sec. 4161]

Matter in *italics* in Code Sec. 4161(b) added by Sec. 1433(a) of the Taxpayer Relief Act of 1997, H.R. 2014, 8/5/97, which struck out:

1. (b) Bows and arrows, etc.

"(1) Bows and arrows.

"There is hereby imposed on the sale by the manufacturer, producer, or importer—

"(A) of any bow which has a draw weight of 10 pounds or more, and

"(B) of any arrow which—

"(i) measures 18 inches overall or more in length, or

"(ii) measures less than 18 inches overall in length but is suitable for use with a bow described in subparagraph (A), a tax equal to 11 percent of the price for which so sold.

"(2) Parts and accessories.

"There is hereby imposed upon the sale by the manufacturer, producer, or importer—

"(A) of any part or accessory suitable for inclusion in or attachment to a bow or arrow described in paragraph (1), and

"(B) of any quiver suitable for use with arrows described in paragraph (1),

a tax equivalent to 11 percent of the price for which so sold.

"(3) Coordination with subsection (a).

"No tax shall be imposed under this subsection with respect to any article taxable under subsection (a)."

Effective Date (Sec. 1433(b), H.R. 2014, 8/5/97) effective for articles sold by the manufacturer, producer, or importer after 9/30/97.

[¶ 3252]   Code Sec. 4222.   Registration.

* * * * * * * * * * *

(b) Exceptions.

(1) Purchases by State and local governments. Subsection (a) shall not apply to any State or local government in connection with the purchase by it of any article if such State or local government complies with such regulations relating to the use of exemption certificates in lieu of registration as the Secretary shall prescribe to carry out the purpose of this paragraph.

(2) [1]*Under regulations.* Subject to such regulations as the Secretary may prescribe for the purpose of this paragraph,[2] the Secretary may relieve the purchaser or the second purchaser, or both, from the requirement of registering under this section.

(3) Certain purchases and sales by the United States. Subsection (a) shall apply to purchases and sales by the United States only to the extent provided by regulations prescribed by the Secretary.

(4) Repealed.

(5) Supplies for vessels or aircraft. Subsection (a) shall not apply to a sale of an article for use by the purchaser as supplies for any vessel or aircraft if such purchaser complies with such regulations relating to the use of exemption certificates in lieu of registration as the Secretary shall prescribe to carry out the purpose of this paragraph.

* * * * * * * * * * *

[For analysis, see ¶ 2224. For committee reports, see ¶ 5289.]

[Endnote Code Sec. 4222]

Matter in *italics* in Code Sec. 4222(b)(2) was added by Sec. 1431(a)(1) and (2) of the Taxpayer Relief Act of 1997, H.R. 2014, 8/5/97, which struck out:

1. "Export"

2. "in the case of any sale or resale for export,"

Effective Date (Sec. 1431(b), H.R. 2014, 8/5/97) effective date of enactment.

[¶ 3253]   Code Sec. 4251.   Imposition of tax.

* * * * * * * * * * *

[1](d) **Treatment of prepaid telephone cards.**

(1) **In general.** For purposes of this subchapter, in the case of communications services acquired by means of a prepaid telephone card—

(A) the face amount of such card shall be treated as the amount paid for such communications services, and

(B) that amount shall be treated as paid when the card is transferred by any telecommunications carrier to any person who is not such a carrier.

(2) **Determination of face amount in absence of specified dollar amount.** In the case of any prepaid telephone card which entitles the user other than to a specified dollar amount of use, the face amount shall be determined under regulations prescribed by the Secretary.

(3) **Prepaid telephone card.** For purposes of this subsection, the term "prepaid telephone card" means any card or other similar arrangement which permits its holder to obtain communications services and pay for such services in advance.

[For analysis, see ¶ 2207. For committee reports, see ¶ 5132.]

[Endnote Code Sec. 4251]
Code Sec. 4251(d), in *italics*, was added by Sec. 1034(a) of the Taxpayer Relief Act of 1997, H.R. 2014, 8/5/97.
1. added subsec. (d)
Effective Date (Sec. 1034(b), H.R. 2014, 8/5/97) effective for amounts paid in calendar months begin. more than 60 days after 8/5/97.

[¶ 3254]   Code Sec. 4261.   Imposition of tax.

[1](a) **In general.** There is hereby imposed on the amount paid for taxable transportation of any person a tax equal to 7.5 percent of the amount so paid.

(b) **Domestic segments of taxable transportation.**

(1) **In general.** There is hereby imposed on the amount paid for each domestic segment of taxable transportation by air a tax in the amount determined in accordance with the following table for the period in which the segment begins:

In the case of segments beginning:	The tax is:
After September 30, 1997, and before October 1, 1998	$ 1.00
After September 30, 1998, and before October 1, 1999	$ 2.00
After September 30, 1999, and before October 1, 2000	$ 2.25
During 2000	$ 2.50
During 2001	$ 2.75
During 2002 or thereafter	$ 3.00

(2) **Domestic segment.** For purposes of this section, the term "domestic segment" means any segment consisting of 1 takeoff and 1 landing and which is taxable transportation described in section 4262(a)(1).

(3) **Changes in segments by reason of rerouting.** If—

(A) transportation is purchased between 2 locations on specified flights, and

(B) there is a change in the route taken between such 2 locations which changes the number of domestic segments, but there is no change in the amount charged for such transportation,

the tax imposed by paragraph (1) shall be determined without regard to such change in route.

(c) **Use of international travel facilities.**

(1) **In general.** There is hereby imposed a tax of $12.00 on any amount paid (whether within or without the United States) for any transportation of any person by air, if such transportation begins or ends in the United States.

(2) **Exception for transportation entirely taxable under subsection (a).** This subsection shall not apply to any transportation all of which is taxable under subsection (a) (determined without regard to sections 4281 and 4282).

(3) Special rule for Alaska and Hawaii. In any case in which the tax imposed by paragraph (1) applies to a domestic segment beginning or ending in Alaska or Hawaii, such tax shall apply only to departures and shall be at the rate of $6.

* * * * * * * * * * * *

²*(e) Special rules.*

(1) Segments to and from rural airports.

(A) *Exception from segment tax.* The tax imposed by subsection (b)(1) shall not apply to any domestic segment beginning or ending at an airport which is a rural airport for the calendar year in which such segment begins or ends (as the case may be).

(B) *Rural airport.* For purposes of this paragraph, the term "rural airport" means, with respect to any calendar year, any airport if—

(i) there were fewer than 100,000 commercial passengers departing by air during the second preceding calendar year from such airport, and

(ii) such airport—

(I) is not located within 75 miles of another airport which is not described in clause (i), or

(II) is receiving essential air service subsidies as of the date of the enactment of this paragraph.

(C) *No phasein of reduced ticket tax.* In the case of transportation beginning before October 1, 1999—

(i) *In general.* Paragraph (5) shall not apply to any domestic segment beginning or ending at an airport which is a rural airport for the calendar year in which such segment begins or ends (as the case may be).

(ii) *Transportation involving multiple segments.* In the case of transportation involving more than 1 domestic segment at least 1 of which does not begin or end at a rural airport, the 7.5 percent rate applicable by reason of clause (i) shall be applied by taking into account only an amount which bears the same ratio to the amount paid for such transportation as the number of specified miles in domestic segments which begin or end at a rural airport bears to the total number of specified miles in such transportation.

(2) Amounts paid outside the United States. In the case of amounts paid outside the United States for taxable transportation, the taxes imposed by subsections (a) and (b) shall apply only if such transportation begins and ends in the United States.

(3) Amounts paid for right to award free or reduced rate air transportation.

(A) *In general.* Any amount paid (and the value of any other benefit provided) to an air carrier (or any related person) for the right to provide mileage awards for (or other reductions in the cost of) any transportation of persons by air shall be treated for purposes of subsection (a) as an amount paid for taxable transportation, and such amount shall be taxable under subsection (a) without regard to any other provision of this subchapter.

(B) *Controlled group.* For purposes of subparagraph (A), a corporation and all wholly owned subsidiaries of such corporation shall be treated as 1 corporation.

(C) *Regulations.* The Secretary shall prescribe rules which reallocate items of income, deduction, credit, exclusion, or other allowance to the extent necessary to prevent the avoidance of tax imposed by reason of this paragraph. The Secretary may prescribe rules which exclude from the tax imposed by subsection (a) amounts attributable to mileage awards which are used other than for transportation of persons by air.

(4) Inflation adjustment of dollar rates of tax.

(A) *In general.* In the case of taxable events in a calendar year after the last nonindexed year, the $3.00 amount contained in subsection (b) and each dollar amount contained in subsection (c) shall be increased by an amount equal to—

(i) such dollar amount, multiplied by

(ii) the cost-of-living adjustment determined under section 1(f)(3) for such calendar year by substituting the year before the last nonindexed year for "calendar year 1992" in subparagraph (B) thereof.

If any increase determined under the preceding sentence is not a multiple of 10 cents, such increase shall be rounded to the nearest multiple of 10 cents.

(B) *Last nonindexed year.* For purposes of subparagraph (A), the last nonindexed year is—

(i) 2002 in the case of the $3.00 amount contained in subsection (b), and

(ii) 1998 in the case of the dollar amounts contained in subsection (c).

(C) *Taxable event.* For purposes of subparagraph (A), in the case of the tax imposed subsection (b), the beginning of the domestic segment shall be treated as the taxable event.

(5) Rates of ticket tax for transportation beginning before October 1, 1999. Subsection (a) shall be applied by substituting for "7.5 percent"—

(A) "9 percent" in the case of transportation beginning after September 30, 1997, and before October 1, 1998, and

(B) "8 percent" in the case of transportation beginning after September 30, 1998, and before October 1, 1999.

[3]*(f)* **Exemption for certain helicopter uses.** No tax shall be imposed under subsection (a) or (b) on air transportation by helicopter for the purpose of—

(1) transporting individuals, equipment, or supplies in the exploration for, or the development or removal of, hard minerals, oil, or gas, or

(2) the planting, cultivation, cutting, or transportation of, or caring for, trees (including logging operations),

but only if the helicopter does not take off from, or land at, a facility eligible for assistance under the Airport and Airway Development Act of 1970, or otherwise use services provided pursuant to section 44509 or 44913(b) or subchapter I of chapter 471 of title 49, United States Code, during such use. In the case of helicopter transportation described in paragraph (1), this subsection shall be applied by treating each flight segment as a distinct flight.

[4]*(g)* **Exemption for air ambulances providing certain emergency medical transportation.** No tax shall be imposed under this section or section 4271 on any air transportation for the purpose of providing emergency medical services—

(1) by helicopter, or

(2) by a fixed-wing aircraft equipped for and exclusively dedicated [5]on that flight to acute care emergency medical services.

[6]*(h)* **Exemption for skydiving uses.** No tax shall be imposed by this section or section 4721 on any air transportation exclusively for the purposes of skydiving.

[7]*(i)* **Application of taxes.**

(1) **In general.** The taxes imposed by this section shall apply to—

(A) transportation beginning during the period—

(i) beginning on the 7th day after the date of the enactment of the Airport and Airway Trust Fund Tax Reinstatement Act of 1997, and

(ii) ending on [8]September 30, 2007, and

(B) amounts paid during such period for transportation beginning after such period.

(2) **Refunds.** If, as of the date any transportation begins, the taxes imposed by this section would not have applied to such transportation if paid for on such date, any tax paid under paragraph (1)(B) with respect to such transportation shall be treated as overpayment.

[For analysis, see ¶ 2201, ¶ 2202, ¶ 2203, ¶ 2206. For committee reports, see ¶ 5129, ¶ 5293.]

[Endnote Code Sec. 4261]

Matter in *italics* in Code Sec. 4261(a), Code Sec. 4261(b), Code Sec. 4261(c), Code Sec. 4261(d), Code Sec. 4261(e), Code Sec. 4261(f) and Code Sec. 4261(g) added by Sec. 1031(c)(1) and (2) of the Taxpayer Relief Act of 1997, H.R. 2014, 8/5/97, which struck out:

1. "(a) In general. There is hereby imposed upon the amount paid for taxable transportation (as defined in section 4262) of any person a tax equal to 10 percent of the amount so paid. In the case of amounts paid outside of the United States for

taxable transportation, the tax imposed by this subsection shall apply only if such transportation begins and ends in the United States.

"(b) Seats, berths, etc. There is hereby imposed upon the amount paid for seating or sleeping accommodations in connection with transportation and with respect to which a tax is imposed by subsection (a), a tax equal to 10 percent of the amount so paid.

"(c) Use of international travel facilities. There is hereby imposed a tax of $6 upon any amount paid (whether within or without the United States) for any transportation of any person by air, if such transportation begins in the United States. This subsection shall not apply to any transportation all of which is taxable under subsection (a) (determined without regard to sections 4281 and 4282)."

2. added subsec. (e)
3. "(e)"
4. "(f)"

Effective Date (Sec. 1031(e)(2), H.R. 2014, 8/5/97) Sec. 1031(e)(2), H.R. 2014, 8/5/97, reads as follows:

"(2) Ticket taxes.

"(A) In general. Except as otherwise provided in this paragraph, the amendments made by subsections (b) and (c) shall apply to transportation beginning on or after October 1, 1997.

"(B) Treatment of amounts paid for tickets purchased before October 1, 1997. The amendments made by subsection (c) shall not apply to amounts paid before October 1, 1997; except that—

"(i) the amendment made to section 4261(c) of the Internal Revenue Code of 1986 shall apply to amounts paid more than 7 days after the 8/5/97 of this Act for transportation beginning on or after October 1, 1997, and

"(ii) the amendment made to section 4263(c) of such Code shall apply to the extent related to taxes imposed under the amendment made to such section 4261(c) on the amounts described in clause (i).

"(C) Amounts paid for right to award mileage awards.

"(i) In general. Paragraph (3) of section 4261(e) of the Internal Revenue Code of 1986 (as added by the amendment made by subsection (c)) shall apply to amounts paid (and other benefits provided) after September 30, 1997.

"(ii) Payments within controlled group. For purposes of clause (i), any amount paid after June 11, 1997, and before October 1, 1997, by 1 member of a controlled group or a right which is described in such section 4261(e)(3) and is furnished by another member of such group after September 30, 1997, shall be treated as paid after September 30, 1997. For purposes of the preceding sentence, all persons treated as as single employer under subsection (a) or (b) of section 52 of such Code shall be treated as members of a controlled group."

Matter in *italics* in Code Sec. 4261(g)(2) added by Sec. 1601(f)(4)(D), H.R. 2014, 8/5/97.
5. added matter in para. (g)(2)

Effective Date (Sec. 1601(j)(1), H.R. 2014, 8/5/97) effective on the 7th calendar day after 8/20/96.

Matter in *italics* in Code Sec. 4261(h) and Code Sec. 4261(i) added by Sec. 1435(a), H.R. 2014, 8/5/97, which struck out:
6. added subsec. (h)
7. "(h)" [as redesignated by Sec. 1031(c)(1), H.R. 2014, 8/5/97]

Effective Date (Sec. 1435(c)(1), H.R. 2014, 8/5/97) effective for amounts paid after 9/30/97.

Matter in *italics* in Code Sec. 4261(h)(1)(A)(ii) added by Sec. 1435(a), H.R. 2014, 8/5/97, which struck out:
8. "September 30, 1997"

Effective Date (Sec. 1031(e)(2)(A), H.R. 2014, 8/5/97) effective for transportation begin. on or after 10/1/97.

[¶ 3255]   Code Sec. 4263.   Special rules.

* * * * * * * * * * *

(c) **Payment of tax.** Where any tax imposed by section 4261 is not paid at the time payment for transportation is made, then, under regulations prescribed by the Secretary, to the extent that such tax is not collected under any other provision of this ¹*subchapter, such tax shall be paid by the carrier providing the initial segment of such transportation which begins or ends in the United States.*

* * * * * * * * * * *

[For analysis, see ¶ 2204. For committee reports, see ¶ 5129.]

[Endnote Code Sec. 4263]

Matter in *italics* in Code Sec. 4263(c) added by Sec. 1031(c)(3) of the Taxpayer Relief Act of 1997, H.R. 2014, 8/5/97, which struck out:
1. "subchapter—

"(1) such tax shall be paid by the person paying for the transportation or by the person using the transportation;

"(2) such tax shall be paid within such time as the Secretary shall prescribe by regulations after whichever of the following first occurs:

"(A) the rights to the transportation expire; or

"(B) the time when the transportation becomes subject to tax; and

"(3) payment of such tax shall be made to the Secretary, to the person to whom the payment for transportation was made, or, in the case of transportation other than transportation described in section 4262(a)(1), to any person furnishing any portion of such transportation."

Effective Date (Sec. 1031(e)(2)(A) and (B), H.R. 2014, 8/5/97) effective for transportation begin. on or after 10/1/97, except as provided in Sec. 1031(e)(2)(B) of this Act, which reads:

"(B) Treatment of amounts paid for tickets purchased before October 1, 1997. The amendments made by subsection (c) shall not apply to amounts paid before October 1, 1997; except that—

"(i) the amendment made to section 4261(c) of the Internal Revenue Code of 1986 shall apply to amounts paid more than 7 days after the 8/5/97 of this Act for transportation beginning on or after October 1, 1997, and

"(ii) the amendment made to section 4263(c) of such Code shall apply to the extent related to taxes imposed under the amendment made to such section 4261(c) on the amounts described in clause (i)."

[¶ 3256]   Code Sec. 4271.   Imposition of tax.

(a) In general. There is hereby imposed upon the amount paid within or without the United States for the taxable transportation (as defined in section 4272) of property a tax equal to 6.25 percent of the amount so paid for such transportation. The tax imposed by this subsection shall apply only to amounts paid to a person engaged in the business of transporting property by air for hire.

* * * * * * * * * * * *

(d) Application of tax.

(1) In general. The tax imposed by subsection (a) shall apply to—

(A) transportation beginning during the period—

(i) beginning on the 7th day after the date of the enactment of the Airport and Airway Trust Fund Tax Reinstatement Act of 1997, and

(ii) ending on ¹*September 30, 2007,* and

(B) amounts paid during such period for transportation beginning after such period.

(2) Refunds. If, as of the date any transportation begins, the taxes imposed by this section would not have applied to such transportation if paid for on such date, any tax paid under paragraph (1)(B) with respect to such transportation shall be treated as an overpayment.

[For analysis, see ¶ 2201. For committee reports, see ¶ 5129.]

[Endnote Code Sec. 4271]

Matter in *italics* in Code Sec. 4271(d)(1)(A)(ii) added by Sec. 1031(b)(2) of the Taxpayer Relief Act of 1997, H.R. 2014, 8/5/97, which struck out:

1. "September 30, 1997"

Effective Date (Sec. 1031(e)(2)(A), H.R. 2014, 8/5/97) effective for transportation begin. on or after 10/1/97.

[¶ 3257]   Code Sec.¹ 4495.   Repealed.

[Endnote Code Sec. 4495]

Code Sec. 4495 was repealed as part of the repeal of Subchapter F, of Chapter 36, of Subtitle D, by Sec. 1432(b)(1) of the Taxpayer Relief Act of 1997, H.R. 2014, date of enactment, which struck out:

1. "SEC. 4495 IMPOSITION OF TAX.

"(a) General rule.

"There is hereby imposed a tax on any removal of a hard mineral resource from the deep seabed pursuant to a deep seabed permit.

"(b) Amount of tax.

"The amount of the tax imposed by subsection (a) on any removal shall be 3.75 percent of the imputed value of the resource so removed.

"(c) Liability for tax.

"The tax imposed by subsection (a) shall be paid by the person to whom the deep seabed permit is issued.

"(d) Time for paying tax.

"The time for paying the tax imposed by subsection (a) shall be the time prescribed by the Secretary by regulations. The time so prescribed with respect to any removal shall be not earlier than the earlier of—

"(1) the commercial use of, or the sale or disposition of, any portion of the resource so removed, or

"(2) the day which is 12 months after the date of the removal of the resource."

Effective Date Effective 8/5/97.

[¶ 3258]   Code Sec.[1] 4496.   Relealed.

[Endnote Code Sec. 4496]

Code Sec. 4496 was repealed as part of the repeal of Subchapter F, of Chapter 36, of Subtitle D, by Sec. 1432(b)(1) of the Taxpayer Relief Act of 1997, H.R. 2014, date of enactment, which struck out:

1. "SEC. 4496. DEFINITIONS.

"(a) Deep seabed permit.

"For purposes of this subchapter, the term 'deep seabed permit' means a permit issued under title I of the Deep Seabed Hard Minerals Resources Act.

"(b) Hard mineral resource.

"For purposes of this subchapter, the term 'hard mineral resource' means any deposit or accretion on, or just below, the surface of the deep seabed of nodules which contain one or more minerals, at least one of which is manganese, nickel, cobalt, or copper.

"(c) Deep seabed.

"For purposes of this subchapter, the term 'deep seabed' means the seabed, and the subsoil thereof to a depth of 10 meters, lying seaward of, and outside—

"(1) the Continental Shelf of any nation; and

"(2) any area of national resource jurisdiction of any foreign nation, if such area extends beyond the Continental Shelf of such nation and such jurisdiction is recognized by the United States.

"(d) Continental Shelf.

"For purposes of this subchapter, the term 'Continental Shelf' means—

"(1) the seabed and subsoil of the submarine areas adjacent to the coast but outside the area of the territorial sea, to a depth of 200 meters or, beyond that limit, to where the depth of the superjacent waters admits of the exploitation of the natural resources of such areas; and

"(2) the seabed and subsoil of similar submarine areas adjacent to the coasts of islands."

Effective Date Effective 8/5/97.

[¶ 3259]   Code Sec.[1] 4497.   Repealed.

[Endnote Code Sec. 4497]

Code Sec. 4497 was repealed as part of the repeal of Subchapter F, of Chapter 36, of Subtitle D, by Sec. 1432(b)(1) of the Taxpayer Relief Act of 1997, H.R. 2014, date of enactment, which struck out:

1. "SEC. 4497. IMPUTED VALUE.

"(a) In general.

"For purposes of this subchapter, the term 'imputed value' means, with respect to any hard mineral resource, 20 percent of the fair market value of the commercially recoverable metals and minerals contained in such resource. Such fair market value shall be determined—

"(1) as of the date of the removal of the hard mineral resource from the deep seabed; and

"(2) as if the metals and minerals contained in such resource were separated from such resource and were in the most basic form for which there is a readily ascertainable market price.

"(b) Commercial recoverability.

"(1) Manganese, nickel, cobalt, and copper. For purposes of subsection (a), manganese, nickel, cobalt, and copper shall be treated as commercially recoverable.

"(2) Minimum quantities and percentages. The Secretary may by regulations prescribe for each metal or mineral quantities or percentages below which the metal or mineral shall be treated as not commercially recoverable.

"(c) Suspension of tax with respect to certain metals and minerals held for later processing.

"(1) Election. The permittee may, in such manner and at such time as may be prescribed by regulations, elect to have the application of the tax suspended with respect to one or more commercially recoverable metals or minerals in the resource which the permittee does not intend to process within one year of the date of extraction. Any metal or mineral affected by such election shall not be taken into account in determining the imputed value of the resource at the time of its removal from the deep seabed. Any suspension under this paragraph with respect to a metal or mineral shall be permanent unless there is a redetermination affecting such metal or mineral under paragraph (2).

"(2) Later computation of tax. If the permittee processes any metal or mineral affected by the election under paragraph (1), or if he sells any portion of the resource containing such a metal or mineral, then the amount of the tax under section 4495 shall be redetermined as if there had been no suspension under paragraph (1) with respect to such metal or mineral. In any such case there shall be added to the increase in tax determined under the preceding sentence an amount equal to the interest (at the underpayment rate established under section 6621) on such increase for the period from the date prescribed for paying the tax on the resources (determined under section 4495(d)) to the date of the processing or sale.

"(d) Determinations of value.

"All determinations of value necessary for the application of this subchapter shall be made by the Secretary (after consultation with other appropriate Federal officials) on the basis of the best available information. Such determinations shall be made under procedures established by the Secretary by regulations."

Effective Date Effective 8/5/97.

[¶ 3260]   Code Sec.¹ 4498.   Repealed.

[Endnote Code Sec. 4498]
   Code Sec. 4498 was repealed as part of the repeal of Subchapter F, of Chapter 36, of Subtitle D, by Sec. 1432(b)(1) of the Taxpayer Relief Act of 1997, H.R. 2014, date of enactment, which struck out:
   1. "SEC. 4498. TERMINATION.
"(a) General rule.
   "The tax imposed by section 4495 shall not apply to any removal from the deep seabed after the earlier of—
   "(1) the date on which an international deep seabed treaty takes effect with respect to the United States, or
   "(2) the date 10 years after the date of the enactment of this subchapter. [Note: 8/5/97 was June 28, 1980]
"(b) International deep seabed treaty.
   "For purposes of subsection (a), the term 'international deep seabed treaty' means any treaty which—
   "(1) is adopted by a United Nations Conference on the Law of the Sea, and
   "(2) requires contributions to an international fund for the sharing of revenues from deep seabed mining."
Effective Date Effective 8/5/97.

[¶ 3261]   Code Sec. 4681.   Imposition of tax.

   (a) General rule. There is hereby imposed a tax on—

   (1) any ozone-depleting chemical sold or used by the manufacturer, producer, or importer thereof, and

   (2) any imported taxable product sold or used by the importer thereof.

   (b) Amount of tax.

   (1) Ozone-depleting chemicals.

   (A) In general. The amount of the tax imposed by subsection (a) on each pound of ozone-depleting chemical shall be an amount equal to—

   (i) the base tax amount, multiplied by

   (ii) the ozone-depletion factor for such chemical.

   ¹(B) Base tax amount. The base tax amount for purposes of subparagraph (A) with respect to any sale or use during any calendar year after 1995 shall be $5.35 increased by 45 cents for each year after 1995.

* * * * * * * * * * * *

[Endnote Code Sec. 4681]
   Matter in *italics* in Code Sec. 4681(b)(1)(B) added by Sec. 1432(c)(1) of the Taxpayer Relief Act of 1997, H.R. 2014, 8/5/97, which struck out:
   1. "(B) Base tax amount. The base tax amount for purposes of subparagraph (A) with respect to any sale or use during a calendar year before 1996 with respect to any ozone-depleting chemical is the amount determined under the following table for such calendar year:

Calendar year:	Base tax amount
1993	3.35
1994	4.35
1995	5.35

   "(C) Base tax amount for later years. The base tax amount for purposes of subparagraph (A) with respect to any sale or use of an ozone-depleting chemical during a calendar year after the last year specified in the table under subparagraph (B) applicable to such chemical shall be the base tax amount for such last year increased by 45 cents for each year after such last year."
Effective Date Effective 8/5/97.

[¶ 3262]   Code Sec. 4682.   Definitions and special rules.

* * * * * * * * * * *

(d) Exceptions.

(1) **Recycling.** No tax shall be imposed by section 4681 on any ozone-depleting chemical which is diverted or recovered in the United States as part of a recycling process (and not as part of the original manufacturing or production process), or on any [1]*recycled Halon-1301 or recycled Halon-2402* imported from any country which is a signatory to the Montreal Protocol on Substances that Deplete the Ozone Layer.

* * * * * * * * * * *

[2]*(g) Chemicals used as propellants in metered-dose inhalers.*

(1) Exemption from tax.

(A) In general. No tax shall be imposed by section 4681 on—

(i) any use of any substance as a propellant in metered-dose inhalers, or

(ii) any qualified sale by the manufacturer, producer, or importer of any substance.

(B) Qualified sale. For purposes of subparagraph (A), the term "qualified sale" means any sale by the manufacturer, producer, or importer of any substance—

(i) for use by the purchaser as a propellant in metered dose inhalers, or

(ii) for resale by the purchaser to a 2d purchaser for such use by the 2d purchaser.

The preceding sentence shall apply only if the manufacturer, producer, and importer, and the 1st and 2d purchasers (if any) meet such registration requirements as may be prescribed by the Secretary.

(2) Overpayments. If any substance on which tax was paid under this subchapter is used by any person as a propellant in metered-dose inhalers, credit or refund without interest shall be allowed to such person in an amount equal to the tax so paid. Amounts payable under the preceding sentence with respect to uses during the taxable year shall be treated as described in section 34(a) for such year unless claim thereof has been timely filed under this paragraph.

* * * * * * * * * * *

[For analysis, see ¶ 2226. For committee reports, see ¶ 5053.]

[Endnote Code Sec. 4682]

Matter in *italics* in Code Sec. 4862(d)(1) added by Sec. 903(a) of the Taxpayer Relief Act of 1997, H.R. 2014, 8/5/97, which struck out:

1. "recycled halon"

Effective Date (Sec. 903(b), H.R. 2014, 8/5/97) effective 8/5/97.

Matter in *italics* in Code Sec. 4682(g) added by Sec. 1432(c)(2), H.R. 2014, 8/5/97, which struck out:

2. "(g) Phase-in of tax on certain substances.

"(1) Treatment for 1990.

"(A) Halons. The term 'ozone-depleting chemical' shall not include halon-1211, halon-1301, or halon-2402 with respect to any sale or use during 1990.

"(B) Chemicals used in rigid foam insulation. No tax shall be imposed by section 4681—

"(i) on the use during 1990 of any substance in the manufacture of rigid foam insulation,

"(ii) on the sale during 1990 by the manufacturer, producer, or importer of any substance—

"(I) for use by the purchaser in the manufacture of rigid foam insulation, or

"(II) for resale by the purchaser to a second purchaser for such use by the second purchaser, or

"(iii) on the sale or use during 1990 by the importer of any rigid foam insulation.

Clause (ii) shall apply only if the manufacturer, producer, and importer, and the 1st and 2d purchasers (if any) meet such registration requirements as may be prescribed by the Secretary.

"(2) Treatment for 1991, 1992, and 1993.

"(A) Halons. The tax imposed by section 4681 during 1991, 1992, or 1993 by reason of the treatment of halon-1211, halon-1301, and halon-2402 as ozone-depleting chemicals shall be the applicable percentage (determined under the following table) of the amount of such tax which would (but for this subparagraph) be imposed.

In the case of	The applicable percentage in the case of sales or use during 1993 is:
Halon-1211	2.49
Halon-1301	0.75
Halon-2402	1.24.

"(B) Chemicals used in rigid foam insulation. In the case of a sale or use during 1991, 1992, or 1993 on which no tax would have been imposed by reason of paragraph (1)(B) had such sale or use occurred during 1990, the tax imposed by section 4681 shall be the applicable percentage (determined in accordance with the following table) of the amount of such tax which would (but for this subparagraph) be imposed.

In the case of sales or use during:	The applicable percentage is:
1991	18
1992	15
1993	7.46.

"(3) Overpayments with respect to chemicals used in rigid foam insulation. If any substance on which tax was paid under this subchapter is used during 1990, 1991, 1992, or 1993 by any person in the manufacture of rigid foam insulation, credit or refund (without interest) shall be allowed to such person an amount equal to the excess of—

"(A) the tax paid under this subchapter on such substance, over

"(B) the tax (if any) which would be imposed by section 4681 if such substance were used for such use by the manufacturer, producer, or importer thereof on the date of its use by such person.

Amounts payable under the preceding sentence with respect to uses during the taxable year shall be treated as described in section 34(a) for such year unless claim therefor has been timely filed under this paragraph.

"(4) Chemicals used as propellants in metered-dose inhalers.

"(A) Tax-exempt.

"(i) In general. No tax shall be imposed by section 4681 on—

"(I) any use of any substance as a propellant in metered-dose inhalers, or

"(II) any qualified sale by the manufacturer, producer, or importer of any substance.

"(ii) Qualified sale. For purposes of clause (i), the term 'qualified sale' means any sale by the manufacturer, producer, or importer of any substance—

"(I) for use by the purchaser as a propellant in metered dose inhalers, or

"(II) for resale by the purchaser to a 2d purchaser for such use by the 2d purchaser.

The preceding sentence shall apply only if the manufacturer, producer and importer, and the 1st and 2d purchasers (if any) meet such registration requirements as may be prescribed by the Secretary.

"(B) Overpayments. If any substance on which tax was paid under this subchapter is used by any person as a propellant in metered-dose inhalers, credit or refund without interest shall be allowed to such person in an amount equal to the tax so paid. Amounts payable under the preceding sentence with respect to uses during the taxable year shall be treated as described in section 34(a) for such year unless claim thereof has been timely filed under this subparagraph.

"(5) Treatment of methyl chloroform. The tax imposed by section 4681 during 1993 by reason of the treatment of methyl chloroform as an ozone-depleting chemical shall be 63.02 percent of the amount of such tax which would (but for this paragraph) be imposed."

Effective Date Effective 8/5/97.

[¶ 3263] Code Sec. 4947. Application of taxes to certain nonexempt trusts.

* * * * * * * * * * * *

(b) Special rules.

* * * * * * * * * * * * *

[1]*(4) Section 507. The provisions of section 507(a) shall not apply to a trust which is described in subsection (a)(2) by reason of a distribution of qualified employer securities (as defined in section 664(g)(4)) to an employee stock ownership plan (as defined in section 4975(e)(7)) in a qualified gratuitous transfer (as defined by section 664(g)).*

[Endnote Code Sec. 4947]

Code Sec. 4947(b)(4), in *italics*, was added by Sec. 1530(c)(9) of the Taxpayer Relief Act of 1997, H.R. 2014, 8/5/97.

1. added para. (b)(4)

Effective Date (Sec. 1530(d), H.R. 2014, 8/5/97) effective for transfers made by trusts to, or for the use of, an employee stock ownership plan after 8/5/97.

[¶ 3264] Code Sec. 4962.   Abatement of first tier taxes in certain cases.

(a) **General rule.** If it is established to the satisfaction of the Secretary that—

(1) a taxable event was due to reasonable cause and not to willful neglect, and

(2) such event was corrected within the correction period for such event,

then any qualified first tier tax imposed with respect to such event (including interest) shall not be assessed and, if assessed, the assessment shall be abated and, if collected, shall be credited or refunded as an overpayment.

(b) **Qualified first tier tax.** For purposes of this section, the term "qualified first tier tax" means any first tier tax imposed by ¹*subchapter A, C, or D* of this chapter, except that such term shall not include the tax imposed by section 4941(a) (relating to initial tax on self-dealing).

* * * * * * * * * * * *

[For analysis, see ¶ 2409. For committee reports, see ¶ 5384.]

[Endnote Code Sec. 4962]

Matter in *italics* in Code Sec. 4962(b) added by Sec. 1603(a) of the Taxpayer Relief Act of 1997, H.R. 2014, 8/5/97, which struck out:

1. "subchapter A or C"

Effective Date (Sec. 1603(c), H.R. 2014, 8/5/97) effective for excess benefit transactions occurring on or after 9/14/95, except as provided in P.L. 104-168, Sec. 1311(d)(2), which reads as follows:

"(2) Binding contracts. The amendments referred to in paragraph (1) shall not apply to any benefit arising from a transactions pursuant to any written contract which was binding on September, 13, 1995, and at all times thereafter before such transaction occurred."

[¶ 3265] Code Sec. 4972.   Tax on nondeductible contributions to qualified employer plans.

* * * * * * * * * * * *

(c) **Nondeductible contributions.** For purposes of this section—

(1) **In general.** The term "nondeductible contributions" means, with respect to any qualified employer plan, the sum of—

(A) the excess (if any) of—

(i) the amount contributed for the taxable year by the employer to or under such plan, over

(ii) the amount allowable as a deduction under section 404 for such contributions (determined without regard to subsection (e) thereof), and

(B) the amount determined under this subsection for the preceding taxable year reduced by the sum of—

(i) the portion of the amount so determined returned to the employer during the taxable year, and

(ii) the portion of the amount so determined deductible under section 404 for the taxable year (determined without regard to subsection (e) thereof).

* * * * * * * * * * * *

(6) **Exceptions.** In determining the amount of nondeductible contributions for any taxable year, there shall not be taken into account—

(A) contributions that would be deductible under section 404(a)(1)(D) if the plan had more than 100 participants if—

(i) the plan is covered under section 4021 of the Employee Retirement Income Security Act of 1974, and

(ii) the plan is terminated under section 4041(b) of such Act on or before the last day of the taxable year, and

[1](B) *so much of the contributions to 1 or more defined contribution plans which are not deductible when contributed solely because of section 404(a)(7) as does not exceed the greater of—*

    (i) *the amount of contributions not in excess of 6 percent of compensation (within the meaning of section 404(a)) paid or accrued (during the taxable year for which the contributions were made) to beneficiaries under the plans, or*

    (ii) *the sum of—*

        (I) *the amount of contributions described in section 401(m)(4)(A), plus*

        (II) *the amount of contributions described in section 402(g)(3)(A).*

If 1 or more defined benefit plans were taken into account in determining the amount allowable as a deduction under section 404 for contributions to any defined contribution plan, subparagraph (B) shall apply only if such defined benefit plans are described in section 404(a)(1)(D). For purposes of subparagraph (B), the deductible limits under section 404(a)(7) shall first be applied to amounts contributed to a defined benefit plan and then to amounts described in subparagraph (B).

* * * * * * * * * * *

[For analysis, see ¶ 911. For committee reports, see ¶ 5313.]

[Endnote Code Sec. 4972]

  Matter in *italics* in Code Sec. 4972(c)(6)(B) added by Sec. 1507(a) of the Taxpayer Relief Act of 1997, H.R. 2014, 8/5/97, which struck out:

  1. "(B) contributions to 1 or more defined contribution plans which are not deductible when contributed solely because of section 404(a)(7), but only to the extent such contributions do not exceed 6 percent of compensation (within the meaning of section 404(a)) paid or accrued (during the taxable year for which the contributions were made) to beneficiaries under the plans."

Effective Date (Sec. 1507(b), H.R. 2014, 8/5/97) effective for tax. yrs. begin. after 12/31/97.

[¶ 3266] Code Sec. 4973. Tax on excess contributions to individual retirement accounts, medical savings accounts, certain section 403(b) contracts, and certain individual retirement annuities.

  (a) Tax imposed. In the case of—

    (1) an individual retirement account (within the meaning of section 408(a)),

    (2) a medical savings account (within the meaning of section 220(d)),[1]

    (3) an individual retirement annuity (within the meaning of section 408(b)), a custodial account treated as an annuity contract under section 403(b)(7)(A) (relating to custodial accounts for regulated investment company stock), [2]*or*

    [3]*(4) an education individual retirement account (as defined in section 530),*

there is imposed for each taxable year a tax in an amount equal to 6 percent of the amount of the excess contributions to such individual's accounts or annuities (determined as of the close of the taxable year). The amount of such tax for any taxable year shall not exceed 6 percent of the value of the account or annuity (determined as of the close of the taxable year). In the case of an endowment contract described in section 408(b), the tax imposed by this section does not apply to any amount allocable to life, health, accident, or other insurance under such contract. The tax imposed by this subsection shall be paid by such individual.

* * * * * * * * * * *

  (d) Excess contributions to medical savings accounts. For purposes of this section, in the case of medical savings accounts (within the meaning of section 220(d)), the term "excess contributions" means the sum of—

    (1) the aggregate amount contributed for the taxable year to the accounts (other than rollover contributions described in section 220(f)(5)) which is neither excludable from gross income under section 106(b) nor allowable as a deduction under section 220 for such year, and

    (2) the amount determined under this subsection for the preceding taxable year, reduced by the sum of—

(A) the distributions out of the accounts which were included in gross income under section 220(f)(2), and

(B) the excess (if any) of—

(i) the maximum amount allowable as a deduction under section 220(b)(1) (determined without regard to section 106(b)) for the taxable year, over

(ii) the amount contributed to the accounts for the taxable year.

For purposes of this subsection, any contribution which is distributed out of the medical savings account in a distribution to which section 220(f)(3) [4-B]*or section 138(c)(3)* applies shall be treated as an amount not contributed.

[5]*(e) Excess contributions to education individual retirement accounts. For purposes of this section—*

(1) In general. In the case of education individual retirement accounts maintained for the benefit of any 1 beneficiary, the term "excess contributions" means—

(A) the amount by which the amount contributed for the taxable year to such accounts exceeds $500, and

(B) any amount contributed to such account for any taxable year if any amount is contributed during such year to a qualified State tuition program for the benefit of such beneficiary.

(2) Special rules. For purposes of paragraph (1), the following contributions shall not be taken into account:

(A) Any contribution which is distributed out of the education individual retirement account in a distribution to which section 530(d)(4)(C) applies.

(B) Any contribution described in section 530(b)(2)(B) to a qualified State tuition program.

(C) Any rollover contribution.

[6]*(f) Excess contributions to Roth IRAs. For purposes of this section, in the case of contributions to a Roth IRA (within the meaning of section 408A(b)), the term "excess contributions" means the sum of—*

(1) the excess (if any) of—

(A) the amount contributed for the taxable year to such accounts (other than a qualified rollover contribution described in section 408A(e)), over

(B) the amount allowable as a contribution under sections 408A (c)(2) and (c)(3), and

(2) the amount determined under this subsection for the preceding taxable year, reduced by the sum of—

(A) the distributions out of the accounts for the taxable year, and

(B) the excess (if any) of the maximum amount allowable as a contribution under sections 408A (c)(2) and (c)(3) for the taxable year over the amount contributed to the accounts for the taxable year.

For purposes of this subsection, any contribution which is distributed from a Roth IRA in a distribution described in section 408(d)(4) shall be treated as an amount not contributed.

[For analysis, see ¶ 301, ¶ 403, ¶ 1201. For committee reports, see ¶ 5005, ¶ 5016, ¶ 5501.]

[Endnote Code Sec. 4973]

Matter in *italics* in Code Sec. 4973(a)(2), Code Sec. 4973(a)(3), and Code Sec. 4973(a)(4), added by Sec. 213(d)(1) of the Taxpayer Relief Act of 1997, H.R. 2014, 8/5/97, which struck out:

1. "or"
2. added matter in para. (a)(3)
3. added para. (a)(4)

Effective Date (Sec. 213(f), H.R. 2014, 8/5/97) effective for tax. yrs. begin. after 12/31/97.

H.R. 2015. Matter in *italics* in Code Sec. 4973(d) added by Sec. 4006(b)(1) of the Balanced Budget Act of 1997, H.R. 2015, 8/5/97.

4_B. added matter in subsec. (d) [H.R. 2015]

Effective Date (Sec. 4006(c), H.R. 2015, 8/5/97) effective for tax. yrs. begin. after 12/31/98.

Code Sec. 4973(e) in *italics* was added by Sec. 213(d)(2), H.R. 2014, 8/5/97:
  5. added subsection (e)
Effective Date (Sec. 213(f), H.R. 2014, 8/5/97) effective for tax. yrs. begin. after 12/31/97.

Code Sec. 4973(f), in *italics*, was added by Sec. 302(b), H.R. 2014, 8/5/97.
  6. added subsection (f)
Effective Date (Sec. 302(f), H.R. 2014, 8/5/97) effective for tax. yrs. begin. after 12/31/97.

[¶ 3267] Code Sec. 4975. Tax on prohibited transactions.

(a) **Initial taxes on disqualified person.** There is hereby imposed a tax on each prohibited transaction. The rate of tax shall be equal to [1]*15 percent* of the amount involved with respect to the prohibited transaction for each year (or part thereof) in the taxable period. The tax imposed by this subsection shall be paid by any disqualified person who participates in the prohibited transaction (other than a fiduciary acting only as such).

(b) **Additional taxes on disqualified person.** In any case in which an initial tax is imposed by subsection (a) on a prohibited transaction and the transaction is not corrected within the taxable period, there is hereby imposed a tax equal to 100 percent of the amount involved. The tax imposed by this subsection shall be paid by any disqualified person who participated in the prohibited transaction (other than a fiduciary acting only as such).

(c) **Prohibited transaction.**

(1) **General rule.** For purposes of this section, the term "prohibited transaction" means any direct or indirect—

(A) sale or exchange, or leasing, of any property between a plan and a disqualified person;

(B) lending of money or other extension of credit between a plan and a disqualified person;

(C) furnishing of goods, services, or facilities between a plan and a disqualified person;

(D) transfer to, or use by or for the benefit of, a disqualified person of the income or assets of a plan;

(E) act by a disqualified person who is a fiduciary whereby he deals with the income or assets of a plan in his own interest or for his own account; or

(F) receipt of any consideration for his own personal account by any disqualified person who is a fiduciary from any party dealing with the plan in connection with a transaction involving the income or assets of the plan.

(2) **Special exemption.** The Secretary shall establish an exemption procedure for purposes of this subsection. Pursuant to such procedure, he may grant a conditional or unconditional exemption of any disqualified person or transaction, orders of disqualified persons or transactions, from all or part of the restrictions imposed by paragraph (1) of this subsection. Action under this subparagraph may be taken only after consultation and coordination with the Secretary of Labor. The Secretary may not grant an exemption under this paragraph unless he finds that such exemption is—

(A) administratively feasible,

(B) in the interests of the plan and of its participants and beneficiaries, and

(C) protective of the rights of participants and beneficiaries of the plan.

Before granting an exemption under this paragraph, the Secretary shall require adequate notice to be given to interested persons and shall publish notice in the Federal Register of the pendency of such exemption and shall afford interested persons an opportunity to present views. No exemption may be granted under this paragraph with respect to a transaction described in subparagraph (E) or (F) of paragraph (1) unless the Secretary affords an opportunity for a hearing and makes a determination on the record with respect to the findings required under subparagraphs (A), (B), and (C) of this paragraph, except that in lieu of such hearing the Secretary may accept any record made by the Secretary of Labor with respect to an application for exemption under section 408(a) of title I of the Employee Retirement Income Security Act of 1974.

(3) Special rule for individual retirement accounts. An individual for whose benefit an individual retirement account is established and his beneficiaries shall be exempt for [sic from] the tax imposed by this section with respect to any transaction concerning such account (which would otherwise be taxable under this section) if, with respect to such transaction, the account ceases to be an individual retirement account by reason of the application of section 408(e)(2)(A) or if section 408(e)(4) applies to such account.

(4) Special rule for medical savings accounts. An individual for whose benefit a medical savings account (within the meaning of section 220(d)) is established shall be exempt from the tax imposed by this section with respect to any transaction concerning such account (which would otherwise be taxable under this section) [2]*if section 220(e)(2) applies to such transaction.*

CAUTION.   Para. (c)(5) is effective for tax. yrs. begin. after 12/31/97.

[3]*(5) Special rule for education individual retirement accounts. An individual for whose benefit an education individual retirement account is established and any contributor to such account shall be exempt from the tax imposed by this section with respect to any transaction concerning such account (which would otherwise be taxable under this section) if section 530(d) applies with respect to such transaction.*

(d) Exemptions.

CAUTION.   The introductory language to subsec. (d), following, is effective for tax. yrs. begin. before 1/1/98. For the introductory language to subsec. (d) effective for tax. yrs. begin. after 12/31/97, see below.

The prohibitions provided in subsection (c) shall not apply to—

CAUTION.   The introductory language to subsec. (d), following, is effective for tax. yrs. begin. after 12/31/97. For the introductory language to subsec. (d) effective for tax. yrs. begin. before 1/1/98, see below.

[4]*Except as provided in subsection (f)(6), the prohibitions* provided in subsection (c) shall not apply to—

(1) any loan made by the plan to a disqualified person who is a participant or beneficiary of the plan if such loan—

(A) is available to all such participants or beneficiaries on a reasonably equivalent basis,

(B) is not made available to highly compensated employees (within the meaning of section 414(q)) in an amount greater than the amount made available to other employees,

(C) is made in accordance with specific provisions regarding such loans set forth in the plan,

(D) bears a reasonable rate of interest, and

(E) is adequately secured;

(2) any contract, or reasonable arrangement, made with a disqualified person for office space, or legal, accounting, or other services necessary for the establishment or operation of the plan, if no more than reasonable compensation is paid therefor;

(3) any loan to a leveraged employee stock ownership plan (as defined in subsection (e)(7)), if—

(A) such loan is primarily for the benefit of participants and beneficiaries of the plan, and

(B) such loan is at a reasonable rate of interest, and any collateral which is given to a disqualified person by the plan consists only of qualifying employer securities (as defined in subsection (e)(8));

(4) the investment of all or part of a plan's assets in deposits which bear a reasonable interest rate in a bank or similar financial institution supervised by the United States or a State, if such bank or other institution is a fiduciary of such plan and if—

(A) the plan covers only employees of such bank or other institution and employees of affiliates of such bank or other institution, or

(B) such investment is expressly authorized by a provision of the plan or by a fiduciary (other than such bank or institution or affiliates thereof) who is expressly empowered by the plan to so instruct the trustee with respect to such investment;

(5) any contract for life insurance, health insurance, or annuities with one or more insurers which are qualified to do business in a State if the plan pays no more than adequate consideration, and if each such insurer or insurers is—

(A) the employer maintaining the plan, or

(B) a disqualified person which is wholly owned (directly or indirectly) by the employer establishing the plan, or by any person which is a disqualified person with respect to the plan, but only if the total premiums and annuity considerations written by such insurers for life insurance, health insurance, or annuities for all plans (and their employers) with respect to which such insurers are disqualified persons (not including premiums or annuity considerations written by the employer maintaining the plan) do not exceed 5 percent of the total premiums and annuity considerations written for all lines of insurance in that year by such insurers (not including premiums or annuity considerations written by the employer maintaining the plan);

(6) the provision of any ancillary service by a bank or similar financial institution supervised by the United States or a State, if such service is provided at not more than reasonable compensation, if such bank or other institution is a fiduciary of such plan, and if—

(A) such bank or similar financial institution has adopted adequate internal safeguards which assure that the provision of such ancillary service is consistent with sound banking and financial practice, as determined by Federal or State supervisory authority, and

(B) the extent to which such ancillary service is provided is subject to specific guidelines issued by such bank or similar financial institution (as determined by the Secretary after consultation with Federal and State supervisory authority), and under such guidelines the bank or similar financial institution does not provide such ancillary service—

(i) in an excessive or unreasonable manner, and

(ii) in a manner that would be inconsistent with the best interests of participants and beneficiaries of employee benefit plans;

(7) the exercise of a privilege to convert securities, to the extent provided in regulations of the Secretary, but only if the plan receives no less than adequate consideration pursuant to such conversion;

(8) any transaction between a plan and a common or collective trust fund or pooled investment fund maintained by a disqualified person which is a bank or trust company supervised by a State or Federal agency or between a plan and a pooled investment fund of an insurance company qualified to do business in a State if—

(A) the transaction is a sale or purchase of an interest in the fund,

(B) the bank, trust company, or insurance company receives not more than reasonable compensation, and

(C) such transaction is expressly permitted by the instrument under which the plan is maintained, or by a fiduciary (other than the bank, trust company, or insurance company, or an affiliate thereof) who has authority to manage and control the assets of the plan;

(9) receipt by a disqualified person of any benefit to which he may be entitled as a participant or beneficiary in the plan, so long as the benefit is computed and paid on a basis which is consistent with the terms of the plan as applied to all other participants and beneficiaries;

(10) receipt by a disqualified person of any reasonable compensation for services rendered, or for the reimbursement of expenses properly and actually incurred, in the performance of his duties with the plan, but no person so serving who already receives full-time pay from an employer or an association of employers, whose employees are participants in the plan or from an employee organization whose members are participants in such plan shall receive compensation from such fund, except for reimbursement of expenses properly and actually incurred;

(11) service by a disqualified person as a fiduciary in addition to being an officer, employee, agent, or other representative of a disqualified person;

(12) the making by a fiduciary of a distribution of the assets of the trust in accordance with the terms of the plan if such assets are distributed in the same manner as provided under section 4044 of title IV of the Employee Retirement Income Security Act of 1974 (relating to allocation of assets);

(13) any transaction which is exempt from section 406 of such Act by reason of section 408(e) of such Act (or which would be so exempt if such section 406 applied to such transaction) or which is exempt from section 406 of such Act by reason of section 408(b)(12) of such Act;

(14) any transaction required or permitted under part 1 of subtitle E of title IV or section 4223 of the Employee Retirement Income Security Act of 1974, but this paragraph shall not apply with respect to the application of subsection (c)(1)(E) or (F); or[5]

CAUTION. Para. (d)(15) and the flush paragraph, following, are effective for tax. yrs. begin. before 1/1/98. For para. (d)(15), effective for tax. yrs. begin. after 12/31/97, see below.

(15) a merger of multiemployer plans, or the transfer of assets or liabilities between multiemployer plans, determined by the Pension Benefit Guaranty Corporation to meet the requirements of section 4231 of such Act, but this paragraph shall not apply with respect to the application of subsection (c)(1)(E) or (F).

The exemptions provided by this subsection (other than paragraphs (9) and (12)) shall not apply to any transaction with respect to a trust described in section 401(a) which is part of a plan providing contributions or benefits for employees some or all of whom are owner-employees (as defined in section 401(c)(3)) in which a plan directly or indirectly lends any part of the corpus or income of the plan to, pays any compensation for personal services rendered to the plan to, or acquires for the plan any property from or sells any property to, any such owner-employee, a member of the family (as defined in section 267(c)(4)) of any such owner-employee, or a corporation controlled by any such owner-employee through the ownership, directly or indirectly, of 50 percent or more of the total combined voting power of all classes of stock entitled to vote or 50 percent or more of the total value of shares of all classes of stock of the corporation. For purposes of the preceding sentence, a shareholder-employee (as defined in section 1379, as in effect on the day before the date of the enactment of the Subchapter S Revision Act of 1982), a participant or beneficiary of an individual retirement account or an individual retirement annuity (as defined in section 408), and an employer or association of employees which establishes such an account or annuity under section 408(c) shall be deemed to be an owner-employee.

CAUTION. Para. (d)(15) and the flush paragraph, following, are effective for tax. yrs. begin. after 12/31/97. For para. (d)(15), effective for tax. yrs. begin. before 1/1/98, see above.

(15) a merger of multiemployer plans, or the transfer of assets or liabilities between multiemployer plans, determined by the Pension Benefit Guaranty Corporation to meet the requirements of section 4231 of such Act, but this paragraph shall not apply with respect to the application of subsection (c)(1)(E) or (F).

CAUTION. The flush language for subsec. (d), following, is repealed for tax. yrs. begin. after 12/31/97.

The exemptions provided by this subsection (other than paragraphs (9) and (12)) shall not apply to any transaction with respect to a trust described in section 401(a) which is part of a plan providing contributions or benefits for employees some or all of whom are owner-employees (as defined in section 401(c)(3)) in which a plan directly or indirectly lends any part of the corpus or income of the plan to, pays any compensation for personal services rendered to the plan to, or acquires for the plan any property from or sells any property to, any such owner-employee, a member of the family (as defined in section 267(c)(4)) of any such owner-employee, or a corporation controlled by any such owner-employee through the ownership, directly or indirectly, of 50 percent or more of the total combined voting power of all classes of stock entitled to vote or 50 percent or more of the total value of shares of all classes of stock of the corporation. For purposes of the preceding sentence, a shareholder-employee (as defined in section

1379, as in effect on the day before the date of the enactment of the Subchapter S Revision Act of 1982), a participant or beneficiary of an individual retirement account or an individual retirement annuity (as defined in section 408), and an employer or association of employees which establishes such an account or annuity under section 408(c) shall be deemed to be an owner-employee.

(e) **Definitions.**

(1) **Plan.** For purposes of this section, the term "plan" means—

(A) a trust described in section 401(a) which forms a part of a plan, or a plan described in section 403(a), which trust or plan is exempt from tax under section 501(a),

(B) an individual retirement account described in section 408(a),

(C) an individual retirement annuity described in section 408(b),

CAUTION. Subparas. (e)(1)(D) and (E), following, are effective for tax. yrs. begin. before 1/1/98. For subparas. (e)(1)(D)-(F), effective for tax. yrs. begin. after 12/31/97, see below.

(D) a medical savings account described in section 220(d), or

(E) a trust, plan, account, or annuity which, at any time, has been determined by the Secretary to be described in any preceding subparagraph of this paragraph.

CAUTION. Subparas. (e)(1)(D)-(F), following, are effective for tax. yrs. begin. after 12/31/97. For subparas. (e)(1)(D) and (E), effective for tax. yrs. begin. before 1/1/98, see above.

(D) a medical savings account described in section 220(d),[6]

[7](E) an education individual retirement account described in section 530, or

[8](F) a trust, plan, account, or annuity which, at any time, has been determined by the Secretary to be described in any preceding subparagraph of this paragraph.

(2) **Disqualified person.** For purposes of this section, the term "disqualified person" means a person who is—

(A) a fiduciary;

(B) a person providing services to the plan;

(C) an employer any of whose employees are covered by the plan;

(D) an employee organization any of whose members are covered by the plan;

(E) an owner, direct or indirect, of 50 percent or more of—

(i) the combined voting power of all classes of stock entitled to vote or the total value of shares of all classes of stock of a corporation,

(ii) the capital interest or the profits interest of a partnership, or

(iii) the beneficial interest of a trust or unincorporated enterprise,

which is an employer or an employee organization described in subparagraph (C) or (D);

(F) a member of the family (as defined in paragraph (6)) of any individual described in subparagraph (A), (B), (C), or (E);

(G) a corporation, partnership, or trust or estate of which (or in which) 50 percent or more of—

(i) the combined voting power of all classes of stock entitled to vote or the total value of shares of all classes of stock of such corporation,

(ii) the capital interest or profits interest of such partnership, or

(iii) the beneficial interest of such trust or estate,

is owned directly or indirectly, or held by persons described in subparagraph (A), (B), (C), (D), or (E);

(H) an officer, director (or an individual having powers or responsibilities similar to those of officers or directors), a 10 percent or more shareholder, or a highly compensated employee (earning 10 percent or more of the yearly wages of an employer) of a person described in subparagraph (C), (D), (E), or (G); or

(I) a 10 percent or more (in capital or profits) partner or joint venturer of a person described in subparagraph (C), (D), (E), or (G).

The Secretary, after consultation and coordination with the Secretary of Labor or his delegate, may by regulation prescribe a percentage lower than 50 percent for subparagraphs (E) and (G) and lower than 10 percent for subparagraphs (H) and (I).

(3) Fiduciary. For purposes of this section, the term "fiduciary" means any person who—

(A) exercises any discretionary authority or discretionary control respecting management of such plan or exercises any authority or control respecting management or disposition of its assets,

(B) renders investment advice for a fee or other compensation, direct or indirect, with respect to any moneys or other property of such plan, or has any authority or responsibility to do so, or

(C) has any discretionary authority or discretionary responsibility in the administration of such plan.

Such term includes any person designated under section 405(c)(1)(B) of the Employee Retirement Income Security Act of 1974.

(4) Stockholdings. For purposes of paragraphs (2)(E)(i) and (G)(i) there shall be taken into account indirect stockholdings which would be taken into account under section 267(c), except that, for purposes of this paragraph, section 267(c)(4) shall be treated as providing that the members of the family of an individual are the members within the meaning of paragraph (6).

(5) Partnerships; trusts. For purposes of paragraphs (2)(E)(ii) and (iii), (G)(ii) and (iii), and (I) the ownership of profits or beneficial interests shall be determined in accordance with the rules for constructive ownership of stock provided in section 267(c) (other than paragraph (3) thereof), except that section 267(c)(4) shall be treated as providing that the members of the family of an individual are the members within the meaning of paragraph (6).

(6) Member of family. For purposes of paragraph (2)(F), the family of any individual shall include his spouse, ancestor, lineal descendant, and any spouse of a lineal descendant.

(7) Employee stock ownership plan. The term "employee stock ownership plan" means a defined contribution plan—

(A) which is a stock bonus plan which is qualified, or a stock bonus and a money purchase plan both of which are qualified under section 401(a), and which are designed to invest primarily in qualifying employer securities; and

(B) which is otherwise defined in regulations prescribed by the Secretary.

A plan shall not be treated as an employee stock ownership plan unless it meets the requirements of section 409(h), section 409(o), and, if applicable, section 409(n) [9]*and section 664(g)* and, if the employer has a registration-type class of securities (as defined in section 409(e)(4)), it meets the requirements of section 409(e).

(8) Qualifying employer security. The term "qualifying employer security" means any employer security within the meaning of section 409(1). If any moneys or other property of a plan are invested in shares of an investment company registered under the Investment Company Act of 1940, the investment shall not cause that investment company or that investment company's investment adviser or principal underwriter to be treated as a fiduciary or a disqualified person for purposes of this section, except when an investment company or its investment adviser or principal underwriter acts in connection with a plan covering employees of the investment company, its investment adviser, or its principal underwriter.

(9) Section made applicable to withdrawal liability payment funds. For purposes of this section—

(A) In general. The term "plan" includes a trust described in section 501(c)(22).

(B) Disqualified person. In the case of any trust to which this section applies by reason of subparagraph (A), the term "disqualified person" includes any person who is a disqualified person with respect to any plan to which such trust is permitted to make payments under section 4223 of the Employee Retirement Income Security Act of 1974.

(f) Other definitions and special rules. For purposes of this section—

(1) Joint and several liability. If more than one person is liable under subsection (a) or (b) with respect to any one prohibited transaction, all such persons shall be jointly and severally liable under such subsection with respect to such transaction.

(2) Taxable period. The term "taxable period" means, with respect to any prohibited transaction, the period beginning with the date on which the prohibited transaction occurs and ending on the earliest of—

(A) the date of mailing a notice of deficiency with respect to the tax imposed by subsection (a) under section 6212,

(B) the date on which the tax imposed by subsection (a) is assessed, or

(C) the date on which correction of the prohibited transaction is completed.

(3) Sale or exchange; encumbered property. A transfer of real or personal property by a disqualified person to a plan shall be treated as a sale or exchange if the property is subject to a mortgage or similar lien which the plan assumes or if it is subject to a mortgage or similar lien which a disqualified person placed on the property within the 10-year period ending on the date of the transfer.

(4) Amount involved. The term "amount involved" means, with respect to a prohibited transaction, the greater of the amount of money and the fair market value of the other property given or the amount of money and the fair market value of the other property received; except that, in the case of services described in paragraphs (2) and (10) of subsection (d) the amount involved shall be only the excess compensation. For purposes of the preceding sentence, the fair market value—

(A) in the case of the tax imposed by subsection (a), shall be determined as of the date on which the prohibited transaction occurs; and

(B) in the case of the tax imposed by subsection (b), shall be the highest fair market value during the taxable period.

(5) Correction. The terms "correction" and "correct" mean, with respect to a prohibited transaction, undoing the transaction to the extent possible, but in any case placing the plan in a financial position not worse than that in which it would be if the disqualified person were acting under the highest fiduciary standards.

CAUTION.   Para. (f)(6), following, is effective for tax. yrs. begin. after 12/31/97.

[10]*(6) Exemptions not to apply to certain transactions.*

(A) In general. In the case of a trust described in section 401(a) which is part of a plan providing contributions or benefits for employees some or all of whom are owner-employees (as defined in section 401(c)(3)), the exemptions provided by subsection (d) (other than paragraphs (9) and (12)) shall not apply to a transaction in which the plan directly or indirectly—

(i) lends any part of the corpus or income of the plan to,

(ii) pays any compensation for personal services rendered to the plan to, or

(iii) acquires for the plan any property from, or sells any property to, any such owner-employee, a member of the family (as defined in section 267(c)(4)) of any such owner-employee, or any corporation in which any such owner-employee owns, directly or indirectly, 50 percent or more of the total combined voting power of all classes of stock entitled to vote or 50 percent or more of the total value of shares of all classes of stock of the corporation.

(B) Special rules for shareholder-employees, etc.

(i) In general. For purposes of subparagraph (A), the following shall be treated as owner-employees:

(I) A shareholder-employee.

(II) A participant or beneficiary of an individual retirement plan (as defined in section 7701(a)(37)).

(III) An employer or association of employees which establishes such an individual retirement plan under section 408(c).

(ii) Exception for certain transactions involving shareholder- employees.—Subparagraph (A)(iii) shall not apply to a transaction which consists of a sale of employer securities to an employee stock ownership plan (as defined in subsection (e)(7)) by a share-

holder- employee, a member of the family (as defined in section 267(c)(4)) of such shareholder-employee, or a corporation in which such a shareholder-employee owns stock representing a 50 percent or greater interest described in subparagraph (A).

(C) Shareholder-employee. For purposes of subparagraph (B), the term "shareholder-employee" means an employee or officer of an S corporation who owns (or is considered as owning within the meaning of section 318(a)(1)) more than 5 percent of the outstanding stock of the corporation on any day during the taxable year of such corporation.

(g) **Application of section.** This section shall not apply—

(1) in the case of a plan to which a guaranteed benefit policy (as defined in section 401(b)(2)(B) of the Employee Retirement Income Security Act of 1974) is issued, to any assets of the insurance company, insurance service, or insurance organization merely because of its issuance of such policy;

(2) to a governmental plan (within the meaning of section 414(d)); or

(3) to a church plan (within the meaning of section 414(e)) with respect to which the election provided by section 410(d) has not been made.

In the case of a plan which invests in any security issued by an investment company registered under the Investment Company Act of 1940, the assets of such plan shall be deemed to include such security but shall not, by reason of such investment, be deemed to include any assets of such company.

(h) **Notification of Secretary of Labor.** Before sending a notice of deficiency with respect to the tax imposed by subsection (a) or (b), the Secretary shall notify the Secretary of Labor and provide him a reasonable opportunity to obtain a correction of the prohibited transaction or to comment on the imposition of such tax.

(i) **Cross reference.** For provisions concerning coordination procedures between Secretary of Labor and Secretary of Treasury with respect to application of tax imposed by this section and for authority to waive imposition of the tax imposed by subsection (b), see section 3003 of the Employee Retirement Income Security Act of 1974.

[For analysis, see ¶ 403, ¶ 908, ¶ 909. For committee reports, see ¶ 5005, ¶ 5156, ¶ 5312.]

[Endnote Code Sec. 4975]

Matter in *italics* in Code Sec. 4975(a) added by Sec. 1074(a) of the Taxpayer Relief Act of 1997, H.R. 2014, 8/5/97, which struck out:

1. "10 percent"

Effective Date (Sec. 1074(b), H.R. 2014, 8/5/97) effective for prohibited transactions occurring after 8/5/97.

Matter in *italics* in Code Sec. 4975(c)(4) added by Sec. 1602(a)(5), H.R. 2014, 8/5/97, which struck out:

2. "if, with respect to such transaction, the account ceases to be a medical savings account by reason of the application of section 220(e)(2) to such account"

Effective Date (Sec. 1602(i), H.R. 2014, 8/5/97) effective for tax. yrs. begin. after 12/31/96.

Code Sec. 4975(c)(5), in *italics*, was added by Sec. 213(b)(2), H.R. 2014, 8/5/97.

3. added paragraph (c)(5)

Effective Date (Sec. 213(e), H.R. 2014, 8/5/97) effective for tax. yrs. begin. after 12/31/97.

Matter in Code Sec. 4975(d) added by Sec. 1506(b)(1)(B)'>, H.R. 2014, 8/5/97, which struck out:

4. "The prohibitions"

5. "The exemptions provided by this subsection (other than paragraphs (9) and (12)) shall not apply to any transaction with respect to a trust described in section 401(a) which is part of a plan providing contributions or benefits for employees some or all of whom are owner-employees (as defined in section 401(c)(3)) in which a plan directly or indirectly lends any part of the corpus or income of the plan to, pays any compensation for personal services rendered to the plan to, or acquires for the plan any property from or sells any property to, any such owner-employee, a member of the family (as defined in section 267(c)(4)) of any such owner-employee, or a corporation controlled by any such owner-employee through the ownership, directly or indirectly, of 50 percent or more of the total combined voting power of all classes of stock entitled to vote or 50 percent or more of the total value of shares of all classes of stock of the corporation. For purposes of the preceding sentence, a shareholder-employee (as defined in section 1379, as in effect on the day before the date of the enactment of the Subchapter S Revision Act of 1982), a participant or beneficiary of an individual retirement account or an individual retirement annuity (as defined in section 408), and an employer or association of employees which establishes such an account or annuity under section 408(c) shall be deemed to be an owner-employee."

Effective Date (Sec. 1506(c), H.R. 2014, 8/5/97) effective for tax. yrs. begin. after 12/31/97.

Matter in *italics* in Code Sec. 4975(e)(1)(D), Code Sec. 4975(e)(1)(E) and Code Sec. 4975(e)(1)(F) added by Sec. 213(b)(1), H.R. 2014, 8/5/97, which struck out:

6. "or"
7. added subparagraph (e)(1)(E)
8. "(E)"
Effective Date (Sec. 213(e), H.R. 2014, 8/5/97) see above.

Matter in *italics* in Code Sec. 4975(e)(7) added by Sec. 1530(c)(10), H.R. 2014, 8/5/97.
9. added matter in para. (e)(7)
Effective Date (Sec. 1530(d), H.R. 2014, 8/5/97) effective for transfers made by trusts to, or for the use of, an employee stock ownership plan after 8/5/97.

Code Sec. 4975(f)(6) was added by Sec. 1506(b)(1)(A), H.R. 2014, 8/5/97.
10. added para. (f)(6)
Effective Date (Sec. 1506(c), H.R. 2014, 8/5/97) effective for tax. yrs. begin after 12/31/97.

[¶ 3268] Code Sec. 4978. Tax on certain dispositions by employee stock ownership plans and certain cooperatives.

(a) Tax on dispositions of securities to which section 1042 applies before close of minimum holding period. If, during the 3-year period after the date on which the employee stock ownership plan or eligible worker-owned cooperative acquired any qualified securities in a sale to which section 1042 applied [1]*or acquired any qualified employer securities in a qualified gratuitous transfer to which section 664(g) applied,* such plan or cooperative disposes of any qualified securities and—

(1) the total number of shares held by such plan or cooperative after such disposition is less than the total number of employer securities held immediately after such sale, or

(2) except to the extent provided in regulations, the value of qualified securities held by such plan or cooperative after such disposition is less than 30 percent of the total value of all employer securities as of such disposition [2]*60 percent of the total value of all employer securities as of such disposition in the case of any qualified employer securities acquired in a qualified gratuitous transfer to which section 664(g) applied),*

there is hereby imposed a tax on the disposition equal to the amount determined under subsection (b).

(b) Amount of tax.

(1) In general. The amount of the tax imposed by subsection (a) shall be equal to 10 percent of the amount realized on the disposition.

(2) Limitation. The amount realized taken into account under paragraph (1) shall not exceed that portion allocable to qualified securities acquired in the sale to which section 1042 applied [3]*or acquired in the qualified gratuitous transfer to which section 664(g) applied* determined as if such securities were disposed of—

(A) first from qualified securities to which section 1042 applied [4]*or to which section 664(g) applied* acquired during the 3-year period ending on the date of the disposition, beginning with the securities first so acquired, and

(B) then from any other employer securities.

If subsection (d) applies to a disposition, the disposition shall be treated as made from employer securities in the opposite order of the preceding sentence.

(3) Distributions to employees. The amount realized on any distribution to an employee for less than fair market value shall be determined as if the qualified security had been sold to the employee at fair market value.

(c) Liability for payment of taxes. The tax imposed by this subsection shall be paid by—

(1) the employer, or

(2) the eligible worker-owned cooperative,

that made the [5]*written statement described in section 664(g)(1)(E) or in section 1042(b)(3) (as the case may be).*

* * * * * * * * * * *

(e) Definitions and special rules. For purposes of this section—

* * * * * * * * * * *

(2) Qualified securities. The term "qualified securities" has the meaning given to such term by section 1 042(c)(1)[6]; *except that such section shall be applied without regard to subparagraph (B) thereof for purposes of applying this section and section 4979A with respect to securities acquired in a qualified gratuitous transfer (as defined in section 664(g)(1)).*

* * * * * * * * * * * *

[Endnote Code Sec. 4978]

Matter in *italics* in Code Sec. 4978(a), Code Sec. 4978(a)(2), Code Sec. 4978(b)(2), Code Sec. 4978(b)(2)(A), Code Sec. 4978(c) and Code Sec. 4978(e)(2) added by Sec. 1530(c)(11)(A) and (B), (c)(12)(A) and (B), (c)(13), and (c)(14) of the Taxpayer Relief Act of 1997, H.R. 2014, 8/5/97, which struck out:

1. added matter in subsec. (a)
2. added matter in para. (a)(2)
3. added matter in para. (b)(2)
4. added matter in subpara. (b)(2)(A)
5. "written statement described in section 1042(b)(3)."
6. "."

Effective Date (Sec. 1530(d), H.R. 2014, 8/5/97) effective for transfers made by trusts to, or for the use of, an employee stock ownership plan after 8/5/97.

[¶ 3269]   Code Sec. 4979A.   Tax on certain prohibited allocations of qualified securities.
[1]*(a) Imposition of tax. If—*

(1) there is a prohibited allocation of qualified securities by any employee stock ownership plan or eligible worker-owned cooperative, or

(2) there is an allocation described in section 664(g)(5)(A),

there is hereby imposed a tax on such allocation equal to 50 percent of the amount involved.

* * * * * * * * * * * *

[2]*(c) Liability for tax. The tax imposed by this section shall be paid by—*

(1) the employer sponsoring such plan, or

(2) the eligible worker-owned cooperative,

which made the written statement described in section 664(g)(1)(E) or in section 1042(b)(3)(B) (as the case may be).

[3]*(d) Special statute of limitations for tax attributable to certain allocations. The statutory period for the assessment of any tax imposed by this section on an allocation described in subsection (a)(2) of qualified employer securities shall not expire before the date which is 3 years from the later of—*

(1) the 1st allocation of such securities in connection with a qualified gratuitous transfer (as defined in section 664(g)(1)), or

(2) the date on which the Secretary is notified of the allocation described in subsection (a)(2).

[4]*(e) Definitions.* Terms used in this section have the same respective meaning as when used in section 4978.

[Endnote Code Sec. 4979A]

Matter in *italics* in Code Sec. 4979A(a), Code Sec. 4979A(c), Code Sec. 4979A(d) and Code Sec. 4979A(e) added by Sec. 1530(c)(15)-(17) of the Taxpayer Relief Act of 1997, H.R. 2014, 8/5/97, which struck out:

1. "(a) Imposition of tax.
"If there is a prohibited allocation of qualified securities by any employee stock ownership plan or eligible worker-owned cooperative, there is hereby imposed a tax on such allocation equal to 50 percent of the amount involved."
2. "(c) Liability for tax.
"The tax imposed by this section shall be paid by—
"(1) the employer sponsoring such plan, or
"(2) the eligible worker-owned cooperative, which made the written statement described in section 1042(b)(3)(B)."
3. added subsec. (d)
4. "(d)"

Effective Date (Sec. 1530(d), H.R. 2014, 8/5/97) effective for transfers made by trusts to, or for the use of, an employee stock ownership plan after 8/5/97.

[¶ 3270]   Code Sec.[1] 4980A.   Repealed.

[For analysis, see ¶ 907. For committee reports, see ¶ 5155.]

[Endnote Code Sec. 4980A]

Code Sec. 4980A was repealed by Sec. 1073(a) of the Taxpayer Relief Act of 1997, H.R. 2014, 8/5/97, which struck out:

1. "SEC. 4980A. TAX ON EXCESS DISTRIBUTIONS FROM QUALIFIED RETIREMENT PLANS.

"(a) General rule. There is hereby imposed a tax equal to 15 percent of the excess distributions with respect to any individual during any calendar year.

"(b) Liability for tax. The individual with respect to whom the excess distributions are made shall be liable for the tax imposed by subsection (a). The amount of the tax imposed by subsection (a) shall be reduced by the amount (if any) of the tax imposed by section 72(t) to the extent attributable to such excess distributions.

"(c) Excess distributions. For purposes of this section—

"(1) In general. The term 'excess distributions' means the aggregate amount of the retirement distributions with respect to any individual during any calendar year to the extent such amount exceeds the greater of—

"(A) $150,000, or

"(B) $112,500 (adjusted at the same time and in the same manner as under section 415(d)).

"(2) Exclusion of certain distributions. The following distributions shall not be taken into account under paragraph (1):

"(A) Any retirement distribution with respect to an individual made after the death of such individual.

"(B) Any retirement distribution with respect to an individual payable to an alternate payee pursuant to a qualified domestic relations order (within the meaning of section 414(p)) if includible in income of the alternate payee.

"(C) Any retirement distribution with respect to an individual which is attributable to the individual's investment in the contract (as defined in section 72(f)).

"(D) Any retirement distribution to the extent not included in gross income by reason of a rollover contribution.

"(E) Any retirement distribution with respect to an individual of an annuity contract the value of which is not includible in gross income at the time of the distribution (other than distributions under, or proceeds from the sale or exchange of, such contract).

"(F) Any retirement distribution with respect to an individual of—

"(i) excess deferrals (and income allocable thereto) under section 402(g)(2)(A)(ii), or

"(ii) excess contributions (and income allocable thereto) under section 401(k)(8) or 408(d)(4) or excess aggregate contributions (and income allocable thereto) under section 401(m)(6).

Any distribution described in subparagraph (B) shall be treated as a retirement distribution to the person to whom paid for purposes of this section.

"(3) Aggregation of payments. If retirement distributions with respect to any individual during any calendar year are received by the individual and 1 or more other persons, all such distributions shall be aggregated for purposes of determining the amount of the excess distributions for the calendar year.

[Caution: Para. (c)(4), following, is effective for tax. yrs. begin. before 1/1/2000. For para. (c)(4) effective for tax. yrs. begin. after 12/31/99, see below. For special rules, see Sec. 1401(c)(2) of P.L. 104-188 reproduced in note following Code Sec. 4980A.]

"(4) Special rule where taxpayer elects income averaging.

If the retirement distributions with respect to any individual during any calendar year include a lump sum distribution to which an election under section 402(d)(4)(B) applies—

"(A) paragraph (1) shall be applied separately with respect to such lump sum distribution and other retirement distributions, and

"(B) the limitation under paragraph (1) with respect to such lump sum distribution shall be equal to 5 times the amount of such limitation determined without regard to this subparagraph.

[Caution: Para. (c)(4), following, is effective for tax. yrs. begin. after 12/31/99. For special rules, see Sec. 1401(c)(2) of P.L. 104-188 reproduced in note following Code Sec. 4980A. For para. (c)(4) effective for tax. yrs. begin. before 1/1/2000, see above.]

"(4) Special one-time election. If the retirement distributions with respect to any individual during any calendar year include a lump sum distribution (as defined in section 402(e)(4)(D)) with respect to which the individual elects to have this paragraph apply—

"(A) paragraph (1) shall be applied separately with respect to such lump sum distribution and other retirement distributions, and

"(B) the limitation under paragraph (1) with respect to such lump sum distribution shall be equal to 5 times the amount of such limitation determined without regard to this subparagraph.

An individual may elect to have this paragraph apply to only one lump-sum distribution.

"(d) Increase in estate tax if individual dies with excess accumulation.

"(1) In general. The tax imposed by chapter 11 with respect to the estate of any individual shall be increased by an amount equal to 15 percent of the individual's excess retirement accumulation.

"(2) No credit allowable. No credit shall be allowable under chapter 11 with respect to any portion of the tax imposed by chapter 11 attributable to the increase under paragraph (1).

"(3) Excess retirement accumulation. For purposes of paragraph (1), the term 'excess retirement accumulation' means the excess (if any) of—

"(A) the value of the individual's interests (other than as a beneficiary, determined after application of paragraph (5)) in qualified employer plans and individual retirement plans as of the date of the decedent's death (or, in the case of an election under section 2032, the applicable valuation date prescribed by such section), over

"(B) the present value (as determined under rules prescribed by the Secretary as of the valuation date prescribed in subparagraph (A)) of a single life annuity with annual payments equal to the limitation of subsection (c) (as in effect for the year in which death occurs and as if the individual had not died).

"(4) Rules for computing excess retirement accumulation. The excess retirement accumulation of an individual shall be computed without regard to—

"(A) any community property law,

"(B) the value of—

"(i) amounts payable to an alternate payee pursuant to a qualified domestic relations order (within the meaning of section 414(p)) if includible in income of the alternate payee, and

"(ii) the individual's investment in the contract (as defined in section 72(f)), and

"(C) the excess (if any) of—

"(i) any interests which are payable immediately after death, over

"(ii) the value of such interests immediately before death.

"(5) Election by spouse to have excess distribution rule apply.

"(A) In general. If the spouse of an individual is the beneficiary of all of the interests described in paragraph (3)(A), the spouse may elect—

"(i) not to have this subsection apply, and

"(ii) to have this section apply to such interests and any retirement distribution attributable to such interests as if such interests were the spouse's.

"(B) De minimis exception. If 1 or more persons other than the spouse are beneficiaries of a de minimis portion of the interests described in paragraph (3)(A)—

"(i) the spouse shall not be treated as failing to meet the requirements of subparagraph (A), and

"(ii) if the spouse makes the election under subparagraph (A), this section shall not apply to such portion or any retirement distribution attributable to such portion.

"(e) Retirement distributions. For purposes of this section—

"(1) In general. The term 'retirement distribution' means, with respect to any individual, the amount distributed during the taxable year under—

"(A) any qualified employer plan with respect to which such individual is or was the employee, and

"(B) any individual retirement plan.

"(2) Qualified employer plan. The term 'qualified employer plan' means—

"(A) any plan described in section 401(a) which includes a trust exempt from tax under section 501(a),

"(B) an annuity plan described in section 403(a), or

"(C) an annuity contract described in section 403(b).

Such term includes any plan or contract which, at any time, has been determined by the Secretary to be such a plan or contract.

"(f) Exemption of accrued benefits in excess of $562,500 on August 1, 1986. For purposes of this section—

"(1) In general. If an election is made with respect to an eligible individual to have this subsection apply, the individual's excess distributions and excess retirement accumulation shall be computed without regard to any distributions or interests attributable to the accrued benefit of the individual as of August 1, 1986.

"(2) Reduction in amounts which may be received without tax. If this subsection applies to any individual—

"(A) Excess distributions. Subsection (c)(1) shall be applied—

"(i) without regard to subparagraph (A), and

"(ii) by reducing (but not below zero) the amount determined under subparagraph (B) thereof by retirement distributions attributable (as determined under rules prescribed by the Secretary) to the individual's accrued benefit as of August 1, 1986.

"(B) Excess retirement accumulation. The amount determined under subsection (d)(3)(B) (without regard to subsection (c)(1)(A)) with respect to such individual shall be reduced (but not below zero) by the present value of the individual's accrued benefit as of August 1, 1986, which has not been distributed as of the date of death.

"(3) Eligible individual. For purposes of this subsection, the term 'eligible individual' means any individual if, on August 1, 1986, the present value of such individual's interests in qualified employer plans and individual retirement plans exceeded $562,500.

"(4) Certain amounts excluded. In determining an individual's accrued benefit for purposes of this subsection, there shall not be taken into account any portion of the accrued benefit—

"(A) payable to an alternate payee pursuant to a qualified domestic relations order (within the meaning of section 414(p)) if includible in income of the alternate payee, or

"(B) attributable to the individual's investment in the contract (as defined in section 72(f)).

"(5) Election. An election under paragraph (1) shall be made on an individual's return of tax imposed by chapter 1 or 11 for a taxable year beginning before January 1, 1989.

"(g) Limitation on application. This section shall not apply to distributions during years beginning after December 31, 1996, and before January 1, 2000, and such distributions shall be treated as made first from amounts not described in subsection (f)."

Effective Date (Sec. 1073(c), H.R. 2014, 8/5/97) Sec. 1073(c), H.R. 2014, 8/5/97, reads as follows:

"(c) Effective dates.

"(1) Excess distribution tax repeal. Except as provided in paragraph (2), the repeal made by subsection (a) shall apply to excess distributions received after December 31, 1996.

"(2) Excess retirement accumulation tax repeal. The repeal made by subsection (a) with respect to Section 4980A(d) of the Internal Revenue Code of 1986 and the amendments made by subsection (b) shall apply to estates of decedents dying after December 31, 1996."

[¶ 3271]   Code Sec. 4980D.   Failure to meet certain group health plan requirements.

(a) **General rule.** There is hereby imposed a tax on any failure of a group health plan to meet the requirements of chapter 100 (relating to group health [1]*plans* requirements).

* * * * * * * * * * *

(c) **Limitations on amount of tax.**

* * * * * * * * * * *

(3) **Overall limitation for unintentional failures.** In the case of failures which are due to reasonable cause and not to willful neglect—

(A) Single employer plans.

(i) In general. In the case of failures with respect to plans other than specified multiple employer health plans, the tax impose by subsection (a) for failures during the taxable year of the employer shall not exceed the amount equal to the lesser of—

(I) 10 percent of the aggregate amount paid or incurred by the employer (or predecessor employer) during the preceding taxable year for group health plans, or

(II) $500,000.

(ii) Taxable years in the case of certain controlled groups. For purposes of this subparagraph, if not all persons who are treated as a single employer for purposes of this section have the same taxable year, the taxable years taken into account shall be determined under principles similar to the principles of section 1561.

(B) Specified multiple employer health plans.

(i) In general. In the case of failures with respect to a specified multiple employer health plan, the tax imposed by subsection (a) for failures during the taxable year of the trust forming part of such plan shall not exceed the amount equal to the lesser of—

(I) 10 percent of the amount paid or incurred by such trust during such taxable year to provide medical care (as defined in section [2]*9832(d)(3)*) directly or through insurance, reimbursement, or otherwise, or

(II) $500,000.

For purposes of the preceding sentence, all plans of which the same trust forms a part shall be treated as 1 plan.

(ii) Special rule for employers required to pay tax. If an employer is assessed a tax imposed by subsection (a) by reason of a failure with respect to a specified multiple employer health plan, the limit shall be determined under subparagraph (A) (and not under this subparagraph) and as if such plan were not a specified multiple employer health plan.

* * * * * * * * * * *

(d) **Tax not to apply to certain insured small employer plans.**

(1) **In general.** In the case of a group health plan of a small employer which provides health insurance coverage solely through a contract with a health insurance issuer, no tax shall be imposed by this section on the employer on any failure [3]*(other than a failure attributable to section 9811)* which is solely because of the health insurance coverage offered by such issuer.

* * * * * * * * * * *

(3) **Health insurance coverage; health insurance issuer.** For purposes of paragraph (1), the terms "health insurance coverage" and "health insurance issuer" have the respective meanings given such terms by section [4]*9832*.

* * * * * * * * * * *

(f) **Definitions.** For purposes of this section—

(1) **Group health plan.** The term "group health plan" has the meaning given such term by section [5]9832(a).

* * * * * * * * * * *

[Endnote Code Sec. 4980D]

Matter in *italics* in Code Sec. 4980D(a), Code Sec. 4980D(c)(3)(B)(i)(I), Code Sec. 4980D(d)(1), Code Sec. 4980D(d)(3), and Code Sec. 4980D(f)(1) added by Sec. 1531(b)(2) of the Taxpayer Relief Act of 1997, H.R. 2014, 8/5/97, which struck out:

1. "plan portability, access, and renewability"
2. "9805(d)(3)"
3. added matter in para. (d)(1)
4. "9805"
5. "9805(a)"

Effective Date (Sec. 1531(c), H.R. 2014, 8/5/97) effective for group health plans for plan yrs. begin. on or after 1/1/98.

* * * * * * * * * * *

[¶ 3272] Code Sec. 4982. Excise tax on undistributed income of regulated investment companies.

* * * * * * * * * * * * *

(e) **Definitions and special rules.** For purposes of this section—

* * * * * * * * * * *

[1](6) *Treatment of gain recognized under section 1296. For purposes of determining a regulated investment company's ordinary income—*

(A) notwithstanding paragraph (1)(C), section 1296 shall be applied as if such company's taxable year ended on October 31, and

(B) any ordinary gain or loss from an actual disposition of stock in a passive foreign investment company during the portion of the calendar year after October 31 shall be taken into account in determining such regulated investment company's ordinary income for the following calendar year.

In the case of a company making an election under paragraph (4), the preceding sentence shall be applied by substituting the last day of the company's taxable year for October 31.

* * * * * * * * * * * *

[Endnote Code Sec. 4982]

Code Sec. 4982(e)(6), in *italics*, was added by Sec. 1122(c)(1) of the Taxpayer Relief Act of 1997, H.R. 2014, 8/5/97.

1. added para. (e)(6)

Effective Date (Sec. 1124, H.R. 2014, 8/5/97) effective for tax. yrs. of United States persons begin. after 12/31/97, and tax. yrs. of foreign corporations end. with or within such tax. yrs. of United States persons.

[¶ 3273] Code Sec. 5008. Abatement, remission, refund, and allowance for loss or destruction of distilled spirits.

* * * * * * * * * * *

(c) **Distilled spirits returned**

(1) **In general.** Whenever any distilled spirits [1]*on which tax has been determined or paid* are returned to the bonded premises of a distilled spirits plant under section 5215(a), the Secretary shall abate or (without interest) credit or refund the tax imposed under section 5001(a)(1) (or the tax equal to such tax imposed under section 7652) on the spirits so returned.

* * * * * * * * * * * *

[For analysis, see ¶ 2227. For committee reports, see ¶ 5277.]

[Endnote Code Sec. 5008]

Matter in *italics* in Code Sec. 5008(c)(1) added by Sec. 1411(a) of the Taxpayer Relief Act of 1997, H.R. 2014, 8/5/97, which struck out:
1. "withdrawn from bonded premises on payment or determination of tax"
Effective Date (Sec. 1411(b), H.R. 2014, 8/5/97) effective on the 1st day of the 1st calendar quarter that begins at least 180 days after 8/5/97.

[¶ 3274] Code Sec. 5041. Imposition and rate of tax.

* * * * * * * * * * * *

(b) Rates of tax.

* * * * * * * * * * * *

(4) On champagne and other sparkling wines, $3.40 per wine gallon;[1]

(5) On artificially carbonated wines, $3.30 per wine gallon[2]; *and*

[3]*(6) On hard cider derived primarily from apples or apple concentrate and water, containing no other fruit product, and containing at least one-half of 1 percent and less than 7 percent alcohol by volume, 22.6 cents per wine gallon.*

(c) Credit for small domestic producers.

(1) Allowance of credit. Except as provided in paragraph (2), in the case of a person who produces not more than 250,000 wine gallons of wine during the calendar year, there shall be allowed as a credit against any tax imposed by this title (other than chapters 2, 21, and 22) of 90 cents per wine gallon on the 1st 100,000 wine gallons of wine (other than wine described in [4]*paragraphs (4) and (6) of subsection (b)*) which are removed during such year for consumption or sale and which have been produced at qualified facilities in the United States.

(2) Reduction in credit. The credit allowable by paragraph (1) shall be reduced (but not below zero) by 1 percent for each 1,000 wine gallons of wine produced in excess of 150,000 wine gallons of wine during the calendar year.

(3) Time for determining and allowing credit. The credit allowable by paragraph (1)—

(A) shall be determined at the same time the tax is determined under subsection (a) of this section, and

(B) shall be allowable at the time any tax described in paragraph (1) is payable as if the credit allowable by this subsection constituted a reduction in the rate of such tax.

(4) Controlled groups. Rules similar to rules of section 5051(a)(2)(B) shall apply for purposes of this subsection.

(5) Denial of deduction. Any deduction under subtitle A with respect to any tax against which a credit is allowed under this subsection shall only be for the amount of such tax as reduced by such credit.

(6) Credit for transferee in bond. If—

(A) wine produced by any person would be eligible for any credit under paragraph (1) if removed by such person during the calendar year,

(B) wine produced by such person is removed during such calendar year by any other person (hereafter in this paragraph referred to as the "transferee") to whom such wine was transferred in bond and who is liable for the tax imposed by this section with respect to such wine, and

(C) such producer holds title to such wine at the time of its removal and provides to the transferee such information as is necessary to properly determine the transferee's credit under this paragraph,

then, the transferee (and not the producer) shall be allowed the credit under paragraph (1) which would be allowed to the producer if the wine removed by the transferee had been removed by the producer on that date.

(7) Regulations. The Secretary may prescribe such regulations as may be necessary to carry out the purposes of this subsection, including regulations—

(A) to prevent the credit provided in this subsection from benefiting any person who produces more than 250,000 wine gallons of wine during a calendar year, and

(B) to assure proper reduction of such credit for persons producing more than 150,000 wine gallons of wine during a calendar year.

(d) Wine gallon. For the purpose of this chapter, the term "wine gallon" means a United States gallon of liquid measure equivalent to the volume of 231 cubic inches. On lesser quantities the tax shall be paid proportionately (fractions of less than one-tenth gallon being converted to the nearest one-tenth gallon, and five-hundredths gallon being converted to the next full one-tenth gallon).

(e) Tolerances. Where the Secretary finds that the revenue will not be endangered thereby, he may by regulation prescribe tolerances (but not greater than ½ of 1 percent) for bottles and other containers, and, if such tolerances are prescribed, no assessment shall be made and no tax shall be collected for any excess in any case where the contents of a bottle or other container are within the limit of the applicable tolerance prescribed.

(f) Illegally produced wine. Notwithstanding subsection (a), any wine produced in the United States at any place other than the bonded premises provided for in this chapter shall (except as provided in section 5042 in the case of tax-free production) be subject to tax at the rate prescribed in subsection (b) at the time of production and whether or not removed for consumption or sale.

[For analysis, see ¶ 2228. For committee reports, see ¶ 5058.]

[Endnote Code Sec. 5041]

Matter in *italics* in Code Sec. 5041(b)(4), Code Sec. 5041(b)(5), Code Sec. 5041(b)(6) and Code Sec. 5041(c)(1) added by Sec. 908(a) and (b) of the Taxpayer Relief Act of 1997, H.R. 2014, 8/5/97, which struck out:
1. "and"
2. "."
3. added paragraph (b)(6)
4. "subsection (b)(4)"

Effective Date (Sec. 908(c), H.R. 2014, 8/5/97) effective 10/1/97.

[¶ 3275]   Code Sec. 5044.   Refund of tax on[1] wine.

(a) General. In the case of any wine produced in the United States and returned to bond[2] under section 5361—

(1) any tax imposed by section 5041 shall, if paid, be refunded or credited, without interest, to the proprietor of the bonded wine cellar to which such wine is delivered; or

(2) if any tax so imposed has not been paid, the person liable for the tax may be relieved of liability therefor,

under such regulations as the Secretary may prescribe. Such regulations may provide that claim for refund or credit under paragraph (1), or relief from liability under paragraph (2), may be made only with respect to minimum quantities specified in such regulations. The burden of proof in all such cases shall be on the applicant.

* * * * * * * * * * *

[For analysis, see ¶ 2227. For committee reports, see ¶ 5277.]

[Endnote Code Sec. 5044]

Matter in Code Sec. 5044 and Code Sec. 5044(a) deleted by Secs. 1416(a) and (b)(2) of the Taxpayer Relief Act of 1997, H.R. 2014, 8/5/97, which struck out:
1. "unmerchantable"
2. "as unmerchantable"

Effective Date (Sec. 1416(c), H.R. 2014, 8/5/97) effective on the 1st day of the 1st calendar quarter that begins at least 180 days after 8/5/97.

[¶ 3276]   Code Sec. 5053.   Exemptions.

* * * * * * * * * * *

[1](f) **Removal for use as distilling material.** *Subject to such regulations as the Secretary may prescribe, beer may be removed from a brewery without payment of tax to any distilled spirits plant for use as distilling material.*

[2](g) **Removals for use of foreign embassies, legations, etc.**

(1) **In general.** *Subject to such regulations as the Secretary may prescribe—*

(A) *beer may be withdrawn from the brewery without payment of tax for transfer to any customs bonded warehouse for entry pending withdrawal therefrom as provided in subparagraph (B), and*

(B) *beer entered into any customs bonded warehouse under subparagraph (A) may be withdrawn for consumption in the United States by, and for the official and family use of, such foreign governments, organizations, and individuals as are entitled to withdraw imported beer from such warehouses free of tax.*
Beer transferred to any customs bonded warehouse under subparagraph (A) shall be entered, stored, and accounted for in such warehouse under such regulations and bonds as the Secretary may prescribe, and may be withdrawn therefrom by such governments, organizations, and individuals free of tax under the same conditions and procedures as imported beer.

(2) **Other rules to apply.** *Rules similar to the rules of paragraphs (2) and (3) of section 5362(e) shall apply for purposes of this subsection.*

[3](h) **Removals for destruction.** *Subject to such regulations as the Secretary may prescribe, beer may be removed from the brewery without payment of tax for destruction.*

[4](i) **Removal as supplies for certain vessels and aircraft.** *For exemption as to supplies for certain vessels and aircraft, see section 309 of the Tariff Act of 1930, as amended (19 U.S.C. 1309).*

[For analysis, see ¶ 2227. For committee reports, see ¶ 5277.]

[Endnote Code Sec. 5053]
Code Sec. 5053(f) in *italics* was added by Sec. 1414(b) of the Taxpayer Relief Act of 1997, H.R. 2014, 8/5/97.
1. added subsec. (f)
Effective Date (Sec. 1414(d), H.R. 2014, 8/5/97) effective the 1st day of the 1st calendar quarter that begins at least 180 days after 8/5/97.

Code Sec. 5053(g) in *italics* was added by Sec. 1418(a), H.R. 2014, 8/5/97.
2. added subsec. (g)
Effective Date (Sec. 1418(b), H.R. 2014, 8/5/97) effective the 1st day of the 1st calendar quarter that begins at least 180 days after 8/5/97.

Code Sec. 5053(h) in *italics* was added by Sec. 1419(a), H.R. 2014, 8/5/97.
3. added subsec. (h)
Effective Date (Sec. 1419(b), H.R. 2014, 8/5/97) effective the 1st day of the 1st calendar quarter that begins at least 180 days after 8/5/97.

Matter in *italics* in Code Sec. 5053(i) was added by Sec. 1414(b), H.R. 2014, 8/5/97, which struck out:
4. "(f)"
Effective Date (Sec. 1414(d), H.R. 2014, 8/5/97) effective the 1st day of the 1st calendar quarter that begins at least 180 days after 8/5/97.

[¶ 3277]   Code Sec. 5055.   Drawback of tax.
On the exportation of beer, brewed or produced in the United States, the brewer thereof shall be allowed a drawback equal in amount to the tax [1]*paid on such beer if there is such proof of exportation as the Secretary may by regulations require.[For analysis, see ¶ 2229. For committee reports, see ¶ 5277.]*

[Endnote Code Sec. 5055]

Matter in *italics* in Code Sec. 5055 added by Sec. 1420(a) of the Taxpayer Relief Act of 1997, H.R. 2014, 8/5/97, which struck out:

1. "found to have been paid on such beer, to be paid on submission of such evidence, records and certificates indicating exportation, as the Secretary may by regulations prescribe. For the purpose of this section, exportation shall include delivery for use as supplies on the vessels and aircraft described in section 309 of the tariff Act of 1930, as amended (19 U.S.C. 1309)."

Effective Date (Sec. 1420(b), H.R. 2014, 8/5/97) effective on the 1st day of the 1st calendar quarter that begins at least 180 days after 8/5/97.

[¶ 3278]   Code Sec. 5056.   Refund and credit of tax, or relief from liability.

* * * * * * * * * * * *

[1]*(c) Beer received at a distilled spirits plant. Any tax paid by any brewer on beer produced in the United States may be refunded or credited to the brewer, without interest, or if the tax has not been paid, the brewer may be relieved of liability therefor, under regulations as the Secretary may prescribe, if such beer is received on the bonded premises of a distilled spirits plant pursuant to the provisions of section 5222(b)(2), for use in the production of distilled spirits.*

[2]*(d)* **Limitations.** No claim under this section shall be allowed (1) unless filed within 6 months after the date of the return, loss, destruction, [3]*rendering unmerchantable, or receipt on the bonded premises of a distilled spirits plant* or (2) if the claimant was indemnified by insurance or otherwise in respect of the tax.

[For analysis, see ¶ 2227. For committee reports, see ¶ 5277.]

[Endnote Code Sec. 5056]

Matter in *italics* in Code Sec. 5056(c) and Code Sec. 5056(d) added by Sec. 1414(c)(1) and (2) of the Taxpayer Relief Act of 1997, H.R. 2014, 8/5/97, which struck out:

1. added subsec. (c)
2. "(c)"
3. "or rendering unmerchantable"

Effective Date (Sec. 1414(d), H.R. 2014, 8/5/97) effective the 1st day of the 1st calendar quarter that begins at least 180 days after 8/5/97.

[¶ 3279]   Code Sec.[1] 5115.   Repealed.

[Endnote Code Sec. 5115]

Code Sec. 5115 was repealed by Sec. 1415(a) of the Taxpayer Relief Act of 1997, H.R. 2014, 8/5/97, which struck out:

1. "SEC. 5115. SIGN REQUIRED ON PREMISES.

"(a) Requirements.

"Every wholesale dealer in liquors who is required to pay special tax as such dealer shall, in the manner and form prescribed by regulations issued by the Secretary, place and keep conspicuously on the outside of the place of such business a sign, exhibiting, in plain and legible letters, the name or firm of the wholesale dealer, with the words: 'wholesale liquor dealer.' The requirements of this subsection will be met by the posting of a sign of the character prescribed herein, but with words conforming to the designation on the dealer's special tax stamp.

"(b) Penalty.

"For penalty for failure to post sign, or for posting sign without paying the special tax, see section 5681."

Effective Date (Sec. 1415(c), H.R. 2014, 8/5/97) effective 8/5/97.

[¶ 3280]   Code Sec. 5175.   Export bonds.

* * * * * * * * * * * *

(c) Cancellation or credit of export bonds. The bonds given under subsection (a) shall be cancelled or credited and the bonds liable under subsection (b) credited [1]*if there is such proof of exportation as the Secretary may by regulations require.*

[For analysis, see ¶ 2229. For committee reports, see ¶ 5277.]

[Endnote Code Sec. 5175]

Matter in *italics* in Code Sec. 5175(c) added by Sec. 1412(a) of the Taxpayer Relief Act of 1997, H.R. 2014, 8/5/97, which struck out:

1. "on the submission of such evidence, records, and certification indicating exportation as the Secretary may by regulations prescribe."

Effective Date (Sec. 1412(b), H.R. 2014, 8/5/97) effective on the 1st day of the 1st calendar quarter that begins at least 180 days after 8/5/97

[¶ 3281]   Code Sec. 5207.   Records and reports.

* * * * * * * * * * *

(c) **Preservation and inspection.** The records required by subsection (a) and a copy of each report required by subsection (b)[1] shall be available for inspection by any internal revenue officer during business hours, and shall be preserved by the person required to keep such records and reports for such period as the Secretary shall by regulations prescribe.

* * * * * * * * * * *

[Endnote Code Sec. 5207]

Matter in Code Sec. 5207(c) deleted by Sec. 1413(a) of the Taxpayer Relief Act of 1997, H.R. 2014, 8/5/97, which struck out:

1. "shall be kept on the premises where the operations covered by the record are carried on and "

Effective Date (Sec. 1413(b), H.R. 2014, 8/5/97) effective on the 1st day of the 1st calendar quarter that begins at least 180 days after 8/5/97.

[¶ 3282]   Code Sec. 5222.   Production, receipt, removal, and use of distilling materials.

* * * * * * * * * * *

(b) **Receipt.** Under such regulations as the Secretary may prescribe, fermented materials to be used in the production of distilled spirits may be received on the bonded premises of a distilled spirits plant authorized to produce distilled spirits as follows—

(1) from the premises of a bonded wine cellar authorized to remove such material by section 5362(c)(6);

[1]*(2) beer conveyed without payment of tax from brewery premises, beer which has been lawfully removed from brewery premises upon determination of tax, or*

(3) cider exempt from tax under the provisions of section 5042(a)(1).

* * * * * * * * * * *

[For analysis, see ¶ 2227. For committee reports, see ¶ 5277.]

[Endnote Code Sec. 5222]

Matter in *italics* in Code Sec. 5222(b)(2) added by Sec. 1414(a) of the Taxpayer Relief Act of 1997, H.R. 2014, 8/5/97, which struck out:

1. "(2) conveyed without payment of tax from contiguous brewery premises where produced; or"

Effective Date (Sec. 1414(d), H.R. 2014, 8/5/97) effective on the 1st day of the 1st calendar quarter that begins at least 180 days after 8/5/97.

[¶ 3283]   Code Sec. 5361.   Bonded wine cellar operations.

In addition to the operations described in section 5351, the proprietor of a bonded wine cellar may, subject to regulations prescribed by the Secretary, on such premises receive[1] taxpaid wine for return to bond, reconditioning, or destruction; prepare for market and store commercial fruit products and by-products not taxable as wines; produce or receive distilling material or vinegar stock; produce (with or without added wine spirits, and without added sugar) or receive on wine premises, subject to tax as wine but not for sale or consumption as beverage wine, (1) heavy bodied blending wines and Spanish-type blending sherries, and (2) other wine products made from natural wine for nonbeverage purposes; and such other operations as may be conducted in a manner that will not jeopardize the revenue or conflict with wine operations. *[For analysis, see ¶ 2227. For committee reports, see ¶ 5277.]*

[Endnote Code Sec. 5361]

In Code Sec. 5361, Sec. 1416(b)(1) of the **Taxpayer Relief Act of 1997**, H.R. 2014, 8/5/97, struck out:

1. "unmerchantable"

Effective Date (Sec. 1416(c), H.R. 2014, 8/5/97) effective on the 1st day of the 1st calendar quarter that begins at least 180 days after 8/5/97.

[¶ 3284]   Code Sec.[1] 5364.

CAUTION.   Code Sec. 5364, following, is effective on the first day of the first calendar quarter begin. at least 180 days after 8/5/97.

Wine imported in bulk.

Wine imported or brought into the United States in bulk containers may, under such regulations as the Secretary may prescribe, be withdrawn from customs custody and transferred in such bulk containers to the premises of a bonded wine cellar without payment of the internal revenue tax imposed on such wine. The proprietor of a bonded wine cellar to which such wine is transferred shall become liable for the tax on the wine withdrawn from customs custody under this section upon release of the wine from customs custody, and the importer, or the person bringing such wine into the United States, shall thereupon be relieved of the liability for such tax. *[For analysis, see ¶ 2227. For committee reports, see ¶ 5277.]*

[Endnote Code Sec. 5364]

Code Sec. 5364 was added by Sec. 1422(a) of the **Taxpayer Relief Act of 1997**, H.R. 2014, 8/5/97.

1. added Code Sec. 5346

Effective Date (Sec. 1422(c), H.R. 2014, 8/5/97) effective on the first day of the first calendar quarter begin. at least 180 days after 8/5/97.

[¶ 3285]   Code Sec. 5384.   Amelioration and sweetening limitations for natural fruit and berry wines.

(a) In general. To natural wine made from berries or fruit other than grapes, pure dry sugar or liquid sugar may be added to the juice in the fermenter, or to the wine after fermentation; but only if such wine has not more than 14 percent alcohol by volume after complete fermentation, or after complete fermentation and sweetening, and a total solids content not in excess of 21 percent by weight; and except that the use under this subsection of liquid sugar shall be limited so that the resultant volume will not exceed the volume which could result from the maximum authorized use of pure dry sugar only.

(b) Ameliorated fruit and berry wines.

* * * * * * * * * * * *

(2) Pure dry sugar or liquid sugar may be used in the production of wines under this subsection for the purpose of correcting natural deficiencies, but not to such an extent as would reduce the natural fixed acid in the corrected juice or wine to five parts per thousand. The quantity of sugar so used shall not exceed the quantity which would have been required to adjust the juice, prior to fermentation, to a total solids content of 25 degrees (Brix). Such sugar shall be added prior to the completion of fermentation of the wine. After such addition of the sugar, the wine or juice shall be treated and accounted for as provided in section 5383(b), covering the production of high acid grape wines, except that—

(A) Natural fixed acid shall be calculated as malic acid for apple wine and as citric acid for other fruit and berry wines, instead of tartaric acid;

(B) Juice adjusted with pure dry sugar or liquid sugar as provided in this paragraph shall be treated in the same manner as original natural juice under the provisions of section

5383(b); except that if liquid sugar is used, the volume of water contained therein must be deducted from the volume of ameliorating material authorized;

(C) Wines made under this subsection shall have a total solids content of not more than 21 percent by weight, whether or not wine spirits have been added; and

(D) Wines made exclusively from [1]*any fruit or berry with a natural fixed acid of 20 parts per thousand or more (before any correction of such fruit or berry)* shall be entitled to a volume of ameliorating material not in excess of 60 percent (in lieu of 35 percent).

[Endnote Code Sec. 5384]

Matter in *italics* in Code Sec. 5384(b)(2)(D) added by Sec. 1417(a) of the Taxpayer Relief Act of 1997, H.R. 2014, 8/5/97, which struck out:

1. "loganberries, currants, or gooseberries,"

Effective Date (Sec. 1417(b), H.R. 2014, 8/5/97) effective on the 1st day of the 1st calendar quarter that begins at least 180 days after 8/5/97.

[¶ 3286]   Code Sec. 5388.   Designation of wines.

* * * * * * * * * * * *

[1]*(c) Use of Semi-Generic Designations.*

(1) In general. Semi-generic designations may be used to designate wines of an origin other than that indicated by such name only if—

(A) there appears in direct conjunction therewith an appropriate appellation of origin disclosing the true place of origin of the wine, and

(B) the wine so designated conforms to the standard of identity, if any, for such wine contained in the regulations under this section or, if there is no such standard, to the trade understanding of such class or type.

(2) Determination of whether name is semi-generic.

(A) In general. Except as provided in subparagraph (B), a name of geographic significance, which is also the designation of a class or type of wine, shall be deemed to have become semi-generic only if so found by the Secretary.

(B) Certain names treated as semi-generic. The following names shall be treated as semi-generic: Angelica, Burgundy, Claret, Chablis, Champagne, Chianti, Malaga, Marsala, Madeira, Moselle, Port, Rhine Wine or Hock, Sauterne, Haut Sauterne, Sherry, Tokay.

[Endnote Code Sec. 5388]

Code Sec. 5388(c), in *italics*, was added by Sec. 910(a) of the Taxpayer Relief Act of 1997, H.R. 2014, 8/5/97.

1. added subsection (c)

Effective Date (Sec. 910(b), H.R. 2014, 8/5/97) effective 8/5/97.

[¶ 3287]   Code Sec.[1] 5418.

CAUTION.   Code Sec. 5418, following, effective on the first day of the first calendar quarter begin. at least 180 days after 8/5/97.

Beer imported in bulk.

Beer imported or brought into the United States in bulk containers may, under such regulations as the Secretary may prescribe, be withdrawn from customs custody and transferred in such bulk containers to the premises of a brewery without payment of the internal revenue tax imposed on such beer. The proprietor of a brewery to which such beer is transferred shall become liable for the tax on the beer withdrawn from customs custody under this section upon release of the beer from customs custody, and the importer, or the person bringing such beer into the United States, shall thereupon be relieved of the liability for such tax.

[For analysis, see ¶ 2227. For committee reports, see ¶ 5277.]

[Endnote Code Sec. 5418]

Code Sec. 5418 was added by Sec. 1421(a) of the Taxpayer Relief Act of 1997, H.R. 2014, 8/5/97.
1. added Code Sec. 5418
Effective Date (Sec. 1421(c), H.R. 2014, 8/5/97) effective on the first day of the first calendar quarter begin. at least 180 days after 8/5/97.

[¶ 3288]   Code Sec. 5681.   Penalty relating to signs.

(a) **Failure to post required sign.** Every person engaged in distilled spirits operations[1] who fails to post the sign required by[2] section 5180(a) shall be fined not more than $1,000, or imprisoned not more than 1 year, or both.

* * * * * * * * * * * *

(c) **Premises where no sign is placed or kept.** Every person who works in any distilled spirits plant [3]*on which no sign required by* section 5180(a) is placed or kept, and every person who knowingly receives at, or carries or conveys any distilled spirits to or from any such distilled spirits plant [4]*or who* knowingly carries or delivers any grain, molasses, or other raw material to any distilled spirits plant on which such a sign is not placed and kept, shall forfeit all vehicles, aircraft, or vessels used in carrying or conveying such property and shall be fined not more than $1,000, or imprisoned not more than 1 year, or both.

* * * * * * * * * * * *

[Endnote Code Sec. 5681]
   Matter in *italics* in Code Sec. 5681(a) and Code Sec. 5681(c) added by Sec. 1415(b)(1), (b)(2)(A) and (b)(2)(B) of the Taxpayer Relief Act of 1997, H.R. 2014, 8/5/97, which struck out:
   1. ", and every wholesale dealer in liquors,"
   2. "section 5115(a) or"
   3. "or wholesale liquor establishment, on which no sign required by section 5115(a) or"
   4. "or wholesale liquor establishment, or who"
Effective Date (Sec. 1415(c), H.R. 2014, 8/5/97) effective 8/5/97.

[¶ 3289]   Code Sec. 5701.   Rate of tax.

CAUTION.   Subsecs. (a)-(g), following, are effective before 1/1/2000. For subsecs. (a)-(h), effective for articles removed (as defined in Code Sec. 5702(k)) after 12/31/99, see below.

(a) **Cigars** On cigars, manufactured in or imported into the United States, there shall be imposed the following taxes:

(1) **Small cigars.** On cigars, weighing not more than 3 pounds per thousand, $1.125 cents per thousand (93.75 cents per thousand on cigars removed during 1991 or 1992);

(2) **Large cigars.** On cigars weighing more than 3 pounds per thousand, a tax equal to

(A) 10.625 percent of the price for which sold but not more than $25 per thousand on cigars removed during 1991 or 1992, and

(B) 12.75 percent of the price for which sold but not more than $30 per thousand on cigars removed after 1992.

Cigars not exempt from tax under this chapter which are removed but not intended for sale shall be taxed at the same rate as similar cigars removed for sale.

(b) **Cigarettes.** On cigarettes, manufactured in or imported into the United States, there shall be imposed the following taxes:

(1) **Small cigarettes.** On cigarettes, weighing not more than 3 pounds per thousand, $12 per thousand ($10 per thousand on cigarettes removed during 1991 or 1992).

(2) **Large cigarettes.** On cigarettes, weighing more than 3 pounds per thousand, $25.20 per thousand ($21 per thousand on cigarettes removed during 1991 or 1992); except that, if more than 6½ inches in length, they shall be taxable at the rate prescribed for cigarettes weighing not more than 3 pounds per thousand, counting each 2¾ inches, or fraction thereof, of the length of each as one cigarette.

(c) Cigarette papers. On each book or set of cigarette papers containing more than 25 papers, manufactured in or imported into the United States, there shall be imposed a tax of 0.75 cent (0.625 cent on cigarette papers removed during 1991 or 1992) for each 50 papers or fractional part thereof; except that, if cigarette papers measure more than 6½ inches in length, they shall be taxable at the rate prescribed, counting each 2¾ inches, or fraction thereof, of the length of each as one cigarette paper.

(d) Cigarette tubes. On cigarette tubes, manufactured in or imported into the United States, there shall be imposed a tax of 1.5 cents (1.25 cents on cigarette tubes removed during 1991 or 1992) for each 50 tubes or fractional part thereof, except that if cigarette tubes measure more than 6½ inches in length, they shall be taxable at the rate prescribed, counting each 2¾ inches, or fraction thereof, of the length of each as one cigarette tube.

(e) Smokeless tobacco. On smokeless tobacco, manufactured in or imported into the United States, there shall be imposed the following taxes:

    (1) Snuff. On snuff, 36 cents (30 cents on snuff removed during 1991 or 1992) per pound and a proportionate tax at the like rate on all fractional parts of a pound.

    (2) Chewing tobacco. On chewing tobacco, 12 cents (10 cents on chewing tobacco removed during 1991 or 1992) per pound and a proportionate tax at the like rate on all fractional parts of a pound.

(f) Pipe tobacco. On pipe tobacco, manufactured in or imported into the United States, there shall be imposed a tax of 67.5 cents (56.25 cents on pipe tobacco removed during 1991 or 1992) per pound (and a proportionate tax at the like rate on all fractional parts of a pound).

(g) Imported tobacco products and cigarette papers and tubes. The taxes imposed by this section on tobacco products and cigarette papers and tubes imported into the United States shall be in addition to any import duties imposed on such articles, unless such import duties are imposed in lieu of internal revenue tax.

    CAUTION.   Subsecs. (a)-(h), following, are effective for articles removed (as defined in Code Sec. 5702(k)) after 12/31/99. For subsecs. (a)-(g), effective before 1/1/2000, see above.

(a) Cigars On cigars, manufactured in or imported into the United States, there shall be imposed the following taxes:

    (1) Small cigars. On cigars, weighing not more than 3 pounds per thousand, [1-B]*$1.828 cents per thousand ($1.594 cents per thousand on cigars removed during 2000 or 2001);*

    (2) Large cigars. On cigars weighing more than 3 pounds per thousand, a tax [2-B]*equal to 20.719 percent ($18.063 percent on cigars removed during 2000 or 2001).*

    Cigars not exempt from tax under this chapter which are removed but not intended for sale shall be taxed at the same rate as similar cigars removed for sale.

(b) Cigarettes. On cigarettes, manufactured in or imported into the United States, there shall be imposed the following taxes:

    (1) Small cigarettes. On cigarettes, weighing not more than 3 pounds per thousand, [3-B]*$19.50 per thousand ($17 per thousand on cigarettes removed during 2000 or 2001).*

    (2) Large cigarettes. On cigarettes, weighing more than 3 pounds per thousand, [4-B]*$40.95 per thousand ($35.70 per thousand on cigarettes removed during 2000 or 2001);* except that, if more than 6½ inches in length, they shall be taxable at the rate prescribed for cigarettes weighing not more than 3 pounds per thousand, counting each 2¾ inches, or fraction thereof, of the length of each as one cigarette.

(c) Cigarette papers. [5-B]*On cigarette papers,* manufactured in or imported into the United States, there shall be imposed a tax of [6-B]*1.22 cents (1.06 cents on cigarette papers removed during 2000 or 2001)* for each 50 papers or fractional part thereof; except that, if cigarette papers measure more than 6½ inches in length, they shall be taxable at the rate prescribed, counting each 2¾ inches, or fraction thereof, of the length of each as one cigarette paper.

(d) Cigarette tubes. On cigarette tubes, manufactured in or imported into the United States, there shall be imposed a tax of [7-B]*2.44 cents (2.13 cents on cigarette tubes removed during 2000 or 2001)* for each 50 tubes or fractional part thereof, except that if cigarette tubes measure more than 6½ inches in length, they shall be taxable at the rate prescribed, counting each 2¾ inches, or fraction thereof, of the length of each as one cigarette tube.

(e) **Smokeless tobacco.** On smokeless tobacco, manufactured in or imported into the United States, there shall be imposed the following taxes:

(1) **Snuff.** On snuff, [8_B]*58.5 cents (51 cents on snuff removed during 2000 or 2001)* per pound and a proportionate tax at the like rate on all fractional parts of a pound.

(2) **Chewing tobacco.** On chewing tobacco, [9_B]*19.5 cents (17 cents on chewing tobacco removed during 2000 or 2001)* per pound and a proportionate tax at the like rate on all fractional parts of a pound.

(f) **Pipe tobacco.** On pipe tobacco, manufactured in or imported into the United States, there shall be imposed a tax of [10_B]*$1.0969 cents (95.67 cents on pipe tobacco removed during 2000 or 2001)* per pound (and a proportionate tax at the like rate on all fractional parts of a pound).

[11_B]*(g) Roll-your-own tobacco. On roll-your-own tobacco, manufactured in or imported into the United States, there shall be imposed a tax of $1.0969 cents (95.67 cents on roll-your-own tobacco removed during 200 or 2001) per pound (and a proportionate tax at the like rate on all fractional parts of a pound).*

[12_B]*(h)* **Imported tobacco products and cigarette papers and tubes.** The taxes imposed by this section on tobacco products and cigarette papers and tubes imported into the United States shall be in addition to any import duties imposed on such articles, unless such import duties are imposed in lieu of internal revenue tax.

[For analysis, see ¶ 2231. For committee reports, see ¶ 5509.]

[Endnote Code Sec. 5701]

H.R. 2015. Matter in *italics* in Code Sec. 5701(a)(1), Code Sec. 5701(a)(2), Code Sec. 5701(b)(1), Code Sec. 5701(b)(2), Code Sec. 5701(c), Code Sec. 5701(d), Code Sec. 5701(e)(1), Code Sec. 5701(e)(2), Code Sec. 5701(f), Code Sec. 5701(g) and Code Sec. 5701(h) added by Sec. 9302(a)(1), (a)(2), (b)(1), (b)(2), (c), (d), (e)(1), (e)(2), (f), (g)(1), (g)(2), and (h)(3) of the Balanced Budget Act of 1997, H.R. 2015, 8/5/97, which struck out:

1_B. "$1.25 cents per thousand (93.75 per thousand on cigars removed during 1991 or 1992)" [H.R. 2015]

2_B. "equal to

"(A) 10.625 percent of the price for which sold but not more than $25 per thousand on cigars removed during 1991 or 1992, and

"12.75 percent of the price for which sold but not more than $30 per thousand on cigars removed after 1992." [H.R. 2015]

3_B. "$12 per thousand ($10 per thousand on cigarettes removed during 1991 or 1992)" [H.R. 2015]

4_B. "$25.20 per thousand ($21 per thousand on cigarettes removed during 1991 or 1992)" [H.R. 2015]

5_B. "On each book or set of cigarette papers containing more than 25 papers," [H.R. 2015]

6_B. "0.75 cent (0.625 cent on cigarette papers removed during 1991 or 1992)" [H.R. 2015]

7_B. "1.5 cents (1.25 cents on cigarette tubes removed during 1991 or 1992)" [H.R. 2015]

8_B. "36 cents (30 cents on snuff removed during 1991 or 1992)" [H.R. 2015]

9_B. "12 cents (10 cents on chewing tobacco removed during 1991 or 1992)" [H.R. 2015]

10_B. "67.5 cents (56.25 cents on pipe tobacco removed during 1991 or 1992)" [H.R. 2015]

11_B. added subsec. (g) [H.R. 2015]

12_B. "(g)" [H.R. 2015]

Effective Date (Sec. 9302(i), H.R. 2015, 8/5/97) Sec. 9302(i), H.R. 2015, 8/5/97, reads as follows:

"(i) Effective date.

"(1) In general. The amendments made by this section shall apply to articles removed (as defined in section 5702(k) of the Internal Revenue Code of 1986, as amended by this section) after December 31, 1999.

"(2) Transitional rule. Any person who—

"(A) on the date of the enactment of this Act is engaged in business as a manufacturer of roll-your-own tobacco or as an importer of tobacco products or cigarette papers and tubes, and

"(B) before January 1, 2000, submits an application under subchapter B of chapter 52 of such Code to engage in such business, may, notwithstanding such subchapter B, continue to engage in such business pending final action on such application. Pending such final action, all provisions of such chapter 52 shall apply to such applicant in the same manner and to the same extent as if such applicant were a holder of a permit under such chapter 52 to engage in such business."

[¶ 3290]   Code Sec. 5702.   Definitions.

* * * * * * * * * * * *

(c) Tobacco products. "Tobacco products" means cigars, cigarettes, smokeless tobacco, ^1_B*pipe tobacco, and roll-your-own tobacco.*

(d) Manufacturer of tobacco products. "Manufacturer of tobacco products" means any person who manufactures cigars, cigarettes, smokeless tobacco ^2_B*pipe tobacco, or roll-your-own to-*bacco except that such term shall not include—

^3_B*(1) a person who produces cigars, cigarettes, smokeless tobacco, pipe tobacco, or roll-your-own tobacco solely for the person's own personal consumption or use, and*

(2) a proprietor of a customs bonded manufacturing warehouse with respect to the operation of such warehouse.

* * * * * * * * * * * *

(k) Removal or remove. "Removal" or "remove" means the removal of tobacco products or cigarette papers or tubes from the factory or from internal revenue bond ^4_B*under section 5704,* as the Secretary shall by regulation prescribe, or release from customs custody, and shall also include the smuggling or other unlawful importation of such articles into the United States.

* * * * * * * * * * * *

^5_B*(p) Roll-your-own tobacco. The term "roll-your-own tobacco" means any tobacco which, because of its appearance, type, packaging, or labeling, is suitable for use and likely to be offered to, or purchased by, consumers as tobacco for making cigarettes.*

[Endnote Code Sec. 5702]

H.R. 2015. Matter in *italics* in Code Sec. 5702(c), Code Sec. 5702(d), Code Sec. 5702(k) and Code Sec. 5702(p) added by Sec. 9302(g)(2), (g)(3)(A), (g)(3)(B)(i)-(ii) and (h)(4) of the Balanced Budget Act of 1997, H.R. 2015, 8/5/97, which struck out:

1_B. "and pipe tobacco" [H.R. 2015]

2_B. "or pipe tobacco" [H.R. 2015]

3_B. "(1) a person who produces cigars, cigarettes, smokeless tobacco, or pipe tobacco solely for his own personal consumption or use; or" [H.R. 2015]

4_B. added matter in subsection (k) [H.R. 2015]

5_B. added subsection (p) [H.R. 2015]

Effective Date (Sec. 9302(i), H.R. 2015, 8/5/97) Sec. 9302(i), H.R. 2015, 8/5/97, reads as follows:

"(i) Effective date.

"(1) In general. The amendments made by this section shall apply to articles removed (as defined in section 5702(k) of the Internal Revenue Code of 1986, as amended by this section) after December 31, 1999.

"(2) Transitional rule. Any person who—

"(A) on the date of the enactment of this Act is engaged in business as a manufacturer of roll-your-own tobacco or as an importer of tobacco products or cigarette papers and tubes, and

"(B) before January 1, 2000, submits an application under subchapter B of chapter 52 of such Code to engage in such business, may, notwithstanding such subchapter B, continue to engage in such business pending final action on such application. Pending such final action, all provisions of such chapter 52 shall apply to such applicant in the same manner and to the same extent as if such applicant were a holder of a permit under such chapter 52 to engage in such business."

[¶ 3291]   Code Sec. 5704.   Exemption from tax.

* * * * * * * * * * * *

(b) Tobacco products and cigarette papers and tubes transferred or removed in bond from domestic factories and export warehouses. A manufacturer or export warehouse proprietor may transfer tobacco products and cigarette papers and tubes, without payment of tax, to the bonded premises of another manufacturer or export warehouse proprietor, or remove such articles, without payment of tax, for shipment to a foreign country, Puerto Rico, the Virgin Islands, or a possession of the United States, or for consumption beyond the jurisdiction of the internal revenue laws of the United States; and manufacturers may similarly remove such articles for use of the United States; in accordance with such regulations and under such bonds as the Secretary shall prescribe. *1_BTobacco products and cigarette papers and tubes may not be transferred or removed under this subsection unless such products or papers and tubes bear such marks, labels, or notices as the Secretary shall by regulations prescribe.*

* * * * * * * * * * * *

[Endnote Code Sec. 5704]

H.R. 2015. Matter in *italics* in Code Sec. 5704(b) added by Sec. 9302(h)(1)(A) of the Balanced Budget Act of 1997, H.R. 2015, 8/5/97.

1_B. added matter in subsection (b) [H.R. 2015]

Effective Date (Sec. 9302(i), H.R. 2015, 8/5/97) Sec. 9302(i), H.R. 2015, 8/5/97, reads as follows:

"(i) Effective date.

"(1) In general. The amendments made by this section shall apply to articles removed (as defined in section 5702(k) of the Internal Revenue Code of 1986, as amended by this section) after December 31, 1999.

"(2) Transitional rule. Any person who—

"(A) on the date of the enactment of this Act is engaged in business as a manufacturer of roll-your-own tobacco or as an importer of tobacco products or cigarette papers and tubes, and

"(B) before January 1, 2000, submits an application under subchapter B of chapter 52 of such Code to engage in such business, may, notwithstanding such subchapter B, continue to engage in such business pending final action on such application. Pending such final action, all provisions of such chapter 52 shall apply to such applicant in the same manner and to the same extent as if such applicant were a holder of a permit under such chapter 52 to engage in such business."

[¶ 3292]   Code Sec. 5712.   Application for permit.

Every person, before commencing business as a manufacturer *1_Bor importer* of tobacco products or as an export warehouse proprietor, and at such other time as the Secretary shall by regulation prescribe, shall make application for the permit provided for in section 5713. The application shall be in such form as the Secretary shall prescribe and shall set forth, truthfully and accurately, the information called for on the form. Such application may be rejected and the permit denied if the Secretary, after notice and opportunity for hearing, find that—

(1) the premises on which it is proposed to conduct the business are not adequate to protect the revenue;*2_B*

3_B(2) the activity proposed to be carried out at such premises does not meet such minimum capacity or activity requirements as the Secretary may prescribe, or

4_B(3) such person (including, in the case of a corporation, any officer, director, or principal stockholder and, in the case of a partnership, a partner) is, by reason of his business experience, financial standing, or trade connections, not likely to maintain operations in compliance with this chapter, or has failed to disclose any material information required or made any material false statement in the application therefor.

[Endnote Code Sec. 5712]

H.R. 2015. Matter in *italics* in Code Sec. 5712 added by Sec. 9302(h)(2)(A) and (h)(5) of the Balanced Budget Act of 1997, H.R. 2015, 8/5/97, which struck out:

1_B. added matter in the introductory paragraph [H.R. 2015]

2_B. "or" [H.R. 2015]

3_B. added paragraph (2) [H.R. 2015]

4. "(2)" [H.R. 2015]

Effective Date (Sec. 9302(i), H.R. 2015, 8/5/97) Sec. 9302(i), H.R. 2015, 8/5/97, reads as follows:

"(i) Effective date.

"(1) In general. The amendments made by this section shall apply to articles removed (as defined in section 5702(k) of the Internal Revenue Code of 1986, as amended by this section) after December 31, 1999.

"(2) Transitional rule. Any person who—

"(A) on the date of the enactment of this Act is engaged in business as a manufacturer of roll-your-own tobacco or as an importer of tobacco products or cigarette papers and tubes, and

"(B) before January 1, 2000, submits an application under subchapter B of chapter 52 of such Code to engage in such business, may, notwithstanding such subchapter B, continue to engage in such business pending final action on such application. Pending such final action, all provisions of such chapter 52 shall apply to such applicant in the same manner and to the same extent as if such applicant were a holder of a permit under such chapter 52 to engage in such business."

[¶ 3293] Code Sec. 5713. Permit.

(a) **Issuance.** A person shall not engage in business as a manufacturer [1-B]*or importer* of tobacco products or as an export warehouse proprietor without a permit to engage in such business. Such permit, conditioned upon compliance with this chapter and regulations issued thereunder, shall be issued in such form and in such manner as the Secretary shall by regulation prescribe, to every person properly qualified under sections 5711 and 5712. A new permit may be required at such other time as the Secretary shall by regulation prescribe.

* * * * * * * * * * * *

[Endnote Code Sec. 5713]

H.R. 2015. Matter in *italics* in Code Sec. 5713(a) added by Sec. 9302(h)(2)(A) of the Balanced Budget Act of 1997, H.R. 2015, 8/5/97.

1_B. added matter in subsec. (a) [H.R. 2015]

Effective Date (Sec. 9302(i), H.R. 2015, 8/5/97) Sec. 9302(i), H.R. 2015, 8/5/97, reads as follows:

"(i) Effective date.

"(1) In general. The amendments made by this section shall apply to articles removed (as defined in section 5702(k) of the Internal Revenue Code of 1986, as amended by this section) after December 31, 1999.

"(2) Transitional rule. Any person who—

"(A) on the date of the enactment of this Act is engaged in business as a manufacturer of roll-your-own tobacco or as an importer of tobacco products or cigarette papers and tubes, and

"(B) before January 1, 2000, submits an application under subchapter B of chapter 52 of such Code to engage in such business, may, notwithstanding such subchapter B, continue to engage in such business pending final action on such application. Pending such final action, all provisions of such chapter 52 shall apply to such applicant in the same manner and to the same extent as if such applicant were a holder of a permit under such chapter 52 to engage in such business."

[¶ 3294] Code Sec. 5721. Inventories.

Every manufacturer [1-B]*or importer* of tobacco products or cigarette papers and tubes, and every export warehouse proprietor, shall make a true and accurate inventory at the time of commencing business, at the time of concluding business, and at such other times, in such manner and form, and to include such items, as the Secretary shall by regulation prescribe. Such inventories shall be subject to verification by any internal revenue officer.

[Endnote Code Sec. 5721]

H.R. 2015. Matter in *italics* in Code Sec. 5721 added by Sec. 9302(h)(2)(A) of the Balanced Budget Act of 1997, H.R. 2015, 8/5/97.

1_B. added matter in subsec. (a) [H.R. 2015]

Effective Date (Sec. 9302(i), H.R. 2015, 8/5/97) Sec. 9302(i), H.R. 2015, 8/5/97, reads as follows:

"(i) Effective date.

"(1) In general. The amendments made by this section shall apply to articles removed (as defined in section 5702(k) of the Internal Revenue Code of 1986, as amended by this section) after December 31, 1999.

"(2) Transitional rule. Any person who—

"(A) on the date of the enactment of this Act is engaged in business as a manufacturer of roll-your-own tobacco or as an importer of tobacco products or cigarette papers and tubes, and

"(B) before January 1, 2000, submits an application under subchapter B of chapter 52 of such Code to engage in such business, may, notwithstanding such subchapter B, continue to engage in such business pending final action on such application. Pending such final action, all provisions of such chapter 52 shall apply to such applicant in the same manner and to the same extent as if such applicant were a holder of a permit under such chapter 52 to engage in such business."

[¶ 3295] Code Sec. 5722. Reports.

Every manufacturer [1-B]*or importer* of tobacco products or cigarette papers and tubes, and every export warehouse proprietor, shall make reports containing such information, in such form, at such times, and for such periods as the Secretary shall by regulation prescribe.

[Endnote Code Sec. 5722]

H.R. 2015. Matter in *italics* in Code Sec. 5722 added by Sec. 9302(h)(2)(A) of the Balanced Budget Act of 1997, H.R. 2015, 8/5/97.

1_B. added matter in Code Sec. 5722[H.R. 2015]

Effective Date (Sec. 9302(i), H.R. 2015, 8/5/97) Sec. 9302(i), H.R. 2015, 8/5/97, reads as follows:

"(i) Effective date.

"(1) In general. The amendments made by this section shall apply to articles removed (as defined in section 5702(k) of the Internal Revenue Code of 1986, as amended by this section) after December 31, 1999.

"(2) Transitional rule. Any person who—

"(A) on the date of the enactment of this Act is engaged in business as a manufacturer of roll-your-own tobacco or as an importer of tobacco products or cigarette papers and tubes, and

"(B) before January 1, 2000, submits an application under subchapter B of chapter 52 of such Code to engage in such business, may, notwithstanding such subchapter B, continue to engage in such business pending final action on such application. Pending such final action, all provisions of such chapter 52 shall apply to such applicant in the same manner and to the same extent as if such applicant were a holder of a permit under such chapter 52 to engage in such business."

[¶ 3296]   Code Sec.¹⁻ᴮ 5754.   Restriction on importation of previously exported tobacco products.

(a) In general. Tobacco products and cigarette papers and tubes previously exported from the United States may be imported or brought into the United States only as provided in section 5704(d). For purposes of this section, section 5704(d), section 5761, and such other provisions as the Secretary may specify by regulations, references to exportation shall be treated as including a reference to shipment to the Commonwealth of Puerto Rico.

(b) Cross reference. For penalty for the sale of tobacco products and cigarette papers and tubes in the United States which are labeled for export, see section 5761(c).

[Endnote Code Sec. 5754]

H.R. 2015. Code Sec. 5754 was added by Sec. 9302(h)(1)(E)(i) of the Balanced Budget Act of 1997, H.R. 2014, 8/5/97.
1_B. added Code Sec. 5754 [H.R. 2015]

Effective Date (Sec. 9302(i), H.R. 2015, 8/5/97) Sec. 9302(i), H.R. 2015, 8/5/97, reads as follows:

"(i) Effective date.

"(1) In general. The amendments made by this section shall apply to articles removed (as defined in section 5702(k) of the Internal Revenue Code of 1986, as amended by this section) after December 31, 1999.

"(2) Transitional rule. Any person who—

"(A) on the date of the enactment of this Act is engaged in business as a manufacturer of roll-your-own tobacco or as an importer of tobacco products or cigarette papers and tubes, and

"(B) before January 1, 2000, submits an application under subchapter B of chapter 52 of such Code to engage in such business, may, notwithstanding such subchapter B, continue to engage in such business pending final action on such application. Pending such final action, all provisions of such chapter 52 shall apply to such applicant in the same manner and to the same extent as if such applicant were a holder of a permit under such chapter 52 to engage in such business."

[¶ 3297]   Code Sec. 5761.   Civil penalties.

(a) Omitting things required or doing things forbidden. Whoever willfully omits, neglects, or refuses to comply with any duty imposed upon him by this chapter, or to do, or cause to be done, any of the things required by this chapter, or does anything prohibited by this chapter, shall in addition to any other penalty provided in this title, be liable to a penalty of $1,000, to be recovered, with costs of suit, in a civil action, except where a penalty under ¹⁻ᴮsubsection (b) or (c) or under section 6651 or 6653 or part II of subchapter A of chapter 68 may be collected from such person by assessment.

* * * * * * * * * * * *

²⁻ᴮ*(c) Sale of tobacco products and cigarette papers and tubes for export. Except as provided in subsections (b) and (d) of section 5704—*

(1) every person who sells, relands, or receives within the jurisdiction of the United States any tobacco products or cigarette papers or tubes which have been labeled or shipped for exportation under this chapter,

(2) every person who sells or receives such relanded tobacco products or cigarette papers or tubes, and

(3) every person who aids or abets in such selling, relanding, or receiving,

shall, in addition to the tax and any other penalty provided in this title, be liable for a penalty equal to the greater of $1,000 or 5 times the amount of the tax imposed by this chapter. All tobacco products and cigarette papers and tubes relanded within the jurisdiction of the United States, and all vessels, vehicles, and aircraft used in such relanding or in removing such products, papers, and tubes from the place where relanded, shall be forfeited to the United States.

[3-B](d) **Applicability of section 6665.** [4-B]*The penalties imposed by subsections (b) and (c)* shall be assessed, collected, and paid in the same manner as taxes, as provided in section 6665(a).

[5-B]*(e)* **Cross references.** For penalty for failure to make deposits or for overstatement of deposits, see section 6656.

[Endnote Code Sec. 5761]

H.R. 2015. Matter in *italics* in Code Sec. 5761(a), Code Sec. 5761(c), Code Sec. 5761(d) and Code Sec. 5761(e) added by Sec. 846(h)(1)(B)-(D) of the Balanced Budget Act of 1997, H.R. 2015, 8/5/97, which struck out:

  1_B. "subsection (b)" [H.R. 2015]
  2_B. added subsection (c) [H.R. 2015]
  3_B. "(c)" [H.R. 2015]
  4_B. "The penalty imposed by subsection (b)" [H.R. 2015]
  5_B. "(d)" [H.R. 2015]

Effective Date (Sec. 9302(i), H.R. 2015, 8/5/97) Sec. 9302(i), H.R. 2015, 8/5/97, reads as follows:

"(i) Effective date.

"(1) In general. The amendments made by this section shall apply to articles removed (as defined in section 5702(k) of the Internal Revenue Code of 1986, as amended by this section) after December 31, 1999.

"(2) Transitional rule. Any person who—

"(A) on the date of the enactment of this Act is engaged in business as a manufacturer of roll-your-own tobacco or as an importer of tobacco products or cigarette papers and tubes, and

"(B) before January 1, 2000, submits an application under subchapter B of chapter 52 of such Code to engage in such business, may, notwithstanding such subchapter B, continue to engage in such business pending final action on such application. Pending such final action, all provisions of such chapter 52 shall apply to such applicant in the same manner and to the same extent as if such applicant were a holder of a permit under such chapter 52 to engage in such business."

[¶ 3298]   Code Sec. 5762.   Criminal penalties.

(a) **Fraudulent offenses.** Whoever, with intent to defraud the United States—

(1) **Engaging in business unlawfully.** Engages in business as a manufacturer [1-B]*or importer* of tobacco products or cigarette papers and tubes, or as an export warehouse proprietor, without filing the bond and obtaining the permit where required by this chapter or regulations thereunder; or

(2) **Failing to furnish information or furnishing false information.** Fails to keep or make any record, return, report, or inventory, or keeps or makes any false or fraudulent record, return, report, or inventory, required by this chapter or regulations thereunder; or

(3) **Refusing to pay or evading tax.** Refuses to pay any tax imposed by this chapter, or attempts in any manner to evade or defeat the tax or the payment thereof; or

(4) **Removing tobacco products or cigarette papers or tubes unlawfully.** Removes, contrary to this chapter or regulations thereunder, any tobacco products or cigarette papers or tubes subject to tax under this chapter; or

(5) **Purchasing, receiving, possessing, or selling tobacco products or cigarette papers or tubes unlawfully.** Violates any provision of section 5751(a)(1) or (a)(2); or

(6) **Destroying, obliterating, or detaching marks, labels, or notices before packages are emptied.** Violates any provision of section 5752;

shall, for each such offense, be fined not more than $10,000, or imprisoned not more than 5 years, or both.

* * * * * * * * * * * *

[Endnote Code Sec. 5762]

H.R. 2015 Matter in *italics* in Code Sec. 5762(a)(1) added by Sec. 9302(h)(2)(A) of the Balanced Budget Act of 1997, H.R. 2014, 8/5/97.

1_B. added matter in para. (a)(1) [H.R. 2015]

Effective Date (Sec. 9302(i), H.R. 2015, 8/5/97) Sec. 9302(i), H.R. 2015, 8/5/97, reads as follows:

"(i) Effective date.

"(1) In general. The amendments made by this section shall apply to articles removed (as defined in section 5702(k) of the Internal Revenue Code of 1986, as amended by this section) after December 31, 1999.

"(2) Transitional rule. Any person who—

"(A) on the date of the enactment of this Act is engaged in business as a manufacturer of roll-your-own tobacco or as an importer of tobacco products or cigarette papers and tubes, and

"(B) before January 1, 2000, submits an application under subchapter B of chapter 52 of such Code to engage in such business, may, notwithstanding such subchapter B, continue to engage in such business pending final action on such application. Pending such final action, all provisions of such chapter 52 shall apply to such applicant in the same manner and to the same extent as if such applicant were a holder of a permit under such chapter 52 to engage in such business."

[¶ 3299]   Code Sec. 5763.   Forfeitures.

* * * * * * * * * * * *

(b) **Personal property of qualified manufacturers,** [1-B]*qualified importers,* **and export warehouse proprietors, acting with intent to defraud.** All tobacco products and cigarette papers and tubes, packages, machinery, fixtures, equipment, and all other materials and personal property on the premises of any qualified manufacturer [2-B]*or importer* of tobacco products or cigarette papers and tubes, or export warehouse proprietor, who, with intent to defraud the United States, fails to keep or make any record, return, report, or inventory, or keeps or makes any false or fraudulent record, return, report, or inventory, required by this chapter; or refuses to pay any tax imposed by this chapter, or attempts in any manner to evade or defeat the tax or the payment thereof; or removes, contrary to any provision of this chapter, any article subject to tax under this chapter, shall be forfeited to the United States.

(c) **Real and personal property of illicit operators.** All tobacco products, cigarette papers and tubes, machinery, fixtures, equipment, and other materials and personal property on the premises of any person engaged in business as a manufacturer [3-B]*or importer* of tobacco products or cigarette papers and tubes, or export warehouse proprietor, without filing the bond or obtaining the permit, as required by this chapter, together with all his right, title, and interest in the building in which such business is conducted, and the lot or tract of ground on which the building is located, shall be forfeited to the United States.

* * * * * * * * * * * *

[Endnote Code Sec. 5763]

H.R. 2015 Matter in *italics* in Code Sec. 5763(b) and Code Sec. 5763(c) added by Sec. 9302(h)(2)(A) and (B) of the Balanced Budget Act of 1997, H.R. 2015, 8/5/97.

1_B. added matter in heading of subsec. (b) [H.R. 2015]

2_B. added matter in subsec. (b) [H.R. 2015]

3_B. added matter in subsec. (c) [H.R. 2015]

Effective Date (Sec. 9302(i), H.R. 2015, 8/5/97) Sec. 9302(i), H.R. 2015, 8/5/97, reads as follows:

"(i) Effective date.

"(1) In general. The amendments made by this section shall apply to articles removed (as defined in section 5702(k) of the Internal Revenue Code of 1986, as amended by this section) after December 31, 1999.

"(2) Transitional rule. Any person who—

"(A) on the date of the enactment of this Act is engaged in business as a manufacturer of roll-your-own tobacco or as an importer of tobacco products or cigarette papers and tubes, and

"(B) before January 1, 2000, submits an application under subchapter B of chapter 52 of such Code to engage in such business, may, notwithstanding such subchapter B, continue to engage in such business pending final action on such application. Pending such final action, all provisions of such chapter 52 shall apply to such applicant in the same manner and to the same extent as if such applicant were a holder of a permit under such chapter 52 to engage in such business."

[¶ 3300]   Code Sec. 6011.   General requirement of return, statement, or list.

* * * * * * * * * * *

(e) Regulations requiring returns on magnetic media, etc.

(1) In general. The Secretary shall prescribe regulations providing standards for determining which returns must be filed on magnetic media or in other machine-readable form. The Secretary may not require returns of any tax imposed by subtitle A on individuals, estates, and trusts to be other than on paper forms supplied by the Secretary.

(2) Requirements of regulations. In prescribing regulations under paragraph (1), the Secretary—

(A) shall not require any person to file returns on magnetic media unless such person is required to file at least 250 returns during the calendar year, and

(B) shall take into account (among other relevant factors) the ability of the taxpayer to comply at reasonable cost with the requirements of such regulations.

[1]*Notwithstanding the preceding sentence, the Secretary shall require partnerships having more than 100 partners to file returns on magnetic media.*

* * * * * * * * * * *

[Endnote Code Sec. 6011]

Matter in *italics* in Code Sec. 6011(e)(2) added by Sec. 1224 of the Taxpayer Relief Act of 1997, H.R. 2014, 8/5/97.
1. added matter in para. (e)(2)

Effective Date (Sec. 1226, H.R. 2014, 8/5/97) effective for partnership tax. yrs. end. on or after 12/31/97.

[¶ 3301]   Code Sec. 6012.   Persons required to make returns of income.

* * * * * * * * * * *

(b) Returns made by fiduciaries and receivers.

* * * * * * * * * * *

[1]*(6) IRA share of partnership income. In the case of a trust which is exempt from taxation under section 408(e), for purposes of this section, the trust's distributive share of items of gross income and gain of any partnership to which subchapter C or D of chapter 63 applies shall be treated as equal to the trust's distributive share of the taxable income of such partnership.*

(c) Certain income earned abroad or from sale of residence. For purposes of this section, gross income shall be computed without regard to the exclusion provided for in section 121 [2]*(relating to gain from sale of principal residence)* and without regard to the exclusion provided for in section 911 (relating to citizens or residents of the United States living abroad).

* * * * * * * * * * *

[For analysis, see ¶ 2306. For committee reports, see ¶ 5213.]

[Endnote Code Sec. 6012]

Code Sec. 6012(b)(6), in *italics*, was added by Sec. 1225 of the Taxpayer Relief Act of 1997, H.R. 2014, date of enactment.

1. added paragraph (b)(6)

Effective Date (Sec. 1226, H.R. 2014, 8/5/97) effective for partnership tax. yrs. end. on or after 12/31/97.

Matter in *italics* in Code Sec. 6012(c) added by Sec. 312(d)(11), H.R. 2014, 8/5/97, which struck out:
2. "(relating to one-time exclusion of gain from sale of principal residence by individual who has attained age 55)"
Effective Date (Sec. 312(d) [sic (e)], H.R. 2014, 8/5/97) effective for sales and exchanges after 5/6/97, except as provided by Sec. 312(d)(2)-(4) [sic (e)(2)-(4)] of this Act, which read as follows:
"(2) Sales before 8/5/97. At the election of the taxpayer, the amendments made by this section shall not apply to any sale or exchange before the date of the enactment of this Act.

"(3) Certain sales within 2 years after 8/5/97. Section 121 of the Internal Revenue Code of 1986 (as amended by this section) shall be applied without regard to subsection (c)(2)(B) thereof in the case of any sale or exchange of property during the 2-year period beginning on the date of the enactment of this Act if the taxpayer held such property on the date of the enactment of this Act and fails to meet the ownership and use requirements of subsection (a) thereof with respect to such property.

"(4) Binding contracts. At the election of the taxpayer, the amendments made by this section shall not apply to a sale or exchange after the date of the enactment of this Act, if—

"(A) such sale or exchange is pursuant to a contract which was binding on such date, or

"(B) without regard to such amendments, gain would not be recognized under section 1034 of the Internal Revenue Code of 1986 (as in effect on the day before the date of the enactment of this Act) on such sale or exchange by reason of a new residence acquired on or before such date or with respect to the acquisition of which by the taxpayer a binding contract was in effect on such date.

This paragraph shall not apply to any sale or exchange by an individual if the treatment provided by section 877(a)(1) of the Internal Revenue Code of 1986 applies to such individual."

[¶ 3302]   Code Sec. 6018.   Estate tax returns.

(a) Returns by executor.

(1) Citizens or residents. In all cases where the gross estate at the death of a citizen or resident exceeds [1]*the applicable exclusion amount in effect under section 2010(c) for the calendar year which includes the date of death,* the executor shall make a return with respect to the estate tax imposed by subtitle B.

* * * * * * * * * * *

(4) [2]Repealed.

(b) Returns by beneficiaries. If the executor is unable to make a complete return as to any part of the gross estate of the decedent, he shall include in his return a description of such part and the name of every person holding a legal or beneficial interest therein. Upon notice from the Secretary such person shall in like manner make a return as to such part of the gross estate.

[For analysis, see ¶ 501. For committee reports, see ¶ 5026.]

[Endnote Code Sec. 6018]

Matter in *italics* in Code Sec. 6018(a)(1) added by Sec. 501(a)(1)(C) of the Revenue Reconciliation Act of 1997, H.R. 2014, 8/5/97, which struck out:

1. "$600,000"

Effective Date (Sec. 501(f), H.R. 2014, 8/5/97) effective for estates of decedents dying, and gifts made, after 12/31/97.

Code Sec. 6018(a)(4) was deleted by Sec. 1073(b)(4), H.R. 2014, 8/5/97, which struck out:

2."(4) Return required if excess retirement accumulation tax. The executor shall make a return with respect to the estate tax imposed by subtitle B in any case where such tax is increased by reason of section 4980A(d)."

Effective Date (Sec. 1073(c)(2), H.R. 2014, 8/5/97) effective for estates of decedents dying after 12/31/96.

[¶ 3303]   Code Sec. 6019.   Gift tax returns.

Any individual who in any calendar year makes any transfer by gift other than—

(1) a transfer which under subsection (b) or (e) of section 2503 is not to be included in the total amount of gifts for such year,[1]

(2) a transfer of an interest with respect to which a deduction is allowed under section 2523, [2]or

[3]*(3) a transfer with respect to which a deduction is allowed under section 2522 but only if—*

(A)

(i) such transfer is of the donor's entire interest in the property transferred, and

(ii) no other interest in such property is or has been transferred (for less than adequate and full consideration in money or money's worth) from the donor to a person, or to a use, not described in subsection (a) or (b) of section 2522, or

(B) such transfer is described in section 2522(d),

shall make a return for such year with respect to the gift tax imposed by subtitle B. *[For analysis, see ¶ 2307. For committee reports, see ¶ 5261.]*

[Endnote Code Sec. 6019]
Matter in *italics* in Code Sec. 6019(1), Code Sec. 6019(2), and Code Sec. 6019(3) added by Sec. 1301(a) of the Taxpayer Relief Act of 1997, H.R. 2014, 8/5/97, which struck out:
1. "or"
2. added matter in para. (2)
3. added para. (3)
Effective Date (Sec. 1301(b), H.R. 2014, 8/5/97) effective for gifts made after 8/5/97.

[¶ 3304] Code Sec. 6031.   Return of partnership income.

* * * * * * * * * * * *

(b) **Copies to partners.** Each partnership required to file a return under subsection (a) for any partnership taxable year shall (on or before the day on which the return for such taxable year was required to be filed) furnish to each person who is a partner or who holds an interest in such partnership as a nominee for another person at any time during such taxable year a copy of such information required to be shown on such return as may be required by regulations. [1]*In the case of an electing large partnership (as defined in section 775), such information shall be furnished on or before the first March 15 following the close of such taxable year.*

* * * * * * * * * * * *

[2]*(e) **Foreign partnerships.***
*(1) **Exception for foreign partnership.** Except as provided in paragraph (2), the preceding provisions of this section shall not apply to a foreign partnership.*
*(2) **Certain foreign partnerships required to file return.** Except as provided in regulations prescribed by the Secretary, this section shall apply to a foreign partnership for any taxable year if for such year, such partnership has—*
(A) gross income derived from sources within the United States, or
(B) gross income which is effectively connected with the conduct of a trade or business within the United States.
The Secretary may provide simplified filing procedures for foreign partnerships to which this section applies.

[For analysis, see ¶ 2302, ¶ 2303. For committee reports, see ¶ 5182, ¶ 5211.]

[Endnote Code Sec. 6031]
Matter in *italics* in Code Sec. 6031(b) was added by Sec. 1223(a) of the Taxpayer Relief Act of 1997, H.R. 2014, 8/5/97.
1. added matter at the end of subsection (b)
Effective Date (Sec. 1226, H.R. 2014, 8/5/97) effective for partnership tax. yrs. end. on or after 12/31/97.

Code Sec. 6031(e), in *italics*, was added by Sec. 1141(a), H.R. 2014, 8/5/97.
2. added subsection (e)
Effective Date (Sec. 1141(c), H.R. 2014, 8/5/97) effective for tax. yrs. begin. after 8/5/97.

[¶ 3305] Code Sec. 6033.   Returns by exempt organizations.

* * * * * * * * * * * *

(b) **Certain organizations described in section 501(c)(3).** Every organization described in section 501(c)(3) which is subject to the requirements of subsection (a) shall furnish annually information, at such time and in such manner as the Secretary may by forms or regulations prescribe, setting forth—

* * * * * * * * * * * *

(10) [1]*the respective amounts (if any) of the taxes imposed on the organization, or any organization manager of the organization, during the taxable year under any of the following provisions (and the respective amounts (if any) of reimbursements paid by the organization*

during the taxable year with respect to taxes imposed on any such organization manager under any of such provisions):

(A) section 4911 (relating to tax on excess expenditures to influence legislation),

(B) section 4912 (relating to tax on disqualifying lobbying expenditures of certain organizations), and

(C) section 4955 (relating to taxes on political expenditures of section 501(c)(3) organizations), [2]*except to the extent that, by reason of section 4962, the taxes imposed under such section are not required to be paid or are credited or refunded,*

[3]*(11) the respective amounts (if any) of—*

(A) the taxes imposed with respect to the organization on any organization manager, or any disqualified person, during the taxable year under section 4958 (relating to taxes on private excess benefit from certain charitable organizations), and

(B) reimbursements paid by the organization during the taxable year with respect to taxes imposed under such section,

except to the extent that, by reason of section 4962, the taxes imposed under such section are not required to be paid or are credited or refunded,

* * * * * * * * * * * *

[For analysis, see ¶ 2305. For committee reports, see ¶ 5384.]

[Endnote Code Sec. 6033]

Matter in *italics* in Code Sec. 6033(b)(10), Code Sec. 6033(b)(10)(C) and Code Sec. 6033(b)(11) added by Sec. 1603(b)(1)(A), (b)(1)(B), and (b)(2) of the Taxpayer Relief Act of 1997, H.R. 2014, 8/5/97, which struck out:

1. "the respective amounts (if any) of the taxes paid by the organization during the taxable year under the following provisions:"

2. added matter in subpara. (b)(10)(C)

3. "(11) the respective amounts (if any) of the taxes paid by the organization, or any disqualified person with respect to such organization, during the taxable year under section 4958 (relating to taxes on private excess benefit from certain charitable organizations),"

Effective Date (Sec. 1603(c), H.R. 2014, 8/5/97) effective for returns for tax. yrs. begin. after 7/30/96.

[¶ 3306]   Code Sec. 6034A.   Information to beneficiaries of estates and trusts.

* * * * * * * * * * * *

[1]*(c) Beneficiary's return must be consistent with estate or trust return or secretary notified of inconsistency.*

(1) In general. A beneficiary of any estate or trust to which subsection (a) applies shall, on such beneficiary's return, treat any reported item in a manner which is consistent with the treatment of such item on the applicable entity's return.

(2) Notification of inconsistent treatment.

(A) In general. In the case of any reported item, if—

(i)   (I) the applicable entity has filed a return but the beneficiary's treatment on such beneficiary's return is (or may be) inconsistent with the treatment of the item on the applicable entity's return, or

(II) the applicable entity has not filed a return, and

(ii) the beneficiary files with the Secretary a statement identifying the inconsistency, paragraph (1) shall not apply to such item.

(B) Beneficiary receiving incorrect information. A beneficiary shall be treated as having complied with clause (ii) of subparagraph (A) with respect to a reported item if the beneficiary—

(i) demonstrates to the satisfaction of the Secretary that the treatment of the reported item on the beneficiary's return is consistent with the treatment of the item on the statement furnished under subsection (a) to the beneficiary by the applicable entity, and

(ii) elects to have this paragraph apply with respect to that item.

(3) Effect of failure to notify. In any case—

(A) described in subparagraph (A)(i)(I) of paragraph (2), and

(B) in which the beneficiary does not comply with subparagraph (A)(ii) of paragraph (2), any adjustment required to make the treatment of the items by such beneficiary consistent with the treatment of the items on the applicable entity's return shall be treated as arising out of mathematical or clerical errors and assessed according to section 6213(b)(1). Paragraph (2) of section 6213(b) shall not apply to any assessment referred to in the preceding sentence.

(4) Definitions. For purposes of this subsection—

(A) Reported item. The term "reported item" means any item for which information is required to be furnished under subsection (a).

(B) Applicable entity. The term "applicable entity" means the estate or trust of which the taxpayer is the beneficiary.

(5) Addition to tax for failure to comply with section. For addition to tax in the case of a beneficiary's negligence in connection with, or disregard of, the requirements of this section, see part II of subchapter A of chapter 68.

[For analysis, see ¶ 2304. For committee reports, see ¶ 5127.]

[Endnote Code Sec. 6034A]

Code Sec. 6034A(c), in *italics*, was added by Sec. 1027(a) of the Taxpayer Relief Act of 1997, H.R. 2014, 8/5/97.
1. added subsec. (c).

Effective Date (Sec. 1027(c), H.R. 2014, 8/5/97) effective for returns of beneficiaries and owners filed after 8/5/97.

[¶ 3307]   Code Sec. 6038.   [1]Information reporting with respect to certain foreign corporations and partnerships.

(a) Requirement.

(1) In general. Every United States person shall furnish, with respect to any foreign business entity which such person controls, such information as the Secretary may prescribe relating to—

(A) the name, the principal place of business, and the nature of business of such entity, and the country under whose laws such entity is incorporated (or organized in the case of a partnership);

(B) in the case of a foreign corporation, its post-1986 undistributed earnings (as defined in section 902(c));

(C) a balance sheet for such entity listing assets, liabilities, and capital;

(D) transactions between such entity and—

(i) such person,

(ii) any corporation or partnership which such person controls, and

(iii) any United States person owning, at the time the transaction takes place—

(I) in the case of a foreign corporation, 10 percent or more of the value of any class of stock outstanding of such corporation, and

(II) in the case of a foreign partnership, at least a 10-percent interest in such partnership; and

(E)

(i) in the case of a foreign corporation, a description of the various classes of stock outstanding, and a list showing the name and address of, and number of shares held by, each United States person who is a shareholder of record owning at any time during the annual accounting period 5 percent or more in value of any class of stock outstanding of such foreign corporation, and

(ii) information comparable to the information described in clause (i) in the case of a foreign partnership.

The Secretary may also require the furnishing of any other information which is similar or related in nature to that specified in the preceding sentence or which the Secretary determines to be appropriate to carry out the provisions of this title.

(2) Period for which information is to be furnished, etc. The information required under paragraph (1) shall be furnished for the annual accounting period of the [2]*foreign business entity* ending with or within the United States person's taxable year. The information so required shall be furnished at such time and in such manner as the Secretary shall by regulations prescribe.

(3) Limitation. No information shall be required to be furnished under this subsection with respect to any [3]*foreign business entity* for any annual accounting period unless such information was required to be furnished under regulations in effect on the first day of such annual accounting period.

(4) Information required from certain shareholders in certain cases. If any foreign corporation is treated as a controlled foreign corporation for any purpose under subpart F of part III of subchapter N of chapter 1, the Secretary may require any United States person treated as a United States shareholder of such corporation for any purpose under subpart F to furnish the information required under paragraph (1).

[4]*(5) Information required from 10-percent partner of controlled foreign partnership. In the case of a foreign partnership which is controlled by United States persons holding at least 10-percent interests (but not any one United States person), the Secretary may require each United States person who holds a 10-percent interest in such partnership to furnish information relating to such partnership, including information relating to such partner's ownership interests in the partnership and allocations to such partner of partnership items.*

(b) Dollar penalty for failure to furnish information.

(1) In general. If any person fails to furnish, within the time prescribed under paragraph (2) of subsection (a), any information with respect to any [5]*foreign business entity* required under paragraph (1) of subsection (a), such person shall pay a penalty of [6]*$10,000* for each annual accounting period with respect to which such failure exists.

(2) Increase in penalty where failure continues after notification. If any failure described in paragraph (1) continues for more than 90 days after the day on which the Secretary mails notice of such failure to the United States person, such person shall pay a penalty (in addition to the amount required under paragraph (1)) of [7]*$10,000* for each 30-day period (or fraction thereof) during which such failure continues with respect to any annual accounting period after the expiration of such 90-day period. The increase in any penalty under this paragraph shall not exceed [8]*$50,000.*

(c) Penalty of reducing foreign tax credit.

(1) In general. If a United States person fails to furnish, within the time prescribed under paragraph (2) of subsection (a), any information with respect to any [9]*foreign business entity* required under paragraph (1) of subsection (a), then—

(A) in applying section 901 (relating to taxes of foreign countries and possessions of the United States) to such United States person for the taxable year, the amount of taxes (other than taxes reduced under subparagraph (B)) paid or deemed paid (other than those deemed paid under section 904(c)) to any foreign country or possession of the United States for the taxable year shall be reduced by 10 percent, and

(B) [10]*in the case of a foreign business entity which is a foreign corporation,* in applying sections 902 (relating to foreign tax credit for corporate stockholder in foreign corporation) and 960 (relating to special rules for foreign tax credit) to any such United States person which is a corporation (or to any person who acquires from any other person any portion of the interest of such other person in any such foreign corporation, but only to the extent of such portion) for any taxable year, the amount of taxes paid or deemed paid by each foreign corporation with respect to which such person is required to furnish information during the annual accounting period or periods with respect to which such information is required under paragraph (2) of subsection (a) shall be reduced by 10 percent.

If such failure continues 90 days or more after notice of such failure by the Secretary to the United States person, then the amount of the reduction under this paragraph shall be 10 percent plus an additional 5 percent for each 3-month period, or fraction thereof, during which such failure to furnish information continues after the expiration of such 90-day period.

(2) Limitation. The amount of the reduction under paragraph (1) for each failure to furnish information with respect to a [11]*foreign business entity* required under subsection (a)(1) shall not exceed whichever of the following amounts is the greater:

(A) $10,000, or

(B) the income of the [12]*foreign business entity* for its annual accounting period with respect to which the failure occurs.

(3) Coordination with subsection (b). The amount of the reduction which (but for this paragraph) would be made under paragraph (1) with respect to any annual accounting period shall be reduced by the amount of the penalty imposed by subsection (b) with respect to such period.

(4) Special rules.

(A) No taxes shall be reduced under this subsection more than once for the same failure.

(B) For purposes of this subsection and subsection (b), the time prescribed under paragraph (2) of subsection (a) to furnish information (and the beginning of the 90-day period after notice by the Secretary) shall be treated as being not earlier than the last day on which (as shown to the satisfaction of the Secretary) reasonable cause existed for failure to furnish such information.

(C) In applying subsections (a) and (b) of section 902, and in applying subsection (a) of section 960, the reduction provided by this subsection shall not apply for purposes of determining the amount of post-1986 undistributed earnings.

(d) Two or more persons required to furnish information with respect to same [13]*foreign business entity*. Where, but for this subsection, two or more United States persons would be required to furnish information under subsection (a) with respect to the same [14]*foreign business entity* for the same period, the Secretary may by regulations provide that such information shall be required only from one person. To the extent practicable, the determination of which person shall furnish the information shall be made on the basis of actual ownership of stock.

(e) Definitions. For purposes of this section—

[15]*(1) Foreign business entity. The term "foreign business entity" means a foreign corporation and a foreign partnership.*

[16]*(2) Control* [17]*of corporation.* A person is in control of a corporation if such person owns stock possessing more than 50 percent of the total combined voting power of all classes of stock entitled to vote, or more than 50 percent of the total value of shares of all classes of stock, of a corporation. If a person is in control (within the meaning of the preceding sentence) of a corporation which in turn owns more than 50 percent of the total combined voting power of all classes of stock entitled to vote of another corporation, or owns more than 50 percent of the total value of the shares of all classes of stock of another corporation, then such person shall be treated as in control of such other corporation. For purposes of this paragraph, the rules prescribed by section 318(a) for determining ownership of stock shall apply; except that—

(A) subparagraphs (A), (B), and (C) of section 318(a)(3) shall not be applied so as to consider a United States person as owning stock which is owned by a person who is not a United States person, and

(B) in applying subparagraph (C) of section 318(a)(2), the phrase "10 percent" shall be substituted for the phrase "50 percent" used in subparagraph (C).

[18]*(3) Partnership-related definitions.*

(A) Control. A person is in control of a partnership if such person owns directly or indirectly more than a 50 percent interest in such partnership.

(B) 50-percent interest. For purposes of subparagraph (A), a 50-percent interest in a partnership is—

(i) an interest equal to 50 percent of the capital interest, or 50 percent of the profits interest, in such partnership, or

(ii) to the extent provided in regulations, an interest to which 50 percent of the deductions or losses of such partnership are allocated.

For purposes of the preceding sentence, rules similar to the rules of section 267(c) (other than paragraph (3)) shall apply,

(C) 10-percent interest. A 10-percent interest in a partnership is an interest which would be described in subparagraph (B) if "10 percent" were substituted for "50 percent" each place it appears.

[19]*(4)* **Annual accounting period.** The annual accounting period of a [20]*foreign business entity* is the annual period on the basis of which such corporation regularly computes its income in keeping its books. In the case of a specified [21]*foreign business entity* (as defined in section 898), the taxable year of such corporation shall be treated as its annual accounting period.

* * * * * * * * * * * *

[For analysis, see ¶ 2312. For committee reports, see ¶ 5182.]

[Endnote Code Sec. 6038]

Matter in *italics* in Code Sec. 6038, Code Sec. 6038(a), Code Sec. 6038(b), Code Sec. 6038(c), Code Sec. 6038(d) and Code Sec. 6038(e) added by Sec. 1142(a)-(e) of the Taxpayer Relief Act of 1997, H.R. 2014, 8/5/97, which struck out:

1. "SEC. 6038. INFORMATION WITH RESPECT TO CERTAIN FOREIGN CORPORATIONS.

"(a) Requirement.

"(1) In general. Every United States person shall furnish, with respect to any foreign corporation which such person controls (within the meaning of subsection (e)(1)), such information as the Secretary may prescribe by regulations relating to—

"(A) the name, the principal place of business, and the nature of business of such foreign corporation, and the country under whose laws incorporated;

"(B) the post-1986 undistributed earnings (as defined in section 902(c)) of such foreign corporation,

"(C) a balance sheet for such foreign corporation listing assets, liabilities, and capital;

"(D) transactions between such foreign corporation and—

"(i) such person,

"(ii) any other corporation which such person controls, and

"(iii) any United States person owning, at the time the transaction takes place, 10 percent or more of the value of any class of stock outstanding of such foreign corporation;

"(E) a description of the various classes of stock outstanding, and a list showing the name and address of, and number of shares held by, each United States person who is a shareholder of record owning at any time during the annual accounting period 5 percent or more in value of any class of stock outstanding of such foreign corporation.

The Secretary may also require the furnishing of any other information which is similar or related in nature to that specified in the preceding sentence or which the Secretary determines to be appropriate to carry out the provisions of this title."

2. "foreign corporation"
3. "foreign corporation"
4. added para. (a)(5)
5. "foreign corporation"
6. "$1,000"
7. "$1,000"
8. "$24,000"
9. "foreign corporation"
10. added matter in subpara. (c)(1)(B)
11. "foreign corporation"
12. "foreign corporation"
13. "foreign corporation"
14. "foreign corporation"
15. added para. (e)(1)
16. "(1)"
17. added matter in the heading of para. (e)(2) [as redesignated]
18. added para. (e)(3)
19. "(2)"
20. "foreign corporation"
21. "foreign corporation"

Effective Date (Sec. 1142(f), H.R. 2014, 8/5/97) effective for annual accounting periods begin. after 8/5/97.

[¶ 3308]   Code Sec. 6038B.   Notice of certain transfers to foreign persons.

(a) In general. Each United States person who—

[1]*(1)* transfers property to—

(A) a foreign corporation in an exchange described in section 332, 351, 354, 355, 356, or 361, or

(B) a foreign partnership in a contribution described in section 721 or in any other contribution described in regulations described by the Secretary,

(2) makes a distribution described in section 336 to a person who is not a United States person,

shall furnish to the Secretary, at such time and in such manner as the Secretary shall by regulations prescribe, such information with respect to such exchange or distribution as the Secretary may require in such regulations.

²*(b) Exceptions for certain transfers to foreign partnerships; special rule.*

(1) Exceptions. Subsection (a)(1)(B) shall apply to a transfer by a United States person to a foreign partnership only if—

(A) the United States person holds (immediately after the transfer) directly or indirectly at least a 10-percent interest (as defined in section 6046A(d)) in the partnership, or

(B) the value of the property transferred (when added to the value of the property transferred by such person or any related person to such partnership or a related partnership during the 12-month period ending on the date of the transfer) exceeds $100,000.

For purposes of the preceding sentence, the value of any transferred property is its fair market value at the time of its transfer.

(2) Special rule. If by reason of an adjustment under section 482 or otherwise, a contribution described in subsection (a)(1) is deemed to have been made, such contribution shall be treated for purposes of this section as having been made not earlier than the date specified by the Secretary.

³*(c) Penalty for failure to furnish information.*

(1) In general. If any United States person fails to furnish the information described in subsection (a) at the time and in the manner required by regulations, such person shall pay a penalty ⁴*equal to 10 percent of the fair market value of the property at the time of the exchange (and, in the case of a contribution described in subsection (a)(1)(B), such person shall recognize gain as if the contributed property had been sold for such value at the time of such contribution).*

(2) Reasonable cause exception. Paragraph (1) shall not apply to any failure if the United States person shows such failure is due to reasonable cause and not to willful neglect.

⁵**(3) Limit on penalty.** The penalty under paragraph (1) with respect to any exchange shall not exceed $100,000 unless the failure with respect to such exchange was due to intentional disregard.

[For analysis, see ¶ 2315. For committee reports, see ¶ 5186.]

[Endnote Code Sec. 6038B]

Matter in *italics* in Code Sec. 6038B(a)(1), Code Sec. 6038B(b), Code Sec. 6038B(c), Code Sec. 6038B(c)(1) and Code Sec. 6038B(c)(3) added by Sec. 1144(a)-(c) of the Taxpayer Relief Act of 1997, H.R. 2014, 8/5/97, which struck out:

1. "(1) transfers property to a foreign corporation in an exchange described in section 332, 351, 354, 355, 356, or 361, or"
2. added subsection (b)
3. "(b)"
4. "equal to 25 percent of the amount of the gain realized on the exchange."
5. added para. (c)(3)

Effective Date (Sec. 1144(d), H.R. 2014, 8/5/97) Sec. 1144(d) of this Act reads as follows:

"(d) Effective date.

"(1) In general. The amendments made by this section shall apply to transfers made after the date of the enactment of this Act.

"(2) Election of retroactive effect. Section 1494(c) of the Internal Revenue Code of 1986 shall not apply to any transfer after August 20, 1996, if the person otherwise required to file a return with respect to such transfer elects to apply the amendments made by this section to transfers after August 20, 1996. The Secretary of the Treasury or his delegate may prescribe simplified reporting under the preceding sentence."

[¶ 3309]   Code Sec. 6039D.   Returns and records with respect to certain fringe benefit plans.

* * * * * * * * * * *

(d) Definitions and special rules. For purposes of this section—

(1) Specified fringe benefit plan. The term "specified fringe benefit plan" means any plan under section 79, 105, 106, 120, 125, 127, [1]*129, or 137.*

(2) Applicable exclusion. The term "applicable exclusion" means, with respect to any specified fringe benefit plan, the section specified under paragraph (1) under which benefits under such plan are excludable from gross income.

(3) Special rule for multiemployer plans. In the case of a multiemployer plan, the plan shall be required to provide any information required by this section which the Secretary determines, on the basis of the agreement between the plan and employer, is held by the plan (and not the employer).

[Endnote Code Sec. 6039D]

Matter in *italics* in Code Sec. 6039D(d)(1) added by Sec. 1601(h)(2)(D)(iii) of the Taxpayer Relief Act of 1997, H.R. 2014, 8/5/97, which struck out:
1. "or 129"
Effective Date (Sec. 1601(j)(1), H.R. 2014, 8/5/97) effective for tax. yrs. begin. after 12/31/96.

[¶ 3310] *Code Sec.*[1] *6039G.* **Information on individuals losing united states citizenship.**

* * * * * * * * * * * *

[Endnote Code Sec. 6039G]

Matter in *italics* in Code Sec. 6039G added by Sec. 1602(h)(1) of the Taxpayer Relief Act of 1997, H.R. 2014, 8/5/97, which struck out:
1. "6039F"
Effective Date (Sec. 1602(i), H.R. 2014, 8/5/97) effective as provided in P.L. 104-191, Sec. 512(c), which reads as follows:
"(c) Effective date. The amendments made by this section shall apply to—
"(1) individuals losing United States citizenship (within the meaning of section 877 of the Internal Revenue Code of 1986) on or after February 6, 1995, and
"(2) long-term residents of the United States with respect to whom an event described in subparagraph (A) or (B) of section 877(e)(1) of such Code occurs on or after such date.
In no event shall any statement required by such amendments be due before the 90th day after the date of the enactment of this Act."

[¶ 3311] Code Sec. 6041A. Returns regarding payments of remuneration for services and direct sales.

* * * * * * * * * * * *

(d) Applications to governmental units.

* * * * * * * * * * * *

[1]*(3) Payments to corporations by federal executive agencies.*

(A) In general. Notwithstanding any regulation prescribed by the Secretary before the date of the enactment of this paragraph, subsection (a) shall apply to remuneration paid to a corporation by any Federal executive agency (as defined in section 6050M(b)).

(B) Exception. Subparagraph (A) shall not apply to—

(i) services under contracts described in section 6050M(e)(3) with respect to which the requirements of section 6050M(e)(2) are met, and

(ii) such other services as the Secretary may specify in regulations prescribed after the date of the enactment of this paragraph.

* * * * * * * * * * * *

[For analysis, see ¶ 2311. For committee reports, see ¶ 5122.]

[Endnote Code Sec. 6041A]

Code Sec. 6041A(d)(3), in *italics*, was added by Sec. 1022(a) of the Taxpayer Relief Act of 1997, H.R. 2014, 8/5/97.
1. added paragraph (d)(3)

Effective Date (Sec. 1022(b), H.R. 2014, 8/5/97) effective for returns the due date for which (determined without regard to any extension) is more than 90 days after 8/5/97.

[¶ 3312] Code Sec. 6045.   Returns of brokers.

* * * * * * * * * * * *

(e) Return required in the case of real estate transactions.

* * * * * * * * * * * *

[1]**(5) Exception for sales or exchanges of certain principal residences.**

(A) In general. Paragraph (1) shall not apply to any sale or exchange of a residence for $250,000 or less if the person referred to in paragraph (2) receives written assurance in a form acceptable to the Secretary from the seller that—

(i) such residence is the principal residence (within the meaning of section 121) of the seller,

(ii) if the Secretary requires the inclusion on the return under subsection (a) of information as to whether there is federally subsidized mortgage financing assistance with respect to the mortgage on residences, that there is no such assistance with respect to the mortgage on such residence, and

(iii) the full amount of the gain on such sale or exchange is excludable from gross income under section 121.

If such assurance includes an assurance that the seller is married, the preceding sentence shall be applied by substituting "$500,000" for "$250,000".

The Secretary may by regulation increase the dollar amounts under this subparagraph if the Secretary determines that such an increase will not materially reduce revenues to the Treasury.

(B) Seller. For purposes of this paragraph, the term "seller" includes the person relinquishing the residence in an exchange.

[2]**(f) Return required in the case of payments to attorneys.**

(1) In general. Any person engaged in a trade or business and making a payment (in the course of such trade or business) to which this subsection applies shall file a return under subsection (a) and a statement under subsection (b) with respect to such payment.

(2) Application of subsection.

(A) In general. This subsection shall apply to any payment to an attorney in connection with legal services (whether or not such services are performed for the payor).

(B) Exception. This subsection shall not apply to the portion of any payment which is required to be reported under section 6041(a) (or would be so required but for the dollar limitation contained therein) or section 6051.

[For analysis, see ¶ 2309, ¶ 2310. For committee reports, see ¶ 5020, ¶ 5121.]

[Endnote Code Sec. 6045]

Code Sec. 6045(e)(5), in *italics*, was added by Sec. 312(c) of the Taxpayer Relief Act of 1997, H.R. 2014, 8/5/97.

1. added para. (e)(5)

Effective Date (Sec. 312(d) [sic (e)], H.R. 2014, 8/5/97) effective for sales and exchanges after 5/6/97, except as provided by Secs. 312(d)(2)-(4) [sic (e)(2)-(4)] of this Act, which read as follows:

"(2) Sales before 8/5/97.—At the election of the taxpayer, the amendments made by this section shall not apply to any sale or exchange before the date of the enactment of this Act.

"(3) Certain sales within 2 years after 8/5/97. Section 121 of the Internal Revenue Code of 1986 (as amended by this section) shall be applied without regard to subsection (c)(2)(B) thereof in the case of any sale or exchange of property during the 2-year period beginning on the date of the enactment of this Act if the taxpayer held such property on the date of the enactment of this Act and fails to meet the ownership and use requirements of subsection (a) thereof with respect to such property.

"(4) Binding contracts.—At the election of the taxpayer, the amendments made by this section shall not apply to a sale or exchange after the date of the enactment of this Act, if—

"(A) such sale or exchange is pursuant to a contract which was binding on such date, or

"(B) without regard to such amendments, gain would not be recognized under section 1034 of the Internal Revenue Code of 1986 (as in effect on the day before the date of the enactment of this Act) on such sale or exchange by reason of a new residence acquired on or before such date or with respect to the acquisition of which by the taxpayer a binding contract was in effect on such date.

This paragraph shall not apply to any sale or exchange by an individual if the treatment provided by section 877(a)(1) of the Internal Revenue Code of 1986 applies to such individual."

Code Sec. 6045(f), in *italics*, was added by Sec. 1021(a), H,R. 2014, 8/5/97.

2. added subsec. (f)

Effective Date (Sec. 1021(c), H.R. 2014, 8/5/97) effective for payments date after 12/31/97.

[¶ 3313]   Code Sec. 6046.   Returns as to organization or reorganization of foreign corporations and as to acquisitions of their stock.

[1]*(a) Requirement of return.*

(1) In general. A return complying with the requirements of subsection (b) shall be made by—

(A) each United States citizen or resident who becomes an officer or director of a foreign corporation if a United States person (as defined in section 7701(a)(30)) meets the stock ownership requirements of paragraph (2) with respect to such corporation,

(B) each United States person—

(i) who acquires stock which, when added to any stock owned on the date of such acquisition, meets the stock ownership requirements of paragraph (2) with respect to a foreign corporation, or

(ii) who acquires stock which, without regard to stock owned on the date of such acquisition, meets the stock ownership requirements of paragraph (2) with respect to a foreign corporation,

(C) each person (not described in subparagraph (B)) who is treated as a United States shareholder under section 953(c) with respect to a foreign corporation, and

(D) each person who becomes a United States person while meeting the stock ownership requirements of paragraph (2) with respect to stock of a foreign corporation.

In the case of a foreign corporation with respect to which any person is treated as a United States shareholder under section 953(c), subparagraph (A) shall be treated as including a reference to each United States person who is an officer or director of such corporation.

(2) Stock ownership requirements. A person meets the stock ownership requirements of this paragraph with respect to any corporation if such person owns 10 percent or more of—

(A) the total combined voting power of all classes of stock of such corporation entitled to vote, or

(B) the total value of the stock of such corporation.

* * * * * * * * * * * *

[For analysis, see ¶ 2314. For committee reports, see ¶ 5188.]

[Endnote Code Sec. 6046]

Matter in *italics* in Code Sec. 6046(a) added by Sec. 1146(a) of the Taxpayer Relief Act of 1997, H.R. 2014, 8/5/97, which struck out:

1. "(a) Requirement of return. A return complying with the requirements of subsection (b) shall be made by—

"(1) each United States citizen or resident who is on January 1, 1963, an officer or director of a foreign corporation, 5 percent or more in value of the stock of which is owned by a United States person (as defined in section 7701(a)(30)), or who becomes such an officer or director at any time after such date,

"(2) each United States person who on January 1, 1963, owns 5 percent or more in value of the stock of a foreign corporation, or who, at any time after such date—

"(A) acquires stock which, when added to any stock owned on January 1, 1963, has a value equal to 5 percent or more of the value of the stock of a foreign corporation, or

"(B) acquires an additional 5 percent or more in value of the stock of a foreign corporation,

"(3) each person (not described in paragraph (2)) who, at any time after January 1, 1987, is treated as a United States shareholder under section 953(c) with respect to a foreign corporation, and

"(4) each person who at any time after January 1, 1963, becomes a United States person while owning 5 percent or more in value of the stock of a foreign corporation.

In the case of a foreign corporation with respect to which any person is treated as a United States shareholder under section 953(c), paragraph (1) shall be treated as including a reference to each United States person who is an officer or director of such corporation."

Effective Date (Sec. 1146(b), H.R. 2014, 8/5/97) effective 1/1/98.

[¶ 3314]   Code Sec. 6046A.   Returns as to interests in foreign partnerships.

(a) **Requirement of return.** Any United States person, except to the extent otherwise provided by regulations—

(1) who acquires any interest in a foreign partnership,

(2) who disposes of any portion of his interest in a foreign partnership, or

(3) whose proportional interest in a foreign partnership changes substantially, shall file a return.

[1]*Paragraphs (1) and (2) shall apply to any acquisition or disposition only if the United States person directly or indirectly holds at least a 10-percent interest in such partnership either before or after such acquisition or disposition, and paragraph (3) shall apply to any change only if the change is equivalent to at least a 10-interest in such partnership.*

* * * * * * * * * * * *

[2]*(d) **10-percent interest.** For purposes of subsection (a), a 10-percent interest in a partnership is an interest described in section 6038(e)(3)(C).*

[3]*(e) **Cross reference.** For provisions relating to penalties for violations of this section, see sections 6679 and 7203.*

[For analysis, see ¶ 2313. For committee reports, see ¶ 5182.]

[Endnote Code Sec. 6046A]

Matter in *italics* in Code Sec. 6046A(a), Code Sec. 6046A(d) and Code Sec. 6046A(e) added by Sec. 1143(a)(1) and (2) of the Taxpayer Relief Act of 1997, H.R. 2014, date of enactment, which struck out:

1. added matter in subsection (a)
2. added subsection (d)
3. "(d)"

Effective Date (Sec. 1143(c), H.R. 2014, 8/5/97) effective for transfers and changes after 8/5/97.

[¶ 3315]   Code Sec. 6048.   Information with respect to certain foreign trusts.

* * * * * * * * * * * *

(b) **United States** [1]*owner of foreign trust.*

(1) **In general.** If, at any time during any taxable year of a United States person, such person is treated as the owner of any portion of a foreign trust under the rules of subpart E of part I of subchapter J of chapter 1, such person shall be responsible to ensure that—

(A) such trust makes a return for such year which sets forth a full and complete accounting of all trust activities and operations for the year, the name of the United States agent for such trust, and such other information as the Secretary may prescribe, and

(B) such trust furnishes such information as the Secretary may prescribe to each United States person (i) who is treated as the owner of any portion of such trust or (ii) who receives (directly or indirectly) any distribution from the trust.

(2) **Trusts not having United States agent.**

(A) In general. If the rules of this paragraph apply to any foreign trust, the determination of amounts required to be taken into account with respect to such trust by a United States person under the rules of subpart E of part I of subchapter J of chapter 1 shall be determined by the Secretary.

(B) United States agent required. The rules of this paragraph shall apply to any foreign trust to which paragraph (1) applies unless such trust agrees (in such manner, subject to such conditions, and at such time as the Secretary shall prescribe) to authorize a United

States person to act as such trust's limited agent solely for purposes of applying sections 7602, 7603, and 7604 with respect to—

(i) any request by the Secretary to examine records or produce testimony related to the proper treatment of amounts required to be taken into account under the rules referred to in subparagraph (A), or

(ii) any summons by the Secretary for such records or testimony.

The appearance of persons or production of records by reason of a United States person being such an agent shall not subject such persons or records to legal process for any purpose other than determining the correct treatment under this title of the amounts required to be taken into account under the rules referred to in subparagraph (A). A foreign trust which appoints an [sic] described in this subparagraph shall not be considered to have an office or a permanent establishment in the United States, or to be engaged in a trade or business in the United States, solely because of the activities of such agent pursuant to this subsection.

(C) Other rules to apply. Rules similar to the rules of paragraphs (2) and (4) of section 6038A(e) shall apply for purposes of this paragraph.

* * * * * * * * * * *

(d) Special rules.

* * * * * * * * * * *

[2]*(5) United States person's return must be consistent with trust return or Secretary notified of inconsistency. Rules similar to the rules of section 6034A(c) shall apply to items reported by a trust under subsection (b)(1)(B) and to United States persons referred to in such subsection.*

[For analysis, see ¶ 2304. For committee reports, see ¶ 5127.]

[Endnote Code Sec. 6048]

Matter in *italics* in Code Sec. 6048(b) heading added by Sec. 1601(i)(1) of the Taxpayer Relief Act of 1997, H.R. 2014, 8/5/97, which struck out:

1. "grantor"

Effective Date (Sec. 1601(j)(1), H.R. 2014, 8/5/97) effective as provided in P.L. 104-188, Sec. 1901(d) which reads as follows:

"(d) Effective dates.

"(1) Reportable events. To the extent related to subsection (a) of section 6048 of the Internal Revenue Code of 1986, as amended by this section, the amendments made by this section shall apply to reportable events (as defined in such section 6048) occurring after the date of the enactment of this Act.

"(2) Grantor trust reporting.— To the extent related to subsection (b) of such section 6048, the amendments made by this section shall apply to taxable years of United States persons beginning after December 31, 1995.

"(3) Reporting by United States — To the extent related to subsection (c) of such section 6048, the amendments made by this section shall apply to distributions received after the date of the enactment of this Act."

Code Sec. 6048(d)(5), in *italics*, was added by Sec. 1027(b), H.R. 2014, 8/5/97.

2. added paragraph (d)(5)

Effective Date (Sec. 1027(c), H.R. 2014, 8/5/97) effective for returns of beneficiaries and owners filed after 8/5/97.

[¶ 3316]   Code Sec. 6050Q.   Certain long-term care benefits.

* * * * * * * * * * *

(b) Statements to be furnished to persons with respect to whom information is required. Every person required to make a return under subsection (a) shall furnish to each individual whose name is required to be set forth in such return a written statement showing—

(1) the name[1], *address, and phone number of the information contact* of the person making the payments, and

(2) the aggregate amount of long-term care benefits paid to the individual which are required to be showing on such return.

The written statement required under the preceding sentence shall be furnished to the individual on or before January 31 of the year following the calendar year for which the return under subsection (a) was required to be made.

* * * * * * * * * * * *

[For analysis, see ¶2317. For committee reports, see ¶5373.]

[Endnote Code Sec. 6050Q]

Matter in *italics* in Code Sec. 6050Q(b)(1) was added by Sec. 1602(d)(1) of the Taxpayer Relief Act of 1997, H.R. 2014, 8/5/97.

1. added matter in paragraph (b)(1)

Effective Date (Sec. 1602(i), H.R. 2014, 8/5/97) effective for benefits paid after 12/31/96.

[¶3317]   Code Sec. 6050R.   Returns relating to certain purchases of fish.

* * * * * * * * * * * *

(c) Statement to be furnished with respect to whom information is required. Every person required to make a return under subsection (a) shall furnish to each person whose name is required to be set forth in such return a written statement showing—

(1) the [1]*name, address, and phone number of the information contact* of the person required to make such a return, and

(2) the aggregate amount of payments to the person required to be shown on the return. The written statement required under the preceding sentence shall be furnished to the person on or before January 31 of the year following the calendar year for which the return under subsection (a) is required to be made.

* * * * * * * * * * * *

[For analysis, see ¶2316. For committee reports, see ¶5356.]

[Endnote Code Sec. 6050R]

Matter in *italics* in Code Sec. 6050R(c)(1) added by Sec. 1501(a)(1) of the Taxpayer Relief Act of 1997, H.R. 2014, 8/5/97, which struck out:

1. "name and address"

Effective Date (Sec. 1601(j)(1), H.R. 2014, 8/5/97) effective for payments made after 12/31/97.

[¶3318]   Code Sec.[1] 6050S.   Returns relating to higher education tuition and related expenses.

(a) In general. Any person—

(1) which is an eligible educational institution which receives payments for qualified tuition and related expenses with respect to any individual for any calendar year, or

[2]*(2) which is engaged in a trade or business and which, in the course of such trade or business—*

(A) makes payments during any calendar year to any individual which constitutes reimbursements or refunds (or similar amounts) of qualified tuition and related expenses of such individual, or

(B) except as provided in regulations, receives from any individual interest aggregating $600 or more for any calendar year on 1 or more qualified educations loans,

shall make the return described in subsection (b) with respect to the individual at such time as the Secretary may by regulations prescribe.

(b) Form and manner of returns. A return is described in this subsection if such return—

(1) is in such form as the Secretary may prescribe,

(2) contains—

(A) the name, address, and TIN of the individual with respect to whom payments [3]*or interest* described in subsection (a) were received from (or were paid to),

1,270

(B) the name, address, and TIN of any individual certified by the individual described in subparagraph (A) as the taxpayer who will claim the individual as a dependent for purposes of the deduction allowable under section 151 for any taxable year ending with or within the calendar year, and

(C) the—

(i) aggregate amount of payments for qualified tuition and related expenses received with respect to the individual described in subparagraph (A) during the calendar year,[4]

(ii) aggregate amount of reimbursements or refunds (or similar amounts) paid to such individual during the calendar year, and

[5]*(iii) aggregate amount of interest received for the calendar year from such individual.*

(D) such other information as the Secretary may prescribe.

(c) Application to governmental units. For purposes of this section—

(1) a governmental unit or any agency or instrumentality thereof shall be treated as a person, and

(2) any return required under subsection (a) by such governmental entity shall be made by the officer or employee appropriately designated for the purpose of making such return.

(d) Statements to be furnished to individuals with respect to whom information is required. Every person required to make a return under subsection (a) shall furnish to each individual whose name is required to be set forth in such return under subparagraph (A) or (B) of subsection (b)(2) a written statement showing—

(1) the name, address, and phone number of the information contact of the person required to make such return, and

(2) the aggregate amounts described in subparagraph (C) of subsection (b)(2).

The written statement required under the preceding sentence shall be furnished on or before January 31 of the year following the calendar year for which the return under subsection (a) was required to be made.

(e) Definitions. For purposes of this section, the terms "eligible educational institution" and "qualified tuition and related expenses" have the meanings given such terms by section 25A [6], *and except as provided in regulations, the term "qualified education loan" has the meaning given such term by section 221(e)(1).*

(f) Returns which would be required to be made by 2 or more persons. Except to the extent provided in regulations prescribed by the Secretary, in the case of any amount received by any person on behalf of another person, only the person first receiving such amount shall be required to make the return under subsection (a).

(g) Regulations. The Secretary shall prescribe such regulations as may be necessary to carry out the provisions of this section. No penalties shall be imposed under part II of subchapter B of chapter 68 with respect to any return or statement required under this section until such time as such regulations are issued.

[For analysis, see ¶ 410. For committee reports, see ¶ 5002.]

[Endnote Code Sec. 6050S]

Code Sec. 6050S was added by Sec. 201(c)(1) of the Taxpayer Relief Act of 1997, H.R. 2014, 8/5/97.

1. added Code Sec. 6050S

Effective Date (Sec. 201(f)(1), H.R. 2014, 8/5/97) effective for expenses paid after 12/31/97 (in tax. yrs. end. after such date), for education furnished in academic periods begin. after 12/31/97.

Matter in *italics* Code Sec. 6050S(a)(2), Code Sec. 6050S(b)(2)(A), Code Sec. 6050S(b)(2)(C)(i), Code Sec. 6050S(b)(2)(C)(iii) and Code Sec. 6050S(e) added by Sec. 202(c)(1), (c)(2)(A), (c)(2)(B), and (c)(3), H.R. 2014, 8/5/97, which struck out:

2. "(2) which is engaged in a trade or business and which, in the course of such trade or business, makes payments during any calendar year to any individual which constitute reimbursements or refunds (or similar amounts) of qualified tuition and related expenses of such individual,"

3. added matter in subpara. (a)(2)(A)

4. "and"

5. added clause (b)(2)(C)(iii)

6. added matter in subsec. (e)

Effective Date (Sec. 202(e), H.R. 2014, 8/5/97) Sec. 202(e), H.R. 2014, 8/5/97, reads as follows:

"(e) Effective date. The amendments made by this section shall apply to any qualified education loan (as defined in section 221(e)(1) of the Internal Revenue Code of 1986, as added by this section) incurred on, before, or after the date of the enactment of this Act, but only with respect to—

"(1) any loan interest payment due and paid after December 31, 1997, and

"(2) the portion of the 60-month period referred to in section 221(d) of the Internal Revenue Code of 1986 (as added by this section) after December 31, 1997."

[¶ 3319]   Code Sec. 6103.   **Confidentiality and disclosure of returns and return information.**

(a) **General rule.** Returns and return information shall be confidential, and except as authorized by this title—

(1) no officer or employee of the United States,

(2) no officer or employee of any State, any local child support enforcement agency, or any local agency administering a program listed in subsection (1)(7)(D) who has or had access to returns or return information under this section, and

(3) no other person (or officer or employee thereof) who has or had access to returns or return information under subsection (e)(1)(D)(iii), paragraph [1-B](6), (12), or (16) of subsection (l), paragraph (2) or (4)(B) of subsection (m), or subsection (n),

shall disclose any return or return information obtained by him in any manner in connection with his service as such an officer or an employee or otherwise or under the provisions of this section. For purposes of this subsection, the term "officer or employee" includes a former officer or employee.

* * * * * * * * * * * *

(d) **Disclosure to State tax officials and State and local law enforcement agencies.**

* * * * * * * * * * * *

[2](5) *Disclosure for certain combined reporting project. The Secretary shall disclose taxpayer identities and signatures for purposes of the demonstration project described in section 967 of the Taxpayer Relief Act of 1997.*

(e) **Disclosure to persons having material interest.**

(1) **In general.** The return of a person shall, upon written request, be open to inspection by or disclosure to—

(A) in the case of the return of an individual—

(i) that individual,

(ii) if property transferred by that individual to a trust is sold or exchanged in a transaction described in section 644, the trustee or trustees, jointly or separately, of such trust to the extent necessary to ascertain any amount of tax imposed upon the trust by section 644,

(iii) the spouse of that individual if the individual and such spouse have signified their consent to consider a gift reported on such return as made one-half by him and one-half by the spouse pursuant to the provisions of section 2513; or

(iv) the child of that individual (or such child's legal representative) to the extent necessary to comply with the provisions of section 1(g)[3];

* * * * * * * * * * * *

(h) **Disclosure to certain Federal officers and employees for purposes of tax administration, etc.**

(1) **Department of the Treasury.** Returns and return information shall, without written request, be open to inspection by or disclosure to officers and employees of the Department of the Treasury whose official duties require such inspection or disclosure for tax administration purposes.

(2) **Department of Justice.** In a matter involving tax administration, a return or return information shall be open to inspection by or disclosure to officers and employees of the Department of Justice (including United States attorneys) personally and directly engaged in, and

solely for their use in, any proceeding before a Federal grand jury or preparation for any proceeding (or investigation which may result in such a proceeding) before a Federal grand jury or any Federal or State court, but only if—

(A) the taxpayer is or may be a party to the proceeding, or the proceeding arose out of, or in connection with, determining the taxpayer's civil or criminal liability, or the collection of such civil liability in respect of any tax imposed under this title;

(B) the treatment of an item reflected on such return is or may be related to the resolution of an issue in the proceeding or investigation; or

(C) such return or return information relates or may relate to a transactional relationship between a person who is or may be a party to the proceeding and the taxpayer which affects, or may affect, the resolution of an issue in such proceeding or investigation.

(3) **Form of request.** In any case in which the Secretary is authorized to disclose a return or return information to the Department of Justice pursuant to the provisions of this subsection—

(A) if the Secretary has referred the case to the Department of Justice, or if the proceeding is authorized by subchapter B of chapter 76, the Secretary may make such disclosure on his own motion, or

(B) if the Secretary receives a written request from the Attorney General, the Deputy Attorney General, or an Assistant Attorney General for a return of, or return information relating to, a person named in such request and setting forth the need for the disclosure, the Secretary shall disclose return or return the information so requested.

(4) **Disclosure in judicial and administrative tax proceedings.** A return or return information may be disclosed in a Federal or State judicial or administrative proceeding pertaining to tax administration, but only—

(A) the taxpayer is a party to the proceeding, or the proceeding arose out of, or in connection with, determining the taxpayer's civil or criminal liability, or the collection of such civil liability, in respect of any tax imposed under this title;

(B) if the treatment of an item reflected on such return is directly related to the resolution of an issue in the proceeding;

(C) if such return or return information directly relates to a transactional relationship between a person who is a party to the proceeding and the taxpayer which directly affects the resolution of an issue in the proceeding; or

(D) to the extent required by order of a court pursuant to section 3500 of title 18, United States Code or rule 16 of the Federal Rules of Criminal Procedure, such court being authorized in the issuance of such order to give due consideration to congressional policy favoring the confidentiality of returns and return information as set forth in this title.

However, such return or return information shall not be disclosed as provided in subparagraph (A), (B), or (C) if the Secretary determines that such disclosure would identify a confidential informant or seriously impair a civil or criminal tax investigation.

[4](5) **Withholding of tax from Social Security benefits.** Upon written request of the payor agency, the Secretary may disclose available return information from the master files of the Internal Revenue Service with respect to the address and status of an individual as a nonresident alien or as a citizen or resident of the United States to the Social Security Administration or the Railroad Retirement Board (whichever is appropriate) for purposes of carrying out its responsibilities for withholding tax under section 1441 from social security benefits (as defined in section 86(d)).

(i) **Disclosure to Federal officers or employees for administration of Federal laws not relating to tax administration.**

* * * * * * * * * * *

(7) **Comptroller general.**

(A) Returns available for inspection. Except as provided in subparagraph (C), upon written request by the Comptroller General of the United States, returns and return information shall be open to inspection by, or disclosure to, officers and employees of the General Accounting Office for the purpose of, and to the extent necessary in, making—

(i) an audit of the Internal Revenue Service or the Bureau of Alcohol, Tobacco and Firearms which may be required by section 713 of title 31, United States Code, or

(ii) any audit authorized by subsection (p)(6),

except that no such officer or employee shall, except to the extent authorized by subsection (f) or (p)(6), disclose to any person, other than another officer or employee of such office whose official duties require such disclosure, any return or return information described in section 4424(a) in a form which can be associated with, or otherwise identify, directly or indirectly, a particular taxpayer, nor shall such officer or employee disclose any other return or return information, except as otherwise expressly provided by law, to any person other than such other officer or employee of such office in a form which can be associated with, or otherwise identify, directly or indirectly, a particular taxpayer.

(B) Audits of other agencies.

(i) In general. Nothing in this section shall prohibit any return or return information obtained under this title by any Federal agency (other than an agency referred to in subparagraph (A)) [5-B]*or by a Trustee as defined in the District of Columbia Retirement Protection Act of 1997,* for use in any program or activity from being open to inspection by, or disclosure to, officers and employees of the General Accounting Office if such inspection or disclosure is—

(I) for purposes of, and to the extent necessary in, making an audit authorized by law of such program or activity, and

(II) pursuant to a written request by the Comptroller General of the United States to the head of such Federal agency.

(ii) Information from secretary. If the Comptroller General of the United States determines that the returns or return information available under clause (i) are not sufficient for purposes of making an audit of any program or activity of a Federal agency (other than an agency referred to in subparagraph (A)), upon written request by the Comptroller General to the Secretary, returns and return information (of the type authorized by subsection (l) or (m) to be made available to the Federal agency for use in such program or activity) shall be open to inspection by, or disclosure to, officers and employees of the General Accounting Office for the purpose of, and to the extent necessary in, making such audit.

(iii) Requirement of notification upon completion of audit. Within 90 days after the completion of an audit with respect to which returns or return information were opened to inspection or disclosed under clause (i) or (ii), the Comptroller General of the United States shall notify in writing the Joint Committee on Taxation of such completion. Such notice shall include—

(I) a description of the use of the returns and return information by the Federal agency involved,

(II) such recommendations with respect to the use of returns and return information by such Federal agency as the Comptroller General deems appropriate, and

(III) a statement on the impact of any such recommendations on confidentiality of returns and return information and the administration of this title.

(iv) Certain restrictions made applicable. The restrictions contained in subparagraph (A) on the disclosure of any returns or return information open to inspection or disclosed under such subparagraph shall also apply to returns and return information open to inspection or disclosed under this subparagraph.

(C) Disapproval by Joint Committee on Taxation. Returns and return information shall not be open to inspection or disclosed under subparagraph (A) or (B) with respect to an audit—

(i) unless the Comptroller General of the United States notifies in writing the Joint Committee on Taxation of such audit, and

(ii) if the Joint Committee on Taxation disapproves such audit by a vote of at least two-thirds of its members within the 30-day period beginning on the day the Joint Committee on Taxation receives such notice.

(8) Repealed.

* * * * * * * * * * *

(k) Disclosure of certain returns and return information for tax administration purposes. [6]**(8) Levies on certain government payments.**

(A) Disclosure of return information in levies on financial management service. In serving a notice of levy, or release of such levy, with respect to any applicable government payment, the Secretary may disclose to officers and employees of the Financial Management Service—

(i) return information, including taxpayer identity information,

(ii) the amount of any unpaid liability under this title (including penalties and interest), and

(iii) the type of tax and tax period to which such unpaid liability relates.

(B) Restriction on use of disclosed information. Return information disclosed under subparagraph (A) may be used by officers and employees of the Financial Management Service only for the purpose of, and to the extent necessary in, transferring levied funds in satisfaction of the levy, maintaining appropriate agency records in regard to such levy or the release thereof, notifying the taxpayer and the agency certifying such payment that the levy has been honored, or in the defense of any litigation ensuing from the honor of such levy.

(C) Applicable government payment. For purposes of this paragraph, the term "applicable government payment" means—

(i) any Federal payment (other than a payment for which eligibility is based on the income or assets (or both) of a payee) certified to the Financial Management Service for disbursement, and

(ii) any other payment which is certified to the Financial Management Service for disbursement and which the Secretary designates by published notice.

CAUTION.   Para. (k)(8) [sic (k)(9)] is effective 9 months after 8/5/97.

[7]*(8) [sic (9)] Disclosure of information to administer section 6311. The Secretary may disclose returns or return information to financial institutions and others to the extent the Secretary deems necessary for the administration of section 6311. Disclosures of information for purposes other than to accept payments by checks or money orders shall be made only to the extent authorized by written procedures promulgated by the Secretary.*

(l) Disclosure of returns and return information for purposes other than tax administration.

* * * * * * * * * * *

(7) Disclosure of return information to Federal, State, and local agencies administering certain programs under the Social Security Act, the Food Stamp Act of 1977 or Title 38, United States Code, or certain housing assistance programs.

* * * * * * * * * * *

(D) Programs to which rule applies. The programs to which this paragraph applies are:

(i) a State program funded under part A of title IV of the Social Security Act;

(ii) medical assistance provided under a State plan approved under title XIX of the Social Security Act;

(iii) supplemental security income benefits provided under title XVI of the Social Security Act, and federally administered supplementary payments of the type described in section 1616(a) of such Act (including payments pursuant to an agreement entered into under section 212(a) of Public Law 93-66);

(iv) any benefits provided under a State plan approved under title I, X, XIV, or XVI of the Social Security Act (as those titles apply to Puerto Rico, Guam, and the Virgin Islands);

(v) unemployment compensation provided under a State law described in section 3304 of this title;

(vi) assistance provided under the Food Stamp Act of 1977;

1,275

(vii) State-administered supplementary payments of the type described in section 1616(a) of the Social Security Act (including payments pursuant to an agreement entered into under section 212(a) of Public Law 93-66);

(viii) (I) any needs-based pension provided under chapter 15 of title 38, United States Code, or under any other law administered by the Secretary of Veterans Affairs;

(II) parents' dependency and indemnity compensation provided under section 1315 of title 38, United States Code;

(III) health-care services furnished under sections 1710(a)(1)(I), 1710(a)(2), 1710(b), and 1712(a)(2)(B) of such title; and

(IV) compensation paid under chapter 11 of title 38, United States Code, at the 100 percent rate based solely on unemployability and without regard to the fact that the disability or disabilities are not rated as 100 percent disabling under the rating schedule.

Only return information from returns with respect to net earnings from self-employment and wages may be disclosed under this paragraph for use with respect to any program described in clause (viii)(IV). Clause (viii) shall not apply after September 30, [8]*2003;* and

(ix) any housing assistance program administered by the Department of Housing and Urban Development that involves initial and periodic review of an applicant's or participant's income, except that return information may be disclosed under this clause only on written request by the Secretary of Housing and Urban Development and only for use by officers and employees of the Department of Housing and Urban Development with respect to applicants for and participants in such programs.

Clause (ix) shall not apply after September 30, 1998.

* * * * * * * * * * * *

(12) Disclosure of certain taxpayer identity information for verification of employment status of medicare beneficiary and spouse of medicare beneficiary.

(A) Return information from Internal Revenue Service. The Secretary shall, upon written request from the Commissioner of Social Security, disclose to the Commissioner available filing status and taxpayer identity information from the individual master files of the Internal Revenue Service relating to whether any medicare beneficiary identified by the Commissioner was a married individual (as defined in section 7703) for any specified year after 1986, and, if so, the name of the spouse of such individual and such spouse's TIN.

(B) Return information from Social Security Administration. The Commissioner of Social Security shall, upon written request from the Administrator of the Health Care Financing Administration, disclose to the Administrator the following information:

(i) The name and TIN of each medicare beneficiary who is identified as having received wages (as defined in section 3401(a)), above an amount (if any) specified by the Secretary of Health and Human Services, from a qualified employer in a previous year.

(ii) For each medicare beneficiary who was identified as married under subparagraph (A) and whose spouse is identified as having received wages, above an amount (if any) specified by the Secretary of Health and Human Services, from a qualified employer in a previous year—

(I) the name and TIN of the medicare beneficiary, and

(II) the name and TIN of the spouse.

(iii) With respect to each such qualified employer, the name, address, and TIN of the employer and the number of individuals with respect to whom written statements were furnished under section 6051 by the employer with respect to such previous year.

(C) Disclosure by Health Care Financing Administration. With respect to the information disclosed under subparagraph (B), the Administrator of the Health Care Financing Administration may disclose—

(i) to the qualified employer referred to in such subparagraph the name and TIN of each individual identified under such subparagraph as having received wages from the employer (hereinafter in this subparagraph referred to as the "employee") for purposes of determining during what period such employee or the employee's spouse may be (or have been) covered under a group health plan of the employer and what benefits are or were covered under the plan (including the name, address, and identifying number of the plan),

(ii) to any group health plan which provides or provided coverage to such an employee or spouse, the name of such employee and the employee's spouse (if the spouse is a medicare beneficiary) and the name and address of the employer, and, for the purpose of presenting a claim to the plan—

(I) the TIN of such employee if benefits were paid under title XVIII of the Social Security Act with respect to the employee during a period in which the plan was a primary plan (as defined in section 1862(b)(2)(A) of the Social Security Act), and

(II) the TIN of such spouse if benefits were paid under such title with respect to the spouse during such period, and

(iii) to any agent of such Administrator the information referred to in subparagraph (B) for purposes of carrying out clauses (i) and (ii) on behalf of such Administrator.

(D) Special rules.

(i) Restrictions on disclosure. Information may be disclosed under this paragraph only for purposes of, and to the extent necessary in, determining the extent to which any medicare beneficiary is covered under any group health plan.

(ii) Timely response to requests. Any request made under subparagraph (A) or (B) shall be complied with as soon as possible but in no event later than 120 days after the date the request was made.

(E) Definitions. For purposes of this paragraph—

(i) Medicare beneficiary. The term "medicare beneficiary" means an individual entitled to benefits under part A, or enrolled under part B, of title XVIII of the Social Security Act, but does not include such an individual enrolled in part A under section 1818.

(ii) Group health plan. The term "group health plan" means any group health plan (as defined in section 5000(b)(1)).

(iii) Qualified employer. The term "qualified employer" means, for a calendar year, an employer which has furnished written statements under section 6051 with respect to at least 20 individuals for wages paid in the year. [9-B]

* * * * * * * * * * * *

[10-B] *(16) Disclosure of return information for purposes of administering the District of Columbia Retirement Protection Act of 1997.*

(A) In general. Upon written request available return information (including such information disclosed to the Social Security Administration under paragraph (1) or (5) of this subsection), relating to the amount of wage income (as defined in section 3121(a) or 3401(a)), the name, address, and identifying number assigned under section 6109, of payors of wage income, taxpayer identity (as defined in subsection 6103(b)(6)), and the occupational status reflected on any return filed by, or with respect to, any individual with respect to whom eligibility for, or the correct amount of, benefits under the District of Columbia Retirement Protection Act of 1997, is sought to be determined, shall be disclosed by the Commissioner of Social Security, or to the extent not available from the Social Security Administration, by the Secretary, to any duly authorized officer or employee of the Department of the Treasury, or a Trustee or any designated officer or employee of a Trustee (as defined in the District of Columbia Retirement Protection Act of 1997), or any actuary engaged by a trustee under the terms of the District of Columbia Retirement Protection Act of 1997, whose official duties require such disclosure, solely for the purpose of, and to the extent necessary in, determining an individual's eligibility for, or the correct amount of, benefits under the District of Columbia Retirement Protection Act of 1997.

(B) Disclosure for use in judicial or administrative proceedings. Return information disclosed to any person under this paragraph may be disclosed in a judicial or administrative

proceeding relating to the determination of an individual's eligibility for, or the correct amount of, benefits under the District of Columbia Retirement Protection Act of 1997.

* * * * * * * * * * * *

(p) Procedure and recordkeeping.

(1) Manner, time, and place of inspections.

* * * * * * * * * * * *

(3) Records of inspection and disclosure.

CAUTION. Subpara. (p)(3)(A), following, is effective before 9 months after 8/5/97. For subpara. (p)(3)(A), effective 9 months after 8/5/97, see below.

(A) System of recordkeeping. Except as otherwise provided by this paragraph, the Secretary shall maintain a permanent system of standardized records or accountings of all requests for inspection or disclosure of returns and return information (including the reasons for and dates of such requests) and of returns and return information inspected or disclosed under this section. Notwithstanding the provisions of section 552a(c) of title 5, United States Code, the Secretary shall not be required to maintain a record or accounting of requests for inspection or disclosure of returns and return information, or of returns and return information inspected or disclosed, under the authority of subsections (c), (e), (h)(1), (3)(A), or (4), (i)(4), or (7)(A)(ii), (k)(1), (2), or (6), (l)(1), (4)(B), (5), (7), (8), (9), (10), (11), (12), (13), (14), [11-B](15), or (16), (m), or (n). The records or accountings required to be maintained under this paragraph shall be available for examination by the Joint Committee on Taxation or the Chief of Staff of such joint committee. Such record or accounting shall also be available for examination by such person or persons as may be, but only to the extent, authorized to make such examination under section 552a(c)(3) of title 5, United States Code.

CAUTION. Subpara. (p)(3)(A), following, is effective 9 months after 8/5/97. For subpara. (p)(3)(A), effective before 9 months after 8/5/97, see above.

(A) System of recordkeeping. Except as otherwise provided by this paragraph, the Secretary shall maintain a permanent system of standardized records or accountings of all requests for inspection or disclosure of returns and return information (including the reasons for and dates of such requests) and of returns and return information inspected or disclosed under this section. Notwithstanding the provisions of section 552a(c) of title 5, United States Code, the Secretary shall not be required to maintain a record or accounting of requests for inspection or disclosure of returns and return information, or of returns and return information inspected or disclosed, under the authority of subsections (c), (e), (h)(1), (3)(A), or (4), (i)(4), or (7)(A)(ii), (k)(1), [12](2), (6), or (8), (l)(1), (4)(B), (5), (7), (8), (9), (10), (11), (12), (13), (14), (15), or (16), (m), or (n). The records or accountings required to be maintained under this paragraph shall be available for examination by the Joint Committee on Taxation or the Chief of Staff of such joint committee. Such record or accounting shall also be available for examination by such person or persons as may be, but only to the extent, authorized to make such examination under section 552a(c)(3) of title 5, United States Code.

(B) Report by the Secretary. The Secretary shall, within 90 days after the close of each calendar year, furnish to the Joint Committee on Taxation a report with respect to, or summary of, the records or accountings described in subparagraph (A) in such form and containing such information as such joint committee or the Chief of Staff of such joint committee may designate. Such report or summary shall not, however, include a record or accounting of any request by the President under subsection (g) for, or the disclosure in response to such request of, any return or return information with respect to any individual who, at the time of such request, was an officer or employee of the executive branch of the Federal Government. Such report or summary, or any part thereof, may be disclosed by such joint committee to such persons and for such purposes as the joint committee may, by record vote of a majority of the members of the joint committee, determine.

(C) Public report on disclosures. The Secretary shall, within 90 days after the close of each calendar year, furnish to the Joint Committee on Taxation for disclosure to the public a report with respect to the records or accountings described in subparagraph (A) which—

(i) provides with respect to each Federal agency, each agency, body, or commission described in subsection (d), (i)(3)(B)(i), or (l)(6), and the General Accounting Office the number of—

(I) requests for disclosure of returns and return information,

(II) instances in which returns and return information were disclosed pursuant to such requests or otherwise,

(III) taxpayers whose returns, or return information with respect to whom, were disclosed pursuant to such requests, and

(ii) describes the general purposes for which such requests were made,

(4) Safeguards. Any Federal agency described in subsection (h)(2), [13]*(h)(5)*, (i)(1), (2), (3), or (5), (j)(1) or (2), [14]*(k)(8)*, (l)(1), (2), (3), (5), (11), (13), or (14), or (o)(1), the General Accounting Office, or any agency, body, or commission described in subsection (d), (i)(3)(B)(i) or (l)(6), (7), (8), (9), (10), [15-B]*(12), or (16), or any other person described in subsection (l)(16)* or (15) shall, as a condition for receiving returns or return information—

(A) establish and maintain, to the satisfaction of the Secretary, a permanent system of standardized records with respect to any request, the reason for such request, and the date of such request made by or of it and any disclosure of return or return information made by or to it;

(B) establish and maintain, to the satisfaction of the Secretary, a secure area or place in which such returns or return information shall be stored;

(C) restrict, to the satisfaction of the Secretary, access to the returns or return information only to persons whose duties or responsibilities require access and to whom disclosure may be made under the provisions of this title;

(D) provide such other safeguards which the Secretary determines (and which he prescribes in regulations) to be necessary or appropriate to protect the confidentiality of the returns or return information;

(E) furnish a report to the Secretary, at such time and containing such information as the Secretary may prescribe, which describes the procedures established and utilized by such agency, body, or commission or the General Accounting Office for ensuring the confidentiality of returns and return information required by this paragraph; and

(F) upon completion of use of such returns or return information—

(i) in the case of an agency, body, or commission described in subsection (d), (i)(3)(B)(i), or (l)(6), (7), (8), [16-B]*(9), or (16), or any other person described in subsection (l)(16)* return to the Secretary such returns or return information (along with any copies made therefrom) or make such returns or return information undisclosable in any manner and furnish a written report to the Secretary describing such manner,

(ii) in the case of an agency described in subsections (h)(2), [17]*(h)(5)*, (i)(1), (2), (3), or (5), (j)(1) or (2), [18]*(k)(8)*, (l)(1), (2), (3), (5), (10), (11), (12), (13), (14) or (15), or (o)(1), or the General Accounting Office, either—

(I) return to the Secretary such returns or return information (along with any copies made therefrom),

(II) otherwise make such returns or return information undisclosable, or

(III) to the extent not so returned or made undisclosable, ensure that the conditions of subparagraphs (A), (B), (C), (D), and (E) of this paragraph continue to be met with respect to such returns or return information, and

(iii) in the case of the Department of Health and Human Services for purposes of subsection (m)(6), destroy all such return information upon completion of its use in providing the notification for which the information was obtained, so as to make such information undisclosable;

except that the conditions of subparagraphs (A), (B), (C), (D), and (E) shall cease to apply with respect to any return or return information if, and to the extent that, such return or return information is disclosed in the course of any judicial or administrative proceeding and made a part of the public record thereof. If the Secretary determines that any such agency, body, or commission[19-B], *including an agency or any other person described in subsection (l)(16),* or the General Accounting Office has failed to, or does not, meet the requirements of this paragraph, he may, after any proceedings for review established under paragraph (7), take such actions as are necessary to ensure such requirements are met, including refusing to disclose returns or return information [20-B]*to such agency, body, or commission, including an agency or any other person described in subsection (l)(16),* or the General Accounting Office until he determines that such requirements have been or will be met. In the case of any agency which receives any mailing address under paragraph (2), (4), (6), or (7) of subsection (m) and which discloses any such mailing address to any agent, or which receives any information under paragraph (6)(A)[21-B], *(12)(B), or (16)* of subsection (l) and which discloses any such information to any agent, [22-B]*or any person including an agent described in subsection (l)(16),* this paragraph shall apply to such agency and each such agent [23-B]*or other person* (except that, in the case of an agent, [24-B]*or any person including an agent described in subsection (l)(16),* any report to the Secretary or other action with respect to the Secretary shall be made or taken through such agency). For purposes of applying this paragraph in any case to which subsection (m)(6) applies, the term "return information" includes related blood donor records (as defined in section 1141(h)(2) of the Social Security Act).

* * * * * * * * * * * *

[For analysis, see ¶ 604, ¶ 2308, ¶ 2319, ¶ 2330, ¶ 2331, ¶ 2332, ¶ 2333. For committee reports, see ¶ 5099, ¶ 5201, ¶ 5205, ¶ 5123, ¶ 5126, ¶ 5250.]

[Endnote Code Sec. 6103]

H.R. 2015. Matter in *italics* in Code Sec. 6103(a)(3) added by Sec. 11024(b)(2) of the Balanced Budget Act of 1997, H.R. 2015, 8/5/97, which struck out:

1_B. "(6) or (12)" [H.R. 2015]

Effective Date Effective 8/5/97.

Code Sec. 6103(d)(5), in *italics,* was added by Sec. 976(c) of the Taxpayer Relief Act of 1997, H.R. 2014, 8/5/97.

2. added para. (d)(5)

Effective Date Effective 8/5/97.

Matter in *italics* in Code Sec. 6103(e)(1)(A)(iv) added by Sec. 1201(b)(2), H.R. 2014, 8/5/97, which struck out:

3. "or 59(j)"

Effective Date (Sec. 1201(c), H.R. 2014, 8/5/97) effective for tax. yrs. begin. after 12/31/97.

Matter in *italics* in Code Sec. 6103(h)(5) added by Sec. 1283(a), H.R. 2014, 8/5/97, which struck out:

4. "(5) Prospective jurors. In connection with any judicial proceeding described in paragraph (4) to which the United States is a party, the Secretary shall respond to a written inquiry from an attorney of the Department of Justice (including a United States attorney) involved in such proceeding or any person (or his legal representative) who is a party to such proceeding as to whether an individual who is a prospective juror in such proceeding has or has not been the subject of any audit or other tax investigation by the Internal Revenue Service. The Secretary shall limit such response to an affirmative or negative reply to such inquiry.

"(6)"

Effective Date (Sec. 1283(c), H.R. 2014, 8/5/97) effective for judicial proceedings commenced after 8/5/97.

H.R. 2015. Matter in *italics* in Code Sec. 6103(i)(7)(B)(i) added by Sec. 11024(b)(3) of the, H.R. 2015, 8/5/97.

5_B. added matter in clause (i)(7)(B)(i) [H.R. 2015]

Effective Date Effective 8/5/97.

Code Sec. 6103(k)(8), in *italics,* was added by Sec. 1026(a), H.R. 2014, 8/5/97.

6. added para. (k)(8)

Effective Date (Sec. 1026(c), H.R. 2014, 8/5/97) effective for levies issued after 8/5/97.

Code Sec. 6103(k)(8) [sic (9)], in *italics,* was added by Sec. 1205(c)(1), H.R. 2014, 8/5/97.

7. added para. (k)(8) [sic (k)(9)]

Effective Date (Sec. 1205(d), H.R. 2014, 8/5/97) effective 9 months after 8/5/97.

Matter in *italics* in Code Sec. 6103(l)(7)(D)(viii) added by Sec. 1023(a), H.R. 2014, 8/5/97, which struck out:

8. "1998"

Effective Date (Sec. 1023(b), H.R. 2014, 8/5/97) effective 8/5/97.

H.R. 2015. Code Sec. 6103(l)(12)(F) was deleted by Sec. 4631(c)(2), H.R. 2015, 8/5/97, which struck out:
9_B. "(F) Termination. Subparagraphs (A) and (B) shall not apply to—
"(i) any request made after September 30, 1998, and
"(ii) any request made before such date for information relating to—
"(I) 1997 or thereafter in the case of subparagraph (A), or
"(II) 1998 or thereafter in the case of subparagraph (B)." [H.R. 2015]
Effective Date Effective 8/5/97.

H.R. 2015. Matter in *italics* in Code Sec. 6103(l)(16), and Code Sec. 6103(p)(3)(A) added by Sec. 11024(b)(1) and (b)(4), H.R. 2015, 8/5/97, which struck out:
10_B. added para. (l)(16) [H.R. 2015]
11_B. "or (15)" [H.R. 2015]
Effective Date Effective 8/5/97

Matter in *italics* in Code Sec. 6103(p)(3)(A) added by Sec. 1026(b)(1)(A), H.R. 2014, 8/5/97, which struck out:
12. "(2), or (6)"
Effective Date (Sec. 1026(c), H.R. 2014, 8/5/97) effective for levies issued after 8/5/97.
This amendment was also made by Sec. 1205(c)(3) of this Act, effective 9 months after 8/5/97.

Matter in *italics* in Code Sec. 6103(p)(4) added by Sec. 1283(b), H.R. 2014, 8/5/97, which struck out:
13. "(h)(6)"
Effective Date (Sec. 1283(c), H.R. 2014, 8/5/97) effective for judicial proceedings commenced after 8/5/97.

Matter in Code Sec. 6103(p)(4) added by Sec. 1026(b)(1)(B), H.R. 2014, 8/5/97.
14. added matter in para. (p)(4)
Effective Date (Sec. 1026(c), H.R. 2014, 8/5/97) effective for levies issued after 8/5/97.

H.R. 2015. Matter in *italics* in Code Sec. 6103(p)(4), Code Sec. 6103(p)(4)(F) and Code Sec. 6103(p)(4)(F)(i) added by Sec. 11024(b)(5) and (b)(6), H.R. 2015, 8/5/97, which struck out:
15_B. "or (12)" [H.R. 2015]
16_B. "or (9)" [H.R. 2015]
Effective Date Effective 8/5/97

Matter in *italics* in Code Sec. 6103(p)(4) added by Sec. 1283, H.R. 2014, 8/5/97, which struck out:
17. "(h)(6)"
Effective Date (Sec. 1283(c), H.R. 2014, 8/5/97) effective for judicial proceedings commenced after 8/5/97.

Matter in Code Sec. 6103(p)(4) added by Sec. 1026(b)(1)(B), H.R. 2014, 8/5/97.
18. added matter in para. (p)(4)
Effective Date (Sec. 1026(c), H.R. 2014, 8/5/97) effective for levies issued after 8/5/97.

Secs. 976(a) and (b), H.R. 2014, 8/5/97, provide:
"(a) In general. The Secretary of the Treasury shall provide for a demonstration project to assess the feasibility and desirability of expanding combined Federal and State tax reporting.
"(b) Description of demonstration project. The demonstration project under subsection (a) shall be—
"(1) carried out between the Internal Revenue Service and the State of Montana for a period ending with the date which is 5 years after the date of the enactment of this Act,
"(2) limited to the reporting of employment taxes, and
"(3) limited to the disclosure of the taxpayer identity (as defined in section 6103(b)(6) of such Code) and the signature of the taxpayer."
H.R. 2015. Matter in *italics* in Code Sec. 6103(p)(4) added by Sec. 11024(b)(7), H.R. 2015, 8/5/97, which struck out:
19_B. added matter in subpara. (p)(4)(F) [H.R. 2015]
20_B. "to such agency, body, or commission" [H.R. 2015]
21_B. "or (12)(B)" [H.R. 2015]
22_B. added matter in subpara. (p)(4)(F) [H.R. 2015]
23_B. added matter in subpara. (p)(4)(F) [H.R. 2015]
24_B. added matter in subpara. (p)(4)(F) [H.R. 2015]
Effective Date Effective 8/5/97

[¶ 3320]   Code Sec. 6111.   Registration of tax shelters.

* * * * * * * * * * * *

[1]*(d) Certain confidential arrangements treated as tax shelters.*
(1) In general. For purposes of this section, the term "tax shelter" includes any entity, plan, arrangement, or transaction—

(A) a significant purpose of the structure of which is the avoidance or evasion of Federal income tax for a direct or indirect participant which is a corporation,

(B) which is offered to any potential participant under conditions of confidentiality, and

(C) for which the tax shelter promoters may receive fees in excess of $100,000 in the aggregate.

(2) Conditions of confidentiality. For purposes of paragraph (1)(B), an offer is under conditions of confidentiality if—

(A) the potential participant to whom the offer is made (or any other person acting on behalf of such participant) has an understanding or agreement with or for the benefit of any promoter of the tax shelter that such participant (or such other person) will limit disclosure of the tax shelter or any significant tax features of the tax shelter, or

(B) any promoter of the tax shelter—

(i) claims, knows, or has reason to know,

(ii) knows or has reason to know that any other person (other than the potential participant) claims, or

(iii) causes another person to claim, that the tax shelter (or any aspect thereof) is proprietary to any person other than the potential participant or is otherwise protected from disclosure to or use by others.

For purposes of this subsection, the term "promoter" means any person or any related person (within the meaning of section 267 or 707) who participates in the organization, management, or sale of the tax shelter.

(3) Persons other than promoter required to register in certain cases.

(A) In general. If—

(i) the requirements of subsection (a) are not met with respect to any tax shelter (as defined in paragraph (1)) by any tax shelter promoter, and

(ii) no tax shelter promoter is a United States person,

then each United States person who discussed participation in such shelter shall register such shelter under subsection (a).

(B) Exception. Subparagraph (A) shall not apply to a United States person who discussed participation in a tax shelter if—

(i) such person notified the promoter in writing (not later than the close of the 90th day after the day on which such discussions began) that such person would not participate in such shelter, and

(ii) such person does not participate in such shelter.

(4) Offer to participate treated as offer for sale. For purposes of subsections (a) and (b), an offer to participate in a tax shelter (as defined in paragraph (1)) shall be treated as an offer for sale.

[2]**(e) Other definitions.** For purposes of this section—

(1) Tax shelter organizer. The term "tax shelter organizer" means—

(A) the person principally responsible for organizing the tax shelter,

(B) if the requirements of subsection (a) are not met by a person described in subparagraph (A) at the time prescribed therefor, any other person who participated in the organization of the tax shelter, and

(C) if the requirements of subsection (a) are not met by a person described in subparagraph (A) or (B) at the time prescribed therefor, any person participating in the sale or management of the investment at a time when the tax shelter was not registered under subsection (a).

(2) Year. The term "year" means—

(A) the taxable year of the tax shelter, or

(B) if the tax shelter has no taxable year, the calendar year.

[3]**(f) Regulations.** The Secretary may prescribe regulations which provide—

(1) rules for the aggregation of similar investments offered by the same person or persons for purposes of applying subsection (c)(4),

(2) that only 1 person shall be required to meet the requirements of subsection (a) in cases in which 2 or more persons would otherwise be required to meet such requirements,

(3) exemptions from the requirements of this section, and

(4) such rules as may be necessary or appropriate to carry out the purposes of this section in the case of foreign tax shelters.

[For analysis, see ¶ 2318. For committee reports, see ¶ 5128, ¶ 5201.]

[Endnote Code Sec. 6111]

Matter in *italics* in Code Sec. 6111(d), Code Sec. 6111(e) and Code Sec. 6111(f) added by Sec. 1028(a) of the Taxpayer Relief Act of 1997, H.R. 2014, 8/5/97, which struck out:

1. added subsec. (d)
2. "(d)"
3. "(e)"

Effective Date (Sec. 1028(e)(1), H.R. 2014, 8/5/97) effective for any tax shelter interests in which are offered to potential participants after the Secretary of the Treasury prescribes guidance with respect to meeting requirements added by such amendments.

[¶ 3321]   Code Sec. 6166.   Extension of time for payment of estate tax where estate consists largely of interest in closely held business.

* * * * * * * * * * *

(b) Definitions and special rules.

* * * * * * * * * * *

(1) **Interest in closely held business.** For purposes of this section, the term "interest in a closely held business" means—

(A) an interest as a proprietor in a trade or business carried on as a proprietorship;

(B) an interest as a partner in a partnership carrying on a trade or business, if—

(i) 20 percent or more of the total capital interest in such partnership is included in determining the gross estate of the decedent, or

(ii) such partnership had 15 or fewer partners; or

(C) stock in a corporation carrying on a trade or business if—

(i) 20 percent or more in value of the voting stock of such corporation is included in determining the gross estate of the decedent, or

(ii) such corporation had 15 or fewer shareholders.

(2) **Rules for applying paragraph (1).** For purposes of paragraph (1)—

(A) Time for testing. Determinations shall be made as of the time immediately before the decedent's death.

(B) Certain interests held by husband and wife. Stock or a partnership interest which—

(i) is community property of a husband and wife (or the income from which is community income) under the applicable community property law of a State, or

(ii) is held by a husband and wife as joint tenants, tenants by the entirety, or tenants in common,

shall be treated as owned by one shareholder or one partner, as the case may be.

(C) Indirect ownership. Property owned, directly or indirectly, by or for a corporation, partnership, estate, or trust shall be considered as being owned proportionately by or for its shareholders, partners, or beneficiaries. For purposes of the preceding sentence, a person shall be treated as a beneficiary of any trust only if such person has a present interest in the trust.

(D) Certain interests held by members of decedent's family. All stock and all partnership interests held by the decedent or by any member of his family (within the meaning of section 267(c)(4)) shall be treated as owned by the decedent.

(3) **Farmhouses and certain other structures taken into account.** For purposes of the 35-percent requirement of subsection (a)(1), an interest in a closely held business which is the business of farming includes an interest in residential buildings and related improvements on

the farm which are occupied on a regular basis by the owner or lessee of the farm or by persons employed by such owner or lessee for purposes of operating or maintaining the farm.

(4) Value. For purposes of this section, value shall be value determined for purposes of chapter 11 (relating to estate tax).

(5) Closely held business amount. For purposes of this section, the term "closely held business amount" means the value of the interest in a closely held business which qualifies under subsection (a)(1).

(6) Adjusted gross estate. For purposes of this section, the term "adjusted gross estate" means the value of the gross estate reduced by the sum of the amounts allowable as a deduction under section 2053 or 2054. Such sum shall be determined on the basis of the facts and circumstances in existence on the date (including extensions) for filing the return of tax imposed by section 2001 (or, if earlier, the date on which such return is filed).

(7) Partnership interests and stock which is not readily tradable.

(A) In general. If the executor elects the benefits of this paragraph (at such time and in such manner as the Secretary shall by regulations prescribe), then—

(i) for purposes of paragraph (1)(B)(i) or (1)(C)(i) (whichever is appropriate) and for purposes of subsection (c), any capital interest in a partnership and any non-readily-tradable stock which (after the application of paragraph (2)) is treated as owned by the decedent shall be treated as included in determining the value of the decedent's gross estate,

(ii) the executor shall be treated as having selected under subsection (a)(3) the date prescribed by section 6151(a), and

(iii) section 6601(j) (relating to [1]2-percent rate of interest) shall not apply.

(B) Non-readily-tradable stock defined. For purposes of this paragraph, the term "non-readily-tradable stock" means stock for which, at the time of the decedent's death, there was no market on a stock exchange or in an over-the-counter market.

(8) Stock in holding company treated as business company stock in certain cases.

(A) In general. If the executor elects the benefits of this paragraph, then—

(i) Holding company stock treated as business company stock. For purposes of this section, the portion of the stock of any holding company which represents direct ownership (or indirect ownership through 1 or more other holding companies) by such company in a business company shall be deemed to be stock in such business company.

(ii) 5-year deferral for principal not to apply. The executor shall be treated as having selected under subsection (a)(3) the date prescribed by section 6151(a).

(iii) [2]2-percent interest rate not to apply. Section 6601(j) (relating to [3]2-percent rate of interest) shall not apply.

(B) All stock must be non-readily-tradable stock. No stock shall be taken into account for purposes of applying this paragraph unless it is non-readily-tradable stock (within the meaning of paragraph (7)(B)).

(C) Application of voting stock requirement of paragraph (1)(C)(i). For purposes of clause (i) of paragraph (1)(C), the deemed stock resulting from the application of subparagraph (A) shall be treated as voting stock to the extent that voting stock in the holding company owns directly (or through the voting stock of 1 or more other holding companies) voting stock in the business company.

(D) Definitions. For purposes of this paragraph—

(i) Holding company. The term "holding company" means any corporation holding stock in another corporation.

(ii) Business company. The term "business company" means any corporation carrying on a trade or business.

* * * * * * * * * * * *

[Endnote Code Sec. 6166]

Matter in *italics* in Code Sec. 6166(b)(7)(A)(iii) and Code Sec. 6166(b)(8)(A)(iii) added by Sec. 503(c)(1) of the Taxpayer Relief Act of 1997, H.R. 2014, 8/5/97, which struck out:

1. "4-percent"
2. "4-percent"
3. "4-percent"

Effective Date (Sec. 503(d), H.R. 2014, 8/5/97) effective for estates of decedents dying after 12/31/97. Sec. 503(d)(2) of this Act provides:

"(2) Election.—In the case of the estate of any decedent dying before January 1, 1998, with respect to which there is an election under section 6166 of the Internal Revenue Code of 1986, the executor of the estate may elect to have the amendments made by this section apply with respect to installments due after the effective date of the election; except that the 2-percent portion of such installments shall be equal to the amount which would be the 4-percent portion of such installments without regard to such election. Such an election shall be made before January 1, 1999 in the manner prescribed by the Secretary of the Treasury and, once made, is irrevocable."

[¶ 3322]   Code Sec. 6211.   Definition of a deficiency.

* * * * * * * * * * * *

[1](c) Coordination with subchapter C. In determining the amount of any deficiency for purposes of this subchapter, adjustments to partnership items shall be made only as provided in subchapter C.

[For analysis, see ¶ 1420. For committee reports, see ¶ 5215, ¶ 5201.]

[Endnote Code Sec. 6211]
Code Sec. 6211(c), in *italics*, was added by Sec. 1231(b) of the Taxpayer Relief Act of 1997, H.R. 2014, 8/5/97.
1. added subsection (c)
Effective Date (Sec. 1231(d), H.R. 2014, 8/5/97) effective for partnership tax. yrs. end. after 8/5/97.

[¶ 3323]   Code Sec. 6212.   Notice of deficiency.

* * * * * * * * * * * *

(c) Further deficiency letters restricted.

(1) General rule. If the Secretary has mailed to the taxpayer a notice of deficiency as provided in subsection (a), and the taxpayer files a petition with the Tax Court within the time prescribed in section 6213(a), the Secretary shall have no right to determine any additional deficiency of income tax for the same taxable year, of gift tax for the same calendar year, of estate tax in respect of the taxable estate of the same decedent, of chapter 41 tax for the same taxable year, of chapter 43 tax for the same taxable year, of chapter 44 tax for the same taxable year, of section 4940 tax for the same taxable year, or of chapter 42 tax (other than under section 4940) with respect to any act (or failure to act) to which such petition relates, except in the case of fraud, and except as provided in section 6214(a) (relating to assertion of greater deficiencies before the Tax Court), in section 6213(b)(1) (relating to mathematical or clerical errors), in section 6851 or 6852 (relating to termination assessments), or in section 6861(c) (relating to the making of jeopardy assessments).

(2) Cross references. For assessment as a deficiency notwithstanding the prohibition of further deficiency letters, in the case of—

(A) Deficiency attributable to change of treatment with respect to itemized deductions, see section 63(e)(3).

(B) Deficiency attributable to gain on involuntary conversion, see section 1033(a)(2)(C) and (D).

[1](C) Deficiency attributable to activities not engaged in for profit, see section 183(e)(4).

For provisions allowing determination of tax in title 11 cases, see section 505(a) of title 11 of the United States Code.

* * * * * * * * * * * *

[Endnote Code Sec. 6212]
Matter in *italics* in Code Sec. 6212(c)(2)(C) added by Sec. 312(d)(12) of the Taxpayer Relief Act of 1997, H.R. 2014, 8/5/97, which struck out:
1. "(C) Deficiency attributable to gain on sale or exchange of principal residence, see section 1034(j).
"(E) [sic (D)]"

Effective Date (Sec. 312(d) [sic (e)], H.R. 2014, 8/5/97) effective for sales and exchanges after 5/6/97, except as provided by Sec. 312(d)(2)-(4) [sic (e)(2)-(4)] of this Act, which read as follows:

"(2) Sales before 8/5/97. At the election of the taxpayer, the amendments made by this section shall not apply to any sale or exchange before the date of the enactment of this Act.

"(3) Certain sales within 2 years after 8/5/97. Section 121 of the Internal Revenue Code of 1986 (as amended by this section) shall be applied without regard to subsection (c)(2)(B) thereof in the case of any sale or exchange of property during the 2-year period beginning on the date of the enactment of this Act if the taxpayer held such property on the date of the enactment of this Act and fails to meet the ownership and use requirements of subsection (a) thereof with respect to such property.

"(4) Binding contracts. At the election of the taxpayer, the amendments made by this section shall not apply to a sale or exchange after the date of the enactment of this Act, if—

"(A) such sale or exchange is pursuant to a contract which was binding on such date, or

"(B) without regard to such amendments, gain would not be recognized under section 1034 of the Internal Revenue Code of 1986 (as in effect on the day before the date of the enactment of this Act) on such sale or exchange by reason of a new residence acquired on or before such date or with respect to the acquisition of which by the taxpayer a binding contract was in effect on such date.

This paragraph shall not apply to any sale or exchange by an individual if the treatment provided by section 877(a)(1) of the Internal Revenue Code of 1986 applies to such individual."

[¶ 3324]   Code Sec. 6213.   Restrictions applicable to deficiencies; petition to Tax Court.

* * * * * * * * * * * *

(g) Definitions. For purposes of this section—

* * * * * * * * * * * *

(2) Mathematical or clerical error. The term "mathematical or clerical error" means—

(A) an error in addition, subtraction, multiplication, or division shown on any return,

(B) an incorrect use of any table provided by the Internal Revenue Service with respect to any return if such incorrect use is apparent from the existence of other information on the return,

(C) an entry on a return of an item which is inconsistent with another entry of the same or another item on such return,

(D) an omission of information which is required to be supplied on the return to substantiate an entry on the return,

(E) an entry on a return of a deduction or credit in an amount which exceeds a statutory limit imposed by subtitle A or B, or chapter 41, 42 43, or 44, if such limit is expressed—

(i) as a specified monetary amount, or

(ii) as a percentage, ratio, or fraction,

and if the items entering into the application of such limit appear on such return,

(F) an omission of a correct taxpayer identification number required under section 32 (relating to the earned income credit) to be included on a return,

CAUTION.   Subparas. (g)(2)(G) and (H), following, are effective prior to amendments by Secs. 101(d)(2) and 201(b), H.R. 2014. For effective dates of such amendments, see notes following this Code Sec. For subparas. (g)(2)(G)-(J) as amended by Secs. 101(d)(2) and 201(b), H.R. 2014, see below.

(G) an entry on a return claiming the credit under section 32 with respect to net earnings from self-employment described in section 32(c)(2)(A) to the extent the tax imposed by section 1401 (relating to self-employment tax) on such net earnings has not been paid, and

(H) an omission of a correct TIN required under section 21 (relating to expenses for household and dependent care services necessary for gainful employment) or section 151 (relating to allowance of deductions for personal exemptions).

CAUTION.   Subparas. (g)(2)(G)-(J), following, are effective as amended by Secs. 101(d)(2) and 201(b), H.R. 2014. For effective dates of such amendments, see notes following this Code Sec. For subparas. (g)(2)(G) and (H) effective prior to amendments by Secs. 101(d)(2) and 202(b), H.R. 2014, see above.

(G) an entry on a return claiming the credit under section 32 with respect to net earnings from self-employment described in section 32(c)(2)(A) to the extent the tax imposed by section 1401 (relating to self-employment tax) on such net earnings has not been paid,[1]

(H) an omission of a correct TIN required under section 21 (relating to expenses for household and dependent care services necessary for gainful employment) or section 151 (relating to allowance of deductions for personal exemptions)[2],[3]

[4]*(I) an omission of a correct TIN required under section 24(e) (relating to child tax credit) to be included on a return[5], and*

[6]*(J) an omission of a correct TIN required under section 25A(g)(1) (relating to higher education tuition and related expenses) to be included on a return.*

CAUTION. Subpara. (g)(2)(J), following [as added by Sec. 1085(a)(3), H.R. 2014], is effective for tax. yrs. begin. after 12/31/96.

[7]*(J) an omission of information required by section 32(k)(2) (relating to taxpayers making improper prior claims of earned income credit).*

* * * * * * * * * * * *

[For analysis, see ¶ 101, ¶ 108, ¶ 401. For committee reports, see ¶ 5001, ¶ 5002, ¶ 5162.]

[Endnote Code Sec. 6213]
Matter in *italics* in Code Sec. 6213(g)(2)(G), Code Sec. 6213(g)(2)(H) and Code Sec. 6213(g)(2)(I) added by Sec. 101(d)(2) of the Taxpayer Relief Act of 1997, H.R. 2014, 8/5/97, which struck out:
1. "and"
2. "."
Effective Date (Sec. 101(e), H.R. 2014, 8/5/97) effective for tax. yrs. begin. after 12/31/97.

Matter in Code Sec. 6213(g)(2)(H) deleted by Sec. 201(b), H.R. 2014, 8/5/97.
3. "and"
Effective Date (Sec. 201(f)(1), H.R. 2014, 8/5/97) effective for expenses paid after 12/31/97 (in tax. yrs. end. after 12/31/97), for education furnished in academic periods begin. after 12/31/97.

Code Sec. 6213(g)(2)(I), in *italics*, was added by Sec. 101(d)(2), H.R. 2014, 8/5/97.
4. added subpara. (g)(2)(I)
Matter in *italics* in Code Sec. 6213(g)(2)(I) and Code Sec. 6213(g)(2)(J) added by Sec. 201(b), H.R. 2014, 8/5/97, which struck out:
5. "."
6. added subpara. (g)(2)(J)
Effective Date (Sec. 201(f)(1), H.R. 2014, 8/5/97) effective for expenses paid after 12/31/97 (in tax. yrs. end. after 12/31/97), for education furnished in academic periods begin. after 12/31/97.

Code Sec. 6213(g)(2)(J), in *italics*, was added by Sec. 1085(a)(3), H.R. 2014, 8/5/97.
7. added subpara. (g)(2)(J)
Effective Date (Sec. 1085(e)(1), H.R. 2014, 8/5/97) effective for tax. yrs. begin. after 12/31/96.

[¶ 3325]   Code Sec. 6221.   Tax treatment determined at partnership level.
Except as otherwise provided in this subchapter, the tax treatment of any partnership [1]*item (and the applicability of any penalty, addition to tax, or additional amount which relates to an adjustment to a partnership item)* shall be determined at the partnership level. *[For analysis, see ¶ 1415. For committee reports, see ¶ 5223.]*

[Endnote Code Sec. 6221]
Matter in *italics* in Code Sec. 6221 added by Sec. 1238(a) of the Taxpayer Relief Act of 1997, H.R. 2014, date of enactment, which struck out:
1. "item"
Effective Date (Sec. 1238(c), H.R. 2014, 8/5/97) effective for partnership tax. yrs. end. after 8/5/97.

[¶ 3326]   Code Sec. 6225.   Assessments made only after partnership level proceedings are completed.

* * * * * * * * * * *

(b) Premature action may be enjoined. Notwithstanding section 7421(a), any action which violates subsection (a) may be enjoined in [1]*the proper court, including the Tax Court. The Tax Court shall have no jurisdiction to enjoin any action or proceeding under this subsection unless a timely petition for a readjustment of the partnership items for the taxable year has been filed and then only in respect of the adjustments that are the subject of such petition.*

* * * * * * * * * * *

[For analysis, see ¶ 1416. For text of committee report, see ¶ 5224.]

[Endnote Code Sec. 6225]

Matter in *italics* in Code Sec. 6225(b) added by Sec. 1239(a) of the Taxpayer Relief Act of 1997, H.R. 2014, 8/5/97, which struck out:

1. "the proper court."

Effective Date (Sec. 1239(f), H.R. 2014, 8/5/97) effective for partnership tax. yrs. end. after 8/5/97.

[¶ 3327]   Code Sec. 6226.   Judicial review of final partnership administrative adjustments.

* * * * * * * * * * *

(b) Petition by partner other than tax matters partner.

* * * * * * * * * * *

[1]*(5) Treatment of premature petitions. If—*

(A) a petition for a readjustment of partnership items for the taxable year involved is filed by a notice partner (or a 5-percent group) during the 90-day period described in subsection (a), and

(B) no action is brought under paragraph (1) during the 60-day period described therein with respect to such taxable year which is not dismissed,

such petition shall be treated for purposes of paragraph (1) as filed on the last day of such 60-day period.

[2]*(6)* **Tax matters partner may intervene.** The tax matters partner may intervene in any action brought under this subsection.

* * * * * * * * * * *

(d) Partner must have interest in outcome.

(1) In order to be party to action. Subsection (c) shall not apply to a partner after the day on which—

(A) the partnership items of such partner for the partnership taxable year became non-partnership items by reason of 1 or more of the events described in subsection (b) of section 6231, or

(B) the period within which any tax attributable to such partnership items may be assessed against that partner expired.

[3]*Notwithstanding subparagraph (B), any person treated under subsection (c) as a party to an action shall be permitted to participate in such action (or file a readjustment petition under subsection (b) or paragraph (2) of this subsection) solely for the purpose of asserting that the period of limitations for assessing any tax attributable to partnership items has expired with respect to such person, and the court having jurisdiction of such action shall have jurisdiction to consider such assertion.*

(2) To file petition. No partner may file a readjustment petition under subsection (b) unless such partner would (after the application of paragraph (1) of this subsection) be treated as a party to the proceeding.

* * * * * * * * * * * *

(f) Scope of judicial review. A court with which a petition is filed in accordance with this section shall have jurisdiction to determine all partnership items of the partnership for the partnership taxable year to which the notice of final partnership administrative adjustment [4]*relates,* the proper allocation of such items among the partners[5], *and the applicability of any penalty, addition to tax, or additional amount which relates to an adjustment to a partnership item.*

* * * * * * * * * * * *

[For analysis, see ¶ 1415, ¶ 1416, ¶ 1418. For text of committee report, see ¶ 5223, ¶ 5224, ¶ 5225.]

[Endnote Code Sec. 6226]

Matter in *italics* in Code Sec. 6226(b)(5) and Code Sec. 6226(b)(6) added by Sec. 1240(a) of the Taxpayer Relief Act of 1997, H.R. 2014, 8/5/97, which struck out:
1. added para. (b)(5)
2. "(5)"

Effective Date (Sec. 1240(b), H.R. 2014, 8/5/97) effective for petitions filed after 8/5/97.

Matter in *italics* in Code Sec. 6226(d)(1) was added by Sec. 1239(b), H.R. 2014, 8/5/97.
3. added matter in paragraph (d)(1)

Effective Date (Sec. 1239(f), H.R. 2014, 8/5/97) effective for partnership tax. yrs. end. after 8/5/97.

Matter in *italics* in Code Sec. 6226(f) added by Sec. 1238(b)(1)(A) and (B), H.R. 2014, 8/5/97, which struck out:
4. "relates and"
5. added matter in subsec. (f)

Effective Date (Sec. 1238(c), H.R. 2014, 8/5/97) effective for tax. yrs. end. after 8/5/97.

[¶ 3328]   Code Sec. 6227.   Administrative adjustment requests.

* * * * * * * * * * *

[1]*(b) Special rule in case of extension of period of limitations under section 6229. The period prescribed by subsection (a)(1) for filing of a request for an administrative adjustment shall be extended—*

(1) for the period within which an assessment may be made pursuant to an agreement (or any extension thereof) under section 6229(b), and

(2) for 6 months thereafter.

[2]*(c)* **Requests by tax matters partner on behalf of partnership.**
(1) Substituted return. If the tax matters partner—

(A) files a request for an administrative adjustment, and

(B) asks that the treatment shown on the request be substituted for the treatment of partnership items on the partnership return to which the request relates,

the Secretary may treat the changes shown on such request as corrections of mathematical or clerical errors appearing on the partnership return.

(2) Requests not treated as substituted returns.

(A) In general. If the tax matters partner files an administrative adjustment request on behalf of the partnership which is not treated as a substituted return under paragraph (1), the Secretary may, with respect to all or any part of the requested adjustments—

(i) without conducting any proceeding, allow or make to all partners the credits or refunds arising from the requested adjustments,

(ii) conduct a partnership proceeding under this subchapter, or

(iii) take no action on the request.

(B) Exceptions. Clause (i) of subparagraph (A) shall not apply with respect to a partner after the day on which the partnership items become nonpartnership items by reason of 1 or more of the events described in subsection (b) of section 6231.

(3) Request must show effect on distributive shares. The tax matters partner shall furnish with any administrative adjustment request on behalf of the partnership revised schedules showing the effect of such request on the distributive shares of the partners and such other information as may be required under regulations.

[3]*(d)* **Other requests.** If any partner files a request for an administrative adjustment (other than a request described in subsection (b)), the Secretary may—

(1) process the request in the same manner as a claim for credit or refund with respect to items which are not partnership items,

(2) assess any additional tax that would result from the requested adjustments,

(3) mail to the partner, under subparagraph (A) of section 6231(b)(1) (relating to items becoming nonpartnership items), a notice that all partnership items of the partner for the partnership taxable year to which such request relates shall be treated as nonpartnership items, or

(4) conduct a partnership proceeding.

[4]*(e)* *Requests with respect to bad debts or worthless securities.* *In the case of that portion of any request for an administrative adjustment which relates to the deductibility by the partnership under section 166 of a debt as a debt which became worthless, or under section 165(g) of a loss from worthlessness of a security, the period prescribed in subsection (a)(1) shall be 7 years from the last day for filing the partnership return for the year with respect to which such request is made (determined without regard to extensions).*

[For analysis, see ¶ 1409, ¶ 1410. For text of committee report, see ¶ 5220, ¶ 5228.]

[Endnote Code Sec. 6227]

Matter in *italics* in Code Sec. 6227(b), Code Sec. 6227(c), and Code Sec. 6227(d) added by Sec. 1236(a) of the Taxpayer Relief Act of 1997, H.R. 2014, date of enactment, which struck out:

1. added subsec. (b)
2. "(b)"
3. "(c)"

Effective Date (Sec. 1236(b), H.R. 2014, 8/5/97) effective for partnership tax. yrs. begin. after 9/3/82. P.L. 97-248, Sec. 407(a)(3) provides:

"(3) The amendments made by sections 402, 403 and 404 [of this Act] shall apply to any partnership taxable year (or in the case of section 6232 of such Code, to any period) ending after the date of the enactment of this Act [9/3/82] if the partnership, each partner, and each indirect partner requests such application and the Secretary of the Treasury or his delegate consents to such application."

Code Sec. 6227(e), in *italics*, was added by Sec. 1243(a), H.R. 2014.

4. added subsec. (e)

Effective Date (Sec. 1243(b), H.R. 2014, 8/5/97) effective for partnership tax. yrs. begin. after 9/3/82. P.L. 97-248Sec. 407(a)(3) reproduced above. Sec. 1243(b) of this Act provides:

"(b) Effective date.—

"(1) In general.—The amendment made by subsection (a) shall take effect as if included in the amendments made by section 402 of the Tax Equity and Fiscal Responsibility Act of 1982.

"(2) Treatment of requests filed before 8/5/97.— In the case of that portion of any request (filed before the date of the enactment of this Act) for an administrative adjustment which relates to the deductibility of a debt as a debt which became worthless or the deductibility of a loss from the worthlessness of a security—

"(A) paragraph (2) of section 6227(a) of the Internal Revenue Code of 1986 shall not apply,

"(B) the period for filing a petition under section 6228 of the Internal Revenue Code of 1986 with respect to such request shall not expire before the date 6 months after the date of the enactment of this Act, and

"(C) such a petition may be filed without regard to whether there was a notice of the beginning of an administrative proceeding or a final partnership administrative adjustment."

[¶ 3329]   Code Sec. 6229.   Period of limitations for making assessments.

* * * * * * * * * * *

(b) Extension by agreement.

(1) In general. The period described in subsection (a) (including an extension period under this subsection) may be extended—

    (A) with respect to any partner, by an agreement entered into by the Secretary and such partner, and

    (B) with respect to all partners, by an agreement entered into by the Secretary and the tax matters partner (or any other person authorized by the partnership in writing to enter into such an agreement), before the expiration of such period.

[1]*(2) Special rule with respect to debtors in title 11 cases. Notwithstanding any other law or rule of law, if an agreement is entered into under paragraph (1)(B) and the agreement is signed by a person who would be the tax matters partner but for the fact that, at the time that the agreement is executed, the person is a debtor in a bankruptcy proceeding under title 11 of the United States Code, such agreement shall be binding on all partners in the partnership unless the Secretary has been notified of the bankruptcy proceeding in accordance with regulations prescribed by the Secretary.*

[2]**(3) Coordination with section 6501(c)(4).** Any agreement under section 6501(c)(4) shall apply with respect to the period described in subsection (a) only if the agreement expressly provides that such agreement applies to tax attributable to partnership items.

* * * * * * * * * * *

(d) Suspension when secretary makes administrative adjustment. If notice of a final partnership administrative adjustment with respect to any taxable year is mailed to the tax matters partner, the running of the period specified in subsection (a) (as modified by other provisions of this section) shall be suspended—

(1) for the period during which an action may be brought under section 6226 [3]*(and, if a petition is filed under section 6226 with respect to such administrative adjustment, until the decision of the court becomes final), and*

(2) for 1 year thereafter.

* * * * * * * * * * *

(f) [4]*Special rules.*

(1) Items becoming nonpartnership items. If, before the expiration of the period otherwise provided in this section for assessing any tax imposed by subtitle A with respect to the partnership items of a partner for the partnership taxable year, such items become nonpartnership items by reason of 1 or more of the events described in subsection (b) of section 6231, the period for assessing any tax imposed by subtitle A which is attributable to such items (or any item affected by such items) shall not expire before the date which is 1 year after the date on which the items become nonpartnership items. The period described in the preceding sentence (including any extension period under this sentence) may be extended with respect to any partner by agreement entered into by the Secretary and such partner.

[5]**(2) Special rule for partial settlement agreements.** *If a partner enters into a settlement agreement with the Secretary with respect to the treatment of some of the partnership items in dispute for a partnership taxable year but other partnership items for such year remain in dispute, the period of limitations for assessing any tax attributable to the settled items shall be determined as if such agreement had not been entered into.*

[6]**(h) Suspension during pendency of bankruptcy proceeding.** *If a petition is filed naming a partner as a debtor in a bankruptcy proceeding under title 11 of the United States Code, the running of the period of limitations provided in this section with respect to such partner shall be suspended—*

(1) for the period during which the Secretary is prohibited by reason of such bankruptcy proceeding from making an assessment, and

(2) for 60 days thereafter.

[For analysis, see ¶ 1411, ¶ 1414. For text of committee report, see ¶ 5217, ¶ 5219.]

[Endnote Code Sec. 6229]

Matter in *italics* in Code Sec. 6229(b)(2) and Code Sec. 6229(b)(3) added by Sec. 1233(c) of the Taxpayer Relief Act of 1997, H.R. 2014, 8/5/97, which struck out:

1. added paragraph (b)(2)
2. "(2)"

Effective Date (Sec. 1233(d)(2), H.R. 2014, 8/5/97) effective for agreements entered into after 8/5/97.

Matter in *italics* in Code Sec. 6229(d)(1) added by Sec. 1233(a), H.R. 2014, 8/5/97, which struck out:

3. "(and, if an action with respect to such administrative adjustment is brought during such period, until the decision of the court in such action becomes final), and"

Effective Date (Sec. 1233(d)(1), H.R. 2014, 8/5/97) effective for the period under Code Sec. 6229 for assessing tax has not expired on or before 8/5/97.

Matter in *italics* in Code Sec. 6229(f), Code Sec. 6229(f)(1) and Code Sec. 6229(f)(2) added by Sec. 1235(a)(1) and (3), H.R. 2014, 8/5/97, which struck out:

4. "(f) Items becoming nonpartnership items. If"
5. added paragraph (f)(2)

Effective Date (Sec. 1235(b), H.R. 2014, 8/5/97) effective for settlements entered into after 8/5/97.

Code Sec. 6229(h), in *italics*, was added by Sec. 1233(b), H.R. 2014, 8/5/97.

6. added subsection (h)

Effective Date (Sec. 1233(d)(1), H.R. 2014, 8/5/97) see above.

[¶ 3330]   Code Sec. 6230.   Additional administrative provisions.

(a) Coordination with deficiency proceedings.

(1) In general. Except as provided in [1]*paragraph (2) or (3)*, subchapter B of this chapter shall not apply to the assessment or collection of any computational adjustment.

(2) Deficiency proceedings to apply in certain cases.

(A) Subchapter B shall apply to any deficiency attributable to—

[2]*(i) affected items which require partner level determinations (other than penalties, additions to tax, and additional amounts that relate to adjustments to partnership items), or*

(ii) items which have become nonpartnership items (other than by reason of section 6231(b)(1)(C)) and are described in section 6231(e)(1)(B).

(B) Subchapter B shall be applied separately with respect to each deficiency described in subparagraph (A) attributable to each partnership.

(C) Notwithstanding any other law or rule of law, any notice or proceeding under subchapter B with respect to a deficiency described in this paragraph shall not preclude or be precluded by any other notice, proceeding, or determination with respect to a partner's tax liability for a taxable year.

[3]*(3) Special rule in case of assertion by partner's spouse of innocent spouse relief.*

(A) Notwithstanding section 6404(b), if the spouse of a partner asserts that section 6013(e) applies with respect to a liability that is attributable to any adjustment to a partnership item [4](including any liability for any penalties, additions to tax, or additional amounts relating to such adjustment), then such spouse may file with the Secretary within 60 days after the notice of computational adjustment is mailed to the spouse a request for abatement of the assessment specified in such notice. Upon receipt of such request, the Secretary shall abate the assessment. Any reassessment of the tax with respect to which an abatement is made under this subparagraph shall be subject to the deficiency procedures prescribed by subchapter B. The period for making any such reassessment shall not expire before the expiration of 60 days after the date of such abatement.

(B) If the spouse files a petition with the Tax Court pursuant to section 6213 with respect to the request for abatement described in subparagraph (A), the Tax Court shall only have jurisdiction pursuant to this section to determine whether the requirements of section

6013(e) have been satisfied. For purposes of such determination, the treatment of partner-ship items [5](and the applicability of any penalties, additions to tax, or additional amounts) *under the settlement, the final partnership administrative adjustment, or the decision of the court (whichever is appropriate) that gave rise to the liability in question shall be conclu-sive.*

(C) Rules similar to the rules contained in subparagraphs (B) and (C) of paragraph (2) shall apply for purposes of this paragraph.

* * * * * * * * * * * *

(c) Claims arising out of erroneous computations, etc.

(1) In general. A partner may file a claim for refund on the grounds that—

(A) the Secretary erroneously computed any computational adjustment necessary—

(i) to make the partnership items on the partner's return consistent with the treatment of the partnership items on the partnership return, or

(ii) to apply to the partner a settlement, a final partnership administrative adjustment, or the decision of a court in an action brought under section 6226 or section 6228(a),[6]

(B) the Secretary failed to allow a credit or to make a refund to the partner in the amount of the overpayment attributable to the application to the partner of a settlement, a final partnership administrative adjustment, or the decision of a court in an action brought under section 6226 or section 6228(a)[7], or

[8]*(C) the Secretary erroneously imposed any penalty, addition to tax, or additional amount which relates to an adjustment to a partnership item.*

(2) Time for filing claim.

[9]*(A) Under paragraph (1)(A) or (C). Any claim under subparagraph (A) or (C) of para-graph (1) shall be filed within 6 months after the day on which the Secretary mails the no-tice of computational adjustment to the partner.*

(B) Under paragraph (1)(B). Any claim under paragraph (1)(B) shall be filed within 2 years after whichever of the following days is appropriate:

(i) the day on which the settlement is entered into,

(ii) the day on which the period during which an action may be brought under section 6226 with respect to the final partnership administrative adjustment expires, or

(iii) the day on which the decision of the court becomes final.

(3) Suit if claim not allowed. If any portion of a claim under paragraph (1) is not allowed, the partner may bring suit with respect to such portion within the period specified in subsec-tion (a) of section 6532 (relating to periods of limitations on refund suits).

(4) No review of substantive issues. For purposes of any claim or suit under this subsec-tion, the treatment of partnership items on the partnership return, under the settlement, under the final partnership administrative adjustment, or under the decision of the court (whichever is appropriate) shall be conclusive. [10]*In addition, the determination under the final partnership administrative adjustment or under the decision of the court (whichever is appropriate) con-cerning the applicability of any penalty, addition to tax, or additional amount which relates to an adjustment to a partnership item shall also be conclusive. Notwithstanding the preceding sentence, the partner shall be allowed to assert any partner level defenses that may apply or to challenge the amount of the computational adjustment.*

[11]*(5) Rules for seeking innocent spouse relief.*

(A) In general. The spouse of a partner may file a claim for refund on the ground that the Secretary failed to relieve the spouse under section 6013(e) from a liability that is attrib-utable to an adjustment to a partnership item [12]*(including any liability for any penalties, ad-ditions to tax, or additional amounts relating to such adjustment).*

(B) Time for filing claim. Any claim under subparagraph (A) shall be filed within 6 months after the day on which the Secretary mails to the spouse the notice of computational adjustment referred to in subsection (a)(3)(A).

(C) Suit if claim not allowed. If the claim under subparagraph (B) is not allowed, the spouse may bring suit with respect to the claim within the period specified in paragraph (3).

(D) Prior determinations are binding. For purposes of any claim or suit under this paragraph, the treatment of partnership items [13](and the applicability of any penalties, additions to tax, or additional amounts) under the settlement, the final partnership administrative adjustment, or the decision of the court (whichever is appropriate) that gave rise to the liability in question shall be conclusive.

(d) Special rules with respect to credits or refunds attributable to partnership items.

* * * * * * * * * * *

(6) Subchapter B of chapter 66 not applicable. Subchapter B of chapter 66 (relating to limitations on credit or refund) shall not apply to any credit or refund of an overpayment attributable to a partnership item[14].

* * * * * * * * * * *

[For analysis, see ¶ 1412, ¶ 1415. For text of committee report, see ¶ 5221, ¶ 5223, ¶ 5224.]

[Endnote Code Sec. 6230]

Matter in *italics* in Code Sec. 6230(a)(1) added by Sec. 1237(c)(1) of the Taxpayer Relief Act of 1997, H.R. 2014, 8/5/97, which struck out:

1. "paragraph (2)"

Effective Date (Sec. 1237(d), H.R. 2014, 8/5/97) effective for partnership tax. yrs. begin. after 9/3/82. P.L. 97-248, Sec. 407(a)(3), provides:

"(3) The amendments made by sections 402, 403 and 404 [of this P.L. 97-248] shall apply to any partnership taxable year (or in the case of section 6232 of such Code, to any period) ending after the date of the enactment of this Act [9/3/82] if the partnership, each partner, and each indirect partner requests such application and the Secretary of the Treasury or his delegate consents to such application."

Matter in *italics* in Code Sec. 6230(a)(2)(A)(i), added by Sec. 1238(b)(2), H.R. 2014, which struck out:

2. " (i) affected items which require partner level determinations, or"

Effective Date (Sec. 1238(c), H.R. 2014, 8/5/97) effective for partnership tax. yrs. end. after 8/5/97.

Code Sec. 6230(a)(3) in *italics* was added by Sec. 1237(a), H.R. 2014.

3. added para. (a)(3)

Effective Date (Sec. 1237(d), H.R. 2014, 8/5/97) effective for partnership tax. yrs. begin. after 9/3/82. P.L. 97-248, Sec. 407(a)(3), reproduced above provides special rules.

Matter in *italics* in Code Sec. 6230(a)(3)(A), Code Sec. 6230(a)(3)(B), Code Sec. 6230(c)(1)(A), Code Sec. 6230(c)(1)(B), Code Sec. 6230(c)(1)(C), Code Sec. 6230(c)(2)(A), and Code Sec. 6230(c)(4) added by Sec. 1238(b)(3)(A), (B), (b)(4), (5), (6), H.R. 2014, which struck out:

4. added "including any liability for any penalty addition to tax, or additional amount relating to such adjustment)" after "partnership item" in subpara. (a)(3)(A) as amended by Sec. 1237(a), of this Act.

5. added "(and the applicability of any penalties, additions to tax, or additional amounts)" after "partnership items" in subpara. (a)(3)(B) as amended by Sec. 1237(a), of this Act.

6. "or"

7. "."

8. added subpara. (c)(1)(C)

9. "(A) Under paragraph (1)(A). Any claim under paragraph (1)(A)"

10. added last two sentences in para. (c)(4).

Effective Date (Sec. 1238(c), H.R. 2014, 8/5/97) effective for partnership tax. yrs. end. after 8/5/97.

Code Sec. 6230(c)(5) in *italics* was added by Sec. 1237(b), H.R. 2014.

11. added para. (c)(5)

Effective Date (Sec. 1237(d), H.R. 2014, 8/5/97) effective for partnership tax. yrs. begin. after 9/3/82. P.L. 97-248, Sec. 407(a)(3), provides special rules, see above.

Matter in Code Sec. 6230(c)(5)(A), and Code Sec. 6230(c)(5)(D), [as added by Sec. 1237(b) of this Act] was added by Sec. 1238(b)(3)(C) and (D), H.R. 2014.

12. added "(including any liability for any penalties, additions to tax, or additional amounts relating to such adjustment)" before the period in subpara. (c)(5)(A) as amended by Sec. 1237(b) of this Act.

13. added "(and the applicability of any penalties, additions to tax, or additional amounts) " after " partnership items" in subpara. (c)(5)(D) as amended by Sec. 1237(b).

Effective Date (Sec. 1238(c), H.R. 2014, 8/5/97) effective for partnership tax. yrs. end. after 8/5/97.

Matter in *italics* in Code Sec. 6230(d)(6) added by Sec. 1239(c)(1), H.R. 2014, which struck out:

14. "(or an affected item)"

Effective Date (Sec. 1239(f), H.R. 2014, 8/5/97) effective for partnership tax. yrs. end. after 8/5/97.

[¶ 3331] Code Sec. 6231. Definitions and special rules.

(a) **Definitions.** For purposes of this subchapter—

(1) **Partnership.**

(A) In general. Except as provided in subparagraph (B), the term "partnership" means any partnership required to file a return under section 6031(a).

(B) Exception for small partnerships.

[1]*(i) In general. The term "partnership" shall not include any partnership having 10 or fewer partners each of whom is an individual (other than a nonresident alien), a C corporation, or an estate of a deceased partner. For purposes of the preceding sentence, a husband and wife (and their estates) shall be treated as 1 partner.*

(ii) Election to have subchapter apply. A partnership (within the meaning of subparagraph (A)) may for any taxable year elect to have clause (i) not apply. Such election shall apply for such taxable year and all subsequent taxable years unless revoked with the consent of the Secretary.

* * * * * * * * * * * *

(f) **Special rule for [2]*deductions, losses, and* credits of foreign partnerships.** Except to the extent otherwise provided in regulations, in the case of any partnership the tax matters partner of which resides outside the United States or the books of which are maintained outside the United States, no [3]*deduction, loss, or* credit shall be allowable to any partner unless section 6031 is complied with for the partnership's taxable year in which such [4]*deduction, loss, or* credit arose at such time as the Secretary prescribes by regulations.

[5]*(g) Partnership return to be determinative of whether subchapter applies.*

(1) Determination that subchapter applies. If, on the basis of a partnership return for a taxable year, the Secretary reasonably determines that this subchapter applies to such partnership for such year but such determination is erroneous, then the provisions of this subchapter are hereby extended to such partnership (and its items) for such taxable year and to partners of such partnership.

(2) Determination that subchapter does not apply. If, on the basis of a partnership return for a taxable year, the Secretary reasonably determines that this subchapter does not apply to such partnership for such year but such determination is erroneous, then the provisions of this subchapter shall not apply to such partnership (and its items) for such taxable year or to partners of such partnership.

[For analysis, see ¶ 1407, ¶ 1408, ¶ 1421. For text of committee report, see ¶ 5182, ¶ 5216, ¶ 5218.]

[Endnote Code Sec. 6231]

Matter in *italics* in Code Sec. 6231(a)(1)(B)(i) added by Sec. 1234(a) of the Taxpayer Relief Act of 1997, H.R. 2014, 8/5/97, which struck out:

1. "(i) In general. The term 'partnership' shall not include any partnership if—

"(I) such partnership has 10 or fewer partners each of whom is a natural person (other than a nonresident alien) or an estate, and

"(II) each partner's share of each partnership item is the same as his share of every other item."

For purposes of the preceding sentence, a husband and wife (and their estates) shall be treated as 1 partner."

Effective Date (Sec. 1234(b), H.R. 2014, 8/5/97) effective for partnership tax. yrs. end. after 8/5/97.

Matter in *italics* in Code Sec. 6231(f) added by Sec. 1141(b)(1) and (2), H.R. 2014, 8/5/97, which struck out:

2. "losses and"

3. "loss or"

4. "loss or"

Effective Date (Sec. 1141(c), H.R. 2014, 8/5/97) effective for tax. yrs. begin. after 8/5/97.

Code Sec. 6231(g) in *italics* was added by Sec. 1232(a), H.R. 2014, 8/5/97.

5. added subsec. (g)

Effective Date (Sec. 1232(b), H.R. 2014, 8/5/97) effective for tax. yrs. end. after 8/5/97.

[¶ 3332] Code Sec.¹ 6234. Declaratory judgment relating to treatment of items other than partnership items with respect to an oversheltered return.

(a) **General rule.** If—

(1) a taxpayer files an oversheltered return for a taxable year,

(2) the Secretary makes a determination with respect to the treatment of items (other than partnership items) of such taxpayer for such taxable year, and

(3) the adjustments resulting from such determination do not give rise to a deficiency (as defined in section 6211) but would give rise to a deficiency if there were no net loss from partnership items,

the Secretary is authorized to send a notice of adjustment reflecting such determination to the taxpayer by certified or registered mail.

(b) **Oversheltered return.** For purposes of this section, the term "oversheltered return" means an income tax return which—

(1) shows no taxable income for the taxable year, and

(2) shows a net loss from partnership items.

(c) **Judicial review in the Tax Court.** Within 90 days, or 150 days if the notice is addressed to a person outside the United States, after the day on which the notice of adjustment authorized in subsection (a) is mailed to the taxpayer, the taxpayer may file a petition with the Tax Court for redetermination of the adjustments. Upon the filing of such a petition, the Tax Court shall have jurisdiction to make a declaration with respect to all items (other than partnership items and affected items which require partner level determinations as described in section 6230(a)(2)(A)(i)) for the taxable year to which the notice of adjustment relates, in accordance with the principles of section 6214(a). Any such declaration shall have the force and effect of a decision of the Tax Court and shall be reviewable as such.

(d) **Failure to file petition.**

(1) **In general.** Except as provided in paragraph (2), if the taxpayer does not file a petition with the Tax Court within the time prescribed in subsection (c), the determination of the Secretary set forth in the notice of adjustment that was mailed to the taxpayer shall be deemed to be correct.

(2) **Exception.** Paragraph (1) shall not apply after the date that the taxpayer—

(A) files a petition with the Tax Court within the time prescribed in subsection (c) with respect to a subsequent notice of adjustment relating to the same taxable year, or

(B) files a claim for refund of an overpayment of tax under section 6511 for the taxable year involved.

If a claim for refund is filed by the taxpayer, then solely for purposes of determining (for the taxable year involved) the amount of any computational adjustment in connection with a partnership proceeding under this subchapter (other than under this section) or the amount of any deficiency attributable to affected items in a proceeding under section 6230(a)(2), the items that are the subject of the notice of adjustment shall be presumed to have been correctly reported on the taxpayer's return during the pendency of the refund claim (and, if within the time prescribed by section 6532 the taxpayer commences a civil action for refund under section 7422, until the decision in the refund action becomes final).

(e) **Limitations period.**

(1) **In general.** Any notice to a taxpayer under subsection (a) shall be mailed before the expiration of the period prescribed by section 6501 (relating to the period of limitations on assessment).

(2) **Suspension when Secretary mails notice of adjustment.** If the Secretary mails a notice of adjustment to the taxpayer for a taxable year, the period of limitations on the making of assessments shall be suspended for the period during which the Secretary is prohibited from making the assessment (and, in any event, if a proceeding in respect of the notice of adjustment is placed on the docket of the Tax Court, until the decision of the Tax Court becomes final), and for 60 days thereafter.

(3) Restrictions on assessment. Except as otherwise provided in section 6851, 6852, or 6861, no assessment of a deficiency with respect to any tax imposed by subtitle A attributable to any item (other than a partnership item or any item affected by a partnership item) shall be made—

(A) until the expiration of the applicable 90-day or 150-day period set forth in subsection (c) for filing a petition with the Tax Court, or

(B) if a petition has been filed with the Tax Court, until the decision of the Tax Court has become final.

(f) Further notices of adjustment restricted. If the Secretary mails a notice of adjustment to the taxpayer for a taxable year and the taxpayer files a petition with the Tax Court within the time prescribed in subsection (c), the Secretary may not mail another such notice to the taxpayer with respect to the same taxable year in the absence of a showing of fraud, malfeasance, or misrepresentation of a material fact.

(g) Coordination with other proceedings under this subchapter.

(1) In general. The treatment of any item that has been determined pursuant to subsection (c) or (d) shall be taken into account in determining the amount of any computational adjustment that is made in connection with a partnership proceeding under this subchapter (other than under this section), or the amount of any deficiency attributable to affected items in a proceeding under section 6230(a)(2), for the taxable year involved. Notwithstanding any other law or rule of law pertaining to the period of limitations on the making of assessments, for purposes of the preceding sentence, any adjustment made in accordance with this section shall be taken into account regardless of whether any assessment has been made with respect to such adjustment.

(2) Special rule in case of computational adjustment. In the case of a computational adjustment that is made in connection with a partnership proceeding under this subchapter (other than under this section), the provisions of paragraph (1) shall apply only if the computational adjustment is made within the period prescribed by section 6229 for assessing any tax under subtitle A which is attributable to any partnership item or affected item for the taxable year involved.

(3) Conversion to deficiency proceeding. If—

(A) after the notice referred to in subsection (a) is mailed to a taxpayer for a taxable year but before the expiration of the period for filing a petition with the Tax Court under subsection (c) (or, if a petition is filed with the Tax Court, before the Tax Court makes a declaration for that taxable year), the treatment of any partnership item for the taxable year is finally determined, or any such item ceases to be a partnership item pursuant to section 6231(b), and

(B) as a result of that final determination or cessation, a deficiency can be determined with respect to the items that are the subject of the notice of adjustment,

the notice of adjustment shall be treated as a notice of deficiency under section 6212 and any petition filed in respect of the notice shall be treated as an action brought under section 6213.

(4) Finally determined. For purposes of this subsection, the treatment of partnership items shall be treated as finally determined if—

(A) the Secretary enters into a settlement agreement (within the meaning of section 6224) with the taxpayer regarding such items,

(B) a notice of final partnership administrative adjustment has been issued and—

(i) no petition has been filed under section 6226 and the time for doing so has expired, or

(ii) a petition has been filed under section 6226 and the decision of the court has become final, or

(C) the period within which any tax attributable to such items may be assessed against the taxpayer has expired.

(h) Special rules if Secretary incorrectly determines applicable procedure.

(1) Special rule if secretary erroneously mails notice of adjustment. If the Secretary erroneously determines that subchapter B does not apply to a taxable year of a taxpayer and consistent with that determination timely mails a notice of adjustment to the taxpayer pursuant to subsection (a) of this section, the notice of adjustment shall be treated as a notice of deficiency under section 6212 and any petition that is filed in respect of the notice shall be treated as an action brought under section 6213.

(2) Special rule if Secretary erroneously mails notice of deficiency. If the Secretary erroneously determines that subchapter B applies to a taxable year of a taxpayer and consistent with that determination timely mails a notice of deficiency to the taxpayer pursuant to section 6212, the notice of deficiency shall be treated as a notice of adjustment under subsection (a) and any petition that is filed in respect of the notice shall be treated as an action brought under subsection (c).

[For analysis, see ¶ 1419. For text of committee report, see ¶ 5215.]

[Endnote Code Sec. 6234]
   Code Sec. 6234 was added by Sec. 1231(a) of the Taxpayer Relief Act of 1997, H.R. 2014, 8/5/97.
   1. added Code Sec. 6234
Effective Date (Sec. 1231(d), H.R. 2014, 8/5/97) effective for partnership tax. yrs. end. after 8/5/97.

[¶ 3333]   Code Sec.[1] 6240.   Application of subchapter.
   (a) General rule. This subchapter shall only apply to electing large partnerships and partners in such partnerships.
   (b) Coordination with other partnership audit procedures.
   (1) In general. Subchapter C of this chapter shall not apply to any electing large partnership other than in its capacity as a partner in another partnership which is not an electing large partnership.
   (2) Treatment where partner in other partnership. If an electing large partnership is a partner in another partnership which is not an electing large partnership—
   (A) subchapter C of this chapter shall apply to items of such electing large partnership which are partnership items with respect to such other partnership, but
   (B) any adjustment under such subchapter C shall be taken into account in the manner provided by section 6242.

[For analysis, see ¶ 1402. For text of committee report, see ¶ 5210.]

[Endnote Code Sec. 6240]
   Code Sec. 6240 was added by Sec. 1222(a) of the Taxpayer Relief Act of 1997, H.R. 2014, 8/5/97.
   1. added Code Sec. 6241
Effective Date (Sec. 1226, H.R. 2014, 8/5/97) effective for partnership tax. yrs. end. on or after 12/31/97.

[¶ 3334]   Code Sec.[1] 6241.   Partner's return must be consistent with partnership return.
   (a) General rule. A partner of any electing large partnership shall, on the partner's return, treat each partnership item attributable to such partnership in a manner which is consistent with the treatment of such partnership item on the partnership return.
   (b) Underpayment due to inconsistent treatment assessed as math error. Any underpayment of tax by a partner by reason of failing to comply with the requirements of subsection (a) shall be assessed and collected in the same manner as if such underpayment were on account of a mathematical or clerical error appearing on the partner's return. Paragraph (2) of section 6213(b) shall not apply to any assessment of an underpayment referred to in the preceding sentence.
   (c) Adjustments not to affect prior year of partners.
   (1) In general. Except as provided in paragraph (2), subsections (a) and (b) shall apply without regard to any adjustment to the partnership item under part II.
   (2) Certain changes in distributive share taken into account by partner.
   (A) In general. To the extent that any adjustment under part II involves a change under section 704 in a partner's distributive share of the amount of any partnership item shown on

the partnership return, such adjustment shall be taken into account in applying this title to such partner for the partner's taxable year for which such item was required to be taken into account.

(B) Coordination with deficiency procedures.

(i) In general. Subchapter B shall not apply to the assessment or collection of any underpayment of tax attributable to an adjustment referred to in subparagraph (A).

(ii) Adjustment not precluded. Notwithstanding any other law or rule of law, nothing in subchapter B (or in any proceeding under subchapter B) shall preclude the assessment or collection of any underpayment of tax (or the allowance of any credit or refund of any overpayment of tax) attributable to an adjustment referred to in subparagraph (A) and such assessment or collection or allowance (or any notice thereof) shall not preclude any notice, proceeding, or determination under subchapter B.

(C) Period of limitations. The period for—

(i) assessing any underpayment of tax, or

(ii) filing a claim for credit or refund of any overpayment of tax,

attributable to an adjustment referred to in subparagraph A shall not expire before the close of the period prescribed by section 6248 for making adjustments with respect to the partnership taxable year involved.

(D) Tiered structures. If the partner referred to in subparagraph (A) is another partnership or an S corporation, the rules of this paragraph shall also apply to persons holding interests in such partnership or S corporation (as the case may be); except that, if such partner is an electing large partnership, the adjustment referred to in subparagraph (A) shall be taken into account in the manner provided by section 6242.

(d) Addition to tax for failure to comply with section. For addition to tax in case of partner's disregard of requirements of this section, see part II of subchapter A of chapter 68.

[For analysis, see ¶ 1403. For text of committee report, see ¶ 5210.]

[Endnote Code Sec. 6241]

Code Sec. 6241 was added by Sec. 1222(a) of the Taxpayer Relief Act of 1997, H.R. 2014, 8/5/97.

1. added Code Sec. 6241

Effective Date (Sec. 1226, H.R. 2014, 8/5/97) effective for partnership tax. yrs. end. on or after 12/31/97.

[¶ 3335]   Code Sec.[1] 6242.   Procedures for taking partnership adjustments into account.

(a) Adjustments flow through to partners for year in which adjustment takes effect.

(1) In general. If any partnership adjustment with respect to any partnership item takes effect (within the meaning of subsection (d)(2)) during any partnership taxable year and if an election under paragraph (2) does not apply to such adjustment, such adjustment shall be taken into account in determining the amount of such item for the partnership taxable year in which such adjustment takes effect. In applying this title to any person who is (directly or indirectly) a partner in such partnership during such partnership taxable year, such adjustment shall be treated as an item actually arising during such taxable year.

(2) Partnership liable in certain cases. If—

(A) a partnership elects under this paragraph to not take an adjustment into account under paragraph (1),

(B) a partnership does not make such an election but in filing its return for any partnership taxable year fails to take fully into account any partnership adjustment as required under paragraph (1), or

(C) any partnership adjustment involves a reduction in a credit which exceeds the amount of such credit determined for the partnership taxable year in which the adjustment takes effect,

the partnership shall pay to the Secretary an amount determined by applying the rules of subsection (b)(4) to the adjustments not so taken into account and any excess referred to in subparagraph (C).

(3) **Offsetting adjustments taken into account.** If a partnership adjustment requires another adjustment in a taxable year after the adjusted year and before the partnership taxable year in which such partnership adjustment takes effect, such other adjustment shall be taken into account under this subsection for the partnership taxable year in which such partnership adjustment takes effect.

(4) **Coordination with part II.** Amounts taken into account under this subsection for any partnership taxable year shall continue to be treated as adjustments for the adjusted year for purposes of determining whether such amounts may be readjusted under part II.

(b) Partnership liable for interest and penalties.

(1) **In general.** If a partnership adjustment takes effect during any partnership taxable year and such adjustment results in an imputed underpayment for the adjusted year, the partnership—

(A) shall pay to the Secretary interest computed under paragraph (2), and

(B) shall be liable for any penalty, addition to tax, or additional amount as provided in paragraph (3).

(2) **Determination of amount of interest.** The interest computed under this paragraph with respect to any partnership adjustment is the interest which would be determined under chapter 67—

(A) on the imputed underpayment determined under paragraph (4) with respect to such adjustment,

(B) for the period beginning on the day after the return due date for the adjusted year and ending on the return due date for the partnership taxable year in which such adjustment takes effect (or, if earlier, in the case of any adjustment to which subsection (a)(2) applies, the date on which the payment under subsection (a)(2) is made).

Proper adjustments in the amount determined under the preceding sentence shall be made for adjustments required for partnership taxable years after the adjusted year and before the year in which the partnership adjustment takes effect by reason of such partnership adjustment.

(3) **Penalties.** A partnership shall be liable for any penalty, addition to tax, or additional amount for which it would have been liable if such partnership had been an individual subject to tax under chapter 1 for the adjusted year and the imputed underpayment determined under paragraph (4) were an actual underpayment (or understatement) for such year.

(4) **Imputed underpayment.** For purposes of this subsection, the imputed underpayment determined under this paragraph with respect to any partnership adjustment is the underpayment (if any) which would result—

(A) by netting all adjustments to items of income, gain, loss, or deduction and by treating any net increase in income as an underpayment equal to the amount of such net increase multiplied by the highest rate of tax in effect under section 1 or 11 for the adjusted year, and

(B) by taking adjustments to credits into account as increases or decreases (whichever is appropriate) in the amount of tax.

For purposes of the preceding sentence, any net decrease in a loss shall be treated as an increase in income and a similar rule shall apply to a net increase in a loss.

(c) Administrative provisions.

(1) **In general.** Any payment required by subsection (a)(2) or (b)(1)(A)—

(A) shall be assessed and collected in the same manner as if it were a tax imposed by subtitle C, and

(B) shall be paid on or before the return due date for the partnership taxable year in which the partnership adjustment takes effect.

(2) **Interest.** For purposes of determining interest, any payment required by subsection (a)(2) or (b)(1)(A) shall be treated as an underpayment of tax.

(3) **Penalties.**

(A) **In general.** In the case of any failure by any partnership to pay on the date prescribed therefor any amount required by subsection (a)(2) or (b)(1)(A), there is hereby imposed on such partnership a penalty of 10 percent of the underpayment. For purposes of the preceding sentence, the term "underpayment" means the excess of any payment required under this section over the amount (if any) paid on or before the date prescribed therefor.

(B) Accuracy-related and fraud penalties made applicable. For purposes of part II of subchapter A of chapter 68, any payment required by subsection (a)(2) shall be treated as an underpayment of tax.

(d) **Definitions and special rules.** For purposes of this section—

(1) **Partnership adjustment.** The term "partnership adjustment" means any adjustment in the amount of any partnership item of an electing large partnership.

(2) **When adjustment takes effect.** A partnership adjustment takes effect—

(A) in the case of an adjustment pursuant to the decision of a court in a proceeding brought under part II, when such decision becomes final,

(B) in the case of an adjustment pursuant to any administrative adjustment request under section 6251, when such adjustment is allowed by the Secretary, or

(C) in any other case, when such adjustment is made.

(3) **Adjusted year.** The term "adjusted year" means the partnership taxable year to which the item being adjusted relates.

(4) **Return due date.** The term "return due date" means, with respect to any taxable year, the date prescribed for filing the partnership return for such taxable year (determined without regard to extensions).

(5) **Adjustments involving changes in character.** Under regulations, appropriate adjustments in the application of this section shall be made for purposes of taking into account partnership adjustments which involve a change in the character of any item of income, gain, loss, or deduction.

(e) **Payments nondeductible.** No deduction shall be allowed under subtitle A for any payment required to be made by an electing large partnership under this section.

[For analysis, see ¶ 1405. For text of committee report, see ¶ 5210.]

[Endnote Code Sec. 6242]
Code Sec. 6242 was added by Sec. 1222(a) of the Taxpayer Relief Act of 1997, H.R. 2014, 8/5/97.
1. added Code Sec. 6242
Effective Date (Sec. 1226, H.R. 2014, 8/5/97) effective for partnership tax. yrs. end. on or after 12/31/97.

[¶ 3336]   Code Sec.[1] 6245.   Secretarial authority.

(a) **General rule.** The Secretary is authorized and directed to make adjustments at the partnership level in any partnership item to the extent necessary to have such item be treated in the manner required.

(b) **Notice of partnership adjustment.**

(1) **In general.** If the Secretary determines that a partnership adjustment is required, the Secretary is authorized to send notice of such adjustment to the partnership by certified mail or registered mail. Such notice shall be sufficient if mailed to the partnership at its last known address even if the partnership has terminated its existence.

(2) **Further notices restricted.** If the Secretary mails a notice of a partnership adjustment to any partnership for any partnership taxable year and the partnership files a petition under section 6247 with respect to such notice, in the absence of a showing of fraud, malfeasance, or misrepresentation of a material fact, the Secretary shall not mail another such notice to such partnership with respect to such taxable year.

(3) **Authority to rescind notice with partnership consent.** The Secretary may, with the consent of the partnership, rescind any notice of a partnership adjustment mailed to such partnership. Any notice so rescinded shall not be treated as a notice of a partnership adjustment, for purposes of this section, section 6246, and section 6247, and the taxpayer shall have no right to bring a proceeding under section 6247 with respect to such notice. Nothing in this subsection shall affect any suspension of the running of any period of limitations during any period during which the rescinded notice was outstanding.

[For analysis, see ¶ 1404. For text of committee report, see ¶ 5210.]

[Endnote Code Sec. 6245]
Code Sec. 6245 was added by Sec. 1222(a) of the Taxpayer Relief Act of 1997, H.R. 2014, 8/5/97.
1. added Code Sec. 6245
Effective Date (Sec. 1226, H.R. 2014, 8/5/97) effective for partnership tax. yrs. end. on or after 12/31/97.

[¶ 3337]   Code Sec.[1] 6246.   Restrictions on partnership adjustments.

(a) **General rule.** Except as otherwise provided in this chapter, no adjustment to any partnership item may be made (and no levy or proceeding in any court for the collection of any amount resulting from such adjustment may be made, begun or prosecuted) before—

(1) the close of the 90th day after the day on which a notice of a partnership adjustment was mailed to the partnership, and

(2) if a petition is filed under section 6247 with respect to such notice, the decision of the court has become final.

(b) **Premature action may be enjoined.** Notwithstanding section 7421(a), any action which violates subsection (a) may be enjoined in the proper court, including the Tax Court. The Tax Court shall have no jurisdiction to enjoin any action under this subsection unless a timely petition has been filed under section 6247 and then only in respect of the adjustments that are the subject of such petition.

(c) **Exceptions to restrictions on adjustments.**

(1) **Adjustments arising out of math or clerical errors.**

(A) In general. If the partnership is notified that, on account of a mathematical or clerical error appearing on the partnership return, an adjustment to a partnership item is required, rules similar to the rules of paragraphs (1) and (2) of section 6213(b) shall apply to such adjustment.

(B) Special rule. If an electing large partnership is a partner in another electing large partnership, any adjustment on account of such partnership's failure to comply with the requirements of section 6241(a) with respect to its interest in such other partnership shall be treated as an adjustment referred to in subparagraph (A), except that paragraph (2) of section 6213(b) shall not apply to such adjustment.

(2) **Partnership may waive restrictions.** The partnership shall at any time (whether or not a notice of partnership adjustment has been issued) have the right, by a signed notice in writing filed with the Secretary, to waive the restrictions provided in subsection (a) on the making of any partnership adjustment.

(d) **Limit where no proceeding begun.** If no proceeding under section 6247 is begun with respect to any notice of a partnership adjustment during the 90-day period described in subsection (a), the amount for which the partnership is liable under section 6242 (and any increase in any partner's liability for tax under chapter 1 by reason of any adjustment under section 6242(a)) shall not exceed the amount determined in accordance with such notice.

[For analysis, see ¶ 1404. For text of committee report, see ¶ 5210.]

[Endnote Code Sec. 6246]
Code Sec. 6246 was added by Sec. 1222(a) of the Taxpayer Relief Act of 1997, H.R. 2014, 8/5/97.
1. added Code Sec. 6246
Effective Date (Sec. 1226, H.R. 2014, 8/5/97) effective for partnership tax. yrs. end. on or after 12/31/97.

[¶ 3338]   Code Sec.[1] 6247.   Judicial review of partnership adjustment.

(a) **General rule.** Within 90 days after the date on which a notice of a partnership adjustment is mailed to the partnership with respect to any partnership taxable year, the partnership may file a petition for a readjustment of the partnership items for such taxable year with—

(1) the Tax Court,

(2) the district court of the United States for the district in which the partnership's principal place of business is located, or

(3) the Claims Court.

(b) **Jurisdictional requirement for bringing action in district court or Claims Court.**

(1) **In general.** A readjustment petition under this section may be filed in a district court of the United States or the Claims Court only if the partnership filing the petition deposits with the Secretary, on or before the date the petition is filed, the amount for which the partnership would be liable under section 6242(b) (as of the date of the filing of the petition) if the partnership items were adjusted as provided by the notice of partnership adjustment. The court may by order provide that the jurisdictional requirements of this paragraph are satisfied where there has been a good faith attempt to satisfy such requirement and any shortfall of the amount required to be deposited is timely corrected.

(2) **Interest payable.** Any amount deposited under paragraph (1), while deposited, shall not be treated as a payment of tax for purposes of this title (other than chapter 67).

(c) **Scope of judicial review.** A court with which a petition is filed in accordance with this section shall have jurisdiction to determine all partnership items of the partnership for the partnership taxable year to which the notice of partnership adjustment relates and the proper allocation of such items among the partners (and the applicability of any penalty, addition to tax, or additional amount for which the partnership may be liable under section 6242(b)).

(d) **Determination of court reviewable.** Any determination by a court under this section shall have the force and effect of a decision of the Tax Court or a final judgment or decree of the district court or the Claims Court, as the case may be, and shall be reviewable as such. The date of any such determination shall be treated as being the date of the court's order entering the decision.

(e) **Effect of decision dismissing action.** If an action brought under this section is dismissed other than by reason of a rescission under section 6245(b)(3), the decision of the court dismissing the action shall be considered as its decision that the notice of partnership adjustment is correct, and an appropriate order shall be entered in the records of the court.

[For analysis, see ¶ 1404. For text of committee report, see ¶ 5210.]

[Endnote Code Sec. 6247]
Code Sec. 6247 was added by Sec. 1222(a) of the Taxpayer Relief Act of 1997, H.R. 2014, 8/5/97.
1. added Code Sec. 6247
Effective Date (Sec. 1226, H.R. 2014, 8/5/97) effective for partnership tax. yrs. end. on or after 12/31/97.

[¶ 3339] Code Sec.[1] 6248.   Period of limitations for making adjustments.

(a) **General rule.** Except as otherwise provided in this section, no adjustment under this subpart to any partnership item for any partnership taxable year may be made after the date which is 3 years after the later of—

(1) the date on which the partnership return for such taxable year was filed, or

(2) the last day for filing such return for such year (determined without regard to extensions).

(b) **Extension by agreement.** The period described in subsection (a) (including an extension period under this subsection) may be extended by an agreement entered into by the Secretary and the partnership before the expiration of such period.

(c) **Special rule in case of fraud, etc.**

(1) **False return.** In the case of a false or fraudulent partnership return with intent to evade tax, the adjustment may be made at any time.

(2) **Substantial omission of income.** If any partnership omits from gross income an amount properly includible therein which is in excess of 25 percent of the amount of gross income stated in its return, subsection (a) shall be applied by substituting "6 years" for "3 years".

(3) **No return.** In the case of a failure by a partnership to file a return for any taxable year, the adjustment may be made at any time.

(4) Return filed by Secretary. For purposes of this section, a return executed by the Secretary under subsection (b) of section 6020 on behalf of the partnership shall not be treated as a return of the partnership.

(d) Suspension when Secretary mails notice of adjustment. If notice of a partnership adjustment with respect to any taxable year is mailed to the partnership, the running of the period specified in subsection (a) (as modified by the other provisions of this section) shall be suspended—

(1) for the period during which an action may be brought under section 6247 (and, if a petition is filed under section 6247 with respect to such notice, until the decision of the court becomes final), and

(2) for 1 year thereafter.

[For analysis, see ¶ 1404. For text of committee report, see ¶ 5210.]

[Endnote Code Sec. 6248]
Code Sec. 6248 was added by Sec. 1222(a) of the Taxpayer Relief Act of 1997, H.R. 2014, 8/5/97.
1. added Code Sec. 6248
Effective Date (Sec. 1226, H.R. 2014, 8/5/97) effective for partnership tax. yrs. end. on or after 12/31/97.

[¶ 3340] Code Sec.[1] 6251.   Administrative adjustment requests.

(a) General rule. A partnership may file a request for an administrative adjustment of partnership items for any partnership taxable year at any time which is—

(1) within 3 years after the later of—

(A) the date on which the partnership return for such year is filed, or

(B) the last day for filing the partnership return for such year (determined without regard to extensions), and

(2) before the mailing to the partnership of a notice of a partnership adjustment with respect to such taxable year.

(b) Secretarial action. If a partnership files an administrative adjustment request under subsection (a), the Secretary may allow any part of the requested adjustments.

(c) Special rule in case of extension under section 6248. If the period described in section 6248(a) is extended pursuant to an agreement under section 6248(b), the period prescribed by subsection (a)(1) shall not expire before the date 6 months after the expiration of the extension under section 6248(b).

[For analysis, see ¶ 1404. For text of committee report, see ¶ 5210.]

[Endnote Code Sec. 6251]
Code Sec. 6251 was added by Sec. 1222(a) of the Taxpayer Relief Act of 1997, H.R. 2014, date of enactment.
1. added Code Sec. 6251
Effective Date (Sec. 1226, H.R. 2014, date of enactment) effective for partnership tax. yrs. end. on or after 12/31/97.

[¶ 3341] Code Sec.[1] 6252.   Judicial review where administrative adjustment request is not allowed in full.

(a) In general. If any part of an administrative adjustment request filed under section 6251 is not allowed by the Secretary, the partnership may file a petition for an adjustment with respect to the partnership items to which such part of the request relates with—

(1) the Tax Court,

(2) the district court of the United States for the district in which the principal place of business of the partnership is located, or

(3) the Claims Court.

(b) Period for filing petition. A petition may be filed under subsection (a) with respect to partnership items for a partnership taxable year only—

(1) after the expiration of 6 months from the date of filing of the request under section 6251, and

(2) before the date which is 2 years after the date of such request.

The 2-year period set forth in paragraph (2) shall be extended for such period as may be agreed upon in writing by the partnership and the Secretary.

(c) Coordination with subpart A.

(1) **Notice of partnership adjustment before filing of petition.** No petition may be filed under this section after the Secretary mails to the partnership a notice of a partnership adjustment for the partnership taxable year to which the request under section 6251 relates.

(2) **Notice of partnership adjustment after filing but before hearing of petition.** If the Secretary mails to the partnership a notice of a partnership adjustment for the partnership taxable year to which the request under section 6251 relates after the filing of a petition under this subsection but before the hearing of such petition, such petition shall be treated as an action brought under section 6247 with respect to such notice, except that subsection (b) of section 6247 shall not apply.

(3) **Notice must be before expiration of statute of limitations.** A notice of a partnership adjustment for the partnership taxable year shall be taken into account under paragraphs (1) and (2) only if such notice is mailed before the expiration of the period prescribed by section 6248 for making adjustments to partnership items for such taxable year.

(d) Scope of judicial review. Except in the case described in paragraph (2) of subsection (c), a court with which a petition is filed in accordance with this section shall have jurisdiction to determine only those partnership items to which the part of the request under section 6251 not allowed by the Secretary relates and those items with respect to which the Secretary asserts adjustments as offsets to the adjustments requested by the partnership.

(e) Determination of court reviewable. Any determination by a court under this section shall have the force and effect of a decision of the Tax Court or a final judgment or decree of the district court or the Claims Court, as the case may be, and shall be reviewable as such. The date of any such determination shall be treated as being the date of the court's order entering the decision.

[For analysis, see ¶ 1404. For text of committee report, see ¶ 5210.]

[Endnote Code Sec. 6252]

Code Sec. 6252 was added by Sec. 1222(a) of the Taxpayer Relief Act of 1997, H.R. 2014, date of enactment.

1. added Code Sec. 6252

Effective Date (Sec. 1226, H.R. 2014, date of enactment) effective for partnership tax. yrs. end. on or after 12/31/97.

[¶ 3342]   Code Sec.[1] 6255.   Definitions and special rules.

(a) **Definitions.** For purposes of this subchapter—

(1) **Electing large partnership.** The term "electing large partnership" has the meaning given to such term by section 775.

(2) **Partnership item.** The term "partnership item" has the meaning given to such term by section 6231(a)(3).

(b) **Partners bound by actions of partnership, etc.**

(1) **Designation of partner.** Each electing large partnership shall designate (in the manner prescribed by the Secretary) a partner (or other person) who shall have the sole authority to act on behalf of such partnership under this subchapter. In any case in which such a designation is not in effect, the Secretary may select any partner as the partner with such authority.

(2) **Binding effect.** An electing large partnership and all partners of such partnership shall be bound—

(A) by actions taken under this subchapter by the partnership, and

(B) by any decision in a proceeding brought under this subchapter.

(c) **Partnerships having principal place of business outside the United States.** For purposes of sections 6247 and 6252, a principal place of business located outside the United States shall be treated as located in the District of Columbia.

(d) Treatment where partnership ceases to exist. If a partnership ceases to exist before a partnership adjustment under this subchapter takes effect, such adjustment shall be taken into account by the former partners of such partnership under regulations prescribed by the Secretary.

(e) Date decision becomes final. For purposes of this subchapter, the principles of section 7481(a) shall be applied in determining the date on which a decision of a district court or the Claims Court becomes final.

(f) Partnerships in cases under title 11 of the United States Code.

(1) Suspension of period of limitations on making adjustment, assessment, or collection. The running of any period of limitations provided in this subchapter on making a partnership adjustment (or provided by section 6501 or 6502 on the assessment or collection of any amount required to be paid under section 6242) shall, in a case under title 11 of the United States Code, be suspended during the period during which the Secretary is prohibited by reason of such case from making the adjustment (or assessment or collection) and—

(A) for adjustment or assessment, 60 days thereafter, and

(B) "(B) for collection, 6 months thereafter. A rule similar to the rule of section 6213(f)(2) shall apply for purposes of section 6246.

(2) Suspension of period of limitation for filing for judicial review. The running of the period specified in section 6247(a) or 6252(b) shall, in a case under title 11 of the United States Code, be suspended during the period during which the partnership is prohibited by reason of such case from filing a petition under section 6247 or 6252 and for 60 days thereafter.

(g) Regulations. The Secretary shall prescribe such regulations as may be necessary to carry out the provisions of this subchapter, including regulations—

(1) to prevent abuse through manipulation of the provisions of this subchapter, and

(2) providing that this subchapter shall not apply to any case described in section 6231(c)(1) (or the regulations prescribed thereunder) where the application of this subchapter to such a case would interfere with the effective and efficient enforcement of this title.

In any case to which this subchapter does not apply by reason of paragraph (2), rules similar to the rules of sections 6229(f) and 6255(f) shall apply.

[For analysis, see ¶ 1402, ¶ 1404, ¶ 1405. For text of committee report, see ¶ 5210.]

[Endnote Code Sec. 6255]

Code Sec. 6255 was added by Sec. 1222(a) of the Taxpayer Relief Act of 1997, H.R. 2014, 8/5/97.

1. added Code Sec. 6255

Effective Date (Sec. 1226, H.R. 2014, 8/5/97) effective for partnership tax. yrs. end. on or after 12/31/97.

[¶ 3343]   *Code Sec.[1] 6311.   Payment of tax by commercially acceptable means.*

(a) Authority to receive. It shall be lawful for the Secretary to receive for internal revenue taxes (or in payment for internal revenue stamps) any commercially acceptable means that the Secretary deems appropriate to the extent and under the conditions provided in regulations prescribed by the Secretary.

(b) Ultimate liability. If a check, money order, or other method of payment, including payment by credit card, debit card, or charge card so received is not duly paid, or is paid and subsequently charged back to the Secretary, the person by whom such check, or money order, or other method of payment has been tendered shall remain liable for the payment of the tax or for the stamps, and for all legal penalties and additions, to the same extent as if such check, money order, or other method of payment had not been tendered.

(c) Liability of banks and others. If any certified, treasurer's, or cashier's check (or other guaranteed draft), or any money order, or any other means of payment that has been guaranteed by a financial institution (such as a credit card, debit card, or charge card transaction which has been guaranteed expressly by a financial institution) so received is not duly paid, the United States shall, in addition to its right to exact payment from the party originally indebted therefor, have a lien for—

(1) the amount of such check (or draft) upon all assets of the financial institution on which drawn,

(2) *the amount of such money order upon all the assets of the issuer thereof, or*

(3) *the guaranteed amount of any other transaction upon all the assets of the institution making such guarantee, and such amount shall be paid out of such assets in preference to any other claims whatsoever against such financial institution, issuer, or guaranteeing institution, except the necessary costs and expenses of administration and the reimbursement of the United States for the amount expended in the redemption of the circulating notes of such financial institution.*

(d) Payment by other means.

(1) Authority to prescribe regulations. *The Secretary shall prescribe such regulations as the Secretary deems necessary to receive payment by commercially acceptable means, including regulations that—*

(A) *specify which methods of payment by commercially acceptable means will be acceptable,*

(B) *specify when payment by such means will be considered received,*

(C) *identify types of nontax matters related to payment by such means that are to be resolved by persons ultimately liable for payment and financial intermediaries, without the involvement of the Secretary, and*

(D) *ensure that tax matters will be resolved by the Secretary, without the involvement of financial intermediaries.*

(2) Authority to enter into contracts. *Notwithstanding section 3718(f) of title 31, United States Code, the Secretary is authorized to enter into contracts to obtain services related to receiving payment by other means where cost beneficial to the Government. The Secretary may not pay any fee or provide any other consideration under such contracts.*

(3) Special provisions for use of credit cards. *If use of credit cards is accepted as a method of payment of taxes pursuant to subsection (a)—*

(A) *a payment of internal revenue taxes (or a payment for internal revenue stamps) by a person by use of a credit card shall not be subject to section 161 of the Truth-in- Lending Act (15 U.S.C. 1666), or to any similar provisions of State law, if the error alleged by the person is an error relating to the underlying tax liability, rather than an error relating to the credit card account such as a computational error or numerical transposition in the credit card transaction or an issue as to whether the person authorized payment by use of the credit card,*

(B) *a payment of internal revenue taxes (or a payment for internal revenue stamps) shall not be subject to section 170 of the Truth-in-Lending Act (15 U.S.C. 1666i), or to any similar provisions of State law,*

(C) *a payment of internal revenue taxes (or a payment for internal revenue stamps) by a person by use of a debit card shall not be subject to section 908 of the Electronic Fund Transfer Act (15 U.S.C. 1693f), or to any similar provisions of State law, if the error alleged by the person is an error relating to the underlying tax liability, rather than an error relating to the debit card account such as a computational error or numerical transposition in the debit card transaction or an issue as to whether the person authorized payment by use of the debit card,*

(D) *the term "creditor" under section 103(f) of the Truth-in-Lending Act (15 U.S.C. 1602(f)) shall not include the Secretary with respect to credit card transactions in payment of internal revenue taxes (or payment for internal revenue stamps), and*

(E) *notwithstanding any other provision of law to the contrary, in the case of payment made by credit card or debit card transaction of an amount owed to a person as the result of the correction of an error under section 161 of the Truth-in-Lending Act (15 U.S.C. 1666) or section 908 of the Electronic Fund Transfer Act (15 U.S.C. 1693f), the Secretary is authorized to provide such amount to such person as a credit to that person's credit card or debit card account through the applicable credit card or debit card system.*

(e) Confidentiality of information.

(1) In general. *Except as otherwise authorized by this subsection, no person may use or disclose any information relating to credit or debit card transactions obtained pursuant to sec-*

tion 6103(k)(8) other than for purposes directly related to the processing of such transactions, or the billing or collection of amounts charged or debited pursuant thereto.

(2) Exceptions.

(A) Debit or credit card issuers or others acting on behalf of such issuers may also use and disclose such information for purposes directly related to servicing an issuer's accounts.

(B) Debit or credit card issuers or others directly involved in the processing of credit or debit card transactions or the billing or collection of amounts charged or debited thereto may also use and disclose such information for purposes directly related to—

(i) statistical risk and profitability assessment;

(ii) transferring receivables, accounts, or interest therein;

(iii) auditing the account information;

(iv) complying with Federal, State, or local law; and

(v) properly authorized civil, criminal, or regulatory investigation by Federal, State, or local authorities.

(3) Procedures. Use and disclosure of information under this paragraph shall be made only to the extent authorized by written procedures promulgated by the Secretary.

(4) Cross reference. For provision providing for civil damages for violation of paragraph (1), see section 7431.

[For analysis, see ¶ 2319. For text of committee report, see ¶ 5205.]

[Endnote Code Sec. 6311]

Code Sec. 6311, in *italics*, was amended by Sec. 1205(a) of the Taxpayer Relief Act of 1997, H.R. 2014, 8/5/97, which struck out:

1. "Sec. 6311. Payment by check or money order.

"(a) Authority to receive. It shall be lawful for the Secretary to receive for internal revenue taxes, or in payment for internal revenue stamps, checks or money orders, to the extent and under the conditions provided in regulations prescribed by the Secretary.

"(b) Check or money order unpaid.

"(1) Ultimate liability. If a check or money order so received is not duly paid, the person by whom such check or money order has been tendered shall remain liable for the payment of the tax or for the stamps, and for all legal penalties and additions, to the same extent as if such check or money order had not been tendered.

"(2) Liability of banks and others. If any certified, treasurer's, or cashier's check (or other guaranteed draft) or any money order so received is not duly paid, the United States shall, in addition to its right to exact payment from the party originally indebted therefor, have a lien for the amount of such check (or draft) upon all the assets of the financial institution on which drawn or for the amount of such money order upon all the assets of the issuer thereof; and such amount shall be paid out of such assets in preference to any other claims whatsoever against such financial institution or issuer except the necessary costs and expenses of administration and the reimbursement of the United States for the amount expended in the redemption of the circulating notes of such financial institution."

Effective Date (Sec. 1205(b), H.R. 2014, 8/5/97) effective 9 months after 8/5/97.

[¶ 3344]   Code Sec. 6331.   Levy and distraint.

* * * * * * * * * * * *

¹*(h) Continuing levy on certain payments.*

(1) In general. The effect of a levy on specified payments to or received by a taxpayer shall be continuous from the date such levy is first made until such levy is released. Notwithstanding section 6334, such continuous levy shall attach to up to 15 percent of any specified payment due to the taxpayer.

(2) Specified payment. For the purposes of paragraph (1), the term "specified payment" means—

(A) any Federal payment other than a payment for which eligibility is based on the income or assets (or both) of a payee,

(B) any payment described in paragraph (4), (7), (9), or (11) of section 6334(a), and

(C) any annuity or pension payment under the Railroad Retirement Act or benefit under the Railroad Unemployment Insurance Act.

²*(i)* **Cross references.**

(1) For provisions relating to jeopardy, see subchapter A of chapter 70.

(2) For proceedings applicable to sale of seized property, see section 6335.

(3) For release and notice of release of levy, see section 6343.

[Endnote Code Sec. 6331]

Matter in *italics* in Code Sec. 6331(h) and Code Sec. 6331(i) added by Sec. 1024(a)(1) and (2) of the Taxpayer Relief Act of 1997, H.R. 2014, 8/5/97, which struck out:

1. added subsec. (h)

2. "(h)"

Effective Date (Sec. 1024(b), H.R. 2014, 8/5/97) effective for levies issued after 8/5/97.

[¶ 3345]   Code Sec. 6334.   Property exempt from levy.

(a) **Enumeration.** There shall be exempt from levy—

* * * * * * * * * * * * *

(13) **Principal residence exempt in absence of certain approval or jeopardy.** Except to the extent provided in subsection (e), the principal residence of the taxpayer (within the meaning of ¹*section 121*).

* * * * * * * * * * *

²*(f) Levy allowed on certain specified payments. Any payment described in subparagraph (B) or (C) of section 6331(h)(2) shall not be exempt from levy if the Secretary approves the levy thereon under section 6331(h).*

³*(g)* **Inflation adjustment.**

(1) **In general.** In the case of any calendar year beginning after 1997, each dollar amount referred to in paragraphs (2) and (3) of subsection (a) shall be increased by an amount equal to—

(A) such dollar amount, multiplied by

(B) the cost-of-living adjustment determined under section 1(f)(3) for such calendar year, by substituting "calendar year 1996" for "calendar year 1992" in subparagraph (B) thereof.

(2) **Rounding.** If any dollar amount after being increased under paragraph (1) is not a multiple of $10, such dollar amount shall be rounded to the nearest multiple of $10.

[Endnote Code Sec. 6334]

Matter in *italics* in Code Sec. 6334(a)(13) added by Sec. 312(d)(1) of the Taxpayer Relief Act of 1997, H.R. 2014, 8/5/97, which struck out:

1. "section 1034"

Effective Date (Sec. 312(d) [sic (e)], H.R. 2014, 8/5/97) effective for sales and exchanges after 5/6/97, except as provided by Secs. 312(d)(2)-(4) [sic (e)(2)-(4)] of this Act, which read as follows:

"(2) Sales before 8/5/97.—At the election of the taxpayer, the amendments made by this section shall not apply to any sale or exchange before the date of the enactment of this Act.

"(3) Certain sales within 2 years after 8/5/97. Section 121 of the Internal Revenue Code of 1986 (as amended by this section) shall be applied without regard to subsection (c)(2)(B) thereof in the case of any sale or exchange of property during the 2-year period beginning on the date of the enactment of this Act if the taxpayer held such property on the date of the enactment of this Act and fails to meet the ownership and use requirements of subsection (a) thereof with respect to such property.

"(4) Binding contracts.—At the election of the taxpayer, the amendments made by this section shall not apply to a sale or exchange after the date of the enactment of this Act, if—

"(A) such sale or exchange is pursuant to a contract which was binding on such date, or

"(B) without regard to such amendments, gain would not be recognized under section 1034 of the Internal Revenue Code of 1986 (as in effect on the day before the date of the enactment of this Act) on such sale or exchange by reason of a new residence acquired on or before such date or with respect to the acquisition of which by the taxpayer a binding contract was in effect on such date.

This paragraph shall not apply to any sale or exchange by an individual if the treatment provided by section 877(a)(1) of the Internal Revenue Code of 1986 applies to such individual."

Matter in *italics* in Code Sec. 6334(f) and Code Sec. 6334(g) added by Sec. 1025(a), H.R. 2014, which struck out:

2. added subsec. (f)

3. "(f)"

Effective Date (Sec. 1025(b), H.R. 2014, 8/5/97) effective for levies issued after 8/5/97.

[¶ 3346]   Code Sec. 6416.   Certain taxes on sales and services.
  (a) Condition to allowance.

* * * * * * * * * * * *

(4) Wholesale distributors to administer credits and refunds of gasoline tax.

(A) In general. For purposes of this subsection, a wholesale distributor who purchases any gasoline on which tax imposed by section 4081 has been paid and who sells the gasoline to its ultimate purchaser shall be treated as the person (and the only person) who paid such tax.

(B) Wholesale distributor. For purposes of subparagraph (A), the term "wholesale distributor" has the meaning given such term by section 4093(b)(2) (determined by substituting "any gasoline taxable under section 4081" for "aviation fuel" therein). [1]*Such term includes any person who makes retail sales of gasoline at 10 or more retail motor fuel outlets.*

  (b) Special cases in which tax payments considered overpayments. Under regulations prescribed by the Secretary, credit or refund (without interest) shall be allowed or made in respect of the overpayments determined under the following paragraphs:

  (1) Price readjustments.

(A) In general. Except as provided in subparagraph (B) or (C), if the price of any article in respect of which a tax, based on such price, is imposed by chapter 31 or 32 , is readjusted by reason of the return or repossession of the article or a covering or container, or by a bona fide discount, rebate, or allowance, including a readjustment for local advertising (but only to the extent provided in section 4216(e)(2) and (3)), the part of the tax proportionate to the part of the price repaid or credited to the purchaser shall be deemed to be an overpayment.

(B) Further manufacture. Subparagraph (A) shall not apply in the case of an article in respect of which tax was computed under section 4223(b)(2); but if the price for which such article was sold is readjusted by reason of the return or repossession of the article, the part of the tax proportionate to the part of such price repaid or credited to the purchaser shall be deemed to be an overpayment.

(C) Adjustment of tire price. No credit or refund of any tax imposed by subsection (a) or (b) of section 4071 shall be allowed or made by reason of an adjustment of a tire pursuant to a warranty or guarantee.

  (2) Specified uses and resales. The tax paid under chapter 32 (or under subsection (a) or (d) of section 4041 in respect of sales or under section 4051) in respect of any article shall be deemed to be an overpayment if such article was, by any person—

(A) exported;

(B) used or sold for use as supplies for vessels or aircraft;

(C) sold to a State or local government for the exclusive use of a State or local government;

(D) sold to a nonprofit educational organization for its exclusive use;

(E) in the case of any tire taxable under section 4071(a), sold to any person for use as described in section 4221(e)(3); or

(F) in the case of gasoline, used or sold for use in the production of special fuels referred to in section 4041.

Subparagraphs (C) and (D) shall not apply in the case of any tax paid under section 4064. In the case of the tax imposed by section 4131, subparagraphs (B), (C), and (D) shall not apply and subparagraph (A) shall apply only if the use of the exported vaccine meets such requirements as the Secretary may by regulations prescribe. This paragraph shall not apply in the case of any tax imposed under section 4041(a)(1) or 4081 on diesel fuel [2]*or kerosene* and any tax paid under section 4091 or 4121.

* * * * * * * * * * * *

(d) Credit on returns. Any person entitled to a refund of tax imposed by chapter 31 or 32, paid to the Secretary may, instead of filing a claim for refund, take credit therefor against taxes imposed by such chapter due on any subsequent return. The preceding sentence shall not apply to the tax imposed by section 4081 in the case of refunds described in section 4081(e) [3]*or to the tax imposed by section 4091 in the case of refunds described in section 4091(d).*

* * * * * * * * * * * *

[For analysis, see ¶ 2215. For text of committee report, see ¶ 5294.]

[Endnote Code Sec. 6416]
Matter in *italics* in Code Sec. 6416(a)(4)(B) added by Sec. 905(a) of the Taxpayer Relief Act of 1997, H.R. 2014, 8/5/97.
1. added matter in subpara. (a)(4)(B)
Effective Date (Sec. 905(b), H.R. 2014, 8/5/97) effective for sales after 8/5/97.

Matter in *italics* in Code Sec. 6416(b)(2) added by Sec. 1032(e)(6), H.R. 2014, 8/5/97.
2. added matter in para. (b)(2)
Effective Date (Sec. 1032(f), H.R. 2014, 8/5/97) effective 7/1/98.

Matter in *italics* in Code Sec. 6416(d) added by Sec. 1436(b), H.R. 2014, 8/5/97.
3. added matter in subsec. (d)
Effective Date (Sec. 1436(c), H.R. 2014, 8/5/97) effective for fuel acquired by the producer after 9/30/97.

[¶ 3347] Code Sec. 6421.   Gasoline used for certain nonhighway purposes, used by local transit systems, or sold for certain exempt purposes.

* * * * * * * * * * * *

(e) Definitions. For purposes of this section—

(1) **Gasoline.** The term "gasoline" has the meaning given to such term by section 4083(a).

(2) **Off-highway business use.**

(A) In general. The term "off-highway business use" means any use by a person in a trade or business of such person or in an activity of such person described in section 212 (relating to production of income) otherwise than as a fuel in a highway vehicle—

(i) which (at the time of such use), is registered, or is required to be registered, for highway use under the laws of any State or foreign country, or

(ii) which, in the case of a highway vehicle owned by the United States, is used on the highway.

(B) Uses in boats.

(i) In general. Except as otherwise provided in this subparagraph, the term "off-highway business use" does not include any use in a motorboat.

(ii) Fisheries and whaling. The term "off-highway business use" shall include any use in a vessel employed in the fisheries or in the whaling business.

[1](iii) Repealed.

(iv) Repealed.

* * * * * * * * * * *

[For analysis, see ¶ 2210. For text of committee report, see ¶ 5052.]

[Endnote Code Sec. 6421]
Code Sec. 6421(e)(2)(B)(iii) and Code Sec. 6421(e)(2)(B)(iv) were deleted by Sec. 902(a) of the Taxpayer Relief Act of 1997, H.R. 2014, 8/5/97, which struck out:
1. ""(iii) Exception for diesel fuel. The term 'off-highway business use' shall include the use of diesel fuel in a boat in the active conduct of—
"(I) a trade or business of commercial fishing or transporting persons or property for compensation or hire, and
"(II) except as provided in clause (iv), any other trade or business.
"(iv) Noncommercial boats. In the case of a boat used predominantly in any activity which is of a type generally considered to constitute entertainment, amusement, or recreation, clause (iii)(II) shall not apply to—
"(I) the taxes under sections 4041(a)(1) and 4081 for the period after December 31, 1993, and before January 1, 2000, and
"(II) so much of the tax under sections 4041(a)(1) and 4081 as does not exceed 4.3 cents per gallon for the period after December 31, 1999."

Effective Date (Sec. 902(c), H.R. 2014, 8/5/97) effective 1/1/98.

[¶ 3348]   Code Sec. 6422.   Cross references.

(1) For limitations on credits and refunds, see subchapter B of chapter 66.

(2) For overpayment in case of adjustments to accrued foreign taxes, see section 905(c).

(3) For credit or refund in case of deficiency dividends paid by a personal holding company, see section 547.

(4) For refund, credit, or abatement of amounts disallowed by courts upon review of Tax Court decision, see section 7486.

[1]*(5)* For refund or redemption of stamps, see chapter 69.

[2]*(6)* For abatement, credit, or refund in case of jeopardy assessments, see chapter 70.

[3]*(7)* For treatment of certain overpayments as having been refunded, in connection with sale of surplus war-built vessels, see section 9(b)(8) of the Merchant Ship Sales Act of 1946 (50 U. S. C. App. 1742).

[4]*(8)* For restrictions on transfers and assignments of claims against the United States, see section 3727 of title 31, United States Code.

[5]*(9)* For set-off of claims against amounts due the United States, see section 3728 of title 31, United States Code.

[6]*(10)* For special provisions relating to alcohol and tobacco taxes, see subtitle E.

[7]*(11)* for [sic]credit or refund in case of deficiency dividends paid by a regulated investment company or real estate investment trust, see section 860.

[8]*(12)* For special rules in the case of a credit or refund attributable to partnership items, see section 6227 and subsections (c) and (d) of section 6230.

[Endnote Code Sec. 6422]

Matter in *italics* in Code Sec. 6422(5), Code Sec. 6422(6), Code Sec. 6422(7), Code Sec. 6422(8), Code Sec. 6422(9), Code Sec. 6422(10), Code Sec. 6422(11), and Code Sec. 6422(12) added by Sec. 1131(c)(3) of the Taxpayer Relief Act of 1997, H.R. 2014, 8/5/97, which struck out:

1. "(5) For abatement or refund of tax on transfers to avoid income tax, see section 1494(b)."

"(6)"

2. "(7)"
3. "(8)"
4. "(9)"
5. "(10)"
6. "(11)"
7. "(12)"
8. "(13)"

Effective Date (Sec. 1131(d), H.R. 2014, 8/5/97) effective 8/5/97.

[¶ 3349]   Code Sec. 6427.   Fuels not used for taxable purposes.

* * * * * * * * * * * *

* * * * * * * * * * * *

(f) Gasoline, diesel fuel, [1]*kerosene,* and aviation fuel used to produce certain alcohol fuels.

(1) **In general.** Except as provided in subsection (k), if any gasoline, diesel fuel, [2]*kerosene,* or aviation fuel on which tax was imposed by section 4081 or 4091 at the regular tax rate is used by any person in producing a mixture described in section 4081(c) or 4091(c)(1)(A) (as the case may be) which is sold or used in such person's trade or business the Secretary shall pay (without interest) to such person an amount equal to the excess of the regular tax rate over the incentive tax rate with respect to such fuel.

(2) **Definitions.** For purposes of paragraph (1)—

(A) Regular tax rate. The term "regular tax rate" means—

(i) in the case of gasoline[3], *diesel fuel, or kerosene,* the aggregate rate of tax imposed by section 4081 determined without regard to subsection (c) thereof, and

(ii) in the case of aviation fuel, the aggregate rate of tax imposed by section 4091 determined without regard to subsection (c) thereof.

(B) Incentive tax rate. The term "incentive tax rate" means—

(i) in the case of gasoline[4], *diesel fuel, or kerosene,* the aggregate rate of tax imposed by section 4081 with respect to fuel described in subsection (c)(2) thereof, and

(ii) in the case of aviation fuel, the aggregate rate of tax imposed by section 4091 with respect to fuel described in subsection (c)(2) thereof.

(3) **Coordination with other repayment provisions.** No amount shall be payable under paragraph (1) with respect to any gasoline, diesel fuel, [5]*kerosene,* or aviation fuel with respect to which an amount is payable under subsection (d), (e), or (l) of this section or under section 6420 or 6421.

(4) **Termination.** This subsection shall not apply with respect to any mixture sold or used after September 30, 1999.

* * * * * * * * * * * *

(i) **Time for filing claims; period covered.**

(1) **General rule.** Except as otherwise provided in this subsection, not more than one claim may be filed under subsection (a), (b), (c), (d), (h), (l) or (q) by any person with respect to fuel used (or a qualified diesel powered highway vehicle purchased) during his taxable year; and no claim shall be allowed under this paragraph with respect to fuel used during any taxable year unless filed by the purchaser not later than the time prescribed by law for filing a claim for credit or refund of overpayment of income tax for such taxable year. For purposes of this paragraph, a person's taxable year shall be his taxable year for purposes of subtitle A.

(2) **Exceptions.**

(A) In general. If $1,000 or more is payable under subsections (a), (b), (d), (h), and (q) to any person with respect to fuel used during any of the first 3 quarters of his taxable year, a claim may be filed under this section with respect to fuel used, during such quarter.

(B) Time for filing claim. No claim filed under this paragraph shall be allowed unless filed on or before the last day of the first quarter following the quarter for which the claim is filed.

(3) **Special rule for alcohol mixture credit.**

(A) In general. A claim may be filed under subsection (f) by any person with respect to gasoline[6], *diesel fuel, or kerosene* used to produce a qualified alcohol mixture (as defined in section 4081(c)(3)) for any period—

(i) for which $200 or more is payable under such subsection (f), and

(ii) which is not less than 1 week.

(B) Payment of claim. Notwithstanding subsection (f)(1), if the Secretary has not paid pursuant to a claim filed under this section within 20 days of the date of the filing of such claim, the claim shall be paid with interest from such date determined by using the overpayment rate and method under section 6621.

(C) Time for filing claim. No claim filed under this paragraph shall be allowed unless filed on or before the last day of the first quarter the earliest quarter included in the claim.

(4) [7]*Special rule for refunds under subsection (l).*

(A) In general. If at the close of any of the 1st 3 quarters of the taxable year of any person, at least $750 is payable under subsection (l) to such person with respect to fuel used during such quarter or any prior quarter during the taxable year (and for which no other claim has been filed), a claim may be filled under subsection (l) with respect to such fuel.

(B) Time for filing claim. No claim filed under this paragraph shall be allowed unless filed during the 1st quarter following the last quarter included in the claim.

(5) **Special rule for vendor refunds.**

(A) In general. A claim may be filed under subsection (l)(5) by any person with respect to fuel sold by such person for any period—

(i) for which $200 or more [8]*($100 or more in the case of kerosene)* is payable under subsection (l)(5), and

(ii) which is not less than 1 week.

Notwithstanding subsection (l)(1), paragraph (3)(B) shall apply to claims filed under the preceding sentence.

(B) Time for filing claim. No claim filed under this paragraph shall be allowed unless filed on or before the last day of the first quarter following the earliest quarter included in the claim.

* * * * * * * * * * * *

(l) Nontaxable uses of diesel fuel and aviation fuel.

(1) **In general.** Except as otherwise provided in this subsection and in subsection (k), if—

(A) any diesel fuel on which tax has been imposed by section 4041 or 4081, or

(B) any aviation fuel on which tax has been imposed by section 4091,

is used by any person in a nontaxable use, the Secretary shall pay (without interest) to the ultimate purchaser of such fuel an amount equal to the aggregate amount of tax imposed on such fuel under section 4041, 4081, or 4091, as the case may be.

(2) **Nontaxable use.** For purposes of this subsection, the term "nontaxable use" means—

(A) in the case of diesel fuel, any use which is exempt from the tax imposed by section 4041(a)(1) other than by reason of a prior imposition of tax, and

(B) in the case of aviation fuel, any use which is exempt from the tax imposed by section 4041(c)(1) other than by reason of a prior imposition of tax.

(3) **Refund of certain taxes on fuel used in diesel-powered trains.** For purposes of this subsection, the term "nontaxable use" includes fuel used in a diesel-powered train. The preceding sentence shall not apply with respect to—

(A) the Leaking Underground Storage Tank Trust Fund financing rate under sections 4041 and 4081, and

(B) so much of the rate specified in section 4081(a)(2)(A) as does not exceed—

(i) 6.8 cents per gallon after September 30, 1993, and before October 1, 1995,

(ii) 5.55 cents per gallon after September 30, 1995, and before October 1, 1999, and

(iii) 4.3 cents per gallon after September 30, 1999.

The preceding sentence shall not apply in the case of fuel sold for exclusive use by a State or any political subdivision thereof.

(4) **No refund of certain taxes on fuel used in commercial aviation.** In the case of fuel used in commercial aviation (as defined in section 4092(b)) (other than supplies for vessels or aircraft within the meaning of section 4221(d)(3)), paragraph (1) shall not apply to so much of the tax imposed by section 4091 as is attributable to—

(A) the Leaking Underground Storage Tank Trust Fund financing rate imposed by such section, and

(B) in the case of fuel purchased after September 30, 1995, as so much of the rate of tax specified in section 4091(b)(1) as does not exceed 4.3 cents per gallon.

(5) **Registered vendors to administer claims for refund of diesel fuel sold to farmers and state and local governments.**

(A) In general. Paragraph (1) shall not apply to diesel fuel used—

(i) on a farm for farming purposes (within the meaning of section 6420(c)), or

(ii) by a State or local government.

(B) Payment to ultimate, registered, vendor. The amount which would (but for subparagraph (A)) have been paid under paragraph (1) with respect to any fuel shall be paid to the ultimate vendor of such fuel, if such vendor—

(i) is registered under section 4101, and

(ii) meets the requirements of subparagraph (A), (B), or (D) of section 6416(a)(1).

CAUTION. Subsec. (l), following, is effective after 6/30/98. For subsec. (l), effective before 7/1/98, see above.

(l) Nontaxable uses of diesel fuel[9], *kerosene,* and aviation fuel.

(1) **In general.** Except as otherwise provided in this subsection and in subsection (k), if—

(A) any diesel fuel[10]*or kerosene* on which tax has been imposed by section 4041 or 4081, or

(B) any aviation fuel on which tax has been imposed by section 4091,

is used by any person in a nontaxable use, the Secretary shall pay (without interest) to the ultimate purchaser of such fuel an amount equal to the aggregate amount of tax imposed on such fuel under section 4041, 4081, or 4091, as the case may be.

(2) Nontaxable use. For purposes of this subsection, the term "nontaxable use" means—

(A) in the case of diesel fuel [11]*or kerosene,* any use which is exempt from the tax imposed by section 4041(a)(1) other than by reason of a prior imposition of tax, and

(B) in the case of aviation fuel, any use which is exempt from the tax imposed by section 4041(c)(1) other than by reason of a prior imposition of tax.

(3) Refund of certain taxes on fuel used in diesel-powered trains. For purposes of this subsection, the term "nontaxable use" includes fuel used in a diesel-powered train. The preceding sentence shall not apply with respect to—

(A) the Leaking Underground Storage Tank Trust Fund financing rate under sections 4041 and 4081, and

(B) so much of the rate specified in section 4081(a)(2)(A) as does not exceed—

(i) 6.8 cents per gallon after September 30, 1993, and before October 1, 1995,

(ii) 5.55 cents per gallon after September 30, 1995, and before October 1, 1999, and

(iii) 4.3 cents per gallon after September 30, 1999.

The preceding sentence shall not apply in the case of fuel sold for exclusive use by a State or any political subdivision thereof.

(4) No refund of certain taxes on fuel used in commercial aviation. In the case of fuel used in commercial aviation (as defined in section 4092(b)) (other than supplies for vessels or aircraft within the meaning of section 4221(d)(3)), paragraph (1) shall not apply to so much of the tax imposed by section 4091 as is attributable to—

(A) the Leaking Underground Storage Tank Trust Fund financing rate imposed by such section, and

(B) in the case of fuel purchased after September 30, 1995, as so much of the rate of tax specified in section 4091(b)(1) as does not exceed 4.3 cents per gallon.

(5) Registered vendors to administer claims for refund of diesel fuel[12]*or kerosene* sold to farmers and state and local governments.

(A) In general. Paragraph (1) shall not apply to diesel fuel[13]*or kerosene* used—

(i) on a farm for farming purposes (within the meaning of section 6420(c)), or

(ii) by a State or local government.

[14]*(B) Sales of kerosene not for use in motor fuel. Paragraph (1)(A) shall not apply to kerosene sold by a vendor—*

(i) for any use if such sale is from a pump which (as determined under regulations prescribed by the Secretary) is not suitable for use in fueling any diesel-powered highway vehicle or train, or

(ii) to the extent provided by the Secretary, for blending with heating oil to be used during periods of extreme or unseasonable cold.

[15]*(C)* Payment to ultimate, registered, vendor. The amount which would (but for [16]*subparagraph (A) or (B))* have been paid under paragraph (1) with respect to any fuel shall be paid to the ultimate vendor of such fuel, if such vendor—

(i) is registered under section 4101, and

(ii) meets the requirements of subparagraph (A), (B), or (D) of section 6416(a)(1).

* * * * * * * * * * *

[For analysis, see ¶ 2208. For text of committee report, see ¶ 5130.]

[Endnote Code Sec. 6427]

Matter in *italics* in Code Sec. 6427(f) heading, Code Sec. 6427(f)(1), Code Sec. 6427(f)(2), Code Sec. 6427(f)(3), Code Sec. 6427(i)(3)(A), Code Sec. 6427(i)(4) heading, Code Sec. 6427(i)(5)(A)(i), Code Sec. 6427(l), Code Sec. 6427(l)(1), Code Sec. 6427(l)(2), Code Sec. 6427(l)(5), Code Sec. 6427(l)(5)(B) and Code Sec. 6427(l)(5)(C) added by Sec. 1032(c)(3)(A)-(E) and (e)(7)-(10) of the Taxpayer Relief Act of 1997, H.R. 2014, 8/5/97, which struck out:

1. added matter in the heading of subsec. (f)

2. added matter in para. (f)(1)

3. "or diesel fuel"

4. "or diesel fuel"
5. added matter in para. (f)(3)
6. "or diesel fuel"
7. "(4) Special rule for nontaxable uses of diesel fuel and aviation fuel taxed under section 4081 or 4091."
8. added matter in clause (i)(5)(A)(i)
9. added matter in the heading of subsec. (l)
10. added matter in para. (l)(1)
11. added matter in para. (l)(2)
12. added matter in the heading of para. (l)(5)
13. added matter in para. (l)(5)
14. added subpara. (l)(5)(B)
15. "(B)"
16. "subparagraph (A)"
Effective Date (Sec. 1032(f), H.R. 2014, 8/5/97) effective 7/1/98.

[¶ 3350]   Code Sec. 6501.   Limitations on assessment and collection.

(a) **General rule.** Except as otherwise provided in this section, the amount of any tax imposed by this title shall be assessed within 3 years after the return was filed (whether or not such return was filed on or after the date prescribed) or, if the tax is payable by stamp, at any time after such tax became due and before the expiration of 3 years after the date on which any part of such tax was paid, and no proceeding in court without assessment for the collection of such tax shall be begun after the expiration of such period. ¹*For purposes of this chapter, the term "return" means the return required to be filed by the taxpayer (and does not include a return of any person from whom the taxpayer has received an item of income, gain, loss, deduction, or credit).*

* * * * * * * * * * * *

(c) **Exceptions.**

* * * * * * * * * * * *

²*(8) Failure to notify Secretary of certain foreign transfers.* In the case of any information which is required to be reported to the Secretary under section 6038, 6038A, 6038B, 6046, 6046A, or 6048, the time for assessment of any tax imposed by this title with respect to any event or period to which such information relates shall not expire before the date which is 3 years after the date on which the Secretary is furnished the information required to be reported under such section.

³*(9) Gift tax on certain gifts not shown on return.* If any gift of property the value of which (or any increase in taxable gifts required under section 2701(d) which) is required to be shown on a return of tax imposed by chapter 12 (without regard to section 2503(b)), and is not shown on such return, any tax imposed by chapter 12 on such gift may be assessed, or a proceeding in court for the collection of such tax may be begun without assessment, at any time. The preceding sentence shall not apply to any item which is disclosed in such return, or in a statement attached to the return, in a manner adequate to apprise the Secretary of the nature of such item. The value of any item which is so disclosed may not be redetermined by the Secretary after the expiration of the period under subsection (a).

* * * * * * * * * * * *

(n) **Cross references.**

(1) For period of limitations for assessment and collection in the case of a joint income return filed after separate returns have been filed, see section 6013(b)(3) and (4).

(2) For extension of period in the case of partnership items (as defined in section 6231(a)(3)), see section 6229.

⁴*(3) For declaratory judgment relating to treatment of items other than partnership items with respect to an oversheltered return, see section 6234.*

[For analysis, see ¶ 522, ¶ 2320, ¶ 2321. For text of committee report, see ¶ 5031, ¶ 5187, ¶ 5251.]

[Endnote Code Sec. 6501]
Matter in *italics* in Code Sec. 6501(a) added by Sec. 1284(a) of the Taxpayer Relief Act of 1997, H.R. 2014, 8/5/97.
1. added matter in subsection (a)
Effective Date (Sec. 1284(b), H.R. 2014, 8/5/97) effective for claims for credit or refund for tax. yrs. end. after 8/5/97.

Matter in *italics* in Code Sec. 6501(c)(8) added by Sec. 1145(a), H.R. 2014, 8/5/97, which struck out:
2. "(8) Failure to notify Secretary under section 6038B. In the case of any tax imposed on any exchange or distribution by reason of subsection (a), (d) or (e) of section 367, the time for assessment of such tax shall not expire before the date which is 3 years after the date on which the Secretary is notified of such exchange or distribution under section 6038B(a)."
Effective Date (Sec. 1145(b), H.R. 2014, 8/5/97) effective for information the due date for reporting of which is after 8/5/97.

Matter in *italics* in Code Sec. 6501(c)(9) added by Sec. 506(b), H.R. 2014, 8/5/97, which struck out:
3. "(9) Gift tax on certain gifts not shown on return. If any gift of property the value of which is determined under section 2701 or 2702 (or any increase in taxable gifts required under section 2701(d)) is required to be shown on a return of tax imposed by chapter 12 (without regard to section 2503(b)), and is not shown on such return, any tax imposed by chapter 12 on such gift may be assessed, or a proceeding in court for the collection of such tax may be begun without assessment, at any time. The preceding sentence shall not apply to any item not shown as a gift on such return if such item is disclosed in such return, or in a statement attached to the return, in a manner adequate to apprise the Secretary of the nature of such item."
Effective Date (Sec. 506(e)(2), H.R. 2014, 8/5/97) effective for gifts made in calendar yrs. end. after 8/5/97.

Code Sec. 6501(n)(3), in *italics*, was added by Sec. 1239(e)(2), H.R. 2014, 8/5/97 [Ed. note. We feel the government intended to add para. (n)(3).
4. added paragraph (n)(3)
Effective Date (Sec. 1239(f), H.R. 2014, 8/5/97) effective for partnership tax. yrs. end. after 8/5/97.

[¶ 3351]   Code Sec. 6503.   Suspension of running of period of limitation.

(a) Issuance of statutory notice of deficiency.

(1) **General rule.** The running of the period of limitations provided in section 6501 or 6502 (or section 6229, but only with respect to a deficiency described in [1]*paragraph (2)(A) or (3) of section 6230(a))* on the making of assessments or the collection by levy or a proceeding in court, in respect of any deficiency as defined in section 6211 (relating to income, estate, gift and certain excise taxes), shall (after the mailing of a notice under section 6212(a)) be suspended for the period during which the Secretary is prohibited from making the assessment or from collecting by levy or a proceeding in court (and in any event, if a proceeding in respect of the deficiency is placed on the docket of the Tax Court, until the decision of the Tax Court becomes final), and for 60 days thereafter.

(2) **Corporation joining in consolidated income tax return.** If a notice under section 6212(a) in respect of a deficiency in tax imposed by subtitle A for any taxable year the period of limitations provided in paragraph (1) of this subsection shall apply in the case of corporations with which such corporation made a consolidated income tax return for such taxable year.

* * * * * * * * * * * *

[Endnote Code Sec. 6503]
Matter in *italics* in Code Sec. 6503(a) added by Sec. 1237(c)(2) of the Taxpayer Relief Act, H.R. 2014, 8/5/97, which struck out:
1. "section 6230(a)(2)(A)"
Effective Date (Sec. 1237(d), H.R. 2014, 8/5/97) effective for partnership tax. yrs. begin. after 9/3/82. P.L. 97-248, Sec. 407(a)(3) provides:
"(3) The amendments made by sections 402, 403 and 404 [of this Act] shall apply to any partnership taxable year (or in the case of section 6232 of such Code, to any period) ending after the date of the enactment of this Act [9/3/82] if the partnership, each partner, and each indirect partner requests such application and the Secretary of the Treasury or his delegate consents to such application."

[¶ 3352]   Code Sec. 6504.   Cross references.

For limitation period in case of—

(1) Adjustments to accrued foreign taxes, see section 905(c).

(2) Change of treatment with respect to itemized deductions where taxpayer and his spouse make separate returns, see section 63(e)(3).

(3) Involuntary conversion of property, see section 1033(a)(2)(C) and (D).

[1]**(4)** Application by fiduciary for discharge from personal liability for estate tax, see section 2204.

[2]**(5)** Insolvent banks and trust companies, see section 7507.

[3]**(6)** Service in a combat zone, etc., see section 7508.

[4]**(7)** Claims against transferees and fiduciaries, see chapter 71.

[5]**(8)** Assessments to recover excessive amounts paid under section 6420 (relating to gasoline used on farms), 6421 (relating to gasoline used for certain nonhighway purposes or by local transit systems), or 6427 (relating to fuels not used for taxable purposes) and assessments of civil penalties under section 6675 for excessive claims under section 6420, 6421, or 6427, see section 6206.

[6]**(9)** Assessment and collection of interest, see section 6601(g).

[7]**(10)** Assessment of civil penalties under section 6694 or 6695, see section 6696(d)(1).

[8]**(11)** Assessments of tax attributable to partnership items, see section 6229.

[Endnote Code Sec. 6504]

Matter in Code Sec. 6504(4), Code Sec. 6504(5), Code Sec. 6504(6), Code Sec. 6504(7), Code Sec. 6504(8), Code Sec. 6504(9), Code Sec. 6504(10), and Code Sec. 6504(11) added by Sec. 312(d)(13) of the Taxpayer Relief Act of 1997, H.R. 2014, 8/5/97, which struck out:

1. "(4) Gain upon sale or exchange of principal residence, see section 1034(j)."
"(5)"

2. "(6)"

3. "(7)"

4. "(8)"

5. "(9)"

6. "(10)"

7. "(11)"

8. "(12)"

Effective Date (Sec. 312(d)[sic (e)], H.R. 2014, 8/5/97) effective for sales and exchanges after 5/6/97, except as provided by Secs. 312(d)(2)-(4) [sic (e)(2)-(4)] of this Act, which read as follows:

"(2) Sales before 8/5/97.—At the election of the taxpayer, the amendments made by this section shall not apply to any sale or exchange before the date of the enactment of this Act.

"(3) Certain sales within 2 years after 8/5/97. Section 121 of the Internal Revenue Code of 1986 (as amended by this section) shall be applied without regard to subsection (c)(2)(B) thereof in the case of any sale or exchange of property during the 2-year period beginning on the date of the enactment of this Act if the taxpayer held such property on the date of the enactment of this Act and fails to meet the ownership and use requirements of subsection (a) thereof with respect to such property.

"(4) Binding contracts.—At the election of the taxpayer, the amendments made by this section shall not apply to a sale or exchange after the date of the enactment of this Act, if—

"(A) such sale or exchange is pursuant to a contract which was binding on such date, or

"(B) without regard to such amendments, gain would not be recognized under section 1034 of the Internal Revenue Code of 1986 (as in effect on the day before the date of the enactment of this Act) on such sale or exchange by reason of a new residence acquired on or before such date or with respect to the acquisition of which by the taxpayer a binding contract was in effect on such date.

This paragraph shall not apply to any sale or exchange by an individual if the treatment provided by section 877(a)(1) of the Internal Revenue Code of 1986 applies to such individual."

[¶ 3353]   Code Sec. 6511.   Limitations on credit or refund.

* * * * * * * * * * * *

(d) Special rules applicable to income taxes. * * *

(3) Special rules relating to foreign tax credit.

(A) Special period of limitation with respect to foreign taxes paid or accrued. If the claim for credit or refund relates to an overpayment attributable to any taxes paid or accrued to any foreign country or to any possession of the United States for which credit is allowed against the tax imposed by subtitle A in accordance with the provisions of section 901 or the provisions of any treaty to which the United States is a party, in lieu of the 3-year period of limitation prescribed in subsection (a), the period shall be 10 years from the date prescribed by law for filing the return [1]*for the year in which such taxes were actually paid or accrued.*

(B) Exception in the case of foreign taxes paid or accrued. In the case of a claim described in subparagraph (A), the amount of the credit or refund may exceed the portion of the tax paid within the period provided in subsection (b) or (c), whichever is applicable, to the extent of the amount of the overpayment attributable to the allowance of a credit for the taxes described in subparagraph (A).

* * * * * * * * * * * *

[2]*(7) Special period of limitation with respect to self-employment tax in certain cases. If—*

(A) the claim for credit or refund relates to an overpayment of the tax imposed by chapter 2 (relating to the tax on self-employment income) attributable to Tax Court determination in a proceeding under section 7436, and

(B) the allowance of a credit or refund of such overpayment is otherwise prevented by the operation of any law or rule of law other than section 7122 (relating to compromises),

such credit or refund may be allowed or made if claim therefor is filed on or before the last day of the second year after the calendar year in which such determination becomes final.

* * * * * * * * * * * *

[For analysis, see ¶ 2322. For text of committee report, see ¶ 5303.]

[Endnote Code Sec. 6511]

Matter in *italics* in Code Sec. 6511(d)(3)(A) added by Sec. 1056(a) of the Taxpayer Relief Act of 1997, H.R. 2014, 8/5/97, which struck out:

1. "for the year with respect to which the claim is made"

Effective Date (Sec. 1056(b), H.R. 2014, 8/5/97) effective for taxes paid or accrued in tax. yrs. begin. after 8/5/97.

Code Sec. 6511(d)(7), in *italics*, was added by Sec. 1454(b)(1), H.R. 2014.

2. added para. (d)(7)

Effective Date (Sec. 1454(c), H.R. 2014, 8/5/97) effective 8/5/97.

[¶ 3354]   Code Sec. 6512.   Limitations in case of petition to Tax Court.

* * * * * * * * * * * *

(b) Overpayment determined by Tax Court.

(1) Jurisdiction to determine. Except as provided by paragraph (3) and by section 7463, if the Tax Court finds that there is no deficiency and further finds that the taxpayer has made an overpayment of income tax for the same taxable year, of gift tax for the same calendar year or calendar quarter, of estate tax in respect of the taxable estate of the same decedent, or of tax imposed by chapter 41, 42, 43, or 44 with respect to any act (or failure to act) to which such petition relates, in respect of which the Secretary determined the deficiency, or finds that there is a deficiency but that the taxpayer has made an overpayment of such tax, the Tax Court shall have jurisdiction to determine the amount of such overpayment, and such amount shall, when the decision of the Tax Court has become final, be credited or refunded to the taxpayer.

(2) Jurisdiction to enforce. If, after 120 days after a decision of the Tax Court has become final, the Secretary has failed to refund the overpayment determined by the Tax Court, together with the interest thereon as provided in subchapter B of chapter 67, then the Tax Court, upon motion by the taxpayer, shall have jurisdiction to order the refund of such overpayment and interest. [1]*An order of the Tax Court disposing of a motion under this paragraph shall be reviewable in the same manner as a decision of the Tax Court, but only with respect to the matters determined in such order.*

(3) Limit on amount of credit or refund. No such credit or refund shall be allowed or made of any portion of the tax unless the Tax Court determines as part of its decision that such portion was paid—

(A) after the mailing of the notice of deficiency,

(B) within the period which would be applicable under section 6511(b)(2), (c), or (d), if on the date of the mailing of the notice of deficiency a claim had been filed (whether or not filed) stating the grounds upon which the Tax Court finds that there is an overpayment, or

(C) within the period which would be applicable under section 6511(b)(2), (c), or (d), in respect of any claim for refund filed within the applicable period specified in section 6511 and before the date of the mailing of the notice of deficiency—

(i) which had not been disallowed before that date,

(ii) which had been disallowed before that date and in respect of which a timely suit for refund could have been commenced as of that date, or

(iii) in respect of which a suit for refund had been commenced before that date and within the period specified in section 6532.

[2]*In the case of a credit or refund relating to an affected item (within the meaning of section 6231(a)(5)), the preceding sentence shall be applied by substituting the periods under sections 6229 and 6230(d) for the periods under section 6551(b)(2), (c), and (d). [3]In a case described in subparagraph (B) where the date of the mailing of the notice of deficiency is during the third year after the due date (with extensions) for filing the return of tax and no return was filed before such date, the applicable period under subsections (a) and (b)(2) of section 6511 shall be 3 years.*

[4]*(4) Denial of jurisdiction regarding certain credits and reductions. The Tax Court shall have no jurisdiction under this subsection to restrain or review any credit or reduction made by the Secretary under section 6402.*

[For analysis, see ¶ 1416, ¶ 2325, ¶ 2326. For text of committee report, see ¶ 5224, ¶ 5249, ¶ 5300.]

[Endnote Code Sec. 6512]

Matter in *italics* in Code Sec. 6512(b)(2) was added by Sec. 1451(a) of the Taxpayer Relief Act of 1997, H.R. 2014, 8/5/97.

1. added matter in para. (b)(2)

Effective Date (Sec. 1451(c), H.R. 2014, 8/5/97) effective 8/5/97.

Matter in *italics* in Code Sec. 6512(b)(3) was added by Sec. 1239(c)(2), H.R. 2014, 8/5/97.

2. added matter in para. (b)(3)

Effective Date (Sec. 1239(f), H.R. 2014, 8/5/97) effective for partnership tax. yrs. end. after 8/5/97.

Matter in *italics* in Code Sec. 6512(b)(3) was added by Sec. 1282(a), H.R. 2014, 8/5/97.

3. added matter in para. (b)(3)

Effective Date (Sec. 1282(b), H.R. 2014, 8/5/97) effective for claims for credit or refund for tax. yrs. end. after 8/5/97.

Code Sec. 6512(b)(4) in *italics* was added by Sec. 1451(b), H.R. 2014, 8/5/97.

4. added para. (b)(4)

Effective Date (Sec. 1451(c), H.R. 2014, 8/5/97) effective 8/5/97.

[¶ 3355]   Code Sec. 6601.   Interest on underpayment, nonpayment, or extensions of time for payment, of tax.

* * * * * * * * * * *

(c) **Suspension of interest in certain income, estate, gift, and certain excise tax cases.** In the case of a deficiency as defined in section 6211 (relating to income, estate, gift and certain excise taxes), if a waiver of restrictions under section 6213(d) on the assessment of such deficiency has been filed, and if notice and demand by the Secretary for payment of such deficiency is not made within 30 days after the filing of such waiver, interest shall not be imposed on such deficiency for the period beginning immediately after such 30th day and ending with the date of notice and demand and interest shall not be imposed during such period on any interest with respect to such deficiency for any prior period. [1]*In the case of a settlement under section 6224(c) which results in the conversion of partnership items to nonpartnership items pursuant to section 6231(b)(1)(C), the preceding sentence shall apply to a computational adjustment resulting from such settlement in the same manner as if such adjustment were a deficiency and such settlement were a waiver referred to in the preceding sentence.*

(d) **Income tax reduced by carryback or adjustment for certain unused deductions.**

(1) **Net operating loss or capital loss carryback.** If the amount of any tax imposed by subtitle A is reduced by reason of a carryback of a net operating loss or net capital loss such reduction in tax shall not affect the computation of interest under this section for the period ending with the filing date for the taxable year in which the net operating loss or net capital loss arises.

[2]*(2) Foreign tax credit carrybacks. If any credit allowed for any taxable year is increased by reason of a carryback of tax paid or accrued to foreign countries or possessions of the United States, such increase shall not affect the computation of interest under this section for the period ending with the filing date for the taxable year in which such taxes were in fact paid or accrued, or, with respect to any portion of such credit carryback from a taxable year attributable to a net operating loss carryback or a capital loss carryback from a subsequent taxable year, such increase shall not affect the computation of interest under this section for the period ending with the filing date for such subsequent taxable year.*

[3]*(3)* **Certain credit carrybacks.**

(A) In general. If any credit allowed for any taxable year is increased by reason of a credit carryback, such increase shall not affect the computation of interest under this section for the period ending with the filing date for the taxable year in which the credit carryback arises, or, with respect to any portion of a credit carryback from a taxable year attributable to a net operating loss carryback, capital loss carryback, or other credit carryback from a subsequent taxable year, such increase shall not affect the computation of interest under this section for the period ending with the filing date for such subsequent taxable year.

(B) Credit carryback defined. For purposes of this paragraph, the term "credit carryback" has the meaning given such term by section 6511(d)(4)(C).

[4]*(4)* **Filing date.** For purposes of this subsection, the term "filing date" has the meaning given such term by section 6611(f)(3)(A).

* * * * * * * * * * *

(j) [5]*2-percent rate on certain portion of estate tax extended under section 6166.*

[6]*(1) In general. If the time for payment of an amount of tax imposed by chapter 11 is extended as provided in section 6166, then in lieu of the annual rate provided by subsection (a)—*

(A) interest on the 2-percent portion of such amount shall be paid at the rate of 2 percent, and

(B) interest on so much of such amount as exceeds the 2-percent portion shall be paid at a rate equal to 45 percent of the annual rate provided by subsection (a).

For purposes of this subsection, the amount of any deficiency which is prorated to install-ments payable under section 6166 shall be treated as an amount of tax payable in install-ments under such section.

(2) 2-percent portion. For purposes of this subsection, the term "2-percent portion" means the lesser of—

(A)

(i) the amount of the tentative tax which would be determined under the rate schedule set forth in section 2001(c) if the amount with respect to which such tentative tax is to be computed were the sum of $1,000,000 and the applicable exclusion amount in effect under section 2010(c), reduced by

(ii) the applicable credit amount in effect under section 2010(c), or

(B) the amount of the tax imposed by chapter 11 which is extended as provided in sec-tion 6166.

CAUTION. Para. (j)(3), following, is effective for estates of decedents dying, and gifts made, before 1/1/98. For paras. (j)(3) and (4), effective for estates of dece-dents dying, and gifts made, after 12/31/97, see below.

(3) Treatment of payments. If the amount of tax imposed by chapter 11 which is ex-tended as provided in section 6166 exceeds the 4-percent portion, any payment of a portion of such amount shall, for purposes of computing interest for periods after such payment, be treated as reducing the 4-percent portion by an amount which bears the same ratio to the amount of such payment as the amount of the 4-percent portion (determined without regard to this paragraph) bears to the amount of the tax which is extended as provided in section 6166.

CAUTION. Paras. (j)(3) and (4), following, are effective for estates of dece-dents dying, and gifts made, after 12/31/97. For para. (j)(3), effective for estates of de-cedents dying, and gifts made, before 1/1/98, see above.

[7]*(3) Inflation adjustment. In the case of estates of decedents dying in a calendar year af-ter 1998, the $1,000,000 amount contained in paragraph (2)(A) shall be increased by an amount equal to—*

(A) $1,000,000, multiplied by

(B) the cost-of-living adjustment determined under section 1(f)(3) for such calendar year by substituting "calendar year 1997" for "calendar year 1992" in subparagraph (B) thereof. If any amount as adjusted under the preceding sentence is not a multiple of $10,000, such amount shall be rounded to the next lowest multiple of $10,000.

[8]*(4) Treatment of payments.* If the amount of tax imposed by chapter 11 which is ex-tended as provided in section 6166 exceeds the 4-percent portion, any payment of a portion of such amount shall, for purposes of computing interest for periods after such payment, be treated as reducing the 4-percent portion by an amount which bears the same ratio to the amount of such payment as the amount of the 4-percent portion (determined without regard to this paragraph) bears to the amount of the tax which is extended as provided in section 6166.

CAUTION. Para. (j)(4), following, is effective for estates of decedents dying after 12/31/97, except as provided in Sec. 503(d)(2) of H.R. 2014, as reproduced in the history. For para. (j)(4), effective for estates of decedents dying, and gifts made, after 12/31/97, see above.

(4) Treatment of payments. If the amount of tax imposed by chapter 11 which is ex-tended as provided in section 6166 exceeds the [9]*2-percent* portion, any payment of a portion of such amount shall, for purposes of computing interest for periods after such payment, be treated as reducing the [10]*2-percent* portion by an amount which bears the same ratio to the amount of such payment as the amount of the [11]*2-percent* portion (determined without regard to this paragraph) bears to the amount of the tax which is extended as provided in section 6166.

(k) No interest on certain adjustments. For provisions prohibiting interest on certain adjust-ments in tax, see section 6205(a).

[For analysis, see ¶ 506, ¶ 1413, ¶ 2402. For text of committee report, see ¶ 5028, ¶ 5147, ¶ 5227.]

[Endnote Code Sec. 6601]

Matter in *italics* in Code Sec. 6601(c) added by Sec. 1242(a) of the Taxpayer Relief Act of 1997, H.R. 2014, 8/5/97.

1. added matter at the end of subsec. (c)

Effective Date (Sec. 1242(b), H.R. 2014, 8/5/97) effective for adjustments with respect to partnership tax. yrs. begin. after 8/5/97.

Matter in *italics* in Code Sec. 6601(d)(2), Code Sec. 6601(d)(3) and Code Sec. 6601(d)(4) added by Sec. 1055(a), H.R. 2014, 8/5/97, which struck out:

2. added para. (d)(2)

3. "(2)"

4. "(3)"

Effective Date (Sec. 1055(c), H.R. 2014, 8/5/97) effective for foreign tax credit carrybacks arising in tax. yrs. begin. after 8/5/97.

Matter in *italics* in Code Sec. 6601(j) heading, Code Sec. 6601(j)(1) and Code Sec. 6601(j)(2) added by Secs. 503(a) and (c)(3), H.R. 2014, 8/5/97, which struck out:

5. "4-percent"

6. "(1) In general. If the time for payment of an amount of tax imposed by chapter 11 is extended as provided in section 6166, interest on the 4-percent portion of such amount shall (in lieu of the annual rate provided by subsection (a)) be paid at the rate of 4 percent. For purposes of this subsection, the amount of any deficiency which is prorated to installments payable under section 6166 shall be treated as an amount of tax payable in installments under such section.

"(2) 4-percent portion. For purposes of this subsection, the term '4-percent portion' means the lesser of—

"(A) $345,800 reduced by the amount of the credit allowable under section 2010(a); or

"(B) the amount of the tax imposed by chapter 11 which is extended as provided in section 6166."

Effective Date (Sec. 503(d), H.R. 2014, 8/5/97) effective for estates of decedents dying after 12/31/97, except as provided by Sec. 503(d)(2) of this Act, which reads as follows:

"(2) Election. In the case of the estate of any decedent dying before January 1, 1998, with respect to which there is an election under section 6166 of the Internal Revenue Code of 1986, the executor of the estate may elect to have the amendments made by this section apply with respect to installments due after the effective date of the election; except that the 2-percent portion of such installments shall be equal to the amount which would be the 4-percent portion of such installments without regard to such election. Such an election shall be made before January 1, 1999 in the manner prescribed by the Secretary of the Treasury and, once made, is irrevocable."

Matter in *italics* in Code Sec. 6601(j)(3) and Code Sec. 6601(j)(4) added by Sec. 501(e), H.R. 2014, date of enactment, which struck out:

7. added para. (j)(3)

8. "(3)"

Effective Date (Sec. 501(f), H.R. 2014, 8/5/97) effective for estates of decedents dying, and gifts made, after 12/31/97.

Matter in *italics* in Code Sec. 6601(j)(4) [as redesignated by Sec. 501(e), H.R. 2014, 8/5/97, see above] was added by Sec. 503(c)(2), H.R. 2014, date of enactment, which struck out:

9. "4-percent"

10. "4-percent"

11. "4-percent"

Effective Date (Sec. 503(d), H.R. 2014, 8/5/97) effective for estates of decedents dying after 12/31/97, except as provided by Sec. 503(d)(2) of this Act, see above.

Sec. 915, H.R. 2014, 8/5/97, relating to the abatement of interest on underpayments by taxpayers in presidentially declared disaster areas, provides:

"Sec. 915. Abatement of interest on underpayments by taxpayers in presidentially declared disaster areas.

"(a) In General.—If the Secretary of the Treasury extends for any period the time for filing income tax returns under section 6081 of the Internal Revenue Code of 1986 and the time for paying income tax with respect to such returns under section 6161 of such Code (and waives any penalties relating to the failure to so file or so pay) for any individual located in a Presidentially declared disaster area, the Secretary shall, notwithstanding section 7508A(b) of such Code, abate for such period the assessment of any interest prescribed under section 6601 of such Code on such income tax.

"(b) Presidentially Declared Disaster Area.—For purposes of subsection (a), the term 'Presidentially declared disaster area' means, with respect to any individual, any area which the President has determined during 1997 warrants assistance by the Federal Government under the Robert T. Stafford Disaster Relief and Emergency Assistance Act.

"(c) Individual.—For purposes of this section, the term 'individual' shall not include any estate or trust.

"(d) Effective Date.—This section shall apply to disasters declared after December 31, 1996."

[¶ 3356]   Code Sec. 6611.   Interest on overpayments.

* * * * * * * * * * * *

(f) Refund of income tax caused by carryback or adjustment for certain unused deductions.

(1) Net operating loss or capital loss carryback. For purposes of subsection (a), if any overpayment of tax imposed by subtitle A results from a carryback of a net operating loss or net capital loss, such overpayment shall be deemed not to have been made prior to the filing date for the taxable year in which such net operating loss or net capital loss arises.

[1]*(2) Foreign tax credit carrybacks. For purposes of subsection (a), if any overpayment of tax imposed by subtitle A results from a carryback of tax paid or accrued to foreign countries or possessions of the United States, such overpayment shall be deemed not to have been made before the filing date for the taxable year in which such taxes were in fact paid or accrued, or, with respect to any portion of such credit carryback from a taxable year attributable to a net operating loss carryback or a capital loss carryback from a subsequent taxable year, such overpayment shall be deemed not to have been made before the filing date for such subsequent taxable year.*

[2]**(3) Certain credit carrybacks.**

(A) In general. For purposes of subsection (a), if any overpayment of tax imposed by subtitle A results from a credit carryback, such overpayment shall be deemed not to have been made before the filing date for the taxable year in which such credit carryback arises, or, with respect to any portion of a credit carryback from a taxable year attributable to a net operating loss carryback, capital loss carryback, or other credit carryback from a subsequent taxable year, such overpayment shall be deemed not to have been made before the filing date for such subsequent taxable year.

(B) Credit carryback defined. For purposes of this paragraph, the term "credit carryback" has the meaning given such term by section 6511(d)(4)(C).

[3]**(4) Special rules for [4]*paragraphs (1), (2), and (3).***

(A) Filing date. For purposes of this subsection, the term "filing date" means the last date prescribed for filing the return of tax imposed by subtitle A for the taxable year (determined without regard to extensions).

(B) Coordination with subsection (e).

(i) In general. For purposes of subsection (e)—

(I) any overpayment described in [5]*paragraph (1), (2), or (3)* shall be treated as an overpayment for the loss year, and

(II) such subsection shall be applied with respect to such overpayment by treating the return for the loss year as not filed before claim for such overpayment is filed.

(ii) Loss year. For purposes of this subparagraph, the term "loss year" means—

(I) in the case of a carryback of a net operating loss or net capital loss, the taxable year in which such loss arises,[6]

[7]*(II) in the case of a carryback of taxes paid or accrued to foreign countries or possessions of the United States, the taxable year in which such taxes were in fact paid or accrued (or, with respect to any portion of such carryback from a taxable year attributable to a net operating loss carryback or a capital loss carryback from a subsequent taxable year, such subsequent taxable year), and*

[8]*(III) in the case of a credit carryback [9](as defined in paragraph (3)(B)), the taxable year in which such credit carryback arises (or, with respect to any portion of a credit carryback from a taxable year attributable to a net operating loss carryback, a capital loss carryback, or other credit carryback from a subsequent taxable year, such subsequent taxable year).*

(C) Application of subparagraph (B) where section 6411(a) claim filed. For purposes of subparagraph (B)(i)(II), if a taxpayer—

(i) files a claim for refund of any overpayment described in [10]*paragraph (1), (2), or (3)* with respect to the taxable year to which a loss or credit is carried back, and

(ii) subsequently files an application under section 6411(a) with respect to such overpayment,

then the claim for overpayment shall be treated as having been filed on the date the application under section 6411(a) was filed.

[11]*(g) No interest until return in processible form.*

(1) For purposes of subsections (b)(3), (e), and (h), a return shall not be treated as filed until it is filed in processible form.

(2) For purposes of paragraph (1), a return is in a processible form if—

(A) such return is filed on a permitted form, and

(B) such return contains—

(i) the taxpayer's name, address, and identifying number and the required signature, and

(ii) sufficient required information (whether on the return or on required attachments) to permit the mathematical verification of tax liability shown on the return.

[12]*(h) Prohibition of administrative review.* For prohibition of administrative review, see section 6406.

[For analysis, see ¶ 2402. For text of committee report, see ¶ 5147.]

[Endnote Code Sec. 6611]

Matter in *italics* in Code Sec. 6611(f)(2), Code Sec. 6611(f)(3), Code Sec. 6611(f)(4), Code Sec. 6611(g) and Code Sec. 6611(h) added by Sec. 1055(b)(1), (b)(2)(A)(i), (b)(2)(A)(ii) and (b)(2)(B)-(D) of the Taxpayer Relief Act of 1997, H.R. 2014, 8/5/97, which struck out:

1. added para. (f)(2)
2. "(2)"
3. "(3)"
4. "paragraphs (1) and (2)"
5. "paragraph (1) or (2)"
6. "and"
7. added subclause (f)(4)(B)(ii)(II)
8. "(II)"
9. added matter in subclause (f)(4)(B)(ii)(III)
10. "paragraph (1) or (2)"
11. "(g) Refund of income tax caused by carryback of foreign taxes. For purposes of subsection (a), if any overpayment of tax results from a carryback of tax paid or accrued to foreign countries or possessions of the United States, such overpayment shall be deemed not to have been paid or accrued prior to the filing date (as defined in subsection (f)(3)) for the taxable year under this subtitle in which such taxes were in fact paid or accrued."
"(h)"
12. "(i)"

Effective Date (Sec. 1055(c), H.R. 2014, 8/5/97) effective for foreign tax credit carrybacks arising in tax. yrs. begin. after 8/5/97.

[¶ 3357]   Code Sec. 6621.   Determination of rate of interest.

(a) **General rule.**

(1) **Overpayment rate.** The overpayment rate established under this section shall be the sum of—

(A) the Federal short-term rate determined under subsection (b), plus

(B) 2 percentage points.

To the extent that an overpayment of tax by a corporation for any taxable period (as defined in [1]*subsection (c)(3), applied by substituting "overpayment" for "underpayment"*) exceeds $10,000, subparagraph (B) shall be applied by substituting "0.5 percentage point" for "2 percentage points".

(2) **Underpayment rate.** The underpayment rate established under this section shall be the sum of—

(A) the Federal short-term rate determined under subsection (b), plus

(B) 3 percentage points.

* * * * * * * * * * * *

(c) Increase in underpayment rate for large corporate underpayments.

(1) In general. For purposes of determining the amount of interest payable under section 6601 on any large corporate underpayment for periods after the applicable date, paragraph (2) of subsection (a) shall be applied by substituting "5 percentage points" for "3 percentage points".

(2) Applicable date. For purposes of this subsection—

(A) In general. The applicable date is the 30th day after the earlier of —

(i) the date on which the 1st letter of proposed deficiency which allows the taxpayer an opportunity for administrative review in the Internal Revenue Service Office of Appeals is sent, or

(ii) the date on which the deficiency notice under section 6212 is sent.

The preceding sentence shall be applied without regard to any such letter or notice which is withdrawn by the Secretary.

(B) Special rules.

(i) Nondeficiency procedures. In the case of any underpayment of any tax imposed by this title to which the deficiency procedures do not apply, subparagraph (A) shall be applied by taking into account any letter or notice provided by the Secretary which notifies the taxpayer of the assessment or proposed assessment of the tax.

(ii) Exception where amounts paid in full. For purposes of subparagraph (A), a letter or notice shall be disregarded if, during the 30-day period beginning on the day on which it was sent, the taxpayer makes a payment equal to the amount shown as due in such letter or notice, as the case may be.

[2](iii) Exception for letters or notices involving small amounts. For purposes of this paragraph, any letter or notice shall be disregarded if the amount of the deficiency or proposed deficiency (or the assessment or proposed assessment) set forth in such letter or notice is not greater than $100,000 (determined by not taking into account any interest, penalties, or additions to tax).

(3) Large corporate underpayment. For purposes of this subsection—

(A) In general. The term "large corporate underpayment" means any underpayment of a tax by a C corporation for any taxable period if the amount of such underpayment for such period exceeds $100,000.

(B) Taxable period. For purposes of subparagraph (A), the term "taxable period" means—

(i) in the case of any tax imposed by subtitle A, the taxable year, or

(ii) in the case of any other tax, the period to which the underpayment relates.

[For analysis, see ¶ 2403. For text of committee report, see ¶ 5306.]

[Endnote Code Sec. 6621]

Matter in *italics* in Code Sec. 6621(a)(1) added by Sec. 1604(b)(1) of the Taxpayer Relief Act of 1997, H.R. 2014, 8/5/97, which struck out:

1. "subsection (c)(3))"

Effective Date (Sec. 1604(b)(4), H.R. 2014, 8/5/97) effective for purposes of determining interest for periods after 12/31/94.

Code Sec. 6621(c)(2)(B)(iii), in *italics*, was added by Sec. 1463(a), H.R. 2014.

2. added clause (c)(2)(B)(iii)

Effective Date (Sec. 1463(b), H.R. 2014, 8/5/97) effective for purposes of determining interest for periods after 12/31/97.

[¶ 3358]   Code Sec. 6652.   Failure to file certain information returns, registration statements, etc.

* * * * * * * * * * * *

(e) Information required in connection with certain plans of deferred compensation; etc. In the case of failure to file a return or statement required under section 6058 (relating to information required in connection with certain plans of deferred compensation), 6047 (relating to information relating to certain trusts and annuity and bond purchase plans), or 6039D (relating to returns and records with respect to certain fringe benefit plans) on the date and in the manner prescribed therefor (determined with regard to any extension of time for filing), unless it is shown that such failure is due to reasonable cause, there shall be paid (on notice and demand by the Secretary and in the same manner as tax) by the person failing so to file, $25 for each day during which such failure continues, but the total amount imposed under this subsection on any person for failure to file any return shall not exceed $15,000. This subsection shall not apply to any return or statement which is an information return described in section 6724(d)(1)(C)(ii) or a payee statement described in [1]*section 6724(d)(2)(Y).*

* * * * * * * * * * * *

(g) Information required in connection with deductible employee contributions. In the case of failure to make a report required by section 219(f)(4) which contains the information required by such section on the date prescribed therefor (determined with regard to any extension of time for filing), there shall be paid (on notice and demand by the Secretary and in the same manner as tax) by the person failing so to file, an amount equal to $25 for each participant with respect to whom there was a failure to file such information, multiplied by the number of years during which such failure continues, but the total amount imposed under this subsection on any person for failure to file shall not exceed $10,000. [2]*No penalty shall be imposed under this subsection on any failure which is shown to be due to reasonable cause and not willful neglect.*

* * * * * * * * * * * *

(k) Failure to make reports required under section 1202. In the case of a failure to make a report required under section 1202(d)(1)(C) which contains the information required by such section on the date prescribed therefor (determined with regard to any extension of time for filing), there shall be paid (on notice and demand by the Secretary and in the same manner as tax) by the person failing to make such report, an amount equal to $50 for each report with respect to which there was such a failure. In the case of any failure due to negligence or intentional disregard, the preceding sentence shall be applied by substituting "$100" for "$50". In the case of a report covering periods in 2 or more years, the penalty determined under preceding provisions of this subsection shall be multiplied by the number of such years. [3]*No penalty shall be imposed under this subsection on any failure which is shown to be due to reasonable cause and not willful neglect.*

* * * * * * * * * * * *

[For analysis, see ¶ 2406. For text of Committee Report see ¶ 5248.]

[Endnote Code Sec. 6652]

Matter in *italics* in Code Sec. 6652(e) added by Sec. 1602(d)(2)(B) of the Taxpayer Relief Act of 1997, H.R. 2014, 8/5/97, which struck out:

1. "section 6724(d)(2)(X)"

Effective Date (Sec. 1602(i), H.R. 2014, 8/5/97) effective for benefits paid after 12/31/96.

Matter in *italics* in Code Sec. 6652(g) and Code Sec. 6652(k) added by Secs. 1281(a) and (b), H.R. 2014, 8/5/97.

2. added matter in subsec. (g)
3. added matter in subsec. (k)

Effective Date (Sec. 1281(e), H.R. 2014, 8/5/97) effective for tax. yrs. begin. after 8/5/97.

[¶ 3359]   Code Sec. 6654.   Failure by individual to pay estimated income tax.

* * * * * * * * * * * *

(d) Amount of required installments. For purposes of this section—

(1) Amount.

* * * * * * * * * * * *

(C) Limitation on use of preceding year's tax.

CAUTION. Clause (d)(1)(C)(i), following, is effective for any installment payment for tax. yrs. begin. before 1/1/98. For clause (d)(1)(C)(i) effective for any installment payment for tax. yrs. begin after 12/31/97, see below.

(i) In general. If the adjusted gross income shown on the return of the individual for the preceding taxable year exceeds $150,000, clause (ii) of subparagraph (B) shall be applied by substituting "110 percent" for "100 percent".

CAUTION. Clause (d)(1)(C)(i), following, is effective for any installment payment for tax. yrs. after before 12/31/97. For clause (d)(1)(C)(i) effective for any installment payment for tax. yrs. begin. before 1/1/98, see above.

[1]*(i) In general. If the adjusted gross income shown on the return of the individual for the preceding taxable year beginning in any calendar year exceeds $150,000, clause (ii) of subparagraph (B) shall be applied by substituting the applicable percentage for "100 percent". For purposes of the preceding sentence, the applicable percentage shall be determined in accordance with the following table:*

If the preceding taxable year begins in:	The applicable percentage is:
1998, 1999, or 2001	105
2001	112
2002 or thereafter	110

This clause shall not apply in the case of a preceding taxable year beginning in calendar year 1997.

* * * * * * * * * * * *

(e) Exceptions.

CAUTION. Para. (e)(1), following, is effective for tax. yrs. begin. before 1/1/98. For para. (e)(1) effective for tax. yrs. begin. after 12/31/97, see below.

(1) Where tax is small amount. No addition to tax shall be imposed under subsection (a) for any taxable year if the tax shown on the return for such taxable year (or, if no return is filed, the tax), reduced by the credit allowable under section 31, is less than $500.

CAUTION. Para. (e)(1), following, is effective for tax. yrs. begin. after 12/31/97. For para. (e)(1) effective for tax. yrs. begin. before 1/1/98, see above.

(1) Where tax is small amount. No addition to tax shall be imposed under subsection (a) for any taxable year if the tax shown on the return for such taxable year (or, if no return is filed, the tax), reduced by the credit allowable under section 31, is less than [2]*$1,000.*

* * * * * * * * * * * *

[For analysis, see ¶ 1802, ¶ 1803. For text of Committee Report see ¶ 5168, ¶ 5202.]

[Endnote Code Sec. 6654]

Matter in *italics* in Code Sec. 6654(c)(1)(C)(i) added by Sec. 1091(a) of the Taxpayer Relief Act of 1997, H.R. 2014, 8/5/97, which stuck out:

1. "(i) In general. If the adjusted gross income shown on the return of the individual for the preceding taxable year exceeds $150,000, clause (ii) of subparagraph (B) shall be applied by substituting '110 percent' for '100 percent'."

Effective Date (Sec. 1091(b), H.R. 2014, 8/5/97) effective for any installment payment for tax. yrs. begin. after 12/31/97.

Matter in *italics* in Code Sec. 6654(e)(1) added by Sec. 1202(a), H.R. 2014, 8/5/97, which struck out:.

2. "$500"

Effective Date (Sec. 1202(b), H.R. 2014, 8/5/97) effective for tax. yrs. begin. after 12/31/97.

Sec. 1(d), H.R. 2014, 8/5/97, provides:

"(d) Waiver of Estimated Tax Penalties.—No addition to tax shall be made under section 6654 or 6655 of the Internal Revenue Code of 1986 for any period before January 1, 1998, for any payment the due date of which is before January 16, 1998, with respect to any underpayment attributable to such period to the extent such underpayment was created or increased by any provision of this Act."

[¶ 3360]   Code Sec. 6655.   Failure by corporation to pay estimated income tax.

* * * * * * * * * * * *

(g) Definitions and special rules.

* * * * * * * * * * * *

(3) Certain tax-exempt organizations. For purposes of this section—

(A) Any organization subject to the tax imposed by section 511, and any private foundation, shall be treated as a corporation subject to tax under section 11.

(B) Any tax imposed by section 511, and any tax imposed by section 1 or 4940 on a private foundation, shall be treated as a tax imposed by section 11.

(C) Any reference to taxable income shall be treated as including a reference to unrelated business taxable income or net investment income (as the case may be).

In the case of any organization described in subparagraph (A), subsection (b)(2)(A) shall be applied by substituting "5th month" for "3rd month", subsection (e)(2)(A) shall be applied by substituting "2 months" for "3 months" in clause (i)(I), the election under clause (i) of subsection (e)(2)(C) may be made separately for each installment, and clause (iii) of subsection (e)(2)(C) shall not apply. [1]*In the case of a private foundation, subsection (c)(2) shall be applied by substituting "May 15" for "April 15".*

* * * * * * * * * * * *

[For analysis, see ¶ 1804. For text of Committee Report see ¶ 5304.]

[Endnote Code Sec. 6655]

Matter in *italics* in Code Sec. 6655(g)(3) added by Sec. 1461(a) of the Taxpayer Relief Act of 1997, H.R. 2014, 8/5/97. 1. added matter in para. (g)(3).
Effective Date (Sec. 1461(b), H.R. 2014, 8/5/97) effective for purposes of determining underpayments of estimated tax for tax. yrs. begin. after 8/5/97.

Sec. 1(d), H.R. 2014, 8/5/97, relating to the waiver of estimated tax penalties, is reproduced in note following Code Sec. 6654.

[¶ 3361]   Code Sec. 6662.   Imposition of accuracy-related penalty.

* * * * * * * * * * * *

(d) Substantial understatement of income tax.

* * * * * * * * * * * *

(2) Understatement.

* * * * * * * * * * * *

(B) Reduction for understatement due to position of taxpayer or disclosed item. The amount of the understatement under subparagraph (A) shall be reduced by that portion of the understatement which is attributable to—

(i) the tax treatment of any item by the taxpayer if there is or was substantial authority for such treatment, or

(ii) any item if—

(I) the relevant facts affecting the item's tax treatment are adequately disclosed in the return or in a statement attached to the return, and

(II) there is a reasonable basis for the tax treatment of such item by the taxpayer.

[1]*For purposes of clause (ii)(II), in no event shall a corporation be treated as having a reasonable basis for its tax treatment of an item attributable to a multiple-party financing transaction if such treatment does not clearly reflect the income of the corporation.*

(C) Special rules in cases involving tax shelters.

* * * * * * * * * * * *

(iii) Tax shelter. For purposes of this subparagraph , the term "tax shelter" means—

(I) a partnership or other entity,

(II) any investment plan or arrangement, or

(III) any other plan or arrangement,

if [2]*a significant purpose* of such partnership, entity, plan, or arrangement is the avoidance or evasion of Federal income tax.

* * * * * * * * * * *

[For analysis, see ¶ 2412. For text of Committee Report see ¶ 5128.]

[Endnote Code Sec. 6662]

Matter in *italics* in Code Sec. 6662(d)(2)(B) and Code Sec. 6662(d)(2)(C)(iii) added by Secs. 1028(c)(1) and (2) of the Taxpayer Relief Act of 1997, H.R. 2014, 8/5/97.

1. added matter in subpara. (d)(2)(B).

2. "the principal purpose"

Effective Date (Sec. 1021(e)(2), H.R. 2014, 8/5/97) effective for items with respect to transactions entered into after 8/5/97.

[¶ 3362]   Code Sec. 6679.   Failure to file returns, etc., with respect to foreign corporations or foreign partnerships.

[1]*(a) Civil penalty.*

(1) In general. In addition to any criminal penalty provided by law, any person required to file a return under section 6035, 6046, or 6046A who fails to file such return at the time provided in such section, or who files a return which does not show the information required pursuant to such section, shall pay a penalty of $10,000, unless it is shown that such failure is due to reasonable cause.

(2) Increase in penalty where failure continues after notification. If any failure described in paragraph (1) continues for more than 90 days after the day on which the Secretary mails notice of such failure to the United States person, such person shall pay a penalty (in addition to the amount required under paragraph (1)) of $10,000 for each 30-day period (or fraction thereof) during which such failure continues after the expiration of such 90-day period. The increase in any penalty under this paragraph shall not exceed $50,000.

(3) Reduced penalty for returns relating to foreign personal holding companies. In the case of a return required under section 6035, paragraph (1) shall be applied by substituting "$1,000" for "$10,000", and paragraph (2) shall not apply.

* * * * * * * * * * *

[For analysis, see ¶ 2411. For text of Committee Report see ¶ 5185.]

[Endnote Code Sec. 6679]

Matter in *italics* in Code Sec. 6679(a) added by Sec. 1143(b) of the Taxpayer Relief Act of 1997, H.R. 2014, 8/5/97, which struck out:

1. "(a) Civil penalty.

"In addition to any criminal penalty provided by law, any person required to file a return under section 6035, 6046 or 6046A who fails to file such return at the time provided in such section, or who files a return which does not show the information required pursuant to such section, shall pay a penalty of $1,000, unless it is shown that such failure is due to reasonable cause."

Effective Date (Sec. 1143(c), H.R. 2014, 8/5/97) effective for transfers and changes after 8/5/97.

[¶ 3363]   Code Sec. 6683.   Failure of foreign corporation to file return of personal holding company tax.

Any foreign corporation which—

(1) is a personal holding company for any taxable year, and

(2) fails to file or to cause to be filed with the Secretary a true and accurate return of the tax imposed by section 541,

shall, in addition to other penalties provided by law, pay a penalty equal to 10 percent of the taxes imposed by chapter 1 (including the tax imposed by section 541) on such foreign corporation for such taxable year. [1]*No penalty shall be imposed under this section on any failure which is shown to be due to reasonable cause and not willful neglect.*

[For analysis, see ¶ 2406. For text of Committee Report see ¶ 5248.]

[Endnote Code Sec. 6683]
   Matter in *italics* in Code Sec. 6683 added by Sec. 1281(c) of the Taxpayer Relief Act of 1997, H.R. 2014, 8/5/97.
   1. added matter in Code Sec. 6683
Effective Date (Sec. 1281(e), H.R. 2014, 8/5/97) effective for tax. yrs. begin. after 8/5/97.

[¶ 3364]   Code Sec. 6693.

   CAUTION.   The heading of Code Sec. 6693, following, is effective before 1/1/98. For the heading of Code Sec. 6693, effective 1/1/98, see below.

   Failure to provide reports on individual retirement accounts or annuities; penalties relating to designated nondeductible contributions.
Code Sec. 6693.

   CAUTION.   The heading of Code Sec. 6693, following, is effective 1/1/98. For the heading of Code Sec. 6693, effective before 1/1/98, see above.

   Failure to provide reports on [1]*certain tax-favored* **accounts or annuities; penalties relating to designated nondeductible contributions.**

   (a) Reports.

   (1) In general. If a person required to file a report under a provision referred to in paragraph (2) fails to file such report at the time and in the manner required by such provision, such person shall pay a penalty of $50 for each failure unless it is shown that such failure is due to reasonable cause.

   CAUTION.   Para. (a)(2), following, is effective prior to amendment by Sec. 211(e)(2)(B) and Sec. 213(c) of H.R. 2014.   For para. (a)(2) in effect after such amendments, see below.   For effective date of such amendments, see notes following this Code Sec.

   (2) Provisions. The provisions referred to in this paragraph are—
      (A) subsections (i) and (l) of section 408 (relating to individual retirement plans), and
      (B) section 220(h) (relating to medical savings accounts).

   CAUTION.   Para. (a)(2), following as amended by Sec. 211(e)(2)(B) and 213(c) of H.R. 2014. For para. (a)(2) in effect prior to such amendments, see above. For effective date of such amendments, see notes following this Code Sec.

   (2) Provisions. The provisions referred to in this paragraph are—
      (A) subsections (i) and (l) of section 408 (relating to individual retirement plans),[2]
      (B) section 220(h) (relating to medical savings accounts)[3],[4]
      [5]*(C) section 529(d) (relating to qualified State tuition programs)*[6], *and*
      [7](D) Section 530(h) (relating to education individual retirement accounts).
   This subsection shall not apply to any report which is an information return described in section 6724(d)(1)(C)(i) or a payee statement described in section 6724(d)(2)(W). [8]*This subsection shall not apply to any report which is an information return described in section 6724(d)(1)(C)(i) or a payee statement described in section 6724(d)(2)(X).*

* * * * * * * * * * *

   (c) Penalties relating to simple retirement accounts.

* * * * * * * * * * * *

   (2) Trustee [9]*and issuer* **penalties.** A trustee [10]*or issuer* who fails—
      (A) to provide 1 or more statements required by the last sentence of section 408(i) shall pay a penalty of $50 for each day on which such failures continue, or
      (B) to provide 1 or more summary descriptions required by section 408(l)(2)(B) shall pay a penalty of $50 for each day on which such failures continue.

* * * * * * * * * * * *

[For analysis, see ¶ 403, ¶ 916, ¶ 1202. For text of Committee Report see ¶ 5005, ¶ 5361, ¶ 5370.]

[Endnote Code Sec. 6693]

Matter in *italics* in Code Sec. 6693 heading, Code Sec. 6693(a)(2)(A) and Code Sec. 6693(a)(2)(B) added by Sec. 211(e)(2)(B) and (C) of the Taxpayer Relief Act of 1997, H.R. 2014, 8/5/97, which struck out:
1. "individual retirement"
2. "and"
3. "."
Effective Date (Sec. 211(f)(1), H.R. 2014, 8/5/97) effective 1/1/98.

In Code Sec. 6693(a)(2)(B), Sec. 213(c), struck out:
4. "and" [as added by Sec. 211(e)(2)(B) of this Act, see above]
Effective Date (Sec. 213(f), H.R. 2014, 8/5/97) effective for tax. yrs. begin. after 12/31/97.

Code Sec. 6693(a)(2)(C) in *italics* was added by Sec. 211(e)(2)(B), H.R. 2014, 8/5/97.
5. added subpara. (a)(2)(C)
Effective Date (Sec. 211(f)(1), H.R. 2014, 8/5/97) effective 1/1/98.

Matter in *italics* in Code Sec. 6693(a)(2)(C) and Code Sec. 6693(a)(2)(D) added by Sec. 213(c), H.R. 2014, 8/5/97, which struck out:
6. "."
7. added subpara. (a)(2)(D)
Effective Date (Sec. 213(f), H.R. 2014, 8/5/97) effective for tax. yrs. begin. after 12/31/97.

Matter in *italics* in Code Sec. 6693(a) added by Sec. 1602(a)(4), H.R. 2014, 8/5/97, which struck out:
8. "This subsection shall not apply to any report which is an information return described in section 6724(d)(1)(C)(i) or a payee statement described in section 6724(d)(2)(W)."
Effective Date (Sec. 1602(i), H.R. 2014, 8/5/97) effective for tax. yrs. begin. after 12/31/96.

Matter in *italics* in Code Sec. 6693(c)(2) added by Sec. 1601(d)(1)(C)(ii)(I) and (II), H.R. 2014, 8/5/97.
9. added matter in the heading of para. (c)(2)
10. added matter in para. (c)(2)
Effective Date (Sec. 1601(j)(1), H.R. 2014, 8/5/97) effective for tax. yrs. begin. after 12/31/96.

[¶ 3365] Code Sec. 6695. Other assessable penalties with respect to the preparation of income tax returns for other persons.

* * * * * * * * * * * *

[1] *(g) Failure to be diligent in determining eligibility for earned income credit. Any person who is an income tax preparer with respect to any return or claim for refund who fails to comply with due diligence requirements imposed by the Secretary by regulations with respect to determining eligibility for, or the amount of, the credit allowable by section 32 shall pay a penalty of $100 for each such failure.*

[For analysis, see ¶ 2410. For text of Committee Report see ¶ 5162.]

[Endnote Code Sec. 6695]

Code Sec. 6695(g) in *italics* was added by Sec. 1085(a)(2) of the Taxpayer Relief Act of 1997, H.R. 2014, 8/5/97.
1. added subsection (g)
Effective Date (Sec. 1085(e)(1), H.R. 2014, 8/5/97) effective for tax. yrs. begin. after 12/31/96.

[¶ 3366] Code Sec. 6707. Failure to furnish information regarding tax shelters.

(a) Failure to register tax shelter.

(1) Imposition of penalty. If a person who is required to register a tax shelter under section 6111(a)—

(A) fails to register such tax shelter on or before the date described in section 6111(a)(1), or

(B) files false or incomplete information with the Secretary with respect to such registration,

such person shall pay a penalty with respect to such registration in the amount determined under [1]*paragraph (2) or (3), as the case may be.* No penalty shall be imposed under the preceding sentence with respect to any failure which is due to reasonable cause.

(2) Amount of penalty. [2]*Except as provided in paragraph (3), the penalty* imposed under paragraph (1) with respect to any tax shelter shall be an amount equal to the greater of—

(A) 1 percent of the aggregate amount invested in such tax shelter, or

(B) $500.

[3]*(3) Confidential arrangements.*

(A) In general. In the case of a tax shelter (as defined in section 6111(d)), the penalty imposed under paragraph (1) shall be an amount equal to the greater of—

(i) 50 percent of the fees paid to all promoters of the tax shelter with respect to offerings made before the date such shelter is registered under section 6111, or

(ii) $10,000.

Clause (i) shall be applied by substituting "75 percent" for "50 percent" in the case of an intentional failure or act described in paragraph (1).

(B) Special rule for participants required to register shelter. In the case of a person required to register such a tax shelter by reason of section 6111(d)(3)—

(i) such person shall be required to pay the penalty under paragraph (1) only if such person actually participated in such shelter,

(ii) the amount of such penalty shall be determined by taking into account under subparagraph (A)(i) only the fees paid by such person, and

(iii) such penalty shall be in addition to the penalty imposed on any other person for failing to register such shelter.

* * * * * * * * * * * *

[For analysis, see ¶ 2318. For text of Committee Report see ¶ 5128.]

[Endnote Code Sec. 6707]

Matter in *italics* in Code Sec. 6707(a)(1)(A) [sic (a)(1) ed note: Amendment cannot be made as stated, but it can be made to para. (a)(1)], Code Sec. 6707(a)(2) and Code Sec. 6707(a)(3) added by Sec. 1028(b), (d)(1) and (d)(2) of the Taxpayer Relief Act of 1997, H.R. 2014, 8/5/97, which struck out:

1. "paragraph (2)"
2. "The penalty"
3. added para. (a)(3)

Effective Date (Sec. 1028(e)(1), H.R. 2014, 8/5/97) effective for any tax shelter (as defined in Code Sec. 6111(d) [as amended by Sec. 1028(a), H.R. 1028, 8/5/97]) interests in which are offered to potential participants after the Secretary of the Treasury prescribes guidance with respect to meeting requirements added by such amendments.

[¶ 3367]   Code Sec. 6715.   Dyed fuel sold for use or used in taxable use.

* * * * * * * * * * * *

(c) Definitions. For purposes of this section—

CAUTION.   Para. (c)(1), following, is effective before 7/1/98. For para. (c)(1), effective after 6/30/98, see below.

(1) Dyed fuel. The term "dyed fuel" means any dyed diesel fuel, whether or not the fuel was dyed pursuant to section 4082.

CAUTION.   Para. (c)(1), following, is effective after 6/30/98. For para. (c)(1), effective before 7/1/98, see above.

(1) Dyed fuel. The term "dyed fuel" means any dyed diesel fuel [1]*or kerosene,* whether or not the fuel was dyed pursuant to section 4082.

* * * * * * * * * * * * *

[For analysis, see ¶ 2208. For text of Committee Report see ¶ 5130.]

[Endnote Code Sec. 6715]

Matter in *italics* in Code Sec. 6715(c)(1) added by Sec. 1032(e)(11) of the Taxpayer Relief Act of 1997, H.R. 2014, 8/5/97.

1. added matter in paragraph (c)(1)

Effective Date (Sec. 1032(f), H.R. 2014, 8/5/97) effective 7/1/98.

[¶ 3368]   Code Sec. 6724.   Waiver; definitions and special rules.

* * * * * * * * * * * *

(d) Definitions. For purposes of this part—

(1) Information return. The term "information return" means—

CAUTION.   Subpara. (d)(1)(A), following, is effective for payments made before 1/1/98. For subpara. (d)(1)(A) effective for payments made after 12/31/97, see below.

(A) any statement of the amount of payments to another person required by—

(i) section 6041(a) or (b) (relating to certain information at source),

(ii) section 6042(a)(1) (relating to payments of dividends),

(iii) section 6044(a)(1) (relating to payments of patronage dividends),

(iv) section 6049(a) (relating to payments of interest),

(v) section 6050A(a) (relating to reporting requirements of certain fishing boat operators),

(vi) section 6050N(a) (relating to payments of royalties), or

(vii) section 6051(d) (relating to information returns with respect to income tax withheld),

CAUTION.   Subpara. (d)(1)(A), following, is effective for payments made after 12/31/97. For subpara. (d)(1)(A) effective for payments made before 1/1/98, see above. These provisions were further amended by H.R. 2014, Sec. 961(b), effective 8/5/97, see history.

(A) any statement of the amount of payments to another person required by—

(i) section 6041(a) or (b) (relating to certain information at source),

(ii) section 6042(a)(1) (relating to payments of dividends),

(iii) section 6044(a)(1) (relating to payments of patronage dividends),

(iv) section 6049(a) (relating to payments of interest),

(v) section 6050A(a) (relating to reporting requirements of certain fishing boat operators),

(vi) section 6050N(a) (relating to payments of royalties),

(vii) section 6051(d) (relating to information returns with respect to income tax withheld),[1]

(viii) section 6050R (relating to returns relating to certain purchases of fish), and [Ed. note: H.R. 2014 does not replace 'and" with "or"][2] *or*

[3]*(ix) section 110(d) (relating to qualified lessee construction allowances for short-term leases),*

(B) any return required by—

(i) section 6041A(a) or (b) (relating to returns of direct sellers),

(ii) section 6045(a) or (d) (relating to returns of brokers),

(iii) section 6050H(a) (relating to mortgage interest received in trade or business from individuals),

CAUTION. Subpara. (d)(1)(B)(iv), following, is effective prior to the 60th day after the date on which the temporary regulations discussed under Sec. 20415(c) of P.L. 103-322 are prescribed. For Sec. 20415(c) of P.L. 103-322, see note following Code Sec. 6724. For subpara. (d)(1)(B)(iv) effective on the 60th day after the date on which the temporary regulations discussed under Sec. 20415(c) of P.L. 103-322 are prescribed, see below.

(iv) section 6050I(a) (relating to cash received in trade or business, etc.),

CAUTION. Subpara. (d)(1)(B)(iv), following, is effective on the 60th day after the date on which the temporary regulations discussed under Sec. 20415(c) of P.L. 103-322 are prescribed. For Sec. 20415(c) of P.L. 103-322, see note following Code Sec. 6724. For subpara. (d)(1)(B)(iv) effective prior to the 60th day after the date on which the temporary regulations discussed under Sec. 20415(c) of P.L. 103-322 are prescribed, see above.

(iv) section 6050I(a) or (g)(1) (relating to cash received in trade or business, etc.),

(v) section 6050J(a) (relating to foreclosures and abandonments of security),

(vi) section 6050K(a) (relating to exchanges of certain partnership interests),

(vii) section 6050L(a) (relating to returns relating to certain dispositions of donated property),

(viii) section 6050P (relating to returns relating to the cancellation of indebtedness by certain financial entities),

CAUTION. Clauses (d)(1)(B)(ix)-(xiv), following, are effective for expenses paid before 1/1/98 (in tax. yrs. end. before 1/1/98), for education furnished in academic periods begin. before 1/1/98. For clauses (d)(1)(B)(ix)-(xv), effective for expenses paid after 12/31/97 (in tax. yrs. end. after 12/31/97), for education furnished in academic periods begin. after 12/31/97, see below.

(ix) section 6050Q (relating to certain long-term care benefits),

(x) section 6052(a) (relating to reporting payment of wages in the form of group [term] life insurance),

(xi) section 6053(c)(1) (relating to reporting with respect to certain tips),

(xii) subsection (b) or (e) of section 1060 (relating to reporting requirements of transferors and transferees in certain asset acquisitions),

(xiii) subparagraph (A) or (C) of subsection (c)(4) of section 4093 (relating to information reporting with respect to tax on diesel and aviation fuels),

(xiv) section 4101(d) (relating to information reporting with respect to fuels taxes), or

CAUTION. Clauses (d)(1)(B)(ix)-(xv)[sic (xvi)], following, are effective for expenses paid after 12/31/97 (in tax. yrs. end. after 12/31/97), for education furnished in academic periods begin. after 12/31/97. For clauses (d)(1)(B)(ix)-(xiv) effective for expenses paid before 1/1/98 (in tax. yrs. end. before 1/1/98), for education furnished in academic periods begin. before 1/1/98, see above.

[4](ix) section 6050S (relating to returns relating to payments for qualified tuition and related expenses),

[5](x) section 6050Q (relating to certain long-term care benefits),

[6](xi) section 6052(a) (relating to reporting payment of wages in the form of group [term] life insurance),

[7](xii) section 6053(c)(1) (relating to reporting with respect to certain tips),

[8](xiii) subsection (b) or (e) of section 1060 (relating to reporting requirements of transferors and transferees in certain asset acquisitions),

[9](xiv) subparagraph (A) or (C) of subsection (c)(4) of section 4093 (relating to information reporting with respect to tax on diesel and aviation fuels),

[10](xv) section 4101(d) (relating to information reporting with respect to fuels taxes), or

(xv) [sic (xvi)] subparagraph (C) of section 338(h)(10) (relating to information required to be furnished to the Secretary in case of elective recognition of gain or loss), and

* * * * * * * * * * *

(2) **Payee statement.** The term "payee statement" means any statement required to be furnished under—

* * * * * * * * * * *

[11]*(R) section 6050R(c) (relating to returns relating to certain purchases of fish),*

(S) section 6051 (relating to receipts for employees),

(T) section 6052(b) (relating to returns regarding payment of wages in the form of group-term life insurance),

(U) section 6053(b) or (c) (relating to reports of tips),

(V) section 6048(b)(1)(B) (relating to foreign trust reporting requirements),

(W) section 4093(c)(4)(B) (relating to certain purchasers of diesel and aviation fuels),

CAUTION.   Subparas. (d)(2)(Y) and (X), following, are effective for expenses paid before 1/1/98 (in tax. yrs. end. before 1/1/98), for education furnished in academic periods begin. before 1/1/98. For subparas. (d)(2)(Y)-(Z) effective for expenses paid after 12/31/97 (in tax. yrs. end. after 12/31/97), for education furnished in academic periods begin. after 12/31/97, see below.

(X) section 408(i) (relating to reports with respect to individual retirement plans) to any person other than the Secretary with respect to the amount of payments made to such person, or

(Y) section 6047(d) (relating to reports by plan administrators) to any person other than the Secretary with respect to the amount of payments made to such person.

CAUTION.   Subparas. (d)(2)(Y)-(Z), following, are effective for expenses paid after 12/31/97 (in tax. yrs. end. after 12/31/97), for education furnished in academic periods begin. after 12/31/97. For subparas. (d)(2)(Y) and (X) effective for expenses paid before 1/1/98 (in tax. yrs. end. before 1/1/98), for education furnished in academic periods begin. before 1/1/98, see above..

(X) section 408(i) (relating to reports with respect to individual retirement plans) to any person other than the Secretary with respect to the amount of payments made to such person,[12]

(Y) section 6047(d) (relating to reports by plan administrators) to any person other than the Secretary with respect to the amount of payments made to such person[13]*, or*

[14]*(Z) section 6050S (relating to returns relating to qualified tuition and related expenses).* Such term also includes any form, statement, or schedule required to be furnished to the recipient of any amount from which tax was required to be deducted and withheld under chapter 3 (or from which tax would be required to be so deducted and withheld but for an exemption under this title or any treaty obligation of the United States).

* * * * * * * * * * *

CAUTION.   Subsec. (e), following, is effective for partnership tax. yrs. end. on or after 12/31/97.

[15]*(e) Special rules for certain partnership returns. In any partnership return under section 6031(a) is required under section 6011(e) to be filed on magnetic media or in other machine-readable form, for purposes of this part, each schedule required to be included with such return with respect to each partner shall be treated as a separate information return.*

[For analysis, see ¶ 410, ¶ 2702. For text of Committee Report see ¶ 5002, ¶ 5208.]

[Endnote Code Sec. 6724]

Matter in *italics* in Code Sec. 6724(d)(1)(A)(vii), Code Sec. 6724(d)(1)(A)(viii), and Code Sec. 6724(d)(1)(A)(ix) added by Sec. 1213(b) of the Taxpayer Relief Act of 1997, H.R. 2014, 8/5/97, which struck out:

1. "or"
2. added matter in clause (d)(1)(A)(viii)
3. added clause (d)(1)(A)(ix)

Effective Date (Sec. 1213(e), H.R. 2014, 8/5/97) effective for leases entered into after 8/5/97.

Matter in *italics* in Code Sec. 6724(d)(1)(B)(ix), Code Sec. 6724(d)(1)(B)(x), Code Sec. 6724(d)(1)(B)(xi), Code Sec. 6724(d)(1)(B)(xii), Code Sec. 6724(d)(1)(B)(xiii), Code Sec. 6724(d)(1)(B)(xiv), and Code Sec. 6724(d)(1)(B)(xv) added by Sec. 201(c)(2)(A), H.R. 2014, which struck out:

4. added clause (d)(1)(B)(ix)
5. "(ix)"
6. "(x)"
7. "(xi)"
8. "(xii)"
9. "(xiii)"
10. "(xiv)"

Effective Date (Sec. 201(f), H.R. 2014, 8/5/97) effective for expenses paid after 12/31/97 (in tax. yrs. end. after 12/31/97), for education furnished in academic periods begin. after 12/31/97.

Matter in *italics* in Code Sec. 6724(d)(2)(R), Code Sec. 6724(d)(2)(S), Code Sec. 6724(d)(2)(T), Code Sec. 6724(d)(2)(U), Code Sec. 6724(d)(2)(V), Code Sec. 6724(d)(2)(W), Code Sec. 6724(d)(2)(X), and Code Sec. 6724(d)(2)(Y) added by Sec. 1602(d)(2)(A), H.R. 2014, which struck out:

11. "(R) section 6051 (relating to receipts for employees),
"(S) section 6050R(c) (relating to returns relating to certain purchases of fish),
"(T) section 6052(b) (relating to returns regarding payment of wages in the form of group-term life insurance),
"(U) section 6053(b) or (c) (relating to reports of tips),
"(U)[sic V] section 4093(c)(4)(B) (relating to certain purchasers of diesel and aviation fuels),
"(V)[sic W] section 6048(b)(1)(B) (relating to foreign trust reporting requirements),
"(W)[sic X] section 408(i) (relating to reports with respect to individual retirement plans) to any person other than the Secretary with respect to the amount of payments made to such person, or
"(X)[sic Y] section 6047(d) (relating to reports to plan administrators) to any person other than the Secretary with respect to the amount of payments made to such person."

Effective Date (Sec. 1602(i), H.R. 2014, 8/5/97) effective for benefits paid after 12/31/96.

Matter in *italics* in Code Sec. 6724(d)(2)(X), Code Sec. 6724(d)(2)(Y), and Code Sec. 6724(d)(2)(Z) added by Sec. 201(c)(2)(B), H.R. 2014, which struck out:

12. "or"
13. "."
14. added subpara. Code Sec. 6724(d)(2)(Z)

Effective Date (Sec. 201(f), H.R. 2014, 8/5/97) effective for expenses paid after 12/31/97 (in tax. yrs. end. after 12/31/97), for education furnished in academic periods begin. after 12/31/97.

Code Sec. 6724(e) was added by Sec. 1223(b), H.R. 2014.
15. added subsec. (e)

Effective Date (Sec. 1226, H.R. 2014, 8/5/97) effective for partnership tax. yrs end. on or after 12/31/97.

[¶ 3369]   Code Sec. 7213.   Unauthorized disclosure of information.

(a) Returns and return information.

* * * * * * * * * * * *

  (2) State and other employees. It shall be unlawful for any person (not described in paragraph (1)) willfully to disclose to any person, except as authorized in this title, any return or return information (as defined in section 6103(b)) acquired by him or another person under subsection (d), (i)(3)(B)(i), (l)(6), (7), (8) , (9), (10), (12), [1]‑B*(15), or (16)* or (m)(2), (4), [2]‑P(5), (6), or (7) of section 6103. Any violation of this paragraph shall be a felony punishable by a fine in any amount not exceeding $5,000, or imprisonment of not more than 5 years, or both, together with the costs of prosecution.

* * * * * * * * * * * *

[For analysis, see ¶ 2407. For text of Committee Report see ¶ 5551.]

[Endnote Code Sec. 7213]

H.R. 2015. Matter in *italics* in Code Sec. 7213(a)(2) added by Sec. 11024(b)(8) of the Balanced Budget Act of 1997, H.R. 2015, 8/5/97, which struck out:

1_B. "or (15)," [H.R. 2015]

Effective Date Effective 8/5/97.

H.R. 1226.

Matter in *italics* in Code Sec. 7213(a)(2) added by Sec. 2(c) of the Taxpayer Browsing Protection Act of 1997, H.R. 1226, 8/5/97.

1_P. added matter in para. (a)(2) [H.R. 1226]

Effective Date (Sec. 2(c), H.R. 1226, 8/5/97) effective for violations occurring on and after 8/5/97.

[¶ 3370] Code Sec.¹⁻ᴾ 7213A.   **Unauthorized inspection of returns or return information.**

(a) Prohibitions.

    (1) Federal employees and other persons. It shall be unlawful for—

      (A) any officer or employee of the United States, or

      (B) any person described in section 6103(n) or an officer or employee of any such person,

    willfully to inspect, except as authorized in this title, any return or return information.

    (2) State and other employees. It shall be unlawful for any person (not described in paragraph (1)) willfully to inspect, except as authorized in this title, any return or return information acquired by such person or another person under a provision of section 6103 referred to in section 7213(a)(2).

(b) Penalty.

    (1) In general. Any violation of subsection (a) shall be punishable upon conviction by a fine in any amount not exceeding $1,000, or imprisonment of not more than 1 year, or both, together with the costs of prosecution.

    (2) Federal officers or employees. An officer or employee of the United States who is convicted of any violation of subsection (a) shall, in addition to any other punishment, be dismissed from office or discharged from employment.

(c) Definitions. For purposes of this section, the terms "inspect", "return", and "return information" have the respective meanings given such terms by section 6103(b).

     [For analysis, see ¶ 2407. For text of Committee Report see ¶ 5551.]

[Endnote Code Sec. 7213A]

   H.R. 1226. Code Sec. 7213A was added by Sec. 2(a) of the Taxpayer Browsing Protection Act of 1997, H.R. 1226, 8/5/97.

   1. added Code Sec. 7213A [H.R. 1226]

Effective Date (Sec. 2(c), H.R. 1226, 8/5/97) effective for violations occurring on and after 8/5/97.

[¶ 3371] Code Sec. 7232.   ¹*Failure to register under section 4101, false representations of registration status, etc.*

Every person who fails to register as required by section 4101, or who in connection with any purchase of ²*any taxable fuel (as defined in section 4083)*, or aviation fuel falsely represents himself to be registered as provided by section 4101, or who willfully makes any false statement in an application for registration under section 4101, shall, upon conviction thereof, be fined not more than $5,000, or imprisoned not more than 5 years, or both, together with the costs of prosecution.

     [For analysis, see ¶ 2208. For text of Committee Report see ¶ 5130.]

[Endnote Code Sec. 7232]

Matter in *italics* in Code Sec. 7232 added by Sec. 1032(d)(12)(A) and (B) of the Taxpayer Relief Act of 1997, H.R. 2014, 8/5/97, which struck out:

1. "SEC. 7232. FAILURE TO REGISTER, OR FALSE STATEMENT BY MANUFACTURER OR PRODUCER OF GASOLINE, DIESEL FUEL, OR AVIATION FUEL."

2. "gasoline, diesel fuel"

Effective Date (Sec. 1032(e), H.R. 2014, 8/5/97) effective 7/1/98.

[¶ 3372] Code Sec. 7421.   Prohibition of suits to restrain assessment or collection.

CAUTION.   Subsec. (a), following, is effective for tax. yrs. end. before 12/31/97. For subsec. (a) effective for tax. yrs. end. on or after 12/31/97, see below.

(a) Tax. Except as provided in sections 6212(a) and (c), 6213(a), [1]*6225(b),*6672(b), 6694(c), and 7426(a) and (b)(1), [2]*7429(b), and 7436,* no suit for the purpose of restraining the assessment or collection of any tax shall be maintained in any court by any person, whether or not such person is the person against whom such tax was assessed.

CAUTION.   Subsec. (a), following, is effective for tax. yrs. end. on or after 12/31/97. For subsec. (a) effective for tax. yrs. end. before 12/31/97, see above.

(a) Tax. Except as provided in sections 6212(a) and (c), 6213(a), 6225(b), [3]*6246(b),* 6672(b), 6694(c), and 7426(a) and (b)(1), 7429(b), and 7436, no suit for the purpose of restraining the assessment or collection of any tax shall be maintained in any court by any person, whether or not such person is the person against whom such tax was assessed.

* * * * * * * * * * *

[For analysis, see ¶ 2329. For text of Committee Report see ¶ 5303.]

[Endnote Code Sec. 7421]

Matter in *italics* in Code Sec. 7421(a) added by Sec. 1239(e)(3) of the Taxpayer Relief Act of 1997, H.R. 2014, 8/5/97.
1. added matter in subsec. (a)
Effective Date (Sec. 1239(f), H.R. 2014, 8/5/97) effective for partnership tax. yrs. end. after 8/5/97.

Matter in *italics* in Code Sec. 7421(a) added by Sec. 1454(b)(2), H.R. 2014, 8/5/97, which struck out:
2. "and 7429(b)"
Effective Date (Sec. 1454(c), H.R. 2014, 8/5/97) effective 8/5/97.

Matter in *italics* in Code Sec. 7421(a) added by Sec. 1222(b)(1), H.R. 2014, 8/5/97.
3. added matter in subsec. (a)
Effective Date (Sec. 1226, H.R. 2014, 8/5/97) effective for partnership tax. yrs. end. on or after 12/31/97.

[¶ 3373] Code Sec. 7430.   Awarding of costs and certain fees.

* * * * * * * * * * *

(b) Limitations.

* * * * * * * * * * *

[1]*(5) [sic (4)] Period for applying to IRS for administrative costs. An award may be made under subsection (a) by the Internal Revenue Service for reasonable administrative costs only if the prevailing party files an application with the Internal Revenue Service for such costs before the 91st day after the date on which the final decision of the Internal Revenue Service as to the determination of the tax, interest, or penalty is mailed to such party.*
(c) Definitions. For purposes of this section—

* * * * * * * * * * *

(4) Prevailing party.

* * * * * * * * * * *

[2]*(D) Special rules for applying net worth requirement. In applying the requirements of section 2412(d)(2)(B) of title 28, United States Code, for purposes of subparagraph (A)(iii) of this paragraph—*
    (i) the net worth limitation in clause (i) of such section shall apply to—
        (I) an estate but shall be determined as of the date of the decedent's death, and

(II) a trust but shall be determined as of the last day of the taxable year involved in the proceeding, and

(ii) individuals filing a joint return shall be treated as separate individuals for purposes of clause *(i)* of such section.

* * * * * * * * * *

(f) Right of appeal.

* * * * * * * * * * *

(2) Administrative proceedings. A decision granting or denying (in whole or in part) an award for reasonable administrative costs under subsection (a) by the Internal Revenue Service shall be subject to [3]*the filing of a petition for review with* the Tax Court under rules similar to the rules under section 7463 (without regard to the amount in dispute). [4]*If the Secretary sends by certified or registered mail a notice of such decision to the petitioner, no proceeding in the Tax Court may be initiated under this paragraph unless such petition is filed before the 91st day after the date of such mailing.*

[5]*(3) Appeal of Tax Court decision. An order of the Tax Court disposing of a petition under paragraph (2) shall be reviewable in the same manner as a decision of the Tax Court, but only with respect to the matters determined in such order.*

[For analysis, see ¶ 2335, ¶ 2336. For text of Committee Report see ¶ 5252, ¶ 5302.]

[Endnote Code Sec. 7430]

Code Sec. 7430(b)(5) [sic (4)], in *italics,* was added by Sec. 1285(b) of the Taxpayer Relief Act of 1997, H.R. 2014, 8/5/97.

1. added para. (b)(5) [sic (b)(4)]

Effective Date (Sec. 1285(d), H.R. 2014, 8/5/97) effective for civil actions or proceedings commenced after 8/5/97.

Code Sec. 7430(c)(4)(d), in *italics,* was added by Sec. 1453(a), H.R. 2014, 8/5/97.

2. added subpara. (c)(4)(D)

Effective Date (Sec. 1453(b), H.R. 2014, 8/5/97) effective for proceedings commenced after 8/5/97.

Matter in *italics* in Code Sec. 7430(f)(2) and Code Sec. 7430(f)(3) added by Sec. 1285(a), (c)(1), and (c)(2), H.R. 2014, 8/5/97, which struck out:

3. "appeal to"

4. added matter in para. (f)(2)

5. added para. (f)(3)

Effective Date (Sec. 1285(d), H.R. 2014, 8/5/97) effective for civil actions or proceedings commenced after 8/5/97.

[¶ 3374]   Code Sec. 7431.   Civil damages for unauthorized [1]*inspection or* **disclosure of returns and return information.**

(a) In General.

(1) [2]*Inspection or disclosure* **by employee of United States.** If any officer or employee of the United States knowingly, or by reason of negligence, [3]*inspects or discloses* any return or return information with respect to a taxpayer in violation of any provision of section 6103, such taxpayer may bring a civil action for damages against the United States in a district court of the United States.

(2) [4]*Inspection or disclosure* **by a person who is not an employee of United States.** If any person who is not an officer or employee of the United States knowingly, or by reason of negligence, [5]*inspects or discloses* any return or return information with respect to a taxpayer in violation of any provision of section 6103, such taxpayer may bring a civil action for damages against such person in a district court of the United States.

[6]*(b) Exceptions.* No liability shall arise under this section with respect to any inspection or disclosure—

(1) which results from a good faith, but erroneous, interpretation of section 6103, or

(2) which is requested by the taxpayer.

(c) Damages. In any action brought under subsection (a), upon a finding of liability on the part of the defendant, the defendant shall be liable to the plaintiff in an amount equal to the sum of—

(1) the greater of—

(A) $1,000 for each act of unauthorized [7-P]*inspection or* disclosure of a return or return information with respect to which such defendant is found liable, or

(B) the sum of—

(i) the actual damages sustained by the plaintiff as a result of such unauthorized [8-P]*inspection or* disclosure, plus

(ii) in the case of a [9-P]*willful inspection or disclosure or an inspection or disclosure* which is the result of gross negligence, punitive damages, plus

* * * * * * * * * * * *

(d) Period for bringing action. Notwithstanding any other provision of law, an action to enforce any liability created under this section may be brought, without regard to the amount in controversy, at any time within 2 years after the date of discovery by the plaintiff of the unauthorized [10-P]*inspection or* disclosure.

[11-P]*(e) Notification of unlawful inspection and disclosure. If any person is criminally charged by indictment or information with inspection or disclosure of a taxpayer's return or return information in violation of—*

(1) paragraph (1) or (2) of section 7213(a),

(2) section 7213A(a), or

(3) subparagraph (B) of section 1030(a)(2) of title 18, United States Code,

the Secretary shall notify such taxpayer as soon as practicable of such inspection or disclosure.

[12-P]*(f) Definitions. For purposes of this section, the terms "inspect", "inspection", "return", and "return information" have the respective meanings given such terms by section 6103(b).*

[13-P]*(g) Extension to information obtained under section 3406. For purposes of this section—*

(1) any information obtained under section 3406 (including information with respect to any payee certification failure under subsection (d) thereof) shall be treated as return information, and

(2) [14-P]*any inspection or use* of such information other than for purposes of meeting any requirement under section 3406 or (subject to the safeguards set forth in section 6103) for purposes permitted under section 6103 shall be treated as a violation of section 6103.

For purposes of subsection (b), the reference to section 6103 shall be treated as including a reference to section 3406.

[1]*(g) [sic (h)] Special rules for information obtained under section 6103(k)(8). For purposes of this section, any reference to section 6103 shall be treated as including a reference to section 6311(e).*

[For analysis, see ¶ 2319, ¶ 2337, ¶ 2408. For text of Committee Report see ¶ 5205, ¶ 5551.]

[Endnote Code Sec. 7431]

H.R. 1226. Matter in *italics* in Code Sec. 7431 heading, Code Sec. 7431(a)(1), Code Sec. 7431(a)(2), Code Sec. 7431(b), Code Sec. 7431(c)(1)(A), Code Sec. 7431(c)(1)(B)(i), Code Sec. 7431(c)(1)(B)(ii), Code Sec. 7431(d), Code Sec. 7431(e), Code Sec. 7431(f), Code Sec. 7431(g) and Code Sec. 7431(g)(2) added by Sec. 3(a)(1), (a)(2), (b), (c), (d)(1)-(4), and (d)(6) of the Taxpayer Browsing Protection Act of 1997, H.R. 2015, 8/5/97, which struck out:

1_P. added matter in the heading of Code Sec. 7431 [H.R. 1226]

2_P. "Disclosure" [H.R. 1226]

3_P. "discloses" [H.R. 1226]

4_P. "Disclosure" [H.R. 1226]

5_P. "discloses" [H.R. 1226]

6_P. "(b) No liability for good faith but erroneous interpretation. No liability shall arise under this section with respect to any disclosure which results from a good faith, but erroneous, interpretation of section 6103." [H.R. 1226]

7_P. added matter in subpara. (c)(1)(A) [H.R. 1226]
8_P. added matter in clause (c)(1)(B)(i) [H.R. 1226]
9_P. "willful disclosure or a disclosure" [H.R. 1226]
10_P. added matter in subsec. (d) [H.R. 1226]
11_P. added subsec. (e) [H.R. 1226]
12_P. "(e) Return; return information. For purposes of this section, the terms 'return' and 'return information' have the respective meanings given such terms in section 6103(b)." [H.R. 1226]
13_P. "(f)" [H.R. 1226]
14_P. "any use" [H.R. 1226]
Effective Date (Sec. 3(e), H.R. 1226, 8/5/97) effective for inspections and disclosures occurring on and after 8/5/97.

Code Sec. 7431(g) [sic (h), in *italics*, was added by Sec. 1205(c)(2) of the Taxpayer Relief Act of 1997, H.R. 2014, 8/5/97.
1. added subsec. (g) [sic (h)]
Effective Date (Sec. 1205(d), H.R. 2014, 8/5/97) effective on the day 9 months after 8/5/97.

[¶ 3375] Code Sec.¹ 7436. Proceedings for determination of employment status.

(a) Creation of remedy. If, in connection with an audit of any person, there is an actual controversy involving a determination by the Secretary as part of an examination that—

(1) one or more individuals performing services for such person are employees of such person for purposes of subtitle C, or

(2) such person is not entitled to the treatment under subsection (a) of section 530 of the Revenue Act of 1978 with respect to such an individual,

upon the filing of an appropriate pleading, the Tax Court may determine whether such a determination by the Secretary is correct. Any such redetermination by the Tax Court shall have the force and effect of a decision of the Tax Court and shall be reviewable as such.

(b) Limitations.

(1) Petitioner. A pleading may be filed under this section only by the person for whom the services are performed.

(2) Time for filing action. If the Secretary sends by certified or registered mail notice to the petitioner of a determination by the Secretary described in subsection (a), no proceeding may be initiated under this section with respect to such determination unless the pleading is filed before the 91st day after the date of such mailing.

(3) No adverse inference from treatment while action is pending. If, during the pendency of any proceeding brought under this section, the petitioner changes his treatment for employment tax purposes of any individual whose employment status as an employee is involved in such proceeding (or of any individual holding a substantially similar position) to treatment as an employee, such change shall not be taken into account in the Tax Court's determination under this section.

(c) Small case procedures.

(1) In general. At the option of the petitioner, concurred in by the Tax Court or a division thereof before the hearing of the case, proceedings under this section may (notwithstanding the provisions of section 7453) be conducted subject to the rules of evidence, practice, and procedure applicable under section 7463 if the amount of employment taxes placed in dispute is $10,000 or less for each calendar quarter involved.

(2) Finality of decisions. A decision entered in any proceeding conducted under this subsection shall not be reviewed in any other court and shall not be treated as a precedent for any other case not involving the same petitioner and the same determinations.

(3) Certain rules to apply. Rules similar to the rules of the last sentence of subsection (a), and subsections (c), (d), and (e), of section 7463 shall apply to proceedings conducted under this subsection.

(d) Special rules.

(1) Restrictions on assessment and collection pending action, etc. The principles of subsections (a), (b), (c), (d) and (f) of section 6213, section 6214(a), section 6215, section 6503(a), section 6512, and section 7481 shall apply to proceedings brought under this section in the same manner as if the Secretary's determination described in subsection (a) were a notice of deficiency.

(2) **Awarding of costs and certain fees.** Section 7430 shall apply to proceedings brought under this section.

(e) **Employment tax.** The term "employment tax" means any tax imposed by subtitle C.

[For analysis, see ¶ 2329. For text of Committee Report see ¶ 5303.]

[Endnote Code Sec. 7436]
Code Sec. 7436 was added by Sec. 1454(a) of the Taxpayer Relief Act of 1997, H.R. 2014, 8/5/97.
1. added Code Sec. 7436
Effective Date (Sec. 1454(c), H.R. 2014, 8/5/97) effective 8/5/97.

[¶ 3376]   Code Sec.[1] 7437.   Cross references.

(1) For determination of amount of any tax, additions to tax, etc., in title 11 cases, see section 505 of title 11 of the United States Code.

(2) For exclusion of tax liability from discharge in cases under title 11 of the United States Code, see section 523 of such title 11.

(3) For recognition of tax liens in cases under title 11 of the United States Code, see sections 545 and 724 of such title 11.

(4) For collection of taxes in connection with plans for individuals with regular income in cases under title 11 of the United States Code, see section 1328 of such title 11.

(5) For provisions permitting the United States to be made party defendant in a proceeding in a State court for the foreclosure of a lien upon real estate where the United States may have claim upon the premises involved, see section 2410 of Title 28 of the United States Code.

(6) For priority of lien of the United States in case of insolvency, see section 3713(a) of title 31, United States Code.

(7) For interest on judgments for overpayments, see section 2411(a) of Title 28 of the United States Code.

(8) For review of a Tax Court decision, see section 7482.

(9) For statute prohibiting suits to replevy property taken under revenue laws, see section 2463 of Title 28 of the United States Code.

[Endnote Code Sec. 7437]
Matter in *italics* in Code Sec. 7437 added by Sec. 1454(a) of the Taxpayer Relief Act of 1997, H.R. 2014, 8/5/97, which struck out:
1. "§7436"
Effective Date (Sec. 1454(c), H.R. 2014, 8/5/97) effective 8/5/97.

[¶ 3377]   Code Sec. 7453.   Rules of practice, procedure, and evidence.
Except in the case of proceedings conducted under [1]*section 7436(c) or 7463*, the proceedings of the Tax Court and its divisions shall be conducted in accordance with such rules of practice and procedure (other than rules of evidence) as the Tax Court may prescribe and in accordance with the rules of evidence applicable in trials without a jury in the United States District Court of the District of Columbia.

[For analysis, see ¶ 2329. For text of Committee Report see ¶ 5303.]

[Endnote Code Sec. 7453]
Matter in *italics* in Code Sec. 7453 added by Sec. 1454(b)(3) of the Taxpayer Relief Act of 1997, H.R. 2014, 8/5/97, which struck out:
1. "section 7463"
Effective Date (Sec. 1454(c), H.R. 2014, 8/5/97) effective 8/5/97.

[¶ 3378]   Code Sec. 7459.   Reports and decisions.

* * * * * * * * * * * *

(c) **Date of decision.** A decision of the Tax Court (except a decision dismissing a proceeding for lack of jurisdiction) shall be held to be rendered upon the date that an order specifying the amount of the deficiency is entered in the records of the Tax Court or, in the case of a declaratory judgment proceeding under part IV of this subchapter or under section 7428 or in the case of an action brought under section 6226¹, *6228(a), or 6234(c)* the date of the court's order entering the decision. If the Tax Court dismisses a proceeding for reasons other than lack of jurisdiction and is unable from the record to determine the amount of the deficiency determined by the Secretary, or if the Tax Court dismisses a proceeding for lack of jurisdiction, an order to that effect shall be entered in the records of the Tax Court, and the decision of the Tax Court shall be held to be rendered upon the date of such entry.

* * * * * * * * * * * *

[For analysis, see ¶ 1404, ¶ 1416. For text of Committee Report see ¶ 5210, ¶ 5224.]

[Endnote Code Sec. 7459]

Matter in *italics* in Code Sec. 7459(c) added by Sec. 1239(e)(1) of the Taxpayer Relief Act of 1997, H.R. 2014, 8/5/97, which struck out:

1. "or section 6228(a)"

Effective Date (Sec. 1239(f), H.R. 2014, 8/5/97) effective for partnership tax. yrs. end. after 8/5/97.

[¶ 3379]   Code Sec.¹ 7477.   Declaratory judgments relating to value of certain gifts.

(a) **Creation of remedy.** In a case of an actual controversy involving a determination by the Secretary of the value of any gift shown on the return of tax imposed by chapter 12 or disclosed on such return or in any statement attached to such return, upon the filing of an appropriate pleading, the Tax Court may make a declaration of the value of such gift. Any such declaration shall have the force and effect of a decision of the Tax Court and shall be reviewable as such.

(b) **Limitations.**

(1) **Petitioner.** A pleading may be filed under this section only by the donor.

(2) **Exhaustion of administrative remedies.** The court shall not issue a declaratory judgment or decree under this section in any proceeding unless it determines that the petitioner has exhausted all available administrative remedies within the Internal Revenue Service.

(3) **Time for bringing action.** If the Secretary sends by certified or registered mail notice of his determination as described in subsection (a) to the petitioner, no proceeding may be initiated under this section unless the pleading is filed before the 91st day after the date of such mailing.

[For analysis, see ¶ 523. For text of Committee Report see ¶ 5031.]

[Endnote Code Sec. 7477]

Code Sec. 7477 was added by Sec. 506(c)(1) of the Taxpayer Relief Act of 1997, H.R. 2014, 8/5/97.
1. added Code Sec. 7477
Effective Date (Sec. 506(e)(1), H.R. 2014, 8/5/97) effective for gifts made after 8/5/97.

[¶ 3380]   Code Sec.¹ 7479.   Declaratory judgments relating to eligibility of estate with respect to installment payments under section 6166.

(a) **Creation of remedy.** In a case of actual controversy involving a determination by the Secretary of (or a failure by the Secretary to make a determination with respect to)—

(1) whether an election may be made under section 6166 (relating to extension of time for payment of estate tax where estate consists largely of interest in closely held business) with respect to an estate, or

(2) whether the extension of time for payment of tax provided in section 6166(a) has ceased to apply with respect to an estate,

upon the filing of an appropriate pleading, the Tax Court may make a declaration with respect to whether such election may be made or whether such extension has ceased to apply. or the amount of such installment payments. Any such declaration shall have the force and effect of a decision of the Tax Court and shall be reviewable as such.

(b) Limitations.

(1) Petitioner. A pleading may be filed under this section, with respect to any estate, only—

(A) by the executor of such estate, or

(B) by any person who has assumed an obligation to make payments under section 6166 with respect to such estate (but only if each other such person is joined as a party).

(2) Exhaustion of administrative remedies. The court shall not issue a declaratory judgment or decree under this section in any proceeding unless it determines that the petitioner has exhausted all available administrative remedies within the Internal Revenue Service. A petitioner shall be deemed to have exhausted its administrative remedies with respect to a failure of the Secretary to make a determination at the expiration of 180 days after the date on which the request for such determination was made if the petitioner has taken, in a timely manner, all reasonable steps to secure such determination.

(3) Time for bringing action. If the Secretary sends by certified or registered mail notice of his determination as described in subsection (a) to the petitioner, no proceeding may be initiated under this section unless the pleading is filed before the 91st day after the date of such mailing.

[For analysis, see ¶ 2328. For text of Committee Report see ¶ 5030.]

[Endnote Code Sec. 7479]
Code Sec. 7479 was added by Sec. 505(a) of the Taxpayer Relief Act of 1997, H.R. 2014, 8/5/97.
1. added Code Sec. 7479
Effective Date (Sec. 505(c), H.R. 2014, 8/5/97) effective for estates of decedents dying after 8/5/97.

[¶ 3381] Code Sec. 7481.   Date when Tax Court decision becomes final.

* * * * * * * * * * *

(b) Nonreviewable decisions. The decision of the Tax Court in a proceeding conducted under [1]*section 7436(c) or 7463* shall become final upon the expiration of 90 days after the decision is entered.

[2]*(c) Jurisdiction over interest determinations.*

(1) In general. Notwithstanding subsection (a), if, within 1 year after the date the decision of the Tax Court becomes final under subsection (a) in a case to which this subsection applies, the taxpayer files a motion in the Tax Court for a redetermination of the amount of interest involved, then the Tax Court may reopen the case solely to determine whether the taxpayer has made an overpayment of such interest or the Secretary has made an underpayment of such interest and the amount thereof.

(2) Cases to which this subsection applies. This subsection shall apply where—

(A)

(i) an assessment has been made by the Secretary under section 6215 which includes interest as imposed by this title, and

(ii) the taxpayer has paid the entire amount of the deficiency plus interest claimed by the Secretary, and

(B) the Tax Court finds under section 6512(b) that the taxpayer has made an overpayment.

(3) Special rules. If the Tax Court determines under this subsection that the taxpayer has made an overpayment of interest or that the Secretary has made an underpayment of interest, then that determination shall be treated under section 6512(b)(1) as a determination of an overpayment of tax. An order of the Tax Court redetermining interest, when entered upon the records of the court, shall be reviewable in the same manner as a decision of the Tax Court.

* * * * * * * * * * * *

[For analysis, see ¶ 2327, ¶ 2329. For text of Committee Report see ¶ 5301, ¶ 5303.]

[Endnote Code Sec. 7481]

Matter in *italics* in Code Sec. 7481(b) added by Sec. 1454(b)(3) of the Taxpayer Relief Act of 1997, H.R. 2014, 8/5/97, which struck out:

1. "section 7463"

Effective Date (Sec. 1454(c), H.R. 2014, 8/5/97) effective 8/5/97.

Matter in *italics* in Code Sec. 7481(c) added by Sec. 1452(a), H.R. 2014, 8/5/97, which struck out:

2. "(c) Jurisdiction over interest determinations. Notwithstanding subsection (a), if—

"(1) an assessment has been made by the Secretary under section 6215 which includes interest as imposed by this title,

"(2) the taxpayer has paid the entire amount of the deficiency plus interest claimed by the Secretary, and

"(3) within 1 year after the date the decision of the Tax Court becomes final under subsection (a), the taxpayer files a petition in the Tax Court for a determination that the amount of interest claimed by the Secretary exceeds the amount of interest imposed by this title,

then the Tax Court may reopen the case solely to determine whether the taxpayer has made an overpayment of such interest and the amount of any such overpayment. If the Tax Court determines under this subsection that the taxpayer has made an overpayment of interest, then that determination shall be treated under section 6512(b)(1) as a determination of an overpayment of tax. An order of the Tax Court redetermining the interest due, when entered upon the records of the court, shall be reviewable in the same manner as a decision of the Tax Court."

Effective Date (Sec. 1452(b), H.R. 2014, 8/5/97) effective 8/5/97.

[¶ 3382]   Code Sec. 7482.   Courts of review.

* * * * * * * * * * * *

(b) Venue.

(1) In general. Except as otherwise provided in paragraphs (2) and (3), such decisions may be reviewed by the United States court of appeals for the circuit in which is located—

(A) in the case of a petitioner seeking redetermination of tax liability other than a corporation, the legal residence of the petitioner,

(B) in the case of a corporation seeking redetermination of tax liability, the principal place of business or principal office or agency of the corporation, or, if it has no principal place of business or principal office or agency in any judicial circuit, then the office to which was made the return of the tax in respect of which the liability arises,

(C) in the case of a person seeking a declaratory decision under section 7476, the principal place of business, or principal office or agency of the employer,

(D) in the case of an organization seeking a declaratory decision under section 7428, the principal office or agency of the organization,[1]

CAUTION.   Subpara. (b)(1)(E), following, is effective for partnership tax. yrs. end. before 12/31/97. For subpara. (b)(1)(E) effective for partnership tax. yrs. end. on or after 12/31/97, see below.

(E) in the case of a petition under section 6226 or 6228(a), the principal place of business of the partnership[2], *or*

CAUTION.   Subpara. (b)(1)(E), following, is effective for partnership tax. yrs. end. on or after 12/31/97. For subpara. (b)(1)(E) effective for partnership tax. yrs. end. before 12/31/97, see above.

(E) in the case of a petition under section 6226[3], 6228(a), 6247, or 6252 the principal place of business of the partnership, or

[4]*(F) in the case of a petition under section 6234(c)—*

(i) the legal residence of the petitioner if the petitioner is not a corporation, and

(ii) the place or office applicable under subparagraph (B) if the petitioner is a corporation.

If for any reason no subparagraph of the preceding sentence applies, then such decisions may be reviewed by the Court of Appeals for the District of Columbia. For purposes of this paragraph, the legal residence, principal place of business, or principal office or agency referred to herein shall be determined as of the time the petition seeking redetermination of tax liability was filed with the Tax Court or as of the time the petition seeking a declaratory decision under section 7428 or 7476, or the petition under section 6226[5], *6228(a) or 6234(c),* was filed with the Tax Court.

* * * * * * * * * * * *

[For analysis, see ¶ 1404, ¶ 1416. For text of Committee Report see ¶ 5210, ¶ 5224.]

[Endnote Code Sec. 7482]

Matter in *italics* in Code Sec. 7482(b)(1) **added** by Sec. 1239(d)(1) of the Taxpayer Relief Act of 1997, H.R. 2014, 8/5/97, which struck out:

1. "or"
2. "."

Effective Date (Sec. 1239(f), H.R. 2014, 8/5/97) effective for partnership tax. yrs. end. after 8/5/97.

3. "or 6228(a)"

Effective Date (Sec. 1226, H.R. 2014, 8/5/97) effective for partnership tax. yrs. end. on or after 12/31/97.

Matter in *italics* in Code Sec. 7482(b)(1) and Code Sec. 7482(b)(1)(F) added by Sec. 1239(d)(1) and (2), H.R. 2014, 8/5/97, which struck out:

4. added subparagraph (b)(1)(F)
5. "or 6228(a)"

Effective Date (Sec. 1239(f), H.R. 2014, 8/5/97) effective for partnership tax. yrs. end. after 8/5/97.

[¶ 3383]   Code Sec. 7485.   Bond to stay assessment and collection.

* * * * * * * * * * * *

CAUTION.   Subsec. (b), following, is effective for partnership tax. yrs. end. before 1/1/98. For subsec. (b), effective for partnership tax. yrs. end. after 12/31/97, see below.

(b) Bond in case of appeal of decision under section 6226 or section 6228(a). The condition of subsection (a) shall be satisfied if a partner duly files notice of appeal from a decision under section 6226 or 6228(a) and on or before the time the notice of appeal is filed with the Tax Court, a bond in an amount fixed by the Tax Court is filed, and with surety approved by the Tax Court, conditioned upon the payment of deficiencies attributable to the partnership items to which that decision relates as finally determined, together with any interest, penalties, additional amounts, or additions to the tax provided by law. Unless otherwise stipulated by the parties, the amount fixed by the Tax Court shall be based upon its estimate of the aggregate liability of the parties to the action.

CAUTION.   Subsec. (b), following, is effective for partnership tax. yrs. end. before 1/1/98. For subsec. (b), effective for partnership tax. yrs. end. after 12/31/97, see below.

(b) [1]*Bond in case of appeal of certain partnership-related decisions.* The condition of subsection (a) shall be satisfied if a partner duly files notice of appeal from a decision under section 6226 [2], *6228(a), 6247, or 6252* and on or before the time the notice of appeal is filed with the Tax Court, a bond in an amount fixed by the Tax Court is filed, and with surety approved by the Tax Court, conditioned upon the payment of deficiencies attributable to the partnership items to which that decision relates as finally determined, together with any interest, [3]*penalties,* additional amounts, or additions to the tax provided by law. Unless otherwise stipulated by the parties, the amount fixed by the Tax Court shall be based upon its estimate of the [4]*aggregate liability of the parties to the action.*

* * * * * * * * * * * *

[For analysis, see ¶ 1404, ¶ 1417. For text of Committee Report see ¶ 5210, ¶ 5226.]

[Endnote Code Sec. 7485]

Matter in *italics* in Code Sec. 7485(b) added by Sec. 1222(b)(4)(A) and (B) of the Taxpayer Relief Act of 1997, H.R. 2014, 8/5/97, which struck out:

1. "(b) Bond in case of appeal of decision under section 6226 or section 6228(a)."
2. "or 6228(a)"

Effective Date (Sec. 1226, H.R. 2014, 8/5/97) effective for partnership tax. yrs. end. after 12/31/97.

Matter in *italics* in Code Sec. 7485(b) added by Sec. 1241(a)(1) and (2), H.R. 2014, 8/5/97, which struck out:

3. added matter in subsec. (b)
4. "aggregate of such deficiencies"

Effective Date (Sec. 1241(b), H.R. 2014, 8/5/97) effective for partnership tax. yrs. begin. after 9/3/82. P.L. 97-248, Sec. 407(a)(3) provides:

"(3) The amendments made by sections 402, 403, and 404 [of this Act] shall apply to any partnership taxable year (or in the case of section 6232 of such Code, to any period) ending after the date of the enactment of this Act [9/3/82] if the partnership, each partner, and each indirect partner requests such application and the Secretary of the Treasury or his delegate consents to such application."

[¶ 3384]   Code Sec.[1] 7508A.   Authority to postpone certain tax-related deadlines by reason of presidentially declared disaster.

(a) In general. In the case of a taxpayer determined by the Secretary to be affected by a Presidentially declared disaster (as defined by section 1033(h)(3)), the Secretary may prescribe regulations under which a period of up to 90 days may be disregarded in determining, under the internal revenue laws, in respect of any tax liability (including any penalty, additional amount, or addition to the tax) of such taxpayer—

(1) whether any of the acts described in paragraph (1) of section 7508(a) were performed within the time prescribed therefor, and

(2) the amount of any credit or refund.

(b) Interest on overpayments and underpayments. Subsection (a) shall not apply for the purpose of determining interest on any overpayment or underpayment.

[For analysis, see ¶ 2334. For text of Committee Report see ¶ 5061.]

[Endnote Code Sec. 7508A]

Code Sec. 7508A was added by Sec. 911(a) of the Taxpayer Relief Act of 1997, H.R. 2014, 8/5/97.

1. added Code Sec. 7508A

Effective Date (Sec. 911(c), H.R. 2014, 8/5/97) effective for any period for performing an act that has not expired before 8/5/97.

Sec. 915, H.R. 2014, 8/5/97, relating to abatement of interest on underpayments by taxpayers in Presidentially declared disaster areas, is reproduced in notes following Code Sec. 6601.

[¶ 3385]   Code Sec. 7518.   Tax incentives relating to Merchant Marine capital construction funds.

* * * * * * * * * * *

(g) Tax treatment of nonqualified withdrawals.

* * * * * * * * * * * *

(6) Nonqualified withdrawals taxed at highest marginal rate.

(A) **In general.** In the case of any taxable year for which there is a nonqualified withdrawal (including any amount so treated under paragraph (5)), the tax imposed by chapter 1 shall be determined—

(i) by excluding such withdrawal from gross income, and

(ii) by increasing the tax imposed by chapter 1 by the product of the amount of such withdrawal and the highest rate of tax specified in section 1 (section 11 in the case of a corporation).

With respect to the portion of any nonqualified withdrawal made out of the capital gain account during a taxable year to which section 1(h) or 1201(a) applies, the rate of tax taken into account under the preceding sentence shall not exceed [1]*20 percent* (34 percent in the case of a corporation).

* * * * * * * * * * *

[For analysis, see ¶ 210. For text of Committee Report see ¶ 5019.]

[Endnote Code Sec. 7518]

Matter in *italics* in Code Sec. 7518(g)(6)(A) added by Sec. 311(c)(2) of the Taxpayer Relief Act of 1997, H.R. 2014, 8/5/97, which struck out:

1. "28 percent"

Effective Date (Sec. 311(d)(1), H.R. 2014, 8/5/97) effective for tax. yrs. end. after 5/6/97.

[¶ 3386] Code Sec. 7519.   Required payments for entities electing not to have required taxable year.

* * * * * * * * * * *

(f) Administrative provisions.

* * * * * * * * * * *

(4) Penalties.

(A) In general. In the case of any failure by any person to pay on the date prescribed therefor any amount required by this section, there shall be imposed on such person a penalty of 10 percent of the underpayment. For purposes of the preceding sentence, the term "underpayment" means the excess of the amount of the payment required under this section over the amount (if any) of such payment paid on or before the date prescribed therefor. [1]*No penalty shall be imposed under this subparagraph on any failure which is shown to be due to reasonable cause and not willful neglect.*

* * * * * * * * * * *

[For analysis, see ¶ 2406. For text of Committee Report see ¶ 5248.]

[Endnote Code Sec. 7519]

Matter in *italics* in Code Sec. 7519(f)(4)(A) added by Sec. 1281(d) of the Taxpayer Relief Act of 1997, H.R. 2014, 8/5/97.

1. added matter in subparagraph (f)(4)(A)

Effective Date (Sec. 1281(e), H.R. 2014, 8/5/97) effective for tax. yrs. begin. after 8/5/97.

[¶ 3387] Code Sec. 7701.   Definitions.

(a) When used in this title, where not otherwise distinctly expressed or manifestly incompatible with the intent thereof—

* * * * * * * * * * *

(4) Domestic. The term "domestic" when applied to a corporation or partnership means created or organized in the United States or under the law of the United States or of any State [1]*unless, in the case of a partnership, the Secretary provides otherwise by regulations.*

* * * * * * * * * * *

(30) United States person. The term "United States person" means—

* * * * * * * * * * *

(E) any trust if—

* * * * * * * * * * *

(ii) one or more United States [2]*persons* have the authority to control all substantial decisions of the trust.

* * * * * * * * * * *

(b) Definition of resident alien and nonresident alien.

* * * * * * * * * * * *

(7) Presence in the United States. For purposes of this subsection—

CAUTION.   Subpara. (b)(7)(A), following, is effective for tax. yrs. begin. before 1/1/98. For subpara. (b)(7)(A), effective for tax. yrs. begin. after 12/31/97, see below.

(A) In general. Except as provided in subparagraph (B) or (C), an individual shall be treated as present in the United States on any day if such individual is physically present in the United States at any time during such day.

CAUTION.   Subpara. (b)(7)(A), following, is effective for tax. yrs. begin. after 12/31/97. For subpara. (b)(7)(A), effective for tax. yrs. begin. before 1/1/98, see above.

(A) In general. Except as provided in subparagraph (B)[3], *(C), or (D)*, an individual shall be treated as present in the United States on any day if such individual is physically present in the United States at any time during such day.

* * * * * * * * * * *

CAUTION.   Subpara. (b)(7)(D), following, is effective for tax. yrs. begin. after 12/31/97.

[4]*(D) Crew members temporarily present. An individual who is temporarily present in the United States on any day as a regular member of the crew of a foreign vessel engaged in transportation between the United States and a foreign country or a possession of the United States shall not be treated as present in the United States on such day unless such individual otherwise engages in any trade or business in the United States on such day.*

* * * * * * * * * * *

[For analysis, see ¶ 529, ¶ 1426, ¶ 1624, ¶ 1628. For text of Committee Report see ¶ 5182, ¶ 5190, ¶ 5196, ¶ 5364.]

[Endnote Code Sec. 7701]

Matter in *italics* in Code Sec. 7701(a)(4) added by Sec. 1151(a) of the Taxpayer Relief Act of 1997, H.R. 2014, 8/5/97.
1. added matter in para. (a)(4)

Effective Date (Sec. 1151(b), H.R. 2014, 8/5/97) effective for partnerships created or organized after the date determined under Code Sec. 7805(b) (without regard to paragraph (2) thereof) with respect to such regulations.

Matter in *italics* in Code Sec. 7701(a)(30)(E)(ii) added by Sec. 1601(i)(3)(A), H.R. 2014, 8/5/97, which struck out:
2. "fiduciaries"

Effective Date (Sec. 1601(j)(1), H.R. 2014, 8/5/97) effective as provided in Sec. 1907(a)(3), P.L. 104-188, 8/20/96, which read as follows:

"(3) Effective date. The amendments made by this subsection shall apply—
"(A) to taxable years beginning after December 31, 1996, or
"(B) at the election of the trustee of a trust, to taxable years ending after the date of the enactment of this Act. Such an election, once made, shall be irrevocable.

To the extent prescribed in regulations by the Secretary of the Treasury or his delegate, a trust which was in existence on August 20, 1996 (other than a trust treated as owned by the grantor under subpart E of part I of subchapter J of chapter 1 of the Internal Revenue code of 1986), and which was treated as a United States person on the day before the date of the enactment of this Act may elect to continue to be treated as a United States person notwithstanding section 7701(a)(30)(E) of such Code."

Matter in *italics* in Code Sec. 7701(b)(7)(A) and Code Sec. 7701(b)(7)(D) added by Sec. 1151(a), H.R. 2014, 8/5/97, which struck out:
3. "or (C)"
4. added subpara. (b)(7)(D)

Effective Date (Sec. 1174(c)(2), H.R. 2014, 8/5/97) effective for tax. yrs. begin. after 12/31/97.

[¶ 3388]   Code Sec. 7702B.   Treatment of qualified long-term care insurance.

* * * * * * * * * * *

(c) **Qualified long-term care services.** For purposes of this section—

* * * * * * * * * * *

(2) **Chronically ill individual.**

* * * * * * * * * * *

(B) Activities for daily living. For purposes of subparagraph (A), each of the following is an activity of daily living:

(i) Eating.

(ii) Toileting.

(iii) Transferring.

(iv) Bathing.

(v) Dressing.

(vi) Continence.

A contract shall not be treated as a qualified long-term care insurance contract unless the determination of whether an individual is a chronically ill individual [1]*described in subparagraph (A)(i)* takes into account at least 5 of such activities.

* * * * * * * * * * *

(g) **Consumer protection provisions.**

* * * * * * * * * * *

(4) **Nonforfeiture requirements.**

* * * * * * * * * * *

(B) Requirements of provision. The nonforfeiture provision required under subparagraph (A) shall meet the following requirements:

* * * * * * * * * * *

(ii) The nonforfeiture provision shall provide for a benefit available in the event of a default in the payment of any premiums and the amount of the benefit may be adjusted subsequent to being initially granted only as necessary to reflect changes in claims, persistency, and interest as reflected in changes in rates for premium paying contracts approved by the [2]*appropriate State regulatory agency* for the same contract form.

(iii) The nonforfeiture provision shall provide at least one of the following:

(I) Reduced paid-up insurance.

(II) Extended term insurance.

(III) Shortened benefit period.

(IV) Other similar offerings approved by the [3]*appropriate State regulatory agency.*

* * * * * * * * * * *

[For analysis, see ¶ 1105, ¶ 1107. For text of Committee Report see ¶ 5371, ¶ 5374.]

[Endnote Code Sec. 7702B]

Matter in *italics* in Code Sec. 7702B(c)(2)(B), Code Sec. 7702B(g)(4)(B)(ii), and Code Sec. 7702B(g)(4)(B)(iii) added by Secs. 1602(b) and (e) of the Taxpayer Relief Act of 1997, H.R. 2014, 8/5/97, which struck out:

1. added matter in subpara. (c)(2)(B)
2. "Secretary"
3. "Secretary"

Effective Date (Sec. 1602(i), H.R. 2014, 8/5/97) effective for contracts issued after 12/31/96.

[¶ 3389]   Code Sec. 7704.   Certain publicly traded partnerships treated as corporations.

* * * * * * * * * * * *

CAUTION.   Subsec. (g), following, is effective for tax. yrs. begin. after 12/31/97.

[1]*(g) Exception for Electing 1987 Partnerships.*

(1) In general. Subsection (a) shall not apply to an electing 1987 partnership.

(2) Electing 1987 partnership. For purposes of this subsection, the term "electing 1987 partnership" means any publicly traded partnership if—

(A) such partnership is an existing partnership (as defined in section 10211(c)(2) of the Revenue Reconciliation Act of 1987),

(B) subsection (a) has not applied (and without regard to subsection (c)(1) would not have applied) to such partnership for all prior taxable years beginning after December 31, 1987, and before January 1, 1998, and

(C) such partnership elects the application of this subsection, and consents to the application of the tax imposed by paragraph (3), for its first taxable year beginning after December 31, 1997.

A partnership which, but for this sentence, would be treated as an electing 1987 partnership shall cease to be so treated (and the election under subparagraph (C) shall cease to be in effect) as of the 1st day after December 31, 1997, on which there has been an addition of a substantial new line of business with respect to such partnership.

(3) Additional tax on electing partnerships.

(A) Imposition of tax. There is hereby imposed for each taxable year on the income of each electing 1987 partnership a tax equal to 3.5 percent of such partnership's gross income for the taxable year from the active conduct of trades and businesses by the partnership.

(B) Adjustments in the case of tiered partnerships. For purposes of this paragraph, in the case of a partnership which is a partner in another partnership, the gross income referred to in subparagraph (A) shall include the partnership's distributive share of the gross income of such other partnership from the active conduct of trades and businesses of such other partnership. A similar rule shall apply in the case of lower-tiered partnerships.

(C) Treatment of tax. For purposes of this title, the tax imposed by this paragraph shall be treated as imposed by chapter 1 other than for purposes of determining the amount of any credit allowable under chapter 1.

(4) Election. An election and consent under this subsection shall apply to the taxable year for which made and all subsequent taxable years unless revoked by the partnership. Such revocation may be made without the consent of the Secretary, but, once so revoked, may not be reinstated.

[For analysis, see ¶ 1427. For text of Committee Report see ¶ 5085.]

[Endnote Code Sec. 7704]

Code Sec. 7704(g), in *italics*, was added by Sec. 964(a) of the Taxpayer Relief Act of 1997, H.R. 2014, 8/5/97.
1. added subsection (g)

Effective Date (Sec. 964(b), H.R. 2014, 8/5/97) effective for tax. yrs. begin. after 12/31/97.

[¶ 3390]   Code Sec. 7872.   Treatment of loans with below-market interest rates.

* * * * * * * * * * * *

(f) Other definitions and special rules. For purposes of this section—

* * * * * * * * * * * * *

(11) Time for determining rate applicable to employee relocation loans.

(A) In general. In the case of any term loan made by an employer to an employee the proceeds of which are used by the employee to purchase a principal residence (within the meaning of [1]*section 121*), the determination of the applicable Federal rate shall be made as of the date the written contract to purchase such residence was entered into.

* * * * * * * * * * *

[Endnote Code Sec. 7872]

Matter in *italics* in Code Sec. 7872(f)(11)(A) added by Sec. 312(d)(1) of the Taxpayer Relief Act of 1997, H.R. 2014, 8/5/97, which struck out:

1. "section 1034"

Effective Date (Sec. 312(d) [sic (e)], H.R. 2014, 8/5/97) effective for sales and exchanges after 5/6/97, except as provided by Secs. 312(d)(2)-(4) [sic (e)(2)-(4)] of this Act, which read as follows:

"(2) Sales before 8/5/97.—At the election of the taxpayer, the amendments made by this section shall not apply to any sale or exchange before the date of the enactment of this Act.

"(3) Certain sales within 2 years after 8/5/97. Section 121 of the Internal Revenue Code of 1986 (as amended by this section) shall be applied without regard to subsection (c)(2)(B) thereof in the case of any sale or exchange of property during the 2-year period beginning on the date of the enactment of this Act if the taxpayer held such property on the date of the enactment of this Act and fails to meet the ownership and use requirements of subsection (a) thereof with respect to such property.

"(4) Binding contracts.—At the election of the taxpayer, the amendments made by this section shall not apply to a sale or exchange after the date of the enactment of this Act, if—

"(A) such sale or exchange is pursuant to a contract which was binding on such date, or

"(B) without regard to such amendments, gain would not be recognized under section 1034 of the Internal Revenue Code of 1986 (as in effect on the day before the date of the enactment of this Act) on such sale or exchange by reason of a new residence acquired on or before such date or with respect to the acquisition of which by the taxpayer a binding contract was in effect on such date.

This paragraph shall not apply to any sale or exchange by an individual if the treatment provided by section 877(a)(1) of the Internal Revenue Code of 1986 applies to such individual."

[¶ 3391]   Code Sec. 9502.   Airport and airway trust fund.

* * * * * * * * * * *

CAUTION.   Subsec. (b), following, is effective for taxes received in the Treasury before 10/1/97. For subsec. (b) effective for taxes received in the Treasury on and after 10/1/97, see below.

(b) Transfers to Airport and Airway Trust Fund. There are hereby appropriated to the Airport and Airway Trust Fund amounts equivalent to—

(1) the taxes received in the Treasury under—

(A) subsections (c) and (e) of section 4041 (relating to aviation fuels),

(B) sections 4261 and 4271 (relating to transportation by air),

(C) section 4081 (relating to gasoline) with respect to aviation gasoline (to the extent that the rate of the tax on such gasoline exceeds 4.3 cents per gallon), and

(D) section 4091 (relating to aviation fuel) to the extent attributable to the Airport and Airway Trust Fund financing rate, and

(2) the amounts determined by the Secretary of the Treasury to be equivalent to the amounts of civil penalties collected under section 47107(n) of title 49, United States Code.

CAUTION.   Subsec. (b), following, is effective for taxes received in the Treasury on and after 10/1/97. For subsec. (b) effective for taxes received in the Treasury before 10/1/97, see above.

(b) Transfers to Airport and Airway Trust Fund. There are hereby appropriated to the Airport and Airway Trust Fund amounts equivalent to—

(1) the taxes received in the Treasury under—

(A) subsections (c) and (e) of section 4041 (relating to aviation fuels),

(B) sections 4261 and 4271 (relating to transportation by air),

(C) section 4081 (relating to gasoline) with respect to aviation gasoline[1], and

(D) section 4091 (relating to aviation fuel)[2], and

(2) the amounts determined by the Secretary of the Treasury to be equivalent to the amounts of civil penalties collected under section 47107(n) of title 49, United States Code.

[3]*There shall not be taken into account under paragraph (1) so much of the taxes imposed by section 4081 and 4091 as are determined at the rates specified in section 4081(a)(2)(B) or 4091(b)(2).*

* * * * * * * * * * * *

(d) Expenditures from airport and airway trust fund.

(1) Airport and airway program. Amounts in the Airport and Airway Trust Fund shall be available, as provided by appropriation Acts, for making expenditures before October 1, 1998, to meet those obligations of the United States—

(A) incurred under title I of the Airport and Airway Development Act of 1970 or of the Airport and Airway Development Act Amendments of 1976 or of the Aviation Safety and Noise Abatement Act of 1979 or under the Fiscal Year 1981 Airport Development Authorization Act or the provisions of the Airport and Airway Improvement Act of 1982 or the Airport and Airway Safety and Capacity Expansion Act of 1987 or the Federal Aviation Administration Research, Engineering, and Development Authorization Act of 1990 or the Aviation Safety and Capacity Expansion Act of 1990 or the Airport and Airway Safety, Capacity, Noise Improvement, and Intermodal Transportation Act of 1992 or the Airport Improvement Program Temporary Extension Act of 1994 or the Federal Aviation Administration Authorization Act of 1994 or the Federal Aviation Reauthorization Act of 1996;

(B) heretofore or hereafter incurred under part A of subtitle VII of title 49, United States Code, which are attributable to planning, research and development, construction, or operation and maintenance of—

(i) air traffic control,

(ii) air navigation,

(iii) communications, or

(iv) supporting services,

for the airway system; or

(C) for those portions of the administrative expenses of the Department of Transportation which are attributable to activities described in subparagraph (A) or (B).

Any reference in subparagraph (A) to an Act shall be treated as a reference to such Act and the corresponding provisions (if any) of title 49, United States Code, as such Act and provisions were in effect on the date of the enactment of the last Act referred to in subparagraph (A).

(2) Transfers from airport and airway trust fund on account of certain refunds. The Secretary of the Treasury shall pay from time to time from the Airport and Airway Trust Fund into the general fund of the Treasury amounts equivalent to the amounts paid after August 31, 1982, in respect of fuel used in aircraft, under section 6420 (relating to amounts paid in respect of gasoline used on farms, 6421 (relating to amounts paid in respect of gasoline used for certain nonhighway purposes), or 6427 (relating to fuels not used for taxable purposes).

(3) Transfers from the airport and airway trust fund on account of certain section 34 credits. The Secretary of the Treasury shall pay from time to time from the Airport and Airway Trust Fund into the general fund of the Treasury amounts equivalent to the credits allowed under section 34 with respect to fuel used after August 31, 1982. Such amounts shall be transferred on the basis of estimates by the Secretary of the Treasury, and proper adjustments shall be made in amounts subsequently transferred to the extent prior estimates were in excess of or less than the credits allowed.

(4) Transfers for refunds and credits not to exceed trust fund revenues attributable to fuel used. The amounts payable from the Airport and Airway Trust Fund under paragraph (2) or (3) shall not exceed the amounts required to be appropriated to such Trust Fund with respect to fuel so used.

(5) Transfers from airport and airway trust fund on account of refunds of taxes on transportation by air. The Secretary of the Treasury shall pay from time to time from the Airport and Airway Trust Fund into the general fund of the Treasury amounts equivalent to the amounts paid after December 31, 1995, under section 6402 (relating to authority to make credits or refunds) or section 6415 (relating to credits or refunds to persons who collected certain taxes) in respect of taxes under sections 4261 and 4271.

⁴*(6) Transfers from the Airport and Airway Trust Fund on account of certain airports.* The Secretary of the Treasury may transfer from the Airport and Airway Trust Fund to the Secretary of Transportation or the Administrator of the Federal Aviation Administration an amount to make a payment to an airport affect by a diversion that is the subject of an administrative action under paragraph (3) or a civil action under paragraph (4) of section 47107(n) of title 49, United States Code.

* * * * * * * * * * *

CAUTION. Subsec. (f), following, is repealed effective for taxes received in the Treasury on or after 10/1/97.

(f) Definition of Airport and Airway Trust Fund financing rate. For purposes of this section—

(1) In general. Except as otherwise provided in this subsection, the Airport and Airway Trust Fund financing rate is—

(A) in the case of fuel used in an aircraft in noncommercial aviation (as defined in section 4041(c)(2)), 17.5 cents per gallon, and

(B) in the case of fuel used in an aircraft other than in noncommercial aviation (as so defined), zero.

(2) Alcohol fuels. If the rate of tax on any fuel is determined under section 4091(c), the Airport and Airway Trust Fund financing rate is the excess (if any) of the rate of tax determined under section 4091(c) over 4.4 cents per gallon (¹% of 4.4 cents per gallon in the case of a rate of tax determined under section 4091(c)(2)).

(3) Termination. Notwithstanding the preceding provisions of this subsection, the Airport and Airway Trust Fund financing rate shall be zero with respect to taxes imposed during any period that the rate of the tax imposed by section 4091(b)(1) is 4.3 cents per gallon.

⁵**(f) Repealed.**

[Endnote Code Sec. 9502]

Matter in *italics* in Code Sec. 9502(b)(1), Code Sec. 9502(b)(1)(C), and Code Sec. 9502(b)(1)(D) added by Sec. 1031(d)(1) of the Taxpayer Relief Act of 1997, H.R. 2014, 8/5/97, which struck out:

1. "(to the extent that the rate of the tax on such gasoline exceeds 4.2 cents per gallon)"
2. "to the extent attributable to the Airport and Airway Trust Fund financing rate"
3. added matter in subsec. (b)

Effective Date (Sec. 1031(e)(3), H.R. 2014, 8/5/97) effective for taxes received by the Treasury on and after 10/1/97.

Matter in *italics* in Code Sec. 9502(d)(6) added by Sec. 1604(g)(5), H.R. 2014, 8/5/97, which struck out:
4. "(5)"

Effective Date Effective 8/5/97.

Code Sec. 9502(f) was deleted by Sec. 1031(d)(2), H.R. 2014, 8/5/97, which struck out:

5. "(f) Definition of Airport and Airway Trust Fund financing rate.

"For purposes of this section—

"(1) In general. Except as otherwise provided in this subsection, the Airport and Airway Trust Fund financing rate is—

"(A) in the case of fuel used in an aircraft in noncommercial aviation (as defined in section 4041(c)(2)), 17.5 cents per gallon, and

"(B) in the case of fuel used in an aircraft other than in noncommercial aviation (as so defined), zero.

"(2) Alcohol fuels. If the rate of tax on any fuel is determined under section 4091(c), the Airport and Airway Trust Fund financing rate is the excess (if any) of the rate of tax determined under section 4091(c) over 4.4 cents per gallon (¹% of 4.4 cents per gallon in the case of a rate of tax determined under section 4091(c)(2)).

"(3) Termination. Notwithstanding the preceding provisions of this subsection, the Airport and Airway Trust Fund financing rate shall be zero with respect to taxes imposed during any period that the rate of the tax imposed by section 4091(b)(1) is 4.3 cents per gallon."

Effective Date (Sec. 1031(e)(3), H.R. 2014, 8/5/97) effective for taxes received by the Treasury on and after 10/1/97.

[¶ 3392]   Code Sec. 9503.   Highway trust fund.

* * * * * * * * * * * *

(b) Transfer to highway trust fund of amounts equivalent to certain taxes.

(1) **In general.** There are hereby appropriated to the Highway Trust Fund amounts equivalent to the taxes received in the Treasury before October 1, 1999, under the following provisions—

* * * * * * * * * * * *

CAUTION.   Subpara. (b)(1)(E), following, is effective before 7/1/98. For subpara. (b)(1)(E), effective after 6/30/98, see below.

(E) section 4081 (relating to tax on gasoline and diesel fuel), and

CAUTION.   Subpara. (b)(1)(E), following, is effective after 6/30/98. For subpara. (b)(1)(E), effective before 7/1/98, see above.

(E) section 4081 (relating to tax on gasoline[1], *diesel fuel, and kerosene*), and

* * * * * * * * * * * *

[2]*(4) Certain taxes not transferred to highway trust fund. For purposes of paragraph (1) and (2), there shall not be taken into account the taxes imposed by—*

(A) section 4041(d),

(B) section 4081 to the extent attributable to the rate specified in section 4081(a)(2)(B),

(C) section 4041 or 4081 to the extent attributable to fuel used in a train,

(D) in the case of fuels used as described in paragraph (4)(D), (5)(B), or (6)(D) of subsection (c), section 4041 or 4081—

(i) with respect to so much of the rate of tax on gasoline or special motor fuels as exceeds 11.5 cents per gallon, and

(ii) with respect to so much of the rate of tax on diesel fuel or kerosene as exceeds 17.5 cents per gallon,

(E) in the case of fuels described in section 4041(b)(2)(A), 4041(k), or 4081(c), section 4041 or 4081 before October 1, 1999, with respect to a rate equal to 2.5 cents per gallon, or

(F) in the case of fuels described in section 4081(c)(2), such section before October 1, 1999, with respect to a rate equal to 2.8 cents per gallon.

(5) General revenue deposits of certain taxes on alcohol mixtures. For purposes of this section, the amounts which would (but for this paragraph) be required to be appropriated under subparagraphs (A) and (E) of paragraph (1) shall be reduced by—

* * * * * * * * * * * *

CAUTION.   Subpara. (b)(5)(B), following, is effective before 7/1/98. For subpara. (b)(5)(B), effective after 6/30/98, see below.

(B) 0.67 cent per gallon in the case of gasoline or diesel fuel used in producing a mixture described in subparagraph (A).

CAUTION.   Subpara. (b)(5)(B), following, is effective after 6/30/98. For subpara. (b)(5)(B), effective before 7/1/98, see above.

(B) 0.67 cent per gallon in the case of gasoline[3], *diesel fuel, or kerosene* used in producing a mixture described in subparagraph (A).

(c) Expenditures from highway trust fund.

* * * * * * * * * * * *

(2) Transfers from highway trust fund for certain repayments and credits.

(A) In general. The Secretary shall pay from time to time from the Highway Trust Fund into the general fund of the Treasury amounts equivalent to—

(i) the amounts paid before July 1, 2000, under—

(I) section 6420 (relating to amounts paid in respect of gasoline used on farms),

(II) section 6421 (relating to amounts paid in respect of gasoline used for certain nonhighway purposes or by local transit systems),

(III) section 6424 (relating to amounts paid in respect of lubricating oil used for certain nontaxable purposes), and

(IV) section 6427 (relating to fuels not used for taxable purposes),

on the basis of claims filed for periods ending before October 1, 1999, and

(ii) the credits allowed under section 34 (relating to credit for certain uses of gasoline, special fuels, and lubricating oil) with respect to gasoline, special fuels, and lubricating oil used before October 1, 1999[4].

The amounts payable from the Highway Trust Fund under this subparagraph or paragraph (3) shall be determined [5]*by taking into account only the portion of the taxes which are deposited in to the Highway Trust Fund.*

* * * * * * * * * * * *

(4) Transfers from the trust fund for motorboat fuel taxes.

* * * * * * * * * * * *

(D) Motorboat fuel taxes. For purposes of this paragraph, the term "motorboat fuel taxes" means the taxes under section 4041(a)(2) with respect to special motor fuels used as fuel in motorboats and under section 4081 with respect to gasoline used as fuel in motorboats, but only to the extent such taxes are [6]*deposited into the Highway Trust Fund.*

* * * * * * * * * * * *

(5) Transfers from the trust fund for small-engine fuel taxes.

* * * * * * * * * * * *

(B) Small-engine fuel taxes. For purposes of this paragraph, the term "small-engine fuel taxes" means the taxes under section 4081 with respect to gasoline used as a fuel in the nonbusiness use of small-engine outdoor power equipment, but only to the extent such taxes are [7]*deposited into the Highway Trust Fund.*

(6) Transfers from trust fund of certain recreational fuel taxes, etc.

* * * * * * * * * * * *

(D) Nonhighway recreational fuel taxes. For purposes of this paragraph, the term "nonhighway recreational fuel taxes" means taxes under section 4041 and 4081 (to the extent [8]*deposited into the Highway Trust Fund)* with respect to—

(i) fuel used in vehicles on recreational trails or back country terrain (including vehicles registered for highway use when used on recreational trails, trail access roads not eligible for funding under title 23, United States Code, or back country terrain), and

(ii) fuel used in campstoves and other nonengine uses in outdoor recreational equipment.

Such term shall not include small-engine fuel taxes (as defined by paragraph (5)) and taxes which are credited or refunded.

* * * * * * * * * * * *

[9]*(7) Limitation on expenditures. Notwithstanding any other provision of law, in calculating amounts under section 157(a) of title 23, United States Code, and sections 1013(c), 1015(a), and 1015(b) of the Intermodal Surface Transportation Efficiency Act of 1991 (Public Law 102-240; 105 Stat. 1914), deposits in the Highway Trust Fund resulting from the amendments made by the Taxpayer Relief Act of 1997 shall not be taken into account.*

* * * * * * * * * * * *

(e) Establishment of mass transit account.

* * * * * * * * * * * *

(2) Transfers to mass transit account. The Secretary of the Treasury shall transfer to the Mass Transit Account the mass transit portion of the amounts appropriated to the Highway Trust Fund under subsection (b) which are attributable to taxes under sections 4041 and 4081, imposed after March 31, 1983. For purposes of the preceding sentence, the term "mass transit portion" means an amount determined at the rate of [10]*2.85 cents* for each gallon with respect to which tax was imposed under section 4041 or 4081.

* * * * * * * * * * * *

(5) Portion of certain transfers to be made from account.

(A) In general. Transfers under paragraphs (2), (3) and (4) of subsection (c) shall be borne by the Highway Account and the Mass Transit Account in proportion to the respective revenues transferred under this section to the Highway Account (after the application of paragraph (2)) and the Mass Transit Account[11].

* * * * * * * * * * *

[12]**(f) Repealed.**

[Endnote Code Sec. 9503]

Matter in *italics* in Code Sec. 9503(b)(1)(E) added by Sec. 1032(e)(13) of the Taxpayer Relief Act of 1997, H.R. 2014, 8/5/97, which struck out:
1. "and diesel fuel"
Effective Date (Sec. 1032(f), H.R. 2014, 8/5/97) effective 7/1/98.

Matter in *italics* in Code Sec. 9503(b)(4) added by Sec. 901(a), H.R. 2014, 8/5/97, which struck out:
2. "(4) Certain additional taxes not transferred to highway trust fund. For purposes of paragraph (1) and (2)—
"(A) there shall not be taken into account the taxes imposed by section 4041(d), and
"(B) there shall be taken into account the taxes imposed by sections 4041 and 4081 only to the extent attributable to the Highway Trust Fund financing rate."
Effective Date (Sec. 901(f), H.R. 2014, 8/5/97) effective for taxes received in the Treasury after 9/30/97.

Matter in *italics* in Code Sec. 9503(b)(5)(B) added by Sec. 1032(e)(14), H.R. 2014, 8/5/97, which struck out:
3. "or diesel fuel"
Effective Date (Sec. 1032(f), H.R. 2014, 8/5/97) effective 7/1/98.

Matter in Code Sec. 9503(c)(2)(A)(ii) deleted by Sec. 1601(f)(2)(A), H.R. 2014, 8/5/97, which struck out:
4. "(or with respect to qualified diesel-powered highway vehicles purchased before January 1, 1999)"
Effective Date (Sec. 1601(j)(1), H.R. 2014, 8/5/97) effective for vehicles purchased after 8/5/97.

Matter in *italics* in Code Sec. 9503(c)(2)(A), Code Sec. 9503(c)(4)(D), Code Sec. 9503(c)(5)(B), Code Sec. 9503(c)(6)(D), Code Sec. 9503(c)(7) and Code Sec. 9503(e)(2) added by Sec. 901(b), (c), (d)(2), and (d)(3), H.R. 2014, 8/5/97, which struck out:
5. "by taking into account only the Highway Trust Fund financing rate applicable to any fuel"
6. "attributable to the Highway Trust Fund financing rate"
7. "attributable to the Highway Trust Fund financing rate"
8. "attributable to the Highway Trust Fund financing rate"
9. added para. (c)(7)
10. "2 cents"
Effective Date (Sec. 901(f), H.R. 2014, 8/5/97) effective for taxes received in the Treasury after 9/30/97.

Matter in *italics* in Code Sec. 9503(e)(5)(A) added by Sec. 1601(f)(2)(B), H.R. 2014, 8/5/97, which struck out:
11. "; except that any such transfers to the extent attributable to section 6427(g) shall be borne only by the Highway Account."
Effective Date (Sec. 1601(j)(1), H.R. 2014, 8/5/97) effective for vehicles purchased after 8/5/97.

Code Sec. 9503(f) deleted by Sec. 901(d)(1), H.R. 2014, 8/5/97, which struck out:
12. "(f) Definition of Highway Trust Fund financing rate. For purposes of this section—
"(1) In general. Except as otherwise provided in this subsection, the Highway Trust Fund financing rate is—
"(A) in the case of gasoline and special motor fuels, 11.5 cents per gallon (14 cents per gallon after September 30, 1995), and
"(B) in the case of diesel fuel, 17.5 cents per gallon (20 cents per gallon after September 30, 1995).
"(2) Certain uses.
"(A) Trains. In the case of fuel used in a train, the Highway Trust Fund financing rate is zero.
"(B) Certain buses. In the case of diesel fuel used in a use described in section 6427(b)(1) (after the application of section 6427(b)(3)), the Highway Trust Fund financing rate is 3 cents per gallon.

"(C) Certain boats. In the case of diesel fuel used in a boat described in clause (iv) of section 6421(e)(2)(B), the Highway Trust Fund financing rate is zero.

"(D) Compressed natural gas. In the case of the tax imposed by section 4041(a)(3), the Highway Trust Fund financing rate is zero.

"(E) Certain other nonhighway uses. In the case of gasoline and special motor fuels used as described in paragraph (4)(D), (5)(B), or (6)(D) of subsection (c), the Highway Trust Fund financing rate is 11.5 cents per gallon; and, in the case of diesel fuel used as described in subsection (c)(6)(D), the Highway Trust Fund financing rate is 17.5 cents per gallon.

"(3) Alcohol fuels.

"(A) In general. If the rate of tax on any fuel is determined under section 4041(b)(2)(A), 4041(k), or 4081(c), the Highway Trust Fund financing rate is the excess (if any) of the rate so determined over—

"(i) 6.8 cents per gallon after September 30, 1993, and before October 1, 1999,

"(ii) 4.3 cents per gallon after September 30, 1999.

In the case of a rate of tax determined under section 4081(c), the preceding sentence shall be applied by increasing the rates specified in clauses (i) and (ii) by 0.1 cent.

"(B) Fuels used to produce mixtures. In the case of a rate of tax determined under section 4081(c)(2), subparagraph (A) shall be applied by substituting rates which are ¹⁰⁄₀ of the rates otherwise applicable under clauses (i) and (ii) of subparagraph (A).

"(C) Partially exempt methanol or ethanol fuel. In the case of a rate of tax determined under section 4041(m), the Highway Trust Fund financing rate is the excess (if any) of the rate so determined over—

"(i) 5.55 cents per gallon after September 30, 1993, and before October 1, 1995, and

"(ii) 4.3 cents per gallon after September 30, 1995.

"(4) Termination. Notwithstanding the preceding provisions of this subsection, the Highway Trust Fund financing rate is zero with respect to taxes received in the Treasury after June 30, 2000."

Effective Date (Sec. 901(f), H.R. 2014, 8/5/97) effective for taxes received in the Treasury after 9/30/97.

[¶ 3393] Code Sec. 9508. Leaking Underground Storage Tank Trust Fund.

* * * * * * * * * * *

(b) Transfers to trust fund. There are hereby appropriated to the Leaking Underground Storage Tank Trust Fund amounts equivalent to—

* * * * * * * * * * *

  CAUTION. Para. (b)(2), following, is effective before 7/1/98. For para. (b)(2), effective after 6/30/98, see below.

(2) taxes received in the Treasury under section 4081 (relating to tax on gasoline and diesel fuel) to the extent attributable to the Leaking Underground Storage Tank Trust Fund financing rate under such section,

  CAUTION. Para. (b)(2), following, is effective after 6/30/98. For para. (b)(2), effective before 7/1/98, see above.

(2) taxes received in the Treasury under section 4081 (relating to tax on gasoline[1], *diesel fuel, and kerosene*) to the extent attributable to the Leaking Underground Storage Tank Trust Fund financing rate under such section,

* * * * * * * * * * *

[Endnote Code Sec. 9508]

Matter in *italics* in Code Sec. 9508(b)(2) added by Sec. 1032(e)(13) of the Taxpayer Relief Act of 1997, H.R. 2014, 8/5/97, which struck out:

1. "and diesel fuel"

Effective Date (Sec. 1032(f), H.R. 2014, 8/5/97) effective 7/1/98.

[¶ 3394] Code Sec. 9801. Increased portability through limitation on preexisting condition exclusions.

* * * * * * * * * * *

(c) Rules relating to crediting previous coverage.

(1) Creditable coverage defined. For purposes of this part, the term "creditable coverage" means, with respect to an individual, coverage of the individual under any of the following:

  (A) A group health plan.

(B) Health insurance coverage.

(C) Part A or part B of title XVIII of the Social Security Act.

(D) Title XIX of the Social Security Act, other than coverage consisting solely of benefits under section 1928.

(E) Chapter 55 of title 10, United States Code.

(F) A medical care program of the Indian Health Service or of a tribal organization.

(G) A State health benefits risk pool.

(H) A health plan offered under chapter 89 of title 5, United States Code.

(I) A public health plan (as defined in regulations).

(J) A health benefit plan under section 5(e) of the Peace Corps Act (22 U.S.C. 2504(e)).

CAUTION. The flush language of para. (c)(1), following, is effective for group health plans for plan yrs. begin. before 1/1/98. For the flush language of para. (c)(1) effective for group health plans for plan yrs. begin. on or after 1/1/98, see below.

Such term does not include coverage consisting solely of coverage of excepted benefits (as defined in section 9805(c)).

CAUTION. The flush language of para. (c)(1), following, is effective for group health plans for plan yrs. begin. on or after 1/1/98. For the flush language of para. (c)(1) effective for group health plans for plan yrs. begin. before 1/1/98, see above.

Such term does not include coverage consisting solely of coverage of excepted benefits (as defined in section [1]9832(c)).

* * * * * * * * * * * *

[Endnote Code Sec. 9801]

Matter in *italics* in Code Sec. 9801(c)(1) added by Sec. 1531(b)(1)(A) of the Taxpayer Relief Act of 1997, H.R. 2014, 8/5/97, which struck out:
   1. "9805(c)"

Effective Date (Sec. 1531(c), H.R. 2014, 8/5/97) effective for group health plans for plan yrs. begin. on or after 1/1/98.

[¶ 3395] Code Sec. 9802. Prohibiting discrimination against individual participants and beneficiaries based on health status.

* * * * * * * * * * * *

[1]*(c) Special rules for church plans.* A church plan (as defined in section 414(e)) shall not be treated as failing to meet the requirements of this section solely because such plan requires evidence of good health for coverage of—

   (1) both any employee of an employer of 10 or less employees (determined without regard to section 414(e)(3)(C)) and any self-employed individual, or

   (2) any individual who enrolls after the first 90 days of initial eligibility under the plan.

   This subsection shall apply to a plan for any year only if the plan included in the provisions described in the preceding sentence on July 15, 1997, and at all times thereafter before the beginning of such year.

   [For analysis, see ¶ 929. For text of Committee Report see ¶ 5354.]

[Endnote Code Sec. 9802]

Code Sec. 9802(c), in *italics*, was added by Sec. 1532(a) of the Taxpayer Relief Act of 1997, H.R. 2014, 8/5/97.
   1. added subsec. (c)

Effective Date (Sec. 1532(b), H.R. 2014, 8/5/97) effective for plan yrs. begin. after 6/30/97.

[¶ 3396] Code Sec.[1] 9811.

CAUTION.   Code Sec. 9811, following, is effective for group health plans for plan yrs. begin. on or after 1/1/98.

Standards relating to benefits for mothers and newborns.

(a) **Requirements for minimum hospital stay following birth.**   (1) **In general.** A group health plan may not—

(A) except as provided in paragraph (2)—

(i) restrict benefits for any hospital length of stay in connection with childbirth for the mother or newborn child, following a normal vaginal delivery, to less than 48 hours, or

(ii) restrict benefits for any hospital length of stay in connection with childbirth for the mother or newborn child, following a caesarean section, to less than 96 hours; or

(B) require that a provider obtain authorization from the plan or the issuer for prescribing any length of stay required under subparagraph (A) (without regard to paragraph (2)).

(2) **Exception.** Paragraph (1)(A) shall not apply in connection with any group health plan in any case in which the decision to discharge the mother or her newborn child prior to the expiration of the minimum length of stay otherwise required under paragraph (1)(A) is made by an attending provider in consultation with the mother.

(b) **Prohibitions.** A group health plan may not—

(1) deny to the mother or her newborn child eligibility, or continued eligibility, to enroll or to renew coverage under the terms of the plan, solely for the purpose of avoiding the requirements of this section;

(2) provide monetary payments or rebates to mothers to encourage such mothers to accept less than the minimum protections available under this section;

(3) penalize or otherwise reduce or limit the reimbursement of an attending provider because such provider provided care to an individual participant or beneficiary in accordance with this section;

(4) provide incentives (monetary or otherwise) to an attending provider to induce such provider to provide care to an individual participant or beneficiary in a manner inconsistent with this section; or

(5) subject to subsection (c)(3), restrict benefits for any portion of a period within a hospital length of stay required under subsection (a) in a manner which is less favorable than the benefits provided for any preceding portion of such stay.

(c) **Rules of construction.**   (1) Nothing in this section shall be construed to require a mother who is a participant or beneficiary—

(A) to give birth in a hospital; or

(B) to stay in the hospital for a fixed period of time following the birth of her child.

(2) This section shall not apply with respect to any group health plan which does not provide benefits for hospital lengths of stay in connection with childbirth for a mother or her newborn child.

(3) Nothing in this section shall be construed as preventing a group health plan from imposing deductibles, coinsurance, or other cost-sharing in relation to benefits for hospital lengths of stay in connection with childbirth for a mother or newborn child under the plan, except that such coinsurance or other cost-sharing for any portion of a period within a hospital length of stay required under subsection (a) may not be greater than such coinsurance or cost-sharing for any preceding portion of such stay.

(d) **Level and type of reimbursements.** Nothing in this section shall be construed to prevent a group health plan from negotiating the level and type of reimbursement with a provider for care provided in accordance with this section.

(f) [sic (e)] **Preemption; exception for health insurance coverage in certain states.** The requirements of this section shall not apply with respect to health insurance coverage if there is a State law (including a decision, rule, regulation, or other State action having the effect of law) for a State that regulates such coverage that is described in any of the following paragraphs:

(1) Such State law requires such coverage to provide for at least a 48-hour hospital length of stay following a normal vaginal delivery and at least a 96-hour hospital length of stay following a caesarean section.

(2) Such State law requires such coverage to provide for maternity and pediatric care in accordance with guidelines established by the American College of Obstetricians and Gynecologists, the American Academy of Pediatrics, or other established professional medical associations.

(3) Such State law requires, in connection with such coverage for maternity care, that the hospital length of stay for such care is left to the decision of (or required to be made by) the attending provider in consultation with the mother.

[*For analysis, see ¶ 1003. For text of Committee Report see ¶ 5353.*]

[Endnote Code Sec. 9811]
Code Sec. 9811 was added by Sec. 1531(a)(4) of the Taxpayer Relief Act of 1997, H.R. 2014, 8/5/97.
1. added Code Sec. 9811
Effective Date (Sec. 1531(c), H.R. 2104, 8/5/97) effective for group health plans for plan yrs. begin. on or after 1/1/98.

[¶ 3397]   Code Sec.[1] 9812.

CAUTION.   Code Sec. 9812, following, is effective for group health plans for plan yrs. begin. on or after 1/1/98.

Parity in the application of certain limits to mental health benefits.

(a) In General.   (1) Aggregate lifetime limits. In the case of a group health plan that provides both medical and surgical benefits and mental health benefits—

(A) No lifetime limit. If the plan does not include an aggregate lifetime limit on substantially all medical and surgical benefits, the plan may not impose any aggregate lifetime limit on mental health benefits.

(B) Lifetime limit. If the plan includes an aggregate lifetime limit on substantially all medical and surgical benefits (in this paragraph referred to as the "applicable lifetime limit"), the plan shall either—

(i) apply the applicable lifetime limit both to the medical and surgical benefits to which it otherwise would apply and to mental health benefits and not distinguish in the application of such limit between such medical and surgical benefits and mental health benefits; or

(ii) not include any aggregate lifetime limit on mental health benefits that is less than the applicable lifetime limit.

(C) Rule in case of different limits. In the case of a plan that is not described in subparagraph (A) or (B) and that includes no or different aggregate lifetime limits on different categories of medical and surgical benefits, the Secretary shall establish rules under which subparagraph (B) is applied to such plan with respect to mental health benefits by substituting for the applicable lifetime limit an average aggregate lifetime limit that is computed taking into account the weighted average of the aggregate lifetime limits applicable to such categories.

(2) Annual limits. In the case of a group health plan that provides both medical and surgical benefits and mental health benefits—

(A) No annual limit. If the plan does not include an annual limit on substantially all medical and surgical benefits, the plan may not impose any annual limit on mental health benefits.

(B) Annual limit. If the plan includes an annual limit on substantially all medical and surgical benefits (in this paragraph referred to as the "applicable annual limit"), the plan shall either—

(i) apply the applicable annual limit both to medical and surgical benefits to which it otherwise would apply and to mental health benefits and not distinguish in the application of such limit between such medical and surgical benefits and mental health benefits; or

(ii) not include any annual limit on mental health benefits that is less than the applicable annual limit.

(C) Rule in case of different limits. In the case of a plan that is not described in subparagraph (A) or (B) and that includes no or different annual limits on different categories of medical and surgical benefits, the Secretary shall establish rules under which subparagraph (B) is applied to such plan with respect to mental health benefits by substituting for the applicable annual limit an average annual limit that is computed taking into account the weighted average of the annual limits applicable to such categories.

(b) **Construction.** Nothing in this section shall be construed—

(1) as requiring a group health plan to provide any mental health benefits; or

(2) in the case of a group health plan that provides mental health benefits, as affecting the terms and conditions (including cost sharing, limits on numbers of visits or days of coverage, and requirements relating to medical necessity) relating to the amount, duration, or scope of mental health benefits under the plan, except as specifically provided in subsection (a) (in regard to parity in the imposition of aggregate lifetime limits and annual limits for mental health benefits).

(c) **Exemptions.**

(1) **Small employer exemption.** This section shall not apply to any group health plan for any plan year of a small employer (as defined in section 4980D(d)(2)).

(2) **Increased cost exemption.** This section shall not apply with respect to a group health plan if the application of this section to such plan results in an increase in the cost under the plan of at least 1 percent.

(d) **Separate Application to Each Option Offered.** In the case of a group health plan that offers a participant or beneficiary two or more benefit package options under the plan, the requirements of this section shall be applied separately with respect to each such option.

(e) **Definitions.** For purposes of this section:

(1) **Aggregate lifetime limit.** The term "aggregate lifetime limit" means, with respect to benefits under a group health plan, a dollar limitation on the total amount that may be paid with respect to such benefits under the plan with respect to an individual or other coverage unit.

(2) **Annual limit.** The term "annual limit" means, with respect to benefits under a group health plan, a dollar limitation on the total amount of benefits that may be paid with respect to such benefits in a 12-month period under the plan with respect to an individual or other coverage unit.

(3) **Medical or surgical benefits.** The term "medical or surgical benefits" means benefits with respect to medical or surgical services, as defined under the terms of the plan, but does not include mental health benefits.

(4) **Mental health benefits.** The term "mental health benefits" means benefits with respect to mental health services, as defined under the terms of the plan, but does not include benefits with respect to treatment of substance abuse or chemical dependency.

(f) **Sunset.** This section shall not apply to benefits for services furnished on or after September 30, 2001.

[For analysis, see ¶ 1102. For text of Committee Report see ¶ 5353.]

[Endnote Code Sec. 9812]

Code Sec. 9812 was added by Sec. 1531(a)(4) of the Taxpayer Relief Act of 1997, H.R. 2014, 8/5/97.

1. added Code Sec. 9812

Effective Date (Sec. 1531(c), H.R. 2014, 8/5/97) effective for group health plans for plan yrs. begin. on or after 1/1/98.

[¶ 3398]   Code Sec.[1] 9831.

CAUTION.   Code Sec. 9831, following, effective for group health plans for plan yrs. begin. on or after 1/1/98. For Code Sec. 9804, effective for group health plans for plan yrs. begin. before 1/1/98, see above.

General exceptions.

(a) **Exception for certain plans.** The requirements of this chapter shall not apply to—

(1) any governmental plan, and

(2) any group health plan for any plan year if, on the first day of such plan year, such plan has less than 2 participants who are current employees.

(b) **Exception for certain benefits.** The requirements of this chapter shall not apply to any group health plan in relation to its provision of excepted benefit described in section [2]*9832(c)(1)*.

(c) **Exception for certain benefits if certain conditions met.**

(1) **Limited, excepted benefits.** The requirements of this chapter shall not apply to any group health plan in relation to its provision of excepted benefits described in section [3]*9832(c)(2)* if the benefits—

(A) are provided under a separate policy, certificate, or contract of insurance; or

(B) are otherwise not an integral part of the plan.

(2) **Noncoordinated, excepted benefits.** The requirements of this chapter shall not apply to any group health plan in relation to its provision of excepted benefits described in section [4]*9832(c)(3)* if all of the following conditions are met:

(A) The benefits are provided under a separate policy, certificate, or contract of insurance.

(B) There is no coordination between the provision of such benefits and any exclusion of benefits under any group health plan maintained by the same plan sponsor.

(C) Such benefits are paid with respect to an event without regard to whether benefits are provided with respect to such an event under any group health plan maintained by the same plan sponsor.

(3) **Supplemental excepted benefits.** The requirements of this chapter shall not apply to any group health plan in relation to its provision of excepted benefits described in section [5]*9832(c)(4)* if the benefits are provided under a separate policy, certificate, or contract of insurance.

[Endnote Code Sec. 9831]

Sec. 1531(a)(2) of the Taxpayer Relief Act of 1997, H.R. 2014, 8/5/97, redesignated Code Sec. 9804 as Code Sec. 9831. Matter in *italics* in Code Sec. 9831(b), Code Sec. 9831(c)(1), Code Sec. 9831(c)(2) and Code Sec. 9831(c)(3) a by Secs. 1531(b)(1)(B)-(E), H.R. 2014.

1. Redesignated Code Sec. 9804 as Code Sec. 9831
2. "9805(c)(1)"
3. "9805(c)(2)"
4. "9805(c)(3)"
5. "9805(c)(4)"

Effective Date (Sec. 1531(c), H.R. 2014, 8/5/97) effective for group health plans for plan yrs. begin. on or after 1/1/98.

[¶ 3399]   Code Sec.[1] 9832.

CAUTION.   Code Sec. 9832, following, is effective for group health plans for plan yrs. begin. on or after 1/1/98. For Code Sec. 9805 effective for group health plans for plan yrs. begin. before 1/1/98, see above.

Definitions.

(a) **Group health plan.** For purposes of this chapter, the term "group health plan" has the meaning given to such term by section 5000(b)(1).

(b) **Definitions relating to health insurance.** For purposes of this chapter—

(1) **Health insurance coverage.**

(A) In general. Except as provided in subparagraph (B), the term "health insurance coverage" means benefits consisting of medical care (provided directly, through insurance or reimbursement, or otherwise) under any hospital or medical service policy or certificate, hospital or medical service plan contract, or health maintenance organization contract offered by a health insurance issuer.

(B) No application to certain excepted benefits. In applying subparagraph (A), excepted benefits described in subsection (c)(1) shall not be treated as benefits consisting of medical care.

(2) Health insurance issuer. The term "health insurance issuer" means an insurance company, insurance service, or insurance organization (including a health maintenance organization, as defined in paragraph (3)) which is licensed to engage in the business of insurance in a State and which is subject to State law which regulates insurance (within the meaning of section 514(b)(2) of the Employee Retirement Income Security Act of 1974, as in effect on the date of the enactment of this section). Such term does not include a group health plan.

(3) Health maintenance organization. The term "health maintenance organization" means—

(A) a Federally qualified health maintenance organization (as defined in section 1301(a) of the Public Health Service Act (42 U.S.C. 300e(a))).

(B) an organization recognized under State law as a health maintenance organization, or

(C) a similar organization regulated under State law for solvency in the same manner and to the same extent as such a health maintenance organization.

(c) Excepted benefits. For purposes of this chapter, the term "excepted benefits" means benefits under one or more (or any combination thereof) of the following:

(1) Benefits not subject to requirements.

(A) Coverage only for accident, or disability income insurance, or any combination thereof.

(B) Coverage issued as a supplement to liability insurance.

(C) Liability insurance, including general liability insurance and automobile liability insurance.

(D) Workers' compensation or similar insurance.

(E) Automobile medical payment insurance.

(F) Credit-only insurance.

(G) Coverage for on-site medical clinics.

(H) Other similar insurance coverage, specified in regulations, under which benefits for medical care are secondary or incidental to other insurance benefits.

(2) Benefits not subject to requirements if offered separately.

(A) Limited scope dental or vision benefits.

(B) Benefits for long-term care, nursing home care, home health care, community-based care, or any combination thereof.

(C) Such other similar, limited benefits as are specified in regulations.

(3) Benefits not subject to requirements if offered as independent, noncoordinated benefits.

(A) Coverage only for a specified disease or illness.

(B) Hospital indemnity or other fixed indemnity insurance.

(4) Benefits not subject to requirements if offered as separate insurance policy. Medicare supplemental health insurance (as defined under section 1882(g)(1) of the Social Security Act), coverage supplemental to the coverage provided under chapter 55 of title 10, United States Code, and similar supplemental coverage provided to coverage under a group health plan.

(d) Other definitions. For purposes of this chapter—

(1) COBRA continuation provision. The term "COBRA continuation provision" means any of the following:

(A) Section 4980B, other than subsection (f)(1) thereof insofar as it relates to pediatric vaccines.

(B) Part 6 of subtitle B of title I of the Employee Retirement Income Security Act of 1974 (29 U.S.C. 1161 *et seq.*), other than section 609 of such Act.

(C) Title XXII of the Public Health Service Act.

(2) Governmental plan. The term "governmental plan" has the meaning given such term by section 414(d).

(3) Medical care. The term "medical care" has the meaning given such term by section 213(d) determined without regard to—

(A) paragraph (1)(C) thereof, and

(B) so much of paragraph (1)(D) thereof as relates to qualified long-term care insurance.

(4) Network plan. The term "network plan" means health insurance coverage of a health insurance issuer under which the financing and delivery of medical care are provided, in whole or in part, through a defined set of providers under contract with the issuer.

(5) Placed for adoption defined. The term "placement", or being "placed", for adoption, in connection with any placement for adoption of a child with any person, means the assumption and retention by such person of a legal obligation for total or partial support of such child in anticipation of adoption of such child. The child's placement with such person terminates upon the termination of such legal obligation.

[Endnote Code Sec. 9832]

Sec. 1531(a)(2) of the Taxpayer Relief Act of 1997, H.R. 2014, 8/5/97, redesignated Code Sec. 9805 as Code Sec. 9832.
1. Redesignated Code Sec. 9805 as Code Sec. 9832
Effective Date (Sec. 1531(c), H.R. 2014, 8/5/97) effective for group health plans for plan yrs. begin. on or after 1/1/98.

[¶ 3400]   Code Sec.[1] 9833.

CAUTION.   Code Sec. 9833, following, is effective for group health plans for plan yrs. begin. on or after 1/1/98. For Code Sec. 9806, effective for group health plans for plan yrs. begin. before 1/1/98, see above.

Regulations.

The Secretary, consistent with section 104 of the Health Care Portability and Accountability Act of 1996, may promulgate such regulations as may be necessary or appropriate to carry out the provisions of this chapter. The Secretary may promulgate any interim final rules as the Secretary determines are appropriate to carry out this chapter.

[Endnote Code Sec. 9833]

Sec. 1531(a)(2) of the Taxpayer Relief Act of 1997, H.R. 2014, 8/5/97, redesignated Code Sec. 9806 as Code Sec. 9833
1. Redesignated Code Sec. 9806 as Code Sec. 9833
Effective Date (Sec. 1531(c), H.R. 2014, 8/5/97) effective for group health plans for plan yrs. begin. on or after 1/1/98.

[¶ 4000]

Act sections of H.R. 2014 or portions thereof that do not amend specific Code Sections are at ¶s 4001-4253. Sections of the Code as amended by H.R. 2014 begin at ¶ 3001.

[¶ 4001]   Sec. 1.   SHORT TITLE; ETC.

(a) Short Title.—This Act may be cited as the "Taxpayer Relief Act of 1997".

(b) Amendment of 1986 Code.—Except as otherwise expressly provided, whenever in this Act an amendment or repeal is expressed in terms of an amendment to, or repeal of, a section or other provision, the reference shall be considered to be made to a section or other provision of the Internal Revenue Code of 1986.

(c) Section 15 Not To Apply.—No amendment made by this Act shall be treated as a change in a rate of tax for purposes of section 15 of the Internal Revenue Code of 1986.

(d) Waiver of Estimated Tax Penalties.—No addition to tax shall be made under section 6654 or 6655 of the Internal Revenue Code of 1986 for any period before January 1, 1998, for any payment the due date of which is before January 16, 1998, with respect to any underpayment attributable to such period to the extent such underpayment was created or increased by any provision of this Act.

(e) Table of Contents.—The table of contents for this Act is as follows:

Sec. 907. Rate of tax on certain special fuels determined on basis of BTU equivalency with gasoline.

Sec. 908. Modification of tax treatment of hard cider.

Sec. 909. Study of feasibility of moving collection point for distilled spirits excise tax.

Sec. 910. Clarification of authority to use semi-generic designations on wine labels.

SUBTITLE B—REVISIONS RELATING TO DISASTERS

Sec. 911. Authority to postpone certain tax-related deadlines by reason of presidentially declared disaster.

Sec. 912. Use of certain appraisals to establish amount of disaster loss.

Sec. 913. Treatment of livestock sold on account of weather-related conditions.

Sec. 914. Mortgage financing for residences located in disaster areas.

Sec. 915. Abatement of interest on underpayments by taxpayers in presidentially declared disaster areas

SUBTITLE C—PROVISIONS RELATING TO EMPLOYMENT TAXES

Sec. 921. Clarification of standard to be used in determining employment tax status of securities brokers.

Sec. 922. Clarification of exemption from self-employment tax for certain termination payments received by former insurance salesmen.

SUBTITLE D—PROVISIONS RELATING TO SMALL BUSINESSES

Sec. 931. Waiver of penalty through June 30, 1998, on small businesses failing to make electronic fund transfers of taxes.

Sec. 932. Clarification of treatment of home office use for administrative and management activities.

Sec. 933. Averaging of farm income over 3 years.

Sec. 934. Increase in deduction for health insurance costs of self- employed individuals.

Sec. 935. Moratorium on certain regulations.

SUBTITLE E—BROWNFIELDS

Sec. 941. Expensing of environmental remediation costs.

SUBTITLE F—EMPOWERMENT ZONES, ENTERPRISE COMMUNITIES, BROWNFIELDS, AND COMMUNITY DEVELOPMENT FINANCIAL INSTITUTIONS

Chapter 1—Additional Empowerment Zones

Sec. 951. Additional empowerment zones.

Chapter 2—New Empowerment Zones

Sec. 952. Designation of new empowerment zones.

Sec. 953. Volume cap not to apply to enterprise zone facility bonds with respect to new empowerment zones.

Sec. 954. Modification to eligibility criteria for designation of future enterprise zones in Alaska or Hawaii.

Chapter 3—Treatment Of Empowerment Zones and Enterprise Communities

Sec. 955. Modifications to enterprise zone facility bond rules for all empowerment zones and enterprise communities.

Sec. 956. Modifications to enterprise zone business definition for all empowerment zones and enterprise communities.

SUBTITLE G—OTHER PROVISIONS

Sec. 961. Use of estimates of shrinkage for inventory accounting.

Sec. 962. Assignment of workmen's compensation liability eligible for exclusion relating to personal injury liability assignments.

Sec. 963. Tax-exempt status for certain State worker's compensation act companies.

Sec. 964. Election for 1987 partnerships to continue exception from treatment of publicly traded partnerships as corporations.

Sec. 965. Exclusion from unrelated business taxable income for certain sponsorship payments.

SUBTITLE H—EXTENSION OF DUTY-FREE TREATMENT UNDER GENERALIZED SYSTEM OF PREFERENCES

TITLE X—REVENUES

SUBTITLE A—FINANCIAL PRODUCTS

SUBTITLE B—CORPORATE ORGANIZATIONS AND REORGANIZATIONS

SUBTITLE C—ADMINISTRATIVE PROVISIONS

SUBTITLE D—EXCISE AND EMPLOYMENT TAX PROVISIONS

[¶ 4002]   Sec. 101.   CHILD TAX CREDIT.

* * * * * * * * * * * *

(e) Effective Date.—The amendments made by this section shall apply to taxable years beginning after December 31, 1997.

[¶ 4003]   Sec. 201.   HOPE AND LIFETIME LEARNING CREDITS.

* * * * * * * * * * * *

(f) Effective Dates.—

(1) In general.—The amendments made by this section shall apply to expenses paid after December 31, 1997 (in taxable years ending after such date), for education furnished in academic periods beginning after such date.

(2) Lifetime learning credit.—Section 25A(a)(2) of the Internal Revenue Code of 1986 shall apply to expenses paid after June 30, 1998 (in taxable years ending after such date), for education furnished in academic periods beginning after such dates.

[¶ 4004]   Sec. 202.   DEDUCTION FOR INTEREST ON EDUCATION LOANS.

* * * * * * * * * * * *

(e) Effective Date.—The amendments made by this section shall apply to any qualified education loan (as defined in section 221(e)(1) of the Internal Revenue Code of 1986, as added by this section) incurred on, before, or after the date of the enactment of this Act, but only with respect to—

(1) any loan interest payment due and paid after December 31, 1997, and

(2) the portion of the 60-month period referred to in section 221(d) of the Internal Revenue Code of 1986 (as added by this section) after December 31, 1997.

[¶ 4005]   Sec. 203.   PENALTY-FREE WITHDRAWALS FROM INDIVIDUAL RETIRE-MENT PLANS FOR HIGHER EDUCATION EXPENSES.

* * * * * * * * * * *

(c) Effective Date.—The amendments made by this section shall apply to distributions after December 31, 1997, with respect to expenses paid after such date (in taxable years ending after such date), for education furnished in academic periods beginning after such date.

[¶ 4006]   Sec. 211.   MODIFICATIONS OF QUALIFIED STATE TUITION PRO-GRAMS.

* * * * * * * * * * *

(f) Effective Dates.—

(1) In general.—Except as otherwise provided in this subsection, the amendments made by this section shall take effect on January 1, 1998.

(2) Expenses to include room and board.—The amendment made by subsection (a) shall take effect as if included in the amendments made by section 1806 of the Small Business Job Protection Act of 1996.

(3) Eligible educational institution.—The amendment made by subsection (b)(2) shall apply to distributions after December 31, 1997, with respect to expenses paid after such date (in taxable years ending after such date), for education furnished in academic periods beginning after such date.

(4) Coordination with education savings bonds.—The amendment made by subsection (c) shall apply to taxable years beginning after December 31, 1997.

(5) Estate and gift tax changes.—

(A) Gift tax changes.—Paragraphs (2) and (5) of section 529(c) of the Internal Revenue Code of 1986, as amended by this section, shall apply to transfers (including designations of new beneficiaries) made after the date of the enactment of this Act.

(B) Estate tax changes.—Paragraph (4) of such section 529(c) shall apply to estates of decedents dying after June 8, 1997.

(6) Transition rule for pre-august 20, 1996 contracts.—In the case of any contract issued prior to August 20, 1996, section 529(c)(3)(C) of the Internal Revenue Code of 1986 shall be applied for taxable years ending after August 20, 1996, without regard to the requirement that a distribution be transferred to a member of the family or the requirement that a change in beneficiaries may be made only to a member of the family.

[¶ 4007]   Sec. 213.   EDUCATION INDIVIDUAL RETIREMENT ACCOUNTS.

* * * * * * * * * * *

(f) Effective Date.—The amendments made by this section shall apply to taxable years beginning after December 31, 1997.

[¶ 4008]   Sec. 221.   EXTENSION OF EXCLUSION FOR EMPLOYER-PROVIDED EDUCATIONAL ASSISTANCE.

* * * * * * * * * * *

(b) Effective Date.—The amendment made by subsection (a) shall apply to taxable years beginning after December 31, 1996.

[¶ 4009]   Sec. 223.   INCREASE IN ARBITRAGE REBATE EXCEPTION FOR GOVERNMENTAL BONDS USED TO FINANCE EDUCATION FACILITIES.

* * * * * * * * * * * *

(b) Effective Date.—The amendments made by this section shall apply to bonds issued after December 31, 1997.

[¶ 4010]   Sec. 224.   CONTRIBUTIONS OF COMPUTER TECHNOLOGY AND EQUIPMENT FOR ELEMENTARY OR SECONDARY SCHOOL PURPOSES.

* * * * * * * * * * * *

(b) Effective Date.—The amendment made by this section shall apply to taxable years beginning after December 31, 1997.

[¶ 4011]   Sec. 225.   TREATMENT OF CANCELLATION OF CERTAIN STUDENT LOANS.

* * * * * * * * * * * *

(b) Effective Date.—The amendments made by this section shall apply to discharges of indebtedness after the date of the enactment of this Act.

[¶ 4012]   Sec. 226.   INCENTIVES FOR EDUCATION ZONES.

* * * * * * * * * * * *

(c) Effective Date.—The amendments made by this section shall apply to obligations issued after December 31, 1997.

[¶ 4013]   Sec. 301.   RESTORATION OF IRA DEDUCTION FOR CERTAIN TAXPAYERS.

* * * * * * * * * * * *

(c) Effective Date.—The amendments made by this section shall apply to taxable years beginning after December 31, 1997.

[¶ 4014]   Sec. 302.   ESTABLISHMENT OF NONDEDUCTIBLE TAX-FREE INDIVIDUAL RETIREMENT ACCOUNTS.

* * * * * * * * * * * *

(f) Effective Date.—The amendments made by this section shall apply to taxable years beginning after December 31, 1997.

[¶ 4015]   Sec. 303.   DISTRIBUTIONS FROM CERTAIN PLANS MAY BE USED WITHOUT PENALTY TO PURCHASE FIRST HOMES.

* * * * * * * * * * * *

(c) Effective Date.—The amendments made by this section shall apply to payments and distributions in taxable years beginning after December 31, 1997.

[¶ 4016]   Sec. 304.   CERTAIN BULLION NOT TREATED AS COLLECTIBLES.

* * * * * * * * * * * *

(b) Effective Date.—The amendment made by this section shall apply to taxable years beginning after December 31, 1997.

[¶ 4017]   Sec. 311.   MAXIMUM CAPITAL GAINS RATES FOR INDIVIDUALS.

* * * * * * * * * * *

(d) Effective Dates.—

(1) In general.—Except as provided in paragraph (2), the amendments made by this section shall apply to taxable years ending after May 6, 1997.

(2) Withholding.—The amendment made by subsection (c)(1) shall apply only to amounts paid after the date of the enactment of this Act.

(e) Election To Recognize Gain on Assets Held on January 1, 2001.—For purposes of the Internal Revenue Code of 1986—

(1) In general.—A taxpayer other than a corporation may elect to treat—

(A) any readily tradable stock (which is a capital asset) held by such taxpayer on January 1, 2001, and not sold before the next business day after such date, as having been sold on such next business day for an amount equal to its closing market price on such next business day (and as having been reacquired on such next business day for an amount equal to such closing market price), and

(B) any other capital asset or property used in the trade or business (as defined in section 1231(b) of the Internal Revenue Code of 1986) held by the taxpayer on January 1, 2001, as having been sold on such date for an amount equal to its fair market value on such date (and as having been reacquired on such date for an amount equal to such fair market value).

(2) Treatment of gain or loss.—

(A) Any gain resulting from an election under paragraph (1) shall be treated as received or accrued on the date the asset is treated as sold under paragraph (1) and shall be recognized notwithstanding any provision of the Internal Revenue Code of 1986.

(B) Any loss resulting from an election under paragraph (1) shall not be allowed for any taxable year.

(3) Election.—An election under paragraph (1) shall be made in such manner as the Secretary of the Treasury or his delegate may prescribe and shall specify the assets for which such election is made. Such an election, once made with respect to any asset, shall be irrevocable.

(4) Readily tradable stock.—For purposes of this subsection, the term "readily tradable stock" means any stock which, as of January 1, 2001, is readily tradable on an established securities market or otherwise.

[¶ 4018]   Sec. 312.   EXEMPTION FROM TAX FOR GAIN ON SALE OF PRINCIPAL RESIDENCE.

* * * * * * * * * * * *

(d) Effective Date.—

(1) In general.—The amendments made by this section shall apply to sales and exchanges after May 6, 1997.

(2) Sales before date of enactment.—At the election of the taxpayer, the amendments made by this section shall not apply to any sale or exchange before the date of the enactment of this Act.

(3) Certain sales within 2 years after date of enactment.— Section 121 of the Internal Revenue Code of 1986 (as amended by this section) shall be applied without regard to subsection (c)(2)(B) thereof in the case of any sale or exchange of property during the 2- year period beginning on the date of the enactment of this Act if the taxpayer held such property on the date of the enactment of this Act and fails to meet the ownership and use requirements of subsection (a) thereof with respect to such property.

(4) Binding contracts.—At the election of the taxpayer, the amendments made by this section shall not apply to a sale or exchange after the date of the enactment of this Act, if—

(A) such sale or exchange is pursuant to a contract which was binding on such date, or

(B) without regard to such amendments, gain would not be recognized under section 1034 of the Internal Revenue Code of 1986 (as in effect on the day before the date of the enactment of this Act) on such sale or exchange by reason of a new residence acquired on or before such date or with respect to the acquisition of which by the taxpayer a binding contract was in effect on such date.

[¶ 4019]   Sec. 313.   ROLLOVER OF GAIN FROM SALE OF QUALIFIED STOCK.

* * * * * * * * * * *

(c) Effective Date.—The amendments made by this section shall apply to sales after the date of enactment of this Act.

[¶ 4020]   Sec. 314.   AMOUNT OF NET CAPITAL GAIN TAKEN INTO ACCOUNT IN COMPUTING ALTERNATIVE TAX ON CAPITAL GAINS FOR CORPORATIONS NOT TO EXCEED TAXABLE INCOME OF THE CORPORATION.

* * * * * * * * * * *

(b) Effective Date.—The amendment made by this section shall apply to taxable years ending after December 31, 1997.

[¶ 4021]   Sec. 401.   EXEMPTION FROM ALTERNATIVE MINIMUM TAX FOR SMALL CORPORATIONS.

* * * * * * * * * * *

(b) Effective Date.—The amendment made by this section shall apply to taxable years beginning after December 31, 1997.

[¶ 4022]   Sec. 403.   MINIMUM TAX NOT TO APPLY TO FARMERS' INSTALLMENT SALES.

* * * * * * * * * * *

(b) Effective Dates.—

(1) In general.—The amendment made by this section shall apply to dispositions in taxable years beginning after December 31, 1987.

(2) Special rule for 1987.—In the case of taxable years beginning in 1987, the last sentence of section 56(a)(6) of the Internal Revenue Code of 1986 (as in effect for such taxable years) shall be applied by inserting "or in the case of a taxpayer using the cash receipts and disbursements method of accounting, any disposition described in section 453C(e)(1)(B)(ii)" after "section 453C(e)(4)".

[¶ 4023]   Sec. 501.   COST-OF-LIVING ADJUSTMENTS RELATING TO ESTATE AND GIFT TAX PROVISIONS.

* * * * * * * * * * *

(f) Effective date.—The amendments made by this section shall apply to the estates of decedents dying, and gifts made, after December 31, 1997.

[¶ 4024]   Sec. 502.   FAMILY-OWNED BUSINESS EXCLUSION.

* * * * * * * * * * *

(c) Effective Date.—The amendments made by this section shall apply to estates of decedents dying after December 31, 1997.

[¶ 4025]   Sec. 503.   MODIFICATIONS TO RATE OF INTEREST ON PORTION OF ESTATE TAX EXTENDED UNDER SECTION 6166.

* * * * * * * * * * *

(d) Effective Date.—

(1) In general.—The amendments made by this section shall apply to estates of decedents dying after December 31, 1997.

(2) Election.—In the case of the estate of any decedent dying before January 1, 1998, with respect to which there is an election under section 6166 of the Internal Revenue Code of 1986, the executor of the estate may elect to have the amendments made by this section apply with respect to installments due after the effective date of the election; except that the 2-percent portion of such installments shall be equal to the amount which would be the 4-percent portion of such installments without regard to such election. Such an election shall be made before January 1, 1999 in the manner prescribed by the Secretary of the Treasury and, once made, is irrevocable.

[¶ 4026]   Sec. 504.   EXTENSION OF TREATMENT OF CERTAIN RENTS UNDER SECTION 2032A TO LINEAL DESCENDANTS.

* * * * * * * * * * *

(c) Effective Date.—The amendments made by this section shall apply with respect to leases entered into after December 31, 1976.

[¶ 4027]   Sec. 505.   CLARIFICATION OF JUDICIAL REVIEW OF ELIGIBILITY FOR EXTENSION OF TIME FOR PAYMENT OF ESTATE TAX.

* * * * * * * * * * *

(c) Effective Date.—The amendments made by this section shall apply to the estates of decedents dying after the date of the enactment of this Act.

[¶ 4028]   Sec. 506.   GIFTS MAY NOT BE REVALUED FOR ESTATE TAX PURPOSES AFTER EXPIRATION OF STATUTE OF LIMITATIONS.

* * * * * * * * * * *

(e) Effective Dates.—

(1) In general.—The amendments made by subsections (a) and (c) shall apply to gifts made after the date of the enactment of this Act.

(2) Subsection (b)—The amendment made by subsection (b) shall apply to gifts made in calendar years ending after the date of the enactment of this Act.

[¶ 4029]   Sec. 507.   REPEAL OF THROWBACK RULES APPLICABLE TO CERTAIN DOMESTIC TRUSTS.

* * * * * * * * * * * *

(c) Effective Dates.—

(1) Accumulation distributions.—The amendments made by subsection (a) shall apply to distributions in taxable years beginning after the date of the enactment of this Act.

(2) Transferred property.—The amendments made by subsection (b) shall apply to sales or exchanges after the date of the enactment of this Act.

[¶ 4030]   Sec. 508.   TREATMENT OF LAND SUBJECT TO A QUALIFIED CONSERVATION EASEMENT.

* * * * * * * * * * * *

(e) Effective Dates.—

(1) Exclusion.—The amendments made by subsections (a) and (b) shall apply to estates of decedents dying after December 31, 1997.

(2) Easements.—The amendments made by subsections (c) and (d) shall apply to easements granted after December 31, 1997.

[¶ 4031]   Sec. 511.   EXPANSION OF EXCEPTION FROM GENERATION-SKIPPING TRANSFER TAX FOR TRANSFERS TO INDIVIDUALS WITH DECEASED PARENTS.

* * * * * * * * * * * *

(c) Effective Date.—The amendments made by this section shall apply to terminations, distributions, and transfers occurring after December 31, 1997.

[¶ 4032]   Sec. 601.   RESEARCH TAX CREDIT.

* * * * * * * * * * * *

(c) Effective Date.—The amendments made by this section shall apply to amounts paid or incurred after May 31, 1997.

[¶ 4033]   Sec. 602.   CONTRIBUTIONS OF STOCK TO PRIVATE FOUNDATIONS.

* * * * * * * * * * * *

(b) Effective Date.—The amendment made by subsection (a) shall apply to contributions made after May 31, 1997.

[¶ 4034]   Sec. 603.   WORK OPPORTUNITY TAX CREDIT.

* * * * * * * * * * * *

(e) Effective date.—The amendments made by this section shall apply to individuals who begin work for the employer after September 30, 1997.

[¶ 4035]   Sec. 604.   ORPHAN DRUG TAX CREDIT.

* * * * * * * * * * * *

(b) Effective Date.—The amendment made by subsection (a) shall apply to amounts paid or incurred after May 31, 1997.

[¶ 4036]   Sec. 701.   TAX INCENTIVES FOR REVITALIZATION OF THE DISTRICT OF COLUMBIA.

* * * * * * * * * * * *

(d) Effective Date.—Except as provided in subsection (c), the amendments made by this section shall take effect on the date of the enactment of this Act.

[¶ 4037]   Sec. 801.   INCENTIVES FOR EMPLOYING LONG-TERM FAMILY ASSISTANCE RECIPIENTS.

* * * * * * * * * * * *

(c) Effective Date.—The amendments made by this section shall apply to individuals who begin work for the employer after December 31, 1997.

[¶ 4038]   Sec. 901.   GENERAL REVENUE PORTION OF HIGHWAY MOTOR FUELS TAXES DEPOSITED INTO HIGHWAY TRUST FUND.

* * * * * * * * * * * *

(e) Delayed Deposits of Highway Motor Fuel Tax Revenues.— Notwithstanding section 6302 of the Internal Revenue Code of 1986, in the case of deposits of taxes imposed by sections 4041 and 4081 (other than subsection (a)(2)(A)(ii)) of the Internal Revenue Code of 1986, the due date for any deposit which would (but for this subsection) be required to be made after July 31, 1998, and before October 1, 1998, shall be October 5, 1998.

(f) Effective Date.—The amendments made by this section shall apply to taxes received in the Treasury after September 30, 1997.

[¶ 4039]   Sec. 902.   REPEAL OF TAX ON DIESEL FUEL USED IN RECREATIONAL BOATS.

* * * * * * * * * * * *

(c) Effective Date.—The amendments made by this section shall take effect on January 1, 1998.

[¶ 4040] Sec. 903. CONTINUED APPLICATION OF TAX ON IMPORTED RE-CYCLED HALON- 1211.

* * * * * * * * * * *

(b) Effective Date.—The amendment made by subsection (a) shall take effect on the date of the enactment of this Act.

[¶ 4041] Sec. 904. UNIFORM RATE OF TAX ON VACCINES.

* * * * * * * * * * *

(d) Effective Date.—The amendments made by this section shall take effect on the day after the date of the enactment of this Act.

(e) Limitation on Certain Credits or Refunds.—For purposes of applying section 4132(b) of the Internal Revenue Code of 1986 with respect to any claim for credit or refund filed before January 1, 1999, the amount of tax taken into account shall not exceed the tax computed under the rate in effect on the day after the date of the enactment of this Act.

[¶ 4042] Sec. 905. OPERATORS OF MULTIPLE GASOLINE RETAIL OUTLETS TREATED AS WHOLESALE DISTRIBUTOR FOR REFUND PURPOSES.

* * * * * * * * * * *

(b) Effective Date.—The amendment made by subsection (a) shall apply to sales after the date of the enactment of this Act.

[¶ 4043] Sec. 906. EXEMPTION OF ELECTRIC AND OTHER CLEAN-FUEL MO-TOR VEHICLES FROM LUXURY AUTOMOBILE CLASSIFICATION.

* * * * * * * * * * *

(c) Effective Date.—The amendments made by this section shall apply to sales and installations occurring after the date of the enactment of this Act.

[¶ 4044] Sec. 907. RATE OF TAX ON CERTAIN SPECIAL FUELS DETERMINED ON BASIS OF BTU EQUIVALENCY WITH GASOLINE.

* * * * * * * * * * *

(c) Effective Date.—The amendments made by this section shall take effect on October 1, 1997.

[¶ 4045] Sec. 908. MODIFICATION OF TAX TREATMENT OF HARD CIDER.

* * * * * * * * * * *

(c) Effective Date.—The amendments made by this section shall take effect on October 1, 1997.

[¶ 4046] Sec. 909. STUDY OF FEASIBILITY OF MOVING COLLECTION POINT FOR DISTILLED SPIRITS EXCISE TAX.

(a) In General.—The Secretary of the Treasury or his delegate shall conduct a study of options for changing the event on which the tax imposed by section 5001 of the Internal Revenue Code of 1986 is determined. One such option which shall be studied is determining such tax on removal from registered wholesale warehouses. In studying each such option, such Secretary shall focus on administrative issues including—

(1) tax compliance,

(2) the number of taxpayers required to pay the tax,

(3) the types of financial responsibility requirements that might be required, and

(4) special requirements regarding segregation of non-tax-paid distilled spirits from other products.

(b) Report.—The report of such study shall be submitted to the Committee on Finance of the Senate and the Committee on Ways and Means of the House of Representatives not later than March 31, 1998.

[¶ 4047] Sec. 910. CLARIFICATION OF AUTHORITY TO USE SEMI-GENERIC DESIGNATIONS ON WINE LABELS.

* * * * * * * * * * * *

(b) Effective Date.—The amendment made by this section shall take effect on the date of the enactment of this Act.

[¶ 4048] Sec. 911. AUTHORITY TO POSTPONE CERTAIN TAX-RELATED DEADLINES BY REASON OF PRESIDENTIALLY DECLARED DISASTER.

* * * * * * * * * * *

(c) Effective Date.—The amendments made by this section shall apply with respect to any period for performing an act that has not expired before the date of the enactment of this Act.

[¶ 4049] Sec. 912. USE OF CERTAIN APPRAISALS TO ESTABLISH AMOUNT OF DISASTER LOSS.

* * * * * * * * * * *

(b) Effective Date.—The amendment made by subsection (a) shall take effect on the date of the enactment of this Act.

[¶ 4050] Sec. 913. TREATMENT OF LIVESTOCK SOLD ON ACCOUNT OF WEATHER-RELATED CONDITIONS.

* * * * * * * * * * *

(c) Effective Date.—The amendments made by this section shall apply to sales and exchanges after December 31, 1996.

[¶ 4051] Sec. 915. ABATEMENT OF INTEREST ON UNDERPAYMENTS BY TAX-PAYERS IN PRESIDENTIALLY DECLARED DISASTER AREAS.

(a) In General.—If the Secretary of the Treasury extends for any period the time for filing income tax returns under section 6081 of the Internal Revenue Code of 1986 and the time for paying income tax with respect to such returns under section 6161 of such Code (and waives any penalties relating to the failure to so file or so pay) for any individual located in a Presidentially declared disaster area, the Secretary shall, notwithstanding section 7508A(b) of such Code, abate for such period the assessment of any interest prescribed under section 6601 of such Code on such income tax.

(b) Presidentially Declared Disaster Area.—For purposes of subsection (a), the term "Presidentially declared disaster area" means, with respect to any individual, any area which the President has determined during 1997 warrants assistance by the Federal Government under the Robert T. Stafford Disaster Relief and Emergency Assistance Act.

(c) Individual.—For purposes of this section, the term "individual" shall not include any estate or trust.

(d) Effective Date.—This section shall apply to disasters declared after December 31, 1996.

[¶ 4052] Sec. 921. CLARIFICATION OF STANDARD TO BE USED IN DETERMINING EMPLOYMENT TAX STATUS OF SECURITIES BROKERS.

(a) In General.—In determining for purposes of the Internal Revenue Code of 1986 whether a registered representative of a securities broker-dealer is an employee (as defined in section 3121(d) of the Internal Revenue Code of 1986), no weight shall be given to instructions from the service recipient which are imposed only in compliance with investor protection standards imposed by the Federal Government, any State government, or a governing body pursuant to a delegation by a Federal or State agency.

(b) Effective Date.—Subsection (a) shall apply to services performed after December 31, 1997.

[¶ 4053] Sec. 922. CLARIFICATION OF EXEMPTION FROM SELF-EMPLOYMENT TAX FOR CERTAIN TERMINATION PAYMENTS RECEIVED BY FORMER INSURANCE SALESMEN.

* * * * * * * * * * * *

(c) Effective Date.—The amendments made by this section shall apply to payments after December 31, 1997.

[¶ 4054] Sec. 931. WAIVER OF PENALTY THROUGH JUNE 30, 1998, ON SMALL BUSINESSES FAILING TO MAKE ELECTRONIC FUND TRANSFERS OF TAXES.

* * * * * * * * * * * *

No penalty shall be imposed under the Internal Revenue Code of 1986 solely by reason of a failure by a person to use the electronic fund transfer system established under section 6302(h) of such Code if—

(1) such person is a member of a class of taxpayers first required to use such system on or after July 1, 1997, and

(2) such failure occurs before July 1, 1998.

[¶ 4055]   Sec. 932.   CLARIFICATION OF TREATMENT OF HOME OFFICE USE FOR ADMINISTRATIVE AND MANAGEMENT ACTIVITIES.

* * * * * * * * * * *

(b) Effective Date.—The amendment made by subsection (a) shall apply to taxable years beginning after December 31, 1998.

[¶ 4056]   Sec. 933.   AVERAGING OF FARM INCOME OVER 3 YEARS.

* * * * * * * * * * *

(c) Effective Date.—The amendments made by this section shall apply to taxable years beginning after December 31, 1997, and before January 1, 2001.

[¶ 4057]   Sec. 934.   INCREASE IN DEDUCTION FOR HEALTH INSURANCE COSTS OF SELF- EMPLOYED INDIVIDUALS.

* * * * * * * * * * *

(b) Effective Date.—The amendment made by this section shall apply to taxable years beginning after December 31, 1996.

[¶ 4058]   Sec. 935.   MORATORIUM ON CERTAIN REGULATIONS.

* * * * * * * * * * *

No temporary or final regulation with respect to the definition of a limited partner under section 1402(a)(13) of the Internal Revenue Code of 1986 may be issued or made effective before July 1, 1998.

[¶ 4059]   Sec. 941.   EXPENSING OF ENVIRONMENTAL REMEDIATION COSTS.

* * * * * * * * * * *

(c) Effective Date.—The amendments made by this section shall apply to expenditures paid or incurred after the date of the enactment of this Act, in taxable years ending after such date.

[¶ 4060]   Sec. 951.   ADDITIONAL EMPOWERMENT ZONES.

(c) Effective Date.—The amendments made by this section shall take effect on the date of the enactment of this Act, except that designations of new empowerment zones made pursuant to such amendments shall be made during the 180-day period beginning on the date of the enactment of this Act. No designation pursuant to such amendments shall take effect before January 1, 2000.

[¶ 4061]   Sec. 953.   VOLUME CAP NOT TO APPLY TO ENTERPRISE ZONE FACILITY BONDS WITH RESPECT TO NEW EMPOWERMENT ZONES.

* * * * * * * * * * *

(b) Effective Date.—The amendment made by this section shall apply to obligations issued after the date of the enactment of this Act.

[¶ 4062]   Sec. 955.   MODIFICATIONS TO ENTERPRISE ZONE FACILITY BOND RULES FOR ALL EMPOWERMENT ZONES AND ENTERPRISE COMMUNITIES.

* * * * * * * * * * *

(c) Effective Date.—The amendments made by this section shall apply to obligations issued after the date of the enactment of this Act.

[¶ 4063]   Sec. 956.   MODIFICATIONS TO ENTERPRISE ZONE BUSINESS DEFINITION FOR ALL EMPOWERMENT ZONES AND ENTERPRISE COMMUNITIES.

* * * * * * * * * * *

(b) Effective Dates.—

(1) In general.—The amendments made by this section shall apply to taxable years beginning on or after the date of the enactment of this Act.

(2) Special rule for enterprise zone facility bonds.—For purposes of section 1394(b) of the Internal Revenue Code of 1986, the amendments made by this section shall apply to obligations issued after the date of the enactment of this Act.

[¶ 4064]   Sec. 961.   USE OF ESTIMATES OF SHRINKAGE FOR INVENTORY ACCOUNTING.

* * * * * * * * * * *

(b) Effective Date.—

(1) In general.—The amendment made by this section shall apply to taxable years ending after the date of the enactment of this Act.

(2) Coordination with section 481.—In the case of any taxpayer permitted by this section to change its method of accounting to a permissible method for any taxable year—

(A) such changes shall be treated as initiated by the taxpayer,

(B) such changes shall be treated as made with the consent of the Secretary of the Treasury, and

(C) the period for taking into account the adjustments under section 481 by reason of such change shall be 4 years.

[¶ 4065]   Sec. 962.   ASSIGNMENT OF WORKMEN'S COMPENSATION LIABILITY ELIGIBLE FOR EXCLUSION RELATING TO PERSONAL INJURY LIABILITY ASSIGNMENTS.

* * * * * * * * * * *

(b) Effective Date.—The amendments made by subsection (a) shall apply to claims under workmen's compensation acts filed after the date of the enactment of this Act.

[¶ 4066]   Sec. 963.   TAX-EXEMPT STATUS FOR CERTAIN STATE WORKER'S COMPENSATION ACT COMPANIES.

* * * * * * * * * * *

(c) Effective Date.—The amendments made by this section shall apply to taxable years beginning after December 31, 1997.

[¶ 4067]   Sec. 964.   ELECTION FOR 1987 PARTNERSHIPS TO CONTINUE EXCEPTION FROM TREATMENT OF PUBLICLY TRADED PARTNERSHIPS AS CORPORATIONS.

* * * * * * * * * * * *

(b) Effective Date.—The amendment made by this section shall apply to taxable years beginning after December 31, 1997.

[¶ 4068]   Sec. 965.   EXCLUSION FROM UNRELATED BUSINESS TAXABLE INCOME FOR CERTAIN SPONSORSHIP PAYMENTS.

* * * * * * * * * * * *

(b) Effective Date.—The amendment made by this section shall apply to payments solicited or received after December 31, 1997.

[¶ 4069]   Sec. 966.   ASSOCIATIONS OF HOLDERS OF TIMESHARE INTERESTS TO BE TAXED LIKE OTHER HOMEOWNERS ASSOCIATIONS.

* * * * * * * * * * * *

(e) Effective Date.—The amendments made by this section shall apply to taxable years beginning after December 31, 1996.

[¶ 4070]   Sec. 967.   ADDITIONAL ADVANCE REFUNDING OF CERTAIN VIRGIN ISLAND BONDS.

* * * * * * * * * * * *

Subclause (I) of section 149(d)(3)(A)(i) of the Internal Revenue Code of 1986 shall not apply to the second advance refunding of any issue of the Virgin Islands which was first advance refunded before June 9, 1997, if the debt provisions of the refunding bonds are changed to repeal the priority first lien requirement of the refunded bonds.

[¶ 4071]   Sec. 968.   NONRECOGNITION OF GAIN ON SALE OF STOCK TO CERTAIN FARMERS' COOPERATIVES.

* * * * * * * * * * * *

(b) Effective Date.—The amendment made by this section shall apply to sales after December 31, 1997.

[¶ 4072]   Sec. 969.   INCREASED DEDUCTIBILITY OF BUSINESS MEAL EXPENSES FOR INDIVIDUALS SUBJECT TO FEDERAL HOURS OF SERVICE.

* * * * * * * * * * * *

(b) Effective Date.—The amendment made by subsection (a) shall apply to taxable years beginning after December 31, 1997.

[¶ 4073]   Sec. 970.   CLARIFICATION OF DE MINIMIS FRINGE BENEFIT RULES TO NO- CHARGE EMPLOYEE MEALS.

* * * * * * * * * * *

(b) Effective Date.—The amendment made by this section shall apply to taxable years beginning after December 31, 1997.

[¶ 4074]   Sec. 971.   EXEMPTION OF THE INCREMENTAL COST OF A CLEAN FUEL VEHICLE FROM THE LIMITS ON DEPRECIATION FOR VEHICLES.

* * * * * * * * * * *

(b) Effective Date.—The amendments made by this section shall apply to property placed in service after the date of enactment of this Act and before January 1, 2005.

[¶ 4075]   Sec. 972.   TEMPORARY SUSPENSION OF TAXABLE INCOME LIMIT ON PERCENTAGE DEPLETION FOR MARGINAL PRODUCTION.

* * * * * * * * * * *

(b) Effective Date.—The amendment made by subsection (a) shall apply to taxable years beginning after December 31, 1997.

[¶ 4076]   Sec. 973.   INCREASE IN STANDARD MILEAGE RATE EXPENSE DEDUCTION FOR CHARITABLE USE OF PASSENGER AUTOMOBILE.

* * * * * * * * * * *

(b) Effective Date.—The amendment made by subsection (a) shall apply to taxable years beginning after December 31, 1997.

[¶ 4077]   Sec. 974.   CLARIFICATION OF TREATMENT OF CERTAIN RECEIVABLES PURCHASED BY COOPERATIVE HOSPITAL SERVICE ORGANIZATIONS.

* * * * * * * * * * *

(b) Effective Date.—The amendment made by subsection (a) shall apply to taxable years beginning after December 31, 1996.

[¶ 4078]   Sec. 975.   DEDUCTION IN COMPUTING ADJUSTED GROSS INCOME FOR EXPENSES IN CONNECTION WITH SERVICE PERFORMED BY CERTAIN OFFICIALS.

* * * * * * * * * * *

(b) Effective Date.—The amendment made by this section shall apply to expenses paid or incurred in taxable years beginning after December 31, 1986.

[¶ 4079] Sec. 976. COMBINED EMPLOYMENT TAX REPORTING DEMONSTRATION PROJECT.

(a) In General.—The Secretary of the Treasury shall provide for a demonstration project to assess the feasibility and desirability of expanding combined Federal and State tax reporting.

(b) Description of Demonstration Project.—The demonstration project under subsection (a) shall be—

(1) carried out between the Internal Revenue Service and the State of Montana for a period ending with the date which is 5 years after the date of the enactment of this Act,

(2) limited to the reporting of employment taxes, and

(3) limited to the disclosure of the taxpayer identity (as defined in section 6103(b)(6) of such Code) and the signature of the taxpayer.

[¶ 4080] Sec. 977. ELECTIVE CARRYBACK OF EXISTING CARRYOVERS OF NATIONAL RAILROAD PASSENGER CORPORATION.

(a) Elective Carryback.—

(1) In general.—If the National Railroad Passenger Corporation (in this section referred to as the "Corporation")—

(A) makes an election under this section for its first taxable year ending after September 30, 1997, and

(B) agrees to the conditions specified in paragraph (2),

(2) Conditions.—

(A) In general.—This section shall only apply to the Corporation if it agrees (in such manner as the Secretary of the Treasury or his delegate may prescribe) to—

(i) except as provided in clause (ii), use any refund of the payment described in paragraph (1) (and any interest thereon) solely to finance qualified expenses of the Corporation, and

(ii) make the payments to non-Amtrak States as described in subsection (c).

(B) Repayment.—

(i) In general.—The Corporation shall repay to the United States any amount not used in accordance with this paragraph and any amount remaining unused as of January 1, 2010.

(ii) Special rules.—For purposes of clause (i)—

(I) no amount shall be treated as remaining unused as of January 1, 2010, if it is obligated as of such date for a qualified expense, and

(II) the Corporation shall not be treated as failing to meet the requirements of clause (i) by reason of investing any amount for a temporary period.

(3) Amount.—For purposes of paragraph (1)—

(A) In general.—The amount determined under this paragraph shall be the lesser of—

(i) 35 percent of the Corporation's existing qualified carryovers, or

(ii) the Corporation's net tax liability for the carryback period.

(B) Dollar limit.—Such amount shall not exceed $2,323,000,000.

(b) Existing Qualified Carryovers; Net Tax Liability.—For purposes of this section—

(1) Existing qualified carryovers.—The term "existing qualified carryovers" means the aggregate of the amounts which are net operating loss carryovers under section 172(b) of the Internal Revenue Code of 1986 to the Corporation's first taxable year ending after September 30, 1997.

(2) Net tax liability for carryback period.—

(A) In general.—The Corporation's net tax liability for the carryback period is the aggregate of the net tax liability of the Corporation's railroad predecessors for taxable years in the carryback period.

(B) Net tax liability.—The term "net tax liability" means, with respect to any taxable year, the amount of the tax imposed by chapter 1 of the Internal Revenue Code of 1986 (or any corresponding provision of prior law) for such taxable year, reduced by the sum of the credits allowable against such tax under such Code (or any corresponding provision of prior law).

(C) Carryback period.—The term "carryback period" means the period—

(i) which begins with the first taxable year of any railroad predecessor beginning before January 1, 1971, for which there is a net tax liability, and

(ii) which ends with the last taxable year of any railroad predecessor beginning before January 1, 1971.

(3) Railroad predecessor.—

(A) In general.—The term "railroad predecessor" means—

(i) any railroad which entered into a contract under section 401 or 404(a) of the Rail Passenger Service Act of 1970 relieving the railroad of its entire responsibility for the provision of intercity rail passenger service, and

(ii) any predecessor thereof.

(B) Consolidated returns.—If any railroad described in subparagraph (A) was a member of an affiliated group which filed a consolidated return for any taxable year in the carryback period, each member of such group shall be treated as a railroad predecessor for such year.

(c) Payments to Non-Amtrak States.—

(1) In general.—Within 30 days after receipt of any refund of any payment described in subsection (a)(1), the Corporation shall pay to each non-Amtrak State an amount equal to 1 percent of the amount of such refund.

(2) Use of payment.—Each non-Amtrak State shall use the payment described in paragraph (1) (and any interest thereon) solely to finance qualified expenses of the State.

(3) Repayment.—A non-Amtrak State shall pay to the United States—

(A) any portion of the payment received by the State under paragraph (1) (and any interest thereon) which is used for a purpose other than to finance qualified expenses of the State or which remains unused as of January 1, 2010, or

(B) if such State ceases to be a non-Amtrak State, the portion of such payment (and any interest thereon) remaining as of the date of the cessation.

(d) Tax Consequences.—

(1) Reduction in carryovers.—If the Corporation elects the application of this section, the Corporation's existing qualified carryovers shall be reduced by an amount equal to the amount determined under subsection (a)(3) divided by 0.35.

(2) Reduction in tax paid by railroad predecessors.—

(A) In general.—The Secretary of the Treasury or his delegate shall appropriately adjust the tax account of each railroad predecessor to reduce the net tax liability of such predecessor for taxable years beginning in the carryback period which is offset by reason of the application of this section.

(B) FIFO ordering rule.—The Secretary shall make the adjustments under subparagraph (A) first for the earliest year in the carryback period and then for each subsequent year in such period.

(C) No effect on other taxpayers.—In no event shall any taxpayer other than the Corporation be allowed a refund or credit by reason of this section.

(D) Waiver of limitations.—If the adjustment under subparagraph (A) is barred by the operation of any law or rule of law, such law or rule of law shall be waived solely for purposes of making such adjustment.

(3) Tax treatment of expenditures.—With respect to any payment by the Corporation of qualified expenses described in subsection (e)(1)(A) during any taxable year from the amount of any refund of the payment described in subsection (a)(1)—

(A) no deduction shall be allowed to the Corporation with respect to any amount paid or incurred which is attributable to such amount, and

(B) the basis of any property shall be reduced by the portion of the cost of such property which is attributable to such amount.

(4) Payments to a non-amtrak state.—No deduction shall be allowed to the Corporation under chapter 1 of the Internal Revenue Code of 1986 for any payment to a non-Amtrak State required under subsection (a)(2)(A)(ii).

(e) Definitions.—For purposes of this section—

(1) Qualified expenses.—The term "qualified expenses" means expenses incurred for—

(A) in the case of the Corporation—

(i) the acquisition of equipment, rolling stock, and other capital improvements, the upgrading of maintenance facilities, and the maintenance of existing equipment, in intercity passenger rail service, and

(ii) the payment of interest and principal on obligations incurred for such acquisition, upgrading, and maintenance, and

(B) in the case of a non-Amtrak State—

(i) the acquisition of equipment, rolling stock, and other capital improvements, the upgrading of maintenance facilities, and the maintenance of existing equipment, in intercity passenger rail service,

(ii) the acquisition of equipment, rolling stock, and other capital improvements, the upgrading of maintenance facilities, and the maintenance of existing equipment, in intercity bus service,

(iii) the purchase of intercity passenger rail services from the Corporation, and

(iv) the payment of interest and principal on obligations incurred for such acquisition, upgrading, maintenance, and purchase.

In the case of a non-Amtrak State which provides its own intercity passenger rail service on the date of the enactment of this paragraph, subparagraph (B) shall be applied by only taking into account clauses (i) and (iv).

(2) Non-amtrak state.—The term "non-Amtrak State" means, with respect to any payment, any State which does not receive intercity passenger rail service from the Corporation at any time during the period beginning on the date of the enactment of this Act and ending on the date of the payment.

(f) Authorizing Reform Required.—

(1) In general.—The Secretary of the Treasury shall not make payment of any refund of any payment described in subsection (a)(1) earlier than the date of the enactment of Federal legislation, other than legislation included in this section, which is enacted after July 29, 1997, and which authorizes reforms of the National Railroad Passenger Corporation.

(2) No interest.—Notwithstanding any other provision of law, if the payment of any refund is delayed by reason of paragraph (1), no interest shall accrue with respect to such payment prior to the 45th day following the date of the enactment of Federal legislation described in paragraph (1).

(3) Estimate of revenue.—For purposes of estimating revenues under budget reconciliation, the impact of this section on Federal revenues shall be determined without regard to this subsection.

[¶ 4081] Sec. 1001. CONSTRUCTIVE SALES TREATMENT FOR APPRECIATED FINANCIAL POSITIONS.

* * * * * * * * * * *

(d) Effective Dates.—

(1) In general.—Except as otherwise provided in this subsection, the amendments made by this section shall apply to any constructive sale after June 8, 1997.

(2) Exception for sales of positions, etc. held before june 9, 1997.—If—

(A) before June 9, 1997, the taxpayer entered into any transaction which is a constructive sale of any appreciated financial position, and

(B) before the close of the 30-day period beginning on the date of the enactment of this Act or before such later date as may be specified by the Secretary of the Treasury, such transaction and position are clearly identified in the taxpayer's records as offsetting,

such transaction and position shall not be taken into account in determining whether any other constructive sale after June 8, 1997, has occurred. The preceding sentence shall cease to apply as of the date such transaction is closed or the taxpayer ceases to hold such position.

(3) Special rule.—In the case of a decedent dying after June 8, 1997, if—

(A) there was a constructive sale on or before such date of any appreciated financial position,

(B) the transaction resulting in such constructive sale of such position remains open (with respect to the decedent or any related person)—

(i) for not less than 2 years after the date of such transaction (whether such period is before or after June 8, 1997), and

(ii) at any time during the 3-year period ending on the date of the decedent's death, and

(C) such transaction is not closed within the 30-day period beginning on the date of the enactment of this Act,

then, for purposes of such Code, such position (and the transaction resulting in such constructive sale) shall be treated as property constituting rights to receive an item of income in respect of a decedent under section 691 of such Code. Section 1014(c) of such Code shall not apply to so much of such position's or property's value (as included in the decedent's estate for purposes of chapter 11 of such Code) as exceeds its fair market value as of the date such transaction is closed.

(4) Election of mark to market by securities traders and traders and dealers in commodities.—

(A) In general.—The amendments made by subsection (b) shall apply to taxable years ending after the date of the enactment of this Act.

(B) 4-year spread of adjustments.—In the case of a taxpayer who elects under subsection (e) or (f) of section 475 of the Internal Revenue Code of 1986 (as added by this section) to change its method of accounting for the taxable year which includes the date of the enactment of this Act—

(i) any identification required under such subsection with respect to securities and commodities held on the date of the enactment of this Act shall be treated as timely made if made on or before the 30th day after such date of enactment, and

(ii) the net amount of the adjustments required to be taken into account by the taxpayer under section 481 of such Code shall be taken into account ratably over the 4-taxable year period beginning with such first taxable year.

[¶ 4082] Sec. 1002. LIMITATION ON EXCEPTION FOR INVESTMENT COMPANIES UNDER SECTION 351.

* * * * * * * * * * *

(b) Effective Date.—

(1) In general.—The amendment made by subsection (a) shall apply to transfers after June 8, 1997, in taxable years ending after such date.

(2) Binding contracts.—The amendment made by subsection (a) shall not apply to any transfer pursuant to a written binding contract in effect on June 8, 1997, and at all times thereafter before such transfer if such contract provides for the transfer of a fixed amount of property.

[¶ 4083] Sec. 1003. GAINS AND LOSSES FROM CERTAIN TERMINATIONS WITH RESPECT TO PROPERTY.

(a) Application of Capital Treatment to Property Other Than Personal Property.—

* * * * * * * * * * *

(2) Effective date.—The amendment made by paragraph (1) shall apply to terminations more than 30 days after the date of the enactment of this Act.

(b) Treatment of Short Sales of Property Which Becomes Substantially Worthless.—

* * * * * * * * * * *

(2) Effective date.—The amendment made by paragraph (1) shall apply to property which becomes substantially worthless after the date of the enactment of this Act.

(c) Application of Capital Treatment, Etc. to Obligations Issued by Natural Persons.—

* * * * * * * * * * *

(2) Effective date.—The amendment made by paragraph (1) shall apply to sales, exchanges, and retirements after the date of enactment of this Act.

[¶ 4084]   Sec. 1004.   DETERMINATION OF ORIGINAL ISSUE DISCOUNT WHERE POOLED DEBT OBLIGATIONS SUBJECT TO ACCELERATION.

* * * * * * * * * * *

(b) Effective Dates.—

(1) In general.—The amendment made by this section shall apply to taxable years beginning after the date of the enactment of this Act.

(2) Change in method of accounting.—In the case of any taxpayer required by this section to change its method of accounting for its first taxable year beginning after the date of the enactment of this Act—

(A) such change shall be treated as initiated by the taxpayer,

(B) such change shall be treated as made with the consent of the Secretary of the Treasury, and

(C) the net amount of the adjustments required to be taken into account by the taxpayer under section 481 of the Internal Revenue Code of 1986 shall be taken into account ratably over the 4-taxable year period beginning with such first taxable year.

[¶ 4085]   Sec. 1005.   DENIAL OF INTEREST DEDUCTIONS ON CERTAIN DEBT INSTRUMENTS.

* * * * * * * * * * *

(b) Effective Date.—

(1) In general.—The amendment made by this section shall apply to disqualified debt instruments issued after June 8, 1997.

(2) Transition rule.—The amendment made by this section shall not apply to any instrument issued after June 8, 1997, if such instrument is—

(A) issued pursuant to a written agreement which was binding on such date and at all times thereafter,

(B) described in a ruling request submitted to the Internal Revenue Service on or before such date, or

(C) described on or before such date in a public announcement or in a filing with the Securities and Exchange Commission required solely by reason of the issuance.

[¶ 4086]   Sec. 1011.   TAX TREATMENT OF CERTAIN EXTRAORDINARY DIVIDENDS.

* * * * * * * * * * *

(d) Effective Dates.—

(1) In general.—The amendments made by this section shall apply to distributions after May 3, 1995.

(2) Transition rule.—The amendments made by this section shall not apply to any distribution made pursuant to the terms of—

(A) a written binding contract in effect on May 3, 1995, and at all times thereafter before such distribution, or

(B) a tender offer outstanding on May 3, 1995.

(3) Certain dividends not pursuant to certain redemptions.—In determining whether the amendment made by subsection (a) applies to any extraordinary dividend other than a dividend treated as an extraordinary dividend under section 1059(e)(1) of the Internal Revenue Code of

1986 (as amended by this Act), paragraphs (1) and (2) shall be applied by substituting "September 13, 1995" for "May 3, 1995".

[¶ 4087]   Sec. 1012.   APPLICATION OF SECTION 355 TO DISTRIBUTIONS IN CONNECTION WITH ACQUISITIONS AND TO INTRAGROUP TRANSACTIONS.

* * * * * * * * * * * *

(d) Effective Dates.—

(1) Section 355 rules.—The amendments made by subsections (a) and (b) shall apply to distributions after April 16, 1997, pursuant to a plan (or series of related transactions) which involves an acquisition described in section 355(e)(2)(A)(ii) of the Internal Revenue Code of 1986 occurring after such date.

(2) Divisive transactions.—The amendments made by subsection (c) shall apply to transfers after the date of the enactment of this Act.

(3) Transition rule.—The amendments made by this section shall not apply to any distribution pursuant to a plan (or series of related transactions) which involves an acquisition described in section 355(e)(2)(A)(ii) of the Internal Revenue Code of 1986 (or, in the case of the amendments made by subsection (c), any transfer) occurring after April 16, 1997, if such acquisition or transfer is—

(A) made pursuant to an agreement which was binding on such date and at all times thereafter,

(B) described in a ruling request submitted to the Internal Revenue Service on or before such date, or

(C) described on or before such date in a public announcement or in a filing with the Securities and Exchange Commission required solely by reason of the acquisition or transfer.

This paragraph shall not apply to any agreement, ruling request, or public announcement or filing unless it identifies the acquirer of the distributing corporation or any controlled corporation, or the transferee, whichever is applicable.

[¶ 4088]   Sec. 1013.   TAX TREATMENT OF REDEMPTIONS INVOLVING RELATED CORPORATIONS.

* * * * * * * * * * * *

(d) Effective Date.—

(1) In general.—The amendments made by this section shall apply to distributions and acquisitions after June 8, 1997.

(2) Transition rule.—The amendments made by this section shall not apply to any distribution or acquisition after June 8, 1997, if such distribution or acquisition is—

(A) made pursuant to a written agreement which was binding on such date and at all times thereafter,

(B) described in a ruling request submitted to the Internal Revenue Service on or before such date, or

(C) described in a public announcement or filing with the Securities and Exchange Commission on or before such date.

[¶ 4089]   Sec. 1014.   CERTAIN PREFERRED STOCK TREATED AS BOOT.

* * * * * * * * * * * *

(f) Effective Date.—

(1) In general.—The amendments made by this section shall apply to transactions after June 8, 1997.

(2) Transition rule.—The amendments made by this section shall not apply to any transaction after June 8, 1997, if such transaction is—

(A) made pursuant to a written agreement which was binding on such date and at all times thereafter,

(B) described in a ruling request submitted to the Internal Revenue Service on or before such date, or

(C) described on or before such date in a public announcement or in a filing with the Securities and Exchange Commission required solely by reason of the transaction.

[¶ 4090]   Sec. 1015.   MODIFICATION OF HOLDING PERIOD APPLICABLE TO DIVIDENDS RECEIVED DEDUCTION.

* * * * * * * * * * *

(c) Effective Date.—

(1) In general.—The amendments made by this section shall apply to dividends received or accrued after the 30th day after the date of the enactment of this Act.

(2) Transitional rule.—The amendments made by this section shall not apply to dividends received or accrued during the 2-year period beginning on the date of the enactment of this Act if—

(A) the dividend is paid with respect to stock held by the taxpayer on June 8, 1997, and all times thereafter until the dividend is received,

(B) such stock is continuously subject to a position described in section 246(c)(4) of the Internal Revenue Code of 1986 on June 8, 1997, and all times thereafter until the dividend is received, and

(C) such stock and position are clearly identified in the taxpayer's records within 30 days after the date of the enactment of this Act.

Stock shall not be treated as meeting the requirement of subparagraph (B) if the position is sold, closed, or otherwise terminated and reestablished.

[¶ 4091]   Sec. 1021.   REPORTING OF CERTAIN PAYMENTS MADE TO ATTORNEYS.

* * * * * * * * * * *

(b) Reporting of Attorneys' Fees Payable to Corporations.—The regulations providing an exception under section 6041 of the Internal Revenue Code of 1986 for payments made to corporations shall not apply to payments of attorneys' fees.

(c) Effective Date.—The amendment made by this section shall apply to payments made after December 31, 1997.

[¶ 4092]   Sec. 1022.   DECREASE OF THRESHOLD FOR REPORTING PAYMENTS TO CORPORATIONS PERFORMING SERVICES FOR FEDERAL AGENCIES.

* * * * * * * * * * *

(b) Effective Date.—The amendment made by this section shall apply to returns the due date for which (determined without regard to any extension) is more than 90 days after the date of the enactment of this Act.

[¶ 4093]   Sec. 1023.   DISCLOSURE OF RETURN INFORMATION FOR ADMINISTRATION OF CERTAIN VETERANS PROGRAMS.

* * * * * * * * * * *

(b) Effective Date.—The amendment made by subsection (a) shall take effect on the date of the enactment of this Act.

[¶ 4094]   Sec. 1024. CONTINUOUS LEVY ON CERTAIN PAYMENTS.

* * * * * * * * * * * *

(b) Effective Date.—The amendment made by subsection (a) shall apply to levies issued after the date of the enactment of this Act.

[¶ 4095]   Sec. 1025. MODIFICATION OF LEVY EXEMPTION.

* * * * * * * * * * * *

(b) Effective Date.—The amendment made by subsection (a) shall apply to levies issued after the date of the enactment of this Act.

[¶ 4096]   Sec. 1026. CONFIDENTIALITY AND DISCLOSURE OF RETURNS AND RETURN INFORMATION.

* * * * * * * * * * * *

(c) Effective Date.—The amendments made by this section shall apply to levies issued after the date of the enactment of this Act.

[¶ 4097]   Sec. 1027. RETURNS OF BENEFICIARIES OF ESTATES AND TRUSTS REQUIRED TO FILE RETURNS CONSISTENT WITH ESTATE OR TRUST RETURN OR TO NOTIFY SECRETARY OF INCONSISTENCY.

* * * * * * * * * * * *

(c) Effective Date.—The amendments made by this section shall apply to returns of beneficiaries and owners filed after the date of the enactment of this Act.

[¶ 4098]   Sec. 1028. REGISTRATION AND OTHER PROVISIONS RELATING TO CONFIDENTIAL CORPORATE TAX SHELTERS.

* * * * * * * * * * * *

(e) Effective Date.—

(1) In general.—Except as provided in paragraph (2), the amendments made by this section shall apply to any tax shelter (as defined in section 6111(d) of the Internal Revenue Code of 1986, as amended by this section) interests in which are offered to potential participants after the Secretary of the Treasury prescribes guidance with respect to meeting requirements added by such amendments.

(2) Modifications to substantial understatement penalty.—The amendments made by subsection (c) shall apply to items with respect to transactions entered into after the date of the enactment of this Act.

[¶ 4099]   Sec. 1031. EXTENSION AND MODIFICATION OF TAXES FUNDING AIRPORT AND AIRWAY TRUST FUND; INCREASED DEPOSITS INTO SUCH FUND.

* * * * * * * * * * * *

(e) Effective Dates.—

(1) Fuel taxes.—The amendments made by subsection (a) shall apply take effect on October 1, 1997.

(2) Ticket taxes.—

(A) In general.—Except as otherwise provided in this paragraph, the amendments made by subsections (b) and (c) shall apply to transportation beginning on or after October 1, 1997.

(B) Treatment of amounts paid for tickets purchased before date of enactment.—The amendments made by subsection (c) shall not apply to amounts paid for a ticket purchased before the date of the enactment of this Act for a specified flight beginning on or after October 1, 1997.

(C) Amounts paid for right to award mileage awards.—

(i) In general.—Paragraph (3) of section 4261(e) of the Internal Revenue Code of 1986 (as added by the amendment made by subsection (c)) shall apply to amounts paid (and other benefits provided) after September 30, 1997.

(ii) Payments within controlled group.—For purposes of clause (i), any amount paid after June 11, 1997, and before October 1, 1997, by 1 member of a controlled group for a right which is described in such section 4261(e)(3) and is furnished by another member of such group after September 30, 1997, shall be treated as paid after September 30, 1997. For purposes of the preceding sentence, all persons treated as a single employer under subsection (a) or (b) of section 52 of such Code shall be treated as members of a controlled group.

(3) Increased deposits into airport and airway trust fund.— The amendments made by subsection (d) shall apply with respect to taxes received in the Treasury on and after October 1, 1997.

(g) Delayed Deposits of Airport Trust Fund Tax Revenues.— Notwithstanding section 6302 of the Internal Revenue Code of 1986—

(1) in the case of deposits of taxes imposed by section 4261 of such Code, the due date for any such deposit which would (but for this subsection) be required to be made after August 14, 1997, and before October 1, 1997, shall be October 10, 1997,

(2) in the case of deposits of taxes imposed by section 4261 of such Code, the due date for any such deposit which would (but for this subsection) be required to be made after August 14, 1998, and before October 1, 1998, shall be October 5, 1998, and

(3) in the case of deposits of taxes imposed by sections 4081(a)(2)(A)(ii), 4091, and 4271 of such Code, the due date for any such deposit which would (but for this subsection) be required to be made after July 31, 1998, and before October 1, 1998, shall be October 5, 1998.

[¶ 4100]   Sec. 1032.   KEROSENE TAXED AS DIESEL FUEL.

* * * * * * * * * * * *

(f) Effective Date.—The amendments made by this section shall take effect on July 1, 1998.

(g) Floor Stock Taxes.—

(1) Imposition of tax.—In the case of kerosene which is held on July 1, 1998, by any person, there is hereby imposed a floor stocks tax of 24.4 cents per gallon.

(2) Liability for tax and method of payment.—

(A) Liability for tax.—A person holding kerosene on July 1, 1998, to which the tax imposed by paragraph (1) applies shall be liable for such tax.

(B) Method of payment.—The tax imposed by paragraph (1) shall be paid in such manner as the Secretary shall prescribe.

(C) Time for payment.—The tax imposed by paragraph (1) shall be paid on or before August 31, 1998.

(3) Definitions.—For purposes of this subsection—

(A) Held by a person.—Kerosene shall be considered as "held by a person" if title thereto has passed to such person (whether or not delivery to the person has been made).

(B) Secretary.—The term "Secretary" means the Secretary of the Treasury or his delegate.

(4) Exception for exempt uses.—The tax imposed by paragraph (1) shall not apply to kerosene held by any person exclusively for any use to the extent a credit or refund of the tax imposed by section 4081 of the Internal Revenue Code of 1986 is allowable for such use.

(5) Exception for fuel held in vehicle tank.—No tax shall be imposed by paragraph (1) on kerosene held in the tank of a motor vehicle or motorboat.

(6) Exception for certain amounts of fuel.—

(A) In general.—No tax shall be imposed by paragraph (1) on kerosene held on July 1, 1998, by any person if the aggregate amount of kerosene held by such person on such date does not exceed 2,000 gallons. The preceding sentence shall apply only if such person submits to the Secretary (at the time and in the manner required by the Secretary) such information as the Secretary shall require for purposes of this paragraph.

(B) Exempt fuel.—For purposes of subparagraph (A), there shall not be taken into account fuel held by any person which is exempt from the tax imposed by paragraph (1) by reason of paragraph (4) or (5).

(C) Controlled groups.—For purposes of this paragraph—

(i) Corporations.—

(I) In general.—All persons treated as a controlled group shall be treated as 1 person.

(II) Controlled group.—The term "controlled group" has the meaning given to such term by subsection (a) of section 1563 of such Code; except that for such purposes the phrase "more than 50 percent" shall be substituted for the phrase "at least 80 percent" each place it appears in such subsection.

(ii) Nonincorporated persons under common control.—Under regulations prescribed by the Secretary, principles similar to the principles of clause (i) shall apply to a group of persons under common control where 1 or more of such persons is not a corporation.

(7) Coordination with section 4081.—No tax shall be imposed by paragraph (1) on kerosene to the extent that tax has been (or will be) imposed on such kerosene under section 4081 or 4091 of such Code.

(8) Other laws applicable.—All provisions of law, including penalties, applicable with respect to the taxes imposed by section 4081 of such Code shall, insofar as applicable and not inconsistent with the provisions of this subsection, apply with respect to the floor stock taxes imposed by paragraph (1) to the same extent as if such taxes were imposed by such section 4081.

[¶ 4101]   Sec. 1034. APPLICATION OF COMMUNICATIONS TAX TO PREPAID TELEPHONE CARDS.

* * * * * * * * * * *

(b) Effective Date.—The amendments made by this section shall apply to amounts paid in calendar months beginning more than 60 days after the date of the enactment of this Act.

[¶ 4102]   Sec. 1041. EXPANSION OF LOOK-THRU RULE FOR INTEREST, ANNUITIES, ROYALTIES, AND RENTS DERIVED BY SUBSIDIARIES OF TAX-EXEMPT ORGANIZATIONS.

* * * * * * * * * * *

(b) Effective Date.—

(1) In general.—Except as provided in paragraph (2), the amendments made by this section shall apply to taxable years beginning after the date of the enactment of this Act.

(2) Binding contracts.—The amendments made by this section shall not apply to any payment made during the first 2 taxable years beginning on or after the date of the enactment of this Act if such payment is made pursuant to a written binding contract in effect on June 8, 1997, and at all times thereafter before such payment.

[¶ 4103] Sec. 1042. TERMINATION OF CERTAIN EXCEPTIONS FROM RULES RELATING TO EXEMPT ORGANIZATIONS WHICH PROVIDE COMMERCIAL-TYPE INSURANCE.

(a) In General.—Subparagraphs (A) and (B) of section 1012(c)(4) of the Tax Reform Act of 1986 shall not apply to any taxable year beginning after December 31, 1997.

(b) Special Rules.—In the case of an organization to which section 501(m) of the Internal Revenue Code of 1986 applies solely by reason of the amendment made by subsection (a)—

(1) no adjustment shall be made under section 481 (or any other provision) of such Code on account of a change in its method of accounting for its first taxable year beginning after December 31, 1997, and

(2) for purposes of determining gain or loss, the adjusted basis of any asset held on the 1st day of such taxable year shall be treated as equal to its fair market value as of such day.

(c) Reserve Weakening After June 8, 1997.—Any reserve weakening after June 8, 1997, by an organization described in subsection (b) shall be treated as occurring in such organization's 1st taxable year beginning after December 31, 1997.

(d) Regulations.—The Secretary of the Treasury or his delegate may prescribe rules for providing proper adjustments for organizations described in subsection (b) with respect to short taxable years which begin during 1998 by reason of section 843 of the Internal Revenue Code of 1986.

[¶ 4104] Sec. 1051. DEFINITION OF FOREIGN PERSONAL HOLDING COMPANY INCOME.

* * * * * * * * * * * *

(c) Effective Date.—The amendments made by this section shall apply to taxable years beginning after the date of the enactment of this Act.

[¶ 4105] Sec. 1052. PERSONAL PROPERTY USED PREDOMINANTLY IN THE UNITED STATES TREATED AS NOT PROPERTY OF A LIKE KIND WITH RESPECT TO PROPERTY USED PREDOMINANTLY OUTSIDE THE UNITED STATES.

* * * * * * * * * * * *

(b) Effective Date.—

(1) In general.—The amendment made by this section shall apply to transfers after June 8, 1997, in taxable years ending after such date.

(2) Binding contracts.—The amendment made by this section shall not apply to any transfer pursuant to a written binding contract in effect on June 8, 1997, and at all times thereafter before the disposition of property. A contract shall not fail to meet the requirements of the preceding sentence solely because—

(A) it provides for a sale in lieu of an exchange, or

(B) the property to be acquired as replacement property was not identified under such contract before June 9, 1997.

[¶ 4106] Sec. 1053. HOLDING PERIOD REQUIREMENT FOR CERTAIN FOREIGN TAXES.

* * * * * * * * * * * *

(c) Effective Date.—The amendments made by this section shall apply to dividends paid or accrued more than 30 days after the date of the enactment of this Act.

[¶ 4107]   Sec. 1054. DENIAL OF TREATY BENEFITS FOR CERTAIN PAYMENTS THROUGH HYBRID ENTITIES.

* * * * * * * * * * * *

(b) Effective Date.—The amendments made by this section shall apply upon the date of enactment of this Act.

[¶ 4108]   Sec. 1055. INTEREST ON UNDERPAYMENTS NOT REDUCED BY FOREIGN TAX CREDIT CARRYBACKS.

* * * * * * * * * * * *

(c) Effective Date.—The amendments made by this section shall apply to foreign tax credit carrybacks arising in taxable years beginning after the date of the enactment of this Act.

[¶ 4109]   Sec. 1056. CLARIFICATION OF PERIOD OF LIMITATIONS ON CLAIM FOR CREDIT OR REFUND ATTRIBUTABLE TO FOREIGN TAX CREDIT CARRYFORWARD.

* * * * * * * * * * * *

(b) Effective Date.—The amendment made by subsection (a) shall apply to taxes paid or accrued in taxable years beginning after the date of the enactment of this Act.

[¶ 4110]   Sec. 1057. REPEAL OF EXCEPTION TO ALTERNATIVE MINIMUM FOREIGN TAX CREDIT LIMIT.

* * * * * * * * * * * *

(b) Effective Date.—The amendment made by this section shall apply to taxable years beginning after the date of the enactment of this Act.

[¶ 4111]   Sec. 1061. ALLOCATION OF BASIS AMONG PROPERTIES DISTRIBUTED BY PARTNERSHIP.

* * * * * * * * * * * *

(b) Effective Date.—The amendment made by subsection (a) shall apply to distributions after the date of the enactment of this Act.

[¶ 4112]   Sec. 1062. REPEAL OF REQUIREMENT THAT INVENTORY BE SUBSTANTIALLY APPRECIATED WITH RESPECT TO SALE OR EXCHANGE OF PARTNERSHIP INTEREST.

* * * * * * * * * * * *

(c) Effective Date.—

(1) In general.—The amendments made by this section shall apply to sales, exchanges, and distributions after the date of the enactment of this Act.

(2) Binding contracts.—The amendments made by this section shall not apply to any sale or exchange pursuant to a written binding contract in effect on June 8, 1997, and at all times thereafter before such sale or exchange.

[¶ 4113]   **Sec. 1063. EXTENSION OF TIME FOR TAXING PRECONTRIBUTION GAIN.**

* * * * * * * * * * * * *

(b) Effective Date.—

(1) In general.—The amendment made by subsection (a) shall apply to property contributed to a partnership after June 8, 1997.

(2) Binding contracts.—The amendment made by subsection (a) shall not apply to any property contributed pursuant to a written binding contract in effect on June 8, 1997, and at all times thereafter before such contribution if such contract provides for the contribution of a fixed amount of property.

[¶ 4114]   **Sec. 1071. PENSION ACCRUED BENEFIT DISTRIBUTABLE WITHOUT CONSENT INCREASED TO $5,000.**

* * * * * * * * * *

(c) Effective Date.—The amendments made by this section shall apply to plan years beginning after the date of the enactment of this Act.

[¶ 4115]   **Sec. 1072. ELECTION TO RECEIVE TAXABLE CASH COMPENSATION IN LIEU OF NONTAXABLE PARKING BENEFITS.**

* * * * * * * * * * * *

(b) Effective Date.—The amendment made by this section shall apply to taxable years beginning after December 31, 1997.

[¶ 4116]   **Sec. 1073. REPEAL OF EXCESS DISTRIBUTION AND EXCESS RETIREMENT ACCUMULATION TAX.**

* * * * * * * * * * * *

(c) Effective Dates.—

(1) Excess distribution tax repeal.—Except as provided in paragraph (2), the repeal made by subsection (a) shall apply to excess distributions received after December 31, 1996.

(2) Excess retirement accumulation tax repeal.—The repeal made by subsection (a) with respect to section 4980A(d) of the Internal Revenue Code of 1986 and the amendments made by subsection (b) shall apply to estates of decedents dying after December 31, 1996.

[¶ 4117]   **Sec. 1074. INCREASE IN TAX ON PROHIBITED TRANSACTIONS.**

* * * * * * * * * * * *

(b) Effective Date.—The amendment made by this section shall apply to prohibited transactions occurring after the date of the enactment of this Act.

[¶ 4118]   **Sec. 1075. BASIS RECOVERY RULES FOR ANNUITIES OVER MORE THAN ONE LIFE.**

* * * * * * * * * * * *

(c) Effective Date.—The amendments made by this section shall apply with respect to annuity starting dates beginning after December 31, 1997.

[¶ 4119]   Sec. 1081. TERMINATION OF SUSPENSE ACCOUNTS FOR FAMILY CORPORATIONS REQUIRED TO USE ACCRUAL METHOD OF ACCOUNTING.

* * * * * * * * * * *

(b) Effective Date.—The amendments made by this section shall apply to taxable years ending after June 8, 1997.

[¶ 4120]   Sec. 1082.   MODIFICATION OF TAXABLE YEARS TO WHICH NET OPERATING LOSSES MAY BE CARRIED.

* * * * * * * * * * *

(c) Effective Date.—The amendments made by this section shall apply to net operating losses for taxable years beginning after the date of the enactment of this Act.

[¶ 4121]   Sec. 1083. MODIFICATIONS TO TAXABLE YEARS TO WHICH UNUSED CREDITS MAY BE CARRIED.

* * * * * * * * * * *

(b) Effective Date.—The amendments made by this section shall apply to credits arising in taxable years beginning after December 31, 1997.

[¶ 4122]   Sec. 1084. EXPANSION OF DENIAL OF DEDUCTION FOR CERTAIN AMOUNTS PAID IN CONNECTION WITH INSURANCE.

* * * * * * * * * * *

(d) Effective Date.—The amendments made by this section shall apply to contracts issued after June 8, 1997, in taxable years ending after such date. For purposes of the preceding sentence, any material increase in the death benefit or other material change in the contract shall be treated as a new contract but the addition of covered lives shall be treated as a new contract only with respect to such additional covered lives. For purposes of this subsection, an increase in the death benefit under a policy or contract issued in connection with a lapse described in section 501(d)(2) of the Health Insurance Portability and Accountability Act of 1996 shall not be treated as a new contract.

[¶ 4123]   Sec. 1085.   IMPROVED ENFORCEMENT OF THE APPLICATION OF THE EARNED INCOME CREDIT.

* * * * * * * * * * *

(e) Effective Dates.—

(1) The amendments made by subsection (a) shall apply to taxable years beginning after December 31, 1996.

(2) The amendments made by subsections (b), (c), and (d) shall apply to taxable years beginning after December 31, 1997.

[¶ 4124]   Sec. 1086. LIMITATION ON PROPERTY FOR WHICH INCOME FORE-CAST METHOD MAY BE USED.

* * * * * * * * * * * *

(c) Effective Date.—The amendment made by this section shall apply to property placed in service after the date of the enactment of this Act.

[¶ 4125]   Sec. 1087. EXPANSION OF REQUIREMENT THAT INVOLUNTARILY CONVERTED PROPERTY BE REPLACED WITH PROPERTY ACQUIRED FROM AN UNRELATED PERSON.

* * * * * * * * * * * *

(b) Effective Date.—The amendment made by this section shall apply to involuntary conversions occurring after June 8, 1997.

[¶ 4126]   Sec. 1088. TREATMENT OF EXCEPTION FROM INSTALLMENT SALES RULES FOR SALES OF PROPERTY BY A MANUFACTURER TO A DEALER.

* * * * * * * * * * * *

(b) Effective Date.—

(1) In general.—The amendment made by this section shall apply to taxable years beginning more than 1 year after the date of the enactment of this Act.

(2) Coordination with section 481.—In the case of any taxpayer required by this section to change its method of accounting for any taxable year—

(A) such changes shall be treated as initiated by the taxpayer,

(B) such changes shall be treated as made with the consent of the Secretary of the Treasury, and

(C) the net amount of the adjustments required to be taken into account under section 481(a) of the Internal Revenue Code of 1986 shall be taken into account ratably over the 4 taxable year period beginning with the first taxable year beginning after the date of the enactment of this Act.

[¶ 4127]   Sec. 1089. LIMITATIONS ON CHARITABLE REMAINDER TRUST ELIGIBILITY FOR CERTAIN TRUSTS.

(a) Limitation on Noncharitable Distributions.—

* * * * * * * * * * * *

(2) Effective date.—The amendment made by paragraph (1) shall apply to transfers in trust after June 18, 1997.

(b) Minimum Charitable Benefit.—

* * * * * * * * * * * *

(6) Effective dates.—

(A) In general.—Except as otherwise provided in this paragraph, the amendments made by this subsection shall apply to transfers in trust after July 28, 1997.

(B) Special rule for certain decedents.—The amendments made by this subsection shall not apply to transfers in trust under the terms of a will (or other testamentary instrument) executed on or before July 28, 1997, if the decedent—

(i) dies before January 1, 1999, without having republished the will (or amended such instrument) by codicil or otherwise, or

(ii) was on July 28, 1997, under a mental disability to change the disposition of his property and did not regain his competence to dispose of such property before the date of his death.

[¶ 4128]　Sec. 1090.　EXPANDED SSA RECORDS FOR TAX ENFORCEMENT.
(a) Expansion of Coordinated Enforcement Efforts of IRS and HHS Office of Child Support Enforcement.—

* * * * * * * * * * *

(3) Coordination between secretaries.—The Secretary of the Treasury and the Secretary of Health and Human Services shall consult regarding the implementation issues resulting from the amendments made by this subsection, including interim deadlines for States that may be able before October 1, 1999, to provide the data required by such amendments. The Secretaries shall report to Congress on the results of such consultation.
(4) Effective date.—The amendments made by this subsection shall take effect on October 1, 1998.
(b) Required Submission of SSN's on Applications.—

* * * * * * * * * * *

(2) Effective dates.—
(A) The amendment made by paragraph (1)(A) shall apply to applications made after the date which is 180 days after the date of the enactment of this Act.
(B) The amendments made by subparagraphs (B) and (C) of paragraph (1) shall apply to information obtained on, before, or after the date of the enactment of this Act.

[¶ 4129]　Sec. 1091.　MODIFICATION OF ESTIMATED TAX SAFE HARBORS.

* * * * * * * * * * *

(b) Effective Date.—The amendment made by this section shall apply with respect to any installment payment for taxable years beginning after December 31, 1997.

[¶ 4130]　Sec. 1101.　CERTAIN INDIVIDUALS EXEMPT FROM FOREIGN TAX CREDIT LIMITATION.

* * * * * * * * * * *

(b) Effective Date.—The amendment made by subsection (a) shall apply to taxable years beginning after December 31, 1997.

[¶ 4131]　Sec. 1102.　EXCHANGE RATE USED IN TRANSLATING FOREIGN TAXES.

* * * * * * * * * * *

(c) Effective Dates.—
(1) In general.—The amendments made by subsections (a)(1) and (b) shall apply to taxes paid or accrued in taxable years beginning after December 31, 1997.
(2) Subsection (a)(2).—The amendment made by subsection (a)(2) shall apply to taxes which relate to taxable years beginning after December 31, 1997.

[¶ 4132]　Sec. 1103.　ELECTION TO USE SIMPLIFIED SECTION 904 LIMITATION FOR ALTERNATIVE MINIMUM TAX.

* * * * * * * * * * *

(b) Effective Date.—The amendment made by this section shall apply to taxable years beginning after December 31, 1997.

[¶ 4133] Sec. 1104. TREATMENT OF PERSONAL TRANSACTIONS BY INDIVIDUALS UNDER FOREIGN CURRENCY RULES.

* * * * * * * * * * *

(b) Effective Date.—The amendments made by this section shall apply to taxable years beginning after December 31, 1997.

[¶ 4134] Sec. 1105. FOREIGN TAX CREDIT TREATMENT OF DIVIDENDS FROM NONCONTROLLED SECTION 902 CORPORATIONS.

* * * * * * * * * * *

(c) Effective Date.—The amendments made by this section shall apply to taxable years beginning after December 31, 2002.

[¶ 4135] Sec. 1111. GAIN ON CERTAIN STOCK SALES BY CONTROLLED FOREIGN CORPORATIONS TREATED AS DIVIDENDS.

* * * * * * * * * * *

(c) Effective Dates.—

(1) The amendment made by subsection (a) shall apply to gain recognized on transactions occurring after the date of the enactment of this Act.

(2) The amendment made by subsection (b) shall apply to distributions after the date of the enactment of this Act.

[¶ 4136] Sec. 1112. MISCELLANEOUS MODIFICATIONS TO SUBPART F.

(a) Section 1248 gain taken into account in determining pro rata share.—

* * * * * * * * * * *

(2) Effective date.—The amendment made by paragraph (1) shall apply to dispositions after the date of the enactment of this Act.

* * * * * * * * * * *

(b) Basis adjustments in stock held by foreign corporation.—

* * * * * * * * * * *

(2) Effective date.—The amendment made by paragraph (1) shall apply for purposes of determining inclusions for taxable years of United States shareholders beginning after December 31, 1997.

* * * * * * * * * * *

(c) Clarification of treatment of branch tax exemptions or reductions.—

* * * * * * * * * * *

(2) Effective date.—The amendment made by paragraph (1) shall apply to taxable years beginning after December 31, 1986.

[¶ 4137]   Sec. 1113.   INDIRECT FOREIGN TAX CREDIT ALLOWED FOR CERTAIN LOWER TIER COMPANIES.

* * * * * * * * * * * *

(c) Effective Date.—

(1) In general.—The amendments made by this section shall apply to taxes of foreign corporations for taxable years of such corporations beginning after the date of enactment of this Act.

(2) Special rule.—In the case of any chain of foreign corporations described in clauses (i) and (ii) of section 902(b)(2)(B) of the Internal Revenue Code of 1986 (as amended by this section), no liquidation, reorganization, or similar transaction in a taxable year beginning after the date of the enactment of this Act shall have the effect of permitting taxes to be taken into account under section 902 of the Internal Revenue Code of 1986 which could not have been taken into account under such section but for such transaction.

[¶ 4138]   Sec. 1124.   EFFECTIVE DATE.

The amendments made by this subtitle shall apply to—

(1) taxable years of United States persons beginning after December 31, 1997, and

(2) taxable years of foreign corporations ending with or within such taxable years of United States persons.

[¶ 4139]   Sec. 1131.   REPEAL OF EXCISE TAX ON TRANSFERS TO FOREIGN ENTITIES; RECOGNITION OF GAIN ON CERTAIN TRANSFERS TO FOREIGN TRUSTS AND ESTATES.

* * * * * * * * * * *

(d) Effective Date.—The amendments made by this section shall take effect on the date of the enactment of this Act.

[¶ 4140]   Sec. 1141.   CLARIFICATION OF APPLICATION OF RETURN REQUIREMENT TO FOREIGN PARTNERSHIPS.

* * * * * * * * * * *

(c) Effective Date.—The amendments made by this section shall apply to taxable years beginning after the date of the enactment of this Act.

[¶ 4141]   Sec. 1142.   CONTROLLED FOREIGN PARTNERSHIPS SUBJECT TO INFORMATION REPORTING COMPARABLE TO INFORMATION REPORTING FOR CONTROLLED FOREIGN CORPORATIONS.

* * * * * * * * * * *

(f) Effective Date.—The amendments made by this section shall apply to annual accounting periods beginning after the date of the enactment of this Act.

[¶ 4142]   Sec. 1143.   MODIFICATIONS RELATING TO RETURNS REQUIRED TO BE FILED BY REASON OF CHANGES IN OWNERSHIP INTERESTS IN FOREIGN PARTNERSHIP.

* * * * * * * * * * *

(c) Effective Date.—The amendments made by this section shall apply to transfers and changes after the date of the enactment of this Act.

[¶ 4143]   Sec. 1144.   TRANSFERS OF PROPERTY TO FOREIGN PARTNERSHIPS SUBJECT TO INFORMATION REPORTING COMPARABLE TO INFORMATION RE-PORTING FOR SUCH TRANSFERS TO FOREIGN CORPORATIONS.

* * * * * * * * * * *

(d) Effective Date.—

(1) In general.—The amendments made by this section shall apply to transfers made after the date of the enactment of this Act.

(2) Election of retroactive effect.—Section 1494(c) of the Internal Revenue Code of 1986 shall not apply to any transfer after August 20, 1996, if all applicable reporting requirements under section 6038B of such Code (as amended by this section) are satisfied. The Secretary of the Treasury or his delegate may prescribe simplified reporting requirements under the preceding sentence.

[¶ 4144]   Sec. 1145.   EXTENSION OF STATUTE OF LIMITATIONS FOR FOREIGN TRANSFERS.

* * * * * * * * * * *

(b) Effective Date.—The amendment made by subsection (a) shall apply to information the due date for the reporting of which is after the date of the enactment of this Act.

[¶ 4145]   Sec. 1146.   INCREASE IN FILING THRESHOLDS FOR RETURNS AS TO ORGANIZATION OF FOREIGN CORPORATIONS AND ACQUISITIONS OF STOCK IN SUCH CORPORATIONS.

* * * * * * * * * * *

(b) Effective Date.—The amendment made by this section shall take effect on January 1, 1998.

[¶ 4146]   Sec. 1151.   DETERMINATION OF FOREIGN OR DOMESTIC STATUS OF PARTNERSHIPS.

* * * * * * * * * * *

(b) Effective Date.—Any regulations issued with respect to the amendment made by subsection (a) shall apply to partnerships created or organized after the date determined under section 7805(b) of the Internal Revenue Code of 1986 (without regard to paragraph (2) thereof) with respect to such regulations.

[¶ 4147]   Sec. 1161.   TRANSITION RULE FOR CERTAIN TRUSTS.

(a) In General.—Paragraph (3) of section 1907(a) of the Small Business Job Protection Act of 1996 is amended by adding at the end the following flush sentence:

(b) Effective Date.—The amendment made by subsection (a) shall take effect as if included in the amendments made by section 1907(a) of the Small Business Job Protection Act of 1996.

[¶ 4148] Sec. 1162. REPEAL OF STOCK AND SECURITIES SAFE HARBOR RE-QUIREMENT THAT PRINCIPAL OFFICE BE OUTSIDE THE UNITED STATES.

* * * * * * * * * * *

(b) Effective Date.—The amendment made by subsection (a) shall apply to taxable years beginning after December 31, 1997.

[¶ 4149] Sec. 1163. MISCELLANEOUS CLARIFICATIONS.

* * * * * * * * * * *

(c) Effective Date.—The amendments made by this section shall take effect on the date of the enactment of this Act.

[¶ 4150] Sec. 1171. TREATMENT OF COMPUTER SOFTWARE AS FSC EXPORT PROPERTY.

* * * * * * * * * * *

(b) Effective Date.—The amendment made by subsection (a) shall apply to gross receipts attributable to periods after December 31, 1997, in taxable years ending after such date.

[¶ 4151] Sec. 1172. ADJUSTMENT OF DOLLAR LIMITATION ON SECTION 911 EXCLUSION.

* * * * * * * * * * *

(b) Effective Date.—The amendment made by this section shall apply to taxable years beginning after December 31, 1997.

[¶ 4152] Sec. 1173. UNITED STATES PROPERTY NOT TO INCLUDE CERTAIN AS-SETS ACQUIRED BY DEALERS IN ORDINARY COURSE OF TRADE OR BUSINESS.

* * * * * * * * * * * * *

(b) Effective Date.—The amendments made by this section shall apply to taxable years of foreign corporations beginning after December 31, 1997, and to taxable years of United States shareholders with or within which such taxable years of foreign corporations end.

[¶ 4153] Sec. 1174. TREATMENT OF NONRESIDENT ALIENS ENGAGED IN IN-TERNATIONAL TRANSPORTATION SERVICES.

* * * * * * * * * * *

(c) Effective Dates.—

(1) In general.—The amendments made by this section shall apply to remuneration for services performed in taxable years beginning after December 31, 1997.

(2) Presence.—The amendment made by subsection (b) shall apply to taxable years beginning after December 31, 1997.

[¶ 4154] Sec. 1175. EXEMPTION FOR ACTIVE FINANCING INCOME.

* * * * * * * * * * *

(c) Effective Date.—The amendments made by this section shall apply to the first full taxable year of a foreign corporation beginning after December 31, 1997, and before January 1, 1999, and to taxable years of United States shareholders with or within which such taxable year of such foreign corporation ends.

[¶ 4155] Sec. 1201. BASIC STANDARD DEDUCTION AND MINIMUM TAX EXEMPTION AMOUNT FOR CERTAIN DEPENDENTS.

* * * * * * * * * * *

(c) Effective Date.—The amendments made by this section shall apply to taxable years beginning after December 31, 1997.

[¶ 4156]   Sec. 1202. INCREASE IN AMOUNT OF TAX EXEMPT FROM ESTIMATED TAX REQUIREMENTS.

* * * * * * * * * * *

(b) Effective Date.—The amendments made by this section shall apply to taxable years beginning after December 31, 1997.

[¶ 4157]   Sec. 1203. TREATMENT OF CERTAIN REIMBURSED EXPENSES OF RURAL MAIL CARRIERS.

* * * * * * * * * * *

(b) Technical Amendment.—Section 6008 of the Technical and Miscellaneous Revenue Act of 1988 is hereby repealed.

(c) Effective Date.—The amendments made by this section shall apply to taxable years beginning after December 31, 1997.

[¶ 4158]   Sec. 1204. TREATMENT OF TRAVELING EXPENSES OF CERTAIN FEDERAL EMPLOYEES ENGAGED IN CRIMINAL INVESTIGATIONS.

* * * * * * * * * * *

(b) Effective Date.—The amendment made by subsection (a) shall apply to amounts paid or incurred with respect to taxable years ending after the date of the enactment of this Act.

[¶ 4159] Sec. 1205. PAYMENT OF TAX BY COMMERCIALLY ACCEPTABLE MEANS.

* * * * * * * * * * *

(d) Effective Date.—The amendments made by this section shall take effect on the day 9 months after the date of the enactment of this Act.

[¶ 4160]   Sec. 1211.   MODIFICATIONS TO LOOK-BACK METHOD FOR LONG-TERM CONTRACTS.

* * * * * * * * * * * *

(c) Effective Date.—

(1) In general.—Except as provided in paragraph (2), the amendments made by this section shall apply to contracts completed in taxable years ending after the date of the enactment of this Act.

(2) Subsection (b).—The amendments made by subsection (b) shall apply for purposes of section 167(g) of the Internal Revenue Code of 1986 to property placed in service after September 13, 1995.

[¶ 4161]   Sec. 1212.   MINIMUM TAX TREATMENT OF CERTAIN PROPERTY AND CASUALTY INSURANCE COMPANIES.

* * * * * * * * * * * *

(b) Effective Date.—The amendment made by subsection (a) shall apply to taxable years beginning after December 31, 1997.

[¶ 4162]   Sec. 1213.   QUALIFIED LESSEE CONSTRUCTION ALLOWANCES FOR SHORT-TERM LEASES.

* * * * * * * * * * * *

(e) Effective Date.—The amendments made by this section shall apply to leases entered into after the date of the enactment of this Act.

[¶ 4163]   Sec. 1221.   SIMPLIFIED FLOW-THROUGH FOR ELECTING LARGE PARTNERSHIPS.

* * * * * * * * * * * *

(c) Effective Date.—The amendments made by this section shall apply to partnership taxable years beginning after December 31, 1997.

[¶ 4164]   Sec. 1226.   EFFECTIVE DATE.

The amendments made by this part shall apply to partnership taxable years ending on or after December 31, 1997.

[¶ 4165]   Sec. 1231.   TREATMENT OF PARTNERSHIP ITEMS IN DEFICIENCY PROCEEDINGS.

* * * * * * * * * * * *

(d) Effective Date.—The amendments made by this section shall apply to partnership taxable years ending after the date of the enactment of this Act.

[¶ 4166]   Sec. 1232. PARTNERSHIP RETURN TO BE DETERMINATIVE OF AUDIT PROCEDURES TO BE FOLLOWED.

* * * * * * * * * * * * *

(b) Effective Date.—The amendment made by this section shall apply to partnership taxable years ending after the date of the enactment of this Act.

[¶ 4167]   Sec. 1233. PROVISIONS RELATING TO STATUTE OF LIMITATIONS.

* * * * * * * * * * *

(d) Effective Dates.—

(1) Subsections (a) and (b).—The amendments made by subsections (a) and (b) shall apply to partnership taxable years with respect to which the period under section 6229 of the Internal Revenue Code of 1986 for assessing tax has not expired on or before the date of the enactment of this Act.

(2) Subsection (c).—The amendment made by subsection (c) shall apply to agreements entered into after the date of the enactment of this Act.

[¶ 4168]   Sec. 1234. EXPANSION OF SMALL PARTNERSHIP EXCEPTION.

* * * * * * * * * * *

(b) Effective Date.—The amendment made by this section shall apply to partnership taxable years ending after the date of the enactment of this Act.

[¶ 4169]   Sec. 1235. EXCLUSION OF PARTIAL SETTLEMENTS FROM 1-YEAR LIMITATION ON ASSESSMENT.

* * * * * * * * * * *

(b) Effective Date.—The amendment made by this section shall apply to settlements entered into after the date of the enactment of this Act.

[¶ 4170]   Sec. 1236. EXTENSION OF TIME FOR FILING A REQUEST FOR ADMINISTRATIVE ADJUSTMENT.

* * * * * * * * * * *

(b) Effective Date.—The amendment made by this section shall take effect as if included in the amendments made by section 402 of the Tax Equity and Fiscal Responsibility Act of 1982.

[¶ 4171]   Sec. 1237. AVAILABILITY OF INNOCENT SPOUSE RELIEF IN CONTEXT OF PARTNERSHIP PROCEEDINGS.

* * * * * * * * * * *

(d) Effective Date.—The amendments made by this section shall take effect as if included in the amendments made by section 402 of the Tax Equity and Fiscal Responsibility Act of 1982.

[¶ 4172]   Sec. 1238.   DETERMINATION OF PENALTIES AT PARTNERSHIP LEVEL.

* * * * * * * * * * * *

(c) Effective Date.—The amendments made by this section shall apply to partnership taxable years ending after the date of the enactment of this Act.

[¶ 4173]   Sec. 1239.   PROVISIONS RELATING TO COURT JURISDICTION, ETC.

* * * * * * * * * * * *

(f) Effective Date.—The amendments made by this section shall apply to partnership taxable years ending after the date of the enactment of this Act.

[¶ 4174]   Sec. 1240.   TREATMENT OF PREMATURE PETITIONS FILED BY NO-TICE PARTNERS OR 5-PERCENT GROUPS.

* * * * * * * * * * * *

(b) Effective Date.—The amendment made by this section shall apply to petitions filed after the date of the enactment of this Act.

[¶ 4175]   Sec. 1241.   BONDS IN CASE OF APPEALS FROM CERTAIN PROCEEDING.

* * * * * * * * * * * *

(b) Effective Date.—The amendment made by this section shall take effect as if included in the amendments made by section 402 of the Tax Equity and Fiscal Responsibility Act of 1982.

[¶ 4176]   Sec. 1242.   SUSPENSION OF INTEREST WHERE DELAY IN COMPUTATIONAL ADJUSTMENT RESULTING FROM CERTAIN SETTLEMENTS.

* * * * * * * * * * * *

(b) Effective Date.—The amendment made by this section shall apply to adjustments with respect to partnership taxable years beginning after the date of the enactment of this Act.

[¶ 4177]   Sec. 1243.   SPECIAL RULES FOR ADMINISTRATIVE ADJUSTMENT REQUESTS WITH RESPECT TO BAD DEBTS OR WORTHLESS SECURITIES.

* * * * * * * * * * * *

(b) Effective Date.—

(1) In general.—The amendment made by subsection (a) shall take effect as if included in the amendments made by section 402 of the Tax Equity and Fiscal Responsibility Act of 1982.

(2) Treatment of requests filed before date of enactment.—In the case of that portion of any request (filed before the date of the enactment of this Act) for an administrative adjustment which relates to the deductibility of a debt as a debt which became worthless or the deductibility of a loss from the worthlessness of a security—

(A) paragraph (2) of section 6227(a) of the Internal Revenue Code of 1986 shall not apply,

(B) the period for filing a petition under section 6228 of the Internal Revenue Code of 1986 with respect to such request shall not expire before the date 6 months after the date of the enactment of this Act, and

(C) such a petition may be filed without regard to whether there was a notice of the beginning of an administrative proceeding or a final partnership administrative adjustment.

[¶ 4178]   Sec. 1246.   CLOSING OF PARTNERSHIP TAXABLE YEAR WITH RESPECT TO DECEASED PARTNER, ETC.

* * * * * * * * * * * * *

(c) Effective Date.—The amendments made by this section shall apply to partnership taxable years beginning after December 31, 1997.

[¶ 4179]   Sec. 1263.   EFFECTIVE DATE.

The amendments made by this part shall apply to taxable years beginning after the date of the enactment of this Act.

[¶ 4180]   Sec. 1271.   REPEAL OF 30-PERCENT GROSS INCOME LIMITATION.

* * * * * * * * * * *

(c) Effective Date.—The amendments made by this section shall apply to taxable years beginning after the date of the enactment of this Act.

[¶ 4181]   Sec. 1281.   REASONABLE CAUSE EXCEPTION FOR CERTAIN PENALTIES.

* * * * * * * * * * *

(e) Effective Date.—The amendments made by this section shall apply to taxable years beginning after the date of the enactment of this Act.

[¶ 4182]   Sec. 1282.   CLARIFICATION OF PERIOD FOR FILING CLAIMS FOR REFUNDS.

* * * * * * * * * * *

(b) Effective Date.—The amendment made by subsection (a) shall apply to claims for credit or refund for taxable years ending after the date of the enactment of this Act.

[¶ 4183]   Sec. 1283.   REPEAL OF AUTHORITY TO DISCLOSE WHETHER PROSPECTIVE JUROR HAS BEEN AUDITED.

* * * * * * * * * * *

(c) Effective Date.—The amendments made by this section shall apply to judicial proceedings commenced after the date of the enactment of this Act.

[¶ 4197] Sec. 1312. TREATMENT UNDER QUALIFIED DOMESTIC TRUST RULES OF FORMS OF OWNERSHIP WHICH ARE NOT TRUSTS.

* * * * * * * * * * *

(b) Effective Date.—The amendments made by this section shall apply to estates of decedents dying after the date of the enactment of this Act.

[¶ 4198] Sec. 1313. OPPORTUNITY TO CORRECT CERTAIN FAILURES UNDER SECTION 2032A.

* * * * * * * * * * *

(b) Effective Date.—The amendment made by subsection (a) shall apply to the estates of decedents dying after the date of the enactment of this Act.

[¶ 4199] Sec. 1314. AUTHORITY TO WAIVE REQUIREMENT OF UNITED STATES TRUSTEE FOR QUALIFIED DOMESTIC TRUSTS.

* * * * * * * * * * *

(b) Effective Date.—The amendment made by this section shall apply to estates of decedents dying after the date of the enactment of this Act.

[¶ 4200] Sec. 1401. INCREASE IN DE MINIMIS LIMIT FOR AFTER-MARKET ALTERATIONS FOR HEAVY TRUCKS AND LUXURY CARS.

* * * * * * * * * * *

(b) Effective Date.—The amendments made by subsection (a) shall apply to installations on vehicles sold after the date of the enactment of this Act.

[¶ 4201] Sec. 1402. CREDIT FOR TIRE TAX IN LIEU OF EXCLUSION OF VALUE OF TIRES IN COMPUTING PRICE.

* * * * * * * * * * *

(c) Effective Date.—The amendments made by this section shall take effect on January 1, 1998.

[¶ 4202] Sec. 1411. CREDIT OR REFUND FOR IMPORTED BOTTLED DISTILLED SPIRITS RETURNED TO DISTILLED SPIRITS PLANT.

* * * * * * * * * * *

(b) Effective Date.—The amendment made by subsection (a) shall take effect on the 1st day of the 1st calendar quarter that begins at least 180 days after the date of the enactment of this Act.

[¶ 4203] Sec. 1412. AUTHORITY TO CANCEL OR CREDIT EXPORT BONDS WITHOUT SUBMISSION OF RECORDS.

* * * * * * * * * * *

(b) Effective Date.—The amendment made by subsection (a) shall take effect on the 1st day of the 1st calendar quarter that begins at least 180 days after the date of the enactment of this Act.

[¶ 4204] Sec. 1413. REPEAL OF REQUIRED MAINTENANCE OF RECORDS ON PREMISES OF DISTILLED SPIRITS PLANT.

* * * * * * * * * * *

(b) Effective Date.—The amendment made by subsection (a) shall take effect on the 1st day of the 1st calendar quarter that begins at least 180 days after the date of the enactment of this Act.

[¶ 4205] Sec. 1414. FERMENTED MATERIAL FROM ANY BREWERY MAY BE RECEIVED AT A DISTILLED SPIRITS PLANT.

* * * * * * * * * * *

(d) Effective Date.—The amendments made by this section shall take effect on the 1st day of the 1st calendar quarter that begins at least 180 days after the date of the enactment of this Act.

[¶ 4206] Sec. 1415. REPEAL OF REQUIREMENT FOR WHOLESALE DEALERS IN LIQUORS TO POST SIGN.

* * * * * * * * * * *

(c) Effective Date.—The amendments made by this section shall take effect on the date of the enactment of this Act.

[¶ 4207] Sec. 1416. REFUND OF TAX TO WINE RETURNED TO BOND NOT LIMITED TO UNMERCHANTABLE WINE.

* * * * * * * * * * *

(c) Effective Date.—The amendments made by this section shall take effect on the 1st day of the 1st calendar quarter that begins at least 180 days after the date of the enactment of this Act.

[¶ 4208] Sec. 1417. USE OF ADDITIONAL AMELIORATING MATERIAL IN CERTAIN WINES.

* * * * * * * * * * *

(b) Effective Date.—The amendment made by this section shall take effect on the 1st day of the 1st calendar quarter that begins at least 180 days after the date of the enactment of this Act.

[¶ 4209] Sec. 1418. DOMESTICALLY PRODUCED BEER MAY BE WITHDRAWN FREE OF TAX FOR USE OF FOREIGN EMBASSIES, LEGATIONS, ETC.

* * * * * * * * * * * *

(b) Effective Date.—The amendment made by subsection (a) shall take effect on the 1st day of the 1st calendar quarter that begins at least 180 days after the date of the enactment of this Act.

[¶ 4210] Sec. 1419. BEER MAY BE WITHDRAWN FREE OF TAX FOR DESTRUCTION.

* * * * * * * * * * * *

(b) Effective Date.—The amendment made by subsection (a) shall take effect on the 1st day of the 1st calendar quarter that begins at least 180 days after the date of the enactment of this Act.

[¶ 4211] Sec. 1420. AUTHORITY TO ALLOW DRAWBACK ON EXPORTED BEER WITHOUT SUBMISSION OF RECORDS.

* * * * * * * * * * * *

(b) Effective Date.—The amendment made by subsection (a) shall take effect on the 1st day of the 1st calendar quarter that begins at least 180 days after the date of the enactment of this Act.

[¶ 4212] Sec. 1421. TRANSFER TO BREWERY OF BEER IMPORTED IN BULK WITHOUT PAYMENT OF TAX.

* * * * * * * * * * * *

(c) Effective Date.—The amendments made by this section shall take effect on the 1st day of the 1st calendar quarter that begins at least 180 days after the date of the enactment of this Act.

[¶ 4213] Sec. 1422. TRANSFER TO BONDED WINE CELLARS OF WINE IMPORTED IN BULK WITHOUT PAYMENT OF TAX.

* * * * * * * * * * * *

(c) Effective Date.—The amendments made by this section shall take effect on the 1st day of the 1st calendar quarter that begins at least 180 days after the date of the enactment of this Act.

[¶ 4214] Sec. 1431. AUTHORITY TO GRANT EXEMPTIONS FROM REGISTRATION REQUIREMENTS.

* * * * * * * * * * * *

(b) Effective Date.—The amendments made by subsection (a) shall take effect on the date of the enactment of this Act.

[¶ 4215]   Sec. 1433.   SIMPLIFICATION OF IMPOSITION OF EXCISE TAX ON AR-ROWS.

* * * * * * * * * * *

(b) Effective Date.—The amendment made by subsection (a) shall apply to articles sold by the manufacturer, producer, or importer after September 30 1997.

[¶ 4216]   Sec. 1434.   MODIFICATIONS TO RETAIL TAX ON HEAVY TRUCKS.

* * * * * * * * * * *

(c) Effective Date.—The amendments made by this section shall take effect on January 1, 1998.

[¶ 4217]   Sec. 1435.   SKYDIVING FLIGHTS EXEMPT FROM TAX ON TRANSPOR-TATION OF PERSONS BY AIR.

* * * * * * * * * * *

(c) Effective Dates.—

(1) Subsection (a).—The amendment made by subsection (a) shall apply to amounts paid after September 30, 1997.

(2) Subsection (b).—The amendment made by subsection (b) shall take effect on October 1, 1997.

[¶ 4218]   Sec. 1436.   ALLOWANCE OR CREDIT OF REFUND FOR TAX-PAID AVIA-TION FUEL PURCHASED BY REGISTERED PRODUCER OF AVIATION FUEL.

* * * * * * * * * * *

(c) Effective Date.—The amendments made by this section shall apply to fuel acquired by the producer after September 30, 1997.

[¶ 4219]   Sec. 1445.   EFFECTIVE DATE.

* * * * * * * * * * *

[¶ 4220]   Sec. 1451.   OVERPAYMENT DETERMINATIONS OF TAX COURT.

* * * * * * * * * * *

(c) Effective Date.—The amendments made by this section shall take effect on the date of the enactment of this Act.

[¶ 4221]   Sec. 1452.   REDETERMINATION OF INTEREST PURSUANT TO MOTION.

* * * * * * * * * * *

(b) Effective Date.—The amendment made by this section shall take effect on the date of the enactment of this Act.

[¶ 4222] Sec. 1453. APPLICATION OF NET WORTH REQUIREMENT FOR AWARDS OF LITIGATION COSTS.

* * * * * * * * * * * *

(b) Effective Date.—The amendment made by this section shall apply to proceedings commenced after the date of the enactment of this Act.

[¶ 4223] Sec. 1454. PROCEEDINGS FOR DETERMINATION OF EMPLOYMENT STATUS.

* * * * * * * * * * * *

(c) Effective Date.—The amendments made by this section shall take effect on the date of the enactment of this Act.

[¶ 4224] Sec. 1461. EXTENSION OF DUE DATE OF FIRST QUARTER ESTIMATED TAX PAYMENT BY PRIVATE FOUNDATIONS.

* * * * * * * * * * * *

(b) Effective Date.—The amendment made by subsection (a) shall apply for purposes of determining underpayments of estimated tax for taxable years beginning after the date of the enactment of this Act.

[¶ 4225] Sec. 1462. CLARIFICATION OF AUTHORITY TO WITHHOLD PUERTO RICO INCOME TAXES FROM SALARIES OF FEDERAL EMPLOYEES.

* * * * * * * * * * * *

(b) Effective Date.—The amendment made by subsection (a) shall take effect on January 1, 1998.

[¶ 4226] Sec. 1463. CERTAIN NOTICES DISREGARDED UNDER PROVISION INCREASING INTEREST RATE ON LARGE CORPORATE UNDERPAYMENTS.

* * * * * * * * * * * *

(b) Effective Date.—The amendment made by subsection (a) shall apply for purposes of determining interest for periods after December 31, 1997.

[¶ 4227] Sec. 1501. MATCHING CONTRIBUTIONS OF SELF-EMPLOYED INDIVIDUALS NOT TREATED AS ELECTIVE EMPLOYER CONTRIBUTIONS.

* * * * * * * * * * * *

(c) Effective Dates.—

(1) Elective deferrals.—The amendment made by subsection (a) shall apply to years beginning after December 31, 1997.

(2) Simple retirement accounts.—The amendment made by subsection (b) shall apply to years beginning after December 31, 1996.

[¶ 4228]   Sec. 1502.   MODIFICATION OF PROHIBITION OF ASSIGNMENT OR ALIENATION.

* * * * * * * * * * * *

(c) Effective Date.—The amendments made by this section shall apply to judgments, orders, and decrees issued, and settlement agreements entered into, on or after the date of the enactment of this Act.

[¶ 4229]   Sec. 1504.   MODIFICATION OF 403(b) EXCLUSION ALLOWANCE TO CONFORM TO 415 MODIFICATIONS.

(a) Definition of compensation.—

* * * * * * * * * * * *

(2) Effective date.—The amendment made by this subsection shall apply to years beginning after December 31, 1997.

(b) Repeal of rules in section 415(e).—The Secretary of the Treasury shall modify the regulations regarding the exclusion allowance under section 403(b)(2) of the Internal Revenue Code of 1986 to reflect the amendment made by section 1452(a) of the Small Business Job Protection Act of 1996. Such modification shall take effect for years beginning after December 31, 1999.

[¶ 4230]   Sec. 1505.   EXTENSION OF MORATORIUM ON APPLICATION OF CERTAIN NONDISCRIMINATION RULES TO STATE AND LOCAL GOVERNMENTS.

* * * * * * * * * * * *

(d) Effective Dates.—

(1) In general.—The amendments made by this section apply to taxable years beginning on or after the date of enactment of this Act.

(2) Treatment for years beginning before date of enactment.—A governmental plan (within the meaning of section 414(d) of the Internal Revenue Code of 1986) maintained by a State or local government or political subdivision thereof (or agency or instrumentality thereof) shall be treated as satisfying the requirements of sections 401(a)(3), 401(a)(4), 401(a)(26), 401(k), 401(m), 403 (b)(1)(D) and (b)(12), and 410 of such Code for all taxable years beginning before the date of enactment of this Act.

[¶ 4231]   Sec. 1506.   CLARIFICATION OF CERTAIN RULES RELATING TO EMPLOYEE STOCK OWNERSHIP PLANS OF S CORPORATIONS.

* * * * * * * * * * * *

(c) Effective Date.—The amendments made by this section shall apply to taxable years beginning after December 31, 1997.

[¶ 4232]   Sec. 1507.   MODIFICATION OF 10-PERCENT TAX FOR NONDEDUCTIBLE CONTRIBUTIONS.

* * * * * * * * * * * *

(b) Effective Date.—The amendments made by this section shall apply to taxable years beginning after December 31, 1997.

[¶ 4233] Sec. 1508. MODIFICATION OF FUNDING REQUIREMENTS FOR CERTAIN PLANS.

(a) Funding Rules for Certain Plans.—Section 769 of the Retirement Protection Act of 1994 is amended by adding at the end the following new subsection:

"(c) Transition Rules for Certain Plans.—

"(1) In general.—In the case of a plan that—

"(A) was not required to pay a variable rate premium for the plan year beginning in 1996;

"(B) has not, in any plan year beginning after 1995 and before 2009, merged with another plan (other than a plan sponsored by an employer that was in 1996 within the controlled group of the plan sponsor); and

"(C) is sponsored by a company that is engaged primarily in the interurban or interstate passenger bus service,

the transition rules described in paragraph (2) shall apply for any plan year beginning after 1996 and before 2010.

"(2) Transition rules.—The transition rules described in this paragraph are as follows:

"(A) For purposes of section 412(l)(9)(A) of the Internal Revenue Code of 1986 and section 302(d)(9)(A) of the Employee Retirement Income Security Act of 1974—

"(i) the funded current liability percentage for any plan year beginning after 1996 and before 2005 shall be treated as not less than 90 percent if for such plan year the funded current liability percentage is at least 85 percent, and

"(ii) the funded current liability percentage for any plan year beginning after 2004 and before 2010 shall be treated as not less than 90 percent if for such plan year the funded current liability percentage satisfies the minimum percentage determined according to the following table:

In the case of a plan year beginning in:	The miniumum percentage is:
2005	86 percent
2006	87 percent
2007	88 percent
2008	89 percent
2009 and thereafter	90 percent

"(B) Sections 412(c)(7)(E)(i)(I) of such Code and 302(c)(7)(E)(i)(I) of such Act shall be applied—

"(i) by substituting '85 percent' for '90 percent' for plan years beginning after 1996 and before 2005, and

"(ii) by substituting the minimum percentage specified in the table contained in subparagraph (A)(ii) for '90 percent' for plan years beginning after 2004 and before 2010.

"(C) In the event the funded current liability percentage of a plan is less than 85 percent for any plan year beginning after 1996 and before 2005, the transition rules under subparagraphs (A) and (B) shall continue to apply to the plan if contributions for such a plan year are made to the plan in an amount equal to the lesser of—

"(i) the amount necessary to result in a funded current liability percentage of 85 percent, or

"(ii) the greater of—

"(I) 2 percent of the plan's current liability as of the beginning of such plan year, or

"(II) the amount necessary to result in a funded current liability percentage of 80 percent as of the end of such plan year.

For the plan year beginning in 2005 and for each of the 3 succeeding plan years, the transition rules under subparagraphs (A) and (B) shall continue to apply to the plan for such plan year only if contributions to the plan for such plan year equal at least the expected increase in current liability due to benefits accruing during such plan year.".

(b) Effective Date.—The amendment made by this section shall apply to plan years beginning after December 31, 1996.

[¶ 4234]   Sec. 1509.   CLARIFICATION OF DISQUALIFICATION RULES RELATING TO ACCEPTANCE OF ROLLOVER CONTRIBUTIONS.

The Secretary of the Treasury or his delegate shall clarify that, under the Internal Revenue Service regulations protecting pension plans from disqualification by reason of the receipt of invalid rollover contributions under section 402(c) of the Internal Revenue Code of 1986, in order for the administrator of the plan receiving any such contribution to reasonably conclude that the contribution is a valid rollover contribution it is not necessary for the distributing plan to have a determination letter with respect to its status as a qualified plan under section 401 of such Code.

[¶ 4235]   Sec. 1510.   NEW TECHNOLOGIES IN RETIREMENT PLANS.

(a) In General.—Not later than December 31, 1998, the Secretary of the Treasury and the Secretary of Labor shall each issue guidance which is designed to—

(1) interpret the notice, election, consent, disclosure, and time requirements (and related recordkeeping requirements) under the Internal Revenue Code of 1986 and the Employee Retirement Income Security Act of 1974 relating to retirement plans as applied to the use of new technologies by plan sponsors and administrators while maintaining the protection of the rights of participants and beneficiaries, and

(2) clarify the extent to which writing requirements under the Internal Revenue Code of 1986 relating to retirement plans shall be interpreted to permit paperless transactions.

(b) Applicability of Final Regulations.—Final regulations applicable to the guidance regarding new technologies described in subsection (a) shall not be effective until the first plan year beginning at least 6 months after the issuance of such final regulations.

[¶ 4236]   Sec. 1521.   INCREASE IN CURRENT LIABILITY FUNDING LIMIT.

* * * * * * * * * * *

(d) Effective Dates.—

(1) In general.—The amendments made by this section shall apply to plan years beginning after December 31, 1998.

(2) Special rule for unamortized balances under existing law.— The unamortized balance (as of the close of the plan year preceding the plan's first year beginning in 1999) of any amortization base established under section 412(c)(7)(D)(iii) of such Code and section 302(c)(7)(D)(iii) of such Act (as repealed by subsection (c)(3)) for any plan year beginning before 1999 shall be amortized in equal annual installments (until fully amortized) over a period of years equal to the excess of—

(A) 20 years, over

(B) the number of years since the amortization base was established.

[¶ 4237]   Sec. 1522.   SPECIAL RULES FOR CHURCH PLANS.

* * * * * * * * * * *

(b) Effective Date.—The amendments made by this section shall apply to years beginning after December 31, 1997.

[¶ 4238] Sec. 1523. REPEAL OF APPLICATION OF UNRELATED BUSINESS IN-COME TAX TO ESOPS.

* * * * * * * * * * *

(b) Effective Date.—The amendments made by this section shall apply to taxable years beginning after December 31, 1997.

[¶ 4239] Sec. 1524. DIVERSIFICATION OF SECTION 401(k) PLAN INVESTMENTS.

* * * * * * * * * * *

(b) Effective Date.—The amendments made by this section shall apply to elective deferrals for plan years beginning after December 31, 1998.

[¶ 4240] Sec. 1525. SECTION 401(K) PLANS FOR CERTAIN IRRIGATION AND DRAINAGE ENTITIES.

* * * * * * * * * * *

(b) Effective Date.—The amendments made by subsection (a) shall apply to years beginning after December 31, 1997.

[¶ 4241] Sec. 1526. PORTABILITY OF PERMISSIVE SERVICE CREDIT UNDER GOVERNMENTAL PENSION PLANS.

* * * * * * * * * * *

(c) Effective Dates.—

(1) In general.—The amendments made by this section shall apply to permissive service credit contributions made in years beginning after December 31, 1997.

(2) Transition rule.—

(A) In general.—In the case of an eligible participant in a governmental plan (within the meaning of section 414(d) of the Internal Revenue Code of 1986), the limitations of section 415(c)(1) of such Code shall not be applied to reduce the amount of permissive service credit which may be purchased to an amount less than the amount which was allowed to be purchased under the terms of the plan as in effect on the date of the enactment of this Act.

(B) Eligible participant.—For purposes of subparagraph (A), an eligible participant is an individual who first became a participant in the plan before the first plan year beginning after the last day of the calendar year in which the next regular session (following the date of the enactment of this Act) of the governing body with authority to amend the plan ends.

[¶ 4242] Sec. 1527. REMOVAL OF DOLLAR LIMITATION ON BENEFIT PAYMENTS FROM A DEFINED BENEFIT PLAN MAINTAINED FOR CERTAIN POLICE AND FIRE EMPLOYEES.

* * * * * * * * * * *

(b) Effective Date.—The amendment made by subsection (a) shall apply to years beginning after December 31, 1996.

[¶ 4243]   Sec. 1528.   SURVIVOR BENEFITS FOR PUBLIC SAFETY OFFICERS KILLED IN THE LINE OF DUTY.

* * * * * * * * * * * *

(b) Effective Date.—The amendments made by this section shall apply to amounts received in taxable years beginning after December 31, 1996, with respect to individuals dying after such date.

[¶ 4244]   Sec. 1529.   TREATMENT OF CERTAIN DISABILITY BENEFITS RECEIVED BY FORMER POLICE OFFICERS OR FIREFIGHTERS.

(a) General Rule.—For purposes of determining whether any amount to which this section applies is excludable from gross income under section 104(a)(1) of the Internal Revenue Code of 1986, the following conditions shall be treated as personal injuries or sickness in the course of employment:

(1) Heart disease.

(2) Hypertension.

(b) Amounts To Which Section Applies.—This section shall apply to any amount—

(1) which is payable—

(A) to an individual (or to the survivors of an individual) who was a full-time employee of any police department or fire department which is organized and operated by a State, by any political subdivision thereof, or by any agency or instrumentality of a State or political subdivision thereof, and

(B) under a State law (as amended on May 19, 1992) which irrebuttably presumed that heart disease and hypertension are work-related illnesses but only for employees separating from service before July 1, 1992; and

(2) which was received in calendar year 1989, 1990, or 1991.

(c) Waiver of Statute of Limitations.—If, on the date of the enactment of this Act (or at any time within the 1-year period beginning on such date of enactment), credit or refund of any overpayment of tax resulting from the provisions of this section is barred by any law or rule of law (including res judicata), then credit or refund of such overpayment shall, nevertheless, be allowed or made if claim therefore is filed before the date 1 year after such date of enactment.

[¶ 4245]   Sec. 1530.   GRATUITOUS TRANSFERS FOR THE BENEFIT OF EMPLOYEES.

* * * * * * * * * * * *

(d) Effective Date.—The amendments made by this section shall apply to transfers made by trusts to, or for the use of, an employee stock ownership plan after the date of the enactment of this Act.

[¶ 4246]   Sec. 1531.   AMENDMENTS TO THE INTERNAL REVENUE CODE OF 1986 TO IMPLEMENT THE NEWBORNS' AND MOTHERS' HEALTH PROTECTION ACT OF 1996 AND THE MENTAL HEALTH PARITY ACT OF 1996.

* * * * * * * * * * * *

(c) Effective Date.—The amendments made by this section shall apply with respect to group health plans for plan years beginning on or after January 1, 1998.

[¶ 4247]   Sec. 1532.   SPECIAL RULES RELATING TO CHURCH PLANS.

* * * * * * * * * * * *

(b) Effective Date.—The amendments made by subsection (a) shall take effect as if included in the amendments made by section 401(a) of the Health Insurance Portability and Accountability Act of 1996.

[¶ 4248]   Sec. 1541.   PROVISIONS RELATING TO PLAN AMENDMENTS.

(a) In General.—If this section applies to any plan or contract amendment—

(1) such plan or contract shall be treated as being operated in accordance with the terms of the plan during the period described in subsection (b)(2)(A), and

(2) such plan shall not fail to meet the requirements of section 411(d)(6) of the Internal Revenue Code of 1986 or section 204(g) of the Employee Retirement Income Security Act of 1974 by reason of such amendment.

(b) Amendments to Which Section Applies.—

(1) In general.—This section shall apply to any amendment to any plan or annuity contract which is made—

(A) pursuant to any amendment made by this title or subtitle H of title X, and

(B) before the first day of the first plan year beginning on or after January 1, 1999.

In the case of a governmental plan (as defined in section 414(d) of the Internal Revenue Code of 1986), this paragraph shall be applied by substituting "2001" for "1999".

(2) Conditions.—This section shall not apply to any amendment unless—

(A) during the period—

(i) beginning on the date the legislative amendment described in paragraph (1)(A) takes effect (or in the case of a plan or contract amendment not required by such legislative amendment, the effective date specified by the plan), and

(ii) ending on the date described in paragraph (1)(B) (or, if earlier, the date the plan or contract amendment is adopted),

the plan or contract is operated as if such plan or contract amendment were in effect, and

(B) such plan or contract amendment applies retroactively for such period.

[¶ 4249]   Sec. 1601.   AMENDMENTS RELATED TO SMALL BUSINESS JOB PROTECTION ACT OF 1996.

* * * * * * * * * * * *

(c) Amendments related to section 1302.—

* * * * * * * * * * * *

(2) Effective date for section 1307.—

(A) Notwithstanding section 1317 of the Small Business Job Protection Act of 1996, the amendments made by subsections (a) and (b) of section 1307 of such Act shall apply to determinations made after December 31, 1996.

(B) In no event shall the 120-day period referred to in section 1377(b)(1)(B) of the Internal Revenue Code of 1986 (as added by such section 1307) expire before the end of the 120-day period beginning on the date of the enactment of this Act.

* * * * * * * * * * * *

(d) Amendments related to section 1316.—

* * * * * * * * * * * *

(4) Clarification of section 1450.—

(A) Section 403(b)(11) of the Internal Revenue Code of 1986 shall not apply with respect to a distribution from a contract described in section 1450(b)(1) of such Act to the extent that such distribution is not includible in income by reason of—

(i) in the case of distributions before January 1, 1998, section 403 (b)(8) or (b)(10) of such Code (determined after the application of section 1450(b)(2) of such Act), and

(ii) in the case of distributions on and after such date, such section 403(b)(1).

(B) This paragraph shall apply as if included in section 1450 of the Small Business Job Protection Act of 1996.

* * * * * * * * * * * * *

(f) Amendments related to subtitle E.—

* * * * * * * * * * * *

(3) Amendments related to section 1607.—

* * * * * * * * * * * *

(C) The amendments made by this paragraph shall apply to sales after the date of the enactment of this Act.

* * * * * * * * * * * *

(g) Amendments related to subtitle G.—

* * * * * * * * * * * * *

(1) Extension of period for claiming refunds for alcohol fuels. —Notwithstanding section 6427(i)(3)(C) of the Internal Revenue Code of 1986, a claim filed under section 6427(f) of such Code for any period after September 30, 1995, and before October 1, 1996, shall be treated as timely filed if filed before the 60th day after the date of the enactment of this Act.

* * * * * * * * * * * *

(h) Amendments related to subtitle H.—

* * * * * * * * * * * *

(1) Amendments related to section 1806.—

* * * * * * * * * * * *

(C) Paragraph (2) of section 1806(c) of the Small Business Job Protection Act of 1996 is amended by striking so much of the first sentence as follows subparagraph (B)(ii) and inserting the following: "then such program (as in effect on August 20, 1996) shall be treated as a qualified State tuition program with respect to contributions (and earnings allocable thereto) pursuant to contracts entered into under such program before the first date on which such program meets such requirements (determined without regard to this paragraph) and the provisions of such program (as so in effect) shall apply in lieu of section 529(b) of the Internal Revenue Code of 1986 with respect to such contributions and earnings.".

* * * * * * * * * * * *

(i) Amendments related to subtitle I.—

* * * * * * * * * * * *

(4) Effective date related to subtitle I.—The Secretary of the Treasury may by regulations or other administrative guidance provide that the amendments made by section 1907(a) of the Small Business Job Protection Act of 1996 shall not apply to a trust with respect to a reasonable period beginning on the date of the enactment of such Act, if—

(A) such trust is in existence on August 20, 1996, and is a United States person for purposes of the Internal Revenue Code of 1986 on such date (determined without regard to such amendments),

(B) no election is in effect under section 1907(a)(3)(B) of such Act with respect to such trust,

(C) before the expiration of such reasonable period, such trust makes the modifications necessary to be treated as a United States person for purposes of such Code (determined with regard to such amendments), and

(D) such trust meets such other conditions as the Secretary may require.

(j) Effective Date.—

(1) In general.—Except as provided in paragraph (2), the amendments made by this section shall take effect as if included in the provisions of the Small Business Job Protection Act of 1996 to which they relate.

(2) Certain administrative requirements with respect to certain pension plans.—The amendment made by subsection (d)(2)(D) shall apply to calendar years beginning after the date of the enactment of this Act.

[¶ 4250]   Sec. 1602.   AMENDMENTS RELATED TO HEALTH INSURANCE PORTABILITY AND ACCOUNTABILITY ACT OF 1996.

* * * * * * * * * * * *

(f) Amendments related to section 501.—

* * * * * * * * * * * *

(4) Subsection (c) of section 501 of the Health Insurance Portability and Accountability Act of 1996 is amended by striking paragraph (3).

(5) Paragraph (2) of section 501(d) of such Act is amended by striking "no additional premiums" and all that follows and inserting the following: "a lapse occurring after October 13, 1995, by reason of no additional premiums being received under the contract.".

* * * * * * * * * * * *

(i) Effective Date.—The amendments made by this section shall take effect as if included in the provisions of the Health Insurance Portability and Accountability Act of 1996 to which such amendments relate.

[¶ 4251]   Sec. 1603.   AMENDMENTS RELATED TO TAXPAYER BILL OF RIGHTS 2.

* * * * * * * * * * * *

(c) Effective Date.—The amendments made by this section shall take effect as if included in the provisions of the Taxpayer Bill of Rights 2 to which such amendments relate.

[¶ 4252]   Sec. 1604.   MISCELLANEOUS PROVISIONS.

(a) Amendments related to Energy Policy Act of 1992.—

* * * * * * * * * * * *

(4) The amendments made by this subsection shall take effect as if included in the amendments made by section 1913 of the Energy Policy Act of 1992.

(b) Amendments related to Uruguay Round Agreement Act.—

* * * * * * * * * * * *

(3) Subparagraph (A) of section 767(d)(3) of the Uruguay Round Agreements Act is amended in the last sentence by striking "(except that" and all that follows through "into account)".

(4) The amendments made by this subsection shall take effect as if included in the sections of the Uruguay Round Agreements Act to which they relate.

(c) Amendment related to Omnibus Budget Reconciliation Act of 1933.—

* * * * * * * * * * * *

(2) The amendment made by paragraph (1) shall apply as if included in the amendments made by section 13321 of the Omnibus Budget Reconciliation Act of 1993, except that such amendment shall not apply—

(A) with respect to property (with an applicable recovery period under section 168(j) of the Internal Revenue Code of 1986 of 6 years or less) held by the taxpayer if the taxpayer claimed the benefits of section 168(j) of such Code with respect to such property on a return filed before

March 18, 1997, but only if such return is the first return of tax filed for the taxable year in which such property was placed in service, or

(B) with respect to wages for which the taxpayer claimed the benefits of section 45A of such Code for a taxable year on a return filed before March 18, 1997, but only if such return was the first return of tax filed for such taxable year.

(d) Amendments related to Tax Reform Act of 1986.—

* * * * * * * * * * * *

(2)(A) Subparagraph (A) of section 833(b)(1) is amended—

* * * * * * * * * * * *

(B) The amendment made by subparagraph (A) shall take effect as if included in the amendments made by section 1012 of the Tax Reform Act of 1986.

(e) Amendment related to Tax Reform Act of 1984.—

* * * * * * * * * * * *

(2) Effective date.—The amendment made by paragraph (1) shall take effect as if included in section 174(b) of the Tax Reform Act of 1984.

(f) Amendments related to Balanced Budget Act of 1997.—

* * * * * * * * * * * *

(3) Section 9302 of the Balanced Budget Act of 1997 is amended by adding at the end the following new subsection:

"(k) Coordination With Tobacco Industry Settlement Agreement.— The increase in excise taxes collected as a result of the amendments made by subsections (a), (e), and (g) of this section shall be credited against the total payments made by parties pursuant to Federal legislation implementing the tobacco industry settlement agreement of June 20, 1997.

(4) The provisions of, and amendments made by, this subsection shall take effect immediately after the sections referred to in this subsection take effect.

* * * * * * * * * * *

[¶ 4253] Sec. 1701. IDENTIFICATION OF LIMITED TAX BENEFITS SUBJECT TO LINE ITEM VETO.

Section 1021(a)(3) of the Congressional Budget and Impoundment Control Act of 1974 shall only apply to—

(1) section 101(c) (relating to high risk pools permitted to cover dependents of high risk individuals);

(2) section 222 (relating to limitation on qualified 501(c)(3) bonds other than hospital bonds);

(3) section 224 (relating to contributions of computer technology and equipment for elementary or secondary school purposes);

(4) section 312(a) (relating to treatment of remainder interests for purposes of provision relating to gain on sale of principal residence);

(5) section 501(b) (relating to indexing of alternative valuation of certain farm, etc., real property);

(6) section 504 (relating to extension of treatment of certain rents under section 2032A to lineal descendants);

(7) section 505 (relating to clarification of judicial review of eligibility for extension of time for payment of estate tax);

(8) section 508 (relating to treatment of land subject to qualified conservation easement);

(9) section 511 (relating to expansion of exception from generation-skipping transfer tax for transfers to individuals with deceased parents);

(10) section 601 (relating to the research tax credit);

(11) section 602 (relating to contributions of stock to private foundations);

(12) section 603 (relating to the work opportunity tax credit);

(13) section 604 (relating to orphan drug tax credit);

(14) section 701 (relating to incentives for revitalization of the District of Columbia) to the extent it amends the Internal Revenue Code of 1986 to create sections 1400 and 1400A (relating to tax-exempt economic development bonds);

(15) section 701 (relating to incentives for revitalization of the District of Columbia) to the extent it amends the Internal Revenue Code of 1986 to create section 1400C (relating to first-time homebuyer credit for District of Columbia);

(16) section 801 (relating to incentives for employing long-term family assistance recipients);

(17) section 904(b) (relating to uniform rate of tax on vaccines) as it relates to any vaccine containing pertussis bacteria, extracted or partial cell bacteria, or specific pertussis antigens;

(18) section 904(b) (relating to uniform rate of tax on vaccines) as it relates to any vaccine against measles;

(19) section 904(b) (relating to uniform rate of tax on vaccines) as it relates to any vaccine against mumps;

(20) section 904(b) (relating to uniform rate of tax on vaccines) as it relates to any vaccine against rubella;

(21) section 905 (relating to operators of multiple retail gasoline outlets treated as wholesale distributors for refund purposes);

(22) section 906 (relating to exemption of electric and other clean-fuel motor vehicles from luxury automobile classification);

(23) section 907(a) (relating to rate of tax on liquefied natural gas determined on basis of BTU equivalency with gasoline);

(24) section 907(b) (relating to rate of tax on methanol from natural gas determined on basis of BTU equivalency with gasoline);

(25) section 908 (relating to modification of tax treatment of hard cider);

(26) section 914 (relating to mortgage financing for residences located in disaster areas);

(27) section 962 (relating to assignment of workmen's compensation liability eligible for exclusion relating to personal injury liability assignments);

(28) section 963 (relating to tax-exempt status for certain State worker's compensation act companies);

(29) section 967 (relating to additional advance refunding of certain Virgin Island bonds);

(30) section 968 (relating to nonrecognition of gain on sale of stock to certain farmers' cooperatives);

(31) section 971 (relating to exemption of the incremental cost of a clean fuel vehicle from the limits on depreciation for vehicles);

(32) section 974 (relating to clarification of treatment of certain receivables purchased by cooperative hospital service organizations);

(33) section 975 (relating to deduction in computing adjusted gross income for expenses in connection with service performed by certain officials) with respect to taxable years beginning before 1991;

(34) section 977 (relating to elective carryback of existing carryovers of National Railroad Passenger Corporation);

(35) section 1005(b)(2)(B) (relating to transition rule for instruments described in a ruling request submitted to the Internal Revenue Service on or before June 8, 1997);

(36) section 1005(b)(2)(C) (relating to transition rule for instruments described on or before June 8, 1997, in a public announcement or in a filing with the Securities and Exchange Commission) as it relates to a public announcement;

(37) section 1005(b)(2)(C) (relating to transition rule for instruments described on or before June 8, 1997, in a public announcement or in a filing with the Securities and Exchange Commission) as it relates to a filing with the Securities and Exchange Commission;

(38) section 1011(d)(2)(B) (relating to transition rule for distributions made pursuant to the terms of a tender offer outstanding on May 3, 1995);

(39) section 1011(d)(3) (relating to transition rule for distributions made pursuant to the terms of a tender offer outstanding on September 13, 1995);

(40) section 1012(d)(3)(B) (relating to transition rule for distributions pursuant to an acquisition described in section 355(e)(2)(A)(ii) of the Internal Revenue Code of 1986 described in a ruling request submitted to the Internal Revenue Service on or before April 16, 1997);

(41) section 1012(d)(3)(C) (relating to transition rule for distributions pursuant to an acquisition described in section 355(e)(2)(A)(ii) of the Internal Revenue Code of 1986 described in a public announcement or filing with the Securities and Exchange Commission) as it relates to a public announcement;

(42) section 1012(d)(3)(C) (relating to transition rule for distributions pursuant to an acquisition described in section 355(e)(2)(A)(ii) of the Internal Revenue Code of 1986 described in a public announcement or filing with the Securities and Exchange Commission) as it relates to a filing with the Securities and Exchange Commission;

(43) section 1013(d)(2)(B) (relating to transition rule for distributions or acquisitions after June 8, 1997, described in a ruling request submitted to the Internal Revenue Service submitted on or before June 8, 1997);

(44) section 1013(d)(2)(C) (relating to transition rule for distributions or acquisitions after June 8, 1997, described in a public announcement or filing with the Securities and Exchange Commission on or before June 8, 1997) as it relates to a public announcement;

(45) section 1013(d)(2)(C) (relating to transition rule for distributions or acquisitions after June 8, 1997, described in a public announcement or filing with the Securities and Exchange Commission on or before June 8, 1997) as it relates to a filing with the Securities and Exchange Commission;

(46) section 1014(f)(2)(B) (relating to transition rule for any transaction after June 8, 1997, if such transaction is described in a ruling request submitted to the Internal Revenue Service on or before June 8, 1997);

(47) section 1014(f)(2)(C) (relating to transition rule for any transaction after June 8, 1997, if such transaction is described in a public announcement or filing with the Securities and Exchange Commission on or before June 8, 1997) as it relates to a public announcement;

(48) section 1014(f)(2)(C) (relating to transition rule for any transaction after June 8, 1997, if such transaction is described in a public announcement or filing with the Securities and Exchange Commission on or before June 8, 1997) as it relates to a filing with the Securities and Exchange Commission;

(49) section 1042(b) (relating to special rules for provision terminating certain exceptions from rules relating to exempt organizations which provide commercial-type insurance);

(50) section 1081(a) (relating to termination of suspense accounts for family corporations required to use accrual method of accounting) as it relates to the repeal of Internal Revenue Code section 447(i)(3);

(51) section 1089(b)(3) (relating to reformations);

(52) section 1089(b)(5)(B)(i) (relating to persons under a mental disability;

(53) section 1171 (relating to treatment of computer software as FSC export property);

(54) section 1175 (relating to exemption for active financing income);

(55) section 1204 (relating to travel expenses of certain Federal employees engaged in criminal investigations);

(56) section 1236 (relating to extension of time for filing a request for administrative adjustment);

(57) section 1243 (relating to special rules for administrative adjustment request with respect to bad debts or worthless securities);

(58) section 1251 (relating to clarification of limitation on maximum number of shareholders);

(59) section 1253 (relating to attribution rules applicable to stock ownership);

(60) section 1256 (relating to modification of earnings and profits rules for determining whether REIT has earnings and profits from non-REIT year);

(61) section 1257 (relating to treatment of foreclosure property);

(62) section 1261 (relating to shared appreciation mortgages);

(63) section 1302 (relating to clarification of waiver of certain rights of recovery);

(64) section 1303 (relating to transitional rule under section 2056A);

(65) section 1304 (relating to treatment for estate tax purposes of short-term obligations held by nonresident aliens);

(66) section 1311 (relating to clarification of treatment of survivor annuities under qualified terminable interest rules);

(67) section 1312 (relating to treatment of qualified domestic trust rules of forms of ownership which are not trusts);

(68) section 1313 (relating to opportunity to correct failures under section 2032A);

(69) section 1414 (relating to fermented material from any brewery may be received at a distilled spirits plant);

(70) section 1417 (relating to use of additional ameliorating material in certain wines);

(71) section 1418 (relating to domestically produced beer may be withdrawn free of tax for use of foreign embassies, legations, etc.);

(72) section 1421 (relating to transfer to brewery of beer imported in bulk without payment of tax);

(73) section 1422 (relating to transfer to bonded wine cellars of wine imported in bulk without payment of tax);

(74) section 1506 (relating to clarification of certain rules relating to employee stock ownership plans of S corporations);

(75) section 1507 (relating to modification of 10-percent tax for nondeductible contributions);

(76) section 1523 (relating to repeal of application of unrelated business income tax to ESOPs);

(77) section 1530 (relating to gratuitous transfers for the benefit of employees);

(78) section 1532 (relating to special rules relating to church plans); and

(79) section 1604(c)(2) (relating to amendment related to Omnibus Budget Reconciliation Act of 1993).

[¶ 4700]

Act sections of H.R. 3103 or portions thereof that do not amend the Code sections are at ¶s 4700-4703. Sections of the Code as amended by H.R. 1226 begin at ¶ 3001.

[¶ 4701]   Sec. 1.   SHORT TITLE.

This Act may be cited as the "Taxpayer Browsing Protection Act".

[¶ 4702]   Sec. 2.   PENALTY FOR UNAUTHORIZED INSPECTION OF TAX RETURNS OR TAX RETURN INFORMATION.

* * * * * * * * * * *

(c) EFFECTIVE DATE.— The amendments made by this section shall apply to violations occurring on and after the date of the enactment of this Act.

[¶ 4703]   Sec. 3.   CIVIL DAMAGES FOR UNAUTHORIZED INSPECTION OF RETURNS AND RETURN INFORMATION; NOTIFICATION OF UNLAWFUL INSPECTION OR DISCLOSURE.

* * * * * * * * * * *

(e) EFFECTIVE DATE.— The amendments made by this section shall apply to inspections and disclosures occurring on and after the date of the enactment of this Act. Speaker of the House of Representatives. Vice President of the United States and President of the Senate.

[¶ 4800]
Act sections of H.R. 2015 or portions thereof that do not amend specific Code Sections are at ¶s 4800-4811. Sections of the Code as amended by H.R. 2015 begin at ¶ 3001.

[¶ 4801] Sec. 1. SECTION 1. SHORT TITLE. This Act may be cited as the "Balanced Budget Act of 1997".

[¶ 4802] Sec. 4006. MEDICARE+CHOICE MSA.

* * * * * * * * * * *

(c) EFFECTIVE DATE.— The amendments made by this section shall apply to taxable years beginning after December 31, 1998.

[¶ 4803] Sec. 4041. TAX TREATMENT OF HOSPITALS WHICH PARTICIPATE IN PROVIDER-SPONSORED ORGANIZATIONS.

* * * * * * * * * * *

(b) EFFECTIVE DATE.— The amendment made by subsection (a) shall take effect on the date of the enactment of this Act.

[¶ 4804] Sec. 5405. EXEMPTION OF SERVICE PERFORMED BY ELECTION WORKERS FROM THE FEDERAL UNEMPLOYMENT TAX.

* * * * * * * * * * *

(b) EFFECTIVE DATE.— The amendments made by this section shall apply with respect to service performed after the date of the enactment of this Act.

[¶ 4805] Sec. 5406. TREATMENT OF CERTAIN SERVICES PERFORMED BY IN-MATES.

* * * * * * * * * * *

(b) EFFECTIVE DATE.— The amendments made by this section shall apply with respect to service performed after January 1, 1994.

[¶ 4806] Sec. 5407. EXEMPTION OF SERVICE PERFORMED FOR AN ELEMENTARY OR SECONDARY SCHOOL OPERATED PRIMARILY FOR RELIGIOUS PURPOSES FROM THE FEDERAL UNEMPLOYMENT TAX.

* * * * * * * * * * *

(b) EFFECTIVE DATE.— The amendments made by this section shall apply with respect to service performed after the date of the enactment of this Act.

[¶ 4807] Sec. 5702. AUTHORIZATION OF APPROPRIATIONS FOR ENFORCE-MENT INITIATIVES RELATED TO THE EARNED INCOME TAX CREDIT.

In addition to any other funds available therefor, there are authorized to be appropriated to the Secretary of the Treasury, for improved application of the earned income credit under section 32 of the Internal Revenue Code of 1986, not more than—

(1) $138,000,000 for fiscal year 1998;

(2) $143,000,000 for fiscal year 1999;

(3) $144,000,000 for fiscal year 2000;

(4) $145,000,000 for fiscal year 2001; and

(5) $146,000,000 for fiscal year 2002.

[¶ 4808] Sec. 9302. INCREASE IN EXCISE TAXES ON TOBACCO PRODUCTS.

* * * * * * * * * * *

(i) EFFECTIVE DATE.—

(1) IN GENERAL.— The amendments made by this section shall apply to articles removed (as defined in section 5702(k) of the Internal Revenue Code of 1986, as amended by this section) after December 31, 1999.

(2) TRANSITIONAL RULE.— Any person who—

(A) on the date of the enactment of this Act is engaged in business as a manufacturer of roll-your-own tobacco or as an importer of tobacco products or cigarette papers and tubes, and

(B) before January 1, 2000, submits an application under subchapter B of chapter 52 of such Code to engage in such business, may, notwithstanding such subchapter B, continue to engage in such business pending final action on such application. Pending such final action, all provisions of such chapter 52 shall apply to such applicant in the same manner and to the same extent as if such applicant were a holder of a permit under such chapter 52 to engage in such business.

(j) FLOOR STOCKS TAXES.—

(1) IMPOSITION OF TAX.— On tobacco products and cigarette papers and tubes manufactured in or imported into the United States which are removed before any tax increase date, and held on such date for sale by any person, there is hereby imposed a tax in an amount equal to the excess of—

(A) the tax which would be imposed under section 5701 of the Internal Revenue Code of 1986 on the article if the article had been removed on such date, over

(B) the prior tax (if any) imposed under section 5701 of such Code on such article.

(2) AUTHORITY TO EXEMPT CIGARETTES HELD IN VENDING MACHINES.— To the extent provided in regulations prescribed by the Secretary, no tax shall be imposed by paragraph (1) on cigarettes held for retail sale on any tax increase date, by any person in any vending machine. If the Secretary provides such a benefit with respect to any person, the Secretary may reduce the $500 amount in paragraph (3) with respect to such person.

(3) CREDIT AGAINST TAX.— Each person shall be allowed as a credit against the taxes imposed by paragraph (1) an amount equal to $500. Such credit shall not exceed the amount of taxes imposed by paragraph (1) on any tax increase date, for which such person is liable.

(4) LIABILITY FOR TAX AND METHOD OF PAYMENT.—

(A) LIABILITY FOR TAX.— A person holding cigarettes on any tax increase date, to which any tax imposed by paragraph

(1) applies shall be liable for such tax.

(B) METHOD OF PAYMENT.— The tax imposed by paragraph (1) shall be paid in such manner as the Secretary shall prescribe by regulations.

(C) TIME FOR PAYMENT.— The tax imposed by paragraph (1) shall be paid on or before April 1 following any tax increase date.

(5) ARTICLES IN FOREIGN TRADE ZONES.— Notwithstanding the Act of June 18, 1934 (48 Stat. 998, 19 U.S.C. 81a) and any other provision of law, any article which is located in a foreign trade zone on any tax increase date, shall be subject to the tax imposed by paragraph (1) if—

(A) internal revenue taxes have been determined, or customs duties liquidated, with respect to such article before such date pursuant to a request made under the 1st proviso of section 3(a) of such Act, or

(B) such article is held on such date under the supervision of a customs officer pursuant to the 2d proviso of such section 3(a).

(6) DEFINITIONS.— For purposes of this subsection—

(A) IN GENERAL.— Terms used in this subsection which are also used in section 5702 of the Internal Revenue Code of 1986 shall have the respective meanings such terms have in such section, as amended by this Act.

(B) TAX INCREASE DATE.— The term "tax increase date" means January 1, 2000, and January 1, 2002.

(C) SECRETARY.— The term "Secretary" means the Secretary of the Treasury or the Secretary's delegate.

(7) CONTROLLED GROUPS.— Rules similar to the rules of section 5061(e)(3) of such Code shall apply for purposes of this subsection.

(8) OTHER LAWS APPLICABLE.— All provisions of law, including penalties, applicable with respect to the taxes imposed by section 5701 of such Code shall, insofar as applicable and not inconsistent with the provisions of this subsection, apply to the floor stocks taxes imposed by paragraph (1), to the same extent as if such taxes were imposed by such section 5701. The Secretary may treat any person who bore the ultimate burden of the tax imposed by paragraph (1) as the person to whom a credit or refund under such provisions may be allowed or made.

[¶ 4809]   Sec. 9304.   IDENTIFICATION OF LIMITED TAX BENEFITS SUBJECT TO LINE ITEM VETO.

Section 1021(a)(3) of the Congressional Budget Act of 1974 shall only apply to 3306(c)(21) of the Internal Revenue Code of 1986 (as added by section 5406 of this Act).

[¶ 4810]   Sec. 11024.   FEDERAL INFORMATION SHARING FOR VERIFICATION OF BENEFIT DETERMINATIONS.

(a) IN GENERAL.— Except with respect to taxpayer returns and return information subject to section 6103 of the Internal Revenue Code of 1986, the Secretary may—

(1) secure directly from any department or agency of the United States information necessary to enable the Secretary to verify or confirm benefit determinations under this subtitle; and

(2) by regulation authorize the Trustee to review such information for purposes of administering this subtitle and the contract.

* * * * * * * * * * *

(c) CONFIDENTIALITY.— The Secretary may issue regulations governing the confidentiality of the information obtained pursuant to subsection (a) and the provisions of law amended by subsection (b).

[¶ 4811]   Sec. 11034.   TREATMENT OF TRUST FUND UNDER CERTAIN LAWS.

(a) INTERNAL REVENUE CODE.— For purposes of the Internal Revenue Code of 1986—

(1) the Trust Fund shall be treated as a trust described in section 401(a) of the Code which is exempt from taxation under section 501(a) of the Code;

(2) any transfer to or distribution from the Trust Fund shall be treated in the same manner as a transfer to or distribution from a trust described in section 401(a) of the Code; and

(3) the benefits provided by the Trust Fund shall be treated as benefits provided under a governmental plan maintained by the District of Columbia.

(b) ERISA.— For purposes of the Employee Retirement Income Security Act of 1974, the benefits provided by the Trust Fund shall be treated as benefits provided under a governmental plan maintained by the District of Columbia.

(c) APPLICATION OF CERTAIN FUTURE AMENDMENTS TO INTERNAL REVENUE CODE.— To the extent that any provision of subpart A of part I of subchapter D of chapter 1 of the Internal Revenue Code of 1986 (26 U.S.C. 401 et seq.) is amended after the date of the enactment of this Act, such provision as amended shall apply to the Trust Fund only to the extent the Secretary determines that application of the provision as amended is consistent with the administration of this subtitle.

Congressional Committee Reports Accompanying the Taxpayer Relief Act of 1997, H.R. 2014.

[¶ 5000]

This section reproduces all important parts of the official explanation of the Taxpayer Relief Act of 1997, H.R. 2014. The material comes from the House, Senate, and the Conference Committee Reports.

The Committee Reports ar arranged in the order of the Act Sections of the Taxpayer Relief Act of 1997, H.R. 2014.

[¶ 5001]   Section 101.   Child and dependent care tax credit - dependents of high risk individuals.

(Code Sec. 24)

[House Report]

Present Law

In general

Present law does not provide tax credits based solely on the taxpayer's number of dependent children. Taxpayers with dependent children, however, generally are able to claim a personal exemption for each of these dependents. The total amount of personal exemptions is subtracted (along with certain other items) from adjusted gross income ("AGI") in arriving at taxable income. The amount of each personal exemption is $2,650 for 1997, and is adjusted annually for inflation. In 1997, the amount of the personal exemption is phased out for taxpayers with AGI in excess of $121,200 for single taxpayers, $151,500 for heads of household, and $181,800 for married couples filing joint returns. These phaseout thresholds are adjusted annually for inflation.

Dependent care credit

A nonrefundable credit against income tax liability is available for up to 30 percent (phased down to 20 percent for individuals with AGI above $28,000) of a limited dollar amount of employment-related child and dependent care expenses for certain qualified individuals;   (1) a dependent child under age 13; (2) a dependent physically or mentally unable to care for him or herself; or (3) a spouse who is physically or mentally unable to care for him or herself. Eligible employment-related expenses are limited to $2,400 if there is one qualifying individual

and $4,800 if there are two or more qualifying individuals. Employment-related expenses are expenses for household services and the care of a qualifying individual, if incurred to enable the taxpayer to be gainfully employed. Employment-related expenses are reduced to the extent the taxpayer has employer-provided dependent care assistance that is excludable from gross income.

Reasons for Change

The Committee believes that the individual income tax structure does not reduce tax liability by enough to reflect a family's reduced ability to pay taxes as family size increases. In part, this is because over the last 50 years the value of the dependent personal exemption has declined in real terms by over one-third. The Committee believes that a tax credit for families with dependent children will reduce the individual income tax burden of those families, will better recognize the financial responsibilities of raising dependent children, and will promote family values.

Explanation of Provision

The bill allows taxpayers a maximum nonrefundable tax credit of $500 ($400 for taxable year 1998) for each qualifying child under the age of 17. A qualifying child is defined as an individual for whom the taxpayer can claim a dependency exemption and who is a son or daughter of the taxpayer (or a descendent of either), a stepson or stepdaughter of the taxpayer or an eligible foster child of the taxpayer. The credit amount is not indexed for inflation.

For taxpayers with modified AGI in excess of certain thresholds, the sum of the otherwise allowable child credit and the otherwise allowable dependent care credit is phased out. Specifically, the sum of the otherwise allowable child credit and then the otherwise allowable dependent care credit is reduced by $25 for each $1,000 of modified AGI (or fraction thereof) in excess of the threshold ("the modified AGI phase-out"). For these purposes modified AGI is computed by increasing the taxpayer's AGI by the amount otherwise excluded from gross income under Code sections 911, 931, or 933 (relating to the exclusion of income of U.S. citizens or residents living abroad; residents of Guam, American Samoa, and the Northern Mariana Islands; and residents of Puerto Rico, respectively). The reduction is applied first to the child credit and then to the dependent care credit. For married taxpayers filing joint returns, the threshold is $110,000. For taxpayers filing single or head of household returns, the threshold is $75,000. For married taxpayers filing separate returns, the threshold is $55,000. These thresholds are not indexed for inflation.

Beginning after 2001, the otherwise allowable child credit would be reduced by one-half of the amount of the taxpayer's otherwise allowable dependent care credit. This reduction to the otherwise allowable child credit would be applied after the application of the modified AGI phase-out to the child and dependent care credits (if applicable). The maximum amount of the child credit for each taxable year (after the reduction, if any, for the dependent care credit after 2001) could not exceed an amount equal to the excess of: (1) the taxpayer's regular income tax liability (net of applicable credits) over (2) the sum of the taxpayer's tentative minimum tax liability (determined without regard to the alternative minimum foreign tax credit) and the earned income credit allowed.

Effective Date

Generally, the child tax credit is effective for taxable years beginning after December 31, 1997.

B. Expand Definition of High-Risk Individuals with Respect to Tax-Exempt State-Sponsored Organizations Providing Health Coverage (sec. 101(b) of the bill and sec. 501(c)(26) of the Code)]

Present Law

Present law provides tax-exempt status to any membership organization that is established by a State exclusively to provide coverage for medical care on a nonprofit basis to certain high-risk individuals, provided certain criteria are satisfied.[1] The organization may provide coverage for medical care either by issuing insurance itself or by entering into an arrangement with a health maintenance organization ("HMO").

High-risk individuals eligible to receive medical care coverage from the organization must be residents of the State who, due to a pre-existing medical condition, are unable to obtain health coverage for such condition through insurance or an HMO, or are able to acquire such coverage only at a rate that is substantially higher than the rate charged for such coverage by the organization. The State must determine the composition of membership in the organization. For example, a State could mandate that all organizations that are subject to insurance regulation by the State must be members of the organization.

Present law further requires the State or members of the organization to fund the liabilities of the organization to the extent that premiums charged to eligible individuals are insufficient to cover such liabilities. Finally, no part of the net earnings of the organization can inure to the benefit of any private shareholder or individual.

Reasons for Change

The Committee believes that including certain children of high-risk individuals in the group of individuals to whom such an organization may provide medical care coverage will assist States in providing medical care coverage for uninsured children.

Explanation of Provision

The provision expands the definition of high-risk individuals to include a child of an

---

1. No inference is intended as to the tax treatment of other types of State-sponsored organizations.

individual who meets the present-law definition of a high-risk individual, subject to certain requirements. The requirements are: (1) the taxpayer is allowed a deduction for a personal exemption for the child for the taxable year; (2) the child has not attained the age of 17 as of the close of the calendar year in which the taxable year of the taxpayer begins; and (3) the child is a son or daughter or the taxpayer (or a dependent of either), a stepson or stepdaughter of the taxpayer, or an eligible foster child of the taxpayer.

Effective Date

The provision is effective for taxable years beginning after December 31, 1997.

[Senate Report]

Present Law

For taxpayers with AGI in excess of certain threshold, the otherwise allowable child credit is phased out. Specifically, the otherwise allowable child credit is reduced by $25 for each $1,000 of modified AGI (or fraction thereof) in excess of the threshold ("the modified AGI phase-out"). For these purposes modified AGI is computed by increasing the taxpayer's AGI by the amount otherwise excluded from gross income under Code sections 911, 931, or 933 (relating to the exclusion of income of U.S. citizens or residents living abroad; residents of Guam, American Samoa, and the Northern Marina Islands; and residents of Puerto Rico, respectively). For married taxpayers filing joint returns, the threshold is $110,000. For taxpayers filing single or head of household returns, the threshold is $75,000. For married taxpayers filing separate returns, the threshold is $55,000. These threshold are not indexed for inflation.

The maximum amount of the child credit for each taxable year can not exceed an amount equal to the excess of: (1) the taxpayer's regular income tax liability (net of applicable credits) over (2) the sum of the taxpayer's tentative minimum tax liability (determined without regard to the alternative minimum foreign tax credit) and one-half of the earned income credit allowed.

[Conference Report]

Conference Agreement

Size of credit

The conference agreement provides a $500 ($400 for taxable year 1998) credit for each qualifying child under the age of 17.

Qualifying child

The conference agreement follows the House bill and the Senate amendment. The conference agreement includes a requirement that the taxpayer include the name and taxpayer identification number (TIN) for each qualifying child. The conference agreement also extends the math and clerical error rule to the child tax credit.

Phaseout

The conference agreement follows the House bill and the Senate amendment with one modification. The modification is to increase the phaseout rate to $50 for each $1,000 of modified AGI (or fraction thereof) in excess of the threshold. The threshold amounts are unchanged from both the House bill and the Senate amendment.

Maximum allowable child credit

In general, in the case of a taxpayer with qualifying children, the amount of the child credit equals $500 times the number of qualifying children.

In the case of a taxpayer with one or two qualifying children, a portion of the child credit may be treated as a supplemental child credit amount. This amount equals the excess of (1) $500 times the number of qualifying children up to the excess of the taxpayer's income tax liability (net of applicable credits other than the earned income credit) over the taxpayer's tentative minimum tax liability (determined without regard to the alternative minimum foreign tax credit) over (2) the sum of the taxpayer's regular income tax liability (net of applicable credits other than the earned income credit) and the employee share of FICA (and one-half of the taxpayer's SECA tax liability, if applicable) reduced by any earned income credit amount. In no case will the total amount of the allowable child credit exceed the amount that would result from its calculation as a nonrefundable personal credit.

In the case of a taxpayer with three or more qualifying children, the maximum amount of the child credit for each taxable year cannot exceed the greater of: (1) the excess of the taxpayer's regular tax liability (net of applicable credits other than the earned income credit) over the taxpayer's tentative minimum tax liability (determined without regard to the alternative minimum foreign tax credit), or (2) an amount equal to the excess of the sum of the taxpayer's regular income tax liability (net of applicable credits other than the earned income credit) and the employee share of FICA (and one-half of the taxpayer's SECA tax liability, if applicable) reduced by the earned income credit. To the extent that the amount determined under (1) is greater than the amount determined under (2), the difference is treated as a supplemental child credit amount.

The conferees anticipate that the Secretary of the Treasury will determine whether a simplified method of calculating the child credit, consistent with the formula described above, can be achieved.

[¶ 5002]   Section 201.   Hope and lifetime learning tax credits.

(Code Sec. 25A, 6050S)

[House Report]

Present Law

Deductibility of education expenses

Taxpayers generally may not deduct education and training expenses. However, a deduction for education expenses generally is allowed under section 162 if the education or training (1) maintains or improves a skill required in a trade or business currently engaged in by the taxpayer, or (2) meets the express requirements of the taxpayer's employer, or requirements of applicable law or regulations, imposed as condition of continued employment (Treas. Reg. sec. 1.162 5). However, education expenses are not deductible if they relate to certain minimum educational requirements or to education or training that enables a taxpayer to begin working in a new trade or business. In the case of an employee, education

Refundable child credit amount

In the case of a taxpayer with three or more qualifying children, if the amount of the allowable child credit as computed under the computation described immediately above exceeds the taxpayer's regular tax liability before the computation, then the excess is a refundable tax credit.

Effective Date

Generally, the child tax credit is effective for taxable years beginning after December 31, 1997.

Senate Amendment

No provision.

Conference Agreement

The conference agreement follows the House bill, with a modification to further expand the definition of high−risk individuals to include the spouse of an individual who meets the present−law definition of a high−risk individual.

expenses (if not reimbursed by the employer) may be claimed as an itemized deduction only if such expenses meet the above-described criteria for deductibility under section 162 and only to the extent that the expenses, along with other miscellaneous deductions, exceed 2 percent of the taxpayer's adjusted gross income (AGI).

Exclusion for employer-provided educational assistance

A special rule allows an employee to exclude from gross income for income tax purposes and from wages for employment tax purposes up to $5,250 annually paid by his or her employer for educational assistance (sec. 127). In order for the exclusion to apply certain requirements must be satisfied, including a requirement that not more than 5 percent of the amounts paid or incurred by the employer during the year for educational assistance under a qualified educational assistance program can be provided for the class of individuals consisting of more than 5-percent owners of the employer and the spouses or dependents of such more than 5-percent owners. This special rule for employer-provided educational assistance expires with respect to courses beginning after June 30, 1997 (and does not apply to graduate level courses beginning after June 30, 1996).

For purposes of the special exclusion, educational assistance means the payment by an employer of expenses incurred by or on behalf of the employee for education of the employee including, but not limited to, tuition, fees, and similar payments, books, supplies, and equipment. Educational assistance also includes the provision by the employer of courses of instruction for the employee (including books, supplies, and equipment). Educational assistance does not include tools or supplies which may be retained by the employee after completion of a course or meals, lodging, or transportation. The exclusion does not apply to any education involving sports, games, or hobbies.

In the absence of the special exclusion, employer-provided educational assistance is excludable from gross income and wages as a working condition fringe benefit (sec. 132(d)) only to the extent the education expenses would be deductible under section 162.

Exclusion for interest earned on savings bonds

Another special rule (sec. 135) provides that interest earned on a qualified U.S. Series EE savings bond issued after 1989 is excludable from gross income if the proceeds of the bond upon redemption do not exceed qualified higher education expenses paid by the taxpayer during the taxable year.[3] "Qualified higher education expenses" include tuition and fees (but not room and board expenses) required for the enrollment or attendance of the taxpayer, the taxpayer's spouse, or a dependent of the taxpayer at certain colleges, universities, or vocational schools. The exclusion provided

by section 135 is phased out for certain higher-income taxpayers, determined by the taxpayer's modified AGI during the year the bond is redeemed. For 1996, the exclusion was phased out for taxpayers with modified AGI between $49,450 and $64,450 ($74,200 and $104,200 for joint returns). To prevent taxpayers from effectively avoiding the income phaseout limitation through issuance of bonds directly in the child's name, section 135(c)(1)(B) provides that the interest exclusion is available only with respect to U.S. Series EE savings bonds issued to taxpayers who are at least 24 years old.

Qualified scholarships

Section 117 excludes from gross income amounts received as a qualified scholarship by an individual who is a candidate for a degree and used for tuition and fees required for the enrollment or attendance (or for fees, books, supplies, and equipment required for courses of instruction) at a primary, secondary, or post-secondary educational institution. The tax-free treatment provided by section 117 does not extend to scholarship amounts covering regular living expenses, such as room and board. There is, however, no dollar limitation for the section 117 exclusion, provided that the scholarship funds are used to pay for tuition and required fees. In addition to the exclusion for qualified scholarships, section 117 provides an exclusion from gross income for qualified tuition reductions for education below the graduate level provided to employees (and their spouses and dependents) of certain educational organizations.[3] Section 117(c) specifically provides that the exclusion for qualified scholarships does not apply to any amount received by a student that represents payment for teaching, research, or other services by the student required as a condition for receiving the scholarship.

Student loan forgiveness

In the case of an individual, section 108(f) provides that gross income subject to Federal income tax does not include any

---

3. If the aggregate redemption amount (i.e., principal plus interest) of all Series EE bonds redeemed by the taxpayer during the taxable year exceeds the qualified education expenses incurred, then the excludable portion of interest income is based on the ratio that the education expenses bears to the aggregate redemption amount (sec. 135(b)).

3. A special rule provides that qualified tuition under section 117(d) may be provided for graduate–level courses in cases of graduate students who are engaged in teaching or research activities for the educational organization (sec. 117(d)(5)).

amount from the forgiveness (in whole or in part) of certain student loans, provided that the forgiveness is contingent on the student's working for a certain period of time in certain professions for any of a broad class of employers (e.g., providing health care services to a nonprofit organization). Student loans eligible for this special rule must be made to an individual to assist the individual in attending an education institution that normally maintains a regular faculty and curriculum and normally has a regularly enrolled body of students in attendance at the place where its education activities are regularly carried on. Loan proceeds may be used not only for tuition and required fees, but also to cover room and board expenses (in contrast to tax-free scholarships under section 117, which are limited to tuition and required fees). In addition, the loan must be made by (1) the United States (or an instrumentality or agency thereof), (2) a State (or any political subdivision thereof), (3) certain tax-exempt public benefit corporations that control a State, county, or municipal hospital and whose employees have been deemed to be public employees under State law, or (4) an educational organization that originally received the funds from which the loan was made from the United States, a State, or a tax-exempt public benefit corporation. Thus, loans made with private, nongovernmental funds are not qualifying student loans for purposes of the section 108(f) exclusion. As with section 117, there is no dollar limitation for the section 108(f) exclusion.

Qualified State prepaid tuition programs

Section 529 (enacted as part of the Small Business Job Protection Act of 1996) provides tax-exempt status to "qualified State tuition programs," meaning certain programs established and maintained by a State (or agency or instrumentality thereof) under which persons may (1) purchase tuition credits or certificates on behalf of a designated beneficiary that entitle the beneficiary to a waiver or payment of qualified higher education expenses of the beneficiary, or (2) make contributions to an account that is established for the purpose of meeting qualified higher education expenses of

the designated beneficiary of the account. "Qualified higher education expenses" are defined as tuition, fees, books, supplies, and equipment required for the enrollment or attendance at a college or university (or certain vocational schools). Qualified higher education expenses do not include room and board expenses. Section 529 also provides that no amount shall be included in the gross income of a contributor to, or beneficiary of, a qualified State tuition program with respect to any distribution from, or earnings under, such program, except that (1) amounts distributed or educational benefits provided to a beneficiary (e.g., when the beneficiary attends college) will be included in the beneficiary's gross income (unless excludable under another Code section) to the extent such amounts or the value of the educational benefits exceed contributions made on behalf of the beneficiary, and (2) amounts distributed to a contributor (e.g., when a parent receives a refund) will be included in the contributor's gross income to the extent such amounts exceed contributions made by that person.[4]

Reasons for Change

To assist low- and middle-income families and students in paying for the costs of post-secondary education, the Committee believes that taxpayers should be allowed to claim a credit against Federal income taxes for certain tuition and related expenses incurred during a student's first two years of attendance (on at least a half-time basis) at a college, university, or certain vocational schools.

Explanation of Provision

In general

Individual taxpayers are allowed to claim a non-refundable HOPE credit against Federal income taxes up to $1,500 per student per year for 50 percent of qualified tuition and related expenses (but not room and board expenses) paid for the first two years of the student's post-secondary education in a degree or certificate program. The qualified tuition and related expenses must be incurred on behalf of the taxpayer, the taxpayer's spouse, or a dependent. The HOPE

---

4. Specifically, section 529(c)(3)(A) provides that any distribution under a qualified State tuition program shall be includible in the gross income of the distributee in the same manner as provided under present-law section 72 to the extent not excluded from gross income under any other provision of the Code.

credit is available with respect to an individual student for two taxable years, provided that the student has not completed the first two years of post-secondary education. Beginning in 1998, the maximum credit amount of $1,500 will be indexed for inflation, rounded down to the closest multiple of $50.[5]

The HOPE credit amount that a taxpayer may otherwise claim is phased out ratably for taxpayers with modified AGI between $40,000 and $50,000 ($80,000 and $100,000 for joint returns). Modified AGI includes amounts otherwise excluded with respect to income earned abroad (or income from Puerto Rico or U.S. possessions). Beginning in 2001, the income phase-out ranges will be indexed for inflation, rounded down to the closest multiple of $5,000.

The HOPE credit is available in the taxable year the expenses are paid, subject to the requirement that the education commence or continue during that year or during the first three months of the next year. Qualified tuition expenses paid with the proceeds of a loan generally are eligible for the HOPE credit (rather than repayment of the loan itself).[6]

Dependent students

A taxpayer may claim the HOPE credit with respect to an eligible student who is not the taxpayer or the taxpayer's spouse (e.g., in cases where the student is the taxpayer's child) only if the taxpayer claims the student as a dependent for the taxable year for which the credit is claimed. If a student is claimed as a dependent by the parent or other taxpayer, the eligible student him- or herself is not entitled to claim a HOPE credit for that taxable year on the student's own tax return. If a parent (or other taxpayer) claims a student as a dependent, any qualified tuition and related expenses paid by the student are treated as

paid by the parent (or other taxpayer) for purposes of the provision.

Election of HOPE credit or proposed deduction for qualified higher education expenses

For each taxable year, a taxpayer may elect with respect to an eligible student either the HOPE credit or the proposed deduction for qualified higher education expenses (described below). Thus, for example, if a parent claims a child as a dependent for a taxable year, then all qualified tuition expenses paid by both the parent and child are deemed paid by the parent, and the parent may claim the HOPE credit (assuming that the AGI phaseout does not apply) on the parent's return. As an alternative, the parent may elect for that taxable year the deduction for qualified higher education expenses with respect to the dependent child (as described below).[7]

Qualified tuition and related expenses

The HOPE credit is available for "qualified tuition and related expenses," meaning tuition, fees, and books required for the enrollment or attendance of an eligible student at an eligible educational institution. Charges and fees associated with meals, lodging, student activities, athletics, insurance, transportation, and similar personal, living or family expenses are not included. The expenses of education involving sports, games, or hobbies are not qualified tuition expenses unless this education is part of the student's degree program.

Qualified tuition and related expenses generally include only out-of-pocket expenses. Qualified tuition and related expenses do not include expenses covered by educational assistance that is not required to be included in the gross income of either the student or the taxpayer claiming the credit. Thus, total qualified tuition and related expenses are reduced by any scholarship or fellowship grants excludable from

---

5. The HOPE credit may not be used to reduce any alternative minimum tax (AMT) liability owed by the taxpayer.
6. The Treasury Department is granted authority to issue regulations providing that the HOPE credit will be recaptured in cases where the student or taxpayer receives a refund of tuition and related expenses with respect to which a credit was claimed in a prior year.
7. For any taxable year, a taxpayer may claim the HOPE credit for qualified tuition and related expenses paid

with respect to one student and also claim the proposed deduction (described below) for higher education expenses paid with respect to one or more other students. If the HOPE credit is claimed with respect to one student for one or two taxable years, then the proposed deduction for higher education expenses may be available with respect to that student for subsequent taxable years.

gross income under present-law section 117 and any other tax-free educational benefits received by the student during the taxable year. No reduction of qualified tuition and related expenses is required for a gift, bequest, devise, or inheritance within the meaning of section 102(a). Under the provision, a HOPE credit is not allowed with respect to any education expense for which a deduction is claimed under section 162 or any other section of the Code.[8]

Eligible student

An eligible student for purposes of the HOPE credit is an individual who is enrolled in a degree, certificate, or other program (including a program of study abroad approved for credit by the institution at which such student is enrolled) leading to a recognized educational credential at an eligible educational institution. The student must pursue a course of study on at least a half-time basis. (In other words, for at least one academic period which begins during the taxable year, the student must carry at least one-half the normal full-time work load for the course of study the student is pursuing.) An eligible student may not have been convicted of a Federal or State felony consisting of the possession or distribution of a controlled substance.

Eligible educational institution

Eligible educational institutions are defined by reference to section 481 of the Higher Education Act of 1965. Such institutions generally are accredited post-secondary educational institutions offering credit toward a bachelor's degree, an associate's degree, or another recognized post-secondary credential. Certain proprietary institutions and post-secondary vocational institutions also are eligible educational institutions. The institution must be eligible to participate in Department of Education student aid programs.

Regulations

The Secretary of the Treasury (in consultation with the Secretary of Education) is granted authority to issue regulations to implement the proposal, including regulations providing appropriate rules for recordkeeping and information reporting. These regulations may address the information reports that eligible educational institutions will be required to file to assist students and the IRS in calculating the amount of the HOPE credit potentially available. Where certain terms are defined by reference to the Higher Education Act of 1965, the Secretary of Education has authority to issue regulations, as well as authority to define other education terms as necessary.

Effective Date

The provision is effective for expenses paid after December 31, 1997, for education furnished in academic periods beginning after such date.

[Conference Report]

Conference Agreement

In general

The conference agreement follows the House bill, except: (1) the HOPE credit rate is 100 percent on the first $1,000 of qualified tuition and fees, and 50 percent on the next $1,000 of qualified tuition and fees;[10] (2) the HOPE credit is available only for tuition and fees required for the enrollment or attendance of an eligible student at an eligible institution, and is not available for expenses incurred to purchase books; and (3) for a taxable year, a taxpayer may elect with respect to an eligible student the HOPE credit, the 20-percent "Lifetime

---

8. In addition, the bill amends present-law section 135 to provide that the amount of qualified higher education expenses taken into account for purposes of that section is reduced by the amount of such expenses taken into account in determining the HOPE credit allowed to any taxpayer with respect to the student for the taxable year.

10. Thus, an eligible student who incurs $1,000 of qualified tuition and fees is eligible (subject to the AGI phaseout) for a $1,000 HOPE credit; and if such a student incurs $2,000 of qualified tuition and fees, then he or she is eligible for a $1,500 HOPE credit. The maximum HOPE credit amount will be indexed for inflation occurring after the year 2000, by increasing the cap on qualified tuition and fees subject to the 100-percent credit rate and the cap on such tuition and fees subject to the 50-percent credit rate (both caps rounded down to the closest multiple of $100). The first taxable year for which the inflation adjustment could be made to increase the cap on qualified tuition and fees will be 2002. In addition, under the conference agreement, the income phase-out ranges for the HOPE credit will be indexed for inflation occurring after the year 2000, rounded down to the closest multiple of $1,000. The first taxable year for which the inflation adjustment could be made to increase the income phase-out ranges will be 2002.

Learning" credit (as described below), or the exclusion from gross income for certain distributions from an education IRA (as provided by the conference agreement).

Lifetime Learning credit for qualified tuition and fees

Allowance of credit

The conference agreement provides that individual taxpayers are allowed to claim a nonrefundable "Lifetime Learning" credit against Federal income taxes equal to 20 percent of qualified tuition and fees incurred during the taxable year on behalf of the taxpayer, the taxpayer's spouse, or any dependents. For expenses paid after June 30, 1998, and prior to January 1, 2003, up to $5,000 of qualified tuition and fees per taxpayer return will be eligible for the 20-percent Lifetime Learning credit (i.e., the maximum credit per taxpayer return will be $1,000). For expenses paid after December 31, 2002, up to $10,000 of qualified tuition and fees per taxpayer return will be eligible for the 20- percent Lifetime Learning credit (i.e., the maximum credit per taxpayer return will be $2,000).

In contrast to the HOPE credit, a taxpayer may claim the Lifetime Learning credit for an unlimited number of taxable years. Also in contrast to the HOPE credit, the maximum amount of the Lifetime Learning credit that may be claimed on a taxpayer's return will not vary based on the number of students in the taxpayer's family.

The Lifetime Learning credit is phased out ratably over the same phaseout range that applies for purposes of the HOPE credit- -i.e., taxpayers with modified AGI between $40,000 and $50,000 ($80,000 and $100,000 for joint returns). The income phase-out ranges will be indexed for inflation occurring after the year 2000, rounded down to the closest multiple of $1,000. The first taxable year for which the inflation adjustment could be made to increase the income phase-out ranges will be 2002.

The Lifetime Learning credit is available in the taxable year the expenses are paid, subject to the requirement that the education commence or continue during that year or during the first three months of the next year. Qualified tuition and fees paid with the proceeds of a loan generally are eligible for the Lifetime Learning credit (rather than repayment of the loan itself).

Dependent students

As with the HOPE credit, a taxpayer may claim the Lifetime Learning credit with respect to a student who is not the taxpayer or the taxpayer's spouse (e.g., in cases where the student is the taxpayer's child) only if the taxpayer claims the student as a dependent for the taxable year for which the credit is claimed. If a student is claimed as a dependent by the parent or other taxpayer, the student him- or herself is not entitled to claim the Lifetime Learning credit for that taxable year on the student's own tax return. If a parent (or other taxpayer) claims a student as a dependent, any qualified tuition and related expenses paid by the student are treated as paid by the parent (or other taxpayer) for purposes of the provision.

Election of Lifetime Learning credit, HOPE credit, or exclusion from gross income for certain distributions from education IRAs.—A taxpayer may claim the Lifetime Learning credit for a taxable year with respect to one or more students, even though the taxpayer also claims a HOPE credit (or claims an exclusion from gross income for certain distributions from qualified State tuition programs or education IRAs) for that same taxable year with respect to other students. If, for a taxable year, a taxpayer claims a HOPE credit with respect to a student (or claims an exclusion for certain distributions from an education IRA with respect to a student), then the Lifetime Learning credit will not be available with respect to that same student for that year (although the Lifetime Learning credit may be available with respect to that same student for other taxable years).

Qualified tuition and fees

The Lifetime Learning credit is available for "qualified tuition and fees," meaning tuition and fees required for the enrollment or attendance of the eligible student at an eligible institution. Charges and fees associated with meals, lodging, student activities, athletics, insurance, transportation, and similar personal, living or family expenses are not included. The 20-percent credit is not available for expenses incurred to purchase books. The expenses of education involving sports, games, or hobbies are not qualified tuition expenses unless this education is part of the student's degree program.

In contrast to the HOPE credit, qualified tuition and fees for purposes of the Lifetime Learning credit include tuition and fees incurred with respect to undergraduate or graduate-level (and professional degree) courses. In addition to allowing a credit for the tuition and fees of a student who attends classes on at least a half-time basis as part of a degree or certificate program, the Lifetime Learning credit also is available with respect to any course of instruction at an eligible educational institution (whether enrolled in by the student on a full-time, half-time, or less than half-time basis) to acquire or improve job skills of the student.

Qualified tuition and fees are defined in the same manner as under the HOPE credit provisions. Thus, qualified tuition and fees generally include only out-of-pocket expenses. Qualified tuition and fees do not include expenses covered by educational assistance that is not required to be included in the gross income of either the student or the taxpayer claiming the credit. Thus, total qualified tuition and fees are reduced by any scholarship or fellowship grants excludable from gross income under present-law section 117 and any other tax-free educational benefits received by the student during the taxable year (such as employer-provided educational assistance excludable under section 127). No reduction of qualified tuition and fees is required for a gift, bequest, devise, or inheritance within the meaning of section 102(a). Under the provision, a Lifetime Learning credit is not allowed with respect to any education expense for which a deduction is claimed under section 162 or any other section of the Code.[12]

Eligible educational institutions

Eligible educational institutions are (as with the HOPE credit) defined by reference to section 481 of the Higher Education Act of 1965. Such institutions generally are accredited post-secondary educational institutions offering credit toward a bachelor's degree, an associate's degree, graduate-level or professional degree, or another recognized post-secondary credential. Certain proprietary institutions and post-secondary vocational institutions also are eligible educational institutions. The institution must be eligible to participate in Department of Education student aid programs.

Regulations

The Secretary of the Treasury (in consultation with the Secretary of Education) is granted authority to issue regulations to implement the provision. The Secretary of the Treasury will have authority to issue regulations providing appropriate rules for record-keeping and information reporting. These regulations may address the information reports that eligible educational institutions will be required to file to assist students and the IRS in calculating the amount of the Lifetime Learning credit potentially available.

Effective Date

The provision is effective for expenses paid after June 30, 1998, for education furnished in academic periods beginning after such date.

[¶ 5003]   Section 202.   Deduction for interest on education loans.

(Code Sec. 221, 222)

[Senate Report]

Present Law

The Tax Reform Act of 1986 repealed the deduction for personal interest. Student loan interest generally is treated as personal interest and thus is not allowable as an itemized deduction from income.

Taxpayers generally may not deduct education and training expenses. However, a deduction for education expenses generally

---

12. In addition, the conference agreement amends present—law section 135 to provide that the amount of qualified higher education expenses taken into account for purposes of that section is reduced by the amount of such expenses taken into account in determining the Lifetime Learning credit claimed by any taxpayer with respect to the student for the taxable year.

is allowed under section 162 if the education or training (1) maintains or improves a skill required in a trade or business currently engaged in by the taxpayer, or (2) meets the express requirements of the taxpayer's employer, or requirements of applicable law or regulations, imposed as a condition of continued employment (Treas. Reg. sec. 1.162-5). Education expenses are not deductible if they relate to certain minimum educational requirements or to education or training that enables a taxpayer to begin working in a new trade or business. In the case of an employee, education expenses (if not reimbursed by the employer) may be claimed as an itemized deduction only if such expenses relate to the employee's current job and only to the extent that the expenses, along with other miscellaneous deductions, exceed two percent of the taxpayer's adjusted gross income (AGI).

Reasons for Change

The Committee is aware that many students incur considerable debt in the course of obtaining undergraduate and graduate education. The Committee believes that permitting a deduction for interest on certain student loans will help to ease the financial burden that such obligations represent.

Explanation of Provision

Under the bill, certain individuals who have paid interest on qualified education loans may claim an above-the-line deduction for such interest expenses, up to a maximum deduction of $2,500 per year. The deduction is allowed only with respect to interest paid on a qualified education loan during the first 60 months in which interest payments are required. Months during which the qualified education loan is in deferral or forbearance do not count against the 60-month period. No deduction is allowed to an individual if that individual is claimed as a dependent on another taxpayer's return for the taxable year. Beginning in 1999, the maximum deduction of $2,500 is indexed for inflation, rounded down to the closest multiple of $50.

A qualified education loan generally is defined as any indebtedness incurred to pay for the qualified higher education expenses of the taxpayer, the taxpayer's spouse, or any dependent of the taxpayer as of the time the indebtedness was incurred in attending (1) post-secondary educational institutions and certain vocational schools defined by reference to section 481 of the Higher Education Act of 1965, or (2) institutions conducting internship or residency programs leading to a degree or certificate from an institution of higher education, a hospital, or a health care facility conducting postgraduate training. Qualified higher education expenses are defined as the student's cost of attendance as defined in section 472 of the Higher Education Act of 1965 (generally, tuition, fees, room and board, and related expenses), reduced by (1) any amount excluded from gross income under section 135 (i.e., United States savings bonds used to pay higher education tuition and fees), (2) any amount distributed from a qualified tuition program or education investment account and excluded from gross income (under the provision described above), and (3) the amount of any scholarship or fellowship grants excludable from gross income under present-law section 117, as well as any other tax-free educational benefits, such as employer-provided educational assistance that is excludable from the employee's gross income under section 127. Such expenses must be paid or incurred within a reasonable period before or after the indebtedness is incurred, and must be attributable to a period when the student is at least a half-time student.

The deduction is phased out ratably for taxpayers with modified adjusted gross income (AGI) between $40,000 and $50,000 ($80,000 and $100,000 for joint returns). Modified AGI includes amounts otherwise excluded with respect to income earned abroad (or income from Puerto Rico or U.S. possessions), and is calculated after application of section 86 (income inclusion of certain Social Security benefits), section 219 (deductible IRA contributions), and section 469 (limitation on passive activity losses and credits).[24] Beginning in 2001, the income phase-out ranges are indexed for in-

---

24. For purposes of sections 86, 135, 219, and 469, adjusted gross income is determined without regard to the deduction for student loan interest.

flation, rounded down to the closest multiple of $5,000.

Any person in a trade or business or any governmental agency that receives $600 or more in qualified education loan interest from an individual during a calendar year must provide an information report on such interest to the IRS and to the payor.

Effective Date

The provision is effective for payments of interest due after December 31, 1996, on any qualified education loan. Thus, in the case of already existing qualified education loans, interest payments qualify for the deduction to the extent that the 60-month period has not expired. For purposes of counting the 60 months, any qualified education loan and all refinancing (that is treated as a qualified education loan) of such loan are treated as a single loan.

[Conference Report]

House Bill

No provision.

Conference Agreement

The conference agreement follows the Senate amendment, except that the maximum deduction is phased in over 4 years, with a $1,000 maximum deduction in 1998, $1,500 in 1999, $2,000 in 2000, and $2,500 in 2001. The maximum deduction amount is not indexed for inflation. In addition, the deduction is phased out ratably for individual taxpayers with modified AGI of $40,000-$55,000 ($60,000- $75,000 for joint returns); such income ranges will be indexed for inflation occurring after the year 2002, rounded down to the closest multiple

of $5,000. Thus, the first taxable year for which the inflation adjustment could be made will be 2003. For purposes of the deduction, modified AGI includes amounts excludable from gross income under section 137 (qualified adoption expenses).[44]

Qualified higher education expenses are defined as the student's cost of attendance as defined in section 472 of the Higher Education Act of 1965 (generally, tuition, fees, room and board, and related expenses), reduced by (1) any amount excluded from gross income under section 135, (2) any amount distributed from an education IRA and excluded from gross income, and (3) the amount of any scholarship or fellowship grants excludable from gross income under present-law section 117, as well as any other tax-free educational benefits, such as employer-provided educational assistance that is excludable from the employee's gross income under section 127.

The conferees expect that the Secretary of Treasury will issue regulations setting forth reporting procedures that will facilitate the administration of this provision. Specifically, such regulations should require lenders separately to report to borrowers the amount of interest that constitutes deductible student loan interest (i.e., interest on a qualified education loan during the first 60 months in which interest payments are required). In this regard, the regulations should include a method for borrower certification to a lender that the loan proceeds are being used to pay for qualified higher education expenses.

The provision is effective for interest payments due and paid after December 31, 1997, on any qualified education loan.

[¶ 5004]   Section 203.   Penalty-free withdrawals from IRAs for higher education expenses.

(Code Sec. 72)

[House Report]

Present Law

An individual may make deductible contributions to an individual retirement ar-

rangement ("IRA") for each taxable year up to the lesser of $2,000 or the amount of the individual's compensation for the year if the individual is not an active participant in an employer-sponsored qualified retirement plan (and, if married, the individual's spouse also is not an active participant). In

---

44. For purposes of section 137, adjusted gross income is determined without regard to the deduction for student loan interest.

the case of a married couple, deductible IRA contributions of up to $2,000 can be made for each spouse (including, for example, a homemaker who does not work outside the home) if the combined compensation of both spouses is at least equal to the contributed amount.

If the individual (or the individual's spouse) is an active participant in an employer-sponsored retirement plan, the $2,000 deduction limit is phased out over certain adjusted gross income ("AGI") levels. The limit is phased out between $40,000 and $50,000 of AGI for married taxpayers, and between $25,000 and $35,000 of AGI for single taxpayers. An individual may make nondeductible IRA contributions to the extent the individual is not permitted to make deductible IRA contributions. Contributions cannot be made to an IRA after age 70½.

Amounts held in an IRA are includible in income when withdrawn (except to the extent the withdrawal is a return of nondeductible contributions). Amounts withdrawn prior to attainment of age 59½ are subject to an additional 10-percent early withdrawal tax, unless the withdrawal is due to death or disability, is made in the form of certain periodic payments, is used to pay medical expenses in excess of 7.5 percent of AGI, or is used to purchase health insurance of an unemployed individual.

Reasons for Change

The Committee believes that it is appropriate and important to allow individuals to withdraw amounts from their IRAs for purposes of paying higher education expenses without incurring an additional 10-percent early withdrawal tax.

Explanation of Provision

The bill provides that the 10-percent early withdrawal tax does not apply to distributions from IRAs (including American Dream IRAs added by the bill) if the taxpayer uses the amounts to pay qualified higher education expenses (including those related to graduate level courses) of the taxpayer, the taxpayer's spouse, or any child, or grandchild of the individual or the individual's spouse.

The penalty-free withdrawal is available for "qualified higher education expenses," meaning tuition, fees, books, supplies, equipment required for enrollment or attendance, and room and board at a post-secondary educational institution (defined by reference to sec 481 of the Higher Education Act of 1965). Qualified higher education expenses are reduced by any amount excludable from gross income under section 135 relating to the redemption of a qualified U.S. savings bond and certain scholarships and veterans benefits.

Effective Date

The provision is effective for distributions after December 31, 1997, with respect to expenses paid after such date for education furnished in academic periods beginning after such date.

[Conference Report]

Senate Amendment

The Senate amendment is the same as the House bill.

Conference Agreement

The conference agreement follows the House bill and the Senate amendment.

[¶ 5005]   Section 211, 213.   Modification of qualified state tuition programs and education on IRAs.

(Code Sec. 529, 530, 25A, 72, 135, 408, 2503, 6693, 4973)

[House Report]

Present Law

Deductibility of education expenses

Taxpayers generally may not deduct education and training expenses. However, a

deduction for education expenses generally is allowed under section 162 if the education or training (1) maintains or improves a skill required in a trade or business currently engaged in by the taxpayer, or (2) meets the express requirements of the taxpayer's employer, or requirements of applicable law or regulations, imposed as a condition of continued employment (Treas.

Reg. sec. 1.162-5). However, education expenses are not deductible if they relate to certain minimum educational requirements or to education or training that enables a taxpayer to begin working in a new trade or business. In the case of an employee, education expenses (if not reimbursed by the employer) may be claimed as an itemized deduction only if such expenses meet the above-described criteria for deductibility under section 162 and only to the extent that the expenses, along with other miscellaneous deductions, exceed 2 percent of the taxpayer's adjusted gross income (AGI).

Exclusion for employer-provided educational assistance

A special rule allows an employee to exclude from gross income for income tax purposes and from wages for employment tax purposes up to $5,250 annually paid by his or her employer for educational assistance (sec. 127). In order for the exclusion to apply certain requirements must be satisfied, including a requirement that not more than 5 percent of the amounts paid or incurred by the employer during the year for educational assistance under a qualified educational assistance program can be provided for the class of individuals consisting of more than 5-percent owners of the employer and the spouses or dependents of such more than 5-percent owners. This special rule for employer-provided educational assistance expires with respect to courses beginning after June 30, 1997 (and does not apply to graduate level courses beginning after June 30, 1996).

For purposes of the special exclusion, educational assistance means the payment by an employer of expenses incurred by or on behalf of the employee for education of the employee including, but not limited to, tuition, fees, and similar payments, books, supplies, and equipment. Educational assistance also includes the provision by the employer of courses of instruction for the employee (including books, supplies, and equipment). Educational assistance does not include tools or supplies which may be retained by the employee after completion of a course

or meals, lodging, or transportation. The exclusion does not apply to any education involving sports, games, or hobbies.

In the absence of the special exclusion, employer-provided educational assistance is excludable from gross income and wages as a working condition fringe benefit (sec. 132(d)) only to the extent the education expenses would be deductible under section 162.

Exclusion for interest earned on savings bonds

Another special rule (sec. 135) provides that interest earned on a qualified U.S. Series EE savings bond issued after 1989 is excludable from gross income if the proceeds of the bond upon redemption do not exceed qualified higher education expenses paid by the taxpayer during the taxable year.[9] "Qualified higher education expenses" include tuition and fees (but not room and board expenses) required for the enrollment or attendance of the taxpayer, the taxpayer's spouse, or a dependent of the taxpayer at certain colleges, universities, or vocational schools. The exclusion provided by section 135 is phased out for certain higher-income taxpayers, determined by the taxpayer's modified AGI during the year the bond is redeemed. For 1996, the exclusion was phased out for taxpayers with modified AGI between $49,450 and $64,450 ($74,200 and $104,200 for joint returns). To prevent taxpayers from effectively avoiding the income phaseout limitation through issuance of bonds directly in the child's name, section 135(c)(1)(B) provides that the interest exclusion is available only with respect to U.S. Series EE savings bonds issued to taxpayers who are at least 24 years old.

Qualified scholarships

Section 117 excludes from gross income amounts received as a qualified scholarship by an individual who is a candidate for a degree and used for tuition and fees required for the enrollment or attendance (or for fees, books, supplies, and equipment required for courses of instruction) at a primary, secondary, or post-secondary educa-

---

9. If the aggregate redemption amount (i.e., principal plus interest) of all Series EE bonds redeemed by the taxpayer during the taxable year exceeds the qualified education expenses incurred, then the excludable portion of interest income is based on the ratio that the education expenses bears to the aggregate redemption amount (sec. 135(b)).

tional institution. The tax-free treatment provided by section 117 does not extend to scholarship amounts covering regular living expenses, such as room and board. There is, however, no dollar limitation for the section 117 exclusion, provided that the scholarship funds are used to pay for tuition and required fees. In addition to the exclusion for qualified scholarships, section 117 provides an exclusion from gross income for qualified tuition reductions for education below the graduate level provided to employees of certain educational organizations.

Section 117(c) specifically provides that the exclusion for qualified scholarships does not apply to any amount received by a student that represents payment for teaching, research, or other services by the student required as a condition for receiving the scholarship.

Student loan forgiveness

In the case of an individual, section 108(f) provides that gross income subject to Federal income tax does not include any amount from the forgiveness (in whole or in part) of certain student loans, provided that the forgiveness is contingent on the student's working for a certain period of time in certain professions for any of a broad class of employers (e.g., providing health care services to a nonprofit organization). Student loans eligible for this special rule must be made to an individual to assist the individual in attending an education institution that normally maintains a regular faculty and curriculum and normally has a regularly enrolled body of students in attendance at the place where its education activities are regularly carried on. Loan proceeds may be used not only for tuition and required fees, but also to cover room and board expenses (in contrast to tax-free scholarships under section 117, which are limited to tuition and required fees). In addition, the loan must be made by (1) the United States (or an instrumentality or agency thereof), (2) a State (or any political subdivision thereof), (3) certain tax-exempt public benefit corporations that control a State, county, or municipal hospital and whose employees have been deemed to be

public employees under State law, or (4) an educational organization that originally received the funds from which the loan was made from the United States, a State, or a tax-exempt public benefit corporation. Thus, loans made with private, nongovernmental funds are not qualifying student loans for purposes of the section 108(f) exclusion. As with section 117, there is no dollar limitation for the section 108(f) exclusion.

Qualified State prepaid tuition programs

Section 529 (enacted as part of the Small Business Job Protection Act of 1996) provides tax-exempt status to "qualified State tuition programs," meaning certain programs established and maintained by a State (or agency or instrumentality thereof) under which persons may (1) purchase tuition credits or certificates on behalf of a designated beneficiary that entitle the beneficiary to a waiver or payment of qualified higher education expenses of the beneficiary, or (2) make contributions to an account that is established for the purpose of meeting qualified higher education expenses of the designated beneficiary of the account. "Qualified higher education expenses" are defined as tuition, fees, books, supplies, and equipment required for the enrollment or attendance at a college or university (or certain vocational schools). Qualified higher education expenses do not include room and board expenses. Section 529 also provides that no amount shall be included in the gross income of a contributor to, or beneficiary of, a qualified State tuition program with respect to any distribution from, or earnings under, such program, except that (1) amounts distributed or educational benefits provided to a beneficiary (e.g., when the beneficiary attends college) will be included in the beneficiary's gross income (unless excludable under another Code section) to the extent such amounts or the value of the educational benefits exceed contributions made on behalf of the beneficiary, and (2) amounts distributed to a contributor (e.g., when a parent receives a refund) will be included in the contributor's gross income to the extent such amounts exceed contributions made by that person.[10]

---

10. Specifically, section 529(c)(3)(A) provides that any distribution under a qualified State tuition program shall be includible in the gross income of the distributee in the same manner as provided under present-law section 72 to the extent not excluded from gross income under any other provision of the Code.

Contributions made to a qualified State tuition program are treated as incomplete gifts for Federal gift tax purposes (sec. 529(c)(2)). Thus, any Federal gift tax consequences are determined at the time that a distribution is made from an account under the program. The waiver (or payment) of qualified higher education expenses of a designated beneficiary by (or to) an educational institution under a qualified State tuition program is treated as a qualified transfer for purposes of present-law section 2503(e). Amounts contributed to a qualified State tuition program (and earnings thereon) are includible in the contributor's estate for Federal estate tax purposes in the event that the contributor dies before such amounts are distributed under the program (sec. 529(c)(4)).

Individual retirement arrangements ("IRAs")

An individual may make deductible contributions to an individual retirement arrangement ("IRA") for each taxable year up to the lesser of $2,000 or the amount of the individual's compensation for the year if the individual is not an active participant in an employer-sponsored qualified retirement plan (and, if married, the individual's spouse also is not an active participant). Contributions may be made to an IRA for a taxable year up to April 15th of the following year. An individual who makes excess contributions to an IRA, i.e., contributions in excess of $2,000, is subject to an excise tax on such excess contributions unless they are distributed from the IRA before the due date for filing the individual's tax return for the year (including extensions). If the individual (or his or her spouse, if married) is an active participant, the $2,000 limit is phased out between $40,000 and $50,000 of adjusted gross income ("AGI") for married couples and between $25,000 and $35,000 of AGI for single individuals.

Present law permits individuals to make nondeductible contributions (up to $2,000 per year) to an IRA to the extent an individual is not permitted to (or does not) make deductible contributions. Earnings on such contributions are includible in gross income when withdrawn.

An individual generally is not subject to income tax on amounts held in an IRA, in-

cluding earnings on contributions, until the amounts are withdrawn from the IRA. Amounts withdrawn from an IRA are includible in gross income (except to the extent of nondeductible contributions). In addition, a 10-percent additional tax generally applies to distributions from IRAs made before age 59 ½, unless the distribution is made (1) on account of death or disability, (2) in the form of annuity payments, (3) for medical expenses of the individual and his or her spouse and dependents that exceed 7.5 percent of AGI, or (4) for medical insurance of the individual and his or her spouse and dependents (without regard to the 7.5 percent of AGI floor) if the individual has received unemployment compensation for at least 12 weeks, and the withdrawal is made in the year such unemployment compensation is received or the following year.

Reasons for Change

To encourage families and students to save for future education expenses, the Committee believes that tax-exempt status should be granted to certain prepaid tuition programs operated by States or private educational institutions and to education investment accounts established by taxpayers on behalf of future students. The Committee further believes that a deduction should be allowed for Federal income tax purposes for earnings withdrawn from such prepaid tuition programs and education investment accounts if the earnings are used pay for qualified higher education expenses of an undergraduate student who is attending a college, university, or certain vocational schools on at least a half-time basis.

Estate and gift tax treatment

For Federal estate and gift tax purposes, any contribution to a qualified tuition program or education investment account will be treated as a completed gift of a present interest from the contributor to the beneficiary at the time of the contribution. Thus, annual contributions—which cannot exceed $5,000 per year in the case of an education investment account or qualified tuition program maintained by one or more private education institutions—will be eligible for the present-law gift tax exclusion provided by Code section 2503(b) and also will be excludable for purposes of the generation-skipping transfer tax (provided that the contribution, when combined with any other contributions made by the donor to that same beneficiary, does not exceed the annual $10,000 gift-tax exclusion limit). Similar gift tax and generation-skipping tax treatment will apply to contributions of up to $10,000 per donor per beneficiary made to a State-sponsored qualified tuition program. Contributions to a qualified tuition program (either a State-sponsored program or one maintained by a private education institution) or to an education investment account will not, however, be eligible for the educational expense exclusion provided by Code section 2503(e). In no event will a distribution from a qualified tuition program or education investment account be treated as a taxable gift.

Transfers or rollovers of credits or account balances from an account benefiting one beneficiary to an account benefiting another beneficiary (or a change in the designated beneficiary) will not be treated as a taxable gift to the extent that the new beneficiary is: (1) a member of the family of the old beneficiary (as defined above), and (2) assigned to the same generation as the old beneficiary (within the meaning of Code section 2651). In all other cases, a transfer from one beneficiary to another beneficiary (or a change in the designated beneficiary) will be treated as a taxable gift from the old beneficiary to the new beneficiary to the extent it exceeds the $10,000 present-law gift tax exclusion. Thus, a transfer of an account from a brother to his sister will not be treated as a taxable gift, whereas a transfer from a father to his son will be treated as a taxable gift (to the extent it exceeds the $10,000 present-law gift tax exclusion).

For estate tax purposes, the value of any interest in a qualified tuition program or education investment account will be includible in the estate of the designated beneficiary. In no event will such interests be includible in the estate of the contributor.

Effective Date

The deduction for qualified higher education expenses, and the expansion of the definition of qualified higher education expenses under sec. 529 to cover room and board expenses, are effective for expenses paid after December 31, 1997, for education furnished in academic periods beginning after such date. The provisions governing the tax-exempt status of qualified tuition plans and education investment accounts generally are effective after December 31, 1997. The gift tax provisions are effective for contributions (or transfers) made after the date of enactment, and the estate tax provisions are effective for decedents dying after June 8, 1997.

[Senate Report]

Explanation of Provision

In general

Under the bill, amounts distributed from qualified tuition programs and certain education investment accounts (referred to as "education IRAs") are excludable from gross income to the extent that the amounts distributed do not exceed qualified higher education expenses of an eligible student incurred during the year the distribution is made.[10] An exclusion is NOT allowed under the bill with respect to an otherwise eligible student if the HOPE credit (as described previously) is claimed with respect to that student for the taxable year the distribution is made.[11]

Under the bill, distributions from a qualified tuition program or education IRA generally will be deemed to consist of distributions of principal (which, under all circumstances, are excludable from gross income) and earnings (which MAY BE excludable from gross income under the bill) by applying the ratio that the aggregate amount of contributions to the program or account for the beneficiary bears to the total balance (or value) of the program or account for the beneficiary at the time the distribution is made.[12] If the qualified higher education expenses of the student for the

---

10. The exclusion will not be a preference item for alternative minimum tax (AMT) purposes.

11. If a HOPE credit was claimed with respect to a student for an earlier taxable year (i.e., the student's first or second year of post-secondary education), the exclu-

sion provided for by the bill may be claimed with respect to that student for a SUBSEQUENT taxable year.

12. Specifically, the bill provides as a general rule that is distributions from a qualified tuition program or educa-

year are at least equal to the total amount of the distribution (i.e., principal and earnings combined) from a qualified tuition program or education IRA, then the earnings in their entirety will be excludable from gross income. If, on the other hand, the qualified higher education expenses of the student for the year are LESS THAN the total amount of the distribution (i.e., principal and earnings combined) from a qualified tuition program or education IRA, then the qualified higher education expenses will be deemed to be paid from a pro-rata share of both the principal and earnings components of the distribution. Thus, in such a case, only a portion of the earnings will be excludable under the bill (i.e., a portion of the earnings based on the ratio that the qualified higher education expenses bear to the total amount of the distribution) and the remaining portion of the earnings will be includible in the gross income of the distributee.[13]

Eligible students

To be an eligible student under the bill, an individual must be at least a half-time student in a degree or certificate undergraduate or graduate program at an eligible educational institution. For this purpose, a student is at least a half-time student if he or she is carrying at least one-half the normal full- time work load for the course of study the student is pursuing. An eligible student may not have been convicted of a Federal or State felony consisting of the possession or distribution of a controlled substance.

Eligible educational institution

Under the bill, eligible educational institutions are defined by reference to section 481 of the Higher Education Act of 1965. Such institutions generally are accredited post-secondary educational institutions of-fering credit toward a bachelor's degree, an associate's degree, a graduate-level or professional degree, or another recognized post-secondary credential. Certain proprietary institutions and post-secondary vocational institutions also are eligible institutions. The institution must be eligible to participate in Department of Education student aid programs.

Qualified higher education expenses

Under the bill, the definition of "qualified higher education expenses" include tuition, fees, books, supplies, and equipment required for the enrollment or attendance of a student at an eligible education institution, as well as room and board expenses (meaning the minimum room and board allowance applicable to the student as determined by the institution in calculating costs of attendance for Federal financial aid programs under sec. 472 of the Higher Education Act of 1965) for any period during which the student is at least a half-time student. Qualified higher education expenses include expenses with respect to undergraduate or graduate-level courses.

Qualified higher education expenses generally include only out-of-pocket expenses. Qualified higher education expenses do not include expenses covered by educational assistance that is not required to be included in the gross income of either the student or the taxpayer claiming the credit. Thus, total qualified higher education expenses are reduced by scholarship or fellowship grants excludable from gross income under present-law section 117, as well as any other tax-free educational benefits, such as employer-provided educational assistance that is excludable from the employee's gross income under section 127. In addition, qualified higher education expenses do not in-

---

tion IRA are includible in gross income to the extent allocable to income on the program or account and are NOT includible in gross income to the extent allocable to the investment (i.e., contributions) in the program or account. However, the bill further provides that, if the HOPE credit is not claimed with respect to the student for the taxable year, then a distribution from a qualified tuition program or education IRA will not be includible in gross income TO THE EXTENT that the distribution does NOT exceed the qualified higher expenses of the student for the year. If a distribution consists of providing in-kind education benefits to the student which, if paid for by the student, would constitute payment of qualified higher education expenses, then no portion of such distribution will be includible in gross income.

]At the time that a final distribution is made for a qualified tuition program or education IRA, the distribution will be deemed to include the full amount of any basis remaining with respect to the program or account.

13. For example, if a $1,000 distribution from a qualified tuition program or education IRA consists of $600 of principal (i.e., contributions) and $400 of earnings, and if the student incurs $750 of qualified higher education expenses during the year, then $300 of the earnings will be excludable from gross income under the bill (i.e., an exclusion will be provided for the pro-rata portion of the earnings, based on the ratio that the $750 of qualified expenses bears to the $1,000 total distribution) and the remaining $100 of earnings will be includible in the distributee's gross income.

clude expenses paid with amounts that are excludible under section 135. No reduction of qualified higher education expenses is required for a gift, bequest, devise, or inheritance within the meaning of section 102(a). If education expenses for a taxable year are deducted under section 162 or any other section of the Code, then such expenses are not qualified higher education expenses under the bill.

Qualified tuition programs and education IRAs

Under the bill, a "qualified tuition program" means any qualified State-sponsored tuition program, defined under section 529 (as modified by the bill), as well as any program established and maintained by one or more eligible educational institutions (which could be private institutions) that satisfy the requirements under section 529 (other than present-law State ownership rule). An "education IRA" means a trust (or custodial account) which is created or organized in the United States exclusively for the purpose of paying the qualified higher education expenses of the account holder and which satisfies certain other requirements.

Contributions to qualified tuition programs or education IRAs may be made only in cash.[14] Such contributions may not be made after the designated beneficiary or account holder reaches age 18. Annual contributions to a qualified tuition program not maintained by a State (i.e., a qualified tuition program operated by one or more private schools) or to an education IRA are limited to $2,000 per beneficiary or account holder, PLUS the amount of any child credit (as provided for by the bill and described above) that is allowed for the taxable year with respect to the beneficiary or account holder.[15] Thus, in the case of any child with respect to whom the maximum $500 child credit is allowed for the taxable year, the contribution limit with respect to such child for the year will be $2,500.[16] Trustees of qualified tuition programs not maintained by a State and trustees of education IRAs are prohibited from accepting contributions to any account on behalf of a beneficiary in excess of $2,500 for any year (except in cases involving certain tax-free rollovers, as described below).[17]

If any balance remaining in an education IRA is not distributed by the time that the account holder becomes 30 years old, then the account will be deemed to be an IRA Plus account (as provided for by the bill and described below) established on behalf of the same account holder.[18] The bill allows (but does not require) tax-free transfers or rollovers of account balances from a qualified tuition program to an IRA Plus account when the beneficiary becomes 30 years old, provided that the funds from the qualified tuition program account are deposited in the IRA Plus account within 60 days after being distributed from the qualified tu-

---

14. The bill allows taxpayers to redeem U.S. Savings Bonds and be eligible for the exclusion under section 135 (as if the proceeds were used to pay qualified higher education expenses) if the proceeds from the redemption are contributed to a qualified tuition program or education IRA on behalf of the taxpayer, the taxpayer's spouse, or a dependent. In such a case, the beneficiary's or account holder's basis in the bond proceeds contributed on his or her behalf to the qualified tuition program or education IRA will be the contributor's basis in the bonds (i.e., the original purchase price paid by the contributor for such bonds). The bill also provides that funds from an education IRA are deemed to be distributed to pay qualified higher education expenses if the funds are used to make contributions to (or purchase tuition credits from) a qualified tuition program for the benefit of the account holder.

15. State-sponsored qualified tuition programs will continue to be governed by the rule contained in present-law section 529(b)(7) that such programs provide adequate safeguards to prevent contributions on behalf of a designated beneficiary in excess of those necessary to provide for the qualified higher education expenses of the beneficiary. State-sponsored qualified tuition programs will NOT be subject to a specific dollar limit on annual contributions that can be made under the program on behalf of a designated beneficiary.

16. The maximum contribution limit for the year is increased even if the child is younger than age 13 — that is, even in cases where the parent is not REQUIRED (under the provision described previously) but may elect to deposit an amount equal to the child credit into a qualified tuition program or education IRA on behalf of the child.

17. The annual $2,000 to $2,500 contribution limit is applied by taking into account all contributions made to any qualified tuition program not maintained by a State AND any education IRA on behalf of a designated individual (but not any contributions made to State-sponsored qualified tuition programs). To the extent contributions exceed the annual contribution limit, an excise tax penalty may be imposed on the contributor under present-law section 4973, unless the excess contributions (and any earnings thereon) are returned to the contributor before the due date for the return for the taxable year during which the excess contribution is made.

18. In such cases, the 5-year holding period applicable to IRA Plus accounts begins with the taxable year in which the education IRA is deemed to be an IRA Plus account.

ition program.[19] In addition, the bill allows tax-free transfers or rollovers of credits or account balances from one qualified tuition program or education IRA account benefiting one beneficiary to another program or account benefiting another beneficiary (as well as redesignations of the named beneficiary), provided that the new beneficiary is a member of the family of the old beneficiary.[20]

Qualified tuition programs and education IRAs (as separate legal entities) will be exempt from Federal income tax, other than taxes imposed under the present-law unrelated business income tax (UBIT) rules.[21]

Under the bill, an additional 10-percent penalty tax will be imposed on any distribution from a qualified tuition program not maintained by a State or from an education IRA to the extent that the distribution exceeds qualified higher education expenses incurred by the taxpayer (and is not made on account of the death, disability, or scholarship received by the designated beneficiary or account holder).[22]

Effective Date

The provision applies to distributions made, and qualified higher education expenses paid, after December 31, 1997, for education furnished in academic periods beginning after such date. The provisions governing contributions to, and the tax-exempt status of, qualified tuition plans and education IRAs generally apply after December 31, 1997.

[Conference Report]

Conference Agreement

Qualified State tuition programs

The conference agreement makes the following modifications to present-law section 529, which governs the tax treatment of qualified

State tuition programs.

Room and board expenses.—The conference agreement expands the definition of "qualified higher education expenses" under section 529(e)(3) to include room and board expenses (meaning the minimum room and board allowance applicable to the student as determined by the institution in calculating costs of attendance for Federal financial aid programs under sec. 472 of the Higher Education Act of 1965) for any period during which the student is at least a half-time student.

Eligible educational institution.—The conference agreement expands the definition of "eligible educational institution" for purposes of section 529 by defining such term by reference to section 481 of the Higher Education Act of 1965. Such institutions generally are accredited post-secondary educational institutions offering credit toward a bachelor's degree, an associate's degree, a graduate-level or professional degree, or another recognized post-secondary credential. Certain proprietary institutions and post-secondary vocational institutions also are eligible institutions. The institution must be eligible to participate in Department of Education student aid programs.

Definition of "member of family".—The conference agreement expands the definition of the term "member of the family" for purposes of allowing tax-free transfers or rollovers of credits or account balances in qualified State tuition programs (and redesignations of named beneficiaries), so that the term means persons described in paragraphs (1) through (8) of section 152(a)— e.g., sons, daughters, brothers, sisters, nephews and nieces, certain in-laws, etc.—and any spouse of such persons.[38]

---

19. In the event of such a rollover, the 5-year holding period applicable to IPA Plus accounts begins with the taxable year in which the rollover occurs.
20. For this purpose, a "member of the family" means persons described in paragraphs (1) through (8) of section 152(a), and any spouse of such persons.
21. An interest in a qualified tuition program is not treated as debt for purposes of the debt-financed property UBIT rules of section 514.
22. Distributions from State-sponsored qualified tuition programs will NOT be subject to this 10-percent additional penalty tax, but will continue to be governed by the present-law section 529(b)(3) role that the State-sponsored programs themselves are required to impose

a "more than de minimis penalty" on any refund of earnings not used for qualified higher education expenses (other than in cases where the refund is made on account of death or disability of, or receipt of a scholarship by, the beneficiary).

38. The conference agreement also provides a special rule that, in the case of any contract issued prior to August 20, 1996 (i.e., the date of enactment of section 529), section 529(c)(3)(C) will be applied without regard to the requirement that a distribution be transferred to a member of the family or the requirement that a change in beneficiaries may be made only to a member of the family.

Prohibition against investment direction.—The conference clarifies the present-law rule contained in section 529(b)(5) that qualified State tuition programs may not allow contributors or designated beneficiaries to direct the investment of contributions to the program (or earnings thereon) by specifically providing that contributors and beneficiaries may not "directly or indirectly" direct the investment of contributions to the program (or earnings thereon).

Interaction with HOPE credit and Lifetime Learning credit.— Under the conference agreement (as under present law), no amount will be includible in the gross income of a contributor to, or beneficiary of, a qualified State tuition program with respect to any contribution to or earnings on such a program until a distribution is made from the program, at which time the earnings portion of the distribution (whether made in cash or in-kind) will be includible in the gross income of the distributee. However, to the extent that a distribution from a qualified State tuition program is used to pay for qualified tuition and fees, the distributee (or another taxpayer claiming the distributee as a dependent) will be able to claim the HOPE credit or Lifetime Learning credit provided for by the conference agreement with respect to such tuition and fees (assuming that the other requirements for claiming the HOPE credit or Lifetime Learning credit are satisfied and the modified AGI phaseout for those credits does not apply).[39]

Effective Date

The modifications to section 529 generally are effective after December 31, 1997. The expansion of the term "qualified higher education expenses" to cover certain room and board expenses is effective as if included in the Small Business Job Protection Act of 1996 (enacted on August 20, 1996).

Education IRAs

The conference agreement generally follows the Senate amendment with respect to the treatment of education IRAs, with the following modifications.

Contribution limit.—Under the conference agreement, annual contributions to education IRAs are limited to $500 per beneficiary. This $500 annual contribution limit for education IRAs is phased out ratably for contributors with modified AGI between $95,000 and $110,000 ($150,000 and $160,000 for joint returns). Individuals with modified AGI above the phase-out range are not allowed to make contributions to an education IRA established on behalf of any other individual.[40]

Qualified expenses.—Education IRAs must be created exclusively for the purpose of paying qualified higher education expenses, meaning post-secondary tuition, fees, books, supplies, equipment, and certain room and board expenses, and not including elementary or secondary school expenses.

Expansion of exclusion for part-time students.—The conference agreement provides that distributions from an education IRA are excludable from gross income to the extent that the distribution does not exceed qualified higher education expenses incurred by the beneficiary during the year the distribution is made, regardless of whether the beneficiary is enrolled at an eligible educational institution on a full-time, half-time, or less than half- time basis. However, room and board expenses (meaning the minimum room and board allowance applicable to the student as determined by the institution in calculating costs of attendance for Federal financial aid programs under sec. 472 of the Higher Education Act of 1965) are qualified higher education expenses only if the student incurring such expenses is enrolled at an eligible educational institution on at least a half-time basis.

---

39. In cases where in-kind benefits are provided to a beneficiary under a qualified State prepaid tuition program, present-law section 529(c)(3)(B) provides that the provision of such benefits is treated as a distribution to the beneficiary. Thus, to the extent such in-kind benefits, if paid for by the beneficiary, would constitute payment of qualified tuition and fees for purposes of the HOPE credit or Lifetime Learning credit, the beneficiary (or another taxpayer claiming the beneficiary as

a dependent) may be able to claim the HOPE credit or Lifetime Learning credit with respect to payments that are deemed to be made by the beneficiary with respect to the in-kind benefit.

40. The conference agreement clarifies that no amount is includible in the gross income of a beneficiary of an education IRA with respect to any contribution to or earnings on such account.

Termination of education IRAs.—Under the conference agreement, any balance remaining in an education IRA at the time a beneficiary becomes 30 years old must be distributed, and the earnings portion of such a distribution will be includible in gross income of the beneficiary and subject to an additional 10-percent penalty tax because the distribution was not for educational purposes. However, as under the Senate amendment, prior to the beneficiary reaching age 30, the conference agreement allows tax-free (and penalty-free) transfers and rollovers of account balances from one education IRA benefiting one beneficiary to another education IRA benefiting a different beneficiary (as well as redesignations of the named beneficiary), provided that the new beneficiary is a member of the family of the old beneficiary.[41]

Interaction with qualified State tuition programs.—The conference agreement provides that no contribution may be made by any person to an education IRA established on behalf of a beneficiary during any taxable year in which any contributions are made by anyone to a qualified State tuition program (defined under sec. 529) on behalf of the same beneficiary.

Interaction with HOPE credit and Lifetime Learning credit.—The conference agreement provides that, in any taxable year in which an exclusion from gross income is claimed with respect to a distribution from an education IRA on behalf of a beneficiary, neither a HOPE credit nor a Lifetime Learning credit may be claimed with respect to educational expenses incurred during that year on behalf of the same beneficiary. The HOPE credit or Lifetime Learning credit will be available in other taxable years with respect to that beneficiary (provided that no exclusion is claimed in such other taxable years for distributions from an education IRA on behalf of the beneficiary and provided that the requirements of the HOPE credit or Lifetime Learning credit are satisfied in such other taxable years).

Effective Date

The provisions governing education IRAs apply to taxable years beginning after December 31, 1997.

Estate and gift tax treatment

The conference agreement follows the House bill with respect to the estate and gift tax treatment of contributions to qualified State tuition programs and education IRAs, except that a special rule is provided in the case of contributions that exceed the annual gift tax exclusion limit (presently $10,000 in the case of an individual or $20,000 in the case of a married couple that splits their gifts, but this amount is scheduled to increase under other provisions of the conference agreement). For such contributions, the contributor may elect to have the contribution treated as if made ratably over a five-year period.

Thus, for Federal estate and gift tax purposes, any contribution to a qualified tuition program or education IRA will be treated as a completed gift of a present interest from the contributor to the beneficiary at the time of the contribution. Annual contributions are eligible for the present-law gift tax exclusion provided by Code section 2503(b) and also are excludable for purposes of the generation-skipping transfer tax (provided that the contribution, when combined with any other contributions made by the donor to that same beneficiary, does not exceed the annual gift- tax exclusion limit of $10,000, or $20,000 in the case of a married couple).

If a contribution in excess of $10,000 ($20,000 in the case of a married couple) is made in one year—which, under the conference agreement, can occur only in the case of a qualified State tuition program and not an education IRA (which cannot receive contributions in excess of $500 per year)—the contributor may elect to have the contribution treated as if made ratably over five years beginning in the year the contribution is made. For example, a $30,000 contribution to a qualified State tuition program would be treated as five annual contributions of $6,000, and the donor could therefore make up to $4,000 in other transfers to the beneficiary each year without payment

---

41. For this purpose, a "member of the family" means—as under the conference agreement modifications to sec-   tion 529—persons described in paragraphs (1) through (8) of section 152(a), and any spouse of such persons.

of gift tax. Under this rule, a donor may contribute up to $50,000 every five years ($100,000 in the case of a married couple) with no gift tax consequences, assuming no other gifts are made from the donor to the beneficiary in the five-year period. A gift tax return must be filed with respect to any contribution in excess of the annual gift-tax exclusion limit, and the election for five-year averaging must be made on the contributor's gift tax return.

If a donor making an over-$10,000 contribution dies during the five-year averaging period, the portion of the contribution that has not been allocated to the years prior to death is includible in the donor's estate. For example, if a donor makes a $40,000 contribution, elects to treat the transfer as being made over a five- year period, and dies the following year, $8,000 would be allocated to the year of contribution, another $8,000 would be allocated to the year of death, and the remaining $24,000 would be includible in the estate.

If a beneficiary's interest is rolled over to another beneficiary, there are no transfer tax consequences if the two beneficiaries are in the same generation. If a beneficiary's interest is rolled over to a beneficiary in a lower generation (e.g., parent to child or uncle to niece), the five-year averaging rule described above may be applied to exempt up to $50,000 of the transfer from gift tax.

The Federal estate and gift tax treatment of educational accounts has no effect on the actual rights and obligations of the parties pursuant to the terms of the contracts under State law.

Effective Date

The gift tax provisions are effective for contributions (or transfers) made after the date of enactment, and the estate tax provisions are effective for decedents dying after June 8, 1997.

[¶ 5007]   Section 221.   Extension of exclusion for employer-provided educational assistance.

(Code Sec. 127)

[(SEC. 221 OF THE BILL AND SEC. 127 OF THE CODE) House Report]

Present Law

Under present law, an employee's gross income and wages do not include amounts paid or incurred by the employer for educational assistance provided to the employee if such amounts are paid or incurred pursuant to an educational assistance program that meets certain requirements. This exclusion is limited to $5,250 of educational assistance with respect to an individual during a calendar year. The exclusion does not apply to graduate level courses beginning after June 30, 1996. The exclusion expires with respect to courses beginning after June 30, 1997. In the absence of the exclusion, educational assistance is excludable from income only if it is related to the employee's current job.

Description of Proposal

The proposal would extend the exclusion for employer-provided educational assis-

tance to courses of instruction beginning before December 31, 1997. As under present law, the exclusion will not apply to graduate-level courses.

Effective Date

The provision would be effective with respect to taxable years beginning after December 31, 1996.

[Conference Report]

Conference Agreement

The conference agreement follows the House bill, with modifications. Under the conference agreement, the exclusion for undergraduate education is extended with respect to courses beginning before June 1, 2000. As under the House bill, the exclusion does not apply with respect to graduate-level courses.

[¶ 5008]   Section 222.   Repeal of limit on qualified 501(c)(3) bonds other than hospital bonds.

(Code Sec. 145)

[House Report]

Present Law

Interest on State and local government bonds generally is excluded from income if the bonds are issued to finance activities carried out and paid for with revenues of these governments. Interest on bonds issued by these governments to finance activities of other persons, e.g., private activity bonds, is taxable unless a specific exception is included in the Code. One such exception is for private activity bonds issued to finance activities of private, charitable organizations described in Code section 501(c)(3) ("section 501(c)(3) organizations") when the activities do not constitute an unrelated trade or business.

Present law treats section 501(c)(3) organizations as private persons; thus, bonds for their use may only be issued as private activity "qualified 501(1)(3) bonds," subject to the restrictions of Code section 145. The most significant of these restrictions limits the amount of outstanding bonds from which a section 501(c)(3) organization may benefit to $150 million. In applying this "$150 million limit," all section 501(c)(3) organizations under common management or control are treated as a single organization. The limit does not apply to bonds for hospital facilities, defined to include only acute care, primarily inpatient, organizations.

[Senate Report]

Reasons for Change

The Committee believes a distinguishing feature of American society is the singular degree to which the United States maintains a private, non-profit sector of private higher education and other charitable institutions in the public service. The Committee believes it is important to assist these private institutions in their advancement of the public good. The Committee finds particularly inappropriate the restrictions of present law which place these section 501(c)(3) organizations at a financial disadvantage relative to substantially identical governmental institutions. For example, a public university generally has unlimited access to tax-exempt bond financing, while a private, non-profit university is subject to a $150 million limitation on outstanding bonds from which it may benefit. The Committee is concerned that this and other restrictions inhibit the ability of America's private, non-profit institutions to modernize their educational facilities. The Committee believes the tax-exempt bond rules should treat more equally State and local governments and those private organizations which are engaged in similar actions advancing the public good.

Explanation of Provision

The $150 million limit is repealed for bonds issued after the date of enactment to finance capital expenditures incurred after date of the enactment.

Effective Date

The provision is effective for bonds issued after the date of enactment to finance capital expenditures incurred after the date of enactment.

[Conference Report]

Conference Agreement

The conference agreement follows the Senate amendment.

Effective Date

The provision is effective for bonds issued after the date of enactment. Because this provision of the conference agreement applies only to bonds issued with respect to capital expenditures incurred after the date of enactment, the $150 million limit will continue to govern issuance of other non-hospital qualified 501(c)(3) bonds (e.g., refunding bonds or new-money bonds for capital expenditures incurred before the date of enactment). Thus, the conferees understand that bond issuers will continue to need Treasury Department guidance on the application of this limit in the future and expect that the Treasury will continue to provide interpretative rules on this limit.

[¶ 5009]   Section 223.   Increase in arbitrage rebate exception for certain bonds.

(Code Sec. 148)

[Senate Report]

Present Law

Generally, all arbitrage profits earned on investments unrelated to the purpose of the borrowing ("nonpurpose investments") when such earnings are permitted must be rebated to the Federal Government.

An exception is provided for bonds issued by governmental units having general taxing powers if the governmental unit (and all subordinate units) issues $5 million or less of governmental bonds during the calendar year ("the small-issuer exception"). This exception does not apply to private activity bonds.

Reasons for Change

The Committee recognizes the need for additional monies to address the needs of our crumbling public school infrastructure. It believes that this provision will reduce the compliance costs of issuers of tax-exempt debt issued for public school construction.

Explanation of Provision

The bill provides that up to $5 million dollars of bonds used to finance public school capital expenditures incurred after December 31, 1997, are excluded from application of the present-law $5 million limit. Thus, small issuers will continue to benefit from the small issue exception from arbitrage rebate if they issue no more than $10 million in governmental bonds per calendar year and no more than $5 million of the bonds is used to finance expenditures other than for public school capital expenditures.

Effective Date

The provision is effective for bonds issued after December 31, 1997.

[Conference Report]

House Bill

No provision.

Conference Agreement

The conference agreement follows the Senate amendment.

[¶ 5010]   Section 224.   Contributions of computer technology and equipment for primary and secondary school purposes.

(Code Sec. 170)

[House Report]

Present Law

In computing taxable income, a taxpayer who itemizes deductions generally is allowed to deduct the fair market value of property contributed to a charitable organization.[20] However, in the case of a charitable contribution of inventory or other ordinary-income property, short-term capital gain property, or certain gifts to private foundations, the amount of the deduction is limited to the taxpayer's basis in the property. In the case of a charitable contribution of tangible personal property, a taxpayer's

deduction is limited to the adjusted basis in such property if the use by the recipient charitable organization is unrelated to the organization's tax-exempt purpose (sec. 170(e)(1)(B)(i)).

Special rules in the Code provide augmented deductions for certain corporate[21] contributions of inventory property for the care of the ill, the needy, or infants (sec. 170(e)(3)) and certain corporate contributions of scientific equipment constructed by the taxpayer, provided the original use of such donated equipment is by the donee for research or research training in the United States in physical or biological sciences

---

20. The amount of the deduction allowable for a taxable year with respect to a charitable contribution may be reduced depending on the type of property contributed, the type of charitable organization to which the property is contributed, and the income of the taxpayer (secs. 170(b) and 170(e)). Corporations are entitled to

claim a deduction for charitable contributions, generally limited to 10 percent of their taxable income (computed without regard to the contributions) for the taxable year.

21. S corporations are not eligible donors for purposes of section 170(e)(3) or section 170(e)(4).

(sec. 170(e)(4)).[22] Under these special rules, the amount of the augmented deduction available to a corporation making a qualified contribution is equal to its basis in the donated property plus one-half of the amount of ordinary income that would have been realized if the property had been sold. However, the augmented deduction cannot exceed twice the basis of the donated property.

Reasons for Change

The Committee believes that providing an incentive for businesses to invest their computer equipment and software for the benefit of primary and secondary school students will help to provide America's schools with the technological resources necessary to prepare both teachers and students for a technologically advanced present and future.

Explanation of Provision

The bill expands the list of qualified contributions that would qualify for the augmented deduction currently available under Code section 170(e)(3) and 170(e)(4). Under the bill, qualified contributions mean gifts of computer technology and equipment (i.e., computer software, computer or peripheral equipment, and fiber optic cable related to computer use) to be used within the United States for educational purposes in any of grades K-12.

Eligible donees are (1) any educational organization that normally maintains a regular faculty and curriculum and has a regularly enrolled body of pupils in attendance at the place where its educational activities are regularly carried on; and (2) Code section 501(c)(3) entities that are organized primarily for purposes of supporting elementary and secondary education. A private foundation also is an eligible donee, pro-

vided that, within 30 days after receipt of the contribution, the private foundation contributes the property to an eligible donee described above.

Qualified contributions are limited to gifts made no later than two years after the date the taxpayer acquired or substantially completed the construction of the donated property. Such donated property could be computer technology or equipment that is inventory or depreciable trade or business property in the hands of the donor. The bill permits payment by the donee organization of shipping, transfer, and installation costs.[23] The special treatment applies only to donations made by C corporations;as under present law section 170(e)(4), S corporations, personal holding companies, and service organizations are not eligible donors.

Effective Date

The provision is effective for contributions made in taxable years beginning after 1997.

[Conference Report]

Senate Amendment

No provision.

Conference Agreement

The conference agreement follows the House bill, except that the provision is sunset after three years. Thus, the provision is effective for contributions made in taxable years beginning after 1997 and before January 1, 2001. In addition, the conference agreement clarifies that the original use of the donated property must commence with the donor or the donee. Accordingly, qualified contributions generally are limited to property that is no more than two years old.

---

22. Eligible donees under section 170(e)(4) are limited to post-secondary educational institutions, scientific research organizations, and certain other organizations that support scientific research.

23. In the case of contributions made through private foundations, the bill permits the payment by the private foundation of shipping, transfer, and installation costs.

[¶ 5011]   Section 225.   Treatment of cancellation of certain student loans.

(Code Sec. 108)

[House Report]

Present Law

In the case of an individual, gross income subject to Federal income tax does not include any amount from the forgiveness (in whole or in part) of certain student loans, provided that the forgiveness is contingent on the student's working for a certain period of time in certain professions for any of a broad class of employers (sec. 108(f)).

Student loans eligible for this special rule must be made to an individual to assist the individual in attending an educational institution that normally maintains a regular faculty and curriculum and normally has a regularly enrolled body of students in attendance at the place where its education activities are regularly carried on. Loan proceeds may be used not only for tuition and required fees, but also to cover room and board expenses (in contrast to tax free scholarships under section 117, which are limited to tuition and required fees). In addition, the loan must be made by (1) the United States (or an instrumentality or agency thereof), (2) a State (or any political subdivision thereof), (3) certain tax-exempt public benefit corporations that control a State, county, or municipal hospital and whose employees have been deemed to be public employees under State law, or (4) an educational organization that originally received the funds from which the loan was made from the United States, a State, or a tax-exempt public benefit corporation. Thus, loans made with private, nongovernmental funds are not qualifying student loans for purposes of the section 108(f) exclusion.

Reasons for Change

The Committee believes that it is appropriate to expand present-law section 108(f), so that certain loan cancellation programs of tax-exempt charitable organizations (e.g., private educational institutions) receive Federal income tax treatment comparable to that provided for similar government-sponsored programs. This provision will promote the establishment of programs that encourage students to use their education and training in valuable community service. In addition, the Committee believes it is appropriate to expand section 108(f) to cover forgiveness of certain Federal direct student loans.

Explanation of Provision

The bill expands section 108(f) so that an individual's gross income does not include forgiveness of loans made by tax-exempt charitable organizations (e.g., educational organizations or private foundations) if the proceeds of such loans are used to pay costs of attendance at an educational institution or to refinance outstanding student loans and the student is not employed by the lender organization. As under present law, the section 108(f) exclusion applies only if the forgiveness is contingent on the student's working for a certain period of time in certain professions for any of a broad class of employers. In addition, in the case of loans made by tax-exempt charitable organizations, the student's work must fulfill a public service requirement. The student must work in an occupation or area with unmet needs and such work must be performed for or under the direction of a tax-exempt charitable organization or a governmental entity.

The exclusion also is expanded to cover forgiveness of direct student loans made through the William D. Ford Federal Direct Loan Program where loan repayment and forgiveness are contingent on the borrower's income level and any unpaid amounts are forgiven in full by the Secretary of Education at the end of a 25-year period. Thus, Federal Direct Loan borrowers who have elected the income-contingent repayment option and who have not repaid their loans in full at the end of a 25-year period would not be required to include the outstanding loan balance in income as a result of the forgiveness of the loan.

Effective Date

The provision applies to discharges of indebtedness after the date of enactment.

[Conference Report]

Senate Amendment

The Senate amendment is the same as the House bill.

Conference Agreement

The conference agreement follows the House bill and the Senate amendment, except that the conference agreement does not include the provision expanding the exclusion to cover forgiveness of direct student loans made through the William D. Ford Federal Direct Loan Program where loan repayment and forgiveness are contingent on the borrower's income level and any unpaid amounts are forgiven in full by the Secretary of Education at the end of a 25-year period.

[¶ 5012]   Section 226.   Incentives for education zones.

(Code Sec. 1397E, 1397F)

[Conference Report]

Present Law

Under present law, interest on bonds issued for general governmental purposes, including public schools, is exempt from Federal income tax.

House Bill

No provision.

Senate Amendment

No provision.

Conference Agreement

Under the conference agreement, certain financial institutions (i.e., banks, insurance companies, and corporations actively engaged in the business of lending money) that hold "qualified zone academy bonds" are entitled to a nonrefundable tax credit in an amount equal to a credit rate (set by the Treasury Department) multiplied by the face amount of the bond. The credit rate applies to all such bonds purchased in each month. A taxpayer holding a qualified zone academy bond is entitled to a credit for each year the taxpayer holds the bond. The credit is includible in gross income, but may be claimed against regular income tax and AMT liability.

The Treasury Department will set the credit rate each month so that such bonds can be issued without discount and without any interest cost to the issuer. The maximum term of the bond issued in a given month also is determined by the Treasury Department so that the present value of the obligation to repay the bond is 50 percent of the face value of the bond. Such present value will be determined using as a discount rate the average annual interest rate of tax-exempt obligations with a term of 10 years or more issued during the month.

"Qualified zone academy bonds" are defined as any bond issued by a State or local government, provided that (1) 95 percent of the proceeds are used for the purpose of renovating, providing equipment to, developing course materials for use at, or training teachers and other school personnel in a "qualified zone academy" and (2) private entities have promised to contribute to the qualified zone academy certain equipment, technical assistance or training, employee services, or other property or services with a value equal to at least 10 percent of the bond proceeds.

A school is a "qualified zone academy" if (1) the school is a public school that provides education and training below the college level, (2) the school operates a special academic program in cooperation with businesses to enhance the academic curriculum and increase graduation and employment rates, and (3) either (a) the school is located in an empowerment zone or enterprise community (including empowerment zones designated or authorized to be designated under the conference agreement), or (b) it is reasonably expected that at least 35 percent of the students at the school will be eligible for free or reduced-cost lunches under the school lunch program established under the National School Lunch Act.

A total of $400 million of "qualified zone academy bonds" may be issued in each of 1998 and 1999. The $800 million aggregate bond cap will be allocated to the

States according to their respective populations of individuals below the poverty line. A State may carry over any unused allocation into subsequent years. Each State, in turn, will allocate the credit to qualified zone academies within such State.

[¶ 5015]   Section 301.   Increase deductible IRA phase-out range and modify active participant rule.

(Code Sec. 219)

[Senate Report]

Present Law

Under present law, an individual may make deductible contributions to an individual retirement arrangement ("IRA") up to the lesser of $2,000 or the individual's compensation if the individual is not an active participant in an employer-sponsored retirement plan (and, if married, the individual's spouse also is not an active participant in such a plan). If the case of a married couple, deductible IRA contributions of up to $2,000 can be made for each spouse (including, for example, a home maker who does not work outside the home) if the combined compensation of both spouses is at least equal to the contributed amount.

If the individual (or the individual's spouse) is an active participant in an employer-sponsored retirement plan, the $2,000 deduction limit is phased out over certain adjusted gross income ("AGI") levels. The limit is phased out between $40,000 and $50,000 of AGI for married taxpayers, and between $25,000 and $35,000 of AGI for single taxpayers. An individual may make nondeductible IRA contributions to the extent the individual is not permitted to make deductible IRA contributions. Contributions cannot be made to an IRA after age 70½.

Amounts held in an IRA are includible in income when withdrawn (except to the extent the withdrawal is a return of non-deductible contributions). Amounts withdrawn prior to attainment of age 59½ are subject to an additional 10-percent early withdrawal tax, unless the withdrawal is due to death or disability, is made in the form of certain periodic payments, is used to pay medical expenses in excess of 7.5 percent of AGI, or is used to purchase health insurance of an unemployed individual.

Effective Date

The provision is effective for bonds issued after 1997.

In general, distributions from an IRA are required to begin at age 70 ½. An excise tax is imposed if the minimum required distributions are not made. Distributions to the beneficiary of an IRA are generally required to begin within 5 years of the death of the IRA owner, unless the beneficiary is the surviving spouse.

A 15-percent excise tax is imposed on excess distributions with respect to an individual during any calendar year from qualified retirement plans, tax-sheltered annuities, and IRAs. In general, excess distributions are defined as the aggregate amount of retirement distributions (i.e., payments from applicable retirement plans) made with respect to an individual during any calendar year to the extent such amounts exceed $160,000 (for 1997) or 5 times that amount in the case of a lump-sum distribution. The dollar limit is indexed for inflation. A similar 15-percent additional estate tax applies to excess retirement accumulations upon the death of the individual. The 15-percent tax on excess distributions (but not the 15-percent additional estate tax) does not apply to distributions in 1997, 1998 or 1999.

IRAs may not be invested in collectibles. A collectible is defined as any piece of art, rug or antique, metal or gem, stamp or coin, alcoholic beverage, or other personal property as specified by the Treasury. This prohibition does not apply to coins issued by a State.

Reasons for Change

The Committee is concerned about the national savings rate, and believes that individuals should be encouraged to save. The Committee believes that the ability to make deductible contributions to an IRA is a significant savings incentive. However, this incentive is not available to all taxpayers under present law. Further, the present-law income threshold for IRA deductions are not indexed for inflation so that fewer Americans will be eligible to make a deductible IRA contribution each year. The Committee believes it is appropriate to encourage individual saving and that deductible IRAs should be available to more individuals.

In addition, the Committee believes that some individuals would be more likely to save if funds set aside in a tax-favored account could be withdrawn without tax after a reasonable holding period for retirement or certain special purposes. Some taxpayers may find such a vehicle more suitable for their savings needs.

The Committee believes that providing an incentive to save for certain special purposes is appropriate. The Committee believes that many Americans may have difficulty saving enough to ensure that they will be able to purchase a home. Home ownership is a fundamental part of the American dream.

The Committee believes that individuals who are unemployed for a substantial period of time should have access to their retirement savings.

The Committee believes that the present-law rules relating to deductible IRAs penalize American homemakers. The Committee believes that an individual should not be precluded from making a deductible IRA contribution merely because his or her

spouse participates in an employer-sponsored retirement plan.

Finally, the Committee believes that IRAs should not be precluded from investing in bullion.

Explanation of Provision

In general

The bill (1) increases the AGI phase-out limits for deductible IRAs, (2) provides that an individual is not considered an active participant in an IRA merely because the individual's spouse is an active participant, (3) provides an exception from the early withdrawal tax for withdrawals for first-time home purchase (up to $10,000) and long-term unemployed individuals, and (4) replaces present-law nondeductible IRAs with a new IRA called the IRA Plus. All individuals may make nondeductible contributions of up to $2,000 annually to an IRA Plus. No income limitations apply to IRA Plus accounts; however, the $2,000 maximum contribution limit is reduced to the extent an individual makes deductible contributions to an IRA. An IRA Plus is an IRA which is designated at the time of establishment as an IRA Plus in the manner prescribed by the Secretary. Qualified distributions from an IRA Plus are not includible in income.

Increase income phase-out ranges for deductible IRAs

The bill increases the AGI phase-out range for deductible IRA contributions as follows:

[In thousands of dollars]

Taxable years beginning in:	Phase-Out Range	
	Single Taxpayers	Joint Returns
1998 and 1999	30,000-40,000	50,000-60,000
2000 and 2001	35,000-45,000	60,000-70,000
2002 and 2003	40,000-50,000	70,000-80,000
2004 and thereafter	50,000-60,000	80,000-100,000

Active participant rule

The bill provides that an individual is not considered an active participant in an employer-sponsored plan merely because the individual's spouse is an active participant.

Effective Date

The provision is effective for taxable years beginning after December 31, 1997.

[Conference Report]

House Bill

No provision.

Conference Agreement

The conference agreement follows the Senate amendment, with modifications.

Under the conference agreement, as under the Senate amendment, an individual is not considered an active participant in an employer-sponsored retirement plan merely because the individual's spouse is an active participant. However, under the conference agreement, the maximum deductible IRA contribution for an individual who is not an active participant, but whose spouse is, is phased out for taxpayers with AGI between $150,000 and $160,000.

Under the conference agreement, the deductible IRA income phase-out limits are increased as follows:

[¶5016] Section 302. Tax-free nondeductible IRAs.

(Code Sec. 408A, 408, 72)

[Senate Report]

Present Law

Under present law, an individual may make deductible contributions to an individual retirement arrangement ("IRA") up to the lesser of $2,000 or the individual's compensation if the individual is not an active participant in an employer-sponsored retirement plan (and, if married, the individual's spouse also is not an active participant in such a plan). If the case of a married couple, deductible IRA contributions of up to $2,000 can be made for each spouse (including, for example, a home maker who does not work outside the home) if the combined compensation of both spouses is at least equal to the contributed amount.

If the individual (or the individual's spouse) is an active participant in an employer-sponsored retirement plan, the $2,000 deduction limit is phased out over certain adjusted gross income ("AGI") levels. The limit is phased out between $40,000 and $50,000 of AGI for married taxpayers, and between $25,000 and $35,000 of AGI for single taxpayers. An individual may make nondeductible IRA contributions to the extent the individual is not permitted to make deductible IRA contributions. Contributions cannot be made to an IRA after age 70½.

The following examples illustrate the income phase-out rules.

Example 1.—Suppose for a year W is an active participant in an employer-sponsored retirement plan, and W's husband, H, is not. Further assume that the combined AGI of H and W for the year is $200,000. Neither W nor H is entitled to make deductible contributions to an IRA for the year.

Example 2.—Same as example 1, except that the combined AGI of W and H is $125,000. H can make deductible contributions to an IRA. However, a deductible contribution could not be made for W.

Amounts held in an IRA are includible in income when withdrawn (except to the extent the withdrawal is a return of non-deductible contributions). Amounts withdrawn prior to attainment of age 59½ are subject to an additional 10-percent early withdrawal tax, unless the withdrawal is due to death or disability, is made in the form of certain periodic payments, is used to pay medical expenses in excess of 7.5 percent of AGI, or is used to purchase health insurance of an unemployed individual.

In general, distributions from an IRA are required to begin at age 70 ½. An excise tax is imposed if the minimum required distributions are not made. Distributions to the beneficiary of an IRA are generally required to begin within 5 years of the death of the IRA owner, unless the beneficiary is the surviving spouse.

A 15-percent excise tax is imposed on excess distributions with respect to an individual during any calendar year from qualified retirement plans, tax-sheltered annuities, and IRAs. In general, excess distributions are defined as the aggregate amount of retirement distributions (i.e., payments from applicable retirement plans) made with respect to an individual during any calendar year to the extent such amounts exceed $160,000 (for 1997) or 5 times that amount in the case of a lump-sum distribution. The dollar limit is indexed for inflation. A similar 15-percent additional estate tax applies to excess retirement accumulations upon the death of the individual. The 15-percent tax on excess distributions (but not the 15-percent additional estate tax) does not apply to distributions in 1997, 1998 or 1999.

IRAs may not be invested in collectibles. A collectible is defined as any piece of art, rug or antique, metal or gem, stamp or coin, alcoholic beverage, or other personal property as specified by the Treasury. This prohibition does not apply to coins issued by a State.

Reasons for Change

The Committee is concerned about the national savings rate, and believes that individuals should be encouraged to save. The Committee believes that the ability to make deductible contributions to an IRA is a significant savings incentive. However, this incentive is not available to all taxpayers under present law. Further, the present-law income threshold for IRA deductions are not indexed for inflation so that fewer Americans will be eligible to make a deductible IRA contribution each year. The Committee believes it is appropriate to encourage individual saving and that deductible IRAs should be available to more individuals.

In addition, the Committee believes that some individuals would be more likely to save if funds set aside in a tax-favored account could be withdrawn without tax after a reasonable holding period for retirement or certain special purposes. Some taxpayers may find such a vehicle more suitable for their savings needs.

The Committee believes that providing an incentive to save for certain special purposes is appropriate. The Committee believes that many Americans may have difficulty saving enough to ensure that they will be able to purchase a home. Home ownership is a fundamental part of the American dream.

The Committee believes that individuals who are unemployed for a substantial period of time should have access to their retirement savings.

The Committee believes that the present-law rules relating to deductible IRAs penalize American homemakers. The Committee believes that an individual should not be precluded from making a deductible IRA contribution merely because his or her spouse participates in an employer-sponsored retirement plan.

Finally, the Committee believes that IRAs should not be precluded from investing in bullion.

Explanation of Provision

In general

The bill (1) increases the AGI phase-out limits for deductible IRAs, (2) provides that an individual is not considered an active participant in an IRA merely because the individual's spouse is an active participant, (3) provides an exception from the early withdrawal tax for withdrawals for first-time home purchase (up to $10,000) and long-term unemployed individuals, and (4) replaces present-law nondeductible IRAs with a new IRA called the IRA Plus. All individuals may make nondeductible contributions of up to $2,000 annually to an IRA Plus. No income limitations apply to IRA Plus accounts; however, the $2,000 maximum contribution limit is reduced to the extent an individual makes deductible contributions to an IRA. An IRA Plus is an IRA which is designated at the time of establishment as an IRA Plus in the manner prescribed by the Secretary. Qualified distributions from an IRA Plus are not includible in income.

IRA Plus accounts

Contributions to IRA Plus accounts.

The maximum annual contribution that may be made to an IRA Plus is the lesser of $2,000 (reduced by deductible IRA contributions) or the individual's compensation for the year. As under the present-law rules relating to deductible IRAs, a contribution of up to $2,000 for each spouse may be made to an IRA Plus provided the combined compensation of the spouses is at least equal to the contributed amount.

Contributions to an IRA Plus may be made even after the individual for whom the account is maintained has attained age 70½.

Taxation of distributions

Qualified distributions from an IRA Plus are not includible in gross income, nor subject to the additional 10-percent tax on early withdrawals. A qualified distribution is a distribution that (1) is made after the 5-taxable year period beginning with the first taxable year in which the individual made a contribution to an IRA Plus,[29] and (2) which is (a) made on or after the date on which the individual attains age 59 ½, (b) made to a beneficiary (or to the individual's estate) on or after the death of the individual, (c) attributable to the individual's being disabled, or (d) a qualified special purpose distribution. Qualified special purpose distributions are distributions that are exempt from the 10- percent early withdrawal tax because they are for first-time homebuyer expenses or long-term unemployed individuals.

Distributions from an IRA Plus that are not qualified distributions are includible in income to the extent attributable to earnings, and subject to the 10-percent early withdrawal tax (unless an exception applies). The same exceptions to the early withdrawal tax that apply to IRAs apply to IRA Plus accounts.

An ordering rule applies for purposes of determining what portion of a distribution that is not a qualified distribution is includible in income. Under the ordering rule, distributions from an IRA Plus are treated as made from contributions first, and all an individual's IRA Plus accounts are treated as a single IRA Plus. Thus, no portion of a distribution from an IRA Plus is treated as attributable to earnings (and therefore includible in gross income) until the total of all distributions from all the individual's IRA Plus accounts exceeds the amount of contributions.

Distributions from an IRA Plus may be rolled over tax free to another IRA Plus.

Conversions of an IRA to an IRA Plus

All or any part of amounts in a present-law deductible or nondeductible IRA may be converted into an IRA Plus. If the conversion is made before January 1, 1999, the amount that would have been includible in gross income if the individual had withdrawn the converted amounts is included in gross income ratably over the 4- taxable year period beginning with the taxable year in which the conversion is made. The early withdrawal tax does not apply to such conversions.[30]

A conversion of an IRA into an IRA Plus can be made in a variety of different ways and without taking a distribution. For example, an individual may make a conversion simply by notifying the IRA trustee. Or, an individual may make the conversion in connection with a change in IRA trustees through a rollover or a trustee-to- trustee transfer. If a part of an IRA balance is converted into an IRA Plus, the IRA Plus amounts may have to be held separately.

Effective Date

The provision is effective for taxable years beginning after December 31, 1997.

[Conference Report]

Conference Agreement

The conference agreement follows the Senate amendment, with modifications. Under the conference agreement, the new IRA is called the "Roth IRA" rather than the IRA Plus. The maximum contribution that can be made to a Roth IRA is phased out for individuals with AGI between $95,000 and $110,000 and for joint filers with AGI between $150,000 and $160,000. Under the conference agreement, distributions to long-term unemployed individuals do not qualify as special purpose distributions. Thus, only first-time homebuyer expenses (as defined under the Senate amendment) qualify as special purpose distributions.

---

29. As is the case with IRAs generally, contributions to an IRA Plus may be made for a year by the due date for the individual's tax return for the year (determined without regard to extensions). In the case of a contribution to an IRA Plus made after the end of the taxable year, the 5-year holding period begins with the tax-

able year to which the contribution relates, rather than the year in which the contribution is actually made.

30. In case of conversions from an IRA to an IRA Plus, the 5- taxable year holding period begins with the taxable year in which the conversion was made.

Under the conference agreement, only taxpayers with AGI of less than $100,000[51] are eligible to roll over or convert an IRA into a Roth IRA.

The conference agreement retains present-law nondeductible IRAs. Thus, an individual who cannot (or does not) make contributions to a deductible IRA or a Roth IRA can make contributions to a nondeductible IRA. In no case can contributions to all an individual's IRAs for a taxable year exceed $2,000.

[¶ 5017]   Section 303.   Modifications of early withdrawal tax.

(Code Sec. 72)

[Senate Report]

Present Law

Under present law, an individual may make deductible contributions to an individual retirement arrangement ("IRA") up to the lesser of $2,000 or the individual's compensation if the individual is not an active participant in an employer-sponsored retirement plan (and, if married, the individual's spouse also is not an active participant in such a plan). If the case of a married couple, deductible IRA contributions of up to $2,000 can be made for each spouse (including, for example, a home maker who does not work outside the home) if the combined compensation of both spouses is at least equal to the contributed amount.

If the individual (or the individual's spouse) is an active participant in an employer-sponsored retirement plan, the $2,000 deduction limit is phased out over certain adjusted gross income ("AGI") levels. The limit is phased out between $40,000 and $50,000 of AGI for married taxpayers, and between $25,000 and $35,000 of AGI for single taxpayers. An individual may make nondeductible IRA contributions to the extent the individual is not permitted to make deductible IRA contributions. Contributions cannot be made to an IRA after age 70½.

Amounts held in an IRA are includible in income when withdrawn (except to the extent the withdrawal is a return of non-deductible contributions). Amounts withdrawn prior to attainment of age 59½ are subject to an additional 10-percent early withdrawal tax, unless the withdrawal is due to death or disability, is made in the form of certain periodic payments, is used to pay medical expenses in excess of 7.5 percent of AGI, or is used to purchase health insurance of an unemployed individual.

In general, distributions from an IRA are required to begin at age 70 ½. An excise tax is imposed if the minimum required distributions are not made. Distributions to the beneficiary of an IRA are generally required to begin within 5 years of the death of the IRA owner, unless the beneficiary is the surviving spouse.

A 15-percent excise tax is imposed on excess distributions with respect to an individual during any calendar year from qualified retirement plans, tax-sheltered annuities, and IRAs. In general, excess distributions are defined as the aggregate amount of retirement distributions (i.e., payments from applicable retirement plans) made with respect to an individual during any calendar year to the extent such amounts exceed $160,000 (for 1997) or 5 times that amount in the case of a lump-sum distribution. The dollar limit is indexed for inflation. A similar 15-percent additional estate tax applies to excess retirement accumulations upon the death of the individual. The 15-percent tax on excess distributions (but not the 15-percent additional estate tax) does not apply to distributions in 1997, 1998 or 1999.

IRAs may not be invested in collectibles. A collectible is defined as any piece of art, rug or antique, metal or gem, stamp or coin, alcoholic beverage, or other personal property as specified by the Treasury. This prohibition does not apply to coins issued by a State.

---

51. For this purpose, AGI is determined before any amount includible in income as a result of the rollover or conversion.

Reasons for Change

The Committee is concerned about the national savings rate, and believes that individuals should be encouraged to save. The Committee believes that the ability to make deductible contributions to an IRA is a significant savings incentive. However, this incentive is not available to all taxpayers under present law. Further, the present-law income threshold for IRA deductions are not indexed for inflation so that fewer Americans will be eligible to make a deductible IRA contribution each year. The Committee believes it is appropriate to encourage individual saving and that deductible IRAs should be available to more individuals.

In addition, the Committee believes that some individuals would be more likely to save if funds set aside in a tax-favored account could be withdrawn without tax after a reasonable holding period for retirement or certain special purposes. Some taxpayers may find such a vehicle more suitable for their savings needs.

The Committee believes that providing an incentive to save for certain special purposes is appropriate. The Committee believes that many Americans may have difficulty saving enough to ensure that they will be able to purchase a home. Home ownership is a fundamental part of the American dream.

The Committee believes that individuals who are unemployed for a substantial period of time should have access to their retirement savings.

The Committee believes that the present-law rules relating to deductible IRAs penalize American homemakers. The Committee believes that an individual should not be precluded from making a deductible IRA contribution merely because his or her spouse participates in an employer-sponsored retirement plan.

Finally, the Committee believes that IRAs should not be precluded from investing in bullion.

Explanation of Provision

In general

The bill (1) increases the AGI phase-out limits for deductible IRAs, (2) provides that an individual is not considered an active participant in an IRA merely because the individual's spouse is an active participant, (3) provides an exception from the early withdrawal tax for withdrawals for first-time home purchase (up to $10,000) and long-term unemployed individuals, and (4) replaces present-law nondeductible IRAs with a new IRA called the IRA Plus. All individuals may make nondeductible contributions of up to $2,000 annually to an IRA Plus. No income limitations apply to IRA Plus accounts; however, the $2,000 maximum contribution limit is reduced to the extent an individual makes deductible contributions to an IRA. An IRA Plus is an IRA which is designated at the time of establishment as an IRA Plus in the manner prescribed by the Secretary. Qualified distributions from an IRA Plus are not includible in income.

Modifications to early withdrawal tax

The bill provides that the 10-percent early withdrawal tax does not apply to withdrawals from an IRA (including an IRA Plus) for (1) up to $10,000 of first-time homebuyer expenses and (2) distributions for long-term unemployed individuals.[27]

Under the bill, qualified first-time homebuyer distributions are withdrawals of up to $10,000 during the individual's lifetime that are used within 120 days to pay costs (including reasonable settlement, financing, or other closing costs) of acquiring, constructing, or reconstructing the principal residence of a first-time homebuyer who is the individual, the individual's spouse, or a child, grandchild, or ancestor of the individual or individual's spouse. A first-time homebuyer is an individual who has not had an ownership interest in a principal residence during the 2-year period ending on the date of acquisition of the principal residence to which the withdrawal relates. The bill requires that the spouse of the individual also meet this requirement as of the date the contract is entered into or construction commences. The date of acqui-

---

27. The bill also provides for penalty-free withdrawals from IRAs for education expenses (see above).

sition is the date the individual enters into a binding contract to purchase a principal residence or begins construction or reconstruction of such a residence. Principal residence is defined as under the provisions relating to the rollover of gain on the sale of a principal residence.

Under the bill, any amount withdrawn for the purchase of a principal residence is required to be used within 120 days of the date of withdrawal. The 10-percent additional income tax on early withdrawals is imposed with respect to any amount not so used. If the 120-day rule cannot be satisfied due to a delay in the acquisition of the residence, the taxpayer may recontribute all or part of the amount withdrawn to an IRA Plus prior to the end of the 120-day period without adverse tax consequences.

Under the bill, the 10-percent early withdrawal tax does not apply to distributions to an individual after separation from employment if the individual has received unemployment compensation for 12 consecutive weeks under any Federal or State unemployment compensation law and the distribution is made during any taxable year during which the unemployment compensation is paid or the succeeding taxable year. This exception does not apply to any distribution made after the individual has been em-

ployed for at least 60 days after the separation of employment. To the extent provided in regulations, the provision applies to a self-employed individual if, under Federal or State law, the individual would have received unemployment compensation but for the fact the individual was self employed.

Effective Date

The provision is effective for taxable years beginning after December 31, 1997.

[Conference Report]

House Bill

The House bill adds an additional exception to the early withdrawal tax for AD IRAs only. The early withdrawal tax does not apply to distributions from an AD IRA for first-time homebuyer expenses, subject to a $10,000 life-time cap.

Effective Date

Taxable years beginning after December 31, 1997.

Conference Agreement

The conference agreement follows the Senate amendment but does not include the provision relating to long-term unemployed individuals.[52]

[¶ 5018]   Section 304.   IRA investments in coin and bullion.

(Code Sec. 408, 408A)

[Senate Report]

Present Law

Under present law, an individual may make deductible contributions to an individual retirement arrangement ("IRA") up to the lesser of $2,000 or the individual's compensation if the individual is not an active participant in an employer-sponsored retirement plan (and, if married, the individual's spouse also is not an active participant in such a plan). If the case of a married couple, deductible IRA contributions of up to $2,000 can be made for each spouse (including, for example, a home maker who

does not work outside the home) if the combined compensation of both spouses is at least equal to the contributed amount.

If the individual (or the individual's spouse) is an active participant in an employer-sponsored retirement plan, the $2,000 deduction limit is phased out over certain adjusted gross income ("AGI") levels. The limit is phased out between $40,000 and $50,000 of AGI for married taxpayers, and between $25,000 and $35,000 of AGI for single taxpayers. An individual may make nondeductible IRA contributions to the extent the individual is not permitted to make deductible IRA contributions. Contributions cannot be made to an IRA after age 70½.

---

52. As under the House bill and Senate amendment, the Conference agreement includes a penalty-free withdrawal provision for education expenses.

Amounts held in an IRA are includible in income when withdrawn (except to the extent the withdrawal is a return of non-deductible contributions). Amounts withdrawn prior to attainment of age 59½ are subject to an additional 10-percent early withdrawal tax, unless the withdrawal is due to death or disability, is made in the form of certain periodic payments, is used to pay medical expenses in excess of 7.5 percent of AGI, or is used to purchase health insurance of an unemployed individual.

In general, distributions from an IRA are required to begin at age 70½. An excise tax is imposed if the minimum required distributions are not made. Distributions to the beneficiary of an IRA are generally required to begin within 5 years of the death of the IRA owner, unless the beneficiary is the surviving spouse.

A 15-percent excise tax is imposed on excess distributions with respect to an individual during any calendar year from qualified retirement plans, tax-sheltered annuities, and IRAs. In general, excess distributions are defined as the aggregate amount of retirement distributions (i.e., payments from applicable retirement plans) made with respect to an individual during any calendar year to the extent such amounts exceed $160,000 (for 1997) or 5 times that amount in the case of a lump-sum distribution. The dollar limit is indexed for inflation. A similar 15-percent additional estate tax applies to excess retirement accumulations upon the death of the individual. The 15-percent tax on excess distributions (but not the 15-percent additional estate tax) does not apply to distributions in 1997, 1998 or 1999.

IRAs may not be invested in collectibles. A collectible is defined as any piece of art, rug or antique, metal or gem, stamp or coin, alcoholic beverage, or other personal property as specified by the Treasury. This prohibition does not apply to coins issued by a State.

Reasons for Change

The Committee is concerned about the national savings rate, and believes that individuals should be encouraged to save. The Committee believes that the ability to make deductible contributions to an IRA is a significant savings incentive. However, this incentive is not available to all taxpayers under present law. Further, the present-law income threshold for IRA deductions are not indexed for inflation so that fewer Americans will be eligible to make a deductible IRA contribution each year. The Committee believes it is appropriate to encourage individual saving and that deductible IRAs should be available to more individuals.

In addition, the Committee believes that some individuals would be more likely to save if funds set aside in a tax-favored account could be withdrawn without tax after a reasonable holding period for retirement or certain special purposes. Some taxpayers may find such a vehicle more suitable for their savings needs.

The Committee believes that providing an incentive to save for certain special purposes is appropriate. The Committee believes that many Americans may have difficulty saving enough to ensure that they will be able to purchase a home. Home ownership is a fundamental part of the American dream.

The Committee believes that individuals who are unemployed for a substantial period of time should have access to their retirement savings.

The Committee believes that the present-law rules relating to deductible IRAs penalize American homemakers. The Committee believes that an individual should not be precluded from making a deductible IRA contribution merely because his or her spouse participates in an employer-sponsored retirement plan.

Finally, the Committee believes that IRAs should not be precluded from investing in bullion.

Explanation of Provision

In general

The bill (1) increases the AGI phase-out limits for deductible IRAs, (2) provides that an individual is not considered an active participant in an IRA merely because the individual's spouse is an active participant, (3) provides an exception from the early withdrawal tax for withdrawals for first-time home purchase (up to $10,000) and long-term unemployed individuals, and (4) replaces present-law nondeductible IRAs with a new IRA called the IRA Plus. All individuals may make nondeductible contributions of up to $2,000 annually to an IRA Plus. No income limitations apply to IRA Plus accounts; however, the $2,000 maximum contribution limit is reduced to the extent an individual makes deductible contributions to an IRA. An IRA Plus is an IRA which is designated at the time of establishment as an IRA Plus in the manner prescribed by the Secretary. Qualified distributions from an IRA Plus are not includible in income.

IRA investments in bullion

Under the bill, IRA assets may be invested in certain bullion. The bill applies to any gold, silver, platinum or palladium bullion of a fineness equal to or exceeding the

minimum fineness required for metals which may be delivered in satisfaction of a regulated futures contract subject to regulation by the Commodity Futures Trading Commission. The provision does not apply unless the bullion is in the physical possession of the IRA trustee.[28]

Effective Date

The provision is effective for taxable years beginning after December 31, 1997.

[Conference Report]

House Bill

No provision.

Conference Agreement

The conference agreement follows the Senate amendment.

[¶ 5019]   Section 311.   Maximum rate of tax on net capital gain on individuals.

(Code Sec. 1, 1250, 1202)

[House Report]

Present Law

In general, gain or loss reflected in the value of an asset is not recognized for income tax purposes until a taxpayer disposes of the asset. On the sale or exchange of capital assets, the net capital gain is taxed at the same rate as ordinary income, except that individuals are subject to a maximum marginal rate of 28 percent of the net capital gain. Net capital gain is the excess of the net long-term capital gain for the taxable year over the net short-term capital loss for the year. Gain or loss is treated as long-term if the asset is held for more than one year.

A capital asset generally means any property except (1) inventory, stock in trade, or property held primarily for sale to customers in the ordinary course of the taxpayer's trade or business, (2) depreciable or real property used in the taxpayer's trade or business, (3) specified literary or artistic property, (4) business accounts or notes receivable, or (5) certain U.S. publications. In addition, the net gain from the disposition

of certain property used in the taxpayer's trade or business is treated as long-term capital gain. Gain from the disposition of depreciable personal property is not treated as capital gain to the extent of all previous depreciation allowances. Gain from the disposition of depreciable real property is generally not treated as capital gain to the extent of the depreciation allowances in excess of the allowances that would have been available under the straight-line method of depreciation.

Reasons for Change

The Committee believes it is important that tax policy be conducive to economic growth. Economic growth cannot occur without saving, investment, and the willingness of individuals to take risks and exploit new market opportunities. The greater the pool of savings, the greater the monies available for business investment in equipment and research. It is through such investment in equipment and new products and services that the United States economy can increase output and productivity. It is through increases in productivity that workers earn higher real wages. Hence, greater

28. The bill does not modify the present-law rule permitting IRAs to be invested in certain State coins.

saving is necessary for all Americans to benefit through a higher standard of living.

The net personal saving rate in the United States has averaged less than 5 percent of gross domestic product (GDP) for the past 15 years. The Committee believes such saving is inadequate to finance the investment that is needed to equip the country's businesses with the equipment and research dollars necessary to create the higher productivity that results in higher real wages for working Americans. A reduction in the taxation of capital gains increases the rate of return on household saving. Testimony by many economists before the Committee generally concluded that increasing the after-tax return to saving should increase the saving rate of American households.

American technological leadership has been enhanced by the willingness of individuals to take the risk of pursuing new businesses exploiting new technologies. Risk taking is stifled if the taxation of any resulting gain is high and the ability to claim losses is limited. The Committee believes it is important to encourage risk taking and believes a reduction in the taxation of capital gains will have that effect.

Reduction in the taxation of capital gains also should improve the efficiency of the capital markets. The taxation of capital gains upon realization encourages investors who have accrued past gains to keep their monies "locked in" to such investments even when better investment opportunities present themselves. All economists that testified before the Committee agreed that reducing the rate of taxation of capital gains would encourage investors to unlock many of these gains. This unlocking will permit more monies to flow to new, highly valued uses in the economy. When monies flow freely, the efficiency of the capital market is improved.

The unlocking effect also has the short-term and long-term effect of increasing revenues to the Federal Government. The current revenue estimating methods employed by the Congress account for this long-term behavioral response. Nevertheless, current Congressional estimates project that revenue losses to the Federal Government will arise from the reduction in the tax rate on capital gains. The Committee observes, however, that the conservative approach embodied in such estimates does not attempt to account for the potential for increased growth in GDP that can result from increased saving and risk taking. Many macroeconomists have concluded that reductions in the taxation of capital gains may increase GDP and wage growth sufficiently that future tax revenues from the taxation of wages and business profits will offset the losses forecast from the sale of capital assets. The potential for future growth and its benefits both for all United States citizens and for future Federal revenues were important considerations for the Committee.

The Committee rejects the narrow view that reductions in the taxation of capital gains benefit primarily higher-income Americans. Taking a longer view, the Committee sees a reduction in the taxation of capital gains as providing potential benefits to all individuals. Most importantly, the Committee stresses that economic growth benefits all Americans. Increased investment leads to greater productivity and leads to higher wages. Traditional attempts to measure the benefit or burden of a tax change do not account for this critical outcome.

Explanation of Provision

Under the bill, the maximum rate of tax on the net capital gain of an individual is reduced from 28 percent to 20 percent. In addition, any net capital gain which otherwise would be taxed at a 15 percent rate is taxed at a rate of 10 percent. These rates apply for purposes of both the regular tax and the minimum tax.

The tax on the net capital gain attributable to any long-term capital gain from the sale or exchange of collectibles will remain at a maximum rate of 28 percent; any long-term capital gain from the sale or exchange of section 1250 property (i.e., depreciable real estate) to the extent the gain would have been treated as ordinary income if the property had been section 1245 property will be taxed at a maximum rate of 26 percent; and the tax treatment of small business stock (as defined in section 1202(c)) will remain unchanged. Gain from the disposition of a collectible which is an indexed asset (described below) will not be eligible for the 28-percent rate unless the taxpayer elects to forego indexing.

Effective Date

The provision applies to taxable years ending after May 6, 1997.

For a taxpayer's year that includes May 7, 1997, the lower rates will not apply to an amount equal the net capital gain determined by including only gain or loss properly taken into account for the portion of the taxable year before May 7, 1997. Any net capital gain not eligible for the lower rates will be subject to the present-law maximum rate of 28 percent. This generally has the effect of applying the lower rates to capital assets sold or exchanged (or installment payments received) on or after May 7, 1997, and subjecting the remaining portion of the net capital gain to a maximum rate of 28 percent.

In the case of gain taken into account by a pass-through entity (i.e., a RIC, a REIT, a partnership, an estate or trust, or a common trust fund), the date taken into account by the entity is the appropriate date for applying the rule in the preceding paragraph. Thus, gain taken into account by a pass-through entity before May 7, 1997 is not eligible for the lower rates.

The provision also changes the 110-percent-of-last-year-liability estimated tax safe harbor to a 109-percent-of-last-year-liability safe harbor for 1997.

[Conference Report]

Conference Agreement

The conference agreement generally follows the House bill and the Senate amendment. The maximum rate of tax on gain attributable to the depreciation of section 1250 property will be 25 percent.

In addition, for taxable years beginning after December 31, 2000, the maximum capital gains rates for assets which are held more than 5 years, are 8 percent and 18 percent (rather than 10 percent and 20 percent). The 18-percent rate only applies to assets the holding period for which begins after December 31, 2000. A taxpayer holding a capital asset or asset used in the taxpayer's trade or business on January 1, 2001, may elect to treat the asset as having been sold on such date for an amount equal to its fair market value, and as having been reacquired for an amount equal to such value. If the election is made, any gain is recognized (and any loss disallowed). The conference agreement allows the Treasury Department to issue regulations coordinating the capital gain provisions with other rules involving the treatment of sales and exchanges by pass- thru entities and of interests therein.

Under the conference agreement, the lower capital gains rates do not apply to the sale or exchange of assets held for 18 months or less, effective for amounts properly taken into account after July 28, 1997. The 28-percent maximum rate will continue to apply to the sale or exchange of capital assets held more than 1 year but not more than 18 months.

[¶ 5020]   Section 312.   Exclusion of gain on sale of principal residence.

(Code Sec. 121, 1034)

[House Report]

Present Law

Rollover of gain

No gain is recognized on the sale of a principal residence if a new residence at least equal in cost to the sales price of the old residence is purchased and used by the taxpayer as his or her principal residence within a specified period of time (sec.

1034). This replacement period generally begins two years before and ends two years after the date of sale of the old residence. The basis of the replacement residence is reduced by the amount of any gain not recognized on the sale of the old residence by reason of this gain rollover rule.

One-time exclusion

In general, an individual, on a one-time basis, may exclude from gross income up to $125,000 of gain from the sale or exchange of a principal residence if the taxpayer (1) has attained age 55 before the sale, and (2) has owned the property and used it as a principal residence for three or more of the five years preceding the sale (sec. 121).

Reasons for Change

Calculating capital gain from the sale of a principal residence is among the most complex tasks faced by a typical taxpayer. Many taxpayers buy and sell a number of homes over the course of a lifetime, and are generally not certain of how much housing appreciation they can expect. Thus, even though most homeowners never pay any income tax on the capital gain on their principal residences, as a result of the rollover provisions and the $125,000 one-time exclusion, detailed records of transactions and expenditures on home improvements must be kept, in most cases, for many decades. To claim the exclusion, many taxpayers must determine the basis of each home they have owned, and appropriately adjust the basis of their current home to reflect any untaxed gains from previous housing transactions. This determination may involve augmenting the original cost basis of each home by expenditures on improvements. In addition to the record-keeping burden this creates, taxpayers face the difficult task of drawing a distinction between improvements that add to basis, and repairs that do not. The failure to account accurately for all improvements leads to errors in the calculation of capital gains, and hence to an under- or over-payment of the capital gains on principal residences. By excluding from taxation capital gains on principal residences below a relatively high threshold, few taxpayers would have to refer to records in determining income tax consequences of transactions related to their house.

To postpone the entire capital gain from the sale of a principal residence, the purchase price of a new home must be greater than the sales price of the old home. This provision of present law encourages some taxpayers to purchase larger and more expensive houses than they otherwise would in order to avoid a tax liability, particularly those who move from areas where housing costs are high to lower-cost areas. This promotes an inefficient use of taxpayer's financial resources.

Present law also may discourage some older taxpayers from selling their homes. Taxpayers who would realize a capital gain in excess of $125,000 if they sold their home and taxpayers who have already used the exclusion may choose to stay in their homes even though the home no longer suits their needs. By raising the $125,000 limit and by allowing multiple exclusions, this constraint to the mobility of the elderly would be removed.

While most homeowners do not pay capital gains tax when selling their homes, current law creates certain tax traps for the unwary that can result in significant capital gains taxes or loss of the benefits of the current exclusion. For example, an individual is not eligible for the one- time capital gains exclusion if the exclusion was previously utilized by the individual's spouse. This restriction has the unintended effect of penalizing individuals who marry someone who has already taken the exclusion. Households that move from a high housing-cost area to a low housing- cost area may incur an unexpected capital gains tax liability. Divorcing couples may incur substantial capital gains taxes if they do not carefully plan their house ownership and sale decisions.

[Senate Report]

Explanation of Provision

Under the bill a taxpayer generally is able to exclude up to $250,000 ($500,000 if married filing a joint return) of gain realized on the sale or exchange of a principal residence. The exclusion is allowed each time a taxpayer selling or exchanging a principal residence meets the eligibility requirements, but generally no more frequently than once every two years. The bill provides that gain would be recognized to the extent of any depreciation allowable with respect to the rental or business use of such principal residence for periods after May 6, 1997.

To be eligible for the exclusion, a taxpayer must have owned the residence and occupied it as a principal residence for at least two of the five years prior to the sale or exchange. A taxpayer who fails to meet these requirements by reason of a change of place of employment, health, or unforeseen circumstances is able to exclude the fraction of the $250,000 ($500,000 if married filing a joint return) equal to the fraction of two years that these requirements are met.

In the case of joint filers not sharing a principal residence, an exclusion of $250,000 is available on a qualifying sale or exchange of the principal residence of one of the spouses. Similarly, if a single taxpayer who is otherwise eligible for an exclusion marries someone who has used the exclusion within the two years prior to the marriage, the bill would allow the newly married taxpayer a maximum exclusion of $250,000. Once both spouses satisfy the eligibility rules and two years have passed since the last exclusion was allowed to either of them, the taxpayers may exclude $500,000 of gain on their joint return.

Under the bill, the gain from the sale or exchange of the remainder interest in the taxpayer's principal residence may qualify for the otherwise allowable exclusion.

Effective Date

The provision is available for all sales or exchanges of a principal residence occurring on or after May 7, 1997, and replaces the present-law rollover and one-time exclusion provisions applicable to principal residences.

A taxpayer may elect to apply present law (rather than the new exclusion) to a sale or exchange (1) made before the date of enactment of the Act, (2) made after the date of enactment pursuant to a binding contract in effect on the date or (3) where the replacement residence was acquired on or before the date of enactment (or pursuant to a binding contract in effect of the date of enactment) and the rollover provision would apply. If a taxpayer acquired his or her current residence in a rollover transaction, periods of ownership and use of the prior residence would be taken into account in determining ownership and use of the current residence.

[Conference Report]

Conference Agreement

The conference agreement generally follows the House bill and the Senate amendment.

The conferees wish to clarify that the provision limiting the exclusion to only one sale every two years by the taxpayer does not prevent a husband and wife filing a joint return from each excluding up to $250,000 of gain from the sale or exchange of each spouse's principal residence provided that each spouse would be permitted to exclude up to $250,000 of gain if they filed separate returns.

[¶ 5021]   Section 313.   Small business stock.

(Code Sec. 1045)

[Conference Report]

Present Law

The Revenue Reconciliation Act of 1993 provided individuals a 50-percent exclusion for the sale of certain small business stock acquired at original issue and held for at least five years. One-half of the excluded gain is a minimum tax preference.

The amount of gain eligible for the 50-percent exclusion by an individual with respect to any corporation is the greater of (1) 10 times the taxpayer's basis in the stock or (2) $10 million.

In order to qualify as a small business, when the stock is issued, the gross assets of the corporation may not exceed $50 million. The corporation also must meet an active trade or business requirement.

House Bill

Under the House bill, the lower capital gains rates do not apply to the includible portion of the gain from the qualifying sale of small business stock. Thus, the maximum rate of regular tax on the sale of small business stock remains at 14 percent.

Conference Agreement

The conference agreement follows the provisions in the House bill. The conference agreement reduces the minimum tax preference from one-half of the excluded gain to 42 percent of such gain.

In addition, the conference agreement allows an individual to roll over tax-free gain from the sale or exchange of qualified small business stock held more than 6 months where the taxpayer uses the proceeds to purchase other qualified small business stock within 60 days of the sale. For purposes of the rollover provision, the replacement stock must meet the active business requirement for the 6-month period following the purchase. Generally, the holding period of the stock purchased will include the holding period of the stock sold, except for purposes of determining whether the 6-month holding period is met. The provision applies to sales after the date of enactment of this Act.

[¶ 5022]   Section 314.   Amount of net capital gain taken into account in computing alternative tax on capital gains for corporations not to exceed taxable income of the corporation.

(Code Sec. 1201)

[House Report]

Present Law

Under present law, the net capital gain of a corporation is taxed at the same rate as ordinary income, and subject to tax at graduated rates up to 35 percent.

Reasons for Change

The Committee believes it is important that tax policy be conducive to economic growth. Economic growth cannot occur without saving, investment, and the willingness of businesses to take risks and exploit new market opportunities. The greater the pool of savings, the greater the monies available for business investment in equipment and research. It is through such investment in equipment and new products and services that the United States economy can increase output and productivity. It is through increases in productivity that workers earn higher real wages. Hence, greater saving is necessary for all Americans to benefit through a higher standard of living.

The Committee observes that net business saving has not increased significantly from its levels of a decade ago. The Committee believes that a lower rate of tax on capital gains will encourage investment, saving, and risk-taking, create new jobs, and promote economic growth.

Explanation of Provision

The bill provides a maximum rate of tax on the net capital gain of a corporation to the extent the gain is attributable to the sale or exchange of property held more than 8 years. The alternative tax is 32 percent on gain attributable to calendar year 1998; 31 percent on gain attributable to calendar year 1999; and 30 percent on gain attributable to calendar years after 1999. The bill also modifies the application of the corporate alternative capital gains tax so that the alternative capital gains tax applies to the lesser of 8-year gain or taxable income. Gain from the disposition of a collectible or attributable to the depreciation of section 1250 property is not eligible for the lower rate.

Effective Date

The provision applies to taxable years ending after December 31, 1997. However, the lower rate does not apply to amounts properly taken into account before January 1, 1998. For fiscal years beginning in 1998 and 1999, the tax is computed by applying the applicable percentage to the 8-year gain for the first portion of the year (or, if less, the 8-year gain for the entire year), but in an amount not to exceed the taxable income for the entire year and then by applying the applicable percentage to an amount equal to the 8-year gain for the entire year (or, if less, taxable income) reduced by the amount taxed at the applicable percentage for the first portion of the year.

In the case of gain taken into account by a corporation from a pass-through entity (i.e., a RIC, a REIT, an S corporation, a partnership, an estate or trust, or a common trust fund), the date taken into account by the entity is the appropriate date for applying the rule in the preceding paragraph.

[Conference Report]

Senate Amendment

No provision.

Conference Agreement

The conference agreement does not include the House bill provision.

The conference agreement provides that the amount of gain subject to the alternative rate of tax under section 1201(a)(2) may not exceed the corporation's taxable income. Because the section 1201 alternative tax does not presently apply, this change has no effect under the rate structure of present law.

[¶ 5023] Section 401. Increase exemption amount applicable to individual alternative minimum tax.

(Code Sec. 55)

[House Report]

Present Law

Present law imposes a minimum tax on an individual to the extent the taxpayer's minimum tax liability exceeds his or her regular tax liability. This alternative minimum tax is imposed upon individuals at rates of (1) 26 percent on the first $175,000 of alternative minimum taxable income in excess of a phased-out exemption amount and (2) 28 percent on the amount in excess of $175,000. The exemption amounts are $45,000 in the case of married individuals filing a joint return and surviving spouses; $33,750 in the case of other unmarried individuals; and $22,500 in the case of married individuals filing a separate return. These exemption amounts are phased-out by an amount equal to 25 percent of the amount that the individual's alternative minimum taxable income exceeds a threshold amount. These threshold amounts are $150,000 in the case of married individuals filing a joint return and surviving spouses; $112,500 in the case of other unmarried individuals; and $75,000 in the case of married individuals filing a separate return, estates, and trusts. The exemption amounts, the threshold phase-out amounts, and the $175,000 breakpoint amount are not indexed for inflation.

Reasons for Change

The Committee is concerned about the projected trend that significantly more individuals with few or no tax preferences and adjustments will become subject to the alternative minimum tax in the near future. This trend is projected, in part, because the exemption amounts applicable to the individual alternative minimum tax are not indexed for inflation, while the standard deduction, personal exemptions, rate brackets and other features of the regular tax are indexed for inflation.

Explanation of Provision

For taxable years beginning in 1999, 2001, 2003, 2005 and 2007, the exemption amounts of the individual alternative minimum tax are increased as follows for each such year: (1) by $1,000 in the case of married individuals filing a joint return and surviving spouses; (2) by $750 in the case of other unmarried individuals; and (3) by $500 in the case of married individuals filing a separate return. For taxable years beginning after 2007, the exemption amounts are indexed for inflation.

Effective Date

The provision is effective for taxable years beginning after December 31, 1998.

[Senate Report]

Explanation of Provision

For taxable years beginning after 2000 and before 2003, the exemption amounts of the individual alternative minimum tax are increased as follows in each year: (1) by $600 in the case of married individuals filing a joint return and surviving spouses; (2) by $450 in the case of other unmarried individuals; and (3) by $300 in the case of married individuals filing separate returns. For taxable years beginning after 2003, the exemption amounts of the individual alternative minimum tax are increased as follows in each year: (1) by $950 in the case of married individuals filing a joint return and surviving spouses; (2) by $700 in the case of other unmarried individuals; and (3) by $475 in the case of married individuals filing separate returns.

Effective Date

[Conference Report]

Conference Agreement

The provision is effective for taxable years beginning after December 31, 2000.

The conference agreement contains neither the House bill nor the Senate amendment.

[¶ 5024]   Section 402.   Repeal alternative minimum tax for small businesses and repeal the depreciation adjustment.

(Code Sec. 56)

[House Report]

Present Law

In general

Present law imposes a minimum tax on an individual or a corporation to the extent the taxpayer's minimum tax liability exceeds its regular tax liability. The individual minimum tax is imposed at rates of 26 and 28 percent on alternative minimum taxable income in excess of a phased-out exemption amount; the corporate minimum tax is imposed at a rate of 20 percent on alternative minimum taxable income in excess of a phased-out $40,000 exemption amount. Alternative minimum taxable income ("AMTI") is the taxpayer's taxable income increased by certain preference items and adjusted by determining the tax treatment of certain items in a manner that negates the deferral of income resulting from the regular tax treatment of those items. In the case of a corporation, in addition to the regular set of adjustments and preferences, there is a second set of adjustments known as the "adjusted current earnings" adjustment.

The most significant alternative minimum tax adjustment relates to depreciation. In computing AMTI, depreciation on property placed in service after 1986 must be computed by using the class lives prescribed by the alternative depreciation system of section 168(g) and either (1) the straight-line method in the case of property subject to the straight-line method under the regular tax or (2) the 150-percent declining balance method in the case of other property. For regular tax purposes, depreciation on tangible personal property generally is computed using shorter recovery periods and more accelerated methods than are allowed for alternative minimum tax purposes.

If a taxpayer is subject to alternative minimum tax in one year, such amount of tax is allowed as a credit in a subsequent taxable year to the extent the taxpayer's regular tax liability exceeds its tentative minimum tax in such subsequent year. If the taxpayer is an individual, this credit is allowed to the extent the taxpayer's alternative minimum tax liability is a result of adjustments that are timing in nature.

Reasons for Change

The Committee believes that the alternative minimum tax inhibits capital formation and business enterprise and is administratively complex. Therefore, the bill deletes the depreciation adjustment for new investment in depreciable property by all businesses and completely repeals the corporate alternative minimum tax for small businesses.

Explanation of Provision

Repeal of the corporate alternative minimum tax for small businesses

The corporate alternative minimum tax is repealed for small business corporations for taxable years beginning after December 31, 1997. A corporation that had average gross receipts of less than $5 million for the three-year period beginning after December 31, 1994, is a small business corporation for any taxable year beginning after December 31, 1997. A corporation that meets the $5 million gross receipts test will continue to be treated as a small business corporation exempt from the alternative minimum tax so long as its average gross receipts do not exceed $7.5 million. A corporation that fails to meet the $7.5 million gross receipts test will become subject to corporate alternative minimum tax only with respect to preferences and adjustments that relate to transactions and investments entered into after the corporation loses its status as a small business corporation.

In addition, the alternative minimum tax credit allowable to a small business corporation may not exceed the corporation's regular tax liability (reduced by other credits) over 25 percent of the corporation's regular tax (reduced by foreign tax credits) in excess of $25,000.

Repeal of the depreciation adjustment

The alternative minimum tax adjustment relating to depreciation is repealed for all taxpayers for property placed in service after December 31, 1998.

Effective Date

Except as provided above, the provision is effective for taxable years beginning after December 31, 1997.

[Conference Report]

Senate Amendment

No provision.

Conference Agreement

The conference agreement generally follows the House bill with respect to the repeal of the corporate alternative minimum tax for small businesses. In addition, for property (including pollution control facilities) placed in service after December 31, 1998, the conference agreement conforms the recovery periods used for purposes of the alternative minimum tax depreciation adjustment to the recovery periods used for purposes of the regular tax under present law.

[¶ 5025]   Section 403.   Repeal installment method adjustment for farmers.

(Code Sec. 56)

[House Report]

Present Law

The installment method allows gain on the sale of property to be recognized as payments are received. Under the regular tax, dealers in personal property are not allowed to defer the recognition of income by use of the installment method on the installment sale of such property. For this purpose, dealer dispositions do not include sales of any property used or produced in the trade or business of farming. For alternative minimum tax purposes, the installment method is not available with respect to the disposition of any property that is the stock in trade of the taxpayer or any other property of a kind which would be properly included in the inventory of the taxpayer if held at year end, or property held by the taxpayer primarily for sale to customers. No explicit exception is provided for installment sales of farm property under the alternative minimum tax.

Reasons for Change

The Committee understands that the Internal Revenue Service ("IRS") takes the position that the installment method may not be used for sales of property produced on a farm for alternative minimum tax purposes. The Committee further understands that the IRS has announced that it generally will not enforce this position for taxable years beginning before January 1, 1997, so long as the farmer changes its method of accounting for installment sales for taxable years beginning afterDecember 31, 1996.[29] The Committee believes that this issue should be clarified in favor of the farmer.

Explanation of Provision

The bill generally provides that for purposes of the alternative minimum tax, farmers may use the installment method of accounting.

Effective Date

The provision generally is effective for dispositions in taxable years beginning after December 31, 1987.

[Conference Report]

Senate Amendment

The Senate amendment is the same as the House bill.

---

29. Notice 97 13, January 28, 1997.

Conference Agreement

The conference agreement follows the House bill and the Senate amendment.

[¶ 5026]   Section 501.   Cost-of-living adjustments relating to estate and gift tax provisions.

(Code Sec. 2010, 6018(a), 2001, 2102, 2505, 2032A, 2503, 2631, 6601)

[House Report]

Present Law

A gift tax is imposed on lifetime transfers by gift and an estate tax is imposed on transfers at death. Since 1976, the gift tax and the estate tax have been unified so that a single graduated rate schedule applies to cumulative taxable transfers made by a taxpayer during his or her lifetime and at death.[30] A unified credit of $192,800 is provided against the estate and gift tax, which effectively exempts the first $600,000 in cumulative taxable transfers from tax (sec. 2010). For transfers in excess of $600,000, estate and gift tax rates begin at 37 percent and reach 55 percent on cumulative taxable transfers over $3 million (sec. 2001(c)). In addition, a 5-percent surtax is imposed upon cumulative taxable transfers between $10 million and $21,040,000, to phase out the benefits of the graduated rates and the unified credit (sec. 2001(c)(2)).[31]

Reasons for Change

The Committee believes that increasing the amount of the estate and gift tax unified credit will encourage saving, promote capital formation and entrepreneurial activity, and help to preserve existing family-owned farms and businesses. The Committee further believes that indexing the unified credit exemption equivalent amount for inflation is appropriate to reduce the transfer tax consequences that result from increases in asset value attributable solely to inflation.

Explanation of Provision

The bill increases the present-law unified credit beginning in 1998, from an effective exemption of $600,000 to an effective ex-

emption of $1,000,000 in 2007. The increase in the effective exemption is phased in according to the following schedule: the effective exemption is $650,000 for decedents dying and gifts made in 1998; $750,000 in 1999; $765,000 in 2000; $775,000 in 2001 through 2004; $800,000 in 2005; $825,000 in 2006; $1 million in 2007. After 2007, the effective exemption is indexed annually for inflation. The indexed exemption amount is rounded to the next lowest multiple of $10,000.

Conforming amendments to reflect the increased unified credit are made (1) to the 5-percent surtax to conform the phase out of the increased unified credit and graduated rates, (2) to the general filing requirements for an estate tax return under section 6018(a), and (3) to the amount of the unified credit allowed under section 2102(c)(3) with respect to nonresident aliens with U.S. situs property who are residents of certain treaty countries.

Effective Date

The provision is effective for decedents dying, and gifts made, after December 31, 1997. *2. INDEXING OF CERTAIN OTHER ESTATE AND GIFT TAX PROVISIONS]*

Present Law

Annual exclusion for gifts.— A taxpayer may exclude $10,000 of gifts of present interests in property made by an individual ($20,000 per married couple) to each donee during a calendar year (sec. 2503).

Special use valuation.— An executor may elect for estate tax purposes to value certain qualified real property used in farming or a closely-held trade or business at its current use value, rather than its "highest and best use" value (sec. 2032A). The max-

---

30. Prior to 1976, separate tax rate schedules applied to the gift tax and the estate tax.
31. Thus, if a taxpayer has made cumulative taxable transfers equaling $21,040,000 or more, his or her average

transfer tax rate is 55 percent. The phaseout has the effect of creating a 60-percent marginal transfer tax rate on transfers in the phaseout range.

imum reduction in value under such an election is $750,000.

Generation-skipping transfer ("GST") tax.— An individual is allowed an exemption from the GST tax of up to $1,000,000 for generation-skipping transfers made during life or at death (sec. 2631).

Installment payment of estate tax.— An executor may elect to pay the Federal estate tax attributable to an interest in a closely held business in installments over, at most, a 14-year period (sec. 6166). The tax on the first $1,000,000 in value of a closely-held business is eligible for a special 4-percent interest rate (sec. 6601(j)).

Reasons for Change

The Committee believes that it is appropriate to index for inflation the annual exclusion for gifts, the ceiling on special use valuation, the generation-skipping transfer tax exemption, and the ceiling on the value of a closely-held business eligible for the special low interest rate, to reduce the transfer tax consequences that result from increases in asset value attributable solely to inflation.

Explanation of Provision

The bill provides that, after 1998, the $10,000 annual exclusion for gifts, the $750,000 ceiling on special use valuation, the $1,000,000 generation-skipping transfer tax exemption, and the $1,000,000 ceiling on the value of a closely-held business eligible for the special low interest rate (as modified below), are indexed annually for inflation. Indexing of the annual exclusion is rounded to the next lowest multiple of $1,000 and indexing of the other amounts is rounded to the next lowest multiple of $10,000.

Effective Date

The proposal is effective for decedents dying, and gifts made, after December 31, 1998.

[Senate Report]

Explanation of Provision

The bill increases the present-law unified credit beginning in 1998, from an effective exemption of $600,000 to an effective ex-

emption of $1,000,000 in 2006. The increase in the effective exemption is phased in according to the following schedule: the effective exemption is $625,000 for decedents dying and gifts made in 1998; $640,000 in 1999; $660,000 in 2000; $675,000 in 2001; $725,000 in 2002; $750,000 in 2003; $800,000 in 2004; $900,000 in 2005; and $1 million in 2006. After 2006, the effective exemption is indexed annually for inflation. The indexed exemption amount is rounded to the next lowest multiple of $10,000.

Conforming amendments to reflect the increased unified credit are made (1) to the 5-percent surtax to conform the phase out of the increased unified credit and graduated rates, (2) to the general filing requirements for an estate tax return under section 6018(a), and (3) to the amount of the unified credit allowed under section 2102(c)(3) with respect to nonresident aliens with U.S. situs property who are residents of certain treaty countries.

[Conference Report]

Conference Agreement

The conference agreement increases the present-law unified credit beginning in 1998, from an effective exemption of $600,000 to an effective exemption of $1,000,000 in 2006. The increase in the effective exemption is phased in according to the following schedule: the effective exemption is $625,000 for decedents dying and gifts made in 1998; $650,000 in 1999; $675,000 in 2000 and 2001; $700,000 in 2002 and 2003; $850,000 in 2004; $950,000 in 2005; and $1 million in 2006 and thereafter. The conference does not index the effective exemption for inflation.

The conference agreement includes the conforming amendments made in the House bill and the Senate amendment.

Effective Date

The provision is effective for decedents dying, and gifts made, after December 31, 1997.

Senate Amendment

The Senate amendment is the same as the House Bill.

Conference Agreement

The conference agreement follows the House bill and the Senate amendment.

[¶ 5027]   Section 502.   Estate tax exclusion for qualified family-owned businesses.

(Code Sec. 2033A)

[Senate Report]

Present Law

There are no special estate tax rules for qualified family-owned businesses. All taxpayers are allowed a unified credit in computing the taxpayer's estate and gift tax, which effectively exempts a total of $600,000 in cumulative taxable transfers from the estate and gift tax (sec. 2010). An executor also may elect, under section 2032A, to value certain qualified real property used in farming or another qualifying closely-held trade or business at its current use value, rather than its highest and best use value (up to a maximum reduction of $750,000). In addition, an executor may elect to pay the Federal estate tax attributable to a qualified closely- held business in installments over, at most, a 14-year period (sec. 6166). The tax attributable to the first $1,000,000 in value of a closely-held business is eligible for a special 4-percent interest rate (sec. 6601(j)).

Reasons for Change

The Committee believes that a reduction in estate taxes for qualified family-owned businesses will protect and preserve family farms and other family-owned enterprises, and prevent the liquidation of such enterprises in order to pay estate taxes. The Committee further believes that the protection of family enterprises will preserve jobs and strengthen the communities in which such enterprises are located.

Explanation of Provision

The bill allows an executor to elect special estate tax treatment for qualified "family-owned business interests" if such interests comprise more than 50 percent of a decedent's estate and certain other requirements are met. In general, the provision excludes the first $1 million of value in qualified family-owned business interests from a decedent's taxable estate.

This new exclusion for qualified family-owned business interests is provided in addition to the unified credit (which presently effectively exempts $600,000 of taxable transfers from the estate and gift tax, and will be increased to an effective exemption of $1,000,000 of taxable transfers under other provisions of the bill), the special-use provisions of section 2032A (which permit the exclusion of up to $750,000 in value of a qualifying farm or other closely-held business from a decedent's estate), and the provisions of section 6166 (which provide for the installment payment of estate taxes attributable to closely held businesses).

Qualified family-owned business interests

For purposes of the bill, a qualified family-owned business interest is defined as any interest in a trade or business (regardless of the form in which it is held) with a principal place of business in the United States if ownership of the trade or business is held at least 50 percent by one family, 70 percent by two families, or 90 percent by three families, as long as the decedent's family owns at least 30 percent of the trade or business. Under the provision, members of an individual's family are defined using the same definition as is used for the special-use valuation rules of section 2032A, and thus include (1) the individual's spouse, (2) the individual's ancestors, (3) lineal descendants of the individual, of the individual's spouse, or of the individual's parents, and (4) the spouses of any such lineal descendants. For purposes of applying the ownership tests in the case of a corporation, the decedent and members of the decedent's family are required to own the requisite percentage of the total combined voting power of all classes of stock entitled to vote AND the requisite percentage of the total value of all shares of all classes of stock of the corporation. In the case of a partnership, the decedent and members of the decedent's family are required to own the requisite percentage of the capital interest, and the requisite percentage of the profits interest, in the partnership.

In the case of a trade or business that owns an interest in another trade or business (i.e., 'tiered entities"), special look- through rules apply. Each trade or business owned (directly or indirectly) by the decedent and members of the decedent's family is separately tested to determine whether that trade or business meets the requirements of a qualified family-owned business interest. In applying these tests, any interest that a trade or business owns in another trade or business is disregarded in determining whether the first trade or business is a qualified family-owned business interest. The value of any qualified family-owned business interest held by an entity is treated as being proportionately owned by or for the entity's partners, shareholders, or beneficiaries. In the case of a multi-tiered entity, such rules are sequentially applied to look through each separate tier of the entity.

For example, if a holding company owns interests in two other companies, each of the three entities will be separately tested under the qualified family-owned business interest rules. In determining whether the holding company is a qualified family-owned business interest, its ownership interest in the other two companies is disregarded. Even if the holding company itself does not qualify as a family-owned business interest, the other two companies still may qualify if the direct and indirect interests held by the decedent and his or her family members satisfy the requisite ownership percentages and other requirements of a qualified family-owned business interest. If either (or both) of the lower-tier entities qualify, the value of the qualified family-owned business interests owned by the holding company are treated as proportionately owned by the holding company's shareholders.

An interest in a trade or business does not qualify if the business's (or a related entity's) stock or securities were publicly-traded at any time within three years of the decedent's death. An interest in a trade or business also does not qualify if more than 35 percent of the adjusted ordinary gross income of the business for the year of the decedent's death was personal holding company income (as defined in section 543). This personal holding company restriction does not apply to banks or domestic building and loan associations.

The value of a trade or business qualifying as a family- owned business interest is reduced to the extent the business holds passive assets or excess cash or marketable securities. Under the bill, the value of qualified family-owned business interests does not include any cash or marketable securities in excess of the reasonably expected day-to-day working capital needs of the trade or business. For this purpose, it is intended that day-to-day working capital needs be determined based on a historical average of the business's working capital needs in the past, using an analysis similar to that set forth in Bardahl Mfg. Corp., 24 T.C.M. 1030 (1965). It is further intended that accumulations for capital acquisitions not be considered "working capital" for this purpose. The value of the qualified family-owned business interests also does not include certain other passive assets. For this purpose, passive assets include any assets that (a) produce dividends, interest, rents, royalties, annuities and certain other types of passive income (as described in sec. 543(a)); (b) are an interest in a trust, partnership or REMIC (as described in sec. 954(c)(1)(B)(ii)); (c) produce no income (as described in sec. 954(c)(1)(B)(iii)); (d) give rise to income from commodities transactions or foreign currency gains (as described in sec. 954(c)(1)(C) and (D)); (e) produce income equivalent to interest (as described in sec. 954(c)(1)(E)); or (f) produce income from notional principal contracts or payments in lieu of dividends (as described in new secs. 954(c)(1)(F) and (G), added elsewhere in the bill). In the case of a regular dealer in property, such property is not considered to produce passive income under these rules, and thus, is not considered to be a passive asset.

Qualifying estates

A decedent's estate qualifies for the special treatment only if the decedent was a U.S. citizen or resident at the time of death, and the aggregate value of the decedent's qualified family- owned business interests that are passed to qualified heirs exceeds 50 percent of the decedent's adjusted gross estate (the "50-percent liquidity test"). For this purpose, qualified heirs include any individual who has been actively employed by the trade or business for at least 10 years prior to the date of the decedent's death, and members of the decedent's family, If a qualified heir is not a citizen of the United States, any qualified family-owned business interest acquired by that heir must be held in a trust meeting requirements similar to those imposed on qualified domestic trusts (under present-law Sec. 2056A(a)), or through certain other security arrangements that meet the satisfaction of the Secretary. The 50- percent liquidity test generally is applied by adding all transfers of qualified family-owned business interests made by the decedent to qualified heirs at the time of the decedent's death, plus certain lifetime gifts of qualified family-owned business interests made to members of the decedent's family, and comparing this total to the decedent's adjusted gross estate. To the extent that a decedent held qualified family-owned business interests in more than one trade or business, all such interests are aggregated for purposes of applying the 50-percent liquidity test.

The 50-percent liquidity test is calculated using a ratio, the numerator and denominator of which are described below.

The numerator is determined by aggregating the value of all qualified family-owned business interests that are includible in the decedent's gross estate and are passed from the decedent to a qualified heir, plus any lifetime transfers of qualified business interests that are made by the decedent to members of the decedent's family (other than the decedent's spouse), provided such interests have been continuously held by members of the decedent's family and were not otherwise includible in the decedent's gross estate. For this purpose, qualified business interests transferred to members of the decedent's family during the decedent's lifetime are valued as of the date of such transfer. This amount is then reduced by all indebtedness of the estate, except for the following: (a) indebtedness on a qualified residence of the decedent (determined in accordance with the requirements for deduct-

ibility of mortgage interest set forth in section 163(h)(3)); (b) indebtedness incurred to pay the educational or medical expenses of the decedent, the decedent's spouse or the decedent's dependents; (c) other indebtedness of up to $10,000.

The denominator is equal to the decedent's gross estate, reduced by any indebtedness of the estate, and increased by the amount of the following transfers, to the extent not already included in the decedent's gross estate: (a) any lifetime transfers of qualified business interests that were made by the decedent to members of the decedent's family (other than the decedent's spouse), provided such interests have been continuously held by members of the decedent's family, plus (b) any other transfers from the decedent to the decedent's spouse that were made within 10 years of the date of the decedent's death, plus (c) any other transfers made by the decedent within three years of the decedent's death, except nontaxable transfers made to members of the decedent's family. The Secretary of Treasury is granted authority to disregard de minimis gifts. In determining the amount of gifts made by the decedent, any gift that the donor and the donor's spouse elected to have treated as a split gift (pursuant to sec. 2513) is treated as made one-half by each spouse for purposes of this provision.

Participation requirements

To qualify for the beneficial treatment provided under the bill, the decedent (or a member of the decedent's family) must have owned and materially participated in the trade or business for at least five of the eight years preceding the decedent's date of death. In addition, each qualified heir (or a member of the qualified heir's family) is required to materially participate in the trade or business for at least five years of any eight-year period within ten years following the decedent's death. For this purpose, "material participation" is defined as under present-law section 2032A (special use valuation) and the regulations promulgated thereunder. See, e.g., Treas. Reg. sec. 20.2032A-3. Under such regulations, no one factor is determinative of the presence of material participation and the uniqueness of the particular industry (e.g., timber, farming, manufacturing, etc.) must be considered.

Physical work and participation in management decisions are the principal factors to be considered. For example, an individual generally is considered to be materially participating in the business if he or she personally manages the business fully, regardless of the number of hours worked, as long as any necessary functions are performed.

If a qualified heir rents qualifying property to a member of the qualified heir's family on a net cash basis, and that family member materially participates in the business, the material participation requirement will be considered to have been met with respect to the qualified heir for purposes of this provision.

Recapture provisions

The benefit of the exclusions for qualified family-owned business interests are subject to recapture if, within 10 years of the decedent's death and before the qualified heir's death, one of the following "recapture events" occurs: (1) the qualified heir ceases to meet the material participation requirements (i.e., if neither the qualified heir nor any member of his or her family has materially participated in the trade or business for at least five years of any eight-year period); (2) the qualified heir disposes of any portion of his or her interest in the family-owned business, other than by a disposition to a member of the qualified heir's family or through a conservation contribution under section 170(h); (3) the principal place of business of the trade or business ceases to be located in the United States; or (4) the qualified heir loses U.S. citizenship. A qualified heir who loses U.S. citizenship may avoid such recapture by placing the qualified family-owned business assets into a trust meeting requirements similar to a qualified domestic trust (as described in present law section 2056A(a)), or through certain other security arrangements.

If one of the above recapture events occurs, an additional tax is imposed on the date of such event. As under section 2032A, each qualified heir is personally liable for the portion of the recapture tax that is imposed with respect to his or her interest in the qualified family-owned business. Thus, for example, if a brother and sister inherit a qualified family-owned business from their father, and only the sister materially participates in the business, her participation will cause both her and her brother to meet the material participation test. If she ceases to materially participate in the business within 10 years after her father's death (and the brother still does not materially participate), the sister and brother would both be liable for the recapture tax; that is, each would be liable for the recapture tax attributable to his or her interest.

The portion of the reduction in estate taxes that is recaptured would be dependent upon the number of years that the qualified heir (or members of the qualified heir's family) materially participated in the trade or business after the decedent's death. If the qualified heir (or his or her family members) materially participated in the trade or business after the decedent's death for less than six years, 100 percent of the reduction in estate taxes attributable to that heir's interest is recaptured; if the participation was for at least six years but less than seven years, 80 percent of the reduction in estate taxes is recaptured; if the participation was for at least seven years but less than eight years, 60 percent is recaptured; if the participation was for at least eight years but less than nine years, 40 percent is recaptured; and if the participation was for at least nine years but less than ten years, 20 percent of the reduction in estates taxes is recaptured. In general, there is no requirement that the qualified heir (or members of his or her family) continue to hold or participate in the trade or business more than 10 years after the decedent's death. As under present-law section 2032A, however, the 10-year recapture period may be extended for a period of up to two years if the qualified heir does not begin to use the property for a period of up to two years after the decedent's death.

If a recapture event occurs with respect to any qualified family-owned business interest (or portion thereof), the amount of reduction in estate taxes attributable to that interest is determined on a proportionate basis. For example, if the decedent's estate included $2 million in qualified family-owned business interests and $1 million of such interests received beneficial treatment under this proposal, one-half of the value of the interest disposed of is deemed to have received the benefits provided under this proposal.

Effective Date

The provision is effective with respect to the estates of decedents dying after December 31, 1997.

[Conference Report]

House Bill

No provision.

Conference Agreement

The conference agreement follows the Senate amendment, except that the exclusion for family-owned business interests may be taken only to the extent that the exclusion for family-owned business interests, plus the amount effectively exempted by the unified credit, does not exceed $1.3 million.

The conferees clarify that a sale or disposition, in the ordinary course of business, of assets such as inventory or a piece of equipment used in the business (e.g., the sale of crops or a tractor) would not result in recapture of the benefits of the qualified family-owned business exclusion.

[¶ 5029]   Section 504.   Estate tax recapture from cash leases of specially-valued property.

(Code Sec. 2032A)

[House Report]

Present Law

A Federal estate tax is imposed on the value of property passing at death. Generally, such property is included in the decedent's estate at its fair market value. Under section 2032A, the executor may elect to value certain "qualified real property" used in farming or other qualifying trade or business at its current use value rather than its highest and best use. If, after the special-use valuation election is made, the heir who acquired the real property ceases to use it in its qualified use within 10 years (15 years for individuals dying before 1982) of the decedent's death, an additional estate tax is imposed in order to "recapture" the benefit of the special-use valuation (sec. 2032A(c)).

Some courts have held that cash rental of specially-valued property after the death of the decedent is not a qualified use under section 2032A because the heirs no longer bear the financial risk of working the property, and, therefore, results in the imposition of the additional estate tax under section 2032A(c). See *Martin v. Commissioner,* 783 F.2d 81 (7th Cir. 1986) (cash lease to unrelated party not qualified use); *Williamson v. Commissioner,* 93 T.C. 242 (1989), aff'd, 974 F.2d 1525 (9th Cir. 1992) (cash lease to family member not a qualified use); *Fisher v. Commissioner,* 65 T.C.M. 2284 (1993) (cash lease to family member not a qualified use); cf. *Minter v. U.S.,* 19 F.3d 426 (8th Cir. 1994) (cash lease to family's farming corporation is qualified use); *Estate of Gavin v. U.S.,* 1997 U.S. App. Lexis 10383 (8th Cir. 1997) (heir's option to pay cash rent or 50 percent crop share is qualified use).

With respect to a decedent's surviving spouse, a special rule provides that the surviving spouse will not be treated as failing to use the property in a qualified use solely because the spouse rents the property to a member of the spouse's family on a net cash basis. (sec. 2032A(b)(5)). Under section 2032A, members of an individual's family include (1) the individual's spouse, (2) the individual's ancestors, (3) lineal descendants of the individual, of the individual's spouse, or of the individual's parents, and (4) the spouses of any such lineal descendants.

Reasons for Change

The Committee believes that cash leasing of farmland among family members is consistent with the purposes of the special-use valuation rules, which are intended to prevent family farms (and other qualifying businesses) from being liquidated to pay estate taxes in cases where members of the decedent's family continue to participate in the business.

Explanation of Provision

The bill provides that the cash lease of specially-valued real property by a lineal descendant of the decedent to a member of the lineal descendant's family, who continues to operate the farm or closely held business, does not cause the qualified use of such property to cease for purposes of imposing the additional estate tax under section 2032A(c).

Effective Date

The provision is effective for cash rentals occurring after December 31, 1976.

[¶ 5028]　Section 503.　Installment payments of estate tax attributable to closely-held businesses.

(Code Sec. 6166, 2053, 6601)

[House Report]

Present Law

In general, the Federal estate tax is due within nine months of a decedent's death. Under Code section 6166, an executor generally may elect to pay the estate tax attributable to an interest in a closely held business in installments over, at most, a 14-year period. If the election is made, the estate may pay only interest for the first four years, followed by up to 10 annual installments of principal and interest. Interest generally is imposed at the rate applicable to underpayments of tax under section 6621 (i.e., the Federal short-term rate plus 3 percentage points). Under section 6601(j), however, a special 4-percent interest rate applies to the amount of deferred estate tax attributable to the first $1,000,000 in value of the closely-held business.

To qualify for the installment payment election, the business must be an active trade or business and the value of the decedent's interest in the closely held business must exceed 35 percent of the decedent's adjusted gross estate. An interest in a closely held business includes: (1) any interest as a proprietor in a business carried on as a proprietorship; (2) any interest in a partnership carrying on a trade or business if the partnership has 15 or fewer partners, or if at least 20 percent of the partnership's assets are included in determining the decedent's gross estate; or (3) stock in a corporation if the corporation has 15 or fewer shareholders, or if at least 20 percent of the value of the voting stock is included in determining the decedent's gross estate.

[Conference Report]

Senate Amendment

The Senate amendment is the same as the House bill.

Conference Agreement

The conference agreement follows the House bill and the Senate amendment.

Reasons for Change

The Committee believes that the installment payment provisions need to be expanded in order to better address the liquidity problems of estates holding farms and closely held businesses, to prevent the liquidation of such businesses in order to pay estate taxes. The Committee further believes that the protection of closely held businesses will preserve jobs and strengthen the communities in which such businesses are located.

In addition, by eliminating the deductibility of interest paid on estate taxes deferred under section 6166 (and reducing the interest rate accordingly), the bill eliminates the need to file annual supplemental estate tax returns and make complex iterative computations to claim an estate tax deduction for interest paid.

Explanation of Provision

The bill extends the period for which Federal estate tax installments can be made under section 6166 to a maximum period of 24 years. If the election is made, the estate pays only interest for the first four years, followed by up to 20 annual installments of principal and interest.

In addition, the bill provides that no interest is imposed on the amount of deferred estate tax attributable to the first $1,000,000 in taxable value of the closely held business (i.e., the first $1,000,000 in value in excess of the effective exemption provided by the unified credit). Thus, for example, in 1998, when the unified credit is increased to provide an effective exemption of $650,000 (as described above), the amount of estate tax attributable to the value of the closely held business between $650,000 and $1,650,000 is eligible for the zero-percent interest rate.

The interest rate imposed on the amount of deferred estate tax attributable to the taxable value of the closely held business in excess of $1,000,000 is reduced to an amount equal to 45 percent of the rate applicable to underpayments of tax. The interest paid on estate taxes deferred under section 6166 is not deductible for estate or income tax purposes.

Effective Date

The provision is effective for decedents dying after December 31, 1997.

[Conference Report]

Senate Amendment

The Senate amendment is the same as the House bill.

Conference Agreement

The conference agreement reduces the 4-percent interest rate to 2 percent, and makes the interest paid on estate taxes deferred under section 6166 non-deductible for estate or income tax purposes. The 2-percent interest rate is imposed on the amount of deferred estate tax attributable to the first $1,000,000 in taxable value of the closely

held business (i.e., the first $1,000,000 in value in excess of the effective exemption provided by the unified credit and any other exclusions).[55] The interest rate imposed on the amount of deferred estate tax attributable to the taxable value of the closely held business in excess of $1,000,000 is reduced to an amount equal to 45 percent of the rate applicable to underpayments of tax.

The conference agreement does not include the provision that extends the repayment period to a maximum period of 24 years or the provision that provides a zero-percent interest rate for a portion of the deferred estate tax attributable to closely held businesses.

Effective Date

The provision is effective for decedents dying after December 31, 1997. Estates deferring estate tax under current law may make a one-time election to use the lower interest rates and forego the interest deduction for installments due after the date of the election (but such estates do not receive the benefit of the increase in the amount eligible for the 6601(j) interest rate- -i.e., only the amount that was previously eligible for the 4-percent rate would be eligible for the 2-percent rate).

[¶ 5030]   Section 505. Clarify eligibility for extension of time for payment of estate tax.

(Code Sec. 7479)

[House Report]

Present Law

In general, the Federal estate tax is due within nine months of a decedent's death. Under Code section 6166, an executor generally may elect to pay the estate tax attributable to an interest in a closely held business in installments over, at most, a 14-year period. If the election is made, the estate may pay only interest for the first four years, followed by up to 10 annual installments of principal and interest. To qualify for the installment payment election, the business must meet certain requirements. If

certain events occur during the repayment period (e.g., the closely held business is sold), full payment of all deferred estate taxes is required at that time.

Under present law, there is limited access to judicial review of disputes regarding initial or continuing eligibility for the deferral and installment election under section 6166. If the Commissioner determines that an estate was not initially eligible for deferral under section 6166, or has lost its eligibility for such deferral, the estate is required to pay the full amount of estate taxes asserted by the Commissioner as being owed in order to obtain judicial review of the Commissioner's determination.

---

55. The $1,000,000 threshold is indexed under other provisions of the bill.

were irrevocable as of March 1, 1984, section 643(f) applies only to contributions to corpus after that date.

Under section 644, if property is sold within two years of its contribution to a trust, the gain that would have been recognized had the contributor sold the property is taxed at the contributor's marginal tax rates. In effect, section 644 treats such gains as if the contributor had realized the gain and then transferred the net after-tax proceeds from the sale to the trust as corpus.

Sections 665 through 668 apply different rules to accumulation distributions from a foreign trust than to accumulation distributions from domestic trusts. If a foreign trust accumulates income, changes its situs so as to become a domestic trust, and then makes a distribution that is deemed to have been made in a year in which the trust was a foreign trust, the distribution is treated as a distribution from a foreign trust for purposes of the accumulation distribution rules. Rev. Rul. 91 6, 1991 1 C.B. 89.

Reasons for Change

The throwback rules and section 644 are intended to eliminate the potential tax reduction arising from taxation at the trust level, rather than the beneficiary or contributor level. When those provisions were enacted, a taxpayer could reduce his or her overall tax liability substantially by transferring property to one or more trusts, so that any income from the property would be taxed at lower income tax rates. In the Tax Reform Act of 1984, Congress curtailed the tax avoidance use of multiple trusts. Moreover, in the Tax Reform Act of 1986, Congress provided a new rate schedule for estates and trusts under which the maximum tax benefit of the graduated rate structure applicable to estates or trusts was reduced substantially to slightly more than $600 per

year for a trust or estate. (Because of indexing of the rate brackets, that benefit has increased to $845 per year per trust or estate.) The Committee has determined that the insignificant potential tax reduction available through the transfer of property to trust no longer warrants the complexity of the throwback rules and section 644.

Explanation of Provision

The bill exempts from the throwback rules amounts distributed by a domestic trust after the date of enactment. The provision also provides that precontribution gain on property sold by a domestic trust no longer is subject to section 644 (i.e., taxed at the contributor's marginal tax rates).

The treatment of foreign trusts, including the treatment of foreign trusts that become domestic trusts, remains unchanged.

Effective Date

The provision with respect to the throwback rules is effective for distributions made in taxable years beginning after the date of enactment. The modification to section 644 applies to sales or exchanges after the date of enactment.

[Conference Report]

Senate Amendment

No provision.

Conference Agreement

The conference agreement follows the House bill, except that the throwback rules continue to apply with respect to (a) foreign trusts, (b) domestic trusts that were once treated as foreign trusts (except as provided in Treasury regulations), and (c) domestic trusts created before March 1, 1984, that would be treated as multiple trusts under sec. 643(f) of the Code.

[¶ 5033]   Section 508.   Reduction in estate tax for certain land subject to permanent conservation easement.

(Code Sec. 2031, 1014, 2032A, 170)

[Senate Report]

Present Law

A deduction is allowed for estate and gift tax purposes for a contribution of a qualified real property interest to a charity (or other qualified organization) exclusively for conservation purposes (secs. 2055(f), 2522(d)). For this purpose, a qualified real property interest means the entire interest of the transferor in real property (other than certain mineral interests), a remainder interest in real property, or a perpetual restriction on the use of real property (sec. 170(h)). A "conservation purpose" is (1) preservation of land for outdoor recreation by, or the education of, the general public, (2) preservation of natural habitat, (3) preservation of open space for scenic enjoyment of the general public or pursuant to a governmental conservation policy, and (4) preservation of historically important land or certified historic structures. Also, a contribution will be treated as "exclusively for conservation purposes" only if the conservation purpose is protected in perpetuity.[33]

A donor making a qualified conservation contribution generally is not allowed to retain an interest in minerals which may be extracted or removed by any surface mining method. However, deductions for contributions of conservation interests satisfying all of the above requirements will be permitted if two conditions are satisfied. First, the surface and mineral estates in the property with respect to which the contribution is made must have been separated before June 13, 1976 (and remain so separated) and, second, the probability of surface mining on the property with respect to which a contribution is made must be so remote as to be negligible (sec. 170(h)(5)(B)).

The same definition of qualified conservation contributions also applies for purposes of determining whether such contributions qualify as charitable deductions for income tax purposes.

Reasons for Change

The Committee believes that a reduction in estate taxes for land subject to a qualified conservation easement will ease existing pressures to develop or sell off open spaces in order to raise funds to pay estate taxes, and will thereby help to preserve environmentally significant land.

Explanation of Provision

Reduction in estate taxes for certain land subject to permanent conservation easement

The provision allows an executor to elect to exclude from the taxable estate 40 percent of the value of any land subject to a qualified conservation easement that meets the following requirements: (1) the land is located within 25 miles of a metropolitan area (as defined by the Office of Management and Budget) or a national park or wilderness area, or within 10 miles of an Urban National Forest (as designated by the Forest Service of the U.S. Department of Agriculture); (2) the land has been owned by the decedent or a member of the decedent's family at all times during the three-year period ending on the date of the decedent's death; and (3) a qualified conservation contribution (within the meaning of section 170(h)) of a qualified real property interest (as generally defined in section 170(h)(2)(C)) was granted by the transferor or a member of his or her family. For purposes of the provision, preservation of a historically important land area or a certified historic structure does not qualify as a conservation purpose. To the extent that the value of such land is excluded from the taxable estate, the basis of such land acquired at death is a carryover basis (i.e., the basis is not stepped-up to its fair market value at death). Debt-financed property is not eligible for the exclusion.

The exclusion amount is calculated based on the value of the property after the conservation easement has been placed on the property. The exclusion from estate

---

33. A member of the transfer's family includes: (1) his or her ancestors; (2) his or her spouse; (3) a lineal descendant of the decedent, the decedent's spouse or the decedent's parents; and (4) the spouse of any of the foregoing lineal descendants.

taxes does not extend to the value of any development rights retained by the decedent or donor, although payment for estate taxes on retained development rights may be deferred for up to two years, or until the disposition of the property, whichever is earlier. For this purpose, retained development rights are any rights retained to use the land for any commercial purpose which is not subordinate to and directly supportive of farming purposes, as defined in section 6420 (e.g., tree farming, ranching, viticulture, and the raising of other agricultural or horticultural commodities).

Maximum benefit allowed

The 40-percent estate tax exclusion for land subject to a qualified conservation easement (described above) may be taken only to the extent that the total exclusion for qualified conservation easements, plus the exclusion for qualified family-owned business interests (described in C., above), does not exceed $1 million. The executor of an estate holding land subject to a qualified conservation easement and/or qualified family-owned business interests is required to designate which of the two benefits is being claimed with respect to each property on which a benefit is claimed.

If the value of the conservation easement is less than 30 percent of (a) the value of the land without the easement, reduced by (b) the value of any retained development rights, then the exclusion percentage is reduced. The reduction in the exclusion percentage is equal to two percentage points for each point that the above ratio falls below 30 percent. Thus, for example, if the value of the easement is 25 percent of the value of the land before the easement less the value of the retained development rights, the exclusion percentage is 30 percent (i.e., the 40 percent amount is reduced by twice the difference between 30 percent and 25 percent). Under this calculation, if the value of the easement is 10 percent or less of the value of the land before the easement less the value of the retained development rights, the exclusion percentage is equal to zero.

Treatment of land subject to a conservation easement for purposes of special-use valuation

The granting of a qualified conservation easement (as defined above) is not treated as a disposition triggering the recapture provisions of section 2032A. In addition, the existence of a qualified conservation easement does not prevent such property from subsequently qualifying for special-use valuation treatment under section 2032A.

Retained mineral interests

The provision also allows a charitable deduction (for income tax purposes or estate tax purposes) to taxpayers making a contribution of a permanent conservation easement on property where a mineral interest has been retained and surface mining is possible, but its probability is "so remote as to be negligible." Present law provides for a charitable deduction in such a case if the mineral interests have been separated from the land prior to June 13, 1976. The provision allows such a charitable deduction to be taken regardless of when the mineral interests had been separated.

Effective Date

The estate tax exclusion applies to decedents dying after December 31, 1997. The rules with respect to the treatment of conservation easements under section 2032A and with respect to retained mineral interests are effective for easements granted after December 31, 1997.

[Conference Report]

House Bill

No provision.

Conference Agreement

The conference agreement follows the Senate amendment, except that the maximum exclusion for land subject to a qualified conservation easement is limited to $100,000 in 1998, $200,000 in 1999, $300,000 in 2000, $400,000 in 2001, and $500,000 in 2002 and thereafter. The exclusion for land subject to a qualified conservation easement may be taken in addition to the maximum exclusion for qualified family-owned business interests (i.e., there is no coordination between the two provisions).

The conference agreement provides that de minimis commercial recreational activity that is consistent with the conservation purpose, such as the granting of hunting and fishing licenses, will not cause the property to fail to qualify under this provision. It is anticipated that the Secretary of the Treasury will provide guidance as to the definition of "de minimis" activities. In addition, the conference agreement makes technical modifications (a) to provide that the definition of farming for purposes of this provision is the same as the definition set forth in section 2032A(e)(5), and (b) to clarify that a post-mortem conservation easement may be placed on the property, as long as the easement has been made no later than the date of the election.

The conferees clarify that debt-financed property is eligible for this provision to the extent of the net equity in the property. For example, if a $1 million property is subject to an outstanding debt balance of $100,000, it is treated in the same manner as a $900,000 property that is not debt-financed.

[¶ 5034]   Section 511.   Modification of generation-skipping transfer tax for transfers to individuals with deceased parents.

(Code Sec. 2651, 2612)

[House Report]

Present Law

Under the "predeceased parent exception", a direct skip transfer to a transferor's grandchild is not subject to the generation skipping transfer ("GST") tax if the child of the transferor who was the grandchild's parent is deceased at the time of the transfer (sec. 2612(c)(2)). This "predeceased parent exception" to the GST tax is not applicable to (1) transfers to collateral heirs, e.g., grandnieces or grandnephews, or (2) taxable terminations or taxable distributions.

Reasons for Change

The Committee believes that a transfer to a collateral relative whose parent is dead should qualify for the predeceased parent exception in situations where the transferor decedent has no lineal heirs, because no motive or opportunity to avoid transfer tax exists. For similar reasons, the Committee believes that transfers to trusts should be permitted to qualify for the predeceased parent exclusion where the parent of the beneficiary is dead at the time that the transfer is first subject to estate or gift tax. The Committee also understands that this treatment will remove a present law impediment to the establishment of charitable lead trusts.

Explanation of Provision

The bill extends the predeceased parent exception to transfers to collateral heirs, provided that the decedent has no living lineal descendants at the time of the transfer. For example, the exception would apply to a transfer made by an individual (with no living lineal heirs) to a grandniece where the transferor's nephew or niece who is the parent of the grandniece is deceased at the time of the transfer.

In addition, the bill extends the predeceased parent exception (as modified by the change in the preceding paragraph) to taxable terminations and taxable distributions, provided that the parent of the relevant beneficiary was dead at the earliest time that the transfer (from which the beneficiary's interest in the property was established) was subject to estate or gift tax. For example, where a trust was established to pay an annuity to a charity for a term for years with a remainder interest granted to a grandson, the termination of the term for years would not be a taxable termination subject to the GST tax if the grandson's parent (who is the son or daughter of the transferor) is deceased at the time the trust was created and the transfer creating the trust was subject to estate or gift tax.

Effective Date

The provision is effective for generation skipping transfers occurring after December 31, 1997.

[Conference Report]

Senate Amendment

The Senate amendment is the same as the House bill.

Conference Agreement

The conference agreement follows the House bill and the Senate amendment.

[¶ 5036]   Section 601.   Research tax credit.

(Code Sec. 41)

[House Report]

Present Law

General rule

Section 41 provides for a research tax credit equal to 20 percent of the amount by which a taxpayer's qualified research expenditures for a taxable year exceeded its base amount for that year. The research tax credit expired and generally will not apply to amounts paid or incurred after May 31, 1997.[34]

A 20-percent research tax credit also applied to the excess of (1) 100 percent of corporate cash expenditures (including grants or contributions) paid for basic research conducted by universities (and certain nonprofit scientific research organizations) over (2) the sum of (a) the greater of two minimum basic research floors plus (b) an amount reflecting any decrease in nonresearch giving to universities by the corporation as compared to such giving during a fixed-base period, as adjusted for inflation. This separate credit computation is commonly referred to as the "university basic research credit" (see sec. 41(e)).

Computation of allowable credit

Except for certain university basic research payments made by corporations, the research tax credit applies only to the extent that the taxpayer's qualified research expenditures for the current taxable year exceed its base amount. The base amount for the current year generally is computed by multiplying the taxpayer's "fixed-base percentage" by the average amount of the taxpayer's gross receipts for the four preceding

years. If a taxpayer both incurred qualified research expenditures and had gross receipts during each of at least three years from 1984 through 1988, then its "fixed-base percentage" is the ratio that its total qualified research expenditures for the 1984–1988 period bears to its total gross receipts for that period (subject to a maximum ratio of .16). All other taxpayers (so-called "start-up firms") are assigned a fixed-base percentage of 3 percent.[35]

In computing the credit, a taxpayer's base amount may not be less than 50 percent of its current-year qualified research expenditures.

To prevent artificial increases in research expenditures by shifting expenditures among commonly controlled or otherwise related entities, research expenditures and gross receipts of the taxpayer are aggregated with research expenditures and gross receipts of certain related persons for purposes of computing any allowable credit (sec. 41(f)(1)). Special rules apply for computing the credit when a major portion of a business changes hands, under which qualified research expenditures and gross receipts for periods prior to the change of ownership of a trade or business are treated as transferred with the trade or business that gave rise to those expenditures and receipts for purposes of recomputing a taxpayer's fixed-base percentage (sec. 41(f)(3)).

Alternative incremental research credit regime

As part of the Small Business Job Protection Act of 1996, taxpayers are allowed to elect an alternative incremental research credit regime. If a taxpayer elects to be subject to this alternative regime, the taxpayer

---

34. When originally enacted, the research tax credit applied to qualified expenses incurred after June 30, 1981. The credit was modified several times and was extended through June 30, 1995. The credit later was extended for the period July 1, 1996, through May 31, 1997 (with a special 11-month extension for taxpayers that elect to be subject to the alternative incremental research credit regime).

35. The Small Business Job Protection Act of 1996 expanded the definition of "start-up firms" under section 41(c)(3)(B)(I) to include any firm if the first taxable year in which such firm had both gross receipts and qualified research expenses began after 1983.

is assigned a three-tiered fixed-base percentage (that is lower than the fixed-base percentage otherwise applicable under present law) and the credit rate likewise is reduced. Under the alternative credit regime, a credit rate of 1.65 percent applies to the extent that a taxpayer's current-year research expenses exceed a base amount computed by using a fixed-base percentage of 1 percent (i.e., the base amount equals 1 percent of the taxpayer's average gross receipts for the four preceding years) but do not exceed a base amount computed by using a fixed-base percentage of 1.5 percent. A credit rate of 2.2 percent applies to the extent that a taxpayer's current-year research expenses exceed a base amount computed by using a fixed-base percentage of 1.5 percent but do not exceed a base amount computed by using a fixed-base percentage of 2 percent. A credit rate of 2.75 percent applies to the extent that a taxpayer's current-year research expenses exceed a base amount computed by using a fixed-base percentage of 2 percent. An election to be subject to this alternative incremental credit regime may be made only for a taxpayer's first taxable year beginning after June 30, 1996, and before July 1, 1997, and such an election applies to that taxable year and all subsequent years (in the event that the credit subsequently is extended by Congress) unless revoked with the consent of the Secretary of the Treasury. If a taxpayer elects the alternative incremental research credit regime for its first taxable year beginning after June 30, 1996, and before July 1, 1997, then all qualified research expenses paid or incurred during the first 11 months of such taxable year are treated as qualified research expenses for purposes of computing the taxpayer's credit.

Eligible expenditures

Qualified research expenditures eligible for the research tax credit consist of: (1) "in-house" expenses of the taxpayer for wages and supplies attributable to qualified research; (2) certain time-sharing costs for computer use in qualified research; and (3) 65 percent of amounts paid by the taxpayer for qualified research conducted on the taxpayer's behalf (so-called "contract research expenses").[36]

To be eligible for the credit, the research must not only satisfy the requirements of present-law section 174 (described below) but must be undertaken for the purpose of discovering information that is technological in nature, the application of which is intended to be useful in the development of a new or improved business component of the taxpayer, and must pertain to functional aspects, performance, reliability, or quality of a business component. Research does not qualify for the credit if substantially all of the activities relate to style, taste, cosmetic, or seasonal design factors (sec. 41(d)(3)). In addition, research does not qualify for the credit if conducted after the beginning of commercial production of the business component, if related to the adaptation of an existing business component to a particular customer's requirements, if related to the duplication of an existing business component from a physical examination of the component itself or certain other information, or if related to certain efficiency surveys, market research or development, or routine quality control (sec. 41(d)(4)).

Expenditures attributable to research that is conducted outside the United States do not enter into the credit computation. In addition, the credit is not available for research in the social sciences, arts, or humanities, nor is it available for research to the extent funded by any grant, contract, or otherwise by another person (or governmental entity).

Relation to deduction

Under section 174, taxpayers may elect to deduct currently the amount of certain research or experimental expenditures incurred in connection with a trade or business, notwithstanding the general rule that business expenses to develop or create an asset that has a useful life extending beyond the current year must be capitalized. However, deductions allowed to a taxpayer

---

36. Under a special rule enacted as part of the Small Business Job Protection Act of 1996, 75 percent of amounts paid to a research consortium for qualified research is treated as qualified research expenses eligible for the research credit (rather than 65 percent under the general rule under section 41(b)(3) governing contract research expenses) if (1) Such research consortium is a tax-exempt organization that is described in section 501(c)(3) (other than a private foundation) or section 501(c)(6) and is organized and operated primarily to conduct scientific research, and (2) such qualified research is conducted by the consortium on behalf of the taxpayer and one or more persons not related to the taxpayer.

under section 174 (or any other section) are reduced by an amount equal to 100 percent of the taxpayer's research tax credit determined for the taxable year. Taxpayers may alternatively elect to claim a reduced research tax credit amount under section 41 in lieu of reducing deductions otherwise allowed (sec. 280C(c)(3)).

Reasons for Change

Businesses may not find it profitable to invest in some research activities because of the difficulty in capturing the full benefits from the research. Costly technological advances made by one firm are often cheaply copied by its competitors. A research tax credit can help promote investment in research, so that research activities undertaken approach the optimal level for the overall economy. Therefore, the Committee believes that, in order to encourage research activities, it is appropriate to reinstate the research tax credit.

Explanation of Provision

The research tax credit is extended for 19 months—i.e., generally for the period June 1, 1997, through December 31, 1998.

Under the provision, taxpayers are permitted to elect the alternative incremental research credit regime under section 41(c)(4) for any taxable year beginning after June 30, 1996, and such election will apply to that taxable year and all subsequent taxable years unless revoked with the consent of the Secretary of the Treasury.

Effective Date

The provision generally is effective for qualified research expenditures paid or incurred during the period June 1, 1997, through December 31, 1998.

A special rule provides that, notwithstanding the general termination date for the research credit of December 31, 1998, if a taxpayer elects to be subject to the alternative incremental research credit regime for its first taxable year beginning after June 30, 1996, and before July 1,1997, the alternative incremental research credit will be available during the entire 30-month period beginning with the first month of such taxa-

ble year—i.e., the equivalent of the 11-month extension provided for by the Small Business Job Protection Act of 1996 plus an additional 19-month extension provided for by this bill. However, to prevent taxpayers from effectively obtaining more than 30-months of research credits from the Small Business Job Protection Act of 1996 and this bill, the 30-month period for taxpayers electing the alternative incremental research credit regime is reduced by the number of months (if any) after June 1996 with respect to which the taxpayer claimed research credit amounts under the regular, 20-percent research credit rules.

[Senate Report]

Senate Amendment

The research tax credit is extended for 24 months—i.e., generally for the period June 1, 1997, through May 31, 1999.

Effective Date

The provision generally is effective for qualified research expenditures paid or incurred during the period June 1, 1997, through December 31, 1999.

A special rule provides that, notwithstanding the general termination date for the research credit of December 31, 1999, if a taxpayer elects to be subject to the alternative incremental research credit regime for its first taxable year beginning after June 30, 1996, and before July 1, 1997, the alternative incremental research credit will be available during the entire 42-month period beginning with the first month of such taxable year — i.e., the equivalent of the 11-month extension provided for by the Small Business Job Protection Act of 1996 PLUS an additional 31-month extension provided for by this bill. However, to prevent taxpayers from effectively obtaining more than 42-months of research credits from the Small Business Job Protection Act of 1996 and this bill, the 42-month period for taxpayers electing the alternative incremental research credit regime is reduced by the number of months (if any) after June 1996 with respect to which the taxpayer claimed research credit amounts under the regular, 20-percent research credit rules.

[Conference Report]

Conference Agreement

Under the conference agreement, the research tax credit is extended for 13 months—i.e., generally for the period June 1, 1997, through June 30, 1998.

Under the provision, taxpayers are permitted to elect the alternative incremental research credit regime under section 41(c)(4) for any taxable year beginning after June 30, 1996, and such election will apply to that taxable year and all subsequent taxable years unless revoked with the consent of the Secretary of the Treasury.

Effective Date

The provision generally is effective for qualified research expenditures paid or incurred during the period June 1, 1997, through June 30, 1998. A special rule provides that, notwithstanding the general termination date for the research credit of June 30, 1998, if a taxpayer elects to be subject to the alternative incremental research credit regime for its first taxable year beginning after June 30, 1996, and before July 1, 1997, the alternative incremental research credit will b e available during the entire 24-month period beginning with the first month of such taxable year—i.e., the equivalent of the 11-month extension provided for by the Small Business Job Protection Act of 1996 plus an additional 13-month extension provided for by the conference agreement. However, to prevent taxpayers from effectively obtaining more than 24-months of research credits from the Small Business Job Protection Act of 1996 and this bill, the 24-month period for taxpayers electing the alternative incremental research credit regime is reduced by the number of months (if any) after June 1996 with respect to which the taxpayer claimed research credit amounts under the regular, 20- percent research credit rules.

[¶ 5037]   Section 602.   Contributions of stock to private foundations.

(Code Sec. 170)

[House Report]

Present Law

In computing taxable income, a taxpayer who itemizes deductions generally is allowed to deduct the fair market value of property contributed to a charitable organization.[37] However, in the case of a charitable contribution of short-term gain, inventory, or other ordinary income property, the amount of the deduction generally is limited to the taxpayer's basis in the property. In the case of a charitable contribution of tangible personal property, the deduction is limited to the taxpayer's basis in such property if the use by the recipient charitable organization is unrelated to the organization's tax-exempt purpose.[38]

In cases involving contributions to a private foundation (other than certain private operating foundations), the amount of the deduction is limited to the taxpayer's basis in the property. However, under a special rule contained in section 170(e)(5), taxpayers are allowed a deduction equal to the fair market value of "qualified appreciated stock" contributed to a private foundation prior to May 31, 1997.[39] Qualified appreciated stock is defined as publicly traded stock which is capital gain property. The fair-market-value deduction for qualified appreciated stock donations applies only to the extent that total donations made by the do-

---

37. The amount of the deduction allowable for a taxable year with respect to a charitable contribution may be reduced depending on the type of property contributed, the type of charitable organization to which the property is contributed, and the income of the taxpayer (secs. 170(b) and 170(e)).

38. As part of the Omnibus Budget Reconciliation Act of 1993, Congress eliminated the treatment of contributions of appreciated property (real, personal, and intangible) as a tax preference for alternative minimum tax (AMT) purposes. Thus, if a taxpayer makes a gift to charity of property (other than short-term gain, inventory, or other ordinary income property, or gifts to pri-

vate foundations) that is real property, intangible property, or tangible personal property the use of which is related to the donee's tax-exempt purpose, the taxpayer is allowed to claim the same fair-market-value deduction for both regular tax and AMT purposes (subject to present-law percentage limitations).

39. The special rule contained in section 170(e)(5), which was originally enacted in 1984, expired January 1, 1995. The Small Business Job Protection Act of 1996 reinstated the rule for 11 months—for contributions of qualified appreciated stock made to private foundations during the period July 1, 1996, through May 31, 1997.

nor to private foundations of stock in a particular corporation did not exceed 10 percent of the outstanding stock of that corporation. For this purpose, an individual is treated as making all contributions that were made by any member of the individual's family.

Reasons for Change

The Committee believes that, to encourage donations to charitable private foundations, it is appropriate to extend the rule that allows a fair market value deduction for certain gifts of appreciated stock to private foundations.

Explanation of Provision

The bill extends the special rule contained in section 170(e)(5) for contributions of qualified appreciated stock made to private foundations during the period June 1, 1997, through December 31, 1998.

Effective Date

The provision is effective for contributions of qualified appreciated stock to private foundations made during the period June 1, 1997, through December 31, 1998.

[Conference Report]

Senate Amendment

The Senate amendment extends the special rule contained in section 170(e)(5) for contributions of qualified appreciated stock made to private foundations during the period June 1, 1997, through May 31, 1999.

Effective Date

The provision is effective for contributions of qualified appreciated stock to private foundations made during the period June 1, 1997, through May 31, 1999.

Conference Agreement

The conference agreement provides that the special rule contained in section 170(e)(5) is extended for the period June 1, 1997, through June 30, 1998. The provision is effective for contributions of qualified appreciated stock to private foundations made during the period June 1, 1997, through June 30, 1998.

[¶ 5038]   Section 603.   Work opportunity tax credit.

(Code Sec. 51)

[C. Work Opportunity Tax Credit (sec. 603 of the bill and sec. 51 of the Code) House Report]

Present Law

In general

The work opportunity tax credit is available on an elective basis for employers hiring individuals from one or more of seven targeted groups. The credit generally is equal to 35 percent of qualified wages. Qualified wages consist of wages attributable to service rendered by a member of a targeted group during the one-year period beginning with the day the individual begins work for the employer. For a vocational rehabilitation referral, however, the period will begin on the day the individual begins work for the employer on or after the beginning of the individual's vocational rehabilitation plan as under prior law.

Generally, no more than $6,000 of wages during the first year of employment is permitted to be taken into account with respect to any individual. Thus, the maximum credit per individual is $2,100. With respect to qualified summer youth employees, the maximum credit is 35 percent of up to $3,000 of qualified first-year wages, for a maximum credit of $1,050.

The deduction for wages is reduced by the amount of the credit. Also, the credit does not reduce alternative minimum tax (AMT) liability.

Targeted groups eligible for the credit

(1) Families receiving AFDC

An eligible recipient is an individual certified by the designated local employment agency as being a member of a family eligible to receive benefits under AFDC or its successor program for a period of at least nine months part of which is during the 9-month period ending on the hiring date. For these purposes, members of the family are defined to include only those individuals taken into account for purposes of determining eligibility for the AFDC or its successor program.

(2) Qualified ex-felon

A qualified ex-felon is an individual certified as: (1) having been convicted of a felony under any State or Federal law, (2) being a member of a family that had an income during the six months before the earlier of the date of determination or the hiring date which on an annual basis is 70 percent or less of the Bureau of Labor Statistics lower living standard, and (3) having a hiring date within one year of release from prison or date of conviction.

(3) High-risk-youth

A high-risk youth is an individual certified as being at least 18 but not 25 on the hiring date and as having a principal place of abode within an empowerment zone or enterprise community (as defined under Subchapter U of the Internal Revenue Code). Qualified wages will not include wages paid or incurred for services performed after the individual moves outside an empowerment zone or enterprise community.

(4) Vocational rehabilitation referral

Vocational rehabilitation referrals are those individuals who have a physical or mental disability that constitutes a substantial handicap to employment and who have been referred to the employer while receiving, or after completing, vocational rehabilitation services under an individualized, written rehabilitation plan under a State plan approved under the Rehabilitation Act of 1973 or under a rehabilitation plan for veterans carried out under Chapter 31 of Title 38, U.S. Code. Certification will be provided by the designated local employment agency upon assurances from the vocational rehabilitation agency that the employee has met the above conditions.

(5) Qualified summer youth employee

Qualified summer youth employees are individuals: (1) who perform services during any 90-day period between May 1 and September 15, (2) who are certified by the des-

ignated local agency as being 16 or 17 years of age on the hiring date, (3) who have not been an employee of that employer before, and (4) who are certified by the designated local agency as having a principal place of abode within an empowerment zone or enterprise community (as defined under Subchapter U of the Internal Revenue Code). As with high-risk youths, no credit is available on wages paid or incurred for service performed after the qualified summer youth moves outside of an empowerment zone or enterprise community. If, after the end of the 90-day period, the employer continues to employ a youth who was certified during the 90-day period as a member of another targeted group, the limit on qualified first-year wages will take into account wages paid to the youth while a qualified summer youth employee.

(6) Qualified Veteran

A qualified veteran is a veteran who is a member of a family certified as receiving assistance under: (1) AFDC for a period of at least nine months part of which is during the 12-month period ending on the hiring date, or (2) a food stamp program under the Food Stamp Act of 1977 for a period of at least three months part of which is during the 12-month period ending on the hiring date. For these purposes, members of a family are defined to include only those individuals taken into account for purposes of determining eligibility for: (i) the AFDC or its successor program, and (ii) a food stamp program under the Food Stamp Act of 1977, respectively.

Further, a qualified veteran is an individual who has served on active duty (other than for training) in the Armed Forces for more than 180 days or who has been discharged or released from active duty in the Armed Forces for a service-connected disability. However, any individual who has served for a period of more than 90 days during which the individual was on active duty (other than for training) is not an eligible employee if any of this active duty occurred during the 60-day period ending on the date the individual was hired by the employer. This latter rule is intended to prevent employers who hire current members of the armed services (or those departed from service within the last 60 days) from receiving the credit.

(7) Families receiving Food Stamps

An eligible recipient is an individual aged 18 but not 25 certified by a designated local employment agency as being a member of a family receiving assistance under a food stamp program under the Food Stamp Act of 1977 for a period of at least six months ending on the hiring date. In the case of families that cease to be eligible for food stamps under section 6(o) of the Food Stamp Act of 1977, the six-month requirement is replaced with a requirement that the family has been receiving food stamps for at least three of the five months ending on the date of hire. For these purposes, members of the family are defined to include only those individuals taken into account for purposes of determining eligibility for a food stamp program under the Food Stamp Act of 1977.

Minimum employment period

No credit is allowed for wages paid unless the eligible individual is employed by the employer for at least 180 days (20 days in the case of a qualified summer youth employee) or 400 hours (120 hours in the case of a qualified summer youth employee).

Expiration date

The credit is effective for wages paid or incurred to a qualified individual who begins work for an employer after September 30, 1996, and before October 1, 1997.

Reasons for Change

The Committee believes that this short-term program with modifications will provide the Congress and the Treasury and Labor Departments an opportunity to assess fully the operation and effectiveness of the credit as a hiring incentive. It will also extend application of the credit to a larger group of eligible individuals pending that evaluation.

Explanation of Provision

The bill extends for one year the work opportunity tax credit and makes four modifications: (1) the minimum employment period is reduced to 120 hours, (2) the credit

percentage is modified so that the percentage is 25% for the first 400 hours and 40% thereafter (assuming the minimum employment period is satisfied with respect to that employee), (3) an otherwise eligible member of a family receiving AFDC benefits satisfies the credit requirements if the family has received AFDC benefits for any 9-month period during the 18-month period ending on the hiring date (this expansion applies whether or not the individual is a qualified veteran), and (4) the credit is allowed against the AMT.

Effective Date

Generally the provisions that extend the work opportunity tax credit and make other modifications to the credit are effective for wages paid or incurred to qualified individuals who begin work for the employer after September 30, 1997, and before October 1, 1998. The provision allowing the credit against the AMT is effective for taxable years beginning after December 31, 1997.

[Conference Report]

Senate Amendment

Extension

The Senate amendment provides a 20-month extension of the work opportunity tax credit.

Targeted categories

Same as the House bill, except the Senate amendment adds SSI beneficiaries as a new category of workers for which the credit is available.

Minimum employment period

Same as the House bill.

Credit percentage

Same as the House bill.

Alternative minimum tax (AMT)

No provision.

Effective Date

The provision is effective for wages paid or incurred to qualified individuals who begin work for the employer after September 30, 1997, and before June 1, 1999.

Conference Agreement

Extension

The conference agreement provides for a 9-month extension of the work opportunity tax credit.

Targeted categories

The conference agreement follows the Senate amendment.

Minimum employment period

The conference agreement follows the House bill and the Senate amendment.

Credit percentage

The conference agreement follows the House bill and the Senate amendment.

Alternative minimum tax (AMT)

The conference agreement does not include the House bill provision.

Effective Date

The conference agreement is generally effective for wages paid to qualified individuals who begin work for an employer after September 30, 1997, and before July 1, 1998.

[¶ 5039]   Section 604.   Orphan drug tax credit.

(Code Sec. 45C)

[d. orphan drug tax credit (sec. 604 of the bill and sec. 45c of the code) House Report]

Present Law

A 50-percent nonrefundable tax credit is allowed for qualified clinical testing expenses incurred in testing of certain drugs for rare diseases or conditions, generally referred to as "orphan drugs." Qualified testing expenses are costs incurred to test an orphan drug after the drug has been approved for human testing by the Food and Drug Administration ("FDA") but before the drug has been approved for sale by the FDA. A rare disease or condition is defined as one that (1) affects less than 200,000 persons in the United States, or (2) affects more than 200,000 persons, but for which there is no reasonable expectation that businesses could recoup the costs of developing a drug for such disease or condition from U.S. sales of the drug. These rare diseases and conditions include Huntington's disease, myoclonus, ALS (Lou Gehrig's disease), Tourette's syndrome, and Duchenne's dystrophy (a form of muscular dystrophy).

As with other general business credits (sec. 38), taxpayers are allowed to carry back unused credits to three years preceding the year the credit is earned (but not to a taxable year ending before July 1, 1996)

and to carry forward unused credits to 15 years following the year the credit is earned. The credit cannot be used to offset a taxpayer's alternative minimum tax liability.

The orphan drug tax credit expired and does not apply to expenses paid or incurred after May 31, 1997.[40]

Reasons for Change

In order to encourage the socially optimal level of research to develop drugs to treat rare diseases and conditions—and because the research and clinical testing of such drugs often must be conducted over several years—the Committee believes that the orphan drug tax credit should be permanently extended.

Explanation of Provision

The orphan drug tax credit provided for by section 45C is permanently extended.

Effective Date

The provision is effective for qualified clinical testing expenses paid or incurred after May 31, 1997.

[Conference Report]

Senate Amendment

The Senate amendment is the same as the House bill.

---

40. The orphan drug tax credit originally was enacted in 1983 and was extended on several occasions. The credit expired on December 31, 1994, and later was reinstated for the period July 1, 1996, through May 31, 1997.

Conference Agreement

The conference agreement follows the House bill and Senate amendment—i.e., the

[¶ 5040]   Section 701. District of Columbia tax incentives.

(Code Sec. 1400, 1400A, 1400B, 1400C)

[House Report]

Present Law

Empowerment zones and enterprise communities

In general

Pursuant to the Omnibus Budget Reconciliation Act of 1993 (OBRA 1993), the Secretaries of the Department of Housing and Urban Development (HUD) and the Department of Agriculture designated a total of nine empowerment zones and 95 enterprise communities on December 21, 1994. As required by law, six empowerment zones are located in urban areas (with aggregate population for the six designated urban empowerment zones limited to 750,000) and three empowerment zones are located in rural areas.[41] Of the enterprise communities, 65 are located in urban areas and 30 are located in rural areas (sec. 1391). Designated empowerment zones and enterprise communities were required to satisfy certain eligibility criteria, including specified poverty rates and population and geographic size limitations (sec. 1392). Portions of the District of Columbia were designated as an enterprise community.

The following tax incentives are available for certain businesses located in empowerment zones: (1) an annual 20-percent wage credit for the first $15,000 of wages paid to a zone resident who works in the zone; (2) an additional $20,000 of expensing under Code section 179 for "qualified zone property" placed in service by an "enterprise zone business" (accordingly, certain businesses operating in empowerment zones are allowed up to $38,000 of expensing for 1997; the allowable amount will increase to

orphan drug tax credit is permanently extended.

$38,500 for 1998); and (3) special tax-exempt financing for certain zone facilities (described in more detail below).

The 95 enterprise communities are eligible for the special tax-exempt financing benefits but not the other tax incentives available in the nine empowerment zones. In addition to these tax incentives, OBRA 1993 provided that Federal grants would be made to designated empowerment zones and enterprise communities.

The tax incentives for empowerment zones and enterprise communities generally will be available during the period that the designation remains in effect, i.e., a 10-year period.

Definition of "qualified zone property"

Present-law section 1397C defines "qualified zone property" as depreciable tangible property (including buildings), provided that: (1) the property is acquired by the taxpayer (from an unrelated party) after the zone or community designation took effect; (2) the original use of the property in the zone or community commences with the taxpayer; and (3) substantially all of the use of the property is in the zone or community in the active conduct of a trade or business by the taxpayer in the zone or community. In the case of property which is substantially renovated by the taxpayer, however, the property need not be acquired by the taxpayer after zone or community designation or originally used by the taxpayer within the zone or community if, during any 24-month period after zone or community designation, the additions to the taxpayer's basis in the property exceed the greater of 100 percent of the taxpayer's basis in the property at the beginning of the period, or $5,000.

---

41. The six designated urban empowerment zones are located in New York City, Chicago, Atlanta, Detroit, Baltimore, and Philadelphia-Camden (New Jersey). The three designated rural empowerment zones are located in Kentucky Highlands (Clinton, Jackson, and Wayne counties, Kentucky), Mid-Delta Mississippi (Bolivar, Holmes, Humphreys, Leflore counties, Mississippi), an Rio Grande Valley Texas (Cameron, Hidalgo, Starr, and Willacy counties, Texas).

Definition of "enterprise zone business"

Present-law section 1397B defines the term "enterprise zone business" as a corporation or partnership (or proprietorship) if for the taxable year: (1) the sole trade or business of the corporation or partnership is the active conduct of a qualified business within an empowerment zone or enterprise community; (2) at least 80 percent of the total gross income is derived from the active conduct of a "qualified business" within a zone or community; (3) substantially all of the business' tangible property is used within a zone or community; (4) substantially all of the business' intangible property is used in, and exclusively related to, the active conduct of such business; (5) substantially all of the services performed by employees are performed within a zone or community; (6) at least 35 percent of the employees are residents of the zone or community; and (7) no more than five percent of the average of the aggregate unadjusted bases of the property owned by the business is attributable to (a) certain financial property, or (b) collectibles not held primarily for sale to customers in the ordinary course of an active trade or business.

A "qualified business" is defined as any trade or business other than a trade or business that consists predominantly of the development or holding of intangibles for sale or license.[42]   In addition, the leasing of real property that is located within the empowerment zone or community to others is treated as a qualified business only if (1) the leased property is not residential property, and (2) at least 50 percent of the gross rental income from the real property is from enterprise zone businesses. The rental of tangible personal property to others is not a qualified business unless substantially all of the rental of such property is by enterprise zone businesses or by residents of an empowerment zone or enterprise community.

Tax-exempt financing rules

Tax-exempt private activity bonds may be issued to finance certain facilities in empowerment zones and enterprise communities. These bonds, along with most private activity bonds, are subject to an annual private activity bond State volume cap equal to $50 per resident of each State, or (if greater) $150 million per State.

Qualified enterprise zone facility bonds are bonds 95 percent or more of the net proceeds of which are used to finance (1) "qualified zone property" (as defined above) the principal user of which is an "enterprise zone business" (also defined above[43]), or (2) functionally related and subordinate land located in the empowerment zone or enterprise community. These bonds may only be issued while an empowerment zone or enterprise community designation is in effect.

The aggregate face amount of all qualified enterprise zone bonds for each qualified enterprise zone business may not exceed $3 million per zone or community. In addition, total qualified enterprise zone bond financing for each principal user of these bonds may not exceed $20 million for all zones and communities.

Taxation of capital gains

In general, gain or loss reflected in the value of an asset is not recognized for income tax purposes until a taxpayer disposes of the asset. On the sale or exchange of capital assets, the net capital gain generally is taxed at the same rate as ordinary income, except that the maximum rate of tax is limited to 28 percent of the net capital gain.[44] Net capital gain is the excess of the net long-term capital gain for the taxable year over the net short-term capital loss for the year. Gain or loss is treated as long-term if the asset is held for more than one year.

Capital losses generally are deductible in full against capital gains. In addition, individual taxpayers may deduct capital losses against up to $3,000 of ordinary income in each year. Any remaining unused capital

---

42. Also, a qualified business does not include certain facilities described in section 144(c)(6)(B) (e.g., massage parlor, hot tub facility, or liquor store) or certain large farms.
43. For purpose of the tax-exempt financing rules, and "enterprise zones Business" also includes a business located in a zone or community which would qualify as

an enterprise zone business if it were separately incorporated.
44. The Revenue Reconciliation Act of 1993 added Code section 12002, which provides a 50-percent exclusion for gain from the sale of certain small business stock acquired at original issue and held for at least five years.

losses may be carried forward indefinitely to another taxable year.

A capital asset generally means any property except (1) inventory, stock in trade, or property held primarily for sale to customers in the ordinary course of the taxpayer's trade or business, (2) depreciable or real property used in the taxpayer's trade or business, (3) specified literary or artistic property, (4) business accounts or notes receivable, and (5) certain publications of the Federal Government.

In addition, the net gain from the disposition of certain property used in the taxpayer's trade or business is treated as long-term capital gain. Gain from the disposition of depreciable personal property is not treated as capital gain to the extent of all previous depreciation allowances. Gain from the disposition of depreciable real property generally is not treated as capital gain to the extent of the depreciation allowances in excess of the allowances that would have been available under the straight-line method.

Individual tax rates

To determine tax liability, an individual taxpayer generally must apply the tax rate schedules (or the tax tables) to his or her taxable income. The rate schedules are broken into several ranges of income, known as income brackets, and the marginal tax rate increases as a taxpayer's income increases. Separate rate schedules apply based on an individual's filing status. For 1997, the individual income tax rate schedules are as follows:

If taxable income is	Then income tax equals
Single individuals	
$0-$24,650	15 percent of taxable income.
$24,651-$59,750	$3,698, plus 28% of the amount over $24,650.
$59,751-$124,650	$13,526, plus 31% of the amount over $59,750.
$124,651-$271,050	$33,645, plus 36% of the amount over $124,650.
Over $271,050	$86,349, plus 39.6% of the amount over $271,050.
Heads of households	
$0-$33,050	15 percent of taxable income.
$33,051-$85,350	$4,958, plus 28% of the amount over $33,050.
$85,351-$138,200	$19,602 plus 31% of the amount over $85,350.
$138,201-$271,050	$35,985, plus 36% of the amount over $138,200.
Over $271,050	$83,811, plus 39.6% of the amount over $271,050.
Married individuals filing joint returns	
$0-$41,200	15 percent of taxable income.
$41,201-$99,600	$6,180, plus 28% of the amount over $41,200.
$99,601-$151,750	$22,532, plus 31% of the amount over $99,600.
$151,751-$271,050	$38,698, plus 36% of the amount over $151,750.
Over $271,050	$81,646, plus 39.6% of the amount over $271,050.
Married individuals filing separate returns	
$0-$20,600	15 percent of taxable income.
$20,601-$49,800	$3,090, plus 28% of the amount over $20,600.
$49,801-$75,875	$11,266, plus 31% of the amount over $49,800.
$75,876-$135,525	$19,349, plus 36% of the amount over $75,875.

Over $135,525	$40,823 plus 39.6% of the amount over $135,525.

Reasons for Change

The Committee believes that the District of Columbia faces two key problems—residents migrating from the District and insufficient economic activity. To this end, the Committee has provided certain tax incentives to reduce the Federal tax burden on certain District residents, and to encourage economic development in those areas of the District where development has been inadequate. However, the Committee is aware that the efficacy of tax incentives to address one or both problems is severely limited absent fundamental structural reform of the District's government and economy. Thus, the availability of the tax incentives is contingent on the passage of other Federal legislation that will implement such critical structural reforms.

Explanation of Provision

Designation of D.C. Enterprise Zone

Certain economically depressed census tracts within the District of Columbia are designated as the "D.C. Enterprise Zone," within which businesses and individual residents are eligible for special tax incentives. The census tracts that compose the D.C. Enterprise Zone are (1) all census tracts that presently are part of the D.C. enterprise community designated under section 1391 (i.e., portions of Anacostia, Mt. Pleasant, Chinatown, and the easternmost part of the District) and (2) all additional census tracts within the District of Columbia where the poverty rate is at least 35 percent. The D.C. Enterprise Zone designation generally will remain in effect for five years for the period from January 1, 1998, through December 31, 2002.[45]

The following tax incentives will take effect only if, prior to January 1, 1998, a Federal law is enacted creating a District of Columbia economic development corporation that is an instrumentality of the District of Columbia government.[46]

Business development incentives

Empowerment zone wage credit, expensing, and tax-exempt financing

The following tax incentives that are available under present law in empowerment zones would be available in the D.C. Enterprise Zone (modified as described below): (1) a 20-percent wage credit for the first $15,000 of wages paid to D.C. Enterprise Zone residents who work in the D.C. Enterprise Zone; (2) an additional $20,000 of expensing under Code section 179 for qualified zone property; and (3) special tax-exempt financing for certain zone facilities.

In general, the wage credit for certain D.C. Enterprise Zone residents who work in the D.C. Enterprise Zone is the same as is available in empowerment zones under present law. However, the wage credit rate remains at 20 percent for the D.C. Enterprise Zone for the period 1998 through 2002 (and does not phase down to 15 percent in the year 2002 as under present-law section 1396). The wage credit is effective for wages paid (or incurred) to a qualified individual after December 31, 1997, and before January 1, 2003.

The increased expensing under Code section 179 is effective for property placed in service in taxable years beginning after December 31, 1997, and before January 1, 2003. Thus, qualified D.C. Zone property placed in service in taxable years beginning in 1998 is eligible for up to $38,500 of expensing.

A qualified D.C. Zone business (defined as under present law section 1394(b)(3)) is permitted to borrow proceeds from the issuance of qualified enterprise zone facility bonds. Such bonds can be issued only by a newly created economic development corporation and are subject to the requirements applicable under present law to enterprise zone facility bonds, except that the amount of outstanding bond proceeds that can be

---

45. The status of certain census tracts within the District as an enterprise community designated under section 1391 also terminates on December 31, 2002.
46. In addition, the bill assumes the enactment of certain modifications to Federal law (other than Federal tax laws contained in the Internal Revenue Code) similar to those proposed by the Administration that would clarify and expand the District's authority to issue revenue bonds.

borrowed by any qualified District business cannot exceed $15 million (rather than $3 million). The special tax-exempt bond provisions apply to bonds issued after December 31, 1997, and prior to January 1, 2003.

Tax credits for equity investments in and loans to businesses located in the District of Columbia

A newly created economic development corporation is authorized to allocate $75 million in tax credits to taxpayers that make certain equity investments in, or loans to, businesses (either corporations or partnerships) engaged in an active trade or business in the District of Columbia. The business need not be located in the D.C. Enterprise Zone, although factors to be considered in the allocation of credits include whether the project would provide job opportunities for low and moderate income residents of the D.C. Enterprise Zone and whether the business is located in the D.C. Enterprise Zone. Eligible businesses are not be required to satisfy the criteria of a qualified D.C. Zone business, described above. Such credits are nonrefundable and can be used to offset a taxpayer's alternative minimum tax (AMT) liability.

Under the bill, the amount of credit cannot exceed 25 percent of the amount invested (or loaned) by the taxpayer. Thus, the economic development corporation may allocate the full $75 million in tax credits to no less than $300 million in equity investments in, or loans, to eligible businesses.

Under the bill, credits may be allocated to loans made to an eligible business only if the business uses the loan proceeds to purchase depreciable tangible property and any functionally related and subordinate land. Credits may be allocated to equity investments only if the equity interest was acquired for cash. Any credits allocated to a taxpayer making an equity investment are subject to recapture if the equity interest is disposed of by the taxpayer within five years. A taxpayer's basis in an equity investment is reduced by the amount of the credit.

The bill applies to credit amounts allocated for taxable years beginning after December 31, 1997, and before January 1, 2003.[47]

Zero percent capital gains rate

The bill provides a zero percent capital gains rate for capital gains from the sale of certain qualified D.C Zone assets held for more than five years. In general, D.C. Zone assets mean stock or partnership interests held in or tangible property held by a D.C. Zone business. For this purpose, a D.C. Zone business is defined as an enterprise zone business under present-law section 1397B.

"D.C. Zone business stock" is stock in a domestic corporation originally issued after December 31, 1997, that, at the time of issuance[48] and during substantially all of the taxpayer's holding period, was a D.C. Zone business, provided that such stock was acquired by the taxpayer on original issue from the corporation solely in exchange for cash[49]. A "D.C. Zone partnership interest" is a domestic partnership interest originally issued after December 31, 1997, that is acquired by the taxpayer from the partnership solely in exchange for cash before January 1, 2003, provided that, at the time such interest was acquired[50] and during substantially all of the taxpayer's holding period, the partnership was a D.C. Zone business. Finally, "D.C. Zone business property" is tangible property acquired by the taxpayer by purchase (within the meaning of present law section 179(d)(2)) after December 31, 1997, and before January 1, 2003, provided that the original use of such property in the D.C. Enterprise Zone commences with the taxpayer and substantially all of the use of such property during substantially all of the taxpayer's holding period was in a D.C. Zone business of the taxpayer.

---

47. As a general business credit, the credit can be carried back three years (but not before January 1, 1998) and forward for fifteen years.
48. In the case of a new corporation, it is sufficient if the corporation is being organized for purposes of being a D.C. Zone business.
49. Qualified D.C. Zone business stock does not include any stock acquired from a corporation which made a

substantial stock redemption or distribution (without a bona fide business purpose therefore) in an attempt to avoid the purposes of the provision. A similar rule applies with respect to qualified D.C. Zone partnership interests.
50. In the case of a new partnership, it is sufficient if the partnership is being formed for purposes of being a D.C. Zone business.

A special rule provides that, in the case of business property that is "substantially renovated," such property need not be acquired by the taxpayer after December 31, 1997, nor need the original use of such property in the D.C. Enterprise Zone commence with the taxpayer. For these purposes, property is treated as "substantially renovated" if, prior to January 1, 2003, additions to basis with respect to such property in the hands of the taxpayer during any 24-month period beginning after December 31, 1997, exceed the greater of (1) an amount equal to the adjusted basis at the beginning of such 24-month period in the hands of the taxpayer, or (2) $5,000. Thus, substantially renovated real estate located in the D.C. Enterprise Zone may constitute D.C. Zone business property. However, the bill specifically excludes land that is not an integral part of a D.C. Zone business from the definition of D.C. Zone business property.

In addition, qualified D.C. Zone assets include property that was a qualified D.C. Zone asset in the hands of a prior owner, provided that at the time of acquisition, and during substantially all of the subsequent purchaser's holding period, either (1) substantially all of the use of the property is in a D.C. Zone business, or (2) the property is an ownership interest in a D.C. Zone business.[51]

In general, gain eligible for the zero percent tax rate means gain from the sale or exchange of a qualified D.C. Zone asset that is (1) a capital asset or (2) property used in the trade or business as defined in section 1231(b). Gain attributable to periods before December 31, 1997, and after December 31, 2007, is not qualified capital gain. No gain attributable to real property, or an intangible asset, which is not an integral part of a D.C. Zone business qualifies for the zero percent rate.

The bill provides that property that ceases to be a qualified D.C. Zone asset because the property is no longer used in (or no longer represents an ownership interest in) a D.C. Zone business after the five-year period beginning on the date the taxpayer acquired such property would continue to be treated as a D.C. Zone asset. Under this rule, the amount of gain eligible for the zero percent capital gains rate cannot exceed the amount which would be qualified capital gain had the property been sold on the date of such cessation.

Special rules are provided for pass-through entities (i.e., ,artnerships, S corporations, regulated investment companies, and common trust funds). In the case of a sale or exchange of an interest in a pass-through entity that was not a D.C. Zone business during substantially all of the period that the taxpayer held the interest, the zero percent capital gains rate applies to the extent that the gain is attributable to amounts that would have been qualified capital gain had the assets been sold for their fair market value on the date of the sale or exchange of the interest in the pass-through entity. This rule applies only if the interest in the pass-through entity were held by the taxpayer for more than five years. In addition, the rule applies only to qualified D.C. Zone assets that were held by the pass-through entity for more than five years, and throughout the period that the taxpayer held the interest in the pass-through entity.

The bill also provides that in the case of a transfer of a qualified D.C. Zone asset by gift, at death, or from a partnership to a partner that held an interest in the partnership at the time that the qualified D.C. Zone asset was acquired, (1) the transferee is to be treated as having acquired the asset in the same manner as the transferor, and (2) the transferee's holding period includes that of the transferor. In addition, rules similar to those contained in section 1202(i)(2) regarding treatment of contributions to capital after the original issuance date and section 1202(j) regarding treatment of certain short positions apply.

Individual resident tax rate reduction

Individuals who have their principal place of abode in any census tract that is part of the D.C. Enterprise Zone are entitled to a 10-percent tax rate on all taxable income that currently is subject to a 15-percent Fed-

---

51. The termination of the D.C. Zone designation will not, by itself, result in property failing to be treated as a qualified D.C. Zone asset. However, capital gain eligi-ble for the zero percent capital gains rate does not include any gain attributable to periods after December 31, 2007.

eral income tax rate. Thus, using the 1997 tax rate schedule, a single taxpayer who resides in the D.C. Enterprise Zone with $24,650 or more of taxable income will receive a Federal income tax reduction of $1,233 under the bill. Married taxpayers who reside in the D.C. Enterprise Zone and file a joint return with taxable income of $41,200 or more of taxable income will receive a Federal income tax reduction of $2,060 under the bill.

The special 10-percent rate provision is in effect for the period 1998–2007.

Effective Date

The D.C. tax incentives generally are effective January 1, 1998, and remain in effect for five years until the termination of the D.C. Enterprise Zone designation on December 31, 2002. However, the zero percent tax rate for capital gains and the special 10-percent rate bracket are effective for the period 1998—2007.

[Senate Report]

Explanation of Provision

The following tax incentives take effect only if, prior to January 1, 1998, a Federal law is enacted creating a District of Columbia economic development corporation that is an instrumentality of the District of Columbia government.

First-time homebuyer credit

The bill provides first-time homebuyers of a principal residence in the District a tax credit of up to $5,000 of the amount of the purchase price. The $5,000 maximum credit amount applies both to individuals and married couples. Married individuals filing separately can claim a maximum credit of $2,500 each. The Secretary of Treasury is directed to prescribe regulations allocating the credit among unmarried purchasers of a residence.[44]

To qualify as a "first-time homebuyer," neither the individual (nor the individual's spouse, if married) can have had a present ownership interest in a principal residence in the District for the one-year period prior to the date of acquisition of the principal residence.[45]

A taxpayer will be treated as a first-time homebuyer with respect to only one residence — i.e., the credit may be claimed one time only. The date of acquisition is the date on which a binding contract to purchase the principal residence is entered into or the date on which construction or reconstruction of such residence commences.

The credit applies to purchases after the date of enactment and before January 1, 2002. Any excess credit may be carried forward indefinitely to succeeding taxable years.

Effective Date

The D.C. first-time homebuyer credit is effective for purchases after the date of enactment and before January 1, 2002. The tax credit for equity investments and loans applies to credit amounts allocated for taxable years beginning after December 31, 1997, and before January 1, 2003. The zero-percent tax rate for capital gains is effective for qualified D.C. assets purchased (or substantially renovated) during the period January 1, 1998, through December 31, 2002, for any gain accruing with respect to such assets after the date or purchase (or substantial renovation).

[Conference Report]

Senate Amendment

Tax credits for equity investments in and loans to businesses located in the District of Columbia

The Senate amendment is the same as the House bill, except that the economic development corporation is authorized to allocate $60 million (rather than $75 million) in credits.

---

44. The provision of the bill that excludes sales of certain personal residences from the real estate transaction reporting requirement would not apply to sales of personal residences in the District of Columbia. In addition, the Committee anticipates that the Secretary of Treasury will require such information as may be necessary to verify eligibility for the D.C. first-time home buyer credit.

45. Special rules apply to members of the Armed Forces and certain individuals with tax homes outside the United States with respect to whom the rollover period available under section 1034 (as in effect prior to the enactment of the bill) is suspended pursuant to sections 1034(h) or (k).

Zero-percent capital gains rate

Like the House bill, the Senate amendment provides a zero- percent capital gains rate for capital gains from the sale of certain qualified D.C. assets held for more than five years. In general, qualified D.C. assets mean stock or partnership interests held in, or tangible property held by, a qualified D.C. business. However; the Senate amendment provides that capital gain from the sale of any D.C. asset acquired during calendar year 1998 shall be subject to tax at a 10 percent rate. A special rule provides that if the basis of any D.C. asset is determined in whole or part by reference to a D.C. asset acquired in 1998, all gain from the sale or exchange of such asset is taxed at the 10 percent rate.

Trust fund for D.C. schools

The Senate amendment provides for a total of $50 million ($5 million for each year 1998 through 2007) to be transferred from Federal income taxes paid by District individual residents to a Trust Fund for D.C. schools. Amounts in the Trust Fund are to be used to pay debt service on qualified D.C. school bonds, which are taxable bonds issued after March 31, 1998, by the District to finance the rehabilitation and repair of District schools.

The Trust Fund for D.C. schools will be funded $5 million per year for 1998 through 2007.

Conference Agreement

The conference agreement follows the House bill in part and the Senate amendment in part.

Designation of D.C Enterprise Zone

The conference agreement includes the House bill provision that designates certain economically depressed census tracts within the District of Columbia as the "D.C. Enterprise Zone," within which businesses and individual residents are eligible for special tax incentives. Under the conference agreement, however, the census tracts that compose the D.C. Enterprise Zone for purposes of the wage credit, expensing, and tax-exempt financing incentives are expanded to include census tracts within the District of Columbia where the poverty rate is not less than 20 percent. Thus, the D.C. Enterprise Zone consists of (1) all census tracts that presently are part of the D.C. enterprise community designated under Code section 1391 (i.e., portions of Anacostia, Mt. Pleasant, Chinatown, and the easternmost part of the District) and (2) all additional census tracts within the District of Columbia where the poverty rate is not less than 20 percent. As under the House bill, the D.C. Enterprise Zone designation generally will remain in effect for five years for the period from January 1, 1998, through December 31, 2002.

Empowerment zone wage credit, expensing, and tax-exempt financing

The conference agreement includes the House bill provision with respect to the tax incentives that are available in the D.C. Enterprise Zone, modified to provide that the wage credit is available with respect to all residents of the District and is not limited to residents of the D.C. Enterprise Zone and to eliminate the requirement that 35 percent of the employees of a qualified "D.C. Zone business" must be residents of the D.C. Enterprise Zone.[26] Thus, the following tax incentives that are available under present law in empowerment zones generally will be available in the D.C. Enterprise Zone: (1) a 20-percent wage credit for the first $15,000 of wages paid to D.C. residents who work in the D.C. Enterprise Zone; (2) an additional $20,000 of expensing under Code section 179 for qualified zone property; and (3) special tax-exempt financing for certain zone facilities.[27] The conference agreement

---

26. The provision of the conference agreement that authorizes the designation of additional empowerment zones also modifies the definition of an enterprise zone business to provide that, in addition to satisfying the other requirements of section 1397B, at least 50 percent (as opposed to 80 percent under present law) of the total gross income of a qualified enterprise zone business must be derived from the active conduct of a "qualified business" within a zone or community. The conference agreement makes certain other modifications to the definition of an enterprise zone business as well. This modified definition of enterprise zone business, determined without regard to the 35-percent zone resident employee requirement, generally applies for purposes of the increased expensing and tax-exempt financing available in the D.C. Enterprise Zone.

27. The provision of the conference agreement that authorizes the designation of additional empowerment zones contains certain modifications to the rules applicable to present-law empowerment zone facility bonds. Such modifications (not including the exception to the volume cap) will apply in the D.C. Enterprise Zone as well.

does not include the provision limiting the special tax-exempt financing benefits to bonds issued by the Economic Development Corporation.

Zero-percent capital gains rate

The conference agreement includes the House bill provision that provides a zero-percent capital gains rate for capital gains from the sale of certain qualified D.C Zone assets held for more than five years. For purposes of the zero-percent capital gains rate, the D.C. Enterprise Zone is defined to include all census tracts within the District of Columbia where the poverty rate is not less than 10 percent.

For purposes of the zero-percent capital gains rate, the definition of qualified "D.C. Zone business" generally is the same as the definition applicable for purposes of the increased expensing described above. However, solely for purposes of the zero-percent capital gains rate, a qualified "D.C. Zone business" must derive at least 80 percent (as opposed to 50 percent) of its total gross income from the active conduct of a "qualified business" within the D.C. Enterprise Zone.

First-time homebuyer tax credit

The conference agreement includes the Senate amendment provision that allows first-time homebuyers of a principal residence in the District a tax credit of up to $5,000 of the amount of the purchase price, except that the credit phases out for individual taxpayers with adjusted gross income between $70,000 and $90,000 ($110,000-$130,000 for joint filers). The conference agreement clarifies that the credit is available with respect to purchases of existing property as well as new construction, and specifies that a taxpayer's basis in a property is reduced by the amount of any homebuyer tax credit claimed with respect to such property. In addition, the conference agreement sunsets the credit after December 31, 2000. Thus, the credit is available with respect to property purchased after the date of enactment and before January 1, 2001.

[¶ 5050]   Section 801.   Welfare-to-work incentives.

(Code Sec. 51A)

[House Report]

Present Law

The work opportunity tax credit is available on an elective basis for employers hiring individuals from one or more of seven targeted groups. The credit generally is equal to 35 percent of qualified wages. Qualified wages consist of wages attributable to service rendered by a member of a targeted group during the one-year period beginning with the day the individual begins work for the employer. For a vocational rehabilitation referral, however, the period will begin on the day the individual begins work for the employer on or after the beginning of the individual's vocational rehabilitation plan as under prior law.

For purposes of the work opportunity tax credit, the targeted groups for which the credit is available include (1) families receiving Aid to Families with Dependent Children (AFDC), (2) qualified ex-felons, (3) high-risk youth, (4) vocational rehabili-

tation referrals, (5) qualified summer youth employees, (6) qualified veterans, and (7) families receiving food stamps.

Generally, no more than $6,000 of wages during the first year of employment is permitted to be taken into account with respect to any individual. Thus, the maximum credit per individual is $2,100. With respect to qualified summer youth employees, the maximum credit is 35 percent of up to $3,000 of qualified first-year wages, for a maximum credit of $1,050. The deduction for wages is reduced by the amount of the credit.

The work opportunity tax credit is effective for wages paid or incurred to a qualified individual who begins work for an employer after September 30, 1996, and before October 1, 1997.

Reasons for Change

One goal of the Personal Responsibility and Work Opportunity Reform Act of 1996 (Public Law 104 193) was to move individuals from welfare to work. The Committee believes that the welfare-to-work credit will provide to employers an additional incentive to hire these categories of individuals. This incentive is intended to ease the transition from welfare to work for the targeted categories of individuals by increasing access to employment. It is also intended to provide certain employee benefits to these individuals to encourage training, health coverage, dependent care and ultimately better job attachment.

Explanation of Provision

The bill provides to employers a credit on the first $20,000 of eligible wages paid to qualified long-term family assistance (AFDC or its successor program) recipients during the first two years of employment. The credit is 35% of the first $10,000 of eligible wages in the first year of employment and 50% of the first $10,000 of eligible wages in the second year of employment. The maximum credit is $8,500 per qualified employee.

Qualified long-term family assistance recipients are: (1) members of a family that has received family assistance for at least 18 consecutive months ending on the hiring date; (2) members of a family that has received family assistance for a total of at least 18 months (whether or not consecutive) after the date of enactment of this credit if they are hired within 2 years after

the date that the 18-month total is reached; and (3) members of a family who are no longer eligible for family assistance because of either Federal or State time limits, if they are hired within 2 years after the Federal or State time limits made the family ineligible for family assistance.

Eligible wages are amounts paid by the employer for the following: (1) educational assistance excludable under a section 127 program (or that would be excludable but for the expiration of section 127); (2) health plan coverage for the employee, but not more than the applicable premium defined under section 4980B(f)(4); and (3) dependent care assistance excludable under section 129.

Effective Date

The provision is effective for wages paid or incurred to a qualified individual who begins work for an employer on or after January 1, 1998 and before May 1, 1999.

[Conference Report]

Senate Amendment

No provision.

Conference Agreement

The conference agreement follows the House bill.

[¶ 5051]   Section 901.   Transfer of general fund highway fuels tax to the Highway Trust Fund.

(Code Sec. 9503)

[Senate Report]

Present Law

Federal excise taxes are imposed on highway motor fuels to finance the Highway Trust Fund (currently, through September 30, 1999): 14 cents per gallon on highway gasoline and special motor fuels, 20 cents per gallon on highway diesel fuel, and 3 cents per gallon on diesel fuel used by intercity buses. Buses pay no Federal gasoline tax. Reduced tax rates apply to ethanol and methanol fuels. In addition, a permanent General Fund tax of 4.3 cents per gallon applies to highway and other motor fuels (other than intercity bus gasoline and recrea-

tional motorboat diesel fuels, which are not subject to the tax, and rail diesel fuel, which pays a General Fund tax of 5.55 cents per gallon).

Amounts equivalent to 2 cents per gallon of the Highway Trust Fund motor fuels tax revenues are credited to the Mass Transit Account of the Trust Fund for capital-related expenditures on mass transit programs; the balance of the highway motor fuels tax revenues are credited to the Highway Account of the Trust Fund for highway- related programs generally.

Transfers are made from the Highway Trust Fund of up to $70 million per fiscal year (through September 30, 1997) to the Boat Safety Account of the Aquatic Resources Trust Fund of amounts equivalent to 11.5 cents per gallon from recreational motorboat gasoline and special motor fuels revenues, plus up to $1 million per fiscal year to the Land and Water Conservation Fund. Any excess revenues attributable to the tax on motorboat fuels is to be transferred from the Highway Trust Fund to the Sport Fish Restoration Account in the Aquatic Resources Trust Fund.

Reasons for Change

The Committee determined that the balance of the existing General Fund excise tax on highway fuels, after the transfer of 0.5 cent per gallon to the new Intercity Passenger Rail Fund established under section 702 of this bill, should be transferred to the Highway Trust Fund to ensure that more funds will be available for needed Highway Trust Fund programs in the future. It is widely suggested by transportation officials and users that there is an urgent need for improved and enhanced highway and transit systems in the nation to meet the needs of a growing transportation system.

Explanation of Provision

The bill transfers the existing General Fund excise tax of 4.3 cents per gallon on motor fuels used in highway transportation to the Highway Trust Fund, beginning on October 1, 1997, except for the temporary transfer of the 0.5 cent per gallon that will go to the Intercity Passenger Rail Fund under section 702 of the bill for the period October 1, 1997 through April 15, 2001. Of the amounts transferred to the Highway Trust fund (3.8 cents or 4.3 cents), 20 percent is to go to the Mass Transit Account and 80 percent to the Highway Account.

The increased deposits to the Highway Trust Fund may not be used to cause an increase in the allocations under section 157 of Title 23 of the U.S. Code or any other increase beyond in direct spending other than by enactment of future legislation in compliance with the Budget Enforcement Act.

Effective Date

The provision is effective on October 1, 1997.

[Conference Report]

House Bill

No provision.

Conference Agreement

Transfer of revenues to Highway Trust Fund.—The conference agreement follows the Senate amendment with a modification to reflect deletion from the agreement of the Senate amendment provision transferring 0.5 cents per gallon of these revenues to a new Intercity Passenger Rail Fund. As under the Senate amendment, revenues from the 4.3-cents-per-gallon tax will be divided between the Highway Trust Fund's Highway Account (3.45 cents per gallon) and Mass Transit Account (0.85 cents per gallon).

Deposit rules for highway motor fuels taxes.—The conference agreement provides that the excise taxes imposed on gasoline (sec. 4081), diesel fuel (sec. 4081), special motor fuels (sec. 4041), and kerosene (sec. 4081) that otherwise would be required to be deposited with the Treasury after July 31, 1998, and before September 30, 1998, are not required to be deposited until October 5, 1998.

[¶ 5052]   Section 902.   Repeal excise tax on diesel fuel used in recreational motorboats.

(Code Sec. 6421, 4041, 4083)

[House Report]

Present Law

Before a temporary suspension through December 31, 1997 was enacted in 1996, diesel fuel used in recreational motorboats was subject to the 24.3-cents-per-gallon diesel fuel excise tax. Revenues from this tax were retained in the General Fund. The tax was enacted by the Omnibus Budget Reconciliation Act of 1993 as a revenue offset for repeal of the excise tax on certain luxury boats.

Reasons for Change

Many marinas have found it uneconomical to carry both undyed (taxed) and dyed (untaxed) diesel fuel because the majority of their market is for uses not subject to tax. As a result, some recreational boaters have experienced difficulty finding fuels. In 1996, Congress suspended imposition of the tax on recreational boating while alternative collection methods were evaluated. No satisfactory alternative has been found; therefore, the Committee determined that competing needs for boat fuel availability and preservation of the integrity of the diesel fuel tax compliance structure are best served by repealing the diesel fuel tax on recreational motorboat use.

Explanation of Provision

The provision repeals the application of the diesel fuel tax to fuel used in recreational motorboats.

Effective Date

The provision is effective for fuel sold after December 31, 1997.

[Conference Report]

Senate Amendment

The Senate amendment is the same as the House bill.

Conference Agreement

The conference agreement follows the House bill and the Senate amendment.

[¶ 5053]   Section 903.   Continued application of tax on imported recycled Halon-1211.

(Code Sec. 4682)

[House Report]

Present Law

An excise tax is imposed on the sale or use by the manufacturer or importer of certain ozone-depleting chemicals (Code sec. 4681). The amount of tax generally is determined by multiplying the base tax amount applicable for the calendar year by an ozone-depleting factor assigned to each taxable chemical. The base tax amount is $6.25 per pound in 1997 and will increase by 45 cents per pound per year thereafter. The ozone-depleting factors for taxable halons are 3 for halon-1211, 10 for halon-1301, and 6 for halon-2402.

Taxable chemicals that are recovered and recycled within the United States are exempt from tax. In addition, exemption is provided for imported recycled halon-1301 and halon-2402 if such chemicals are imported from countries that are signatories to the Montreal Protocol on Substances that Deplete the Ozone Layer. Present law further provides that exemption is to be provided for imported recycled halon-1211, for such chemicals imported from countries that are signatories to the Montreal Protocol on Substances that Deplete the Ozone Layer after December 31, 1997.

Reasons for Change

The Committee understands that in response to the profit incentive created by the higher price for ozone-depleting chemicals that has resulted from the tax on these chemicals, entrepreneurs have developed and are marketing a substitute for halon-1211 that is not ozone depleting. The Committee believes permitting imported recycled halon-1211 to compete in the market tax free may destroy this entrepreneurial and environmental success story.

Explanation of Provision

The bill repeals the present-law exemption for imported recycled halon-1211.

Effective Date

The provision is effective on the date of enactment.

[Conference Report]

Senate Amendment

No provision.

Conference Agreement

The conference agreement follows the House bill.

[¶ 5054]   Section 904.   Uniform rate of excise tax on vaccines.

(Code Sec. 4131, 4132)

[House Report]

Present Law

Under section 4131, a manufacturer's excise tax is imposed on the following vaccines routinely recommended for administration to children: DPT (diphtheria, pertussis, tetanus,), $4.56 per dose; DT (diphtheria, tetanus), $0.06 per dose; MMR (measles, mumps, or rubella), $4.44 per dose; and polio, $0.29 per dose. In general, if any vaccine is administered by combining more than one of the listed taxable vaccines, the amount of tax imposed is the sum of the amounts of tax imposed for each taxable vaccine. However, in the case of MMR and its components, any component vaccine of MMR is taxed at the same rate as the MMR-combined vaccine.

Amounts equal to net revenues from this excise tax are deposited in the Vaccine Injury Compensation Trust Fund to finance compensation awards under the Federal Vaccine Injury Compensation Program for individuals who suffer certain injuries following administration of the taxable vaccines. This program provides a substitute Federal, "no fault" insurance system for the State-law tort and private liability insurance systems otherwise applicable to vaccine manufacturers. All persons immunized after September 30, 1998, with covered vaccines must pursue compensation under this Federal program before bringing civil tort actions under State law.

Reasons for Change

The Committee understands that the present-law tax rates applicable to taxable vaccines were chosen to reflect estimated probabilities of adverse reactions and the severity of the injury that might result from such reactions. The Committee understands that medical researchers believe that there is insufficient data to support fine gradations of estimates of potential harm from the various different childhood vaccines. In the light of this scientific assessment, the Committee believes some simplicity can be achieved by taxing such vaccines at the same rate per dose.

The Committee further believes it is appropriate to review the list of taxable vaccines from time to time as medical science advances. The Center for Disease Control has recommended that the vaccines for HIB (hemophilus influenza type B), Hepatitis B, and varicella (chickenpox) be widely administered among the nation's children. In light of the growing number of immunizations using these vaccines, the Committee adds these vaccines to the list of taxable vaccines.

Explanation of Provision

The bill replaces the present-law excise tax rates, that differ by vaccine, with a single rate tax of $0.84 per dose on any listed vaccine component. Thus, the bill provides that the tax applied to any vaccine that is a combination of vaccine components is 84 cents times the number of components in the combined vaccine. For example, the MMR vaccine is to be taxed at a rate of $2.52 per dose and the DT vaccine is to be taxed at rate of $1.68 per dose.

In addition, the provision adds three new taxable vaccines to the present-law taxable vaccines: (1) HIB (hemophilus influenza type B); (2) Hepatitis B; and (3) varicella (chickenpox). The three newly listed vaccines also are subject to the 84-cents per dose excise tax.

Effective Date

The provision is effective for vaccine purchases after September 30, 1997. No tax is to be collected or refunds permitted for amounts held for sale on October 1, 1997.

[Senate Report]

Explanation of Provision

The bill replaces the present-law excise tax rates, that differ by vaccine, with a single rate tax of $0.84 per dose on any listed vaccine component. Thus, the bill provides that the tax applied to any vaccine that is a combination of vaccine components is 84 cents times the number of components in the combined vaccine. For example, the MMR vaccine is to be taxed at a rate of $2.52 per dose and the DT vaccine is to be taxed at rate of $1.68 per dose.

In addition, the provision adds three new taxable vaccines to the present-law taxable vaccines: (1) HIB (haemophilus influenza type B); (2) Hepatitis B; and (3) varicella (chicken pox). The three newly listed vaccines also are subject to the 84-cents per dose excise tax.

Lastly, the Committee directs the Secretary of the Treasury to undertake a study of the efficacy of the new flat-rate vaccine tax system as a means to finance the Vaccine Injury Compensation Trust Fund. Among other issues that the Secretary might find pertinent, the Committee directs the Secretary to explore the following questions. For each taxable vaccine, how does the magnitude of the tax compare to the total price of the vaccine that is charged to the patient (or the patient's insurance company)? Have any changes in the prices of taxable vaccines that might have resulted from the changes in tax enacted by this bill altered the use of taxable vaccines (i.e., what is the price elasticity of demand for the various taxable vaccines)? Does scientific evidence exist to permit a vaccine tax structure that reflects possibly different medical risks from the different vaccines? Does the flat-rate structure generate savings in compliance costs for taxpayers and administrative cost savings for the Internal Revenue Service? The Committee welcomes recommendations regarding possible changes in this tax structure. However, the Committee reminds the Secretary that determination of the tax base and the tax rate are the constitutional prerogative of the Congress and that recommendations for delegation of such authority to the executive branch are inappropriate. The results of the study are to be reported to the Senate Committee on Finance and the House Committee on Ways and Means by September 30, 1999.

Effective Date

The provision is effective for vaccine purchases after September 30, 1997. No floor stocks tax is to be collected or refunds permitted for amounts held for sale on October 1, 1997. Returns to the manufacturer occurring on or after October 1, 1997, are assumed to be returns of vaccines to which the new rates of tax apply.

[Conference Report]

Conference Agreement

The conference agreement generally follows the House bill and the Senate amendment by imposing a uniform rate of tax, but at a rate of $0.75 per dose on any listed vaccine component. The conference agreement also adds the HIB (haemophilus influenza type B), Hepatitis B, and varicella (chickenpox) vaccines to the list of taxable vaccines.

The conference agreement does not require the Secretary to study the new vaccine tax structure.

Effective Date

The provision is effective for sales after the date of enactment. No floor stocks tax is to be collected, or floor stocks refunds permitted, for vaccines held on the effective date. For the purpose of determining the amount of refund of tax on a vaccine returned to the manufacturer or importer, for vaccines returned after the date of enactment and before January 1, 1999, the amount of tax assumed to have been paid on the initial purchase of the returned vaccine shall not exceed $0.75 per dose.

[¶ 5055]   Section 905.   Treat certain gasoline "chain retailers" as wholesale distributors under the gasoline excise tax refund rules.

(Code Sec. 6416)

[House Report]

Present Law

Gasoline is taxed at 18.3 cents per gallon upon removal from a registered pipeline or barge terminal facility. The position holder in the terminal at the time of removal is liable for payment of the tax. Certain uses of gasoline, including use by States and local governments, are exempt from tax. In general, these exemptions are realized by refunds to the exempt users of tax paid by the party that removed the gasoline from a terminal facility. Present law includes an exception to the general rule that refunds are made to consumers in the case of gasoline sold to States and local governments and certain other exempt users. In those cases, wholesale distributors sell the gasoline net of tax previously paid and receive the refunds. The term wholesale distributor includes only persons that sell gasoline to producers, retailers, or to users in bulk quantities. Retailers do not qualify as wholesale distributors, regardless of their size.

Reasons for Change

During recent years, States and local governments increasingly have purchased gasoline for their fleets by credit card purchases from retail outlets. Previously, these purchases were through bulk deliveries to tanks supplying private pumps at government installations. Currently, wholesale distributors are eligible to claim gasoline tax refunds on behalf of these customers. The Committee determined that allowing retail businesses of comparable size would adapt the gasoline tax rules to current market conditions without creating new opportunities for tax evasion.

Explanation of Provision

The definition of wholesale distributor is expanded to include certain "chain retailers"—retailers who own and make retail sales from 10 or more retail gasoline outlets. This modification conforms the definition of wholesale distributor to that which existed before 1987 when the point of collection of the gasoline tax was moved from the wholesale distribution level to removal from a terminal facility.

Effective Date

The provision is effective after September 30, 1997.

[Conference Report]

Senate Amendment

No provision.

Conference Agreement

The conference agreement follows the House bill.

[¶ 5056]   Section 906.   Exemption of electric and other clean-fuel motor vehicle from luxury automobile classification.

(Code Sec. 4001, 4003)

[House Report]

Present Law

Present law imposes an excise tax on the sale of automobiles whose price exceeds a designated threshold, currently $34,000. The excise tax is imposed at a rate of 8-percent for 1997 on the excess of the sales price above the designated threshold. The 8-percent rate declines by one percentage point per year until reaching 3 percent in 2002, and no tax thereafter. The $34,000 threshold is indexed for inflation. The present-law index of $34,000 is the result of adjusting a $30,000 threshold specified in the Code for inflation occurring after 1990 (sec. 4001(e)).

The tax generally applies only to the first retail sale after manufacture, production, or importation of an automobile. It does not apply to subsequent sales of taxable automobiles. A 10-percent tax is imposed on the separate purchase of vehicle and parts and accessories therefor when the sum of the separate purchases exceeds the luxury tax threshold (sec. 4003).[52]

The tax under section 4001 applies to sales before January 1, 2003. The tax under section 4003 has no termination date.[53]

Reasons for Change

The Committee believes that the price of a clean-burning fuel vehicle or an electric vehicle does not necessarily represent the consumer's purchase of a luxury good in

---

52. The rate of tax under section 4003 is not determined by reference to section 4001. However, a technical correction under the bill (Title XV) conforms the tax rate applicable under section 4003 to that applicable under section 4001.

53. A technical correction under the bill (Title XV) conforms the expiration date of the tax under section 4003 to the expiration date under section 4001.

the sense intended with the enactment of the luxury excise tax on automobiles in the Omnibus Budget Reconciliation Act of 1990. Rather, the higher price of such vehicles often represents the cost of the technology required to produce an automobile designed to provide certain environmental benefits. The Committee believes the cost of this technology should not be considered a luxury for the purpose of the luxury excise tax on automobiles. Therefore, the Committee believes it is appropriate to modify the threshold above which the luxury automobile excise tax applies in the case of certain clean-burning fuel vehicles and electric vehicles.

Explanation of Provision

The bill modifies the threshold above which the luxury excise tax on automobiles will apply for each of two identified classes of automobiles both in the case of a purchase of a vehicle and in the case of the separate purchase of a vehicle and parts and accessories therefor. First, for an automobile that is not a clean-burning fuel vehicle to which retrofit parts and components are installed to make the vehicle a clean-burning vehicle (as defined under sec. 179A(c)(1)(A)), the threshold would be $30,000, as adjusted for inflation under present law, plus an amount equal to the increment to the retail value of the automobile attributable to the retrofit parts and components installed. For example, assume that in 1997, after the date of enactment, an individual purchases a clean-burning fuel vehicle for $43,000. Further assume that had the individual purchased the identical vehicle, without having had certain components replaced to qualify it as clean burning, the

price paid would have been $39,000. The incremental increase in the price of the vehicle due to the installation of the qualified property is $4,000, and the luxury tax would be applied for the amount paid above a threshold of $38,000 (the $34,000 base threshold applicable for 1997 plus $4,000 for the value of the incremental components). The tax would apply to $5,000 of the sales price ($43,000 less the $38,000 threshold).

In the case of a passenger vehicle designed to be propelled primarily by electricity and built by an original equipment manufacturer, the threshold applicable for any year is modified to equal 150 percent of $30,000 with the result increased for inflation occurring after 1990 and rounded to next lowest multiple of $2,000.

For all other vehicles, the threshold remains equal to that provided under present law.

Effective Date

The provision is effective for sales and installations occurring on or after the date of enactment.

[Conference Report]

Senate Amendment

No provision.

Conference Agreement

The conference agreement follows the House bill, with a modification to the effective date that provides that the provision is effective for sales and installations occurring after the date of enactment.

[¶ 5057]   Section 907.   Tax certain alternative fuels based on energy equivalency to gasoline.

(Code Sec. 4041)

[Senate Report]

Present Law

Excise taxes are imposed on gasoline, diesel fuel, and special motor fuels used in highway vehicles. 4.3 cents per gallon of each of these taxes is retained in the General Fund, with the balance of the revenues being dedicated to one or more Trust Funds.

The tax on gasoline is 18.3 cents per gallon; the tax on diesel fuel is 24.3 cents per gallon; and the tax on special motor fuels generally is 18.3 cents per gallon. Taxable special motor fuels include liquefied petroleum gas ("propane"), liquefied natural gas ("LNG"), methanol from natural gas, and compressed natural gas ("CNG"). Special rates apply to methanol from natural gas (exempt from 7 cents of the 14- cents-per-gallon Highway Trust Fund component of the special motor fuels tax), and compressed natural gas (exempt from the entire Highway Trust Fund component of the tax).

In general, these four special motor fuels contain less energy (i.e., fewer Btu's) per gallon than does gasoline.

Reasons for Change

The largest portion of the excise tax on propane, LNG, and methanol from natural gas is imposed to finance Federal highway programs through the Highway Trust Fund. A basic principle of the highway taxes is that users of the highway system should be taxed in relation to their use of the system. Adjusting the tax rates on these three special motor fuels is consistent with that principle because consumers must purchase more gallons of these lower-energy-content fuels than gallons of gasoline to travel the same number of miles.

Explanation of Provision

The tax rates on propane, LNG, and methanol from natural gas are adjusted to

reflect the respective energy equivalence of the fuels to gasoline.

Propane   13.6 cents

Methanol 9.15 cents

Liquified natural gas 11.9 cents

After September 39, 1999, these three fuels will be taxed based on Btu equivalency to gasoline's 4.3–cents–per–gallon rate. No change is made to the current reduced tax rate on compressed natural gas.

Effective Date

The provision is effective for fuels sold or used after September 30, 1997.

[Conference Report]

Conference Agreement

The conference agreement follows the Senate amendment.

[¶ 5058]   Section 908.   Provide a lower rate of alcohol excise tax on certain hard ciders.

(Code Sec. 5041)

[Senate Report]

Present Law

Distilled spirits are taxed at a rate of $13.50 per proof gallon; beer is taxed at a rate of $18 per barrel (approximately 58 cents per gallon); and still wines of 14 percent alcohol or less are taxed at a rate of $1.07 per wine gallon. Higher rates of tax are applied to wines with greater alcohol content and sparkling wines.

Certain small wineries may claim a credit against the excise tax on wine of 90 cents per wine gallon on the first 100,000 gallons of wine produced annually. Certain small breweries pay a reduced tax of $7.00 per barrel (approximately 22.6 cents per gallon) on the first 60,000 barrels of beer produced annually.

Apple cider containing alcohol ("hard cider") is classified and taxed as wine.

Reasons for Change

The Committee understands that as an alcoholic beverage, hard cider competes more as a substitute for beer than as a substitute for table wine. If most consumers of alcoholic beverages choose between hard cider and beer, rather than between hard cider and wine, taxing hard cider at tax rates imposed on other wine products may distort consumer choice and unfairly disadvantage producers of hard cider in the market place. The Committee also understands that producers of hard cider generally are small businesses and has concluded that it would improve market efficiency and fairness to tax this beverage at a rate equivalent to the tax imposed on the production of beer by small brewers.

Explanation of Provision

The bill adjusts the tax rate on apple cider having an alcohol content of no more than seven percent to 22.6 cents per gallon for those persons who produce more than

100,000 gallons of apple cider during a calendar year. The tax rate applicable to apple cider produced by persons who produce 100,000 gallons or less in a calendar year will remain as under present law and those persons may continue to claim the credit permitted for small wineries. Apple cider production will continue to be counted in determining whether other production of a producer qualifies for the tax credit for small producers. The bill does not change the classification of qualifying apple cider as wine.

[¶ 5059]   Section 909.   Study feasibility of moving collection point for distilled spirits excise tax.

(Code Sec. 5001)

[Senate Report]

Present Law

Distilled spirits are subject to tax at $13.50 per proof gallon. (A proof gallon is a liquid gallon consisting of 50 percent alcohol.) In the case of domestically produced distilled spirits and distilled spirits imported in to the United States in bulk containers for domestic bottling, the tax is imposed on removal of the beverage from the distillery (without regard to whether a sale occurs at that time). Bottled distilled spirits that are imported into the United States comprise approximately 15 percent of the current market for these beverages; tax is imposed on these imports when the distilled spirits are removed from the first customs bonded warehouse in which they are deposited upon entry into the United States.

In the case of certain distilled spirits products, a tax credit for alcohol derived from fruit is allowed. This credit reduces the effective tax paid on those beverages. The credit is determined when the tax is paid (i.e., at the distillery or on importation).

Explanation of Provision

The Treasury Department is directed to study options for changing the point at which the distilled spirits excise tax is collected. One of the options evaluated should be collecting the tax at the point at which the distilled spirits are removed from registered wholesale warehouses. As part of this

Effective Date

The provision is effective for hard cider removed after September 30, 1997.

[Conference Report]

House Bill

No provision.

Conference Agreement

The conference agreement follows the Senate amendment.

study, the Treasury is to focus on administrative issues associated with the identified options, including the effects on tax compliance. For example, the Treasury is to evaluate the actual compliance record of wholesale dealers that currently paid the excise tax on imported bottled distilled spirits, and the compliance effects of allowing additional wholesale dealers to be distilled spirits taxpayers. The study also is to address the number of taxpayers involved, the types of financial responsibility requirements that might be needed, any special requirements regarding segregation of non-tax-paid distilled spirits from other products carried by the potential new taxpayers. The study further is to review the effects of the options on Treasury staffing and other budgetary resources as well as projections of the time between when tax currently is collected and the time when tax otherwise would be collected.

The study is required to be completed and transmitted to the Committee on Finance and the Committee on Ways and Means no later than January 31, 1998.

[Conference Report]

House Bill

No provision.

Conference Agreement

The conference agreement follows the Senate amendment with a modification delaying the due date of the study to March 31, 1998.

[¶ 5060]   Section 910.   Codify Treasury Department regulations regulating wine labels.

(Code Sec. 5388)

[Senate Report]

Present Law

The Code includes provisions regulating the labeling of wine when it is removed from a winery for marketing. In general, the regulations under these provisions allow the use of semi-generic names for wine that reflect geographic identifications understood in the industry, provided that the labels include clear indication of any deviation from that which is generally understood in the source of the grapes or the process by which the wine is produced.

Reasons for Change

The Committee determined that the Treasury Department regulations governing the use of semi-generic designations such as "Chablis" and "burgundy" in wine labeling should be codified to add clarity to the existing Code provisions.

Explanation of Provision

The current Treasury Department regulations governing the use of semi-generic wine designations which reflect geographic origin are codified into the Code's wine labeling provisions.

Effective Date

The provision is effective on the date of enactment.

[Conference Report]

House Bill

No provision.

Conference Agreement

The conference agreement follows the Senate amendment with a modification deleting the Secretary of the Treasury's discretion to eliminate currently listed semi-generic names.

[¶ 5061]   Section 911.   Authority to postpone certain tax-related deadlines by reason of presidentially declared disaster.

(Code Sec. 7508A)

[House Report]

Present Law

In the case of a Presidentially declared disaster, the Secretary of the Treasury has the authority to postpone some (but not all) tax-related deadlines.

Reasons for Change

The Committee believes that the Secretary should have the authority to postpone additional tax-related deadlines.

Explanation of Provision

The bill provides that, in the case of a taxpayer determined to be affected by a Presidentially declared disaster, the Secretary may specify that, for a period of up to 90 days, certain taxpayer deadlines are post-poned. The deadlines that may be postponed are the same as are postponed by reason of service in a combat zone. The provision does not apply for purposes of determining interest on any overpayment or underpayment.

Effective Date

The provision is effective for any period for performing an act that has not expired before the date of enactment.

[Conference Report]

Senate Amendment

No provision.

Conference Agreement

The conference agreement follows the House bill, except that it is applicable to all deadlines (not just taxpayer deadlines).

[¶ 5062]   Section 912.   Use of certain appraisals to establish amount of disaster loss.

(Code Sec. 165)

[House Report]

Present Law

In order to claim a disaster loss, a taxpayer must establish the amount of the loss. This may, for example, be done through the use of an appraisal.

Reasons for Change

The Committee believes that no impediment should exist to utilizing alternate types of acceptable appraisals.

Explanation of Provision

The bill provides that nothing in the Code should be construed to prohibit Treasury from issuing guidance providing that an ap-praisal for the purpose of obtaining a Federal loan or Federal loan guarantee as the result of a Presidentially declared disaster may be used to establish the amount of a disaster loss.

Effective Date

The provision is effective on the date of enactment.

[Conference Report]

Senate Amendment

No provision.

Conference Agreement

The conference agreement follows the House bill.

[¶ 5063]   Section 913.   Treatment of livestock sold on account of weather-related conditions.

(Code Sec. 451, 1033)

[House Report]

Present Law

In general, cash-method taxpayers report income in the year it is actually or constructively received. However, present law contains two special rules applicable to livestock sold on account of drought conditions. Code section 451(e) provides that a cash-method taxpayer whose principal trade or business is farming who is forced to sell livestock due to drought conditions may elect to include income from the sale of the livestock in the taxable year following the taxable year of the sale. This elective deferral of income is available only if the taxpayer establishes that, under the taxpayer's usual business practices, the sale would not have occurred but for drought conditions that resulted in the area being designated as eligible for Federal assistance. This exception is generally intended to put taxpayers who receive an unusually high amount of income in one year in the position they would have been in absent the drought.

In addition, the sale of livestock (other than poultry) that is held for draft, breeding, or dairy purposes in excess of the number of livestock that would have been sold but for drought conditions is treated as an involuntary conversion under section 1033(e). Consequently, gain from the sale of such livestock could be deferred by reinvesting the proceeds of the sale in similar property within a two-year period.

Reasons for Change

The Committee believes that the present-law exceptions to gain recognition for livestock sold on account of drought should apply to livestock sold on account of floods and other weather-related conditions as well.

Explanation of Provision

The bill amends Code section 451(e) to provide that a cash-method taxpayer whose principal trade or business is farming and who is forced to sell livestock due not only to drought (as under present law), but also to floods or other weather-related conditions, may elect to include income from the sale of the livestock in the taxable year following the taxable year of the sale. This elective deferral of income is available only if the taxpayer establishes that, under the taxpayer's usual business practices, the sale would not have occurred but for the drought, flood or other weather-related conditions that resulted in the area being designated as eligible for Federal assistance.

In addition, the bill amends Code section 1033(e) to provide that the sale of livestock (other than poultry) that are held for draft, breeding, or dairy purposes in excess of the number of livestock that would have been sold but for drought (as under present law), flood or other weather-related conditions is treated as an involuntary conversion.

[¶ 5064]   Section 914.   Mortgage bond financing for residences located in Presidentially declared disaster areas.

(Code Sec. 143)

[House Report]

Present Law

Qualified mortgage bonds are private activity tax-exempt bonds issued by States and local governments acting as conduits to provide mortgage loans to first-time home buyers who satisfy specified income limits and who purchase homes that cost less than statutory maximums.

Present law waives the three buyer targeting requirements for a portion of the loans made with proceeds of a qualified mortgage bond issue if the loans are made to finance homes in statutorily prescribed economically distressed areas.

Reasons for Change

The Committee believes that availability of mortgage subsidy financing may help survivors of Presidentially declared disasters rebuild their homes.

Explanation of Provision

The bill waives the first time home buyer requirement, the income limits, and the purchase price limits for loans to finance homes in certain Presidentially declared disaster areas. The waiver applies only during the one-year period following the date of the disaster declaration.

Effective Date

The provision applies to sales and exchanges after December 31, 1996.

[Conference Report]

Senate Amendment

The Senate amendment is the same as the House bill.

Conference Agreement

The conference agreement follows the House bill and the Senate amendment.

Effective Date

The provision applies to loans financed with bonds issued after December 31, 1996, and before January 1, 2000.

[Conference Report]

Senate Amendment

The Senate amendment is the same as the House bill except for the effective date.

Effective Date

The provision applies to loans financed with bonds issued after December 31, 1996, and before January 1, 1999.

Conference Agreement

The conference agreement allows the waivers of the first- time home buyer requirement, the income limits, and the purchase price limits for loans to finance homes in certain Presidentially declared disaster areas. The waiver applies only during the two-year period following the date of disaster declaration.

Effective Date

The provision applies to loans financed with bonds issued after December 31, 1996 and before January 1, 1999 (i.e., is the same as the Senate amendment).

[¶ 5065]   Section 915.   Requirement to abate interest by reason of Presidentially declared disaster.

(Code Sec. 6601)

[Conference Report]

Present Law

In the case of a Presidentially declared disaster, the Secretary of the Treasury has the authority to postpone some tax- related deadlines, but there is no authority to abate interest.

House Bill

No provision.

Senate Amendment

The Senate amendment requires the IRS to abate interest for the same period of time for which the IRS has provided an extension of time to file tax returns and pay taxes for individuals located in Presidentially declared disaster areas during 1997.

Effective Date

Disasters occurring in 1997.

Conference Agreement

The conference agreement follows the Senate amendment.

[¶ 5066]   Section 921.   Clarification of standard to be used in determining tax status of retail securities brokers.

(Code Sec. 3121)

[House Report]

Present Law

Under present law, whether a worker is an employee or independent contractor is generally determined under a common-law facts and circumstances test. An employer-employee relationship is generally found to exist if the service recipient has not only the right to control the result to be accomplished by the work, but also the means by which the result is to be accomplished. The Internal Revenue Service ("IRS") generally takes the position that the presence and extent of instructions is important in reaching a conclusion as to whether a business retains the right to direct and control the methods by which a worker performs a job, but that it is also important to consider the weight to be given those instructions if they are imposed by the business only in compliance with governmental or governing body regulations. The IRS training manual provides that if a business requires its workers to comply with rules established by a third party (e.g., municipal building codes related to construction), the fact that such rules are imposed should be given little weight in determining the worker's status.

Reasons for Change

Brokerage houses are required to monitor compliance with certain investor protection laws. The Committee believes that such monitoring should not be taken into account in determining the status of a broker for Federal tax purposes.

Explanation of Provision

Under the bill, in determining the status of a registered representative of a broker-dealer for Federal tax purposes, no weight may be given to instructions from the service recipient which are imposed only in compliance with governmental investor protection standards or investor protection standards imposed by a governing body pursuant to a delegation by a Federal or State agency.

Effective Date

The provision is effective with respect to services performed after December 31, 1997. No inference is intended that the treatment under the proposal is not present law.

[Senate Report]

Reasons for Change

Broker-dealers are required to supervise the activities of their affiliated registered representatives in order to comply with

State and Federal investor protection laws. The Committee believes that compliance with duty-to-supervise requirements does not constitute evidence of control for purposes of the common-law test for determining worker classification.

[Conference Report]

Senate Amendment

Same as the House bill, except that the provision applies only for Federal income tax purposes.

Effective Date

Same as the House bill.

Conference Agreement

The conference agreement follows the House bill.

[¶ 5067]   Section 922.   Clarification of exemption from self-employment tax for certain termination payments received by former insurance salesmen.

(Code Sec. 1402)

[House Report]

Present Law

As part of the Federal Insurance Contributions Act ("FICA") a tax is imposed on employees and employers. The tax consists of two parts: old-age, survivor, and disability insurance ("OASDI") and Medicare Hospital Insurance ("HI"). For wages paid in 1997, the OASDI tax rate is 6.2 percent of wages up to $65,400 (indexed for inflation) on both the employer and employee. The HI tax rate on both the employer and the employee is 1.45 percent of wages (with no wage cap).

Similarly, under the self-employment contributions act ("SECA"), taxes are imposed on an individual's net earnings from self employment. In general, net earnings from self employment means the gross income derived by an individual from any trade or business carried on by such individual, less the deductions allowed which are attributable to such trade or business. The SECA tax rate is the same as the combined employer and employee FICA rates (i.e., 12.4 percent for OASDI and 2.9 percent for HI) and the maximum amount of earnings subject to the OASDI portion of SECA taxes is coordinated with and is set at the same level as the maximum level of wages and salaries subject to the OASDI portion of FICA taxes. There is no limit on the amount of self-employment income subject to the HI portion of the tax.

Certain insurance salesmen are independent contractors and therefore subject to tax under SECA.

Under case law, certain payments received by a former insurance salesmen who had sold insurance as an independent contractor are not net earnings from self employment and therefore are not subject to SECA. See, e.g., *Jackson v. Comm'r*, 108 TC XXNo. 10 (1997); *Gump v. U.S.*, 86 F. 3d 1126 (CA FC 1996); *Milligan v. Comm'r*, 38 F. 3d 1094 (9th Cir. 1994).

Reasons for Change

Clarifying the SECA tax treatment of certain payments would provide greater certainty to taxpayers and would reduce the need for further litigation.

Explanation of Provision

The bill codifies case law by providing that net earnings from self employment do not include any amount received during the taxable year from an insurance company on account of services performed by such individual as an insurance salesman for such company if (1) such amount is received after termination of the individual's agreement to perform services for the company, (2) the individual performs no services for the company after such termination and before the close of the taxable year, (3) the amount of the payment depends solely on policies sold by the individual during the last year of the agreement and the extent to which such policies remain in force for some period after such termination, and does not depend on the length of service or overall earnings from services performed for the company, and (4) the payments are conditioned upon the salesman agreeing not to compete with the company for at least one year following such termination.

The bill will also amend the Social Security Act to provide that such termination payments are not treated as earnings for purposes of determining social security benefits.

No inference is intended with respect to the SECA tax treatment of payments that are not described in the proposal.

Effective Date

The provision is effective with respect to payments after December 31, 1997. No inference is intended that the proposal is not present law.

[Conference Report]

Senate Amendment

No provision.

Conference Agreement

The conference agreement follows the House bill, with clarifications with respect to the requirement as to the amount of the payments. The conference agreement clarifies that the provision applies if the amount of the payment depends primarily on policies sold by or credited to the account of the individual during the last year of the service agreement and/or the extent to which such policies remain in force for some period after such termination and does not depend on length of service or overall earnings. The conference agreement clarifies that the eligibility for the payment can be based on length of service or overall earnings.

[¶ 5068]   Section 931.   Delay imposition of penalties for failure to make payments electronically through EFTPS until after December 31, 1998.

(Code Sec. 6302)

[House Report]

Present Law

Employers are required to withhold income taxes and FICA taxes from wages paid to their employees. Employers also are liable for their portion of FICA taxes, excise taxes, and estimated payments of their corporate income tax liability.

The Code requires the development and implementation of an electronic fund transfer system to remit these taxes and convey deposit information directly to the Treasury (Code sec. 6302(h)[55]). The Electronic Federal Tax Payment System ("EFTPS") was developed by Treasury in response to this requirement.[56] Employers must enroll with one of two private contractors hired by the Treasury. After enrollment, employers generally initiate deposits either by telephone or by computer.

The new system is phased in over a period of years by increasing each year the percentage of total taxes subject to the new EFTPS system. For fiscal year 1994, 3 percent of the total taxes are required to be made by electronic fund transfer. These percentages increased gradually for fiscal years 1995 and 1996. For fiscal year 1996, the percentage was 20.1 percent (30 percent for excise taxes and corporate estimated tax payments). For fiscal year 1997, these percentages increased significantly, to 58.3 percent (60 percent for excise taxes and corporate estimated tax payments). The specific implementation method required to achieve the target percentages is set forth in Treasury regulations. Implementation began with the largest depositors.

Treasury had originally implemented the 1997 percentages by requiring that all employers who deposit more than $50,000 in 1995 must begin using EFTPS by January 1, 1997. The Small Business Job Protection Act of 1996 provided that the increase in the required percentages for fiscal year 1997

---

55. This requirement was enacted in 1993 (sec. 523 of P.L. 103 182).
56. Treasury had earlier developed TAXLINK as the prototype for EFTPS. TAXLINK has been operational for

several years; EFTPS is currently operational. Employers currently using TAXLINK will ultimately be required to participate in EFTPS.

(which, pursuant to Treasury regulations, was to take effect on January 1, 1997) will not take effect until July 1, 1997.[57] This was done to provide additional time prior to implementation of the 1997 requirements so that employers could be better informed about their responsibilities.

On June 2, 1997, the IRS announced[58] that it will not impose penalties through December 31, 1997, on businesses that make timely deposits using paper federal tax deposit coupons while converting to the EFTPS system.

[Senate Report]

Reasons for Change

The Committee believes that it is necessary to provide small businesses with additional time prior to implementation of the

requirements so that these employers may be better informed about their responsibilities.

Explanation of Provision

The bill provides that no penalty shall be imposed solely by reason of a failure to use EFTPS prior to July 1, 1998, if the taxpayer was first required to use the EFTPS system on or after July 1, 1997.

Effective Date

The provision is effective on the date of enactment.

[Conference Report]

Conference Agreement

The conference agreement follows the Senate amendment.

[¶ 5069]   Section 932.   Home office deduction: clarification of definition of principal place of business.

(Code Sec. 280A)

[House Report]

Present Law

A taxpayer's business use of his or her home may give rise to a deduction for the business portion of expenses related to operating the home (e.g., a portion of rent or depreciation and repairs). Code section 280A(c)(1) provides, however, that business deductions generally are allowed only with respect to a portion of a home that is used exclusively and regularly in one of the following ways: (1) as the principal place of business for a trade or business; (2) as a place of business used to meet with patients, clients, or customers in the normal course of the taxpayer's trade or business; or (3) in connection with the taxpayer's trade or business, if the portion so used constitutes a separate structure not attached to the dwelling unit. In the case of an employee, the Code further requires that the business use of the home must be for the convenience of the employer (sec. 280A(c)(1)).[59] These rules apply to houses,

apartments, condominiums, mobile homes, boats, and other similar property used as the taxpayer's home (sec. 280A(f)(1)). Under Internal Revenue Service (IRS) rulings, the deductibility of expenses incurred for local transportation between a taxpayer's home and a work location sometimes depends on whether the taxpayer's home office qualifies under section 280A(c)(1) as a principal place of business (see Rev. Rul. 94 47, 1994 29 I.R.B. 6).

Prior to 1976, expenses attributable to the business use of a residence were deductible whenever they were "appropriate and helpful to the taxpayer's business. In 1976, Congress adopted section 280A, in order to provide a narrower scope for the home office deduction, but did not define the term 'principal place of business.' In Commissioner v. Soliman, 113 S.Ct. 701 (1993), the Supreme Court reversed lower court rulings and upheld an IRS interpretation of section 280A that disallowed a home office deduction for a self-employed anesthesiologist who practiced at several hospitals but was not provided office space at the hospitals. Although

---

57. Sec. 1809 of P.L. 104-188.
58. IR 97-32.
59. If an employer provides access to suitable space on the employer's premises for the conduct by an employee of particular duties, then, if the employee opts to con-

duct such duties at home as a matter of personal preference, the employee's use of the home office is not "for the convenience of the employer." See e.g., *W. Michael Mathes*, (1990) T.C. Memo 1990 483.

the anesthesiologist used a room in his home exclusively to perform administrative and management activities for his profession (i.e., he spent two or three hours a day in his home office on bookkeeping, correspondence, reading medical journals, and communicating with surgeons, patients, and insurance companies), the Supreme Court upheld the IRS position that the 'principal place of business' for the taxpayer was not the home office, because the taxpayer performed the 'essence of the professional service' at the hospitals.[60] Because the taxpayer did not meet with patients at his home office and the room was not a separate structure, a deduction was not available under the second or third exception under section 280A(c)(1) (described above).

Section 280A(c)(2) contains a special rule that allows a home office deduction for business expenses related to a space within a home that is used on a regular (even if not exclusive) basis as a storage unit for the inventory or product samples of the taxpayer's trade or business of selling products at retail or wholesale, but only if the home is the sole fixed location of such trade or business.

Home office deductions may not be claimed if they create (or increase) a net loss from a business activity, although such deductions may be carried over to subsequent taxable years (sec. 280A(c)(5)).

Reasons for Change

The Committee believes that the Supreme Court's decision in Soliman unfairly denies a home office deduction to a growing number of taxpayers who manage their business activities from their homes. Thus, the statutory modification adopted by the Committee will reduce the present-law bias in favor of taxpayers who manage their business activities from outside their home, thereby enabling more taxpayers to work efficiently at home, save commuting time and expenses, and spend additional time with their families. Moreover, the statutory modification is an appropriate response to the computer and information revolution, which has made it

more practical for taxpayers to manage trade or business activities from a home office.

Explanation of Provision

Section 280A is amended to specifically provide that a home office qualifies as the "principal place of business" if (1) the office is used by the taxpayer to conduct administrative or management activities of a trade or business and (2) there is no other fixed location of the trade or business where the taxpayer conducts substantial administrative or management activities of the trade or business. As under present law, deductions will be allowed for a home office meeting the above two-part test only if the office is exclusively used on a regular basis as a place of business by the taxpayer and, in the case of an employee, only if such exclusive use is for the convenience of the employer.

Thus, under the bill, a home office deduction is allowed (subject to the present-law "convenience of the employer" rule governing employees) if a portion of a taxpayer's home is exclusively and regularly used to conduct administrative or management activities for a trade or business of the taxpayer, who does not conduct substantial administrative or management activities at any other fixed location of the trade or business, regardless of whether administrative or management activities connected with his trade or business (e.g., billing activities) are performed by others at other locations. The fact that a taxpayer also carries out administrative or management activities at sites that are not fixed locations of the business, such as a car or hotel room, will not affect the taxpayer's ability to claim a home office deduction under the bill. Moreover, if a taxpayer conducts some administrative or management activities at a fixed location of the business outside the home, the taxpayer still will be eligible to claim a deduction so long as the administrative or management activities conducted at any fixed location of the business outside the home are not substantial (e.g., the taxpayer occasionally does minimal paperwork at another fixed location

---

60. In response to the Supreme Court's decision in *Soliman*, the IRS revised its *Publication 587, Business Use of Your Home*, to more closely follow the comparative analysis used in *Soliman* by focusing on the following two primary factors in determining whether

a home office is a taxpayer's principal place of business: (1) the relative importance of the activities performed at each business location; and (2) the amount of time spent at each location.

of the business). In addition, a taxpayer's eligibility to claim a home office deduction under the bill will not be affected by the fact that the taxpayer conducts substantial non-administrative or non-management business activities at a fixed location of the business outside the home (e.g., meeting with, or providing services to, customers, clients, or patients at a fixed location of the business away from home).

If a taxpayer in fact does not perform substantial administrative or management activities at any fixed location of the business away from home, then the second part of the test will be satisfied, regardless of whether or not the taxpayer opted not to use an office away from home that was available for the conduct of such activities. However, in the case of an employee, the question whether an employee chose not to use suitable space made available by the employer for administrative activities is relevant to determining whether the present-law convenience of the employer' test is satisfied. In cases where a taxpayer's use of a home office does not satisfy the provision's two-part test, the taxpayer nonetheless may be able to claim a home office deduction under the present-law 'principal place of business exception or any other provision of section 280A.

Effective Date

The provision applies to taxable years beginning after December 31, 1997.

[Conference Report]

Senate Amendment

No provision.

Conference Agreement

The conference agreement follows the House bill, except that the provision is effective for taxable years beginning after December 31, 1998.

[¶ 5070]   Section 933. Income averaging for farmers.

(Code Sec. 480A)

[Conference Report]

Present Law

The ability for an individual taxpayer to reduce his or her tax liability by averaging his or her income over a number of years was repealed by the Tax Reform Act of 1986.

House Bill

No provision.

Senate Amendment

An individual taxpayer is allowed to elect to compute his or her current year tax liability by averaging, over the prior three- year period, all or a portion of his or her taxable income from the trade of business of farming.

Effective Date

The provision is effective for taxable years beginning after the date of enactment and before January 1, 2001.

Conference Agreement

The conference agreement includes the Senate amendment with modifications. The conference agreement clarifies that the provision operates such that an electing eligible taxpayer (1) designates all or a portion of his or her taxable income from the trade or business of farming from the current year as "elected farm income;" (2) allocates one-third of such "elected farm income" to each of the prior three taxable years; and (3) determines his or her current year section 1 tax liability by determining the sum of (a) his or her current year section 1 liability without the elected farm income allocated to the three prior taxable years plus (b) the increases in the section 1 tax for each of the three prior taxable years by taking into account the allocable share of the elected farm income for such years. If a taxpayer elects the operation the provision for a taxable year, the allocation of elected farm income among taxable years pursuant to the election shall apply for purposes of any election in a subsequent taxable year.

The provision does not apply for employment tax purposes, or to an estate or a trust. Further, the provision does not apply for purposes of the alternative minimum tax under section 55. Finally, the provision does not require the recalculation of the tax liability of any other taxpayer, including a minor child required to use the tax rates of his or her parents under section 1(g).

The election shall be made in the manner prescribed by the Secretary of the Treasury and, except as provided by the Secretary, shall be irrevocable. In addition, the Secretary of the Treasury shall prescribe such regulations as are necessary to carry out the purposes of the provision, including regulations regarding the order and manner in which items of income, gain, deduction, loss, and credits (and any limitations thereon) are to be taken into account for purposes of the provision and the application of the provision to any short taxable year. It is expected that such regulations will deny the multiple application of items that carryover from one taxable year to the next (e.g., net operating loss or tax credit carryovers).

The provision applies to taxable years beginning after December 31, 1997, and before January 1, 2001.

[¶ 5071]   Section 934.   Increase deduction for health insurance costs of self-employed individuals.

(Code Sec. 162)

[Conference Report]

Present Law

Under present law, self-employed individuals are entitled to deduct the amount paid for health insurance for the self-employed individual and the individual's spouse and dependents as follows: the deduction is 40 percent in 1997; 45 percent in 1998 through 2002; 50 percent in 2003; 60 percent in 2004; 70 percent in 2005; and 80 percent in 2006 and thereafter. The deduction for health insurance expenses of self-employed individuals is not available for any month in which the taxpayer is eligible to participate in a subsidized health plan maintained by the employer of the taxpayer or the taxpayer's spouse.

Under present law employees can exclude from income 100 percent of employee-provided health insurance.

House Bill

No provision.

Senate Amendment

The Senate amendment permits self-employed individuals to deduct a higher percentage of the amount paid for health insurance as follows: the deduction is 50 percent in 1997 and 1998; 60 percent in 1999 through 2002; 70 percent in 2003; 80 percent in 2004; 85 percent in 2005; 90 percent in 2006; and 100 percent in 2007 and all years thereafter.

Effective Date

The provision is effective for taxable years beginning after December 31, 1996.

Conference Agreement

The conference agreement follows the Senate amendment, with modifications. Under the conference agreement, the self-employed health deduction is phased up as follows: the deduction is 40 percent in 1997, 45 percent in 1998 and 1999, 50 percent in 2000 and 2001, 60 percent in 2002, 80 percent in 2003 through 2005, 90 percent in 2006, and 100 percent in 2007 and thereafter.

[¶ 5072]   Section 935.   Moratorium on regulations; self-employment taxes of limited partners.

(Code Sec. 1402)

[House Report]

Generalized System of Preferences (sec. 971 of the bill)

Section 971 of the bill reauthorizes Title V of the Trade Act of 1974, as mended Generalized System of Preferences, "GSP") for two years to expire on May 31, 1999.

Prior Law

Title V of the Trade Act of 1974, as amended, (Generalized System of Preferences), grants authority to the President to provide duty-free treatment on imports of eligible articles from designated beneficiary developing countries, subject to specific conditions and limitations. To qualify for GSP privileges each beneficiary country is subject to various mandatory and discretionary eligibility criteria. Import sensitive products are ineligible for GSP. The President's authority to grant GSP benefits expired on May 31, 1997.

Explanation of Provision

The bill reauthorizes the GSP program for two years, to expire on May 31, 1999. The bill provides for refunds, upon request of the importer, of any duty paid between May 31, 1997, and the date of enactment.

Effective Date

The provision is effective upon date of enactment.

[E. Sense of the Senate Regarding Self-Employment Taxes of Limited Partners (sec. 734 of the Senate amendment) Conference Report]

Present Law

Under the Self-Employment Contributions Act, taxes are imposed on an individual's net earnings from self employment. A limited partner's net earnings from self employment include guaranteed payments made to the individual for services actually rendered and do not include a limited partner's distributive share of the income or loss of the partnership. The Department of the Treasury has issued proposed regula-

tions defining a limited partner for this purpose. These regulations provide, among other things, that an individual is not a limited partner if the individual participates in the partnership business for more than 500 hours during the taxable year. The regulations are proposed to be effective beginning with the individual's first taxable year beginning on or after the date the regulations are published as final regulations in the Federal Register.

House Bill

No provision.

Senate Amendment

It is the Sense of the Senate that the Department of the Treasury should withdraw the proposed regulations defining limited partner, and that the Congress should determine the tax law governing self-employment income.

Conference Agreement

The conference agreement provides that any regulations relating to the definition of a limited partner for self-employment tax purposes shall not be issued or effective before July 1, 1998.

[Conference Report]

Under present law, an individual taxpayer generally is subject to an addition to tax for any underpayment of estimated tax. An individual generally does not have an underpayment of estimated tax if he or she makes timely estimated tax payments at least equal to: (1) 100 percent of the tax shown on the return of the individual for the preceding year (the "100 percent of last year's liability safe harbor") or (2) 90 percent of the tax shown on the return for the current year. The 100 percent of last year's liability safe harbor is modified to be a 110 percent of last year's liability safe harbor for any individual with an AGI of more than $150,000 as shown on the return for the preceding taxable year.

House Bill

The House bill changes the 110 percent of last year's liability safe harbor to be a

109 percent of last year's liability safe harbor for taxable years beginning in 1997 and a 105 percent of last year's liability safe harbor for taxable years beginning in 1998.

Senate Amendment

No provision.

Conference Agreement

The conference agreement changes the 110 percent of last year's liability safe harbor to be a 100 percent of last year's liability safe harbor for taxable years beginning in 1998, a 105 percent of last year's liability safe harbor for taxable years beginning in 1990, 2000, and 2001, and a 112 percent of last year's liability safe harbor for taxable years beginning in 2002. In addition, no estimated tax penalties will be imposed under section 6654 or 6655 for any period before January 1, 1998, for any payment the due date of which is before January 16, 1998, with respect to an underpayment to the extent the underpayment is created or increased by a provision of the Act.

[Conference Report]

Senate Amendment

No provision.

Conference Agreement

The conference agreement follows the House bill, with a modification to extend the GSP reauthorization through June 30, 1998.

[¶ 5073]   Section 941.   Expensing of environmental remeditaion costs.

(Code Sec. 198)

[Senate Report]

Present Law

Code section 162 allows a deduction for ordinary and necessary expenses paid or incurred in carrying on any trade or business. Treasury Regulations provide that the cost of incidental repairs which neither materially add to the value of property nor appreciably prolong its life, but keep it in an ordinarily efficient operating condition, may be deducted currently as a business expense. Section 263(a)(1) limits the scope of section 162 by prohibiting a current deduction for certain capital expenditures. Treasury Regulations define "capital expenditures" as amounts paid or incurred to materially add to the value, or substantially prolong the useful life, of property owned by the taxpayer, or to adapt property to a new or different use. Amounts paid for repairs and maintenance do not constitute capital expenditures. The determination of whether an expense is deductible or capitalizable is based on the facts and circumstances of each case.

Treasury regulations provide that capital expenditures include the costs of acquiring or substantially improving buildings, machinery, equipment, furniture, fixtures and similar property having a useful life substantially beyond the current year. In *IN-*DOPCO, Inc. v. Commissioner*, 112 S. Ct. 1039 (1992), the Supreme Court required the capitalization of legal fees incurred by a taxpayer in connection with a friendly takeover by one of its customers on the grounds that the merger would produce signi ficant economic benefits to the taxpayer extending beyond the current year; capitalization of the costs thus would match the expenditures with the income produced. Similarly, the amount paid for the construction of a filtration plant, with a life extending beyond the year of completion, and as a permanent addition to the taxpayer's mill property, was a capital expenditure rather than an ordinary and necessary current business expense. *Woolrich Woolen Mills v. United States*, 289 F.2d 444 (3d Cir. 1961).

Although Treasury regulations provide that expenditures that materially increase the value of property must be capitalized, they do not set forth a method of determining how and when value has been increased. In *Plainfield-Union Water Co. v. Commissioner*, 39 T.C. 333 (1962), nonacq., 1964-2 C.B. 8, the U.S. Tax Court held that increased value was determined by comparing the value of an asset after the expenditure with its value before the condition necessitating the expenditure. The Tax Court stated that "an expenditure which returns property to the state it was in before the situation prompting the expenditure arose, and which does not make the relevant property more valuable, more useful, or longer-lived, is usually deemed a deductible repair."

In several Technical Advice Memoranda (TAM), the Internal Revenue Service (IRS) declined to apply the *Plainfield Union* valuation analysis, indicating that the analysis represents just one of several alternative methods of determining increases in the value of an asset. In TAM 9240004 (June 29, 1992), the IRS required certain asbestos removal costs to be capitalized rather than expensed. In that instance, the taxpayer owned equipment that was manufactured with insulation containing asbestos; the taxpayer replaced the asbestos insulation with less thermally efficient, non-asbestos insulation. The IRS concluded that the expenditures resulted in a material increase in the value of the equipment because the asbestos removal eliminated human health risks, reduced the risk of liability to employees resulting from the contamination, and made the property more marketable. Similarly, in TAM 9411002 (November 19, 1993), the IRS required the capitalization of expenditures to remove and replace asbestos in connection with the conversion of a boiler room to garage and office space. However, the IRS permitted deduction of costs of encapsulating exposed asbestos in an adjacent warehouse.

In 1994, the IRS issued Rev. Rul. 94-38, 1994-1 C.B. 35, holding that soil remediation expenditures and ongoing water treatment expenditures incurred to clean up land and water that a taxpayer contaminated with hazardous waste are deductible. In this ruling, the IRS explicitly accepted the *Plainfield Union* valuation analysis.[64] However, the IRS also held that costs allocable to constructing a groundwater treatment facility are capital expenditures.

In 1995, the IRS issued TAM 9541005 (October 13, 1995) requiring a taxpayer to capitalize certain environmental study costs, as well as associated consulting and legal fees. The taxpayer acquired the land and conducted activities causing hazardous waste contamination. After the contamination, but before it was discovered, the com-

pany donated the land to the county to be developed into a recreational park. After the county discovered the contamination, it reconveyed the land to the company for $1. The company incurred the costs in developing a remediation strategy. The IRS held that the costs were not deductible under section 162 because the company acquired the land in a contaminated state when it purchased the land from the county. In January, 1996, the IRS revoked and superseded TAM 9541005 (PLR 9627002). Noting that the company's contamination of the land and liability for remediation were unchanged during the break in ownership by the county, the IRS concluded that the break in ownership should not, in and of itself, operate to disallow a deduction under section 162.

Reasons for Change

To encourage the cleanup of contaminated sites, as well as to eliminate uncertainty regarding the appropriate treatment of environmental remediation expenditures for Federal tax law purposes, the Committee believes that it is appropriate to provide clear and consistent rules regarding the Federal tax treatment of certain environmental remediation expenses.

Explanation of Provision

The bill provides that taxpayers could elect to treat certain environmental remediation expenditures that would otherwise be chargeable to capital account as deductible in the year paid or incurred. The deduction applies for both regular and alternative minimum tax purposes. The expenditure must be incurred in connection with the abatement or control of hazardous substances at a qualified contaminated site. In general, any expenditure for the acquisition of depreciable property used in connection with the abatement or control of hazardous substances at a qualified contaminated site does not constitute a qualified environmental remediation expenditure. However, depreciation deductions allowable for such property which would otherwise be allocated to the site under the principles set forth in

---

64. Rev. Rul. 94-38 generally rendered moot the holding in TAM 9315004 (December 17, 1992) requiring a taxpayer to capitalize certain costs associated with the remediation of soil contaminated with polychlorinated biphenyls (PCBs).

Comm'r v. Idaho Power Co.[65] and section 263A are treated as qualified environmental remediation expenditures.

A "qualified contaminated site" generally is any property that (1) is held for use in a trade or business, for the production of income, or as inventory; (2) is certified by the appropriate State environmental agency to be located within a targeted area; and (3) contains (or potentially contains) a hazardous substance (so-called "brownfields"). Targeted areas would mean (1) empowerment zones and enterprise communities (as designated under present law and the D.C. Enterprise Zone designated under the bill); and (2) sites announced before February, 1997, as being subject to one of the 76 Environmental Protection Agency (EPA) Brownfields Pilots.

Both urban and rural sites qualify. However, sites that are identified on the national priorities list under the Comprehensive Environmental Response, Compensation, and Liability Act of 1980 (CERCLA) cannot be targeted areas. Appropriate State environmental agencies are designated by the EPA; if no State agency is designated, the EPA is responsible for providing the certification. Hazardous substances generally are defined by reference to sections 101(14) and 102 of CERCLA, subject to additional limitations applicable to asbestos and similar substances within buildings, certain naturally occurring substances such as radon, and certain other substances released into drinking water supplies due to deterioration through ordinary use.

The bill further provides that, in the case of property to which a qualified environmental remediation expenditure otherwise would have be capitalized, any deduction allowed under the bill would be treated as a depreciation deduction and the property would be treated as subject to section 1245. Thus, deductions for qualified environmental remediation expenditures would be subject to recapture as ordinary income upon sale or other disposition of the property.

Effective Date

The provision applies to eligible expenditures incurred after the date of enactment.

[Conference Report]

House Bill

No provision.

Conference Agreement

The conference agreement follows the Senate amendment, except that the definition of "targeted areas" is expanded to include population census tracts with a poverty rate of 20 percent or more and certain industrial and commercial areas that are adjacent to such census tracts. Thus, targeted areas generally would include: (1) empowerment zones and enterprise communities as designated under present law and under the conference agreement.[51] (including any supplemental empowerment zone designated on December 21, 1994); (2) sites announced before February 1997, as being subject to one of the 76 Environmental Protection Agency (EPA) Brownfields Pilots; (3) any population census tract with a poverty rate of 20 percent or more; and (4) certain industrial and commercial areas that are adjacent to tracts described in (3) above.

With respect to certification of targeted areas, the conference agreement provides that the chief executive officer of a State may, in consultation with the Administrator of the EPA, designate an appropriate State environmental agency. If no State environmental agency is so designated within 60 days of the date of enactment, the appropriate environmental agency for such State shall be designated by the Administrator of the EPA.

---

65. *Comm'r v. Idaho Power Co.*, 418 U.S. 1 (1974) (holding that equipment depreciation allocable to the taxpayer's construction of capital facilities must be capitalized under section 263(a)(1)).

51. Thus, the 20 additional empowerment zones authorized to be designated under the conference agreement as well as the D.C. Enterprise Zone established under the conference agreement are "targeted areas" for purposes of this provision.

[¶ 5074]   Section 951-956.   Designation of additional empowerment zones; modification of empowerment zone and enterprise community criteria.

(Code Sec. 1391, 1392, 1396, 1394, 1397B)

[Conference Report]

Present Law

In general

Pursuant to the Omnibus Budget Reconciliation Act of 1993 (OBRA 1993), the Secretaries of the Department of Housing and Urban Development (HUD) and the Department of Agriculture designated a total of nine empowerment zones and 95 enterprise communities on December 21, 1994. As required by law, six empowerment zones are located in urban areas (with aggregate population for the six designated urban empowerment zones limited to 750,000) and three empowerment zones are located in rural areas.[52] Of the enterprise communities, 65 are located in urban areas and 30 are located in rural areas (sec. 1391). Designated empowerment zones and enterprise communities were required to satisfy certain eligibility criteria, including specified poverty rates and population and geographic size limitations (sec. 1392).

The following tax incentives are available for certain businesses located in empowerment zones: (1) a 20-percent wage credit for the first $15,000 of wages paid to a zone resident who works in the zone; (2) an additional $20,000 of section 179 expensing for "qualified zone property" placed in service by an "enterprise zone business" (accordingly, certain businesses operating in empowerment zones are allowed up to $38,000 of expensing for 1997); and (3) special tax-exempt financing for certain zone facilities (described in more detail below).

The 95 enterprise communities are eligible for the special tax-exempt financing benefits but not the other tax incentives available in the nine empowerment zones. In addition to these tax incentives, OBRA 1993 provided that Federal grants would be made to designated empowerment zones and enterprise communities.

The tax incentives for empowerment zones and enterprise communities generally will be available during the period that the designation remains in effect, i.e., a 10-year period.

Reasons for Change

In view of the unique characteristics of the States of Alaska and Hawaii, and the economically depressed areas within those States, the Committee believes that the generally applicable criteria for empowerment zones and enterprise communities should be modified in the event that Congress decides to provide for additional designations of such zones or communities.

Definition of "qualified zone property"

Present-law section 1397C defines "qualified zone property" as depreciable tangible property (including buildings), provided that: (1) the property is acquired by the taxpayer (from an unrelated party) after the zone or community designation took effect; (2) the original use of the property in the zone or community commences with the taxpayer; and (3) substantially all of the use of the property is in the zone or community in the active conduct of a trade or business by the taxpayer in the zone o r community. In the case of property which is substantially renovated by the taxpayer, however, the property need not be acquired by the taxpayer after zone or community designation or originally used by the taxpayer within the zone or community if, during any 24-month period after zone or community designation, the additions to the taxpayer's basis in the property exceed 100 percent of the taxpayer's basis in the property at the beginning of the period, or $5,000 (whichever is greater).

52. The six designated urban empowerment zones are located in New York City, Chicago, Atlanta, Detroit, Baltimore, and Philadelphia–Camden (New Jersey). The three designated rural empowerment zones are located in Kentucky Highlands (Clinton, Jackson, and Wayne counties, Kentucky) Mid–Delta Mississippi (Bolivar, Holmes, Humphreys, Leflore counties, Mississippi), and Rio Grande Valley Texas (Cameron, Hidalgo, Starr, and Willacy counties, Texas).

Definition of "enterprise zone business

Present-law section 1397B defines the term "enterprise zone business" as a corporation or partnership (or proprietorship) if for the taxable year: (1) the sole trade or business of the corporation or partnership is the active conduct of a qualified business within an empowerment zone or enterprise community; (2) at least 80 percent of the total gross income is derived from the active conduct of a "qualified business" within a zone or community; (3) substantially all of the business's tangible property is used within a zone or community; (4) substantially all of the business's intangible property is used in, and exclusively related to, the active conduct of such business; (5) substantially all of the services performed by employees are performed wi thin a zone or community; (6) at least 35 percent of the employees are residents of the zone or community; and (7) no more than five percent of the average of the aggregate unadjusted bases of the property owned by the business is attributable to (a) certain financial property, or (b) collectibles not held primarily for sale to customers in the ordinary course of an active trade or business.

A "qualified business" is defined as any trade or business other than a trade or business that consists predominantly of the development or holding of intangibles for sale or license.[53] In addition, the leasing of real property that is located within the empowerment zone or community to others is treated as a qualified business only if (1) the leased property is not residential property, and (2) at least 50 percent of the gross rental income from the real property is from enterprise zone businesses. The rental of tangible personal property to others is not a qualified business unless substantially all of the rental of such property is by enterprise zone businesses or by residents of an empowerment zone or enterprise community.

Tax-exempt financing rules

Tax-exempt private activity bonds may be issued to finance certain facilities in em-powerment zones and enterprise communities. These bonds, along with most private activity bonds, are subject to an annual private activity bond State volume cap equal to $50 per resident of each State, or (if greater) $150 million per State.

Qualified enterprise zone facility bonds are bonds 95 percent or more of the net proceeds of which are used to finance (1) "qualified zone property" (as defined above) the principal user of which is an "enterprise zone business" (also defined above[54]), or (2) functionally related and subordinate land located in the empowerment zone or enterprise community. These bonds may only be issued while an empowerment zone or enterprise community designation is in effect.

The aggregate face amount of all qualified enterprise zone bonds for each qualified enterprise zone business may not exceed $3 million per zone or community. In addition, total qualified enterprise zone bond financing for each principal user of these bonds may not exceed $20 million for all zones and communities.

House Bill

No provision.

Conference Agreement

The conference agreement follows the Senate amendment. In addition, the conference agreement provides for the designation of 20 additional empowerment zones pursuant to slightly expanded eligibility criteria, and includes certain modifications to the definition of an enterprise zone business and the tax-exempt financing rules.

Two additional empowerment zones with same tax incentives as previously designated empowerment zones

Under the conference agreement, the Secretary of HUD is authorized to designate two additional empowerment zones located in urban areas (thereby increasing to eight the total number of empowerment zones located in urban areas) with respect to which

---

53. Also, a qualified business does not include certain facilities described in section 144(c)(6)(B)(e.g., massage parlor, hot tub facility, or liquor store) or certain large farms.

54. For purposes of the tax-exempt financing rules, an "enterprise zone business" also includes a business lo-cated in a zone or community which would qualify as an enterprise zone business if it were separately incorporated.

generally apply the same tax incentives (i.e., the wage credit, additional expensing, and special tax-exempt financing) as are available within the empowerment zones authorized by the Omnibus Budget Reconciliation Act of 1993 (OBRA 1993). The wage credit available in the two new urban empowerment zones is modified slightly to provide that the percentage of wages taken into account for purposes of determining the wage credit is 20 percent for 2000-2004, 15 percent for 2005, 10 percent for 2006, and 5 percent for 2007. No wage credit is available in the two new urban empowerment zones after 2007.

The two additional empowerment zones are subject to the same eligibility criteria under present-law section 1392 that applies to the original six urban empowerment zones. In order to permit designation of these two additional empowerment zones, the conference agreement increases the present-law 750,000 aggregate population cap applicable to empowerment zones located in urban areas to a cap of one million aggregate population for the eight urban empowerment zones.

The two empowerment zones must be designated within 180 days after the date of enactment. However, the designations will not take effect before January 1, 2000, and generally will remain in effect for 10 years.

Designation of additional empowerment zones

The conference agreement authorizes the Secretaries of HUD and Agriculture to designate an additional 20 empowerment zones (no more than 15 in urban areas and no more than five in rural areas).[55] With respect to these additional empowerment zones, the present-law eligibility criteria are expanded slightly. First, the square mileage limitations of present law (i.e., 20 square miles for urban areas and 1,000 for rural areas) are expanded to allow the empowerment zones to include an additional 2,000 acres. This additional acreage, which could be developed for commercial or industrial

purposes, is not subject to the poverty rate criteria and could be divided among up to three noncontiguous parcels. In addition, the present-law requirement that at least half of the nominated area consist of census tracts with poverty rates of 35 percent or more does not apply. Thus, under present-law section 1392(a)(4), at least 90 percent of the census tracts within a nominated area must have a poverty rate of 25 percent or more, and the remaining census tracts must have a poverty rate of 20 percent or more.[56] For this purpose, census tracts with populations under 2,000 are treated as satisfying the 25-percent poverty rate criteria if (1) at least 75 percent of the tract is zoned for commercial or industrial use and (2) the tract is contiguous to one or more other tracts that actually have a poverty rate of 25 percent or more.

Within the 20 additional empowerment zones, qualified "enterprise zone businesses" are eligible to receive up to $20,000 of additional section 179 expensing[57] and to utilize special tax-exempt financing benefits. The "brownfields tax incentive provided under the conference agreement also is available within all designated empowerment zones. Businesses within the 20 additional empowerment zones are not, however, eligible to receive the present-law wage credit available within the 11 other designated empowerment zones (i.e., the wage credit would be available only in the nine present-law zones and two new urban empowerment zones designated under the conference agreement).

The 20 additional empowerment zones are required to be designated before 1999, and the designations generally will remain in effect for 10 years.

Modification of definition of enterprise zone business

The conference agreement modifies the present-law requirement of section 1397B that an entity may qualify as an "enterprise zone business" only if (in addition to the other present-law criteria) at least 80 percent of the total gross income of such entity

---

55. Under the conference agreement, areas located within Indian reservations are eligible for designation as empowerment zones.

56. In lieu of the poverty criteria, outmigration may be taken into account in designating one rural empowerment zone.

57. However, the additional section 179 expensing is not available within the additional 2,000 acres allowed to be included under the conference agreement within an empowerment zone.

is derived from the active conduct of a qualified business within an empowerment zone or enterprise community. The conference agreement liberalizes this present-law requirement by reducing the percentage threshold so that an entity could qualify as an enterprise zone business if at least 50 percent of the total gross income of such entity is derived from the active conduct of a qualified business within an empowerment zone or enterprise community (assuming that the other criteria of section 1397B are satisfied).

In addition, section 1397B is modified so that rather than requiring that "substantially all" tangible and intangible property (and employee services) of an enterprise zone business be used (and performed) within a designated zone or community, a "substantial portion" of tangible and intangible property (and employee services) of an enterprise zone business would be required to be used (and performed)) within a designated zone or community. Moreover, the conference agreement further amends the section 1397B rule governing intangible assets so that a substantial portion of an entity's intangible property must be used in the active conduct of a qualified business within a zone or community, but there is no need (as under present law) to determine whether the use of such assets is "exclusively related to" such business. However, the present-law rule of section 1397B(d)(4) continues to apply, such that a "qualified business" would not include any trade or business consisting predominantly of the development or holding or intangibles for sale or license. The conference agreement also clarifies that an enterprise zone business that leases to others commercial property within a zone or community may rely on a lessee's certification that the lessee is an enterprise zone business. Finally, the conference agreement provides that the rental to others of tangible personal property shall be treated as a qualified business if and only if at least 50 percent of the rental of such property is by enterprise zone businesses or by residents of a zone or community (rather than the present-law requirement that "substantially all" tan-

gible personal property rentals of an enterprise zone business satisfy this test).

This modified "enterprise zone business" definition applies to all previously designated empowerment zones and enterprise communities, the two urban empowerment zones designated under the conference agreement, as well as to the 20 additional empowerment zones authorized to be designated pursuant to the conference agreement.[58]

Tax-exempt financing rules

Exceptions to volume cap

The conference agreement allows "new empowerment zone facility bonds" to be issued for qualified enterprise zone businesses in the 20 additional empowerment zones. These bonds are not subject to the State private activity bond volume caps or the special limits on issue size applicable to qualified enterprise zone facility bonds under present law. The maximum amount of these bonds that can be issued is limited to $60 million per rural zone, $130 million per urban zone with a population of less than 100,000, and $230 million per urban zone with a population of 100,000 or more. Changes to certain rules applicable to both empowerment zone facility bonds and qualified enterprise community facility bonds

Qualified enterprise zone businesses located in newly designated empowerment zones, as well as those located in previously designated empowerment zones and enterprise communities, would be eligible for special tax-exempt bond financing under present-law rules, subject to the modifications described below (and the exception to the volume cap described above for newly designated empowerment zones).

The conference agreement waives until the end of a "startup period" the requirement that 95 percent or more of the proceeds of bond issue be used by a qualified enterprise zone business. With respect to each property, the startup period ends at the beginning of the first taxable year beginning more than two years after the later of (1) the date of the bond issue financing such

---

58. In addition, the modifications to the enterprise zone business definition will apply for purposes of defining a "D.C. Zone business" under certain provisions of the

conference agreement that provide certain tax incentives for the District of Columbia.

property, or (2) the date the property was placed in service (but in no event more than three years after the date of bond issuance). This waiver is only available if, at the beginning of the startup period, there is a reasonable expectation that the use by a qualified enterprise zone business would be satisfied at the end of the startup period and the business makes bona fide efforts to satisfy the enterprise zone business definition.

The conference agreement also waives the requirements of an enterprise zone business (other than the requirement that at least 35 percent of the business' employees be residents of the zone or community) for all years after a prescribed testing period equal to first three taxable years after the startup period.

Finally, the conference agreement relaxes the rehabilitation requirement for financing existing property with qualified enterprise zone facility bonds. In the case of property which is substantially renovated by the taxpayer, the property need not be acquired by the taxpayer after zone or community designation or originally used by the taxpayer within the zone if, during any 24- month period after zone or community designation,

the additions to the taxpayer's basis in the property exceeded 15 percent of the taxpayer's basis at the beginning of the period, or $5,000 (whichever is greater).

Effective Date

The two additional urban empowerment zones (within which generally are available the same tax incentives as are available in the empowerment zones designated pursuant to OBRA 1993) must be designated within 180 days after enactment, but the designation will not take effect before January 1, 2000. The 20 additional empowerment zones (within which the wage credit is not available) are to be designated after enactment but prior to January 1, 1999. For purposes of the additional section 179 expensing available within empowerment zones, the modifications to the definition of "enterprise zone business" are effective for taxable years beginning on or after the date of enactment.

The changes to the tax-exempt financing rules are effective for qualified enterprise zone facility bonds and the new empowerment zone facility bonds issued after the date of enactment.

[¶ 5082]   Section 961.   Use of estimates of shrinkage for inventory accounting.

(Code Sec. 471)

[House Report]

Present Law

Section 471(a) provides that "(w)henever in the opinion of the Secretary the use of inventories is necessary in order clearly to determine the income of any taxpayer, inventories shall be taken by such taxpayer on such basis as the Secretary may prescribe as conforming as nearly as may be to the best accounting practice in the trade or business and as most clearly reflecting income." Where a taxpayer maintains book inventories in accordance with a sound accounting system, the net value of the inventory will be deemed to be the cost basis of the inventory, provided that such book inventories are verified by physical inventories at reasonable intervals and adjusted to conform therewith.[61] The physical count is used to

determine and adjust for certain items, such as undetected theft, breakage, and bookkeeping errors, collectively referred to as "shrinkage."

Some taxpayers verify and adjust their book inventories by a physical count taken on the last day of the taxable year. Other taxpayers may verify and adjust their inventories by physical counts taken at other times during the year. Still other taxpayers take physical counts at different locations at different times during the taxable year (cycle counting).

If a physical inventory is taken at year-end, the amount of shrinkage for the year is known. If a physical inventory is not taken at year-end, shrinkage through year-end will have to be based on an estimate, or not taken into account until the following year. In the first decision in *Dayton Hudson v.*

---

61. Treas. reg. sec. 1:471 2(d).

Commissioner,[62] the U.S. Tax Court held that a taxpayer's method of accounting may include the use of an estimate of shrinkage occurring through year-end, provided the method is sound and clearly reflects income. In the second decision in *Dayton Hudson v. Commissioner,*[63] the U.S. Tax Court adhered to this holding. However, the U.S. Tax Court in the second decision determined that this taxpayer had not established that its method of accounting clearly reflected income. Other cases decided by the U.S. Tax Court[64] have held that taxpayers' methods of accounting that included shrinkage estimates do clearly reflect income.

The U.S. Tax Court in the second *Dayton Hudson* opinion noted that "(i)n most cases, generally accepted accounting principles (GAAP), consistently applied, will pass muster for tax purposes. The Supreme Court has made clear, however, that GAAP does not enjoy a presumption of accuracy that must be rebutted by the Commissioner."

Reasons for Change

The Committee believes that inventories should be kept in a manner that clearly reflects income. The Committee also believes that it is inappropriate to require a physical count of a taxpayer's entire inventory to be taken exactly at year-end, provided that physical counts are taken on a regular and consistent basis. Where physical inventories are not taken at year-end, the Committee believes that income will be more clearly reflected if the taxpayer makes a reasonable estimate of the shrinkage occurring through year-end, rather than simply ignoring it.

The Committee believes that a taxpayer should have the opportunity to change its method of accounting to a method that keeps inventories using shrinkage estimates, so long as such method is sound and clearly reflects income. The Committee does not believe that it is appropriate to deny a taxpayer access to such a method solely because its current, acceptable method of accounting does not utilize shrinkage estimates.

Explanation of Provision

The bill provides that a method of keeping inventories will not be considered unsound, or to fail to clearly reflect income, solely because it includes an adjustment for the shrinkage estimated to occur through year-end, based on inventories taken other than at year-end. Such an estimate must be based on actual physical counts. Where such an estimate is used in determining ending inventory balances, the taxpayer is required to take a physical count of inventories at each location on a regular and consistent basis. A taxpayer is required to adjust its ending inventory to take into account all physical counts performed through the end of its taxable year.

Effective Date

The provision is effective for taxable years ending after the date of enactment.

A taxpayer is permitted to change its method of accounting by this section if the taxpayer is currently using a method that does not utilize estimates of inventory shrinkage and wishes to change to a method for inventories that includes shrinkage estimates based on physical inventories taken other than at year-end. Such a change is treated as a voluntary change in method of accounting, initiated by the taxpayer with the consent of the Secretary of the Treasury, provided the taxpayer changes to a permissible method of accounting. The period for taking into account any adjustment required under section 481 as a result of such a change in method is 4 years.

No inference is intended by the Committee by the adoption of this provision with regard to the validity of any method of accounting for inventories under present law.

[Conference Report]

Senate Amendment

The Senate amendment is the same as the House bill.

Conference Agreement

The conference agreement follows the House bill and the Senate amendment, with the following clarifications regarding safe

---

62. 101 T.C. 462 (1993).
63. T.C. Memo (filed June 11, 1997).

64. *Wal-Mart v. Commissioner,* T.C. Memo 1997-1 and *Kroger v. Commissioner,* T.C. Memo 1997 2.

harbor methods for the estimation of inventory shrinkage.

In general.—

The conferees expect that the Secretary of the Treasury will issue guidance establishing one or more safe harbor methods for the estimation of inventory shrinkage that will be deemed to result in a clear reflection of income, provided such safe harbor method is consistently applied and the taxpayer's inventory methods otherwise satisfy the clear reflection of income standard.

Safe harbors applicable to retail trade.— In the case of taxpayers primarily engaged in retail trade (the resale of personal property to the general public), where physical inventories are normally taken at each location at least annually, the conferees anticipate that a safe harbor method will be established that will use a historical ratio of shrinkage to sales, multiplied by total sales between the date of the last physical inventory and year-end. This historical ratio is based on the actual shrinkage established by all physical inventories taken during the most recent three taxable years and the sales for related periods. The historical ratio should be separately determined for each store or department in a store of the taxpayer. The historical ratio, or estimated

shrinkage determined using the historical ratio, cannot be adjusted by judgmental or other factors (e.g., floors or caps). The conferees expect that estimated shrinkage determined in accordance with the consistent application of the safe harbor method will not be required to be recalculated, through a lookback adjustment or otherwise, to reflect the results of physical inventories taken after year-end.

In the case of a new store or department in a store that has not verified shrinkage by a physical inventory in each of the most recent three taxable years, the historical ratio is the average of the historical ratios of the retailer's other stores or departments. Retailers using last in, first out (LIFO) methods of inventory are expected to be required to allocate shrinkage among their various inventory pools in a reasonable and consistent manner.

The conferees expect that procedures will be provided allowing an automatic election of such method of accounting for a taxpayer's first taxable year ending after the date of enactment. Any adjustment required by section 481 as a result of the change in method of accounting generally will be taken into account over a period of four years.

[¶ 5083]   Section 962.   Assignment of workmen's compensation liability eligible for exclusion relating to personal injury liability assignments.

(Code Sec. 130)

[House Report]

Present Law

Under present law, an exclusion from gross income is provided for amounts received for agreeing to a qualified assignment to the extent that the amount received does not exceed the aggregate cost of any qualified funding asset (sec. 130). A qualified assignment means any assignment of a liability to make periodic payments as damages (whether by suit or agreement) on account of a personal injury or sickness (in a case involving physical injury or physical sickness), provided the liability is assumed from a person who is a party to the suit or agreement, and the terms of the assignment

satisfy certain requirements. Generally, these requirements are that (1) the periodic payments are fixed as to amount and time; (2) the payments cannot be accelerated, deferred, increased, or decreased by the recipient; (3) the assignee's obligation is no greater than that of the assignor; and (4) the payments are excludable by the recipient under section 104(a)(2) as damages on account of personal injuries or sickness. Present law provides a separate exclusion under section 104(a)(1) for the recipient of amounts received under workmen's compensation acts as compensation for personal injuries or sickness, but a qualified assignment under section 130 does not include the assignment of a liability to make such payments.

Reasons for Change

Structured settlement arrangements are essentially conduit arrangements in which the assignor of a liability, the assignee (the structured settlement company) and the claimant (recipient of benefits) share the economic benefit of the exclusion from income provided under present law. The Committee understands that some workmen's compensation payments involve periodic payments (rather than lump sum payments). The Committee was persuaded that additional economic security would be provided to workmen's compensation claimants who receive periodic payments if the payments are made through a structured settlement arrangement, where the payor is generally is subject to State insurance company regulation that is aimed at maintaining solvency of the company, in lieu of being made directly by self-insuring employers that may not be subject to comparable solvency-related regulation.

Explanation of Provision

The provision extends the exclusion for qualified assignments under Code section 130 to amounts assigned for assuming a liability to pay compensation under any workmen's compensation act. The provision requires that the assignee assume the liability from a person who is a party to the workmen's compensation claim, and requires that the periodic payment be excludable from the recipient's gross income under section 104(a)(1), in addition to the requirements of present law.

Effective Date

The provision is effective for workmen's compensation claims filed after the date of enactment.

[Conference Report]

Senate Amendment

No provision.

Conference Agreement

The conference agreement follows the House bill.

[¶ 5084]   Section 963.   Tax-exempt status for certain state workers compensation act companies.

(Code Sec. 501)

[House Report]

Present Law

In general, the Internal Revenue Service ("IRS") takes the position that organizations that provide insurance for their members or other individuals are not considered to be engaged in a tax-exempt activity. The IRS maintains that such insurance activity is either (1) a regular business of a kind ordinarily carried on for profit, or (2) an economy or convenience in the conduct of members' businesses because it relieves the members from obtaining insurance on an individual basis.

Certain insurance risk pools have qualified for tax exemption under Code section 501(c)(6). In general, these organizations (1) assign any insurance policies and administrative functions to their member organizations (although they may reimburse their members for amounts paid and expenses); (2) serve an important common business interest of their members; and (3) must be membership organizations financed, at least in part, by membership dues.

State insurance risk pools may also qualify for tax exempt status under section 501(c)(4) as social welfare organizations or under section 115 as serving an essential governmental function of a State. In seeking qualification under section 501(c)(4), insurance organizations generally are constrained by the restrictions on the provision of "commercial-type insurance" contained in section 501(m). Section 115 generally provides that gross income does not include income derived from the exercise of any essential governmental function and accruing to a State or any political subdivision thereof. However, the IRS may be reluctant to rule that particular State risk-pooling entities satisfy the section 501(c)(4) or 115 requirements for tax-exempt status.

Reasons for Change

The Committee believes that eliminating uncertainty concerning the eligibility of certain State workmen's compensation act companies for tax-exempt status will assist States in ensuring workmen's compensation coverage for uninsured employers with respect to employees in the State.

Explanation of Provision

The provision clarifies the tax-exempt status of any organization that is created by State law, and organized and operated exclusively to provide workmen's compensation insurance and related coverage that is incidental to workmen's compensation insurance,[65] and that meets certain additional requirements. The workmen's compensation insurance must be required by State law, or be insurance with respect to which State law provides significant disincentives if it is not purchased by an employer (such as loss of exclusive remedy or forfeiture of affirmative defenses such as contributory negligence). The organization must provide workmen's compensation to any employer in the State (for employees in the State or temporarily assigned out-of-State) seeking such insurance and meeting other reasonable requirements. The State must either extend its full faith and credit to debt of the organization or provide the initial operating capital of such organization. For this purpose, the initial operating capital can be provided by providing the proceeds of bonds issued by a State authority; the bonds may be repaid through exercise of the State's taxing authority, for example. For periods after the date of enactment, the assets of the organization must revert to the State upon dissolution. Finally, the majority of the board of directors (or comparable oversight body) of the organization must be appointed by an official of the executive branch of the State or by the State legislature, or by both.

Effective Date

The provision is effective for taxable years beginning after December 31, 1997. No inference is intended as to the status of such organizations under present law.

---

65. Related coverage that is incidental to workmen's compensation insurance includes liability under Federal workmen's compensation laws, for example.

[Conference Report]

Conference Agreement

The conference agreement follows the House bill and the Senate amendment with modifications.

The conference agreement modifies the full-faith-and- credit portion of the requirement that the State must extend its full faith and credit to debt of the organization (or provide the initial operating capital of such organization). Under the conference agreement, the State must extend its full faith and credit to the initial debt of the organization.

The conference agreement also modifies the requirement relating to reversion of assets to the State upon dissolution. The conference agreement requires that, in the case of periods after the date of enactment, either the assets of the organization must revert to the State upon dissolution, or State law must not permit the dissolution of the organization, absent an act of the State legislature. Should dissolution of the organization become permissible under applicable State law, then the requirement that the assets of the organization revert to the State upon dissolution applies.

Many organizations described in the provision have been operating as organizations that are exempt from tax (e.g., as an organization that is exempt from tax because it is serving an essential governmental function of a State). No inference is intended that organizations described in the provision are not exempt from tax under present law. In addition, no inference is intended that the benefit plans of such organizations are not properly maintained by the organization. It is anticipated that Federal regulatory agencies will take appropriate action to address transition issues faced by organizations to conform to their benefit plans under the provision. For example, it is intended that an organization that has been maintaining a section 457 plan as an agency or instrumentality of a State could (without creating any inference with respect to present- law treatment) freeze future contributions to the section 457 plan and establish a retirement arrangement (e.g., a section 401(k) plan) that is consistent with the treatment of the organization as a tax- exempt employer under the provision.

[¶ 5085]   Section 964.   Election for 1987 partnerships to continue exception from treatment of publicly traded partnerships as corporations.

(Code Sec. 7704)

[House Report]

A publicly traded partnership generally is treated as a corporation for Federal tax purposes (sec. 7704). An exception to the rule treating the partnership as a corporation applies if 90 percent of the partnership's gross income consists of "passive-type income," which includes (1) interest (other than interest derived in a financial or insurance business, or certain amounts determined on the basis of income or profits), (2) dividends, (3) real property rents (as defined for purposes of the provision), (4) gain from the sale or other disposition of real property, (5) income and gains relating to minerals and natural resources (as defined for purposes of the provision), and (6) gain from the sale or disposition of a capital asset (or certain trade or business property) held for the production of income of the foregoing types (subject to an exception for certain commodities income).

The exception for publicly traded partnerships with "passive-type income" does not apply to any partnership that would be described in section 851(a) of the Code (relating to regulated investment companies, or "RICs"), if that partnership were a domestic corporation. Thus, a publicly traded partnership that is registered under the Investment Company Act of 1940 generally is treated as a corporation under the provision. Nevertheless, if a principal activity of the partnership consists of buying and selling of commodities (other than inventory or property held primarily for sale to customers) or futures, forwards and options with respect to commodities, and 90 percent of the partnership's income is such income, then the partnership is not treated as a corporation.

A publicly traded partnership is a partnership whose interests are (1) traded on an established securities market, or (2) readily tradable on a secondary market (or the substantial equivalent thereof).

Treasury regulations provide detailed guidance as to when an interest is treated as readily tradable on a secondary market or the substantial equivalent. Generally, an interest is so treated "if, taking into account all of the facts and circumstances, the partners are readily able to buy, sell, or exchange their partnership interests in a manner that is comparable, economically, to trading on an established securities market" (Treas. Reg. sec. 1.7704 1(c)(1)).

When the publicly traded partnership rules were enacted in 1987, a 10-year grandfather rule provided that the provisions apply to certain existing partnerships only for taxable years beginning after December 31, 1997.[66] An existing publicly traded partnership is any partnership, if (1) it was a publicly traded partnership on December 17, 1987, (2) a registration statement indicating that the partnership was to be a publicly traded partnership was filed with the Securities and Exchange Commission with respect to the partnership on or before December 17, 1987, or (3) with respect to the partnership, an application was filed with a State regulatory commission on or before December 31, 1987, seeking permission to restructure a portion of a corporation as a publicly traded partnership. A partnership that otherwise would be treated as an existing publicly traded partnership ceases to be so treated as of the first day after December 17, 1987, on which there has been an addition of a substantial new line of business with respect to such partnership. A rule is provided to coordinate this grandfather rule with the exception to the rule treating the partnership as a corporation applies if 90 percent of the partnership's gross income consists of passive-type income. The coordination rule provides that passive-type income exception applies only after the grandfather rule ceases to apply (whether by

---

66. Omnibus Budget Reconciliation Act of 1987 (P.L. 100 203), sec. 10211(c).

passage of time or because the partnership ceases to qualify for the grandfather rule).

Effective Date

The provision is effective for taxable years beginning after December 31, 1997.

[Senate Report]

Reasons for Change

The Committee believes that, in important respects, publicly traded partnerships generally resemble corporations and should be subject to tax as corporations, so long as the current corporate income tax applies to corporate entities. Nevertheless, in the case of certain publicly traded partnerships that were existing on December 17, 1987, and that are treated as partnerships under the grandfather rule until December 31, 1997, it is appropriate to permit the continuation of their status as partnerships, so long as they elect to be subject to a tax that is intended to approximate the corporate tax they would pay if they were treated as corporations for Federal tax purposes.

Explanation of Provision

In the case of an existing publicly traded partnership that elects under the provision to be subject to a tax on gross income from the active conduct of a trade or business, the rule of present law treating a publicly traded partnership as a corporation does not apply. An existing publicly traded partnership is any publicly traded partnership that is not treated as a corporation, so long as such treatment is not determined under the passive-type income exception of Code section 7704(c)(1). The el ection to be subject

to the tax on gross trade or business income, once made, remains in effect until revoked by the partnership, and cannot be reinstated.

The tax is 3.5 percent of the partnership's gross income from the active conduct of a trade or business. The partnership's gross trade or business income includes its share of gross trade or business income of any lower-tier partnership. The tax imposed under the provision may not be offset by tax credits.

[Conference Report]

Conference Agreement

The conference agreement follows the Senate amendment, with technical modifications. The conference agreement clarifies that the provision applies to any electing 1987 partnership, which means any publicly traded partnership, if (1) it is an existing partnership within the meaning of section 10211(c)(2) of the 1987 Act, (2) it has not been treated as a corporation for taxable years beginning after December 31, 1987, and before January 1, 1998 (and would not have been treated as a corporation even without regard to section 7704(c), the exception for partnerships with "passive-type" income), and (3) the partnership elects under the provision to be subject to a tax on gross income from the active conduct of a trade or business. An electing 1987 partnership ceases to be treated as such as of the first day after December 31, 1997, on which there has been the addition of a substantial new line of business with respect to the partnership.

[¶ 5086]   Section 965.   Exclusion from unrelated business taxable income for certain sponsorship payments.

(Code Sec. 513)

[House Report]

Present Law

Although generally exempt from Federal income tax, tax-exempt organizations are subject to the unrelated business income tax ("UBIT") on income derived from a trade or business regularly carried on that is not

substantially related to the performance of the organization's tax-exempt functions (secs. 511 514). Contributions or gifts received by tax-exempt organizations generally are not subject to the UBIT. However, present-law section 513(c) provides that an activity (such as advertising) does not lose its identity as a separate trade or business merely because it is carried on within a larger complex of other endeavors.[67] If a tax-exempt organization receives sponsorship payments in connection with an event or other activity, the solicitation and receipt of such sponsorship payments may be treated as a separate activity. The Internal Revenue Service (IRS) has taken the position that, under some circumstances, such sponsorship payments are subject to the UBIT.[68]

Reasons for Change

In order to reduce the uncertainty regarding the treatment for UBIT purposes of corporate sponsorship payments received by tax-exempt organizations, the Committee believes that it is appropriate to distinguish sponsorship payments for which the donor receives no substantial return benefit other than the use or acknowledgment of the donor's name or logo as part of a sponsored event (which should not be subject to the UBIT) from payments made in exchange for advertising provided by the recipient organization (which should be subject to the UBIT).

Explanation of Provision

Under the bill, qualified sponsorship payments received by a tax-exempt organization (or State college or university described in section 511(a)(2)(B)) are exempt from the UBIT.

"Qualified sponsorship payments" are defined as any payment made by a person engaged in a trade or business with respect to which the person will receive no substantial return benefit other than the use or acknowledgment of the name or logo (or product lines) of the person's trade or business in connection with the organization's activities.[69] Such a use or acknowledgment does not include advertising of such person's products or services—meaning qualitative or comparative language, price infor-

mation or other indications of savings or value, or an endorsement or other inducement to purchase, sell, or use such products or services. Thus, for example, if, in return for receiving a sponsorship payment, an organization promises to use the sponsor's name or logo in acknowledging the sponsor's support for an educational or fundraising event conducted by the organization, such payment will not be subject to the UBIT. In contrast, if the organization provides advertising of a sponsor's products, the payment made to the organization by the sponsor in order to receive such advertising will be subject to the UBIT (provided that the other, present-law requirements for UBIT liability are satisfied).

The bill specifically provides that a qualified sponsorship payment does not include any payment where the amount of such payment is contingent, by contract or otherwise, upon the level of attendance at an event, broadcast ratings, or other factors indicating the degree of public exposure to an activity. However, the fact that a sponsorship payment is contingent upon an event actually taking place or being broadcast, in and of itself, will not cause the payment to fail to be a qualified sponsorship payment. Moreover, mere distribution or display of a sponsor's products by the sponsor or the tax-exempt organization to the general public at a sponsored event, whether for free or for remuneration, will be considered to be "use or acknowledgment" of the sponsor's product lines (as opposed to advertising), and thus will not affect the determination of whether a payment made by the sponsor is a qualified sponsorship payment.

The provision does not apply to the sale of advertising or acknowledgments in tax-exempt organization periodicals. For this purpose, the term "periodical" means regularly scheduled and printed material published by (or on behalf of) the payee organi-

---

67. See *United States v. American College of Physicians*, 475 U.S. 834 (1986) (holding that activity of selling advertising in medical journal was not substantially related to the organization's exempt purposes and, as a separate business under section 513(c), was subject to tax).

68. See Prop. Treas. Reg. sec. 1.513-4 (issued January 19, 1993, EE 7492, IRB 1993-7, 71). These proposed regulations generally exclude from the UBIT financial arrangements under which the tax-exempt organization provides so-called "institutional" or "good will" advertising to a sponsor (i.e., arrangements under which a

sponsor's name, logo, or product line is acknowledged by the tax-exempt organization). However, specific product advertising (e.g., "comparative or qualitative descriptions of the sponsor's products") provided by a tax-exempt organization on behalf of a sponsor is not shielded from the UBIT under the proposed regulations.

69. In determining whether a payment is a qualified sponsorship payment, it is irrelevant whet her the sponsored activity is related or unrelated to the organization's exempt purpose.

zation that is not related to and primarily distributed in connection with a specific event conducted by the payee organization. For example, the provision will not apply to payments that lead to acknowledgments in a monthly journal, but will apply if a sponsor receives an acknowledgment in a program or brochure distributed at a sponsored event.

The provision specifically provides that, to the extent that a portion of a payment would (if made as a separate payment) be a qualified sponsorship payment, such portion of the payment will be treated as a separate payment. Thus, if a sponsorship payment made to a tax-exempt organization entitles the sponsor to both product advertising and use or acknowledgment of the sponsor's name or logo by the organization, then the UBIT will not apply to the amount of such payment that exceeds the fair market value of the product advertising provided to the sponsor. Moreover, the provision of facilities, services or other privileges by an exempt organization to a sponsor or the sponsor's designees (e.g., complimentary tickets, pro-am playing spots in golf tournaments, or receptions for major donors) in connection with a sponsorship payment will not affect the determination of whether the payment is a qualified sponsorship payment. Rather, the provision of such goods or services will be evaluated as a separate transaction in determining whether the organization has unrelated business taxable income from the event. In general, if such services or facilities do not constitute a substantial return benefit or if the provision of such services or facilities is a related business activity, then the payments attributable to such services or facilities will not be subject to the UBIT. Moreover, just as the provision of facilities, services or other privileges by a tax-exempt organization to a sponsor or the sponsor's designees (complimentary tickets, pro-am playing spots in golf tournaments, or receptions for major donors) will be treated as a separate transaction that does not affect the determination of whether a sponsorship payment is a qualified sponsorship payment, a sponsor's receipt of a license to use an intangible asset (e.g., trademark, logo, or designation) of the tax-

exempt organization likewise will be treated as separate from the qualified sponsorship transaction in determining whether the organization has unrelated business taxable income.

The exemption provided by the provision will be in addition to other present-law exceptions from the UBIT (e.g., the exceptions for activities substantially all the work for which is performed by volunteers and for activities not regularly carried on). No inference is intended as to whether any sponsorship payment received prior to 1998 was subject to the UBIT.

Effective Date

The provision applies to qualified sponsorship payments solicited or received after December 31, 1997.

[Conference Report]

Senate Amendment

The Senate amendment is the same as the House bill.

Conference Agreement

The conference agreement follows the House bill and Senate amendment, except that the conference agreement clarifies that the qualified sponsorship payment provision does not apply to payments that entitle the payor to the use or acknowledgment of the payor's trade or business name or logo (or product lines) in tax-exempt organization periodicals. Similarly, the qualified sponsorship payment provision does not apply to payments made in connection with "qualified convention or trade show activities," as defined in present-law section 513(d)(3). Such payments are outside the qualified sponsorship payment provision's safe-harbor exclusion, and, therefore, will be governed by present-law rules that determine whether the payment is subject to the UBIT. Thus, for example, payments that entitle the payor to a depiction of the payor's name or logo in a tax-exempt organization periodical may or may not be subject to the UBIT depending on the application of present-law rules regarding periodical advertising and nontaxable donor recognition.[45]

---

45. For guidance regarding the treatment of periodical advertising under the UBIT, see section 513(c); *United States v. American College of Physicians*, 475 U.S.

834 (1986); Treas. Reg. 1.51301(d)(4)(iv), Example 7; Rev. Rul. 82-139, 1982-2 C.B. 108; Rev. Rul. 74-38,

As a further clarification, the conferees intend that, as provided under Prop. Treas. Reg. sec. 1.513-4, the use of promotional logos or slogans that are an established part of the sponsor's identity would not, by itself, constitute advertising for purposes of determining whether a payment is a qualified sponsorship payment.

[¶ 5089]   Section 966.   Associations of holders of timeshare interests to be taxed like other homeowners associations.

(Code Sec. 528)

[House Report]

Present Law

Taxation of homeowners associations making the section 528 election. —

Under present law (sec. 528), condominium management associations and residential real estate management associations may elect to be taxable at a 30 percent rate on their "homeowners association income" if they meet certain income, expenditure, and organizational requirements. "Homeowners association income" is the excess of the association's gross income, excluding "exempt function income," over allowable deductions directly connected with non-exempt function gross income. "Exempt function income" includes membership dues, fees, and assessments for a common activity undertaken by association members or owners of residential units in the condominium or subdivision. Homeowners association income includes passive income (e.g., interest and dividends) earned on reserves and fees for use of association property (e.g., swimming pools, meeting rooms, etc.).

For an association to qualify for this treatment, (1) at least 60 percent of the association's gross income must consist of membership dues, fees, or assessments on owners, (2) at least 90 percent of its expenditures must be for the acquisition, management, maintenance, or care of "association property," and (3) no part of its net earnings can inure to the benefit of any private shareholder. "Association property" means: (1) property held by the association; (2) property commonly held by association members; (3) property within the association privately held by association members; and (4) property held by a governmental unit for the benefit of association members. In addition to these statutory requirements, Treasury regulations require that the units of the association be used for residential purposes. Use is not a residential use if the unit is occupied by a person or series of persons less than 30 days for more than half of the association's taxable year. Treas. reg. sec. 1.528-4(d).

Taxation of homeowners associations not making the section 528 election. —

Homeowners associations that do not (or cannot) make the section 528 election are taxed either as a tax-exempt social welfare organization under section 501(c)(4) or as a regular C corporation. In order for an organization to qualify as a tax-exempt social welfare organization, the organization must meet the following three requirements: (1) the association must serve a "community" which bears a reasonable, recognizable relationship to an area ordinarily identified as a governmental subdivision or unit; (2) the association may not conduct activities directed to exterior maintenance of any private residence, and (3) common areas of association facilities must be for the use and enjoyment of the general public (Rev. Rul. 74 99, 1974-1 C.B. 131).

Non-exempt homeowners associations are taxed as C corporations, except that (1) the association may exclude excess assessments that it refunds to its members or applies to the subsequent year's assessments (Rev. Rul. 70 604, 1970-2 C.B. 9); (2) gross income does not include special assessments

---

1974-1 C.B. 144; PLR 9137049; and PLR 9234002. For guidance regarding the treatment of donor acknowledgments under the UBIT, see Rev. Rul. 76-93, 1976-1 C.B. 170; PLR 8749085; and PLR 9044071. In the interest of administrative convenience, the conferees encourage the Treasury Department to permit tax-exempt entities to provide combined reporting of payments that are both qualified sponsorship payments and nontaxable payments made in exchange for donor acknowledgments in a periodical or in connection with a qualified convention or trade show. In addition, to the extent tax-exempt entities are required to allocate portions of payments, the conferees encourage the Treasury Department to minimize the reporting burden associated with any such allocation.

held in a special bank account (Rev. Rul. 75-370, 75-2 C.B. 25), and (3) assessments for capital improvements are treated as non-taxable contributions to capital (Rev. Rul. 75-370, 1975-2 C.B. 25).

Taxation of timeshare associations. —

Under present law, timeshare associations are taxed as regular C corporations because (1) they cannot meet the requirement of the Treasury regulations for the section 528 election that the units be used for residential purposes (i.e., the 30-day rule) and they have relatively large amount of services performed for its owners (e.g., maid and janitorial services) and (2) they cannot meet any of requirements of Rev. Rul. 74 99 for tax-exempt status under section 501(c)(4).

[Senate Report]

Reasons for Change

The committee understands that the IRS recently has challenged the exclusions from gross income of timeshare associations of refunds of excess assessments, special assessments held in a segregated account, and capital assessments as contributions to capital. See P.L.R. 9539001 (June 8, 1995). The committee believes that the activities of timeshare associations are sufficiently similar to those of homeowners associations that they should be similarly taxed. Accordingly, the committee bill would extend the rules for the taxation of homeowners associations to timeshare associations, except that the rate of tax on timeshare associations is 32 percent, instead of the 30-percent rate that applies to homeowner's associations.

Explanation of Provision

The bill amends section 528 to permit timeshare associations to qualify for taxation under that section. Timeshare associations would have to meet the requirements of section 528 (e.g., the 60 percent gross income, 90 percent expenditure, and the non-profit organizational and operational requirements). Timeshare associations electing to be taxed under section 528 are subject to a tax on their "timeshare association income" at a rate of 32 percent.

60-Percent Test

A qualified timeshare association must receive at least 60 percent of its income from membership dues, fees and assessments from owners of either (a) timeshare rights to use of, or (b) timeshare ownership in, property the timeshare association.

90-Percent Test

At least 90 percent of the expenditures of the timeshare association must be for the acquisition, management, maintenance, or care of "association property," and activities provided by the association to, or on behalf of, members of the timeshare association. "Activities provided to or on behalf of members of the [timeshare] association" includes events located on association property (e.g., member's meetings at the association's meeting room, parties at the association's swimming pool, golf lessons on association's golf range, transportation to and from association property, etc.).

Organizational and Operational Tests

No part of the net earnings of the timeshare association can inure to the benefit (other than by acquiring, constructing, or providing management, maintenance, and care of property of the timeshare association or rebate of excess membership dues, fees, or assessments) of any private shareholder or individual. A member of a qualified timeshare association must hold a timeshare right to use (or timeshare ownership in) real property of the association. Property of a timeshare association includes property in which a timeshare association or members of the association have rights arising out of recorded easements, covenants, and other recorded instruments to use property related to the timeshare project. A qualified timeshare association cannot be a condominium management association. Lastly, the timeshare association must elect to be taxed under section 528.

Effective Date

The provision is effective for taxable years beginning after December 31, 1996.

[Conference Report]

Conference Agreement

The conference agreement follows the Senate amendment.

[¶5090]   Section 967.   Modifications of advance refunding rules for certain tax-exempt bonds issued by the Virgin Islands.

(Code Sec. 149)

[House Report]

Present Law

Advance refundings

Generally a governmental bond originally issued after December 31, 1985, may be advance refunded one time. An advance refunding is any refunding where all of the refunded bonds are not redeemed within 90 days after the refunding bonds are issued.

Virgin Island bonds

Under present law, the Virgin Islands is required to secure its bonds with a priority first lien claim on specified revenue streams rather than being permitted to issue multiple bond issues secured on a parity basis by a common pool of revenues. Under a proposed non-tax law change, the priority lien requirement would be repealed.

Reasons for Change

The Committee believes that an additional advance refunding is appropriate in light of changed circumstances with respect to these bonds.

Explanation of Provision

One additional advance refunding would be allowed for governmental bonds issued by the Virgin Islands that were advance refunded before June 9, 1997, if the Virgin Islands debt provisions are changed to repeal the current priority first lien requirement.

Effective Date

The provision is effective on the date of enactment.

[Conference Report]

Senate Amendment

No provision.

Conference Agreement

The conference agreement follows the House bill.

[¶5091]   Section 968.   Nonrecognition of gain on sale of stock to certain farmers' cooperatives.

(Code Sec. 1042)

[House Report]

Present Law

Under present law, if certain requirements are satisfied, a taxpayer may defer recognition of gain on the sale of qualified securities to an employee stock ownership plan ("ESOP") or a eligible worker-owed cooperative to the extent that the taxpayer reinvests the proceeds in qualified replacement property (sec. 1042). Gain is recognized when the taxpayer disposes of the qualified replacement property. One of the requirements that must be satisfied for deferral to apply is that, immediately after the sale, the ESOP must own at least 30 percent of the stock of the corporation issuing the qualified securities. In general, qualified securities are securities issued by a domestic C corporation that has no stock outstanding that is readily tradeable on an established securities market. Deferral treatment does not apply to gain on the sale of qualified securities by a C corporation.

Reasons for Change

The Committee believes it appropriate to facilitate the transfer of refiners and processors to farmers' cooperatives.

Explanation of Provision

The bill extends the deferral provided under section 1042 to the sale of stock of a qualified refiner or processor to an eligible farmer's cooperative. A qualified refiner or processor is a domestic corporation substantially all of the activities of which consist of the active conduct of the trade or business of refining or processing agricultural or horticultural products and which purchases more than one-half of such products to be refined or processed from farmers who make up the cooperative which is purchasing the stock or the cooperative. An eligible farmers' cooperative is an organization which is treated as a cooperative for Federal income tax purposes and which is engaged in the marketing of agricultural or horticultural products.

The deferral of gain is available only if, immediately after the sale, the eligible farmers' cooperative owns 100 percent of the qualified refiner or processor. The provision applies even if the stock of the qualified refiner or processor is publicly traded. In addition, the bill applies to gain on the sale of stock by a C corporation.

Effective Date

The provision applies to sales after December 31, 1997.

[Conference Report]

Senate Amendment

No provision.

Conference Agreement

The conference agreement follows the House bill, with the modification that the requirement that the refiner or processor purchase more than one-half of the products to be refined or processed from farmers who make up the cooperative which is purchasing the stock or the cooperative must be satisfied for at least one year prior to the sale.

[¶ 5092]   Section 969.   Increased deductibility of business meal expenses for individuals subject to federal hours of service.

(Code Sec. 274)

[House Report]

Present Law

Ordinary and necessary business expenses, as well as expenses incurred for the production of income, are generally deductible, subject o a number of restrictions and limitations. Generally, the amount allowable as a deduction for food and beverage is limited to 50 percent of the otherwise deductible amount. Exceptions to this 50 percent rule are provided for food and beverages provided to crew members of certain vessels and offshore oil or gas platforms or drilling rigs.

Reasons for Change

Individuals subject to the hours of service limitations of the Department of Transportation are frequently forced to eat meals away from home in circumstances where their choice is limited, prices comparatively high and the opportunity for lavish meals remote. The Committee believes that it is appropriate to allow a higher percentage of the cost of food and beverages consumed while away from home by these individuals to be deducted than is allowed under the general rule.

Explanation of Provision

The bill increases to 80 percent the deductible percentage of the cost of food and beverages consumed while away from home by an individual during, or incident to, a period of duty subject to the hours of service limitations of the Department of Transportation.

Individuals subject to the hours of service limitations of the Department of Transportation include:

(1) certain air transportation employees such as pilots, crew, dispatchers, mechanics, and control tower operators pursuant to Federal Aviation Administration regulations,

(2) interstate truck operators and interstate bus drivers pursuant to Department of Transportation regulations,

(3) certain railroad employees such as engineers, conductors, train crews, dispatchers and control operations personnel pursuant to Federal Railroad Administration regulations, and

(4) certain merchant mariners pursuant to Coast Guard regulations.

The increase in the deductible percentage is phased in according to the following schedule:

Taxable years beginning in:	Deductible earnings
1998, 1999	55
2000, 2001	60
2002, 2003	65
2004, 2005	70
2006, 2007	75
2008 and thereafter	80

Effective Date

The provision is effective for taxable years beginning after 1997.

[Conference Report]

Senate Amendment

The Senate amendment is the same as the House bill.

Conference Agreement

The conference agreement follows the House bill and the Senate amendment.

[¶ 5093]   Section 970.   Clarification of de minimus fringe benefit rules to no-charge employee meals.

(Code Sec. 132)

[Senate Report]

Present Law

In general, subject to several exceptions, only 50 percent of business meal and entertainment expenses are allowed as a deduction (sec. 274(n)). Under one exception, the value of meals that are excludable from employees' incomes as a de minimis fringe benefit (sec. 132) are fully deductible by the employer.

In addition, the courts that have considered the issue have held that if meals are provided for the convenience of the employer pursuant to section 119 they are fully deductible (*Boyd Gaming Corp. v. Commissioner*[67] and *Gold Coast Hotel & Casino v. I.R.S*[68]).

Reasons for Change

The Committee believes that it is consistent with the case law to provide for full deductibility of business meals that are excludible from employees' incomes because they are provided for the convenience of the employer.

Explanation of Provision

The bill provides that meals that are excludable from employees' incomes because they are provided for the convenience of the employer pursuant to section 119 of the Code are excludable as a de minimis fringe benefit and therefore are fully deductible by the employer. No inference is intended as to whether such meals are fully deductible under present law.

Effective Date

The provision is effective for taxable years beginning after December 31, 1997.

[Conference Report]

House Bill

No provision.

Senate Amendment

The Senate amendment provides that meals that are excludable from employees' incomes because they are provided for the convenience of the employer pursuant to section 119 of the Code are excludable as a de minimis fringe benefit and therefore are fully deductible by the employer, provided they satisfy the relevant section 132 require-

---

67. 106 T.C. No. 19 (May 23, 1996).
68. U.S.D.C. Nev. CV-5-94-1146-HDM(LRL) (September 26, 1996).

ments. No inference is intended as to whether such meals are fully deductible under present law.

The Senate amendment also increases to 80 percent the deductible percentage of the cost of food and beverages consumed by workers at remote seafood processing facilities located in the United States north of 53 degrees north latitude. A seafood processing facility is remote when there are insufficient eating facilities in the vicinity of the employer's premises.[48]

The increase in the deductible percentage is phased in according to the following schedule:

Effective Dates

The provisions are effective for taxable years beginning after 1997.

Conference Agreement

The conference agreement follows the Senate amendment as to meals provided pursuant to section 119. Because food and beverages consumed by workers at these specified remote seafood processing facilities are provided for the convenience of the employer pursuant to section 119 and therefore will be deductible under the Senate amendment provision as to meals provided pursuant to section 119 (provided they satisfy the relevant section 132 requirements), the conference agreement does not include the Senate amendment provision relating to remote seafood processors because it is subsumed by the section 119 provision.

[¶ 5094]   Section 971.   Exemption of the incremental cost of a clean fuel vehicle from the limits on depreciation for vehicles.

(Code Sec. 280F)

[House Report]

Present Law

The amount the taxpayer may claim as a depreciation deduction for any passenger automobile is limited to: $2,560 for the first taxable year in the recovery period; $4,100 for the second taxable year in the recovery period; $2,450 for the third taxable year in the recovery period; and $1,475 for each succeeding taxable year in the recovery period. Each of the dollar limitations is indexed for inflation after October 1987 by automobile component of the Consumer Price Index. Consequently, the limitations applicable for 1997 are $3,160, $5,000, $3,050, and $1,775.

Reasons for Change

The Committee believes that the price of a clean-burning fuel vehicle or an electric vehicle does not necessarily represent the consumer's purchase of a luxury. Rather, the higher price of such vehicles often represents the cost of the technology required to produce an automobile designed to pro-

vide certain environmental benefits. The Committee believes the cost of this technology should not be considered a luxury for the purpose of the limitation on depreciation that may be claimed on passenger automobiles. Therefore, the Committee believes it is appropriate to modify the limitation on depreciation that may be claimed on passenger automobiles in the case of certain clean-burning fuel vehicles and electric vehicles.

Explanation of Provision

The bill modifies the section 280F limitation on depreciation in the case of qualified clean-burning fuel vehicles and certain electric vehicles. With respect to qualified clean-burning fuel vehicles, those that are modified to permit such vehicle to be propelled by a clean burning fuel, the bill generally modifies present-law by applying the current limitation to that portion of the vehicles cost not represented by the installed qualified clean-burning fuel property. The taxpayer may claim an amount otherwise allowable as a depreciation deduction on the installed qualified clean-burning fuel, without regard to the 280F limitation. Generally, this has the same effect as only subjecting

---

48. See Treas. Reg. Sec. 1.119-1(a)(2)(ii)(c) and 1.119-1(f) (Example 7).

the cost of the vehicle before modification to the sec. 280F limitations.

For example, assume that in 1997, after the date of enactment, a taxpayer purchases a clean-burning fuel vehicle for $43,000. Further assume that had the taxpayer purchased the identical vehicle, without having had certain components replaced to qualify it as clean burning, the price paid would have been $39,000. The cost of the qualified retrofit parts and components is $4,000. The depreciation that the taxpayer may claim for this vehicle in any year is the depreciation that could be claimed under present law section 280F for that portion of the vehicle worth $39,000, plus the depreciation that can be claimed under section 168 for the $4,000 worth of qualified retrofit parts and components.

In the case of a passenger vehicle designed to be propelled primarily by electricity and built by an original equipment manufacturer, the base-year limitation amounts of $2,560 for the first taxable year in the recovery period, $4,100 for the second taxable year in the recovery period, $2,450 for the third taxable year in the recovery period, and $1,475 for each succeeding taxable year in the recovery period are tripled to $7,680, $12,300, $7,350, and $4,425, respectively, and then adjusted for inflation after October 1987 by the automobile component of the Consumer Price Index.

Effective Date

The provision is effective for property placed in service on or after the date of enactment and before January 1, 2005.

[Conference Report]

Senate Amendment

No provision.

Conference Agreement

The conference agreement follows the House bill, with a modification to the effective date that provides that the provision is effective for property placed in service after the date of enactment and before January 1, 2005.

[¶ 5095]   Section 972.   Temporary suspension of taxable income limit on percentage depletion for marginal production.

(Code Sec. 613A)

[House Report]

Present Law

The Code permits taxpayers to recover their investments in oil and gas wells through depletion deductions (sec. 613A). In the case of certain properties, the deductions may be determined using the percentage depletion method. Among the limitations that apply in calculating percentage depletion deductions is a restriction that these deductions may not exceed 65 percent of the taxpayer's taxable income (excluding, for this purpose, percentage depletion net operating loss carrybacks, and capital loss carrybacks). If a portion of percentage depletion deductions are disallowed by this limitation, the disallowed amount may be deducted in the following year.

Specific percentage depletion rules apply to oil and gas production from "marginal" properties. Marginal production is defined as domestic crude oil and natural gas production from stripper well property or from property substantially all of the production from which during the calendar year is heavy oil. Stripper well property is property from which the average daily production is 15 barrel equivalents or less, determined by dividing the average daily production of domestic crude oil and domestic natural gas from producing wells on the property for the calendar year by the number of wells.

Reasons for Change

The Committee determined that a limited modification of the net income limit for marginal oil and gas production is an appropriate part of overall national energy security policy.

Explanation of Provision

The 65-percent-of-net-income limitation is suspended for domestic oil and gas production from marginal properties during taxable years beginning after December 31, 1997, and before January 1, 2000.

Effective Date

The provision is effective on the date of enactment.

[Senate Report]

Explanation of Provision

The 100-percent-of-net-income property limitation does not apply for any taxable year beginning in a calendar year in which the annual average wellhead price per barrel for crude oil (within the meaning of section 29(d)(2)(C)) is below $14 per barrel.

Effective Date

The provision is effective for taxable years beginning after December 31, 1997.

[¶ 5096]   Section 973.   Increase in standard mileage rate expense deduction for charitable use of passenger automobile.

(Code Sec. 170)

[Senate Report]

Present Law

In general, individuals who itemize their deductions may deduct charitable contributions. For purposes of computing the charitable deduction for the use of a passenger automobile, the standard mileage rate is 12 cents per mile (sec. 170(i)).

Reasons for Change

The Committee believes that this rate should be increased and indexed for inflation.

Explanation of Provision

The bill increases this mileage rate to 15 cents per mile. This rate is indexed for inflation, rounded down to the nearest whole cent.

[¶ 5097]   Section 974.   Clarification of certain receivables purchased by cooperative service organizations.

(Code Sec. 501)

[Senate Report]

Present Law

Section 501(e) provides that an organization organized on a cooperative basis by tax-exempt hospitals will itself be tax-ex-

[Conference Report]

Conference Agreement

The 100-percent-of-net-income property limitation is suspended for domestic oil and gas production from marginal properties during taxable years beginning after December 31, 1997, and before January 1, 2000.

Effective Date

The provision is effective on the date of enactment.

Effective Date

The increase to 15 cents is effective for taxable years beginning after December 31, 1997. The indexation is effective for inflation occurring after 1997. Accordingly, the first adjustment for indexing will occur in 1999 to reflect inflation in 1998.

[Conference Report]

House Bill

No provision.

Conference Agreement

The conference agreement increases this mileage rate to 14 cents per mile (not indexed for inflation), effective for taxable years beginning after December 31, 1997.

empt if the organization is operated solely to perform, on a centralized basis, one or more of certain enumerated services for its members. These services are: data processing, purchasing (including the purchase of insurance on a group basis), warehousing, billing and collection, food, clinical, industrial engineering, laboratory, printing, communications, record center, and personnel services. An organization does not qualify under section 501(e) if it performs services other than the enumerated services. (Treas. reg. sec. 1.501(e)(-1(c)).

Reasons for Change

The Committee believes that it is important to clarify that permissible billing and collection services that can be carried out by hospital cooperative services organizations under section 501(e) include the purchase of patron accounts receivable on a recourse basis.

Explanation of Provision

The bill clarifies that, for purposes of section 501(e), billing and collection services include the purchase of patron accounts receivable on a recourse basis. Thus,

hospital cooperative service organizations are permitted to advance cash on the basis of member accounts receivable, provided that each member hospital retains the risk of non-payment with respect to its accounts receivable.

Effective Date

The provision is effective for taxable years beginning after December 31, 1996. No inference is intended with respect to taxable years prior to the effective date.

[Conference Report]

House Bill

No provision.

Conference Agreement

The conference agreement follows the Senate amendment.

[¶ 5098]   Section 975.   Deduction in computing adjusted gross income for expenses in connection with service performed by certain officials.

(Code Sec. 62)

[Senate Report]

Present Law

Under present law, individuals may generally deduct ordinary and necessary business expenses in determining adjusted gross income ("AGI"). This deduction does not apply in the case of an individual performing services as an employee. Employee business expenses are generally deductible only as a miscellaneous itemized deduction, i.e., only to the extent all the taxpayer's miscellaneous itemized deductions exceed 2 percent of the taxpayer's AGI. Employee business expenses are not allowed as a deduction for alternative minimum tax purposes.

Reasons for Change

The Committee is aware that certain State and local government officials are compensated (in whole or in part) on a fee basis to provide certain services to the government. These officials hire employees and incur expenses in connection with their official duties. These expenses may be subject, under present law, to the 2- percent floor on item-

ized deductions. The Committee believes these expenses should be deductible.

Explanation of Provision

Under the bill, employee business expenses relating to service as an official of a State or local government (or political subdivision thereof) are deductible in computing AGI ("above the line"), provided the official is compensated in whole or in part on a fee basis. Consequently, such expenses are also deductible for minimum tax purposes.

Effective Date

The provision applies to expenses paid or incurred in taxable years beginning after December 31, 1997.

[Conference Report]

House Bill

No provision.

Conference Agreement

The conference agreement follows the Senate amendment.

Effective Date

The conference agreement is effective with respect to expenses paid or incurred in taxable years beginning after December 31, 1986.

[¶ 5099]   Section 976.   Combined employment tax reporting demonstration project.

(Code Sec. 6103)

[Senate Report]

Present Law

Traditionally, Federal tax forms are filed with the Federal government and State tax forms are filed with individual states. This necessitates duplication of items common to both returns. Some States have recently been working with the IRS to implement combined State and Federal reporting of certain types of items on one form as a way of reducing the burdens on taxpayers. The State of Montana and the IRS have cooperatively developed a system to combine State and Federal employment tax reporting o n one form. The one form would contain exclusively Federal data, exclusively State data, and information common to both: the taxpayer's name, address, TIN, and signature.

The Internal Revenue Code prohibits disclosure of tax returns and return information, except to the extent specifically authorized by the Internal Revenue Code (sec. 6103). Unauthorized disclosure is a felony punishable by a fine not exceeding $5,000 or imprisonment of not more than five years, or both (sec. 7213). An action for civil damages also may be brought for unauthorized disclosure (sec. 7431). No tax information may be furnished by the Internal Revenue Service ("IRS") to another agency unless the other agency establishes procedures satisfactory to the IRS for safeguarding the tax information it receives (sec. 6103(p)).

Implementation of the combined Montana-Federal employment tax reporting project has been hindered because the IRS interprets section 6103 to apply that provision's restrictions on disclosure to information common to both the State and Federal portions of the combined form, although these restrictions would not apply to the State with respect to the State's use of State-requested information if that information were supplied separately to both the State and the IRS.

Reasons for Change

The Committee believes it is appropriate to permit a demonstration project to assess the feasibility and desirability of expanding combined reporting in the future.

Explanation of Provisions

The bill permits implementation of a demonstration project to assess the feasibility and desirability of expanding combined reporting in the future. There are several limitations on the demonstration project. First, it is limited to the State of Montana and the IRS. Second, it is limited to employment tax reporting. Third, it is limited to disclosure of the name, address, TIN, and signature of the taxpayer, which is information common to both the Montana and Federal portions of the combined form. Fourth, it is limited to a period of five years.

Effective Date

The provision is effective on the date of enactment, and will expire on the date five years after the date of enactment.

[Conference Report]

House Bill

No provision.

Conference Agreement

The conference agreement follows the Senate amendment, with a technical modification providing a cross-reference to the provision in section 6103 of the Code.

[¶ 5100]   Section 977.   Elective Carryback of Existing Carryovers of National Railroad Passengers.

(Code Sec. 172)

[Senate Report]

Present Law

Separate Federal excise taxes are imposed on specified transportation motor fuels. Taxable fuels include gasoline, diesel fuel, and special motor fuels used for highway transportation, gasoline and diesel fuel used in motorboats, diesel fuel used in trains, fuels used in inland waterway transportation, and aviation fuel (gasoline and jet fuel). Motor fuels used by all of these transportation sectors are subject to a permanent 4.3-cents-per-gallon excise tax, enacted by the Omnibus Budget Reconciliation Act of 1993. Revenues from the 4.3-cents-per-gallon excise tax are retained in the General Fund of the Treasury.

The aggregate tax rate varies for each transportation sector. For example, diesel fuel used in trains is subject to an aggregate General Fund tax rate of 5.55 cents per gallon. Transportation sectors that benefit from Federal public works and environmental programs also are subject to additional tax rates (beyond the 4.3-cents-per-gallon General Fund rate) to finance Federal Trust Funds established as a financing source for those programs. All motor fuels excise taxes other than the 4.3-cents-per-gallon General Fund excise tax are temporary (i.e., have scheduled expiration dates). Table 1, below, shows the tax rates applicable to various transportation sectors, by Trust Fund and General Fund component.

TABLE 1.—PRESENT-LAW FEDERAL MOTOR FUELS EXCISE TAX RATES ON VARIOUS TRANSPORTATION SECTORS
(Rates shown in cents per gallon)

Transportation sector	Trust fund	General fund	Total tax
Highway Transportation:			
In general (trucks, automobiles):			
Gasoline	14.0	4.3	18.3
Diesel fuel	20.0	4.3	24.3
Special motor fuels	14.0	4.3	18.3
Private intercity bus:			
Gasoline	(*)	(*)	
Diesel fuel	3.0	4.3	7.3
Rail Transportation	(*)	5.55	5.55
Water Transportation:			
Inland Waterway	20.0	4.3	24.3
Recreational boats:			
Gasoline	14.0	4.3	18.3
Diesel fuel	52(*)	(*)	
Air Transportation:			
Commercial aviation	(*)	4.3	4.3
Noncommercial aviation:			
Gasoline	15.0	4.3	19.3
Jet fuel	17.5	4.3	21.8

(*) No tax

Reasons for Change

The Committee believes that the provision of viable intercity passenger rail service is an important national objective. At present, that objective is threatened by capital needs of the principal passenger rail service provider. Accordingly, the bill provides for transfer of a portion of transportation

---

52. A General Fund tax rate of 24.3 cents per gallon, enacted in 1993 to be effective through December 31, 1999, was suspended through December 31, 1997, by the Small Business Job Protection Tax Act of 1996. Another proposal in the Chairman's Mark would repeal this tax on diesel fuel used in recreational motorboats.

motor fuels tax revenues to promote needed modernization of passenger rail service facilities.

Explanation of Provision

Intercity Rail Fund provisions

Senate Amendment

The Senate amendment dedicates net revenues from 0.5 cent per gallon of the 4.3-cents-per gallon transportation motor fuels excise tax to a new Intercity Passenger Rail Fund ("Rail Fund") to finance capital improvements of National Railroad Passenger Corporation (Amtrak) and certain transportation activities in States not receiving Amtrak service. Dedicated revenues are those from fuels taxes imposed from October 1, 1997 through April 15, 2001.

Amounts deposited in the Rail Fund are divided between Amtrak and States not receiving Amtrak passenger rail service to finance obligations incurred after September 30, 1997, and before April 16, 2001. Although transfers to the Rail Fund and authority to enter into new obligations would terminate after April 15, 2001, monies deposited in the Fund will remain available to satisfy outstanding obligations.

Each State not receiving Amtrak rail service will receive an allocation each fiscal year not exceeding one percent of the lesser of (1) Rail Fund revenues for the year or (2) the aggregate amount appropriated from the Rail Fund for the year. Allocations to these non-Amtrak States will be pro-rated on a monthly basis if Amtrak service is provided in the State during a portion of a fiscal year.

The Senate amendment also expands the purposes for which non-Amtrak States may use Rail Fund monies to include: (1) local transit needs such as transportation for the elderly and handicapped; (2) rail/highway crossing safety projects (generally financed through the Highway Trust Fund); (3) certain capital expenditures of smaller freight railroads; and (4) certain rural airport capital expenditures.

Pursuant to section 207 of H. Con. Res. 84, of the total revenues raised in the bill, the amounts equal to the amounts deposited

in the Intercity Passenger Rail Fund each year, are dedicated to finance that Fund.

Rail Fund spending is subject to appropriation, and is provided for under provisions of the Fiscal Year 1998 Budget Resolution.

Tax treatment of Rail Fund expenditures

Amounts received from the Rail Fund by Amtrak and other taxable entities are not included in gross income when received. However, the basis of any property financed with the monies will be reduced by the tax-free amounts received, and no deduction will be allowed for any expenditures attributable to those amounts.

Effective Date

The provision is effective on the date of enactment.

[Conference Report]

House Bill

No provision.

Conference Agreement

The conference agreement follows the approach of the Senate amendment with modifications. The conference agreement provides elective procedures that allows Amtrak to consider the tax attributes of its predecessors, those railroads that were relieved of their responsibility to provide intercity rail passenger service as a result of the Rail Passenger Service Act of 1970, in the use of its net operating losses. The benefit allowable under these procedures is limited to the least of: (1) 35 percent of Amtrak's existing qualified carryovers, (2) the net tax liability for the carryback period, or (3) $2,323,000,000. One half of the amount so calculated will be treated as a payment of the tax imposed by chapter 1 of the Internal Revenue Code of 1986 for each of the first two taxable years ending after the date of enactment.

The existing qualified carryovers are the net operating loss carryovers that are available under section 172(b) in Amtrak's first taxable year ending after September 30, 1997. The net tax liability for the carryback period is the aggregate of the net tax liability of Amtrak's railroad predecessors for all taxable years beginning before January 1,

1971, for which there is a net Federal tax liability. Amtrak's railroad predecessors are those railroads that were relieved of their responsibility to provide intercity rail passenger service as a result of the Rail Passenger Service Act of 1970, and their predecessors. In the case of a railroad predecessor who joined in the filing of a consolidated tax return, the net tax liability of the predecessor will be the net tax liability of the consolidated group.

The net operating losses of Amtrak are required to be reduced by an amount equal to the amount obtained by Amtrak under this provision, divided by 0.35. The Secretary of the Treasury is to adjust, as he deems appropriate, the tax account of each predecessor railroad for the carryback period to reflect the utilization of the net operating losses. The amount of the adjustment is equal to the amount of the benefit and is to be taken into consideration on the tax accounts of the predecessor railroads on a first-in, first-out basis, starting with balances for the earliest year for which any predecessor railroad has a net tax liability. No additional refund to any taxpayer other than Amtrak is to be allowed as a result of these adjustments.

The availability of the elective procedures is conditioned on Amtrak (1) agreeing to make payments of one percent (1%) of the amount it receives to each of the non-Amtrak States to offset certain transportation related expenditures and (2) using the balance for certain qualified expenses. Non-Amtrak States are those States that are not receiving Amtrak service at any time during the period beginning on the date of enactment and ending on the date of payment.

No deduction is allowed with respect to any qualified expense whose payment is attributable to the proceeds made available as a result of this provision. The basis of any property must be reduced by the portion of its cost that is attributable to such proceeds. An item of cost or expense is attributable to such proceeds if it is (1) paid from the proceeds of the refund or (2) to the extent the principal and interest of any borrowings are paid from the proceeds of the refund, from the proceeds of such borrowings.

Amtrak's earnings and profits will be increased by the amount of the refund. However, the conferees expect that this amount will not be included in adjusted current earnings for alternative minimum tax purposes, consistent with Treas. Reg. sec. 1.56(g)- 1(c)(4) (ii).

Effective Date

The provision is effective on the date of enactment. However, no refund shall be made as a result of this provision earlier than the date of enactment of Federal legislation which authorizes reforms of Amtrak. No interest shall accrue with respect to the payment of any refund until 45 days after the later of (1) the enactment of such reform legislation, or (2) the filing by Amtrak of a Federal income tax return which includes the election to use the procedures described in this provision.

[¶ 5111]   Section 1001(a).   Constructive Sales Treatment for Appreciated Financial Positions.

(Code Sec. 1259, 1092, 475)

[House Report]

Present Law

In general, gain or loss is taken into account for tax purposes when realized. Gain or loss generally is realized with respect to a capital asset at the time the asset is sold, exchanged, or otherwise disposed of. Gain or loss is determined by comparing the amount realized with the adjusted basis of the particular property sold. In the case of corporate stock, the basis of shares purchased at different dates or different prices generally is determined by reference to the actual lot sold if it can be identified. Special rules under the Code can defer or accelerate recognition in certain situations.

The recognition of gain or loss is postponed for open transactions. For example, in the case of a "short sale" (i.e., when a taxpayer sells borrowed property such as stock and closes the sale by returning identical property to the lender), no gain or loss on the transaction is recognized until the closing of the borrowing.

Transactions designed to reduce or eliminate risk of loss on financial assets generally do not cause realization. For example, a taxpayer may lock in gain on securities by entering into a "short sale against the box," i.e., when the taxpayer owns securities that are the same as, or substantially identical to, the securities borrowed and sold short. The form of the transaction is respected for income tax purposes and gain on the substantially identical property is not recognized at the time of the short sale. Pursuant to rules that allow specific identification of securities delivered on a sale, the taxpayer can obtain open transaction treatment by identifying the borrowed securities as the securities delivered. When it is time to close out the borrowing, the taxpayer can choose to deliver either the securities held or newly-purchased securities. The Code provides rules only to prevent taxpayers from using short sales against the box to accelerate loss or to convert short-term capital gain into long-term capital gain or long-term capital loss into short-term capital loss (sec. 1233(b)).

Taxpayers also can lock in gain on certain property by entering into offsetting positions in the same or similar property. Under the straddle rules, when a taxpayer realizes a loss on one offsetting position in actively-traded personal property, the taxpayer generally can deduct this loss only to the extent the loss exceeds the unrecognized gain in the other positions in the straddle. In addition, rules similar to the short sale rules prevent taxpayers from changing the tax character of gains and losses recognized on the offsetting positions in a straddle (sec. 1092).

Taxpayers may engage in other arrangements, such as "futures contracts," "forward contracts," "equity swaps" and other "notional principal contracts" where the risk of loss and opportunity for gain with respect to property are shifted to another party (the counterparty'). These arrangements do not result in the recognition of gain by the taxpayer.

The Code accelerates the recognition of gains and losses in certain cases. For example, taxpayers are required each year to mark to market certain regulated futures contracts, foreign currency contracts, non-equity options, and dealer equity options, and to take any capital gain or loss thereon into account as 40 percent short-term gain and 60 percent long-term gain (sec. 1256).

Reasons for Change

In general, a taxpayer cannot completely eliminate risk of loss (and opportunity for gain) with respect to property without disposing of the property in a taxable transaction. In recent years, however, several financial transactions have been developed or popularized which allow taxpayers to substantially reduce or eliminate their risk of loss (and opportunity for gain) without a taxable disposition. Like most taxable dispositions, many of these transactions also provide the taxpayer with cash or other property in return for the interest that the taxpayer has given up.

One of these transactions is the "short sale against the box." In such a transaction, a taxpayer borrows and sells shares identical to the shares the taxpayer holds. By holding two precisely offsetting positions, the taxpayer is insulated from economic fluctuations in the value of the stock. While the short against the box is in place, the taxpayer generally can borrow a substantial portion of the value of the appreciated long stock so that, economically, the transaction strongly resembles a sale of the stock held.

Other transactions that have been used by taxpayers to transfer risk of loss (and opportunity for gain) involve entering into notional principal contracts or futures or forward contracts to deliver the same stock. For example, a taxpayer holding appreciated stock may enter into an "equity swap" which requires the taxpayer to make payments equal to the dividends and any increase in the stock's value for a specified period, and entitles the taxpayer to receive payments equal to any depreciation in value. The terms of such swaps also frequently entitle the shareholder to receive payments during the swap period of a market rate of return (e.g., the Treasury-bill rate) on a notional principal amount equal to the value of the shareholder's appreciated stock, making the transaction strongly resemble a taxable exchange of the appreciated stock for an interest-bearing asset.

[Senate Report]

Explanation of Provision

General rule

The bill requires a taxpayer to recognize gain (but not loss) upon entering into a constructive sale of any appreciated position in stock, a partnership interest or certain debt instruments as if such position were sold, assigned or otherwise terminated at its fair market value on the date of the constructive sale.

If the requirements for a constructive sale are met, the taxpayer would recognize gain in a constructive sale as if the position were sold at its fair market value on the date of the sale and immediately repurchased. Except as provided in Treasury regulations, a constructive sale would generally not be treated as a sale for other Code purposes. An appropriate adjustment in the basis of the appreciated financial position would be made in the amount of any gain realized on a constructive sale, and a new holding period of such position would begin as if the taxpayer had acquired the position on the date of the constructive sale.

A taxpayer is treated as making a constructive sale of an appreciated position when the taxpayer (or, in certain circumstances, a person related to the taxpayer) does one of the following: (1) enters into a short sale of the same property, (2) enters into an offsetting notional principal contract with respect to the same property, or (3) enters into a futures or forward contract to deliver the same property. A constructive sale under any part of the definition occurs if the two positions are in property that, although not the same, is substantially identical. In addition, in the case of an appreciated financial position that is a short sale, a notional principal contract or a futures or forward contract, the holder is treated as making a constructive sale when it acquires the same property as the underlying property for the position. Finally, to the extent provided in Treasury regulations, a taxpayer is treated as making a constructive sale when it enters into one or more other transactions, or acquires one or more other positions, that have substantially the same effect as any of the transactions described.

The positions of two related persons are treated as together resulting in a constructive sale if the relationship is one described in section 267 or section 707(b) and the transaction is entered into with a view toward avoiding the purposes of the provision.

Whether any part of the constructive sale definition is met by one or more appreciated financial positions and offsetting transactions generally will be determined as of the date the last of such positions or transactions is entered into. More than one appreciated financial position or more than one offsetting transaction can be aggregated to determine whether a constructive sale has occurred. For example, it is possible that no constructive sale would result if one appreciated financial position and one offsetting transaction were considered in isolation, but that a constructive sale would result if the appreciated financial position were considered in combination with two transactions. Where the standard for a constructive sale is met with respect to only a pro rata portion of a taxpayer's appreciated financial position (e.g., some, but not all, shares of stock), that portion would be treated as constructively sold under the provision. If there is a constructive sale of less than all of any type of property held by the taxpayer, the specific property deemed sold would be determined under the rules governing actual sales, after adjusting for previous constructive sales under the bill. Under the regulations to be issued by the Treasury, either a taxpayer's appreciated financial position or its offsetting transaction might in some circumstances be disaggregated on a nonpro rata basis for purposes of the constructive sale determination.

The bill provides an exception from constructive sale treatment for any transaction that is closed before the end of the 30th day after the close of the taxable year in which it was entered into. This exception does not apply, however, where a transaction is closed during the last 60 days of the taxable year or within 30 days thereafter (the "90-day period") unless (1) the taxpayer holds the appreciated financial position to which the transaction relates (e.g., the stock where the offsetting transaction is a short sale) through-out the 60-day period beginning on the date the transaction is closed and (2) at no time during such 60-day period is the taxpayer's risk of loss reduced (under the principles of section 246(c)(4)) by holding positions with respect to substantially similar or related property. These requirements do not apply to a transaction that is closed during the 90-day period where a similar transaction is reopened during such period, so long as the reopened transaction is closed during the 90-day period and the requirements of the previous sentence are met after such closing.

A transaction that has resulted in a constructive sale of an appreciated financial position (e.g., a short sale) is not treated as resulting in a constructive sale of another appreciated financial position so long as the taxpayer holds the position which was treated as constructively sold. However, when that position is assigned, terminated or disposed of by the taxpayer, the taxpayer immediately thereafter is treated as entering into the transaction that resulted in the constructive sale (e.g., the short sale) if it remains open at that time. Thus, the transaction can cause a constructive sale of another appreciated financial position at any time thereafter. For example, assume a taxpayer holds two appreciated stock positions and one offsetting short sale, and the taxpayer identifies the short sale as offsetting one of the stock positions. If the taxpayer then sells the stock position that was identified, the identified short position would cause a constructive sale of the taxpayer's other stock position at that time.

Definitions

An appreciated financial position is defined as any position with respect to any stock, debt instrument, or partnership interest, if there would be gain upon a taxable disposition of the position for its fair market value. A "position" is defined as an interest, including a futures or forward contract, short sale, or option. An exception is provided for debt instruments that are not convertible and the interest on which is either fixed, payable at certain variable rates (Treas. reg. sec. 1.860G-1-(a)(3)) or is based on certain interest payments on a pool of mortgages. Other debt instruments, including those identified as part of a hedging or straddle transaction, are appreciated financial positions.

A notional principal contract is treated as an offsetting notional principal contract, and thus, results in a constructive sale of an appreciated financial position, if it requires the holder of the appreciated financial position to pay (or provide a contractual credit for) all or substantially all of the investment yield and appreciation on the position for a specified period and also gives the holder a right to be reimbursed for (or receive credit for) all or substantially all of any decline in value of the position.

A forward contract results in a constructive sale of an appreciated financial position only if the forward contract provides for delivery of a substantially fixed amount of property and a substantially fixed price. Thus, a forward contract providing for delivery of an amount of property, such as shares of stock, that is subject to significant variation under the contract terms does not result in a constructive sale.

A constructive sale does not include a transaction involving an appreciated financial position that is marked to market, including positions governed by section 475 (mark to market for securities dealers) or section 1256 (mark to market for futures contracts, options and currency contracts). Nor does a constructive sale include any contract for sale of an appreciated financial position which is not a "marketable security" (as defined in section 453(f)) if the contract settles within one-year after the date it is entered into.

Treasury guidance

The bill provides regulatory authority to the Treasury to treat as constructive sales certain transactions that have substantially the same effect as those specified (i.e., short sales, offsetting notional principal contracts and futures or forward contracts to deliver the same or substantially similar property).

It is anticipated that the Treasury will use the provision's authority to treat as constructive sales other financial transactions that, like those specified in the provision, have the effect of eliminating substantially all of the taxpayer's risk of loss and opportunity for income or gain with respect to the appreciated financial position. Because this standard requires reduction of both risk of loss and opportunity for gain, it is intended that transactions that reduce only risk of loss or only opportunity for gain will not be covered. Thus, for example, it is not intended that a taxpayer who holds an appreciated financial position in stock will be treated as having made a constructive sale when the taxpayer enters into a put option with an exercise price equal to the current market price (an "at the money" option). Because such an option reduces only the taxpayer's risk of loss, and not its opportunity for gain, the above standard would not be met.

For purposes of the provision, it is not intended that risk of loss and opportunity for gain be considered separately. Thus, if a transaction has the effect of eliminating a PORTION of the taxpayer's risk of loss and a PORTION of the taxpayer's opportunity for gain with respect to an appreciated financial position which, taken together, are substantially all of the taxpayer's risk of loss and opportunity for gain, it is intended that Treasury regulations will treat this transaction as a constructive sale of the position.

It is anticipated that the Treasury regulations, when issued, will provide specific standards for determining whether several common transactions will be treated as constructive sales. One such transaction is a "collar." In a collar, a taxpayer commits to an option requiring him to sell a financial position at a fixed price (the "call strike price") and has the right to have his position purchased at a lower fixed price (the "put strike price"). For example, a shareholder may enter into a collar for a stock currently trading at $100 with a put strike price of $95 and a call strike price of $110. The effect of the transaction is that the seller has transferred the rights to all gain above the $110 call strike price and all loss below the $95 put strike price; the seller has retained all risk of loss and opportunity for gain in the range price between $95 and $110. A collar can be a single contract or can be effected by using a combination of put and call options.

In order to determine whether collars have substantially the same effect as the transactions specified in the provision, it is anticipated that Treasury regulations will provide specific standards that take into ac-count various factors with respect to the appreciated financial position, including its volatility. Similarly, it is expected that several aspects of the collar transaction will be relevant, including the spread between the put and call prices, the period of the transaction, and the extent to which the taxpayer retains the right to periodic payments on the appreciated financial position (e.g., the dividends on collared stock). The Committee expects that the Treasury regulations with respect to collars will be applied prospectively, except in cases to prevent abuse.

Another common transaction for which a specific regulatory standard may be appropriate is a so-called "in-the-money" option, i.e., a put option where the strike price is significantly above the current market price or a call option where the strike price is significantly below the current market price. For example, if a shareholder purchases a put option exercisable at a future date (a so-called "European" option) with a strike price of $120 with respect to stock currently trading at $100, the shareholder has eliminated all risk of loss on the position for the option period and assured himself of all gain on the stock for any appreciation up to $120. In determining whether such a transaction will be treated as a constructive sale, it is anticipated that Treasury regulations will provide a specific standard that takes into account many of the factors described above with respect to collars, including the yield and volatility of the stock and the period and other terms of the option.

For collars, options and some other transactions, one approach that Treasury might take in issuing regulations is to rely on option prices and option pricing models. The price of an option represents the payment the market requires to eliminate risk of loss (for a put option) and to purchase the right to receive yield and gain (for a call option). Thus, option pricing offers one model for quantifying both the total risk of loss and opportunity for gain with respect to an appreciated financial position, as well as the proportions of these total amounts that the taxpayer has retained.

In addition to setting specific standards for treatment of these and other transactions, it may be appropriate for Treasury regulations to establish "safe harbor" rules for common financial transactions that do not result in constructive sale treatment. An example might be a collar with a sufficient spread between the put and call prices, a sufficiently limited period and other relevant terms such that, regardless of the particular characteristics of the stock, the collar probably would not transfer substantially all risk of loss and opportunity for gain.

Effective Date

The provision is effective for constructive sales entered into after June 8, 1997. A special rule is provided for transactions before this date which would have been constructive sales under the provision. The positions in such a transaction will not be taken into account in determining whether a constructive sale after June 8, 1997, has occurred, provided that the taxpayer identifies the offsetting positions of the earlier transaction within 30 days after the date of enactment. The special rule will cease to apply on the date the taxpayer ceases to hold any of the offsetting positions so identified.

In the case of a decedent dying after June 8, 1997, if (1) a constructive sale of an appreciated financial position (as defined in the provision) occurred before such date, (2) the transaction remains open for not less than two years, and (3) the transaction is not closed in a taxable transaction within 30 days after the date of enactment, such position (and any property related to it, under the principles of the provision) will be treated as property constituting rights to receive income in respect of a decedent under section 691.

[Conference Report]

Conference Agreement

The conference agreement follows the Senate amendment with the following modifications.

A trust instrument that is actively traded is generally treated as stock for purposes of determining whether the instrument is an appreciated financial position. The conference agreement provides that a trust instrument will not be treated as stock if substantially all (by value) of the property held by the trust is debt that qualifies for the exception to the definition of appreciated financial position for certain debt instruments. In addition, the conference agreement clarifies that only debt instruments that entitle the holder to receive an unconditional principal amount qualify for the exception.

The conference agreement modifies the exception to constructive sale treatment for transactions that are closed in the 90-day period ending with the 30th day after the close of the taxable year by applying similar requirements to all transactions closed prior to such day. Under the conference agreement, the exception is available only if, for the 60 days after closing a transaction, (1) the taxpayer holds the appreciated financial position and (2) at no time is the taxpayer's risk of loss reduced by holding certain other positions. If a transaction that is closed is reestablished in a substantially similar position, the exception applies provided that the reestablished position is closed prior to the end of the 30th day after the close of the taxable year and the above two requirements are met after such closing.

The conferees also wish to clarify some aspects of the application of the provision. The conferees do not intend that an agreement that is not a contract for purposes of applicable contract law will be treated as a forward contract. Thus, contingencies to which the contract is subject will generally be taken into account.

The conferees intend that the constructive sale provision generally will apply to transactions that are identified hedging or straddle transactions under other Code provisions (secs. 1092(a)(2), (b)(2) and (e), 1221 and 1256(e)). Where either position in such an identified transaction is an appreciated financial position and a constructive sale of such position results from the other position, the conferees intend that the constructive sale will be treated as having occurred immediately before the identified transaction. The constructive sale will not, however, prevent qualification of the transaction as an identified hedging or straddle transaction. Where, after the establishment of such an identified transaction, there is a constructive sale of either position in the transaction, gain will generally be recognized and accounted for under the relevant hedging or straddle provision. However, the conferees intend that future Treasury regulations may except certain transactions from the constructive sale provision where the gain recognized would be deferred under an identified hedging or straddle provision (e.g. Treas. reg. sec. 1.446-4(b)).

The conferees wish to clarify certain other aspects of the Treasury's regulatory authority under the provision. The conferees urge that the Treasury issue prompt guidance, including safe harbors, with respect to common transactions entered into by taxpayers.

The legislative history to both the House bill and the Senate amendment describe "collar" transactions and recommend that Treasury regulations provide standards for determining which collar transactions result in constructive sales. The conferees expect that these Treasury regulations with respect to collars will be applied prospectively, except in cases to prevent abuse.

The legislative history states that, under the regulations to be issued by the Treasury, either a taxpayer's appreciated financial position or an offsetting transaction may in certain circumstances be considered on a disaggregated basis for purposes of the constructive sale determination. The conferees wish to clarify that this authority is intended to be used only where such disaggregated treatment reflects the economic reality of the transaction and is administratively feasible. For example, one transaction for which disaggregated treatment might be appropriate is an equity swap that references a small group of stocks, where the transaction is entered into by a taxpayer owning only one of the stocks.[1]

Effective Date

The conference agreement modifies the special rule for decedents dying after June 8, 1997, to require that a position be open at some time during the three-year period ending on the decedent's death. Thus, no amount will be treated as income in respect of a decedent under the rule unless this requirement is met, as well as the requirements that the transaction remains open for not less than two years and that the transaction is not closed within 30 days after the

date of enactment. Finally, the conference agreement modifies the special rule to provide that gain with respect to a position that accrues after the transaction is closed will not be included in income in respect of a decedent.

[House Report]

Present Law

A dealer in securities must compute its income pursuant to a mark-to-market method of accounting (sec. 475). Any security that is inventory must be included in inventory at its fair market value, and any security that is not inventory and that is held at year end is treated as sold for its fair market value. There is an exception to mark-to-market treatment for any security identified as held for investment or not held for sale to customers (or a hedge of such a security). For this purpose, a "dealer in securities" is a person who (1) regularly purchases securities from or sells securities to customers in the ordinary course of a trade or business, or (2) regularly offers to enter into, assume, offset, assign or otherwise terminate positions in securities with customers in the ordinary course of a trade or business. For this purpose, "security" means any stock in a corporation; any partnership or beneficial ownership interest in a widely-held or publicly-traded partnership or trust; any note, bond, debenture, or other evidence of indebtedness; an interest rate, currency or equity notional principal contract; any evidence of an interest in, or a derivative financial instrument of any security described above; and certain positions identified as hedges of any of the above. Any gain or loss taken into account under these provisions generally is treated as ordinary gain or loss.

Traders in securities generally are taxpayers who engage in a trade or business involving active sales or exchanges of securities on the market, rather than to customers. The mark-to-market treatment applicable to securities dealers does not apply to traders in securities or to dealers in other property.

1.

]A standard similar to that of Treas. reg. 1.246-5 would be appropriate for determining whether the relationship be-

tween the stock and the group of stocks shorted is sufficient for constructive sale purposes.

Reasons for Change

Mark-to-market accounting generally provides a clear reflection of income with respect to assets that are traded in established markets. For market-valued assets, mark-to-market accounting imposes few burdens and offers few opportunities for manipulation. Securities and exchange-traded commodities have determinable market values, and securities traders and commodities traders and dealers regularly calculate year-end values of their assets in determining their income for financial statement purposes. Many commodities dealers also utilize year-end values in adjusting their inventory using the lower-of-cost-or-market method for Federal income tax purposes.

Explanation of Provision

The bill allows securities traders and commodities traders and dealers to elect application of the mark-to-market accounting rules, which apply only to securities dealers under present law. All securities held by an electing taxpayer in connection with a trade or business as a securities trader, and all commodities held by an electing taxpayer in connection with a trade or business as a commodities dealer or trader, are subject to mark-to-market treatment. The taxpayer is allowed to identify property not held in connection with its trade or business as not subject to the election. As for securities dealers under present law, gain or loss recognized by an electing taxpayer under the provision is ordinary gain or loss.

With respect to a commodities dealer, all of the provisions of present law section 475 apply as if commodities were securities. Commodities for purposes of the provision would include only commodities of a kind customarily dealt in on an organized commodities exchange. It is anticipated that Treasury regulations will provide that section 475(c)(4), which prevents a dealer from treating certain notional principal contracts and other derivative financial instruments as held for investment, will apply only to contacts and instruments referenced to commodities in the case of a commodities dealer.

For securities traders, some of the provisions of present law section 475 apply, but others that are specific to dealers do not.

For example, because a securities trader does not hold inventory, the mark-to-market rules for inventory are not applicable to traders. In addition, securities that are not held in connection with the trade or business of a securities trader are excluded from mark-to-market treatment if the trader identifies the securities in the trader's records before the close of the day on which they are acquired under rules similar to those of section 475(b)(2) for dealers. The provisions applicable to securities traders apply to commodities traders as if commodities were securities.

The election is to be made separately with respect to the taxpayer's entire business as (1) a securities trader, (2) a commodities trader, or (3) a commodities dealer. Thus, a taxpayer that is both a commodities dealer and a securities trader may make the election with respect to one business, but not the other. The election will be made in the time and manner prescribed by the Secretary of the Treasury and will be effective for the taxable year for which it is made and all subsequent taxable years, unless revoked with the consent of the Secretary.

Effective Date

The provision would apply to taxable years of securities traders ending after the date of enactment. For a taxpayer making the election, the adjustments required under section 481 as a result of the change in accounting method are required to be taken into account ratably over a four-year period.

For elections made for the first taxable year ending after the date of enactment, the taxpayer must identify the securities or commodities to which the election will apply within 30 days of the date of enactment.

[Conference Report]

Senate Amendment

The Senate amendment is the same as the House bill.

Conference Agreement

The conference agreement follows the House bill and Senate amendment with the following modifications.

The conference agreement clarifies that if a securities trader elects application of the provision, all securities held in connection with its trade or business will generally be subject to mark-to-market accounting. An exception is provided for securities that have no connection with activities as a trader and that are identified on the day acquired (or at such other times as provided in Treasury regulations). The conferees do not intend that an electing taxpayer can mark-to-market loans made to customers or receivables or debt instruments acquired from customers that are not received or acquired in connection with a trade or business as a securities trader. Because the conferees are concerned about issues of taxpayer selectivity, the conferees intend that an electing taxpayer must be able to demonstrate by clear and convincing evidence that a security bears no relation to activities as a trader in order to be identified as not subject to the mark-to-market regime. Any security that hedges another security that is held in connection with the taxpayer's trade or business as a trader will be treated as so held. Any position that is properly subject to the mark-to-market regime will not be taken into account for purposes of the constructive sale rules of section 1259. Similar rules apply to commodities traders.

The conference agreement expands the definition of a commodity for purposes of the provision to include any commodity that is actively traded (within the meaning of section 1092(d)(1)), any option, forward contract, futures contract, short position, notional principal contract or derivative instrument that references such a commodity, and any other evidence of an interest in such a commodity. Also included are positions that hedge the listed items and that are identified by the taxpayer under rules similar to the rules for securities.

The conferees anticipate that Treasury regulations applying section 475(b)(4), which prevents a dealer from treating certain notional principal contracts and other derivative financial instruments as held for investment, will in the case of a commodities trader or dealer apply only to contracts and instruments referenced to commodities.

Effective Date

The conferees wish to clarify that the special rule with respect to the section 481 adjustment applies only to taxpayers making the election for the taxable year which includes the date of enactment. Any elections made thereafter will be governed by rules and procedures established by the Secretary of the Treasury.

[¶ 5112]   Section 1002.   Limitation on exception for investment companies under section 351.

(Code Sec. 351)

[Senate Report]

Present Law

A contribution of property to a corporation does not result in gain or loss to the contributing shareholder if the contributor is part of a group of contributors who own 80 percent of the voting stock of each class of stock entitled to vote. A contribution of property to a partnership generally does not result in recognition of gain or loss to the contributing partner.

Certain Code sections provide exceptions to the general rule for deferral of pre-contribution gain and loss. Gain or loss is recognized upon a contribution by a shareholder to a corporation that is an investment company (sec. 351(e)(1)). Gain, but not loss, is recognized upon a contribution by a partner to a partnership that would be treated as an investment company if the partnership were a corporation (sec. 721(b)). Under Treasury regulations, a contribution of property by a shareholder to a corporation, or by a partner to a partnership, is treated as a transfer to an investment company only if (1) the contribution results, directly or indirectly, in a diversification of the transferor's interests, and (2) the transferee is (a) a regulated investment company ("RIC"), (b) a real estate investment trust ("REIT"), or (c) a corporation more than 80 percent of the assets of which by value (excluding cash and nonconvertible debt instruments) are readily marketable stocks or securities or interests in RICs or REITs that are held for investment (Treas. reg. Sec. 1.351-1(c)(1)).

Reasons for Change

Under present law and regulations, a partnership or a corporation is not treated as an investment company even though more than 80 percent of its assets are a combination of readily marketable stock and securities and other high-quality investment assets of determinable values, such as non-convertible debt instruments, notional principal contracts, foreign currency and interests in metals. Thus, under present law, a partner may contribute stock, securities or other assets to an investment partnership, and a shareholder may contribute such assets to a corporation (e.g., a RIC) and, without current taxation, receive an interest in an entity that is essentially a pool of high-quality investment assets. Where, as a result of such a transaction, the partner or shareholder has diversified or otherwise changed the nature of the financial assets in which it has an interest, the transaction has the effect of a taxable exchange. Of particular concern to the Committee is the reappearance of so-called "swap funds," which are partnerships or RICs that are structured to fall outside the definition of an investment company, and thereby allow contributors to make tax-free contributions of stock and securities in exchange for an interest in an entity that holds similar assets.

Explanation of Provision

The bill modifies the definition of an investment company for purposes of determining whether a transfer of property to a partnership or corporation results in gain recognition (secs. 351(e) and 721(b)) by requiring that certain assets be taken into account for purposes of the definition, in addition to readily marketable stock and securities as under present law.

Under the bill, an investment company includes a RIC or REIT as under present law. In addition, under the bill, an investment company includes any corporation or partnership if more than 80 percent of its assets by value consist of money, stocks and other equity interests in a corporation, evidences of indebtedness, options, forward or futures contracts, notional principal contracts or derivatives, foreign currency, certain interests in precious metals, interests in REITs, RICs, common trust funds and publicly- traded partnerships or other interests in non-corporate entities that are convertible into or exchangeable for any of the assets listed. Other assets that count toward the 80-percent test are an interest in an entity substantially all of the assets of which are assets listed, and to the extent provided in Treasury regulations, interests in other entities, but only to the extent of the value of the interest that is attributable to assets listed.[69] Finally, the bill grants regulatory authority to the Treasury to add other assets to the list set out in the provision, or, under certain circumstances, to remove items from the list.

The bill is intended to change only the types of assets considered in the definition of an investment company in the present Treasury regulations (Treas. reg. sec. 1.351-1(c)(1)(ii)) and not to override the other provisions of those regulations. For example, the bill does not override (1) the requirement that only assets held for investment are considered for purposes of the definition (Treas. reg. sec. 1.351-1(c)(3)), (2) the rule treating the assets of a subsidiary as owned proportionally by a parent owning 50 percent or more of its stock (Treas. reg. sec. 1.351-1(c)(4)), (3) the requirement that the investment company determination consider any plan with regard to an entity's assets in existence at the time of transfer (Treas. reg. Sec. 1.351-1(c)(2),[70] and (4) the requirement that a contribution of property to an investment company result

---

69. Until such regulations are issued, it is intended that the Treasury regulations promulgated under the similar provisions of section 731(c)(2) generally will apply. Specifically, it is intended that an entity will meet the "substantially all" requirement if 90 percent or more of its assets are listed assets (Treas. reg. sec. 1.731-2(c)(3)(i)). Similarly, with respect to partnerships and the non-corporate entities, it is intended that, where 20 percent or more (but less than 90 percent) of the entity's assets consist of listed assets, a pro rata portion

of the interest in the entity will be treated as a listed asset. (Treas. reg. sec. 1.731-2(c)(3)(ii).

70. Although money is counted toward the 80-percent test under the bill, this provision in the regulations should have the effect that where money is contributed and, pursuant to a plan, assets not treated as stock or securities under the bill are either purchased or contributed by other parties, the investment company determination would be made only on the basis of the entity's assets after such events.

in diversification in order for gain to be recognized (Treas. reg. sec. 1.351-1(c)(1)(i)).

Effective Date

The provision applies to all transfers after June 8, 1997, in taxable years ending after such date. An exception is provided for transfers of a fixed amount of securities made pursuant to a binding written contract in effect on June 8, 1997, and at all times thereafter until the transfer.

[Conference Report]

Conference Agreement

The conference agreement is the same as the Senate amendment.

[¶ 5113]   Section 1003.   Gains and losses from certain termination with respect to property.

(Code Sec. 1233, 1234A)

[Senate Report]

Present Law

Treatment of gains and losses

Gain from the "sale or other disposition" is the excess of the amount realized therefrom over its adjusted basis; loss is the excess of adjusted basis over the amount realized. The definition of capital gains and losses in section 1222 requires that there be a "sale or exchange" of a capital asset.[71] The U.S. Supreme Court has held that the term "sale or exchange" is a narrower term than "sale or other disposition."[72] Thus, it is possible from there to be a taxable income from the sale or other disposition of an asset without that gain being treated as a capital gain.

Treatment of capital gains and losses

Long-term capital gains of individuals are subject to a maximum rate of tax of 28 percent.[73] Capital losses of individuals are allowed to the extent of capital gains or the lower of those gains or $3,000.

Long-term capital gains of corporations are subject to the same rate of tax as ordinary income.[74] Capital losses of corporations are allowed only to the extent of the corporation's capital gains; excess capital losses may be carried back to the 3 preceding years and carried forward for the succeeding years.

In the case of gains and losses from the sale or exchange of property used in a trade or business, net gains generally are treated as capital gain while net losses are treated as ordinary losses (sec. 1231).

Court decisions interpreting the "sale or exchange" requirement

There has been a considerable amount of litigation dealing with whether modifications of legal relationships between taxpayers is to be treated as a "sale or exchange." For example, in *Douglass Fairbanks v. U.S.*, 306 U.S. 436 (1939), the U.S. Supreme Court held that gain realized on the redemption of bonds before their maturity is not entitled to capital gain treatment because the redemption was not a "sale or exchange".[75] Several court decisions interpreted the "sale or exchange" requirement to mean that a disposition, that occurs as a result of a lapse, cancellation, or abandonment, is not a sale or exchange of a capital asset, but produces ordinary income or loss. For example, in *Commissioner v. Pittston Co.*, 252 F. 2d 344 (2d Cir), cert. denied, 357 U.S. 919

---

71. Code section 1221 defines a capital asset to mean property held by the taxpayer other than (1) property properly includible in inventory of the taxpayer or primarily held for sale to customers in the ordinary course of the taxpayer's trade or business, (2) depreciable and real property used in the taxpayer's trade of business, (3) a copyright, a literary musical; or artistic composition, letter or memorandum, or similar property that was created by the taxpayer (or whose basis is determined, in whole or in part, the basis of the creator, (4) accounts or notes receivable acquired in the ordinary course of the taxpayer's trade or business, and (5) a publication of the United States Government which was received from the Government other than by sale.

72. *Helvering v. William Flaccus Oak Leather Co.*, 313 U.S. 247 (1941).

73. See bill section 311, which provides an alternative tax rates on long-term capital gains of 10 percent or 20 percent for taxpayers otherwise marginal bracket is 15 percent or greater than 15 percent, respectively.

74. See bill section 321, which provides an alternative tax rate of 30 percent on corporate capital gains an assets held lower than 5 years.

75. The result in this case was overturned by enactment in 1934 of the predecessor of present law sec. 1271(a), see below. See section 117 of the Revenue Act of 1934, 28 Stat. 680, 714-715.

(1958), the taxpayer was treated as receiving ordinary income from amounts received for acquisition from the mine owner of a contract that the taxpayer had made with mine owner to buy all of the coal mined at a particular mine for a period of 10 years on the grounds that the payments were in lieu of subsequent profits that would have been taxed as ordinary income. Similarly, *Commissioner v. Starr Brothers,* 205 F. 2d 673 (1953), the Second Circuit held that a payment that a retail distributor received from a manufacturer in exchange for waiving a contract provision prohibiting the manufacturer from selling to the distributor's competition was not a sale or exchange. Likewise, in *General Artists Corp. v. Commissioner,* 205 F. 2d 360, cert. denied 346 U.S. 866 (1953), the Second Circuit held that amounts received by a booking agent for cancellation of a contract to be the exclusive agent of a singer was not a sale or exchange. In *National-Standard Company v. Commissioner,* 749 F. 2d 369, the Sixth Circuit held that a loss incurred the transfer of foreign currency to discharge the taxpayer's liability was an ordinary loss, since transfer was not a "sale or exchange" of that currency. More recently, in *Stoller v. Commissioner,* 994 F. 2d 855, 93-1 U.S.T.C. par. 50349 (1993), the Court of Appeals for the District of Columbia held, in a transaction that preceded the effective date of section 1234A, that losses incurred on the cancellation of forward contracts to buy and sell short-term Government securities that formed a straddle were ordinary because the cancellation of the contracts was not a "sale or exchange."

The U.S. Tax Court has held that the abandonment of property subject to non-recourse indebtedness is a "sale" and, therefore, any resulting loss is a capital loss. *Freeland v. Commissioner,* 74 T.C. 970 (1980); *Middleton v. Commissioner,* 77 T.C. 310 (1981), aff'd per curiam 693 F.2d 124 (11th Cir. 1982); and *Yarbro v. Commissioner,* 45 T.C.M. 170, aff'd. 737 F.2d 479 (5th Cir. 1984), cert. denied, 105 S.Ct. 959.

Extinguishment treated as sale or exchange

The Internal Revenue Code contains provisions that deem certain transactions to be a sale or exchange and, therefore, any resulting gain or loss is to be treated as a capital gain or loss. These rules generally provide for "sale or exchange" treatment as a way of extending capital gain or loss treatment of those transactions. Under one special provision, gains and losses attributable to the cancellation, lapse, expiration, or other termination of a right or obligation with respect to certain personal property are treated as gains or losses from the sale of a capital asset (sec. 1234A). Personal property subject to this rule is (1) personal property of a type which is actively traded[76] and which is, or would be on acquisition, a capital asset in the hands of the taxpayer (other than stock that is not part of straddle or of a corporation that is not formed or availed of to take positions which offset positions in personal property of its shareholders) and (2) a "section 1256 contract"[77] which is capital asset in the hands of the taxpayer.[78] Section 1234A does not apply to the retirement of a debt instrument.

---

76. Treasury Regulations generally define "actively traded" as any personal property for which there is an established financial market. In addition, those regulations provided that "notional principal contract constitutes personal property of a type that is actively traded if contracts based on the same or substantially similar specified indices are purchased, sold, or entered into on an established financial market" and that "rights and obligations of a party to a notional principal contract are rights and obligations with respect to personal property and constitute an interest is personal property." Treas. Reg. sec. 1.092(d)-1(c).

77. A "Section 1256 contract" means (i) any regulated futures contract, (2) foreign currency contract, (3) nonequity option, or (4) dealer equity option.

78. The present law provisions (sec. 1234A) which treats cancellation, lapse, expiration, or other termination of a right or obligation with respect to personal property as a sale of a capital asset was added by Congress in 1981 when Congress adopted a number of provisions dealing with tax straddles. There are two components or "legs" to a straddle, where the value of one leg changes inversely with the value of the other leg. Without a special role, taxpayers were able to "leg-out" of the loss leg of the straddle, while retaining the gain leg, resulting the creation of an ordinary loss. In 1981, Congress believed that the effective ability of taxpayer to elect the character of a gain or loss leg of a straddle was unwarranted and provided the present law rule that a cancellation, lapse, expiration or other termination of a right is a sale or exchange. However, since straddles were the focus the 1981 legislation, that legislation was limited to types of property which were the subject of straddles, i.e., personal property (other than stock) of a type which is actively traded which is, or would be on acquisition, a capital asset in the hands of the taxpayer. The provision subsequently was extended to section 1256 contracts.

Retirement of debt obligations treated as sale or exchange

Amounts received on the retirement of any debt instrument are treated as amounts received in exchange therefor (sec. 1271(a)(1)). In addition, gain on the sale or exchange of a debt instrument with OID[79] generally is treated as ordinary income to the extent of its OID if there was an intention at the time of its issuance to call the debt instrument before maturity (sec. 1271(a)(2)). These rules do not apply to (1) debt issued by a natural person or (2) debt issued before July 2, 1982, by a noncorporate or nongovernment issuer. As a result of this exemption, the character of gain or loss realized on retirement of an obligation issued by a natural person under present law is governed by case law.

Reasons for Change

Extinguishment treated as sale or exchange

In general, the Committee believes that present law is deficient since it (1) taxes similar economic transactions differently, (2) effectively provides some, but not all, taxpayers with an election, and (3) its lack of certainty makes the tax laws unnecessarily difficult to administer.

The Committee believes that some transactions, such as settlements of contracts to deliver a capital asset, are economically equivalent to a sale or exchange of such contracts since the value of any asset is the present value of the future income that such asset will produce. In addition, to the extent that present law treats modifications of property rights as not being a sale or exchange, present law effectively provides, in many cases, taxpayers with an election to treat the transaction as giving rise to capital gain, subject to more favorable rates than ordinary income, or an ordinary loss that can offset higher-taxed ordinary income and not be subject to limitations on use of capital losses. The effect of an election can be achieved by selling the property right if the resulting transaction results in a gain or providing for the extinguishment of the property right if the resulting transaction results in a loss.

Courts have given different answers as to whether transactions which terminate contractual interests are treated as a "sale or exchange." This lack of uniformity has caused uncertainty to both taxpayers and the Internal Revenue Service in the administration of the tax laws.

Accordingly, the Committee bill treats the cancellation, lapse, expiration, or other termination of a right or obligation with respect to property which is (or on acquisition would be) a capital asset in the hands of the taxpayer to all types of property as a "sale or exchange." A major effect of the Committee bill would be to remove the effective ability of a taxpayer to elect the character of gains and losses from certain transactions. Another significant effect of the Committee bill would be to reduce the uncertainty concerning the tax treatment of modifications of property rights.

Character of gain on retirement of debt obligations issued by natural persons. —

Similar objections can be raised about the rule which exempts debt of natural persons from the deemed sale or exchange rule applicable to debt of other taxpayers. The Committee believes that the debt of natural persons and other taxpayers is sufficiently economically similar to be similarly taxed upon their retirement. Accordingly, the Committee believes that the exception to the deemed sale or exchange rule on retirement of debt of a natural person should be repealed.

Explanation of Provision

Extension of relinquishment rule to all types of property

The bill extends to all types of property the rule which treats gain or loss from the cancellation, lapse, expiration, or other termination of a right or obligation with respect to property which is (or on acquisition

---

79. The issuer of a debt instrument with OID generally accrues and deducts the discount, as interest, over the life of the obligation even though the amount of such interest is not paid until the debt matures. The holder of such a debt instrument also generally includes the OID in income as it accrues as interest on an accrual basis.

The mandatory inclusion of OID in income does not apply, among other exceptions, to debt obligations issued by natural persons before March 2, 1984, and loans of less than $10,000 between natural persons if such loan is not made in the ordinary course of business of the lender (secs. 1272(a)(2)(D) and (E)).

would be) a capital asset in the hands of the taxpayer.

By definition, the extension of the "sale or exchange rule" of present law section 1234A to all property will only affect property that is not personal property which is actively traded on an established exchange. Thus, the committee bill will apply to (1) interests in real property and (2) non-actively traded personal property. An example of the first type of property interest that will be affected by the committee bill is the tax treatment of amounts received to release a lessee from a requirement that the premise be restored on termination of the lease.[80] An example of the second type of property interest that is affected by the committee bill is the forfeiture of a down payment under a contract to purchase stock.[81] The committee bill does not affect whether a right is "property" or whether property is a "capital asset."

Character of gain or loss on retirement of debt obligations issued by natural persons

The committee bill repeals the provision that exempts debt obligations issued by natural persons effective for obligations issued after June 8, 1997. In addition, the committee bill terminates the grandfather of debt issued before July 2, 1982, by noncorporations or nongovernments and by natural persons before June 9, 1997, from the rule which treats gain or loss realized on retirement of such debt as gain or loss realized on an exchange effective for obligations acquired after June 8, 1997, unless the acquirer's basis in the obligation is a carryover basis (i.e., the basis is determined soley by reference to the basis from whom the acquirer acquired the obligation). Thus, under the bill, gain or loss on the retirement of such debt will be capital gain or loss.

Effective Date

Extension of relinquishment rule to all types of property

The extension of the extinguishment rule applies to terminations occurring more than 30 days after the date of enactment of the provision.

Character of gain or loss on retirement of debt obligations issued by natural persons, etc. —

The provision is effective for dispositions after the date of enactment. Thus, any gain or loss occurring after the date of enactment on (1) an obligation of a natural person issued after June 8, 1997, or (2) an obligation issued by a natural person on or before that date to which section 1271(b) currently applies and which is acquired after that date other than in a carryover basis transaction will be treated as a gain or loss from the exchange of the obligation.

[Conference Report]

Conference Agreement

The conference agreement generally follows the Senate amendment.

In addition, the conference agreement provides that if a taxpayer enters into a short sale of property and such property becomes substantially worthless, the taxpayer shall recognize gain as if the short sale were closed when the property becomes substantially worthless. The conference agreement also extends the statute of limitations with respect to such gain recognition to the earlier of: (1) three years after the Treasury Secretary is notified that the position has become substantially worthless; or (2) six years after the date of filing of the income tax return for the taxable year during which the position became substantially worthless. To the extent provided in Treasury regulations, similar gain recognition rules shall apply to any option with respect to property, any offsetting notional principal contract with respect to property, any futures or forward contract to deliver property, or with respect to any similar transaction or position that becomes substantially worthless. The provision applies to property that becomes substantially worthless after the date of enactment of the Act. No inference is intended as to the proper treatment of these or similar transactions or positions under present law.

---

80. See *Billy Rose Diamond Horseshoe, Inc. v. Commissioner,* 448 F.2d 549 (1971), where the Second Circuit held that payments were not entitled to capital gain treatment because there was no sale or exchange. See also, Sirbo Holdings, Inc. v. Commissioner, 509 F.2d 1220 (2d Cir. 1975).

81. See U.S. Freight Co. v. U.S. F.2d 887 (Ct. Cl. 1970), holding that forfeiture was an ordinary loss.

[¶ 5114]   Section 1004.   Determination of original issue discount where pooled debt obligations subject to acceleration.

(Code Sec. 272)

[House Report]

Present Law

Inclusion of interest income, in general

A taxpayer generally must include in gross income the amount of interest received or accrued within the taxable year on indebtedness held by the taxpayer. If the principal amount of an indebtedness may be paid without interest by a specified date (as is the case with certain credit card balances), under present law, the holder of the indebtedness is not required to accrue interest until after the specified date has passed.

Original issue discount

The holder of a debt instrument with original issue discount ("OID") generally accrues and incudes in gross income, as interest, the OID over the life of the obligation, even though the amount of the interest may not be received until the maturity of the instrument.

The amount of OID with respect to a debt instrument is the excess of the stated redemption price at maturity over the issue price of the debt instrument. The stated redemption price at maturity includes all amounts payable at maturity. The amount of OID in a debt instrument is allocated over the life of the instrument through a series of adjustments to the issue price for each accrual period. The adjustment to the issue price is determined by multiplying the adjusted issue price (i.e., the issue price increased by adjustments prior to the accrual period) by the instrument's yield to maturity, and then subtracting the interest payable during the accrual period. Thus, in order to compute the amount of OID and the portion of OID allocable to a period, the stated redemption price at maturity and the time of maturity must be known. Issuers of OID instruments accrue and deduct the amount of OID as interest expense in the same manner as the holder.

Special rules for determining the amount of OID allocated to a period apply to certain instruments that may be subject to pre-

payment. First, if a borrower can reduce the yield on a debt by exercising a prepayment option, the OID rules assume that the borrower will prepay the debt. In addition, in the case of (1) any regular interest in a REMIC, (2) qualified mortgages held by a REMIC, or (3) any other debt instrument if payments under the instrument may be accelerated by reason of prepayments of other obligations securing the instrument, the daily portions of the OID on such debt instruments are determined by taking into account an assumption regarding the prepayment of principal for such instruments.

Reasons for Change

Interest income generally accrues over the period an amount is borrowed and repaid. Certain debt instruments, such as credit card receivables, do not require the debtors to pay interest if they pay their accounts by a specified date. The operation of the OID and interest accrual rules of present law provide that, in such instances, the holder of the debt may assume that the debtors will remit their balances in a timely manner and thus avoid the interest charges. In a the case of a large pool of such debt instruments, this prepayment assumption, as applied to all debtors in the pool, is unrealistic and may result in the mismeasurement of income with respect to the interest charged to those debtors that do not prepay their account balances.

Explanation of Provision

The bill applies the special OID rule applicable to any regular interest in a REMIC, qualified mortgages held by a REMIC, or certain other debt instruments to any pool of debt instruments the payments on which may be accelerated by reason of prepayments. Thus, under the bill, if a taxpayer holds a pool of credit card receivables that require interest to be paid if the borrowers do not pay their accounts by a specified date, the taxpayer would be required to accrue interest or OID on such pool based upon a reasonable assumption regarding the timing of the payments of the accounts in the pool. In cases where the payments in the pool occur soon after year end and before the taxpayer files its tax return for such year end, the taxpayer may accrue interest based on its actual experience rather than based upon reasonable assumptions.

The bill operates as follows. Assume that a calendar year taxpayer issues credit cards, the terms of which provide that if charges for a calendar month are paid within 30 days after the close of the month, no interest will accrue with respect to such charges. However, if the balances are not paid within this 30-day grace period, interest will accrue from the date of the charge until the balance is paid. Further assume that the taxpayer issues a significant number of such credit cards and the card holders incur charges of $10 million in December 1997. Under present law (depending upon the taxpayer's accounting method), the taxpayer is not required to include any interest income in 1997 with respect to the December charges because it is possible that all the credit card holders will pay off the $10 million cumulative December balance by January 30, 1998, and therefore will not be subject to interest with respect to such charges. If some of the credit card holders do not pay their December charges by January 30, 1998, the balances of those holders will be subject to interest charges under the terms of the credit cards and the taxpayer would accrue such interest in income in 1998. Under the bill, the taxpayer, in computing its 1997 taxable income, would be required to make a reasonable assumption as to what portion of the $10 million balances will not be paid off within the 30-day grace period and would be required to accrue interest income through December 31, 1997, with respect to such portion. The taxpayer would then adjust such accrual in 1998 to reflect the extent to which such prepayment assumption reflected the actual payments received in January.

In addition, the Secretary of the Treasury is authorized to provide appropriate exemptions from the provision, including exemptions for taxpayers that hold a limited amount of debt instruments, such as small retailers.

Effective Date

The provision is effective for taxable years beginning after the date of enactment. If a taxpayer is required to change its method of accounting under the bill, such change would be treated as initiated by the taxpayer with the consent of the Secretary of the Treasury and any section 481 adjustment would be included in income ratably over a four-year period. It is understood that some taxpayers presently use a method of accounting similar to the method required to be used under the bill and have asked the Secretary of the Treasury for permission to change to a different method for pre-effective date years. So as not to require taxpayers to change methods of accounting multiple times, it is expected that the Secretary would not grant these pending requests.

[Conference Report]

Senate Amendment

No provision.

Conference Agreement

The conference agreement generally follows the House bill, with modifications. The conference agreement applies to any pool of debt instruments the yield on which may be affected by reason of prepayments. In addition, the conferees wish to clarify that it is within the discretion of the Secretary of the Treasury to grant changes of methods of accounting that are pending for pre-effective date years.

[¶ 5115]   Section 1005.   Denial of Interest Deductions on Certain Debt Instruments.

(Code Sec. 163)

[House Report]

Present Law

Whether an instrument qualifies for tax purposes as debt or equity is determined

under all the facts and circumstances based on principles developed in case law. If an instrument qualifies as equity, the issuer generally does not receive a deduction for dividends paid and the holder generally includes such dividends in income (although corporate holders generally may obtain a dividends-received deduction of at least 70 percent of the amount of the dividend). If an instrument qualifies as debt, the issuer may receive a deduction for accrued interest and the holder generally includes interest in income, subject to certain limitations.

Original issue discount ("OID") on a debt instrument is the excess of the stated redemption price at maturity over the issue price of the instrument. An issuer of a debt instrument with OID generally accrues and deducts the discount as interest over the life of the instrument even though interest may not be paid until the instrument matures. The holder of such a debt instrument also generally includes the OID in income on an accrual basis.

Reasons for Change

The Committee is concerned that corporate taxpayers may issue instruments denominated as debt but that more closely resemble equity transactions for which an interest deduction is not appropriate.

Explanation of Provision

Under the bill, no deduction is allowed for interest or OID on an instrument issued by a corporation (or issued by a partnership to the extent of its corporate partners) that is payable in stock of the issuer or a related party (within the meaning of sections 267(b) and 707(b)), including an instrument a substantial portion of which is mandatorily convertible or convertible at the issuer's option into stock of the issuer or a related party. In addition, an instrument is be treated as payable in stock if a substantial portion of the principal or interest is required to be determined, or may be determined at the option of the issuer or related party, by reference to the value of stock of the issuer or related party. An instrument also is treated as payable in stock if it is part of an arrangement designed to result in such payment of the instrument with or by reference to such stock, such as in the case of certain issuances of a forward contract in connection with the issuance of debt, nonrecourse debt that is secured principally by such stock, or certain debt instruments that are convertible at the holder's option when it is substantially certain that the right will be exercised. For example, it is not expected that the provision will affect debt with a conversion feature where the conversion price is significantly higher than the market price of the stock on the issue date of the debt. The bill does not affect the treatment of a holder of an instrument.

The bill is not intended to affect the characterization of instruments as debt or equity under present law; and no inference is intended as to the treatment of any instrument under present law.

Effective Date

The provision is effective for instruments issued after June 8, 1997, but will not apply to such instruments (1) issued pursuant to a written agreement which was binding on such date and at all times thereafter, (2) described in a ruling request submitted to the Internal Revenue Service on or before such date, or (3) described in a public announcement or filing with the Securities and Exchange Commission on or before such date.

[Conference Report]

Senate Amendment

No provision.

Conference Agreement

The conference agreement follows the House bill. The conference agreement clarifies that for purposes of the provision, principal or interest shall be treated as required to be paid in, converted to, or determined with reference to the value of equity if it may be so required at the option of the holder or a related party and there is a substantial certainty that the option will be exercised.

[¶ 5116]   Section 1011.   Require Gain Recognition for Certain Extraordinary Dividends.

(Code Sec. 1059)

[House Report]

Present Law

A corporate shareholder generally can deduct at least 70 percent of a dividend received from another corporation. This dividends received deduction is 80 percent if the corporate shareholder owns at least 20 percent of the distributing corporation and generally 100 percent if the shareholder owns at least 80 percent of the distributing corporation.

Section 1059 of the Code requires a corporate shareholder that receives an "extraordinary dividend" to reduce the basis of the stock with respect to which the dividend was received by the nontaxed portion of the dividend. Whether a dividend is "extraordinary" is determined, among other things, by reference to the size of the dividend in relation to the adjusted basis of the shareholder's stock. Also, a dividend resulting from a non pro rata redemption or a partial liquidation is an extraordinary dividend. If the reduction in basis of stock exceeds the basis in the stock with respect to which an extraordinary dividend is received, the excess is taxed as gain on the sale or disposition of such stock, but not until that time (sec. 1059(a)(2)). The reduction in basis for this purpose occurs immediately before any sale or disposition of the stock (sec. 1059(d)(1)(A)). The Treasury Department has general regulatory authority to carry out the purposes of the section.

Except as provided in regulations, the extraordinary dividend provisions do not apply to result in a double reduction in basis in the case of distributions between members of an affiliated group filing consolidated returns, where the dividend is eliminated or excluded under the consolidated return regulations. Double inclusion of earnings and profits (i.e., from both the dividend and from gain on the disposition of stock

with a reduced basis) also should generally be prevented.[15] Treasury regulations provide for application of the provision when a corporation is a partner in a partnership that receives a distribution.[16]

In general, a distribution in redemption of stock is treated as a dividend, rather than as a sale of the stock, if it is essentially equivalent to a dividend (sec. 302). A redemption of the stock of a shareholder generally is essentially equivalent to a dividend if it does not result in a meaningful reduction in the shareholder's proportionate interest in the distributing corporation. Section 302(b) also contains several specific tests (e.g., a substantial reduction computation and a termination test) to identify redemptions that are not essentially equivalent to dividends. The determination whether a redemption is essentially equivalent to a dividend includes reference to the constructive ownership rules of section 318, including the option attribution rules of section 318(a)(4). The rules relating to treatment of cash or other property received in a reorganization contain a similar reference (sec. 356(a)(2)).

Reasons for Change

Corporate taxpayers have attempted to dispose of stock of other corporations in transactions structured as redemptions, where the redeemed corporate shareholder apparently expects to take the position that the transactions are dividends that qualify for the dividends received deduction. Thus, the redeemed corporate shareholder attempts to exclude from income a substantial portion of the amount received. In some cases, it appears that the taxpayers' interpretations of the option attribution rules of section 318(a)(4) are important to the taxpayers' contentions that their interests in the distributing corporation are not meaningfully reduced, and are, therefore, dividends.[17] Some taxpayers may argue that certain options have sufficient economic reality that

---

15. See H Rept. 99 841, II 166, 99th Cong. 2d Sess. (September 18, 1986).
16. See Treas. reg. sec. 1.701 2(f), Example (2).
17. For example, it has been reported that Seagram Corporation intends to take the position that the corporate

dividends-received deduction will eliminate tax on significant distributions received from DuPont Corporation in a redemption of almost all the DuPont stock held by Seagram, coupled with the issuance of certain

they should be recognized as stock ownership for purposes of determining whether a taxpayer has substantially reduced its ownership.

Even in the absence of options, the present law rules dealing with extraordinary dividends may permit inappropriate deferral of gain recognition when the portion of the distribution that is excluded due to the dividends received deduction exceeds the basis of the stock with respect to which the extraordinary dividend is received.

Explanation of Provision

Under the bill, except as provided in regulations, a corporate shareholder recognizes gain immediately with respect to any redemption treated as a dividend (in whole or in part) when the nontaxed portion of the dividend exceeds the basis of the shares surrendered, if the redemption is treated as a dividend due to options being counted as stock ownership.[18]

In addition, the bill requires immediate gain recognition whenever the basis of stock with respect to which any extraordinary dividend was received is reduced below zero. The reduction in basis of stock would be treated as occurring at the beginning of the ex-dividend date of the extraordinary dividend to which the reduction relates.

Reorganizations or other exchanges involving amounts that are treated as dividends under section 356 of the Code are treated as redemptions for purposes of applying the rules relating to redemptions under section 1059(e). For example, if a recapitalization or other transaction that involves a dividend under section 356 has the effect of a non pro rata redemption or is treated as a dividend due to options being counted as stock, the rules of section 1059 apply. Redemptions of shares, or other extraordinary dividends on shares, held by a partnership will be subject to section 1059 to the extent there are corporate partners

(e.g., appropriate adjustments to the basis of the shares held by the partnership and to the basis of the corporate partner's partnership interest will be required).

Under continuing section 1059(g) of present law, the Treasury Department is authorized to issue regulations where necessary to carry out the purposes and prevent the avoidance of the provision.

Effective Date

The provision generally is effective for distributions after May 3, 1995, unless made pursuant to the terms of a written binding contract in effect on May 3, 1995 and at all times thereafter before such distribution, or a tender offer outstanding on May 3, 1995.[19] However, in applying the new gain recognition rules to any distribution that is not a partial liquidation, a non pro rata redemption, or a redemption that is treated as a dividend by reason of options, September 13, 1995 is substituted for May 3, 1995 in applying the transition rules.

No inference is intended regarding the tax treatment under present law of any transaction within the scope of the provision, including transactions utilizing options.

In addition, no inference is intended regarding the rules under present law (or in any case where the treatment is not specified in the provision) for determining the shares of stock with respect to which a dividend is received or that experience a basis reduction.

[Conference Report]

Senate Amendment

The Senate amendment is the same as the House bill.

Conference Agreement

The conference agreement follows the House bill and the Senate amendment.

---

rights to reacquire DuPont stock. (See, e.g., Landro and Shapiro, "Hollywood Shuffle," Wall Street Journal, pp. A1 and A11 (April 7, 1995); Sloan, "For Seagram and DuPont, a Tax Deal that No One Wants to Brandy About," Washington Post, p. D3 (April 11, 1995); Sheppard, "Can Seagram Bail Out of DuPont without Capital Gain Tax," Tax Notes Today, (April 10, 1995, 95 TNT 75 4).

18. Thus, for example, where a portion of such a distribution would not have been treated as a dividend due to

insufficient earnings and profits, the rule applies to the portion treated as a dividend.

19. Thus, for example, in the case of a distribution prior to the effective date, the provisions of present law would continue to apply, including the provisions of present-law sections 1059(a) and 1059(d)(1), requiring reduction in basis immediately before any sale or disposition of the stock, and requiring [recognition] of gain at the time of such sale or disposition.

[¶ 5117]   Section 1012.   Application of section 355 to distributions in connection with acquisitions and to intragroup transactions.

(Code Sec. 355, 318, 351, 358, 368)

[House Report]

Present Law

A corporation generally is required to recognize gain on the distribution of property (including stock of a subsidiary) as if such property had been sold for its fair market value. The shareholders generally treat the receipt of property as a taxable event as well. Section 355 of the Internal Revenue Code provides an exception to this rule for certain "spin-off" type distributions of stock of a controlled corporation, provided that various requirements are met, including certain restrictions relating to acquisitions and dispositions of stock of the distributing corporation ("distributing") or the controlled corporation ("controlled") prior and subsequent to a distribution.

In cases where the form of the transaction involves a contribution of assets to the particular controlled corporation that is distributed in connection with the distribution, there are specific Code requirements that distributing corporation's shareholders own "control" of the distributed corporation immediately after the distribution. Control is defined for this purpose as 80 percent of the voting power of all classes of stock entitled to vote and 80 percent of each other class of stock. (Sections 368(a)(1)(D), 368(c), and 351(a) and (c)). In addition, it is a requirement for qualification of any section 355 distribution that the distributing corporation distribute control of the controlled corporation (defined by reference to the same 80-percent test).[20] Present law has the effect of imposing more restrictive requirements on certain types of acquisitions or other transfers following a distribution if the company involved is the controlled corporation rather than the distributing corporation.

[Senate Report]

Reasons for Change

The Committee believes that section 355 was intended to permit the tax-free division of existing business arrangements among existing shareholders. In cases in which it is intended that new shareholders will acquire ownership of a business in connection with a spin off, the transaction more closely resembles a corporate level disposition of the portion of the business that is acquired.

The Committee also believes that the difference in treatment of certain transactions following a spin-off, depending upon whether the distributing or controlled corporation engages in the transaction, should be minimized.

The Committee also is concerned that spin-off transactions within a single corporate group can have the effect of avoiding other present law rules that create or recapture excess loss accounts in affiliated groups filing consolidated returns.[88]

Such intra-group distributions also can have the effect of permitting possibly inappropriate basis increases (or preventing basis decreases) following a distribution, due to the differences between the basis allocation rules that govern spin-offs and those

---

20. If a controlled corporation is acquired after a distribution, an issue may arise whether under step-transaction concepts, the acquisition can be viewed as having occurred before the distribution, with the result that the distributing corporation would not be viewed as having distributed the necessary 80 percent control. The Internal Revenue Service has indicated that it will not rule on requests for section 355 treatment in cases in which there have been negotiations, agreements, or arrangements with respect to transactions or events which, if consummated before the distribution, would result in the distribution of stock or securities of a corporation which is not "controlled" by the distributing corporation. Rev. Proc. 96 39, 1996 33 I.R.B. 11; see also Rev. Rul. 96 30, 1996 1 C.B. 36; Rev. Rul. 70 225, 1970 1 C.B. 80.

88. Excess loss accounts in consolidation generally are created when a subsidiary corporation makes a distribution (or has a loss that is used by other members of the group) that exceeds the parent's basis in the stock of the subsidiary. In general, such excess loss accounts in consolidation are permitted to be deferred rather than causing immediate taxable gain. Nevertheless, they are recaptured when a subsidiary leaves the group or in certain other situations. However, such excess loss accounts are not recaptured in certain cases where there is an internal spinoff prior to the subsidiary leaving the group. See Treas. reg. sec. 1.150-219(g). In addition, an excess loss account may not be created at all in certain cases that are similar economically to a distribution that would reduce the stock basis of the distributing subsidiary corporation, if the distribution from the subsidiary is structured to meet the form of a section 355 distribution.

that apply to other distributions. In the case of an affiliated group not filing a consolidated return, it is also possible that section 355 distributions could in effect permit similar inappropriate basis results.

Explanation of Provision

The bill adopts additional restrictions under section 355 on acquisitions and dispositions of the stock of the distributing or controlled corporation.

Under the bill, if either the controlled or distributing corporation is acquired pursuant to a plan or arrangement in existence on the date of distribution, gain is recognized by the other corporation as of the date of the distribution.

In the case of an acquisition of a controlled corporation, the amount of gain recognized by the distributing corporation is the amount of gain that the distributing corporation would have recognized had stock of the controlled corporation been sold for fair market value on the date of distribution. In the case of an acquisition of the distributing corporation, the amount of gain recognized by the controlled corporation is the amount of net gain that the distributing corporation would have recognized had it sold its assets for fair market value immediately after the distribution. This gain is treated as long-term capital gain. No adjustment to the basis of the stock or assets of either corporation is allowed by reason of the recognition of the gain.

Whether a corporation is acquired is determined under rules similar to those of present law section 355(d), except that acquisitions would not be restricted to "purchase" transactions. Thus, an acquisition occurs if one or more persons acquire 50 percent or more of the vote or value of the stock of the controlled or distributing corporation pursuant to a plan or arrangement. For example, assume a corporation ("P") distributes the stock of its wholly owned subsidiary ("S") to its shareholders. If, pursuant to a plan or arrangement, 50 percent or more of the vote or value of either P or S is acquired by one or more persons, the bill proposal requires gain recognition by the corporation not acquired. Except as provided in Treasury regulations, if the assets of the distributing or controlled corporation are ac-

quired by a successor in a merger or other transaction under section 368(a)(1) (A), (C) or (D) of the Code, the shareholders (immediately before the acquisition) of the corporation acquiring such assets are treated as acquiring stock in the corporation from which the assets were acquired. Under Treasury regulations, other asset transfers also could be subject to this rule. However, in any transaction, stock received directly or indirectly by former shareholders of distributing or controlled, in a successor or new controlling corporation of either, is not treated as acquired stock if it is attributable to such shareholders stock in distributing or controlled that was not acquired as part of a plan or arrangement to acquire 50 percent or more of such successor or other corporation.

Acquisitions occurring within the four-year period beginning two years before the date of distribution are presumed to have occurred pursuant to a plan or arrangement. Taxpayers can avoid gain recognition by showing that an acquisition occurring during this four-year period was unrelated to the distribution.

The bill does not apply to distributions that would otherwise be subject to section 355(d) of present law, which imposes corporate level tax on certain disqualified distributions.

The bill does not apply to a distribution pursuant to a title 11 or similar case.

The Treasury Department is authorized to prescribe regulations as necessary to carry out the purposes of the proposal, including regulations to provide for the application of the proposal in the case of multiple transactions.

Except as provided in Treasury regulations, in the case of distributions of stock within an affiliated group of corporations (as defined in section 1504(a)), section 355 does not apply to any distribution of the stock of one member of the group to another member if it is part of a transaction that results in an acquisition that would be taxable to either the distributing or the controlled corporation.

In addition, in the case of any distribution of stock of one member of an affiliated group of corporations to another member, the Secretary of the Treasury is authorized under section 358(c) to provide adjustments to the basis of any stock in a corporation which is a member of such group, to reflect appropriately the proper treatment of such distribution.

As one example, the Secretary of the Treasury may consider providing rules that require a carryover basis within the group for the stock of the distributed corporation (including a carryover of an excess loss account, if any, in a consolidated return) and that also provide a reduction in the basis of the stock of the distributing corporation to reflect the change in the value and basis of the distributing corporation's assets. The Treasury Department may determine that the aggregate stock basis of distributing and controlled after the distribution may be adjusted to an amount that is less than the aggregate basis of the stock of the distributing corporation before the distribution, to prevent inappropriate potential for artificial losses or diminishment of gain on disposition of any of the corporations involved in the spin off.

The bill also modifies certain rules for determining control immediately after a distribution in the case of certain divisive transactions in which a controlled corporation is distributed and the transaction meets the requirements of section 355. In such cases, under section 351 and modified section 368(a)(2)(H) with respect to certain reorganizations under section 368(a)(1)(D), those shareholders receiving stock in the distributed corporation are treated as in control of the distributed corporation immediately after the distribution if they hold stock representing a greater than 50 percent interest in the vote and value of stock of the distributed corporation.

The bill does not change the present-law requirement under section 355 that the distributing corporation must distribute 80 percent of the voting power and 80 percent of each other class of stock of the controlled corporation. It is expected that this requirement will be applied by the Internal Revenue Service taking account of the provisions of the bill regarding plans that permit certain types of planned restructuring of the distributing corporation following the distri-

bution, and to treat similar restructurings of the controlled corporation in a similar manner. Thus, the 80-percent control requirement is expected to be administered in a manner that would prevent the tax-free spin-off of a less-than-80-percent controlled subsidiary, but generally would not impose additional restrictions on post-distribution restructurings of the controlled corporation if such restrictions would not apply to the distributing corporation.

Effective Date

The bill is generally effective for distributions after April 16, 1997. However, the part of the bill providing a greater- than-80 per cent control requirement immediately after certain section 351 and 368(a)(1)(D) distributions will be effective for transfers after the date of enactment.

The bill will not apply to a distribution after April 16, 1997 that is part of an acquisition that would otherwise cause gain recognition to the distributing or controlled corporation under the bill, if such acquisition is (1) made pursuant to a written agreement which was binding on April 16, 1997 and at all times thereafter; (2) described in a ruling request submitted to the Internal Revenue Service on or before such date; or (3) described on or before such date in a public announcement or in a filing with the Securities and Exchange Commission ("SEC") required solely by reason of the distribution or acquisition. Any written agreement, ruling request, or public announcement or SEC filing is not within the scope of these transition provisions unless it identifies the acquiror of the distributing corporation or of any controlled corporation, whichever is applicable.

The part of the bill providing a greater-than-50-percent control provision for certain transfers after the date of enactment will not apply if such transfer meets the requirements of (1), (2), or (3) of the preceding paragraph.

[Conference Report]

Conference Agreement

The conference agreement follows the Senate amendment with additional modifications.

Amount and timing of gain recognition under section 355(e)

Under the conference agreement, in the case of an acquisition of either the distributing corporation or the controlled corporation, the amount of gain recognized is the amount that the distributing corporation would have recognized had the stock of the controlled corporation been sold for fair market value on the date of the distribution. Such gain is recognized immediately before the distribution. As under the House bill and Senate amendment, no adjustment to the basis of the stock or assets of either corporation is allowed by reason of the recognition of the gain.[13]

Acquisitions resulting in gain recognition

Under the conference agreement, as under the House bill and Senate amendment, the gain recognition provisions of section 355(e) apply when one or more persons acquire 50 percent or more of the voting power or value of the stock of either the distributing corporation or the controlled corporation, pursuant to a plan or series of related transactions.

The conference agreement provides certain additions and clarifications to identify cases that do not cause gain recognition under the provisions of section 355(e).

Single affiliated group

Under the conference agreement, a plan (or series of related transactions) is not one that will cause gain recognition if, immediately after the completion of such plan or transactions, the distributing corporation and all controlled corporations are members of a single affiliated group of corporations (as defined in section 1504 without regard to subsection (b) thereof).

Example 1: P corporation is a member of an affiliated group of corporations that includes subsidiary corporation S and subsidiary corporation S1. P owns all the stock of S. S owns all the stock of S1. P corporation is merged into unrelated X corporation in a transaction in which the former shareholders of X corporation will own 50 percent or

more of the vote or value of the stock of surviving X corporation after the merger. As part of the plan of merger, S1 will be distributed by S to X, in a transaction that otherwise qualifies under section 355. After this distribution, S, S1, and X will remain members of a single affiliated group of corporations under section 1504 (without regard to whether any of the corporations is a foreign corporation, an insurance company, a tax exempt organization, or an electing section 936 company). Even though there has been an acquisition of P, S, and S1 by X, and a distribution of S1 by S that is part of a plan or series of related transactions, the plan is not treated as one that requires gain recognition on the distribution of S1 to X. This is because the distributing corporation S and the controlled corporation S1 remain within a single affiliated group after the distribution (even though the P group has changed ownership).

Continuing direct or indirect ownership

The conference agreement clarifies that an acquisition does not require gain recognition if the same persons own 50 percent or more of both corporations, directly or indirectly (rather than merely indirectly, as in the House bill and Senate amendment), before and after the acquisition and distribution, provided the stock owned before the acquisition was not acquired as part of a plan (or series of related transactions) to acquire a 50-percent or greater interest in either distributing or controlled.

Example 2: Individual A owns all the stock of P corporation. P owns all the stock of a subsidiary corporation, S. Subsidiary S is distributed to individual A in a transaction that otherwise qualifies under section 355. As part of a plan, P then merges with corporation X, also owned entirely by individual A. There is not an acquisition that requires gain recognition under the provision, because individual A owns directly or indirectly 100 percent of all the stock of both X, the successor to P, and S before and after the transaction.[14] The same result would occur if P were contributed to a

---

13. There is no intention to limit the otherwise applicable Treasury regulatory authority under section 336(e) of the Code. There is also no intention to limit the otherwise applicable provisions of section 1367 with respect

to the effect on shareholder stock basis of gain recognized by an S corporation under this provision

14. The example assumes that A did not acquire his or her stock in P as part of a plan or series of related transac-

holding company, all the stock of which is owned by A.

The conference agreement, following the House bill and Senate amendment, continues to provide that except as provided in Treasury regulations, certain other acquisitions are not taken into account. For example, under section 355(e)(3)(A), the following other types of acquisitions of stock are not subject to the provision, provided that the stock owned before the acquisition was not acquired pursuant to a plan or series of related transactions to acquire a 50- percent or greater ownership interest in either distributing or controlled:

First, the acquisition of stock in the controlled corporation by the distributing corporation (as one example, in the case of a drop-down of property by the distributing corporation to the corporation to be distributed in exchange for the stock of the controlled corporation);

Second, the acquisition by a person of stock in any controlled corporation by reason of holding stock or securities in the distributing corporation (as one example, the receipt by a distributing corporation shareholder of controlled corporation stock in a distribution—including a split-off distribution in which a shareholder that did not own 50 percent of the stock of distributing owns 50 percent or more of the stock of controlled); and

Third, the acquisition by a person of stock in any successor corporation of the distributing corporation or any controlled corporation by reason of holding stock or securities in such distributing or controlled corporation (for example, the receipt by former shareholders of distributing of 50 percent or more of the stock of a successor corporation in a merger of distributing).

As under the House bill and Senate amendment, a public offering of sufficient size can result in an acquisition that causes gain recognition under the provision.

Attribution

The conference agreement also modifies the attribution rule for determining when an acquisition has occurred. Rather than apply section 355(d)(8)(A), which attributes stock owned by a corporation to a corporate shareholder only if that shareholder owns 10 percent of the corporation, the conference agreement provides that, except as provided in regulations, section 318(a)(2)(C) applies without regard to the amount of stock ownership of the corporation.

Example 3: Assume the facts are the same as in the immediately preceding example except that corporations P and X are each owned by the same 20 individual 5-percent shareholders (rather than wholly by individual A). The transaction described in the previous example, in which S is spun off by P to P's shareholders and P is acquired by X, would not cause gain recognition, because the same shareholders would own directly or indirectly 50 percent or more of the stock of each corporation both before and after the transaction.

Section 355(f)

The conference agreement follows the Senate amendment in providing that, except as provided in Treasury regulations, section 355 (or so much of section 356 as relates to section 355) shall not apply to the distribution of stock from one member of an affiliated group of corporations (as defined in section 1504(a)) to another member of such group (an "intragroup spin-off") if such distribution is part of a plan (or series of related transactions) described in subsection (e)(2)(A)(ii), pursuant to which one or more persons acquire directly or indirectly stock representing a 50-percent or greater interest in the distributing corporation or any controlled corporation.

Example 4: P corporation owns all the stock of subsidiary corporation S. S owns all the stock of subsidiary corporation T. S distributes the stock of T corporation to P as part of a plan or series of related transactions in which P then distributes S to its shareholders and then P is merged into unrelated X corporation. After the merger, former shareholders of X corporation own 50 percent or more of the voting power or value of the stock of the merged corpora-

---

tions that results in the direct or indirect ownership of 50 percent or more of S or P separately by A. If A's stock in P was acquired as part of such a plan, the

transaction would be one requiring gain recognition on the spin-off of S.

tion. Because the distribution of T by S is part of a plan or series of related transactions in which S is distributed by P outside the P affiliated group and P is then acquired under section 355(e), section 355 in its entirety does not apply to the intragroup spin-off of T to P, under section 355(f). Also, the distribution of S by P is subject to section 355(e).

The conference agreement clarifies that, in determining whether an acquisition described in subsection (e)(2)(A)(ii) occurs, all the provisions of new subsection 355(e) are applied. For example, an intragroup spin-off in connection with an overall transaction that does not cause gain recognition under section 355(e) because it is described in section 355(e)(2)(C), or because of section 355(e)(3), is not subject to the rule of section 355(f).

The Treasury Department has regulatory authority to vary the result that the intragroup distribution under section 355(f) does not qualify for section 355 treatment. In this connection, the Treasury Department could by regulation eliminate some or all of the gain recognition required under section 355(f) in connection with the issuance of regulations that would cause appropriate basis results with respect to the stock of S and T in the above example so that concerns regarding present law section 355 basis rules (described below in connection with section 358(c)) would be eliminated.[15]

Treasury regulatory authority under section 358(c)

As under the Senate amendment, the conference agreement provides that in the case of any distribution of stock of one member of an affiliated group of corporations to another member under section 355 ("intragroup spin-off"), the Secretary of the Treasury is authorized under section 358(c) to provide adjustments to the basis of any stock in a corporation which is a member of such group, to reflect appropriately the proper treatment of such distribution. It is understood that the approach of any such regulations applied to intragroup spin-offs that do not involve an acquisition may also

be applied under the Treasury regulatory authority to modify the rule of section 355(f) as may be appropriate.

The conferees believe that the concerns relating to basis adjustments in the case of intragroup spin offs are essentially similar, whether or not an acquisition is currently intended as part of a plan or series of related transactions. The concerns include the following. First, under present law consolidated return regulations, it is possible that an excess loss account of a lower tier subsidiary may be eliminated. This creates the potential for the subsidiary to leave the group without recapture of the excess loss account, even though the group has benefitted from the losses or distributions in excess of basis that led to the existence of the excess loss account.

Second, under present law, a shareholder's stock basis in its stock of the distributing corporation is allocated after a spin- off between the stock of the distributing and controlled corporations, in proportion to the relative fair market values of the stock of those companies. If a disproportionate amount of asset basis (as compared to value) is in one of the companies (including but not limited to a shift of value and basis through a borrowing by one company and contribution of the borrowed cash to the other), present law rules under section 358(c) can produce an increase in stock basis relative to asset basis in one corporation, and a corresponding decrease in stock basis relative to asset basis in the other company. Because the spin-off has occurred within the corporate group, the group can continue to benefit from high inside asset basis either for purposes of sale or depreciation, while also choosing to benefit from the disproportionately high stock basis in the other corporation. If, for example, both corporations were sold at a later date, a prior distribution can result in a significant decrease in the amount of gain recognized than would have occurred if the two corporations had been sold together without a prior spin off (or separately, without a prior spin-off).

Example 5: P owns all the stock of S1 and S1 owns all the stock of S2. P's basis

---

15. Examples of approaches that the Treasury Department may consider are discussed in connection with section 358(c), *infra*.)

in the stock of S1 is 50; the inside asset basis of S1's assets is 50; and the total value of S1's stock and assets (including the value of S2) is 150. S1's basis in the stock of S2 is 0; the inside basis of S2's assets is 0; and the value of S2's stock and assets is 100. If S1 were sold, holding S2, the total gain would be 100. S1 distributes S2 to P in a section 355 transaction. After this spin-off, under present law, P's basis in the stock of S1 is approximately 17 (50/150 times the total 50 stock basis in S1 prior to the spin-off) and the inside asset basis of S1 is 50. P's basis in the stock of S2 is 33 (100/150 times the total 50 stock basis in S1 prior to the spin-off) and the inside asset basis of S2 is 0. After a period of time, S2 can be sold for its value of 100, with a gain of 67 rather than 100. Also, since S1 remains in the corporate group, the full 50 inside asset basis can continue to be used. S1's assets could be sold for 50 with no gain or loss. Thus, S1 and S2 can be sold later at a total gain of 67, rather than the total gain of 100 that would have occurred had they been sold without the spin-off.

As one variation on the foregoing concern, taxpayers have attempted to utilize spin-offs to extract significant amounts of asset value and basis, (including but not limited to transactions in which one corporation decreases its value by incurring debt, and increases the asset basis and value of the other corporation by contributing the proceeds of the debt to the other corporation) without creation of an excess loss account or triggering of gain, even when the extraction is in excess of the basis in the distributing corporation's stock.

The Treasury Department may promulgate any regulations necessary to address these concerns and other collateral issues. As one example, the Treasury Department may consider providing rules that require a carryover basis within the group (or stock basis conforming to asset basis as appropriate) for the distributed corporation (including a carryover of an excess loss account, if any, in a consolidated return). Similarly, the Treasury Department may provide a reduction in the basis of the stock of the distributing corporation to reflect the change in the value and basis of the distributing corporation's assets. The Treasury Department may determine that the aggregate stock basis of distributing and controlled after the distribution may be adjusted to an amount that is less than the aggregate basis of the stock of the distributing corporation before the distribution, to prevent inappropriate potential for artificial losses or diminishment of gain on disposition of any of the corporations involved in the spin-off. The Treasury Department may provide separate regulations for corporations in affiliated groups filing a consolidated return and for affiliated groups not filing a consolidated return, as appropriate to each situation.

Effective Date

The conferees wish to clarify certain aspects of the effective date and transitional relief under the provision.

First, the conference agreement clarifies that an acquisition of stock that occurs on or before April 16, 1997 will not cause gain recognition under the provision, even if there is a distribution after that date that is part of a plan or series of related transactions that would otherwise be subject to the provision.

Second, any contract that is in fact binding under State law as of April 16, 1997, even though not written, is eligible for transition relief. It would be expected, in such a case, that some form of contemporaneous written evidence of such contract would be in existence. As one example, if under State law acceptance of the terms and conditions of a contract by a corporate board of directors creates a binding contract with an acquiror, then such contract, and the terms and conditions presented to the board, could satisfy the requirement for binding contract transitional relief under the conference agreement. If there was such an offer and acceptance on or before April 16, 1997 and a ruling request filed on or before April 16, 1997, with respect to a proposed spin-off and acquisition, which identifies the acquiror as one of a list of prospective acquirors, then the transaction may be eligible for relief under the transition rules.

Finally, with respect to the Treasury Department regulatory authority under section 358(c) as applied to intragroup spin-off transactions that are not part of a plan or series of related transactions under new section 355(f), the conferees expect that any

Treasury regulations will be applied prospectively, except in cases to prevent abuse.

[¶ 5118]   Section 1013.   Reform tax treatment of certain corporate stock transfers.

(Code Sec. 304, 1059)

[House Report]

Present Law

Under section 304, if one corporation purchases stock of a related corporation, the transaction generally is recharacterized as a redemption. In determining whether a transaction so recharacterized is treated as a sale or a dividend, reference is made to the changes in the selling corporation's ownership of stock in the issuing corporation (applying the constructive ownership rules of section 318(a) with modifications under section 304(c)). Sales proceeds received by a corporate transferor that are characterized as a dividend may qualify for the dividends received deduction under section 243, and such dividend may bring with it foreign tax credits under section 902. Section 304 does not apply to transfers of stock between members of a consolidated group.

Section 1059 applies to "extraordinary dividends," including certain redemption transactions treated as dividends qualifying for the dividends received deduction. If a redemption results in an extraordinary dividend, section 1059 generally requires the shareholder to reduce its basis in the stock of the redeeming corporation by the nontaxed portion of such dividend.

Reasons for Change

Section 304 is directed primarily at preventing a controlling shareholder from claiming basis recovery and capital gain treatment on transactions that result in a withdrawal of earnings from corporate solution. There concerns are most relevant where the shareholder is an individual. Different concerns may be present if the shareholder is a corporation, due in part to the presence of the dividends received deduction. A corporation often may prefer a transaction to be characterized as a dividend, as opposed to a sale or exchange. Accordingly, a corporation may intentionally seek to apply section 304 to a transaction which is in substance a sale or exchange. Corporations that are related for purposes of section 304 need not be 80-percent controlled by a common parent. The separate rules for corporations filing a consolidated return, that would generally reduce basis for untaxed dividends received, do not apply. Furthermore, in some situations where the selling corporation does not in fact own any stock of the acquiring corporation before or after the transaction (except by attribution), it is possible that current law may lead to inappropriate results.

As one example, in certain related-party sales the selling corporation may take the position that its basis in any shares of stock it may have retained (or possibly in any shares of the acquiring corporation that it may own) need not be reduced by the amount of its dividends received deduction. This could result in an inappropriate shifting of basis. The result can be artificial reduction of gain or creation of loss on disposition of any such retained shares.

As one example, assume that domestic corporation X owns 70 percent of the shares of domestic corporation S and all the shares of domestic corporation B. S owns all the shares of domestic corporation T with a basis of $100. Assume that corporation B has sufficient earnings and profits so that any distribution of property would be treated as a dividend. Assume that S sells all but one of its shares in T to B for $99, their fair market value. Under present law, the transfer is treated as a redemption of shares of B, which redemption is treated as dividend to S because, even though S in fact owns no shares of B, it is deemed to own all the shares of B before and after the transaction through attribution from X. Taxpayers may contend that the one share of T retained (worth $1) retains the entire original basis of $100. Although S has received $99 from B for its other shares of T, and has not paid full tax on that receipt due to the dividends received deduction, S may now attempt to claim a $99 loss on disposing of the remaining share of T.

In international cases, a U.S. corporation owned by a foreign corporation may inappropriately claim foreign tax credits from a section 304 transaction. For example, if a foreign-controlled domestic corporation sells the stock of a subsidiary to a foreign sister corporation, the domestic corporation may take the position that it is entitled to credit foreign taxes that were paid by the foreign sister corporation. See Rev. Rul. 92 86, 1992 2 C.B. 199; Rev. Rul. 91 5, 1991 1 C.B. 114. However, if the foreign sister corporation had actually distributed its earnings and profits to the common foreign parent, no foreign tax credits would have been available to the domestic corporation.

Explanation of Provision

Under the bill, to the extent that a section 304 transaction is treated as a distribution under section 301, the transferor and the acquiring corporation are treated as if (1) the transferor had transferred the stock involved in the transaction to the acquiring corporation in exchange for stock of the acquiring corporation in a transaction to which section 351(a) applies, and (2) the acquiring corporation had then redeemed the stock it is treated as having issued. Thus, the acquiring corporation is treated for all purposes as having redeemed the stock it is treated as having issued to the transferor. In addition, the bill amends section 1059 so that, if the section 304 transaction is treated as a dividend to which the dividends received deduction applies, the dividend is treated as an extraordinary dividend in which only the basis of the transferred shares would be taken into account under section 1059.

Under the bill, a special rule applies to section 304 transactions involving acquisitions by foreign corporations. The bill limits the earnings and profits of the acquiring foreign corporation that are taken into account in applying section 304. The earnings and profits of the acquiring foreign corporation to be taken into account will not exceed the portion of such earnings and profits that (1) is attributable to stock of such acquiring corporation held by a corporation or individual who is the transferor (or a person related thereto) and who is a U.S. shareholder (within the meaning of sec, 951(b)) of such corporation, and (2) was accumulated during periods in which such stock was owned by such person while such acquiring corporation was a controlled foreign corporation. For purposes of this rule, except as otherwise provided by the Secretary of the Treasury, the rules of section 1248(d) (relating to certain exclusions from earnings and profits) would apply. The Secretary of the Treasury is to prescribe regulations as appropriate, including regulations determining the earnings and profits that are attributable to particular stock of the acquiring corporation.

No inference is intended as to the treatment of any transaction under present law.

Effective Date

The provision is effective for distributions or acquisitions after June 8, 1997 except that the provision will not apply to any such distribution or acquisition (1) made pursuant to a written agreement which was binding on such date and at all times thereafter, (2) described in a ruling request submitted to the Internal Revenue Service on or before such date, or (3) described in a public announcement or filing with the Securities and Exchange Commission on or before such date.

[Conference Report]

Senate Amendment

The Senate amendment is the same as the House bill.

Conference Agreement

The conference agreement follows the House Bill and the Senate amendment.

[¶ 5119]   Section 1014.   Certain preferred stock treated as "boot."

(Code Sec. 351, 354, 355, 356, 1036)

[House Report]

Present Law

In reorganization transactions within the meaning of section 368 and certain other re- tructurings, no gain or loss is recognized except to the extent "other property" (often called "boot") is received, that is, property other than certain stock, including preferred stock. Thus, preferred stock can be re- ceived tax-free in a reorganization. Upon the receipt of "other property," gain but not loss can be recognized. A special rule permits debt securities to be received tax- free, but only to the extent debt securities of no lesser principal amount are surren- dered in the exchange. Other than this debt- for-debt rule, similar rules generally apply to transactions described in section 351.

Reasons for Change

Certain preferred stocks have been widely used in corporate transactions to afford tax- payers non-recognition treatment, even though the taxpayer may receive relatively secure instruments in exchange for rela- tively risky instruments.

As one example, a shareholder of a cor- poration that is to be acquired for cash may not wish to recognize gain on a sale of his or her stock at that time. Transactions are structured so that a new holding company is formed, to which the shareholder contrib- utes common stock of the company to be acquired, and receives in exchange a pre- ferred stock. The acquiring corporation con- tributes cash to a holding company, which uses the cash to acquire the stock of the other shareholders. In the final acquisition structure, the shareholder who received the preferred stock may also have the additional benefit that the holding company, in which the shareholder now owns preferred stock, may itself own highly secure investments. (Similar results might also be obtained if the corporation to be acquired recapitalized by issuing the preferred stock in exchange for the common stock of the shareholder.) Features such as puts and calls may effec- tively determine the period within which to- tal payment is to occur. In the case of an

individual shareholder, the preferred stock may be puttable or redeemable only at death, in which case the shareholder obtains a basis step-up and never recognizes gain on the transaction.

Similarly, as another type of example, so called "auction rate" preferred stock has a mechanism to reset the dividend rate on preferred stock so that it tracks changes in interest rates over the term of the instru- ment, thus diminishing any risk that the "principal" amount of stock would change if interest rates changed.

The Committee believes that when such preferred stock instruments are received in certain exchange transactions, it is appropri- ate to view such instruments as taxable con- sideration since the investor has often ob- tained a more secure form of investment.

Explanation of Provision

The bill amends the relevant provisions (secs. 351, 354, 355, 356 and 1036) to treat certain preferred stock as "other property" (i.e., "boot") subject to certain exceptions. Thus, when a taxpayer exchanges property for this preferred stock in a transaction that qualifies under either section 351, 355, 368, or 1036, gain but not loss is recognized.

The bill applies to preferred stock (i.e., stock that is limited and preferred as to div- idends and does not participate, including through a conversion privilege, in corporate growth to any significant extent), where (1) the holder has the right to require the issuer or a related person (within the meaning of secs. 267(b) and 707(b)) to redeem or purchase the stock, (2) the issuer or a re- lated person is required to redeem or purchase the stock, (3) the issuer (or a re- lated person) has the right to redeem or purchase the stock and, as of the issue date, it is more likely than not that such right will be exercised, or (4) the dividend rate on the stock varies in whole or in part (directly or indirectly) with reference to interest rates, commodity prices, or other similar indices, regardless of whether such varying rate is provided as an express term of the stock (for example, in the case of an adjustable rate stock) or as a practical result of other aspects of the stock (for example, in the case of auction rate stock). For this purpose, the rules of (1), (2), and (3) apply if the right or obligation may be exercised within 20 years of the date the instrument is issued and such right or obligation is not subject to a contingency which, as of the issue date, makes remote the likelihood of the redemption or purchase. In addition, if neither the stock surrendered nor the stock received in the exchange is stock of a corporation any class of stock of which (or of a related corporation) is publicly traded, a right or obligation is disregarded if it may be exercised only upon the death, disability, or mental incompetency of the holder. Also, a right or obligation is disregarded in the case of stock transferred in connection with the performance of services if it may be exercised only upon the holder's separation from service.

The following exchanges are excluded from this gain recognition: (1) certain exchanges of preferred stock for comparable preferred stock of the same or lesser value; (2) an exchange of preferred stock for common stock; (3) certain exchanges of debt securities for preferred stock of the same or lesser value; and (4) exchanges of stock in certain recapitalizations of family-owned corporations. For this purpose, a family-owned corporation is defined as any corporation if at least 50 percent of the total voting power and value of the stock of such corporation is owned by members of the same family for five years preceding the recapitalization. In addition, a recapitalization does not qualify for the exception if the same family does not own 50 percent of the total voting power and value of the stock throughout the three-year period following the recapitalization. Members of the same family are defined by reference to the definition in section 447(e). Thus, a family includes children, parents, brothers, sisters, and spouses, with a limited attribution for directly and indirectly owned stock of the corporation. Shares held by a family member are treated as not held by a family member to the extent a non-family member had a right, option or agreement to acquire the shares (directly or indirectly, for example, through redemptions by the issuer), or with respect to shares as to which a family member has reduced its risk of loss with respect to the share, for example, through an

equity swap. Even though the provision excepts certain family recapitalizations, the special valuation rules of section 2701 for estate and gift tax consequences continue to apply.

An exchange of nonqualified preferred stock for nonqualified preferred stock in an acquiring corporation may qualify for tax-free treatment under section 354, but not section 351. In cases in which both sections 354 and 351 may apply to a transaction, section 354 generally will apply for purposes of this proposal. Thus, in that situation, the exchange would be tax free.

The Treasury Secretary has regulatory authority to (1) apply installment sale-type rules to preferred stock that is subject to this proposal in appropriate cases and (2) prescribe treatment of preferred stock subject to this provision under other provisions of the Code (e.g., secs. 304, 306, 318, and 368(c)). Until regulations are issued, preferred stock that is subject to the proposal shall continue to be treated as stock under other provisions of the Code.

Effective Date

The provision is effective for transactions after June 8, 1997, but will not apply to such transactions (1) made pursuant to a written agreement which was binding on such date and at all times thereafter, (2) described in a ruling request submitted to the Internal Revenue Service on or before such date, or (3) described in a public announcement or filing with the Securities and Exchange Commission on or before such date.

[Conference Report]

Senate Amendment

The Senate amendment is the same as the House bill.

Conference Agreement

The conference agreement follows the House bill and the Senate amendment with certain clarifications.

The conference agreement clarifies that nonqualified preferred stock is treated as "boot" under section 351(b). The transferor receiving such stock thus is not treated as receiving nonrecognition treatment under section 351(a). However, the nonqualified preferred stock continues to be treated as stock received by a transferor for purposes of qualification of a transaction under section 351(a), unless and until regulations may provide otherwise.

Thus, for example, if A contributes appreciated property to new corporation X for all the common stock (representing 90 percent of the value and all the voting power) of X stock and B contributes cash for nonqualified preferred stock representing 10 percent of the value of X stock, B has received "boot," but the preferred stock is still treated as stock for purposes of sections 351(a) and 368(c), unless and until Treasury Regulations are issued requiring a different result. Thus, the transaction qualifies for non-recognition under section 351. If B had received other stock in addition to nonqualified preferred stock, B would be required to recognize gain only to the extent of the fair market value of the nonqualified preferred stock B receives.

The conference agreement also clarifies the treatment of certain conversion or exchange rights, by deleting any statutory reference to the existence of a "conversion privilege." The conferees wish to clarify that in no event will a conversion privilege into stock of the issuer automatically be considered to constitute participation in corporate growth to any significant extent. The conferees also wish to clarify that stock that is convertible or exchangeable into stock of a corporation other than the issuer (including, for example, stock of a parent corporation or other related corporation) is not considered to be stock that participates in corporate growth to any significant extent for purposes of the provision.

[¶ 5120]   Section 1015.   Modification of Holding Period applicable to Dividends Received Deduction.

(Code Sec. 246)

[House Report]

Present Law

If an instrument issued by a U.S. corporation is classified for tax purposes as stock, a corporate holder of the instrument generally is entitled to a dividends received deduction for dividends received on that instrument. This deduction is 70 percent of dividends received if the recipient owns less than 20 percent (by vote and value) of stock of the payor. If the recipient owns more than 20 percent of the stock the deduction is increased to 80 percent. If the recipient owns more than 80 percent of the payor's stock, the deduction is further increased to 100 percent for qualifying dividends.

The dividends-received deduction is allowed to a corporate shareholder only if the shareholder satisfies a 46-day holding period for the dividend-paying stock (or a 91-day period for certain dividends on preferred stock). The 46- or 91-day holding period generally does not include any time in which the shareholder is protected from the risk of loss otherwise inherent in the ownership of an equity interest. The holding period must be satisfied only once, rather than with respect to each dividend received.

Reasons for Change

Under present law, dividend-paying stocks can be marketed to corporate investors with accompanying attempts to hedge or relieve the holder from risk for much of the holding period of the stock, after the initial holding period has been satisfied. In addition, because of the limited application of section 1059 of the Code requiring basis reduction, many investors whose basis includes a price paid with the expectation of a dividend may be able to sell the stock after the receipt of a dividend not subject to tax at an artificial loss, even though the holder may actually have been relieved of the risk of loss for much of the period it has held the stock.

The Committee believes that no deduction for a distribution on stock should be allowed when the owner of stock does not bear the risk of loss otherwise inherent in the ownership of an equity interest at a time proximate to the time the distribution is made.

Explanation of Provision

The bill provides that a taxpayer is not entitled to a dividends-received deduction if the taxpayer's holding period for the dividend-paying stock is not satisfied over a period immediately before or immediately after the taxpayer becomes entitled to receive the dividend.

[Senate Report]

Effective Date

The provision is generally effective for dividends paid or accrued after the 30th day after the date of the enactment of the bill. However, the provision will not apply to dividends received within two years of the date of enactment if (1) the dividend is paid with respect to stock held on June 8, 1997, and all times thereafter until the dividend is received; (2) the stock is continuously subject to a position described in section 246(c)(4) on June 8, 1997, and all times thereafter until the dividend is received; and (3) such stock and related position is identified by the taxpayer within 30 days after enactment of this Act. A stock will not be considered to be continuously subject to a position if such position is sold, closed or otherwise terminated and is reestablished.

[Conference Report]

Conference Agreement

The conference agreement follows the Senate amendment.

[¶ 5121]   Section 1021.   Reporting of certain payments made to attorneys.

(Code Sec. 6045)

[House Report]

Present Law

Information reporting is required by persons engaged in a trade or business and making payments in the course of that trade or business of "rent, salaries, wages, * * * or other fixed or determinable gains, profits, and income" (Code sec. 6041(a)). Treas. reg. sec. 1.6041 1(d)(2) provides that attorney's fees are required to be reported if they are paid by a person in a trade or business in the course of a trade or business. Reporting is required to be done on Form 1099 Misc. If, on the other hand, the payment is a gross amount and it is not known what portion is the attorney's fee, no reporting is required on any portion of the payment.

Reasons for Change

The provision will have a positive impact on compliance with the tax laws by requiring additional information reporting. Although some might consider it inappropriate to single out payments to one profession for additional information reporting, requiring reporting is appropriate in this instance because attorneys are generally the only professionals who receive this type of payment, a portion of which may be income to them and a portion of which may belong to their client.

Explanation of Provision

The provision requires gross proceeds reporting on all payments to attorneys made by a trade or business in the course of that trade or business. It is anticipated that gross proceeds reporting would be required on Form 1099 B (currently used by brokers to report gross proceeds). The only exception to this new reporting requirement would be for any payments reported on either Form 1099 Misc under section 6041 (reports of payment of income) or on Form W 2 under section 6051 (payments of wages).

In addition, the present exception in the regulations exempting from reporting any payments made to corporations will not apply to payments made to attorneys. Treasury regulation section 1.6041 3(c) exempts payments to corporations generally (although payments to most corporations providing medical services must be reported). Reporting will be required under both Code sections 6041 and 6045 (as proposed) for payments to corporations that provide legal services. The exception of Treasury regulation section 1.6041 3(g) exempting from reporting payments of salaries or profits paid or distributed by a partnership to the individual partners would continue to apply to both sections (since these amounts are required to reported on Form K 1).

First, the provision applies to payments made to attorneys regardless of whether the attorney is the exclusive payee. Second, payments to law firms are payments to attorneys, and therefore are subject to this reporting provision. Third, attorneys are required to promptly supply their TINs to persons required to file these information reports, pursuant to section 6109. Failure to do so could result in the attorney being subject to penalty under section 6723 and the payments being subject to backup withholding under section 3406. Fourth, the IRS should administer this provision so that there is no overlap between reporting under section 6041 and reporting under section 6045. For example, if two payments are simultaneously made to an attorney, one of which represents the attorney's fee and the second of which represents the settlement with the attorney's client, the first payment would be reported under section 6041 and

the second payment would not be reported under either section 6041 or section 6045, since it is known that the entire payment represents the settlement with the client (and therefore no portion of it represents income to the attorney).

Effective Date

The provision is effective for payments made after December 31, 1997. Consequently, the first information reports will be filed with the IRS (and copies will be provided to recipients of the payments) in 1999, with respect to payments made in 1998.

[Conference Report]

Senate Amendment

No provision.

Conference Agreement

The conference agreement follows the House bill.

[¶ 5122]   Section 1022. Information reporting on persons receiving contract payments from certain Federal agencies.

(Code Sec. 6041A)

[House Report]

Present Law

A service recipient (i.e., a person for whom services are performed) engaged in a trade or business who makes payments of remuneration in the course of that trade or business to any person for services performed must file with the IRS an information return reporting such payments (and the name, address, and taxpayer identification number of the recipient) if the remuneration paid to the person during the calendar year is $600 or more (sec. 6041A(a)). A similar statement must also be furnished to the person to whom such payments were made (sec. 6041A(e)). Treasury regulations explicitly exempt from this reporting requirement payments made to a corporation (Treas. reg. sec. 1.6041A 1(d)(2)).

The head of each Federal executive agency must file an information return indicating the name, address, and taxpayer identification number (TIN) of each person (including corporations) with which the agency

enters into a contract (sec. 6050M). The Secretary of the Treasury has the authority to require that the returns be in such form and be made at such time as is necessary to make the returns useful as a source of information for collection purposes. The Secretary is given the authority both to establish minimum amounts for which no reporting is necessary as well as to extend the reporting requirements to Federal license grantors and subcontractors of Federal contracts. Treasury regulations provide that no reporting is required if the contract is for $25,000 or less (Treas. reg. sec. 1.6050M 1(c)(1)(i)).

Reasons for Change

Lowering the information reporting threshold from $25,000 to $600 will improve compliance because additional, small-dollar value contracts will be reported.

Explanation of Provision

The provision requires reporting of all payments of $600 or more made by a Federal executive agency to any person (including a corporation) for services. In addition, the provision requires that a copy of the information return be sent by the Federal agency to the recipient of the payment. An exception is provided for certain classified or confidential contracts.

Effective Date

The provision is effective for returns the due date for which (without regard to extensions) is more than 90 days after the date of enactment.

[¶ 5123]   Section 1023. Disclosure of tax return information for administration of certain veterans programs.

(Code Sec. 6103)

[House Report]

Present Law

The Internal Revenue Code prohibits disclosure of tax returns and return information, except to the extent specifically authorized by the Internal Revenue Code (sec. 6103). Unauthorized disclosure is a felony punishable by a fine not exceeding $5,000 or imprisonment of not more than five years, or both (sec. 7213). An action for civil damages also may be brought for unauthorized disclosure (sec. 7431). No tax information may be furnished by the Internal Revenue Service ("IRS") to another agency unless the other agency establishes procedures satisfactory to the IRS for safeguarding the tax information it receives (sec. 6103(p)).

Among the disclosures permitted under the Code is disclosure to the Department of Veterans Affairs ("DVA") of self-employment tax information and certain tax information supplied to the Internal Revenue Service and Social Security Administration by third parties. Disclosure is permitted to assist DVA in determining eligibility for, and establishing correct benefit amounts under, certain of its needs-based pension, health care, and other programs (sec. 6103(1)(7)(D)(viii)). The income tax returns filed by the veterans themselves are not disclosed to DVA.

The DVA is required to comply with the safeguards currently contained in the Code

[Conference Report]

Senate Amendment

The Senate amendment is the same as the House bill.

Conference Agreement

The conference agreement follows the House bill and the Senate amendment.

and in section 1137(c) of the Social Security Act (governing the use of disclosed tax information). These safeguards include independent verification of tax data, notification to the individual concerned, and the opportunity to contest agency findings based on such information.

The DVA disclosure provision is scheduled to expire after September 30, 1998.

Reasons for Change

It is appropriate to permit disclosure of otherwise confidential tax information to ensure the correctness of government benefits payments.

Explanation of Provision

The provision permanently extends the DVA disclosure provision.

Effective Date

The provision is effective on the date of enactment.

[Conference Report]

Senate Amendment

The Senate amendment is the same as the House bill.

Conference Agreement

The conference agreement extends the DVA disclosure provision through September 30, 2003.

[¶ 5124]   Section 1024.   Continuous Levy on certain payments.

(Code Sec. 6331)

[House Report]

Present Law

If any person is liable for any internal revenue tax and does not pay it within 10 days after notice and demand[22] by the IRS, the IRS may then collect the tax by levy upon all property and rights to property belonging to the person,[23] unless there is an explicit statutory restriction on doing so. A levy is the seizure of the person's property or rights to property. Property that is not cash is sold pursuant to statutory requirements.[24]

In general, a levy does not apply to property acquired after the date of the levy,[25] regardless of whether the property is held by the taxpayer or by a third party (such as a bank) on behalf of a taxpayer. Successive seizures may be necessary if the initial seizure is insufficient to satisfy the liability.[26] The only exception to this rule is for salary and wages.[27] A levy on salary and wages is continuous from the date it is first made until the date it is fully paid or becomes unenforceable. A minimum exemption is provided for salary and wages.[28] It is computed on a weekly basis by adding the value of the standard deduction plus the aggregate value of personal exemptions to which the taxpayer is entitled, divided by 52.[29] For a family of four for taxable year 1996, the weekly minimum exemption is $325.[30]

Reasons for Change

The extension of the continuous levy provisions will substantially ease the administrative burdens of collecting taxes by levy. The Committee anticipates that taxpayers who already comply with the tax laws will have a positive view of increased collections of taxes owed by taxpayers who have not complied with the tax laws.

Explanation of Provision

The provision amends the Code to provide that a continuous levy is also applicable to non-means tested recurring Federal payments. This is defined as a Federal payment for which eligibility is not based on the income and/or assets of a payee. For example, Social Security payments, which are subject to levy under present law, would become subject to continuous levy.

In addition, the provision provides that this levy would attach up to 15 percent of any specified payment due the taxpayer. This rule explicitly replaces the other specifically enumerated exemptions from levy in the Code. A continuous levy of up to 15 percent would also apply to unemployment benefits and means-tested public assistance.

The bill also permits the disclosure of otherwise confidential tax return information to the Treasury Department's Financial Management Service only for the purpose of, and to the extent necessary in, implementing these levy provisions.

Effective Date

The provision is effective for levies issued after the date of enactment.

[Conference Report]

Senate Amendment

The Senate amendment is the same as the House bill.

Conference Agreement

The conference agreement follows the House bill and the Senate amendment.

---

22. Notice and demand is the notice given to a person liable for tax stating that the tax has been assessed and demanding that payment be made. The notice and demand must be mailed to the person's last known address or left at the person's dwelling or usual place of business (Code sec. 6303).
23. Code sec. 6331.
24. Code secs. 6335, 6343.

25. Code sec. 6331(b).
26. Code sec. 6331(c).
27. Code sec. 6331(e).
28. Code sec. 6334(a)(9).
29. Code sec. 6334(d).
30. Standard deduction of $6,700 plus four personal exemptions at $2,550 each equals $16,900, which when divided by 52 equals $325.

[¶ 5125]   Section 1025.   Modifications of Levy Exemptions.

(Code Sec. 6334)

[b. Modifications of levy exemptions House Report]

Present Law

The Code exempts from levy workmen's compensation payments[31] and annuity or pension payments under the Railroad Retirement Act and benefits under the Railroad Unemployment Insurance Act[32] described above, unemployment benefits[33] and means-tested public assistance.[34]

Reasons for Change

The Committee believes that if wages are subject to levy, wage replacement payments should also be subject to levy. In addition, the Committee believes that it is inappropriate to exempt from levy one type of annuity or pension payment while most other types of these payments are subject to levy.

Explanation of Provision

The provision provides that the following property is not exempt from levy if the Secretary of the Treasury (or his delegate) approves the levy of such property: (1) workmen's compensation payments, (2) annuity or pension payments under the Railroad Retirement Act and benefits under the Railroad Unemployment Insurance Act, (3) unemployment benefits, and   (4) means-tested public assistance.

Effective Date

The provision applies to levies issued after the date of enactment.

[Conference Report]

Senate Amendment

The Senate amendment is the same as the House bill, except that it does not apply to annuity or pension payments under the Railroad Retirement Act and benefits under the Railroad Unemployment Insurance Act.

Conference Agreement

The conference agreement follows the House bill.

[¶ 5127]   Section 1027.   Returns of Beneficiaries of Estates and Trusts Required to File Returns Consistent with Estate or Trust Return or to Notify Secretary of Inconsistency.

(Code Sec. 6034A, 6048)

[House Report]

Present Law

An S corporation is required to file a return for the taxable year and is required to furnish to its shareholders a copy of certain information shown on such return. The shareholder is required to file its return in a manner that is consistent with the information received from the S corporation, unless the shareholder files with the Secretary of the Treasury a notification of inconsistent treatment (sec. 6037(c)). Similar rules apply in the case of partnerships and their partners (sec. 6222).

The fiduciary of an estate or trust that is required to file a return for any taxable year is required to furnish to beneficiaries certain information shown on such return (generally via a Schedule K-1) (sec. 6034A). In addition, a U.S. person that is treated as the owner of any portion of a foreign trust is required to ensure that the trust files a return for the taxable year and furnishes certain required information to each U.S. person who is treated as an owner of a portion of the trust or who receives any distribution from the trust (sec. 6048(b)). However, rules comparable to the consistency rules that apply to S corporation shareholders and partners in partnerships are not specified in the case of beneficiaries of estates and trusts.

Reasons for Change

Both partners in partnerships and shareholders of S corporations are required either

---

31. Code sec. 6334(a)(7).
32. Code sec. 6334(a)(6).

33. Sec. 6334(a)(4).
34. Sec. 6334(a)(11).

to file their returns on a basis that is consistent with the information received from the partnership or S corporation or to identify any inconsistent treatment. The Committee believes that it is appropriate to apply such requirement also to beneficiaries of estates and trusts.

Explanation of Provision

Under the bill, a beneficiary of an estate or trust is required to file its return in a manner that is consistent with the information received from the estate or trust, unless the beneficiary files with its return a notification of inconsistent treatment identifying the inconsistency.

Effective Date

The provision is effective for returns filed after date of enactment.

Senate Amendment

The Senate amendment is the same as the House bill.

Conference Agreement

The conference agreement follows the House bill and the Senate amendment.

[¶ 5128]   Section 1028.   Registration of confidential corporate tax shelters and substantial understatement penalty.

(Code Sec. 6111, 6662, 6707)

[House Report]

Present Law

Tax shelter registration

An organizer of a tax shelter is required to register the shelter with the Internal Revenue Service (IRS) (sec. 6111). If the principal organizer does not do so, the duty may fall upon any other participant in the organization of the shelter or any person participating in its sale or management. The shelter's identification number must be furnished to each investor who purchases or acquires an interest in the shelter. Failure to furnish this number to the tax shelter investors will subject the organizer to a $100 penalty for each such failure (sec. 6707(b)).

A penalty may be imposed against an organizer who fails without reasonable cause to timely register the shelter or who provides false or incomplete information with respect to it. The penalty is the greater of one percent of the aggregate amount invested in the shelter or $500. Any person claiming any tax benefit with respect to a shelter must report its registration number on her return. Failure to do so without reasonable cause will subject that person to a $250 penalty (sec. 6707(b)(2)).

A person who organizes or sells an interest in a tax shelter subject to the registration rule or in any other potentially abusive plan

or arrangement must maintain a list of the investors (sec. 6112). A $50 penalty may be assessed for each name omitted from the list. The maximum penalty per year is $100,000 (sec. 6708).

For this purpose, a tax shelter is defined as any investment that meets two requirements. First, the investment must be (1) required to be registered under a Federal or state law regulating securities, (2) sold pursuant to an exemption from registration requiring the filing of a notice with a Federal or state agency regulating the offering or sale of securities, or (3) a substantial investment. Second, it must be reasonable to infer that the ratio of deductions and 350 percent of credits to investment for any investor (i.e., the tax shelter ratio) may be greater than two to one as of the close of any of the first five years ending after the date on which the investment is offered for sale. An investment that meets these requirements will be considered a tax shelter regardless of whether it is marketed or customarily designated   as a tax shelter (sec. 6111(c)(1)).

Accuracy-related penalty

The accuracy-related penalty, which is imposed at a rate of 20 percent, applies to the portion of any underpayment that is attributable to (1) negligence, (2) any substantial understatement of income tax, (3) any substantial valuation misstatement, (4) any substantial overstatement of pension liabilities, or (5) any substantial estate or gift tax valuation understatement.

The substantial understatement penalty applies in the following manner. If the correct income tax liability of a taxpayer for a taxable year exceeds that reported by the taxpayer by the greater of 10 percent of the correct tax or $5,000 ($10,000 in the case of most corporations), then a substantial understatement exists and a penalty may be imposed equal to 20 percent of the underpayment of tax attributable to the understatement. In determining whether a substantial understatement exists, the amount of the understatement is reduced by any portion attributable to an item if (1) the treatment of the item on the return is or was supported by substantial authority, or (2) facts relevant to the tax treatment of the item were adequately disclosed on the return or on a statement attached to the return and there was a reasonable basis for the tax treatment of the item. Special rules apply to tax shelters.

With respect to tax shelter items of non-corporate taxpayers, the penalty may be avoided only if the taxpayer establishes that, in addition to having substantial authority for his position, he reasonably believed that the treatment claimed was more likely than not the proper treatment of the item. This reduction in the penalty is unavailable to corporate tax shelters. The reduction in the understatement for items disclosed on the return is inapplicable to both corporate and non-corporate tax shelters. For this purpose, a tax shelter is a partnership or other entity, plan, or arrangement the principal purpose of which is the avoidance or evasion of Federal income tax.

The Secretary may waive the penalty with respect to any item if the taxpayer establishes reasonable cause for his treatment of the item and that he acted in good faith.

Reasons for Change

The provision will improve compliance with the tax laws by giving the Treasury Department earlier notification than it generally receives under present law of transactions that may not comport with the tax laws. In addition, the provision will improve compliance by discouraging taxpayers from entering into questionable transactions. Also, the provision will improve economic efficiency, because investments that are not economically motivated, but that are instead tax-motivated, may reduce the supply of capital available for economically motivated activities, which could cause a loss of economic efficiency.

Explanation of Provision

Tax shelter registration

The provision requires a promoter of a corporate tax shelter to register the shelter with the Secretary. Registration is required not later than the next business day after the day when the tax shelter is first offered to potential users. If the promoter is not a U.S. person, or if a required registration is not otherwise made, then any U.S. participant is required to register the shelter. An exception to this special rule provides that registration would not be required if the U.S. participant notifies the promoter in writing not later than 90 days after discussions began that the U.S. participant will not participate in the shelter and the U.S. person does not in fact participate in the shelter.

A corporate tax shelter is any investment, plan, arrangement or transaction (1) a significant purpose of the structure of which is tax avoidance or evasion by a corporate participant, (2) that is offered to any potential participant under conditions of confidentiality, and (3) for which the tax shelter promoters may receive total fees in excess of $100,000.

A transaction is offered under conditions of confidentiality if: (1) an offeree (or any person acting on its behalf) has an understanding or agreement with or for the benefit of any promoter to restrict or limit its disclosure of the transaction or any significant tax features of the transaction; or (2) the promoter claims, knows or has reason to know (or the promoter causes another person to claim or otherwise knows or has reason to know that a party other than the potential offeree claims) that the transaction (or one or more aspects of its structure) is proprietary to the promoter or any party other than the offeree, or is otherwise protected from disclosure or use. The promoter includes specified related parties.

Registration will require the submission of information identifying and describing the tax shelter and the tax benefits of the tax shelter, as well as such other information as the Treasury Department may require.

Tax shelter promoters are required to maintain lists of those who have signed confidentiality agreements, or otherwise have been subjected to nondisclosure requirements, with respect to particular tax shelters. In addition, promoters must retain lists of those paying fees with respect to plans or arrangements that have previously been registered (even though the particular party may not have been subject to confidentiality restrictions).

All registrations will be treated as taxpayer information under the provisions of section 6103 and will therefore not be subject to any public disclosure.

The penalty for failing to timely register a corporate tax shelter is the greater of $10,000 or 50 percent of the fees payable to any promoter with respect to offerings prior to the date of late registration (i.e., this part of the penalty does not apply to fee payments with respect to offerings after late registration). A similar penalty is applicable to actual participants in any corporate tax shelter who were required to register the tax shelter but did not. With respect to participants, however, the 50-percent penalty is based only on fees paid by that participant. Intentional disregard of the requirement to register by either a promoter or a participant increases the 50-percent penalty to 75 percent of the applicable fees.

Substantial understatement penalty

The provision makes two modifications to the substantial understatement penalty. The first modification affects the reduction in the amount of the understatement which is attributable to an item if there is a reasonable basis for the treatment of the item. The provision provides that in no event would a corporation have a reasonable basis for its tax treatment of an item attributable to a multi-party financing transaction if such treatment does not clearly reflect the income of the corporation. No inference is intended that such a multi-party financing transaction could not also be a tax shelter as defined

under the modification described below or under present law.

The second modification affects the special tax shelter rules, which define a tax shelter as an entity the principal purpose of which is the avoidance or evasion of Federal income tax. The provision instead provides that a significant purpose (rather than the principal purpose) of the entity must be the avoidance or evasion of Federal income tax for the entity to be considered a tax shelter. This modification conforms the definition of tax shelter for purposes of the substantial understatement penalty to the definition of tax shelter for purposes of these new confidential corporate tax shelter registration requirements.

Treasury report

The provision also directs the Treasury Department, in consultation with the Department of Justice, to issue a report to the tax-writing committees on the following tax shelter issues: (1) a description of enforcement efforts under section 7408 of the Code (relating to actions to enjoin promoters of abusive tax shelters) with respect to corporate tax shelters and the lawyers, accountants, and others who provide opinions (whether or not directly addressed to the taxpayer) regarding aspects of corporate tax shelters; (2) an evaluation of whether the penalties regarding corporate tax shelters are generally sufficient; and (3) an evaluation of whether confidential tax shelter registration should be extended to transactions where the investor (or potential investor) is not a corporation. The report is due one year after the date of enactment.

Effective Date

The tax shelter registration provision applies to any tax shelter offered to potential participants after the date the Treasury Department issues guidance with respect to the filing requirements. The modifications to the substantial understatement penalty apply to items with respect to transactions entered into after the date of enactment.

[Conference Report]

Senate Amendment

The Senate amendment is the same as the House bill.

Conference Agreement

The conference agreement follows the House bill and the Senate amendment.

[¶ 5129]   Section 1031.   Extension and Modification of Airport and Airway Trust Fund Excise Taxes.

(Code Sec. 4261, 4081, 4091, 4041, 4271, 9502, 4263)

[House Report]

Present Law

Present law imposes a variety of excise taxes on air transportation to finance the Airport and Airway Trust Fund programs administered by the Federal Aviation Administration (the "FAA"). In general, the full cost of FAA capital programs is financed from the Airport and Airway Trust Fund, while only a portion of FAA operational expenses is Trust Fund-financed. Overall, the portion of total FAA expenditures that has been financed from the Trust Fund has declined from 75 percent through the early 1990s to 62 percent for the 1997 fiscal year. The balance is financed by general taxpayers, rather than directly by program users. Each of the Airport and Airway Trust Fund excise taxes is scheduled to expire after September 30, 1997.

Commercial air passenger transportation taxes

Domestic air passenger transportation is subject to an ad valorem excise tax equal to 10 percent of the amount paid for the transportation. Taxable domestic air transportation includes both travel within the United States and certain travel between the United States and points in Canada or Mexico that are within 225 miles of the U.S. border (the "225-mile zone").

Special rules apply to air transportation between the continental United States and Alaska or Hawaii and between Alaska and Hawaii. The portion of such transportation which is not within the United States (e.g., the portion over the Pacific Ocean between the continental West Coast and Hawaii) is not subject to the 10-percent air passenger excise tax.[101] The 10-percent excise tax applies in full, however, to air transportation within the States of Alaska and Hawaii.

International air passenger transportation is subject to a $6 departure excise tax imposed on passengers departing the United States for other countries. No tax is imposed on passengers arriving in the United States from other countries. International transportation is defined to include separate domestic flights that connect to international flights, provided that stopover time at any point within the United States does not exceed 12 hours. Thus, these "domestic legs" associated with international transportation (e.g., a flight from Los Angeles to New York from which the passenger boards a connecting flight to London) are exempt from the 10-percent ad valorem excise tax otherwise imposed on such transportation between two domestic points.

There is no special tax rate for flight segments to or from small, rural airports. Application of the 10-percent tax to transportation sold through credit card frequent flyer award and similar arrangements is unclear.

Passengers are liable for the tax; air carrier liability is only for collection and remittance to the government. Air carriers deposit collected taxes semimonthly, generally no later than the 10th day of the second semimonthly period after the transportation is deemed sold. In general, both the domestic and international air passenger transportation excise taxes are imposed without regard to whether the transportation is purchased within the United States. An exception provides that travel between the United States and the 225-mile zone is subject to the ad valorem domestic tax only if it is purchased within the United States.

The Code requires all advertising for taxable air passenger transportation either (1) to state the fare on a tax-inclusive basis or

---

101. The $6 per passenger international departure excise tax, described below, does apply to this transportation.

(2) if the Federal tax is stated separately, to state the amount of the tax at least as prominently as the underlying airline fare and to identify that amount as "user taxes to pay for airport construction and airway safety and operations" (sec. 7275(b)).

The amount of air passenger transportation excise tax collected from a passenger must be stated separately on the ticket.

Commercial air cargo transportation

Domestic air cargo transportation is subject to a 6.25-percent ad valorem excise tax. This tax, like the air passenger excise taxes, is imposed on the consumer, with the transportation provider being required to collect and remit the tax to the Federal Government. However, there is no requirement that the tax be stated separately on shipping invoices.

Noncommercial aviation

Noncommercial aviation, or transportation on private aircraft which is not "for hire," is subject to excise taxes imposed on fuel in lieu of the commercial air passenger ticket and air cargo excise taxes. The current Airport and Airway Trust Fund tax rates on these fuels are 15 cents per gallon on aviation gasoline and 17.5 cents per gallon on jet fuel.

The aviation gasoline excise tax is imposed on removal of the fuel from a registered terminal facility (the same point as the highway gasoline excise tax). The jet fuel excise tax is imposed on sale of the fuel by a wholesale distributor. Many larger airports have dedicated pipeline facilities that directly service aircraft; in such a case, the tax effectively is imposed at the retail level. The person removing the gasoline from a terminal facility or the wholesale distributor of the jet fuel is liable for these taxes.

General Fund aviation fuels excise tax

Fuels used in air transportation are subject to a 4.3-cents-per-gallon excise tax, receipts from which are retained in the General Fund. This fuels tax is identical to taxes also imposed on motor fuels used in other transportation sectors, including highway, inland waterway, and rail.

Deposit of air transportation excise taxes

Under present law, the air passenger ticket and freight excise taxes are collected from passengers and freight shippers by the commercial air carriers. The air carriers then remit the funds to the Treasury Department; however, the air carriers are not required to remit monies immediately. Excise tax returns are filed quarterly (similar to annual income tax returns) with taxes being deposited on a semi-monthly basis (similar to estimated income taxes). For air transportation sold during a semi-monthly period, air carriers may elect to treat the taxes as collected on the last day of the first week of the second following semi-monthly period. Under these "deemed collected" rules, for example, the taxes on air transportation sold between August 1 and August 15, are treated as collected by the air carriers on or before September 7, with the amounts generally being deposited with the Treasury Department by September 10. A special rule requires certain amounts deemed collected during the second half of September to be deposited by September 29.

Semi-monthly deposits and quarterly excise tax returns also are required with respect to the fuels excise taxes imposed on air transportation.

Overflight user fees

Non-tax user fees are imposed on air transportation (both commercial and noncommercial aviation) that travels through airspace for which the United States provides air traffic control services, but that neither lands in nor takes off from a point in the United States. These fees are imposed and collected by the FAA with respect to mileage actually flown, and apply both to travel within U.S. territorial airspace and to travel within international oceanic airspace for which the United States is responsible for providing air traffic control services.

Reasons for Change

The Committee determined that provisions to ensure a long-term, stable funding source for the Airport and Airway Trust Fund should be enacted at this time. As illustrated by the recent events when a shortfall in fiscal year 1997 FAA funding was narrowly averted by an emergency extension of the present-law excise taxes through September 30, 1997, longer-term assurance of these funding needs is imperative. Therefore, the bill extends (with certain modifications) the current Airport and Airway excise taxes for a 10-year period, a move that is believed will resolve, for this period, concerns about the availability of adequate user tax revenues to fund the portion of FAA programs to be appropriated from the Airport and Airway Trust Fund.

The Committee determined limited modifications to the current passenger excise tax structure are warranted. First, the structure of the tax is modified to include a reduced ad valorem rate and a fixed dollar amount tax rate applicable to all revenue passengers. In addition, the Committee determined that the perceived fairness of the passenger air transportation excise taxes will be improved if certain currently untaxed payments and passengers were required to contribute to the financing of the FAA programs from which they benefit. In furtherance of this goal, the bill extends the tax to internationally arriving passengers and clarifies that the tax applies to payments to airlines (and related parties) from credit card and other companies in exchange for the right to award frequent flyer or other reduced air travel rights.

Explanation of Provision

Extension of Airport and Airway Trust Fund taxes

The Airport and Airway Trust Fund excise taxes, as modified below, are extended for 10 years, for the period October 1, 1997, through September 30, 2007. The taxes that are extended include the domestic and international air passenger excise taxes, the air cargo excise tax, and the noncommercial aviation fuels taxes. Gross receipts from these taxes will continue to be deposited in the Airport and Airway Trust Fund.

Modification of commercial air passenger transportation taxes

Modify tax rates. —

The current 10-percent domestic air passenger excise tax is changed to a tax equal to the total of 7.5 percent of the gross amount paid by the passenger for the transportation plus a $2.00 fixed dollar amount per flight segment. The fixed dollar amount per flight segment will be increased each January 1 for a four-year period, as follows:

	Per flight segment charge
Calendar year:	
1999	$2.25
2000	2.50
2001	2.75
2002	3.00

Beginning on January 1, 2003, and each January 1 thereafter, the fixed dollar amount per flight segment will be indexed annually for inflation occurring after 2001, measured by changes in the Consumer Price Index (the "CPI") rounded to the nearest 10 cents. Inflation adjustments will be effective for transportation provided beginning after December 31, 2002, and in each subsequent calendar year.

The term "flight segment" is defined as transportation involving a single take-off and a single landing.[35] The bill provides that there is no change in the number of flight segments for which a passenger is charged (increase or decrease) in the case of transportation routing changes initiated by the air carrier, provided there is no change in the fare charged. Generally, this rule applies to flight changes for travel between the same origin and destination as a result of, e.g., aircraft mechanical problems. The rule similarly covers itinerary changes such as a diversion to another intermediate or destination airport as a result of inclement weather conditions.

All transportation between points within the 48 contiguous States (and within Hawaii

---

35. For example, travel from New York to San Francisco, with an intermediate stop in Chicago, would consist of two flight segments (without regard to whether the passenger changed aircraft in Chicago).

or Alaska), other than domestic segments associated with international transportation, is subject to tax at the 7.5 percent and $2.00 rates.

The current $6 international departure tax is increased to $15.50 per departure, and an identical $15.50 per passenger tax is imposed on arrivals in the United States from international locations. The international departure and arrival taxes are indexed for inflation occurring after 1997, measured by changes in the CPI rounded to the nearest 10 cents. Inflation adjustments will be effective for transportation provided beginning after December 31, 1998, and each subsequent calendar year.

As under present law, certain air transportation between the United States and points within the 225-mile zone of Canada or Mexico is taxed as domestic transportation subject to the 7.5 percent and $2.00 rates. The present-law rules classifying transportation between the 48 contiguous States and Alaska or Hawaii (or between those States) as part domestic and part international are retained, without change, other than a clarification that a single flight segment between the 48 contiguous States and Alaska or Hawaii (or between those States) is subject to only one $15.50 per passenger international tax despite the fact that the flight both departs into and arrives from international airspace.

Extension of tax to certain currently exempt passengers

As described above, passengers arriving in the United States from other countries, who currently are the only group of travelers whose transportation is subject neither to an excise tax nor a user fee for U.S.-provided aviation services, are subject to tax on their arriving international flights.

Clarification further is provided that any amounts paid to air carriers (in cash or in kind) for the right to award or otherwise distribute free or reduced-rate air transportation are treated as amounts paid for taxable air transportation, subject to the 7.5 percent ad valorem tax rate. Examples of such taxable amounts include (1) payments for frequent flyer miles purchased by credit card companies, telephone companies, rental car companies, television networks, restaurants

and hotels, and other businesses for distribution to their customers and others and (2) amounts received by airlines pursuant to joint venture credit card or other marketing arrangements. The Treasury Department is authorized specifically to disregard accounting allocations or other arrangements which have the effect of reducing artificially the base to which the 7.5-percent tax is applied. No inference is intended from this provision as to the proper treatment of these payments under present law.

Liability for tax

The present-law provision imposing liability for the tax on passengers (with transportation providers being liable for collecting and remitting revenues to the Federal Government) are modified to impose secondary liability on air carriers. As with the current tax, the aggregate tax will continue to be required to be stated separately on passenger tickets.

Transfer of 4.3-cents-per-gallon fuels excise tax to Airport and Airway Trust Fund

The 4.3-cents-per-gallon excise tax on aviation gasoline and jet fuel will be deposited in the Airport and Airway Trust Fund, rather than in the General Fund, beginning with fuels sold or removed after September 30, 1997.

Modify air passenger excise tax deposit rules

The deposit rules with respect to the commercial air passenger excise taxes are modified to permit payment of these taxes that otherwise would have been required to be deposited during the period August 15, 1997 through September 30, 1997, to be deposited on October 10, 1997.

Effective Date

These provisions generally are effective on the date of enactment, for air transportation beginning after September 30, 1997.

Present law requires transportation providers to continue collecting the commercial aviation excise taxes (at the current rates) on transportation to be provided after September 30, 1997, if the transportation is purchased before October 1, 1997. The bill requires transportation providers to collect the taxes at the modified rates for transportation purchased after the date of enactment for travel beginning after September 30, 1997.

The extension of the general aviation fuels excise taxes is effective for fuels removed or sold after September 30, 1997.

The provision clarifying application of the commercial air passenger excise tax to certain amounts paid for the right to award air transportation is effective for amounts paid (or benefits transferred) after September 30, 1997, except payments (or transfers) between related parties occurring after June 11, 1997 and before October 1, 1997, are subject to tax if the payments relate to rights to transportation to be awarded or otherwise distributed after September 30, 1997.

The provisions transferring certain General Fund fuels tax revenues and modifying the commercial air passenger excise tax deposit rules are effective on the date of enactment.

[Senate Report]

Reasons for Change

The Committee determined that limited modifications to the current passenger excise tax structure are warranted to improve the perceived fairness of these taxes. First, the Committee was very concerned that, under present law, passengers traveling in international transportation pay significantly less tax for transportation involving comparable FAA services than do entirely domestic passengers. The Committee believes it unfair for American families traveling domestically on, e.g., family vacations, to be required to subsidize persons engaged in this international travel. In particular, the Committee is extremely concerned that domestic passengers flying on entirely domestic flights currently are exempt from tax if they connect to or from another, international flight while passengers on the same flight who do not go on to or arrive from an international destination are fully taxed. Similarly, the Committee believes it is inappropriate that passengers arriving in the

United States should not pay any tax for the FAA services they receive. To achieve greater equity in the air transportation user taxes, the bill extends the tax to internationally arriving passengers, reclassifies domestic segments of international travel as domestic transportation, and clarifies that the tax applies to payments to airlines (and related parties) from credit card and other companies in exchange for the right to award frequent flyer miles or other reduced air travel rights.

The Committee further believes that continued availability of air transportation services to rural areas is an important national objective. Accordingly, the bill provides a special, reduced tax rate for flight segments to and from smaller rural airports.

Explanation of Provisions

Modification of commercial air passenger transportation taxes. Tax on international arrivals and departures; treatment of domestic flight segments associated with international travel

The current $6 international departure tax is increased to $8 per departure, and an identical $8 per passenger tax is imposed on arrivals in the United States from international locations. The definition of international transportation is modified to eliminate domestic flight segments associated with that travel (which are taxed the same as other domestic transportation under the bill). Thus, the $8 per passenger tax applies to all uninterrupted flight segments between a point in the United States and a point in a foreign country.

Special rules applicable to certain Transportation

Transportation between the 48 contiguous States and Alaska or Hawaii (or between those States) remains subject to the special rules provided in present law. Thus, this transportation is taxed on apportioned mileage in U.S. territorial airspace plus $6 per passenger per one-way flight.[102] Clarification is provided that only one $6 per passenger tax is imposed on a single flight seg-

---

102. This special rule also applies to domestic segments between the contiguous 48 states and Alaska or Hawaii which are associated with international arrivals or departures to or from those States. Thus, the flight segment between the 48 contiguous States and Alaska or

Hawaii is subject to a tax of $6 plus 10 percent of the apportioned mileage in U.S. territorial airspace, and the flight segment between Alaska or Hawaii and a foreign country is subject to the new $8 international arrival and departure tax rate.

ment (despite the fact that such a flight segment technically constitutes both an international departure and an international arrival).

Additionally, the current special provisions governing transportation between the United States and points within the 225-mile zone of Canada or Mexico are retained, with that transportation being taxed on the same basis as other domestic transportation in the circumstances provided under present law (as modified by the provisions of the bill recharacterizing certain domestic flight segments associated with international transportation).

A further special rule is provided for certain flight segments to or from qualified rural airports. A qualified rural airport is an airport that (1) in the second preceding calendar year had fewer than 100,000 commercial passenger enplanements (i.e., departures), and (2) either (a) is not located within 75 miles of another airport that had more than 100,000 such passenger enplanements in that year, or (b) is eligible for payments under the Federal "essential air services" program (as in effect on the date of enactment). Flight segments to or from a qualified rural airport are subject to a reduced, 7.5- percent ad valorem rate (in lieu of the general 10-percent rate).[103] The term flight segment is defined as transportation involving a single take-off and a single landing. In the case of transportation involving multiple flight segments, the portion of the fare allocable to the rural segment is determined based on the number of Great Circle miles in the rural flight segment as compared to the aggregate number of miles in all of the flight segments. This is the same calculation that is used in apportioning international transportation between taxable international travel and associated domestic flight segments.

Clarification further is provided that any amounts paid to air carriers (in cash or in kind) for the right to award or otherwise distribute free or reduced-rate air transportation are treated as amounts paid for taxable air transportation, subject to the 10- percent ad valorem tax rate.

[Conference Report]

Senate Amendment

Transfer of General Fund fuels tax

No provision.

Conference Agreement

Extension.—

The conference agreement follows the House bill and the Senate amendment (i.e., extends the present-law Airport and Airway Trust Fund excise taxes for 10 years, subject to the modifications described below).

Commercial passenger tax modifications.—

The conference agreement follows the House bill's domestic passenger tax structure with the following modifications to the rates:

October 1, 1997 - September 30, 1998 — 9 percent of the fare, plus $1 per domestic flight segment

October 1, 1998 - September 30, 1999 — 8 percent of the fare, plus $2 per domestic flight segment

September 30, 1999-December 31, 1999 — 7.5 percent of the fare, plus $2.25 per domestic flight segment

After December 31, 1999, the ad valorem rate will remain at 7.5 percent. The domestic flight segment component of the tax will increase to $2.50 (January 1, 2000-December 31, 2000), to $2.75 (January 1, 2001-December 31, 2001), and to $3 (January 1, 2002- December 31, 2002). Beginning on January 1, 2003, the $3 rate will be indexed to the CPI as under the House bill.

The conference agreement follows the Senate amendment on the treatment of certain domestic flight segments to and from qualified rural airports, with a modification. Under the conference agreement, the tax rate on these flight segments will be 7.5 percent of fare, with no flight segment rate being imposed on eligible flight segments.

The conference agreement follows the House bill and the Senate amendment provi-

---

103. The Treasury Department is directed to publish an annual list of qualified rural airports, based on passenger enplanements for the requisite calendar year.

sions extending the tax on international departures and expanding that tax to include international arrivals, with a modification setting the tax rate on both international departures and arrivals at $12 per passenger (indexed to the CPI beginning on January 1, 1999, as under the House bill). The conferees believe this increased tax level is consistent with the user tax principles of the Airport and Airway Trust Fund taxes which include the recovery from international passengers of a greater percentage of the costs those passengers impose on FAA-programs than are collected by the present-law international departure tax, so that purely domestic passengers and the General Fund will not be required to subsidize the costs imposed by international travelers to the extent occurring under present law.

The conference agreement does not include the provision of the Senate amendment extending tax to domestic flights that connect to or from international flights. Rather, those flights will continue to be tax-free when the flights constitute segments of uninterrupted international transportation (i.e., the scheduled interval at any intermediate stop does not exceed 12 hours). If an intermediate stop exceeds 12 hours, subsequent domestic segments are taxed as domestic transportation.

The conference agreement follows the Senate amendment provision retaining the $6 per passenger rate applicable to the international airspace component of flights between the 48 contiguous States and Alaska or Hawaii (or to flights between Alaska and Hawaii). For example, a passenger traveling from Los Angeles to Honolulu in December 1997 would be taxed at 9 percent of the fare applicable to U.S. territorial miles plus $1 per flight segment plus $6. As with the general $12 international arrival and departure rate, this $6-per-passenger rate will be indexed to the CPI beginning on January 1, 1999.

The conference agreement follows the House bill and Senate amendment provisions clarifying that the air passenger excise tax applies to payments to air carriers (and related parties) for the right to award air travel benefits. The tax rate is 7.5 percent. Examples of such taxable payments include (1) payments for frequent flyer miles (including other rights to air transportation) purchased by credit card companies, telephone companies, rental car companies, television networks, restaurants and hotels, air carriers and related parties, and other businesses, and (2) amounts received by air carriers (or related parties) pursuant to joint venture credit card or other marketing arrangements. The conference agreement includes an exception to this general rule in the case of payments for air transportation rights between corporations that are members of a 100 percent commonly owned controlled group (e.g., transportation purchased from an air carrier by a 100 percent commonly owned corporation operating a frequent flyer award program for the air carrier).

The conferees are aware that consumers accrue mileage awards from numerous sources, including actual air travel as well as programs giving rise to taxable payments under this provision of the conference agreement. Once awarded to consumers, these miles are commingled in the consumer's account such that any miles used for a specific purpose may not be traceable to the source which gave rise to them. The conference agreement authorizes the Treasury Department to develop regulations excluding from the tax base a portion of otherwise taxable payments, if any, with respect to awarded frequent flyer miles if the Treasury determines that a portion properly can be allocated (traced) to miles which are used by consumers for purposes other than air transportation. Miles that are unused should not be treated as used for purposes other than air transportation. As part of any rulemaking process it undertakes, the Treasury is authorized to review airline frequent flyer programs and other information from all available sources, including industry and third-party data, in determining whether mileage awards can be adequately traced to support tax-base allocations based on the ultimate use of the awards. The conferees intend that an adjustment to the tax base will be prescribed only if the Treasury finds a consistent pattern of non-air transportation usage by consumers at levels indicating that significant mileage awarded pursuant to payments taxable under this provision is being used for purposes other than air transportation. In making any such adjustment, the Treasury Department should treat mileage used for non-air transportation purposes as coming first from mileage awarded to consumers from actual air travel (and other sources not subject to tax under this provision).

The conference agreement follows the House bill and the Senate amendment provisions extending secondary liability for the passenger taxes to air carriers.

The conference agreement includes the provision of the House bill changing certain commercial air passenger excise tax deposit dates for taxes otherwise due after August 14, 1997, and before October 1, 1997, to October 10, 1997. Additionally, the conference agreement provides that deposits of commercial air passenger taxes that otherwise would be required after August 14,

1998, and before October 1, 1998, will be due on October 5, 1998. Deposits of the commercial air cargo and aviation fuels taxes that otherwise would be required to be made after July 31, 1998, and before October 1, 1998, will be due on October 5, 1998.

Transfer of General Fund fuels tax revenues.—

The conference agreement includes the House bill provision transferring gross receipts from the 4.3-cents-per-gallon general fund tax on aviation fuels to the Airport and Airway Trust Fund.

Effective Date

The conference agreement follows the House bill.

[¶ 5130]   **Section 1032.   Kerosene Taxed as Diesel Fuel.**

(Code Sec. 4083, 4082, 4081, 4101, 6427, 4093, 6416, 6715, 7232, 9503, 9508)

[House Report]

Present Law

Diesel fuel used as a transportation motor fuel generally is taxed at 24.3 cents per gallon. This tax is collected on all diesel fuel upon removal from a pipeline or barge terminal unless the fuel is indelibly dyed and is destined for a nontaxable use. Diesel fuel also commonly is used as heating oil; diesel fuel used as heating oil is not subject to tax. Certain other uses also are exempt from tax, and some transportation uses (e.g., rail and intercity buses) are taxed at reduced rates. Both exemptions and reduced-rates are realized through refund claims if undyed diesel fuel is used in a qualifying use.

Aviation gasoline and jet fuel (both commercial and noncommercial use) currently are subject to a 4.3-cents-per-gallon General Fund tax rate. In addition, through September 30, 1997, gasoline and jet fuel used in noncommercial aviation are subject to an additional 15-cents-per- gallon rate (gasoline) and 17.5-cents-per-gallon rate (jet fuel) for the Airport and Airway Trust Fund. These combined rates produce an aggregate tax of 21.8 cents per gallon on noncommer-

cial aviation jet fuel and 19.3 cents per gallon on noncommercial aviation gasoline.

The tax on non-gasoline aviation fuel is imposed on the sale of the fuel by a "producer," typically a wholesale distributor. Thus, this tax is imposed at a point in the fuel distribution chain subsequent to removal from a terminal facility. Kerosene is used both as a transportation fuel and as an aviation fuel. Kerosene also is blended with diesel fuel destined both for taxable (highway) and nontaxable (heating oil) uses to, among other things, prevent gelling of the diesel fuel in colder temperatures. Under present law, kerosene is not subject to excise tax unless it is blended with taxable diesel fuel or is sold for use as aviation fuel. When kerosene is blended with dyed diesel fuel to be used in a nontaxable use, the dye concentration of the fuel mixture must be adjusted to ensure that it meets Treasury Department requirements for untaxed, dyed diesel fuel.

Clear, low-sulphur kerosene (K 1) also is used in space heaters, and often is sold for this purpose at retail service stations. As with other heating oil uses, kerosene used in space heaters, is not subject to Federal excise tax. Although heating oil often has minor amounts of kerosene blended with it in colder weather, this blending typically occurs before removal of the fuel from the terminal facilities where Federal excise taxes are imposed. However, it may be necessary during periods of extreme or unseasonably cold weather to add kerosene to heating oil after its removal from the terminal. Other nontaxable uses of kerosene include feedstock use in the petrochemical industry.

Reasons for Change

The Internal Revenue Service has discovered significant evidence that kerosene is being blended with taxable highway diesel fuel during periods when the blending is not necessary due to colder weather conditions. Some wholesale distributors of diesel fuel also have suggested that their competitors have not been paying the tax on the kerosene that they blend with diesel fuel for highway use. These reports of increased use of kerosene as a taxable highway fuel without payment of tax coincided with implementation of enhanced diesel fuel tax compliance measures that have significantly reduced opportunities to evade that tax. The Committee determined therefore, that these same compliance measures should be extended to kerosene.

Explanation of Provision

The diesel fuel-excise tax rules are extended to kerosene. Thus, kerosene is be taxed when it is removed from a registered terminal unless it is indelibly dyed and destined for a nontaxable use. However, aviation-grade kerosene that is removed from the terminal by a registered producer of aviation fuel is not subject to the dyeing requirement and would be taxed under the present law rules applicable to aviation fuel. Feedstock kerosene that a registered industrial user receives by pipeline or vessel also is exempt from the dyeing requirement. Other feedstock kerosene would be exempt from the dyeing requirement to the extent and under conditions (including satisfaction of registration and certification requirements) prescribed by Treasury Department regulation.

To accommodate State safety regulations that require the use of clear (K 1) kerosene in certain space heaters, a refund procedure would be provided under which registered ultimate vendors may claim refunds of the tax paid on kerosene sold for that use. In addition, the Internal Revenue Service is given discretion to refund to a registered ultimate vendor the tax paid on kerosene that is blended with heating oil for use during periods of extreme or unseasonable cold.

Effective Date

The provision is effective for kerosene removed from terminal facilities after June 30, 1998. Appropriate floor stocks taxes will be imposed on kerosene held beyond the point of taxation on July 1, 1998.

[Conference Report]

Senate Amendment

No provision.

Conference Agreement

The conference agreement follows the House bill with modifications. First, registration as a terminal facility eligible to handle non-tax-paid diesel fuel and kerosene is conditional on the facility offering its customers dyeing for nontaxable sales of diesel fuel and kerosene. Second, the minimum amount for vendor refunds of tax paid on kerosene is reduced from $200 to $100. Third, the Treasury Department is given regulatory authority to allow tax-free sales of kerosene to wholesale dealers that (a) satisfy such registration and other compliance measures as Treasury may prescribe and (b) sell kerosene exclusively to retailers eligible for refunds with respect to undyed kerosene sold by them for a nontaxable use.

[¶ 5131]   Section 1033.   Restoration of Leaking Underground Storage Tank Trust Fund Taxes.

(Code Sec. 4081)

[House Report]

Present Law

Before January 1, 1996, an excise tax of 0.1 cent per gallon was imposed on gasoline, diesel fuel (including train diesel fuel), special motor fuels (other than liquefied petroleum gas), aviation fuels, and inland waterways fuels. Revenues from the tax were dedicated to the Leaking Underground Storage Tank Trust Fund to finance cleanups of leaking underground storage tanks.

Reasons for Change

The Committee determined that the Leaking Underground Storage Tank Trust Fund excise tax should be reinstated for a 5-year period to ensure the availability of funds to pay cleanup costs of leaking underground storage tanks.

Explanation of Provision

The bill reinstates for a 5-year period the prior-law Leaking Underground Storage Tank Trust Fund excise tax.

Effective Date

The provision is effective on the date of enactment.

[Senate Report]

Explanation of Provision

The bill reinstates the prior-law Leaking Underground Storage Tank Trust Fund excise tax through September 30, 2007.

Effective Date

The provision is effective on October 1, 1997.

[Conference Report]

Conference Agreement

The conference agreement follows the House bill and Senate amendment with a modification to the reinstatement period. The modified period is October 1, 1997, through March 31, 2005.

[¶ 5132]   Section 1034.   Communications Tax on Prepaid Telephone Cards.

(Code Sec. 4251)

[House Report]

Present Law

A 3-percent excise tax is imposed on amounts paid for local and toll (long-distance) telephone service and teletypewriter exchange service. The tax is collected by the provider of the service from the consumer (business and personal service).

Reasons for Change

The Committee understands that communication service providers sometimes sell units of long-distance service to third parties who, in turn, resell or distribute these units of long-distance telephone service to the ultimate customer in the form of prepaid telephone cards or similar arrangements. The Committee believes that such payments clearly represent payments for long-distance telephone service and clarifies that such payments are subject to the communications excise tax.

Explanation of Provision

The bill provides that any amounts paid to communications service providers (in cash or in kind) for the right to award or otherwise distribute free or reduced-rate long-distance telephone service are treated as amounts paid for taxable communication services, subject to the 3-percent ad valorem tax rate. Examples of such taxable amounts include (1) prepaid telephone cards offered through service stations, convenience stores and other businesses to their customers and others and (2) amounts received by communication service providers pursuant to joint venture credit card or other marketing arrangements. The Treasury Department is authorized specifically to disregard accounting allocations or other arrangements which have the effect of reducing artificially the base to which the 3-percent tax is applied. No inference is intended from this provision as to the proper treatment of these payments under present law.

[Senate Report]

Examples of such taxable amounts include (1) prepaid telephone cards offered through service stations, convenience stores and other businesses to their customers and others (e.g., employees) and (2) amounts received by telephone carriers pursuant to joint venture credit card or other marketing arrangements.

For example, company A, which is a telephone carrier that owns telephone transmission and switching equipment and generally offers telephone service to the public, may sell a block of long- distance message units to company B for X dollars. Company B owns no transmission or switching equipment, but rather acts as a reseller of long distance telephone services and also is a telephone carrier. Company B, in turn, resells all or part of the long-distance message units purchased from Company A to Company C for Y dollars. Company C operates a chain of convenience stores. Company C resells some of the long-distance message units in the form of prepaid telephone cards to its convenience store customers and also makes some of the message units available to its employees as a benefit by the free distribution of such prepaid telephone cards to the employees. The amount Y will be considered an amount paid for telecommunications services subject to the 3-percent telephone excise tax. Alternatively, if company C had purchased the block of message units directly from company A for X dollars, the amount X will be considered an amount paid for telecommunications services subject to the 3-percent telephone excise tax.

Effective Date

The provision is effective for amounts paid on or after the date of enactment.

[Conference Report]

Conference Agreement

The conference agreement follows the House bill and the Senate amendment with technical modifications. The conference agreement clarifies that any amounts paid to communications service providers (in cash or in kind) for the right to award or otherwise distribute free or reduced-rate telephone service (i.e., local or toll telephone service) are treated as amounts paid for taxable communication services, subject to the 3-percent ad valorem tax rate.

The conference agreement also clarifies that the base to which the communications tax applies in the case of prepaid telephone cards and similar arrangements is the retail value of the service provided by the use of the card or arrangement. The conferees understand that prepaid telephone cards are offered to the public in two forms. The first type of prepaid telephone card can be called a "dollar value card." In this case, the final customer purchases a card or account which allows him to utilize $X worth of telephone service provided by an underlying telecommunications carrier. In this case, following the House bill and the Senate amendment, the conference agreement provides that the 3-percent communications excise tax apply to the value X at the time the prepaid telephone card is sold by a telecommunications carrier to a person who is not a telecommunications carrier.

The second type of prepaid telephone card can be called a "unit card" or a "minute card." In this case the final customer purchases a card or account which allows him to use Y number of units or minutes of telephone service provided by an underlying telecommunications carrier. The conferees intend that the tax applicable to such cards be based on the retail value of the telephone service offered to a consumer and the conference agreement grants the Treasury Department regulatory authority to determine the appropriate retail value. Presently, the Federal Communications Commission generally requires telecommunications carriers to file a tariff listing the prices of their various service offerings including the price of units or minutes offered via prepaid telephone cards. In this case, following the House bill and the Senate amendment, the conference agreement provides that the 3-percent communications excise tax will apply to Y (the number of units or minutes) multiplied by the tariffed price of those units or minutes at the time the prepaid telephone card is sold by a telecommunications carrier to a person who is not a telecommunications carrier. The conferees recognize that such a tariffed value may not in all cases correspond to the over-the- counter price that a final customer may pay for the card. However, the conferees believe that looking to the tariffed price, at present, is the best way to achieve neutral treatment of "dollar cards" and "unit" or "minute cards." The conferees understand that not all prepaid telephone cards may have an underlying tariff that applies to that particular card. In such cases, the conferees intend that tariffs for comparable telephone service be applied if applicable. The conferees believe that tariffs should continue to be filed for service offered via prepaid telephone cards, but if, in the future, tariff filings are not generally filed the conference agreement authorizes the Treasury Department to determine the appropriate retail value of the units or minutes of service offered on such cards.

The conferees understand that sometimes a communications service provider may require certain customers to prepay for their service as assurance that payment is made by the customer for services to be provided. The conferees do not consider such arrangements to constitute payment for communications services for the purposes of this provision if the customer is entitled to a full refund, in cash, for the value of any unused service. The conferees consider such arrangements to be deposits to assure payment of service to be provided in the future.

No inference is intended from this provision as to the proper treatment of payments received by communications service providers for prepaid telephone cards and amounts received by communication service providers pursuant to joint venture credit card or other marketing arrangements under present law.

Effective Date

The conference agreement modifies the effective date so that the provision is effective for cards sold on or after the first day of the month which commences more than 60 days after the date of enactment.

[¶ 5133]   Section 1035.   Extension of Federal unemployment surtax.

(Code Sec. 3301)

[Senate Report]

Present Law

The Federal Unemployment Tax Act (FUTA) imposes a 6.2- percent gross tax rate on the first $7,000 paid annually by covered employers to each employee. Employers in States with programs approved by the Federal Government and with no delinquent Federal loans may credit 5.4-percentage points against the 6.2-percent tax rate, making the minimum, net Federal unemployment tax rate 0.8 percent. Since all States have approved programs, 0.8 percent is the Federal tax rate that generally applies. This Federal revenue finances administration of the system, half of the Federal-State extended benefits program, and a Federal account for State loans. The States use the revenue turned back to them by the 5.4 percent credit to finance their regular State programs and half of the Federal-State extended benefits program.

In 1976, Congress passed a temporary surtax of 0.2 percent of taxable wages to be added to the permanent FUTA tax rate. Thus, the current 0.8 percent FUTA tax rate has two components: a permanent tax rate of 0.6 percent, and a temporary surtax rate of 0.2 percent. The temporary surtax has been subsequently extended through 1998.

Reasons for Change

The Committee believes that the surtax extension will increase the Federal Unemployment Trust Fund to provide a cushion against future expenditures. The monies retained in the Federal Unemployment Account of the Federal Unemployment Trust Fund can then be used to make loans to the 53 State Unemployment Compensation benefit accounts as needed.

Explanation of Provision

The bill extends the temporary surtax rate through December 31, 2007. The bill also increases the limit from 0.25 percent to 0.50 percent of covered wages on the Federal

Unemployment Account (FUA) in the Unemployment Trust Fund.

Effective Date

The provision is effective for labor performed on or after January 1, 1999.

[¶ 5141] Section 1041. Extension of UBIT Rules and Modification of Control Test.

(Code Sec. 512)

[House Report]

Present Law

In general, interest, rents, royalties and annuities are excluded from unrelated taxable business income (UBTI) of tax-exempt organizations. However, section 512(b)(13) treats otherwise excluded rent, royalty, annuity, and interest income as UBTI if such income is received from a taxable or tax-exempt subsidiary that is 80 percent controlled by the parent tax-exempt organization.[37] In the case of a stock subsidiary, the 80 percent control test is met if the parent organization owns 80 percent or more of the voting stock and all other classes of stock of the subsidiary.[38] In the case of a non-stock subsidiary, the applicable Treasury regulations look to factors such as the representation of the parent corporation on the board of directors of the nonstock subsidiary, or the power of the parent corporation to appoint or remove the board of directors of the subsidiary.[39]

The control test under section 512(b)(13) does not, however, incorporate any indirect ownership rules.[40] Consequently, rents,

No provision.

Conference Agreement

The conference agreement follows the Senate amendment.

royalties, annuities and interest derived from second-tier subsidiaries generally do not constitute UBTI to the tax-exempt parent organization.[41]

Reasons for Change

Section 512(b)(13) was enacted to prevent subsidiaries of tax-exempt organizations from reducing their otherwise taxable income by borrowing, leasing, or licensing assets from a tax-exempt parent organization at inflated levels. Because section 512(b)(13) was narrowly drafted, organizations were able to circumvent its application through, for example, the issuance of 21 percent of nonvoting stock with nominal value to a separate friendly party or through the use of tiered or brother/sister subsidiaries. The Committee believes that the modifications to the control requirement and inclusion of attribution rules will ensure that section 512(b)(13) operate consistent with its intended purpose.

Explanation of Provision

The bill modifies the test for determining control for purposes of section 512(b)(13). Under the bill, "control" means (in the case of a stock corporation) ownership by vote

---

37.

]For this purpose, a "controlled organization" is defined under section 368(c). Under present law, rent, royalty. annuity, and interest payments are treated as UBTI when received by the parent organization based on the percentage of the subsidiary's income that is UBTI (either in the hands of the subsidiary if the subsidiary is tax-exempt, or in the hands of the parent organization if the subsidiary is taxable).
38. Treas. reg. sec. 1.512(b) 1(1)(4)(I)(a).
39. Treas. reg. sec. 1.512(b) 1(1)(4)(I)(b).
40.

]See PLR 9338003 (June 16, 1993) (holding that because no indirect ownership rules are applicable under section 512(b)(13), rents paid by a second-tier taxable subsidi-

ary are not UBTI to a tax-exempt parent organization). In contrast, an example of an indirect ownership rule can be found in Code section 318. Section 318(a)(2)(C) provides that if 50 percent or more in value of the stock in a corporation is owned, directly or indirectly, by or for any person, such person shall be considered as owning the stock owned, directly or indirectly by or for such corporation, in the proportion the value of the person's stock ownership bears to the total value of all stock in the corporation.
41.

]See PLR 9542045 (July 28, 1995) (holding that first-tier holding company and second-tier operating subsidiary were organized with bona fide business functions and were not agents of the tax-exempt parent organization; therefore, rents, royalties, and interest received by tax-exempt parent organization from second-tier subsidiary were not UBTI).

or value of more than 50 percent of the stock. In the case of a partnership or other entity, control means ownership of more than 50 percent of the profits, capital or beneficial interests.

In addition, the bill applies the constructive ownership rules of section 318 for purposes of section 512(b)(13). Thus, a parent exempt organization is deemed to control any subsidiary in which it holds more than 50 percent of the voting power or value, directly (as in the case of a first-tier subsidiary) or indirectly (as in the case of a second-tier subsidiary).

The bill also makes technical modifications to the method provided in section 512(b)(13) for determining how much of an interest, rent, annuity, or royalty payment made by a controlled entity to a tax-exempt organization is includible in the latter organization's UBTI. Such payments are subject to the unrelated business income tax to the extent the payment reduces the net unrelated income (or increases any net unrelated loss) of the controlled entity.

Effective Date

The modification of the control test to one based on vote or value, the application of the constructive ownership rules of section 318, and the technical modifications to

the flow-through method apply to taxable years beginning after the date of enactment. The reduction of the ownership threshold for purposes of the control test from 80 percent to more than 50 percent applies to taxable years beginning after December 31, 1998.

[Conference Report]

Senate Amendment

The Senate amendment is the same as the House bill.

Conference Agreement

The conference agreement follows the House bill and the Senate amendment, except that the effective date is modified to provide temporary transition relief for certain payments. The provision does not apply to payments made during the first two taxable years beginning on or after the date of enactment if such payments are made pursuant to a binding written contract in effect as of June 8, 1997, and at all times thereafter before such payment. In addition, the conference agreement does not include the delayed application of the reduction of the ownership threshold for purposes of the control test from 80 percent to more than 50 percent.

[¶ 5142]   Section 1042.   Repeal Grandfather Rule with Respect to Certain Insurers' Pension Business.

(Code Sec. 501)

[House Report]

Present Law

Present law provides that an organization described in sections 501(c) (3) or (4) of the Code is exempt from tax only if no substantial part of its activities consists of providing commercial-type insurance. When this rule was enacted in 1986, certain treatment (described below) applied to Blue Cross and Blue Shield organizations providing health insurance that (1) were in existence on August 16, 1986; (2) were determined at any time to be tax-exempt under a determination that had not been revoked; and (3) were tax-exempt for the last taxable year beginning before January 1, 1987 (when the pre-

sent-law rule became effective), provided that no material change occurred in the structure or operations of the organizations after August 16, 1986, and before the close of 1986 or any subsequent taxable year.

The treatment applicable to such organizations, which became taxable organizations under the provision, is as follows. A special deduction applies with respect to health business equal to 25 percent of the claims and expenses incurred during the taxable year less the adjusted surplus at the beginning of the year. An exception is provided for such organizations from the application of the 20-percent reduction in the deduction for increases in unearned premiums that applies generally to property and casualty insurance companies. A fresh start was provided with respect to changes in accounting methods resulting from the change from tax-exempt to taxable status. Thus, no adjustment was made under section 481 on account of an accounting method change. Such an organization was required to compute its ending 1986 loss reserves without artificial changes that would reduce 1987 income. Thus, any reserve weakening after August 16, 1986 was treated as occurring in the organization's first taxable year beginning after December 31, 1986. The basis of such an organization's assets was deemed to be equal to the amount of the assets' fair market value on the first day of the organization's taxable year beginning after December 31, 1986, for purposes of determining gain or loss (but not for determining depreciation or for other purposes).

Grandfather rules were provided in the 1986 Act relating to the provision. It was provided that the provision does not apply to that portion of the business of the Teachers Insurance Annuity Association-College Retirement Equities Fund which is attributable to pension business, nor does the provision apply with respect to that portion of the business of Mutual of America which is attributable to pension business. Pension business means the administration of any plan described in section 401(a) of the Code which includes a trust exempt from tax under section 501(a), and plan under which amounts are contributed by an individual's employer for an annuity contract described in section 403(b) of the Code, any individual retirement plan described in section 408 of the Code, and any eligible deferred compensation plan to which section 457(a) of the Code applies.

Reasons for Change

The Committee is concerned that the continued tax-exempt status of certain organizations that engage in insurance activities gives such organizations an unfair competitive advantage. The Committee believes that the provision of insurance at a price sufficient to cover the costs of insurance generally constitutes an activity that is commercial. Thus, the Committee believes, it is no longer appropriate to continue the grandfather rule that permits certain organizations to retain tax-exempt status with respect to pension business that constitutes commercial-type insurance.

Explanation of Provision

The provision repeals the grandfather rules applicable to that portion of the business of the Teachers Insurance Annuity Association-College Retirement Equities Fund which is attributable to pension business and to that portion of the business of Mutual of America which is attributable to pension business. The Teachers Insurance Annuity Association and College Retirement Equities Fund and Mutual of America are to be treated for Federal tax purposes as life insurance companies.

A fresh start is provided with respect to changes in accounting methods resulting from the change from tax-exempt to taxable status. Thus, no adjustment is made under section 481 on account of an accounting method change. The Teachers Insurance Annuity Association and College Retirement Equities Fund and Mutual of America are required to compute ending 1997 loss reserves without artificial changes that would reduce 1998 income. Thus, any reserve weakening after June 8, 1997, is treated as occurring in the organization's first taxable year beginning after December 31, 1997. The basis of assets of Teachers Insurance Annuity Association and College Retirement Equities Fund and Mutual of America is deemed to be equal to the amount of the assets' fair market value on the first day of the organization's taxable year beginning after December 31, 1997, for purposes of determining gain or loss (but not for determining depreciation or for other purposes).

Effective Date

The provision is effective for taxable years beginning after December 31, 1997.

[Conference Report]

Senate Amendment

The Senate amendment is the same as the House bill, except that the Senate amendment repeals only the grandfather rule applicable to that portion of the business of Mutual of America which is attributable to pension business.

Conference Agreement

The conference agreement follows the House bill.

[¶ 5143]   Section 1051.   Definition of Foreign Personal Holding Company Income.

(Code Sec. 954)

[House Report]

Present Law

Under the subpart F rules, the U.S. 10-percent shareholders of a controlled foreign corporation ("CFC") are subject to U.S. tax currently on certain income earned by the CFC, whether or not such income is distributed to the shareholders. The income subject to current inclusion under the subpart F rules includes, among other things, "foreign personal holding company income."

Foreign personal holding company income generally consists of the following: dividends, interest, royalties, rents and annuities; net gains from sales or exchanges of (1) property that gives rise to the foregoing types of income, (2) property that does not give rise to income, and (3) interests in trusts, partnerships, and REMICs; net gains from commodities transactions; net gains from foreign currency transactions; and income that is equivalent to interest. Income from notional principal contracts referenced to commodities, foreign currency, interest rates, or indices thereon is treated as foreign personal holding company income; income from equity swaps or other types of notional principal contracts is not treated as foreign personal holding company income. Income derived from transfers of debt securities (but not equity securities) pursuant to the rules governing securities lending transactions (sec. 1058) is treated as foreign personal holding company income.

Income earned by a CFC that is a regular dealer in the property sold or exchanged generally is excluded from the definition of foreign personal holding company income. However, no exception is available for a CFC that is a regular dealer in financial instruments referenced to commodities.

A U.S. shareholder of a passive foreign investment company ("PFIC") is subject to U.S. tax and an interest charge with respect to certain distributions from the PFIC and gains on dispositions of the stock of the PFIC, unless the shareholder elects to include in income currently for U.S. tax purposes its share of the earnings of the PFIC. A foreign corporation is a PFIC if it satisfies either a passive income test or a passive assets test. For this purpose, passive income is defined by reference to foreign personal holding company income.

Reasons for Change

The Committee understands that income from notional principal contracts and stock-lending transactions is economically equivalent to types of income that are treated as foreign personal holding company income under present law. Accordingly, the Committee believes that the categories of foreign personal holding company income should be expanded to cover such income. In addition, the Committee believes that an exception from the foreign personal holding company income rules should be available for dealers in financial instruments referenced to commodities.

Explanation of Provision

The bill treats net income from all types of notional principal contracts as a new category of foreign personal holding company income. However, income, gain, deduction or loss from a notional principal contract entered into to hedge an item of income in another category of foreign personal holding company income is included in that other category.

The bill treats payments in lieu of dividends derived from equity securities lending transactions pursuant to section 1058 as another new category of foreign personal holding company income.

The bill provides an exception from foreign personal holding company income for certain income, gain, deduction, or loss from transactions (including hedging transactions) entered into in the ordinary course of a CFC's business as a regular dealer in property, forward contracts, options, notional principal contracts, or similar financial instruments (including instruments referenced to commodities).

These modifications to the definition of foreign personal holding company income apply for purposes of determining a foreign corporation's status as a PFIC.

Effective Date

The provision applies to taxable years beginning after the date of enactment.

[Senate Report]

Present Law

Under the subpart F rules, the U.S. 10-percent shareholders of a controlled foreign corporation ("CFC") are subject to U.S. tax currently on certain income earned by the CFC, whether or not such income is distributed to the shareholders. The income subject to current inclusion under the subpart F rules includes, among other things, "foreign personal holding company income."

Foreign personal holding company income generally consists of the following: dividends, interest, royalties, rents and annuities; net gains from sales or exchanges of (1) property that gives rise to the foregoing types of income, (2) property that does not give rise to income, and (3) interests in trusts, partnerships, and REMICs; net gains from commodities transactions; net gains from foreign currency transactions; and income that is equivalent to interest. Income from notional principal contracts referenced to commodities, foreign currency, interest rates, or indices thereon is treated as foreign personal holding company income; income from equity swaps or other types of notional principal contracts is not treated as foreign personal holding company income. Income derived from transfers of debt securities (but not equity securities) pursuant to the rules governing securities lending transactions (sec. 1058) is treated as foreign personal holding company income.

Income earned by a CFC that is a regular dealer in the property sold or exchanged generally is excluded from the definition of foreign personal holding company income. However, no exception is available for a CFC that is a regular dealer in financial instruments referenced to commodities.

[820] A U.S. shareholder of a passive foreign investment company ("PFIC") is subject to U.S. tax and an interest charge with respect to certain distributions from the PFIC and gains on dispositions of the stock of the PFIC, unless the shareholder elects to include in income currently for U.S. tax purposes its share of the earnings of the PFIC. A foreign corporation is a PFIC if it satisfies either a passive income test or a passive assets test. For this purpose, passive income is defined by reference to foreign personal holding company income.

Reasons for Change

The Committee understands that income from notional principal contracts and stock-lending transactions is economically equivalent to types of income that are treated as foreign personal holding company income under present law. Accordingly, the Committee believes that the categories of foreign personal holding company income should be expanded to cover such income. In addition, the Committee believes that an exception from the foreign personal holding company income rules should be available for dealers in financial instruments referenced to commodities.

Explanation of Provision

The bill treats net income from all types of notional principal contracts as a new category of foreign personal holding company income. However, income, gain, deduction or loss from a notional principal contract entered into to hedge an item of income in another category of foreign personal holding company income is included in that other category.

[823] The bill treats payments in lieu of dividends derived from equity securities lending transactions pursuant to section 1058 as another new category of foreign personal holding company income.

[824] The bill provides an exception from foreign personal holding company income for certain income, gain, deduction, or loss from transactions (including hedging transactions) entered into in the ordinary course of a CFC's business as a regular dealer in property, forward contracts, options, notional principal contracts, or similar financial instruments (including instruments referenced to commodities).

These modifications to the definition of foreign personal holding company income apply for purposes of determining a foreign corporation's status as a PFIC.

Effective Date

The provision applies to taxable years beginning after the date of enactment.

[Conference Report]

Senate Amendment

The Senate amendment is the same as the House bill.

Conference Agreement

The conference agreement follows the House bill and the Senate amendment. The conferees wish to clarify the treatment of notional principal contracts under the provision. Although net income from notional principal contracts is added as a new category of foreign personal holding company income, amounts with respect to a notional principal contract entered into to hedge an item described in another category of foreign personal holding company income are taken into account under the rules of such other category. In this regard, gains and losses from transactions in inventory property are covered by an exclusion from the category of personal holding company income for net gains from property transactions; income from a notional principal contract entered into to hedge inventory property is taken into account under such category and thus similarly is excluded from foreign personal holding company income.

[¶ 5144]   Section 1052.   Like-kind Exchange Rules For Personal Property Used Inside/Outside the U.S.

(Code Sec. 1031)

[House Report]

Present Law

Like-kind exchanges

An exchange of property, like a sale, generally is a taxable event. However, no gain or loss is recognized if property held for productive use in a trade or business or for investment is exchanged for property of a "like-kind" which is to be held for productive use in a trade or business or for investment (sec. 1031). In general, any kind of real estate is treated as of a like-kind with other real property as long as the properties are both located either within or both outside the United States. In addition, certain types of property, such as inventory, stocks and bonds, and partnership interests, are not eligible for nonrecognition treatment under section 1031.

If section 1031 applies to an exchange of properties, the basis of the property received in the exchange is equal to the basis of the property transferred, decreased by any money received by the taxpayer, and further adjusted for any gain or loss recognized on the exchange.

Application of depreciation rules

Tangible personal property that is used predominantly outside the United States generally is accorded a less favorable depreciation regime than is property that is used predominantly within the United States. Thus, under present law, if a taxpayer exchanges depreciable U.S. property with a low adjusted basis (relative to its fair market value) for similar property situated outside the United States, the adjusted basis of the acquired property will be the same as the adjusted basis of the relinquished property, but the depreciation rules applied to such acquired property generally will be different than the rules that were applied to the relinquished property.

Reasons for Change

The Committee believes that the depreciation rules applicable to foreign- and domestic-use are sufficiently dissimilar so as to treat such property as not "like-kind" property for purposes of section 1031.

Explanation of Provision

The bill provides that personal property predominantly used within the United States and personal property predominantly used outside the United States are not "like-kind" properties. For this purpose, the use of the property surrendered in the exchange will be determined based upon the use during the 24 months immediately prior to the exchange. Similarly, for section 1031 to apply, property received in the exchange must continue in the same use (i.e., foreign or domestic) for the 24 months immediately after the exchange.

The 24-month period is reduced to such lesser time as the taxpayer held the property, unless such shorter holding period is a result of a transaction (or series of transactions) structured to avoid the purposes of the provision. Property described in section 168(g)(4) (generally, property used both within and without the United States that is eligible for accelerated depreciation as if used in the United States) will be treated as property predominantly used in the United States.

Effective Date

The provision is effective for exchanges after June 8, 1997, unless the exchange is pursuant to a binding contract in effect on

such date and all times thereafter. A contract will not fail to be considered to be binding solely because (1) it provides for a sale in lieu of an exchange or (2) either the property to be disposed of as relinquished property or the property to be acquired as replacement property (whichever is applicable) was not identified under the contract before June 9, 1997.

[Conference Report]

Senate Amendment

The Senate amendment is the same as the House bill.

Conference Agreement

The conference agreement follows the House bill and the Senate amendment.

[¶ 5145]   Section 1053. Holding Period Requirement For Foreign Tax Credit With Respect to Dividends.

(Code Sec. 901, 853)

[House Report]

Present Law

A U.S. person that receives a dividend from a foreign corporation generally is entitled to a credit for income taxes paid to a foreign government on the dividend, regardless of the U.S. person's holding period for the foreign corporation's stock. A U.S. corporation that receives a dividend from a foreign corporation in which it has a 10-percent or greater voting interest may be entitled to a credit for the foreign taxes paid by the foreign corporation, also without regard to the U.S. shareholder's holding period for the corporation's stock (sections 902 and 960).

As a consequence of the foreign tax credit limitations of the Code, certain taxpayers are unable to utilize their creditable foreign taxes to reduce their U.S. tax liability. U.S. shareholders that are tax-exempt receive no U.S. tax benefit for foreign taxes paid on dividends they receive.

[Senate Report]

Reasons for Change

The Committee believes that when a U.S. person sells inventory to its U.S. customers,

the resulting income is inherently domestic, regardless of the site of the particular transaction. The Committee believes that income from sales of inventory property by a U.S. resident to another U.S. resident for use in the United States should be treated as income from U.S. sources, without regard to where the sale occurs.

Explanation of Provision

Under the bill, income from a sale of inventory property by a U.S. resident to another U.S. resident for use, consumption, or disposition in the United States is treated as U.S. source income, if the sale is not attributable to an office or other fixed place of business maintained by the seller outside the United States.

Effective Date

The provision is effective for taxable years beginning after date of enactment.

[Conference Report]

Senate Amendment

The Senate amendment is the same as the House bill with one modification. Under the Senate amendment, the special rule for contracts to sell stock does not apply to indirect foreign tax credits of a RIC shareholder.

Conference Agreement

The conference agreement generally follows the Senate amendment with one modification. The conference agreement grants regulatory authority to the Secretary of the Treasury to treat certain foreign taxes as not subject to the provision. The conferees anticipate that this authority may be used to address internal withholding taxes imposed by a foreign country on persons that do business in the foreign country.

[¶ 5146]   Section 1054.   Denial of Treaty Benefits for Certain Payments Through Hybrid Entities.

(Code Sec. 894)

[House Report]

Present Law

Nonresident alien individuals and foreign corporations (collectively, foreign persons) that are engaged in business in the United States are subject to U.S. tax on the income from such business in the same manner as a U.S. person. In addition, the United States imposes tax on certain types of U.S. source income, including interest, dividends and royalties, of foreign persons not engaged in business in the United States. Such tax is imposed on a gross basis and is collected through withholding. The statutory rate of this withholding tax is 30 percent. However, most U.S. income tax treaties provide for a reduction in rate, or elimination, of this withholding tax. Treaties generally provide for different applicable withholding tax rates for different types of income. Moreover, the applicable withholding tax rates differ among treaties. The specific withholding tax rates pursuant to a treaty are the result of negotiations between the United States and the treaty partner.

The application of the withholding tax is more complicated in the case of income derived through an entity, such as a limited liability company, that is treated as a partnership for U.S. tax purposes but may be treated as a corporation for purposes of the tax laws of a treaty partner. The Treasury regulations include specific rules that apply in the case of income derived through an entity that is treated as a partnership for U.S. tax purposes. In the case of a payment of an item of U.S. source income to a U.S. partnership, the partnership is required to impose the withholding tax to the extent the item of income is includible in the distributive share of a partner who is a foreign person. Tax-avoidance opportunities may arise in applying the reduced rates of withholding tax provided under a treaty to cases involving income derived through a limited liability company or other hybrid entity (e.g., an entity that is treated as a partnership for U.S. tax purposes but as a corporation for purposes of the treaty partner's tax laws). Regulations that have been proposed but not yet finalized would address this issue in the case of an item received by a foreign entity by allowing an interest holder in that entity to claim a reduced rate of withholding tax with respect to that item under a treaty only if the treaty partner requires the interest holder to include in income its distributive share of the entity's income on a flow-through basis. Prop. Treas. Reg. Sec. 1.1441 6(b)(4). This provision in the proposed regulations does not apply in the case of a U.S. entity.

Reasons for Change

The Committee is concerned about the potential tax-avoidance opportunities available for foreign persons that invest in the United States through hybrid entities. In particular, the Committee understands that the interaction of the tax laws and the applicable tax treaty may provide a business structuring opportunity that would allow Canadian corporations with U.S. subsidiaries to avoid both U.S. and Canadian income taxes with respect to those U.S. operations. The Committee believes that such tax-avoidance opportunities should be eliminated.

Explanation of Provision

The bill limits the availability of a reduced rate of withholding tax pursuant to an income tax treaty in order to prevent tax avoidance. Under the bill, a foreign person is entitled to a reduced rate of withholding tax under a treaty with a foreign country on an item of income derived through an entity that is a partnership (or is otherwise treated as transparent) for U.S. tax purposes only if such item is treated for purposes of the taxation laws of such foreign country as an item of income of such person. This rule does not apply if the treaty itself contains a provision addressing the applicability of the treaty in the case of income derived through a partnership. Moreover, the rule does not apply if the foreign country imposes tax on an actual distribution of such item of income from such partnership to such person. In this regard, the foreign country will be considered to impose tax on a distribution even though such tax may be reduced or eliminated by reason of deductions or credits otherwise available to the taxpayer.

This bill addresses a potential tax-avoidance opportunity for Canadian corporations with U.S. subsidiaries that arises because of the interaction between the U.S. tax law, the Canadian tax law, and the income tax treaty between the United States and Canada. Through the use of a U.S. limited liability company, which is treated as a partnership for U.S. tax purposes but as a corporation for Canadian tax purposes, a payment of interest (which is deductible for U.S. tax purposes) may be converted into a dividend (which is excludable for Canadian tax purposes). Accordingly, interest paid by a U.S. subsidiary through a U.S. limited liability company to a Canadian parent corporation would be deducted by the U.S. subsidiary for U.S. tax purposes and would be excluded by the Canadian parent corporation for Canadian tax purposes; the only tax on such interest would be a U.S. withholding tax, which may be imposed at a reduced rate of 10 percent (rather than the full statutory rate of 30 percent) pursuant to the income tax treaty between the United States and Canada. Under the bill, withholding tax is imposed at the full statutory rate of 30 percent in such case. The bill would not apply if the U.S.-Canadian income tax treaty is amended to include a provision reaching a similar result. In this regard, the United States and Canada recently negotiated a proposed protocol that would amend the provision in the treaty governing cross-border social security payments and this issue could be addressed in the context of that protocol or an additional protocol. Moreover, the

bill would not apply if Canada were to impose tax on the Canadian parent on dividends received from the U.S. limited liability company.

Effective Date

The provision is effective upon date of enactment.

[Conference Report]

Conference Agreement

The conference agreement generally follows the House bill with a modification to provide regulatory authority to address the availability of treaty benefits in situations that involve hybrid entities but that are not covered by the denial of benefits specifically provided by the provision.

Under the conference agreement, a foreign person is not entitled to a reduced rate of withholding tax under a treaty with a foreign country on an item of income derived through an entity that is treated as a partnership (or is otherwise treated as fiscally transparent) for U.S. tax purposes if (i) such item is not treated for purposes of the taxation laws of such foreign country as an item of income of such person, (ii) the foreign country does not impose tax on an actual distribution of such item of income from such entity to such person, and (iii) the treaty itself does not contain a provision addressing the applicability of the treaty in the case of income derived through a partnership or other fiscally transparent entity. In addition, the conference agreement grants the Secretary of the Treasury authority to prescribe regulations to determine, in situations other than the situation specifically described in the statutory provision, the extent to which a taxpayer shall not be entitled to benefits under an income tax treaty of the United States with respect to any payment received by, or income attributable to activities of, an entity that is treated as a partnership for U.S. federal income tax purposes (or is otherwise treated as fiscally transparent for such purposes) but is treated as fiscally non- transparent for purposes of the tax laws of the jurisdiction of residence of the taxpayer.

The conferees note that on June 30, 1997 the Secretary issued proposed and temporary regulations addressing the availability of treaty benefits in cases involving hybrid entities. The conferees believe that these regulations are consistent with the provision in the conference agreement. The conferees also believe that the provision in the conference agreement and the temporary and proposed regulations are consistent with U.S.

treaty obligations. Such provision and such regulations represent interpretations of U.S. treaties clarifying those situations involving hybrid entities in which taxpayers are entitled to treaty benefits and those situations in which they are not.

[¶ 5147]   Section 1055.   Interest on Underpayments and Foreign Tax Credit Carrybacks.

(Code Sec. 6601, 6611)

[House Report]

Present Law

U.S. persons may credit foreign taxes against U.S. tax on foreign source income. The amount of foreign tax credits that can be claimed in a year is subject to a limitation that prevents taxpayers from using foreign tax credits to offset U.S. tax on U.S. source income. Separate limitations are applied to specific categories of income. The amount of creditable taxes paid or accrued in any taxable year which exceeds the foreign tax credit limitation is permitted to be carried back two years and carried forward five years.

For purposes of the computation of interest on overpayments of tax, if an overpayment for a taxable year results from a foreign tax credit carryback from a subsequent taxable year, the overpayment is deemed not to arise prior to the filing date for the subsequent taxable year in which the foreign taxes were paid or accrued (sec. 6611(g)). Accordingly, interest does not accrue on the overpayment prior to the filing date for the year of the carryback that effectively created such overpayment. In Fluor Corp. v. United States, 35 Fed. Cl. 520 (1996), the court held that in the case of an underpayment of tax (rather than an overpayment) for a taxable year that is eliminated by a foreign tax credit carryback from a subsequent taxable year, interest does not accrue on the underpayment that is eliminated by the foreign tax credit carryback. The Government has filed an appeal in the Fluor case.

Reasons for Change

The Committee believes that the application of the interest rules in the case of a de-

ficiency that is reduced or eliminated by a foreign tax credit carryback must be consistent with the application of the interest rules in the case of an overpayment that is created by a foreign tax credit carryback. The Committee believes that in such cases the deficiency cannot be considered to have been eliminated, and the overpayment cannot be considered to have been created, until the filing date for the taxable year in which the foreign tax credit carryback arises. Accordingly, interest should continue to accrue on the deficiency through such date. In addition, the Committee believes that it is appropriate to clarify the interest rules that apply in the case of a foreign tax credit carryback that is itself triggered by another carryback from a subsequent year.

Explanation of Provision

Under the bill, if an underpayment for a taxable year is reduced or eliminated by a foreign tax credit carryback from a subsequent taxable year, such carryback does not affect the computation of interest on the underpayment for the period ending with the filing date for such subsequent taxable year in which the foreign taxes were paid or accrued. The bill also clarifies the application of the interest rules of both section 6601 and section 6611 in the case of a foreign tax credit carryback that is triggered by a net operating loss or net capital loss carryback; in such a case, a deficiency is not considered to have been reduced, and an overpayment is not considered to have been created, until the filing date for the subsequent year in which the loss carryback arose. No inference is intended regarding the computation of interest under present law in the case of a foreign tax credit carryback (including a foreign tax credit carryback that is triggered by a net operating loss or net capital loss carryback).

Effective Date

The provision is effective for foreign taxes actually paid or accrued in taxable years beginning after date of enactment.

[Conference Report]

Senate Amendment

The Senate amendment is the same as the House bill.

[¶ 5148]   Section 1056.   Limitations Period Relating to Foreign Tax Credit Claims.

(Code Sec. 6511)

[House Report]

Present Law

U.S. persons may credit foreign taxes against U.S. tax on foreign source income. The amount of foreign tax credits that can be claimed in a year is subject to a limitation that prevents taxpayers from using foreign tax credits to offset U.S. tax on U.S. source income. Separate limitations are applied to specific categories of income. The amount of creditable taxes paid or accrued in any taxable year which exceeds the foreign tax credit limitation is permitted to be carried back two years and carried forward five years.

For purposes of the period of limitations on filing claims for credit or refund, in the case of a claim relating to an overpayment attributable to foreign tax credits, the limitations period is ten years from the filing date for the taxable year with respect to which the claim is made. The Internal Revenue Service has taken the position that, in the case of a foreign tax credit carryforward, the period of limitations is determined by reference to the year in which the foreign taxes were paid or accrued (and not the year to which the foreign tax credits are carried) (Rev. Rul. 84 125, 1984 2 C.B. 125). However, the court in Ampex Corp. v. United States, 620 F.2d 853 (1980), held that, in the case of a foreign tax credit carryforward, the period of limitations is determined by reference to the year to which the

foreign tax credits are carried (and not the year in which the foreign taxes were paid or accrued).

Reasons for Change

The Committee believes that it is appropriate to identify clearly the date on which the ten-year period of limitations for claims with respect to foreign tax credits begins.

Explanation of Provision

Under the bill, in the case of a claim relating to an overpayment attributable to foreign tax credits, the limitations period is determined by reference to the year in which the foreign taxes were paid or accrued (and not the year to which the foreign tax credits are carried). No inference is intended regarding the determination of such limitations period under present law.

Effective Date

The provision is effective for foreign taxes paid or accrued in taxable years beginning after date of enactment.

[Conference Report]

Senate Amendment

The Senate amendment is the same as the House bill.

Conference Agreement

The conference agreement follows the House bill and the Senate amendment.

Conference Agreement

The conference agreement follows the House bill and the Senate amendment.

[¶ 5149]   Section 1057.   Repeal of Exception to Alternative Minimum Foreign Tax Credit Limit

(Code Sec. 59)

[Senate Report]

Present Law

Present law imposes a minimum tax on a corporation to the extent the taxpayer's minimum tax liability exceeds its regular tax liability. The corporate minimum tax is imposed at a rate of 20 percent on alternative minimum taxable income in excess of a phased-out $40,000 exemption amount.

The combination of the taxpayer's net operating loss carryover and foreign tax credits cannot reduce the taxpayer's alternative minimum tax liability by more than 90 percent of the amount determined without these items.

The Omnibus Budget Reconciliation Act of 1989 ("1989 Act") provided a special exception to the limitation on the use of the foreign tax credit against the tentative minimum tax. In order to qualify for this exception, a corporation must meet four requirements. First, more than 50 percent of both the voting power and value of the stock of the corporation must be owned by U.S. persons who are not members of an affiliated group which includes such corporation. Second, all of the activities of the corporation must be conducted in one foreign country with which the United States has an income tax treaty in effect and such treaty must provide for the exchange of information between such country and the United States. Third, the corporation generally must dis-

tribute to its shareholders all current earnings and profits (except for certain amounts utilized for normal maintenance or capital expenditures related to its existing business). Fourth, all of such distributions which are received by U.S. persons must be utilized by such persons in a U.S. trade or business. This exception applies to taxable years beginning after March 31, 1990 (with a proration rule effective for certain taxable years which include March 31, 1990).

Reasons for Change

The committee believes that taxpayers should be treated the same with respect to the foreign tax credit limitation of the alternative minimum tax.

Explanation of Provision

The special exception regarding the use of foreign tax credits for purposes of the alternative minimum tax, as provided by the 1989 Act, is repealed.

Effective Date

The provision is effective for taxable years beginning after the date of enactment.

[Conference Report]

House Bill

No provision.

Conference Agreement

The conference agreement follows the Senate amendment.

[¶ 5150]   Section 1061.   Basis Allocation of Properties Distributed by a Partnership.

(Code Sec. 732)

[House Report]

Present Law

In general

The partnership provisions of present law generally permit partners to receive distributions of partnership property without rec-

ognition of gain or loss (sec. 731).[50] Rules are provided for determining the basis of the distributed property in the hands of the distributee, and for allocating basis among multiple properties distributed, as well as for determining adjustments to the distributee partner's basis in its partnership interest. Property distributions are tax-free to a partnership. Adjustments to the basis of the

---

50. Exceptions to this nonrecognition rule apply: (1) when money (and the fair market value of marketable securi- ties) received exceeds a partner's adjusted basis in the partnership sec. 731(a)(1)); (2) when only money, in-

partnership's remaining undistributed assets are not required unless the partnership has made an election that requires basis adjustments both upon partnership distributions and upon transfers of partnership interests (sec. 754).

Partner's basis in distributed properties and partnership interest

Present law provides two different rules for determining a partner's basis in distributed property, depending on whether or not the distribution is in liquidation of the partner's interest in the partnership. Generally, a substituted basis rule applies to property distributed to a partner in liquidation. Thus, the basis of property distributed in liquidation of a partner's interest is equal to the partner's adjusted basis in its partnership interest (reduced by any money distributed in the same transaction) (sec. 732(b)).

By contrast, generally, a carryover basis rule applies to property distributed to a partner other than in liquidation of its partnership interest, subject to a cap (sec. 732(a)). Thus, in a non-liquidating distribution, the distributee partner's basis in the property is equal to the partnership's adjusted basis in the property immediately before the distribution, but not to exceed the partner's adjusted basis in its partnership interest (reduced by any money distributed in the same transaction). In a non-liquidating distribution, the partner's basis in its partnership interest is reduced by the amount of the basis to the distributee partner of the property distributed and is reduced by the amount of any money distributed (sec. 733).

Allocating basis among distributed properties

In the event that multiple properties are distributed by a partnership, present law provides allocation rules for determining their bases in the distributee partner's hands. An allocation rule is needed when the substituted basis rule for liquidating distributions applies, in order to assign a portion of the partner's basis in its partnership interest to each distributed asset. An allocation rule is also needed in a non-liquidating distribution of multiple assets when the total carryover basis would exceed the partner's basis in its partnership interest, so a portion of the partner's basis in its partnership interest is assigned to each distributed asset.

Present law provides for allocation in proportion to the partnership's adjusted basis. The rule allocates basis first to unrealized receivables and inventory items in an amount equal to the partnership's adjusted basis (or if the allocated basis is less than partnership basis, then in proportion to the partnership's basis), and then among other properties in proportion to their adjusted bases to the partnership (sec. 732(c)).[51] Under this allocation rule, in the case of a liquidating distribution, the distributee partner can have a basis in the distributed property that exceeds the partnership's basis in the property.

Reasons for Change

The rule providing that distributee partners allocate basis in proportion to the partnership's adjusted basis in the distributed property gives rise to problems in application.[52] The Committee is concerned that the present-law rule permits basis shifting transactions in which basis is allocated so as

---

ventory and unrealized receivables are received in liquidation of partner's interest and loss is realized (sec., 731 (a)(2)); (3) to certain disproportionate distributions involving inventory and unrealized receivables (sec. 751(b)); and (4) to certain distributions relating to contributed property (secs. 704(c) and 737). In addition, if a partner engages in a transaction with a partnership other than in its capacity as a member of the partnership, the transaction generally is considered as occurring between the partnership and one who is not a partner (sec. 707).

51. A special rule allows a partner that acquired a partnership interest by transfer within two years of a distribution to elect to allocate the basis of property received in the distribution as if the partnership had a section 754 election in effect (sec. 732(d)). The special rule also allows the Service to require such an allocation where the value at the time of transfer of the property

received exceeds 110 percent of its adjusted basis to the partnership (sec. 732(d)). Tres. Reg. sec. 1.732 1(d)(4) generally requires the application of section 732(d) where the allocation of basis under section 732(c) upon a liquidation of the partner's interest would have resulted in a shift of basis from non-depreciable property to depreciable property.

52. "The failure of these rules to take fair market value into account puts a high premium on tax planning in connection with in-kind liquidating distributions. Allocation of the portion of the basis in excess of the partnerships basis in the distributed assets according to their relative market values would be a conceptually sound approach, and would eliminate the strange results and manipulation possibilities . . . ." W. McKee, W. Nelson and R. Whitmire, Federal Taxation of Partnerships and Partners (3rd ed. 1997), para. 19.06.

to increase basis artificially, giving rise to inflated depreciation deductions or artificially large losses, for example. The Committee believes that these problems would be significantly reduced by taking into account the fair market value of property distributed by a partnership for purposes of allocating basis in the hands of the distributee partner.

Explanation of Provision

The provision modifies the basis allocation rules for distributee partners. It allocates a distributee partner's basis adjustment among distributed assets first to unrealized receivables and inventory items in an amount equal to the partnership's basis in each such property (as under present law).

Under the provision, basis is allocated first to the extent of each distributed property's adjusted basis to the partnership. Any remaining basis adjustment, if an increase, is allocated among properties with unrealized appreciation in proportion to their respective amounts of unrealized appreciation (to the extent of each property's appreciation), and then in proportion to their respective fair market values. For example, assume that a partnership with two assets, A and B, distributes them both in liquidation to a partner whose basis in its interest is 55. Neither asset consists of inventory or unrealized receivables. Asset A has a basis to the partnership of 5 and a fair market value of 40, and asset B has a basis to the partnership of 10 and a fair market value of 10. Under the provision, basis is first allocated to asset in the amount of 5 and to asset B in the amount of 10 (their adjusted bases to the partnership). The remaining basis adjustment is an increase totaling 40 (the partner's 55 basis minus the partnership's total basis in distributed assets of 15). Basis is then allocated to asset A in the amount of 35, its unrealized appreciation, with no allocation to asset B attributable to unrealized appreciation because its fair market value equals the partnership's adjusted basis. The remaining basis adjustment of 5 is allocated in the ratio of the assets' fair market values, i.e., 4 to asset A (for a total basis of 44) and 1 to asset B (for a total basis of 11).

If the remaining basis adjustment is a decrease, it is allocated among properties with unrealized depreciation in proportion to their respective amounts of unrealized depreciation (to the extent of each property's depreciation), and then in proportion to their respective adjusted bases (taking into account the adjustments already made). A remaining basis adjustment that is a decrease arises under the provision when the partnership's total adjusted basis in the distributed properties exceeds the amount of the partner's basis in its partnership interest, and the latter amount is the basis to be allocated among the distributed properties. For example, assume that a partnership with two assets, C and D, distributes them both in liquidation to a partner whose basis in its partnership interest is 20. Neither asset consists of inventory or unrealized receivables. Asset C has a basis to the partnership of 15 and a fair market value of 15, and asset D has a basis to the partnership of 15 and a fair market value of 5. Under the provision, basis is first allocated to the extent of the partnership's basis in each distributed property, or 15 to each distributed property, for a total of 30. Because the partner's basis in its interest is only 20, a downward adjustment of 10 (30 minus 20) is required. The entire amount of the 10 downward adjustment is allocated to the property D, reducing its basis to 5. Thus, the basis of property C is 15 in the hands of the distributee partner, and the basis of property D is 5 in the hands of the distributee partner.

Effective Date

The provision applies to partnership distributions after the date of enactment.

[Conference Report]

Senate Amendment

The Senate amendment is the same as the House bill.

Conference Agreement

The conference agreement follows the House bill and the Senate amendment.

[¶5151] Section 1062. Treatment of Partnership Inventory

(Code Sec. 751, 724, 731, 732, 735)

[House Report]

Present Law

Under present law, upon the sale or exchange of a partnership interest, any amount received that is attributable to unrealized receivables, or to inventory that has substantially appreciated, is treated as an amount realized from the sale or exchange of property that is not a capital asset (sec. 751(a)).

Present law provides a similar rule to the extent that a distribution is treated as a sale or exchange of a partnership interest. A distribution by a partnership in which a partner receives substantially appreciated inventory or unrealized receivables in exchange for its interest in certain other partnership property (or receives certain other property in exchange for its interest in substantially appreciated inventory or unrealized receivables) is treated as a taxable sale or exchange of property, rather than as a nontaxable distribution (sec. 751(b)).

For purposes of these rules, inventory of a partnership generally is treated as substantially appreciated if the fair market value of the inventory exceeds 120 percent of adjusted basis of the inventory to the partnership (sec. 751(d)(1)(A)). In applying this rule, inventory property is excluded from the calculation if a principal purpose for acquiring the inventory property was to avoid the rules relating to inventory (sec. 751(d)(1)(B)).

Reasons for Change

The substantial appreciation requirement with respect to inventory of a partnership has been criticized as both ineffective at insulating partnerships from the potential complexity of the disproportionate distribution rules of section 751(b), and also ineffective at properly treating income attributable to inventory as ordinary income under the section 751 rules for partnerships with profit margins below 20 percent.[53] Because the Committee believes that income attributable to inventory should be treated as ordinary income, the bill repeals the substantial appreciation requirement with respect to inventory, in the case of partnership sales, exchanges and distributions.

Explanation of Provision

The provision eliminates the requirement that inventory be substantially appreciated in order to give rise to ordinary income under the rules relating to sales and exchanges of partnership interests and certain partnership distributions. This conforms the treatment of inventory to the treatment of unrealized receivables under these rules.

Effective Date

The provision is effective for sales, exchanges, and distributions after the date of enactment.

[Conference Report]

Senate Amendment

The Senate amendment is the same as the House bill.

Conference Agreement

The conference agreement follows the House bill and the Senate amendment, with modifications. The conference agreement repeals the requirement that inventory be substantially appreciated only with respect to sales or exchanges of partnership interests under section 751 (a) of the Code, but not with respect to distributions under section 751(b) of the Code. Thus, present law is retained with respect to distributions governed by section 751(b).

Effective Date

The conference agreement follows the House bill and the Senate amendment, with a modification. The conference agreement

---

53. The 1984 ALI study on partnership rules referred to the substantial appreciation requirement as subject to manipulation and tax planning (American Law Institute, Federal Income Tax Project: Subchapter K: Proposals on the Taxation of Partners (R. Cohen, reporter, 1984), 26. In 1993 the definition of substantially appreciated inventory was modified, and the present-law test relat-ing to a principal purpose of avoidance was added (Omnibus Budget Reconciliation Act of 1993, P.L. 103 66, sec. 13206(e)(1)). Nevertheless, the substantial appreciation requirement is still criticized as ineffective (W. McKee, W. Nelson and R. Whitmire, Federal Taxation of Partners and Partnerships, (3rd ed. 1997) sec. 16.04[2]).

provides that the provision is effective for sales, exchanges, and distributions after the date of enactment, except that the provision does not apply to any sale or exchange pursuant to a written binding contract in effect on June 8, 1997, and at all times thereafter before such sale or exchange.

[¶ 5152]   Section 1063.   Time for Taxing Pre-Contribution Gain With Respect to Appreciated Property.

(Code Sec. 704, 737)

[House Report]

Present Law

Under present law, if a partner contributes appreciated property to a partnership, no gain is recognized to the contributing partner at the time of the contribution. The contributing partner's basis in its partnership interest is increased by the basis of the contributed property at the time of the contribution. The pre-contribution gain is reflected in the difference between the partner's capital account and its basis in its partnership interest ("book/tax differential"). Income, gain, loss, and deduction with respect to the contributed property must be shared among the partners so as to take account of the variation between the basis of the property to the partnership and its fair market value at the time of contribution (sec. 704(c)(1)(A)).

If the property is subsequently distributed to another partner within 5 years of the contribution, the contributing partner generally recognizes gain as if the property had been sold for its fair market value at the time of the distribution (sec. 704(c)(1)(B)). Similarly, the contributing partner generally includes pre-contribution gain in income to the extent that the value of other property distributed by the partnership to that partner exceeds its adjusted basis in its partnership interest, if the distribution by the partnership is made within 5 years after the contribution of the appreciated property (sec. 737).

If a partnership distributes property to a partner, the partner does not recognize gain except to the extent any money (including marketable securities) received in the distribution exceeds the partner's basis for its partnership interest (sec. 731(a)). In addition, a partnership does not recognize gain on a distribution to a partner (sec. 731(b)).

Reasons for Change

The Committee is concerned that the inconsistency in treatment of partnership sales and partnership distributions of property contributed by partners makes it possible for partners to circumvent the rule requiring pre-contribution gain on contributed property to be allocated to the contributing partner. In order to limit the inconsistency and to reduce opportunities for circumventing this rule, the Committee believes that the contributing partner should recognize pre-contribution gain when the contributed property is distributed to another partner, or the partnership distributes to the contributing partner other property whose value exceeds that partner's basis in its partnership interest, within 10 years after the contribution of the appreciated property.

Explanation of Provision

The provision extends to 10 years the period in which a partner recognizes pre-contribution gain with respect to property contributed to a partnership.

Effective Date

The provision is effective for property contributed to a partnership after June 8, 1997.

[Conference Report]

Senate Amendment

No provision.

Conference Agreement

The conference agreement follows the House bill, with a modification. The conference agreement extends to 7 years the period in which a partner recognizes pre-contribution gain with respect to property contributed to a partnership. Thus, under the conference agreement, a partner that contributes appreciated property to a partnership generally recognizes pre-contribution gain in the event that the partnership distributes the contributed property to another partner, or distributes to the contributing partner other property whose value exceeds that partner's basis in its partnership interest, if the distribution occurs within 7 years after the contribution to the partnership.

[¶ 5153]   Section 1071.   Cash Out of Certain Accrued Benefits.

(Code Sec. 411, 417, 457)

[House Report]

Present Law

Under present law, in the case of an employee whose plan participation terminates, a qualified plan may involuntarily "cash out" the benefit (i.e., pay out the balance to the credit of a plan participant without the participant's consent, and, if applicable, the consent of the participant's spouse) if the present value of the benefit does not exceed $3,500. If a benefit is cashed out under this rule and the participant subsequently returns to employment covered by the plan, then service taken into account in computing benefits payable under the plan after the return need not include service with respect to which benefits were cashed out unless the employee "buys back" the benefit. Generally, a cash-out distribution from a qualified plan to a plan participant can be rolled over, tax free, to an IRA or to another qualified plan.

Reasons for Change

The Committee believes that the limit on involuntary cash-outs should be raised to $5,000 in recognition of the effects of inflation and the value of small benefits payable under a qualified pension plan.

[Conference Report]

House Bill

The House bill increases the limit on involuntary cash outs from $3,500 to $5,000. The $5,000 amount is adjusted for inflation beginning after 1998 in $50 increments.

Senate Amendment

The Senate amendment is the same as the House bill, except the Senate amendment also makes a corresponding change to title I of ERISA and provides that the $5,000 amount is adjusted for inflation beginning after 1997 in $50 increments.

Conference Agreement

The conference agreement follows the House bill and the Senate amendment, except that the conference agreement does not increase the $5,000 limit for inflation.

[¶ 5154]   Section 1072.   Election to Receive Taxable Cash Compensation in Lieu of Nontaxable Parking Benefits.

(Code Sec. 132)

[Senate Report]

Present Law

Under present law, up to $165 per month of employer- provided parking is excludable from gross income. In order for the exclusion to apply, the parking must be provided in addition to and not in lieu of any compensation that is otherwise payable to the employee. Employer-provided parking cannot be provided as part of a cafeteria plan.

Reasons for Change

The Committee believes that the present-law rules relating to employer-provided parking result in an overutilization of parking as a fringe benefit. By permitting employers to offer cash compensation in lieu of parking, the Committee believes that employees will be more likely to elect to receive cash compensation, which will increase the electing employees' taxable income. In addition, the election to take cash may promote sound energy policy by increasing the use of mass transit and reduce the amount of commuting by car.

Explanation of Provision

Under the bill, no amount is includible in the income of an employee merely because the employer offers the employee a choice between cash and employer-provided parking. The amount of cash offered is includible in income only if the employee chooses the cash instead of parking.

Effective Date

The provision is effective with respect to taxable years beginning after December 31, 1997.

[¶ 5155]   Section 1073.   Repeal of Excess Distribution and Excess Retirement Accumulation Taxes.

(Code Sec. 4980A, 691, 2013, 2503, 6018)

[Senate Report]

Present Law

Under present law, a 15-percent excise tax is imposed on excess distributions from qualified retirement plans, tax-sheltered annuities, and IRAs. Excess distributions are generally the aggregate amount of retirement distributions from such plans during any calendar year in excess of $160,000 (for 1997) or 5 times that amount in the case of a lump-sum distribution. The 15-percent excise tax does not apply to distributions received in 1997, 1998, and 1999.

An additional 15-percent estate tax is imposed on an individual's excess retirement accumulations. Excess retirement accumulations are generally the balance in retirement plans in excess of the present value of a benefit that would not be subject to the 15-percent tax in excess distributions.

Reasons for Change

The excess distribution and retirement accumulation taxes are designed to limit the overall tax-deferred savings by individuals, as well as to help ensure that tax-favored retirement vehicles are used primarily for retirement purposes. The Committee believes that the limits on contributions and benefits applicable to each type of vehicle are sufficient limits on tax-deferred savings. Additional penalties are unnecessary, and may also deter individuals from saving.

The excess accumulation and distribution taxes also inappropriately penalize favorable investment returns.

Explanation of Provision

The bill repeals both the 15-percent excise tax on excess distributions and the 15-percent estate tax on excess retirement accumulations.

Effective Date

The provision repealing the excess distribution tax is effective with respect to excess distributions received after December 31, 1996. The repeal of the excess accumulation tax is effective with respect to decedents dying after December 31, 1996.

[Conference Report]

House Bill

No provision.

Conference Agreement

The conference agreement follows the Senate amendment.

[Conference Report]

House Bill

No provision.

Conference Agreement

The conference agreement follows the Senate amendment.

[¶ 5156]   Section 1074.   Tax on Prohibited Transactions.

(Code Sec. 4975)

[Senate Report]

Present Law

Present law prohibits certain transactions (prohibited transactions) between a qualified plan and a disqualified person in order to prevent persons with a close relationship to the qualified plan from using that relationship to the detriment of plan participants and beneficiaries. A two-tier excise tax is imposed on prohibited transactions. The initial level tax was equal to 10- percent of the amount involved with respect to the transaction. If the transaction is not corrected within a certain period, a tax equal to 100 percent of the amount involved may be imposed.

Reasons for Change

The Committee believes it is appropriate to increase the initial level prohibited transaction tax to discourage disqualified persons from engaging in such transactions.

Explanation of Provision

The bill increases the initial-level prohibited transaction tax from 0-percent to 15-percent. No changes were made to the prohibited transaction provisions of title I of the Employee Retirement Income Security Act of 1974, as amended ("ERISA").

Effective Date

The provision is effective with respect to prohibited transactions occurring after the date of enactment.

[Conference Report]

House Bill

No provision.

Conference Agreement

The conference agreement follows the Senate amendment.

[¶ 5157]   Section 1075.   Basis Recovery Rules

(Code Sec. 72)

[Senate Report]

Present Law

Under present law, amounts received as an annuity under a tax-qualified pension plan generally are includible in income in the year received, except to the extent the amount received represents return of the recipient's investment in the contract (i.e., basis). The portion of each annuity payment that represents a return of basis generally is determined by a simplified method. Under this method, the portion of each annuity payment that is a return to basis is equal to the employee's total basis as of the annuity starting date, divided by the number of anticipated payments under a specified table, shown below. The number of anticipated payments listed in the table is based on the age of the primary annuitant on the annuity starting date.

Age of primary annuitant: ---- Number of Payments

Age	Number of Payments
55 or less	360
56-60	310
61-65	260
66-70	210
71 or more	160

If the number of payments is fixed under the terms of the annuity, that number is used instead of the number of anticipated payments listed in the table. The simplified method is not available if the primary annuitant has attained age 75 on the annuity starting date unless there are fewer than 5 years of guaranteed payments under the annuity. If, in connection with commencement of annuity payments, the recipient receives a lump-sum payment that is not part of the annuity stream, such payment is taxable under the rules relating to annuities (sec. 72) as if received before the annuity starting date, and the investment in the contract used to calculate the simplified exclusion ratio for the annuity payments is reduced by the amount of the payment. In no event is the total amount excluded from income as nontaxable return of basis greater than the recipient's total investment in the contract.

Reasons for Change

The table for determining anticipated payments does not differ depending on whether the annuity is payable in the form of a single life annuity or a joint and survivor annuity. Applying the table for single life annuities to joint and survivor annuities understates the expected payments under a joint and survivor annuity.

Explanation of Provision

Under the bill, the present-law table would apply to benefits based on the life of one annuitant. A separate table would apply to benefits based on the life of more than one annuitant, as follows:

Combined age of annuitants:---Number of payments

110 or less-----------------------410
111-120---------------------------360
121-130---------------------------310
131-140---------------------------260

141 and over---------------------210

Effective Date

The provision is effective with respect to annuity starting dates beginning after December 31, 1997.

[Conference Report]

Conference Agreement

The conference agreement follows the Senate amendment. As under the Senate amendment, a separate table applies to benefits based on the life of more than one annuitant.

The conference agreement clarifies that the new table applies to benefits based on the life of more than one annuitant, even if the amount of the annuity varies by annuitant. Thus, for example, the new table applies to a 50-percent joint and survivor annuity. The new table does not apply to an annuity paid on a single life merely because it has additional features, e.g., a term certain.

[¶5158]   Section 1081. Phase out suspense accounts for certain large farm corporations.

(Code Sec. 447)

[House Report]

Present Law

A corporation (or a partnership with a corporate partner) engaged in the trade or business of farming must use an accrual method of accounting for such activities unless such corporation (or partnership), for each prior taxable year beginning after December 31, 1975, did not have gross receipts exceeding $1 million. If a farm corporation is required to change its method of accounting, the section 481 adjustment resulting from such change is included in gross income ratably over a 10-year period, beginning with the year of change. This rule does not apply to a family farm corporation.

A provision of the Revenue Act of 1987 ("1987 Act") requires a family corporation (or a partnership with a family corporation as a partner) to use an accrual method of accounting for its farming business unless,

for each prior taxable year beginning after December 31, 1985, such corporation (and any predecessor corporation) did not have gross receipts exceeding $25 million. A family corporation is one where at 50 percent or more of the stock of the corporation is held by one (or in some limited cases, two or three) families.

A family farm corporation that must change to an accrual method of accounting as a result of the 1987 Act provision is to establish a suspense account in lieu of including the entire amount of the section 481 adjustment in gross income. The initial balance of the suspense account equals the lesser of (1) the section 481 adjustment otherwise required for the year of change, or (2) the section 481 adjustment computed as if the change in method of accounting had occurred as of the beginning of the taxable year preceding the year of change.

The amount of the suspense account is required to be included in gross income if the corporation ceases to be a family corporation. In addition, if the gross receipts of the corporation attributable to farming for any taxable year decline to an amount below the lesser of (1) the gross receipts attributable to farming for the last taxable year for which an accrual method of accounting was not required, or (2) the gross receipts attributable to farming for the most recent taxable year for which a portion of the suspense account was required to be included in income, a portion of the suspense account is required to be included in gross income.

[Senate Report]

Reasons for Change

The committee believes that an accrual method of accounting more accurately measures the economic income of a corporation than does the cash receipts and disbursements method and that changes from one method of accounting to another should be taken into account under section 481. However, the committee believes that it may be appropriate for a family farm corporation to retain the use of the cash method of accounting until such corporation reaches a certain size. At that time, the corporation should be subject to tax accounting rules to which other corporations are so subject. In addition, the committee believes that the present-law suspense account provision applicable to large family farm corporations may effectively provide an exclusion for, rather than a deferral of, amounts otherwise properly taken into account under section 481 upon the required change in the method of accounting for such corporations. However, the committee recognizes that requiring the recognition of previously established suspense accounts may impose liquidity concerns upon some farm corporations. Thus, the committee provides an extended period over which existing suspense accounts must be restored to income and provides further deferral where the corporation has insufficient income for the year.

Explanation of Provision

The bill repeals the ability of a family farm corporation to establish a suspense account when it is required to change to an accrual method of accounting. Thus, under the bill, any family farm corporation required to change to an accrual method of

accounting would restore the section 481 adjustment applicable to the change in gross income ratably over a 10-year period beginning with the year of change.

In addition, any taxpayer with an existing suspense account is required to restore the account into income ratably over a 20-year period beginning in the first taxable year beginning after June 8, 1997, subject to the present-law requirements to restore such accounts more rapidly. The amount required to be restored to income for a taxable year pursuant to the 20-year spread period shall not exceed the net operating loss of the corporation for the year (in the case of a corporation with a net operating loss) or 50 percent of the net income of the taxpayer for the year (for corporations with taxable income). For this purpose, a net operating loss or taxable income is determined without regard to the amount restored to income under the bill. Any reduction in the amount required to be restored to income is taken into account ratably over the remaining years in the 20-year period or, if applicable, after the end of the 20-year period. Amounts that extend beyond the 20-year period remain subject to the net operating loss and 50-percent-of-taxable income rules.

Finally, the present-law requirement that a portion of a suspense account be restored to income if the gross receipts of the corporation diminishes is repealed.

Effective Date

The provision is effective for taxable years ending after June 8, 1997.

[Conference Report]

Senate Amendment

The Senate amendment is the same as the House bill.

In addition, the Senate amendment repeals the present-law requirement to accelerate the recovery of suspense accounts when the gross receipts of the taxpayer decreases.

Conference Agreement

The conference agreement follows the Senate amendment. In addition, the conferees wish to clarify that in the case of a family farm corporation that elects to be an S corporation for a taxable year, the net operating loss and 50 percent of taxable income limitations shall be determined by taking into account all the items of income, gain, deduction and loss of the corporation, whether or not such items are separately stated under section 1366.

[¶ 5159]   Section 1082.   Modify new operating loss carryback and carryforward rules.

(Code Sec. 172)

[House Report]

Present Law

The net operating loss ("NOL") of a taxpayer (generally, the amount by which the business deductions of a taxpayer exceeds its gross income) may be carried back three years and carried forward 15 years to offset taxable income in such years. A taxpayer may elect to forgo the carryback of an NOL. Special rules apply to real estate investment trusts ("REITs") (no carrybacks), specified liability losses (10-year carryback), and excess interest losses (no carrybacks).

[Senate Report]

Reason for Change

The committee recognizes that while Federal income tax reporting requires a taxpayer to report income and file returns based on a 12-month period, the natural business cycle of a taxpayer may exceed 12 months. However, the committee believes that allowing a two-year carryback of NOLs is sufficient to account for these business cycles, particularly since (1) many deductions allowed for tax purposes relate to future, rather than past, income streams and (2) certain deductions that do relate to past income streams are granted special, longer carryback periods under present law (which are retained by the bill).

Explanation of Provision

The bill limits the NOL carryback period to two years and extends the NOL carryfor-

ward period to 20 years. The bill does not apply to the carryback rules relating to REITs, specified liability losses, excess interest losses, and corporate capital losses.

The bill does not apply to NOLs arising from casualty losses of individual taxpayers. In addition, the bill does not apply to NOLs attributable to losses incurred in Presidentially declared disaster areas by taxpayers engaged in a farming business or a small business. For this purpose, a "small business" means any trade or business (including one conducted in or through a corporation, partnership, or sole proprietorship) the average annual gross receipts (as determined under sec. 448(c)) of which are $5 million or less, and a "farming business" is defined as in section 263A(e)(4).

Effective Date

The provision is effective for NOLs for taxable years beginning after the date of enactment. The provision does not apply to NOLs carried forward from prior taxable years.

[Conference Report]

Senate Amendment

The Senate amendment follows the House bill. In addition, the Senate amendment preserves the 3-year carryback for NOLs of farmers and small businesses attributable to losses incurred in Presidentially declared disaster areas.

Conference Agreement

The conference agreement follows the Senate amendment.

[¶ 5160]   Section 1083.   Modify general business credit carryback and carryforward rules.

(Code Sec. 39)

[Conference Report]

Present Law

A qualified taxpayer is allowed to claim the rehabilitation credit, the energy credit, the reforestation credit, the work opportunity credit, the alcohol fuels credit, the research credit, the low-income housing credit, the enhanced oil recovery credit, the disabled access credit, the renewable electricity production credit, the empowerment zone employment credit, the Indian employment credit, the employer social security credit, and the orphan drug credit (collectively, known as the general business credit), subject to certain limitations based on tax liability for the year. Unused general business credits generally may be carried back three years and carried forward 15 years to offset tax liability of such years, subject to the same limitations.

House Bill

No provision.

Senate Amendment

The Senate amendment limits the carryback period for the general business credit to one year and extends the carryforward period to 20 years.

Effective Date

The provision is effective for taxable years beginning after December 31, 1997.

Conference Agreement

The conference agreement includes the Senate amendment with a clarification that the provision is effective for credits arising in taxable years beginning after December 31, 1997.

[¶ 5161]   Section 1084.   Expand the limitations on deductibility of premiums and interest with respect to life insurance, endowment and annuity contracts.

(Code Sec. 264, 805, 807, 812, 832, 265)

[House Report]

Present Law

Exclusion of inside buildup and amounts received by reason of death

No Federal income tax generally is imposed on a policyholder with respect to the earnings under a life insurance contract ("inside buildup").[45] Further, an exclusion from Federal income tax is provided for amount received under a life insurance contract paid by reason of the death of the insured (sec. 101(a)).

Premium deduction limitation

No deduction is permitted for premiums paid on any life insurance policy covering the life of any officer or employee, or of any person financially interested in any trade or business carried on by the taxpayer, when the taxpayer is directly or indirectly a beneficiary under such policy (sec. 264(a)(1)).

45.

]This favorable tax treatment is available only if a life insurance contract meets certain requirements designed to limit the investment character of the contract (sec. 7702). Distributions from a life insurance contract (other than a modified endowment contract) that are made prior to the death of the insured generally are includible in income, to the extent that the amounts distributed exceed the taxpayer's basis in the contract; such distributions generally are treated first as a tax-free recovery of basis, and then as income (sec. 72(e)). In the case of a modified endowment contract, however, in general, distributions are treated as income first, loans are treated as distributions (i.e., income rather

than basis recovery first), and an additional 10 percent tax is imposed on the income portion of distributions made before age 59 ½ and in certain other circumstances (secs. 72(e) and (v)). A modified endowment contract is a life insurance contract that does not meet a statutory "7-pay" test, i.e., generally is funded more rapidly than 7 annual level premiums (sec. 7702A). Certain amounts received under a life insurance contract on the life of a terminally or chronically ill individual, and certain amounts paid for the sale or assignment to viatical settlement provider of a life insurance contract on the life of terminally ill or chronically ill individual, are treated as excludable as if paid of the death of insured (sec. 101(g)).

Interest deduction disallowance with respect to life insurance

Present law provides generally that no deduction is allowed for interest paid or accrued on any indebtedness with respect to one or more life insurance contracts or annuity or endowment contracts owned by the taxpayer covering any individual who is or was (1) an officer or employee of, or (2) financially interested in, any trade or business currently or formerly carried on by the taxpayer (the "COLI" rules).

This interest deduction disallowance rule generally does not apply to interest on debt with respect to contracts purchased on or before June 20, 1986; rather, an interest deduction limit based on Moody's Corporate Bond Yield Average—Monthly Average Corporates applies in the case of such contract.[46]

An exception to this interest disallowance rule is provided for interest on indebtedness with respect to life insurance policies covering up to 20 key persons. A key person is an individual who is either an officer or a 20-percent owner of the taxpayer. The number of individuals that can be treated as key persons may not exceed the greater of (1) 5 individuals, or (2) the lesser of 5 percent of the total number of officers and employees of the taxpayer, or 20 individuals. For determining who is a 20-percent owner, all members of a controlled group are treated as one taxpayer. Interest paid or accrued on debt with respect to a contract covering a key person is deductible only to the extent the rate of interest does not exceed Moody's Corporate Bond Yield Average—Monthly Average Corporates for each month beginning after December 31, 1995, that interest is paid or accrued.

The foregoing interest deduction limitation was added in 1996 to existing interest deduction limitations with respect to life insurance and similar contracts.[47]

Interest deduction limitation with respect to tax-exempt interest income

Present law provides that no deduction is allowed for interest on debt incurred or continued to purchase or carry obligations the interest on which is wholly exempt from Federal income tax (sec. 265(a)(2)). In addition, in the case a financial institution, a proration rule provides that no deduction is allowed for that portion of the taxpayer's interest that is allocable to tax-exempt interest (sec. 265(b)). The portion of the interest deduction that is disallowed under this rule generally is the portion determined by the ratio of the taxpayer's (1) average adjusted bases of tax-exempt obligations acquired after August 7, 1986, to (2) the average adjusted bases for all of the taxpayer's assets (sec. 265(b)(2)).[48]

Reasons for Change

The Committee understands that, under applicable State laws, the holder of a life insurance policy generally is required to have an insurable interest in the life of the insured individual only when the policyholder purchases the life insurance policy. The Committee understands that under State laws relating to insurable interests, a taxpayer generally has an insurable interest in the lives of its debtors. Further, rules governing permitted investments of financial institutions may allow the institutions to acquire cash value life insurance covering the lives of debtors, as well as the lives of individuals with other relationships to the taxpayer such as shareholders, employees or officers. In addition, insurable interest laws in many States have been expanded in re-

---

46. Phase-in rules apply generally with respect to otherwise deductible interest paid or accrued after December 31, 1995, and before January 1, 1999, in the case of debt incurred before January 1, 1996. In addition, transition rules apply.

47. Since 1942, a limitation has applied to the deductibility of interest with respect to single premium contracts (sec. 264(a)(2)). For this purpose, a contract is treated as a single premium contract if (1) substantially all the premiums on the contract are paid within a period of 4 years from the date on which the contract is purchased, or (2) and amount is deposited with the insurer for payment of a substantial number of future premiums on the contract. Further, under a limitation added in 1964, no deduction is allowed for any amount paid or

accrued on debt incurred or continued to purchase or carry a life insurance, endowment, or annuity contract pursuant to a plan of purchase that contemplates the systematic direct or indirect borrowing of part or all the increases in the cash value of the contract (sec. 264(a)(3)). An exception to the latter rule is provided, permitting deductibility of interest on bona fide debt that is part of such a plan, if no part of 4 of the annual premiums due during the first 7 years is paid by means of debt (the "4-out-of-7 rule") (sec. 264(a)(1)). In addition to the specific disallowance rules of section 264, generally applicable principles of tax law apply.

48. Special rules apply for certain tax-exempt obligations of small issuers (sec. 265(b)(3)).

cent years, and States could decide in the future to expand further the range of persons in whom a taxpayer has an insurable interest.

For example, a business could purchase cash value life insurance on the lives of its debtors, and increase the investment in these contracts as the debt diminishes and even after the debt is repaid. If a mortgage lender can (under applicable State law and banking regulations) buy a cash value life insurance policy on the lives of mortgage borrowers, the lender may be able to deduct premiums or interest on debt with respect to such a contract, if no other deduction disallowance rule or principle of tax law applies to limit the deductions. The premiums or interest could be deductible even after the individual's mortgage loan is sold to another lender or to a mortgage pool. If the loan were sold to a second lender, the second lender might also be able to buy a cash value life insurance contract on the life of the same borrower, and to deduct premiums or interest with respect to that contract. The Committee bill addresses this issue by providing that no deduction is allowed for premiums on any life insurance policy, or endowment or annuity contract, if the taxpayer is directly or indirectly a beneficiary under the policy or contract, and by providing that no deduction is allowed for interest paid or accrued on any indebtedness with respect to life insurance policy, or endowment or annuity contract, covering the life of any individual.

In addition, the Committee understands that taxpayers may be seeking new means of deducting interest on debt that in substance funds the tax-free inside build-up of life insurance, annuity and endowment contracts.[49] The Committee believes that present law was not intended to promote tax arbitrage by allowing financial or other business that have the ongoing ability to borrow funds from depositors, bondholders, investors or other lenders to concurrently invest a portion of their assets in cash value life insurance contracts, or endowment or annuity contracts. Therefore, the bill provides that, for taxpayers other than natural persons, no deduction is allowed for the

portion of the taxpayer's interest expense that is allocable to unborrowed policy cash surrender values of any life insurance policy or annuity or endowment contract issued after June 8, 1997.

Explanation of Provision

Expansion of premium deduction limitation to individuals in whom taxpayer has an insurable interest

Under the provision, the present-law premium deduction limitation is modified to provide that no deduction is permitted for premiums paid on any life insurance, annuity or endowment contract, if the taxpayer is directly or indirectly a beneficiary under the contract.

Expansion of interest disallowance to individuals in whom taxpayer has insurable interest

Under the provision, no deduction is allowed for interest paid or accrued on any indebtedness with respect to life insurance policy, or endowment or annuity contract, covering the life of any individual. Thus, the provision limits interest deductibility in the case of such a contract covering any individual in whom the taxpayer has an insurable interest when the contract is first issued under applicable State law, except as otherwise provided under present law with respect to key persons and pre-1986 contracts.

Pro rata disallowance of interest on debt to fund life insurance

In the case of a taxpayer other than a natural person, no deduction is allowed for the portion of the taxpayer's interest expense that is allocable to unborrowed policy cash surrender values with respect to any life insurance policy or annuity or endowment contract issued after June 8, 1997. Interest expense is so allocable based on the ratio of (1) the taxpayer's average unborrowed policy cash values of life insurance policies, and annuity and endowment contracts, issued after June 8, 1997, to (2) the average adjusted bases for all assets of the taxpayer. This rule does not apply to any policy or contract owned by an entity engaged in a trade or business, covering any individual

---

49. See "Fannie Mae Designing a Program to Link Life Insurance, Loans," Washington Post, p. E3, February 8, 1997; "Fannie Mae Considers Whether to Bestow Mortgage Insurance," Wall St. Journal, p. C1, April 22, 1997.

who is an employee, officer or director of the trade or business at the time first covered by the policy or contract. Such a policy or contract is not taken into account in determining unborrowed policy cash values.

The unborrowed policy cash values means the cash surrender value of the policy or contract determined without regard to any surrender charge, reduced by the amount of any loan with respect to the policy or contract. The cash surrender value is to be determined without regard to any other contractual or noncontractual arrangement that artificially depresses the cash value of a contract.

If a trade or business (other than a sole proprietorship or a trade or business of performing services as an employee) is directly or indirectly the beneficiary under any policy or contract, then the policy or contract is treated as held by the trade or business. For this purpose, the amount of the unborrowed cash value is treated as not exceeding the amount of the benefit payable to the trade or business. In the case of a partnership or S corporation, the provision applies at the partnership or corporate level. The amount of the benefit is intended to take into account the amount payable to the business under the contract (e.g., as a death benefit) or pursuant to another agreement (e.g., under a split dollar agreement). The amount of the benefit is intended also to include any amount by which liabilities of the business would be reduced by payments under the policy or contract (e.g., when payments under the policy reduce the principal or interest on a liability owed to or by the business).

As provided in regulations, the issuer or policyholder of the life insurance policy or endowment or annuity contract is required to report the amount of the amount of the unborrowed cash value in order to carry out this rule.

If interest expense is disallowed under other provisions of section 264 (limiting interest deductions with respect to life insurance policies or endowment or annuity contracts) or under section 265 (relating to tax-exempt interest), then the disallowed interest expense is not taken into account under this provision, and the average adjusted bases of assets is reduced by the amount of debt, interest on which is so disallowed. The provision is applied before present-law rules relating to capitalization of certain expenses where the taxpayer produces property (sec. 263A).

An aggregation rule is provided, treating related persons as one for purposes of the provision.

The provision does not apply to any insurance company subject to tax under subchapter L of the Code. Rather, the rules reducing certain deductions for losses incurred, in the case of property and casualty companies, and reducing reserve deductions or dividends received deductions of life insurance companies, are modified to take into account the increase in cash values of life insurance policies or annuity or endowment contracts held by insurance companies.

Effective Date

The provisions apply with respect to contracts issued after June 8, 1997. For this purpose, a material increase in the death benefit or the material change in the contract causes the contract to be treated as a new contract. To the extent of additional covered lives under a contract after June 8, 1997, the contract is treated as a new contract. In the case of an increase in the death benefit of a contract that is converted to extended term insurance pursuant to nonforfeiture provisions, in a transaction to which section 501(d)(2) of the Health Insurance Portability and Accountability Act of 1996 applies, the contract is not treated as a new contract.

[Conference Report]

Senate Amendment

The Senate amendment is the same as the House bill.

Conference Agreement

The conference agreement follows the House bill and the Senate amendment, with modifications.

Expansion of premium deduction limitation to individuals in whom taxpayer has an insurable interest

The conference agreement provides that the premium deduction limitation does not apply to premiums with respect to any annuity contract described in section 72(s)(5) (relating to certain qualified pension plans, certain retirement annuities, individual retirement annuities, and qualified funding assets), nor to premiums with respect to any annuity to which section 72(u) applies (relating to current taxation of income on the contract in the case of an annuity contract held by a person who is not a natural person).

Expansion of interest disallowance to individuals in whom taxpayer has insurable interest

The conference agreement specifies the treatment of certain interest to which the provision of the bill providing for expansion of interest disallowance to individuals in whom taxpayer has insurable interest otherwise would apply. The conference agreement provides that in the case of a transfer for valuable consideration of a life insurance contract or any interest therein described in section 101(a)(2), the amount of the death benefit excluded from gross income under section 101(a) may not exceed an amount equal to the sum of the actual value of the consideration, premiums, interest disallowed as a deduction under new section 264(a)(4), and other amounts subsequently paid by the transferee. Thus, under the provision, in the case of the transfer for value of a life insurance contract, the interest with respect to the contract that otherwise would be disallowed under new section 264(a)(4) is capitalized, reducing the amount included in income by the transferee upon receipt by the transferee of the amounts paid by reason of the death of the insured.

Pro rata disallowance of interest on debt to fund life insurance

Under the pro rata interest disallowance provision of the bill, the conference agreement provides that interest expense is allocable to unborrowed policy cash values based on the ratio of (1) the taxpayer's average unborrowed policy cash values of life insurance policies, and annuity and endowment contracts, issued after June 8, 1997, to (2) the sum of (a) in the case of assets that are life insurance policies or annuity or endowment contracts, the average unborrowed policy cash values, and (b) in the case of other assets, the average adjusted bases for all such other assets of the taxpayer.

Under the pro rata interest disallowance rule, the conference agreement expands the exception for any policy or contract owned by an entity engaged in a trade or business, covering an individual who is an employee, officer or director of the trade or business at the time first covered. Under the conference agreement, the exception applies to any policy or contract owned by an entity engaged in a trade or business, which covers one individual who (at the time first insured under the policy or contract) is (1) a 20- percent owner of the entity, or (2) an individual (who is not a 20- percent owner) who is an officer, director or employee of the trade or business. The exception also applies in the case of a joint-life policy or contract under which the sole insureds are a 20-percent owner and the spouse of the 20-percent owner. A joint-life contract under which the sole insureds are a 20-percent owner and his or her spouse is the only type of policy or contract with more than one insured that comes within the exception. Thus, for example, if the insureds under a contract include an individual described in the exception (e.g., an employee, officer, director, or 20-percent owner) and any individual who is not described in the exception (e.g., a debtor of the entity), then the exception does not apply to the policy or contract. For purposes of this exception, a 20-percent owner has the same meaning as under present-law section 264(d)(4). In addition, the conference agreement provides that the pro rata interest disallowance rule does not apply to any annuity contract to which section 72(u) applies (relating to current taxation of income on the contract in the case of an annuity contract held by a person who is not a natural person). The conference agreement provides that any policy or contract that is not subject to the pro rata interest disallowance rule by reason of this exception (for 20-percent owners, their spouses, employees, officers and directors, and in the case of an annuity contract to which section

72(u) applies) is not taken into account in the applying the ratio to determine the portion of the taxpayer's interest expense that is allocable to unborrowed policy cash values.

The conferees wish to clarify that the aggregation rule (treating related persons as one for purposes of the provision) is intended to prevent taxpayers from avoiding the pro rata interest limitation by owning life insurance, endowment or annuity contracts, while incurring interest expense through a related person.

Treatment of insurance companies

The conference agreement modifies the rules of the provision relating to the reduction of certain deductions of insurance companies. For purposes of those rules, an increase in the policy cash value for any policy or contract is (1) the amount of the increase in the adjusted cash value, reduced by (2) the gross premiums received with respect to the policy or contract during the taxable year, and increased by (3) distributions under the policy or contract to which

section 72(e) apply (other than amounts includable in the policyholder's gross income). For this purpose, the adjusted cash value means the cash surrender value of the policy or contract, increased by (1) commissions payable with respect to the policy or contract for the taxable year, and (2) asset management fees, surrender and mortality charges, and any other fees or charges, specified in regulations, which are imposed (or would be imposed if the policy or contract were surrendered or canceled) with respect to the policy or contract for the taxable year.

Effective Date

The conferees wish to clarify the rule under the effective date providing that the addition of covered lives is treated as a new contract only with respect to such additional covered lives. It is intended that this rule apply with respect to a master or group policy or contract, not with respect to a joint-life policy or contract (i.e., a policy or contract that insures more than one individual).

[¶ 5162]   Section 1085.   Earned income credit compliance provisions.

(Code Sec. 32, 6213, 6695)

[House Report]

Overview

Certain eligible low-income workers are entitled to claim a refundable earned income credit on their income tax return. A refundable credit is a credit that not only reduces an individual's tax liability but allows refunds to the individual in excess of income tax liability. The amount of the credit an eligible individual may claim depends upon whether the individual has one, more than one, or no qualifying children, and is determined by multiplying the credit rate by the individual's[54] earned income up to an earned income amount. The maximum amount of the credit is the product of the credit rate and the earned income amount. The credit is reduced by the amount of the alternative minimum tax ("AMT") the taxpayer owes for the year. The credit is

phased out above certain income levels. For individuals with earned income (or AGI, if greater) in excess of the beginning of the phaseout range, the maximum credit amount is reduced by the phaseout rate multiplied by the amount of earned income (or AGI, if greater) in excess of the beginning of the phaseout range. For individuals with earned income (or AGI, if greater) in excess of the end of the phaseout range, no credit is allowed. The definition of AGI used for phasing out the earned income credit disregards certain losses. The losses disregarded are: (1) net capital losses (if greater than zero); (2) net losses from trusts and estates; (3) net losses from nonbusiness rents and royalties; and (4) 50 percent of the net losses from business, computed separately with respect to sole proprietorships (other than in farming), sole proprietorships in farming, and other businesses. Also, an individual is not eligible for the earned income credit if the

---

54.

]In the case of a married individual who files a joint return with his or her spouse, the income for purposes of these tests is the combined income of the couple.

aggregate amount of "disqualified income" of the taxpayer for the taxable year exceeds $2,250. Disqualified income is the sum of: (1) interest (taxable and tax-exempt); (2) dividends; (3) net rent and royalty income (if greater than zero); (4) capital gain net income; and (5) net passive income (if greater than zero) that is not self-employment income. The earned income amount, the phaseout amount and the disqualified income amount are indexed for inflation.

The parameters for the credit depend upon the number of qualifying children the individual claims. For 1997, the parameters are given in the following table:

PRESENT-LAW EARNED INCOME CREDIT PARAMETERS

	Two or more qualifying children	One qualifying child	No qualifying children
Credit rate (percent)	40.00	34.00	7.65
Earned income amount	$ 9,140	$ 6,500	$4,340
Maximum credit	$ 3,656	$ 2,210	$ 332
Phaseout begins	$11,930	$11,930	$5,430
Phaseout rate (percent)	21.06	15.98	7.65
Phaseout ends........................	$29,290	$25,760	$9,770

In order to claim the credit, an individual must either have a qualifying child or meet other requirements. A qualifying child must meet a relationship test, an age test, an identification test, and a residence test. In order to claim the credit without a qualifying child, an individual must not be a dependent and must be over age 24 and under age 65.

[House Report]

Present Law

The accuracy-related penalty, which is imposed at a rate of 20 percent, applies to the portion of any underpayment that is attributable to (1) negligence, (2) any substantial understatement of income tax, (3) any substantial valuation overstatement, (4) any substantial overstatement of pension liabilities, or (5) any substantial estate or gift tax valuation understatement (sec. 6662). Negligence includes any careless, reckless, or intentional disregard of rules or regulations, as well as any failure to make a reasonable attempt to comply with the provisions of the Code.

The fraud penalty, which is imposed at a rate of 75 percent, applies to the portion of any underpayment that is attributable to fraud (sec. 6663).

Neither the accuracy-related penalty nor the fraud penalty is imposed with respect to any portion of an underpayment if it is shown that there was a reasonable cause for that portion and that the taxpayer acted in good faith with respect to that portion.

Reason for Change

The Committee believes that taxpayers who fraudulently claim the EIC or recklessly or intentionally disregard EIC rules or regulations should be penalized for doing so.

Explanation of Provision

A taxpayer who fraudulently claims the earned income credit (EIC) is ineligible to claim the EIC for a subsequent period of 10 years. In addition, a taxpayer who erroneously claims the EIC due to reckless or intentional disregard of rules or regulations is ineligible to claim the EIC for a subsequent period of two years. These sanctions are in addition to any other penalty imposed under present law. The determination of fraud or of reckless or intentional disregard of rules or regulations are made in a deficiency proceeding (which provides for judicial review).

Effective Date

The provision is effective for taxable years beginning after December 31, 1996.

Senate Amendment

The Senate amendment is the same as the House bill.

Conference Agreement

The conference agreement follows the House bill and the Senate amendment.

[House Report]

Present Law

If an individual fails to provide a correct TIN and claims the EIC, such omission is treated as a mathematical or clerical error. Also, if an individual who claims the EIC with respect to net earnings from self employment fails to pay the proper amount of self-employment tax on such net earnings, the failure is treated as a mathematical or clerical error for purposes of the amount of EIC claimed. Generally, taxpayers have 60 days in which they can either provide a correct TIN or request that the IRS follow the current-law deficiency procedures. If a taxpayer fails to respond within this period, he or she must file an amended return with a correct TIN or clarify that any self-employment tax has been paid in order to obtain the EIC originally claimed.

The IRS must follow deficiency procedures when investigating other types of questionable EIC claims. Under these procedures, contact letters are first sent to the taxpayer. If the necessary information is not provided by the taxpayer, a statutory notice of deficiency is sent by certified mail, notifying the taxpayer that the adjustment will be assessed unless the taxpayer files a petition in Tax Court within 90 days. If a petition is not filed within that time and there is no other response to the statutory notice, the assessment is made and the EIC is denied.

Reason for Change

The Committee believes that the requirement of additional information to determine EIC eligibility is prudent for taxpayers who have incorrectly claimed the EIC in the past.

[House Report]

Present Law

There are several penalties that apply in the case of an understatement of tax that is caused by an income tax return preparer. First, if any part of an understatement of tax on a return or claim for refund is attributable to a position for which there was not a realistic possibility of being sustained on its merits and if any person who is an income tax return preparer with respect to such return or claim for refund knew (or reasonably should have known) of such position and such position was not disclosed or was frivolous, then that return preparer is subject to a penalty of $250 with respect to that return or claim (sec. 6694(a)). The penalty is not imposed if there is reasonable cause for the understatement and the return preparer acted in good faith. In addition, if any part of an understatement of tax on a return or claim for refund is attributable to a willful attempt by an income tax return preparer to understate the tax liability of another person or to any reckless or intentional disregard of rules or regulations by an income tax return preparer, then the income tax return preparer is subject to a penalty of $1,000 with respect to that return or claim (sec. 6694(b)).

Also, a penalty for aiding and abetting the understatement of tax liability is imposed in cases where any person aids, assists in, procures, or advises with respect to the preparation or presentation of any portion of a return or other document if (1) the person knows or has reason to believe that the return or other document will be used in connection with any material matter arising under the tax laws, and (2) the person knows that if the portion of the return or other document were so used, an understatement of the tax liability of another person would result (sec. 6701).

Additional penalties are imposed on return preparers with respect to each failure to (1) furnish a copy of a return or claim for refund to the taxpayer, (2) sign the return or claim for refund, (3) furnish his or her identifying number, (4) retain a copy or list of the returns prepared, and (5) file a correct information return (sec. 6695). The penalty is $50 for each failure and the total penalties imposed for any single type of failure for any calendar year are limited to $25,000.

Reason for Change

The Committee believes that more thorough efforts by return preparers are important to improving EIC compliance.

Explanation of Provision

Return preparers are required to fulfill certain due diligence requirements with respect to returns they prepare claiming the EIC. The penalty for failure to meet these requirements is $100. This penalty is in addition to any other penalty imposed under present law.

Effective Date

The provision is effective for taxable years beginning after December 31, 1996.

[Conference Report]

Senate Amendment

The Senate amendment is the same as the House bill.

Conference Agreement

The conference agreement follows the House bill and the Senate amendment.

[

House Bill

Under the House bill, a taxpayer who has been denied the EIC as a result of deficiency procedures is ineligible to claim the EIC in subsequent years unless evidence of eligibility for the credit is provided by the taxpayer. To demonstrate current eligibility, the taxpayer is required to meet evidentiary requirements established by the Secretary of the Treasury. Failure to provide this information when claiming the EIC is treated as a mathematical or clerical error. If a taxpayer is recertified a s eligible for the credit, the taxpayer is not required to provide this information in the future unless the IRS again denies the EIC as a result of a deficiency procedure. Ineligibility for the EIC under the provision is subject to review by the courts.

Effective Date

The provision is effective for taxable years beginning after December 31, 1996.

Senate Amendment

The Senate amendment is the same as the House bill.

Conference Agreement

The conference agreement follows the House bill and the Senate amendment.

[

Senate Amendment

The Senate amendment is the same as the House bill.

Conference Agreement

The conference agreement follows the House bill and the Senate amendment.

[Conference Report]

Present Law

The EIC is phased out above certain income levels. For individuals with earned income (or AGI, if greater) in excess of the beginning of the phaseout range, the maximum credit amount is reduced by the phaseout rate multiplied by the amount of earned income (or AGI, if greater) in excess of the beginning of the phaseout range. For individuals with earned income (or AGI, if greater) in excess of the end of the phaseout range, no credit is allowed. The definition of AGI used for the phase out of the earned income credit disregards certain losses. The losses disregarded are: (1) net capital losses (if greater than zero); (2) net losses from trusts and estates; (3) net losses from non-business rents and royalties; and (4) 50 percent of the net losses from business, computed separately with respect to sole proprietorships (other than in farming), sole proprietorships in farming, and other businesses.

House Bill

No provision.

Senate Amendment

No provision.

Conference Agreement

The conference agreement modifies the definition of AGI used for phasing out the credit by adding two items of nontaxable income and changing the percentage of certain losses disregarded. The two items added are: (1) tax-exempt interest, and (2) nontaxable distributions from pensions, annuities, and individual retirement arrangements (but only if not rolled over into similar vehicles during the applicable rollover period). The conference agreement also increases the amount of net losses from businesses, computed separately with respect to sole proprietorships (other than farming), sole proprietorships in farming, and other businesses disregarded from 50 percent to 75 percent.

Effective Date

The provision is effective for taxable years beginning after December 31, 1997.

[¶ 5163]   Section 1086.   Eligibility for income forecast method.

(Code Sec. 167, 168)

[House Report]

Present Law

A taxpayer generally recovers the cost of property used in a trade or business through depreciation or amortization deductions over time.Tangible property generally is depreciated under the modified Accelerated Cost Recovery System ("MACRS") of section 168, which applies specific recovery periods and depreciation methods to the cost of various types of depreciable property. Intangible property generally is amortized under section 197, which applies a 15-year recovery period and the straight-line method to the cost of applicable property.

MACRS does not apply to certain property, including any motion picture film, video tape, or sound recording or to other any property if the taxpayer elects to exclude such property from MACRS and the taxpayer applies a unit-of-production method or other method of depreciation not expressed in a term of years. Section 197 does not apply to certain intangible property, including property produced by the taxpayer or any interest in a film, sound recording, video tape, book or similar property not acquired in transaction (or a series of related transactions) involving the acquisition of assets constituting a trade or business or substantial portion thereof. Thus, the cost of a film, video tape, or similar property that is produced by the taxpayer or is acquired on a "stand-alone" basis by the taxpayer may not be recovered under either the MACRS depreciation provisions or under the section 197 amortization provisions. The cost of such property may be depreciated under the "income forecast" method.

The income forecast method is considered to be a method of depreciation not expressed in a term of years. Under the income forecast method, the depreciation deduction for a taxable year for a property is determined by multiplying the cost of the property (less estimated salvage value) by a fraction, the numerator of which is the income generated by the property during the year and the denominator of which is the total forecasted or estimated income to be derived from the property during its useful life. The income forecast method is available to any property if (1) the taxpayer elects to exclude such property from MACRS and (2) for the first taxable year for which depreciation is allowable, the property is properly depreciated under such method. The income forecast method has been held to be applicable for computing depreciation deductions for motion picture films, television films and taped shows, books, patents, master sound recordings and video games.[55] Most recently, the income forecast method has been held applicable to consumer durable property subject to short-term "rent-to-own" leases.[56]

55.

]See, e.g., Rev. Rul. 60-358, 1960-2 C.B. 68; Rev. Rul. 64 273, 1964 2 C.B. 62; Rev. Rul. 79-285, 1979-2 C.B. 91; and Rev. Rul. 89-62, 1989-1 C.B. 78.

56.

]See, ABC Rentals of San Antonio v. Comm., No. 95 9008 (10th Cir. 9/27/96), where the Tenth Circuit decision reversed the holding of ABC Rentals of San Antonio v.

Comm., 68 TCM 1362 (1994) and held that consumer durable property subject to short-term, "rent-to-own" leases were eligible for the income forecast method. For decisions supporting the Tax Court memorandum decision denying eligibility for certain tangible personal property, see El Charro TV Rental v. Comm., No. 95   60301 (5th Cir., 1995) (rent-to-own property not eligible) and Carland, Inc. v. Comm., 90 T.C. 505 (1988), aff'd on this issue, 909 F.2d 1101 (8th Cir., 1990) (railroad rolling stock subject to a lease not eligible).

Reasons for Change

Depreciation allowances attempt to measure the decline in the value of property due to wear, tear, and obsolescence and to match the cost recovery for the property with the income stream produced by the property. The Committee believes that the income forecast method of depreciation is, in theory, an appropriate method to match the recovery of cost of property with the income stream produced by the property. However, when compared to MACRS, the income forecast method involves significant complexities, including the determination of the income estimated to be generated by the property, the determination of the residual value of the property, and the application of the look-back method. Thus, the Committee believes that the availability of the income forecast method should be limited to instances where the economic depreciation of the property cannot be adequately reflected by the passage of time alone or where the income stream from the property is sufficiently unpredictable or uneven such that the application of another method of depreciation may result in the distortion of income. In addition, because the income forecast method is elective, the Committee is concerned about taxpayer selectivity. Finally, the Committee provides a MACRS class life for consumer durables subject to rent-to-own contracts, in order to avoid future controversies with respect to the proper treatment of such property.

Explanation of Provision

The bill clarifies the types of property to which the income forecast method may be applied. Under the bill, the income forecast method is available to motion picture films, television films and taped shows, books, patents, master sound recordings, copyrights, and other such property as designated by the Secretary of the Treasury. It is expected that the Secretary will exercise this authority such that the income forecast method will be available to property the economic depreciation of which cannot be adequately measured by the passage of time alone or to property the income from which is sufficiently unpredictable or uneven so as to result in the distortion of income. The mere fact that property is subject to a lease should not make the property eligible for the income forecast method. The income forecast method is not be applicable to property to which section 197 applies.

In addition, consumer durables subject to rent-to-own contracts are provided a three-year recovery period and a four-year class life for MACRS purposes (and would not be eligible for the income forecast method). Such property generally is described in Rev. Proc. 95-38, 1995-34 I.R.B. 25.

Effective Date

The provision is effective for property placed in service after the date of enactment.

[Conference Report]

Senate Amendment

The Senate amendment is the same as the House bill.

Conference Agreement

The conference agreement generally follows the House bill and the Senate amendment, with modifications to depreciation applicable to qualified rent-to-own property. First, the conference agreement provides that the special 3-year recovery period may apply to any property generally used in the home for personal, but not business, use. The conferees understand that certain rent-to-own property, including computer and peripheral equipment, may be used in the home for either personal or business purposes, and the taxpayer may not be aware of how its customers may use the property. So as not to increase the administrative burdens of taxpayers, the conferees intend that if such dual-use property does not represent a significant portion of a taxpayer's leasing property and if such other leasing property predominantly is qualified rent-to-own property, then such dual-use property generally also would be qualified rent-to-own property. However, if such dual-use property represents a significant portion of the taxpayer's leasing property, the conferees intend that the burden of proof be placed on the taxpayer to show that such property is qualified rent-to-own property.

In addition, the conference agreement modifies the definition of "rent-to-own contract" to include leases that provide for decreasing regular periodic payments.

Finally, the conferees wish to clarify that the 3-year recovery period provided under the provision only applies to property subject to leases and no inference is intended as to whether any arrangement constitutes a lease for tax purposes.

[¶ 5164]   Section 1087.   Modify the exception to the related perty rule of section 1033 for individuals to only provide an exception for de minimis amounts.

(Code Sec. 1033)

[House Report]

Present Law

Under section 1033, gain realized by a taxpayer from certain involuntary conversions of property is deferred to the extent the taxpayer purchases property similar or related in service or use to the converted property within a specified replacement period of time. Pursuant to a provision of Public Law 104 7, subchapter C corporations (and certain partnerships with corporate partners) are not entitled to defer gain under section 1033 if the replacement property or stock is purchased from a related person. A person is treated as related to another person if the person bears a relationship to the other person described in section 267(b) or 707(b)(1). An exception to this related party rule provides that a taxpayer could purchase replacement property or stock from a related person and defer gain under section 1033 to the extent the related person acquired the replacement property or stock from an unrelated person within the replacement period.

Reasons for Change

The Committee believes that, except for de minimis cases, individuals should be subject to the same rules with respect to the acquisition of replacement property from a related person as are other taxpayers.

Explanation of Provision

The bill expands the present-law denial of the application of section 1033 to any other taxpayer (including an individual) that acquires replacement property from a related party (as defined by secs. 267(b) and 707(b)(1)) unless the taxpayer has aggregate realized gain of $100,000 or less for the taxable year with respect to converted property with aggregate realized gains. In the case of a partnership (or S corporation), the annual $100,000 limitation applies to both the partnership (or S corporation) and each partner (or shareholder).

Effective Date

The provision applies to involuntary conversions occurring after June 8, 1997.

[Conference Report]

Senate Amendment

The Senate amendment is the same as the House bill.

Conference Agreement

The conference agreement follows the House bill and the Senate amendment.

[¶ 5165]   Section 1088.   Repeal of exception for certain sales by manufacturers to dealer.

(Code Sec. 811)

[House Report]

Present Law

In general, the installment sales method of accounting may not be used by dealers in personal property. Present law provides an exception which permits the use of the installment method for installment obligations arising from the sale of tangible personal property by a manufacturer of the property (or an affiliate of the manufacturer) to a dealer,[57] but only if the dealer is obligated to make payments of principal only when the dealer resells (or rents) the property, the manufacturer has the right to repurchase the property at a fixed (or ascertainable) price

---

57. *I.e,* the sale of the property must be intended to be for resale or leasing by the dealer.

after no longer than a nine month period following the sale to the   dealer, and certain other conditions are met. In order to meet the other conditions, the aggregate face amount of the installment obligations that otherwise qualify for the exception must equal at least 50 percent of the total sales to dealers that gave rise to such receivables (the "fifty percent test") in both the taxable year and the preceding taxable year, except that, if the taxpayer met all of the requirements for the exception in the preceding taxable year, the taxpayer would not be treated as failing to meet the fifty percent test before the second consecutive year in which the taxpayer did not actually meet the test. For purposes of applying the fifty percent test, the aggregate face amount of the taxpayer's receivables is computed using the weighted average of the taxpayer's receivables outstanding at the end of each month during the taxpayer's taxable year. In addition, these requirements must be met by the taxpayer in its first taxable year beginning after October 22, 1986, except that obligations issued before that date are treated as meeting the applicable requirements if such obligations were conformed to the requirements of the provision within 60 days of that date.

Reasons for Change

The Committee believes that the special exception that permitted certain dealers to use the installment method is no longer necessary or appropriate and the installment sale method of accounting should not be available to such dealers. Accordingly, the Committee bill repeals that exception.

Explanation of Provision

The bill repeals the exception that permits the use of the installment method of accounting for certain sales by manufacturers to dealers.

Effective Date

The provision is effective for taxable years beginning after the date of enactment. Any resulting adjustment from a required change in accounting will be includible ratably over the 4-year taxable years beginning after that date.

[Conference Report]

Senate Amendment

The Senate amendment is the same as the House bill, except for the effective date.

Effective Date

The provision is effective for taxable years beginning one year after the date of enactment. Any resulting adjustment from a required change in accounting will be includible ratably over the 4 taxable years beginning after that date.

Conference Agreement

The conference agreement follows the Senate amendment.

[¶ 5166]   Section 1089.   Treatment of charitable remainder trusts with greater than 50 percent annual payout.

(Code Sec. 664, 2055)

[Senate Report]

Present Law

In general

Sections 170(f), 2055(e)(2) and 2522(c)(2) disallow a charitable deduction for income, estate or gift tax purposes,respectively, where the donor transfers an interest in property to a charity (e.g., a remainder) while also either retaining an interest in that prosperity (e.g., an income in-

terest) or transferring an interest in that property to a noncharity for less than full and adequate consideration. Exceptions to this general rule are provided for (1) remainder interests in charitable remainder annuity trusts, charitable remainder unitrusts, pooled income funds, farms, and personal residences; (2) present interests in the form of a guaranteed annuity or a fixed percentage of the annual value of the property, (3) an undivided portion of the donor's entire interest in the property, and (4) a qualified conservation easement.

Charitable remainder annuity trusts and charitable remainder unitrusts

A charitable remainder annuity trust is a trust which is required to pay, at least annually, a fixed dollar amount at least 5 percent of the initial value of the trust to a non-charity for the life of an individual or period of less than 20 years, with the remainder passing to charity. A charitable remainder unitrust is a trust which generally is required to pay, at least annually, a fixed percentage of the fair market value of the trust's assets determined at least annually to a non-charity for the life of an individual or period less than 20 years, with the remainder passing to charity. Sec. 664(d).

Distributions from a charitable remainder annuity trust or charitable remainder unitrust are treated in the following order as: (1) ordinary income to the extent of the trust's current and previously undistributed ordinary income for the trust's year in which the distribution occurred, (2) capital gains to the extent of the trust's current capital gain and previously undistributed capital gain for the trust's year in which the distribution occurred; (3) other income (e.g., tax-exempt income) to the extent of the trust's current and previously undistributed other income for the trust's year in which the distribution occurred, and (4) corpus. Sec. 664(b).

Distributions are includible in the income of the beneficiary for the year that the annuity or unitrust amount is required to be distributed even though the annuity or unitrust amount is not distributed until after the close of the trust's taxable year. Treas. Reg. sec. 1.664-1(d)(4).

Reasons for Change

The Committee is concerned that the interplay of the rules governing the timing of income from distributions from charitable remainder trusts (i.e., Treas. Reg. sec. 1.664-1(d)(4)) and the rules governing the character of distributions (i.e., sec. 664(b)) have created opportunities for abuse where the required annual payments are a large portion of the trust and realization of income and gain can be postponed until a year later than the accrual of such large payments. For example, some taxpayers have been creating charitable remainder unitrusts with a required annual payout of 80 percent of the trust's assets and then funding the trust with highly appreciated nondividend paying stock which the trust sells in a year subsequent to when the required distribution is includible in the beneficiary's income, and using proceeds from that sale to pay the required distribution attributable to the prior year. Those taxpayers have treated the distribution of 80 percent of the trust's assets attributable to the trust's first required distribution as non-taxable distributions of corpus because the trust had not realized any income in its first taxable year. The Committee believes that such treatment is abusive and is inconsistent with the purpose of the charitable remainder trust rules. In order to limit this kind of abuse, the Committee bill provides that a trust cannot be a charitable remainder trust if the required payout is greater than 50 percent of the initial fair market value of the trusts assets (in the case of a charitable remainder annuity trust) or 50 percent of the annual value of the trusts assets (in the case of a charitable remainder unitrust).

On April 18, 1997, the Treasury Department proposed regulations providing additional rules under sections 664 and 2702 to address the abuse described above and other perceived abuses involving distributions from charitable remainder trusts. One of those proposed rules would require that payment of any required annuity or unitrust amount by a charitable remainder trust be made by the close of the trust's taxable year in which such payments are due. See Prop. Treas. Reg. secs. 1.664-2(a)(1)(i) and 1.664-3(a)(1)(i). The Committee intends that the provision of the Committee bill does not limit or alter the validity of the regulations proposed by the Treasury Department on April 18, 1997, or the Treasury Department's authority to address this or other abuses of the rules governing the taxation of charitable remainder trusts or their beneficiaries.

Explanation of Provision

Under the provision, a trust would not qualify as charitable remainder annuity trust if the annuity for a year is greater than 50 percent of the initial fair market value of the trust's assets or a trust would not qualify as a charitable remainder unitrust if the percentage of assets that are required to be distributed at least annually is greater than 50 percent. Any trust that fails this 50 percent rule will not be a charitable remainder trust whose taxation is governed under section 664, but will be treated as a complex trust and, accordingly, all of its income will be taxed to its beneficiaries or to the trust.

Effective Date

The provision applies to transfers to a trust made after June 18, 1997.

[Conference Report]

House Bill

No provision.

Conference Agreement

The conference agreement follows the Senate amendment with a modification that requires that the value of the charitable remainder with respect to any transfer to a qualified charitable remainder annuity trust or charitable remainder unitrust be at least 10 percent of the net fair market value of such property transferred in trust on the date of the contribution to the trust. The 10-percent test is measured on each transfer to the charitable remainder trust and, consequently, a charitable remainder trust which meets the 10- percent test on the date of transfer will not subsequently fail to meet that test if interest rates have declined between the trust's creation and the death of a measuring life. Similarly, where a charitable remainder trust is created for the joint lives of two individuals with a remainder to charity, the trust will not cease to qualify as a charitable remainder trust because the value of the charitable remainder was less than 10 percent of the trust's assets at the first death of those two individuals. The conference agreement provides several additional rules in order to provide relief for trusts that do not meet the 10-percent rule.

First, where a transfer is made after July 28, 1997, to a charitable remainder trust that fails the 10-percent test, the trust is treated as meeting the 10-percent requirement if the governing instrument of the trust is changed by reformation, amendment, construction, or otherwise to meet such requirement by reducing the payout rate or duration (or both) of any noncharitable beneficiary's interest to the extent necessary to satisfy such require-

ment so long as the reformation is commenced within the period permitted for reformations of charitable remainder trusts under section 2055(e)(3). The statute of limitations applicable to a deficiency of any tax resulting from reformation of the trust shall not expire before the date one year after the Treasury Department is notified that the trust has been reformed. In substance, this rule relaxes the requirements of section 2055(e)(3)(B) to the extent necessary for the reformation for the trust to meet the 10-percent requirement.

Second, a transfer to a trust will be treated as if the transfer never had been made where a court having jurisdiction over the trust subsequently declares the trust void (because, e.g., the application of the 10 percent rule frustrates the purposes for which the trust was created) and judicial proceedings to revoke the trust are commenced within the period permitted for reformations of charitable remainder trusts under section 2055(e)(3). Under this provision, the effect of "unwinding" the trust is that any transactions made by the trust with respect to the property transferred (e.g., income earned on the assets transferred to the trust and capital gains generated by the sales of the property transferred) would be income and capital gain of the donor (or the donor's estate if the trust was testamentary), and the donor (or the donor's estate if the trust was testamentary) would not be permitted a charitable deduction with respect to the transfer. The statute of limitations applicable to a deficiency of any tax resulting from "unwinding" the trust shall not expire before the date one year after the Treasury Department is notified that the trust has been revoked.

Third, where an additional contribution is made after July 28, 1997, to a charitable remainder unitrust created before July 29, 1997, and that unitrust would not meet the 10-percent requirement with respect to the additional contribution, the conference agreement provides that such additional contribution will be treated, under regulations to be issued by the Secretary of the Treasury, as if it had been made to a new trust that does not meet the 10-percent requirement, but which does not affect the status of the original unitrust as a charitable remainder trust.

The conferees intend that this provision of the conference agreement not limit or alter the validity of regulations proposed by the Treasury Department on April 18, 1997, or the Treasury Department's authority to address abuses of the rules governing the taxation of charitable remainder trusts or their beneficiaries.

Effective Date

The requirement that the payout rate not exceed 50 percent applies to transfers to a trust made after June 18, 1997.

The requirement that the value of the charitable remainder with respect to any

transfer to a qualified remainder trust be at least 10 percent of the fair market value of the assets transferred in trust applies to transfers to a trust made after July 28, 1997. However, the 10-percent requirement does not apply to a charitable remainder trust created by a testamentary instrument (e.g., a will or revocable trust) executed before July 29, 1997, if the instrument is not modified after that date and the settlor dies before January 1, 1999, or could not be modified after July 28, 1997, because the settlor was under a mental disability on that date (i.e., July 28, 1997) and all times thereafter.

[¶ 5167]   Section 1090.   Expanded SSA records for tax enforcement.

(Code Sec.)

[Expanded SSA records for tax enforcement. Conference Report]

Present Law

Under the Family Support Act of 1988, States must require each parent to furnish their social security number (SSN) for birth records. Parents can apply directly to the Social Security Administration (SSA) for an SSN for their child; or, in most states, they may apply for the child's SSN when obtaining a birth certificate. On an individual's SSN application, the SSA currently requires the mother's maiden name but not her SSN.

House Bill

No provision.

Senate Amendment

No provision.

Conference Agreement

SSA is required to obtain social security numbers (SSNs) of both parents on minor children's applications for SSNs. The SSA will provide this information to the IRS as part of the Data Master File ("DM-1 file"). The conferees anticipate that the IRS will use the information to identify questionable claims for the earned income credit, the dependent exemption, and other tax benefits, before tax refunds are paid out.

Effective Date

The provision is effective on the date of enactment.

[¶ 5170]   Section 1101.   Exemption From Foreign Tax Credit Limitation For Certain Individuals.

(Code Sec. 904)

[House Report]

Present Law

In order to compute the foreign tax credit, a taxpayer computes foreign source taxable income and foreign taxes paid in each of the applicable separate foreign tax credit limitation categories. In the case of an individual, this requires the filing of IRS Form 1116.

In many cases, individual taxpayers who are eligible to credit foreign taxes may have only a modest amount of foreign source gross income, all of which is income from investments. Taxable income of this type ordinarily is includible in the single foreign tax credit limitation category for passive income. However, under certain circumstances, the Code treats investment-type income (e.g., dividends and interest) as income in one of several other separate limitation categories (e.g., high withholding tax interest income or general limitation in-

come). For this reason, any taxpayer with foreign source gross income is required to provide sufficient detail on Form 1116 to ensure that foreign source taxable income from investments, as well as all other foreign source taxable income, is allocated to the correct limitation category.

Reasons for Change

The Committee believes that a significant number of individuals are entitled to credit relatively small amounts of foreign tax imposed at modest effective tax rates on foreign source investment income. For taxpayers in this class, the applicable foreign tax credit limitations typically exceed the amounts of taxes paid. Therefore, exempting these taxpayers from the foreign tax credit limitation rules significantly reduces the complexity of the tax law without significantly altering actual tax liabilities. At the same time, however, the Committee believes that this exemption should be limited to those cases where the taxpayer receives a payee statement showing the amount of the foreign source income and the foreign tax.

Explanation of Provision

The bill allows individuals with no more than $300 ($600 in the case of married persons filing jointly) of creditable foreign taxes, and no foreign source income other than passive income, an exemption from the foreign tax credit limitation rules. (The

Committee intends that an individual electing this exemption will not be required to file Form 1116 in order to obtain the benefit of the foreign tax credit.) An individual making this election is not entitled to any carryover of excess foreign taxes to or from a taxable year to which the election applies.

For purposes of this election, passive income generally is defined to include all types of income that is foreign personal holding company income under the subpart F rules, plus income inclusions from foreign personal holding companies and passive foreign investment companies, provided that the income is shown on a payee statement furnished to the individual. For purposes of this election, creditable foreign taxes include only foreign taxes that are shown on a payee statement furnished to the individual.

Effective Date

The provision applies to taxable years beginning after December 31, 1997.

[Conference Report]

Senate Amendment

The Senate amendment is the same as the House bill.

Conference Agreement

The conference agreement follows the House bill and the Senate amendment.

[¶ 5171]   Section 1102.   Translation of Foreign Taxes.

(Code Sec. 986, 989)

[House Report]

Present Law

Translation of foreign taxes

Foreign income taxes paid in foreign currencies are required to be translated into U.S. dollar amounts using the exchange rate as of the time such taxes are paid to the foreign country or U.S. possession. This rule applies to foreign taxes paid directly by U.S. taxpayers, which taxes are creditable in the year paid or accrued, and to foreign taxes paid by foreign corporations that are deemed paid by a U.S. corporation that is a shareholder of the foreign corporation, and hence creditable, in the year that the U.S.

corporation receives a dividend or has an income inclusion from the foreign corporation.

Redetermination of foreign taxes

For taxpayers that utilize the accrual basis of accounting for determining creditable foreign taxes, accrued and unpaid foreign tax liabilities denominated in foreign currencies are translated into U.S. dollar amounts at the exchange rate as of the last day of the taxable year of accrual. If a difference exists between the dollar value of accrued foreign taxes and the dollar value of those taxes when paid, a redetermination of foreign taxes arises. A foreign tax redetermination may occur in the case of a refund of foreign taxes. A foreign tax redetermination

also may arise because the amount of foreign currency units actually paid differs from the amount of foreign currency units accrued. In addition, a redetermination may arise due to fluctuations in the value of the foreign currency relative to the dollar between the date of accrual and the date of payment.

As a general matter, a redetermination of foreign tax paid or accrued directly by a U.S. person requires notification of the Internal Revenue Service and a redetermination of U.S. tax liability for the taxable year for which the foreign tax was claimed as a credit. The Treasury regulations provide exceptions to this rule for de minimis cases. In the case of a redetermination of foreign taxes that qualify for the indirect (or "deemed-paid") foreign tax credit under sections 902 and 960, the Treasury regulations generally require taxpayers to make appropriate adjustments to the payor foreign corporation's pools of earnings and profits and foreign taxes.

[Senate Report]

Reasons for Change

The Committee believes that the administrative burdens associated with the foreign tax credit can be reduced significantly by permitting foreign taxes to be translated using reasonably accurate average translation rates for the period in which the tax payments are made. This approach will reduce, sometimes substantially, the number of translation calculations that are required to be made. In addition, the Committee believes that taxpayers that are on the accrual basis of accounting for purposes of determining creditable foreign taxes should be permitted to translate those taxes into U.S. dollar amounts in the year to which those taxes relate, and should not be required to make adjustments or redetermination to those translated amounts, if actual tax payments are made within a reasonably short period of time after the close of such year. Moreover, the Committee believes that it is appropriate to use an average exchange rate for the taxable year with respect to which such foreign taxes relate for purposes of translating those taxes. On the other hand, the Committee believes that a foreign tax not paid within a reasonably short period after the close of the year to which the taxes

relate should not be treated as a foreign tax for such year. By drawing a bright line between those foreign tax payment delays that do and do not require a redetermination, the Committee believes that a reasonable degree of certainty and clarity will be added to the law in this area.

Explanation of Provision

Translation of foreign taxes

Translation of certain accrued foreign taxes

With respect to taxpayers that take foreign income taxes into account when accrued, the bill generally provides for foreign taxes to be translated at the average exchange rate for the taxable year to which such taxes relate. This rule does not apply (1) to any foreign income tax paid after the date two years after the close of the taxable year to which such taxes relate, (2) with respect to taxes of an accrual-basis taxpayer that are actually paid in a taxable year prior to the year to which they relate, or (3) to tax payments that are denominated in an inflationary currency (as defined by regulations).

Translation of all other foreign taxes

Under the bill, foreign taxes not eligible for application of the preceding rule generally are translated into U.S. dollars using the exchange rates as of the time such taxes are paid. The bill provides the Secretary of the Treasury with authority to issue regulations that would allow foreign tax payments to be translated into U.S. dollar amounts using an average exchange rate for a specified period.

Redetermination of foreign taxes

Under the bill, a redetermination is required if: (1) accrued taxes when paid differ from the amounts claimed as credits by the taxpayer, (2) accrued taxes are not paid before the date two years after the close of the taxable year to which such taxes relate, or (3) any tax paid is refunded in whole or in part. Thus, for example, the bill provides that if at the close of the second taxable year after the taxable year to which an accrued tax relates, any portion of the tax so accrued has not yet been paid, a foreign tax redetermination under section 905(c) is required for the amount representing the unpaid portion of that accrued tax. In other words, the previous accrual of any tax that is unpaid as of that date is denied. In cases where a redetermination is required, as under present law, the bill specifies that the taxpayer must notify the Secretary, who will redetermine the amount of the tax for the year or years affected. In the case of indirect foreign tax credits, regulatory authority is granted to prescribe appropriate adjustments to the foreign corporation's pool of post-1986 foreign income taxes in lieu of such a redetermination.

The bill provides specific rules for the treatment of accrued taxes that are paid more than two years after the close of the taxable year to which such taxes relate. In the case of the direct foreign tax credit, any such taxes subsequently paid are taken into account for the taxable year to which such taxes relate, but would be translated into U.S. dollar amounts using the exchange rates in effect as of the time such taxes are paid. In the case of the indirect foreign tax credit, any such taxes subsequently paid are taken into account for the taxable year in which paid, and would be translated into U.S. dollar amounts using the exchange rates as of the time such taxes are paid.

For example, assume that in year 1 a taxpayer accrues 1,000 units of foreign tax that relate to year 1 and that give rise to a foreign tax credit under section 901 and assume that the currency involved is not inflationary. Further assume that as of the end of year 1 the tax is unpaid. In this case, the bill provides that the taxpayer translates 1,000 units of accrued foreign tax into U.S. dollars at the average exchange rate for year

1. If the 1,000 units of tax are paid by the taxpayer in either year 2 or year 3, no redetermination of foreign tax is required. If any portion of the tax so accrued remains unpaid as of the end of year 3, however, the taxpayer is required to redetermine its foreign tax accrued in year 1 to eliminate the accrued but unpaid tax, thereby reducing its foreign tax credit for such year. If the taxpayer pays the disallowed taxes in year 4, the taxpayer again redetermines its foreign taxes (and foreign tax credit) for year 1, but the taxes paid in year 4 are translated into U.S. dollars at the exchange rate for year 4.

Effective Date

The provision generally is effective for foreign taxes paid (in the case of taxpayers using the cash basis for determining the foreign tax credit) or accrued (in the case of taxpayers using the accrual basis for determining the foreign tax credit) in taxable years beginning after December 31, 1997. The provision's changes to the foreign tax redetermination rules apply to foreign taxes which relate to taxable years beginning after December 31, 1997.

[Conference Report]

Conference Agreement

The conference agreement follows the Senate amendment with one modification. The conference agreement clarifies that the regulatory authority applicable in the case of indirect foreign tax credits allows, in lieu of a redetermination of taxes, appropriate adjustments to the pools of post-1986 foreign income taxes and the pools of post-1986 undistributed earnings.

[¶ 5172]   Section 1103.   Simplified Foreign Tax Credit Limitation For Alternative Minimum Tax.

(Code Sec. 59)

[House Report]

Present Law

Computing foreign tax credit limitations requires the allocation and apportionment of deductions between items of foreign source income and items of U.S. source income. Foreign tax credit limitations must be computed both for regular tax purposes and for purposes of the alternative minimum tax

(AMT). Consequently, the allocation and apportionment of deductions must be done separately for regular tax foreign tax credit limitation purposes and AMT foreign tax credit limitation purposes.

Reasons for Change

The process of allocating and apportioning deductions for purposes of calculating the regular and AMT foreign tax credit limitations can be complex. Taxpayers that have allocated and apportioned deductions for regular tax purposes generally must reallocate and reapportion the same deductions for AMT foreign tax credit purposes, based on assets and income that reflect AMT adjustments (including depreciation). However, the differences between regular taxable income and alternative minimum taxable income often are relevant primarily to U.S. source income. The Committee believes that permitting taxpayers to use foreign source regular taxable income in computing their AMT foreign tax credit limitation would provide an appropriate simplification of the necessary computations by eliminating the need to reallocate and reapportion every deduction.

Explanation of Provision

The provision permits taxpayers to elect to use as their AMT foreign tax credit limitation fraction the ratio of foreign source regular taxable income to entire alternative minimum taxable income, rather than the ratio of foreign source alternative minimum taxable income to entire alternative minimum taxable income. Under this election, foreign source regular taxable income is used, however, only to the extent it does not exceed entire alternative minimum taxable income. In the event that foreign source regular taxable income does exceed entire alternative minimum taxable income, and the taxpayer has income in more than one foreign tax credit limitation category, the

Committee intends that the foreign source taxable income in each such category generally would be reduced by a pro rata portion of that excess.

The election is available only in the first taxable year beginning after December 31, 1997 for which the taxpayer claims an AMT foreign tax credit. The Committee intends that a taxpayer will be treated, for this purpose, as claiming an AMT foreign tax credit for any taxable year for which the taxpayer chooses to have the benefits of the foreign tax credit and in which the taxpayer is subject to the alternative minimum tax or would be subject to the alternative minimum tax but for the availability of the AMT foreign tax credit. The election, once made, will apply to all subsequent taxable years, and may be revoked only with the consent of the Secretary of the Treasury.

Effective Date

The provision applies to taxable years beginning after December 31, 1997.

[Conference Report]

Senate Amendment

The Senate amendment is the same as the House bill.

Conference Agreement

The conference agreement follows the House bill and the Senate amendment.

[¶ 5173]   Section 1104.   Treatment of Personal Trasactions in Foreign Currency.

(Code Sec. 988)

[House Report]

Present Law

When a U.S. taxpayer makes a payment in a foreign currency, gain or loss (referred to as "exchange gain or loss") generally arises from any change in the value of the foreign currency relative to the U.S. dollar between the time the currency was acquired (or the obligation to pay was incurred) and the time that the payment is made. Gain or loss results because foreign currency, unlike the U.S. dollar, is treated as property for Federal income tax purposes.

Exchange gain or loss can arise in the course of a trade or business or in connection with an investment transaction. Exchange gain or loss also can arise where foreign currency was acquired for personal use. For example, the IRS has ruled that a taxpayer who converts U.S. dollars to a foreign currency for personal use while traveling abroad realizes exchange gain or loss on reconversion of appreciated or depreciated foreign currency (Rev. Rul. 74-7, 1974 1 C.B. 198).

Prior to the Tax Reform Act of 1986 ("1986 Act"), most of the rules for determining the Federal income tax consequences of foreign currency transactions were embodied in a series of court cases and revenue rulings issued by the IRS. Additional rules of limited application were provided by Treasury regulations. Pre-1986 law was believed to be unclear regarding the character, the timing of recognition, and the source of gain or loss due to fluctuations in the exchange rate of foreign currency. The 1986 Act provided a comprehensive set of rules for the U.S. tax treatment of transactions involving foreign currencies.

However, the 1986 Act provisions designed to clarify the treatment of currency transactions, primarily found in section 988 of the Code, apply to transactions entered into by an individual only to the extent that expenses attributable to such transactions are deductible under section 162 (as a trade or business expense) or section 212 (as an expense of producing income). Therefore, the principles of pre-1986 law continue to apply to personal currency transactions.

Reasons for Change

An individual who lives or travels abroad generally cannot use U.S. dollars to make all of the purchases incident to daily life. If an individual must treat foreign currency in this instance as property giving rise to U.S.-dollar income or loss every time the individual, in effect, "barters the foreign currency for goods or services, the U.S. individual living in or visiting a foreign country will have a significant administrative burden that may bear little or no relation to whether U.S.-dollar measured income has increased or decreased. The Committee believes that individuals should be given relief from the requirement to keep track of exchange gains on a transaction-by-transaction basis in de minimis cases.

Explanation of Provision

If an individual acquires foreign currency and disposes of it in a personal transaction and the exchange rate changes between the acquisition and disposition of such currency, the provision applies nonrecognition treatment to any resulting exchange gain, provided that such gain does not exceed $200. The provision does not change the treatment of resulting exchange losses. The Committee understands that under other Code provisions such losses typically are not deductible by individuals (e.g., sec. 165(c)).

Effective Date

The provision applies to taxable years beginning after December 31, 1997.

[Conference Report]

Senate Amendment

The Senate amendment is the same as the House bill.

Conference Agreement

The conference agreement follows the House bill and the Senate amendment with one modification. The conference agreement clarifies that transactions entered into in connection with a business trip constitute personal transactions for purposes of this provision. Exchange gain resulting from such transactions is eligible for nonrecognition treatment under this provision.

[¶ 5174]   Section 1105.   Foreign Tax Credit Limitation For 10/50 Company Dividends.

(Code Sec. 904)

[House Report]

Present Law

U.S. persons may credit foreign taxes against U.S. tax on foreign source income. The amount of foreign tax credits that can be claimed in a year is subject to a limitation that prevents taxpayers from using foreign tax credits to offset U.S. tax on U.S. source income. Separate limitations are applied to specific categories of income.

Special foreign tax credit limitation rules apply in the case of dividends received from a foreign corporation in which the taxpayer owns at least 10 percent of the stock by vote and which is not a controlled foreign corporation (a so-called "10/50 company"). Dividends received by the taxpayer from each 10/50 company are subject to a separate foreign tax credit limitation.

Reasons for Change

The Committee finds that the present-law rule that subjects the dividends received from each so-called 10/50 company to a separate foreign tax credit limitation imposes a substantial record-keeping burden on companies and has the additional negative effect of discouraging minority-position joint ventures abroad. Indeed, the Committee is aware that recent academic research suggests that the present-law requirements may distort the form and amount of overseas investment undertaken by U.S.-based enterprises. The research findings suggest that the present-law limitation "greatly reduces the attractiveness of joint ventures to American investors, particularly ventures in low-tax foreign countries. Aggregate data indicate that U.S. participation in international joint ventures fell sharply after [enactment of present law] in 1986. The decline in U.S. joint venture activity is most pronounced in low-tax countries. * * * Moreover, joint ventures in low-tax countries use more debt and pay greater royalties to their U.S. parents after 1986, which reflects their incentives to economize on dividend payments."[58]

Explanation of Provision

Under the bill, a single foreign tax credit limitation generally applies to dividends received by the taxpayer from all 10/50 companies. However, separate foreign tax credit limitations continue to apply to dividends received by the taxpayer from each 10/50 company that qualifies as a passive foreign investment company. Regulatory authority is granted to provide rules regarding the treatment of distributions out of earning and profits for periods prior to the taxpayer's acquisition of such stock. To the extent the regulations treat distributions from a foreign corporation out of earnings and profits for pre-acquisition periods as subject to a separate foreign tax credit limitation, it is expected that the regulations would allow the taxpayer to elect to apply that separate foreign tax credit limitation (rather than the limitation applicable to dividends from all 10/50 companies) also to distributions out of post-acquisition earnings and profits of such corporation.

Effective Date

The provision is effective for taxable years beginning after December 31, 2001.

[Conference Report]

Senate Amendment

No provision.

Conference Agreement

The conference agreement generally provides for look-through treatment to apply in characterizing dividends from 10/50 companies for foreign tax credit limitation purposes. Under the conference agreement, any dividend from a 10/50 company paid out of earnings and profits accumulated in a taxable year beginning after December 31, 2002 is treated as income in a foreign tax credit limitation category in proportion to the ratio of the earnings and profits attributable to income in such foreign tax credit limitation category to the total earnings and profits. Regulatory authority is granted to provide rules regarding the treatment of distributions out of earning and profits for periods prior to the taxpayer's acquisition of such stock.

In the case of dividends from a 10/50 company paid out of earnings and profits accumulated in a taxable year beginning before January 1, 2003, the conference agreement provides that a *single* foreign tax credit limitation generally applies to all such dividends from all 10/50 companies. However, separate foreign tax credit limitations continue to apply to any such dividends received by the taxpayer from each 10/50 company that qualifies as a passive foreign investment company. Regulatory authority is granted to provide rules regarding the treatment of distributions out of earning and profits for periods prior to the taxpayer's acquisition of such stock.

Effective Date

The provision is effective for taxable years beginning after December 31, 2002.

58.

]The Committee believes that the joint venture can be an efficient way for American business to exploit its know-how and technology in foreign markets. If the present-law limitation is discouraging such joint ventures or altering the structure of new ventures, the ability of American business to succeed abroad may be diminished. The Committee believes it is appropriate to modify the present-law limitation to promote simplicity and the ability of American business to compete abroad.

[¶ 5175]   Section 1111-1113.   Controlled Foreign Corporations.

(Code Sec. 964, 902, 904, 951, 952, 960, 961)

[House Report]

Present Law

If an upper-tier controlled foreign corporation ("CFC") sells stock of a lower-tier CFC, the gain generally is included in the income of U.S. 10-percent shareholders as subpart F income and such U.S. shareholder's basis in the stock of the first-tier CFC is increased to account for the inclusion. The inclusion is not characterized for foreign tax credit limitation purposes by reference to the nature of the income of the lower-tier CFC; instead it generally is characterized as passive income.

For purposes of the foreign tax credit limitations applicable to so-called 10/50 companies, a CFC is not treated as a 10/50 company with respect to any distribution out of its earnings and profits for periods during which it was a CFC and, except as provided in regulations, the recipient of the distribution was a U.S. 10-percent shareholder in such corporation.

If subpart F income of a lower-tier CFC is included in the gross income of a U.S. 10-percent shareholder, no provision of present law allows adjustment of the basis of the upper-tier CFC's stock in the lower-tier CFC.

The subpart F income earned by a foreign corporation during its taxable year is taxed to the persons who are U.S. 10-percent shareholders of the corporation on the last day, in that year, on which the corporation is a CFC. In the case of a U.S. 10-percent shareholder who acquired stock in a CFC during the year, such inclusions are reduced by all or a portion of the amount of dividends paid in that year by the foreign corporation to any person other than the acquiror with respect to that stock.

As a general rule, subpart F income does not include income earned from sources within the United States if the income is effectively connected with the conduct of a U.S. trade or business by the CFC. This general rule does not apply, however, if the income is exempt from, or subject to a reduced rate of, U.S. tax pursuant to a provision of a U.S. treaty.

A U.S. corporation that owns at least 10 percent of the voting stock of a foreign corporation is treated as if it had paid a share of the foreign income taxes paid by the foreign corporation in the year in which the foreign corporation's earnings and profits become subject to U.S. tax as dividend income of the U.S. shareholder. A U.S. corporation also may be deemed to have paid taxes paid by a second- or third-tier foreign corporation if certain conditions are satisfied.

Reasons for Change

The Committee believes that complexities are caused by uncertainties and gaps in the present statutory schemes for taxing gains on dispositions of stock in CFCs as dividend income or subpart F income. The Committee believes that it is appropriate to reduce complexities by rationalizing these rules.

The Committee also understands that certain arbitrary limitations placed on the operation of the indirect foreign tax credit may have resulted in taxpayers undergoing burdensome and sometimes costly corporate restructuring. In other cases, there is concern that these limitations may have contributed to decisions by U.S. companies against acquiring foreign subsidiaries. The Committee deems it appropriate to ease these restrictions.

Explanation of Provision

Lower-tier CFCs

Characterization of gain on stock disposition

Under the bill, if a CFC is treated as having gain from the sale or exchange of stock in a foreign corporation, the gain is treated as a dividend to the same extent that it would have been so treated under section 1248 if the CFC were a U.S. person. This provision, however, does not affect the determination of whether the corporation whose stock is sold or exchanged is a CFC.

Thus, for example, if a U.S. corporation owns 100 percent of the stock of a foreign corporation, which owns 100 percent of the stock of a second foreign corporation, then under the bill, any gain of the first corporation upon a sale or exchange of stock of the second corporation is treated as a dividend for purposes of subpart F income inclusions to the U.S. shareholder, to the extent of earnings and profits of the second corporation attributable to periods in which the first foreign corporation owned the stock of the second foreign corporation while the latter was a CFC with respect to the U.S. shareholder.

Gain on disposition of stock in a related corporation created or organized under the laws of, and having a substantial part of its assets in a trade or business in, the same foreign country as the gain recipient, even if recharacterized as a dividend under the proposal, is not excluded from foreign personal holding company income under the same-country exception that applies to actual dividends.

Under the bill, for purposes of this rule, a CFC is treated as having sold or exchanged stock if, under any provision of subtitle A of the Code, the CFC is treated as having gain from the sale or exchange of such stock. Thus, for example, if a CFC distributes to its shareholder stock in a foreign corporation, and the distribution results in gain being recognized by the CFC under section 311(b) as if the stock were sold to the shareholder for fair market value, the bill makes clear that, for purposes of this rule, the CFC is treated as having sold or exchanged the stock.

The bill also repeals a provision added to the Code by the Technical and Miscellaneous Revenue Act of 1988 that, except as provided by regulations, requires a recipient of a distribution from a CFC to have been a U.S. 10-percent shareholder of that CFC for the period during which the earnings and profits which gave rise to the distribution were generated in order to avoid treating the distribution as one coming from a 10/50 company. Thus, under the bill, a CFC is not treated as a 10/50 company with respect to any distribution out of its earnings and profits for periods during which it was a CFC, whether or not the recipient of the distribution was a U.S. 10-percent shareholder of the corporation when the earnings and profits giving rise to the distribution were generated.

Adjustments to basis of stock

Under the bill, when a lower-tier CFC earns subpart F income, and stock in that corporation is later disposed of by an upper-tier CFC, the resulting income inclusion of the U.S. 10-percent shareholders, under regulations, is to be adjusted to account for previous inclusions, in a manner similar to the adjustments provided to the basis of stock in a first-tier CFC. Thus, just as the basis of a U.S. 10-percent shareholder in a first-tier CFC rises when subpart F income is earned and falls when previously taxed income is distributed, so as to avoid double taxation of the income on a later disposition of the stock of that company, the subpart F income from gain on the disposition of a lower-tier CFC generally is reduced by income inclusions of earnings that were not subsequently distributed by the lower-tier CFC.

For example, assume that a U.S. person is the owner of all of the stock of a first-tier CFC which, in turn, is the sole shareholder of a second-tier CFC. In year 1, the second-tier CFC earns $100 of subpart F income which is included in the U.S. person's gross income for that year. In year 2, the first-tier CFC disposes of the second-tier CFC's stock and recognizes $300 of income with respect to the disposition. All of that income constitutes subpart F foreign personal holding company income. Under the bill, the Secretary is granted regulatory authority to reduce the U.S. person's year 2 subpart F inclusion by $100—the amount of year 1 subpart F income of the second-tier CFC that was included, in that year, in the U.S. person's gross income. Such an adjustment, in effect, allows for a step-up in the basis of the stock of the second-tier CFC to the extent of its subpart F income previously included in the U.S. person's gross income.

Subpart F inclusions in year of acquisition

If a U.S. 10-percent shareholder acquires the stock of a CFC from another U.S. 10-percent shareholder during a taxable year of the CFC in which it earns subpart F income, the proposal reduces the acquiror's subpart F income inclusion for that year by a portion of the amount of the dividend deemed (under sec. 1248) to be received by the transferor. The portion by which the inclusion is reduced (as is the case if a dividend was paid to the previous owner of the stock) does not exceed the lesser of the amount of dividends with respect to such stock deemed received (under sec. 1248) by other persons during the year or the amount determined by multiplying the subpart F income for the year by the proportion of the year during which the acquiring shareholder did not own the stock.

Treatment of U.S. income earned by a CFC

Under the bill, an exemption or reduction by treaty of the branch profits tax that would be imposed under section 884 on a CFC does not affect the general statutory exemption from subpart F income that is granted for U.S. source effectively connected income. For example, assume a CFC earns income of a type that generally would be subpart F income, and that income is earned from sources within the United States in connection with business operations therein. Further assume that repatriation of that income is exempted from the U.S. branch profits tax under a provision of an applicable U.S. income tax treaty. The bill provides that, notwithstanding the treaty's effect on the branch tax, the income is not treated as subpart F income as long as it is not exempt from U.S. taxation (or subject to a reduced rate of tax) under any other treaty provision.

Extension of indirect foreign tax credit

The bill extends the application of the indirect foreign tax credit (secs. 902 and 960) to taxes paid or accrued by certain fourth-, fifth-, and sixth-tier foreign corporations. In general, three requirements are required to be satisfied by a foreign company at any of these tiers to qualify for the credit. First, the company must be a CFC. Second, the U.S. corporation claiming the credit under section 902(a) must be a U.S. shareholder (as defined in sec. 951(b)) with respect to the foreign company. Third, the

product of the percentage ownership of voting stock at each level from the U.S. corporation down must equal at least 5 percent. The bill limits the application of the indirect foreign tax credit below the third tier to taxes paid or incurred in taxable years during which the payor is a CFC. Foreign taxes paid below the sixth tier of foreign corporations remain ineligible for the indirect foreign tax credit.

Effective Dates

Lower-tier CFCs

The provision that treats gains on dispositions of stock in lower-tier CFCs as dividends under section 1248 principles applies to gains recognized on transactions occurring after the date of enactment.

The provision that expands look-through treatment, for foreign tax credit limitation purposes, of dividends from CFCs is effective for distributions after the date of enactment.

The provision that provides for regulatory adjustments to U.S. shareholder inclusions, with respect to gains of CFCs from dispositions of stock in lower-tier CFCs is effective for determining inclusions for taxable years of U.S. shareholders beginning after December 31, 1997. Thus, the bill permits regulatory adjustments to an inclusion occurring after the effective date to account for income that was previously taxed under the subpart F provisions either prior to or subsequent to the effective date.

Subpart F inclusions in year of acquisition

The provision that permits dispositions of stock to be taken into consideration in determining a U.S. shareholder's subpart F inclusion for a taxable year is effective with respect to dispositions occurring after the date of enactment.

Treatment of U.S. source income earned by a CFC

The provision concerning the effect of treaty exemptions from, or reductions of, the branch profits tax on the determination of subpart F income is effective for taxable years beginning after December 31, 1986.

Extension of indirect foreign tax credit

The provision that extends application of the indirect foreign tax credit to certain CFCs below the third tier is effective for foreign taxes paid or incurred by CFCs for taxable years of such corporations beginning after the date of enactment.

In the case of any chain of foreign corporations, the taxes of which would be eligible for the indirect foreign tax credit, under present law or under the bill, but for the denial of indirect credits below the third or sixth tier, as the case may be, no liquidation, reorganization, or similar transaction in a taxable year beginning after the date of enact-ment will have the effect of permitting taxes to be taken into account under the indirect foreign tax credit provisions of the Code which could not have been taken into account under those provisions but for such transaction.

[*Conference Report*]

Senate Amendment

The Senate amendment is the same as the House bill.

Conference Agreement

The conference agreement follows the House bill and the Senate amendment.

[¶ 5178]   Section 1121-1124.   Passive Foreign Investment Companies

(Code Sec. 1296, 1297)

[House Report]

Present Law

Overview

U.S. citizens and residents and U.S. corporations (collectively, "U.S. persons") are taxed currently by the United States on their worldwide income, subject to a credit against U.S. tax on foreign income based on foreign income taxes paid with respect to such income. A foreign corporation generally is not subject to U.S. tax on its income from operations outside the United States.

Income of a foreign corporation generally is taxed by the United States when it is repatriated to the United States through payment to the corporation's U.S. shareholders, subject to a foreign tax credit. However, a variety of regimes imposing current U.S. tax on income earned through a foreign corporation have been reflected in the Code. Today the principal anti-deferral regimes set forth in the Code are the controlled foreign corporation rules of subpart F (secs. 951 964) and the passive foreign investment company rules (secs. 1291 1297). Additional anti-deferral regimes set forth in the Code are the foreign personal holding company rules (secs. 551 558); the personal holding company rules (secs. 541 547); the accumulated earnings tax (secs. 531 537); and the foreign investment company and electing foreign investment company rules (secs. 1246 1247). The anti-deferral regimes included in the Code overlap such that a given taxpayer may be subject to multiple sets of anti-deferral rules.

Controlled foreign corporations

A controlled foreign corporation (CFC) is defined generally as any foreign corporation if U.S. persons own more than 50 percent of the corporation's stock (measured by vote or value), taking into account only those U.S. persons that own at least 10 percent of the stock (measured by vote only) (sec. 957). Stock ownership includes not only stock owned directly, but also stock owned indirectly or constructively (sec. 958).

Certain income of a CFC (referred to as "subpart F income") is subject to current U.S. tax. The United States generally taxes the U.S. 10-percent shareholders of a CFC currently on their pro rata shares of the subpart F income of the CFC. In effect, the Code treats those U.S. shareholders as having received a current distribution out of the CFC's subpart F income. Such shareholders also are subject to current U.S. tax on their pro rata shares of the CFC's earnings invested in U.S. property. The foreign tax credit may reduce the U.S. tax on these amounts.

Passive foreign investment companies

The Tax Reform Act of 1986 established an anti-deferral regime for passive foreign investment companies (PFICs). A PFIC is any foreign corporation if (1) 75 percent or more of its gross income for the taxable year consists of passive income, or (2) 50 percent or more of the average fair market value of its assets consists of assets that produce, or are held for the production of, passive income. For purposes of applying the PFIC asset test, the assets of a CFC are required to be measured using adjusted basis; the assets of a foreign corporation that is not a CFC are measured using fair market value unless the corporation elects to use adjusted basis. Two alternative sets of income inclusion rules apply to U.S. persons that are shareholders in a PFIC. One set of rules applies to PFICs that are "qualified electing funds," under which electing U.S. shareholders include currently in gross income their respective shares of the PFIC's total earnings, with a separate election to defer payment of tax, subject to an interest charge, on income not currently received. The second set of rules applies to PFICs that are not qualified electing funds ("non-qualified funds"), under which the U.S. shareholders pay tax on income realized from the PFIC and an interest charge that is attributable to the value of deferral.

Overlap between subpart F and the PFIC provisions

A foreign corporation that is a CFC is also a PFIC if it meets the passive income test or the passive asset test described above. In such a case, the 10-percent U.S. shareholders are subject both to the subpart F provisions (which require current inclusion of certain earnings of the corporation) and to the PFIC provisions (which impose an interest charge on amounts distributed from the corporation and gains recognized upon the disposition of the corporation's stock, unless an election is made to include currently all of the corporation's earnings).

Reasons for Change

The anti-deferral rules for U.S. persons owning stock in foreign corporations are very complex. Moreover, the interactions between the anti-deferral regimes cause additional complexity. The overlap between the subpart F rules and the PFIC provisions is of particular concern to the Committee. The PFIC provisions, which do not require a threshold level of ownership by U.S. per-

sons, apply where the U.S.-ownership requirements of subpart F are not satisfied. However, the PFIC provisions also apply to a U.S. shareholder that is subject to the current inclusion rules of subpart F with respect to the same corporation. The Committee believes that the additional complexity caused by this overlap is unnecessary.

The Committee also understands that the interest-charge method for income inclusion provided in the PFIC rules is a substantial source of complexity for shareholders of PFICs. Even without eliminating the interest-charge method, significant simplification can be achieved by providing an alternative income inclusion method for shareholders of PFICs. Further, some taxpayers have argued that they would have preferred choosing the current-inclusion method afforded by the qualified fund election, but were unable to do so because they could not obtain the necessary information from the PFIC. Accordingly, the Committee believes that a mark-to-market election would provide PFIC shareholders with a fair alternative method for including income with respect to the PFIC.

Explanation of Provision

Elimination of overlap between subpart F and the PFIC provisions

In the case of a PFIC that is also a CFC, the bill generally treats the corporation as not a PFIC with respect to certain 10-percent shareholders. This rule applies if the corporation is a CFC (within the meaning of section 957(a)) and the shareholder is a U.S. shareholder (within the meaning of section 951(b)) of such corporation (i.e., if the shareholder is subject to the current inclusion rules of subpart F with respect to such corporation). Moreover, the rule applies for that portion of the shareholder's holding period with respect to the corporation's stock which is after December 31, 1997 and during which the corporation is a CFC and the shareholder is a U.S. shareholder. Accordingly, a shareholder that is subject to current inclusion under the subpart F rules with respect to stock of a PFIC that is also a CFC generally is not subject also to the PFIC provisions with respect to the same stock. The PFIC provisions continue to apply in the case of a PFIC that is also a CFC to shareholders that are not subject to subpart F (i.e., to shareholders that are U.S. persons and that own (directly, indirectly, or constructively) less than 10 percent of the corporation's stock by vote).

If a shareholder of a PFIC is subject to the rules applicable to nonqualified funds before becoming eligible for the special rules provided under the proposal for shareholders that are subject to subpart F, the stock held by such shareholder continues to be treated as PFIC stock unless the shareholder makes an election to pay tax and an interest charge with respect to the unrealized appreciation in the stock or the accumulated earnings of the corporation.

If, under the bill, a shareholder is not subject to the PFIC provisions because the shareholder is subject to subpart F and the shareholder subsequently ceases to be subject to subpart F with respect to the corporation, for purposes of the PFIC provisions, the shareholder's holding period for such stock is treated as beginning immediately after such cessation. Accordingly, in applying the rules applicable to PFICs that are not qualified electing funds, the earnings of the corporation are not attributed to the period during which the shareholder was subject to subpart F with respect to the corporation and was not subject to the PFIC provisions.

Mark-to-market election

The bill allows a shareholder of a PFIC to make a mark-to-market election with respect to the stock of the PFIC, provided that such stock is marketable (as defined below). Under such an election, the shareholder includes in income each year an amount equal to the excess, if any, of the fair market value of the PFIC stock as of the close of the taxable year over the shareholder's adjusted basis in such stock. The shareholder is allowed a deduction for the excess, if any, of the adjusted basis of the PFIC stock over its fair market value as of the close of the taxable year. However, deductions are allowable under this rule only to the extent of any net mark-to-market gains with respect to the stock included by the shareholder for prior taxable years.

Under the bill, this mark-to-market election is available only for PFIC stock that is

"marketable." For this purpose, PFIC stock is considered marketable if it is regularly traded on a national securities exchange that is registered with the Securities and Exchange Commission or on the national market system established pursuant to section 11A of the Securities and Exchange Act of 1934. In addition, PFIC stock is considered marketable if it is regularly traded on any exchange or market that the Secretary of the Treasury determines has rules sufficient to ensure that the market price represents a legitimate and sound fair market value. Any option on stock that is considered marketable under the foregoing rules is treated as marketable, to the extent provided in regulations. PFIC stock also is treated as marketable, to the extent provided in regulations, if the PFIC offers for sale (or has outstanding) stock of which it is the issuer and which is redeemable at its net asset value in a manner comparable to a U.S. regulated investment company (RIC).

In addition, the bill treats as marketable any PFIC stock owned by a RIC that offers for sale (or has outstanding) any stock of which it is the issuer and which is redeemable at its net asset value. The bill treats as marketable any PFIC stock held by any other RIC that otherwise publishes net asset valuations at least annually, except to the extent provided in regulations. It is believed that even for RICs that do not make a market in their own stock, but that do regularly report their net asset values in compliance with the securities laws, inaccurate valuation may bring exposure to legal liabilities, and this exposure may ensure the reliability of the values such RICs assign to the PFIC stock they hold.

The shareholder's adjusted basis in the PFIC stock is adjusted to reflect the amounts included or deducted under this election. In the case of stock owned indirectly by a U.S. person through a foreign entity (as discussed below), the basis adjustments for mark-to-market gains and losses apply to the basis of the PFIC in the hands of the intermediary owner, but only for purposes of the subsequent application of the PFIC rules to the tax treatment of the indirect U.S. owner. In addition, similar basis adjustments are made to the adjusted basis of the property actually held by the U.S.

person by reason of which the U.S. person is treated as owning PFIC stock.

Amounts included in income pursuant to a mark-to-market election, as well as gain on the actual sale or other disposition of the PFIC stock, is treated as ordinary income. Ordinary loss treatment also applies to the deductible portion of any mark-to-market loss on PFIC stock, as well as to any loss realized on the actual sale or other disposition of PFIC stock to the extent that the amount of such loss does not exceed the net mark-to-market gains previously included with respect to such stock. The source of amounts with respect to a mark-to-market election generally is determined in the same manner as if such amounts were gain or loss from the sale of stock in the PFIC.

An election to mark to market applies to the taxable year for which made and all subsequent taxable years, unless the PFIC stock ceases to be marketable or the Secretary of the Treasury consents to the revocation of such election.

Under constructive ownership rules, U.S. persons that own PFIC stock through certain foreign entities may make this election with respect to the PFIC. These constructive ownership rules apply to treat PFIC stock owned directly or indirectly by or for a foreign partnership, trust, or estate as owned proportionately by the partners or beneficiaries, except as provided in regulations. Stock in a PFIC that is thus treated as owned by a person is treated as actually owned by that person for purposes of again applying the constructive ownership rules. In the case of a U.S. person that is treated as owning PFIC stock by application of this constructive ownership rule, any disposition by the U.S. person or by any other person that results in the U.S. person being treated as no longer owning the PFIC stock, as well as any disposition by the person actually owning the PFIC stock, is treated as a disposition by the U.S. person of the PFIC stock.

In addition, a CFC that owns stock in a PFIC is treated as a U.S. person that may make the election with respect to such PFIC stock. Any amount includible (or deductible) in the CFC's gross income pursuant to this mark-to-market election is treated as foreign personal holding company income (or a deduction allocable to foreign personal holding company income). The source of such amounts, however, is determined by reference to the actual residence of the CFC.

In the case of a taxpayer that makes the mark-to-market election with respect to stock in a PFIC that is a nonqualified fund after the beginning of the taxpayer's holding period with respect to such stock, a coordination rule applies to ensure that the taxpayer does not avoid the interest charge with respect to amounts attributable to periods before such election. A similar rule applies to RICs that make the mark-to-market election under this bill after the beginning of their holding period with respect to PFIC stock (to the extent that the RIC had not previously marked to market the stock of the PFIC).

Except as provided in the coordination rules described above, the rules of section 1291 (with respect to nonqualified funds) do not apply to a shareholder of a PFIC if a mark-to-market election is in effect for the shareholder's taxable year. Moreover, in applying section 1291 in a case where a mark-to-market election was in effect for any prior taxable year, the shareholder's holding period for the PFIC stock is treated as beginning immediately after the last taxable year for which such election applied.

A special rule applicable in the case of a PFIC shareholder that becomes a U.S. person treats the adjusted basis of any PFIC stock held by such person on the first day of the year in which such shareholder becomes a U.S. person as equal to the greater of its fair market value on such date or its adjusted basis on such date. Such rule applies only for purposes of the mark-to-market election.

Effective Date

The provision is effective for taxable years of U.S. persons beginning after December 31, 1997, and taxable years of foreign corporations ending with or within such taxable years of U.S. persons.

Senate Amendment

The Senate amendment is the same as the House bill.

Conference Agreement

The conference agreement follows the House bill and the Senate amendment with one modification to the rules regarding the measurement of assets for purposes of applying the PFIC asset test. Under the conference agreement, if the stock of a foreign corporation is publicly traded for the taxable year, the PFIC asset test is applied using fair market value for purposes of measuring the PFIC's assets. For this purpose, the stock of a foreign corporation is treated as publicly traded if such stock is readily tradeable on a national securities exchange that is registered with the Securities and Exchange Commission, the national market system established pursuant to section 11A of the Securities and Exchange Act of 1934, or any other exchange or market that the Secretary of the Treasury determines has rules sufficient to ensure that the market

price represents a sound fair market value. Because the PFIC asset test is applied based on quarterly measurements of the corporation's assets, it is intended that a corporation the stock of which is publicly traded on each such quarterly measurement date during the taxable year will be eligible for this asset measurement rule for such taxable year. In applying the PFIC asset test, it is intended that the total value of a publicly-traded foreign corporation's assets generally will be treated as equal to the sum of the aggregate value of its outstanding stock plus its liabilities.

The conference agreement does not change the rules applicable to non-publicly-traded foreign corporations for purposes of the measurement of assets in applying the PFIC asset test. Accordingly, CFCs that are not publicly traded continue to be required to measure their assets using adjusted basis, and any other foreign corporations that are not publicly traded continue to measure their assets using fair market value unless they elect to use adjusted basis.

[¶ 5182]   Section 1131, 1141, 1142. Simplify Formation and Operation of International Joint Ventures.

(Code Sec. 684, 1035, 6231)

Present Law

Under section 1491, an excise tax generally is imposed on transfers of property by a U.S. person to a foreign corporation as paid-in surplus or as a contribution to capital or to a foreign partnership, estate or trust. The tax is 35 percent of the amount of gain inherent in the property transferred but not recognized for income tax purposes at the time of the transfer. However, several exceptions to the section 1491 excise tax are available. Under section 1494(c), a substantial penalty applies in the case of a failure to report a transfer described in section 1491.

Section 367 applies to require gain recognition upon certain transfers by U.S. persons to foreign corporations. Under section 367(d), a U.S. person that contributes intangible property to a foreign corporation is

treated as having sold the property to the corporation and is treated as receiving deemed royalty payments from the corporation. These deemed royalty payments are treated as U.S. source income. A U.S. person may elect to apply similar rules to a transfer of intangible property to a foreign partnership that otherwise would be subject to the section 1491 excise tax.

A foreign partnership may be required to file a partnership return. If a foreign partnership fails to file a required return, losses and credits with respect to the partnership may be disallowed to the partnership. A U.S. person that acquires or disposes of an interest in a foreign partnership, or whose proportional interest in the partnership changes substantially, may be required to file an information return with respect to such event.

A partnership generally is considered to be a domestic partnership if it is created or organized in the United States or under the laws of the United States or any State. A foreign partnership generally is any partnership that is not a domestic partnership.

[Senate Report]

Reasons for Change

The Committee understands that the present-law rules imposing an excise tax on certain transfers of appreciated property to a foreign entity unless the requirements for an exception from such excise tax are satisfied operate as a trap for the unwary. The Committee further understands that the special source rule of present law for deemed royalty payments with respect to a transfer of an appreciated intangible to a foreign corporation was intended to discourage such transfers. The Committee believes that the imposition of enhanced information reporting obligations with respect to both foreign partnerships and foreign corporations would eliminate the need for both of these sets of rules.

Explanation of Provision

The bill repeals the sections 1491-1494 excise tax and information reporting rules that apply to certain transfers of appreciated property by a U.S. person to a foreign entity. Instead of the excise tax that applies under present law to transfers to a foreign estate or trust, gain recognition is required upon a transfer of appreciated property by a U.S. person to a foreign estate or trust. Instead of the excise tax that applies under present law to certain transfers to foreign corporations, regulatory authority is granted under section 367 to deny nonrecognition treatment to such a transfer in a transaction that is not otherwise described in section 367. Instead of the excise tax that applies under present law to transfers to foreign partnerships, regulatory authority is granted to provide for gain recognition on a transfer of appreciated property to a partnership in cases where such gain otherwise would be transferred to a foreign partner. In addition, regulatory authority is granted to deny the nonrecognition treatment that is provided under section 1035 to certain exchanges of insurance policies, where the transfer is to a foreign person.

The bill repeals the rule that treats as U.S. source income any deemed royalty arising under section 367(d). Under the bill, in the case of a transfer of intangible property to a foreign corporation, the deemed royalty payments under section 367(d) are treated as foreign source income to the same extent that an actual royalty payment would be considered to be foreign source income. Regulatory authority is granted to provide similar treatment in the case of a transfer of intangible property to a foreign partnership.

The bill provides detailed information reporting rules in the case of foreign partnerships. A foreign partnership generally is required to file a partnership return for a taxable year if the partnership has U.S. source income or is engaged in a U.S. trade or business, except to the extent provided in regulations.

Under the bill, reporting rules similar to those applicable under present law in the case of controlled foreign corporations apply in the case of foreign partnerships. A U.S. partner that controls a foreign partnership is required to file an annual information return with respect to such partnership. For this purpose, a U.S. partner is considered to control a foreign partnership if the partner holds a more than 50 percent interest in the capital, profits, or, to the extent provided in regulation s, losses, of the partnership. Similar information reporting also will be required from a U.S. 10-percent partner of a foreign partnership that is controlled by U.S. 10-percent partners. A $10,000 penalty applies to a failure to comply with these reporting requirements; additional penalties of up to $50,000 apply in the case of continued noncompliance after notification by the Secretary of the Treasury. Under the bill, the penalties for failure to report information with respect to a controlled foreign corporation are conformed with these penalties.

Under the bill, reporting by a U.S. person of an acquisition or disposition of an interest in a foreign partnership, or a change in the person's proportional interest in the partnership, is required only in the case of acquisitions, dispositions, or changes involving at least a 10-percent interest. A $10,000 penalty applies to a failure to comply with these reporting requirements; additional penalties of up to $50,000 apply in the case of continued noncompliance after notification by the Secreta ry. Under the bill, the penalties for failure to report information with respect to a foreign corporation are conformed with these penalties.

Under the bill, reporting rules similar to those applicable under present law in the case of transfers by U.S. persons to foreign corporations apply in the case of transfers to foreign partnerships. These reporting rules apply in the case of a transfer to a foreign partnership only if the U.S. person holds at least a 10- percent interest in the partnership or the value of the property transferred by such person to the partnership during a 12- month period exceeded $100,000. A penalty equal to 10 percent of the value of the property transferred applies to a failure to comply with these reporting requirements. Under the bill, the penalty under present law for failure to report transfers to a foreign corporation is conformed with this penalty. In the case of a transfer to a foreign partnership, failure to comply also results in gain recognition with respect to the property transferred.

Under the bill, in the case of a failure to report required information with respect to a foreign corporation, partnership, or trust, the statute of limitations with respect to any event or period to which such information relates not expire before the date that is three years after the date on which such information is provided.

Under the bill, regulatory authority is granted to provide rules treating a partnership as a domestic or foreign partnership, where such treatment is more appropriate, without regard to where the partnership is created or organized. It is expected that a recharterization of a partnership under such regulations will be based only on material factors such as the residence of the partners and the extent to which the partnership is engaged in business in the United States or earns U.S. source income. It also is expected that such regulations will provide guidance regarding the determination of whether an entity that is a partnership for Federal income tax purposes is to be considered to be created or organized in the United States or under the law of the United States or any State.

Effective Date

The provisions with respect to the repeal of sections 1491-1494 are effective upon date of enactment. The provisions with respect to the source of a deemed royalty under section 367(d) also are effective for transfers made and royalties deemed received after date of enactment.

The provisions regarding information reporting with respect to foreign partnerships generally are effective for partnership taxable years beginning after date of enactment. The provisions regarding information reporting with respect to interests in, and transfers to, foreign partnerships are effective for transfers to, and changes in interest in, foreign partnerships after date of enactment. Taxpayers may elect to apply these rules to transfers made after August 20, 1996 (and thereby avoid a penalty under section 1494(c)) and the Secretary may prescribe simplified reporting requirements for these cases. The provision with respect to the statute of limitations in the case of noncompliance with reporting requirements is effective for information returns due after date of enactment.

The provision granting regulatory authority with respect to the treatment of partnerships as foreign or domestic is effective for partnership taxable years beginning after date of enactment.

[Conference Report]

Conference Agreement

The conference agreement generally follows the Senate amendment with modifications.

The conference agreement clarifies that, for purposes of the requirement of gain recognition upon a transfer of appreciated property by a U.S. person to a foreign estate or trust, a U.S. trust that becomes a foreign trust is treated as having transferred all of its assets to a foreign trust.

The conference agreement further clarifies that, in the case of a transfer by a U.S. person to a foreign corporation as paid- in surplus or as a contribution to capital in a transaction not otherwise described in section 367 (e.g., a capital contribution by a non-shareholder), regulatory authority is granted under section 367 to treat such transfer as a fair market value sale and to require gain recognition thereon.

For purposes of the information reporting rules applicable to a U.S. partner that controls a foreign partnership, the conference agreement clarifies that a partner's interest in a partnership is determined with application of constructive ownership rules similar to those provided in section 267(c) (other than paragraph (3)).

Finally, the conference agreement provides that regulations issued under the grant of regulatory authority to provide rules treating a partnership as a domestic or foreign partnership will apply only to partnerships created or organized after the date such regulations are filed with the Federal

Register (or, if earlier, the date of a public notice substantially describing the expected contents of the regulations). Accordingly, regulations issued under this grant of regulatory authority will not be applied to reclassify pre-existing partnerships. In connection with this regulatory authority, the conferees wish to make clear that it is intended that the general rule for classifying a partnership as domestic or foreign will continue to be the place where the partnership is created or organized (or the laws under which it is created or organized), and that the regulations are expected to provide a different classification result only in unusual cases. The conferees also expect that any regulations will avoid period-by-period reclassifications of partnerships.

[¶ 5188]   Section 1146.   Modification of Reporting Threshold for Stock Ownership of a Foreign Corporation.

(Code Sec. 6046)

[House Report]

Present Law

Several provisions of the Code require U.S. persons to report information with respect to a foreign corporation in which they are shareholders or officers or directors. Sections 6038 and 6035 generally require every U.S. citizen or resident who is an officer, or director, or who owns at least 10 percent of the stock, of a foreign corporation that is a controlled foreign corporation or a foreign personal holding company to file Form 5471 annually.

Section 6046 mandates the filing of information returns by certain U.S. persons with respect to a foreign corporation upon the occurrence of certain events. U.S. persons required to file these information returns are those who acquire 5 percent or more of the value of the stock of a foreign corporation, others who become U.S. persons while owning that percentage of the stock of a foreign corporation, and U.S. citizens and residents who are officers or directors of foreign corporations with such U.S. ownership.

A failure to file the required information return under section 6038 may result in

monetary penalties or reduction of foreign tax credit benefits. A failure to file the required information returns under sections 6035 or 6046 may result in monetary penalties.

Reasons for Change

The Committee believes that it is appropriate to make the stock ownership threshold at which reporting with respect to an ownership interest in a foreign corporation is required generally parallel to the thresholds that apply in the case of other annual information reporting with respect to foreign corporations. The Committee believes that increasing the threshold for such reporting from 5 percent to 10 percent will reduce the compliance burdens on taxpayers.

Explanation of Provision

The bill increases the threshold for stock ownership of a foreign corporation that results in information reporting obligations under section 6046 from 5 percent (based on value) to 10 percent (based on vote or value).

Effective Date

The provision is effective for reportable transactions occurring after December 31, 1997.

[Conference Report]

Senate Amendment

The Senate amendment is the same as the House bill.

[¶ 5190]   Section 1161.   Trust Transition Rules.

(Code Sec. 7701)

[House Report]

Present Law

Under rules enacted with the Small Business Job Protection Act of 1996, a trust is considered to be a U.S. trust if two criteria are met. First, a court within the United States must be able to exercise primary supervision over the administration of the trust. Second, U.S. fiduciaries of the trust must have the authority to control all substantial decisions of the trust. A trust that does not satisfy both of these criteria is considered to be a foreign trust. These rules for defining a U.S. trust generally are effective for taxable years of a trust that begin after December 31, 1996. A trust that qualified as a U.S. trust under prior law could fail to qualify as a U.S. trust under these new criteria.

Reasons for Change

The change in the criteria for qualification as a U.S. trust could cause large numbers of existing domestic trusts to become foreign trusts, unless they are able to make

Conference Agreement

The conference agreement follows the House bill and the Senate amendment.

the modifications necessary to satisfy the new criteria. The Committee believes that an election is appropriate for those existing domestic trusts that prefer to continue to be subject to tax as U.S. trusts.

Explanation of Provision

Under the bill, the Secretary of the Treasury is granted authority to allow nongrantor trusts that had been treated as U.S. trusts under prior law to elect to continue to be treated as U.S. trusts, notwithstanding the new criteria for qualification as a U.S. trust.

Effective Date

The provision is effective for taxable years beginning after December 31, 1996.

[Conference Report]

Senate Amendment

The Senate amendment is the same as the House bill.

Conference Agreement

The conference agreement follows the House bill and the Senate amendment.

[¶ 5191]   Section 1162.   Simplification of Stock and Securities Trading Safe Harbor.

(Code Sec. 864)

[House Report]

Present Law

A non-resident alien individual or foreign corporation that is engaged in a trade or business within the United States is subject to U.S. taxation on its net income that is effectively connected with the trade or business, at graduated rates of tax. Under a "safe harbor" rule, foreign persons that trade in stocks or securities for their own accounts are not treated as engaged in a U.S. trade or business for this purpose.

For a foreign corporation to qualify for the safe harbor, it must not be a dealer in stock or securities. In addition, if the principal business of the foreign corporation is trading in stock or securities for its own account, the safe harbor generally does not apply if the principal office of the corporation is in the United States.

For foreign persons who invest in securities trading partnerships, the safe harbor applies only if the partnership is not a dealer in stock and securities. In addition, if the principal business of the partnership is trading stock or securities for its own account, the safe harbor generally does not apply if the principal office of the partnership is in the United States.

Under Treasury regulations which apply to both corporations and partnerships, the determination of the location of the entity's principal office turns on the location of various functions relating to operation of the entity, including communication with investors and the general public, solicitation and acceptance of sales of interests, and maintenance and audits of its books of account (Treas. reg. sec. 1.864 2(c)(2)(iii)). Under the regulations, the location of the entity's principal office does not depend on the location of the entity's management or where investment decisions are made.

Reasons for Change

The stock and securities trading safe harbor serves to promote foreign investment in U.S. capital markets. The Committee understands that the principal office rule operates simply to shift certain administrative functions with respect to securities trading—and the associated jobs—offshore. The Committee believes that the elimination of this rule would facilitate the foreign investment in U.S. markets that the safe harbor was designed to promote.

Because the location of a partnership's or foreign corporation's principal office is determined by the location of certain administrative functions rather than the location of management and investment decisions, the requirement of a foreign principal office is met even if only administrative functions are performed abroad.

Explanation of Provision

The bill modifies the stock and securities trading safe harbor by eliminating the requirement for both partnerships and foreign corporations that trade stock or securities for their own account that the entity's principal office not be within the United States.

Effective Date

The provision is effective for taxable years beginning after December 31, 1997.

[Conference Report]

Senate Amendment

The Senate amendment is the same as the House bill.

Conference Agreement

The conference agreement follows the House bill and the Senate amendment.

[¶ 5192]   Section 1163.   Determination of Foreign Taxes Deemed Paid.

(Code Sec. 902, 904)

[House Report]

Present Law

Under section 902, a domestic corporation that receives a dividend from a foreign corporation in which it owns 10 percent or more of the voting stock is deemed to have paid a portion of the foreign taxes paid by such foreign corporation. The domestic corporation that receives a dividend is deemed to have paid a portion of the foreign corporation's post-1986 foreign income taxes based on the ratio of the amount of such dividend to the foreign corporation's post-1986 undistributed earnings. The foreign corporation's post-1986 foreign income taxes is the sum of the foreign income taxes with respect to the taxable year in which the dividend is distributed plus certain foreign income taxes with respect to

prior taxable years (beginning after December 31, 1986).

Reasons for Change

The Committee believes that it is appropriate to clarify the determination of foreign taxes deemed paid for purposes of the indirect foreign tax credit.

Explanation of Provision

The bill clarifies that, for purposes of the deemed paid credit under section 902 for a taxable year, a foreign corporation's post-1986 foreign income taxes includes foreign income taxes with respect to prior taxable years (beginning after December 31, 1986) only to the extent such taxes are not attributable to dividends distributed by the foreign corporation in prior taxable years. No inference is intended regarding the determination of foreign taxes deemed paid under present law.

Effective Date

The provision is effective on date of enactment.

Senate Amendment

The Senate amendment is the same as the House bill.

Conference Agreement

The conference agreement follows the House bill and the Senate amendment.

Present Law

Under section 904, separate foreign tax credit limitations apply to various categories of income. Two of these separate limitation categories are passive income and financial services income. For purposes of the separate foreign tax credit limitation applicable to passive income, certain income that is treated as high-taxed income is excluded from the definition of passive income. For purposes of the separate foreign tax credit limitation applicable to financial services income, the definition of financial services income generally incorporates passive income as defined for purposes of the separate limitation applicable to passive income.

Reasons for Change

The Committee believes that it is appropriate to clarify that high-taxed income is not excluded from the separate foreign tax credit limitation for financial services income.

Explanation of Provision

The bill clarifies that the exclusion of income that is treated as high-taxed income does not apply for purposes of the separate foreign tax credit limitation applicable to financial services income. No inference is intended regarding the treatment of high-taxed income for purposes of the separate foreign tax credit limitation applicable to financial services income under present law.

Effective Date

The provision is effective on date of enactment.

[Conference Report]

Senate Amendment

The Senate amendment is the same as the House bill.

Conference Agreement

The conference agreement follows the House bill and the Senate amendment.

[¶ 5193]   Section 1171.   Treatment of computer software as Foreign sales corp. export property.

(Code Sec. 927)

[House Report]

Present Law

Under special tax provisions that provide an export benefit, a portion of the foreign trade income of an eligible foreign sales corporation ("FSC") is exempt from Federal income tax. Foreign trade income is defined as the gross income of an FSC that is attributable to foreign trading gross receipts. The term "foreign trading gross receipts" includes the gross receipts of an FSC from the sale, lease, or rental of export property and from services related and subsidiary to such sales, leases, or rentals.

For purposes of the FSC rules, export property is defined as property (1) which is manufactured, produced, grown, or extracted in the United States by a person other than an FSC; (2) which is held primarily for sale, lease, or rental in the ordinary conduct of a trade or business by or to an FSC for direct use, consumption, or disposition outside the United States; and (3) not more than 50 percent of the fair market value of which is attributable to articles imported into the United States. Intangible property generally is excluded from the definition of export property for purposes of the FSC rules; this exclusion applies to copyrights other than films, tapes, records, or similar reproductions for commercial or home use. The temporary Treasury regulations provide that a license of a master recording tape for reproduction outside the United States is not excluded from the definition of export property (Treas. Reg. sec. 1.927(a) 1T(f)(3)). The statutory exclusion for intangible property does not contain any specific reference to computer software. However, the temporary Treasury regulations provide that a copyright on computer software does not constitute export property, and that standardized, mass marketed computer software constitutes export property if such software is not accompanied by a right to reproduce for external use (Treas. Reg. sec. 1.927(a) 1T(f)(3)).

Reasons for Change

For purposes of the FSC provisions, films, tapes, records and similar reproductions explicitly are included within the definition of export property. In light of technological developments, the Committee believes that computer software is virtually indistinguishable from the enumerated films, tapes, and records. Accordingly, the Committee believes that the benefits of the FSC provisions similarly should be available to computer software.

Explanation of Provision

The bill provides that computer software licensed for reproduction abroad is not excluded from the definition of export property for purposes of the FSC provisions.

Accordingly, computer software that is exported with a right to reproduce is eligible for the benefits of the FSC provisions. In light of the rapid innovations in the computer and software industries, the Committee intends that the term "computer software" be construed broadly to accommodate technological changes in the products produced by both industries. No inference is intended regarding the qualification as export property of computer software licensed for reproduction abroad under present law.

[Conference Report]

Senate Amendment

The Senate amendment is the same as the House bill, with a modification to the effective date.

Effective Date

The provision applies to gross receipts from computer software licenses attributable to periods after December 31, 1997. Accordingly, in the case of a multi-year license, the provision applies to gross receipts attributable to the period of such license that is after December 31, 1997.

Conference Agreement

The conference agreement follows the Senate amendment.

[¶ 5194]   Section 1172.   Increase Dollar Limitation on section 911 Exclusion.

(Code Sec. 911)

[House Report]

Present Law

U.S. citizens generally are subject to U.S. income tax on all their income, whether derived in the United States or elsewhere. A U.S. citizen who earns income in a foreign country also may be taxed on such income by that foreign country. A credit against the U.S. income tax imposed on foreign source income is allowed for foreign taxes paid on such income.

U.S. citizens living abroad may be eligible to exclude from their income for U.S. tax purposes certain foreign earned income and foreign housing costs. In order to qualify for these exclusions, a U.S. citizen must

be either (1) a bona fide resident of a foreign country for an uninterrupted period that includes an entire taxable year or (2) present overseas for 330 days out of any 12 consecutive month period. In addition, the taxpayer must have his or her tax home in a foreign country.

The exclusion for foreign earned income generally applies to income earned from sources outside the United States as compensation for personal services actually rendered by the taxpayer. The maximum exclusion for foreign earned income for a taxable year is $70,000.

The exclusion for housing costs applies to reasonable expenses, other than deductible interest and taxes, paid or incurred by or on behalf of the taxpayer for housing for the taxpayer and his or her spouse and dependents in a foreign country. The exclusion amount for housing costs for a taxable year is equal to the excess of such housing costs for the taxable year over an amount computed pursuant to a specified formula.

The combined earned income exclusion and housing cost exclusion may not exceed the taxpayer's total foreign earned income. The taxpayer's foreign tax credit is reduced by the amount the credit that is attributable to excluded income.

Reasons for Change

The Committee recognizes that for U.S. businesses to be effective competitors overseas it is necessary to dispatch U.S. citizens or residents to sites of foreign operations. Being stationed abroad typically imposes additional financial burdens on the employee and his family. These burdens may arise from maintaining two homes (one in the United States and one abroad), additional personal travel to maintain family ties, or the added expenses of living in a foreign location that has a high cost of living. Businesses often remunerate their employees for these additional burdens by paying higher wages. Because the increased remuneration is offset by larger burdens, the remuneration does not truly reflect an increase in economic well being. The Committee, therefore, believes that the exclusion of section 911 is a simple way to prevent taxpayers from facing an increased tax burden when there has been no increase in economic well being by accepting an overseas assignment.

The Committee further observes that the present-law $70,000 exclusion has remained unchanged for the past 10 years, while the extra costs from working abroad have increased with worldwide inflation. The Committee, therefore, believes it is appropriate to increase the exclusion permitted under section 911. In addition, as a rough measure for the increased burden that may be expected to arise from future inflation, the Committee believes it is appropriate to index the level of the section 911 exclusion amount to future changes in the domestic cost of living.

Explanation of Provision

Under the bill, the $70,000 limitation on the exclusion for foreign earned income is increased to $80,000, in increments of $2,000 each year beginning in 1998. Under the bill, the limitation on the exclusion for foreign earned income then is indexed for inflation beginning in 2008 (for inflation after 2006).

Effective Date

The provision is effective for taxable years beginning after December 31, 1997.

[Conference Report]

Senate Amendment

No provision.

Conference Agreement

The conference agreement follows the House bill.

[¶ 5195]   Section 1173.   Treatment of Certain Securities Positions Under Subpart F.

(Code Sec. 956)

[Senate Report]

Present Law

Under the rules of subpart F (secs. 951-964), the U.S. 10- percent shareholders of a controlled foreign corporation (CFC) are required to include in income currently for U.S. tax purposes certain earnings of the CFC, whether or not such earnings are distributed currently to the shareholders. The U.S. 10-percent shareholders of a CFC are subject to current U.S. tax on their shares of certain income earned by the CFC (referred to as "subpart F income"). The U.S. 10-percent shareholders also are subject to current U.S. tax on their shares of the CFC's earnings to the extent invested by the CFC in certain U.S. property.

A shareholder's current income inclusion with respect to a CFC's investment in U.S. property for a taxable year is based on the CFC's average investment in U.S. property for such year. For this purpose, the U.S.

property held by the CFC must be measured as of the close of each quarter in the taxable year. U.S. property generally is defined to include tangible property located in the United States, stock of a U.S. corporation, obligations of a U.S. person, and the right to use certain intellectual property in the United States. Exceptions are provided for, among other things, obligations of the United States, U.S. bank deposits, certain trade or business obligations, and stock or debts of certain unrelated U.S. corporations.

Reasons for Change

The Committee believes that guidance is needed regarding the treatment of certain transactions entered into by securities dealers in the ordinary course of business under the investment in U.S. property provisions of subpart F. The Committee believes that deposits of collateral or margin in the ordinary course of business should not give rise to an income inclusion as an investment in U.S. property under the provisions of subpart F. Similarly, the Committee believes that repurchase agreements entered into in the ordinary course of business should not give rise to an income inclusion as an investment in U.S. property.

Explanation of Provision

The bill provides two additional exceptions from the definition of U.S. property for purposes of the subpart F rules. Both exceptions relate to transactions entered into by a securities or commodities dealer in the ordinary course of its business as a securities or commodities dealer.

The first exception covers the deposit of collateral or margin by a securities or commodities dealer, or the receipt of such a deposit by a securities or commodities dealer, if such deposit is made or received on commercial terms in the ordinary course of the dealer's business as a securities or commodities dealer. This exception applies to deposits of margin or collateral for securities

loans, notional principal contracts, options contracts, forward contracts, futures contracts, and any other financial transaction with respect to which the Secretary of the Treasury determines that the posting of collateral or margin is customary.

The second exception covers repurchase agreement transactions and reverse repurchase agreement transactions entered into by or with a securities or commodities dealer in the ordinary course of its business as a securities or commodities dealer. The exception applies only to the extent that the obligation under the transaction does not exceed the fair market value of readily marketable securities transferred or otherwise posted as collateral.

Effective Date

The provision is effective for taxable years of foreign corporations beginning after December 31, 1997, and taxable years of U.S. shareholders with or within which such taxable years of foreign corporations end.

[Conference Report]

House Bill

No provision.

Conference Agreement

The conference agreement generally follows the Senate amendment. Under the conference agreement, for purposes of these two additional exceptions under section 956, the term "dealer in commodities" means futures commission merchants and dealers in commodities within the meaning of the new definition that is added to section 475 by the conference agreement. In addition, the conferees wish to clarify that the addition of these two exceptions under section 956 is not intended to create any inference regarding the treatment of an obligation of a U.S. person to return stock that is borrowed pursuant to a securities loan.

[¶ 5196]   Section 1174.   Nonresident Alien Engaged in International Transport.

(Code Sec. 861, 863, 7701)

[Senate Report]

Present Law

Nonresident alien individuals generally are subject to U.S. taxation and withholding on their U.S. source income. Compensation for labor and personal services performed within the United States is considered U.S. source unless such income qualifies for a de minimis exception. To qualify for the exception, the compensation paid to a nonresident alien individual must not exceed $3,000, the compensation must reflect services performed on behalf of a foreign employer, and the individual must be present in the United Sates for not more than 90 days during the taxable year. Special rules apply to exclude certain items from the gross income of a nonresident alien. An exclusion applies to gross income derived by a nonresident alien individual from the international operation of a ship if the country in which such individual is resident provides a reciprocal exemption for U.S. residents. However, this exclusion does not apply to income from personal services performed by an individual crew member on board a ship. Consequently, wages exceeding $3,000 in a taxable year that are earned by nonresident alien individual crew members of a foreign ship while the vessel is within U.S. territory are subject to income taxation by the United States.

U.S. residents are subject to U.S. tax on their worldwide income. In general, a non-U.S. citizen is considered to be a resident of the United States if the individual (1) has entered the United States as a lawful permanent U.S. resident or (2) is present in the United States for 31 or more days during the current calendar year and has been present in the United States for a substantial period of time — 183 or more days — during a three-year period computed by weighting toward the present year (the "substantial presence test"). An individual generally is treated as present in the United States on any day if such individual is physically present in the United States at any time during the day. Certain categories of individuals (e.g., foreign government employees and certain students) are not treated as U.S. residents even if they are present in the United States for the requisite period of time. Crew members of a foreign vessel who are on board the vessel while it is stationed within U.S. territorial waters are treated as present in the United States.

Reasons for Change

The Committee understands that U.S. tax rules impose a significant compliance burden on nonresident alien individuals who are present in the United States for short periods of time as members of the regular crew of a foreign vessel and who may not be permitted to leave such vessel during those periods. The Committee believes that an exemption from U.S. tax is appropriate for the income earned by a nonresident alien individual from personal services performed as a member of the regular crew of a foreign vessel. Moreover, the Committee believes that such an individual's presence in the United States as a regular crew member of a foreign vessel should not be taken into account for purposes of determining whether the individual is treated as a resident alien for U.S. tax purposes.

Explanation of Provision

The bill treats gross income of a nonresident alien individual, who is present in the United States as a member of the regular crew of a foreign vessel, from the performance of personal services in connection with the international operation of a ship as income from foreign sources. Thus, such income is exempt from U.S. income and withholding tax. However, such persons are not excluded for purposes of applying the minimum participation standards of section 410 to a plan of the employer. In addition, for purposes of determining whether an individual is a U.S. resident under the substantial presence test, the bill provides that the days that such individual is present as a member of the regular crew of a foreign vessel are disregarded.

Effective Date

The provision is effective for taxable years beginning after December 31, 1997.

[*Conference Report*]

House Bill

No provision.

Conference Agreement

The conference agreement generally follows the Senate amendment with modifications. The conference agreement provides that the treatment of income of a nonresident alien crew member of a foreign vessel as foreign source income will not apply for purposes of the pension rules and certain employee benefit provisions. The conference agreement further provides that, for purposes of determining whether an individual is a U.S. resident under the substantial presence test, any day that such individual is present as a member of the regular crew of a foreign vessel is disregarded only if the individual does not otherwise engage in trade or business within the United States on such day.

[¶ 5197]   Section 1175.   Exemption for active financing income.

(Code Sec. 954)

[Senate Report]

Present Law

Under the subpart F rules, certain U.S. shareholders of a controlled foreign corporation ("CFC") are subject to U.S. tax currently on certain income earned by the CFC, whether or not such income is distributed to the shareholders. The income subject to current inclusion under the subpart F rules includes, among other things, "foreign personal holding company income" and insurance income. The U.S. 10-percent shareholders of a CFC also are subject to current inclusion with respect to their shares of the CFC's foreign base company services income (i.e., income derived from services performed for a related person outside the country in which the CFC is organized).

Foreign personal holding company income generally consists of the following: dividends, interest, royalties, rents and annuities; net gains from sales or exchanges of (1) property that gives rise to the preceding types of income, (2) property that does not give rise to income, and (3) interests in trusts, partnerships, and REMICs; net gains from commodities transactions; net gains from foreign currency transactions; and income that is equivalent to interest.

Insurance income suspect to current inclusion under the subpart F rules includes any income of a CFC attributable to the issuing or reinsuring of any insurance or annuity contract in connection with risks located in a country other than the CFC's country of organization. Subpart F insurance income also includes income attributable to an insurance contract in connection with risks located within the CFC's country of organization, as the result of an arrangement under which another corporation receives a substantially equal amount of consideration for insurance of other-country risks. Investment income of a CFC that is allocable to any insurance or annuity contract related to risks located outside the CFC's country of organization is taxable as subpart F insurance income (Prop. Treas. reg. sec. 1.953-1(a)). Investment income allocable to risks located within the CFC's country of organization generally is taxable as foreign personal holding company income.

Reasons for Change

The subpart F rules historically have been aimed at requiring current inclusion by the U.S. shareholders of income of a CFC that is either passive or easily movable. Prior to the enactment of the 1986 Act, exceptions from foreign personal holding company income were provided for income derived in the conduct of a banking, financing, or similar business or derived from certain investments made by an insurance company. The Committee is concerned that the 1986 Act's repeal of these exceptions has resulted in the extension of the subpart F provisions to income that is neither passive nor easily moveable. The Committee believes that the provision of exceptions from foreign personal holding company income for income from the active conduct of an insurance, banking, financing or similar business is appropriate.

Explanation of Provision

The bill provides a temporary exception from foreign personal holding company income for subpart F purposes for certain income that is derived in the active conduct of an insurance, banking, financing or similar business. Such exception is applicable only for taxable years beginning in 1998

Under the bill, foreign personal holding company income does not include income that is derived in or incident to the active conduct of a banking, financing or similar business by a CFC that is predominantly engaged in the active conduct of such business. For this purpose, income derived in the active conduct of a banking, financing, or similar business generally is determined under the principles applicable in determining financial services income for foreign tax credit limitation purposes. More over, the Secretary of the Treasury shall prescribe regulations applying look-through treatment in characterizing for this purpose dividends, interest, income equivalent to interest, rents, and royalties from related persons. A CFC is considered to be predominantly engaged in the active conduct of a banking, financing, or similar business if (1) more than 70 percent of its gross income is derived from transactions with unrelated persons and more than 20 percent of its gross income from that business is derived from transactions with unrelated persons located within the country in which the CFC is organized or incorporated, or (2) the CFC is predominantly engaged in the active conduct of a banking or securities business, or is a qualified bank or securities affiliate, as defined for purposes of the passive foreign investment company provisions.

Under the bill, foreign personal holding company income also does not include certain investment income of a qualifying insurance company with respect to risks located within the CFC's country of organization. These exceptions apply to income derived from investments of assets equal to the total of (1) unearned premiums and reserves ordinary and necessary for the proper conduct of the CFC's insurance business, (2) one-third of premiums earned during the taxable year on insurance contracts regulated in the country in which sold as property, casualty, or health insurance con-

tracts, and (3) the greater of $10 million or 10 percent of reserves for insurance contracts regulated in the country in which sold as life insurance or annuity contracts. For this purpose, a qualifying insurance company is an entity that is subject to regulation as an insurance company under the laws of its country of incorporation and that realizes at least 50 percent of its gross income (other than income from investments) from premiums related to risks located within such country. The bill's exceptions for insurance investment income do not apply to investment income which is received by the CFC from a related person. Similarly, the exceptions do not apply to investment income that is attributable directly or indirectly to the insurance or reinsurance of risks of related persons. The bill does not change the rule of present law that investment income of a CFC that is attributable to the issuing or reinsuring any insurance or annuity contract related to risks outside of its country of organization is taxable as Subpart F insurance income.

The bill also provides an exception from foreign base company services income for income derived from services performed in connection with the active conduct of a banking, financing, insurance or similar business by a CFC that is predominantly engaged in the active conduct of such business.

Effective Date

The provision applies only to taxable years of foreign corporations beginning in 1998, and to taxable years of United States shareholders with or within which such taxable years of foreign corporations end.

[Conference Report]

House Bill

No provision.

Conference Agreement

The conference agreement generally follows the Senate amendment with modifications.

Under the conference agreement, the temporary exception from foreign personal holding company income applies to income that is derived in the active conduct of a banking, financing or similar business by a

CFC that is predominantly engaged in the active conduct of such business. For this purpose, income derived in the active conduct of a banking, financing, or similar business generally is determined under the principles applicable in determining financial services income for foreign tax credit limitation purposes. However, in the case of a corporation that is engaged in the active conduct of a banking or securities business, the income that is eligible for this exception is determined under the principles applicable in determining the income which is treated as nonpassive income for purposes of the passive foreign investment company provisions. The conferees generally intend that the income of a corporation engaged in the active conduct of a banking or securities business that is eligible for this exception is the income that is treated as nonpassive under the regulations proposed under section 1296(b). See Prop. Treas. Reg. secs. 1.1296-4 and 1.1296-6. In this regard, the conferees intend that eligible income will include income or gains with respect to foreclosed property which is incident to the active conduct of a banking business.

For purposes of the temporary exception, a corporation is considered to be predominantly engaged in the active conduct of a banking, financing, or similar business if it is engaged in the active conduct of a banking or securities business or is a qualified bank affiliate or qualified securities affiliate. In this regard, the conferees intend that a corporation will be considered to be engaged in the active conduct of a banking or securities business if the corporation would be treated as so engaged under the regulations proposed under section 1296(b); the conferees further intend that qualified bank affiliates and qualified securities affiliates will be as determined under such proposed regulations. See Prop. Treas. Reg. secs. 1.1296-4 and 1.1296-6.

Alternatively, a corporation is considered to be engaged in the active conduct of a banking, financing or similar business if more than 70 percent of its gross income is derived from such business from transactions with unrelated persons located within the country under the laws of which the corporation is created or organized. For this purpose, income derived by a qualified business unit of a corporation from transactions with unrelated persons located in the country in which the qualified business unit maintains its principal office and conducts substantial business activity is treated as derived by the corporation from transactions with unrelated persons located within the country in which the corporation is created or organized. A person other than a natural person is considered to be located within the country in which it maintains an office through which it engages in a trade or business and by which the transaction is effected. A natural person is treated as located within the country in which such person is physically located when such person enters into the transaction.

The conference agreement provides a temporary exception from foreign personal holding company income for certain investment income of a qualifying insurance company with respect to risks located within the CFC's country of creation or organization. The rules of this provision of the conference agreement differ from the rules of present-law section 953 of the Code, which determines the subpart F inclusions of a U.S. shareholder relating to insurance income of a CFC. Such insurance income under section 953 generally is computed in accordance with the rules of subchapter L of the Code. The conferees believe that review of the rules of this provision would be appropriate when final guidance under section 953 is published by the Treasury Department.

The conference agreement provides a temporary exception for income (received from a person other than a related person) from investments made by a qualifying insurance company of its reserves or 80 percent of its unearned premiums (as defined for purposes of the provision). For this purpose, in the case of contracts regulated in the country in which sold as property, casualty, or health insurance contracts, unearned premiums and reserves mean unearned premiums and reserves for losses incurred determined using the methods and interest rates that would be used if the qualifying insurance company were subject to tax under subchapter L of the Code. Thus, for this purpose, unearned premiums are determined in accordance with section 832(b)(4), and reserves for losses incurred are determined in accordance with section 832(b)(5) and 846 of the Code (as well as any other rules applicable to a U.S. property and casualty insurance company with respect to such amounts).

In the case of a contract regulated in the country in which sold as a life insurance or annuity contract, the following three alternative rules for determining reserves are provided under the conference agreement. It is intended that any one of the three rules may be elected with respect to a particular line of business.

First, reserves for such contracts may be determined generally under the rules applicable to domestic life insurance companies under subchapter L of the Code, using the methods there specified, but substituting for the interest rates in Code section 807(d)(2)(B) an interest rate determined for the country in which the qualifying insurance company was created or organized, calculated in the same manner as the mid-term applicable Federal interest rate ("AFR") (within the meaning of section 1274(d)).

Second, the reserves for such contracts may be determined generally using a preliminary term foreign reserve method, except that the interest rate to be used is the interest rate determined for the country in which the qualifying insurance company was created or organized, calculated in the same manner as the mid-term AFR. If a qualifying insurance company uses such a preliminary term method with respect to contracts insuring risks located in the country in which the company is created or organized, then such method is the method that applies for purposes of this election.

Third, reserves for such contracts may be determined to be equal to the net surrender value of the contract (as defined in section 807(e)(1)(A)).

In no event may the reserve for any contract at any time exceed the foreign statement reserve for the contract, reduced by any catastrophe or deficiency reserve. This rule applies whether the contract is regulated as a property, casualty, health, life insurance, annuity, or any other type of contract.

The conference agreement also provides a temporary exception for income from investment of assets equal to (1) one-third of premiums earned during the taxable year on insurance contracts regulated in the country in which sold as property, casualty, or health insurance contacts, and (2) the greater of 10 percent of reserves, or, in the case of a qualifying insurance company that is a startup company, $10 million. For this purpose, a startup company is a company (including any predecessor) that has not been engaged in the active conduct of an insurance business for more than 5 years. It is intended that the 5-year period commences when the foreign company first is engaged in the active conduct of an insurance business. If the foreign company was formed before being acquired by the U.S. shareholder, the 5-year period commences when the acquired company first was engaged in the active conduct of an insurance business. The conferees intend that in the event of the acquisition of a book of business from another company through an assumption or indemnity reinsurance transaction, the period commences when the acquiring company first engaged in the active conduct of an insurance business, except that if more than a substantial part (e.g., 80 percent) of the business of the ceding company is acquired, then the 5-year period commences when the ceding company first engaged in the active conduct of an insurance business. In addition, it is not intended that reinsurance transactions among related persons be used to multiply the number of 5-year periods.

To prevent the shifting of relatively high-yielding assets to generate investment income that qualifies under this temporary exception, the conference agreement provides that, under rules prescribed by the Secretary, income is allocated to contracts as follows. In the case of contracts that are separate-account-type contracts (including variable contracts not meeting the requirements of section 817), only the income specifically allocable to such contracts is taken into account. In the case of other contracts, income not specifically allocable is allocated ratably among such contracts.

The conference agreement modifies the definition of a qualifying insurance company. Under the conference agreement, a qualifying insurance company means any entity which: (1) is regulated as an insurance company under the laws of the country in which it is incorporated; (2) derives at least 50 percent of its net written premiums from the insurance or reinsurance of risks situated within its country of incorporation; and (3) is engaged in the active conduct of an insurance business and would be subject to tax under subchapter L if it were a domestic corporation.

The conference agreement clarifies that this provision does not apply to investment income (includable in the income of a U.S. shareholder of a CFC pursuant to section 953) allocable to contracts that insure related party risks or risks located in a country other than the country in which the qualifying insurance company is created or organized.

Finally, the conference agreement provides an anti-abuse rule applicable for purposes of these temporary exceptions from foreign personal holding company income. For purposes of applying these exceptions, items with respect to a transaction or series of transactions shall be disregarded if one of the principal purposes of the transaction or transactions is to qualify income or gain for these exceptions, including any change in the method of computing reserves or any other transaction or transactions one of the principal purposes of which is the accelera-

tion or deferral of any item in order to claim the benefits of these exceptions.

The conferees recognize that insurance, banking, financing, and similar businesses are businesses the active conduct of which involves the generation of income, such as interest and dividends, of a type that generally is treated as passive for purposes of subpart F. For purposes of this temporary provision, the conferees intend to delineate the income derived in the active conduct of such businesses, while retaining the present-law anti- deferral rules of subpart F with respect to income not derived in the active conduct of these financial services businesses. However, the conferees recognize that the line between income derived in the active conduct of such businesses and income otherwise derived by entities so engaged can be difficult to draw. The conferees believe that the issues of the determination of income derived in the active conduct of such businesses and the potential mobility of the business activity and income recognition of insurance, banking, financing, and similar businesses require further study. In the event that it becomes necessary to consider a possible extension of the provision in the future, the conferees would invite the comments of taxpayers and the Treasury Department regarding these issues.

[¶ 5201]   Section 1201.   Modifications to standard deduction of dependents; AMT treatment of certain minor children.

(Code Sec. 63, 59, 6103)

[House Report]

Present Law

Standard deduction of dependents. —The standard deduction of a taxpayer for whom a dependency exemption is allowed on another taxpayer's return can not exceed the lesser of (1) the standard deduction for an individual taxpayer (projected to be $4,250 for 1998) or (2) the greater of $500 (indexed)[1] or the dependent's earned income (sec. 63(c)(5)).

Taxation of unearned income of children under age 14. —The tax on a portion of the

unearned income (e.g., interest and dividends) of a child under age 14 is the additional tax that the child's custodial parent would pay if the child's unearned income were included in that parent's income. The portion of the child's unearned income which is taxed at the parent's top marginal rate is the amount by which the child's unearned income is more than the sum of (1) $500[2] (indexed) plus (2) the greater of (a) $500[3] (indexed) or (b) the child's itemized deductions directly connected with the production of the unearned income (sec. 1(g)).

---

1. The indexed amount is projected to be $700 for 1998
2. Projected to be $700 for 1998.

3. Projected to be $700 for 1998.

Alternative minimum tax ("AMT") exemption for children under age 14. —Single taxpayers are entitled to an exemption from the alternative minimum tax ("AMT") of $33,750. However, in the case of a child under age 14, his exemption from the AMT, in substance, is the unused alternative minimum tax exemption of the child's custodial parent, limited to sum of earned income and $1,400 (sec. 59(j)).

Reasons for Change

The Committee believes that significant simplification of the existing income tax system can be achieved by providing larger exemptions such that taxpayers with incomes less than the exemption are not required to compute and pay any tax. The Committee particularly believes that the present-law exemptions of dependent children are too small.

Explanation of Provision

Standard deduction of dependents. —The bill increases the standard deduction for a taxpayer with respect to whom a dependency exemption is allowed on another taxpayer's return to the lesser of (1) the standard deduction for individual taxpayers or (2) the greater of: (a) $500[4] (indexed for inflation as under present law), or (b) the individual's earned income plus $250. The $250 amount is indexed for inflation after 1998.

Alternative minimum tax exemption for children under age 14. —The bill increases the AMT exemption amount for a child under age 14 to the lesser of (1) $33,750 or (2) the sum of the child's earned income plus $5,000. The $5,000 amount is indexed for inflation after 1998.

Effective Date

The provision is effective for taxable years beginning after December 31, 1997.

[Conference Report]

Senate Amendment

The Senate amendment is the same as the House bill.

Conference Agreement

The conference agreement follows the House bill and the Senate amendment.

[¶ 5202]   Section 1202.   Increase de minimis threshold for estimated tax to $1,000 for individuals.

(Code Sec. 6654)

[House Report]

Present Law

An individual taxpayer generally is subject to an addition to tax for any underpayment of estimated tax (sec. 6654). An individual generally does not have an underpayment of estimated tax if he or she makes timely estimated tax payments at least equal to: (1) 100 percent of the tax shown on the return of the individual for the preceding year (the "100 percent of last year's liability safe harbor") or (2) 90 percent of the tax shown on the return for the current year. The 100 percent of last year's liability safe harbor is modified to be a 110 percent of last year's liability safe harbor for any individual with an AGI of more than $150,000 as shown on the return for the preceding taxable year. Income tax withholding from wages is considered to be a payment of estimated taxes. In general, payment of estimated taxes must be made quarterly. The addition to tax is not imposed where the total tax liability for the year, reduced by any withheld tax and estimated tax payments, is less than $500.

Reasons for Change

Raising the individual estimated tax de minimis threshold will simplify the tax laws for a number of taxpayers.

Explanation of Provision

The bill increases the $500 individual estimated tax de minimis threshold to $1,000.

Effective Date

The provision is effective for taxable years beginning after December 31, 1997.

4. Projected to be $700 for 1998.

[Conference Report]

Senate Amendment

The Senate amendment is the same as the House bill.

Conference Agreement

The conference agreement follows the House bill and the Senate amendment.

[¶5203]   Section 1203.   Treatment of certain reimbursed expenses of rural letter carriers' vehicles.

(Code Sec. 162)

[House Report]

Present Law

A taxpayer who uses his or her automobile for business purposes may deduct the business portion of the actual operation and maintenance expenses of the vehicle, plus depreciation (subject to the limitations of sec. 280F). Alternatively, the taxpayer may elect to utilize a standard mileage rate in computing the deduction allowable for business use of an automobile that has not been fully depreciated. Under this election, the taxpayer's deduction equals the applicable rate multiplied by the number of miles driven for business purposes and is taken in lieu of deductions for depreciation and actual operation and maintenance expenses

An employee of the U.S. Postal Service may compute his deduction for business use of an automobile in performing services involving the collection and delivery of mail on a rural route by using, for all business use mileage, 150 percent of the standard mileage rate.

Rural letter carriers are paid an equipment maintenance allowance (EMA) to compensate them for the use of their personal automobiles in delivering the mail. The tax consequences of the EMA are determined by comparing it with the automobile expense deductions that each carrier allowed to claim (using either the actual expenses method or the 150 percent of the standard mileage rate). If the EMA exceeds the allowable automobile expense deductions, the excess generally is subject to tax. If the EMA falls short of the allowable automobile expense deductions, a deduction is allowed only to the extent that the sum of this shortfall and all other miscellaneous itemized deductions exceeds two percent of the taxpayer's adjusted gross income.

Reasons for Change

The filing of tax returns by rural letter carriers can be complex. Under present law, those who are reimbursed at more than the 150 percent rate must report their reimbursement as income and deduct their expenses as miscellaneous itemized deductions (subject to the two-percent floor). Permitting the income and expenses to wash, so that neither will have to be reported on the rural letter carrier's tax return, will simplify these tax returns.

Explanation of Provision

The bill repeals the special rate for Postal Service employees of 150 percent of the standard mileage rate. In its place, the bill requires that the rate of reimbursement provided by the Postal Service to rural letter carriers be considered to be equivalent to their expenses. The rate of reimbursement that is considered to be equivalent to their expenses is the rate of reimbursement contained in the 1991 collective bargaining agreement, which may be increased by no more than the rate of inflation.

Effective Date

The provision is effective for taxable years beginning after December 31, 1997.

[Conference Report]

Senate Amendment

The Senate amendment is the same as the House bill.

Conference Agreement

The conference agreement follows the House bill and the Senate amendment.

[¶ 5204]   Section 1204. Travel expenses of Federal employees participating in a Federal criminal investigation.

(Code Sec. 162)

[House Report]

Present Law

Unreimbursed ordinary and necessary travel expenses paid or incurred by an individual in connection with temporary employment away from home (e.g., transportation costs and the cost of meals and lodging) are generally deductible, subject to the two-percent floor on miscellaneous itemized deductions. Travel expenses paid or incurred in connection with indefinite employment away from home, however, are not deductible. A taxpayer's employment away from home in a single location is indefinite rather than temporary if it lasts for one year or more; thus, no deduction is permitted for travel expenses paid or incurred in connection with such employment (sec. 162(a)). If a taxpayer's employment away from home in a single location lasts for less than one year, whether such employment is temporary or indefinite is determined on the basis of the facts and circumstances.

Reasons for Change

The Committee believes that it would be inappropriate if this provision in the tax laws were to be a hindrance to the investigation of a Federal crime.

Explanation of Provision

The one-year limitation with respect to deductibility of expenses while temporarily away from home does not include any period during which a Federal employee is certified by the Attorney General (or the Attorney General's designee) as traveling on behalf of the Federal Government in a temporary duty status to investigate or provide support services to the investigation of a Federal crime. Thus, expenses for these individuals during these periods are fully deductible, regardless of the length of the period for which certification is given (provided that the other requirements for deductibility are satisfied).

Effective Date

The provision is effective for amounts paid or incurred with respect to taxable years ending after the date of enactment.

[Conference Report]

Senate Amendment

The Senate amendment is the same as the House bill.

Conference Agreement

The conference agreement follows the House bill and the Senate amendment.

[¶ 5205]   Section 1205. Payment of taxes by commercially acceptable means.

(Code Sec. 6311, 6103, 7431)

[House Report]

Present Law

Payment of taxes may be made by checks or money orders, to the extent and under the conditions provided by Treasury regulations (sec. 6311).

Reasons for Change

Additional payment mechanisms (such as credit cards, debit cards, and charge cards) have become commonly used and reliable forms of payment. Some taxpayers may find paying taxes by these mechanisms more convenient than paying by check or money order.

Explanation of Provision

In general

The Internal Revenue Service (IRS) is engaged in a long-term modernization of its information systems, the Tax Systems Modernization (TSM) Program. This modernization is intended to address deficiencies in the current IRS information systems and to plan effectively for future information system needs and requirements. The systems changes are designed to reduce the burden on taxpayers, generate additional revenue through improved voluntary compliance, and achieve productivity gains throughout the IRS. One key element of this program is electronic filing of tax returns.

At the present time, increasing reliance is being placed upon electronic funds transfers for payment of obligations. In light of this the IRS seeks to integrate these payment methods in its TSM program,including electronic filing of returns, as well as into its traditional collection functions. The bill allows the IRS to accept payment by any commercially acceptable means that the Secretary deems appropriate, to the extent and under the conditions provided in Treasury regulations.This will include, for example, electronic funds transfers, including those arising from credit cards, debit cards, and charge cards.

The IRS contemplates that it will proceed to negotiate contracts to implement this provision with one or more private sector credit and debit card systems. The bill provides that the Federal Government may pay fees with respect to any such contracts only out of amounts specifically appropriated for that purpose.

Billing error resolution

In the course of processing these transactions, it will be necessary to resolve billing errors and other disputes. The Internal Revenue Code contains mechanisms for the determination of tax liability, defenses and other taxpayer protections, and the resolution of disputes with respect to those liabilities. The Truth-in-Lending Act contains provisions for determination of credit card liabilities, defenses and other consumer protections, and the resolution of disputes with respect to these liabilities.

The bill excludes credit card, debit card, and charge card issuers and processing mechanisms from the resolution of tax liability, but makes IRS subject to the Truth-in-Lending provisions insofar as those provisions impose obligations and responsibilities with regard to the "billing error" resolution process. It is not intended that consumers obtain additional ways to dispute their tax liabilities under the Truth-in-Lending provisions.

The bill also specifically includes the use of debit cards in this provision and provides that the corresponding defenses and "billing

error" provisions of the Electronic Fund Transfer Act will apply in a similar manner.

The bill adds new section 6311(d)(3) to the Code. This section describes the circumstances under which section 161 of the Truth-in-Lending Act ("TILA") and section 908 of the Electronic Fund Transfer Act ("EFTA") apply to disputes that may arise in connection with payments of taxes made by credit card or debit card. Subsections (A) through (C) recognize that "billing errors" relating to the credit card account, such as an error arising from a credit card transaction posted to a cardholder's account without the cardholder's authorization an amount posted to the wrong cardholder's account, or an incorrect amount posted to a cardholder's account as a result of a computational error or numerical transposition, are governed by the billing error provisions of section 161 of TILA. Similarly, subsections 6311(d)(3) (A- (C) provide that errors such as those described above which arise in connection with payments of internal revenue taxes made by debit card, are governed by section 908 of EFTA.

The Internal Revenue Code provides that refunds are only authorized to be paid to the person who made the overpayment (generally the taxpayer). Subsection 6311(d)(3)(E), however, provides that where a taxpayer is entitled to receive funds as a result of the correction of billing error made under section 161 of TILA in connection with a credit card transaction, or under section 908 of EFTA in connection with a debit card transaction, the IRS is authorized to utilize the appropriate credit card or debit card system to initiate a credit to the taxpayer's credit card or debit card account. The IRS may, therefore, provide such funds through the taxpayer's credit card or debit card account rather than directly to the taxpayer.

On the other hand, subsections 6311(d)(3)(A)-(C) provide that any alleged error or dispute asserted by a taxpayer concerning the merits of the taxpayer's underlying tax liability or tax return is governed solely by existing tax laws, and is not subject to section 161 or section 170 of TILA, section 908 of EFTA, or any similar provisions of State law. Absent the exclusion from section 170 of TILA, in a collection action brought against the cardholder by the card issuer the cardholder might otherwise assert as a defense that the IRS had incorrectly computed his tax liability. A collection action initiated by a credit card issuer against the taxpayer/cardholder will be an inappropriate vehicle for the determination of a taxpayer's tax liability, especially since the United States will not be a party to such an action.

Similarly, without the exclusion from section 161 of TILA and section 908 of EFTA, a taxpayer could contest the merits of his tax liability by putting the charge which appears on the credit card bill in dispute. Pursuant to TILA or EFTA, the taxpayer's card issuer will have to investigate the dispute, thereby finding itself in the middle of a dispute between the IRS and the taxpayer. It is believed that it is improper to attempt to resolve tax disputes through the billing process. It is also noted that the taxpayer retains the traditional, existing remedies for resolving tax disputes, such as resolving the dispute administratively with the IRS, filing a petition with the Tax Court after receiving a statutory notice of deficiency, or paying the disputed tax and filing a claim for refund (and subsequently filing a refund suit if the claim is denied or not acted upon).

Creditor status

The TILA imposes various responsibilities and obligations on creditors. Although the definition of the term "creditor" set forth in 15 U.S.C. sec. 1602 is limited, and will generally not include the IRS, in the case of an open-end credit plan involving a credit card, the card issuer and any person who honors the credit card are, pursuant to 15 U.S.C. sec. 1602(f), creditors.

In addition, 12 CFR sec. 226.12(e) provides that the creditor must transmit a credit statement to the card issuer within 7 business days from accepting the return or forgiving the debt. There is a concern that the response deadlines otherwise imposed by 12 CFR sec. 226.12(e), if applicable, will be difficult for the IRS to comply with (given the volume of payments the IRS is likely to receive in peak periods). This could subject the IRS to unwarranted damage actions. Consequently, the bill generally provides an exception to creditor status for the IRS.

Privacy protections

The bill also addresses privacy questions that arise from the IRS' participation in credit card processing systems. It is believed that taxpayers expect that the maximum possible protection of privacy will be accorded any transactions they have with the IRS. Accordingly, the bill provides the greatest possible protection of taxpayers' privacy that is consistent with developing and operating an efficient tax administration system. It is expected that the principle will be fully observed in the implementation of this provision.

A key privacy issue is the use and redisclosure of tax information by financial institutions for purposes unrelated to the processing of credit card charges, i.e., marketing and related uses. To accept credit card charges by taxpayers, the IRS will have to disclose tax information to financial institutions to obtain payment and to resolve billing disputes. To obtain payment, the IRS will have to disclose, at a minimum, information on the "credit slip," i.e., the dollar amount of the payment and the taxpayer's credit card number.

The resolution of billing disputes may require the disclosure of additional tax information to financial institutions. In most cases, providing a copy of the credit slip and verifying the transaction amount will be sufficient. Conceivably, financial institutions could require some information regarding the underlying liability even where the dispute concerns a "billing dispute" matter. This additional information will not necessarily be shared as widely as the initial payment data. In lieu of disclosing further information, the IRS may elect to allow disputed amounts to be charged back to the IRS and to reinstate the corresponding tax liability.

Despite the language in most cardholder agreements that permits redisclosure of credit card transaction information, the public may be largely unaware of how widely that information is shared. For example, some financial institutions may share credit, payment, and purchase information with private credit bureaus, who, in turn, may sell this information to direct mail marketers, and others. Without use and redisclosure restrictions, taxpayers may discover that some traditionally confidential tax information might be widely disseminated to direct mail marketers and others.

It is intended that credit or debit card transaction information will generally be restricted to those uses necessary to process payments and resolve billing errors, as well as other purposes that are specified in the statute. The bill directs the Secretary to issue published procedures on what constitutes authorized uses and disclosures. It is anticipated that the Secretary's published procedures will prohibit the use of transaction information for marketing tax-related services by the issuer or any marketing that targets only those who use their credit card to pay their taxes. It is also anticipated that the published procedures will prohibit the sale of transaction information to a third party.

Effective Date

The provision is effective nine months after the date of enactment. The IRS may, in this interim period, conduct internal tests and negotiate with card issuers, but may not accept credit or debit cards for payment of tax liability.

[Conference Report]

Senate Amendment

No provision.

Conference Agreement

The conference agreement follows the House bill, except that the requirement that a separate appropriation be made for payment by the IRS of credit card fees is deleted, and a prohibition on the payment by the IRS of any fee or the provision of any other consideration is added.

[¶ 5207]   Section 1212. Minimum tax treatment of certain property and casualty insurance companies.

(Code Sec. 56)

[House Report]

Present Law

Present law provides that certain property and casualty insurance companies may elect to be taxed only on taxable investment income for regular tax purposes (sec. 831(b)). Eligible property and casualty insurance companies are those whose net written premiums (or if greater, direct written premiums) for the taxable year exceed $350,000 but do not exceed $1,200,000.

Under present law, all corporations including insurance companies are subject to an alternative minimum tax. Alternative minimum taxable income is increased by 75 percent of the excess of adjusted current earnings over alternative minimum taxable income (determined without regard to this adjustment and without regard to net operating losses).

Reasons for Change

The Committee believes that property and casualty companies small enough to be eligible to simplify their regular tax computa-

tion by electing to be taxed only on taxable investment income should be accorded comparable simplicity in the calculation of their alternative minimum tax. Under present law, the simplicity under the regular tax is nullified because electing companies must calculate underwriting income for tax purposes under the alternative minimum tax. The provision thus simplifies the entire Federal income tax calculation for a group of small taxpayers whom Congress has previously determined merit a simpler tax calculation.

Explanation of Provision

The bill provides that a property and casualty insurance company that elects for regular tax purposes to be taxed only on taxable investment income determines its adjusted current earnings under the alternative minimum tax without regard to any amount not taken into account in determining its gross investment income under section 834(b). Thus, adjusted current earnings of an electing company is determined without regard to underwriting income (or underwriting expense, as provided in sec. 56(g)(4)(B)(I)(II)).

Effective Date	Conference Agreement

Effective Date

The provision is effective for taxable years beginning after December 31, 1997.

[Conference Report]

Senate Amendment

The Senate amendment is the same as the House bill.

Conference Agreement

The conference agreement follows the House bill and the Senate amendment.

[¶ 5208]   Section 1213.   Treatment of construction allowances provided to lessees.

(Code Sec. 110, 6724, 168)

[House Report]

Present Law

Depreciation allowances for property used in a trade or business generally are determined under the modified Accelerated Cost Recovery System ("MACRS") of section 168. Depreciation allowances for improvements made on leased property are determined under MACRS, even if the MACRS recovery period assigned to the property is longer than the term of the lease (sec. 168(i)(8)).[70] This rule applies regardless whether the lessor or lessee places the leasehold improvements in service.[71] If a leasehold improvement constitutes an addition or improvement to nonresidential real property already placed in service, the improvement is depreciated using the straight-line method over a 39-year recovery period, beginning in the month the addition or improvement was placed in service (secs. 168 (b)(3), (c)(1), (d)(2), and (I)(6)). A lessor of leased property that disposes of a leasehold improvement that was made by the lessor for the lessee of the property may take the adjusted basis of the improvement into account for purposes of determining gain or loss if the improvement is irrevocably disposed of or abandoned by the lessor at the termination of the lease (sec. 168(i)(8)).

The gross income of a lessor of real property does not include any amount attributable to the value of buildings erected, or other improvements made by, a lessee that revert to the lessor at the termination of a lease (sec. 109).

Issues have arisen as to the proper treatment of amounts provided to a lessee by a lessor for property to be constructed and used by the lessee pursuant to the lease ("construction allowances"). Incentive payments have been includible in income as accessions to wealth.[72]   However, a coordinated issue paper issued by the Internal Revenue Service on October 8, 1996, provides that amounts received by a lessee from a lessor and expended by the lessee on assets owned by the lessor were not includible in the lessee's income. The issue paper provides that tax ownership is determined by applying a "benefits and burdens of ownership" test and includes an examination of the following factors: (1) whether legal title passes; (2) how the parties treat the transaction; (3) whether an equity interest was acquired in the property; (4) whether the contract creates present obligations on the seller to execute and deliver a deed and on the buyer to make payments; (5) whether the right of possession is vested; (6) who pays property taxes; (7) who bears the risk of loss or damage to the property; (8) who receives the profits from the operation and

---

70. The Tax Reform Act of 1986 modified the Accelerated cost Recovery System ("ACRS") to institute MACRS. Prior to the adoption of ACRS by the Economic Recovery Act of 1981, taxpayers were allowed to depreciate the various components of a building a separate assets with separate useful lives. The use of component depreciation was repealed upon the adoption of ACRS. The denial of component depreciation also applies under MACRS, as provided by the Tax Reform Act of 1986.

71. Former Code sections 168(f)(6) and 178 provided that in certain circumstances, a lessee could recover the cost of leasehold improvements made over the remaining term of the lease. These provisions were repealed by the Tax Reform Act of 1986.

72. *John B. White, Inc. v. Comm.*, 55 T.C. 729 (1971), aff'd per curiam 458 F. 2d 989 (3d Cir.), cert. denied, 409 U.S. 876 (1972).

sale of the property; (9) who carries insurance with respect to the property; (10) who is responsible for replacing the property; and (11) who has the benefits of any remainder interests in the property.

Reasons for Change

The Committee understands that it is common practice for a lessor to custom improve retail space for the use by a lessee pursuant to a lease. Such leasehold improvements generally may be provided by the lessor constructing the improvements to the lessee's specifications. Alternatively, the lessee may receive a construction allowance from the lessor pursuant to the lease in order to build or improve the property. The Committee believes that the tax treatment of either case should be the same. The Committee understands that the IRS paper on this issue reaches a similar conclusion in cases where the lessor is treated as the tax owner of the constructed or improved property. However, the Committee is concerned that the traditional factors cited by the IRS in making the determination of who is the tax owner of the property may be applied differently by the lessor and the lessee and may lead to controversies between the IRS and taxpayers. Thus, the bill provides a safe harbor such that it will be assumed that a construction allowance is used to construct or improve lessor property (and is properly excludible by the lessee) when long-lived property is constructed and used pursuant to a short-term lease. In addition, the bill provides safeguards to ensure that lessors and lessees consistently treat the property subject to the construction allowance as nonresidential real property.

Explanation of Provision

The bill provides that the gross income of a lessee does not include amounts received in cash (or treated as a rent reduction) from a lessor under a short-term lease of retail space for the purpose of the lessee's construction or improvement of qualified long-term real property for use in the lessee's trade or business at such retail space. The exclusion only applies to the extent the allowance does not exceed the amount expended by the lessee on the construction or improvement of qualified long-term real property. For this purpose, "qualified long-term real property" means nonresidential

real property that is part of, or otherwise present at, retail space used by the lessee and that reverts to the lessor at the termination of the lease. A "short-term lease" means a lease or other agreement for the occupancy or use of retail space for a term of 15 years or less (as determined pursuant to sec. 168(i)(3)). "Retail space" means real property leased, occupied, or otherwise used by the lessee in its trade or business of selling tangible personal property or services to the general public.

The bill provides that lessor will treat the amounts expended on the construction allowance as nonresidential real property. However, the lessee's exclusion is not dependent upon the lessor's treatment of the property as nonresidential real property.

The bill contains reporting requirements to ensure that both the lessor and lessee treat such amounts as nonresidential real property. Under regulations the lessor and the lessee, shall, at such times and in such manner as provided by the regulations, furnish to the Secretary of the Treasury information concerning the amounts received (or treated as a rent reduction), the amounts expended on qualified long-term real property, and such other information as the Secretary deems necessary to carry out the provisions of the bill. It is expected that the Secretary, in promulgating such regulations, will attempt to minimize the administrative burdens of taxpayers while ensuring compliance with the bill.

Effective Date

The provision applies to leases entered into after the date of enactment. No inference is intended as to the treatment of amounts that are not subject to the provision.

[Conference Report]

Senate Amendment

The Senate amendment is the same as the House bill.

Conference Agreement

The conference agreement generally follows the House bill and the Senate amendment, with a clarification of the coordination of the provision and present-law rule that allows lessors to take losses with respect to certain leasehold improvements abandoned at the end of the term of the lease (sec. 168(i)(8)). In addition, the conferees wish to emphasize that no inference is intended as to the treatment of amounts

that are not subject to the provision, and that the provisions of the IRS issue paper and present law (including case law) will continue to apply where applicable.

[¶ 5206]   Section 1211.   Modifications to look-back method for long-term contracts.

(Code Sec. 460)

[House Report]

Present Law

Taxpayers engaged in the production of property under a long-term contract generally must compute income from the contract under the percentage of completion method. Under the percentage of completion method, a taxpayer must include in gross income for any taxable year an amount that is based on the product of (1) the gross contract price and (2) the percentage of the contract completed as of the end of the year. The percentage of the contract completed as of the end of the year is determined by comparing costs incurred with respect to the contract as of the end of the year with estimated total contract costs.

Because the percentage of completion method relies upon estimated, rather than actual, contract price and costs to determine gross income for any taxable year, a "look-back method" is applied in the year a contract is completed in order to compensate the taxpayer (or the Internal Revenue Service) for the acceleration (or deferral) of taxes paid over the contract term. The first step of the look-back method is to reapply the percentage of completion method using actual contract price and costs rather than estimated contract price and costs. The second step generally requires the taxpayer to recompute its tax liability for each year of the contract using gross income as reallocated under the look-back method. If there is any difference between the recomputed tax liability and the tax liability as previously determined for a year, such difference is treated as a hypothetical underpayment or overpayment of tax to which the taxpayer

applies a rate of interest equal to the overpayment rate, compounded daily.[5] The taxpayer receives (or pays) interest if the net amount of interest applicable to hypothetical overpayments exceeds (or is less than) the amount of interest applicable to hypothetical underpayments.

The look-back method must be reapplied for any item of income or cost that is properly taken into account after the completion of the contract.

The look-back method does not apply to any contract that is completed within two taxable years of the contract commencement date and if the gross contract price does not exceed the lesser of (1) $1 million or (2) one percent of the average gross receipts of the taxpayer for the preceding three taxable years. In addition, a simplified look-back method is available to certain pass-through entities and, pursuant to Treasury regulations, to certain other taxpayers. Under the simplified look-back method, the hypothetical underpayment or overpayment of tax for a contract year generally is determined by applying the highest rate of tax applicable to such taxpayer to the change in gross income as recomputed under the look-back method.

Reasons for Change

Present law may require multiple applications of the look-back method with respect to a single contract or may otherwise subject contracts to the look-back method even though amounts necessitating the look-back calculations are de minimis relative to the aggregate contract income. In addition, the use of multiple interest rates complicates the mechanics of the look-back calculation. The

---

5.

   ]The overpayment rate equals the applicable Federal short-term rate plus two percentage points. This rate is ad-

justed quarterly by the IRS. Thus, in applying the look-back method for a contract year, a taxpayer may be required to use five different interest rates.

Committee wishes to address these concerns.

Explanation of Provision

Election not to apply the look-back method for de minimis amounts

The provision provides that a taxpayer may elect not to apply the look-back method with respect to a long-term contract if for each prior contract year, the cumulative taxable income (or loss) under the contract as determined using estimated contract price and costs is within 10 percent of the cumulative taxable income (or loss) as determined using actual contract price and costs.

Thus, under the election, upon completion of a long-term contract, a taxpayer would be required to apply the first step of the look-back method (the reallocation of gross income using actual, rather than estimated, contract price and costs), but is not required to apply the additional steps of the look-back method if the application of the first step resulted in de minimis changes to the amount of income previously taken into account for each prior contract year.

The election applies to all long-term contracts completed during the taxable year for which the election is made and to all long-term contracts completed during subsequent taxable years, unless the election is revoked with the consent of the Secretary of the Treasury.

Example 1. —A taxpayer enters into a three-year contract and upon completion of the contract, determines that annual net income under the contract using actual contract price and costs is $100,000, $150,000, and $250,000, respectively, for Years 1, 2, and 3 under the percentage of completion method. An electing taxpayer need not apply the look-back method to the contract if it had reported cumulative net taxable income under the contract using estimated contract price and costs of between $90,000 and $110,000 as of the end of Year 1; and between $225,000 and $275,000 as of the end of Year 2.

Election not to reapply the look-back method

The provision provides that a taxpayer may elect not to reapply the look-back method with respect to a contract if, as of the close of any taxable year after the year the contract is completed, the cumulative taxable income (or loss) under the contract is within 10 percent of the cumulative look-back income (or loss) as of the close of the most recent year in which the look-back method was applied (or would have applied but for the other de minimis exception described above). In applying this rule, amounts that are taken into account after completion of of the contract are not discounted.

Thus, an electing taxpayer need not apply or reapply the look-back method if amounts that are taken into account after the completion of the contract are de minimis.

The election applies to all long-term contracts completed during the taxable year for which the election is made and to all long-term contracts completed during subsequent taxable years, unless the election is revoked with the consent of the Secretary of the Treasury.

Example 2. —A taxpayer enters into a three-year contract and reports taxable income of $12,250, $15,000 and $12,750, respectively, for Years 1 through 3 with respect to the contract. Upon completion of the contract, cumulative look-back income with respect to the contract is $40,000, and 10 percent of such amount is $4,000. After the completion of the contract, the taxpayer incurs additional costs of $2,500 in each of the next three succeeding years (Years 4, 5, and 6) with respect to the contract. Under the provision, an electing taxpayer does not reapply the look-back method for Year 4 because the cumulative amount of contract taxable income ($37,500) is within 10 percent of contract look-back income as of the completion of the contract ($40,000). However, the look-back method must be applied for Year 5 because the cumulative amount of contract taxable income ($35,000) is not within 10 percent of contract look-back income as of the completion of the contract ($40,000). Finally, the taxpayer does not reapply the look-back method for Year 6 because the cumulative amount of contract taxable income ($32,500) is within 10 percent of contract look-back income as of the last application of the look-back method ($35,000).

Interest rates used for purposes of the look-back method

The provision provides that for purposes of the look-back method, only one rate of interest is to apply for each accrual period. An accrual period with respect to a taxable year begins on the day after the return due date (determined without regard to extensions) for the taxable year and ends on such return due date for the following taxable year. The applicable rate of interest is the overpayment rate in effect for the calendar quarter in which the accrual period begins.

Effective Date

The provision applies to contracts completed in taxable years ending after the date of enactment. The change in the interest rate calculation also applies for purposes of the look-back method applicable to the income forecast method of depreciation for property placed in service after September 13, 1995.

[Conference Report]

Senate Amendment

The Senate amendment is the same as the House bill.

Conference Agreement

The conference agreement follows the House bill and the Senate amendment.

[¶ 5209]   Section 1221. Simplified flow-through for electing large partnerships.

(Code Sec. 771, 772, 773, 774, 775, 776, 777)

[House Report]

Present Law

Treatment of partnerships in general

A partnership generally is treated as a conduit for Federal income tax purposes. Each partner takes into account separately his distributive share of the partnership's items of income, gain, loss, deduction or credit. The character of an item is the same as if it had been directly realized or incurred by the partner. Limitations affecting the computation of taxable income generally apply at the partner level.

The taxable income of a partnership is computed in the same manner as that of an individual, except that no deduction is permitted for personal exemptions, foreign taxes, charitable contributions, net operating losses, certain itemized deductions, or depletion. Elections affecting the computation of taxable income derived from a partnership are made by the partnership, except for certain elections such as those relating to discharge of indebtedness income and the foreign tax credit.

Capital gains

The net capital gain of an individual is taxed generally at the same rates applicable to ordinary income, subject to a maximum marginal rate of 28 percent. Net capital gain is the excess of net long-term capital gain over net short-term capital loss. Individuals with a net capital loss generally may deduct up to $3,000 of the loss each year against ordinary income. Net capital losses in excess of the $3,000 limit may be carried forward indefinitely.

A special rule applies to gains and losses on the sale, exchange or involuntary conversion of certain trade or business assets (sec. 1231). In general, net gains from such assets are treated as long-term capital gains but net losses are treated as ordinary losses.

A partner's share of a partnership's net short-term capital gain or loss and net long-term capital gain or loss from portfolio investments is separately reported to the partner. A partner's share of a partnership's net gain or loss under section 1231 generally is also separately reported.

Deductions and credits

Miscellaneous itemized deductions (e.g., certain investment expenses) are deductible only to the extent that, in the aggregate, they exceed two percent of the individual's adjusted gross income.

In general, taxpayers are allowed a deduction for charitable contributions, subject to certain limitations. The deduction allowed an individual generally cannot exceed 50 percent of the individual's adjusted gross income for the taxable year. The deduction allowed a corporation generally cannot exceed 10 percent of the corporation's taxable income. Excess contributions are carried forward for five years.

A partner's distributive share of a partnership's miscellaneous itemized deductions and charitable contributions is separately reported to the partner.

Each partner is allowed his distributive share of credits against his taxable income.

Foreign taxes

The foreign tax credit generally allows U.S. taxpayers to reduce U.S. income tax on foreign income by the amount of foreign income taxes paid or accrued with respect to that income. In lieu of electing the foreign tax credit, a taxpayer may deduct foreign taxes. The total amount of the credit may not exceed the same proportion of the taxpayer's U.S. tax which the taxpayer's foreign source taxable income bears to the taxpayer's worldwide taxable income for the taxable year.

Unrelated business taxable income

Tax-exempt organizations are subject to tax on income from unrelated businesses. Certain types of income (such as dividends, interest and certain rental income) are not treated as unrelated business taxable income. Thus, for a partner that is an exempt organization, whether partnership income is unrelated business taxable income depends on the character of the underlying income. Income from a publicly traded partnership, however, is treated as unrelated business taxable income regardless of the character of the underlying income.

Special rules related to oil and gas activities

Taxpayers involved in the search for and extraction of crude oil and natural gas are subject to certain special tax rules. As a result, in the case of partnerships engaged in such activities, certain specific information is separately reported to partners.

A taxpayer who owns an economic interest in a producing deposit of natural resources (including crude oil and natural gas) is permitted to claim a deduction for depletion of the deposit as the minerals are extracted. In the case of oil and gas produced in the United States, a taxpayer generally is permitted to claim the greater of a deduction for cost depletion or percentage depletion. Cost depletion is computed by multiplying a taxpayer's adjusted basis in the depletable property by a fraction, the numerator of which is the amount of current year production from the property and the denominator of which is the property's estimated reserves as of the beginning of that year. Percentage depletion is equal to a specified percentage (generally, 15 percent in the case of oil and gas) of gross income from production. Cost depletion is limited to the taxpayer's basis in the depletable property; percentage depletion is not so limited. Once a taxpayer has exhausted its basis in the depletable property, it may continue to claim percentage depletion deductions (generally referred to as "excess percentage depletion").

Certain limitations apply to the deduction for oil and gas percentage depletion. First, percentage depletion is not available to oil and gas producers who also engage (directly or indirectly) in significant levels of oil and gas retailing or refining activities (so-called "integrated producers" of oil and gas). Second, the deduction for percentage depletion may be claimed by a taxpayer only with respect to up to 1,000 barrels-per-day of production. Third, the percentage depletion deduction may not exceed 100 percent of the taxpayer's net income for the taxable year from the depletable oil and gas property. Fourth, a percentage depletion deduction may not be claimed to the extent that it exceeds 65 percent of the taxpayer's pre-percentage depletion taxable income.

In the case of a partnership that owns depletable oil and gas properties, the depletion allowance is computed separately by the partners and not by the partnership. In computing a partner's basis in his partnership interest, basis is increased by the partner's share of any partnership-related excess percentage depletion deductions and is decreased (but not below zero) by the partner's total amount of depletion deductions attributable to partnership property.

Intangible drilling and development costs ("IDCs") incurred with respect to domestic oil and gas wells generally may be deducted at the election of the taxpayer. In the case of integrated producers, no more than 70 percent of IDCs incurred during a taxable year may be deducted. IDCs not deducted are capitalized and generally are either added to the property's basis and recovered through depletion deductions or amortized on a straight-line basis over a 60-month period.

The special treatment granted to IDCs incurred in the pursuit of oil and gas may give rise to an item of tax preference or (in the case of corporate taxpayers) an adjusted current earnings ("ACE") adjustment for the alternative minimum tax. The tax preference item is based on a concept of "excess IDCs." In general, excess IDCs are the excess of IDCs deducted for the taxable year over the amount of those IDCs that would have been deducted had they been capitalized and amortized on a straight-line basis over 120 months commencing with the month production begins from the related well. The amount of tax preference is then computed as the difference between the excess IDC amount and 65 percent of the taxpayer's net income from oil and gas (computed without a deduction for excess IDCs). For IDCs incurred in taxable years beginning after 1992, the ACE adjustment related to IDCs is repealed for taxpayers other than integrated producers. Moreover, beginning in 1993, the IDC tax preference generally is repealed for taxpayers other than integrated producers. In this case, however, the repeal of the excess IDC preference may not result in more than a 40 percent reduction (30 percent for taxable years beginning in 1993) in the amount of the taxpayer's alternative minimum taxable income computed as if that preference had not been repealed.

Passive losses

The passive loss rules generally disallow deductions and credits from passive activities to the extent they exceed income from passive activities. Losses not allowed in a taxable year are suspended and treated as current deductions from passive activities in the next taxable year. These losses are allowed in full when a taxpayer disposes of the entire interest in the passive activity to an unrelated person in a taxable transaction. Passive activities include trade or business activities in which the taxpayer does not materially participate. (Limited partners generally do not materially participate in the activities of a partnership.) Passive activities also include rental activities (regardless of the taxpayer's material participation).[6] Portfolio income (such as interest and dividends), and expenses allocable to such income, are not treated as income or loss from a passive activity.

The $25,000 allowance also applies to low-income housing and rehabilitation credits (on a deduction equivalent basis), regardless of whether the taxpayer claiming the credit actively participates in the rental real estate activity generating the credit. In addition, the income phaseout range for the $25,000 allowance for rehabilitation credits is $200,000 to $250,000 (rather than $100,000 to $150,000). For interests acquired after December 31, 1989 in partnerships holding property placed in service after that date, the $25,000 deduction-equivalent allowance is permitted for the low-income housing credit without regard to the taxpayer's income.

A partnership's operations may be treated as multiple activities for purposes of the passive loss rules. In such case, the partnership must separately report items of income and deductions from each of its activities.

Income, loss and other items from a publicly traded partnership are treated as separate from income and loss from any other publicly traded partnership, and also as separate from any income or loss from passive activities.

6.

]An individual who actively participates in a rental real estate activity and holds at least a 10-percent interest may

deduct up to $25,000 of passive losses. The $25,000 amount phases out as the individual's income increases from $100,000 to $150,000.

The Omnibus Budget Reconciliation Act of 1993 added a rule, effective for taxable years beginning after December 31, 1993, treating a taxpayer's rental real estate activities in which he materially participates as not subject to limitation under the passive loss rules if the taxpayer meets eligibility requirements relating to real property trades or businesses in which he performs services (sec. 469(c)(7)). Real property trade or business means any real property development, redevelopment, construction, reconstruction, acquisition, conversion, rental, operation, management, leasing, or brokerage trade or business. An individual taxpayer generally meets the eligibility requirements if (1) more than half of the personal services the taxpayer performs in trades or business during the taxable year are performed in real property trades or businesses in which the taxpayer materially participates, and (2) such taxpayer performs more than 750 hours of services during the taxable year in real property trades or businesses in which the taxpayer materially participates.

REMICs

A tax is imposed on partnerships holding a residual interest in a real estate mortgage investment conduit ("REMIC"). The amount of the tax is the amount of excess inclusions allocable to partnership interests owned by certain tax-exempt organizations ("disqualified organizations") multiplied by the highest corporate tax rate.

Contribution of property to a partnership

In general, a partner recognizes no gain or loss upon the contribution of property to a partnership. However, income, gain, loss and deduction with respect to property contributed to a partnership by a partner must be allocated among the partners so as to take into account the difference between the basis of the property to the partnership and its fair market value at the time of contribution. In addition, the contributing partner must recognize gain or loss equal to such difference if the property is distributed to another partner within five years of its contribution (sec. 704(c)), or if other property is distributed to the contributor within the five year period (sec. 737).

Election of optional basis adjustments

In general, the transfer of a partnership interest or a distribution of partnership property does not affect the basis of partnership assets. A partnership, however, may elect to make certain adjustments in the basis of partnership property (sec. 754). Under a section 754 election, the transfer of a partnership interest generally results in an adjustment in the partnership's basis in its property for the benefit of the transferee partner only, to reflect the difference between that partner's basis for his interest and his proportionate share of the adjusted basis of partnership property (sec. 743(b)). Also under the election, a distribution of property to a partner in certain cases results in an adjustment in the basis of other partnership property (sec. 734(b)).

Terminations

A partnership terminates if either (1) all partners cease carrying on the business, financial operation or venture of the partnership, or (2) within a 12-month period 50 percent or more of the total partnership interests are sold or exchanged (sec. 708).

Reasons for Change

The requirement that each partner take into account separately his distributive share of a partnership's items of income, gain, loss, deduction and credit can result in the reporting of a large number of items to each partner. The schedule K 1, on which such items are reported, contains space for more than 40 items. Reporting so many separately stated items is burdensome for individual investors with relatively small, passive interests in large partnerships. In many respects such investments are indistinguishable from those made in corporate stock or mutual funds, which do not require reporting of numerous separate items.

In addition, the number of items reported under the current regime makes it difficult for the Internal Revenue Service to match items reported on the K 1 against the partner's income tax return. Matching is also difficult because items on the K 1 are often modified or limited at the partner level before appearing on the partner's tax return.

By significantly reducing the number of items that must be separately reported to partners by an electing large partnership, the provision eases the reporting burden of partners and facilitates matching by the IRS. Moreover, it is understood that the Internal Revenue Service is considering restricting the use of substitute reporting forms by large partnerships. Reduction of the number of items makes possible a short standardized form.

Explanation of Provisions

In general

The bill modifies the tax treatment of an electing large partnership (generally, any partnership that elects under the provision, if the number of partners in the preceding taxable year is 100 or more) and its partners. The provision provides that each partner takes into account separately the partner's distributive share of the following items, which are determined at the partnership level: (1) taxable income or loss from passive loss limitation activities; (2) taxable income or loss from other activities (e.g., portfolio income or loss); (3) net capital gain or loss to the extent allocable to passive loss limitation activities and other activities; (4) tax-exempt interest; (5) net alternative minimum tax adjustment separately computed for passive loss limitation activities and other activities; (6) general credits; (7) low-income housing credit; (8) rehabilitation credit; (9) credit for producing fuel from a nonconventional source; (10) creditable foreign taxes and foreign source items; and (11) any other items to the extent that the Secretary determines that separate treatment of such items is appropriate.[7] Separate treatment may be appropriate, for example, should changes in the law necessitate such treatment for any items.

Under the bill, the taxable income of an electing large partnership is computed in the same manner as that of an individual, except that the items described above are separately stated and certain modifications are made. These modifications include disallowing the deduction for personal exemptions, the net operating loss deduction and certain itemized deductions.[8] All limitations and other provisions affecting the computation of taxable income or any credit (except for the at risk, passive loss and itemized deduction limitations, and any other provision specified in regulations) are applied at the partnership (and not the partner) level.

All elections affecting the computation of taxable income or any credit generally are made by the partnership.

Capital gains

Under the bill, netting of capital gains and losses occurs at the partnership level. A partner in a large partnership takes into account separately his distributive share of the partnership's net capital gain or net capital loss.[9] Such net capital gain or loss is treated as long-term capital gain or loss.

Any excess of net short-term capital gain over net long-term capital loss is consolidated with the partnership's other taxable income and is not separately reported.

A partner's distributive share of the partnership's net capital gain is allocated between passive loss limitation activities and other activities. The net capital gain is allocated to passive loss limitation activities to the extent of net capital gain from sales and exchanges of property used in connection with such activities, and any excess is allocated to other activities. A similar rule ap-

---

7.

]In determining the amounts required to be separately taken into account by a partner, those provisions of the large partnership rules governing computations of taxable income are applied * * * separately with respect to that partner by taking into account that partner's distributive share of the partnership's items of income, gain, loss, deduction or credit. This rule permits partnerships to make otherwise valid special allocations of partnership items to partners.
8.

]An electing large partnership is allowed a deduction under section 212 for expenses incurred for the production of income, subject to 70-percent disallowance. No income from an electing large partnership is treated as fishing or farming income.
9.

]The term "net capital gain" has the same meaning as in section 1222(11). The term "net capital loss" means the excess of the losses from sales or exchanges of capital assets over the gains from sales or exchanges of capital assets. Thus, the partnership cannot offset any portion of capital losses against ordinary income.

plies for purposes of allocating any net capital loss.

Any gains and losses of the partnership under section 1231 are netted at the partnership level. Net gain is treated as long-term capital gain and is subject to the rules described above. Net loss is treated as ordinary loss and consolidated with the partnership's other taxable income.

Deductions

The bill contains two special rules for deductions. First, miscellaneous itemized deductions are not separately reported to partners. Instead, 70 percent of the amount of such deductions is disallowed at the partnership level;[10] the remaining 30 percent is allowed at the partnership level in determining taxable income, and is not subject to the two- percent floor at the partner level.

Second, charitable contributions are not separately reported to partners under the bill. Instead, the charitable contribution deduction is allowed at the partnership level in determining taxable income, subject to the limitations that apply to corporate donors.

Credits in general

Under the bill, general credits are separately reported to partners as a single item. General credits are any credits other than the low-income housing credit, the rehabilitation credit and the credit for producing fuel from a nonconventional source. A partner's distributive share of general credits is taken into account as a current year general business credit. Thus, for example, the credit for clinical testing expenses is subject to the present law limitations on the general business credit. The refundable credit for gasoline used for exempt purposes and the refund or credit for undistributed capital gains of a regulated investment company are allowed to the partnership, and thus are not separately reported to partners.

In recognition of their special treatment under the passive loss rules, the low-income housing and rehabilitation credits are separately reported.[11] In addition, the credit for producing fuel from a nonconventional source is separately reported.

The bill imposes credit recapture at the partnership level and determines the amount of recapture by assuming that the credit fully reduced taxes. Such recapture is applied first to reduce the partnership's current year credit, if any; the partnership is liable for any excess over that amount. Under the bill, the transfer of an interest in an electing large partnership does not trigger recapture.

Foreign taxes

The bill retains present-law treatment of foreign taxes. The partnership reports to the partner creditable foreign taxes and the source of any income, gain, loss or deduction taken into account by the partnership. Elections, computations and limitations are made by the partner.

Tax-exempt interest

The bill retains present-law treatment of tax-exempt interest. Interest on a State or local bond is separately reported to each partner.

Unrelated business taxable income

The bill retains present-law treatment of unrelated business taxable income. Thus, a tax-exempt partner's distributive share of partnership items is taken into account separately to the extent necessary to comply with the rules governing such income.

Passive losses

Under the bill, a partner in an electing large partnership takes in an electing to account separately his distributive share of the partnership's taxable income or loss from passive loss limitation activities. The term "passive loss limitation activity" means any activity involving the conduct of a trade or

---

10.

]The 70 percent figure is intended to approximate the amount of such deductions that would be denied at the partner level as a result of the two-percent floor.
11.

]It is understood that the rehabilitation and low-income housing credits which are subject to the same passive loss

rules (i.e., in the case of the low-income housing credit, where the partnership interest was acquired or the property was placed in service before 1990) could be reported together on the same line.

business (including any activity treated as a trade or business under sec. 469(c)(5) or (6)) and any rental activity. A partner's share of an electing large partnership's taxable income or loss from passive loss limitation activities is treated as an item of income or loss from the conduct of a trade or business which is a single passive activity, as defined in the passive loss rules. Thus, an electing large partnership generally is not required to separately report items from multiple activities.

A partner in an electing large partnership also takes into account separately his distributive share of the partnership's taxable income or loss from activities other than passive loss limitation activities. Such distributive share is treated as an item of income or expense with respect to property held for investment. Thus, portfolio income (e.g., interest and dividends) is reported separately and is reduced by portfolio deductions and allocable investment interest expense.

In the case of a partner holding an interest in an electing large partnership which is not a limited partnership interest, such partner's distributive share of any items are taken into account separately to the extent necessary to comply with the passive loss rules. Thus, for example, income of an electing large partnership is not treated as passive income with respect to the general partnership interest of a partner who materially participates in the partnership's trade or business.

Under the bill, the requirement that the passive loss rule be separately applied to each publicly traded partnership (sec. 469(k) of the Code) continues to apply.

Alternative minimum tax

Under the bill, alternative minimum tax ("AMT") adjustments and preferences are combined at the partnership level. An electing large partnership would report to partners a net AMT adjustment separately computed for passive loss limitation activities and other activities. In determining a partner's alternative minimum taxable income, a partner's distributive share of any net AMT adjustment is taken into account instead of making separate AMT adjustments with respect to partnership items. The net AMT adjustment is determined by using the adjustments applicable to individuals (in the case of partners other than corporations), and by using the adjustments applicable to corporations (in the case of corporate partners). Except as provided in regulations, the net AMT adjustment is treated as a deferral preference for purposes of the section 53 minimum tax credit.

Discharge of indebtedness income

If an electing large partnership has income from the discharge of any indebtedness, such income is separately reported to each partner. In addition, the rules governing such income (sec. 108) are applied without regard to the large partnership rules. Partner-level elections under section 108 are made by each partner separately. Thus, for example, the large partnership provisions do not affect section 108(d)(6), which provides that certain section 108 rules apply at the partner level, or section 108(b)(5), which provides for an election to reduce the basis of depreciable property. The large partnership provisions also do not affect the election under 108(c) (added by the Omnibus Budget Reconciliation Act of 1993) to exclude discharge of indebtedness income with respect to qualified real property business indebtedness.

REMICs

For purposes of the tax on partnerships holding residual interests in REMICs, all interests in an electing large partnership are treated as held by disqualified organizations. Thus, an electing large partnership holding a residual interest in a REMIC is subject to a tax equal to the excess inclusions multiplied by the highest corporate rate. The amount subject to tax is excluded from partnership income.

Election of optional basis adjustments

Under the bill, an electing large partnership may still elect to adjust the basis of partnership assets with respect to transferee partners. The computation of an electing large partnership's taxable income is made without regard to the section 743(b) adjustment. As under present law, the section 743(b) adjustment is made only with respect to the transferee partner. In addition, an electing large partnership is permitted to adjust the basis of partnership property under section 734(b) if property is distributed to a partner, as under present law.

Terminations

The bill provides that an electing large partnership does not terminate for tax purposes solely because 50 percent of its interests are sold or exchanged within a 12-month period.

Partnerships and partners subject to large partnership rules

Definition of electing large partnership

An "electing large partnership" is any partnership that elects under the provision, if the number of partners in the preceding taxable year is 100 or more. The number of partners is determined by counting only persons directly holding partnership interests in the taxable year, including persons holding through nominees; persons holding indirectly (e.g., through another partnership) are not counted. Regulations may provide, however, that if the number of partners in any taxable year falls below 100, the partnership may not be treated as an electing large partnership. The election applies to the year for which made and all subsequent years and cannot be revoked without the Secretary's consent.

Special rules for certain service partnerships

An election under this provision is not effective for any partnership if substantially all the partners are: (1) individuals performing substantial services in connection with the partnership's activities, or personal service corporations the owner-employees of which perform such services; (2) retired partners who had performed such services; or (3) spouses of partners who had performed such services. In addition, the term "partner" does not include any individual performing substantial services in connection with the partnership's activities and holding a partnership interest, or an individual who formerly performed such services and who held a partnership interest at the time the individual performed such services.

Exclusion for commodity partnerships

An election under this provision is not effective for any partnership the principal activity of which is the buying and selling of commodities (not described in sec. 1221(1)), or options, futures or forwards with respect to commodities.

Special rules for partnerships holding oil and gas properties

Simplified reporting treatment of electing large partnerships with oil and gas activities

The bill provides special rules for electing large partnerships with oil and gas activities that operate under the simplified reporting regime. These partnerships are collectively referred to herein as "oil and gas large partnerships." Generally, the bill provides that an oil and gas large partnership reports information to its partners under the general simplified large partnership reporting regime described above. To prevent the extension of percentage depletion deductions to persons excluded therefrom under present law, however, certain partners are treated as disqualified persons under the bill.

The treatment of a disqualified person's distributive share of any item of income, gain, loss, deduction, or credit attributable to any partnership oil or gas property is determined under the bill without regard to the special rules applicable to large partnerships. Thus, an oil and gas large partnership reports information related to oil and gas activities to a partner who is a disqualified person in the same manner and to the same extent that it reports such information to that partner under present law. The simplified reporting rules of the bill, however, apply with respect to reporting such a partner's share of items not related to oil and gas activities.

The bill defines two categories of taxpayers as disqualified persons. The first category encompasses taxpayers who do not qualify for the deduction for percentage depletion under section 613A (i.e., integrated producers of oil and gas). The second category includes any person whose average daily production of oil and gas (for purposes of determining the depletable oil and natural gas quantity under section 613A(c)(2)) is at least 500 barrels for its taxable year in which (or with which) the partnership's taxable year ends. In making this computation, all production of domestic crude oil and natural gas attributable to the partner is taken into account, including such partner's proportionate share of any production of the large partnership.

A taxpayer that falls within a category of disqualified person has the responsibility of notifying any large partnership in which it holds a direct or indirect interest (e.g., through a pass-through entity) of its status as such. Thus, for example, if an integrated producer owns an interest in a partnership which in turn owns an interest in an oil and gas large partnership, it is responsible for providing the management of the electing large partnership information regarding its status as a disqualified person and details regarding its indirect interest in the electing large partnership.

Under the bill, an oil and gas large partnership computes its deduction for oil and gas depletion under the general statutory rules (subject to certain exceptions described below) under the assumptions that the partnership is the taxpayer and that it qualifies for the percentage depletion deduction. The amount of the depletion deduction, as well as other oil and gas related items, generally are reported to each partner (other than to partners who are disqualified persons) as components of that partner's distributive share of taxable income or loss from passive loss limitation activities. The bill provides that in computing the partnership's oil and gas percentage depletion deduction, the 1,000-barrel-per-day limitation does not apply. In addition, an oil and gas large partnership is allowed to compute percentage depletion under the bill without applying the 65-percent-of-taxable-income limitation under section 613A(d)(1).

As under present law, an election to deduct IDCs under section 263(c) is made at the partnership level. Since the bill treats those taxpayers required by the Code (sec. 291) to capitalize 30 percent of IDCs as disqualified persons, an oil and gas large partnership may pass through a full deduction of IDCs to its partners who are not disqualified persons. In contrast to present law, an oil and gas large partnership also has the responsibility with respect to its partners who are not disqualified persons for making an election under section 59(e) to capitalize and amortize certain specified IDCs. Partners who are disqualified persons are permitted to make their own separate section 59(e) elections under the bill.

Consistent with the general reporting regime for electing large partnerships, the bill provides that a single AMT adjustment (under either corporate or non-corporate principles, as the case may be) is made and reported to the partners (other than disqualified persons) of an oil and gas large partnership as a separate item. This separately-reported item is affected by the limitation on the repeal of the tax preference for excess IDCs. For purposes of computing this limitation, the bill treats an oil and gas large partnership as the taxpayer. Thus, the limitation on repeal of the IDC preference is applied at the partnership level and is based on the cumulative reduction in the partnership's alternative minimum taxable income resulting from repeal of that preference.

The bill provides that in making partnership-level computations, any item of income, gain, loss, deduction, or credit attributable to a partner who is a disqualified person is disregarded. For example, in computing the partnership's net income from oil and gas for purposes of determining the IDC preference (if any) to be reported to partners who are not disqualified persons as part of the AMT adjustment, disqualified persons' distributive shares of the partnership's net income from oil and gas are not to be taken into account.

Regulatory authority

The Secretary of the Treasury is granted authority to prescribe such regulations as may be appropriate to carry out the purposes of the provisions.

Effective Date

The provisions generally apply to partnership taxable years beginning after December 31, 1997.

[Conference Report]

Senate Amendment

The Senate amendment is the same as the House bill.

Conference Agreement

The conference agreement follows the House bill and the Senate amendment.

[¶ 5210]   Section 1222.   Simplified audit ptocedures for electing large partnerships.

(Code Sec. 6240, 6241, 6242, 6245, 6246, 6247, 6248, 6251, 6252)

[House Report]

Present Law

In general

Prior to 1982, regardless of the size of a partnership, adjustments to a partnership's items of income, gain, loss, deduction, or credit had to be made in separate proceedings with respect to each partner individually. Because a large partnership sometimes had many partners located in different audit districts, adjustments to items of income, gains, losses, deductions, or credits of the partnership had to be made in numerous actions in several jurisdictions, sometimes with conflicting outcomes.

The Tax Equity and Fiscal Responsibility Act of 1982 ("TEFRA") established unified audit rules applicable to all but certain small (10 or fewer partners) partnerships. These rules require the tax treatment of all "partnership items" to be determined at the partnership, rather than the partner, level. Partnership items are those items that are more appropriately determined at the partnership level than at the partner level, as provided by regulations.

Under the TEFRA rules, a partner must report all partnership items consistently with the partnership return or must notify the IRS of any inconsistency. If a partner fails to report any partnership item consistently with the partnership return, the IRS may make a computational adjustment and immediately assess any additional tax that results.

Administrative proceedings

Under the TEFRA rules, a partner must report all partnership items consistently with the partnership return or must notify the IRS of any inconsistency. If a partner fails

to report any partnership item consistently with the partnership return, the IRS may make a computational adjustment and immediately assess any additional tax that results.

The IRS may challenge the reporting position of a partnership by conducting a single administrative proceeding to resolve the issue with respect to all partners. But the IRS must still assess any resulting deficiency against each of the taxpayers who were partners in the year in which the understatement of tax liability arose.

Any partner of a partnership can request an administrative adjustment or a refund for his own separate tax liability. Any partner also has the right to participate in partnership-level administrative proceedings. A settlement agreement with respect to partnership items binds all parties to the settlement.

Tax Matters Partner

The TEFRA rules establish the "Tax Matters Partner" as the primary representative of a partnership in dealings with the IRS. The Tax Matters Partner is a general partner designated by the partnership or, in the absence of designation, the general partner with the largest profits interest at the close of the taxable year. If no Tax Matters Partner is designated, and it is impractical to apply the largest profits interest rule, the IRS may select any partner as the Tax Matters Partner.

Notice requirements

The IRS generally is required to give notice of the beginning of partnership-level administrative proceedings and any resulting administrative adjustment to all partners whose names and addresses are furnished to the IRS. For partnerships with more than 100 partners, however, the IRS generally is not required to give notice to any partner whose profits interest is less than one percent.

Adjudication of disputes concerning partnership items

After the IRS makes an administrative adjustment, the Tax Matters Partner (and, in limited circumstances, certain other partners) may file a petition for readjustment of partnership items in the Tax Court, the district court in which the partnership's principal place of business is located, or the Claims Court.

Statute of limitations

The IRS generally cannot adjust a partnership item for a partnership taxable year if more than 3 years have elapsed since the later of the filing of the partnership return or the last day for the filing of the partnership return.

Reasons for Change

Present audit procedures for large partnerships are inefficient and more complex than those for other large entities. The IRS must assess any deficiency arising from a partnership audit against a large number of partners, many of whom cannot easily be located and some of whom are no longer partners. In addition, audit procedures are cumbersome and can be complicated further by the intervention of partners acting individually.

Explanation of Provision

The bill creates a new audit system for electing large partnerships. The provision defines "electing large partnership" the same way for audit and reporting purposes (generally, any partnership that elects under the reporting provisions, if the number of partners in the preceding taxable year is 100 or more).

As under present law, electing large partnerships and their partners are subject to unified audit rules. Thus, the tax treatment of "partnership items" are determined at the partnership, rather than the partner, level. The term "partnership items" is defined as under present law.

Unlike present law, however, partnership adjustments generally will flow through to the partners for the year in which the ad-justment takes effect. Thus, the current-year partners' share of current-year partnership items of income, gains, losses, deductions, or credits will be adjusted to reflect partnership adjustments that take effect in that year. The adjustments generally will not affect prior-year returns of any partners (except in the case of changes to any partner's distributive shares).

In lieu of flowing an adjustment through to its partners, the partnership may elect to pay an imputed underpayment. The imputed underpayment generally is calculated by netting the adjustments to the income and loss items of the partnership and multiplying that amount by the highest tax rate (whether individual or corporate). A partner may not file a claim for credit or refund of his allocable share of the payment. A partnership may make this election only if it meets requirements set forth in Treasury regulations designed to ensure payment (for example, in the case of a foreign partnership).

Regardless of whether a partnership adjustment flows through to the partners, an adjustment must be offset if it requires another adjustment in a year after the adjusted year and before the year the offsetted adjustment takes effect. For example, if a partnership expensed a $1,000 item in year 1, and it was determined in year 4 that the item should have been capitalized and amortized ratably over 10 years, the adjustment in year 4 would be $700, apart from any interest or penalty. (The $900 adjustment for the improper deduction would be offset by $200 of adjustments for amortization deductions.) The year 4 partners would be required to include an additional $700 in income for that year. The partnership may ratably amortize the remaining $700 of expenses in years 4 10.

In addition, the partnership, rather than the partners individually, generally is liable for any interest and penalties that result from a partnership adjustment. Interest is computed for the period beginning on the return due date for the adjusted year and ending on the earlier of the return due date for the partnership taxable year in which the adjustment takes effect or the date the partnership pays the imputed underpayment. Thus, in the above example, the partnership would be liable for 4 years' worth of interest (on a declining principal amount).

Penalties (such as the accuracy and fraud penalties) are determined on a year-by-year basis (without offsets) based on an imputed underpayment. All accuracy penalty criteria and waiver criteria (such as reasonable cause, substantial authority, etc.) are determined as if the partnership were a taxable individual. Accuracy and fraud penalties are assessed and accrue interest in the same manner as if asserted against a taxable individual.

Any payment (for Federal income taxes, interest, or penalties) that an electing large partnership is required to make is non-deductible.

If a partnership ceases to exist before a partnership adjustment takes effect, the former partners are required to take the adjustment into account, as provided by regulations. Regulations are also authorized to prevent abuse and to enforce efficiently the audit rules in circumstances that present special enforcement considerations (such as partnership bankruptcy).

Administrative proceedings

Under the electing large partnership audit rules, a partner is not permitted to report any partnership items inconsistently with the partnership return, even if the partner notifies the IRS of the inconsistency. The IRS may treat a partnership item that was reported inconsistently by a partner as a mathematical or clerical error and immediately assess any additional tax against that partner.

As under present law, the IRS may challenge the reporting position of a partnership by conducting a single administrative proceeding to resolve the issue with respect to all partners. Unlike under present law, however, partners will have no right individually to participate in settlement conferences or to request a refund.

Partnership representative

The bill requires each electing large partnership to designate a partner or other person to act on its behalf. If an electing large partnership fails to designate such a person, the IRS is permitted to designate any one of

the partners as the person authorized to act on the partnership's behalf. After the IRS's designation, an electing large partnership could still designate a replacement for the IRS-designated partner.

Notice requirements

Unlike under present law, the IRS is not required to give notice to individual partners of the commencement of an administrative proceeding or of a final adjustment. Instead, the IRS is authorized to send notice of a partnership adjustment to the partnership itself by certified or registered mail. The IRS could give proper notice by mailing the notice to the last known address of the partnership, even if the partnership had terminated its existence.

Adjudication of disputes concerning partnership items

As under present law, an administrative adjustment could be challenged in the Tax Court, the district court in which the partnership's principal place of business is located, or the Claims Court. However, only the partnership, and not partners individually, can petition for a readjustment of partnership items. partnership, the court with which the petition is filed will have

If a petition for readjustment of partnership items is filed by the jurisdiction to determine the tax treatment of all partnership items of the partnership for the partnership taxable year to which the notice of partnership adjustment relates, and the proper allocation of such items among the partners. Thus, the court's jurisdiction is not limited to the items adjusted in the notice.

Statute of limitations

Absent an agreement to extend the statute of limitations, the IRS generally could not adjust a partnership item of an electing large partnership more than 3 years after the later of the filing of the partnership return or the last day for the filing of the partnership return. Special rules apply to false or fraudulent returns, a substantial omission of income, or the failure to file a return. The IRS would assess and collect any deficiency of a partner that arises from any adjustment to a partnership item subject to the limitations period on assessments and collection applicable to the year the adjustment takes effect (secs. 6248, 6501 and 6502).

Regulatory authority

The Secretary of the Treasury is granted authority to prescribe regulations as may be necessary to carry out the simplified audit procedure provisions, including regulations to prevent abuse of the provisions through manipulation. The regulations may include rules that address transfers of partnership interests, in anticipation of a partnership adjustment, to persons who are tax-favored (e.g., corporations with net operating losses, tax-exempt organizations, and foreign partners) or persons who are expected to be unable to pay tax (e.g., shell corporations). For example, if prior to the time a partnership adjustment takes effect, a taxable partner transfers a partnership interest to a nonresident alien to avoid the tax effect of the partnership adjustment, the rules may provide, among other things, that income related to the partnership adjustment is treated as effectively connected taxable income, that the partnership adjustment is treated as taking effect before the partnership interest was transferred, or that the former partner is treated as a current partner to whom the partnership adjustment is allocated.

Effective Date

The provision applies to partnership taxable years beginning after December 31, 1997.

[Conference Report]

Senate Amendment

The Senate amendment is the same as the House bill.

[¶ 5211]   Section 1223. Due date for furnishing information to partners of electing large partnerships.

(Code Sec. 6031, 6724)

[House Report]

Present Law

A partnership required to file an income tax return with the Internal Revenue Service must also furnish an information return to each of its partners on or before the day on which the income tax return for the year is required to be filed, including extensions. Under regulations, a partnership must file its income tax return on or before the fifteenth day of the fourth month following the end of the partnership's taxable year (on or before April 15, for calendar year partnerships). This is the same deadline by which most individual partners must file their tax returns.

Reasons for Change

Information returns that are received on or shortly before April 15 (or later) are difficult for individuals to use in preparing their tax returns (or in computing their payments) that are due on that date.

Explanation of Provision

The bill provides that an electing large partnership must furnish information returns to partners by the first March 15 following the close of the partnership's taxable year. Electing large partnerships are those partnerships subject to the simplified reporting and audit rules (generally, any partnership that elects under the reporting provision, if the number of partners in the preceding taxable year is 100 or more).

The provision also provides that, if the partnership is required to provide copies of the information returns to the Internal Revenue Service on magnetic media, each schedule (such as each Schedule K 1) with respect to each partner is treated as a separate information return with respect to the corrective periods and penalties that are generally applicable to all information returns.

Effective Date

The provision is effective for partnership taxable years beginning after December 31, 1997.

[Conference Report]

Senate Amendment

The Senate amendment is the same as the House bill.

Conference Agreement

The conference agreement follows the House bill and the Senate amendment.

[¶ 5212]   Section 1224.   Partnership returns required on magnetic media.

(Code Sec. 6011)

[House Report]

Present Law

Partnerships are permitted, but not required, to provide the tax return of the partnership (Form 1065), as well as copies of the schedules sent to each partner (Form K 1), to the Internal Revenue Service on magnetic media.

Reasons for Change

Most entities that file large numbers of documents with the Internal Revenue Service must do so on magnetic media. Conforming the reporting provisions for partnerships to the generally applicable information reporting rules will facilitate integration of partnership information into already existing data systems.

[¶ 5213]   Section 1225.   Treatment of partnership items of individual retirement arrangements.

(Code Sec. 6012)

[House Report]

Present Law

Return filing requirements

An individual retirement account ("IRA") is a trust which generally is exempt from taxation except for the taxes imposed on income from an unrelated trade or business. A fiduciary of a trust that is exempt from taxation (but subject to the taxes imposed on income from an unrelated trade or business) generally is required to file a return on behalf of the trust for a taxable year if the trust has gross income of $1,000 or more included in computing unrelated business taxable income for that year (Treas. Reg. sec. 1.6012-3(a)(5)).

Explanation of Provision

The bill provides generally that any partnership is required to provide the tax return of the partnership (Form 1065), as well as copies of the schedule sent to each partner (Form K 1), to the Internal Revenue Service on magnetic media. An exception is provided for partnerships with 100 or fewer partners.

Effective Date

The provision is effective for partnership taxable years beginning after December 31, 1997.

[Conference Report]

Senate Amendment

The Senate amendment is the same as the House bill.

Conference Agreement

The conference agreement follows the House bill and the Senate amendment.

Unrelated business taxable income is the gross income (including gross income from a partnership) derived by an exempt organization from an unrelated trade or business, less certain deductions which are directly connected with the carrying on of such trade or business (sec. 512(a)(1). In calculating unrelated business taxable income, exempt organizations (including IRAs) generally also are permitted a specific deduction of $1,000 (sec. 512(b)(12)).

Unified audits of partnerships

All but certain small partnerships are subject to unified audit rules established by the Tax Equity and Fiscal Responsibility Act of 1982. These rules require the tax treatment of all "partnership items" to be determined at the partnership, rather than the partner, level. Partnership items are those items that are more appropriately determined at the partnership level than at the partner level, including such items as gross income and deductions of the partnership.

Reasons for Change

Under present law, tax returns often must be filed for IRAs that have no taxable income and, consequently, no tax liability. The filing of these returns by taxpayers, and the processing of these returns by the IRS, impose significant costs. Imposing this burden is unnecessary to the extent that the income of the IRA has been derived from an interest in a partnership that is subject to partnership-level audit rules. In these circumstances, the appropriateness of any deductions may be determined at the partnership level, and an additional filing is unnecessary to facilitate this determination.

Explanation of Provision

The bill modifies the filing threshold for an IRA with an interest in a partnership that is subject to the partnership-level audit rules. A fiduciary of such an IRA could

treat the trust's share of partnership taxable income as gross income, for purposes of determining whether the trust meets the $1,000 gross income filing threshold. A fiduciary of an IRA that receives taxable income from a partnership that is subject to partnership-level audit rules of less than $1,000 (before the $1,000 specific deduction) is not required to file an income tax return if the IRA does not have any other income from an unrelated trade or business.

Effective Date

The provision applies to taxable years beginning after December 31, 1997.

[Conference Report]

Senate Amendment

The Senate amendment is the same as the House bill.

Conference Agreement

The conference agreement follows the House bill and the Senate amendment.

[¶ 5215] Section 1231. Treatment of partnership items in deficiency proceedings.

(Code Sec. 6234, 6211)

[House Report]

Present Law

Partnership proceedings under rules enacted in TEFRA[12] must be kept separate from deficiency proceedings involving the partners in their individual capacities. Prior to the Tax Court's opinion in *Munro v. Commissioner,* 92 T.C. 71 (1989), the IRS computed deficiencies by assuming that all items that were subject to the TEFRA partnership procedures were correctly reported on the taxpayer's return. However, where the losses claimed from TEFRA partnerships were so large that they offset any proposed adjustments to nonpartnership items, no deficiency could arise from a non-TEFRA proceeding, and if the partnership losses were subsequently disallowed in a partnership proceeding, the non-TEFRA adjustments might be uncollectible because

of the expiration of the statute of limitations with respect to nonpartnership items.

Faced with this situation in *Munro,* the IRS issued a notice of deficiency to the taxpayer that presumptively disallowed the taxpayer's TEFRA partnership losses for computational purposes only. Although the Tax Court ruled that a deficiency existed and that the court had jurisdiction to hear the case, the court disapproved of the methodology used by the IRS to compute the deficiency. Specifically, the court held that partnership items (whether income, loss, deduction, or credit) included on a taxpayer's return must be completely ignored in determining whether a deficiency exists that is attributable to nonpartnership items.

Reasons for Change

The opinion in *Munro* creates problems for both taxpayers and the IRS. For example, a taxpayer would be harmed in the case where he has invested in a TEFRA partner-

---

12. Tax Equity and Fiscal Responsibility Act of 1982.

ship and is also subject to the deficiency procedures with respect to nonpartnership item adjustments, since computing the tax liability without regard to partnership items will have the same effect as if the partnership items were disallowed. If the partnership items were losses, the effect will be a greatly increased deficiency for the nonpartnership items. If, when the partnership proceedings are completed, the taxpayer is ultimately allowed any part of the losses, the taxpayer will receive part of the increased deficiency back in the form of an overpayment. However, in the interim, the taxpayer will have been subject to assessment and collection of a deficiency inflated by items still in dispute in the partnership proceeding. In essence, a taxpayer in such a case would be deprived of a prepayment forum with respect to the partnership item adjustments. The IRS would be harmed if a taxpayer's income is primarily from a TEFRA partnership, since the IRS may be unable to adjust nonpartnership items such as medical expense deductions, home mortgage interest deductions or charitable contribution deductions because there would be no deficiency since, under *Munro,* the income must be ignored.

Explanation of Provision

The bill overrules *Munro* and allow the IRS to return to its prior practice of computing deficiencies by assuming that all TEFRA items whose treatment has not been finally determined had been correctly reported on the taxpayer's return. This eliminates the need to do special computations that involve the removal of TEFRA items from a taxpayer's return, and will restore to taxpayers a prepayment forum with respect to the TEFRA items. In addition, the provision provides a special rule to address the factual situation presented in *Munro* .

Specifically, the bill provides a declaratory judgment procedure in the Tax Court for adjustments to an oversheltered return. An oversheltered return is a return that shows no taxable income and a net loss from TEFRA partnerships. In such a case, the IRS is authorized to issue a notice of adjustment with respect to non-TEFRA items, notwithstanding that no deficiency would result from the adjustment. However,

the IRS could only issue such a notice if a deficiency would have arisen in the absence of the net loss from TEFRA partnerships.

The Tax Court is granted jurisdiction to determine the correctness of such an adjustment as well as to make a declaration with respect to any other item for the taxable year to which the notice of adjustment relates, except for partnership items and affected items which require partner-level determinations. No tax is due upon such a determination, but a decision of the Tax Court is treated as a final decision, permitting an appeal of the decision by either the taxpayer or the IRS. An adjustment determined to be correct would thus have the effect of increasing the taxable income that is deemed to have been reported on the taxpayer's return. If the taxpayer's partnership items were then adjusted in a subsequent proceeding, the IRS has preserved its ability to collect tax on any increased deficiency attributable to the nonpartnership items.

Alternatively, if the taxpayer chooses not to contest the notice of adjustment within the 90-day period, the bill provides that when the taxpayer's partnership items are finally determined, the taxpayer has the right to file a refund claim for tax attributable to the items adjusted by the earlier notice of adjustment for the taxable year. Although a refund claim is not generally permitted with respect to a deficiency arising from a TEFRA proceeding, such a rule is appropriate with respect to a defaulted notice of adjustment because taxpayers may not challenge such a notice when issued since it does not require the payment of additional tax.

In addition, the bill incorporates a number of provisions intended to clarify the coordination between TEFRA audit proceedings and individual deficiency proceedings. Under these provisions, any adjustment with respect to a non-partnership item that caused an increase in tax liability with respect to a partnership item would be treated as a computational adjustment and assessed after the conclusion of the TEFRA proceeding. Accordingly, deficiency procedures do not apply with respect to this increase in tax liability, and the statute of limitations applicable to TEFRA proceedings is controlling.

Effective Date

The provision is effective for partnership taxable years ending after the date of enactment.

[Conference Report]

Senate Amendment

The Senate amendment is the same as the House bill.

Conference Agreement

The conference agreement follows the House bill and the Senate amendment.

[¶ 5216]   Section 1232.   Partnership return to be determinative of audit procedures to be followed.

(Code Sec. 6231)

[House Report]

Present Law

TEFRA established unified audit rules applicable to all partnerships, except for partnerships with 10 or fewer partners, each of whom is a natural person (other than a nonresident alien) or an estate, and for which each partner's share of each partnership item is the same as that partner's share of every other partnership item. Partners in the exempted partnerships are subject to regular deficiency procedures.

Reasons for Change

The IRS often finds it difficult to determine whether to follow the TEFRA partnership procedures or the regular deficiency procedures. If the IRS determines that there were fewer than 10 partners in the partnership but was unaware that one of the partners was a nonresident alien or that there was a special allocation made during the year, the IRS might inadvertently apply the wrong procedures and possibly jeopardize any assessment. Permitting the IRS to rely on a partnership's return would simplify the IRS' task.

Explanation of Provision

The bill permits the IRS to apply the TEFRA audit procedures if, based on the partnership's return for the year, the IRS reasonably determines that those procedures should apply. Similarly, the provision permits the IRS to apply the normal deficiency procedures if, based on the partnership's return for the year, the IRS reasonably determines that those procedures should apply.

Effective Date

The provision is effective for partnership taxable years ending after the date of enactment.

[Conference Report]

Senate Amendment

The Senate amendment is the same as the House bill.

Conference Agreement

The conference agreement follows the House bill and the Senate amendment.

[¶ 5217]   Section 1233.   Provisions relating to statute of limitations. a. Suspend statute when an untimely petition is filed

(Code Sec. 6229)

[House Report]

Present Law

In a deficiency case, section 6503(a) provides that if a proceeding in respect of the deficiency is placed on the docket of the Tax Court, the period of limitations on assessment and collection is suspended until the decision of the Tax Court becomes final, and for 60 days thereafter. The counterpart to this provision with respect to TEFRA cases is contained in section

6229(d). That section provides that the period of limitations is suspended for the period during which an action may be brought under section 6226 and, if an action is brought during such period, until the decision of the court becomes final, and for 1 year thereafter. As a result of this difference in language, the running of the statute of limitations in a TEFRA case will only be tolled by the filing of a timely petition whereas in a deficiency case, the statute of limitations is tolled by the filing of any petition, regardless of whether the petition is timely.

Reasons for Change

Under present law, if an untimely petition is filed in a TEFRA case, the statute of limitations can expire while the case is still pending before the court. To prevent this from occurring, the IRS must make assessments against all of the investors during the pendency of the action and if the action is in the Tax Court, presumably abate such assessments if the court ultimately determines that the petition was timely. These steps are burdensome to the IRS and to taxpayers.

Explanation of Provision

The bill conforms the suspension rule for the filing of petitions in TEFRA cases with the rule under section 6503(a) pertaining to deficiency cases. Under the provision, the statute of limitations in TEFRA cases is suspended by the filing of any petition under section 6226, regardless of whether the petition is timely or valid, and the suspension will remain in effect until the decision of the court becomes final, and for one year thereafter. Hence, if the statute of limitations is open at the time that an untimely petition is filed, the limitations period would no longer continue to run and possibly expire while the action is pending before the court.

Effective Date

The provision is effective with respect to all cases in which the period of limitations has not expired under present law as of the date of enactment.

Senate Amendment

The Senate amendment is the same as the House bill.

Conference Agreement

The conference agreement follows the House bill and the Senate amendment.

ii. Suspend statute of limitations during bankruptcy proceedings (sec. 1233(b) of the bill and sec. 6229 of the Code)

Present Law

The period for assessing tax with respect to partnership items generally is the longer of the periods provided by section 6229 or section 6501. For partnership items that convert to nonpartnership items, section 6229(f) provides that the period for assessing tax shall not expire before the date which is 1 year after the date that the items become nonpartnership items. Section 6503(h) provides for the suspension of the limitations period during the pendency of a bankruptcy proceeding. However, this provision only applies to the limitations periods provided in sections 6501 and 6502.

Under present law, because the suspension provision in section 6503(h) applies only to the limitations periods provided in section 6501 and 6502, some uncertainty exists as to whether section 6503(h) applies to suspend the limitations period pertaining to converted items provided in section 6229(f) when a petition naming a partner as a debtor in a bankruptcy proceeding is filed. As a result, the limitations period provided in section 6229(f) may continue to run during the pendency of the bankruptcy proceeding, notwithstanding that the IRS is prohibited from making an assessment against the debtor because of the automatic stay provisions of the Bankruptcy Code.

Reasons for Change

The ambiguity in present law makes it difficult for the IRS to adjust partnership items that convert to nonpartnership items by reason of a partner going into bankruptcy. In addition, any uncertainty may result in increased requests for the bankruptcy court to lift the automatic stay to permit the IRS to make an assessment with respect to the   converted items.

Explanation of Provision

The bill clarifies that the statute of limitations is suspended for a   partner who is named in a bankruptcy petition. The suspension period is   for the entire period during which the IRS is prohibited by reason of the bankruptcy proceeding from making an assessment, and for 60 days   thereafter. The provision does not purport to create any inference as to   the proper interpretation of present law.

Effective Date

The provision is effective with respect to all cases in which the   period of limitations has not expired under present law as of the date   of enactment.

Senate Amendment

The Senate amendment is the same as the House bill.

Conference Agreement

The conference agreement follows the House bill and the Senate amendment.

iii. Extend statute of limitations for bankrupt TMPs (sec. 1233(c) of the bill and sec. 6229 of the Code)

Present Law

Section 6229(b)(1)(B) provides that the statute of limitations is   extended with respect to all partners in the partnership by an agreement   entered into between the tax matters partner (TMP) and the IRS. However,   Temp. Treas. Reg. secs. 301.6231(a)(7) 1T(l)(4) and 301.6231(c) 7T(a)   provide that upon the filing of a petition naming a partner as a debtor   in a bankruptcy proceeding, that partner's partnership items convert to   nonpartnership items, and if the debtor was the tax matters partner,   such status terminates. These rules are necessary because of the automatic stay provision contained in 11 U.S.C. sec. 362(a)(8). As a   result, if a consent to extend the statute of limitations is signed by a   person who would be the TMP but for the fact that at the time that the agreement is executed

the person was a debtor in a bankruptcy proceeding, the consent would not be binding on the other partners because the person signing the agreement was no   longer the TMP at the time that the agreement was executed.

Reasons for Change

The IRS is not automatically notified of bankruptcy filings and   cannot easily determine whether a taxpayer is in bankruptcy, especially   if the audit of the partnership is being conducted by one district and   the taxpayer resides in another district, as is frequently the situation   in TEFRA cases. If the IRS does not discover that a person signing a   consent is in bankruptcy, the IRS may mistakenly rely on that consent.   As a result, the IRS may be precluded from assessing any tax attributable to partnership item adjustments with respect to any of the   partners in the partnership.

Explanation of Provision

The bill provides that unless the IRS is notified of a bankruptcy   proceeding in accordance with regulations, the IRS can rely on a statute   extension signed by a person who is the tax matters partner but for the   fact that said person was in bankruptcy at the time that the person signed the agreement. Statute extensions granted by a bankrupt TMP in   these cases are binding on all of the partners in the partnership. The   provision is not intended to create any inference as to the proper   interpretation of present law.

Effective Date

The provision is effective for extension agreements entered into   after the date of enactment.

[Conference Report]

Senate Amendment

The Senate amendment is the same as the House bill.

Conference Agreement

The conference agreement follows the House bill and the Senate amendment.

[¶ 5218]   Section 1234.   Expansion of small partnership exception.

(Code Sec. 6231)

[House Report]

Present Law

TEFRA established unified audit rules applicable to all partnerships, except for partnerships with 10 or fewer partners, each of whom is a natural person (other than a nonresident alien) or an estate, and for which each partner's share of each partnership item is the same as that partner's share of every other partnership item. Partners in the exempted partnerships are subject to regular deficiency procedures.

Reasons for Change

The mere existence of a C corporation as a partner or of a special allocation does not warrant subjecting the partnership and its partners of an otherwise small partnership to the TEFRA procedures.

Explanation of Provision

The bill permits a small partnership to have a C corporation as a partner or to specially allocate items without jeopardizing its exception from the TEFRA rules. However, the provision retains the prohibition of present law against having a flow-through entity (other than an estate of a deceased partner) as a partner for purposes of qualifying for the small partnership exception.

Effective Date

The provision is effective for partnership taxable years ending after the date of enactment.

[Conference Report]

Senate Amendment

The Senate amendment is the same as the House bill.

Conference Agreement

The conference agreement follows the House bill and the Senate amendment.

[¶ 5219]   Section 1235.   Exclusion of partial settlements from 1-year limitation on assessment.

(Code Sec. 6229)

[House Report]

Present Law

The period for assessing tax with respect to partnership items generally is the longer of the periods provided by section 6229 or section 6501. For partnership items that convert to nonpartnership items, section 6229(f) provides that the period for assessing tax shall not expire before the date which is 1 year after the date that the items become nonpartnership items. Section 6231(b)(1)(C) provides that the partnership items of a partner for a partnership taxable year become nonpartnership items as of the date the partner enters into a settlement agreement with the IRS with respect to such items.

Reasons for Change

When a partial settlement agreement is entered into, the assessment period for the

items covered by the agreement may be different than the assessment period for the remaining items. This fractured statute of limitations poses a significant tracking problem for the IRS and necessitates multiple computations of tax with respect to each partner's investment in the partnership for the taxable year.

Explanation of Provision

The bill provides that if a partner and the IRS enter into a settlement agreement with respect to some but not all of the partnership items in dispute for a partnership taxable year and other partnership items remain in dispute, the period for assessing any tax attributable to the settled items is determined as if such agreement had not been entered into. Consequently, the limitations period that is applicable to the last item to be resolved for the partnership taxable year is controlling with respect to all disputed partnership items for the partnership taxable year. The provision does not purport to create any inference as to the proper interpretation of present law.

Effective Date

The provision is effective for settlements entered into after the date of enactment.

[¶ 5220]   Section 1236.   Extension of time for filing a request for administrative adjustment.

(Code Sec. 6227)

[House Report]

Present Law

If an agreement extending the statute is entered into with respect to a non-TEFRA statute of limitations, that agreement also extends the statute of limitations for filing refund claims (sec. 6511(c)). There is no comparable provision for extending the time for filing refund claims with respect to partnership items subject to the TEFRA partnership rules.

Reasons for Change

The absence of an extension for filing refund claims in TEFRA proceedings hinders taxpayers that may want to agree to extend the TEFRA statute of limitations but want to preserve their option to file a refund claim later.

[¶ 5221]   Section 1237.

(Code Sec. 6230, 6503)

[House Report]

Present Law

In general, an innocent spouse may be relieved of liability for tax, penalties and interest if certain conditions are met (sec. 6013(e)). However, existing law does not provide the spouse of a partner in a TEFRA partnership with a judicial forum to raise the innocent spouse defense with respect to any tax or interest that relates to an investment in a TEFRA partnership.

[Conference Report]

Senate Amendment

The Senate amendment is the same as the House bill.

Conference Agreement

The conference agreement follows the House bill and the Senate amendment.

Explanation of Provision

The bill provides that if a TEFRA statute extension agreement is entered into, that agreement also extends the statute of limitations for filing refund claims attributable to partnership items or affected items until 6 months after the expiration of the limitations period for assessments.

Effective Date

The provision is effective as if included in the amendments made by section 402 of the Tax Equity and Fiscal Responsibility Act of 1982.

[Conference Report]

Senate Amendment

The Senate amendment is the same as the House bill.

Conference Agreement

The conference agreement follows the House bill and the Senate amendment.

Reasons for Change

Providing a forum in which to raise the innocent spouse defense with respect to liabilities attributable to adjustments to partnership items (including penalties, additions to tax and additional amounts) would make the innocent spouse rules more uniform.

Explanation of Provision

The bill provides both a prepayment forum and a refund forum for raising the innocent spouse defense in TEFRA cases.

With respect to a prepayment forum, the provision provides that within 60 days of the date that a notice of computational adjustment relating to partnership items is mailed to the spouse of a partner, the spouse could request that the assessment be abated. Upon receipt of such a request, the assessment is abated and any reassessment will be subject to the deficiency procedures. If an abatement is requested, the statute of limitations does not expire before the date which is 60 days after the date of the abatement. If the spouse files a petition with the Tax Court, the Tax Court only has jurisdiction to determine whether the requirements of section 6013(e) have been satisfied. In making this determination, the treatment of the partnership items that gave rise to the liability in question is conclusive.

Alternatively, the bill provides that the spouse of a partner could file a claim for refund to raise the innocent spouse defense. The claim has to be filed within 6 months from the date that the notice of computational adjustment is mailed to the spouse. If the claim is not allowed, the spouse could file a refund action. For purposes of any claim or suit under this provision, the treatment of the partnership items that gave rise to the liability in question is conclusive.

Effective Date

The provision is effective as if included in the amendments made by section 402 of the Tax Equity and Fiscal Responsibility Act of 1982.

[Conference Report]

Senate Amendment

The Senate amendment is the same as the House bill.

Conference Agreement

The conference agreement follows the House bill and the Senate amendment.

[¶ 5223]   Section 1238.   Determination of penalties at partnership level.

(Code Sec. 6221, 6226, 6230)

[House Report]

Present Law

Partnership items include only items that are required to be taken into account under the income tax subtitle. Penalties are not partnership items since they are contained in the procedure and administration subtitle. As a result, penalties may only be asserted against a partner through the application of the deficiency procedures following the completion of the partnership-level proceeding.

Reasons for Change

Many penalties are based upon the conduct of the taxpayer. With respect to partnerships, the relevant conduct often occurs at the partnership level. In addition, applying penalties at the partner level through the deficiency procedures following the conclusion of the unified proceeding at the partnership level increases the administrative burden on the IRS and can significantly increase the Tax Court's inventory.

Explanation of Provision

The bill provides that the partnership-level proceeding is to include a determination of the applicability of penalties at the partnership level. However, the provision allows partners to raise any partner-level defenses in a refund forum.

Effective Date

The provision is effective for partnership taxable years ending after the date of enactment.

[Conference Report]

Senate Amendment

The Senate amendment is the same as the House bill.

Conference Agreement

The conference agreement follows the House bill and the Senate amendment, with technical modifications.

[¶ 5224]   Section 1239. Provisions relating to Tax Court jurisdiction.

(Code Sec. 6225, 6226, 6230, 6512, 7482, 7459, 6501, 7421)

[House Report]

Present Law

Improper assessment and collection activities by the IRS during the 150-day period for filing a petition or during the pendency of any Tax Court proceeding, "may be enjoined in the proper court." Present law may be unclear as to whether this includes the Tax Court.

For a partner other than the Tax Matters Partner to be eligible to file a petition for redetermination of partnership items in any court or to participate in an existing case, the period for assessing any tax attributable to the partnership items of that partner must not have expired. Since such a partner would only be treated as a party to the action if the statute of limitations with respect to them was still open, the law is unclear whether the partner would have standing to assert that the statute of limitations had expired with respect to them.

Reasons for Change

Clarifying the Tax Court's jurisdiction simplifies the resolution of tax cases.

Explanation of Provision

The bill clarifies that an action to enjoin premature assessments of deficiencies attributable to partnership items may be brought in the Tax Court. The provision also permits a partner to participate in an action or file a petition for the sole purpose of asserting that the period of limitations for assessing any tax attributable to partnership items has expired for that person. Additionally, the provision clarifies that the Tax Court has overpayment jurisdiction with respect to affected items.

Effective Date

The provision is effective for partnership taxable years ending after the date of enactment.

[Conference Report]

Senate Amendment

The Senate amendment is the same as the House bill.

Conference Agreement

The conference agreement follows the House bill and the Senate amendment, with technical modifications.

[¶ 5225]   Section 1240. Treatment of premature petitions filed by notice partners or 5-percent groups.

(Code Sec. 6226)

[House Report]

Present Law

The Tax Matters Partner is given the exclusive right to file a petition for a readjustment of partnership items within the 90-day period after the issuance of the notice of a final partnership administrative adjustment (FPAA). If the Tax Matters Partner does not file a petition within the 90-day period, certain other partners are permitted to file a petition within the 60-day period after the close of the 90-day period. There are ordering rules for determining which action goes forward and for dismissing other actions.

Reasons for Change

A petition that is filed within the 90-day period by a person who is not the Tax Matters Partner is dismissed. Thus, if the Tax Matters Partner does not file a petition within the 90-day period and no timely and valid petition is filed during the succeeding 60-day period, judicial review of the adjustments set forth in the notice of FPAA is foreclosed and the adjustments are deemed to be correct.

Explanation of Provision

The bill treats premature petitions filed by certain partners within the 90-day period as being filed on the last day of the following 60-day period under specified circumstances, thus affording the partnership with an opportunity for judicial review that is not available under present law.

Effective Date

The provision is effective with respect to petitions filed after the date of enactment.

[¶ 5226]   Section 1241.   Bonds in case of appeals from certain proceedings.

(Code Sec. 7485)

[House Report]

Present Law

A bond must be filed to stay the collection of deficiencies pending the appeal of the Tax Court's decision in a TEFRA proceeding. The amount of the bond must be based on the court's estimate of the aggregate deficiencies of the partners.

Reasons for Change

The Tax Court cannot easily determine the aggregate changes in tax liability of all of the partners in a partnership who will be affected by the Court's decision in the proceeding. Clarifying the calculation of the bond amount would simplify the Tax Court's task.

Explanation of Provision

The bill clarifies that the amount of the bond should be based on the Tax Court's estimate of the aggregate liability of the parties to the action (and not all of the partners in the partnership). For purposes of this provision, the amount of the bond could be estimated by applying the highest individual rate to the total adjustments determined by the Tax Court and doubling that amount to take into account interest and penalties.

Effective Date

The provision is effective as if included in the amendments made by section 402 of the Tax Equity and Fiscal Responsibility Act of 1982.

[Conference Report]

Senate Amendment

The Senate amendment is the same as the House bill.

Conference Agreement

The conference agreement follows the House bill and the Senate amendment.

[Conference Report]

Senate Amendment

The Senate amendment is the same as the House bill.

Conference Agreement

The conference agreement follows the House bill and the Senate amendment.

[¶ 5227]   Section 1242.   Suspension of interest where delay in computational adjustment resulting from certain settlements.

(Code Sec. 6601)

[House Report]

Present Law

Interest on a deficiency generally is suspended when a taxpayer executes a settlement agreement with the IRS and waives the restrictions on assessments and collections, and the IRS does not issue a notice and demand for payment of such deficiency within 30 days. Interest on a deficiency that results from an adjustment of partnership items in TEFRA proceedings, however, is not suspended.

Reasons for Change

Processing settlement agreements and assessing the tax due takes a substantial amount of time in TEFRA cases. A taxpayer is not afforded any relief from interest during this period.

Explanation of Provision

The bill suspends interest where there is a delay in making a computational adjustment relating to a TEFRA settlement.

Effective Date

The provision is effective with respect to adjustments relating to taxable years beginning after the date of enactment.

[Conference Report]

Senate Amendment

The Senate amendment is the same as the House bill.

Conference Agreement

The conference agreement follows the House bill and the Senate amendment.

[¶ 5228]   Section 1243. Special rules for administrative adjustment requests with respect to bad debts or worthless securities.

(Code Sec. 6227)

[House Report]

Present Law

The non-TEFRA statute of limitations for filing a claim for credit or refund generally is the later of (1) three years from the date the return in question was filed or (2) two years from the date the claimed tax was paid, whichever is later (sec. 6511(b)). However, an extended period of time, seven years from the date the return was due, is provided for filing a claim for refund of an overpayment resulting from a deduction for a worthless security or bad debt (sec. 6511(d)).

Under the TEFRA partnership rules, a request for administrative adjustment ("RAA") must be filed within three years after the later of (1) the date the partnership return was filed or (2) the due date of the partnership return (determined without regard to extensions) (sec. 6227(a)(1)). In addition, the request must be filed before a final partnership administrative adjustment ("FPAA") is mailed for the taxable year (sec. 6227(a)(2)). There is no special provision for extending the time for filing an RAA that relates to a deduction for a worthless security or an entirely worthless bad debt.

Reasons for Change

Whether and when a stock or debt becomes worthless is a question of fact that may not be determinable until after the year in which it appears the loss has occurred. An extended statute of limitations allows partners in a TEFRA partnership the same opportunity to file a delayed claim for refund in these difficult factual situations as other taxpayers are permitted.

Further, on past occasions, the IRS issued FPAAs that did not adjust the partnership's tax return. This action created wasteful paperwork, and may have, in some cases truncated the appeals rights of individual partners. A special rule is necessary to permit partners who may have been adversely impacted by this past practice of the IRS to avail themselves of the extended period irrespective of whether an FPAA has been issued.

Explanation of Provision

The bill extends the time for the filing of an RAA relating to the deduction by a partnership for a worthless security or bad debt. In these circumstances, in lieu of the three-year period provided in sec. 6227(a)(1), the period for filing an RAA is seven years from the date the partnership return was due with respect to which the request is made (determined without regard to extensions). The RAA is still required to be filed before the FPAA is mailed for the taxable year.

Effective Date

The provision is effective as if included in the amendments made by section 402 of the Tax Equity and Fiscal Responsibility Act of 1982.

[Conference Report]

Senate Amendment

The Senate amendment is the same as the House bill.

Conference Agreement

The conference agreement follows the House bill and the Senate amendment.

[¶ 5229]   Section 1246.   Closing of partnership taxable year with respect to deceased partner.

(Code Sec. 706)

[House Report]

Present Law

The partnership taxable year closes with respect to a partner whose entire interest is sold, exchanged, or liquidated. Such year, however, generally does not close upon the death of a partner. Thus, a decedent's entire share of items of income, gain, loss, deduction and credit for the partnership year in which death occurs is taxed to the estate or successor in interest rather than to the decedent on his or her final income tax return. See Estate of Hesse v. Commissioner , 74 T.C. 1307, 1311 (1980).

Reasons for Change

The rule leaving open the partnership taxable year with respect to a deceased partner was adopted in 1954 to prevent the bunching of income that could occur with respect to a partnership reporting on a fiscal year other than the calendar year. Without this rule, as many as 23 months of income might have been reported on the partner's final return. Legislative changes occurring since 1954 have required most partnerships to adopt a calendar year, reducing the possibility of bunching. Consequently, income and deductions are better matched if the partnership taxable year closes upon a partner's death and partnership items are reported on the decedent's last return.

Present law closes the partnership taxable year with respect to a deceased partner only if the partner's entire interest is sold or exchanged pursuant to an agreement existing at the time of death. By closing the taxable year automatically upon death, the provision reduces the need for such agreements.

Explanation of Provision

The bill provides that the taxable year of a partnership closes with respect to a partner whose entire interest in the partnership terminates, whether by death, liquidation or otherwise. The bill does not change present law with respect to the effect upon the partnership taxable year of a transfer of a partnership interest by a debtor to the debtor's estate (under Chapters 7 or 11 of Title 11, relating to bankruptcy).

Effective Date

The provision applies to partnership taxable years beginning after December 31, 1997.

[Conference Report]

Senate Amendment

The Senate amendment is the same as the House bill.

Conference Agreement

The conference agreement follows the House bill and the Senate amendment.

[¶ 5230]   Section 1251-1263.   Modifications of rules for real estate investment trusts.

(Code Sec. 856, 857)

[House Report]

Present Law

Overview

In general, a real estate investment trust ("REIT") is an entity that receives most of its income from passive real estate related investments and that receives conduit treatment for income that is distributed to shareholders. If an entity meets the qualifications for REIT status, the portion of its income that is distributed to the investors each year generally is taxed to the investors without being subjected to a tax at the REIT level; the REIT generally is subject to a corporate tax only on the income that it retains and on certain income from property that qualifies as foreclosure property.

Election to be treated as a REIT

In order to qualify as a REIT, and thereby receive conduit treatment, an entity must elect REIT status. A newly-electing entity generally cannot have earnings and profits accumulated from any year in which the entity was in existence and not treated as a REIT (sec. 857(a)(3)). To satisfy this requirement, the entity must distribute, during its first REIT taxable year, any earnings and profits that were accumulated in non-REIT years. For this purpose, distributions by the entity generally are treated as being made from the most recently accumulated earnings and profits.

Taxation of REITs

Overview

In general, if an entity qualifies as a REIT by satisfying the various requirements described below, the entity is taxable as a corporation on its "real estate investment trust taxable income" ("REITTI"), and also is taxable on certain other amounts (sec. 857). REITTI is the taxable income of the REIT with certain adjustments (sec. 857(b)(2)). The most significant adjustment is a deduction for dividends paid. The allowance of this deduction is the mechanism by which the REIT becomes a conduit for income tax purposes.

Capital gains

A REIT that has a net capital gain for a taxable year generally is subject to tax on such capital gain under the capital gains tax regime generally applicable to corporations (sec. 857(b)(3)). However, a REIT may diminish or eliminate its tax liability attributable to such capital gain by paying a "capital gain dividend" to its shareholders (sec. 857(b)(3)(C)). A capital gain dividend is any dividend or part of a dividend that is designated by the payor REIT as a capital gain dividend in a written notice mailed to shareholders. Shareholders who receive capital gain dividends treat the amount of such dividends as long-term capital gain regardless of their holding period of the stock (sec. 857(b)(3)(C)).

A regulated investment company ("RIC"), but not a REIT, may elect to retain and pay income tax on net long-term capital gains it received during the tax year. If a RIC makes this election, the RIC shareholders must include in their income as long-term capital gains their proportionate share of these undistributed long-term capital gains as designated by the RIC. The shareholder is deemed to have paid the shareholder's share of the tax, which can be credited or refunded to the shareholder. Also, the basis of the shareholder's shares is increased by the amount of the undistributed long-term capital gains (less the amount of capital gains tax paid by the RIC) included in the shareholder's long-term capital gains.

Income from foreclosure property

In addition to tax on its REITTI, a REIT is subject to tax at the highest rate of tax paid by corporations on its net income from foreclosure property (sec. 857(b)(4)). Net income from foreclosure property is the excess of the sum of gains from foreclosure property that is held for sale to customers in the ordinary course of a trade or business and gross income from foreclosure property (other than income that otherwise would qualify under the 75-percent income test described below) over all allowable deductions directly connected with the production of such income.

Foreclosure property is any real property or personal property incident to such real property that is acquired by a REIT as a result of default or imminent default on a lease of such property or indebtedness secured by such property, provided that (unless acquired as foreclosure property), such property was not held by the REIT for sale to customers (sec. 856(e)). A property generally may be treated as foreclosure property for a period of two years after the date the property is acquired by the REIT. The IRS may grant extensions of the period for treating the property as foreclosure property if the REIT establishes that an extension of the grace period is necessary for the orderly liquidation of the REIT's interest in the property. The grace period cannot be extended beyond six years from the date the property is acquired by the REIT.

Property will cease to be treated as foreclosure property if, after 90 days after the date of acquisition, the REIT operates the foreclosure property in a trade or business other than through an independent contractor from whom the REIT does not derive or receive any income (sec. 856(e)(4)(C)).

Income or loss from prohibited transactions

In general, a REIT must derive its income from passive sources and not engage in any active trade or business. Accordingly, in addition to the tax on its REITTI and on its net income from foreclosure property, a 100 percent tax is imposed on the net income of a REIT from "prohibited transactions" (sec. 857(b)(6)). A prohibited transaction is the sale or other disposition of property described in section 1221(1) of the Code (property held for sale in the ordinary course of a trade or business) other than foreclosure property. Thus, the 100 percent tax on prohibited transactions helps to ensure that the REIT is a passive entity and may not engage in ordinary retailing activities such as sales to customers of condominium units or subdivided lots in a development project. A safe harbor is provided for certain sales that otherwise might be considered prohibited transactions (sec. 857(b)(6)(C)). The safe harbor is limited to seven or fewer sales a year or, alternatively, any number of sales provided that the aggregate adjusted basis of the property sold does not exceed 10 percent of the aggregate basis of all the REIT's assets at the beginning of the REIT's taxable year.

Requirements for REIT status

A REIT must satisfy four tests on a year-by-year basis: organizational structure, source of income, nature of assets, and distribution of income. These tests are intended to allow conduit treatment in circumstances in which a corporate tax otherwise would be imposed, only if there really is a pooling of investment arrangement that is evidenced by its organizational structure, if its investments are basically in real estate assets, and if its income is passive income from real estate investment, as contrasted with income from the operation of business involving real estate. In addition, substantially all of the entity's income must be passed through to its shareholders on a current basis.

Organizational structure requirements

To qualify as a REIT, an entity must be for its entire taxable year a corporation or an unincorporated trust or association that would be taxable as a domestic corporation but for the REIT provisions, and must be managed by one or more trustees (sec. 856(a)). The beneficial ownership of the entity must be evidenced by transferable shares or certificates of ownership. Except for the first taxable year for which an entity elects to be a REIT, the beneficial ownership of the entity must be held by 100 or more persons, and the entity may not be so closely held by individuals that it would be treated as a personal holding company if all its adjusted gross income constituted personal holding company income. A REIT is disqualified for any year in which it does not comply with regulations to ascertain the actual ownership of the REIT's outstanding shares.

Income requirements

Overview

In order for an entity to qualify as a REIT, at least 95 percent of its gross income generally must be derived from certain passive sources (the "95-percent test"). In addition, at least 75 percent of its income generally must be from certain real estate sources (the "75-percent test"), including rents from real property.

In addition, less than 30 percent of the entity's gross income may be derived from gain from the sale or other disposition of stock or securities held for less than one year, real property held less than four years (other than foreclosure property, or property subject to an involuntary conversion within the meaning of sec. 1033), and property that is sold or disposed of in a prohibited transaction (sec. 856(c)(4)).

Definition of rents

For purposes of the income requirements, rents from real property generally include rents from interests in real property, charges for services customarily rendered or furnished in connection with the rental of real property, whether or not such charges are separately stated, and rent attributable to personal property that is leased under or in connection with a lease of real property, but only if the rent attributable to such personal property does not exceed 15 percent of the total rent for the year under the lease (sec. 856(d)(1)).

Services provided to tenants are regarded as customary if, in the geographic market within which the building is located, tenants in buildings that are of a similar class (for example, luxury apartment buildings) are customarily provided with the service. The furnishing of water, heat, light, and air conditioning, the cleaning of windows, public entrances, exits, and lobbies, the performance of general maintenance, and of janitorial and cleaning services, the collection of trash, the furnishing of elevator services, telephone answering services, incidental storage space, laundry equipment, watchman or guard service, parking facilities and swimming pool facilities are examples of services that are customarily furnished to tenants of a particular class of buildings in many geographical marketing areas (Treas. Reg. sec. 1.856 4(b)).

In addition, amounts are not treated as qualifying rent if received from certain parties in which the REIT has an ownership interest of 10 percent or more (sec. 856(d)(2)(B)). For purposes of determining the REIT's ownership interest in a tenant, the attribution rules of section 318 apply, except that 10 percent is substituted for 50 percent where it appears in subparagraph (C) of section 318(a)(2) and 318(a)(3) (sec. 856(d)(5)).

Finally, where a REIT furnishes or renders services to the tenants of rented property, amounts received or accrued with respect to such property generally are not treated as qualifying rents unless the services are furnished through an independent contractor (sec. 856(d)(2)(C)). A REIT may furnish or render a service directly, however, if the service would not generate unrelated business taxable income under section 512(b)(3) if provided by an organization described in section 511(a)(2). In general, an independent contractor is a person who does not own more than a 35 percent interest in the REIT, and in which no more than a 35 percent interest is held by persons with a 35 percent or greater interest in the REIT (sec. 856(d)(3)).

Hedging instruments

Interest rate swaps or cap agreements that protect a REIT from interest rate fluctuations on variable rate debt incurred to acquire or carry real property are treated as securities under the 30-percent test and payments under these agreements are treated as qualifying under the 95-percent test (sec. 856(c)(6)(G)).

Treatment of shared appreciation mortgages

For purposes of the income requirements for qualification as a REIT, and for purposes of the prohibited transaction provisions, any income derived from a "shared appreciation provision" is treated as gain recognized on the sale of the "secured property." For these purposes, a shared appreciation provision is any provision that is in connection with an obligation that is held by the REIT and secured by an interest in real property, which provision entitles the REIT to receive a specified portion of any gain realized on the sale or exchange of such real property (or of any gain that would be realized if the property were sold on a specified date). Secured property for these purposes means the real property that secures the obligation that has the shared appreciation provision.

In addition, for purposes of the income requirements for qualification as a REIT, and for purposes of the prohibited transactions provisions, the REIT is treated as holding the secured property for the period during which it held the shared appreciation provision (or, if shorter, the period during which the secured property was held by the person holding such property), and the secured property is treated as property described in section 1221(1) if it is such property in the hands of the obligor on the obligation to which the shared appreciation provision relates (or if it would be such property if held by the REIT). For purposes of the prohibited transaction safe harbor, the REIT is treated as having sold the secured property at the time that it recognizes income on account of the shared appreciation provision, and any expenditures made by the holder of the secured property are treated as made by the REIT.

Asset requirements

To satisfy the asset requirements to qualify for treatment as a REIT, at the close of each quarter of its taxable year, an entity must have at least 75 percent of the value of its assets invested in real estate assets, cash and cash items, and government securities (sec. 856(c)(5)(A)). Moreover, not more than 25 percent of the value of the entity's assets can be invested in securities of any one issuer (other than government securities and other securities described in the preceding sentence). Further, these securities may not comprise more than five percent of the entity's assets or more than 10 percent of the outstanding voting securities of such issuer (sec. 856(c)(5)(B)). The term real estate assets is defined to mean real property (including interests in real property and mortgages on real property) and interests in REITs (sec. 856(c)(6)(B)).

REIT subsidiaries

Under present law, all the assets, liabilities, and items of income, deduction, and credit of a "qualified REIT subsidiary" are treated as the assets, liabilities, and respective items of the REIT that owns the stock of the qualified REIT subsidiary. A subsidiary of a REIT is a qualified REIT subsidiary if and only if 100 percent of the subsidiary's stock is owned by the REIT at all times that the subsidiary is in existence. If at any time the REIT ceases to own 100 percent of the stock of the subsidiary, or if the REIT ceases to qualify for (or revokes an election of) REIT status, such subsidiary is treated as a new corporation that acquired all of its assets in exchange for its stock (and assumption of liabilities) immediately before the time that the REIT ceased to own 100 percent of the subsidiary's stock, or ceased to be a REIT as the case may be.

Distribution requirements

To satisfy the distribution requirement, a REIT must distribute as dividends to its shareholders during the taxable year an amount equal to or exceeding (i) the sum of 95 percent of its REITTI other than net capital gain income and 95 percent of the excess of its net income from foreclosure property over the tax imposed on that income minus (ii) certain excess noncash income (described below).

Excess noncash items include (a) the excess of the amounts that the REIT is required to include in income under section 467 with respect to certain rental agreements involving deferred rents, over the amounts that the REIT otherwise would recognize under its regular method of accounting, (2) in the case of a REIT using the cash method of accounting, the excess of the amount of original issue discount and coupon interest that the REIT is required to take into account with respect to a loan to which section 1274 applies, over the amount of money and fair market value of other property received with respect to the loan, and (3) income arising from the disposition of a real estate asset in certain transactions that failed to qualify as like-kind exchanges under section 1031.

Reasons for Change

The REIT serves as a means whereby numerous small investors can have a practical opportunity to invest in a diversified portfolio of real estate assets and have the benefit of professional management. The Committee believes that the asset requirements of present law ensure that a REIT acts as a pass-through entity for taxpayers wishing to invest in real estate. Therefore, the Committee finds the 30-percent gross income test unnecessary and administratively burdensome. The Committee further finds that financial markets have changed over the past decade such that interest risk can be managed by many strategies other than swaps and caps. Recognizing these developments in the financial markets, the Committee believes it necessary to modify the classification of income from certain hedging instruments to provide flexibility to REITs in managing risk for their shareholders. The Committee also believes that, as a pass-through entity, REITs should be permitted to retain the proceeds of realized capital gains in a manner comparable to that accorded to RICs.

Explanation of Provisions

Overview

The bill modifies many of the provisions relating to the requirements for qualification as, and the taxation of, a REIT. In particular, the modifications relate to the general requirements for qualification as a REIT, the taxation of a REIT, the income requirements for qualification as a REIT, and certain other provisions.

[Conference Report]

Senate Amendment

The Senate amendment is identical to the House bill.

Conference Agreement

The conference agreement follows the House bill and the Senate amendment. In addition, the conference agreement extends, to the definition of an independent contractor under section 856(d)(3), the modification to the attribution to partnerships of section 318(a)(3)(A) so that attribution occurs only when a partner owns a 25-percent or greater interest in the partnership. Thus, a person providing services will not fail to be an in-dependent contractor (and, therefore, amounts received or accrued by the REIT with respect to the property will not be treated as non-qualifying rents) where the REIT's shares are owned by a partnership and a partner owning a directly and indirectly a less-than-25-percent interest in the partnership also owns an interest in a contractor. Similarly, a contractor will not fail to be an independent contractor where owners of the REIT and owners of the contractor are partners in a partnership and either the owners of the REIT or owners of the tenant are directly and indirectly less-than-25-percent partners in the partnership.

Effective Date

The conference agreement is effective for taxable years beginning after the date of enactment.

[¶ 5247]   Section 1271.   Repeal of the 30-percent ("Short-short") Test for Regulated Invetsment Companies.

(Code Sec. 851)

[House Report]

Present Law

To qualify as a Regulated Investment Company (RIC), a company must derive less than 30 percent of its gross income from the sale or other disposition of stock or securities held for less than 3 months (the "30-percent test" or "short-short rule").

Reasons for Change

The short-short rule restricts the investment flexibility of RICs. The rule can, for example, limit a RIC's ability to "hedge" its investments (e.g., to use options to protect against adverse market moves).

The rule also burdens a RIC with significant recordkeeping, compliance, and administration costs. The RIC must keep track of the holding periods of assets and the rela-tive percentages of short-term gain that it realizes throughout the year. The Committee believes that the short-short test places unnecessary limitations upon a RIC's activities.

[Senate Report]

Explanation of Provision

The 30-percent test (or short-short rule) is repealed.

Effective Date

The provision is effective for taxable years beginning after December 31, 1997.

[Conference Report]

Conference Agreement

The conference agreement follows the House bill and the Senate amendment effective for taxable years beginning after the date of enactment.

[¶ 5248] Section 1281. Reasonable Cause exception for Additional Penalties.

(Code Sec. 6652, 6683, 7519)

[House Report]

Present Law

Many penalties in the Code may be waived if the taxpayer establishes reasonable cause. For example, the accuracy-related penalty (sec. 6662) may be waived with respect to any item if the taxpayer establishes reasonable cause for his treatment of the item and that he acted in good faith (sec. 6664(c)).

Reasons for Change

The Committee believes that it is appropriate to provide a reasonable cause exception for several additional penalties where one does not currently exist.

Explanation of Provision

The bill provides that the following penalties may be waived if the failure is shown to be due to reasonable cause and not willful neglect: (1) the penalty for failure to make a report in connection with deductible employee contributions to a retirement savings plan (sec. 6652(g)); (2) the penalty for failure to make a report as to certain small business stock (sec. 6652(k)); (3) the penalty for failure of a foreign corporation to file a return of personal holding company tax (sec. 6683); and (4) the penalty for failure to make required payments for entities electing not to have the required taxable year (sec. 7519).

Effective Date

The provision is effective for taxable years beginning after the date of enactment.

[Conference Report]

Senate Amendment

The Senate amendment is the same as the House bill.

Conference Agreement

The conference agreement follows the House bill and the Senate amendment.

[¶ 5249] Section 1282. Clarification of period for filing claims for refunds.

(Code Sec. 6512)

[House Report]

Present Law

The Code contains a series of limitations on tax refunds. Section 6511 of the Code provides both a limitation on the time period in which a claim for refund can be made (section 6511(a)) and a limitation on the amount that can be allowed as a refund (section 6511(b)).

Section 6511(a) provides the general rule that a claim for refund must be filed within 3 years of the date of the return or 2 years of the date of payment of the taxes at issue, whichever is later.

Section 6511(b) limits the refund amount that can be covered: if a return was filed, a taxpayer can recover amounts paid within 2 years before the claim. Section 6512(b)(3) incorporates these rules where taxpayers who challenge deficiency notices in Tax Court are found to be entitled to refunds.

In Commissioner v. Lundy, 116 S. Ct. 647 (1996), the taxpayer had not filed a return, but received a notice of deficiency within 3 years after the date the return was due and challenged the proposed deficiency in Tax Court. The Supreme Court held that the taxpayer could not recover overpayments attributable to withholding during the tax year, because no return was filed and the 2-year "look back" rule applied. Since overwithheld amounts are deemed paid as of the date the taxpayer's return was first due (i.e., more than 2 years before the notice of deficiency was issued), such overpayments could not be recovered. By contrast, if the same taxpayer had filed a return on the date the notice of deficiency was issued, and then claimed a refund, the 3-year "look back" rule would apply, and the taxpayer could have obtained a refund of the overwithheld amounts.

Reasons for Change

The Committee believes that it is appropriate to eliminate this disparate treatment.

Explanation of Provision

The bill permits taxpayers who initially fail to file a return, but who receive a notice of deficiency and file suit to contest it in Tax Court during the third year after the return due date, to obtain a refund of excessive amounts paid within the 3-year period prior to the date of the deficiency notice.

Effective Date

The provision applies to claims for refund with respect to tax years ending after the date of enactment.

[¶ 5250]   Section 1283.   Repeal of authority to disclose whether a prospective juror has been audited.

(Code Sec. 6103)

[House Report]

Present Law

In connection with a civil or criminal tax proceeding to which the United States is a party, the Secretary must disclose, upon the written request of either party to the lawsuit, whether an individual who is a prospective juror has or has not been the subject of an audit or other tax investigation by the Internal Revenue Service (sec. 6103(h)(5)).

Reasons for Change

This disclosure requirement, as it has been interpreted by several recent court decisions, has created significant difficulties in the civil and criminal tax litigation process. First, the litigation process can be substantially slowed. It can take the Secretary a considerable period of time to compile the information necessary for a response (some courts have required searches going back as far as 25 years). Second, providing early release of the list of potential jurors to defendants (which several recent court decisions have required, to permit defendants to obtain disclosure of the information from the Secretary) can provide an opportunity for harassment and intimidation of potential jurors in organized crime, drug, and some tax protester cases. Third, significant judicial resources have been expended in inter-

[Conference Report]

Senate Amendment

The Senate amendment is the same as the House bill.

Conference Agreement

The conference agreement follows the House bill and the Senate amendment.

preting this procedural requirement that might better be spent resolving substantive disputes. Fourth, differing judicial interpretations of this provision have caused confusion. In some instances, defendants convicted of criminal tax offenses have obtained reversals of those convictions because of failures to comply fully with this provision.

Explanation of Provision

The bill repeals the requirement that the Secretary disclose, upon the written request of either party to the lawsuit, whether an individual who is a prospective juror has or has not been the subject of an audit or other tax investigation by the Internal Revenue Service.

Effective Date

The provision is effective for judicial proceedings commenced after the date of enactment.

[Conference Report]

Senate Amendment

The Senate amendment is the same as the House bill.

Conference Agreement

The conference agreement follows the House bill and the Senate amendment.

[¶ 5251]   Section 1284.   C;arify statute of limitations for items from pass-through entities.

(Code Sec. 6501)

[House Report]

Present Law

Pass through entities (such as S corporations, partnerships, and certain trusts) generally are not subject to income tax on their taxable income. Instead, these entities file information returns and the entities' shareholders (or beneficial owners) report their pro rata share of the gross income and are liable for any taxes due.

Some believe that, prior to 1993, it may have been unclear as to whether the statute of limitations for adjustments that arise from distributions from passthrough entities should be applied at the entity or individual level (i.e., whether the 3-year statute of limitations for assessments runs from the time that the entity files its information return or from the time that a shareholder timely files his or her income tax return). In 1993, the Supreme Court held that the limitations period for assessing the income tax liability of an S corporation shareholder runs from the date the shareholder's return is filed (Bufferd v. Comm., 113 S. Ct. 927 (1993)).

Reasons for Change

Uncertainty regarding the correct statute of limitations hinders the resolution of factual and legal issues and creates needless litigation over collateral matters.

Explanation of Provision

The bill clarifies that the return that starts the running of the statute of limitations for a taxpayer is the return of the taxpayer and not the return of another person from whom the taxpayer has received an item of income, gain, loss, deduction, or credit.

Effective Date

The provision is effective for taxable years beginning after the date of enactment.

[Conference Report]

Senate Amendment

The Senate amendment is the same as the House bill.

Conference Agreement

The conference agreement follows the House bill and the Senate amendment.

[¶ 5252]   Section 1285.   Awarding of administrative costs and attorneys fees.

(Code Sec. 7430)

[House Report]

Present Law

Any person who substantially prevails in any action brought by or against the United States in connection with the determination, collection, or refund of any tax, interest, or penalty may be awarded reasonable administrative costs incurred before the IRS and reasonable litigation costs incurred in connection with any court proceeding.

No time limit is specified for the taxpayer to apply to the IRS for an award of administrative costs. In addition, no time limit is specified for a taxpayer to appeal to the Tax Court an IRS decision denying an award of administrative costs. Finally, the procedural rules for adjudicating a denial of administrative costs are unclear.

Reasons for Change

The proper procedures for applying for a cost award are uncertain in some instances. Clarifying these procedures will decrease litigation over these procedural issues and will provide for expedited settlement of these claims.

Explanation of Provision

The bill provides that a taxpayer who seeks an award of administrative costs must apply for such costs within 90 days of the date on which the taxpayer was determined to be a prevailing party. The bill also provides that a taxpayer who seeks to appeal an IRS denial of an administrative cost award must petition the Tax Court within 90 days after the date that the IRS mails the denial notice.

The bill clarifies that dispositions by the Tax Court of petitions relating only to administrative costs are to be reviewed in the same manner as other decisions of the Tax Court.

Effective Date

The provision is effective with respect to costs incurred in civil actions or proceedings commenced after the date of enactment.

[¶ 5261] Section 1301. Gifts to Charities Exempt from Gift Tax Filing Requirements.

(Code Sec. 6019)

[House Report]

Present Law

A gift tax generally is imposed on lifetime transfers of property by gift (sec. 2501). In computing the amount of taxable gifts made during a calendar year, a taxpayer generally may deduct the amount of any gifts made to a charity (sec. 2522). Generally, this charitable gift deduction is available for outright gifts to charity, as well as gifts of certain partial interests in property (such as a remainder interest). A gift of a partial interest in property must be in a prescribed form in order to qualify for the deduction.

Individuals who make gifts in excess of $10,000 to any one donee during the calendar year generally are required to file a gift tax return (sec. 6019). This filing requirement applies to all gifts, whether charitable or noncharitable, and whether or not the gift qualifies for a gift tax charitable deduction. Thus, under current law, a gift tax return is required to be filed for gifts to charity in excess of $10,000, even though no gift tax is payable on the transfer.

Reasons for Change

Because a charitable gift does not give rise to a gift tax liability, many donors are unaware of the requirement to file a gift tax return for charitable gifts in excess of $10,000. Failure to file a gift tax return under these circumstances could expose the donor to penalties. The bill eliminates this potential trap for the unwary.

Explanation of Provision

The bill provides that gifts to charity are not subject to the gift tax filing requirements of section 6019, as long as the entire value of the transferred property qualifies for the gift tax charitable deduction under section 2522. The filing requirements for gifts of partial interests in property remain unchanged.

Effective Date

The provision is effective for gifts made after the date of enactment.

[Conference Report]

Senate Amendment

The Senate amendment is the same as the House bill.

Conference Agreement

The conference agreement follows the House bill and the Senate amendment, with a technical clarification that the property given to charity must be the donor's entire interest in the property.

[Conference Report)]

Senate Amendment

No provision.

Conference Agreement

The conference agreement follows the House bill.

[¶ 5262]   Section 1302.   Clarification of Waiver of Certain Rights of Recovery.

(Code Sec. 2207A, 2207B)

[House Report]

Present Law

For estate and gift tax purposes, a marital deduction is allowed for qualified terminable interest property (QTIP). Such property generally is included in the surviving spouse's gross estate upon his or her death. The surviving spouse's estate is entitled to recover the portion of the estate tax attributable to inclusion of QTIP from the person receiving the property, unless the spouse directs otherwise by will (sec. 2207A).

For this purpose, a will provision specifying that all taxes shall be paid by the estate is sufficient to waive the right of recovery.

A decedent's gross estate includes the value of previously transferred property in which the decedent retains enjoyment or the right to income (sec. 2036). The estate is entitled to recover from the person receiving the property a portion of the estate tax attributable to the inclusion (sec. 2207B). This right may be waived only by a provision in the will (or revocable trust) specifically referring to section 2207B.

Reasons for Change

It is understood that persons utilizing standard testamentary language often inadvertently waive the right of recovery with respect to QTIP. Similarly, persons waiving a right to contribution are unlikely to refer to the code section granting the right. Accordingly, allowing the right of recovery

(or right of contribution) to be waived only by specific reference should simplify the drafting of wills by better conforming with the testator's likely intent.

Explanation of Provision

The bill provides that the right of recovery with respect to QTIP is waived only to the extent that language in the decedent's will or revocable trust specifically so indicates (e.g., by a specific reference to QTIP, the QTIP trust, section 2044, or section 2207A). Thus, a general provision specifying that all taxes be paid by the estate is no longer sufficient to waive the right of recovery.

The bill also provides that the right of contribution for property over which the decedent retained enjoyment or the right to income is waived by a specific indication in the decedent's will or revocable trust, but specific reference to section 2207B is no longer required.

Effective Date

The provision applies to decedents dying after the date of enactment.

[Conference Report]

Senate Amendment

The Senate amendment is the same as the House bill.

Conference Agreement

The conference agreement follows the House bill and the Senate amendment.

[¶ 5263]   Section 1303.   Transitional Rule Under Section 2056A.

(Code Sec. 2056A)

[House Report]

Present Law

A "marital deduction" generally is allowed for estate and gift tax purposes for the value of property passing to a spouse. The Technical and Miscellaneous Revenue Act of 1988 ("TAMRA") denied the marital deduction for property passing to an alien spouse outside a qualified domestic

trust ("QDT"). An estate tax generally is imposed on corpus distributions from a QDT.

TAMRA defined a QDT as a trust that, among other things, required all trustees be U.S. citizens or domestic corporations. This provision was modified in the Omnibus Budget Reconciliation Acts of 1989 and 1990 to require that at least one trustee be a U.S. citizen or domestic corporation and that no corpus distribution be made unless such trustee has the right to withhold any estate tax imposed on the distribution (the "withholding requirement").

Reasons for Change

Wills drafted under the TAMRA rules must be revised to conform with the withholding requirement, even though both the TAMRA rule and its successor ensure that a U.S. trustee is personally liable for the estate tax on a QDT. Reinstatement of the TAMRA rule for wills drafted in reliance upon it reduces the number of will revisions necessary to comply with statutory changes, thereby simplifying estate planning.

Explanation of Provision

Certain trusts created before the enactment of the Omnibus Budget Reconciliation Act of 1990 are treated as satisfying the withholding requirement if the governing instruments require that all trustees be U.S. citizens or domestic corporations.

Effective Date

The provision applies as if included in the Omnibus Budget Reconciliation Act of 1990.

[Conference Report]

Senate Amendment

The Senate amendment is the same as the House bill.

Conference Agreement

The conference agreement follows the House bill and the Senate amendment.

[¶ 5264]   Section 1304.   Treatment for Estate Tax Purposes of Short-term Obligations Held by Non-resident Aliens.

(Code Sec. 2105)

[House Report]

Present Law

The United States imposes estate tax on assets of noncitizen nondomiciliaries that were situated in the United States at the time of the individual's death. Debt obligations of a U.S. person, the United States, a political subdivision of a State, or the District of Columbia are considered property located within the United States if held by a nonresident not a citizen of the United States (sec. 2014(c)).

Special rules apply to treat certain bank deposits and debt instruments the income from which qualifies for the bank deposit interest exemption and the portfolio interest exemption as property from without the United States despite the fact that such items are obligations of a U.S. person, the United States, a political subdivision of a State, or the District of Columbia (sec. 2105(b)). Income from such items is exempt from U.S. income tax in the hands of the nonresident recipient (secs. 871(h) and 871(I)(2)(A)). The effect of these special rules is to exclude these items from the U.S. gross estate of a nonresident not a citizen of the United States. However, because of an amendment to section 871(h) made by the Tax Reform Act of 1986, these special rules no longer cover obligations that generate short-term OID income despite the fact that such income is exempt from U.S. income tax in the hands of the nonresident recipient (sec. 871(g)(1)(B)(I)).

Reasons for Change

The Committee believes that the income and estate tax treatments of short-term OID obligations held by nonresident aliens should conform. A purpose of exempting short-term OID income derived by nonresident aliens from U.S. income tax is to enhance the ability of U.S. borrowers to raise funds from foreign lenders, and such purpose is hindered by the lack of a corresponding exemption for U.S. estate tax. Moreover, to the extent the interest from such an obligation is exempt from U.S. income tax, the inclusion of the instrument in the nonresident noncitizen's U.S. estate would be a trap for the unwary.

Explanation of Provision

The bill provides that any debt obligation, the income from which would be eligible for the exemption for short-term OID under section 871(g)(1)(B)(I) if such income were received by the decedent on the date of his death, is treated as property located outside of the United States in determining the U.S.

estate tax liability of a nonresident not a U.S. citizen. No inference is intended with respect to the estate tax treatment of such obligations under present law.

Effective Date

The provision is effective for estates of decedents dying after the date of enactment.

[¶ 5265]   Section 1305.   Certain Revocable Trusts Treated as Part of Estate.

(Code Sec. 2652)

[House Report]

Present Law

Both estates and revocable inter vivos trusts can function to settle the affairs of a decedent and distribute assets to heirs. In the case of revocable inter vivos trusts, the grantor transfers property into a trust which is revocable during his or her lifetime. Upon the grantor's death, the power to revoke ceases and the trustee then performs the settlement functions typically performed by the executor of an estate. While both estates and revocable trusts perform essentially the same function after the testator or grantor's death, there are a number of ways in which an estate and a revocable trust operate differently. First, there can be only one estate per decedent while there can be more than one revocable trust. Second, estates are in existence only for a reasonable period of administration; revocable trusts can perform the same settlement functions as an estate, but may continue in existence thereafter as testamentary trusts.

Numerous differences presently exist between the income tax treatment of estates and revocable trusts, including: (1) estates are allowed a charitable deduction for amounts permanently set aside for charitable purposes while post death revocable trusts are allowed a charitable deduction only for amounts paid to charities; (2) the active participation requirement the passive loss rules under section 469 is waived in the case of estates (but not revocable trusts) for two years after the owner's death; and (3) estates can qualify for section 194 amortization of reforestation expenditures, while trusts do not.

Senate Amendment

The Senate amendment is the same as the House bill.

Conference Agreement

The conference agreement follows the House bill and the Senate amendment.

Reasons for Change

The use of revocable trusts may offer certain non-tax advantages for estate planning as compared to a traditional estate plan. There are several differences, however, between the Federal tax treatment of revocable trusts and an estate. These differences may discourage individuals from utilizing revocable trusts for estate planning where they might otherwise be appropriate or efficient. Accordingly, in an effort to minimize these tax differences, the Committee believes it is appropriate to allow an election to treat a revocable trust as part of the decedent's estate during a reasonable period of administration.

Explanation of Provision

The bill provides an irrevocable election to treat a qualified revocable trust as part of the decedent's estate for Federal income tax purposes. This elective treatment is effective from the date of the decedent's death until two years after his or her death (if no estate tax return is required) or, if later, six months after the final determination of estate tax liability (if an estate tax return is required). The election must be made by both the executor of the decedent's estate (if any) and the trustee of the revocable trust no later than the time required for filing the income tax return of the estate for its first taxable year, taking into account any extensions. A conforming change is made to section 2652(b) for generation-skipping transfer tax purposes.

For this purpose, a qualified revocable trust is any trust (or portion thereof) which was treated under section 676 as owned by the decedent with respect to whom the election is being made, by reason of a power in the grantor (i.e., trusts that are treated as owned by the decedent solely by reason of a power in a nonadverse party would not qualify).

As described below, the separate share rule may apply when a qualified revocable trust is treated as part of the decedent's estate.

Effective Date

The provision applies to decedents dying after the date of enactment.

[¶ 5266]   Section 1306.   Distributions During First 65 Days of Taxable Year of Estate.

(Code Sec. 663)

[House Report]

Present Law

In general, trusts and estates are treated as conduits for Federal income tax purposes; income received by a trust or estate that is distributed to a beneficiary in the trust or estate's taxable year "ending with or within" the taxable year of the beneficiary is taxable to the beneficiary in that year; income that is retained by the trust or estate is initially taxable to the trust or estate. In the case of distributions of previously accumulated income by trusts (but not estates), there may be additional tax under the so-called "throwback" rules if the beneficiary to whom the distributions were made has marginal rates higher than those of the trust. Under the "65-day rule," a trust may elect to treat distributions paid within 65 days after the close of its taxable year as paid on the last day of its taxable year. The 65-day rule is not applicable to estates.

Reasons for Change

In order to minimize the tax differences between estates and revocable trusts, the

[Conference Report]

Senate Amendment

No provision.

Conference Agreement

The conference agreement follows the House bill.

Committee believes that the 65-day rule should be allowed to estates as well as to trusts.

Explanation of Provision

The bill extends application of the 65-day rule to distributions by estates. Thus, an executor can elect to treat distributions paid within 65 days after the close of the estate's taxable year as having been paid on the last day of such taxable year.

Effective Date

The provision applies to taxable years beginning after the date of enactment.

[Conference Report]

Senate Amendment

The Senate amendment is the same as the House bill.

Conference Agreement

The conference agreement follows the House bill and the Senate amendment.

[¶ 5267]   Section 1307.   Seperate share rules available for estates.

(Code Sec. 663)

[House Report]

Present Law

Trusts with more than one beneficiary must use the "separate share" rule in order

to provide different tax treatment of distributions to different beneficiaries to reflect the income earned by different shares of the trust's corpus.[17] Treasury regulations provide that "[t]he application of the separate share rule . . . will generally depend upon whether distributions of the trust are to be made in substantially the same manner as if separate trusts had been created. . . . Separate share treatment will not be applied to a trust or portion of a trust subject to a power to distribute, apportion, or accumulate income or distribute corpus to or for the use of one or more beneficiaries within a group or class of beneficiaries, unless the payment of income, accumulated income, or corpus of a share of one beneficiary cannot affect the proportionate share of income, accumulated income, or corpus of any shares of the other beneficiaries, or unless substantially proper adjustment must thereafter be made under the governing instrument so that substantially separate and independent shares exist." (Treas. Reg. sec. 1.663(c) 3). The separate share rule presently does not apply to estates.

Reasons for Change

The Committee understands that estates typically do not have separate shares. Nonetheless, where separate shares do exist in an estate, the inapplicability of the separate share rule to estates may result in one beneficiary or class of beneficiaries being taxed on income payable to, or accruing to, a separate beneficiary or class of beneficiaries. Accordingly, the Committee believes that a more equitable taxation of an estate and its beneficiaries would be achieved with the application of the separate share rule to an estate where, under the provisions of the decedent's will or applicable local law, there are separate shares in the estate.

Explanation of Provision

The bill extends the application of the separate share rule to estates. There are separate shares in an estate when the governing instrument of the estate (e.g., the will and applicable local law) creates separate economic interests in one beneficiary or class of beneficiaries such that the economic interests of those beneficiaries (e.g., rights to income or gains from specified items of property) are not affected by economic interests accruing to another separate beneficiary or class of beneficiaries. For example, a separate share in an estate would exist where the decedent's will provides that all of the shares of a closely-held corporation are devised to one beneficiary and that any dividends paid to the estate by that corporation should be paid only to that beneficiary and any such dividends would not affect any other amounts which that beneficiary would receive under the will. As in the case of trusts, the application of the separate share rule is mandatory where separate shares exist.

Effective Date

The provision applies to decedents dying after the date of enactment.

[Conference Report]

Senate Amendment

The Senate amendment is the same as the House bill.

Conference Agreement

The conference agreement follows the House bill and the Senate amendment.

[¶ 5268]   Section 1308. Executor of estate and beneficiaries treated as related persons for disallowance of losses, etc.

(Code Sec. 267, 1239)

[House Report]

Present Law

Section 267 disallows a deduction for any loss on the sale of an asset to a person related to the taxpayer. For the purposes of section 267, the following parties are re-lated persons: (1) a trust and the trust's grantor, (2) two trusts with the same grantor, (3) a trust and a beneficiary of the trust, (4) a trust and a beneficiary of another trust, if both trusts have the same grantor, and (5) a trust and a corporation the stock of which is more than 50 percent owned by the trust or the trust's grantor.

---

17. Application for the separate share rule is not elective; it is mandatory if there are separate shares in the trust.

Section 1239 disallows capital gain treatment on the sale of depreciable property to a related person. For purposes of section 1239, a trust and any beneficiary of the trust are treated as related persons, unless the beneficiary's interest is a remote contingent interest. Neither section 267 or section 1239 presently treat an estate and a beneficiary of the estate as related persons.

Reasons for Change

The Committee believes that the disallowance rules under sections 267 and 1239 with respect to transactions between related parties should apply to an estate and a beneficiary of that estate for the same reasons that such rules apply to a trust and a beneficiary of that trust.

Explanation of Provision

Under the bill, an estate and a beneficiary of that estate are treated as related persons

for purposes of sections 267 and 1239, except in the case of a sale or exchange in satisfaction of a pecuniary bequest.

Effective Date

The provision applies to taxable years beginning after the date of enactment.

[Conference Report]

Senate Amendment

The Senate amendment is the same as the House bill.

Conference Agreement

The conference agreement follows the House bill and the Senate amendment.

[¶ 5269]   Section 1309.   Treatment of funeral trusts.

(Code Sec. 685)

[House Report]

Present Law

A pre-need funeral trust is an arrangement where an individual purchases funeral services or merchandise from a funeral home in advance of the individual's death. The individual enters into a contract with the provider of such services or merchandise whereby the individual selects the services or merchandise to be provided upon his or her death, and agrees to pay for them in advance of his or her death. Such amounts (or a portion thereof) are held in trust during the individual's lifetime and are paid to the seller upon the individual's death.

Under present law, pre-need funeral trusts generally are treated as grantor trusts, and the annual income earned by such trusts is taxed to the purchaser/grantor of the trust. Rev. Rul. 87 127. Any amount received from the trust by the seller (as payment for services or merchandise) is includible in the gross income of the seller.

Reasons for Change

To the extent that pre-need funeral trusts are treated as grantor trusts under present law, numerous individual taxpayers are required to account for the earnings of such trusts on their tax returns, even though the earnings with respect to any one taxpayer may be small. The Committee believes that this recordkeeping burden on individuals could be eased, and that compliance with the tax laws would be improved, if such trusts instead were taxed at the entity level, with one simplified annual return filed by the trustee reporting the aggregate income from all such trusts administered by the trustee.

Explanation of Provision

The bill allows the trustee of a pre-need funeral trust to elect special tax treatment for such a trust, to the extent the trust would otherwise be treated as a grantor trust. A qualified funeral trust is defined as one which meets the following requirements: (1) the trust arises as the result of a contract between a person engaged in the trade or business of providing funeral or burial services or merchandise and one or more individuals to have such services or property provided upon such individuals' death; (2) the only beneficiaries of the trust are individuals who have entered into contracts to have such services or merchandise provided upon their death; (3) the only contributions to the trust are contributions by or for the benefit of the trust beneficiaries; (4) the trust's only purpose is to hold and invest funds that will be used to make payments for funeral or burial services or merchandise for the trust beneficiaries; and (5) the trust has not accepted contributions totaling more than $7,000 by or for the benefit of any individual. For this purpose, "contributions" include all amounts transferred to the trust, regardless of how denominated in the contract. Contributions do not, however, include income or gain earned with respect to property in the trust. For purposes of applying the $7,000 limit, if a purchaser has more than one contract with a single trustee (or related trustees), all such trusts are treated as one trust. Similarly, if the Secretary of Treasury determines that a purchaser has entered into separate contracts with unrelated trustees to avoid the $7,000 limit described above, the Secretary may require that such trusts be treated as one trust. For contracts entered into after 1998, the $7,000 limit is indexed annually for inflation.

The trustee's election to have this provision apply to a qualified funeral trust is to be made separately with respect to each purchaser's trust. It is anticipated that the Department of Treasury will issue prompt guidance with respect to the simplified reporting requirements so that if the election is made, a single annual trust return may be filed by the trustee, separately listing the amount of income earned with respect to each purchaser. If the election is made, the trust is not treated as a grantor trust and the amount of tax paid with respect to each purchaser's trust is determined in accordance with the income tax rate schedule generally applicable to estates and trusts (Code sec. 1(e)), but no deduction is allowed under section 642(b). The tax on the annual earnings of the trust is payable by the trustee.

As under present law, amounts received from the trust by the seller are treated as payments for services and merchandise and are includible in the gross income of the seller. No gain or loss is recognized to the beneficiary of the trust for payments from the trust to the beneficiary upon cancellation of the contract, and the beneficiary takes a carryover basis in any assets received from the trust upon cancellation.

Effective Date

The provision is effective for taxable years beginning after the date of enactment.

[Conference Report]

Senate Agreement

The Senate amendment is the same as the House bill.

Conference Agreement

The conference agreement follows the House bill and the Senate amendment with modifications that would (1) allow the provision to be applied to contracts purchased by one individual to have funeral or burial services or merchandise provided for another individual upon that individual's death (to the extent that such arrangements would otherwise be treated as grantor trusts), and (2) allow the election to be made for taxable years ending after the date of enactment.

Effective Date

The provision is effective for taxable years ending after the date of enactment.

[¶ 5270]   Section 1310.   Adjustments for gifts within 3 years of decedent's death.

(Code Sec. 2035)

[House Report]

Present Law

The first $10,000 of gifts of present interests to each donee during any one calendar year are excluded from Federal gift tax.

The value of the gross estate includes the value of any previously transferred property if the decedent retained the power to revoke the transfer (sec. 2038). The gross estate also includes the value of any property with respect to which such power is relinquished during the three years before death (sec. 2035). There has been significant litigation as to whether these rules require that certain transfers made from a revocable trust within three years of death be includible in the gross estate. See, e.g., Jalkut Estate v. Commissioner , 96 T.C. 675 (1991) (transfers from revocable trust includible in gross estate); McNeely v. Commissioner , 16 F.3d 303 (8th Cir. 1994) (transfers from revocable trust not includible in gross estate); Kisling v. Commissioner , 32 F.3d 1222 (8th Cir. 1994) (acq.) (transfers from revocable trust not includible in gross estate).

Reasons for Change

The inclusion of certain property transferred during the three years before death is directed at transfers that would otherwise reduce the amount subject to estate tax by more than the amount subject to gift tax, disregarding appreciation between the times of gift and death. Because all amounts transferred from a revocable trust are subject to the gift tax, the Committee believes that inclusion of such amounts is unnecessary where the transferor has retained no power over the property transferred out of the trust. The Committee believes that clarifying these rules statutorily will lend certainty to these rules.

Explanation of Provision

The provision codifies the rule set forth in the McNeely and Kisling cases to provide that a transfer from a revocable trust (i.e., a trust described under section 676) is treated as if made directly by the grantor. Thus, an annual exclusion gift from such a trust is not included in the gross estate. The provision also revises section 2035 to improve its clarity.

Effective Date

The provision applies to decedents dying after the date of enactment.

[Conference Report]

Senate Amendment

The Senate amendment is the same as the House bill.

Conference Agreement

The conference agreement follows the House bill and the Senate amendment. The provision is not intended to modify the result reached in the Kisling case.

[¶ 5271]   Section 1311.   Clarification of treatment of survivor annuities under qualified terminable interest rules.

(Code Sec. 2056)

[House Report]

Present Law

Community property

Under state community property laws, each spouse owns an undivided one-half interest in each community property asset. In community property jurisdictions, a nonparticipant spouse may be treated as having a vested community property interest in either his or her spouse's qualified plan, individual retirement arrangement ("IRA"), or simplified employee pension ("SEP") plan.

Transfer tax treatment of qualified plans

In the Retirement Equity Act of 1984 ("REA"), qualified retirement plans were required to provide automatic survivor benefits (1) in the case of a participant who retires under the plan, in the form of a qualified joint and survivor annuity, and (2) in the case of a vested participant who dies before the annuity starting date and who has a surviving spouse, in the form of a preretirement survivor annuity. A participant generally is permitted to waive such annuities, provided he or she obtains the written consent of his or her spouse.

The Tax Reform Act of 1986 repealed the estate tax exclusion, formerly contained in sections 2039(c) and 2039(d), for certain interests in qualified plans owned by a nonparticipant spouse attributable to community property laws and made certain other changes to conform the transfer tax treatment of qualified and nonqualified plans.

As a result of these changes made by REA and the Tax Reform Act of 1986, the transfer tax treatment of married couples residing in a community property state is unclear where either spouse is covered by a qualified plan.

Reasons for Change

The Committee believes that survivorship interests in annuities in community property States should be accorded similar treatment to the tax treatment of interests in such annuities in non-community property States. Accordingly, the bill would clarify that the transfer at death of a survivorship interest in an annuity to a surviving spouse will be a deductible marital transfer under the QTIP rules regardless of whether the decedent's annuity interest arose out of his or her employment or arose under community property laws by reason of the employment of his or her spouse.

Explanation of Provision

The bill clarifies that the marital deduction is available with respect to a nonparticipant spouse's interest in an annuity attributable to community property laws where he or she predeceases the participant spouse. Under the bill, the nonparticipant spouse's interest in an annuity arising under the community property laws of a State that passes to the surviving participant spouse may qualify for treatment as QTIP under section 2056(b)(7).

The provision is not intended to create an inference regarding the treatment under present law of a transfer to a surviving spouse of the decedent spouse's interest in an annuity arising under community property laws.

Effective Date

The provision applies to decedents dying, or waivers, transfers and disclaimers made, after the date of enactment.

[Conference Report]

Senate Amendment

The Senate amendment is the same as the House bill.

Conference Agreement

The conference agreement follows the House bill and the Senate amendment. The provision is not intended to modify the result of the Supreme Court's decision in *Boggs v. Boggs, 117 S.Ct. 1754 (1997).*

[¶ 5272]   Section 1312.   Treatment under qualified domestic trust rules of forms of ownership which are not trusts.

(Code Sec. 2056A)

[House Report]

Present Law

A marital deduction generally is allowed for estate and gift tax purposes for the value of property passing to a spouse. The marital deduction is not available for property passing to an alien spouse outside a qualified domestic trust ("QDT"). An estate tax generally is imposed on corpus distributions from a QDT.

Trusts are not permitted in some countries. (e.g., many civil law countries).[19]

As a result, it is not possible to create a QDT in those countries.

---

19. Note that in some civil law States (e.g., Louisiana) an entity similar to a trust, called a usufruct, exists.

Reasons for Change

The estate of a decedent with a nonresident spouse should not be precluded from qualifying for the marital deduction in situations where the use of a trust is prohibited by another country. Accordingly, the Committee believes it is appropriate to grant regulatory authority to allow qualification for the marital deduction in such situations where the Treasury Department determines that another similar arrangement allows the U.S. to retain jurisdiction and provides adequate security for the payment of U.S. transfer taxes on subsequent transfers by the surviving spouse of the property transferred by the decedent.

Explanation of Provision

The bill provides the Treasury Department with regulatory authority to treat as trusts legal arrangements that have substantially the same effect as a trust. It is anticipated that such regulations, if any, would only permit a marital deduction with respect to non-trust arrangements under which the U.S. would retain jurisdiction and adequate

security to impose U.S. transfer tax on transfers by the surviving spouse of the property transferred by the decedent. Possible arrangements could include the adoption of a bilateral treaty that provides for the collection of U.S. transfer tax from the noncitizen surviving spouse or a closing agreement process under which the surviving spouse waives treaty benefits, allows the U.S. to retain taxing jurisdiction and provides adequate security with respect to such transfer taxes.

Effective Date

The provision applies to decedents dying after the date of enactment.

[Conference Report]

Senate Amendment

The Senate amendment is the same as the House bill.

Conference Agreement

The conference agreement follows the House bill and the Senate amendment.

[¶ 5273]   Section 1313.   Opportunity to correct certain failures under section 2032A.

(Code Sec. 2032A)

[House Report]

Present Law

For estate tax purposes, an executor may elect to value certain real property used in farming or other closely held business operations at its current use value rather than its highest and best use (sec. 2032A). A written agreement signed by each person with an interest in the property must be filed with the election.

In 1984, section 2032A was amended to provide that if an executor makes a timely election that substantially complies with Treasury regulations, but fails to provide all required information or the signatures of all persons required to enter into the agreement, the executor may supply the missing information within a reasonable period of time (not exceeding 90 days) after notification by the Treasury Department.

Treasury regulations require that a notice of election and certain information be filed with the Federal estate tax return (Treas. Reg. sec. 20.2032A 8). The administrative policy of the Treasury Department is to disallow current use valuation elections unless the required information is supplied.

Reasons for Change

It is understood that executors commonly fail to include with the filed estate tax return a recapture agreement signed by all persons with an interest in the property or all information required by Treasury regulations. It is believed that allowing such signatures or information to be supplied later is consistent with the legislative intent of section 2032A and eases return filing.

Explanation of Provision

The bill extends the procedures allowing subsequent submission of information to any executor who makes the election and submits the recapture agreement, without regard to compliance with the Treasury regulations. Thus, the bill allows the current use valuation election if the executor supplies the required information within a reasonable period of time (not exceeding 90 days) after notification by the IRS. During that time period, the bill also allows the addition of signatures to a previously filed agreement.

The Committee believes that the Treasury Department has taken an unnecessarily restrictive view of the 1984 amendment to section 2032A and intends no inference that the Treasury Department lacks the power, under the law in effect prior to the date of enactment, to correct the situation addressed by this provision. The Committee intends that, with respect to technically defective 2032A elections made prior to the date of enactment, prior law should be applied in a manner consistent with the provision.

Effective Date

The provision applies to decedents dying after the date of enactment.

[Conference Report]

Senate Amendment

The Senate amendment is the same as the House bill.

Conference Agreement

The conference agreement follows the House bill and the Senate amendment.

[¶ 5274]   Section 1314.   Authority to waive requirement of United States trustee for qualified domestic trusts.

(Code Sec. 2056A)

[House Report]

Present Law

In order for a trust to be a QDT, a U.S. trustee must have the power to approve all corpus distributions from the trust. In some countries, trusts cannot have any U.S. trustees. As a result, trusts established in those countries cannot qualify as a QDT.

Reasons for Change

The estate of a decedent with a nonresident spouse should not be precluded from qualifying for the marital deduction in situations where the use of a U.S. trustee is prohibited by another country. Accordingly, the Committee believes it is appropriate to grant regulatory authority to allow qualification for the marital deduction in such situations where the Treasury Department determines that the U.S. can retain jurisdiction and other adequate security has been provided for the payment of U.S. transfer taxes on subsequent transfers by the surviving spouse of the property transferred by the decedent.

Explanation of Provision

In order to permit the establishment of a QDT in those situations where a country prohibits a trust from having a U.S. trustee, the bill provides the Treasury Department with regulatory authority to waive the requirement that a QDT have a U.S. trustee. It is anticipated that such regulations, if any, provide an alternative mechanism under which the U.S. would retain jurisdiction and adequate security to impose U.S. transfer tax on transfers by the surviving spouse of the property transferred by the decedent. For example, one possible mechanism would be a closing agreement process under which the surviving spouse waives treaty benefits, allows the U.S. to retain taxing jurisdiction and provides adequate security with respect to such transfer taxes.

Effective Date

The provision applies to decedents dying after the date of enactment.

[Conference Report]

Senate Amendment

The Senate amendment is the same as the House bill.

Conference Agreement

The conference agreement follows the House bill and the Senate amendment.

[¶5275]   Section 1401.   Increase de minimis limit for after-market alterations subject to heavy truck and luxury automobile excise taxes.

(Code Sec. 4001, 4051)

[House Report]

Present Law

An excise tax is imposed on retail sales of truck chassis and truck bodies suitable for use in a vehicle with a gross vehicle weight of over 33,000 pounds. The tax is equal to 12 percent of the retail sales price. An excise tax also is imposed on retail sales of luxury automobiles. The tax currently is equal to 8 percent of the amount by which the retail sales price exceeds an inflation-adjusted $30,000 base. (The rate is scheduled to be reduced by 1 percentage point per year through 2002, and the tax is not imposed after 2002.) Anti-abuse rules prevent the avoidance of these taxes through separate purchases of major component parts. With certain exceptions, tax at the rate applicable to the vehicle is imposed on the subsequent installation of parts and accessories within six months after purchase of a taxable vehicle. The exceptions include a de minimis exception for parts and accessories with an aggregate price that does not exceed $200 (or such other amount as Treasury may by regulation prescribe).

Reasons for Change

Retailers are generally responsible for taxes on truck chassis and bodies and luxury automobiles. In the case of a subsequent installation, however, the owner or operator of the vehicle is responsible for paying the tax attributable to the installation and the installer is secondarily liable. Increasing the de minimis amount should significantly reduce the number of return filers and relieve many persons from the administrative burden of filing an excise tax return reporting a very small amount of tax.

Explanation of Provision

The tax on subsequent installation of parts and accessories does not apply to parts and accessories with an aggregate price that does not exceed $1,000. Parts and accessories installed on a vehicle on or before that date are taken into account in determining whether the $1,000 threshold is exceeded. If the aggregate price of the pre-effective date parts and accessories does not exceed $200, they will not be subject to tax unless the aggregate price of all additions exceeds $1,000.

Effective Date

The increase in the threshold for taxing after-market additions under the heavy truck and luxury car excise taxes is effective on January 1, 1998.

[Conference Report]

Senate Amendment

The Senate amendment is the same as the House bill.

Conference Agreement

The conference agreement follows the House bill and the Senate amendment.

[¶5276]   Section 1402.   Modify treatment of tires under the heavy highway vehicle retail excise tax.

(Code Sec. 4051)

[House Report]

Present Law

A 12-percent retail excise tax is imposed on certain heavy highway trucks and trailers, and on highway tractors. A separate manufacturers' excise tax is imposed on tires weighing more than 40 pounds. This tire tax is imposed as a fixed dollar amount which varies based on the weight of the tire. Because tires are taxed separately, the value of tires installed on a highway vehicle is excluded from the 12-percent excise tax on heavy highway vehicles. The determination of value is factual and has given rise to numerous tax audit challenges.

Reasons for Change

Allowing a credit for the tire tax actually paid on truck tires will simplify the application of the retail truck tax.

Explanation of Provision

The current exclusion of the value of tires installed on a taxable highway vehicle is repealed. Instead, a credit for the amount of manufacturers' excise tax actually paid on the tires is allowed.

Effective Date

The provision is effective after December 31, 1997.

[¶ 5277]   Section 1411-1422.   Provisions related to distilled spirits, wines, and beer.

(Code Sec. 5008, 5044, 5053, 5055, 5115, 5175, 5207, 5222, 5418)

[House Report]

Present Law

Imported distilled spirits returned to plant

Excise tax that has been paid on domestic distilled spirits is credited or refunded if the spirits are later returned to bonded premises. Tax is imposed on imported bottled spirits when they are withdrawn from customs custody, but the tax is not refunded or credited if the spirits are later returned to bonded premises.

Cancellation of export bonds

An exporter that withdraws distilled spirits from bonded warehouses for export or transportation to a customs bonded warehouse without the payment of tax must furnish a bond to cover the withdrawal. The required bonds are canceled "on the submission of such evidence, records, and certification indicating exportation as the Secretary may by regulations prescribe."

Location of records of distilled spirits plant

Proprietors of distilled spirits plants are required to maintain records and reports relating to their production, storage, denaturation, and processing activities on the premises where the operations covered by the record are carried on.

[Conference Report]

Senate Amendment

The Senate amendment is the same as the House bill.

Conference Agreement

The conference agreement follows the House bill and the Senate amendment.

Transfers from brewery to distilled spirits plant

A distilled spirits plant may receive on its bonded premises beer to be used in the production of distilled spirits only if the beer is produced on contiguous brewery premises.

Sign not required for wholesale dealers

Wholesale liquor dealers are required to post a sign identifying the firm as such. Failure to do so is subject to a penalty.

Refund on returns of merchantable wine

Excise tax paid on domestic wine that is returned to bond as unmerchantable is refunded or credited, and the wine is once again treated as wine in bond on the premises of a bonded wine cellar.

Increased sugar limits for certain wine

Natural wines may be sweetened to correct high acid content. For most wines, however, sugar cannot constitute more than 35 percent (by volume) of the combined sugar and juice used to produce the wine. Up to 60 percent sugar may be used in wine made from loganberries, currants, and gooseberries. If the amount of sugar used exceeds the applicable limitation, the wine must be labeled "substandard."

Beer withdrawn for embassy use

Imported beer to be used for the family and official use of representatives of foreign governments or public international organizations may be withdrawn from customs bonded warehouses without payment of excise tax. No similar exemption applies to domestic beer withdrawn from a brewery or entered into a bonded customs warehouse for the same authorized use.

Beer withdrawn for destruction

Removals of beer from a brewery are exempt from tax if the removal is for export, because the beer is unfit for beverage use, for laboratory analysis, research, development and testing, for the brewer's personal or family use, or as supplies for certain vessels and aircraft.

Drawback on exported beer

A domestic producer that exports beer may recover the tax (receive a "drawback") found to have been paid on the exported beer upon the "submission of such evidence, records and certificates indicating exportation" required by regulations.

Imported beer transferred in bulk to brewery and imported wine transferred in bulk to wineries

Imported beer and wine are subject to tax when removed from customs custody.

Reasons for Change

Until 1980, the method of collecting alcohol excise taxes required the regular presence of Treasury Department inspectors at alcohol production facilities. In 1980, the method of collecting tax was changed to a bonded premises system under which examinations and collection procedures are similar to those used in connection with other Federal excise taxes.

A number of reporting and recordkeeping requirements need to be modified to conform to the current collection system. Appropriate modification will allow the Bureau of Alcohol, Tobacco, and Firearms to administer alcohol excise taxes more efficiently and relieve taxpayers of unnecessary paperwork burdens.

The current rules under which the Code permits tax-free removals of alcoholic beverages (or allows a credit or refund of tax on a return to bonded premises) result in inappropriate disparities in the treatment of different types of alcoholic beverages. In addition, these rules unduly limit available options for complying with environmental and other laws that regulate the destruction and disposition of alcoholic beverages.

Under the bonded premises system, these rules can be liberalized without jeopardizing the collection of tax revenues.

Other provisions of current law (i.e., the sign requirement and the sugar limits for certain wine) are outdated and should be repealed or revised.

Explanation of Provisions

Imported distilled spirits returned to plant

Refunds or credits of the tax are available for imported bottled spirits that are returned to distilled spirits plants.

Cancellation of export bonds

The certification requirement is relaxed to allow the bonds to be canceled if there is such proof of exportation as the Secretary may require.

Location of records of distilled spirits plant

Records and reports are permitted to be maintained elsewhere other than on the plant premises.

Transfers from brewery to distilled spirits plant

Beer may be brought from any brewery for use in the production of spirits. Such beer is exempt from excise tax, subject to Treasury regulations.

Sign not required for wholesale dealers

The requirement that a sign be posted is repealed.

Refund on returns of merchantable wine. —A refund or credit is available in the case of all domestic wine returned to bond, whether or not unmerchantable.

Increased sugar limits for certain wine

Up to 60 percent sugar is permitted in any wine made from juice, such as cranberry or plum juice, with an acid content of 20 or more parts per thousand.

Beer withdrawn for embassy use

Subject to Treasury's regulatory authority, an exemption similar to that currently available for imported beer is provided for domestic beer.

Beer withdrawn for destruction

An exemption from tax is added for removals for destruction, subject to Treasury regulations.

Drawback on exported beer

The certification requirement is relaxed to allow a drawback of tax paid if there is such proof of exportation as the Secretary may by regulations require.

Imported beer transferred in bulk to brewery and imported wine transferred in bulk to wineries

Subject to Treasury regulations, beer imported in bulk may be withdrawn from customs custody and transferred in bulk to a brewery without payment of tax. The proprietor of the brewery to which the beer is transferred or of the winery to which the wine is transferred will be liable for the tax imposed on the withdrawal from customs custody and the importer will be relieved of liability.

Effective Date

The provision to repeal the requirement that wholesale liquor dealers post a sign outside their place of business takes effect on the date of enactment. The other provisions take effect on the first day of the calendar quarter that begins at least 90 days after the date of enactment.

[Conference Report]

Senate Amendment

The Senate amendment is the same as the House bill.

Conference Agreement

The conference agreement follows the House bill and the Senate amendment, with a modification delaying the effective date of certain provisions from the first day of the calendar quarter that begins at least 90 days after the date of enactment to the first day of the quarter beginning at least 180 days after such date.

[¶5289]   Section 1431.   Authority for Internal Revenue Service to grant exemptions from excise tax regulation requirements.

(Code Sec. 4222)

[House Report]

Present Law

The Code exempts certain types of sales (e.g., sales for use in further manufacture, sales for export, and sales for use by a State or local government or a nonprofit educational organization) from excise taxes imposed on manufacturers and retailers. These exemptions generally apply only if the seller, the purchaser, and any person to whom the article is resold by the purchaser (the second purchaser) are registered with the Internal Revenue Service. The IRS can waive the registration requirement for the purchaser and second purchaser in some but not all cases.

Reasons for Change

Allowing the IRS to waive the registration requirement for purchasers and second purchasers in all cases will permit more ef-

ficient administration of the exemptions and reduce paperwork burdens on taxpayers.

Explanation of Provision

The IRS is authorized to waive the registration requirement for purchasers and second purchasers in all cases.

Effective Date

The provision applies to sales made pursuant to waivers issued after the date of enactment.

[Conference Report]

Senate Amendment

The Senate amendment is the same as the House bill.

Conference Agreement

The conference agreement follows the House bill and the Senate amendment.

[¶ 5290]   Section 1432. Repeal of excise tax deadwood provisions.

(Code Sec. 4051, 4495, 4496, 4497, 4498, 4681, 4682)

[House Report]

Present Law

The Code includes a provision relating to a temporary reduction in the tax on piggy-back trailers sold before July 18, 1985, and provisions relating to the tax on the removal of hard minerals from the deep seabed before June 28, 1990.

An excise tax is imposed on the sale or use by the manufacturer or importer of certain ozone-depleting chemicals (sec. 4681). The amount of the tax generally is determined by multiplying the base tax amount applicable for the calendar year by an ozone-depleting factor assigned to each taxable chemical. The base tax amount was $5.80 per pound in 1996 and will increase by 45 cents per pound per year thereafter. The Code contains provisions for special rates of tax applicable to years before 1996 (e.g., sec. 4282(g)(1), (2), (3), and (5)).

Reasons for Change

The elimination of out-of-date, "dead-wood" provisions will simplify the Code by removing unneeded Code sections.

Explanation of Provision

These provisions are repealed, as "dead-wood".

Effective Date

The provisions are effective on the date of enactment.

[Conference Report]

Senate Amendment

The Senate amendment is the same as the House bill.

Conference Agreement

The conference agreement follows the House bill and the Senate amendment.

[¶ 5291]   Section 1433. Simplification of imposition of excise tax on arrows.

(Code Sec. 4161)

[Senate Report]

Present Law

An 11-percent manufacturer's excise tax is imposed on bows having a draw weight of more than 10 pounds and on arrows that either are greater than 18 inches in length or are suitable for use with a taxable bow. The tax is imposed on the manufacturer's sales price of the completed arrow.

Reasons for Change

Imposing the excise tax on the component parts of the arrow before they are shipped to the assembler of the arrow will improve compliance with, and collection of, the tax by reducing the potential number of tax collection points.

Explanation of Provision

Under the bill, the current excise tax on arrows tax is replaced with a manufacturer's excise tax on the four component parts of the arrow: shafts, points, nocks, and vanes. The tax rate is increased to 12.4 percent of the value of each of these four components to offset the reduction in aggregate value subjected to tax compared to present-law valuation of the completed arrow.

Effective Date

The provision is effective for arrow components sold after September 30, 1997.

[Conference Report]

House Bill

No provision.

Conference Agreement

The conference agreement follows the Senate amendment.

[¶ 5292]   Section 1434.   Modifications to heavy highway vehicle retail excise tax.

(Code Sec. 4051, 4052)

[Senate Report]

Present Law

A 12-percent retail excise tax is imposed on certain heavy highway trucks and trailers, and on highway tractors. Small trucks (those with a gross vehicle weight not over 33,000 pounds) and lighter trailers (those with a gross vehicle weight not over 26,000 pounds) are exempt from the tax. The tax applies to the first retail sale of a new or remanufactured vehicle. The determination under present law of whether a particular modification to an existing vehicle constitutes remanufacture (taxable) or a repair (nontaxable) is factual and generally is based on whether the function of the vehicle is changed or, in the case of worn vehicles, whether the cost of the modification exceeds 75 percent of the value of the modified vehicle.

No tax is imposed on trucks, tractors, and trailers when they are sold for resale or long-term lease, if the purchaser is registered with the Treasury Department. In such cases, purchasers are liable for the tax when the vehicle is sold or leased. The tax is based on the sales price in the transaction to which it applies.

Reasons for Change

Clarification is needed concerning the application of the 75-percent of value threshold in determining whether repairs to a wrecked vehicle constitutes remanufacture. A certification requirement for resales of trucks, tractors, and trailers will simplify administration of the tax.

Explanation of Provision

The bill makes two changes to the heavy vehicle excise tax:

(1)   Clarification is provided that the 75-percent of value threshold applies in determining whether repairs to a wrecked vehicle constitute remanufacture; and

(2)   The registration requirement currently applicable to certain sales of trucks, tractors, and trailers for resale is replaced with a certification requirement.

Effective Date

The provision is effective after December 31, 1997.

[Conference Report]

Conference Agreement

The conference agreement follows the Senate amendment.

[¶ 5293]   Section 1435.   Skydiving flights exempt from tax on transportation of persons by air.

(Code Sec. 4261, 4041)

[Senate Report]

Present Law

Commercial passenger aviation, or air transportation for which a fare is charged, is subject to a 10-percent ad valorem excise tax for the Airport and Airway Trust Fund. General aviation, or air transportation which is not "for hire" is subject to a fuels tax for the Trust Fund. In the case of skydiving flights, questions have arisen as to when the flight is commercial aviation subject to the ticket tax and when it is noncommercial aviation subject to the fuels tax. In general, if instruction is offered, the flight is general

aviation. Otherwise, the flight is treated as commercial aviation. Many skydiving flights carry both persons receiving instruction and others not receiving instruction.

Reasons for Change

The tax treatment of skydiving flights as commercial or noncommercial needs to be clarified.

Explanation of Provision

The bill specifies that flights which are exclusively dedicated to skydiving are taxed as noncommercial aviation flights, regardless of whether instruction is offered to any of the passengers.

Effective Date

The provision is effective for flights beginning after September 30, 1997.

[Conference Report]

House Bill

No provision.

Conference Agreement

The conference agreement follows the Senate amendment.

[¶ 5294] Section 1436. Eliminate double taxation of certain aviation fuels sold to producers by "fixed base operators".

(Code Sec. 4091)

[Senate Report]

Present Law

Section 4091 imposes a tax on the sale of aviation fuel by any producer (defined to include a wholesale distributor). Fuel sold at many rural airports is sold by retail dealers who do not qualify as wholesale distributors. This fuel is purchased by the retailers tax-paid. In certain instances, fuel which has been purchased tax- paid by a retailer will be re-sold to a producer, e.g., to enable the producer to serve one of its customers at the airport. When this fuel is resold at retail by the pro ducer, a second tax is imposed. The Code contains no provision allowing a refund of the first tax in such cases.

Reasons for Change

Permitting a refund of the tax previously paid on aviation fuel when a producer resells the fuel and pays tax on the resale will improve the fairness of the tax collection for such fuel.

Explanation of Provision

The bill will permit a refund of the tax previously paid on aviation fuel when a producer acquires the fuel, resells it, and pays tax on the second sale.

Effective Date

The provision is effective for fuel sold after September 30, 1997.

[Conference Report]

House Bill

No provision.

Conference Agreement

The conference agreement follows the Senate amendment, with a clarification that the provision applies to tax-paid fuel purchased by registered producers after September 30, 1997.

[¶ 5295] Section 1441. Repeal of $100,000 limitation on unspent proceeds under 1-year exception from rebate.

(Code Sec. 148)

[House Report]

Present Law

Subject to limited exceptions, arbitrage profits from investing bond proceeds in investments unrelated to the governmental purpose of the borrowing must be rebated to the Federal Government. No rebate is required if the gross proceeds of an issue are spent for the governmental purpose of the borrowing within six months after issuance.

This six-month exception is deemed to be satisfied by issuers of governmental bonds (other than tax and revenue anticipation notes) and qualified 501(c)(3) bonds if (1) all proceeds other than an amount not exceeding the lesser of five percent or $100,000 are so spent within six months and (2) the remaining proceeds are spent within one year after the bonds are issued.

Reasons for Change

Exemption of interest paid on State and local bonds from Federal income tax provides an implicit subsidy to State and local governments for their borrowing costs. The principal Federal policy concern underlying the arbitrage rebate requirement is to discourage the earlier and larger than necessary issuance of tax-exempt bonds to take advantage of the opportunity to profit by investing funds borrowed at low-cost tax-exempt rates in higher yielding taxable investments. If at least 95 percent of the proceeds of an issue is spent within six months, and the remainder is spent within one year, opportunities for such arbitrage profit are significantly limited.

Explanation of Provision

The $100,000 limit on proceeds that may remain unspent after six months for certain governmental and qualified 501(c)(3) bonds otherwise exempt from the rebate requirement is deleted. Thus, if at least 95 percent

of the proceeds of these bonds is spent within six months after their issuance, and the remainder is spent within one year, the six-month exception is deemed to be satisfied.

Effective Date

The provision applies to bonds issued after the date of enactment.

[Conference Report]

Senate Amendment

The Senate amendment is the same as the House bill.

Conference Agreement

The conference agreement follows the House bill and the Senate amendment.

[¶ 5296]   Section 1442.   Exception from rebate for earnings on bona fide debt service fund under construction bond rules.

(Code Sec. 148)

[House Report]

Present Law

In general, arbitrage profits from investing bond proceeds in investments unrelated to the governmental purpose of the borrowing must be rebated to the Federal Government. An exception is provided for certain construction bond issues if the bonds are governmental bonds, qualified 501(c)(3) bonds, or exempt-facility private activity bonds for governmentally-owned property.

This exception is satisfied only if the available construction proceeds of the issue are spent at minimum specified rates during the 24-month period after the bonds are issued. The exception does not apply to bond proceeds invested after the 24-month expenditure period as part of a reasonably required reserve or replacement fund, a bona fide debt service fund, or to certain other investments (e.g., sinking funds). Issuers of these construction bonds also may elect to comply with a penalty regime in lieu of rebating arbitrage profits if they fail to satisfy the exception's spending requirements.

Reasons for Change

Bond proceeds invested in a bona fide debt service fund generally must be spent at least annually for current debt service. The short-term nature of investments in such funds results in only limited potential for generating arbitrage profits. If the spending requirements of the 24-month rebate exception are satisfied, the administrative complexity of calculating rebate on these proceeds outweighs the other Federal policy concerns addressed by the rebate requirement.

Explanation of Provision

The bill exempts earnings on bond proceeds invested in bona fide debt service funds from the arbitrage rebate requirement and the penalty requirement of the 24-month exception if the spending requirements of that exception are otherwise satisfied.

Effective Date

The provision applies to bonds issued after the date of enactment.

[Conference Report]

Senate Amendment

The Senate amendment is the same as the House bill.

Conference Agreement

The conference agreement follows the House bill and the Senate amendment.

[¶ 5297]   Section 1443.   Repeal of debt service–based limitation on investment in certain nonpurpose investments.

(Code Sec. 148)

[House Report]

Present Law

Issuers of all tax-exempt bonds generally are subject to two sets of restrictions on investment of their bond proceeds to limit arbitrage profits. The first set requires that tax-exempt bond proceeds be invested at a yield that is not materially higher (generally defined as 0.125 percentage points) than the bond yield ("yield restrictions"). Exceptions are provided to this restriction for investments during any of several "temporary periods" pending use of the proceeds and, throughout the term of the issue, for proceeds invested as part of a reasonably required reserve or replacement fund or a "minor" portion of the issue proceeds.

Except for temporary periods and amounts held pending use to pay current debt service, present law also limits the amount of the proceeds of private activity bonds (other than qualified 501(c)(3) bonds) that may be invested at materially higher yields at any time during a bond year to 150 percent of the debt service for that bond year. This restriction affects primarily investments in reasonably required reserve or replacement funds. Present law further restricts the amount of proceeds from the sale of bonds that may be invested in these reserve funds to ten percent of such proceeds.

The second set of restrictions requires generally that all arbitrage profits earned on investments unrelated to the governmental purpose of the borrowing be rebated to the Federal Government ("arbitrage rebate"). Arbitrage profits include all earnings (in excess of bond yield) derived from the investment of bond proceeds (and subsequent earnings on any such earnings).

Reasons for Change

The 150-percent of debt service limit was enacted before enactment of the arbitrage rebate requirement and the ten-percent limit on the size of reasonably required reserve or replacement funds. It was intended to eliminate arbitrage-motivated activities available from investment of such reserve funds. Provided that comprehensive yield restriction and arbitrage rebate requirements and the present-law overall size limit on reserve funds are maintained, the 150-percent of debt service yield restriction limit is duplicative.

Explanation of Provision

The bill repeals the 150-percent of debt service yield restriction.

Effective Date

The provision applies to bonds issued after the date of enactment.

[Conference Report]

Senate Amendment

The Senate amendment is the same as the House bill.

Conference Agreement

The conference agreement follows the House bill and the Senate amendment.

[¶ 5298]   Section 1444.   Repeal of expired provisions relating to student loan bonds.

(Code Sec. 148)

[House Report]

Present Law

Present law includes two special exceptions to the arbitrage rebate and pooled financing temporary period rules for certain qualified student loan bonds. These exceptions applied only to bonds issued before January 1, 1989.

Explanation of Provision

These special exceptions are deleted as "deadwood."

Effective Date

The provision applies to bonds issued after the date of enactment. It has no effect on bonds issued prior to the date of enactment.

[Conference Report]

Senate Amendment

The Senate amendment is the same as the House bill.

Conference Agreement

The conference agreement follows the House bill and the Senate amendment.

[¶ 5300]   Section 1451.   Overpayment determinations of Tax Court.

(Code Sec. 6512)

[House Report]

Present Law

The Tax Court may order the refund of an overpayment determined by the Court, plus interest, if the IRS fails to refund such overpayment and interest within 120 days after the Court's decision becomes final. Whether such an order is appealable is uncertain.

In addition, it is unclear whether the Tax Court has jurisdiction over the validity or merits of certain credits or offsets (e.g., providing for collection of student loans, child support, etc.) made by the IRS that reduce or eliminate the refund to which the taxpayer was otherwise entitled.

Reasons for Change

Clarification of the jurisdiction of the Tax Court and the ability to appeal orders of the Tax Court would provide for greater certainty for taxpayers and the government in conducting cases before the Tax Court. Clarification will also reduce litigation.

Explanation of Provision

The bill clarifies that an order to refund an overpayment is appealable in the same manner as a decision of the Tax Court. The bill also clarifies that the Tax Court does not have jurisdiction over the validity or merits of the credits or offsets that reduce or eliminate the refund to which the taxpayer was otherwise entitled.

Effective Date

The provision is effective on the date of enactment.

[Conference Report]

Senate Amendment

The Senate amendment is the same as the House bill.

Conference Agreement

The conference agreement follows the House bill and the Senate amendment.

[¶ 5301]   Section 1452.   Redetermination of interest pursuant to motion.

(Code Sec. 7481)

[House Report]

Present Law

A taxpayer may seek a redetermination of interest after certain decisions of the Tax Court have become final by filing a petition with the Tax Court.

Reasons for Change

It would be beneficial to taxpayers if a proceeding for a redetermination of interest supplemented the original deficiency action brought by the taxpayer to redetermine the deficiency determination of the IRS. A motion, rather than a petition, is a more appropriate pleading for relief in these cases.

Explanation of Provision

The bill provides that a taxpayer must file a "motion" (rather than a "petition") to seek a redetermination of interest in the Tax Court.

Effective Date

The provision is effective on the date of enactment.

[Conference Report]

Senate Amendment

The Senate amendment is the same as the House bill.

Conference Agreement

The conference agreement follows the House bill and the Senate amendment. In clarifying the Tax Court's jurisdiction over interest determinations, the conferees do not intend to limit any other remedies that taxpayers may currently have with respect to such determinations, including in particular refund proceedings relating solely to the amount of interest due.

[¶ 5302]   Section 1453.   Application of net worth requirement for awards of litigation costs.

(Code Sec. 7430)

[House Report]

Present Law

Any person who substantially prevails in any action brought by or against the United States in connection with the determination, collection, or refund of any tax, interest, or penalty may be awarded reasonable administrative costs incurred before the IRS and reasonable litigation costs incurred in connection with any court proceeding. A person who substantially prevails must meet certain net worth requirements to be eligible for an award of administrative or litigation costs. In general, only an individual whose net worth does not exceed $2,000,000 is eligible for an award, and only a corporation or partnership whose net worth does not exceed $7,000,000 is eligible for an award. (The net worth determination with respect to a partnership or S corporation applies to all actions that are in substance partnership actions or S corporation actions, including

unified entity-level proceedings under sections 6226 or 6228, that are nominally brought in the name of a partner or a shareholder.)

Reasons for Change

Although the net worth requirements are explicit for individuals, corporations, and partnerships, it is not clear which net worth requirement is to apply to other potential litigants. It is also unclear how the individual net worth rules are to apply to individuals filing a joint tax return. Clarifying these rules will provide certainty for potential claimants and will decrease needless litigation over procedural issues.

Explanation of Provision

The bill provides that the net worth limitations currently applicable to individuals also apply to estates and trusts. The bill also provides that individuals who file a joint tax return shall be treated as separate individuals for purposes of computing the net worth limitations.

Effective Date

The provision applies to proceedings commenced after the date of enactment.

[Conference Report]

Conference Agreement

The conference agreement follows the House bill and the Senate amendment with respect to estates and trusts. The conference agreement follows the Senate amendment with respect to individuals.

[¶ 5303]   Section 1454.   Tax Court jurisdiction for determination of employment status.

(Code Sec. 7436, 7437)

[House Report]

Present Law

The Tax Court is a court of limited jurisdiction, established under Article I of the Constitution. The Tax Court only has the jurisdiction that is expressly conferred on it by statute (sec. 7442).

Reasons for Change

It will be advantageous to taxpayers to have the option of going to the Tax Court to resolve certain disputes regarding employment status.

[Senate Report]

Explanation of Provision

The bill provides that, in connection with the audit of any person, if there is an actual controversy involving a determination by the IRS as part of an examination that (a) one or more individuals performing services for that person are employees of that person or (b) that person is not entitled to relief under section 530 of the Revenue Act of 1978, the Tax Court would have jurisdiction to determine whether the IRS is correct. For example, one way the IRS could make the required determination is through a mechanism similar to the employment tax early referral procedures.[146] A failure to agree would also be considered a determination for this purpose.

The bill provides for de novo review (rather than review of the administrative record). Assessment and collection of the tax would be suspended while the matter is pending in the Tax Court. Any determination by the Tax Court would have the force and effect of a decision of the Tax Court and would be reviewable as such; accordingly, it would be binding on the parties. Awards of costs and certain fees (pursuant to section 7430) would be available to eligible taxpayers with respect to Tax Court det erminations pursuant to this proposal. The bill also provides a number of procedural rules to incorporate this new jurisdiction within the existing procedures applicable in the Tax Court.

Effective Date

The provision takes effect on the date of enactment.

[Conference Report]

Conference Agreement

The conference agreement follows the House bill and the Senate amendment, with additional technical modifications.

---

146. See Announcement 96-13 and Announcement 97-52.

[¶ 5304]   Section 1461.   Extension of due date of first quarter estimated tax payment by private foundations.

(Code Sec. 6655)

[House Report]

Present Law

Under section 4940, tax-exempt private foundations generally are required to pay an excise tax equal to two percent of their net investment income for the taxable year. Under section 6655(g)(3), private foundations are required to pay estimated tax with respect to their excise tax liability under section 4940 (as well as any unrelated business income tax (UBIT) liability under section 511).[21] Section 6655(c) provides that this estimated tax is payable in quarterly installments and that, for calendar-year foundations, the first quarterly installment is due on April 15th. Under section 6655(I), foundations with taxable years other than the calendar year must make their quarterly estimated tax payments no later than the dates in their fiscal years that correspond to the dates applicable to calendar-year foundations.

Reasons for Change

Because a private foundation's estimated tax payments are determined, in part, by reference to the foundation's tax liability for the preceding year, the due date of a foundation's first-quarter estimated tax payment should be the same date for filing the foundation's annual return (Form 990 PF) for the preceding year.

Explanation of Provision

The bill amends section 6655(g)(3) to provide that a calendar-year foundation's first-quarter estimated tax payment is due on May 15th (which is the same day that its annual return, Form 990 PF, for the preceding year is due). As a result of the operation of present-law section 6655(I), fiscal-year foundations will be required to make their first-quarter estimated tax payment no later than the 15th day of the fifth month of their taxable year.

Effective Date

The provision applies to taxable years beginning after the date of enactment.

[Conference Report]

Senate Amendment

The Senate amendment is the same as the House bill.

Conference Agreement

The conference agreement follows the House bill and the Senate amendment.

[¶ 5305]   Section 1462.   Withholding of Commonwealth income taxes from the wages of Federal employees.

(Code Sec. 5517)

[House Report]

Present Law

If State law provides generally for the withholding of State income taxes from the wages of employees in a State, the Secretary of the Treasury shall (upon the request of the State) enter into an agreement with the State providing for the withholding of State income taxes from the wages of Federal employees in the State. For this purpose, a State is a State, territory, or possession of the United States. The Court of Appeals for the Federal Circuit recently held in Romero v. United States (38 F.3d 1204 (1994)) that Puerto Rico was not encompassed within this definition; consequently, the court invalidated an agreement between the Secretary of the Treasury and Puerto Rico that provided for the withholding of Puerto Rico income taxes from the wages of Federal employees.

---

21. Generally, the amount of the first quarter payment must be at least 25 percent of the lesser of (1) the preceding year's tax liability, as shown on he foundation's Form 990 PF, or (2) 95 percent of the foundation's current-year tax liability.

Reasons for Change

The Committee believes that employees of the United States should be in no better or worse position than other employees vis-a-vis local withholding.

Explanation of Provision

The bill makes any Commonwealth eligible to enter into an agreement with the Secretary of the Treasury that would provide for income tax withholding from the wages of Federal employees.

Effective Date

The provision is effective January 1, 1998.

[Conference Report]

Senate Amendment

The Senate amendment is the same as the House bill.

Conference Agreement

The conference agreement follows the House bill and the Senate amendment.

[¶ 5306]   Section 1463.   Certain notices disregarded under provision increasing interest rate on large corporate underpayments.

(Code Sec. 6621)

[House Report]

Present Law

The interest rate on a large corporate underpayment of tax is the Federal short-term rate plus five percentage points. A large corporate underpayment is any underpayment by a subchapter C corporation of any tax imposed for any taxable period, if the amount of such underpayment for such period exceeds $100,000. The large corporate underpayment rate generally applies to periods beginning 30 days after the earlier of the date on which the first letter of proposed deficiency, a statutory notice of deficiency, or a nondeficiency letter or notice of assessment or proposed assessment is sent. For this purpose, a letter or notice is disregarded if the taxpayer makes a payment equal to the amount shown on the letter or notice within that 30 day period.

Reasons for Change

The large corporate underpayment rate generally applies if the underpayment of tax for a taxable period exceeds $100,000, even if the initial letter or notice of deficiency, proposed deficiency, assessment, or proposed assessment is for an amount less than $100,000. Thus, for example, under present

law, a nondeficiency notice relating to a relatively minor mathematical error by the taxpayer may result in the application of the large corporate underpayment rate to a subsequently identified income tax deficiency.

Explanation of Provision

For purposes of determining the period to which the large corporate underpayment rate applies, any letter or notice is disregarded if the amount of the deficiency, proposed deficiency, assessment, or proposed assessment set forth in the letter or notice is not greater than $100,000 (determined by not taking into account any interest, penalties, or additions to tax).

Effective Date

The provision is effective for purposes of determining interest for periods after December 31, 1997.

[Conference Report]

Senate Amendment

The Senate amendment is the same as the House bill.

Conference Agreement

The conference agreement follows the House bill and the Senate amendment.

[¶ 5307]   Section 1501. Matching contributions of self–employed individuals not treated as elective employer contributions.

(Code Sec. 402, 408)

[Senate Report]

Present Law

A qualified cash or deferred arrangement (a "section 401(k) plan") is a type of tax-qualified pension plan under which employees can elect to make pre-tax contributions. An employee's annual elective contributions are subject to a dollar limit ($9,500 for 1997). Employers may make matching contributions based on employees' elective contributions. In the case of employers, such matching contributions are not subject to the $9,500 limit on elective contributions.

Under present law, matching contributions made for a self- employed individual are generally treated as additional elective contributions by the self-employed individual who receives the matching contribution. Accordingly, elective contributions and matching contributions for such self-employed individual are subject to the section 401(k) limits on elective contributions.

Reasons for Change

The Committee believes it is appropriate to treat self- employed individuals in the same manner as other employees with regard to the limitations on matching contributions.

Explanation of Provision

The bill provides that matching contributions for self- employed individuals are treated the same as matching contributions for employees, i.e., they are not treated as elective contributions and are not subject to the elective contribution limit.

Effective Date

The provision is effective for years beginning after December 31, 1997.

[Conference Report]

House Bill

No provision.

Conference Agreement

The conference agreement follows the Senate amendment, and clarifies that the provision does not apply to qualified matching contributions that are treated as elective contributions for purposes of satisfying the ADP test.

Effective Date

Same as the Senate amendment, except that the conference agreement provides that the provision is effective for years beginning after December 31, 1996, in the case of SIMPLE retirement plans.

[¶ 5308]   Section 1502. Modification of prohibition of assignment or alienation.

(Code Sec. 401)

[Senate Report]

Present Law

Under present law, amounts held in a qualified retirement plan for the benefit of a participant are not, except in very limited circumstances, assignable or available to personal creditors of the participant. A plan may permit a participant, at such time as benefits under the plan are in pay status, to make a voluntary revocable assignment of an amount not in excess of 10-percent of any benefit payment, provided the purpose is not to defray plan administration costs. In addition, a plan may comply with a quali-

fied domestic relations order issued by a state court requiring benefit payments to former spouses or other "alternate payees" even if the participant is not in pay status.

There is no specific exception under the Employee Retirement Income Security Act of 1974, as amended ("ERISA") or the Internal Revenue Code which would permit the offset of a participant's benefit against the amount owed to a plan by the participant as a result of a breach of fiduciary duty to the plan or criminality involving the plan. Courts have been divided in their interpretation of the prohibition on assignment or alienation in these cases. Some courts have ruled that there is no exception in ER-

ISA for the offset of a participant's benefit to make a plan whole in the case of a fiduciary breach. Other courts have reached a different result and permitted an offset of a participant's benefit for breach of fiduciary duties.

Reasons for Change

The Committee believes that the assignment and alienation rules should be clarified by creating a limited exception that permits participants' benefits under a qualified plan to be reduced under certain circumstances including the participant's breach of fiduciary duty to the plan.

Explanation of Provision

The bill permits a participant's benefit in a qualified plan to be reduced to satisfy liabilities of the participant to the plan due to (1) the participant being convicted of committing a crime involving the plan, (2) a civil judgment (or consent order or decree) entered by a court in an action brought in connection with a violation of the fiduciary provisions of ERISA, or (3) a settlement agreement between the Secretary of Labor or the Pension Benefit Guaranty Corporation and the participant in connection with a violation of the fiduciary provisions of

ERISA. The court order establishing such liability must require that the participant's benefit in the plan be applied to satisfy the liability. If the participant is married at the time his or her benefit under the plan is offset to satisfy the liability, spousal consent to such offset is required unless the spouse is also required to pay an amount to the plan in the judgment, order, decree or settlement or the judgment, order, decree or settlement provides a 50-percent survivor annuity for the spouse. The bill will make the corresponding changes to ERISA.

Effective Date

The provision is effective for judgments, orders, and decrees issued, and settlement agreements entered into, on or after the date of enactment.

[Conference Report]

House Bill

No provision.

Conference Agreement

The conference agreement follows the Senate amendment. The conference agreement clarifies that an offset is includible in income on the date of the offset.

[¶ 5309]   Section 1503. Elimination of paperwork burdens on plans.

(Code Sec.)

[Senate Report]

Present Law

Under present law, employers are required to prepare summary plan descriptions of employee benefit plans ("SPDs"), and summaries of material modifications to such plans ("SMMs"). The SPDs and SMMs generally provide information concerning the benefits provided by the plan and the participants' rights and obligations under the plan. The SPDs and SMMs must be furnished to plan participants and beneficiaries and filed with the Secretary of Labor.

Reasons for Change

The Committee believes it is appropriate to alleviate the cost and burden of paperwork associated with employee benefit plans.

Explanation of Provision

The bill eliminates the requirement that SPDs and SMMs be filed with the Secretary of Labor. Employers would be required to furnish these documents to the Secretary of Labor upon request. A civil penalty could be imposed by the Secretary of Labor on the plan administrator for failure to comply with such requests. The penalty would be up to $100 per day of failure, up to a maximum of $1,000 per request. No penalty would be imposed if the failure was due to matters reasonably outside the control o f the plan administrator.

Effective Date

The provision is effective on the date of enactment.

[Conference Report]

House Bill

No provision.

[¶ 5310]   Section 1504.   Modification of 403(b) exclusion allowance to conform to 415 modifications.

(Code Sec. 403, 415)

[Senate Report]

Present Law

Under present law, annual contributions to a section 403(b) annuity cannot exceed the exclusion allowance. In general, the exclusion allowance for a taxable year is the excess, if any, of (1) 20 percent of the employee's includible compensation multiplied by his or her years of service, over (2) the aggregate employer contributions for an annuity excludable for any prior taxable years. Includible compensation means the amount of compensation from the employer that is includible in gross income for the most recent year that can be counted as a year of service.

Alternatively, an employee may elect to have the exclusion allowance determined under the rules relating to tax-qualified defined contribution plans (sec. 415). Under those rules, the maximum annual addition that can be made to a defined contribution plan is the lesser of (1) $30,000 or 25 percent of compensation. For years beginning after December 31, 1996, compensation for this purpose includes certain elective deferrals of the employee. An overall limitation applies if the employee is a participant in both a defined contribution plan and a defined benefit plan of the same employer. This overall limitation may further reduce the maximum annual addition that could be made to a defined contribution plan. The overall limitation is repealed with respect to years beginning after December 31, 1999. Existing Treasury regulations relating to the alternative method of determining the exclusion allowance refer to the overall limit.

Reasons for Change

The exclusion allowance for tax-sheltered annuities should be modified to reflect re-

Conference Agreement

The conference agreement follows the Senate amendment.

cent changes to the corresponding limits on benefits under tax-qualified plans.

Explanation of Provision

The provision conforms the section 403(b) exclusion allowance to the section 415 limits by providing that includible compensation includes elective deferrals (and similar pre-tax contributions) of the employee.

The Secretary of the Treasury is directed to revise the regulations regarding the exclusion allowance to reflect the fact that the overall limit on benefits and contributions is repealed (sec. 415(e)). The revised regulations are to be effective for limitation years beginning after December 31, 1999.

The revised regulations are to be effective for limitation years beginning after December 31, 1999.

Effective Date

The modification to the definition of includible compensation is effective for years beginning after December 31, 1997. The direction to the Secretary is effective on the date of enactment.

[Conference Report]

House Bill

No provision

Conference Agreement

The conference agreement follows the Senate amendment, with the clarification that the revised Treasury regulations are to be effective for years (rather than limitation years) beginning after December 31, 1999. In addition, the conference agreement clarifies that the revised regulations are to relate to the election to have the exclusion allowance determined under section 415.

[¶ 5311]   Section 1505.   Extension of moratorium on application of certain nondiscrimination rles to state and local governments.

(Code Sec. 401, 410, 403)

[House Report]

Present Law

Under present law, the rules applicable to governmental plans require that such plans satisfy certain nondiscrimination and minimum participation rules. In general, the rules require that a plan not discriminate in favor of highly compensated employees with regard to the contribution and benefits provided under the plan, participation in the plan, coverage under the plan, and compensation taken into account under the plan. The nondiscrimination rules apply to all governmental plans; qualified retirement plans (including cash or deferred arrangements (sec. 401(k) plans) in effect before May 6, 1986) and annuity plans (sec. 403(b) plans).

For purposes of satisfying the nondiscrimination rules, the Internal Revenue Service has issued several Notices which extended the effective date for compliance for governmental plans. Governmental plans will be required to comply with the nondiscrimination rules beginning with plan years beginning on or after the later of January 1, 1999, or 90 days after the opening of the first legislative session beginning on or after January 1, 1999, of the governing body with authority to amend the plan, if that body does not meet continuously. For plan years beginning before the extended effective date, governmental plans are deemed to satisfy the nondiscrimination requirements

Reasons for Change

The Committee believes that, because of the unique circumstances applicable to governmental plans and the complexity of com-

pliance, the moratorium on compliance with the nondiscrimination rules should be made permanent.

Explanation of Provision

The bill provides that governmental plans will be exempt from the nondiscrimination and minimum participation rules.

Effective Date

The provision is effective for taxable years beginning on and after the date of enactment.

[Conference Report]

Senate Amendment

The Senate amendment is the same as the House bill.

Conference Agreement

The conference agreement follows the House bill and the Senate amendment and clarifies that the exemption from the nondiscrimination and participation rules includes exemption from the ACP and ADP tests. The conference agreement provides that a cash or deferred arrangement under a governmental plan is treated as a qualified cash or deferred arrangement even though the ADP test is not in fact satisfied. Thus, for example, elective contributions made by a government employer on behalf of an employee are not treated as distributed or made available to the employee (in accordance with section 402(e)(3) of the Code).

Effective Date

Same as the House bill and Senate amendment.

[¶ 5312]   Section 1506.   ESOPS maintained by S corporations.

(Code Sec. 409, 4975)

[House Report]

Under present law, an S corporation can have no more than 75 shareholders. For taxable years beginning after December 31, 1997, certain tax-exempt organizations, in-

cluding employee stock ownership plans ("ESOPs") can be a shareholder of an S corporation.

ESOPs are generally required to make distributions in the form of employer securities. If the employer securities are not readily tradable, the employee has a right to require the employer to buy the securities. In the case of an employer whose bylaws or charter restricts ownership of substantially all employer securities to employees or a pension plan, the plan may provide that benefits are distributed in the form of cash. Such a plan may distribute employer securities, if the employee has a right to require the employer to purchase the securities.

ESOPs are subject to certain prohibited transaction rules designed to prohibit certain transactions between the plan and certain persons close to the plan. A number of statutory exceptions are provided to the prohibited transaction rules, including exceptions for loans between the plan and plan participants and certain sales of stock to the ESOP. These statutory exceptions do not apply to shareholder-employees of S corporations. However, such individuals can obtain an administrative exception from such rules from the Department of Labor.

Reasons for Change

It is possible that an S corporation may lose its status as such if the ESOP is required to give stock to plan participants, rather than cash equal to the value of the stock. Changes to the prohibited transactions rules are appropriate to facilitate the maintenance of an ESOP by an S corporation.

Explanation of Provision

The bill provides that ESOPs of S corporations may distribute cash to plan participants as long as the employee has a right to require the employer to purchase the securities (as under the present-law rules). In addition, the bill extends the exception to certain prohibited transactions rules to S corporations.

Effective Date

The provision is effective for taxable years beginning after December 31, 1997.

[Conference Report]

House Bill

The House bill provides that ESOPs of S corporations may distribute cash to plan participants as long as the employee has a right to require the employer to purchase employer securities (as under the present-law rules). In addition, the House bill extends the Code's statutory exceptions to certain prohibited transactions rules to shareholder employees of S corporations.

Effective Date

The provision is effective for taxable years beginning after December 31, 1997.

Senate Amendment

The Senate amendment is the same as the House bill with respect to the provision that permits ESOPs of S corporations to distribute stock in certain cases.

The Senate amendment provides that the sale of stock by a shareholder employee of an S corporation is not a prohibited transaction under the Code or ERISA.

Effective Date

Same as the House bill.

Conference Agreement

The conference agreement follows the House bill and the Senate amendment with respect to the provision permitting ESOPs maintained by S corporations to distribute employer securities in certain circumstances.

The conference agreement follows the Senate amendment with respect to the provision relating to prohibited transaction rules, as modified. Under the conference agreement, the statutory exceptions do not fail to apply merely because a transaction involves the sale of employer securities to an ESOP maintained by an S corporation by a shareholder employee, a family member of the shareholder employee, or a corporation controlled by the shareholder employee. Thus, the statutory exemptions for such a transaction (including the exemption for a loan to the ESOP to acquire employer securities in connection with such a sale or a guarantee of such a loan) apply.

Effective Date

Same as the House bill and the Senate amendment.

[¶ 5313]   Section 1507.   Modification of 10–percent tax for non–deductible contrubitions.

(Code Sec. 4972)

[Senate Report]

Present Law

Under present law, contributions to qualified pension plans are deductible within certain limits. In the case of a single- employer defined benefit plan which has more than 100 participants during the year, the maximum amount deductible is not less than the plan's unfunded current liability as determined under the minimum funding rules. Limits are also imposed on the amount of annual deductible contributions if an employer sponsors both a defined benefit plan and a defined contribution plan that covers some of the same employees. Under the combined plan limitation, the total deduction for all plans for a plan year is generally limited to the greater of (1) 25 percent of compensation or (2) the contribution necessary to meet the minimum funding requirements of the defined benefit plan for the year.

A 10-percent nondeductible excise tax is imposed on contributions that are not deductible. This excise tax does not apply to contributions to one or more defined contribution plans that are nondeductible because they exceed the combined plan deduction limit to the extent such contributions do not exceed 6 percent of compensation in the year for which the contribution is made.

Reasons for Change

The Committee believes that present law unfairly penalizes employers by imposing an excise tax on employer plan contributions that are required to be made and that are not deductible because the employer is fully funding its pension plan. In particular, the Committee does not believe that the excise tax on nondeductible contributions should be imposed when an employer is required to make contributions attributable to elective deferrals under a section 401(k) plan and employer matching contributions.

Explanation of Provision

The bill adds an additional exception to the 10-percent excise tax on nondeductible contributions. Under the provision, the excise tax does not apply to contributions to one or more defined contribution plans that are not deductible because they exceed the combined plan deduction limit to the extent such contributions do not exceed the amount of the employer's matching contributions plus the elective deferral contributions to a section 401(k) plan.

Effective Date

The provision is effective with respect to taxable years beginning after December 31, 1997.

[Conference Report]

House Bill

No provision.

Conference Agreement

The conference agreement follows the Senate amendment.

[¶ 5314]   Section 1508.   Modification of funding requirements for certain plans.

(Code Sec. 412)

[Senate Report]

Present Law

Under present law, defined benefit pension plans are required to meet certain minimum funding rules. Underfunded plans are required to satisfy certain faster funding requirements. In general, these additional requirements do not apply in the case of plans with a funded current liability percentage of at least 90 percent.

The Pension Benefit Guaranty Corporation ("PBGC") insures benefits under most defined benefit pension plans in the event the plan is terminated with insufficient assets to pay for plan benefits. The PBGC is funded in part by a flat-rate premium per plan participant, and a variable rate premium based on plan underfunding.

Reasons for Change

Certain interstate bus companies have pension plans that are closed to new participants and the participants in these plans have demonstrated mortality significantly greater than that predicted by the mortality tables that the plans are required to use for minimum funding purposes. As a result, the sponsors of such plans are required to make contributions that cause the plan to be substantially overfunded. The Committee believes it appropriate to modify the minimum funding requirements for such plans, while at the same time ensuring that pension benefits are adequately funded.

Explanation of Provision

The bill modifies the minimum funding requirements in the case of certain plans. The bill applies in the case of plans that (1) were not required to pay a variable rate PBGC premium for the plan year beginning in 1996, (2) do not, in plan years beginning after 1995 and before 2009, merge with another plan (other than a plan sponsored by an employer that was a member of the controlled group of the employer in 1996), and (3) are sponsored by a company that is engaged primarily in the interurban or interstate passenger bus service.

The bill treats a plan to which it applies as having a funded current liability percentage of at least 90 percent for plan years beginning after 1996 and before 2005. For plan years beginning after 2004, the funded current liability percentage will be deemed to be at least 90 percent if the actual funded current liability percentage is at least as follows:

Plan year beginning in:	Minimum percentage
2005	86
2006	87
2007	88
2008	89
2009 and thereafter	90

If the funded current liability percentage falls below 85 percent for a plan year beginning before 2005, the rule described above still applies if contributions for any such year are made to the plan in an amount equal to the lesser of: (1) the amount necessary to bring the funded current liability percentage to 85 percent, or (2) the greater of (a) 2 percent of the plan's current liability as of the beginning of such plan year or (b) the amount necessary to bring the funded current liability percentage to 80 percent as of the end of such plan year.

The relief from the minimum funding requirements applies for the plan year beginning in 2005, 2006, 2007, and 2008 only if contributions to the plan equal at least the expected increase in current liability due to benefits accruing during the plan year.

Effective Date

The provision is effective with respect to contributions due after December 31, 1997.

[Conference Report]

House Bill

No provision.

Senate Amendment

Conference Agreement

The conference agreement follows the Senate amendment.

Effective Date

The provision is effective with respect to plan years beginning after December 31, 1996.

[¶ 5315]   Section 1509.   Clarification of disqualification rules relating to acceptance of rollover contributuions.

(Code Sec. 402)

[Senate Report]

Present Law

Under present law, a qualified retirement plan that accepts rollover contributions from other plans will not be disqualified because the plan making the distribution is, in fact, not qualified at the time of the distribution, if, prior to accepting the rollover, the receiving plan reasonably concluded that the distributing plan was qualified. The receiving plan can reasonably conclude that the distributing plan was qualified if, for example, prior to accepting the rollover, the distributing plan provided a statement that the distributing plan had a favorable determination letter issued by the Internal Revenue Service ("IRS"). The receiving plan is not required to verify this information.

Reasons for Change

In order to encourage employers to accept rollovers from other qualified retirement plans, the Committee believes that the receiving plans should be insulated from disqualification based on the subsequent qualified status of the distributing plan.

Explanation of Provision

The bill clarifies the circumstances under which a qualified plan could accept rollover contributions without jeopardizing its qualified status. Under the provision, if the trustee of the plan making the distribution notifies the recipient plan that the distributing plan is intended to be a qualified plan, the plan receiving the rollover will not be disqualified if the distributing plan was not in fact a qualified plan.

Effective Date

The provision is effective for rollover contributions made after December 31, 1997.

[Conference Report]

House Bill

No provision.

Conference Agreement

The conference agreement follows the Senate amendment, as modified. Under the conference agreement, the Secretary of the Treasury is directed to clarify that, under its regulations protecting plans from disqualification because they receive invalid rollover contributions, it is not necessary for a distributing plan to have a determination letter in order for the administrator of the receiving plan to reasonably conclude that a contribution is a valid rollover.

[¶ 5316]   Section 1510.   New technologies in retirement plans.

(Code Sec.)

[Senate Report]

Present Law

Under present law it is not clear if sponsors of employee benefit plans may use new technologies (telephonic response systems, computers, email) to satisfy the various ERISA requirements for notice, election, consent, record keeping, and participant disclosure.

Reasons for Change

The Committee believes it is appropriate to review existing guidance for purposes of permitting the use of new technologies for notice and record keeping requirements for retirement plans.

Explanation of Provision

The bill directs the Secretaries of the Treasury and Labor to each issue guidance facilitating the use of new technology for plan purposes. The guidance will be designed to (1) interpret the notice, election, consent, disclosure, and time requirements (and related recordkeeping requirements) under the Internal Revenue Code of 1986 ("IRC") and the Employee Retirement Income Security Act of 1974, as amended ("ERISA") relating to retirement plans as applied to the use of new technologies by plan sponsors and administrators while maintaining the protection of the rights of participants and beneficiaries, and (2) clarify the extent to which writing requirements under the IRC shall be interpreted to permit paperless transactions.

Effective Date

The provision is effective on the date of enactment and requires that the guidance be issued not later than December 31, 1998.

[¶ 5343]   Section 1521.   Increase in full funding limit.

(Code Sec. 412)

[Conference Report]

Present Law

Under present law, defined benefit pension plans are subject to minimum funding requirements. In addition, there is a maximum limit on contributions that can be made to a plan, called the full funding limit. The full funding limit is the lesser of a plan's accrued liability and 150 percent of current liability. In general, current liability is all liabilities to plan participants and beneficiaries. Current liability represents benefits accrued to date, whereas the accrued liability full funding limit is based on projected benefits. Under IRS rules, amounts that cannot be contributed because of the current liability full funding limit are amortized over 10 years.

House Bill

No provision.

Senate Amendment

The Senate amendment increases the 150-percent of full funding limit as follows: 155 percent for plan years beginning in 1999 or 2000, 160 percent for plan years beginning

[Conference Report]

House Bill

No provision.

Conference Agreement

The conference agreement follows the Senate amendment.

in 2001 or 2002, 165 percent for plan years beginning in 2003 and 2004, and 170 percent for plan years beginning in 2005 and thereafter.

In addition, under the provision, amounts that cannot be contributed due to the current liability full funding limit are amortized over 20 years. Amounts that could not be contributed because of such full funding limit and that have not been amortized as of the last day of the plan year beginning in 1998 are amortized over this 20-year period.

Effective Date

Plan years beginning after December 31, 1998.

Conference Agreement

The conference agreement follows the Senate amendment, with the modification that, with respect to amortization bases remaining at the end of the 1998 plan year, the 20-year amortization period is reduced by the number of years since the amortization base had been established. The conference agreement also clarifies that no amortization is required with respect to funding methods that do not provide for amortization bases.

[¶ 5344]   Section 1522.   Special rules for church plans.

(Code Sec. 414)

[Senate Report]

Present Law

Under present law, contributions made to retirement plans by ministers who are self-

employed are deductible to the extent such contributions do not exceed certain limitations applicable to retirement plans. These limitations include the limit on elective deferrals, the exclusion allowance, and the limit on annual additions to a retirement plan.

Reasons for Change

The Committee believes that the unique characteristics of church plans and the procedures associated with contributions made by ministers who are self-employed create particular problems with respect to plan administration.

Explanation of Provision

The bill provides that in the case of a contribution made on behalf of a minister who is self-employed to a church plan, the contribution will be excludable from the income of the minister to the extent that the contribution would be excludable if the minister was an employee of a church and the contribution was made to the plan.

Effective Date

The provision is effective for years beginning after December 31, 1997.

House Bill

No provision.

Conference Agreement

The conference agreement follows the Senate amendment. The provision does not alter present law under which amounts contributed for a minister in connection with section 403(b), either by the minister's actual employer or by any church or convention or association of churches that is treated as the minister's employer under section 414(e), are excluded from the minister's income, and amounts contributed in accordance with section 403(b) by the minister (whether the minister is an employee or is self-employed) are deductible by the minister as provided in section 404 taking into account the other special rules of section 414(e).

Present Law

Under present law ministers who are employed by an organization other than a church are treated as if employed by the church and may participate in the retirement plan sponsored by the church. If the organization also sponsors a retirement plan, such plan does not have to include the ministers as employees for purposes of satisfying the nondiscrimination rules applicable to qualified plans provided the organization is not eligible to participate in the church plan.

Reasons for Change

The Committee believes it is appropriate to extend the same relief to other non-church organizations that may be eligible to participate in a church plan but elect not to do so. Such organizations will not be required to treat ministers as employees for purposes of satisfying the nondiscrimination rules applicable to their retirement plan.

Explanation of Provision

The bill provides that if a minister is employed by an organization other than a church and the organization is not otherwise participating in the church plan then, the minister does not have to be included as an employee under the retirement plan of the organization for purposes of the nondiscrimination rules.

Effective Date

The provision is effective for years beginning after December 31, 1997.

[Conference Report]

House Bill

No provision.

Conference Agreement

The conference agreement follows the Senate amendment.

[¶ 5345]   Section 1523.   Repeal application of UBIT to ESOPs of S corporations.

(Code Sec. 512)

[Senate Report]

Present Law

Under present law, for taxable years beginning after December 31, 1997, certain tax-exempt organizations, including employee stock ownership plans ("ESOPs") can be a shareholder of an S corporation. Items of income or loss of the S corporation will flow through to qualified tax-exempt shareholders as unrelated business taxable income ("UBTI"), regardless of the source of the income.

Reasons for Change

The Committee believes that treating S corporation income as UBTI is not appropriate because such amounts would be subject to tax at the ESOP level, and also again when benefits are distributed to ESOP participants.

Explanation of Provision

The bill repeals the provision treating items of income or loss of an S corporation as unrelated business taxable income in the case of an employee stock ownership plan that is an S corporation shareholder.

Effective Date

The provision is effective for taxable years beginning after December 31, 1997.

[Conference Report]

House Bill

No provision.

Conference Agreement

The conference agreement follows the Senate amendment, and clarifies that the repeal of the provision treating items of income or loss of an S corporation as unrelated business taxable income applies only with respect to employer securities held by an employee stock ownership plan (as defined in section 4975(e)(7) of the Code) maintained by an S corporation.

[¶ 5346]   Section 1524.   Diversification in section 401(k) plan investments.

(Code Sec.)

[Conference Report]

Present Law

The Employee Retirement Income Security Act of 1974, as amended ("ERISA") prohibits certain employee benefit plans from investing more than 10 percent of the plan's assets in the securities and real property of the employer who sponsors the plan. The 10 percent limitation does not apply to "eligible individual account plans" that specifically authorize such investments. Generally, eligible individual account plans are defined contribution plans, including plans containing a cash or deferred arrangement ("401(k) plans"). The assets of such plans may be invested in employer securities and real property without regard to the 10-percent limitation.

House Bill

No provision.

Senate Amendment

The Senate amendment provides that the term "eligible individual account plan" does not include the portion of a plan that consists of elective deferrals (and earnings on the elective deferrals) made under section 401(k) if elective deferrals equal to more than 1 percent of a participant's compensation are required to be invested in employer securities at the direction of a person other than the participant. Such portion of the plan is treated as a separate plan subject to the 10-percent limitation on investment in employer securities and real property.

The Senate amendment does not apply to an individual account plan if the value of the assets of all individual account plans maintained by the employer does not exceed

10 percent of the value of the assets of all pension plans maintained by the employer. The Senate amendment does not apply to an employee stock ownership plan as defined in sections 409(a) and 4975(e)(7) of the Internal Revenue Code.

Effective Date

The provision is effective with respect to employer securities and employer real property acquired after the beginning of the first plan year beginning after the 90th day after the date of enactment. The provision does not apply to employer securities and real property acquired pursuant to a binding written contract to acquire such securities or real property in effect on the date of enactment and at all times thereafter.

Conference Agreement

The conference agreement follows the Senate amendment, with modifications. The conference agreement clarifies that the provision applies if elective deferrals equal to more than 1 percent of an employee's eligible compensation are required to be invested in employer securities and employer real property. Eligible compensation is compensation that is eligible to be deferred. As

under the Senate amendment, if the 1 percent threshold is exceeded, then the portion of the plan that consists of elective deferrals (and earnings thereon) is still treated as an individual account plan as long as elective deferrals (and earnings thereon) are not required to be invested in employer securities and employer real property.

The conference agreement provides that multiemployer plans are not taken into account in determining whether the value of the assets of all individual account plans maintained by the employer does not exceed 10 percent of the value of the assets of all pension plans maintained by the employer. The conference agreement provides that the provision does not apply to an employee stock ownership plan as defined in section 4975(e)(7) of the Internal Revenue Code.

Effective Date

Under the conference agreement, the provision is effective with respect to elective deferrals in plan years beginning after December 31, 1998 (and earnings thereon). The provision does not apply with respect to earnings on elective deferrals for years beginning before January 1, 1999.

[¶ 5347]   Section 1525.   Cash or deferred arrangements for irrigationand drainage entities.

(Code Sec. 401)

[House Report]

Present Law

Under present law, taxable and tax-exempt employers may maintain qualified cash or deferred arrangements. State and local government organizations generally are prohibited from establishing qualified cash or deferred arrangements ("section 401(k) plans"). This prohibition does not apply to qualified cash or deferred arrangements adopted by a State or local government before May 6, 1986.

Mutual irrigation or ditch companies are exempt from tax if at least 85 percent of the income of the company consists of amounts collected from members for the sole purpose of meeting losses and expenses.

Reasons for Change

The Committee believes that all mutual irrigation and ditch companies and water districts should be permitted to maintain a qualified cash or deferred arrangement, regardless of whether the company or district is a tax-exempt or taxable entity or part of a State or local government.

Explanation of Provision

Under the bill, mutual irrigation or ditch companies and districts organized under the laws of a State as a municipal corporation for the purpose of irrigation, water conservation or drainage (or a national association of such organizations) are permitted to maintain qualified cash or deferred arrangements, even if the company or district is a State or local government organization.

Effective Date

The provision is effective with respect to years beginning after December 31, 1997.

[Conference Report]

Senate Amendment

No provision.

[¶ 5348]   Section 1526.   Portability of permissive service credit under government pension plans.

(Code Sec. 415)

[Conference Report]

Present Law

Under present law, limits are imposed on the contributions and benefits under qualified pension plans (Code sec. 415). Certain special rules apply in the case of State and local governmental plans.

In the case of a defined contribution plan, the limit on annual additions is the lesser of $30,000 or 25 percent of compensation. Annual additions include employer contributions, as well as after-tax employee contributions. In the case of a defined benefit pension plan, the limit on the annual retirement benefit is the lesser of (1) 100 percent of compensation or (2) $125,000 (indexed for inflation). The 100 percent of compensation limitation does not apply in the case of State and local governmental pension plans.

Amounts contributed by employees to a State or local governmental plan are treated as made by the employer if the employer "picks up" the contribution.

[House Report]

Reasons for Change

Many State and local government plans facilitate portability of pension benefits by permitting employees to purchase credit for service with another governmental employer and for certain other service as provided in the plan. The Committee believes it appropriate to modify the limits on contributions and benefits to encourage portability of benefits between governmental plans.

Conference Agreement

The conference agreement follows the House bill.

Explanation of Provision

Under the bill, in applying the defined benefit pension plan limit, the annual benefit under a State or local governmental plan includes the accrued benefit derived from contributions to purchase permissive service credit. Such contributions are not taken into account in determining annual additions.

Permissive service credit means credit for a period of service recognized by the governmental plan if the employee contributes to the plan an amount (as determined by the plan) which does not exceed the amount necessary to fund the accrued benefit attributable to such period of service. The bill does not affect the treatment of "pick up" contributions.

Effective Date

The provision is effective with respect to years beginning after December 31, 1997.

Senate Amendment

No provision.

Conference Agreement

The conference agreement follows the House bill, with modifications. Under the conference agreement, contributions by a participant in a State or local governmental plan to purchase permissive service credits are subject to one of two limits. Either (1) the accrued benefit derived from all contributions to purchase permissive service credit must be taken into account in determining whether the defined benefit pension plan limit is satisfied, or (2) all such contributions must be taken into account in determining whether the $30,000 limit on annual additions is met for the year (taking into account any other annual additions of the par-

ticipant). Under the first alternative, a plan will not fail to satisfy the reduced defined benefit pension plan limit that applies in the case of early retirement due to the accrued benefit derived from the purchase of permissive service credits. These limits may be applied on a participant-by-participant basis. That is, contributions to purchase permissive service credits by all participants in the same plan do not have to satisfy the same limit.

Under the conference agreement, permissive service credit is defined as under the House bill. Thus, it is credit for a period of service that is recognized by the governmental plan only if the employee voluntarily contributes to the plan an amount (as determined by the plan) which does not exceed the amount necessary to fund the benefit attributable to the period of service and which is in addition to the regular employee contributions, if any, under the plan. Section 415 is violated if more than 5 years of permissive service credit is purchased for "nonqualified service". In addition, section 415 is violated if nonqualified service is taken into account for an employee who has less than 5 years of participation under the plan. Nonqualified service is service other than service (1) as a Federal, State, or local government employee, (2) as an employee of an association representing Federal, State or local government employees, (3) as an employee of an educational institution which provides elementary or secondary education, or (4) for military service. Service under (1), (2) or (3) is not qualified if it enables a participant to receive a retirement benefit for the same service under more than one plan.

The conference agreement provides that in the case of any repayment of contribu-

tions and earnings to a governmental plan with respect to an amount previously refunded upon a forfeiture of service credit under the plan (or another plan maintained by a State or local government employer within the same State) any such repayment shall not be taken into account for purposes of section 415 and service credit obtained as a result of the repayment shall not be considered permissive service credit.

The provision is not intended to affect the application of "pick up" contributions to purchase permissive service credit or the treatment of pick up contributions under section 415. The provision does not apply to purchases of service credit for qualified military service under the rules relating to veterans' reemployment rights (sec. 414(u)).

Effective Date

In general, the conference agreement is effective with respect to contributions to purchase permissive service credits made in years beginning after December 31, 1997.

The conference agreement provides a transition rule for plans that provided for the purchase of permissive service credit prior to enactment of this Act. Under this rule, the defined contribution limits will not reduce the amount of permissive service credit of an eligible participant allowed under the terms of the plan as in effect on the date of enactment. For this purpose an eligible participant is an individual who first became a participant in the plan before the first plan year beginning after the last day of the calendar year in which the next regular session (following the date of the enactment of this Act) of the governing body with authority to amend the plan ends.

[¶ 5349]   Section 1527.   Removal of dollar limitaion on benefit payments from a defined benefit plan for police and fire employees.

(Code Sec. 415)

[Conference Report]

Present Law

Under present law, limits are imposed on the contributions and benefits under qualified pension plans. Certain special rules ap-

ply in the case of State and local governmental plans.

In the case of a defined benefit pension plan, the limit on the annual retirement benefit is the lesser of (1) 100 percent of compensation or (2) $125,000 (for 1997, indexed for inflation). The 100 percent of compensation limitation does not apply in

the case of State and local governmental pension plans. In general, the dollar limit is reduced if benefits begin before social security retirement age and increased if benefits begin after social security retirement age. In the case of State and local government plans, the dollar limit is not reduced unless benefits begin before age 62 and in any case is not less than $75,000, and the dollar limit is increased if benefits begin after age 65. In the case of certain police and fire department employees, the dollar limit cannot be reduced below $50,000 (indexed), regardless of the age at which benefits commence.

House Bill

No provision.

Senate Amendment

The dollar limit on defined benefit plans does not apply to individuals who receive the special rule for certain police and fire department employees under present law.

Effective Date

Years beginning after December 31, 1996.

Conference Agreement

The conference agreement follows the Senate amendment, with the clarification that the exception from the dollar limit for police and fire department employees only applies to the reduction for early retirement benefits. Thus, the defined benefit plan dollar limit continues to apply, but is not reduced in the case of early retirement. As under present law, the dollar limit is increased for such employees if benefits begin after age 65.

Effective Date

Same as the Senate amendment.

[¶ 5350]   Section 1528.   Exemption from tax upon death of a policy officer in the line of duty.

(Code Sec. 138)

[House Report]

Present Law

Survivors of military service personnel (such as those killed in combat) are generally entitled to survivor benefits (38 U.S.C. sec. 1310). These survivor benefits are generally exempt from taxation (38 U.S.C. sec. 5301). Survivor means the surviving spouse or surviving dependent child of the military service personnel.

Survivor annuity benefits paid under a governmental retirement plan to a survivor of a law enforcement officer killed in the line of duty are generally includible in income. Amounts contributed to the plan by the officer and previously included in the officer's income would not be includible in the survivor's income.

Reasons for Change

The Committee believes that it is appropriate to apply to the survivors of law enforcement officers who are killed in the line of duty the rules regarding the taxation of certain survivor benefits provided to survivors of military personnel.

Explanation of Provision

The bill generally provides that an amount paid as a survivor annuity on account of the death of a law enforcement officer who is killed in the line of duty will be excludable from income to the extent the survivor annuity is attributable to the officer's service as a law enforcement officer. The survivor annuity must be provided under a governmental plan to the surviving spouse (or former spouse) of the law enforcement officer or to a child of the officer.

Effective Date

The provision applies to amounts received in taxable years beginning after December 31, 1996, with respect to individuals dying after that date.

[Conference Report]

Senate Amendment

The Senate amendment is the same as the House bill except that the provision applies to public safety officers killed in the line of duty. Public safety officers include law enforcement officers, firefighters, rescue squad or ambulance crew.

Conference Agreement

The conference agreement follows the Senate amendment. The conference agreement clarifies that the provision does not apply with respect to the death of a public safety officer if it is determined by the appropriate supervising authority that (1) the death was caused by the intentional misconduct of the officer or by the officers intention to bring about the death, (2) the officer was voluntarily intoxicated at the time of death, (3) the officer was performing his or her duties in a grossly negligent manner at the time of death, or (4) the actions of the individual to whom payment is to be made were a substantial contributing factor to the death of the officer.

[¶ 5351]   Section 1529.   Treatment of certain disability payments to public safety employees.

(Code Sec. 104)

[House Report]

Present Law

Under present law, amounts received under a workmen's compensation act as compensation for personal injuries or sickness incurred in the course of employment are excluded from gross income. Compensation received under a workmen's compensation act by the survivors of a deceased employee also are excluded from gross income. Nonoccupational death and disability benefits are not excludable from income as workmen's compensation benefits.

Reasons for Change

The Committee is aware that some State plans were structured so that the exclusion for workers' compensation benefits was not applicable, and that some benefit recipients mistakenly thought the exclusion applied. The Committee believes it appropriate to provide relief in such cases.

Explanation of Provision

Under the bill, certain payments made on behalf of full-time employees of any police or fire department organized and operated by a State (or any political subdivision, agency, or instrumentality thereof) are excludable from income. The bill applies to payments made on account of heart disease or hypertension of the employee and that were received in 1989, 1990, 1991 pursuant to a State law as amended on May 19, 1992, which irrebuttably presumed that heart disease and hypertension are work-related illnesses, but only for employees separating from service before July 1, 1992.

The bill provides that claims for refund or credit for overpayment of tax resulting from the provision could be filed up to 1 year after the date of enactment, without regard to the otherwise applicable statute of limitations.

Effective Date

The provision is effective on the date of enactment.

[Conference Report]

Senate Amendment

The Senate amendment is the same as the House bill, except that the provision applies to amounts payable under a State law (as in existence on July 1, 1992) which irrebuttably presumed that heart disease and hypertension are work-related illnesses, but only for employees separating from service before such date.

Effective Date

Same as the House bill.

Conference Agreement

The conference agreement follows the House bill.

[¶ 5352]   Section 1530.   Gratuitous transfers for the benefit of employees.

(Code Sec. 664, 4975, 401, 415)

[House Report]

Present Law

Employee stock ownership plans

An employee stock ownership plan ("ESOP") is a qualified stock bonus plan or a combination stock bonus and money purchase pension plan under which employer securities are held for the benefit of employees. The securities, which are held by one or more tax-exempt trusts under the plan, may be acquired through direct employer contributions or with the proceeds of a loan to the trust (or trusts).

Charitable remainder trusts

A deduction is allowed for Federal estate tax purposes for transfers by a decedent to charitable, religious, scientific, etc. organizations (Code sec. 2055(a)). In the case of a transfer of a remainder interest to a charity, the remainder interest must be in a charitable remainder trust (Code sec. 2055(e)). A charitable remainder trust generally is a trust that is required to pay, no less often than annually, a fixed dollar amount (charitable remainder annuity trust) or a fixed percentage of the fair market value of the trust's assets determined at least annually (charitable remainder unitrust) to noncharitable beneficiaries, and the remainder of the trust (i.e., after termination of the annuity or unitrust amounts) to a charitable, religious, scientific, etc. organization (Code sec. 664).

Reasons for Change

The Committee believes it appropriate to encourage certain transfers of stock to an ESOP.

Explanation of Provision

In general

The bill permits certain limited transfers of qualified employer securities by charitable remainder trusts to ESOPs without adversely affecting the status of the charitable remainder trusts under Code section 664. As a result, the bill provides that a qualified gratuitous transfer of employer securities to an ESOP is deductible from the gross estate of a decedent under Code section 2055 to the extent of the present value of the remainder interest. In addition, an ESOP will not fail to be a qualified plan because it complies with the requirements with respect to a qualified gratuitous transfer.

Qualified gratuitous transfer

In order for a transfer of securities to be a "qualified gratuitous transfer," the following requirements must be satisfied: (1) the securities transferred must previously have passed from the decedent to a charitable remainder trust; (2) at the time of the transfer to the ESOP, family members of the decedent own (directly or indirectly) no more than 10 percent of the value of the outstanding stock of the company; (3) immediately after the transfer to the ESOP, the ESOP owns at least 60 percent[54] of the value of outstanding stock of the company; and (4) the plan meets certain requirements. In order to prevent erosion of the 60-percent ownership requirements, an excise tax is imposed on the employer maintaining the ESOP with respect to certain dispositions of the transferred stock within 3 years of the transfer.

The provision applies in cases in which the ESOP was in existence on August 1, 1996, and the decedent dies on or before December 31, 1998. The provision does not fail to apply merely because the ESOP is amended after August 1, 1996, for example, in order to conform to the requirements of the provision.

Plan requirements

In order for a transfer to qualify as a gratuitous transfer, the ESOP must contain certain provisions. First, the plan must provide that plan participants are entitled to direct the manner in which stock transferred are to be voted (with respect to all matters). Transferred securities that have not yet been allocated to participants must be voted by a trustee that is not a 5-percent

---

54. The 60-percent requirement is determined assuming that outstanding options have been exercised.

owner of the company or a family member of the decedent.

Second, the plan must provide that participants have the right to receive distributions in the form of stock and that the participant can require the employer to repurchase any shares distributed under a fair valuation formula. For this purpose, a valuation formula is not considered fair if it takes into account a discount for minority interests.

Finally, the plan must provide that, if the plan is terminated before all the transferred stock has been allocated, the remaining stock is to be transferred to one or more charitable organizations. The employer is subject to an excise tax designed to recapture the estate taxes that would have been due had the transfer to the ESOP not occurred if the plan is terminated and any unallocated shares are not transferred to charitable organizations.

Treatment of transferred stock and allocation rules

No deduction is permitted under section 404 of the Code with respect to securities transferred from the charitable remainder trust. The nondiscrimination requirements (sec. 401(a)(4)) normally applicable to qualified plans must be satisfied with respect to the securities transferred. The ESOP is required to treat the securities transferred as employer securities, except for purposes of determining the amount of deductible contributions to the plan otherwise permitted by the employer. The ESOP is required to allocate the transferred securities up to the limit on contributions and benefits (sec. 415) after allocating any other employer contributions for the year; any transferred securities that can not be al-

located because of the section 415 limits would be held in a suspense account and allocated in the same manner in subsequent years. Transferred securities are not taken into account in determining whether any other contributions satisfy the section 415 limit. Further, securities transferred to an ESOP by a charitable remainder trust cannot be allocated to the account of (1) any family member of the decedent, or (2) any employee owning more than 5 percent of any class of outstanding stock of the corporation issuing the securities (or a member of a controlled group of corporations) or the total value of any class of outstanding stock of any such corporation. The employer is subject to an excise tax if impermissible allocations are made.

Definition of qualified employer securities

Qualified employer securities include only employer securities (within the meaning of sec. 409(l) of the Code), which are issued by a domestic corporation that has no outstanding stock that is readily tradable on an established securities market and that has only one class of stock.

Effective Date

The bill applies to transfers made to trusts to, or for the use of, an ESOP after the date of enactment.

[Conference Report]

Senate Amendment

No provision.

Conference Agreement

The conference agreement follows the House bill.

[¶ 5353]   Section 1531.   Newborns' and mothers' health protection; mental health parity.

(Code Sec. 9811, 9812)

[Conference Report]

Present Law

The Newborns' and Mothers' Health Protection Act of 1996 amended the Employee Retirement Income Security Act ("ERISA")

and the Public Health Service Act to impose certain requirements on group health plans with respect to coverage of newborns and mothers, including a requirement that a group health plan cannot restrict benefits for a hospital stay in connection with childbirth for the mother or newborn to less than 48 hours following a normal vaginal delivery or less than 96 hours following a cesarean section. These provisions are effective with respect to plan years beginning on or after January 1, 1998.

The Mental Health Parity Act of 1996 amended ERISA and the Public Health Service Act to provide that group health plans that provide both medical and surgical benefits and mental health benefits cannot impose limits on mental health benefits that are not imposed on substantially all medical and surgical benefits. The provisions of the Mental Health Parity Act are effective with respect to plan years beginning on or after January 1, 1998, but do not apply to benefits for services furnished on or after September 30, 2001.

The Internal Revenue Code requires that group health plans meet certain requirements with respect to limitations on exclusions of preexisting conditions and that group health plans not discriminate against individuals based on health status. An excise tax of $100 per day during the period of noncompliance is imposed on the employer sponsoring the plan if the plan fails to meet these requirements. The maximum tax that can be imposed during a taxable year cannot exceed the lesser of 10 percent of the employer's group health plan expenses for the prior year or $500,000. No tax is imposed if the Secretary determines that the employer did not know, and exercising reasonable diligence would not have known, that the failure existed.

House Bill

No provision.

Senate Amendment

No provision.

Conference Agreement

The conference agreement incorporates into the Internal Revenue Code the provisions of the Newborns' and Mothers' Health Protection Act of 1996 and the Mental Health Parity Act of 1996 relating to group health plans. Failures to comply with such provisions are subject to the present-law excise tax applicable to failures to comply with present-law group health plan requirements.

Effective Date

The provisions are effective with respect to plan years beginning on or after January 1, 1998.

[¶ 5354]   Section 1532.   Church plan exception to prohibition on discrimination against individuals based on health status.

(Code Sec. 9802)

[Conference Report]

Present Law

Under the Health Insurance Portability and Accountability Act ("HIPAA"), group health plans generally may not establish rules for eligibility based on any of the following factors relating to an individual or a dependent of the individual: (1) health status, (2) medical condition, (3) claims experience, (4) receipt of health care, (5) medical history, (6) genetic information, (7) evidence of insurability, or (8) disability. In addition, a group health plan may not charge an individual a greater premium based on any of such factors.

A excise tax is imposed on the failure of a group plan to satisfy the nondiscrimination rule. In general, the excise tax is imposed on the employer sponsoring the plan and is equal to $100 per day per individual as long as the plan is not in compliance.

House Bill

No provision.

Senate Amendment

No provision.

Conference Agreement

The conference agreement provides that certain church plans are not treated as violating the nondiscrimination requirement merely because the plan requires evidence of good health in order for an individual to enroll in the plan for (1) individuals who are employees of employers with 10 or fewer and for self-employed individuals or (2) any individual who enrolls after the first 90 days of eligibility under the plan. The provision applies to a church plan for a year if the plan included such provisions requiring evidence of good health on July 15, 1997, and at all times thereafter before the beginning of the year.

Effective Date

The provision is effective as if included in HIPAA.

[¶ 5355] Section 1541. Date for adoption of plan amendments.

(Code Sec.)

[Conference Report]

Present Law

Plan amendments to reflect amendments to the law generally must be made by the time prescribed by law for filing the income tax return of the employer for the employer's taxable year in which the change in law occurs.

House Bill

No provision.

Senate Amendment

No provision.

Conference Agreement

The conference agreement provides that any amendments to a plan or annuity contract required to be made by the Act are not

required to be made before the first day of the first plan year beginning on or after January 1, 1999. In the case of a governmental plan, the date for amendments is extended to the first plan year beginning on or after January 1, 2001. The conference agreement also provides that if an amendment is made pursuant to the Act (whether or not the amendment is required) before the date for required plan amendments, the plan or contract is operated in a manner consistent with the amendment during a period and the amendment is effective retroactively to such period (1) the plan or contract will not fail to be treated as operated in accordance with its terms for such period merely because it is operated in a manner consistent with the amendment, and (2) the plan will not fail to meet the anti-cutback provisions applicable to qualified retirement plans by reason of such a plan amendment.

[¶ 5356] Section 1601(a). Returns relating to purchases of fish.

(Code Sec. 6050R)

[House Report]

Present Law

Every person engaged in the trade or business of purchasing fish for resale must file an informational return reporting its purchases from any person that is engaged in the trade or business of catching fish which are in excess of $600 for any calendar year. Persons filing such an informational return relating to the purchase of fish must furnish a statement showing the name and address of the person filing the return, as well as the amount shown on the return, to each person whose name is required to be disclosed on the return.

Explanation of Provision

Every person filing an informational return relating to the purchase of fish must

furnish a statement showing the phone number of the person filing the return, as well as such person's name, address and the amount shown on the return, to each person whose name is required to be disclosed on the return.

Conference Report]

Senate Amendment

The Senate Amendment is the same as the House bill.

Conference Agreement

The conference agreement follows the House bill and the Senate amendment.

[¶ 5357]   Section 1601(c).   Charitable remainder trusts not eligible to be electing small business trusts.

(Code Sec. 1361)

[House Report]

Present Law

Under present law, an electing small business trust may be a shareholder in an S corporation. In order to qualify for this treatment, all beneficiaries of the electing small business trust generally must be individuals or estates eligible to be S corporation shareholders. An exempt trust may not qualify as an electing small business trust.

DESCRIPTION OF PROVISION

The provision clarifies that charitable remainder annuity trusts and charitable remainder unitrusts may not be electing small business trusts.

Conference Report]

Senate Amendment

The Senate Amendment is the same as the House bill.

Conference Agreement

The conference agreement follows the House bill and the Senate amendment.

[¶ 5358]   Section 1601(c).   Clarify the effective date for post-termination transition period provision.

(Code Sec.)

[House Report]

Present Law

Distributions made by a former S corporation during its post-termination period are treated in the same manner as if the distributions were made by an S corporation (e.g., treated by shareholders as nontaxable distributions to the extent of the accumulated adjustment account). Distributions made after the post-termination period are generally treated as made by a C corporation (i.e., treated by shareholders as taxable dividends to the extent of earnings and profits).

The "post-termination period" is the period beginning on the day   after the last day of the last taxable year of the S corporation and ending on the later of: (1) a date that is one year later, or (2) the   due date for filing the return for the last taxable year and the 120-day period beginning on the date of a determination that the corporation's S corporation election had terminated for a previous taxable year.

The Small Business Act expanded the post-termination period to   include the 120-day period beginning on the date of any determination   pursuant to an audit of the

taxpayer that follows the termination of the S corporation's election and that adjusts a subchapter S item of income, loss or deduction of the S corporation during the S period. In addition, the definition of "determination" was expanded to include a final disposition of the Secretary of the Treasury of a claim for refund and, under regulations, certain agreements between the Secretary and any person, relating to the tax liability of the person. The Small Business Act provision was effective for taxable years beginning after December 31, 1996.

Explanation of Provision

The technical correction clarifies that the effective date for the   Small Business Act provision affecting the post-termination transition period is for determinations after December 31, 1996, not for   determinations with respect to taxable years beginning after December   31, 1996. However, in no event will the post-termination transition period expanded by the Small Business Act end before the end of the 120-day period beginning after the date of enactment of this Act. *Conference Report]*

Senate Amendment

The Senate Amendment is the same as the House bill.

Conference Agreement

The conference agreement follows the House bill and the Senate amendment.

[¶ 5359]   Section 1601(c).   Treatment of qualified subchapter S subsidiaries.

(Code Sec. 1361)

[House Report]

Present Law

Pursuant to a provision of the Small Business Act, an S corporation is allowed to own a qualified subchapter S subsidiary. The term "qualified subchapter S subsidiary" means a domestic corporation that (1) is not an ineligible corporation (i.e., a corporation that would be eligible to be an S corporation if the stock of the corporation were held directly by the shareholders of its parent S corporation) if 100 percent of the stock of the subsidiary were held by its S corporation parent and (2) which the parent elects to treat as a qualified subchapter S subsidiary. Under the election, for all purposes of the Code, the qualified subchapter S subsidiary is not treated as a separate corporation and all the assets, liabilities, and items of income, deduction, and credit of the subsidiary are treated as the assets, liabilities, and items of income, deduction, and credit of the parent S corporation.

The legislative history of the provision provides that if an election is made to treat an existing corporation as a qualified subchapter S subsidiary, the subsidiary will be deemed to have liquidated under sections 332 and 337 immediately before the election is effective.

Explanation of Provision

The technical correction provides that the Secretary of the Treasury may provide, by regulations, instances where the separate corporate existence of a qualified subchapter S subsidiary may be taken into account for purposes of the Code. Thus, if an S corporation owns 100 percent of the stock of a bank (as defined in sec. 581) and elects to treat the bank as a qualified subchapter S subsidiary, it is expected that Treasury regulations would treat the bank as a separate legal entity for purposes of those Code provisions that apply specifically to banks (e.g., sec. 582).

Treasury regulations also may provide exceptions to the general rule that the qualified subchapter S subsidiary election is treated as a deemed section 332 liquidation of the subsidiary in appropriate cases. In addition, if the effect of a qualified subchapter S subsidiary election is to invalidate an election to join in the filing of a consolidated return for a group of subsidiaries that formerly joined in such filing, Treasury regulations may provide guidance as to the consolidated return effects of the S election. *Conference Report]*

Senate Amendment

The Senate Amendment is the same as the House bill.

Conference Agreement

The conference agreement follows the House bill and the Senate amendment.

[¶ 5360]   Section 1601(d).   Salary reduction simplified employee pensions ("SARSEPS").

(Code Sec. 408)

[House Report]

Present Law

SARSEPs were repealed for years beginning after December 31, 1996, unless the SARSEP was established before January 1, 1997. Consequently, an employer was not permitted to establish a SARSEP after December 31, 1996. SARSEPs established before January 1, 1997, may continue to receive contributions under the rules in effect prior to January 1, 1997.

Explanation of Provision

The bill amends Code section 408(k)(6) to clarify that new employees of an employer hired after December 31, 1996, may participate in a SARSEP of an employer established before January 1, 1997. *Conference Report]*

Senate Amendment

The Senate Amendment is the same as the House bill.

Conference Agreement

The conference agreement follows the House bill and the Senate amendment.

[¶ 5361]   Section 1601(d).   SIMPLE retirement plans.

(Code Sec. 408, 6693, 401, 404)

[House Report]

Reporting requirements for SIMPLE IRAs.

Present Law

A trustee of an individual retirement account and the issuer of an   individual retirement annuity must furnish reports regarding the account or annuity to the individual for whom the account or annuity is maintained not later than January 31 of the calendar year following the year to which the reports relate. In the case of a SIMPLE IRA, such reports are to be furnished within 30 days after each calendar year.

Explanation of Provision

The bill conforms the time for providing reports for SIMPLE IRAs to   that for IRA reports generally. Thus, the bill would provide that the   report required to be furnished to the individual under a SIMPLE IRA would be provided within 31 days after each calendar year. *Conference Report]*

Senate Amendment

The Senate Amendment is the same as the House bill.

Conference Agreement

The conference agreement follows the House bill and the Senate amendment.

b. Notification requirement for SIMPLE IRAs (sec.   1501(d)(1)(C) of the bill and secs. 408(l)(2) and 6693(c) of the Code)]

Present Law

The trustee of any SIMPLE IRA is required to provide the employer   maintaining the arrangement a summary plan description containing basic   information about the plan. At least once a year, the trustee is also   required to furnish an account statement to each individual maintaining   a SIMPLE account. In addition, the trustee is required to file an annual   report with the Secretary. A trustee who fails to provide any of such   reports or descriptions will be subject to a penalty of $50 per day until such failure is corrected, unless the failure is due to reasonable cause.

Explanation of Provision

The bill provides that issuers of annuities for SIMPLE IRAs have the   same reporting requirements as SIMPLE IRA trustees.

c. Maximum dollar limitation for SIMPLE IRAs (sec.   1501(d)(1)(D) of the bill and sec. 408(p) of the Code)]

Present Law

The Small Business Act created a simplified retirement plan for small   business called the savings incentive match plan for employees   ("SIMPLE") retirement plan. A SIMPLE plan can be either an individual   retirement arrangement ("IRA") for each employee or part of a qualified cash or deferred arrangement ("a 401(k) plan"). A SIMPLE IRA   permits employees to make elective contributions up to $6,000 per year   to their IRA. The employer is required to satisfy one of two contribution formulas. Under the matching contribution formula, the   employer generally is required to match employee elective contributions on a dollar-for-dollar basis up to 3 percent of the employee's compensation, unless the employer elects a lower percentage matching contribution (but not less than 1 percent of each employee's compensation). Alternatively, an employer is permitted to elect, in lieu of making matching contributions, to make a 2 percent of compensation nonelective contribution on behalf of each eligible employee. The employer contribution amounts are contributed to the employee's IRA. The maximum contribution limitation to an IRA is $2,000.

Explanation of Provision

The bill provides that in the case of a SIMPLE IRA, the $2,000 maximum limitation applicable to IRAs is increased to the limitations in effect for contributions made under a qualified salary reduction arrangement. This includes employee elective contributions and required employer contributions.
Conference Report]

Senate Amendment

The Senate Amendment is the same as the House bill.

Conference Agreement

The conference agreement follows the House bill and the Senate amendment. *d. Application of exclusive plan requirement for SIMPLE IRAs to noncollectively bargained employees (sec. 1501(d)(1)(E) of the bill and sec. 408(p)(2)(D) of the Code)]*

Present Law

A SIMPLE IRA will be treated as a qualified salary reduction arrangement provided the employer does not maintain a qualified plan during the same time period the SIMPLE IRA is maintained. Collectively bargained employees can be excluded from participation in the SIMPLE IRA and may be covered under a plan established by the employer as a result of a good faith bargaining agreement.

Explanation of Provision

The bill provides that an employer who maintains a plan for collectively bargained employees is permitted to maintain a SIM-PLE IRA for noncollectively bargained employees. *Conference Report]*

Senate Amendment

The Senate Amendment is the same as the House bill.

Conference Agreement

The conference agreement follows the House bill and the Senate amendment. *e. Application of exclusive plan requirement for SIMPLE IRAs in the case of mergers and acquisitions (sec. 1501(d)(1)(F) of the bill and sec. 408(p)(2) of the Code)]*

Present Law

Only employers who employ 100 or fewer employees who received compensation for the preceding year of at least $5,000 are eligible to establish a SIMPLE IRA. An eligible employer maintaining a SIMPLE IRA who fails to be an eligible employer due to an acquisition, disposition or similar transaction is treated as an eligible employer for the 2 years following the last year the employer was eligible provided rules similar to the special coverage rules of section 410(b)(6)(C)(i) apply. There is no parallel provision with respect to an employer who, because of an acquisition, disposition or similar transaction, maintains a qualified plan and a SIMPLE IRA at the same time.

Explanation of Provision

The bill provides that if an employer maintains a qualified plan and a SIM-PLE IRA in the same year due to an acquisition, disposition or similar transaction the SIMPLE IRA is treated as a qualified salary reduction arrangement for the year of the transaction and the following calendar year.
Conference Report]

Senate Amendment

The Senate Amendment is the same as the House bill.

Conference Agreement

The conference agreement follows the House bill and the Senate amendment.

Top-heavy exemption for SIMPLE 401(k) arrangements (sec. 1501(d)(2)(A) of the bill and sec. 401(k)(11)(D) of the Code).

Present Law

A plan meeting the SIMPLE 401(k) requirements for any year is not treated as a top-heavy plan under section 416 for the year. This rule was intended to apply only to SIMPLE 401(k)s, and not other plans maintained by the employer.

Explanation of Provision

The bill provides that the top-heavy exemption applies to a plan which permits only contributions required to satisfy the SIMPLE 401(k) requirements. *Conference Report]*

Senate Amendment

The Senate Amendment is the same as the House bill.

Conference Agreement

The conference agreement follows the House bill and the Senate amendment.

Cost of living adjustments for SIMPLE 401(k) arrangements (sec. 1501(d)(2)(B) of the bill and sec. 401(k)(11) of the Code)

Present Law

The $6,000 limit on deferrals to a SIMPLE IRA is subject to a cost-of-living adjustment. There is no parallel provision applicable to a SIMPLE 401(k) arrangement.

Explanation of Provision

The bill provides that the $6,000 limit on elective deferrals under a SIMPLE 401(k) arrangement will be adjusted at the same time and in the same manner as for SIMPLE IRAs. *Conference Report]*

Senate Amendment

The Senate Amendment is the same as the House bill.

Conference Agreement

The conference agreement follows the House bill and the Senate amendment.

Employer deduction for SIMPLE 401(k) arrangements (sec. 1501(d)(2)(C) of the bill and sec. 404(a)(3) of the Code).

Present Law

Contributions paid by an employer to a profit sharing or stock bonus plan are deductible by the employer for a taxable year to the extent the contributions do not exceed 15-percent of the compensation otherwise paid or accrued during the taxable year to the participants under the plan. Contributions paid by an employer to a profit sharing or stock bonus plan that are not deductible because they are in excess of the 15-percent limitation are subject to a 10-percent excise tax payable by the employer making the contribution.

Explanation of Provision

The bill provides that to the extent that contributions paid by an employer to a SIMPLE 401(k) arrangement satisfy the contribution requirements of section 401(k)(11)(B), such contributions is deductible by the employer for the taxable year.

Conference Report]

Senate Amendment

The Senate Amendment is the same as the House bill.

Conference Agreement

The conference agreement follows the House bill and the Senate amendment.

Notification and election periods for SIMPLE 401(k) arrangements (sec. 1501(d)(2)(D) of the bill and sec. 401(k)(11) of the Code).

Present Law

An employer maintaining a SIMPLE 401(k) arrangement is required to make a matching contribution for employees making elective deferrals of up to 3-percent of compensation (or, alternatively, elect to make a 2-percent of compensation nonelective contribution on behalf of all eligible employees). An employer electing to make a 2-percent nonelective contribution is required to notify all employees of such election within a reasonable period of time before the 60th day before the beginning of the year.

An employer maintaining a SIMPLE IRA is required to notify each employee of the employee's opportunity to make or modify salary reduction contributions as well as the contribution alternative chosen by the employer within a reasonable period of time before the employee's election period. The employee's election period is the 60-day period before the beginning of any year (and the 60-day period before the first day such employee is eligible to participate).

Explanation of Provision

The bill extends the employer notice and employee election requirements of SIMPLE IRAs to SIMPLE 401(k) arrangements.

Effective Date

The bill is effective with respect to calendar years beginning after the date of enactment.
Conference Report]

Senate Amendment

The Senate Amendment is the same as the House bill.

Conference Agreement

The conference agreement follows the House bill and the Senate amendment.

[¶ 5362] Section 1601(e). Measurement of earnings of controlled foreign corporations.

(Code Sec. 956)

[House Report]

Present Law

U.S. 10-percent shareholders of a controlled foreign corporation (CFC) are subject to current U.S. tax on their pro rata shares of the CFC's earnings invested in United States property. For this purpose, earnings include both current earnings and profits (not including a deficit) referred to in section 316(a)(1) and accumulated earnings and profits referred to in section 316(a)(2). It could be argued that this definition of earnings takes current year earnings into account twice.

Explanation of Provision

The technical correction clarifies that accumulated earnings and profits of a CFC

taken into account for purposes of determining the CFC's earnings invested in United States property do not include current earnings (which are taken into account separately). A similar technical correction to the definition of earnings for purposes of prior-law section 956A (relating to a CFC's earnings invested in excess passive assets) was enacted with the Small Business Job Protection Act of 1996 (section 1703(i)(2)). *Conference Report]*

Senate Amendment

The Senate Amendment is the same as the House bill.

Conference Agreement

The conference agreement follows the House bill and the Senate amendment.

[¶ 5363] Section 1601(i). Transfers to foreign trusts at fair market value.

(Code Sec. 679)

[House Report]

Present Law

A U.S. person who transfers property to a foreign trust which has U.S. beneficiaries generally is treated as the owner of such trust. However, this rule does not apply

where the U.S. person transfers property to a trust in exchange for fair market value consideration. In determining whether the U.S. person receives fair market value consideration, obligations of certain related persons are not taken into account. For this purpose, related persons include the trust, any grantor or beneficiary of the trust, and certain persons who are related to any such grantor or beneficiary.

Explanation of Provision

The technical correction clarifies that, for purposes of determining whether a U.S. person's transfer to a trust is for fair market value consideration, the related persons whose obligations are disregarded include any owner of the trust and certain persons

who are related to   any such owner. *Conference Report]*

Senate Amendment

The Senate Amendment is the same as the House bill.

Conference Agreement

The conference agreement follows the House bill and the Senate amendment.

[¶ 5364]   Section 1601(j).   Treatment of trust as U.S. person.

(Code Sec. 641, 7701)

[House Report]

Present Law

A trust is considered to be a U.S. person if two criteria are met.   First, a court within the United States must be able to exercise primary supervision over the administration of the trust. Second, one or more U.S. fiduciaries must have the authority to control all substantial decisions of the trust.

These criteria regarding the treatment of a trust as a U.S. person are effective for taxable years beginning after December 31, 1996. The   Internal Revenue Service announced procedures under which a U.S. trust in existence on August 20, 1996 may continue to file returns as a U.S. trust for taxable years beginning after December 31, 1996. To qualify   for such treatment, the trustee (1) must initiate modification of the trust to conform to the new criteria by the due date for filing the trust's return for its first taxable year beginning after 1996, (2) must complete the modification within two years of such date, and (3) must   attach the required statement to the trust returns for the taxable years beginning after 1996.[1]

Explanation of Provision

The technical correction clarifies that a trust is treated as a U.S. person as long as

one or more U.S. persons have the authority to control all substantial decisions of the trust (and a U.S. court can exercise   primary supervision). Accordingly, the fact that a substantial decision of the trust is controlled by a U.S. person who is not a fiduciary would not cause the trust not to be treated as a U.S. person. In addition, the technical correction clarifies that a trust that is a foreign trust under these criteria is not considered to be present or resident in the United States at any time. Finally, the technical correction provides   the Secretary of Treasury with authority to allow reasonable time for   U.S. trusts in existence on August 20, 1996 to make modifications in order to comply with the new criteria for treatment of a trust as a U.S. person. *Conference Report]*

Senate Amendment

The Senate Amendment is the same as the House bill.

Conference Agreement

The conference agreement follows the House bill and the Senate amendment.

---

1. Notice 96 65, I.R.B. 1996 52. See Joint Committee on Taxation,   "General Explanation of Tax Legislation

Enacted in the 104th Congree" (JCS 12 96), December 12, 1996, pp. 277 278.

[¶ 5365]   Section 1601(f).   Treatment of certain reserves of thrift institutions.

(Code Sec. 593, 1374)

[House Report]

Present Law

A provision of the Small Business Act repealed the percentage-of-taxable income method for deducting bad debts applicable to thrift institutions. The portion of the section 481(a) adjustment applicable to pre-1988 reserves of an institution required to change its method of accounting generally is not restored to income unless the institution makes a distribution to which section 593(e) applies. Section 593(e) provides that if a institution makes a nonliquidating distribution in an amount in excess of its post-1951 accumulated earnings and profits, such excess will be treated as a distribution of the post-1987 reserve for bad debts, requiring recapture of such amount.

Another provision of the Small Business Act allows a bank or a thrift institution to elect to be treated as an S corporation so long as the entity does not use a reserve method of accounting for bad debts. The earnings of an S corporation increase the corporation's accumulated adjustments account, but do not increase its accumulated earnings and profits (sec. 1368). In addition, any net unrealized built-in gains of a C corporation that converts to S corporation status that are recognized during the 10-year period beginning with the date of such conversion generally are subject to corporate-level tax (sec. 1374). Section 481(a) adjustments taken into account during the 10-year period generally are subject to section 1374.

Explanation of Provision

The bill provides rules to clarify the section 593(e) treatment of pre-1988 bad debt reserves of thrift and former thrift institutions that become S corporations. The technical corrections provide that (1) the accumulated adjustments account of an S corporation would be treated the same as post-1951 earnings and profits for purposes of section 593(e) and (2) section 593(e) would apply irrespective of section 1374 (e.g., distributions that trigger section 593(e) would be subject to corporate-level recapture even if such distributions occur after the 10-year period of section 1374).

Conference Report]

Senate Amendment

The Senate Amendment is the same as the House bill.

Conference Agreement

The conference agreement follows the House bill and the Senate amendment.

[¶ 5366]   Section 1601(f).   "FASIT" technical corrections.

(Code Sec. 860L)

[House Report]

Present Law

In general

A "financial asset securitization investment trust" ("FASIT") is designed to facilitate the securitization of debt obligations such as credit card receivables, home equity loans, and auto loans. A FASIT generally is not taxable; the FASIT's taxable income or net loss flows through to the owner of the FASIT.

The ownership interest of a FASIT generally is required to be entirely held by a single domestic C corporation. In addition, a FASIT generally must hold only qualified debt obligations, and certain other specified assets, and is subject to certain restrictions on its activities. An entity that qualifies as a FASIT can issue instruments (called "regular interests") that meet certain specified requirements and treat those instruments as debt for Federal income tax purposes. In general, those requirements must be met "after the startup date." Instruments bearing yields to maturity over 5 percentage points above the yield to maturity on specified United States government obligations (i.e., "high-yield interests") may be held only by domestic C corporations that are not exempt from income tax.

Income from prohibited transactions

The owner of a FASIT is required to pay a penalty excise tax equal to 100 percent of net income derived from (1) an asset that is not a permitted asset, (2) any disposition of an asset other than a permitted disposition, (3) any income attributable to loans originated by the FASIT, and (4) compensation for services (other than fees for a waiver, amendment, or consent under permitted assets not acquired through foreclosure). A permitted disposition is any disposition of any permitted asset (1) arising from complete liquidation of a class of regular interests (i.e., a qualified liquidation)[2]; (2) incident to the foreclosure, default, or imminent default of the asset; (3) incident to the bankruptcy or insolvency of the FASIT; (4) necessary to avoid a default on any indebtedness of the FASIT attributable to a default (or imminent default) on an asset of the FASIT; (5) to facilitate a cleanup call; (6) to substitute a permitted debt instrument for another such instrument; or (7) in order to reduce over-collateralization where a principal purpose of the disposition was not to avoid recognition of gain arising from an increase in its market value after its acquisition by the FASIT.

Definition of "FASIT"

For an entity or arrangement to qualify as a FASIT, substantially all of its assets must consist of the following "permitted assets": (1) cash and cash equivalents; (2) certain permitted debt instruments; (3) certain foreclosure property; (4) certain instruments or contracts that represent a hedge or guarantee of debt held or issued by the FASIT; (5) contract rights to acquire permitted debt instruments or hedges; (6) a regular interest in another FASIT; and (7) a regular interest in a REMIC. A FASIT must meet the asset test at the 90th day after its formation and at all times thereafter. Permitted assets may be acquired at any time by a FASIT, including any time after its formation.

Explanation of Provision

Definition of regular interest

The bill provides that the requirement of a "regular interest" must be met "on or after the startup date," instead of just "after the startup date."

Correction of cross reference

The bill corrects an incorrect cross reference in section 860L(d) from section 860L(c)(2) to section 860L(b)(2).

Tax on prohibited transactions

The bill provides that the tax on prohibited transactions would not apply to dispositions of foreclosure property or hedges using the similar exception applicable to REMICs. *Conference Report]*

Senate Amendment

The Senate Amendment is the same as the House bill.

Conference Agreement

The conference agreement follows the House bill and the Senate amendment.

[¶ 5367]   Section 1601(h).   Qualified State tuition plans.

(Code Sec. 529)

[House Report]

Present Law

Section 529 provides tax-exempt status to certain qualified State tuition programs and provides rules for the tax treatment of distributions from such programs. Section 529 was effective on the date of enactment of the Small Business Job Protection Act of 1996, but a special transition rule provides that if (1) a State maintains (on the date of enactment) a program under which persons may purchase tuition credits on behalf of, or make contributions for educational expenses of, a designated beneficiary, and (2) such program meets the requirements of a qualified State tuition program before the later of (a) one year after the date of enactment, or (b) the first day of the first calendar quarter after the close of the first regular session of the State legislature that begins after the

---

2. For this purpose, a "qualified liquidation" has the same meaning as it does purposes of the exemption from the tax on prohibited transactions of a real estate mortgage investment conduit ("REMIC") in section 860F(a)(4).

date of enactment, then the provisions of the Small Business Act will apply to contributions (and earnings allocable thereto) made before the date the program meets the requirements of a qualified State tuition program, without regard to whether the requirements of a qualified State tuition program are satisfied with respect to such contributions and earnings (e.g., even if the interest in the tuition or educational savings program covers not only qualified higher education expenses but also room and board expenses).

Explanation of Provision

The provision clarifies that, if a State program under which persons may purchase tuition credits comes into compliance with the requirements of a "qualified State tuition program" as defined in section 529

[¶ 5368]   Section 1601(h).   Adoption credit.

(Code Sec. 23)

[House Report]

Present Law

Taxpayers are allowed a maximum nonrefundable tax credit against income tax liability of $5,000 per child for qualified adoption expenses ($6,000 in the case of certain domestic adoptions) paid or incurred by the taxpayer. Qualified adoption expenses are reasonable and necessary adoption fees, court costs, attorneys' fees, and other expenses that are directly related to the legal adoption of an eligible child.

Otherwise qualified adoption expenses paid or incurred in one taxable year are not taken into account for purposes of the credit until the next taxable year unless the expenses are paid or incurred in the year the adoption becomes final.

[¶ 5369]   Section 1601(h).   Phaseout of adoption assistance exclusion.

(Code Sec. 137)

[House Report]

Present Law

The adoption tax credit and the exclusion for employer provided adoption assistance are generally phased out ratably for taxpay-

within a specified time period, then such program will be treated as a qualified State tuition program with respect to any contributions (and earnings allocable thereto) made pursuant to a contract entered into under the program before the date on which the program comes into compliance with the present-law requirements of a qualified State tuition program under section 529. *Conference Report]*

Senate Amendment

The Senate Amendment is the same as the House bill.

Conference Agreement

The conference agreement follows the House bill and the Senate amendment.

Explanation of Provision

The technical correction conforms the treatment of otherwise qualified adoption expenses paid or incurred in years after the year the adoption becomes final to the treatment of expenses paid or incurred in the year the adoption becomes final. Another technical correction repeals as "deadwood" an ordering rule inadvertently included in the credit. *Conference Report]*

Senate Amendment

The Senate Amendment is the same as the House bill.

Conference Agreement

The conference agreement follows the House bill and the Senate amendment.

ers with modified adjusted gross income (AGI) above $75,000, and are fully phased out at $115,000 of modified AGI. For these purposes modified AGI is computed by increasing the taxpayer's AGI by the amount otherwise excluded from gross income under Code sections 911, 931, or 933 (relating to the exclusion of income of U.S. citizens or residents living abroad; residents of Guam, American Samoa, and the Northern Mariana Islands, and residents of Puerto Rico, respectively).

Explanation of Provision

The technical correction conforms the phaseout range of the adoption assistance exclusion to the phaseout range of the credit for qualified adoption expenses.

[¶ 5370]   Section 1602(a).   Medical savings accounts.

(Code Sec. 220)

[House Report]

a. Additional tax on distributions not used for medical purposes.

Present Law

Under present law, distributions from a medical savings account ("MSA") that are not used for medical expenses are includible in gross income and subject to a 15-percent additional tax unless the distribution is after age 65 or death or on account of disability. A similar additional 10-percent tax is imposed on early withdrawals from individual retirement arrangements and qualified pension plans. The 10-percent additional tax on early withdrawals is not treated as tax liability for purposes of the minimum tax. No such rule applies to the 15-percent additional tax applicable to MSAs.

Explanation of Provision

The bill provides that the 15-percent tax on nonmedical withdrawals from an MSA is not treated as tax liability for purposes of the minimum tax.

Senate Amendment

The Senate amendment is the same as the House bill.

Conference Agreement

The conference agreement follows the House bill and the Senate amendment.

b. Definition of permitted coverage

Present Law

Under present law, in order to be eligible to have an MSA an individual must be covered under a high deductible health plan and

Conference Report]

Senate Amendment

The Senate amendment is the same as the House bill.

Conference Agreement

The conference agreement follows the House bill and the Senate amendment.

no other health plan, except for plans that provide certain permitted coverage. Medicare supplemental plans are one of the types of permitted coverage, even though an individual covered by Medicare is not eligible to have an MSA.

Explanation of Provision

Under the bill, Medicare supplemental plans would be deleted from the types of permitted coverage an individual may have and still qualify for an MSA.

Senate Amendment

The Senate amendment is the same as the House bill.

Conference Agreement

The conference agreement follows the House bill and the Senate amendment.

c. Taxation of distributions

Present Law

Under present law, in order to be eligible to have a medical savings account ("MSA") an individual must be covered under a high deductible health plan and no other health plan, except for plans that provide certain permitted coverage and must be either (1) a self-employed individual, or (2) employed by a small employer. Distributions from an MSA for the medical expenses of the MSA account holder and his or her spouse or dependents are generally excludable from income. However, in any year for which a contribution is made to an MSA, withdrawals from the MSA are excludable from income only if the individual for whom the expenses were incurred was an eligible individual for the month in which the expenses were incurred. This rule is designed to ensure that MSAs are used in conjunction with a high deductible plan and that they are not primarily used by other individuals who have health plans that are not high deductible plans.

Explanation of Provision

The bill would clarify that, in any year for which a contribution is made to an MSA, withdrawals from the MSA are excludable from income only if the individual for whom the expenses were incurred was covered under a high deductible health plan (and no other health plan except for plans that provide certain permitted coverage) in the month in which the expenses were incurred. That is, the individual for whom the expenses were incurred does not have to be self employed or employed by a small employer in order for a withdrawal for medical expenses to be excludible.

Senate Amendment

The Senate amendment is the same as the House bill.

Conference Agreement

The conference agreement follows the House bill and the Senate amendment.

d. Penalty for failure to provide required reports

Present Law

Trustees of an MSA are required to provide such reports to the Secretary and the account holder as the Secretary may require. A penalty of $50 applies with respect to each failure to provide a required report. Under present law, separate penalties apply to information returns required by the Code.

Explanation of Provision

The bill provides that the $50 penalty does not apply to information returns.

Senate Amendment

The Senate amendment is the same as the House bill.

Conference Agreement

The conference agreement follows the House bill and the Senate amendment.

[¶ 5371]   Section 1602(b).   Definition of chronically ill individual under a qualified long-term care insurance contract.

(Code Sec. 7702B)

[House Report]

Present Law

Under the long-term care insurance rules, a chronically ill individual is one who has been certified within the previous 12 months by a licensed health care practitioner as (1) being unable to perform (without substantial assistance) at least 2 activities of daily living for at least 90 days due to a loss of functional capacity, (2) having a level of disability similar (as determined under regulations prescribed by the Secretary in consultation with the Secretary of Health and Human Services) to the level of disability described above, or (3) requiring substantial supervision to protect the individual from threats to health and safety due to severe cognitive impairment. A contract is not treated as a qualified long-term care

insurance contract unless the determination of whether an individual is a chronically ill individual takes into account at least 5 of such activities.

Explanation of Provision

The technical correction clarifies that the five-activity requirement—i.e., that the number of activities of daily living that are taken into account not be less than five—applies only for purposes of the first of three alternative definitions of a chronically ill individual (Code sec. 7702B(c)(2)(A)(i)), that is, by reason of the individual being unable to perform (without substantial assistance) at least 2 activities of daily living for at least 90 days due to a loss of functional capacity. Thus, the requirement does not apply to the determination of whether an individual is a chronically ill individual either (1) by virtue of severe cognitive impairment, or (2) if the insured satisfies a standard (if any) that is not based upon activities of daily living, as determined under regulations.

Senate Amendment

The Senate amendment is the same as the House bill.

[¶ 5372]   Section 1602(c).   Deduction for long-term care insurance of self employed individuals.

(Code Sec. 162)

[House Report]

Present Law

Present law provides that the deduction for health insurance expenses of a self-employed individual is not available for a month for which the individual is eligible to participate in any subsidized health plan maintained by any employer of the individual or the individual's spouse. Present law also provides that in the case of a qualified long-term care insurance contract, only eligible long-term care premiums (as defined for purposes of the medical expense deduction) are taken into account in determining the deduction for health insurance expenses of a self-employed individual.

Explanation of Provision

The technical correction applies the rules for the deduction for health insurance ex-

Conference Agreement

The conference agreement follows the House bill and the Senate amendment.

penses of a self-employed individual separately with respect to (1) plans that include coverage for qualified long-term care services or that are qualified long-term care insurance contracts, and (2) plans that do not include such coverage and are not such contracts. Thus, the provision clarifies that the fact that an individual is eligible for employer-subsidized health insurance does not affect the ability of such an individual to deduct long-term care insurance premiums, so long as the individual is not eligible for employer-subsidized long-term care insurance.

Senate Amendment

The Senate amendment is the same as the House bill.

Conference Agreement

The conference agreement follows the House bill and the Senate amendment.

[¶ 5373]   Section 1602(d).   Applicability of reporting requirements of long-term care contracts and accelerated death benefits.

(Code Sec. 6050Q)

[House Report]

Present Law

Present law provides that amounts (other than policyholder dividends or premium refunds) received under a long-term care insurance contract generally are excludable as amounts received for personal injuries and sickness, subject to a dollar cap on per diem contracts only. If the aggregate amount of periodic payments under all qualified long-term care contracts exceeds the dollar cap for the period, then the amount of such excess payments is excludable only to the extent of the individual's costs (that

are not otherwise compensated for by insurance or otherwise) for long-term care services during the period.

Present law also provides an exclusion from gross income as an amount paid by reason of the death of an insured for (1) amounts received under a life insurance contract and (2) amounts received for the sale or assignment of any portion of the death benefit under a life insurance contract to a qualified viatical settlement provider, provided that the insured under the life insurance contract is either terminally ill or chronically ill (the accelerated death benefit rules).

A payor of long-term care benefits (defined for this purpose to include any amount paid under a product advertised, marketed or offered as long-term care insurance), and a payor of amounts treated as subject to reporting under the accelerated death benefit rules, is required to report to the IRS the aggregate amount of such benefits paid to any individual during any calendar year, and the name, address and taxpayer identification number of such individual. A payor is also required to report the name, address, and taxpayer identification number of the chronically ill individual on account of whose condition the amounts are paid, and whether the contract under which the amount is paid is a per diem-type contract. A copy of the report must be provided to the payee by January 31 following the year of payment, showing the name of the payor and the aggregate amount of benefits paid to the individual during the calendar year.

Failure to file the report or provide the copy to the payee is subject to the generally applicable penalties for failure to file similar information reports.

Explanation of Provision

The technical correction clarifies that the reporting requirements include the need to report the address and phone number of the information contact. This conforms these reporting requirements to the requirements of the Taxpayer Bill of Rights 2.

Senate Amendment

The Senate amendment is the same as the House bill.

Conference Agreement

The conference agreement follows the House bill and the Senate amendment.

[¶ 5374]   Section 1602(e).   Consumer protection provisions for long-term care insurance contracts.

(Code Sec. 7702B)

[House Report]

Present Law

The long-term care insurance rules of present law include consumer protection provisions (sec. 7702B(g)). Among these provisions is a requirement that the issuer of a contract offer to the policyholder a nonforfeiture provision that meets certain requirements. The requirements include a rule that the nonforfeiture provision shall provide for a benefit available in the event of a default in the payment of any premiums and the amount of the benefit may be adjusted subsequent to being initially granted only as necessary to reflect changes in claims, persistency, and interest as reflected in changes in rates for premium paying policies approved by the Secretary for the same contract form.

Explanation of Provision

The technical correction clarifies that the nonforfeiture provision shall provide for a benefit available in the event of a default in the payment of any premiums and the amount of the benefit may be adjusted subsequent to being initially granted only as necessary to reflect changes in claims, persistency, and interest as reflected in changes in rates for premium paying policies approved by the appropriate State regulatory authority (not by the Secretary) for the same contract form.

Senate Amendment

The Senate amendment is the same as the House bill.

Conference Agreement

The conference agreement follows the House bill and the Senate amendment.

[¶ 5375]   Section 1602(f).

(Code Sec. 264)

[House Report]

Present Law

No deduction is allowed for interest paid or accrued on any indebtedness with respect to one or more life insurance policies or annuity or endowment contracts owned by the taxpayer covering any individual who is (1) an officer or employee of, or (2) is financially interested in, any trade or business carried on by the taxpayer (the COLI rule). An exception is provided for interest on indebtedness with respect to life insurance policies covering up to 20 key persons, subject to an interest rate cap.

Explanation of Provision

The technical correction is intended to prevent unintended avoidance of the COLI rule by clarifying that the rule relates to life insurance policies or annuity or endowment contracts covering any individual who (1)

is or was an officer or employee of, or (2) is or was financially interested in, any trade or business carried on currently or formerly by the taxpayer. Thus, for example, the provision would clarify the treatment of interest on debt with respect to contracts covering former employees of the taxpayer. As another example, the provision would clarify the treatment of interest on debt with respect to a business formerly conducted by the taxpayer and transferred to an affiliate of the taxpayer. No inference is intended as the interpretation of this provision under prior law.

Senate Amendment

The Senate amendment is the same as the House bill.

Conference Agreement

The conference agreement follows the House bill and the Senate amendment.

[¶ 5376] Section 1602(f). Applicable period for purposes of applying the interest rate for a variable rate contract under the COLI rules.

(Code Sec. 264)

[House Report]

Present Law

No deduction is allowed for interest paid or accrued on any indebtedness with respect to one or more life insurance policies or annuity or endowment contracts owned by the taxpayer covering any individual who is (1) an officer or employee of, or (2) is financially interested in, any trade or business carried on by the taxpayer. An exception is provided for interest on indebtedness with respect to life insurance policies covering up to 20 key persons, subject to an interest rate cap.

This provision generally does not apply to interest on debt with respect to contracts purchased on or before June 20, 1986. If the policy loan interest rate under such a contract does not provide for a fixed rate of interest, then interest on such a contract paid or accrued after December 31, 1995, is allowable only to the extent the rate of interest for each fixed period selected by the taxpayer does not exceed Moody's Corpo-

rate Bond Yield Average—Monthly Average Corporates, for the third month preceding the first month of the fixed period. The fixed period must be 12 months or less.

Explanation of Provision

The technical correction provides that an election of an applicable period for purposes of applying the interest rate for a variable rate contract can be made no later than the 90th date after the date of enactment of the proposal, and applies to the taxpayer's first taxable year ending on or after October 13, 1995. If no election is made, the applicable period is the policy year. The policy year is the 12-month period beginning on the anniversary date of the policy.

Senate Amendment

The Senate amendment is the same as the House bill.

Conference Agreement

The conference agreement follows the House bill and the Senate amendment.

[¶ 5377]   Section 1602(f).   Definition of 20-percent owner for purposes of key person exception under COLI rule.

(Code Sec. 264)

[House Report]

Present Law

No deduction is allowed for interest paid or accrued on any indebtedness with respect to one or more life insurance policies or annuity or endowment contracts owned by the taxpayer covering any individual who is (1) an officer or employee of, or (2) is financially interested in, any trade or business carried on by the taxpayer. An exception is provided for interest on indebtedness with respect to life insurance policies covering up to 20 key persons, subject to an interest rate cap.

A key person is an individual who is either an officer or a 20-percent owner of the taxpayer. The number of individuals that can be treated as key persons may not exceed the greater of (1) 5 individuals, or (2) the lesser of 5 percent of the total number of officers and employees of the taxpayer, or 20 individuals. Employees are to be full-time employees, for this purpose. A 20-percent owner is an individual who directly owns 20 percent or more of the total combined voting power of the corporation. If the taxpayer is not a corporation, the statute states that a 20-percent owner is an individual who directly owns 20 percent or more of the capital or profits interest of the employer.

Explanation of Provision

The technical correction clarifies that, in determining a key person, if the taxpayer is not a corporation, a 20-percent owner is an individual who directly owns 20 percent or more of the capital or profits interest of the taxpayer.

Senate Amendment

The Senate amendment is the same as the House bill.

Conference Agreement

The conference agreement follows the House bill and the Senate amendment.

[¶ 5378]   Section 1602(f).   Effective date of interest rate cap on key persons and pre-1986 contracts under the COLI rule.

(Code Sec.)

[House Report]

Present Law

No deduction is allowed for interest paid or accrued on any indebtedness with respect to one or more life insurance policies or annuity or endowment contracts owned by the taxpayer covering any individual who is (1) an officer or employee of, or (2) is financially interested in, any trade or business carried on by the taxpayer. An exception is provided for interest on indebtedness with respect to life insurance policies covering up to 20 key persons, subject to an interest rate cap.

This provision generally does not apply to interest on debt with respect to contracts purchased on or before June 20, 1986. If the policy loan interest rate under such a contract does not provide for a fixed rate of interest, then interest on such a contract paid or accrued after December 31, 1995, is allowable only to the extent the rate of interest for each fixed period selected by the taxpayer does not exceed Moody's Corporate Bond Yield Average—Monthly Average Corporates, for the third month preceding the first month of the fixed period. The fixed period must be 12 months or less.

The interest rate cap on key persons and pre-1986 contracts is effective with respect to interest paid or accrued for any month beginning after December 31, 1995. Another part of the provision provides that the interest rate cap on key employees and pre-1986 contracts applies to interest paid or accrued after October 13, 1995.

Explanation of Provision

The technical correction clarifies that, under the COLI rule, the interest rate cap on key persons and pre-1986 contracts applies to interest paid or accrued for any month beginning after December 31, 1995. This technical correction eliminates the discrepancy between the October and the December dates in the grandfather rule for pre-1986 contracts.

[¶ 5379]   Section 1602(f).   Clarification of contract lapses under effective date provisions of the COLI rule.

(Code Sec.)

[House Report]

Present Law

No deduction is allowed for interest paid or accrued on any indebtedness with respect to one or more life insurance policies or annuity or endowment contracts owned by the taxpayer covering any individual who is (1) an officer or employee of, or (2) is financially interested in, any trade or business carried on by the taxpayer. An exception is provided for interest on indebtedness with respect to life insurance policies covering up to 20 key persons, subject to an interest rate cap.

Additional limitations are imposed on the deductibility of interest with respect to single premium contracts, and interest on debt incurred or continued to purchase or carry a life insurance, endowment, or annuity contract pursuant to a plan of purchase that contemplates the systematic direct or indirect borrowing of part or all of the increases in the cash value of the contract. An exception to the latter rule is provided, permitting deductibility of interest on bona fide debt that is part of such a plan, if no part of 4 of the annual premiums due during the first 7 years is paid by means of debt (the "4-out-of-7" rule).

Present law provides that the COLI rule is phased in. In connection with the phase-in rule, a transition rule provides that any amount included in income during 1996, 1997, or 1998, that is received under a contract described in the provision on the complete surrender, redemption or maturity of the contract or in full discharge of the obligation under the contract that is in the nature of a refund of the consideration paid for the contract, is includable ratably over the first 4 taxable years beginning with the taxable year the amount would otherwise have been includable. The lapse of a contract after October 13, 1995, due to nonpayment of premiums does not cause interest paid or accrued prior to January 1, 1999, to be nondeductible solely by reason of (1) failure to meet the 4-out-of-7 rule of present law, or (2) causing the contract to be treated as a single premium contract within the meaning of section 264(b)(1). This lapse provision states that the relief is provided in the following case: solely by reason of no additional premiums being received by reason of a lapse.

Senate Amendment

The Senate amendment is the same as the House bill.

Conference Agreement

The conference agreement follows the House bill and the Senate amendment.

Explanation of Provision

The technical correction clarifies that, under the transition relief provided under the COLI rule, the 4-out-of-7 rule and the single premium rule of present law are not to apply solely by reason of a lapse occurring by reason of no additional premiums being received under the contract after October 13, 1995.

Senate Amendment

The Senate amendment is the same as the House bill.

Conference Agreement

The conference agreement follows the House bill and the Senate amendment.

[¶ 5380]   Section 1602(g).   Requirement of gain recognition on certain exchanges.

(Code Sec. 877, 2107)

[House Report]

Present Law

Under the expatriation tax provisions in section 877, special tax treatment applies to certain former U.S. citizens and former long-term U.S. residents for 10 years following the date of loss of U.S. citizenship or U.S. residency status. Gain recognition is required on certain exchanges of property following loss of U.S. citizenship or U.S. residency status, unless a gain recognition agreement is entered into. In addition, regulatory authority is granted to apply this rule to the 15-year period beginning 5 years before the loss of U.S. citizenship or U.S. residency status.

Explanation of Provision

The technical correction clarifies that the period to which the general rule requiring gain recognition on certain exchanges applies is the 10-year period that begins on the date of loss of U.S. citizenship or U.S. residency status. In addition, the technical correction clarifies that in the case of an exchange occurring during the 5-year period before the loss of U.S. citizenship or U.S. residency status, any gain required to be recognized under regulations is to be recognized immediately after the date of such loss of U.S. citizenship.

Senate Amendment

The Senate amendment is the same as the House bill.

Conference Agreement

The conference agreement follows the House bill and the Senate amendment.

Present Law

Under the expatriation tax provisions in section 877, special tax treatment applies to certain former U.S. citizens and former long-term U.S. residents for 10 years following the date of loss of U.S. citizenship or U.S. residency status. The running of this period with respect to gain on the sale or exchange of any property is suspended for any period during which the individual's risk of loss with respect to the property is substantially diminished.

Explanation of Provision

The technical correction clarifies that the period to which the rule suspending such period in the case of a substantial diminution of risk of loss applies is the 10-year period that begins on the date of loss of U.S. citizenship or U.S. residency status.

Senate Amendment

The Senate amendment is the same as the House bill.

Conference Agreement

The conference agreement follows the House bill and the Senate amendment.

Present Law

Under the expatriation tax provisions in section 877, special tax treatment applies to certain former U.S. citizens and former long-term U.S. residents for 10 years following the date of loss of U.S. citizenship or U.S. residency status. Special rules apply in the case of certain contributions of U.S. property by such an individual to a foreign corporation during such period.

Explanation of Provision

The technical correction clarifies that the period to which the rule regarding certain contributions to foreign corporations applies is the 10-year period that begins on the date of loss of U.S. citizenship or U.S. residency status. The technical correction also clarifies that the rule applies in the case of property the income from which, immediately before the contribution, was from U.S. sources.

Senate Amendment

The Senate amendment is the same as the House bill.

Conference Agreement

The conference agreement follows the House bill and the Senate amendment.

Present Law

Under the expatriation tax provisions in section 2107, special estate tax treatment applies to certain former U.S. citizens and former long-term U.S. residents who die within 10 years following the date of loss of U.S. citizenship or U.S. residency status. Special rules provide a credit against the U.S. estate tax for foreign estate taxes paid with respect to property that is includible in the decedent's U.S. estate solely by reason of the expatriation estate tax provisions.

Explanation of Provision

The technical correction clarifies the formula for determining the amount of the foreign tax credit allowable against U.S. estate taxes on property includible in the decedent's U.S. estate solely by reason of the expatriation estate tax provisions. The credit for the estate taxes paid to any foreign country generally is limited to the lesser of (1) the foreign estate taxes attributable to the property includible in the decedent's U.S. estate solely by reason of the expatriation estate tax provisions or (2) the U.S. estate tax attributable to property that is subject to estate tax in such foreign country and is includible in the decedent's U.S. estate solely by reason of the expatriation tax provisions. The amount of taxes attributable to such property is determined on a pro rata basis.

Senate Amendment

The Senate amendment is the same as the House bill.

Conference Agreement

The conference agreement follows the House bill and the Senate amendment.

[¶ 5384]   Section 1603.   Reasonable cause abatement for first-tier intermediate sanctions excise tax.

(Code Sec. 4962, 6033)

[House Report]

Present Law

Section 4958 imposes penalty excise taxes as an intermediate sanction in cases where organizations exempt from tax under sections 501(c)(3) or 501(c)(4) (other than private foundations) engage in an "excess benefit transaction." The excise tax may be imposed on certain disqualified persons (i.e., insiders) who improperly benefit from an excess benefit transaction and on organization managers who participate in such a transaction knowing that it is improper.

A disqualified person who benefits from an excess benefit transaction is subject to a first-tier penalty tax equal to 25 percent of the amount of the excess benefit. Organization managers who participate in an excess benefit transaction knowing that it is improper are subject to a first-tier penalty tax of 10 percent of the amount of the excess benefit. Additional second-tier taxes equal to 200 percent of the amount of the excess benefit may be imposed on a disqualified person if there is no correction of the transaction within a specified time period.

Under section 4962, the IRS has the authority to abate certain first-tier taxes if the taxable event was due to reasonable cause and not to willful neglect and the event was corrected within the applicable correction period. First-tier taxes which may be abated include, among others, the taxes imposed under sections 4941 (on acts of self-dealing between private foundations and disqualified persons), 4942 (for failure by private foundations to distribute a minimum amount of income), and 4943 (on private foundations with excess business holdings).

In enacting the new excise taxes on excess benefit transactions, Congress explicitly intended to provide the IRS with abatement authority under section 4962.[3] However, the abatement rules of section 4962 apply only to qualified first-tier taxes imposed by subchapter A or C of Chapter 42. The section 4958 excise tax is located in subchapter D of Chapter 42. The failure to cross reference subchapter D in section 4962 means that IRS does not have such

---

3. See Ways and Means Committee Report 104 506 accompanying H.R. 2377, p. 59.

abatement authority with respect to the section 4958 excise taxes.

Explanation of Provision

The bill amends section 4962(b) to include a cross-reference to first-tier taxes imposed by subchapter D (i.e., the section 4958 excise taxes on excess benefit transactions). Thus, the IRS has authority to abate the first-tier excise taxes on excess benefit transactions in cases where it is established that the violation was due to reasonable cause and not due to willful neglect and the transaction at issue was corrected within the specified period.

Present Law

Section 4958 imposes penalty excise taxes as an intermediate sanction in cases where organizations exempt from tax under sections 501(c)(3) or 501(c)(4) (other than private foundations) engage in an "excess benefit transaction." The excise tax may be imposed on certain disqualified persons (i.e., insiders) who improperly benefit from an excess benefit transaction and on organization managers who participate in such a transaction knowing that it is improper. No tax is imposed on the organization itself with respect under section 4958.

Section 4911 imposes an excise tax penalty on excess lobbying expenditures made by public charities. The tax is imposed on the organization itself. Section 4912 imposes a penalty excise tax on certain public charities that make disqualifying lobbying expenditures and section 4955 imposes a penalty excise tax on political expenditures of section 501(c)(3) organizations. Both of these penalty taxes are imposed not only on the affected organization, but also on organization managers who agree to an expenditure knowing that it is improper.

Under section 4962, the IRS has the authority to abate certain first-tier taxes if the taxable event was due to reasonable cause and not to willful neglect and the event was corrected within the applicable correction period. First-tier taxes which may be abated include, among others, the taxes imposed under section 4955.[4]

Under section 6033(b)(10), 501(c)(3) organizations are required to report annually on Form 990 any amounts paid by the organization under section 4911, 4912, and 4955. Thus, although sections 4912 and 4955 impose excise taxes on organization managers, organizations technically are not required to report any such excise taxes paid by such managers.

In addition, under section 6033(b)(11), an organization exempt from tax under section 501(c)(3) must report on Form 990 any amount of excise tax on excess benefit transactions paid by the organization, or any disqualified person with respect to such organization, during the taxable year. The Code does not explicitly require the reporting of any excess benefit excise taxes paid by an organization manager solely in his or her capacity as such (i.e., an organization manager might also be a disqualified person with respect to an excess benefit transaction, in which case any tax paid would be reported).

Explanation of Provision

The bill makes the reporting requirements of section 6033(b)(10) and (11) consistent with the excise tax penalty provisions to which they relate. Thus, section 6033(b)(10) is amended to require 501(c)(3) organizations to report any amounts of tax imposed under sections 4911, 4912, and 4955 on the organization or any organization manager of the organization. In addition, the bill requires reporting with respect to any reimbursements paid by an organization with respect to taxes imposed under sections 4912 or 4955 on any organization manager of the organization. Section 6033(b)(11) is amended to require 501(c)(3) organizations to report any amounts of tax imposed under section 4958 on any organization manager or any disqualified person, as well as any reimbursements of section 4958 excise tax liability paid by the organization to such organization managers or disqualified persons.

In addition, the bill clarifies that no reporting is required under sections 6033(b)(10) or (11) in the event a first-tier penalty excise tax imposed under section

---

4. A separate provision in the bill makes a technical correction to section 4962(b) to permit the abatement of first-tier penalty excise taxes imposed under section 4958.

4955 or section 4958 is abated by the IRS pursuant to its authority under section 4962.

Senate Amendment

The Senate amendment is the same as the House bill.

Conference Agreement

The conference agreement follows the House bill and the Senate amendment.

[¶ 5385]   Section 1604(b).   Correction of GATT interest and mortality rate provisions in the Retirement Protection Act.

(Code Sec. 415)

[House Report]

Present Law

The Retirement Protection Act of 1994, enacted as part of the implementing legislation for the General Agreements on Tariffs and Trade ("GATT"), modified the actuarial assumptions that must be used in adjusting benefits and limitations under section 415. In general, in adjusting a benefit that is payable in a form other than a straight life annuity and in adjusting the dollar limitation if benefits begin before age 62, the interest rate to be used cannot be less than the greater of 5 percent or the rate specified by the plan. Under GATT, the benefit is payable in a form subject to the requirements of section 417(e)(3), then the interest rate on 30-year Treasury securities is substituted for 5 percent. Also under GATT, for purposes of adjusting any limit or benefit, the mortality table prescribed by the Secretary must be used. This provision of GATT was generally effective as of the first day of the limitation year beginning in 1995.

The Small Business Act conformed the effective date of these changes to the effective date of similar changes by providing generally that, in the case of a plan that was adopted and in effect before December, 8, 1994, the GATT change is not effective with respect to benefits accrued before the earlier of (1) the later of the date a plan amendment applying the amendments is adopted or made effective or (2) the first

day of the first limitation year beginning after December 31, 1999. The Small Business Act provides that "Determinations under section 415(b)(2)(E) before such earlier date are to be made with respect to such benefits on the basis of such section as in effect on December 7, 1994 (except that the modification made by section 1449(b) of the Small Business Job Protection Act of 1996 shall be taken into account), and the provisions of the plan as in effect on December 7, 1994, but only if such provisions of the plan meet the requirements of such section (as so in effect)."

Explanation of Provision

The provision in the Small Business Act was intended to permit plans to apply pre-GATT law under section 415(b)(2)(E) for a transition period. The bill conforms the statute to this intent by providing that determinations under section 415(b)(2)(E) before such earlier date are to be made with respect to such benefits on the basis of such section as in effect on December 7, 1994 and the provisions of the plan as in effect on December 7, 1994, but only if such provisions of the plan meet the requirements of such section (as so in effect).

Senate Amendment

The Senate amendment is the same as the House bill.

Conference Agreement

The conference agreement follows the House bill and the Senate amendment.

[¶ 5386]   Section 1604(e).   Related parties determined by reference to section 267.

(Code Sec. 267)

[Senate Report]

Present Law

Section 267 disallows loses arising in transactions between certain defined related parties. In the case of related corporations, such losses may be deferred. Several Code provisions, in defining related parties, often incorporate the relationships described in section 267 by cross-reference to such section.

[¶ 5387] Technical Corrections.

(Code Sec.)

[House Bill]

The House bill contains technical, clerical, and conforming amendments to the Small Business Job Protection Act of 1996, the Health Insurance Portability and Accountability Act of 1996, the Taxpayer Bill of Rights 2, and other recently enacted tax legislation.

Senate Amendment

The Senate amendment is the same as the House bill, except that the Senate amendment (1) does not contain the provision that defines the term "former reservations in Oklahoma" for purposes of section 168(j)(6) (relating to certain tax benefits provided with reference to activities occurring on Indian reservations) and (2) makes certain clarifications to the provisions relating to church plans included in the Small Business Job Protection Act of 1996.

Conference Agreement

The conference agreement follows the House bill and the Senate amendment. Thus, the conference agreement contains both the provision in the House bill relating to the definition of the term "former reservations in Oklahoma" and the provisions in the Senate amendment relating to church plans.

Explanation of Provision

Any provision of the Internal Revenue Code of 1986 that refers to a relationship that would result in loss disallowance under section 267 also refers to relationships where loss is deferred, where such relationship is applicable to the provision.

Senate Amendment

The Senate amendment is the same as the House bill.

Conference Agreement

The conference agreement follows the House bill and the Senate amendment.

In addition, the conference agreement makes the following additions, modifications, and clarifications relating to technical correction provisions.

(1)   The conference agreement amends section 205(c) of the Employee Retirement Income Security Act (as amended by the Small Business Job Protection Act of 1996) to clarify that the reference to "the Secretary" is to the Secretary of the Treasury.

(2)   The conference agreement clarifies that, for purposes of the section 833 deduction, liabilities incurred during the taxable year under cost-plus contracts are added to claims incurred under section 833(b)(1)(A)(i). Similarly, for purposes of the section 833 deduction, expenses incurred during the taxable year in connection with cost-plus contracts are added to expenses incurred under section 833(b)(1)(A)(ii). The provision is effective as if included in the Tax Reform Act of 1986.

(3)   The conference agreement provides that the technical correction provisions clarifying the phased reduction in luxury excise tax rates for automobiles will be effective for sales after the date of enactment of this Act.

(4)   The conference agreement clarifies that, under the transition relief provided under the company-owned life insurance

rule, the 4-out-of-7 rule and the single premium rule of present law are not to apply solely by reason of a lapse occurring after October 13, 1995, by reason of no additional premiums being received under the contract.

[¶ 5388]   Section 1604(c).   Clarify definition of Indian reservation under section 168(j)(6).

(Code Sec. 168)

[House Report]

Present Law

Section 168(j)(6) provides for accelerated depreciation for certain property located on Indian reservations. For this purpose, provides that the term "Indian reservation" means a reservation as defined in either (a) section 3(d) of the Indian Financing Act of 1974 (25 U.S.C. 1452(d)), or (b) section 4(10) of the Indian Child Welfare Act of 1978 (25 U.S.C. 1903(10)). In addition, section 45A (which provides for an incremental Indian employment credit) incorporates by reference the same definition of "Indian reservation" contained in section 168(j)(6). Section 3(d) of the Indian Financing Act of 1974 includes not only officially designated Indian reservations and public domain Indian allotments, but also all "former Indian reservations in Oklahoma," which covers most of the State of Oklahoma even though parts of such "former Indian reservations" may no longer have a significant nexus to an Indian tribe.

Explanation of Provision

For purposes of the section 168(j)(6) definition of "Indian reservation," the term "former reservations in Oklahoma" is defined as lands that are (1) within the jurisdictional area of an Oklahoma Indian tribe as determined by the Secretary of the Interior, and (2) recognized by such Secretary as an area eligible for trust land status under 25 C.F.R. Part 51.

Effective Date

The provision generally is effective as if included in the Omnibus Budget Reconciliation Act of 1993 (i.e., the technical correction applies to property placed in service and wages paid on or after January 1, 1994). However, the provision does not apply to wages claimed on any original return filed prior to March 18, 1997, nor does it apply to property placed in service with a 10-year life or less (without regard to section 168(j)) if accelerated depreciation under section 168(j) was claimed with respect to such property on an original return filed prior to March 18, 1997.

Senate Amendment

The Senate amendment does not contain the provision that defines the term "former reservations in Oklahoma" for purposes of section 168(j)(6) (relating to certain tax benefits provided with reference to activities occurring on Indian reservations.

Conference Agreement

The conference agreement follows the House bill.

[¶ 5389]   Section 1701.   Identification of limited tax benefits subject to the Line Item Veto Act.

[Conference Report]

The Line Item Veto Act amended the Congressional Budget and Impoundment Act of 1974 to grant the President the limited authority to cancel specific dollar amounts of discretionary budget authority, certain new direct spending, and limited tax benefits. The Line Item Veto Act provides that the Joint Committee on Taxation is required to examine any revenue or reconciliation bill or joint resolution that amends the Internal Revenue Code of 1986 prior to its filing by a conference committee in order to determine whether or not the bill or joint resolution contains any limited tax benefits and to provide a statement to the conference committee that either (1) identifies each limited tax benefit contained in the bill or resolution, or (2) states that the bill or resolution contains no limited tax benefits. The conferees determine whether or not to include the Joint Committee's statement in the conference report. If the conference report includes the information from the Joint Committee on Taxation identifying provisions that are limited tax benefits, then the President may cancel one or more of those, but only those, provisions that have been identified. If such a conference report contains a statement from the Joint Committee on Taxation that none of the provisions in the conference report are limited tax benefits, then the President has no authority to cancel any of the specific tax provisions, because there are no tax provisions that are eligible for cancellation under the Line Item Veto Act.

The conference report contains a list of provisions that have been identified by the Joint Committee on Taxation as limited tax benefits within the meaning of the Line Item Veto Act. These provisions are listed below

(1) Sec. 101(c) (relating to high risk pools permitted to cover dependents of high risk individuals)

(2) Sec. 222 (relating to limitation on qualified 501(c)(3) bonds other than hospital bonds)

(3) Sec. 224 (relating to contributions of computer technology and equipment for elementary or secondary school purposes)

(4) Sec. 312(a) (relating to treatment of remainder interests for purposes of provision relating to gain from sale of principal residence)

(5) Sec. 501(b) (relating to indexing of alternative valuation of certain farm, etc., real property)

(6) Sec. 504 (relating to extension of treatment of certain rents under section 2032A to lineal descendants)

(7) Sec. 505 (relating to clarification of judicial review of eligibility for extension of time for payment of estate tax) 100 or fewer taxpayers benefit; no exception applies

(8) Sec. 508 (relating to treatment of land subject to qualified conservation easement)

(9) Sec. 511 (relating to expansion of exception from generation-skipping transfer tax for transfers to individuals with deceased parents)

(10) Sec. 601 (relating to the research tax credit)

(11) Sec. 602 (relating to contributions of stock to private foundations)

(12) Sec. 603 (relating to the work opportunity tax credit)

(13) Sec. 604 (relating to orphan drug tax credit)

(14) Sec. 701 (relating to incentives for revitalization of the District of Columbia) to the extent it amends the Internal Revenue Code of 1986 to create sections 1400 and 1400A (relating to tax-exempt economic development bonds)

(15) Sec. 701 (relating to incentives for revitalization of the District of Columbia) to the extent it amends the Internal Revenue Code of 1986 to create section 1400C (relating to first-time homebuyer credit for District of Columbia)

(16) Sec. 801 (relating to incentives for employing long-term family assistance recipients)

(17) Sec. 904(b) (relating to uniform rate of tax on vaccines) as it relates to any vaccine containing pertussis bacteria, extracted or partial cell bacteria, or specific pertussis antigens

(18) Sec. 904(b) (relating to uniform rate of tax on vaccines) as it relates to any vaccine against measles

(19) Sec. 904(b) (relating to uniform rate of tax on vaccines) as it relates to any vaccine against mumps

(20) Sec. 904(b) (relating to uniform rate of tax on vaccines) as it relates to any vaccine against rubella

(21) Sec. 905 (relating to operators of multiple retail gasoline outlets treated as wholesale distributors for refund purposes)

(22) Sec. 906 (relating to exemption of electric and other clean-fuel motor vehicles from luxury automobile classification)

(23) Sec. 907(a) (relating to rate of tax on liquified natural gas determined on basis of BTU equivalency with gasoline)

(24) Sec. 907(b) (relating to rate of tax on methanol from natural gas determined on basis of BTU equivalency with gasoline)

(25) Sec. 908 (relating to modification of tax treatment of hard cider)

(26) Sec. 914 (relating to mortgage financing for residences located in disaster areas)

(27) Sec. 962 (relating to assignment of workmen's compensation liability eligible for exclusion relating to personal injury liability assignments)

(28) Sec. 963 (relating to tax-exempt status for certain State worker's compensation act companies)

(29) Sec. 967 (relating to additional advance refunding of certain Virgin Island bonds)

(30) Sec. 968 (relating to nonrecognition of gain on sale of stock to certain farmers' cooperatives)

(31) Sec. 971 (relating to exemption of the incremental cost of a clean fuel vehicle from the limits on depreciation for vehicles)

(32) Sec. 974 (relating to clarification of treatment of certain receivables purchased by cooperative hospital service organizations)

(33) Sec. 975 (relating to deduction in computing adjusted gross income for expenses in connection with service performed by certain officials) with respect to taxable years beginning before 1991

(34) Sec. 977 (relating to elective carryback of existing carryovers of National Railroad Passenger Corporation)

(35) Sec. 1005(b)(2)(B) (relating to transition rule for instruments described in a ruling request submitted to the Internal Revenue Service on or before June 8, 1997)

(36) Sec. 1005(b)(2)(C) (relating to transition rule for instruments described on or before June 8, 1997, in a public announcement or in a filing with the Securities and Exchange Commission) as it relates to a public announcement

(37) Sec. 1005(b)(2)(C) (relating to transition rule for instruments described on or before June 8, 1997, in a public announcement or in a filing with the Securities and Exchange Commission) as it relates to a filing with the Securities and Exchange Commission

(38) Sec. 1011(d)(2)(B) (relating to transition rule for distributions made pursuant to the terms of a tender offer outstanding on May 3, 1995)

(39) Sec. 1011(d)(3) (relating to transition rule for distributions made pursuant to the terms of a tender offer outstanding on September 13, 1995)

(40) Sec. 1012(d)(3)(B) (relating to transition rule for distributions pursuant to an acquisition described in section 355(e)(2)(A)(ii) of the Internal Revenue Code of 1986 described in a ruling request submitted to the Internal Revenue Service on or before April 16, 1997)

(41) Sec. 1012(d)(3)(C) (relating to transition rule for distributions pursuant to an acquisition described in section 355(e)(2)(A)(ii) of the Internal Revenue Code of 1986 described in a public announcement or filing with the Securities and Exchange Commission) as it relates to a public announcement

(42) Sec. 1012(d)(3)(C) (relating to transition rule for distributions pursuant to an acquisition described in section 355(e)(2)(A)(ii) of the Internal Revenue Code of 1986 described in a public announcement or filing with the Securities and Exchange Commission) as it relates to a filing with the Securities and Exchange Commission

(43) Sec. 1013(d)(2)(B) (relating to transition rule for distributions or acquisitions after June 8, 1997, described in a ruling request submitted to the Internal Revenue Service submitted on or before June 8, 1997)

(44) Sec. 1013(d)(2)(C) (relating to transition rule for distributions or acquisitions after June 8, 1997, described in a public announcement or filing with the Securities and Exchange Commission on or before June 8, 1997) as it relates to a public announcement

(45) Sec. 1013(d)(2)(C) (relating to transition rule for distributions or acquisitions after June 8, 1997, described in a public announcement or filing with the Securities and Exchange Commission on or before June 8, 1997) as it relates to a filing with the Securities and Exchange Commission

(46) Sec. 1014(f)(2)(B) (relating to transition rule for any transaction after June 8, 1997, if such transaction is described in a ruling request submitted to the Internal Revenue Service on or before June 8, 1997)

(47) Sec. 1014(f)(2)(C) (relating to transition rule for any transaction after June 8, 1997, if such transaction is described in a

public announcement or filing with the Securities and Exchange Commission on or before June 8, 1997) as it relates to a public announcement

(48) Sec. 1014(f)(2)(C) (relating to transition rule for any transaction after June 8, 1997, if such transaction is described in a public announcement or filing with the Securities and Exchange Commission on or before June 8, 1997) as it relates to a filing with the Securities and Exchange Commission

(49) Sec. 1042(b) (relating to special rules for provision terminating certain exceptions from rules relating to exempt organizations which provide commercial-type insurance)

(50) Sec. 1081(a) (relating to termination of suspense accounts for family corporations required to use accrual accounting) as it relates to the repeal of Internal Revenue Code section 447(i)(3)

(51) Sec. 1089(b)(3) (relating to reformations)

(52) Sec. 1089(b)(5)(B)(i) (relating to persons under a mental disability)

(53) Sec.1171 (relating to treatment of computer software as FSC export property)

(54) Sec. 1175 (relating to exemption for active financing income)

(55) Sec. 1204 (relating to travel expenses of Federal employees doing criminal investigations)

(56) Sec. 1236 (relating to extension of time for filing a request for administrative adjustment)

(57) Sec. 1243 (relating to special rules for administrative adjustment request with respect to bad debts or worthless securities)

(58) Sec. 1251 (relating to clarification on limitation on maximum number of shareholders)

(59) Sec. 1253 (relating to attribution rules applicable to tenant ownership)

(60) Sec. 1256 relating to modification of earnings and profits rules for determining whether REIT has earnings and profits from non-REIT years)

(61) Sec. 1257 (relating to treatment of foreclosure property)

(62) Sec. 1261 (relating to shared appreciation mortgages)

(63) Sec. 1302 (relating to clarification of waiver of certain rights of recovery)

(64) Sec. 1303 (relating to transitional rule under section 2056A)

(65) Sec. 1304 (relating to treatment for estate tax purposes of short-term obligations held by nonresident alien)

(66) Sec. 1311 (relating to clarification of treatment of survivor annuities under qualified terminable interest rules)

(67) Sec. 1312 (relating to treatment of qualified domestic trust rules of forms of ownership which are not trusts)

(68) Sec. 1313 (relating to opportunity to correct failures under section 2032A)

(69) Sec. 1414 (relating to fermented material from any brewery may be received at a distilled spirits plant)

(70) Sec. 1417 (relating to use of additional ameliorating material in certain wines)

(71) Sec. 1418 (relating to domestically produced beer may be withdrawn free of tax for use of foreign embassies, legations, etc.)

(72) Sec. 1421 (relating to transfer to brewery of beer imported in bulk without payment of tax)

(73) Sec. 1422 (relating to transfer to bonded wine cellars of wine imported in bulk without payment of tax)

(74) Sec. 1506 (relating to clarification of certain rules relating to employee stock ownership plans of S corporations)

(75) Sec. 1507 (relating to modification of 10 percent tax for nondeductible contributions)

(76) Sec. 1523 (relating to repeal of application of unrelated business income tax to ESOPs)

(77) Sec. 1530 (relating to gratuitous transfers for the benefit of employees)

(78) Sec. 1532 (relating to special rules relating to church plans)

(79) Sec. 1604(c)(2) (relating to amendment related to Omnibus Budget Reconciliation Act of 1993)

[¶ 5390]   Section 1601(d).   Treatment of Indian tribal governments under section 403(b).

(Code Sec. 403)

[House Report]

Present Law

Any 403(b) annuity contract purchased in a plan year beginning before January 1, 1995, by an Indian tribal government is treated as purchased by an entity permitted to maintain a tax- sheltered annuity plan. Such contracts may be rolled over into a section 401(k) plan maintained by the Indian tribal government in accordance with the rollover rules of section 403(b)(8).

Explanation of Provision

The bill clarifies that an employee participating in a 403(b) annuity contract of the Indian tribal government would be permitted to roll over amounts from such contract to a section 401(k) plan maintained by the Indian tribal government whether or not the annuity contract is terminated.

Senate Amendment

The Senate amendment is the same as the House bill.

Conference Agreement

The conference agreement follows the House bill and the Senate amendment.

Congressional Committee Reports Accompanying the Balanced Budget Act of 1997, H.R. 2015

[¶ 5500]

This section reproduces all important parts of the official explanation of the Balanced Budget Act of 1997, H.R. 2015. The material comes from the House, Senate, and Conference Committee Reports.

The Committee Reports are arranged in the order of the Act Sections of the Balanced Budget Act of 1997, H.R. 2015.

[¶ 5501]   Section 4006.   Medicare choice/Medicare Plus MSAS.

[House Report—Budget]

Current Law

Under present law, the value of Medicare coverage and benefits is not includable in taxable income.

Individuals who itemize deductions may deduct amounts paid during the taxable year (if not reimbursed by insurance or otherwise) for medical expenses of the taxpayer and the taxpayer's spouse and dependents (including expenses for insurance providing medical care) to the extent that the total of such expenses exceeds 7.5 percent of the taxpayer's adjusted gross income ("AGI").

Within limits, contributions to a medical savings account ("MSA") are deductible in determining AGI if made by an eligible individual and are excludable from gross income and wages for employment tax purposes if made by the employer of an eligible individual.[1] Individuals covered under Medicare are not eligible to have an MSA.

Earnings on amounts in an MSA are not currently includable in income. Distributions from an MSA for medical expenses of the MSA account holder and his or her spouse or dependents are not includable in income. For this purpose, medical expenses are defined as under the itemized deduction for medical expenses, except that medical expenses do not include any insurance premiums other than premiums for long-term care insurance, continuation coverage (so-called "COBRA coverage"), or premiums for coverage while an individual is receiving unemployment compensation. Distributions not used for medical expenses are subject to an additional 15 percent tax unless the distribution is made after age 65, death, or disability.

Under present law, there are no provisions for MedicarePlus medical savings accounts ("MedicarePlus MSAs").

Explanation of provision.

Under the bill, individuals who are eligible for Medicare are permitted to choose either the traditional Medicare program or a MedicarePlus MSA plan. To the extent an individual chooses such a plan, the Secretary of Health and Human Services makes a specified contribution directly into a MedicarePlus MSA designated by such individual. Only contributions by the Secretary of Health and Human Services can be made to a MedicarePlus MSA and such contributions are not included in the taxable income of the MedicarePlus MSA holder. Income earned on amounts held in a MedicarePlus MSA are not currently includable in taxable income. Withdrawals from a MedicarePlus MSA are excludable from taxable income if used for the qualified medical expenses of the MedicarePlus MSA holder. Withdrawals from a MedicarePlus MSA that are not used for the qualified medical expenses of the account holder are includable in income and may be subject to an additional tax (described below).

---

1. The number of MSAs which can be established is subject to a cap.

Definition of MedicarePlus MSAs.

In general a MedicarePlus MSA is an MSA that is designated as MedicarePlus MSA and to which only the contribution that can be made are those by the Secretary of Health and Human Services.[2] Thus a MedicarePlus MSA is a tax-exempt trust (or a custodial account) created exclusively for the purpose of paying the qualified medical expenses of the account holder that meets requirements similar to those applicable to individual retirement arrangements ("IRAs").[3] The trustee of a MedicarePlus MSA can be a bank, insurance company, or other person that demonstrates to the satisfaction of the Secretary of the treasury that the manner in which such person will administer the trust will be consistent with applicable requirements.

A MedicarePlus MSA trustee would be required to make such reports as may be required by the Secretary of the Treasury. A $50 penalty would be imposed for each failure to file without reasonable cause.

Taxation of distributions from a MedicarePlus MSA.

Distributions from a MedicarePlus MSA that are used to pay the qualified medical expenses of the account holder would be excludable from taxable income regardless of whether the account holder is enrolled in the MedicarePlus MSA plan at the time of the distribution.[4] Qualified medical expenses are defined as under the rules relating to the itemized deduction for medical expenses. However, for this purpose, qualified medical expenses would not include any insurance premiums other than premiums for long-term care insurance, continuation insurance (so-called "COBRA coverage"), or premium for coverage while an individual is receiving unemployment compensation. Distributions from a MedicarePlus MSA that are excludable from gross income under the provision can not be taken into account for purposes of the itemized deduction for medical expenses.

Distributions for purposes other than qualified medical expenses are includable in taxable income. An additional tax of 50 percent applies to the extent the total distributions for purposes other than qualified medical expenses in a taxable year exceed the amount by which the value of the MedicarePlus MSA as of December 31, of the preceding taxable year exceeds 60 percent of the deductible of the plan under which the individual is covered. The additional tax does not apply to distributions on account of the disability or death of the account holder. Direct trustee-to-trustee transfers could be made from one MedicarePlus MSA to another MedicarePlus MSA without income inclusion.

The provision includes a corrective mechanism so that if contributions for a year are erroneously made by the Secretary of Health and Human Services, such erroneous contributions can be returned to the Secretary of Health and Human Services (along with any attributable earnings) from the MedicarePlus MSA without tax consequence to the account holder.

Treatment of MedicarePlus MSA at death.

If the beneficiary of a MedicarePlus MSA is not the account holder's spouse, the MedicarePlus MSA is no longer treated as a MedicarePlus MSA and the value of the MedicarePlus MSA on the account holder's date of death is included in the taxable income of the beneficiary for the taxable year in which the death occurred (under the rules applicable to MSAs generally). If the account holder fails to name a beneficiary, the value of the MedicarePlus MSA on the account holder's date of death is to be included in the taxable income of the account holder's final income tax return (under the rules applicable to MSA generally).

---

2. Medicare Plus MSAs are not taken into account for purposes of the cap on non-MedicarePlus MSAs, nor are they subject to that cap.

3. For example, no MedicarePlus MSA assets could be invested in life insurance contracts, MedicarePlus MSA assets could not be commingled with other property except in a common trust fund or common investment fund, and an account holder's interest in a MedicarePlus MSA would be nonforfeitable. In addition, if

an account holder engages in a prohibited transaction with respect to a MedicarePlus MSA or pledges assets in a MedicarePlus MSA, rules similar to those for IRAs would apply, and any amounts treated as distributed to the account holder under such rules would be treated as not used for qualified medical expenses.

4. Under the provision, medical expenses of the account holder's spouse or dependents would not be treated as qualified medical expenses.

In all cases, the value of the MedicarePlus MSA is included in the account holder's gross estate for estate tax purposes.

Reason for Change.

The Committee believes that introduction of significant innovations from the private sector, coupled with the full transfer of responsibility for health care choices to enrollees who choose to participate in private sector health plans, will be effective in tempering the growth of Medicare spending while providing opportunities for beneficiaries to improve upon the traditional government-defined Medicare benefit package. In addition, the Committee believes that senior citizens should be provided with greater power over their own health care choices and expenses.

Effective Date

The provision is effective with respect to taxable years beginning after December 31, 1998.

[Senate Report]

Present Law

Medical Savings Accounts are not currently an option for Medicare beneficiaries.

Reason for Change

The intention of this act is to give Medicare beneficiaries the same choices for health care delivery as the private sector currently has, including Medical Savings Accounts. In addition, Medical Savings Accounts coupled with high-deductible insurance policies discourage over-utilization of health care items and services and therefore help to slow the growth in health care spending.

Committee Provision

Medicare beneficiaries will be able toelect as a Medicare Choice option, a medical savings account high deductible insurance policy in combination with a medical savings account. The high deductible insurance policy must provide reimbursement for at least the items and services covered under Medicare Parts A and B--but only after the enrollee incurs countable expenses equal to the amount of an annual deductible of not more than $2,250 and not less than

$1,500 in 1999, updated annually by an inflation factor.

To the extent an individual chooses such a plan, the Secretary of Health and Human Services would pay the premium of the high deductible insurance policy and also make an annual contribution to the beneficiary's medical savings account equal to the difference between the premium of the insurance policy and the Medicare Choice capitation rate in the beneficiary's county. Only contributions by the Secretary of Health and Human Services could be made to a Medicare Choice MSA and such contributions would not be included in the taxable income of the Medicare Choice MSA holder.

Contributions to the enrollee's MSA can be used by the enrollee to pay for any medical care they choose. Withdrawals from Medicare Choice MSAs are excludable from taxable income if used for qualified medical expenses regardless of whether an account holder is enrolled in an MSA Plan at the time of the distribution. Withdrawals for purposes other than qualified medical expenses are includable in taxable income. An additional tax of 50% of the amount includible in taxable income applies to the extent total distributions for purposes other than qualified medical expenses in a taxable year exceed the amount by which the value of the MSA (as of December 31 of the preceding taxable year) exceeds 60 percent of the MSA plan's deductible.

Any MSA plan purchased by a Medicare beneficiary must include a cap on out-of-pocket costs of $3,000.

The demonstration will be limited to the first 100,000 Medicare beneficiaries who enroll and new enrollments will not be permitted after January 1, 2003.

An exception to the enrollment and date limits listed above will be made for individuals who already have tax-deductible MSAs upon turning 65. These individuals will be permitted to retain qualified MSAs under Medicare Choice without respect to this demonstration's limit on enrollment or sunset date.

Effective Date

January 1, 1998.

[Conference Report]

Conference Agreement

The conference agreement follows the House bill and the Senate amendment.

[¶ 5502]   Section 4041.   Tax treatment of hospitals which participate in provider-sponsored organizations.

(Code Sec. 501)

[House Report—Budget]

Current law

To qualify as a charitable tax-exempt organization described in Internal Revenue Code (the "Code") section 501(c)(3), an organization must be organized and operated exclusively for religious, charitable, scientific, testing for public safety, literary, or educational purposes, or to foster international sports competition, or for the prevention of cruelty to children or animals. Although section 501(c)(3) does not specifically mention furnishing medical care and operating a nonprofit hospital, such activities have long been considered to further charitable purposes, provided that the organization benefits the community as a whole.

No part of the net earnings of a 501(c)(3) organization may inure to the benefit of any private shareholder or individual. No substantial part of the activities of a 501(c)(3) organization may consist of carrying on propaganda, or otherwise attempting to influence legislation, and such organization may not participate in, or intervene in, any political campaign on behalf of (or in opposition to) any candidate for public office. In addition, under section 501(m), an organization described in section 501(c)(3) or 501(c)(4) is exempt from tax only if no substantial part of its activities consists of providing commercial-type insurance.

A tax-exempt organization may, subject to certain limitations, enter into a joint venture or partnership with a for-profit organization without affecting its tax-exempt status. Under current ruling practice, the IRS examines the facts and circumstances of each arrangement to determine (1) whether the venture itself and the participation of the tax-exempt organization therein furthers a charitable purpose, and (2) whether the sharing of profits and losses or other aspects of the arrangement entail improper private inurement or more than incidental private benefit.[1]

Explanation of provision

The provision provides that an organization does not fail to be treated as organized and operated exclusively for a charitable purpose for purposes of Code section 501(c)(3) solely because a hospital which is owned and operated by such organization participates in a provider-sponsored organization ("PSO") (as defined in section 1845(a)(1) of the Social Security Act), whether or not such PSO is exempt from tax. Thus, participation by a hospital in a PSO (whether taxable or tax-exempt) is deemed to satisfy the first part of the inquiry under current IRS ruling practice.[2]

The provision does not change present-law restrictions on private inurement and private benefit. However, the provision provides that any person with a material financial interest in such a PSO shall be treated as a private shareholder or individual with respect to the hospital for purposes of applying the private inurement prohibition in Code section 501(c)(3). Accordingly, the facts and circumstances of each PSO arrangement are evaluated to determine whether the arrangement entails impermissible private inurement or more than incidental private benefit (e.g., where there is a disproportionate allocation of profits and

1. See IRS General Counsel Memorandum 39862; Announcement 92 83, 1992 22 I.R.B. 59 (IRS Audit Guidelines for Hospitals). Even where no prohibited private inurement exists, however, more than incidental private benefits conferred on individuals may result in the organization not being operated "exclusively" for an exempt purpose. See, e.g., American Campaign *Academy v. Commissioner,* 92 T.C. 1053 (1989).

2. The qualification of a hospital as a tax-exempt charitable organization under section 501(c)(3) is determined as under present law. See Rev. Rul. 69 545, 1969 2 C.B. 117.

losses to the non-exempt partners, the tax-exempt partner makes loans to the joint venture that are commercially unreasonable, the tax-exempt partner provides property or services to the joint venture at less than fair market value, or a non-exempt partner receives more than reasonable compensation for the sale of property or services to the joint venture).

The provision does not change present-law restrictions on lobbying and political activities. In addition, the restrictions of Code section 501(m) on the provision of commercial-type insurance continue to apply.

[¶ 5503]   Section 4631.   Permanent extension of certain secondary payer provisions.

[House Report—Budget]

Current Law

Generally, Medicare is the primary payer, that is, it pays health claims first, with an individual's private or other public plan filling in some or all of the coverage gaps. In certain cases, the individual's other coverage pays first, while Medicare is the secondary payer. This is known as the Medicare secondary payer (MSP) program. The MSP provisions apply to group health plans for the working aged, large group health plans for the disabled, and employer health plans (regardless of size) for the end-stage renal disease (ESRD) population for 18 months. The MSP provisions for the disabled expire October 1, 1998. The MSP provisions for the ESRD population apply for 12 months, except the period is extended to 18 months for the February 1, 1991-October 1, 1998 period.

The law authorizes a data match program which is intended to identify potential secondary payer situations. Medicare beneficiaries are matched against data contained in the Social Security Administration and Internal Revenue Service files to identify cases where a working beneficiary (or working spouse) may have employer-based health insurance coverage.

Reason for change

The provision is necessary to ensure that certain providers not lose tax-exempt status simply because they join or form a PSO.

Effective date

The provision is effective on the date of enactment.

[Conference]

The Senate amendment is the same as the House bill.

Conference Agreement

The conference agreement follows the House bill and the Senate amendment.

Explanation of Provision

The provision would make permanent the provisions relating to the disabled and the data match program.

The provision would extend application of the MSP provisions for the ESRD population for 30 months. This would apply to items and services furnished on or after enactment with respect to periods beginning on or after the date that is 18 months prior to enactment.

[Senate Report]

Reasons for Change

The Committee provision would provide for improved operation of the secondary payer program.

Committee Provision

The Committee provision would:

(a) Make permanent law that Medicare is the secondary payer for disabled beneficiaries who have employer-provided health insurance; and make permanent law and extend to 30 months the period of time employer health insurance is the primary payer for ESRD beneficiaries;

(b) Make the data match program authority permanent law; and

(c) Specify that the U.S. could seek to recover payments if the request for payments was submitted to the entity required or responsible to pay within three years from the date the item or service was furnished. This provision would apply notwithstanding any other claims filing time limits that may apply under an employer group health plan. The provision would apply to items and services furnished after 1990. The provision should not be construed as permitting any waiver of the 3-year requirement in the case of items and services furnished more than 3 years before enactment.

The provision would permit recovery from third party administrators of primary plans. However, recovery would not be permitted where the third-party administrator would not be able to recover the amount at issue from the employer or group health plan for whom it provides administrative services due to the insolvency or bankruptcy of the employer or plan.

The provision would clarify that the beneficiary is not liable in Medicare secondary payer recovery cases unless the benefits were paid directly to the beneficiary.

Effective Date

Generally on enactment.

[¶ 5504]   Section 5405. Exemption of service performed by election workers from the federal unemployment tax.

(Code Sec. 3121)

[House Report—Budget]

Present law

The Federal Unemployment Tax Act generally requires States to cover under their unemployment compensation laws work performed in the employment of a State or local government. Only certain enumerated exceptions are allowed.

Explanation of provision

The proposal would exempt from FUTA taxes and UI benefits work performed as an election official or election worker. This exemption would apply only if the annual wages received by the individual for such service is less than $1,000.

Reason for change

The Committee believes that short-term employment as an election official or election worker should not be used as the basis for participation in the unemployment compensation system.

Effective date

Date of enactment.

[¶ 5506]   Section 5406. Treatment of certain services performed by inmates.

(Code Sec. 3121)

[House Report—Budget]

Present law

The Federal Unemployment Tax Act (FUTA) imposes a 6.2 percent gross tax rate on the first $7,000 of wages paid annually by covered employers to each employee. Generally, wages are defined to include all remuneration for employment unless specifically exempted. There is no exemption for wages paid to persons committed to penal institutions. However, in the requirement of FUTA that States cover State and local employment, an exception is permitted for government wages paid to inmates.

Explanation of provision

The proposal would exempt wages paid to persons committed to penal institutions from the definition of wages for FUTA tax purposes. These persons would also be ineligible to claim unemployment benefits with respect to such wages.

Reason for change

The Committee provision prevents a person committed to a penal institution from qualifying for unemployment insurance benefits. The Committee also intends that if a

State has denied unemployment benefits to a person because the person's qualifying wages were earned while the person was committed to a penal institution, before or after the effective date of this change, that such denial of unemployment benefits does not place that State's law out of conformity with Federal law and does not prevent certification of that State's law by the Secretary of Labor pursuant to section 3304 of the Internal Revenue Code of 1986.

Effective date

The proposal would be effective with respect to service performed after March 26, 1996.

[Senate Report]

Present Law

Federal law requires UI coverage for most nongovernmental employment, and employers have to pay taxes under the Federal Unemployment Tax Act (FUTA) for their employees. Federal law also requires state UI programs to cover jobs in state and local government agencies. Each governmental employer reimburses the state UI program for the cost of any unemployment benefits paid to its workers.

Federal law does except certain employment from this mandatory coverage. One exception permits states to exclude from coverage services performed for a govern-

mental agency by inmates of custodial or penal institutions. However, any work performed by inmates by private employers through work-release programs or other cooperative arrangements between prison authorities and private employers does not come under this exception. Further, there is no exception to FUTA coverage of private employers for jobs held by inmates of penal institutions. Thus, it is possible for a prison inmate on work-release to earn UI coverage that may be used to claim UI benefits, if the inmate, when released, is unemployed and available for work.

Reasons for Change

The Committee provision exempts services performed by inmates who participate in prison work programs from unemployment taxes and benefits.

Committee Provisions

The Committee provision will prevent the payment of unemployment compensation benefits to former prisoners who became "unemployed" when they were released and were no longer participating in a prison work program. Inmates who provide services directly to the prison are already exempt from unemployment taxes. This would extend the same treatment to inmates who participate in other work programs while in prison.

[¶ 5507]   Section 5407.   Exemption of service performed for an elementary or secondary school operated primarily for religious purposes from the federal unemployment tax.

(Code Sec. 3121)

[House Report—Budget]

Present law

The Federal Unemployment Tax Act requires States to cover under their unemployment compensation laws certain nonprofit organizations designated under FUTA. Specifically, FUTA exempts service performed in the employ of: (1) a church or convention or association of churches, or (2) an organization which is operated primarily for religious purposes and which is operated, supervised, controlled, or principally supported by a church or convention or as-

sociation of churches. Individuals who are in the employ of entities with a religious orientation which are not affiliated with a particular church, or convention or association of churches are not exempt.

Explanation of provision

The proposal would exempt from both the FUTA tax and UI benefits work performed in an elementary or secondary school which is operated primarily for religious purposes. This exemption would be available to such schools even though they are not operated, supervised, controlled, or principally supported by a church or convention or association of churches. Persons performing such service would also be ineligible to claim benefits with respect to such wages.

Reason for change

The Committee believes that employees of certain schools with a religious orientation should be treated similarly for FUTA tax purposes regardless of the school's affiliation, or lack thereof, with a particular church, or convention, or association of churches.

Effective date

Date of enactment.

Congressional Committee Reports Accompanying the Taxpayer Browsing Protection Act of 1997, H.R. 1226

[¶ 5550]

This section reproduces all important parts of the official explanation of the Taxpayer Browsing Act of 1997, H.R. 1226. The material comes from the House Committee Report.

[¶ 5551]   Section 2 and 3.   **Criminal and civil penalties for unauthorized inspection of returns.**

(Code Sec. 7213A, 7431)

[House Report]

Present Law

The Internal Revenue Code prohibits disclosure of tax returns and return information, except to the extent specifically authorized by theInternal Revenue Code (sec. 6103). Unauthorized willful disclosure is afelony punishable by a fine not exceeding $5,000 or imprisonment of not more than five years, or both (sec. 7213). An action for civil damages also may be brought for unauthorized disclosure (sec. 7431).

There is no explicit criminal penalty in the Internal Revenue Code for unauthorized inspection (absent subsequent disclosure) of tax returns and return information. Such inspection is, however, explicitlyprohibited by the Internal Revenue Service ("IRS").[1] In a recent case, an individual was convicted of violating the Federal wire fraud statute (18 U.S.C. 1343 and 1346) and a Federal computer fraud statute (18 U.S.C. 1030) for unauthorized inspection. However, the U.S. First Circuit Court of Appeals overturned this conviction.[2]   Unauthorized inspection of information of any department or agency of the United States (including the IRS) via computer was made a crime under 18 U.S.C. 1030 by the Economic Espionage Act of 1996.[3] This provision does not apply to unauthorized inspection of paper documents.

Reasons for Change

The Committee believes that it is important to have a criminal penalty in the Inter-
nal Revenue Code to punish this type of behavior. The Committee also believes that it is appropriate to provide for civil damages for unauthorized inspection parallel to civil damages for unauthorized disclosure.

Explanation of Provisions

Criminal penalties (sec. 2 of the bill and new sec. 7213A of the Code)

The bill creates a new criminal penalty in the Internal Revenue Code. The penalty is imposed for willful inspection (except as authorized by the Code) of any tax return or return information by any Federal employee or IRS contractor. The penalty also applies to willful inspection (except as authorized) by any State employee or other person who acquired the tax return or return information under specific provisions of section 6103. Upon conviction, the penalty is a fine in any amount not exceeding $1,000,[4] or imprisonment of not more than 1 year, or both, together with the costs of prosecution. In addition, upon conviction, an officer or employee of the United States would be dismissed from office or discharged from employment.

The Congress views any unauthorized inspection of tax return information as a very serious offense; this new criminal penalty reflects that view. The Congress also believes that unauthorized inspection warrants very serious personnel sanctions against IRS employees who engage in unauthorized inspection, and that it is appropriate to fire employees who do this.

---

1. IRS Declaration of Privacy Principles, May 9, 1994.
2. *U.S. v. Czubinski*, DTR 2/25/97, p. K 2.
3. P.L. 104 294, sec. 201 (October 11, 1996).
4. Pursuant to 18 U.S.C. sec. 3571 (added by the Sentencing Reform Act of 1984), the amount of the fine is not more than the greater of the amount specified in this new Code section or $100,000.

Civil damages (sec. 3 of the bill and sec. 7431 of the Code)

The bill amends the provision providing for civil damages for unauthorized disclosure by also providing for civil damages for unauthorized inspection. Damages are available for unauthorized inspection that occurs either knowingly or by reason of negligence. Accidental or inadvertent inspection that may occur (such as, for example, by making an error in typing in a TIN) would not be subject to damages because it would not meet this standard. The bill also provides that no damages are available to a taxpayer if that taxpayer requested the inspection or disclosure.

The bill also requires that, if any person is criminally charged by indictment or information with inspection or disclosure of a taxpayer's return or return information in violation of section 7213(a) or (b), section 7213A (as added by the bill), or 18 USC section 1030 (a)(2)(B), the Secretary notify that taxpayer as soon as practicable of the inspection or disclosure.

Effective date

The bill is effective for violations occurring on or after the date of enactment.

¶ 6000. Act Section Cross Reference Table
* denotes Budget Act
† denotes Privacy Act

Act §	Code §	Topic	Generally effective date	Analysis ¶	Com Rep ¶
1(c)	None	Tax rate changes made by '97 Act are not subject to "tax-straddle" computation	Aug. 5, '97	2701	
1(d)	None	No penalty for underpayment of pre-'98 estimated tax caused by '97 Act	Aug. 5, '97	1801	5168
2(a) †	7213A	Criminal penalty imposed on "browsing" of tax returns or return information	Violations occurring on or after Aug. 5, '97	2407	5551
2(b)(1) †	7213(a)(2)	Criminal penalty imposed on "browsing" of tax returns or return information	Violations occurring on or after Aug. 5, '97	2407	5551
3(a) †	7431(a)	Civil damages made available for unauthorized inspection of returns or return information	Inspections and disclosures occurring on or after Aug. 5, '97	2408	5551
3(b) †	7431(e)	IRS required to notify taxpayers of unlawful inspection or disclosure of their returns or return information	Inspections and disclosures occurring on or after Aug. 5, '97	2337	5551
3(c) †	7431(b)	Civil damages made available for unauthorized inspection of returns or return information	Inspections and disclosures occurring on or after Aug. 5, '97	2408	5551
3(d)(1) and (2) †	7431(c)	Civil damages made available for unauthorized inspection of returns or return information	Inspections and disclosures occurring on or after Aug. 5, '97	2408	5551

Act §	Code §	Topic	Generally effective date	Analysis ¶	Com Rep ¶
3(d)(3) †	7431(f)	Civil damages made available for unauthorized inspection of returns or return information	Inspections and disclosures occurring on or after Aug. 5, '97	2408	5551
101(a)	24	Child tax credit of up to $400 in '98, $500 in '99 and later years, for each qualifying child under age 17	Tax years beginning after Dec. 31, '97	101	5001
101(b)	32(m)(3)	Child tax credit of up to $400 in '98, $500 in '99 and later years, for each qualifying child under age 17	Tax years beginning after Dec. 31, '97	101	5001
101(c)	501(c)(26)	Tax-exempt state-sponsored high risk pools can provide health care coverage to spouse and children of high risk individual	Tax years beginning after Dec. 31, '97	1305	5001
101(d)(2)	6213(g)(2)(I)	Child tax credit of up to $400 in '98, $500 in '99 and later years, for each qualifying child under age 17	Tax years beginning after Dec. 31, '97	101	5001
201(a)	25A	"Hope Scholarship Credit," up to $1,500 per year, and "Lifetime Learning Credit," up to $1,000 per year, allowed for higher education expenses	Expenses paid after Dec. 31, '97	401	5002
201(b)	6213(g)(2)	"Hope Scholarship Credit," up to $1,500 per year, and "Lifetime Learning Credit," up to $1,000 per year, allowed for higher education expenses	Expenses paid after Dec. 31, '97	401	5002
201(c)(1)	6050S	Educational institutions receiving, and businesses paying, higher education expenses must furnish information returns	Expenses paid after Dec. 31, '97	410	5002
201(c)(2)(A)	6724(d)(1)(B)(ix)	Educational institutions receiving, and businesses paying, higher education expenses must furnish information returns	Expenses paid after Dec. 31, '97	410	5002

Act §	Code §	Topic	Generally effective date	Analysis ¶	Com Rep ¶
201(c)(2)(B)	6724(d)(2)(Z)	Educational institutions receiving, and businesses paying, higher education expenses must furnish information returns	Expenses paid after Dec. 31, '97	410	5002
201(d)	135(d)(2)	Higher education expenses used to compute exclusion of redemption proceeds of U.S. savings bonds must be reduced by higher education expenses for which Hope/Lifetime Learning credit is claimed	Expenses paid after Dec. 31, '97	409	5002
202(a)	221	Above-the-line deduction allowed for up to $1,000 of interest paid on higher education loans in '98, increasing over four years to $2,500 for interest paid in 2001	Any loan interest payment due and paid after Dec. 31, '97	402	5003
202(b)	62(a)(17)	Above-the-line deduction allowed for up to $1,000 of interest paid on higher education loans in '98, increasing over four years to $2,500 for interest paid in 2001	Any loan interest payment due and paid after Dec. 31, '97	402	5003
203	72(t)	No penalty for early withdrawal of IRA funds to pay higher education expenses	Distributions made after '97	304	5004
211(a)	529(e)(3)	Qualified state tuition program expanded	Jan. 1, '98	406	5005
211(b)(1)	529(e)	Tax treatment of contributions to and distributions from qualified tuition programs modified	Jan. 1, '98	405	5005
211(b)(2)	529(e)(5)	Qualified state tuition program expanded	Jan. 1, '98	406	5005
211(b)(3)	529(c)	Tax treatment of contributions to and distributions from qualified tuition programs modified	Jan. 1, '98	405	5005
211(e)	135(c)(2)(C)	Tax treatment of contributions to and distributions from qualified tuition programs modified	Jan. 1, '98	405	5005
211(e)(2)(A)	529(d)	Qualified state tuition program expanded	Jan. 1, '98	406	5005

Act §	Code §	Topic	Generally effective date	Analysis ¶	Com Rep ¶
213(a)	530	Tax-exempt education IRAs allowed	Tax years beginning after Dec. 31, '97	403	5005
213(b)	4975(c)	Tax-exempt education IRAs allowed	Tax years beginning after Dec. 31, '97	403	5005
213(c)	6693	Tax-exempt education IRAs allowed	Tax years beginning after Dec. 31, '97	403	5005
213(d)	4973(e)	Tax-exempt education IRAs allowed	Tax years beginning after Dec. 31, '97	403	5005
221	127(d)	Exclusion for employer-provided educational assistance extended through 2000	Years beginning after Dec. 31, '96	404	5007
222(a)	145(b)(1)	$150 million limitation on 501(c)(3) bonds repealed	Aug. 5, '97	2505	5008
223(a)	148(f)(4)(D)(vii)	Up to $5 million in bonds used to finance public school capital expenditures after '97 exempted from arbitrage rebate requirements	Bonds issued after Dec. 31, '97	2502	5009
224(a)	170(e)(6)	Corporate gifts of computer technology and equipment to elementary and secondary schools before 2000 get charitable deduction tax break	Tax years beginning after '97	1512	5010
225	108(f)	Exclusion from income for cancellation of student loans expanded to cover cancellation of loans under nongovernment sponsored programs	Aug. 5, '97	103	5011
226(a)	1397E	Certain financial institutions holding qualified zone academy bonds are entitled to nonrefundable tax credit	Obligations issued after Dec. 31, '97	705	5012
301(a)	219(g)(3)(B)	Increased availability of IRA deductions for active pension plan participants and spouses	Taxable years beginning after Dec. 31, '97	302	5015
301(b)	219(g)	Increased availability of IRA deductions for active pension plan participants and spouses	Taxable years beginning after Dec. 31, '97	302	5015

Act §	Code §	Topic	Generally effective date	Analysis ¶	Com Rep ¶
302(a)	408A	New nondeductible Roth IRA allows tax-free withdrawal of earnings	Taxable years beginning after Dec. 31, '97	301	5016
302(b)	4973(b)	New nondeductible Roth IRA allows tax-free withdrawal of earnings	Taxable years beginning after Dec. 31, '97	301	5016
302(c)	219(c)(1)(B)	New nondeductible Roth IRA allows tax-free withdrawal of earnings	Taxable years beginning after Dec. 31, '97	301	5016
302(d)	408(i)	New nondeductible Roth IRA allows tax-free withdrawal of earnings	Taxable years beginning after Dec. 31, '97	301	5016
303	72(t)	No penalty for early withdrawal of IRA funds for "first-time homebuyers"— $10,000 lifetime limitation	Payments and distributions made after '97	303	5017
304(a)	408(m)(3)	Individual retirement accounts and individually-directed plan accounts may be invested in certain bullion	Tax years beginning after Dec. 31, '97	305	5018
311(a)	1(h)	Capital gains tax rates for individuals reduced from 28% to 20% and 15% to 10% for post-May 6, '97 gains	Tax years ending after May 6, '97, but without regard to pre-May 7, '97 gains	201	5019
311(b)	55(b)(3)	Alternative minimum tax rate on net capital gain for non-corporate taxpayers reduced from 26%/28% to 20% or 10%	Tax years ending after May 6, '97, but without regard to pre-May 7, '97 gains	602	5019
311(b)(2)(B)	57(a)(7)	AMT preference for portion of gain on sale of qualified small business stock reduced from 50% to 42%	Tax years ending after May 6, '97	605	5019
311(c)(2)	7518(g)(6)(A)	Tax on nonqualified withdrawals from capital gain account under Merchant Marine capital construction fund reduced from 28% to 20%	Tax years ending after May 6, '97	210	5019

Act §	Code §	Topic	Generally effective date	Analysis ¶	Com Rep ¶
311(c)(3)	904(b)(2)(C)	IRS can modify rule for determining foreign source income attributable to capital gains to properly reflect capital gain rate differential and computation of net capital gain	For tax years ending after May 6, '97	1608	
312(a)	121	Replacement of rollover rules and the one-time exclusion that applied to sales of a principal residence with an exclusion of gain of up to $250,000 ($500,000 for joint filers)	Sales and exchanges after May 6, '97	102	5020
312(b)	1034	Replacement of rollover rules and the one-time exclusion that applied to sales of a principal residence with an exclusion of gain of up to $250,000 ($500,000 for joint filers)	Sales and exchanges after May 6, '97	102	5020
312(c)	6045(e)	Sales and exchanges of certain principal residences exempted from real estate reporting requirements	Sales and exchanges after May 6, '97	2309	5020
313(a)	1045	Elective rollover of gain from qualified small business stock to other qualified small business stock	Sales after Aug. 5, '97	206	5021
313(b)(2)	1223(15)	Elective rollover of gain from qualified small business stock to other qualified small business stock	Sales after Aug. 5, '97	206	5021
314(a)	1201(a)(2)	Amount of net capital gain taken into account in computing alternative tax on net capital gain for corporations is limited to taxable income	Tax years ending after Dec. 31, '97	603	5022
401(a)	55(e)	Alternative minimum tax (AMT) repealed for small corporations after '97	Tax years beginning after Dec. 31, '97	601	5023
402(a)	56(a)(1)(A)(i)	The alternative minimum tax adjustment for depreciation of property placed in service after '98 is computed using the 150% declining balance method (and switching to the straight line method)	Aug. 5, '97	606	5024

Act §	Code §	Topic	Generally effective date	Analysis ¶	Com Rep ¶
402(b)	56(a)(5)	The AMT adjustment for pollution control facilities is determined for facilities placed in service after '98 by using straight line depreciation	Aug. 5, '97	610	5024
403(a)	56(a)(6)	Alternative minimum tax on installment sales repealed retroactively for dispositions in tax years beginning after '87	Dispositions in tax years beginning after Dec. 31, '87	607	5025
501(a)(1)(A)	2010(a)	Exemption equivalent amount of unified estate and gift tax credit is increased to $1 million on a phased-in schedule through 2006	Applies to estates of decedents dying, and gifts made, after Dec. 31, '97	501	5026
501(a)(1)(B)	2010(c)	Exemption equivalent amount of unified estate and gift tax credit is increased to $1 million on a phased-in schedule through 2006	Applies to estates of decedents dying, and gifts made, after Dec. 31, '97	501	5026
501(a)(1)(C)	6018(a)(1)	Exemption equivalent amount of unified estate and gift tax credit is increased to $1 million on a phased-in schedule through 2006	Applies to estates of decedents dying, and gifts made, after Dec. 31, '97	501	5026
501(a)(1)(D)	2001(c)(2)	Exemption equivalent amount of unified estate and gift tax credit is increased to $1 million on a phased-in schedule through 2006	Applies to estates of decedents dying, and gifts made, after Dec. 31, '97	501	5026
501(a)(1)(E)	2102(c)(3)(A)	Exemption equivalent amount of unified estate and gift tax credit is increased to $1 million on a phased-in schedule through 2006	Applies to estates of decedents dying, and gifts made, after Dec. 31, '97	501	5026
501(a)(2)	2505(a)(1)	Exemption equivalent amount of unified estate and gift tax credit is increased to $1 million on a phased-in schedule through 2006	Applies to estates of decedents dying, and gifts made, after Dec. 31, '97	501	5026

Act §	Code §	Topic	Generally effective date	Analysis ¶	Com Rep ¶
501(b)	2032A(a)(3)	$750,000 limit on estate tax special use valuation reduction will be adjusted for inflation after '98	Applies to estates of decedents dying in a calendar year after '98	502	5026
501(c)(3)	2503(b)(2)	Gift tax annual exclusion of $10,000 will be adjusted for inflation after '98	Applies to gifts made in a calendar year after '98	503	5026
501(d)	2631(c)	Generation-skipping transfer exemption of $1 million will be adjusted for inflation after '98	Applies to individuals who die in any calendar year after '98	504	5026
501(e)	6601(j)(3)	Estate tax benefit of qualified family-owned business exclusion may be recaptured if certain events occur	Applies to estates of decedents dying after Dec. 31, '97	506	5028
502(a)	2033A	Estate tax exclusion allowed for qualified family-owned business interests—exclusion amount, plus exemption equivalent of unified credit, can't exceed $1.3 million	Applies to estates of decedents dying after Dec. 31, '97	505	5027
502(a)	2033A(f)	Estate tax benefit of qualified family-owned business exclusion may be recaptured if certain events occur	Applies to estates of decedents dying after Dec. 31, '97	506	5027
502(a)	2033A(g)	Estate tax benefit of qualified family-owned business exclusion may be recaptured if certain events occur	Applies to estates of decedents dying after Dec. 31, '97	506	5027
503(a)	6601(j)(1)	Estate tax benefit of qualified family-owned business exclusion may be recaptured if certain events occur	Applies to estates of decedents dying after Dec. 31, '97	506	5028
503(a)	6601(j)(2)	Estate tax benefit of qualified family-owned business exclusion may be recaptured if certain events occur	Applies to estates of decedents dying after Dec. 31, '97	506	5028

Act §	Code §	Topic	Generally effective date	Analysis ¶	Com Rep ¶
503(b)(1)	2053(c)(1)(D)	Estate tax benefit of qualified family-owned business exclusion may be recaptured if certain events occur	Applies to estates of decedents dying after Dec. 31, '97	506	5028
503(b)(2)(A)	163(k)	Estate tax benefit of qualified family-owned business exclusion may be recaptured if certain events occur	Applies to estates of decedents dying after Dec. 31, '97	506	5028
503(b)(2)(B)	163(h)(2)(E)	Estate tax benefit of qualified family-owned business exclusion may be recaptured if certain events occur	Applies to estates of decedents dying after Dec. 31, '97	506	5028
504(a)	2032A(c)(7)	Lineal descendant's inter-family cash lease of specially-valued property won't trigger recapture estate tax	For leases entered into after Dec. 31, '76	510	5029
504(b)	2032A(b)(5)(A)	Lineal descendant's inter-family cash lease of specially-valued property won't trigger recapture estate tax	For leases entered into after Dec. 31, '76	510	5029
505	7479	Tax Court authorized to issue declaratory judgments on eligibility for deferral of estate tax from closely-held business	Estates of decedents dying after Aug. 5, '97	2328	5030
506(a)	2001(f)	Gifts may not be revalued for estate tax purposes after gift tax statute of limitations expires	For gifts made after Aug. 5, '97	521	5031
506(b)	6501(c)(9)	Statute of limitations will not run on inadequately disclosed gift	For gifts made in calendar years after Aug. 5, '97	522	5031
506(c)(1)	7477	Donor may petition the Tax Court for a declaratory judgment relating to the value of certain gifts	For gifts made after Aug. 5, '97	523	5031
506(d)	2504(c)	Gifts may not be revalued for estate tax purposes after gift tax statute of limitations expires	For gifts made after Aug. 5, '97	521	5031

Act §	Code §	Topic	Generally effective date	Analysis ¶	Com Rep ¶
507(a)(1)	665(c)	Throwback rules repealed for U.S. trusts	For distributions made in tax years beginning after Aug. 5, '97	530	5032
507(b)(1)	644	Special rule for gain on property transferred to trust at less than fair market value is repealed	For sales or exchanges after the Aug. 5, '97	531	5032
508(a)	2031(c)	Estate tax exclusion for up to 40% of value of land subject to qualified conservation easement	For estates of decedents dying after Dec. 31, '97	517	5033
508(b)	1014(a)(4)	No step–up in basis for land subject to a qualified conservation easement that is excluded from the gross estate	For estates of decedents dying after Dec. 31, '97	518	5033
508(c)	2032A(c)(8)	Qualified conservation contribution is not a disposition for estate tax special use valuation purposes	For easements granted after Dec. 31, '97	519	5033
508(d)	170(h)(5)(B)(ii)	Income and estate tax charitable deduction for a qualified conservation contribution where a mineral interest has been retained	For easements granted after Dec. 31, '97	520	5033
511(a)	2651(e)	"Deceased parent exception" to generation–skipping transfer (GST) tax is expanded	For generation–skipping transfers occurring after Dec. 31, '97	525	5034
511(b)(1)	2612(c)(2)	"Deceased parent exception" to generation–skipping transfer (GST) tax is expanded	For generation–skipping transfers occurring after Dec. 31, '97	525	5034
511(b)(2)	2612(c)(3)	"Deceased parent exception" to generation–skipping transfer (GST) tax is expanded	For generation–skipping transfers occurring after Dec. 31, '97	525	5034
601(a)(1)	41(h)(1)	Research credit is retroactively restored and extended until June 30, '98	Amounts paid or incurred after May 31, '97	706	5036

Act §	Code §	Topic	Generally effective date	Analysis ¶	Com Rep ¶
601(b)(1)	41(c)(4)(B)	Research credit is retroactively restored and extended until June 30, '98	Amounts paid or incurred after May 31, '97	706	5036
602(a)	170(e)(5)(D)(ii)	Full deduction for contributions of qualified appreciated stock to private foundations restored for period June 1, '97 to June 30, '98	Contributions made after May 31, '97	107	5037
603(a)(1)	51(c)(4)(B)	Work opportunity credit is modified and extended through June 30, '98	Individuals who begin work for the employer after Sept. 30, '97, but before July 1, '98	702	5038
603(b)(1)	51(d)(2)(A)	Work opportunity credit is modified and extended through June 30, '98	Individuals who begin work for the employer after Sept. 30, '97, but before July 1, '98	702	5038
603(b)(2)	51(d)(3)(A)	Work opportunity credit is modified and extended through June 30, '98	Individuals who begin work for the employer after Sept. 30, '97, but before July 1, '98	702	5038
603(c)(1)	51(d)(1)(H)	Work opportunity credit is modified and extended through June 30, '98	Individuals who begin work for the employer after Sept. 30, '97, but before July 1, '98	702	5038
603(c)(2)	51(d)(9)	Work opportunity credit is modified and extended through June 30, '98	Individuals who begin work for the employer after Sept. 30, '97, but before July 1, '98	702	5038

Act §	Code §	Topic	Generally effective date	Analysis ¶	Com Rep ¶
603(d)(1)	51(a)	Work opportunity credit is modified and extended through June 30, '98	Individuals who begin work for the employer after Sept. 30, '97, but before July 1, '98	702	5038
603(d)(2)	51(i)(3)	Work opportunity credit is modified and extended through June 30, '98	Individuals who begin work for the employer after Sept. 30, '97, but before July 1, '98	702	5038
604(a)	45C	Orphan drug tax credit is retroactively restored and permanently extended	Amounts paid or incurred after May 31, '97	707	5039
701(a)	1400	Designation of DC Enterprise Zone as an empowerment zone	Aug. 5, '97	2601	5040
701(a)	1400A	Tax-exempt bonds for District of Columbia	Aug. 5, '97	2604	5040
701(a)	1400B	Zero percent capital gains rate applies to certain sales of DC Zone assets held for more than five years	Aug. 5, '97	2602	5040
701(a)	1400C	$5,000 credit for first-time home buyers in the District of Columbia	Aug. 5, '97	2603	5040
701(b)(1)	39(d)(8)	Designation of DC Enterprise Zone as an empowerment zone	Aug. 5, '97	2601	5040
801(a)	51A	New welfare-to-work credit is available to employers of long-term family assistance recipients	Individuals who begin work for the employer after Dec. 31, '97, but before May 1, '99	704	5050
901(e) and 1031(g)(3)	6302	Deposit due dates for certain fuel excise taxes delayed	July 31, '98	2217	5051
902(a)	6421(e)(2)(B)	Suspended excise tax on diesel fuel used in recreational motorboats is repealed	Jan. 1, '98	2210	5052

Act §	Code §	Topic	Generally effective date	Analysis ¶	Com Rep ¶
902(b)(1)	4041(a)(1)(A)	Suspended excise tax on diesel fuel used in recreational motorboats is repealed	Jan. 1, '98	2210	5052
902(b)(3)	4083(a)(3)	Suspended excise tax on diesel fuel used in recreational motorboats is repealed	Jan. 1, '98	2210	5052
903(a)	4682(d)(1)	Scheduled exemption from ozone-depleting-chemicals tax for imported recycled halon-1211 is repealed	Aug. 5, '97	2226	5053
904(a)	4131(b)	Uniform vaccine excise tax rate replaces various vaccine-specific rates; three new vaccines taxed	Day after Aug. 5, '97	2223	5054
904(b)	4132(a)(1)	Uniform vaccine excise tax rate replaces various vaccine-specific rates; three new vaccines taxed	Day after Aug. 5, '97	2223	5054
904(c)	4132(a)	Uniform vaccine excise tax rate replaces various vaccine-specific rates; three new vaccines taxed	Day after Aug. 5, '97	2223	5054
904(e)	4132(b)	Uniform vaccine excise tax rate replaces various vaccine-specific rates; three new vaccines taxed	Day after Aug. 5, '97	2223	5054
905(a)	6416(a)(4)(B)	Multiple-outlet gasoline retailers may claim gasoline tax refunds	Sales after Aug. 5, '97	2214	5055
906(a)	4001(a)	Purchase price triggering imposition of luxury excise tax is increased for electric and other clean-burning fuel vehicles	For sales and installations occurring after Aug. 5, '97	2218	5056
906(b)(1)	4001(e)(1)	Purchase price triggering imposition of luxury excise tax is increased for electric and other clean-burning fuel vehicles	For sales and installations occurring after Aug. 5, '97	2218	5056
906(b)(3)	4003(a)(1)(A)	Purchase price triggering imposition of luxury excise tax is increased for electric and other clean-burning fuel vehicles	For sales and installations occurring after Aug. 5, '97	2218	5056

Act §	Code §	Topic	Generally effective date	Analysis ¶	Com Rep ¶
906(b)(4)	4003(a)(2)(B)	Purchase price triggering imposition of luxury excise tax is increased for electric and other clean-burning fuel vehicles	For sales and installations occurring after Aug. 5, '97	2218	5056
907(a)(1)	4041(a)(2)	Tax rates on propane, liquefied natural gas and methanol produced from natural gas decreased	Oct. 1, '97	2212	5057
907(a)(2)	4041(d)(1)	Tax rates on propane, liquefied natural gas and methanol produced from natural gas decreased	Oct. 1, '97	2212	5057
907(b)	4041(m)(1)(A)(i)	Tax rates on propane, liquefied natural gas and methanol produced from natural gas decreased	Oct. 1, '97	2212	5057
908(a)	5041(b)(6)	Alcohol excise tax on hard cider reduced	Oct. 1, '97	2228	5058
908(b)	5041(c)	Alcohol excise tax on hard cider reduced	Oct. 1, '97	2228	5058
910(a)	5388(c)	Regs on geographic appellations codified; sign-posting requirement for wholesale liquor dealers repealed; up to 60% added sugar allowed in acidic wines	various	2230	5277, 5060
911	7508A	IRS authority to extend tax deadlines for taxpayers affected by Presidentially-declared disasters expanded	With respect to periods for performing acts that have not expired before Aug. 5, '97	2334	5061
912(a)	165(i)(4)	IRS authorized to permit appraisals used to get federal disaster relief to also be used to establish amount of disaster loss	Aug. 5, '97	111	5062
913(a)(1)	451(e)(1)	Cash basis farmers may elect to defer gain from forced sales of livestock due to floods or other weather-related conditions	Sales and exchanges after Dec. 31, '96	2101	5063
913(b)(1)	1033(e)	Forced sales of livestock due to floods or other weather conditions are treated as involuntary conversions	Sales and exchanges after Dec. 31, '96	2102	5063

Act §	Code §	Topic	Generally effective date	Analysis ¶	Com Rep ¶
914	143(k)(11)	First-time home buyer, purchase price, and mortgagor's income requirements waived for mortgage bond financing for residences located in disaster areas	Bonds issued after Dec. 31, '96 and before Jan. 1, '99	2501	5064
915	None	Interest abated when due date for tax extended in '97 disaster areas	Disasters declared after Dec. 31, '96	2401	5065
921(a)	3121(d)	In determining the employment status of retail securities brokers, instructions to ensure compliance with government investor protection standards are disregarded	For services performed after Dec. 31, '97	1902	5066
922(a)	1402(k)	Exemption from self-employment tax for termination payments received by former insurance salesmen	Payments made after Dec. 31, '97	1903	5067
931	None	Penalty for failure by small businesses to make electronic tax deposits waived through June 30, '98	Aug. 5, '97	2405	5068
932(a)	280A(c)(1)	Limit on basic standard deduction for certain dependents increased from greater of $500 (indexed) or earned income to greater of $500 (indexed) or earned income plus $250 (indexed)	Tax years beginning after Dec. 31, '98	113	5069
933	1301	Farm income averaging over a three-year period is permitted for individuals	Tax years beginning after Dec. 31, '97 and before Jan. 1, 2001	2103	5070
934(a)	162(l)(1)(B)	Percentage of health insurance costs deductible by self-employeds gradually increased to 100% by 2007	Tax years beginning after Dec. 31, '96	1103	5071
935	None	Prohibition issued on regulatory definition of a limited partner for self-employment tax purposes	Aug. 5, '97	1906	

Act §	Code §	Topic	Generally effective date	Analysis ¶	Com Rep ¶
941	198	Election to treat certain environmental remediation costs as deductible ("brownfields")	Expenditures paid or incurred after Aug. 5, '97 in tax years ending after Aug. 5, '97	808	5073
951(a)	1391(b)(2)	Authorization of two additional urban empowerment zones meeting the same criteria and eligible for the same tax incentives as existing empowerment zones	Aug. 5, '97, except that designations of new empowerment zones will be made in the 180-day period after Aug. 5, '97, and no designation takes effect before Jan. 1, 2000	2607	5081
951(b)(2)	1396(b)(2)	Authorization of two additional urban empowerment zones meeting the same criteria and eligible for the same tax incentives as existing empowerment zones	Aug. 5, '97, except that designations of new empowerment zones will be made in the 180-day period after Aug. 5, '97, and no designation takes effect before Jan. 1, 2000	2607	5081
952(a)	1391(g)	Authorization of 20 new empowerment zones meeting different eligibility criteria and eligible for different tax incentives	Upon designations to be made after Aug. 5, '97 but before Jan. 1, '99	2606	5081
952(b)	1396(e)	Authorization of 20 new empowerment zones meeting different eligibility criteria and eligible for different tax incentives	Upon designations to be made after Aug. 5, '97 but before Jan. 1, '99	2606	5081

Act §	Code §	Topic	Generally effective date	Analysis ¶	Com Rep ¶
952(c)	1397A(c)	Authorization of 20 new empowerment zones meeting different eligibility criteria and eligible for different tax incentives	Upon designations to be made after Aug. 5, '97 but before Jan. 1, '99	2606	5081
953(a)	1394(f)	State private activity bond volume caps and $3 million/$20 million limits on issue amounts do not apply to new empowerment zone facility bonds	Obligations issued after Aug. 5, '97	2609	5081
954	1392(d)	Empowerment zone and enterprise community eligibility criteria for nominated areas in Alaska or Hawaii are relaxed	Aug. 5, '97	2614	5081
955(a)	1394(b)(3)	Enterprise zone facility bond rules are modified	Obligations issued after Aug. 5, '97	2608	5081
955(b)	1394(b)(2)	Enterprise zone facility bond rules are modified	Obligations issued after Aug. 5, '97	2608	5081
956(a)	1397B(b)	Definition of business entity for enterprise zone business rules is liberalized	Tax years beginning on or after Aug. 5, '97	2610	5081
956(a)	1397B(c)	Definition of qualified proprietorship for enterprise zone business rules is liberalized	Tax years beginning on or after Aug. 5, '97	2611	5081
956(a)(4)	1397B(d)	Property rental rules are modified for enterprize zone business definition	Tax years beginning on or before Aug. 5, '97	2612	5081
956(a)(6)	1397B(f)	Treatment of businesses straddling census tract lines for enterprise zone business definition	Tax years beginning on or after Aug. 5, '97	2613	5081
961(a)	471(b)	Rules for estimating inventory shrinkage are provided	Tax years ending after Aug. 5, '97	2005	5082
962(a)	130(c)	Exclusion for amounts received for agreeing to a qualified assignment is extended to amounts received for assuming a workers' compensation liability	Claims filed after Aug. 5, '97	2705	5083

Act §	Code §	Topic	Generally effective date	Analysis ¶	Com Rep ¶
963(a)	501(c)(27)(B)	Certain state workmen's compensation act companies are tax–exempt	For tax years after Dec. 31, '97	1306	5084
964(a)	7704(g)	"Electing 1987 partnerships" continue exception from treatment as corporations but must pay 3.5% tax on gross income	Tax years beginning after Dec. 31, '97	1427	5085
965(a)	513(i)	"Qualified sponsorship payments" excluded from UBIT	Payments solicited or received after Dec 31, '97.	1301	5086
966(a)(1)	528(c)(1)	Timeshare associations may elect to be taxed like other homeowner associations	Tax years beginning after Dec. 31, '96	2706	5089
966(a)(2)	528(c)(4)	Timeshare associations may elect to be taxed like other homeowner associations	Tax years beginning after Dec. 31, '96	2706	5089
966(b)	528(d)(3)	Timeshare associations may elect to be taxed like other homeowner associations	Tax years beginning after Dec. 31, '96	2706	5089
966(c)	528(c)(5)	Timeshare associations may elect to be taxed like other homeowner associations	Tax years beginning after Dec. 31, '96	2706	5089
967	149(d)(3)(A)(i)(I)	Certain Virgin Islands bonds allowed one additional refinancing if Virgin Islands priority first lien requirement is repealed	Aug. 5, '97	2506	5090
968	1042(g)	Gain may be deferred on the sale to eligible farmers' cooperatives of stock of qualified agricultural refiners or processors	Sales after Dec. 31, '97	208	5091
969(a)	274(n)(3)	Business meals deduction increased from 50% to 80% (over 10 years) for individuals subject to DOT hours of service limitations	Tax years beginning after Dec. 31, '97	117	5092
970(a)	132(e)(2)	Clarification of de minimis fringe benefit rules to no–charge employee meals	For tax years beginning after Dec. 31, '97	1001	5093

Act §	Code §	Topic	Generally effective date	Analysis ¶	Com Rep ¶
971(a)	280F(a)(1)(C)	Luxury automobile depreciation limits are removed for clean-fuel vehicle property and tripled for electric vehicles	Property placed in service after Aug. 5, '97, but before Jan. 1, 2005	802	5094
972	613A(c)(6)(H)	100%-of-net-income limitation on percentage depletion is suspended for production from marginal oil and gas wells after '97 and before 2000	Tax years beginning after Dec. 31, '97	2704	5095
973(a)	170(i)	Standard mileage rate for computing charitable deduction for use of a car is increased from 12¢ to 14¢ per mile	Tax years beginning after Dec. 31, '97	106	5096
974(a)	501(e)(1)(A)	Cooperative hospital service organizations may purchase patient account receivables	Taxable years beginning after Dec. 31, '96	1303	5097
975(a)	62(a)(2)(C)	Above-the-line (and therefore an AMT) deduction for business expenses of state and local government officials who are compensated on a fee basis	Expenses paid or incurred in tax years beginning after Dec. 31, '86	116	5098
976(a)	None	Five-year test of joint Montana-Federal employment tax reporting is authorized	Aug. 5, '97	2308	5099
976(b)	None	Five-year test of joint Montana-Federal employment tax reporting is authorized	Aug. 5, '97	2308	5099
976(c)	6103(d)(5)	Five-year test of joint Montana-Federal employment tax reporting is authorized	Aug. 5, '97	2308	5099
1001(a)	1259	Constructive sales treatment for appreciated financial positions	Any constructive sale after June 8, '97	202	5111
1001(b)	475(e)	Commodities dealers and traders in securities and commodities can elect the mark-to-market rules	Tax years ending after Aug. 5, '97	2001	5111
1001(b)	475(f)	Commodities dealers and traders in securities and commodities can elect the mark-to-market rules	Tax years ending after Aug. 5, '97	2001	5111

Act §	Code §	Topic	Generally effective date	Analysis ¶	Com Rep ¶
1002	351(e)(1)	Expanded definition of investment company for purposes of transfers to partnerships and controlled corporations	Transfers after June 8, '97	1504	5112
1003(a)(1)	1234A(1)	Sale treatment for cancellations, lapses, expirations and other terminations is expanded to all property which is a capital asset	Terminations more than 30 days after Aug. 5, '97	204	5113
1003(b)(1)	1233(h)	Substantial worthlessness of short sale property is a gain recognition event; regs are to provide similar rules for other transactions similar to short sales	Property which becomes substantially worthless after Aug. 5, '97	203	5113
1003(c)	1271(b)	Sale-or-exchange treatment for retirement of debt instruments is expanded to include instruments issued by natural persons	Sales, exchanges and retirements after Aug. 5, '97 for obligations issued by individuals issued or purchased after June 8, '97 and for sales, exchanges and retirements after Aug. 5, '97 for obligations issued before July 2, '82 by an issuer which isn't a corporation or government (or political subdivision) which are purchased after June 8, '97	205	5113
1004(a)	1272(a)(6)(C)	Interest must be accrued on credit card receivables during payment grace period	Tax years beginning after Aug. 5, '97	2006	5114

Act §	Code §	Topic	Generally effective date	Analysis ¶	Com Rep ¶
1005(a)	163(l)	No deduction for interest on corporate debt payable in stock of the issuer or a related party	Debt instruments issued after June 8, '97	1511	5115
1011	1059	Treatment of extraordinary dividends amended	Distributions after May 3, '95	1503	5116
1012(a)	355(e)	Rules for tax-free divisions modified	Distributions after April 16, '97 and transfers after Aug. 5, '97	1501	5117
1012(b)(1)	355(f)	Rules for tax-free divisions modified	Distributions after April 16, '97 and transfers after Aug. 5, '97	1501	5117
1012(b)(2)	358(g)	Rules for tax-free divisions modified	Distributions after April 16, '97 and transfers after Aug. 5, '97	1501	5117
1012(c)(1)	351(c)	Rules for tax-free divisions modified	Distributions after April 16, '97 and transfers after Aug. 5, '97	1501	5117
1012(c)(2)	368(a)(2)(H)	Rules for tax-free divisions modified	Distributions after April 16, '97 and transfers after Aug. 5, '97	1501	5117
1013(a)	304(a)(1)	Treatment of dividend from related-party stock purchase amended	Distributions or acquisitions after June 8, '97	1505	5118
1013(b)	1059(e)(1)(A)(iii)	Treatment of dividend from related-party stock purchase amended	Distributions or acquisitions after June 8, '97	1505	5118
1013(c)	304(b)(5)	Treatment of dividend from related-party stock purchase amended	Distributions or acquisitions after June 8, '97	1505	5118
1014(a)	351(g)	Certain preferred stock treated as boot	Transactions after June 8, '97	1502	5119

Act §	Code §	Topic	Generally effective date	Analysis ¶	Com Rep ¶
1014(b)	354(a)(2)(C)	Certain preferred stock treated as boot	Transactions after June 8, '97	1502	5119
1014(c)	355(a)(3)(D)	Certain preferred stock treated as boot	Transactions after June 8, '97	1502	5119
1014(d)	356(e)	Certain preferred stock treated as boot	Transactions after June 8, '97	1502	5119
1014(e)(3)	1036(c)	Certain preferred stock treated as boot	Transactions after June 8, '97	1502	5119
1015	246(c)	Holding period for dividends-received deduction modified	Dividends received or accrued after the 30th day after Aug. 5, '97	1509	5120
1021(a)	6045(f)	Information reporting required for trade or business payments to attorneys after '97	Payments made after Dec. 31, '97	2310	5121
1022(a)	6041A(d)	Information reporting required for federal agency payments of $600 or more to corporations	Returns with due dates (determined without regard to any extension) more than 90 days after Aug. 5, '97	2311	5122
1023(a)	6103(l)(7)(D)	Rules on disclosure of return information to Veterans Affairs Department extended through 2003	Aug. 5, '97	2332	5123
1024(a)	6331(h)	IRS may levy on certain wage replacement and annuity payments	Levies issued after Aug. 5, '97	2324	5124, 5125
1025(a)	6334(f)	IRS may levy on certain wage replacement and annuity payments	Levies issued after Aug. 5, '97	2324	5124, 5125
1026(a)	6103(k)	IRS authorized to disclose return information when levying on certain federal payments	Levies issued after Aug. 5, '97	2331	5126

2,922

Act §	Code §	Topic	Generally effective date	Analysis ¶	Com Rep ¶
1026(b)(1)(A)	6103(p)(3)(A)	IRS authorized to disclose return information when levying on certain federal payments	Levies issued after Aug. 5, '97	2331	5126
1026(b)(1)(B)	6103(p)(4)	IRS authorized to disclose return information when levying on certain federal payments	Levies issued after Aug. 5, '97	2331	5126
1027(a)	6034A(c)	Estate and trust beneficiaries must report items in manner consistent with estate or trust return or notify IRS of inconsistency	Returns of beneficiaries and owners filed after Aug. 5, '97	2304	5127
1027(b)	6048(d)	Estate and trust beneficiaries must report items in manner consistent with estate or trust return or notify IRS of inconsistency	Returns of beneficiaries and owners filed after Aug. 5, '97	2304	5127
1028(a)	6111(d)	Tax shelter registration requirements extended to certain "confidential corporate tax shelters"	Tax shelter interests offered after IRS issues guidance	2318	5128
1028(a)	6111(e)	Tax shelter registration requirements extended to certain "confidential corporate tax shelters"	Tax shelter interests offered after IRS issues guidance	2318	5128
1028(b)	6707(a)	Tax shelter registration requirements extended to certain "confidential corporate tax shelters"	Tax shelter interests offered after IRS issues guidance	2318	5128
1028(c)(1)	6662(d)(2)(B)	Substantial understatement penalty modified	Transactions entered into after Aug. 5, '97	2412	5128
1028(c)(2)	6662(d)(2)(C)(iii)	Substantial understatement penalty modified	Transactions entered into after Aug. 5, '97	2412	5128
1031(a)(1)	4091(b)(3)(A)(ii)	Airport and airway trust fund taxes extended through Sept. 30, 2007	Oct. 1, '97	2201	5129
1031(a)(2)	4081(d)(2)(B)	Airport and airway trust fund taxes extended through Sept. 30, 2007	Oct. 1, '97	2201	5129

Act §	Code §	Topic	Generally effective date	Analysis ¶	Com Rep ¶
1031(a)(3)	4041(c)(3)(B)	Airport and airway trust fund taxes extended through Sept. 30, 2007	Oct. 1, '97	2201	5129
1031(b)(1)	4261(g)(1)(A)(ii)	Airport and airway trust fund taxes extended through Sept. 30, 2007	Oct. 1, '97	2201	5129
1031(b)(2)	4271(d)(1)(A)(ii)	Airport and airway trust fund taxes extended through Sept. 30, 2007	Oct. 1, '97	2201	5129
1031(c)(1)	4261(a)	Domestic air passenger transportation tax restructured; tax imposed on right to make mileage awards	Transportation beginning after Sept. 30, '97	2202	5129
1031(c)(1)	4261(b)	Domestic air passenger transportation tax restructured; tax imposed on right to make mileage awards	Transportation beginning after Sept. 30, '97	2202	5129
1031(c)(1)	4261(c)	Air passenger tax on international departures increased; international arrivals taxed	Transportation beginning after Sept. 30, '97	2203	5129
1031(c)(2)	4261(e)	Domestic air passenger transportation tax restructured; tax imposed on right to make mileage awards	Transportation beginning after Sept. 30, '97	2202	5129
1031(c)(2)	4261(e)(4)	Air passenger tax on international departures increased; international arrivals taxed	Transportation beginning after Sept. 30, '97	2203	5129
1031(c)(3)	4263(c)	Air carriers made secondarily liable for passenger air transportation taxes; due date for certain deposits of passenger and property air transportation taxes delayed	Transportation beginning after Sept. 30, '97	2204	5129
1031(g)	6302	Air carriers made secondarily liable for passenger air transportation taxes; due date for certain deposits of passenger and property air transportation taxes delayed	Transportation beginning after Sept. 30, '97	2204	5129
1032(a)	4083(a)	Diesel fuel removal-at-terminal excise tax rules generally made applicable to kerosene	July 1, '98	2208	5130
1032(b)	4081(a)(2)(A)(iii)	Diesel fuel removal-at-terminal excise tax rules generally made applicable to kerosene	July 1, '98	2208	5130

Act §	Code §	Topic	Generally effective date	Analysis ¶	Com Rep ¶
1032(c)(1) and 1032(c)(2)	4082	Diesel fuel removal-at-terminal excise tax rules generally made applicable to kerosene	July 1, '98	2208	5130
1032(c)(3)	6427(l)	Diesel fuel removal-at-terminal excise tax rules generally made applicable to kerosene	July 1, '98	2208	5130
1032(c)(3)(E)	6427(i)(5)(A)(i)	Diesel fuel removal-at-terminal excise tax rules generally made applicable to kerosene	July 1, '98	2208	5130
1032(d)	4101(e)	Diesel fuel removal-at-terminal excise tax rules generally made applicable to kerosene	July 1, '98	2208	5130
1032(e)(4)	4083(b)	Diesel fuel removal-at-terminal excise tax rules generally made applicable to kerosene	July 1, '98	2208	5130
1032(e)(7) and 1032(e)(8)	6427(f)	Diesel fuel removal-at-terminal excise tax rules generally made applicable to kerosene	July 1, '98	2208	5130
1032(e)(9)	6427(i)(3)(A)	Diesel fuel removal-at-terminal excise tax rules generally made applicable to kerosene	July 1, '98	2208	5130
1032(e)(11)	6715(c)(1)	Diesel fuel removal-at-terminal excise tax rules generally made applicable to kerosene	July 1, '98	2208	5130
1032(e)(12)(A)	7232	Diesel fuel removal-at-terminal excise tax rules generally made applicable to kerosene	July 1, '98	2208	5130
1032(g)	None	Floor stocks tax imposed on kerosene held on July 1, '98	July 1, '98	2209	5130
1033	4081(d)(3)	Leaking underground storage tank trust fund financing tax reimposed	Oct. 1, '97	2211	5131
1034(a)	4251(d)	Prepaid telephone cards and similar arrangements are subject to communications excise tax	Amounts paid in calendar months beginning more than 60 days after Aug. 5, '97	2207	5132
1035	3301	FUTA surtax extended through 2007	For labor performed on or after Jan. 1, '99	1905	5133
1041	512(b)(13)	UBTI rules apply to second-tier subsidiaries; control test changed	Aug. 5, '97	1302	5141

Act §	Code §	Topic	Generally effective date	Analysis ¶	Com Rep ¶
1042	None	Grandfather rule with respect to pension business of TIAA-CREF and Mutual of America is repealed	Tax years beginning after '97	937	5142
1051(a)(1)	954(c)(1)(F)	Definition of foreign personal holding company income expanded	Tax years starting after Aug. 5, '97	1609	5143
1051(a)(1)	954(c)(1)(G)	Definition of foreign personal holding company income expanded	Tax years starting after Aug. 5, '97	1609	5143
1051(a)(2)	954(c)(1)(B)	Definition of foreign personal holding company income expanded	Tax years starting after Aug. 5, '97	1609	5143
1051(b)	954(c)(2)(C)	Definition of foreign personal holding company income expanded	Tax years starting after Aug. 5, '97	1609	5143
1052(a)	1031(h)(2)	Personal property used predominantly in the U.S. is treated as not property of a like-kind with respect to personal property used predominantly outside the U.S. for purposes of the like-kind exchange rules	Transfers after June 8, '97, in tax years ending after June 8, '97	209	5144
1053(a)	901(k)	Holding period requirement for certain foreign taxes	Dividends paid or accrued more than 30 days after Aug. 5, '97.	1604	5145
1053(b)	853(c)	Holding period requirement for certain foreign taxes	Dividends paid or accrued more than 30 days after Aug. 5, '97.	1604	5145
1054	894(c)	Treaty benefits denied for certain payments through hybrid entities	Aug. 5, '97	1625	5146
1055(a)	6601(d)(2)	Interest accrual period with respect to tax underpayment not reduced by foreign tax credit carryback	Foreign tax credit carrybacks arising in tax years beginning after Aug. 5, '97	2402	5147

Act §	Code §	Topic	Generally effective date	Analysis ¶	Com Rep ¶
1055(b)(1)	6611(f)(2)	Interest accrual period with respect to tax underpayment not reduced by foreign tax credit carryback	Foreign tax credit carrybacks arising in tax years beginning after Aug. 5, '97	2402	5147
1055(b)(2)	6611(f)(4)(B)(ii)(II)	Interest accrual period with respect to tax underpayment not reduced by foreign tax credit carryback	Foreign tax credit carrybacks arising in tax years beginning after Aug. 5, '97	2402	5147
1056(a)	6511(d)(3)(A)	Limitations period on refund claim attributable to foreign tax credit begins on due date of return for year in which foreign taxes were paid or accrued	Taxes paid or accrued in tax years beginning after Aug. 5, '97	2323	5148
1057(a)	59(a)(2)(C)	Exception for certain domestic corporations from limitation on use of foreign tax credits to reduce alternative minimum tax is repealed	Tax years beginning after Aug. 5, '97	609	5149
1061	732(c)	Allocation of basis among properties distributed by partnerships	Partnership distributions after Aug. 5, '97	1422	5150
1062(a)	751(a)(2)	Allocation of basis among properties distributed by partnerships	Partnership sales, exchanges, and distributions after Aug. 5, '97.	1422	5151
1062(b)(1)(A)	751(b)(1)	Allocation of basis among properties distributed by partnerships	Partnership sales, exchanges, and distributions after Aug. 5, '97.	1422	5151
1063(a)	704(c)(1)(B)	Seven-year period for taxing pre-contribution gain or loss	Property contributed to a partnership after June 8, '97	1424	5152

Act §	Code §	Topic	Generally effective date	Analysis ¶	Com Rep ¶
1063(a)	737(b)(1)	Seven-year period for taxing pre-contribution gain or loss	Property contributed to a partnership after June 8, '97	1424	5152
1071(a)(1)	411(a)(11)(A)	Maximum involuntary pension "cash-out" amount increased from $3,500 to $5,000	Plan years beginning after Aug. 5, '97	902	5153
1071(a)(2)	417(e)	Maximum involuntary pension "cash-out" amount increased from $3,500 to $5,000	Plan years beginning after Aug. 5, '97	902	5153
1071(a)(2)	457(e)(9)	Maximum involuntary pension "cash-out" amount increased from $3,500 to $5,000	Plan years beginning after Aug. 5, '97	902	5153
1072(a)	132(f)(4)	Election to receive taxable cash compensation in place of nontaxable parking benefits	Tax years beginning after Dec. 31, '97	1003	5154
1073(a)	4980A	Repeal of excess distribution and excess retirement accumulation tax	After Dec. 31, '96	907	5155
1074(a)	4975(a)	First-tier excise tax on prohibited transactions increased from 10% to 15%	For prohibited transactions after Aug. 5, '97	908	5156
1075(a)	72(d)(1)(B)(iv)	Separate table provided for figuring basis recovery for annuities based on more than one life	Annuity starting dates beginning after '97	903	5157
1075(b)	72(d)(1)(B)(iii)	Separate table provided for figuring basis recovery for annuities based on more than one life	Annuity starting dates beginning after '97	903	5157
1081	447(i)(3)	Suspense accounts prohibited for family corporations required to change to the accrual method of accounting for farming income	Tax years ending after June 8, '97	2104	5158
1081	447(i)(4)	Suspense accounts prohibited for family corporations required to change to the accrual method of accounting for farming income	Tax years ending after June 8, '97	2104	5158

Act §	Code §	Topic	Generally effective date	Analysis ¶	Com Rep ¶
1081	447(i)(5)	Suspense accounts prohibited for family corporations required to change to the accrual method of accounting for farming income	Tax years ending after June 8, '97	2104	5158
1082(a)	172(b)(1)(A)	NOL carryback period reduced from three to two years; carryforward period extended from 15 to 20 years	Tax years beginning after Aug. 5, '97	1510	5159
1082(b)	172(b)(1)(F)	NOL carryback period reduced from three to two years; carryforward period extended from 15 to 20 years	Tax years beginning after Aug. 5, '97	1510	5159
1083(a)	39(a)	Carryback period for unused business credits reduced from 3 years to 1; carryforward period extended from 15 years to 20	Credits arising in tax years beginning after Dec. 31, '97	701	5160
1084(a)(1)	264(a)(1)	Rules disallowing premium and interest deductions on life insurance of officers and employees extended to life insurance on debtors and others	Contracts issued after June 8, '97	710	5161
1084(a)(2)	264(b)	Rules disallowing premium and interest deductions on life insurance of officers and employees extended to life insurance on debtors and others	Contracts issued after June 8, '97	710	5161
1084(a)(2)	264(d)	"Applicable period" changed for interest-rate cap rules on pre-'86 key person life insurance contracts	Interest paid or accrued after Oct. 13, '95	715	5376
1084(a)(2)	264(d)	For company-owned life insurance (COLI) rules, noncorporate "key person" definition clarified to refer to taxpayer, not employer	Interest paid or accrued after Oct. 13, '95	712	5377
1084(b)(1)	264(a)(4)	Rules disallowing premium and interest deductions on life insurance of officers and employees extended to life insurance on debtors and others	Contracts issued after June 8, '97	710	5161

Act §	Code §	Topic	Generally effective date	Analysis ¶	Com Rep ¶
1084(b)(2)	101(a)(2)	Nondeductible interest on transferred company-owned life insurance policies taken into account in determining amount of excludible death benefits under those policies	Contracts issued after June 8, '97	711	5161
1084(c)	264(f)	No deduction for interest allocable to unborrowed policy cash values ("inside build-up") on life insurance contracts	Contracts issued after June 8, '97	708	5161
1085(a)(1)	32(k)	No earned income credit allowed for ten years for taxpayers who fraudulently claimed credit (two years for taxpayers who recklessly claimed credit)	Tax years beginning after Dec. 31 '96	108	5162
1085(a)(2)	6695(g)	$100 penalty for lack of due diligence by preparers of returns claiming earned income credit	Tax years beginning after Dec. 31 '96.	2410	5162
1085(a)(3)	6213(g)(2)(J)	No earned income credit allowed for ten years for taxpayers who fraudulently claimed credit (two years for taxpayers who recklessly claimed credit)	Tax years beginning after Dec. 31 '96	108	5162
1085(b)	32(c)(5)(B)(iv)	Definition of AGI for phasing out the earned income credit is modified by increasing the percentage of certain losses disregarded from 50% to 75%, and adding tax-exempt interest and nontaxable pension and annuity distributions	Tax years beginning after Dec. 31, '97	109	5162
1085(c)	32(c)(2)(B)(v)	Workfare payments not included in earned income for earned income credit purposes	Tax years beginning after Dec. 31, '97	110	5162
1085(d)(3)	32(c)(5)(B)(v)	Definition of AGI for phasing out the earned income credit is modified by increasing the percentage of certain losses disregarded from 50% to 75%, and adding tax-exempt interest and nontaxable pension and annuity distributions	Tax years beginning after Dec. 31, '97	109	5162

Act §	Code §	Topic	Generally effective date	Analysis ¶	Com Rep ¶
1085(d)(3)	32(c)(5)(B)(vi)	Definition of AGI for phasing out the earned income credit is modified by increasing the percentage of certain losses disregarded from 50% to 75%, and adding tax-exempt interest and nontaxable pension and annuity distributions	Tax years beginning after Dec. 31, '97	109	5162
1085(d)(4)	32(c)(5)(B)	Definition of AGI for phasing out the earned income credit is modified by increasing the percentage of certain losses disregarded from 50% to 75%, and adding tax-exempt interest and nontaxable pension and annuity distributions	Tax years beginning after Dec. 31, '97	109	5162
1086(a)	167(g)(6)	Property qualifying for the income forecast method of depreciation is limited; rent-to-own consumer durables are ineligible	Property placed in service after Aug. 5, '97	801	5163
1086(b)(1)	168(3(A)(iii)	Qualified rent-to-own property is designated as MACRS 3-year property with a 4-year class life	Property placed in service after Aug. 5, '97	803	5163
1086(b)(2)	168(g)(3)(B)	Qualified rent-to-own property is designated as MACRS 3-year property with a 4-year class life	Property placed in service after Aug. 5, '97	803	5163
1086(b)(3)	168(i)(14)	Qualified rent-to-own property is designated as MACRS 3-year property with a 4-year class life	Property placed in service after Aug. 5, '97	803	5163
1087(a)	1033(i)	Involuntary conversion nonrecognition rules exception for replacement property acquired from a related party is expanded to cover all taxpayers	Involuntary conversions occurring after June 8, '97	207	5164
1088(a)	None	Repeal of exception to the installment sale rules for sales of property by a manufacturer to a dealer	Tax years beginning more than one year after Aug. 5, '97	2002	5165

Act §	Code §	Topic	Generally effective date	Analysis ¶	Com Rep ¶
1089	664(d)	Limitation on charitable remainder trust (CRT) eligibility for trusts with greater than 50% payout and less than 10% charitable remainder	For transfers in trust after June 18, '97	532	5166
1089(b)(3)	2055(e)(3)(J)	Limitation on charitable remainder trust (CRT) eligibility for trusts with greater than 50% payout and less than 10% charitable remainder	For transfers in trust after June 18, '97	532	5166
1091(a)	6654(d)(1)(C)(i)	Estimated tax 110%-of-prior-year's-tax safe harbor for high income individuals changed to 100% for '98, 105% for '99–2001, 112% for 2002	Tax years ending after Dec. 31, '97	1803	5168
1101(a)	904(j)	Certain individuals exempt from foreign tax credit limitation	Tax years starting after Dec. 31, '97.	1602	5170
1102(a)(1)	986(a)	Translation of foreign taxes simplified	Tax years starting after Dec. 31, '97.	1605	5171
1102(a)(2)	905(c)	Translation of foreign taxes simplified	Tax years starting after Dec. 31, '97.	1605	5171
1102(b)(1)	986(a)(3)	Translation of foreign taxes simplified	Tax years starting after Dec. 31, '97.	1605	5171
1102(b)(2)	989(c)(6)	Translation of foreign taxes simplified	Tax years starting after Dec. 31, '97.	1605	5171
1103(a)	59(a)(3)	Simplified foreign tax credit limitation may be elected for alternative minimum tax purposes	Tax years beginning after Dec. 31, '97	608	5172
1104(a)	988(e)	Simplification of treatment of personal transactions in foreign currency	Tax years starting after Dec. 31, '97.	1623	5173
1105(a)(1)	904(d)(1)(E)	Certain individuals exempt from foreign tax credit limitation	Tax years beginning after Dec. 31, 2002.	1602	5174
1105(a)(2)	904(d)(2)(E)	Certain individuals exempt from foreign tax credit limitation	Tax years beginning after Dec. 31, 2002.	1602	5174

Act §	Code §	Topic	Generally effective date	Analysis ¶	Com Rep ¶
1105(a)(3)	904(d)(2)(C)(iii)(II)	Certain individuals exempt from foreign tax credit limitation	Tax years beginning after Dec. 31, 2002.	1602	5174
1105(a)(3)	904(d)(2)(D)	Certain individuals exempt from foreign tax credit limitation	Tax years beginning after Dec. 31, 2002.	1602	5174
1105(b)	904(d)(4)	Certain individuals exempt from foreign tax credit limitation	Tax years beginning after Dec. 31, 2002.	1602	5174
1111(a)	964(e)	Gain on certain stock sales by CFCs treated as dividends	Aug. 5, '97	1612	5175
1111(b)	904(d)(2)(E)(i)	Gain on certain stock sales by CFCs treated as dividends	Aug. 5, '97	1612	5175
1112(a)	951(a)(2)	Gain on certain stock sales by CFCs treated as dividends	Dispositions after Aug. 5, '97	1612	5175
1112(b)	961(c)	Adjustments to basis of stock in lower-tier CFCs	Tax years beginning after Dec. 31, '97	1614	5175
1112(c)	952(b)	Treatment of exemptions from branch profits tax clarified	Tax years beginning after Dec. 31, '86	1615	5175
1113(a)	902(b)	Indirect foreign tax credit extended to sixth-tier corporations	Tax years beginning after Aug. 5, '97	1601	5175
1113(b)	960(a)(1)	Indirect foreign tax credit extended to sixth-tier corporations	Tax years beginning after Aug. 5, '97	1601	5175
1121	1296(e)	10% U.S. shareholders of a CFC are not subject to PFIC rules	Tax years of U.S. persons beginning after Dec. 31, '97.	1617	5178
1122(a)	1296	Mark-to-market election for PFIC stock	Tax years of U.S. persons beginning after Dec. 31, '97 and tax years of foreign corporations ending with or within such tax years of U.S. persons.	1618	5178

Act §	Code §	Topic	Generally effective date	Analysis ¶	Com Rep ¶
1123(a)	1297(e)	Valuation of assets for passive foreign investment company determination	Tax years of U.S. persons beginning after Dec. 31. '97.	1619	5178
1131(a)	1491	Transfer of property to foreign estate, trust, corporation or partnership triggers gain; excise tax on transfers to foreign entities repealed	Aug. 5, '97	1629	5182
1131(a)	1492	Transfer of property to foreign estate, trust, corporation or partnership triggers gain; excise tax on transfers to foreign entities repealed	Aug. 5, '97	1629	5182
1131(a)	1494	Transfer of property to foreign estate, trust, corporation or partnership triggers gain; excise tax on transfers to foreign entities repealed	Aug. 5, '97	1629	5182
1131(b)	684	Transfer of property to foreign estate, trust, corporation or partnership triggers gain; excise tax on transfers to foreign entities repealed	Aug. 5, '97	1629	5182
1131(b)(1)	1035(c)	Transfer of property to foreign estate, trust, corporation or partnership triggers gain; excise tax on transfers to foreign entities repealed	Aug. 5, '97	1629	5182
1131(b)(4)	367(d)(2)	U.S. source treatment of deemed royalties repealed	Aug. 5, '97	1630	5182
1131(b)(5)	367(d)(3)	U.S. source treatment of deemed royalties repealed	Aug. 5, '97	1630	5182
1131(b)(5)	721(d)	U.S. source treatment of deemed royalties repealed	Aug. 5, '97	1630	5182
1131(c)	1057	Transfer of property to foreign estate, trust, corporation or partnership triggers gain; excise tax on transfers to foreign entities repealed	Aug. 5, '97	1629	5182
1141(a)	6031(e)	Return requirements of foreign partnerships clarified	Tax years beginning after Aug. 5, '97	2303	5182
1141(b)	6231(f)	Deductions denied to partners of nonfiling partnerships with non-U.S. tax matters partner or books kept outside U.S.	Tax years beginning after Aug. 5, '97	1421	5182

Act §	Code §	Topic	Generally effective date	Analysis ¶	Com Rep ¶
1142(a)	6038(a)(1)	U.S. partners that control foreign partnerships subject to information reporting	Annual accounting periods beginning after Aug. 5, '97	2312	5182
1142(b)	6038(e)	U.S. partners that control foreign partnerships subject to information reporting	Annual accounting periods beginning after Aug. 5, '97	2312	5182
1142(c)	6038(b)	U.S. partners that control foreign partnerships subject to information reporting	Annual accounting periods beginning after Aug. 5, '97	2312	5182
1142(d)	6038(a)(5)	U.S. partners that control foreign partnerships subject to information reporting	Annual accounting periods beginning after Aug. 5, '97	2312	5182
1143(a)(1)	6046A(a)	Change of interest in foreign partnership need not be reported unless change involves 10% interest	Transfers and changes after Aug. 5, '97	2313	5182
1143(a)(2)	6046A(d)	Change of interest in foreign partnership need not be reported unless change involves 10% interest	Transfers and changes after Aug. 5, '97	2313	5182
1143(b)	6679(a)	Penalty for failure to file certain information returns relating to foreign partnerships and corporations increased from $1,000 to $10,000; additional penalties imposed on continuing failures	Transfers and changes after Aug. 5, '97	2411	5185
1144(a)	6038B(a)(1)	U.S. persons must report contributions to foreign partnerships	Transfers made after Aug. 5, '97	2315	5186
1144(b)	6038B(b)	U.S. persons must report contributions to foreign partnerships	Transfers made after Aug. 5, '97	2315	5186
1144(c)(1)	6038B(b)(1)	U.S. persons must report contributions to foreign partnerships	Transfers made after Aug. 5, '97	2315	5186
1144(c)(2)	6038B(b)(3)	U.S. persons must report contributions to foreign partnerships	Transfers made after Aug. 5, '97	2315	5186

Act §	Code §	Topic	Generally effective date	Analysis ¶	Com Rep ¶
1145(a)	6501(c)(8)	Assessment limitations period stays open where information returns aren't filed with respect to certain foreign transactions	Information returns due after Aug. 5, '97	2320	5187
1146(a)	6046(a)	Reporting threshold for stock ownership in a foreign corporation increased from 5% to 10%	Jan. 1, '98	2314	5188
1151(a)	7701(a)(4)	IRS regs can treat a domestic partnership as a foreign partnership	For partnerships created after regulations are filed or a notice published	1426	5182
1161(a)	7701(a)(30)(E)	IRS regs can allow nongrantor trusts to elect to continue to be U.S. trusts despite '96 Act provision that would treat them as foreign	Tax years beginning after Dec. 31, '96	529	5190
1162(a)	864(b)(2)(A)(ii)	Simplification of the stock and securities trading safe harbor for foreign corporations	Tax years starting after Dec. 31, '97	1620	5191
1163(a)	902(c)(2)(B)	Clarification of determination of foreign taxes deemed paid	Aug. 5, '97	1606	5192
1163(b)	904(d)(2)(C)(i)(II)	Clarification of foreign tax credit limitation for financial services income	Aug. 5, '97	1607	5192
1171	927(a)(2)(B)	FSC export property treatment extended to computer software licensed for reproduction abroad	Gross receipts attributable to periods after Dec. 31, '97, in tax years ending after that date.	1621	5193
1172	911(b)(2)	Increase in dollar limitation on foreign earned income exclusion	Tax years starting after Dec. 31, '97.	1622	5194

Act §	Code §	Topic	Generally effective date	Analysis ¶	Com Rep ¶
1173(a)	956(c)(2)	U.S. property does not include certain assets acquired by a dealer in securities or commodities in the ordinary course of a trade or business	Tax years of foreign corporations beginning after Dec. 31, '97, and to tax years of U.S. shareholders with or within which such tax years of foreign corporations end.	1611	5195
1174(a)(1)	861(a)(3)	Nonresident alien crew member's income not U.S. source income	Tax years beginning after Dec. 31, '97	1624	5196
1174(a)(2)	863(c)(2)(B)	Nonresident alien crew member's income not U.S. source income	Tax years beginning after Dec. 31, '97	1624	5196
1174(b)	7701(b)(7)(D)	Nonresident alien crew member's income not U.S. source income	Tax years beginning after Dec. 31, '97	1624	5196
1175(a)	954(h)	Temporary exception from foreign personal holding company income for active financing income	Tax years of foreign corporations beginning after Dec. 31, '97 and before Jan. 1, '99, and tax years of U.S. shareholders with or within such tax years of foreign corporations end.	1610	5197

Act §	Code §	Topic	Generally effective date	Analysis ¶	Com Rep ¶
1175(b)	954(e)(2)	Temporary exception from foreign personal holding company income for active financing income	Tax years of foreign corporations beginning after Dec. 31, '97 and before Jan. 1, '99, and tax years of U.S. shareholders with or within such tax years of foreign corporations end.	1610	5197
1201(a)(1)	63(c)(5)	Limit on basic standard deduction for certain dependents increased from greater of $500 (indexed) or earned income to greater of $500 (indexed) or earned income plus $250 (indexed)	Tax years beginning after Dec. 31, '97	113	5201
1201(a)(2)	63(c)(4)	Limit on basic standard deduction for certain dependents increased from greater of $500 (indexed) or earned income to greater of $500 (indexed) or earned income plus $250 (indexed)	Tax years beginning after Dec. 31, '97	113	5201
1201(b)(1)	59(j)	Limit on AMT exemption for under-age-14 child increased from sum of earned income plus twice the $500 limit on basic standard deduction to sum of earned income plus $5,000; limit on child's AMT repealed	Tax years beginning after Dec. 31, '97	604	5201
1201(b)(2)	6103(e)(1)(A)(iv)	Limit on AMT exemption for under-age-14 child increased from sum of earned income plus twice the $500 limit on basic standard deduction to sum of earned income plus $5,000; limit on child's AMT repealed	Tax years beginning after Dec. 31, '97	604	5201
1202(a)	6654(e)(1)	Increase in de minimis threshold for individuals' estimated taxes	Tax years beginning after Dec. 31, '97	1802	5202

Act §	Code §	Topic	Generally effective date	Analysis ¶	Com Rep ¶
1203(a)	162(o)	Rural mail carriers can exclude full equipment maintenance allowance; 150% standard mileage rate deduction repealed	For tax years beginning after Dec. 31, '97	105	5203
1204(a)	162(a)	One-year limit on away-from-home travel expenses doesn't apply to certified federal investigators	For amounts paid or incurred for tax years ending after Aug. 5, '97	115	5204
1205(a)	6311	Methods by which taxes may be paid expanded	Nine months after Aug. 5, '97	2319	5205
1205(c)(1)	6103(k)(8)	Methods by which taxes may be paid expanded	Nine months after Aug. 5, '97	2319	5205
1205(c)(2)	7431(g)	Methods by which taxes may be paid expanded	Nine months after Aug. 5, '97	2319	5205
1205(c)(3)	6103(p)(3)(A)	Methods by which taxes may be paid expanded	Nine months after Aug. 5, '97	2319	5205
1211(a)	460(b)(6)	Look-back method as applied to long-term contracts isn't required in de minimis situations	Contracts completed in tax years ending after Aug. 5, '97	2003	5206
1211(b)(1)	460(b)(2)(C)	Interest calculation changed in the look-back methods used in long-term contract accounting and in income forecast depreciation	For long-term contract accounting, contracts completed in tax years ending after Aug. 5, '97. For income forecast depreciation, property placed in service after Sept. 13, '95	2004	5206

Act §	Code §	Topic	Generally effective date	Analysis ¶	Com Rep ¶
1211(b)(2)	460(b)(7)	Interest calculation changed in the look-back methods used in long-term contract accounting and in income forecast depreciation	For long-term contract accounting, contracts completed in tax years ending after Aug. 5, '97. For income forecast depreciation, property placed in service after Sept. 13, '95	2004	5206
1212(a)	56(g)(4)(B)(i)	Property and casualty insurance companies electing to be taxed only on taxable investment income compute ACE for AMT purposes without regard to underwriting income or expenses	Tax years beginning after Dec. 31, '97	611	5207
1213(a)	110	Income exclusion of construction allowances received by lessees for qualified lessee construction related to short-term leases of retail space	Leases entered into after Aug. 5, '97	2702	5208
1213(b)	6724(d)(1)(A)(ix)	Income exclusion of construction allowances received by lessees for qualified lessee construction related to short-term leases of retail space	Leases entered into after Aug. 5, '97	2702	5208
1221(a)	771	Simplified flow-through for electing large partnerships	Partnership tax years beginning after Dec. 31, '97	1401	5209
1221(a)	772	Simplified flow-through for electing large partnerships	Partnership tax years beginning after Dec. 31, '97	1401	5209
1221(a)	773	Simplified flow-through for electing large partnerships	Partnership tax years beginning after Dec. 31, '97	1401	5209
1221(a)	774	Simplified flow-through for electing large partnerships	Partnership tax years beginning after Dec. 31, '97	1401	5209

Act §	Code §	Topic	Generally effective date	Analysis ¶	Com Rep ¶
1221(a)	775	Simplified flow-through for electing large partnerships	Partnership tax years beginning after Dec. 31, '97	1401	5209
1221(a)	775(a)	Consistency rules and audit procedures for electing large partnerships	Partnership tax years ending after Dec. 30, '97	1402	5210
1221(a)	776	Simplified flow-through for electing large partnerships	Partnership tax years beginning after Dec. 31, '97	1401	5209
1221(a)	777	Simplified flow-through for electing large partnerships	Partnership tax years beginning after Dec. 31, '97	1401	5209
1222(a)	6240	Consistency rules and audit procedures for electing large partnerships	Partnership tax years ending after Dec. 30, '97	1402	5210
1222(a)	6241	Consistency rules for electing large partnerships	Partnership tax years ending after Dec. 30, '97	1403	5210
1222(a)	6242	Procedures for taking partnership adjustments into account under the electing large partnership audit procedures	Partnership tax years ending after Dec. 30, '97	1405	5210
1222(a)	6245	Partnership-level adjustments under the electing large partnership audit procedures	Partnership tax years ending after Dec. 30, '97	1404	5210
1222(a)	6246	Partnership-level adjustments under the electing large partnership audit procedures	Partnership tax years ending after Dec. 30, '97	1404	5210
1222(a)	6247	Partnership-level adjustments under the electing large partnership audit procedures	Partnership tax years ending after Dec. 30, '97	1404	5210
1222(a)	6248	Partnership-level adjustments under the electing large partnership audit procedures	Partnership tax years ending after Dec. 30, '97	1404	5210
1222(a)	6251	Partnership-level adjustments under the electing large partnership audit procedures	Partnership tax years ending after Dec. 30, '97	1404	5210

Act §	Code §	Topic	Generally effective date	Analysis ¶	Com Rep ¶
1222(a)	6252	Partnership-level adjustments under the electing large partnership audit procedures	Partnership tax years ending after Dec. 30, '97	1404	5210
1222(a)	6255(a)	Consistency rules and audit procedures for electing large partnerships	Partnership tax years ending after Dec. 30, '97	1402	5210
1222(a)	6255(b)	Partnership-level adjustments under the electing large partnership audit procedures	Partnership tax years ending after Dec. 30, '97	1404	5210
1222(a)	6255(c)	Partnership-level adjustments under the electing large partnership audit procedures	Partnership tax years ending after Dec. 30, '97	1404	5210
1222(a)	6255(d)	Procedures for taking partnership adjustments into account under the electing large partnership audit procedures	Partnership tax years ending after Dec. 30, '97	1405	5210
1222(a)	6255(e)	Partnership-level adjustments under the electing large partnership audit procedures	Partnership tax years ending after Dec. 30, '97	1404	5210
1222(a)	6255(f)	Partnership-level adjustments under the electing large partnership audit procedures	Partnership tax years ending after Dec. 30, '97	1404	5210
1222(a)	6255(g)	Consistency rules and audit procedures for electing large partnerships	Partnership tax years ending after Dec. 30, '97	1402	5210
1222(b)(2)	7459(c)	Partnership-level adjustments under the electing large partnership audit procedures	Partnership tax years ending after Dec. 30, '97	1404	5210
1222(b)(3)	7482(b)(1)(E)	Partnership-level adjustments under the electing large partnership audit procedures	Partnership tax years ending after Dec. 30, '97	1404	5210
1222(b)(4)	7485(b)	Partnership-level adjustments under the electing large partnership audit procedures	Partnership tax years ending after Dec. 30, '97	1404	5210
1223(a)	6031(b)	Electing large partnerships must file K-1s by Mar. 15	Partnership tax years ending after Dec. 30, '97	2302	5211

Act §	Code §	Topic	Generally effective date	Analysis ¶	Com Rep ¶
1223(b)	6724(e)	Large partnerships' tax returns must be filed on magnetic media and are subject to information return reporting penalties	Partnership tax years ending after Dec. 30, '97	2301	5211, 5212
1224	6011(e)(2)	Large partnerships' tax returns must be filed on magnetic media and are subject to information return reporting penalties	Partnership tax years ending after Dec. 30, '97	2301	5211, 5212
1225	6012(b)(6)	Unrelated business income tax return requirements for IRAs liberalized	Partnership tax years ending after Dec. 30, '97	2306	5213
1231(a)	6234	New set of deficiency procedures provided for certain returns of partners that show no taxable income	Partnership tax years ending after Aug. 5, '97	1419	5215
1231(b)	6211(c)	Clarification of treatment of partnership items for purposes of computing amount of deficiency under non-partnership deficiency procedures	Partnership tax years ending after Aug. 5, '97	1420	5215
1232(a)	6231(g)	IRS can rely on partnership return in determining whether to use partnership audit procedures	Partnership tax years ending after Aug. 5, '97	1407	5216
1233(a)	6229(d)(1)	Statute of limitations for partnership proceedings suspended by untimely partnership petition and by partner's bankruptcy petition	Partnership tax years for which the partnership assessment limitations period has not expired on or before Aug. 5, '97	1411	5217
1233(b)	6229(h)	Statute of limitations for partnership proceedings suspended by untimely partnership petition and by partner's bankruptcy petition	Partnership tax years for which the partnership assessment limitations period has not expired on or before Aug. 5, '97	1411	5217

Act §	Code §	Topic	Generally effective date	Analysis ¶	Com Rep ¶
1233(c)	6229(b)	Statute of limitations for partnership proceedings suspended by untimely partnership petition and by partner's bankruptcy petition	Partnership tax years for which the partnership assessment limitations period has not expired on or before Aug. 5, '97	1411	5217
1234(a)	6231(a)(1)(B)(i)	Small partnership exception to unified partnership audit procedures expanded	Tax years ending after Aug. 5, '97	1408	5218
1235(a)	6229(f)	Partial settlements excluded from one-year limitation on assessment	Settlements entered into after Aug. 5, '97	1414	5219
1236(a)	6227(b)	Extension of assessment period automatically extends time for filing request for administrative adjustment	Partnership tax years beginning after Sept. 3, '82	1409	5220
1237(a)	6230(a)(3)	Innocent spouse relief extended to unified partnership proceedings	Partnership tax years beginning after Sept. 3, '82	1412	5221
1237(b)	6230(c)(5)	Innocent spouse relief extended to unified partnership proceedings	Partnership tax years beginning after Sept. 3, '82	1412	5221
1237(c)	6230(a)(1)	Innocent spouse relief extended to unified partnership proceedings	Partnership tax years beginning after Sept. 3, '82	1412	5221
1238(a)	6221	Certain penalties to be determined at partnership level under unified partnership audit procedures	Partnership tax years ending after Aug. 5, '97	1415	5223
1238(b)	6226(f)	Certain penalties to be determined at partnership level under unified partnership audit procedures	Partnership tax years ending after Aug. 5, '97	1415	5223
1238(b)	6230(a)	Certain penalties to be determined at partnership level under unified partnership audit procedures	Partnership tax years ending after Aug. 5, '97	1415	5223

Act §	Code §	Topic	Generally effective date	Analysis ¶	Com Rep ¶
1238(b)	6230(c)	Certain penalties to be determined at partnership level under unified partnership audit procedures	Partnership tax years ending after Aug. 5, '97	1415	5223
1238(b)(3)	6230(a)(3)	Innocent spouse relief extended to unified partnership proceedings	Partnership tax years beginning after Sept. 3, '82	1412	5221
1238(b)(3)(D)	6230(c)(5)	Innocent spouse relief extended to unified partnership proceedings	Partnership tax years beginning after Sept. 3, '82	1412	5221
1239(a)	6225(b)	Tax Court jurisdiction extended in partnership proceedings	Partnership tax years ending after Aug. 5, '97	1416	5224
1239(b)	6226(d)(1)	Tax Court jurisdiction extended in partnership proceedings	Partnership tax years ending after Aug. 5, '97	1416	5224
1239(c)(1)	6230(d)(6)	Tax Court jurisdiction extended in partnership proceedings	Partnership tax years ending after Aug. 5, '97	1416	5224
1239(c)(2)	6512(b)(3)	Tax Court jurisdiction extended in partnership proceedings	Partnership tax years ending after Aug. 5, '97	1416	5224
1239(d)(1)	7482(b)(1)(F)	Tax Court jurisdiction extended in partnership proceedings	Partnership tax years ending after Aug. 5, '97	1416	5224
1239(e)(1)	7459(c)	Tax Court jurisdiction extended in partnership proceedings	Partnership tax years ending after Aug. 5, '97	1416	5224
1240(a)	6226(b)(5)	Premature petitions for judicial review filed by notice partners or 5% groups may be treated as timely	Petitions filed after Aug. 5, '97	1418	5225
1241(a)	7485(b)	Calculation of bond amount for stay of assessment and collection pending appeal of Tax Court decision in partnership proceeding is modified	Partnership tax years beginning after Sept. 3, '82	1417	5226

2,945

Act §	Code §	Topic	Generally effective date	Analysis ¶	Com Rep ¶
1242(a)	6601(c)	Interest suspended where IRS delays notice and demand with respect to computational adjustment relating to partnership settlement	Adjustments for partnership tax years beginning after Aug. 5, '97	1413	5227
1243(a)	6227(e)	Time for filing administrative adjustment requests relating to bad debts or worthless securities extended	Partnership tax years beginning after Sept. 3, '82	1410	5228
1246(a)	760(c)(2)(A)	Partnership tax year closes with respect to interest of deceased partner	Partnership tax years beginning after Dec. 31, '97.	1425	5229
1251(a)(1)	857(a)(2)	Failure by REIT to maintain shareholder records results in monetary penalties, not disqualification	Tax years beginning after Aug. 5, '97	1703	5230
1251(a)(1)	857(a)(3)	Distributions by newly electing REITs to reduce pre-REIT earnings and profits are deemed to reduce earliest acquired earnings and profits before current earnings and profits	For tax years beginning after Aug. 5, '97	1714	5230
1251(a)(1)	857(a)(3)	Failure by REIT to maintain shareholder records results in monetary penalties, not disqualification	Tax years beginning after Aug. 5, '97	1703	5230
1251(a)(2)	857(f)	Failure by REIT to maintain shareholder records results in monetary penalties, not disqualification	Tax years beginning after Aug. 5, '97	1703	5230
1251(b)(1)	856(k)	Requirement that REIT not be closely held is met where adequate shareholder records are maintained and REIT has no knowledge to contrary	Tax years beginning after Aug. 5, '97	1704	5230
1251(b)(2)	856(a)(6)	Requirement that REIT not be closely held is met where adequate shareholder records are maintained and REIT has no knowledge to contrary	Tax years beginning after Aug. 5, '97	1704	5230
1252(a)	856(d)(2)(C)	REITs may render de minimis amount of tenant services and still treat income from property as rent	Tax years beginning after Aug. 5, '97	1705	5230

Act §	Code §	Topic	Generally effective date	Analysis ¶	Com Rep ¶
1252(b)	856(d)(7)	REITs may render de minimis amount of tenant services and still treat income from property as rent	Tax years beginning after Aug. 5, '97	1705	5230
1253	856(d)(5)	For purposes of applying the related party test or the independent contractor test to REIT rental income, the attribution rules apply to partnerships only where a partner owns 25% or more interest in the partnership	Tax years beginning after Aug. 5, '97	1713	5230
1254(a)	857(b)(3)(D)	REITs may elect to retain capital gains and pass-through to shareholders credit for capital gains taxes paid like RICs	For tax years beginning after Aug. 5, '97	1701	5230
1254(b)(1)	857(b)(7)(A)	REITs may elect to retain capital gains and pass-through to shareholders credit for capital gains taxes paid like RICs	For tax years beginning after Aug. 5, '97	1701	5230
1254(b)(2)	852(b)(3)(D)(iii)	Increase in shareholder's basis for undistributed capital gains passed through a RIC is adjusted	Tax years beginning after Aug. 5, '97	1702	5230
1255(a)(2)	856(c)(4)	Repeal of requirement that no more than 30% of REIT's gross income can be derived from sales or other dispositions	Tax years beginning after Aug. 5, '97	1709	5230
1255(a)(2)	856(c)(8)	Repeal of requirement that no more than 30% of REIT's gross income can be derived from sales or other dispositions	Tax years beginning after Aug. 5, '97	1709	5230
1255(a)(3)	856(c)	Repeal of requirement that no more than 30% of REIT's gross income can be derived from sales or other dispositions	Tax years beginning after Aug. 5, '97	1709	5230
1255(b)(1)	856(c)(6)(G)	Favorable treatment of REIT income from interest rate swaps and caps is extended to income from all types of hedging agreements	For tax years beginning after Aug. 5, '97	1708	5230

Act §	Code §	Topic	Generally effective date	Analysis ¶	Com Rep ¶
1256	857(d)(3)	Distributions by newly electing REITs to reduce pre-REIT earnings and profits are deemed to reduce earliest acquired earnings and profits before current earnings and profits	For tax years beginning after Aug. 5, '97	1714	5230
1257(a)(1)	856(e)(2)	Election by REIT to treat real estate as foreclosure property made revocable, election grace periods extended, definition of independent contractor conformed	Tax years beginning after Aug. 5, '97	1706	5230
1257(a)(2)	856(e)(3)	Election by REIT to treat real estate as foreclosure property made revocable, election grace periods extended, definition of independent contractor conformed	Tax years beginning after Aug. 5, '97	1706	5230
1257(b)	856(e)(5)	Election by REIT to treat real estate as foreclosure property made revocable, election grace periods extended, definition of independent contractor conformed	Tax years beginning after Aug. 5, '97	1706	5230
1257(c)	856(e)(4)	Election by REIT to treat real estate as foreclosure property made revocable, election grace periods extended, definition of independent contractor conformed	Tax years beginning after Aug. 5, '97	1706	5230
1258	856(c)(6)(G)	Favorable treatment of REIT income from interest rate swaps and caps is extended to income from all types of hedging agreements	For tax years beginning after Aug. 5, '97	1708	5230
1259	857(e)(2)(B)	REIT's "excess noncash income" includes coupon interest and OID under both cash and accrual methods, as well as income from debt cancellation	Tax years beginning after Aug. 5, '97	1707	5230
1259	857(e)(2)(C)	REIT's "excess noncash income" includes coupon interest and OID under both cash and accrual methods, as well as income from debt cancellation	Tax years beginning after Aug. 5, '97	1707	5230

Act §	Code §	Topic	Generally effective date	Analysis ¶	Com Rep ¶
1260	857(b)(6)(C)(iii)	REIT property that is involuntarily converted is excluded from prohibited transaction 100% tax	Tax years beginning after Aug. 5, '97	1710	5230
1261(a)	856(j)(4)	REITs provided safe harbor from prohibited transaction tax for shared appreciation mortgages disposed of under bankruptcy court jurisdiction	For tax years beginning after Aug. 5, '97	1712	5230
1261(b)	856(j)(4)(A)	REITs provided safe harbor from prohibited transaction tax for shared appreciation mortgages disposed of under bankruptcy court jurisdiction	For tax years beginning after Aug. 5, '97	1712	5230
1262	856(i)(2)	Existing corporation in which a REIT acquires a 100% ownership interest is a qualified subsidiary	Tax years beginning after Aug. 5, '97	1711	5230
1271	851(b)(3)	30% gross income limitation (short-short test) for RICs is repealed	Tax years beginning after Aug. 5, '97	1715	5247
1281(a)	6652(g)	Reasonable cause exception provided for various civil penalties	Tax years beginning after Aug. 5, '97	2406	5248
1281(b)	6652(k)	Reasonable cause exception provided for various civil penalties	Tax years beginning after Aug. 5, '97	2406	5248
1281(c)	6683	Reasonable cause exception provided for various civil penalties	Tax years beginning after Aug. 5, '97	2406	5248
1281(d)	7519(f)(4)(A)	Reasonable cause exception provided for various civil penalties	Tax years beginning after Aug. 5, '97	2406	5248
1282(a)	6512(b)(3)	Nonfilers can get Tax Court refund of overpayments paid within three years before deficiency notice	Claims for credit or refund for tax years ending after Aug. 5, '97	2326	5249
1283(a)	6103(h)(5)	Repeal of IRS authority to disclose whether prospective juror has been audited	Judicial proceedings commenced after Aug. 5, '97	2330	5250
1284(a)	6501(a)	Limitations period for passthrough items starts running with filing of taxpayer's return	Tax years beginning after Aug. 5, '97	2321	5251

Act §	Code §	Topic	Generally effective date	Analysis ¶	Com Rep ¶
1285(a)	7430(f)(3)	Taxpayers' right to seek administrative cost awards from IRS subjected to time limits	Civil actions or proceedings commenced after Aug. 5, '97	2336	5252
1285(b)	7430(b)(5)	Taxpayers' right to seek administrative cost awards from IRS subjected to time limits	Civil actions or proceedings commenced after Aug. 5, '97	2336	5252
1285(c)	7430(f)(2)	Taxpayers' right to seek administrative cost awards from IRS subjected to time limits	Civil actions or proceedings commenced after Aug. 5, '97	2336	5252
1301(a)	6019(3)	Gift tax return requirement eliminated for many charitable donations	Gifts made after Aug. 5, '97	2307	5261
1302(a)	2207A(a)(2)	Recovery right for QTIP and retained life estate property waived only if specific intent indicated	Applies to estates of decedents dying after Aug. 5, '97	513	5262
1302(b)	2207B(a)(2)	Recovery right for QTIP and retained life estate property waived only if specific intent indicated	Applies to estates of decedents dying after Aug. 5, '97	513	5262
1303	None	Trusts created before Nov. 5, '90 are treated as meeting the qualified domestic trust (QDOT) requirements if they meet the QDOT requirements that were in effect before Nov. 5, '90	Applies to estates of decedents dying after Nov. 10, '88	516	5263
1304(a)	2105(b)(4)	Certain short-term obligations held by nonresident aliens are not subject to U.S. estate tax	Applies to estates of decedents dying after Aug. 5, '97	511	5264
1305(a)	646	Election to treat revocable trust as part of estate for income and generation–skipping transfer (GST) tax purposes	For estates of decedents dying after Aug. 5, '97	526	5265

Act §	Code §	Topic	Generally effective date	Analysis ¶	Com Rep ¶
1305(b)	2652(b)(1)	Election to treat revocable trust as part of estate for income and generation–skipping transfer (GST) tax purposes	For estates of decedents dying after Aug. 5, '97	526	5265
1306	663(b)	Election to treat distributions during first 65 days of estate's tax year as made in previous tax year	For tax years beginning after Aug. 5, '97	527	5266
1307(a)	663(c)	Separate share rule is extended to estates	For estates of decedents dying after Aug. 5, '97	528	5267
1308(a)	267(b)	Estate and beneficiaries treated as related for loss and capital gain treatment on sale of depreciable property	Tax years beginning after Aug. 5, '97	211	5268
1308(b)	1239(b)	Estate and beneficiaries treated as related for loss and capital gain treatment on sale of depreciable property	Tax years beginning after Aug. 5, '97	211	5268
1309(a)	685	Election to have income of qualified funeral trust taxed to the trust	For tax years ending after Aug. 5, '97	533	5269
1310(a)	2035(e)	Annual exclusion gifts from revocable trusts within three years of grantor's death are not includible in gross estate	Applies to estates of decedents dying after Aug. 5, '97	524	5270
1311(a)	2056(b)(7)(C)	Nonparticipant spouse's community property interest in annuity qualifies as QTIP	Applies to estates of decedents dying after Aug. 5, '97	512	5271
1312(a)	2056A(c)(3)	Entities other than trusts may be eligible for qualified domestic trust (QDOT) treatment	Applies to estates of decedents dying after Aug. 5, '97	514	5272
1313(a)	2032A(d)(3)	Rules for correcting special use valuation elections eased	Applies to estates of decedents dying after Aug. 5, '97	509	5273
1314(a)	2056A(a)(1)(A)	IRS given authority to waive U.S. trustee requirement for qualified domestic trusts (QDOTs)	Estates of decedents dying after Aug. 5, '97	515	5274

Act §	Code §	Topic	Generally effective date	Analysis ¶	Com Rep ¶
1401(a)	4003(a)(3)(C)	De minimis exceptions to retail heavy truck and luxury taxes on separate purchase and installation of parts and accessories are increased	Installations on vehicles sold after Aug. 5, '97	2220	5275
1401(a)	4051(b)(2)(B)	De minimis exceptions to retail heavy truck and luxury taxes on separate purchase and installation of parts and accessories are increased	Installations on vehicles sold after Aug. 5, '97	2220	5275
1402(a)	4051(e)	Exclusion of tire value from retail heavy truck excise tax replaced by credit for manufacturers' excise tax on tires	Jan. 1, '98	2221	5276
1402(b)	4052(b)(1)(B)(iii)	Exclusion of tire value from retail heavy truck excise tax replaced by credit for manufacturers' excise tax on tires	Jan. 1, '98	2221	5276
1411(a)	5008(c)(1)	Tax-free removal of alcoholic beverages from bonded premisesand refund or credit on return to bonded premises allowed	The first day of the first calendar quarter beginning at least 180 days after Aug. 5, '97.	2227	5277
1412(a)	5175(c)	Alcoholic beverage taxes paperwork and administration eased	The first day of the first calender quarter beginning at least 180 says after Aug. 5, '97	2229	5277
1413(a)	5027(c)	Alcoholic beverage taxes paperwork and administration eased	The first day of the first calender quarter beginning at least 180 says after Aug. 5, '97	2229	5277
1414(a)	5222(b)(2)	Tax-free removal of alcoholic beverages from bonded premisesand refund or credit on return to bonded premises allowed	The first day of the first calendar quarter beginning at least 180 days after Aug. 5, '97.	2227	5277

Act §	Code §	Topic	Generally effective date	Analysis ¶	Com Rep ¶
1414(b)	5053(f)	Tax-free removal of alcoholic beverages from bonded premisesand refund or credit on return to bonded premises allowed	The first day of the first calendar quarter beginning at least 180 days after Aug. 5, '97.	2227	5277
1414(c)(1)	5056(c)	Tax-free removal of alcoholic beverages from bonded premisesand refund or credit on return to bonded premises allowed	The first day of the first calendar quarter beginning at least 180 days after Aug. 5, '97.	2227	5277
1414(c)(2)	5056(d)	Tax-free removal of alcoholic beverages from bonded premisesand refund or credit on return to bonded premises allowed	The first day of the first calendar quarter beginning at least 180 days after Aug. 5, '97.	2227	5277
1415(a)	5115	Regs on geographic appellations codified; sign-posting requirement for wholesale liquor dealers repealed; up to 60% added sugar allowed in acidic wines	various	2230	5277, 5060
1416(a)	5044(a)	Tax-free removal of alcoholic beverages from bonded premisesand refund or credit on return to bonded premises allowed	The first day of the first calendar quarter beginning at least 180 days after Aug. 5, '97.	2227	5277
1416(b)(1)	5361	Tax-free removal of alcoholic beverages from bonded premisesand refund or credit on return to bonded premises allowed	The first day of the first calendar quarter beginning at least 180 days after Aug. 5, '97.	2227	5277
1417(a)	5384(b)(2)(D)	Regs on geographic appellations codified; sign-posting requirement for wholesale liquor dealers repealed; up to 60% added sugar allowed in acidic wines	various	2230	5277, 5060

Act §	Code §	Topic	Generally effective date	Analysis ¶	Com Rep ¶
1418(a)	5053(g)	Tax-free removal of alcoholic beverages from bonded premisesand refund or credit on return to bonded premises allowed	The first day of the first calendar quarter beginning at least 180 days after Aug. 5, '97.	2227	5277
1419(a)	5053(h)	Tax-free removal of alcoholic beverages from bonded premisesand refund or credit on return to bonded premises allowed	The first day of the first calendar quarter beginning at least 180 days after Aug. 5, '97.	2227	5277
1420(a)	5055	Alcoholic beverage taxes paperwork and administration eased	The first day of the first calender quarter beginning at least 180 says after Aug. 5, '97	2229	5277
1421(a)	5418	Tax-free removal of alcoholic beverages from bonded premisesand refund or credit on return to bonded premises allowed	The first day of the first calendar quarter beginning at least 180 days after Aug. 5, '97.	2227	5277
1422(a)	5364	Tax-free removal of alcoholic beverages from bonded premisesand refund or credit on return to bonded premises allowed	The first day of the first calendar quarter beginning at least 180 days after Aug. 5, '97.	2227	5277
1431(a)	4222(b)(2)	IRS authority to waive purchaser registration requirements for excise-tax-free sales is expanded	Aug. 5, '97	2224	5289
1433(a)	4161(b)	Manufacturers' tax on completed arrows is replaced with tax on arrow's component parts	Articles sold by the manufacturer, producer or importer after Sept. 30, '97	2225	5291

Act §	Code §	Topic	Generally effective date	Analysis ¶	Com Rep ¶
1434(a)	4052(f)	Retail heavy truck tax modified for wrecked vehicle remanufacturing and resale registration requirement replaced with certification procedure	Jan. 1, '98	2222	5292
1434(b)(1)	4052(d)	Retail heavy truck tax modified for wrecked vehicle remanufacturing and resale registration requirement replaced with certification procedure	Jan. 1, '98	2222	5292
1434(b)(2)	4052(g)	Retail heavy truck tax modified for wrecked vehicle remanufacturing and resale registration requirement replaced with certification procedure	Jan. 1, '98	2222	5292
1435(a)	4261(h)	Skydiving flights are exempted from air transportation taxes; fel used in such flights taxed as fuel used in non-commercial aviation	Oct. 1, '97	2206	5293
1435(b)	4041(c)(2)	Skydiving flights are exempted from air transportation taxes; fel used in such flights taxed as fuel used in non-commercial aviation	Oct. 1, '97	2206	5293
1436(a)	4091(d)	Registered aviation fuel producers who buy and resell tax-paid fuel are allowed a refund to prevent double taxation	Fuel acquired by the producer after Sept. 30, '97	2215	5294
1436(b)	6416(d)	Registered aviation fuel producers who buy and resell tax-paid fuel are allowed a refund to prevent double taxation	Fuel acquired by the producer after Sept. 30, '97	2215	5294
1441	148(f)(4)(B)(ii)(I)	Arbitrage bond rebate requirement: repeal of $100,000 limitation on unspent proceeds under six-month spending exception; exemption for earnings on bona fide debt service funds under construction issue exception	Bonds issued after Aug. 5, '97	2504	5295, 5296

Act §	Code §	Topic	Generally effective date	Analysis ¶	Com Rep ¶
1442	148(f)(4)(C)(xvii)	Arbitrage bond rebate requirement: repeal of $100,000 limitation on unspent proceeds under six-month spending exception; exemption for earnings on bona fide debt service funds under construction issue exception	Bonds issued after Aug. 5, '97	2504	5295, 5296
1443	148(d)	Repeal of 150%-of-debt-service limit on investment in nonpurpose investments under arbitrage bond rules	Bonds issued after Aug. 5, '97	2503	5297
1444(a)	148(c)(2)(B)	Repeal as deadwood two exceptions to arbitrage rebate and temporary period pooled financing rules for qualified student loan bonds issued before '89	Bonds issued after Aug. 5, '97	2507	5298
1444(b)	148(f)(4)(E)	Repeal as deadwood two exceptions to arbitrage rebate and temporary period pooled financing rules for qualified student loan bonds issued before '89	Bonds issued after Aug. 5, '97	2507	5298
1451(a)	6512(b)(2)	Tax Court order requiring IRS to refund overpayment may be appealed; Tax Court jurisdiction over refund offset is limited	Aug. 5, '97	2325	5300
1451(b)	6512(b)(4)	Tax Court order requiring IRS to refund overpayment may be appealed; Tax Court jurisdiction over refund offset is limited	Aug. 5, '97	2325	5300
1452(a)	7481(c)	Taxpayers may motion, instead of petition, for interest redeterminations in Tax Court; Tax Court given jurisdiction over IRS interest underpayments	Aug. 5, '97	2327	5301
1453(a)	7430(c)(4)(D)	Net worth requirements for awards of litigation, etc. costs to estates, trusts, and joint return filers clarified	Proceedings commenced after Aug. 5, '97	2335	5302
1454(a)	7436	Tax Court given jurisdiction to review certain IRS determinations of employment status	Aug. 5, '97	2329	5303

Act §	Code §	Topic	Generally effective date	Analysis ¶	Com Rep ¶
1454(b)	6511(d)(7)	Special limitations period for credits or refunds for self-employment taxes resulting from Tax Court employment status cases	Aug. 5, '97	2322	5303
1454(b)(2)	7421(a)	Tax Court given jurisdiction to review certain IRS determinations of employment status	Aug. 5, '97	2329	5303
1454(b)(3)	7453	Tax Court given jurisdiction to review certain IRS determinations of employment status	Aug. 5, '97	2329	5303
1454(b)(3)	7481(b)	Tax Court given jurisdiction to review certain IRS determinations of employment status	Aug. 5, '97	2329	5303
1461(a)	6655(g)(3)	Extension of private foundation's first quarter estimated tax payment due date	For tax years beginning after Aug. 5, '97	1804	5304
1462(a)	None	Commonwealth income taxes can be withheld from federal employees' wages	Jan. 1, '98	2703	5305
1463(a)	6621(c)(2)(B)(iii)	Notices involving less than $100,000 disregarded under rule increasing interest rate on large corporate underpayments	Interest for periods after Dec. 31, '97	2403	5306
1501(a)	402(g)(9)	Matching contributions of self-employed individuals are not treated as elective employer contributions	Years beginning after Dec. 31, '97	933	5307
1501(b)	408(p)(8)	Matching contributions of self-employed individuals are not treated as elective employer contributions	Years beginning after Dec. 31, '97	933	5307
1502(b)	401(a)(13)(C)	Judgment or settlement amounts for certain participant crimes and ERISA violations may be offset against his benefits	Judgments, orders, and decrees issued, and settlements entered into, on or after Aug. 5, '97	904	5308

Act §	Code §	Topic	Generally effective date	Analysis ¶	Com Rep ¶
1503	None	ERISA plan descriptions, summary plan descriptions, and material modifications no longer filed with DOL, except on request	Aug. 5, '97	935	5309
1504(a)(1)	403(b)(3)	Exclusion allowance rules for 403(b) annuities modified to conform to earlier Code Sec. 415 changes	Years beginning after Dec. 31, '97	925	5310
1504(b)	None	Exclusion allowance rules for 403(b) annuities modified to conform to earlier Code Sec. 415 changes	Years beginning after Dec. 31, '97	925	5310
1505(a)(1)	401(a)(5)	Qualified plan nondiscrimination and minimum participation rules made permanently inapplicable to state and local governmental plans	Tax years beginning on or after Aug. 5, '97	924	5311
1505(a)(2)	401(a)(26)(H)	Qualified plan nondiscrimination and minimum participation rules made permanently inapplicable to state and local governmental plans	Tax years beginning on or after Aug. 5, '97	924	5311
1505(a)(3)	410(c)(2)	Qualified plan nondiscrimination and minimum participation rules made permanently inapplicable to state and local governmental plans	Tax years beginning on or after Aug. 5, '97	924	5311
1505(b)	401(k)(3)(G)	Qualified plan nondiscrimination and minimum participation rules made permanently inapplicable to state and local governmental plans	Tax years beginning on or after Aug. 5, '97	924	5311
1505(c)	403(b)(12)(C)	Qualified plan nondiscrimination and minimum participation rules made permanently inapplicable to state and local governmental plans	Tax years beginning on or after Aug. 5, '97	924	5311
1506(a)	409(h)(2)(B)	Certain cash distributions permitted by ESOPs maintained by S corporations	Taxable years beginning after Dec. 31, 1997	910	5312
1506(b)(1)	4975(f)(6)	Statutory exemptions from prohibited transaction rules extended to S corporations	Taxable years beginning after Dec. 31, 1997	909	5312

Act §	Code §	Topic	Generally effective date	Analysis ¶	Com Rep ¶
1507(a)	4972(c)(6)(B)	New exception to 10-percent excise tax on nondeductible contributions for contributions to 401(k) plan	Tax years after '97	911	5313
1508	None	Transitional relief for certain bus companies from some minimum funding requirements	Plan years beginning after Dec. 31, '96	928	5314
1509	None	Qualified retirement plans may receive rollovers from plans intended to have a qualified trust	Aug. 5, '97	901	5315
1510	None	Congress directs IRS and DOL to facilitate retirement plan administrators' use of electronic technologies	Aug. 5, '97	936	5316
1521(a)	412(c)(7)(A)(i)(I)	Increase in current liability funding limit and new special amortization rule	Plan years beginning after Dec. 31, '98	931	5343
1521(a)	412(c)(7)(F)	Increase in current liability funding limit and new special amortization rule	Plan years beginning after Dec. 31, '98	931	5343
1521(c)(1)	412(b)(2)(E)	Increase in current liability funding limit and new special amortization rule	Plan years beginning after Dec. 31, '98	931	5343
1522(a)(1)	414(e)(5)(C)	Exclusion of ministers from discrimination testing of non-church retirement plans is expanded	Years beginning after '97	926	5344
1522(a)(2)	415(e)(5)(E)	Contributions to church plan on behalf of self-employed minister are excluded from income	Years beginning after '97	927	5344
1523(a)	512(e)(3)	UBIT no longer applies to S corporation ESOPs	Taxable years beginning after Dec. 31, '97	912	5345
1524	None	ERISA limit on investments in employer securities applies to 401(k) plan deferrals	Plan years beginning after '98	934	5346
1525	401(k)(7)(B)(iv)	Rural irrigation and water conservation entities can have 401(k) plans	Years beginning after Dec. 31 '97	930	5347
1526(a)	415(n)	Limits on contributions for purchasing permissive service credit under governmental plans	Years beginning after Dec. 31, '97	923	5348

Act §	Code §	Topic	Generally effective date	Analysis ¶	Com Rep ¶
1526(b)	415(k)	Limits on contributions for purchasing permissive service credit under governmental plans	Years beginning after Dec. 31, '97	923	5348
1527(a)	415(b)(2)(G)	Dollar limitation on defined benefit plan payments is no longer reduced for police and firefighters whose benefits begin before age 65	Years beginning after Dec. 31, '96	922	5349
1528(a)	101(h)	Tax exemption for annuities paid to survivors of public safety officers killed in the line of duty	Amounts received in tax years beginning after Dec. 31, '96, with respect to officers dying after that date	104	5350
1529	None	Retroactive exclusion from certain retired firefighters' and police officers' income for amounts received because of heart disease or hypertension	Aug. 5, '97	1002	5351
1530(b)	664(d)	Limited transfer of qualified employer securities by charitable remainder trusts to ESOPs is permitted	Aug. 5, '97	938	5352
1530(b)	664(g)	Limited transfer of qualified employer securities by charitable remainder trusts to ESOPs is permitted	Aug. 5, '97	938	5352
1530(c)(7)	2055(a)	Limited transfer of qualified employer securities by charitable remainder trusts to ESOPs is permitted	Aug. 5, '97	938	5352
1531(a)(4)	9811	Election to receive taxable cash compensation in place of nontaxable parking benefits	Plan years beginning after Dec. 31, '97	1003	5353
1531(a)(4)	9812	Mental health benefits under group health plans to have parity with medical benefits	For plan years beginning after Dec. 31, '97	1102	5353
1532	9802(c)	Certain church health plans can discriminate based on health status	Plan years beginning after June 30, '97	929	5354

Act §	Code §	Topic	Generally effective date	Analysis ¶	Com Rep ¶
1541	None	Window period for amending plans and annuity contracts to reflect the '97 Act	Aug. 5, '97	932	5355
1601(a)(1)	6050R(c)(1)	Information return requirements for purchasers of fish for resale expanded	Payments made after Dec. 31, '97	2316	5356
1601(b)	52(c)	Work opportunity credit not allowed to tax-exempt organizations	Individuals who begin work for the employer after Sept. 30, '96	703	
1601(c)(1)	1361(e)(1)(B)(iii)	Charitable remainder trusts may not be electing small business trust shareholders	Tax years beginning after Dec. 31, '96	1506	5357
1601(c)(2)(A)	None	Effective date of '96 Act changes to post-termination transition period (PTTP) of S corporations	Determination after Dec. 31, '96	1507	5358
1601(c)(2)(B)	None	Effective date of '96 Act changes to post-termination transition period (PTTP) of S corporations	Determination after Dec. 31, '96	1507	5358
1601(c)(3)	1361(b)(3)(A)	Treatment of qualified Subchapter S subsidiaries (QSSSs) as separate corporations	Tax years beginning after Dec. 31, '96	1508	5359
1601(d)(1)(A)	408(i)	Trustees' SIMPLE IRA reports to individuals now due on Jan. 31	Tax years beginning after Dec. 31, '96	917	5361
1601(d)(1)(C)(i)	408(l)(2)(B)	Notification requirements and penalties for SIMPLE IRAs apply also to issuers of SIMPLE IRA annuities	Tax years beginning after Dec. 31, '96	916	5361
1601(d)(1)(C)(ii)	6693(c)(2)	Notification requirements and penalties for SIMPLE IRAs apply also to issuers of SIMPLE IRA annuities	Tax years beginning after Dec. 31, '96	916	5361
1601(d)(1)(D)	408((p)(8)	Maximum dollar limitation on IRA contributions conformed to allow maximum contributions to SIMPLE IRAs	Tax years beginning after Dec. 31, '96	915	5361

Act §	Code §	Topic	Generally effective date	Analysis ¶	Com Rep ¶
1601(d)(1)(E)	408(p)(2)(D)(i)	Employers that maintain a plan for collectively bargained employees can maintain a SIMPLE plan for noncollectively bargained employees	Tax years beginning after Dec. 31, '96	913	5361
1601(d)(1)(F)	408(p)2)(D)(iii)	Grace period for employers that maintain both a qualified plan and a SIMPLE plan as a result of a merger or acquisition	Tax years beginning after Dec. 31, '96	914	5361
1601(d)(2)(A)	401(k)(11)(D)(ii)	Only SIMPLE 401(k) plans are exempt from the top-heavy rules	Tax years beginning after Dec. 31, '96	921	5361
1601(d)(2)(B)	401(k)(11)(E)	Limit on contributions to SIMPLE 401(k) plans will be adjusted for changes in the cost-of-living	Tax years beginning after Dec. 31, '96	919	5361
1601(d)(2)(C)	404(a)(3)(A)	Employer contributions to SIMPLE 401(k) plans are not subject to the 15 percent limits on contributions to profit-sharing or stock bonus plans	Tax years beginning after Dec. 31, '96	918	5361
1601(d)(2)(D)	401(k)(11)(B)(iii)	Employers must provide timely notice of SIMPLE 401(k) plan elective contribution rules to eligible employees	Calendar years beginning after Aug. 5, '97	920	5361
1601(d)(4)	None	Permissible rollovers from certain 403(b) plans maintained by Indian tribal governments	Aug. 20, '96	906	5390
1601(d)(6)(A)	414(e)(5)(A)	Rules on self-employed ministers clarified	Years beginning after Dec. 31, '96	1901	5344
1601(d)(6)(B)	403(b)(1)(A)	Rules on self-employed ministers clarified	Years beginning after Dec. 31, '96	1901	5344
1601(e)	956(b)(1)(A)	Clarification of earnings and profits definition for purposes of CFC rules	Tax years of CFCs beginning after '96, and tax years of U.S. shareholders within which or with which such years end	1616	5362

Act §	Code §	Topic	Generally effective date	Analysis ¶	Com Rep ¶
1601(f)(3)(A)	4001(f)	Luxury tax on separate installation of auto parts and accessories is conformed to tax on auto sales	Sales after Aug. 5, '97	2219	5387
1601(f)(3)(B)	4001(g)	Luxury tax on separate installation of auto parts and accessories is conformed to tax on auto sales	Sales after Aug. 5, '97	2219	5387
1601(f)(4)(A)(i)	4041(l)	Exemption from air transportation of persons tax for fixed-wing aircraft used for emergency medical services applied retroactively to aviation fuel taxes; definition of fixed-wing aircraft is modified	Aug. 27, '96	2205	
1601(f)(4)(D)	4261(f)	Exemption from air transportation of persons tax for fixed-wing aircraft used for emergency medical services applied retroactively to aviation fuel taxes; definition of fixed-wing aircraft is modified	Aug. 27, '96	2205	
1601(f)(4)(F)	None	Exemption from floor stocks tax on aviation fuel held on Aug. 27, '96 is retroactively expanded	Aug. 27, '96	2216	
1601(f)(5)(A)	593(e)(1)(A)	Rules modified on recapture of bad debt reserve by thrift institutions	Tax years beginning after Dec. 31, '95	1717	5365
1601(f)(5)(B)	1374(d)(7)	Rules modified on recapture of bad debt reserve by thrift institutions	Tax years beginning after Dec. 31, '95	1717	5365
1601(f)(6)(A)	860L(b)(1)	Rules for regular interests in FASITs apply to interests issued on or after the starting date	Sep. 1, '97	1718	5366
1601(f)(6)(C)	860L(e)(2)(B)	Certain transactions exempted from FASIT prohibited transaction rules	Sep. 1, '97	1719	5366
1601(f)(6)(D)	860L(e)(3)(A)	Certain transactions exempted from FASIT prohibited transaction rules	Sep. 1, '97	1719	5366
1601(f)(6)(E)	860L(e)(3)(D)	Certain transactions exempted from FASIT prohibited transaction rules	Sep. 1, '97	1719	5366

Act §	Code §	Topic	Generally effective date	Analysis ¶	Com Rep ¶
1601(g)(1)	None	Period for claiming refund for gasoline or diesel fuel used to produce alcohol fuel for period Sept. 30, '95 through Oct. 1, '96 is extended	Jan. 1, '94	2213	
1601(h)(1)(B)	529(e)(1)(C)	Definition of "designated beneficiary" expanded for purposes of rules on qualified state tuition programs	Tax years ending after Aug. 20, '96	407	5367
1601(h)(1)(C)	None	State program under which persons may purchase tuition credits will be treated as a qualified state tuition program if it meets the qualified state tuition program requirements within a specified time period	Tax years ending after Aug. 20, '96	408	5367
1601(h)(2)(A)	23(a)(2)	Adoption expense credit allowed for expenses paid after the year adoption becomes final and conformed to exclusion for employer adoption assistance payments	Tax years beginning after Dec. 31, '96	112	5368, 5369
1601(h)(2)(B)	23(b)(2)(B)	Adoption expense credit allowed for expenses paid after the year adoption becomes final and conformed to exclusion for employer adoption assistance payments	Tax years beginning after Dec. 31, '96	112	5368, 5369
1601(h)(2)(C)	137(b)(1)	Adoption expense credit allowed for expenses paid after the year adoption becomes final and conformed to exclusion for employer adoption assistance payments	Tax years beginning after Dec. 31, '96	112	5368, 5369
1601(h)(2)(D)(i)	414(n)(3)(C)	Adoption expense credit allowed for expenses paid after the year adoption becomes final and conformed to exclusion for employer adoption assistance payments	Tax years beginning after Dec. 31, '96	112	5368, 5369
1601(h)(2)(D)(ii)	414(t)(2)	Adoption expense credit allowed for expenses paid after the year adoption becomes final and conformed to exclusion for employer adoption assistance payments	Tax years beginning after Dec. 31, '96	112	5368, 5369

Act §	Code §	Topic	Generally effective date	Analysis ¶	Com Rep ¶
1601(h)(2)(D)(iii)	6039D(d)(1)	Adoption expense credit allowed for expenses paid after the year adoption becomes final and conformed to exclusion for employer adoption assistance payments	Tax years beginning after Dec. 31, '96	112	5368, 5369
1601(i)(2)	679(a)(3)(C)	Obligations issued by owner are disregarded in determining whether transfer to foreign trust is for fair market value	Property transfers made after Feb. 6, '95	1627	5363
1601(i)(3)(A)	7701(a)(30)(E)	Definition of trust as U.S. person clarified	Tax years beginning after '96	1628	5364
1601(i)(3)(B)	641(b)	Definition of trust as U.S. person clarified	Tax years beginning after '96	1628	5364
1602(a)	220	Changes to MSA rules on coverage, distributions, and reporting requirements	Taxable years beginning after Dec. 31, '96	1202	5370
1602(a)	26(b)(2)(P)	Changes to MSA rules on coverage, distributions, and reporting requirements	Taxable years beginning after Dec. 31, '96	1202	5370
1602(a)	6693(a)	Changes to MSA rules on coverage, distributions, and reporting requirements	Taxable years beginning after Dec. 31, '96	1202	5370
1602(b)	7702B(c)(2)	Definition of "chronically ill" individual modified for qualified long-term care insurance contracts	For contracts issued after Dec. 31, '96	1105	5371
1602(c)	162(l)(2)(B)	Self-employeds can deduct long-term care premiums even if they participate in employer-provided health plan (if the plan doesn't include long-term care coverage)	Tax years beginning after Dec. 31, '96	1104	5372
1602(d)(1)	6050Q(b)(1)	Information return requirements for payors of long-term care benefits expanded	Benefits paid after Dec. 31, '96	2317	5373
1602(e)	7702B(g)(4)(B)	Long-term care insurance contract nonforfeiture provisions subject to state regulatory approval	For contracts issued after '96	1107	5374

Act §	Code §	Topic	Generally effective date	Analysis ¶	Com Rep ¶
1602(f)(1)	264(a)(4)	Limit on deductibility of interest to carry COLI policies extended to policies covering taxpayer's former officers or employees and persons formerly financially interested in taxpayer's current or former trade or business	Interest paid or accrued after Oct. 13, '95	709	5375
1602(f)(2)	264(d)(2)(B)(ii)	"Applicable period" changed for interest-rate cap rules on pre-'86 key person life insurance contracts	Interest paid or accrued after Oct. 13, '95	715	5376
1602(f)(3)	264(d)(4)(B)	For company-owned life insurance (COLI) rules, noncorporate "key person" definition clarified to refer to taxpayer, not employer	Interest paid or accrued after Oct. 13, '95	712	5377
1602(f)(4)	264(d)(2)(A)	Interest paid or accrued after Dec. 31, '95, on pre-June 21, '86 COLI contracts is subject to '96 Health Act grandfather rules—conflict with Oct. 13, '95 date eliminated	Interest paid or accrued after Oct. 13, '95	714	5378
1602(f)(5)	264(a)(2)	"Lapse" safe harbor rules for single-premium and "plan of purchase" life insurance contract rules corrected to refer to lapses occurring because of failure to pay premiums, rather than failure to pay premiums occurring because of lapses	Interest paid or accrued after Oct. 13, '95	713	5379
1602(f)(5)	264(c)(1)	"Lapse" safe harbor rules for single-premium and "plan of purchase" life insurance contract rules corrected to refer to lapses occurring because of failure to pay premiums, rather than failure to pay premiums occurring because of lapses	Interest paid or accrued after Oct. 13, '95	713	5379
1602(g)(1)	877(d)(2)(B)	Expatriate tax rules clarified	For individuals giving up U.S. citizenship or U.S. residency after Feb. 5, '95	1626	5380

Act §	Code §	Topic	Generally effective date	Analysis ¶	Com Rep ¶
1602(g)(2)	877(d)(2)(D)	Expatriate tax rules clarified	For individuals giving up U.S. citizenship or U.S. residency after Feb. 5, '95	1626	5380
1602(g)(3)	877(d)(3)	Expatriate tax rules clarified	For individuals giving up U.S. citizenship or U.S. residency after Feb. 5, '95	1626	5380
1602(g)(4)	877(d)(4)(A)	Expatriate tax rules clarified	For individuals giving up U.S. citizenship or U.S. residency after Feb. 5, '95	1626	5380
1602(g)(6)(A)	2107(c)(2)(B)(i)	Expatriate tax rules clarified	For individuals giving up U.S. citizenship or U.S. residency after Feb. 5, '95	1626	5380
1602(g)(6)(B)	2107(c)(2)(C)	Expatriate tax rules clarified	For individuals giving up U.S. citizenship or U.S. residency after Feb. 5, '95	1626	5380
1603(a)	4962(b)	IRS authorized to make reasonable cause abatements of first-tier penalty taxes on charitable organization excess benefit transactions	Excess benefit transactions occurring after Sept. 13, '95	2409	5384
1603(b)(1)	6033(b)(10)	Reporting by public charities on excise tax penalties coordinated with the penalties	Returns for tax years beginning after July 30, '96	2305	5384
1603(b)(2)	6033(b)(11)	Reporting by public charities on excise tax penalties coordinated with the penalties	Returns for tax years beginning after July 30, '96	2305	5384

Act §	Code §	Topic	Generally effective date	Analysis ¶	Com Rep ¶
1604(a)(1)	263(a)(1)(H)	Amounts expensed as the cost of qualified clean-fuel vehicle property and qualified clean-fuel refueling property deducted in connection with clean-fuel vehicles are not capital expenditures	Property placed in service after June 30, '93	807	
1604(a)(2)	312(k)(3)(B)	Amounts deducted in connection with clean-fuel vehicles amortized over five years in computing earnings and profits	Qualified clean-fuel property placed in service after June 30, '93	1514	
1604(a)(3)	1245(a)(2)(C)	Qualified rent-to-own property is designated as MACRS 3-year property with a 4-year class life	Property placed in service after June 30, '93	803	5163
1604(a)(3)	1245(a)(3)(C)	Qualified rent-to-own property is designated as MACRS 3-year property with a 4-year class life	Property placed in service after June 30, '93	803	5163
1604(b)(1)	6621(a)(1)	Definition of "taxable period" for reduced interest rate on large corporate overpayments corrected	Periods after Dec. 31, '94	2404	
1604(b)(3)	None	Interest and mortality rate rules in Retirement Protection Act of '94 corrected	Dec. 8, '94	905	5385
1604(c)(1)	168(j)(6)	Definition of Indian reservation clarified for depreciation and incremental credit purposes	Property placed in service after Dec. 31, '93	806	5388
1604(d)(2)(A)	833(b)(1)	Deduction for Blue Cross and Blue Shield organizations clarified to include cost-plus contract liabilities and expenses	Tax years beginning after Dec. 31, '86	1106	5387
1604(e)	267(f)(4)	Loss deferrals under the Code Sec. 267 related party rules are treated as loss disallowances for purposes of the non-Code Sec. 267 related party rules	Transactions after Dec. 31, '83 in tax years ending after Dec. 31, '83	212	5386
4006(a) *	138	Medicare eligible individuals may choose "Medicare+Choice MSAs" as a Medicare option	Taxable years beginning after Dec. 31, '98	1201	5501

Act §	Code §	Topic	Generally effective date	Analysis ¶	Com Rep ¶
4006(b)(1)	4973(d)	Medicare eligible individuals may choose "Medicare+Choice MSAs" as a Medicare option	Taxable years beginning after Dec. 31, '98	1201	5501
4006(b)(2)	220(b)	Medicare eligible individuals may choose "Medicare+Choice MSAs" as a Medicare option	Taxable years beginning after Dec. 31, '98	1201	5501
4041 *	501(o)	Hospitals will not loose tax-exempt status by participating in a provider-sponsored organization ("PSO")	Aug. 5, '97	1304	5502
4631(c)(2) *	6103(l)(12)(F)	Medicare secondary payer program disclosure rules made permanent	Aug. 5, '97	2333	5503
5406(a)(3) *	3306(c)(21)	Wages paid for services by inmates in a penal institution are exempt from FUTA tax	Service performed after Jan. 1, '94	1904	5506
9302(a) *	5701(b)	Taxes on cigarettes and other tobacco products rise	Products removed after Dec. 31, '99	2231	5509
9302(b) *	5701(a)	Taxes on cigarettes and other tobacco products rise	Products removed after Dec. 31, '99	2231	5509
9302(c) *	5701(c)	Taxes on cigarettes and other tobacco products rise	Products removed after Dec. 31, '99	2231	5509
9302(d) *	5701(d)	Taxes on cigarettes and other tobacco products rise	Products removed after Dec. 31, '99	2231	5509
9302(f) *	5701(f)	Taxes on cigarettes and other tobacco products rise	Products removed after Dec. 31, '99	2231	5509
9302(g) *	5701(g)	Taxes on cigarettes and other tobacco products rise	Products removed after Dec. 31, '99	2231	5509
9302(j) *	None	Taxes on cigarettes and other tobacco products rise	Products removed after Dec. 31, '99	2231	5509

Act §	Code §	Topic	Generally effective date	Analysis ¶	Com Rep ¶
11024(b)	6103(a)(3)	Disclosure of return information authorized for purposes of administering District of Columbia retirement provisions	Oct 1, '97 or, if later, the date certified by the District of Columbia Financial Responsibility and Management Assistance Authority	2605	
11024(b)	6103(i)(7)	Disclosure of return information authorized for purposes of administering District of Columbia retirement provisions	Oct 1, '97 or, if later, the date certified by the District of Columbia Financial Responsibility and Management Assistance Authority	2605	
11024(b)	6103(l)	Disclosure of return information authorized for purposes of administering District of Columbia retirement provisions	Oct 1, '97 or, if later, the date certified by the District of Columbia Financial Responsibility and Management Assistance Authority	2605	
11024(b)	6103(p)	Disclosure of return information authorized for purposes of administering District of Columbia retirement provisions	Oct 1, '97 or, if later, the date certified by the District of Columbia Financial Responsibility and Management Assistance Authority	2605	

Act §	Code §	Topic	Generally effective date	Analysis ¶	Com Rep ¶
11024(b)	7213(a)(2)	Disclosure of return information authorized for purposes of administering District of Columbia retirement provisions	Oct 1, '97 or, if later, the date certified by the District of Columbia Financial Responsibility and Management Assistance Authority	2605	
11034*	None	D.C. Federal Pension Liability Trust Fund to be treated as qualified plan	Aug. 5, '97	939	

¶ 6001. Code Section Cross Reference Table
* denotes Budget Act
† denotes Privacy Act

Code §	Act §	Topic	Generally effective date	Analysis ¶	Com Rep ¶
1(h)	311(a)	Capital gains tax rates for individuals reduced from 28% to 20% and 15% to 10% for post-May 6, '97 gains	Tax years ending after May 6, '97, but without regard to pre-May 7, '97 gains	201	5019
23(a)(2)	1601(h)(2)(A)	Adoption expense credit allowed for expenses paid after the year adoption becomes final and conformed to exclusion for employer adoption assistance payments	Tax years beginning after Dec. 31, '96	112	5368, 5369
23(b)(2)(B)	1601(h)(2)(B)	Adoption expense credit allowed for expenses paid after the year adoption becomes final and conformed to exclusion for employer adoption assistance payments	Tax years beginning after Dec. 31, '96	112	5368, 5369
24	101(a)	Child tax credit of up to $400 in '98, $500 in '99 and later years, for each qualifying child under age 17	Tax years beginning after Dec. 31, '97	101	5001
25A	201(a)	"Hope Scholarship Credit," up to $1,500 per year, and "Lifetime Learning Credit," up to $1,000 per year, allowed for higher education expenses	Expenses paid after Dec. 31, '97	401	5002
26(b)(2)(P)	1602(a)	Changes to MSA rules on coverage, distributions, and reporting requirements	Taxable years beginning after Dec. 31, '96	1202	5370
32(c)(2)(B)(v)	1085(c)	Workfare payments not included in earned income for earned income credit purposes	Tax years beginning after Dec. 31, '97	110	5162

Code §	Act §	Topic	Generally effective date	Analysis ¶	Com Rep ¶
32(c)(5)(B)	1085(d)(4)	Definition of AGI for phasing out the earned income credit is modified by increasing the percentage of certain losses disregarded from 50% to 75%, and adding tax-exempt interest and nontaxable pension and annuity distributions	Tax years beginning after Dec. 31, '97	109	5162
32(c)(5)(B)(iv)	1085(b)	Definition of AGI for phasing out the earned income credit is modified by increasing the percentage of certain losses disregarded from 50% to 75%, and adding tax-exempt interest and nontaxable pension and annuity distributions	Tax years beginning after Dec. 31, '97	109	5162
32(c)(5)(B)(v)	1085(d)(3)	Definition of AGI for phasing out the earned income credit is modified by increasing the percentage of certain losses disregarded from 50% to 75%, and adding tax-exempt interest and nontaxable pension and annuity distributions	Tax years beginning after Dec. 31, '97	109	5162
32(c)(5)(B)(vi)	1085(d)(3)	Definition of AGI for phasing out the earned income credit is modified by increasing the percentage of certain losses disregarded from 50% to 75%, and adding tax-exempt interest and nontaxable pension and annuity distributions	Tax years beginning after Dec. 31, '97	109	5162
32(k)	1085(a)(1)	No earned income credit allowed for ten years for taxpayers who fraudulently claimed credit (two years for taxpayers who recklessly claimed credit)	Tax years beginning after Dec. 31 '96	108	5162
32(m)(3)	101(b)	Child tax credit of up to $400 in '98, $500 in '99 and later years, for each qualifying child under age 17	Tax years beginning after Dec. 31, '97	101	5001
39(a)	1083(a)	Carryback period for unused business credits reduced from 3 years to 1; carryforward period extended from 15 years to 20	Credits arising in tax years beginning after Dec. 31, '97	701	5160

Code §	Act §	Topic	Generally effective date	Analysis ¶	Com Rep ¶
39(d)(8)	701(b)(1)	Designation of DC Enterprise Zone as an empowerment zone	Aug. 5, '97	2601	5040
41(c)(4)(B)	601(b)(1)	Research credit is retroactively restored and extended until June 30, '98	Amounts paid or incurred after May 31, '97	706	5036
41(h)(1)	601(a)(1)	Research credit is retroactively restored and extended until June 30, '98	Amounts paid or incurred after May 31, '97	706	5036
45C	604(a)	Orphan drug tax credit is retroactively restored and permanently extended	Amounts paid or incurred after May 31, '97	707	5039
51(a)	603(d)(1)	Work opportunity credit is modified and extended through June 30, '98	Individuals who begin work for the employer after Sept. 30, '97, but before July 1, '98	702	5038
51(c)(4)(B)	603(a)(1)	Work opportunity credit is modified and extended through June 30, '98	Individuals who begin work for the employer after Sept. 30, '97, but before July 1, '98	702	5038
51(d)(1)(H)	603(c)(1)	Work opportunity credit is modified and extended through June 30, '98	Individuals who begin work for the employer after Sept. 30, '97, but before July 1, '98	702	5038
51(d)(2)(A)	603(b)(1)	Work opportunity credit is modified and extended through June 30, '98	Individuals who begin work for the employer after Sept. 30, '97, but before July 1, '98	702	5038

Code §	Act §	Topic	Generally effective date	Analysis ¶	Com Rep ¶
51(d)(3)(A)	603(b)(2)	Work opportunity credit is modified and extended through June 30, '98	Individuals who begin work for the employer after Sept. 30, '97, but before July 1, '98	702	5038
51(d)(9)	603(c)(2)	Work opportunity credit is modified and extended through June 30, '98	Individuals who begin work for the employer after Sept. 30, '97, but before July 1, '98	702	5038
51(i)(3)	603(d)(2)	Work opportunity credit is modified and extended through June 30, '98	Individuals who begin work for the employer after Sept. 30, '97, but before July 1, '98	702	5038
51A	801(a)	New welfare-to-work credit is available to employers of long-term family assistance recipients	Individuals who begin work for the employer after Dec. 31, '97, but before May 1, '99	704	5050
52(c)	1601(b)	Work opportunity credit not allowed to tax-exempt organizations	Individuals who begin work for the employer after Sept. 30, '96	703	
55(b)(3)	311(b)	Alternative minimum tax rate on net capital gain for non-corporate taxpayers reduced from 26%/28% to 20% or 10%	Tax years ending after May 6, '97, but without regard to pre-May 7, '97 gains	602	5019
55(e)	401(a)	Alternative minimum tax (AMT) repealed for small corporations after '97	Tax years beginning after Dec. 31, '97	601	5023

Code §	Act §	Topic	Generally effective date	Analysis ¶	Com Rep ¶
56(a)(1)(A)(i)	402(a)	The alternative minimum tax adjustment for depreciation of property placed in service after '98 is computed using the 150% declining balance method (and switching to the straight line method)	Aug. 5, '97	606	5024
56(a)(5)	402(b)	The AMT adjustment for pollution control facilities is determined for facilities placed in service after '98 by using straight line depreciation	Aug. 5, '97	610	5024
56(a)(6)	403(a)	Alternative minimum tax on installment sales repealed retroactively for dispositions in tax years beginning after '87	Dispositions in tax years beginning after Dec. 31, '87	607	5025
56(g)(4)(B)(i)	1212(a)	Property and casualty insurance companies electing to be taxed only on taxable investment income compute ACE for AMT purposes without regard to underwriting income or expenses	Tax years beginning after Dec. 31, '97	611	5207
57(a)(7)	311(b)(2)(B)	AMT preference for portion of gain on sale of qualified small business stock reduced from 50% to 42%	Tax years ending after May 6, '97	605	5019
59(a)(2)(C)	1057(a)	Exception for certain domestic corporations from limitation on use of foreign tax credits to reduce alternative minimum tax is repealed	Tax years beginning after Aug. 5, '97	609	5149
59(a)(3)	1103(a)	Simplified foreign tax credit limitation may be elected for alternative minimum tax purposes	Tax years beginning after Dec. 31, '97	608	5172
59(j)	1201(b)(1)	Limit on AMT exemption for under-age-14 child increased from sum of earned income plus twice the $500 limit on basic standard deduction to sum of earned income plus $5,000; limit on child's AMT repealed	Tax years beginning after Dec. 31, '97	604	5201

Code §	Act §	Topic	Generally effective date	Analysis ¶	Com Rep ¶
62(a)(2)(C)	975(a)	Above-the-line (and therefore an AMT) deduction for business expenses of state and local government officials who are compensated on a fee basis	Expenses paid or incurred in tax years beginning after Dec. 31, '86	116	5098
62(a)(17)	202(b)	Above-the-line deduction allowed for up to $1,000 of interest paid on higher education loans in '98, increasing over four years to $2,500 for interest paid in 2001	Any loan interest payment due and paid after Dec. 31, '97	402	5003
63(c)(4)	1201(a)(2)	Limit on basic standard deduction for certain dependents increased from greater of $500 (indexed) or earned income to greater of $500 (indexed) or earned income plus $250 (indexed)	Tax years beginning after Dec. 31, '97	113	5201
63(c)(5)	1201(a)(1)	Limit on basic standard deduction for certain dependents increased from greater of $500 (indexed) or earned income to greater of $500 (indexed) or earned income plus $250 (indexed)	Tax years beginning after Dec. 31, '97	113	5201
72(d)(1)(B)(iii)	1075(b)	Separate table provided for figuring basis recovery for annuities based on more than one life	Annuity starting dates beginning after '97	903	5157
72(d)(1)(B)(iv)	1075(a)	Separate table provided for figuring basis recovery for annuities based on more than one life	Annuity starting dates beginning after '97	903	5157
72(t)	203	No penalty for early withdrawal of IRA funds to pay higher education expenses	Distributions made after '97	304	5004
72(t)	303	No penalty for early withdrawal of IRA funds for "first-time homebuyers" — $10,000 lifetime limitation	Payments and distributions made after '97	303	5017
101(a)(2)	1084(b)(2)	Nondeductible interest on transferred company-owned life insurance policies taken into account in determining amount of excludible death benefits under those policies	Contracts issued after June 8, '97	711	5161

Code §	Act §	Topic	Generally effective date	Analysis ¶	Com Rep ¶
101(h)	1528(a)	Tax exemption for annuities paid to survivors of public safety officers killed in the line of duty	Amounts received in tax years beginning after Dec. 31, '96, with respect to officers dying after that date	104	5350
108(f)	225	Exclusion from income for cancellation of student loans expanded to cover cancellation of loans under nongovernment sponsored programs	Aug. 5, '97	103	5011
110	1213(a)	Income exclusion of construction allowances received by lessees for qualified lessee construction related to short-term leases of retail space	Leases entered into after Aug. 5, '97	2702	5208
121	312(a)	Replacement of rollover rules and the one-time exclusion that applied to sales of a principal residence with an exclusion of gain of up to $250,000 ($500,000 for joint filers)	Sales and exchanges after May 6, '97	102	5020
127(d)	221	Exclusion for employer-provided educational assistance extended through 2000	Years beginning after Dec. 31, '96	404	5007
130(c)	962(a)	Exclusion for amounts received for agreeing to a qualified assignment is extended to amounts received for assuming a workers' compensation liability	Claims filed after Aug. 5, '97	2705	5083
132(e)(2)	970(a)	Clarification of de minimis fringe benefit rules to no-charge employee meals	For tax years beginning after Dec. 31, '97	1001	5093
132(f)(4)	1072(a)	Election to receive taxable cash compensation in place of nontaxable parking benefits	Tax years beginning after Dec. 31, '97	1003	5154
135(c)(2)(C)	211(e)	Tax treatment of contributions to and distributions from qualified tuition programs modified	Jan. 1, '98	405	5005

Code §	Act §	Topic	Generally effective date	Analysis ¶	Com Rep ¶
135(d)(2)	201(d)	Higher education expenses used to compute exclusion of redemption proceeds of U.S. savings bonds must be reduced by higher education expenses for which Hope/Lifetime Learning credit is claimed	Expenses paid after Dec. 31, '97	409	5002
137(b)(1)	1601(h)(2)(C)	Adoption expense credit allowed for expenses paid after the year adoption becomes final and conformed to exclusion for employer adoption assistance payments	Tax years beginning after Dec. 31, '96	112	5368, 5369
138	4006(a)*	Medicare eligible individuals may choose "Medicare+Choice MSAs" as a Medicare option	Taxable years beginning after Dec. 31, '98	1201	5501
143(k)(11)	914	First-time home buyer, purchase price, and mortgagor's income requirements waived for mortgage bond financing for residences located in disaster areas	Bonds issued after Dec. 31, '96 and before Jan. 1, '99	2501	5064
145(b)(1)	222(a)	$150 million limitation on 501(c)(3) bonds repealed	Aug. 5, '97	2505	5008
148(c)(2)(B)	1444(a)	Repeal as deadwood two exceptions to arbitrage rebate and temporary period pooled financing rules for qualified student loan bonds issued before '89	Bonds issued after Aug. 5, '97	2507	5298
148(d)	1443	Repeal of 150%-of-debt-service limit on investment in nonpurpose investments under arbitrage bond rules	Bonds issued after Aug. 5, '97	2503	5297
148(f)(4)(B)(ii)(I)	1441	Arbitrage bond rebate requirement: repeal of $100,000 limitation on unspent proceeds under six-month spending exception; exemption for earnings on bona fide debt service funds under construction issue exception	Bonds issued after Aug. 5, '97	2504	5295, 5296

Code §	Act §	Topic	Generally effective date	Analysis ¶	Com Rep ¶
148(f)(4)(C)(xvii)	1442	Arbitrage bond rebate requirement: repeal of $100,000 limitation on unspent proceeds under six-month spending exception; exemption for earnings on bona fide debt service funds under construction issue exception	Bonds issued after Aug. 5, '97	2504	5295, 5296
148(f)(4)(D)(vii)	223(a)	Up to $5 million in bonds used to finance public school capital expenditures after '97 exempted from arbitrage rebate requirements	Bonds issued after Dec. 31, '97	2502	5009
148(f)(4)(E)	1444(b)	Repeal as deadwood two exceptions to arbitrage rebate and temporary period pooled financing rules for qualified student loan bonds issued before '89	Bonds issued after Aug. 5, '97	2507	5298
149(d)(3)(A)(i)(I)	967	Certain Virgin Islands bonds allowed one additional refinancing if Virgin Islands priority first lien requirement is repealed	Aug. 5, '97	2506	5090
162(a)	1204(a)	One-year limit on away-from-home travel expenses doesn't apply to certified federal investigators	For amounts paid or incurred for tax years ending after Aug. 5, '97	115	5204
162(l)(1)(B)	934(a)	Percentage of health insurance costs deductible by self-employeds gradually increased to 100% by 2007	Tax years beginning after Dec. 31, '96	1103	5071
162(l)(2)(B)	1602(c)	Self-employeds can deduct long-term care premiums even if they participate in employer-provided health plan (if the plan doesn't include long-term care coverage)	Tax years beginning after Dec. 31, '96	1104	5372
162(o)	1203(a)	Rural mail carriers can exclude full equipment maintenance allowance; 150% standard mileage rate deduction repealed	For tax years beginning after Dec. 31, '97	105	5203

Code §	Act §	Topic	Generally effective date	Analysis ¶	Com Rep ¶
163(h)(2)(E)	503(b)(2)(B)	Estate tax benefit of qualified family-owned business exclusion may be recaptured if certain events occur	Applies to estates of decedents dying after Dec. 31, '97	506	5028
163(k)	503(b)(2)(A)	Estate tax benefit of qualified family-owned business exclusion may be recaptured if certain events occur	Applies to estates of decedents dying after Dec. 31, '97	506	5028
163(l)	1005(a)	No deduction for interest on corporate debt payable in stock of the issuer or a related party	Debt instruments issued after June 8, '97	1511	5115
165(i)(4)	912(a)	IRS authorized to permit appraisals used to get federal disaster relief to also be used to establish amount of disaster loss	Aug. 5, '97	111	5062
167(g)(6)	1086(a)	Property qualifying for the income forecast method of depreciation is limited; rent-to-own consumer durables are ineligible	Property placed in service after Aug. 5, '97	801	5163
168(3(A)(iii)	1086(b)(1)	Qualified rent-to-own property is designated as MACRS 3-year property with a 4-year class life	Property placed in service after Aug. 5, '97	803	5163
168(g)(3)(B)	1086(b)(2)	Qualified rent-to-own property is designated as MACRS 3-year property with a 4-year class life	Property placed in service after Aug. 5, '97	803	5163
168(i)(14)	1086(b)(3)	Qualified rent-to-own property is designated as MACRS 3-year property with a 4-year class life	Property placed in service after Aug. 5, '97	803	5163
168(j)(6)	1604(c)(1)	Definition of Indian reservation clarified for depreciation and incremental credit purposes	Property placed in service after Dec. 31, '93	806	5388
170(e)(5)(D)(ii)	602(a)	Full deduction for contributions of qualified appreciated stock to private foundations restored for period June 1, '97 to June 30, '98	Contributions made after May 31, '97	107	5037

Code §	Act §	Topic	Generally effective date	Analysis ¶	Com Rep ¶
170(e)(6)	224(a)	Corporate gifts of computer technology and equipment to elementary and secondary schools before 2000 get charitable deduction tax break	Tax years beginning after '97	1512	5010
170(h)(5)(B)(ii)	508(d)	Income and estate tax charitable deduction for a qualified conservation contribution where a mineral interest has been retained	For easements granted after Dec. 31, '97	520	5033
170(i)	973(a)	Standard mileage rate for computing charitable deduction for use of a car is increased from 12¢ to 14¢ per mile	Tax years beginning after Dec. 31, '97	106	5096
172(b)(1)(A)	1082(a)	NOL carryback period reduced from three to two years; carryforward period extended from 15 to 20 years	Tax years beginning after Aug. 5, '97	1510	5159
172(b)(1)(F)	1082(b)	NOL carryback period reduced from three to two years; carryforward period extended from 15 to 20 years	Tax years beginning after Aug. 5, '97	1510	5159
198	941	Election to treat certain environmental remediation costs as deductible ("brownfields")	Expenditures paid or incurred after Aug. 5, '97 in tax years ending after Aug. 5, '97	808	5073
219(c)(1)(B)	302(c)	New nondeductible Roth IRA allows tax-free withdrawal of earnings	Taxable years beginning after Dec. 31, '97	301	5016
219(g)	301(b)	Increased availability of IRA deductions for active pension plan participants and spouses	Taxable years beginning after Dec. 31, '97	302	5015
219(g)(3)(B)	301(a)	Increased availability of IRA deductions for active pension plan participants and spouses	Taxable years beginning after Dec. 31, '97	302	5015
220	1602(a)	Changes to MSA rules on coverage, distributions, and reporting requirements	Taxable years beginning after Dec. 31, '96	1202	5370

Code §	Act §	Topic	Generally effective date	Analysis ¶	Com Rep ¶
220(b)	4006(b)(2)	Medicare eligible individuals may choose "Medicare+Choice MSAs" as a Medicare option	Taxable years beginning after Dec. 31, '98	1201	5501
221	202(a)	Above-the-line deduction allowed for up to $1,000 of interest paid on higher education loans in '98, increasing over four years to $2,500 for interest paid in 2001	Any loan interest payment due and paid after Dec. 31, '97	402	5003
246(c)	1015	Holding period for dividends-received deduction modified	Dividends received or accrued after the 30th day after Aug. 5, '97	1509	5120
263(a)(1)(H)	1604(a)(1)	Amounts expensed as the cost of qualified clean-fuel vehicle property and qualified clean-fuel refueling property deducted in connection with clean-fuel vehicles are not capital expenditures	Property placed in service after June 30, '93	807	
264(a)(1)	1084(a)(1)	Rules disallowing premium and interest deductions on life insurance of officers and employees extended to life insurance on debtors and others	Contracts issued after June 8, '97	710	5161
264(a)(2)	1602(f)(5)	"Lapse" safe harbor rules for single-premium and "plan of purchase" life insurance contract rules corrected to refer to lapses occurring because of failure to pay premiums, rather than failure to pay premiums occurring because of lapses	Interest paid or accrued after Oct. 13, '95	713	5379
264(a)(4)	1084(b)(1)	Rules disallowing premium and interest deductions on life insurance of officers and employees extended to life insurance on debtors and others	Contracts issued after June 8, '97	710	5161

Code §	Act §	Topic	Generally effective date	Analysis ¶	Com Rep ¶
264(a)(4)	1602(f)(1)	Limit on deductibility of interest to carry COLI policies extended to policies covering taxpayer's former officers or employees and persons formerly financially interested in taxpayer's current or former trade or business	Interest paid or accrued after Oct. 13, '95	709	5375
264(b)	1084(a)(2)	Rules disallowing premium and interest deductions on life insurance of officers and employees extended to life insurance on debtors and others	Contracts issued after June 8, '97	710	5161
264(c)(1)	1602(f)(5)	"Lapse" safe harbor rules for single-premium and "plan of purchase" life insurance contract rules corrected to refer to lapses occurring because of failure to pay premiums, rather than failure to pay premiums occurring because of lapses	Interest paid or accrued after Oct. 13, '95	713	5379
264(d)	1084(a)(2)	"Applicable period" changed for interest-rate cap rules on pre-'86 key person life insurance contracts	Interest paid or accrued after Oct. 13, '95	715	5376
264(d)	1084(a)(2)	For company-owned life insurance (COLI) rules, noncorporate "key person" definition clarified to refer to taxpayer, not employer	Interest paid or accrued after Oct. 13, '95	712	5377
264(d)(2)(A)	1602(f)(4)	Interest paid or accrued after Dec. 31, '95, on pre-June 21, '86 COLI contracts is subject to '96 Health Act grandfather rules—conflict with Oct. 13, '95 date eliminated	Interest paid or accrued after Oct. 13, '95	714	5378
264(d)(2)(B)(ii)	1602(f)(2)	"Applicable period" changed for interest-rate cap rules on pre-'86 key person life insurance contracts	Interest paid or accrued after Oct. 13, '95	715	5376
264(d)(4)(B)	1602(f)(3)	For company-owned life insurance (COLI) rules, noncorporate "key person" definition clarified to refer to taxpayer, not employer	Interest paid or accrued after Oct. 13, '95	712	5377

Code §	Act §	Topic	Generally effective date	Analysis ¶	Com Rep ¶
264(f)	1084(c)	No deduction for interest allocable to unborrowed policy cash values ("inside build-up") on life insurance contracts	Contracts issued after June 8, '97	708	5161
267(b)	1308(a)	Estate and beneficiaries treated as related for loss and capital gain treatment on sale of depreciable property	Tax years beginning after Aug. 5, '97	211	5268
267(f)(4)	1604(e)	Loss deferrals under the Code Sec. 267 related party rules are treated as loss disallowances for purposes of the non-Code Sec. 267 related party rules	Transactions after Dec. 31, '83 in tax years ending after Dec. 31, '83	212	5386
274(n)(3)	969(a)	Business meals deduction increased from 50% to 80% (over 10 years) for individuals subject to DOT hours of service limitations	Tax years beginning after Dec. 31, '97	117	5092
280A(c)(1)	932(a)	Limit on basic standard deduction for certain dependents increased from greater of $500 (indexed) or earned income to greater of $500 (indexed) or earned income plus $250 (indexed)	Tax years beginning after Dec. 31, '98	113	5069
280F(a)(1)(C)	971(a)	Luxury automobile depreciation limits are removed for clean-fuel vehicle property and tripled for electric vehicles	Property placed in service after Aug. 5, '97, but before Jan. 1, 2005	802	5094
304(a)(1)	1013(a)	Treatment of dividend from related-party stock purchase amended	Distributions or acquisitions after June 8, '97	1505	5118
304(b)(5)	1013(c)	Treatment of dividend from related-party stock purchase amended	Distributions or acquisitions after June 8, '97	1505	5118
312(k)(3)(B)	1604(a)(2)	Amounts deducted in connection with clean-fuel vehicles amortized over five years in computing earnings and profits	Qualified clean-fuel property placed in service after June 30, '93	1514	

Code §	Act §	Topic	Generally effective date	Analysis ¶	Com Rep ¶
351(c)	1012(c)(1)	Rules for tax-free divisions modified	Distributions after April 16, '97 and transfers after Aug. 5, '97	1501	5117
351(e)(1)	1002	Expanded definition of investment company for purposes of transfers to partnerships and controlled corporations	Transfers after June 8, '97	1504	5112
351(g)	1014(a)	Certain preferred stock treated as boot	Transactions after June 8, '97	1502	5119
354(a)(2)(C)	1014(b)	Certain preferred stock treated as boot	Transactions after June 8, '97	1502	5119
355(a)(3)(D)	1014(c)	Certain preferred stock treated as boot	Transactions after June 8, '97	1502	5119
355(e)	1012(a)	Rules for tax-free divisions modified	Distributions after April 16, '97 and transfers after Aug. 5, '97	1501	5117
355(f)	1012(b)(1)	Rules for tax-free divisions modified	Distributions after April 16, '97 and transfers after Aug. 5, '97	1501	5117
356(e)	1014(d)	Certain preferred stock treated as boot	Transactions after June 8, '97	1502	5119
358(g)	1012(b)(2)	Rules for tax-free divisions modified	Distributions after April 16, '97 and transfers after Aug. 5, '97	1501	5117
367(d)(2)	1131(b)(4)	U.S. source treatment of deemed royalties repealed	Aug. 5, '97	1630	5182
367(d)(3)	1131(b)(5)	U.S. source treatment of deemed royalties repealed	Aug. 5, '97	1630	5182
368(a)(2)(H)	1012(c)(2)	Rules for tax-free divisions modified	Distributions after April 16, '97 and transfers after Aug. 5, '97	1501	5117

2,986

Code §	Act §	Topic	Generally effective date	Analysis ¶	Com Rep ¶
401(a)(5)	1505(a)(1)	Qualified plan nondiscrimination and minimum participation rules made permanently inapplicable to state and local governmental plans	Tax years beginning on or after Aug. 5, '97	924	5311
401(a)(13)(C)	1502(b)	Judgment or settlement amounts for certain participant crimes and ERISA violations may be offset against his benefits	Judgments, orders, and decrees issued, and settlements entered into, on or after Aug. 5, '97	904	5308
401(a)(26)(H)	1505(a)(2)	Qualified plan nondiscrimination and minimum participation rules made permanently inapplicable to state and local governmental plans	Tax years beginning on or after Aug. 5, '97	924	5311
401(k)(3)(G)	1505(b)	Qualified plan nondiscrimination and minimum participation rules made permanently inapplicable to state and local governmental plans	Tax years beginning on or after Aug. 5, '97	924	5311
401(k)(7)(B)(iv)	1525	Rural irrigation and water conservation entities can have 401(k) plans	Years beginning after Dec. 31 '97	930	5347
401(k)(11)(B)(iii)	1601(d)(2)(D)	Employers must provide timely notice of SIMPLE 401(k) plan elective contribution rules to eligible employees	Calendar years beginning after Aug. 5, '97	920	5361
401(k)(11)(D)(ii)	1601(d)(2)(A)	Only SIMPLE 401(k) plans are exempt from the top-heavy rules	Tax years beginning after Dec. 31, '96	921	5361
401(k)(11)(E)	1601(d)(2)(B)	Limit on contributions to SIMPLE 401(k) plans will be adjusted for changes in the cost-of-living	Tax years beginning after Dec. 31, '96	919	5361
402(g)(9)	1501(a)	Matching contributions of self-employed individuals are not treated as elective employer contributions	Years beginning after Dec. 31, '97	933	5307
403(b)(1)(A)	1601(d)(6)(B)	Rules on self-employed ministers clarified	Years beginning after Dec. 31, '96	1901	5344

Code §	Act §	Topic	Generally effective date	Analysis ¶	Com Rep ¶
403(b)(3)	1504(a)(1)	Exclusion allowance rules for 403(b) annuities modified to conform to earlier Code Sec. 415 changes	Years beginning after Dec. 31, '97	925	5310
403(b)(12)(C)	1505(c)	Qualified plan nondiscrimination and minimum participation rules made permanently inapplicable to state and local governmental plans	Tax years beginning on or after Aug. 5, '97	924	5311
404(a)(3)(A)	1601(d)(2)(C)	Employer contributions to SIMPLE 401(k) plans are not subject to the 15 percent limits on contributions to profit-sharing or stock bonus plans	Tax years beginning after Dec. 31, '96	918	5361
408((p)(8)	1601(d)(1)(D)	Maximum dollar limitation on IRA contributions conformed to allow maximum contributions to SIMPLE IRAs	Tax years beginning after Dec. 31, '96	915	5361
408(i)	1601(d)(1)(A)	Trustees' SIMPLE IRA reports to individuals now due on Jan. 31	Tax years beginning after Dec. 31, '96	917	5361
408(i)	302(d)	New nondeductible Roth IRA allows tax-free withdrawal of earnings	Taxable years beginning after Dec. 31, '97	301	5016
408(l)(2)(B)	1601(d)(1)(C)(i)	Notification requirements and penalties for SIMPLE IRAs apply also to issuers of SIMPLE IRA annuities	Tax years beginning after Dec. 31, '96	916	5361
408(m)(3)	304(a)	Individual retirement accounts and individually-directed plan accounts may be invested in certain bullion	Tax years beginning after Dec. 31, '97	305	5018
408(p)(2)(D)(i)	1601(d)(1)(E)	Employers that maintain a plan for collectively bargained employees can maintain a SIMPLE plan for noncollectively bargained employees	Tax years beginning after Dec. 31, '96	913	5361
408(p)(8)	1501(b)	Matching contributions of self-employed individuals are not treated as elective employer contributions	Years beginning after Dec. 31, '97	933	5307
408(p)2)(D)(iii)	1601(d)(1)(F)	Grace period for employers that maintain both a qualified plan and a SIMPLE plan as a result of a merger or acquisition	Tax years beginning after Dec. 31, '96	914	5361

Code §	Act §	Topic	Generally effective date	Analysis ¶	Com Rep ¶
408A	302(a)	New nondeductible Roth IRA allows tax-free withdrawal of earnings	Taxable years beginning after Dec. 31, '97	301	5016
409(h)(2)(B)	1506(a)	Certain cash distributions permitted by ESOPs maintained by S corporations	Taxable years beginning after Dec. 31, 1997	910	5312
410(c)(2)	1505(a)(3)	Qualified plan nondiscrimination and minimum participation rules made permanently inapplicable to state and local governmental plans	Tax years beginning on or after Aug. 5, '97	924	5311
411(a)(11)(A)	1071(a)(1)	Maximum involuntary pension "cash-out" amount increased from $3,500 to $5,000	Plan years beginning after Aug. 5, '97	902	5153
412(b)(2)(E)	1521(c)(1)	Increase in current liability funding limit and new special amortization rule	Plan years beginning after Dec. 31, '98	931	5343
412(c)(7)(A)(i)(I)	1521(a)	Increase in current liability funding limit and new special amortization rule	Plan years beginning after Dec. 31, '98	931	5343
412(c)(7)(F)	1521(a)	Increase in current liability funding limit and new special amortization rule	Plan years beginning after Dec. 31, '98	931	5343
414(e)(5)(A)	1601(d)(6)(A)	Rules on self-employed ministers clarified	Years beginning after Dec. 31, '96	1901	5344
414(e)(5)(C)	1522(a)(1)	Exclusion of ministers from discrimination testing of non-church retirement plans is expanded	Years beginning after '97	926	5344
414(n)(3)(C)	1601(h)(2)(D)(i)	Adoption expense credit allowed for expenses paid after the year adoption becomes final and conformed to exclusion for employer adoption assistance payments	Tax years beginning after Dec. 31, '96	112	5368, 5369
414(t)(2)	1601(h)(2)(D)(ii)	Adoption expense credit allowed for expenses paid after the year adoption becomes final and conformed to exclusion for employer adoption assistance payments	Tax years beginning after Dec. 31, '96	112	5368, 5369

Code §	Act §	Topic	Generally effective date	Analysis ¶	Com Rep ¶
415(b)(2)(G)	1527(a)	Dollar limitation on defined benefit plan payments is no longer reduced for police and firefighters whose benefits begin before age 65	Years beginning after Dec. 31, '96	922	5349
415(e)(5)(E)	1522(a)(2)	Contributions to church plan on behalf of self-employed minister are excluded from income	Years beginning after '97	927	5344
415(k)	1526(b)	Limits on contributions for purchasing permissive service credit under governmental plans	Years beginning after Dec. 31, '97	923	5348
415(n)	1526(a)	Limits on contributions for purchasing permissive service credit under governmental plans	Years beginning after Dec. 31, '97	923	5348
417(e)	1071(a)(2)	Maximum involuntary pension "cash-out" amount increased from $3,500 to $5,000	Plan years beginning after Aug. 5, '97	902	5153
447(i)(3)	1081	Suspense accounts prohibited for family corporations required to change to the accrual method of accounting for farming income	Tax years ending after June 8, '97	2104	5158
447(i)(4)	1081	Suspense accounts prohibited for family corporations required to change to the accrual method of accounting for farming income	Tax years ending after June 8, '97	2104	5158
447(i)(5)	1081	Suspense accounts prohibited for family corporations required to change to the accrual method of accounting for farming income	Tax years ending after June 8, '97	2104	5158
451(e)(1)	913(a)(1)	Cash basis farmers may elect to defer gain from forced sales of livestock due to floods or other weather-related conditions	Sales and exchanges after Dec. 31, '96	2101	5063
457(e)(9)	1071(a)(2)	Maximum involuntary pension "cash-out" amount increased from $3,500 to $5,000	Plan years beginning after Aug. 5, '97	902	5153

Code §	Act §	Topic	Generally effective date	Analysis ¶	Com Rep ¶
460(b)(2)(C)	1211(b)(1)	Interest calculation changed in the look-back methods used in long-term contract accounting and in income forecast depreciation	For long-term contract accounting, contracts completed in tax years ending after Aug. 5, '97. For income forecast depreciation, property placed in service after Sept. 13, '95	2004	5206
460(b)(6)	1211(a)	Look-back method as applied to long-term contracts isn't required in de minimis situations	Contracts completed in tax years ending after Aug. 5, '97	2003	5206
460(b)(7)	1211(b)(2)	Interest calculation changed in the look-back methods used in long-term contract accounting and in income forecast depreciation	For long-term contract accounting, contracts completed in tax years ending after Aug. 5, '97. For income forecast depreciation, property placed in service after Sept. 13, '95	2004	5206
471(b)	961(a)	Rules for estimating inventory shrinkage are provided	Tax years ending after Aug. 5, '97	2005	5082
475(e)	1001(b)	Commodities dealers and traders in securities and commodities can elect the mark-to-market rules	Tax years ending after Aug. 5, '97	2001	5111
475(f)	1001(b)	Commodities dealers and traders in securities and commodities can elect the mark-to-market rules	Tax years ending after Aug. 5, '97	2001	5111
501(c)(26)	101(c)	Tax-exempt state-sponsored high risk pools can provide health care coverage to spouse and children of high risk individual	Tax years beginning after Dec. 31, '97	1305	5001

Code §	Act §	Topic	Generally effective date	Analysis ¶	Com Rep ¶
501(c)(27)(B)	963(a)	Certain state workmen's compensation act companies are tax–exempt	For tax years after Dec. 31, '97	1306	5084
501(e)(1)(A)	974(a)	Cooperative hospital service organizations may purchase patient account receivables	Taxable years beginning after Dec. 31, '96	1303	5097
501(o)	4041*	Hospitals will not loose tax-exempt status by participating in a provider-sponsored organization ("PSO")	Aug. 5, '97	1304	5502
512(b)(13)	1041	UBTI rules apply to second-tier subsidiaries; control test changed	Aug. 5, '97	1302	5141
512(e)(3)	1523(a)	UBIT no longer applies to S corporation ESOPs	Taxable years beginning after Dec. 31, '97	912	5345
513(i)	965(a)	"Qualified sponsorship payments" excluded from UBIT	Payments solicited or received after Dec 31, '97.	1301	5086
528(c)(1)	966(a)(1)	Timeshare associations may elect to be taxed like other homeowner associations	Tax years beginning after Dec. 31, '96	2706	5089
528(c)(4)	966(a)(2)	Timeshare associations may elect to be taxed like other homeowner associations	Tax years beginning after Dec. 31, '96	2706	5089
528(c)(5)	966(c)	Timeshare associations may elect to be taxed like other homeowner associations	Tax years beginning after Dec. 31, '96	2706	5089
528(d)(3)	966(b)	Timeshare associations may elect to be taxed like other homeowner associations	Tax years beginning after Dec. 31, '96	2706	5089
529(c)	211(b)(3)	Tax treatment of contributions to and distributions from qualified tuition programs modified	Jan. 1, '98	405	5005
529(d)	211(e)(2)(A)	Qualified state tuition program expanded	Jan. 1, '98	406	5005
529(e)	211(b)(1)	Tax treatment of contributions to and distributions from qualified tuition programs modified	Jan. 1, '98	405	5005

Code §	Act §	Topic	Generally effective date	Analysis ¶	Com Rep ¶
529(e)(1)(C)	1601(h)(1)(B)	Definition of "designated beneficiary" expanded for purposes of rules on qualified state tuition programs	Tax years ending after Aug. 20, '96	407	5367
529(e)(3)	211(a)	Qualified state tuition program expanded	Jan. 1, '98	406	5005
529(e)(5)	211(b)(2)	Qualified state tuition program expanded	Jan. 1, '98	406	5005
530	213(a)	Tax-exempt education IRAs allowed	Tax years beginning after Dec. 31, '97	403	5005
593(e)(1)(A)	1601(f)(5)(A)	Rules modified on recapture of bad debt reserve by thrift institutions	Tax years beginning after Dec. 31, '95	1717	5365
613A(c)(6)(H)	972	100%-of-net-income limitation on percentage depletion is suspended for production from marginal oil and gas wells after '97 and before 2000	Tax years beginning after Dec. 31, '97	2704	5095
641(b)	1601(i)(3)(B)	Definition of trust as U.S. person clarified	Tax years beginning after '96	1628	5364
644	507(b)(1)	Special rule for gain on property transferred to trust at less than fair market value is repealed	For sales or exchanges after the Aug. 5, '97	531	5032
646	1305(a)	Election to treat revocable trust as part of estate for income and generation–skipping transfer (GST) tax purposes	For estates of decedents dying after Aug. 5, '97	526	5265
663(b)	1306	Election to treat distributions during first 65 days of estate's tax year as made in previous tax year	For tax years beginning after Aug. 5, '97	527	5266
663(c)	1307(a)	Separate share rule is extended to estates	For estates of decedents dying after Aug. 5, '97	528	5267
664(d)	1089	Limitation on charitable remainder trust (CRT) eligibility for trusts with greater than 50% payout and less than 10% charitable remainder	For transfers in trust after June 18, '97	532	5166

Code §	Act §	Topic	Generally effective date	Analysis ¶	Com Rep ¶
664(d)	1530(b)	Limited transfer of qualified employer securities by charitable remainder trusts to ESOPs is permitted	Aug. 5, '97	938	5352
664(g)	1530(b)	Limited transfer of qualified employer securities by charitable remainder trusts to ESOPs is permitted	Aug. 5, '97	938	5352
665(c)	507(a)(1)	Throwback rules repealed for U.S. trusts	For distributions made in tax years beginning after Aug. 5, '97	530	5032
679(a)(3)(C)	1601(i)(2)	Obligations issued by owner are disregarded in determining whether transfer to foreign trust is for fair market value	Property transfers made after Feb. 6, '95	1627	5363
684	1131(b)	Transfer of property to foreign estate, trust, corporation or partnership triggers gain; excise tax on transfers to foreign entities repealed	Aug. 5, '97	1629	5182
685	1309(a)	Election to have income of qualified funeral trust taxed to the trust	For tax years ending after Aug. 5, '97	533	5269
704(c)(1)(B)	1063(a)	Seven-year period for taxing pre-contribution gain or loss	Property contributed to a partnership after June 8, '97	1424	5152
721(d)	1131(b)(5)	U.S. source treatment of deemed royalties repealed	Aug. 5, '97	1630	5182
732(c)	1061	Allocation of basis among properties distributed by partnerships	Partnership distributions after Aug. 5, '97	1422	5150
737(b)(1)	1063(a)	Seven-year period for taxing pre-contribution gain or loss	Property contributed to a partnership after June 8, '97	1424	5152
751(a)(2)	1062(a)	Allocation of basis among properties distributed by partnerships	Partnership sales, exchanges, and distributions after Aug. 5, '97.	1422	5151

Code §	Act §	Topic	Generally effective date	Analysis ¶	Com Rep ¶
751(b)(1)	1062(b)(1)(A)	Allocation of basis among properties distributed by partnerships	Partnership sales, exchanges, and distributions after Aug. 5, '97.	1422	5151
760(c)(2)(A)	1246(a)	Partnership tax year closes with respect to interest of deceased partner	Partnership tax years beginning after Dec. 31, '97.	1425	5229
771	1221(a)	Simplified flow-through for electing large partnerships	Partnership tax years beginning after Dec. 31, '97	1401	5209
772	1221(a)	Simplified flow-through for electing large partnerships	Partnership tax years beginning after Dec. 31, '97	1401	5209
773	1221(a)	Simplified flow-through for electing large partnerships	Partnership tax years beginning after Dec. 31, '97	1401	5209
774	1221(a)	Simplified flow-through for electing large partnerships	Partnership tax years beginning after Dec. 31, '97	1401	5209
775	1221(a)	Simplified flow-through for electing large partnerships	Partnership tax years beginning after Dec. 31, '97	1401	5209
775(a)	1221(a)	Consistency rules and audit procedures for electing large partnerships	Partnership tax years ending after Dec. 30, '97	1402	5210
776	1221(a)	Simplified flow-through for electing large partnerships	Partnership tax years beginning after Dec. 31, '97	1401	5209
777	1221(a)	Simplified flow-through for electing large partnerships	Partnership tax years beginning after Dec. 31, '97	1401	5209
833(b)(1)	1604(d)(2)(A)	Deduction for Blue Cross and Blue Shield organizations clarified to include cost-plus contract liabilities and expenses	Tax years beginning after Dec. 31, '86	1106	5387

Code §	Act §	Topic	Generally effective date	Analysis ¶	Com Rep ¶
851(b)(3)	1271	30% gross income limitation (short-short test) for RICs is repealed	Tax years beginning after Aug. 5, '97	1715	5247
852(b)(3)(D)(iii)	1254(b)(2)	Increase in shareholder's basis for undistributed capital gains passed through a RIC is adjusted	Tax years beginning after Aug. 5, '97	1702	5230
853(c)	1053(b)	Holding period requirement for certain foreign taxes	Dividends paid or accrued more than 30 days after Aug. 5, '97.	1604	5145
856(a)(6)	1251(b)(2)	Requirement that REIT not be closely held is met where adequate shareholder records are maintained and REIT has no knowledge to contrary	Tax years beginning after Aug. 5, '97	1704	5230
856(c)	1255(a)(3)	Repeal of requirement that no more than 30% of REIT's gross income can be derived from sales or other dispositions	Tax years beginning after Aug. 5, '97	1709	5230
856(c)(4)	1255(a)(2)	Repeal of requirement that no more than 30% of REIT's gross income can be derived from sales or other dispositions	Tax years beginning after Aug. 5, '97	1709	5230
856(c)(6)(G)	1255(b)(1)	Favorable treatment of REIT income from interest rate swaps and caps is extended to income from all types of hedging agreements	For tax years beginning after Aug. 5, '97	1708	5230
856(c)(6)(G)	1258	Favorable treatment of REIT income from interest rate swaps and caps is extended to income from all types of hedging agreements	For tax years beginning after Aug. 5, '97	1708	5230
856(c)(8)	1255(a)(2)	Repeal of requirement that no more than 30% of REIT's gross income can be derived from sales or other dispositions	Tax years beginning after Aug. 5, '97	1709	5230
856(d)(2)(C)	1252(a)	REITs may render de minimis amount of tenant services and still treat income from property as rent	Tax years beginning after Aug. 5, '97	1705	5230

Code §	Act §	Topic	Generally effective date	Analysis ¶	Com Rep ¶
856(d)(5)	1253	For purposes of applying the related party test or the independent contractor test to REIT rental income, the attribution rules apply to partnerships only where a partner owns 25% or more interest in the partnership	Tax years beginning after Aug. 5, '97	1713	5230
856(d)(7)	1252(b)	REITs may render de minimis amount of tenant services and still treat income from property as rent	Tax years beginning after Aug. 5, '97	1705	5230
856(e)(2)	1257(a)(1)	Election by REIT to treat real estate as foreclosure property made revocable, election grace periods extended, definition of independent contractor conformed	Tax years beginning after Aug. 5, '97	1706	5230
856(e)(3)	1257(a)(2)	Election by REIT to treat real estate as foreclosure property made revocable, election grace periods extended, definition of independent contractor conformed	Tax years beginning after Aug. 5, '97	1706	5230
856(e)(4)	1257(c)	Election by REIT to treat real estate as foreclosure property made revocable, election grace periods extended, definition of independent contractor conformed	Tax years beginning after Aug. 5, '97	1706	5230
856(e)(5)	1257(b)	Election by REIT to treat real estate as foreclosure property made revocable, election grace periods extended, definition of independent contractor conformed	Tax years beginning after Aug. 5, '97	1706	5230
856(i)(2)	1262	Existing corporation in which a REIT acquires a 100% ownership interest is a qualified subsidiary	Tax years beginning after Aug. 5, '97	1711	5230
856(j)(4)	1261(a)	REITs provided safe harbor from prohibited transaction tax for shared appreciation mortgages disposed of under bankruptcy court jurisdiction	For tax years beginning after Aug. 5, '97	1712	5230

Code §	Act §	Topic	Generally effective date	Analysis ¶	Com Rep ¶
856(j)(4)(A)	1261(b)	REITs provided safe harbor from prohibited transaction tax for shared appreciation mortgages disposed of under bankruptcy court jurisdiction	For tax years beginning after Aug. 5, '97	1712	5230
856(k)	1251(b)(1)	Requirement that REIT not be closely held is met where adequate shareholder records are maintained and REIT has no knowledge to contrary	Tax years beginning after Aug. 5, '97	1704	5230
857(a)(2)	1251(a)(1)	Failure by REIT to maintain shareholder records results in monetary penalties, not disqualification	Tax years beginning after Aug. 5, '97	1703	5230
857(a)(3)	1251(a)(1)	Distributions by newly electing REITs to reduce pre-REIT earnings and profits are deemed to reduce earliest acquired earnings and profits before current earnings and profits	For tax years beginning after Aug. 5, '97	1714	5230
857(a)(3)	1251(a)(1)	Failure by REIT to maintain shareholder records results in monetary penalties, not disqualification	Tax years beginning after Aug. 5, '97	1703	5230
857(b)(3)(D)	1254(a)	REITs may elect to retain capital gains and pass-through to shareholders credit for capital gains taxes paid like RICs	For tax years beginning after Aug. 5, '97	1701	5230
857(b)(6)(C)(iii)	1260	REIT property that is involuntarily converted is excluded from prohibited transaction 100% tax	Tax years beginning after Aug. 5, '97	1710	5230
857(b)(7)(A)	1254(b)(1)	REITs may elect to retain capital gains and pass-through to shareholders credit for capital gains taxes paid like RICs	For tax years beginning after Aug. 5, '97	1701	5230
857(d)(3)	1256	Distributions by newly electing REITs to reduce pre-REIT earnings and profits are deemed to reduce earliest acquired earnings and profits before current earnings and profits	For tax years beginning after Aug. 5, '97	1714	5230

Code §	Act §	Topic	Generally effective date	Analysis ¶	Com Rep ¶
857(e)(2)(B)	1259	REIT's "excess noncash income" includes coupon interest and OID under both cash and accrual methods, as well as income from debt cancellation	Tax years beginning after Aug. 5, '97	1707	5230
857(e)(2)(C)	1259	REIT's "excess noncash income" includes coupon interest and OID under both cash and accrual methods, as well as income from debt cancellation	Tax years beginning after Aug. 5, '97	1707	5230
857(f)	1251(a)(2)	Failure by REIT to maintain shareholder records results in monetary penalties, not disqualification	Tax years beginning after Aug. 5, '97	1703	5230
860L(b)(1)	1601(f)(6)(A)	Rules for regular interests in FASITs apply to interests issued on or after the starting date	Sep. 1, '97	1718	5366
860L(e)(2)(B)	1601(f)(6)(C)	Certain transactions exempted from FASIT prohibited transaction rules	Sep. 1, '97	1719	5366
860L(e)(3)(A)	1601(f)(6)(D)	Certain transactions exempted from FASIT prohibited transaction rules	Sep. 1, '97	1719	5366
860L(e)(3)(D)	1601(f)(6)(E)	Certain transactions exempted from FASIT prohibited transaction rules	Sep. 1, '97	1719	5366
861(a)(3)	1174(a)(1)	Nonresident alien crew member's income not U.S. source income	Tax years beginning after Dec. 31, '97	1624	5196
863(c)(2)(B)	1174(a)(2)	Nonresident alien crew member's income not U.S. source income	Tax years beginning after Dec. 31, '97	1624	5196
864(b)(2)(A)(ii)	1162(a)	Simplification of the stock and securities trading safe harbor for foreign corporations	Tax years starting after Dec. 31, '97	1620	5191
877(d)(2)(B)	1602(g)(1)	Expatriate tax rules clarified	For individuals giving up U.S. citizenship or U.S. residency after Feb. 5, '95	1626	5380

Code §	Act §	Topic	Generally effective date	Analysis ¶	Com Rep ¶
877(d)(2)(D)	1602(g)(2)	Expatriate tax rules clarified	For individuals giving up U.S. citizenship or U.S. residency after Feb. 5, '95	1626	5380
877(d)(3)	1602(g)(3)	Expatriate tax rules clarified	For individuals giving up U.S. citizenship or U.S. residency after Feb. 5, '95	1626	5380
877(d)(4)(A)	1602(g)(4)	Expatriate tax rules clarified	For individuals giving up U.S. citizenship or U.S. residency after Feb. 5, '95	1626	5380
894(c)	1054	Treaty benefits denied for certain payments through hybrid entities	Aug. 5, '97	1625	5146
901(k)	1053(a)	Holding period requirement for certain foreign taxes	Dividends paid or accrued more than 30 days after Aug. 5, '97.	1604	5145
902(b)	1113(a)	Indirect foreign tax credit extended to sixth-tier corporations	Tax years beginning after Aug. 5, '97	1601	5175
902(c)(2)(B)	1163(a)	Clarification of determination of foreign taxes deemed paid	Aug. 5, '97	1606	5192
904(b)(2)(C)	311(c)(3)	IRS can modify rule for determining foreign source income attributable to capital gains to properly reflect capital gain rate differential and computation of net capital gain	For tax years ending after May 6, '97	1608	
904(d)(1)(E)	1105(a)(1)	Certain individuals exempt from foreign tax credit limitation	Tax years beginning after Dec. 31, 2002.	1602	5174

Code §	Act §	Topic	Generally effective date	Analysis ¶	Com Rep ¶
904(d)(2)(C)(i)(II)	1163(b)	Clarification of foreign tax credit limitation for financial services income	Aug. 5, '97	1607	5192
904(d)(2)(C)(iii)(II)	1105(a)(3)	Certain individuals exempt from foreign tax credit limitation	Tax years beginning after Dec. 31, 2002.	1602	5174
904(d)(2)(D)	1105(a)(3)	Certain individuals exempt from foreign tax credit limitation	Tax years beginning after Dec. 31, 2002.	1602	5174
904(d)(2)(E)	1105(a)(2)	Certain individuals exempt from foreign tax credit limitation	Tax years beginning after Dec. 31, 2002.	1602	5174
904(d)(2)(E)(i)	1111(b)	Gain on certain stock sales by CFCs treated as dividends	Aug. 5, '97	1612	5175
904(d)(4)	1105(b)	Certain individuals exempt from foreign tax credit limitation	Tax years beginning after Dec. 31, 2002.	1602	5174
904(j)	1101(a)	Certain individuals exempt from foreign tax credit limitation	Tax years starting after Dec. 31, '97.	1602	5170
905(c)	1102(a)(2)	Translation of foreign taxes simplified	Tax years starting after Dec. 31, '97.	1605	5171
911(b)(2)	1172	Increase in dollar limitation on foreign earned income exclusion	Tax years starting after Dec. 31, '97.	1622	5194
927(a)(2)(B)	1171	FSC export property treatment extended to computer software licensed for reproduction abroad	Gross receipts attributable to periods after Dec. 31, '97, in tax years ending after that date.	1621	5193
951(a)(2)	1112(a)	Gain on certain stock sales by CFCs treated as dividends	Dispositions after Aug. 5, '97	1612	5175
952(b)	1112(c)	Treatment of exemptions from branch profits tax clarified	Tax years beginning after Dec. 31, '86	1615	5175
954(c)(1)(B)	1051(a)(2)	Definition of foreign personal holding company income expanded	Tax years starting after Aug. 5, '97	1609	5143

Code §	Act §	Topic	Generally effective date	Analysis ¶	Com Rep ¶
954(c)(1)(F)	1051(a)(1)	Definition of foreign personal holding company income expanded	Tax years starting after Aug. 5, '97	1609	5143
954(c)(1)(G)	1051(a)(1)	Definition of foreign personal holding company income expanded	Tax years starting after Aug. 5, '97	1609	5143
954(c)(2)(C)	1051(b)	Definition of foreign personal holding company income expanded	Tax years starting after Aug. 5, '97	1609	5143
954(e)(2)	1175(b)	Temporary exception from foreign personal holding company income for active financing income	Tax years of foreign corporations beginning after Dec. 31, '97 and before Jan. 1, '99, and tax years of U.S. shareholders with or within such tax years of foreign corporations end.	1610	5197
954(h)	1175(a)	Temporary exception from foreign personal holding company income for active financing income	Tax years of foreign corporations beginning after Dec. 31, '97 and before Jan. 1, '99, and tax years of U.S. shareholders with or within such tax years of foreign corporations end.	1610	5197
956(b)(1)(A)	1601(e)	Clarification of earnings and profits definition for purposes of CFC rules	Tax years of CFCs beginning after '96, and tax years of U.S. shareholders within which or with which such years end	1616	5362

Code §	Act §	Topic	Generally effective date	Analysis ¶	Com Rep ¶
956(c)(2)	1173(a)	U.S. property does not include certain assets acquired by a dealer in securities or commodities in the ordinary course of a trade or business	Tax years of foreign corporations beginning after Dec. 31, '97, and to tax years of U.S. shareholders with or within which such tax years of foreign corporations end.	1611	5195
960(a)(1)	1113(b)	Indirect foreign tax credit extended to sixth-tier corporations	Tax years beginning after Aug. 5, '97	1601	5175
961(c)	1112(b)	Adjustments to basis of stock in lower-tier CFCs	Tax years beginning after Dec. 31, '97	1614	5175
964(e)	1111(a)	Gain on certain stock sales by CFCs treated as dividends	Aug. 5, '97	1612	5175
986(a)	1102(a)(1)	Translation of foreign taxes simplified	Tax years starting after Dec. 31, '97.	1605	5171
986(a)(3)	1102(b)(1)	Translation of foreign taxes simplified	Tax years starting after Dec. 31, '97.	1605	5171
988(e)	1104(a)	Simplification of treatment of personal transactions in foreign currency	Tax years starting after Dec. 31, '97.	1623	5173
989(c)(6)	1102(b)(2)	Translation of foreign taxes simplified	Tax years starting after Dec. 31, '97.	1605	5171
1014(a)(4)	508(b)	No step–up in basis for land subject to a qualified conservation easement that is excluded from the gross estate	For estates of decedents dying after Dec. 31, '97	518	5033
1031(h)(2)	1052(a)	Personal property used predominantly in the U.S. is treated as not property of a like-kind with respect to personal property used predominantly outside the U.S. for purposes of the like-kind exchange rules	Transfers after June 8, '97, in tax years ending after June 8, '97	209	5144

Code §	Act §	Topic	Generally effective date	Analysis ¶	Com Rep ¶
1033(e)	913(b)(1)	Forced sales of livestock due to floods or other weather conditions are treated as involuntary conversions	Sales and exchanges after Dec. 31, '96	2102	5063
1033(i)	1087(a)	Involuntary conversion nonrecognition rules exception for replacement property acquired from a related party is expanded to cover all taxpayers	Involuntary conversions occurring after June 8, '97	207	5164
1034	312(b)	Replacement of rollover rules and the one-time exclusion that applied to sales of a principal residence with an exclusion of gain of up to $250,000 ($500,000 for joint filers)	Sales and exchanges after May 6, '97	102	5020
1035(c)	1131(b)(1)	Transfer of property to foreign estate, trust, corporation or partnership triggers gain; excise tax on transfers to foreign entities repealed	Aug. 5, '97	1629	5182
1036(c)	1014(e)(3)	Certain preferred stock treated as boot	Transactions after June 8, '97	1502	5119
1042(g)	968	Gain may be deferred on the sale to eligible farmers' cooperatives of stock of qualified agricultural refiners or processors	Sales after Dec. 31, '97	208	5091
1045	313(a)	Elective rollover of gain from qualified small business stock to other qualified small business stock	Sales after Aug. 5, '97	206	5021
1057	1131(c)	Transfer of property to foreign estate, trust, corporation or partnership triggers gain; excise tax on transfers to foreign entities repealed	Aug. 5, '97	1629	5182
1059	1011	Treatment of extraordinary dividends amended	Distributions after May 3, '95	1503	5116
1059(e)(1)(A)(iii)	1013(b)	Treatment of dividend from related-party stock purchase amended	Distributions or acquisitions after June 8, '97	1505	5118

Code §	Act §	Topic	Generally effective date	Analysis ¶	Com Rep ¶
1201(a)(2)	314(a)	Amount of net capital gain taken into account in computing alternative tax on net capital gain for corporations is limited to taxable income	Tax years ending after Dec. 31, '97	603	5022
1223(15)	313(b)(2)	Elective rollover of gain from qualified small business stock to other qualified small business stock	Sales after Aug. 5, '97	206	5021
1233(h)	1003(b)(1)	Substantial worthlessness of short sale property is a gain recognition event; regs are to provide similar rules for other transactions similar to short sales	Property which becomes substantially worthless after Aug. 5, '97	203	5113
1234A(1)	1003(a)(1)	Sale treatment for cancellations, lapses, expirations and other terminations is expanded to all property which is a capital asset	Terminations more than 30 days after Aug. 5, '97	204	5113
1239(b)	1308(b)	Estate and beneficiaries treated as related for loss and capital gain treatment on sale of depreciable property	Tax years beginning after Aug. 5, '97	211	5268
1245(a)(2)(C)	1604(a)(3)	Qualified rent-to-own property is designated as MACRS 3-year property with a 4-year class life	Property placed in service after June 30, '93	803	5163
1245(a)(3)(C)	1604(a)(3)	Qualified rent-to-own property is designated as MACRS 3-year property with a 4-year class life	Property placed in service after June 30, '93	803	5163
1259	1001(a)	Constructive sales treatment for appreciated financial positions	Any constructive sale after June 8, '97	202	5111

Code Section Table

Code §	Act §	Topic	Generally effective date	Analysis ¶	Com Rep ¶
1271(b)	1003(c)	Sale-or-exchange treatment for retirement of debt instruments is expanded to include instruments issued by natural persons	Sales, exchanges and retirements after Aug. 5, '97 for obligations issued by individuals issued or purchased after June 8, '97 and for sales, exchanges and retirements after Aug. 5, '97 for obligations issued before July 2, '82 by an issuer which isn't a corporation or government (or political subdivision) which are purchased after June 8, '97	205	5113
1272(a)(6)(C)	1004(a)	Interest must be accrued on credit card receivables during payment grace period	Tax years beginning after Aug. 5, '97	2006	5114
1296	1122(a)	Mark-to-market election for PFIC stock	Tax years of U.S. persons beginning after Dec. 31, '97 and tax years of foreign corporations ending with or within such tax years of U.S. persons.	1618	5178
1296(e)	1121	10% U.S. shareholders of a CFC are not subject to PFIC rules	Tax years of U.S. persons beginning after Dec. 31, '97.	1617	5178

Code §	Act §	Topic	Generally effective date	Analysis ¶	Com Rep ¶
1297(e)	1123(a)	Valuation of assets for passive foreign investment company determination	Tax years of U.S. persons beginning after Dec. 31. '97.	1619	5178
1301	933	Farm income averaging over a three-year period is permitted for individuals	Tax years beginning after Dec. 31, '97 and before Jan. 1, 2001	2103	5070
1361(b)(3)(A)	1601(c)(3)	Treatment of qualified Subchapter S subsidiaries (QSSSs) as separate corporations	Tax years beginning after Dec. 31, '96	1508	5359
1361(e)(1)(B)(iii)	1601(c)(1)	Charitable remainder trusts may not be electing small business trust shareholders	Tax years beginning after Dec. 31, '96	1506	5357
1374(d)(7)	1601(f)(5)(B)	Rules modified on recapture of bad debt reserve by thrift institutions	Tax years beginning after Dec. 31, '95	1717	5365
1391(b)(2)	951(a)	Authorization of two additional urban empowerment zones meeting the same criteria and eligible for the same tax incentives as existing empowerment zones	Aug. 5, '97, except that designations of new empowerment zones will be made in the 180-day period after Aug. 5, '97, and no designation takes effect before Jan. 1, 2000	2607	5081
1391(g)	952(a)	Authorization of 20 new empowerment zones meeting different eligibility criteria and eligible for different tax incentives	Upon designations to be made after Aug. 5, '97 but before Jan. 1, '99	2606	5081
1392(d)	954	Empowerment zone and enterprise community eligibility criteria for nominated areas in Alaska or Hawaii are relaxed	Aug. 5, '97	2614	5081
1394(b)(2)	955(b)	Enterprise zone facility bond rules are modified	Obligations issued after Aug. 5, '97	2608	5081

Code §	Act §	Topic	Generally effective date	Analysis ¶	Com Rep ¶
1394(b)(3)	955(a)	Enterprise zone facility bond rules are modified	Obligations issued after Aug. 5, '97	2608	5081
1394(f)	953(a)	State private activity bond volume caps and $3 million/$20 million limits on issue amounts do not apply to new empowerment zone facility bonds	Obligations issued after Aug. 5, '97	2609	5081
1396(b)(2)	951(b)(2)	Authorization of two additional urban empowerment zones meeting the same criteria and eligible for the same tax incentives as existing empowerment zones	Aug. 5, '97, except that designations of new empowerment zones will be made in the 180-day period after Aug. 5, '97, and no designation takes effect before Jan. 1, 2000	2607	5081
1396(e)	952(b)	Authorization of 20 new empowerment zones meeting different eligibility criteria and eligible for different tax incentives	Upon designations to be made after Aug. 5, '97 but before Jan. 1, '99	2606	5081
1397A(c)	952(c)	Authorization of 20 new empowerment zones meeting different eligibility criteria and eligible for different tax incentives	Upon designations to be made after Aug. 5, '97 but before Jan. 1, '99	2606	5081
1397B(b)	956(a)	Definition of business entity for enterprise zone business rules is liberalized	Tax years beginning on or after Aug. 5, '97	2610	5081
1397B(c)	956(a)	Definition of qualified proprietorship for enterprise zone business rules is liberalized	Tax years beginning on or after Aug. 5, '97	2611	5081
1397B(d)	956(a)(4)	Property rental rules are modified for enterprize zone business definition	Tax years beginning on or before Aug. 5, '97	2612	5081

Code §	Act §	Topic	Generally effective date	Analysis ¶	Com Rep ¶
1397B(f)	956(a)(6)	Treatment of businesses straddling census tract lines for enterprise zone business definition	Tax years beginning on or after Aug. 5, '97	2613	5081
1397E	226(a)	Certain financial institutions holding qualified zone academy bonds are entitled to nonrefundable tax credit	Obligations issued after Dec. 31, '97	705	5012
1400	701(a)	Designation of DC Enterprise Zone as an empowerment zone	Aug. 5, '97	2601	5040
1400A	701(a)	Tax-exempt bonds for District of Columbia	Aug. 5, '97	2604	5040
1400B	701(a)	Zero percent capital gains rate applies to certain sales of DC Zone assets held for more than five years	Aug. 5, '97	2602	5040
1400C	701(a)	$5,000 credit for first-time home buyers in the District of Columbia	Aug. 5, '97	2603	5040
1402(k)	922(a)	Exemption from self-employment tax for termination payments received by former insurance salesmen	Payments made after Dec. 31, '97	1903	5067
1491	1131(a)	Transfer of property to foreign estate, trust, corporation or partnership triggers gain; excise tax on transfers to foreign entities repealed	Aug. 5, '97	1629	5182
1492	1131(a)	Transfer of property to foreign estate, trust, corporation or partnership triggers gain; excise tax on transfers to foreign entities repealed	Aug. 5, '97	1629	5182
1494	1131(a)	Transfer of property to foreign estate, trust, corporation or partnership triggers gain; excise tax on transfers to foreign entities repealed	Aug. 5, '97	1629	5182
2001(c)(2)	501(a)(1)(D)	Exemption equivalent amount of unified estate and gift tax credit is increased to $1 million on a phased-in schedule through 2006	Applies to estates of decedents dying, and gifts made, after Dec. 31, '97	501	5026

Code §	Act §	Topic	Generally effective date	Analysis ¶	Com Rep ¶
2001(f)	506(a)	Gifts may not be revalued for estate tax purposes after gift tax statute of limitations expires	For gifts made after Aug. 5, '97	521	5031
2010(a)	501(a)(1)(A)	Exemption equivalent amount of unified estate and gift tax credit is increased to $1 million on a phased-in schedule through 2006	Applies to estates of decedents dying, and gifts made, after Dec. 31, '97	501	5026
2010(c)	501(a)(1)(B)	Exemption equivalent amount of unified estate and gift tax credit is increased to $1 million on a phased-in schedule through 2006	Applies to estates of decedents dying, and gifts made, after Dec. 31, '97	501	5026
2031(c)	508(a)	Estate tax exclusion for up to 40% of value of land subject to qualified conservation easement	For estates of decedents dying after Dec. 31, '97	517	5033
2032A(a)(3)	501(b)	$750,000 limit on estate tax special use valuation reduction will be adjusted for inflation after '98	Applies to estates of decedents dying in a calendar year after '98	502	5026
2032A(b)(5)(A)	504(b)	Lineal descendant's inter-family cash lease of specially-valued property won't trigger recapture estate tax	For leases entered into after Dec. 31, '76	510	5029
2032A(c)(7)	504(a)	Lineal descendant's inter-family cash lease of specially-valued property won't trigger recapture estate tax	For leases entered into after Dec. 31, '76	510	5029
2032A(c)(8)	508(c)	Qualified conservation contribution is not a disposition for estate tax special use valuation purposes	For easements granted after Dec. 31, '97	519	5033
2032A(d)(3)	1313(a)	Rules for correcting special use valuation elections eased	Applies to estates of decedents dying after Aug. 5, '97	509	5273
2033A	502(a)	Estate tax exclusion allowed for qualified family-owned business interests—exclusion amount, plus exemption equivalent of unified credit, can't exceed $1.3 million	Applies to estates of decedents dying after Dec. 31, '97	505	5027

Code §	Act §	Topic	Generally effective date	Analysis ¶	Com Rep ¶
2033A(f)	502(a)	Estate tax benefit of qualified family-owned business exclusion may be recaptured if certain events occur	Applies to estates of decedents dying after Dec. 31, '97	506	5027
2033A(g)	502(a)	Estate tax benefit of qualified family-owned business exclusion may be recaptured if certain events occur	Applies to estates of decedents dying after Dec. 31, '97	506	5027
2035(e)	1310(a)	Annual exclusion gifts from revocable trusts within three years of grantor's death are not includible in gross estate	Applies to estates of decedents dying after Aug. 5, '97	524	5270
2053(c)(1)(D)	503(b)(1)	Estate tax benefit of qualified family-owned business exclusion may be recaptured if certain events occur	Applies to estates of decedents dying after Dec. 31, '97	506	5028
2055(a)	1530(c)(7)	Limited transfer of qualified employer securities by charitable remainder trusts to ESOPs is permitted	Aug. 5, '97	938	5352
2055(e)(3)(J)	1089(b)(3)	Limitation on charitable remainder trust (CRT) eligibility for trusts with greater than 50% payout and less than 10% charitable remainder	For transfers in trust after June 18, '97	532	5166
2056(b)(7)(C)	1311(a)	Nonparticipant spouse's community property interest in annuity qualifies as QTIP	Applies to estates of decedents dying after Aug. 5, '97	512	5271
2056A(a)(1)(A)	1314(a)	IRS given authority to waive U.S. trustee requirement for qualified domestic trusts (QDOTs)	Estates of decedents dying after Aug. 5, '97	515	5274
2056A(c)(3)	1312(a)	Entities other than trusts may be eligible for qualified domestic trust (QDOT) treatment	Applies to estates of decedents dying after Aug. 5, '97	514	5272

3,011

Code §	Act §	Topic	Generally effective date	Analysis ¶	Com Rep ¶
2102(c)(3)(A)	501(a)(1)(E)	Exemption equivalent amount of unified estate and gift tax credit is increased to $1 million on a phased-in schedule through 2006	Applies to estates of decedents dying, and gifts made, after Dec. 31, '97	501	5026
2105(b)(4)	1304(a)	Certain short-term obligations held by nonresident aliens are not subject to U.S. estate tax	Applies to estates of decedents dying after Aug. 5, '97	511	5264
2107(c)(2)(B)(i)	1602(g)(6)(A)	Expatriate tax rules clarified	For individuals giving up U.S. citizenship or U.S. residency after Feb. 5, '95	1626	5380
2107(c)(2)(C)	1602(g)(6)(B)	Expatriate tax rules clarified	For individuals giving up U.S. citizenship or U.S. residency after Feb. 5, '95	1626	5380
2207A(a)(2)	1302(a)	Recovery right for QTIP and retained life estate property waived only if specific intent indicated	Applies to estates of decedents dying after Aug. 5, '97	513	5262
2207B(a)(2)	1302(b)	Recovery right for QTIP and retained life estate property waived only if specific intent indicated	Applies to estates of decedents dying after Aug. 5, '97	513	5262
2503(b)(2)	501(c)(3)	Gift tax annual exclusion of $10,000 will be adjusted for inflation after '98	Applies to gifts made in a calendar year after '98	503	5026
2504(c)	506(d)	Gifts may not be revalued for estate tax purposes after gift tax statute of limitations expires	For gifts made after Aug. 5, '97	521	5031
2505(a)(1)	501(a)(2)	Exemption equivalent amount of unified estate and gift tax credit is increased to $1 million on a phased-in schedule through 2006	Applies to estates of decedents dying, and gifts made, after Dec. 31, '97	501	5026

Code §	Act §	Topic	Generally effective date	Analysis ¶	Com Rep ¶
2612(c)(2)	511(b)(1)	"Deceased parent exception" to generation–skipping transfer (GST) tax is expanded	For generation–skipping transfers occurring after Dec. 31, '97	525	5034
2612(c)(3)	511(b)(2)	"Deceased parent exception" to generation–skipping transfer (GST) tax is expanded	For generation–skipping transfers occurring after Dec. 31, '97	525	5034
2631(c)	501(d)	Generation-skipping transfer exemption of $1 million will be adjusted for inflation after '98	Applies to individuals who die in any calendar year after '98	504	5026
2651(e)	511(a)	"Deceased parent exception" to generation–skipping transfer (GST) tax is expanded	For generation–skipping transfers occurring after Dec. 31, '97	525	5034
2652(b)(1)	1305(b)	Election to treat revocable trust as part of estate for income and generation–skipping transfer (GST) tax purposes	For estates of decedents dying after Aug. 5, '97	526	5265
3121(d)	921(a)	In determining the employment status of retail securities brokers, instructions to ensure compliance with government investor protection standards are disregarded	For services performed after Dec. 31, '97	1902	5066
3301	1035	FUTA surtax extended through 2007	For labor performed on or after Jan. 1, '99	1905	5133
3306(c)(21)	5406(a)(3)*	Wages paid for services by inmates in a penal institution are exempt from FUTA tax	Service performed after Jan. 1, '94	1904	5506
4001(a)	906(a)	Purchase price triggering imposition of luxury excise tax is increased for electric and other clean-burning fuel vehicles	For sales and installations occurring after Aug. 5, '97	2218	5056
4001(e)(1)	906(b)(1)	Purchase price triggering imposition of luxury excise tax is increased for electric and other clean-burning fuel vehicles	For sales and installations occurring after Aug. 5, '97	2218	5056

Code §	Act §	Topic	Generally effective date	Analysis ¶	Com Rep ¶
4001(f)	1601(f)(3)(A)	Luxury tax on separate installation of auto parts and accessories is conformed to tax on auto sales	Sales after Aug. 5, '97	2219	5387
4001(g)	1601(f)(3)(B)	Luxury tax on separate installation of auto parts and accessories is conformed to tax on auto sales	Sales after Aug. 5, '97	2219	5387
4003(a)(1)(A)	906(b)(3)	Purchase price triggering imposition of luxury excise tax is increased for electric and other clean-burning fuel vehicles	For sales and installations occurring after Aug. 5, '97	2218	5056
4003(a)(2)(B)	906(b)(4)	Purchase price triggering imposition of luxury excise tax is increased for electric and other clean-burning fuel vehicles	For sales and installations occurring after Aug. 5, '97	2218	5056
4003(a)(3)(C)	1401(a)	De minimis exceptions to retail heavy truck and luxury taxes on separate purchase and installation of parts and accessories are increased	Installations on vehicles sold after Aug. 5, '97	2220	5275
4041(a)(1)(A)	902(b)(1)	Suspended excise tax on diesel fuel used in recreational motorboats is repealed	Jan. 1, '98	2210	5052
4041(a)(2)	907(a)(1)	Tax rates on propane, liquefied natural gas and methanol produced from natural gas decreased	Oct. 1, '97	2212	5057
4041(c)(2)	1435(b)	Skydiving flights are exempted from air transportation taxes; fel used in such flights taxed as fuel used in non-commercial aviation	Oct. 1, '97	2206	5293
4041(c)(3)(B)	1031(a)(3)	Airport and airway trust fund taxes extended through Sept. 30, 2007	Oct. 1, '97	2201	5129
4041(d)(1)	907(a)(2)	Tax rates on propane, liquefied natural gas and methanol produced from natural gas decreased	Oct. 1, '97	2212	5057

Code §	Act §	Topic	Generally effective date	Analysis ¶	Com Rep ¶
4041(l)	1601(f)(4)(A)(i)	Exemption from air transportation of persons tax for fixed-wing aircraft used for emergency medical services applied retroactively to aviation fuel taxes; definition of fixed-wing aircraft is modified	Aug. 27, '96	2205	
4041(m)(1)(A)(i)	907(b)	Tax rates on propane, liquefied natural gas and methanol produced from natural gas decreased	Oct. 1, '97	2212	5057
4051(b)(2)(B)	1401(a)	De minimis exceptions to retail heavy truck and luxury taxes on separate purchase and installation of parts and accessories are increased	Installations on vehicles sold after Aug. 5, '97	2220	5275
4051(e)	1402(a)	Exclusion of tire value from retail heavy truck excise tax replaced by credit for manufacturers' excise tax on tires	Jan. 1, '98	2221	5276
4052(b)(1)(B)(iii)	1402(b)	Exclusion of tire value from retail heavy truck excise tax replaced by credit for manufacturers' excise tax on tires	Jan. 1, '98	2221	5276
4052(d)	1434(b)(1)	Retail heavy truck tax modified for wrecked vehicle remanufacturing and resale registration requirement replaced with certification procedure	Jan. 1, '98	2222	5292
4052(f)	1434(a)	Retail heavy truck tax modified for wrecked vehicle remanufacturing and resale registration requirement replaced with certification procedure	Jan. 1, '98	2222	5292
4052(g)	1434(b)(2)	Retail heavy truck tax modified for wrecked vehicle remanufacturing and resale registration requirement replaced with certification procedure	Jan. 1, '98	2222	5292
4081(a)(2)(A)(iii)	1032(b)	Diesel fuel removal-at-terminal excise tax rules generally made applicable to kerosene	July 1, '98	2208	5130

Code §	Act §	Topic	Generally effective date	Analysis ¶	Com Rep ¶
4081(d)(2)(B)	1031(a)(2)	Airport and airway trust fund taxes extended through Sept. 30, 2007	Oct. 1, '97	2201	5129
4081(d)(3)	1033	Leaking underground storage tank trust fund financing tax reimposed	Oct. 1, '97	2211	5131
4082	1032(c)(1) and 1032(c)(2)	Diesel fuel removal-at-terminal excise tax rules generally made applicable to kerosene	July 1, '98	2208	5130
4083(a)	1032(a)	Diesel fuel removal-at-terminal excise tax rules generally made applicable to kerosene	July 1, '98	2208	5130
4083(a)(3)	902(b)(3)	Suspended excise tax on diesel fuel used in recreational motorboats is repealed	Jan. 1, '98	2210	5052
4083(b)	1032(e)(4)	Diesel fuel removal-at-terminal excise tax rules generally made applicable to kerosene	July 1, '98	2208	5130
4091(b)(3)(A)(ii)	1031(a)(1)	Airport and airway trust fund taxes extended through Sept. 30, 2007	Oct. 1, '97	2201	5129
4091(d)	1436(a)	Registered aviation fuel producers who buy and resell tax-paid fuel are allowed a refund to prevent double taxation	Fuel acquired by the producer after Sept. 30, '97	2215	5294
4101(e)	1032(d)	Diesel fuel removal-at-terminal excise tax rules generally made applicable to kerosene	July 1, '98	2208	5130
4131(b)	904(a)	Uniform vaccine excise tax rate replaces various vaccine-specific rates; three new vaccines taxed	Day after Aug. 5, '97	2223	5054
4132(a)	904(c)	Uniform vaccine excise tax rate replaces various vaccine-specific rates; three new vaccines taxed	Day after Aug. 5, '97	2223	5054
4132(a)(1)	904(b)	Uniform vaccine excise tax rate replaces various vaccine-specific rates; three new vaccines taxed	Day after Aug. 5, '97	2223	5054
4132(b)	904(e)	Uniform vaccine excise tax rate replaces various vaccine-specific rates; three new vaccines taxed	Day after Aug. 5, '97	2223	5054

Code Section Table

Code §	Act §	Topic	Generally effective date	Analysis ¶	Com Rep Code ¶
4161(b)	1433(a)	Manufacturers' tax on completed arrows is replaced with tax on arrow's component parts	Articles sold by the manufacturer, producer or importer after Sept. 30, '97	2225	5291
4222(b)(2)	1431(a)	IRS authority to waive purchaser registration requirements for excise-tax-free sales is expanded	Aug. 5, '97	2224	5289
4251(d)	1034(a)	Prepaid telephone cards and similar arrangements are subject to communications excise tax	Amounts paid in calendar months beginning more than 60 days after Aug. 5, '97	2207	5132
4261(a)	1031(c)(1)	Domestic air passenger transportation tax restructured; tax imposed on right to make mileage awards	Transportation beginning after Sept. 30, '97	2202	5129
4261(b)	1031(c)(1)	Domestic air passenger transportation tax restructured; tax imposed on right to make mileage awards	Transportation beginning after Sept. 30, '97	2202	5129
4261(c)	1031(c)(1)	Air passenger tax on international departures increased; international arrivals taxed	Transportation beginning after Sept. 30, '97	2203	5129
4261(e)	1031(c)(2)	Domestic air passenger transportation tax restructured; tax imposed on right to make mileage awards	Transportation beginning after Sept. 30, '97	2202	5129
4261(e)(4)	1031(c)(2)	Air passenger tax on international departures increased; international arrivals taxed	Transportation beginning after Sept. 30, '97	2203	5129
4261(f)	1601(f)(4)(D)	Exemption from air transportation of persons tax for fixed-wing aircraft used for emergency medical services applied retroactively to aviation fuel taxes; definition of fixed-wing aircraft is modified	Aug. 27, '96	2205	
4261(g)(1)(A)(ii)	1031(b)(1)	Airport and airway trust fund taxes extended through Sept. 30, 2007	Oct. 1, '97	2201	5129

Code Section Table

Code §	Act §	Topic	Generally effective date	Analysis ¶	Com Rep ¶
4261(h)	1435(a)	Skydiving flights are exempted from air transportation taxes; fel used in such flights taxed as fuel used in non-commercial aviation	Oct. 1, '97	2206	5293
4263(c)	1031(c)(3)	Air carriers made secondarily liable for passenger air transportation taxes; due date for certain deposits of passenger and property air transportation taxes delayed	Transportation beginning after Sept. 30, '97	2204	5129
4271(d)(1)(A)(ii)	1031(b)(2)	Airport and airway trust fund taxes extended through Sept. 30, 2007	Oct. 1, '97	2201	5129
4682(d)(1)	903(a)	Scheduled exemption from ozone-depleting-chemicals tax for imported recycled halon-1211 is repealed	Aug. 5, '97	2226	5053
4962(b)	1603(a)	IRS authorized to make reasonable cause abatements of first-tier penalty taxes on charitable organization excess benefit transactions	Excess benefit transactions occurring after Sept. 13, '95	2409	5384
4972(c)(6)(B)	1507(a)	New exception to 10-percent excise tax on nondeductible contributions for contributions to 401(k) plan	Tax years after '97	911	5313
4973(b)	302(b)	New nondeductible Roth IRA allows tax-free withdrawal of earnings	Taxable years beginning after Dec. 31, '97	301	5016
4973(d)	4006(b)(1)	Medicare eligible individuals may choose "Medicare+Choice MSAs" as a Medicare option	Taxable years beginning after Dec. 31, '98	1201	5501
4973(e)	213(d)	Tax-exempt education IRAs allowed	Tax years beginning after Dec. 31, '97	403	5005
4975(a)	1074(a)	First-tier excise tax on prohibited transactions increased from 10% to 15%	For prohibited transactions after Aug. 5, '97	908	5156
4975(c)	213(b)	Tax-exempt education IRAs allowed	Tax years beginning after Dec. 31, '97	403	5005

Code §	Act §	Topic	Generally effective date	Analysis ¶	Com Rep ¶
4975(f)(6)	1506(b)(1)	Statutory exemptions from prohibited transaction rules extended to S corporations	Taxable years beginning after Dec. 31, 1997	909	5312
4980A	1073(a)	Repeal of excess distribution and excess retirement accumulation tax	After Dec. 31, '96	907	5155
5008(c)(1)	1411(a)	Tax-free removal of alcoholic beverages from bonded premisesand refund or credit on return to bonded premises allowed	The first day of the first calendar quarter beginning at least 180 days after Aug. 5, '97.	2227	5277
5027(c)	1413(a)	Alcoholic beverage taxes paperwork and administration eased	The first day of the first calender quarter beginning at least 180 says after Aug. 5, '97	2229	5277
5041(b)(6)	908(a)	Alcohol excise tax on hard cider reduced	Oct. 1, '97	2228	5058
5041(c)	908(b)	Alcohol excise tax on hard cider reduced	Oct. 1, '97	2228	5058
5044(a)	1416(a)	Tax-free removal of alcoholic beverages from bonded premisesand refund or credit on return to bonded premises allowed	The first day of the first calendar quarter beginning at least 180 days after Aug. 5, '97.	2227	5277
5053(f)	1414(b)	Tax-free removal of alcoholic beverages from bonded premisesand refund or credit on return to bonded premises allowed	The first day of the first calendar quarter beginning at least 180 days after Aug. 5, '97.	2227	5277
5053(g)	1418(a)	Tax-free removal of alcoholic beverages from bonded premisesand refund or credit on return to bonded premises allowed	The first day of the first calendar quarter beginning at least 180 days after Aug. 5, '97.	2227	5277

Code §	Act §	Topic	Generally effective date	Analysis ¶	Com Rep ¶
5053(h)	1419(a)	Tax-free removal of alcoholic beverages from bonded premisesand refund or credit on return to bonded premises allowed	The first day of the first calendar quarter beginning at least 180 days after Aug. 5, '97.	2227	5277
5055	1420(a)	Alcoholic beverage taxes paperwork and administration eased	The first day of the first calender quarter beginning at least 180 says after Aug. 5, '97	2229	5277
5056(c)	1414(c)(1)	Tax-free removal of alcoholic beverages from bonded premisesand refund or credit on return to bonded premises allowed	The first day of the first calendar quarter beginning at least 180 days after Aug. 5, '97.	2227	5277
5056(d)	1414(c)(2)	Tax-free removal of alcoholic beverages from bonded premisesand refund or credit on return to bonded premises allowed	The first day of the first calendar quarter beginning at least 180 days after Aug. 5, '97.	2227	5277
5115	1415(a)	Regs on geographic appellations codified; sign-posting requirement for wholesale liquor dealers repealed; up to 60% added sugar allowed in acidic wines	various	2230	5277, 5060
5175(c)	1412(a)	Alcoholic beverage taxes paperwork and administration eased	The first day of the first calender quarter beginning at least 180 says after Aug. 5, '97	2229	5277
5222(b)(2)	1414(a)	Tax-free removal of alcoholic beverages from bonded premisesand refund or credit on return to bonded premises allowed	The first day of the first calendar quarter beginning at least 180 days after Aug. 5, '97.	2227	5277

Code §	Act §	Topic	Generally effective date	Analysis ¶	Com Rep ¶
5361	1416(b)(1)	Tax-free removal of alcoholic beverages from bonded premises and refund or credit on return to bonded premises allowed	The first day of the first calendar quarter beginning at least 180 days after Aug. 5, '97.	2227	5277
5364	1422(a)	Tax-free removal of alcoholic beverages from bonded premises and refund or credit on return to bonded premises allowed	The first day of the first calendar quarter beginning at least 180 days after Aug. 5, '97.	2227	5277
5384(b)(2)(D)	1417(a)	Regs on geographic appellations codified; sign-posting requirement for wholesale liquor dealers repealed; up to 60% added sugar allowed in acidic wines	various	2230	5277, 5060
5388(c)	910(a)	Regs on geographic appellations codified; sign-posting requirement for wholesale liquor dealers repealed; up to 60% added sugar allowed in acidic wines	various	2230	5277, 5060
5418	1421(a)	Tax-free removal of alcoholic beverages from bonded premises and refund or credit on return to bonded premises allowed	The first day of the first calendar quarter beginning at least 180 days after Aug. 5, '97.	2227	5277
5701(a)	9302(b)*	Taxes on cigarettes and other tobacco products rise	Products removed after Dec. 31, '99	2231	5509
5701(b)	9302(a)*	Taxes on cigarettes and other tobacco products rise	Products removed after Dec. 31, '99	2231	5509
5701(c)	9302(c)*	Taxes on cigarettes and other tobacco products rise	Products removed after Dec. 31, '99	2231	5509
5701(d)	9302(d)*	Taxes on cigarettes and other tobacco products rise	Products removed after Dec. 31, '99	2231	5509
5701(f)	9302(f)*	Taxes on cigarettes and other tobacco products rise	Products removed after Dec. 31, '99	2231	5509

Code §	Act §	Topic	Generally effective date	Analysis ¶	Com Rep ¶
5701(g)	9302(g)*	Taxes on cigarettes and other tobacco products rise	Products removed after Dec. 31, '99	2231	5509
6011(e)(2)	1224	Large partnerships' tax returns must be filed on magnetic media and are subject to information return reporting penalties	Partnership tax years ending after Dec. 30, '97	2301	5211, 5212
6012(b)(6)	1225	Unrelated business income tax return requirements for IRAs liberalized	Partnership tax years ending after Dec. 30, '97	2306	5213
6018(a)(1)	501(a)(1)(C)	Exemption equivalent amount of unified estate and gift tax credit is increased to $1 million on a phased-in schedule through 2006	Applies to estates of decedents dying, and gifts made, after Dec. 31, '97	501	5026
6019(3)	1301(a)	Gift tax return requirement eliminated for many charitable donations	Gifts made after Aug. 5, '97	2307	5261
6031(b)	1223(a)	Electing large partnerships must file K-1s by Mar. 15	Partnership tax years ending after Dec. 30, '97	2302	5211
6031(e)	1141(a)	Return requirements of foreign partnerships clarified	Tax years beginning after Aug. 5, '97	2303	5182
6033(b)(10)	1603(b)(1)	Reporting by public charities on excise tax penalties coordinated with the penalties	Returns for tax years beginning after July 30, '96	2305	5384
6033(b)(11)	1603(b)(2)	Reporting by public charities on excise tax penalties coordinated with the penalties	Returns for tax years beginning after July 30, '96	2305	5384
6034A(c)	1027(a)	Estate and trust beneficiaries must report items in manner consistent with estate or trust return or notify IRS of inconsistency	Returns of beneficiaries and owners filed after Aug. 5, '97	2304	5127
6038(a)(1)	1142(a)	U.S. partners that control foreign partnerships subject to information reporting	Annual accounting periods beginning after Aug. 5, '97	2312	5182

Code §	Act §	Topic	Generally effective date	Analysis ¶	Com Rep ¶
6038(a)(5)	1142(d)	U.S. partners that control foreign partnerships subject to information reporting	Annual accounting periods beginning after Aug. 5, '97	2312	5182
6038(b)	1142(c)	U.S. partners that control foreign partnerships subject to information reporting	Annual accounting periods beginning after Aug. 5, '97	2312	5182
6038(e)	1142(b)	U.S. partners that control foreign partnerships subject to information reporting	Annual accounting periods beginning after Aug. 5, '97	2312	5182
6038B(a)(1)	1144(a)	U.S. persons must report contributions to foreign partnerships	Transfers made after Aug. 5, '97	2315	5186
6038B(b)	1144(b)	U.S. persons must report contributions to foreign partnerships	Transfers made after Aug. 5, '97	2315	5186
6038B(b)(1)	1144(c)(1)	U.S. persons must report contributions to foreign partnerships	Transfers made after Aug. 5, '97	2315	5186
6038B(b)(3)	1144(c)(2)	U.S. persons must report contributions to foreign partnerships	Transfers made after Aug. 5, '97	2315	5186
6039D(d)(1)	1601(h)(2)(D)(iii)	Adoption expense credit allowed for expenses paid after the year adoption becomes final and conformed to exclusion for employer adoption assistance payments	Tax years beginning after Dec. 31, '96	112	5368, 5369
6041A(d)	1022(a)	Information reporting required for federal agency payments of $600 or more to corporations	Returns with due dates (determined without regard to any extension) more than 90 days after Aug. 5, '97	2311	5122
6045(e)	312(c)	Sales and exchanges of certain principal residences exempted from real estate reporting requirements	Sales and exchanges after May 6, '97	2309	5020

Code §	Act §	Topic	Generally effective date	Analysis ¶	Com Rep ¶
6045(f)	1021(a)	Information reporting required for trade or business payments to attorneys after '97	Payments made after Dec. 31, '97	2310	5121
6046(a)	1146(a)	Reporting threshold for stock ownership in a foreign corporation increased from 5% to 10%	Jan. 1, '98	2314	5188
6046A(a)	1143(a)(1)	Change of interest in foreign partnership need not be reported unless change involves 10% interest	Transfers and changes after Aug. 5, '97	2313	5182
6046A(d)	1143(a)(2)	Change of interest in foreign partnership need not be reported unless change involves 10% interest	Transfers and changes after Aug. 5, '97	2313	5182
6048(d)	1027(b)	Estate and trust beneficiaries must report items in manner consistent with estate or trust return or notify IRS of inconsistency	Returns of beneficiaries and owners filed after Aug. 5, '97	2304	5127
6050Q(b)(1)	1602(d)(1)	Information return requirements for payors of long-term care benefits expanded	Benefits paid after Dec. 31, '96	2317	5373
6050R(c)(1)	1601(a)(1)	Information return requirements for purchasers of fish for resale expanded	Payments made after Dec. 31, '97	2316	5356
6050S	201(c)(1)	Educational institutions receiving, and businesses paying, higher education expenses must furnish information returns	Expenses paid after Dec. 31, '97	410	5002
6103(a)(3)	11024(b)	Disclosure of return information authorized for purposes of administering District of Columbia retirement provisions	Oct 1, '97 or, if later, the date certified by the District of Columbia Financial Responsibility and Management Assistance Authority	2605	
6103(d)(5)	976(c)	Five-year test of joint Montana-Federal employment tax reporting is authorized	Aug. 5, '97	2308	5099

Code §	Act §	Topic	Generally effective date	Analysis ¶	Com Rep ¶
6103(e)(1)(A)(iv)	1201(b)(2)	Limit on AMT exemption for under-age-14 child increased from sum of earned income plus twice the $500 limit on basic standard deduction to sum of earned income plus $5,000; limit on child's AMT repealed	Tax years beginning after Dec. 31, '97	604	5201
6103(h)(5)	1283(a)	Repeal of IRS authority to disclose whether prospective juror has been audited	Judicial proceedings commenced after Aug. 5, '97	2330	5250
6103(i)(7)	11024(b)	Disclosure of return information authorized for purposes of administering District of Columbia retirement provisions	Oct 1, '97 or, if later, the date certified by the District of Columbia Financial Responsibility and Management Assistance Authority	2605	
6103(k)	1026(a)	IRS authorized to disclose return information when levying on certain federal payments	Levies issued after Aug. 5, '97	2331	5126
6103(k)(8)	1205(c)(1)	Methods by which taxes may be paid expanded	Nine months after Aug. 5, '97	2319	5205
6103(l)	11024(b)	Disclosure of return information authorized for purposes of administering District of Columbia retirement provisions	Oct 1, '97 or, if later, the date certified by the District of Columbia Financial Responsibility and Management Assistance Authority	2605	
6103(l)(7)(D)	1023(a)	Rules on disclosure of return information to Veterans Affairs Department extended through 2003	Aug. 5, '97	2332	5123

Code §	Act §	Topic	Generally effective date	Analysis ¶	Com Rep ¶
6103(l)(12)(F)	4631(c)(2)*	Medicare secondary payer program disclosure rules made permanent	Aug. 5, '97	2333	5503
6103(p)	11024(b)	Disclosure of return information authorized for purposes of administering District of Columbia retirement provisions	Oct 1, '97 or, if later, the date certified by the District of Columbia Financial Responsibility and Management Assistance Authority	2605	
6103(p)(3)(A)	1026(b)(1)(A)	IRS authorized to disclose return information when levying on certain federal payments	Levies issued after Aug. 5, '97	2331	5126
6103(p)(3)(A)	1205(c)(3)	Methods by which taxes may be paid expanded	Nine months after Aug. 5, '97	2319	5205
6103(p)(4)	1026(b)(1)(B)	IRS authorized to disclose return information when levying on certain federal payments	Levies issued after Aug. 5, '97	2331	5126
6111(d)	1028(a)	Tax shelter registration requirements extended to certain "confidential corporate tax shelters"	Tax shelter interests offered after IRS issues guidance	2318	5128
6111(e)	1028(a)	Tax shelter registration requirements extended to certain "confidential corporate tax shelters"	Tax shelter interests offered after IRS issues guidance	2318	5128
6211(c)	1231(b)	Clarification of treatment of partnership items for purposes of computing amount of deficiency under non-partnership deficiency procedures	Partnership tax years ending after Aug. 5, '97	1420	5215
6213(g)(2)	201(b)	"Hope Scholarship Credit," up to $1,500 per year, and "Lifetime Learning Credit," up to $1,000 per year, allowed for higher education expenses	Expenses paid after Dec. 31, '97	401	5002

Code §	Act §	Topic	Generally effective date	Analysis ¶	Com Rep ¶
6213(g)(2)(I)	101(d)(2)	Child tax credit of up to $400 in '98, $500 in '99 and later years, for each qualifying child under age 17	Tax years beginning after Dec. 31, '97	101	5001
6213(g)(2)(J)	1085(a)(3)	No earned income credit allowed for ten years for taxpayers who fraudulently claimed credit (two years for taxpayers who recklessly claimed credit)	Tax years beginning after Dec. 31 '96	108	5162
6221	1238(a)	Certain penalties to be determined at partnership level under unified partnership audit procedures	Partnership tax years ending after Aug. 5, '97	1415	5223
6225(b)	1239(a)	Tax Court jurisdiction extended in partnership proceedings	Partnership tax years ending after Aug. 5, '97	1416	5224
6226(b)(5)	1240(a)	Premature petitions for judicial review filed by notice partners or 5% groups may be treated as timely	Petitions filed after Aug. 5, '97	1418	5225
6226(d)(1)	1239(b)	Tax Court jurisdiction extended in partnership proceedings	Partnership tax years ending after Aug. 5, '97	1416	5224
6226(f)	1238(b)	Certain penalties to be determined at partnership level under unified partnership audit procedures	Partnership tax years ending after Aug. 5, '97	1415	5223
6227(b)	1236(a)	Extension of assessment period automatically extends time for filing request for administrative adjustment	Partnership tax years beginning after Sept. 3, '82	1409	5220
6227(e)	1243(a)	Time for filing administrative adjustment requests relating to bad debts or worthless securities extended	Partnership tax years beginning after Sept. 3, '82	1410	5228
6229(b)	1233(c)	Statute of limitations for partnership proceedings suspended by untimely partnership petition and by partner's bankruptcy petition	Partnership tax years for which the partnership assessment limitations period has not expired on or before Aug. 5, '97	1411	5217

Code §	Act §	Topic	Generally effective date	Analysis ¶	Com Rep ¶
6229(d)(1)	1233(a)	Statute of limitations for partnership proceedings suspended by untimely partnership petition and by partner's bankruptcy petition	Partnership tax years for which the partnership assessment limitations period has not expired on or before Aug. 5, '97	1411	5217
6229(f)	1235(a)	Partial settlements excluded from one-year limitation on assessment	Settlements entered into after Aug. 5, '97	1414	5219
6229(h)	1233(b)	Statute of limitations for partnership proceedings suspended by untimely partnership petition and by partner's bankruptcy petition	Partnership tax years for which the partnership assessment limitations period has not expired on or before Aug. 5, '97	1411	5217
6230(a)	1238(b)	Certain penalties to be determined at partnership level under unified partnership audit procedures	Partnership tax years ending after Aug. 5, '97	1415	5223
6230(a)(1)	1237(c)	Innocent spouse relief extended to unified partnership proceedings	Partnership tax years beginning after Sept. 3, '82	1412	5221
6230(a)(3)	1237(a)	Innocent spouse relief extended to unified partnership proceedings	Partnership tax years beginning after Sept. 3, '82	1412	5221
6230(a)(3)	1238(b)(3)	Innocent spouse relief extended to unified partnership proceedings	Partnership tax years beginning after Sept. 3, '82	1412	5221
6230(c)	1238(b)	Certain penalties to be determined at partnership level under unified partnership audit procedures	Partnership tax years ending after Aug. 5, '97	1415	5223
6230(c)(5)	1237(b)	Innocent spouse relief extended to unified partnership proceedings	Partnership tax years beginning after Sept. 3, '82	1412	5221

Code §	Act §	Topic	Generally effective date	Analysis ¶	Com Rep ¶
6230(c)(5)	1238(b)(3)(D)	Innocent spouse relief extended to unified partnership proceedings	Partnership tax years beginning after Sept. 3, '82	1412	5221
6230(d)(6)	1239(c)(1)	Tax Court jurisdiction extended in partnership proceedings	Partnership tax years ending after Aug. 5, '97	1416	5224
6231(a)(1)(B)(i)	1234(a)	Small partnership exception to unified partnership audit procedures expanded	Tax years ending after Aug. 5, '97	1408	5218
6231(f)	1141(b)	Deductions denied to partners of nonfiling partnerships with non-U.S. tax matters partner or books kept outside U.S.	Tax years beginning after Aug. 5, '97	1421	5182
6231(g)	1232(a)	IRS can rely on partnership return in determining whether to use partnership audit procedures	Partnership tax years ending after Aug. 5, '97	1407	5216
6234	1231(a)	New set of deficiency procedures provided for certain returns of partners that show no taxable income	Partnership tax years ending after Aug. 5, '97	1419	5215
6240	1222(a)	Consistency rules and audit procedures for electing large partnerships	Partnership tax years ending after Dec. 30, '97	1402	5210
6241	1222(a)	Consistency rules for electing large partnerships	Partnership tax years ending after Dec. 30, '97	1403	5210
6242	1222(a)	Procedures for taking partnership adjustments into account under the electing large partnership audit procedures	Partnership tax years ending after Dec. 30, '97	1405	5210
6245	1222(a)	Partnership-level adjustments under the electing large partnership audit procedures	Partnership tax years ending after Dec. 30, '97	1404	5210
6246	1222(a)	Partnership-level adjustments under the electing large partnership audit procedures	Partnership tax years ending after Dec. 30, '97	1404	5210
6247	1222(a)	Partnership-level adjustments under the electing large partnership audit procedures	Partnership tax years ending after Dec. 30, '97	1404	5210

Code §	Act §	Topic	Generally effective date	Analysis ¶	Com Rep ¶
6248	1222(a)	Partnership-level adjustments under the electing large partnership audit procedures	Partnership tax years ending after Dec. 30, '97	1404	5210
6251	1222(a)	Partnership-level adjustments under the electing large partnership audit procedures	Partnership tax years ending after Dec. 30, '97	1404	5210
6252	1222(a)	Partnership-level adjustments under the electing large partnership audit procedures	Partnership tax years ending after Dec. 30, '97	1404	5210
6255(a)	1222(a)	Consistency rules and audit procedures for electing large partnerships	Partnership tax years ending after Dec. 30, '97	1402	5210
6255(b)	1222(a)	Partnership-level adjustments under the electing large partnership audit procedures	Partnership tax years ending after Dec. 30, '97	1404	5210
6255(c)	1222(a)	Partnership-level adjustments under the electing large partnership audit procedures	Partnership tax years ending after Dec. 30, '97	1404	5210
6255(d)	1222(a)	Procedures for taking partnership adjustments into account under the electing large partnership audit procedures	Partnership tax years ending after Dec. 30, '97	1405	5210
6255(e)	1222(a)	Partnership-level adjustments under the electing large partnership audit procedures	Partnership tax years ending after Dec. 30, '97	1404	5210
6255(f)	1222(a)	Partnership-level adjustments under the electing large partnership audit procedures	Partnership tax years ending after Dec. 30, '97	1404	5210
6255(g)	1222(a)	Consistency rules and audit procedures for electing large partnerships	Partnership tax years ending after Dec. 30, '97	1402	5210
6302	1031(g)	Air carriers made secondarily liable for passenger air transportation taxes; due date for certain deposits of passenger and property air transportation taxes delayed	Transportation beginning after Sept. 30, '97	2204	5129
6302	901(e) and 1031(g)(3)	Deposit due dates for certain fuel excise taxes delayed	July 31, '98	2217	5051

Code §	Act §	Topic	Generally effective date	Analysis ¶	Com Rep ¶
6311	1205(a)	Methods by which taxes may be paid expanded	Nine months after Aug. 5, '97	2319	5205
6331(h)	1024(a)	IRS may levy on certain wage replacement and annuity payments	Levies issued after Aug. 5, '97	2324	5124, 5125
6334(f)	1025(a)	IRS may levy on certain wage replacement and annuity payments	Levies issued after Aug. 5, '97	2324	5124, 5125
6416(a)(4)(B)	905(a)	Multiple-outlet gasoline retailers may claim gasoline tax refunds	Sales after Aug. 5, '97	2214	5055
6416(d)	1436(b)	Registered aviation fuel producers who buy and resell tax-paid fuel are allowed a refund to prevent double taxation	Fuel acquired by the producer after Sept. 30, '97	2215	5294
6421(e)(2)(B)	902(a)	Suspended excise tax on diesel fuel used in recreational motorboats is repealed	Jan. 1, '98	2210	5052
6427(f)	1032(e)(7) and 1032(e)(8)	Diesel fuel removal-at-terminal excise tax rules generally made applicable to kerosene	July 1, '98	2208	5130
6427(i)(3)(A)	1032(e)(9)	Diesel fuel removal-at-terminal excise tax rules generally made applicable to kerosene	July 1, '98	2208	5130
6427(i)(5)(A)(i)	1032(c)(3)(E)	Diesel fuel removal-at-terminal excise tax rules generally made applicable to kerosene	July 1, '98	2208	5130
6427(l)	1032(c)(3)	Diesel fuel removal-at-terminal excise tax rules generally made applicable to kerosene	July 1, '98	2208	5130
6501(a)	1284(a)	Limitations period for passthrough items starts running with filing of taxpayer's return	Tax years beginning after Aug. 5, '97	2321	5251
6501(c)(8)	1145(a)	Assessment limitations period stays open where information returns aren't filed with respect to certain foreign transactions	Information returns due after Aug. 5, '97	2320	5187
6501(c)(9)	506(b)	Statute of limitations will not run on inadequately disclosed gift	For gifts made in calendar years after Aug. 5, '97	522	5031

Code Section Table

Code §	Act §	Topic	Generally effective date	Analysis ¶	Com Rep ¶
6511(d)(3)(A)	1056(a)	Limitations period on refund claim attributable to foreign tax credit begins on due date of return for year in which foreign taxes were paid or accrued	Taxes paid or accrued in tax years beginning after Aug. 5, '97	2323	5148
6511(d)(7)	1454(b)	Special limitations period for credits or refunds for self-employment taxes resulting from Tax Court employment status cases	Aug. 5, '97	2322	5303
6512(b)(2)	1451(a)	Tax Court order requiring IRS to refund overpayment may be appealed; Tax Court jurisdiction over refund offset is limited	Aug. 5, '97	2325	5300
6512(b)(3)	1239(c)(2)	Tax Court jurisdiction extended in partnership proceedings	Partnership tax years ending after Aug. 5, '97	1416	5224
6512(b)(3)	1282(a)	Nonfilers can get Tax Court refund of overpayments paid within three years before deficiency notice	Claims for credit or refund for tax years ending after Aug. 5, '97	2326	5249
6512(b)(4)	1451(b)	Tax Court order requiring IRS to refund overpayment may be appealed; Tax Court jurisdiction over refund offset is limited	Aug. 5, '97	2325	5300
6601(c)	1242(a)	Interest suspended where IRS delays notice and demand with respect to computational adjustment relating to partnership settlement	Adjustments for partnership tax years beginning after Aug. 5, '97	1413	5227
6601(d)(2)	1055(a)	Interest accrual period with respect to tax underpayment not reduced by foreign tax credit carryback	Foreign tax credit carrybacks arising in tax years beginning after Aug. 5, '97	2402	5147
6601(j)(1)	503(a)	Estate tax benefit of qualified family-owned business exclusion may be recaptured if certain events occur	Applies to estates of decedents dying after Dec. 31, '97	506	5028

Code §	Act §	Topic	Generally effective date	Analysis ¶	Com Rep ¶
6601(j)(2)	503(a)	Estate tax benefit of qualified family-owned business exclusion may be recaptured if certain events occur	Applies to estates of decedents dying after Dec. 31, '97	506	5028
6601(j)(3)	501(e)	Estate tax benefit of qualified family-owned business exclusion may be recaptured if certain events occur	Applies to estates of decedents dying after Dec. 31, '97	506	5028
6611(f)(2)	1055(b)(1)	Interest accrual period with respect to tax underpayment not reduced by foreign tax credit carryback	Foreign tax credit carrybacks arising in tax years beginning after Aug. 5, '97	2402	5147
6611(f)(4)(B)(ii)(II)	1055(b)(2)	Interest accrual period with respect to tax underpayment not reduced by foreign tax credit carryback	Foreign tax credit carrybacks arising in tax years beginning after Aug. 5, '97	2402	5147
6621(a)(1)	1604(b)(1)	Definition of "taxable period" for reduced interest rate on large corporate overpayments corrected	Periods after Dec. 31, '94	2404	
6621(c)(2)(B)(iii)	1463(a)	Notices involving less than $100,000 disregarded under rule increasing interest rate on large corporate underpayments	Interest for periods after Dec. 31, '97	2403	5306
6652(g)	1281(a)	Reasonable cause exception provided for various civil penalties	Tax years beginning after Aug. 5, '97	2406	5248
6652(k)	1281(b)	Reasonable cause exception provided for various civil penalties	Tax years beginning after Aug. 5, '97	2406	5248
6654(d)(1)(C)(i)	1091(a)	Estimated tax 110%-of-prior-year's-tax safe harbor for high income individuals changed to 100% for '98, 105% for '99–2001, 112% for 2002	Tax years ending after Dec. 31, '97	1803	5168
6654(e)(1)	1202(a)	Increase in de minimis threshold for individuals' estimated taxes	Tax years beginning after Dec. 31, '97	1802	5202

Code §	Act §	Topic	Generally effective date	Analysis ¶	Com Rep ¶
6655(g)(3)	1461(a)	Extension of private foundation's first quarter estimated tax payment due date	For tax years beginning after Aug. 5, '97	1804	5304
6662(d)(2)(B)	1028(c)(1)	Substantial understatement penalty modified	Transactions entered into after Aug. 5, '97	2412	5128
6662(d)(2)(C)(iii)	1028(c)(2)	Substantial understatement penalty modified	Transactions entered into after Aug. 5, '97	2412	5128
6679(a)	1143(b)	Penalty for failure to file certain information returns relating to foreign partnerships and corporations increased from $1,000 to $10,000; additional penalties imposed on continuing failures	Transfers and changes after Aug. 5, '97	2411	5185
6683	1281(c)	Reasonable cause exception provided for various civil penalties	Tax years beginning after Aug. 5, '97	2406	5248
6693	213(c)	Tax-exempt education IRAs allowed	Tax years beginning after Dec. 31, '97	403	5005
6693(a)	1602(a)	Changes to MSA rules on coverage, distributions, and reporting requirements	Taxable years beginning after Dec. 31, '96	1202	5370
6693(c)(2)	1601(d)(1)(C)(ii)	Notification requirements and penalties for SIMPLE IRAs apply also to issuers of SIMPLE IRA annuities	Tax years beginning after Dec. 31, '96	916	5361
6695(g)	1085(a)(2)	$100 penalty for lack of due diligence by preparers of returns claiming earned income credit	Tax years beginning after Dec. 31 '96.	2410	5162
6707(a)	1028(b)	Tax shelter registration requirements extended to certain "confidential corporate tax shelters"	Tax shelter interests offered after IRS issues guidance	2318	5128
6715(c)(1)	1032(e)(11)	Diesel fuel removal-at-terminal excise tax rules generally made applicable to kerosene	July 1, '98	2208	5130

Code §	Act §	Topic	Generally effective date	Analysis ¶	Com Rep ¶
6724(d)(1)(A)(ix)	1213(b)	Income exclusion of construction allowances received by lessees for qualified lessee construction related to short-term leases of retail space	Leases entered into after Aug. 5, '97	2702	5208
6724(d)(1)(B)(ix)	201(c)(2)(A)	Educational institutions receiving, and businesses paying, higher education expenses must furnish information returns	Expenses paid after Dec. 31, '97	410	5002
6724(d)(2)(Z)	201(c)(2)(B)	Educational institutions receiving, and businesses paying, higher education expenses must furnish information returns	Expenses paid after Dec. 31, '97	410	5002
6724(e)	1223(b)	Large partnerships' tax returns must be filed on magnetic media and are subject to information return reporting penalties	Partnership tax years ending after Dec. 30, '97	2301	5211, 5212
7213(a)(2)	11024(b)	Disclosure of return information authorized for purposes of administering District of Columbia retirement provisions	Oct 1, '97 or, if later, the date certified by the District of Columbia Financial Responsibility and Management Assistance Authority	2605	
7213(a)(2)	2(b)(1) †	Criminal penalty imposed on "browsing" of tax returns or return information	Violations occurring on or after Aug. 5, '97	2407	5551
7213A	2(a) †	Criminal penalty imposed on "browsing" of tax returns or return information	Violations occurring on or after Aug. 5, '97	2407	5551
7232	1032(e)(12)(A)	Diesel fuel removal-at-terminal excise tax rules generally made applicable to kerosene	July 1, '98	2208	5130
7421(a)	1454(b)(2)	Tax Court given jurisdiction to review certain IRS determinations of employment status	Aug. 5, '97	2329	5303

Code §	Act §	Topic	Generally effective date	Analysis ¶	Com Rep ¶
7430(b)(5)	1285(b)	Taxpayers' right to seek administrative cost awards from IRS subjected to time limits	Civil actions or proceedings commenced after Aug. 5, '97	2336	5252
7430(c)(4)(D)	1453(a)	Net worth requirements for awards of litigation, etc. costs to estates, trusts, and joint return filers clarified	Proceedings commenced after Aug. 5, '97	2335	5302
7430(f)(2)	1285(c)	Taxpayers' right to seek administrative cost awards from IRS subjected to time limits	Civil actions or proceedings commenced after Aug. 5, '97	2336	5252
7430(f)(3)	1285(a)	Taxpayers' right to seek administrative cost awards from IRS subjected to time limits	Civil actions or proceedings commenced after Aug. 5, '97	2336	5252
7431(a)	3(a) †	Civil damages made available for unauthorized inspection of returns or return information	Inspections and disclosures occurring on or after Aug. 5, '97	2408	5551
7431(b)	3(c) †	Civil damages made available for unauthorized inspection of returns or return information	Inspections and disclosures occurring on or after Aug. 5, '97	2408	5551
7431(c)	3(d)(1) and (2) †	Civil damages made available for unauthorized inspection of returns or return information	Inspections and disclosures occurring on or after Aug. 5, '97	2408	5551
7431(e)	3(b) †	IRS required to notify taxpayers of unlawful inspection or disclosure of their returns or return information	Inspections and disclosures occurring on or after Aug. 5, '97	2337	5551
7431(f)	3(d)(3) †	Civil damages made available for unauthorized inspection of returns or return information	Inspections and disclosures occurring on or after Aug. 5, '97	2408	5551

Code §	Act §	Topic	Generally effective date	Analysis ¶	Com Rep ¶
7431(g)	1205(c)(2)	Methods by which taxes may be paid expanded	Nine months after Aug. 5, '97	2319	5205
7436	1454(a)	Tax Court given jurisdiction to review certain IRS determinations of employment status	Aug. 5, '97	2329	5303
7453	1454(b)(3)	Tax Court given jurisdiction to review certain IRS determinations of employment status	Aug. 5, '97	2329	5303
7459(c)	1222(b)(2)	Partnership-level adjustments under the electing large partnership audit procedures	Partnership tax years ending after Dec. 30, '97	1404	5210
7459(c)	1239(e)(1)	Tax Court jurisdiction extended in partnership proceedings	Partnership tax years ending after Aug. 5, '97	1416	5224
7477	506(c)(1)	Donor may petition the Tax Court for a declaratory judgment relating to the value of certain gifts	For gifts made after Aug. 5, '97	523	5031
7479	505	Tax Court authorized to issue declaratory judgments on eligibility for deferral of estate tax from closely-held business	Estates of decedents dying after Aug. 5, '97	2328	5030
7481(b)	1454(b)(3)	Tax Court given jurisdiction to review certain IRS determinations of employment status	Aug. 5, '97	2329	5303
7481(c)	1452(a)	Taxpayers may motion, instead of petition, for interest redeterminations in Tax Court; Tax Court given jurisdiction over IRS interest underpayments	Aug. 5, '97	2327	5301
7482(b)(1)(E)	1222(b)(3)	Partnership-level adjustments under the electing large partnership audit procedures	Partnership tax years ending after Dec. 30, '97	1404	5210
7482(b)(1)(F)	1239(d)(1)	Tax Court jurisdiction extended in partnership proceedings	Partnership tax years ending after Aug. 5, '97	1416	5224

Code §	Act §	Topic	Generally effective date	Analysis ¶	Com Rep ¶
7485(b)	1222(b)(4)	Partnership-level adjustments under the electing large partnership audit procedures	Partnership tax years ending after Dec. 30, '97	1404	5210
7485(b)	1241(a)	Calculation of bond amount for stay of assessment and collection pending appeal of Tax Court decision in partnership proceeding is modified	Partnership tax years beginning after Sept. 3, '82	1417	5226
7508A	911	IRS authority to extend tax deadlines for taxpayers affected by Presidentially-declared disasters expanded	With respect to periods for performing acts that have not expired before Aug. 5, '97	2334	5061
7518(g)(6)(A)	311(c)(2)	Tax on nonqualified withdrawals from capital gain account under Merchant Marine capital construction fund reduced from 28% to 20%	Tax years ending after May 6, '97	210	5019
7519(f)(4)(A)	1281(d)	Reasonable cause exception provided for various civil penalties	Tax years beginning after Aug. 5, '97	2406	5248
7701(a)(4)	1151(a)	IRS regs can treat a domestic partnership as a foreign partnership	For partnerships created after regulations are filed or a notice published	1426	5182
7701(a)(30)(E)	1161(a)	IRS regs can allow nongrantor trusts to elect to continue to be U.S. trusts despite '96 Act provision that would treat them as foreign	Tax years beginning after Dec. 31, '96	529	5190
7701(a)(30)(E)	1601(i)(3)(A)	Definition of trust as U.S. person clarified	Tax years beginning after '96	1628	5364
7701(b)(7)(D)	1174(b)	Nonresident alien crew member's income not U.S. source income	Tax years beginning after Dec. 31, '97	1624	5196
7702B(c)(2)	1602(b)	Definition of "chronically ill" individual modified for qualified long-term care insurance contracts	For contracts issued after Dec. 31, '96	1105	5371

Code §	Act §	Topic	Generally effective date	Analysis ¶	Com Rep ¶
7702B(g)(4)(B)	1602(e)	Long-term care insurance contract nonforfeiture provisions subject to state regulatory approval	For contracts issued after '96	1107	5374
7704(g)	964(a)	"Electing 1987 partnerships" continue exception from treatment as corporations but must pay 3.5% tax on gross income	Tax years beginning after Dec. 31, '97	1427	5085
9802(c)	1532	Certain church health plans can discriminate based on health status	Plan years beginning after June 30, '97	929	5354
9811	1531(a)(4)	Election to receive taxable cash compensation in place of nontaxable parking benefits	Plan years beginning after Dec. 31, '97	1003	5353
9812	1531(a)(4)	Mental health benefits under group health plans to have parity with medical benefits	For plan years beginning after Dec. 31, '97	1102	5353
None	1(c)	Tax rate changes made by '97 Act are not subject to "tax-straddle" computation	Aug. 5, '97	2701	
None	1(d)	No penalty for underpayment of pre-'98 estimated tax caused by '97 Act	Aug. 5, '97	1801	5168
None	1032(g)	Floor stocks tax imposed on kerosene held on July 1, '98	July 1, '98	2209	5130
None	1042	Grandfather rule with respect to pension business of TIAA-CREF and Mutual of America is repealed	Tax years beginning after '97	937	5142
None	1088(a)	Repeal of exception to the installment sale rules for sales of property by a manufacturer to a dealer	Tax years beginning more than one year after Aug. 5, '97	2002	5165
None	11034*	D.C. Federal Pension Liability Trust Fund to be treated as qualified plan	Aug. 5, '97	939	
None	1303	Trusts created before Nov. 5, '90 are treated as meeting the qualified domestic trust (QDOT) requirements if they meet the QDOT requirements that were in effect before Nov. 5, '90	Applies to estates of decedents dying after Nov. 10, '88	516	5263

Code Section Table

Code §	Act §	Topic	Generally effective date	Analysis ¶	Com Rep ¶
None	1462(a)	Commonwealth income taxes can be withheld from federal employees' wages	Jan. 1, '98	2703	5305
None	1503	ERISA plan descriptions, summary plan descriptions, and material modifications no longer filed with DOL, except on request	Aug. 5, '97	935	5309
None	1504(b)	Exclusion allowance rules for 403(b) annuities modified to conform to earlier Code Sec. 415 changes	Years beginning after Dec. 31, '97	925	5310
None	1508	Transitional relief for certain bus companies from some minimum funding requirements	Plan years beginning after Dec. 31, '96	928	5314
None	1509	Qualified retirement plans may receive rollovers from plans intended to have a qualified trust	Aug. 5, '97	901	5315
None	1510	Congress directs IRS and DOL to facilitate retirement plan administrators' use of electronic technologies	Aug. 5, '97	936	5316
None	1524	ERISA limit on investments in employer securities applies to 401(k) plan deferrals	Plan years beginning after '98	934	5346
None	1529	Retroactive exclusion from certain retired firefighters' and police officers' income for amounts received because of heart disease or hypertension	Aug. 5, '97	1002	5351
None	1541	Window period for amending plans and annuity contracts to reflect the '97 Act	Aug. 5, '97	932	5355
None	1601(c)(2)(A)	Effective date of '96 Act changes to post-termination transition period (PTTP) of S corporations	Determination after Dec. 31, '96	1507	5358
None	1601(c)(2)(B)	Effective date of '96 Act changes to post-termination transition period (PTTP) of S corporations	Determination after Dec. 31, '96	1507	5358
None	1601(d)(4)	Permissible rollovers from certain 403(b) plans maintained by Indian tribal governments	Aug. 20, '96	906	5390

Code §	Act §	Topic	Generally effective date	Analysis ¶	Com Rep ¶
None	1601(f)(4)(F)	Exemption from floor stocks tax on aviation fuel held on Aug. 27, '96 is retroactively expanded	Aug. 27, '96	2216	
None	1601(g)(1)	Period for claiming refund for gasoline or diesel fuel used to produce alcohol fuel for period Sept. 30, '95 through Oct. 1, '96 is extended	Jan. 1, '94	2213	
None	1601(h)(1)(C)	State program under which persons may purchase tuition credits will be treated as a qualified state tuition program if it meets the qualified state tuition program requirements within a specified time period	Tax years ending after Aug. 20, '96	408	5367
None	1604(b)(3)	Interest and mortality rate rules in Retirement Protection Act of '94 corrected	Dec. 8, '94	905	5385
None	915	Interest abated when due date for tax extended in '97 disaster areas	Disasters declared after Dec. 31, '96	2401	5065
None	9302(j) *	Taxes on cigarettes and other tobacco products rise	Products removed after Dec. 31, '99	2231	5509
None	931	Penalty for failure by small businesses to make electronic tax deposits waived through June 30, '98	Aug. 5, '97	2405	5068
None	935	Prohibition issued on regulatory definition of a limited partner for self-employment tax purposes	Aug. 5, '97	1906	
None	976(a)	Five-year test of joint Montana-Federal employment tax reporting is authorized	Aug. 5, '97	2308	5099
None	976(b)	Five-year test of joint Montana-Federal employment tax reporting is authorized	Aug. 5, '97	2308	5099

¶ 6002. Code Sections Amended by '97 Act
(including conforming amendments)
* denotes Budget Act
† denotes Privacy Act

Code Sec.	Act Sec.	Code Sec.	Act Sec.
1(h)	311(a)	45C(e)	604(a)
15	1(c)	51(a)	603(d)(1)
23(a)(2)	1601(h)(2)(A)	51(c)(4)(B)	603(a)
23(b)(2)(B)	1601(h)(2)(B)	51(d)(1)(F), (G)	603(c)(1)
24	101(a)	51(d)(1)(H)	603(c)(1)
24	101(d)(3)	51(d)(2)(A)	603(b)(1)
25(e)(7)	312(d)(1)	51(d)(3)(A)	603(b)(2)
25A	201(a)	51(d)(9)-(11)	603(c)(2)
25A	201(e)	51(i)(3)	603(d)(2)
26(b)(2)(E)-(P)	213(e)(1)	51A	801(a)
26(b)(2)(N), (O)	1602(a)(1)	51A	801(b)
26(b)(2)(P)	1602(a)(1)	52(c)	1601(b)
30A	1601(f)(1)(A)	52(d)(9)	603(c)(2)
30A	1601(f)(1)(B)	55(b)(1)(A)(ii)	311(b)(2)(A)
32	5702 *	55(b)(3)	311(b)(1)
32(c)(2)(B)(iii), (iv)	1085(c)	55(c)(1)	1601(f)(1)(C)
32(c)(2)(B)(v)	1085(c)	55(e)	401(a)
32(c)(4)	312(d)(2)	56(a)(1)(A)(i)	402(a)
32(c)(5)(B)	1085(d)(4)	56(a)(5)	402(b)
32(c)(5)(B)(iii)	1085(d)(1)	56(a)(6)	403(a)
32(c)(5)(B)(iv)	1085(b)	56(a)(7), (8)	403(a)
32(c)(5)(B)(iv)(III)	1085(d)(2)	56(e)(1)(A)	312(d)(1)
32(c)(5)(B)(v)-(vi)	1085(d)(3)	56(e)(3)(B)(i)	312(d)(1)
32(k), (l)	1085(a)(1)	56(g)(4)(B)(i)	1212(a)
32(m)	101(b)	57(a)(7)	311(b)(2)(B)
39(a)(1)	1083(a)(1)	59(a)(2)(C)	1057(a)
39(a)(2)	1083(a)(2)	59(a)(3)	1103(a)
39(d)(8)	701(b)(1)	59(j)	1201(b)(1)
41(c)(4)(B)	601(b)(1)	62(a)(17)	202(b)
41(h)(1)	601(a)(1)	62(a)(2)(C)	975(a)
41(h)(1)	601(a)(2)	63(c)(4)	1201(a)(2)(A)
45C(b)(1)	601(b)(2)	63(c)(4)(B)	1201(a)(2)(B)

Code Sec.	Act Sec.	Code Sec.	Act Sec.
63(c)(5)	1201(a)(1)	148(f)(4)(B)(ii)(I)	1441
72(d)(1)(B)(iii)	1075(b)(1)	148(f)(4)(C)(xvii)	1442
72(d)(1)(B)(iii)	1075(b)(2)	148(f)(4)(D)(vii)	223(a)
72(d)(1)(B)(iv)	1075(a)	148(f)(4)(E)	1444(b)
72(t)(2)(E)	203(a)	149(d)(3)(A)(i)(I)	967
72(t)(2)(F)	303(a)	162(a)	1204(a)
72(t)(7)	203(b)	162(l)(1)(B)	934(a)
72(t)(8)	303(b)	162(l)(2)(B)	1602(c)
101(a)(2)	1084(b)(2)	162(o)	1203(a)
101(h)	1528(a)	163(h)(2)(E)	503(b)(2)(B)
104	1529(a)	163(h)(4)(A)(i)(I)	312(d)(1)
108(f)(2)(B)	225(a)(1)	163(j)(2)(B)(iii)	1604(g)(1)
108(f)(2)(D)	225(a)(1)	163(k)	503(b)(2)(A)
108(f)(3)	225(a)(2)	163(l)	1005(a)
110	1213(a)	165(i)(4)	912(a)
121	312(d)(14)	167(g)(6)	1086(a)
121	312(a)	168(e)(3)(A)(i), (ii)	1086(b)(1)
127(d)	221(a)	168(e)(3)(A)(iii)	1086(b)(1)
130(c)	962(a)(1)	168(g)(3)(B)	1086(b)(2)
130(c)(1)	962(a)(2)	168(i)(14)	1086(b)(3)
130(c)(2)(D)	962(a)(3)	168(i)(8)(C)	1213(c)
132(e)(2)	970(a)	168(j)(6)	1604(c)(1)
132(f)(4)	1072(a)	170(e)(5)(D)(ii)	602(a)
135	1601(h)(1)(C)	170(e)(6)	224(a)
135(c)(2)(C)	213(e)(2)	170(h)(5)(B)(ii)	508(d)
135(c)(2)(C)	211(c)	170(i)	973(a)
135(d)(2), (3)	201(d)	172(b)(1)(A)(i)	1082(a)(1)
137(b)(1)	1601(h)(2)(C)	172(b)(1)(A)(ii)	1082(a)(2)
138	4006(a) *	172(b)(1)(F)	1082(b)
138	4006(b)(3) *	198	941(a)
143(i)(1)(C)(i)(I)	312(d)(1)	198	941(b)
143(k)(11)	914	216(e)	312(d)(4)
143(m)(6)(A)	312(d)(3)	219(c)(1)(B)(ii)	302(c)
145(b)(5)	222	219(g)(1)	301(b)(1)
148(c)(2)(B)	1444(a)	219(g)(2)(A)(ii)	301(a)(2)
148(c)(2)(C)-(E)	1444(a)	219(g)(3)(B)	301(a)(1)
148(d)(3)	1443	219(g)(7)	301(b)(2)

Code Sec.	Act Sec.	Code Sec.	Act Sec.
220(b)(7)	4006(b)(2) *	351(c)	1012(c)(1)
220(c)(3)(A)	1602(a)(2)	351(e)(1)	1002(a)
220(c)(3)(B)-(D)	1602(a)(2)	351(g)	1014(a)
220(d)(2)(C)	1602(a)(3)	354(a)(2)(B)	1014(e)(1)
221	202(a)	354(a)(2)(C)	1014(b)
221	202(d)	354(a)(3)(A)	1014(e)(2)
222	202(d)	355(a)(3)(C)	1014(e)(1)
246(c)(1)(A)	1015(a)	355(a)(3)(D)	1014(c)
246(c)(2)	1015(b)(1)	355(a)(4)(A)	1014(e)(2)
246(c)(3)(A)	1015(b)(2)	355(e)	1012(a)
246(c)(3)(B)	1015(b)(2)	355(f)	1012(b)(1)
246(c)(3)(C)	1015(b)(2)	356(e), (f)	1014(d)
263(a)(1)(F), (G)	1604(a)(1)	358(g)	1012(b)(2)
263(a)(1)(H)	1604(a)(1)	367(d)(2)(C)	1131(b)(4) sic [(c)]
264	1602(f)(4)	367(d)(3)	1131(b)(5)(A) sic [(c)]
264	1602(f)(5)	367(f)	1131(b)(2) sic [(c)]
264(a)(1)	1084(a)(1)	368(a)(2)(H)	1012(c)(2)
264(a)(4)	1084(b)(1)	401	11034 *
264(a)(4)	1602(f)(1)	401(a)(1)	1530(c)(1)
264(b)-(d)	1084(a)(2)	401(a)(13)(C)-(D)	1502(b)
264(d)(4)(B)	1602(f)(3)	401(a)(26)(H)	1505(a)(2)
264(d)(4)(B)(ii)	1602(f)(2)	401(a)(5)(G)	1505(a)(1)
264(f)	1084(c)	401(k)(11)(B)(iii)	1601(d)(2)(D)
265(b)(4)(A)	1084(c) [sic (e)]	401(k)(11)(D)(ii)	1601(d)(2)(A)
267(b)(11), (12)	1308(a)	401(k)(11)(E)	1601(d)(2)(B)
267(b)(13)	1308(a)	401(k)(3)(G)	1505(b)
267(f)(4)	1604(e)(1)	401(k)(7)(B)(iii)	1525(a)(1)
274	1203(b)	401(k)(7)(B)(iv)	1525(a)(1)
274(n)(3)	969(a)	401(k)(7)(B)(v)	1525(a)(2)
280A(c)(1)	932(a)	401(m)(11)	1601(d)(3)
280A(d)(4)(A)	312(d)(1)	402	1509
280F(a)(1)(C)	971(a)	402(g)(9)	1501(a)
304(a)(1)	1013(a)	403(b)(1)(A)(i), (ii)	1601(d)(6)(B)
304(b)(5)	1013(c)	403(b)(1)(A)(iii)	1601(d)(6)(B)
312(k)(3)(B)	1604(a)(2)(A)	403(b)(11)	1601(d)(4)
312(k)(3)(B)	1604(a)(2)(B)	403(b)(12)(C)	1505(c)
318(b)(8)	1142(e)(3)	403(b)(3)	1504(a)(1)

Code Sec.	Act Sec.	Code Sec.	Act Sec.
404(a)(3)(A)(i)	1601(d)(2)(C)(i)	414(q)(7)	1601(d)(7)
404(a)(3)(A)(ii)	1601(d)(2)(C)(ii)	414(t)(2)	1601(h)(2)(D)(ii)
404(a)(9)(C)	1530(c)(2)	415	1504(b)
408(i)	302(d)(1)	415(b)(2)(G)	1527(a)
408(i)	302(d)(2)	415(c)(6)	1530(c)(3)
408(i)	1601(d)(1)(A)	415(e)(6)	1530(c)(4)(A)
408(k)(6)(H)	1601(d)(1)(B)	415(e)(6)	1530(c)(4)(B)
408(l)(2)(B)	1601(d)(1)(C)(i)(I)	415(k)(3)	1526(b)
408(l)(2)(B)(i)	1601(d)(1)(C)(i)(II)	415(n)	1526(a)
408(m)(3)	304(a)	417(e)(1)	1071(a)(2)(A)
408(p)(2)(D)(i)	1601(d)(1)(E)	417(e)(1)	1071(a)(2)(B)
408(p)(2)(D)(iii)	1601(d)(1)(F)	417(e)(2)	1071(a)(2)(A)
408(p)(5)	1601(d)(1)(G)	417(e)(2)	1071(a)(2)(B)
408(p)(8)	1501(b)	447(i)(3), (4)	1081(a)
408(p)(8)	1601(d)(1)(D)	447(i)(5), (6)	1081(a)
408A	302(e)	451(e)	913(a)(2)
408A	302(a)	451(e)(1)	913(a)(1)
409(h)(2)	1506(a)(2)(A)	453C	1088(a)
409(h)(2)	1506(a)(2)(B)	457(e)(9)	1071(a)(2)(A)
409(h)(2)(B)	1506(a)(1)	457(e)(9)(A)	1071(a)(2)(B)
410(c)(2)	1505(a)(3)	460(b)(2)(C)	1211(b)(1)
411	1541	460(b)(6)	1211(a)
411	1604(b)(3)	460(b)(7)	1211(b)(2)
411(a)(11)(A)	1071(a)(1)	464(f)(3)(B)(i)	312(d)(1)
411(a)(7)(B)	1071(a)(2)(A)	471(b)	961(a)
412	1508(a)	475(e)-(f)	1001(b)
412(b)(2)(C), (D)	1521(c)(1)	501(c)(26)	101(c)
412(b)(2)(E)	1521(c)(1)	501(c)(27)	963(b)
412(c)(7)(A)(i)(I)	1521(a)(A) [sic (a)(1)]	501(c)(27)(A)-(C)	963(b)
412(c)(7)(D)(i), (ii)	1521(c)(3)(A)	501(c)(27)(B)	963(a)
412(c)(7)(D)(iii)	1521(c)(3)(A)	501(c)(27)(B)(i), (ii)	963(b)
412(c)(7)(F)	1521(a)(B) [sic (a)(2)]	501(c)(27)(C)(i), (ii)	963(b)
412(m)(5)(E)(ii)(II)	1604(b)(2)(A)	501(e)(1)(A)	974(a)
414(e)(5)(A)	1601(d)(6)(A)	501(o)	4041(a)*
414(e)(5)(C)	1522(a)(1)	512(a)(3)(D)	312(d)(5)
414(e)(5)(E)	1522(a)(2)	512(b)(13)	1041(a)
414(n)(3)(C)	1601(h)(2)(D)(i)	512(e)(1)	1601(c)(4)(D)

Code Sec.	Act Sec.	Code Sec.	Act Sec.
512(e)(2)	1601(c)(4)(A)	646	1305(a)
512(e)(3)	1523(a)	646	1305(c)
513(i)	965(a)	663(b)	1306(a)
528(b)	966(d)	663(b)(2)	1306(b)
528(c)(1)	966(a)(1)(A)	663(c)	1307(a)(1)
528(c)(1)(B)(i), (ii)	966(a)(1)(B)	663(c)	1307(a)(2)
528(c)(1)(B)(iii)	966(a)(1)(B)	663(c)	1307(b)
528(c)(1)(C)	966(a)(1)(C)	664(d)(1)(A)	1089(a)(1)
528(c)(4)	966(a)(2)	664(d)(1)(B)	1530(c)(5)
528(c)(5)	966(c)	664(d)(1)(B), (C)	1089(b)(1)
528(d)(3)(A), (B)	966(b)	664(d)(1)(C)	1530(a)
528(d)(3)(C)	966(b)	664(d)(1)(D)	1089(b)(1)
529	211(f)(6)	664(d)(2)(A)	1089(a)(1)
529	1601(h)(1)(C)	664(d)(2)(B)	1530(c)(5)
529(b)(5)	211(b)(4)	664(d)(2)(B), (C)	1089(b)(2)
529(c)(2)	211(b)(3)(A)(i)	664(d)(2)(C)	1530(a)
529(c)(3)(A)	211(d)	664(d)(2)(D)	1089(b)(2)
529(c)(4)	211(b)(3)(B)	664(d)(4)	1089(b)(4)
529(c)(5)	211(b)(3)(A)(ii)	664(g)	1530(b)
529(d)	211(e)(2)(A)	665(b)	507(a)(2)
529(e)(1)(B)	1601(h)(1)(A)	665(c)	507(a)(1)
529(e)(1)(C)	1601(h)(1)(B)	665(d)(1)	1604(g)(2)
529(e)(2)	211(b)(1)	674(b)(4)	1530(c)(6)
529(e)(3)	211(a)	679(a)(3)(C)(ii)	1601(i)(2)
529(e)(5)	211(b)(2)	679(a)(3)(C)(iii)	1601(i)(2)
530	213(a)	684	1131(b)
530	213(e)(3)	684	1131(c)(6) sic [(d)]
532(b)(4)	1122(d)(1)	685	1309(a)
542(c)(10)	1122(d)(1)	685	1309(b)
551(f)	1122(d)(2)	691(c)(1)(C)	1073(b)(1)
593(e)(1)(A)	1601(f)(5)(A)	704(c)(1)(B)	1063(a)
613A(c)(6)(H)	972(a)	706(b)(5)	507(b)(2)
641(b)	1601(i)(3)(B)	706(c)(2)	1246(b)
644	507(b)(1)	706(c)(2)(A)	1246(a)
644	507(b)(3)	721(c)	1131(b)(3) sic [(c)]
645	507(b)(1)	721(d)	1131(b)(5)(B) sic [(c)]
645	507(b)(3)	724(d)(2)	1062(b)(3)

Code Sec.	Act Sec.	Code Sec.	Act Sec.
731(a)(2)(B)	1062(b)(3)	851(b)(4)	1271(a)
731(c)(6)	1062(b)(3)	851(c)	1271(b)(2)
732(c)	1061(a)	851(d)	1271(b)(3)
732(c)(1)(A)	1062(b)(3)	851(e)(1)	1271(b)(4)
735(a)(2)	1062(b)(3)	851(e)(4)	1271(b)(5)
735(c)(1)	1062(b)(3)	851(g)	1271(b)(6)
737(b)(1)	1063(a)	851(g)(3)	1271(b)(7)
751(a)(2)	1062(a)	851(h)	1271(b)(6)
751(b)(1)(A)-(B)	1062(b)(1)(A)	852(b)(10)	1122(c)(2)
751(b)(3)	1062(b)(1)(B)	852(b)(3)(D)(iii)	1254(b)(2)
751(d)	1062(b)(2)	852(c)	1122(c)(3)
771	1221(a)	853(c)	1053(b)
772	1221(a)	856(a)(6)	1251(b)(2)
773	1221(a)	856(c)(3)	1255(a)(1)
774	1221(a)	856(c)(4)	1255(a)(2)
775	1221(a)	856(c)(5)(G)	1255(b)(1)
776	1221(a)	856(c)(5)(G)	1258
777	1221(a)	856(c)(5)-(7)	1255(a)(3)
805(a)(4)(C)(ii)	1084(b)(1)(A) [sic (d)]	856(c)(8)	1255(a)(2)
805(a)(4)(D)(iii)	1084(b)(1)(B) [sic (d)]	856(d)(2)	1252(a)
805(a)(4)(F)	1084(b)(1)(C) [sic (d)]	856(d)(5)	1253
807(a)(2)(B)	1084(b)(2)(A) [sic (d)]	856(d)(7)	1252(b)
807(b)(1)(B)	1084(b)(2)(B) [sic (d)]	856(e)(2)	1257(a)(1)
812(d)(1)(B), (C)	1084(b)(3) [sic (d)]	856(e)(3)	1257(a)(2)(A)
812(d)(1)(D)	1084(b)(3) [sic (d)]	856(e)(3)	1257(a)(2)(B)
814(h)	1131(c)(1) sic [(d)]	856(e)(4)	1257(c)
817(h)(2)(A)	1271(b)(8)(A)	856(e)(5)	1257(b)
817(h)(2)(B)	1271(b)(8)(B)	856(i)(2)	1262
832(b)(5)(B)(i), (ii)	1084(b)(4) [sic (d)]	856(j)(4)	1261(a)
832(b)(5)(B)(iii)	1084(b)(4) [sic (d)]	856(j)(5)(A)(ii)	1261(b)
833	1042	856(k)	1251(b)(1)
833(b)(1)(A)(i)	1604(d)(2)(A)(i)	857(a)(2)	1251(a)(1)
833(b)(1)(A)(ii)	1604(d)(2)(A)(ii)	857(a)(3)	1251(a)(1)
851(b)(2)	1271(a)	857(b)(3)(D)	1254(a)
851(b)(3)	1271(b)(1)(A)	857(b)(5)	1255(b)(2)
851(b)(3)	1271(b)(1)(B)	857(b)(6)(C)	1255(b)(3)
851(b)(3)	1271(a)	857(b)(6)(C)(iii)(I)	1260

Code Sec.	Act Sec.	Code Sec.	Act Sec.
857(b)(6)(C)(iii)(II)	1260	904(d)(2)(C)(i)(II)	1163(b)
857(b)(7)(A)(i)	1254(b)(1)	904(d)(2)(C)(iii)(II)	1105(a)(3)
857(d)(3)	1256	904(d)(2)(D)	1105(a)(3)
857(e)(2)(B)	1259(1)	904(d)(2)(E)(i)	1111(b)
857(e)(2)(C)	1259(2)	904(d)(2)(E)(iv)	1105(a)(2)
857(e)(2)(C)	1259(3)	904(d)(4), (5)	1105(b)
857(e)(2)(C)	1259(4)	904(j)	1101(a)
857(e)(2)(D)	1259(4)	905(c)	1102(a)(2)
857(f)	1251(a)(2)	911(b)(2)(A)	1172(a)(1)
860L(b)(1)(A)	1601(f)(6)(A)	911(b)(2)(D)	1172(a)(2)
860L(d)(2)	1601(f)(6)(B)	927(a)(2)(B)	1171(a)
860L(e)(2)(A)	1601(f)(6)(E)(ii)	951(a)(2)	1112(a)(1)
860L(e)(2)(B)	1601(f)(6)(C)	952(b)	1112(c)(1)
860L(e)(3)(A)	1601(f)(6)(D)	954(c)(1)(B)	1051(a)(2)(A)
860L(e)(3)(D)	1601(f)(6)(E)(i)	954(c)(1)(B)	1051(a)(2)(B)
861(a)(3)	1174(a)(1)	954(c)(1)(F)-(G)	1051(a)(1)
863(c)(2)(B)	1174(a)(2)	954(c)(2)(C)	1051(b)
864(b)(2)(A)(ii)	1162(a)	954(e)(2)(A), (B)	1175(b)
877(d)(2)(B)	1602(g)(1)	954(e)(2)(C)	1175(b)
877(d)(2)(D)	1602(g)(2)	954(h)	1175(a)
877(d)(3)	1602(g)(3)	956(b)(1)(A)	1601(e)
877(d)(4)(A)	1602(g)(4)(B)	956(c)(2)(H), (I)	1173(a)
877(d)(4)(A)	1602(g)(4)(C)	956(c)(2)(J)-(K)	1173(a)
877(d)(4)(A)(i)	1602(g)(4)(A)	960(a)(1)	1113(b)
877(e)(1)	1602(h)(3)	961(c)	1112(b)(1)
894(c)	1054(a)	964(e)	1111(a)
901(k)	1053(a)	986(a)	1102(a)(1)
901(k)(4)	1142(e)(4)	986(a)(3)	1102(b)(1)
902(b)	1113(a)(1)	988(e)	1104(a)
902(c)(2)(B)	1163(a)	989(b)	1102(b)(3)
902(c)(3)	1113(a)(2)(D)	989(c)(4), (5)	1102(b)(2)
902(c)(3)	1113(a)(2)(C)	989(c)(6)	1102(b)(2)
902(c)(3)(B)(i)	1113(a)(2)(A)	1014(a)(1)-(3)	508(b)
902(c)(3)(B)(ii), (iii)	1113(a)(2)(A)	1014(a)(4)	508(b)
902(c)(4)(B)	1113(a)(2)(B)	1016(a)(23)	313(b)(1)(A)
904(b)(2)(C)	311(c)(3)	1016(a)(23)	313(b)(1)(B)
904(d)(1)(E)	1105(a)(1)	1016(a)(25), (26)	701(b)(2)

Code Sec.	Act Sec.	Code Sec.	Act Sec.
1016(a)(27)	701(b)(2)	1250(e)(3)	312(d)(10)(B)
1016(a)(7)	312(d)(6)	1259	1001(c)
1031(h)	1052(a)	1259	1001(a)
1033(e)	913(b)(1)	1271(b)	1003(c)(1)
1033(e)	913(b)(2)	1272(a)(6)(C)(i), (ii)	1004(a)
1033(h)(4)	312(d)(1)	1272(a)(6)(C)(iii)	1004(a)
1033(i)	1087(a)	1274(c)(3)(B)	312(d)(1)
1033(k)(3)	312(d)(7)	1291(a)(3)(A)	1122(b)(3)
1034	312(b)	1291(d)	1122(b)(2)
1034	312(d)(15)	1291(d)(1)	1122(b)(1)
1035(c)	1131(b)(1) sic [(c)]	1293(a)(1)	1122(d)(3)
1036(b)	1014(e)(3)	1293(d)	1122(d)(3)
1038(e)	312(d)(8)	1296	1122(a)
1042(g)	968(a)	1296(e)	1121
1045	313(a)	1297	1122(a)
1045	313(b)(3)	1297(a)	1123(b)(1)
1057	1131(c)(2) sic [(d)]	1297(a)	1123(b)(2)
1057	1131(c)(5) sic [(d)]	1297(b)(3)	1122(d)(4)
1059(a)(2)	1011(a)	1297(e)	1123(a)
1059(d)(1)	1011(c)	1298(b)(1)	1122(e)
1059(d)(3)	1604(d)(1)	1301	933(a)
1059(e)(1)	1011(b)	1361(b)(1)(B)	1601(c)(4)(C)
1059(e)(1)(A)(iii)	1013(b)	1361(b)(3)(A)	1601(c)(3)
1092(f)(2)	1271(b)(9)	1361(c)(7)	1601(c)(4)(B)
11024(a)-(b)	11024(c) *	1361(e)(1)(B)(i), (ii)	1601(c)(1)
1201(a)(2)	314(a)	1361(e)(1)(B)(iii)	1601(c)(1)
1223(15)	313(b)(2)	1374(d)(7)	1601(f)(5)(B)
1223(7)	312(d)(9)	1377	1601(c)(2)(A)
1231	311(e)	1377(b)(1)(B)	1601(c)(2)(B)
1233(h)	1003(b)(1)	1391(b)(2)	951(a)(1)
1234A(1)	1003(a)(1)	1391(b)(2)	951(a)(2)
1239(b)(2)	1308(b)	1391(b)(2)	951(a)(3)
1239(b)(3)	1308(b)	1391(c)	952(d)(2)
1245(a)(2)(C)	1604(a)(3)	1391(e)	952(d)(1)
1245(a)(3)(C)	1604(a)(3)	1391(f)	952(d)(1)
1250(d)(7)	312(d)(10)(A)	1391(g)	952(a)
1250(d)(9), (10)	312(d)(10)(A)	1392(d)	954

Code Sec.	Act Sec.	Code Sec.	Act Sec.
1394(b)(2)	955(b)	2032A(c)(7)(E)	504(a)
1394(b)(3)	955(a)	2032A(c)(8)	508(c)
1394(f)	953(a)	2032A(d)(3)	1313(a)
1396(b)	951(b)(1)	2033A	502(a)
1396(b)(2)	951(b)(2)	2033A	502(b)
1396(e)	952(b)	2035	1310(a)
1397A(c)	952(c)	2035	1310(b)
1397B(b)	956(a)(2)	2053(c)(1)(B)	1073(b)(3)
1397B(b)(2)	956(a)(1)	2053(c)(1)(D)	503(b)(1)
1397B(b)(4)	956(a)(3)	2055(a)(3)	1530(c)(7)(i) [sic (A)]
1397B(c)	956(a)(2)	2055(a)(4)	1530(c)(7)(ii) [sic (B)]
1397B(c)(1)	956(a)(1)	2055(a)(5)	1530(c)(7)(iii) [sic (C)]
1397B(c)(3)	956(a)(3)	2055(e)(3)(G)	1089(b)(5)
1397B(d)(2)	956(a)(4)	2055(e)(3)(J)	1089(b)(3)
1397B(d)(3)	956(a)(5)	2056(b)(7)(C)	1311(a)
1397B(f)	956(a)(6)	2056(b)(8)	1530(c)(8)
1397E	226(a)	2056A	1303(a)
1397F	226(b)(2)	2056A(a)(1)(A)	1314(a)
1400	701(a)	2056A(c)(3)	1312(a)
1400A	701(a)	2102(c)(3)(A)	501(a)(1)(E)
1400B	701(a)	2105(b)(2)	1304(a)
1400C	701(a)	2105(b)(3)	1304(a)
1402	935	2105(b)(4)	1304(a)
1402(k)	922(a)	2107(c)(2)(B)(i)	1602(g)(6)(A)
1441(g)	1604(g)(3)	2107(c)(2)(C)	1602(g)(6)(B)
1445(e)(1)	311(c)(1)	2207A(a)(2)	1302(a)
1491	1131(a)	2207B(a)(2)	1302(b)
1492	1131(a)	2501(a)(3)(C)	1602(g)(5)
1494	1131(a)	2503(b)	501(c)(1)
2001(c)(2)	501(a)(1)(D)	2503(b)	501(c)(2)
2001(f)	506(a)	2503(b)(2)	501(c)(3)
2010(a)	501(a)(1)(A)	2504(c)	506(d)
2010(c)	501(a)(1)(B)	2505(a)(1)	501(a)(2)
2013(g)	1073(b)(2)	2523(g)(1)	1604(g)(4)
2031(c)	508(a)	2612(c)(2)	511(b)(1)
2032A(a)(3)	501(b)	2612(c)(2)	511(b)(2)
2032A(b)(5)(A)	504(b)	2612(c)(3)	511(b)(1)

Code Sec.	Act Sec.	Code Sec.	Act Sec.
2631(c)	501(d)	4051(b)(2)(B)	1401(a)
2651(e)	511(a)	4051(d)	1432(a)
2652(b)(1)	1305(b)	4051(e)	1402(a)
3121	921	4051(e)	1432(a)
3301(1)	1035(1)	4052(b)(1)(B)(ii)	1402(b)
3301(2)	1035(2)	4052(b)(1)(B)(iii)	1402(b)
3306	9304*	4052(b)(1)(B)(iv)	1402(b)
3306(19)	5406(a)(1)*	4052(d)	1434(b)(1)
3306(20)	5406(a)(2)*	4052(f)	1434(a)
3306(21)	5406(a)(3)*	4052(g)	1434(b)(2)
3309(b)(1)(A)	5407(a)(1)*	4081	1032(g)
3309(b)(1)(C)	5407(a)(2)*	4081	1601(f)(4)(E)
3309(b)(3)(D)	5405(a)(1)*	4081	1601(f)(4)(F)
3309(b)(3)(E)	5405(a)(2)*	4081(a)(2)(A)(iii)	1032(b)
3309(b)(3)(F)	5405(a)(3)*	4081(d)(2)(B)	1031(a)(2)
4001(a)	906(a)	4081(d)(3)	1033
4001(e)	906(b)(1)	4082	1032(e)(3)(A)
4001(f)	906(b)(2)	4082	1032(e)(3)(B)
4001(f)	1601(f)(3)(A)(i)	4082(a)	1032(c)(1)
4001(f)	1601(f)(3)(A)(ii)	4082(c)	1032(c)(1)
4001(g)	1601(f)(3)(B)	4082(d)	1032(c)(1)
4003(a)(1)(A)	906(b)(3)	4082(d), (e)	1032(c)(2)
4003(a)(2)(B)	906(b)(4)	4083(a)(3)	902(b)(3)
4003(a)(3)(C)	1401(a)	4083(a)[(1)](A), (B)	1032(a)
4041(a)(1)(A)	902(b)(1)(A)	4083(a)[(1)](C)	1032(a)
4041(a)(1)(A)	902(b)(1)(B)	4083(b)	1032(e)(4)
4041(a)(1)(D)	902(b)(2)	4091	1601(f)(4)(E)
4041(a)(2)	907(a)(1)	4091	1601(f)(4)(F)
4041(a)(2)	1032(e)(1)	4091(b)(3)(A)(ii)	1031(a)(1)
4041(a)(2)	1601(f)(4)(B)	4091(d)	1436(a)
4041(c)(1)	1032(e)(2)	4092(b)	1601(f)(4)(C)
4041(c)(2)	1435(b)	4093(a)	1032(e)(5)
4041(c)(3)(B)	1031(a)(3)	4101(e)	1032(d)
4041(d)(1)	907(a)(2)	4131(b)	904(a)
4041(l)	1601(f)(4)(A)(i)	4132	904(e)
4041(l)	1601(f)(4)(A)(ii)	4132(a)(1)	904(b)
4041(m)(1)(A)	907(b)	4132(a)(2)-(5)	904(c)

Code Sec.	Act Sec.	Code Sec.	Act Sec.
4132(a)(6)-(8)	904(c)	4975(f)(6)	1506(b)(1)(A)
4161(b)	1433(a)	4978(a)	1530(c)(11)(A)
4222(b)(2)	1431(a)(1)	4978(a)(2)	1530(c)(11)(B)
4222(b)(2)	1431(a)(2)	4978(b)(2)	1530(c)(12)(A)
4251(d)	1034(a)	4978(b)(2)(A)	1530(c)(12)(B)
4261	1031(g)	4978(c)	1530(c)(13)
4261(a)-(c)	1031(c)(1)	4978(e)(2)	1530(c)(14)
4261(e)-(g)	1031(c)(2)	4979A(a)	1530(c)(15)
4261(g)	1601(f)(4)(D)	4979A(c)	1530(c)(16)
4261(g)(1)(A)(ii)	1031(b)(1)	4979A(d)	1530(c)(17)
4261(h)	1435(a)	4980A	1073(a)
4263(c)	1031(c)(3)	4980D(a)	1531(b)(2)(A)
4271(d)(1)(A)(ii)	1031(b)(2)	4980D(c)(3)(B)(i)(I)	1531(b)(2)(B)
4495	1432(b)(1)	4980D(d)(1)	1531(b)(2)(C)
4496	1432(b)(1)	4980D(d)(3)	1531(b)(2)(D)
4497	1432(b)(1)	4980D(f)(1)	1531(b)(2)(E)
4498	1432(b)(1)	4982(e)(6)	1122(c)(1)
4681(b)(1)(B), (C)	1432(c)(1)	5001	909
4682(d)(1)	903(a)	5008(c)(1)	1411(a)
4682(g)	1432(c)(2)	5041(b)(4), (5)	908(a)
4947(b)(4)	1530(c)(9)	5041(b)(6)	908(a)
4962(b)	1603(a)	5041(c)(1)	908(b)
4972(c)(6)(B)	1507(a)	5044	1416(b)(2)
4973(a)(2)	213(d)(1)	5044	1416(b)(3)
4973(a)(3)	213(d)(1)	5044(a)	1416(a)
4973(a)(4)	213(d)(1)	5053(f)	1414(b)
4973(d)	4006(b)(1) *	5053(g)	1418(a)
4973(e)	213(d)(2)	5053(h)	1419(a)
4973(f) [(b)]	302(b)	5055	1420(a)
4975(a)	1074(a)	5056(c)	1414(c)(1)
4975(c)(4)	1602(a)(5)	5056(d)	1414(c)(2)
4975(c)(5)	213(b)(2)	5115	1415(a)
4975(d)	1506(b)(1)(B)(i)	5115	1415(b)(3)
4975(d)	1506(b)(1)(B)(ii)	5175(c)	1412(a)
4975(e)(1)(D)	213(b)(1)	5207(c)	1413(a)
4975(e)(1)(E)	213(b)(1)	5222(b)(2)	1414(a)
4975(e)(7)	1530(c)(10)	5361	1416(b)(1)

Code Sec.	Act Sec.	Code Sec.	Act Sec.
5364	1422(a)	5761(c)-(d)	9302(h)(1)(B) *
5364	1422(b)	5761(d)	9302(h)(1)(D) *
5384(b)(2)(D)	1417(a)	5762(a)(1)	9302(h)(2)(A) *
5388(c)	910(a)	5763(b)	9302(h)(2)(A) *
5418	1421(a)	5763(b)	9302(h)(2)(B) *
5418	1421(b)	5763(c)	9302(h)(2)(A) *
5681(a)	1415(b)(1)	6011(e)(2)	1224
5681(c)	1415(b)(2)(A)	6012(b)(6)	1225
5681(c)	1415(b)(2)(B)	6012(c)	312(d)(11)
5701	1604(f)(3)	6018(a)(1)	501(a)(1)(C)
5701	9302(j) *	6018(a)(4)	1073(b)(4)
5701(a)(1)	9302(b)(1) *	6019(1)	1301(a)
5701(a)(2)	9302(b)(2) *	6019(2)	1301(a)
5701(b)(1)	9302(a)(1) *	6019(3)	1301(a)
5701(b)(2)	9302(a)(2) *	6031(b)	1223(a)
5701(c)	9302(c) *	6031(e)	1141(a)
5701(c)	9302(h)(3) *	6033(b)(10)	1603(b)(1)(A)
5701(d)	9302(d) *	6033(b)(10)(C)	1603(b)(1)(B)
5701(e)(1)	9302(e)(1) *	6033(b)(11)	1603(b)(2)
5701(e)(2)	9302(e)(2) *	6034A(c)	1027(a)
5701(f)	9302(f) *	6038	1142(a)
5701(g)	9302(g)(1) *	6038	1142(e)(5)
5701(p)	9302(g)(2) *	6038(a)(2)	1142(e)(1)(A)
5702(c)	9302(g)(3)(A) *	6038(a)(3)	1142(e)(1)(A)
5702(d)	9302(g)(3)(B)(i) *	6038(a)(5)	1142(d)
5702(d)(1)	9302(g)(3)(B)(ii) *	6038(b)	1142(c)(1)(A)
5702(k)	9302(h)(4) *	6038(b)	1142(e)(1)(B)
5704	9302(h)(1)(A) *	6038(b)(2)	1142(c)(1)(B)
5712	9302(h)(2)(A) *	6038(c)	1142(e)(1)(C)
5712(1)	9302(h)(5) *	6038(c)(1)(B)	1142(e)(2)
5712(2)	9302(h)(5) *	6038(d)	1142(e)(1)(D)
5713(a)	9302(h)(2)(A) *	6038(e)(1)	1142(b)(1)(B)
5721	9302(h)(2)(A) *	6038(e)(1), (2)	1142(b)(1)(A)
5722	9302(h)(2)(A) *	6038(e)(2)	1142(b)(2)
5754	9302(h)(1)(E)(i) *	6038(e)(3)	1142(b)(1)(C)
5754	9302(h)(1)(E)(ii) *	6038(e)(4)	1142(e)(1)(E)
5761(a)	9302(h)(1)(C) *	6038B(a)(1)	1144(a)

Code Sec.	Act Sec.	Code Sec.	Act Sec.
6038B(b)	1144(b)	6103(l)(16)	11024(b)(1) *
6038B(b)(1)	1144(c)(1)	6103(l)(7)(D)(viii)	1023(a)
6038B(b)(3)	1144(c)(2)	6103(p)(3)(A)	1026(b)(1)(A)
6039D(d)(1)	1601(h)(2)(D)(iii)	6103(p)(3)(A)	1205(c)(3)
6039F	1602(h)(1)	6103(p)(3)(A)	11024(b)(4) *
6039F and G	1602(h)(2)	6103(p)(4)	1026(b)(1)(B)
6041	1021(b)	6103(p)(4)	1283(b)
6041A(d)(3)	1022(a)	6103(p)(4)	11024(b)(5) *
6045(e)(5)	312(c)	6103(p)(4)(F)	11024(b)(7) *
6045(f)	1021(a)	6103(p)(4)(F)(i)	11024(b)(6) *
6046(a)	1146(a)	6111(d), (e)	1028(a)
6046A(a)	1143(a)(1)	6166(b)(7)(A)(iii)	503(c)(1)
6046A(d)	1143(a)(2)	6166(b)(8)(A)(iii)	503(c)(1)
6048(b)	1601(i)(1)	6211(c)	1231(b)
6048(d)(5)	1027(b)	6212(c)(2)(C)	312(d)(12)
6050Q(b)(1)	1602(d)(1)	6212(c)(2)(E)	312(d)(12)
6050R(c)(1)	1601(a)(1)	6213(g)(2)(G)	101(d)(2)
6050S	201(c)(1)	6213(g)(2)(H)	101(d)(2)
6050S	201(c)(3)	6213(g)(2)(H)	201(b)
6050S(a)(2)	202(c)(1)	6213(g)(2)(H), (I)	1085(a)(3)
6050S(b)(2)(A)	202(c)(2)(A)	6213(g)(2)(I)	101(d)(2)
6050S(b)(2)(C)(i)	202(c)(2)(B)	6213(g)(2)(I)	201(b)
6050S(b)(2)(C)(ii)	202(c)(2)(B)	6213(g)(2)(J)	201(b)
6050S(b)(2)(C)(iii)	202(c)(2)(B)	6213(g)(2)(J)	1085(a)(3)
6050S(e)	202(c)(3)	6221	1238(a)
6103	976(a)	6225(b)	1239(a)
6103	976(b)	6226(b)(5)	1240(a)
6103	11024(a) *	6226(d)(1)	1239(b)
6103(a)(3)	11024(b)(2) *	6226(f)	1238(b)(1)(A)
6103(d)(5)	976(c)	6226(f)	1238(b)(1)(B)
6103(e)(1)(A)(iv)	1201(b)(2)	6227(b), (c)	1236(a)
6103(h)(5)	1283(a)	6227(e)	1243(a)
6103(h)(6)	1283(a)	6229	1235(a)(2)
6103(i)(7)(B)(i)	11024(b)(3) *	6229(b)(2)	1233(c)
6103(k)(8)	1026(a)	6229(d)(1)	1233(a)
6103(k)(8)	1205(c)(1)	6229(f)	1235(a)(1)
6103(l)(12)(F)	4631(c)(2) *	6229(f)(2)	1235(a)(3)

Code Sec.	Act Sec.	Code Sec.	Act Sec.
6229(h)	1233(b)	6334(f)	1025(a)
6230(a)(1)	1237(c)(1)	6416(a)(4)(B)	905(a)
6230(a)(2)(A)(i)	1238(b)(2)	6416(b)(2)	1032(e)(6)
6230(a)(3)	1237(a)	6416(d)	1436(b)
6230(a)(3)(A)	1238(b)(3)(A)	6421(e)(2)(B)(iii), (iv)	902(a)
6230(a)(3)(B)	1238(b)(3)(B)	6422(5)	1131(c)(3) sic [(d)]
6230(c)(1)(A), (B)	1238(b)(4)	6422(6)-(13)	1131(c)(3) sic [(d)]
6230(c)(1)(C)	1238(b)(4)	6427	1601(g)(1)
6230(c)(2)(A)	1238(b)(5)	6427(f)	1032(e)(7)
6230(c)(4)	1238(b)(6)	6427(f)(1)	1032(e)(7)
6230(c)(5)	1237(b)	6427(f)(2)	1032(e)(8)
6230(c)(5)(A)	1238(b)(3)(C)	6427(f)(3)	1032(e)(7)
6230(c)(5)(D)	1238(b)(3)(D)	6427(i)(3)(A)	1032(e)(9)
6230(d)(6)	1239(c)(1)	6427(i)(4)	1032(e)(10)
6231(a)(1)(B)(i)	1234(a)	6427(i)(5)(A)(i)	1032(c)(3)(E)
6231(f)	1141(b)(1)	6427(l)	1032(c)(3)(D)
6231(f)	1141(b)(2)	6427(l)(1)	1032(c)(3)(A)
6231(g)	1232(a)	6427(l)(2)	1032(c)(3)(A)
6234	1231(c)	6427(l)(5)	1032(c)(3)(A)
6234	1231(a)	6427(l)(5)(B)	1032(c)(3)(B)
6240	1222(a)	6427(l)(5)(C)	1032(c)(3)(C)
6241	1222(a)	6501(a)	1284(a)
6242	1222(a)	6501(c)(8)	1145(a)
6245	1222(a)	6501(c)(9)	506(b)
6246	1222(a)	6501(o)(3)	1239(e)(2)
6247	1222(a)	6503(a)	1237(c)(2)
6248	1222(a)	6504(4)	312(d)(13)
6251	1222(a)	6504(5)-(12)	312(d)(13)
6252	1222(a)	6511(d)(3)(A)	1056(a)
6255	1222(a)	6511(d)(7)	1454(b)(1)
6302	901(e)	6512(b)(2)	1451(a)
6302	931	6512(b)(3)	1239(c)(2)
6311	1205(a)	6512(b)(3)	1282(a)
6311	1205(b)	6512(b)(4)	1451(b)
6331(h)	1024(a)(1)	6601	915
6331(h)	1024(a)(2)	6601(c)	1242(a)
6334(a)(13)	312(d)(1)	6601(d)(2), (3)	1055(a)

Code Sec.	Act Sec.	Code Sec.	Act Sec.
6601(j)	503(c)(3)	6695(g)	1085(a)(2)
6601(j)(1), (2)	503(a)	6707(a)(1)(A)	1028(d)(2)
6601(j)(3)	501(e)	6707(a)(2)	1028(d)(1)
6601(j)(4)	503(c)(2)	6707(a)(3)	1028(b)
6611(f)(2), (3)	1055(b)(1)	6715(c)(1)	1032(e)(11)
6611(f)(4)	1055(b)(2)(A)(i)	6724(d)(1)(A)(ix)	1213(b)
6611(f)(4)	1055(b)(2)(A)(ii)	6724(d)(1)(A)(vii), (viii)	1213(b)
6611(f)(4)(B)(ii)(I)	1055(b)(2)(B)	6724(d)(1)(B)(ix)-(xiv)	201(c)(2)(A)
6611(f)(4)(B)(ii)(II)	1055(b)(2)(B)	6724(d)(2)(R)-(Y)	1602(d)(2)(A)
6611(f)(4)(B)(ii)(III)	1055(b)(2)(C)	6724(d)(2)(W)	201(c)(2)(B)
6611(g)	1055(b)(2)(D)	6724(d)(2)(X)	201(c)(2)(B)
6611(h), (i)	1055(b)(2)(D)	6724(d)(2)(Z)	201(c)(2)(B)
6621(a)(1)	1604(b)(1)	6724(e)	1223(b)
6621(c)(2)(B)(iii)	1463(a)	7213(a)(2)	2(b)(1) †
6652(e)	1602(d)(2)(B)	7213(a)(2)	11024(b)(8) *
6652(g)	1281(a)	7213A	2(a) †
6652(k)	1281(b)	7213A	2(b)(2) †
6654	1(d)	7232	1032(e)(12)(A)
6654(d)(1)(C)(i)	1091(a)	7232	1032(e)(12)(B)
6654(e)(1)	1202(a)	7232	1032(e)(12)(C)
6655	1(d)	7421(a)	1222(b)(1)
6655(g)(3)	1461(a)	7421(a)	1454(b)(2)
6662(d)(2)(B)	1028(c)(1)	7421(a)	1239(e)(3)
6662(d)(2)(C)(iii)	1028(c)(2)	7430(b)(5)	1285(b)
6679(a)	1143(b)	7430(c)(4)(D)	1453(a)
6683	1281(c)	7430(f)(2)	1285(c)(1)
6693	211(e)(2)(C)	7430(f)(2)	1285(c)(2)
6693	211(e)(2)(D)	7430(f)(3)	1285(a)
6693(a)	1602(a)(4)	7431	3(d)(4) †
6693(a)(2)(A)	211(e)(2)(B)	7431	3(d)(5) †
6693(a)(2)(B)	211(e)(2)(B)	7431(a)(1)	3(a)(1) †
6693(a)(2)(B)	213(c)	7431(a)(1)	3(a)(2) †
6693(a)(2)(C)	213(c)	7431(a)(2)	3(a)(1) †
6693(a)(2)(C)	211(e)(2)(B)	7431(a)(2)	3(a)(2) †
6693(a)(2)(D)	213(c)	7431(b)	3(c) †
6693(c)(2)	1601(d)(1)(C)(ii)(I)	7431(c)(1)(A)	3(d)(1) †
6693(c)(2)	1601(d)(1)(C)(ii)(II)	7431(c)(1)(B)(i)	3(d)(1) †

Code Sec.	Act Sec.	Code Sec.	Act Sec.
7431(c)(1)(B)(ii)	3(d)(2) †	7701(b)(7)(D)	1174(b)(1)
7431(d)	3(d)(1) †	7702B(c)(2)(B)	1602(b)
7431(e),(f)	3(b) †	7702B(g)(4)(B)(ii)	1602(e)
7431(f)	3(d)(3) †	7702B(g)(4)(B)(iii)	1602(e)
7431(g)	1205(c)(2)	7704(g)	964(a)
7431(g)(2)	3(d)(6) †	7872(f)(11)(A)	312(d)(1)
7436	1454(a)	9502(b)(1)	1031(d)(1)(C)
7436	1454(b)(4)	9502(b)(1)(C)	1031(d)(1)(A)
7453	1454(b)(3)	9502(b)(1)(D)	1031(d)(1)(B)
7459(c)	1222(b)(2)	9502(d)	1604(g)(5)
7459(c)	1239(e)(1)	9502(f)	1031(d)(2)
7477	506(c)(2)	9503(b)(1)(E)	1032(e)(13)
7477	506(c)(1)	9503(b)(4)	901(a)
7479	505(a)	9503(b)(5)(B)	1032(e)(14)
7479	505(b)	9503(c)(2)(A)	901(d)(2)
7481(b)	1454(b)(3)	9503(c)(2)(A)(ii)	1601(f)(2)(A)
7481(c)	1452(a)	9503(c)(4)(D)	901(d)(3)
7482(b)(1)	1239(d)(2)	9503(c)(5)(B)	901(d)(3)
7482(b)(1)(D), (E)	1239(d)(1)	9503(c)(6)(D)	901(d)(3)
7482(b)(1)(E)	1222(b)(3)	9503(c)(7)	901(c)
7482(b)(1)(F)	1239(d)(1)	9503(e)(2)	901(b)
7485(b)	1222(b)(4)(A)	9503(e)(5)(A)	1601(f)(2)(B)
7485(b)	1241(a)(1)	9503(f)	901(d)(1)
7485(b)	1241(a)(2)	9508(b)(2)	1032(e)(13)
7485(b)	1222(b)(4)(B)	9801(c)(1)	1531(b)(1)(A)
7508A	911(b)	9802(c)	1532(a)
7508A	911(a)	9804	1531(a)(2)
7508A	915	9805	1531(a)(2)
7518(g)(6)(A)	311(c)(2)	9811	1531(a)(4)
7519(f)(4)(A)	1281(d)	9812	1531(a)(4)
7701	1161(a)	9831(b)	1531(b)(1)(B)
7701	1601(i)(4)	9831(c)(1)	1531(b)(1)(C)
7701(a)(30)(E)(ii)	1601(i)(3)(A)	9831(c)(2)	1531(b)(1)(D)
7701(a)(4)	1151(a)	9831(c)(3)	1531(b)(1)(E)
7701(b)(7)(A)	1174(b)(2)		

¶ 6003. '97 Act Sections Amending Code
(including conforming amendments)

* denotes Budget Act
† denotes Privacy Act

Act Sec.	Code Sec.	Act Sec.	Code Sec.
1(c)	15	201(c)(2)(A)	6724(d)(1)(B)(ix)-(xiv)
1(d)	6654	201(c)(2)(B)	6724(d)(2)(W)
1(d)	6655	201(c)(2)(B)	6724(d)(2)(X)
2(a) †	7213A	201(c)(2)(B)	6724(d)(2)(Z)
2(b)(1) †	7213(a)(2)	201(c)(3)	6050S
2(b)(2) †	7213A	201(d)	135(d)(2), (3)
3(a)(1) †	7431(a)(1)	201(e)	25A
3(a)(1) †	7431(a)(2)	202(a)	221
3(a)(2) †	7431(a)(1)	202(b)	62(a)(17)
3(a)(2) †	7431(a)(2)	202(c)(1)	6050S(a)(2)
3(b) †	7431(e),(f)	202(c)(2)(A)	6050S(b)(2)(A)
3(c) †	7431(b)	202(c)(2)(B)	6050S(b)(2)(C)(i)
3(d)(1) †	7431(c)(1)(A)	202(c)(2)(B)	6050S(b)(2)(C)(ii)
3(d)(1) †	7431(c)(1)(B)(i)	202(c)(2)(B)	6050S(b)(2)(C)(iii)
3(d)(1) †	7431(d)	202(c)(3)	6050S(e)
3(d)(2) †	7431(c)(1)(B)(ii)	202(d)	221
3(d)(3) †	7431(f)	202(d)	222
3(d)(4) †	7431	203(a)	72(t)(2)(E)
3(d)(5) †	7431	203(b)	72(t)(7)
3(d)(6) †	7431(g)(2)	211(a)	529(e)(3)
101(a)	24	211(b)(1)	529(e)(2)
101(b)	32(m)	211(b)(2)	529(e)(5)
101(c)	501(c)(26)	211(b)(3)(A)(i)	529(c)(2)
101(d)(2)	6213(g)(2)(G)	211(b)(3)(A)(ii)	529(c)(5)
101(d)(2)	6213(g)(2)(H)	211(b)(3)(B)	529(c)(4)
101(d)(2)	6213(g)(2)(I)	211(b)(4)	529(b)(5)
101(d)(3)	24	211(c)	135(c)(2)(C)
201(a)	25A	211(d)	529(c)(3)(A)
201(b)	6213(g)(2)(H)	211(e)(2)(A)	529(d)
201(b)	6213(g)(2)(I)	211(e)(2)(B)	6693(a)(2)(A)
201(b)	6213(g)(2)(J)	211(e)(2)(B)	6693(a)(2)(B)
201(c)(1)	6050S	211(e)(2)(B)	6693(a)(2)(C)

Act Sec.	Code Sec.	Act Sec.	Code Sec.
211(e)(2)(C)	6693	303(b)	72(t)(8)
211(e)(2)(D)	6693	304(a)	408(m)(3)
211(f)(6)	529	311(a)	1(h)
213(a)	530	311(b)(1)	55(b)(3)
213(b)(1)	4975(e)(1)(D)	311(b)(2)(A)	55(b)(1)(A)(ii)
213(b)(1)	4975(e)(1)(E)	311(b)(2)(B)	57(a)(7)
213(b)(2)	4975(c)(5)	311(c)(1)	1445(e)(1)
213(c)	6693(a)(2)(B)	311(c)(2)	7518(g)(6)(A)
213(c)	6693(a)(2)(C)	311(c)(3)	904(b)(2)(C)
213(c)	6693(a)(2)(D)	311(e)	1231
213(d)(1)	4973(a)(2)	312(a)	121
213(d)(1)	4973(a)(3)	312(b)	1034
213(d)(1)	4973(a)(4)	312(c)	6045(e)(5)
213(d)(2)	4973(e)	312(d)(1)	25(e)(7)
213(e)(1)	26(b)(2)(E)-(P)	312(d)(1)	56(e)(1)(A)
213(e)(2)	135(c)(2)(C)	312(d)(1)	56(e)(3)(B)(i)
213(e)(3)	530	312(d)(1)	143(i)(1)(C)(i)(I)
221(a)	127(d)	312(d)(1)	163(h)(4)(A)(i)(I)
222	145(b)(5)	312(d)(1)	280A(d)(4)(A)
223(a)	148(f)(4)(D)(vii)	312(d)(1)	464(f)(3)(B)(i)
224(a)	170(e)(6)	312(d)(1)	1033(h)(4)
225(a)(1)	108(f)(2)(B)	312(d)(1)	1274(c)(3)(B)
225(a)(1)	108(f)(2)(D)	312(d)(1)	6334(a)(13)
225(a)(2)	108(f)(3)	312(d)(1)	7872(f)(11)(A)
226(a)	1397E	312(d)(2)	32(c)(4)
226(b)(2)	1397F	312(d)(3)	143(m)(6)(A)
301(a)(1)	219(g)(3)(B)	312(d)(4)	216(e)
301(a)(2)	219(g)(2)(A)(ii)	312(d)(5)	512(a)(3)(D)
301(b)(1)	219(g)(1)	312(d)(6)	1016(a)(7)
301(b)(2)	219(g)(7)	312(d)(7)	1033(k)(3)
302(a)	408A	312(d)(8)	1038(e)
302(b)	4973(f) [(b)]	312(d)(9)	1223(7)
302(c)	219(c)(1)(B)(ii)	312(d)(10)(A)	1250(d)(7)
302(d)(1)	408(i)	312(d)(10)(A)	1250(d)(9), (10)
302(d)(2)	408(i)	312(d)(10)(B)	1250(e)(3)
302(e)	408A	312(d)(11)	6012(c)
303(a)	72(t)(2)(F)	312(d)(12)	6212(c)(2)(C)

Act Sec.	Code Sec.	Act Sec.	Code Sec.
312(d)(12)	6212(c)(2)(E)	503(c)(3)	6601(j)
312(d)(13)	6504(4)	504(a)	2032A(c)(7)(E)
312(d)(13)	6504(5)-(12)	504(b)	2032A(b)(5)(A)
312(d)(14)	121	505(a)	7479
312(d)(15)	1034	505(b)	7479
313(a)	1045	506(a)	2001(f)
313(b)(1)(A)	1016(a)(23)	506(b)	6501(c)(9)
313(b)(1)(B)	1016(a)(23)	506(c)(1)	7477
313(b)(2)	1223(15)	506(c)(2)	7477
313(b)(3)	1045	506(d)	2504(c)
314(a)	1201(a)(2)	507(a)(1)	665(c)
401(a)	55(e)	507(a)(2)	665(b)
402(a)	56(a)(1)(A)(i)	507(b)(1)	644
402(b)	56(a)(5)	507(b)(1)	645
403(a)	56(a)(6)	507(b)(2)	706(b)(5)
403(a)	56(a)(7), (8)	507(b)(3)	644
501(a)(1)(A)	2010(a)	507(b)(3)	645
501(a)(1)(B)	2010(c)	508(a)	2031(c)
501(a)(1)(C)	6018(a)(1)	508(b)	1014(a)(1)-(3)
501(a)(1)(D)	2001(c)(2)	508(b)	1014(a)(4)
501(a)(1)(E)	2102(c)(3)(A)	508(c)	2032A(c)(8)
501(a)(2)	2505(a)(1)	508(d)	170(h)(5)(B)(ii)
501(b)	2032A(a)(3)	511(a)	2651(e)
501(c)(1)	2503(b)	511(b)(1)	2612(c)(2)
501(c)(2)	2503(b)	511(b)(1)	2612(c)(3)
501(c)(3)	2503(b)(2)	511(b)(2)	2612(c)(2)
501(d)	2631(c)	601(a)(1)	41(h)(1)
501(e)	6601(j)(3)	601(a)(2)	41(h)(1)
502(a)	2033A	601(b)(1)	41(c)(4)(B)
502(b)	2033A	601(b)(2)	45C(b)(1)
503(a)	6601(j)(1), (2)	602(a)	170(e)(5)(D)(ii)
503(b)(1)	2053(c)(1)(D)	603(a)	51(c)(4)(B)
503(b)(2)(A)	163(k)	603(b)(1)	51(d)(2)(A)
503(b)(2)(B)	163(h)(2)(E)	603(b)(2)	51(d)(3)(A)
503(c)(1)	6166(b)(7)(A)(iii)	603(c)(1)	51(d)(1)(F), (G)
503(c)(1)	6166(b)(8)(A)(iii)	603(c)(1)	51(d)(1)(H)
503(c)(2)	6601(j)(4)	603(c)(2)	51(d)(9)-(11)

Act Sec.	Code Sec.	Act Sec.	Code Sec.
603(c)(2)	52(d)(9)	906(b)(3)	4003(a)(1)(A)
603(d)(1)	51(a)	906(b)(4)	4003(a)(2)(B)
603(d)(2)	51(i)(3)	907(a)(1)	4041(a)(2)
604(a)	45C(e)	907(a)(2)	4041(d)(1)
701(a)	1400	907(b)	4041(m)(1)(A)
701(a)	1400A	908(a)	5041(b)(4), (5)
701(a)	1400B	908(a)	5041(b)(6)
701(a)	1400C	908(b)	5041(c)(1)
701(b)(1)	39(d)(8)	909	5001
701(b)(2)	1016(a)(25), (26)	910(a)	5388(c)
701(b)(2)	1016(a)(27)	911(a)	7508A
801(a)	51A	911(b)	7508A
801(b)	51A	912(a)	165(i)(4)
901(a)	9503(b)(4)	913(a)(1)	451(e)(1)
901(b)	9503(e)(2)	913(a)(2)	451(e)
901(c)	9503(c)(7)	913(b)(1)	1033(e)
901(d)(1)	9503(f)	913(b)(2)	1033(e)
901(d)(2)	9503(c)(2)(A)	914	143(k)(11)
901(d)(3)	9503(c)(4)(D)	915	6601
901(d)(3)	9503(c)(5)(B)	915	7508A
901(d)(3)	9503(c)(6)(D)	921	3121
901(e)	6302	922(a)	1402(k)
902(a)	6421(e)(2)(B)(iii), (iv)	931	6302
902(b)(1)(A)	4041(a)(1)(A)	932(a)	280A(c)(1)
902(b)(1)(B)	4041(a)(1)(A)	933(a)	1301
902(b)(2)	4041(a)(1)(D)	934(a)	162(l)(1)(B)
902(b)(3)	4083(a)(3)	935	1402
903(a)	4682(d)(1)	941(a)	198
904(a)	4131(b)	941(b)	198
904(b)	4132(a)(1)	951(a)(1)	1391(b)(2)
904(c)	4132(a)(2)-(5)	951(a)(2)	1391(b)(2)
904(c)	4132(a)(6)-(8)	951(a)(3)	1391(b)(2)
904(e)	4132	951(b)(1)	1396(b)
905(a)	6416(a)(4)(B)	951(b)(2)	1396(b)(2)
906(a)	4001(a)	952(a)	1391(g)
906(b)(1)	4001(e)	952(b)	1396(e)
906(b)(2)	4001(f)	952(c)	1397A(c)

Act Sec.	Code Sec.	Act Sec.	Code Sec.
952(d)(1)	1391(e)	968(a)	1042(g)
952(d)(1)	1391(f)	969(a)	274(n)(3)
952(d)(2)	1391(c)	970(a)	132(e)(2)
953(a)	1394(f)	971(a)	280F(a)(1)(C)
954	1392(d)	972(a)	613A(c)(6)(H)
955(a)	1394(b)(3)	973(a)	170(i)
955(b)	1394(b)(2)	974(a)	501(e)(1)(A)
956(a)(1)	1397B(b)(2)	975(a)	62(a)(2)(C)
956(a)(1)	1397B(c)(1)	976(a)	6103
956(a)(2)	1397B(b)	976(b)	6103
956(a)(2)	1397B(c)	976(c)	6103(d)(5)
956(a)(3)	1397B(b)(4)	1001(a)	1259
956(a)(3)	1397B(c)(3)	1001(b)	475(e)-(f)
956(a)(4)	1397B(d)(2)	1001(c)	1259
956(a)(5)	1397B(d)(3)	1002(a)	351(e)(1)
956(a)(6)	1397B(f)	1003(a)(1)	1234A(1)
961(a)	471(b)	1003(b)(1)	1233(h)
962(a)(1)	130(c)	1003(c)(1)	1271(b)
962(a)(2)	130(c)(1)	1004(a)	1272(a)(6)(C)(i), (ii)
962(a)(3)	130(c)(2)(D)	1004(a)	1272(a)(6)(C)(iii)
963(a)	501(c)(27)(B)	1005(a)	163(l)
963(b)	501(c)(27)	1011(a)	1059(a)(2)
963(b)	501(c)(27)(A)-(C)	1011(b)	1059(e)(1)
963(b)	501(c)(27)(B)(i), (ii)	1011(c)	1059(d)(1)
963(b)	501(c)(27)(C)(i), (ii)	1012(a)	355(e)
964(a)	7704(g)	1012(b)(1)	355(f)
965(a)	513(i)	1012(b)(2)	358(g)
966(a)(1)(A)	528(c)(1)	1012(c)(1)	351(c)
966(a)(1)(B)	528(c)(1)(B)(i), (ii)	1012(c)(2)	368(a)(2)(H)
966(a)(1)(B)	528(c)(1)(B)(iii)	1013(a)	304(a)(1)
966(a)(1)(C)	528(c)(1)(C)	1013(b)	1059(e)(1)(A)(iii)
966(a)(2)	528(c)(4)	1013(c)	304(b)(5)
966(b)	528(d)(3)(A), (B)	1014(a)	351(g)
966(b)	528(d)(3)(C)	1014(b)	354(a)(2)(C)
966(c)	528(c)(5)	1014(c)	355(a)(3)(D)
966(d)	528(b)	1014(d)	356(e), (f)
967	149(d)(3)(A)(i)(I)	1014(e)(1)	354(a)(2)(B)

Act Sec.	Code Sec.	Act Sec.	Code Sec.
1014(e)(1)	355(a)(3)(C)	1031(d)(1)(C)	9502(b)(1)
1014(e)(2)	354(a)(3)(A)	1031(d)(2)	9502(f)
1014(e)(2)	355(a)(4)(A)	1031(g)	4261
1014(e)(3)	1036(b)	1032(a)	4083(a)[(1)](A), (B)
1015(a)	246(c)(1)(A)	1032(a)	4083(a)[(1)](C)
1015(b)(1)	246(c)(2)	1032(b)	4081(a)(2)(A)(iii)
1015(b)(2)	246(c)(3)(A)	1032(c)(1)	4082(a)
1015(b)(2)	246(c)(3)(B)	1032(c)(1)	4082(c)
1015(b)(2)	246(c)(3)(C)	1032(c)(1)	4082(d)
1021(a)	6045(f)	1032(c)(2)	4082(d), (e)
1021(b)	6041	1032(c)(3)(A)	6427(l)(1)
1022(a)	6041A(d)(3)	1032(c)(3)(A)	6427(l)(2)
1023(a)	6103(l)(7)(D)(viii)	1032(c)(3)(A)	6427(l)(5)
1024(a)(1)	6331(h)	1032(c)(3)(B)	6427(l)(5)(B)
1024(a)(2)	6331(h)	1032(c)(3)(C)	6427(l)(5)(C)
1025(a)	6334(f)	1032(c)(3)(D)	6427(l)
1026(a)	6103(k)(8)	1032(c)(3)(E)	6427(i)(5)(A)(i)
1026(b)(1)(A)	6103(p)(3)(A)	1032(d)	4101(e)
1026(b)(1)(B)	6103(p)(4)	1032(e)(1)	4041(a)(2)
1027(a)	6034A(c)	1032(e)(2)	4041(c)(1)
1027(b)	6048(d)(5)	1032(e)(3)(A)	4082
1028(a)	6111(d), (e)	1032(e)(3)(B)	4082
1028(b)	6707(a)(3)	1032(e)(4)	4083(b)
1028(c)(1)	6662(d)(2)(B)	1032(e)(5)	4093(a)
1028(c)(2)	6662(d)(2)(C)(iii)	1032(e)(6)	6416(b)(2)
1028(d)(1)	6707(a)(2)	1032(e)(7)	6427(f)
1028(d)(2)	6707(a)(1)(A)	1032(e)(7)	6427(f)(1)
1031(a)(1)	4091(b)(3)(A)(ii)	1032(e)(7)	6427(f)(3)
1031(a)(2)	4081(d)(2)(B)	1032(e)(8)	6427(f)(2)
1031(a)(3)	4041(c)(3)(B)	1032(e)(9)	6427(i)(3)(A)
1031(b)(1)	4261(g)(1)(A)(ii)	1032(e)(10)	6427(i)(4)
1031(b)(2)	4271(d)(1)(A)(ii)	1032(e)(11)	6715(c)(1)
1031(c)(1)	4261(a)-(c)	1032(e)(12)(A)	7232
1031(c)(2)	4261(e)-(g)	1032(e)(12)(B)	7232
1031(c)(3)	4263(c)	1032(e)(12)(C)	7232
1031(d)(1)(A)	9502(b)(1)(C)	1032(e)(13)	9503(b)(1)(E)
1031(d)(1)(B)	9502(b)(1)(D)	1032(e)(13)	9508(b)(2)

Act Sec.	Code Sec.	Act Sec.	Code Sec.
1032(e)(14)	9503(b)(5)(B)	1062(b)(3)	735(c)(1)
1032(g)	4081	1063(a)	704(c)(1)(B)
1033	4081(d)(3)	1063(a)	737(b)(1)
1034(a)	4251(d)	1071(a)(1)	411(a)(11)(A)
1035(1)	3301(1)	1071(a)(2)(A)	411(a)(7)(B)
1035(2)	3301(2)	1071(a)(2)(A)	417(e)(1)
1041(a)	512(b)(13)	1071(a)(2)(A)	417(e)(2)
1042	833	1071(a)(2)(A)	457(e)(9)
1051(a)(1)	954(c)(1)(F)-(G)	1071(a)(2)(B)	417(e)(1)
1051(a)(2)(A)	954(c)(1)(B)	1071(a)(2)(B)	417(e)(2)
1051(a)(2)(B)	954(c)(1)(B)	1071(a)(2)(B)	457(e)(9)(A)
1051(b)	954(c)(2)(C)	1072(a)	132(f)(4)
1052(a)	1031(h)	1073(a)	4980A
1053(a)	901(k)	1073(b)(1)	691(c)(1)(C)
1053(b)	853(c)	1073(b)(2)	2013(g)
1054(a)	894(c)	1073(b)(3)	2053(c)(1)(B)
1055(a)	6601(d)(2), (3)	1073(b)(4)	6018(a)(4)
1055(b)(1)	6611(f)(2), (3)	1074(a)	4975(a)
1055(b)(2)(A)(i)	6611(f)(4)	1075(a)	72(d)(1)(B)(iv)
1055(b)(2)(A)(ii)	6611(f)(4)	1075(b)(1)	72(d)(1)(B)(iii)
1055(b)(2)(B)	6611(f)(4)(B)(ii)(I)	1075(b)(2)	72(d)(1)(B)(iii)
1055(b)(2)(B)	6611(f)(4)(B)(ii)(II)	1081(a)	447(i)(3), (4)
1055(b)(2)(C)	6611(f)(4)(B)(ii)(III)	1081(a)	447(i)(5), (6)
1055(b)(2)(D)	6611(g)	1082(a)(1)	172(b)(1)(A)(i)
1055(b)(2)(D)	6611(h), (i)	1082(a)(2)	172(b)(1)(A)(ii)
1056(a)	6511(d)(3)(A)	1082(b)	172(b)(1)(F)
1057(a)	59(a)(2)(C)	1083(a)(1)	39(a)(1)
1061(a)	732(c)	1083(a)(2)	39(a)(2)
1062(a)	751(a)(2)	1084(a)(1)	264(a)(1)
1062(b)(1)(A)	751(b)(1)(A)-(B)	1084(a)(2)	264(b)-(d)
1062(b)(1)(B)	751(b)(3)	1084(b)(1)	264(a)(4)
1062(b)(2)	751(d)	1084(b)(2)	101(a)(2)
1062(b)(3)	724(d)(2)	1084(c)	264(f)
1062(b)(3)	731(a)(2)(B)	1084(b)(1)(A) [sic (d)]	805(a)(4)(C)(ii)
1062(b)(3)	731(c)(6)	1084(b)(1)(B) [sic (d)]	805(a)(4)(D)(iii)
1062(b)(3)	732(c)(1)(A)	1084(b)(1)(C) [sic (d)]	805(a)(4)(F)
1062(b)(3)	735(a)(2)	1084(b)(2)(A) [sic (d)]	807(a)(2)(B)

Act Sec.	Code Sec.	Act Sec.	Code Sec.
1084(b)(2)(B) [sic (d)]	807(b)(1)(B)	1102(b)(1)	986(a)(3)
1084(b)(3) [sic (d)]	812(d)(1)(B), (C)	1102(b)(2)	989(c)(4), (5)
1084(b)(3) [sic (d)]	812(d)(1)(D)	1102(b)(2)	989(c)(6)
1084(b)(4) [sic (d)]	832(b)(5)(B)(i), (ii)	1102(b)(3)	989(b)
1084(b)(4) [sic (d)]	832(b)(5)(B)(iii)	1103(a)	59(a)(3)
1084(c) [sic (e)]	265(b)(4)(A)	1104(a)	988(e)
1085(a)(1)	32(k), (l)	1105(a)(1)	904(d)(1)(E)
1085(a)(2)	6695(g)	1105(a)(2)	904(d)(2)(E)(iv)
1085(a)(3)	6213(g)(2)(H), (I)	1105(a)(3)	904(d)(2)(C)(iii)(II)
1085(a)(3)	6213(g)(2)(J)	1105(a)(3)	904(d)(2)(D)
1085(b)	32(c)(5)(B)(iv)	1105(b)	904(d)(4), (5)
1085(c)	32(c)(2)(B)(iii), (iv)	1111(a)	964(e)
1085(c)	32(c)(2)(B)(v)	1111(b)	904(d)(2)(E)(i)
1085(d)(1)	32(c)(5)(B)(iii)	1112(a)(1)	951(a)(2)
1085(d)(2)	32(c)(5)(B)(iv)(III)	1112(b)(1)	961(c)
1085(d)(3)	32(c)(5)(B)(v)-(vi)	1112(c)(1)	952(b)
1085(d)(4)	32(c)(5)(B)	1113(a)(1)	902(b)
1086(a)	167(g)(6)	1113(a)(2)(A)	902(c)(3)(B)(i)
1086(b)(1)	168(e)(3)(A)(i), (ii)	1113(a)(2)(A)	902(c)(3)(B)(ii), (iii)
1086(b)(1)	168(e)(3)(A)(iii)	1113(a)(2)(B)	902(c)(4)(B)
1086(b)(2)	168(g)(3)(B)	1113(a)(2)(C)	902(c)(3)
1086(b)(3)	168(i)(14)	1113(a)(2)(D)	902(c)(3)
1087(a)	1033(i)	1113(b)	960(a)(1)
1088(a)	453C	1121	1296(e)
1089(a)(1)	664(d)(1)(A)	1122(a)	1296
1089(a)(1)	664(d)(2)(A)	1122(a)	1297
1089(b)(1)	664(d)(1)(B), (C)	1122(b)(1)	1291(d)(1)
1089(b)(1)	664(d)(1)(D)	1122(b)(2)	1291(d)
1089(b)(2)	664(d)(2)(B), (C)	1122(b)(3)	1291(a)(3)(A)
1089(b)(2)	664(d)(2)(D)	1122(c)(1)	4982(e)(6)
1089(b)(3)	2055(e)(3)(J)	1122(c)(2)	852(b)(10)
1089(b)(4)	664(d)(4)	1122(c)(3)	852(c)
1089(b)(5)	2055(e)(3)(G)	1122(d)(1)	532(b)(4)
1091(a)	6654(d)(1)(C)(i)	1122(d)(1)	542(c)(10)
1101(a)	904(j)	1122(d)(2)	551(f)
1102(a)(1)	986(a)	1122(d)(3)	1293(a)(1)
1102(a)(2)	905(c)	1122(d)(3)	1293(d)

Act Sec.	Code Sec.	Act Sec.	Code Sec.
1122(d)(4)	1297(b)(3)	1142(e)(1)(E)	6038(e)(4)
1122(e)	1298(b)(1)	1142(e)(2)	6038(c)(1)(B)
1123(a)	1297(e)	1142(e)(3)	318(b)(8)
1123(b)(1)	1297(a)	1142(e)(4)	901(k)(4)
1123(b)(2)	1297(a)	1142(e)(5)	6038
1131(a)	1491	1143(a)(1)	6046A(a)
1131(a)	1492	1143(a)(2)	6046A(d)
1131(a)	1494	1143(b)	6679(a)
1131(b)	684	1144(a)	6038B(a)(1)
1131(b)(1) sic [(c)]	1035(c)	1144(b)	6038B(b)
1131(b)(2) sic [(c)]	367(f)	1144(c)(1)	6038B(b)(1)
1131(b)(3) sic [(c)]	721(c)	1144(c)(2)	6038B(b)(3)
1131(b)(4) sic [(c)]	367(d)(2)(C)	1145(a)	6501(c)(8)
1131(b)(5)(A) sic [(c)]	367(d)(3)	1146(a)	6046(a)
1131(b)(5)(B) sic [(c)]	721(d)	1151(a)	7701(a)(4)
1131(c)(1) sic [(d)]	814(h)	1161(a)	7701
1131(c)(2) sic [(d)]	1057	1162(a)	864(b)(2)(A)(ii)
1131(c)(3) sic [(d)]	6422(5)	1163(a)	902(c)(2)(B)
1131(c)(3) sic [(d)]	6422(6)-(13)	1163(b)	904(d)(2)(C)(i)(II)
1131(c)(5) sic [(d)]	1057	1171(a)	927(a)(2)(B)
1131(c)(6) sic [(d)]	684	1172(a)(1)	911(b)(2)(A)
1141(a)	6031(e)	1172(a)(2)	911(b)(2)(D)
1141(b)(1)	6231(f)	1173(a)	956(c)(2)(H), (I)
1141(b)(2)	6231(f)	1173(a)	956(c)(2)(J)-(K)
1142(a)	6038	1174(a)(1)	861(a)(3)
1142(b)(1)(A)	6038(e)(1), (2)	1174(a)(2)	863(c)(2)(B)
1142(b)(1)(B)	6038(e)(1)	1174(b)(1)	7701(b)(7)(D)
1142(b)(1)(C)	6038(e)(3)	1174(b)(2)	7701(b)(7)(A)
1142(b)(2)	6038(e)(2)	1175(a)	954(h)
1142(c)(1)(A)	6038(b)	1175(b)	954(e)(2)(A), (B)
1142(c)(1)(B)	6038(b)(2)	1175(b)	954(e)(2)(C)
1142(d)	6038(a)(5)	1201(a)(1)	63(c)(5)
1142(e)(1)(A)	6038(a)(2)	1201(a)(2)(A)	63(c)(4)
1142(e)(1)(A)	6038(a)(3)	1201(a)(2)(B)	63(c)(4)(B)
1142(e)(1)(B)	6038(b)	1201(b)(1)	59(j)
1142(e)(1)(C)	6038(c)	1201(b)(2)	6103(e)(1)(A)(iv)
1142(e)(1)(D)	6038(d)	1202(a)	6654(e)(1)

Act Sec.	Code Sec.	Act Sec.	Code Sec.
1203(a)	162(o)	1222(b)(4)(B)	7485(b)
1203(b)	274	1223(a)	6031(b)
1204(a)	162(a)	1223(b)	6724(e)
1205(a)	6311	1224	6011(e)(2)
1205(b)	6311	1225	6012(b)(6)
1205(c)(1)	6103(k)(8)	1231(a)	6234
1205(c)(2)	7431(g)	1231(b)	6211(c)
1205(c)(3)	6103(p)(3)(A)	1231(c)	6234
1211(a)	460(b)(6)	1232(a)	6231(g)
1211(b)(1)	460(b)(2)(C)	1233(a)	6229(d)(1)
1211(b)(2)	460(b)(7)	1233(b)	6229(h)
1212(a)	56(g)(4)(B)(i)	1233(c)	6229(b)(2)
1213(a)	110	1234(a)	6231(a)(1)(B)(i)
1213(b)	6724(d)(1)(A)(vii), (viii)	1235(a)(1)	6229(f)
		1235(a)(2)	6229
1213(b)	6724(d)(1)(A)(ix)	1235(a)(3)	6229(f)(2)
1213(c)	168(i)(8)(C)	1236(a)	6227(b), (c)
1221(a)	771	1237(a)	6230(a)(3)
1221(a)	772	1237(b)	6230(c)(5)
1221(a)	773	1237(c)(1)	6230(a)(1)
1221(a)	774	1237(c)(2)	6503(a)
1221(a)	775	1238(a)	6221
1221(a)	776	1238(b)(1)(A)	6226(f)
1221(a)	777	1238(b)(1)(B)	6226(f)
1222(a)	6240	1238(b)(2)	6230(a)(2)(A)(i)
1222(a)	6241	1238(b)(3)(A)	6230(a)(3)(A)
1222(a)	6242	1238(b)(3)(B)	6230(a)(3)(B)
1222(a)	6245	1238(b)(3)(C)	6230(c)(5)(A)
1222(a)	6246	1238(b)(3)(D)	6230(c)(5)(D)
1222(a)	6247	1238(b)(4)	6230(c)(1)(A), (B)
1222(a)	6248	1238(b)(4)	6230(c)(1)(C)
1222(a)	6251	1238(b)(5)	6230(c)(2)(A)
1222(a)	6252	1238(b)(6)	6230(c)(4)
1222(a)	6255	1239(a)	6225(b)
1222(b)(1)	7421(a)	1239(b)	6226(d)(1)
1222(b)(2)	7459(c)	1239(c)(1)	6230(d)(6)
1222(b)(3)	7482(b)(1)(E)	1239(c)(2)	6512(b)(3)
1222(b)(4)(A)	7485(b)		

Act Sec.	Code Sec.	Act Sec.	Code Sec.
1239(d)(1)	7482(b)(1)(D), (E)	1258	856(c)(5)(G)
1239(d)(1)	7482(b)(1)(F)	1259(1)	857(e)(2)(B)
1239(d)(2)	7482(b)(1)	1259(2)	857(e)(2)(C)
1239(e)(1)	7459(c)	1259(3)	857(e)(2)(C)
1239(e)(2)	6501(o)(3)	1259(4)	857(e)(2)(C)
1239(e)(3)	7421(a)	1259(4)	857(e)(2)(D)
1240(a)	6226(b)(5)	1260	857(b)(6)(C)(iii)(I)
1241(a)(1)	7485(b)	1260	857(b)(6)(C)(iii)(II)
1241(a)(2)	7485(b)	1261(a)	856(j)(4)
1242(a)	6601(c)	1261(b)	856(j)(5)(A)(ii)
1243(a)	6227(e)	1262	856(i)(2)
1246(a)	706(c)(2)(A)	1271(a)	851(b)(3)
1246(b)	706(c)(2)	1271(a)	851(b)(2)
1251(a)(1)	857(a)(2)	1271(a)	851(b)(4)
1251(a)(1)	857(a)(3)	1271(b)(1)(A)	851(b)(3)
1251(a)(2)	857(f)	1271(b)(1)(B)	851(b)(3)
1251(b)(1)	856(k)	1271(b)(2)	851(c)
1251(b)(2)	856(a)(6)	1271(b)(3)	851(d)
1252(a)	856(d)(2)	1271(b)(4)	851(e)(1)
1252(b)	856(d)(7)	1271(b)(5)	851(e)(4)
1253	856(d)(5)	1271(b)(6)	851(g)
1254(a)	857(b)(3)(D)	1271(b)(6)	851(h)
1254(b)(1)	857(b)(7)(A)(i)	1271(b)(7)	851(g)(3)
1254(b)(2)	852(b)(3)(D)(iii)	1271(b)(8)(A)	817(h)(2)(A)
1255(a)(1)	856(c)(3)	1271(b)(8)(B)	817(h)(2)(B)
1255(a)(2)	856(c)(4)	1271(b)(9)	1092(f)(2)
1255(a)(2)	856(c)(8)	1281(a)	6652(g)
1255(a)(3)	856(c)(5)-(7)	1281(b)	6652(k)
1255(b)(1)	856(c)(5)(G)	1281(c)	6683
1255(b)(2)	857(b)(5)	1281(d)	7519(f)(4)(A)
1255(b)(3)	857(b)(6)(C)	1282(a)	6512(b)(3)
1256	857(d)(3)	1283(a)	6103(h)(5)
1257(a)(1)	856(e)(2)	1283(a)	6103(h)(6)
1257(a)(2)(A)	856(e)(3)	1283(b)	6103(p)(4)
1257(a)(2)(B)	856(e)(3)	1284(a)	6501(a)
1257(b)	856(e)(5)	1285(a)	7430(f)(3)
1257(c)	856(e)(4)	1285(b)	7430(b)(5)

Act Sec.	Code Sec.	Act Sec.	Code Sec.
1285(c)(1)	7430(f)(2)	1411(a)	5008(c)(1)
1285(c)(2)	7430(f)(2)	1412(a)	5175(c)
1301(a)	6019(1)	1413(a)	5207(c)
1301(a)	6019(2)	1414(a)	5222(b)(2)
1301(a)	6019(3)	1414(b)	5053(f)
1302(a)	2207A(a)(2)	1414(c)(1)	5056(c)
1302(b)	2207B(a)(2)	1414(c)(2)	5056(d)
1303(a)	2056A	1415(a)	5115
1304(a)	2105(b)(2)	1415(b)(1)	5681(a)
1304(a)	2105(b)(3)	1415(b)(2)(A)	5681(c)
1304(a)	2105(b)(4)	1415(b)(2)(B)	5681(c)
1305(a)	646	1415(b)(3)	5115
1305(b)	2652(b)(1)	1416(a)	5044(a)
1305(c)	646	1416(b)(1)	5361
1306(a)	663(b)	1416(b)(2)	5044
1306(b)	663(b)(2)	1416(b)(3)	5044
1307(a)(1)	663(c)	1417(a)	5384(b)(2)(D)
1307(a)(2)	663(c)	1418(a)	5053(g)
1307(b)	663(c)	1419(a)	5053(h)
1308(a)	267(b)(11), (12)	1420(a)	5055
1308(a)	267(b)(13)	1421(a)	5418
1308(b)	1239(b)(2)	1421(b)	5418
1308(b)	1239(b)(3)	1422(a)	5364
1309(a)	685	1422(b)	5364
1309(b)	685	1431(a)(1)	4222(b)(2)
1310(a)	2035	1431(a)(2)	4222(b)(2)
1310(b)	2035	1432(a)	4051(d)
1311(a)	2056(b)(7)(C)	1432(a)	4051(e)
1312(a)	2056A(c)(3)	1432(b)(1)	4495
1313(a)	2032A(d)(3)	1432(b)(1)	4496
1314(a)	2056A(a)(1)(A)	1432(b)(1)	4497
1401(a)	4003(a)(3)(C)	1432(b)(1)	4498
1401(a)	4051(b)(2)(B)	1432(c)(1)	4681(b)(1)(B), (C)
1402(a)	4051(e)	1432(c)(2)	4682(g)
1402(b)	4052(b)(1)(B)(iii)	1433(a)	4161(b)
1402(b)	4052(b)(1)(B)(ii)	1434(a)	4052(f)
1402(b)	4052(b)(1)(B)(iv)	1434(b)(1)	4052(d)

Act Sec.	Code Sec.	Act Sec.	Code Sec.
1434(b)(2)	4052(g)	1506(b)(1)(B)(i)	4975(d)
1435(a)	4261(h)	1506(b)(1)(B)(ii)	4975(d)
1435(b)	4041(c)(2)	1507(a)	4972(c)(6)(B)
1436(a)	4091(d)	1508(a)	412
1436(b)	6416(d)	1509	402
1441	148(f)(4)(B)(ii)(I)	1521(a)(A) [sic (a)(1)]	412(c)(7)(A)(i)(I)
1442	148(f)(4)(C)(xvii)	1521(a)(B) [sic (a)(2)]	412(c)(7)(F)
1443	148(d)(3)	1521(c)(1)	412(b)(2)(C), (D)
1444(a)	148(c)(2)(B)	1521(c)(1)	412(b)(2)(E)
1444(a)	148(c)(2)(C)-(E)	1521(c)(3)(A)	412(c)(7)(D)(i), (ii)
1444(b)	148(f)(4)(E)	1521(c)(3)(A)	412(c)(7)(D)(iii)
1451(a)	6512(b)(2)	1522(a)(1)	414(e)(5)(C)
1451(b)	6512(b)(4)	1522(a)(2)	414(e)(5)(E)
1452(a)	7481(c)	1523(a)	512(e)(3)
1453(a)	7430(c)(4)(D)	1525(a)(1)	401(k)(7)(B)(iii)
1454(a)	7436	1525(a)(1)	401(k)(7)(B)(iv)
1454(b)(1)	6511(d)(7)	1525(a)(2)	401(k)(7)(B)(v)
1454(b)(2)	7421(a)	1526(a)	415(n)
1454(b)(3)	7453	1526(b)	415(k)(3)
1454(b)(3)	7481(b)	1527(a)	415(b)(2)(G)
1454(b)(4)	7436	1528(a)	101(h)
1461(a)	6655(g)(3)	1529(a)	104
1463(a)	6621(c)(2)(B)(iii)	1530(a)	664(d)(1)(C)
1501(a)	402(g)(9)	1530(a)	664(d)(2)(C)
1501(b)	408(p)(8)	1530(b)	664(g)
1502(b)	401(a)(13)(C)-(D)	1530(c)(1)	401(a)(1)
1504(a)(1)	403(b)(3)	1530(c)(2)	404(a)(9)(C)
1504(b)	415	1530(c)(3)	415(c)(6)
1505(a)(1)	401(a)(5)(G)	1530(c)(4)(A)	415(e)(6)
1505(a)(2)	401(a)(26)(H)	1530(c)(4)(B)	415(e)(6)
1505(a)(3)	410(c)(2)	1530(c)(5)	664(d)(1)(B)
1505(b)	401(k)(3)(G)	1530(c)(5)	664(d)(2)(B)
1505(c)	403(b)(12)(C)	1530(c)(6)	674(b)(4)
1506(a)(1)	409(h)(2)(B)	1530(c)(7)(i) [sic (A)]	2055(a)(3)
1506(a)(2)(A)	409(h)(2)	1530(c)(7)(ii) [sic (B)]	2055(a)(4)
1506(a)(2)(B)	409(h)(2)	1530(c)(7)(iii) [sic (C)]	2055(a)(5)
1506(b)(1)(A)	4975(f)(6)	1530(c)(8)	2056(b)(8)

Act Sec.	Code Sec.	Act Sec.	Code Sec.
1530(c)(9)	4947(b)(4)	1601(c)(4)(D)	512(e)(1)
1530(c)(10)	4975(e)(7)	1601(d)(1)(A)	408(i)
1530(c)(11)(A)	4978(a)	1601(d)(1)(B)	408(k)(6)(H)
1530(c)(11)(B)	4978(a)(2)	1601(d)(1)(C)(i)(I)	408(l)(2)(B)
1530(c)(12)(A)	4978(b)(2)	1601(d)(1)(C)(i)(II)	408(l)(2)(B)(i)
1530(c)(12)(B)	4978(b)(2)(A)	1601(d)(1)(C)(ii)(I)	6693(c)(2)
1530(c)(13)	4978(c)	1601(d)(1)(C)(ii)(II)	6693(c)(2)
1530(c)(14)	4978(e)(2)	1601(d)(1)(D)	408(p)(8)
1530(c)(15)	4979A(a)	1601(d)(1)(E)	408(p)(2)(D)(i)
1530(c)(16)	4979A(c)	1601(d)(1)(F)	408(p)(2)(D)(iii)
1530(c)(17)	4979A(d)	1601(d)(1)(G)	408(p)(5)
1531(a)(2)	9804	1601(d)(2)(A)	401(k)(11)(D)(ii)
1531(a)(2)	9805	1601(d)(2)(B)	401(k)(11)(E)
1531(a)(4)	9811	1601(d)(2)(C)(i)	404(a)(3)(A)(i)
1531(a)(4)	9812	1601(d)(2)(C)(ii)	404(a)(3)(A)(ii)
1531(b)(1)(A)	9801(c)(1)	1601(d)(2)(D)	401(k)(11)(B)(iii)
1531(b)(1)(B)	9831(b)	1601(d)(3)	401(m)(11)
1531(b)(1)(C)	9831(c)(1)	1601(d)(4)	403(b)(11)
1531(b)(1)(D)	9831(c)(2)	1601(d)(6)(A)	414(e)(5)(A)
1531(b)(1)(E)	9831(c)(3)	1601(d)(6)(B)	403(b)(1)(A)(i), (ii)
1531(b)(2)(A)	4980D(a)	1601(d)(6)(B)	403(b)(1)(A)(iii)
1531(b)(2)(B)	4980D(c)(3)(B)(i)(I)	1601(d)(7)	414(q)(7)
1531(b)(2)(C)	4980D(d)(1)	1601(e)	956(b)(1)(A)
1531(b)(2)(D)	4980D(d)(3)	1601(f)(1)(A)	30A
1531(b)(2)(E)	4980D(f)(1)	1601(f)(1)(B)	30A
1532(a)	9802(c)	1601(f)(1)(C)	55(c)(1)
1541	411	1601(f)(2)(A)	9503(c)(2)(A)(ii)
1601(a)(1)	6050R(c)(1)	1601(f)(2)(B)	9503(e)(5)(A)
1601(b)	52(c)	1601(f)(3)(A)(i)	4001(f)
1601(c)(1)	1361(e)(1)(B)(i), (ii)	1601(f)(3)(A)(ii)	4001(f)
1601(c)(1)	1361(e)(1)(B)(iii)	1601(f)(3)(B)	4001(g)
1601(c)(2)(A)	1377	1601(f)(4)(A)(i)	4041(l)
1601(c)(2)(B)	1377(b)(1)(B)	1601(f)(4)(A)(ii)	4041(l)
1601(c)(3)	1361(b)(3)(A)	1601(f)(4)(B)	4041(a)(2)
1601(c)(4)(A)	512(e)(2)	1601(f)(4)(C)	4092(b)
1601(c)(4)(B)	1361(c)(7)	1601(f)(4)(D)	4261(g)
1601(c)(4)(C)	1361(b)(1)(B)	1601(f)(4)(E)	4081

Act Sec.	Code Sec.	Act Sec.	Code Sec.
1601(f)(4)(E)	4091	1602(d)(1)	6050Q(b)(1)
1601(f)(4)(F)	4081	1602(d)(2)(A)	6724(d)(2)(R)-(Y)
1601(f)(4)(F)	4091	1602(d)(2)(B)	6652(e)
1601(f)(5)(A)	593(e)(1)(A)	1602(e)	7702B(g)(4)(B)(ii)
1601(f)(5)(B)	1374(d)(7)	1602(e)	7702B(g)(4)(B)(iii)
1601(f)(6)(A)	860L(b)(1)(A)	1602(f)(1)	264(a)(4)
1601(f)(6)(B)	860L(d)(2)	1602(f)(2)	264(d)(4)(B)(ii)
1601(f)(6)(C)	860L(e)(2)(B)	1602(f)(3)	264(d)(4)(B)
1601(f)(6)(D)	860L(e)(3)(A)	1602(f)(4)	264
1601(f)(6)(E)(i)	860L(e)(3)(D)	1602(f)(5)	264
1601(f)(6)(E)(ii)	860L(e)(2)(A)	1602(g)(1)	877(d)(2)(B)
1601(g)(1)	6427	1602(g)(2)	877(d)(2)(D)
1601(h)(1)(A)	529(e)(1)(B)	1602(g)(3)	877(d)(3)
1601(h)(1)(B)	529(e)(1)(C)	1602(g)(4)(A)	877(d)(4)(A)(i)
1601(h)(1)(C)	135	1602(g)(4)(B)	877(d)(4)(A)
1601(h)(1)(C)	529	1602(g)(4)(C)	877(d)(4)(A)
1601(h)(2)(A)	23(a)(2)	1602(g)(5)	2501(a)(3)(C)
1601(h)(2)(B)	23(b)(2)(B)	1602(g)(6)(A)	2107(c)(2)(B)(i)
1601(h)(2)(C)	137(b)(1)	1602(g)(6)(B)	2107(c)(2)(C)
1601(h)(2)(D)(i)	414(n)(3)(C)	1602(h)(1)	6039F
1601(h)(2)(D)(ii)	414(t)(2)	1602(h)(2)	6039F and G
1601(h)(2)(D)(iii)	6039D(d)(1)	1602(h)(3)	877(e)(1)
1601(i)(1)	6048(b)	1603(a)	4962(b)
1601(i)(2)	679(a)(3)(C)(ii)	1603(b)(1)(A)	6033(b)(10)
1601(i)(2)	679(a)(3)(C)(iii)	1603(b)(1)(B)	6033(b)(10)(C)
1601(i)(3)(A)	7701(a)(30)(E)(ii)	1603(b)(2)	6033(b)(11)
1601(i)(3)(B)	641(b)	1604(a)(1)	263(a)(1)(F), (G)
1601(i)(4)	7701	1604(a)(1)	263(a)(1)(H)
1602(a)(1)	26(b)(2)(N), (O)	1604(a)(2)(A)	312(k)(3)(B)
1602(a)(1)	26(b)(2)(P)	1604(a)(2)(B)	312(k)(3)(B)
1602(a)(2)	220(c)(3)(A)	1604(a)(3)	1245(a)(2)(C)
1602(a)(2)	220(c)(3)(B)-(D)	1604(a)(3)	1245(a)(3)(C)
1602(a)(3)	220(d)(2)(C)	1604(b)(1)	6621(a)(1)
1602(a)(4)	6693(a)	1604(b)(2)(A)	412(m)(5)(E)(ii)(II)
1602(a)(5)	4975(c)(4)	1604(b)(3)	411
1602(b)	7702B(c)(2)(B)	1604(c)(1)	168(j)(6)
1602(c)	162(l)(2)(B)	1604(d)(1)	1059(d)(3)

Act Sec.	Code Sec.	Act Sec.	Code Sec.
1604(d)(2)(A)(i)	833(b)(1)(A)(i)	9302(g)(3)(A) *	5702(c)
1604(d)(2)(A)(ii)	833(b)(1)(A)(ii)	9302(g)(3)(B)(i) *	5702(d)
1604(e)(1)	267(f)(4)	9302(g)(3)(B)(ii) *	5702(d)(1)
1604(f)(3)	5701	9302(h)(1)(A) *	5704
1604(g)(1)	163(j)(2)(B)(iii)	9302(h)(1)(B) *	5761(c)-(d)
1604(g)(2)	665(d)(1)	9302(h)(1)(C) *	5761(a)
1604(g)(3)	1441(g)	9302(h)(1)(D) *	5761(d)
1604(g)(4)	2523(g)(1)	9302(h)(1)(E)(i) *	5754
1604(g)(5)	9502(d)	9302(h)(1)(E)(ii) *	5754
4006(a) *	138	9302(h)(2)(A) *	5712
4006(b)(1) *	4973(d)	9302(h)(2)(A) *	5713(a)
4006(b)(2) *	220(b)(7)	9302(h)(2)(A) *	5721
4006(b)(3) *	138	9302(h)(2)(A) *	5722
4041(a) *	501(o)	9302(h)(2)(A) *	5762(a)(1)
4631(c)(2) *	6103(l)(12)(F)	9302(h)(2)(A) *	5763(b)
5405(a)(1) *	3309(b)(3)(D)	9302(h)(2)(A) *	5763(c)
5405(a)(2) *	3309(b)(3)(E)	9302(h)(2)(A) *	5763(b)
5405(a)(3) *	3309(b)(3)(F)	9302(h)(2)(B) *	5701(c)
5406(a)(1) *	3306(19)	9302(h)(3) *	5702(k)
5406(a)(2) *	3306(20)	9302(h)(4) *	5712(1)
5406(a)(3) *	3306(21)	9302(h)(5) *	5712(2)
5407(a)(1) *	3309(b)(1)(A)	9302(h)(5) *	5701
5407(a)(2) *	3309(b)(1)(C)	9302(j) *	3306
5702 *	32	9304 *	6103
9302(a)(1) *	5701(b)(1)	11024(a) *	6103(l)(16)
9302(a)(2) *	5701(b)(2)	11024(b)(1) *	6103(a)(3)
9302(b)(1) *	5701(a)(1)	11024(b)(2) *	6103(i)(7)(B)(i)
9302(b)(2) *	5701(a)(2)	11024(b)(3) *	6103(p)(3)(A)
9302(c) *	5701(c)	11024(b)(4) *	6103(p)(4)
9302(d) *	5701(d)	11024(b)(5) *	6103(p)(4)(F)(i)
9302(e)(1) *	5701(e)(1)	11024(b)(6) *	6103(p)(4)(F)
9302(e)(2) *	5701(e)(2)	11024(b)(7) *	7213(a)(2)
9302(f) *	5701(f)	11024(b)(8) *	11024(a)-(b)
9302(g)(1) *	5701(g)	11024(c) *	401
9302(g)(2) *	5701(p)	11034 *	

¶ 6004. FTC 2d ¶s affected by '97 Act

FTC 2d ¶	Analysis ¶	FTC 2d ¶	Analysis ¶	FTC 2d ¶	Analysis ¶
A-1104 *et seq.*	2701	D-1004	603	E-6545	1706
A-2600 *et seq.*	116	D-1322	1427	E-6546	1712
A-2604	105	D-1323	1427	E-6553	1711
A-2700 *et seq.*	116	D-1452	912	E-6553.1	1711
A-2707 *et seq.*	116	D-1452.1	1508	E-6602	1707
A-2809	113	D-1479.1	1506	E-6603	1707
A-2811	113	D-1655	1717	E-6614	1710, 1712
A-3501	101	D-1788	1507	E-6615	1714
A-4203	109	D-2263	1509	E-6616	1701
A-4216	110	D-4100	1303	E-6617	1701
A-4401.1	112	D-5106	2706	E-6619	1701
A-4402	112	D-5700 *et seq.*	2706	E-6620	1703, 1704
A-6032	1903	D-6251	408	E-6622	1714
A-6156.1	1906	D-6252	407	E-7304	1718
A-8104	601	D-6258	405	E-7357	1719
A-8107	604	D-6259	407	E-9458	603
A-8115	601, 602	D-6260	406	F-1004, F-4010	1502
A-8124	604	D-6322	1305	F-1302	1504
A-8126	608	D-6341 *et seq.*	1306	F-1906	2706
A-8128	609	D-6429	2305	F-1907	2706
A-8132	601	D-6651	2305	F-2707	1501
A-8209	606	D-6651 *et seq.*	2409	F-4608	1501
A-8228	610	D-6800	1301, 1302	F-4707	1501
A-8242	607	D-6921	2306	F-6501	1630
A-8310	116	D-6928	603	F-10304	1514
A-8316	605	D-8201	2305, 2409	F-11710 *et seq.*	1505
A-8404	611	E-3108	1513	F-11904	212
A-8405	611	E-3111	1513	G-1573	2406
B-1800 *et seq.*	1403	E-3318	1717	G-2707	211
B-1900	1401	E-4821 *et seq.*	1716	G-3156	2003
B-3125	1424	E-4826	1716	G-3157	2003
B-3507	1421	E-4950 *et seq.*	1716	G-3161	2004
B-3700	1422	E-5535 *et seq.*	1716	G-3166	2003
B-3900	1423	E-5625	1106	G-3167	2003
B-3901	201	E-5627	937	G-3171	2004
B-4200	1425	E-6006	1715	G-3204	2003
C-1000 *et seq.*	526	E-6155	1702	G-4751	212
C-2016	531	E-6511	1704	G-5120	2005
C-2711	528	E-6515	1709	G-6611	2002
C-2713	527	E-6517	1709	G-6736 *et seq.*	2002
C-4107.1	212	E-6522	1708	G-7047	1623
C-5215	533	E-6527	1713	H-1325.1 *et seq.*	1101, 1102
C-5602	1628	E-6531	1713	H-1325.14	929
C-5602.1	529	E-6538	1706	H-1325.15	929
C-5603	1627	E-6540	1706	H-1326	1201
C-7000 *et seq.*	526	E-6541	1706	H-1355	1002

FTC 2d ¶	Analysis ¶	FTC 2d ¶	Analysis ¶	FTC 2d ¶	Analysis ¶
H-1451	112	H-12259	201, 305	J-3377	2606, 2607
H-1821	1001	H-12352	914	J-3379	2606
H-1931	1001	H-12353	913	J-3384	2606
H-2064	404	H-12357	915, 919	J-3387	2606, 2614
H-3303	902	H-12378	920	J-3400 et seq.	2502
H-4035 et seq.	710	H-12420	924	J-3446	2504
H-4109	710			J-3448	2504
		H-12436	906	J-3462 et seq.	2502
H-4260	1902	H-12439	925		
H-4300 et seq.	2329	H-12443	925	J-3614	2507
H-4760	1904	H-12457	925	J-3620	2503
H-4801	1905	H-12500	1202	J-3621	2507
H-5406	924			J-3660	2506
		H-12501	908	J-4343 et seq.	2006
H-5754	924	H-12566	909		
H-5957.1	905	I-1403 et seq.	204	J-4729 et seq.	711
H-5957.2	905	I-1409 et seq.	204	J-5000 et seq.	104
H-5960	922	I-1800 et seq.	205	J-5307.1	713
H-6104	924			J-5401	405
		I-1900 et seq.	205	J-5833	2705
H-6512	924	I-3060	209		
H-6526	933	I-3504	211	J-5834	2705
H-7301	932	I-3527	211	J-7508	103
H-7510	902	I-3733.1	207	K-2141.2	1105
H-7629	931			K-2141.3	1107
		I-4600 et seq.	102	K-3160	1512
H-7629.1	928	I-4700 et seq.	102		
H-7644.1	928	I-5110	201	K-3176	107
H-8201	904	I-5117 et seq.	603	K-3261 et seq.	532
H-8251.2	901	I-6001	201	K-3283	938
H-8701	902			K-3291 et seq.	532
		I-7500	202	K-3324	938
H-8751	932	I-7619	204		
H-8969	930	I-7650	2001	K-3478 et seq.	517, 519
H-9051	924	I-7700	202	K-3503	520
H-9087	918, 919,	I-7706	203	K-3629	106
	920, 921			K-5351	709, 710
H-9152	933	I-8703	211	K-5353	712
		I-9100.1	206		
H-9155	933	I-10106	805	K-5354 et seq.	714
H-9329	910	I-10204	804	K-5355	715
H-9556	926, 927,	J-1360	210	K-5510 et seq.	402
	1901			K-5513	508
H-10202	918	J-3015 et seq.	409	K-5570 et seq.	713
H-10214	918	J-3017	405		
		J-3018	406	K-5580 et seq.	713
H-10300	918	J-3187	2501	K-5790	1511
H-10303.2	911	J-3191	2501	L-1300 et seq.	114
H-11012	903			L-1811	115
H-11101	303, 304	J-3193	2501	L-1911	105
H-11300	907	J-3211	2501		
		J-3248.2	2505	L-2135	117
H-12103	208	J-3280	212	L-2141	117
H-12201	915	J-3350 et seq.	2604	L-3402	710
H-12215	302			L-3510	1103, 1104
H-12238	301	J-3353	2608	L-3900 et seq.	116
		J-3354	2608		

FTC 2d ¶	Analysis ¶	FTC 2d ¶	Analysis ¶	FTC 2d ¶	Analysis ¶
L-4700 *et seq.*	116	N-2420	212	R-2058.1	405
L-5800 *et seq.*	807	N-2431	1401	R-2202	524
L-6151	808			R-2457	513
L-6154	808	N-2700 *et seq.*	2704	R-5200 *et seq.*	519
L-6155	808	N-7028	212		
		O-1006.1	1426	R-5204	502
L-6157	808	O-1057	1624	R-5254	509
L-8204	803	O-1102	1622	R-5307.1	510
L-8205	803			R-5450	508
L-8214	801	O-1840 *et seq.*	1621	R-5451	508
L-8807	806	O-1894	1621		
		O-2200	1618	R-5701	938
L-9403	803	O-2201	1617	R-5766 *et seq.*	532
L-9926	212	O-2202	1619	R-6203	514, 515,
L-9950	2606				516
L-9955	2610	O-2432	1609	R-6439	513
L-9956	2611	O-2432 *et seq.*	1610	R-7005	521
		O-2448	1609		
L-9958	2612	O-2546	1611, 1616	R-7008, R-7102	501
L-9959	2612	O-2602	1615	R-7041	907
L-10004	802			R-7080	514
L-10012	802	O-2609.2	1613	R-7101	507
L-10704	801	O-2613	1614	R-8017	511
		O-2800.1	1613		
L-10704.1	801	O-3600 *et seq.*	1610	R-8028	501
L-10705 *et seq.*	801	O-3701	1629	R-8033.5	1626
L-10707.4	2004			R-9514	525
L-15202	704	O-4000 *et seq.*	1604	R-9551	504
L-15202.1	704	O-4325	1607	S-1302	2301
		O-4332	1603		
L-15208	704	O-4343	1612	S-2010	2306
L-15209	701, 704	O-4351	1612	S-2201	2307
L-15300 *et seq.*	706			S-2301	501
L-15600.1	707	O-4401	1602	S-2710	2302
L-15630	2606	O-4404	1608	S-2717.1	2303
		O-4800 *et seq.*	1604		
L-15632	2607	O-4804	1601	S-2857.1	2305
L-15635	704	O-4901	1601	S-2857.2	2305
L-15684	806			S-3399.1	916
L-16925	212	O-5003	1606	S-3399.2	916
L-17775	702, 703,	O-5300 *et seq.*	1605	S-3399.3	916, 917
	704	O-10204	511		
		O-10220	511	S-3441	2317
L-17776	702	O-10226	511	S-3442	2317
L-17777	702			S-3585 *et seq.*	2312
L-17778	702	O-10516	1620	S-3593.2	2312
L-17779	702	O-10931.1	1624	S-3597 *et seq.*	2312
L-17785	702	O-11712	1626		
		O-11713	1626	S-3602	2314
L-17785.1	702	P-5101	1503	S-3606	2314
L-18100	101, 1202			S-3607	2314
M-2000 *et seq.*	111	P-5103	1503	S-3643	2313
M-4301	1510	P-5108	1503	S-3643.1	1421
N-1031	2101	Q-1910.1	405		
		Q-5002	503	S-3656, S-3659,	2311
N-1045	2104	Q-5255.1	405	S-3660	
N-1047	2104			S-3675	2310
N-1216	2102	Q-8005; R-7101	501, 505	S-3676	2310

FTC 2d ¶	Analysis ¶	FTC 2d ¶	Analysis ¶	FTC 2d ¶	Analysis ¶
S-3681	2311	T-2202	1409, 1410	U-3421	2327
S-3695.1	2316	T-2206 *et seq.*	1410	U-3600 *et seq.*	2329
S-3800	2309	T-2211	1404, 1417	U-5201	1416
S-4400 *et seq.*	2318	T-2215	1404, 1406	V-1002	2401
S-4413	2318	T-2222	1406, 1418	V-1110	2403
S-5001	2401	T-2228	1418	V-1111	2403
S-5200 *et seq.*	1801	T-2231	1418	V-1220	2402
S-5204.1	1803	T-2232	1418	V-1656.1	2405
S-5266	1802	T-2236	1416	V-1762	2301
S-5301	1803	T-2240	1415	V-1764	2406
S-5320 *et seq.*	1801	T-2242	1404, 1417	V-1803 *et seq.*	410
S-5422	1804	T-2251	1415	V-1803, V-1804, V-1805	2301
S-5711.0	2217	T-2254	1416	V-1814 *et seq.*	410
S-5711.1	2217	T-2261.1	1412	V-1901.2	2315, 2411
S-5719	2204	T-2262	1415	V-1919	2406
S-5721	2204	T-3406	1413	V-1950	2312
S-5722	2217	T-3622	101	V-1955.1	1202
S-5722.1	2217	T-3628	108	V-1955.2	916
S-5754	2319	T-4001	522	V-1956	2406
S-5851	2401	T-4015 *et seq.*	1416	V-2000	108
S-6009	507	T-4020	2321	V-2154	2412
S-6200	2605	T-4021	2321	V-2178	2412
S-6205	2605	T-4023	2321	V-2630	2410
S-6206	2605	T-4101	522	V-3304	2337, 2605
S-6302	604	T-4146	2320	V-3305	2337
S-6325	2331	T-4147 *et seq.*	522	V-5200 *et seq.*	2324
S-6348	2330	T-4222	522	V-7332	1411
S-6352	2605	T-4316	1411	V-8506 *et seq.*	2335
S-6362	2332	T-4320	1411, 1414	W-1501	2201, 2211
S-6363	2333	T-4323	1411	W-1501.1	2208, 2211
S-6411	2331, 2605	T-4419	1406, 1409, 1411	W-1509	2208
S-6501	2319, 2408	T-6001	2325	W-1515.1	2210
S-6506	2408	T-7501	1410, 2322	W-1515.2	2208
T-1801.1 *et seq.*	2329	T-7552	1410	W-1515.4	2208
T-2100 *et seq.*	1402, 1405, 2306	T-7569	2323	W-1522.1	2208
T-2101	1404	T-7570	2323	W-1551	2210
T-2101 *et seq.*	1415	T-7578	1416, 2326	W-1564	2214
T-2103	1406, 1407, 1408	T-7578.1	2326	W-1564.2 *et seq.*	2208
T-2137	1411	U-1282	2335	W-1564.3 *et seq.*	2208
T-2156	1404	U-1283, U-1283.1	2335	W-1565	2208
T-2157	1418	U-1285	2336	W-1566	2208, 2213
T-2160	1404, 1418	U-1286	2336	W-1601	2208
T-2161	1418	U-1287	2336	W-1607	2201, 2208, 2211
T-2172	1404	U-1289	2336	W-1617	2205
T-2201	1406	U-2108	2328	W-1625	2208
T-2201 *et seq.*	1409	U-2133	2325	W-1647.06	2216
		U-2301	2334	W-1707	2210, 2211

FTC 2d ¶	Analysis ¶	FTC 2d ¶	Analysis ¶	FTC 2d ¶	Analysis ¶
W-1707.1	2208	W-2952	2223	W-4328	2226
W-1711	2211, 2212	W-2953	2223	W-5001	2207
W-1713	2201, 2208, 2211	W-2971	2218, 2219	W-5101	2201, 2203
		W-2972	2218	W-5103	2201, 2202
W-1720	2211	W-2980	2218, 2219	W-5103.1	2202
W-1724	2210	W-2983	2220		
W-1726	2212			W-5103.2	2202
W-1728	2205	W-3118	2220	W-5125	2202
		W-3135	2222	W-5126	2202
W-2261	2224	W-3140	2221	W-5141	2205
W-2416	2215	W-3163	2222	W-5146	2204
W-2417	2215	W-3201	2211		
W-2751 *et seq.*	2225			W-5201	2201

¶ 6005. USTR ¶s affected by '97 Act

USTR ¶	Analysis ¶	USTR ¶	Analysis ¶	USTR ¶	Analysis ¶
14	201	1454.02	2505	4014	924, 932
154.02	2701	1474.02	212	4014.14	904
264	101	1484 et seq.	2502	4014.17	930, 933
264.01	1202	1484.03	2503	4014.171	933
324.01	109	1484.04	2504, 2507	4014.173	924
324.05	110	1493.03	2506	4014.1735	918, 919, 920, 921
384	704	1514	101		
394	704	1624.067	116	4014.19	924
394.01	701	1624.130	115	4014.21	924
414 et seq.	706	1624.403	1103, 1104	4014.25	924
45A4	806	1627.117	808	4014.27	901
45C4	707	1627.177(3)	808	4024	933
514	702, 704	1634	402, 508	4024.02	903
524	703	1654.520	111	4034.04	906, 924, 925
534	601	1674.100	801, 2004		
554	601	1684	801	4044.08	918
554.01	602	1684.01	803, 806	4044.12	918
564	607, 611	1684.03	803	4084.01	301, 915
564.01	606, 610	1704.37	106	4084.03	201, 305
564.02	116	1704.42	107, 1512	4084.06	913, 914, 915, 916, 917, 919, 920, 933
574	605	1704.45	517, 519		
594	604, 608, 609	1724.31	1510		
		1794.05	2606		
624 et seq.	116	2194.01	302	4094.10	910
624.02	105	2204.02	1202	4104.1021	924
634	113, 116	2434.04	1509	4114.15	902
674 et seq.	116	2634	807	4114.45	932
724 et seq.	104	2644	709, 710, 712, 713, 714, 715	4124.07	931
724.22	303, 304			4124.10	928
902.01	1604			4144.13	926, 927, 1901
1014.02	711	2654	1513		
1044.01	1002	269A4	212	4154.03	905, 922
1084.04	103	2744.01	117	4174.06	902
1214	102	2744.17	105	4444	2406
1245.08	1201	280A4.014	114	4474	2104
1274	404	280C4	704	4514.176	2101
1304.01	2705	280F4	802	4534	2002
1324.01	1001	3044.03	1505	4534.17	211
1324.06	1001	3124.04	1514	453C8.400	2002
1354 et seq.	409	3514.05	1501	4574	902
1354.02	406	3514.06	1504	4604	2003, 2004
1374	112	3544.06, 3515.04	1502	4714	2005
1434.012	2501	3554.01	1501	4714.21	2005
1434.013	2501	3,674.03	1630	4754	2001
1434.014	2501	3684.13	1501	5014.07	1304
1444.01	212	3854	1511	5014.10	1303

USTR ¶	Analysis ¶	USTR ¶	Analysis ¶	USTR ¶	Analysis ¶
5014.13	2706	8644.01	1620	13,944	2604, 2608
5014.39	1305	8714	511, 1624	13,964	704, 2606,
5114	603	8774	1626		2607
5124	1301, 1302,	9024.01	1601	13,97A4	2610, 2611,
	2306	9024.03	1606		2612
5284	2706	9044.01	1602, 1603,	14,024	1903
5294	406, 407,		1607, 1608,	14,024.16	1906
	408		1612	14,914	1629
5294.02	405	9114.06	1622	20,014	501
5294.03	405	9214.02	1621	20,104	507
5514	1610	9514.01	1613	20,32A4	502, 509,
5934.01	1717	9524.01	1615		510
6134.009	2704	9544.02	1609, 1610	2032A4	519
				20,385.01(15)	524
613A4	212	9564.01	1611, 1616	20,534	508
6314.04	212	9604	1604	20,554	938
6409	526	9614.01	1614	20,554.16	532
6434.10	212	9864.01	1605	20,56A4	514, 516
6444	531	9884.01	1623	20,56A4.01	515
6634.01	528	10,314	209	21,024	501
6634.03	527	10,334.08	2102	21,054	511
6644.01	532, 938	10,334.221	207	21,074.02	1626
6794	1627	10,344	102	21,214 et seq.	1402, 1405
7024	1401	10,424	208	22,07A4	513
7034	1401	10,594	1503	22,07B4	513
7044.09	1424	10,924	202	25,034	503
7064.02	1425	12,014	603	25034	405
7324.01	1422	12,024	206	25,045	521, 522
7374	1424	12,214	201	25,224	2307
7514	201, 1423	12,224.07	204	26,124	525
8054	1716	12,224.22	204	26,314	504
8074	1716	12,334.01	202, 203	27,044.02	211
8124	1716	1234A4	204	33,014	1904
8324.01	1716	12,354.06	211	34,014.37	1902
8334	1106	12,394.01	211	34,014.375	2329
8514.03	1715	12,454.01	805	35,014.07	1905
8524.02	1702	12,454.05	804	40,014	2218, 2219
8564.01	1704	12,714	205	40,034	2218, 2219,
8564.03	1708, 1709	12,714.01	2006		2220
8564.04	1713	12,914.01	1619	40,414	2201, 2208,
8564.07	1711	12,914.02	1618		2210, 2211,
8564.08	1712	12,914.04	1618		2212
8564.11	1706	12,914.05	1617	40,414.01	2208
8574.01	1701, 1703,	13,614.03	912, 1506	40,414.09	2205
	1710, 1714	13,614.05	1508	40,424	2211
8574.03	1707	13,744.01	1717	40,514	2220, 2221,
860A4.05	1401	13,774	1507		2222
860H4.01	1718, 1719	13,914	2606, 2607,	40,814	2201, 2208,
8614.15	1624		2614		2210, 2211

USTR ¶	Analysis ¶	USTR ¶	Analysis ¶	USTR ¶	Analysis ¶
40,814.01	2208	61,034.02	2331, 2605	65,114.10	1410
40,824	2208	61,034.03	2605	65,114.12	2323
40,914	2201, 2205,	61,034.06	2332, 2333,	65,115.12	2323
	2208, 2211,		2605	65,124	1416, 2325,
	2215, 2216	61,034.08	604		2326
41,314	2223	61,035.10(43)	2330	66,014	507, 2401
41,614	2225	61,114	2318	66,014.02	1413
		61,124	2318	66,014.03	2402
42,214	2224	61,614	2401		
42,514	2207	62,134.02	108	66,214	2403
42,614.01	2201, 2202,			66,524	2406
	2203	62134.02	101	66,544 et seq.	1802
42,614.02	2205	62,214 et seq.	1415, 2306	66,544	1801, 1803
42,614.03	2202, 2204	62,214	1404	66,554	1804
		62,214.01	1403		
42,714	2201	62,214.02	1404, 1406,	66,555	1801
44,614	211		1418	66,564.01	2405
46,814.01	2226			66,624	108
49,584	2305, 2409	62,214.03	1404	66,624.04	2412
49,614	2409	62,214.04	1416	66,834	2406
		62,214.05	1406, 1415,		
49,624	2305		1416, 1418	66,934	916, 1202
49,724	911, 918	62,214.06	1406, 1409,	66,944	2410
49,754	908, 909		1410	66,984	2301
49,80A4	907	62,214.07	1410	67,214	410, 2301
4980D4	1101, 1102			67,224	410
		62,214.08	1406, 1409,		
58,814	212		1411, 1414	67,244	410
60,114.07	2301	62,214.09	1415, 1416	72,134	2337, 2605
60,124.04	2306	62,214.10	1406, 1407,	74,304.01	2335
60,134.05	2335		1408	74,304.02	2336
60,184	501	62,314	1421	74,314	2319, 2408
60,194	2307	63,014	2204, 2217		
60,314	2302, 2303			74,424	2328
60,334	2305	63,114	2319	74,814	2327
60,384	2312	63,314.03	2324	74,824	1416
60,38B4	2315	64,024	2325	74,824.10	1404, 1417
		64,164	2214, 2215	75,184	210
60,414.05	2310	64,204.2	2210		
60,41A4	2311			76,557	2329
60,454.04	2309	64,274	2208	77,014.45	529, 1628
60,464	2314	64,274.01	2208, 2213	7702B4	1107
60,46A4	2313, 2411	65,014	522	77,02B4.01	1105
		65,014.04	2321	77,044.03	1427
60,50M4.01	2311	65,014.05	522		
60,50Q4	2317			79,006.03	211
60,50R4	2316	65,014.28(d)	2320	98,024	929
60,814	2401	65,034	1411, 1415	20,104; 25,054	501, 505
61,034	2605	65,114.01	1410, 2322	66,544(h)	1803
61,034.01	2331				

¶ 6006. TaxDesk ¶ s affected by '97 Act

TaxDesk ¶	Analysis ¶	TaxDesk ¶	Analysis ¶	TaxDesk ¶	Analysis ¶
11,803	2101	23,332	201	28,413	933
11,813	2104	23,737, 23,754	1501	28,418	924
13,160	1001	24,336 et seq.	1505	28,420	933
13,369.2 et seq.	112	24,661	206	28,606	924
13,377	1001	24,901	201	28,617	932
13,676	404	25,664 et seq.	116	28,635	932
14,110	903	25,809 et seq.	114	28,751	908, 909
14,312	305	26,520 et seq.	807	28,800	1201, 1202
14,405	901	26,623	803	29,213	115
14,453	902	26,624	803	29,317	105
14,552	303, 304	26,708	806	29,455	117
14,560	907	26,753	803	29,753	704
14,650 et seq.	104	26,761	802	30,402	710
14,877 et seq.	711	26,767	802	30,459	1103
15,308 et seq.	2006	26,804	801	30,811	808
15,810	2501	26,805 et seq.	801	31,351	1511
15,813	2503, 2504,	26,806.4	2004	31,400 et seq.	402
	2507	26,866	212	31,402	508
15,813 et seq.	2502	26,870	2606, 2610,	31,681	709, 710
15,814	2506		2611	31,682	712
17,123	1514	26,871	2612	31,683	714, 715
17,306	1701	27,101	2704	31,684	710
18,207	2705	27,124	1401	31,685	713
18,806	103	27,126	212	31,720 et seq.	713
19,060	1624	27,855 et seq.	710	31,750 et seq.	713
19,104	1622	28,062	910	32,902	2319
21,622	1503	28,070	924, 925	33,169	1512
22,122 et seq.	204	28,156	931	33,176	107
22,128 et seq.	204	28,182	918	33,211	532, 938
22,151	205	28,194	918	33,272	106
22,308.3	804	28,200	918	34,634	1105, 1107
22,308.5	805	28,203.2	911	35,150 et seq.	116
22,360	209	28,268	905	35,601	1510
22,388	603	28,271	922	36,910	111
22,580	102	28,331	913, 914	38,051	707
22,650	102	28,333	915, 919	38,052	704
22,793	211	28,340	920	38,053	704
22,806	211	28,345	916	38,058	704
22,840	202	28,346	916, 917	38,059	701, 704
22,890	202	28,350	301	38,070	702, 703
22,893	203	28,352	302	38,071	702, 704
22,974.4	207	28,388	915	38,072	702
23,105	1502	28,394	201, 305	38,079	702
23,212	1504	28,403	924	38,080	702
23,236	2706	28,403.1	918, 919,	38,401 et seq.	706
23,237	2706		920, 921	38,412	2606

TaxDesk ¶	Analysis ¶	TaxDesk ¶	Analysis ¶	TaxDesk ¶	Analysis ¶
38,413	2607	59,101	201	69,681	610
38,416	704	59,250	1425	69,702	605
38,432	704	59,608	2302	69,712	116
38,433	806	59,625	2301		
39,401	1603	60,066	1509	69,803	611
39,404	1606	60,920 et seq.	1801	73,102	503
39,412	1602			74,404; 78,181	501, 505
39,437	1605	60,991	2706	74,601	2307
43,408	2406	61,116.1	1506	76,302	524
44,542	2003	61,485.1	1507, 1508	76,439	513
44,546	2003	63,117	511	77,137	509
44,549	2004	63,118	511	77,141	502
44,555	2003	63,305	1624	77,153	519
44,556	2003	64,166	1620	77,158	510
44,559	2004	64,471	1626		
44,582	2003	65,101	526	77,636	508
45,113	2005	65,122	531	77,637	508
46,609	2002			77,710	938
53,217	1002	65,446	528	77,759 et seq.	532
53,510	1902	65,448	527	77,829	514, 515,
		65,711	533		516
53,700 et seq.	2329	65,752	1627	77,926	513
55,052	1905	65,806	529, 1628	78,055	521, 522
55,102	1904			78,058; 78,182	501
55,986	2405	65,905	2306	78,121	907
56,070 et seq.	116	66,101	526	78,151	514
56,072	1104	66,606	1803		
56,101	105	67,060	1304	78,181	507
56,120 et seq.	116	67,073	1303	78,351	501
56,160 et seq.	116			78,606	501
56,208	113	67,230	406	79,101	525
		67,231	408	79,106	504
56,240	101	67,232	407		
56,822	2701	67,239	407	80,312	2325
56,904	109	67,288	1305	80,601	1410, 2322
56,908	110			80,646	1410
56,959.1 et seq.	112	67,650	2305, 2409	80,660	2323
		68,102	603	80,661	2323
56,961	101	68,106	1302		
57,046	2401	68,112	2306	80,668	2326
57,093	1412, 2335	68,118	1301	80,743	2325
57,130 et seq.	1801			81,401, 81,405	2311
57,135	1803	68,566	2305, 2409	81,406	2310
		68,854	2706	81,418	2310
57,186	1802	68,901	1804		
57,622	704	69,104	604	81,439	2309
57,653	1906	69,152	602	81,553	2312
58,400	1401			81,620	2311
58,410	1403	69,153	601	81,700 et seq.	2318
		69,155	604	81,708	2318
58,818	1424	69,302	608		
58,907	1421, 2303	69,304	609	82,500	2306
58,950	1422	69,401	601	82,501 et seq.	1402, 1405,
59,100	1423	69,657	607		1415
		69,659	606	82,504	1406, 1407,
					1408

TaxDesk ¶	Analysis ¶	TaxDesk ¶	Analysis ¶	TaxDesk ¶	Analysis ¶
82,508	1404	82,533	1415, 1416	85,314	2402
82,511	1411	82,534	1416	86,125 *et seq.*	410
82,512	1418	82,538	1406, 1411	86,125, 86,126	2301
82,518	1406	82,540	1411	86,133 *et seq.*	410
82,519	1404	83,615	101	86,137	916
82,520	1406	83,616	108	86,143	2312
82,520 *et seq.*	1409	83,801	522	86,145	2411
82,521	1409, 1410	83,803	1416, 2321	86,148	2411
82,522	1404, 1417	83,805	2321	86,153	410
82,522 *et seq.*	1410	83,806	2321	86,164	410, 2317
82,523	1406, 1416,	83,812	522	86,300	108
	1418	83,844	1411, 1414	86,316	2412
82,526	1418	83,846	1411	86,700	2410
82,528	1404, 1417	85,105	2403	88,551	2314
82,530	1415	85,106	507	90,201	2324
82,532	1415	85,311	1413	1354 *et seq.*	409

¶ 6007. PCA ¶s affected by '97 Act

PCA ¶	Analysis ¶	PCA ¶	Analysis ¶	PCA ¶	Analysis ¶
23,207	924	28,403	933	35,553	914
23,505	924	28,406	933	35,554	913
23,708.1	905	28,630	910	35,558	915, 919
23,708.2	905	29,007	926, 927,	35,579	920
23,711	922		1901	36,021	924
23,905	924	30,303	918	36,037	906
24,613	924	30,315	918	36,040	925
24,627	933	30,401	918	36,044	925
25,302	932	30,404.2	911	36,058	925
25,511	902	32,113	903	40,404	902
25,630	931	32,202	303, 304	51,211	904
25,645.1	928	32,701	907	53,802	908
26,602	904			53,867	909
26,652.2	901	33,204	208		
27,202	902	34,123	1905	54,111	934
27,302	932	34,252	907	56,153.1	916
28,120	930	35,101	301	56,153.2	916
28,202	924	35,102	915	56,153.3	916, 917
28,238	918, 919,	35,116	302	56,174.3A	916
	920, 921	35,160	305	56,210	935

¶ 6008. PE ¶s affected by '97 Act

PE ¶	Analysis ¶	PE ¶	Analysis ¶	PE ¶	Analysis ¶
72-4.22	303, 304	404-4.08	918	414-4.13	926, 927, 1901
219-4.01	302	404-4.12	918		
401-4	924, 932	408-4.01	301, 915	415-4.03	905, 922
401-4.14	904	408-4.03	305	417-4.06	902
401-4.17	930, 933	408-4.06	913, 914,	457-4	902
401-4.19	924		915, 916,		
401-4.21	924		917, 919,	1042-4	208
401-4.25	924		920, 933	3501-4.07	1905
401-4.27	901			4972-4	911, 918
401-4.171	933	409-4.10	910	4975-4	908, 909
401-4.173	924	410-4.1021	924	4980A-4	907
401-4.1735	919, 920, 921	411-4.15	902		
402-4	933	411-4.45	932	6693-4	916
402-4.02	903	412-4.07	931	9802-4	929
403-4.04	906, 924, 925	412-4.10	928	ER101-4	935
				ER407-4.07	934

¶ 6009. EP ¶s affected by '97 Act

EPTC/EPA ¶	Analysis ¶	EPTC/EPA ¶	Analysis ¶	EPTC/EPA ¶	Analysis ¶
41,514 et seq.	532	44,302	938	46,092	504
41,536	938	44,367 et seq.	532	47,161.1	405
41,544	532	44,554	514, 515,		
41,577	938		516	48,203	503
41,734 et seq.	517, 519	44,740	513	48,276.1	405
		44,906	521	80,051 et seq.	526
41,759	520			83,052	501
43,159.1	405	44,909; 45,103	501	83,210	507
43,253	524	45,002	907		
43,329	513	45,051	514	85,001 et seq.	526
44,001 et seq.	519	45,102	507	85,067	531
		45,102; 48,555	501, 505	85,362	528
44,005	502	45,518	511	85,364	527
44,055	509	45,529	501	85,686	533
44,108.1	510	46,045	525	87,151 et seq.	522
44,201	508				
44,202	508				

¶ 6010. Table of Action Alert Items

Date	Action	Topic	Analysis ¶
30 days after Aug. 5, '97	A corporation which has owned stock in another corporation continuously since June 8, '97, which stock has been subject to a diminished risk of loss by virtue of holding another position at all times since such date, should clearly identify the stock and the position on its books or records within 30 days after Aug. 5, '97 in order to be entitled to the two-year transition rule for the more stringent holding period requirement applicable to the dividends received deduction.	Holding period for dividends-received deduction modified	1509
30 days after Aug. 5, '97	For many taxpayers, the last day on which there can occur a cancellation, lapse, expiration or other termination (of a right or obligation with respect to real property interests, non-actively traded personal property or certain stock) eligible to give rise to an ordinary loss, rather than a capital loss, is 30 days after Aug. 5, '97.	Sale treatment for cancellations, lapses, expirations and other terminations is expanded to all property which is a capital asset	204
30 days after Aug. 5, '97	Securities and commodities traders and dealers in commodities must identify the securities or commodities, to which the election to be subject to the mark-to-market rules will apply, within 30 days of Aug. 5, '97.	Commodities dealers and traders in securities and commodities can elect the mark-to-market rules	2001
30 days after Aug. 5, '97	Within 30 days of Aug. 5, '97, the taxpayer must identify any transaction or position entered into before June 9, '97 which is a constructive sale of any appreciated financial position in order for that transaction to be grandfathered under the transitional rules that apply to constructive sales of appreciated financial positions.	Constructive sales treatment for appreciated financial positions	202

Date	Action	Topic	Analysis ¶
90 days after Aug. 5, '97	For purposes of deducting interest on debt incurred with respect to company-owned life insurance policies, endowment or annuity contracts on key persons, the election to use an "applicable period" different from the 12-month policy year period specified by Code Sec. 264(e)(2)(B)(ii) (as redesignated) must be made no later than the 90th day after Aug. 5, '97.	"Applicable period" changed for interest-rate cap rules on pre-'86 key person life insurance contracts	715
365 days after Aug. 5, '97	Claims for credit or refund should be filed in the one-year period beginning on Aug. 5, '97.	Retroactive exclusion from certain retired firefighters' and police officers' income for amounts received because of heart disease or hypertension	1002
June 30, '98	Taxpayers who want to get a deduction for the full fair market value of qualified appreciated stock contributed to a private foundation must have the foundation in existence and make the contribution by June 30, '98.	Full deduction for contributions of qualified appreciated stock to private foundations restored for period June 1, '97 to June 30, '98	107
June 30, '98	The last day a taxpayer can employ a qualifying individual and be eligible to get a credit for that individual is June 30, '98.	Work opportunity credit is modified and extended through June 30, '98	702
Dec. 31, '98	A taxpayer who wants to use the simplified limitation to compute the AMT foreign tax credit must elect to do so for the taxpayer's first tax year that begins after Dec. 31,'97 for which the taxpayer claims an AMT foreign tax credit.	Simplified foreign tax credit limitation may be elected for alternative minimum tax purposes	608
Dec. 31, '98	Calendar-year taxpayers holding a pool of debt instruments the yield on which may be reduced by reason of prepayments who are required to change their method of accounting for interest earned on those instruments to conform to the requirements of Code Sec. 1272(a)(6)(C)(iii) must file the change request no later than Dec. 31, '98.	Interest must be accrued on credit card receivables during payment grace period	2006

Action Alert Items

Date	Action	Topic	Analysis ¶
Dec. 31, '98	If the estate of a decedent dying before Jan. 1, '98 has elected under Code Sec. 6166 to make installment payments of the estate tax attributable to a closely held business interest, the estate may elect, before Jan. 1, '99, to have the amendments made by the '97 Act apply with respect to installments due after the effective date of the election to have the '97 Act amendments apply.	Interest imposed on estate tax deferred under Code Sec. 6166 is reduced	507
Jan. 1, '99	In '98, all or any part of a regular IRA may be converted into a Roth IRA and receive special tax treatment.	New nondeductible Roth IRA allows tax-free withdrawal of earnings	301
Apr. 30, '99	The last day for hiring an employee with respect to whom the welfare-to-work credit is allowable is Apr. 30, '99.	New welfare-to-work credit is available to employers of long-term family assistance recipients	704

INDEX

References are to paragraph numbers

Tables

NOTES

NOTES

NOTES

NOTES

NOTES

NOTES

NOTES

NOTES

NOTES

NOTES